SENIOR HIGH SCHOOL LIBRARY CATALOG

FIFTEENTH EDITION

STANDARD CATALOG SERIES

JULIETTE YAAKOV, GENERAL EDITOR

CHILDREN'S CATALOG

FICTION CATALOG

**MIDDLE AND JUNIOR HIGH SCHOOL
LIBRARY CATALOG**

PUBLIC LIBRARY CATALOG

SENIOR HIGH SCHOOL LIBRARY CATALOG

SENIOR HIGH SCHOOL LIBRARY CATALOG

FIFTEENTH EDITION

EDITED BY

JULIETTE YAAKOV

SCHOOL OF EDUCATION
CURRICULUM LABORATORY
UM-DEARBORN

NEW YORK AND DUBLIN
THE H. W. WILSON COMPANY
1997

Printed in the United States of America

ISBN 0-8242-0921-4

PREFACE

Senior High School Library Catalog is a selective list of fiction and nonfiction books for young adults, along with review sources and other professional aids for librarians and school media specialists. It includes analytical entries for parts of books and a list of recommended resources available on CD-ROM. Annual supplements to this volume will be published in 1998, 1999, 2000, and 2001.

History. The first edition of the Catalog was published in 1926 as an author-title list, followed by a fuller version in 1928 that also included a subject index and analytical entries. Since the appearance of the second edition in 1932, the Catalog has been published regularly every five years. Initially it was called *Standard Catalog for High School Libraries,* but when *Junior High School Library Catalog* (now *Middle and Junior High School Library Catalog*) was introduced in 1965, its scope was changed. It became *Senior High School Library Catalog* with the ninth edition in 1967.

Preparation. The voting list for the Catalog was compiled with the assistance of an advisory committee of distinguished librarians. The committee reevaluated the titles from the previous edition and its supplements, and proposed many new works. The list that resulted from its deliberations was then submitted to a representative group of librarians with experience in the needs of young adults. These consultants elected the titles included. In most cases their vote incorporates the judgment of a number of their colleagues.

Scope and Purpose. The Catalog lists books for young people in grades nine through twelve. With this edition a separate section listing essential reference works published on CD-ROM has been added. The availability of a CD-ROM version of a print equivalent continues to be indicated in the entry for the print version in the Classified List. Sources for the librarian or school media specialist include works on the history and development of young adult literature; literary criticism; bibliographies; selection aids; guides to the operation of media centers; periodicals relating to library science and education; and review media.

The fifteenth edition includes 5,432 titles and 10,344 analytical entries. Four annual supplements, which will expand the total coverage by several thousand additional titles, are intended for use with this volume. Libraries and media centers serving large systems and those with special curriculum needs or user groups will wish to supplement this list further. Schools that must accommodate students reading below their grade level may find it helpful to consult the latest edition of *Middle and Junior High School Library Catalog* and its supplements. To augment the fiction list the reader is referred to *Fiction Catalog* and its supplements.

Books listed were published or distributed in the United States. A small number of out-of-print titles that were considered essential to a well-rounded collection have been retained at the suggestion of the advisory committee. They are noted as o.p. All other titles were in print at the time of listing. Original paperback editions are included and information is provided on paperback reprints of hardcover editions. Those concerned about the durability of paperbound editions may wish to utilize a commercial rebinding service.

The goal of the advisory committee was to support the secondary school curriculum for both the college- and non-college-bound student, and to identify quality high-interest materials. The committee expanded the folklore section to reflect the extensive use of folk tales in senior-high-level social studies and multicultural education. It also attempted to increase the representation of authors in the fiction section. In so doing, it limited the works of individual authors to those it considered most significant for the present-day high school student. The convention of citing the first book in a fiction series in full with brief listings for other works in the series has been retained. Notes indicate the availability of large print editions, and identify sequels or companion volumes.

The advisory committee found that many books in geography and history were outdated and that topical materials were unavailable in some areas of the arts. Committee members were also concerned about the potential for inaccuracies in works about AIDS and other health-related topics given the rapidity of scientific advances. For recent information in all of these areas the committee recommends consulting the supplements to the Catalog, current reference tools, periodical articles, and electronic media.

The Catalog excludes the following: textbooks; nonprint materials, with the exception of CD-ROMs; periodicals, except for professional materials; and non-English-language items, except for dictionaries and bilingual works. Also excluded are items that date quickly, such as works about specific vocations or computer software versions.

Organization. The Catalog consists of four parts. Part 1, the Classified Catalog, is arranged according to the Dewey Decimal Classification. Items have been classified according to the twelfth abridged edition. Sections for fiction and story collections follow the nonfiction classes. Within classes, arrangement is by main entry, with complete bibliographical information supplied for each book. Prices have been obtained from publishers and are as current as possible. Suggested subject headings based on *Sears List of Subject Headings,* a descriptive annotation, and an evaluation, frequently from a quoted source, are also included.

Part 2, the Author, Title, Subject, and Analytical Index, serves as a comprehensive key to the classified list. Analytical entries, which provide indexing for parts of works, are an important feature of the Catalog. Subject analytics afford access to parts of books not covered by subject headings for the whole, while author and title analytics provide an approach to anthologies and collections, especially of stories and tales. They aid in maximizing use of the library's holdings.

Part 3, Select List of Recommended CD-ROM Reference Works, is new to the Catalog. It consists chiefly of interactive multimedia resources of high quality and reference value for which there is not a print equivalent.

Part 4, Directory of Publishers and Distributors, includes fuller information about the publishers of the books listed.

The section that follows, Directions for Use of the Catalog, contains more detailed information about the purpose, content and arrangement of the Catalog.

Acknowledgments. The H. W. Wilson Company is indebted to the publishers who supplied copies of their books and information about editions and prices. This Catalog could not have been published without the efforts of the advisory committee and the consultants who gave so generously of their time and expertise. Their names appear below.

The advisory committee comprised:

Betty Carter, Chair
  Associate Professor
  School of Library and Information Studies
  Texas Woman's University
  Denton, Tex.

Frances B. Bradburn, Chief Consultant
  Information Technology Evaluation Services
  Public Schools of N.C.
  Raleigh, N.C.

Michael Cart, Writer, Lecturer & Consultant
    on Young Adult Literature
  Studio City, Calif.

Catherine M. Clancy, Head
  Young Adult Services
  General Library
  Boston Public Library
  Boston, Mass.

Carol Fox, Library Media Specialist
  El Dorado High School
  El Dorado, Kan.

Judy T. Nelson, Children's Librarian—Lead
  Bellevue Regional Library
  Bellevue, Wash.

Hazel Rochman, Assistant Editor
  Books for Youth
  Booklist
  American Library Association
  Chicago, Ill.

The following consultants participated in the voting:

Beryl Eber, Principal Librarian
  Manhattan Borough Office
  New York Public Library
  New York, N.Y.

Deanna Draper, Coordinator
  Library Media Department
  Sunset High School
  Beaverton, Ore.

Judy Druse, Curriculum/Media Librarian
  Washburn University
  Topeka, Kan.

Mary Joan Egan, Director of Libraries
  Burnt Hills-Ballston Lake Central Schools
  Burnt Hills, N.Y.

Betty A. Hutsler, Library Media Coordinator
  Frederick County Public Schools
  Winchester, Va.

Joy L. Lowe, Associate Professor of Library
    Science
  Louisiana Tech University
  Ruston, La.

Carol McCarthy, Library Director
  Tower Hill School
  Wilmington, Del.

Jan Rogers, Media Director
  Griffin-Spaulding Board of Education
  Griffin, Ga.

Beverly Shinn, Librarian
  The Burack School
  Brookline High School
  Brookline, Mass.

Judy G. Westerman, Director
  Division of Library and Media Services
  Pittsburgh Public Schools
  Pittsburgh, Pa.

DIRECTIONS FOR USE OF THE CATALOG

Senior High School Library Catalog is arranged in four parts: Part 1. Classified Catalog; Part 2. Author, Title, Subject, and Analytical Index; Part 3. Select List of Recommended CD-ROM Reference Works; Part 4. Directory of Publishers and Distributors.

USES OF THE CATALOG

Senior High School Library Catalog is designed to serve these purposes:

As an aid in purchasing. Information concerning publisher, ISBN, price, and availability, along with the descriptive and evaluative annotations, is intended to assist in the selection and ordering of titles. Arrangement of the Classified Catalog according to the Dewey Decimal Classification expedites the process of identifying elements of the local collection that should be updated or strengthened. A separate section lists recommended reference works published in CD-ROM format. Evaluation of the suitability of a particular work will take into account the special character of the students, the school, and community that the collection serves. It is inadvisable, of course, to rely upon a single source for materials selection.

As a reference aid. Reference work and user service are facilitated by information about sequels and companion volumes, by the descriptive and critical annotations in the Classified Catalog, and by the subject approach in the Index. Analytical entries augment the local catalog by providing access to parts of composite works.

As an aid in verification of information. Full bibliographical data, recommended subject headings based upon *Sears List of Subject Headings,* a suggested classification derived from the *Abridged Dewey Decimal Classification and Relative Index,* and notes that describe publication history and available editions are provided.

As an aid in curriculum support. The classified approach, subject indexing, and annotations are helpful in identifying materials appropriate for classroom use.

As an aid in collection maintenance. In addition to recently published works, the Catalog includes titles listed in the previous edition and its supplements that were reelected because they have retained their usefulness. This information affects decisions to rebind, replace, or discard materials in the local collection.

As an instructional aid. The Catalog supports courses that deal with book selection.

DESCRIPTION OF THE CATALOG
Part 1. Classified Catalog

The Classified Catalog is arranged with the nonfiction books first, classified by the Dewey Decimal Classification in numerical order from 000 to 999. Individual biographies are classed at 92 and follow the 920's (collective biography). Two sections follow the nonfiction: Fiction, denoted by the symbol "Fic," and Story Collections, denoted by "S C."

An Outline of Classification, which serves as a table of contents to the Classified Catalog, is reproduced on page 2. Many books may properly be classified in more than one discipline. If a particular title is not found where it might be expected, the Index should be consulted to determine if the work is classified elsewhere.

Within classes, works are arranged alphabetically under main entry, usually the author. An exception is made for works of individual biography, classed in 92, which are arranged alphabetically under the name of the person written about.

Following is an example of an entry along with a brief description of typical components of entries:

> **Character** above all; ten presidents from FDR
> to George Bush; edited by Robert A. Wilson.
> Simon & Schuster 1996 256p $23; pa $12
>
> **920**
>
> 1. Presidents—United States 2. United States—Politics
> and government—1900-1999 (20th century)
> ISBN 0-684-81411-0; 0-684-82709-3 (pa) LC 95-44827
>
> This is a collection of essays that aims to explore the
> character of ten modern presidents
>
> "The authors of these essays are all historians who have
> written impressive biographies of presidents. . . . Every
> essayist abounds with arch style and cogent insights." Booklist

When a book is entered under title, the first word of the title is printed in bold face type. When the entry is under personal author, the name of the author is inverted and printed in bold face type. Names are given in conformity with *Anglo-American Cataloguing Rules,* 2nd edition, 1988 revision, with 1993 Amendments. The title is followed by the subtitle, responsibility statement, edition, and publisher. For further information about the publisher, refer to the Directory of Publishers and Distributors. Given next are the date of publication, pagination, illustration note, series note, price and binding. Prices stated were current when the Catalog went to press. As time passes they should be confirmed with the publisher.

The figure printed in bold face following the body of the entry is the classification number derived from the *Abridged Dewey Decimal Classification.* Numbered terms are recommended subject headings for the book. In some instances subject headings assigned to the entire book will not show that portions of the book deal with more specific topics. In such cases subject analytic entries are made. An analytic entry under the heading for each of the ten presidents discussed in the sample entry will be found in the Index. All subject headings are based on *Sears List of Subject Headings.*

The ISBN (International Standard Book Number) or ISSN (International Standard Serial Number), which facilitate ordering, and the Library of Congress control (card) number are provided when available.

Notes supply additional information about the book. Most entries include both a note describing the book's content and a critical note, which is useful in evaluating books for selection and in determining which of several works on the same subject is best suited for the individual reader. Other notes describe special features, sequels, companion volumes, editions available, and publication history.

Part 2. Author, Title, Subject, and Analytical Index

The Index is an alphabetical list of all the books entered in the Catalog. Each book is entered under author; title, if distinctive; and subject, with added entries as appropriate. Also included are subject, author, and title analytics for parts of composite works. The classification number in bold face type is the key to the location of the main entry of the book in the Classified Catalog. Works classed in 92, individual biography, will be found under the name of the person written about.

Entries are also made under headings that indicate form or publication characteristics such as "Large print books." Books that are also published in a CD-ROM version are listed under "CD-ROM." The user interested in electronic resources should also consult Part 3, Select List of Recommended CD-ROM Reference Works, for CD-ROMs that do not have a print equivalent.

"See" references are made from forms of names or subjects not used as headings. "See also" references are made to related or more specific headings.

Following are examples of Index entries for the book cited above:

Title	**Character** above all	**920**
Editor	**Wilson, Robert A.**	
	(ed) Character above all. See	
	Character above all	**920**
Subject	**Presidents**	
	United States	
	Character above all	**920**
Subject Analytic	**Truman, Harry S., 1884-1972**	
	See/See also pages in the following books	
	Character above all	**920**

Examples of other types of entries:

Author	**Mitton, Jacqueline**	
	Gems of Hubble	**520**
Joint author	**Maran, Stephen P.**	
	(jt. auth) Mitton, J. Gems of Hubble	
		520
Compiler	**Vail, Ken**	
	(comp) Jazz milestones. See Jazz	
	milestones	**781.65**
Author analytic	**Kingston, Maxine Hong**	
	A sea worry	
	In American dragons: twenty-five	
	Asian American voices p112-17	**810.8**
Title analytic	A sea worry. Kingston, M. H.	
	In American dragons: twenty-five Asian	
	American voices p112-17	**810.8**

Part 3. Select List of Recommended CD-ROM Reference Works

The resources on this list are largely interactive multimedia for which there is no print equivalent. The list is highly selective and is limited to items of superior quality and reference value. Entries in the Classified Catalog for books that are also available in a CD-ROM version contain a note to that effect.

Bibliographic information includes the title, edition, publisher's name and address, date, an indication that the work has sound capability and is in color, and price. A system requirements note and a descriptive annotation follow. Versions, prices and system requirements of electronic media are subject to frequent change and should be checked with the publisher.

Part 4. Directory of Publishers and Distributors

This Directory provides the full name, address, telephone number, and other pertinent information about the publisher or distributor of the books listed.

CONTENTS

PART 1

CLASSIFIED CATALOG

Outline of Classification

Reproduced below is the Second Summary of the Dewey Decimal Classification.* Part 1 of the Catalog is arranged according to this classification, and the outline thus serves as a table of contents for it. Fiction (Fic) and Story collections (S C) have been added at the end of the summary. These sections follow the 999's.

000 Generalities
010 Bibliography
020 Library & information sciences
030 General encyclopedic works
040
050 General serials & their indexes
060 General organizations & museology
070 News media, journalism, publishing
080 General collections
090 Manuscripts & rare books

100 Philosophy & psychology
110 Metaphysics
120 Epistemology, causation, humankind
130 Paranormal phenomena
140 Specific philosophical schools
150 Psychology
160 Logic
170 Ethics (Moral philosophy)
180 Ancient, medieval, Oriental philosophy
190 Modern Western philosophy

200 Religion
210 Natural theology
220 Bible
230 Christian theology
240 Christian moral & devotional theology
250 Christian orders & local church
260 Christian social theology
270 Christian church history
280 Christian denominations & sects
290 Other & comparative religions

300 Social sciences
310 General statistics
320 Political science
330 Economics
340 Law
350 Public administration
360 Social services; association
370 Education
380 Commerce, communications, transport
390 Customs, etiquette, folklore

400 Language
410 Linguistics
420 English & Old English
430 Germanic languages   German
440 Romance languages   French
450 Italian, Romanian, Rhaeto-Romanic
460 Spanish & Portuguese languages
470 Italic languages   Latin
480 Hellenic languages   Classical Greek
490 Other languages

500 Natural sciences & mathematics
510 Mathematics
520 Astronomy & allied sciences
530 Physics
540 Chemistry & allied sciences
550 Earth sciences
560 Paleontology   Paleozoology
570 Life sciences
580 Botanical sciences
590 Zoological sciences

600 Technology (Applied sciences)
610 Medical sciences   Medicine
620 Engineering & allied operations
630 Agriculture
640 Home economics & family living
650 Management & auxiliary services
660 Chemical engineering
670 Manufacturing
680 Manufacture for specific uses
690 Buildings

700 The arts
710 Civic & landscape art
720 Architecture
730 Plastic arts   Sculpture
740 Drawing & decorative arts
750 Painting & paintings
760 Graphic arts   Printmaking & prints
770 Photography & photographs
780 Music
790 Recreational & performing arts

800 Literature & rhetoric
810 American literature in English
820 English & Old English literatures
830 Literatures of Germanic languages
840 Literatures of Romance languages
850 Italian, Romanian, Rhaeto-Romanic
860 Spanish & Portuguese literatures
870 Italic literatures   Latin
880 Hellenic literatures   Classical Greek
890 Literatures of other languages

900 Geography & history
910 Geography & travel
920 Biography, genealogy, insignia
930 History of ancient world
940 General history of Europe
950 General history of Asia   Far East
960 General history of Africa
970 General history of North America
980 General history of South America
990 General history of other areas

Fic Fiction
S C Story collections

* Reproduced from Edition 12 of the Dewey Decimal Classification, published in 1990, by permission of Forest Press, a division of OCLC Online Computer Library Center, owner of copyright.

SENIOR HIGH SCHOOL LIBRARY CATALOG
FIFTEENTH EDITION
CLASSIFIED CATALOG

000 GENERALITIES

001.3 Humanities

The **Columbia** dictionary of modern literary and cultural criticism; Joseph Childers and Gary Hentzi, general editors. Columbia Univ. Press 1995 362p $49.50; pa $19.50 **001.3**
1. Humanities—Dictionaries 2. Criticism—Dictionaries
ISBN 0-231-07242-2; 0-231-07243-0 (pa)
LC 94-42535
"The more than 450 definitions in this book are aimed at helping those not formally trained in theory or criticism. The definitions clarify key terms, chiefly in structuralism, semiotics, and post-structuralism. . . . Useful cross references enable the reader to explore related concepts, as do references to key sources at the end of entries." Libr J
For a fuller review see: Booklist, June 1, 1995

001.4 Research. Grants, prizes, scholarships

Student contact book; how to find low-cost, expert information on today's issues for: term papers, debates, research projects, and more! Annette Novallo, editor; Joyce Jakubiak and Joseph M. Palmisano, associate editors. Gale Res. 1993 xxviii, 657p il pa $35 **001.4**
1. Research 2. Associations—Directories 3. Information services—Directories
ISBN 0-8103-8876-6
"Designed to help novice researchers, this volume offers two types of resources: access to 'live' information via interviews with people at organizations and individual experts, and access to publications. It lists over 800 organizations that answer inquiries and offer free or low-cost publications, as well as more than 200 professional rosters and other directories that will connect students to experts." SLJ

001.9 Controversial knowledge

Aaseng, Nathan, 1953-
Science versus pseudoscience. Watts 1994 144p il lib bdg $22.70 **001.9**
1. Science
ISBN 0-531-11182-2
LC 93-30014
"An Impact book"

After identifying ten characteristics of science the author discusses ESP, near-death experiences, miracle cures, creationism, astrology, UFO's and other pseudosciences
Includes bibliography

Bryan, C. D. B. (Courtlandt Dixon Barnes)
Close encounters of the fourth kind; alien abduction, UFOs, and the conference at M.I.T. Knopf 1995 476p $25 **001.9**
1. Unidentified flying objects
ISBN 0-679-42975-1
Also available in paperback from Penguin Bks.
This is an "account of a five-day conference on UFO abductions held at the Massachusetts Institute of Technology in 1992." Publ Wkly
"Bryan is a conscientious and objective journalist, carefully guiding the reader through the pros, cons, and complexities of this bizarre, otherworldly topic." Booklist

Clark, Jerome
Encyclopedia of strange and unexplained physical phenomena. Gale Res. 1993 xxvi, 395p il $60 **001.9**
1. Science 2. Curiosities and wonders
ISBN 0-8103-8843-X
LC 93-16958
"In his introduction, Clark places topics such as Big Foot, crop circles, sea serpents, unidentified flying objects, the Loch Ness Monster, and the Yeti into scientific and sociological context. . . . The book is arranged alphabetically by topic and includes noted investigators, societies, and cross references." Libr J
"Young adults and adults with an interest in physical anomalies will find this to be a very complete source of information about common and little known occurrences." Voice Youth Advocates

Earth energies; by the editors of Time-Life Books. Time-Life Bks. 1991 144p il (Mysteries of the unknown) $9.95 **001.9**
1. Parapsychology 2. Earth 3. Nature
LC 90-20666
Text and numerous illustrations survey spirituality based on the natural world. Among the topics discussed are grain circles, the power of trees and the art of Feng Shui
Includes bibliography

O'Neill, Catherine, 1950-
Amazing mysteries of the world. National Geographic Soc. 1983 101p il maps $12.50; lib bdg $12.50 **001.9**
1. Curiosities and wonders
ISBN 0-87044-497-2; 0-87044-502-2 (lib bdg)
LC 83-13444
"Books for world explorers"
Discusses such mystifying phenomena as the auroras, black holes, and Bigfoot
"The first chapter makes it clear that the book explains how scientists continually search for answers to the world's mysteries. The pictures, an outstanding feature of the book, are well labeled and explained. A thorough index and a list of additional reading materials round out the volume." SLJ

Reader's Digest mysteries of the unexplained. Reader's Digest Assn. 1983 c1982 320p il maps $35 **001.9**
1. Curiosities and wonders
ISBN 0-89577-146-2
LC 82-60791
"Covering the gamut from prophecies to UFOs, most of the accounts in this large-format book have appeared elsewhere, but here they are presented in an attractive 'Digest' format. A couple of redeeming features make this book stand out from others that attempt to do much the same thing: First, the source material for every item is listed with the item itself; second, the book contains an excellent index." Libr J
Includes bibliography

Ritchie, David, 1952-
UFO; the definitive guide to unidentified flying objects and related phenomena. Facts on File 1994 264p il maps $40 **001.9**
1. Unidentified flying objects
ISBN 0-8160-2894-X
LC 93-31037
"Arranged in alphabetical order by subject, the entries include accounts of UFO sightings, both unexplained and hoaxes. Also included are other phenomena such as the appearance of the Virgin Mary at Fatima and accounts of encounters with demons by early church writers. . . . Ritchie's work is an interesting interpretation of some very puzzling phenomena." Booklist

Sagan, Carl, 1934-1996
The demon-haunted world; science as a candle in the dark. Random House 1996 457p $25.95; pa $14 **001.9**
1. Science
ISBN 0-394-53512-X; 0-345-40946-9 (pa)
LC 95-34076
"Using basic tools of science—empiricism, rationalism, and experimentation—Sagan debunks . . . common fallacies of pseudoscience. In doing so, he speculates as to how such beliefs arise." Libr J
Sagan "links today's aliens with yesterday's demons in this lithe, well-supported, sometimes quite wry, and altogether refreshing performance." Booklist
Includes bibliographical references

Stein, Gordon
Encyclopedia of hoaxes; foreword by Martin Gardner. Gale Res. 1993 xxi, 347p il $55 **001.9**
1. Impostors and imposture 2. Errors
ISBN 0-8103-8414-0
"Several hundred hoaxes are arranged here under such subjects as archaeology, business, education, history, law, literature, photography, and travel. . . . Hoaxes as old as the Piltdown Man and as recent as Milli Vanilli are described. . . . For secondary school and public library reference collections." Booklist

002   The book

Olmert, Michael
The Smithsonian book of books. Smithsonian Bks. 1992 319p il $49.95 **002**
1. Books—History
ISBN 0-89599-030-X
LC 91-39590
Topics covered in this heavily illustrated work include the history of books and manuscripts, "the evolution of the printing industry, libraries, medieval illumination and modern illustration, the book trade (including book fairs and bookstores), problems with bookworms, . . . and methods of conservation." Libr J

003   Systems

Lampton, Christopher
Science of chaos. Watts 1992 126p il lib bdg $22 **003**
1. Chaos (Science) 2. Computers
ISBN 0-531-12513-0
LC 91-40896
"A Venture book"
A discussion of a scientific theory, formed with the help of computers, which proposes the existence of patterns and order in the seeming chaos and unpredictability of the physical world
"Here is a book that deals logically and carefully with the concept of cause-and-effect as it occurs in the world of science. . . . All things considered, this book is far more than the simple 'let's make a science project' book. It is an adult approach to the world of physics in both a real and an academic sense." Voice Youth Advocates
Includes bibliographical references

Peak, David
Chaos under control; the art and science of complexity; [by] David Peak, Michael Frame. Freeman, W.H. 1994 408p il pa $24.95 **003**
1. Chaos (Science)
ISBN 0-7167-2429-4
LC 94-3092
This overview of the science of complex systems examines fractals, chaos, the Butterfly Effect, self-organization and emergent properties and connects them to other areas of intellectual pursuit in the arts and humanities
Includes bibliographical references

004 Data processing. Computer science

Barron, Ann E.

The Internet and instruction; activities and ideas; [by] Ann E. Barron, Karen S. Ivers. Libraries Unlimited 1996 159p il pa $26.50   **004**
1. Internet (Computer network) 2. Computer assisted instruction
ISBN 1-56308-331-0   LC 95-46690

This resource "provides instructional ideas and guidelines for integration of the Internet into the research process, curriculum, and the classroom. . . . Detailed graphics and configurations enhance the text, which is interspersed with Internet addresses . . . and further references. Content areas are the focus of chapters on the curricula of science and mathematics, language arts, social studies and geography, music and art; provided are a plethora of motivational activities, e-mail exchanges, reproducible lesson plans and masters—cutting across interdisciplinary lines and readily-adaptable to all grade levels." Voice Youth Advocates

Billings, Charlene W., 1941-

Supercomputers; shaping the future. Facts on File 1995 132p il (Facts on File science sourcebooks) $17.95   **004**
1. Supercomputers
ISBN 0-8160-3096-0   LC 94-44111

This work gives "a brief overview of computer development and [focuses] on the megamachines that are the fastest and most powerful computers in the world. Billings details several special projects involving weather, medicine, astronomy, and other realms, explaining how supercomputers can be used to simulate and test research designs. . . . [This book] will provide valuable information for student projects and papers." Booklist
Includes glossary and bibliography

Campbell-Kelly, Martin

Computer; a history of the information machine; [by] Martin Campbell Kelly and William Aspray. Basic Bks. 1996 342p il $28; pa $15   **004**
1. Computers 2. Electronic data processing
ISBN 0-465-02989-2; 0-465-02990-6 (pa)
    LC 96-2098

"The authors trace an unbroken line from the typewriters, adding and record-keeping machines of 1890s America to today's business-oriented computers. They tell how English mathematician Charles Babbage's failed dream of building his 'Analytical Engine,' a full-scale calculator, in the 1830s was realized a century later when IBM built the first fully automatic computing machine at Harvard University." Publ Wkly

"Focusing on Americans and U.S. companies (the dominant players), the book is easily read and highly informative. Terms are clearly defined and examples clearly drawn, with up-to-date bibliographical references." Libr J

Consumer

reports guide to personal computers; [by] Olen R. Pearson and the editors of Consumer Reports Books. Consumer Repts. Bks. il pa $8.95   **004**
1. Microcomputers

Annual. First published 1990 with title: Personal computer buying guide

This guide provides tips on: assessing your computer needs; shopping for the right computer; figuring out software and hardware requirements; becoming computer literate. Brand-name ratings of desktop computers, software for children, monitors and printers are included

CyberHound's

guide to Internet databases. Gale Res. $99   **004**
1. Internet (Computer network)—Directories
ISSN 1081-2385

Annual. First published 1995 with title: Gale guide to Internet databases. Editors vary

This "guide attempts to identify and describe . . . domestic and international databases that reach a broad audience over the Internet. Entries are arranged alphabetically, with detailed access and retrieval information. . . . Entries are copiously annotated and provide details of database content and scope. A variety of indexing makes this work more useful than most in finding relevant databases." Libr J [review of 1995 edition]

Downing, Douglas

Dictionary of computer and Internet terms; [by] Douglas A. Downing, Michael A. Covington, Melody Mauldin Covington. Barron's Educ. Ser. il pa $9.95   **004**
1. Computers—Dictionaries 2. Internet (Computer network)

First published 1986 with title: Dictionary of computer terms. (5th edition 1996) Frequently revised

This work defines approximately 1,700 computer terms. Topics explained "include finding information with search tools on the Web, creating a home page with HTML, communicating via e-mail, tuning in to multimedia applications, and the technical details involved in connecting a computer with a modem to other computers and the Internet." Publisher's note

Freedman, Alan

The computer glossary; the complete illustrated dictionary. AMACOM il pa $24.95   **004**
1. Computers—Dictionaries 2. Electronic data processing—Dictionaries

First published by Computer Language Co. (7th edition, 1995) Periodically revised

This work contains more than 5,300 computer terms, abbreviations, and acronyms. Topics covered include: systems design, programming, communications, LANs, computer graphics, desktop publishing, multimedia, PCs, Macintoshes and workstations

Gates, Bill, 1955-

The road ahead; [by] Bill Gates with Nathan Myhrvold, and Peter Rinearson. Viking 1995 286p il $29.95; pa $15.95   **004**
 1. Microsoft Corporation 2. Information networks 3. Computer industry 4. Telecommunication
ISBN 0-670-77289-5; 0-14-026040-4 (pa)
         LC 95-43803
Includes multimedia CD-ROM
 Gates discusses his career as cofounder and chairperson of Microsoft Corporation and presents speculations on the role of information networks in the future
 "Although many of Gates's predictions are not new, readers will find the book thought-provoking as well as entertaining." Christ Sci Monit

Guide to free computer materials. Educators Progress Service, 214 Center St., Randolph, WI 53956 pa $38.95   **004**
 1. Computer software 2. Free material
Annual. First published 1983
 "Some 250 free computer brochures, programs, booklets, demonstration software, and catalogs are listed in each annual. The materials, classified according to type or field (e.g., hardware, software, systems, business, communications), are nonevaluative. Indexed by title, subject, and source." Nichols. Guide to Ref Books for Sch Media Cent. 4th edition

The **Information** highway; Charles P. Cozic, book editor. Greenhaven Press 1996 208p (Current controversies) lib bdg $19.95; pa $11.95 **004**
 1. Internet (Computer network) 2. Telecommunication
ISBN 1-56510-375-0 (lib bdg); 1-56510-374-2 (pa)
         LC 95-35486
 The first topic in this volume "attempts to define the 'information highway.' The others explain how to develop it, whether it's good or bad for society, and whether and how to regulate it." SLJ
 "Students writing research papers, involved in debates, or simply interested in the topic will find this offering in the Current Controversies series an invaluable resource." Booklist
Includes bibliographical references

Internet connections; a librarian's guide to dial-up access and use; [by] Mary E. Engle [et al.] [2nd ed] American Lib. Assn. 1995 268p il pa $24
          004
 1. Internet (Computer network) 2. Library information networks
ISBN 0-8389-7793-6   LC 95-18790
First published 1993
 This guide gives an overview of the Internet; a list of dial-up service providers and their services; and information on Internet resources and applications, including Telnet and WWW. Appendices list electronic serials, library-oriented listservs, and Internet organizations
Includes bibliography

Margolis, Philip E.

Random House personal computer dictionary. 2nd ed. Random House 1996 xxi, 528p il pa $15
          004
 1. Microcomputers—Dictionaries
ISBN 0-679-76424-0   LC 95-45508
Also available with computer disk for Windows pa $24.95
First published 1991
 "The rapid growth of the computer industry and its role in our lives has prompted this . . . dictionary of computerese. Margolis includes 28 tables, 86 figures, plenty of cross-references, and more than 1,900 terms, making this book utterly indispensable." Booklist

McGraw-Hill encyclopedia of personal computing; Stan Gibilisco, editor in chief. McGraw-Hill 1995 1216p il $89.95 **004**
 1. Microcomputers—Dictionaries
ISBN 0-07-023718-2   LC 95-17260
 This guide to terms and phrases associated with personal computing "is arranged in alphabetical order from Abscissa to Zooming. . . . Line drawings illustrate many entries. . . . An appendix lists abbreviations and acronyms with their meanings. . . . This is a welcome addition to computer reference collections and a highly recommended purchase for all libraries, high school and up." Booklist

Miller, Elizabeth B.

The Internet resource directory for K-12 teachers and librarians. Libraries Unlimited pa $25
          004
 1. Internet (Computer network) 2. Information systems—Directories
Annual. First published 1994 for 1994-1995
 This directory "provides details on accessing more than 400 discussion groups, electronic books and newspapers, lesson plans, and a variety of other teaching resources by E-mail, gopher, telnet, and FTP. . . . The directory proper is arranged under broad curricular areas plus resources for educators, reference, and school library media applications. Each of these is further divided by narrower disciplines. . . . Recommended for all school library media centers." Booklist

Stoll, Clifford

Silicon snake oil; second thoughts on the information highway. Doubleday 1995 247p hardcover o.p. paperback available $14 **004**
 1. Computers and civilization 2. Internet (Computer network) 3. Information science
ISBN 0-385-41994-5 (pa)   LC 95-2537
 In this critique of the information highway the author contends that "virtual reality is no substitute for the real thing; computers alter our thinking processes; they isolate us and minimize social interactions; they are expensive and difficult to use; and they become obsolete in a few years. The Internet is a disorganized waste land, and E-mail isn't as good as the U.S. Postal Service. In chapter 11, Stoll expresses fear for the future of libraries." Booklist

Using the Internet, online services & CD-ROMS for writing research and term papers; edited by Charles Harmon. Neal-Schuman 1996 167p il (Neal-Schuman net-guide series) pa $29.95
004
1. Report writing 2. Dissertations 3. Research 4. CD-ROM 5. Internet (Computer network)
ISBN 1-555-70238-4   LC 95-51155
"A step-by-step guide on how to research and write a paper using only electronic resources. Harmon examines potential resources, such as electronic indexes, CD-ROMs, and the Internet; he also goes into the complete research process from formulating a thesis to finding and evaluating online sources to notetaking and preparing the final copy. The author ends with a valuable chapter on how to cite the various forms of electronic resources in notes and in a bibliography." SLJ

Webster's New World dictionary of computer terms; compiled by Donald Spencer. Macmillan pa $9.95   **004**
1. Computers—Dictionaries 2. Electronic data processing—Dictionaries
First edition compiled by Laura Darcy and Louise Boston published 1983 by Simon & Schuster. (5th edition 1994) Frequently revised
This dictionary defines "more than 5,000 of the most frequently used computer terms. Headwords range from 'A: drive' to 'zooming,' with almost any conceivable computer-related term in between. . . . A useful desk reference for all levels of readers." Choice [review of 1992 edition]

006   Special computer methods

Weiss, Ann E., 1943-
Virtual reality; a door to cyberspace. 21st Cent. Bks. (NY) 1996 128p il lib bdg $17.98   **006**
1. Virtual reality
ISBN 0-8050-3722-5   LC 95-34444
The author offers an "introduction to the emerging virtual reality technology and examines the various approaches to a computer-generated dimension. She questions what actually constitutes virtual reality. . . . She provides examples of current applications of virtual reality in fields from medicine to the military and the predominance of entertainment-related research and development. She also probes the dark side of virtual reality raising questions about its possible promotion of violence, mind control, and threat to social interaction." Voice Youth Advocates
"This title is useful and interesting for both reports and general reading." SLJ
Includes bibliography

006.6   Computer graphics

Dillon, Patrick M.
Multimedia technology from A to Z; by Patrick M. Dillon and David C. Leonard. Oryx Press 1995 xxvii, 225p pa $25   **006.6**
1. Multimedia systems
ISBN 0-89774-892-1   LC 94-37853
"More than 1,000 terms pertaining to multimedia are defined in this . . . resource. An introduction attempts to explain what is encompassed in the term 'multimedia.'. . . Each alphabetical segment begins with a quotation pertaining to multimedia, communication, and/or technology. Abbreviations are defined, as well as words and phrases. Definitions are short and nontechnical." Book Rep

Multi-media; the complete guide. DK Pub. 1996 192p il $24.95   **006.6**
1. Multimedia systems
ISBN 0-7894-0422-2   LC 95-30090
This guide "explains the hardware, software, and industry driving the complex combination of multimedia technologies. The volume's five chapters describe, in turn, the wide variety of software and applications, such as CD-ROM encyclopedias and 3-D programs; the basics of personal computers; the historical developments that led to today's capabilities; the human side of the technology and the development of a product that includes animation, video, and sound; and the Internet capabilities for multimedia. Appended to the book are a listing of distributors of the products mentioned, an index, and a glossary." Sci Books Films

011   General bibliographies

American reference books annual. Libraries Unlimited $95   **011**
1. Reference books—Bibliography 2. Reference books—Reviews
ISSN 0065-9959
Five-year cumulative index available for 1990-1994
Annual. First published 1970
Editor: 1970- Bohdan S. Wynar
"Each issue covers the reference book output (including reprints) of the previous year (i.e., the 1970 volume covers 1969 publications). Offers descriptive and evaluative notes (many of them signed by contributors), with references to selected reviews. Classed arrangement; author-subject-title index." Guide to Ref Books. 11th edition

Guide to reference books; edited by Robert Balay; associate editor, Vee Friesner Carrington; with special editorial assistance by Murray S. Martin. 11th ed. American Lib. Assn. 1996 xxvii, 2020p $275   **011**
1. Reference books—Bibliography
ISBN 0-8389-0669-9   LC 95-26322
First published 1902
Nearly 16,000 entries provide details on general reference works and on reference books in the humanities, so-

Guide to reference books—*Continued*

cial and behavioral sciences, history and area studies, and science, technology, and medicine. Electronic resources are included

For a review see: Booklist, May 1, 1996

Magazines for libraries; for the general reader and school, junior college, college, university, and public libraries; [edited by] Bill Katz and Linda Sternberg Katz. Bowker $155   **011**

1. Periodicals—Bibliography

ISSN 0000-0914

First published 1969. (8th edition 1995) Frequently revised

"Annotated classified guide to recommended periodicals for the general reader and school, college, and public libraries. Provides comparative evaluations and grade- and age-level recommendations for all periodicals included." N Y Public Libr. Book of How & Where to Look It Up

The Reader's adviser. Bowker 6v ea $110; set $500   **011**

1. Books and reading—Best books 2. Literature—Bio-bibliography 3. Reference books—Bibliography

ISSN 0094-5943

Also available CD-ROM version

First published 1921 with title: The Bookman's manual. Title varies. (14th edition 1994) Frequently revised

Contents: v1 The best in reference books, British literature, and American literature; v2 The best in world literature; v3 The best in social sciences, history, and the arts; v4 The best in philosophy and religion; v5 The best in science, technology, and medicine; v6 Indexes

"Designed primarily for the bookseller and librarian, this is an up-to-date, standard work useful in any library." Sheehy. Guide to Ref Books. 10th edition

Recommended reference books for small and medium-sized libraries and media centers. Libraries Unlimited $45   **011**

1. Reference books—Bibliography 2. Reference books—Reviews

ISSN 0277-5948

Annual. First published 1981

Editor: 1981- Bohdan S. Wynar

Each annual volume includes reviews of about 550 titles chosen by the editor as the most valuable reference titles published during the previous year

"Where budget restrictions are a consideration, this is an invaluable asset; for small libraries, a superior selection/acquisitions tool. Highly recommended." Voice Youth Advocates

Words on cassette. Bowker 2v set $149.95   **011**

1. Sound recordings—Bibliography

Annual. First published 1992 in one volume. Formed by the merger of On cassette and Words on tape

This work "lists spoken-word audiocassettes in many and varied subject areas. . . . Information on each includes reader's name, author, title, playing time, number of cassettes, purchase/rental price, order number, and publisher. Many titles have an annotation." Nichols. Guide to Ref Books for Sch Media Cent. 4th edition

011.6   General bibliographies of works for specific kinds of users

Best books for senior high readers; John T. Gillespie, editor. Bowker 1991 931p $55   **011.6**

1. Young adults' literature—Bibliography 2. Books and reading—Best books

ISBN 0-8352-3021-X   LC 91-26666

"This volume annotates material appropriate for grades 10-12 (ages 15-18). . . . 10,805 titles are mentioned in 9,979 annotated entries. . . . Entries include author, title, grade level, publication date, publisher, price, and ISBN. Annotations of a sentence or two describe the book. Each entry concludes with the Dewey classification number; some cite reviews." Booklist

Books for you; an annotated booklist for senior high school students. National Council of Teachers of English (NCTE bibliography series) pa $21.95   **011.6**

1. Young adults' literature—Bibliography 2. Books and reading—Best books

ISSN 1051-4740

First published 1945. (1995 edition) Frequently revised. Editors vary

This bibliography of over 1,000 titles is arranged by subject into 35 thematic chapters. More than 150 titles of multicultural interest are included. Each entry provides bibliographic information, a summary of contents, and mention of any awards the book has won. Includes a publisher's directory

Criscoe, Betty L., 1940-

Award-winning books for children and young adults. Scarecrow Press 1990-1993 2v v1 $37.50; v2 $79.50   **011.6**

1. Literary prizes 2. Children's literature—Bibliography 3. Young adults' literature—Bibliography 4. Books and reading—Best books

ISBN 0-8108-2336-5 (v1); 0-8108-2597-X (v2)

Volume one covers the year 1989; volume two covers the years 1990-1991

An alphabetical listing of awards giving "the name and address of the sponsoring organization, information about the award and its history, [an] annotation of the book or description of the individual's achievements, and a picture of the book's cover or of the award winner." Booklist

"A valuable selection tool. . . . For small libraries unable to afford more than one or two reviewing periodicals or journals, this is worth careful consideration." SLJ

Magazines for young people; [edited] by Bill Katz and Linda Sternberg Katz. 2nd ed. Bowker 1991 361p $38   **011.6**

1. Periodicals—Bibliography

ISBN 0-8352-3009-0

First published 1987 with title: Magazines for school libraries

"This guide evaluates over 1,100 magazines appropriate for preschool through high school levels. The titles include curriculum-related periodicals, others of general interest, and professional journals directed toward educa-

Magazines for young people—*Continued*
tors. An introduction and core list of titles preface each of the 60 subject areas. Entries contain the beginning year of publication; frequency; cost; address; presence of illustrations, advertising, and an index; circulation; availability in other formats; indexing elsewhere; inclusion of book reviews; and suggested library level. The evaluations indicate strength, weaknesses, and political bias." Nichols. Guide to Ref Books for Sch Media Cent. 4th edition

Middle and junior high school library catalog; edited by Anne Price and Juliette Yaakov; editorial staff: John Greenfieldt [et al.] 7th ed. Wilson, H.W. 1995 988p $175   **011.6**
1. Classified catalogs 2. School libraries—Catalogs
ISBN 0-8242-0880-3   LC 95-38272
"Standard catalog series"
First published 1965 with title: Junior high school library catalog
Kept up to date by annual supplements which are included in price of main volume
Expanding its coverage to include material for the middle grades, the seventh edition of the catalog includes 4,224 titles and nearly 5,000 analytical entries of books for the middle school grades through grade nine. Entries contain full bibliographic information, Dewey Decimal Classification number, subject headings, descriptive, and when available, critical annotations

Miller-Lachmann, Lyn, 1956-
Our family, our friends, our world; an annotated guide to significant multicultural books for children and teenagers. Bowker 1992 710p il $49.95   **011.6**
1. Children's literature—Bibliography 2. Young adults' literature—Bibliography 3. Minorities—Bibliography
ISBN 0-8352-3025-2   LC 91-24549
This is an annotated guide to some 1,000 books for children and teens, published between 1970 and 1990, "that focus on cultures, identities, and histories of minority groups in the U.S. and Canada as well as cultures from the rest of the world." Booklist
"With its clear and informative background information, convenient format, and extensive scope, this book is a valuable tool—a must for every professional collection that supports a collection of literature for young people." Voice Youth Advocates

New York Public Library
Books for the teen age. New York Public Lib. pa $6   **011.6**
1. Young adults' literature—Bibliography 2. Books and reading—Best books
Annual. First published 1929
A list of some 1,250 books of interest to teenagers arranged in broad categories. Many of the titles address current concerns

Outstanding books for the college bound; choices for a generation; [pub. in assn. with] Young Adult Library Services Association; Marjorie Lewis, editor. American Lib. Assn. 1996 217p pa $22   **011.6**
1. College students 2. Books and reading—Best books
ISBN 0-8389-3456-0   LC 96-5086
Supersedes the compilation with same title published 1984
This "bibliography brings together all the books chosen between 1959 and 1994 by the specially appointed YALSA committees. More than 1,000 books are arranged by genre (the arts, biography, fiction, nonfiction, now/current, and poetry), with brief reader annotations; they are then arranged by year of appearance on the list (just author and title here)." Booklist
"For young people who want to prepare for college in an increasingly competitive environment, this list can serve as a road map to people, places and things that they want to know more about, or where they don't feel confident." Voice Youth Advocates

Rochman, Hazel
Against borders; promoting books for a multicultural world. American Lib. Assn. 1993 288p il pa $25   **011.6**
1. Young adults' literature—Bibliography 2. Books and reading 3. Multiculturalism—Bibliography 4. Minorities—Bibliography
ISBN 0-8389-0601-X   LC 93-17840
"Starting with her personal immigrant's journey from South Africa to the U.S., Rochman's essays focus on using books across cultures. The second part of the book is made up of bibliographies—many of them updated and expanded from *Booklist*—on specific ethnic groups and cultural issues." Booklist
"The subject access by ethnic group and nationality will prove useful for doing reader's advisory work as well as developing units on ethnic and cultural identity." SLJ

Totten, Herman L., 1938-
Culturally diverse library collections for youth; [by] Herman L. Totten, Carolyn Garner, Risa W. Brown. Neal-Schuman 1996 220p pa $35   **011.6**
1. Minorities—Bibliography 2. Young adults' literature—Bibliography
ISBN 1-55570-141-8   LC 96-1020
This volume includes "books and videos about African American, Hispanic, Asian, and Native American cultures. Nonfiction, biography, folk tales, reference books, and scholarly works are covered. Each title is annotated with full bibliographic data and suggested ages and grades. Relevant adult ethnic books are also evaluated for use in school." Publisher's note
For a review see: Booklist, Oct. 15, 1996

The Young adult reader's adviser; general editor, Myra Immell; consulting editor, Marion Sader. Bowker 1992 2v il set $79.95   **011.6**
1. Young adults' literature—Bibliography 2. Books and reading—Best books
ISBN 0-8352-3068-6   LC 92-3232
A junior companion volume to The Reader's adviser, entered in class 011

The Young adult reader's adviser—*Continued*

Contents: v1 The best in literature and language arts, mathematics and computer science; v2 The best in social sciences and history, science and health

This reference work "parallels the courses of study in American schools and closely follows the needs of curricula. It's a bibliographic tool, a critical compendium, and a biographical encyclopedia. . . . Full bibliographic information is included." SLJ

Zvirin, Stephanie

The best years of their lives; a resource guide for teenagers in crisis. 2nd ed. American Lib. Assn. 1996 154p il pa $25   **011.6**

1. Adolescence—Bibliography

ISBN 0-8389-0686-9   LC 96-14446

First published 1992

A selective, annotated bibliography of fiction, non-fiction and video self-help works for teenagers. Topics addressed include: pregnancy, suicide, sexual abuse, learning disabilities, sexuality, violence, safety and health

"Highly recommended; an essential purchase for all public libraries and school libraries serving youth aged ten to eighteen." J Youth Serv Libr

015.73 Bibliographies and catalogs of works issued or printed in the United States

Books in print. Bowker 9v set $510   **015.73**

1. Bibliography

ISSN 0068-0214

Also available CD-ROM version Books in print plus

Annual. First published 1948

Updated by Books in print Supplement (3v) published annually in Spring, available at $260 (ISSN 0000-0310)

Contents: v1-4 Authors; v5-8 Titles; v9 Publishers

Lists titles available during the current year from American publishers, supplying such information as authors, co-authors, title, price, publisher, year of publication, and International Standard Book Numbers of cooperating publishers

Kelly, Melody S.

Using government documents; a how-to-do it manual for school librarians. Neal-Schuman 1992 160p (How-to-do-it manuals for school and public librarians) $32.50   **015.73**

1. Government publications—United States—Bibliography

ISBN 1-55570-106-X   LC 92-11729

"The body of the text is a listing of recommended documents for school libraries, organized by curricular headings such as English Language Arts, Social Studies, and Mathematics, subdivided by school level." SLJ

This volume "contains a wealth of information for elementary, middle, and high school librarians which will allow them to build extensive and relatively inexpensive sets of materials available from a wide range of federal agencies and departments." Voice Youth Advocates

Subject guide to Books in print. Bowker 5v set $369.95   **015.73**

1. Subject catalogs 2. Bibliography

ISSN 0000-0159

Also available on CD-ROM as part of Books in print plus

Annual. First published 1957

This companion publication to Books in print, lists titles currently available from United States publishers indexing them under LC subject headings

United States. Superintendent of Documents

U.S. Government books; publications for sale by the Government Printing Office. U.S. Govt. Ptg. Office gratis   **015.73**

1. Government publications—United States—Bibliography

First published 1982. Issued irregularly

This catalog contains annotations of hundreds of currently available Government publications, organized into subject categories. Each entry includes date, pages, GPO stock number, and price

Vertical file index; guide to pamphlets and references to current topics. Wilson, H.W. pa $50 per year   **015.73**

1. Pamphlets—Bibliography 2. Pamphlets—Indexes

ISSN 0042-4439

First published 1932 with title: Vertical file service catalog. Issued monthly except August

"A list of free and inexpensive pamphlets, booklets, leaflets, and similar material considered to be of interest to general libraries. Subjects range from those suitable for school libraries to specialized technical reports. Arranged alphabetically by subject headings (deemed suitable for vertical file use) with title index." Guide to Ref Books. 11th edition

016 Bibliographies and catalogs of works on specific subjects or in specific disciplines

Kister, Kenneth F., 1935-

Kister's best encyclopedias; a comparative guide to general and specialized encyclopedias. 2nd ed. Oryx Press 1994 506p $50.25   **016**

1. Encyclopedias and dictionaries—Bibliography

ISBN 0-89774-744-5   LC 94-11282

First published 1986 with title: Best encyclopedias

"An excellent source that surveys and evaluates more than 1,000 encyclopedias, both print and electronic. While the emphasis is on works in English, major foreign-language encyclopedias are covered as well. Includes a title/topic index and a directory of publishers and distributors." Guide to Ref Books. 11th edition

Includes bibliographical references

Miller-Lachmann, Lyn, 1956-
Global voices, global visions; a core collection of multicultural books. Bowker 1995 xxxv, 870p maps $55   **016**
1. Culture—Bibliography 2. Multiculturalism—Bibliography 3. Modern civilization—Bibliography
ISBN 0-8352-3291-3   LC 95-36829
This volume contains annotations of some "1,700 recommended works on multicultural topics for adults and mature high-school students dealing with ethnic groups from all regions of the world. Arranged by region, each of the 15 chapters contains a map and a signed introduction to the literature of the area. This is followed by the bibliography arranged in subdivisions of fiction, drama, and poetry; nonfiction; and biography." Booklist
"This book is written for an adult audience but it is a valuable resource for high school teachers and librarians who want to find titles that will provide a realistic look at minorities in the United States and cultures around the world." Voice Youth Advocates

016.3054 Bibliographies of women

Bauermeister, Erica
500 great books by women; a reader's guide; [by] Erica Bauermeister, Jesse Larsen, and Holly Smith. Penguin Bks. 1994 425p pa $12.95
                                         016.3054
1. Women—Bibliography 2. Women authors—Bibliography
ISBN 0-14-017590-3   LC 94-15989
"Representing diverse voices and cultures ranging from the thirteenth century to the contemporary period, the 500 works by women recommended in this guide are those that the compilers 'found to be thought-provoking, beautiful, and satisfying.' Among the selections are works by Aphra Behn, Jane Austen, Marguerite Duras, Barbara Tuchman, Gail Godwin, and Amy Tan. To be considered for inclusion, books had to be written in prose, available in English, and in print." Booklist

016.3058 Bibliographies of racial, ethnic, national groups

Glover, Denise Marie
Voices of the spirit; sources for interpreting the African-American experience; [by] Denise M. Glover. American Lib. Assn. 1995 211p pa $28
                                         016.3058
1. African Americans—History—Bibliography
ISBN 0-8389-0639-7   LC 94-29139
"This annotated bibliography on African American history includes several types of resources, including books, traveling exhibits available from the Smithsonian Institution, and videotapes. Classic works by nineteenth-century pioneers in African American history are listed, as well as those by . . . contemporary scholars. . . . [This work] will be useful in school media centers and community college libraries; public libraries will want a copy, too." Booklist

Williams, Helen Elizabeth, 1933-
Books by African-American authors and illustrators for children and young adults. American Lib. Assn. 1991 270p $7   **016.3058**
1. Children's literature—Bibliography 2. Young adults' literature—Bibliography 3. African American authors 4. Illustrators
ISBN 0-8389-0570-6   LC 91-13931
"Annotated descriptive bibliography containing over 1250 books written and illustrated by African-Americans and published between 1900 and 1990. The titles are divided into three sections by reading/interest level (preK-gr 4; gr 5-8; gr 9+), with the majority for senior high school level and above. A final chapter highlights 53 black illustrators and their work." SLJ
"The amount of information given is impressive and is well-organized and usable by students and teachers." Voice Youth Advocates

016.3637 Bibliographies of environmental problems and services

Dwyer, James R., 1949-
Earth works; recommended fiction and nonfiction about nature and the environment for adults and young adults; [by] Jim Dwyer. Neal-Schuman 1996 507p pa $39.95   **016.3637**
1. Environmental protection—Bibliography
ISBN 1-55570-194-9   LC 94-36284
Dwyer "lists 2600 entries, including about 1000 fiction titles, that were in print as of March 1995. The nonfiction titles are arranged into seven chapters by such topics as specific environments (deserts, rainforests), activities and issues (water supply, energy), and, in the largest section, environmental action (deep ecology, green business). The fiction titles are arranged by such topics as animals, ecofeminism, and the New West. . . . Entries offer standard bibliographic information . . . a two- to three-sentence annotation discussing the scope of the work, and reading level for young adult titles." Libr J

016.3713 Bibliographies of instructional materials

El-hi textbooks and serials in print. Bowker $155
                                         016.3713
1. Textbooks—Bibliography 2. Periodicals—Bibliography
ISSN 0000-0825
Also available on CD-ROM as part of Books in print plus
Annual. Title varies
"Index to textbooks, dictionaries, encyclopedias, maps, atlases, professional books, teaching aids and auxiliary AV materials for grades K-12, plus adult and special education. Subject index contains grade and reading level; also author and title indexes and series index. Lists information not in 'Books in Print.'" N Y Public Libr. Ref Books for Child Collect. 2d edition

Videos for understanding diversity; a core selection and evaluative guide; Gregory I. Stevens, editor; assisted by Sarah Parker Scotchmer. American Lib. Assn. 1993 217p il pa $35   **016.3713**
1. Videotapes—Catalogs 2. Audiovisual materials—Bibliography 3. Multicultural education
ISBN 0-8389-0612-5   LC 93-2662
Each of the 126 videos selected "deals with one or more themes, including race, ethnicity, gender, religion, culture, life stages, and stereotypes. Although some are well known (e.g. *The Autobiography of Miss Jane Pittman, Torch Song Trilogy*), most of these videos would remain unknown and unused were it not for this guide." Am Ref Books Annu, 1994

016.5   Bibliographies of science

Science Books & Films. American Assn. for the Advancement of Science $40 per year   **016.5**
1. Science—Bibliography—Periodicals 2. Books—Reviews 3. Audiovisual materials—Reviews
ISSN 0098-342X
Nine issues a year. First published 1965 with title: Science Books, a quarterly review
"This magazine is an indispensable tool for librarians in all types of libraries who wish to make informed collection development decisions in the area of science. . . . Arranged by Dewey decimal class numbers, the reviews cover books, audiovisual (AV) materials, and even software." Katz. Mag for Libr. 8th edition

016.8   Bibliographies of literature

Adamson, Lynda G.
Recreating the past; a guide to American and world historical fiction for children and young adults. Greenwood Press 1994 xxii, 494p $55
                                          016.8
1. Children's literature—Bibliography 2. Young adults' literature—Bibliography 3. Historical fiction—Bibliography
ISBN 0-313-29008-3   LC 94-14435
This work consists of 20 separate annotated bibliographies of historical fiction. Coverage is international. Each section is arranged alphabetically by author and includes publication information, a summary and reading and interest levels
This "will be especially useful for teachers and media specialists in interdisciplinary and whole language settings." SLJ

Anatomy of wonder 4; a critical guide to science fiction; edited by Neil Barron. Bowker 1995 xxiv, 912p $39   **016.8**
1. Science fiction—Bibliography 2. Science fiction—History and criticism
ISBN 0-8352-3288-3   LC 94-42363
First published 1976
This volume evaluates and provides summaries of some 2100 adult and young adult science fiction titles published through early 1994. Included also are sections on reference sources; films and television shows; science fiction art, comics and magazines; and a core collection checklist

Burgess, Michael, 1948-
Reference guide to science fiction, fantasy, and horror. Libraries Unlimited 1992 403p $55 **016.8**
1. Science fiction—Bibliography 2. Fantasy fiction—Bibliography 3. Horror fiction—Bibliography
ISBN 0-87287-611-X   LC 91-44853
"This title provides a crisp and clear introduction to the entire domain of reference works that deal with perhaps the most exciting of modern literature genres. Every type of reference source known . . . is succinctly described and intelligently evaluated. Included is a very practical 'Core Collections' listing that recommends individual works appropriate for libraries. . . . This reference book is now the standard guide to the field." Am Libr

Fiction catalog; edited by Juliette Yaakov and John Greenfieldt. 13th ed. Wilson, H.W. 1996 973p $115   **016.8**
1. Fiction—Bibliography 2. Fiction—Indexes
ISBN 0-8242-0894-3   LC 96-151775
"Standard catalog series"
First published 1908
Kept up to date by annual supplements, which are included in price of main catalog
"A standard annotated bibliography of . . . classical and popular fiction. Serves both as a selection aid and as a source for identifying outstanding works of fiction. Entries, arranged alphabetically by author, contain full bibliographic information and brief descriptive summaries, along with excerpts from critical reviews. Includes out-of-print titles and a special section for large-print books. Title and subject indexes." Ref Sources for Small & Medium-sized Libr. 5th edition

Genre favorites for young adults; a collection of Booklist columns; edited by Sally Estes. Booklist Publs. 1993 64p pa $7.95   **016.8**
1. Young adults' literature—Bibliography
ISBN 0-8389-5755-2
"Offers a compilation of popular young adult bibliographies with a wide-ranging appeal for a variety of tastes and maturity levels. The bibliographies focus on genre reading—using not only traditional categories like humor and romance, but also such popular subgenres as school stories and survival tales." Publisher's note

Hartman, Donald K.
Historical figures in fiction; [by] Donald K. Hartman and Gregg Sapp. Oryx Press 1994 352p $53.25   **016.8**
1. Historical fiction—Bibliography 2. Young adults' literature—Bibliography 3. Characters and characteristics in literature
ISBN 0-89774-718-6   LC 94-15105
This "book lists 4200 English-language novels published after 1940 in which 1500 historical figures appear as major characters. The body of the book is arranged alphabetically by the name of the historical figure. . . . Each name entry includes the person's dates and a brief biographical description, then lists the novels in which that person is a character. Citations for the novels give author, title, publisher, date, notes about the reading level, awards won, and as many as six reviews." Libr J
"This impressively researched work has a definite place in the professional library." Book Rep

Helbig, Alethea

This land is our land; a guide to multicultural literature for children and young adults; [by] Alethea K. Helbig and Agnes Regan Perkins. Greenwood Press 1994 401p $49.95 **016.8**
1. Young adults' literature—Bibliography 2. Children's literature—Bibliography 3. Minorities—Bibliography
ISBN 0-313-28742-2   LC 94-16124
An annotated bibliography of 570 books published from 1985 through 1993 focusing on the fiction, poetry and oral traditions of African, Asian, Hispanic and Native Americans
"Libraries and curriculum resource centers will want to consider *This Land is Our Land* for its currency and comprehensive coverage of quality multicultural literature for children." Booklist

Herald, Diana Tixier

Genreflecting; a guide to reading interests in genre fiction. 4th ed. Libraries Unlimited 1995 xxvi, 367p $38 **016.8**
1. Fiction—Bibliography 2. Fiction—History and criticism 3. Books and reading
ISBN 1-56308-354-X   LC 95-7633
First published 1982 under the authorship of Betty Rosenberg
This volume covers "such popular genres as crime, adventure, romance, science fiction, fantasy, and horror, defining each along with its many subgenres and listing good books in each category. . . . Besides information on authors and titles, there is background material on each genre (anthologies, bibliographies and encyclopedias, history and criticism, organizations, publishers, etc.) Highly recommended where information on genre fiction is sought." Booklist

Holsinger, M. Paul

The ways of war; the era of World War II in children's and young adult fiction: an annotated bibliography. Scarecrow Press 1995 487p $57.50 **016.8**
1. World War, 1939-1945—Literature and the war—Bibliography 2. Young adults' literature—Bibliography 3. Children's literature—Bibliography 4. War stories—Bibliography
ISBN 0-8108-2925-X   LC 94-20484
This annotated bibliography analyzes 750 fiction books that deal with World War II. Entries are arranged alphabetically by author and include reading level as well as quality rating. There is a title index and a geographical and thematic index
"Teachers and students have a valuable resource here in finding specific books to help with their understanding of a complex period in world history." Voice Youth Advocates

Jacob, Merle

To be continued; an annotated guide to sequels; by Merle Jacob and Hope Apple. Oryx Press 1995 364p $53.75 **016.8**
1. Fiction—Bibliography
ISBN 0-89774-842-5   LC 95-3283
"Jacob and Apple list 1,257 series of English-language adult fiction, excluding mysteries, 'that tell a continuing story or are united by a regional, social, or philosophical theme.' For each novel in a series, they provide author, series title (if any), title, bibliographical information, brief plot summary, genre, and subject headings." Libr J
"For libraries where a print source has to serve as the readers' advisor, this book will be a lifesaver." Booklist

Kies, Cosette N., 1936-

Supernatural fiction for teens; more than 1300 good paperbacks to read for wonderment, fear, and fun; [by] Cosette Kies. 2nd ed. Libraries Unlimited 1992 267p pa $25 **016.8**
1. Young adults' literature—Bibliography 2. Supernatural in literature—Bibliography 3. Paperback books—Bibliography 4. Books and reading—Best books 5. Fantasy fiction—Bibliography
ISBN 0-87287-940-2   LC 91-45469
First published 1987
"Alphabetically arranged by author, entries include bibliographic information, a brief annotation, a code indicating reading level . . . notes on movie versions, and classification of book." Nichols. Guide to Ref Books for Sch Media Cent. 4th edition

Peck, David R.

American ethnic literatures; native American, African American, Chicano/Latino, and Asian American writers and their backgrounds: an annotated bibliography. Salem Press 1992 218p (Magill bibliographies) **016.8**
1. American literature—American Indian authors—Bibliography 2. American literature—African American authors—Bibliography 3. American literature—Hispanic American authors—Bibliography 4. American literature—Asian American authors—Bibliography
    LC 92-12897
Available in hardcover from Scarecrow Press $40 (ISBN 0-8108-2792-1)
"Peck briefly introduces the four ethnic literatures; pulls together and annotates secondary sources, important background studies, reference works, journals, teaching guides, and comparative literature studies; and lists full-length primary works by their authors. . . . Coverage is limited to works in English, including some bilingual texts. Very highly recommended for all libraries." Choice

Reginald, R., 1948-

Science fiction and fantasy literature, 1975-1991; a bibliography of science fiction, fantasy, and horror fiction books and nonfiction monographs; associate editors, Mary A. Burgess, Daryl F. Mallett; editorial assistants and advisors, Scott Alan Burgess [et al.] Gale Res. 1992 1512p $199 **016.8**
1. Science fiction—Bibliography 2. Fantastic fiction—Bibliography 3. Horror fiction—Bibliography
ISBN 0-8103-1825-3   LC 92-28219
Companion volume to the author's Science fiction and fantasy literature: a checklist, 1700-1974 (1979)
This is "an alphabetical listing of authors and their works. Excluded are stage plays, poetry, songs, and

Reginald, R., 1948——_Continued_
graphic novels and comic books, but nonfiction works
about the field and compilations of sf art are included.
Each author entry notes titles, place of publication, publisher, date, pagination, binding, type (novel, collection,
anthology, television/movie adaptation, nonfiction), and
series." Libr J

Smith, Myron J.
Cloak and dagger fiction; an annotated guide to
spy thrillers; [by] Myron J. Smith, Jr. and Terry
White; foreword by Julian Rathbone; preface by
Joe Poyer. 3rd ed. Greenwood Press 1995 xl, 849p
(Bibliographies and indexes in American literature)
$95   **016.8**
1. Spies in literature—Bibliography 2. Fiction—Bibliography
ISBN 0-313-27700-1   LC 94-22017
First published 1976 by Scarecrow Press with title:
Cloak-and-dagger bibliography
This is "a 5,807-entry annotated bibliography arranged
by author. . . . Most of the titles were published since
1940. With the exception of a key work listed at the beginning of some authors' entries along with biographical
notes, annotations are descriptive of plot but are not
evaluative. Symbols following many annotations indicate
if a title exists exclusively in paperback, portrays no
graphic sexuality, is suitable for young adults, features
humor, or uses a historical plot, setting, or characters."
Booklist

Spencer, Pamela G.
What do young adults read next? a reader's
guide to fiction for young adults. Gale Res. 1994
816p $55   **016.8**
1. Young adults' literature—Bibliography 2. Books
and reading—Best books 3. Fiction—Bibliography
ISBN 0-8103-8887-1   LC 93-49806
New edition in preparation
More than 1500 titles chosen to reflect reading interests of sixth-to-twelfth graders are featured. "Each entry
provides authors name, book title, publication data,
recommended grade levels, subject(s), major characters
with brief descriptions, time period, locale, a brief plot
summary, citations to reviews, a selection of other books
by the author, and an annotated list of 'other books you
might like.'" Booklist

What do I read next? a reader's guide to current
genre fiction, fantasy, western, romance, horror,
mystery, science fiction; [by] Neil Barron [et
al.] Gale Res. $105   **016.8**
1. Fiction—Bibliography
ISSN 1052-2212
Also available CD-ROM version
Annual. First published 1991 for 1989-1990
A guide to locating new fiction titles in specific
genres. Arranged by author within six genre sections,
each entry provides publisher and publication date, series
name, major characters, time period, geographic setting,
review citations, and related books

016.80881   Bibliographies of poetry collections

Katz, William A., 1924-
The Columbia Granger's guide to poetry
anthologies; [by] William Katz, Linda Sternberg
Katz, Esther Crain. 2nd enl ed. Columbia Univ.
Press 1995 c1994 xxxiv, 440p $75   **016.80881**
1. Poetry—Collections—Bibliography
ISBN 0-231-10104-X   LC 94-6482
Also available as part of Columbia Granger's world of
poetry on CD-ROM, which also includes Granger's index
to poetry and the Columbia Granger's index to poetry
First published 1990
The authors provide critical annotations for all 800 an-
thologies indexed in the seventh and eighth editions of
Granger's index to poetry and the ninth and tenth edi-
tions of Columbia Granger's index to poetry

016.813   Bibliographies of American fiction

Coffey, Rosemary K.
America as story; historical fiction for middle
and secondary schools; [by] Rosemary K. Coffey,
Elizabeth F. Howard. 2nd ed. American Lib. Assn.
1997 xxi, 216p pa $25   **016.813**
1. Historical fiction—Bibliography 2. American fiction—Bibliography 3. United States—History—Fiction—Bibliography
ISBN 0-8389-0702-4   LC 96-43453
First published 1988 under the authorship of Elizabeth
F. Howard
"This is an annotated bibliography of approximately
200 recommended titles arranged by historical period.
Coded according to appropriate reading levels, the entries
include annotations, comments on what readers will learn
about historical events, and suggestions for reports and
activities." Publisher's note

Kutenplon, Deborah
Young adult fiction by African American
writers, 1968-1993; a critical and annotated guide;
[by] Deborah Kutenplon, Ellen Olmstead. Garland
1995 xlviii, 367p il (Garland reference library of
the humanities) $60   **016.813**
1. Young   adults'   literature—Bibliography
2. American fiction—Bibliography 3. African Americans in literature—Bibliography
ISBN 0-8153-0873-6   LC 95-20051
This volume covers some 200 titles by close to 50
African American authors. The main body of the book is
an annotated bibliography, alphabetical by author, with
individual works arranged by publication date. Each annotation explores themes, plot, character development,
handling of issues, and quality of writing. Readership
recommendations are provided

Modern women writers; Matthew J. Bruccoli and Judith Baughman, series editors; foreword by Mary Ann Wimsatt. Facts on File 1994 100p (Essential bibliography of American fiction) $19.95; pa $9.95 **016.813**
1. American fiction—Women authors—Bibliography
ISBN 0-8160-3000-6; 0-8160-3001-4 (pa)

LC 93-8642

Based on Bibliography of American fiction, 1919-1988 (1991) and Bibliography of American fiction, 1866-1918 (1993)

This volume "focuses on 10 authors, including Edith Wharton, Flannery O'Connor, and Eudora Welty. . . . [Following an] introductory paragraph about the author, the bibliographic portion of each entry is divided into sections that list bibliographies, primary works, biographies, interviews, and critical studies. Manuscript collections and concordances are also identified when appropriate." Booklist

VanMeter, Vandelia
America in historical fiction; a bibliographic guide; [by] Vandelia L. VanMeter. Libraries Unlimited 1997 280p $38.50 **016.813**
1. Historical fiction—Bibliography 2. American fiction—Bibliography 3. United States—History—Fiction—Bibliography
ISBN 1-56308-496-1 LC 96-34745
"Arranged in major chronological divisions of U.S. history, the annotated entries include standard bibliographic information, time period, subject, location, research base (if known), and whether the title is more appropriate for mature students or younger secondary students." Publisher's note

016.9 Bibliographies of geography and history

Khorana, Meena
Africa in literature for children and young adults; an annotated bibliography of English-language books. Greenwood Press 1994 l, 313p (Bibliographies and indexes in world literature) $65 **016.9**
1. Children's literature—Bibliography 2. Young adults' literature—Bibliography 3. Africa in literature—Bibliography
ISBN 0-313-25488-5 LC 94-34223
"Lists and critically annotates 700 titles about Africa by Western and African authors, published in or translated into English, 1873-1994. The evaluations include a plot or theme summary but also point out any bias found. The volume has six chapters by region: general books, North Africa, West Africa, East Africa, Central Africa, and Southern Africa, each chapter further subdivided by genre." Choice
For a fuller review see: Booklist, April 15, 1995

016.94053 Bibliographies of World War II, 1939-1945

Stephens, Elaine C., 1943-
Learning about—the Holocaust; literature and other resources for young people; [by] Elaine C. Stephens, Jean E. Brown, Janet E. Rubin. Library Professional Publs. 1995 198p $29.50; pa $18.50 **016.94053**
1. Holocaust, 1933-1945—Bibliography
ISBN 0-208-02398-4; 0-208-02408-5 (pa)

LC 95-31545

"This book furnishes annotated lists of materials on the Holocaust that are appropriate for kindergarten through high school. Chapters cover a variety of genres and formats, including nonfiction, photo-essays, maps, personal narratives, poetry, and drama. The authors also present materials that address the aftermath of the Holocaust and its implications for contemporary society. Each chapter provides an overview, questions to ponder, annotated entries with age levels and teaching ideas, and lists of additional resources." SLJ

016.97004 Bibliographies of North American native races

Kuipers, Barbara J.
American Indian reference and resource books for children and young adults. 2nd ed. Libraries Unlimited 1995 230p pa $27.50 **016.97004**
1. Indians of North America—Bibliography
ISBN 1-563-08258-6 LC 95-10008
First published 1991
This bibliography "is laid out in Dewey order, with reference books first, then subject order following. . . . Many series are listed as well as individual biographies of famous and not-so-famous Native Americans." Voice Youth Advocates
"Beautifully organized, meticulous, and with the inclusion of many issues involving American Indian students and their specific needs." J Youth Serv Libr

020.5 Library and information sciences—Serial publications

Library Journal. Bowker $99.50 **020.5**
1. Library science—Periodicals 2. Libraries—Periodicals
ISSN 0363-0277
Semimonthly February through June and September through November. Monthly January, July, August and December. First published 1876
Each issue "delivers news, timely articles, commentary, and hundreds of reviews of books, CD-ROMs, videos, audiotapes, and professional readings. Special issues include the Fall and Spring book announcements issues and the annual buying guide. No other library science periodical matches LJ for timeliness and reviewing sources. An essential purchase for any library collection." Katz. Mag for Libr. 8th edition

021.7   Promotion of libraries, information centers

Barteluk, Wendy D. M., 1945-
Library displays on a shoestring; 3-dimensional techniques for promoting library services. Scarecrow Press 1993 119p il $27.50   **021.7**
1. Libraries—Exhibitions
ISBN 0-8108-2662-3   LC 93-4813
"Barteluk shares the inexpensive ways she has discovered to accomplish professional looking displays. . . . Careful directions are included for each idea so that even the most insecure are eager to attempt their own display. Many of her materials are free or low cost and can be reused. . . . Highly recommended for schools and public libraries." Voice Youth Advocates
Includes bibliographical references

Schaeffer, Mark
Library displays handbook. Wilson, H.W. 1991 250p il $42   **021.7**
1. Libraries—Exhibitions 2. Public relations—Libraries
ISBN 0-8242-0801-3   LC 90-49442
"Schaeffer presents techniques for the design and lettering of signs, posters, wall displays, bulletin boards, and exhibits, discussing such up-to-date means to those end products as computer-generated graphics, including clip art. Many sample projects are carefully presented step-by-step, and appendixes provide materials sources, computer software suggestions, further reading suggestions." Booklist

025.1   Library administration

Woolls, E. Blanche
The school library media manager; [by] Blanche Woolls. Libraries Unlimited 1994 336p (Library science text series) $38.50; pa $31.50   **025.1**
1. School libraries 2. Instructional materials centers
ISBN 1-56308-304-3; 1-56308-318-3 (pa)
      LC 94-27627
Replaces The school library media center, by Emanuel T. Prostano and Joyce S. Prostano
Following a brief history of school library media programs the author covers various "aspects of library management; staff (professional and clerical), facility, collection, budget, marketing the program, evaluation, cooperation or networking, and planning for the future." Publisher's note
Includes bibliographical references

025.2   Collection development and acquisitions

Boardman, Edna M.
Censorship; the problem that won't go away. Linworth Pub. 1993 various paging il (Professional growth series) $17.95   **025.2**
1. Libraries—Censorship 2. School libraries
ISBN 0-938865-18-8   LC 93-153093
The author discusses "the issues, circumstances, problems, and intimidation of censorship and clearly articulates procedures for dealing with challenges. . . . Several essential documents are appended: sample selection policies, a flow chart delineating selection procedures, reconsideration forms, and ALA and AASL documents on intellectual freedom issues. The three-hole-punched workbook format helps the book function easily as a handbook and guidebook for dealing with censors." SLJ
Includes bibliographical references

Dewey, Patrick R., 1949-
303 CD-ROMs to use in your library; descriptions, evaluations, and practical advice. American Lib. Assn. 1996 xxii, 238p pa $30
    025.2
1. CD-ROM—Reviews 2. Libraries—Special collections
ISBN 0-8389-0666-4   LC 95-23607
"Opening with a short description of general software and hardware requirements for the use of CD-ROMs, this volume contains 303 CD-ROM reviews arranged by subject. . . . Each review follows a standard format listing the title of the CD-ROM, vendor, cost, hardware/software requirements, and comments. Some reviews are only a couple of sentences in length while others run to more than a page. . . . The book concludes with vendor addresses and a glossary." Libr J
Includes bibliographical references

Reichman, Henry, 1947-
Censorship and selection; issues and answers for schools. rev ed. American Lib. Assn.; American Assn. of School Adm. 1993 172p pa $20   **025.2**
1. Censorship 2. School libraries 3. Academic freedom
ISBN 0-8389-0620-6   LC 93-19711
First published 1988
This "book deals with censorship and selection in schools on four levels: theoretical, statistical, legal, and practical. Described are the differences between censorship and selection, the motives for censorship and the dangers of self-censorship. . . . This book is an excellent resource for all educators." Voice Youth Advocates
Includes bibliographical references

Sorrow, Barbara
CD-ROM for librarians and educators; a guide to over 800 instructional resources; by Barbara Head Sorrow and Betty S. Lumpkin. 2nd ed. McFarland & Co. 1996 405p pa $45   **025.2**
1. CD-ROM—Reviews 2. Libraries—Special collections
ISBN 0-7864-0176-1   LC 96-15652
First published 1993

Sorrow, Barbara—*Continued*

This "book consists of brief sketches of and basic information on . . . databases grouped by subject matter alphabetically from *aerospace* to *stories*. Each entry includes name, hardware requirements, producer, grade level, etc. Supplemental information includes a list of vendor addresses." Booklist

Symons, Ann K.

Protecting the right to read; a how-to-do-it manual for school and public librarians; [by] Ann K. Symons, Charles Harmon; illustrations by Pat Race. Neal-Schuman 1995 211p il (How-to-do-it manuals for librarians) pa $39.95   **025.2**
1. Libraries—Censorship 2. Intellectual freedom
ISBN 1-55570-216-3   LC 95-42444
"The authors take readers from discussion of the policies and principles of intellectual freedom to considerations specific to school and public libraries to the protection of freedom on the Internet. . . . Appendixes consist of reprints of documents put out by the ALA and the Minnesota Coalition Against Censorship." Book Rep
"Intellectual freedom issues and guiding principles get a thorough and comprehensive treatment. . . . An essential book." Voice Youth Advocates
Includes bibliographical references

025.3   Bibliographic analysis and control

Anglo-American cataloguing rules, 2d ed., 1988 revision; prepared under the direction of the Joint Steering Committee for Revision of AACR, a committee of the American Library Association [et al.]; the Australian Committee on Cataloguing, the British Library; edited by Michael Gorman and Paul W. Winkler. American Lib. Assn. 1988 xxv, 677p + packet of 1993 amendments $65; pa $50; loose-leaf $100   **025.3**
1. Cataloging
ISBN   0-8389-3346-7;   0-8389-3360-2   (pa); 0-8389-3361-0 (loose-leaf)   LC 88-19349
Also available separately 1993 amendments in loose-leaf format $15 (ISBN 0-8389-3431-5)
First published 1967
"These rules are designed for use in the construction of catalogues and other lists in general libraries of all sizes. . . . The rules cover the description of, and the provision of access points for, all library materials commonly collected at the present time. . . . Part I deals with the provision of information describing the item being catalogued and part II deals with the determination and establishment of headings (access points) under which the descriptive information is to be presented to catalogue users, and with the making of references to those headings." General Introduction

Byrne, Deborah J.

MARC manual; understanding and using MARC records. Libraries Unlimited 1991 260p pa $29.50   **025.3**
1. MARC formats 2. Cataloging
ISBN 0-87287-813-9   LC 90-13413
New edition in preparation
"This book presents a detailed and often technical description of the development, structure, coding, storage media, and present and potential uses of the MARC record." Libr J
Includes bibliographical references

Gorman, Michael, 1941-

The concise AACR2, 1988 revision. American Lib. Assn. 1989 161p pa $28   **025.3**
1. Anglo-American cataloguing rules 2. Cataloging
ISBN 0-8389-3362-9   LC 89-15110
Based on Anglo-American cataloguing rules, 2nd edition, 1988 revision entered above
"Many smaller libraries will find this volume more helpful than the complete *AACR2*, although some may eventually progress to the full set of rules. . . . Capitalization rules, glossary and comparative table of *AACR2* and *Concise AACR2* rules appended." Booklist

Intner, Sheila S., 1935-

Standard cataloging for school and public libraries; [by] Sheila S. Intner and Jean Weihs. 2nd ed. Libraries Unlimited 1996 278p il lib bdg $32.50   **025.3**
1. Cataloging 2. Classification—Books
ISBN 1-56308-349-3   LC 95-53186
First published 1990
This explains the Anglo-American Cataloging Rules (AACR2), Sears and Library of Congress subject headings, Dewey decimal and Library of Congress classification systems, MARC format, large computer networks, policy manuals, and how to manage a cataloging department
"The beauty of this manual is in clear discussions and backgrounds for every major area, phase, rule, and detail." Book Rep
Includes glossary and bibliography

025.4   Subject analysis and control

Dewey, Melvil, 1851-1931

Abridged Dewey decimal classification and relative index; devised by Melvil Dewey. ed 13, edited by Joan S. Mitchell, Julianne Beall, Winton E. Matthews, Jr., Gregory R. New. Forest Press (Albany) 1997 1023p $90   **025.4**
1. Dewey Decimal Classification
ISBN 0-910608-59-8   LC 97-10791
First abridged edition published 1894
The 13th Abridged Edition is an abridgement of the four volume 21st Edition. Adapted to the needs of small and growing libraries, the 13th Abridged Edition is designed primarily for school and public libraries with collections of up to 20,000 titles

Dewey, Melvil, 1851-1931—*Continued*
Dewey decimal classification and relative index;
devised by Melvil Dewey. ed 21, edited by Joan
S. Mitchell, Julianne Beall, Winton E. Matthews,
Jr., Gregory R. New. Forest Press (Albany) 1996
4v set $325   **025.4**
1. Dewey Decimal Classification
ISBN 0-910608-50-4   LC 96-7393
Also available CD-ROM version
First published anonymously in 1876
Contents: v1 Introduction, tables; v2-3 Schedules; v4
Relative index, manual

**Library of Congress. Cataloging Policy and
Support Office**
Library of Congress subject headings; prepared
by the Cataloging Policy and Support Office,
Library Services. Library of Congress 4v set $200
    025.4
1. Subject headings
Also available CD-ROM version
This work contains the headings and cross-references
established and applied by the Library of Congress
Annual. Variant title: Subject headings used in the
dictionary catalogs of the Library of Congress. Issued
previously by the Subject Cataloging Division and later
by the Office for Subject Cataloging Policy

Sears list of subject headings. 16th ed, edited by
Joseph Miller. Wilson, H.W. 1997 lii, 786p
$54   **025.4**
1. Subject headings
ISBN 0-8242-0920-6
Also available Canadian companion to 15th edition
$24 (ISBN 0-8242-0879-X)
First published 1923 with title: List of subject headings for small libraries, by Minnie Earl Sears
In addition to more than 300 new subject headings
this edition updates the suggested classification numbers
to conform to the new 13th edition of the Abridged
Dewey Decimal Classification. The list reflects subject
simplification and a revision of subdivision policy. Headings in the field of religions have been revised to avoid
sectarian bias

025.5   Services to users

The **American** Library Association guide to
information access; a complete research
handbook and directory; Sandy Whiteley, editor.
Random House 1994 xxv, 533p $35; pa $19
    025.5
1. Reference services (Libraries) 2. Information systems 3. Research
ISBN 0-679-43060-1; 0-679-75075-4 (pa)
    LC 94-10861
The editors cover "sources of information, the electronic revolution in information dissemination, and 36
topics—ranging from genealogy to multiculturalism—
chosen to reflect the questions librarians are most frequently asked. . . . Whiteley and her impressive list of
contributors have done a good job; this handbook could
evolve into an extremely useful tool." Libr J

The **New** York Public Library book of how and
where to look it up; Sherwood Harris,
editor-in-chief. Prentice-Hall 1991 382p
hardcover o.p. paperback available $14   **025.5**
1. Reference books—Bibliography 2. Research 3. Libraries—Handbooks, manuals, etc.
ISBN 0-671-89264-9 (pa)   LC 91-25660
"A Stonesong Press book"
This work "is a mixture of bibliographic and directory
information. . . . The book consists of six sections, covering Reference Books, Telephone, Government, and Picture sources, Special Collections, and Electronic
Databases. . . . Within each category, entries are alphabetical by subject. . . . Virtually all entries are
annotated. . . . It will prove an outstanding purchase for
small libraries, and larger ones will welcome it as a
ready reference tool at the public service desk." Libr J

Skills for life: library information literacy for
grades 9-12; Paul Rux, editor. Linworth Pub.
1993 various paging (Professional growth series)
loose-leaf $36.95   **025.5**
1. Bibliographic instruction 2. School libraries—Activity projects
ISBN 0-938865-21-8   LC 93-39622
A publication of the Book Report and Library Talk
This notebook contains a sample of library skills lesson plans for school library media specialists to use with
high school students

027.62   Libraries for children and young adults

Edwards, Margaret A., 1902-1988
The fair garden and the swarm of beasts; the
library and the young adult; with a foreword by
Patty Campbell. repr ed. American Lib. Assn.
1994 xxvii, 156p il pa $20   **027.62**
1. Young adults' library services 2. Books and reading
ISBN 0-8389-0635-4   LC 94-14269
A reprint, with a new preface, of the title first published 1969 by Hawthorn Bks.
The author "describes methods of working with young
adults, the training of young adult librarians and work in
the public schools, and provides information on book selection, book talks and displays." Wis Libr Bull [review
of 1969 edition]
"Edwards focuses intently on books and reading . . .
and her advice on bringing books and teens together remains sensible and inspiring. . . . Campbell's preface
traces Edward's career [and] examines the changing picture of youth librarianship and literature written for
teens." Bull Cent Child Books

Excellence in library services to young adults; the
nation's top programs; edited by Mary K.
Chelton; [pub. in assn. with] American Library
Association President's Committee for Customer
Service to Youth. American Lib. Assn. 1994
76p il pa $22   **027.62**
1. Young adults' library services
ISBN 0-8389-3440-4   LC 94-15407
This highlights "youth services programs from
throughout the United States, selected by a committee

Excellence in library services to young adults—
Continued

appointed by ALA's . . . Past President, Hardy R. Franklin." Publisher's note

"Both inspiring and practical, the top YA library programs outlined here don't require huge outlays of capital and exhaustive grant writing. Chelton's thought-provoking introduction sets the scene for the book: the vision is grounded in the daily realities of school and public library work, in respect for teenagers, and in commitment to making a difference in the community." Booklist

Includes bibliographical references

027.6205 Libraries for children and young adults—Serial publications

Journal of Youth Services in Libraries. American Lib. Assn. $40 per year   027.6205
1. Young adults' library services—Periodicals 2. Children's libraries—Periodicals 3. Books—Reviews
ISSN 0894-2498

Quarterly. Formerly Top of the News

"This publication provides news, columns, bibliographic essays, refereed feature articles, and reviews of professional reading. . . . Typical of ALA-sponsored journals, this one is of high quality and highly recommended for school and public library professional collections." Katz. Mag for Libr. 8th edition

VOYA: Voice of Youth Advocates. Scarecrow Press $38.50 per year   027.6205
1. Young adults' library services—Periodicals 2. Young adults' literature—Periodicals 3. Books—Reviews
ISSN 0160-4201

Bimonthly. First published 1978

This "continues to be an attractive journal devoted to library service to young adults. . . . The majority of each issue is devoted to concise reviews of material for young adults. *VOYA* regularly confronts controversial issues and provides an important forum for practitioners working with young people. . . . Highly recommended for both school and public libraries." Katz. Mag for Libr. 8th edition

027.8 School libraries

American Association of School Librarians
Information power; guidelines for school library media programs; prepared by the American Association of School Librarians and Association for Educational Communications and Technology. American Lib. Assn.; Association for Educ. Communications & Technology 1988 171p il pa $15   027.8
1. School libraries 2. Instructional materials centers
ISBN 0-8389-3352-1   LC 88-3480

Replaces Media programs: district and school, published 1975

"The book begins with the mission statement—to ensure that students and staff are effective users of ideas

and information—and lists five challenges that library media specialists face. Following are individual chapters, complete with helpful bibliographies, that discuss programs; roles and responsibilities; leadership, planning, and management; personnel; resources and equipment; facilities; and district, regional and state leadership." Booklist

Assessment and the school library media center; editor, Carol Collier Kuhlthau; associate editors, M. Elspeth Goodin and Mary Jane McNally. Libraries Unlimited 1994 152p pa $20   027.8
1. Bibliographic instruction 2. Instructional materials centers
ISBN 1-56308-211-X   LC 94-27290

This book is a compilation of articles addressing the impact of school library media programs on student learning. Among the topics discussed are new methods of assessment, and the instructional role of the library media specialist

Includes bibliographical references

Automation for school libraries; how to do it from those who have done it; edited by Teresa Thurman Day, Bruce Flanders, Gregory Zuck. American Lib. Assn. 1994 138p il pa $18   027.8
1. School libraries—Automation
ISBN 0-8389-0637-0   LC 94-15406

This book addresses "the areas of automation systems, peripheral equipment and, most important, funding. Also included are practical advice, case experiences, model procedures and basic facts. . . . Whether you are a computer hacker or brand new at the game, this title will fill a void on your professional shelf." Book Rep

Includes glossary and bibliography

Craver, Kathleen W.
School library media centers in the 21st century; changes and challenges. Greenwood Press 1994 xxxi, 179p $35   027.8
1. School libraries 2. Instructional materials centers
ISBN 0-313-29100-4   LC 94-5146

The author has compiled "statistics, studies, and examples in this discussion of school library media centers (SLMCs) of the future. She devotes chapters to technological, economic, employment, educational, social/behavioral, instructional, and organizational/managerial trends; she presents eight challenges for the media specialist. The emphasis here is . . . on technology." Voice Youth Advocates

"This is a 'must-read' for practicing and potential school library media specialists." SLJ

Includes bibliographical references

Loertscher, David V., 1940-
Taxonomies of the school library media program; illustrated by Mark Loertscher. Libraries Unlimited 1988 336p il pa $26.50   027.8
1. School libraries 2. Instructional materials centers
ISBN 0-87287-662-4   LC 87-35367

"The author provides a detailed look at the role of the teacher, the student, the administrator, and the media

Loertscher, David V., 1940——*Continued*
specialist. There are charts of library skills; research
skills; technology skills; and the grade levels for awareness, mastery, and maintenance of these skills. . . . This
book presents a wealth of information and illustrations.
. . . All school library media specialists should have access to it." Voice Youth Advocates

Moody, Regina B.
Coming to terms; subject search strategies in the
school library media center. Neal-Schuman 1995
178p il pa $29.95　　　**027.8**
　1. School libraries 2. Instructional materials centers
3. Bibliographic instruction
　ISBN 1-55570-225-2　　　LC 94-37893
This is "a book of detailed lesson plans to teach
searching skills for the library catalog (paper or auto-
mated), indexes, databases and online searching. . . .
These lesson plans are sequential for each unit and offer
objectives, presentation, and excellent visual aids. . . .
This book contains a wealth of ideas with clever means
of delivering information which can be less than stimulating to many students." Voice Youth Advocates
　Includes bibliography

Morris, Betty J.
Administering the school library media center.
3rd ed, by Betty J. Morris with John T. Gillespie
and Diana L. Spirt. Bowker 1992 567p il $45
　　　　　027.8
　1. School libraries 2. Instructional materials centers
　ISBN 0-8352-3092-9　　　LC 92-9186
First published 1973 under the authorship of John T.
Gillespie and Diane L. Spirt with title: Creating a school
media program
　The chapters cover "all aspects of library/media center
work. The budgeting, planning, developing, selecting,
and maintaining of a collection are detailed; . . . also
considered are policy and procedure statements, the physical plant layout, and the new technologies. . . . The authors have done an admirable job of fielding problems
and anticipating new situations. Recommended." Voice
Youth Advocates
　Includes bibliographical references

Skaggs, Gayle, 1952-
Off the wall! school year bulletin boards and
displays for the library. McFarland & Co. 1995
142p il pa $24.50　　　**027.8**
　1. School libraries 2. Libraries—Exhibitions 3. Bulletin boards
　ISBN 0-7864-0116-8　　　LC 95-5693
Arranged to correlate with the school year, this "guide
contains more than 100 bulletin board and display ideas.
. . . Skaggs has concentrated on ideas that can be inex-
pensively made and assembled fairly quickly." Booklist
　"This is a handy aid for quick displays and to stimulate further creative ideas." Voice Youth Advocates

Stein, Barbara L.
Running a school library media center; a
how-to-do-it manual for librarians; [by] Barbara L.
Stein, Risa W. Brown. Neal-Schuman 1992 143p
il (How-to-do-it manuals for school and public
librarians) $35　　　**027.8**
　1. School libraries 2. Instructional materials centers
　ISBN 1-55570-100-0　　　LC 92-317
"Information is organized into nine chapters which
cover topics ranging from goal setting and budgeting to
ordering materials to programming. Appendices contain
lists of sources, a learning skills inventory, sample job
descriptions, and Library Bill of Rights information."
Voice Youth Advocates
　Includes bibliographical references

Van Orden, Phyllis J.
The collection program in schools; concepts,
practices, and information sources. 2nd ed.
Libraries Unlimited 1995 376p il $42.50; pa
$32.50　　　**027.8**
　1. School libraries
　ISBN 1-56308-120-2; 1-56308-334-5 (pa)
　　　　　LC 94-32233
　First published 1988
This "book is divided into three parts. The first section covers the librarian's role within the school and the
community, aspects of the collection program, and concerns with censorship and intellectual freedom. . . . Part
Two lists types of materials available and selection
criteria specific to format. . . . Part Three identifies selection tools and offers suggestions for collection maintenance and evaluation." Book Rep

Vandergrift, Kay E., 1940-
Power teaching; a primary role of the school
library media specialist. American Lib. Assn. 1994
171p (School library media programs: Focus on
trends and issues) pa $22　　　**027.8**
　1. School libraries—Activity projects 2. Bibliographic
instruction
　ISBN 0-8389-3435-8　　　LC 93-35565
Topics covered include "the librarian's role as teacher,
research and evaluation strategies, webbing as a path to
organization, staff development, workshop initiatives, and
self evaluation." Voice Youth Advocates
　"Though not a pick-up-and-do book, this is an excellent source for the librarian who wants information from
the cutting edge." Book Rep
　Includes bibliographical references

The **Virtual** school library; gateway to the
information superhighway; editor, Carol Collier
Kuhlthau; associate editors, M. Elspeth Goodin
and Mary Jane McNally. Libraries Unlimited
1996 161p pa $24　　　**027.8**
　1. School libraries 2. Information systems
　ISBN 1-56308-336-1　　　LC 95-52601
This collection of articles discussing various aspects
and applications of a virtual school library focuses on
four major themes: the technologies available; approaches
to learning in an electronic environment; examples of im-
plementation for school, district and state level libraries;
new directions in education for school media specialists
　Includes bibliographical references

027.805 School libraries—Serial publications

The Book Report; the journal for junior and senior high school librarians. Linworth Pub. $44 per year   **027.805**
1. School libraries—Periodicals 2. Books—Reviews
ISSN 0731-4388
Five times a school year. First published 1982
Each issue "includes a theme section, with several articles built around the theme. . . . The many reviews of books and media are well written and insightful. Regular features include a computer column and booktalking. This publication . . . is a very useful one for junior high and high school librarians." Katz. Mag for Libr. 8th edition

School Library Journal; for children's, young adult, & school librarians. Bowker $87.50 per year   **027.805**
1. School libraries—Periodicals 2. Books—Reviews
ISSN 0362-8930
Monthly. First published 1954 with title: Junior Libraries. Subtitle varies
"This is the leading magazine for children's and young adults' librarians working in public and school libraries. The feature articles are well written and timely. The contents include a calendar of events, news from the field, notes on people, columns including 'Up for Discussion,' and 'Teens & Libraries,' as well many reviews— of professional reading, books for children and young adults, audiovisuals, and computer software. . . . This is an essential professional journal for school and public librarians." Katz. Mag for Libr. 8th edition

School Library Media Quarterly. American Lib. Assn. $40 per year   **027.805**
1. School libraries—Periodicals 2. Instructional materials centers—Periodicals
ISSN 0278-4823
Quarterly. First published 1972 as a successor to School Libraries with title: School Media Quarterly
"Journal of the American Association of School Librarians"
This journal provides "feature articles that are well edited and timely; news of the association and of school library related legislation; reviews of professional reading, software, and audiovisuals, and annual AASL conference coverage. This is essential for school library professional collections." Katz. Mag for Libr. 8th edition

028 Reading and use of other information media

Diefendorf, Elizabeth
The New York Public Library's books of the century; illustrations by Diana Bryan. Oxford Univ. Press 1996 229p il $14.95; pa $8.95   **028**
1. Books and reading—Best books
ISBN 0-19-510897-3; 0-19-511790-5 (pa)
                                    LC 95-52685
"To celebrate its centennial, the New York Public Library exhibited works selected from titles recommended by its librarians. Diefendorf, the curator of the exhibit, has put together this list of classics that have had deep or enduring influence, whether for good or not, or attracted millions of readers. This work collects the approximately 175 exhibition titles into 11 categories, such as Landmarks of Modern Literature and Favorites of Childhood and Youth, and briefly describes each work, noting its significance." Libr J

Krashen, Stephen D.
The power of reading; insights from the research; [by] Stephen Krashen. Libraries Unlimited 1993 119p pa $15   **028**
1. Reading 2. Literacy
ISBN 1-56308-006-0   LC 92-15096
The author "outlines and 'proves' via . . . research reports how Free Voluntary Reading (FVR), the use of in-school free reading programs, is beneficial to children's reading comprehension, writing style, vocabulary, spelling, and grammatical development. . . . This book will be useful for teachers and librarians (media specialists) who need solid data and numbers to take to their library directors or principals." Voice Youth Advocates
Includes bibliographical references

Rochman, Hazel
Tales of love and terror; booktalking the classics, old and new. American Lib. Assn. 1987 120p pa $22   **028**
1. Books and reading 2. Literature—Stories, plots, etc.
ISBN 0-8389-0463-7   LC 86-32285
"Rochman's booktalks begin with themes of nearly universal interest, such as love and terror, to provide a framework for brief descriptions of a dozen or more titles. . . . Later chapters . . . demonstrate how a single book may relate to many different themes, and describe the range of books which might be used." Publisher's note
"Both experienced and new booktalkers will find a wealth of ideas in *Tales of Love and Terror*. . . . [It] should be a part of every young adult librarian's professional collection." SLJ

028.1 Reviews of books and other media

Bodart, Joni Richards
100 world-class thin books; or, What to read when your book report is due tomorrow! Libraries Unlimited 1993 204p $27.50   **028.1**
1. Young adults' literature—Bibliography 2. Report writing 3. Books and reading—Best books
ISBN 0-87287-986-0   LC 92-2351
"The books described here are all 200 pages or shorter and are suitable for middle or high school students. . . . Each entry provides bibliographic information, subject areas covered, description of characters, a short booktalk, major ideas or themes, book report ideas, and booktalk ideas. Indexes include author, title, curriculum area, genre, readability and subject." Book Rep

Book review digest. Wilson, H.W. service basis
028.1
1. Books—Reviews
ISSN 0006-7326
Also available CD-ROM version
All annual cumulations 1905-to date available
Published monthly, except February and July. Quarterly cumulations. Permanent bound annual cumulations
This work "provides excerpts from, and citations to, reviews of adult and juvenile fiction and nonfiction, trade books, and reference books. . . . Entries, arranged alphabetically by author or title (as appropriate), give author, title, paging, price, publisher and year, ISBN, a descriptive introduction to the book, age or grade level (for juvenile works), suggested Sears subject headings, and LC card number. Reviewing information includes citations of reviews, name of reviewers, approximate length of each review, and up to four review excerpts chosen to provide a balance of opinion." Nichols. Guide to Ref Books for Sch Media Cent. 4th edition
An author/title index covering 1975-1984 is available for $65 (ISBN 0-8242-0729-7); index covering 1905-1974 is o.p.

Book review index. Gale Res. **028.1**
1. Books—Reviews—Indexes
ISSN 0524-0581
3 issues per year. Began publication in 1965. Frequency varies. Annual cumulations available for $240 each
"This comprehensive index cites all reviews appearing in more than 500 popular and professional periodicals. Included are adult and juvenile fiction, nonfiction, and reference books—some 132,000 review citations for about 74,000 new books each year. Arranged alphabetically by author, *BRI* gives only author, title, and the review. There is a title index. No descriptive summaries or excerpts from reviews, such as those found in *Book Review Digest*, are offered; nor is any subject access provided." Nichols. Guide to Ref Books for Sch Media Cent. 4th edition
Master cumulations covering 1965-1984 and 1985-1992 available each $1,315

Booklist. American Lib. Assn. $69.50 per year
028.1
1. Books—Reviews 2. Books and reading—Best books
ISSN 0006-7385
Semimonthly September through June; monthly July and August. First published 1905 with title: A.L.A. Booklist. Merged with Subscription Books Bulletin in 1956
The Reference Books Bulletin section is also available separately in an annual cumulation for $26
"Intended chiefly as a guide for librarians in public and school libraries, each issue covers titles in five major areas: forthcoming titles, adult books, books for youth, audiovisual media, and reference books. . . . Because of its selectivity, its early reviews, and its broad coverage of popular non-print media, *Booklist* is essential reading for public, school, and many academic libraries." Katz. Mag for Libr. 8th edition

Carter, Betty, 1944-
Best books for young adults; the selections, the history, the romance. American Lib. Assn. 1994 214p il pa $28 **028.1**
1. Young adults' literature—Bibliography 2. Books and reading—Best books
ISBN 0-8389-3439-0 LC 94-2640
"In this overview of the annual Best Books for Young Adults lists chosen by a committee of the Young Adult Library Services Association of the ALA, Carter discusses the history of the list and addresses such issues as . . . how the list should be used in schools and libraries. A final section includes annotated bibliographies of titles chosen from 1966-93." Booklist
"A valuable resource for any middle school, junior high, high school, or public library." Voice Youth Advocates

Kliatt; reviews of selected paperback books, educational software and audiobooks. , 33 Bay State Rd., Wellesley, Mass. 02181 $36 per year
028.1
1. Paperback books—Reviews 2. Young adults' literature—Periodicals
ISSN 1065-8602
Six issues per year. First published 1967. Former titles: Kliatt Young Adult Paperback Book Guide; Kliatt Paperback Book Guide
This is "a review service devoted chiefly to paperback books, whether reprints, reissues, or originals. Reference books suitable for high school libraries, audiobooks, and educational software are also included. Each review is coded for reading level and difficulty. . . . A recommended selection tool for junior high, high school and YA librarians." Katz. Mag for Libr. 8th edition

028.5 Reading and use of other information media by children and young adults

Booktalk! 2-5. Wilson, H.W. 1985-1993 4v pa ea $32 **028.5**
1. Books and reading
ISBN 0-8242-0716-5 (v2); 0-8242-0764-5 (v3); 0-8242-0835-8 (v4); 0-8242-0836-6 (v5)
Original Booktalk! published 1980 o.p.
Edited by Joni Richards Bodart
Volume 2 explains what booktalks are and contains 250 examples; volume 3 offers 500 booktalks and has a combined index to booktalks in volumes 2-3; volume 4 is a collection of 350 booktalks and 5 articles which appeared in the Booktalker section of Wilson Library Bulletin between September 1989 and May 1992; volume 5 adds 320 more talks and 4 articles on booktalking

Booktalking the award winners; edited by Joni Richards Bodart. Wilson, H.W. pa ea $32
028.5
1. Books and reading—Best books 2. Children's literature—Stories, plots, etc. 3. Young adults' literature—Stories, plots, etc.
Also available Booktalking the award winners: young adult retrospective volume pa $32 (ISBN 0-8242-0877-3) and Index to the Wilson Booktalking series pa $27 (ISBN 0-8242-0905-2)

Booktalking the award winners—*Continued*

Annual. First published 1994 for 1992-1993

Each volume of this series is composed of 200-300 booktalks on children's and young adult titles which have won national-level awards during the previous year. Among the awards represented are the Caldecott, Carnegie and Newbery medals, the Coretta Scott King Book Award and the Scott O'Dell Award for Historical Fiction. Bibliographies by author, by age level, and by theme and genre are included

Cart, Michael

From romance to realism; 50 years of growth and change in young adult literature. HarperCollins Pubs. 1996 312p $24.95   028.5

1. Young adults' literature—History and criticism 2. American fiction—History and criticism 3. Books and reading 4. Realism in literature

ISBN 0-06-024289-2   LC 95-31734

"Cart devotes the first half of the book, 'That Was Then,' to a discussion of the genre's history, and the second half, 'This Is Now,' focuses on contemporary literature and current issues. Throughout, he deals competently with both broad generic tendencies and specific texts, including some interesting explorations of the merits and the flaws of major young-adult authors. His distinctly personal, often colloquial voice makes a refreshing contrast to bland literary surveys." Bull Cent Child Books

Includes bibliography

Carter, Betty, 1944-

Nonfiction for young adults; from delight to wisdom; by Betty Carter and Richard F. Abrahamson. Oryx Press 1990 233p il maps $32.50   028.5

1. Young adults' literature 2. Books and reading

ISBN 0-89774-555-8   LC 90-7046

"The chapters on the evaluation and uses of nonfiction are interspersed with author interviews. . . . The selection criteria developed are detailed and practical. The chapters focus on interest, accuracy, content, style, organization, format, and uses. Each chapter also gives many examples of familiar titles that are useful in the curriculum as well as titles that will work well in reader's advisory." Voice Youth Advocates

Includes bibliography

Dear author; students write about the books that changed their lives; collected by Weekly reader's Read magazine; introduction by Lois Lowry. Conari Press 1995 186p pa $9.95
                028.5

1. Letters 2. Books and reading

ISBN 1-57324-003-6   LC 95-14455

Also available in hardcover from Borgo Press

A collection of letters from students to an assortment of authors both past and present about the impact of their work on the lives of their readers

"The letters themselves are well written, thought-provoking, and likely to stimulate curiosity about the titles mentioned. Teachers could use this collection to help motivate their students or to use as examples of letter-writing." SLJ

Masterplots II: juvenile and young adult fiction series; edited by Frank N. Magill. Salem Press 1991 4v set $365   028.5

1. Children's literature—Stories, plots, etc. 2. Young adults' literature—Stories, plots, etc.

ISBN 0-89356-579-2   LC 91-4509

Focusing "on fiction that is of interest to readers aged 10 to 18 . . . [this set] covers more than 500 titles. . . . The selection criteria are exceptionally broad, allowing for the inclusion of children's classics, works written for a general audience but of particular interest to children and young adults, those from past eras, and those of contemporary writers." Am Ref Books Annu, 1992

Includes bibliographical references

Masterplots II: juvenile and young adult literature series supplement; edited by Frank N. Magill; project editor, Tracy Irons-Georges. Salem Press 1997 3v set $275   028.5

1. Children's literature—Stories, plots, etc. 2. Young adults' literature—Stories, plots, etc.

ISBN 0-89356-916-X   LC 96-39759

Supplements the Juvenile and young adult fiction series and the Juvenile and young adult biography series (1993) o.p.; includes for the first time poetry collections, plays, short-story collections, and books on art, history, sociology, and science for young readers; the cumulative indexes cover the contents of the earlier series as well as those covered in the supplement

Includes bibliographical references

Nilsen, Alleen Pace

Literature for today's young adults; [by] Alleen Pace Nilsen, Kenneth L. Donelson. 4th ed. HarperCollins College Pubs. 1993 626p il $45.50
                028.5

1. Young adults' literature—History and criticism 2. Books and reading

ISBN 0-673-46652-3   LC 92-42250

First published 1980 with authors' names in reverse order

The authors survey the field of young adult literature and its literary aspects, and discuss books and authors by genre, the psychology of the adolescent, the teaching of literature in schools, the history of young adult books, evaluation criteria, and include annotated lists of books, films, and magazines

This is "an authoritative and useful resource for youth librarians and a basic tool for the teaching of YA literature." Booklist

Includes bibliographical references

Sherman, Gale W.

Rip-roaring reads for reluctant teen readers; [by] Gale W. Sherman, Bette D. Ammon. Libraries Unlimited 1993 164p il pa $22.50   028.5

1. Books and reading 2. Young adults' literature—Bibliography

ISBN 1-56308-094-X   LC 93-6439

Divided into separate sections for junior high school and high school students, this work "provides booktalks and related activities for 40 contemporary YA titles that will grab reluctant readers. . . . For each title, there's in-

Sherman, Gale W.—*Continued*
formation about the author and about book reviews in major journals; then there's a brief plot summary and two kinds of talks. . . . With a style that's immediate, informal, open, and always enthusiastic, this hands-on resource will be welcomed by librarians and teachers who want to share the pleasure of good books." Booklist
Includes bibliographical references

028.505   Children's reading—Serial publications

The **ALAN** Review. National Council of Teachers of English $15 per year   **028.505**
1. Books—Reviews 2. Young adults' literature—Periodicals
ISSN 0882-2840
Three issues per year. First published 1973
Published by the Assembly on Literature for Adolescents, National Council of Teachers of English
This publication "is unique in being devoted entirely to adolescent literature. Each issue contains 'Clip and File' reviews of approximately twenty new hardbacks or paperbacks and includes [several] feature articles, news announcements, and occasional in-depth reviews of professional books." Donelson. Literature for Today's Young Adults

031   American general encyclopedic works

Academic American encyclopedia. Grolier 21v il maps apply to publisher for price   **031**
1. Encyclopedias and dictionaries
Also available CD-ROM version, The Grolier multimedia encyclopedia
First published 1980 by Aretê Publishing Company. Frequently revised
This "is a current, accurate, well-written set that, according to its editors, devotes almost equal space to the humanities, sciences, and social sciences. As the name implies, it attempts to reflect the current curricula of American schools and colleges. . . . Highly recommended for high schools but can serve as a supplementary set for upper elementary and middle schools." Nichols. Guide to Ref Books for Sch Media Cent. 4th edition
For a review see: Booklist, Sept. 15, 1996

Collier's encyclopedia; with bibliography and index. Collier, P.F. 24v il maps apply to publisher for price   **031**
1. Encyclopedias and dictionaries
Also available CD-ROM version
First published 1949-1951 by Crowell-Collier Educational Corporation. Frequently revised
Supplemented by: Collier's yearbook
"An adult encyclopedia suitable for junior and senior high school students as well as the adult reader. Almost all articles are signed by scholars of international renown. . . . The arts, humanities, social sciences, and biography are particularly represented in articles that in-

clude integrated subtopics. . . . Objectivity is consistent in the set's handling of controversial topics." Ref Sources for Small & Medium-sized Libr. 5th edition
For a review see: Booklist, Sept. 15, 1996

The **Columbia** encyclopedia; edited by Barbara A. Chernow and George A. Vallasi; consultants: Peter J. Awn [et al.] 5th ed. Columbia Univ. Press; distributed by Houghton Mifflin 1993 3048p il maps $59.95   **031**
1. Encyclopedias and dictionaries
ISBN 0-395-62438-X   LC 92-26989
Also available CD-ROM version
First published 1935. Fourth edition published with title: The New Columbia encyclopedia
This single-volume general encyclopedia, "provides international coverage of basic knowledge, yet it remains, in the words of the editors, an 'American encyclopedia written for American readers.'" Libr J

Compton's encyclopedia and fact-index. Compton's Learning 26v il maps apply to publisher for price   **031**
1. Encyclopedias and dictionaries
Also available CD-ROM version, Compton's interactive encyclopedia
First published 1922 with title: Compton's pictured encyclopedia. Frequently revised
Supplemented by: Compton yearbook
"An encyclopedia for young adults, ages nine through eighteen, for home and school use, with emphasis on practical and curriculum-related information. Among the . . . contributors are scholars, writers, and notable librarians. Arrangement is letter by letter and each volume . . . is divided into two parts. The illustrated 'Fact Index' at the back refers the readers to text and illustrations in the volume at hand and to information contained elsewhere in the set." Ref Sources for Small & Medium-sized Libr. 5th edition
For a review see: Booklist, Sept. 15, 1996

The **Concise** Columbia encyclopedia. 3rd ed. Columbia Univ. Press; distributed by Houghton Mifflin 1994 973p il maps $49.95; pa $19.95
          031
1. Encyclopedias and dictionaries
ISBN 0-395-62439-8; 0-395-75184-5 (pa)
          LC 94-16721
First published 1983
"This edition was condensed from the fifth edition of the *Columbia Encyclopedia*. . . . Although its coverage of historical figures, geography, politics, and sports is stronger than that of popular culture, it fulfills its goal of presenting many facts to a wide audience in a useful and eminently readable fashion for a modest price. An ideal home reference tool: also useful in small public, school, and academic libraries." Choice

The **Dorling** Kindersley visual encyclopedia. Dorling Kindersley 1995 456p il $44.95   **031**
1. Encyclopedias and dictionaries
ISBN 1-56458-985-4   LC 94-45785
"A one-volume encyclopedia that attempts to partner straightforward, high-quality factual information with a plethora of visual aids to instruct and intrigue readers.

The Dorling Kindersley visual encyclopedia—
Continued

The tome is divided into 11 subject areas." SLJ

This work "differs from visual dictionaries in that it is more than a collection of labeled pictures; there is considerable text as well. . . . The diversity and clarity of illustrations and the effort to lure readers by humor and tantalizing facts are commendable." Booklist

The Encyclopedia Americana. Grolier 30v il maps apply to publisher for price   **031**
1. Encyclopedias and dictionaries
Also available CD-ROM version
First published 1829. Frequently revised
Supplemented by: The Americana annual
"An encyclopedia suitable for junior and senior high school students as well as adults and college-level students. A broad base of scholarship supports the authority of *Americana*. . . . The sciences, mathematics, American history, and the social sciences are particularly well developed. Practical as well as historical and theoretical aspects of subjects are covered. Continuous revision ensures that content is reasonably current. The text is clear, concise, and understandable." Ref Sources for Small & Medium-size Libr. 5th edition
For a review see: Booklist, Sept. 15, 1996

Hirsch, E. D. (Eric Donald), 1928-
The dictionary of cultural literacy; [by] E. D. Hirsch, Jr., Joseph F. Kett, James Trefil. 2nd ed, rev and updated. Houghton Mifflin 1993 619p il maps $24.95   **031**
1. Civilization—Dictionaries 2. English language—Dictionaries 3. United States—Civilization—Dictionaries
ISBN 0-395-65597-8   LC 93-19568
Also available CD-ROM version
First published 1988
This dictionary of general cultural information is divided into twenty-three sections, each dealing with a major field of knowledge. Within each section entries identify ideas, events, and individuals. More than 250 maps, charts and illustrations accompany the text

The Larousse desk reference; edited by James Hughes. Larousse; distributed by Larousse Kingfisher Chambers 1995 800p il maps $39.95   **031**
1. Encyclopedias and dictionaries
ISBN 1-85697-568-1   LC 94-37198
This "desk reference has seven thematic units: 'Earth and the Universe,' 'Life on Earth,' 'People,' 'History,' 'Science and Technology,' 'Arts and Culture,' and 'International World.' Each section contains a chronology, charts and tables, a glossary, and . . . biographies. . . . There are color maps for every country of the world." Booklist

The Macmillan visual desk reference; [by] the Diagram Group. Macmillan 1993 various paging il maps $29.95   **031**
1. Encyclopedias and dictionaries
ISBN 0-02-531310-X   LC 91-38184
This work "arranges information in eight thematic chapters (e.g., 'Sports,' 'The Arts,' 'Communications')

covering 1,100 key topics. Things are explained visually with 4,000 charts, graphs, tables, and diagrams and with minimal text." Booklist

The New Encyclopaedia Britannica. Encyclopaedia Britannica 32v il maps apply to publisher for price   **031**
1. Encyclopedias and dictionaries
Also available CD-ROM version, Britannica CD
First published 1768 in England; in the United States 1902. Now published with the editorial advice of the University of Chicago. First published with current title 1974. Frequently revised
"In three sections: Propaedia, or outline of knowledge; Macropaedia, with longer in-depth articles covering major topics; and Micropaedia, with shorter A-to-Z ready reference entries. *Britannica's* reputation as the basic encyclopedia for all libraries and reference collections is based on the writing and knowledge of thousands of expert contributors and consultants. Updated between major editions by the Britannica *Book of the Year*." NY Public Libr Book of How & Where to Look It Up
For a review see: Booklist, Feb. 1, 1997

The World Book encyclopedia. World Bk. 22v il maps apply to publisher for price   **031**
1. Encyclopedias and dictionaries
Also available CD-ROM version, The World Book multimedia encyclopedia
First published 1917-1918 by Field Enterprises. Frequently revised
Supplemented by: The World Book year book; another available annual supplement is Science year
"Curriculum-oriented, this superior encyclopedia is well-edited and produced to meet the reference and informational needs of students from grade four through high school. Long standing tradition of excellence for readability, accuracy, authoritativeness, objectivity, judicious and extensive use of outstanding graphics and timeliness." N Y Public Libr. Ref Books for Child Collect
For a review see: Booklist, Sept. 15, 1996

031.02 American books of miscellaneous facts

Ash, Russell
The top 10 of everything. DK Pub. il $24.95; pa $16.95   **031.02**
1. Curiosities and wonders
Annual. First published 1994
Ash "has amassed thousands of statistics on topics of popular interest, listing the 10 most (or least) common, popular, expensive, or best in each category. . . . The wide range of categories reported spans from the natural sciences (the Earth, universe, and human body), to entertainment (music, stage, radio, sports, and travel). Bright, splashy, full-color photos enliven the columnar text, as do relevant 'Did you know' sidebars. . . . A browser's dream." SLJ

Cole, Sylvia
The Facts on File dictionary of 20th-century allusions; from atom bomb to Ziegfeld girls; [by] Sylvia Cole, Abraham H. Lass. Facts on File 1990 287p $24.95　　　　**031.02**
　　1. Allusions
　　ISBN 0-8160-1915-0　　　　LC 90-41796
"The authors have compiled information on significant people (real and fictional), places, events, phrases, literary works, terms, etc., to form an excellent one-volume encyclopedia. First the reference is defined by its original significance; it is then followed by an explanation of what it has come to mean today. Most entries conclude with a quoted allusion." SLJ

Feldman, David, 1950-
When do fish sleep? and other imponderables of everyday life; illustrated by Kassie Schwan. Harper & Row 1989 260p il hardcover o.p. paperback available $11　　　　**031.02**
　　1. Questions and answers
　　ISBN 0-06-092011-4 (pa)　　　　LC 89-45038
"Feldman offers answers to such 'imponderables' as Why are rented bowling shoes so ugly? and Why do doctors tap on our backs during physical exams? Delightful and informative browsing fare." Booklist

Why do clocks run clockwise? and other imponderables; mysteries of everyday life; explained by David Feldman; illustrated by Kas Schwan. Harper & Row 1987 251p il hardcover o.p. paperback available $11　　　　**031.02**
　　1. Questions and answers
　　ISBN 0-06-091515-3 (pa)　　　　LC 87-45045
The author "answers such recurring questions as 'What causes the ringing sound in your ears?' 'Why do nurses wear white?' and 'Why doesn't a "two-by-four" measure two inches by four inches?' Feldman answers them as authoritatively and truthfully as he can, relying on as trustworthy sources as he can find and sometimes, when the query submits to no single answer, fielding several different probable responses." Booklist

Why do dogs have wet noses? and other imponderables of everyday life; illustrated by Kassie Schwan. HarperPerennial 1990 249p il hardcover o.p. paperback available $11　　　　**031.02**
　　1. Questions and answers
　　ISBN 0-06-092111-0 (pa)　　　　LC 89-46529
"Feldman poses such questions as, 'Why are racquetballs blue?' 'How did the football get its strange shape?' . . . The answers are supplied with the consultation of experts." Booklist

Information please almanac. Houghton Mifflin il maps $24.95; pa $10.95　　　　**031.02**
　　1. Almanacs 2. Statistics 3. United States—Statistics
　　ISSN 0073-7860
Annual. First published 1947 by Doubleday. Publisher varies
"Statistical and factual material organized by subject area; contains special articles by experts. Illustrated, with a color map section and detailed index." N Y Public Libr. Book of How & Where to Look It Up

Kane, Joseph Nathan, 1899-
Famous first facts: a record of first happenings, discoveries, and inventions in American history. 4th ed expanded & rev. Wilson, H.W. 1981 1350p $80　　　　**031.02**
　　1. Encyclopedias and dictionaries 2. United States—History—Dictionaries
　　ISBN 0-8242-0661-4　　　　LC 81-3395
　　New edition in preparation
　　First published 1933
"This unusual work focuses on 'firsts' on the North American continent (1,007 to date) that concern a wide range of subjects (e.g., events, inventions, discoveries)—9,000 in all. Arrangement is by subject with appropriate cross-references and concise explanations for each entry. Indexing is by year and month/date of occurrence, names of persons directly and indirectly involved, and location of the event." Nichols. Guide to Ref Books for Sch Media Cent. 4th edition

Krantz, Les
The peoplepedia; the ultimate reference on the American people; [by] Les Krantz and Jim McCormick. Holt & Co. 1996 474p il (Henry Holt reference book) $35　　　　**031.02**
　　1. Encyclopedias and dictionaries 2. United States—Statistics 3. United States—Biography
　　ISBN 0-8050-3727-6　　　　LC 95-8948
"The book is divided into three sections. Part 1, 'The American Mindset,' covers what U.S. citizens think about issues from morality to feminism to faith healing. Part 2, 'The American Collective,' is subdivided into 11 chapters, each dealing with broad areas of U.S. life, such as education, families, populations, sexuality, possessions, and more. Last, part 3 consists of short biographical entries of people who were active in their professions during the writing of this book. . . . This reference resource is recommended for public libraries [and] high school libraries." Am Ref Books Annu, 1997

The **New York** Public Library desk reference. 2nd ed. Prentice Hall General Ref. 1993 930p il maps $40　　　　**031.02**
　　1. Encyclopedias and dictionaries
　　ISBN 0-671-85014-8　　　　LC 93-18299
　　"A Stonesong Press book"
　　First published 1989 by Webster's New World
Divided into twenty-six chapters, this reference features charts, tables, lists, and illustrations providing information in such categories as signs and symbols, mathematics and science basics, the arts, grammar and punctuation, etiquette, personal finance, first aid, and household tips

Panati, Charles, 1943-
Extraordinary origins of everyday things. Harper & Row 1987 463p il hardcover o.p. paperback available $16　　　　**031.02**
　　1. Curiosities and wonders
　　ISBN 0-06-096419-7 (pa)　　　　LC 87-213
　　Paperback edition has title: Panati's extraordinary origins of everyday things

Panati, Charles, 1943——*Continued*

This work "explores the history of over 500 things, from superstitions, magazines, games, and holidays to household objects such as Kleenex, buttons, graham crackers, and wallpaper. . . . Serious researchers will appreciate the references in the 20-page bibliographic essay. . . . Fun to browse through as well as necessary for reference." Am Libr

The **People's** almanac presents The twentieth century; the definitive compendium of astonishing events, amazing people, and strange-but-true facts; [by] David Wallechinsky. Little, Brown 1995 835p il $24.95; pa $17.95
031.02

1. Almanacs 2. Curiosities and wonders
ISBN 0-316-92095-9; 0-316-92056-8 (pa)
LC 95-11568

"Seven hundred signed entries grouped under 20 subject headings reflect the century in a series of fractured glimpses, sometimes cynically, often amusingly, always entertainingly. Emphasis is on the final two-thirds of the century. Coverage is quirky (only four presidents are profiled) but broad in scope, and most entries have something memorable to impart." Libr J

The **Practical** guide to practically everything; Peter Bernstein & Christopher Ma, editors. Random House 1995 1006p il pa $13.95
031.02

1. Almanacs 2. Consumer education
ISBN 0-679-75491-1

This guide to miscellaneous information, scheduled for annual revision, is "categorized into 14 general chapters, such as money, health, education, house and garden, facts of life, computers, and autos. In selecting material, the authors looked for 'authoritative information and expert views on all the subjects that could really make a difference in your daily life.'" Libr J

Reader's Digest book of facts. 3rd rev ed. Reader's Digest Assn. 1995 432p il maps $30
031.02

1. Encyclopedias and dictionaries
ISBN 0-89577-692-8
LC 95-10117

First published 1985 in the United Kingdom; first United States edition 1987

This book is divided into the following categories: people, places, science and technology, animals and plants, arts and entertainment, the earth, and the universe

Sutton, Caroline

More how do they do that? wonders of the modern world explained; [by] Caroline Sutton and Kevin Markey. Morrow 1992 256p il hardcover o.p. paperback available $9
031.02

1. Questions and answers
ISBN 0-688-13221-9 (pa)
LC 92-22201

Companion volumes How do they do that? (ISBN 0-688-01111-X) and How did they do that? (ISBN 0-688-05935-X) available in paperback for $9 each

"Readers will learn how the *New York Times* writes its headlines, how antilock brakes work, how bubbles get into seltzer water, how calories in food are calculated,

how shredded wheat is made, and more. . . . This is a fun book recommended for secondary school and public libraries which collect trivia titles." Libr J
Includes bibliographical references

Tesar, Jenny E.

The new view almanac; the first all-visual resource of vital facts and statistics! computer graphics by David C. Bell; text by Jenny Tesar; Bruce S. Glassman, editor. Blackbirch Press 1996 608p il maps lib bdg $29.95; pa $19.95 **031.02**

1. Almanacs 2. United States—Statistics
ISBN 1-56711-123-8 (lib bdg); 1-56711-124-6 (pa)
LC 95-40618

This almanac contains over 2000 "color and black-and-white charts, tables, maps, and graphs. . . . It successfully conveys trends in topical subjects and should prove popular with visually oriented secondary school and undergraduate students." Libr J

The **Universal** almanac. Andrews & McMeel maps $22.95; pa $12.95 **031.02**
1. Almanacs
ISSN 1045-9820

Annual. First published 1989 for 1990

"The subjects covered are: the year in review, the U.S. both historically and currently, other world nations, sports, science and the arts. Since its coverage varies slightly from other almanacs, this title will not be redundant. Because of its format, it is easier to use than other almanacs and will be a primary source for young researchers." SLJ

The **World** almanac and book of facts. World Almanac Bks. il maps $27.95; pa $9.95 **031.02**
1. Almanacs 2. Statistics 3. United States—Statistics
ISSN 0084-1382

Also available CD-ROM version

Annual. First published 1868. Publisher varies

"This is the most comprehensive and well-known of almanacs. . . . Contains a chronology of the year's events, consumer information, historical anniversaries, annual climatological data, and forecasts. Color section has flags and maps. Includes detailed index." N Y Public Libr. Book of How & Where to Look It Up

032.02 English books of miscellaneous facts

Guinness book of records. Facts on File il $22.95
032.02

1. Curiosities and wonders
ISSN 0300-1679

Also available CD-ROM version

Annual. First published 1955 in the United Kingdom; in the United States 1962. Variant title: Guinness book of world records

Editors vary

"A compendium of information concerning the longest, shortest, tallest, deepest, fastest, etc., in relation to natural features, manmade structures, people, events and achievements (in sports, politics, arts and entertainment), etc., grouped in topical sections." Guide to Ref Books. 11th edition

051 American general serial publications and their indexes

Readers' guide to periodical literature. Wilson, H.W. $200 per year   **051**
1. Periodicals—Indexes
ISSN 0034-0464
Also available CD-ROM version
First published 1900. Semi-monthly in September, October, December, March, April and June; monthly in January, February, May, July, August and November. Permanent bound annual cumulations
A free pamphlet How to use the Reader's guide to periodical literature, is available upon request
A cumulative author and subject index to over 200 periodicals. Coverage includes computers, business, health, fashion, politics, education, science, sports, arts and literature with criticism of individual dramatic works, videodiscs and videotapes, operas, ballets, musicals, movies, phonograph records, dance, and television and radio programs
"This is a modern index of the best type." Sheehy. Guide to Ref Books. 10th edition

060.4 General rules of order (Parliamentary procedure)

Robert, Henry Martyn, 1837-1923
The Scott, Foresman Robert's Rules of order newly revised. a new and enl ed, by Sarah Corbin Robert, with the assistance of Henry M. Robert III, William J. Evans. Scott, Foresman $16.95 **060.4**
1. Parliamentary practice
A simplified paperback version with title: The new Robert's Rules of order, by Mary A. De Vries, is available from New Am. Lib.
First published 1876 as: Pocket manual of rules of order for deliberate assemblies. Later editions have title: Robert's Rules of order
"Long the standard compendium of parliamentary law, explaining methods of organizing and conducting the business of societies, conventions, and other assemblies. Includes convenient charts and tables." Ref Sources for Small & Medium-sized Libr. 5th edition

069 Museum science

America's Smithsonian; celebrating 150 years. Smithsonian Institution Press 1996 238p il $45; pa $24.95   **069**
1. Smithsonian Institution 2. United States—Civilization 3. Popular culture—United States
ISBN 1-56098-697-2; 1-56098-699-9 (pa)
                                          LC 95-49181
This companion volume to the Smithsonian's exhibition of treasures from their collection is divided "into sections that mark human exploration and discovery, human creativity and imagination, and a celebration of both momentous events and everyday lives." Libr J

Conaway, James, 1941-
The Smithsonian; 150 years of adventure, discovery, and wonder. Smithsonian Bks.; Knopf 1995 432p il $60   **069**
1. Smithsonian Institution
ISBN 0-679-44175-1   LC 95-17667
"Conaway's photo-rich celebration-tribute lets armchair travellers visit one of our country's best-loved and most fascinating institutions and learn its history." Booklist

070.1 News media

Cloud, Stanley
The Murrow boys; pioneers on the front lines of broadcast journalism; [by] Stanley Cloud and Lynne Olson. Houghton Mifflin 1996 445p il $27.95   **070.1**
1. Broadcast journalism 2. Journalists
ISBN 0-395-68084-0   LC 95-44939
This is a study of various CBS correspondents. Edward R. Murrow "hired and supervised a hard-working group of radio reporters who covered Europe before and during the war, including Charles Collingwood, Eric Sevaried, William L. Shirer and Howard K. Smith." N Y Times Book Rev
"*The Murrow Boys* is written with page-turning verve; the largely egocentric, hard-drinking cast is presented in detail with all warts exposed." Libr J
Includes bibliographical references

070.4 Journalism

Lande, Nathaniel
Dispatches from the front; news accounts of American wars, 1776-1991. Holt & Co. 1995 416p il (Henry Holt reference book) $35   **070.4**
1. Reporters and reporting 2. United States—Military history
ISBN 0-8050-3664-4   LC 95-13277
The author "has chosen nearly 90 works dating back to the Revolutionary War, by such familiar recent names as Ernie Pyle, John Hersey, Edward R. Murrow, David Halberstam, and Vietnam-era Peter Arnett." Libr J
"Lande's exhaustive compilation is not only fascinating reading but a great example of the ongoing bond, albeit an often reluctant one, between soldiers and the press." Booklist
Includes bibliographical references

070.5 Publishing

Blake, Barbara Radke
Creating newsletters, brochures, and pamphlets; a how-to-do-it manual; [by] Barbara Radke Blake, Barbara L. Stein. Neal-Schuman 1992 129p il (How-to-do-it manuals for school and public librarians) $35   **070.5**
1. Newsletters 2. Pamphlets 3. Public relations—Libraries
ISBN 1-55570-107-8   LC 92-1370
"The authors give suggestions for simple typewriter-pasteup newsletters as well as information on desktop

Blake, Barbara Radke—*Continued*
publishing and using commercial facilities. Particularly
useful are basic writing and design recommendations.
. . . The positive tone of the book, the practical advice,
and the realistic examples leave the reader thinking 'I
can do this' and 'I want to do this.'" Voice Youth Advocates

Includes glossary and bibliographical references

Greenfeld, Howard
Books: from writer to reader. rev ed. Crown
1989 197p il o.p.   **070.5**
1. Books 2. Book industries 3. Printing
                                    LC 88-11876
First published 1976
"Greenfeld takes the reader from a writer working
with publishers and agents, through every phase in the
creation of a book (editing, designing, layout, printing,
binding, selling). . . . [A] compassionate and accurate
portrayal." Voice Youth Advocates

Includes glossary and bibliography

071   Journalism and newspapers—
North America

Bates, Douglas
The Pulitzer Prize; the inside story of America's
most prestigious award; by J. Douglas Bates. Carol
Pub. Group 1991 291p $19.95   **071**
1. Pulitzer, Joseph, 1847-1911 2. Pulitzer Prizes
ISBN 1-55972-070-0   LC 91-13659
"A Birch Lane Press book"
A "look at the history, mechanics, and politics of
American journalism's best-known award. . . . The author also investigates the story behind the story as he
tells why certain sure winners were passed over, and he
describes the constant controversies within certain categories." Booklist

Includes bibliography

New York Times Company
The New York Times Index. New York Times
$1220 per year; includes 3 quarterly cumulations
and annual cumulation   **071**
ISSN 0147-538X
This index "has provided coverage since 1851. It is
currently in a dictionary arrangement with cross-
references to names and related topics. Entries,
chronologically arranged with topics, include brief abstracts of the news stories, which often can be used instead of the actual newspaper accounts. Book and theater
reviews are grouped in a separate section." Nichols.
Guide to Ref Books for Sch Media Cent. 4th edition

Senna, Carl, 1944-
The black press and the struggle for civil rights.
Watts 1993 160p il (African-American experience)
lib bdg $21.40; pa $6.95   **071**
1. African American newspapers 2. African Americans—Civil rights 3. United States—Race relations
ISBN 0-531-11036-2; 0-531-15693-1 (pa)
                                    LC 93-17558
"Senna traces the evolution of the black press from
1827 to the present with specific and detailed attention

to its role in African Americans' struggle for civil rights.
The book is a solid, academic contribution for students
of history and journalism. Especially interesting are the
chapters that deal with slavery, the Civil War, and Reconstruction." SLJ

Includes bibliography

080   General collections

Essay and general literature index. Wilson, H.W.
$150 per year   **080**
1. Essays—Indexes 2. Literature—Indexes
ISSN 0014-083X
Also available CD-ROM version
Works indexed, 1900-1969 which cites the 9,917 titles
analyzed in the first seven permanent cumulations is
available for $43 (ISBN 0-8242-0503-0)
Basic volume and permanent seven year (1934-1954)
and five year (1955-1989) cumulative volumes available
at $225 each
Continues the "A.L.A. index to general literature."
The basic volume published 1934 covered the period
1900-1933. Kept up to date by semi-annual supplements,
cumulating annually, with five year permanent cumulations
"This subject-author index provides access to essays
and articles in collections and anthologies published in
English. It emphasizes the humanities and social sciences
but analyzes some collections in science and other areas.
Literature receives special attention, making this an excellent source for criticism of authors around the world."
Nichols. Guide to Ref Books for Sch Media Cent. 4th
edition

Great treasury of Western thought; a compendium
    of important statements on man and his
    institutions by the great thinkers in Western
    history; edited by Mortimer J. Adler & Charles
    Van Doren. Bowker 1977 xxv, 1771p $49.50
                                                      080
1. Quotations
ISBN 0-8352-0833-8   LC 77-154
"Quotations are often long ones, the average lengths
being about 100 words. . . . Arranged in twenty chapters
(Man, Family, Love, Emotion, Mind, Knowledge, etc.)
with introductory notes for each chapter and subsection.
Overall subject and proper name index." Sheehy. Guide
to Ref Books. 10th edition

098   Prohibited works, forgeries,
hoaxes

Hit list: frequently challenged books for young
    adults; prepared by the Intellectual Freedom
    Committee of the Young Adult Library Services
    Association; with the assistance of Merri M.
    Monks and Donna Reidy Pistolis. American Lib.
    Assn. 1996 92p pa $22   **098**
1. Books—Censorship—Bibliography
ISBN 0-8389-3459-5   LC 96-14418
Also available Hit list: frequently challenged books for
children
First published 1989

Hit list: frequently challenged books for young adults—*Continued*

"Entries range from classics ('Huckleberry Finn') to popular adult literature (Stephen King) to titles by critically-acclaimed young adult authors like Chris Crutcher and Walter Dean Myers. Each includes an even-handed summary of the plot and its controversial aspects; reviews and sources of information about the author; awards and recommended lists on which the book appears; media versions; and examples of challenges. It is fascinating reading on the academic level. But more important, the book provides a model for responding intelligently and calmly to challenges. . . . This is an essential tool for school and public library staff." Voice Youth Advocates

Noble, William, 1932-

Bookbanning in America; who bans books?— and why? Eriksson 1990 349p $21.95; pa $14.95
098

1. Books—Censorship
ISBN 0-8397-1080-1; 0-8397-1081-X (pa)
LC 90-3413

The author "quotes from transcripts of trials, school board meetings, and interviews with librarians, educators, and parents. Striving for balance, he presents both sides of the censorship issue." Booklist

"A useful entry point for individuals beginning elementary research on censorship. Recommended for most public and high school libraries." Choice

Includes bibliographical references

100 PHILOSOPHY AND PSYCHOLOGY

Falcone, Vincent J., 1934-

Great thinkers, great ideas; an introduction to Western thought. 2nd ed. Cranbury Publs. 1992 c1988 274p il pa $9.95
100

1. Philosophy 2. Political science 3. Economics
ISBN 0-9629323-1-0
LC 92-7554

First published 1988 by North River Press; with new introduction

This volume presents some of the basic ideas and concepts put forward by important thinkers from Plato to Jean Paul Sartre

Includes bibliographical references

Masterpieces of world philosophy; edited by Frank N. Magill; selection by John K. Roth; with an introduction by John K. Roth. Harper & Row 1990 684p $45
100

1. Philosophy
ISBN 0-06-016430-1
LC 89-46545

This book "examines and summarizes nearly one hundred influential works through critical essays that focus on their themes and major points. Based on the . . . five-volume reference, *World Philosophy* [1982] each essay explains the historical background of the work, the life of its author, and its influence on modern thought. Alternate views of the philosopher's ideas are provided through reviews of important critical works." Publisher's note

103 Philosophy—Encyclopedias and dictionaries

The **Cambridge** dictionary of philosophy; general editor, Robert Audi. Cambridge Univ. Press 1995 xxviii, 882p il $89.95; pa $27.95 **103**

1. Philosophy—Dictionaries
ISBN 0-521-40224-7; 0-521-48328-X (pa)
LC 95-13775

This "source provides short biographical entries for many philosophers from both eastern and western traditions and covers a vast number of philosophical terms, topics, and themes. There are numerous cross-references, and the volume ends with an 'Index of Selected Names Not Occurring as Headwords.' The latter is particularly valuable in that it links specific philosophers to theories and key ideas associated with their work." Choice

The **Encyclopedia** of philosophy; Paul Edwards, editor in chief. Free Press 1973 c1967 8v in 4 $450 **103**

1. Philosophy—Dictionaries
ISBN 0-02-909200-0

A reissue of the title first published 1967 in eight volumes

This is a "clear, readable compendium of articles by authorities in many areas; includes Eastern and Western thought." N Y Public Libr. Book of How & Where to Look It Up

The **Encyclopedia** of philosophy: Supplement; Donald M. Borchert, editor in chief. Macmillan 1996 xxxii, 775p $125 **103**

1. Philosophy—Dictionaries
ISBN 0-02-864629-0
LC 95-47988

This volume updates the above entry

"The supplement is not intended to be used on its own. Rather, it 'presupposes and builds on the work embodied in the Encyclopedia' and is selective of topics chosen for inclusion. Overview articles on areas within the discipline of philosophy update the user on developments since the publication of the encyclopedia. . . . Nearly one-half of the personal entries in the supplement are new and include such philosophers as Saul Kripke, John Rawls, and George Henrik von Wright. . . . The supplement includes a comprehensive index to both itself and the encyclopedia, and cross-referencing in the supplement is made to entries in both works." Booklist

109 Philosophy—History

Adler, Mortimer Jerome, 1902-

The great ideas; a lexicon of Western thought. Macmillan 1992 xxxviii, 957p $45 **109**

1. Philosophy—History
ISBN 0-02-500573-1
LC 92-127

Originally published 1952 as v2-3 of Great books of the Western world

This work is a collection of 102 philosophical essays in which Adler synthesizes the ideas of the great philosophers from ancient to modern times. The foreword contains a new essay in which Adler addresses the "cultural delusion of the twentieth century"

Includes bibliographical references

Durant, William James, 1885-1981
The story of philosophy; the lives and opinions of the great philosophers; by Will Durant. [2nd ed] Simon & Schuster 1933 412p hardcover o.p. paperback available $15   **109**
1. Philosophy—History 2. Philosophers
ISBN 0-671-20159-X (pa)
First published 1926
A selective account of western thinkers from Socrates and Kant to Schopenhauer and Dewey
Includes glossary and bibliography

Jaspers, Karl, 1883-1969
The great philosophers. Harcourt Brace & Co. 1962-1994 4v v1-2 o.p. v3-4 ea $29.95   **109**
1. Philosophy—History 2. Philosophers
Analyzed in Essay and general literature index
Originally published in Germany
v1-2 edited by Hannah Arendt; translated by Ralph Manheim; v3-4 edited by Michael Ermarth and Leonard H. Ehrlich; translated by Edith Ehrlich and Leonard H. Ehrlich
Contents: v1 The foundations: The paradigmatic individuals; Socrates; Buddha; Confucius; Jesus. The seminal founders of philosophical thought: Plato; Augustine; Kant (o.p.); v2 The original thinkers: Anaximander; Heraclitus; Parmenides; Plotinus; Anselm; Nicholas of Cusa; Spinoza; Lao-Tzu; and Nagarjuna (o.p.); v3 Xenophanes; Democritus; Empedocles; Bruno; Epicurus; Bohme; Schelling; Leibniz; Aristotle; Hegel (ISBN 0-15-136942-9); v4 The disturbers: Descartes; Pascal; Lessing; Kierkegaard; Nietzsche; philosophers in other realms: Einstein; Weber; Marx (ISBN 0-15-136943-7)
"Extracts the living essence of each philosopher's wisdom in these highly individualistic critiques." Publ Wkly
Includes bibliographical references

Russell, Bertrand, 1872-1970
A history of Western philosophy; and its connection with political and social circumstances from the earliest times to the present day. Simon & Schuster 1945 xxiii, 895p hardcover o.p. paperback available $22   **109**
1. Philosophy—History 2. Philosophers
ISBN 0-671-20158-1 (pa)
Analyzed in Essay and general literature index
Originally designed and partly delivered as lectures at the Barnes Foundation in Pennsylvania
Contents: Ancient philosophy; Catholic philosophy; Modern philosophy. A summary is given of the main contributions of each period
"My purpose is to exhibit philosophy as an integral part of social and political life; not as the isolated speculations of remarkable individuals." Preface

Solomon, Robert C.
A short history of philosophy; [by] Robert C. Solomon, Kathleen M. Higgins. Oxford Univ. Press 1996 329p $27.50; pa $14.95   **109**
1. Philosophy—History
ISBN 0-19-508647-3; 0-19-510196-0 (pa)
                                      LC 95-12578
"This general history of philosophy . . . focuses on Western philosophy, but also discusses non-Western

philosophical traditions. The authors cover major philosophers and movements as well as minor but interesting figures. They treat serious religious thought as philosophical, and include information about the Jewish, Christian, and other religious traditions." Publisher's note
"This is a fine overview of the subject that any interested reader will find rewarding." Libr J
Includes bibliographical references

133   Parapsychology and occultism

Cavendish, Richard
The world of ghosts and the supernatural. Facts on File 1994 160p il maps $24.95   **133**
1. Parapsychology 2. Occultism 3. Supernatural
ISBN 0-8160-3209-2   LC 94-15743
"In concise entries, Cavendish examines fact and fiction about the world of ghosts and the supernatural, touching on such varied subjects as the Tower of London, funeral rites in India, and the poet Wilfred Owen. An entertaining work for circulating or reference." Booklist

Encyclopedia of occultism & parapsychology; edited by J. Gordon Melton. 4th ed. Gale Res. 1996 2v set $315   **133**
1. Occultism—Dictionaries 2. Parapsychology—Dictionaries
ISBN 0-8103-5487-X
First published 1978 under the editorship of Leslie Shepard
"A compendium of information on the occult sciences, magic, demonology, superstitions, spiritism, mysticism, metaphysics, psychical science, and parapsychology, with biographical and bibliographical notes and comprehensive indexes." Title page

Man, myth, & magic; the illustrated encyclopedia of mythology, religion, and the unknown; editor in chief, Richard Cavendish. rev ed. Marshall Cavendish 1995 21v il lib bdg set $549.95   **133**
1. Occultism—Dictionaries 2. Mythology—Dictionaries 3. Religion—Dictionaries
ISBN 1-85435-731-X   LC 94-10784
Originally issued in the United Kingdom in installments; first United States edition published 1970 in 24 volumes
This encyclopedia covers subject categories in mythology, world religions, and the supernatural, with special emphasis on anthropology, art and symbolism, and history
"High-school and public libraries . . . will find this encyclopedia valuable." Booklist

The Mysterious world; by the editors of Time-Life Books. Time-Life Bks. 1992 144p il maps (Mysteries of the unknown) $9.95   **133**
1. Parapsychology
                                      LC 92-20196
This book surveys beliefs in supernatural phenomena in many parts of the world including ghosts, magic and mysticism, monsters, UFOs, spiritualism, and the occult
Includes bibliography

Paranormal phenomena: opposing viewpoints; Terry O'Neill, book editor; Stacey Tipp, assistant editor. Greenhaven Press 1991 238p il lib bdg $19.95; pa $11.95   **133**
1. Parapsychology
ISBN 0-89908-487-7 (lib bdg); 0-89908-462-1 (pa)
LC 90-24081

"Opposing viewpoints series"

Presents opposing viewpoints on the existence of paranormal phenomena such as extrasensory perception, unidentified flying objects, and the prediction of the future

"An above-average overview of the field of parapsychology." SLJ

Includes bibliography

133.1   Apparitions

Classic American ghost stories; 200 years of ghost lore from the Great Plains, New England, the South, and the Pacific Northwest; edited by Deborah A. Downer. August House 1990 214p $19.95; pa $12.95   **133.1**
1. Ghosts
ISBN 0-87483-115-6; 0-87483-118-0 (pa)
LC 90-34782

"Editor Deborah Downer brings together stories from newspapers, journals, and magazines, none of which were written as fictitious. An index references story locations by city and state." Publisher's note

Guiley, Rosemary Ellen
The encyclopedia of ghosts and spirits. Facts on File 1992 374p il $40; pa $20   **133.1**
1. Ghosts—Dictionaries 2. Parapsychology—Dictionaries
ISBN 0-8160-2140-6; 0-8160-2846-X (pa)
LC 91-37427

This "compendium of the supernatural documents the fascinating world of ghosts, goblins, and spirits. In over 400 alphabetical entries, the author provides descriptions of and explanations for strange spiritual phenomena, apparitions, and other ghostly events, including both those based in folk traditions and those investigated by scientific method. . . . In addition, the work also provides numerous biographical sketches of persons involved in the reporting or debunking of ghosts and psychical research. Some entries are illustrated and each entry ends with a short bibliography for further study." Am Libr

Norman, Michael, 1947-
Historic haunted America; [by] Michael Norman and Beth Scott. TOR Bks. 1995 445p $24.95; pa $7.99   **133.1**
1. Ghosts
ISBN 0-312-85752-7; 0-8125-6436-7 (pa)
LC 95-23291

Companion volume to Haunted America (1994)
"A Tom Doherty Associates book"

"Having traversed the United States and Canada to garner eyewitness accounts of ghostly sightings and habitats, the authors present . . . [an] assortment of earthly visitations by restless spirits of bygone eras residing in such common locales as homes, theaters, plantations, open fields, schools, and railroad cars. . . . Mesmerizing, spine-tingling—and not to be missed by any folklore collection." Libr J

Includes bibliographical references

133.3   Divinatory arts

Schimmel, Annemarie
The mystery of numbers. Oxford Univ. Press 1993 314p il $25; pa $12.95   **133.3**
1. Symbolism of numbers
ISBN 0-19-506303-1; 0-19-508919-7 (pa)
LC 90-22456

Based on a German work by Franz Carl Endres

Schimmel "covers everything from the origins of our Arabic numbers to modern superstitions and number games, stopping off to explore the Gnostics, mysticism, and Islam. The author continues with a detailed description of the various meanings and symbolism associated with each individual number up to 40, and then includes assorted descriptions from 42-10,000. Each of these chapters is fascinating and includes much detail taken from religion, mythology, daily life, and scientific observation." SLJ

Includes bibliographic references

133.4   Demonology and witchcraft

Guiley, Rosemary Ellen
The encyclopedia of witches and witchcraft. Facts on File 1989 488p il $45; pa $22.95 **133.4**
1. Witchcraft—Dictionaries
ISBN 0-8160-1793-X; 0-8160-2268-2 (pa)
LC 89-11776

This volume contains over 500 essay "entries on modern Wiccan philosophy, practices, and beliefs plus a wealth of historical information on the various witch trials in Europe and America during the persecution of folk magic practitioners, midwives, and healers. . . . It also offers an impressive collection of current biographies of contemporary 20th-century witches." Libr J

Includes bibliography

Hansen, Chadwick, 1926-
Witchcraft at Salem. Braziller 1969 252p il $17.95; pa $11.95   **133.4**
1. Witchcraft 2. Salem (Mass.)—History
ISBN 0-8076-0492-5; 0-8076-1137-9 (pa)

The author examines the practice of witchcraft and its effect upon the people of colonial New England

Includes bibliography

Hill, Frances, 1943-
A delusion of Satan; the full story of the Salem witch trials. Doubleday 1995 269p il map $23.95   **133.4**
1. Trials 2. Witchcraft 3. Salem (Mass.)—History
ISBN 0-385-47255-2   LC 95-12900

As Hill tells the "tale about how a group of girls accused innocent women from all walks of life of practic-

Hill, Frances, 1943——*Continued*
ing witchcraft, thus instigating a year of mass hysteria and causing the death of 25 people, she emphasizes the harshness, sterility, and repressiveness of seventeenth-century New England Puritan life." Booklist
Includes bibliographical references

Karlsen, Carol F., 1940-
The devil in the shape of a woman; witchcraft in colonial New England. Norton 1987 360p o.p.; Vintage Bks. paperback available $13   **133.4**
1. Witchcraft 2. New England—History—1600-1775, Colonial period
ISBN 0-679-72184-3 (pa)   LC 87-16615
The author presents a "social history of witchcraft in Puritan New England (1620-1725). She unearths detailed evidence which demonstrates that prosecuted and accused witches generally were older, married women who had violated the religious and/or economic Puritan social hierarchy. . . . A well-written, provocative addition to the recent scholarship on New England witchcraft." Libr J
Includes bibliographical references

133.5   Astrology

Lewis, James R.
The astrology encyclopedia. Gale Res. 1994 xxvii, 603p il maps $45; pa $19.95   **133.5**
1. Astrology—Dictionaries
ISBN 0-8103-8900-2; 0-8103-9460-X (pa)
          LC 94-3067
This encyclopedia "presents 780 alphabetically arranged entries. . . . The focus here is almost entirely on natal astrology, which deals with individual personalities, as opposed to mundane astrology, which is concerned with nations and political events. . . . Entries ranging in length from one sentence to more than 15 pages include dozens of historical and contemporary astrologers, hundreds of astronomical bodies (mostly asteroids), and technical terms of astrology and astronomy." Booklist
"Recommended for all libraries." Libr J

133.9   Spiritualism

What survives? contemporary explorations of life after death; edited by Gary Doore. Tarcher, J.P. 1990 287p pa $13.95   **133.9**
1. Future life 2. Death 3. Materialism
ISBN 0-87477-583-3   LC 90-35084
"This collection of original writing explores the questions, Is there life after death? and, if so, What's it like? Essays on reincarnation, communication with the dead, and panoramic vision are included in the discussion of evidence for an afterlife." Booklist
Includes bibliographical references

140   Specific philosophical schools

Constructing a life philosophy: opposing viewpoints; David L. Bender, book editor. Greenhaven Press il lib bdg $19.95; pa $11.95   **140**
1. Life 2. Philosophy
          LC 92-40706
"Opposing viewpoints series"
First published 1971. (6th edition 1993) Periodically revised
This volume presents a variety of approaches for exploring the meaning of life. Religious, moral, and ethical concerns are stressed
Includes bibliographical references

150.19   Psychological systems, schools, viewpoints

Bettelheim, Bruno
Freud and man's soul. Knopf 1983 111p hardcover o.p. paperback available $9   **150.19**
1. Freud, Sigmund, 1856-1939 2. Psychoanalysis
ISBN 0-394-71036-3 (pa)   LC 82-47809
The author argues that Freud was a great humanist and that mistranslation of his work has lead American psychoanalysis astray

Freud, Sigmund, 1856-1939
The basic writings of Sigmund Freud; translated and edited by A.A. Brill. Modern Lib. 1995 c1938 973p $20   **150.19**
1. Psychoanalysis
ISBN 0-679-60166-X   LC 95-13411
A reissue of the 1938 edition
Contents: Psychopathology of everyday life; The interpretation of dreams; Three contributions to the theory of sex; Wit and its relations to the unconscious; Totem and taboo; The history of the psychoanalytic movement

Rogers, Carl R. (Carl Ransom), 1902-1987
A way of being. Houghton Mifflin 1980 395p hardcover o.p. paperback available $11.95 **150.19**
1. Psychology 2. Humanism
ISBN 0-395-75530-1 (pa)   LC 80-20275
The author offers a "collection of papers, talks, autobiographical sketches and vignettes of patients' experiences in workshops and therapy." Publ Wkly
"This is a book rich in theoretical insights and experiential sharing, and full of invigorating optimism." Libr J
Includes bibliography

Skinner, B. F. (Burrhus Frederic), 1904-1990
About behaviorism. Knopf 1974 256p hardcover o.p. paperback available $9   **150.19**
1. Behaviorism
ISBN 0-394-71618-3 (pa)
The author defines, analyzes and defends the science of behaviorism with chapters exploring the causes of behavior, operant behavior, verbal behavior, thinking, causes and reasons, knowledge, emotion and self
Includes bibliography

150.9 Psychology—Historical and geographic treatment

Fancher, Raymond E.
Pioneers of psychology. 3rd ed. Norton 1996
511p il pa $13.95   **150.9**
1. Psychology—History 2. Psychologists
ISBN 0-393-96994-0   LC 96-6403
First published 1979
The author traces the evolution of psychology through the work of leading psychologists from Descartes, Gall and Kant to James, Piaget, Skinner and Pascal. Includes a chapter on artificial intelligence, beginning with Pascal's "Pascaline" and proceeding through the machines and programs of Leibniz, Babbage, Turing, and Newell, Shaw, and Simon
Includes bibliographical references

152.14 Visual perception

Elkins, James, 1955-
The object stares back; on the nature of seeing.
Simon & Schuster 1996 271p il $24   **152.14**
1. Perception 2. Vision
ISBN 0-684-80095-0   LC 95-44872
The author forges a "synthesis of art history, biology, neurology, psychology, and his own assiduous and penetrating observations in an effort to understand more about how the eye and mind work in tandem. Almost unnervingly accurate and gratifyingly frank about our habits of sight, Elkins describes and analyzes such rarely examined phenomena as how objects change when you look at them; how we are changed by what we see; how we both see and are seen; and how much we don't see." Booklist
Includes bibliographical references

152.4 Emotions and feelings

Dentemaro, Christine
Straight talk about anger; [by] Christine Dentemaro and Rachel Kranz. Facts on File 1995
148p $17.95; pa $9.95   **152.4**
1. Anger
ISBN 0-8160-3079-0; 0-8160-3551-2 (pa)
    LC 94-34591
"The authors probe biological reactions associated with anger and present situations that may serve as provocations. There are excellent discussions of hidden anger and passive-aggressive behavior, strategies for constructive release of anger, and valuable suggestions for using it as an ally to correct injustice." SLJ
Includes bibliography

Emotions; by the editors of Time-Life Books.
Time-Life Bks. 1994 144p il (Journey through the mind and body) $19.95   **152.4**
1. Emotions
    LC 94-8885
This volume "investigates the full range of human emotions and their physical manifestations. Why we

blush when embarrassed and laugh at a funny story. How our body responds to love and fear." Publisher's note
Includes bibliographical references

Fromm, Erich, 1900-1980
The art of loving. Harper & Row 1956
hardcover o.p. paperback available $11   **152.4**
1. Love
ISBN 0-06-091594-3 (pa)
Also available in hardcover from Borgo Press
"World perspectives"
"Dr. Fromm discusses love in all its aspects, not only romantic love, so surrounded by false conceptions, but also the love of parents for children, brotherly love, erotic love, self-love and love of God." Publisher's note
Includes bibliographical references

Lorenz, Konrad
On aggression; translated by Marjorie Kerr Wilson. Harcourt Brace Jovanovich 1966 306p
hardcover o.p. paperback available $9.95   **152.4**
1. Aggressiveness (Psychology) 2. Comparative psychology
ISBN 0-15-668741-0 (pa)
"A Helen and Kurt Wolff book"
Original German edition published 1963 in Austria
The author examines aggression in animals and humans, noting both the positive and destructive manifestations of such behavior
Includes bibliography

153 Conscious mental processes and intelligence

Arendt, Hannah
The life of the mind. Harcourt Brace Jovanovich
1981 2v in 1 pa $14   **153**
1. Intellect 2. Philosophy 3. Free will and determinism
ISBN 0-15-651992-5
First published 1978 as two separate volumes with titles: v1 Thinking and v2 Willing
An exploration of the nature of mind and thought. Among the concepts discussed are: appearance versus reality, free will, determinism, and necessity
Includes bibliographical references

Metos, Thomas H., 1932-
The human mind; how we think and learn.
Watts 1990 128p il lib bdg $22   **153**
1. Brain 2. Thought and thinking 3. Psychology of learning
ISBN 0-531-10885-6   LC 90-34960
"A Venture book"
Describes how the human brain and nervous system function and examines recent theories on the origins of intelligence
"Interestingly written, the book could be read completely for its informational value or consulted as a quick reference." SLJ
Includes glossary and bibliography

Sagan, Carl, 1934-1996
The dragons of Eden; speculations on the evolution of human intelligence. Random House 1977 263p il $10.95　　**153**
1. Intellect 2. Brain 3. Genetics
ISBN 0-394-41045-9　　LC 76-53472
Also available in paperback from Ballantine Bks.
In this study of human intellect "Sagan is principally preoccupied with the neocortex, with its left hemisphere, responsible for language and logic, a right hemisphere in charge of intuition and spatial dimension, and a corpus callosum that mediates and synthesizes the two." Atl Mon
"Sagan is an excellent popularizer: he has a talent for making complex scientific ideas comprehensible to intelligent and curious young adults." SLJ
Includes glossary and bibliography

153.1　Memory and learning

Noll, Richard
The encyclopedia of memory and memory disorders; [by] Richard Noll and Carol Turkington. Facts on File 1994 265p $45　　**153.1**
1. Memory—Dictionaries
ISBN 0-8160-2610-6　　LC 94-1590
This volume "contains more than 700 alphabetically arranged entries summarizing the current knowledge of memory research. The entries range from a few short sentences to several pages in length. . . . The material is broad in scope, including profiles of noted researchers; clinical terms and concepts; descriptions of diseases and disorders; and information on drugs and mnemonic therapies related to memory." Libr J
For a fuller review see: Booklist, Feb. 15, 1995

153.3　Imagination and imagery. Creativity

Grudin, Robert
The grace of great things; creativity and innovation. Ticknor & Fields 1990 257p o.p.; Houghton Mifflin paperback available $12.95
　　153.3
1. Creative ability
ISBN 0-395-58868-5 (pa)　　LC 89-77195
"The author examines art, teaching, literature, philosophy, and related disciplines, looking at the process of innovation itself and using concise examples from the work of Plato, Rilke, F.L. Wright, etc. . . . A beautifully written book that is highly recommended." Libr J
Includes bibliographical references

153.6　Communication

Fast, Julius, 1918-
Body language. Evans & Co. 1970 192p o.p.; Pocket Bks. paperback available $5.99　　**153.6**
1. Body language
ISBN 0-671-67325-4 (pa)
This book discusses the "science of kinesics, the use of non-verbal communication through the means of body

movements which may support or contradict our verbal expressions." Best Sellers
Includes bibliography

154　Subconscious and altered states and processes

Secrets of the inner mind; by the editors of Time-Life Books. Time-Life Bks. 1993 144p il (Journey through the mind and body) $19.95
　　154
1. Dreams 2. Creative ability 3. Extrasensory perception 4. Mind and body
　　LC 93-31415
This book explores "questions about the human mind and brain, including the wellsprings of imagination and creativity and the nature, function and meaning—if any—of dreams. Looks at evidence for and against the so-called sixth sense, or extra-sensory perceptions." Publisher's note
Includes glossary and bibliographical references

154.6　Sleep phenomena

Parker, Julia, 1932-
Parkers' complete book of dreams; [by] Julia & Derek Parker. Dorling Kindersley 1995 208p il $24.95　　**154.6**
1. Dreams
ISBN 1-56458-855-6　　LC 94-27918
This guide covers the history as well as theories concerning the meaning of dreaming. Advice is given on how to record and improve the ability to recall specific dreams
"There are many books on this subject, but few are as readable, colorful, and inviting as this one." SLJ

155　Differential and developmental psychology

Stefoff, Rebecca, 1951-
Friendship and love; introduction by C. Everett Koop. Chelsea House 1989 102p il (Encyclopedia of health) lib bdg $19.95　　**155**
1. Friendship 2. Love
ISBN 0-7910-0039-7　　LC 88-30032
Defines the different levels of friendship, love, and intimacy and discusses their role in leading a healthy life
This volume "reads almost like a psychology or sociology textbook. However, quality writing, with clear explanations and examples, redeems it." SLJ
Includes glossary and bibliography

155.2   Individual psychology

The **Enigma** of personality; by the editors of Time-Life Books. Time-Life Bks. 1994 144p il (Journey through the mind and body) $19.95
155.2
1. Personality
LC 93-44200
Among the topics discussed in this work are the biological factors that shape personality; psychological types; personality disorders; and reshaping the personality through means such as therapeutic drugs and psychotherapy
Includes glossary and bibliography

Steinem, Gloria
Revolution from within; a book of self-esteem. Little, Brown 1992 377p $22.95   **155.2**
1. Self-esteem 2. Feminism
ISBN 0-316-81240-4   LC 91-11356
The author discusses the importance of self-esteem and offers practical advice on ways of acquiring it
Steinem's "book unfolds like a flower: it offers literature, art, nature, meditation, and connectedness as ways of finding and exploring the self. . . . Her focus is women, but she is clear that what she has to say is for men, too, and she is neither strident nor dismissive." Libr J
Includes bibliography

155.5   Psychology of young adults

Bode, Janet
Truce: ending the sibling war. Watts 1991 125p lib bdg $22.70   **155.5**
1. Brothers and sisters
ISBN 0-531-10996-8 (lib bdg)   LC 90-47322
Explores the sometimes poor relationships of children and teens with their brothers and sisters, focusing especially on ways to end conflict and improve relations by changing attitudes and behavior
"On the whole the book is impressive because it is non-judgmental and sympathetic, and candid without any trace of titillation or dramatization." Bull Cent Child Books
Includes bibliography

Galbraith, Judy
The gifted kids' survival guide; a teen handbook; [by] Judy Galbraith and Jim Delisle; edited by Pamela Espeland. revised, expanded and updated ed. Free Spirit 1996 295p il pa $14.95
155.5
1. Gifted children
ISBN 1-57542-003-1   LC 96-29430
First published 1983 by Wetherall Publishing Company
Examines issues that are of concern for young people who have been labeled "gifted," discussing what the label means, intelligence testing, educational options, and relationships with parents and friends. Includes first-person essays on being gifted
Includes bibliographical references

Hayden, Torey L.
The tiger's child; [by] Torey Hayden. Scribner 1995 256p $21   **155.5**
1. Child abuse 2. Emotionally disturbed children 3. Child psychology
ISBN 0-02-549150-4   LC 94-36740
Also available in paperback from Avon Bks.
"A Lisa Drew book"
This continues the story of the autistic abandoned girl recorded in the author's One child (1980). "Here, Hayden describes in detail what happened to Sheila from the age of six to 16. . . . Throughout this time, she keeps track of Sheila, torn between her professional knowledge of what constitutes appropriate treatment for the young woman and her instinct to be the good mother." Libr J

155.6   Psychology of adults

Landau, Elaine
The beauty trap. New Discovery Bks. 1994 128p lib bdg $13.95   **155.6**
1. Personal grooming 2. Women—Psychology
ISBN 0-02-751389-0   LC 93-29641
"An Open book"
"Defining the beauty trap as 'a way of thinking that asserts that a woman's true value and desirability are essentially tied to the way she looks,' this book explores ways in which society and the media promote that attitude and, consequently diminish the female self-image." SLJ
This is "an important book about a subject that touches every teenage girl and the people who care about her." Booklist
Includes bibliographical references

155.9   Environmental psychology

Bettelheim, Bruno
Surviving, and other essays. Knopf 1979 432p hardcover o.p. paperback available $16   **155.9**
1. Adjustment (Psychology) 2. Social psychology
ISBN 0-394-74264-8 (pa)   LC 78-20388
Analyzed in Essay and general literature index
These essays cover topics such as the Holocaust, education, sexual mores, violence, and contemporary youth
Includes bibliographical references

Bode, Janet
Death is hard to live with; teenagers and how they cope with loss; art by Stan Mack. Delacorte Press 1993 178p il $16.95; pa $3.99   **155.9**
1. Death 2. Bereavement
ISBN 0-385-31041-2; 0-440-21929-9 (pa)
LC 92-32409
This book explores death "from both the cultural and the emotional perspective. Viewpoints of therapists and representatives from religious communities, as well as insights from specialists (a forensic expert, a funeral director, and so on), entwine with teenagers' moving personal stories." Booklist
"A sane, sensitive exploration of a difficult subject." Horn Book
Includes bibliography

Death and dying: opposing viewpoints; William Dudley, book editor. Greenhaven Press 1992 236p il $19.95; pa $11.95 **155.9**
1. Death
ISBN 0-89908-192-4; 0-89908-167-3 (pa)
LC 92-6667
"Opposing viewpoints series"
Replaces the edition published 1980 under editorship of David L. Bender and Richard Hagen
Following the usual series format, "the areas of concern addressed include the determination of death, the best treatment for the terminally ill, how dying patients can control the decision to end treatment, coping with grief, and life after death." Booklist
Includes bibliographical references

DiGiulio, Robert C., 1949-
Straight talk about death and dying; [by] Robert DiGiulio, Rachel Kranz. Facts on File 1995 134p $17.95; pa $9.95 **155.9**
1. Death 2. Bereavement
ISBN 0-8160-3078-2; 0-8160-3553-9 (pa)
LC 95-2488
The authors "utilize three fictionalized situations in which adolescents deal with death, grief, and mourning. These continuing scenarios serve as introductions to each chapter and act as guides through the bereavement process." SLJ
"The clear, cogent text is accessible to a range of readers, and its potential audience extends to any adult who deals with teenagers on a regular basis." Voice Youth Advocates

Feldman, Robert S. (Robert Stephen), 1947-
Understanding stress. Watts 1992 94p il lib bdg $22 **155.9**
1. Stress (Psychology)
ISBN 0-531-12531-9
LC 91-38158
"A Venture book"
This book "deals with a variety of issues relating to stress such as: the causes and consequences, treatment, and preventative measures. Further, the text provides examples of stress and stressful situations and mechanisms to avoid and deal with the situations." Appraisal
"A useful index, a list of organizations, and books for further reading are also included. Whether researching the topic for personal reasons or for a school assignment, readers will welcome this book." SLJ

Gootman, Marilyn E., 1944-
When a friend dies; a book for teens about grieving & healing. Free Spirit 1994 107p pa $7.95 **155.9**
1. Death 2. Bereavement
ISBN 0-915793-66-0
LC 93-37992
This book "aids teenagers who are grieving the loss of a friend, someone of their own generation. The reader is addressed alternately by the author and by teenagers who have experienced such a loss. . . . The young mourner accesses what he or she needs from the book through the questions that are the table of contents." Voice Youth Advocates
Includes bibliographical references

Gordon, James Samuel
Stress management; introduction by C. Everett Koop. Chelsea House 1990 111p il (Encyclopedia of health) lib bdg $19.95 **155.9**
1. Stress (Psychology)
ISBN 0-7910-0042-7
LC 89-25293
Discusses various aspects of stress management, including the nature and biology of stress, ecological and psychosocial aspects, techniques for stress reduction, and stress management programs
"A well-organized, useful series entry that describes the physiology involved in more detail than do most other teenage books on the subject." Booklist
Includes glossary and bibliography

Gravelle, Karen
Teenagers face to face with bereavement; [by] Karen Gravelle, Charles Haskins. Messner 1989 134p hardcover o.p. paperback available $5.95 **155.9**
1. Death 2. Bereavement
ISBN 0-671-65975-8 (pa)
LC 89-3133
In this work the authors ask seventeen teenagers, "all of whom have lost a relative or a close friend, to tell their stories. These responses are discussed . . . from the points of view of teens and counselors, as are difficult situations which may follow a death." Booklist
"The young people speak honestly and earnestly, offering coping strategies that worked for them. Both interviewees and compilers offer hope and comfort." SLJ
Includes bibliography

Grollman, Earl A.
Straight talk about death for teenagers; how to cope with losing someone you love. Beacon Press 1993 146p hardcover o.p. paperback available $9.95 **155.9**
1. Death 2. Bereavement
ISBN 0-8070-2501-1 (pa)
LC 92-34540
"Grollman explains the grieving process to teenagers in a poetic, reflective way, gently, but firmly guiding his readers through the painful process of dealing with loss of a parent, sibling, or friend. He suggests survival techniques that emphasize self-understanding and use of whatever support services are available in their communities." Book Rep

Kübler-Ross, Elisabeth
Living with death and dying. Macmillan 1981 181p il hardcover o.p. paperback available $9 **155.9**
1. Death 2. Terminal care
ISBN 0-02-086490-6 (pa)
LC 80-26984
The author argues that caring for, and living with the terminally ill need not be a solely negative experience

On death and dying. Macmillan 1991 c1969 260p $50; pa $10 **155.9**
1. Death
ISBN 0-02-567111-1; 0-02-089141-5 (pa)
LC 90-22561
A reissue of the title first published 1969
A look at the psychological, sociological and theological issues faced by the terminally ill and their caregivers
Includes bibliographical references

Maloney, Michael, 1944-

Straight talk about anxiety and depression; [by] Michael Maloney and Rachel Kranz. Facts on File 1991 121p lib bdg $16.95   **155.9**

1. Stress (Psychology) 2. Depression (Psychology)

ISBN 0-8160-2434-0   LC 90-23858

Discusses the different types of stress that can affect teenagers, the anxiety and depression that may result, and ways of coping with these situations

"This is one of a handful of books that takes teenage stress seriously." Booklist

Newman, Susan

Don't be S.A.D.: a teenage guide to handling stress, anxiety & depression. Messner 1991 121p il hardcover o.p. paperback available $8.95 **155.9**

1. Stress (Psychology) 2. Depression (Psychology)

ISBN 0-671-72611-0 (pa)   LC 91-24471

"This guide, using actual stories of teenagers who are dealing with situations that cause stress, anxiety, and depression, is divided into three main sections, each concerned with one of the three problems. . . . Some of the problems discussed include being overextended with activities, having an abusive parent, substance abuse, teen pregnancy, and serious illness. . . . This is a good book with basic advice on how to deal with stress, anxiety, and depression." Voice Youth Advocates

Includes bibliographical references

158   Applied psychology

Bode, Janet

Trust & betrayal; real life stories of friends and enemies. Delacorte Press 1995 161p $15.95   **158**

1. Friendship 2. Human relations

ISBN 0-385-32105-8   LC 94-21415

"Through group and individual conversations, Bode lets teens tell their own stories about their experiences with and concerns about peer relationships. Topics include sexual harassment, attention deficit disorder, computer bulletin board dating, homosexuality, gangs, handicapped accessibility, suicide, teen pregnancy, and abusive relationships." Book Rep

"This title gives today's YAs . . . [a] realistic, up-to-date book that speaks to their needs." SLJ

Hill, Margaret, 1915-

Coping with family expectations. Rosen Pub. Group 1990 153p lib bdg $15.95   **158**

1. Human relations 2. Family life

ISBN 0-8239-1159-4   LC 90-34018

Discusses family expectations of individuals, how they can be too harsh, too few, or too mild, how they develop and affect the individual, and how they can be understood and handled

Includes bibliography

174   Economic, professional, occupational ethics

Biomedical ethics: opposing viewpoints; Terry O'Neill, book editor. Greenhaven Press 1994 312p il lib bdg $19.95; pa $11.95   **174**

1. Medical ethics 2. Bioethics

ISBN 1-56510-062-X (lib bdg); 1-56510-061-1 (pa)

LC 93-7260

"Opposing viewpoints series"

Replaces the edition published 1987 under the editorship of Julie S. Bach

Presents opposing viewpoints on biomedical ethics issues such as genetic engineering, organ transplants, medical use of fetal tissue, and reproductive technology

Includes bibliographical references

Business ethics; Tamara Roleff, book editor. Greenhaven Press 1996 105p (At issue) lib bdg $12.95; pa $9.44   **174**

1. Business ethics

ISBN 1-56510-385-8 (lib bdg); 1-56510-384-X (pa)

LC 95-39052

"Essays drawn from book chapters and magazine articles debate the validity of corporate giving, American CEO salary packages, and some multinational businesses' overseas policies. The authors, all well known in the field of business, offer carefully honed perspectives on these issues." Booklist

Includes bibliographical references

Ethics; Carol Wekesser, book editor. Greenhaven Press 1995 269p (Current controversies) lib bdg $19.95; pa $11.95   **174**

1. Business ethics

ISBN 1-56510-231-2 (lib bdg); 1-56510-230-4 (pa)

LC 94-28195

"Essays discuss people's motivation to behave ethically, whether there is a lack of professional ethics in America, whether such practices benefit society, whether modern biomedical practices are ethical, and how to promote ethical behavior." SLJ

Includes bibliographical references

Genetic engineering: opposing viewpoints; Carol Wekesser, book editor. Greenhaven Press 1995 240p lib bdg $19.95; pa $11.95   **174**

1. Genetic engineering 2. Bioethics

ISBN 1-56510-359-9 (lib bdg); 1-56510-358-0 (pa)

LC 95-241

Replaces the edition published 1990 under the editorship of William Dudley

"Opposing viewpoints series"

This collection of articles presents various points of view about genetic engineering including whether or not it benefits society, its effects on agriculture and healthcare, whether or not it should be regulated, and the accuracy of DNA fingerprinting

Includes bibliographical references

The **Human** Genome Project and the future of health care; edited by Thomas H. Murray, Mark A. Rothstein, and Robert F. Murray, Jr. Indiana Univ. Press 1996 248p il (Medical ethics series) $29.95 **174**
1. Human Genome Project 2. Medical genetics 3. Medical ethics
ISBN 0-253-33213-3 LC 96-1718

Scientists, lawyers and scholars, present an "account of the legal, medical, ethical, and policy issues many (if not all) of us will be wrestling with, on both a personal and a public level, as a result of current genetic research." Libr J

"Well balanced in the subjects it discusses, the book serves as an excellent tool for the identification of topics for public debate." Sci Books Films

Includes bibliographical references

Mabie, Margot C. J.
Bioethics and the new medical technology. Atheneum Pubs. 1993 162p $15 **174**
1. Medical ethics 2. Bioethics
ISBN 0-689-31637-2 LC 92-22642

Examines some of the ethical questions raised by the capabilities of modern medicine

"Topics include gene therapy, organ donation and transplant, abortion, prenatal diagnostic testing in connection with the decision to terminate a pregnancy, euthanasia, surrogate motherhood, and assisted suicide. . . . Thought-provoking reading for anyone." Book Rep

Includes glossary and bibliography

176 Ethics of sex and reproduction

Reproductive technologies; Carol Wekesser, editor. Greenhaven Press 1996 191p (Current controversies) lib bdg $19.95; pa $11.95 **176**
1. Reproduction
ISBN 1-56510-377-7 (lib bdg); 1-56510-376-9 (pa) LC 95-35484

Among the issues discussed are "surrogate motherhood, creating pregnancy in post-menopausal women, genetic testing, and regulation of the reproductive technology industry." SLJ

Includes bibliographical references

177 Ethics of social relations

Goldberg, M. Hirsh
The book of lies; schemes, scams, fakes, and frauds that have changed the course of history and affect our daily lives; illustrations by Ray Driver. Morrow 1990 269p il hardcover o.p. paperback available $8 **177**
1. Truthfulness and falsehood
ISBN 0-688-10743-5 (pa) LC 89-29099

"In an interesting perspective on the 'game of lies' that has become an accepted part of our lives, Goldberg examines deceptions throughout history as well as those that pervade Hollywood images, corporate structures, the political arena, tall tales, and relationships with the opposite sex." Booklist

Includes bibliographical references

179 Other ethical norms

Animal rights and welfare; edited by Jeanne Williams. Wilson, H.W. 1991 168p (Reference shelf, v63 no4) pa $15 **179**
1. Animal rights 2. Animal experimentation
ISBN 0-8242-0815-3 LC 91-19053

The articles in the first section of this book trace the development of the animal-rights movement. The second section examines the confrontation between animal-rights activists and medical researchers over the use of animals in scientific experiments. The third section covers other groups that have been targeted by activists, such as the fur industry, the poultry industry, and hunters

Animal rights: opposing viewpoints; Andrew Harnack, book editor. Greenhaven Press 1996 240p lib bdg $24.94; pa $14.44 **179**
1. Animal rights
ISBN 1-56510-399-8 (lib bdg); 1-56510-398-X (pa) LC 95-52147

Replaces the edition published 1990 under the editorship of Janelle Rohr

"Opposing viewpoints series"

This collection of articles presents varying viewpoints regarding animal rights, animal experimentation, using animals for food, genetic engineering of farm animals, protection of wildlife, and disagreements within the animal rights movement

Includes bibliographical references

Arguing euthanasia; the controversy over mercy killing, assisted suicide, and the "right to die"; edited by Jonathan D. Moreno. Simon & Schuster 1995 251p pa $11 **179**
1. Euthanasia 2. Medical ethics
ISBN 0-684-80760-2 LC 95-9581

"A Touchstone book"

This book features "viewpoints from both sides of this emotionally charged question as well as voices from the gravely ill and their loved ones." Publisher's note

Catalano, Julie
Animal welfare; introduction by Russell E. Train. Chelsea House 1994 111p il (Earth at risk) lib bdg $19.95 **179**
1. Animal welfare 2. Animal rights
ISBN 0-7910-1591-2 LC 93-26841

The author "presents a short history of man's highly ambivalent relationship with animals both wild and domestic from the Stone Age to the present. . . . The subject spawning the most controversy is the use of animals in various forms of scientific research. . . . The pros and cons of factory farming are presented, as well as the ramifications of a population explosion among pet animals in the United States." Voice Youth Advocates

Includes bibliographical references

Euthanasia: opposing viewpoints; Carol Wekesser, book editor. Greenhaven Press 1995 214p il lib bdg $22.45; pa $11.95 **179**
1. Euthanasia
ISBN 1-56510-244-4 (lib bdg); 1-56510-243-6 (pa) LC 94-41046

"Opposing viewpoints series"

Euthanasia: opposing viewpoints—*Continued*

Replaces the edition published 1989 under the editorship of Neal Bernards

Dr. Jack Kevorkian is among the contributors to this collection of articles which debate ethical and legal aspects of euthanasia, including such issues as physician-assisted euthanasia and treatment of severely handicapped newborns

Includes bibliography

Finsen, Lawrence

The animal rights movement in America; from compassion to respect; [by] Lawrence Finsen and Susan Finsen. Twayne Pubs. 1994 309p il (Social movements past and present) $27.95; pa $15.95
                                        179

1. Animal rights movements
ISBN 0-8057-3883-5; 0-8057-3884-3 (pa)
                                      LC 93-41223

"The Finsens profile the various animal-rights groups and their philosophies, goals, and actions. . . . They treat in particular detail several of the most active and influential animal-rights organizations, including People for the Ethical Treatment of Animals and the Animal Liberation Front. . . . Though the authors acknowledge their bias in favor of animal rights . . . theirs remains an excellent primer on a growing political movement." Booklist

Includes bibliographical references

Gay, Kathlyn

The right to die; public controversy, private matter. Millbrook Press 1993 128p il (Issue and debate) lib bdg $15.90
                                        179

1. Right to die 2. Euthanasia
ISBN 1-56294-325-1   LC 92-32201

A discussion of the debate concerning the right-to-die issue, including past and present views on euthanasia, the controversial subject of assisted suicide, and the legal ramifications

"The right to die will continue to be a hotly debated topic . . . and this book is a great place to start for information." SLJ

Includes bibliography

Hendin, Herbert

Suicide in America. new & expanded ed. Norton 1995 312p $23
                                        179

1. Suicide
ISBN 0-393-03688-X   LC 94-20554

First published 1982

The author maintains that treatment of seriously suicidal people is possible and that current social policy toward suicide is guided by misconception. Euthanasia and assisted suicide are discussed

Includes bibliographical references

Landau, Elaine

The right to die. Watts 1993 96p il lib bdg $22.70
                                        179

1. Terminal care 2. Right to die
ISBN 0-531-13015-0   LC 93-10800

The author examines "patient rights in determining treatment; the true definition of death; the concept of living wills and durable powers of attorney; denial of treatment for severely disabled infants; quality of life; young adult rights versus parental choice in cases of terminal illness; and suicide and euthanasia." SLJ

"Landau's balanced examination of this controversial and emotionally charged issue will provide readers with information that is not readily available in other sources." Booklist

Includes bibliography

McCoy, J. J. (Joseph J.), 1917-

Animals in research; issues and conflicts. Watts 1993 128p lib bdg $21.40
                                        179

1. Animal experimentation 2. Animal rights movements
ISBN 0-531-13023-1   LC 92-21117

"An Impact book"

The author "summarizes the controversy surrounding the use of animals in medical research, product testing, and educational demonstrations. The book includes coverage of the various laws and guidelines that govern the use of animals, as well as an outline of the various groups concerned with animal welfare." Bull Cent Child Books

McCoy "does an excellent job of presenting a reasoned account of both viewpoints in the disagreement over animal experimentation. . . . The book provides a good basis for initiating student discussions of this explosive and divisive issue." Appraisal

Includes bibliography

Sherry, Clifford J.

Animal rights; a reference handbook. ABC-CLIO 1994 240p (Contemporary world issues) $39.50
                                        179

1. Animal rights 2. Animal welfare
ISBN 0-87436-733-6   LC 94-7168

"The first quarter presents an overview and chronology of the animal rights movement, followed by biographical sketches of key figures. Included is a section on federal laws dealing with the protection of animals, and a summary of animal rights litigation. . . . The remainder of the volume is composed of lists of various types of resources for further information." Libr J

Singer, Peter

Animal liberation. 2nd ed. New York Review of Bks.; distributed by Random House 1990 320p il $19.95
                                        179

1. Animal rights 2. Vegetarianism
ISBN 0-394-58390-6   LC 89-43160

Also available in paperback from Avon Bks.

First published 1975

The author argues against the use of animals for experimentation and as a source of food. He also describes the history of the animal rights movement

"This is a necessary purchase for any animal rights collection." Libr J

Includes bibliographical references

Singer, Peter—*Continued*
Rethinking life & death; the collapse of our traditional ethics. St. Martin's Press 1995 256p $22.95; pa $14.95 **179**
1. Medical ethics 2. Animal rights
ISBN 0-312-11880-5; 0-312-14401-6 (pa)
LC 94-45534
The author argues "for a change in attitudes toward abortion, euthanasia, fetal transplants and animal rights. He considers that 20th-century advances in medicine, technology and anthropology have made traditional Judeo-Christian ethics irrelevant and hypocritical." Publ Wkly
"This is a book sure to provoke heated controversy." Booklist
Includes bibliographical references

181   Oriental philosophy

Confucius
The wisdom of Confucius; edited and translated with notes by Lin Yutang. Modern Lib. 1994 290p $14.50 **181**
1. Chinese philosophy
ISBN 0-679-60123-6
A reissue of the Modern Library edition published 1938
A selection of writings by the Chinese political and ethical philosopher who advocated a form of rationalism based on humanity, reverence for ancient sages, and government by personal virtue

Creel, Herrlee Glessner, 1905-1994
Chinese thought from Confucius to Mao Tsê-tung. University of Chicago Press 1953 292p hardcover o.p. paperback available $13.95 **181**
1. Chinese philosophy
ISBN 0-226-12030-9 (pa)
This history of Chinese philosophy and thought features discussions of: Confucius, Mo Tzu, Menacius, Hsün Tzu, Taoism, Buddhism, and Neo-Confucianism
Includes bibliography

Great thinkers of the Eastern world; the major thinkers and the philosophical and religious classics of China, India, Japan, Korea, and the world of Islam; edited by Ian P. McGreal. HarperCollins Pubs. 1995 505p $45 **181**
1. Oriental philosophy 2. Asia—Religion
ISBN 0-06-270085-5 LC 94-19418
Companion volume Great thinkers of the western world entered in class 190
"This book serves as a brief introduction to the major ideas of more than 100 'great thinkers' of Eastern civilization. Included are philosophers (e.g., China's Confucius), mystic theologians (India's Aurobindo), and political and social thinkers (Ghandi and Mao Tse-tung). The coverage moves chronologically within each country as well as within Islam. Provided for each thinker is basic biographical information, a brief listing of 'major ideas,' a four-to-five page discussion of these ideas, and a brief bibliography for further reading." Choice

184   Platonic philosophy

Hare, R. M. (Richard Mervyn)
Plato. Oxford Univ. Press 1982 82p (Past masters series) hardcover o.p. paperback available $7.95 **184**
1. Plato
ISBN 0-19-287585-X (pa) LC 83-159441
The author examines the chief Platonic concepts in their political and intellectual context
Includes bibliography

185   Aristotelian philosophy

Adler, Mortimer Jerome, 1902-
Aristotle for everybody; difficult thought made easy; by Mortimer J. Adler. Macmillan 1978 206p hardcover o.p. paperback available $12.95 **185**
1. Aristotle, 384-322 B.C.
ISBN 0-02-064111-7 (pa) LC 78-853
Adler traces "in the simplest language and with occasional modern analogues, the logic and growth of Aristotle's basic doctrines." Publ Wkly
Includes bibliographical references

Barnes, Jonathan
Aristotle. Oxford Univ. Press 1983 c1982 101p (Past masters series) hardcover o.p. paperback available $7.95 **185**
1. Aristotle, 384-322 B.C.
ISBN 0-19-287581-7 (pa) LC 83-159918
This "book is structured into 20 short essays on subjects ranging from Aristotle's biography, to overviews on logic, psychology, and ethics, to specialized topics such as causes, teleology, and empiricism." Choice
Includes bibliography

190   Modern Western philosophy

Great thinkers of the Western world; edited by Ian P. McGreal. HarperCollins Pubs. 1992 572p $45; pa $14 **190**
1. Philosophy 2. Theology 3. Science
ISBN 0-06-270026-X; 0-06-272017-1 (pa)
LC 91-38362
"The major ideas and classic works of more than 100 outstanding Western philosophers, physical and social scientists, psychologists, religious writers, and theologians." Title page
"This guide to 116 selected authors . . . spans the ancient Greeks to the first half of the twentieth century. . . . It is arranged chronologically by the birthdate of the writer. Each entry contains birth and death dates, a list of the author's major ideas, an essay of three to five pages, and a short annotated list of secondary sources." Booklist

191   North American philosophy

Baker, James Thomas
Ayn Rand; [by] James T. Baker. Twayne Pubs.
1987 168p (Twayne's United States authors series)
$21.95   **191**
1. Rand, Ayn, 1905-1982
ISBN 0-8057-7497-1   LC 86-29569
The author "gives a good sketch of Rand's life, routine summaries of her books, and very useful outlines of
her themes and theories and of the published attacks on
and defenses of her work. Libraries in which Rand's
books thrive would do well to add this commentary."
Booklist
Includes bibliography

193   German and Austrian philosophy

Nietzsche, Friedrich Wilhelm, 1844-1900
The portable Nietzsche; selected and translated,
with an introduction, prefaces, and notes, by
Walter Kaufmann. Viking 1954 687p hardcover
o.p. paperback available $14.95   **193**
ISBN 0-14-015062-5 (pa)
"The Viking portable library"
Includes the complete texts of: Thus spoke Zarathustra, Twilight of the idols, The antichrist, and Nietzsche
contra Wagner. Selections from other works, notes and
letters complete the volume

200   RELIGION

Lynch, Patricia Ann
Christianity. Facts on File 1991 128p (World
religions) $17.95   **200**
1. Christianity
ISBN 0-8160-2441-3   LC 90-25325
"The story of the world's most widespread religion,
beginning with its history and customs, and tracing its
historical spread. Includes an overview of how Christianity is practiced throughout the world today." Publisher's
note
Includes bibliographical references

Wise women; over two thousand years of spiritual
writing by women; edited by Susan Cahill.
Norton 1996 xxiii, 395p $27.50   **200**
1. Spiritual life 2. Women—Religious life
ISBN 0-393-03946-3   LC 95-40575
This anthology includes material "drawn from diverse
traditions, genres, and places. . . . Each selection is prefaced by a brief biographical-historical introduction that
locates the selection without presuming to tell readers
how to interpret it. . . . More than half the book is devoted to material from the twentieth century." Booklist
"Cahill's collection of poems, stories, and essays is a
rich and powerful testimony to the liberating power of
divine love and justice in the lives of women." Libr J
Includes bibliographical references

200.3   Religion—Encyclopedias and dictionaries

The **Encyclopedia** of religion; Mircea Eliade,
editor in chief. Complete and unabridged ed.
Macmillan 1993 16v in 8 il set $600   **200.3**
1. Religion—Dictionaries
ISBN 0-02-897135-3   LC 93-37017
First published 1987 in 16 volumes
"Treats theoretical (e.g., doctrines, myths, theologies,
ethics), practical (e.g., cults, sacraments, meditations),
and sociological (e.g., religious groups, ecclesiastical
forms) aspects of religion; includes extensive coverage of
non-Western religions. Signed articles by some 1,400
contributors worldwide end with bibliographies. Many
composite entries treat two or more related topics. . . .
Has quickly become the standard work." Guide to Ref
Books. 11th edition

The **HarperCollins** dictionary of religion; general
editior, Jonathan Z. Smith; associate editor,
William Scott Green; area editors, Jorunn
Jacobsen Buckley [et al.]; with the American
Academy of Religion. HarperSanFrancisco 1995
154p il maps $45   **200.3**
1. Religion—Dictionaries 2. Religions—Dictionaries
ISBN 0-06-067515-2   LC 95-37024
"The 3200-plus articles are written by a team of 327
religion scholars, experts in their respective fields. . . .
In addition to the standard alphabetically arranged articles on persons, holy days, rituals, deities, scriptures,
etc., there are ten major articles dealing with ancient and
modern religious traditions and one on the study of religion." Libr J
For a fuller review see: Booklist, April 15, 1996

200.9   Religion—Historical and geographic treatment

Encyclopedia of the American religious
experience; studies of traditions and movements;
Charles H. Lippy and Peter W. Williams,
editors. Scribner 1988 3v set $295   **200.9**
1. United States—Religion
ISBN 0-684-18062-6   LC 87-4781
Analyzed in Essay and general literature index
This "set traces the effect of particular religions on
American history and the influence of American culture
on the growth of various religions and religious move-
ments." Publisher's note
This encyclopedia represents "the best of current
scholarship. Excellent for students and the general reader.
Extensive bibliographies, cross-references, and cross-
disciplinary analyses." N Y Public Libr. Book of How &
Where to Look It Up

Melton, J. Gordon
The encyclopedia of American religions. Gale
Res. $195   **200.9**
1. United States—Religion—Dictionaries 2. Sects—
Dictionaries
Companion volume to The Encyclopedia of American
religions: religious creeds, entered in class 291

Melton, J. Gordon—*Continued*
First published 1978 by McGrath Publishing Company. (5th edition 1996) Periodically revised
This study of religious and spiritual bodies in the United States provides information on approximately 1,600 groups, ranging from Adventists to Zen Buddhists

Queen, Edward L.
Encyclopedia of American religious history; by Edward L. Queen II, Stephen R. Prothero, and Gardiner H. Shattuck, Jr.; foreword by Martin E. Marty. Facts on File 1995 2v set $99 **200.9**
1. United States—Religion—Dictionaries
ISBN 0-8160-2406-5 LC 95-2487
This resource contains more than 500 articles on American religious history from pre-Colonial times to the present. Includes topics on Buddhism, Islam, Judaism, and alternative religions, as well as Christianity
For a review see: Booklist, March 1, 1996

213 Creation

Eve, Raymond A., 1946-
The creationist movement in modern America; [by] Raymond A. Eve, Francis B. Harrold. Twayne Pubs. 1990 234p (Social movements past and present) lib bdg $25.95; pa $15.95 **213**
1. Creation 2. Evolution
ISBN 0-8057-9741-6 (lib bdg); 0-8057-9742-4 (pa)
LC 90-40090
"The authors examine creationism from a sociological perspective, analyzing its roots, ideology, and the nature and tactics of its supporters. This penetrating study of the origin, success, and probable future of creationist groups offers a valuable perspective on an issue often clouded with accusations and obfuscations." Booklist
Includes bibliographical references

220 Bible

ABC's of the Bible. Reader's Digest Assn. 1991 336p il maps $32 **220**
1. Bible—Miscellanea
ISBN 0-89577-375-9 LC 90-45962
At head of title: Reader's Digest
This "book is divided into eight chapters, covering everything Biblical from creation, everyday life, miracles and the supernatural, significant persons, and messiahs, to the history of the Bible as a book. The chapters are divided into sections, each headed by a question, followed by an answer. Explanatory boxes appear throughout." Voice Youth Advocates
"This very readable reference is an easy one for YAs to use." SLJ

220.3 Bible—Encyclopedias and topical dictionaries

The **HarperCollins** Bible dictionary; general editor, Paul J. Achtemeier; associate editors, Roger S. Boraas [et al.] with the Society of Biblical Literature. HarperSanFrancisco 1996 xxiv, 1256p il $45 **220.3**
1. Bible—Dictionaries
ISBN 0-06-060037-3 LC 96-25424
First published 1985 with title: Harper's Bible dictionary
This volume features a "two-column format, with 16 single-column articles interspersed throughout (including 'Art in the Biblical Period,' 'Jesus Christ,' and 'The Temple'), and it is well illustrated. Many of the longer articles include a brief bibliography. . . . Though not a flawless work (e.g., the article 'Manasseh' treats only the 14th king of Judah but neither the patriarch nor the tribe of Israel that also bear the name), it is outstanding in terms of scholarship and writing." Libr J

The **Oxford** companion to the Bible; edited by Bruce M. Metzger, Michael D. Coogan. Oxford Univ. Press 1993 xxi, 874p il maps $55 **220.3**
1. Bible—Dictionaries
ISBN 0-19-504645-5 LC 93-19315
This volume "contains more than 700 signed entries treating the formation, transmission, circulation, socio-historical situation, interpretation, theology, uses, and influence of the Bible." Libr J
"The many contributors read as a veritable who's who among biblical scholars. Although this companion is not meant to be an exhaustive reference, it is a highly reliable guide." Booklist

220.5 Bible—Modern versions

Bible
The Holy Bible; containing the Old and New Testaments; translated out of the original tongues; and with the former translations diligently compared and revised by King James's special command, 1611. Oxford Univ. Press prices vary
220.5

Available in various bindings and editions
The authorized or King James Version originally published 1611

The Holy Bible: new revised standard version; containing the Old and New Testaments with the Apocryphal/Deuterocanonical books. Nelson, T. maps prices vary **220.5**

Available in various bindings in regular and large print editions
This version first published 1989
"Intended for public reading, congregational worship, private study, instruction, and meditation, it attempts to be as literal as possible while following standard American English usage, avoids colloquialism, and prefers simple, direct terms and phrases." Sheehy. Guide to Ref Books. 10th edition. suppl

Bible—*Continued*

Holy Bible: the new King James Version; containing the Old and New Testaments. Nelson, T. prices vary   **220.5**

Available in various editions and bindings
This version first published 1982
"Protestant. This edition replaces 17th Century verb forms and second person pronouns. Updates archaic terms. Psalms and Job appear as poetry." N Y Public Libr. Ref Books for Child Collect. 2d edition

The new American Bible; with revised New Testament; translated from the original languages, with critical use of all the ancient sources by members of the Catholic Biblical Association of America; sponsored by the Bishops' Committee of the Confraternity of Christian Doctrine. Benziger 1987 1347, 513, 16p maps $8.75   **220.5**
ISBN 0-02-641640-9
First published 1970 by Kenedy
"Roman Catholic version based on modern English translations; replaces the Douay edition." N Y Public Libr. Book of How & Where to Look It Up

The new Jerusalem Bible. Doubleday maps prices vary   **220.5**

Available in various editions and bindings
First published in this format 1966 with title: The Jerusalem Bible
General editor: Henry Wansbrough
"Derives from the French version edited at the Dominican Ecole Biblique de Jerusalem and known as 'La Bible de Jerusalem.' The introductions and notes are 'a direct translation from the French, though revised and brought up to date in some places' but translation of the Biblical text goes back to the original languages." Sheehy. Guide to Ref Books. 10th edition

The revised English Bible. Oxford Univ. Press; Cambridge Univ. Press 1989 prices vary   **220.5**

Available in various bindings with and without the Apocrypha
A revised edition of: The new English Bible, first published 1970
This version is based upon a re-examination of the original Greek, Hebrew, and Aramaic texts, and is written in contemporary English

220.6   Bible—Interpretation and criticism

Porter, J. R. (Joshua Roy), 1921-
The illustrated guide to the Bible. Oxford Univ. Press 1995 288p il maps $35   **220.6**
1. Bible—History of Biblical events 2. Palestine—Civilization
ISBN 0-19-521159-6   LC 95-7696
Examines the Biblical narratives in their historical, social, archaeological, and mythological contexts and pro-

vides a section with a book-by-book summary of the Bible
Includes bibliographical references

220.9   Bible—Geography, history, biography, stories

Aharoni, Yohanan, 1919-1976
The Macmillan Bible atlas; [by] Yohanan Aharoni and Michael Avi-Yonah; designed and prepared by Carta. completely rev 3rd ed, [by] Anson F. Rainey, Ze'ev Safrai. Macmillan 1993 unp il maps $35   **220.9**
1. Bible—Geography—Maps 2. Bible—History of biblical events 3. Palestine—Maps
ISBN 0-02-500605-3   LC 92-27895
First published 1968
This atlas contains over 200 maps and depicts events from 3,000 B.C. to A.D. 200 including migrations, conquests, economic developments, archeological excavations, and church growth. It incorporates Egyptian, Assyrian, Greek, and Roman resources in addition to recent biblical studies

Calvocoressi, Peter
Who's who in the Bible. Viking 1987 xxxi, 269p maps $19.95; pa $13.95   **220.9**
1. Bible—Biography
ISBN 0-670-81188-2; 0-14-051212-8 (pa)
LC 87-50540
"This work provides profiles, ranging in length from a sentence to several pages, of some 450 biblical characters. It is unusual in discussing the literature, visual arts, and music associated with many of these characters." Libr J

Oxford Bible atlas; edited by Herbert G. May; with the assistance of G.N.S. Hunt; in consultation with R.W. Hamilton. 3rd ed, rev for the 3rd ed by John Day. Oxford Univ. Press 1984 144p il maps $31.25; pa $17.95   **220.9**
1. Bible—Geography
ISBN 0-19-143452-3; 0-19-143451-5 (pa)
LC 84-10052
First published 1962
"An introductory essay supported by 50 photos and two chronological tables surveys the geography and climate of the area, and traces the history of the Israelites from 1025 B.C. to the fall of Jerusalem in A.D. 70. The map section contains 26 revised colored maps showing topography, climate, historical periods, and archaeological sites." Wynar. Guide to Ref Books for Sch Media Cent. 3d edition

Reader's Digest atlas of the Bible; an illustrated guide to the Holy Land. Reader's Digest Assn. 1982 c1981 256p il maps $30   **220.9**
1. Bible—Geography 2. Bible—History of biblical events 3. Middle East—Antiquities
ISBN 0-89577-097-0   LC 80-53426
Editor: Joseph L. Gardner

Reader's Digest atlas of the Bible—*Continued*
This volume "serves as a historical atlas and a companion to the Bible. The extensive text (more than half of the volume) includes a narrative chronology of biblical events, information relating to the geography and history of Palestine, captions, and boxed, supplemental information. . . . Other features are a 30-page gazetteer identifying 900 villages and towns, a list of readings, a key to biblical quotations, and an index." Wynar. Guide to Ref Books for Sch Media Cent. 3d edition

Rogerson, J. W. (John William), 1935-
Atlas of the Bible; [by] John Rogerson. Facts on File 1985 237p il maps $45   **220.9**
1. Bible—Geography 2. Bible—History of biblical events
ISBN 0-8160-1207-5   LC 84-25980
This volume "treats the subject geographically rather than historically. . . . Part one of the book is devoted to a discussion of the composition and transmission of biblical literature, while part two presents an outline of biblical history and a pictographic account of the Bible in art. But the discussion of the geography of the Bible in part three constitutes by far the largest portion of his study." Booklist
This atlas is "an admirably brisk and comprehensive presentation of an enormous amount of information." Atl Mon

Who's who in the Bible. Reader's Digest Assn. 1994 480p il maps $32   **220.9**
1. Bible—Biography
ISBN 0-89577-618-9   LC 94-17591
"More than 500 people, Aaron to Job's friend Zophar, are profiled in the alphabetical entries. . . . At the head of each biography is the pronunciation, original language, and meaning (if known) of the name; following is a summary and interpretation of that person's story, complete with biblical citations and cross-references in 'bold' type to related entries." Publisher's note
For a review see: Booklist, Feb. 1, 1995

221.5 Bible. Old Testament— Modern versions

Bible. O.T.
The Old Testament: King James Version; with an introduction by George Steiner. Knopf 1996 li, 1382p $35   **221.5**
ISBN 0-679-45102-1   LC 96-22789
"Everyman's library"
An edition of the classic translation of the Old Testament into the language of seventeenth-century England. Steiner's introduction provides a look at the historical, social, political, literary and philosophical impact of the King James version

221.9 Bible. Old Testament— Geography, history, biography, stories

Heaton, Eric William
Everyday life in Old Testament times; [by] E. W. Heaton; illustrated from drawings by Marjorie Quennell. Scribner 1956 240p il maps o.p. **221.9**
1. Bible. O.T. 2. Palestine—Social life and customs
A study on daily life of the Israelites during the period 1250-586 B.C.

225.9 Bible. New Testament— Geography, history, biography, stories

Bouquet, Alan Coates
Everyday life in New Testament times; [by] A. C. Bouquet; illustrated from drawings by Marjorie Quennell. Scribner 1954 c1953 235p il maps o.p.
225.9
1. Bible. N.T.—Antiquities 2. Palestine—Social life and customs
A look at how people lived in Palestine under Roman rule

232.9 Family and life of Jesus

Bishop, Jim, 1907-1987
The day Christ died; [introduction by Paul L. Maier] HarperSanFrancisco 1991 c1957 272p pa $11   **232.9**
1. Jesus Christ—Crucifixion
ISBN 0-06-060816-1   LC 90-42233
A reissue with new introduction of the title first published 1957
An hour-by-hour account of the Last Supper, trial and crucifixion
Includes bibliography

248 Christian experience, practice, life

Lewis, C. S. (Clive Staples), 1898-1963
The Screwtape letters. Macmillan 1943   **248**
1. Christian life 2. Satire
Hardcover and paperback editions available from various publishers
An exchange of letters between an experienced devil and his apprentice nephew

252   Texts of sermons

✓ **King, Martin Luther, 1929-1968**
Strength to love; [by] Martin Luther King, Jr.
Harper & Row 1963 146p o.p.; Fortress Press
paperback available $10   **252**
1. Sermons
ISBN 0-8006-1441-0 (pa)
Also available Walker & Co. large print edition
A collection of sermons addressing social injustice and
racism
Includes bibliography

270   Christian church history

Chadwick, Owen
A history of Christianity. St. Martin's Press
1996 304p il $35   **270**
1. Church history
ISBN 0-312-13807-5   LC 96-2631
"A Thomas Dunne book"
This overview of Christianity is "illustrated, with the
text and pictures working well together to give the reader
a clear meaning of basic Christian concepts. . . . The
facts are correct, the time lines are accurate, the voice is
that of a lover of Christian history rather than a purely
academic scholar." Libr J

The **Oxford** illustrated history of Christianity;
edited by John McManners. Oxford Univ. Press
1990 724p il maps $55; pa $27.50   **270**
1. Church history
ISBN 0-19-822928-3; 0-19-285259-0 (pa)
     LC 90-30280
"A collection of 19 essays written by noted individuals and arranged in chronological order from first-century
Christianity to projections about the future of the religion. Approximately 350 illustrations complement the selections. . . . The thorough index includes ideas and
movements as well as proper names, guiding readers to
both text and illustrations. While not easy reading, this
is an excellent research source." SLJ
Includes bibliographical references

270.6   Christian church— Reformation

The **Oxford** encyclopedia of the Reformation;
Hans J. Hillerbrand, editor in chief. Oxford
Univ. Press 1996 4v set $450   **270.6**
1. Reformation 2. Doctrinal theology 3. Europe—
Church history 4. Sixteenth century
ISBN 0-19-506493-3   LC 95-24520
This work contains "1200-plus articles on standard
figures or topics such as the Church, Luther, the Bible,
Loyola, the Council of Trent, and predestination, as well
as such varied topics as America, art, education, literacy,
printing, Jews, medicine, music, marriage, and popular
religion." Libr J
For a fuller review see: Booklist, March 1, 1996

280   Christian denominations and sects

Mead, Frank Spencer, 1898-1982
Handbook of denominations in the United
States; [by] Frank S. Mead. Abingdon Press
$15.95   **280**
1. Sects 2. United States—Religion
First published 1957. (10th edition 1995) Periodically
revised
Current edition edited by Samuel S. Hill
"History and present structure of Christian religious
bodies in the United States. Reports on doctrines of dif-
ferent churches. Includes bibliography and index." N Y
Public Libr. Book of How & Where to Look It Up

282   Roman Catholic Church

The **HarperCollins** encyclopedia of Catholicism;
general editor, Richard P. McBrien; associate
editors, Harold W. Attridge [et al.]
HarperSanFrancisco 1995 xxxviii, 1349p il maps
$45   **282**
1. Catholic Church—Dictionaries
ISBN 0-06-065338-8   LC 94-39972
"This encyclopedic dictionary contains 4700 entries by
277 experts. . . . Broad-ranging topics in Catholic theology, history, culture, art, canon law, literature, etc., are
replete with cross references, photos, maps, tables, diagrams, and charts." Libr J
For a fuller review see: Booklist, Sept. 1, 1995

289.7   Mennonite churches

Amish roots; a treasury of history, wisdom, and
lore; [edited by] John A. Hostetler. Johns
Hopkins Univ. Press 1989 319p il $39; pa
$16.95   **289.7**
1. Amish
ISBN 0-8018-3769-3; 0-8018-4402-9 (pa)
     LC 88-31688
This is a compilation of "writing by and about the
Amish from journals and letters, family and farm records, newspaper stories, poems, songs and stories. Ranging from the observations of the first Anabaptist immigrants in the 1700s to the present, the over 150 entries—
commenting on church, family life, work, school and the
rich Amish agricultural heritage—form a remarkably
complete portrait." Publ Wkly
Includes bibliography

Hostetler, John A., 1918-
Amish society. 4th ed. Johns Hopkins Univ.
Press 1993 435p il maps $47; pa $14.95   **289.7**
1. Amish
ISBN 0-8018-4441-X; 0-8018-4442-8 (pa)
     LC 92-19304
First published 1963
This book discusses the sectarian origins of the
Amish, immigration history, family and community life,
population trends, farming practices, technological inno-
vations, education, medicine and the effects of govern-
ment regulation
Includes bibliographical references

Seitz, Ruth Hoover

Amish ways; photography by Blair Seitz. RB Bks. 1991 117p il $24.95 **289.7**

1. Amish

ISBN 1-879441-77-2   LC 90-063838

"The author and photographer take readers on a journey through three Amish settlements—Lancaster County, Pa., eastern Ohio, and Ontario, Canada—describing the family life, art, schooling, and businesses of the Amish people. A selection of 150 color photographs, supplemented by eight informative essays provide a wonderful overview of this fascinating sect." SLJ

291   Comparative religion and religious mythology

Bulfinch, Thomas, 1796-1867

Bulfinch's mythology   **291**

1. Mythology 2. Folklore—Europe 3. Chivalry

Hardcover and paperback editions available from various publishers

First combined edition published 1913 by Crowell. Originally published in three separate volumes 1855, 1858 and 1862 respectively

Contents: The age of fable; The age of chivalry; Legends of Charlemagne

"The basic work on classical mythology. Includes information on Greek, Roman, Norse, Egyptian, Asian, Germanic myths, as well as the Arthurian cycle and other heroic epics." N Y Public Libr. Ref Books for Child Collect

Campbell, Joseph, 1904-1987

The masks of God. Viking 1959-1968 4v hardcover o.p. paperbacks available ea $15.95

291

1. Mythology 2. Mythology in literature

Contents: v1 Primitive mythology (ISBN0-14-019443-6); v2 Oriental mythology (ISBN 0-14-019442-8); v3 Occidental mythology (ISBN 0-14-019441-X); v4 Creative mythology (ISBN 0-14-019440-1)

In the first three volumes the author deals "with the anonymous mythological past; in . . . [the final volume he shifts] the emphasis to individual creators of modern myths—from Dante to James Joyce, Thomas Mann, and T.S. Eliot." Libr J

Includes bibliographies

The power of myth; [by] Joseph Campbell, with Bill Moyers; Betty Sue Flowers, editor. Doubleday 1988 231p il $35; pa $24.95   **291**

1. Mythology 2. Religious art and symbolism 3. Spiritual life

ISBN 0-385-24773-7; 0-385-24774-5 (pa)

LC 88-4218

This companion to a public television series records a series of conversations between the author of The Hero With A Thousand Faces and Bill Moyers. Campbell reflects on themes and symbols from world religions and mythologies and explores their relevance for his own spiritual journey

"Campbell is the hero on his own voyage of discovery. This well-bound book on lovely paper with helpful illustrations from art is highly recommended for all libraries." Choice

Earhart, H. Byron

Religions of Japan; many traditions within one sacred way. Harper & Row 1984 142p il (Religious traditions of the world) pa $12   **291**

1. Japan—Religion

ISBN 0-06-062112-5   LC 84-47722

"The author first presents a brief historical background on Japanese culture and society and then discusses the country's religious traditions." Booklist

Includes glossary and bibliography

Eastern mysteries; by the editors of Time-Life Books. Time-Life Bks. 1991 160p il (Mysteries of the unknown) $9.95   **291**

1. Asia—Religion

LC 90-11281

An illustrated look at Asiatic religion, spirituality and mysticism. The book also explores the growing appeal of Eastern faiths in the Western world

Includes bibliography

Eastern wisdom; an illustrated guide to the religions and philosophies of the East; C. Scott Littleton, general editor. Holt & Co. 1996 176p il maps (Henry Holt reference book) $30   **291**

1. Oriental philosophy 2. Asia—Religion

ISBN 0-8050-4647-X   LC 95-38082

This guide contains "sections by scholars, who explain Hinduism, Buddhism, Confucianism, Taoism, and Shinto. . . . Terms are defined parenthetically within the text and more fully in a general glossary, and many captioned color photographs assist understanding and capture interest." Libr J

For a fuller review see: Booklist, July, 1996

Eerdmans' handbook to the world's religions. rev ed. Eerdmans 1994 464p il maps pa $24   **291**

1. Religions 2. Religion

ISBN 0-8028-0853-0

First published 1982

This "volume has eight parts: religion as a phenomenon; ancient religions (e.g., those of ancient Egypt, Greece, and Rome); primal religions (e.g., those of sub-Saharan Africa, the Americas, and Oceania); Eastern religions (e.g., Hinduism, Buddhism); Judaism and Islam; Christianity; the context of modern religion (e.g., secularism, pluralism, and so on); and a 'rapid fact-finder'. . . . In these sections, the history, beliefs, and practices of religions are treated, and charts systematically present information on festivals, religious subdivisions, and pantheons. A general index concludes the handbook." Am Ref Books Annu, 1996

Eliot, Alexander

The universal myths; heros, gods, tricksters, and others; with contributions by Joseph Campbell and Mircea Eliade. New Am. Lib. 1990 310p pa $12.95   **291**

1. Mythology

ISBN 0-452-01027-6   LC 89-38161

"A Meridian book"

Eliot, Alexander—*Continued*

First published 1976 by McGraw Hill with title: Myths

This volume provides a "retelling of so-called universal myths, which Eliot and associates have drawn from various cultures worldwide and organized by commonality of theme. . . . It is Eliot's contention that the ubiquity of such myths argues strongly for the essential oneness of humankind. Essays by Joseph Campbell and Mircea Eliade bolster this view." Booklist

Includes bibliographical references

The **Encyclopedia** of American religions: religious creeds; J. Gordon Melton, editor. Gale Res. 1988-1994 2v ea $145   291
1. Creeds 2. Doctrinal theology
ISBN 0-8103-2132-7 (v1); 0-8103-5491-8 (v2)
LC 87-30384

"A compilation of more than 450 creeds, confessions, statements of faith, and summaries of doctrine of religious and spiritual groups in the United States and Canada." Title page

Volume two: J. Gordon Melton with James Sauer

"Not intended to replace other sources, this volume emphasizes contemporaneity by including only creeds currently acknowledged. Texts are arranged by the 'religious family' groupings used in Melton's *Encyclopedia of American Religions* [entered in class 200.9]. A superb reference that also makes fascinating reading; highly recommended." Libr J

Frazer, Sir James George, 1854-1941

The golden bough; a study in magic and religion. 1 volume abridged ed. Macmillan 1958 c1950 864p hardcover o.p. paperback available $16   291
1. Mythology 2. Religions 3. Superstition
ISBN 0-02-095570-7 (pa)

Also available in hardcover from Buccaneer Bks.

An abridged edition of the twelve volume work on the anthropology of religion published by Macmillan 1907-15

The author argues that religion arose from myths, superstitions, and fables

Includes bibliographical references

The new golden bough; a new abridgment of the classic work; edited and with notes and foreword by Theodor H. Gaster. Phillips 1959 xxx, 738p $49.95   291
1. Mythology 2. Religions 3. Superstition
ISBN 0-87599-036-3

Also available in paperback from New Am. Lib.

First published with imprint Criterion Books

This edition is based on the 12 volumes of The golden bough and its supplements with revisions, new commentary and annotations

"A comparative study of world religions, magic, vegetation and fertility beliefs and rites, kingship, taboos, totemism and the like." New Century Handb of Engl Lit

Includes bibliographical references

Kaplan, David E., 1955-

The cult at the end of the world; the terrifying story of the Aum doomsday cult, from the subways of Tokyo to the nuclear arsenals of Russia; [by] David E. Kaplan & Andrew Marshall. Crown 1996 310p il $25   291
1. Aum Shinrikyo (Sect) 2. Terrorism
ISBN 0-517-70543-5   LC 96-168693

"By the time Japan's bizarre Aum Shinrikyo cult launched its 1995 nerve-gas attack on the Tokyo subway system, killing 12 and injuring thousands, the wealthy religious sect, which received generous tax breaks, had a global network of at least 37 companies, according to this exhaustively researched page-turner. Aum had acquired powerful lasers and was planning a military assault on Japan's parliament so that its bearded, near-blind leader, Shoko Asahara, a fanatical admirer of Hitler, could install himself as head of a new religious state." Publ Wkly

Leeming, David Adams, 1937-

The world of myth. Oxford Univ. Press 1990 362p il $27.50; pa $14.95   291
1. Mythology
ISBN 0-19-505601-9; 0-19-507475-0 (pa)
LC 89-48070

In this "volume the myths of various types are divided into four sections: of the cosmos, of the gods, of the hero, and of places and objects. . . . This work does not and is not meant to rival that of Joseph Campbell, but it will be useful to general readers or as a high school or college introductory text." Libr J

Includes bibliographical references

Melton, J. Gordon

Encyclopedic handbook of cults in America. rev & updated ed. Garland 1992 407p (Religious information systems series) $65; pa $18.95   291
1. Cults
ISBN 0-8153-0502-8; 0-8153-1140-0 (pa)
LC 92-11540

First published 1986

"The opening chapter surveys the topic of cults as alternative religion and is followed by sections reviewing thirty-seven movements active today. Counter-cult groups are discussed and an excellent section on violence and cults ends the book. Well written, thoroughly documented and indexed." Ref Sources for Small & Medium-sized Libr. 5th edition [review of 1986 edition]

Includes bibliographical references

Monroe, Charles E.

World religions; an introduction. Prometheus Bks. 1995 439p hardcover o.p. paperback available $15.95   291
1. Religion—History 2. Church history
ISBN 0-87975-942-9 (pa)   LC 94-40049

"Among the religions examined are: Prehistoric Cosmic Religions, the River Valley Religions of Ancient Egypt, the Greek gods, Taoism, Hinduism, Buddhism, Sikhism, Zoroastrianism, Judaism, Islam, and Christianity—with a special emphasis on Catholicism." Publisher's

Monroe, Charles E.—*Continued*
note
"A thoughtful and lucidly written reference book. Monroe's informed, insightful observations and comparisons reveal his lifetime of thinking and teaching about the world's varied religious practices." SLJ
Includes bibliographical references

Porterfield, Kay Marie
Straight talk about cults. Facts on File 1995 151p $16.95   **291**
1. Cults
ISBN 0-8160-3115-0   LC 94-37296
"Porterfield defines cults, distinguishes between those that are dangerous and those that are nonthreatening, and looks at their special appeal to teens. She combines vignettes of impressionable young people joining cults with a detailed and fair analysis of what makes them vulnerable to the groups' enticements, how they become entrapped, and how new recruits are molded into obedient members." SLJ
Includes bibliographical references

Religions on file; by the Diagram Group. Facts on File 1990 various paging il maps $155   **291**
1. Religions
ISBN 0-8160-2224-0   LC 89-48398
A looseleaf "collection of charts, diagrams, and maps that cover a wide range of the world's great faiths, both those practiced today and those followed in the past." Foreword

Religious cults in America; edited by Robert Emmet Long. Wilson, H.W. 1994 171p (Reference shelf, v66 no4) pa $15   **291**
1. Branch Davidians 2. Cults
ISBN 0-8242-0855-2   LC 94-16329
A collection of articles discussing the cult phenomena in the United States. Particular emphasis is placed on an examination of handling of the Branch Davidian confrontation in Waco
Includes bibliographical references

World mythology; Roy Willis, general editor; foreword by Robert Walter. Holt & Co. 1993 311p il maps (Henry Holt reference book) $45; pa $22.50   **291**
1. Mythology
ISBN 0-8050-2701-7; 0-8050-4913-4 (pa)
LC 93-3045
This book describes "the myths of Egypt, the Middle East, India, China, Tibet, Mongolia, Japan, Greece, Rome, the Celtic lands, Northern and Eastern Europe, the Arctic, North and South America, Mesoamerica, Africa, Australia, Oceania, and Southeast Asia." Libr J

The **World's** religions; understanding the living faiths; consultant editor, Peter B. Clarke. Reader's Digest Assn. 1993 220p il maps $35   **291**
1. Religions
ISBN 0-89577-501-8   LC 93-22323
This work "examines the great living faiths of the world, including Judaism, Christianity, Islam, Buddhism,

Hinduism, Sikhism, Shinto, and China's religious tradition. It tells how the major religions began and traces their development from their origins to the present." Publisher's note
Includes bibliography

291.03 Comparative religion— Encyclopedias and dictionaries

Ann, Martha
Goddesses in world mythology; [by] Martha Ann, Dorothy Myers Imel. ABC-CLIO 1993 xx, 655p il $75   **291.03**
1. Gods and goddesses—Dictionaries 2. Mythology—Dictionaries
ISBN 0-87436-715-8   LC 93-31496
"The authors present more than 9500 goddesses, nymphs, demons, and deified women from cultures around the world. Divided alphabetically into 15 geographical regions, entries identify goddesses by their various historical incarnations." Libr J

Cotterell, Arthur
The Macmillan illustrated encyclopedia of myths and legends. Macmillan 1989 260p il maps hardcover o.p. paperback available $24.95 **291.03**
1. Mythology—Dictionaries 2. Legends—Dictionaries
ISBN 0-02-86051-8 (pa)   LC 89-8282
"Enhanced by a variety of illustrations, this comprehensive, readable reference guide to the world of myths and legends includes the themes and characters important to world literature, mythology, and anthropology. A handy cross-referenced 'micropedia' is appended." Booklist
Includes bibliography

The **Dictionary** of world myth; general editor: Peter Bentley. Facts on File 1995 240p il maps $22.95; pa $14.95   **291.03**
1. Mythology—Dictionaries
ISBN 0-8160-3300-5; 0-8160-3325-0 (pa)
LC 94-44700
Published in the United Kingdom with title: The Hutchinson dictionary of world myth
This illustrated volume provides "coverage of global mythology, such as Middle Eastern, Chinese, Indian, African, North American, Slavic, Japanese, South and Central American, and Southeast Asian mythic traditions, both past and present. . . . Highlighted feature panels scattered throughout the book focus on universal themes, such as afterlife, chaos, flood myths and the origins of death." Publisher's note

Larousse dictionary of beliefs and religions; editor, Rosemary Goring; consultant editor, Frank Whaling. Larousse (London); distributed by Larousse Kingfisher Chambers 1994 605p il $30; pa $14.95   **291.03**
1. Religion—Dictionaries 2. Religions—Dictionaries
ISBN 0-7523-5000-5; 0-7523-0000-8 (pa)
LC 94-191416
First published 1992 in the United Kingdom with title: Chambers dictionary of beliefs and religions

Larousse dictionary of beliefs and religions—
Continued

"Entries cover current and historical religions and their beliefs in a single alphabetic arrangement. There are numerous cross references and an appendix that groups entry headings according to major religious traditions and a few other broad topics." Libr J

Leeming, David Adams, 1937-
Encyclopedia of creation myths; [by] David Adams Leeming with Margaret Adams Leeming. ABC-CLIO 1994 330p il $60   **291.03**
1. Creation—Dictionaries 2. Mythology—Dictionaries
ISBN 0-87436-739-5   LC 94-7169
"Alphabetized entries compare and contrast various aspects of creation mythology from many cultures. . . . Entries range in length from one sentence to several pages; some entire myths are reproduced. . . . Of special interest to story tellers, it will be useful for units on mythology, comparative cultures or religions, and classical studies." Book Rep

Mercatante, Anthony S.
The Facts on File encyclopedia of world mythology and legend. Facts on File 1988 807p il $95   **291.03**
1. Mythology—Dictionaries 2. Folklore—Dictionaries
3. Legends—Dictionaries
ISBN 0-8160-1049-8   LC 84-21218
"A comprehensive reference on world mythologies covered in thematic, biographical, and narrative essays." N Y Public Libr. Book of How & Where to Look It Up

291.3   Public worship and other religious practices

How to be a perfect stranger; a guide to etiquette in other people's religious ceremonies; edited by Arthur J. Magida. Jewish Lights Pub. 1996-1997 2v ea $24.95   **291.3**
1. Etiquette 2. Rites and ceremonies
ISBN 1-879045-39-7 (v1); 1-879045-63-X (v2)
    LC 95-37474
The first volume considers "'mainstream' American religious custom in congregations of the Assemblies of God, Baptists, Buddhists, Episcopalians, Hindus, Muslims, Jews, Methodists, Mormons and others. [The second] volume explores the religious ceremonies of less mainstream faiths, such as the African American Methodist Church, Baha'i, the Church of the Nazarene, the Mennonites and the Amish, the Sikhs and the Pentecostal Church of God." Publ Wkly
For a fuller review of volume one see: Booklist, Feb. 15. 1996

Kelly, Aidan A.
Religious holidays and calendars; an encyclopaedic handbook; by Aidan Kelly, Peter Dresser, and Linda M. Ross. Omnigraphics 1993 163p $64   **291.3**
1. Religious holidays 2. Calendars
ISBN 1-55888-348-7   LC 92-41189
Arranged in two sections, this book begins with a history of calendars. "The largest part of the book [a cata-

log of religious holidays] presents approximately 300 entries in alphabetical order ranging in length from one sentence to more than one page. Each entry contains the name of the holiday, the date on which it is celebrated, and a brief discussion of its history and current practice. . . . This convenient compilation should be given purchase consideration by high school, public, and undergraduate libraries." Booklist

292   Classical religion and religious mythology

Adkins, Lesley
Dictionary of Roman religion; [by] Lesley Adkins & Roy A. Adkins. Facts on File 1996 288p il $40   **292**
1. Rome—Religion—Dictionaries
ISBN 0-8160-3005-7   LC 95-8355
This dictionary "provides more than 1,400 brief definitions and descriptions of deities, myths, and persons; cult sites and practices, and terminology and technology drawn from the religions of the Roman Republic and Empire. . . . Although the entries decidedly emphasize archaeology and art history . . . they are clearly and concisely written and refreshingly free of the unexplicated jargon or terminology that can intimidate novices." Choice

Asimov, Isaac, 1920-1992
Words from the myths; decorations by William Barss. Houghton Mifflin 1961 225p il o.p.; New Am. Lib. paperback available $3.95   **292**
1. Classical mythology 2. English language—Etymology
ISBN 0-451-16252-8 (pa)
The author's "informal retelling and discussion of the myths to point out the scores of words rooted in mythology and to explain their usage in the English language provide a fresh look at the myths and a better understanding of the words and expressions derived from them." Booklist

Bell, Robert E., 1926-
Women of classical mythology; a biographical dictionary. ABC-CLIO 1991 462p $60   **292**
1. Classical mythology—Dictionaries 2. Gods and goddesses—Dictionaries
ISBN 0-87436-581-3   LC 91-26649
Also available in paperback from Oxford Univ. Press
This "dictionary contains the names of both notable and not so notable women of classical myth who are not easily found in other convenient sources on myth. . . . The biographical entries, ranging from a single sentence to three pages in length, are easily understood and provide sufficient information for further study." Choice

Daly, Kathleen N.
Greek and Roman mythology A to Z; a young reader's companion. Facts on File 1992 132p il map lib bdg $19.95   **292**
1. Classical mythology—Dictionaries
ISBN 0-8160-2151-1   LC 91-43037
"Over 400 entries explore the characters, places, legends, and epics of Greek and Roman mythology. The

Daly, Kathleen N.—*Continued*
format is accessible, making the book useful for school assignments, as well as enjoyable for general reading. Each entry provides a clear definition, and retells the stories associated with the character or place. The broad coverage, ample cross-references, and extensive index enable readers to recognize the many connections and interrelationships between characters and myths." SLJ

Fleischman, Paul
Dateline: Troy; collages by Gwen Frankfeldt & Glenn Morrow. Candlewick Press 1996 79p il $15.99   292
1. Trojan War 2. Classical mythology
ISBN 1-56402-469-5   LC 95-36356
The author juxtaposes a "redaction of the legendary conflagration at Troy with newspaper clippings that report events ranging from World War I to sociological experiments on babies' reactions to unattractive women. Each page of text faces such clippings, selected to highlight relevant themes." Publ Wkly
"Fleischman's precision of language reflects the stately perspective of a Homeric story but also, ironically, the distance of modern news reporting styles, which makes the parallels of content even more uncanny. A thought-provoking book, classically austere in design, with a partnership of text and illustration unusual in young adult [literature]." Bull Cent Child Books

Graves, Robert, 1895-1985
Greek myths   292
1. Classical mythology
Hardcover and paperback editions available from various publishers
First published 1955 by Penguin Bks.
A collection of the author's interpretations of Greek myths based on anthropological and archaeological findings

Hamilton, Edith, 1867-1963
Mythology; illustrated by Steele Savage. Little, Brown 1942 497p il $24.95   292
1. Classical mythology 2. Norse mythology
ISBN 0-316-34114-2
Also available in paperback from New Am. Lib.
A retelling of Greek, Roman and Norse myths

293 Germanic religion and religious mythology

Daly, Kathleen N.
Norse mythology A to Z; a young reader's companion. Facts on File 1991 116p il (Mythology A to Z) $19.95   293
1. Norse mythology—Dictionaries
ISBN 0-8160-2150-3   LC 90-25678
More than 400 alphabetically listed entries identify and explain the characters, events, and important places of Norse mythology
"The book would be most useful to those who are already reading Norse myths and who may require more information or clarification of terms, places, and characters." Am Ref Books Annu, 1992

294.3 Buddhism

Wangu, Madhu Bazaz
Buddhism. Facts on File 1993 128p il (World religions) $17.95   294.3
1. Buddhism
ISBN 0-8160-2442-1   LC 92-33177
Presents the story of Buddhism's origins and growth through the centuries, discussing its basic philosophy and the evolution of the three major schools of Buddhist thought
Includes bibliographical references

294.5 Hinduism

Wangu, Madhu Bazaz
Hinduism. Facts on File 1991 128p (World religions) $17.95   294.5
1. Hinduism
ISBN 0-8160-2447-2   LC 90-25431
Presents the history, customs, and beliefs of Hinduism, describing the mysteries and myths that sustained its growth over the centuries
Includes bibliographical references

Yoga, mind & body; [by] Sivananda Yoga Vedanta Center. DK Pub. 1996 168p il $24.95
294.5
1. Yoga
ISBN 0-7894-0447-8   LC 95-44387
"Five main principles of yoga based on the tenet of 'simple living and high thinking' are introduced. Each one is explained and illustrated in a separate section of the book. The chapter on proper exercise is the longest section and goes through a complete workout session with full-color photographs and drawings of each position. The mental and physical benefits of each position are listed as well as possible problems, and variations for different skill levels. The chapter on vegetarian diet has 20 pages of recipes." SLJ

296 Judaism

The **Encyclopedia** of Judaism; editor-in-chief Geoffrey Wigoder. Macmillan 1989 768p il $75
296
1. Judaism—Dictionaries
ISBN 0-02-628410-3   LC 89-8184
"A large, comprehensive work that covers, in clear and concise entries, Jewish culture, Judaism as a religion, and the history of the Jewish people. Illustrated, with a glossary." N Y Public Libr. Book of How & Where to Look It Up

Gates, Fay Carol
Judaism. Facts on File 1991 128p (World religions) $17.95   296
1. Judaism
ISBN 0-8160-2444-8   LC 90-25436
An account of the history and rituals of Judaism, examining such areas as sacred use of the Hebrew language and the role of the faith in establishing the contemporary nation of Israel
Includes bibliographical references

Jacobs, Louis
The Jewish religion; a companion. Oxford Univ.
Press 1995 641p $45   **296**
1. Judaism—Dictionaries
ISBN 0-19-826463-1   LC 95-3203
"Jacobs deals with topics ranging from personalities in
the Bible to Jewish thinkers of the present day; he includes customs, traditions, and Jewish ideas on topics as
diverse as adoption and astrology. The author also considers Jewish attitudes towards ecology, insanity, and
even worrying. The text is readable and interesting; there
is no need to have any grounding in Hebrew language or
terminology. High school students asked to examine historical issues associated with Judaism or to understand
Judaic allusions in literature will find this work invaluable." SLJ
Includes bibliographical references

296.1   Judaism—Sources

The **Book** of legends. Sefer ha-aggadah; legends
from the Talmud and Midrash; edited by Hayim
Nahman Bialik and Yehoshua Hana Ravnitzky;
translated by William G. Braude; introduction
by David Stern. Schocken Bks. 1992 xxii, 897p
$75   **296.1**
1. Aggada 2. Midrash 3. Jewish legends
ISBN 0-8052-4113-2   LC 91-52700
This is a "thematic anthology of nonlegal rabbinic literature on all aspects of human life (e.g., creation, redemption, wisdom, clothing, folk medicine studied
through Jewish stories, parables, sayings, homilies, and
anecdotes). The translation by Braude is clear, lucid, and
readable and includes interpolations that increase the
sense and comprehension of the text." Libr J

297   Islam and religions originating in it

Gordon, Matthew
Islam; by Matthew S. Gordon. Facts on File
1991 128p (World religions) $17.95   **297**
1. Islam
ISBN 0-8160-2443-X   LC 90-24830
An overview of Islam chronicling the religion's impact historically and in the modern world and discussing
its origins, basic beliefs, structure, places of worship, and
rites of passage
Includes bibliographical references

Koran
The Koran   **297**

Available in various bindings and editions
"The sacred scripture of Islam, regarded by Muslims
as the Word of God, and except in sūra I.—which is a
prayer to God—and some few passages in which Muhammad or the angels speak in the first person, the
speaker throughout is God." Ency Britannica

Lippman, Thomas W.
Understanding Islam; an introduction to the
Muslim world. 2nd rev ed. Penguin Bks. 1995
198p pa $10.95   **297**
1. Islam
ISBN 0-452-01160-4   LC 95-24015
"A Meridian book"
First published 1982
The author explains fundamental Islamic beliefs and
practices. The life and work of Mohammed is examined
in depth
Includes bibliographical references

The **Muslim** almanac; a reference work on the
history, faith, culture, and peoples of Islam;
Azim A. Nanji, editor. Gale Res. 1996 xxxv,
581p il map $75   **297**
1. Islam 2. Islamic countries
ISBN 0-8103-8924-X   LC 95-17324
This "basic reference on Islam contains 39 chapters,
each contributed by a recognized scholar and each discussing a broad topic area of Islamic history, belief, or
culture. Chapters conclude with useful topical bibliographies. A general bibliography, a chronology of Islamic
history, and a glossary of Islamic terms also appear."
Libr J

299   Other religions

Bierhorst, John
The mythology of Mexico and Central America.
Morrow 1990 239p il maps $17; pa $10   **299**
1. Indians of Mexico—Religion 2. Indians of Central
America—Religion
ISBN 0-688-06721-2; 0-688-11280-3 (pa)
     LC 90-5879
The author collects twenty basic myths of the Aztec
and Mayan people and examines their influence on the
culture and political life of the region
Includes glossary and bibliography

The mythology of North America. Morrow 1985
259p il maps $16   **299**
1. Indians of North America—Religion
ISBN 0-688-04145-0   LC 85-281
The author presents a region-by-region approach to
North American Indian mythology and folklore
"The description, history, and recounting of tales flow
together smoothly. Bierhorst's usual fine scholarship and
meticulous attention to sources are evident in the extensive notes section and introduction." Horn Book
Includes bibliography

The mythology of South America. Morrow 1988
269p il maps $16; pa $9   **299**
1. Indians of South America—Religion
ISBN 0-688-06722-0; 0-688-10739-7 (pa)
     LC 87-26237
Discusses Indian mythology of various regions of
South America, describing origins, comparing similar
tales, and presenting some of the myths themselves

Gill, Sam D., 1943-
Dictionary of Native American mythology; [by] Sam D. Gill, Irene F. Sullivan. ABC-CLIO 1992 xxx, 425p il maps $69.50 **299**
1. Indians of North America—Religion—Dictionaries
ISBN 0-87436-621-6 LC 92-27053
Also available in paperback from Oxford Univ. Press
"The authors have included entries representing more than 150 Native American language groups. . . . For each of the alphabetically arranged entries, tribal source and culture area are included. A collection of vivid black-and-white illustrations is reprinted. A comprehensive bibliography and index by tribe complete this excellent reference work." Libr J

Hartz, Paula
Taoism; [by] Paula R. Hartz. Facts on File 1993 128p il (World religions) $17.95 **299**
1. Taoism
ISBN 0-8160-2448-0 LC 91-43018
This is a "survey of one of China's three great religious traditions, offering [an] explanation of Taoism's basic outlook and [an] account of its metamorphosis from a mystical way of life to a religion of monastic orders and secular hierarchies." Publisher's note
Includes bibliographical references

Hirschfelder, Arlene B.
The encyclopedia of Native American religions; [by] Arlene Hirschfelder, Paulette Molin. Facts on File 1991 367p il maps $50 **299**
1. Indians of North America—Religion—Dictionaries
ISBN 0-8160-2017-5 LC 91-21145
"The entries in this encyclopedia provide descriptions of religious ceremonies and terminology; biographies of native American religious leaders, missionaries, and others who have influenced the practice of these religions; summaries of major court cases affecting native religious practices; healing and other ceremonial practices that are spiritual rather than religious in nature; and some . . . mythology. . . . This encyclopedia is quite readable and informative. It will be useful in any high school that has a religion curriculum or studies native American culture." Booklist
Includes bibliography

Hoobler, Thomas
Confucianism; by Thomas and Dorothy Hoobler. Facts on File 1993 128p il (World religions) $17.95 **299**
1. Confucianism
ISBN 0-8160-2445-6 LC 92-33178
Describes how the teachings of Confucius evolved from a social order to a religion, infusing all phases of Chinese life for 2000 years
Includes bibliographical references

Native American myths and legends; editorial consultant, Colin F. Taylor. Smithmark Pubs. 1994 144p il $16.98 **299**
1. Indians of North America—Religion
ISBN 0-8317-6290-X LC 94-8904
"Nine specific chapters, each by a different hand or hands, describe Native American cultures of the Arctic,

subarctic, both northern coasts, California, the plains, the plateau and basin near the western mountains, the Southeast, and the Southwest. Myths are retold as part of each chapter, but emphasis is upon the defining characteristics of the represented cultures." Booklist
Includes bibliographical references

Piggott, Juliet
Japanese mythology. new rev ed. Bedrick Bks. 1983 c1982 144p il map (Library of the world's myths and legends) $24.95; pa $14.95 **299**
1. Japanese mythology
ISBN 0-911745-09-2; 0-87226-251-0 (pa)
LC 83-71480
First published 1969 in the United Kingdom; this edition first published 1982
This presentation of Japanese mythology is illustrated with about 50 color photographs of temples and artifacts and over 100 black-and-white photographs
Includes bibliography

The **Spirit** world; by the editors of Time-Life Books. Time-Life Bks. 1992 176p il (American Indians) $19.95 **299**
1. Indians of North America—Religion 2. Indians of North America—Rites and ceremonies
LC 92-7592
This work explores creation myths, magical rituals, medical practices and other aspects of the spiritual life of various Native American peoples. There are many color photographs depicting artifacts and modern ceremonies, as well as historic black-and-white photographs
Includes bibliography

Warner, Elizabeth, 1940-
Heroes, monsters and other worlds from Russian mythology; text by Elizabeth Warner; illustrations by Alexander Koshkin. Bedrick Bks. 1996 c1985 132p il (World mythology series) $22.50 **299**
1. Slavic mythology
ISBN 0-87226-925-6 LC 95-31349
First published 1985 in the United Kingdom
This "book is divided into three types of tales: 'bylinas' which are ancient heroes; 'skazkas' are pure fantasy such as Babayaga and the Ivans; and 'bylichkas' are the spirits of the supernatural. . . . Also printed is the Russian alphabet with English pronunciation." Voice Youth Advocates
"The individual stories are great for sharing, and the collection is an excellent resource for cross-curricular studies of Russian history and culture." Booklist
Includes bibliographical references

300 SOCIAL SCIENCES

301 Sociology and anthropology

Encyclopedia of sociology; Edgar F. Borgatta, editor-in-chief, Marie L. Borgatta, managing editor. Macmillan 1992 4v il set $375 **301**
1. Sociology—Dictionaries
ISBN 0-02-897051-9 LC 91-37827
"The first comprehensive encyclopedia for general sociology, intended for a broad audience. 370 lengthy,

Encyclopedia of sociology—*Continued*
signed articles, two to 18 pages in length, concluding
with bibliographies, and written by 339 national and international sociologists. Includes classic topics, as well as
those reflecting emerging fields. Omits biographical entries. Sample entries: Social problems, Homelessness,
Family violence, Feminist theory. Entries are cross-
referenced and arranged alphabetically. Lists of articles,
authors, institutions. Most references from 1970-90. Detailed cross-referenced subject index." Guide to Ref
Books. 11th edition

Jary, David
The HarperCollins dictionary of sociology; [by]
David Jary and Julia Jary. HarperPerennial 1991
601p il hardcover o.p. paperback available $16
301
1. Sociology—Dictionaries
ISBN 0-06-461036-5 (pa)   LC 91-55446
"Containing more than 1,200 entries representing the
major concepts, theories, subdisciplines, thinkers, and
methods of sociology, this dictionary is a useful interme-
diate-level source. . . . The writing is clear and succinct,
with a minimum of jargon or embellishment. The emphasis is on history and philosophy with less on methodology, recent developments, and applied fields." Choice

302 Social interaction

Salzman, Marian, 1959-
150 ways teens can make a difference; by
Marian Salzman and Teresa Reisgies; with Maribel
Becker [et al.] Peterson's Guides 1991 191p pa
$7.95   302
1. Voluntarism
ISBN 1-56079-093-8   LC 91-2965
Teenagers discuss the rewarding and sometimes frustrating experiences of being a volunteer, including their
commitment and accomplishments, parental support, and
how they incorporate volunteer activities into their busy
high school schedules
"An excellent, upbeat handbook for those who want to
improve the world by volunteering." SLJ

302.2 Communication

Becker, Udo
The Continuum encyclopedia of symbols;
translated by Lance W. Garmer. Continuum 1994
345p il $39.50   302.2
1. Signs and symbols
ISBN 0-8264-0644-0   LC 94-11000
In this volume "more than 1,500 entries are arranged
alphabetically, along with 800 illustrations, most of them
in black and white, with an insert of colorplates. . . .
Readers will find symbolic meanings for common objects, such as the rose, cross, and numbers, as well as the
Greek god Tyche, valerian weed, and ancient mythical
giant Ymir. Exploring a wealth of objects and concepts,
this encyclopedia traces symbols to their cultural, religious, or mythological origins in 50-100 words." Booklist

Biedermann, Hans, 1930-
Dictionary of symbolism; translated by James
Hulbert. Facts on File 1992 465p il $45   302.2
1. Signs and symbols
ISBN 0-8160-2593-2   LC 91-44933
Also available in paperback from New Am. Lib.
Original German edition, 1989
This dictionary "incorporates symbols that originated
in Asia, Africa, Europe and the 'New World'. There are
almost 600s entries from mythology, fairy tale, psychology, religion, and sociology, plus historical and legendary
figures. With 2000 black-and-white illustrations, the book
is highly attractive. The symbols are accompanied by
thorough interpretations based on various sources." SLJ

Lebow, Irwin
Information highways and byways; from the
telegraph to the 21st century. IEEE Press 1995
307p il pa $34.95   302.2
1. Communication—History
ISBN 0-7803-1073-X   LC 94-45457
"Lebow describes the inventions chronologically, beginning with the telegraph in 1844. In addition to detailing how the inventions came about, he discusses legal
problems, patent applications, and entrepreneurs who
backed the products. . . . Inventions include the telephone, the wireless radio, vacuum tubes, television and
satellite transmission as well as computers from
UNIVAC to the most recent." Book Rep
Includes bibliographical references

Liungman, Carl G., 1938-
Dictionary of symbols. ABC-CLIO 1991 596p il
$67.50   302.2
1. Signs and symbols 2. Picture writing
ISBN 0-87436-610-0   LC 91-36657
Also available in paperback from Norton
Original Swedish edition, 1974
This book "allows students to locate a symbol by defining just four of its visual characteristics from a set of
common descriptors. Included are symbols used in design, decoration, architecture, logos, and more. Extensive
cross-references for meanings, words, names of sign systems, and names of symbols are included." SLJ

Morris, Desmond
Bodytalk; the meaning of human gestures.
Crown Trade Paperbacks 1994 231p il pa $14
302.2
1. Body language
ISBN 0-517-88355-4   LC 94-30719
"Morris and his researchers have identified more than
600 gestures that are used internationally and locally to
indicate emotions, attitudes, and messages. Not linked to
sign language, these gestures are informal and are used
in conversation or in lieu of words. Each gesture is classified by the major body part involved (e.g., eye wink or
thumb hitch). Then, the meaning, action, and background
are spelled out, accompanied by a helpful drawing."
Booklist

302.23 Media (Means of communication)

Fallows, James M.
Breaking the news; how the media undermine American democracy; [by] James Fallows. Pantheon Bks. 1996 296p $23; pa $12   302.23
1. Journalism 2. Mass media
ISBN 0-679-44209-X; 0-679-75856-9 (pa)
LC 95-31467
The author "argues that growing bottomline pressure—on newspapers struggling to survive, and on TV newscasters for ratings—has made reporting a cynical game increasingly dominated by image over substance and by overpaid star reporters. . . . Buttressed by a wealth of examples, Fallows's points are well taken." Publ Wkly
Includes bibliographical references

Mass media: opposing viewpoints; William Barbour, book editor. Greenhaven Press 1994 306p lib bdg $19.95; pa $11.95   302.23
1. Mass media
ISBN 1-56510-107-3 (lib bdg); 1-56510-106-5 (pa)
LC 93-30960
"Opposing viewpoints series"
Replaces the edition published 1988 under the editorship of Neal Bernards
Politicians, sociologists and journalists discuss media bias, government regulation, advertising, and politics
Includes bibliography

McLuhan, Marshall, 1911-1980
Understanding media; the extensions of man; introduction by Lewis H. Lapham. MIT Press 1994 xxiii, 365p pa $14.95   302.23
1. Mass media 2. Communication 3. Technology and civilization
ISBN 0-262-63159-8   LC 94-27722
Also available in paperback from New Am. Lib.
A reissue of the title first published 1964 by McGraw-Hill
The premise of the book is that the form of any medium, rather than its content determines what is being communicated. The author examines the various media to show how their forms effect "the patterning of human associations"
Includes bibliographical references

The **Media** and politics; Paul A. Winters, book editor. Greenhaven Press 1996 80p (At issue) lib bdg $12.95; pa $7.95   302.23
1. Mass media 2. United States—Politics and government—1989-
ISBN 1-56510-383-1 (lib bdg); 1-56510-382-3 (pa)
LC 95-39053
This volume "focuses on the effectiveness of the media during the 1992 Presidential campaign. The differences between the 'old' and 'new' media are also evaluated. . . . Topics include how the media may misrepresent politicians' messages, using alternative media to encourage voter participation and how much real influence the media have on elections." Voice Youth Advocates
Includes bibliographical references

Minow, Newton Norman, 1926-
Abandoned in the wasteland; children, television, and the First Amendment; [by] Newton N. Minow and Craig L. LaMay. Hill & Wang 1995 237p $20; pa $11   302.23
1. Television and children 2. Television
ISBN 0-8090-2311-3; 0-8090-1589-7 (pa)
LC 95-1113
This book argues "that the congressional mandate that broadcasters serve the public interest demands (among other things) excellent, educational programming for children—a challenge that is not being met. By failing in this, the authors maintain, programmers are receiving the 'quid' of free access to the airwaves without providing the 'quo,' and the resulting programming is harmful to children." San Francisco Rev Books
"The authors make a strong argument that educational opportunities are going unrealized by programs created for the main purpose of peddling toys." N Y Times Book Rev
Includes bibliographical references

Weiner, Richard, 1927-
Webster's New World dictionary of media and communications. rev and updated. Macmillan 1996 676p $39.95   302.23
1. Mass media—Dictionaries 2. Communication—Dictionaries
ISBN 0-02-860611-6   LC 96-12949
First published 1990
"Briefly defines words from a variety of fields, including sales and advertising, broadcasting and publishing, and computers and computer graphics. Also lists and describes leading companies, and trade and professional associations." Guide to Ref Books. 11th edition

302.3 Social interaction within groups

Hinojosa, Maria, 1961-
Crews: gang members talk to Maria Hinojosa; photographs by German Perez. Harcourt Brace & Co. 1995 168p il $17; pa $9   302.3
1. Gangs
ISBN 0-15-292873-1; 0-15-200283-4 (pa)
LC 94-12173
A "look at Latino gang members in New York City. Shank, Coki, Cindy, Tre, Smooth b, and their friends answer the interviewer's questions to reveal lives driven overwhelmingly by some common threads: the need for acceptance, suppressed anger, dysfunctional families, poverty, violence, and drugs. . . . Hinojosa's open-ended questioning style encourages young men and women to tell their own stories." SLJ

303.3 Social coordination and control

Gillam, Scott

Discrimination; prejudice in action. Enslow Pubs. 1995 128p il (Multicultural issues) lib bdg $18.95   **303.3**

1. Discrimination 2. Prejudices

ISBN 0-89490-643-7   LC 94-38962

This book "briefly explores racial, gender, age, sex, and disability discrimination. Each chapter presents compelling demonstrations of current discriminatory practices, along with solid background information and suggestions for creating change. . . . This offering is a good starting point for young researchers." SLJ

Includes glossary and bibliography

Huxley, Aldous, 1894-1963

Brave new world revisited. Harper & Row 1958 147p hardcover o.p. paperback available $6 **303.3**

1. Propaganda 2. Totalitarianism 3. Brainwashing 4. Culture

ISBN 0-06-080984-1 (pa)

Also available in hardcover from Amereon

In response to his 1932 novel Brave new world [entered in Fiction section] "Huxley reconsiders his prophecies and fears that some of these may be coming true much sooner than he thought." Oxford Companion to Engl Lit. 5th edition

Kronenwetter, Michael

Prejudice in America; causes and cures. Watts 1993 144p lib bdg $22.70   **303.3**

1. Prejudices

ISBN 0-531-11163-6   LC 93-1598

"Citing examples of racial, religious and ethnic prejudice, the book leads the reader to examine the issue from the perspective of the victim. Separate chapters deal with causes, stereotypes and the learning of prejudice. How we can learn to break out of the cycle is discussed in the next three chapters. Kronenwetter does an admirable job of presenting a highly controversial topic in a manner that is not didactic but raises the reader's level of consciousness." Book Rep

Includes bibliographical references

Miller, Maryann, 1943-

Coping with a bigoted parent. Rosen Pub. Group 1992 157p il lib bdg $15.95   **303.3**

1. Prejudices 2. Discrimination 3. Toleration 4. Parent and child

ISBN 4-8239-1345-7   LC 91-32739

"Miller addresses the nature of bigotry, prejudice, and discrimination and discusses how teens can deal with these traits in themselves and in others, including their parents." SLJ

Includes bibliographical references

303.4 Social change

Anderson, Terry H., 1946-

The movement and the sixties. Oxford Univ. Press 1995 500p il $30; pa $16.95   **303.4**

1. Radicalism 2. Protests, demonstrations, etc. 3. United States—Social conditions

ISBN 0-19-507409-2; 0-19-510457-9 (pa)

LC 94-16344

This "book is a national study of U.S. social activism from 1960 to 1973, focusing on how 'the Movement' was experienced by participants and exploring why this activism arose when it did, how it developed, and what it accomplished." Booklist

Anderson's "sweeping study is a valuable, refreshingly unbiased reassessment of the '60s legacy." Publ Wkly

Includes bibliographical references

Burns, Stewart

Social movements of the 1960s; searching for democracy. Twayne Pubs. 1990 215p il (Social movements past and present) lib bdg $25.95; pa $15.95   **303.4**

1. Civil rights 2. Radicalism 3. Feminism 4. Social movements

ISBN 0-8057-9737-8 (lib bdg); 0-8057-9738-6 (pa)

LC 89-24644

This is "a history of the black freedom movement in the deep South, the student-oriented New Left with emphasis on Vietnamese War protests, and the women's movement. . . . Burns concludes his study with an analysis of the movements and consideration of ways in which they might have been more effective." SLJ

"Written largely from the words of the participants, this study is an excellent introduction to the social turmoil of the 1960s." Choice

Includes bibliographical references

Lubar, Steven D.

InfoCulture; the Smithsonian book of information age inventions; [by] Steven Lubar. Houghton Mifflin 1993 408p il $34.95   **303.4**

1. National Museum of American History (U.S.) 2. Telecommunication—History

ISBN 0-395-57042-5   LC 93-4815

Based on an exhibit at the Smithsonian Institution's National Museum of American History

"Lubar examines the origins and development of technology and how our infoculture—information, communications, and entertainment technologies—affects our daily lives. A well-documented work, brimming with illustrations that will attract researchers and readers seriously interested in technology." Booklist

Includes bibliographical references

Naisbitt, John

Megatrends; ten new directions transforming our lives. Warner Bks. 1982 290p hardcover o.p. paperback available $6.50   **303.4**

1. Social change 2. United States—Social conditions

ISBN 0-446-35681-6 (pa)   LC 82-6959

"Among the ten 'Megatrends' Naisbitt describes are: a global economy edging out national economies; a

Naisbitt, John—*Continued*
north-to-south population shift; a move from an industrial to an information-based society. Naisbitt advocates that such trends should influence planning. . . . Fascinating reading." Libr J
Includes bibliographical references

Megatrends 2000; ten new directions for the 1990's; [by] John Naisbitt and Patricia Aburdene. Morrow 1990 384p $21.95 **303.4**
1. Social change 2. United States—Social conditions
ISBN 0-688-07224-0   LC 89-13301
Also available in paperback from Avon Bks.

The authors "examine what they see as ten 'millennial megatrends.' . . . They are: the global economy; a renaissance in arts; the emergence of free-market socialism; global lifestyles and cultural nationalism; the privatization of the welfare state; rise of the Pacific Rim; the decade of women in leadership; the age of biology; the religious revival; . . . [and] the triumph of the individual." Christ Sci Monit
"A thought-provoking resource for history, government, and debate students." SLJ
Includes bibliographical references

Toffler, Alvin
Future shock. Random House 1970 505p $18.95
303.4
1. Social change 2. Technology and civilization 3. Modern civilization—1950-
ISBN 0-394-42586-3
Also available in paperback from Bantam Bks.
According to the author, "future shock is 'the dizzying disorientation brought on by the premature arrival of the future.' . . . Toffler outlines some interesting strategies for survival, writing in a clear popular style." Publ Wkly
Includes bibliography

Powershift; knowledge, wealth, and violence at the edge of the 21st century. Bantam Bks. 1990 xxii, 585p hardcover o.p. paperback available $7.99 **303.4**
1. Social change 2. Power (Social sciences) 3. Modern civilization—1950-
ISBN 0-553-29215-3 (pa)   LC 90-1068
The author "argues that the control of knowledge has become the principal means to create wealth and power. Aided by the widespread use of computers and other communications technologies, this 'powershift,' Toffler predicts, will dramatically alter the world's political balance." Libr J
Includes bibliography

303.49   Social forecasts

21st century earth: opposing viewpoints; Oliver W. Markley and Walter R. McCuan, editors. Greenhaven Press 1996 288p il lib bdg $19.95; pa $11.95 **303.49**
1. Twenty-first century 2. Human ecology 3. Forecasting
ISBN 1-56510-415-3 (lib bdg); 1-56510-414-5 (pa)
LC 95-39051
"Opposing viewpoints series"

This book "deals with an assortment of forecasts for the near future. The first section, 'How will demographic trends affect humanity?' includes discussion of overpopulation, the gap between haves and have-nots, and teens vs. senior citizen as the dominant age-group. The impacts of new technologies and trends that might affect the global ecology are addressed." SLJ
"Students researching topics for speeches, science, social studies, and persuasive essay assignments on futuristic topics will find the readings and their supplemental bibliographies invaluable." Booklist

America beyond 2001: opposing viewpoints; Oliver W. Markley & Walter R. McCuan, editors. Greenhaven Press 1995 312p lib bdg $19.95; pa $11.95 **303.49**
1. Twenty-first century 2. United States—Social conditions 3. Technology and civilization 4. Forecasting
ISBN 1-56510-293-2 (lib bdg); 1-56510-292-4 (pa)
LC 94-46738
"Opposing viewpoints series"
This collection of articles "on America in the near future focuses strongly on technology and how it will affect the family, education, economics, and the environment." Booklist
Includes bibliographical references

Asimov, Isaac, 1920-1992
The march of the millennia; a key to looking at history; by Isaac Asimov and Frank White. Walker & Co. 1991 196p $18.95; pa $12.95 **303.49**
1. Technology and civilization 2. Civilization—History 3. Forecasting
ISBN 0-8027-1122-7; 0-8027-7391-5 (pa)
LC 90-38086
"Asimov and White provide a millennium-by-millennium view of how cultures have developed, from the discovery of agriculture to the atom bomb. . . . The final chapter is an attempt to peek into the future and examine issues that may alter the momentum—energy use, population growth, etc. An excellent overview and springboard for creating interest in history." Booklist

303.6   Social conflict

Archer, Jules
Rage in the streets; mob violence in America. Browndeer Press 1994 175p il $16.95 **303.6**
1. Violence 2. United States—Social conditions
ISBN 0-15-277691-5   LC 93-5710
"The events described span from colonial times to the present and include the Boston Tea Party, protests by northerners against the Civil War, labor union struggles in the '30s, civil rights struggles in the '50s, student protests in the '60s, the 1992 L.A. riots and even riots during rock concerts and sporting events. . . . The text is clear, concise and will hold readers' interest. In addition, it will be a valuable supplement to history and sociology curriculums." SLJ
Includes bibliographical references

Arendt, Hannah
On revolution   303.6
1. Revolutions
Hardcover and paperback editions available from various publishers
First published 1963 by Viking
The author "believes that war and revolution are the central facts of our time. But while war may become obsolete through nuclear terror, revolution seems likely to persist as the order of the day, and those who understand revolution may well be the masters of the future." Atl Mon

On violence. Harcourt Brace Jovanovich 1970 106p hardcover o.p. paperback available $7 **303.6**
1. Violence
ISBN 0-15-669500-6 (pa)
The author "argues that violence is not creative, that it is the opposite of power, and that it stems from the frustration of the basic human power, to act. . . . [Her] answer to the problem of violence is participatory democracy." Libr J
Includes bibliographical references

Atkins, Stephen E.
Terrorism; a reference manual. ABC-CLIO 1992 199p (Contemporary world issues) $39.50 **303.6**
1. Terrorism
ISBN 0-87436-670-4   LC 92-28530
This survey discusses the philosophy, theory and forms of terrorism from 1894-1992. Includes brief biographies and a directory of terrorist groups
"Although the writing style is dry, it is still clear, understandable, and, given the emotionally charged material, remarkably unbiased." SLJ

DiCanio, Margaret
The encyclopedia of violence; origins, attitudes, consequences. Facts on File 1993 404p $45
                                             303.6
1. Violence—Dictionaries
ISBN 0-8160-2332-8   LC 92-39721
"Topics include battered women, child abuse, gun control, arson, campus violence, DNA fingerprinting, mass murderers and serial killers, post-traumatic stress disorder, and sports violence. . . . Overall, this book is an excellent one-volume reference for the money and should be on both school and public library shelves." Book Rep

Long, David E.
The anatomy of terrorism. Free Press 1990 244p $27.95   **303.6**
1. Terrorism
ISBN 0-02-919345-1   LC 90-33634
An "examination of terrorist operations, characteristics, strategies, and motivations. . . . Leading terrorist groups are profiled in the appendix." Booklist
"Far from condoning violence, Long sketches a somber reality rather than resorting to clichés. Essential reading for its erudition, sharp analysis, and intellectual honesty." Libr J
Includes bibliographical references

Sherrow, Victoria
Violence and the media. Millbrook Press 1996 160p il (Issue and debate) lib bdg $16.40 **303.6**
1. Violence 2. Mass media
ISBN 1-56294-549-1   LC 95-22286
The author "presents a historical overview of violence, and describes how it is handled by the mass media and how it has pervaded our popular culture. She includes an evenhanded assessment of the effects of violence on viewers, particularly on young people, and looks at what can be done to address the problem. The well-documented text is readable and right on target." SLJ
Includes bibliographical references

Violence in the media; Carol Wekesser, book editor. Greenhaven Press 1995 192p (Current controversies) lib bdg $19.95; pa $11.95 **303.6**
1. Violence 2. Mass media
ISBN 1-56510-237-1 (lib bdg); 1-56510-236-3 (pa)
                                        LC 94-43377
A look at the moral, social, political, and legal implications of violence in mass media. John Leonard, Irving Kristol, Robert Scheer, Barbara Ehrenreich and Virginia I. Postrel are among the contributors
Includes bibliographical references

Violence: opposing viewpoints; Scott Barbour, book editor, Karin L. Swisher, book editor. Greenhaven Press 1996 306p lib bdg $19.95; pa $11.95   **303.6**
1. Violence 2. Family violence
ISBN 1-56510-355-6 (lib bdg); 1-56510-354-8 (pa)
                                        LC 95-35628
"Opposing viewpoints series"
Replaces Violence in America, published 1990 under the editorship of Janelle Rohr
This "book begins by examining both sides of the question, 'Is violence a serious problem in America?' It discusses some of the possible causes and devotes particular attention to the problems of domestic and youth violence. The final section includes debates on policies to reduce violence, the use of anti-crime measures, increased gun control, and increased incarceration." SLJ
Includes bibliographical references

304.2   Human ecology

Commoner, Barry, 1917-
Making peace with the planet. Pantheon Bks. 1990 292p o.p.; New Press (NY) paperback available $11.95   **304.2**
1. Pollution 2. Human influence on nature 3. Environmental protection 4. Nature conservation
ISBN 1-56584-012-7 (pa)   LC 89-43241
Also available in hardcover from P. Smith
The author offers an "analysis of our contemporary environmental crisis, using the metaphor of a war between the natural ecosphere and the human-made technosphere." Libr J
"Visionary yet specific, his urgent essay is a blueprint of our possible future and a beacon for the environmental struggles of the '90s." Publ Wkly
Includes bibliographical references

Erickson, Jon, 1948-
The human volcano; population growth as geologic force. Facts on File 1995 210p il maps (Changing earth) $24.95 **304.2**
1. Human influence on nature 2. Population 3. Pollution
ISBN 0-8160-3130-4 LC 94-32148
"Likening the effects of the current population explosion to those of a volcanic eruption, this volume traces the damage that human expansion has caused: resource depletion, climatic change, global pollution, habitat destruction, and more." Publisher's note
Includes bibliographical references

Gore, Albert, Jr.
Earth in the balance; ecology and the human spirit; [by] Al Gore. Houghton Mifflin 1992 407p il maps $22.95 **304.2**
1. Human ecology 2. Environmental protection
ISBN 0-395-57821-3 LC 91-42676
Also available in paperback from New Am. Lib.
In this discussion of the global environment and civilization the author "argues that only a radical rethinking of our relationship with nature can save the earth's ecology for future generations." Publisher's note
"A passionate yet clearheaded exposition of a worldwide crisis. . . . The book may seem daunting to some, but its 3-part, 15-chapter structure, which allows readers to browse at will, should make it accessible enough to most YAs." SLJ
Includes bibliography

Leakey, Richard E., 1944-
The sixth extinction; patterns of life and the future of humankind; [by] Richard Leakey and Roger Lewin. Doubleday 1995 271p il $24.95; pa $14 **304.2**
1. Evolution 2. Human influence on nature 3. Mass extinction of species
ISBN 0-385-42497-3; 0-395-46809-1 (pa)
LC 95-18286
The authors contend that "human beings, by destroying tropical rain forests and driving tens of thousands of species into extinction, are dangerously reducing biodiversity, damaging ecosystems and possibly precipitating the next major mass extinction." Publ Wkly
Leakey and Lewin "present a powerful message based on years of observation and fieldwork." Libr J
Includes bibliographical references

304.6 Population

Cohen, Joel E.
How many people can the earth support? Norton 1995 532p $30 **304.6**
1. Population 2. Forecasting
ISBN 0-393-03862-9 LC 95-6133
This is an "overview of the history of human population, the factors theorized to modulate its growth, and the methods used to project the future number of the teeming multitude. . . . A cogent presentation for open-minded nondemographers seeking to make informed opinions rather than ratifying preconceived ideas." Booklist
Includes bibliography

Doyle, Rodger
The atlas of contemporary America; portrait of a nation—politics, economy, environment, ethnic and religious diversity, health issues, demographic patterns, quality of life, crime, personal freedoms. Facts on File 1994 unp maps $45 **304.6**
1. United States—Population—Maps 2. United States—Statistics
ISBN 0-8160-2545-2 LC 90-675147
This book "transforms the raw data of the 1990 census and other statistics into a revealing look at life in late 20th-century United States. The seven chapters cover such broad subjects as demographics, politics, health, and the economy." Libr J
"School librarians as well as social studies and science teachers will revel in the abundance of interesting data put forth in this atlas." SLJ

Ehrlich, Paul R.
The population explosion; [by] Paul R. Ehrlich & Anne H. Ehrlich. Simon & Schuster 1990 320p hardcover o.p. paperback available $12 **304.6**
1. Population 2. Human ecology
ISBN 0-671-73294-3 (pa) LC 89-48263
In this follow-up to the author's The population bomb (1968), Ehrlich and his co-author examine "the detonation of and fall out from the overpopulation of the Earth. The dimensions of the problem . . . are up-dated to include global warming, rain forest destruction, ozone depletion, and AIDS. The authors clearly portray the magnitude of the problem and offer viable solutions. This is an important book." Libr J
Includes bibliographical references

Henwood, Douglas
The state of the U.S.A. atlas; the changing face of American life in maps and graphics; [by] Doug Henwood. Simon & Schuster 1994 127p maps $30; pa $17 **304.6**
1. United States—Population—Maps 2. United States—Statistics
ISBN 0-671-79696-8; 0-671-79695-X (pa)
LC 94-14142
"A Touchstone book"
The maps in this work are divided into four topical sections: Demographics, Economy, Society, and Government. The author "utilizes pie charts and a wide variety of other (often entertaining) graphic devices to illustrate aspects of the mapped topics. . . . A wide variety of socioeconomic topics are covered: working women, poverty, voting rates, value of Pentagon contracts, percentage not covered by health insurance, etc." Booklist

Mattson, Mark T.
Atlas of the 1990 census. Macmillan 1992 168p il maps $110 **304.6**
1. United States—Census—Maps 2. United States—Population—Maps
ISBN 0-02-897302-X LC 92-24006
"This work is organized into six sections containing maps that graphically depict the statistical results of the 1990 census of population and housing. Population includes density, age, sex, death and birth rates, etc. Information about households depicts families, marital status, female-headed, nonfamily, etc." Booklist

Population: opposing viewpoints; Charles F.
Hohm, book editor, Lori Justine Jones, assistant
editor. Greenhaven Press 1995 240p il lib bdg
$19.95; pa $11.95   **304.6**
1. Population
ISBN 1-56510-215-0 (lib bdg); 1-56510-214-2 (pa)
    LC 94-41042
"Opposing viewpoints series"
Considers opposing opinions on various issues concerning world population including problems of rapid
growth, the effects of population on the environment, and
ways of decreasing human fertility
Includes bibliography

Roberts, Sam
Who we are; a portrait of America based on the
latest U.S. census. Times Bks. 1994 c1993 306p
maps hardcover o.p. paperback available $13
    304.6
1. United States—Population 2. United States—Census
ISBN 0-8129-2526-2 (pa)   LC 92-56842
"By analyzing 1990 census results (and comparing
them with results from previous years), Roberts points
out surprising changes in American society as well as
troubling echoes from previous eras. He touches on the
aging of the U.S. population and on racial and economic
discrimination. . . . His informative summary of the census also describes how it was compiled." Booklist

United Nations. Statistical Office
Demographic yearbook. U.N. Publs. $125
    304.6
1. Population—Statistics
Annual. First issue for 1948 published 1949. Text in
English and French
"Official compilation of international demographic
data in such fields as area and population, natality, mor-
tality, marriage, divorce, and international migration.
Each year some aspect of demographic statistics is treat-
ed intensively." Ref Sources for Small & Medium-sized
Libr. 5th edition

305.23   Young people

Abner, Allison, 1959-
Finding our way; the teen girls' survival guide;
[by] Allison Abner & Linda Villarosa.
HarperPerennial 1995 319p il pa $13   **305.23**
1. Life skills 2. Teenagers 3. Girls
ISBN 0-06-095114-1   LC 95-35964
This life skills book for teenage girls includes such
topics as body image, puberty, sexual development, birth
control, relationships with friends and family, and nutrition
"This candid book is one of the best resources for
young women to come out in a long time. The tone is
light but not flip . . . judiciously used comments from
teens personalize the reading, and there's an obvious attempt to encompass multicultural difference." Booklist
Includes bibliographical references

Bass, Ellen
Free your mind; the book for gay, lesbian, and
bisexual youth—and their allies; [by] Ellen Bass
and Kate Kaufman. HarperPerennial 1996 xxi,
417p il pa $14   **305.23**
1. Homosexuality
ISBN 0-06-095104-4   LC 96-4157
"The book's six sections address: self-discovery and
coming out, dealing with friends and first love, dealing
with family, defending and asserting oneself in school,
finding solace in spirituality, and locating community
support. . . . Of course, the book will infuriate those
who give homosexuality no quarter and also, on account
of its safe-sex counsel." Booklist
Includes bibliographical references

The **Best** of Free Spirit; five years of
award-winning news & views on growing up;
by the Free Spirit editors. Free Spirit 1995 234p
il pa $24.95   **305.23**
1. Youth—United States 2. Education—United States
ISBN 0-915793-91-1   LC 95-13014
"This work compiles the 'best of' essays from the
Free Spirit Newsletter. Free Spirit was published during
the school year from 1987-1992 and was designed to
provide a forum for discussion for kids 'growing up' and
the issues etc., that go along with adolescence. Contributors included teachers, psychologists, specialists, and
most importantly, young readers of the newsletter. Topics
cover school-related issues (back-to-school, study skills,
school survival) and personal issues (self-
awareness/esteem, family and friends, creativity, and
sports and hobbies)." Voice Youth Advocates
Includes bibliographical references

Bode, Janet
Beating the odds; stories of unexpected
achievers; drawings by Stan Mack. Watts 1991
126p il lib bdg $22.70   **305.23**
1. Life skills 2. Success
ISBN 0-531-10985-2   LC 91-14215
Also available Thorndike Press large print edition
Profiles a series of young people who overcame seemingly impossible odds—drugs, poverty, sexual abuse—
and not only survived but became successes in their own
right
"Sandwiched between these inspiring first-person stories . . . are comments by specialists on how to cope
with stress, set goals, and get help. Even teens with nothing more pressing in their lives than getting a date for
Saturday's dance will gain a new perspective by reading
these accounts. To kids in troubled straits, Bode's book
will be a lifeline." Booklist
Includes bibliography

Due, Linnea A., 1948-
Joining the tribe; growing up gay & lesbian in
the '90s; [by] Linnea Due. Anchor Bks. (NY)
1995 xliv, 272p il pa $12.95   **305.23**
1. Homosexuality
ISBN 0-385-47500-4   LC 95-7643
"Due aims to explain what it's like to be young and
gay in different towns and cities throughout the country.

Due, Linnea A., 1948——*Continued*
In chapters that resemble Sunday-newspaper human-interest interviews, she lets young people tell their stories." Booklist
"A brilliant, heartrending book of youth lives based on superb ethnographic interviews." Voice Youth Advocates

Fenwick, Elizabeth, 1935-
Adolescence; the survival guide for parents and teenagers; [by] Elizabeth Fenwick & Tony Smith; photographs by Barnabas Kindersley. Dorling Kindersley 1994 c1993 286p il $19.95; pa $14.95
305.23
1. Adolescence 2. Parent and child
ISBN 1-56458-330-9; 0-7894-0635-7 (pa)
LC 93-15780
First published 1993 in the United Kingdom
This volume covers parent/teen issues "including physical development, communication, school problems, sexuality, risky behavior, emotional problems, and teen illness and health." Voice Youth Advocates
"A needed resource for parents and teens—there aren't many alternatives." BAYA Book Rev
Includes bibliographical references

Hawes, Joseph M.
The children's rights movement; a history of advocacy and protection. Twayne Pubs. 1991 169p il (Social movements past and present) $30; pa $15.95
305.23
1. Children—Civil rights
ISBN 0-8057-9747-5; 0-8057-9748-3 (pa)
LC 91-10922
The author presents an "overview of the 'many disparate social actions' that might pass as a children's rights 'movement.' Hawes begins his narrative with the 'stubborn child' law (1641); he continues through (among other significant happenings) the founding of the Society for the Prevention of Cruelty to Children (1875), the creation of the U.S. Children's Bureau (1912), the establishment of the Children's Defense League (1973), and the ACLU's stance on behalf of child welfare victims in 1990." Libr J
Includes bibliographical references

Kinnear, Karen L.
Violent children; a reference handbook. ABC-CLIO 1995 251p (Contemporary world issues) $39.50
305.23
1. Violence 2. Juvenile delinquency
ISBN 0-87436-786-7
LC 95-6457
This volume provides a "survey of the resources available on violent children and a guide to further research on the topic. After a general overview, additional chapters provide a chronology of significant events pertaining to violent children, biographical sketches of individuals who have played or are currently playing key roles in the area of child violence, and statistical information on the extent of violent acts committed by youth." Voice Youth Advocates
For a fuller review see: Booklist, Oct. 1, 1995

Kohl, Candice, 1950-
The string on a roast won't catch fire in the oven; an A-Z encyclopedia of common sense for the newly independent young adult. Gylantic 1993 174p il pa $12.95
305.23
1. Life skills
ISBN 1-880197-07-3
LC 93-3961
A survival guide for young adults out on their own, discussing apartments, job hunting, budgets, laundry, taxes, sexual relations, cars, and food
The author "provides a lot of practical advice. The information is well laid out on each page. Summary lists and illustrations make the book appealing. A list of recommended reading is included in each chapter. A good introduction to living on one's own." Voice Youth Advocates

Kotlowitz, Alex
There are no children here; the story of two boys growing up in the other America. Doubleday 1991 324p hardcover o.p. paperback available $12.95
305.23
1. Children—United States 2. Family 3. Public housing 4. Chicago (Ill.)—Social conditions
ISBN 0-385-26556-5 (pa)
LC 90-45225
"Kotlowitz traces two years in the lives of ten-year-old Lafeyette and seven-year-old Pharoah Rivers as they struggle to beat the odds and grow up in one of Chicago's worst housing projects." Libr J
"Young people everywhere will be moved by the author's account." Booklist
Includes bibliographical references

Kuklin, Susan
Speaking out; teenagers take on race, sex, and identity. Putnam 1993 165p il hardcover o.p. paperback available $8.95
305.23
1. Teenagers 2. Human relations
ISBN 0-399-22532-3 (pa)
LC 92-44288
This "is a collection of interviews with students from all different races and backgrounds, discussing their experiences in dealing with prejudice and racial stereotypes. . . . Many of these testimonies are heart-breaking, some are uplifting, some are terrifying; every single one is memorable." Voice Youth Advocates

Lewis, Sydney, 1952-
"A totally alien life-form"; teenagers. New Press (NY) 1996 363p $25
305.23
1. Teenagers
ISBN 1-56584-282-0
LC 96-5574
In these interviews the "teens, who range in age from 13 to 19, are mainly city kids, though a few are from small towns and suburbs. Their backgrounds and experiences differ more than expected. . . . They speak often about family, self-image, and the future, and about drugs and violence in their homes, schools, and communities." Booklist

Orenstein, Peggy
Schoolgirls; young women, self-esteem, and the confidence gap; by Peggy Orenstein in association with the American Association of University Women. Doubleday 1994 xxix, 335p hardcover o.p. paperback available $12.95   **305.23**
1. Adolescence 2. Girls 3. Self-esteem
ISBN 0-385-42576-7 (pa)   LC 94-9883
"Troubled by the 1990 American Association of University Women report on the loss of self-esteem by American girls between the ages of nine and 15, journalist Orenstein sought the human stories behind the statistics. She worked for a year with girls from two California schools, interviewing students, their families, teachers, and the administrators of the two schools." Libr J
Includes bibliographical references

Ousseimi, Maria
Caught in the crossfire; growing up in a war zone. Walker & Co. 1995 128p il $19.95; lib bdg $20.85   **305.23**
1. War
ISBN 0-8027-8363-5; 0-8027-8364-3 (lib bdg)   LC 94-44457
"Each of the five chapters is devoted to quotes from interviews with young survivors of brutal fighting in Lebanon, El Salvador, Mozambique, Bosnia-Herzegovina and the urban battleground of drugs and gangs in Washington, D.C. Background on the complicated political circumstances leading to the conflicts is provided. Accounts of rapes and wholesale executions of villagers make this grim reading. The author's focus is the emotional effects of devastation and displacement on these powerful victims. Recommend this book with caution for those readers mature enough to handle such a difficult subject." Child Book Rev Serv
Includes bibliographical references

Pratt, Jane
For real; the uncensored truth about America's teenagers; by Jane Pratt and Kelli Pryor. Hyperion 1995 317p pa $9.95   **305.23**
1. Teenagers 2. Adolescent psychology 3. Youth—United States
ISBN 0-7868-8064-3   LC 94-46189
In this book the authors "give 25 teens, selected from a wide range of socioeconomic and ethnic groups, a chance to tell their stories. Pratt's respect for teens is clear, and although some of the kids suffer from the effects of poverty, prejudice, parental divorce, peer rejection, and substance abuse, the overall sensibility of these youngsters is a combination of resiliency and hope." Booklist
Includes bibliographical references

Two teenagers in twenty; writings by gay and lesbian youth; edited by Ann Heron. Alyson Publs. 1994 185p hardcover o.p. paperback available $9.95   **305.23**
1. Homosexuality 2. Lesbians
ISBN 1-55583-282-2 (pa)   LC 94-9761
First published 1983 with title: One teenager in ten

"A collection of forty-three essays written by American gay teens for gay teens. The authors (twenty female, twenty-three male, ages twelve to twenty-four), describe how they learned to accept their homosexuality and gain their self respect." Voice Youth Advocates
"Adults who work with young people in any capacity, as well as heterosexual young adults, will benefit from reading the book." Horn Book Guide

West, Elliott, 1945-
Growing up in twentieth-century America; a history and reference guide. Greenwood Press 1996 378p il $49.95   **305.23**
1. Children—United States 2. United States—Social life and customs
ISBN 0-313-28801-1   LC 95-38652
"Chapters cover the years 1900-1920, 1920-1940, 1940-1960, and 1960 to the present. Each includes a substantial section on the six selected topics: home, play, work, school, health, and the law. A bibliographical essay with sections corresponding to the topics covered plus personal reflections precedes the notes in every chapter." Book Rep
"Students researching the roles and significance of childhood in American society will find a well-balanced, informative assessment. . . . Photographs enhance the text." Voice Youth Advocates

305.26   Late adulthood

An **Aging** population: opposing viewpoints; Charles P. Cozic, book editor. Greenhaven Press 1996 216p il lib bdg $19.95; pa $11.95 **305.26**
1. Elderly—United States
ISBN 1-56510-395-5 (lib bdg); 1-56510-394-7 (pa)   LC 95-49646
"Opposing viewpoints series"
"Economic burdens, social security, Medicare, quality of life, the outlook for retirees, Alzheimer's disease, and age bias are among the topics debated here. An introduction tells of the mixed backgrounds of the people whose points of view have been included in the essays, and emphasizes that both professional and lay opinions need to be sought when seriously considering the ramifications of these issues." SLJ
Includes bibliographical references

Terkel, Studs, 1912-
Coming of age; the story of our century by those who've lived it. New Press (NY) 1995 xxvi, 468p $25   **305.26**
1. Elderly—United States
ISBN 1-56584-284-7   LC 95-3806
Also available in paperback from St. Martin's Press
For this oral history "Terkel interviewed 69 individuals who have come of age in the latter part of the 20th century. The youngest is 70, the oldest, 99. Some are well known (artist Jacob Lawrence, actress Uta Hagen, economist John Kenneth Galbraith); others live out of the limelight (a farm workers' organizer, a retired bank president, a librarian)." Libr J
"The people interviewed for 'Coming of Age,' though

Terkel, Studs, 1912—*Continued*
diverse in their life histories, are an inordinately like-minded crowd, and the language spoken here is pure Terkel: the voice of the embattled old liberal shaking his stick at the 20th century." N Y Times Book Rev
Includes bibliographical references

305.3 Men and women. Sex role

Male/female roles: opposing viewpoints; Jonathan S. Petrikin, book editor. Greenhaven Press 1995 312p il lib bdg $19.95; pa $11.95   **305.3**
1. Sex role
ISBN 1-56510-174-X (lib bdg); 1-56510-175-8 (pa)
LC 94-4975
"Opposing viewpoints series"
Replaces the edition published 1989 under the editorship of Neal Bernards and Terry O'Neill
Robert Bly and Susan Faludi are among the authors who are represented in this collection which "considers how sex roles are established, whether the roles of both men and women have changed for the better, how work affects the family, and the future of male/female relationships." Booklist
Includes bibliography

305.4 Women

Beauvoir, Simone de, 1908-1986
The second sex; translated and edited by H.M. Parshley. Knopf 1993 lv, 786p $20; pa $14
305.4
1. Women
ISBN 0-679-42016-9; 0-679-72451-6 (pa)
LC 92-54303
"Everyman's library"
Original French edition, 1949; this translation first published 1953
This "thorough analysis of women's secondary status in society, became a classic of feminist literature." Reader's Ency. 3d edition

Becker, Susan D.
The origins of the Equal Rights Amendment; American feminism between the wars. Greenwood Press 1981 300p (Contributions in women's studies) lib bdg $55   **305.4**
1. National Woman's Party 2. Women's rights 3. Women's movement
ISBN 0-313-22818-3   LC 80-23633
"The idea and text of an equal rights amendment were first formulated in the early 1920s by Alice Paul's National Woman's Party. . . . This study describes in detail the NWP programs and personalities, placing them in the context of the women's rights movement as a whole." Libr J
Includes bibliography

Brown, Dorothy M. (Dorothy Marie), 1932-
Setting a course: American women in the 1920s. Twayne Pubs. 1987 302p il (American women in the twentieth century) lib bdg $24.95; pa $11.95
305.4
1. Women—United States—History
ISBN 0-8057-9906-0 (lib bdg); 0-8057-9908-7 (pa)
LC 86-22898
The author characterizes "the decade between the end of World War I and the beginning of the Depression as one in which the newly enfranchised American woman began mapping an arduous, unpredictable route toward self-definition and freedom of choice. . . . The economic, political, religious, and cultural milieu is well documented." Booklist
Includes bibliography

Celebrating women's history; a women's history month resource book; Mary Ellen Snodgrass, editor; foreword by Mary Ruthsdotter. Gale Res. 1995 517p il $44.95   **305.4**
1. Women—History
ISBN 0-7876-0605-7   LC 95-43315
This guide "contains 300 activities and projects that can be done with a variety of age groups, from pre-k through adults. Activities are grouped by subject, including cinema, health, library research, speech and debate, and sports. They range from games and contests to cooking projects and arts and crafts. . . . For each project is noted the age/grade level or audience, procedure, budget, sources (mostly books and videos), and related activities. An appendix lists sources of multimedia, museums, archives, newsletters, publishers, etc. . . . *Celebrating Women's History* will be useful all year round." Booklist

Cullen-DuPont, Kathryn
The encyclopedia of women's history in America. Facts on File 1995 339p $48   **305.4**
1. Women—United States—History 2. Feminism—Dictionaries
ISBN 0-8160-2625-4   LC 95-4308
This reference work "covers people, significant events, organizations, legislation, court cases, and issues affecting women. . . . Rounding out the more than 500 entries are appendixes containing the complete texts of 34 documents ranging from a 1647 request for suffrage to a 1992 court case. . . . High-school and public libraries that want to beef up their collections on women's history will find *The Encyclopedia of Women's History in America*

De Pauw, Linda Grant
Founding mothers; women in America in the Revolutionary era; wood engravings by Michael McCurdy. Houghton Mifflin 1975 228p il $16.95; pa $5.95   **305.4**
1. Women—United States—History 2. Women—Social conditions 3. United States—Social life and customs—1600-1775, Colonial period
ISBN 0-395-21896-9; 0-395-70109-0 (pa)
LC 75-17031
"Viewing roles of women who lived during the Revolutionary era from a contemporary feminist perspective

De Pauw, Linda Grant—*Continued*
. . . [the author] examines Black, white and Native American women as well as women of all social classes, including slaves." SLJ
Includes bibliography

Fast, Timothy
The women's atlas of the United States; [by] Timothy H. Fast & Cathy Carroll Fast. rev ed. Facts on File 1995 246p il maps $75   **305.4**
1. Women—United States 2. Women—Social conditions
ISBN 0-8160-2970-9   LC 94-29084
First published 1986 under the authorship of Anne Gibson and Timothy Fast
This "resource covers a wide variety of contemporary women's sociological issues: demographics, education, employment, child care, health, crime, and politics. Usually statistics are presented for the entire state via large, easy-to-read maps or graphs utilizing bright, distinctive colors. Symbols are effectively used to heighten interest. Accounting for perhaps one-third of the book, the narration explains and efficiently elaborates on the data presented. . . . An excellent resource, and a must-purchase wherever women's studies are a part of the curriculum." SLJ

Feminism: opposing viewpoints; Carol Wekesser, book editor. Greenhaven Press 1995 239p lib bdg $19.95; pa $11.95   **305.4**
1. Feminism 2. Women's rights
ISBN 1-56510-178-2 (lib bdg); 1-56510-179-0 (pa)
LC 94-4974
"Opposing viewpoints series"
Replaces the edition published 1986 under the editorship of Andrea Hinding
This book "begins with a historical perspective of the women's movement and a discussion of 19th-century feminism. Topics also include feminism's effects on women, society, and its future and goals." SLJ
Includes bibliography

Franck, Irene M.
The women's desk reference; by Irene Franck & David Brownstone. Viking 1993 840p il hardcover o.p. paperback available $11.95   **305.4**
1. Women—United States
ISBN 0-14-017046-4 (pa)   LC 93-17515
"Subjects range from legislation and social problems to health issues, history, and literature. The first section contains 1500 alphabetically arranged entries, which often have a list of books and agencies for additional information. . . . The second section provides text to documents such as the Declaration of Sentiments and Resolution, statistical charts, books by women, and a timeline of women's history." Libr J

Women's world; a timeline of women in history; [by] Irene Franck & David Brownstone. HarperPerennial 1995 654p il pa $22.50   **305.4**
1. Women—History
ISBN 0-06-273336-2   LC 94-31298
This chronology of women's history "covers prehistory through the early 1990s, proceeding first by era and

then by year after 1830. . . . The book is divided into four large areas—politics/war/law, religion/education/everyday life, science/technology/medicine, and arts/literature—and . . . includes more than 50 sidebars generally offering short excerpts from contemporary writing." Libr J
For a fuller review see: Booklist, Oct. 1, 1995

Friedan, Betty
The feminine mystique. 20th anniversary ed. Norton 1983 xxviii, 452p $17.50   **305.4**
1. Women—United States 2. Feminism
ISBN 0-393-01775-3   LC 83-11375
Also available in paperback from Dell
First published 1963
An "analysis of the dilemma facing the educated American woman; the post-war emphasis on the feminine image of the role as wife and mother has caused the American woman to lose her identity, says the author." Cincinnati Public Libr
Includes bibliographical references

Garza, Hedda
Latinas; Hispanic women in the United States. Watts 1994 192p il maps (Hispanic experience in the Americas) lib bdg $22.70   **305.4**
1. Hispanic Americans
ISBN 0-531-11186-5   LC 94-30598
"This overview of Latino history from Spanish colonization through the present focuses on women's political and economic oppression and highlights the work of Latina activists such as Lucy Parsons and Luisa Moreno." Bull Cent Child Books
Includes bibliographical references

Gay, Kathlyn
Rights and respect; what you need to know about gender bias and sexual harassment. Millbrook Press 1995 128p lib bdg $16.40 **305.4**
1. Sexual harassment
ISBN 1-56294-493-2   LC 94-45501
Describes sexual harassment in school and at work, explains the relationship of harassment to sex discrimination, and explores methods of preventing gender bias and harassment
"Student researchers will appreciate the balanced presentation, with its meticulous documentation, extensive bibliography, and resource listing." Booklist

Gies, Frances
Women in the Middle Ages; [by] Frances and Joseph Gies. Crowell 1978 264p il o.p.; HarperCollins Pubs. paperback available $12.50
305.4
1. Women—Europe 2. Middle Ages—History
ISBN 0-06-092304-0 (pa)   LC 77-25832
"From Blanche of Castile to a peasant farmer's wife, this book describes the lives of a group of women in the Middle Ages who represent all classes and a variety of occupations. [Accounts of] an abbess, a clothmaker, a merchant's wife are . . . drawn from household records,

Gies, Frances—*Continued*
letters, and secondary sources." Libr J
"A remarkably well-balanced presentation of the changing role played by women during the long centuries usually lumped together under the designation 'Middle Ages.'" Choice
Includes bibliography

Greenspan, Karen
The timetables of women's history; a chronology of the most important people and events in women's history. Simon & Schuster 1994 459p il $35; pa $21   **305.4**
1. Women—History
ISBN 0-671-67150-2; 0-684-81579-6 (pa)
LC 94-41762
This chronology contains essays which "include biographical sketches and topics such as housework, dowry, pornography, Renaissance artists, women in early Islam, and the feminization of poverty." Libr J
For a fuller review see: Booklist, April 1, 1995

Jones, Constance, 1961-
Sexual harassment. Facts on File 1996 280p (Library in a book) $24.95   **305.4**
1. Sexual harassment
ISBN 0-8160-3273-4   LC 95-18508
This volume includes a definition and history of sexual harassment, a discussion of relevant court cases, a chronology and biographical listings, a lengthy annotated bibliography, a list of organizations and agencies, and appendices of laws and court rulings regarding sexual harassment

Landau, Elaine
Sexual harassment. Walker & Co. 1993 93p $14.95; lib bdg $15.85   **305.4**
1. Sexual harassment
ISBN 0-8027-8265-5; 0-8027-8266-3 (lib bdg)
LC 92-43748
Examines the varied forms that sexual harassment can take, discusses instances of harassment in both work and school settings, and offers suggestions on how to handle such situations
"This will be very helpful both for reports and for individual reading. It is a concise, well-done introduction." Voice Youth Advocates
Includes bibliography

Lanker, Brian
I dream a world: portraits of black women who changed America; photographs and interviews by Brian Lanker; edited by Barbara Summers; foreword by Maya Angelou. Stewart, Tabori & Chang 1989 167p il $40; pa $24.95   **305.4**
1. African American women
ISBN 1-55670-063-6; 1-55670-092-X (pa)
LC 88-32697
"A doubled-paged format of photographs, brief biographical information, and first-person accounts of women from all walks of life. . . . The book can function as

art, history, literature, or social commentary. Though Barbara Jordan, Alice Walker, and Priscilla Williams inspired this white man's project, many other women provide the names he needed to produce the final 75. Amazingly beautiful and moving." Libr J

Making waves: an anthology of writings by and about Asian American women; edited by Asian Women United of California. Beacon Press 1989 481p il hardcover o.p. paperback available $19   **305.4**
1. Asian Americans 2. Women—United States
ISBN 0-8070-5905-6 (pa)   LC 88-47661
This volume "contains seven thematic sections: immigration, war, work, generations, identity, injustice, and activism. . . . Essays focus on women in broadcasting, in organization building, and as resisting the matchmaking tradition. . . . This collection offers, for everyone, valuable insights about the American experience." Choice
Includes bibliographical references

Mills, Kay
From Pocahontas to power suits; everything you need to know about women's history in America. Penguin Bks. 1995 325p pa $10.95   **305.4**
1. Women—United States—History
ISBN 0-452-27152-5   LC 94-34521
"In a question-and-answer format, this celebration of women in America's history touches on everything from civil rights and women in the workplace to education, the arts, and sports. A stimulating resource for women's studies and American history classes." Booklist
Includes bibliographical references

Peavy, Linda Sellers, 1943-
Pioneer women; the lives of women on the frontier; by Linda Peavy and Ursula Smith. Smithmark Pubs. 1996 144p il $15.98   **305.4**
1. Frontier and pioneer life—West (U.S.) 2. Women—West (U.S.)
ISBN 0-8317-7220-4
An illustrated exploration of women's lives on the Western frontier. Marriages between Anglo men and Indian and Hispanic women are examined as are the lives of women who found employment outside the homestead as teachers, physicians and journalists
"YAs seeking primary source material for women's studies and on the westward movement will find this exceptional collection of journals, letters, oral histories, and rarely seen photographs an outstanding resource." Booklist

Schneider, Dorothy
American women in the Progressive Era, 1900-1920; [by] Dorothy Schneider & Carl J. Schneider. Facts on File 1993 276p il $27.95
305.4
1. Women—United States—History 2. Progressive movement, 1900-1915
ISBN 0-8160-2513-4   LC 92-22588
Also available in paperback from Anchor Bks.

Schneider, Dorothy—*Continued*

"The story of women's continuous struggle for equality during the early 20th century is presented in this well-researched book that offers copious statistics as documentation. Primary sources, diaries, letters, magazines, and photographs bring the era to life." SLJ

Includes bibliographical references

Steinem, Gloria

Outrageous acts and everyday rebellions. 2nd ed, with a new preface and notes by the author. Holt & Co. 1995 xxii, 406p pa $12.95   **305.4**
1. Feminism
ISBN 0-8050-4202-4   LC 95-31711
"An Owl book"
First published 1983

"Twenty years are spanned in this selected and edited collection of Steinem's writings. . . . [The topics range from] personal accounts of political leaders and individual women (including Marilyn Monroe and Jackie Onassis) to general theoretical material regarding the feminist movement to articles addressing specific feminist issues." Libr J

Includes bibliographical references

We are your sisters; black women in the 19th century; edited by Dorothy Sterling. Norton 1984 xx, 535p il hardcover o.p. paperback available $14.95   **305.4**
1. African American women 2. Women—United States—History 3. African Americans—History
ISBN 0-393-30252-0 (pa)   LC 83-11469

The editor has created a "documentary of the experience of black women in 19th-century America. In accounts culled from personal correspondence, court papers, memoirs and other primary sources, including transcripts of more than 1,000 interviews with former slaves, the often heroic conduct of these women is conveyed." N Y Times Book Rev

"Useful for assignments [this book] is also a pleasure to read, and is highly recommended for its wealth of information as well as a source of enlightenment about the past contributions of American black women." SLJ

Includes bibliography

What is sexual harassment? Karin L. Swisher, book editor. Greenhaven Press 1995 91p (At issue) lib bdg $12.95; pa $7.95   **305.4**
1. Sexual harassment
ISBN 1-56510-299-1 (lib bdg); 1-56510-266-5 (pa)
LC 94-28345

Essays examine the social, legal and political implications of sexual harassment in the business world and academia. Mona Charen, Katie Roiphe and Ellen Goodman are among the contributors

Includes bibliographical references

Women in the classical world; image and text; [by] Elaine Fantham [et al.] Oxford Univ. Press 1994 430p il maps $35; pa $19.95   **305.4**
1. Women—History
ISBN 0-19-506727-4; 0-19-509862-5 (pa)
LC 92-47284

This volume chronicles "the lives of women both famous and anonymous, aristocratic and indentured, wor-

shiped and abused. The result is a unique illustrated chronological survey of women's lives built upon a foundation of vivid cultural and social history and laced with poetry, anecdotes, and original interpretations." Booklist

Includes bibliographical references

Women's issues; edited by Robin Brown. Wilson, H.W. 1993 154p (Reference shelf, v65 no5) pa $15   **305.4**
1. Women—United States 2. Sex discrimination 3. Women—Employment
ISBN 0-8242-0844-7   LC 93-4940

The articles in this collection are grouped under the following headings: Women in the workplace; Sexual harassment; Work and the family; The new politics

Women's lives in medieval Europe: a sourcebook; edited by Emilie Amt. Routledge 1993 347p il hardcover o.p. paperback available $16.95   **305.4**
1. Women—Europe 2. Europe—History—476-1492
ISBN 0-415-90628-8 (pa)   LC 92-12815

"Excerpts from primary sources provide information regarding the daily lives of European women from A.D. 500 to 1500. Following an overview of the times . . . the materials are arranged chronologically. They trace a heritage of ideas, describing living conditions of noblewomen, workers, religious sects, and outsiders. Full bibliographic information precedes each entry. Although religious texts, public law, and regulations constitute a large portion of the documents, materials written by women are included when possible. YAs interested in the subject . . . will have their knowledge expanded, and they'll be able to meet many primary-source research requirements." SLJ

The **Women's** rights movement: opposing viewpoints; Brenda Stalcup, book editor. Greenhaven Press 1996 263p (American history series) lib bdg $19.95; pa $11.95   **305.4**
1. Women's rights
ISBN 1-56510-367-X (lib bdg); 1-56510-366-1 (pa)
LC 95-51244

This collection of articles presents early debates on women's rights, varying viewpoints on the women's liberation movement, and historical evaluations of the women's suffrage movement

Includes bibliographical references

Woolf, Virginia, 1882-1941

A room of one's own. Harcourt Brace Jovanovich 1991 c1929 125p $15.95; pa $5.95   **305.4**
1. Women—Social conditions 2. Women authors 3. Women—Great Britain
ISBN 0-15-178733-6; 0-15-678733-4 (pa)
LC 91-17953

"An HBJ modern classic"
A reissue of the title first published 1929

"Woolf begins by announcing her basic thesis: that 'a woman must have money and a room of her own if she is to write fiction.' . . . She then examines the educational, social, and financial disadvantages and prejudices which have thwarted women writers throughout (English) history." Camb Guide to Lit in Engl

The **Young** Oxford history of women in the United States. Oxford Univ. Press 1994-1995 11v il lib bdg ea $22 **305.4**
1. Women—United States—History 2. Women—Social conditions 3. United States—Social conditions

Contents: v1 The tried and the true, by J. Demos; v2 The colonial mosaic, by R. E. Jakoubek; v3 The limits of independence, by M. Salmon; v4 Breaking new ground, by M. Goldberg; v5 An unfinished battle, by H. Sigerman; v6 Laborers for liberty, by H. Sigerman; v7 New paths to power, by K. M. Smith; v8 From ballots to breadlines, by S. Deutsch; v9 Pushing the limits, by E. T. May; v10 The road to equality, by W. H. Chafe; v11 Supplement and index

"The series lives up to its stated aim of presenting American history with a social and cultural slant that emphasizes the roles of women. . . . The accomplishments of well-known figures . . . are presented alongside the lives of 1950s white suburban housewives, 1940s Chicana unionists, 1880s African American tobacco warehouse workers, 1870s Chinese immigrants forced into prostitution, and many more." Voice Youth Advocates

305.8 Racial, ethnic, national groups

The **African** American almanac. Gale Res. il $165 **305.8**
1. African Americans
ISSN 1071-8710

First edition under the editorship of Harry A. Ploski published 1967 by Bellwether with title: The Negro almanac. (7th edition 1997) Periodically revised

Current editor: L. Mpho Mabunda

"Reference covering the cultural and political history of Black Americans. Includes generous amount of statistical information and biographies of Black Americans, both historical and contemporary." N Y Public Libr. Book of How & Where to Look It Up

The **African** American encyclopedia; editor: Michael W. Williams. Marshall Cavendish 1993 6v il maps set $449.95 **305.8**
1. African Americans—Dictionaries
ISBN 1-85435-545-7 LC 93-141

Also available two volume supplement $149.95 (ISBN 0-7614-0563-1)

"Consists of long topical entries (usually one to three pages), and shorter entries, of one to three paragraphs, primarily devoted to personalities. Covers a wide variety of individuals, including politicians, sports figures, entertainers, military, and civil rights leaders, as well as historical persons. Suggested readings accompany many of the longer entries. Photographs with approximately one-half the entries." Guide to Ref Books. 11th edition

Asante, Molefi K., 1942-
The historical and cultural atlas of African Americans; [by] Molefi K. Asante, Mark T. Mattson. Macmillan 1991 198p il maps $110; pa $28 **305.8**
1. African Americans—History
ISBN 0-02-897021-7; 0-02-897029-2 (pa)
LC 90-46410

This "book offers encyclopedic treatment of the African-American experience from African origins to present-day social and economic realities. In addition to the printed text . . . the book contains numerous photographs, diagrams, and charts. But what distinguishes the work from similar sources . . . is its 65 informative and clearly drawn maps." Libr J

The **Asian-American** almanac; a reference work on Asians in the United States; Susan Gall, managing editor; Irene Natividad, executive editor. Gale Res. 1995 834p il $95 **305.8**
1. Asian Americans
ISBN 0-8103-9193-7 LC 95-8520

This volume "covers 15 major Asian American groups/nationalities. . . . Noteworthy chapters include those that discuss prominent Asian Americans and historic Asian American landmarks, and reprinted texts of speeches. . . . Overall, this is a very good resource." Choice

Baldwin, James, 1924-1987
The fire next time. Modern Lib. 1995 105p $12.50; pa $9 **305.8**
1. African Americans 2. Black Muslims 3. United States—Race relations
ISBN 0-679-60151-1; 0-679-74472-X (pa)
LC 94-23228

A reissue of the title first published 1963 by Dial Press

"Through a study of the emergent Black Muslims and a remembrance of his own experience as a preacher, Baldwin prophesies to the white world: wake up or be destroyed; 'God gave Noah the rainbow sign, no more water, the fire next time.'" Benet's Reader's Ency of Am Lit

No name in the street. Dial Press 1972 197p o.p.; Dell paperback available $5.99 **305.8**
1. African Americans 2. United States—Race relations
ISBN 0-440-36461-2 (pa)

In this personal statement on American political and social history, the author discusses his self-exile, the deaths of many black leaders, and gives reasons for his increasingly militant participation in the civil rights movement

Nobody knows my name; more notes of a native son. Dial Press 1961 241p o.p.; Vintage Bks. paperback available $10 **305.8**
1. African Americans 2. United States—Race relations
ISBN 0-679-74473-8 (pa)

In this collection of first-person essays, the author deals with the "relationship between black and white and

Baldwin, James, 1924-1987—*Continued*
between the writer and society. Drawing on his own experiences and observations in the U.S. and Europe he writes of American majorities and minorities . . . [and] novelists Richard Wright and Norman Mailer." Booklist

Notes of a native son. 3rd ed. Beacon Press 1990 xxxvi, 175p pa $12   **305.8**
1. African Americans 2. United States—Race relations
ISBN 0-8070-6431-9   LC 90-52598
First published 1955
Contents: Autobiographical notes; Everybody's protest novel; Many thousands gone; Carmen Jones: the dark is light enough; The Harlem ghetto; Journey to Atlanta; Notes of a native son; Encounter on the Seine: black meets brown; A question of identity; Equal in Paris; Stranger in the village

Bennett, Lerone, 1928-
Before the Mayflower: a history of black America; by Lerone Bennett, Jr. Johnson il maps $25   **305.8**
1. African Americans—History
Also available in paperback from Penguin Bks.
First published 1962. Periodically revised
The author traces the history of black America from its African origins, through slavery and Reconstruction, to the role of blacks in contemporary society
Includes bibliography

The **Black** Americans: a history in their own words, 1619-1983; edited by Milton Meltzer. Crowell 1984 306p il lib bdg $15.89; pa $9.95   **305.8**
1. African Americans—History
ISBN 0-690-04418-6 (lib bdg); 0-06-446055-X (pa)
     LC 83-46160
This is a revised and updated edition of In their own words: a history of the American Negro, edited by Milton Meltzer and published in three volumes, 1964-1967
A history of black people in the United States, as told through letters, speeches, articles, eyewitness accounts, and other documents

Black firsts; 2,000 years of extraordinary achievement; edited by Jessie Carney Smith, with Casper L. Jordan, Robert L. Johns; foreword by Johnetta B. Cole. Gale Res. 1994 529p il $39.95; pa $16.95   **305.8**
1. African Americans—History
ISBN 0-8103-8902-9; 0-8103-9490-1 (pa)
     LC 93-44155
Also available junior version with title African American breakthroughs (1995) published by U.X.L.
"Who was the first black woman elected to a political office in the U.S.? Who was the first black player drafted by a professional basketball team?. . . . These are only a few of the almost 3,000 entries in 15 chapters that cover areas such as arts and entertainment, business, government, the military, civil rights, religion, and sports. A chronological chapter arrangement with many illustrations enhances the appeal of this browsable volume. . . . This is a particularly useful source for locating Black History Month information." Am Libr
Includes bibliographical references

Black history month resource book; Mary Ellen Snodgrass, editor; foreword by Bertha Calloway. Gale Res. 1993 xx, 430p $45   **305.8**
1. African Americans—History
ISBN 0-8103-9151-1   LC 93-25964
This book describes activities for Black History Month, "arranged in such subject areas as art and architecture, cooking, genealogy, math, religion and ethics, sewing and fashion, speech and drama, and storytelling. The subject areas of the typical elementary and secondary curriculum are well represented." Booklist
Includes bibliographical references

Carnes, Jim
Us and them; a history of intolerance in America; preface by Justice Harry A. Blackmun; illustrations by Herbert Tauss. Oxford Univ. Press 1996 131p il $22   **305.8**
1. Prejudices 2. Fanaticism 3. United States—Race relations 4. Ethnic relations
ISBN 0-19-510378-5   LC 95-11367
"Working chronologically, this history examines the prejudice against and persecution of various groups since the English colonies were established in America. Each of the fourteen chapters focuses on a specific incident— Mary Dyer's harassment and banishment for her Quaker faith, the Florida riots that destroyed the African-American town of Rosewood, the drowning of a gay man in Maine—and includes first-person accounts and relevant official documents." Bull Cent Child Books
This book "should get widespread use, both for classroom discussion and for personal reading." Booklist
Includes bibliographical references

Cleaver, Eldridge, 1935-
Soul on ice; with an introduction by Maxwell Geismar. McGraw-Hill 1968 210p o.p.; Dell paperback available $6.50   **305.8**
1. African Americans
ISBN 0-440-21128-X (pa)
"A Ramparts book"
In a collection of essays and open letters written from California's Folsom State Prison, the author writes about the forces which shaped his life
There are sections "on the Watts riots, on Cleaver's religious conversion, on the black man's stake in the Vietnam War, on fellow-writers and white women." Saturday Rev

Cockcroft, James D.
The Hispanic struggle for social justice. Watts 1994 160p il (Hispanic experience in the Americas) lib bdg $22.70   **305.8**
1. Hispanic Americans
ISBN 0-531-11185-7   LC 94-22968
The author examines the ethnic history of Mexican Americans, Puerto Ricans, and other Latinos in terms of national issues of labor, immigration, civil rights, and feminism
Includes bibliographical references

Cockcroft, James D.—*Continued*

Latinos in the making of the United States. Watts 1995 191p il (Hispanic experience in the Americas) lib bdg $22.70   **305.8**
1. Hispanic Americans
ISBN 0-531-11209-8   LC 94-23933
"'Latinos' in this work include Mexican Americans, Puerto Ricans, Cubans and immigrants from Latin America. Cockcroft emphasizes the vital part Latinos have played in the history of our nation while pointing out the discrimination these groups have faced. . . . Documentation is thorough and much of this material is rarely found in books for high school students. Useful for fact finding in history, minority studies and economics classes." Book Rep

Crouch, Stanley

The all-American skin game; or, The decoy of race; the long and short of it, 1990-1994. Pantheon Bks. 1995 267p $24; pa $12   **305.8**
1. African Americans 2. United States—Race relations
ISBN 0-679-44202-2; 0-679-77660-5 (pa)
LC 95-10142
Analyzed in Essay and general literature index
"In this collection of essays on race in American culture and society, Crouch comments on the blues, the jazz of Miles Davis & Dizzy Gillespie, and the movies." Libr J
These essays are informed by the author's "keen analytical mind that, at times, transcends the liberal or conservative labels." Booklist
Includes bibliographical references

Dalton, Harlon L.

Racial healing; confronting the fear between blacks and whites. Doubleday 1995 246p $22.50; pa $12   **305.8**
1. United States—Race relations
ISBN 0-385-47516-0; 0-385-47517-9 (pa)
LC 95-18882
The author explores "the issue of race in America. . . . Race always has mattered greatly in America, Dalton says, and the sooner we muster the courage to face the debilitating issues surrounding it and work through the awkwardness of discussing the issues, the sooner healing can occur." Christ Sci Monit
Includes bibliographical references

Davidson, Art, 1943-

Endangered peoples; foreword by Rigoberta Menchú; photographs by Art Wolfe and John Isaac; book design by Charles Fuhrman. Sierra Club Bks. 1993 195p il $30; pa $20   **305.8**
1. Ethnology
ISBN 0-87156-457-2; 0-87156-423-8 (pa)
LC 93-22026
"More than a colorfully photographed profile of various endangered cultures—for example the Ainus of Japan and the Samis of Russia—this attractive large-format volume personalizes each culture through Davidson's own impressions and recollections." Booklist

Davidson, Osha Gray

The best of enemies; race and redemption in the new South. Scribner 1996 336p il $25   **305.8**
1. Ku Klux Klan 2. Southern States—Race relations
ISBN 0-684-19759-6   LC 95-45543
"The growing friendship between a black civil rights advocate and a member of the Ku Klux Klan is set against the racist anger and struggle of the 1960s in Durham, North Carolina." Booklist

Davis, Marilyn P.

Mexican voices/American dreams; an oral history of Mexican immigration to the United States. Holt & Co. 1990 446p $29.95; pa $15.95   **305.8**
1. Mexican Americans 2. United States—Immigration and emigration
ISBN 0-8050-1216-8; 0-8050-1859-X (pa)
LC 90-31640
"From the perilous crossing of the border itself to the gut-wrenching recognition of the economic reality in the two countries, these accounts reveal a whole spectrum of emotions, from misery to acceptance to hope." Booklist
Includes glossary

A **Documentary** history of the Negro people in the United States; edited by Herbert Aptheker. Citadel Press 1989-1994 7v   **305.8**
1. African Americans—History 2. African Americans—Civil rights
Apply to publisher for price and availability
Volume one first published 1951; published as a 3 volume set 1969-1974
Contents: v1 From colonial times through the Civil War; v2 From the Reconstruction to the founding of the N.A.A.C.P.; v3 1910-1932; v4 1933-1945; v5 1945-1951 From the end of World War II to the Korean War; v6 1951-1959 From the Korean War to the emergence of Martin Luther King, Jr.; v7 1960-1968 From the Alabama protests to the death of Martin Luther King, Jr.
This is a compilation of documents, including articles, essays, pamphlets, diary excerpts, speeches, letters, etc., written by African Americans. The arrangement is largely chronological

Douglass, Frederick, 1817?-1895

Frederick Douglass, in his own words; edited by Milton Meltzer; illustrated by Stephen Alcorn. Harcourt Brace & Co. 1995 220p il $22   **305.8**
1. Slavery—United States 2. African Americans—History
ISBN 0-15-229492-9   LC 94-14524
"Sixty-six speeches, encompassing a span of 40 years, are chronologically divided into sections devoted to before, during, and after the Civil War. A brief descriptive annotation introduces each speech, noting its date, place delivered, and circumstances surrounding its presentation. The selections, mainly two to three pages in length, afford a rich resource for report writers, orators, and debaters." SLJ
Includes bibliographical references

Du Bois, W. E. B. (William Edward Burghardt), 1868-1963

The Oxford W. E. B. Du Bois reader; edited by Eric J. Sundquist. Oxford Univ. Press 1996 680p pa $19.95   **305.8**

1. African Americans 2. United States—Race relations

ISBN 0-19-509178-7   LC 95-21307

This reader covers Du Bois's "writing career, from the 1890s through the early 1960s. The volume selects key essays and longer works that portray the range of Du Bois's thought on such subjects as African American culture, the politics and sociology of American race relations, art and music, black leadership, gender and women's rights, Pan-Africanism and anti-colonialism, and Communism in the U.S. and abroad." Publisher's note

Includes bibliographical references

The souls of black folk; essays and sketches; by W.E. Burghardt Du Bois   **305.8**

1. African Americans

Hardcover and paperback editions available from various publishers

First published 1903 by McClurg

"A collection of fifteen essays and sketches by W.E.B. Du Bois. In it he describes the lives of African American farmers, sketches the role of music in their churches, details the history of the Freedman's Bureau, discusses the career of Booker T. Washington, and advocates a commitment to higher education for the most talented African American youth." Benet's Reader's Ency of Am Lit

W.E.B. Du Bois: a reader; edited by David Levering Lewis. Holt & Co. 1995 801p $35; pa $16.95   **305.8**

1. African Americans 2. Africa

ISBN 0-8050-3263-0; 0-8050-3264-9 (pa)

     LC 94-23482

"A John Macrae book"

This is a selection of essays, speeches, book excerpts and magazine articles on subjects ranging from race and civil rights issues to Africa, Pan-Africanism and imperialism

Includes bibliographical references

Dyson, Michael Eric

Between God and gangsta rap; bearing witness to black culture. Oxford Univ. Press 1996 xx, 218p $25   **305.8**

1. African Americans—Social conditions 2. African American arts

ISBN 0-19-509898-6   LC 95-20779

This "book comprises a series of essays following three themes: Testimonials, or lives of contemporary black men; Lessons, or the politics of black culture, from the Panthers to the current Congress; Songs of Celebration, which cross musical and cultural lines, from gospel to pop and gangsta rap. . . . [A] timely account." Libr J

East to America: Korean American life stories; [edited by] Elaine H. Kim, Eui-Young Yu. New Press (NY) 1996 xxii, 386p map $25   **305.8**

1. Korean Americans

ISBN 1-56584-297-9   LC 95-32555

Contains edited transcriptions of interviews conducted by Kim and Yu presented as oral histories

"These 38 interviews include a Korean adopted as a baby by white Americans, a rap artist, a journalist, a gay activist, several inner-city shop owners, a widow, an abused wife, and a charity volunteer. The book's usefulness lies in exposing students, especially those of Korean descent, to Korean-Americans' recent history, culture, and heritage. It can also serve as background reading for multicultural issues." SLJ

Encyclopedia of African-American culture and history; edited by Jack Salzman, David Lionel Smith, Cornel West. Macmillan 1996 5v il set $425   **305.8**

1. African Americans—Dictionaries

ISBN 0-02-897345-3   LC 95-33607

With coverage beginning with the arrival in 1619 of the first slaves from Africa, this set provides a "survey of both the contributions to and the problems of blacks in American society. The 2,300 signed entries treat North America only. . . . Two-thirds of the entries are biographies treating such important historical figures as Sojourner Truth and Frederick Douglass and such contemporary people as Marian Wright Edelman and Colin Powell. . . . Many well-known scholars are contributors: James Cone, John Hope Franklin, David Levering Lewis, C. Eric Lincoln, and Eric Foner, for example." Booklist

Encyclopedia of cultural anthropology; editors, David Levinson, Melvin Ember. Holt & Co. 1996 4v set $395   **305.8**

1. Ethnology—Dictionaries

ISBN 0-8050-2877-3   LC 95-37237

This encyclopedia "has been developed to emphasize the cross-cultural perspective, holistic approach, and practice of fieldwork that demark cultural anthropology. . . . The 340 lengthy entries mainly comprise subjects, theoretical constructs, geographical/cultural areas, cultural groups, and important organizations related to anthropology." Libr J

For a fuller review see: Booklist, June 1 & 15, 1996

Encyclopedia of multiculturalism; editor, Susan Auerbach. Marshall Cavendish 1993 6v il set $449.95   **305.8**

1. Multiculturalism—Dictionaries 2. Minorities—Dictionaries

ISBN 1-85435-670-4   LC 93-23405

This encyclopedia "covers the ethnic groups of African Americans, American Indians, Inuets and Aluets, Asian and Pacific Islanders, European and Middle Eastern Americans, Jewish Americans, and Latinos. It also focuses on issues faced by groups such as women, gays and lesbians, the elderly, and the disabled. . . . Articles range from a few hundred words to several pages in length." Book Rep

For a fuller review see: Booklist, May 1, 1994

Fernández-Shaw, Carlos M.
The Hispanic presence in North America from 1492 to today; translated by Alfonso Bertodano Stourton and others. Facts on File 1991 xxi, 375p il maps $45   **305.8**
1. Hispanic Americans—History 2. Spanish Americans—History 3. United States—Civilization
ISBN 0-8160-2133-3   LC 91-10786
Also available Spanish language edition
An abridged and updated version of the 1987 Spanish edition
"This book traces the history and continuing Spanish influence in each state. Greater emphasis and separate chapters are devoted to states with a large Hispanic presence or those formerly administered by Spain. The regional section is preceded by a lengthy introduction to Spain's role in U.S. history: exploration, colonization, religion, culture, economy, and the law." Libr J

Franklin, John Hope, 1915-
From slavery to freedom; a history of African Americans; [by] John Hope Franklin, Alfred A. Moss, Jr. Knopf il maps $45   **305.8**
1. African Americans—History 2. Slavery—United States
Also available in paperback from McGraw-Hill
First published 1947. (7th edition 1994) Periodically revised
A survey of African-American history from slavery to the present
Includes bibliography

Gale encyclopedia of multicultural America; contributing editor, Rudolph J. Vecoli; edited by Judy Galens, Anna Sheets, Robyn V. Young. Gale Res. 1995 2v il set $125   **305.8**
1. Ethnic groups—Dictionaries 2. Minorities—Dictionaries
ISBN 0-8103-9163-5   LC 95-23341
"This two-volume reference work examines 101 different ethnic groups in the United States, ranging from migrant groups to certain distinct religions. . . . Generally ten to 20 pages long, the signed original articles by recognized scholars contain a general history of the group, a description of the area or country of origin, and an examination of a variety of different aspects of the group's experience in the United States. The entries are excellent summary articles that also include handbook-type information such as addresses of organizations." Libr J
For a fuller review see: Booklist, Dec. 1, 1995

Garza, Hedda
African Americans and Jewish Americans; a history of struggle. Watts 1995 208p il (African-American experience) lib bdg $22.70   **305.8**
1. African Americans 2. Jews and Gentiles 3. United States—Race relations
ISBN 0-531-11217-9   LC 95-18838
"Overview of the relations between Blacks and Jews in the U.S. through history. . . . Garza draws on a wide range of excellent, fully-documented sources. She shows that both groups have suffered racism and both have fought against it for themselves and for each other. She's candid about prejudice in the country today, including the blame-the-victim backlash and anti-Semitism." Booklist
Includes bibliographical references

Gates, Henry Louis
The future of the race; by Henry Louis Gates, Jr. and Cornel West. Knopf 1996 196p $20; pa $12   **305.8**
1. Du Bois, W. E. B. (William Edward Burghardt), 1868-1963 2. African Americans—Social conditions 3. African Americans—Intellectual life 4. United States—Race relations
ISBN 0-679-44405-X; 0-679-76378-3 (pa)
    LC 96-14450
"Gates and West explore the challenge of W.E.B. DuBois's famous essay 'The Talented Tenth' and consider the future of African American society in light of it. . . . The authors examine the responsibility of the successful and talented black middle and upper classes to uplift the impoverished. . . . The text includes DuBois's 'The Talented Tenth' and, reprinted for the first time, his 1948 critique of it." Libr J
Includes bibliographical references

Gay, Kathlyn
"I am who I am"; speaking out about multiracial identity. Watts 1995 144p lib bdg $22.70   **305.8**
1. Multiculturalism 2. United States—Race relations
ISBN 0-531-11214-4   LC 94-39206
"Gay weaves together many sources, often first-person accounts of specific incidents, to present information on racial prejudice and its sociohistorical origins, the experiences of racially mixed families, media stereotypes, how other world societies cope with racism and multiracial people, and finally, the ways and means of creating and maintaining harmony." SLJ
Includes bibliographical references

Glazer, Nathan
Beyond the melting pot; the Negroes, Puerto Ricans, Jews, Italians, and Irish of New York City; by Nathan Glazer and Daniel Patrick Moynihan. 2nd ed. MIT Press 1970 xcviii, 363p hardcover o.p. paperback available $17.50   **305.8**
1. Minorities 2. New York (N.Y.)—Foreign population
ISBN 0-262-57022-X (pa)
First published 1963
A study of the different levels of achievement of the five major ethnic groups of New York City in education, business, and politics
Includes bibliographical references

Griffin, John Howard, 1920-1980
Black like me. 2nd ed, with a new epilogue by the author. Houghton Mifflin 1977 208p o.p.; New Am. Lib. paperback available $5.99   **305.8**
1. African Americans—Southern States 2. Prejudices
ISBN 0-451-19203-6 (pa)   LC 76-47690
First published 1961

Griffin, John Howard, 1920-1980—*Continued*

The author, "who is white, a Catholic, and a Texan, conceived and carried out the unusual notion of blackening his skin with a newly developed pigment drug and traveling through the Deep South as a Negro. This book, part of which appeared in the Negro magazine Sepia, is a journal account of that experience." New Yorker

Growing up Jewish; an anthology; edited and with an introduction by Jay David; foreword by TK. Morrow 1996 249p $22   **305.8**

1. Jews—United States

ISBN 0-688-12824-6   LC 95-26106

"This volume of excerpts contains stories and essays about being Jewish and young in 20th-century America. Despite the anti-Semitism and poverty they detail, the personal anecdotes and descriptions are fascinating windows into other people's joys and successes." Libr J

Growing up Jewish in America; an oral history; [compiled by] Myrna Katz Frommer and Harvey Frommer. Harcourt Brace & Co. 1995 xxi, 264p il $25   **305.8**

1. Jews—United States

ISBN 0-15-100132-4   LC 95-19620

The compilers "mix the experiences of some 100 interviewees—a good fraction of them writers or Jewish community officials—into a rich mosaic portrait. . . . Interviewees discuss politicization, the impact of the Holocaust, the effects of Zionism and the ongoing tensions about assimilation and anti-Semitism. . . . An accessible introduction to the varieties of the American Jewish experience." Publ Wkly

Includes bibliographical references

Hacker, Andrew

Two nations; black and white, separate, hostile, unequal. Scribner 1992 257p il $24.95   **305.8**

1. African Americans—Social conditions 2. United States—Race relations

ISBN 0-684-19148-2   LC 91-34003

Also available in paperback from Ballantine Bks.

The author discusses race in the United States, addressing such questions as "how we define and divide people into races; what it is like to be black in America; and why white Americans react as they do to people of African ancestry. . . . Hacker goes on to analyze such problems as crime, unemployment, family instability, and the role of race in politics." Publisher's note

"The real value of this book, despite its wealth of data, is in Mr. Hacker's calm, analytical eye, his unblinking view of American history and his unwillingness to accept cant and 'common sense' as facts." N Y Times Book Rev

Includes bibliography

Harley, Sharon

The timetables of African-American history; a chronology of the most important people and events in African-American history. Simon & Schuster 1995 400p il $35; pa $21   **305.8**

1. African Americans—History

ISBN 0-671-79524-4; 0-684-81578-8 (pa)

LC 94-22571

This work "is arranged by year; under each date events are listed across the page under such categories as

Education; Laws and Legal Actions; Religion; Arts; Science, Technology, and Medicine; and Sports." Booklist

"These timetables would be an excellent addition to any collection of African American studies as a ready reference source or a starting point for further research." Libr J

Harvard encyclopedia of American ethnic groups; Stephan Thernstrom, editor; Ann Orlov, managing editor, Oscar Handlin, consulting editor. Belknap Press 1980 xxv, 1076p maps $115   **305.8**

1. Ethnic groups—Dictionaries 2. Minorities—Dictionaries

ISBN 0-674-37512-2   LC 80-17756

"Defining *ethnic* in the widest possible way, this book contains substantial articles on American ethnic groups. Origins, migration and settlement, history in America, socioeconomic structure, religion and politics, and many other topics are addressed. Includes demographic information, individual bibliographies, and appendices." N Y Public Libr. Book of How & Where to Look It Up

Hoobler, Dorothy

The African American family album; [by] Dorothy and Thomas Hoobler; introduction by Phylicia Rashad. Oxford Univ. Press 1995 127p il (American family albums) $19.95; lib bdg $22.95   **305.8**

1. African Americans

ISBN 0-19-509460-3; 0-19-508128-5 (lib bdg)

LC 94-34697

"Beginning with life in pre-colonial Africa, the Hooblers make superb use of personal histories, autobiographies, slave narratives, and other original documents to paint a vivid picture of life in medieval Africa, in Africa during the slave trade, and of the lives of slaves and former slaves in the U.S. Readers are introduced to a complex set of historical events, presented in a simple, yet moving manner. . . . An excellent addition to any collection." SLJ

Includes bibliography

The Chinese American family album; [by] Dorothy and Thomas Hoobler; introduction by Bette Bao Lord. Oxford Univ. Press 1994 128p il map (American family albums) $19.95; lib bdg $22.95   **305.8**

1. Chinese Americans

ISBN 0-19-509123-X; 0-19-508130-7 (lib bdg)

LC 93-11873

"This sourcebook on the Chinese immigrant experience is divided into six topics: the homeland, the voyage to America, arrival in America, first-generation life, the integration of . . . generations, and Chinese Americans today. The authors introduce each chapter with a summary essay, then let the immigrants and their descendents speak for themselves in excerpts from oral reminiscences, written histories, and fiction spanning the years from the Gold Rush to the 1980s. Period photographs and drawings, maps, and sidebars enhance the text. The result resembles a well-organized, handsomely designed scrapbook. . . . A valuable resource." SLJ

Includes bibliography

Hoobler, Dorothy—*Continued*

The Cuban American family album; [by] Dorothy and Thomas Hoobler; introduction by Oscar Hijuelos. Oxford Univ. Press 1996 127p il (American family albums) $19.95; lib bdg $22.95
305.8
1. Cuban Americans
ISBN 0-19-510340-8; 0-19-508132-3 (lib bdg)
LC 95-38103
Interviews, excerpts from diaries and letters, newspaper accounts, profiles of famous individuals, and pictures from family albums portray the Cuban American experience
Includes bibliography

The German American family album; [by] Dorothy and Thomas Hoobler; introductions by Werner Klemperer. Oxford Univ. Press 1996 127p il (American family albums) $19.95; lib bdg $22.95
305.8
1. German Americans
ISBN 0-19-510341-6; 0-19-508133-1 (lib bdg)
LC 95-14448
Traces the history of German immigrants to the United States through letters, diaries and newspaper accounts
Includes bibliography

The Irish American family album; [by] Dorothy and Thomas Hoobler; introduction by Joseph P. Kennedy II. Oxford Univ. Press 1995 128p il (American family albums) $19.95; lib bdg $22.95
305.8
1. Irish Americans
ISBN 0-19-509461-1; 0-19-508127-7 (lib bdg)
LC 94-19569
"Selections from diaries, letters, interviews, newspaper and magazine articles, and books provide an arresting picture of what it has meant to be of Irish heritage in America. . . . Topics such as prejudice, working conditions and labor unions; politics; and the importance of family, friends, and the Catholic Church are touched upon." SLJ
Includes bibliography

The Italian American family album; [by] Dorothy and Thomas Hoobler; introduction by Governor Mario M. Cuomo. Oxford Univ. Press 1994 127p il map (American family albums) $19.95; lib bdg $22.95
305.8
1. Italian Americans
ISBN 0-19-509124-8; 0-19-508126-9 (lib bdg)
LC 93-46918
This volume includes selections from "diaries, letters, and oral histories. . . . Each of the six chapters begins with background information and then goes on to discuss life in the old country, coming to America, first impressions, working, forming a new life, and becoming a part of America." SLJ
Includes bibliography

The Japanese American family album; [by] Dorothy and Thomas Hoobler. Oxford Univ. Press 1995 127p il map (American family albums) $19.95; lib bdg $22.95
305.8
1. Japanese Americans
ISBN 0-19-509934-6; 0-19-508131-5 (lib bdg)
LC 94-43466
"Organized chronologically, this book captures the broad sweep of the Japanese-American experience. Each of the six chapters offers a succinct historical presentation followed by first-person accounts. Relying on oral histories and original documents, both pictorial and written, the Hooblers have truly humanized historical events." SLJ
Includes bibliography

The Jewish American family album; [by] Dorothy and Thomas Hoobler; introduction by Mandy Patinkin. Oxford Univ. Press 1995 127p il (American family albums) $19.95; lib bdg $22.95
305.8
1. Jews—United States
ISBN 0-19-509935-4; 0-19-508135-8 (lib bdg)
LC 94-43460
This volume "begins with a five-page thumbnail sketch of Jewish history from Abraham to the rise of the State of Israel. Successive chapters detail Jewish life in 'the old country', immigration to America, and the contributions Jews have made to their new homeland." Book Rep
"What makes this title unique is the high quality of the carefully researched and varied historical information and the Hooblers' judicious selection of primary-source excerpts, many of which are by well-known writers, politicians, and celebrities." SLJ
Includes bibliography

The Mexican American family album; [by] Dorothy and Thomas Hoobler; introduction by Henry G. Cisneros. Oxford Univ. Press 1994 127p il (American family albums) $19.95; lib bdg $22.95
305.8
1. Mexican Americans
ISBN 0-19-509459-X; 0-19-508129-3 (lib bdg)
LC 94-7785
"Using almost exclusively first-person accounts, the Hooblers present vignettes of history, culture, and experience from the first Mexican American settlers to the Chicano Movement. . . . Gathered together, these accounts present a powerful portrait of a strong people, rich in history and culture. A must for multicultural studies." Book Rep
Includes bibliography

Hornsby, Alton, Jr.
Chronology of African-American history; significant events and people from 1619 to the present. Gale Res. 1991 xlvii, 526p il $60 **305.8**
1. African Americans—History
ISBN 0-8103-7093-X
LC 91-17303
New edition in preparation
This chronology "begins in 1619 with the arrival of the first Africans to be brought forcibly to America and concludes in the summer of 1990. An introductory sec-

Hornsby, Alton, Jr.—*Continued*

tion presents some African history and a discussion of the effect each U.S. president has had on African-American society. The main-section entries are brief yet informative." Libr J

Includes bibliography

Interracial America: opposing viewpoints; Bonnie Szumski, book editor. Greenhaven Press 1996 237p lib bdg $19.95; pa $11.95 **305.8**
1. United States—Race relations
ISBN 1-56510-393-9 (lib bdg); 1-56510-392-0 (pa)
LC 95-52626

"Opposing viewpoints series"

A collection of articles debating issues relating to race relations in America including affirmative action, interracial families, racism and poverty, and whether or not racial differences should be emphasized

Includes bibliographical references

Jackson, Kennell A.

America is me; 170 fresh questions and answers on black American history; [by] Kennell Jackson. HarperCollins Pubs. 1996 446p $27.50; pa $14 **305.8**
1. African Americans—History 2. Questions and answers
ISBN 0-06-017036-0; 0-06-092785-2 (pa)
LC 95-48927

This book "answers approximately 200 questions about African American history and culture. Arranged chronologically, the book covers a wide variety of subjects on the most significant issues in African American history, thought, and politics. . . . *America Is Me* performs the important task of providing . . . up-to-date information . . . on African American persons, events, and achievements. It will prove an invaluable resource." Booklist

Includes bibliographical references

Japanese American history; an A-to-Z reference from 1868 to the present; Brian Niiya, editor; foreword by Daniel K. Inouye. Facts on File 1993 386p il $45 **305.8**
1. Japanese Americans
ISBN 0-8160-2680-7 LC 92-35753

Published in association with the Japanese American National Museum

This resource "provides an overview of Japanese immigration; a chronology of major events that have affected Japanese Americans; and encyclopedic entries of people, places, vocabulary, and historical happenings." SLJ

The **Latino** encyclopedia; editors, Richard Chabrán and Rafael Chabrán. Marshall Cavendish 1995 6v set $459.95 **305.8**
1. Hispanic Americans—Dictionaries
ISBN 0-7614-0125-3 LC 95-13144

This "encyclopedia covers all Caribbean and Latin American populations in the United States. Organized in traditional encyclopedic format, with 1910 separate articles, 1000 illustrations, and 11 appendixes, it describes people, organizations, history, culture, economics, politics, and other aspects of Latino life." Libr J

"This is an excellent addition to middle-through high-school and public library reference collections. It will be especially useful at report-writing time." Booklist

Nationalism and ethnic conflict; Charles P. Cozic, book editor. Greenhaven Press 1994 288p map (Current controversies) lib bdg $19.95; pa $11.95 **305.8**
1. Nationalism 2. Ethnic relations
ISBN 1-56510-080-8 (lib bdg); 1-56510-079-4 (pa)
LC 93-19854

A collection of "pro and con essays and articles on the benefits of nationalism, the historical and current causes of ethnic violence around the world, and the question of intervention by outside nations. . . . A challenging but nonetheless excellent resource for research or debate students." SLJ

Includes bibliographical references

Perseverance; by the editors of Time-Life Books; with a foreword by Henry Louis Gates, Jr. Time-Life Bks. 1993 254p il maps (African Americans: voices of triumph) $29.95 **305.8**
1. African Americans—History 2. Slavery—United States 3. African Americans—Civil rights
LC 93-19566

This illustrated look at the role of blacks in American history begins with an account of the Songhai Empire in West Africa. The following chapters describe slavery and abolition, blacks as pioneers in the West, blacks in the military, and the civil rights movement

Includes bibliography

Race relations: opposing viewpoints; Paul A. Winters, book editor. Greenhaven Press 1995 239p lib bdg $19.95; pa $11.95 **305.8**
1. United States—Race relations
ISBN 1-56510-357-2 (lib bdg); 1-56510-356-4 (pa)
LC 95-9016

"Opposing viewpoints series"

This volume "explores such topics as the efficacy of Affirmative Action programs, whether or not America's justice system discriminates against African Americans, and the relations among Black, Asian, and Latino political powerbases. . . . Thoughtfully arranged with excellent book and periodical bibliographies, this title will prove useful for report writers and debators." SLJ

Sachar, Howard Morley, 1928-

A history of the Jews in America; by Howard M. Sachar. Knopf 1992 1051p hardcover o.p. paperback available $20 **305.8**
1. Jews—United States
ISBN 0-679-74530-0 (pa) LC 91-4261

The author examines "two different subjects. One is the rich, sometimes dark, ultimately triumphant story of Jews in the United States. The other is the relation between American Jews and Israel. . . . [This is] not only good history but a contribution to the current debate over American-Israeli relations." N Y Times Book Rev

Includes bibliographical references

Takaki, Ronald T., 1939-
Strangers from a different shore; a history of Asian Americans; [by] Ronald Takaki. Little, Brown 1989 570p il o.p.; Penguin Bks. paperback available $13.95 **305.8**
1. Asian Americans
ISBN 0-14-013885-4 (pa)   LC 89-2816
"This popular history of Asian Americans . . . based frequently on primary sources, shows how they have made their presence felt in America from the early 1800s." Libr J
"Takaki, himself the son of a Japanese immigrant to Hawaii, tells this story with passion and eloquence, his narrative encompassing a diverse group that includes Chinese, Japanese, Filipinos, Koreans, Vietnamese, Laotians, Cambodians, and Asian Indians. An excellent popular history with a far-ranging epic sweep." Booklist
Includes bibliographical references

Terkel, Studs, 1912-
Race; how blacks and whites think and feel about the American obsession. New Press (NY) 1992 403p $24.95 **305.8**
1. United States—Race relations
ISBN 1-56584-000-3   LC 91-66864
Also available in paperback from Anchor Bks.
In this "oral history, Terkel explores Americans' inner feelings and values pertaining to the subject of race. . . . His study is primarily centered in Chicago, but the people chosen to be interviewed represent a broad spectrum of society. . . . Terkel demonstrates how very skilled he is at drawing out interviewees' intrinsic feelings pertaining to race." Libr J

Ungar, Sanford J.
Fresh blood; the new American immigrants. Simon & Schuster 1995 399p $25 **305.8**
1. Immigrants 2. United States—Immigration and emigration
ISBN 0-684-80860-9   LC 95-19405
In this look at immigrant communities the author recounts "the human tales that are ignored when Americans, and their politicians, turn their anger against immigrants. . . . He concentrates on such relatively unknown groups as the Laotian Hmong in the Minneapolis-St. Paul area; the Mashadi Jews of Iran, now living in Queens; Washington's Ethiopians and Eritreans; and 'second wave' Poles and Irish migrating to already well-established ethnic neighborhoods in Chicago and Boston. Through his eyes we experience the conflicts felt by nearly all immigrants between group loyalty and the seductions of assimilation." N Y Times Book Rev
Includes bibliographical references

The **Young** Oxford history of African Americans; Robin D. G. Kelley and Earl Lewis, general editors. Oxford Univ. Press 1994-1997 11v il maps set $231 **305.8**
1. African Americans—History 2. United States—Race relations
ISBN 0-19-508502-7
Contents: v1 The first passage, by C. A. Palmer; v2 Strange new land, by P. H. Wood; v3 Revolutionary citi-

zens, by D. C. Littlefield; v4 Let my people go, by D. G. White; v5 Break those chains at last, by N. Frankel; v6 Though justice sleeps, by B. Bair; v7 A chance to make good, by J. R. Grossman; v8 From a raw deal to a new deal? by J. W. Trotter; v9 We changed the world, by V. Harding; v10 Into the fire, by R. D. G. Kelley; v11 Biographical supplement and index, by D. M. Freund and M. McQuirter
This set "provides an in-depth examination of African-American involvement in every historical period from the Spanish explorers through the L. A. riots of 1992 and their aftermath. Each book has a detailed time-line, a thorough index and an extensive list for further reading." Child Book Rev Serv

305.9 Occupational and miscellaneous groups

Homosexuality: opposing viewpoints; William Dudley, book editor. Greenhaven Press 1993 216p il lib bdg $19.95; pa $11.95 **305.9**
1. Homosexuality
ISBN 0-89908-481-8 (lib bdg); 0-89908-456-7 (pa)
          LC 92-40705
"Opposing viewpoints series"
Presents opposing viewpoints on such aspects of homosexuality as what causes it, how society should treat homosexuals, and whether sexual orientation can be changed
Includes bibliographical references

Pollack, Rachel
The journey out; a guide for and about lesbian, gay, and bisexual teens; by Rachel Pollack and Cheryl Schwartz. Viking 1995 148p $14.99; pa $6.99 **305.9**
1. Homosexuality 2. Lesbians 3. Bisexuality
ISBN 0-670-85845-5; 0-14-037254-7 (pa)
          LC 95-14276
Suggests how gay, lesbian, and bisexual teenagers may discover their sexual orientation, find self-acceptance, come out, cope with prejudice, and deal with religious and political issues
The authors "include copious quotes from gay or bisexual teens and supply an extensive list of sources of additional information and help, including community centers, crisis hotlines and supportive religious organizations. An explicit discussion of sexually transmitted diseases concludes with basic facts about AIDS. . . . A candid, accessible resource." Publ Wkly
Includes bibliography

306 Culture and institutions

American values: opposing viewpoints; Charles P. Cozic, book editor. Greenhaven Press 1995 307p il lib bdg $19.95; pa $11.95 **306**
1. Social values 2. United States—Moral conditions
ISBN 1-56510-242-8 (lib bdg); 1-56510-241-X (pa)
          LC 94-41912
"Opposing viewpoints series"
Replaces the edition published 1989 under the editorship of David L. Bender

American values: opposing viewpoints—*Continued*

Among the topics debated in this collection are the work ethic, moral conduct, family values, religious values, and materialism

Includes bibliography

Culture wars: opposing viewpoints; Fred Whitehead, book editor. Greenhaven Press 1994 216p il lib bdg $19.95; pa $11.95   **306**
1. Multiculturalism 2. United States—Civilization
ISBN 1-56510-101-4 (lib bdg); 1-56510-100-6 (pa)
    LC 93-8512

"Opposing viewpoints series"

This collection of articles "explores the various cultural differences which are prevalent in the United States. . . . Both sides of each issue are presented by authors such as Ishmael Reed and Mortimer Adler. The specific topics include political correctness, Madonna, and the National Endowment for the Arts. The information is clear and concise, with both sides of each argument given equal time. 'Culture Wars' is a valuable resource for students as well as teachers." Voice Youth Advocates

Includes bibliographical references

Encyclopedia of world cultures; David Levinson, editor in chief. Hall, G.K. & Co. 1991-1996 10v maps set $1100   **306**
1. Ethnology—Dictionaries
ISBN 0-8161-1840-X   LC 90-49123
v1 North America, Timothy J. O'Leary, David Levinson, volume editors; v2 Oceania, Terence E. Hays, volume editor; v3 South Asia, Paul Hockings, volume editor; v4 Europe (central, western, and southeastern Europe), Linda A. Bennett, volume editor; v5 East and Southeast Asia, Paul Hockings, volume editor; v6 Russia and Eurasia, China, Paul Friedrich and Norma Diamond, volume editors; v7 South America, Johannes Wilbert, volume editor; v8 Middle America and the Caribbean, James W. Dow, volume editor; v9 Africa and the Middle East, John Middleton and Amal Rassam, volume editors; v10 Indexes, David Levinson, volume editor

This set includes "more than 1,500 cultural groups. Descriptions of these 20th century cultures vary in length from several paragraphs to several pages. Each signed entry contains the following elements: culture name, ethnonym, history and cultural relations, settlements, economy, Kinship, marriage and family, sociopolitical organization, religion and expressive culture, and bibliography." Guide to Ref Books. 11th edition

306.4   Specific aspects of culture

Coca-Cola culture; icons of pop; series editors, Roger Rosen and Patra McSharry Sevastiades. Rosen Pub. Group 1993 170p il (Icarus world issues series) lib bdg $16.95; pa $8.95   **306.4**
1. Popular culture—United States
ISBN 0-8239-1593-X (lib bdg); 0-8239-1594-8 (pa)
    LC 93-23495
This is a "collection of nine essays and one work of fiction focusing on the ways in which America's products, from cigarettes to movies to Disney World, have influenced the way other countries perceive the U.S.—and

themselves in relation to us—as well as the way we perceive ourselves. Each of the contributions is well written, and the editors have done a nice job of choosing a variety of perspectives and styles to keep the younger reader interested and the viewpoints fresh." Booklist

Includes glossary and bibliography

Genetics & society; edited by Penelope Barker. Wilson, H.W. 1995 189p (Reference shelf, v67 no3) pa $15   **306.4**
1. Genetics 2. Genetic engineering
ISBN 0-8242-0870-6   LC 95-10332
A collection of articles grouped as follows: Genetics and medicine; Ethical, social, and legal issues raised by advances in medical genetics; Genetics and industry

Includes bibliographical references

306.7   Institutions pertaining to relations of the sexes

Human sexuality: opposing viewpoints; Brenda Stalcup, book editor. Greenhaven Press 1995 258p il lib bdg $19.95; pa $11.95   **306.7**
1. Sexual behavior
ISBN 1-56510-246-0 (lib bdg); 1-56510-245-2 (pa)
    LC 94-41913

"Opposing viewpoints series"

A collection of debates about such topics as the determination of gender identity, the establishment of sex norms, and society's changing views of sexuality

Includes bibliography

Landau, Elaine

Interracial dating and marriage. Messner 1993 102p il lib bdg $13.98; pa $7.95   **306.7**
1. Dating (Social customs) 2. Interracial marriage
ISBN 0-671-75258-8 (lib bdg); 0-671-75261-8 (pa)
    LC 92-44814
"Landau begins with a chapter tracing the difficult, even dangerous, history of interracial attachments in the United States, from colonial to contemporary times. She focuses mainly on the interrelationships of African-Americans and of Japanese-Americans with whites. The book is composed of interviews with teens and adults who are, have been, or at some time may be involved in or affected by such relationships. The subjects represent many backgrounds, male and female." SLJ

Includes bibliographical references

Sexual values: opposing viewpoints; Charles P. Cozic, book editor. Greenhaven Press 1995 286p il lib bdg $19.95; pa $11.95   **306.7**
1. Sexual ethics
ISBN 1-56510-211-8 (lib bdg); 1-56510-210-X (pa)
    LC 94-4978

"Opposing viewpoints series"

Replaces the edition published 1989 under the editorship of Lisa Orr

The articles in this collection debate "the issues of whether sex is eroding moral values, how gay and lesbians should be regarded by society, pornography, sexual values for children, and if sexual behavior is changing in America." Booklist

Includes bibliography

306.8 Marriage and family

Boyden, Jo
Families; celebration and hope in a world of change. Facts on File 1993 175p il $29.95 **306.8**
1. Family
ISBN 0-8160-2992-X   LC 93-4617
"A Gaia original"
Published in cooperation with Unesco
This volume identifies "economic, social and political issues that weigh on the survival of families around the globe. . . . Effects of war, industrialization, drugs and alcohol, poverty, poor health, the work place and much more are all considered as they affect the quality of family life." Book Rep
"Students in world cultures, sociology, family living, and government classes may gain greater appreciation of both the commonalities and differences in living situations around the globe. A gold mine of material to think about and discuss." SLJ
Includes bibliographical references

The **Family** in America: opposing viewpoints; Viqi Wagner, book editor; Karin L. Swisher, assistant editor. Greenhaven Press 1992 264p il lib bdg $19.95; pa $11.95   **306.8**
1. Family
ISBN 0-89908-194-0 (lib bdg); 0-89908-169-X (pa)
LC 92-8150
"Opposing viewpoints series"
Presents differing views on such family-related topics as reproduction, divorce, working mothers, and government assistance
Includes bibliographical references

Gravelle, Karen
Teenage fathers; [by] Karen Gravelle and Leslie Peterson. Messner 1992 102p hardcover o.p. paperback available $5.95   **306.8**
1. Teenage fathers
ISBN 0-671-72851-2 (pa)   LC 91-29670
Explores various aspects of teenage fatherhood through the experiences of thirteen teenage fathers
This is "a dramatic, eye-opening portrayal of what teen fathers face when their desires and expectations collide with reality. The text is an excellent bet for marriage and the family classes, sure to leave readers of both sexes thinking about the consequences of their actions." Booklist
Includes bibliography

Lang, Paul
Teen fathers; [by] Paul Lang and Susan S. Lang. Watts 1995 128p (Changing family) lib bdg $22.70   **306.8**
1. Teenage fathers
ISBN 0-531-11216-0   LC 95-1349
Discusses issues related to teenage fatherhood, including costs to children and society, strategies for coping, acknowledging paternity, and minority fathers. Includes resource list of organizations, books, articles, and videotapes

"This title will be an important addition on the topic of teen fatherhood. It's both a resource and a compelling, well-written treatment of a seldom-examined problem." SLJ

Lindsay, Jeanne Warren
Teenage couples, caring, commitment and change; how to build a relationship that lasts. Morning Glory Press 1995 206p il $15.95; pa $9.95   **306.8**
1. Unmarried couples 2. Teenagers 3. Love 4. Marriage
ISBN 0-930934-92-X; 0-930934-93-8 (pa)
LC 94-37983
This book discusses relationships. "Topics include choosing a partner, changes brought about by living together, communication, sexual part of the relationship, jealousy, [and] partner abuse." Publisher's note
"Lindsay does a good job of explaining to teenagers some of the ways in which [partnership] can be accomplished." Booklist
Includes bibliographical references

Teenage couples, coping with reality; dealing with money, in-laws, babies and other details of daily life. Morning Glory Press 1995 190p il $15.95; pa $9.95   **306.8**
1. Marriage 2. Family life 3. Unmarried couples 4. Teenagers
ISBN 0-930934-87-3; 0-930934-86-5 (pa)
LC 94-36860
The author offers "counsel on the day-to-day aspects of being part of a couple. One of the best chapters concerns life with in-laws; others deal with budgeting, working, parenting styles, and pregnancy. . . . The operative word here is partnership, and Lindsay does a good job of explaining to teenagers some of the ways in which this can be accomplished." Booklist
Includes bibliographical references

Menzel, Peter
Material world; a global family portrait; introduction by Paul Kennedy; text by Charles C. Mann; photo editing by Sandra Eisert. Sierra Club Bks. 1994 255p il map $35; pa $20   **306.8**
1. Family—Pictorial works 2. Cross cultural studies
ISBN 0-87156-437-8; 0-87156-430-0 (pa)
LC 94-8588
This work contains "color photographic portraits of 30 families with their material possessions arrayed nearby. Each family represents one of 30 different countries— some poor, some rich—and each approximates what World Bank and UN statisticians deemed to be 'average' for its country." Libr J
"This fascinating work will be used as a reference tool for reports because of the concise, well-documented statistical data included, but it will be picked up as often by curious browsers drawn by the intimate look at our neighbors on planet Earth." Voice Youth Advocates
Includes bibliographical references

Packer, Alex J., 1951-
Bringing up parents; the teenager's handbook; edited by Pamela Espeland; illustrated by Harry Pulver, Jr. Free Spirit 1992 264p il pa $14.95
306.8
1. Parent and child 2. Conflict of generations 3. Family
ISBN 0-915793-48-2 LC 92-36625
Discusses ways that teenagers can improve their relationship with their parents and help each other develop mutual trust and respect
"While not above coddling or resorting to caustic humor (and even an occasional insult) to attract teen readers, Packer . . . has put together a serious, practical book that parents as well as teenagers should read." Booklist

Popenoe, David, 1932-
Life without father; compelling new evidence that fatherhood and marriage are indispensable for the good of children and society. Kessler Bks. 1996 275p $25
306.8
1. Father and child 2. Fathers 3. Single parent family 4. United States—Social conditions
ISBN 0-684-82297-0 LC 95-46233
This is a study of fatherhood. The author finds that "children from single-parent families are more prone to poverty, juvenile delinquency, and dropping out of school than their two-parent counterparts. The chief cause: lack of a father role model and difficulties of single-parent supervision." Libr J
Includes bibliographical references

306.89 Separation and divorce

Bolick, Nancy O'Keefe
How to survive your parents' divorce. Watts 1994 126p (Changing family) lib bdg $22.70
306.89
1. Children of divorced parents 2. Divorce
ISBN 0-531-11054-0 LC 94-15075
This book contains "excerpts from interviews with various junior and senior high students who are children of divorced parents. Between their statements, Bolick weaves analyses of the meaning she perceives behind their words, evaluates their feelings and behaviors, and suggests applications for readers experiencing similar circumstances. A summary chapter ties together the young people's recommendations with professional tips and guidance." SLJ
Includes bibliographical references

307.7 Specific kinds of communities

America's cities: opposing viewpoints; Charles P. Cozic, book editor. Greenhaven Press 1993 264p il lib bdg $19.95; pa $11.95
307.7
1. Cities and towns—United States
ISBN 0-89908-195-9 (lib bdg); 0-89908-170-3 (pa)
LC 92-40708
"Opposing viewpoints series"

An anthology of articles debating issues related to America's cities, including the decline of the cities, measures to improve urban housing, the reduction of homelessness and urban crime, and how cities can be improved
Includes bibliographical references

310.5 General statistics—Serial publications

The **Statesman's** year-book; statistical and historical annual of the states of the world. St. Martin's Press $100
310.5
1. Statistics 2. Political science
ISSN 0081-4601
Annual. First published 1864
"Descriptive and statistical information about international organizations and countries of the world—brief history, area, political status, economy, etc." N Y Public Libr. Ref Books for Child Collect. 2d edition
"The most useful of all the general yearbooks; indispensable in any type of library." Guide to Ref Books. 11th edition

Statistical abstract of the world. Gale Res. maps $60
310.5
1. Statistics
ISSN 1077-1360
Annual. First published 1994
"Topics include geography, population/demographics, health, ethnicity, crime, science and technology, government, finance, trade, economy, manufacturing, energy, military expenditures, and human rights observances. . . . The 30-page appendix explains the sources, definitions, and limitations of the data." Libr J

United Nations. Statistical Office
Statistical yearbook. U.N. Publs. $120
310.5
1. Statistics
Also available CD-ROM version
First published 1948. Text in English and French
An annual giving statistics under the following headings: Population; Manpower; Production summary; Agriculture; Forestry; Fishing; Mining, quarrying; Manufacturing; Construction; Electricity, gas, consumption; Transport; Communications; Internal trade; External trade; Balance of payments; International economic aid; Wages and prices; National income; Public finance; Housing statistics; Education, culture

317.3 General statistics of the United States

CQ's state fact finder; rankings across America. Congressional Quarterly $78.95; pa $44.95
317.3
1. United States—Statistics
Annual. First published 1993 under the authorship of Victoria Van Son. Authors vary
"This guide provides data, state by state, under such headings as *Business and Economy, Education, Energy,*

CQ's state fact finder—*Continued*

Health, Population, Recreation, Social Services, and *Transportation.* . . . A second section of the book rearranges the data by state, so that the user can go directly to a particular state and see where it ranks in each of 325 areas. . . . This is a must purchase for all academic, high-school, and public libraries, where information like this is sure to be in demand." Booklist

Includes bibliographical references

United States. Bureau of the Census

Statistical abstract of the United States. U.S. Govt. Ptg. Office prices vary **317.3**
1. United States—Statistics 2. Statistics
Annual. First published for the year 1878
"Compendium of statistics on the social, political and economic organization of the U.S. presented in tables. Lists other sources of such information." N Y Public Libr. Ref Books for Child Collect. 2d edition

320 Political science

Machiavelli, Niccolò, 1469-1527

The prince **320**
1. Political science 2. Political ethics
Hardcover and paperback editions available from various publishers
Written in 1513
"A handbook of advice on the acquisition, use, and maintenance of political power, dedicated to Lorenzo de Medici." Haydn. Thesaurus of Book Dig

Paine, Thomas, 1737-1809

Collected writings. Library of Am. 1995 906p $35 **320**
1. Political science
ISBN 1-883011-03-5 LC 94-25756
Contents: Common sense; The crisis and other pamphlets, articles and letters; Rights of man; The age of reason
Includes bibliographical references

The rights of man **320**
1. Political science 2. France—History—1789-1799, Revolution
Hardcover and paperback editions available from various publishers
First published 1791-1792
A political work "defending the French Revolution against attacks made on it by Edmund Burke. In it Paine argues that civil government exists only through a contract with a majority of the people for the safeguarding of the individual, and that if man's 'natural rights' are interfered with by the government, revolution is permissible." Reader's Ency

Rights of man [and] Common sense. Knopf 1994 lii, 306p $17 **320**
1. Political science 2. France—History—1789-1799, Revolution
ISBN 0-679-43314-7 LC 94-5989
"Everyman's library"

This volume combines Rights of man with Common sense which was "published anonymously at Philadelphia (Jan. 10, 1776). . . . Over 100,000 copies were sold by the end of March, and it is generally considered the most important literary influence on the movement for independence." Oxford Companion to Am Lit. 5th edition

Includes bibliographical references

320.1 The state

Hobbes, Thomas, 1588-1679

Leviathan **320.1**
1. Political science 2. State, The
Hardcover and paperback editions available from various publishers
First published 1651
"A treatise on the origin and ends of government. . . . This work, a defense of secular monarchy, written while the Puritan Commonwealth ruled England, contains Hobbes's famous theory of the sovereign state." Reader's Ency

Social contract; essays by Locke, Hume, and Rousseau; with an introduction by Sir Ernest Barker. Oxford Univ. Press 1980 xliv, 307p pa $14.95 **320.1**
1. Political science 2. State, The
ISBN 0-19-500309-8
Also available in hardcover from Greenwood Press
First published 1947 in the United Kingdom; 1948 in the United States
Contents: An essay concerning the true original, extent and end of civil government, by J. Locke; Of the original contract, by D. Hume; The social contract, by J. Rousseau

This book contains three major essays dealing with the social contract theory of government, first published 1690, 1748 and 1762 respectively. The introduction by Sir Ernest Barker discusses the history and transformations of the theory before focusing on the ideas of the three authors

320.4 Structure and functions of government

Politics in America: opposing viewpoints; Stacey L. Tipp, book editor; Carol Wekesser, book editor. Greenhaven Press 1992 214p il lib bdg $19.95; pa $11.95 **320.4**
1. United States—Politics and government
ISBN 0-89908-189-4 (lib bdg); 0-89908-164-9 (pa) LC 91-42803
"Opposing viewpoints series"
Presents opposing viewpoints on various issues involving United States politics, including the quality of political leadership, voter participation, and political parties and ideologies
"The study questions and choices of viewpoints indicate an effort to promote critical thinking rather than to present a thorough analysis of the topics. Each article is illustrated with a political cartoon and/or a chart. Debate teams will find [this] quite useful." SLJ

Includes glossary and bibliography

320.5   Political ideologies

Islam: opposing viewpoints; Paul A. Winters, book editor. Greenhaven Press 1995 311p il maps lib bdg $19.95; pa $11.95   **320.5**
1. Islam and politics
ISBN 1-56510-248-7 (lib bdg); 1-56510-247-9 (pa)
    LC 94-41044
"Opposing viewpoints series"
A discussion of the political implications of fundamentalist Islamic movements. Terrorism and the status of women are emphasized
Includes glossary and bibliography

Laqueur, Walter, 1921-
Fascism; past, present, future. Oxford Univ. Press 1996 263p $25   **320.5**
1. Fascism
ISBN 0-19-509245-7   LC 95-17612
"Part 1 examines historical fascism's 'ideology, its specific features, the reasons that it received the support of many millions, and how it came to power;' part 2 sketches fascist, right-wing extremist, neofascist, and radical nationalist populist movements that have emerged since World War II, noting their similarities to and differences from Hitler's and Mussolini's regimes; and part 3 considers 'clerical fascism, that is, radical Islam and similar trends in other religions' and extremist groups in formerly communist states. Laqueur analyzes these subjects judiciously." Booklist
Includes bibliographical references

321   Systems of governments and states

More, Sir Thomas, Saint, 1478-1535
Utopia   **321**
1. Utopias
Hardcover and paperback editions available from various publishers
Originally published 1516 in Latin; 1551 in English
In his study of the ideal state, "More assigns the narrative to a Raphael Hythloday ('Hythloday' is Greek for 'talker of nonsense'). . . . Book I treats of the evils of the world and asserts the need for an ideal commonwealth, which Book II describes." Haydn. Thesaurus of Book Dig

321.8   Democratic systems

The **Encyclopedia** of democracy; Seymour Martin Lipset, editor in chief. Congressional Quarterly 1995 4v il maps set $395   **321.8**
1. Democracy—Dictionaries
ISBN 0-87187-675-2   LC 95-34217
"Articles are alphabetically arranged by topic, with tables of contents by subject and author; a detailed index to the entire encyclopedia is printed at the end of each volume. . . . A third of the last volume reprints modern English texts of 20 documents chosen for their importance to the development of democracy. . . . A good addition to any reference collection." Choice
For a fuller review see: Booklist, March 1, 1996

321.9   Authoritarian systems

Arendt, Hannah
Origins of totalitarianism. new ed with added prefaces. Harcourt Brace Jovanovich 1973 xliii, 527p pa $15   **321.9**
1. Totalitarianism 2. Imperialism 3. Antisemitism
ISBN 0-15-670153-7
Also available as three separate paperbacks with titles: Antisemitism; Imperialism; Totalitarianism
"A Harvest book"
First published 1951 in the United Kingdom with title: The burden of our time
In this book, the author documents her "belief that Nazism and Communism had their roots in the anti-Semitism and imperialism of the 19th century." Reader's Ency
Includes bibliography

322.4   Political action groups

Chalmers, David Mark
Hooded Americanism: the history of the Ku Klux Klan. 3rd ed. Duke Univ. Press 1987 c1981 477p il lib bdg $41.95; pa $19.95   **322.4**
1. Ku Klux Klan
ISBN 0-8223-0730-8 (lib bdg); 0-8223-0772-3 (pa)
    LC 86-29133
First published 1965 by Doubleday; this is a reissue of the 1981 edition published by Watts
This book recounts the history of the Klan. It describes the sociological and psychological forces behind the Klan, and sets forth its dogmas
"The book is written in a breezy, journalistic style. . . . Especially instructive and sobering is Chalmers' account of the role of the Klan in politics." J Am Hist
Includes bibliography

Gandhi, Mahatma, 1869-1948
Gandhi on non-violence; selected texts from Mohandas K. Gandhi's Non-violence in peace and war; edited with an introduction by Thomas Merton. New Directions 1965 82p pa $5.95
    322.4
1. Passive resistance 2. India—Politics and government
ISBN 0-8112-0097-3
"A New Directions paperbook"
In an introductory essay Merton "considers Gandhi's ideas, not in relation to their Indian context, but in terms of their applicability to all men's lives. Brief quotations from Gandhi's writings make up most of the book." Asia: a Guide to Paperbacks

Kronenwetter, Michael
United they hate; white supremacist groups in America. Walker & Co. 1992 133p il $14.95; lib bdg $15.85   **322.4**
1. Racism 2. Fanaticism
ISBN 0-8027-8162-4; 0-8027-8163-2 (lib bdg)
    LC 91-39778
Chronicles the development of white supremacy hate groups and analyzes their philosophies, personalities, mo-

Kronenwetter, Michael—*Continued*
tives, and weaknesses

"The historical survey is clear and well-organized, as is the picture of contemporary groups ranging from the Klan to LaRouche followers to skinheads." Bull Cent Child Books

Includes bibliography

Landau, Elaine

The white power movement; America's racist hate groups. Millbrook Press 1993 96p il lib bdg $17.40 **322.4**

1. Racism 2. Fanaticism

ISBN 1-56294-327-8   LC 92-40920

Explores the origins and development of racist hate groups in the United States, such as the Ku Klux Klan and the skinheads

This "is a powerful, clearly written, well-organized book." SLJ

Includes bibliography

Meltzer, Milton, 1915-

Ain't gonna study war no more: the story of America's peace seekers. Harper & Row 1985 282p il o.p.   **322.4**

1. Pacifism 2. Draft resisters

LC 84-48337

Presents a history of pacifism and those who have protested against war, concentrating on war resistance in the United States, from colonial days up to the current movement against nuclear arms

The author's "clear, provocative interpretation will disturb many, frighten some, inspire others. In all libraries it should stand alongside more traditional histories as an impetus to young people's development of their own ideas." Voice Youth Advocates

Includes bibliography

323   Civil and political rights

Civil liberties: opposing viewpoints; Charles P. Cozic, book editor. Greenhaven Press 1994 240p il lib bdg $19.95; pa $11.95   **323**

1. Civil rights

ISBN 1-56510-058-1 (lib bdg); 1-56510-057-3 (pa)

LC 93-16419

"Opposing viewpoints series"

Replaces the edition published 1988 under the editorship of Julie S. Bach

This volume "includes various opposing points of view on the right to privacy, freedom of expression, separation of church and state, and the protection of civil liberties. Each chapter has a preface that includes thought-provoking questions. Lively cartoons are well placed throughout the text." SLJ

Includes bibliographical references

Social justice: opposing viewpoints; Carol Wekesser, book editor; Karin Swisher & Janelle Rohr, assistant editors. Greenhaven Press 1990 264p il lib bdg $19.95; pa $11.95   **323**

1. Civil rights 2. Minorities 3. United States—Social policy

ISBN 0-89908-482-6 (lib bdg); 0-89908-457-5 (pa)

LC 90-42855

"Opposing viewpoints series"

Observers present differing views on issues of economic and social justice in the United States, focusing especially on the question of just treatment of minorities and women

Includes bibliographical references

Walker, Samuel, 1942-

In defense of American liberties: a history of the ACLU. Oxford Univ. Press 1990 479p il $27.95; pa $12.95   **323**

1. American Civil Liberties Union

ISBN 0-19-504539-4; 0-19-507141-7 (pa)

LC 89-32843

"Walker recounts the ACLU's stormy history since its founding in 1920 to fight for free speech. He explores its involvement in some of the most famous causes in American history, including the Scopes 'Monkey Trial,' the internment of Japanese-Americans during World War II, the Cold War anti-Communist witch hunts, and the civil rights movement." Publisher's note

Includes bibliography

323.1   Civil and political rights of nondominant aggregates

Bullard, Sara

Free at last; a history of the Civil Rights Movement and those who died in the struggle; introduction by Julian Bond. Oxford Univ. Press 1993 112p il map $22.95; pa $10.95   **323.1**

1. African Americans—Civil rights 2. United States—Race relations

ISBN 0-19-508381-4; 0-19-509450-6 (pa)

LC 92-38174

An illustrated history of the civil rights movement, including a timeline and profiles of forty people who gave their lives in the movement

Includes bibliography

Cagin, Seth

We are not afraid; the story of Goodman, Schwerner, and Chaney and the civil rights campaign for Mississippi; [by] Seth Cagin and Philip Dray. Macmillan 1988 500p il o.p.   **323.1**

1. Chaney, James Earl, 1943-1964 2. Schwerner, Michael Henry, 1939-1964 3. Goodman, Andrew, 1943-1964 4. African Americans—Civil rights 5. Mississippi—Race relations

LC 87-24069

This is an account of the murder of three civil rights workers who went to Mississippi in the summer of 1964

Cagin, Seth—*Continued*

to help blacks register to vote

"Cagin and Dray do a fantastic job of dramatizing this terrible story. The commitment of the young men, the anguish of their families, and the effect their deaths had on fellow civil rights workers are emotionally recounted. But this book also succeeds as a thorough and accurate history of the civil rights movement." Voice Youth Advocates

The **Civil** rights movement: opposing viewpoints; William Dudley, book editor. Greenhaven Press 1996 288p (American history series) lib bdg $19.95; pa $11.95 **323.1**
1. African Americans—Civil rights
ISBN 1-56510-369-6 (lib bdg); 1-56510-368-8 (pa)
LC 95-48244

A collection of articles addressing the history, aims and achievements of the American civil rights movement. Includes contributions by Earl Warren, Marcus Garvey, Charlayne Hunter, Roy Wilkins, David J. Garrow, and others

Includes bibliography

Deloria, Vine

The nations within: the past and future of American Indian sovereignty; [by] Vine Deloria, Jr., Clifford M. Lytle. Pantheon Bks. 1984 293p pa $11.96 **323.1**
1. Indians of North America—Government relations
ISBN 0-394-72566-2 LC 84-42663

The authors examine the "controversy surrounding self-government for the American Indian nations. . . . The book also considers the Indian Civil Rights Act, the concept of self-determination, and proposals for the future of Indian nations and sovereignty." Libr J

"A first-rate study, extremely well written." Choice
Includes bibliography

Durham, Michael S., 1935-

Powerful days; the civil rights photography of Charles Moore; text by Michael S. Durham; introduction by Andrew Young. Stewart, Tabori & Chang; Eastman Kodak. Professional Photography Div. 1990 207p il o.p. **323.1**
1. Moore, Charles 2. African Americans—Civil rights—Pictorial works 3. Southern States—Race relations—Pictorial works
LC 90-10327

This is a photographic record of leaders and events in the civil rights campaign of the 1950s and 1960s

"Disturbing yet inspiring, the 180 duotones presented here are a needed and welcome document of a struggle that still continues." Libr J

The **Eyes** on the prize civil rights reader; documents, speeches, and firsthand accounts from the black freedom struggle, 1954-1990; general editors, Clayborne Carson [et al.] Penguin Bks. 1991 764p pa $16.95 **323.1**
1. African Americans—Civil rights 2. United States—Race relations
ISBN 0-14-015403-5 LC 91-9507

First published 1987 with title: Eyes on the prize: America's civil rights years, a reader and guide

"Including excerpts from a 1990 address by Nelson Mandela, the speech 'I See the Promised Land' delivered by Martin Luther King, Jr., on the night before his death, and selections from Black Panther founding father Huey Newton's 'Revolutionary Suicide,' this anthology of primary-source material is recommended for all high school collections." Booklist

Includes bibliographical references

Grossman, Mark

The ABC-CLIO companion to the civil rights movement. ABC-CLIO 1993 263p il $55 **323.1**
1. African Americans—Civil rights 2. United States—Race relations
ISBN 0-87436-696-8 LC 93-38425

This work "is designed to provide concise information on the key leaders, court decisions, legislation, institutions, concepts, organizations, events, heroes and martyrs, and even the opposition. The approximately 450 alphabetically arranged entries are usually one paragraph in length, but longer when necessary." Booklist

"This book is a must for middle and high school libraries and all public libraries." Voice Youth Advocates

Hampton, Henry

Voices of freedom; an oral history of the civil rights movement from the 1950s through the 1980s; [by] Henry Hampton and Steve Fayer with Sarah Flynn. Bantam Bks. 1990 692p hardcover o.p. paperback available $18.95 **323.1**
1. African Americans—Civil rights 2. United States—Race relations
ISBN 0-553-35232-6 (pa) LC 89-18297

This companion to the PBS series "'Eyes on the Prize,' composed of interviews done originally for the TV program, is a riveting document of the civil rights movement of the 1960s and 1970s. The text is arranged in a chronological sequence that reconstructs major events from the murder of Emmett Till in Mississippi in 1955 and the Little Rock integration crisis to the affirmative action cases of the 1970s." Booklist

Includes bibliographical references

King, Martin Luther, 1929-1968

Stride toward freedom; the Montgomery story; by Martin Luther King, Jr. Harper & Row 1958 230p il hardcover o.p. paperback available $12 **323.1**
1. African Americans—Civil rights 2. African Americans—Segregation 3. Montgomery (Ala.)—Race relations
ISBN 0-06-250490-8 (pa)

An account of the bus boycott organized by Montgomery blacks in December, 1955, to protest discriminatory practices

A testament of hope; the essential writings of Martin Luther King, Jr.; edited by James Melvin Washington. Harper & Row 1986 xxvi, 676p hardcover o.p. paperback available $22.50 **323.1**
1. African Americans—Civil rights 2. United States—Race relations
ISBN 0-06-064691-8 (pa) LC 85-45370

"King's most important writings are gathered together in one source. The arrangement is topical: philosophy,

King, Martin Luther, 1929-1968—*Continued*
sermons and public addresses, essays, interviews and excerpts of his books. The material within each of these categories is arranged chronologically. Included are Dr. King's writings on nonviolence, integration and politics." SLJ

Includes bibliography

Where do we go from here: chaos or community? [by] Martin Luther King, Jr. Harper & Row 1967 209p o.p.; Beacon Press paperback available $14   **323.1**
1. African Americans—Civil rights 2. United States—Race relations 3. African Americans—History
ISBN 0-8070-0571-1 (pa)
The author reaffirms his belief in the power of nonviolence to achieve full citizenship for black people in America and defines his attitude toward the Black Power movement and the white backlash
Includes bibliographical references

Why we can't wait; [by] Martin Luther King, Jr. Harper & Row 1964 178p il o.p.; New Am. Lib. paperback available $5.99   **323.1**
1. African Americans—Civil rights 2. Birmingham (Ala.)—Race relations
ISBN 0-451-62754-7 (pa)
The author first reviews the background of the 1963 civil rights demands. He then describes the strategy of the Birmingham campaign and outlines future action

Patterson, Charles, 1935-
The civil rights movement. Facts on File 1995 138p il (Social reform movements) $17.95   **323.1**
1. African Americans—Civil rights
ISBN 0-8160-2968-7   LC 95-3027
This "account begins with a discussion of the legacy of slavery, putting into perspective the denial of basic human rights to African Americans. Patterson follows the course of the civil rights movement into the early 1970s, focusing on key turning points. . . . A credible and sympathetic examination of an important part of American history." SLJ
Includes bibliography

Seeger, Pete
Everybody says freedom; [by] Pete Seeger, Bob Reiser; including many songs collected by Guy and Candie Carawan. Norton 1989 266p il music hardcover o.p. paperback available $18.95   **323.1**
1. African Americans—Civil rights 2. African American music
ISBN 0-393-30604-6 (pa)   LC 88-23341
This narrative of the American civil rights movement of the 1960s "is illustrated with music and words to three dozen songs. . . . Profiles of 15 people active in the movement, anecdotes about . . . others, and a chronological outline/commentary on events from 1955 to 1968 are linked by the songs." Libr J
Includes discography and bibliography

Wexler, Sanford
The civil rights movement; an eyewitness history; introduction by Julian Bond. Facts on File 1993 356p il maps (Eyewitness history series) $45   **323.1**
1. African Americans—Civil rights 2. United States—Race relations
ISBN 0-8160-2748-X   LC 92-28674
Uses speeches, articles, and other writings of those involved to trace the history of the civil rights movement in the United States, primarily from 1954 to 1965
"This very readable source deserves a place in every public and middle and high school library, though it may fit better in the circulating collection." Booklist
Includes bibliographical references

Williams, Juan
Eyes on the prize: America's civil rights years, 1954-1965; [by] Juan Williams with the Eyes on the prize production team; introduction by Julian Bond. Viking 1987 300p il hardcover o.p. paperback available $14.95   **323.1**
1. African Americans—Civil rights 2. United States—Race relations
ISBN 0-14-009653-1 (pa)   LC 86-40271
"A Robert Lavelle book"
"This companion volume to the PBS TV series of the same name is an . . . account of black America's struggle for social and political equality, covering the civil rights battle from the landmark Brown v. Board of Education decision in 1954 to the Selma protest marches, and Voting Rights Act of 1965." Libr J
"Highly recommended both as a socio-historical document and as a heartfelt, poignant remembrance of a movement and its activists." Booklist
Includes bibliographical references

323.3 Civil and political rights of other social aggregates

Shapiro, Joseph P.
No pity; people with disabilities forging a new civil rights movement. Times Bks. 1993 372p $25; pa $15   **323.3**
1. Handicapped—Civil rights 2. Discrimination
ISBN 0-8129-1964-5; 0-8129-2412-6 (pa)
                                               LC 92-34751
The author explores "the thoughts, fears, and facts behind the disability rights movement. The premise throughout this compelling historical account is that there is no pity or tragedy in disability—it is society's myths, fears, and stereotypes that make being disabled difficult. . . . For those interested in gaining a basic understanding of the disability rights movement, the title is well organized, thorough in research, and thought-provoking." Libr J

Includes bibliographical references

323.44   Freedom of action (Liberty)

Alderman, Ellen
The right to privacy; [by] Ellen Alderman and Caroline Kennedy. Knopf 1995 405p $26.95; pa $14   **323.44**
1. Right of privacy
ISBN 0-679-41986-1; 0-679-74434-7 (pa)
         LC 95-14286
"The authors consider a welter of legal and ethical dilemmas involving the clashing interests of people who wish to be left alone and employers, police and the press, whose job may make them intrusive. The use of metal detectors and drug tests in schools and workplaces, women's right to abortion and contraception, people suing to squelch reporting by the media, patients' right to refuse further medical treatment or to undergo assisted suicide, and claims against voyeurs are among the issues and conflicts discussed." Publ Wkly
"Students may find topics for further research, seek to clarify or advance their legal understanding, or just dip in for the stories." SLJ
Includes bibliography

Censorship. Wilson, H.W. 1990 161p (Reference shelf, v62 no3) pa $15   **323.44**
1. Censorship
ISBN 0-8242-0792-0   LC 90-39571
A collection of articles exploring various aspects of the censorship debate in the United States and Great Britain
Includes bibliographical references

Censorship: opposing viewpoints; Byron L. Stay, book editor. Greenhaven Press 1997 192p lib bdg $19.95; pa $11.95   **323.44**
1. Censorship
ISBN 1-56510-508-7 (lib bdg); 1-56510-507-9 (pa)
         LC 96-29030
Replaces the edition published 1990 under the editorship of Lisa Orr
This volume presents "arguments on all sides of the current censorship debate in schools and libraries, on the Internet, and in the entertainment media. . . . There are arguments for and against antipornography laws, campus speech codes, and the use of the V-chip, as well as discussions of basic questions of whether there should be limits to free speech." Booklist
Includes bibliographical references

Free speech; Bruno Leone, book editor. Greenhaven Press 1994 236p (Current controversies) lib bdg $19.95; pa $11.95   **323.44**
1. Freedom of speech
ISBN 1-56510-078-6 (lib bdg); 1-56510-077-8 (pa)
         LC 93-19855
A collection of articles debating issues related to free speech such as censorship, restrictions on the press, pornography, and libel
"A particularly timely volume, especially as the forces of political correctness have been running headlong into the anticensorship, pro-free speech movement." SLJ
Includes bibliographical references

Fromm, Erich, 1900-1980
Escape from freedom. Farrar & Rinehart 1941 305p o.p.; Holt & Co. paperback available $12
         323.44
1. Freedom 2. Social psychology 3. Totalitarianism
ISBN 0-8050-3149-9 (pa)
"A searching inquiry into the meaning of freedom for modern man. . . . The author stresses the role of psychological factors in the social process, interpreting the historical development of freedom in terms of man's awareness of himself as a significant separate being." Libr J
Includes bibliographical references

Intellectual freedom manual; compiled by the Office for Intellectual Freedom of the American Library Association. American Lib. Assn. il pa $35   **323.44**
1. Intellectual freedom 2. Libraries—Censorship
First published 1974. (5th edition 1996) Periodically revised
This guide to preserving intellectual freedom includes: ALA interpretations to the Library Bill of Rights; recommendations for special libraries and specific situations; information about legal decisions affecting school and public libraries; a section on the ALA's Intellectual Freedom Action Network
Includes bibliographical references

Lang, Susan S.
Censorship; [by] Susan S. Lang and Paul Lang. Watts 1993 126p il lib bdg $22.70   **323.44**
1. Censorship 2. Freedom of speech
ISBN 0-531-10999-2   LC 92-41707
"With many specific examples—from cigarette advertising and rap lyrics to the Pentagon Papers and Madonna—the Langs present an overview of a wide range of issues relating to First Amendment rights. . . . A good starting point for class discussion and personal reading." Booklist
Includes bibliography

Marsh, Dave
50 ways to fight censorship; and important facts to know about the censors; by Dave Marsh and friends. Thunder's Mouth Press 1991 128p il pa $5.95   **323.44**
1. Censorship
ISBN 1-56025-011-9   LC 91-3209
"Marsh proffers practical ways for anyone of school age on up to defend freedom of speech. . . . Each suggestion's entry includes a rationale for doing it, how-to advice, and, often as not, both the story of someone who succeeded at it and a little list of helpful resources." Booklist

324   The political process

Running for president; the candidates and their images; editor Arthur M. Schlesinger, Jr.; associate editors Fred L. Israel, David J. Frent. Simon & Schuster 1994 2v il set $175   **324**
1. Presidents—United States—Election 2. United States—Politics and government
ISBN 0-13-303371-6   LC 93-46386
"A Harold Steinberg book"

Running for president—*Continued*
Contents: v1 1789-1896; v2 1900-1992
"This source covers campaign images and the fun of presidential campaigns. For each election, a spirited essay written by an expert political historian and/or journalist details what tactics each candidate or political party employed to appeal to the electorate. Winners, losers, and third-party candidates are included here." Am Libr
This "resource will be relished by high school and college students, public historians, and collectors of political memorabilia alike." Libr J

324.025 The political process— Directories

Political handbook of the world. CSA Publs. $115
324.025
1. Political science—Handbooks, manuals, etc. 2. Political parties
ISSN 0193-175X
First published 1927 with title: A political handbook of Europe. Variant title: Political handbook and atlas of the world. Publisher and frequency vary
Current editors: Arthur S. Banks, Alan J. Day and Thomas C. Muller
"Treats the independent countries of the world in alphabetically-arranged entries that usually give a description of the country and information on its government and politics, heads of state, political parties, legislature, cabinet, news media, and intergovernmental representation. Also contains a section on intergovernmental organizations. Appendixes include chronologies of major international events and conferences. Geographic/organization name and personal name indexes." Guide to Ref Books. 11th edition

324.2 Political parties

Political parties & elections in the United States; an encyclopedia; general editor, L. Sandy Maisel; associate editor, Charles Bassett. Garland 1991 2v il (Garland reference library of social science) set $150
324.2
1. Political parties—Dictionaries 2. Elections—United States
ISBN 0-8240-7975-2
LC 91-6940
"In an encyclopedic format, this book covers dates, parties, and people important to the U.S. electoral process, including candidates for national, state, and city offices, presidents, vice-presidents, cabinet members, speakers of the house, majority and minority leaders, and party chairs. . . . Every one of the over 1,200 articles is signed and includes a bibliography." Am Libr

Wattenberg, Martin P., 1956-
The decline of American political parties, 1952-1994. Harvard Univ. Press 1996 244p il pa $17.75
324.2
1. Political parties 2. United States—Politics and government
ISBN 0-674-19434-9
LC 95-39297
First published 1984 covering the years 1952-1980

The author argues that more and more voters are choosing candidates based on personal qualities than on political parties. He bases his findings upon presidential election statistics of the period covered
Includes bibliographical references

324.6 Election systems and procedures; suffrage

Congressional Quarterly's guide to U.S. elections. 3rd ed. Congressional Quarterly 1994 1543p $290
324.6
1. Elections—United States
ISBN 0-87187-996-4
LC 94-19015
First published 1975
"An impressive compilation of data on presidential, gubernatorial, and congressional elections drawn from many sources, including 'Historical election returns file' of the Inter-University Consortium for Political and Social Research. Divided into sections covering political parties; presidential elections; gubernatorial elections; Senate elections; and House elections." Guide to Ref Books. 11th edition

Frost-Knappman, Elizabeth
Women's suffrage in America; an eyewitness history; [by] Elizabeth Frost and Kathryn Cullen-DuPont. Facts on File 1992 452p il (Eyewitness history series) $45
324.6
1. Women—Suffrage 2. Women—United States—History
ISBN 0-8160-2309-3
LC 91-31177
Chronicles the struggle of American women for the right to vote, from 1800 to their victory in 1920. Includes quotations from contemporary witnesses through memoirs, letters, and other documents of the period
This is "a lively and important sourcebook for students of American political and cultural history." SLJ
Includes bibliographical references

Havel, James T.
U.S. presidential candidates and the elections; a biographical and historical guide. Macmillan Lib. Ref. USA 1996 2v set $175
324.6
1. Presidents—United States—Election 2. Politicians—United States
ISBN 0-02-897134-5
LC 96-12074
"The first volume, 'The Candidates,' contains an alphabetically arranged list of individuals who have sought the office of the presidency and vice-presidency, with the spectrum of diversity extending from George Bush to Lawrence Welk (Democratic presidential candidate, 1976). Entries give standard information (birth, death, education, children, organizational membership, and so forth) and a current mailing address when appropriate. . . . The second volume, 'The Elections,' provides a summary of each election, highlighting important events, parties, conventions, and platforms. Results from primary, general, and electoral college balloting are also given." Am Ref Books Annu, 1997
"Havel is unique in providing information on many obscure candidates who never made it on a ballot." Booklist

Morin, Isobel V., 1928-
Impeaching the president. Millbrook Press 1996
159p il lib bdg $16.40   **324.6**
1. Impeachments 2. Presidents—United States
ISBN 1-56294-668-4   LC 95-43820
Analyzes the Constitution's provision for impeachment
and its relevance to the presidencies of Andrew Jackson,
Andrew Johnson, Richard Nixon, and Ronald Reagan
"Morin clearly recounts the history behind each of
these situations and explains the relevant constitutional
implications which tipped the balance of action one way
or the other. Gray boxed sidebars, political cartoons, and
photographs clarify just what was at stake during each of
these political crises." Voice Youth Advocates
Includes bibliographical references

Presidential elections, 1789-1992. Congressional
Quarterly 1995 274p il maps pa $30.95   **324.6**
1. Presidents—United States—Election
ISBN 0-87187-857-7   LC 94-45937
"Sections about the origin of the electoral college, an
analysis of popular voting, and the evolution of conventions and the party system are . . . presented and are accompanied by tables and narratives of voting since 1789,
organized by date, state, and candidates. Also included
are a useful directory of presidential and vice presidential
candidates and the text of major election laws." Libr J
Includes bibliographical references

White, Theodore H., 1915-1986
The making of the president, 1960. Atheneum
Pubs. 1961 400p   **324.6**
1. Nixon, Richard M. (Richard Milhous), 1913-1994
2. Kennedy, John F. (John Fitzgerald), 1917-1963
3. Presidents—United States—Election 4. United
States—Politics and government—1953-1961
Available in hardcover from Buccaneer Bks.
Volumes covering the elections of 1964, 1968, and
1972 are o.p.
A chronological account of the 1960 Presidential cam-
paign "beginning with the first primaries in New Hampshire and Wisconsin and continuing through Inauguration
Day, and into the White House." New Repub

325.73   Immigration to the United States

Andryszewski, Tricia, 1956-
Immigration; newcomers and their impact on the
United States. Millbrook Press 1995 112p il (Issue
and debate) lib bdg $16.40   **325.73**
1. United States—Immigration and emigration
ISBN 1-56294-499-1   LC 94-21834
The author "gives reasons for current emigration patterns and then sketches the history of immigration to the
U.S. and the official reactions it has provoked. The second half of the book is devoted to the present situation:
the impact of the stream of newcomers on the economy,
the handling of illegal aliens, the policy of granting political asylum, and of establishing quotas." SLJ
"The numerous personal insights from immigrants and
extensive foot-noted statistics from a wide variety of impressive sources provide a balance that makes this both
informative and readable." Booklist

Arguing immigration; the debate over the
changing face of America; edited by Nicolaus
Mills; with essays by Toni Morrison [et al.]
Simon & Schuster 1994 223p pa $12   **325.73**
1. United States—Immigration and emigration
ISBN 0-671-89558-3   LC 94-21821
"A Touchstone book"
"This collection of 18 essays includes some original
pieces with others reprinted from publications like the
National Review, the New York Times and Dissent. . . .
Among the more interesting are those by novelist Toni
Morrison, writing about the scorning of native born
blacks by immigrants . . . Richard Rodriguez, arguing
that immigrants work harder than Californians; and Jack
Miles, musing darkly on post-Rodney King Los Ange-
les." Publ Wkly

Bode, Janet
New kids on the block: oral histories of
immigrant teens. Watts 1989 126p map lib bdg
$22.70   **325.73**
1. United States—Immigration and emigration
2. Children of immigrants
ISBN 0-531-10794-9   LC 89-32543
"Most of the subjects have escaped from war, repression, or poverty; all share a carefully qualified admiration for their adopted country. The narratives are distinct
in both voice and personal detail, with varying attitudes
towards the invariable cultural clashes between old ways
and new." Bull Cent Child Books
"This is a wonderful collection, outstanding nonfiction, and a useful resource for school assignments."
Voice Youth Advocates
Includes bibliography

Daniels, Roger
Coming to America; a history of immigration
and ethnicity in American life. HarperCollins Pubs.
1990 450p il maps hardcover o.p. paperback
available $16   **325.73**
1. Minorities 2. United States—Immigration and emigration
ISBN 0-06-092100-5 (pa)   LC 89-46524
"After discussing the topic of immigration in general
and sociological theories of why people migrate between
countries, Daniel discusses each racial or national group
that came to the United States during the various eras of
the nation's history." SLJ
"Both comprehensive and detailed, this lively history
. . . will give good high school readers cocurricular material on immigration as well as background about their
individual roots." Booklist
Includes bibliographical references

Illegal immigration; William Barbour, book editor.
Greenhaven Press 1994 222p (Current
controversies) lib bdg $19.95; pa $11.95
                                             325.73
1. Illegal aliens 2. United States—Immigration and
emigration
ISBN 1-56510-072-7 (lib bdg); 1-56510-071-9 (pa)
                                        LC 93-1808
"An anthology of articles representing a variety of
viewpoints about the seriousness of the problem, whether

Illegal immigration—*Continued*

it adversely affects the U.S., the treatment of illegal immigrants, and how the government should respond. They are drawn from books, periodicals, and newspapers from 1992 and later. The selections, while helpful to report writers and debaters, tend to be dense and dry." SLJ

Includes bibliographical references

Illegal immigration: opposing viewpoints; Charles P. Cozic, book editor. Greenhaven Press 1997 207p lib bdg $19.95; pa $11.95   325.73
1. Illegal aliens 2. United States—Immigration and emigration
ISBN 1-56510-514-1 (lib bdg); 1-56510-513-3 (pa)
LC 96-22686
"Opposing viewpoints series"
Replaces the edition published 1990 with title: Immigration: opposing viewpoints, under the editorship of William Dudley

"Contributors examine questions regarding economics, human rights, and race in the following chapters: Would new measures targeting illegal immigrants be fair? Do illegal immigrants harm America? How should America respond to illegal immigration? Are illegal immigrants being victimized?" Publisher's note

Includes bibliographical references

Immigration; edited by Robert Emmet Long. Wilson, H.W. 1996 185p (Reference shelf, v68 no1) pa $15   325.73
1. Illegal aliens 2. United States—Immigration and emigration
ISBN 0-8242-0886-2   LC 95-52085
Among the topics examined in this compilation of articles are problems at the Mexico-U.S. border, Cuban refugees and California's Proposition 187

Includes bibliographical references

Immigration: opposing viewpoints; Teresa O'Neill, book editor. Greenhaven Press 1992 312p il maps (American history series) lib bdg $19.95; pa $11.95   325.73
1. United States—Immigration and emigration
ISBN 1-56510-007-7 (lib bdg); 1-56510-006-9 (pa)
LC 92-21794
"Opposing viewpoints series"
"This title covers a selection of opposing and 'representative opinions' about the impact of immigration on American history. It concentrates primarily on the period 1820-1920, when 35 million people came to the United States. . . . A fine resource for students doing reports or preparing debates, the book also contains a detailed chronology and a lengthy annotated bibliography of adult materials, with many primary sources." SLJ

Immigration to the U.S.; edited by Robert Emmet Long. Wilson, H.W. 1992 202p (Reference shelf, v64 no4) pa $15   325.73
1. United States—Immigration and emigration
ISBN 0-8242-0828-5   LC 92-28399
The articles in this compilation are grouped under the following headings: Refugees from the Caribbean and Central America; The flow of immigration from Mexico; Migration from Southeast Asia; and The question of immigration policy

Includes bibliography

Kennedy, John F. (John Fitzgerald), 1917-1963

A nation of immigrants; introduction by Robert F. Kennedy. rev and enl ed. Harper & Row 1964 111p il map hardcover o.p. paperback available $11   325.73
1. United States—Immigration and emigration
2. United States—Foreign population
ISBN 0-06-091367-3 (pa)
Also available in hardcover from Borgo Press
A reissue of a booklet written 1958 for the "One Nation Library" series of the Anti-Defamation League of B'nai B'rith

"An account of the struggles of successive waves of immigrants, their contributions to America, and their repeated triumphs over prejudice and discrimination. Expounds the need for an enlargement of our immigration laws." Guide to Read in Am Hist

Includes bibliography

Leinwand, Gerald

American immigration; should the open door be closed? Watts 1995 144p il lib bdg $22.70
325.73
1. United States—Immigration and emigration
ISBN 0-531-13038-X   LC 95-3303
"An Impact book"
This is a "history of immigration, with the first three chapters parallel to material found in most high school history texts. The chronological division of these chapters is standard: 1607-1820, 1820-1920, and 1920-1965. The next three chapters focus on the contemporary setting, that is, immigration after 1965; political refugees and illegal immigrants; and the current debate over restricting immigration." Sci Books Films
"A well-written book that will provide the secondary student with solid information on the ever-changing face of immigration." Book Rep

Includes glossary and bibliography

326   Slavery and emancipation

King, Wilma, 1942-

Stolen childhood; slave youth in nineteenth-century America. Indiana Univ. Press 1995 253p il $27.95   326
1. Slavery—United States 2. African American children 3. African Americans—History 4. United States—History—1800-1899 (19th century)
ISBN 0-253-32904-3   LC 94-49163
The author "traces how those born into slavery grew old almost instantly, before their time, suffering atrocities akin to those of war-ravaged populations. She examines family, work, play, religion, punishment, and escape in a pioneering survey to assess our understanding of slavery from the experiences and perspectives of those under 21 years of age." Libr J
"With moral authority and appreciation for the telling anecdote, Wilma King takes up the neglected story of black slave children in the American South." Christ Sci Monit

Includes bibliographical references

Lester, Julius

To be a slave; illustrated by Tom Feelings. Dial Bks. for Young Readers 1968 160p il $15.99
    326

1. Slavery—United States

ISBN 0-8037-8955-6

"Through the words of the slave, interwoven with strongly sympathetic commentary, the reader learns what it is to be another man's property; how the slave feels about himself; and how he feels about others. Every aspect of slavery, regardless of how grim, has been painfully and unrelentingly described." Read Ladders for Hum Relat. 6th edition

Includes bibliography

Slavery: opposing viewpoints; William Dudley, book editor. Greenhaven Press 1992 310p il maps (American history series) lib bdg $19.95; pa $11.95
    326

1. Slavery—United States

ISBN 1-56510-013-1 (lib bdg); 1-56510-012-3 (pa)
    LC 92-21796

A collection of texts arguing the moral, economic, political and constitutional aspects of slavery in the United States

Includes bibliography

327   International relations

The New world order: opposing viewpoints; Matthew Polesetsky, book editor; William Dudley, assistant editor. Greenhaven Press 1991 261p il lib bdg $19.95; pa $11.95
    327

1. World politics—1965- 2. United States—Foreign relations

ISBN 0-89908-183-5 (lib bdg); 0-89908-158-4 (pa)
    LC 91-12374

"Opposing viewpoints series"

Debates topics relating to today's changing world order such as the role of the U.S. in the world, the role of economics, military conflict, the end of the Cold War, and the roles of the UN and NATO

Includes bibliography

327.1   General topics of international relations

Carter, Jimmy, 1924-

Talking peace; a vision for the next generation. rev ed. Dutton Children's Bks. 1995 205p il maps $18.99
    327.1

1. Peace 2. International relations 3. United States—Foreign relations

ISBN 0-525-45517-5
    LC 95-40247

Also available in paperback from Puffin Bks.

First published 1993

Carter discusses the various factors involved in peace negotiations and conflict resolution, examining such elements as the living conditions of citizens in peacetime and wartime and the effect of international relations on innocent citizens. The former president writes in detail

about Camp David, his work in Atlanta and his peace missions to Korea, Haiti, Bosnia, and Sudan

"This book shows that a determined, committed individual can make a difference and, with its specific suggestions for ways to become involved, it will appeal to young people who are interested in promoting peace." SLJ

Includes bibliographical references

Nuclear proliferation: opposing viewpoints; Charles P. Cozic, book editor; Karin L. Swisher, assistant editor. Greenhaven Press 1992 234p il map lib bdg $19.95; pa $11.95
    327.1

1. Nuclear weapons 2. Arms control

ISBN 1-56510-005-0 (lib bdg); 1-56510-004-2 (pa)
    LC 92-23065

"Opposing viewpoints series"

Presents differing opinions on the threat of nuclear proliferation, the need for arms control, the role of NATO, the elimination of nuclear weapons, and other related topics

"The material is up-to-date and provides enlightening background for students. . . . The editors do a good job of contrasting alarmist and partisan positions with more moderate ones." SLJ

Includes glossary and bibliographies

327.12   Espionage and subversion

Melton, H. Keith (Harold Keith), 1944-

The ultimate spy book; forewords by William E. Colby and Oleg Kalugin. DK Pub. 1996 176p il $29.95
    327.12

1. Espionage 2. Intelligence service

ISBN 0-7894-0443-5
    LC 95-44054

This "book includes spy history, equipment, techniques, weaponry, recruitment, training, and individual profiles of spies." Voice Youth Advocates

"A wealth of information about the practice of spying, illustrated with a variety of well-captioned photographs, reproductions, charts, and sketches." SLJ

Includes bibliographical references

O'Toole, G. J. A. (George J. A.), 1936-

The encyclopedia of American intelligence and espionage; from the Revolutionary War to the present. Facts on File 1988 539p il $50 **327.12**

1. American espionage—Dictionaries

ISBN 0-8160-1011-0
    LC 87-30361

A "work on the history of American intelligence and espionage. Some 700 alphabetically arranged entries, varying in length from a few lines to several pages, cover major figures in the field (some 500 entries), American intelligence organizations and their roles in 9 wars, topics (e.g., covert action, cryptography), events or incidents (e.g., Bay of Pigs), and a few terms. A list of abbreviations, 150 black-and-white illustrations, a 10-page bibliography, and an index are included." Nichols. Guide to Ref Books for Sch Media Cent. 4th edition

327.73 United States—Foreign relations

American foreign policy: opposing viewpoints; Carol Wekesser, book editor. Greenhaven Press 1993 239p il lib bdg $19.95; pa $11.95 **327.73**
1. United States—Foreign relations
ISBN 0-89908-199-1 (lib bdg); 0-89908-174-6 (pa)
LC 92-40707
"Opposing viewpoints series"
Replaces the edition published 1987 under the editorship of Neal Bernards and Lynn Hall
This volume "looks at several broad questions of policy, devoting sections to goals, relations with allies, intervention in regional conflicts, the merits of foreign aid, and our changing relationship with the countries of the former USSR. . . . A resource that will be in demand for debaters and report writers." SLJ
Includes bibliographical references

Cartoon history of United States foreign policy; by the editors of the Foreign Policy Association; with an introduction by Daniel P. Moynihan. Foreign Policy Assn. 1975-1991 2v **327.73**
1. United States—Foreign relations—Cartoons and caricatures 2. American wit and humor
Volume covering the years 1945 to the present by Nancy King published by Pharos Bks.
Contents: [v1] 1776-1976 pa $9.95 (ISBN 0-688-07976-8); [v2] From 1945 to the present pa $12.95 (ISBN 0-88687-534-X)
These volumes contain a selection of American political cartoons, arranged chronologically. Among the cartoonists represented are Bill Mauldin, Herblock, John Fischetti, Pat Oliphant, Don Wright, and Mike Peters

The **Cold** War: opposing viewpoints; William Dudley, book editor. Greenhaven Press 1992 312p il map (American history series) lib bdg $19.95; pa $11.95 **327.73**
1. World politics—1945-1991 2. United States—Foreign relations
ISBN 1-56510-009-3 (lib bdg); 1-56510-008-5 (pa)
LC 92-21797
A collection of papers discussing various military and political implications of the Cold War. Douglas MacArthur, Barry Goldwater, J. William Fulbright, Lyndon B. Johnson and Charles Krauthammer are among the authors represented
Includes bibliography

Dolan, Edward F., 1924-
Shaping U.S. foreign policy; profiles of twelve secretaries of state; [by] Edward F. Dolan, Margaret M. Scariano. Watts 1996 128p il (Democracy in action) lib bdg $22.70 **327.73**
1. Cabinet officers 2. Statesmen 3. United States—Foreign relations
ISBN 0-531-11264-0 LC 95-49390
"This book examines the contributions of 12 Secretaries of State ranging from James Madison, who arranged the Louisiana Purchase, to Henry Kissinger. . . . Dolan and Scariano begin each chapter with a brief bio-

graphical introduction and then describe how the Secretary made some change in either the size of the country or its relations with other nations. The authors are positive about the men and their accomplishments and do not discuss more critical interpretations of their actions." SLJ
Includes bibliographical references

328.73 The legislative process in the United States

Barone, Michael
The almanac of American politics; [by] Michael Barone and Grant Ujifusa with Richard E. Cohen. National Journal il maps $64.95; pa $49.95
328.73
1. United States. Congress 2. United States—Politics and government 3. Almanacs
First published 1972 by Gambit. (1996 edition) Frequently revised
Subtitle and publisher vary
"The senators, the representatives and the governors; their records and elections results, their states and districts." Subtitle
"A political overview for each state (with a map of election districts) is followed by information on its governor, senators, and representatives (with district-by-district background and analysis). Includes brief biographies; office addresses and telephone numbers; election results; and (for legislators) committees, interest group ratings, and key votes. Usually offers a variety of additional information (e.g., demographics; campaign finance; Senate, House, and Joint committees and members)." Guide to Ref Books. 11th edition

Birnbaum, Jeffrey H., 1956-
The lobbyists; how influence peddlers get their way in Washington. Times Bks. 1992 334p hardcover o.p. paperback available $15 **328.73**
1. Lobbying 2. Business and politics 3. United States—Politics and government
ISBN 0-8129-2314-6 (pa) LC 92-53673
"Focusing on the activities of several of the more than 80,000 lobbyists who represent corporate, trade, and special interests, Birnbaum defines the lobbyist's role, techniques, corporate concerns, and impact on legislation considered during 1989 and 1990." Booklist
This is "a highly disturbing account, calculated to open the eyes of the uninitiated reader to the realities of the political process. . . . This work deserves a wide and thoughtful readership." Libr J
Includes bibliographical references

Christianson, Stephen G.
Facts about the Congress; with an introduction by Richard Allan Baker. Wilson, H.W. 1996 xxvii, 635p il $55 **328.73**
1. United States. Congress 2. United States—Politics and government
ISBN 0-8242-0883-8 LC 95-53691
This volume describes "the structure, function, and history of both houses of the U.S. Congress. An opening

Christianson, Stephen G.—*Continued*

section discusses how the Congress operates in the passage of legislation, including the details of its committee and subcommittee structure, leadership and seniority, and relations with the President. The main part of the book consists of chapters devoted to the activities of every Congress, from the First (1789-1791) to the One Hundred Fourth (1995)." Publisher's note

Includes glossary and bibliographical references

Congress A to Z; a ready reference encyclopedia. 2nd ed. Congressional Quarterly 1993 547p il maps $139   **328.73**
1. United States. Congress
ISBN 0-87187-826-7   LC 93-25926
First published 1988

This volume "provides basic information on the structure and work of Congress. Most entries are no more than a page or so in length and include biographies, committee descriptions and roles, and brief definitions (e.g., *cloakrooms, debt limit, enacting clause*). A number of essays, ranging from five to seven pages in length, deal with broader topics, such as the budget process, ethics, leadership, and the Watergate scandal. Black-and-white illustrations are logically placed throughout the text." Am Ref Books Annu, 1994

Includes bibliographical references

Congress and the Nation; a review of government and politics. Congressional Quarterly 1965-1993 8v il maps v1 o.p.; v2-8 ea $215   **328.73**
1. United States. Congress 2. Legislation 3. United States—Politics and government—1900-1999 (20th century)
Contents: v1 1945-1964 o.p.; v2 1965-1968 (ISBN 0-87187-004-5); v3 1969-1972 (ISBN 0-87187-055-X); v4 1973-1976 (ISBN 0-87187-112-2); v5 1977-1980 (ISBN 0-87187-216-1); v6 1981-1984 (ISBN 0-87187-334-6); v7 1985-1988 (ISBN 0-87187-532-2); v8 1989-1992 (0-87187-789-9)

"Overview and detailed coverage of presidential, legislative, and political events in every major subject area." N Y Public Libr. Book of How & Where to Look It Up

Congressional Quarterly's guide to Congress. Congressional Quarterly il $249   **328.73**
1. United States. Congress
First published 1971 with title: Congressional Quarterly's guide to the Congress of the United States.(4th edition 1991) Periodically revised

"Covers history and workings of Congress, with biographical data on all members." N Y Public Libr. Book of How & Where to Look It Up

Congressional Quarterly's politics in America. CQ Press il maps $94.95; pa $55.95   **328.73**
1. United States. Congress 2. Elections—United States
Also available CD-ROM version
Biennial. First published 1981
Current editor: Phil Duncan

Profiles each current member of Congress, providing political background, statistical information, committee assignments, etc.

The **Encyclopedia** of the United States Congress; edited by Donald C. Bacon, Roger H. Davidson, Morton Keller. Simon & Schuster 1995 4v il set $355   **328.73**
1. United States. Congress
ISBN 0-13-276361-3   LC 94-21203

This "set contains eight lengthy essays and over 1000 shorter, alphabetically arranged entries on a wide range of topics such as the inner workings of Congress, landmark legislation, relationships with the other branches of government, the legislative process, and a storehouse of additional information." Libr J

For a fuller review see: Booklist, Aug. 1995

Greenberg, Ellen

The House and Senate explained; the people's guide to Congress. Norton 1996 173p il $19.95; pa $12   **328.73**
1. United States. Congress
ISBN 0-393-03984-6; 0-393-31496-0 (pa)
                                                      LC 96-12291
Revised edition of the House & Senate explained published 1986

"Greenberg simplifies, explains, and presents the legislative branch in ways that bring clarity to confusion. She begins with the basics—how both the House and Senate are physically organized. . . . A typical congressional day is outlined and a pithy explanation of the steps from a bill to law is offered. An excellent reference source, the book includes a full index and sections on written and Internet accesses to the government." SLJ

How Congress works. 2nd ed. Congressional Quarterly 1991 157p il pa $27.95   **328.73**
1. United States. Congress
ISBN 0-87187-598-5   LC 91-11116
First published 1983

This book explains the rules and procedures followed in the House and Senate and includes changes made during the 1980s

Includes bibliographical references

Ritchie, Donald A.

The young Oxford companion to the Congress of the United States. Oxford Univ. Press 1993 239p il $40   **328.73**
1. United States. Congress 2. United States—Politics and government—Dictionaries
ISBN 0-19-507777-6   LC 93-6466

"Ritchie offers brief entries on individual House and Senate members and congressional powers, traditions, and procedures. Biographies are limited to a sampling of those who have earned historical recognition. . . . Readers will find clear definitions of concepts such as checks and balances, filibusters, incumbents, etc., as well as enjoy the more anecdotal entries." SLJ

United States. Congress

Official Congressional directory. U.S. Govt. Ptg. Office $43; pa $23   **328.73**
1. United States. Congress—Biography 2. United States. Congress—Directories
Biennial

United States. Congress—*Continued*
"Covers biographical information, committee assignments of members of Congress, and officers of Congress." N Y Public Libr. Book of How & Where to Look It Up

The **World** almanac of U.S. politics. World Almanac Bks. $29.95; pa $18.95   **328.73**
1. United States—Politics and government 2. Almanacs
ISSN 1043-1535
Biennial. First published 1989
"This useful, inexpensive work provides factual and descriptive information about federal, state, and local governments. Brief essays treat such topics as the electoral college, budget process, campaign financing, and political parties. Also covered are federal agencies; popular government programs; congressional committees; and concise biographies of members of Congress, cabinet members, federal judges, and important executive branch persons." Nichols. Guide to Ref Books for Sch Media Cent. 4th edition

330   Economics

Galbraith, John Kenneth, 1908-
The affluent society. 4th ed. Houghton Mifflin 1984 xxxvii, 291p hardcover o.p.; New Am. Lib. reprint available $4.95   **330**
1. Economics 2. United States—Economic conditions—1900-1999 (20th century)
ISBN 0-451-62394-0 (pa)   LC 84-12880
First published 1958
The author surveys the economic upheavals that have changed the economic climate of the world. He also discusses the proper goals and management of a modern society and the question of how the production and distribution of wealth should be organized
Includes bibliographical references

Heilbroner, Robert L.
Economics explained; everything you need to know about how the economy works and where it's going; [by] Robert Heilbroner and Lester Thurow. rev & updated [ed] Simon & Schuster 1994 285p il pa $12   **330**
1. Economics 2. United States—Economic conditions
ISBN 0-671-88422-0   LC 93-21329
"A Touchstone book"
First published 1982 by Prentice-Hall
This "primer on economics . . . targets those with little or no background in the subject, clearly explaining concepts such as the GNP, deficit spending, and price systems. It also provides an overview of the history of economic thought by contrasting the theories of Adam Smith, Karl Marx, and John Maynard Keynes. While economic theories are often likely to be colored by political or moral values, the authors readily identify opinions or statements that may be controversial." Booklist
Includes bibliographical references

330.1   Economic systems and theories

Heilbroner, Robert L.
The worldly philosophers; the lives, times, and ideas of the great economic thinkers. Simon & Schuster pa $14   **330.1**
1. Economists 2. Economics
First published 1953. (6th edition 1986) Periodically revised
The author traces the story of economics and the great economists from Adam Smith, Malthus, Ricardo, the Utopians, Marx, Veblen and Keynes to those working with the problems of our contemporary world
Includes bibliography

Smith, Adam, 1723-1790
The wealth of nations   **330.1**
1. Economics
Hardcover and paperback editions available from various publishers
First published 1776
Variant title: An inquiry into the nature and causes of the wealth of nations
This treatise "is the first comprehensive treatment of the whole subject of political economy, and is remarkable for its breadth of view. . . . [In it, the author presents an] attack on the mercantile system, and an advocacy of freedom of commerce and industry." Oxford Companion to Engl Lit. 5th edition

330.9   Economic situation and conditions

The **Third** World: opposing viewpoints; Jonathan S. Petrikin, book editor. Greenhaven Press 1995 288p il lib bdg $19.95; pa $11.95   **330.9**
1. Developing countries
ISBN 1-56510-250-9 (lib bdg); 1-56510-249-5 (pa)
LC 94-41911
"Opposing viewpoints series"
Replaces the edition published 1989 under the editorship of Janelle Rohr
Presents opposing opinions on such questions concerning the Third World as why it is poor, how it can achieve economic development, and what forms of government would best serve its needs
Includes bibliography

330.973   United States—Economic conditions

Galbraith, John Kenneth, 1908-
The Great Crash, 1929; with a new introduction by the author. Houghton Mifflin 1988 xx, 206p il hardcover o.p. paperback available $12.95
        330.973
1. United States—Economic conditions—1919-1933
2. Economic depressions 3. Business cycles
ISBN 0-395-47805-7 (pa)   LC 88-134280
First published 1955

Galbraith, John Kenneth, 1908—_Continued_

Beginning with the bull market of Coolidge and Hoover and continuing through the stock market crash, the author analyzes its causes and speculates about the chances of another crash

Includes bibliographical references

Meltzer, Milton, 1915-

Brother, can you spare a dime? the Great Depression, 1929-1933; illustrated with contemporary prints & photographs. Facts on File 1991 130p il maps (Library of American history) $17.95   **330.973**

1. United States—Economic conditions—1919-1933
2. Economic depressions 3. United States—Social conditions

ISBN 0-8160-2372-7   LC 90-39760

Also available in paperback from New Am. Lib.

First published 1969 by Knopf

"Meltzer focuses on the human reactions to the events of the Great Depression, and as such, draws heavily on first-hand accounts of those who experienced them." SLJ

"Young people reading the narratives and essays here can begin to understand the importance and relevance of this time in history. Very highly recommended." Voice Youth Advocates

Includes bibliography

331.1   Labor force and market

Affirmative action; A.E. Sadler, book editor. Greenhaven Press 1996 94p (At issue) lib bdg $12.95; pa $7.95   **331.1**

1. Affirmative action programs

ISBN 1-56510-387-4 (lib bdg); 1-56510-386-6 (pa)
                LC 95-39058

"This anthology includes eight previously published articles which provide a variety of viewpoints about affirmative action. . . . The first half of the book is devoted to arguments in favor of affirmative action and the second half to arguments against it. . . . [This book] will provide students with a good starting place when faced with a term paper assignment." Voice Youth Advocates

Includes bibliographical references

331.2   Compensation and other conditions of employment

Terkel, Studs, 1912-

Working; people talk about what they do all day and how they feel about what they do. Pantheon Bks. 1974 xlix, 589p o.p.; Ballantine Bks. paperback available $6.95   **331.2**

1. Labor—United States 2. Work 3. United States—Social conditions

ISBN 0-345-32569-9 (pa)

Also available in paperback from New Press (NY)

Based on interviews, this study describes the working lives and feelings of people engaged in occupations ranging from interstate truck driver to stockbroker to bookbinder to corporation president

This "is not a dry, academic treatise but a sensitive portrayal of the experience of working, with all its pain, tension, frustrations, and occasional satisfactions." Best Sellers

331.3   Workers of specific age groups

Meltzer, Milton, 1915-

Cheap raw material. Viking 1994 167p il $14.99
                331.3

1. Children—Employment

ISBN 0-670-83128-X   LC 93-31478

A "discourse on child labor which starts with a history of practices including slavery, servitude, apprenticeship, and the early period of industrialization. [The author] moves next to the recent child labor abuses cited in fast-food chains, farming, and industrial home work. . . . Although Meltzer tries to prove, through example, systemic and systematic abuse and exploitation of child workers in this country and worldwide, he succeeds primarily when he talks of farm laborers and children in less regulated countries such as India and Mexico. . . . Meltzer's research is commendable and his sources are well documented." Bull Cent Child Books

331.4   Women workers

America's working women; a documentary history, 1600 to the present; edited by Rosalyn Baxandall and Linda Gordon, with Susan Reverby. rev and updated. Norton 1995 356p il hardcover o.p. paperback available $12.95
                331.4

1. Women—Employment

ISBN 0-393-31262-3 (pa)   LC 94-32194

First published 1976 by Random House

"This chronologically arranged anthology presents an . . . overview of the changing roles and contributions of woman at home, in the fields, and in today's workplace." Booklist

Includes bibliographical references

Dash, Joan

We shall not be moved; the women's factory strike of 1909. Scholastic 1996 165p il $15.95
                331.4

1. Women—Employment 2. Labor unions 3. Strikes

ISBN 0-590-48409-5   LC 95-19404

Describes the conditions that gave rise to efforts to secure better working conditions for the women working in the garment industry in early twentieth-century New York and led to the formation of the Women's Trade Union League and the first women's strike in 1909

"Dash brings a novelist's skill to her descriptions of Lower East Side streets, and she conveys the general excitement of the movement by focusing on key individuals, memorably presenting them as impassioned agents for social change." Publ Wkly

Includes bibliography

Gluck, Sherna Berger

Rosie the Riveter revisited; women, the war, and social change. Twayne Pubs. 1987 282p (Twayne's oral history series) $22.95 **331.4**

1. Women—Employment 2. World War, 1939-1945—Women 3. World War, 1939-1945—War work 4. Airplane industry

ISBN 0-8057-9022-5 LC 86-31852

Also available in paperback from New Am. Lib.

This book is the outgrowth of an oral history project in which forty-five former southern California women aircraft workers were interviewed. Ten of their life histories are presented here

"In near unanimity, these women say that war work taught them they could do just about anything, including men's work. . . . This book presents a solid lesson in the interconnectedness of public policy and women's private spheres." N Y Times Book Rev

Includes bibliography

Sexual harassment; Carol Wekesser, senior editor; Karin L. Swisher, book editor; Christina Pierce, assistant editor. Greenhaven Press 1992 208p il (Current controversies) lib bdg $19.95; pa $11.95 **331.4**

1. Sexual harassment

ISBN 1-56510-021-2 (lib bdg); 1-56510-020-4 (pa)
LC 92-23593

A collection of excerpts and articles from a variety of sources addressing various aspects of sexual harassment. Anita Hill, Barbara Kantrowitz, Daniel Goleman and Naomi Wolf are among the contributors

"For teenagers researching the issue, the book is a real find, and the annotated table of contents makes research even easier." Booklist

Includes bibliography

331.5 Special categories of workers other than by age or sex

Ashabranner, Brent K., 1921-

Dark harvest: migrant farmworkers in America; [by] Brent Ashabranner; photographs by Paul Conklin. Linnet Bks. 1993 c1985 150p il lib bdg $18.50 **331.5**

1. Migrant labor 2. Agricultural laborers

ISBN 0-208-02391-7 LC 93-33170

A reissue of the title first published 1985 by Dodd, Mead

A "look at the world of the migrant worker, accompanied by powerful black-and-white photographs. Includes interviews with workers, their children, their employers and those who work in social programs to assist them. While optimistic about the progress that has been made, such as Head Start childcare centers, Ashabranner emphasizes the prejudice, injustice and indifference that still prevail." Soc Educ

Includes bibliography

Oldman, Mark

Student advantage guide to America's top internships; [by] Mark Oldman and Samer Hamadeh. Random House il pa $20 **331.5**

ISSN 1073-5801

Annual. First published 1993 with title: Student access guide to America's top 100 internships

At head of title: The Princeton Review

This "resource lists internships for graduates, college and high school students, minorities, and adult career changers. Arranged by individual company, each entry provides such pertinent information as pay, quality of life at the job site, prerequisites, and deadlines for application. Company history and mission are also stated. Indexes detail selection criteria, scholarships, type of internship, and location. Easy to use and informative." SLJ

331.7 Labor by industry and occupation

Dictionary of occupational titles; [by the] U.S. Department of Labor, Employment and Training Administration, U.S. Employment Service. 4th ed, rev 1991. U.S. Govt. Ptg. Office 1991 2v set pa $40 **331.7**

1. Occupations

ISBN 0-16-032357-6 LC 91-601686

Hardcover and paperback editions also available from various publishers

First published 1939-1944

"Offers standardized descriptions of job content and structure for about 20,000 occupations. Grouped by occupations to emphasize similarities and variations. Detailed classed arrangement indexed alphabetically by occupation and industry group. Glossary." Guide to Ref Books. 11th edition

The **Encyclopedia** of careers and vocational guidance. Ferguson, J.G. 4v il set $149.95 **331.7**

1. Occupations 2. Vocational guidance

Also available CD-ROM version

First published 1967 (10th edition 1996). Periodically revised. Editors vary

"Entries describe educational and training requirements, duties, salaries, and prospects. Each volume contains a complete index of the job titles in all four volumes; v. 4 has an index of jobs by Dictionary of occupational titles number. . . . Appendixes list organizations that assist in training and job placement for disabled and other special groups and provide information on internships, apprenticeships, and special training programs." Guide to Ref Books. 11th edition

Field, Shelly

100 best careers for the 21st century. Macmillan 1996 304p pa $15.95 **331.7**

1. Vocational guidance 2. Occupations 3. Employment forecasting

ISBN 0-02-860595-0 LC 95-52518

"An Arco book"

First published 1992 by Prentice Hall with title: 100 best careers for the year 2000

Field, Shelly—*Continued*

This "guide describes scores of attractive job opportunities in the career areas expected to grow fastest, among them: hospitality and travel, education, conservation and the environment, medical technology and health care, home business, and many more." Publisher's note

Jones, Lawrence K.

Job skills for the 21st century; a guide for students. Oryx Press 1996 209p il pa $29.95

                  331.7

1. Vocational guidance 2. Employment forecasting

ISBN 0-89774-956-1   LC 95-42438

This is a "skills-improvement and career-guidance manual for teens. Emphasizing the foundation skills of reading, writing, math, listening, and speaking, Jones includes a multitude of actual job scenes, with workers describing what they do. Readers are also given a chance to assess their own skills, personality types, and aptitudes and are given suggestions for setting goals, learning new skills, and honing decision-making, problem-solving, and other skills. . . . A good choice for career-development collections." Booklist

Mitchell, Joyce Slayton, 1933-

The College Board guide to jobs and career planning. 2nd ed. College Entrance Examination Bd. 1994 331p pa $14   **331.7**

1. Occupations 2. Vocational guidance

ISBN 0-87447-467-1   LC 94-166980

First published 1990

Spine title: Guide to jobs and career planning

"The first three parts of this career guide deal with the importance of planning ahead. . . . The fourth, and last, section divides over 100 occupations into career groups. . . . One nice feature of this career guide is that in the fourth section young people who have been in their jobs for a few years briefly tell the reader what their jobs are really like." Voice Youth Advocates

Specialty occupational outlook: professions; Joyce Jakubiak, editor. Gale Res. 1995 254p $49.95

                  331.7

1. Professions 2. Vocational guidance

ISBN 0-8103-9644-0

Revised and updated editions projected to follow new editions of Occupational outlook handbook

This volume "covers 150 professional jobs not included in the *Occupational Outlook Handbook* (OOH). These include financial planners, animal breeders, geophysicists, broadcast engineers, and coaches. The format is almost exactly that of OOH. . . . Recommended for all libraries with career resource material." Booklist

Specialty occupational outlook: trade & technical; Joyce Jakubiak, editor. Gale Res. 1996 252p $49.95   **331.7**

1. Industrial arts 2. Vocational guidance

ISBN 0-8103-9645-9

Revised and updated editions projected to follow new editions of Occupational outlook handbook

"Based on the US Department of Labor's popular *Occupational Outlook handbook* (1949-), this new career planning directory provides guidance concerning 150 occupations in the trade and technical fields that are not covered in the government publication. The types of careers covered range from the common (biological technician or legal secretary) to the relatively rare (apiarist or fire spotter). . . . Each entry describes the nature of the work, working conditions, employment, training and qualifications, job outlook, earnings, related occupations, and sources of additional information." Choice

Unger, Harlow G., 1931-

But what if I don't want to go to college? a guide to success through alternative education. Facts on File 1992 178p lib bdg $19.95; pa $10.95

                  331.7

1. Occupational training 2. Vocational education 3. Vocational guidance

ISBN 0-8160-2534-7 (lib bdg); 0-8160-2836-2 (pa)

                  LC 91-3186

This guide "defines and relays the advantages and disadvantages of the ten basic kinds of vocational education. . . . Descriptions of a variety of jobs in many career areas are included as well as agencies and organizations to contact for accreditation and other information, guidance for resume and letter preparation, and tips for successful interviewing. . . . A great choice for serious students who plan to follow a different route than their pre-collegiate peers." SLJ

United States. Bureau of Labor Statistics

Occupational outlook handbook. U.S. Govt. Ptg. Office il $38; pa $32   **331.7**

1. Occupations 2. Vocational guidance

Also available CD-ROM version

Biennial. First published 1949. Supplemented by Occupational Outlook Quarterly, subscription $9.50

"Gives information on employment trends and outlook in more than 800 occupations. Indicates nature of work, qualifications, earnings and working conditions, entry level jobs, where to go for more information, etc." Guide to Ref Books. 11th edition

331.8   Labor unions and labor-management relations

Meltzer, Milton, 1915-

Bread—and roses: the struggle of American labor, 1865-1915. Facts on File 1991 167p il maps (Library of American history) $17.95   **331.8**

1. Labor unions—History 2. United States—Social conditions

ISBN 0-8160-2371-9   LC 90-39759

First published 1967 by Knopf

Uses original source material to portray the momentous changes that took place in American labor, industry, and trade-unionism following the Civil War. Focuses on the work environment in this early age of mass production and mechanization, and shows how abusive conditions often led to labor unrest

Includes glossary and bibliography

332.4 Money

Rendon, Marion
Straight talk about money; [by] Marion Rendon and Rachel Kranz. Facts on File 1992 112p $16.95
332.4
1. Money 2. Personal finance
ISBN 0-8160-2612-2   LC 91-36586
Discusses money, the economy, ways of earning and saving money, and its significance in society
"Well organized and easy to read, the text provides current information and a balanced examination of issues that surround the subject, and readers will appreciate the authors' sound, straightforward advice." Booklist

333.7 Natural resources and energy

Amdur, Richard
Wilderness preservation; introduction by Russell E. Train. Chelsea House 1993 110p il (Earth at risk) lib bdg $19.95   **333.7**
1. Wilderness areas 2. Conservation of natural resources 3. Environmental protection
ISBN 0-7910-1580-7   LC 92-10594
This book discusses the degradation or destruction of wilderness areas and possible ways to save them. The spotted owl controversy, mining in Yellowstone Park, and oil exploration in Alaska's Arctic National Wildlife refuge are explored in detail
Includes glossary and bibliography

Goldberg, Jake
Economics and the environment; introduction by Russell E. Train. Chelsea House 1993 119p il map (Earth at risk) lib bdg $19.95   **333.7**
1. Environmental protection
ISBN 0-7910-1594-7   LC 92-10593
Examines the role of economics in preserving or destroying the environment and conflicts between companies and environmentalists
"This book is well written and very readable." Sci Books Films
Includes glossary and bibliography

Naar, Jon
This land is your land; a guide to North America's endangered ecosystems; [by] Jon Naar and Alex J. Naar. HarperPerennial 1992 388p il maps pa $15   **333.7**
1. Ecology 2. Environmental protection
ISBN 0-06-096882-6   LC 91-50508
This book discusses the major ecosystems of North America, the hazards they face, and what can be done to protect and restore them. Using a case-history approach, the authors document the conditions of endangered rivers, lakes and wetlands; grasslands, forests, and deserts; and national parks, wildlife refuges and other public lands. Appended is a resources section which contains an annotated directory of environmental organizations and summaries of pending legislation
Includes glossary and bibliographical references

333.75 Forest lands

The **Conservation** atlas of tropical forests: Africa; edited by Jeffrey A. Sayer, Caroline S. Harcourt, N. Mark Collins; editorial assistant: Clare Billington; map editor: Mike Adam. Simon & Schuster 1992 288p il maps $128.50
333.75
1. Rain forests 2. Africa—Maps 3. Human influence on nature 4. Conservation of natural resources
ISBN 0-13-175332-0   LC 91-39120
Published for the World Conservation Union
This atlas provides an analysis of Africa's "ecological history, superb maps based on satellite imagery of country-by-country forest resources, and a discussion of biodiversity, conservation areas, and initiatives for conservationists. . . . An excellent single-volume source, this is highly recommended." Libr J

333.79 Energy

Energy alternatives; Charles P. Cozic, book editor; Matthew Polesetsky, book editor. Greenhaven Press 1991 176p il (Current controversies) lib bdg $19.95; pa $11.95   **333.79**
1. Renewable energy resources
ISBN 0-89908-577-6 (lib bdg); 0-89908-583-0 (pa)
LC 91-24387
A collection of articles offering opinions for and against such energy issues as whether fossil fuels should be replaced, the uses of nuclear power, alternatives to gasoline-powered cars, and the need for a national energy policy
"As a primary source of information for debates or papers, it will be useful. Names and addresses of several of the advocacy groups are appended." SLJ
Includes bibliographical references

333.91 Water

Allaby, Michael, 1933-
Water; its global nature. Facts on File 1992 208p il maps (Elements) $35   **333.91**
1. Water
ISBN 0-8160-2526-6   LC 92-227976
"A comprehensive overview that describes water's basic properties and varieties, as well as its essential role in all life forms on Earth. Its fantastic motions as evidenced in rivers, currents, and tides are explained, along with its influence on weather and climate. Humankind's many uses of this precious resource and the inherent problems of worldwide pollution are also highlighted." SLJ
Includes glossary and bibliography

Water: opposing viewpoints; Carol Wekesser, book editor. Greenhaven Press 1994 191p lib bdg $19.95; pa $11.95   **333.91**
1. Water supply 2. Acid rain 3. Pollution
ISBN 1-56510-064-6 (lib bdg); 1-56510-063-8 (pa)
LC 93-12374
"Opposing viewpoints series"

Water: opposing viewpoints—*Continued*
This collection of articles presents opposing viewpoints on issues relating to water, including managing the water supply, acid rain, and government regulations
Includes bibliographical references

333.95 Biological resources

Cohen, Daniel, 1936-
The modern ark; saving endangered species. Putnam 1995 120p il $15.95   333.95
1. Endangered species 2. Wildlife conservation
ISBN 0-399-22442-4   LC 94-34007
"Cohen tells the stories of modern efforts to save certain endangered species: the red wolf, California condor, black-footed ferret, peregrine falcon, golden lion tamarin, Arabian oryx, panda, and cheetah. . . . The stories reflect the realities of saving a species, including politics, economics, pollution, loss of habitat, disease, biological and technological know-how, and luck. The first and last chapters concentrate on the increasing involvement of zoos in programs designed to save species from extinction." Booklist
Includes bibliographical references

Saving wildlife; a century of conservation; general editor, Donald Goddard; research editor, Sam Swope; foreword by Peter Matthiessen; epilogue by William Conway. Abrams 1995 286p il $49.50   333.95
1. NYZS/The Wildlife Conservation Society 2. Wildlife conservation 3. Endangered species 4. Nature conservation
ISBN 0-8109-3674-7   LC 94-22874
Published in association with the Wildlife Conservation Society
"This history of the first 100 years of the New York Zoological Society, renamed the Wildlife Conservation Society in 1992, is told primarily through photographs and excerpts from the writings of some of those most influential in the development of the society's role from mere provider of the Bronx Zoo to the leader in international conservation research and education." Libr J
"This is a book for zoo-goers, animal lovers and everyone concerned with preserving wildlife." Publ Wkly

Turner, Tom
Sierra Club; 100 years of protecting nature. Abrams 1991 288p il maps $49.50   333.95
1. Sierra Club 2. Nature conservation
ISBN 0-8109-3820-0   LC 91-9866
Published in association with the Sierra Club
This "book details, in text and photographs, the history of one of America's oldest conservation groups. . . . Nearly 300 photographs from some of the world's foremost nature photographers, including Ansel Adams and Philip Hyde, make this volume a remarkable chronicle of the environmental movement." Libr J
Includes bibliographical references

335 Socialism and related systems

Ebenstein, Alan D.
Today's isms; socialism, capitalism, fascism, communism; [by] Alan D. Ebenstein, William Ebenstein, Edwin Fogelman. Prentice-Hall il pa $21.45   335
1. Communism 2. Fascism 3. Socialism 4. Capitalism
First published 1954 (10th edition 1994). Frequently revised
A look at the basic principles, history, and policies of fascist, communist, socialist and capitalist forms of government
Includes bibliography

335.4 Marxian systems

Marx, Karl, 1818-1883
The Communist manifesto of Karl Marx and Friedrich Engels   335.4
1. Communism
Hardcover and paperback editions available from various publishers
First published 1848
This document "analyzes history in terms of class conflict, predicts the imminent overthrow of the ruling bourgeoisie by the oppressed proletariat, and envisions a resulting classless society in which personal property would be abolished. The 'Manifesto' calls upon the proletariat of the world to unite and strengthen itself for this final revolution." Reader's Ency
Includes bibliography

336.3 Public borrowing, debt, expenditure

Balancing the federal budget; edited by J.W. Aros. Wilson, H.W. 1996 154p (Reference shelf, v68 no2) pa $15   336.3
1. Budget—United States 2. Deficit financing
ISBN 0-8242-0887-0   LC 96-6130
A compilation of articles offering a range of opinions on the national debt, federal deficits, and the budget's impact on social programs like Medicare and welfare
Includes bibliographical references

338.1 Agriculture. Food supply

Goldberg, Jake
The disappearing American farm. Watts 1995 128p il lib bdg $22.70   338.1
1. Family farms 2. Agriculture—United States
ISBN 0-531-11261-6   LC 95-49386
Describes the problems in American agriculture due to technological innovation, gives a history of American agriculture to explain the origins of the crisis, and outlines the limitations of government farm programs and policies

Goldberg, Jake—*Continued*
to cope

The author explains "issues in such a way as to make them both understandable and interesting to teen readers. . . . Goldberg has done an outstanding job on an extremely complex topic." Voice Youth Advocates

Includes bibliographical references

Kluger, Richard

Ashes to ashes; America's hundred-year cigarette war, the public health, and the unabashed triumph of Philip Morris. Knopf 1996 807p $35

338.1

1. Philip Morris, Inc. 2. Smoking 3. Tobacco habit 4. Tobacco industry

ISBN 0-394-57076-6   LC 95-42103

"From the Native American usage of tobacco through the law-suits of the 1990s, Kluger follows the industry's agricultural and labor practices, technical advances, and marketing campaigns; he also considers research on tobacco's deleterious health effects and the tobacco control movement. Significant personalities and events such as the invention of the cigarette-rolling machine are featured. . . . Suitable for readers of high school age on up, this book belongs in every library." Libr J

Includes bibliography

Patent, Dorothy Hinshaw

The vanishing feast; how dwindling genetic diversity threatens the world's food supply. Harcourt Brace & Co. 1994 180p il $17.95

338.1

1. Biological diversity 2. Conservation of natural resources 3. Agriculture

ISBN 0-15-292867-7   LC 94-2227

The author "explains the process of genetic engineering and how it threatens the small farmer, the environment, thousands of life forms, and the world's food supply. She stresses the importance of natural diversity in order for species to survive year after year under varying conditions and discusses current efforts to preserve it." SLJ

"This is well written and very informative about a little touched area of the ecology crisis. It could be extremely useful in reports or for those really interested in genetics and/or ecology." Voice Youth Advocates

Includes glossary and bibliographical references

Raeburn, Paul

The last harvest; the genetic gamble that threatens to destroy American agriculture. Simon & Schuster 1995 269p $24

338.1

1. Plant breeding 2. Farm produce 3. Agriculture—United States 4. Biological diversity

ISBN 0-684-80365-8   LC 95-7369

Also available in paperback from University of Neb. Press

The author discusses "the disappearance of the genetic diversity needed for the future improvement of crop plants that are the mainstay of U.S. and world agriculture." Sci Books Films

"Whether or not America is on the verge of agricul-

tural catastrophe, Raeburn certainly furnishes information useful to readers concerned with the biological vulnerabilities in America's complicated food production complex." Booklist

Includes bibliographical references

338.7 Business enterprises and their structure

Love, John F.

McDonald's: behind the arches. rev ed. Bantam Bks. 1995 486p il pa $12.95

338.7

1. Kroc, Ray 2. McDonald's Corp. 3. Food industry

ISBN 0-553-34759-4   LC 95-11540

First published 1986

A history of the hugely successful fast food franchise corporation. McDonald's founder Ray Kroc is profiled

338.973 United States—Economic policy

Anderson, Rolf

Atlas of the American economy; an illustrated guide to industries and trends. CQ Press 1994 176p il $40.95

338.973

1. Industry 2. Economic forecasting 3. United States—Economic conditions

ISBN 1-56802-001-5   LC 94-23105

This work "is divided into four parts. The first, 'The Big Picture,' provides an overview of the U.S. economy; an assessment of 'The Big Trends' follows. Part 3, 'The Basic Industries,' devotes one page each to data on approximately 70 industries. . . . Part 4, 'Notes and Sources,' comprises a hefty 40 percent of the book and is the only section that includes analytical text." Libr J

Economics in America: opposing viewpoints; Terry O'Neill, Karin Swisher, book editors. Greenhaven Press 1992 258p il lib bdg $19.95; pa $11.95

338.973

1. United States—Economic policy

ISBN 0-89908-187-8 (lib bdg); 0-89908-162-2 (pa)

LC 91-42802

"Opposing viewpoints series"

Replaces the edition published 1986

Articles in this volume debate "the state of the U.S. economy, the budget deficit, taxation, the banking system, and the future of American labor. . . . Good curriculum support material for students in a variety of classes." Booklist

Includes glossary and bibliography

340 Law

Encyclopedia of the American judicial system; studies of the principal institutions and process of law; Robert J. Janosik, editor. Scribner 1987 3v set $305

340

1. Law—United States 2. Administration of justice 3. United States—Constitutional law

ISBN 0-684-17807-9   LC 87-4742

Analyzed in Essay and general literature index

Encyclopedia of the American judicial system—
Continued

These essays are "arranged in six sections: legal history, substantive law, institutions and personnel, process and behavior, constitutional law and issues, and methodology. The first section proceeds chronologically from the colonial period through the Burger court. The other sections are arranged alphabetically. . . . Intended for lay readers as well as students and researchers." Libr J

Garza, Hedda

Barred from the bar; a history of women in the legal profession. Watts 1996 224p il (Women then—women now) lib bdg $22.70; pa $9   **340**

1. Women lawyers 2. Sex discrimination

ISBN 0-531-11265-9 (lib bdg); 0-531-15795-4 (pa)

LC 95-49391

The author chronicles "the stormy history of women lawyers and jurists in America, starting with the problematic treatment of women under colonial law and ending with an examination of the contemporary status of the profession. Enroute, she covers a great deal of detailed and little-discussed territory, describing the efforts of various 'firsts': first woman admitted to the bar, first woman to practice before the Supreme Court, first African-American woman lawyer, etc." Bull Cent Child Books

"Full of anecdotal detail, this well-researched and well-documented chronicle . . . will appeal to students drawn to law as a career as well as to women's-studies buffs." SLJ

Includes bibliographical references

340.03   Law—Dictionaries

Black, Henry Campbell, 1860-1927

Black's law dictionary. West $33.75   **340.03**

1. Law—Dictionaries

Also available in an abridged paperback edition $21.25 (ISBN 0-314-88536-6)

First published 1891 with title: A dictionary of law (6th edition 1990). Periodically revised to bring terms up to date

"Definitions of the terms and phrases of American and English jurisprudence, ancient and modern." Subtitle

"This comprehensive work is the standard U.S. law dictionary. . . . Many entries include references to cases or statutes. Appendixes include a table of abbreviations and the text of the U.S. Constitution." Guide to Ref Books. 11th edition

341.23   United Nations

Jacobs, William Jay

Search for peace; the story of the United Nations. Scribner 1994 144p $14.95   **341.23**

1. United Nations

ISBN 0-684-19652-2   LC 93-27149

"After describing Woodrow Wilson's dream of a League of Nations, Jacobs discusses the founding and structure of the UN, covers its peacekeeping efforts over the years, outlines the work of its specialized agencies, and speculates on directions for a 'new world order.'" SLJ

"Commemorating the fiftieth anniversary of the United Nations, this volume is intelligent, comprehensive, and well written." Booklist

Includes bibliographical references

Patterson, Charles, 1935-

The Oxford 50th anniversary book of the United Nations. Oxford Univ. Press 1995 237p il lib bdg $40   **341.23**

1. United Nations

ISBN 0-19-508280-X   LC 94-35280

The author "discusses the earliest attempts at international cooperation, the League of Nations, and the wartime Allied meetings that led to the creation of the UN in 1945. Its internal structure is described in the areas of international peace and security, disarmament, economic development, social issues, human rights, and international law. The text is illustrated with black-and-white photographs from news sources and UN archives." SLJ

Includes bibliography

United Nations. Dept. of Public Information

Everyone's United Nations. U.N. Publs. $9.95   **341.23**

1. United Nations

First published 1948 with title: Everyman's United Nations (10th edition 1986). Periodically revised

This tenth edition is a self-contained volume, covering all 40 years of the Organization's existence. It focuses on the period 1978-1985." Title page

"A basic reference work describing the work of the U.N. and the 18 intergovernmental agencies associated with it. Pt. 1 describes the structure of the U.N., pt. 2 its work. The latter part has chapters on U.N. functions, such as peacemaking, human rights, etc. Appendixes include the U.N. Charter, the Statute of the International Court of Justice, and the Universal Declaration of Human Rights. Index by author and subject." Guide to Ref Books. 11th edition

The United Nations' role in world affairs; edited by Donald Altschiller. Wilson, H.W. 1993 218p (Reference shelf, v65 no2) pa $15   **341.23**

1. United Nations 2. International relations

ISBN 0-8242-0841-2   LC 93-21142

This collection of articles, excerpts from books and addresses is divided in four sections: overview of the United Nations; reform and finance; views from the United States and abroad; the United Nations and its critics

Includes bibliography

342   Constitutional and administrative law

Affirmative action; edited by Donald Altschiller. Wilson, H.W. 1991 168p (Reference shelf, v63 no3) pa $15   **342**

1. Affirmative action programs

ISBN 0-8242-0813-7   LC 91-14134

A collection of articles discussing the legal aspects of affirmative action, the prospects of affirmative action in

Affirmative action—*Continued*

the work place, the impact of affirmative action on student admissions and faculty recruitment in U.S. colleges and universities, various attitudes held by whites, and personal reflections of some who have been affected by affirmative action

Includes bibliography

Alderman, Ellen

In our defense: the Bill of Rights in action; [by] Ellen Alderman, Caroline Kennedy. Morrow 1990 430p il $22.95 **342**
1. United States. Supreme Court 2. United States. Constitution. 1st-10th amendments 3. Civil rights 4. United States—Constitutional law
ISBN 0-688-07801-X LC 90-48844
Also available in paperback from Avon Bks.

This "book considers 20 or so Supreme Court cases, the verdicts of which pivot on one of the first Ten Amendments to the U.S. Constitution. The cases chosen are not the landmark, precedent-setting ones with which most people are familiar. Instead, readers will find normal people who, because of circumstance, victimization, or character flaws, end up having their stories studied by the highest court in the land. . . . The writing is clear, direct, and often poignant. There are photographs of some of the protagonists that add to the down-to-earth character of this study." SLJ

Includes bibliographical references

Barker, Lucius Jefferson, 1928-

Civil liberties and the Constitution; cases and commentaries; [by] Lucius J. Barker, Twiley W. Barker, Jr. Prentice-Hall pa $55.25 **342**
1. United States. Supreme Court 2. Civil rights 3. United States—Constitutional law
First published 1970 (7th edition 1994). Frequently revised

Topics covered include: Civil liberties in a political-social context; religious liberty; freedom of expression, assembly, and association; the rights of the accused; racial and sexual discrimination; political participation; and the right to privacy

Includes bibliography

Bartholomew, Paul Charles, 1907-

Summaries of leading cases on the Constitution; by Paul C. Bartholomew and Joseph F. Menez. Littlefield, Adams pa $21.95 **342**
1. United States. Supreme Court 2. United States—Constitutional law
First published 1954 (13th edition 1990). Periodically revised

This volume presents summaries of major cases concerning constitutional law that have been decided by the Supreme Court since its establishment. It is written for students and laypersons

Beard, Charles Austin, 1874-1948

An economic interpretation of the Constitution of the United States; [by] Charles A. Beard; with a new introduction by Forrest McDonald. Free Press 1986 c1935 liii, 330p map hardcover o.p. paperback available $14.95 **342**
1. United States—Constitutional law 2. United States—Constitutional history 3. United States—Economic conditions
ISBN 0-02-902480-3 (pa) LC 86-7675
A reissue of the title first published 1913 by Macmillan

In this treatise, Beard "examines the motives of the makers of the Constitution and claims that as men of property they were chiefly interested in constructing a charter to protect their wealth." Herzberg. Reader's Ency of Am Lit

Includes bibliography

The Bill of Rights: opposing viewpoints; William Dudley, book editor. Greenhaven Press 1994 311p (American history series) lib bdg $19.95; pa $11.95 **342**
1. United States. Constitution. 1st-10th amendments 2. Civil rights 3. United States—Constitutional law
ISBN 1-56510-088-3 (lib bdg); 1-56510-087-5 (pa) LC 93-4575

This volume presents differing views on various civil rights issues arising from contemporary interpretations of constitutional intent

Includes bibliographical references

Biskupic, Joan

The Supreme Court and individual rights; [by] Joan Biskupic and Elder Witt. 3rd ed. Congressional Quarterly 1997 360p il pa $34.95 **342**
1. United States. Supreme Court 2. Civil rights 3. United States—Constitutional law
ISBN 1-56802-239-5 LC 96-8220
First published 1979

This volume "examines the impact of Court decisions on the rights and freedoms of the individual through the 1995-1996 term. Focusing primarily on the twentieth century, the book provides full coverage of the freedoms outlined in the Bill of Rights, the right to vote and to engage in political participation, the individual's right to due process under the law, and modern equality issues such as affirmative action and rights allowed illegal immigrants to the United States." Publisher's note

Includes glossary and bibliographical references

Bowen, Catherine Drinker, 1897-1973

Miracle at Philadelphia; the story of the Constitutional Convention, May to September, 1787; foreword by Warren E. Burger. Little, Brown 1986 c1966 346p hardcover o.p. paperback available $14.95 **342**
1. United States. Constitutional Convention (1787) 2. United States—Constitutional history
ISBN 0-316-10398-5 (pa) LC 86-205421
"An Atlantic Monthly Press book"
A reissue of the title first published 1966

Bowen, Catherine Drinker, 1897-1973—Continued

"Writing from sources—delegates' letters and diaries; contemporary reports; James Madison's faithful minutes—Catherine Drinker Bowen draws [a] . . . picture of the men, issues and background of the Constitutional Convention held at Philadelphia in the hot summer of 1787." Publ Wkly

Includes bibliographical references

Burger, Warren E., 1907-1995

It is so ordered; a constitution unfolds. Morrow 1995 242p $22   **342**

1. United States—Constitutional history 2. United States—Constitutional law

ISBN 0-688-09595-X   LC 94-36252

Former Chief Justice Burger provides "accounts of 14 cases, mostly fundamental early ones like *Marbury v. Madison*

Corwin, Edward Samuel, 1878-1963

Edward S. Corwin's The Constitution and what it means today; [by] Edward S. Corwin. 14th ed. Princeton Univ. Press 1978 673p pa $21.95 **342**

1. United States. Constitution 2. United States—Constitutional law

ISBN 0-691-02758-7   LC 78-53809

First published 1920

An exposition of the various clauses of the Constitution showing the difference between the original meaning and intention and the present interpretation

Includes bibliographical references

Encyclopedia of the American Constitution; Leonard W. Levy, editor-in-chief; Kenneth L. Karst, associate editor; Dennis J. Mahoney, assistant editor. Macmillan 1986 4v + suppl (1991)   **342**

1. United States—Constitutional law

LC 86-3038

Also available CD-ROM version

Reissued 1990 in a two volume set; available with Supplement I for $350 (ISBN 0-02-897256-2)

"Articles are alphabetically arranged, and run from one paragraph to several pages in length. . . . Entries track the development of issues such as abortion, civil disobedience, and capital punishment. . . . Also included are Supreme Court decisions, key congressional bills, and events, such as the Whiskey Rebellion, which influenced the development of the Constitution. Biographical sketches include . . . Supreme Court Justices, Presidents, framers of the Constitution, and constitutional scholars." SLJ

The Federalist; edited, with introduction and notes, by Jacob E. Cooke. Wesleyan Univ. Press 1982 c1961 xxx, 672p pa $24   **342**

1. United States. Constitution

ISBN 0-8195-6077-4   LC 82-2815

A reissue of the 1961 edition

"From 27 Oct. 1787 to 2 April 1788, 77 essays were published in the semi-weekly 'Independent Journal' of New York, entitled 'The Federalist' and signed first 'A Citizen of New York' then 'Publius.' Eight more were added when they were collected in book form [in 1789]. . . . They were so acute and massively learned in their exposition of the true intent of the Constitution, that even the courts have accepted them as authoritative comments in doubtful cases; and they are held by all the civilized world as among the noblest storehouses of political philosophy in existence. A classic textbook of political science." Ency Americana

Friendly, Fred W.

The Constitution—that delicate balance; [by] Fred W. Friendly, Martha J.H. Elliott. Random House 1984 339p il $24.95   **342**

1. United States. Supreme Court 2. United States—Constitutional law

ISBN 0-394-54074-3   LC 84-42656

"The focus is on the conflicts behind 16 major Supreme Court cases, and each chapter is a lucid, informative account of such controversial issues as abortion, school prayer, the insanity plea and the treatment of illegal aliens. By tracing each conflict back in time . . . the authors allow us to follow its evolution and court efforts to balance individual and societal rights." Publ Wkly

Includes bibliography

Hentoff, Nat

Free speech for me—but not for thee; how the American left and right relentlessly censor each other. HarperCollins Pubs. 1992 405p hardcover o.p. paperback available $13   **342**

1. Freedom of speech 2. Censorship

ISBN 0-06-099510-6 (pa)   LC 92-52550

"An Aaron Asher book"

This is a collection of pieces from the author's weekly columns in The Village Voice and The Washington Post

"Anyone sitting down to read [this book] should be prepared for a hard but rewarding experience. . . . Its importance lies in its accounting, in rich detail, of the major assaults upon our freedom to think, read, write and speak that have taken place since the days of Joseph McCarthy. It is exceptional, too, in that it contains mostly eyewitness material." N Y Times Book Rev

The Living U.S. Constitution. 3rd rev ed, by Jacob W. Landynski. Penguin Bks. 1995 xx, 492p pa $14.95   **342**

1. United States. Supreme Court 2. United States—Constitutional law 3. United States—Constitutional history

ISBN 0-452-01147-7   LC 94-24753

"A Meridian book"

First published 1953 by Praeger

"Historical background, landmark Supreme Court decisions: with introductions, indexed guide, pen portraits of the signers." Title page

Renstrom, Peter G., 1943-

Constitutional law and young adults. 2nd ed rev and updated. ABC-CLIO 1996 497p $55   **342**

1. United States—Constitutional law

ISBN 0-87436-850-2   LC 96-28831

First published 1992

Renstrom, Peter G., 1943—*Continued*
"Assuming the reader is not familiar with federal law, Renstrom painstakingly dissects each legal concept to provide an idea of the evolving status of civil rights and demonstrate the importance of the Constitution and the uniqueness of the U.S. judicial system." Booklist
Includes bibliographical references

The **Supreme** Court and the Constitution; readings in American Constitutional history; edited by Stanley I. Kutler. Norton pa $22.25   **342**
1. United States. Supreme Court 2. United States—Constitutional history
First published 1969 by Houghton Mifflin. Periodically revised
This work includes extracts of judicial cases which have had significance for constitutional law. Arrangement is chronological, further subdivided by topical categories

Vile, John R.
Encyclopedia of constitutional amendments, proposed amendments, and amending issues, 1789-1995. ABC-CLIO 1996 427p lib bdg $60
    342
1. United States—Constitutional law 2. United States—Constitutional history
ISBN 0-87436-783-2   LC 96-19540
"In over 400 alphabetically arranged entries, the author provides a history and analysis of the 27 existing amendments to the U.S. Constitution and the nearly 11,000 amendments that have been proposed. Biographical entries [are included]. . . . Supreme Court decisions . . . are reviewed and explained. Subject-matter essays covering topics such as reproductive rights, slavery, and school prayer add depth and accessibility." Libr J
For a fuller review see: Booklist, Dec. 1, 1996

343   Military, public property, public finance, tax, trade, industrial law

Krohn, Lauren
Consumer protection and the law; a dictionary. ABC-CLIO 1995 358p (Contemporary legal issues) $39.50   **343**
1. Consumer protection
ISBN 0-87436-763-8   LC 95-36285
"Krohn accomplishes encyclopedic treatment of the laws, the jargon, the key concepts, significant individuals, and the history. . . . Court cases are fully cited and bolded references within an entry indicate the item is treated fully elsewhere." Libr J
For a fuller review see: Booklist, May 1, 1996

344   Social, labor, welfare, & related law

Layman, Nancy S., 1942-
Sexual harassment in American secondary schools; a legal guide for administrators, teachers, and students. Contemporary Res. Assocs. 1994 207p $50; pa $18.95   **344**
1. Sexual harassment 2. Secondary education—Law and legislation
ISBN 0-935061-57-6; 0-935061-52-5 (pa)
    LC 93-11323
In this exploration of sexual harassment as it applies to schools the author provides "examples of this type of discriminating behavior, and explains how to file a claim and proceed with a complaint under various acts. . . . Layman also provides information on establishing a policy for school districts to eradicate sexual harassment. In addition, she gives sample policies which could be modified to suit the needs of one's own school district." Voice Youth Advocates
Includes bibliographical references

Marshall, Eliot
Legalization; a debate. Chelsea House 1988 121p il (Encyclopedia of psychoactive drugs) lib bdg $19.95   **344**
1. Drugs—Law and legislation
ISBN 1-55546-229-4   LC 87-23271
"Legalization is debated specifically for marijuana, but a discussion of drugs in general widens the perspective. The history of drug legislation is traced through the Anti-Drug Abuse Act of 1986. Alcohol is covered in detail because aspects of Prohibition are used in arguments both for and against legalization of other drugs." SLJ
Includes bibliography

Tushnet, Mark V., 1945-
Brown v. Board of Education; the battle for integration. Watts 1995 143p il (Historic Supreme Court cases) lib bdg $22   **344**
1. Brown, Oliver 2. Topeka (Kan.). Board of Education 3. Segregation in education 4. African Americans—Civil rights
ISBN 0-531-11230-6   LC 95-13013
Describes the people playing major roles in the battle for desegregation, the smaller court cases that led up to Brown v. The Board of Education, and the results and repercussions of the case
Includes bibliographical references

345   Criminal law

Aymar, Brandt
A pictorial history of the world's greatest trials; from Socrates to Jean Harris; [by] Brandt Aymar and Edward Sagarin. new enl ed. Bonanza Bks. 1985 405p il $12.98   **345**
1. Trials—History
ISBN 0-517-46793-3   LC 84-27413
First published 1974 by Crown with title: Laws and trials that created history

Aymar, Brandt—*Continued*

Commentary on trials that span over two millenia, including those of Socrates, Galileo, Andrew Johnson, Oscar Wilde, Sacco and Vanzetti, Jomo Kenyatta, Eichmann, Leopold and Loeb, Angela Davis, and Jean Harris. The events leading up to the trial, as well as the trial and aftermath, are described, including excerpts of transcripts and photographs

Includes bibliography

Criminal justice: opposing viewpoints; Michael D. Biskup, book editor. Greenhaven Press 1993 213p lib bdg $19.95; pa $11.95   **345**

1. Administration of criminal justice

ISBN 0-89908-624-1 (lib bdg); 0-89908-623-3 (pa)

"Opposing viewpoints series"

Presents opposing viewpoints on such aspects of criminal justice as reforms, the rights of the accused, crime victim's rights, lawyers, and the abuse of police authority

"A well-researched and fact-filled tool for critical thinking. The book challenges readers to examine their own opinions and assumptions by offering carefully balanced writings by prominent spokespeople and professionals in the field." SLJ

Includes bibliography

Criminal sentencing; edited by Robert Emmet Long. Wilson, H.W. 1995 152p (Reference shelf, v67 no1) pa $15   **345**

1. Administration of criminal justice 2. Capital punishment—United States 3. Crime

ISBN 0-8242-0868-4   LC 95-2365

Among the topics addressed in this compilation of articles are: crime among the young, mandatory sentencing, prison expansion, and the death penalty

Includes bibliographical references

√ **Haskins, James, 1941-**

The Scottsboro Boys. Holt & Co. 1994 118p $15.95   **345**

1. Scottsboro case 2. Trials

ISBN 0-8050-2206-6   LC 93-42331

"In 1931 in Alabama, false accusations led to the arrest of nine African-American boys and men for the alleged rapes of two white women. The story of their arrest and consequent trials is . . . documented in this . . . chronicle of racial injustice." Horn Book Guide

"The brief but historically accurate book should be in every school library and young adult collection in public libraries." Voice Youth Advocates

Includes bibliographical references

Wice, Paul B.

Miranda v. Arizona; "You have the right to remain silent--". Watts 1996 158p il (Historic Supreme Court cases) lib bdg $22   **345**

1. Miranda, Ernesto 2. Trials 3. Law—United States

ISBN 0-531-11250-0   LC 95-45284

Wice "begins with the crime for which a young man named Ernest Miranda was accused, the rape and kidnapping of a young woman. . . . He confessed and was eventually tried and convicted. The Supreme Court ruled that since he had not been informed of his rights against self-incrimination and to have a lawyer present, the confession was invalid. The author discusses other aspects of the case, including other court cases involving self-incrimination, the opinions of the Supreme Court justices who overturned the conviction, and the interpretation of the fifth amendment of the U.S. Constitution." SLJ

Includes bibliographical references

346   Private law

Hempelman, Kathleen A.

Teen legal rights; a guide for the '90s. Greenwood Press 1994 236p il $39.95   **346**

1. Youth—Law and legislation

ISBN 0-313-28760-0   LC 93-37509

"Topical chapters, covering everything from emancipation and students' rights to matters of sexual privacy, personal appearance, and treatment in juvenile court, are presented in question-answer form, with a minimum of legal jargon." Booklist

"An outstanding resource for any library which serves the youth of today." Voice Youth Advocates

Includes glossary and bibliographical references

346.04   Property law

Bruwelheide, Janis H., 1948-

The copyright primer for librarians and educators. 2nd ed. American Lib. Assn.; National Educ. Assn. 1995 151p pa $25   **346.04**

1. Fair use (Copyright) 2. Libraries—Law and legislation 3. School libraries—Law and legislation

ISBN 0-8389-0642-7   LC 95-17840

First published 1987 under the authorship of Mary Hutchings Reed

"Brief discussions of key copyright areas and concepts are followed by question-answer sections. . . . The topics range from general copyright information to fair use; copying under Section 108, for classrooms, for reserve rooms to off-air taping and 'home-use only' videocassettes and libraries; databases, computer software, multimedia, and Internet to distance education." Voice Youth Advocates

"Clearly written, packed with information, and well indexed. . . . Appendixes are a gold mine of useful addresses, phone numbers, copyright publications, Internet resources, and landmark court decisions." Libr J

Simpson, Carol Mann, 1949-

Copyright for school libraries; a practical guide. Linworth Pub. 1994 various paging (Professional growth series) pa $19.95   **346.04**

1. Fair use (Copyright) 2. School libraries—Law and legislation

ISBN 0-938865-31-5   LC 93-50802

This book "begins with a brief history of copyright liability and fair use provisions. In separate sections, the author looks at liability and fair use as they apply to print materials, audiovisual works, and computer software. Samples of school district compliance agreements, warning notices (to be posted at photocopiers and other

Simpson, Carol Mann, 1949——*Continued*
duplicating devices), off-air taping logs, and reprint permission requests follow." Publisher's note

"Simpson's tone and attitude are professional, knowledgeable, and geared to a building-level school library media specialist. A must-purchase for school libraries." Booklist

Includes bibliographical references

347 Civil procedure and courts

Abramson, Jeffrey B.
We, the jury; the jury system and the ideal of democracy; [by] Jeffrey Abramson. Basic Bks. 1994 308p hardcover o.p. paperback available $14
347
1. Jury 2. Administration of justice
ISBN 0-465-09116-4 (pa)   LC 94-11580
The author "discusses historical and contemporary court cases that exemplify or nullify a democratic model of consensus through deliberation. He also examines the new mandatory cross-section representation for juries, scientific jury selection, legitimization of state power through juries, and a common justice above social divisions." Libr J
Includes bibliographical references

Baum, Lawrence
The Supreme Court. CQ Press $37.95; pa $24.95
347
1. United States. Supreme Court
First published 1981. (5th edition 1995) Periodically revised
This book provides an introduction to various aspects of the Supreme Court, including the selection of justices, types of cases chosen, and factors influencing the decisions rendered
Includes glossary and bibliography

Jost, Kenneth
The Supreme Court yearbook. Congressional Quarterly $34.95; pa $24.95
347
1. United States. Supreme Court
ISSN 1054-2701
Annual. First published 1991 under the authorship of Joan Biskupic. Current yearbook by Kenneth Jost
A review of the actions of the Supreme Court. Each volume "summarizes every case decided during the [most recent] term, excerpts the most important rulings, and previews the next term's most significant cases. A helpful explanation of how the Court works, a glossary of legal terms, and brief biographies of the justices round out the volumes. A truly unique source." Am Libr

The **Legal** system: opposing viewpoints; Tamara Roleff, book editor. Greenhaven Press 1996 210p lib bdg $19.95; pa $11.95
347
1. Administration of justice 2. Jury
ISBN 1-56510-405-6 (lib bdg); 1-56510-404-8 (pa)
LC 95-49643
"Opposing viewpoints series"
This collection of articles examines the jury system, the civil and criminal justice systems, litigation, and how the media affect the administration of justice
Includes glossary and bibliographical references

Lewis, Anthony, 1927-
Gideon's trumpet. Random House 1964 262p hardcover o.p. paperback available $11
347
1. Gideon, Clarence Earl 2. United States. Supreme Court 3. Law—United States
ISBN 0-679-72312-9 (pa)
An account of the case of a Florida man convicted of burglary which brought about a historic decision of the Supreme Court decreeing that in all states a defendant is entitled to counsel
Includes bibliographical references

Lindop, Edmund
The changing Supreme Court. Watts 1995 176p il (Democracy in action) lib bdg $22.70
347
1. United States. Supreme Court
ISBN 0-531-11224-1   LC 95-13842
Focusing on changes in membership and perspective over the past forty years, this book examines how the Supreme Court has attempted to provide stable interpretation of the Constitution in such issues as abortion, civil rights, due process, capital punishment, and religion
Includes bibliographical references

The **Oxford** companion to the Supreme Court of the United States; editor in chief, Kermit L. Hall; editors, James W. Ely, Jr., Joel B. Grossman, William M. Wiecek. Oxford Univ. Press 1992 xx, 1032p il $55
347
1. United States. Supreme Court
ISBN 0-19-505835-6   LC 92-3863
"An encyclopedia of constitutional law, the Supreme Court, and the American judicial system, with more than 1,000 signed alphabetically arranged entries. Ranging in length from one paragraph to a 30-page History of the Court, articles cover major cases, terms and legal concepts, constitutional law issues, and justices and other historical figures. Illustrated with portraits of justices." Guide to Ref Books. 11th edition

Paddock, Lisa
Facts about the Supreme Court of the United States; historical overview by Paul Barrett. Wilson, H.W. 1996 xxx, 569p il $55
347
1. United States. Supreme Court
ISBN 0-8242-0896-X   LC 95-53202
"A New England Pub. Assocs. book"
A look at the organization, function and history of the Supreme Court. The chronological arrangement places each Court, its justices, and individual cases in historical context. Includes a glossary of legal terms and concepts
Includes bibliography

Patrick, John J.
The young Oxford companion to the Supreme Court of the United States. Oxford Univ. Press 1994 368p il maps $41.75
347
1. United States. Supreme Court
ISBN 0-19-507877-2   LC 93-6467
This volume "profiles all justices from John Jay . . . to Ruth Bader Ginsburg. Also covered are significant cases ranging from early landmarks such as *Marbury v.*

Patrick, John J.—*Continued*
Madison to more recent ones such as *Brown v. Board of Education*. Several 1993 rulings are included. Definitions of terms help explain the operation of the Court, from how cases are accepted to how opinions are written." Book Rep
"Will definitely help answer many court-related reference questions and aid report writers." Voice Youth Advocates
Includes bibliographical references

The **Supreme** Court A to Z; a ready reference encyclopedia; Elder Witt, advisory editor. rev ed. Congressional Quarterly 1994 528p (CQ's encyclopedia of American government) $139; pa $89.95　　　**347**
1. United States. Supreme Court
ISBN 1-56802-053-8; 1-56802-007-4 (pa)
　　　　　　　　　　　　　　　　LC 94-29912

First published 1993
"Contains some 300 brief articles on the Court, including doctrinal issues, procedures, and a few major cases. Biographies of justices are accompanied by portraits. Other illustrations include photographs of litigants whose names have become synonymous with constitutional doctrines. Appendixes provide a Court chronology and the text of the Constitution." Guide to Ref Books. 11th edition

Wice, Paul B.
Gideon v. Wainwright and the right to counsel. Watts 1995 128p il (Historic Supreme Court cases) lib bdg $22　　　**347**
1. Gideon, Clarence Earl 2. Wainwright, Louie L. 3. Legal assistance to the poor
ISBN 0-531-11231-4　　　　　　　LC 95-11290
Discusses the principle of the right to counsel for all defendants, the case of Gideon v. Wainwright, and the significance of the Supreme Court's decision regarding that principle
Includes bibliographical references

Zerman, Melvyn Bernard, 1930-
Beyond a reasonable doubt: inside the American jury system. Crowell 1981 217p il o.p.　　　**347**
1. Jury
　　　　　　　　　　　　　　　　LC 80-2451
The author "describes the way the jury system began in the fourth century B.C. (in Greece) and how it evolved into its present form and function. He uses some actual cases to illustrate both the drama of the trial courtroom and the unpredictability of juries, and he discusses every aspect of the system that a prospective juror might find useful, from the way a jury is chosen to the pronouncement of sentence and the aftermath of a trial." Bull Cent Child Books
Includes bibliography

353　Administration of United States federal and state governments

United States government manual; Office of the Federal Register, National Archives and Records Service, General Services Administration. Superintendent of Docs. pa $33　　　**353**
1. United States—Politics and government—Handbooks, manuals, etc.
ISSN 0092-1904
Annual. First published 1935. Variant title: United States government organization manual
"Official handbook of the Federal government describing the purposes and programs of most Government agencies and listing the top personnel." N Y Public Libr. Ref Books for Child Collect. 2d edition

353.03　President and vice-president

Guide to the presidency; Michael Nelson, editor. 2nd ed. Congressional Quarterly 1996 2v il set $299　　　**353.03**
1. Presidents—United States
ISBN 1-56802-018-X　　　　　　　LC 96-18543
First published 1989 with title: Congressional Quarterly's guide to the presidency
This set covers "presidential origins and development; selection and removal; presidential powers; the president and the public; the White House and the executive branch; the chief executive and Congress, the Supreme Court, and the bureaucracy; and biographies of the presidents and vice presidents." Publisher's note
Includes bibliographical references

The **Inaugural** addresses of twentieth-century American presidents; edited by Halford Ryan. Praeger Pubs. 1993 324p (Praeger series in political communication) $59.95　　　**353.03**
1. Presidents—United States 2. United States—Politics and government—1900-1999 (20th century)
ISBN 0-275-94039-X　　　　　　　LC 92-34950
This volume presents "essays on all 20th-century inaugural addresses. Topics analyzed include the content of each speech, its composition process, the president's delivery of the text, and the public's reaction. . . . Of particular interest are the chapters discussing why Nixon's and Reagan's second addresses, as well as Carter's inaugural, are regarded as failures. Clinton's address did not make it into this volume. Overall, the book is an excellent addition to the field of political communications." Libr J
Includes bibliographical references

Pious, Richard M., 1944-
The young Oxford companion to the presidency of the United States. Oxford Univ. Press 1994 304p il $44.50　　　**353.03**
1. Presidents—United States—Dictionaries 2. United States—Politics and government—Dictionaries
ISBN 0-19-507799-7　　　　　　　LC 93-19908
An alphabetical listing and explanation of terms relating to the Presidency, including the White House, presi-

Pious, Richard M., 1944—*Continued*
dential history, powers, policymaking, agencies, theories, advisors, accountability, and elections. Includes biographical information on the presidents and vice-presidents

"Small black-and-white photos, political cartoons, or drawings accompany many of the articles. Cross-references are abundant. Suggested reading often rounds out specific articles. Time lines, charts, lists of addresses, and a bibliography are appended. An outstanding [volume] for browsing and research." Booklist

The **Presidency** A to Z; a ready reference encyclopedia; Michael Nelson, advisory editor. rev ed. Congressional Quarterly 1994 574p il (CQ's encyclopedia of American government) $139; pa $89.95   **353.03**
1. Presidents—United States—Dictionaries
ISBN 1-56802-056-2; 1-56802-006-6 (pa)
LC 94-17668
First published 1992

"Approximately 300 entries describe the background of the presidents, their public experiences, daily and family life, powers and life in the White House, and deaths. Extensive essays explore concepts relating to the presidency such as Constitutional powers, the budget process, diplomatic activity, the cabinet, and the relationship of the presidency to Congress and the courts." Libr J

The **Presidents** speak; the inaugural addresses of the American presidents from Washington to Clinton; [compiled by] Davis Newton Lott. Holt & Co. 1994 434p il (Henry Holt reference book) $35   **353.03**
1. Presidents—United States
ISBN 0-8050-3305-X
LC 94-9616
First published 1961 with title: The inaugural addresses of the American presidents from Washington to Kennedy

This work provides "a capsule biography of each president, an overview of what was happening in the U.S. and the world at the time of the election and the inauguration, statistical insight into the election results, and a portrait of each president at the time he took office. Most important, however, and what makes this book special, are the annotations of the speeches. . . . *The President's Speak* will be appreciated by anyone doing ready reference, in-depth research, or browsing." Booklist

Includes bibliographical references

Ragsdale, Lyn, 1954-
Vital statistics on the presidency; Washington to Clinton. Congressional Quarterly 1996 455p il $49.95; pa $34.95   **353.03**
1. Presidents—United States
ISBN 1-56802-050-3; 1-56802-049-X (pa)
LC 95-33031
First published 1988 with title: The elusive executive, under the authorship of Gary King and Lyn Ragsdale

This statistical exploration of the presidency contains 160 figures and tables; "they are supplemented by nine interpretive essays on broad themes, such as presidential selection, elections, public opinion, policy making, and relations with Congress. Some of the tables offer comparative data back to the early 1800s, while others focus

on recent presidencies. . . . This very useful reference work will complement the standard sources on American government." Libr J
Includes bibliographical references

Speeches of the American presidents; edited by Janet Podell, Steven Anzovin. Wilson, H.W. 1988 xxv, 820p il $65   **353.03**
1. Presidents—United States 2. Speeches 3. United States—History—Sources
ISBN 0-8242-0761-0
LC 87-29833
This volume "contains 180 speeches of the 40 Presidents, from Washington through Reagan. . . . Most speeches are included in their entirety, while some of the longer ones are excerpted. Each speech is prefaced by date, place, and historical context. . . . These easily accessible speeches will serve as primary sources in fulfillment of teachers' requirements for history assignments." SLJ

353.9   State governments

The **Book** of the states. Council of State Govts. $79   **353.9**
1. State governments
ISSN 0068-0125
Also available CD-ROM version
Biennial. Began publication 1935

"In addition to general articles on various aspects of state government, this source provides many statistical and directory data, the principal state officials, and such information as the nickname, motto, flower, bird, song, and tree of each state." Ref Sources for Small & Medium-sized Libr. 5th edition

355   Military science

Black, Jeremy
The Cambridge illustrated atlas of warfare: Renaissance to revolution, 1492-1792. Cambridge Univ. Press 1996 192p il maps $39.95   **355**
1. Military history 2. Military art and science 3. Renaissance—Maps
ISBN 0-521-47033-1
LC 95-36852
Color maps illustrate this "study of warfare during the early modern period, ranging from the European Renaissance to the American Revolution. . . . Feature boxes describe key events, important military confrontations, individual tacticians, battle strategies and weapons." Publisher's note
Includes bibliographical references

The **Cambridge** illustrated history of warfare; the triumph of the West; edited by Geoffrey Parker. Cambridge Univ. Press 1995 408p il maps $39.95   **355**
1. Military art and science 2. War 3. Western civilization
ISBN 0-521-44073-4
LC 95-15180
"This book is a comprehensive history of the Western (European) way of war, spanning ancient Greece to today's modern methods and policies of destruction. . . .

The Cambridge illustrated history of warfare—
Continued
The text is superbly supported by numerous and handy sidebars providing details, insights, and anecdotes." Libr J

Includes glossary and bibliography

Davis, Paul K., 1952-
Encyclopedia of invasions and conquests from ancient times to the present. ABC-CLIO 1996 443p il maps $60   355
1. Military history—Dictionaries
ISBN 0-87436-782-4   LC 96-49452
"The book is organized chronologically into sections ('The Ancient World,' 'The Age of Empires,' and so on). Within each section, entries are organized alphabetically by the name of the invading/conquering empire. Each entry is numbered; at the beginning of each section is a world or regional map with the site of each invasion marked by the corresponding number. Some entries are broad-brush summaries, others offer detailed accounts of specific battles. All contain interesting information, quotations from primary source documents, or observations from the author. Cross-references, a reference list for each entry, and a comprehensive bibliography are included." Am Ref Books Annu, 1997

Dupuy, R. Ernest (Richard Ernest), 1887-1975
The Harper encyclopedia of military history; from 3500 BC to the present; [by] R. Ernest Dupuy and Trevor N. Dupuy. 4th ed. HarperCollins Pubs. 1993 xxi, 1654p il maps $70
355
1. Military history—Dictionaries
ISBN 0-06-270056-1   LC 92-17853
First published 1970 with title: The encyclopedia of military history
"Wars, warfare, and military affairs are treated in a series of chronologically and geographically arranged chapters. Covers through the late 1980s with a few entries for 1990-91. Exhaustive general index for names and events with separate index sections for battles and sieges and for wars." Guide to Ref Books. 11th edition

Hooper, Nicholas, 1956-
The Cambridge illustrated atlas of warfare: the Middle Ages; [by] Nicholas Hooper & Matthew Bennett. Cambridge Univ. Press 1995 192p il maps $39.95   355
1. Europe—History—476-1492—Maps 2. Military art and science 3. Middle Ages—Maps
ISBN 0-521-44049-1   LC 95-36851
This is a "survey of medieval warfare from the accession of Charlemagne (768) to the end of the third War of the Roses (1487). Geographical coverage is restricted to Western Europe and the Mediterranean basin (including 'Latin Christendom'). The full-color maps of regional campaigns and specific battles are supplemented by informative text, an extensive essay and parallel chronological tables by region." Libr J
For a fuller review see: Booklist, June 1, 1996

How to prepare for the Armed Forces test—ASVAB; Armed Services Vocational Aptitude Battery; compiled by the Editorial Department of Barron's Educational Series, Inc. Barron's Educ. Ser. il pa $12.95   355
1. United States—Armed forces—Examinations
First published 1984. (4th edition 1992) Frequently revised
Cover title: Barron's how to prepare for the ASVAB Armed Forces test
This study guide includes practice examinations and a review of pertinent subject areas

Kagan, Donald
On the origins of war and the preservation of peace. Doubleday 1995 606p maps hardcover o.p. paperback available $15.95   355
1. War 2. Military history
ISBN 0-385-42375-6 (pa)   LC 94-12250
The author examines hostilities between world powers through "five case studies: the Athens-Sparta war, the Second Punic War, World Wars I and II, and the world war that wasn't—the Cuban missile crisis. As causal factors, Kagan emphasizes a 'Thucydidean triad' of honor, fear, and interest. The triad grows out of the inherently anarchial character of international systems, which are fundamentally shifting patterns of power. . . . An incisive series of stimulating studies." Booklist
Includes bibliographical references

Kappraff, Ronald M.
ASVAB basics; [by] Ronald Kappraff, Ronald Bronk. [rev ed] Prentice-Hall 1994 290p il $11
355
1. United States—Armed forces—Examinations
ISBN 0-671-84787-2   LC 93-50770
"An Arco book"
First published 1990
At head of title: Arco
This study guide includes practice examinations and a review of pertinent subject areas

Keegan, John, 1934-
A history of warfare. Knopf 1993 432p il maps $30; pa $15   355
1. Military history 2. War
ISBN 0-394-58801-0; 0-679-73082-6 (pa)
LC 93-14884
The author "examines the origins and nature of warfare, the ethos of the primitive and modern warrior and the development of weapons and defenses from the battle of Megiddo (1469 B.C.) into the nuclear age." Publ Wkly
"I do not know a work in which such an encyclopedic range of military knowledge is so well arranged, for while the general outline is chronological, Mr. Keegan does not hesitate to leap the centuries and continents to illustrate a point or make a telling comparison." Natl Rev
Includes bibliography

Stanley, Sandra Carson
Women in the military. Messner 1993 138p il
lib bdg $14.98; pa $8.95   355
1. Women in the armed forces 2. United States—
Armed forces
ISBN 0-671-75549-8 (lib bdg); 0-671-75550-1 (pa)
                                   LC 93-22312
"A history of females serving in wars and a discussion
of the development of women's service units in the
Navy, Army, Air Force, Marines, and Coast Guard. Information on the requirements and roles of enlisted personnel, officers, and service academies includes entrance
levels, salaries, duties, restrictions on females, and advancement potential. . . . This is a detailed, well-
documented look at military service and is an excellent
place to begin research on the topic." SLJ
Includes glossary and bibliographical references

Toffler, Alvin
War and anti-war; survival at the dawn of the
21st century; [by] Alvin and Heidi Toffler. Little,
Brown 1993 302p $22.95   355
1. Military art and science
ISBN 0-316-85024-1   LC 93-20789
Also available in paperback from Warner Bks.
"Seeing the phenomena of war as related to the level
of technology and production in society, [the authors] focus on the 'Third Wave' form of war as exemplified by
the Gulf War. . . . [They] discuss how the new production technology has transformed war from the 'Second
Wave' warfare (i.e, the Vietnam-era military) to a new
era of 'smart bombs' and 'intelligent' weapons systems.
. . . Despite its occasional glibness, the Tofflers' work
is recommended as a stimulus to thinking about the future of global military and political conflict." Libr J
Includes bibliographical references

Warfare in the ancient world; edited and
introduced by Sir John Hackett. Facts on File
1990 c1989 256p il maps $35   355
1. Military art and science 2. Military history
ISBN 0-8160-2459-6   LC 90-31106
"Coverage extends to all regions of the ancient world
and includes period-by-period analyses of all facets of
warfare, among them: the organization, tactics, armor,
and weaponry of armies." Publisher's note
Includes bibliographical references

Warry, John, 1916-
Warfare in the classical world; an illustrated
encyclopedia of weapons, warriors, and warfare in
the ancient civilisations of Greece and Rome.
University of Okla. Press 1995 224p il maps pa
$19.95   355
1. Military art and science 2. Military history
ISBN 0-8061-2794-5   LC 95-18643
A reissue of the title first published 1980 by St. Martin's Press
"The many and various technologies of war developed
and employed by the Greeks and Romans are shown
along with the political and social arenas of the times.
. . . Famous leaders—Alexander the Great, Julius Caesar, Bulla, Hannibal, and Pompey—are presented in
mini-biographies with synopses of conditions that provoked war. . . . Useful for history and classical studies,
and a terrific read." SLJ

355.8 Military equipment and supplies

Bull, Stephen
20th-century arms and armor; foreword by
Harry G. Summers. Facts on File 1996 224p il $35
                                         355.8
1. Military weapons 2. Armor
ISBN 0-8160-3349-8   LC 95-12020
Text and numerous illustrations "document the development of light weaponry from the end of the nineteenth
century to the present day. In seven chapters, author Stephen Bull discusses each major combat situation and the
effect our growing grasp on technology has had on the
weaponry involved." Publisher's note
Includes bibliographical references

An historical guide to arms & armor; edited by
Tony North. Facts on File 1991 224p il $35
                                         355.8
1. Weapons 2. Armor
ISBN 0-8160-2620-3   LC 91-36681
The author "has compiled an evolutionary history of
small arms (swords, knives, pistols, and rifles) and armor
(helmets and body armor) beginning with the Graeco-
Roman world and ending with the advent of World War
I. The history is supported with over 300 photographs,
mostly from works of art and individual pieces in European art museums." Libr J

356 Foot forces and warfare

Sullivan, George
Elite warriors; the special forces of the United
States and its allies. Facts on File 1995 132p il
$19.95   356
1. Armed forces
ISBN 0-8160-3110-X   LC 94-41247
"Six chapters of this book are devoted to the specialized military units of the United States, with one each
for Great Britain, Germany and Israel. The remaining
chapter covers special forces of five Western European
nations. Descriptions of each unit include its military
mission, historical background, and rigorous training.
Stories of successful actions undertaken by that unit are
provided." Book Rep
"Excellent for reports and a much needed addition on
military science." SLJ
Includes bibliographical references

358 Air and other specialized forces and warfare

Taylor, C. L.
Chemical and biological warfare; [by] C.L.
Taylor and L.B. Taylor, Jr. rev ed. Watts 1992
128p il lib bdg $22.70   358
1. Chemical warfare 2. Biological warfare
ISBN 0-531-13029-0   LC 92-17083
"An Impact book"

Taylor, C. L.—*Continued*

First published 1985

This book includes "Saddam Hussein's use of chemical and biological (CB) weapons against the Kurds, the threat of the weapons' use in the Persian Gulf conflict, and measures taken in the past two years to eliminate CB weapons production and deployment. . . . The subject is marvelous for debate or for informational or persuasive speeches, and the thoroughly documented text, which includes a detailed bibliography, is a good place for students to begin their research." Booklist

358.4   Air forces and warfare

Flintham, Victor

Air wars and aircraft; a detailed record of air combat, 1945 to the present. Facts on File 1990 415p il maps $40   **358.4**

1. Military aeronautics 2. Military airplanes 3. Military history

ISBN 0-8160-2356-5   LC 89-23382

This "reference work presents capsule descriptions of every armed conflict of the postwar era in which air power played a part. . . . Political backgrounds as well as air operations are given. The material is accurate and highly detailed. . . . Each section concludes with a technical section on aircraft, including colors and markings." Libr J

Includes glossary and bibliographical references

359   Sea (Naval) forces and warfare

Symonds, Craig L.

The Naval Institute historical atlas of the U.S. Navy; cartography by William J. Clipson. Naval Inst. Press 1995 241p il maps $45   **359**

1. United States—Naval history—Maps

ISBN 1-55750-797-X   LC 94-22911

This naval atlas "is divided into 10 sections, covering from the American Revolution to the Gulf War. . . . Good, brief coverage of important naval battles accounts for most of the discussion, but the author also suggests political concerns serving to impede or expedite development of the U.S. naval force from its beginnings in October 1775. . . . Entries are based on sound scholarship, reflecting the author's disinterestedness, and he is able to make complex operations understandable and interesting to laypersons." Booklist

Van der Vat, Dan

Stealth at sea; the history of the submarine. Houghton Mifflin 1995 c1994 374p $30   **359**

1. Submarines

ISBN 0-395-65242-1   LC 94-40105

"Covering the early development of submersible craft in a prologue and nuclear submarines (which he considers radioactive dinosaurs in the post-cold war era) in an epilogue, van der Vat focuses most of the book on the two world wars." Booklist

The author "has written a comprehensive volume that will delight submarine buffs." Publ Wkly

Includes bibliographical references

361   General social problems and welfare

Meltzer, Milton, 1915-

Who cares? millions do—a book about altruism. Walker & Co. 1994 164p il $15.95; lib bdg $16.85   **361**

1. Altruism 2. Social action 3. Voluntarism

ISBN 0-8027-8324-4; 0-8027-8325-2 (lib bdg)

LC 94-4082

Profiles of "altruistic organizations such as CARE, the Peace Corps, Habitat for Humanity, and Volunteers of America as well as individual humanitarians such as Oskar Schindler, Eugene Lang (who promised college educations to 61 New York sixth-graders), and Jean-Henri Dunant (founder of the Red Cross) are all gathered together in a single volume." Booklist

This "work may be the best and most comprehensive history of voluntarism ever written for young adults." Voice Youth Advocates

Includes bibliographical references

361.3   Social work

Fiffer, Steve

50 ways to help your community; a handbook for change; [by] Steve Fiffer and Sharon Sloan Fiffer. Doubleday 1994 205p pa $7.95   **361.3**

1. Voluntarism 2. Social action

ISBN 0-385-47234-X   LC 93-37989

"A Main Street book"

This work contains "profiles of innovative volunteer programs that have been initiated by ordinary citizens that can be easily replicated. Topics include: Individual and Community Initiatives, Student and School Initiatives and Employee and Corporate Initiatives." Publisher's note

361.6   Governmental welfare action

Kronenwetter, Michael

Welfare state America; safety net or social contract? Watts 1993 127p il lib bdg $22.70   **361.6**

1. Public welfare

ISBN 0-531-13010-X   LC 92-35880

"An Impact book"

Examines the welfare system in the United States from its inception during the 1930s to the present, discussing its various programs, problems that have occurred, and efforts to reform it

"Students looking for a brief, clearly written history of welfare and a discussion of its pro's and con's will find this a useful resource." Voice Youth Advocates

Includes bibliography

LeVert, Marianne
The welfare system; help or hindrance to the poor? Millbrook Press 1995 112p il (Issue and debate) lib bdg $16.40 **361.6**
1. Public welfare 2. United States—Social conditions
ISBN 1-56294-455-X   LC 94-21815
The author "begins by outlining the American system of welfare from colonial times to the signing of the Social Security Act by Roosevelt in 1935. Current government assistance programs, especially the highly publicized Aid to Families with Dependent Children (AFDC), are explained. Societal issues including single-parent families, teenage pregnancy, drug addiction, racism and workfare are analyzed, as are proposed reforms." Book Rep

This "is a remarkably clear, balanced, and comprehensive look at the hot topic of welfare reform." Booklist

Includes glossary and bibliographical references

361.7 Private welfare action. Fund raising

Fremon, Celeste
Father Greg and the homeboys; the extraordinary journey of Father Greg Boyle and his work with the Latino gangs of East L.A. Hyperion 1995 307p $24.95 **361.7**
1. Boyle, Gregory J. 2. Church work with youth 3. Juvenile delinquency 4. Gangs 5. Los Angeles (Calif.)—Social conditions
ISBN 0-7868-6089-8   LC 94-45196
The author describes Father Boyle's "efforts to redirect lives: finding jobs and decent alternative schooling and offering unqualified support and love for kids whose homes are so emotionally impoverished or destructive that gang affiliation is a surrogate family tie. . . . Interspersed with the descriptive narrative are first-person vignettes from some of the young people." Libr J

"This is a heartfelt study of the gangland culture and a tribute to a man who has had a measure of success redeeming some of its members." Booklist

362.1 Physical illness. Medical care

Burkett, Elinor
The gravest show on earth; America in the age of AIDS. Houghton Mifflin 1995 399p $24.95 **362.1**
1. AIDS (Disease)
ISBN 0-395-74537-3   LC 95-9021
"Burkett critiques the roles of scientists, physicians, politicians, gay activists, fundamentalists, pharmaceutical companies, and media figures as they jump on the AIDS bandwagon for personal and political advancement." Libr J

This is "acerbic, compelling and morally acute." Publ Wkly

Includes bibliographical references

Corea, Gena
The invisible epidemic; the story of women and AIDS. HarperCollins Pubs. 1992 356p il hardcover o.p. paperback available $12 **362.1**
1. AIDS (Disease) 2. Women—Diseases
ISBN 0-06-092191-9 (pa)   LC 91-58369
The author "charges that the medical establishment in this country has vastly underreported and misdiagnosed cases of AIDS in women, thereby shortening the lives of infected women and falsely suggesting to the rest of the female population—especially middle-class women—that their chance of contracting the disease is relatively small." N Y Times Book Rev

Includes bibliographical references

Ford, Michael Thomas
The voices of AIDS; twelve unforgettable people talk about how AIDS has changed their lives. Morrow Junior Bks. 1995 225p $15; pa $6.99 **362.1**
1. AIDS (Disease)
ISBN 0-688-05322-X; 0-688-05323-8 (pa)
LC 95-10629
This book contains "personal interviews with YAs who are HIV-positive, friends and relatives of AIDS patients, and AIDS educators and activists. Readers will be inspired by the determination and tenacity of those who are speaking out and their dedication to this critical cause. Between the interviews are brief passages of information about HIV and AIDS." SLJ

Includes bibliographical references

Freudenheim, Ellen
Healthspeak; a complete dictionary of America's health care system. Facts on File 1996 310p $35
362.1
1. Medical care—Dictionaries
ISBN 0-8160-3210-6   LC 95-10965
"Over 2,000 nonclinical terms, ranging over many issues and industries, from AIDS to insurance, public health to pharmaceuticals, law to medicine, from managed care to mental health are included in this book. While most of the terms are briefly defined, several hundred are treated in essay form." Introduction

Health care in America: opposing viewpoints; Carol Wekesser, book editor. Greenhaven Press 1994 264p lib bdg $19.95; pa $11.95 **362.1**
1. Medical care 2. Health insurance
ISBN 1-56510-135-9 (lib bdg); 1-56510-134-0 (pa)
LC 93-30963
"Opposing viewpoints series"
Replaces The Health crisis: opposing viewpoints, published 1989 under the editorship of Bonnie Szumski
Various aspects of American health care are discussed including the health care crisis, the role of physicians, alternative medicine, health care reform, and increased regulation

Includes bibliography

Kaufman, Miriam

Easy for you to say; Q & As for teens living with chronic illness or disability. Key Porter Bks.; distributed by Firefly Bks. (Buffalo) 1995 292p pa $15.95   **362.1**

1. Diseases 2. Physically handicapped
ISBN 1-55013-619-4

This work "aimed exclusively at teens who are disabled or who have a chronic illness, focuses on individual needs. Written by a Canadian physician who works with adolescents, it is filled with very personal, even courageous questions from teens with varied medical conditions—from spina bifida to cystic fibrosis, to kidney disease. There are a few fairly general chapters—on family dynamics, friendship, and recreation. But the best sections concern medical issues and sexuality." Booklist

Kelly, Pat

Coping when you or a friend is HIV-positive. Rosen Pub. Group 1995 118p $15.95   **362.1**

1. AIDS (Disease)
ISBN 0-614-05422-2   LC 95-8556

"After a brief explanation of the syndrome, Kelly talks about myths and facts and explains how to be tested and what the results mean. She gives suggestions about dealing with health-care professionals, friends, and relatives. She discusses responsibilities and rights, general health tips, treatment, and prevention." SLJ

The author "addresses a weighty topic in clear, non-judgmental language. Information, resources, and reassurance are provided for teens and adults. Case studies personalize an important text which should be readily available to all teenagers." Voice Youth Advocates

Includes bibliographical references

Landau, Elaine

Alzheimer's disease. Watts 1996 112p il lib bdg $22   **362.1**

1. Alzheimer's disease
ISBN 0-531-11268-3   LC 95-48848

"A Venture book"

"The author opens with true stories, some ending tragically, and continues with questions and answers and descriptions of the stages of the progressive disease—loss of memory, panic, paranoia, and decline in physical condition. Landau also describes treatment currently used. . . . A major part of the book discusses research concerning the cause of the illness and treatments that may help to retard its progress." Booklist

"The writing is crisp and well organized. . . . The material will be useful for reports as well as for families touched by the disease." SLJ

Includes bibliographical references

LeVert, Suzanne

Teens face to face with chronic illness. Messner 1993 129p hardcover o.p. paperback available $7.95   **362.1**

1. Diseases
ISBN 0-671-74541-7 (pa)   LC 92-45819

This book presents "profiles of 13 young people who deal with a variety of chronic illnesses including hemo-philia, HIV, arthritis, asthma, cancer, leukemia, diabetes, epilepsy, and heart disease. The discussion is divided into four parts, the first of which outlines the nature of the diseases. Other sections present information about daily challenges relating to parents, siblings, friends, and members of the opposite sex, as well as self-esteem and dealing with the attitudes of others." SLJ

Includes glossary and bibliography

Sherrow, Victoria

The U.S. health care crisis; the fight over access, quality, and cost. Millbrook Press 1994 144p il (Issue and debate) lib bdg $16.40   **362.1**

1. Medical care—Costs
ISBN 1-56294-364-2   LC 93-51508

The author outlines "the history of hospitals and medical care in the United States and the way their improvement has led to higher costs. The debates over access to health care and whether or not it is a 'right' are explored, and Sherrow details the various attempts to contain costs through the use of HMOs and medical plans. The concluding chapter discusses the (recently defeated) Clinton health care plan." Bull Cent Child Books

"While the nature of much of this material will date quickly, it provides a good solid overview of the health care crisis, how it evolved, and foreign models which may provide future direction." Voice Youth Advocates

Includes bibliographical references

Shilts, Randy

And the band played on; politics, people, and the AIDS epidemic. St. Martin's Press 1987 xxiii, 630p o.p.; Penguin Bks. paperback available $16.95   **362.1**

1. AIDS (Disease)
ISBN 0-14-011369-X (pa)   LC 87-16528

A "chronicle of the five-year political, scientific, and social battle to force government, the medical and blood-bank establishments, the news media, and gay men to take AIDS seriously." Booklist

"Shilts successfully weaves comprehensive investigative reporting and commercial page-turner pacing, political intrigue and personal tragedy into a landmark work." Publ Wkly

Includes bibliographical references

The **Spread** of AIDS; Daniel A. Leone, editor. Greenhaven Press 1997 96p (At issue) lib bdg $12.95; pa $7.95   **362.1**

1. AIDS (Disease)
ISBN 1-56510-538-9 (lib bdg); 1-56510-537-0 (pa)
                                   LC 96-42912

"This collection of 16 uncut articles, drawn mainly from recent books and periodicals, focuses on controversies surrounding measures that are being taken (or are being considered) to control the AIDS epidemic. . . . Each article contains an introduction establishing the authority of the author or source and a brief statement of the issue to be discussed in subsequent text. Articles are followed by bibliographic references and a list of organizations to contact for further information." SLJ

362.2   Mental and emotional illnesses and disturbances

Mental illness: opposing viewpoints; William Barbour, editor. Greenhaven Press 1995 312p il lib bdg $19.95; pa $11.95   **362.2**
1. Mental illness
ISBN 1-56510-209-6 (lib bdg); 1-56510-208-8 (pa)
LC 94-4977

"Opposing viewpoints series"

This anthology of articles examines mental illness, its causes and treatment. Includes chapters on society's response to the homeless mentally ill and the legal system's role in dealing with mental illness

Includes glossary and bibliography

Suicide; edited by Robert Emmet Long. Wilson, H.W. 1995 162p (Reference shelf, v67 no2) pa $15   **362.2**
1. Suicide
ISBN 0-8242-0869-2   LC 95-11850

The articles in the first section of this compilation discuss adolescent and young adult suicide. The second section covers Nancy Cruzan and the Right to Die movement. The last two sections discuss Dr. Jack Kevorkian and assisted suicide

Includes bibliographical references

Suicide: opposing viewpoints; Michael D. Biskup, book editor; Carol Wekesser, assistant editor. Greenhaven Press 1992 188p il lib bdg $22.50; pa $11.95   **362.2**
1. Suicide
ISBN 0-89908-193-2 (lib bdg); 0-89908-168-1 (pa)
LC 92-6093

"Opposing viewpoints series"

Presents opposing viewpoints on various aspects of suicide, including individual rights, physician-assisted suicide, and prevention

"This is a superb source for reports, discussion, and debates. YAs will find it stimulating and thought-provoking." SLJ

Includes bibliographies

362.29   Substance abuse

Alcoholism; Carol Wekesser, book editor. Greenhaven Press 1994 250p (Current controversies) lib bdg $19.95; pa $11.95   **362.29**
1. Alcoholism
ISBN 1-56510-074-3 (lib bdg); 1-56510-073-5 (pa)
LC 93-22396

"Discussions address whether or not alcohol dependency is a disease, the most effective treatments, whether advertisements encourage abuse, and if adult children of alcoholics benefit from recovery groups. Since opinions presented vary widely, the information will be valuable to debaters and others seeking support for one of the positions on the questions presented." SLJ

Includes bibliography

Berger, Gilda
Alcoholism and the family. Watts 1993 123p (Changing family) lib bdg $22.70   **362.29**
1. Alcoholism 2. Family
ISBN 0-531-12548-3   LC 93-10898

This book "is divided into chapters that describe what alcoholism is, the causes of alcoholism, the effect alcoholic parents have on their children as well as chapters on adult children of alcoholics and how alcoholism contributes to a dysfunctional family. The last chapters include information on prevention, treatment, and recovery." Voice Youth Advocates

"A comprehensive, clearly written survey of the illness." SLJ

Includes bibliography

Chemical dependency: opposing viewpoints; Carol Wekesser, book editor. Greenhaven Press 1997 192p lib bdg $19.95; pa $11.95   **362.29**
1. Substance abuse
ISBN 1-56510-552-4 (lib bdg); 1-56510-551-6 (pa)
LC 96-48030

"Opposing viewpoints series"

Replaces the edition published 1991 under the editorship of Charles P. Cozic and Karin Swisher

Articles debate the following issues: How great a problem is chemical dependency? What causes chemical dependency? What treatments are effective for chemical dependency? Should drug laws be reformed?

Includes bibliographical references

Drug abuse: opposing viewpoints; Karin L. Swisher, book editor; Katie de Koster, assistant editor. Greenhaven Press 1994 261p il lib bdg $19.95; pa $11.95   **362.29**
1. Drug abuse
ISBN 1-56510-060-3 (lib bdg); 1-56510-059-X (pa)
LC 93-12375

"Opposing viewpoints series"

Replaces the edition published 1988 under the editorship of Julie S. Bach

This title "examines ways that drug abuse, and the resulting social problems, might be eradicated. The five chapters each contain four to six articles written by experts in such fields as medicine, government, law, education, and business. . . . This book offers a useful, up-to-date presentation on an issue of great importance." Voice Youth Advocates

Includes bibliography

Encyclopedia of drugs and alcohol; Jerome H. Jaffe, editor in chief. Macmillan Lib. Ref. USA 1995 4v il set $340   **362.29**
1. Drug abuse—Dictionaries 2. Substance abuse—Dictionaries 3. Alcoholism—Dictionaries
ISBN 0-02-897185-X   LC 95-2321

This work presents 725 articles on "legal and illegal drug and alcohol use and abuse. . . . [Topics discussed include] the history of the use of various substances, specific substances and their chemical properties, treatment programs and activist groups, and the societal impact of such phenomena as addicted babies, drugs in the workplace, substance abuse and AIDS, and drunken driving. . . . This encyclopedia contains material on the topics students are interested in researching and covers many aspects of those subjects." Booklist

Landau, Elaine

Hooked; talking about addiction. Millbrook Press 1995 64p il lib bdg $15.90   **362.29**

1. Substance abuse

ISBN 1-56294-469-X   LC 94-41680

A "discussion of addictive behavior that explains causes and effects and the recovery process. In first-person confessions, teens talk about experiences not only with alcohol, drugs, and gambling, but with excessive studying and exercising." SLJ

"The grainy, dark photographs add little, but the anecdotal text is a good jumping-off point for students who want to learn about addictions. A list of further reading and addresses of help organizations are included." Booklist

Teenage drinking. Enslow Pubs. 1994 104p il (Issues in focus) lib bdg $18.95   **362.29**

1. Teenagers—Alcohol use 2. Alcoholism

ISBN 0-89490-575-9   LC 94-40

The author "covers drinking and driving, factors that predispose teens to alcoholism, available assistance, and warning signs to which peers and families should be alert. She provides information on current efforts by schools, federal, state, and local agencies to prevent and to treat teen alcoholism. . . . The text is well organized and easy to understand. There is a good mix of statistical and medical information and human-interest material. . . . This title is highly readable and informative." SLJ

Includes bibliography

Seixas, Judith S.

Children of alcoholism; a survivor's manual; by Judith S. Seixas and Geraldine Youcha. Crown 1985 c1984 208p o.p.; HarperCollins Pubs. paperback available $12   **362.29**

1. Children of alcoholics 2. Alcoholics

ISBN 0-06-097020-0 (pa)   LC 84-17450

The authors "describe the loneliness and fear of children growing up in an alcoholic family. . . . They also discuss overt behaviors a child may be exposed to or witness, such as spouse and child abuse, incest, and other forms of violence. They deal as well with how children try to understand the 'why' of what has happened, and how they develop coping skills and may finally get help. A useful addition to a fast growing area of self-help literature." Libr J

Includes bibliography

Statistics on alcohol, drug & tobacco use; Timothy L. Gall and Daniel M. Lucas, editors; Carl G. Leukefeld, contributing editor. Gale Res. 1996 238p il $55   **362.29**

1. Drinking of alcoholic beverages 2. Drug abuse 3. Tobacco habit

ISBN 0-7876-0526-3   LC 95-32413

"A selection of statistical charts, graphs, and tables about alcohol, drug, and tobacco use from a variety of published sources with explanatory comments." Title page

"This compilation of statistics on the prevalence and adverse effects of substance abuse is divided into three sections—one each for alcohol, tobacco, and illegal drugs. . . . There is no other reference work that combines all of these topics in one, easy-to-use volume; thus it may prove useful for high school or small public libraries." Libr J

Includes glossary

362.4   Problems of and services to people with physical disabilities

Cheney, Glenn Alan

Teens with physical disabilities; real-life stories of meeting the challenges. Enslow Pubs. 1995 112p il (Issues in focus) lib bdg $18.95   **362.4**

1. Physically handicapped

ISBN 0-89490-625-9   LC 94-3603

"A collection of autobiographical sketches by teens living with the challenges of physical disabilities. Rheumatoid arthritis, muscular dystrophy, blindness, deafness, cerebral palsy, and paralysis resulting from a gunshot wound are all discussed." SLJ

"A tremendously valuable source of information for learning about the experiences of teens with physical disabilities." Voice Youth Advocates

Includes bibliography

362.5   Problems of and services to the poor

Fantasia, Rick

Homelessness: a sourcebook; [by] Rick Fantasia and Maurice Isserman. Facts on File 1994 356p il $45   **362.5**

1. Homeless persons—Dictionaries

ISBN 0-8160-2571-1   LC 92-37762

"This sourcebook is primarily a dictionary, explaining 500 items, persons, policies, organizations, court decisions, laws, etc., relevant to the topic of homelessness. Lengthy appendixes list organizations, some 1990 census figures, and an 84-page report, 'A Status Report of Hunger and Homelessness in America's Cities: 1993.'" Libr J

For a fuller review see: Booklist, Oct. 15, 1994

Hombs, Mary Ellen

American homelessness; a reference handbook. 2nd ed. ABC-CLIO 1994 272p (Contemporary world issues) $39.50   **362.5**

1. Homeless persons

ISBN 0-87436-725-5   LC 94-33788

First published 1990

This volume "consists of a chronology from December 1976 to March 1994, biographical sketches, facts and statistics, and federal legislation. Also included are lists of organizations, associations, government agencies, and print and non-print resources." Book Rep

Includes glossary

The **Homeless:** opposing viewpoints; Tamara Roleff, book editor. Greenhaven Press 1995 240p il lib bdg $19.95; pa $11.95   **362.5**

1. Homeless persons

ISBN 1-56510-361-0 (lib bdg); 1-56510-360-2 (pa)
LC 95-19809

"Opposing viewpoints series"

The Homeless: opposing viewpoints—*Continued*
Replaces the edition published 1990 under the editorship of Lisa Orr

This collection groups essays into five chapters: Is homelessness a serious problem? What are the causes of homelessness? How can society help the homeless? What housing options would benefit the homeless? How can government help the homeless?

"An indispensable companion to the number of other titles currently available on the subject." SLJ

Includes bibliographical references

The Homeless problem; edited by Matthew A. Kraljic. Wilson, H.W. 1992 162p (Reference shelf, v64 no2) pa $15   **362.5**
1. Homeless persons
ISBN 0-8242-0826-9   LC 92-5909

A collection of articles looking at the problem of homelessness from a variety of perspectives. Causes of homelessness and various suggestions for social and political responses are suggested

Includes bibliographical references

Poverty: opposing viewpoints; David L. Bender & Bruno Leone, series editors; Katie de Koster, book editor; Bruno Leone, assistant editor. Greenhaven Press 1994 288p il lib bdg $19.95; pa $11.95   **362.5**
1. Poverty 2. United States—Economic conditions 3. Public welfare
ISBN 1-56510-066-2 (lib bdg); 1-56510-065-4 (pa)
LC 93-22397
"Opposing viewpoints series"

Replaces the edition published 1988 under the editorship of William Dudley

A collection of articles debating issues related to poverty in America, including its causes, how it affects minorities, government policies, and how poverty can be reduced

Includes bibliographical references

362.7   Problems of and services to young people

Adoption: opposing viewpoints; Andrew Harnack, book editor. Greenhaven Press 1995 306p lib bdg $19.95; pa $11.95   **362.7**
1. Adoption
ISBN 1-56510-213-4 (lib bdg); 1-56510-212-6 (pa)
LC 94-41043
"Opposing viewpoints series"

Debates issues concerning the adoption of children, presenting arguments both in favor of and against adopting

Includes bibliography

Aitkens, Maggi
Kerry, a teenage mother; photographs by Rob Levine. Lerner Publs. 1994 48p il lib bdg $18.95
362.7
1. Teenage mothers
ISBN 0-8225-2556-9   LC 94-897
"Aitkens describes 18-year-old Kerry's life since her daughter [Vanessa's] birth 15 months earlier, reflecting

both the positive and the negative changes." SLJ

"This book is a great value to teenagers, single parents, teachers, social workers, psychologists, and other professionals in the health care field." Sci Books Films

Includes bibliographical references

America's children: opposing viewpoints; Carol Wekesser, book editor. Greenhaven Press 1991 263p il lib bdg $19.95; pa $11.95   **362.7**
1. Child welfare 2. Children—United States 3. United States—Social conditions 4. Education—United States
ISBN 0-89908-486-9 (lib bdg); 0-89908-461-3 (pa)
LC 90-24085
"Opposing viewpoints series"

Experts debate what school policies would help children, how to protect children from abuse, the effects of working parents on children, and if children are disproportionately poor in the United States

Includes bibliographical references

Bode, Janet
Kids still having kids; people talk about teen pregnancy; art by Stan Mack. Watts 1992 191p il lib bdg $22.70   **362.7**
1. Unmarried mothers 2. Teenage pregnancy 3. Teenage mothers
ISBN 0-531-11132-6   LC 92-14175
First published 1980 with title: Kids having kids

Presents interviews with teenage mothers and provides information about adoption, parenting, abortion, and foster care

"The information is medically correct and up-to-date, emotionally on target, and delivered in an easy to understand manner." Voice Youth Advocates

Includes glossary and bibliography

Child abuse: opposing viewpoints; Katie de Koster, book editor; Karin L. Swisher, assistant editor. Greenhaven Press 1994 288p il lib bdg $19.95; pa $11.95   **362.7**
1. Child abuse
ISBN 1-56510-056-5 (lib bdg); 1-56510-055-7 (pa)
LC 93-9240
"Opposing viewpoints series"

A discussion of issues related to child abuse, including what causes this form of abuse, and is it possible to justly prosecute it in the courts

"Illustrated with a few editorial cartoons and some graphs, thought-provokingly written with objectivity, and appended with lists of organizations to contact and questions for further discussion, *Child Abuse* is a solid work on a timely topic." SLJ

Includes bibliographical references

Davies, Nancy Millichap
Foster care. Watts 1994 112p il (Changing family) lib bdg $22.70   **362.7**
1. Foster home care
ISBN 0-531-11081-8   LC 93-23237
"This book surveys the many aspects of foster care: the reasons for foster care, the duties of foster parents, the types of foster homes, the caseworkers and the laws governing foster care." Publisher's note

Includes bibliographical references

Dolan, Edward F., 1924-
Child abuse. rev ed. Watts 1992 127p lib bdg
$22.70   **362.7**
1. Child abuse
ISBN 0-531-11042-7   LC 92-11355
First published 1980
Investigates the various forms of child abuse and the
sources of help that are available for victims and abusers
"This book should be of help to anyone seeking infor-
mation whether for general information, a report or per-
sonal reasons." Voice Youth Advocates
Includes bibliography

Teenagers and compulsive gambling. Watts
1994 140p lib bdg $22.70   **362.7**
1. Compulsive gambling
ISBN 0-531-11100-8   LC 93-31956
In this book, "which includes a history of gambling in
the world and the current state of gambling in the U.S.,
the author describes the personality traits of the compulsive gambler and, using individual stories, shows how
one can recover from this addiction." Publisher's note
Includes bibliographical references

Frankel, Bernard
Straight talk about teenage suicide; [by] Bernard
Frankel and Rachel Kranz. Facts on File 1994
138p $16.95   **362.7**
1. Suicide
ISBN 0-8160-2987-3   LC 93-38381
"Topics covered include 'cluster' suicides, myths, danger signals, and appropriate responses by peers. Also discussed is the effect on teens of the communal
rootlessness and personal isolation of contemporary society." SLJ
"This book clearly examines the concerns of today's
teens without preaching, judging or talking down. It is a
timely and valuable addition to any library serving young
people." Book Rep

Gravelle, Karen
Where are my birth parents? a guide for teenage
adoptees; [by] Karen Gravelle & Susan Fischer.
Walker & Co. 1993 132p $14.95; lib bdg $15.95;
pa $8.95   **362.7**
1. Birthparents 2. Adoption
ISBN 0-8027-8257-4; 0-8027-8258-2 (lib bdg);
0-8027-7453-9 (pa)   LC 92-34586
Discusses how and why adopted children may try to
locate and get to know their birth parents and examines
possible psychological benefits and problems associated
with the process
"This is a straightforward, easily readable, and reas-
suring book that many young people will find helpful to
read even if they choose not to search as teens, or at all.
An extensive list of search and support groups, registries,
and counseling centers is included, along with a bibliography and index." Bull Cent Child Books

Hayden, Torey L.
Ghost girl; the true story of a child in peril and
the teacher who saved her. Little, Brown 1991
307p o.p.; Avon Bks. paperback available $5.99
                        362.7
1. Child abuse 2. Satanism
ISBN 0-380-71681-X (pa)   LC 90-19944
This is the "story of a young special education teacher
who suspects that one of her students, a young girl who
is habitually hunched over and mute, may be the victim
of sexual abuse and a black magic cult. A gripping account for mature teens." Booklist

Johnson, Joan J., 1942-
Teen prostitution. Watts 1992 192p il lib bdg
$22.70   **362.7**
1. Juvenile prostitution
ISBN 0-531-11099-0   LC 92-15231
Discusses the nature and causes of teen prostitution
"This is probably the most thorough treatment of the
topic available for this audience; in addition, it is well
researched, nonsensational, and evenhanded. Johnson
manages to present teenage prostitutes and their desperate plight with clarity and sympathy. The judicious blend
of factual material and personal narrative provides good
pacing and a human face to all the numbers." SLJ
Includes bibliography

Kinnear, Karen L.
Childhood sexual abuse; a reference handbook.
ABC-CLIO 1995 333p (Contemporary world
issues) $39.50   **362.7**
1. Child sexual abuse
ISBN 0-87436-691-7   LC 95-40065
The author's "introduction provides information on
myths about childhood sexual abuse, the scope of the
problem, the perpetrators, the causes, effects, prevention,
false memories, ritual abuse, and more. . . . A section
on 'Facts and Statistics, Documents and Legislation'
gives information on prevalence and incidence, on signs
and symptoms, excerpts from federal legislation, and two
U.S. Supreme Court cases." Libr J
Includes bibliographical references

Kozol, Jonathan
Amazing grace; the lives of children and the
conscience of a nation. Crown 1995 286p $24
                        362.7
1. Poor—New York (N.Y.) 2. Socially handicapped
children 3. Inner cities
ISBN 0-517-79999-5   LC 95-23163
Also available in paperback from HarperPerennial
In this "book, Mr. Kozol travels the Mott Haven section of the Bronx, one of the poorest neighborhoods in
the nation, where he visits with children, their parents
and ministers, talking with them about their lives and
about what they perceive as their place in the world." N
Y Times Book Rev
Kozol's "powerfully understated report takes us inside
rat-infested homes that are freezing in winter, overcrowded schools, dysfunctional clinics, soup kitchens. . . .
While his narrative offers no specific solutions, it forcefully drives home his conviction: a civilized nation cannot allow this situation to continue." Publ Wkly
Includes bibliographical references

Kuklin, Susan

What do I do now? talking about teenage pregnancy. Putnam 1991 179p il o.p. **362.7**

1. Teenage mothers 2. Teenage pregnancy

LC 90-45775

"Kuklin interviewed teens of both sexes and their families from many racial, ethnic, and socioeconomic backgrounds, as well as medical and counseling personnel. . . . From these interviews and her observations of a Planned Parenthood unit, an adoption agency, a facility that performs abortions, and a hospital clinic, she presents in a clear and detailed style the pros and cons of options available to pregnant teens and their consequences. . . . Solid information, soberly presented, without moralization or strident activism." SLJ

Includes glossary and bibliography

Levy, Barrie

In love and in danger; a teen's guide to breaking free of abusive relationships. Seal Press 1993 107p pa $8.95 **362.7**

1. Dating (Social customs) 2. Aggressiveness (Psychology)

ISBN 1-878067-26-5   LC 92-41914

Describes the experiences of teens who have had abusive dating relationships and gives advice on how to end the cycle of abuse and forge healthy and loving, violence-free relationships

"By not being judgmental or sensational in the discussions of what is going on in a teen's personal relationships, the author lends a calm, sane, unbiased voice to the subject. . . . Levy's book is one of the few nonfiction titles that speaks specifically to teens, in teen language, and very movingly." Voice Youth Advocates

Liptak, Karen

Adoption controversies. Watts 1993 158p il (Changing family) lib bdg $22.70 **362.7**

1. Adoption

ISBN 0-531-13032-0   LC 93-19810

"Liptak explores various controversial aspects including options for unwed, pregnant teens, open versus closed adoption, agency versus private adoptions, transracial adoptions, foster care, special needs adoptions, rights of birth fathers and searches for biological parents or children. Surrogate mothering is briefly addressed." Book Rep

"This is a good, basic source of up-to-date information and a good starting point whether for personal use or research." Voice Youth Advocates

Includes glossary and bibliography

Luker, Kristin

Dubious conceptions; the politics of teenage pregnancy. Harvard Univ. Press 1996 283p $24.95 **362.7**

1. Teenage pregnancy 2. Unmarried mothers

ISBN 0-674-21702-0   LC 95-52833

The author contends "that, while most teen pregnancies occur out of wedlock, the majority of illegitimate infants are borne by older women. . . . She demonstrates that poor teenage women are the most likely to become pregnant and that pregnancy is a measure of poverty, not a cause." Libr J

"A provocative examination of an issue of major interest to anyone concerned about or working with adolescents." Voice Youth Advocates

Includes bibliography

Mather, Cynthia L. (Cynthia Lynn), 1955-

How long does it hurt? a guide to recovering from incest and sexual abuse for teenagers, their friends, and their families; [by] Cynthia L. Mather with Kristina E. Debye; illustrations by Judy Wood; foreword by Eliana Gil. Jossey-Bass 1994 265p il pa $16.50 **362.7**

1. Incest 2. Child sexual abuse

ISBN 1-55542-674-3   LC 94-12536

The authors present information on how to identify and expose abuse and then focus on overcoming the confusion and self-doubt that ensues. Includes discussion of going to court, the possibility of forgiving offenders, and developing a confident and informed view of sex

Mufson, Susan

Straight talk about child abuse; [by] Susan Mufson and Rachel Kranz. Facts on File 1991 104p $16.95 **362.7**

1. Child abuse

ISBN 0-8160-2376-X   LC 90-39758

A guide for teens discussing the pervasive problem of child abuse in all forms, its effects, and possible solutions. A resource section provides lists of hotlines, associations, and agencies that offer assistance

"This book's strength lies not so much in its solid information . . . but in its encouragement for teens facing abuse in their own lives or in the lives of others. A reaffirming guide that presents realistic options." SLJ

Pohl, Constance

Transracial adoption; children and parents speak; by Constance Pohl and Kathy Harris. Watts 1992 142p il lib bdg $22.70 **362.7**

1. Interracial adoption

ISBN 0-531-11134-2   LC 92-10991

Explores the issues related to interracial and international adoptions, using interviews with black, biracial, Asian, and Hispanic young people who were adopted into white or biracial families

"The strength of this volume is its profiles of adoptees and families, which illustrate the bureaucratic nature of the problems. . . . This work will have older teens and adults thinking about race, and about family." SLJ

Includes glossary and bibliography

Switzer, Ellen Eichenwald, 1923-

Anyplace but here; young, alone, and homeless: what to do; [by] Ellen Switzer. Atheneum Pubs. 1992 161p il $14.95 **362.7**

1. Runaway teenagers

ISBN 0-689-31694-1   LC 92-15

Examines the problems that lead young people to live on the streets and what life is like for them there. Also

Switzer, Ellen Eichenwald, 1923——_Continued_
provides information on how they can get help

"A combination of anecdotal stories, personal experiences, facts, laws pertaining to minors, and a few statistics make for a highly readable yet informative treatment." SLJ

362.82   Problems of and services to families

Domestic violence; Karin L. Swisher, book editor. Greenhaven Press 1995 96p (At issue) lib bdg $12.95; pa $9.44   **362.82**
1. Family violence
ISBN 1-56510-381-5 (lib bdg); 1-56510-380-7 (pa)
LC 95-24176

Contributors to this volume debate the nature and extent of domestic violence and how it can be reduced
Includes bibliography

Family violence; A.E. Sadler, book editor. Greenhaven Press 1996 205p (Current controversies) lib bdg $19.95; pa $11.95
362.82
1. Family violence
ISBN 1-56510-371-8 (lib bdg); 1-56510-370-X (pa)
LC 95-35485

Topics such as "child abuse, abusive parenting, verbal battering, spanking, violence against women, sexual abuse, abuse of the elderly, domestic violence against gays, as well as other pertinent themes are explored by a wide range of writers and public health professionals. The well-organized format includes article summaries, short quotes in boldface throughout, and an extensive list of educational, counseling, and research organizations with descriptions of their services." SLJ
Includes bibliographical references

Kosof, Anna
Battered women; living with the enemy. Watts 1994 110p il (Women then—women now) lib bdg $22.70; pa $12   **362.82**
1. Abused women
ISBN 0-531-11203-9 (lib bdg); 0-531-15755-5 (pa)
LC 94-29529

Kosof offers "an in-depth look at the psychology of battery, both from the victim's and the perpetrator's point of view, paying some attention to the history of police intervention and the effects of domestic violence on dependent children." SLJ
Includes bibliographical references

McCue, Margi Laird
Domestic violence; a reference handbook. ABC-CLIO 1995 273p (Contemporary world issues) $39.95   **362.82**
1. Family violence
ISBN 0-87436-762-X   LC 95-44080
"A broad and in-depth view of spousal abuse, particularly the abuse of women by men with whom they have or have had an intimate relationship. Reactions to the problem are discussed, including the responses of men, women, the community, and sociologists. A chronology of events, laws, and legislation provides a historical context within which domestic violence can be understood, while a section of biographical sketches features individuals who have been influential in securing rights for women. . . . Men as victims and violence in same-sex relationships are also discussed." SLJ
Includes bibliographical references and filmography

362.83   Problems of and services to women

Violence against women; Bruno Leone, executive editor; Karin L. Swisher, Carol Wekesser, book editors; William Barbour, assistant editor. Greenhaven Press 1994 320p (Current controversies) lib bdg $19.95; pa $11.95
362.83
1. Abused women 2. Violence
ISBN 1-56510-070-0 (lib bdg); 1-56510-069-7 (pa)
LC 93-1807

Articles present opposing opinions on the seriousness of violence against women, including issues of rape, domestic violence, sexual harassment, and pornography
"A most comprehensive resource, particularly for students preparing for a speech or debate." SLJ
Includes bibliographical references

362.87   Problems of and services to victims of political oppression

Sawyer, Kem Knapp
Refugees; seeking a safe haven. Enslow Pubs. 1995 128p il (Multicultural issues) lib bdg $17.95
362.87
1. Refugees
ISBN 0-89490-663-1   LC 94-41425
The author begins with a "historical overview of displaced persons after World War I and II and then describes the past and present efforts of refugee-aid groups. Her discussions encompass many countries in different parts of the world (e.g., Haiti, Cuba, Bosnia, Somalia, Burma, and Cambodia), but do not include China, Iraq, Iran, Libya, and Nigeria. . . . Sawyer emphasizes the difficulties of intervention, especially in relation to issues of sovereignty. A clear, dispassionate analysis." SLJ
Includes bibliography

362.88   Problems of and services to victims of crimes

Booher, Dianna Daniels
Rape: what would you do if ...? rev ed. Messner 1991 133p lib bdg $13.98; pa $6.95   **362.88**
1. Rape
ISBN 0-671-74538-7 (lib bdg); 0-671-74546-8 (pa)
LC 91-10066

First published 1981

Booher, Dianna Daniels—*Continued*

The author "explores the different motivations of rapists, demonstrates strategies for tricking each kind of would-be assaulter, and tells how to fight to escape. The last two sections cover the aftermath of rape and encourage girls to decide . . . that they will report rape if it happens to them." SLJ

"This book covers all of these [above mentioned] areas thoroughly in clear, easy-to-read language. Quizzes and life examples help to make this book an excellent resource on the subject." Voice Youth Advocates

Includes bibliography

Brownmiller, Susan

Against our will; men, women and rape. Simon & Schuster 1975 472p o.p.; Fawcett Bks. paperback available $12.50   **362.88**

1. Rape

ISBN 0-449-90820-8 (pa)

A "history of rape, including psychological, sociopolitical, and legal perspectives. . . . The material is well documented and compellingly presented." Choice

Mufson, Susan

Straight talk about date rape; [by] Susan Mufson and Rachel Kranz. Facts on File 1993 123p $16.95
362.88

1. Rape 2. Dating (Social customs)

ISBN 0-8160-2863-X   LC 92-41681

"The authors outline the extent of the problem and give its complexities their due by discussing the principal myths and misapprehensions that surround both date and acquaintance rape. The tone is matter of fact—there's no accusatory language or stridency—and although the book's main focus is on women as victims, the authors also offer some discussion about men as targets." Booklist

Includes bibliographical references

Parrot, Andrea

Coping with date rape & acquaintance rape. rev ed. Rosen Pub. Group 1995 174p lib bdg $15.95
362.88

1. Rape 2. Dating (Social customs)

ISBN 0-8239-2141-7

First published 1988

The author contends that "teens are especially vulnerable to being raped because of their dating environment. This book provides steps that they can take to prevent rape and recommends where rape victims can go for help." Publisher's note

363.1   Public safety programs

Nader, Ralph

Collision course; the truth about airline safety; [by] Ralph Nader, Wesley J. Smith. TAB Bks. 1993 xxiii, 378p $21.95; pa $14.95   **363.1**

1. Aeronautics—Safety measures

ISBN 0-8306-4271-4; 0-07-045987-8 (pa)

LC 93-8266

The authors discuss "the Federal Aviation Administration and other government agencies; air-traffic control;

the commercial aircraft fleet; airports; the impact of human and economic factors; the impact of weather on air safety. . . . A solidly researched, constructive analysis." Booklist

Read, Piers Paul, 1941-

Ablaze; the story of the heroes and victims of Chernobyl. Random House 1993 362p il o.p.
363.1

1. Chernobyl Nuclear Accident, Chernobyl, Ukraine, 1986 2. Radioactive pollution

LC 92-56840

Read provides a "history of the Soviet atomic system and the activities of the separate, sometimes antagonistic, bureaucracies that controlled it. His conversations with local informants have led him to conclude that Chernobyl, by thoroughly shaking the faith of citizens in the efficiency of their authorities, was a major cause of the fall of Gorbachev and the collapse of the Soviet Union. That last point may be debatable, but Mr. Read's account as a whole is both informative and cautionary." Atl Mon

363.2   Police services

Denenberg, Barry

The true story of J. Edgar Hoover and the FBI. Scholastic 1993 202p il $13.95; pa $5.99   **363.2**

1. Hoover, J. Edgar (John Edgar), 1895-1972 2. United States. Federal Bureau of Investigation

ISBN 0-590-43168-4; 0-590-44157-4 (pa)

LC 91-8021

"Denenberg shows how Hoover took over a poorly funded, amateurish agency, and upgraded both the quality of the agents and the methods and techniques they use. He also shows how Hoover manipulated the press and the public, refused to acknowledge the Mafia, obsessed over communism, and used FBI surveillance capability to intimidate people inside and outside of government." SLJ

"This is an extraordinary book; with it, Denenberg reaches the highest standards for excellence in nonfiction." Voice Youth Advocates

Includes bibliography

Fisher, David, 1946-

Hard evidence; how detectives inside the FBI's sci-crime lab have helped solve America's toughest cases. Simon & Schuster 1995 316p $23
363.2

1. FBI Laboratory 2. Criminal investigation

ISBN 0-671-79369-1   LC 94-46293

Also available in paperback from Dell

The author "describes the work of the FBI Crime Laboratory—regarding explosives, firearms, hairs and fibers, toxicology, etc.—and how it has been used to solve problematic cases. Writing with the FBI's cooperation, Fisher tends to accept at face value their judgments in some controversial cases—Sacco and Vanzetti, Alger Hiss, the Lindbergh baby kidnapping, and the JFK assassination. Nevertheless, his enthusiasm for the progress in processing the faintest crime-scene clues is not misplaced." Libr J

Kessler, Ronald

The FBI; inside the world's most powerful law enforcement agency. Pocket Bks. 1993 492p il hardcover o.p. paperback available $6.99   **363.2**

1. United States. Federal Bureau of Investigation

ISBN 0-671-78658-X (pa)   LC 93-5207

"Kessler details how the bureau solved prominent cases such as Watergate and the World Trade Center bombing; covered up many detrimental internal cases; and introduced and employed ultra-modern forensic technologies for criminal investigations." Libr J

Includes glossary and bibliography

Miller, Maryann, 1943-

Everything you need to know about dealing with the police. Rosen Pub. Group 1995 64p il (Need to know library) lib bdg $15.95   **363.2**

1. Police 2. Helping behavior

ISBN 0-8239-1875-0   LC 94-18526

This book provides an "overview of situations teens might face. Specific areas of discussion look at how law enforcement operates, traffic tickets, police harassment, ethics, police and community cooperative projects, being searched, teens' rights, dialing 911, and dealing with confrontations." SLJ

Includes bibliographical references

363.3 Other aspects of public safety

Kruschke, Earl R. (Earl Roger), 1934-

Gun control; a reference handbook. ABC-CLIO 1995 408p il (Contemporary world issues) $39.50   **363.3**

1. Firearms—Law and legislation

ISBN 0-87436-695-X   LC 95-10450

"Pertinent historical cases and laws, both Constitutional and state; biographical vignettes of seminal figures in the gun-control debate; a philosophical chronology from Plato to the present; and an annotated bibliography of print resources contribute to this useful tool for research projects." SLJ

Includes glossary

363.4 Controversies related to public morals and customs

Abortion; edited by Janet Podell. Wilson, H.W. 1990 231p (Reference shelf, v62 no4) pa $15   **363.4**

1. Abortion

ISBN 0-8242-0793-9   LC 90-12924

Highlights both sides of the controversial abortion debate, with presentation of the ethical, political and legal views espoused by the pro-choice movement and the anti-abortion camp

Includes bibliography

The **Abortion** controversy; book editors, Charles Cozic & Jonathan Petrikin. Greenhaven Press 1995 284p (Current controversies) lib bdg $19.95; pa $11.95   **363.4**

1. Abortion

ISBN 1-56510-229-0 (lib bdg); 1-56510-228-2 (pa)

LC 94-28196

"An examination of the legal and moral aspects of the abortion debate that gives both sides of the argument via previously published essays and articles. . . . Authors addressing these topics include journalists, lawyers, theologians, Supreme Court justices, activists, physicians, and philosophers." SLJ

Includes bibliographical references

Abortion: opposing viewpoints; Tamara L. Roleff, book editor. Greenhaven Press 1997 216p lib bdg $19.95; pa $11.95   **363.4**

1. Abortion

ISBN 1-56510-506-0 (lib bdg); 1-56510-505-2 (pa)

LC 96-17342

"Opposing viewpoints series"

Replaces the edition published 1991 under the editorship of Charles P. Cozic and Stacey L. Tipp

Contributors explore the ethical, religious, legal, social and medical questions raised by the abortion debate. Research using aborted fetal tissue is also discussed

Includes bibliographical references

Day, Nancy

Abortion; debating the issue. Enslow Pubs. 1995 128p il (Issues in focus) lib bdg $18.95   **363.4**

1. Abortion

ISBN 0-89490-645-3   LC 94-40697

Discusses the pros and cons of the abortion issue and gives statistics on abortion in the United States and other countries

"This is a excellent reference source for term papers." Baya Book Rev

Includes bibliographical references

Drugs in America; edited by Robert Emmet Long. Wilson, H.W. 1993 250p (Reference shelf, v65 no4) pa $15   **363.4**

1. Drug traffic 2. Drug abuse 3. Drugs—Law and legislation

ISBN 0-8242-0843-9   LC 93-16881

The articles in the first section of this book concern the government's efforts in the war on drugs. The second section focuses on the Latin American countries that supply cocaine and heroin for U.S. consumption. Section three discusses cocaine and crack, and the last section covers the issue of legalizing drugs

Gambling; edited by Andrew Riconda. Wilson, H.W. 1995 202p (Reference shelf, v67 no4) pa $15   **363.4**

1. Gambling

ISBN 0-8242-0871-4   LC 95-22719

This collection of articles about gambling is divided into four sections: An overview; The gambler's world; A case study: the Indian reservation; When gambling becomes a problem

Includes bibliographical references

Gambling; Charles P. Cozic, Paul A. Winters [book editors] Greenhaven Press 1995 208p (Current controversies) lib bdg $19.95; pa $11.95 **363.4**

1. Gambling

ISBN 1-565-10235-5 (lib bdg); 1-565-10234-7 (pa)

LC 94-43378

An anthology providing opposing viewpoints as to whether gambling is ethical, if it benefits economies, if government should regulate Indian gambling, how it affects sports, and if compulsive gambling is a serious problem

Includes bibliographical references

Legalizing drugs; Karin L. Swisher, book editor. Greenhaven Press 1995 128p (At issue) lib bdg $12.95; pa $7.95 **363.4**

1. Drugs—Law and legislation

ISBN 1-56510-379-3 (lib bdg); 1-56510-378-5 (pa)

LC 95-24105

James Q. Wilson, A. M. Rosenthal, Max Frankel and Barbara Ehrenreich are among the contributors examining the implications of drug decriminalization

Includes bibliography

363.7 Environmental problems and services

Andryszewski, Tricia, 1956-

What to do about nuclear waste. Millbrook Press 1995 128p il lib bdg $16.40 **363.7**

1. Radioactive waste disposal 2. Nuclear power plants—Environmental aspects

ISBN 1-56294-577-7 LC 94-44662

The author discusses "the problem of handling long-lived, highly poisonous waste that cannot be safely neutralized. She briefly describes the history of nuclear power and weapons production, but focuses on the various proposals for waste transportation and disposal. . . . Her writing style is clear and the organization is quite logical; she neither downplays nor sensationalizes the dramatic facts." SLJ

Includes glossary and bibliographical references

Carson, Rachel, 1907-1964

Silent spring; with an introduction by Al Gore. Houghton Mifflin 1994 xxvi, 368p il hardcover o.p. paperback available $13 **363.7**

1. Pesticides—Environmental aspects 2. Pesticides and wildlife

ISBN 0-395-68329-7 (pa) LC 95-109031

Also available G.K. Hall large print edition. Companion volume Silent spring revisited available from American Chemical Soc.

A reissue with new introduction of the title first published 1962

In The silent spring, Carson "contended that the indiscriminate use of weed killers and insecticides constituted a hazard to wildlife and to human beings. Her provocative work inspired many subsequent environmental studies." Reader's Ency. 4th edition

Includes bibliographical references

Dashefsky, H. Steven

Environmental literacy; everything you need to know about saving our planet. Random House 1993 298p il pa $13 **363.7**

1. Environmental protection—Dictionaries

ISBN 0-679-74774-5 LC 92-56808

This "is an alphabetical dictionary-encyclopedia of terms, phrases, people, organizations (with addresses), acronyms, and legislative acts. The information is presented clearly and is written for those with little or no formal education in the environmental sciences. . . . This work should be purchased by all libraries for its thorough coverage, ease of use, and excellent price." Libr J

The **Dictionary** of ecology and environmental science; Henry W. Art, general editor; foreword by F. Herbert Bormann; contributing editors, Daniel Botkin [et al.] Holt & Co. 1993 632p il (Henry Holt reference book) $60 **363.7**

1. Environment—Dictionaries 2. Ecology—Dictionaries

ISBN 0-8050-2079-9 LC 92-38526

"Over 8000 entries dealing with the environmental sciences and ecology are included, with definitions that are for the most part clear and concise. There are some entries for environmental laws and organizations but none for individuals, and the numerous *See* references are helpful." Libr J

The **Encyclopedia** of the environment; Ruth A. Eblen and William R. Eblen, editors. Houghton Mifflin 1994 846p il maps $49.95 **363.7**

1. Environmental protection—Dictionaries

ISBN 0-395-55041-6 LC 94-13669

This volume stresses the "humanistic concepts as espoused by the late Pulitzer Prize-winning author and pioneer environmentalist, René Dubos. . . . The work has over 550 alphabetically arranged entries as well as many maps, charts, and tables. Following each entry is a list of suggestions for further reading." Libr J

The **Environment:** opposing viewpoints; A.E. Sadler, editor. Greenhaven Press 1996 216p il lib bdg $19.95; pa $11.95 **363.7**

1. Environmental protection 2. Human ecology

ISBN 1-56510-397-1 (lib bdg); 1-56510-396-3 (pa)

LC 95-51743

"Opposing viewpoints series"

Replaces the edition published 1991 with title: The environmental crisis: opposing viewpoints, under the editorship of Neal Bernards

"This anthology includes the following chapters: Is there an environmental crisis? How serious is air and water pollution? Is the American lifestyle bad for the environment? Is ecological conservation bad for the economy? How should the environment be protected?" Publisher's note

Includes bibliographical references

Environmental career directory; a practical, one-stop guide to getting a job preserving the environment; Bradley J. Morgan and Joseph M. Palmisano, editors; Diane M. Sawinski, associate editor. Gale Res. 1993 348p $39   **363.7**
1. Environmental protection—Vocational guidance
ISBN 0-8103-9153-8
A guide to careers in such fields as forestry and wildlife management and air and water quality control

Environmental encyclopedia; William P. Cunningham [et al.] editors. Gale Res. 1994 xxi, 981p il maps (Gale environmental library) $200   **363.7**
1. Environmental protection—Dictionaries 2. Ecology—Dictionaries 3. Earth sciences—Dictionaries
ISBN 0-8103-8856-1   LC 94-177482
The over 1,200 "articles on disasters, organizations, terms, legislation, environmentalists, public policy, processes, animals and recycling will serve the student, policy maker, voter, educator, and activist. Well-chosen black- and-white photos enhance adjacent essays that clarify issues and environmental problems." Am Libr

Environmental policy in the 1990s; reform or reaction? edited by Norman J. Vig, Michael E. Kraft. 3rd ed. CQ Press 1997 416p $41.95; pa $29.95   **363.7**
1. Environmental policy—United States 2. United States—Politics and government—1989-
ISBN 1-56802-242-5; 1-56802-165-8 (pa)
    LC 96-9490
First published 1990
This volume "puts 25 years of environmental policy development in context by examining the institutional framework for making policy, the role of environmentalism and public opinion in shaping policy, the search for more efficient policy solutions, and the impact of global environmental imperatives." Publisher's note
Includes bibliographical references

Feldman, Andrew J.
The Sierra Club green guide; everybody's desk reference to environmental information. Sierra Club Bks. 1996 282p pa $25   **363.7**
1. Environmental protection—Directories
ISBN 0-87156-402-5   LC 95-2438
"This guide annotates more than 1,000 print and electronic sources. . . . In chapters by topics (energy, waste, water, etc.) [the author] describes government clearinghouses, organizations, online services, directories and other reference books, and periodicals. A second part of the book lists similar sources for 'green living' topics—education, grants, shopping, travel, etc." Booklist

Gale environmental almanac; [edited by] Russ Hoyle; foreword by Russell E. Train. Gale Res. 1993 xx, 684p il maps $85   **363.7**
1. Environmental protection 2. Environmental policy—United States
ISBN 0-8103-8877-4   LC 93-37699
This volume "is divided into 13 chapters on subjects such as the history of the American conservation move-

ment, environmental regulation, environmental science, and environmental business. Each chapter contains a well-written essay (30 to 80 pages long) by a journalist or academic in environmental studies, a bibliography, and numerous excellent photographs." Libr J

Gay, Kathlyn
Air pollution. Watts 1991 144p il lib bdg $22.70   **363.7**
1. Air pollution
ISBN 0-531-13002-9   LC 91-17780
"An Impact book"
Examines the growing problem of air pollution, its effect on the ozone and stratosphere and what we can do to improve air quality
"This book would be useful for those students interested in the environment, as well as those needing current information for research." Appraisal
Includes glossary and bibliography

Saving the environment; debating the costs. Watts 1996 128p lib bdg $22.70   **363.7**
1. Environmental policy—United States 2. Environmental protection
ISBN 0-531-11263-2   LC 95-49389
The author discusses "the major environmental issues facing society today, with particular emphasis on the struggle to balance the economic and environmental concerns of each. Individual property rights versus environmental protection of land and native species, clean air and clean water regulation versus jobs, global versus national environmentalism, unfunded mandates, and risk assessment are all addressed." Booklist
"The topic is well researched, fully documented and rich in detail." Voice Youth Advocates
Includes bibliographical references

The **Greenhouse** effect; edited by Matthew A. Kraljic. Wilson, H.W. 1992 155p (Reference shelf, v64 no3) pa $15   **363.7**
1. Greenhouse effect
ISBN 0-8242-0827-7   LC 92-5990
A collection of reprinted articles from various sources concerning the greenhouse effect, its measurement and causes, consequences and possible solutions
Includes bibliography

Grossman, Mark
The ABC-CLIO companion to the environmental movement. ABC-CLIO 1994 445p il (ABC-CLIO companions to key issues in American history and life) $55   **363.7**
1. Environmental protection—Dictionaries 2. Environmental policy—Dictionaries
ISBN 0-87436-732-8   LC 94-36186
This volume "spans American environmental awareness from early naturalists such as Audubon up through current legislation. . . . Concise definitions are given for terms such as 'acid rain,' 'biodiversity,' and 'endangered species.'" Libr J
Includes bibliographical references

Mowrey, Marc

Not in our back yard; the people and events that shaped America's modern environmental movement; [by] Marc Mowrey and Tim Redmond. Morrow 1993 496p $27.50   **363.7**

1. Environmental policy—United States 2. Earth Day
ISBN 0-688-10644-7   LC 93-24393

"From Earth Day, 1970, to Earth Day, 1990, the authors trace the history of the environmental movement, profiling an activist in each chapter in a way that enables readers to relate more easily to the problems involved in the struggle. A book that will interest armchair reader and activist alike." Booklist

Newton, David E.

Global warming; a reference handbook. ABC-CLIO 1993 183p (Contemporary world issues) $39.50   **363.7**

1. Greenhouse effect
ISBN 0-87436-711-5   LC 93-24821

This work "includes a chronology of global warming from 2.5 million years ago to the present; a group of biographical sketches of important people in the field; a section of statistical information; a directory of organizations; a list of state programs; an annotated bibliography of books, reports, nonprint sources, and computer programs [and] a glossary." Libr J

"This is a well-written, unbiased book. . . . It would be a good resource for high-school libraries as well as academic and public libraries." Booklist

Pollution; book editor, Charles P. Cozic. Greenhaven Press 1994 224p il (Current controversies) lib bdg $19.95; pa $11.95 **363.7**

1. Pollution 2. Environmental protection
ISBN 1-56510-076-X (lib bdg); 1-56510-075-1 (pa)
                 LC 93-4552

"The contributors debate the seriousness of pollution and how it can be remedied. Chapters include: How Effective Is the Environmental Protection Agency? Are Corporations Polluting the Environment? How Serious a Problem Is Air Pollution? Is Recycling an Effective Way to Reduce Pollution?" Publisher's note

Includes bibliographical references

Stefoff, Rebecca, 1951-

The American environmental movement. Facts on File 1995 146p il (Social reform movements) $17.95   **363.7**

1. Environmental movement
ISBN 0-8160-3046-4   LC 94-33393

The author uses a chronological approach to outline "the development of Euro-American attitudes toward the land. Contrasting Native Americans' lifestyles with those of the rapacious colonists and settlers, she also introduces such early conservationists as Thomas Jefferson. Other chapters depict the development of American industry and the devastated landscapes it created; early naturalists; the rise of the wilderness movement and its champion, Theodore Roosevelt; and later conservationists. Particularly insightful are the author's accounts of Rachel Carson's work and of the origins and evolution of the National Wildlife Federation and other organizations." SLJ

The **True** state of the planet; Ronald Bailey, editor. Free Press 1995 472p il pa $15.95

                 363.7

1. Environmental policy 2. Environmental protection
ISBN 0-02-874010-6   LC 95-937

"A project of the Competitive Enterprise Institute"

Bailey "enlists a dozen scientists to explain what is and isn't known about the changing environment. . . . The prominent green organizations adhere to regulatory and prohibitionist principles; whereas this set of writers favor the private management of resources, believing that to be the path to green benefits and material wealth. Prescriptions aside, this info-rich work is crammed with tabular data about biodiversity, pesticides, and air quality and is supported by a guarded, foot-noted text." Booklist

Includes bibliographical references

363.8 Food supply

Hunger; Scott Barbour, book editor, William Dudley, assistant editor. Greenhaven Press 1995 224p (Current controversies) lib bdg $19.95; pa $11.95   **363.8**

1. Food supply 2. Food relief 3. Hunger
ISBN 1-56510-239-8 (lib bdg); 1-56510-238-X (pa)
                 LC 94-43376

An anthology providing opposing viewpoints as to the causes and politics of world hunger, how to improve world food production, and whether wealthy nations should aid hungry populations

Includes bibliographical references

363.9 Population problems

Gay, Kathlyn

Pregnancy; private decisions, public debates. Watts 1993 112p (Women then—women now) lib bdg $22.70   **363.9**

1. Birth control
ISBN 0-531-11167-9   LC 93-29456

"Controversies examined include abortion; fetal personhood; the impact of medical technology on individuals' choices; and the social mores affecting attitudes toward reproduction, surrogacy, and employment policies. The book concludes with a statement of some global reproductive concerns." SLJ

Includes glossary and bibliography

364 Criminology

Crime and criminals: opposing viewpoints; Paul A. Winters, book editor. Greenhaven Press 1995 285p il lib bdg $19.95; pa $11.95   **364**

1. Crime 2. Criminals
ISBN 1-56510-176-6 (lib bdg); 1-56510-177-4 (pa)
                 LC 94-4976

"Opposing viewpoints series"

Replaces the edition published 1989 under the editorship of William Dudley

Crime and criminals: opposing viewpoints—
Continued

"Chapters explore questions about the causes of crime and effective methods of prevention, gun control, programs for young offenders, and the effects of Americans' fear of crime. Essays explore a range of viewpoints from politically liberal through conservative. . . . A good classroom resource." Voice Youth Advocates

Includes bibliographical references

Meltzer, Milton, 1915-

Crime in America. Morrow Junior Bks. 1990 170p il $12.95　　**364**

1. Crime

ISBN 0-688-08513-X　　LC 90-5698

Discusses various aspects of crime in America, including crime in the streets, battered family members, the Mob, and law enforcement

"The brisk pace and competent synthesis of ideas, facts, and explanation result in a clear, comprehensive overview of an enormous subject." Horn Book

Includes glossary and bibliography

364.1　Criminal offenses

Banking scandals: the S&Ls and BCCI; edited by Robert Emmet Long. Wilson, H.W. 1993 122p (Reference shelf, v65 no3) pa $15　　**364.1**

1. Bank of Credit and Commerce International SA 2. Savings and loan associations

ISBN 0-8242-0842-0　　LC 93-16882

The articles in the first two sections of this compilation discuss the Savings and Loan industry collapse and subsequent government bailout. The last two sections cover the illegal activities of the Bank of Credit and Commerce International

Includes bibliographical references

Bugliosi, Vincent

Helter skelter; the true story of the Manson murders; [by] Vincent Bugliosi with Curt Gentry. 25th anniversary ed. Norton 1994 528p il $25　　**364.1**

1. Manson, Charles, 1934- 2. Homicide

ISBN 0-393-08700-X　　LC 94-20957

Also available in paperback from Bantam Bks.

A reissue of the title published 1974

"This book by the prosecutor at the Tate-LaBianca murder trial tells the inside story of the Manson Family murders, the investigations, and the trial. . . . The title refers to the Beatles song 'Helter Skelter' which Manson interpreted to mean a coming war between races. He planned the killings as a means of getting that war under way." Libr J

Capote, Truman, 1924-1984

In cold blood; a true account of a multiple murder and its consequences. Modern Lib. 1992 410p $15.50; pa $12　　**364.1**

1. Hickock, Richard, 1931-1965 2. Smith, Perry, 1928-1965 3. Homicide

ISBN 0-679-60023-X; 0-679-74558-0 (pa)

LC 92-50211

Also available G.K. Hall large print edition

First published 1966

"Truman Capote called his account of the 1959 murder of a Kansas farm family a nonfiction novel. Using information he collected through interviews with townspeople and the killers, Capote created a vivid portrait of the criminals and graphically described the crime, the criminals' escape to Mexico, capture, trial, appeals, and hanging." Benet's Reader's Ency of Am Lit

Duncan, Lois, 1934-

Who killed my daughter? Delacorte Press 1992 289p il hardcover o.p. paperback available $5.99

364.1

1. Arquette, Kaitlyn Clare, 1970-1989 2. Homicide

ISBN 0-440-21342-8 (pa)　　LC 92-89

"Duncan, a highly acclaimed author of young adult literature, here tells the story of her agonizing search for her daughter's murderers. The police wrote off the crime as a 'random shooting,' but Duncan could not accept that verdict and set about her own investigation of what really happened." Libr J

"Readers critical of either Duncan's contacts with paranormals or her talking to God and to her dead daughter may be put off by the book, but many will be sympathetic to this mother's plight." Publ Wkly

Gangs: opposing viewpoints; Charles P. Cozic, book editor. Greenhaven Press 1995 191p lib bdg $19.95; pa $11.95　　**364.1**

1. Gangs

ISBN 1-56510-363-7 (lib bdg); 1-56510-362-9 (pa)

LC 95-9015

"Opposing viewpoints series"

A collection of articles debating issues relating to gangs in America, including what encourages gang behavior, how serious a problem they are, how they can be controlled, and how gang members view themselves

"The views and opinions presented are thought-provoking, alarming, and moving." Voice Youth Advocates

Includes bibliographical references

Greene, Laura, 1935-

Wildlife poaching; [by] Laura Offenhartz Greene. Watts 1994 142p il lib bdg $22　　**364.1**

1. Poaching

ISBN 0-531-13007-X　　LC 94-21035

"A Venture book"

The author discusses "the problems of game poaching from a historical perspective and explores the differences between big-game hunting in North America and in Africa and Asia. She also deals with poaching of other kinds, including the poaching of water and air, and includes a good deal of information (nearly one third of the text) on prevention. . . . This book will be a valuable addition to environmental studies collections." Booklist

Includes bibliographical references

Hall, Rob

Rape in America; a reference handbook. ABC-CLIO 1995 202p (Contemporary world issues) $39.50 **364.1**

1. Rape

ISBN 0-87436-730-1   LC 95-12102

"This handbook presents an overview of the historical and social context of rape in America. Major law enforcement, judicial system, and correctional system trends in dealing with both the rapist and the victim are discussed. Also included are an analysis of the types and motivations of rapists, a psychological profile of rapists, and a statistical profile of rape victims." Publisher's note

"The final chapter on 'Reference Materials' offers a good list of well-annotated print matter and audiovisual materials. . . . The author has provided some good insights into the depth of problems concerned with this crime. It is a valuable resource." Voice Youth Advocates

Hate crimes; Paul A. Winters, book editor. Greenhaven Press 1996 208p (Current controversies) lib bdg $19.95; pa $11.95 **364.1**

1. Hate crimes

ISBN 1-56510-373-4 (lib bdg); 1-56510-372-6 (pa)
LC 95-23817

Contributors address the moral, social, political and legal aspects of attempts to regulate hate crimes

Includes bibliography

Hilts, Philip J.

Smokescreen; the truth behind the tobacco industry cover-up. Addison-Wesley 1996 253p il $22 **364.1**

1. Tobacco industry 2. Smoking 3. Tobacco habit

ISBN 0-201-48836-1   LC 96-23187

The author "sketches an industry conspiracy to minimize public awareness of the dangers of smoking. As internal corporate documents leaked to Hilts show, while industry officials claim they don't manipulate levels of addictive nicotine in cigarettes, they have done so for years and this makes the firms increasingly vulneralbe to lawsuits. Hilt's documents also reveal, chillingly, how tobacco companies target youths, their most crucial market." Publ Wkly

Includes bibliographical references

Korem, Danny

Suburban gangs; the affluent rebels; Dan Korem. International Focus Press 1994 281p il $19.95 **364.1**

1. Gangs

ISBN 0-9639103-1-0   LC 94-96794

The author discusses "the steadily rising numbers of youths from affluent homes who, like their inner-city cohorts, choose delinquent, occultic, or ideological gang-based activity as a way of life. European and American youths are joining gangs to escape the reality of life in severely dysfunctional, often abusive home situations." Libr J

"Korem will enlighten many readers with his thoughtful and instructive approach to a growing and troubling social problem." Booklist

Includes bibliographical references

Larson, Erik

Lethal passage; how the travels of a single handgun expose the roots of America's gun crisis. Crown 1994 272p $21 **364.1**

1. Elliot, Nicholas 2. Firearms—Law and legislation 3. Homicide

ISBN 0-517-59677-6   LC 93-34560

Also available in paperback from Vintage Bks.

"Larson's text consists of two interwoven strands. One is the story of the day 16-year-old Nicholas Elliot brought his gun to school and murdered a teacher [and] wounded another. . . . The other relates Larson's discoveries about the gun trade and its regulation as he tracked the course by which the gun, a nasty semiautomatic, came to Elliot." Booklist

This book "sometimes suffers for its hyperbolic rhetoric—as when it suggests that 'Nicholas in effect carried with him the good wishes of an industry and a culture.' But its argument that too many unqualified people are carrying guns in America today is persuasive." N Y Times Book Rev

Includes bibliographical references

Lindop, Edmund

Assassinations that shook America. Watts 1992 141p il lib bdg $22.70 **364.1**

1. Assassination 2. Presidents—United States—Assassination

ISBN 0-531-11049-4   LC 92-15082

"Lindop recounts the events leading to and the repercussions resulting from the assassination of Abraham Lincoln, James Garfield, William McKinley, Huey Long, John Kennedy, Martin Luther King, Jr., and Robert Kennedy. In separate chapters, the author places each man within the historical and political context of his time and indicates how his presence and his death affected the world surrounding him." Booklist

"Lindop's text provides a useful summary of the achievements of those included. . . . Report writers and budding historians should find this of interest." Voice Youth Advocates

Includes bibliography

Rape on campus; Bruno Leone, book editor. Greenhaven Press 1995 120p (At issue) lib bdg $12.95; pa $7.95 **364.1**

1. Rape 2. Dating (Social customs) 3. College students—Sexual behavior

ISBN 1-56510-296-7 (lib bdg); 1-56510-263-0 (pa)
LC 94-42400

"Coverage is broad and includes radical and revisionist feminists' views of rape; campus rape-control strategies; and a discussion of the Violations Against Women Act, which classifies rape motivated by gender bias as a civil-rights offense. The only caveat is that the issues are college-related, and the arguments are complicated and sophisticated." SLJ

Includes bibliographical references

Sifakis, Carl

Hoaxes and scams; a compendium of deceptions, ruses, and swindles. Facts on File 1993 308p il $45; pa $19.95   **364.1**

1. Impostors and imposture 2. Swindlers and swindling 3. Fraud

ISBN 0-8160-2569-X; 0-8160-3026-X (pa)

LC 92-34347

"An encyclopedia of the planned and unplanned fraudulent claims that have been accepted throughout history. . . . Concise, well-written entries give the history of the deceits, why the public was vulnerable to them, and their effects. Cartoons, diagrams, and black-and-white photographs add interest. . . . This volume will appeal to teens intrigued by crime and deception." SLJ

364.3   Offenders

Bode, Janet

Hard time; a real life look at juvenile crime and violence; [by] Janet Bode and Stan Mack. Delacorte Press 1996 218p il $16.95   **364.3**

1. Juvenile delinquency 2. Crime 3. Violence

ISBN 0-385-32186-4   LC 95-40598

Young people whose lives have been impacted by violence and crime, either as perpetrators or as victims, tell their stories. Also includes comments from concerned adults who work with these teens

This volume "is well organized, engrossing, and informative, and it provides glimpses of hope for those wishing to leave violence behind." SLJ

Includes glossary and bibliographical references

The **Gunfighters**; by the editors of Time-Life Books; with text by Paul Trachtman. Time-Life Bks. 1974 238p il map (Old West) o.p.   **364.3**

1. Thieves 2. Frontier and pioneer life—West (U.S.)

This book describes the exploits of such western gunfighters as Jesse and Frank James, Butch Cassidy, and Billy the Kid. The apprehension of outlaws by sheriffs and marshalls, and the exercise of frontier justice by courts and by vigilance committees are also discussed

Includes bibliography

Humes, Edward

No matter how loud I shout; a year in the life of Juvenile Court. Simon & Schuster 1996 399p $24   **364.3**

1. Juvenile courts 2. Juvenile delinquency

ISBN 0-684-81194-4   LC 95-53327

"Humes profiles five teenagers living in a dark, violent world with a revolving door that leads from juvenile court to group homes to jail. Including moving passages in the teens' own words, this is a riveting look at America's lost youth." Booklist

Includes bibliographical references

Lang, Susan S.

Teen violence. Watts 1991 175p il lib bdg $22   **364.3**

1. Juvenile delinquency 2. Violence

ISBN 0-531-11057-5   LC 91-549

Examines the causes and manifestations of violence among teenagers in America and discusses possible solutions

"Lang presents a well researched overview of this problem. . . . Highly recommended for all libraries." Voice Youth Advocates

Includes bibliography

Marshall, Joseph E., Jr.

Street soldier; one man's struggle to save a generation, one life at a time; [by] Joseph Marshall, Jr. and Lonnie Wheeler. Delacorte Press 1996 xxvii, 305p $22.95   **364.3**

1. Omega Boys Club 2. Juvenile delinquency 3. Youth—United States

ISBN 0-385-31430-2   LC 95-35958

"Marshall, a former schoolteacher, now heads San Francisco's Omega Boys Club, which he founded in 1987 to help young people at risk. Working with three other 'street soldiers,' he is fighting drugs, guns and unemployment, which he deems the chief causes of misery in the ghetto. . . . He rejoices in the successes of his converts, dozens of whom are now in college, and laments dropouts from the club, of which there are many. Marshall stresses in this compelling call to arms that simply because you can't save everybody doesn't mean you can't save somebody." Publ Wkly

Newton, David E.

Teen violence; out of control. Enslow Pubs. 1995 112p (Issues in focus) lib bdg $18.95 **364.3**

1. Juvenile delinquency 2. Violence

ISBN 0-89490-506-6   LC 95-6943

This overview of teenage violence includes "sections on the biological bases for violence and the nature-versus-nurture debate, two subjects not always included in books on the topic. Newton also provides information on the ways that teens are punished for violent crimes and what's being done to prevent teen violence." Booklist

Includes bibliographical references

364.6   Penology

The **Death** penalty: opposing viewpoints; Paul A. Winters, book editor. Greenhaven Press 1997 192p il lib bdg $19.95; pa $11.95   **364.6**

1. Capital punishment

ISBN 1-56510-510-9 (lib bdg); 1-56510-509-5 (pa)

LC 96-22575

"Opposing viewpoints series"

Replaces the edition published 1991 under the editorship of Carol Wekesser

"Helen Prejean, Harry A. Blackmun, Antonin Scalia, and others explore the current debate over the morality and constitutionality of capital punishment." Publisher's note

Includes bibliographical references

365 Penal and related institutions

America's prisons: opposing viewpoints; Charles P. Cozic, book editor. Greenhaven Press 1997 199p lib bdg $19.95; pa $11.95   **365**
1. Prisons—United States
ISBN 1-56510-550-8 (lib bdg); 1-56510-549-4 (pa)
              LC 96-47990
"Opposing viewpoints series"
Replaces the edition published 1991 under the editorship of Stacey L. Tipp
Articles "discuss the growth of America's prisons and debate the treatment and punishment of criminal offenders. Contributors examine questions regarding prison conditions, prison sentences, and prisoner rights." Publisher's note
Includes bibliographical references

Kosof, Anna
Prison life; the crisis today. Watts 1995 144p il lib bdg $22.70   **365**
1. Prisons—United States
ISBN 0-531-10984-4   LC 95-14886
Discusses issues such as the youth offender, women in prison, the new challenge posed by AIDS, the impact of drugs, and alternatives to the present system
Includes bibliographical references

Solzhenitsyn, Aleksandr, 1918-
The Gulag archipelago, 1918-1956; an experiment in literary investigation; [Pts] I-VII. Harper & Row 1974-1978 3v il maps o.p.; Westview Press paperback available 3v set $54
              365
1. Political prisoners 2. Soviet Union—Politics and government
ISBN 0-8133-3294-X (pa)
"A 'literary investigation' of the network of Soviet prison camps as they existed between 1918 and 1956. . . . A mixture of autobiography, history, and analysis, the relentlessly grim picture of life inside the camps forms the basis for an attack not only on Stalinism and Leninism but also on the whole process of substituting Western rational and secular ideas for Russia's traditional mysticism." Reader's Ency. 4th edition

369.4 Young people's societies

Erickson, Judith B.
Directory of American youth organizations. Free Spirit pa $21.95   **369.4**
1. Youth—Societies—Directories
ISSN 1044-4440
"A Do something! book"
Biennial. First published 1983 by Father Flanagan's Boys' Home
"Provides an annotated guide to over 400 clubs, groups, troops, teams, societies, lodges, and other organizations for children and young adults. All groups listed are national in scope, nonprofit, and conducted under adult supervision. Each organization listed includes name, national headquarters, address, telephone number, and a brief descriptive annotation. Arrangement is by group focus: hobbies, special interest, sports, school subjects, religious, patriotic, political, social, conservation, agriculture, and career interests." Am Ref Books Annu, 1991

369.43 Boy Scouts

Boy Scouts of America
Fieldbook. 3rd ed. Boy Scouts of Am. 1984 630p il maps pa $16.25   **369.43**
1. Boy Scouts—Handbooks, manuals, etc. 2. Outdoor life
ISBN 0-8395-3200-8   LC 84-72053
First edition by James E. West and William Hillcourt published 1944 with title: Scout field book
This "is a worthwhile guide for those involved in outdoor activities as well as Boy Scouts. The volume addresses hiking, camping, mountaineering, horseback riding, cross-country skiing, swimming, orienteering, canoeing, fitness conditioning, first aid, and outdoor safety. The concise text is supplemented by clear black-and-white and color photographs." Nichols. Guide to Ref Books for Sch Media Cent. 4th edition

370.1 Education—Philosophy

Dewey, John, 1859-1952
Democracy and education; an introduction to the philosophy of education. Macmillan 1916 434p o.p.; Free Press paperback available $15.95 **370.1**
1. Education—Philosophy
ISBN 0-02-907370-7 (pa)
"The author's aim here is to detect and state the ideas implied in a democratic society and to apply those ideas to the problems of education." Boston Transcr

370.19 Education—Social aspects

Dolan, Edward F., 1924-
Illiteracy in America; [by] Edward F. Dolan and Margaret M. Scariano. Watts 1995 128p lib bdg $22.70   **370.19**
1. Literacy
ISBN 0-531-11178-4   LC 93-29528
"An Impact book"
This book "covers the history of illiteracy in the U.S. and places an emphasis on the problem today. Possible cause, costs to society, and remedial programs are introduced. The situation globally, especially in the developing world, is presented as well. . . . The writing is well balanced and straightforward." SLJ
Includes bibliography

The **High-school** student's guide to study, travel, and adventure abroad; by Council on International Educational Exchange. St. Martin's Press pa $13.95   **370.19**
1. Education—Directories 2. Foreign study—Directories
First published 1987 under the authorship of Marjorie Adoff Cohen with title: The teenager's guide to study,

The High-school student's guide to study, travel, and adventure abroad—*Continued*
travel, and adventure abroad. (5th edition 1995) Periodically revised

"High school students seeking interesting activities abroad will value this handbook. It lists over 150 organized programs with information on sponsors, housing, supervision, costs, and comments by past participants." Nichols. Guide to Ref Books for Sch Media Cent. 4th edition

Kozol, Jonathan
Death at an early age; the destruction of the hearts and minds of Negro children in the Boston public schools. Houghton Mifflin 1967 240p o.p.; New Am. Lib. paperback available $11.95 **370.19**
1. Discrimination in education 2. Public schools—Boston (Mass.) 3. African Americans—Education
ISBN 0-452-26292-5 (pa)
National Book Award winner, 1968
The author relates his experience as a fourth-grade teacher in 1964 at a predominantly black Boston school, emphasizing poorly trained teachers, biased text books, overcrowded conditions, prejudiced school administrators, and their effects upon the students
Includes bibliographical references

Illiterate America. Anchor Press/Doubleday 1985 270p o.p.; New Am. Lib. paperback available $12.95 **370.19**
1. Literacy 2. Education—Social aspects
ISBN 0-452-26203-8 (pa)   LC 84-20487
The author's "statistics show that one-third of Americans are semiliterate at best, and he finds inadequacies in existing literacy programs. Advocating societal empowerment of the victims of illiteracy, the development of relevant subject matter, and the use of neighborhood facilities, he names elements of successful literacy programs." Booklist
"Passionate and disturbing, 'Illiterate America' is both a consciousness raiser and a primer for action focused on America's 'invisible minority.'" Libr J

370.25   Education—Directories

The **Handbook** of private schools; an annual descriptive survey of independent education. Sargent Pubs. il maps $90 **370.25**
1. Private schools—Directories 2. Education—United States—Directories
ISSN 0072-9884
First published 1915 with title: Handbook of the best private schools of the United States and Canada
"Describes more than 1,700 boarding and day schools, providing information on age and grade ranges, whether co-educational or for boys or girls, enrollment, faculty size and background, academic orientation and curriculum, and where graduates attend college. 'Features classified' section lists institutions offering military programs, elementary boarding divisions, programs for students with learning differences, international and bilingual schools, and schools with more than 500 or fewer than 100 students. Index of institutions." Guide to Ref Books. 11th edition

Patterson's American education. Educational Directories $83 **370.25**
1. Education—United States—Directories
ISSN 0079-0230
Annual. First published 1904 by the American Education Company with title: Patterson's College and school directory of the United States and Canada. Title, coverage and arrangement varies. Currently published in two parts: (1) Secondary schools; (2) Schools classified
"The first part lists public, private, and Catholic junior high school and high school districts, and combined elementary and secondary districts. Arranged by state, beginning with addresses of officials of state departments of education; then by community; then by district, with names of top officials; then by individual schools, giving names, addresses, and phone numbers of principals. Has separate listings of schools in U.S. territories; Catholic, Seventh-day Adventist, and Lutheran school superintendents; and educational associations and societies. The second part consists of a directory of schools classified by specialty." Guide to Ref Books. 11th edition

370.9   Education—Historical and geographic treatment

Education in America: opposing viewpoints; Charles P. Cozic, book editor. Greenhaven Press 1992 288p il lib bdg $19.95; pa $11.95 **370.9**
1. Education—United States
ISBN 0-89908-188-6 (lib bdg); 0-89908-163-0 (pa)
    LC 91-42495
"Opposing viewpoints series"
Issues covered include an extended school year, standardized testing, national teacher certification, merit pay, school vouchers, multiculturalism, bilingual education, and religion in public education
"A valuable collection of well-chosen, readable articles that bring most of today's major educational issues into focus." SLJ
Includes bibliography

Postman, Neil
The end of education; redefining the value of school. Knopf 1995 209p $23; pa $12 **370.9**
1. Education—United States
ISBN 0-679-43006-7; 0-679-75031-2 (pa)
    LC 94-46605
"The volume initially investigates American education in the earlier part of this century, when 'we knew what schools were for.' Part 2 shifts focus to contemporary education, describing the underlying conceptions of today's schools and considering economic utility, consumerism, technology, and separatism. . . . Postman responds creatively to the problems of 'modernity,' holding out hope for regaining a sense of purpose and respect for learning." Choice
"Beautifully written, breathtakingly high-minded, this is Postman's best book on American education." Booklist
Includes bibliographical references

Unger, Harlow G., 1931-
Encyclopedia of American education. Facts on File 1996 3v set $175   **370.9**
1. Education—United States—Dictionaries
ISBN 0-8160-2994-6   LC 95-41694
"Nearly 2,500 alphabetical entries cover broad subjects such as administration, history, reform, organizations, programs, and tests; not to mention the complex ones, such as church-and-state conflicts. Profiles of leading educators are also included. Each clearly written entry provides an overview plus a bibliography of additional sources. Volume 3 contains a comprehensive bibliography, organized into 41 major subject areas. The cross-references, the detailed index, and the four appendixes add usefulness to the text, helping to make this a truly outstanding reference source on American education." Am Libr

371.3025 Audio and visual materials—Directories

AV market place. Bowker il pa $157.50
                    371.3025
1. Audiovisual materials—Directories
ISSN 1044-0445
Annual. First published 1969 with title: Audiovisual market place. Subtitle varies
"The complete business directory of products & services for the audio video industry including: audio visual, computer systems, film, video, programming, with industry yellow pages." Title page
This volume identifies thousands of "companies that create, supply, or distribute an extraordinary range of audiovisual equipment and services. An index of . . . products and services is cross-referenced to companies in the main body. The products, services, and company index identifies all firms geographically. . . . Companies are also indexed by name." Nichols. Guide to Ref Books for Sch Media Cent. 4th edition

371.305 Methods of instruction and study—Serial publications

Media & Methods; multimedia products, technologies & programs for K-12 school districts. American Society of Educators, 1429 Walnut St., Philadelphia, PA 19102 $33.50 per year   **371.305**
1. Audiovisual education—Periodicals
ISSN 0025-6897
Five times a school year. First published 1965. Subtitle varies
"The majority of articles discuss how to use media to motivate students and enhance the learning experience for both teacher and pupil. Innovative uses of media are always presented, such as applications for videodiscs in the classroom, using film and video in the curriculum, integrated learning systems, and teaching global studies with online communication. Articles on the selection and evaluation of equipment are also abundant." Katz. Mag for Libr. 8th edition

371.9 Special education

Cohen, Leah Hager
Train go sorry; inside a deaf world. Houghton Mifflin 1994 296p il $22.95   **371.9**
1. Lexington School for the Deaf (New York, N.Y.)
2. Deaf—Means of communication
ISBN 0-395-63625-6   LC 93-2291
Also available in paperback from Vintage Bks.
"Cohen draws upon her experiences as the hearing grandchild of deaf immigrants to combine personal stories of hearing-impaired individuals with related aspects of deaf culture. Using her first home and her father's place of employment, the Lexington School for the Deaf in New York City, to connect characters and experiences, she shares tales of activities familiar to young adults." Libr J
"Well organized and beautifully written." Booklist

Conroy, Pat
The water is wide; illustrated with photographs by William and Paul Keyserling. Houghton Mifflin 1972 306p il o.p.; Bantam Bks. paperback available $6.50   **371.9**
1. Socially handicapped children 2. African Americans—Education 3. Public schools—South Carolina
ISBN 0-553-26893-7 (pa)
"A young white teacher goes to an island off the coast of South Carolina to teach a group of functionally illiterate black children. Yamacraw Island is backward and primitive, a world for the most part left untouched by the 20th Century. . . . By ignoring the textbooks and concentrating on meaningful situations and dialogue . . . he begins to make headway. He also, unfortunately arouses the ire of the powers that be and, after fierce struggle, is fired." Libr J

Cummings, Rhoda Woods
The survival guide for teenagers with LD* (*learning differences); by Rhoda Cummings and Gary Fisher; edited by Pamela Espeland; illustrated by L.K. Hansen. Free Spirit 1993 190p il pa $11.95   **371.9**
1. Learning disabilities 2. Life skills
ISBN 0-915793-51-2   LC 93-6798
Includes information and advice on "such topics as legal rights, getting a job, independent living, school, friendship, dating, health, sexuality, and planning for the future. An entire chapter is devoted to the crucial task of teaching the reader how to be his/her own advocate." Voice Youth Advocates
"This is a very positive book that will be helpful to counselors and LD teachers as well as students and their parents." SLJ
Includes bibliographical references

Kozol, Jonathan
Savage inequalities; children in America's schools. Crown 1991 262p $20   **371.9**
1. Public schools 2. Socially handicapped children 3. Segregation in education
ISBN 0-517-58221-X   LC 91-17574
Also available in paperback from HarperPerennial

Kozol, Jonathan—*Continued*
In 1988, Kozol "visited schools in over 30 neighborhoods, including East St. Louis, Harlem, the Bronx, Chicago, Jersey City, and San Antonio. In this account, he concludes that real integration has seriously declined and education for minorities and the poor has moved backwards by at least several decades." Libr J

"Jonathan Kozol has written an impassioned book, laced with anger and indignation, about how our public education system scorns so many of our children. 'Savage Inequalities' is also an important book, and warrants widespread attention." N Y Times Book Rev

Includes bibliographical references

Quinn, Patricia O.
Adolescents and ADD; gaining the advantage. Magination Press 1995 81p il pa $12.95   **371.9**
1. Attention deficit disorder
ISBN 0-945354-70-3   LC 95-25301
The author "defines Attention Deficit Disorder (ADD), explains diagnostic criteria, and discusses treatments. . . . She uses a question-and-answer format throughout much of the book, anticipating virtually any question readers may have. . . . Teens may particularly appreciate the inclusion of first-person accounts by ADD youths, as they share practical coping strategies, including developing time management skills." SLJ

372.1   Generalities of elementary schools

Kidder, Tracy
Among schoolchildren. Houghton Mifflin 1989 340p o.p.; Avon Bks. paperback available $11
372.1
1. Teaching 2. Elementary education
ISBN 0-380-71089-7 (pa)   LC 89-34378
Also available Thorndike Press large print edition
"A Richard Todd book"
"Christine Zajac teaches fifth grade in a racially mixed school in a poor district of Holyoke, Mass. About half of her students are Hispanic; many come from broken homes. Through Kidder's . . . re-creation of Zajac's daily round, we come to know her students' fears and inmost strivings; we also share this teacher's frustrations, loneliness and the rush of satisfaction that comes with helping students learn." Publ Wkly
"A warm, honest, refreshingly positive look inside a classroom. Essential for most libraries." Libr J
Includes bibliography

372.6   Language arts. Storytelling

De Vos, Gail, 1949-
Storytelling for young adults; techniques and treasury. Libraries Unlimited 1991 169p $24.50
372.6
1. Young adults' library services 2. Books and reading 3. Storytelling
ISBN 0-87287-832-5   LC 91-6856
"From a discussion of how YAs benefit from storytelling and techniques for storytelling to this age group, de

Vos describes some original ways classroom activities and library programs can be enhanced with storytelling. An annotated bibliography of good stories by subject is included along with some sample stories, many retold by the author." Voice Youth Advocates

373   Secondary education

Dunnahoo, Terry
How to survive high school; a student's guide; illustrated by Tom Huffman. Watts 1993 111p il lib bdg $22.70; pa $6.95   **373**
1. High schools
ISBN 0-531-11135-0 (lib bdg); 0-531-15705-9 (pa)
LC 92-41700
The author provides "advice on getting adequate sleep and nutrition, handling stress and rejection, setting goals, and dealing with educational labels and vocational school recruiters. Throughout this dose of straight talk, the tone conveys respect for teens. . . . All libraries serving adolescents should have at least one copy of this refreshing title." SLJ
Includes bibliography

Mayer, Barbara, 1939-
How to succeed in high school. VGM Career Horizons 1992 157p pa $8.95   **373**
1. Study skills 2. High schools
ISBN 0-8442-8121-2   LC 91-15316
First published 1981 with title: The high school survival guide
This guide is intended "to help YAs assess themselves and learn how to study effectively. There is information about high school, peer pressure, and ways to accomplish success. Mayer includes specific suggestions and methods for improving grades, outlines obstacles that students may encounter and ways to overcome them, and encourages teens to look to the future." SLJ
"Mayer writes well and students will enjoy her style, which is direct, open, and informative." Voice Youth Advocates

373.2   Types and levels of secondary education

Peterson's private secondary schools. Peterson's il pa $29.95   **373.2**
1. Private schools—Directories 2. Education—United States—Directories
Annual. First published 1980. Title varies
"Describes more than 1,600 American and foreign boarding and day schools including schools that serve children with special needs. Outlines each institution's setting; enrollment by sex, race, grade, and geographic origin; faculty size and educational background; facilities; subjects offered; special programs; graduation requirements; tuition; admissions procedures; and where the graduates go to college." Guide to Ref Books. 11th edition

376   Education of women

Hanmer, Trudy J.

The gender gap in schools; girls losing out. Enslow Pubs. 1996 112p il (Issues in focus) lib bdg $17.95   **376**

1. Sex discrimination 2. Women—Education

ISBN 0-89490-718-2   LC 95-43831

Hanmer "explores issues of self-esteem, eating disorders, sexual harassment, scientific thinking, and standardized tests. . . . The author shows how teachers, male and female alike, treat female students differently than male peers from preschool through college. One chapter gives the history of female education in the United States and the place of females in math and science courses. . . . This is an important, well-documented book that should make female students aware of when and how they are being treated differently. A list of organizations that deal with gender bias is included." SLJ

Includes bibliographical references

378   Higher education

✓ The **Black** student's guide to college success; edited by Ruby D. Higgins [et al.]; foreword by Louis W. Sullivan. Greenwood Press 1993 357p $39.95; pa $35   **378**

1. African Americans—Education 2. Colleges and universities—United States

ISBN 0-313-28604-3; 0-313-29432-1 (pa)

LC 92-21362

This guide offers "advice on how to succeed in college, college success stories, and a college and university directory." Libr J

Includes bibliographical references

Davidson, Wilma

Writing a winning college application essay; [by] Wilma Davidson & Susan McCloskey. Peterson's 1996 125p il pa $9.95   **378**

1. College applications

ISBN 1-56079-601-4   LC 96-21954

At head of title: Peterson's practically painless guide

This book guides students "through each stage of planning, composing, revising, and polishing their essays. Using actual applicant essays, it provides examples, comments on their strengths and shortcomings, and traces the progress of several essays from first through final drafts. . . . References include a 'writer's survival kit' for avoiding common grammar, style, and mechanics mistakes and answers to frequently asked questions." Publisher's note

Includes glossary and bibliographical references

DiSalvo, Jack

College admissions for the high school athlete; [by] Jack DiSalvo and Theresa Foy DiGeronimo. Facts on File 1993 161p $21.95; pa $9.95   **378**

1. Colleges and universities—Entrance requirements 2. Athletes 3. College applications

ISBN 0-8160-2760-9; 0-8160-2816-8 (pa)

LC 93-16811

This volume "shows students how to put their high school academic and athletic records to work for them when applying for college admissions and scholarships. It covers such challenges as: setting goals, contacting college coaches, understanding the rules set by the National Collegiate Athletic Association (NCAA) and other groups, taking campus visits, compiling application packets, finding financial aid, making the final choice." Publisher's note

Dobkin, Rachel

The college woman's handbook; educating ourselves; [by] Rachel Dobkin & Shana Sippy; illustrations by Virginia Halstead. Workman 1995 640p il pa $14.95   **378**

1. Women—Education 2. College students 3. Colleges and universities—United States

ISBN 1-56305-559-7   LC 95-106

This "handbook provides practical advice on a wide range of topics from academic and career issues to health and sexuality. The text opens by focusing on academics: courses and registration, choosing a major, grading issues, how to study, financial aid, and more. It then proceeds to discuss personal finances, housing, health, and nutrition. The chapter entitled 'Getting Ready for the Real World' contains many helpful tips on job hunting, writing résumés and cover letters, researching job opportunities, and interviewing." Libr J

"Librarians who are asked survival questions, parents sending their children to college, college counseling centers, and those seeing friends off to college, would do well to use this lively, provocative, and honest handbook." Choice

Includes bibliographical references

Gottesman, Greg

College survival; [by] Greg Gottesman and friends. 4th ed. Macmillan 1996 246p il pa $10.95   **378**

1. College students 2. Colleges and universities—United States

ISBN 0-02-861068-7   LC 96-12705

First published 1991

At head of title: ARCO

Written by students for students and illustrated with cartoons, this guide presents ideas for coping with college life. Such subjects as clothing, choosing classes, time management, test-taking, dating, and roommates are addressed. A tear-out checklist is included

Hayden, Thomas C.

Peterson's handbook for college admissions; the essential family guide to selecting colleges, visits and interviews, applications, financial aid, the freshman year. 4th ed. Peterson's 1995 279p il pa $14.95   **378**

1. College choice 2. Colleges and universities—Entrance requirements

ISBN 1-56079-428-3   LC 95-33208

First published 1981 by Atheneum Pubs.

"Topics covered include setting priorities and goals in evaluating colleges, using on-line information and other state-of-the-art tools in school selection, making the most of college visits and interviews, preparing for the SAT and ACT tests, understanding the new financial aid guidelines, writing effective application essays, and more." Publisher's note

Lewis, Erica-Lee

Help yourself: handbook for college-bound students with learning disabilities. Random House 1996 236p il pa $20   **378**

1. Learning disabilities 2. College students

ISBN 0-679-76461-5

At head of title: The Princeton Review

This guide covers SAT tests, the admissions process, choice of school and financial aid applications

Nourse, Kenneth A.

How to write your college application essay. VGM Career Horizons 1994 95p pa $12.95   **378**

1. College applications

ISBN 0-8442-4169-5   LC 92-37909

The author "gives examples of essays and tells YAs what admissions counselors are seeking when reading them. . . . One chapter discusses the five-paragraph theme and how to write an essay using this technique. There are several books recommended which will help YAs with their grammar, punctuation, and style. Another chapter gives tips on what to include and what to avoid. Nourse also tells YAs what to do if they do not like any of the suggested essay topics. A good addition to complement your collection of college catalogs, SAT study aids and financial aid guides." Voice Youth Advocates

Paul, William Henry, 1948-

Getting in; an inside look at the admissions process; [by] Bill Paul. Addison-Wesley 1995 260p $20   **378**

1. Colleges and universities—Entrance requirements

ISBN 0-201-62256-4   LC 95-18675

This book "focuses on admissions at a highly selective university. . . . The volume also follows several high school honor students through each step of the process and presents advice from an experienced high school guidance counselor. The book should be helpful to students seeking admission to selective universities, as well as parents and guidance counselors." Libr J

Includes bibliographical references

Robbins, Wendy H.

The portable college adviser; a guide for high school students. Watts 1996 176p il lib bdg $22; pa $9   **378**

1. Colleges and universities—United States 2. College choice

ISBN 0-531-11257-8 (lib bdg); 0-531-15790-3 (pa)   LC 95-47026

"Robbins guides students through the college selection process, including high-school course choices, standardized test preparation, and campus visits and interviews. She also offers advice on applications, financial aid, decision making, and the transition from high school to college." Booklist

"The text is accessible and attractive with highlighted paragraphs, numbered lists and boxed inserts. . . . All high school library media centers should have this guide, and ideally, all prospective college students should have personal copies as well." Book Rep

Includes bibliographical references

Study abroad. Unesco Press; distributed by UNIPUB pa $24   **378**

1. Foreign study—Directories 2. Scholarships

ISSN 0081-895X

First published 1948. Frequently revised

"Lists, for 124 countries, financial aid and courses for foreign students, with information on scholarships, fellowships, and other assistance for study, teaching, research, training, and observation; university-level and short courses; continuing education and training programs; and student employment opportunities." Guide to Ref Books. 11th edition

Worthington, Janet Farrar

The ultimate college survival guide; [by] Janet Farrar Worthington, Ronald Farrar. Peterson's 1995 250p il pa $11.95   **378**

1. College students 2. Colleges and universities—United States

ISBN 1-560-79396-1   LC 94-42142

"This guide speaks directly to first time college entrants. Packed with information, there are thirteen chapters that cover topics such as homesickness, rooming with a stranger, studying and test taking, how to address and communicate with professors, and socializing. Accompanying the traditional chapters this guide incorporates sidebars of additional information. The sidebars contain helpful hints from students, statistics, and explanations of college terminology." Voice Youth Advocates

378.1   Generalities of higher education

ACT, American College Testing Program. Macmillan il pa $24.95   **378.1**

1. ACT assessment 2. Colleges and universities—Entrance requirements

Frequently revised. Authors and title vary

At head of title: Arco

Authors of current edition: Joan U. Levy, Norman Levy

This guide provides subject reviews and practice tests with answers. Study-planning software is included in 1997 edition

Brownstein, Samuel C., 1909-1996

How to prepare for SAT I; [by] Samuel C. Brownstein, Mitchel Weiner [and] Sharon Weiner Green. Barron's Educ. Ser. pa $12.95   **378.1**

1. Scholastic aptitude test 2. Colleges and universities—Entrance requirements

Also available with computer disk for $29.95

Study guides for SAT II subject tests are also available at various prices

First published 1954. Title varies

This guide includes a review of skills, test-taking strategies, and sample tests with answers

Cracking the SAT II [subject tests] Random House il pa ea $17   **378.1**

1. Scholastic aptitude test 2. Colleges and universities—Entrance requirements

At head of title: The Princeton Review

Cracking the SAT II [subject tests]—*Continued*

These guides provide test-taking strategies and sample tests for the following subjects: biology, chemistry, English, French, history, math, physics, and Spanish

Gruber, Gary R.

Gruber's complete preparation for the new SAT. HarperPerennial pa $15.95   **378.1**

1. Scholastic aptitude test 2. Colleges and universities—Entrance requirements

First published 1985 with title: Gruber's complete preparation for the SAT by Critical Thinking Book Co. (7th edition 1996) Frequently revised

The author explains the principles behind the test, reviews necessary skills and develops test-taking strategies. Sample tests with answers are provided

How to prepare for the ACT, American College Testing Assessment Program; [by] George Ehrenhaft [et al.] Barron's Educ. Ser. il pa $12.95   **378.1**

1. ACT assessment 2. Colleges and universities—Entrance requirements

Also available with computer disk for $29.95

First published 1972 with title: Barron's how to prepare for the American College Testing Program (ACT). (10th edition 1995) Frequently revised. Editors vary

A guide to achieving higher scores on the ACT which includes subject reviews and practice exams with answers

Includes bibliography

Preparation for the SAT and PSAT; general editor, Edward J. Deptula. Macmillan pa $24.95   **378.1**

1. Scholastic aptitude test 2. Colleges and universities—Entrance requirements

Frequently revised. Title and editors vary

At head of title: Arco

Seventeenth edition, 1997 includes study-planning software

Provides a review of verbal and quantitative skills and includes practice exams with answers

Robinson, Adam

Cracking the SAT & PSAT; by Adam Robinson and John Katzman. Random House pa $18 **378.1**

1. Scholastic aptitude test 2. Colleges and universities—Entrance requirements

ISSN 1049-6238

Also available with sample tests on computer disk and on CD-ROM for $29.95

Annual. First published 1986 with title: Cracking the system, the SAT

At head of title: The Princeton Review

This volume provides practical advice on how to prepare for the PSAT and SAT college entrance exams. The various types of questions are discussed and samples are provided with full explanations of the correct answers

378.3   Student finances

Athletic scholarships; a complete guide. Conway Greene 1994 561p pa $20.95   **378.3**

1. Athletes 2. Scholarships 3. College sports

ISBN 1-884669-05-0

New edition in preparation

This "is a comprehensive guide to scholarships at more than 1,000 institutions, from National Collegiate Athletic Association (NCAA) Division 1-A level programs to National Association of Intercollegiate Athletes (NAIA) schools. NJCAA (junior colleges) are also listed. . . . Entries are arranged alphabetically by the school name and are easy to read. Indexes are by institution, by sport (for men's and women's), and by state/city. Coverage is not just for the major sports, but includes sports such as wrestling, hockey, fencing, dance, and crew—in all, nearly 60 sports." Recomm Ref Books for Small & Medium-sized Libr & Media Cent, 1996

Berry, Lemuel, Jr.

Minority financial aid directory; a guide to more than 4,000 educational scholarships, loans, grants, and fellowships for African Americans, Asian Americans, Hispanic Americans, Native Americans, and other minorities. Kendall/Hunt 1995 732p pa $45.95   **378.3**

1. Student aid 2. Minorities—Education—Directories

ISBN 0-8403-9944-8   LC 95-141590

In this directory "'awards' are broadly interpreted to include fellowships, grants, internships, loans, and scholarships for both undergraduate and graduate programs. Separate access to awards is provided for Asian Americans, African Americans, Hawaiians, Hispanic Americans, Japanese Americans, Native Alaskans, Native Americans, Native Pacific Islanders, and Puerto Ricans. These are broken down by discipline. . . . Basic information is provided in each entry: name of the agency, criteria for award, amount available, application deadline, and contact person." Booklist

Includes bibliographical references

Kirby, Debra M.

Fund your way through college; uncovering 1,700 great opportunities in undergraduate financial aid; [by] Debra M. Kirby with Christa Brelin. rev ed. Gale Res. 1994 731p $45   **378.3**

1. Scholarships 2. Student loan funds

ISBN 0-8103-9396-4

First published 1992

This is a guide to scholarships and loans available from associations, foundations, corporations, religious groups, and other special interest groups. The main section is arranged alphabetically by the name of the sponsoring organization. Entries include names of the awards, selection criteria, funds available, application details, and deadlines

Ordovensky, Pat

Financial aid for college; a quick guide to everything you need to know, with the new 1996 forms! rev & updated [ed] Peterson's 1995 154p il pa $8.95   **378.3**

1. Student aid 2. Scholarships

ISBN 1-56079-568-9   LC 95-32627

First published 1994

At head of title: USA today

This book describes loans, scholarships, grants, work-study programs and tuition-free colleges; it also includes sample financial aid forms and answers by college admission and financial aid officers to various questions

Peterson's college money handbook. Peterson's
    Guides pa $26.95   **378.3**

1. College costs 2. Student loan funds 3. Scholarships

ISSN 0894-9395

Includes a Windows/Mac-formatted disk

Annual. First published 1983. Variant title: Paying less for college

"Arranged alphabetically and covering more than $36 billion in institutional, state, and federal aid, this . . . book includes profiles of more than 1,600 colleges and universities and the need -and non-need-based scholarships they offer. It answers commonly asked questions about financial aid and provides a step-by-step explanation of the financial aid application process." Publisher's note

Schlachter, Gail A.

Directory of financial aids for minorities; [by] Gail Ann Schlachter, R. David Weber. Reference Service Press $47.50   **378.3**

1. Student aid 2. Minorities—Education—Directories

ISSN 0738-4122

Biennial. First published 1984

"Chapters by type of award (scholarships, loans, grants, internships, etc.) are divided into sections: minorities in general, Asian Americans, Black Americans, Hispanic Americans, and Native Americans. Organized alphabetically by name of sponsoring agency within each section. Additional chapters provide information on state sources of information on educational benefits and list reference sources on financial aid." Guide to Ref Sources. 11th edition

Directory of financial aids for women; [by] Gail Ann Schlachter. Reference Service Press $45
                                              378.3

1. Scholarships 2. Women—Education

ISSN 0732-5215

Biennial. First published 1978

Describes "scholarships, fellowships, loans, grants, awards, and internships designed primarily or exclusively for women. . . . Lists state sources of educational benefits and offers an annotated bibliography of directories that list general financial aid programs. Program title, sponsoring organization, geographic, subject, and filing date indexes." Ref Sources for Small & Medium-sized Libr. 5th edition

Financial aid for the disabled and their families; [by] Gail Ann Schlachter, R. David Weber. Reference Service Press $39.50   **378.3**

1. Scholarships 2. Physically handicapped

Biennial. First published 1988

"Provides information on a wide range of funding needs in such areas as education, career development, research, and travel. Includes multiple indexes; cross-referenced." N Y Public Libr. Book of How & Where to Look It Up

High school senior's guide to merit and other no-need funding; [by] Gail Ann Schlachter, R. David Weber. Reference Service Press $25.95
                                              378.3

1. Scholarships 2. Student aid

First published 1996

The authors focus on "middle-class students who don't qualify for need-based scholarships. They list scholarships based on academic record, artistic ability, religious or ethnic background, etc., that are granted by associations, labor unions, foundations, and other private groups. . . . Entries note eligibility, amount of award, duration, number of awards granted, and deadline." Booklist

"This well-designed survey takes some of the confusion out of the process and presents current information." SLJ

378.73 Institutions of higher education—United States

American universities and colleges. De Gruyter
    lib bdg $149.95   **378.73**

1. Colleges and universities—United States—Directories 2. Education—United States—Directories

ISSN 0066-0922

First published 1928. (14th edition 1992) Frequently revised

Sponsored by the American Council on Education

This directory "describes more than 1,900 accredited schools offering baccalaureate or higher degrees. Its main section, arranged by state, presents narrative data for each college, covering its history, institutional structure and control, admissions and degree requirements, enrollment and degrees conferred, fees and financial arrangements, numbers of teachers in specific departments and degrees they hold, library collections, and student life (dormitories, intercollegiate athletics, car regulations, surrounding communities). Another section lists institutions offering professional degrees at baccalaureate, masters, and doctoral levels, arranged alphabetically by course of study." Guide to Ref Books. 11th edition

Barron's profiles of American colleges. Barron's
    Educ. Ser. pa $23.95   **378.73**

1. Colleges and universities—United States—Directories 2. Education—United States—Directories

ISSN 1065-5026

First published 1964. (21st edition 1996) Periodically revised

Includes computer disks for Windows and Macintosh

"A comprehensive guide to more than 1,550 American colleges and universities, including some Canadian and

Barron's profiles of American colleges—*Continued*

Mexican institutions and American-operated schools abroad. . . . One section, Index of college majors, was published separately as v.2 from 1982-92. Arranged alphabetically by state; index of colleges." Guide to Ref Books. 11th edition

✓ **Black** American colleges & universities; profiles of two-year, four-year, & professional schools; Levirn Hill, editor; introduction by Reginald Wilson. Gale Res. 1994 xli, 796p il maps $60

378.73

1. African Americans—Education 2. Colleges and universities—United States—Directories

ISBN 0-8103-9166-X   LC 94-3898

"This volume profiles 118 two-year, four-year, and professional programs at historically and/or predominantly black colleges and universities. Entries are grouped by state and provide such information as admission and graduation requirements, cost, financial aid, degrees offered, student body, faculty profiles, special programs, and notable alumni. . . . The directory should be very helpful to students interested in attending a predominantly black college or university." Libr J

Cass & Birnbaum's guide to American colleges; for students, parents, and counselors; by James Cass and Max Birnbaum. HarperCollins Pubs. pa $19.95   **378.73**

1. Colleges and universities—United States—Directories 2. Education—United States—Directories

ISSN 1075-3443

Biennial. First published 1964 with title: Comparative guide to American colleges. Editors and title vary

"Emphasizes career-oriented considerations of college selection, with special attention to career counseling and job placement programs, and a Selectivity index categorizing colleges according to their students' academic potential as suggested by SAT and ACT scores, ranks in high school classes, etc." Guide to Ref Books. 11th edition

The College blue book. Macmillan 5v maps lib bdg set $225   **378.73**

1. Colleges and universities—United States—Directories 2. Education—United States—Directories

ISSN 0069-5572

Also available CD-ROM version

Biennial. First published 1923

"The five-volume set contains: 'College Narrative Descriptions'; 'Tabular Data'; 'Degrees Offered by College and Subject'; 'Occupational Education'; and 'Scholarships, Fellowships, Grants and Loans.' . . . The set provides comprehensive and up-to-date information on a wide range of post-secondary education opportunities." Wynar. Guide to Ref Books for Sch Media Cent. 3d edition

College Entrance Examination Board

The college handbook. College Entrance Examination Bd. pa $21.95   **378.73**

1. Colleges and universities—United States—Directories 2. Education—United States—Directories

Annual. First published 1941 by Ginn with title: Annual handbook

This work offers "detailed information for college-bound students on such subjects as freshman admissions requirements and procedures, enrollment, majors, expenses, financial aid, and many other areas of interest." N Y Public Libr. Book of How & Where to Look It Up

Index of majors and graduate degrees. College Entrance Examination Bd. pa $15.95   **378.73**

1. Colleges and universities—United States—Directories 2. Colleges and universities—Curricula

Annual. First published 1977 with title: The college handbook index of majors. Variant title: Index of majors

"Directory of colleges offering specific majors at bachelors, master, doctoral, professional, associate, and certificate levels. Lists of institutions and the degree levels offered for each major are arranged alphabetically by major, then by state. A section on specialized academic programs lists schools that offer cooperative education, dual majors, independent study, study abroad." Guide to Ref Books. 11th edition

Includes glossary

Custard, Edward T.

The complete book of colleges. Random House il pa $25   **378.73**

1. Colleges and universities—United States—Directories 2. Education—United States—Directories

ISSN 1088-8594

Annual. Replaces The big book of colleges, published 1995

At head of title: The Princeton Review student advantage guide

This guide to 1,200 North American colleges includes "academic programs and requirements, majors offered, faculty and student body profiles (including retention and graduation figures), services and facilities, extracurriculars, athletics, costs and financial aid, and admissions." Publisher's note

Fiske, Edward B.

The Fiske guide to colleges. Times Bks. pa $19   **378.73**

1. Colleges and universities—United States—Directories 2. Education—United States—Directories

Annual. First published 1982 with title: The New York Times selective guide to colleges

This guide to over 300 of the best colleges and universities nationwide includes information on admissions, costs, financial aid, housing, social life, and academic strengths and weaknesses

Lovejoy's college guide. Macmillan $45; pa $21.95   **378.73**

1. Colleges and universities—United States—Directories 2. Education—United States—Directories

ISSN 0076-132X

First published 1940 by Simon & Schuster with title: So you're going to college, compiled by Clarence E. Lovejoy. (23rd edition 1995) Frequently revised

"Lovejoy's provides profiles of more than 2,500 four-year and two-year colleges and universities, along with admissions requirements, application procedures, tuition figures, selectivity rankings, and information on many other topics." N Y Public Libr. Book of How & Where to Look It Up

Mitchell, Robert, 1959-
    The multicultural student's guide to colleges; what every African-American, Asian-American, Hispanic, and Native American applicant needs to know about America's top schools. rev ed. Noonday Press 1996 745p pa $25   **378.73**
    1. Colleges and universities—United States—Directories 2. Minorities—Education
    ISBN 0-374-52476-9
    First published 1993
    This work consists of "a combination of tabular and narrative information on each of about two hundred colleges and universities in the United States. . . . Tabular data includes the sort of information in any college guide, as well as items such as non-white freshman admissions, retention rate of non-white students, academic support services, notable non-white alumni, and non-white administrators." Voice Youth Advocates

Peterson's colleges with programs for students with learning disabilities. Peterson's Guides pa $32.95   **378.73**
    1. Learning disabilities 2. Colleges and universities—United States—Directories
    Packaged with computer disk
    Biennial. First published 1985 with title: Peterson's guide to colleges with programs for learning-disabled students
    "Profiles more than 800 two-year and four-year colleges offering special services and programs and includes information on graduate-level options, financial aid, and special services at U.S. and Canadian schools. It's divided into two main sections: one with colleges that have comprehensive programs and the other with schools that make a number of services available." Publisher's note

Peterson's guide to four-year colleges. Peterson's Guides il maps pa $24.95   **378.73**
    1. Colleges and universities—United States—Directories 2. Education—United States—Directories
    ISSN 0894-9336
    Annual. First published 1966 as part of Peterson's annual guide to undergraduate study
    Includes a Windows or Mac computer disk
    "In two major sections: (1) half-page entries for some 2,000 institutions, with details of enrollment, admission requirements, expenses, housing, student aid, and programs offered; (2) two-page in-depth descriptions of more than 800 institutions, prepared by their officials, which emphasize campus environment, student activities, and lifestyle. Indexes: major, entrance difficulty, cost, and name of institution." Guide to Ref Books. 11th edition

Peterson's guide to two-year colleges. Peterson's Guides il pa $21.95   **378.73**
    1. Colleges and universities—United States—Directories 2. Education—United States—Directories
    ISSN 0894-9328
    Annual. First published 1966 as part of Peterson's annual guide to undergradute study
    "Describes 1,400 accredited institutions in the U.S. and its territories awarding the associate degree as their most popular undergraduate offering, plus some non-degree-granting schools. The latter are usually branch campuses of multi-campus systems that offer the first two years of college, transferrable to degree-granting institutions. In addition to the usual information on admission and graduation requirements, programs, costs, etc., treats considerations peculiar to junior colleges, giving advice on profiting from two-year colleges and transferring to four-year schools, statistics on students transferring from individual colleges, and a list by major of colleges offering associate degree programs." Guide to Ref Books. 11th edition

Peterson's register of higher education. Peterson's Guides pa $49.95   **378.73**
    1. Colleges and universities—United States—Directories
    ISSN 1046-2406
    Annual. First published 1988 with title: Peterson's higher education directory
    "Arranged alphabetically by institution; brief entries provide not only the usual data on tuition, enrollment, and similar concerns, but also, e.g., information on computer facilities and names of affiliated research organizations and of such personnel as deans and development officers. Appendixes list major government higher education agencies, accrediting bodies, associations, and consortia, and another section lists recent institutional changes such as newly-adopted college names and school closings." Guide to Ref Books. 11th edition

Spencer, Janet
    Visiting college campuses; by Janet Spencer and Sandra Maleson. Random House il maps pa $20   **378.73**
    1. College choice 2. Colleges and universities—United States
    Annual. First published 1993 with title: The complete guide to college visits by Carol Pub. Group
    At head of title: The Princeton Review
    This volume presents travel information for colleges in the U.S. "Arranged by state, sections begin with a map showing the colleges mentioned and a mileage matrix of the distances between colleges and major cities. The entry for a college begins with a calendar of the typical school year. The address and telephone number of the admissions office is given, followed by information about tours, interviews, class visits, overnight dorm accommodations, and directions on getting to the campus by car, bus, plane, etc. The entry ends with information about off-campus accommodations and tourist attractions." Booklist [review of 1993 edition]

379 Government regulation, control, support of education

Preserving intellectual freedom; fighting censorship in our schools; edited by Jean E. Brown. National Council of Teachers of English 1994 252p pa $24.95   **379**
    1. Academic freedom 2. Censorship 3. Literature—Study and teaching
    ISBN 0-8141-3671-0   LC 94-19860
    This collection of essays "treats censorship solely from the perspective of English teachers, who have con-

Preserving intellectual freedom—*Continued*
cerns about and a stake in intellectual freedom just as librarians do. . . . Some, such as 'The Censorship of Young Adult Literature' and 'Intellectual Freedom and the Student,' are especially interesting because they discuss several specific works. 'What Do I Do Now? Where to Turn When You Face a Censor' is particularly useful in that it discusses anticensorship groups with which many librarians may not be familiar." Booklist
Includes bibliographical references

382 International commerce (Foreign trade)

Miller, E. Willard (Eugene Willard), 1915-
America's international trade; a reference handbook; [by] E. Willard Miller, Ruby M. Miller. ABC-CLIO 1995 325p (Contemporary world issues) $39.50   **382**
1. International trade 2. United States—Commerce 3. United States—Commercial policy
ISBN 0-87436-770-0   LC 95-14135
"This handbook examines issues of global trade from a U.S. standpoint, covering trade agreements, objectives, growth, balance, laws, and organizations. Short, descriptive entries provide an adequate introduction for neophytes and students." Libr J
Includes glossary and bibliographical references

384.3 Computer communication

The **Information** revolution; edited by Donald Altschiller. Wilson, H.W. 1995 241p (Reference shelf, v67 no5) pa $15   **384.3**
1. Information systems
ISBN 0-8242-0872-2   LC 95-23641
The articles in this compilation examine the history and future of the information superhighway; the economic impact of the information revolution; legal and legislative debates over ownership and privacy issues; and cultural and social issues arising from new communications technology
Includes bibliographical references

387.2 Ships

Macaulay, David, 1946-
Ship. Houghton Mifflin 1993 96p il $19.95; pa $8.95   **387.2**
1. Shipwrecks 2. Underwater exploration 3. Caribbean region—Antiquities
ISBN 0-395-52439-3; 0-395-74518-7 (pa)
                                      LC 92-1346
This book "opens with an underwater find in the Caribbean and, in story and illustration, follows the work of marine archeologists in studying the wreck. As part of the background research in Spain, one of the team finds a diary recording the building of a caravel in 1504. The rest of the book contains a 'translation' of the diary with accompanying illustrations. Though a fictional account, the narrative gives a good feel for the maritime technology of the early 16th century." Sci Books Films

389 Metrology and standardization

Darton, Michael
The Macmillan dictionary of measurement; [by] Mike Darton and John Clark. Macmillan 1994 538p il maps $27.50   **389**
1. Weights and measures—Dictionaries
ISBN 0-02-525750-1   LC 93-47005
In this dictionary, some 35 categories of terms are covered, such as mathematics, engineering, "music, sports, geological time, and military rank. The alphabetically arranged entries range from a few words to a page or more. The subject field from which the term is taken is given, and frequently its origin as well. Charts and graphs are used when [needed]." Booklist

391 Costume and personal appearance

Baker, Patricia
Fashions of a decade, The 1940s; original illustrations by Robert Price. Facts on File 1992 64p il $16.95   **391**
1. Costume
ISBN 0-8160-2467-7   LC 91-10326
Chronicles clothing trends of the 1940s and the influence of World War II on styles of dress, availability of many fabrics, and the new ideas of "designers at war"
Includes glossary and bibliography

Fashions of a decade, The 1950s; original illustrations by Robert Price. Facts on File 1991 64p il $16.95   **391**
1. Costume
ISBN 0-8160-2468-5   LC 90-46333
Surveys the fads, fashions, trends, and cultural and intellectual preoccupations of the 1950s
Includes glossary and bibliography

Calasibetta, Charlotte Mankey
Fairchild's dictionary of fashion. 2nd ed. Fairchild Publs. 1988 749p il $60   **391**
1. Fashion design—Dictionaries 2. Costume—Dictionaries
ISBN 0-87005-635-2   LC 88-80198
First published 1975
"This work provides 15,000 definitions along with about 500 well-executed line drawings and another 500 biographical sketches of designers." Ref Sources for Small & Medium-sized Libr. 5th edition

Carnegy, Vicky
Fashions of a decade, The 1980s; original illustrations by Robert Price. Facts on File 1990 64p il $16.95   **391**
1. Costume
ISBN 0-8160-2471-5   LC 90-30895
A pictorial survey chronicling the international clothing fashions of the 1980s

Carnegy, Vicky—*Continued*

This "provides an accessible overview of [the] decade, placing fashion trends within their appropriate political and historical contexts. . . . Browsers and fashion design students alike will be intrigued." Booklist
Includes glossary and bibliography

Connikie, Yvonne

Fashions of a decade, The 1960s; original illustrations by Robert Price. Facts on File 1990 64p il $16.95   **391**
1. Costume
ISBN 0-8160-2469-3   LC 90-30896
A pictorial survey chronicling the international fashions of the 1960s
This is "not for serious students of fashion, but will be fun for browsers and those interested in an introduction to the concept of clothing design in the context of contemporary events." SLJ
Includes glossary and bibliography

Costantino, Maria

Fashions of a decade, The 1930s; original illustrations by Robert Price. Facts on File 1992 64p il $16.95   **391**
1. Costume
ISBN 0-8160-2466-9   LC 91-10327
Chronicles trends in 1930s styles such as lower hemlines and broader shoulders; the introduction of synthetic fabrics; and new views of fitness, health, and personal beauty
Includes glossary and bibliography

Ewing, Elizabeth

History of twentieth century fashion. 3rd ed. Barnes & Noble Bks. 1986 278p il o.p.   **391**
1. Costume—History 2. Fashion—History
     LC 86-3502
First published 1974 in the United Kingdom; 1975 in the United States by Scribner
"The author looks behind the fashion scene for a deeper understanding of the social, economic and technical changes which have caused a revolution in our attitudes toward dress. . . . Over 280 drawings and photographs [portray the] changes and sharp contrasts between succeeding periods and designs." Publisher's note
Includes bibliography

Feldman, Elane

Fashions of a decade, The 1990s; original illustrations by Robert Price. Facts on File 1992 64p il $16.95   **391**
1. Costume
ISBN 0-8160-2472-3
A pictorial survey of the 1990s fashion trends
"The major flaw is that the book understandably includes only two years' worth of information; certainly the years 1992-1999 deserve treatment before a volume may purport to be about the entire decade." SLJ
Includes glossary and bibliography

Herald, Jacqueline

Fashions of a decade, The 1920s; original illustrations by Robert Price. Facts on File 1991 64p il $16.95   **391**
1. Costume
ISBN 0-8160-2465-0   LC 90-46334
Surveys the fads, fashions, trends, and cultural and intellectual preoccupations of the 1920s
"Students interested in fashion and societal changes, as well as those in need of a good outline reference, will find [this volume] . . . helpful." Booklist
Includes glossary and bibliography

Fashions of a decade, The 1970s. Facts on File 1992 64p il $16.95   **391**
1. Costume
ISBN 0-8160-2470-7   LC 91-44209
This volume in the series looks at how the fashions of the 1970s reflected the social, historical and cultural events of that decade
This "includes chapters on 'Black is Beautiful,' 'Dressed to Clash,' 'Trash Culture,' etc. . . . An abundance of full-color and black-and-white illustrations and photographs amplify the text with generally appropriate placement and captions." SLJ
Includes glossary and bibliography

Holkeboer, Katherine Strand

Patterns for theatrical costumes; garments, trims, and accessories from ancient Egypt to 1915. Prentice-Hall 1984 342p il o.p.; Drama Bk. Pubs. paperback available $29.95   **391**
1. Costume 2. Sewing
ISBN 0-89676-125-8 (pa)   LC 83-27057
Each design "includes black-and-white drawings of the completed garment, pattern pieces for enlarging embellishments to be copied, and, when necessary, illustrations of how to wear the particular costume. A few special costumes—clergy, animals, oriental—are featured as are notes on constructing important accessories." Booklist
Includes bibliography

Kennett, Frances

Ethnic dress; [by] Frances Kennett with Caroline MacDonald-Haig. Facts on File 1995 192p il maps $40   **391**
1. Costume
ISBN 0-8160-3136-3   LC 94-37638
"Costumes of the many cultures that do not adhere to . . . Western dress are featured in 500 color photos. Included is everyday clothing as well as costumes for festivals and holidays. Wrapping blankets, sarongs, headdresses, face veils, and head and face decorations are shown. Organization by regions of the world makes for easy use." Book Rep
Includes glossary and bibliography

Lister, Margot

Costume; an illustrated survey from ancient times to the twentieth century. Plays 1968 346p il $32.50   **391**
1. Costume—History
ISBN 0-8238-0096-2
"A comprehensive reference work on costume from the old Egyptian kingdom to 1914, effectively illustrated

Lister, Margot—*Continued*
with line drawings. Attention to details such as hair style, footwear, jewelry, colors and materials, suggestions for constructing the garments, and inclusion of the dress of all classes of society give it practical value. . . . A glossary and list of authorities are included." Booklist

Paterek, Josephine
Encyclopedia of American Indian costume. ABC-CLIO 1994 516p il maps $79.50   **391**
1. Indians of North America—Costume
ISBN 0-87436-685-2   LC 93-39337
Paterek describes "the clothing used for everyday, war, rites, and ceremonies for men, women, and children in hundreds of tribes in diverse climates stretching over centuries. Well-organized text and 400 drawings and authentic photos plus the cultural essays prefacing the 10 regional groupings and each tribe put the costumes in historical, social, and geographic context. Appendixes cover terminology and the materials used in clothing. The excellent bibliographies in this classic work both document and encourage further reading." Am Libr

Payne, Blanche, 1896-1972
The history of costume; from ancient Mesopotamia through the twentieth century; [by] Blanche Payne, Geitel Winakor, Jane Farrell-Beck; drawings by Elizabeth Curtis. 2nd ed. HarperCollins Pubs. 1992 659p il maps   **391**
1. Costume—History
LC 91-16113
Available in hardcover from Watson-Guptill $65 (ISBN 0-8230-4958-2)
First published 1965
"For each period there is brief consideration of the historical background, followed by descriptions—with many photographs and line drawings—of both men's and women's costumes. Some attention is given to footwear, hair styles, and accessories." Guide to Ref Books. 11th edition
Includes bibliographical references

Peacock, John, 1943-
The chronicle of Western fashion; from ancient times to the present day. Abrams 1991 224p il $35
391
1. Costume—History 2. Fashion—History
ISBN 0-8109-3953-3   LC 90-1053
Published in the United Kingdom with title: The chronicle of Western costume
A survey of "Western costume from ancient Egypt to 1980. Presented chronologically, the 8 to 10 illustrations per page are lavishly colored and use color schemes appropriate to each period. All illustrations are labeled with country of origin and wearer's societal status. Every century is followed up by concise captions corresponding to the illustrations. Included is an illustrated glossary." Booklist
Includes bibliographical references

Wilcox, R. Turner, 1888-1970
The dictionary of costume. Scribner 1969 406p il $60   **391**
1. Costume—Dictionaries
ISBN 0-684-15150-2   LC 68-12503
"This fully illustrated dictionary of historic costume covers all facets on a worldwide basis. The entries are primarily succinct descriptions of items of clothing." Ref Sources for Small & Medium-sized Libr. 5th edition
Includes bibliography

Folk and festival costume of the world. Scribner 1965 unp il $55   **391**
1. Costume
ISBN 0-684-15379-3   LC 65-23986
"Traditional costumes from 150 countries, described and illustrated in black and white." N Y Public Libr. Ref Books for Child Collect. 2d edition
Includes bibliography

Yarwood, Doreen
Fashion in the Western world, 1500-1900. Drama Bk. Pubs. 1992 176p il $29.95   **391**
1. Fashion—History 2. Costume—History
ISBN 0-89676-118-5   LC 92-239581
Illustrated with "line drawings and photographs, the book traces the succession of styles of women's, men's, and children's dress and accessories against their contemporary social and cultural background as well as the technological developments in fabrics and the manufacture and care of garments." Publisher's note
Includes bibliographical references

393 Death customs

El Mahdy, Christine
Mummies, myth and magic in ancient Egypt. Thames & Hudson 1989 192p il map hardcover o.p. paperback available $15.95   **393**
1. Mummies 2. Egypt—Antiquities
ISBN 0-500-27579-3 (pa)   LC 89-50542
This volume addresses the origins, nature and significance of the practice of mummification in ancient Egypt. It also examines the attitudes toward mummies in later historical times and discusses the work of modern researchers
"A lavishly illustrated, thoroughly entertaining history." Booklist
Includes glossary and bibliography

394.2 Customs—Special occasions

The **American** book of days; compiled and edited by Jane M. Hatch. 3rd ed. Wilson, H.W. 1978 xxvi, 1214p $87   **394.2**
1. Holidays 2. Festivals—United States
ISBN 0-8242-0593-6   LC 78-16239
First edition by George W. Douglas, published 1937
"Emphasis is on historical events relating to the founding and development of the U.S. and major religious and public holidays; descriptive articles; chronological order with detailed index by topic, key people and events." N Y Public Libr. Ref Books for Child Collect. 2d edition

Chase's calendar of events. Contemporary Bks.
$49.95   **394.2**
1. Calendars 2. Holidays 3. Almanacs
ISSN 0740-5286

Annual. First published 1958 with title: Chase's calendar of annual events, under the editorship of William D. and Helen M. Chase. Variant title: Chase's annual events

"Day-by-day listing of national and state holidays, religious observances, special events, festivals and fairs, and historical anniversaries and birthdays. Covers U.S. events primarily, but some international occasions and anniversaries are included." N Y Public Libr. Book of How & Where to Look It Up

The **Folklore** of American holidays; Hennig Cohen and Tristram Potter Coffin, editors. 2nd ed. Gale Res. 1991 xxxi, 509p $95   **394.2**
1. Holidays 2. Festivals—United States 3. Folklore—United States
ISBN 0-8103-7602-4   LC 91-14994
First published 1987

"A compilation of more than 500 beliefs, legends, superstitions, proverbs, riddles, poems, songs, dances, games, plays, pageants, fairs, foods, and processions associated with over 120 American calendar customs and festivals." Title page

"This is a massive compilation. . . . The entries, in calendar arrangement, range from less than one-half page to 30 (Christmas) and include ideas for holiday programs. A five-part index provides access by subject; ethnic and geographial areas; collectors, informants, and translators; song titles and first lines; and motifs and tale types." Nichols. Guide to Ref Books for Sch Media Cent. 4th edition

The **Folklore** of world holidays; Margaret Read MacDonald, editor. Gale Res. 1992 xxix, 739p $95   **394.2**
1. Holidays 2. Festivals 3. Folklore
ISBN 0-8103-7577-X   LC 91-38032

"This compilation explains the folklore surrounding 340 holidays in over 150 countries, excluding the United States. The contents section lists holidays in chronological order, and countries are arranged below each holiday." Libr J

Includes bibliographical references

Holidays and anniversaries of the world; Jennifer Mossman, editor. 2nd ed. Gale Res. 1990 xxix, 1080p $95   **394.2**
1. Holidays 2. Historical chronology
ISBN 0-8103-4870-5   LC 90-127165
First published 1985

"A comprehensive catalogue containing detailed information of every month and day of the year, with extensive coverage of holidays, anniversaries, fasts and feasts, holy days, days of the saints, the blesseds, and other days of heortological significance, birthdays of the famous, important dates in history, and special events and their sponsors." Title page

Holidays and festivals index; a descriptive guide to information on more than 3,000 holidays . . .; edited by Helene Henderson and Barry Puckett. Omnigraphics 1995 cv, 782p $75
                               394.2
1. Holidays—Indexes 2. Festivals—Indexes
ISBN 0-7808-0012-5   LC 94-39351

"This volume indexes 26 reference books that provide information on more than 3,000 holidays, festivals, celebrations, commemorative days, feasts, and fasts in more than 150 countries. . . . The volume begins with a list of legal holidays by state and country; a dictionary of words relating to periods of time, . . . descriptions of calendar systems, an annotated bibliography of the sources indexed, and a list of additional sources. The entries are arranged alphabetically by English name with alternate forms of foreign names of the holiday in parentheses." Booklist

Santino, Jack
All around the year; holidays and celebrations in American life. University of Ill. Press 1994 xxi, 227p il $24.95; pa $14.95   **394.2**
1. Holidays 2. Festivals 3. United States—Social life and customs
ISBN 0-252-02049-9; 0-252-06516-6 (pa)
                               LC 93-1516

"A look at contemporary American culture as seen through our observance of commemorative and communal festivals and holidays—including local, regional multicultural, religious, and occupational celebrations." Booklist

Includes bibliographical references

Thompson, Sue Ellen, 1948-
Holidays, festivals, and celebrations of the world dictionary; detailing more than 1,400 observances from all 50 states and more than 100 nations; compiled by Sue Ellen Thompson and Barbara W. Carlson. Omnigraphics 1994 lxii, 536p $62 **394.2**
1. Holidays 2. Festivals
ISBN 1-55888-768-7   LC 93-6220
New edition in preparation

"A compendious reference guide to popular, ethnic, religious, national, and ancient holidays, festivals, celebrations, commemorations, holy days, feasts, and fasts, supplemented by a special section on calendar systems, tables of state and national public holidays, special indexes of chronological, cultural and ethnic, geographic, historical, religious, and sports holidays, and a general and key-word index." Title page

395   Etiquette (Manners)

Dresser, Norine
Multicultural manners; new rules of etiquette for a changing society. Wiley 1996 285p pa $14.95
                                  395
1. Etiquette 2. Manners and customs
ISBN 0-471-11819-2   LC 96-139921

"From body language and table manners to classroom behavior and gift giving, this guide to etiquette provides

Dresser, Norine—*Continued*
fascinating information about relations in our multicultural society." Booklist
Includes bibliographical references

Martin, Judith, 1938-
Miss Manners' guide to excruciatingly correct behavior; illustrated by Gloria Kamen. Atheneum Pubs. 1982 745p il o.p.; Warner Bks. paperback available $17.99   **395**
1. Etiquette
ISBN 0-446-38632-4 (pa)   LC 81-69135
"A humorously presented, but determinedly correct, guide to modern social behavior. Incorporates questions and answers from the United Feature Syndicate column by 'Miss Manners.'" Guide to Ref Books. 11th edition

Post, Elizabeth L.
Emily Post's teen etiquette; [by] Elizabeth L. Post and Joan M. Coles. HarperPerennial 1995 177p il pa $11   **395**
1. Etiquette
ISBN 0-06-273337-0   LC 95-18503
Replaces Emily Post talks with teens about manners and etiquette (1986)
"Practical, commonsense advice on dealing with your family, communicating with others, mealtime manners, your appearance, social survival (friendship and dating), money, and getting a job. The basics of how to write a thank you note and which fork to use are covered as well as dealing with call waiting and beepers. The family section recognizes divorce and stepfamilies as well as situations involving abuse." Voice Youth Advocates

Post, Peggy, 1945-
Emily Post's etiquette. HarperCollins Pubs. il $35   **395**
1. Etiquette
First published 1922 under the authorship of Emily Post. Periodically revised and updated. Title varies. 11th-15th editions revised by Elizabeth L. Post; 16th edition 1997 revised by Peggy Post
"The classic reference for which fork to use has been expanded to include such modern situations as dating, living together, second marriages, and co-ed business traveling." N Y Public Libr. Book of How & Where to Look It Up

398 Folklore

Bettelheim, Bruno
The uses of enchantment; the meaning and importance of fairy tales. Knopf 1976 328p hardcover o.p. paperback available $12   **398**
1. Fairy tales—History and criticism 2. Child psychology
ISBN 0-679-72393-5 (pa)
"Premising that unlike other childhood literature, fairy tales function as a necessary aid to emotional growth, a noted child psychologist analyzes some of the old favor-

ites in terms of such concepts as sibling rivalry, the onset of puberty, the threat of adult prerogatives, and reveals how folktales help children accomplish the psychological tasks of development common to the human race." Booklist
"An indispensable handbook for those concerned with child development and children's literature, and fascinating reading for anyone interested in human psychology." Libr J

Bunson, Matthew
The vampire encyclopedia. Crown 1993 303p il hardcover o.p. paperback available $16   **398**
1. Vampires—Dictionaries
ISBN 0-517-88100-4 (pa)   LC 92-42005
This "is an A-Z arrangement of more than 2000 entries drawn from folklore, literature, and popular culture. Entries range in length from a line to over a page, with a few tables (film, literature, etc.) running to several pages. *See* and *See also* references are frequent, . . . appendixes list more novels and anthologies, major works consulted, and vampire societies." Libr J

√ **Deloria, Vine**
Red earth, white lies; Native Americans and the myth of scientific fact; [by] Vine Deloria, Jr. Scribner 1995 286p $23   **398**
1. Indians of North America—Folklore 2. Science—Philosophy 3. Religion and science
ISBN 0-684-80700-9   LC 95-9401
The author "takes the scientific community to task for insisting on uniformity of opinion within academia while neglecting Native oral traditions about such events as the peopling of the Western Hemisphere and the disappearance of the giant animals of Pleistocene era. While many will challenge Deloria's arguments, the author's insistence that scientists investigate non-Western knowledge in their search for the truth echoes a cry heard through Native American communities." Libr J
Includes bibliography

Nigg, Joe
Wonder beasts; tales and lore of the phoenix, the griffin, the unicorn, and the dragon. Libraries Unlimited 1995 160p il $24.50   **398**
1. Animals—Folklore
ISBN 1-56308-242-X   LC 94-46797
The author "has compiled material ranging from Herodotus, Ovid, Pliny the Elder, to Chinese and Native American folk tales, and fantasies by Edith Nesbit. Each entry is carefully documented and a reference list at the end provides dozens of full citations for those who'd like to delve deeper. Wonder Beasts will be useful to students who are researching myth and folklore, and to librarians and scholars who are looking for a comprehensive source list on the topic." Voice Youth Advocates

Skal, David J.
V is for Vampire; the A-to-Z guide to everything undead. Penguin Bks. 1996 288p il pa $15.95   **398**
1. Vampires
ISBN 0-452-27173-8   LC 95-15522
This is a "compendium of vampire-related films, rock groups, personalities, novels, themes, and related topics."

Skal, David J.—*Continued*
Booklist

"This book is sure to entertain the pop culture set interested in the creatures of the night." Voice Youth Advocates

398.03   Folklore—Encyclopedias and dictionaries

Funk & Wagnalls standard dictionary of folklore, mythology, and legend; Maria Leach, editor; Jerome Fried, associate editor. Harper & Row 1984 1236p il hardcover o.p. paperback available $40   **398.03**
1. Folklore—Dictionaries 2. Legends—Dictionaries 3. Mythology—Dictionaries
ISBN 0-06-250511-4 (pa)   LC 72-78268

This is a reissue, with minor corrections, of a title first published 1949-1950 in two volumes

"A comprehensive encyclopedia and dictionary dealing with the gods, heroes, tales, motifs, customs, beliefs, songs, dances, games, proverbs, etc., of the cultures of the world, including survey articles with bibliographies on regions and on special subjects (ballad, dance, fairy tale, national mythologies, etc.), written and signed by specialists." Guide to Ref Books. 11th edition

Jones, Alison
Larousse dictionary of world folklore. Larousse (London); distributed by Larousse Kingfisher Chambers 1995 493p il $27.50; pa $14.95
                398.03
1. Folklore—Dictionaries
ISBN 0-7523-0012-1; 0-7523-0043-1 (pa)

"From the *abatwas* of southern Africa to the zombies of Haiti, more than 1,500 references to folkloric motifs and archetypes from around the world are gathered in this well-written and easy-to-use volume. . . . The main text is augmented by four appendixes: a bibliography of suggested reading, a biographical guide to 37 significant folklorists, a worldwide directory of folklore-related museums, and a calendar of festivals and events." Choice

For a fuller review see: Booklist, Feb. 1, 1996

398.2   Folk literature

Sagas, romances, legends, ballads, and fables in prose form, and fairy tales, folk tales, and tall tales are included here, instead of with the literature of the country of origin, to keep the traditional material together and to make it more readily accessible. Modern fairy tales are classified with Fiction, Story collections (SC)

✓ **African** folktales; traditional stories of the black world; selected and retold by Roger D. Abrahams. Pantheon Bks. 1983 354p il hardcover o.p. paperback available $17   **398.2**
1. Folklore—Africa
ISBN 0-394-72117-9 (pa)   LC 83-2474

"The Pantheon fairy tale and folklore library"

This collection contains almost one hundred tales gleaned from the storytelling traditions of Africa, south of the Sahara

Includes bibliography

American folklore; an encyclopedia; edited by Jan Harold Brunvand. Garland 1996 794p il (Garland reference library of the humanities) $95   **398.2**
1. Folklore—United States—Dictionaries 2. North America—Social life and customs—Dictionaries
ISBN 0-8153-0751-9   LC 95-53734

This volume contains "more than 500 articles covering American and Canadian folklore from holidays, festivals, and rituals to crafts, music, dance, and occupations. Well-chosen black-and-white photographs illustrate many aspects of our rich folklife tradition. Twenty-three ethnic groups receive lengthy articles describing their traditional and contemporary folklore—with the exception of Native Americans." Am Libr

For a fuller review see: Booklist, Aug. 1996

Includes bibliographical references

✓ **Arab** folktales; translated and edited by Inea Bushnaq. Pantheon Bks. 1986 xxviii, 386p hardcover o.p. paperback available $18   **398.2**
1. Arabs—Folklore
ISBN 0-394-75179-5 (pa)   LC 85-9569

"Ranging throughout the Arab world from Africa to the Middle East, this collection contains animal stories, tales of mischief and trickery, ghost and magic stories, and religious and moral instructions." Booklist

"The importance of [this] book is not only in the pleasure and delight it gives but in the way it participates in the retrieval of a cultural heritage by making that culture available to today's English-language reader." N Y Times Book Rev

Includes bibliography

✓ **Asian-Pacific** folktales and legends; edited by Jeannette L. Faurot. Simon & Schuster 1995 252p pa $12   **398.2**
1. Folklore—Asia
ISBN 0-684-81197-9   LC 95-31549

"A Touchstone book"

"The 65 myths and folktales in this volume are gathered from the rich heritage of legends in eight East and Southeast Asian countries, with the largest number of stories coming from China (17). The editor herself translates or retells 14 of the Chinese stories for this collection, while the others are reprinted from existing anthologies. . . . The collection gives a quick, multinational overview of some favorite Asian legends." Libr J

Best-loved folktales of the world; selected and with an introduction by Joanna Cole; illustrated by Jill Karla Schwarz. Doubleday 1983 xxiv, 792p il pa $15.95   **398.2**
1. Folklore 2. Fairy tales
ISBN 0-385-18949-4   LC 81-43288

"200 tales from widely ranging countries of the world make up this diversified collection. . . . Familiar classics and lesser known stories are arranged geographically by region, but access can also be obtained through an index of categories, which is appended. Here, users can find tales through motifs, such as trickster heroes, giants and ogres, fables with a moral, quests, and magical helpers." Booklist

Best-loved stories told at the National Storytelling Festival; selected by the National Association for the Preservation and Perpetuation of Storytelling. National Storytelling Press 1991 223p hardcover o.p. paperback available $14.95
398.2

1. Folklore 2. Fairy tales 3. Storytelling—Collections
ISBN 0-87999-100-4 (pa)   LC 91-30058

Companion volume More best-loved stories told at the National Storytelling Festival available for $24.95 (ISBN 1-87999-109-8); pa $14.95 (ISBN 1-87999-108-X)

A collection of thirty-seven traditional and adapted folk and fairy tales, original tales, true narratives, and ghost stories, told at the annual National Storytelling Festival from 1973 to 1990. Includes information about the storytellers, the tales, and the background of the festival

Dolan, Edward F., 1924-
The Old farmer's almanac book of weather lore; the fact and fancy behind weather predictions, superstitions, old-time sayings, and traditions; foreword by Willard Scott. Yankee Bks. 1988 224p il o.p.   **398.2**

1. Weather—Folklore

LC 88-14018

The author "discusses weather phenomena, noting that much of the lore originated with farmers and seafarers. Everybody knows the one about the wooly-bear caterpillar, for example: the width of its brown band foretells the severity of the coming winter. Dolan notes that this prediction is usually accurate, and that scientists can't explain why. He also gives a formula for determining the temperature at any given moment by counting cricket chirps. All this is agreeable trivia." Publ Wkly
Includes bibliography

Edmonds, Margot
Voices of the winds: native American legends; [by] Margot Edmonds, Ella E. Clark. Facts on File 1989 368p il $29.95   **398.2**

1. Indians of North America—Legends
ISBN 0-8160-2067-1   LC 89-35431

"Traditional stories from 60 Native cultures of North America are prefaced by brief headnotes. Sources include government documents, periodicals, histories, and field research." Libr J

"Edmonds and Clark have produced a mammoth sampling . . . that will attract teenagers interested in folklore, as well as those pursuing native American studies." Booklist
Includes bibliography

Favorite folktales from around the world; edited by Jane Yolen. Pantheon Bks. 1986 498p hardcover o.p. paperback available $18 **398.2**

1. Folklore 2. Fairy tales
ISBN 0-394-75188-4 (pa)   LC 86-42644

"Selections include tales from the American Indians, the brothers Grimm, Italo Calvino's Italian folk-tales, as well as stories from Iceland, Afghanistan, Scotland, and many other countries. Yolen provides each section with a relevant introduction, often including historical and literary factors, thus alerting readers as to what to look for." SLJ

Guiley, Rosemary Ellen
Atlas of the mysterious in North America. Facts on File 1994 unp il maps $35; pa $17.95 **398.2**

1. Folklore—United States
ISBN 0-8160-2876-1; 0-8160-2882-6 (pa)

LC 93-41985

Contents: Power points and sacred places; Earthworks and mounds; Stoneworks; Haunted places; Ghost lights; Phantom and mystery ships; Water monsters; Mysterious creatures

"Sections are broken down by state and Canadian province and then alphabetically by site. For states or regions with heavy concentrations of sites, there is a detailed map. Each chapter has a brief description of the sites listed. Notes on sites vary from a line or two to several paragraphs." Booklist
Includes bibliographical references

Hearne, Betsy Gould
Beauties and beasts; by Betsy Hearne; illustrated by Joanne Caroselli. Oryx Press 1993 179p il (Oryx multicultural folktale series) pa $23.50
398.2

1. Fairy tales 2. Folklore 3. Mythology
ISBN 0-89774-729-1   LC 93-16

"The theme of a lonely beast who is transformed by the magic of human love is threaded throughout world-wide variations of the 'Beauty and the Beast' folktale. Author Betsy G. Hearne presents 28 versions of the beloved fable with minimal adaptations from around the world." Publisher's note

"Professionals will be very grateful for this sensitively written, thoughtful, and accessible interpretive collection." J Youth Serv Libr
Includes bibliography

Irish folktales; edited by Henry Glassie. Pantheon Bks. 1985 353p il hardcover o.p. paperback available $17   **398.2**

1. Folklore—Ireland
ISBN 0-394-74637-6 (pa)   LC 85-42841

A compilation of "more than 100 short Irish folktales that encompass such familiar themes as animals, ghosts, poets, mischievous fairies, religion, and, of course, Irish history. Taken together, these tales, which successfully capture the voice of the teller while avoiding excessive dialect, provide a valuable overview of the rich Irish folk tradition." Booklist
Includes bibliography

Lester, Julius
Black folktales; illustrated by Tom Feelings. Baron, R.W. 1969 159p il o.p.; Grove Press paperback available $9.95   **398.2**

1. Blacks—Folklore 2. Folklore—Africa
ISBN 0-8021-3242-1 (pa)

"Lester gives 12 African and Afro-American folk tales such twentieth-century touches as the Lord's reading of the 'TV Guide' and the mention of Rap Brown and Aretha Franklin but his sprightly versions retain the spirit and shape of the original story. . . . These stories of creation, love, folk heroes, and everyday people have a direct simplicity and laconic humor that is both effective and appealing." Booklist

Malory, Sir Thomas, 15th cent.

Le morte d'Arthur   **398.2**
1. Arthur, King
Hardcover and paperback editions available from various publishers
Originally published 1485
"The work is a skillful selection and blending of materials taken from the mass of Arthurian legends. The central story consists of two main elements: the reign of King Arthur ending in catastrophe and the dissolution of the Round Table; and the quest of the Holy Grail." Oxford Companion to Engl Lit

Picard, Barbara Leonie, 1917-

Tales of ancient Persia; retold from the Shah-N-ama of Firdausi by Barbara Leonie Picard; illustrated by Victor G. Ambrus. Oxford Univ. Press 1993 173p il (Oxford myths and legends) pa $12.95   **398.2**
1. Folklore—Iran
ISBN 0-19-274154-3
First published 1972 in the United Kingdom
These stories are from the first half of the Iranian epic poem the Book of Kings, by Firdausi. This book "begins with the creation of the world by Ormuzd, or Ahura Mazda, and the introduction into it of evil and falsehood by Ahrimän, but the bulk of the stories are concerned with the great hero Rustem." Times Lit Suppl

Pourrat, Henri, 1887-1959

French folktales; from the collection of Henri Pourrat; selected by C.G. Bjurström; translated and with an introduction by Royall Tyler. Pantheon Bks. 1989 xxvi, 484p il (Pantheon fairy tale & folklore library) hardcover o.p. paperback available $17   **398.2**
1. Folklore—France
ISBN 0-679-74833-4 (pa)   LC 89-42560
This is a selection of stories from Le Trésor des Contes, a collection of folk and fairy tales from the Auvergne
These "stories range from brief jokes and fables to elaborate tales of adventure and enchantment. . . . The selection is unusually rich and varied." Christ Sci Monit
Includes bibliography

Pyle, Howard, 1853-1911

The story of King Arthur and his knights; written and illustrated by Howard Pyle. Scribner 1984 312p il $21   **398.2**
1. Arthur, King 2. Arthurian romances
ISBN 0-684-14814-5   LC 84-50167
Also available in paperback from Dover Publs.
A reissue of the title first published 1903
The first of a four-volume series retelling the Arthurian legends
This is an account of the times "when Arthur, son of Uther-Pendragon, was Overlord of Britain and Merlin was a powerful enchanter, when the sword Excalibur was forged and won, when the Round Table came into being." Publisher's note

The story of Sir Launcelot and his companions. Scribner 1985 340p il   **398.2**
1. Lancelot (Legendary character) 2. Arthurian romances
Available in paperback from Dover Publs.
A reissue of the title first published 1907
This third book of the series follows "Sir Launcelot's adventures as he rescues Queen Guinevere from the clutches of Sir Mellegrans, does battle with the Worm of Corbin, wanders as a madman in the forest and is finally returned to health by the Lady Elaine." Best Sellers

The story of the champions of the Round Table; written and illustrated by Howard Pyle. Scribner 1984 328p il $19.95   **398.2**
1. Arthurian romances
ISBN 0-684-18171-1
Also available in paperback from Dover Publs.
A reissue of the title first published 1905
Contents: The story of Launcelot; The book of Sir Tristram; The book of Sir Percival
"Pyle's second volume of Arthurian legends will be of interest to motivated students of literature and history, as well as useful in professional collections for comparisons and source work. In spite of the archaic language . . . the narrative depth and graphic force . . . will draw in readers." Booklist

The story of the Grail and the passing of Arthur. Scribner 1985 258p il $19.95   **398.2**
1. Arthur, King 2. Arthurian romances 3. Grail—Fiction
ISBN 0-684-18483-4   LC 85-40302
Also available in paperback from Dover Publs.
A reissue of the title first published 1910
This fourth volume of the series follows the adventures of Sir Geraint, Galahad's quest for the holy Grail, the battle between Launcelot and Gawaine, and the slaying of Mordred

√ A **Treasury** of African folklore; the oral literature, traditions, myths, legends, epics, tales, recollections, wisdom, sayings, and humor of Africa; [compiled] by Harold Courlander. Crown 1975 617p il o.p.; Marlowe & Co. paperback available $14.95   **398.2**
1. Folklore—Africa
ISBN 0-56924-816-8 (pa)
"Originating with the familiar Yoruba, Iausa, and Amhara peoples as well as with other African tribes the selections, reprinted from literary sources or recorded from individual contributors, convey affinities within cultures and at the same time illustrate particularized, sometimes unique forms and themes within a shared inheritance." Booklist
Includes bibliography

√ The **White** deer and other stories told by the Lenape; edited by John Bierhorst. Morrow 1995 137p il $15   **398.2**
1. Delaware Indians—Legends
ISBN 0-688-12900-5   LC 94-30962
"These short tales were written down or tape-recorded by Native Americans at various times during the twenti-

The White deer and other stories told by the Lenape—*Continued*

eth century. Bierhorst adds an informative introduction describing Lenape history and storytelling practice. The tales of origins, lost children, boy heroes, tricksters, and prophecy will also interest adult storytellers." Horn Book Guide

Includes glossary and bibliographical references

World folktales; [edited by] Atelia Clarkson & Gilbert B. Cross. Scribner 1980 450p o.p.

398.2

1. Folklore

LC 79-20921

"A Scribner resource collection"

"The volume presents an approach to 'the complex study of folklore narrative' with discussions of the use of folklore in a classroom or a library and includes sixty-six representative examples of folk tales from around the world. The annotation for each tale comments on tale type and principal motifs." Horn Book

Includes bibliography

Yiddish folktales; edited by Beatrice Silverman Weinreich; translated by Leonard Wolf. Pantheon Bks. 1988 xxxii, 413p il (Pantheon fairy tale & folklore library) hardcover o.p. paperback available $18

398.2

1. Jews—Folklore

ISBN 0-679-73097-4 (pa)   LC 88-42594

Published in cooperation with Yivo Institute for Jewish Research

A "collection of Yiddish folktales divided into various categories, including allegories, children's tales, humor, legends, and the supernatural. The more than 200 selections from the world of Eastern European Jewry are drawn from the archives of the YIVO Institute of Jewish Research. . . . [This work] brings the Yiddish culture of long ago vividly to life." Booklist

398.9 Proverbs

The **Oxford** dictionary of English proverbs; with an introduction by Joanna Wilson. 3rd ed, revised by F. P. Wilson. Oxford Univ. Press 1970 930p $55

398.9

1. Proverbs

ISBN 0-19-869118-1

First published 1935. The first two editions were compiled by William George Smith

Proverbs are "alphabetized under significant words (usually the first). . . . Liberal cross references are included from all other significant words, usually with enough of the phrase so that it is readily identifiable. . . . Dated references are given for each proverb to the earliest uses and sources found, with variant usages at succeeding times, shown by examples from literature." Guide to Ref Books. 11th edition

Titelman, Gregory Y.

Random House dictionary of popular proverbs & sayings; [by] Gregory Titelman. Random House 1996 468p $30

398.9

1. Proverbs

ISBN 0-679-44554-4   LC 95-52189

This dictionary contains 1,500 expressions. Each proverb or saying is given a definition; a discussion of its origins; a list of variants; and examples from a variety of sources

For a review see: Booklist, July, 1996

400 LANGUAGE

Crystal, David, 1941-

The Cambridge encyclopedia of language. Cambridge Univ. Press 1987 472p il maps $64.95; pa $32.95

400

1. Language and languages

ISBN 0-521-26438-3; 0-521-42443-7 (pa)

LC 86-32637

"Thematic sections cover subjects such as sounds, speech development, and language families, and include numerous illustrations, graphs, charts, and abbreviations, a table of world languages, and bibliographies of suggested readings. Language, author/name, and subject indexes." Guide to Ref Books. 11th edition

Katzner, Kenneth

The languages of the world; Kenneth Katzner. New ed. Routledge 1995 378p pa $16.95   **400**

1. Language and languages

ISBN 0-415-11809-3   LC 94-24228

First published 1975 by Funk & Wagnalls

After presenting an overview of the major language families the author describes specific languages arranged by geographical areas. A country-by-country language survey completes the volume

This is "an essential tool for linguists. Literature buffs will also appreciate the passages (with translations) included here in the original language and in the native script if the language uses a nonroman alphabet." Am Ref Books Annu, 1997

Includes bibliographical references

412 Etymology

Hayakawa, S. I.

Language in thought and action; [by] S.I. Hayakawa and Alan R. Hayakawa. 5th ed. Harcourt Brace Jovanovich 1990 287p il $28.50; pa $11

412

1. Semantics 2. Thought and thinking 3. English language

ISBN 0-15-550120-8; 0-15-648240-1 (pa)

LC 89-84371

First published 1939 with title: Language in action

The author analyzes the nature of language, discusses the processes of thinking and writing, and gives advice on thinking and writing clearly

Includes bibliography

413 Dictionaries

The **Macmillan** visual dictionary. multilingual ed. Macmillan 1994 959p il $60   **413**

1. Picture dictionaries 2. Polyglot dictionaries

ISBN 0-02-578115-4   LC 94-15016

Also available in English-language and abridged editions

This terminology-oriented dictionary is "organized into forty-two chapters and includes such subjects as astronomy, the animal kingdom, the human being, sports, and health and safety. Specific objects as well as features of these objects are named in detail in English, Spanish, French, and German. It also includes individual indexes in the four different languages. . . . With over 3,500 computer-generated illustrations and more than 25,000 terms in four different languages, it will prove to be a valuable reference for school librarians." Voice Youth Advocates

419 Verbal language not spoken and written

Butterworth, Rod R.

Signing made easy; a complete program for learning sign language. Includes sentence drills and exercises for increased comprehension and signing skill; [by] Rod R. Butterworth and Mickey Flodin. Putnam Pub. Group 1989 224p il pa $11.95   **419**

1. Sign language

ISBN 0-399-51490-2   LC 88-23878

"A Perigee book"

"Presented in a large-format . . . design, the book is organized into general subject areas such as Family and Friends, Work, Food, and Travel. Each chapter builds progressively on the vocabulary and grammar of the previous lesson." Publisher's note

Costello, Elaine

Random House American sign language dictionary; illustrated by Lois Lenderman, Paul M. Setzer, Linda C. Tom. Random House 1994 xxxiv, 1067p il $50   **419**

1. Sign language

ISBN 0-394-58580-1

Costello "has compiled over 5000 signs in this massive dictionary. Each sign is illustrated with a full-torso picture showing hand configuration and movement, and both the common and alternate meanings are given where necessary. Arranged like a typical dictionary, this work is easy to use and very detailed." Libr J

Signing; how to speak with your hands; illustrated by Lois A. Lehman. rev ed. Bantam Bks. 1995 xx, 262p il pa $16.95   **419**

1. Sign language

ISBN 0-553-37539-3   LC 94-46156

First published 1983

An illustrated introduction to American Sign Language (ASL) and its different uses by both the hearing and the deaf

Includes bibliographical references

Riekehof, Lottie L.

The joy of signing; the illustrated guide for mastering sign language and the manual alphabet. 2nd ed. Gospel Pub. House 1987 352p il $18.95   **419**

1. Sign language

ISBN 0-88243-520-5   LC 86-80173

First published 1963 with title: Talk to the deaf

This manual presents over 1300 signs used for communicating with deaf adults, and provides basic vocabulary needed for entering interpreter training programs. Signs are arranged in 25 categories with an alphabetical index. For each sign there is a line drawing, description of how to make sign, origin (concept) and notes on usage

Includes bibliography

Sternberg, Martin L. A.

American sign language: a comprehensive dictionary; illustrated by Herbert Rogoff. Harper & Row 1981 xlv, 1132p il $75   **419**

1. Sign language

ISBN 0-06-270052-9   LC 75-25066

Also available CD-ROM version; an abridged paperback edition is also available

This guide "contains some 5000 alphabetically arranged entries, each providing a pronunciation guide, grammatical notes, and a description and illustration of the appropriate sign and its formation. Extensive bibliography with a subject index, and seven foreign language indexes." Ref Sources for Small & Medium-sized Libr. 5th edition

Includes bibliography

420 English and Old English

Crystal, David, 1941-

The Cambridge encyclopedia of the English language. Cambridge Univ. Press 1995 489p il maps $54.95   **420**

1. English language

ISBN 0-521-40179-8   LC 94-23918

This "volume is divided into six broad topics that cover the English language's history, vocabulary, grammar, writing and speech systems, usage, and acquisition. Within these major topics, the book is divided into logical subtopics and finally into the basic unit of the text—the two-page spread. . . . The clear and spirited text is stunning, enhanced with over 500 illustrations, making this a particularly rich reference work and a browser's dream." Libr J

For a fuller review see: Booklist, July 1995

McCrum, Robert

The story of English; [by] Robert McCrum, William Cran, Robert MacNeil. new & rev ed. Penguin Bks. 1993 c1992 394p il maps pa $22.95   **420**

1. English language—History

ISBN 0-14-015405-1   LC 92-20181

First published 1986 by Viking; present edition first published 1992 in the United Kingdom

McCrum, Robert—*Continued*

This book is a companion to the PBS series on the history of the English language. The book discusses the development of the language in British, Scots, Irish, American, Australian, Canadian and black Englishes and the modern evolution of English and English-based Creoles in former British colonies

Includes bibliographical references

The **Oxford** companion to the English language; edited by Tom McArthur; managing editor, Feri McArthur. Oxford Univ. Press 1992 xxvii, 1184p il $55   **420**

1. English language

ISBN 0-19-214183-X

"This Oxford companion—part dictionary, part usage guide, part linguistic encyclopedia—offers the broadest range of reference information to be found in any single source. Included are entries on grammar, prosody, language acquisition, and sexist language, on every nation where English is widely spoken, and on writers and lexicographers whose works have significantly affected the development of the language—about 5,000 entries all told." Am Libr

421.03 Written and spoken codes of standard English—Dictionaries

The **Barnhart** abbreviations dictionary; edited by Robert K. Barnhart. Wiley 1995 xxi, 434p $34.95   **421.03**

1. Abbreviations—Dictionaries 2. Signs and symbols 3. Acronyms

ISBN 0-471-57146-6   LC 96-115251

"This dictionary provides more than 60,000 entries for currently used abbreviations. . . . Two distinct parts form this work. The first is the list of abbreviation headwords with explanatory material. . . . The second part consists of a reverse list of words, phrases, and written symbols with current abbreviation forms. . . . [This work] belongs on ready reference shelves in academic and public libraries." Choice

Kleinedler, Steven Racek

NTC's dictionary of acronyms and abbreviations; compiled by Steven Racek Kleinedler; edited by Richard A. Spears. National Textbook 1993 311p $16.95; pa $12.95   **421.03**

1. Acronyms 2. Abbreviations—Dictionaries

ISBN 0-8442-5160-7; 0-8442-5376-6 (pa)

LC 93-188151

This is a "guide to approximately 2,100 acronyms, initialisms, blends, clippings and abbreviations. . . . The differences among these terms are defined in a brief introduction. This work provides a selection of 'shortened forms' one is most likely to encounter in newspapers, directions, instructions, and on packaging, as well as acronyms for major governmental organizations." Booklist

Webster's guide to abbreviations. Merriam-Webster 1985 383p $6.50   **421.03**

1. Abbreviations—Dictionaries

ISBN 0-87779-072-8   LC 85-15286

This guide contains "some 7,700 abbreviations and approximately 12,000 words and phrases that are most of-ten abbreviated in general reading and writing. Part 1 arranges abbreviations in one alphabetical sequence. . . . The second part, a reverse list, enters words and phrases, followed by their abbreviations." Wynar. Guide to Ref Books for Sch Media Cent. 3d edition

422.03 Etymology of standard English—Dictionaries

The **Barnhart** dictionary of etymology; Robert K. Barnhart, editor; Sol Steinmetz, managing editor. Wilson, H.W. 1988 xxvii, 1284p $64   **422.03**

1. English language—Etymology—Dictionaries

ISBN 0-8242-0745-9   LC 87-27994

"Avoiding abbreviations and technical terminology, and gracefully blending linguistic and historic fact based on the most current American scholarship, this dictionary traces the origin of over 30,000 words in American English. For scholar and lay reader alike." Libr J

Hendrickson, Robert, 1933-

The Facts on File encyclopedia of word and phrase origins. Facts on File 1987 581p $50

    422.03

1. English language—Etymology—Dictionaries 2. English language—Terms and phrases

ISBN 0-8160-1012-9   LC 86-2067

Also available in a paperback edition from Holt & Co. with title: The Henry Holt encyclopedia of word and phrase origins

"This is a collection of stories, speculative though entertaining, behind 7500 English words and phrases. . . . The stories are fascinating, but the book is marred by many misspellings, particularly in the quotations from German." Libr J

Merriam-Webster's word histories. Merriam-Webster 1993 c1989 526p $21.95; pa $9.95   **422.03**

1. English language—Etymology—Dictionaries

ISBN 0-87779-148-1; 0-87779-603-3 (pa)

LC 93-22569

Replaces Webster's word histories, published 1989

This volume presents entries that discuss the origins of some 1500 English words

The **Oxford** dictionary of English etymology; edited by C. T. Onions; with the assistance of G. W. S. Friedrichsen and R. W. Burchfield. Oxford Univ. Press 1966 1024p $65   **422.03**

1. English language—Etymology—Dictionaries

ISBN 0-19-861112-9

Also available in a concise edition pa $15.95 (ISBN 0-19-283098-8)

"Authoritative work tracing the history of common English words back to their Indo-European roots." Ref Sources for Small & Medium-sized Libr. 5th edition

Rees, Nigel, 1944-

Dictionary of catchphrases. Cassell; distributed by Sterling 1995 230p hardcover o.p. paperback available $10.95   **422.03**

1. English language—Etymology—Dictionaries 2. English language—Terms and phrases

ISBN 0-304-34788-4 (pa)   LC 95-189181

A "guide to over 1200 popular expressions from all over the English-speaking world. 'Calling all cars,' 'A funny thing happened to me on the way . . .,' 'Is everybody happy?,' 'no comment,' and other well-known phrases are collected here. A boon for projects on the origins of words and for ESL students." SLJ

For a fuller review see: Booklist, Feb. 15, 1996

Tuleja, Tad, 1944-

Foreignisms; a dictionary of foreign expressions commonly (and not so commonly) used in English. Macmillan 1988 205p hardcover o.p. paperback available $9.95   **422.03**

1. English language—Foreign words and phrases—Dictionaries

ISBN 0-02-038020-8 (pa)   LC 88-21563

Provides "spellings, pronunciations, and the meanings of confusing Latin, French, Italian, and other foreign terms. Beyond a genial 'A-Z' listing of definitions, Tuleja offers special sections on popular expressions, subdivided by nationality or purpose. . . . Handy for reference or casual enlightenment." Booklist

Word mysteries & histories; from quiche to humble pie; by the editors of The American Heritage Dictionaries; with illustrations by Barry Moser; foreword by Robert Claiborne. Houghton Mifflin 1986 308p il hardcover o.p. paperback available $9.95   **422.03**

1. English language—Etymology—Dictionaries

ISBN 0-395-40264-6 (pa)   LC 86-10455

"The editors of the American Heritage dictionaries have prepared a fine repast for the etymological gourmand. Inspired by queries from the dictionaries' readers, these discussions of the origin and usage of such unusual words as *fizzle, jackanapes, posh,* and *sunbeam* are served up with witty elegance. Enhanced by Barry Moser's woodcuts, this volume is a thesaurus in the earliest sense of the term—'a treasury of words.'" Booklist

423   English language—Dictionaries

The **American** Heritage college dictionary. 3rd ed. Houghton Mifflin 1993 xxxiv, 1630p il maps $18.95; thumb-indexed $22.95   **423**

1. English language—Dictionaries

ISBN 0-395-66917-0; 0-395-44638-4 (thumb-indexed)   LC 92-42124

First published 1975 as an abridgement of The American Heritage dictionary of the English language

This dictionary is derived from the third edition of The American Heritage dictionary of the English language. It "has 185,000 words (200,000 definitions) and about 15,000 new words and meanings, nearly the same as the parent work. . . . Most of the usage and regional notes and the synonym paragraphs from the parent work are found in this version. Biographical and geographic entries are in the main A-Z sequence." Booklist

Bartlett's Roget's thesaurus. Little, Brown 1996 xxxii, 1415p $18.95   **423**

1. English language—Synonyms and antonyms

ISBN 0-316-10138-9   LC 96-18343

This work includes "more than 350,000 terms and phrases in an easy-to-use format . . . [this is] a thesaurus that reflects the current state of American English, including terminology from the worlds of composers and television, with such sub-categories as 'Living Things,' 'The Arts,' 'Feelings.' But what really makes the book a joy to use is the tremendously useful lists—everything from phobias to styles and periods of furniture." Am Libr

For a fuller review see: Booklist, April 15, 1996

The **Concise** Oxford dictionary of current English. Oxford Univ. Press $27.50; thumb-indexed $29.95   **423**

1. English language—Dictionaries (thumb-indexed)

First published 1911 under the editorship of H. W. Fowler and F. G. Fowler. (9th edition 1995) Periodically revised

This work contains approximately 120,000 entries, including derivatives, compounds and abbreviations. It includes explanatory notes on pronunciation, grammatical inflection and etymology

Dorling Kindersley ultimate visual dictionary. Dorling Kindersley 1994 640p il $39.95   **423**

1. Picture dictionaries 2. English language—Dictionaries

ISBN 1-56458-648-0   LC 94-11173

A "dictionary that uses more than 6,000 full-color photographs, illustrations, and cross sections to explore most aspects of the natural world: the universe, prehistoric Earth, architecture, and much more. Arranged by subject but indexed in great detail." SLJ

Glazier, Stephen

Random House word menu. [newly rev & updated ed] Random House 1997 xxix, 767p $35   **423**

1. English language—Synonyms and antonyms 2. English language—Terms and phrases

ISBN 0-679-44963-9   LC 96-27251

First published 1992

This work classifies approximately 75,000 words into seven general categories: nature; science and technology; domestic life; institutions; arts and leisure; language; the human condition

Kipfer, Barbara Ann

Roget's 21st century thesaurus in dictionary form; the essential reference for home, school, or office. Dell 1992 978p hardcover o.p. paperback available $12.95   **423**

1. English language—Synonyms and antonyms

ISBN 0-385-31255-5 (pa)   LC 91-37916

"Produced by The Philip Lief Group, Inc."

This thesaurus "follows the now-popular dictionary format for its 17,000 main entries (*abandon-zoom*) and provides other innovations as well. The part of speech,

Kipfer, Barbara Ann—*Continued*

very brief definition, synonyms (over 450,000), and references to an 837-term Concept Index are indicated for each entry. . . . The lexicographer-author's selections reflect contemporary usage, gender sensitivity, and recently evolved words." Libr J

Laird, Charlton, 1901-

Webster's New World thesaurus; Charlton Laird and the editors of Webster's New World dictionaries; Michael Agnes, editor in chief. 3rd ed. Macmillan 1997 882p thumb-indexed $17.95; $16; pa $12   423

1. English language—Synonyms and antonyms
ISBN 0-02-861320-1 (thumb-indexed); 0-02-860337-0; 0-02-860336-2 (pa)   LC 96-2072
"A Webster's New World book"

First published 1948 by Holt with title: Laird's promptory; first published with present title 1971

This alphabetically arranged thesaurus contains more than 300,000 synonyms and derived terms of commonly used words and phrases. Includes information on usage and idioms. Brief definitions are included

McCutcheon, Marc

Roget's superthesaurus. Writer's Digest Bks. 1995 609p $22.99   423

1. English language—Synonyms and antonyms
ISBN 0-89879-658-X   LC 94-34221

In addition to synonyms and antonyms, this work features a reverse dictionary function, vocabulary-builder words with pronunciation keys and sample sentences, and quotations. The more than 325,000 entries are arranged alphabetically

"A great desk reference that will provide variety, precision, and clarity for all writers." SLJ

Merriam-Webster's collegiate dictionary. 10th ed. Merriam-Webster 1993 1559p   423

1. English language—Dictionaries

LC 93-20206

Prices vary according to binding

First published 1898. Previous edition had title: Webster's ninth new collegiate dictionary

"Includes 160,000 entries (211,000 definitions), 35,000 verbal illustrations and illustrative quotations, 35,000 etymologies, 4,400 usage paragraphs and notes, and 700 black-and-white drawings. . . . Abbreviations, foreign words and phrases, biographical and geographic names, signs, symbols, and a handbook of style conclude the volume." Booklist

Merriam-Webster's collegiate thesaurus. Merriam-Webster 1993 868p $17.95   423

1. English language—Synonyms and antonyms
ISBN 0-87779-169-4   LC 93-3177
Also available CD-ROM version

First published 1976 with title: Webster's collegiate thesaurus

"Employs a conventional dictionary arrangement, and gives synonyms, related terms, idiomatic equivalents, antonyms, and contrasted words as applicable. Cross-references in small capitals." Guide to Ref Books. 11th edition

Merriam-Webster's dictionary of synonyms. Merriam-Webster thumb-indexed $21.95   423

1. English language—Synonyms and antonyms

First published 1942 with title: Webster's dictionary of synonyms. (1993 edition) Periodically revised

"This synonym dictionary is an outstanding work. . . . Synonyms and similar words, alphabetically arranged, are carefully defined, discriminated, and illustrated with thousands of quotations. The entries also include antonyms and analogous words." Nichols. Guide to Ref Books for Sch Media Cent. 4th edition

Metaphors dictionary; Elyse Sommer, executive editor; Dorrie Weiss, associate editor. Gale Res. 1995 xliv, 833p $65   423

1. English language—Terms and phrases
ISBN 0-8103-9149-X   LC 94-36728

This is a collection of 6,500 metaphors, from ancient times to the present, organized in more than 500 subject categories

For a review see: Booklist, April 1, 1995

Oxford American dictionary; [compiled by] Eugene Ehrlich [et al.] Oxford Univ. Press 1980 816p $19.95   423

1. English language—Dictionaries 2. Americanisms
ISBN 0-19-502795-7   LC 80-16510

This work, "which contains in the neighborhood of 70,000 entries, offers brief but very clear definitions, numerous illustrative examples, and about 600 frankly prescriptive usage notes." Kister's Best Dict for Adults & Young People

The **Oxford** desk dictionary: American edition; edited by Laurence Urdang. Oxford Univ. Press 1995 691p il $12.95   423

1. English language—Dictionaries
ISBN 0-19-509153-1   LC 95-10393

In this dictionary "entries were selected from the most often used terms in the language and include those in the new areas of technology, medicine, and business. Definitions include traditional pronunciation guides, derivatives, and etymologies. Some phrases are included, but there are no sentence examples." SLJ

The **Oxford** dictionary of new words; a popular guide to words in the news; compiled by Sara Tulloch. Oxford Univ. Press 1991 322p hardcover o.p. paperback available $10.95   423

1. English language—Dictionaries 2. New words—Dictionaries
ISBN 0-19-283077-5 (pa)   LC 91-18814

In this "dictionary, about 2000 contemporary words and phrases are given international Phonetic Alphabet pronunciation, one or more definitions, accounts of origin and usage, and readable, useful summaries of their background. All the information provided is first-rate. Examples of usage are quoted, with citations, and a set of 11 'subject icons' highlight graphically the fields of interest (business, drugs, music, etc.) in which the terms operate." Libr J

Random House compact unabridged dictionary. special 2nd ed. Random House 1996 xxvi, 2230p il maps $50 **423**

1. English language—Dictionaries

ISBN 0-679-45026-2   LC 95-26318

Also available CD-ROM version; book with CD-ROM version inserted $64.95 (ISBN 0-679-44991-4)

First published 1987

This work includes over 315,000 entries and 2,400 spot maps and illustrations. An addenda section includes new words and definitions not found in the main A-Z section. Charts, tables and a basic manual of style complete the volume

Random House unabridged dictionary; Stuart Berg Flexner, editor in chief; Leonore Crary Hauck, managing editor. 2nd ed newly rev & updated. Random House 1993 xlii, 2478p il maps $100 **423**

1. English language—Dictionaries

ISBN 0-679-42917-4   LC 93-84591

Also available CD-ROM version

First published 1966 with title: Random House dictionary of the English language

Entries reflect current usage of words, and include date of first use, pronunciation, syntax, usage, and etymology. Brief biographical entries are included. Supplementary sections include signs and symbols used in various fields; a directory of colleges and universities; concise bilingual dictionaries for French, German, Italian, and Spanish; a manual of style; and a full-color atlas

Random House Webster's college dictionary. 2nd ed. Random House 1997 xxvii, 1535p il maps $23.95 **423**

1. English language—Dictionaries

ISBN 0-679-45570-1   LC 97-903

First published 1991 as a successor to The Random House college dictionary

This dictionary is comprised of over 160,000 entries and 175,000 definitions. New words current to the mid-1990s are included. Also contains usage notes, biographical and geographical entries and 8 pages of world maps

Random House Webster's college thesaurus; original edition edited by Jess Stein and Stuart Berg Flexner. rev & updated [ed], by Fraser Sutherland. Random House 1997 792p $18 **423**

1. English language—Synonyms and antonyms

ISBN 0-679-45280-X   LC 96-29480

First published 1984 with title: Random House thesaurus. College ed.

Based on Reader's digest family word finder

An alphabetical listing of main-entry word lists which group together synonyms and antonyms by meaning. Also included are sample sentences for every main entry (and for each meaning)

Roget A to Z; edited by Robert L. Chapman. HarperCollins Pubs. 1994 763p $17; pa $10 **423**

1. English language—Synonyms and antonyms

ISBN 0-06-270058-8; 0-06-272059-7 (pa)

LC 94-9501

This is a version of Roget's international thesaurus in which the entries have been rearranged in an alphabetical format

Roget's II; the new thesaurus; by the editors of The American Heritage dictionaries. 3rd ed. Houghton Mifflin 1995 1200p $16.95 **423**

1. English language—Synonyms and antonyms

ISBN 0-395-68722-5   LC 94-42879

First published 1980

This work's "alphabetical sequence of headwords supplemented by a category index and plentiful cross-references supplies an array of colorful and vivid synonyms that will be helpful for writers who do not have the time to engage in the long process of using a classified or category-indexed thesaurus." Booklist

Roget's international thesaurus. 5th ed, edited by Robert L. Chapman. HarperCollins Pubs. 1992 1139p $18.95; thumb indexed $19.95; pa $13.50 **423**

1. English language—Synonyms and antonyms

ISBN 0-06-270046-4; 0-06-270014-6 (thumb indexed); 0-06-272037-6 (pa)   LC 92-7615

First copyright edition published 1911 with title: The standard thesaurus of English words and phrases classified and arranged so as to facilitate the expression of ideas and assist in literary composition

"Roget's 150-year-old plan of organizing words within eight broad classes has been revised by Chapman to create a simpler, more natural, and contemporary arrangement of 15 new classes." Libr J

Third Barnhart dictionary of new English; [edited by] Robert K. Barnhart, Sol Steinmetz with Clarence L. Barnhart. Wilson, H.W. 1990 xxi, 565p $52 **423**

1. New words—Dictionaries 2. English language—Dictionaries

ISBN 0-8242-0796-3   LC 90-33483

Revised edition of: The Second Barnhart dictionary of new English, published 1980

This work "treats 12,000 new words, abbreviations, and acronyms 'which have come into the common or working vocabulary of the English-speaking world' during the past 30 years. . . . Definitions are as simple and brief as possible, since the *Dictionary* relies on documented quotations to bring out the full meaning of a word. . . . Some entries include explanatory notes regarding usage, word formation, or relevant cultural or historical facts. Pronunciation is given only for difficult or unfamiliar words. . . . Highly recommended." Booklist

Urdang, Laurence

The Oxford desk thesaurus: American edition. Oxford Univ. Press 1995 600p $12.95   **423**

1. English language—Synonyms and antonyms 2. Americanisms

ISBN 0-19-509960-5   LC 95-10395

This "is a condensation of the *Oxford Thesaurus: American Edition* and groups synonyms together when one word has different senses. The editors aim to avoid misunderstandings by using the term in a sentence for each sense. There is no index, although there is cross referencing to indicate which synonyms are used as main entries themselves." SLJ

The Oxford thesaurus: American edition. Oxford Univ. Press 1992 1005p $19.95   **423**

1. English language—Synonyms and antonyms 2. Americanisms

ISBN 0-19-507354-1   LC 91-3938

"This thesaurus contains 650,000 words. The main A-Z section presents headwords selected on the basis of their frequency of use in the language. . . . Entries include part-of-speech designations followed by numbered synonym lists. Each numbered list groups synonyms by sense and is illustrated by an example sentence. . . . Spellings of words are those preferred by American writers, with frequently used American variants also indicated." Booklist

"A great choice for high-school students as it provides both the simplicity of the dictionary format and the comprehensiveness of the old *Roget's*." SLJ

Webster's II new college dictionary. Houghton Mifflin 1995 xxii, 1514p il $18.95   **423**

1. English language—Dictionaries

ISBN 0-395-70869-9   LC 95-5833

At head of title on cover: Riverside

"This new dictionary is an expanded and updated version of *Webster's II New Riverside University Dictionary* (1984). Calling itself a 'user's dictionary,' it aims for accuracy, ease of use, and brevity. Usage notes, word histories, and synonym paragraphs are given within entries. . . . Appendixes include abbreviations, biographical names, geographical names, foreign words and phrases, colleges, concise style guide, forms of address, tables of measurements, periodic table of elements, and signs and symbols." Choice

Webster's third new international dictionary of the English language; unabridged. Merriam-Webster il   **423**

1. English language—Dictionaries

Prices vary according to binding

Original edition by Noah Webster published 1828 with title: An American dictionary of the English language. Has also appeared under various other titles. First published with present title 1961. (1993 edition) Frequently reprinted with additions and changes to keep it up to date

Young, Sue

The new comprehensive American rhyming dictionary. Morrow 1991 622p o.p.; Avon Bks. paperback available $14   **423**

1. English language—Rhyme—Dictionaries 2. Americanisms

ISBN 0-380-71392-6 (pa)   LC 90-19165

Also available in paperback from Avon Bks.

This book contains over 65,000 words and phrases categorized by sound, rather than spelling. It includes many colloquialisms and slang expressions

427   English language variations

Dictionary of American regional English; Frederic G. Cassidy, chief editor. Belknap Press 1985-1996 3v maps   **427**

1. English language—Dictionaries 2. Americanisms

The first three volumes of a projected five volume work

Contents: v1 Introduction and A-C $73.50 (ISBN 0-674-20511-1); v2 D-H $70 (ISBN 0-674-20512-X); v3 I-O $75 (ISBN 0-674-20519-7)

This dictionary "offers detailed information on nonstandard, regional, or folk American speech. . . . Entries do not merely define, but include part of speech, pronunciation, variant forms, etymology, geographic range, usage, cross-references, editorial notes, and dated quotations defining the word. Where appropriate, a computer-generated map . . . illustrates the regional distribution of a word. When it is completed . . . this work will definitely take its place beside the OED as a classic." Am Libr

Juba to jive; a dictionary of African-American slang; edited and with an introduction by Clarence Major. Penguin Bks. 1994 xxxv, 548p pa $16.95   **427**

1. African Americans—Language 2. English language—Slang 3. Americanisms

ISBN 0-14-051306-X   LC 93-11748

First published 1970 by International Pubs. with title: Dictionary of Afro-American slang

This dictionary "covers the four areas of African-American slang: early rural Southern slang, which started during slavery; the sinner-man/black musician period between 1900 and 1960; the street slang out of which rap and hip hop emerged; and working-class language." Publisher's note

"This book reflects the varied worlds of black slang from the witty 1940s phrase 'straight up six o'clock girl' for a very thin woman to the grim euphemism 'dime bag' for $10 worth of marijuana or morphine. There is plenty of prison, drug, and crime slang, with words and phrases to offend every sensibility. . . . A necessary purchase for any special collection on African Americans or slang and unconventional English." Booklist

Lewin, Esther

The thesaurus of slang; [by] Esther Lewin and Albert E. Lewin. rev and expanded ed. Facts on File 1994 456p $50   **427**

1. English language—Slang 2. English language—Synonyms and antonyms

ISBN 0-8160-2898-2   LC 93-42890

First published 1988

Lewin, Esther—*Continued*

This work "lists 12,000 standard English words with 165,000 synonyms gathered from newspapers, magazines, books, television, radio, industry and conversations. Other sources include ad copywriters, adolescents, technical workers, politicians and writers." Book Rep

Includes bibliographical references

The **Oxford** dictionary of modern slang; [by] John Ayto, John Simpson. Oxford Univ. Press 1992 299p $25; pa $9.95   **427**
1. English language—Slang
ISBN 0-19-866181-9; 0-19-280007-8 (pa)
            LC 93-108616

This dictionary defines "more than 5,000 slang terms currently or recently in use in the English-speaking world. . . . Entries give the date of earliest written use and include indicators that tell where or among what group a slang term originated or is used. Surprisingly, ODMS is divided evenly between US and UK-Commonwealth slang." Choice

Partridge, Eric, 1894-1979

A concise dictionary of slang and unconventional English; edited by Paul Beale; from: A Dictionary of slang and unconventional English, by Eric Partridge. Macmillan 1990 xxvi, 534p $35   **427**
1. English language—Slang
ISBN 0-02-605350-0   LC 90-38042
Based on the eighth edition of A dictionary of slang and unconventional English, entered below

First published 1989 in the United Kingdom

"This concise version omits words, phrases, and senses that are known to have originated prior to this century; approximately 1,500 new expressions coined in the 1980s have been added. . . . The emphasis seems to be on British and Commonwealth words. . . . Entries include (to varying degrees) part-of-speech designations, register, definitions, date information, and sources in which early recording of the word can be found. Interesting essays on various topics, also with a British and Commonwealth slant, conclude this volume." Booklist

Includes bibliographical references

A dictionary of slang and unconventional English; colloquialisms and catch-phrases, solecisms and catachreses, nicknames, vulgarisms and such Americanisms as have been naturalized. Macmillan   **427**
1. English language—Slang 2. Americanisms
First published 1937. (8th edition 1984 $75 0-02-594980-2)

Entries are "in one alphabet; front matter includes a helpful note, 'Arrangement Within Entries.' Entries trace, in a way that recalls the 'Oxford English Dictionary,' the development of terms and usages." Booklist

"Partridge remains essential for all reference collections, an irresistable distraction to browsers." Am Ref Books Annu, 1986

Random House historical dictionary of American slang; J. E. Lighter, editor; assistant editors, J. Ball, J. O'Connor. v1: A-G. Random House 1994 lxiv, 1006p $55   **427**
1. English language—Slang 2. Americanisms
ISBN 0-394-54427-7   LC 94-9721
Volume one of a projected three volume set; volume two in preparation

In this dictionary "terms are not only defined but their etymological development is traced chronologically through dated citations. . . . Lighter's dictionary represents a major contribution to lexicographic scholarship. It belongs in every serious reference collection." Libr J

Spears, Richard A.

NTC's American idioms dictionary. 2nd ed. National Textbook 1994 532p $16.95; pa $12.95   **427**
1. Americanisms 2. English language—Idioms 3. Americanisms
ISBN 0-8442-0825-6; 0-8442-0826-4 (pa)
            LC 94-190451
First published 1987

This dictionary defines over 8,000 contemporary expressions and provides examples of their usage. Access by keyword is provided through a phrase-finder index

428   Standard English usage

Fowler, H. W.

The new Fowler's modern English usage; first edited by H.W. Fowler. 3rd ed, edited by R.W. Burchfield. Oxford Univ. Press 1996 xxiii, 864p $25   **428**
1. English language—Etymology 2. English language—Idioms 3. English language—Usage
ISBN 0-19-869126-2   LC 97-108626
First published 1926 with title: A dictionary of modern English usage

"In a simple, alphabetical arrangement, the third edition covers grammar, syntax, style, word choice, and advice on usage." Libr J

Merriam-Webster's dictionary of English usage. Merriam-Webster 1994 978p $21.95   **428**
1. English language—Usage
ISBN 0-87779-132-5   LC 93-19289
First published 1989 with title: Webster's dictionary of English usage

This guide looks at English usage from both historical and contemporary perspectives. Over 20,000 quotations illustrate the discussion of usage issues. Provides explanations of how accomplished writers have dealt with usage problems. Grammar, spelling and punctuation points are also covered

Includes bibliographical references

Random House English language desk reference. Random House 1995 621p $18   **428**
1. English language—Grammar 2. English language—Usage
ISBN 0-679-43898-X   LC 94-42297
"Organized to provide quick access to information, this resource covers grammar, usage, punctuation, and

Random House English language desk reference—*Continued*

vocabulary building, and provides a thesaurus, a rhyming dictionary, definitions, and a ready-reference guide to such commonly sought after facts as the names and terms of office of the U.S. presidents. . . . Also of interest will be the section on 'Avoiding Sexist Language.'" SLJ

For a fuller review see: Booklist, Oct. 1, 1995

Rowh, Mark

How to improve your grammar and usage. Watts 1994 95p (Speak out, write on!) lib bdg $22.70; pa $6.95 **428**

1. English language—Grammar 2. English language—Usage

ISBN 0-531-11177-6 (lib bdg); 0-531-15729-6 (pa)
LC 93-31276

"Rowh stresses the importance of good grammar for success in school and in the 'real world' of work, as well as appropriate times to use formal and/or informal language. . . . The well-organized presentation includes numerous examples of acceptable and unacceptable usage. Such handbooks tend to be dry in style; this resource is informative, clear, and actually interesting." SLJ

Includes bibliographical references

Wilson, Kenneth G. (Kenneth George), 1923-

The Columbia guide to standard American English. Columbia Univ. Press 1993 482p $31.50; pa $16.95 **428**

1. English language—Dictionaries 2. English language—Usage 3. Americanisms

ISBN 0-231-06988-X; 0-231-06989-8 (pa)
LC 92-37887

"The 6,500 entries in this book provide a unique approach to spoken and written English. Wilson diagrams five levels of speech, from intimate to oratorical, and three levels of writing, from informal to formal. His descriptive discussion of usage is intended to assist in making choices. . . . Cross references are numerous, and a helpful guide to pronunciation is included." Am Libr

433   German language—Dictionaries

Cassell's German-English, English-German dictionary; completely revised by Harold T. Betteridge. Macmillan 2v in 1 $25; thumb-indexed $27 **433**

1. German language—Dictionaries
(thumb-indexed)

Also available in a concise edition for $13.95 (ISBN 0-02-522650-9)

First compiled 1888 by Elizabeth Weir and published by Heath. Periodically revised. Previous American editions published by Funk & Wagnalls with title: The New Cassell's German dictionary

This dictionary incorporates "many new words and usages. Gives phonetic transcriptions of headwords. One of the most useful bilingual dictionaries." Guide to Ref Books. 11th edition

443   French language—Dictionaries

French-English, English-French dictionary. unabridged ed. Larousse (Paris); distributed by Larousse Kingfisher Chambers 1994 c1993 1042p maps $50 **443**

1. French language—Dictionaries
ISBN 2-03-420100-0
General editor, Faye Carney

This dictionary "includes proper nouns, geographical references, popular slang, and many new French words that are culturally Swiss, Belgian, and French-Canadian. Each entry includes the phonetic spelling of the word, the part of speech, and its usage. . . . It also includes eight pages of color maps highlighting the French language, culture, and heritage." Choice

Harrap's new collegiate French and English dictionary; edited by Peter Collin [et al.] National Textbook; distributed by French & Spanish 1983 983, 798p $39.95 **443**

1. French language—Dictionaries
ISBN 0-8288-0780-9

A one volume abridgment of the four-volume Harrap's new standard French and English dictionary published 1980; this edition published in the United Kingdom with title: Harrap's shorter French and English dictionary

This dictionary covers "all varieties of both languages, and it represents a satisfactory fusion of the scientific approach to language with sensitivity to literary values." Times Lit Suppl

Larousse concise French-English, English-French dictionary. Larousse (Paris); distributed by Larousse Kingfisher Chambers 1994 c1993 555, 629, xliip $16.95; pa $10.95 **443**

1. French language—Dictionaries
ISBN 2-03-420300-3; 2-03-420500-6 (pa)
General editor, Catherine E. Love

This dictionary contains over 90,000 references and 120,000 translations. Includes coverage of idioms, grammatical constructions, abbreviations, acronyms, computer terms, and proper nouns

The **Oxford-Hachette** French dictionary; French-English, English-French; edited by Marie-Hélène Corréard, Valerie Grundy. Oxford Univ. Press 1994 lx, 1943p il thumb-indexed $39.95 **443**

1. French language—Dictionaries
ISBN 0-19-864519-8
LC 95-160279
Also available CD-ROM version

Also available The compact Oxford-Hachette French dictionary $25 (ISBN 0-19-864329-2)

This dictionary, drawing on two databases of current French and English, contains more than 350,000 words and phrases and over 500,000 translations

This work also contains "pages providing sample letters of invitation in French, the acceptance or declining of invitations, applications for jobs, typical job advertisements and the abbreviations used in them, and a curriculum vitae in French. These are immensely helpful additions that previous dictionaries have not offered." Am Ref Books Annu, 1996

Petit Larousse illustré. Larousse (Paris); distributed by French & Spanish il maps $95 **443**
1. French language—Dictionaries
Annual. First published 1906. Title varies
Earlier editions by Pierre Larousse, published with title: Nouveau petit Larousse illustré, and Petit Larousse. Frequently revised to keep up to date with new words and accepted expressions. Text in French

Standard French-English, English-French dictionary. new ed. Larousse (Paris); distributed by Larousse Kingfisher Chambers 1995 c1994 xxi, 996p $29.95 **443**
1. French language—Dictionaries
ISBN 2-03-420260-0 LC 94-73275
General editor, Faye Carney
This dictionary contains approximately 220,000 references and 400,000 translations. Includes special sections on language usage that explain idiomatic expressions in specific situations

453 Italian language—Dictionaries

Cassell's Italian dictionary: Italian-English, English-Italian; compiled by Piero Rebora with the assistance of Francis M. Guercio and Arthur L. Hayward. Macmillan $21; thumb-indexed $24.95 **453**
1. Italian language—Dictionaries
First published 1958 in the United Kingdom with title: Cassell's Italian-English, English-Italian dictionary. Periodically revised. Previous United States editions published by Funk & Wagnalls
"A general dictionary of the Italian language as currently written and spoken." Ref Sources for Small & Medium-sized Libr. 5th edition

463 Spanish language—Dictionaries

The **American** Heritage Larousse Spanish dictionary; Spanish/English; English/Spanish. Houghton Mifflin 1986 xxx, 532, 572p $22.95 **463**
1. Spanish language—Dictionaries
ISBN 0-395-32429-7 LC 86-7202
Also available in a concise edition for $17.95 (ISBN 0-395-43412-2)
Based on The American Heritage Dictionary and the Pequeño Larousse, this work includes 120,000 words and phrases representing American English and Latin American Spanish usage

Cassell's Spanish-English, English-Spanish dictionary; completely revised by Anthony Gooch, Angel García de Paredes. Macmillan $19.95; thumb-indexed $22.95 **463**
1. Spanish language—Dictionaries
Also available in a concise edition for $13 (ISBN 0-02-522660-6)
First published 1959 in the United KIngdom. First American edition published 1960 by Funk & Wagnalls with title: Cassell's Spanish dictionary. Periodically revised

This dictionary emphasizes the Spanish of Latin America, and includes both classical and literary Spanish as well as the language of the modern Spanish-speaking world

Larousse concise Spanish-English, English-Spanish dictionary. Larousse (Paris); distributed by Larousse Kingfisher Chambers 1994 c1993 550, 642, xxviiip $17.95; pa $10.95 **463**
1. Spanish language—Dictionaries
ISBN 2-03-420400-X; 2-03-420600-2 (pa)
LC 93-86204
General editor, Catherine E. Love
This new Spanish dictionary is intended to provide solutions to reading present-day Spanish. It includes common abbreviations and acronyms, proper names, business terms and computer terms

Larousse English-Spanish Spanish-English dictionary; [general ed.: Elvira D. Moragas] new ed. Larousse (Paris); distributed by Larousse Kingfisher Chambers 1996 xxiii, 665, xxii, 717p $29.95 **463**
1. Spanish language—Dictionaries
ISBN 2-03-420280-5
With over 160,000 references and 260,000 translations this dictionary covers general, professional and literary vocobulary. Abbreviations, acronyms and proper nouns are included. Contains special sections on language usage arranged alphabetically in main dictionary text

473 Latin language—Dictionaries

Cassell's Latin dictionary; Latin-English, English-Latin; by D. P. Simpson. Macmillan thumb-indexed $24.95 **473**
1. Latin language—Dictionaries
Also available in a concise edition for $12.95 (ISBN 0-02-522630-4)
First published 1854. This edition first published 1959. Periodically revised. Previous United States editions published by Funk & Wagnalls with title: Cassell's New Latin dictionary
"As are all Cassell's dictionaries, this is a standard work and a good choice for libraries that require a basic Latin dictionary. The 30,000 entries include geographical and proper names, etymological notes, and illustrative quotations." Nichols. Guide to Ref Books for Sch Media Cent. 4th edition

Oxford Latin dictionary; edited by P. G. W. Glare. Oxford Univ. Press 1982 xxiii, 2126p $250 **473**
1. Latin language—Dictionaries
ISBN 0-19-864224-5 LC 82-8162
"An important scholarly work; the standard reference for Classical Latin. Treats classical Latin from its beginnings to the end of the second century CE and includes words from both literary and nonliterary sources. Etymological notes are brief; quotations illustrating usage are arranged in chronological order." Guide to Ref Books. 11th edition

491.7 East Slavic languages. Russian

The **Oxford** English-Russian dictionary; edited by P. S. Falla. Oxford Univ. Press 1984 1052p hardcover o.p. paperback available $29.95
491.7
1. Russian language—Dictionaries
ISBN 0-19-864192-3 (pa)   LC 83-17344
Companion volume to The Oxford Russian-English dictionary, by Marcus Wheeler
This dictionary includes over 90,000 "English words, phrases, and items. The editor has paid special attention to correct translation of colloquial and idiomatic language. His explanatory glosses enable the user to select the appropriate Russian equivalents of English words. He has also included the more important or familiar Americanisms." Am Ref Books Annu, 1985

The **Oxford** Russian dictionary; English-Russian, edited by Paul Falla; Russian-English, edited by Marcus Wheeler and Boris Unbegaun. rev and updated throughout, by Colin Howlett. Oxford Univ. Press 1993 1340p $49.95; pa $11.95
491.7
1. Russian language—Dictionaries
ISBN 0-19-864189-3; 0-19-864526-0 (pa)
LC 94-127368
New edition in preparation
"Amalgamation, harmonization and updating of The Oxford Russian-English dictionary (1972-, second edition 1984) and The Oxford English-Russian dictionary (1984)." pv
This dictionary "contains more than 18,000 words and 290,000 translations. . . . Colloquial terms, idioms, and general scientific and technological terms are included. The emphasis is on current usage. Transcriptions of Russian into the International Phonetic Alphabet are a new feature." Booklist

495.1 Chinese language

A **New** English-Chinese dictionary; edited by Zheng Yi Li [et al.] 2nd rev ed. Wiley 1985 1613p hardcover o.p. paperback available $64.95
495.1
1. Chinese language—Dictionaries
ISBN 0-471-80897-0 (pa)
Also available from French & Spanish
"Originally published in 1950 (Shanghai) with a first revision appearing in 1957 (Peking), this current volume presents more than 120,000 entries including abbreviations, compounds, and derivatives for a total of 6 million words in all." Choice

495.6 Japanese language

Merriam-Webster's Japanese-English learner's dictionary. Merriam-Webster 1993 1121p il $27.95
495.6
1. Japanese language—Dictionaries
ISBN 0-87779-164-3   LC 93-27294
Published in collaboration with Kenkyusha Limited

"This dictionary is designed for use by students at all levels and by business professionals who intend to master practical modern Japanese. Each Japanese entry, which [has] accent marks, is shown in roman letters, then by the standard writing in *hiragana* or *katakana*; this is followed, where appropriate, by another writing in parentheses that contains *kanji*, and then the English equivalent is given. Model sentences and phrases are provided for most entries." Am Ref Books Annu, 1994

Nelson, Andrew Nathaniel
The modern reader's Japanese-English character dictionary; [by] Andrew Nelson. [2nd] rev ed. Tuttle 1966 1108p $69.95
495.6
1. Japanese language—Dictionaries
ISBN 0-8048-0408-7
First published 1962
New edition in preparation
"Indispensable for English-speaking students of Japanese until they are able to use Japanese words. Based on the Radical Priority System; presents 4775 characters and 671 variants for a total of 5446 numbered entries plus cross-references. Covers current and common usage as well as older words still encountered in modern literature." Ref Sources for Small & Medium-sized Libr. 5th edition

The **Oxford-Duden** pictorial English-Japanese dictionary. Oxford Univ. Press 1983 864p il hardcover o.p. paperback available $21.95
495.6
1. Japanese language—Dictionaries 2. Picture dictionaries
ISBN 0-19-860119-0 (pa)   LC 83-163303
"This topically arranged picture dictionary will be of value chiefly to Japanese speakers engaged in the conversion of English into Japanese (though, with some limitations, thanks to its English and Japanese indexes, it can serve as a regular bilingual dictionary as well). . . . Needless to say, the entries are largely nouns (or nominal phrases). Within the narrow domain of its usability, a fine piece of lexicography." Libr J

500 NATURAL SCIENCES AND MATHEMATICS

Asimov, Isaac, 1920-1992
Frontiers II; more recent discoveries about life, earth, space, and the universe; [by] Isaac and Janet Asimov. Dutton 1993 369p hardcover o.p. paperback available $11.95
500
1. Science 2. Universe
ISBN 0-452-27229-7 (pa)   LC 93-221
Companion volume Frontiers available in paperback for $12.95 (ISBN 0-452-26634-3)
"A Truman Talley book"
"This second compilation of Isaac Asimov's syndicated science column includes 125 articles, approximately 30 of which were contributed by his wife Janet after her husband's death in 1992. Arranged in sections concerning life sciences, astronomy, particle physics and general technology news, the 1500-word essays offer lively, though brief, discussions." Publ Wkly

Baker, William Lynn
Dancing honeybees and other natural wonders of
science; an illustrated compendium. Contemporary
Bks. 1994 96p il maps pa $9.95   **500**
1. Science 2. Natural history
ISBN 0-8092-3552-8   LC 94-26009
In this illustrated work based on the author's weekly
newspaper column "mysteries of natural science are explained in simple ways for readers, young and old, on a
wide range of topics." Sci Books Films
Includes bibliographical references

Barnes-Svarney, Patricia
The New York Public Library science desk
reference. Macmillan 1995 668p il maps $39.95
     500
1. Science 2. Technology
ISBN 0-02-860403-2   LC 94-40445
"A Stonesong Press book"
"Thirteen chapters cover major divisions of science
(e.g., astronomy, biology, chemistry, computer and environmental sciences, technology) listing basic facts, formulas, terms, and processes. One additional chapter lists
'useful resources' such as books, organizations, museums, zoos, national parks, and planetariums." Libr J
For a fuller review see: Booklist, Dec. 1, 1995

Ehrlich, Robert, 1938-
What if you could unscramble an egg? Rutgers
Univ. Press 1996 222p il $25.95   **500**
1. Science 2. Questions and answers
ISBN 0-8135-2254-4   LC 95-18316
In a question and answer format, the author "takes
readers on journeys into seemingly fantastic realms that
yet are anchored to reality by solid and penetrating scientific knowledge. The subjects of inquiry range from biology to physics to materials and constants." Booklist
Includes bibliographical references

Hazen, Robert M., 1948-
Science matters: achieving scientific literacy;
[by] Robert M. Hazen and James Trefil.
Doubleday 1991 294p il hardcover o.p. paperback
available $12.95   **500**
1. Science
ISBN 0-385-26108-X (pa)   LC 90-3786
"This book attempts to acquaint the educated (or mis-
educated) layperson with the major concepts of modern
science. . . . Although many concepts are, perforce,
oversimplified, offering the reader only a superficial understanding of some of them, this book is a step in the
right direction." Libr J
Includes bibliography

Kuttner, Paul
Science's trickiest questions; 402 questions that
will stump, amuse, and surprise. Holt & Co. 1994
285p pa $10.95   **500**
1. Science
ISBN 0-8050-2873-0   LC 94-5954
"An Owl book"

This book presents "queries in the areas of astronomy,
biology, chemistry, mathematics, botany, and medicine."
Publisher's note
"For those who like to ponder some of the fascinating
facts, conditions, and relationships that are a part of the
natural world, this compendium of questions and answers
can serve as a stimulating resource tool." Sci Books
Films

Roberts, Royston M.
Serendipity: accidental discoveries in science.
Wiley 1989 270p il (Wiley science editions)
hardcover o.p. paperback available $16.95   **500**
1. Science
ISBN 0-471-60203-5 (pa)   LC 88-33638
This volume "contains diverse stories of accidental
discoveries in medicine, chemical elements, astronomy,
and technologies. Among them are teflon, DNA, antibod-
ies, and safety glass. The well-written articles are supported by black-and-white photographs and drawings."
Nichols. Guide to Ref Books for Sch Media Cent. 4th
edition
Includes bibliography

Sagan, Carl, 1934-1996
Broca's brain; reflections on the romance of
science. Random House 1979 347p $14.95   **500**
1. Science 2. Philosophy
ISBN 0-394-50169-1   LC 78-21810
Also available in paperback from Ballantine Bks.
"Sagan considers a variety of themes within the context of contemporary scientific developments, including
the quest for extraterrestrial life, popular science, and religious questions, as well as numerous concerns more
immediate to his own specialty, astronomy." Libr J
The author "is a lucid, logical writer with a gift for
explaining science to the layman and infecting the reader
with his own boundless enthusiasm and curiosity." Natl
Rev
Includes bibliographical references

Science and technology desk reference; 1,500
answers to frequently-asked or
difficult-to-answer questions; [by] the Carnegie
Library of Pittsburgh Science and Technology
Department. Gale Res. 1993 741p il $45   **500**
1. Science 2. Technology
ISBN 0-8103-8884-7   LC 92-75423
Also available in paperback with title: The Handy science answer book
This work "consists of approximately 1,500 questions
and answers arranged within broad subject chapters. Entries include: an entry number; the question and answer
(some with a table or illustration), and up to three source
citations with full bibliographic data for follow-up research. Approximately 100 line drawings and charts help
illustrate selected answers. Subjects covered include the
animal world, astronomy, chemistry, the earth, the environment, health and medicine." Publisher's note

The **Way** science works. Macmillan 1996 288p il
$35   **500**
1. Science 2. Technology
ISBN 0-02-860822-4   LC 95-19702
"The book is organized in two parts. The first has sev-
en chapters with two-page spreads explaining how 94

The Way science works—*Continued*
things work, ranging from nuclear power to compact disc. . . . The second part of the book, 'Principles,' surveys 30 scientific principles, also in a two-page format." Booklist

Includes bibliographical references

501 Science—Philosophy and theory

Horgan, John
The end of science; facing the limits of knowledge in the twilight of the scientific age. Addison-Wesley 1996 308p $24 **501**
1. Science—Philosophy 2. Science—History
ISBN 0-201-62679-9 LC 96-4374
"Helix books"
"This book investigates a serious question concerning empirical inquiry: Is there a limit to the discovery of theories about nature? The ongoing success of scientific research suggests that a final (ultimate), comprehensive, testable, and effective theory explaining the unity of all reality may soon be forthcoming. Exploring this possibility, Horgan . . . introduces the reader to a wide spectrum of opinion, from Francis Crick, Karl Popper, Stephen Hawking, Richard Dawkins, Stanley Miller, Margin Minksy, Frank Tippler, and Edward Wilson, among others." Libr J
Includes bibliography

502 Science—Miscellany

Oleksy, Walter G., 1930-
Science and medicine; by Walter Oleksy. Facts on File 1995 136p il (Information revolution) $17.95 **502**
1. Information systems 2. Science—Data processing 3. Medicine—Data processing
ISBN 0-8160-3076-6 LC 94-44109
Examines how computer technology affects the acquisition and application of scientific knowledge in such fields as astronomy, archaeology, medicine, and physics
"The source of Oleksy's information is largely telephone interviews with scientists themselves, giving the book a vitality and vigor of style. The researchers effectively convey their enthusiasm about their work. This volume will be valuable to students writing reports, and will be enjoyable reading for computer enthusiasts." SLJ
Includes bibliographical references

Stewart, Gail, 1949-
Microscopes; bringing the unseen world into focus; by Gail B. Stewart. Lucent Bks. 1992 96p il (Encyclopedia of discovery and invention) lib bdg $17.95 **502**
1. Microscopes
ISBN 1-56006-211-8 LC 92-17316
The author "traces the development of the microscope from Antonie van Leeuwenhoek's discovery of bacteria in the 17th century to today's use of scanning electronic microscopes. In addition to history, readers are given good explanations of how different kinds of lenses and scopes work, accompanied by well-labeled diagrams. New technology is covered, and several scientists are quoted about the future of microscopic research." SLJ
Includes glossary and bibliography

503 Science—Encyclopedias and dictionaries

Ardley, Neil, 1937-
Dictionary of science; written by Neil Ardley. Dorling Kindersley 1994 192p il $19.95 **503**
1. Science—Dictionaries 2. Technology—Dictionaries
ISBN 1-56458-349-X LC 93-29811
This illustrated dictionary is divided into sections on scientific investigation, matter, atoms, time and space, force, motion and machines, transportation, energy, light, heat, sound, magnetism and electricity, electronics and computing, communications, chemical changes, chemical compounds, chemical industry and mathematics. It also lists plane and solid shapes, abbreviations, and scientists

The **Dictionary** of science; edited by Peter Lafferty and Julian Rowe. Simon & Schuster 1994 678p il maps $45 **503**
1. Science—Dictionaries
ISBN 0-13-304718-0 LC 94-39128
First published 1993 in the United Kingdom with title: The Hutchison dictionary of science
This volume's "5,000 entries range from a few lines to a page or so. There are chronologies of great events and boxed full-page progress reports for the various sciences. Medicine is covered, as are technology, computers, and environmental science, but the social sciences are not. A dozen science puzzles are scattered throughout the book with answers at the back." Booklist
"This fine dictionary for students and general readers presents the rich world of science in an interesting, informative, and readily understandable manner while remaining concise and factual." Libr J

Gibilisco, Stan
The concise illustrated dictionary of science and technology. TAB Bks. 1993 520p il maps $36.95; pa $24.95 **503**
1. Science—Dictionaries 2. Technology—Dictionaries
ISBN 0-8306-4152-1; 0-8306-4153-X (pa)
LC 92-22545
This reference "includes more than 5,000 terms that students will encounter in their reading, such as *pie graph, greenhouse effect, integrated circuit, power plant, creationism,* and *group therapy.* The definitions are nonthreatening and easy to follow and include the most common terms from astronomy, chemistry, earth science, engineering, life science, mathematics, and physics. A few biographical entries are included, and some common abbreviations are entered in the main alphabet." Booklist

Illustrated dictionary of science; advisory editor, Michael Allaby. Facts on File 1995 256p il maps $29.95 **503**
1. Science—Dictionaries
ISBN 0-8160-3253-X LC 94-24272
"An Andromeda book"

Illustrated dictionary of science—*Continued*

First published 1988 with title: The Encyclopedic dictionary of science

This dictionary covers "physics, biology, medicine, geology, physical geography, astronomy, and technology. . . . More than 5,000 terms are defined. In addition to coverage of current terms, a significant number of entries provide information on the history of concepts. More than 700 biographical entries survey people from ancient times to the present. . . . Written in clear, nonspecialist language, the *Illustrated Dictionary of Science* will be useful for quick reference." Booklist

Larousse dictionary of science and technology; general editor, Peter M. B. Walker. Larousse (London); distributed by Larousse Kingfisher Chambers 1995 1236p il $45   **503**
1. Science—Dictionaries 2. Technology—Dictionaries
ISBN 0-7523-0010-5

First published 1988 with title: Chambers science and technology dictionary. Variant title: Cambridge dictionary of science and technology

"Subjects featured include astronomy, chemistry, computing, electronics, engineering, geology, life sciences, math, physical sciences, and technology. Over 40,000 terms and 500 small black-and-white illustrations are presented. . . . Appendixes cover everything from the periodic table to a chronology of inventions." Libr J

McGraw-Hill concise encyclopedia of science & technology; Sybil P. Parker, editor in chief. 3rd ed. McGraw-Hill 1994 lxxvi, 2241p il $115.50   **503**
1. Science—Dictionaries 2. Technology—Dictionaries
ISBN 0-07-045560-0   LC 94-16592

First published 1984

A condensed version of the McGraw-Hill encyclopedia of science & technology

This volume "contains some 7,900 alphabetically arranged articles . . . with more than 1,600 photographs and line drawings. An analytical index aids in locating information for topics that do not have their own entries. There are also 15 appendixes covering such topics as the Greek alphabet, conversion tables, the periodic table of elements, mathematical notations, a geological time scale, and biographical listings. This is an excellent, affordable one-volume encyclopedia that is highly recommended for all libraries that do not own the multivolume set." Booklist

McGraw-Hill encyclopedia of science & technology; an international reference work in twenty volumes including an index. McGraw-Hill 20v set $2111.25   **503**
1. Science—Dictionaries 2. Technology—Dictionaries
Also available CD-ROM version

First published 1960 in fifteen volumes. (8th edition 1996) Periodically revised. Starting with sixth edition set has been expanded to twenty volumes

This work provides "ready-reference information in all areas of modern science and technology. . . . The entries are broad survey articles written for the nonspecialist by an authority in the field. . . . The *McGraw-Hill Encyclopedia of Science and Technology* offers the most comprehensive selection of accurate scientific information for a broad, general audience." Topical Ref Books

Supplemented by: McGraw-Hill yearbook of science & technology

The **New** book of popular science. Grolier 6v il maps $239   **503**
1. Science—Dictionaries 2. Technology—Dictionaries 3. Natural history—Dictionaries

First published 1924 with title: The Book of popular science. Frequently revised

The information in this set is classified under such broad categories as astronomy and space science, computers and mathematics, earth sciences, energy, environmental sciences, physical sciences, general biology, plant life, animal life, mammals, human sciences and technology

Uvarov, E. B. (Eugene Boris), 1910-
The Penguin dictionary of science; [by] E.B. Uvarov and Alan Isaacs. Penguin Bks. il pa $13.95   **503**
1. Science—Dictionaries

First published 1943. (7th edition 1993) Periodically revised. Variant title: The Facts on File dictionary of science

This dictionary includes " entries in the fields of physics, chemistry, mathematics, and astronomy, with some additional terms from interdisciplinary sciences. The definitions are clear and concise." Malinowsky. Best Sci & Technol Ref Books for Young People

Van Nostrand's scientific encyclopedia. Van Nostrand Reinhold 2v set $249.95   **503**
1. Science—Dictionaries 2. Technology—Dictionaries

First published 1938. (8th edition 1995) Frequently revised

"Animal life; biosciences; chemistry; earth and atmospheric sciences; energy source and power technology; mathematics and information sciences; materials and engineering sciences, medicine, anatomy, and physiology; physics; plant science; space and planetary sciences." Subtitle. 7th edition

"This work is an invaluable source of concise, ready-reference information." Topical Ref Books

505   Science—Serial publications

General science index. Wilson, H.W. service basis   **505**
1. Science—Periodicals—Indexes
ISSN 0162-1963
Also available CD-ROM version

First published July 1978. Monthly, except June and December, with quarterly and bound annual commulations

"A cumulative subject index to more than 100 English-language general science periodicals not completely covered by other abstracts and indexes. In addition, an author listing of citations to book reviews follows the main body of the index. No other author entries are included." Guide to Ref Books. 11th edition

507 Science—Education and related topics

Brown, Robert J., 1907-
333 more science tricks & experiments. TAB Bks. 1984 228p il hardcover o.p. paperback available $10.95 **507**
1. Science—Experiments 2. Scientific recreations
ISBN 0-8306-1835-X (pa)   LC 84-8878
This companion volume to the title entered below contains additional ideas for scientific projects

333 science tricks & experiments. TAB Bks. 1984 199p il $15.95; pa $10.95 **507**
1. Science—Experiments 2. Scientific recreations
ISBN 0-8306-0825-7; 0-8306-1825-2 (pa)
LC 84-8875
"Science students will find ideas for projects involving basic scientific principles, including inertia, gravity, magnetism, and the mysteries of chemistry, in this well-illustrated work." Booklist

Grand, Gail L., 1943-
Student science opportunities; your guide to over 300 exciting national programs, competitions, internships, and scholarships. Wiley 1994 292p pa $14.95 **507**
1. Science—Study and teaching 2. Science—Competitions
ISBN 0-471-31088-3   LC 93-23412
This is a guide to summer science "programs offered throughout the U.S. Although most take place on university campuses, other sites include an archaeological dig, an uninhabited barrier island, an Alaskan ice field, and the U.S. Space and Rocket Center. . . . There is also information about science competitions during the school year, scholarship opportunities, resources available to women and minorities, and national agencies that sponsor programs." Booklist
"This valuable resource should be in every middle and high school in the United States." Sci Books Films

Krieger, Melanie Jacobs
How to excel in science competitions. Watts 1991 143p il (Experimental science series) lib bdg $21.40 **507**
1. Science—Competitions
ISBN 0-531-11004-4   LC 91-17790
"Krieger opens with chapters on reasons for competing, profiles of student researchers, and how to get started. She moves on to consider the research project, paper, abstract, presentation, and concludes with a discussion of what to expect from judges. Thorough appendixes list major competitions, rules, winning project titles, summer training programs, and a sample Westinghouse Science Talent Search entry form." SLJ
Includes bibliography

507.8 Science—Use of apparatus and equipment in study and teaching

Bochinski, Julianne Blair, 1966-
The complete handbook of science fair projects; illustrations by Judy J. Bochinski-DiBiase. rev ed. Wiley 1996 221p il $27.95; pa $14.95 **507.8**
1. Science projects
ISBN 0-471-12378-1; 0-471-12377-3 (pa)
LC 95-22791
First published 1991
"The book starts with a section on how to conduct an experiment, record and evaluate results, and then put it all together in an informative and appealing display. . . . Besides the 50 experiments described, an additional 400 ideas are suggested in Appendix A. Other appendices list suppliers of scientific materials and science fairs on a state-by-state and country basis. This inexpensive and useful collection is highly recommended." Sci Books Films
Includes glossary

Gardner, Robert, 1929-
Experimenting with science in sports. Watts 1993 128p il lib bdg $22; pa $6.95 **507.8**
1. Science—Experiments 2. Sports
ISBN 0-531-12543-2; 0-531-15682-6 (pa)
LC 92-37994
"A Venture book"
Discusses how such principles of physics as force, gravity, and momentum apply to a variety of athletic actions, with experiments for the reader to try
"All the experiments are clearly described and the problems convincingly discussed. Generally, the book is clearly written and well illustrated." Appraisal
Includes bibliography

Robert Gardner's challenging science experiments. Watts 1993 174p il (Experimental science series) lib bdg $19.86; pa $6.95 **507.8**
1. Science—Experiments
ISBN 0-531-11090-7 (lib bdg); 0-531-15671-0 (pa)
LC 92-21116
Presents easy-to-prepare scientific experiments that demonstrate principles of physics, chemistry, astronomy, and biology
"The reader is in the hands of the master teacher, one whose depth of feeling for, as well as knowledge of, science sets an inspiring example. . . . The experiments all have roots in commonplace observations and the experience of nature, which they illuminate with satisfying and sometimes startling effects." Sci Books Films
Includes bibliography

More science experiments on file; experiments, demonstrations, and projects for school and home. Facts on File 1991 various paging il $165 **507.8**
1. Science—Experiments
ISBN 0-8160-2196-1   LC 90-47449
This companion volume to the title entered below contains approximately 85 additional experiments

Newton, David E.

Making and using scientific equipment. Watts 1993 157p il (Experimental science series) lib bdg $21.40; pa $6.95   **507.8**
1. Scientific apparatus and instruments
ISBN 0-531-11176-8 (lib bdg); 0-531-15663-X (pa)
     LC 92-38039

Describes the function of scientific equipment used in the fields of physics, meteorology, biology, and earth science and provides instructions for constructing these instruments

"The author has produced an excellent book that is both fun and educational." Sci Books Films

Includes bibliography

Science experiments on file; experiments, demonstrations, and projects for school and home. Facts on File 1988 various paging il $161.25   **507.8**
1. Science—Experiments
ISBN 0-8160-1888-X   LC 88-3883

"Eighty-four inexpensive, innovative, reproductible experiments in the categories of earth science, biology, physical science/chemistry, and physics are included. . . . Each experiment includes introductions, time and materials needed, safety precautions, procedures, and analysis. . . . Experiments are aimed at students in grades six through twelve and were prepared by a group of science teachers who have received awards from the National Science Foundation." Am Libr

Science fairs and projects, 7-12; a collection of articles reprinted from Science and Children, Science Scope, the Science Teacher. National Science Teachers Assn. 1988 70p il $9.50
     507.8
1. Science projects 2. Science—Study and teaching
ISBN 0-87355-072-2   LC 89-208795

This book includes "sample entry, judging, and reporting forms and hand-outs, master planning schedules . . . profiles of successful fairs, and a . . . section on alternatives to the traditional science fair." Publisher's note

508   Natural history

The Curious naturalist. National Geographic Soc. 1991 288p il $32   **508**
1. Natural history 2. Nature study 3. Ecology
ISBN 0-87044-861-7   LC 91-27559

Series of essays on various ecosystems that includes "woodlands, grasslands, deserts, mountains, streams, lakes, ponds and bogs, sandy shores and coastal wetlands, rocky shores, and sky. Each essay is a narrative by a naturalist visitor to the ecosystem who presents observations, information, and musings about the plants and animals that occur there." Appraisal

"A useful addition to ecology and natural science collections." SLJ

Includes bibliography

Darwin, Charles, 1809-1882

The voyage of the Beagle   **508**
1. Beagle Expedition (1831-1836) 2. Natural history 3. South America—Description
Available in paperback from NAL/Dutton and Penguin Bks.

First published 1839 with title: Journal of researches into the geology and natural history of the various countries visited by H.M.S. Beagle

This journal records the author's five year voyage around the world as naturalist aboard H.M.S. Beagle. The trip was influential in the formulation of Darwin's theories of evolution. During the journey he collected data on wildlife, geological formations, weather, and local customs

Discovering the wonders of our world. Reader's Digest Assn. 1994 456p il maps $30   **508**
1. Natural history 2. Wilderness areas
ISBN 0-276-42108-6

At head of title: Reader's Digest
Editor: Noel Buchanan

This is a continent-by-continent guide to the natural wonders of the world. The Sahara, the Ngorogoro Crater, the Matterhorn and Mount Fuji are among the nearly 140 wilderness spots described in text, color photographs, illustrations, diagrams and maps

Durrell, Gerald M., 1925-1995

The amateur naturalist; [by] Gerald Durrell with Lee Durrell. Knopf 1983 320p il o.p.; McKay, D. paperback available $25   **508**
1. Nature study
ISBN 0-679-72837-6 (pa)   LC 83-47940

This guide describes field observation and experiments in a variety of natural habitats, beginning with the backyard and moving on to meadows, woodlands, marshlands, the seashore, and other environments

Includes glossary and bibliography

Few, Roger

The atlas of wild places; in search of the Earth's last wildernesses. Facts on File 1994 240p il $35   **508**
1. Natural history 2. Wilderness areas
ISBN 0-8160-3168-1   LC 94-11375

This is "a book of photos and short supporting articles covering 53 of the wildest locations still remaining on earth. The survey is world-wide, including everything from remote polar regions to the Okefenokee Swamp in Georgia." Book Rep

"This combination of gorgeous photographs and readable text provides teens with an excellent introduction to many of the world's remaining wilderness areas." SLJ

Forgotten Edens; exploring the world's wild places; photographic essays by Frans Lanting; text essays by Christine K. Eckstrom; prepared by the Book Division, National Geographic Society. National Geographic Soc. 1993 202p il maps $16   **508**
1. Natural history
ISBN 0-87044-866-8   LC 92-42371

This volume portrays the natural history of Borneo, South Georgia on the edge of Antarctica, Hawaii, Madagascar, and Okavango in Africa's Kalahari Basin

"This gorgeous book describes, in equally compelling text and photos, five of the most spectacular surviving wildernesses on earth." Voice Youth Advocates

Gould, Stephen Jay, 1941-
Bully for brontosaurus; reflections in natural history. Norton 1991 540p il hardcover o.p. paperback available $13.95   **508**
1. Natural history 2. Evolution
ISBN 0-393-30857-X (pa)   LC 91-6916
A collection of essays from the author's monthly columns in Natural History magazine
"These pithy essays focus on evolution and the workings of science. Gould's fans . . . will find these works fascinating, literate, and often challenging—vintage Gould." Libr J

Dinosaur in a haystack; reflections in natural history. Harmony Bks. 1995 480p il $25   **508**
1. Natural history
ISBN 0-517-70393-9   LC 95-51333
Analyzed in Essay and general literature index
In this collection the author "relates anecdotes from the history of science and demonstrates their relevance to contemporary scientific disputes and social trends." Libr J
"A discovery awaits in every essay—in every haystack—which solidifies Gould as one of the most eloquent science popularizers writing today." Booklist
Includes bibliography

The flamingo's smile; reflections in natural history. Norton 1985 476p il hardcover o.p. paperback available $12.95   **508**
1. Natural history
ISBN 0-393-30375-6 (pa)   LC 85-4916
In this collection "the theme is history, both natural and human. . . . The essays are marked by Gould's usual careful scholarship and erudition and clear and nontechnical language." Sci Books Films
Includes bibliography

Islands; consulting editors, Robert E. Stevenson, Frank H. Talbot. Rodale Press 1994 160p il maps (Illustrated library of the earth) $35   **508**
1. Islands
ISBN 0-87596-632-2   LC 93-36352
This work contains a description "of all types of islands, including continental, volcanic, and coral islands, and a discussion of the sociology of the human populations inhabiting these islands. . . . The strongest emphasis is on the geology of islands, followed by natural history and, to some degree, meteorology. . . . A series of superb diagrams accompanies the superb photography." Sci Books Films

Nature projects on file; [by] the Diagram Group. Facts on File 1992 various paging il $155
                    508
1. Natural history 2. Environmental protection 3. Science projects
ISBN 0-8160-2705-6   LC 91-40846
This "is a looseleaf collection of hands-on experiments that are designed for independent investigation. Topics include: the earth, weather, animals, plants, ecology, pollution, energy, and environmental quality. . . . Since the pages are designed for photocopying, the series could be very appropriately used for a school system resource, from which teachers could select and duplicate timely

experiments. . . . The hands-on activities are varied, creative, interesting, and challenging. . . . The materials required are simple, inexpensive, and easily procured. Safety is stressed constantly." Sci Books Films

Our awesome earth; its mysteries and its splendors; prepared by the Special Publications Division, National Geographic Society, Washington, D.C. National Geographic Soc. 1986 199p il $16   **508**
1. Natural history 2. Earth sciences
ISBN 0-87044-545-6   LC 85-23733
An exploration of the dominant ecosystems of the world: the seas, forests, grasslands, deserts, and mountains, and the plants and animals which have adapted to each. Featured are the volcanoes of Indonesia, the Serengeti grasslands, the rain forests of Costa Rica, and the Sahara
Includes bibliography

Rexer, Lyle
American Museum of Natural History; 125 years of expedition and discovery; [by] Lyle Rexer and Rachel Klein; foreword by Edward O. Wilson. Abrams 1995 256p il maps $49.95   **508**
1. American Museum of Natural History
ISBN 0-8109-1965-6   LC 95-6108
This illustrated text explores the museum's many archaeological, anthropological and paleontological holdings
The illustrations "include everything from a fascinating engraving depicting an early conception for the museum in which entrance was to be underground from Central Park, to hand-colored lantern slides, to photographs of and by such great scientific explorers as Roy Chapman Andrews and Carl Akeley, to modern colorplates of beautiful items from the museum's collection. Great browsing, great reading." Booklist
Includes bibliographical references

Seff, Philip
Our fascinating earth; [by] Philip Seff and Nancy R. Seff. rev ed. Contemporary Bks. 1996 324p il map pa $16.95   **508**
1. Natural history 2. Curiosities and wonders
ISBN 0-8092-3249-9   LC 95-49402
First published 1990
This "is a collection of articles compiled from the author's syndicated newspaper column that discuss the causes of bizarre happenings and unusual phenomena. . . . The scope and range of events and information included are immense, covering a broad range of physical and cultural phenomena. . . . This is fascinating reading." Sci Books Films
Includes bibliography

The **Walker's** companion; [by] Elizabeth Ferber [et al.]; with illustrations by Cathy Johnson. Time-Life Bks. 1995 288p il maps (Nature Company guide) $29.95   **508**
1. Natural history—North America 2. Walking 3. Hiking

                    LC 95-4551
This illustrated text guides hikers through mountain, forest, grassland, desert, wetland, and seashore habitats.

The Walker's companion—*Continued*
Tips are included on finding trails, choosing equipment, keeping journals, and photographing wildlife

Wood, Robert Muir
Atlas of the natural world. Facts on File 1990 64p il maps (World contemporary issues) $17.95   **508**
1. Natural history—Maps 2. Physical geography—Maps
ISBN 0-8160-2131-7   LC 89-675217
Text and maps depict and explain the natural world and the structure and processes of the Earth
"The drawings, graphs, and maps are excellent and provide information in a vivid, visual way." Booklist
Includes glossary

509 Science—Historical and geographic treatment

Alic, Margaret
Hypatia's heritage; a history of women in science from antiquity through the nineteenth century. Beacon Press 1986 230p il hardcover o.p. paperback available $13.75   **509**
1. Women scientists
ISBN 0-8070-6731-8 (pa)   LC 86-47510
This book contains "accounts of the lives and work of Egyptian and Babylonian chemists, Greco-Egyptian mathematicians and natural philosophers, . . . medieval alchemists and cosmologists, 17th- and 18th-century geologists, astronomers, physicians, physicists." Science
Includes bibliography

Asimov, Isaac, 1920-1992
Asimov's Chronology of science and discovery. updated & il [ed] HarperCollins Pubs. 1994 790p il $37.50   **509**
1. Science—History 2. Inventions—History
ISBN 0-06-270113-4   LC 94-2504
First published 1989
This offers information on landmark scientific events and places these achievements in the context of concurrent political, social, and cultural events

Great scientific achievements. Salem Press 1994 10v il (Twentieth century) set $250   **509**
1. Science—History—Dictionaries 2. Technology—History—Dictionaries
ISBN 0-89356-860-0   LC 94-1829
"A Magill book from the editors of Salem Press"
Contents: v1 1880-1905; v2 1906-1916; v3 1917-1929; v4 1929-1938; v5 1938-1949; v6 1950-1958; v7 1958-1964; v8 1964-1973; v9 1973-1982; v10 1982-1994
This set "covers 21 disciplines, including agriculture, astronomy, biology, computer science, food science, transportation, and weapons technology. . . . Each entry runs three pages and includes a half- or full-page illustration." Booklist
"Useful to both students and teachers in middle or high school mathematics, science, and history classes." Book Rep

Hellemans, Alexander, 1946-
The timetables of science; a chronology of the most important people and events in the history of science; [by] Alexander Hellemans and Bryan Bunch. Simon & Schuster 1988 656p hardcover o.p. paperback available $20   **509**
1. Science—History
ISBN 0-671-73328-1 (pa)   LC 88-23920
Companion volume The timetables of technology, entered under Bunch, Bryan H., class 609
"Contains over 10,000 entries organized chronologically and by discipline, interspersed with more than 100 short essays on science and technology and nine overviews of the main periods of scientific history. Indexed by subject and name." N Y Public Libr. Book of How & Where to Look It Up

Mount, Ellis, 1921-
Milestones in science and technology; the ready reference guide to discoveries, inventions, and facts; by Ellis Mount and Barbara A. List. 2nd ed. Oryx Press 1994 206p il $34.50   **509**
1. Science 2. Technology 3. Inventions
ISBN 0-89774-671-6   LC 93-25679
First published 1987
"Thumbnail alphabetical entries—1,250 in all—that present scientific history are neatly laid out, easy to read, and of popular interest. The scope is broad, including pure and applied sciences." SLJ
Includes bibliographical references

Spangenburg, Ray, 1939-
The history of science from the ancient Greeks to the scientific revolution; [by] Ray Spangenburg and Diane K. Moser. Facts on File 1993 166p il $18.95   **509**
1. Science—History
ISBN 0-8160-2739-0   LC 92-33180
Surveys the early history of science, discussing the philosophical underpinnings developed by Greek thinkers, continuing through the developments of the Middle Ages and the Renaissance, and concluding with the discoveries of the seventeenth century
"Very well written and thoroughly understandable, the book succeeds hugely in its objective to introduce the development of science in an interesting fashion to the intended audience without patronizing or oversimplifying." Sci Books Films
Includes bibliographical references

The history of science in the 18th century; [by] Ray Spangenburg and Diane K. Moser. Facts on File 1993 xx, 156p $18.95   **509**
1. Science—History
ISBN 0-8160-2740-4   LC 92-41500
"Astronomy, geology, chemistry, electricity, natural history, and the life sciences are discussed in the context of social and political developments and the industrial revolution. From the vast scope of scientific activity that this century offers, the authors have chosen judiciously and fairly. The vignettes present enough biographical and contextual information to make them interesting and colorful, yet convey the important contributions of the men and women discussed." Sci Books Films
Includes bibliographical references

Spangenburg, Ray, 1939——Continued

The history of science in the nineteenth century; by Ray Spangenburg and Diane K. Moser. Facts on File 1994 142p il $18.95   **509**
1. Science—History
ISBN 0-8160-2741-2   LC 93-10576
Examines the role of science in the Industrial Revolution, its establishment as a popular discipline, and discoveries in the areas of atoms and the elements, chemistry, evolution, and energy
This "is a valuable resource." Voice Youth Advocates
Includes bibliographical references

The history of science from 1895 to 1945; [by] Ray Spangenburg and Diane K. Moser. Facts on File 1994 164p il $21.25   **509**
1. Science—History
ISBN 0-8160-2742-0   LC 93-26820
The first part of this "science survey covers developments in the physical sciences in the first half of the twentieth century. . . . The second part of the book deals with the life sciences: microbiology, biochemistry, genetics, and archaeology, with each science linked with the lives of scientists studying it." Booklist
Includes bibliographical references

The history of science from 1946 to the 1990s; [by] Ray Spangenburg and Diane K. Moser. Facts on File 1994 176p il $18.95   **509**
1. Science—History
ISBN 0-8160-2743-9   LC 93-46058
The authors provide "descriptions of complex scientific theories and lines of research in the latter part of the 20th century—but only in the natural sciences: physics (new particles, lasers, and superconductors), astronomy (quasars, black holes, cosmology, dark matter, planetary geology, and SETI), geology (evolution, plate tectonics, and environmental change), and biology (DNA, biotechnology, the human genome, and retroviruses)." Sci Books Films
Includes bibliographical references

510   Mathematics

Boyer, Carl B. (Carl Benjamin), 1906-
A history of mathematics; revised by Uta C. Merzbach. 2nd ed. Wiley 1989 762p il $75.75; pa $32.95   **510**
1. Mathematics—History
ISBN 0-471-09763-2; 0-471-54397-7 (pa)
LC 89-5325
First published 1969
"This good general history of mathematics is understandable to the student as well as authoritative for the mathematician." Malinowsky. Best Sci & Technol Ref Books for Young People
Includes bibliographies

Burington, Richard Stevens
Handbook of mathematical tables and formulas. 5th ed. McGraw-Hill 1973 500p $66.75   **510**
1. Mathematics—Tables
ISBN 0-07-009015-7
First published 1933 by Handbook Pubs.

This handbook "is designed for use by students and workers in mathematics, engineering, physics, chemistry, and other fields. The first part includes a summary of the more important formulas and theorems. . . . Part 2 consists of tables. . . . There is a section containing references, a glossary of symbols, and index of numerical tables, and a subject index. Useful as a handbook for high school." Wynar. Guide to Ref Books for Sch Media Cent. 3d edition

Gardner, Robert, 1929-
Math in science and nature; finding patterns in the world around us; by Robert Gardner and Edward A. Shore. Watts 1994 144p il lib bdg $19.90   **510**
1. Mathematics 2. Science projects
ISBN 0-531-11196-2   LC 94-26878
"The first chapter introduces concepts—graphing especially—and provides practice problems. Gardner and Shore go on to mix classic demonstrations, such as Ohm's Law and the behavior of a pendulum, with contemporary issues such as greenhouse warming and energy conservation. An entire chapter is devoted to examples from sports; others explore music and sailing. Formulae and calculations cover basic algebra, geometry, statistics, graphing, and trigonometry. Household materials or tables of data are the basis for each experiment." SLJ
Includes bibliographical references

Gullberg, Jan
Mathematics; from the birth of numbers; technical illustrations, Pär Gullberg. Norton 1997 xxiii, 1093p il $50   **510**
1. Mathematics—History
ISBN 0-393-04002-X   LC 96-13428
The author "aims to cure math phobia by plunging the reader into mathematical thinking and activity, whether the topic is algebra, geometry, set theory, symbolic logic, topology, fractals, probability theory or differential equations." Publ Wkly
This book contains a "wealth of historical anecdotes, literary quotations, artwork, light verse, and even cartoons sprinkled liberally through the pages. Perhaps because he is himself a well-practiced amateur in the field rather than a professional, Gullberg anticipates perfectly the perplexities of the average reader. Simplified derivations and numerous examples will clear up most of the hard points." Booklist
Includes bibliographical references

Jacobs, Harold R.
Mathematics, a human endeavor; a book for those who think they don't like the subject. 3rd ed. Freeman, W.H. 1994 678p il $52.95   **510**
1. Mathematics
ISBN 0-7167-2426-X   LC 93-37458
Also available in a teachers edition with instruction manual, workbook, etc.
First published 1970
Contents: Mathematical ways of thinking; Number sequences; Functions and their graphs; Large numbers and logarithms; Symmetry and regular figures; Mathematical curves; Methods of counting; The mathematics of chance; An introduction to statistics; Topics in topology
Includes bibliographical references

Math on file; the Diagram Group. Facts on File 1995 various paging $155   **510**
1. Mathematics
ISBN 0-8160-2936-9   LC 95-23089
This looseleaf collection includes "54 projects covering the major areas of mathematics: number theory, algebra, geometry, trigonometry, probability, functions, and calculus. The geometry section is the largest with 19 projects. The activities can be used as individual assignments or as class activities. The materials required are items normally found in a math classroom." Book Rep
Includes glossary

Stewart, Ian, 1945-
Nature's numbers; the unreal reality of mathematical imagination. Basic Bks. 1995 164p (Science masters series) $20   **510**
1. Mathematics
ISBN 0-465-07273-9   LC 95-10238
The author "conveys some sense of the basic nature of mathematics without using equations or numbers. After dealing with some very general considerations, he offers several examples of the application of mathematics in the physical and biological sciences. The entire work is well written and constitutes an excellent popularization of a discipline notoriously hard to describe to lay readers." Libr J
Includes bibliographical references

Thomas, David A. (David Allen), 1946-
Math projects in the computer age. Watts 1995 176p il (Projects for young scientists) lib bdg $20.50   **510**
1. Mathematics—Data processing 2. Science projects
ISBN 0-531-11213-6   LC 94-42037
This book offers projects in fractal geometry, matrix algebra, mathematical friezes, and graph theory
The author "provides generally satisfactory introductions to each area of study, as well as a list of resources for further information on the topics of each chapter." Sci Book Films
Includes bibliographical references

Tobias, Sheila
Overcoming math anxiety. rev and expanded. Norton 1993 260p il $23; pa $12.95   **510**
1. Mathematics
ISBN 0-393-03577-8; 0-393-31307-7 (pa)
LC 93-3648
First published 1978
The author explains common misconceptions about mathematical concepts, analyzes what makes math seem difficult, discusses alleged sex differences in brain function in relation to math, and describes math programs aimed at women
Includes bibliographical references

510.3   Mathematics—Encyclopedias and dictionaries

Borowski, E. J. (Ephraim J.)
The HarperCollins dictionary of mathematics; [by] E.J. Borowski and J.M. Borwein, with the assistance of J.F. Bowers, A. Robertson, and M. McQuillan. HarperPerennial 1991 659p il hardcover o.p. paperback available $18   **510.3**
1. Mathematics—Dictionaries
ISBN 0-06-461019-5 (pa)   LC 90-55995
Spine title: Mathematics
"The major objective of this work . . . is to provide a dictionary of mathematical terms for students of mathematics at all levels. . . . In-depth explanations and examples cover more than 4,000 entries and all the major subjects. More than 400 diagrams illustrated such concepts as four-color theorem, hyperbolic function, and correlation. Also included are biographies of major mathematicians with detailed descriptions of their contributions to the field. . . . This book covers a wide range of technical terms from both pure and applied mathematics, going beyond basic definitions to provide helpful explanations and examples." Am Ref Books Annu, 1993

Downing, Douglas
Dictionary of mathematics terms. 2nd ed. Barron's Educ. Ser. 1995 303p il pa $10.95
      510.3
1. Mathematics—Dictionaries
ISBN 0-8120-3097-4   LC 95-12039
First published 1987
"Some of the general subjects included are arithmetic; algebra; geometry; analytical geometry; trigonometry; calculus, including some topics in multivariable calculus; probability and statistics; and logic. Information on several mathematicians who have made major contributions to the field is also given." Am Ref Books Annu, 1996

Mathematics dictionary; [edited by Robert C.] James [and Glenn] James; contributors, Armen A. Alchian [et al.] 5th ed. Van Nostrand Reinhold 1992 548p il $42.95; pa $29.95
      510.3
1. Mathematics—Dictionaries
ISBN 0-442-00741-8; 0-442-01241-1 (pa)
LC 92-6757
First published 1942 by Digest Press
"Provides definitions of terms and phrases in pure and applied mathematics; brief biographical entries. . . . Contains sections on Denominate numbers, Mathematical symbols, Differentiation formulas, and Integral tables. Indexes in French, German, Russian, and Spanish." Guide to Ref Books. 11th edition

510.7 Mathematics—Education and related topics

Zaslavsky, Claudia, 1917-
Fear of math; how to get over it and get on with your life. Rutgers Univ. Press 1994 264p il $37; pa $14.95   **510.7**
1. Mathematics—Study and teaching
ISBN 0-8135-2090-8; 0-8135-2099-1 (pa)
     LC 93-43904
The author explores the causes for many people's phobia about the study and use of mathematics and provides tips for easing the anxiety. Also includes a discussion of math and minorities. Teaching strategies are suggested
Includes bibliographical references

513 Arithmetic

Clawson, Calvin C.
The mathematical traveler; exploring the grand history of numbers. Plenum Press 1994 307p il (Language of science) $25.95   **513**
1. Numbers 2. Counting
ISBN 0-306-44645-6   LC 94-2740
Clawson "explores the history and science of numbers, detailing the development of simple to advanced numerical concepts." Booklist
The author's "presentation is clear and compelling for the serious lay reader." SciTech Book News
Includes glossary and bibliographical references

Humez, Alexander
Zero to lazy eight; the romance of numbers; [by] Alexander Humez, Nicholas Humez, and Joseph Maguire. Simon & Schuster 1993 228p il $21; pa $11   **513**
1. Numerals 2. Mathematics
ISBN 0-671-74282-5; 0-671-74281-7 (pa)
     LC 93-13204
This book comprises "essays on numbers 1 through 13 (plus zero and infinity) [that] discuss the linguistic roots of numerical expressions and related folklore, idioms, and mathematical diversions. For instance, the chapter on number 6 starts with the expression 'six of one and half a dozen of the other' and goes on to discuss ways of talking about symmetry and equality, puns and jokes (linguistic mapping), mathematical mapping, set theory, syllogisms, and socialism." Libr J

Kogelman, Stanley
The only math book you'll ever need; [by] Stanley Kogelman and Barbara R. Heller. rev ed. Facts on File 1994 xx, 268p il $22.95   **513**
1. Mathematics
ISBN 0-8160-2767-6   LC 93-10539
Also available in paperback from HarperCollins
First published 1986
Step-by-step operations are reviewed in problems encountered on a daily basis such as comparing credit cards, evaluating investments, estimating interest rates, and converting area measurements

515 Analysis. Calculus

Berlinski, David, 1942-
A tour of the calculus. Pantheon Bks. 1995 331p il $27.50; pa $14   **515**
1. Calculus
ISBN 0-679-42645-0; 0-679-74788-5 (pa)
     LC 95-4042
This is an introduction to "the foundations of calculus. It is in part an informal history of the subject; the author interweaves the historical fragments with expository sections that [seek to] explain the concepts from a modern viewpoint." Libr J
"Berlinski tangibly grounds the abstract notions, so that attentive readers can ease into and grasp the several full-blown proofs he sets forth." Booklist

520 Astronomy and allied sciences

Asimov, Isaac, 1920-1992
Isaac Asimov's guide to earth & space. Random House 1991 285p il o.p.; Fawcett Bks. paperback available $4.99   **520**
1. Astronomy 2. Earth
ISBN 0-449-22059-1 (pa)   LC 91-11097
Written as if "Asimov were chatting with an interesting but unsophisticated companion, this guide covers a wide range: ancient history; new discoveries; specific properties of the sun, moon, stars and Earth; as well as general information about the universe." Voice Youth Advocates
"Although most of this is familiar ground to regular readers of scientific books and magazines, it is a fine introduction to modern astronomical theory for the intellectually curious high school student or intelligent but scientifically illiterate adult." Libr J

The secret of the universe. Doubleday 1991 c1990 240p o.p.; Pinnacle Bks. (NY) paperback available $4.50   **520**
1. Solar system 2. Universe
ISBN 1-55817-658-6 (pa)   LC 90-38309
In this collection of essays "complex phenomena such as quasars, gravitational lenses, fusion, and the greenhouse effect are detailed in easy-to-read passages. Also, the book is sprinkled with well-written anecdotes regarding a number of key physicists, and astronomers. . . . An index, however, would have made the volume a more valuable reference." Sci Books Films

Barbree, Jay
A journey through time; exploring the universe with the Hubble Space Telescope; by Jay Barbree and Martin Caidin; foreword by John H. Glenn, Jr.; designed by William A. Sponn. Penguin Studio 1995 232p il $29.95   **520**
1. Hubble Space Telescope 2. Outer space—Exploration
ISBN 0-670-86018-2   LC 95-6758
Color photographs illustrate this "account of the initial failure of the Hubble optical system and its repair by a skilled and daring team of astronauts." Libr J

Berman, Bob

Secrets of the night sky; the most amazing things in the universe you can see with the naked eye; illustrations by Alan McKnight. Morrow 1995 320p il $23   **520**

1. Astronomy
ISBN 0-688-12727-4   LC 94-21604
Also available in paperback from HarperPerennial

Berman discusses a "variety of interesting celestial objects and how to view some of them and reviews a number of important concepts of physical science and how they are related to the objects we are able to see through binoculars and small telescopes. . . . Fun to read, with virtually all the astronomical subject information timely and generally accurate." Sci Books Films

Includes bibliographical references

The **Cambridge** illustrated history of astronomy; edited by Michael Hoskin. Cambridge Univ. Press 1997 392p il maps $39.95   **520**

1. Astronomy—History
ISBN 0-521-41158-0   LC 95-40923
This volume traces the story of astronomy from prehistoric times to the space age

"This volume is a triumph: authoritative, current, elegantly written, lavishly illustrated, thoughtfully and aesthetically designed, and handsomely executed. If there is to be only one history of astronomy on one's bookshelf, this is the one to have." Sci Books Films

Includes glossary and bibliography

Levy, David H., 1948-

Skywatching; consultant editor, John O'Byrne. Time-Life Bks. 1995 c1994 288p il (Nature Company guide) $29.95   **520**

1. Astronomy
                                        LC 95-8609
This illustrated guide covers such topics as "the history of astronomy, types of stars and other celestial objects of interest to skywatchers, and techniques and equipment for the amateur. The core of the book features a series of seasonal sky charts to be used in conjunction with a generous alphabetical arrangement of constellation maps." Libr J

Includes glossary and bibliography

Mitton, Jacqueline

Gems of Hubble; text by Jacqueline Mitton and Stephen P. Maran. Cambridge Univ. Press 1996 123p il pa $13.95   **520**

1. Astronomy 2. Stars 3. Hubble Space Telescope
ISBN 0-521-57100-6   LC 96-15179
"The book showcases (with appropriate scientific comment) some 60 of the telescope's finest pictures. . . . Truly, this is a star-studded book of extraordinary interest." Sci Books Films

North, John David

The Norton history of astronomy and cosmology. Norton 1994 xxvii, 697p il maps (Norton history of science) $35; pa $18.95 **520**

1. Astronomy—History 2. Universe
ISBN 0-393-03656-1; 0-393-31193-7 (pa)
First published in the United Kingdom with title: The Fontana history of astronomy and cosmology

This volume "surveys facts and ideas about the universe from prehistoric observations, ancient mythologies, and rational speculations to space exploration, radio astronomy, and modern cosmogony. . . . North focuses on recent advances in instruments (telescope, spectroscope, antenna, camera, rocket) and new theories in physics that have brought about remarkable discoveries in astronomy (quasars, pulsars, supernovae) and dynamic models in cosmology." Libr J

"North manages to pack an enormous amount of material into a surprisingly readable and extremely useful text." Booklist

Parker, Barry R.

Chaos in the cosmos; the stunning complexity of the universe; [by] Barry Parker. Plenum Press 1996 307p il $28.95   **520**

1. Astrophysics 2. Chaos (Science)
ISBN 0-306-45261-8   LC 96-1482
"The first half of the text gives a general overview of the history of astronomy, leading off with a very thorough history of the development of chaos. . . . The second half deals specifically with the issue of the chaotic nature of our solar system, before moving on to the larger context of galaxies and cosmology. . . . This text truly covers a wide range of topics, but does so in a careful, easy-to-understand manner." Sci Books Films

Includes bibliographical references

Sagan, Carl, 1934-1996

Cosmos. Random House 1980 365p il hardcover o.p. paperback available $30   **520**

1. Astronomy 2. Universe
ISBN 0-394-71596-9 (pa)   LC 80-5286
Also available in hardcover from P. Smith and in paperback from Ballantine Bks.

Based on C. Sagan's 13-part television series

This is an "account, mostly in chronological order, of the great human efforts at scientific accomplishment. . . . Here are 13 chapters, beginning with a rapid overview of the cosmic ocean in which we live and ending with a discussion of our choice to preserve our planet or destroy it in a nuclear holocaust." Christ Century

Includes bibliography

Pale blue dot; a vision of the human future in space. Random House 1994 429p il $35; pa $22
                                        520

1. Outer space—Exploration
ISBN 0-679-43841-6; 0-679-76486-0 (pa)
                                        LC 94-18121
"In a tour of our solar system, galaxy and beyond . . . Sagan meshes a history of astronomical discovery, a cogent brief for space exploration and an overview of life. . . . His exploration of our place in the universe is illustrated with photographs, relief maps and paintings, including high-resolution images made by *Voyager 1* and *2*, as well as photos taken by the *Galileo* spacecraft, the Hubble Space Telescope and satellites orbiting Earth." Publ Wkly

"Teenagers need to read and ponder the facts Sagan carefully and systematically presents. This book is meant for them." Book Rep

Includes bibliographical references

Vogt, Gregory
Space exploration projects for young scientists. Watts 1995 144p il (Projects for young scientists) lib bdg $22 **520**
1. Space sciences 2. Outer space—Exploration 3. Science projects
ISBN 0-531-11233-0 LC 95-23328
Suggests projects demonstrating such outer space principles and phenomena as gravity wells, rocket propulsion, and planetary motion
Includes bibliographical references

520.3 Astronomy—Encyclopedias and dictionaries

The **Facts** on File dictionary of astronomy; edited by Valerie Illingworth. 3rd ed. Facts on File 1994 520p il $27.95; pa $14.95 **520.3**
1. Astronomy—Dictionaries
ISBN 0-8160-3184-3; 0-8160-3185-1 (pa)
LC 94-26275
First published 1979
This "is a resource for astronomical, as well as scientific and mathematical, terms. It contains more than 3,500 entries with some 100 b&w diagrams, ranging from the Airy disc to the Willstrop telescope. . . . The text is authoritative and relatively easy to understand." Book Rep

McGraw-Hill encyclopedia of astronomy; editors in chief, Sybil P. Parker, Jay M. Pasachoff. 2nd ed. McGraw-Hill 1993 531p il maps $75.50
520.3
1. Astronomy—Dictionaries
ISBN 0-07-045314-4 LC 92-40523
First published 1983
"A subset of the multi-volume *McGraw-Hill Encyclopedia of Science & Technology* . . . this work consists of 225 alphabetically arranged topical articles written by prominent astronomers and other specialists from around the world. The focus is on physical rather than descriptive aspects of astronomy, with an underlying theme being the study of the heavens through electromagnetic radiation. . . . Although the text is presented at a fairly advanced level, it is clearly written." Dority. Guide to Ref Books for Small & Medium-sized Libr. 1984-1994
Includes bibliographical references

521 Celestial mechanics

Goodstein, David L., 1939-
Feynman's lost lecture; the motion of planets around the sun; [by] David L. Goodstein and Judith R. Goodstein. Norton 1996 191p il $35
521
1. Feynman, Richard Phillips 2. Universe 3. Astrophysics
ISBN 0-393-03918-8 LC 95-38719
Includes audio CD
This "book consists of four chapters. The first and largest is a brief history of the establishment of the Co-

pernican cosmology, which Feynman gave as a lecture to the freshman class at Caltech. Feynman then revisits the work of Isaac Newton and the watershed proof of the Scientific Revolution that separated the ancient world from the modern. There is also a chapter with some wonderful reminiscences of Feynman." Libr J
Includes bibliography

522 Techniques, equipment, materials of astronomy

Florence, Ronald
The perfect machine; building the Palomar telescope. HarperCollins Pubs. 1994 451p il $27.50; pa $14 **522**
1. Mount Wilson and Palomar Observatories 2. Telescopes 3. Astronomy
ISBN 0-06-018205-9; 0-06-092670-8 (pa)
LC 93-46374
This describes the construction of the 200 inch telescope on Mount Palomar in California, conceived and overseen by astronomer George Hale
"An engaging tale, with enough dramatic disappointments, cliff-hanging crises, and clashing personalities to remind the reader that this is a world away from being a dry, technical report." Booklist
Includes bibliographical references

Miller, Robert, 1948-
Making & enjoying telescopes; 6 complete projects & a stargazer's guide; [by] Robert Miller & Kenneth Wilson. Sterling 1995 160p il $27.95; pa $14.95 **522**
1. Telescopes—Design and construction 2. Astronomy
ISBN 0-8069-1277-4; 0-8069-1278-2 (pa)
LC 95-4592
"A Sterling/Lark book"
This guide for the backyard astronomer provides basic information, offers activity ideas, and gives construction details and assembly drawings for six telescopes
"The procedures are laid out in an easy-to-follow technique. The book includes a rich gallery of illustrated telescopes that amateurs have built. This gallery is a welcome addition as a source of ideas." Sci Books Films
Includes bibliographical references

Porcellino, Michael R.
Through the telescope; a guide for the amateur astronomer. TAB Bks. 1989 342p il $22.95; pa $19.95 **522**
1. Astronomy
ISBN 0-8306-1459-1; 0-8306-3159-3 (pa)
LC 89-34641
This guide covers the use of the telescope and other tools of the astronomer, and provides instruction for observing the planets, the moon, stars, and other objects. Sky charts are also included
Includes bibliography

523 Specific celestial bodies and phenomena

The **Cambridge** atlas of astronomy; edited by Jean Audouze and Guy Israël. 3rd ed. Cambridge Univ. Press 1994 470p il $95 **523**
1. Astronomy
ISBN 0-521-43438-6   LC 95-112181
First published 1985

This volume presents information on aspects of "planetary science, astronomy, astrophysics, and cosmology. . . . [It covers] developments such as the Magellan mission to Venus, the Voyager mission to Neptune, [and] the Hubble Space Telescope." Sci Books Films

This is "arguably the best and most complete available collection of astronomical photographs and graphic illustrations. The 30 authors (all French professional astronomers) have written the terse and information-packed text to accompany the superb pictorial material, and the editors have succeeded in making it suprisingly uniform. This is one of the very few books that will be enjoyed by all lovers of astronomy, from the casually interested . . . to the professionals who want reasonably reliable and quite detailed, up-to-date information on areas outside their specialties." Choice

Chartrand, Mark R.
The Audubon Society field guide to the night sky; astronomical charts by Wil Tirion. Knopf 1991 714p il maps $19   **523**
1. Astronomy
ISBN 0-679-40852-5   LC 91-52708
"A Chanticleer Press edition. The Audubon Society field guide series"

This guide "begins with monthly star charts and constellation star charts . . . then gives photographs of the constellations; and finally, provides detailed information on each constellation including stars, galaxies, and nebulae. . . . Other information includes hints on observing the sky; dates of solar and lunar eclipses, meteor showers, and comets, and the Messier catalog. . . . Students interested in astronomy will find lots of observing tips and information." Voice Youth Advocates

Includes bibliography

Gallant, Roy A.
National Geographic picture atlas of our universe. rev ed. National Geographic Soc. 1995 c1994 284p il $25; lib bdg $23.95   **523**
1. Astronomy 2. Universe
ISBN 0-7922-2731-X; 0-7922-2956-8 (lib bdg)
First published 1980

This guide to astronomy includes chapters on the solar system, space technology, and astronomical phenomena, illustrated with maps, photographs, and diagrams

Kals, W. S.
Stars and planets; the Sierra Club guide to sky watching and direction finding. Sierra Club Bks. 1990 244p il maps pa $15   **523**
1. Astronomy 2. Stars 3. Planets
ISBN 0-87156-671-0   LC 90-33711

This guide shows how to locate bright stars, planets, and constellations with the naked eye. Among the features are constellation maps, a calendar for phases of the moon and positions of the visible planets to the year 2000, how to get compass directions from the sun and stars, and a pronouncing gazeteer

Moeschl, Richard
Exploring the sky; projects for beginning astronomers. rev ed. Chicago Review Press 1993 413p il pa $16.95   **523**
1. Astronomy 2. Science projects
ISBN 1-55652-160-X   LC 92-18863
"A Ziggurat book"
First published 1989

"The author takes the reader from the universe as seen by early man right up to our own space age. Included on the journey are mythology, history (and the women and men who made it), and scientific theories. All of this information is woven into a series of 72 fully explained projects." Book Rep
Includes glossary and bibliography

Moore, Patrick
Stargazing; astronomy without a telescope. Barron's Educ. Ser. 1985 176p il maps $21.95
          523
1. Astronomy
ISBN 0-8120-5644-2   LC 85-6091

"This guide for finding celestial objects with the naked eye provides copious star charts and maps as aids to the identification of constellations, important stars, and other objects. There are separate sets of maps for viewers in the southern and northern hemispheres, and in equatorial regions." Libr J

"Information is presented in prose that is clear, concise, nontechnical, and readily comprehensible." Booklist

Norton's 2000.0; star atlas and reference handbook (epoch 2000.0); edited by Arthur P. Norton. 18th ed, rev under the editorship of Ian Ridpath. Wiley 1989 179p il maps $44.95 **523**
1. Astronomy 2. Stars—Atlases
ISBN 0-582-03163-X   LC 89-12226
First published 1910. Variant titles: A star atlas and telescopic handbook; A star atlas and reference handbook

"The familiar features of this standard atlas of practical astronomy have been retained, but all maps have been redrawn to standard epoch 2000.0. Map projections have been standardized and computer-verified. The reference section has been rewritten and expanded." Guide to Ref Books. 11th edition

Pasachoff, Jay M.
A field guide to the stars and planets; [by] Jay M. Pasachoff, Donald H. Menzel; with monthly star maps and atlas charts by Wil Tirion. 3rd ed. Houghton Mifflin 1992 502p il maps $24.95; pa $16.95   **523**
1. Astronomy
ISBN 0-395-53764-9; 0-395-53759-2 (pa)
          LC 92-17556

"The Peterson field guide series"
First published 1964 with authors' names in reverse order

Pasachoff, Jay M.—*Continued*

This guide contains 72 star maps, 52 atlas charts, and numerous color photographs from NASA space missions
Includes bibliographical references

Schaaf, Fred

Seeing the sky; 100 projects, activities, and explorations in astronomy; with illustrations by Doug Myers. Wiley 1990 212p il (Wiley science editions) hardcover o.p. paperback available $18.95

523

1. Astronomy
ISBN 0-471-51067-1 (pa) LC 89-70673
"Focusing on celestial bodies and sky phenomena, this hands-on introduction to the science of astronomical observation details more than 100 projects and experiments." Booklist
Includes bibliographical references

The **Universe** explained; the earth-dweller's guide to the mysteries of space; Colin A. Ronan [editor] Holt & Co. 1994 192p il (Henry Holt reference book) $35

523

1. Astronomy 2. Universe
ISBN 0-8050-3488-9 LC 94-16294
"Drawing on telescopes, satellites, computer imagery, and . . . current theories, this book examines the interlinked relationships of the cosmos. . . . Five major sections concentrate on the universe from our observatory Earth, the planets, the sun and stars, nebulae and galaxies, and how it all works. . . . A welcome addition to any collection for budding scientist or curious information seeker." Booklist

523.1 The universe; space, galaxies, quasars

Barrow, John D., 1952-

The origin of the universe. Basic Bks. 1994 150p il (Science masters series) $20

523.1

1. Universe 2. Astrophysics
ISBN 0-465-05354-8 LC 94-6343
The author explains current theories in cosmology including the big bang, the inflationary universe, wormholes and the origin of physical constants
"The attentive reader will be rewarded with a gigantic feast for continued contemplation, especially if one comes to the book with fundamental concepts of astronomy and physics well in hand. . . . This is an extremely stimulating book." Sci Books Films
Includes bibliographical references

Boslough, John

Stephen Hawking's universe. Morrow 1985 158p il hardcover o.p. paperback available $7.95

523.1

1. Hawking, S. W. (Stephen W.) 2. Universe
ISBN 0-688-06270-9 (pa) LC 84-4673
Also available in paperback from Avon Bks.
Published in the United Kingdom with title: Beyond the black hole

This book presents a profile of the English physicist along with a transcript of one of his lectures
"Boslough captures the essence of Hawking's contributions to the fundamentals and the applications of physics to astronomy and cosmology. . . . Any reader at any level with an interest in the ideas of science will enjoy reading this man's views of the physical universe." Choice

Dauber, Philip M.

The three big bangs; comet crashes, exploding stars, and the creation of the universe; [by] Philip M. Dauber and Richard A. Muller. Addison-Wesley 1996 207p il $25

523.1

1. Universe 2. Catastrophes (Geology) 3. Supernovas
ISBN 0-201-40752-3 LC 95-24451
The authors "identify and describe the three main events that brought life to planet Earth. They begin 65 million years ago when a comet or asteroid slammed into the earth and so disrupted the balance of life that two-thirds of all planet and animal species, including the dinosaurs, became extinct. . . . The next crucial occurence the authors discuss is the explosion of a giant star, a supernova that brought into being all the chemical elements essential to life. . . . Finally, they get to the ultimate big bang, the original and nearly inconceivable explosion that created not only matter, but space itself, and maybe even time." Booklist
Includes bibliographical references

Hawking, S. W. (Stephen W.)

Black holes and baby universes and other essays; [by] Stephen Hawking. Bantam Bks. 1993 182p hardcover o.p. paperback available $13.95

523.1

1. Universe 2. Science—Philosophy
ISBN 0-553-37411-7 (pa) LC 93-8269
Analyzed in Essay and general literature index
A collection of essays and speeches ranging from autobiographical sketches to theoretical discussions of black holes, relativity and quantum mechanics
Hawking's essays "will appeal to science-minded YAs." Booklist

A brief history of time; from the big bang to black holes; [by] Stephen W. Hawking; introduction by Carl Sagan; illustrations by Ron Miller. Bantam Bks. 1988 198p il $26.95; pa $14.95

523.1

1. Universe
ISBN 0-553-05340-X; 0-533-34614-8 (pa)
LC 87-33333
This book is an "attempt to simplify and outline some of the most complex and compelling ideas in modern science. The first five chapters are an introduction for the general reader. . . . Where Hawking really hits his stride is in the last six chapters. This is where he describes his own discoveries and work on black holes, the origin and fate of the universe, the arrow of time, and the unification of physical theories. Here the reader really gets an insight into Hawking's mind, and the ideas he puts forth are fascinating." Sci Books Films

Jastrow, Robert, 1925-
God and the astronomers. 2nd ed. Norton 1992
149p il $18.95   **523.1**
1. Universe 2. Astronomy 3. Religion and science
ISBN 0-393-85005-6   LC 92-32186
First published 1978
The author considers the theological implications of
the big bang theory of creation, and summarizes the evidence for the theory including the relativity theory, the
life story of stars, and the discovery of the retreat of the
galaxies. Includes chapters by a Catholic astronomer and
a Jewish theologian with their viewpoints on the origin
and destiny of the universe
Includes bibliographical references

Red giants and white dwarfs. new ed. Norton
1990 269p il pa $11.95   **523.1**
1. Universe
ISBN 0-393-85004-8   LC 91-135759
Companion volumes The enchanted loom (1981) and
Until the sun dies, entered in class 577
First published 1967
The book describes "the birth and death of stars and
planets and the emergence of intelligent life. . . . [It] includes the latest findings on the origin and probable fate
of the universe, giant black holes and quasars, the exploration of the moon and Mars, and travel to other stars.
The author's observations of Darwin, Rutherford and oth-
er pioneer scientists [are included]." Publisher's note
Includes bibliography

Kolb, Rocky
Blind watchers of the sky; the people and ideas
that shaped our view of the universe.
Addison-Wesley 1996 338p il $25   **523.1**
1. Universe 2. Solar system
ISBN 0-201-48992-9   LC 95-41438
The author "presents a popular history of astronomy
and scientific cosmology from Tycho Brahe to the sec-
ond half of the 20th century." Libr J
Includes bibliographical references

Price, Huw, 1953-
Time's arrow & Archimedes' point; new
directions for the physics of time. Oxford Univ.
Press 1996 306p $25   **523.1**
1. Time 2. Physics—Philosophy
ISBN 0-19-510095-6   LC 95-25508
The author discusses various issues in physics, aiming
to pick "out from each a connection with the asymmetry
of time. The selected topics include irreversibility in
thermodynamics, the causal behavior of radiation, the origin of the universe, and measurement in quantum mechanics." Choice
"Price's book is a useful addition to the literature on
time." New Sci
Includes bibliography

523.2   Solar system

Mammana, Dennis
Other suns, other worlds? the search for extra
solar planetary systems; [by] Dennis L. Mammana
and Donald W. McCarthy. St. Martin's Press 1996
227p il $23.95   **523.2**
1. Planets 2. Solar system
ISBN 0-312-14021-5   LC 95-40391
This recounts the history of astronomers' search for
planets beyond our solar system
"If you would like to know just where we stand in
trying to answer the questions, 'Are we alone?' you will
enjoy this book." Libr J

523.4   Planets

Beebe, Reta F.
Jupiter; the giant planet; [by] Reta Beebe. 2nd
ed. Smithsonian Institution Press 1997 261p il
(Smithsonian library of the solar system) pa
$16.95   **523.4**
1. Jupiter (Planet)
ISBN 1-560-98731-6 ($29.95); 1-560-98685-9 (pa)
                                        LC 96-38604
The author describes the history of discoveries about
Jupiter, its atmosphere and interior composition. Includes
findings from the 1994 collision of Comet Shoemaker-
Levy/9 and observations of the Galileo probe
Includes bibliographical references

Watters, Thomas R.
Planets. Macmillan 1995 256p il maps
(Smithsonian guides) $24.95; pa $18   **523.4**
1. Planets
ISBN 0-02-860404-0; 0-02-860405-9 (pa)
                                        LC 94-44718
"A Latimer book"
Features of this guide include full-color photographs
and illustrations of the planets, astronomical concepts and
current technology; a chapter which compares the planets; a timeline of interplanetary missions; and an illustrated glossary
"Whether for browsing or for a school assignment,
this state-of-the-knowledge summary is viable until the
current generation of missions—to Mars and Jupiter—unveil their discoveries in the late 1990s." Booklist
Includes bibliography

523.5   Meteoroids, solar wind, zodiacal light

Hutchison, Robert, 1938-
Meteorites; [by] Robert Hutchison & Andrew
Graham. Sterling 1993 60p il pa $12.95   **523.5**
1. Meteorites
ISBN 0-8069-0489-5   LC 93-15955
This book "describes the fundamental characteristics
of meteorites. . . . Discussions of asteroids, the origin of

Hutchison, Robert, 1938—*Continued*
the planets of the solar system, meteorite impacts, and future research in the field are included." Sci Books Films

"The text is direct, interesting, and free of mind-numbing chemistry and physics formulas. . . . Fifty per cent of the book is made up of photographs and diagrams; most are in full color. . . . An exceptionally well-done summary." SLJ
Includes glossary

523.6 Comets

The **Great** comet crash; the impact of comet Shoemaker-Levy 9 on Jupiter; edited by John R. Spencer and Jacqueline Mitton. Cambridge Univ. Press 1995 118p il map $24.95   **523.6**
1. Comets 2. Jupiter (Planet)
ISBN 0-521-48274-7   LC 95-42372
This book documents the discovery and the "impact of the fragments of the comet Shoemaker-Levy 9 with Jupiter . . . [and] is told in the words of those who played key roles in the [event]." Sci Books Films

Sagan, Carl, 1934-1996
Comet; [by] Carl Sagan and Ann Druyan. Random House 1985 398p il $27.50   **523.6**
1. Comets 2. Halley's comet
ISBN 0-394-54908-2   LC 85-8308
"The authors explore the myth and science of comets in a lavishly illustrated, slightly oversize volume that is both fascinating and authoritative." Booklist
Includes bibliography

Yeomans, Donald K.
Comets; a chronological history of observation, science, myth, and folklore. Wiley 1991 485p il (Wiley science editions) $35   **523.6**
1. Comets
ISBN 0-471-61011-9   LC 90-12657
This is a "history of comet research from the ancient Greeks and Chinese to the observational results obtained during Halley's Comet's latest visit in 1986. [Yeomans'] story makes fascinating reading for all comers until the narrative reaches the present century, wherein the scientific details become formidable for those lacking a good background in the physical sciences. However, lay readers can surely understand at least the general import of recent discoveries." Libr J
Includes bibliographical references

523.7 Sun

Wentzel, Donat G., 1934-
The restless sun. Smithsonian Institution Press 1989 279p il $29.95   **523.7**
1. Sun 2. Astrophysics
ISBN 0-87474-982-4   LC 88-18491
This book presents, "without recourse to mathematics, phenomena scientists spend their lives unraveling. Lumi-

nosity, solar chemistry, nuclear fusion, solar winds, and the Van Allen belts are a few of the complex subjects well described by illustrations and text. Later chapters consider the sun's effects upon the weather and climate of Earth." Booklist
Includes bibliography

523.8 Stars

Bakich, Michael E.
The Cambridge guide to the constellations. Cambridge Univ. Press 1995 320p il maps $34.95; pa $19.95   **523.8**
1. Constellations
ISBN 0-521-46520-6; 0-521-44921-9 (pa)
                                      LC 94-4678
"This book is the ultimate constellation reference book that brings together a variety of information about constellations, including: the size, visibility and relative brightness of all eighty-eight constellations; former location of extinct constellations; the number of visible stars in each constellation, and more." Univ Press Books for Public and Second Sch Libr
"The author has produced a very useful book of manageable size." Choice
Includes bibliographical references

Goldsmith, Donald
Supernova! the exploding star of 1987. St. Martin's Press 1989 221p il $15.95   **523.8**
1. Supernovas
ISBN 0-312-02647-1   LC 88-29861
"This book discusses the astronomical and physical significance of a supernova in one of our closest neighboring galaxies. Essentially, Goldsmith gives us a summary, in ordinary language, of the scientific methodology used and the major published papers associated with this astronomical event." Libr J
Includes glossary and bibliography

526 Mathematical geography

Sobel, Dava
Longitude; the true story of a lone genius who solved the greatest scientific problem of his time. Walker & Co. 1995 184p $19   **526**
1. Harrison, John, 1693-1776 2. Longitude
ISBN 0-8027-1312-2   LC 95-17402
Also available in paperback from Penguin Bks.
"In 1714, Britain's Parliament offered the modern equivalent of $12 to anybody who could develop a means of determining longitude at sea. While the likes of Isaac Newton and Edmund Halley sought to calculate longitude by celestial measurement, John Harrison, an uneducated clockmaker, solved the problem with his invention of the chronometer. Science writer Sobel tells this story in a way that enables readers 'to see the globe anew.'" Libr J
Includes bibliographical references

529   Chronology

Encyclopedia of time; edited by Samuel L. Macey. Garland 1994 xxiv, 699p il (Garland reference library of social science) $95   **529**
1. Time—Dictionaries
ISBN 0-8153-0615-6   LC 93-43355
Companion volume to Time: a bibliographic guide (1991)

"Macey includes approximately 360 articles written by specialists in the interdisciplinary field of time studies. This volume relates time to diverse interesting topics, from how time affects allergies to how several famous authors' fascination with time added to their literary success. The index provides entry by both author and subject, and articles are amply cross-referenced." Choice

Gardner, Robert, 1929-
Experimenting with time. Watts 1995 160p il maps lib bdg $20.60   **529**
1. Time 2. Science projects
ISBN 0-531-12554-8   LC 95-1471
"A Venture book"
"This volume contains a challenging combination of the history of human concepts of time and experiments or projects that investigate ways of understanding and measuring time. The book explores how scientists view time and how they apply their concepts in many situations." Sci Books Films
Includes bibliographical references

530   Physics

McGraw-Hill encyclopedia of physics; Sybil P. Parker, editor in chief. 2nd ed. McGraw-Hill 1993 1624p il $95.50   **530**
1. Physics—Dictionaries
ISBN 0-07-051400-3   LC 92-43215
First published 1983
"Most of the material in this volume has been published previously in the McGraw-Hill encyclopedia of science & technology, seventh edition." Verso of title page
This volume contains articles covering major branches of physics including acoustics, atomic physics, particle physics, molecular physics, nuclear physics, electricity, fluid mechanics, optics, relativity, and solid state physics
Includes bibliographies

530.1   Physics—Theories and mathematical physics

Calder, Nigel, 1931-
Einstein's universe. Viking 1979 154p il o.p.; Penguin Bks. paperback available $11.95   **530.1**
1. Relativity (Physics) 2. Astrophysics 3. Universe
ISBN 0-14-005499-5 (pa)   LC 78-26087
"Calder undertakes to explain the theory of relativity to the layman without using mathematics. . . . Einstein's theory of general relativity . . . is presented first; the historically earlier special relativity theory . . . is introduced late in the book. Calder goes on to discuss developments in science that have borne out Einstein's deductions." Libr J

"The author writes with competence and simplicity. It is a proper tribute to the man who revolutionized our ideas of space, time, and motion." Choice

Einstein, Albert, 1879-1955
The meaning of relativity; including the Relativistic theory of the non-symmetric field. 5th ed. Princeton Univ. Press 1956 166p $39.50
   530.1
1. Relativity (Physics)
ISBN 0-691-08007-0
First published 1922. Translated by Edwin Plimpton Adams, Ernst G. Straus and Bruria Kaufman
The Stafford Little lectures of Princeton University, May 1921
"Though few can understand it, most readers in physics and librarians in charge of science collections know this book as one of the landmarks of modern knowledge. . . . The book is not intended for general reading. Instead it is addressed to . . . [those whose training enables] them to understand the mathematical expressions of relativity." N Y Public Libr. New Tech Books

Guillen, Michael
Five equations that changed the world; the power and poetry of mathematics. Hyperion 1995 277p $22.95; pa $12.95   **530.1**
1. Physics 2. Mathematics
ISBN 0-7868-6103-7; 0-7868-8187-9 (pa)
     LC 95-15199
The author "devotes this work to discussions of five significant equations in physics and the individuals who developed them. The individuals are Isaac Newton (Universal gravitation), Daniel Bernoulli (hydrodynamic pressure), Michael Faraday (thermodynamics), Rudolf Clausius (thermodynamics), and Albert Einstein (special relativity), Guillen sets their work in the context of the science of their times." Libr J
"A seamless blend of dramatic biography and mathematical documentary that links the personal with the scientific." Publ Wkly

Hawking, S. W. (Stephen W.)
The nature of space and time; [by] Stephen Hawking and Roger Penrose. Princeton Univ. Press 1996 141p il (Isaac Newton Institute series of lectures) $24.95   **530.1**
1. Space and time 2. Quantum theory 3. Astrophysics
ISBN 0-691-03791-4   LC 95-35582
This volume "takes the form of a debate between Hawking and Penrose at Cambridge in 1994. At the center of the discussion is a pair of powerful theories: the quantum theory of fields and the general theory of relativity. The issue is how—if at all—one can merge the two into a quantum theory of gravity. . . . A substantial background in theoretical physics is needed for full comprehension." Libr J
Includes bibliographical references

Lindley, David
Where does the weirdness go? why quantum mechanics is strange, but not as strange as you think. Basic Bks. 1996 251p il $24; pa $13

530.1

1. Quantum theory 2. Physics—Philosophy
ISBN 0-465-06785-9; 0-465-06786-7 (pa)

LC 96-1049

An overview of quantam mechanics for the general reader. Lindley "leads the reader through several important experiments, the Einstein-Podolsky-Rosen paradox, Bell's theorem, the Schrödinger's cat thought experiment, and the theories of Bohm and Everett, among others. . . . A thorough bibliography appropriate for a wide range of levels of sophistication is included." Choice
Includes bibliographical references

Osserman, Robert
Poetry of the universe; a mathematical exploration of the cosmos. Anchor Bks. (NY) 1995 210p il hardcover o.p. paperback available $10

530.1

1. Relativity (Physics) 2. Mathematics 3. Universe
ISBN 0-385-47429-6 (pa)

LC 94-27971

The author examines the theory "that space has curvature and is not flat. . . . [Topics discussed include] ancient measurements of the earth, . . . the nineteenth-century German mathematicians Carl Fried Gauss and George Friedrich Riemann, [and] the shape of the *retroverse*, as the author tags our celestial view back into time and on toward invented abstract multidimensional shapes dubbed *manifolds*." Booklist
Includes bibliographical references

Thorne, Kip S.
Black holes and time warps; Einstein's outrageous legacy. Norton 1994 619p il $30; pa $14.95

530.1

1. Physics 2. Relativity (Physics) 3. Astrophysics
4. Black holes (Astronomy)
ISBN 0-393-03505-0; 0-393-31276-3 (pa)

LC 93-2014

This book is "about black holes, white holes, wormholes, parallel universes, time travel, 10-dimensional space-time, the origin and fate of the universe and a lot of other subjects dear to science fiction fans." N Y Times Book Rev
"This volume, a model of style, format and illustration, will speak eloquently to the readership, ranging widely in scientific literacy and interest, that such theoretical physics writers as Hawking and Feynman have established." Publ Wkly
Includes glossary and bibliographical references

534 Sound and related vibrations

Gardner, Robert, 1929-
Experimenting with sound. Watts 1991 128p il lib bdg $22

534

1. Sound—Experiments
ISBN 0-531-12503-3

LC 91-4012

"A Venture book"

The author provides "activities for students who want to investigate the properties of sound, including speed of sound, resonance, sound frequency and intensity, and acoustics. . . . The experiments vary in complexity, and some will require specialized equipment." Booklist
"These experiments are too quick to be recommended for in depth science projects, but for clear illustrations of sound, it is a wonderful book." BAYA Book Rev
Includes bibliography

537 Electricity and electronics

Wong, Ovid K.
Experimenting with electricity and magnetism. Watts 1993 128p il lib bdg $22; pa $6.95

537

1. Electricity—Experiments 2. Magnetism—Experiments
ISBN 0-531-12547-5 (lib bdg); 0-531-15681-8 (pa)

LC 92-37672

"A Venture book"
"The principles and properties of electricity and magnetism are explored through forty-three experiments in this project book, most dealing with electricity." Voice Youth Advocates
"Clear, step-by-step instructions are neatly laid out; black-and-white illustrations show the materials required. Cautionary notes are included within the instructions." SLJ
Includes bibliographical references

538 Magnetism

Verschuur, Gerrit L., 1937-
Hidden attraction; the history and mystery of magnetism. Oxford Univ. Press 1993 256p il $25; pa $14.95

538

1. Magnetism
ISBN 0-19-506488-7; 0-19-510655-5 (pa)

LC 92-37690

The author "uses the history of magnetism to illustrate the development of scientific theory and method, from natural phenomena rooted in superstition to the accurate simulations of modern science. An informative study, with details about such scientists as Michael Faraday and James Maxwell and their pioneering work." Booklist
Includes bibliographical references

539 Modern physics

Clark, John O. E. (John Owen Edward), 1937-
Matter and energy; physics in action; by J.O.E. Clark. Oxford Univ. Press 1994 160p il (New encyclopedia of science) $35

539

1. Physics 2. Matter 3. Force and energy
ISBN 0-19-521085-9

LC 94-16054

This "encyclopedia explains the many fascinating aspects of matter and energy, based on the most up-to-date findings. Richly illustrated and uniquely user-friendly, the encyclopedia features 48 essays, each devoted to a fundamental theme in physics." Univ Press Books for Public and Second Sch Libr

539.7   Atomic and nuclear physics

Asimov, Isaac, 1920-1992
Atom; journey across the subatomic cosmos; illustrated by D.F. Bach. Dutton 1991 319p il hardcover o.p. paperback available $14.95   **539.7**
  1. Atoms 2. Nuclear physics
  ISBN 0-452-26834-6 (pa)   LC 90-21343
  "A Truman Talley book"
  "Within the first five pages, Asimov introduces the concept of atomism, reviews the history of philosophical arguments on the subject, and summarizes the first application of the scientific method to the subject. . . . In a logical, orderly, and comprehensible fashion, the progress of knowledge about the atom (including its components and interactions) is revealed. The relationship of subatomic particles to various forms of energy, and even the structure of the universe, is explained without involving math above the grade school level. [An] excellent book." Sci Books Films

Boorse, Henry A. (Henry Abraham), 1904-
The atomic scientists; a biographical history; [by] Henry A. Boorse, Lloyd Motz, and Jefferson Hane Weaver. Wiley 1989 472p il (Wiley science editions) $27.95   **539.7**
  1. Nuclear physics 2. Atomic theory
  ISBN 0-471-50455-6   LC 88-35181
  "Boorse and company trace the history of atomic science. Lucretius, the Roman poet whose 'De Rerum Natura' passed Greek atomic theory to scientists of the Enlightenment, is by far the most ancient entrant, and the Nobel laureate high energy physicists C. N. Yang and T. D. Lee, the newest. . . . Each [biography] includes a small portrait and concentrates upon the individual's scientific achievements. Personal particulars are largely ignored or treated perfunctorily. In keeping with the development of physical knowledge, the prose becomes increasingly, but never too, technical." Booklist
  Includes bibliographical references

540   Chemistry and allied sciences

CRC handbook of chemistry and physics; a ready-reference book of chemical and physical data. CRC Press $110   **540**
  1. Chemistry—Tables 2. Physics—Tables
  Also available in a student edition pa $49.95
  First published 1913. (77th edition 1996) Periodically revised
  A "reference book containing much-used information on mathematics, chemistry, and physics, including tables, physical constants of chemical elements and compounds, definitions, formulae, etc." AAAS Sci Book List for Young Adults
  Includes bibliographical references

Hoffmann, Roald, 1937-
Chemistry imagined; reflections on science; [by] Roald Hoffmann and Vivian Torrence; with a foreword by Carl Sagan and a commentary by Lea Rosson DeLong. Smithsonian Institution Press 1993 168p il hardcover o.p. paperback available $19.95   **540**
  1. Chemistry
  ISBN 0-56098-539-9 (pa)   LC 92-31996
  This overview combines history, anecdote, poetry and art in an examination of chemistry from alchemy to synthetics
  "A well-written, entertaining, and enjoyable book that presents chemistry from an entirely different perspective." SLJ
  Includes bibliographical references

Lange's handbook of chemistry. McGraw-Hill $110   **540**
  1. Chemistry—Tables
  First published 1934. (14th edition 1996) Periodically revised
  Editors, 1934-1967: Norbert Adolph Lange and Gordon M. Forker; 1973- John A. Dean
  "This excellent chemical handbook covers just chemistry. It is divided into nine sections of values, formulas, facts, figures, and data: 'Mathematics,' 'General Information and Conversion Tables,' 'Atomic and Molecular Structure,' 'Inorganic Chemistry, Analytical Chemistry,' 'Electrochemistry,' 'Organic Chemistry,' 'Spectroscopy,' 'Thermal Properties,' 'Physical Properties,' and 'Miscellaneous Chemical Information.'" Malinowsky. Best Sci & Technol Ref Books for Young People

540.3   Chemistry—Encyclopedias and dictionaries

The **Facts** on File dictionary of chemistry; edited by John Daintith. rev & expanded ed. Facts on File 1988 249p il hardcover o.p. paperback available $12.95   **540.3**
  1. Chemistry—Dictionaries
  ISBN 0-8160-2367-0 (pa)   LC 88-45477
  First published 1981
  This reference work includes about 2,500 cross-referenced entries that identify terms, reactions, techniques, and applications likely to need definition by high school students and undergraduates

540.7   Chemistry—Education and related topics

VanCleave, Janice Pratt
Janice VanCleave's A+ projects in chemistry; winning experiments for science fairs and extra credit. Wiley 1993 233p il $24.95; pa $12.95
                                              540.7
  1. Chemistry—Experiments 2. Science projects
  ISBN 0-471-58631-5; 0-471-58630-7 (pa)
                                          LC 93-10588
  Provides step-by-step instructions for thirty advanced chemistry experiments suitable for science fairs

VanCleave, Janice Pratt—*Continued*
"The topics are interesting and appropriate for students who read well, follow instructions well, and are independently responsible." Sci Books Films
Includes glossary

540.9 Chemistry—Historical and geographic treatment

Brock, W. H. (William Hodson)
The Norton history of chemistry; [by] William H. Brock. Norton 1993 c1992 744p il (Norton history of science) $35; pa $15.95 **540.9**
1. Chemistry—History
ISBN 0-393-03536-0; 0-393-31043-4 (pa)
LC 93-19054
First published 1992 in the United Kingdom with title: The Fontana history of chemistry
This is a "survey of chemistry's rich heritage from its early beginnings in alchemy and iatrochemistry to its emergence in the 18th and 19th centuries as a more empirical and systematic science. A generous treatment of 20th-century chemistry explores the worlds of Linus Pauling, Robert Woodward, and others. Each chapter is devoted to a significant development in chemistry's history." Libr J
"Suitable for reference or for advanced students." Booklist
Includes bibliographical references

541.2 Theoretical chemistry

Atkins, P. W. (Peter William), 1940-
The periodic kingdom; a journey into the land of the chemical elements. Basic Bks. 1995 161p il (Science masters series) $20 **541.2**
1. Chemical elements 2. Periodic law
ISBN 0-465-07265-8
LC 95-7362
"Depicting the periodic table of elements as a map, Atkins explores the territories that it represents, from metallic 'deserts' to the hydrogen 'island.' Basic chemistry has never been presented in a more creative and readily comprehensible manner." Libr J
Includes bibliographical references

541.3 Physical chemistry

Allaby, Michael, 1933-
Fire; the vital source of energy. Facts on File 1993 208p il (Elements) $35 **541.3**
1. Fire
ISBN 0-8160-2714-5
LC 92-47224
Illustrated with photographs and drawings, this work presents an overview of fire in all its forms, both useful and destructive

546 Inorganic chemistry

Aldersey-Williams, Hugh
The most beautiful molecule; the discovery of the buckyball. Wiley 1995 340p il $24.95 **546**
1. Buckminsterfullerene
ISBN 0-471-10938-X
LC 95-12422
"One of the most exciting developments in chemistry is the discovery, in 1985, of a complex form of carbon. The molecule, called fullerenes (or 'buckyballs') because of their resemblance to R. Buckminster Fuller's geodesic domes, has been the subject of intense research, as recounted here." Libr J
Includes bibliographical references

Newton, David E.
The chemical elements. Watts 1994 96p il lib bdg $19.70 **546**
1. Chemical elements
ISBN 0-531-12501-7
LC 93-30044
"A Venture book"
"Introduction to the history and organization of the periodic table. Discusses the concept of the elements and atomic structure. Examines the properties and uses of the alkali metals, the halogens, hydrogen and the noble gases, common metals, the lanthanides and actinides, nonmetals, and metalloids." Publisher's note
Includes glossary and bibliography

549 Mineralogy

Chesterman, Charles W.
The Audubon Society field guide to North American rocks and minerals; scientific consultant, Kurt E. Lowe. Knopf 1979 c1978 850p il $19 **549**
1. Mineralogy 2. Rocks
ISBN 0-394-50269-8
LC 78-54893
"Pocket guide providing color photos and descriptions of some 232 mineral species and forty types of rocks. Includes guide to mineral environments, glossary, bibliography, and indexes by name and locality." ALA. Ref Sources for Small & Medium-sized Libr. 5th edition

Hochleitner, Rupert
Minerals; identifying, learning about, and collecting the most beautiful minerals and crystals; 500 color photos by the author and the staff of Lapis, 300 drawings of crystals by the author, 14 color drawings by Marlene Gemke. Barron's Educ. Ser. 1994 237p il (Barron's nature guide) pa $14.95 **549**
1. Mines and mineral resources
ISBN 0-8120-1777-3
LC 93-40790
This guide identifies "approximately 300 minerals by using two key tests: streak and hardness. Hochleitner's opening definition of what minerals are leads into a discussion of various properties: hardness, tenacity, density, streak, color, and cleavage. This is followed by sections on crystal forms, origins, modes of occurrence, and gemstones." Booklist
Includes glossary and bibliographical references

Pellant, Chris
Rocks, minerals & fossils of the world; photographs by Roger Phillips & Chris Pellant. Little, Brown 1990 175p il hardcover o.p. paperback available $17.95   **549**
1. Mineralogy 2. Rocks 3. Fossils
ISBN 0-316-69796-6 (pa)   LC 89-63627
"Some 150 rocks are classified by type—igneous, metamorphic, or sedimentary. Identifying characteristics (crystal shape, color, luster, cleavage, and hardness) are provided for over 250 minerals. Fossils, which receive the most attention, are organized by such types as trilobites, corals, and crinoids. The work's strength lies in its beautiful photographs, which are equally useful for identification." Nichols. Guide to Ref Books for Sch Media Cent. 4th edition
Includes bibliographical references

Pough, Frederick H. (Frederick Harvey), 1906-
A field guide to rocks and minerals. 5th ed, photographs by Jeff Scovil. Houghton Mifflin 1996 396p il $27.95; $17.95   **549**
1. Mineralogy 2. Rocks
ISBN 0-395-72778-2; 0-395-72777-4
LC 94-49005
"The Peterson field guide series"
First published 1953
"Sponsored by the National Audubon Society, the National Wildlife Federation, and the Roger Tory Peterson Institute"
This illustrated guide utilizes traditional identification methods and includes discussions of crystallography, mineralogy and home laboratory techniques
Includes bibliographical references

550   Earth sciences

Allaby, Michael, 1933-
Earth; our planet and its resources. Facts on File 1993 208p il (Elements) $35   **550**
1. Geophysics 2. Earth
ISBN 0-8160-2713-7   LC 92-47225
This illustrated work explores the geology, geography, and ecosystems of the world

Erickson, Jon, 1948-
Quakes, eruptions, and other geologic cataclysms. Facts on File 1994 198p il maps (Changing earth) $24.95   **550**
1. Natural disasters
ISBN 0-8160-2949-0   LC 93-43587
"A one-volume encyclopedia that provides succinct, factual descriptions of almost all aspects of the Earth's dynamic activity. Appropriate black-and-white photographs abound; clear line diagrams and maps illustrate subjects and occurrences that are difficult to visualize and are not easily found elsewhere. An excellent geological resource." SLJ
Includes bibliographical references

Planet earth. Time-Life Bks. 1992 151p il maps (Understanding science & nature) $18.95   **550**
1. Earth sciences
LC 92-270
Questions and answers explore the shape and structure of the Earth, continental drift and plate tectonics, earthquakes, volcanoes, oceans, and other aspects of our world

Smith, Bruce G.
Geology projects for young scientists; [by] Bruce Smith and David Mckay. Watts 1992 144p il maps (Projects for young scientists) $22; pa $6.95   **550**
1. Geology—Experiments 2. Science projects
ISBN 0-531-11012-5; 0-531-15651-6 (pa)
LC 91-43705
Projects and experiments explore such aspects of the Earth as its age, plate tectonics, earthquakes, and hydrogeology
Includes bibliographical references

550.3   Earth sciences—
Encyclopedias and dictionaries

Encyclopedia of earth sciences; E. Julius Dasch, editor in chief. Macmillan Lib. Ref. USA 1996 2v il maps set $200   **550.3**
1. Earth sciences—Dictionaries
ISBN 0-02-883000-8   LC 96-11302
Spine title: Macmillan encyclopedia of earth sciences
"This two-volume set covers not only the sciences of the solid earth, the oceanographic and atmospheric sciences, and the biological sciences, but also the study of the solar system and its place in the galaxy and the universe. Well written and indexed, this encyclopedia will find an audience with both high school and college students as well as with decison makers and the interested layperson." Am Libr
For a fuller review see: Booklist, Nov. 1, 1996

Farndon, John
Dictionary of the earth. Dorling Kindersley 1994 192p il $19.95   **550.3**
1. Earth sciences—Dictionaries 2. Geology—Dictionaries
ISBN 0-7894-0049-9   LC 94-35497
This work, which defines 2000 terms, is "arranged by themes such as 'Soil' and 'Seas & Oceans.' One section treats the human impact on the earth (i.e., pollution, flood management). Biographies of more than 70 earth science pioneers precede the index." Booklist

551.1 Gross structure and properties of the earth

Erickson, Jon, 1948-
Craters, caverns, and canyons; delving beneath the earth's surface. Facts on File 1992 200p il maps (Changing earth) $24.95   551.1
1. Earth sciences
ISBN 0-8160-2590-8   LC 92-15626
This illustrated look at structural geology and petrology includes chapters on meteorite impacts; craters; caves and caverns; canyons and valleys; basins; volcanic rifts; earthquake faults; and ground failures
Includes glossary and bibliographical references

Vogel, Shawna
Naked Earth; the new geophysics. Dutton 1995 217p $21.95; pa $11.95   551.1
1. Geophysics 2. Earth—Internal structure
ISBN 0-525-93771-4; 0-452-27162-2 (pa)
LC 94-23784
In this survey of geophysics "Vogel evokes a dynamic underworld of powerful currents of liquid rock; colliding tectonic plates; fossil volcanoes that have spewed out natural diamonds; and 30-foot-tall mineral chimneys soaring above the Pacific Ocean floor, natural warm-water vents for dispersing heat from Earth's core. This is top-notch science journalism." Publ Wkly

551.2 Volcanoes, earthquakes, thermal waters and gases

Bolt, Bruce A., 1930-
Earthquakes. newly rev & expanded ed. Freeman, W.H. 1993 331p il $19.95   551.2
1. Earthquakes
ISBN 0-7167-2236-4   LC 92-18504
First published 1978
"Major sections include (1) what one feels in an earthquake and accounts of select major quakes; (2) how earthquakes are measured; (3) faults and the inside of the earth; (4) causes of earthquakes; (5) earthquakes and volcanoes, and tidal waves and water; (6) events preceding earthquakes; (7) self-protection in earthquakes; (8) building for earthquake resistance; and (9) eight appendixes filled with essential earthquake intelligence and calculations. A glossary and select bibliography are included. Illustrations are especially attractive, simple, and powerful." Choice

Earthquakes and geological discovery. Scientific Am. Lib. 1993 229p il maps $32.95   551.2
1. Earthquakes
ISBN 0-7167-5040-6   LC 93-12636
This book "describes how and why scientists trace seismic activity and measure the extent and patterns of seismic waves. Through analysis of numerous earthquakes, both historical and present, [the author] illustrates that basic geological lessons are learned in almost every occurrence of these highly varied events." Publisher's note
Includes bibliography

Bryan, T. Scott
Geysers: what they are and how they work. Roberts Rinehart Pubs. 1990 24p il map pa $5.95
551.2
1. Geysers
ISBN 0-911797-74-2   LC 91-143449
This book describes "what geysers are, where they are found, how they differ from hot springs, their types, their geology, how they erupt, and what causes changes in their activity. . . . The book is clearly written, accurate, and informative." Sci Books Films
Includes bibliographical references

Carson, Rob, 1950-
Mount St. Helens: the eruption and recovery of a volcano; with selected photographs by Geff Hinds, Cheryl Haselhorst and Gary Braasch. Sasquatch Bks. 1990 160p il hardcover o.p. paperback available $19.95   551.2
1. Mount Saint Helens (Wash.)
ISBN 0-912365-32-3 (pa)   LC 90-31009
The author "describes the eruption of Mount St. Helens in 1980, and goes on to report what has happened in the devastated area since then. . . . Mr. Carson has a lively story to tell and does it well. The photographs . . . provide beauty as well as information." Atl Mon

Decker, Robert Wayne, 1927-
Volcanoes; [by] Robert Decker, Barbara Decker. rev & updated ed. Freeman, W.H. 1989 285p il maps pa $19.95   551.2
1. Volcanoes
ISBN 0-7167-1851-0   LC 89-31441
First published 1981
This book discusses active volcanoes of the world, the effects of recent eruptions, and advances in forecasting techniques. Included also are several color plates showing various volcanoes in full eruption
Includes glossary and bibliography

Levy, Matthys
Why the earth quakes; [by] Matthys Levy and Mario Salvadori; illustrations by Michael Lilly. Norton 1995 215p il maps $25; pa $13   551.2
1. Volcanoes 2. Earthquakes
ISBN 0-393-03774-6; 0-393-31527-4 (pa)
LC 95-1021
Levy and Salvadori "use examples from history to explore how human-made structures fare in the wake of earthquakes and volcanic eruptions. The authors briefly explain the nature of the earth, then discuss modern engineering solutions for keeping buildings upright during earthquakes." Libr J
This is a "popularly written, illustrated account, suitable for science students and other interested readers." Booklist
Includes glossary and bibliographical references

Ritchie, David, 1952-

The encyclopedia of earthquake and volcanoes.
Facts on File 1994 232p il maps $40   **551.2**

1. Earthquakes—Dictionaries 2. Volcanoes—Dictionaries

ISBN 0-8160-2659-9   LC 93-7670

This volume presents 632 alphabetically arranged entries relating to "volcanic eruptions, earthquakes, and faults plus pertinent geological terms (seismology) and concepts. . . . There is sure to be interest in this book in middle-school, high-school, public, and academic libraries." Booklist

Thro, Ellen

Volcanoes of the United States. Watts 1992
112p il maps lib bdg $22   **551.2**

1. Volcanoes

ISBN 0-531-12522-X   LC 91-36002

"A Venture book"

Explores volcanoes and volcanic activity in the United States, discussing the study of volcanoes, their effect on the environment, and volcanic hazards and risks

"Thro is a fine writer—her enticing and simple style will appeal to all age levels. Her introductory description of the 1980 eruption of Mount St. Helens has a captivating journalistic flair. Comments on the role of humans and technology in volcano-related research and a section called 'How to Become a Volcanologist' are perceptive and innovative." Sci Books Films

Includes glossary and bibliography

551.3   Surface and exogenous processes and their agents

Desonie, Dana

Cosmic collisions; foreword by David H. Levy and Carolyn and Eugene Shoemaker. Holt & Co. 1996 127p il map (Scientific American focus book) $22.50; pa $9.95   **551.3**

1. Asteroids 2. Catastrophes (Geology)

ISBN 0-8050-3843-4; 0-8050-3844-2 (pa)

LC 95-24460

"Desonie details the history of impacts in the formation of the Earth and the solar system, and delves into the debate over future impacts and the chances of successfully defending our planet." Publisher's note

Includes bibliographical references

Erickson, Jon, 1948-

Glacial geology; how ice shapes the land. Facts on File 1996 248p il maps (Changing earth) $24.95   **551.3**

1. Glaciers 2. Ice Age

ISBN 0-8160-3355-2   LC 95-35271

"After introducing the general concepts of glaciology, the geological study of ice, Erickson outlines the major historical ice ages. . . . Other chapters explore the current interglacial period; causes and effects of glaciation; continental glaciers, including the polar ice caps and Greenland; the Arctic and Antarctica; glacial structures, both on land and undersea; and glacial deposits, remnants of which survive in the strangest places." Publisher's note

Includes glossary and bibliography

551.46   Hydrosphere. Oceanography

Carson, Rachel, 1907-1964

The sea around us; [by] Rachel L. Carson; introduction by Ann H. Zwinger; afterword by Jeffrey S. Levinton. Oxford Univ. Press 1989 xxvii, 250p $24.95; pa $9.95   **551.46**

1. Ocean

ISBN 0-19-506186-1; 0-19-506997-8 (pa)

LC 89-16333

First published 1951; revised edition published 1961; this is a reissue of the 1979 edition which added the introduction and afterword

Beginning with a description of how the earth acquired its oceans, the book covers such topics as how life began in the primeval sea, the hidden lands, the life discovered in the abyss by highly delicate sounding apparatus, currents and tides, the formation of volcanic islands, and mineral resources

Includes bibliography

Erickson, Jon, 1948-

Marine geology; undersea landforms and life forms. Facts on File 1996 243p il maps (Changing earth) $24.95   **551.46**

1. Submarine geology 2. Marine biology

ISBN 0-8160-3354-4   LC 95-22109

"Erickson explains how the ocean's dynamics affect and are affected by the extravagantly sculptured ocean floor as he describes this vast, mysterious, and decidedly inhuman realm within the context of geologic history as well as the history of deep-sea research and exploration." Booklist

Includes bibliographical references

Groves, Donald G.

The oceans: a book of questions and answers; [by] Don Groves. Wiley 1989 203p il maps (Wiley nature editions) pa $14.95   **551.46**

1. Oceanography

ISBN 0-471-60712-6   LC 88-32625

"In question-and-answer format, [this book] recounts some of the history of ocean exploration and the ships used to sail above and below the surface." Booklist

Includes glossary and bibliography

551.48   Hydrology

Palmer, Tim

America by rivers. Island Press (Covelo) 1996
336p il maps $28   **551.48**

1. Rivers 2. Water conservation 3. Boats and boating

ISBN 1-55963-263-1   LC 96-14421

Palmer writes about "the rivers of America. Each of his ten chapters deals with a region's rivers, including unique features, facts (such as length, flowrate, and dams), current environmental and biological conditions, and cultural context. Palmer, who has been canoeing and rafting rivers for 25 years, shares his personal experience on a particular waterway in each region." SLJ

Includes bibliography

551.5 Meteorology

Allaby, Michael, 1933-
How the weather works. Reader's Digest Assn. 1995 192p il maps $24   **551.5**
1. Weather 2. Meteorology
ISBN 0-89577-612-X   LC 94-43156
"The first five sections explain the individual elements of weather such as clouds, rain, and wind, how they interact to form weather patterns and climates, and give brief historical information on the discovery of major weather concepts. . . . [Included are] approximately 100 simple projects which are used to demonstrate the concepts described. . . . The last section gives detailed directions for building a home weather forecasting station and describes weather forecasting including how to read weather maps." Voice Youth Advocates
Includes glossary

The **Encyclopedia** of climatology; edited by John E. Oliver, Rhodes W. Fairbridge. Van Nostrand Reinhold 1987 986p il maps (Encyclopedia of earth sciences) $139.95   **551.5**
1. Meteorology—Dictionaries 2. Climate—Dictionaries
ISBN 0-87933-009-0   LC 86-11173
This work "covers an impressive range of topics in climatology, each in considerable detail. . . . There are 213 signed entries, arranged alphabetically. . . . The reading level of the text tends to be somewhat technical." Topical Ref Books

Lockhart, Gary
The weather companion; an album of meteorological history, science, legend, and folklore. Wiley 1988 230p il maps (Wiley science editions) pa $16.95   **551.5**
1. Meteorology 2. Weather
ISBN 0-471-62079-3   LC 88-6884
This "is a compendium of weather lore, facts, history, and science and covers everything from ancient myths to current research." Sci Teach
Includes bibliography

Newton, David E.
The ozone dilemma; a reference handbook. ABC-CLIO 1995 195p (Contemporary world issues) $39.50   **551.5**
1. Ozone layer
ISBN 0-87436-719-0   LC 95-18722
"Beginning with a historical overview of the awareness of the ozone layer's importance and recent changes in it, Newton continues with scientific explanations of how it is being depleted. Also included are brief biographies of people involved in the study of ozone and in the politics of its protection." SLJ
Includes glossary and bibliographical references

Weather; [by] William J. Burroughs [et al.]; consultant editor, Richard Whitaker. Time-Life Bks. 1996 288p il (Nature Company guide) $29.95   **551.5**
1. Weather
LC 95-20621
Contents: The nature of weather, by R. Whitaker; Understanding the weather, by E. Vallier-Talbot; Weather-watching through the ages, by B. Crowder; Forecasting today, by W. J. Burroughs; Changing weather, by W. J. Burroughs; Humankind and the weather, by W. J. Burroughs; Adapting to the weather, by T. Robertson; The weather in action, by R. Whitaker; Resources directory
Includes glossary and bibliography

551.55 Atmospheric disturbances and formations

Fisher, David E., 1932-
The scariest place on Earth; eye to eye with hurricanes. Random House 1994 250p il $23
551.55
1. Hurricanes
ISBN 0-679-43566-2   LC 94-1810
The author gives a "detailed, scientific explanation of hurricanes—what they are, how they form and wreak havoc and how we might modify or avoid them. Interspersed is an account of his experiences during Hurricane Andrew in 1992." Publ Wkly
"Riveting and informative reading." Libr J
Includes bibliographical references

551.6 Climatology and weather

Carpenter, Clive, 1938-
The changing world of weather. Facts on File 1991 191p il maps $22.95   **551.6**
1. Climate 2. Weather
ISBN 0-8160-2521-5   LC 90-46709
A guide to understanding weather, especially "how human behavior influences weather, e.g., greenhouse effect, tropical rainforest, population, etc. With its recent data; numerous color photographs; clear, practical diagrams; and detailed index, this is excellent supplementary material for students who have completed an introductory unit on the topic. All regions of the Earth are well represented, but more examples come from Europe than elsewhere. A fresh perspective and new insight for researchers." SLJ

Encyclopedia of climate and weather; Stephen H. Schneider, editor in chief. Oxford Univ. Press 1996 2v il maps set $195   **551.6**
1. Climate 2. Weather
ISBN 0-19-509485-9   LC 95-31019
This "is an alphabetical arrangement of over 300 short articles . . . on everything from clouds and tornadoes to human influences on weather and climate (e.g., acid rain, deforestation, and effects of aerosols on the ozone layer). . . . The set contains over 400 black-and-white line drawings, photographs, charts, and maps, as well as a glossary." Libr J
For a fuller review see: Booklist, July 1996

Laskin, David, 1953-

Braving the elements; the stormy history of American weather. Doubleday 1995 241p il $23.95
551.6

1. United States—Climate
ISBN 0-385-46955-1   LC 95-19851

The author presents a "history of our weather and our interpretations of it, covering everything from spiritual perspectives—weather as signs from God—to our obsession with televised forecasts. Laskin articulates the myriad ways weather affects us, from the obvious, such as the destructiveness of hurricanes, to more subtle manifestations, such as how it influences our moods." Booklist

Includes bibliographical references

Ludlum, David M., 1910-1997

The Audubon Society field guide to North American weather. Knopf 1991 656p il maps $19
551.6

1. Weather forecasting
ISBN 0-679-40851-7   LC 91-52707
"A Chanticleer Press edition"

"The opening essays provide in-depth information on topics such as clouds, snowstorms, floods, etc. About half of the book is comprised of labelled, high-quality photographs. The third section gives description, environment, season, range, and significance of each type of weather. Clear diagrams, simple definitions, and a readable text make this an excellent selection." SLJ

Includes glossary

Pearce, E. A.

The Times Books world weather guide; [by] E.A. Pearce and Gordon Smith. updated ed. Times Bks. 1990 480p maps pa $17.95
551.6

1. Meteorology 2. Weather
ISBN 0-8129-1881-9   LC 90-50319
First published 1984

"Seasonal weather conditions for almost 500 cities worldwide make up the content of this volume, ... The introductory material contains explanations of weather conditions, charts of heat and humidity, the windchill index, and a glossary of terms. The main body of the work, arranged by continent and then by nation and city, includes a survey of the country's climate, followed by charts for cities." Nichols. Guide to Ref Books for Sch Media Cent. 4th edition

Watson, Benjamin A.

Acts of God; the Old farmer's almanac unpredictable guide to weather and natural disasters; [by] Benjamin A. Watson and the editors of the Old farmer's almanac. Random House 1993 246p il $20
551.6

1. Weather—Folklore 2. Natural disasters
ISBN 0-679-73794-4   LC 92-42605

Watson "has compiled an extensive collection of scientific information, anecdotes and folklore, facts and figures, as well as practical tips on what to do in case of severe weather. The articles are short and interesting." Book Rep

Williams, Jack, 1936-

The weather book. Vintage Bks. 1992 212p il maps pa $19
551.6

1. Weather 2. United States—Climate
ISBN 0-679-73669-7   LC 91-50697
At head of title: USA today

This illustrated book contains information about U.S. weather and climate, including storms, precipitation, and forecasting. Profiles of atmospheric scientists and an explanation of the greenhouse effect are included

Includes bibliography

551.7   Historical geology

Erickson, Jon, 1948-

Ice ages: past and future. TAB Bks. 1990 177p il $22.95; pa $15.95
551.7

1. Ice Age
ISBN 0-8306-8463-8; 0-8306-3463-0 (pa)
LC 89-48455

This "is a comprehensive analysis of the earth's origins that examines the causes and effects of ice ages and glaciers and competently discusses major environmental concerns such as global warming." Booklist

Includes glossary and bibliography

The **Historical** atlas of the earth; a visual exploration of the earth's physical past; general editors, Roger Osborne and Donald Tarling; consultant editor, Stephen Jay Gould; additional contributions by G.A.L. Johnson. Holt & Co. 1996 192p il maps (Henry Holt reference book) $45
551.7

1. Stratigraphic geology 2. Fossils
ISBN 0-8050-4552-X   LC 95-79328

Organized around the "divisions of geologic time [this volume] tracks continental drift as inferred from fossils, paleomagnetism, radioactive dating, or glaciation. The editors portray the evidence in two-page color spreads devoted to a specific topic, for instance, rocks such as coal or limestone that characterize ancient epochs. . . . [This is an] excellent info-jammed atlas." Booklist

Includes bibliographical references

Johnson, Kirk R.

Prehistoric journey; a history of life on earth; [by] Kirk R. Johnson and Richard K. Stucky. Roberts Rinehart Pubs. 1995 144p il $39.95; pa $19.95
551.7

1. Stratigraphic geology 2. Fossils 3. Evolution
ISBN 1-57098-056-X; 1-57098-045-4 (pa)
LC 95-69271

"This chronology begins 600 million years ago with illustrations of sea organisms such as translucent Ediacaria, Mawsonites, and Kimberella, and it ends with a photo of Lucy, an early hominid. . . . Eight areas where the authors collected fossils are described as the sites must have looked when they were living ecosystems." Book Rep

"The authors have turned out a readable and understandable text. What makes this such a terrific book, especially for students, is the format. The illustations are splendidly done." SLJ

Includes glossary and bibliography

Smith, Norman F., 1920-
Millions and billions of years ago; dating our earth and its life. Watts 1993 127p il lib bdg $22
551.7
1. Earth—Age 2. Stratigraphic geology
ISBN 0-531-12533-5   LC 92-42744
"A Venture book"
"The author "discusses the dating methods used by generations of archaeologists and scientists as they searched for ever more accurate means of measurement." Booklist
"This book is well suited to introduce the lay person to the extreme antiquity of Earth and the universe. It is written in a narrative style that should be accessible to early secondary students, as well as intriguing to adult readers." Sci Books Films
Includes glossary and bibliography

553.2   Carbonaceous materials

Grimaldi, David A.
Amber; window to the past. Abrams 1996 216p il maps $49.50   **553.2**
1. Amber
ISBN 0-8109-1966-4   LC 95-651
Published in association with the American Museum of Natural History
The author combines "the natural history of amber with coverage of its uses throughout history in art and sculpture. He discusses the properties of various types of amber, its most common localities, the types of life it typically preserves, and examples of past forgeries." Libr J
"This lavish book captures both the beauty and the strangeness of amber: the beauty, in glorious, honey-toned color images of some of the world's most exquisite amber artifacts; the strangeness, in close-ups of leaf fragments, tiny feathers, or whole bees buried among bubbles of ancient air. The text, meanwhile, is solid and comprehensive." Booklist
Includes bibliographical references

553.7   Water

Gardner, Robert, 1929-
Experimenting with water. Watts 1993 144p il lib bdg $19.14   **553.7**
1. Water 2. Science—Experiments
ISBN 0-531-12549-1   LC 93-15586
"A Venture book"
Provides instructions for experiments and activities involving water
This "is a valuable resource for the science/math teacher or student. . . . The black and white photos are excellent, diagrams and graphs easy to interpret, and illustrations helpful." Voice Youth Advocates
Includes bibliography

553.8   Gems

Arem, Joel E., 1943-
Color encyclopedia of gemstones. 2nd ed. Van Nostrand Reinhold 1987 248p il   **553.8**
1. Precious stones
          LC 86-26759
Available from Chapman & Hall
First published 1977
"This well-written encyclopedia covers over 200 gemstones, giving chemical formula, crystal structure, colors, luster, hardness, density, cleavage, optics, spectral data, luminescence, and size. The color photography is outstanding, capturing the cut and brilliance of each gem." Malinowsky. Best Sci & Technol Ref Books for Young People
Includes bibliography

Holden, Martin
The encyclopedia of gems and minerals; consulting editor, E.A. Mathez; principal photography by the British Museum (Natural History), with line drawings from Viktor Goldschmidt's Atlas der Krystallformen. Facts on File 1991 303p il $45   **553.8**
1. Gems—Dictionaries 2. Mineralogy—Dictionaries
ISBN 0-8160-2177-5   LC 91-7782
"A Friedman Group book"
This reference source "pulls together into one book data usually found in a variety of references. It is a perfect balance between an encyclopedia and a rock-identification handbook. Alphabetically arranged, it allows readers to look up groups of or individual minerals and their physical properties." SLJ

560   Paleontology. Paleozoology

Erickson, Jon, 1948-
A history of life on earth; understanding our planet's past. Facts on File 1995 244p il maps (Changing earth) $24.95   **560**
1. Stratigraphic geology
ISBN 0-8160-3131-2   LC 94-25290
Among the topics covered in this look at historical geology and paleontology are the coelocanth, greenstone belts containing gold deposits, and the continent of Gondwanaland
"The book is very technical and will require a highly motivated reader to elicit information that may be very difficult to find in other resources. . . . I recommend this book for those libraries who wish to provide a high quality reference with answers that would generally require multiple books." Voice Youth Advocates
Includes glossary and bibliographical references

An introduction to fossils and minerals; seeking clues to the earth's past. Facts on File 1992 184p il maps (Changing earth) $24.95   **560**
1. Fossils 2. Mineralogy 3. Geology
ISBN 0-8160-2587-8   LC 91-34390
"The volume begins by detailing the earth's early history, then explains how fossils are used as clues to the

Erickson, Jon, 1948——*Continued*
earth's past, how they tell us about evolution and the rise
and extinction of species, and how they are laid down in
the earth's rocks. . . . The book also discusses the formation of crystals and minerals, how they grow, and how
to identify and classify them. The volume concludes with
information on . . . where and how to collect fossils and
minerals." Publisher's note
  The book is "quite comprehensive. . . . Outstanding,
clear diagrams and various charts and maps clarify the
material." SLJ
  Includes glossary and bibliography

Hecht, Jeff
  Vanishing life; the mystery of mass extinctions.
Scribner 1993 149p il maps $15.95   **560**
  1. Mass extinction of species
  ISBN 0-684-19331-0   LC 92-41713
  The author "incorporates the latest dinosaur discoveries on the phenomenon of mass extinction. He explores
the geological evidence and interpretation and various
theories while recognizing a wide variety of possibilities." BAYA
  "Hecht raises as many provocative questions about ancient and modern extinctions as he answers, and science
teachers can easily use any of them as a starting point
for student research or discussion." Booklist
  Includes glossary and bibliography

Palmer, Douglas
  Fossils. DK Pub. 1996 160p il maps (Pockets)
pa $6.95   **560**
  1. Fossils
  ISBN 0-7894-0606-3   LC 95-42178
  Introduces the world of fossils including information
on where they are found, how they are formed, and how
they are classified; also describes many of the various
kinds
  This is an "attractively illustrated 'pocket' book. . . .
The taxonomy that makes up two-thirds of the book is
useful and interesting." Sci Books Films
  Includes glossary

Thompson, Ida
  The Audubon Society field guide to North
American fossils; with photographs by Townsend
P. Dickinson; visual key by Carol Nehring. Knopf
1982 846p il maps flexible bdg $19   **560**
  1. Fossils
  ISBN 0-394-52412-8   LC 81-84772
  "A Chanticleer Press edition. The Audubon Society
field guide series"
  "This softbound field guide to fossils is divided into
a section of color photographs followed by a section of
detailed descriptions. It covers 420 fossils of marine and
freshwater invertebrates, insects, plants, and vertebrates
that are likely to be found by the amateur." Malinowsky.
Best Sci & Technol Ref Books for Young People

567.9   Fossil reptiles. Dinosaurs

Fastovsky, David E.
  The evolution and extinction of the dinosaurs;
[by] David E. Fastovsky, David B. Weishampel;
with original illustrations by Brian Regal.
Cambridge Univ. Press 1996 460p il maps $44.95
          567.9
  1. Dinosaurs 2. Evolution
  ISBN 0-521-44496-9   LC 95-6002
  "This book is arranged as a series of essays on select-
ed topics about dinosaurs, such as 'The Mesozoic Era:
Back to the Past,' 'Ankylosauria: Mass and Gas,' and
'Pachycephalosauria: Head-to-Head, with Malice Afore-
thought.'" Book Rep
  "Challenging but very well written and informative."
Libr J

Horner, John R.
  The complete T. rex; by John R. Horner and
Don Lessem. Simon & Schuster 1993 239p il
hardcover o.p. paperback available $15   **567.9**
  1. Dinosaurs
  ISBN 0-671-89154-2 (pa)   LC 93-211
  "Horner and Lessem bring together some of the many
theories about *T. rex*. They start the book with the 1988
discovery of the most complete *T. rex* skeleton ever
found. . . . The rest of the book considers how the
toothsome giant may have lived. . . . [The authors] are
obviously at ease with their subject and produce one of
the more entertaining, informative dinosaur tomes of recent years." Booklist
  Includes bibliographical references

Lessem, Don
  The Dinosaur Society's dinosaur encyclopedia;
[by] Don Lessem & Donald F. Glut; illustrations
by Tracy Ford [et al.]; scientific advisors, Peter
Dodson, Catherine Forster and Anthony Fiorillo.
Random House 1993 xli, 533p il $25   **567.9**
  1. Dinosaurs—Dictionaries
  ISBN 0-679-41770-2
  "Each entry is arranged alphabetically by genus and
gives pronunciation, species, order, suborder, family,
name origin (such as the Latinized name of the discover-
er), size, period, place, and diet. Most entries contain further explanatory paragraphs that note the type and number of skeleton fragments that have been identified. . . .
This source is highly recommended for public and school
libraries." Booklist

Norell, Mark
  Discovering dinosaurs in the American Museum
of Natural History; [by] Mark A. Norell, Eugene
S. Gaffney, Lowell Dingus; foreword by Angela
Milner. Knopf 1995 xx, 204p il maps $35   **567.9**
  1. American Museum of Natural History 2. Dinosaurs
  ISBN 0-679-43386-4   LC 94-46225
  "A Peter N. Nevraumont book"

Norell, Mark—*Continued*

"This book describes the new Hall of Dinosaurs at New York City's American Museum of Natural History . . . and gives the history of the paleontological expeditions sponsored by the museum." Libr J

"Handsomely illustrated by 167 photos and maps, some in color, this volume takes us into a new world of dinosaurs." Publ Wkly

Officer, Charles B.

The great dinosaur extinction controversy; [by] Charles Officer & Jake Page. Addison-Wesley 1996 209p il (Helix books) $25   **567.9**
  1. Mass extinction of species 2. Dinosaurs
  ISBN 0-201-48384-X   LC 96-3809

"Officer has long been an opponent of the 1980 Alvarez theory that a meteoritic impact caused the demise of the dinosaurs. He and Page prefer the 'hypothesis' that global cooling and darkening due to excessive volcanism was the cause of the latest Cretaceous (K-T) extinction." Choice

Includes bibliographical references

Psihoyos, Louis

Hunting dinosaurs; [by] Louie Psihoyos with John Knoebber. Random House 1994 267p il maps $40; pa $23   **567.9**
  1. Dinosaurs
  ISBN 0-679-43124-1; 0-679-76420-8 (pa)
          LC 94-10010

The authors "lead readers on a trek from bone quarries to laboratories to exhibit halls. Traveling around the world, carrying the skull of 19th-century bone hunter Edward Drinker Cope as credential and charm, they interview leading fossil hunters, including Bob Bakker, Jack Horner, Paul Sereno and John Ostrum." Publ Wkly

"Part road show, part instruction, and wholly fun, this hilarious pictorial layout will instantly seize the attentions of the *T. rex*-loving young, and convulse their elders in the bargain." Booklist

Includes bibliographical references

Russell, Dale A.

An odyssey in time: the dinosaurs of North America. NorthWord Press 1989 240p il maps o.p.; University of Toronto Press paperback available $24.95   **567.9**
  1. Dinosaurs
  ISBN 0-8020-7718-8 (pa)   LC 90-134085

Published in association with National Museum of Natural Sciences

This is an overview "of the ecology and social dynamics of selected dinosaurs, especially as represented in North American fossil sites. Illustrations include photographs of these sites and paintings of dinosaurs." Libr J

"Russell has produced one of the few original contributions to the popular literature on dinosaurs, as well as an insight into the nature of the terrestrial fossil record." New Sci

Includes bibliography

Spalding, David A. E.

Dinosaur hunters. Prima Pub. 1993 310p il maps hardcover o.p. paperback available $14.95   **567.9**
  1. Dinosaurs
  ISBN 1-55958-590-0 (pa)   LC 93-15319

This history of the quest for dinosaur fossils examines field techniques, major discoveries and interpretations of findings. William Buckland, John Horner and Dale Russell are among the researchers profiled

Includes bibliographical references

Wallace, Joseph, 1957-

The American Museum of Natural History's book of dinosaurs and other ancient creatures. Simon & Schuster 1994 144p il $25   **567.9**
  1. Fossils 2. Dinosaurs
  ISBN 0-671-86590-0   LC 93-46353

This "book is a companion to exhibits at the American Museum of National History in New York. . . . It relates the history of museum-sponsored expeditions of the past that were led by such noted paleontologists as Barnum Brown and Roy Chapman Andrews. Specimens from the collection are shown along with the stories of their discovery and acquisition." Libr J

Includes bibliographical references

Wilford, John Noble

The riddle of the dinosaur; drawings by Douglas Henderson. Knopf 1985 304p il hardcover o.p. paperback available $13   **567.9**
  1. Dinosaurs
  ISBN 0-394-74392-X (pa)   LC 85-40015

The author "traces some of the scientific debates about dinosaurs: which creatures were their ancestors, their rivals, their descendants? Were they hot- or cold-blooded, fast or slow, smart or dumb, sociable or solitary?" N Y Times Book Rev

"Wilford tells the tales and elucidates the theoretical controversies in superlative popular style." Booklist

Includes bibliography

573.2 Evolution and genetics of humankind

Blueprint for life; by the editors of Time-Life Books. Time-Life Bks. 1993 144p il (Journey through the mind and body) $18.95   **573.2**
  1. Genetics 2. Heredity

          LC 93-21603

This volume offers "an introduction to inheritance, an explanation of modern genetic techniques, and an examination of the issue of nature versus nurture. . . . Most of the ground that an interested nonscientist from junior high school age up ought to know, or would like to know, is covered accurately." Sci Books Films

Includes glossary and bibliographical references

Bodmer, W. F. (Walter Fred), 1936-

The book of man; the Human Genome Project and the quest to discover our genetic heritage; [by] Walter Bodmer and Robin McKie. Scribner 1995 c1994 259p il maps $27.50   **573.2**

1. Human Genome Project 2. Genetic mapping
ISBN 0-684-80102-7   LC 94-38081

Also available in paperback from Oxford Univ. Press

First published 1994 in the United Kingdom with subtitle: The quest to discover our genetic heritage

This book discusses the Human Genome Project and contains "information on how human genes are mapped and why this mapping is important in medical, evolutionary, and sociological terms." Libr J

This "is highly readable, clear and accurate." New Sci

The **Cambridge** encyclopedia of human evolution; edited by Steve Jones, Robert Martin and David Pilbeam; executive editor, Sarah Bunney; foreword by Richard Dawkins. Cambridge Univ. Press 1993 506p il maps $100; pa $34.95   **573.2**

1. Human origins 2. Evolution
ISBN 0-521-32370-3; 0-521-46786-1 (pa)
     LC 92-18037

"This encyclopedia of the human species places modern man in evolutionary perspective, showing the descent of humankind from Mitochondrial Eve and its relationship to other living primates. Genetics, fossils, biology, brain function, disease, the biology, evolution, and ecology of humans and other modern primates are the major themes arranged topically in this encyclopedia. Excellent black-and-white photos, drawings, tables, and maps complement a work with over 70 contributors." Am Lib

Johanson, Donald C.

Lucy: the beginnings of humankind; [by] Donald C. Johanson and Maitland A. Edey. Simon & Schuster 1981 409p il hardcover o.p. paperback available $14   **573.2**

1. Human origins 2. Fossil mammals
ISBN 0-671-72499-1 (pa)   LC 80-21759

In November 1974 at a place called Hadar in Ethiopia Donald Johanson "discovered the partial skeleton of an extremely primitive female, erect-walking primate or hominid. . . . The skeleton received the name 'Lucy.' Much later, Lucy received the scientific name, Australopithecus afarensis, and it was determined she was some 3.5 million years old. . . . This book is Johanson's own story of the events leading up to and subsequent to Lucy's discovery." Best Sellers

Includes bibliography

Lucy's child: the discovery of a human ancestor; [by] Donald Johanson and James Shreeve. Morrow 1989 318p il maps o.p.; Avon Bks. paperback available $12.50   **573.2**

1. Human origins 2. Fossil mammals
ISBN 0-380-71234-2 (pa)   LC 89-9461

This is an account of archaeological excavations in Tanzania in 1986 during which a Homo habilis specimen was uncovered

"Although the descriptions of digging fossils are rich in detail and dialogue, . . . it becomes clear that the

book's real value lies elsewhere, in the lengthy digressions. There Mr. Johanson provides a lively review of the latest thinking about human origins." N Y Times Book Rev

Includes bibliography

Jones, Steve, 1944-

The language of genes; solving the mysteries of our genetic past, present and future. Doubleday 1994 272p hardcover o.p. paperback available $14   **573.2**

1. Genetics
ISBN 0-385-47428-8 (pa)   LC 93-44626

First published 1993 in the United Kingdom

"Based on a series of BBC radio lectures about genetics, this volume examines genetic changes, natural selection, inherited differences, and other related topics in a knowledgeable, yet nonscholarly fashion. For older science students." Booklist

Includes bibliographical references

Kitcher, Philip, 1947-

The lives to come; the genetic revolution and human possibilities. Simon & Schuster 1996 381p il $25   **573.2**

1. Human Genome Project 2. Genetics
ISBN 0-684-80055-1   LC 95-41523

In the first section of this book the author "writes on how genetic testing is done, the ethics of genetic testing, sequencing DNA, the various types of genetic therapy, and the possible uses and misuses of information on genetics, including the forensic use of such information. . . . The second section is an argument for what Kitcher calls utopian eugenics—the practice of modifying the human gene pool for the good of as many as possible." Sci Books Films

Includes bibliographical references

Leakey, Richard E., 1944-

The origin of humankind; [by] Richard Leakey. Basic Bks. 1994 171p il maps (Science masters series) $20; pa $10   **573.2**

1. Human origins
ISBN 0-465-03135-8; 0-465-05313-0 (pa)
     LC 94-3617

"Leakey summarizes the evolution of theories, from Darwin's to his own, in the process demonstrating the scientific method in action. . . . Covering the taxonomy of skeletons and craniums, shapes of tools, and the first sprouts of art and culture, Leakey knowledgeably points the enthralled neophyte to the wide avenues of future discoveries." Booklist

This "is a worthwhile addition to many kinds of libraries—public, general, science, biological, and psychological." Sci Books Films

Includes bibliographical references

Leakey, Richard E., 1944——*Continued*

Origins; what new discoveries reveal about the emergence of our species and its possible future; [by] Richard E. Leakey and Roger Lewin. Dutton 1977 264p il hardcover o.p. paperback available $11.95 **573.2**
1. Human origins 2. Evolution
ISBN 0-14-015336-5 (pa) LC 77-77941
The authors piece "together the scientific puzzle of human origins, as [they discuss] early predecessors of modern man and [study] species survival and development as part of the process of biological evolution. This volume uses a highly visual approach and an informal textual style." Booklist
Includes bibliographical references

Origins reconsidered; in search of what makes us human; [by] Richard Leakey and Roger Lewin. Doubleday 1992 375p il hardcover o.p. paperback available $14.95 **573.2**
1. Human origins 2. Evolution
ISBN 0-385-46792-3 (pa) LC 92-6661
"Leakey and Lewin discuss how conceptions of human anatomical and behavioral development have been radically altered within the last 12 years by new discoveries and research in other fields. They review the developments and assert Leakey's own hypotheses based on these discoveries. . . . This is an engrossing book written for the layperson, fully explaining anthropological terms and theories when necessary. It's a solid introduction to current theory concerning human development." SLJ

Lee, Thomas F.

The Human Genome Project; cracking the genetic code of life. Plenum Press 1991 323p il $24.50 **573.2**
1. Human Genome Project 2. Genetic mapping
ISBN 0-306-43965-4 LC 91-21358
The author "gives some history, explains what genes and DNA are and what they do, describes maps and markers, and then turns to an examination of the Human Genome Project: its plans, people, potential products, funding, and ethics." Booklist
Includes glossary and bibliography

Milner, Richard

The encyclopedia of evolution; humanity's search for its origins; foreword by Stephen Jay Gould. Facts on File 1990 481p il $45 **573.2**
1. Human origins—Dictionaries 2. Evolution—Dictionaries
ISBN 0-8160-1472-8 LC 90-3344
Also available in paperback from Holt & Co.
"Short entries (500-1000 words) explain theories and present capsule biographies of significant people. They also discuss controversial ideas. . . . Many entries end with brief bibliographies of books and articles by and/or about the subject." Libr J
"Milner delineates his subject matter with clarity, intelligence, and humor." Booklist

Stanley, Steven M.

Children of the Ice Age; how a global catastrophe allowed humans to evolve. Harmony Bks. 1996 278p il maps $25 **573.2**
1. Human origins 2. Ice Age
ISBN 0-517-58867-6 LC 96-4979
The author "proposes that the onset of the modern Ice Age altered Africa's landscape, drastically reducing its woodlands and ultimately prompting *Australopithecus* to abandon trees, which finally provided the opportunity for a larger brain to evolve—possible only when our ancestors freed their hands to care for immature offspring. . . . This fascinating, eminently readable book is sure to arouse controversy but contributes thought-provoking arguments." Libr J
Includes bibliography

Tudge, Colin

The time before history; 5 million years of human impact. Scribner 1996 366p il maps $27.50; pa $14 **573.2**
1. Human origins 2. Evolution 3. Mammals
ISBN 0-684-80726-2; 0-684-83052-3 (pa)
LC 95-42026
Tudge "begins by putting time into perspective so that we can understand how vast is our past; he helps us see that all evolution is part of a bigger whole—an unfolding process affected by shifting continents, climactic changes, and our own impact on the planet and its ecosystems. . . . He defines our origins in a biological, as well as historical context and applies the lessons that we should learn from our mistakes as well as our achievements to provide a blueprint for the future." Libr J
"With majestic sweep and subtle wit, . . . Tudge brings an astonishing perspective to the story of humanity." Publ Wkly
Includes bibliographical references

Walker, Alan

The wisdom of the bones; in search of human origins; [by] Alan Walker and Pat Shipman. Knopf 1996 338p il maps $26 **573.2**
1. Human origins 2. Evolution 3. Fossil man
ISBN 0-679-42624-8 LC 95-37525
"In 1984 Walker, along with colleague Richard Leakey and their 'hominidgang' of experienced Kenyan excavators, discovered a near-intact fossil of *Homo erectus*. The find was a veritable trove of theory-busting information, which the authors take up after recounting the scientists who preceded Walker in investigating the species. . . . A fluidly presented portrait of the people and process of paleoanthropology." Booklist
Includes bibliographical references

573.3 Prehistoric humankind

Tattersall, Ian

The last Neanderthal; the rise, success, and mysterious extinction of our closest human relatives. Macmillan 1995 208p il maps $39.95
573.3
1. Fossil man
ISBN 0-02-616351-9 LC 95-16621
"A Peter N. Nevraumont book"

Tattersall, Ian—*Continued*

Drawing on recent findings and new techniques of analyzing the human fossil record, the author "conveys the essentials of the technical literature to the public. These consist of methods by which Neanderthal sites are dated, what inferences may be drawn from the fossils' anatomy, and for background, a narrative of current knowledge about the hominid line. Abundant full-page photos of specimens and archaeological digs cement Tattersall's clarity on the topic, making this an immeasurable aid to students and armchair anthropologists alike." Booklist

Includes bibliography

574 Biology

Hoagland, Mahlon B., 1921-

The way life works; [by] Mahlon Hoagland, Bert Dodson. Times Bks. 1995 xxi, 233p il $35; pa $7   574

1. Life (Biology)

ISBN 0-8129-2020-1; 0-8129-2667-6 (pa)

LC 94-48780

Hoagland's text and Dodson's illustrations "present the mechanics of everything from DNA to neural circuits and evolution. As they move from discussion of 16 key patterns in life to chapters titled 'Energy,' 'Information,' 'Feedback,' 'Community,' and 'Evolution,' Hoagland and Dodson link the mechanics of the invisible world of molecules to the observable working world of plants and animals, water and light, and human beings and even machines. There is a lively sense of discovery here that makes this an ideal book for young people as well as adults." Booklist

Includes bibliographical references

Lovelock, James

The ages of Gaia; a biography of our living earth. Norton 1988 xx, 252p il hardcover o.p. paperback available $12   574

1. Biology—Philosophy 2. Biosphere 3. Life (Biology)

ISBN 0-393-31239-9 (pa)

LC 87-36567

"A volume of the Commonwealth Fund Book Program, under the editorship of Lewis Thomas."

"Gaia is the Greek goddess of the earth. For James Lovelock she is the embodiment of a hypothesis: the earth is not merely the abode of life but is a single living organism. He proposes that all living species are components of that organism, as cells are components of the human body." N Y Times Book Rev

Includes bibliographical references

Margulis, Lynn, 1938-

Five kingdoms; an illustrated guide to the phyla of life on earth; [by] Lynn Margulis, Karlene V. Schwartz. 2nd ed. Freeman, W.H. 1988 376p il hardcover o.p. paperback available $38.95   574

1. Biology

ISBN 0-7167-1912-6 (pa)

LC 87-210

Also available CD-ROM version from Springer-Verlag

First published 1982

"After a general discussion of life based on cells, each kingdom is described and includes a phylogeny showing the possible evolutionary relationships that occur among the phyla of that kingdom. It is arranged from the simplest to the most complex. A list of the better known genera of the phylum being discussed is given and followed by an illustration and fully labeled anatomic drawing of a representative species. The most typical habitat on earth is indicated for each phylum. This is a good introductory guide." Malinowsky. Best Sci & Technol Ref Books for Young People

Includes bibliography

Thomas, Lewis, 1913-1993

The lives of a cell; notes of a biology watcher. Viking 1974 153p hardcover o.p. paperback available $10.95   574

1. Biology—Philosophy

ISBN 0-14-004743-3 (pa)

In this collection of twenty-nine short essays "the author does not confine his scientist's eye to a microscope. He takes a much wider view of the world, looking at insect behavior and the possibility of intelligent life in outer space or bird songs and the evolution of language. He also offers a modest proposal for saving ourselves from nuclear self-destruction." Time

Includes bibliography

VanCleave, Janice Pratt

Janice VanCleave's A+ projects in biology; winning experiments for science fairs and extra credit. Wiley 1993 217p il $24.95; pa $12.95   574

1. Biology—Experiments 2. Science projects

ISBN 0-471-58629-3; 0-471-58628-5 (pa)

LC 93-13306

A collection of experiments and projects exploring various aspects of biology

"The topics are presented clearly together with simple line drawings. . . . Science teachers looking for relatively 'low-tech,' hands-on activities will find [this book] helpful." Sci Books Films

Includes glossary

574.03 Biology—Encyclopedias and dictionaries

Burnie, David

Dictionary of nature. Dorling Kindersley 1994 192p il $19.95   574.03

1. Biology—Dictionaries

ISBN 1-56458-473-9

LC 93-30696

"Arranged thematically rather than alphabetically, the dictionary takes readers through topics such as cells, evolution, plants, animals, and ecology, covering more than 2,000 concepts. Each main heading consists of one to two pages of information, including a broad introduction and a series of definitions and explanations. . . . If applicable, a brief biography of a scientist linked to that subject is included. Topics are illustrated with three dimensional models, diagrams, and photographs." Am Ref Books Annu, 1995

Concise encyclopedia biology; translated and revised by Thomas A. Scott. De Gruyter 1996 1287p il $99.95   **574.03**
1. Biology—Dictionaries
ISBN 3-11-010661-2   LC 95-39080
Original German edition, 1986
"The more than 7000 entries (along with 1200 figures, formulas, and tables) range from a few lines to several pages and cover all fields of biology: anatomy, biochemistry, botany, ecology, genetics, molecular biology, physiology, and zoology. The book is especially good on various groups of plants and animals, and although persons are not given individual entries names appear in longer entries." Libr J
For a fuller review see: Booklist, Aug., 1996

Encyclopedia of life sciences. Marshall Cavendish 1996 11v set $449.95   **574.03**
1. Biology—Dictionaries 2. Life sciences—Dictionaries
ISBN 0-7614-0254-3   LC 95-18950
An encyclopedia covering the disciplines of zoology, botany, evolutionary science, medicine, physiology, human anatomy, cytology, and genetics
For a review see: Booklist, July, 1996

574.5 Ecology

Ackerman, Diane
The rarest of the rare; vanishing animals, timeless worlds. Random House 1995 xxi, 184p $23   **574.5**
1. Endangered species 2. Rare animals
ISBN 0-679-40346-9   LC 95-8499
In these essays the author "tells of her adventures in several relatively isolated habitats of several endangered animal species: monk seals in Hawaii, golden lion tamarins in the Brazilian rain forest, short-tailed albatrosses on a Japanese volcanic island, and monarch butterflies in southern California. For each of the habitats Ackerman has recruited the company of one or more biologically sophisticated guides." Choice
"Every species that is endangered or becomes extinct deserve so poetic a chronicler as Ackerman." Libr J

Agosta, William C.
Bombardier beetles and fever trees; a close-up look at chemical warfare and signals in animals and plants; [by] William Agosta. Addison-Wesley 1996 224p il $25   **574.5**
1. Chemicals 2. Ecology
ISBN 0-201-62658-6   LC 95-9533
The author offers an "introduction to the chemicals that occur naturally in plants and animals. Classifying these substances as warfare agents, lifestyle components, or message senders, he includes a wide variety of examples for each. . . . A secondary theme is Agosta's emphasis on the importance of nature's chemicals to humans in pharmaceutical and other applications. He also briefly touches on ecological and environmental matters that influence the present and future of many of the organisms." Libr J

"Rarely does such a complex subject get so lucid a treatment as in this book; and rarely does such a lucid treatment comprise such perfect prose . . . and unequivocally factual and interesting-to-read material." Sci Books Films
Includes bibliographical references

Buchmann, Stephen
The forgotten pollinators; [by] Stephen L. Buchmann and Gary Paul Nabhan; with a foreword by Edward O. Wilson; illustrations by Paul Mirocha. Island Press (Covelo) 1996 xx, 292p il $25   **574.5**
1. Fertilization of plants 2. Biological diversity 3. Ecology
ISBN 1-55963-352-2   LC 96-802
The authors explore the "link between plants and their pollinators. It is a disturbing story of disappearing insects and diminishing plant reproduction, owing to overuse of pesticide and fragmented habitat. The authors combine anecdotes from the field with discussions of ecology, entomology, botany, crop science and the economics of pollination." Publ Wkly
Includes bibliographical references

Conrad, Jim
Discover nature in the garden; things to know and things to do; illustrations by Jim Conrad. Stackpole Bks. 1996 234p il maps pa $14.95
                     574.5
1. Garden ecology 2. Nature study 3. Gardening
ISBN 0-8117-2442-5   LC 95-46473
This volume is divided "into three main sections—plants, animals, and ecology. . . . In the first section, Conrad explains the composition of plants, types of fruits and seeds, and the photosynthesis process. . . . The section on animals is divided into chapters on insects, earthworms, birds, and moles. Backyard ecology focuses on interrelationships in the garden and offers data on composting, soil, plant diseases, and pest control." Booklist
Includes bibliographical references

Dashefsky, H. Steven
Environmental science; high-school science fair experiments; illustrations by Janice Lebeyka. TAB Bks. 1994 177p il $19.95; pa $12.60   **574.5**
1. Environment 2. Science projects 3. Ecology—Experiments
ISBN 0-8306-4587-X; 0-8306-4586-1 (pa)
                     LC 93-34615
"Includes projects on applied ecology, soil ecosystems, energy, aquatic ecosystems, and potential solutions to environmental problems." Booklist
"A clear, concise introduction to environmental science and an introduction to scientific research start the potential researcher off in the right direction." Book Rep
Includes bibliographical references

Deserts; the encroaching wilderness: a world conservation atlas; edited by Tony Allan and Andrew Warren; introduction by Mostafa Tolba. Oxford Univ. Press 1993 176p il maps $39.95
       574.5

1. Desert ecology 2. Nature conservation
ISBN 0-19-520941-9   LC 92-31992
This "book covers all aspects of deserts: their physical features, plant and animal life, human inhabitants, oil and mineral resources, desertification, and conservation. The book's longest chapter gives individual attention to each of the world's major deserts and desert regions. *Deserts* is liberally (and beautifully) illustrated with striking color photographs and maps. The text and illustrations work well together to provide a brief but excellent introduction to the subject." Libr J

Duffy, Trent
The vanishing wetlands. Watts 1994 159p il lib bdg $19.70   574.5

1. Wetlands 2. Human influence on nature
ISBN 0-531-13034-7   LC 93-26332
"An Impact book"
The author "provides defining specifics on what wetlands are, why they are vanishing, and what may be done to preserve them." Booklist
"This book is a sound and satisfactory primer on the topic. The writing is direct enough for the younger researcher and sophisticated enough for the higher level student." Book Rep
Includes glossary and bibliography

Ecology. Time-Life Bks. 1992 151p il (Understanding science & nature) $17.95 **574.5**
1. Ecology
       LC 91-39877

Questions and answers present information about the distribution of plants and animals, the relationships among living things, and the food chain

Encyclopedia of endangered species; edited by Mary Emanoil; in association with IUCN-the World Conservation Union, Species Survival Commission. Gale Res. 1994 1230p il maps $95
       574.5

1. Endangered species—Dictionaries
ISBN 0-8103-8857-X
"This book contains synopses of 700 endangered species. . . . There are eight broad taxonomic sections arranged by family and genus. . . . The accounts are clearly written, with sections on description and biology, habitat and current distribution, and conservation measures." Am Ref Books Annu, 1995

Endangered species: opposing viewpoints; Brenda Stalcup, book editor. Greenhaven Press 1995 264p lib bdg $19.95; pa $11.95   574.5
1. Endangered species
ISBN 1-56510-365-3 (lib bdg); 1-56510-364-5 (pa)
       LC 95-239
"Opposing viewpoints series"
This collection of articles presents varying viewpoints on issues relating to endangered species, including how serious a problem extinction is, whether or not endan-

gered species can be preserved, and whether or not they should take priority over jobs, development, and property rights, what U.S. policy should be in other countries, and whether or not humans are an endangered species
Includes bibliographical references

Flegg, Jim
Deserts; miracle of life. Facts on File 1993 160p il $29.95   574.5
1. Deserts
ISBN 0-8160-2902-4   LC 92-46603
The author "defines what a desert is and, chapter by chapter, describes the surprising variety of life forms that find sustenance in an inhospitable environment. . . . He also devotes a chapter to human desert dwellers, describing their nomadic lifestyle and the way cultures have been formed around the struggle for moisture and food. Flegg's knowledge seems boundless, his style scholarly but readable." Book Rep
Includes bibliographical references

Forsyth, Adrian
Portraits of the rainforest; photographs by Michael and Patricia Fogden. Camden House (Camden East); distributed by Firefly Bks. (Buffalo) 1990 156p il hardcover o.p. paperback available $24.95   574.5
1. Rain forest ecology
ISBN 0-921820-99-2 (pa)   LC 91-190043
"Portraits both in supple prose and exquisite, up-close color photographs record the diversity of life in the rain forests of Costa Rica and Peru." Am Libr
Includes bibliography

Gay, Kathlyn
Rainforests of the world; a reference handbook. ABC-CLIO 1993 219p il maps (Contemporary world issues) $39.50   574.5
1. Rain forest ecology
ISBN 0-87436-712-3   LC 93-39619
"The volume examines the reasons for the forests' destruction, the effects of deforestation on indigenous plant and animal life as well as the entire planet, and what policies and actions are currently being taken to stop the clearing efforts. Annotated listings of organizations and print and nonprint resources are included." Publisher's note
"A fine reference source for basic information." Voice Youth Advocates
Includes glossary

Gibbons, Whit, 1939-
Keeping all the pieces; perspectives on natural history and the environment. Smithsonian Institution Press 1993 xx, 182p pa $16.95 **574.5**
1. Ecology 2. Natural history 3. Human ecology
ISBN 1-56098-224-1   LC 93-2037
The author examines the relationships among organisms and their environments. He also discusses human population growth and environmental degradation
"This very well-written and readable book is likely to stimulate interest in ecology and our environment and make readers think more about our role in preserving the natural world." Sci Books Films

Kricher, John C.
A field guide to eastern forests: North America;
text and photographs by John C. Kricher;
illustrated by Gordon Morrison. Houghton Mifflin
1988 368p il $22.95; pa $16.95   **574.5**
1. Forest ecology
ISBN 0-395-35346-7; 0-395-47953-3 (pa)
                                        LC 87-35247
"The Peterson field guide series"
"Sponsored by the National Audubon Society, the National Wildlife Federation, and the Roger Tory Peterson
Institute"
This "field guide introduces the forests of the eastern
half of the United States, treating each of twenty-seven
forest types as a complex ecological system. . . . Sixty
plates of Kricher's photographs and Morrison's drawings,
many in color, depict major plant and animal species."
Wilson Libr Bull

Mann, Charles C.
Noah's choice; the future of endangered species;
[by] Charles C. Mann, Mark L. Plummer. Knopf
1995 302p $25   **574.5**
1. Endangered species 2. Wildlife conservation
ISBN 0-679-42002-9   LC 94-25807
The authors discuss the Endangered Species Act and
the choices necessary to balance human needs against the
preservation of biodiversity
"The writing is clear and entertaining, and the authors'
key argument—that the Endangered Species Act doesn't
allow for enough flexibility based on values—is compelling, cogent, and highly controversial." Libr J
Includes bibliographical references

Maser, Chris
Forest primeval; the natural history of an
ancient forest. Sierra Club Bks. 1989 xxi, 282p il
hardcover o.p. paperback available $12   **574.5**
1. Forest ecology
ISBN 0-87156-548-X (pa)   LC 89-31775
"Maser describes the growth and development of a
stretch of Oregon forest through a number of chronological steps. . . . Within the text are sections that look
briefly into the lives of many species of animals and
plants common to that type of environment. Readers will
find much biological and natural history information
woven into a hypothetical account of a piece of old-
growth forest. The author enriches this accounting by his
own personal experiences and scientific background."
Choice
Includes glossary and bibliography

Newman, Arnold, 1918-
Tropical rainforest; a world survey of our most
valuable and endangered habitat with a blueprint
for its survival; foreword by Mildred E. Mathias.
Facts on File 1990 256p il $45   **574.5**
1. Rain forest ecology
ISBN 0-8160-1944-4   LC 90-3484
The author "explains the dynamics of rain forests and
their contribution to the environment, as well as the reasons for their alarmingly rapid destruction. His descrip-

tions of the diversity, complexity, and fecundity of the
forests are accompanied by splendid color photographs."
Booklist
Includes bibliography

The **Official** World Wildlife Fund guide to
endangered species of North America. Beacham
Pub. 1990-1994 4v il v1-2 set $195; v3-4 ea
$85   **574.5**
1. Nature conservation 2. Endangered species 3. Rare
animals 4. Rare plants
ISBN 0-933833-17-2 (v1-2); 0-933833-29-6 (v3);
0-933833-33-4 (v4)
Contents: v1 Plants, mammals; v2 Birds, reptiles, amphibians, fishes, mussels, crustaceans, snails, insects &
arachnids; v3 Species listed August 1989 to December
1991; v4 Species listed December 1991 to July 1994
"An examination of plant and animal species that have
been officially declared 'endangered' or 'threatened' by
the United States Congress. . . . Each article includes a
locator map showing primary habitats, a short bibliography, and contact organizations for more information."
SLJ

Quinn, John R.
Wildlife survivors; the flora and fauna of
tomorrow. TAB Bks. 1993 208p il $21.95; pa
$12.95   **574.5**
1. Adaptation (Biology) 2. Natural selection 3. Human influence on nature
ISBN 0-8306-4346-X; 0-8306-4345-1 (pa)
                                        LC 93-21037
The author discusses "many of the plants and animals
in the United States that thrive despite urban sprawl and
degraded habitats. Outlined are nine types of land-use
environments and the kinds of wildlife they may harbor.
. . . Nature lovers, teachers, librarians, and wildlife professionals dealing with the public may well want this
book on their shelves. The author's admiration of these
hardy breeds permeates both pictures and text." Sci
Books Films
Includes bibliographical references

Rainis, Kenneth G.
Environmental science projects for young
scientists. Watts 1994 160p il (Projects for young
scientists) lib bdg $22   **574.5**
1. Environment 2. Science projects 3. Ecology—Experiments
ISBN 0-531-11194-6   LC 94-26876
These "projects bring readers into direct contact with
their local environment to learn how it works and what
makes it thrive. Many of the activities directly benefit
the environment. Others focus on giving readers enough
information and experience to come up with their own
ways of helping out." Publisher's note
Includes bibliographical references

Stanley, Steven M.
Extinction. Scientific Am. Lib. 1987 242p il
$32.95   **574.5**
1. Extinct animals 2. Fossil plants
ISBN 0-7167-5014-7   LC 86-22027
This "volume traces the history and causation of epi-
sodic mass extinctions of marine and terrestrial organ-

Stanley, Steven M.—*Continued*

isms since the Precambrian [period], as revealed by evidence in the fossil record." Choice

This work "has a well-organized, well-written text supported by many generously sized and excellent illustrations." Sci Books Films

Includes bibliography

Terborgh, John, 1936-

Diversity and the tropical rain forest. Scientific Am. Lib. 1992 242p il maps $32.95   **574.5**

1. Rain forest ecology 2. Nature conservation

ISBN 0-7167-5030-9   LC 91-30053

Spine title: Diversity and the rain forest

The author provides "information on how diverse the plant species are in the tropical rain forest, and includes an examination of both horizontal and vertical distribution of the plants. Animal diversity is also examined (emphasis on vertebrates, especially mammals), as well as the reasons for this diversity." Choice

"An authoritative, up-to-date, and superbly organized and illustrated collation of thinking. . . . This is a 'must read' for those who can, should, or want to affect the future of tropical forests. . . . Written in a popular vein, the book should also appeal to a wide range of natural history buffs, teachers, and students." Sci Books Films

Wetlands in danger; a world conservation atlas; edited by Patrick Dugan; introduction by David Bellamy. Oxford Univ. Press 1993 187p il maps $48.75   **574.5**

1. Marsh ecology 2. Nature conservation

ISBN 0-19-520942-7   LC 93-21729

This volume "divides the world's regions into 19 sections and discusses each region's wetlands. A color map is included for each region. A few other chapters define wetlands, discuss their value and characteristic plant and animal life, deal with wetland loss and its consequences, and touch upon some conservation issues. . . . This book is a solid choice for public, high school, and academic undergraduate libraries." Libr J

The World's wild shores; prepared by the Special Publications Division, National Geographic Society, Washington, D.C. National Geographic Soc. 1990 199p il map $12.95; lib bdg $12.95   **574.5**

1. Seashore ecology

ISBN 0-87044-716-5; 0-87044-721-1 (lib bdg)

LC 89-13952

Illustrated with numerous color photographs, this book discusses the ecology of coastlines around the world in five major climate zones

"Skillful integration of historical, geographical, cultural, economic, ecological, and factual information makes for interesting and captivating reading." Appraisal

Includes bibliography

574.6   Economic biology

Foster, Steven, 1957-

A field guide to venomous animals and poisonous plants; North America, North of Mexico; [by] Steven Foster and Roger A. Caras. Houghton Mifflin 1994 244p il $22.95; pa $15.95   **574.6**

1. Poisonous animals 2. Poisonous plants

ISBN 0-395-51594-7; 0-395-35292-4 (pa)

LC 94-1641

"The Peterson field guide series"

Sponsored by National Audubon Society, National Wildlife Federation, and Roger Tory Peterson Institute

This guide includes "90 animals from the mildly irritating to the deadly venomous: stinging and biting insects, scorpions and spiders, mammals, and reptiles, with an emphasis on snakes. More than 250 plants are described: wildflowers, weeds and exotic aliens, shrubs, trees, ferns, and mushrooms. The list includes plants that often cause allergies or dermatitis, such as Poison Ivy, as well as those that are toxic to eat." Publisher's note

Includes glossary and bibliographical references

574.87   Cytology (Cell biology)

Drlica, Karl

Understanding DNA and gene cloning; a guide for the curious. 3rd ed. Wiley 1997 329p il pa $28.95   **574.87**

1. Molecular cloning 2. Recombinant DNA 3. Genetic engineering

ISBN 0-471-13774-X   LC 96-23077

First published 1984

This overview of genetic research and engineering explores: basic molecular biology, manipulation of DNA, insights obtained from gene cloning, and human genetics. The author also suggests ways to protect yourself from the discrimination that may arise from the release of genetic information. A chapter on retroviruses is included

Includes glossary and bibliography

574.9   Geographic treatment of organisms

Durrell, Gerald M., 1925-1995

My family & other animals. Viking 1957 c1956 273p hardcover o.p. paperback available $7.95

574.9

1. Natural history—Corfu Island (Greece)

ISBN 0-14-001399-7 (pa)

Also available in hardcover from P. Smith

First published 1956 in the United Kingdom

As a boy Durrell spent five years with his family on the island of Corfu. The friendly islanders gave him strange and wonderful animals for his collection. Interspersed with descriptions of the island and its wildlife are amusing accounts of the exploits of the Durrell family

Quammen, David, 1948-
The song of the dodo; island biogeography in an age of extinctions; maps by Kris Ellingsen. Scribner 1996 702p maps $32.50 **574.9**
1. Islands 2. Endangered species 3. Biogeography
ISBN 0-684-80083-7 LC 95-44972
The author "discusses the development of island biogeography and how it can inform current environmental situations and practices. He uses numerous examples and personal experiences of islands from around the world and their unique animals, as well as interviews with the scientists who study them, to explore evolution, extinction, and ecology." Libr J
Includes bibliography

574.92 Aquatic biology. Marine biology

Brower, Kenneth, 1944-
Realms of the sea. National Geographic Soc. 1991 278p il $35 **574.92**
1. Marine biology 2. Ocean
ISBN 0-87044-855-2 LC 91-11113
An introductory chapter explains the basics of the physical ocean. Text and full-color photographs then explore the natural history of five marine habitats
Includes bibliography

Carson, Rachel, 1907-1964
The edge of the sea; with illustrations by Bob Hines. Houghton Mifflin 1955 276p il hardcover o.p. paperback available $12.95 **574.92**
1. Marine biology 2. Seashore
ISBN 0-395-28519-4 (pa)
"The seashores of the world may be divided into three basic types: the rugged shores of rock, the sand beaches, and the coral reefs and all their associated features. Each has its typical community of plants and animals. The Atlantic coast of the United States [provides] clear examples of each of these types. I have chosen it as the setting for my pictures of shore life." Preface

Holing, Dwight
Coral reefs; photographers, Frank Balthis [et al.] Silver Burdett Press 1994 39p il map (Close up: a focus on nature) $14.95; pa $7.95 **574.92**
1. Coral reefs and islands
ISBN 0-382-24857-0; 0-382-24858-9 (pa)
LC 94-30868
First published 1990 by Blake Pub.
The author provides "a description of coral reefs and the polyps that build them. Also covered is a discussion of the other plants and animals that live along a reef but do not contribute to the building of the structure." Sci Books Films
Includes glossary and bibliography

Ocean planet; writings and images of the sea; original text by Peter Benchley; edited by Judith Gradwohl. Abrams 1995 192p il $39.95 **574.92**
1. Marine ecology 2. Ocean
ISBN 0-8109-3677-1 LC 94-23265
Published by Abrams and Times Mirror Magazines in association with the Smithsonian Institution

This companion to a Smithsonian exhibition is a "collection of writings by a diverse group of authors, including Benjamin Franklin, William Beebe, Joseph Conrad, Rachel Carson, Loren Eisley, Farley Mowat, and John McPhee. The excerpts are grouped under four topics: 'Visions of the Sea,' 'Seafarers,' 'Discovery,' and 'Oceans in Peril.' Each of these sections is introduced by essayist, novelist, and reporter Benchley. Numerous photographs illustrate the complexity of the problems impacting the ocean environment and the interdependence of all forms of life." Choice
"The photographs may lead some readers to consider this a coffee-table book, but the text is worth reading and conveys the intended message." Libr J

Sammon, Rick
Seven underwater wonders of the world. Thomasson-Grant 1992 180p il map $29.95
574.92
1. Marine biology 2. Marine resources 3. Coral reefs and islands
ISBN 0-934738-78-5 LC 92-6413
Text and numerous photography portrait the ecosystems of the Belize Barrier Reef, Lake Baikal, the Northern Red sea, the Galapagos archipelago, the Great Barrier Reef, deep ocean vents and Palau
Includes bibliographical references

Stafford-Deitsch, Jeremy
Reef; a safari through the coral world; photographs and text by Jeremy Stafford-Deitsch. Sierra Club Bks. 1991 200p il hardcover o.p. paperback available $20 **574.92**
1. Coral reefs and islands 2. Marine ecology
ISBN 0-87156-541-2 (pa) LC 90-25432
This volume offers underwater photographs and a commentary on the natural history of coral reefs
This book has "an interesting, informative text highlighted with spectacular full-color photographs. . . . Science, photography, and nature students will gain useful information from this attractive title." SLJ
Includes glossary and bibliography

574.999 Astrobiology

Angelo, Joseph A.
The extraterrestrial encyclopedia; by Joseph A. Angelo, Jr. rev and updated. Facts on File 1991 240p il $40 **574.999**
1. Life on other planets—Dictionaries 2. Interstellar communication—Dictionaries
ISBN 0-8160-2276-3 LC 90-22192
First published 1985
This sourcebook covers topics ranging from basic astronomy to some of the more speculative theories on UFOs and life on other planets

575   Evolution and genetics

Erickson, Jon, 1948-
Dying planet; the extinction of species. TAB Bks. 1991 188p il $23.95; pa $14.95   **575**
1. Extinct animals 2. Evolution
ISBN 0-8306-6726-1; 0-8306-7726-7 (pa)
LC 91-9277
"This book traces the extinction of species from the origin of life to the present. The intervening history is devoted to chapters on geology, the major extinctions, the evolution of species, the causes and effects of extinction, the ice ages, and the greenhouse effect. It is a serious account of a very urgent problem." Appraisal
Includes glossary and bibliography

Evolution of life. Time-Life Bks. 1992 151p il (Understanding science & nature) $17.95   **575**
1. Evolution
LC 92-8227
Questions and answers present information about the theory and process of evolution

Lewin, Roger
Thread of life; the Smithsonian looks at evolution. Smithsonian Bks. 1982 256p il maps $35   **575**
1. Evolution
ISBN 0-89599-010-5   LC 82-16834
"Lewin begins with an overview of the geological history and the background of modern evolutionary theory. He then explores the origin of life and life in the sea." Sci Books Films
"A profusion of handsome—sometimes startling—color photos, augmented by charts, diagrams, drawings, and paintings, enriches this cohesive popularization of evolution." Booklist

575.01   Evolution and genetics— Theories

Bowler, Peter J.
Darwinism. Twayne Pubs. 1993 118p (Twayne's studies in intellectual and cultural history) $27.75; pa $15.95   **575.01**
1. Darwin, Charles, 1809-1882 2. Evolution 3. Natural selection
ISBN 0-8057-8613-9; 0-8057-8638-4 (pa)
LC 93-431
The author "defines Darwinism and sets it in the context of nineteenth-century thought. He illustrates its relation to Lyell's *Principles of Geology* (1830) . . . explains the important distinction between Lamarckian evolution and natural selection; and traces the various religious reactions to Darwinism. . . . [He also provides an] assessment of the many uses and abuses of Darwinism." Publisher's note
Includes bibliographical references

Darwin, Charles, 1809-1882
The Darwin reader; edited by Mark Ridley. 2nd ed. Norton 1996 315p il pa $12.95   **575.01**
1. Evolution 2. Natural selection
ISBN 0-393-96967-3   LC 95-50297
First published in the United Kingdom with title: The essential Darwin; first Norton edition published 1987
This collection presents excerpts from Darwin's most important works including Origin of the species, The descent of man and Coral reef. Illustrations are taken from the original editions
Includes bibliographical references

The essential Darwin; Robert Jastrow, general editor; selections and commentary by Kenneth A. Korey. Little, Brown 1984 327p il (Masters of modern science series) $19.95   **575.01**
1. Evolution 2. Natural selection
ISBN 0-316-45826-0   LC 84-15502
"This book presents excerpts from Darwin's most important writings: 'The Voyage of the Beagle,' 'The Origin of Species,' 'The Descent of Man,' and his autobiography. Included in the text are critical evaluations that put Darwin into modern perspective in light of the most recent scientific findings. A fine, well-rounded introduction to Darwin's scientific contributions." Booklist
Includes bibliography

The portable Darwin; edited, with an introduction, notes, and epilogue by Duncan M. Porter and Peter W. Graham. Penguin Bks. 1993 xxii, 561p il pa $13.95   **575.01**
1. Evolution 2. Natural selection
ISBN 0-14-015109-5   LC 93-17106
"The Viking portable library"
This collection of Darwin's writings includes five chapters from The origin of species; excerpts from The voyage of the Beagle, The descent of man, and The variation of animals and plants under domestication; scientific papers, travel writings, and letters
Includes bibliography

576   Microbiology

Dashefsky, H. Steven
Microbiology: 49 science fair projects; illustrations by Debra Ellinger. TAB Bks. 1994 176p il (Science fair projects) hardcover o.p. paperback available $10.95   **576**
1. Microbiology—Experiments 2. Science projects
ISBN 0-07-015660-3 (pa)   LC 93-48718
In these projects students "explore microscopic populations in such places as air conditioning filters, vacuum cleaners, food, and insect bodies. They also test several methods of controlling microbe growth, including ultra-violet light and various commercially produced antibacterial substances. The author carefully describes the skills needed to complete an activity successfully." Sci Child
"A commendable learning experience." SLJ

Dashefsky, H. Steven—*Continued*

Microbiology: high-school science fair experiments. TAB Bks. 1995 169p il $21.95; pa $12.95 **576**

1. Microbiology—Experiments 2. Science projects
ISBN 0-07-015663-8; 0-07-015664-6 (pa)
LC 94-23117

"The focus in this book is on experiments that apply natural products to affect the growth of microbes. This involves learning about microorganisms. Each experiment contains a paragraph on background information; one on an overview of the project, including a list of materials, a set of procedures, and an analysis; and one on how to expand the experiment, including suggestions for related research. . . . Each section is concise and has good illustrations." Sci Books Films

Includes glossary and bibliography

Dixon, Bernard

Power unseen; how microbes rule the world. Freeman, W.H. 1994 237p il hardcover o.p. paperback available $13.95 **576**

1. Microbiology
ISBN 0-7167-4550-X (pa)
LC 93-37697

"In a collection of 75 brief essays, Dixon provides information on a wide variety of microbes, including the bacteria that help to clean up oil spills and molds that are used in manufacturing cheese. . . . [This book] is valuable for its broad overview, which illustrates the diversity found in the field of microbiology." Libr J

Includes bibliography

Henig, Robin Marantz

A dancing matrix; voyages along the viral frontier. Knopf 1993 269p il $23 **576**

1. Viruses 2. Medicine—Research
ISBN 0-394-58878-9
LC 92-16443

"This account of contemporary viral research is as engrossing as it is informative. Henig lucidly explains current theories on the nature of viruses, the origins of AIDS, and the disease-generating impact of human encroachment on the environment." Booklist

Includes bibliography

Sagan, Dorion, 1959-

Garden of microbial delights; a practical guide to the subvisible world; [by] Dorion Sagan, Lynn Margulis. Kendall/Hunt 1993 232p il $36.95 **576**

1. Microbiology
ISBN 0-8403-8529-3
LC 93-77830

First published 1988 by Harcourt Brace Jovanovich

This "introduction to microbial organisms, including bacteria, protoctista, and fungi, looks at their history, structure, and function, and provides identification guidelines. The many black-and-white illustrations and oversize format make this attractive reference/cocurricular material for science students." Booklist

Includes bibliographical references

577 General nature of life

Asimov, Isaac, 1920-1992

Beginnings; the story of origins—of mankind, life, the earth, the universe. Walker & Co. 1987 284p il o.p.; Berkley Bks. paperback available $5.99 **577**

1. Life—Origin 2. Human origins
ISBN 0-425-11586-0 (pa)
LC 87-15325

The author "traces the ancestry of humankind, starting with historical times and moving backward to find the origins of ancient man, hominids, mammals, chordates." Libr J

Jastrow, Robert, 1925-

Until the sun dies. Norton 1977 172p il $12.95 **577**

1. Life—Origin 2. Universe 3. Astronomy
ISBN 0-393-06415-8
LC 77-5613

Companion volumes The enchanted loom (1981) and Red giants and white dwarfs, entered in class 523.1

"The author's story starts with the riddle of creation some 20 billion years ago, then moves swiftly forward through the creation of the galaxies and the formation of our planet. Jastrow continues from molecular evolution through the first cell, to the age of dinosaurs and mammals, and finally to the emergence of the human race." Sci Books Films

Margulis, Lynn, 1938-

What is life? [by] Lynn Margulis and Dorion Sagan; foreword by Niles Eldredge. Simon & Schuster 1995 207p il $40 **577**

1. Life (Biology) 2. Biology—Philosophy 3. Biological diversity 4. Life—Origin
ISBN 0-684-81326-2
LC 94-44213

"A Peter N. Nevraumont book"

"Continuing Margulis's contention that organelles within cells, such as mitochondria, were originally free-living organisms that fused with others to form complex cells and bodies, the authors extend this concept to the Earth as a superorganism. Although following traditional evolutionary pathways, the authors argue that life has played a role in its own evolution. Designed for the general reader, this book could be used to interest students who are less than excited by standard biology textbooks, as well as by teachers who may derive new approaches." Choice

Includes bibliographical references

Sagan, Carl, 1934-1996

Shadows of forgotten ancestors; a search for who we are; [by] Carl Sagan, Ann Druyan. Random House 1992 505p hardcover o.p. paperback available $14 **577**

1. Life—Origin 2. Evolution
ISBN 0-345-38472-5 (pa)
LC 92-50155

The authors "trace the roots of the *Homo sapiens* family tree down to life at its tiniest. . . . As Sagan and Druyan move up the evolutionary ladder from microorganisms to more complex creatures including insects,

Sagan, Carl, 1934-1996—*Continued*

snakes, fish, birds, and primates, they track the emergence of sexuality, survival tactics, instinct, and thinking, all sparked by the basic interplay between heredity and environment." Booklist

"Despite a preference for the overly dramatic phrase at the expense of scientific clarity, the argument is coherent throughout." Libr J

Includes bibliographical references

581   Botany

Bleifeld, Maurice

Botany projects for young scientists. Watts 1992 144p il (Projects for young scientists) lib bdg $19.14; pa $6.95   **581**

1. Botany—Experiments 2. Science projects

ISBN 0-531-11046-X (lib bdg); 0-531-15650-8 (pa)
LC 91-43704

"This book is geared for the high school biology student faced with a science fair or term project. . . . Chapters are divided up by topics (Plant Structures, Heredity, Ecology, etc.) and within each chapter, projects range from simple . . . to difficult. . . . Most of the projects are appropriate and do-able in terms of scientific techniques and methods, and the hypotheses are 'real' enough to make the projects interesting." Voice Youth Advocates

Includes bibliography

Dashefsky, H. Steven

Botany; high-school science fair experiments. TAB Bks. 1995 158p il $21.95; pa $12.95   **581**

1. Botany—Experiments 2. Science projects

ISBN 0-07-015684-0; 0-07-015685-9 (pa)
LC 94-34890

"The book is divided into three sections, progressing from an introduction to botany to detailed explanations of specific projects. The projects, adapted from actual entries in the International Science and Engineering Fair, address a wide variety of questions, including those dealing with the environment. . . . The book is clearly organized into several sections and contains a great deal of pertinent information. Dashefsky's writing style is clear and lucid." Appraisal

Includes glossary and bibliography

Gray, Asa, 1810-1888

Gray's Manual of botany. 8th (centennial) ed, largely rewritten and expanded by Merritt Lyndon Fernald; with assistance of specialists in some groups. American Bk. Co. 1950 lxiv, 1632p il o.p.; Dioscorides Press reprint available $59.95   **581**

1. Plants

ISBN 0-931146-09-7

First published 1848 by J. Munroe and Company with title: A manual of the botany of the northern United States

"A handbook of the flowering plants and ferns of the Central and Northeastern United States and adjacent Canada." Subtitle

"This standard work contains many basic botanical data as well as descriptions of some 8000 species of plants. This material includes a synopsis of the orders and families of vascular plants, a summary of the families, a glossary, and indexes to the Latin, English, French-Canadian, and colloquial." Murphey. How & Where to Look It Up

Hershey, David R.

Plant biology science projects. Wiley 1995 165p il (Best science projects for young adults) pa $12.95   **581**

1. Botany—Experiments 2. Plants—Experiments 3. Science projects

ISBN 0-471-04983-2   LC 94-12934

"The introduction provides a guide to scientific experimentation with explanations of the metric system, descriptions of instruments and equipment, and excellent planning guidelines. The activities are divided into five broad areas—seeds, plants and water, light and photosynthesis, soils and fertilizers, and hydroponics; the author provides background information, sources for further research, and a bibliography for each section." SLJ

Includes glossary

Hyam, R. (Roger)

Plants and their names: a concise dictionary; [by] R. Hyam, R. Pankhurst. Oxford Univ. Press 1995 545p $32   **581**

1. Botany—Dictionaries 2. Popular plant names

ISBN 0-19-866189-4   LC 94-5024

"The dictionary describes families (511) and genera (2,169); lists species (5,500 only), with at least one for each genus entry; lists specific epiphytes (2,600) and their meanings; and catalogs and cross-references synonyms (names that are no longer accepted) to accepted names. Common names (6000), also cross-referenced, are included as well. A small glossary is added that includes abbreviations used." Sci Books Films

581.5   Botany—Ecology

Attenborough, David, 1926-

The private life of plants; a natural history of plant behaviour. Princeton Univ. Press 1995 320p il $29.95   **581.5**

1. Plants 2. Botany

ISBN 0-691-00639-3   LC 95-17514

In this companion to the BBC television series, the author claims "that plants 'must grapple with much the same problems as animals, including ourselves,' and describes these endeavors in chapters on traveling, feeding and growing, flowering, social struggle, living together, and surviving. Other popularizations have covered the same basic territory, but rarely in such a captivating way." Libr J

Reading, Susan

Plants of the tropics; written by Susan Reading. Facts on File 1990 62p il map (Plant life) $15.95
581.5

1. Tropical plants 2. Rain forest ecology

ISBN 0-8160-2423-5   LC 90-32397

This book "offers a tour of the rain forest, noting the variety of plants, their means of survival, their partnership with animals, and the ongoing destruction of the ecosystem. . . . An inviting and informative introduction." Booklist

Includes bibliographical references

581.6   Economic botany

Bown, Deni

Encyclopedia of herbs & their uses. Dorling Kindersley 1995 424p il $39.95   **581.6**

1. Herbs 2. Herb gardening

ISBN 0-7894-0184-3   LC 95-8171

At head of title: The Herb Society of America

An introductory section in this reference work covers plant classification and legal restrictions on herbs, herb history, myth, and legend. Following are sections on designing an herb garden, uses of herbs, herbs in the wild described by continent, an herb catalog including full botanical descriptions, and an herb dictionary including information on uses, growing and harvesting. Over 1000 plants are described, and the book is illustrated with more than 1500 photographs

Includes bibliographical references

Bremness, Lesley

Herbs. Dorling Kindersley 1993 304p il (Eyewitness handbooks) $29.95; pa $17.95 **581.6**

1. Herbs

ISBN 1-56458-497-6; 1-56458-496-8 (pa)

    LC 93-26815

This pictorial guide to 700 species of herbs "is divided into six parts: trees, shrubs, herbaceous perennials, annuals and biennials, vines, and other herbs (including fungi and non-seed-bearing plants)." Booklist

"As a browser's delight, a useful herbal handbook, or a quick reference source, this is a welcome addition to any library with a perennially popular herbs section." Libr J

Lewington, Anna

Plants for people; foreword by Anita Roddick. Oxford Univ. Press 1990 232p il $41.75   **581.6**

1. Economic botany

ISBN 0-19-520840-4   LC 90-52979

This book "traces the use of plants in cosmetics, foods, buildings, furniture, medicine, transportation, and recreation. Easy to read and entertaining, it has practical, scientific information along with beautiful drawings and/or photographs of the plants. . . . A competently done book that will fill a gap in many high school collections." SLJ

Westbrooks, Randy G., 1953-

Poisonous plants of eastern North America; by Randy G. Westbrooks, James W. Preacher. University of S.C. Press 1986 xx, 226p il $21.95
581.6

1. Poisonous plants

ISBN 0-87249-442-X   LC 86-1669

This guide examines native and cultivated plants that are poisonous to humans, either by ingestion or by skin contact. Color photographs and concise descriptions as well as information on toxicity and symptoms is provided

Includes bibliography

582.13   Herbaceous flowering plants

Coffey, Timothy

The history and folklore of North American wildflowers; foreword by Stephen Foster. Facts on File 1993 xxiv, 356p il $40   **582.13**

1. Wild flowers 2. Economic botany 3. Medical botany

ISBN 0-8160-2624-6   LC 92-18392

Also available in paperback from Houghton Mifflin

"Entries discuss about 700 plants from over 90 families. Plants featured were those used by the Indians and/or colonists. Arrangement is by family according to evolutionary development. . . . For each of the entries, basic information includes the common name, the Latin name and its translation, and any vernacular names. One or more paragraphs quote what various writers have observed about the plant." Booklist

"This book brings together a wealth of information that is otherwise scattered throughout many obscure sources." Libr J

Niering, William A.

The Audubon Society field guide to North American wildflowers: eastern region; [by] William A. Niering and Nancy C. Olmstead; visual key by Susan Rayfield and Carol Nehring. Knopf 1979 863p il $19   **582.13**

1. Wild flowers

ISBN 0-394-50432-1   LC 78-20383

"A Chanticleer Press edition"

"Covers the area east of the Rockies and east of the Big Bend area of Texas to the Atlantic. Color photographs together with family and species descriptions make this a most useful field guide." Sci News

Peterson, Roger Tory, 1908-1996

A field guide to wildflowers of northeastern and north-central North America; a visual approach arranged by color, form, and detail; by Roger Tory Peterson and Margaret McKenny. Houghton Mifflin 1968 xxviii, 420p il map hardcover o.p. paperback available $16.95   **582.13**

1. Wild flowers

ISBN 0-395-18325-1 (pa)

Also available in abridged form in paperback with title: Peterson first guide to wildflowers of northeastern and north-central North America, by Roger Tory Peterson

Peterson, Roger Tory, 1908-1996—*Continued*

"The Peterson field guide series"

A "guide to the most frequently encountered flowering plants of Northeastern and North-central North America. There are 1344 illustrations, many in color, of nearly 1300 species. . . . The material is accurate and the authors have used only a small number of technical terms. This guide is invaluable to those interested in the natural history of eastern North America." Sci Books

Includes glossary

Spellenberg, Richard

The Audubon Society field guide to North American wildflowers: western region; visual key by Susan Rayfield and Carol Nehring. Knopf 1979 862p il $19   **582.13**

1. Wild flowers

ISBN 0-394-50431-3   LC 78-20384

"A Chanticleer Press edition"

This is an illustrated guide to wildflowers found from Alaska through California. Subjects are arranged by color and shape to facilitate identification. More than 600 species are covered in detail with notes on 400 others

Familiar flowers of North America: eastern region; Ann H. Whitman, editor. Knopf 1986 192p il pa $4.95   **582.13**

1. Wild flowers

ISBN 0-394-74843-3   LC 86-045587

Familiar flowers of North America: western region; Ann H. Whitman, editor. Knopf 1986 192p il pa $4.95   **582.13**

1. Wild flowers

ISBN 0-394-74844-1   LC 86-045586

"Chanticleer Press editions. The Audubon Society pocket guides"

"Eighty gorgeous color plates, arranged by the color and shape of the flower, fill the main section of [each of these] truly pocket-size field [guides]. Each entry also includes a line drawing, a description of the plant's habitat and range, and a paragraph explaining its place among other flowers and its folklore or history. . . . Appendices include a brief glossary and an alphabetic and a family index." BAYA Book Rev

582.16   Trees

Collingwood, G. H. (George Harris), 1890-1958

Knowing your trees; by G. H. Collingwood and Warren D. Brush, revised and edited by Devereux Butcher. American Forestry Assn. il maps $9.50   **582.16**

1. Trees—United States

First published 1937. Revised with each printing

"Discusses in detail the characteristics of 188 species of trees that grow in the United States and explains the importance of trees. Photos show winter and summer forms of trees, with detail of leaves, flowers, fruit, and bark. A map for each species shows its distribution; a map of the 10 hardiness zones is on the inside front cover." Wynar. Guide to Ref Books for Sch Media Cent. 3d edition

Familiar trees of North America: eastern region; Ann H. Whitman, editor; Jerry F. Franklin, John Farrand, Jr., consultants. Knopf 1986 192p il pa $9   **582.16**

1. Trees—North America

ISBN 0-394-74851-4   LC 86-045585

Familiar trees of North America: western region; Ann H. Whitman, editor; Jerry F. Franklin, John Farrand, Jr., consultants. Knopf 1986 192p il pa $9   **582.16**

1. Trees—North America

ISBN 0-394-74852-2   LC 86-045584

"Chanticleer Press editions. The Audubon Society pocket guides"

Each of these pocket field guides covers eighty trees commonly found in the region indicated. "Each color plate is accompanied by a black silhouette of the tree and a small photo of its bark as well as a written description of its characteristics, its habitat and range, and its history and uses. . . . Introductory essays and illustrations provide a key to tree identification. Appendices include descriptions of tree families and an index to common and botanical names." BAYA Book Rev

Jonas, Gerald, 1935-

The living earth book of North American trees; foreword by Ed Zahniser. Reader's Digest Assn. 1993 216p il maps $30   **582.16**

1. Trees—North America

ISBN 0-89577-488-7   LC 93-2633

"A Reader's Digest living earth book"

"The first two chapters go over tree ecology, anatomy, and physiology. The rest of the book describes how the pre-Columbian Americans used trees, and then follows the European settlers as they moved across the country, consuming an apparently infinite resource, up through present day conservation efforts and environmental threats to our remaining forests. The information is encyclopedic, over 400 photographs are striking, and the writing style is often elegant." Voice Youth Advocates

Walker, Laurence C., 1924-

Forests; a naturalist's guide to trees and forest ecology. Wiley 1990 288p il (Wiley nature editions) $14.95   **582.16**

1. Trees—United States 2. Forest ecology

ISBN 0-471-52108-6   LC 89-70675

The author "covers the many different species of trees that grow in the U.S. and provides hands-on projects that encourage readers to experience and observe nature directly." Booklist

Includes glossary and bibliography

589.2 Fungi

McKnight, Kent H.
A field guide to mushrooms, North America; [by] Kent H. McKnight and Vera B. McKnight; illustrations by Vera B. McKnight. Houghton Mifflin 1987 429p il $21.95; pa $16.95   **589.2**
1. Mushrooms
ISBN 0-395-42101-2; 0-395-42102-0 (pa)
LC 86-27799
"The Peterson field guide series"
"Sponsored by the National Audubon Society and the National Wildlife Federation"
"More than 500 species [of mushrooms] are described and depicted. . . . Edibility of each species is noted and signified by marginal pictograms both in the text and on the colorplates. . . . Appended: a genial chapter of recipes by Anne Dow, glossary, selected references, and index." Booklist

590.74 Zoological museums, collections, exhibits

Page, Jake
Smithsonian's new zoo. Smithsonian Institution Press 1990 208p il $29.95   **590.74**
1. National Zoological Park (U.S.) 2. Wildlife conservation
ISBN 0-87474-734-1   LC 89-29626
This "volume describes the changing role of zoos in the world as reflected by the Smithsonian's . . . National Zoological Park in Washington, D.C. . . . and its many satellite programs around the world. . . . The book's captivating photography and sometimes casual style help present its important message." Sci Books Films
Includes bibliographical references

Zoo: the modern ark; photographs by Franz Maier; text by Jake Page; preface by Gerald Durrell. Facts on File 1990 190p il $35   **590.74**
1. Zoos
ISBN 0-8160-2345-X   LC 89-29634
"Ten of the world's finest zoos are highlighted, three of which are in the United States: the Bronx Zoo in New York, the San Diego Zoo, and the National Zoological Park in Washington, D.C. An appendix also lists the major zoos of the world and gives their particular strengths. An excellent source." SLJ
Includes glossary and bibliography

591 Zoology

Bailey, Jill
Animal life; form and function in the animal kingdom. Oxford Univ. Press 1994 160p il (New encyclopedia of science) $35   **591**
1. Zoology
ISBN 0-19-521084-0   LC 94-16055
"This user-friendly encyclopedia provides a wealth of knowledge about the animal world. Topics as varied as the diversity of species, basic life processes, feeding, movement, growth and reproduction, and communication are all given lively, authoritative treatments." Univ Press Books for Public and Second Sch Libr

Dashefsky, H. Steven
Zoology: 49 science fair projects. TAB Bks. 1994 xxi, 169p il (Science fair projects) $19.95; pa $11.95   **591**
1. Zoology—Experiments 2. Science projects
ISBN 0-07-015682-4; 0-07-015683-2 (pa)
LC 94-12060
"The introduction explains how to organize projects and gives brief background material about the animal kingdom and the classification system. Grouped into nine broad areas—behavior, the senses, growth, etc.—each project includes an overview, a list of needed materials, clearly written instructions, hints on drawing conclusions, and suggestions for further study." SLJ
Students "will find a fascinating array of projects, quite varied in difficulty, to choose from." Booklist

Zoology: high school science fair experiments. TAB Bks. 1995 145p il $21.95; pa $12.95   **591**
1. Zoology—Experiments 2. Science projects
ISBN 0-07-015686-7; 0-07-015687-5 (pa)
LC 94-29631
"Dashefsky offers 20 experiments about human and nonhuman form of life. . . . Helpful chapters on the scientific method, zoology basics, and research tips set the stage nicely for the experiments, which fall into four categories: people-related, biocides, animal lives, and animals and the environment." Booklist
Includes glossary and bibliography

Hidden worlds of wildlife; prepared by the Special Publications Division, National Geographic Society. National Geographic Soc. 1990 199p il map $16   **591**
1. Animals
ISBN 0-87044-791-2   LC 90-13348
This book describes wildlife in various remote habitats around the world, including Namibia, the American tropics, the Yukon, New Guinea, New Zealand and the Antarctic
Includes bibliography

The **Illustrated** encyclopedia of wildlife; wildlife consultant, Mary Corliss Pearl. Grey Castle Press; distributed by Encyclopaedia Britannica Educ. Corp. 1991 15v il maps $495   **591**
1. Zoology
ISBN 1-55905-052-7   LC 90-3750
First published 1989 in the United Kingdom
Contents: v1-5 The mammals; v6-8 The birds; v9 Reptiles and amphibians; v10 The fishes; v11-14 The invertebrates; v15 The invertebrates and index
"Organized systematically by zoological classification, the set is divided by class. . . . Each chapter covers anatomy, behavior, habitat, and evolution and is profusely illustrated with full-color photographs and drawings which highlight the behaviors discussed in the text." SLJ
"As a comprehensive source on international wildlife, this set has wide appeal for both students and adults. The scope of the set is broader than is implied by the title." Booklist

591.1 Physiology of animals

Waterman, Talbot H. (Talbot Howe), 1914-
Animal navigation. Scientific Am. Lib. 1989
243p il maps $32.95   **591.1**
1. Animal locomotion 2. Animals—Migration
ISBN 0-7167-5024-4   LC 88-15811
This discussion of animal migration and navigation
"includes both invertebrates and vertebrates. . . . The diversity of organisms is paralleled by discussions of the
multiplicity of navigational aids, such as biological
clocks, magnetic fields, memory and neural maps, and
polar space sense. The many graphs, charts, and color
photographs are breathtaking." Choice
Includes bibliography

591.3 Development and maturation of animals

The Encyclopedia of animal evolution; edited by
R.J. Berry and A. Hallam. Facts on File 1987
144p il maps o.p.   **591.3**
1. Evolution 2. Fossils
LC 87-8940
"An Equinox book"
This volume discusses "paleontology, the origin of
life, homology, adaptation, mechanisms of evolution, humankind and evolution, and controversies about evolution." Choice
"High-school and college biology students will find it
a useful supplement for clarifying puzzling concepts. A
glossary of scientific terms plus a carefully selected bibliography of additional readings also help to make this a
useful book." Sci Books Films

Parker, Steve
Animal babies; a habitat-by-habitat guide to how
wild animals grow. Rodale Press 1993 176p il
maps $35   **591.3**
1. Animal babies
ISBN 0-87596-595-4   LC 93-28287
The author "presents by habitat 55 species of animals.
. . . Nine habitats . . . are considered, and each section
includes a map indicating the species covered and where
they are located. For each species, Parker devotes two
pages, offering clear definitions, high-quality illustrations,
and boxed 'Factfiles' that summarize key information
about each animal baby." Libr J

591.4 Anatomy and morphology of animals

Animal anatomy on file; by the Diagram Group.
Facts on File 1990 unp $155   **591.4**
1. Comparative anatomy
ISBN 0-8160-2244-5   LC 89-29772
This looseleaf volume "contains 250 photocopiable
charts and diagrams of the major divisions of the animal
kingdom. . . . The diagramatic plates illustrate the external form, the skeleton, various body systems, muscles,

and major organs. . . . Almost 50 species of animals are
illustrated, including the bat, cat, dog, dolphin, pigeon,
kangaroo, and pig. Biology students doing reports will
find the book useful. Art students also may find it helpful when they need a really clear external view of a particular animal." SLJ

Berman, William
How to dissect; exploring with probe and
scalpel. 4th ed. Arco 1984 223p il hardcover o.p.
paperback available $11   **591.4**
1. Dissection 2. Anatomy
ISBN 0-671-76342-3 (pa)   LC 83-27510
First published 1978
"This 'how-to' book covers the dissection of 11 commonly used organisms—six invertebrates, four chordates,
and an angiosperm. The introductory chapter explains the
various dissecting tools and important technical terms.
The remaining chapters supply background information
on the organism to be dissected, materials needed, and
the protocol for dissection." Sci Teach

591.5 Ecology of animals

Adams, Douglas, 1952-
Last chance to see; [by] Douglas Adams and
Mark Carwardine. Harmony Bks. 1991 220p il $20
591.5
1. Endangered species
ISBN 0-517-58215-5   LC 90-42756
Also available in paperback from Ballantine Bks.
This volume recounts the authors' worldwide expeditions in search of endangered species in their native habitats. The komodo dragon, northern white rhinoceros,
mountain gorilla, kakapo, baiji dolphin, and rodrigues
fruit bat are described

Agosta, William C.
Chemical communication; the language of
pheromones. Scientific Am. Lib. 1992 179p il
$32.95   **591.5**
1. Animal communication
ISBN 0-7167-5036-8   LC 92-9412
This work "covers organisms from water molds to humans and informs readers of the diverse ways chemicals
are used for communication—as sex attractants, in aggre-
gation, in egg laying, and more. . . . The writing is clear
and lively, the illustrations are helpful and attractive.
. . . The book is excellent overall and should appeal to
the advanced high school student, the interested lay reader, and educators of all kinds." Sci Books Films
Includes glossary and bibliography

Benyus, Janine M.

Beastly behaviors; a zoo lover's companion: what makes whales whistle, cranes dance, pandas turn somersaults, and crocodiles roar: a watcher's guide to how animals act and why; illustrations by Juan Carlos Barberis. Addison-Wesley 1992 366p il hardcover o.p. paperback available $15.95

591.5

1. Animal behavior 2. Zoos
ISBN 0-201-62482-6 (pa)   LC 92-5381

This "guide details the physical characteristics and basic behaviors . . . of more than 20 captive animals, such as elephants, whales, flamingos, and crocodiles." Booklist

"This is one of the best books published on animal behavior for the general reader. . . . [It] is highly recommended for its ability to convey concise yet readable information." Libr J

Includes bibliography

Bergman, Charles

Wild echoes: encounters with the most endangered animals in North America. McGraw-Hill 1990 322p il o.p.; Alaska Northwest Bks. paperback available $12.95   **591.5**

1. Endangered species
ISBN 0-88240-404-0 (pa)   LC 89-12271

The author "uses accounts of endangered species as a way of looking at how humans perceive their position in nature. He considers the cases of wolves, California condors, Florida panthers, manatees, and whales. . . . In general this is a thoughful work that asks important questions. . . . Appended: list of extinctions in the U.S. and its territories, list of relevant organizations, select bibliography." Booklist

Endangered wildlife of the world. Marshall Cavendish 1993 11v il maps set $399.95 **591.5**

1. Endangered species—Dictionaries 2. Wildlife conservation—Dictionaries
ISBN 1-85435-489-2   LC 92-14974

"This encyclopedia profiles animal species listed as either 'endangered,' 'threatened,' or 'vulnerable' by both the U.S. Fish and Wildlife Service's Endangered Species List and the International Union for the Conservation of Nature and Natural Resources' 'Red List.' . . . Each entry lists the species' common and scientific name and reports size, diet, longevity, habitat, range, and other facts, while a narrative essay further describes the species and efforts to conserve it." Libr J

"The set is visually attractive, the information is as complete as possible, and the text is readable and well presented. . . . A solid, easily used reference." Booklist

The **Grolier** world encyclopedia of endangered species. Grolier Educ. Corp. 1993 10v il maps lib bdg set $339   **591.5**

1. Endangered species—Dictionaries 2. Wildlife conservation—Dictionaries
ISBN 0-7172-7192-7   LC 92-54833

Revised, updated, and redesigned from a Japanese edition published 1988

Contents: v1-2 Africa; v3-4 Asia; v5 North America; v6-7 South America; v8 Oceania; v9 Oceania, Europe; v10 Index

"Describes over 600 species threatened with extinction, and provides information on where, when, and why each species is in danger, and what measures, if any, have been taken or are planned to defend it." Publisher's note

"A major feature of the work is the more than 700 color photographs ranging in size from a quarter-page to double-page spreads. Every attempt was made to photograph the species in its native habitat. The pictures are clear; the colors, vibrant." Booklist

Hart, Stephen

The language of animals; foreword by Franz B.M. de Waal. Holt & Co. 1996 126p il (Scientific American focus book) $22.50; pa $9.95   **591.5**

1. Animal communication
ISBN 0-8050-3839-6; 0-8050-3840-X (pa)

LC 95-34585

This study of animal communication examines "the dancing of bees and the sound of crickets, schooling fish, birdsong and elephant song, dolphin research, and the reported progress made with chimps, gorillas, and other primates." Publisher's note

"This is an easy, anecdotal introduction with plenty of factoids and some interesting details on how experiments in animal behavior are constructed." Publ Wkly

Includes bibliographical references

Masson, J. Moussaieff (Jeffrey Moussaieff), 1941-

When elephants weep; the emotional lives of animals; [by] Jeffrey Moussaieff Masson and Susan McCarthy. Delacorte Press 1995 xxiii, 291p il $23.95; pa $13.95   **591.5**

1. Animal intelligence 2. Animal behavior
ISBN 0-385-31425-6; 0-385-31428-0 (pa)

LC 94-23819

The authors gather "the evidence to date for the existence of emotions and, hence, something approaching human consciousness in animals." Booklist

"An excellent resource in psychology, this title will also be a useful addition for animal research. Its clear and conversational style makes it interesting for general readers as well." SLJ

Includes bibliographical references

Murie, Olaus Johan, 1889-1963

A field guide to animal tracks; text and illustrations by Olaus J. Murie. 2nd ed. Houghton Mifflin 1975 c1974 xxi, 375p il $24.95; pa $15.95

591.5

1. Animal tracks
ISBN 0-395-19978-6; 0-395-18323-5 (pa)
"The Peterson field guide series"
First published 1954

"Murie's handbook is recognized as the classic work on the subject. . . . The illustrated guide describes the tracks, droppings, and marks left on bones and leaves by an army of wild animals—bats, bears, rabbits, reptiles, moles, weasels, and others. A fascinating collection of miscellaneous information about the habits of these creatures is part of the descriptive text." Wynar. Ref Books in Paperb, 2d edition

The **Oxford** companion to animal behavior; edited by David McFarland; foreword by Niko Tinbergen. Oxford Univ. Press 1982 c1981 657p il $52.25   **591.5**
1. Animal behavior
ISBN 0-19-866120-7   LC 82-80431
This work contains over 200 articles written by specialists for laymen on physical and psychological aspects of animal behavior, on animals' relations to each other, to their environment and to man, and on the study of their behavior. Only a few personal entries for important scientists, such as Darwin, Lorenz, and Pavlov, are included. Length of entries ranges from a few paragraphs to several pages
"An excellent source of basic information on animal behavior." Topical Ref Books
Includes bibliography

Patent, Dorothy Hinshaw
How smart are animals? Harcourt Brace Jovanovich 1990 189p il $17.95   **591.5**
1. Animal intelligence
ISBN 0-15-236770-5   LC 89-24581
Discusses recent research on levels of intelligence in both wild and domestic animals
"A focused, objective work about animal intelligence, stressing the difficulties of first defining and then measuring it. . . . For young scientists or students looking for research paper ideas, this book is an excellent starting point to pique curiosity about animal learning studies." SLJ
Includes glossary and bibliography

Robinson, Michael
Zoo animals; [by] Michael H. Robinson, David Challinor, with Holly Webber. Macmillan 1995 256p il maps (Smithsonian guides) $24.95; pa $18   **591.5**
1. Habitat (Ecology) 2. Animals 3. Zoos
ISBN 0-02-860406-7; 0-02-860407-5 (pa)
                    LC 94-48288
"A Latimer book"
"The first section of the book explores animal communities and introduces key concepts—such as biosphere as a system, food chains, competition and predation, and symbiosis. It also traces the evolution of zoos, from the first assemblages of barred cages to today's modern zoos that create naturalistic environments to house animals. The seven following chapters profile animals by habitat. . . . Each section explores animal behavior in the wild, and the relationships of species with one another." Publisher's note
Includes glossary and bibliography

591.6 Economic zoology

Nichol, John, 1939-
Bites and stings; the world of venomous animals. Facts on File 1989 160p il $21.50 **591.6**
1. Poisonous animals
ISBN 0-8160-2233-X   LC 89-32853
"Topics covered include the natural history of venomous animals, venoms and antivenoms, venomous animals

and religion, snake charmers, venomous animals in the modern world, bites and stings, and conservation. . . . In addition to thoroughly covering reptiles, the author does a commendable job of covering all other major groups of animals with venomous species." Sci Books Films
Includes bibliography

591.9 Geographic treatment of animals

Stouffer, Marty
Marty Stouffer's wild America. Times Bks. 1988 392p il $30   **591.9**
1. Animals—North America
ISBN 0-8129-1610-7   LC 87-26564
This work "focuses on the habits and habitats of creatures rare and endangered as well as common and familiar. Birth, predation, mating, and death . . . are discussed." Publisher's note

591.92 Marine zoology

Ellis, Richard, 1938-
Monsters of the sea. Knopf 1994 429p il $35
                    591.92
1. Marine animals 2. Sea monsters
ISBN 0-679-40639-5   LC 93-48180
This is an "examination of the natural history and mythology of marine animals. Augmented with facts and 150 illustrations, the book covers everything from the Loch Ness monster, sea serpents and mermaids, to manatees, squid, whales, octopus and shark." Book Rep
"Always striving for accuracy, Ellis has a healthy strain of skepticism and a marvelously wry sense of humor. These qualities shape this thoroughly enjoyable and extensively researched study." Booklist
Includes bibliographical references

The **Encyclopedia** of aquatic life; edited by Keith Banister and Andrew Campbell. Facts on File 1985 349, xxxiiip il $45   **591.92**
1. Marine animals 2. Freshwater animals
ISBN 0-8160-1257-1   LC 85-10245
"An Equinox book"
"The articles are arranged in three main sections: fishes, aquatic invertebrates, and sea mammals. Each section begins with an overview of the animals to be discussed, then individual taxonomic groups are covered." Topical Ref Books

592 Invertebrates

Aaseng, Nathan, 1953-
Invertebrates. Watts 1993 110p il lib bdg $19.14
                    592
1. Invertebrates
ISBN 0-531-12550-5   LC 93-4093
"A Venture book"

Aaseng, Nathan, 1953—— *Continued*

Discusses animals with no backbones, including protozoans, sponges, worms, mollusks, arachnids, and arthropods

"Each chapter contains interesting, pertinent information describing the animals presented and emphasizing the similarities and differences among the species." Book Rep

Includes glossary and bibliography

Animals without backbones; [by] Ralph Buchsbaum [et al.] 3rd ed. University of Chicago Press 1987 572p il $41.25; pa $23.95

592

1. Invertebrates

ISBN 0-226-07873-6; 0-226-07874-4 (pa)

LC 86-7046

First published 1938

An introduction to the structure and behavior of "jellyfishes, corals, flatworms, squids, starfishes, spiders, grasshoppers, and the other invertebrates that make up ninety-seven percent of the animal kingdom. . . . Eschewing pure morphology, the authors use each group of animals to introduce one or more biological principles." Publisher's note

Includes bibliography

Meinkoth, Norman August, 1913-

The Audubon Society field guide to North American seashore creatures; [by] Norman A. Meinkoth. Knopf 1981 799p il maps flexible bdg $19

592

1. Invertebrates 2. Marine biology

ISBN 0-394-51993-0

LC 81-80828

"A Chanticleer Press edition. The Audubon Society field guide series"

This "unique field guide covers some 850 marine invertebrate animals living in or around the shallow waters of the temperate seacoasts of the United States and Canada. Excellent color photographs are grouped at the beginning of the book, followed by text that gives, for each animal, a short description, common and scientific names, habitat, range, and comments." Malinowsky. Best Sci & Technol Ref Books for Young People

594   Mollusks and mollusk-like animals

Abbott, R. Tucker (Robert Tucker), 1919-1995

A field guide to shells; Atlantic and Gulf coasts and the West Indies; [by] R. Tucker Abbott and Percy A. Morris; photographs by R. Tucker Abbott. 4th ed. Houghton Mifflin 1995 xxxiii, 350p il $26.95; pa $16.95

594

1. Shells 2. Mollusks

ISBN 0-395-69780-8; 0-395-69779-4 (pa)

LC 94-14421

"The Peterson field guide series"

First published 1947 under the authorship of Percy A. Morris with title: A field guide to the shells of our Atlantic Coast

Sponsored by the National Audubon Society, the National Wildlife Federation and the Roger Tory Peterson Institute

"The introduction discusses how pollution and habitat destruction have changed the practices of collectors in order to protect species. It continues with tips on how and where to collect, preparation for display, arrangement, and labeling of shells. An explanation of nomenclature rules follows, and commonalities of mollusks are discussed. The species, 780 in number, are described in clear text. . . . Color plates visually depict the shells and clarify the detailed text descriptions." Am Ref Books Annu, 1996

Includes glossary and bibliography

Douglass, Jackie Leatherbury

Peterson first guide to shells of North America; illustrations by John Douglass. Houghton Mifflin 1989 128p il pa $4.95

594

1. Shells

ISBN 0-395-49604-7

LC 88-32884

"Shell collectors will enjoy the basic descriptions of shell types. Douglass has included the 'most colorful, not necessarily the most common, shells.' . . . Filled with precise color drawings and concise identification information." Booklist

Morris, Percy A.

A field guide to Pacific coast shells; including shells of Hawaii and the Gulf of California. 2d ed rev and enl. Houghton Mifflin 1974 c1966 xxxiii, 279p il $21.95; pa $15.95

594

1. Shells 2. Mollusks

ISBN 0-395-08029-0; 0-395-18322-7 (pa)

"The Peterson field guide series"

First published 1952 with title: A field guide to shells of the Pacific coast and Hawaii

The book is divided into three parts. The first part covers the marine shells occurring from Alaska to southern California; the second includes the Gulf of California; and the third part deals with the shells of Hawaii

Includes glossary and bibliography

Wye, Kenneth R.

The encyclopedia of shells. Facts on File 1991 288p il $45

594

1. Shells

ISBN 0-8160-2702-1

LC 91-12191

"Over 1000 types of shells are illustrated in color photographs. . . . Distribution, habitat depth, and relative availability to collectors are explained in descriptions. Coverage is worldwide with extensive representation from the Far East, including many shells rarely seen by casual shell collectors." Libr J

595.4   Arachnids

Hillyard, P. D.

The book of the spider; from arachnophobia to the love of spiders; by Paul Hillyard. Random House 1996 c1994 218p il $25

595.4

1. Spiders

ISBN 0-679-40881-9

First published 1994 in the United Kingdom

Hillyard, P. D.—*Continued*

The author "discusses the spider in folklore, literature, history, and science. . . . There are chapters on arachnophobia, spider venom and bites, webs and silk, and conservation. A chapter on folklore, myths, and literature includes excerpts from the Bible, Shakespeare, Walt Whitman, E.B. White (*Charlotte's Web*), and many others." Libr J

Includes bibliographical references

595.7   Insects

Arnett, Ross H., Jr.

Simon and Schuster's guide to insects; by Ross H. Arnett, Jr., and Richard L. Jacques, Jr. Simon & Schuster 1981 511p il hardcover o.p. paperback available $15   **595.7**

1. Insects

ISBN 0-671-25014-0 (pa)   LC 80-29485

"A Fireside book"

This field guide identifies 350 insect species found in North America. Entries include information about the habits and biology of each species, as well as the scientific and common names of the species and its impact on the environment. Also included is a history of the study of insects, and instructions for collecting insects

Includes glossary

Berenbaum, May R.

Bugs in the system; insects and their impact on human affairs. Addison-Wesley 1995 377p il $25; pa $15   **595.7**

1. Insects

ISBN 0-201-62499-0; 0-201-40824-4 (pa)

    LC 94-14032

"Helix books"

The author describes "both the good and bad aspects of the interaction between humans and insects, but the focus is on the good." Publisher's note

"A book written with imagination, humor, and skill, and one that will be excellent for assignments." SLJ

Includes bibliographical references

Borror, Donald Joyce, 1907-1988

A field guide to the insects of America north of Mexico; by Donald J. Borror and Richard E. White; color and shaded drawings by Richard E. White; line drawings by the authors. Houghton Mifflin 1970 404p il hardcover o.p. paperback available $17   **595.7**

1. Insects

ISBN 0-395-18523-8 (pa)

Also available in abridged form in paperback with title: Peterson first guide to insects of North America, by Christopher W. Leahy

"The Peterson field guide series"

This book aids in the "identification of the more common of the 88,000 species that have been identified in North America. . . . The last part of the book consists of insect orders with descriptions of the order and the families in them." Sci Books

The **Encyclopedia** of insects; edited by Christopher O'Toole. Facts on File 1986 141p il $29.95   **595.7**

1. Insects

ISBN 0-8160-1358-6   LC 85-29226

"An Equinox book"

"The emphasis is placed on recent advances in our understanding of the ecology, behavior, morphology, and evolution of each group. Excellent color photographs and illustrations accompany the text. All species are identified by family and scientific name as well as common name." Choice

Includes glossary and bibliography

Hoyt, Erich, 1950-

The earth dwellers; adventures in the land of ants. Simon & Schuster 1996 319p il $24; pa $13   **595.7**

1. Wilson, Edward O., 1929- 2. Brown, William L. 3. Ants

ISBN 0-684-81086-7; 0-684-83045-0 (pa)

    LC 95-45885

"A description of the life cycles of several species of ants found at La Selva Biological Station in Costa Rica is combined with biographical sketches of myrmecologists William L. Brown . . . and Edward O. Wilson." SLJ

"An informative and entertaining account of ant societies and the scientists who study them." Publ Wkly

Includes bibliographical references

Milne, Lorus Johnson, 1912-

The Audubon Society field guide to North American insects and spiders; [by] Lorus and Margery Milne; visual key by Susan Rayfield. Knopf 1980 989p il flexible bdg $19   **595.7**

1. Insects 2. Spiders

ISBN 0-394-50763-0   LC 80-7620

"A Chanticleer Press edition. The Audubon Society field guide series"

The authors "have based their field guide on 702 excellent color photographs (75 of which are of spiders and other arachnids). In addition to some general information, the text (two thirds of the book) is made up of brief comments on each kind of arthropod pictured." Choice

Includes glossary

Pyle, Robert Michael

The Audubon Society field guide to North American butterflies; visual key by Carol Nehring and Jane Opper. Knopf 1981 916p il $19   **595.7**

1. Butterflies

ISBN 0-394-51914-0   LC 80-84240

"A Chanticleer Press edition. The Audubon Society field guide series"

This guide "introduces more than 600 species of North American butterfly, including those native to the Hawaiian Islands. A section of brilliant color plates (more than 1,000 of them) featuring butterflies in their natural habitats, follows a general introduction and notes on text organization and use." Booklist

Includes glossary

Taylor, Barbara, 1954-
Butterflies & moths; written by Barbara Taylor.
DK Pub. 1996 160p il maps pa $6.95   **595.7**
1. Butterflies 2. Moths
ISBN 0-7894-0605-5   LC 95-42177
"DK pockets"
Provides information on the behavior, appearance,
habitats, and identification of butterflies and moths in
various environments
Includes glossary

Waldbauer, Gilbert
Insects through the seasons. Harvard Univ. Press
1996 289p il $24.95   **595.7**
1. Moths
ISBN 0-674-45488-X   LC 95-35171
"Waldbauer uses the yearly cycle of the cecropia moth
as a base to which he periodically returns while presenting an impressive array of the tactics the moth's fellow
insects and arthropod relatives use to live and thrive."
Booklist
"The scientific information is excellent and the writing
is fascinating." Sci Books Films
Includes bibliographical references

White, Richard E.
A field guide to the beetles of North America;
text and illustrations by Richard E. White.
Houghton Mifflin 1983 368p il hardcover o.p.
paperback available $16.95   **595.7**
1. Beetles
ISBN 0-395-33953-7 (pa)   LC 83-60
"The Peterson field guide series"
The author "supplies general information on collecting, preparing, and identifying beetles, as well as discussions of beetle structure, growth, development, and their
scientific classification. There follows a text-and-picture
identification guide arranged by suborder and superfami-
ly. A section of color plates is also included." Booklist
Includes glossary and bibliography

Wootton, Anthony, 1935-
Insects of the world. Facts on File 1984 224p il
$25.95   **595.7**
1. Insects
ISBN 0-87196-991-2   LC 83-25425
The text includes "insect evolution, distribution, morphology, metamorphosis, reproduction, coloration, and
migration. The final chapter covers nomenclature and
classification." Sci Books Films
"Lavish illustrations and an easy conversational style
communicate much detailed information that will be useful to high school biology students." Booklist
Includes glossary and bibliography

596   Vertebrates

Aaseng, Nathan, 1953-
Vertebrates. Watts 1993 112p il lib bdg $19.14
                                          596
1. Vertebrates
ISBN 0-531-12551-3   LC 93-13391
"A Venture book"

Examines fish, reptiles, mammals, and other animals
with backbones, noting both their similarities and their
differences
"Well written and readable." SLJ
Includes glossary and bibliography

597   Cold-blooded vertebrates.
Fishes

The **Audubon** Society field guide to North
American fishes, whales, and dolphins; [by]
Herbert T. Boschung, Jr. [et al.]; visual key by
Carol Nehring and Jordan Verner. Knopf 1983
848p il flexible bdg $19   **597**
1. Fishes—North America 2. Whales 3. Dolphins
ISBN 0-394-53405-0   LC 83-47962
"A Chanticleer Press edition. The Audubon Society
field guide series"
This guide has "a first section containing excellent
photographs of 529 marine and freshwater fishes and 45
cetacean species found in or near North America north
of Mexico, and a second section giving brief descriptions
of each species. . . . The well-organized and well-
written text includes descriptions of physical features,
habitat, range (generally with a small map), and related
or similar species." Choice
Includes glossary

Eschmeyer, William N.
A field guide to Pacific coast fishes of North
America; from the Gulf of Alaska to Baja
California; [by] William N. Eschmeyer, Earl S.
Herald; illustrations by Howard Hammann;
Katherine P. Smith, associate illustrator. Houghton
Mifflin 1983 336p il map $21.95; pa $16.95
                                          597
1. Fishes—North America
ISBN 0-395-26873-7; 0-395-33188-9 (pa)
                                      LC 82-11989
"The Peterson field guide series"
"Sponsored by the National Audubon Society and Na-
tional Wildlife Federation"
"A comprehensive, well-illustrated, nearly jargon-free
field guide that describes the more than 500 marine fish
species likely to be found in depths, less than 650 feet,
from the Gulf of Alaska to Baja California." Sci Books
Films
Includes bibliography

Filisky, Michael, 1947-
Peterson first guide to fishes of North America;
illustrated by Sarah Landry. Houghton Mifflin
1989 128p il pa $4.95   **597**
1. Fishes—North America
ISBN 0-395-50219-5   LC 88-32887
"For those who enjoy fishing, scuba diving, or visiting
aquariums, Filisky's is a helpful introduction to common
fish species and fish shapes. . . . Filled with precise col-
or drawings and concise identification information."
Booklist

Page, Lawrence M.
A field guide to freshwater fishes: North America north of Mexico; [by] Lawrence M. Page, Brooks M. Burr; illustrations by Eugene C. Beckham III, John Parker Sherrod, Craig W. Ronto. Houghton Mifflin 1991 432p il maps $24.95; pa $16.95   **597**
1. Fishes—North America
ISBN 0-395-35307-6; 0-395-53933-1 (pa)
         LC 90-42049
"The Peterson field guide series"
Sponsored by the National Audubon Society, the National Wildlife Federation, and the Roger Tory Peterson Institute
This guide "covers all 790 species known in North America north of Mexico. Over 700 illustrations, most in color, show identifying marks. Also includes 377 distribution maps and additional line drawings of key details." Publisher's note
Includes glossary and bibliography

597.6   Amphibians

Behler, John L.
The Audubon Society field guide to North American reptiles and amphibians; [by] John L. Behler, F. Wayne King. Knopf 1979 743p il flexible bdg $19   **597.6**
1. Reptiles 2. Amphibians
ISBN 0-394-50824-6   LC 79-2217
"A Chanticleer Press edition. The Audubon Society field guide series"
"Photographs of the reptiles and amphibians are arranged in six main groups: salamanders, frogs and toads, crocodilians, turtles, lizards, and snakes, then subarranged by color. The marine turtles of coastal waters are also included. The text describes each of the species and gives common and scientific names, description, voice, breeding, habitat, subspecies, range, and descriptive comments." Malinowsky. Best Sci & Technol Ref Books for Young People

Conant, Roger, 1909-
A field guide to reptiles and amphibians, eastern and central North America; [by] Roger Conant and Joseph T. Collins; illustrated by Isabelle Hunt Conant and Tom R. Johnson. 3rd ed. Houghton Mifflin 1991 450p il maps $24.95; pa $16.95   **597.6**
1. Reptiles 2. Amphibians
ISBN 0-395-37022-1; 0-395-58389-6 (pa)
         LC 90-21053
"The Peterson field guide series"
First published 1958 with title: A field guide to reptiles and amphibians of the United States and Canada east of the 100th meridian
Sponsored by the National Audubon Society, the National Wildlife Federation, and the Roger Tory Peterson Institute
This guide describes 595 species and subspecies. Full-color illustrations and drawings highlight key details and over 300 distribution maps show ranges
Includes glossary and bibliography

Peterson first guide to reptiles and amphibians; [by] Roger Conant, Robert C. Stebbins, Joseph T. Collins. Houghton Mifflin 1992 128p il pa $4.95   **597.6**
1. Reptiles 2. Amphibians
ISBN 0-395-62232-8   LC 91-33016
This is a guide to identification of reptile and amphibian species
This is "easy to use. The information is accurate and easy to understand. . . . Useful for browsing as well as for identification in the field." Voice Youth Advocates

The **Encyclopedia** of reptiles and amphibians; edited by Tim R. Halliday and Kraig Adler. Facts on File 1986 143p il $27.95   **597.6**
1. Reptiles 2. Amphibians
ISBN 0-8160-1359-4   LC 85-29249
"An Equinox book"
"This encyclopedia includes entries for representative species of all the families in Reptilia and Amphibia. The descriptions are very accurate and concise, with excellent illustrations. Range maps are included." Malinowsky. Best Sci & Technol Ref Books for Young People
Includes glossary and bibliography

Stebbins, Robert C. (Robert Cyril), 1915-
A field guide to western reptiles and amphibians; text and illustrations by Robert C. Stebbins. 2nd ed rev. Houghton Mifflin 1985 336p il hardcover o.p. paperback available $16.95   **597.6**
1. Reptiles 2. Amphibians
ISBN 0-395-38253-X (pa)   LC 84-25125
"The Peterson field guide series"
First published 1966
Sponsored by the National Audubon Society and National Wildlife Federation
"Field marks of all species in western North America, including Baja California." Title page
This field guide features over 240 species, most accompanied by illustration and distribution map. Coverage includes Baja California and information on reptile reproduction
Includes bibliography

597.8   Anura (Salientia)

Mattison, Christopher
Frogs & toads of the world. Facts on File 1987 191p il $24.95   **597.8**
1. Frogs 2. Toads
ISBN 0-8160-1602-X   LC 87-15615
"Chapters review classification, morphology, physiology, ecology (including interaction with man), and reproductive strategies. The central theme throughout is the amazing diversity of Anuran life styles." Sci Books Films
Includes bibliography

597.9 Reptiles

Dow, Lesley
Alligators and crocodiles. Facts on File 1990
68p il maps (Great creatures of the world) $17.95
597.9
1. Alligators 2. Crocodiles
ISBN 0-8160-2273-9   LC 90-31570
Discusses the biological features of alligators and
crocodiles, their habitats, lifestyles, and history
The book is "highlighted by abundant clear, full-color
(and, at times, full-page) photographs and excellent
drawings, interspersed with diagrams and maps." SLJ

Ernst, Carl H.
Turtles of the world; [by] Carl H. Ernst and
Roger W. Barbour. Smithsonian Institution Press
1989 313p il hardcover o.p. paperback available
$24.95   597.9
1. Turtles
ISBN 1-56098-212-8 (pa)   LC 88-29727
"The book covers 12 families, 87 genera, and 257
species in a logical and systematic order. In order to use
the many identification keys to the families, genera, and
species, the text provides discussion and illustrations of
the bones and the scutes of the plastron and carapace as
well as the skull. The material is covered thoroughly."
Sci Books Films
Includes glossary and bibliography

Mattison, Christopher
The encyclopedia of snakes; [by] Chris
Mattison. Facts on File 1995 256p il maps $35
597.9
1. Snakes
ISBN 0-8160-3072-3   LC 95-2501
This study of snakes covers "their taxonomy, mor-
phology, habitats, diet, reproduction, and protective
mechanisms. Especially interesting are the discussions of
the snake's relationship with humans in myth and reality.
Color photographs illustrate the discussion throughout."
Booklist
Includes bibliographical references

Mehrtens, John M.
Living snakes of the world in color. Sterling
1987 480p il $65   597.9
1. Snakes
ISBN 0-8069-6460-X   LC 87-9932
This book presents more than 500 "color photographs
of captive snakes, each with a one-page description of
the reptile's geographic range, ecological niche, and captive care requirements. Special precautions are noted for
venomous species." Libr J
"This is an interesting introduction to the living snakes
of the world. . . . The information is not only accurate
but well presented." Sci Books Films
Includes glossary

Snakes; a natural history; edited by Roland
Bauchot. Sterling 1994 220p il maps $39.95
597.9
1. Snakes
ISBN 0-8069-0654-5   LC 93-43892
This volume discusses "the biology, ecology, and geographic extent of serpents, including their physiology,
evolutionary trends, reproduction, unique mode of locomotion, habitat, and lifestyle. . . . Unwarranted fear of
snakes is allayed, snake legends are explained, and human relations with snakes down through the ages are
critically reviewed." Booklist
Includes bibliographical references

598 Birds

The **Atlas** of bird migration; tracing the great
journeys of the world's birds; general editor,
Jonathan Elphick; foreword by Thomas E.
Lovejoy. Random House 1995 180p il maps $35
598
1. Birds—Migration
ISBN 0-679-43827-0   LC 94-29378
"A Marshall edition"
"About 100 representative species are depicted and every layout consists of a two-page spread devoted to one
of them; an illustration of the bird is backed by a map
showing its nesting and resting sites and its annual cross-
continental flyways. . . . Attractive and informative, this
atlas will appeal to a broad library constituency, from the
student report-writer to the adult binocular-wearer."
Booklist
Includes bibliographical references

Birding; [by] Joseph Forshaw [et al.]; consultant
editor, Terence Lindsey. Time-Life Bks. 1995
c1994 288p il (Nature Company guide) $29.95
598
1. Bird watching
                                      LC 95-8608
"Three introductory chapters cover the basics of avian
biology, attracting birds to one's yard, and field observation techniques. Arranged by habitat, brief descriptive accounts (one or two per page) of about 200 common
North American species make up the bulk of the work."
Libr J
This work is "set apart from the plethora of other
books on the subject by its comprehensiveness, innovative format, and color illustrations." Sci Books Films
Includes glossary and bibliography

Birds of prey; Ian Newton, consulting editor;
illustrations by Tony Pyrzakowski. Facts on File
1990 240p il maps $40   598
1. Birds of prey
ISBN 0-8160-2182-1   LC 90-33303
"Coverage is given to all meat-eating birds (except
owls, which are not considered raptors). . . . Field guide
drawings of all major raptors are provided, with details
about each bird's appearance, size, diet, and range." SLJ
Includes bibliography

Book of North American birds. Reader's Digest Assn. 1990 576p il maps $32.95   **598**
1. Birds—North America
ISBN 0-89577-351-1   LC 89-70261
This book "consists of over 450 page-length species accounts which feature a . . . color painting, a half-page anecdotal narrative essay, a range map, a drawing, plus small sections detailing the bird's identification, habitat, and food. Smaller accounts (three per page) for 117 scarcer birds follow the full-page ones. Appended is a 40-page section with thumbnail sketches of the best birding areas in the United States and Canada." Libr J
Includes bibliography

Brooks, Bruce, 1950-
On the wing; the life of birds: from feathers to flight. Scribner 1989 192p il o.p.   **598**
1. Birds
LC 89-4200
An "introduction to birds that explores many facets of their adaptation and behavior, including flight, nest building, and methods of communication." Booklist
"This attractive, enticing book is a companion to the PBS series *Nature*. . . . Interspersed throughout the text are 150 excellent color photos reinforcing points made by Brooks." Libr J
Includes bibliography

Davis, Lloyd S.
Penguin; a season in the life of the Adélie penguin; recorded in words and photographs by Lloyd Spencer Davis. Harcourt Brace & Co. 1994 76p il $18.95   **598**
1. Penguins 2. Antarctic regions
ISBN 0-15-200070-4   LC 93-36407
Davis "endows an Adélie penguin with a human voice, thereby enabling him to be the spokesperson for his kind and for a land that has no native people to tell its tales. . . . Combined with excellent-quality full-color and black-and-white photographs, the narrative achieves a fine feel for this hostile land and its inhabitants, and ultimately a respect and caring for what will happen to them." SLJ

Ehrlich, Paul R.
The birder's handbook; a field guide to the natural history of North American birds: including all species that regularly breed north of Mexico; [by] Paul R. Ehrlich, David S. Dobkin, Daryl Wheye. Simon & Schuster 1988 xxx, 785p il hardcover o.p. paperback available $17   **598**
1. Birds—North America
ISBN 0-671-65989-8 (pa)   LC 87-32404
This volume contains "basic information on each of the 646 species of birds in North America, enriched by 250 short essays on all aspects of avian behavior and biology. This book is a companion volume to any illustrated field guide." Am Libr
Includes bibliography

Encyclopedia of birds; edited by Christopher M. Perrins and Alex. L.A. Middleton. Facts on File 1985 xxxi, 445p il maps $45   **598**
1. Birds
ISBN 0-8160-1150-8   LC 84-26024
"An Equinox book"
This work "presents an overview of the world's living bird groups. . . . Illustrations are great in number. The full-color drawings are nicely presented, as are the range maps and drawings showing general size compared to humans." Topical Ref Books
Includes glossary and bibliography

Field guide to the birds of North America. 2nd ed. National Geographic Soc. 1987 464p il maps pa $21   **598**
1. Birds—North America
ISBN 0-87044-692-4   LC 86-33249
First published 1983
An identification guide to more than 800 species of North American birds. Arranged in family groups, the information for each species includes a full-color illustration, a range map, common and scientific names, measurement, and a description of plumage, distinctive songs and calls, behavior, abundance, and habitat

Gerrard, Jonathan M., 1947-
The bald eagle; haunts and habits of a wilderness monarch; [by] Jon M. Gerrard and Gary R. Bortolotti. Smithsonian Institution Press 1988 177p il (Smithsonian nature book) hardcover o.p. paperback available $13.95   **598**
1. Bald eagle
ISBN 0-87474-451-2 (pa)   LC 87-26530
Describes the morphology, behavior, flight patterns, hunting, migration, nesting, development, and growth of bald eagles
Includes bibliography

Peterson, Roger Tory, 1908-1996
A field guide to the birds; a completely new guide to all the birds of eastern and central North America; text and illustrations by Roger Tory Peterson; maps by Virginia Marie Peterson. 4th ed, completely rev and enl. Houghton Mifflin 1980 384p il maps $24.95; pa $16.95   **598**
1. Birds—North America
ISBN 0-395-26621-1; 0-395-26619-X (pa)
LC 80-14304
New edition in preparation
Also available CD-ROM version that covers birds throughout North America
"The Peterson field guide series"
First published 1934
"Sponsored by the National Audubon Society and National Wildlife Federation"
This guide to birds found east of the Rocky Mountains contains colored illustrations painted by the author, with description of each species on the facing page. Views of young birds and seasonal variations in plumage are included. Birds are arranged in eight major groups of body shape. There are also 390 colored maps showing summer and winter range

Peterson, Roger Tory, 1908-1996—*Continued*

A field guide to western birds; text and illustrations by Roger Tory Peterson; maps by Virginia Marie Peterson. 3rd ed, completely rev and enl. Houghton Mifflin 1989 432p il maps $22.95; pa $16.95 **598**
1. Birds—West (U.S.)
ISBN 0-395-51749-4; 0-395-51424-X (pa)
LC 89-31517
"The Peterson field guide series"
First published 1941
"A completely new guide to field marks of all species found in North America west of the 100th meridian and north of Mexico." Title page
Sponsored by the National Audubon Society, the National Wildlife Federation, and the Roger Tory Peterson Institute
This guide illustrates over 1,000 birds (700 species) on 165 color plates. In addition, over 400 distribution maps are included

Rosair, David

Photographic guide to the shorebirds of the world; [by] David Rosair, David Cottridge. Facts on File 1995 175p il $29.95 **598**
1. Water birds—Pictorial works
ISBN 0-8160-3309-9
LC 95-2502
First published in the United Kingdom with title: Hamlyn photographic guide to the waders of the world
"The discussion of each species gives the range; the adult breeding, nonbreeding, and juvenile plumage; in-flight characteristics; calls; habits and behavior; and movements. Currently there are 212 recognized species of waders, and all are treated by the authors. There are more than 700 color photographs." Choice
For a fuller review see: Booklist, Feb. 1, 1996
Includes bibliographical references

Savage, Candace, 1949-

Peregrine falcons; foreword by Adrian Forsyth. Sierra Club Bks. 1992 145p il $30; pa $20 **598**
1. Falcons
ISBN 0-87156-504-8; 0-87156-461-0 (pa)
LC 92-2681
This "study of the peregrine includes a map showing the species' worldwide distribution and a history of falconry. The photographs depict every stage in the life history of the peregrine. The dangers of chemical invasion in the food supply of the peregrine and how it has depleted the falcon population and continues to affect man's environment is the main message of this Sierra Club Book. . . . Young adults will be able to use this book for research and they may be captivated by the stunning photographs." Voice Youth Advocates
Includes bibliography

Sparks, John

Owls; their natural and unnatural history; [by] John Sparks and Tony Soper; illustrated by Robert Gillmor. [new rev ed] Facts on File 1989 240p il o.p.; Sterling paperback available $19.95 **598**
1. Owls
ISBN 0-7153-0423-2 (pa)
LC 89-30364
First published 1970 by Taplinger

This book describes the behavior, anatomy, and paleontological history of owls, and includes folklore and ancient verse about owls
A "delightful book for the general audience, replete with . . . superb-quality photographs, easily read print, and enjoyable text extracted from more than 80 sources." Sci Books Films
Includes bibliography

Weiner, Jonathan

The beak of the finch; a story of evolution in our time. Knopf 1994 332p il $27.50; pa $13 **598**
1. Grant, Peter R., 1936- 2. Grant, B. Rosemary 3. Finches 4. Evolution
ISBN 0-679-40003-6; 0-679-73337-X (pa)
LC 93-36755
"This is an account of Peter and Rosemary Grant's research on the microevolutionary modifications that occur in finch beaks as they adapt to environmental changes. Analysis of data collected from 18,000 birds on a Galápagos island over 21 years conclusively demonstrates that the pressures of natural selection are currently altering wild populations." Libr J
"Compelling fare for students with a scientific bent, either for curricular or personal reading." Booklist
Includes bibliographical references

599 Mammals

Burt, William Henry, 1903-1987

A field guide to the mammals; text and maps by William Henry Burt; illus. by Richard Philip Grossenheider. 3d ed. Houghton Mifflin 1976 xxv, 289p il maps $24.95; pa $16.95 **599**
1. Mammals
ISBN 0-395-24082-4; 0-395-24084-0 (pa)
Also available in abridged form in paperback with title: Peterson first guide to mammals of North America, by Peter Alden
"The Peterson field guide series"
First published 1952
"Sponsored by the National Audubon Society and National Wildlife Federation"
"Field marks of all North American species found north of Mexico." Title page
"This field guide covers 380 species of mammals, including whales, dolphins, and porpoises. Each one is described in detail and most are depicted in color photographs and additional black-and-white sketches. Range maps are included. The description includes information on distinguishing marks, habitat, litter size, appearance of young, specimen tracks, and representations of nests." Malinowsky. Best Sci & Technol Ref Books for Young People

The Encyclopedia of mammals; edited by David Macdonald. Facts on File 1984 895, xlviiip il $80 **599**
1. Mammals
ISBN 0-87196-871-1
LC 84-1631
"The 700 entries in this beautifully written encyclopedia cover all of the major species, giving basic evolution-

The Encyclopedia of mammals—*Continued*

ary facts, appearance, social patterns, and environmental concerns. The unique charts show the relative size of each animal compared to man. Other information includes the average body size, gestation period, longevity, and distribution." Malinowsky. Best Sci & Technol Ref Books for Young People

Includes glossary

Grzimek's encyclopedia of mammals. McGraw-Hill 1990 5v il set $583.50   **599**
1. Mammals
ISBN 0-07-909508-9   LC 89-12542
Original German edition, 1988
"Arranged by subclasses and orders; each category includes an introduction, information on phylogeny and evolution of the group, detailed information about many species, and bibliographies. Good for summary accounts of the basic biology of each group and of selected individual species. Excellent photographs." Guide to Ref Books. 11th edition

Mammals of Australia; edited by Ronald Strahan. Smithsonian Institution Press 1996 c1995 756p il maps $75   **599**
1. Mammals
ISBN 1-56098-673-5   LC 95-71108
First published 1983 in Australia with title: Complete book of Australian mammals
This "covers all species of mammals, native and introduced, exclusive of whales, known to have existed in Australia since the arrival of Europeans. . . . Each brief, signed account includes identification, size, habitat, reproduction, conservation, a range map, selected references, and, for nearly all, one or more excellent color photos." Libr J

Includes bibliographical references

Melham, Tom, 1946-
Alaska's wildlife treasures; prepared by the Book Division, National Geographic Society. National Geographic Soc. 1994 200p il $16   **599**
1. Animals 2. Natural history—Alaska
ISBN 0-87044-977-X   LC 94-8008
Text and numerous full-color photographs explore the diversity of Alaska's flora and fauna
Includes bibliographical references

Walker, Ernest P. (Ernest Pillsbury), 1891-1969
Walker's mammals of the world. 5th ed, by Ronald M. Nowak. Johns Hopkins Univ. Press 1991 2v il set $89.95   **599**
1. Mammals
ISBN 0-8018-3970-X   LC 91-27011
First published 1964
"An authoritative, systematic compendium of scientifically reliable information on mammals that attempts to provide a photograph of a living representative of every genus. In this edition, that photo coverage has been greatly expanded, and the text has been completely revised to reflect current scientific knowledge. The first edition concluded with a separately classified bibliographic volume, which the library may wish to retain. In

this fifth edition, specific references include some 3500 titles. A world distribution chart refers to identification and natural history information in the text. A classic work." Ref Sources for Small & Medium-sized Libr. 5th edition

Includes bibliographical references

Whitaker, John O., Jr.
The Audubon Society field guide to North American mammals; [by] John O. Whitaker, Jr.; Robert Elman, text consultant; visual key by Carol Nehring. Knopf 1980 745p il flexible bdg $19
     599
1. Mammals
ISBN 0-394-50762-2   LC 79-3525
"A Chanticleer Press edition. The Audubon Society field guide series"
"This field guide, describing the mammals of North America found north of Mexico, is notable for the use of attractive color photographs to illustrate most species. . . . There is considerable information on the habits of individual species in the text of this compact but substantial volume. . . . It also includes animal distribution maps, lists of diagnostic characters, and notes on habitat." Libr J

Wild animals of North America. rev ed. National Geographic Soc. 1987 406p il (Natural science library)   **599**
1. Mammals
     LC 87-12182
Available in revised printing (1995) $40 (ISBN 0-7922-2958-4)
First published 1960
Discusses the characteristics and evolution of mammals in general, then examines more than 200 common species found in North America. Over 400 color illustrations and 74 maps are included
Includes bibliography

599.4   Bats

Fenton, M. Brock (Melville Brockett), 1943-
Bats. Facts on File 1992 207p il $45   **599.4**
1. Bats
ISBN 0-8160-2679-3   LC 92-4787
"This book discusses the origins of bats, their anatomy, echolocation capabilities, eating habits, social organization, and classification. It also includes chapters on bats and public health, bat conservation, mankind's images of bats, and vampire bats. The many color photographs and illustrations contribute to making this an attractive, interesting, and informative volume." Libr J
Includes bibliography

Hill, John Edwards
Bats; a natural history; [by] John E. Hill and James D. Smith. University of Tex. Press 1984 243p il maps o.p.   **599.4**
1. Bats
     LC 83-51654
"Published in co-operation with the British Museum of Natural History"

Hill, John Edwards—*Continued*

"Chapters cover anatomy, origin and evolution, flight, feeding, reproduction, echolocation, and ecology. . . . [Hill also discusses] bat systematic biology and the relationships of people and bats." Choice

This "is an excellent account for the professional biologist, lay person, and student." Sci Books Films

Includes bibliography

599.5 Cetaceans and sirenians

Bonner, W. Nigel (William Nigel)

Whales of the world; [by] Nigel Bonner. Facts on File 1989 191p il $27.95   **599.5**

1. Whales 2. Dolphins

ISBN 0-8160-1734-4   LC 88-33315

This "survey of the cetacean species—their evolution, behavioral patterns, physical characteristics, and reaction to their environment—also examines . . . such topical issues as the whale's exploitation for scientific research and commercial entertainment, pollution, and commercial fishing and hunting." Booklist

This book "is complete and accurate in its coverage and goes into great depth without being overly technical." Sci Books Films

Includes bibliography

Carwardine, Mark

Whales, dolphins, and porpoises; illustrated by Martin Camm; editorial consultants: Peter Evans, Mason Weinrich. Dorling Kindersley 1995 256p il maps (Eyewitness handbooks) $29.95; flexible bdg $17.95   **599.5**

1. Whales 2. Dolphins 3. Porpoises

ISBN 1-56458-621-9; 1-56458-620-0 (flexible bdg)

    LC 94-33301

This book is "arranged by species. Each entry has a drawing of the animal; drawings of body parts, such as teeth and fins; and a map showing the distribution of the species. Information is given on status, population size, threats to survival, birth and adult weight, and diet. The introduction discusses cetacean behavior and where and how to observe the animals. An identification key helps in distinguishing among various species." Booklist

"A book with efficient organization, concise information, and loads of illustrations." SLJ

Includes bibliographical references

Connor, Richard C.

The lives of whales and dolphins; by Richard C. Connor and Dawn Micklethwaite Peterson. Holt & Co. 1994 233p il maps $25; pa $15.95   **599.5**

1. Whales 2. Dolphins

ISBN 0-8050-1950-2; 0-8050-4565-1 (pa)

    LC 93-46665

At head of title: From the American Museum of Natural History

This is an account of "sea creatures, detailing their habits, movements, and particularly their intelligence and modes of communication. Based on the latest research, the book points out how human behavior is linked to the survival and conservation of these fantastic mammals. A colorful addition to any science collection." SLJ

Hall, Howard

A charm of dolphins; writer & principal photographer, Howard Hall; additional photographers, Frank Balthis [et al.] Silver Burdett Press 1994 43p il (Close up: a focus on nature) $21; pa $7.95   **599.5**

1. Dolphins

ISBN 0-382-24880-5; 0-382-24881-3 (pa)

    LC 94-31820

This illustrated book answers "such questions as What is a dolphin? Where do dolphins live? and Why do dolphins jump? All other aspects are also covered—diving, reproduction, how dolphins communicate, etc. The last part of the book discusses the fact that dolphins are in danger of becoming extinct if certain conditions continue to exist." Sci Books Films

Leatherwood, Stephen

The Sierra Club handbook of whales and dolphins; by Stephen Leatherwood and Randall R. Reeves; illustrated by Larry Foster. Sierra Club Bks. 1983 302p il hardcover o.p. paperback available $18   **599.5**

1. Whales 2. Dolphins

ISBN 0-87156-340-1 (pa)   LC 83-388

An identification guide to 76 species giving names and derivation, special features, description, global distribution and status of endangerment

"Immense in detail and scope, this handbook is virtually an encyclopedia of marine mammals. . . . A fine introduction to the subject." SLJ

Includes bibliography

Paine, Stefani, 1946-

The world of the Arctic whales; belugas, bowheads, and narwhals; photographs by John Ford. Sierra Club Bks. 1995 116p il map $26

    599.5

1. Whales

ISBN 0-87156-378-9   LC 95-1168

"Paine discusses diet, mating, birth, and death, concluding with the historical ecological impact humans have had on the whales from the Inuit fisherman to the wholesale commercial hunters of today. Technical jargon is kept to a minimum, and the author's style is informative and engaging." SLJ

Includes bibliographical references

Whales, dolphins, and porpoises; consulting editors, Richard Harrison, M.M. Bryden; illustrations by Tony Pyrzakowski. Facts on File 1988 240p il $35   **599.5**

1. Whales 2. Dolphins 3. Porpoises

ISBN 0-8160-1977-0   LC 88-11700

This work "covers the distribution, ecology, evolution, and kinds of whales along with their anatomy, adaptations to aquatic environments, reproduction and development, behavior, intelligence, relations with humans in captivity and in the wild, whales in art and in literature, and the International Whaling Commission. The writing is clear and enjoyable. . . . The illustrations are finely executed." Sci Books Films

Includes bibliography

Whales, dolphins, and porpoises; prepared by the Book Division, National Geographic Society. National Geographic Soc. 1995 232p il $40
                                                                 599.5

1. Whales 2. Dolphins 3. Porpoises
ISBN 0-7922-2952-5   LC 95-20916

In this heavily illustrated volume, contributors examine: whale hunting, research and conservation; the habitat of the deep-diving toothed whales; the behavior of humpbacks, grays and baleens; the social structures, intelligence and echolocating abilities of dolphins and porpoises

Includes bibliography

599.6   Paenungulata

Caras, Roger A.
A most dangerous journey; the life of an African elephant; with photographs by the author. Dial Bks. 1995 189p il $15.99   **599.6**
1. Elephants
ISBN 0-8037-1880-2   LC 95-2548

The author "follows the elephant Ndovu, a composite based on Caras' own observations and the research of others, from birth to adulthood—depicting a life filled with natural disasters and deadly encounters with human beings. An ardent conservationist, Caras harshly criticizes poachers and condemns corrupt officials and military officers who profit from ivory." Booklist

"This is a touching and rewarding work that can be read not only for information but also as a great story." SLJ

Chadwick, Douglas H.
The fate of the elephant. Sierra Club Bks. 1992 492p hardcover o.p. paperback available $14
                                                                 599.6

1. Elephants 2. Wildlife conservation
ISBN 0-87156-495-5 (pa)   LC 92-4520

The author "examines the major threats to the survival of the world's largest land mammal in a book filled with facts and anecdotes. Natural history buffs as well as readers concerned about the environment will enjoy this glimpse of the elephant's evolution and impact on global ecology." Booklist
Includes bibliography

599.74   Carnivores

Adamson, Joy, 1910-1980
Born free; a lioness of two worlds. Pantheon Bks. 1987 220p il $11.95; pa $15   **599.74**
1. Lions 2. Kenya—Description
ISBN 0-679-56141-2; 0-394-74635-X (pa)
                                    LC 86-42972

Also available in hardcover from Buccaneer Bks.
A reissue of the title first published 1960

The "story of a lioness who bridged the gulf between two worlds, that of the jungle and of man. The author and her husband, a Kenya game warden, reared a cub to kill and fend for herself when she was returned to the jungle. At the same time they were able to preserve the bond of confidence and affection established with her as a pet." Cincinnati Public Libr

Alderton, David
Foxes, wolves, and wild dogs of the world; photographs by Bruce Tanner. Facts on File 1994 192p il $27.95   **599.74**
1. Foxes 2. Wolves
ISBN 0-8160-2954-7   LC 92-46595

"More than half the book discusses individual species based on their geographical distribution; maps show the locations of the habitats of each group. . . . The text is scientific but easily understood. It would be a good reference book in any high school library that needs a book on the subject." Book Rep
Includes bibliographical references

Wild cats of the world; photographs by Bruce Tanner. Facts on File 1993 192p il maps $25.95
                                                                 599.74

1. Wild cats
ISBN 0-8160-2736-6   LC 92-38774

"A broad, comprehensive overview of the world's wild felines. The first half of the book covers the animals' anatomy, way of life, and interaction with humans. The second half is a species-by-species look at the specific cats. A map and a description indicates where they can be found. The author's ecological concerns are evident throughout. The full-color photographs are detailed and intriguing and amount to perhaps a third of the book." SLJ
Includes bibliography

Bonner, W. Nigel (William Nigel)
The natural history of seals. Facts on File 1990 196p il $25.95   **599.74**
1. Seals (Animals)
ISBN 0-8160-2336-0   LC 89-37620

Describes the natural history of this popular animal, focusing on its behavior, relationship to man, and prospects for survival

"The book is well illustrated, both in black and white and in color. The chapter on conservation and seals is helpful." Sci Books Films
Includes bibliography

Seals and sea lions of the world. Facts on File 1994 224p il maps $27.95   **599.74**
1. Seals (Animals)
ISBN 0-8160-2955-5   LC 92-46594

This study provides an "account of the facts and figures on seal populations on every continent. . . . The evolution, size, reproductive data, social structure, future of the three families of Pinnipedia are the main thrust of the book. The book closes with a discussion of the threats to seals from humans, organochlorines and petroleum." Appraisal

"The volume is profusely illustrated, mostly with fine color photos, the majority of which were taken by the author. . . . This is a good book for classwork and supplemental reading for courses in zoology, biology, and life sciences for senior high school up." Sci Books Films
Includes bibliographical references

Busch, Robert

The wolf almanac; [by] Robert H. Busch. Lyons & Burford 1995 226p il maps $27.95 **599.74**

1. Wolves

ISBN 1-55821-351-1   LC 95-59

This guide to the evolution of wolves discusses "their biology, their history, their conservation, wolves as big game and wolves as pets." Publisher's note

The author "bases his discussion of wolf behavior on observations and data provided by leading wolf researchers, and this information helps to bridge the gap between myth and reality. Well written and organized, this book includes 16 pages of color photographs." Libr J

Includes bibliographical references

Catton, Chris

Pandas. Facts on File 1990 152p il maps $24.95 **599.74**

1. Giant panda

ISBN 0-8160-2331-X   LC 89-23401

Beginning with a chapter on the "history of Western acquaintance with the giant panda . . . this book progresses logically through the anatomy, physiology, behavior, and required environment of the species. A few color plates and numerous clear black-and-white drawings and maps illustrate the text. . . . Useful for research on the panda specifically, this could also stimulate thinking on animal preservation in general." SLJ

Includes bibliographical references

Domico, Terry

Bears of the world; photographs by Terry Domico and Mark Newman. Facts on File 1988 189p il $29.95 **599.74**

1. Bears

ISBN 0-8160-1536-8   LC 88-3881

"After a once-over-lightly about ursine development and capabilities . . . Domico devotes successive chapters to the American black, brown, polar, 'tropical,' Asian black, and panda species." Booklist

Includes bibliography

Grady, Wayne, 1948-

The world of the coyote. Sierra Club Bks. 1994 143p il hardcover o.p. paperback available $18 **599.74**

1. Coyotes

ISBN 0-87156-376-2 (pa)   LC 94-1464

An illustrated look at coyote taxonomy, social organization, reproduction and hunting behavior

"While many facts are included, they will not overwhelm high school readers—the writing style is conversational enough to hold their interest. Conservation-minded students will also be interested in the discussion of the relationship between humans and coyotes and efforts to control the animal's numbers and range." Book Rep

Includes bibliographical references

Grambo, Rebecca L., 1963-

The world of the fox. Sierra Club Bks. 1995 109p il $25 **599.74**

1. Foxes

ISBN 0-87156-377-0   LC 95-1167

Also published with title: The nature of foxes

Text and numerous illustrations reveal the full range of fox life. The author also covers the portrayal of foxes in folklore, myth and literature

Includes bibliographical references

Great cats; consulting editors, John Seidensticker, and Susan Lumpkin; illustrations, Frank Knight. Rodale Press 1991 240p il maps (Majestic creatures of the wild) $40 **599.74**

1. Wild cats

ISBN 0-87857-965-6   LC 90-29179

"Thirty-eight contributing editors from around the world have written informative chapters about cat species, about the image of cats perpetuated in the art and culture of various civilizations, about cats' survival in zoos and in the wild, and about the outlook for preserving threatened species. Public and secondary school libraries will find this book a useful reference source. . . . The essays make this volume a nice addition to circulating collections, as well." Libr J

McCall, Karen, 1950-

Cougar; ghost of the Rockies; [by] Karen McCall and Jim Dutcher; foreword by Wallace Stegner; introduction by Maurice Hornocker. Sierra Club Bks. 1992 146p il hardcover o.p. paperback available $20 **599.74**

1. Pumas

ISBN 0-87156-463-7 (pa)   LC 92-3691

Also available in hardcover from P. Smith

This "book on the largest extant wild native American cat is the accompaniment to Dutcher's film on the same subject. As much an account of wildlife moviemaking as of the animal, it unfolds the parallel stories of one female cougar and her offspring and of the filming of the same cats. . . . Any popular natural history library will be graced by [its] beauty, enriched by [its] information." Booklist

Includes bibliography

Paine, Stefani, 1946-

The world of the sea otter; text by Stefani Paine; photographs by Jeff Foott. Sierra Club Bks. 1993 132p il hardcover o.p. paperback available $18 **599.74**

1. Otters

ISBN 0-87156-375-4 (pa)   LC 93-2820

"The first half of the book examines the sea otter, its habitat, diet, and way of life. The second half is a discussion of the effects of humans and their pollution on these creatures." SLJ

"This book is a work of art—from the attractive format, to the superb color photos, to the clear writing. . . . Students will find this a rich source of information for reports and research papers." Book Rep

Includes bibliography

Savage, Candace, 1949-

Wild cats; lynx, bobcats, mountain lions. Sierra Club Bks. 1993 136p il maps hardcover o.p. paperback available $20 **599.74**

1. Wild cats

ISBN 0-87156-424-6 (pa)   LC 93-2821

Full-color photographs accompany a text that examines the habitat, diet and hunting techniques of the lynx,

Savage, Candace, 1949——_Continued_
bobcat and mountain lion
   Includes bibliography

   The world of the wolf. Sierra Club Bks. 1996
114p il maps $27.50   **599.74**
   1. Wolves
   ISBN 0-87156-899-3   LC 96-17673
   A revised and updated version of Wolves, published
1989 by Sierra Club Bks.
   This discusses the relationship between wolves and
people, wolf pack structure, sex roles, communication,
hunting, and current conservation strategies
   Includes bibliographical references

Schaller, George B.
   The last panda. University of Chicago Press
1993 xx, 291p il maps hardcover o.p. paperback
available $13.95   **599.74**
   1. Giant panda
   ISBN 0-226-73629-6 (pa)   LC 92-18869
   "Schaller, who spent five years studying the panda in
its natural habitat, recounts the various factors that have
placed it in peril . . . and outlines a realistic plan to preserve it." Libr J
   "Recommended highly for curricular study of endangered species and wildlife conservation." Booklist
   Includes bibliographical references

Steinhart, Peter
   The company of wolves. Knopf 1995 374p il
maps $27.50   **599.74**
   1. Wolves
   ISBN 0-679-41881-4   LC 94-26913
   This is "an examination of the relationship between
humans and wolves in the wolves' last refuges in the
Arctic and in places where the two species live together
again as wolves move into new areas, either through
their own natural movements or through attempts at
reintroduction. Steinhart . . . speaks with wolf biologists,
wildlife managers, trappers, ranchers, Native Americans,
and others." Libr J
   "Steinhart's book should be used in any high school
where students study how biology, government and social responsibility correlate. It is an excellent presentation
of several sides of a complex problem." Book Rep
   Includes bibliographical references

Thomas, Elizabeth Marshall, 1931-
   The tribe of tiger; cats and their culture;
illustrated by Jared Taylor Williams. Simon &
Schuster 1994 240p il hardcover o.p. paperback
available $12   **599.74**
   1. Cats 2. Tigers 3. Lions
   ISBN 0-684-80454-9 (pa)   LC 94-20195
   Also available G.K. Hall large print edition
   The author offers a "look into the lives of various
members of the cat family—small and large, domestic
and wild, Old World and New. She begins with the evolution and spread of different feline species, explaining
the physiology and behavior of cats, including house
cats, as meat eaters, that is, in the light of their hunting

instincts. She then examines the changes over a period of
more than 30 years in the culture . . . of different lion
communities in several parts of Africa. In conclusion,
she discusses the need for tiger conservation." Booklist
   Includes bibliographical references

Ward, Paul, 1959-
   Wild bears of the world; [by] Paul Ward and
Suzanne Kynaston. Facts on File 1995 191p il
maps $25.95   **599.74**
   ISBN 0-8160-3245-9   LC 95-12487
   This book "starts by explaining how and why bears
have meant so much from early in our evolutionary history. . . . It then describes the bears' position and
uniqueness among carnivores, introduces the living species, charts their evolutionary history, tells how they live,
what they eat, how they cope with their habitats, and
looks at their behavior. It concludes with a re-
examination of the interrelationship they have with us."
Publisher's note
   Includes glossary and bibliography

599.8   Primates

Galdikas, Biruté
   Reflections of Eden; my years with the
orangutans of Borneo; [by] Biruté M.F. Galdikas.
Little, Brown 1995 408p il maps $24.95; pa
$13.95   **599.8**
   1. Orangutan 2. Borneo—Description
   ISBN 0-316-30181-7; 0-316-30186-8 (pa)
      LC 94-22948
   The author discusses her life in Borneo and her research into the lives of the orangutans of Borneo's rain
forest
   "Highly recommended for all libraries, this book will
inspire young scientists and enthrall anyone interested in
orangutans and the rigors of modern field research." Libr
J

Preston-Mafham, Rod
   Primates of the world; [by] Rod and Ken
Preston-Mafham. Facts on File 1992 191p il
$25.95   **599.8**
   1. Primates
   ISBN 0-8160-2745-5   LC 91-34964
   "A look at over 60 species and subspecies of lemurs,
monkeys, and apes. The book details their social systems, breeding, habitats, food needs, communication
styles as well as the primates' threatened relationship
with humans in the life chain. Based on the most recent
zoological research and filled with excellent photographs,
this is a timely addition to science collections." SLJ

599.88 Apes

Fossey, Dian
Gorillas in the mist. Houghton Mifflin 1983
326p il hardcover o.p. paperback available $10.95
599.88
1. Gorillas
ISBN 0-685-06802-1 (pa)   LC 82-23332
This book "recounts some of the events of the thirteen
years that I have spent with the mountain gorillas in their
natural habitat and includes data from the fifteen years
of continuing field study." Preface
Includes bibliography

Goodall, Jane, 1934-
The chimpanzees of Gombe; patterns of
behavior. Belknap Press 1986 673p il $47.50
599.88
1. Chimpanzees 2. Gombe Stream National Park
(Tanzania)
ISBN 0-674-11649-6   LC 85-20030
This book is based on the author's and her students'
observation of chimpanzees in the Gombe National Park
in Tanzania. It is an attempt to provide synthesis of
twenty-five years of research on these primates
This "densely written book covers almost every aspect
of [chimpanzee] behavior observed in the wild. . . .
Goodall's book will be a major source for decades and
must be considered an essential holding for any life science collection." Choice
Includes bibliography

In the shadow of man; photographs by Hugo
van Lawick. rev ed. Houghton Mifflin 1988 297p
il map pa $14.95   **599.88**
1. Chimpanzees
ISBN 0-395-33145-5   LC 87-36965
First published 1971
The author describes the chimpanzee group she stud-
ied during ten years of field observation in the Gombe
Stream Chimpanzee Reserve in Tanzania
Includes bibliography

Through a window; my thirty years with the
chimpanzees of Gombe. Houghton Mifflin 1990
268p il map hardcover o.p. paperback available
$12.95   **599.88**
1. Chimpanzees
ISBN 0-395-59925-3 (pa)   LC 90-36974
This continuation of the study entered above "tells two
stories: first of how the chimps of Gombe in Tanzania
have grown, changed and died, and second, how Goodall
and her dedicated group of Tanzanian observers have
survived the rigours of the past thirty years. It is beautifully written, and evokes both sympathy and understanding of these animals." Times Lit Suppl

Nichols, Michael K., 1953-
The great apes; between two worlds;
photographs and essays by Michael Nichols;
contributions by Jane Goodall, George B. Schaller,
Mary G. Smith; prepared by the Book Division,
National Geographic Society. National Geographic
Soc. 1993 200p il maps $35   **599.88**
1. Apes 2. Chimpanzees 3. Gorillas 4. Orangutan
ISBN 0-87044-947-8   LC 93-2261
"Nichols describes the current status of gorillas,
orangutans, chimpanzees, and bonobos (pygmy chimpanzees) in the wild and in captivity, bringing us up-to-date
on field studies by Jane Goodall, Birute Galdikas, and
other researchers." Libr J
"This book is an attractive browsing item that will
also be useful in biology, ecology, or psychology classes." Book Rep

600 TECHNOLOGY (APPLIED SCIENCES)

Frontline of discovery; science on the brink of
tomorrow; prepared by the Book Division,
National Geographic Society. National
Geographic Soc. 1994 200p il $16   **600**
1. Science 2. Inventions
ISBN 0-87044-979-6   LC 94-38077
Contributors explore new discoveries and applications
in biology, material science, climatology and space sciences

How in the world? Reader's Digest Assn. 1990
448p il $32   **600**
1. Technology 2. Science 3. Curiosities and wonders
ISBN 0-89577-353-8   LC 90-30663
"How astronauts navigate in space, how the Great
Pyramids were built, and how the soft centers are put in
pieces of chocolate are among the many questions answered in this fascinating book. . . . A treasure trove of
information that can be read for pleasure or as a starting
point for research papers or projects." SLJ

Macaulay, David, 1946-
The way things work. Houghton Mifflin 1988
384p il $29.95   **600**
1. Technology 2. Machinery 3. Inventions
ISBN 0-395-42857-2   LC 88-11270
Also available CD-ROM version
In a "combination of illustration and text, Macaulay
introduces the science behind mechanization as he explains the functioning of familiar devices, ranging in variety from camshafts to computers." Booklist
Includes glossary

603 Technology—Encyclopedias and dictionaries

Oxford illustrated encyclopedia of invention and technology; edited by Monty Finniston. Oxford Univ. Press 1992 391p il $52.25   **603**
1. Inventions—Dictionaries 2. Technology—Dictionaries
ISBN 0-19-869138-6

This work "covers the world's engineering achievements and traces the development of technology from the earliest civilizations to the present. Major inventors, concepts and inventions are described in entries arranged alphabetically, ranging from a few sentences to over a thousand words. Illustrations and explanatory diagrams accompany many entries." Libr J

608 Inventions and patents

Brown, Travis, 1926-
Historical first patents; the first United States patent for many everyday things. Scarecrow Press 1994 216p il $39.50   **608**
1. Patents—History 2. Inventions—History
ISBN 0-8108-2898-7   LC 94-14814

This "is an overview of over 80 granted U.S. patent applications, with emphasis on the familiar: Howe, Whitney, Bell, and others whose names are closely associated with a specific device. Each entry consists of the historical developments leading to the invention, a biographical description of the inventor, and the story of the creation of the invention itself. A patent drawing accompanies most entries." Libr J
For a fuller review see: Booklist, Jan. 1, 1995
Includes bibliography

Karnes, Frances A.
Girls & young women inventing; twenty true stories about inventors plus how you can be one yourself; [by] Frances A. Karnes and Suzanne M. Bean; edited by Rosemary Wallner. Free Spirit 1995 168p il pa $12.95   **608**
1. Women inventors 2. Inventions
ISBN 0-915793-89-X   LC 95-16300

"Part one relates in first-person narrative the development of inventions in such diverse areas as conservation, safety, convenience, and fun. . . . Part two focuses on how to be an inventor with practical advice on getting started, developing sketches, and patenting and marketing ideas. The final part contains resource information about organizations and associations, a bibliography, inspiring quotes, and a chronological listing of female inventors. Illustrated with photos and diagrams, this book will be useful for any would-be inventor." Voice Youth Advocates

Park, Robert, 1927-
The inventor's handbook; how to develop, protect, & market your invention. 2nd ed. Betterway Publs. 1990 230p il pa $14.95   **608**
1. Inventions 2. Patents
ISBN 1-55870-149-4   LC 89-18348
First published 1986

This handbook "covers all the steps in the inventing process, from the initial creative phase to prototyping; from financing to production to marketing." Publisher's note

609 Technology—Historical and geographic treatment

Bunch, Bryan H.
The timetables of technology; a chronology of the most important people and events in the history of technology; [by] Bryan Bunch and Alexander Hellemans. Simon & Schuster 1993 490p $35; pa $20   **609**
1. Technology—History
ISBN 0-671-76918-9; 0-671-88767-X (pa)
          LC 93-27734
Companion volume The timetables of science, entered under Hellemans, Alexander, class 509
"A Hudson Group book"
This is a "comprehensive overview of technological developments. The major categories change over time from General, Agricultural/Construction, Communications/Transportation, Food & Agriculture, and Tools/Materials to General, Communications, Electronics & Computers, Energy, Food & Shelter, Materials, Medical Technology, Tools & Devices, and Transportation, reflecting the development and increasing importance of new technologies. There are introductory textual sections, substantial annotations of points of interest, and extensive indexes." Libr J

Cardwell, D. S. L. (Donald Stephen Lowell)
The Norton history of technology; [by] Donald Cardwell. Norton 1994 565p il (Norton history of science) $35; pa $18.95   **609**
1. Technology—History
ISBN 0-393-03652-9; 0-393-31192-9 (pa)
First published in the United Kingdom with title: The Fontana history of technology
"Cardwell begins with the earliest manifestation of technology, the simple yet ingenuous tools of our first ancestors, and works his way to satellites and computers. His . . . spirited discussion covers all the expected milestones, such as the invention of the printing press and the steam engine, but also emphasizes the perfection of such basic and influential tools as the clock." Booklist
Includes bibliographical references

Flatow, Ira
They all laughed; from lightbulbs to lasers, the fascinating stories behind the great inventions that have changed our lives. HarperCollins Pubs. 1992 238p il hardcover o.p. paperback available $11   **609**
1. Inventions
ISBN 0-06-092415-2 (pa)   LC 91-58336
The author has put together an "overview of how some of our more interesting scientific discoveries and inventions have come to be. From teflon to lasers, from xerography to velcro, he humorously describes the often

Flatow, Ira—*Continued*
serendipitous events leading to the particular break-through. The treatment is enthusiastic and lighthearted and not organized in any thematic or chronological fashion. It's a quick read and informative." Libr J
Includes bibliographical references

Inventors and discoverers; changing our world. National Geographic Soc. 1988 320p il $35
                                                                          609
1. Inventions—History 2. Technology—History
ISBN 0-87044-751-3   LC 88-22375
"The text is divided into categories such as steam, electricity, materials, imaging, and computers, with each section highlighting the major contributions in its area and focusing on inventors as much as the inventions. In addition, the book places both people and machines in the context of their eras and social times." Booklist
"Each chapter and section is technically sound and exceptionally readable." Appraisal

James, Peter
Ancient inventions; [by] Peter James & Nick Thorpe. Ballantine Bks. 1994 xxiii, 672p il $29.95; pa $17.50   609
1. Inventions—History 2. Technology—History
ISBN 0-345-36476-7; 0-345-40102-6 (pa)
                                      LC 94-7738
The authors "define the ancient period as the time before A.D. 1492, analyzing the evolution of inventions from brain surgery to playing cards, and putting into perspective the accomplishments of many diverse cultures while laying to rest some 'distorted Western views of history.'" Booklist
This "is thoroughly researched and profusely illustrated; it is doubtful that anyone could examine it without coming away enlightened in one of its broadly ranging areas." Libr J
Includes bibliographical references

Karwatka, Dennis
Technology's past; America's industrial revolution and the people who delivered the goods. Prakken Publs. 1996 262p il pa $24.95   609
1. Inventions—History 2. Inventors 3. Technology—History
ISBN 0-911168-91-5   LC 95-72938
"This volume profiles 76 Americans who influenced technology in the United States from the Industrial Revolution through the beginning years of World War II. . . . Biographies are three pages long and are arranged chronologically by the birth date of the inventor. . . . The final section of the book covers four areas of technology: computers, television, manned space flight, robotics." Book Rep
"This is a readable, well-documented selection." SLJ
Includes bibliographies

Macdonald, Anne L., 1920-
Feminine ingenuity; women and invention in America; [by] Anne Macdonald. Ballantine Bks. 1992 xxiv, 514p il hardcover o.p. paperback available $14   609
1. Women inventors 2. Inventions
ISBN 0-345-38314-1 (pa)   LC 91-55502
Focusing on "American women patent holders, MacDonald details women's inventions while simultaneously chronicling the history of the women's movement. A well-documented survey for women's history and technology collections." Booklist
Includes bibliographical references

Williams, Trevor Illtyd
The history of invention. Facts on File 1987 352p il $40   609
1. Technology—History 2. Inventions—History
ISBN 0-8160-1788-3   LC 87-8880
The author "presents a history of technology in five sections: ancient civilizations, the rise of Islam to 1500, Renaissance to the birth of industrialism, early twentieth century to World War II, and postwar civilization to the frontiers of science." Appraisal
"Well written and well illustrated, this book also contains an excellent biographical dictionary of inventors through the ages. I recommend it for young adults and general audiences." Sci Books Films
Includes bibliography

World of invention; Bridget Travers, editor; Jeffrey Muhr, assistant editor. Gale Res. 1993 770p il $75   609
1. Inventions
ISBN 0-8103-8375-6
In this reference work "more than 1100 alphabetically arranged entries describe significant developments from the Industrial Revolution to the present, focusing not on how things work but on how they came to be. Directed toward an audience of high school students and other lay readers, concise information is presented in a nontechnical manner." Libr J

610 Medical sciences. Medicine

Check, William A.
The mind-body connection; introduction by C. Everett Koop. Chelsea House 1990 111p il (Encyclopedia of health) lib bdg $19.95   610
1. Health 2. Mind and body
ISBN 0-7910-0068-0   LC 89-20968
Discusses the connection between the body and the mind examining such topics as how the brain and the immune system work together and the influence of thoughts and emotions on physical health
Includes glossary and bibliography

O'Neil, Karen E.

Health and medicine projects for young scientists. Watts 1993 127p il (Projects for young scientists) lib bdg $19.14; pa $6.95   **610**

1. Medicine—Experiments 2. Science projects

ISBN 0-531-11050-8 (lib bdg); 0-531-15668-0 (pa)

LC 92-42745

Provides instructions for experiments demonstrating medical principles and explains how similar investigations have helped find cures or treatments for serious illnesses

"This is exactly the type of resource material that can lead students into the most intriguing aspects of scientific investigation." Sci Books Films

Includes bibliography

610.3 Medical sciences— Encyclopedias and dictionaries

The **American** Medical Association encyclopedia of medicine; medical editor, Charles B. Clayman. Random House 1989 1184p il $45   **610.3**

1. Medicine—Dictionaries

ISBN 0-394-56528-2   LC 88-29693

"The main section (more than 5,000 entries) includes symptoms, disorders, anatomy and physiology, medical tests, surgical procedures, and drugs, and is illustrated by flow charts, diagrams, etc. References in the text that refer to headworks of other articles are italicized. Also has a directory of self-help organizations and a drug glossary that cross-references brand and generic drug names and gives page numbers for related entries." Guide to Ref Books. 11th edition

Black's medical dictionary. Barnes & Noble Bks. $130.75   **610.3**

1. Medicine—Dictionaries

First published 1906. (1996 edition) Frequently revised

Editors vary; current editor: C. W. H. Havard

The intention of this work is to "describe medical practice as clearly and concisely as possible. . . . Its entries are exceptionally well written and informative, often explaining disease from a patient's perspective rather than a practitioner's." Am Ref Books Annu, 1989

Isler, Charlotte

The Watts teen health dictionary; by Charlotte Isler and Alwyn T. Cohall; illustrations by David Kelley. Watts 1996 191p il $24.95   **610.3**

1. Medicine—Dictionaries 2. Health—Dictionaries 3. Teenagers

ISBN 0-531-11236-5   LC 95-22166

This "dictionary covers diseases and their therapies, guidelines for healthy living, and health concerns and issues. Black-and-white line drawings illustrate many entries. Few books written for teens are written so concisely and yet are so thorough when covering such items as sports injuries, what to expect in a physical exam, emotional disorders, and diagnostic techniques. . . . Excellent appendixes include hotlines, medications, street drugs, health-care specialists and what they treat, books for teens . . . and an illustrated first aid manual." Booklist

Includes bibliography

Macmillan health encyclopedia. Macmillan 1993 9v il set $360   **610.3**

1. Health 2. Medicine

ISBN 0-02-897439-5   LC 92-28939

Contents: v1 Body systems; v2 Communicable diseases; v3 Noncommunicable diseases and disorders; v4 Nutrition and fitness; v5 Emotional and mental health; v6 Sexuality and reproduction; v7 Drugs, alcohol, and tobacco; v8 Safety and environmental health; v9 Health care systems; cumulative index

"Written specifically for adolescents, this . . . is an interdisciplinary, curriculum-related source. It supports and supplements course work in health, science, biology, psychology, home economics, and physical education. . . . [This work] satisfies the need for health information that is reliable, accurate, and clear." Booklist

Magill's medical guide, health and illness; [by] the editors of Salem Press. Salem Press 1995 3v il set $270   **610.3**

1. Medicine—Dictionaries

ISBN 0-89356-712-4   LC 94-44709

Also available supplementary volumes, published 1996 and numbered v4-6, set $240 (ISBN 0-89356-716-7)

"This three-volume set features 375 articles on the major disorders of the human body. . . . Every entry identifies the body part or system affected by the disorder and the type of specialist who deals with the problem; also provided is a short, dictionary-style definition. About two-thirds of the essays have a longer additional section that discusses causes and symptoms as well as treatment and therapy." Libr J

For a fuller review see: Booklist, Oct. 1, 1995

Merck manual of diagnosis and therapy. Merck & Co. $35   **610.3**

1. Medicine—Handbooks, manuals, etc.

First published 1899. (1994 edition) Periodically revised

"A one-volume reference that attempts to cover all but the most obscure diseases. Sections are organized by type of disease or medical specialty." N Y Public Libr. Book of How & Where to Look It Up

Merriam-Webster's medical desk dictionary. Merriam-Webster 1993 26a, 790p $24.95 **610.3**

1. Medicine—Dictionaries

ISBN 0-87779-125-2   LC 93-7965

First published 1986 with title: Webster's medical desk dictionary

This medical dictionary features "part-of-speech labels, pronunciation respelling for all entries, British spellings where needed . . . prefixes, suffixes, and combining forms, an essay on the history of medical English, and over 1,000 biographies of men and women whose names have become part of the medical vocabulary." Publisher's note

The **Oxford** medical companion; edited by John Walton (Lord Walton of Detchant), Jeremiah A. Barondess, and Stephen Lock. Oxford Univ. Press 1994 xxi, 1038p il $65   **610.3**

1. Medicine—Dictionaries

ISBN 0-19-262355-9   LC 94-30681

First published 1986 in two volumes with title: The Oxford companion to medicine

The Oxford medical companion—*Continued*
This "can best be described as a combination medical dictionary and encyclopedia covering the social as well as the clinical aspects of medicine . . . containing more than 8,000 alphabetically arranged entries. Entries range in length from one-sentence definitions of medical terms to 182 lengthy articles on broad medical and medically related topics. . . . There is much that is of interest here for the browsing reader, students, and medical practitioners." Booklist

Stedman's medical dictionary. Williams & Wilkins $44.95 **610.3**
1. Medicine—Dictionaries
First published 1911. (1995 edition) Frequently revised
"A vocabulary of medicine and its allied sciences, with pronunciation and derivations." Title page
In addition to general medicine this dictionary covers dentistry, veterinary medicine, biochemistry and other related fields

610.69 Medical personnel

My first year as a doctor; real world stories from America's M.D.'s; edited by Melissa Ramsdell. Walker & Co. 1994 xx, 124p $19.95; pa $9.95 **610.69**
1. Physicians 2. Medicine
ISBN 0-8027-1290-8; 0-8027-7418-0 (pa)
LC 94-4990
Also available in paperback from NAL/Dutton
This is a "collection of eighteen doctors' personal accounts of their first year of practice. . . . Some of the areas of medicine are family practice, surgery, research, and emergency treatment. The reasons for their choices are very individual. . . . This book is an excellent suggestion to the YA with the school career assignment. It should also be one of the must reads for students considering medicine as a vocation." Voice Youth Advocates

610.9 Medical sciences—Historical and geographic treatment

Bourdillon, Hilary
Women as healers; a history of women and medicine. Cambridge Univ. Press 1988 48p il (Women in history) pa $10.95 **610.9**
1. Women in medicine
ISBN 0-521-31090-3
LC 88-6146
"A brief overview of the role women have played in the development of the science and profession of medicine in the Western world." Booklist
This book "offers detail in text and sufficient illustrations for its size. Within its limited scope, this concise history is a fair and well-informed survey." Sci Books Films
Includes glossary and bibliography

611 Human anatomy, cytology, histology

The **Color** atlas of human anatomy; edited by Vanio Vannini and Giuliano Pogliani; translated and revised by Richard T. Jolly. Beekman House 1980 107p il o.p.; Harmony Bks. paperback available $12 **611**
1. Human anatomy
ISBN 0-517-54514-4 (pa)
LC 80-68640
Original Italian edition, 1979
This illustrated guide presents a multidimensional view of various body systems

Gray's anatomy; the anatomical basis of medicine and surgery. Churchill Livingstone $175 **611**
1. Human anatomy
First published 1858. (38th edition 1995) Frequently revised. Publisher varies. Variant title: Gray's anatomy of the human body
A comprehensive standard reference work with illustrations, descriptions and definitions
"Holds its place as a major and authoritative text on systematic anatomy. Recommended." Annals of Internal Medicine

Human body on file: anatomy; [by] The Diagram Group. Facts on File 1996 unp il $165 **611**
1. Human anatomy
ISBN 0-8160-3527-X
Companion volume to Human body on file: physiology, entered in class 612
First published 1983 with title: The human body. Present edition incorporates the original material plus the images in the update volume (available separately $60 ISBN 0-8160-5528-8)
"The work consists of black-and-white line drawings of the various systems/parts of the human body. All are clearly labeled with numbers keyed to terms which appear below each drawing. . . . Purchasers may make copies of any part by any means for nonprofit educational or private use without obtaining any further permission or payment of fees. This is an excellent source for anyone studying or teaching anatomy at any basic level, particularly in K-12 and junior colleges." Booklist [review of 1983 edition]

Leonardo, da Vinci, 1452-1519
Leonardo on the human body; [by] Leonardo da Vinci. Dover Publs. 1983 506p il pa $18.95 **611**
1. Human anatomy
ISBN 0-486-24483-0
LC 82-18285
First published 1952 by H. Schuman with title: Leonardo Da Vinci on the human body
This volume includes 215 black-and-white plates containing some 1200 illustrations. Each plate is accompanied by explanatory notes

612 Human physiology

Bodyclock; the effects of time on human health; edited by Martin Hughes, Milo Keynes. Facts on File 1989 191p il $24.95   **612**
1. Physiology 2. Biological rhythms
ISBN 0-8160-2223-2   LC 89-11690
"Opening with a 'Lifespan Health Chart' that briefly describes normal developmental milestones, Hughes continues with a more comprehensive but still brief overview of the various body systems." SLJ
Includes bibliographical references

Burnie, David
The concise encyclopedia of the human body. Dorling Kindersley 1995 160p il $19.95   **612**
1. Human anatomy 2. Physiology
ISBN 0-7894-0204-1   LC 95-15134
"Arranged thematically by major body systems, this volume succinctly explains and illustrates over 2000 basic terms and concepts in human biology and physiology. . . . A final chapter gives brief biographical information on over 100 doctors and biologists, and some individuals are highlighted within relevant subject areas. Full-color drawings, diagrams, models, photographs, and electron micrographs are clearly labeled and add to the textual information." SLJ

Human body. Time-Life Bks. 1992 152p il (Understanding science & nature) $18.95   **612**
1. Physiology 2. Human anatomy
LC 91-36143
This heavily illustrated volume uses a question and answer format to discuss the anatomy and function of the human body

The **Human** body: an illustrated guide to its structure, function, and disorders; editor-in-chief, Charles Clayman. Dorling Kindersley 1995 240p il $29.95   **612**
1. Physiology 2. Human anatomy
ISBN 1-56458-992-7   LC 94-37165
"This body atlas uses current medical illustration techniques to provide unique views of human anatomical features. Color-enhanced microscope photographs and computer-generated images accompany detailed drawings to illustrate various organs, demonstrate body functions, and depict problems or complications. The introduction explains various types of medical illustration such as computerized tomography, ultrasound, and magnetic resonance imaging." Booklist
"This absolutely stunning book succeeds immeasurably as a guide to the human body." Sci Books Films

The **Human** body explained; a guide to understanding the incredible living machine; Philip Whitfield, general editor. Holt & Co. 1995 192p il (Henry Holt reference book) $40   **612**
1. Physiology 2. Human anatomy
ISBN 0-8050-3752-7   LC 95-86
"This guide to the body is organized in five interconnected sections that examine body functions both in terms of day-to-day existence and in the grand scheme of things, that is, the adaptability and survival of our species. . . . All the major organs and systems of the body are explained, both textually and visually, in extraordinary detail, making this an invaluable resource." Booklist
Includes bibliographical references

Human body on file: physiology; [by] The Diagram Group. Facts on File 1996 unp il $165   **612**
1. Physiology 2. Human anatomy
ISBN 0-8160-3415-X   LC 95-42852
This companion volume to Human body on file: anatomy (entered in class 611) presents the physiological processes of the body and shows how the body's systems and components function when healthy or when experiencing problems

The **Incredible** machine. National Geographic Soc. 1986 384p il $35   **612**
1. Physiology 2. Human anatomy
ISBN 0-87044-619-3   LC 85-29731
A collection of "essays detailing the operation of the world's most incredible machine—the human body. The authors integrate recent scientific findings . . . in their engrossing coverage of reproduction, nutrition, the brain, the effects of aging, and the nervous, circulatory, and immune systems." Booklist
"It is the illustrations (399 excellent photos, 44 paintings and diagrams) that make this a special reference tool. . . . A valuable resource for science classes on all grade levels." SLJ
Includes bibliography

Kittredge, Mary, 1949-
The human body: an overview; introduction by C. Everett Koop. Chelsea House 1990 144p il (Encyclopedia of health) lib bdg $19.95   **612**
1. Physiology 2. Human anatomy
ISBN 0-7910-0019-2   LC 89-9877
This book begins with "a brief outline of the various scientists and discoveries that have led to our current understanding of the functions of the body. From there, the workings of the body are divided by systems; each is examined and explained. . . . Finally, a short chapter titled 'The Body of the Future' touches on some of the current developments in medical practice and technology." SLJ
Includes glossary and bibliography

Repair and renewal; by the editors of Time-Life Books. Time-Life Bks. 1994 144p il (Journey through the mind and body) $17.95   **612**
1. Physiology 2. Wounds and injuries 3. Growth
LC 94-18844
This illustrated look at the human body's capacity for regeneration explores how damaged cells, tissues and bones are able to renew themselves
Includes glossary and bibliography

Xenakis, Alan P.

Why doesn't my funny bone make me laugh? sneezes, hiccups, butterflies, and other funny feelings explained. Villard Bks. 1993 183p il hardcover o.p. paperback available $10   **612**

1. Physiology 2. Medicine

ISBN 0-679-75946-8 (pa)   LC 92-56802

"Beginning with belching and continuing alphabetically through a variety of bodily responses, Xenakis examines in brief, accessible chapters the various ways our bodies 'speak' to us everyday. A resource for trivia as well as information." Booklist

612.1 Blood and circulation

Avraham, Regina

The circulatory system; introduction by C. Everett Koop. Chelsea House 1989 110p il (Encyclopedia of health) lib bdg $19.95   **612.1**

1. Cardiovascular system 2. Blood—Circulation

ISBN 0-7910-0013-3   LC 88-20260

This book "gives a brief history of the study of the heart, and discusses in detail the anatomy and working of the circulatory system, common heart problems, and the prevention and treatment of heart disease; it concludes with the latest breakthroughs, methods of future treatment, and recommended health habits. . . . Highly recommended." Voice Youth Advocates

Includes glossary and bibliography

612.2 Respiration

Kittredge, Mary, 1949-

The respiratory system; introduction by C. Everett Koop. Chelsea House 1989 105p il (Encyclopedia of health) lib bdg $19.95   **612.2**

1. Respiration

ISBN 0-7910-0026-5   LC 88-14069

Kittredge discusses the way various animals breathe, the functioning of the human respiratory system, respiratory diseases, and dangers to the respiratory system due to pollution and smoking

Includes glossary and bibliography

612.3 Digestion

Avraham, Regina

The digestive system; introduction by C. Everett Koop. Chelsea House 1989 99p il (Encyclopedia of health) lib bdg $19.95   **612.3**

1. Digestion

ISBN 0-7910-0015-X   LC 88-34175

The author "discusses the normal biology of the alimentary tract, describes common digestive disorders and their treatment, and ends with practical suggestions for maintaining a healthy digestive system." Sci Books Films

Includes glossary and bibliography

Galperin, Anne

Nutrition; introduction by C. Everett Koop. Chelsea House 1991 119p il (Encyclopedia of health) lib bdg $19.95   **612.3**

1. Nutrition

ISBN 0-7910-0024-9   LC 90-44364

Examines the basics of good nutrition by studying the categories of nutrients, their functions in the body, and problems of diet and nutritional deficiencies

Includes glossary and bibliography

612.4 Secretion, excretion, related functions

Little, Marjorie

The endocrine system; introduction by C. Everett Koop. Chelsea House 1990 111p il (Encyclopedia of health) lib bdg $19.95   **612.4**

1. Endocrine glands 2. Hormones

ISBN 0-7910-0016-8   LC 89-25314

Describes the basic features of the endocrine system, the structure and function of its glands and hormones, and the causes and treatment of endocrine disorders

This "is a useful resource for students studying the functions of the human body and will be a worthwhile purchase for libraries needing materials in the area." Voice Youth Advocates

Includes glossary and bibliography

Young, John K.

Hormones: molecular messengers. Watts 1994 96p il lib bdg $19.70   **612.4**

1. Hormones 2. Endocrine glands

ISBN 0-531-12545-9   LC 92-40503

"A Venture book"

Provides an introduction to the endocrine system, focusing on the human body's major hormones and the organs affected by them

"Young weaves a great deal of medical information into the text, often revealing fascinating facts about discoveries. . . . An excellent resource." Booklist

Includes glossary and bibliography

612.6 Reproduction, development, maturation

Avraham, Regina

The reproductive system; introduction by C. Everett Koop. Chelsea House 1991 125p il (Encyclopedia of health) lib bdg $19.95   **612.6**

1. Reproduction 2. Sex education

ISBN 0-7910-0025-7   LC 90-1721

Discusses aspects of reproduction, including heredity, pregnancy, and contraception, and explains the stages of growth from fertilization to birth

"The book is written so that it can be understood easily by the average nonscientist, and the material itself is accurate and up to date." Sci Books Films

Includes glossary and bibliography

Medina, John J., 1956-
The clock of ages; why we age—how we age—winding back the clock. Cambridge Univ. Press 1996 332p il $24.95   **612.6**
1. Aging
ISBN 0-521-46244-4   LC 95-40712
This "biological explanation of the aging process explores the changes that occur in the human body as it approaches death." Book Rep
"This is the best biology book written for the lay public to appear in many years." Libr J
Includes bibliographical references

Morowitz, Harold J.
The facts of life; science and the abortion controversy; [by] Harold J. Morowitz and James S. Trefil. Oxford Univ. Press 1992 179p il $25; pa $9.95   **612.6**
1. Embryology 2. Reproduction 3. Abortion
ISBN 0-19-507927-2; 0-19-509046-2 (pa)
LC 92-16343
In this discussion of the biological facts of human embryology and abortion the authors "make it clear that they do not believe that the abortion debate can be reduced to a question of scientific fact. The point is to make sure that you are using truthful biological concepts to support your position on abortion. . . . The concepts discussed are not overly technical, so most people . . . will have no trouble understanding the biology that is involved. . . . It is well written and informative." Sci Books Films
Includes bibliography

Nilsson, Lennart, 1922-
A child is born. completely new ed, text by Lars Hamberger. Delacorte Press 1990 213p il $27.50
612.6
1. Pregnancy 2. Embryology 3. Childbirth
ISBN 0-385-30237-1   LC 90-33633
"A Merloyd Lawrence book"
Original Swedish edition, 1965; first United States edition, 1966
"Sections of the text include a general consideration of male and female reproductive anatomy and physiology, the processes of ovulation and fertilization, fetal development, and labor and delivery. . . . The illustrations and accompanying captions are first rate." Appraisal

Stoppard, Miriam
The breast book. DK Pub. 1996 208p il $24.95
612.6
1. Breast
ISBN 0-7894-0420-6   LC 95-44848
This book "contains advice and information on breast anatomy, self-examination, breast feeding, the breast as a sexual organ, cosmetic surgery, developmental changes in the breast—both benign and threatening—and diseases of the breast and their treatment." Libr J
Includes bibliographical references

Vaughan, Christopher
How life begins; the science of life in the womb; illustrations: Marni Fylling. Times Bks. 1996 290p il $23   **612.6**
1. Pregnancy 2. Embryology 3. Childbirth
ISBN 0-8129-2103-8   LC 94-48779
"Vaughan describes fetal growth and the technology that has allowed doctors to follow the development of human life from single cell to birth." Booklist
"An informative guide for expectant parents and the scientifically curious." Publ Wkly

612.7   Motor functions and skin (integument), hair, nails

Allstetter, William D.
Speech and hearing; introduction by C. Everett Koop. Chelsea House 1991 111p il (Encyclopedia of health) lib bdg $19.95   **612.7**
1. Speech 2. Hearing
ISBN 0-7910-0029-X   LC 90-1718
Examines the vital mechanisms of human communication, speech and hearing, through a discussion of the body's role in these functions
"The information is well organized and accurate. . . . [The book has] many photographs, drawings, and diagrams to enhance the text." Voice Youth Advocates
Includes glossary and bibliography

Feinberg, Brian
The musculoskeletal system; introduction by C. Everett Koop. Chelsea House 1993 111p il (Encyclopedia of health) lib bdg $19.95   **612.7**
1. Musculoskeletal system
ISBN 0-7910-0028-1   LC 92-21956
An examination of the musculoskeletal system, including its structure, functions, and disorders
Includes glossary and bibliography

612.8   Nervous functions. Sensory functions

Coren, Stanley
Sleep thieves; an eye-opening exploration into the science and mysteries of sleep. Free Press 1996 304p $24   **612.8**
1. Sleep
ISBN 0-684-82304-7   LC 95-51549
The author "explores the basic body cycles and their effects on sleep, and he describes the human 'internal clock'. . . . His main theme, though, is sleep deprivation." Booklist
"This is a well-written, easy-to-understand book on a complex scientific subject to which everyone can relate." Libr J
Includes bibliographical references

Edelson, Edward, 1932-

The nervous system; introduction by C. Everett Koop. Chelsea House 1991 111p il (Encyclopedia of health) lib bdg $19.95 **612.8**
1. Nervous system
ISBN 0-7910-0023-0 LC 90-1723
Discusses the nervous system and its components and how they function
Includes glossary and bibliography

Sleep; introduction by C. Everett Koop. Chelsea House 1991 109p il (Encyclopedia of health) lib bdg $19.95 **612.8**
1. Sleep
ISBN 0-7910-0092-3 LC 91-9279
Examines the function of sleep in both humans and animals. Discusses REM sleep, dreams, insomnia, narcolepsy, and other sleep disorders
"This brief book is a factual, well-written historical and current overview of sleep research." Sci Books Films
Includes glossary and bibliography

Hobson, J. Allan

Sleep. Scientific Am. Lib. 1989 213p il $32.95; pa $19.95 **612.8**
1. Sleep
ISBN 0-7167-5050-3; 0-7167-6014-2 (pa)
LC 88-37027
This study of sleep in humans and animals "embraces concepts from a variety of scientific disciplines, including neurology, psychology, and ethology. . . . This book is highly recommended to those interested in a general overview of current topics in sleep and dream research." Sci Books Films
Includes bibliography

Hubel, David (David Hunter), 1926-

Eye, brain, and vision. Scientific Am. Lib. 1988 240p il hardcover o.p. paperback available $19.95 **612.8**
1. Eye 2. Vision
ISBN 0-7167-6009-6 (pa) LC 87-23506
This book provides a look at the eye, the brain, and the physiologic processes involved in seeing
There is "considerable detail in this treatise, which gives a comprehensive overview of current vision research while maintaining an engaging style that carries the reader through a complex subject." Sci Books Films
Includes bibliography

Ornstein, Robert E. (Robert Evan), 1942-

The amazing brain; [by] Robert Ornstein and Richard F. Thompson; illustrated by David Macaulay. Houghton Mifflin 1984 182p il hardcover o.p. paperback available $15.95 **612.8**
1. Brain
ISBN 0-395-40800-8 (pa) LC 84-12907
This "book presents a selected group of topics dealing with the evolution, anatomy, and function of the human brain." Choice
"While the text is accessible to advanced high-school students, it is the illustrations that separate this book from others." SLJ

Powledge, Tabitha M.

Your brain; how you got it and how it works. Scribner 1994 210p il $14.95 **612.8**
1. Brain
ISBN 0-684-19659-X LC 94-14273
The author explains "the development and workings of the brain, the effects of drugs and alcohol on the brain, and the ways in which the brain becomes damaged or diseased." Publisher's note
Powledge "presents difficult material in a readable, concise manner and uses fine examples from common experience to illustrate complicated terms and processes." Booklist
Includes glossary and bibliographical references

613 Promotion of health

Carlson-Finnerty, LaVonne

Environmental health; introduction by C. Everett Koop. Chelsea House 1994 111p il (Encyclopedia of health) lib bdg $19.95 **613**
1. Environmental health
ISBN 0-7910-0082-6 LC 93-20245
Examines the issues and concerns of environmental pollutants and hazards
Includes glossary and bibliography

The **Good** Housekeeping illustrated guide to women's health; comprehensive information and advice about medical and life-style issues facing women today; Kathryn A. Cox, medical editor; Genell J. Subak-Sharpe, editorial editor; Diane M. Goetz, managing editor; Briar Lee Mitchell, illustrator. Hearst Bks. 1995 351p il $25 **613**
1. Women—Health and hygiene
ISBN 0-688-12116-0 LC 94-9284
This guide covers "common illnesses, from AIDS to yeast infections. With the focus on care and prevention, there is information on the aging process, including common physical and psychological changes, fitness, nutrition, breast exams, and conquering fatigue. Other significant issues covered include workplace hazards and how to react to and recover from violent attacks." Booklist
Includes glossary

Health and fitness: opposing viewpoints; Scott Barbour, Karin L. Swisher, book editor[s] Greenhaven Press 1996 188p il $19.95; pa $11.95 **613**
1. Health 2. Medical care
ISBN 1-565-10403-X; 1-565-10402-1 (pa)
LC 96-7203
"Opposing viewpoints series"
"Among the specific issues addressed are the benefits and risks of meat and milk consumption, vitamins, exercise, weight-loss treatments, and various alternative therapies. A discussion of the health-care industry completes the book. Each article is preceded by the author's credentials, a synopsis of the opinion expressed, and several questions to consider while reading. . . . No easy answers will result from persuing these pages, but readers' thinking will be challenged and stimulated." SLJ
Includes bibliographies

Health on file; [by] Victoria Chapman & Associates. Facts on File 1995 various paging il $155 **613**
1. Health
ISBN 0-8160-2993-8   LC 94-7097
This is a looseleaf collection of materials which "can be reproduced and distributed as classroom materials. Topics include: mental health; social & family health; growth & development; food & nutrition; personal health; substance abuse; diseases & disorders; consumer health; and environmental health. Current issues such as AIDS, wellness, refusal skills and conflict resolution are covered." Book Rep

McCoy, Kathleen, 1945-
The new teenage body book; [by] Kathy McCoy & Charles Wibbelsman; illustrations by Bob Stover. thoroughly rev and updated. Body Press/Perigee 1992 286p pa $15   **613**
1. Adolescence 2. Hygiene 3. Sex education
ISBN 0-399-51725-1   LC 91-35962
First published 1979 by Pocket Bks. with title: The teenage body book, and with authors' names in reverse order
A handbook for teenagers discussing such topics as the male and female bodies, health, grooming, emotions, various aspects of sex, eating disorders, depression, drugs, and sexually transmitted diseases
This book is "among the most thorough and objective broad-scope self-help books available to teenagers." SLJ
Includes bibliographical references

The **New** our bodies, ourselves; a book by and for women. Updated and expanded for the 1990s. Simon & Schuster 1992 751p il pa $20   **613**
1. Women—Health and hygiene 2. Women—Psychology
ISBN 0-671-79176-1   LC 92-1627
Also available in hardcover from P. Smith
"A Touchstone book"
First published 1971 with title: Our bodies, ourselves
"This encyclopedia of women's health is organized by broad subject areas: relationships and sexuality, fertility, childbearing, aging. Each chapter has comprehensive information about the subject, quotations from women who have experience with the condition, notes and references and referrals for further information. . . . It is an outstanding resource written by and for women with accessible information for all collections." Libr J
Includes bibliographical references

The **PDR** family guide to women's health and prescription drugs. Medical Economics Data 1994 891p il pa $24.95   **613**
1. Women—Health and hygiene 2. Drugs
ISBN 1-56363-086-9
"An overview of the diseases and disorders that threaten women constitutes the first part of the book. They are arranged into sections: the reproductive system; general health concerns (heart disease, AIDS, headaches, plastic surgery); fertility and family planning, pregnancy, menopause; emotional problems (stress, depression, eating disorders); and cancer. The second part provides readers with detailed information on medicines their doctors are most likely to prescribe. . . . All librarians (high school and up) will want to make room for this title in their reference collections." Booklist

Slap, Gail B.
Teenage health care; the first comprehensive family guide for the preteen to young adult years; [by] Gail B. Slap and Martha M. Jablow; foreword by Benjamin Spock. Pocket Bks. 1994 xxvi, 530p il pa $14   **613**
1. Youth—Health and hygiene
ISBN 0-671-75412-2   LC 94-10427
The authors "describe bodily systems and what can go wrong with them . . . they also discuss other matters affecting teens: eating disorders, sexual promiscuity, sexual abuse, alcohol and drug use, contraception, pregnancy. Because the authors have chosen not to sermonize, teenagers will probably find the book appealing. Also included is an extensive list of resources and a glossary." Publ Wkly

Staying healthy in a risky environment; the New York University Medical Center family guide; Arthur C. Upton, medical editor, Eden Graber, editor; Lewis Goldfrank [et al.], editorial board. Simon & Schuster 1993 811p il $32.50   **613**
1. Environmental health
ISBN 0-671-76815-8   LC 93-2634
"A one-volume encyclopedia of environmental hazards and advice for preventing disease resulting from exposure to them. Written from a public health perspective that emphasizes consumer action, the book . . . [discusses] environmental issues, distinguishing serious health hazards from minor threats, and advising readers how to control unhealthy exposure to hazardous substances. . . . This handbook is an essential consumer reference." Booklist
Includes bibliographical references

The **Women's** complete healthbook; [by] the American Medical Women's Association; medical editors, Susan C. Stewart, Roselyn Payne Epps. Delacorte Press 1995 708p $39.95; pa $21.95   **613**
1. Women—Health and hygiene
ISBN 0-385-31382-9; 0-440-50723-5 (pa)
LC 94-36851
"Diet and nutrition, anatomy and physiology, sexuality and sexually transmitted diseases, exercise, emergency first aid, and diseases affecting women are among the topics covered. The text is easy to understand, and the illustrations are clear. There are no bibliographies, but referrals to organizations are provided. The chapter on medication, which explains the effects of gender differences on drugs, is outstanding." Libr J

613.2 Dietetics

Krizmanic, Judy
A teen's guide to going vegetarian; illustrations by Matthew Wawiorka; foreword by T. Colin Campbell. Viking 1994 218p il $14.99; pa $7.99

613.2

1. Vegetarianism 2. Nutrition
ISBN 0-670-85114-0; 0-14-036589-3 (pa)

LC 94-7790

The author "examines the relationship of vegetarianism to animal rights, environmental issues and even women's rights. She goes on to explore the difficulties that teens may encounter and even the resistance from friends and family to accept the dietary changes. . . . Krizmanic concentrates on the proper approach to the vegetarian diet and the substitutions that must be made to insure good health." Voice Youth Advocates

"Breezy, upbeat, conversational writing enlivens this book." SLJ

Includes glossary and bibliographical references

LeBow, Michael D.
Overweight teenagers; don't bear the burden alone; foreword by J. Kevin Thompson. Insight Bks. 1995 250p il $23.95

613.2

1. Obesity 2. Reducing
ISBN 0-306-45047-X

LC 95-24649

"Because he understands the stereotypes and the cycle of ridicule and self-hate that often accompanies obesity, LeBow ministers to the psyche as well as the appetite, as he talks about everything from setting goals, drafting a contract, and recording progress to keeping the weight off once it's gone." Booklist

Includes bibliographical references

Messina, Virginia
The vegetarian way; healthy eating for you and your family; [by] Virginia and Mark Messina. Crown 1996 390p $35; pa $24

613.2

1. Vegetarianism
ISBN 0-517-70427-7; 0-517-88275-2 (pa)

LC 95-34599

The authors contend "that going meatless lowers the risk of heart disease, cancer, diabetes and other diseases. . . . For beginners, they offer a nine-step program for getting started, with recipes and sections on meal planning and food buying. The special needs of pregnant women and nursing mothers, infants, children, teenagers and seniors are addressed, as are those of diabetics, athletes and the overweight." Publ Wkly

Nardo, Don, 1947-
Vitamins and minerals; introduction by C. Everett Koop. Chelsea House 1994 111p il (Encyclopedia of health) lib bdg $19.95

613.2

1. Vitamins 2. Nutrition
ISBN 0-7910-0032-X

LC 93-26204

"An introduction to basic nutritional principles for today's students. Each vitamin and mineral is discussed, its food sources and recommended daily allowance, and the results of overdose. In addition, effects of vitamin and mineral deficiencies (with accompanying photos), healthy eating habits, and eating disorders complete this overview. . . . An excellent, up-to-date resource for public and school libraries." Voice Youth Advocates

Includes glossary and bibliography

Salter, Charles A., 1947-
The vegetarian teen. Millbrook Press 1991 112p il $16.40

613.2

1. Vegetarianism 2. Diet 3. Nutrition
ISBN 1-56294-048-1

"A Teen nutrition book"

The author discusses vegetarianism and "explains how to go about it through planning well-balanced meals. He addresses some of the problems of teenagers that may arise, such as what do you do when everyone goes for burgers and you order salad. . . . There is a short recipe section." BAYA Book Rev

"An introduction to vegetarianism that is enthusiastic but also considerate of the nutritional needs of teenagers." Booklist

Includes bibliography

Tver, David F.
The nutrition and health encyclopedia; [by] David F. Tver and Percy Russell. 2nd ed. Van Nostrand Reinhold 1989 639p il $49.95

613.2

1. Nutrition 2. Health—Dictionaries
ISBN 0-442-23397-3

LC 88-33957

First published 1981

Terms in nutrition and health are arranged in dictionary format; appendixes include tables and lists, charts, cross-references

613.6 Promotion of health—Special topics

Olsen, Larry Dean, 1939-
Outdoor survival skills. 5th ed. Chicago Review Press 1990 224p il pa $11.95

613.6

1. Wilderness survival
ISBN 1-55652-084-0

LC 89-49670

Also available in paperback from Simon & Schuster
First published 1967 by Brigham Young Univ.

"Olsen presents explicit instructions for such wilderness survival tactics and skills as shelter construction, fire building, and food procurement. A useful resource for backpackers and other outdoor adventurers." Booklist

613.7 Physical fitness

Baechle, Thomas R., 1943-
Fitness weight training; [by] Tom R. Baechle, Roger W. Earle. Human Kinetics 1995 169p il (Fitness spectrum series) pa $14.95

613.7

1. Weight lifting 2. Physical fitness
ISBN 0-87322-445-0

LC 94-28361

The authors "provide an overview of weight-training benefits compared to other fitness regimes, offer guide-

Baechle, Thomas R., 1943——*Continued*
lines for equipment selection, and discuss whether one needs to join a fitness club. . . . The sample exercise programs are color coded for easy reference and graduated to ensure progress with minimal risk of injury or undue strain." Booklist

Kennedy, Robert, 1938-
Bodybuilding basics. Sterling 1991 128p il pa $10.95   **613.7**
1. Bodybuilding
ISBN 0-8069-7392-7   LC 90-28701
First published 1984 with title: Start bodybuilding
The author "starts with medically sound principles, continues with the latest information on proper nutrition, and then gives a thorough explanation of recommended techniques. A surefire winner for reluctant readers." SLJ

Micheli, Lyle J., 1940-
Healthy runner's handbook; [by] Lyle J. Micheli with Mark Jenkins. Human Kinetics 1996 253p il pa $16.95   **613.7**
1. Running 2. Sports medicine 3. Wounds and injuries
ISBN 0-88011-524-6   LC 95-26222
"Covers 31 injuries." On cover
The authors present "techniques for preventing, diagnosing, caring for, and rehabilitating common running injuries. . . . A chapter devoted to female runners' special concerns (skeletal injuries, eating disorders, and hormonal problems) and another on nutrition round out an excellent resource." Booklist

Peterson, James A., 1943-
Strength training for women; [by] James A. Peterson, Cedric X. Bryant, Susan L. Peterson. Human Kinetics 1995 155p il pa $15.95   **613.7**
1. Weight lifting 2. Physical fitness 3. Women—Health and hygiene
ISBN 0-87322-752-2   LC 94-47646
This handbook describes a variety of weight training styles with instructions and demonstrational photographs and covers such topics as nutrition and overcoming inhibitions
The authors offer "sound advice and encouragement to those interested in this sport." Voice Youth Advocates

Soft workouts; low-impact exercise. Time-Life Bks. 1988 144p il (Fitness, health, and nutrition) $17.27   **613.7**
1. Exercise 2. Physical fitness
                                            LC 87-33604
This guide to physical fitness incorporates illustrations and descriptions of low-impact exercises, including some to be performed in water. Guidelines for planning a personal exercise program, advice on nutrition, and recipes are appended

White, Timothy P.
The wellness guide to lifelong fitness; by Timothy P. White and the editors of the University of California at Berkeley wellness letter. Rebus 1993 476p il $29.95   **613.7**
1. Exercise 2. Physical fitness
ISBN 0-929661-08-7   LC 93-19083
At head of title: University of California at Berkeley
A "comprehensive guide to overall physical well-being. More than 1,000 full-color photographs are used to illustrate the proper techniques for aerobic walking, running, cycling, swimming, stretching, and strength training. Unlike many illustrations in fitness books, these photos are actually helpful—carefully designed to clearly demonstrate arm, leg, and body positions. . . . A superb book." Booklist

613.9 Birth control and sex hygiene

Bell, Ruth
Changing bodies, changing lives; a book for teens on sex and relationships; [by] Ruth Bell and other co-authors of Our bodies, ourselves and Ourselves and our children, together with members of the Teen-Book-Project. rev & updated. Random House 1987 254p il $29.95; pa $12.95   **613.9**
1. Sex education
ISBN 0-394-56499-5; 0-394-75541-3 (pa)
                                            LC 87-42649
First published 1980
"A monumental, encyclopedic discussion of sexual and emotional change during the teen years." SLJ

Fenwick, Elizabeth, 1935-
How sex works; a clear, comprehensive guide for teenagers to emotional, physical, and sexual maturity; [by] Elizabeth Fenwick & Richard Walker. Dorling Kindersley 1994 96p il $14.95; pa $9.95   **613.9**
1. Sex education
ISBN 1-56458-505-0; 0-7894-0634-9 (pa)
                                            LC 93-37638
The authors give an "explanation of the body changes, feelings, and decisions that all young people face during the teen years. Issues such as sexual abuse, AIDS, pregnancy, contraception, and sexual preference are clearly addressed with enough information for teens to make their own decisions as to how to deal with them. The book is illustrated throughout with photos, drawings, and diagrams that help to clarify and explain the subject." Voice Youth Advocates

Moe, Barbara A.
Everything you need to know about sexual abstinence; [by] Barbara Moe. Rosen Pub. Group 1996 64p il (Need to know library) lib bdg $15.95   **613.9**
1. Celibacy 2. Sex education 3. Youth—Sexual behavior
ISBN 0-8239-2104-2   LC 95-21957
Presents facts about human sexuality and discusses the choices teenagers face in deciding whether or not to be sexually active
Includes bibliographical references

Teenage sexuality: opposing viewpoints; Karin L. Swisher, book editor; Terry O'Neill & Bruno Leone, assistant editors. Greenhaven Press 1994 236p il lib bdg $19.95; pa $11.95   **613.9**
1. Sex education
ISBN 1-56510-103-0 (lib bdg); 1-56510-102-2 (pa)
LC 93-30962
"Opposing viewpoints series"
Replaces the edition published 1988 under the editorship of Neal Bernards
Issues covered include teenagers' attitudes about sex, teen pregnancy, sex education, and teenage homosexuality
"Graphics are clear, well chosen, and liberally placed throughout the text. The writing styles are smooth and the reading levels are accessible. . . . A good addition to balanced collection, and a solid research resource." SLJ
Includes bibliographies

Winikoff, Beverly
The contraceptive handbook; a guide to safe and effective choices; [by] Beverly Winikoff, Suzanne Wymelenberg, and the editors of Consumer Reports Books. Consumer Repts. Bks. 1992 248p il $18.95   **613.9**
1. Birth control
ISBN 0-89043-430-1   LC 92-98
The authors "present basic facts about anatomy and physiology and the latest information about barrier methods, pills, intrauterine devices, male and female sterilization, and natural methods of contraception. They discuss the advantages, disadvantages, costs, and methods of obtaining each type of contraceptive. . . . Thorough, objective coverage makes *The Contraceptive Handbook* an excellent choice for all collections." Libr J
Includes bibliography

614   Forensic medicine, incidence & prevention of disease

Grauer, Neil A.
Medicine and the law; [by] Neil Grauer; introduction by C. Everett Koop. Chelsea House 1989 119p il (Encyclopedia of health) lib bdg $19.95   **614**
1. Medical jurisprudence
ISBN 0-7910-0088-5   LC 89-10027
This book provides a "general overview of issues from euthanasia, animal rights, and abortion to genetic engineering, surrogate motherhood, and medical malpractice. . . . The information is solid, and the style and format have the accessibility of a magazine article, with lots of illustrations and subheads." Booklist
Includes glossary and bibliography

Lampton, Christopher
DNA fingerprinting. Watts 1991 111p il lib bdg $22.70   **614**
1. DNA fingerprints
ISBN 0-531-13003-7   LC 91-16533
"An Impact book"

Examines the procedures and uses of DNA fingerprinting as a method of identification in forensic science
"A lively, well-organized introduction to a specific, sometimes controversial area of forensic science." Booklist
Includes glossary and bibliography

Thomas, Peggy
Talking bones; the science of forensic anthropology. Facts on File 1995 136p il (Facts on File science sourcebooks) $17.95   **614**
1. Forensic anthropology
ISBN 0-8160-3114-2   LC 94-44110
Introduces the history, technology, and importance of the science of using human remains to solve crimes. Actual forensic cases are included
"Not only does this book give interesting and somewhat gory facts about forensics, it provides students with an understanding of how this science benefits our society." Book Rep
Includes glossary and bibliographical references

614.4   Incidence of and public measures to prevent disease

Encyclopedia of plague and pestilence; editor, George C. Kohn. Facts on File 1995 408p $45   **614.4**
1. Epidemics—Dictionaries 2. Medicine—History
ISBN 0-8160-2758-7   LC 94-23135
"Alphabetical entries give geographical and historical information about major outbreaks from the past to the present. Each article gives the particulars of the disease: when and where it started, how and why it occurred and spread, whom it affected, and what was the outcome or significance." Book Rep
"A book that will enrich science, social studies, English, and other classes, as well as inform general readers." SLJ

Giblin, James, 1933-
When plague strikes; the Black Death, smallpox, AIDS; by James Cross Giblin; woodcuts by David Frampton. HarperCollins Pubs. 1995 212p $14.95; lib bdg $14.89; pa $6.95   **614.4**
1. Plague 2. Smallpox 3. AIDS (Disease) 4. Epidemics
ISBN 0-06-025854-3; 0-06-025864-0 (lib bdg); 0-06-446195-5 (pa)   LC 94-39881
"Giblin takes a look back to ancient Egypt, to the Dark Ages, and to the age of the smallpox epidemics and finds intriguing historic parallels. Then he traces what is known about the *AIDS* epidemic from its earliest suspected case to the present. Giblin closes his study with the report of a new plague, a mutation of the hantavirus, which seems to be ready to continue to wreck havoc on populations worldwide." Book Rep
The author "writes with simplicity and drama about three terrible plagues and about the suffering, bigotry, and humanity of people, then and now." Booklist
Includes bibliographical references

Karlen, Arno
Man and microbes; disease and plagues in history and modern times. Putnam 1995 266p $24.95   614.4
1. Epidemics 2. Communicable diseases
ISBN 0-87477-759-3   LC 94-36164
Also available in paperback from Simon & Schuster
"A Jeremy P. Tarcher/Putnam book"
Karlen presents a "report on the current global crisis of new and resurgent diseases. Covering cholera, leprosy, cancer, AIDS, viral encephalitis, lethal Ebola fever, streptococcal 'flesh-eating' infections and a host of other killers, he shows how the present wave of diseases arose with drastic environmental change, wars, acceleration of travel, the breakdown of public health measures, and microbial adaptation." Publ Wkly
"An excellent research source." SLJ
Includes bibliographical references

614.5 Incidence & prevention of specific diseases

Leavitt, Judith Walzer
Typhoid Mary; captive to the public's health. Beacon Press 1996 331p il $25   614.5
1. Typhoid Mary, d. 1938 2. Typhoid fever 3. Public health
ISBN 0-8070-2102-4   LC 95-43486
"The story of Mary Mallon, the Irish immigrant cook who later became known as 'Typhoid Mary,' dramatically illustrates the conflict between the needs of an individual and the needs of society. . . . Leavitt . . . has examined the medical, legal, and social perspectives of the early 20th century as she endeavors to understand Mallon's situation, her reactions to her isolation, and the reaction of the media and of the public. Leavitt concludes her book with an interesting discussion of the relevance of Mallon's story to recent public health concerns." Libr J
Includes bibliographical references

Preston, Richard
The hot zone. Random House 1994 300p $23
                                            614.5
1. Ebola virus 2. Animal experimentation
ISBN 0-679-43094-6   LC 94-13415
Also available in paperback from Anchor Bks.
This book is a "reconstruction of what happened in the winter of 1989, when Ebola virus broke out in a monkey quarantine facility at Reston, Va., . . . and threatened to spark an American epidemic." N Y Times Book Rev
"YAs interested in science or fans of Stephen King or Michael Crichton will find this a fast-paced medical chiller right to the last disturbing page." SLJ

Ryan, Frank, 1944-
The forgotten plague; how the battle against tuberculosis was won—and lost. Little, Brown 1993 c1992 460p il hardcover o.p. paperback available $15.95   614.5
1. Tuberculosis
ISBN 0-316-76381-0 (pa)   LC 92-46893
"Including information on the relationship between AIDS and TB, Ryan looks at the research into this new threat and discusses what is allowing the disease to regain momentum." Booklist
"A compelling picture of the process of scientific research as well as a troubling look at an emerging public health crisis, Ryan's book is recommended for all libraries." Libr J
Includes bibliographical references

615 Pharmacology and therapeutics

Check, William A.
Drugs & perception; [by] William Check. Chelsea House 1988 111p il (Encyclopedia of psychoactive drugs) lib bdg $19.95   615
1. Drugs 2. Perception
ISBN 1-55546-214-6   LC 87-29501
Explains the effects of psychoactive drugs on the senses including such experiences as distorted self-image, paranoia, damage to the sensory organs, and confusion of reality and illusion
Includes bibliography

Facklam, Margery, 1927-
Healing drugs; the history of pharmacology; [by] Margery and Howard Facklam. Facts on File 1992 120p il (Facts on File science sourcebooks) lib bdg $17.95   615
1. Pharmacology
ISBN 0-8160-2627-0   LC 92-9198
Traces the history of pharmacology, from the early days of leeches and simple plants to modern research into drugs to work against cancer
"An excellent introduction to the subject." SLJ
Includes glossary and bibliography

Gilbert, Richard J.
Caffeine, the most popular stimulant. Chelsea House 1986 154p il (Encyclopedia of psychoactive drugs) lib bdg $19.95   615
1. Caffeine
ISBN 0-87754-756-4   LC 85-25970
A discussion of caffeine's influence on the human body and mind
"Gilbert's brief list of further readings includes some possibly hard-to-come-by material, but his index is good; his glossary will be helpful; and captioned black-and-white photographs add interest." Booklist

Kittredge, Mary, 1949-
Prescription and over-the-counter drugs; introduction by C. Everett Koop. Chelsea House 1989 110p il (Encyclopedia of health) lib bdg $19.95
615
1. Drugs 2. Nonprescription drugs
ISBN 0-7910-0062-1   LC 88-34173
Following a history of the use of drugs in medicine, this book includes chapters covering the sources and manufacture of drugs, how they work in the human body, and what current drug research implies for the future. Appended are sources of further information, and a checklist of common prescription and OTC drugs
Includes glossary and bibliography

The **Merck** index; an encyclopedia of chemicals, drugs and biologicals. Chapman & Hall il $45
615
1. Materia medica—Indexes 2. Drugs—Indexes
Also available CD-ROM version
First published 1889. (12th edition 1996) Periodically revised
"Technical descriptions of the preparation, properties, uses, commercial names, and toxicity of drugs and medicines." N Y Public Libr. Book of How & Where to Look It Up

Rodgers, Joann Ellison
Drugs & sexual behavior. Chelsea House 1988 92p il (Encyclopedia of psychoactive drugs) lib bdg $19.95
615
1. Drugs 2. Sexual behavior
ISBN 1-55546-215-4   LC 87-23272
Discusses the sexual responses of the human body as they are affected by hormones and various kinds of drugs including alcohol, psychotropic drugs, and supposed aphrodisiacs
Includes glossary and bibliography

Theodore, Alan
The origins & sources of drugs. Chelsea House 1988 120p il (Encyclopedia of psychoactive drugs) lib bdg $19.95
615
1. Drugs
ISBN 1-55546-234-0   LC 87-35233
Describes the characteristics and effects of various drugs derived from plants
Includes bibliography

Zimmerman, David R.
Zimmerman's Complete guide to nonprescription drugs. 2nd ed. Gale Res. 1992 lix, 1125p $45; pa $19.95
615
1. Nonprescription drugs
ISBN 0-8103-8874-X; 0-8103-9421-9 (pa)
LC 92-32693
First published 1983 by Harper & Row with title: The essential guide to nonprescription drugs
"Written for general readers. Arranged alphabetically by therapeutic categories such as cold and cough remedies, antihistamines, smoking deterrents, sun-screens, etc. Detailed table of contents; general index; symptoms index." Guide to Ref Books. 11th edition

615.8 Specific therapies and kinds of therapies

Gilbert, Susan K.
Medical fakes and frauds; introduction by C. Everett Koop. Chelsea House 1989 101p il (Encyclopedia of health) lib bdg $19.95   **615.8**
1. Quacks and quackery
ISBN 0-7910-0090-7   LC 88-30184
Describes fraudulent remedies and their peddlers over the centuries, probes the reasons people are easily deceived, and offers advice on how to avoid falling prey to false promises
"The purpose of this book is to inform the public of the dangers of medical frauds. This aim is well achieved through the author's journalistic style as she relates a number of case histories from the recent past. Excellent illustrations accompany the text." Sci Books Films
Includes glossary and bibliography

Kusinitz, Marc
Folk medicine; introduction by C. Everett Koop. Chelsea House 1991 110p il (Encyclopedia of health) lib bdg $19.95   **615.8**
1. Traditional medicine
ISBN 0-7910-0083-4   LC 91-19627
A look at how folk medicine varies in different cultures and how it affects modern medicine
Includes glossary and bibliography

Stewart, Gail, 1949-
Alternative healing; opposing viewpoints. Greenhaven Press 1990 111p il (Great mysteries) lib bdg $16.95   **615.8**
1. Alternative medicine
ISBN 0-89908-083-9   LC 90-3807
Examines the arguments for and against alternative healing methods such as psychic and natural healing, self-healing, and faith healing
Includes bibliographical references

616 Diseases

Biddle, Wayne
A field guide to germs. Holt & Co. 1995 196p il $22.50
616
1. Microbiology 2. Germ theory of disease
ISBN 0-8050-3531-1   LC 94-48204
Also available in paperback from Anchor Bks.
"Relaying essential information about the 100 most prevalent, powerful, or literarily famous microbiological malefactors in dictionary-encyclopedia style, Biddle injects social and political history into the exposition to provide fuller understanding of germs, their roles in society, their histories, and their current statuses. . . . Eminently entertaining, the book yet has the serious purpose of showing how concerns other than science and the relief of human suffering have affected the course of medical history." Booklist
Includes bibliographical references

Brynie, Faith Hickman, 1946-

Genetics & human health; a journey within; illustrated by Sharon Lane Holm. Millbrook Press 1995 128p il lib bdg $16.40   **616**

1. Medical genetics

ISBN 1-56294-545-9   LC 94-25832

The author provides an "explanation of the relationship between genetics and diseases. . . . Brynie tells about Mendel, Crick and Watson, and Wexler, showing how their discoveries built on existing knowledge. She describes inherited diseases, some of which are more prevalent than others (cystic fibrosis, Marfan's syndrome, sickle-cell anemia, Huntington's disease), personalizing the discussion with individual cases and mentioning famous victims when appropriate." SLJ

Includes glossary and bibliographical references

Drlica, Karl

Double-edged sword; the promises and risks of the genetic revolution; [by] Karl A. Drlica. Addison-Wesley 1994 242p il $20; pa $13   **616**

1. Medical genetics 2. Genetic engineering

ISBN 0-201-40982-8 (pa)   LC 94-14033

"Drlica's goal with this book is to educate the general reader in the intricacies of genetic testing, prenatal screening, gene therapy, and screening for predisposition to cancer. Compelling case histories are used to introduce each topic, and ethical issues are addressed throughout." Sci Books Films

Includes glossary and bibliographical references

Edelson, Edward, 1932-

Birth defects; introduction by C. Everett Koop. Chelsea House 1992 111p il (Encyclopedia of health) lib bdg $19.95   **616**

1. Birth defects

ISBN 0-7910-0058-3   LC 91-27448

This introduction looks at hereditary, chromosomal and environmental conditions that lead to birth defects. Problems related to alcohol, drugs and medications are addressed

Includes glossary and bibliography

Kittredge, Mary, 1949-

Pain; introduction by C. Everett Koop. Chelsea House 1992 111p il (Encyclopedia of health) lib bdg $19.95   **616**

1. Pain

ISBN 0-7910-0072-9   LC 91-3739

Discusses what pain is, how it happens, kinds of pain, some common pains, drugs to treat pain, and pain relief without drugs

Includes glossary and bibliography

Microorganisms from smallpox to Lyme disease; readings from Scientific American magazine; edited by Thomas D. Brock. Freeman, W.H. 1990 173p il maps pa $16.95   **616**

1. Microbiology 2. Communicable diseases

ISBN 0-7167-2084-1   LC 89-17205

Articles explore "the benefits and limits of prevention and cure and discuss malaria and trypanosomiasis and the difficulties encountered in developing therapeutic drugs to target protozoa-caused illnesses." Publisher's note

Includes bibliographical references

Nourse, Alan Edward, 1928-

The virus invaders; [by] Alan E. Nourse. Watts 1992 96p il lib bdg $22   **616**

1. Viruses

ISBN 0-531-12511-4   LC 91-36650

"A Venture book"

Explores different viruses and our body's defenses against them

"Historical events unfold to illustrate beautifully the role of the scientific method in solving the mysteries of viruses—what they are, how they are discovered, and how they cause disease. Analogies and action-packed adjectives and nouns will keep young readers actively involved in unraveling the mysteries of these 'tiny tyrants.' . . . Overall, the book is recommended highly, both for general knowledge and as supplement material for the classroom." Sci Books Films

Includes bibliographical references

Radetsky, Peter

The invisible invaders; the story of the emerging age of viruses. Little, Brown 1991 415p il $22.95; pa $14.95   **616**

1. Viruses

ISBN 0-316-73216-8; 0-316-73217-6 (pa)

    LC 90-6612

This book presents "the history, nature and operation of viruses responsible for AIDS, cancer and other lethal diseases." Publ Wkly

"Radetsky succeeds in his aim to inform and intrigue general readers while remaining 'absolutely accurate in terms of the workings of these invisible invaders and the people who spend their lives dealing with them.' This fascinating and important book is highly recommended." Libr J

Includes bibliography

Roueché, Berton, 1911-1994

The medical detectives. New Am. Lib. 1991 c1988 421p pa $13.95   **616**

1. Medicine

ISBN 0-452-26588-6   LC 90-14267

Companion volume The man who grew two breasts: and other true tales of medical detection available in paperback for $10.95 (ISBN 0-452-27410-9)

"A Truman Talley book"

A collection of medical investigative articles pulled from The New Yorker between 1947-1988. Some of the articles were previously published in the 1980 Times Books edition

Wynbrandt, James

The encyclopedia of genetic disorders and birth defects; [by] James Wynbrandt and Mark D. Ludman. Facts on File 1991 xxi, 426p il $50

616

1. Birth defects—Dictionaries 2. Medical genetics—Dictionaries 3. Growth disorders—Dictionaries

ISBN 0-8160-1926-6   LC 89-48278

This encyclopedia gives "explanations of the physical characteristics and mode of inheritance of genetic disorders. . . . Explanations include information on prognosis, incidence in the population, prenatal diagnosis, and interesting background information concerning discovery and name." Booklist

"A readable book with a wealth of information for students of biology and psychology. It has well-written and clearly cited source entries, and gives excellent background on genetic problems." SLJ

Includes bibliography

Yancey, Diane

The hunt for hidden killers; ten cases of medical mystery. Millbrook Press 1994 127p il lib bdg $15.90

616

1. Medicine

ISBN 1-56294-389-8   LC 93-16638

Describes how doctors and public health investigators work to unravel the mysteries surrounding unusual symptoms, unexplained poisonings, and outbreaks of rare or previously unknown diseases

"An excellent resource for health classes, this book could possibly be used for science fair ideas as well." Book Rep

Includes glossary and bibliography

616.02   Domestic medicine and medical emergencies

American Medical Association family medical guide; medical editor, Charles B. Clayman. rev & updated 3rd ed. Random House 1994 880p il $37.50

616.02

1. Medicine 2. Health self-care

ISBN 0-679-41290-5   LC 94-2116

First published 1982

"Aimed at general readers, this guide is in four main sections: general discussion of the healthy body, self-diagnosis symptom charts with visual aids to diagnosis, diseases and other disorders and problems, and caring for the sick, including a section on accidents and emergencies. Glossary and subject index." Guide to Ref Books. 11th edition

The American Medical Association handbook of first aid & emergency care; developed by the American Medical Association; medical editors: Stanley M. Zydlo, Jr., James A. Hill; illustrations by Larry Frederick. rev ed. Random House 1990 332p il (American Medical Association home reference library) pa $10

616.02

1. First aid

ISBN 0-679-72959-3   LC 89-43545

First published 1980

"A general introduction to procedures is followed by an alphabetical section that has entries on diseases and injuries, giving background information, symptoms, a list of what to do, immediate action to take, and continual care." Nichols. Guide to Ref Books for Sch Media Cent. 4th edition

Kittredge, Mary, 1949-

Emergency medicine; introduction by C. Everett Koop. Chelsea House 1991 111p il (Encyclopedia of health) lib bdg $19.95

616.02

1. Emergency medicine 2. First aid

ISBN 0-7910-0063-X   LC 90-1715

Describes emergency medicine, those who provide it, a variety of emergency situations, and possible prevention tips

"YAs should find this an interesting and easy read. This is a fine addition to any health education course." Voice Youth Advocates

Includes glossary and bibliography

The New Good Housekeeping family health and medical guide. rev ed. Hearst Bks. 1989 788p il $24.95

616.02

1. Health 2. Medicine

ISBN 0-688-06164-8   LC 88-11257

First published 1980 with title: Good Housekeeping family health & medical guide

This book "includes lengthy discussions of life stages and health, promoting wellness, and first aid, in addition to brief essays covering specific diseases, types of health-care providers, tests, and procedures. . . . Medical terms are explained parenthetically." Libr J

Includes bibliographical references

616.07   Pathology

Clark, William R., 1938-

At war within; the double-edged sword of immunity. Oxford Univ. Press 1995 276p $22

616.07

1. Immunity

ISBN 0-19-509286-4   LC 94-45134

The author combines discussion of AIDS, allergies, tuberculosis and other subjects in this overview of the immune system. "Devoting each chapter to a unique malady or condition, he provides the details needed to understand our immune structure, particularly when it unravels and turns on itself. These details do not overwhelm the general reader's grasp of the topic; instead they support it. Clark's presentation is straightforward, arranged well, and includes historical background." Libr J

Includes bibliography

Edelson, Edward, 1932-

The immune system; introduction by C. Everett Koop. Chelsea House 1989 103p il (Encyclopedia of health) lib bdg $19.95

616.07

1. Immunity

ISBN 0-7910-0021-4   LC 89-743

"Edelson writes clearly about microbiology, beginning with the structure of cells and the development of anti-

Edelson, Edward, 1932——Continued
bodies. He talks about allergies . . . autoimmune disease, immune deficiency diseases like 'AIDS,' and developments in genetic engineering." Booklist
Includes glossary and bibliography

Murphy, Wendy B.
Nuclear medicine; [by] Wendy and Jack Murphy. Chelsea House 1994 111p il (Encyclopedia of health) lib bdg $19.95   **616.07**
1. Nuclear medicine
ISBN 0-7910-0070-2   LC 92-44342
Reviews the history of nuclear medicine beginning with the discovery of the X-ray and follows the evolution of the field to the present, using specific medical problems in examples of how the technology works
"The book provides enough information for the reader to be a partner with the doctor in getting the best treatment." Sci Books Films
Includes glossary and bibliography

Nuland, Sherwin B.
How we die; reflections on life's final chapter. Knopf 1994 278p $24; pa $13   **616.07**
1. Death
ISBN 0-679-41461-4; 0-679-74244-1 (pa)
                                        LC 93-24590
Also available large print edition for $23 (ISBN 0-679-75690-6)
The author provides "information on the clinical, biological and emotional details of deaths resulting from heart disease, stroke, cancer, AIDS, Alzheimer's disease, old age, accidents, suicide, euthanasia and murder or violent physical assault." Publ Wkly
"Nuland is one of those rare physicians who know a great deal about a great deal, not only medicine but also its history and, beyond that, literature and the humanities." Commentary

Pinckney, Cathey
The patient's guide to medical tests; [by] Cathey Pinckney and Edward R. Pinckney. 3rd ed. Facts on File 1986 385p $27.95   **616.07**
1. Diagnosis
ISBN 0-8160-1292-X   LC 82-21129
First published 1978 in paperback by Pocket Books with title: The encyclopedia of medical tests
This book's primary emphasis is "educating the patient-consumer about the purpose and effectiveness of more than 1,200 of the most common medical tests—and the relative benefits, risks, and costs of these tests." Booklist

616.1   Diseases of the cardiovascular system

Arnold, Caroline, 1944-
Heart disease. Watts 1990 111p il lib bdg $22
                                        616.1
1. Heart—Diseases
ISBN 0-531-10884-8   LC 90-33609
"A Venture book"

The author discusses "the symptoms, prevention, and treatment of such infectious diseases as rheumatic fever and bacterial endocarditis, as well as atherosclerosis, angina, and congestive heart failure. . . . Arnold's concise, fluid writing competently imparts well-researched, up-to-date information." Booklist
Includes glossary and bibliography

Beshore, George W.
Sickle cell anemia; [by] George Beshore. Watts 1994 94p il lib bdg $19.90   **616.1**
1. Sickle cell anemia
ISBN 0-531-12510-6   LC 94-15513
"A Venture book"
"An overview of a hereditary blood disorder that primarily affects people of African and Mediterranean descent. Beshore relates its history, and explains how the disease is passed from one generation to another. He discusses how to live with sickle cell anemia, as well as the new treatments and ongoing research." SLJ
"A valuable resource for general information and research." Booklist
Includes bibliographical references

616.2   Diseases of the respiratory system

Aaseng, Nathan, 1953-
The common cold and the flu. Watts 1992 95p il lib bdg $22   **616.2**
1. Influenza 2. Cold (Disease)
ISBN 0-531-12537-8   LC 92-15137
"A Venture book"
Discusses the causes, symptoms, methods of prevention, and treatment of two common ailments, colds and flus
Includes bibliographical references

Kittredge, Mary, 1949-
The common cold; introduction by C. Everett Koop. Chelsea House 1989 104p il (Encyclopedia of health) lib bdg $19.95   **616.2**
1. Cold (Disease)
ISBN 0-7910-0060-5   LC 89-10009
Explains the common cold, including symptoms, causes, treatments, and prevention
"Good for research, this book deals with a common illness in a very interesting and comprehensive way." Voice Youth Advocates
Includes glossary and bibliography

616.4   Diabetes

Little, Marjorie
Diabetes; introduction by C. Everett Koop. Chelsea House 1990 111p il (Encyclopedia of health) lib bdg $19.95   **616.4**
1. Diabetes
ISBN 0-7910-0061-3   LC 90-1720
"Little begins with a historical overview of the disease and concludes with a look at what the future may yield.

Little, Marjorie—*Continued*

The bulk of the text explains two types of diabetes, the complications that may occur if they go undiagnosed and untreated, and the ways in which self-health monitoring enables those who have diabetes to get on with their lives." Booklist

Includes glossary and bibliography

616.5 Diseases of the skin, hair, nails

Bergfeld, Wilma F., 1938-

A woman doctor's guide to skin care; essential facts and up-to-the minute information on keeping skin healthy at any age; by Wilma F. Bergfeld, with Shelagh Ryan Masline. Hyperion 1995 207p pa $9.95   **616.5**

1. Skin—Care and hygiene

ISBN 0-7868-8100-3   LC 95-1576

This offers "advice on the care and treatment of the skin, hair and nails. Diet, skin care at different ages, cancer, infections and cosmetic products are among the topics covered. Medical advice . . . is included, as well as information on choosing over-the-counter shampoos, soaps and cosmetics based on skin and hair types." Publ Wkly

Includes glossary and bibliographical references

MacKie, Rona M.

Healthy skin; the facts. Oxford Univ. Press 1992 148p il $19.95   **616.5**

1. Skin—Care and hygiene

ISBN 0-19-262246-3   LC 91-39238

This book "explains how the skin is structured and how it works, before giving information on healthy skin and the prevention of skin disease." Univ Press Books for Public and Second Sch Libr

Turkington, Carol

Skin deep; an A-Z of skin disorders, treatments and health; [by] Carol A. Turkington and Jeffrey S. Dover; medical illustrations by Birck Cox. Facts on File 1996 404p il $40   **616.5**

1. Skin

ISBN 0-8160-3071-5   LC 95-10187

"Skin diseases and injuries are defined, causes and symptoms are given, and diagnostic methods and treatments are described. Cosmetic treatment procedures such as laser resurfacing are covered. There are articles on skin care, types of soaps, cosmetics, aging skin, skin problems associated with AIDS, allergies, baldness, and skin cancer." Booklist

Walzer, Richard A., 1930-

Treating acne; [by] Richard A. Walzer and the editors of Consumer Reports Books. Consumer Repts. Bks. 1992 100p il $16.95   **616.5**

1. Acne

ISBN 0-89043-449-2   LC 91-40262

This overview of acne discusses its causes, various self-help treatments, seeing a dermatologist, choosing the right cosmetics, and methods available for repairing scars

Includes glossary

616.8 Diseases of the nervous system and mental disorders

Aaseng, Nathan, 1953-

Cerebral palsy. Watts 1991 95p il lib bdg $19.14   **616.8**

1. Cerebral palsy

ISBN 0-531-12529-7   LC 91-18558

"A Venture book"

"Aaseng discusses the causes, prevention, detection, and treatment of cerebral palsy. . . . He presents a brief history of it, then looks at its different forms and manifestations. . . . The material is well presented and easy to understand. . . . A limited list of organizations and readings, over half of which are personal accounts or works of fiction, is appended." Booklist

Killilea, Marie

Karen. Prentice-Hall 1952 314p   **616.8**

1. Killilea, Karen 2. Cerebral palsy

Available in hardcover from Buccaneer Bks.

The mother of Karen, a child with cerebral palsy, tells of Karen's first years and describes the beginnings of the United Cerebral Palsy Association

This "is a wonderful story of human courage, patience, and triumph." N Y Times Book Rev

Followed by With love from Karen (1963)

Kittredge, Mary, 1949-

Headaches; introduction by C. Everett Koop. Chelsea House 1989 102p il (Encyclopedia of health) lib bdg $19.95   **616.8**

1. Headache

ISBN 0-7910-0064-8   LC 88-34222

"This volume deals with the history, anatomy, physiology, and pharmacology of different types of headache. The author distills the vast amount of information available on these topics into a brief tour around the periphery of the subject, and various experts are briefly quoted." Sci Books Films

"This is a well-organized book." Sci Teach

Includes glossary and bibliography

Sacks, Oliver W.

The man who mistook his wife for a hat and other clinical tales; [by] Oliver Sacks. Summit Bks. 1985 233p il o.p.; Perennial Lib. paperback available $13   **616.8**

1. Nervous system—Diseases

ISBN 0-06-097079-0 (pa)   LC 85-17220

Also available in hardcover from P. Smith

"Sacks introduces the reader to real people who suffer from a variety of neurological syndromes which includes symptoms such as amnesia, uncontrolled movements, and musical hallucinations. Sacks recounts their stories in a riveting, compassionate, and thoughtful manner." Libr J

Includes bibliography

Shuman, Robert

Living with multiple sclerosis; a handbook for families; [by] Robert Shuman and Janice Schwartz; foreword by Robert J. Slater. Collier Bks. 1994 235p pa $10   **616.8**

1. Multiple sclerosis

ISBN 0-02-082026-7   LC 93-47116

First published 1988 by Scribner with title: Understanding multiple sclerosis

This handbook "addresses the problems that families must face together and provides advice on how to alleviate the psychological pressures of the illness; confront economic, career, and sexual issues; and handle periods of remission that offset episodes of ill health." Publisher's note

Includes bibliographical references

616.85 Neuroses, disorders of personality and intellect, speech and language disorders

Abraham, Suzanne

Eating disorders; the facts; [by] Suzanne Abraham and Derek Llewellyn-Jones. 3rd ed. Oxford Univ. Press 1992 201p il hardcover o.p. paperback available $17.95   **616.85**

1. Eating disorders

ISBN 0-19-262759-7 (pa)   LC 91-47619

First published 1984

This work focuses on diagnosis and treatment of anorexia nervosa, bulimia and obesity

Includes bibliographical references

Antonello, Jean

Breaking out of food jail; how to free yourself from diets and problem eating once and for all. Simon & Schuster 1996 288p il pa $11   **616.85**

1. Eating disorders 2. Women—Psychology

ISBN 0-684-81193-6   LC 96-820

"A Fireside book"

This guide "outlines ways to break loose from a 'feast and famine' cycle of eating and develop a normal relationship with food. For older, diet-conscious teens and students investigating the subject of nutrition." Booklist

Ashley, Joyce

Overcoming stage fright in everyday life. Potter 1996 171p $23   **616.85**

1. Fear 2. Public speaking

ISBN 0-517-70465-X   LC 96-410

This guide to overcoming anxiety of public speaking in business, professional, and personal situations offers case histories and exercises in relaxation, probing childhood memories, and confronting emotions, and advice on seeking professional help

Includes bibliography

Axline, Virginia M.

Dibs: in search of self; personality development in play therapy. Houghton Mifflin 1964 186p o.p.; Ballantine Bks. paperback available $5.99   **616.85**

1. Child psychology

ISBN 0-345-33925-8 (pa)

"A clinical psychologist informally re-creates . . . the dialog and events of her play-therapy sessions with a severely withdrawn five-year-old boy from an intellectual but unloving home." Booklist

Boskind-White, Marlene

Bulimarexia; the binge/purge cycle; [by] Marlene Boskind-White, William C. White, Jr. 2nd ed. Norton 1987 284p hardcover o.p. paperback available $12.95   **616.85**

1. Bulimia

ISBN 0-383-30117-6 (pa)   LC 86-23733

First published 1983

The authors discuss "findings about the psychological consequences of binge-ing, the relationship of dieting to eating disorders, and the need for nutritional counseling. In addition to group therapy, treatment of individuals, families, and couples is covered. The negative aspects of pharmacological ('magic bullet') cures are discussed." Publisher's note

Includes bibliography

Cassell, Dana K.

Encyclopedia of obesity and eating disorders; [by] Dana K. Cassell with Félix E. F. Larocca. Facts on File 1994 259p $45   **616.85**

1. Eating disorders—Dictionaries 2. Obesity—Dictionaries

ISBN 0-8160-1985-1   LC 92-18289

The 400 entries cover "the most common varieties of obesity, anorexia and bulimia disorders, and several lesser-known disorders. Related topics such as drugs, diets, organizations (such as Overeaters Anonymous), surgeries (gastric bubble), and short biographies of researchers important in obesity and eating disorder research are also included." Book Rep

This "offers a broad overview of a complex subject in a way that is readily accessible to lay readers. It provides brief answers for ready-reference purposes and serves as a starting point for further research." Booklist

Controlling eating disorders with facts, advice, and resources; Raymond Lemberg, consulting editor. Oryx Press 1992 xxi, 218p pa $29.50   **616.85**

1. Eating disorders

ISBN 0-89774-691-0   LC 91-42850

A discussion of "eating disorders, their causes, descriptions, health and psychological effects, and treatments. Lembert also includes a directory of facilities and programs state by state, an extensive bibliography . . . and a list of organizations devoted to this problem. Not only an excellent volume for research, the book has a positive tone that will encourage those personally affected by eating disorders." SLJ

Cush, Cathie, 1957-
Depression. Raintree Steck-Vaughn 1994 80p il
(Teen hot line) lib bdg $24.26   **616.85**
  1. Depression (Psychology)
  ISBN 0-8114-3529-6   LC 93-14252
  The author discusses a variety of issues related to
teenage depression, including personal relationships and
pressures, substance abuse, suicide, running away, and
how to get help and develop coping skills
  Includes bibliography

Doctor, Ronald M.
The encyclopedia of phobias, fears, and
anxieties; [by] Ronald M. Doctor and Ada P.
Kahn. Facts on File 1989 487p $50   **616.85**
  1. Phobias—Dictionaries 2. Fear—Dictionaries
  ISBN 0-8160-1798-0   LC 88-31057
  "Arranged alphabetically, the *Encyclopedia* offers psychological, pharmacological, diagnostic, and historical information in entries varying in length from a few lines
to a few pages and concludes with a brief index and an
extensive bibliography. Authoritative yet easier to use
than existing resources, this guide's clear presentation
makes it useful to both the layperson and the professional." Am Libr

Epstein, Rachel S.
Eating habits and disorders; introduction by C.
Everett Koop. Chelsea House 1990 109p il
(Encyclopedia of health) lib bdg $19.95   **616.85**
  1. Eating disorders
  ISBN 0-7910-0048-6   LC 89-22120
  Describes the types of eating disorders and discusses
their possible causes, effects, and treatment
  This "is an appropriate selection for an overview of
the subject, and can readily be used for research and
self-help." Voice Youth Advocates
  Includes glossary and bibliography

Hales, Dianne R., 1950-
Depression; [by] Dianne Hales; introduction by
C. Everett Koop. Chelsea House 1989 101p il
(Encyclopedia of health) lib bdg $19.95   **616.85**
  1. Depression (Psychology)
  ISBN 0-7910-0046-X   LC 88-34176
  Explores some causes of depression, ways to over-
come this illness, and where and when to seek help
  "The presentation is factual as well as insightful and
offers a plethora of useful information. Perhaps the great-
est strength of the book is the clarity of the writing. . . .
Useful anecdotes will help victims view this disorder in
a realistic fashion." Sci Books Films
  Includes glossary and bibliography

Hesse-Biber, Sharlene Janice
Am I thin enough yet? the cult of thinness and
the commercialization of identity; [by] Sharlene
Hesse-Biber. Oxford Univ. Press 1996 191p il $25
                                          616.85
  1. Eating disorders 2. Women—Psychology
  ISBN 0-19-508241-9   LC 95-11812
  "Hesse-Biber examines the socioeconomic forces affecting body perception, emphasizing the differences between men's and women's perceptions of their bodies.
. . . She provides therapeutic options for those seeking
to overcome weight obsessions, eating disorders, and the
mind-body dichotomy that a culture that values minds
more than bodies uses for social control and oppression."
Booklist
  Includes bibliographical references

Hyde, Margaret Oldroyd, 1917-
The violent mind; [by] Margaret O. Hyde &
Elizabeth Held Forsyth. Watts 1991 125p il lib
bdg $22   **616.85**
  1. Violence
  ISBN 0-531-11060-5   LC 91-18566
  Discusses the biological roots of violence, how it can
reflect a troubled mind, and how such mental problems
can be prevented or treated
  "A well-researched and balanced study of violence in
our society. Hyde provides solid statistical material along
with insights to the causes of violence. . . . The contents
are clearly presented with an excellent mix of vignette
case histories and factual material. In both scope and
writing style, the book is for sophisticated high school
students." SLJ
  Includes glossary and bibliography

Kolodny, Nancy J.
When food's a foe; how to confront and
conquer eating disorders; Nancy J. Kolodny. rev &
updated. Little, Brown 1992 198p il pa $9.95
                                          616.85
  1. Anorexia nervosa 2. Bulimia
  ISBN 0-316-50181-6   LC 91-37304
  First published 1987
  "Kolodny presents information about self-image and
eating disorders; how habits become addictions; facts
about anorexia, bulimia and bulimarexia; and ways to
confront the problems. A variety of contemporary comic
strips dot the text. . . . Personal experience letters and
incidents are used to convince readers that changes in behavior can be made." SLJ
  Includes bibliographical references

Maloney, Michael, 1944-
Straight talk about eating disorders; [by]
Michael Maloney and Rachel Kranz. Facts on File
1991 122p $16.95   **616.85**
  1. Eating disorders
  ISBN 0-8160-2414-6   LC 90-49707
  Describes compulsive eating, bulimia, and anorexia
and discusses the mixed messages given to women and
girls about eating, weight, diet, and looks, and how these
messages can be destructive
  This book "provides a clear picture of each of the
three types of eating disorders, endeavouring to give
readers a basis for judging their own or a friend's or
family member's behavior. . . . Teenagers with an interest in psychology may well be fascinated by connections
the authors make." Booklist

McCoy, Kathleen, 1945-
Life happens; a teenager's guide to friends, failure, sexuality, love, rejection, addiction, peer pressure, families, loss, depression, change, and other challenges of living; [by] Kathy McCoy and Charles Wibbelsman. Berkley Pub. Group 1996 213p pa $11   **616.85**
1. Depression (Psychology) 2. Stress (Psychology)
ISBN 0-399-51987-4   LC 95-9647
"A Perigee book"
The authors "explore what they call 'common crises' and suggest, in an expanded checklist form, ways to get past problems and move on with life. . . . [Topics include] the death of a family member, teen pregnancy, the end of a romantic relationship, being homosexual, having an alcoholic parent. . . . What makes this book valuable is its success in trimming each subject to manageable proportions without undue oversimplification." Booklist

Moe, Barbara A.
Coping with eating disorders; [by] Barabara Moe. Rosen Pub. Group 1991 145p lib bdg $15.95   **616.85**
1. Eating disorders
ISBN 0-8239-1343-0   LC 91-11742
Describes the different kinds of eating disorders, what can cause them, and what can be done about them
The author's "writing is competent without being clinical, which makes this book approachable by younger readers. . . . One major positive feature of this title is Moe's ability to draw the reader into the text with the use of numerous case studies." Voice Youth Advocates
Includes bibliography

Morrison, Jaydene
Coping with ADD/ADHD; attention deficit disorder/attention deficit hyperactivity disorder. Rosen Pub. Group 1996 96p il lib bdg $15.95   **616.85**
1. Attention deficit disorder
ISBN 0-8239-2070-4   LC 95-41284
Identifies the syndrome of attention deficit disorder and discusses the appropriate treatment and counseling
"Morrison's tone is optimistic throughout as she stresses various coping mechanisms and the value of a positive attitude. Specific case studies add a personal touch to the narrative." SLJ
Includes glossary and bibliography

Nardo, Don, 1947-
Anxiety and phobias; introduction by C. Everett Koop. Chelsea House 1992 111p il (Encyclopedia of health) lib bdg $19.95   **616.85**
1. Phobias 2. Stress (Psychology)
ISBN 0-7910-0041-9   LC 91-22876
Defines anxieties and phobias and discusses their causes and treatment
Includes glossary and bibliography

Patterson, Charles, 1935-
Eating disorders. Raintree Steck-Vaughn 1995 80p il (Teen hot line) lib bdg $24.26   **616.85**
1. Eating disorders
ISBN 0-8114-3813-9   LC 94-32116
"General information is followed by specific chapters on anorexia, bulimia, compulsive overeating, and treatment. Self-diagnosis quizzes and lists of symptoms and physical effects are highlighted." SLJ
"The quality of the information presented and the professional manner in which the disorders are discussed are impressive. . . . This book can be vitally important in helping young people clarify issues pertaining to the various eating disorders and in giving them direction for getting help." Sci Books Films
Includes bibliographical references

Porterfield, Kay Marie
Straight talk about post-traumatic stress disorder; coping with the aftermath of trauma. Facts on File 1996 135p $17.95; pa $9.95   **616.85**
1. Post-traumatic stress disorder
ISBN 0-8160-3258-0; 0-8160-3552-0 (pa)
    LC 95-21006
An in-depth discussion of the condition known to psychologists as post-traumatic stress disorder or PTSD, including possible causes, symptoms, treatment, the process of recovery, and sources of help
Includes bibliography

Roesch, Roberta
The encyclopedia of depression; introduction by Ewald Horwath. Facts on File 1991 263p $45   **616.85**
1. Depression (Psychology)—Dictionaries
ISBN 0-8160-1936-3   LC 90-3576
This volume offers some five hundred entries discussing depression disorders, drugs, organizations and individuals
"An excellent resource for high school libraries, alphabetically arranged. In addition to the well-written and clearly cited source entries, the book gives a complete overview of the problem of depression." SLJ
Includes bibliography

Sacker, Ira M.
Dying to be thin; [by] Ira M. Sacker and Marc A. Zimmer. Warner Bks. 1987 266p il pa $14.99   **616.85**
1. Anorexia nervosa 2. Bulimia
ISBN 0-446-38417-8   LC 87-10590
Provides information on seeking help for anorexics, bulemics, and their families
Includes bibliography

Sherman, Roberta Trattner, 1949-
Bulimia; a guide for family and friends; [by] Roberta Trattner Sherman, Ron A. Thompson. Lexington Bks. 1990 155p $18.95   **616.85**
1. Bulimia
ISBN 0-669-24503-8   LC 90-34377
"The authors examine the causes (societal, familial, individual); explore behaviors, thoughts and emotions; and

Sherman, Roberta Trattner, 1949——*Continued*
present treatment options. The format is question and answer, and the style is very readable. At the end of each chapter is a list of helpful suggestions." SLJ
Includes bibliography

Silverstein, Alvin
So you think you're fat? all about obesity, anorexia nervosa, bulimia nervosa, and other eating disorders; [by] Alvin & Virginia B. Silverstein with Robert Silverstein. HarperCollins Pubs. 1991 215p lib bdg $14.89   **616.85**
  1. Obesity 2. Eating disorders
  ISBN 0-06-021642-5   LC 90-40761
"This is a comprehensive discussion of understanding weight loss and gain, plus the influence of good eating habits. Chapters include topics on food addiction, dangers of obesity, making a diet work, getting help, anorexia nervosa, and bulimia nervosa." BAYA Book Rev
"The approach is straightforward, compassionate, and avoids being condescending. The advice given is sensible." Voice Youth Advocates
Includes bibliography

Sonder, Ben, 1954-
Eating disorders; when food turns against you. Watts 1993 96p lib bdg $22.70   **616.85**
  1. Eating disorders
  ISBN 0-531-11175-X   LC 92-37547
This book examines such eating disorders as bulimia and anorexia nervosa. "Societal expectations and pressures regarding body image and weight, personality traits that contribute to inappropriate 'relationships' with food, and biological causes of obesity are discussed." Book Rep
"The material is presented clearly, concisely, and in a nonjudgmental, impersonal manner that will make it particularly appropriate for student research." Booklist
Includes glossary and bibliography

Webb, Margot, 1934-
Coping with compulsive behavior. Rosen Pub. Group 1994 107p lib bdg $15.95   **616.85**
  1. Compulsive behavior
  ISBN 0-8239-1604-9   LC 93-29403
Discusses different kinds of compulsive behaviors and their underlying causes, coping with people who have compulsive traits, and where and how compulsive teens can get help
Includes bibliography

616.86   Substance abuse (Drug abuse)

Berger, Gilda
Addiction. rev ed. Watts 1992 176p il lib bdg $22.70   **616.86**
  1. Substance abuse
  ISBN 0-531-11144-X   LC 92-17093
First published 1982

Discusses the phenomenon of compulsive dependence on such pleasure-giving substances as drugs, alcohol, tobacco, caffeine, and food, as well as causes of, treatments for, and societal attitudes toward such addictions
"This book is straight-forward concerning the causes and effects of the physical, psychological and social factors that influence chemical dependency." Voice Youth Advocates
Includes bibliographical references

Crack. rev ed, by Nancy Levitin. Watts 1994 128p il lib bdg $22.70   **616.86**
  1. Crack (Drug) 2. Drug abuse
  ISBN 0-531-11188-1   LC 94-23309
"An Impact book"
First published 1987
This discussion of the danger of crack "devotes space to information about the manufacture and sale of coca leaves that are later processed into crack. There is also information about international efforts to control the shipping of cocaine into this country. . . . This book will be useful for social studies or economics classes because of its information about international issues." Book Rep
Includes glossary and bibliography

Cohen, Susan, 1938-
A six-pack and a fake I.D.: teens look at the drinking question; by Susan and Daniel Cohen. Evans & Co. 1986 150p $13.95   **616.86**
  1. Teenagers—Alcohol use
  ISBN 0-87131-459-2   LC 85-25337
The authors "explain what alcohol is and what it does to the body. They treat facts, myths, and laws associated with drinking and include an intriguing capsule history of alcohol acceptance in the U.S. . . . A chapter describing various alcohol-related associations/organizations (MADD, SADD, etc.) rounds out the treatment." Booklist
Includes bibliography

The **Encyclopedia** of drug abuse; [edited by] Robert O'Brien [et al.] 2nd ed. Facts on File 1992 xxvii, 500p il $50   **616.86**
  1. Drug abuse—Dictionaries
  ISBN 0-8160-1956-8   LC 89-71531
First published 1984
An alphabetically arranged "compendium of biological, legal, medical and social factors of the drug problem." Publisher's note
This "is a good introduction for those beginning research and a fine ready-reference source for definitions, referrals, and statistics." Booklist

Engel, Joel, 1952-
Addicted: kids talking about drugs in their own words; foreword by Michael L. Peck. TOR Bks. 1989 174p hardcover o.p. paperback available $3.95   **616.86**
  1. Drug abuse 2. Youth—Drug use
  ISBN 0-8125-9446-0 (pa)
"Ten personal narratives by teens involved in drug and alcohol abuse. Peer pressure, self-hatred, isolation, shyness, sexual abuse, divorce, and anti-authoritarian urges

Engel, Joel, 1952——Continued

are themes that emerge time after time in each autobiographical tale. Parents who didn't notice the signs of abuse until it was too late are also woefully prevalent. Painful and horrifying as the stories are, they all come with endings of hard-earned sobriety." SLJ

Go ask Alice; Author anonymous. Prentice-Hall
1971 159p $15 **616.86**
1. Drug addiction
ISBN 0-671-66458-1
Also available in paperback from Avon Bks.

Based on an actual diary this is the "story of a fifteen-year-old, white, middle-class girl unsuspectingly introduced to LSD who immediately becomes an avid user of any drug available. . . . A brief epilog tells of her death from an unexplained overdose." Booklist

"An important book, this deserves as wide a readership as libraries can give it." SLJ

Hermes, William J.

Marijuana; its effects on mind and body; [by] William J. Hermes, Anne Galperin. Chelsea House 1992 119p il (Encyclopedia of psychoactive drugs) lib bdg $19.95 **616.86**
1. Marijuana 2. Drug abuse
ISBN 0-87754-754-8 LC 91-17766
First published 1985 under the authorship of Miriam Cohen

Discusses the scientific, social, and personal aspects of marijuana, examining its history, cultural impact, psychological and physical effects, dangers, and legal status

Substance abuse; introduction by C. Everett Koop. Chelsea House 1993 119p il (Encyclopedia of health) lib bdg $19.95 **616.86**
1. Substance abuse 2. Drug abuse
ISBN 0-7910-0078-8 LC 92-1625
Examines such substances as prescription drugs, marijuana, psychedelics, and heroin, discusses their functions and effects, and describes substance addiction and methods of treatment

"This book is a goldmine of basic information for students needing sources for reports, or those after an overview of the subject." Voice Youth Advocates
Includes glossary and bibliography

Porterfield, Kay Marie

Focus on addictions; a reference handbook. ABC-CLIO 1992 242p (Teenage perspectives) $39.50 **616.86**
1. Substance abuse 2. Compulsive behavior
ISBN 0-87436-674-7 LC 92-26623
"This reference handbook covers addiction in its broadest sense, to include not only physically addicting substances but also obsessive-compulsive disorders, impulse control problems, eating disorders, and problems caused by living in an addictive family. The focus is on the similarities in self-destructive behaviors. Each chapter contains a clearly written narrative defining a particular addiction and briefly covering causes, results, and treatment." SLJ
Includes bibliographical references

Ryan, Elizabeth A. (Elizabeth Anne), 1943-

Straight talk about drugs and alcohol. rev ed. Facts on File 1995 152p $16.95; pa $9.95
616.86
1. Drug abuse 2. Alcoholism
ISBN 0-8160-3249-1; 0-8160-3549-0 (pa)
LC 94-41726
First published 1989

In this discussion of drug and alcohol abuse "Ryan uses the stories of several teenagers to prove her points. . . . After looking at some general information about drug use, there is a chapter on the physical effects of drinking. Both long term and short term effects are discussed. The same format is used to discuss other drugs such as marijuana, cocaine, amphetamines, etc. . . . There is also information about where to find help if YAs have a drug problem or need more information." Voice Youth Advocates

"A good source of well-written, precise material that covers the most important aspects of addictions." SLJ
Includes bibliography

Silverstein, Herma

Alcoholism. Watts 1990 126p il lib bdg $22
616.86
1. Alcoholism
ISBN 0-531-10879-1 LC 90-12578
"A Venture book"

Discusses how alcohol affects the body and the lives of both alcoholics and those closest to them

"The disease theory of alcoholism is defined and thoroughly explained in this well written and readable book. . . . Contemporary photographs illustrate strong images of the disease. . . . It is highly recommended for its clear presentation of a complicated theory and Silverstein's sensitive style which never preaches or condescends to the reader." Voice Youth Advocates
Includes bibliography

Weil, Andrew

From chocolate to morphine; everything you need to know about mind-altering drugs; [by] Andrew Weil and Winifred Rosen. rev & updated. Houghton Mifflin 1993 240p il pa $13.95 **616.86**
1. Psychotropic drugs
ISBN 0-395-66079-3 LC 92-31727
First published 1983 with title: Chocolate to morphine

"Neither condoning nor condemning drug use, the authors cover a wide range of available substances, from coffee to marijuana, from antihistamines to psychedelics, from steroids to the new 'smart drugs.' Besides describing the likely effects of each drug, the authors discuss precautions and alternatives." Publisher's note

"Because drug use (legal or illegal) is not condemned, this volume may be considered unorthodox by some. . . . Aimed at young people, their parents and teachers, this book offers an alternative way of looking at drug use." Libr J
Includes glossary and bibliographical references

Winger, Gail
Valium and other tranquilizers. Chelsea House 1992 125p il (Encyclopedia of psychoactive drugs) lib bdg $19.95   **616.86**
1. Valium 2. Drug abuse
ISBN 0-87754-759-9
First published 1986 with title: Valium: the tranquil trap
This book examines the nature, effects, and dangers of use and abuse of Valium and related anti-anxiety drugs
Includes glossary and bibliography

616.89   Mental disorders

Gutkind, Lee
Stuck in time; the tragedy of childhood mental illness. Holt & Co. 1993 253p $25; pa $14.95
616.89
1. Adolescent psychiatry 2. Child psychiatry 3. Mentally ill children
ISBN 0-8050-1469-1; 0-8050-3808-6 (pa)
LC 92-45087
"A series of interviews with mentally ill teens, social workers, and psychiatrists [is] combined with Gutkind's carefully written text. . . . Frustrations with the medical, governmental, and health-care bureaucracies; the ever-present social stigma, the financial system; and the overwhelming difficulties of dealing with the mentally ill child in a family setting on a day-to-day basis are all addressed." SLJ

Lundy, Allan
Diagnosing and treating mental illness; introduction by C. Everett Koop. Chelsea House 1990 136p il (Encyclopedia of health) lib bdg $19.95   **616.89**
1. Mental illness
ISBN 0-7910-0047-8   LC 89-22119
Discusses the types of mental illness and describes how they are diagnosed and treated
"This is a complex topic to be covered in so few pages, but the author has succeeded in giving factual information and insights into common mental illness." Voice Youth Advocates
Includes glossary and bibliography

Smith, Douglas W., 1949-
Schizophrenia. Watts 1993 95p il lib bdg $18.43
616.89
1. Schizophrenia 2. Mental illness
ISBN 0-531-12514-9   LC 92-21140
"A Venture book"
In this examination of schizophrenia the author describes the "history, symptoms, and theories about the causes of the disease. He includes case studies and a comparison of treatments past and present, and speculates on the future." SLJ
"The text is well written and chapters well organized for the reader searching for report material or simply wanting more information about this baffling disorder." Appraisal
Includes glossary and bibliography

Veggeberg, Scott
Medication of the mind; foreword by Richard Restak. Holt & Co. 1996 128p il (Scientific American focus book) $22.50; pa $9.95   **616.89**
1. Psychiatry 2. Mental illness—Drug therapy
ISBN 0-8050-3841-8; 0-8050-3842-6 (pa)
LC 95-34584
A discussion of "the use of drugs and other medical techniques to treat and manage psychiatric illness. . . . Other topics [covered] include health-care costs, gene therapy, and . . . research on the possible physical and genetic components of schizoprenia, violence, alcoholism, and homosexuality." Publisher's note
Includes bibliographical references

Young, Patrick
Schizophrenia; introduction by C. Everett Koop. Chelsea House 1988 114p il (Encyclopedia of health) lib bdg $19.95   **616.89**
1. Schizophrenia
ISBN 0-7910-0052-4   LC 88-1052
"Young looks at disease characteristics, describes some of the more familiar symptoms . . . and discusses different categories of the illness. . . . He goes on to consider biological, psychological, and social theories related to cause and risk factors, turning finally to some of the breakthroughs in medical science. . . . Young has put together a sensitive and informative introduction to a devastating mental health concern, made more affecting by the inclusion of commentary by some of the illness' victims." Booklist
Includes glossary and bibliography

616.9   Other diseases

Gottfried, Robert S., 1949-
The black death; natural and human disaster in medieval Europe. Free Press 1983 203p hardcover o.p. paperback available $16.95   **616.9**
1. Plague
ISBN 0-02-912370-4 (pa)   LC 82-48745
This history examines the social and economic effects of the plague that ravished Europe from 1347 to 1351
Includes bibliography

Harding, Richard M.
Survival in space; medical problems of manned spaceflight; [by] Richard Harding. Routledge 1989 227p il $22   **616.9**
1. Space medicine 2. Space flight
ISBN 0-415-00253-2   LC 88-32091
The author "covers everything from the stresses of acceleration on lift-off through the problems of prolonged weightlessness and personal hygiene in a zero-gravity environment. He also provides a historical overview of the piloted spaceflights to date from the medical point of view and offers a special section on women in space." Booklist
Includes glossary and bibliography

Kusinitz, Marc

Tropical medicine; introduction by C. Everett Koop. Chelsea House 1990 111p il (Encyclopedia of health) lib bdg $19.95　　　**616.9**

1. Tropical medicine

ISBN 0-7910-0079-6　　　LC 89-70819

This book "describes the causes, symptoms, treatments, and preventive measures of such illnesses [as tuberculosis, bubonic plague, and leprosy] and describes the areas in which they are endemic. The book also discusses the efforts of government officials, relief agencies, and tropical peoples who are battling tropical diseases." Publisher's note

Includes glossary and bibliography

Mactire, Sean P.

Lyme disease and other pest-borne illnesses. Watts 1992 111p il lib bdg $22　　　**616.9**

1. Lyme disease

ISBN 0-531-12523-8　　　LC 91-40895

"A Venture book"

Describes the causes, symptoms, and treatment of Lyme disease and examines other pest-borne diseases

"The author has achieved a relatively good balance in describing the nature of these diseases and their associated means of transmission, treatment, and prevention. The book is appropriate for young adults. The writing is straightforward and clear, and the descriptions of signs and symptoms, treatments, and approaches to treatment are brief, but functional." Sci Books Films

Includes bibliographical references

Shader, Laurel

Mononucleosis and other infectious diseases; [by] Laurel Shader and Jon Zonderman; introduction by C. Everett Koop. Chelsea House 1989 111p il (Encyclopedia of health) lib bdg $19.95　　　**616.9**

1. Communicable diseases

ISBN 0-7910-0069-9　　　LC 88-34186

Examines various infectious diseases, including mononucleosis, chicken pox, and infections of the respiratory, gastrointestinal, and genitourinary systems

The authors "have succeeded in gathering the highlights of medical advancements as they apply to this area. . . . Overall, readers will find a great deal of good information in a no-nonsense style." Voice Youth Advocates

Includes bibliography

Wax, Nina

Occupational health; introduction by C. Everett Koop. Chelsea House 1994 111p il (Encyclopedia of health) lib bdg $19.95　　　**616.9**

1. Occupational health and safety

ISBN 0-7910-0089-3　　　LC 93-3903

This book "discusses the development and current status of legal and governmental protection of workers. The causes and symptoms of various diseases that afflict different professions are examined, as well as what both government agencies and private industries are doing to prevent such diseases." Publisher's note

Includes glossary and bibliography

616.95　Venereal diseases

Brodman, Michael

Straight talk about sexually transmitted diseases; [by] Michael Brodman, John Thacker, and Rachel Kranz. Facts on File 1993 138p il $17.95　**616.95**

1. Sexually transmitted diseases

ISBN 0-8160-2864-8　　　LC 93-20411

Provides information about such sexually transmitted diseases as gonorrehea, syphilis, herpes, chlamydia, and AIDS, and how they can be prevented and treated

"The authors are nonjudgmental but emphasize the ethical responsibility one has to oneself and one's partner to disclose previous and current sexual practices that could put another person at risk." Booklist

Includes glossary and bibliography

616.97　Diseases of the immune system

Aaseng, Nathan, 1953-

Autoimmune diseases. Watts 1995 112p il lib bdg $22　　　**616.97**

1. Diseases

ISBN 0-531-12553-X　　　LC 94-49443

"A Venture book"

"Aaseng defines the term and goes into detail about 9 of the more than 40 diseases now categorized or suspected to be autoimmune. He explains how the immune system works and outlines current theories, research, and efforts to find prevention and cures." SLJ

"The black-and-white photos, helpful illustrations, and celebrity anecdotes serve to break up the scientific text, create immediacy, and maintain reader interest." Booklist

Includes glossary and bibliographical references

Allergies; the complete guide to diagnosis, treatment, and daily management; [by] Stuart Young, Bruce S. Dobozin, Margaret Miner, and the editors of Consumer Reports Books. Consumer Repts. Bks. 1992 308p $22.95

616.97

1. Allergy

ISBN 0-89043-362-3　　　LC 91-40481

This book covers all types of allergies, including asthma, food and drug allergies, hay fever, and skin disorders. It provides information on the various diagnostic tests and on treatment options. The book also discusses ways to allergy-proof the home and to otherwise avoid potential allergens. Common over-the-counter remedies are evaluated and treatment scams are pointed out

Includes bibliography

Ford, Michael Thomas

100 questions and answers about AIDS; a guide for young people. New Discovery Bks. 1992 202p il $14.95　　　**616.97**

1. AIDS (Disease)

ISBN 0-02-735424-5　　　LC 92-15072

"An Open door book"

Ford, Michael Thomas—*Continued*

Answers 100 common questions about AIDS, what causes it, how it is spread, and how to protect yourself from getting it. Includes interviews with four young people living with HIV infection

"According to the demands of the topic, the text contains explicit details; the tone is matter-of-fact and nonjudgemental. Diagrams are included, e.g., step-by-step instructions on how to put on a condom or clean a syringe. . . . While Ford suggests reading through the answers to all the questions for a thorough understanding of the topic, it is possible to gain a great deal of information by just browsing." SLJ

Gallo, Robert C.

Virus hunting; AIDS, cancer, and the human retrovirus: a story of scientific discovery. Basic Bks. 1991 352p hardcover o.p. paperback available $15 **616.97**

1. AIDS (Disease) 2. Medicine—Research
ISBN 0-465-09815-0 (pa)   LC 90-55600
"A New Republic book"

The author describes his biomedical research of the cancer-causing retrovirus, how it led to the discovery of the AIDS virus, and the political and ethical controversies surrounding AIDS research

"Laypersons well acquainted with AIDS literature will have little trouble reading the book. . . . Less motivated readers may be put off by Gallo's impersonal, professional tone as much as by the complexity of the material. But have no doubt about it, this is *the* book about the science of AIDS." Booklist

Grmek, Mirko D.

History of AIDS; emergence and origin of a modern pandemic; translated by Russell C. Maulitz and Jacalyn Duffin. Princeton Univ. Press 1990 279p $44; pa $16.95 **616.97**

1. AIDS (Disease)
ISBN 0-691-08552-8; 0-691-02477-4 (pa)
LC 90-32514

Original French edition, 1989

In this "medical and social history of the disease, Dr. Grmek . . . speculates about the prehistory of AIDS, before its seemingly sudden appearance from nowhere in 1981. He argues that while today's runaway epidemic is a new phenomenon, the viruses that cause AIDS have infected people for many decades, if not for centuries." N Y Times Book Rev

Includes bibliography

LeVert, Marianne

AIDS; a handbook for the future. Millbrook Press 1996 160p lib bdg $16.90 **616.97**

1. AIDS (Disease)
ISBN 1-56294-660-9   LC 96-3186

"Combining personal vignettes, blocked quotes and important information, and bulleted facts about the illness and its prevention, the book covers the history, medical implications, and basic facts about AIDS, including abstinence and safer sex strategies." Booklist

"LeVert does an outstanding job of organizing a great deal of historical material and current, technical AIDS-awareness information into a readable form." SLJ

Includes glossary and bibliography

Newman, Gerald, 1939-

Allergies; [by] Gerald Newman and Eleanor Newman Layfield. Watts 1992 110p il lib bdg $22 **616.97**

1. Allergy
ISBN 0-531-12516-5   LC 91-33862
"A Venture book"

"Covering a variety of topics related to the subject, this volume outlines the chemistry of allergic reactions and discusses symptoms of allergic diseases, treatments, and research. Each of the four types of allergens are described in depth. A discussion of what to expect when seeing the doctor for treatment concludes the book. Information is concise, accessible, and clearly presented." SLJ

Includes bibliographical references

Sonder, Ben, 1954-

Epidemic of silence; the facts about women and AIDS. Watts 1995 111p (Women then—women now) lib bdg $22.70 **616.97**

1. AIDS (Disease) 2. Women—Diseases
ISBN 0-531-11243-8   LC 95-6500

The author "examines the particular issues that arise from women's experiences with HIV and discusses how our understandings of the disease must adapt. This title also provides readers with [a] . . . look into the lives of AIDS pioneers who have fought for women's voices to be heard." Publisher's note

Includes bibliographical references

616.99 Tumors and cancers

Cancer sourcebook for women; edited by Alan R. Cook and Peter D. Dresser. Omnigraphics 1996 xxix, 495p il (Health reference series) $75 **616.99**

1. Cancer 2. Women—Diseases
ISBN 0-7808-0076-1   LC 95-36875

"Basic information about specific forms of cancer that effect women, featuring facts about breast cancer, cervical cancer, ovarian cancer, cancer of the uterus and uterine sarcoma, cancer of the vagina, and cancer of the vulva; statistical and demographic data; treatments, self-help management suggestions, and current research initiatives" Title page

"The discussions of treatment modalities, risk factors, and current research provide valuable material for decision-making. . . . This volume will be of great benefit to those seeking guidance about cancers." Libr J

Includes bibliographical references

Landau, Elaine

Breast cancer. Watts 1995 112p il lib bdg $22 **616.99**

1. Breast cancer
ISBN 0-531-11242-X   LC 95-3831
"A Venture book"

The author "explains symptoms, self-examinations, and medical examinations and emphasizes the many benefits of early detection. Various treatments for breast cancer, including different kinds of surgery, radiation therapy, hormone treatment, and chemotherapy are detailed." Publisher's note

Includes glossary and bibliography

Rodgers, Joann Ellison

Cancer; introduction by C. Everett Koop. Chelsea House 1990 108p il (Encyclopedia of health) lib bdg $19.95   **616.99**

1. Cancer

ISBN 0-7910-0059-1   LC 89-17417

"Rodgers starts with an historical perspective and proceeds to explain causes, types, treatment, and cures, devoting a chapter to young people." SLJ

This book is "highly recommended and will be very useful, particularly in a resource-based instruction situation." Voice Youth Advocates

Includes glossary and bibliography

Vogel, Carole Garbuny

Will I get breast cancer? questions & answers for teenage girls. Messner 1995 c1994 191p il lib bdg $14.95; pa $7.95   **616.99**

1. Breast cancer

ISBN 0-671-88046-2 (lib bdg); 0-671-88047-0 (pa) LC 94-21979

Coverage ranges "from basic breast physiology, cancer cell formation, and factors that determine who gets breast cancer, to how breast cancer is diagnosed and treated, how to cope when someone close has breast cancer and what the future holds for breast cancer research and patients." Voice Youth Advocates

"An excellent glossary rounds out a fine book on the subject, one of a very few for YAs, that not only always keeps its teenage audience in mind, but also presents the facts without patronizing or pretending." Booklist

Includes bibliography

Weinberg, Robert A.

Racing to the beginning of the road; the search for the origin of cancer. Harmony Bks. 1996 270p $27.50   **616.99**

1. Cancer

ISBN 0-517-59118-9   LC 96-4109

The author "tells the story of the race in cancer studies that took place during the 40 years after World War II. . . . His fascinating and lucid history climaxes with the 1986 demonstration of the keys that unlocked the origin of cancer—the relationships between oncogenes and tumor-suppressing genes." Booklist

617.1   Wounds and injuries

Aaseng, Nathan, 1953-

Head injuries; [by] Nathan Aaseng and Jay Aaseng. Watts 1996 112p il lib bdg $22   **617.1**

1. Brain—Wounds and injuries

ISBN 0-531-11267-5   LC 95-44988

"Nathan Aaseng's experience with his son, Jay, who suffered a head injury at the age of 13, serves as a jumping-off point for a discussion of what happens when brain injuries occur, what scientists know and don't know about the effects of such accidents, and the emotional and behavioral problems that may develop." Booklist

"The writing is well organized and very complete.

. . . The diagrams are clear and descriptive, and the black-and-white photos, especially of CT scans, are instructive. A well-done and sensitive treatment of a little-discussed topic." SLJ

Includes glossary and bibliography

Conquering athletic injuries; [by] American Running and Fitness Association; Paul M. Taylor, Diane K. Taylor, editors. Leisure Press 1988 326p il pa $22.95   **617.1**

1. Sports medicine 2. Physical fitness

ISBN 0-88011-305-7   LC 87-33905

This volume discusses the prevention, treatment and rehabilitation of athletic injuries. Provides information on shoulder bursitis, shin splints, hamstring injuries, muscle cramps, and ingrown toenails

Includes bibliography

Edelson, Edward, 1932-

Sports medicine; introduction by C. Everett Koop. Chelsea House 1988 107p il (Encyclopedia of health) lib bdg $19.95; pa $9.95   **617.1**

1. Sports medicine

ISBN 0-7910-0030-3 (lib bdg); 0-7910-0470-8 (pa) LC 88-2568

A "guide to sports injuries—how they occur and how to prevent, recognize, and treat them. . . . Edelson considers directly and without condescension the untrained and the amateur as well as the serious athlete on a rigorous schedule. He discusses what happens to the body during exercise; gives advice on diet, equipment, and training programs; and describes danger signs and treatment for a range of injuries from blisters and shin splints to potentially fatal heatstroke." Booklist

Includes glossary and bibliography

617.6   Dentistry

Siegel, Dorothy Schainman

Dental health; [by] Dorothy Siegel; introduction by C. Everett Koop. Chelsea House 1993 111p il (Encyclopedia of health) lib bdg $19.95   **617.6**

1. Dentistry 2. Teeth

ISBN 0-7910-0014-1   LC 92-45205

This overview of dental care includes a discussion of the basic anatomy of the teeth, jaws and gums. Oral hygiene and advances in dental technology are reviewed

Includes glossary and bibliography

617.7   Ophthalmology

Samz, Jane

Vision; introduction by C. Everett Koop. Chelsea House 1990 103p il (Encyclopedia of health) lib bdg $19.95   **617.7**

1. Eye 2. Vision disorders

ISBN 0-7910-0031-1   LC 89-71160

This exploration of the physical mechanisms of vision covers disorders of the eye, tools and procedures of optometrists and the phenomenon of optical illusions

Includes glossary and bibliography

617.8   Otology and audiology

Mango, Karin N., 1936-
Hearing loss. Watts 1991 144p il lib bdg $22
                                                    617.8
1. Deaf
ISBN 0-531-12519-X   LC 90-19746
"A Venture book"
Describes the conditions and varying degrees of hearing loss and deafness, and discusses methods by which the hearing-impaired can communicate with others
Includes bibliographical references

617.9   Transplantation of tissue and organs

Kittredge, Mary, 1949-
Organ transplants; introduction by C. Everett Koop. Chelsea House 1989 106p il (Encyclopedia of health) lib bdg $19.95   **617.9**
1. Transplantation of organs, tissues, etc.
ISBN 0-7910-0071-0   LC 88-14098
An "overview of the history and procedure of organ transplantation. . . . A chapter each [is] devoted to which organs can be transplanted, how organs and recipients are matched, immune-system rejection, the case history of a kidney recipient, ethical issues, and the future of transplantation. It is smoothly written, with enough dialogue and points of interest to keep readers involved. Medical terms are defined in both the text and in the glossary." SLJ
Includes bibliography

Reybold, Laura
Everything you need to know about the dangers of tattooing and body piercing. Rosen Pub. Group 1996 64p il (Need to know library) lib bdg $15.95
                                                    617.9
1. Body piercing 2. Tattooing
ISBN 0-8239-2151-4   LC 95-20227
Presents a history of body piercing and tattooing before discussing the risks and consequences involved
This "is a timely title on a current popular-culture phenomenon. . . . While Reybold provides much accurate information about issues to consider and questions to ask of practitioners to preserve health, her disapproval of these practices is obvious throughout." SLJ
Includes glossary and bibliography

618.2   Obstetrics

Hales, Dianne R., 1950-
Pregnancy and birth; [by] Dianne Hales; introduction by C. Everett Koop. Chelsea House 1989 106p il (Encyclopedia of health) lib bdg $19.95   **618.2**
1. Pregnancy 2. Childbirth
ISBN 0-7910-0040-0   LC 88-38283
This work discusses "pregnancy from conception through the nine months of prenatal development and la-

bor and delivery." Sci Books Films
"This is a good source for students researching such topics as test tube babies; surrogate mothers; artificial insemination; the effect of drugs, alcohol, and smoking on pregnant women and their unborn babies; prenatal testing; and statistics about teenage mothers and their children. This is not an advice book." Voice Youth Advocates
Includes glossary and bibliography

Lindsay, Jeanne Warren
Your pregnancy and newborn journey; how to take care of yourself and your newborn if you're a pregnant teen; [by] Jeanne Warren Lindsay and Jean Brunelli. Morning Glory Press 1991 191p il (Teens parenting) $19; pa $9.95   **618.2**
1. Teenage pregnancy 2. Teenage mothers
ISBN 0-930934-51-2; 0-930934-50-4 (pa)
                                                    LC 91-3712
This "begins by briefly exploring options (abortion isn't considered) open to pregnant teens, then follows the course of pregnancy through the first days of infant development. Fathers and mothers . . . add personal voices, while the authors discuss everything from adoption and prenatal care to contraception." Booklist
Includes bibliography

618.3   Diseases and complications of pregnancy

Corser, Kira, 1951-
When the bough breaks; pregnancy and the legacy of addiction; Kira Corser, photography and narratives; Frances Payne Adler, poetry and narratives; foreword by Jennifer Howse. NewSage Press 1993 112p il $39.95; pa $22.95   **618.3**
1. Pregnancy 2. Substance abuse 3. Children of drug addicts 4. Abused women
ISBN 0-939165-20-1; 0-939165-19-8 (pa)
                                                    LC 93-5611
This is an "arrangement of text and photographs. The text includes first-person narratives based on the words of mothers formerly addicted to drugs or alcohol, and of others—health professionals, teachers, family members—involved in some way with the mothers or their children, as well as poems . . . by Adler to reflect the women's lives." Women's Rev Books
"This is a collection of poignant, raw, and searing memories that are agonizing to read." SLJ

Luke, Barbara
Every pregnant woman's guide to preventing premature birth; a program for reducing the sixty proven risks that can lead to prematurity. Times Bks. 1995 239p il $23   **618.3**
1. Pregnancy
ISBN 0-8129-2472-X   LC 95-12213
This book addresses "prematurity, its possible causes, and its long-term emotional and financial effects. [The author] offers a personal risk assessment covering a woman's family background, obstetrical and gynecologi-

Luke, Barbara—_Continued_
cal history, home and work environments, lifestyle, and
nutrition to ascertain the stresses that might cause early
contractions and labor." Booklist
Includes bibliographical references

618.92   Pediatrics

Gravelle, Karen
Understanding birth defects. Watts 1990 126p il
lib bdg $22.70   **618.92**
1. Birth defects
ISBN 0-531-10955-0   LC 90-32658
This "survey explains the causes of birth defects and
how to prevent and treat such conditions. It includes a
discussion of low birth weight, which is not really a birth
defect, but is often a problem for teenage mothers. Diseases are grouped and discussed by causes. . . . Using
fictional cases, Gravelle explains genetic counseling and
prenatal care . . . and new theories and treatments are
presented." SLJ
"A sensitive yet straightforward account that will be
of value to student researchers." Booklist
Includes glossary and bibliography

Knox, Jean McBee
Learning disabilities; introduction by C. Everett
Koop. Chelsea House 1989 100p il (Encyclopedia
of health) lib bdg $19.95; pa $7.95   **618.92**
1. Learning disabilities
ISBN 0-7910-0049-4 (lib bdg); 0-7910-0529-1 (pa)
                              LC 88-34174
The author "discusses the nature, possible causes, and
treatment of learning disabilities, how they are diagnosed, and whom they affect." Sci Books Films
This book "needs to be on the list for those who work
. . . in all fields of education and social work, as well
as those in the medical field, students who suspect something is the matter, and parents." Voice Youth Advocates
Includes glossary and bibliography

620   Engineering and allied operations

Freiman, Fran Locher
Failed technology; true stories of technological
disasters; [by] Fran Locher Freiman & Neil
Schlager. U.X.L 1995 2v il set $39.95   **620**
1. Technology 2. Disasters 3. Engineering
ISBN 0-8103-9794-3   LC 96-129100
A survey of "forty-five technological disasters of the
twentieth century. . . . Subjects covered include: ships
and submarines; airships, aircraft and spacecraft; automobiles; dams and bridges; nuclear plants; and chemical,
environmental, and medical disasters. A chronological list
places events historically. . . . This set is especially well
written taking what could be a dry subject and presenting
it in a way that makes it difficult to put down." Voice
Youth Advocates

Goodwin, Peter, 1951-
More engineering projects for young scientists.
Watts 1994 126p il (Projects for young scientists)
lib bdg $14.35   **620**
1. Engineering—Experiments 2. Physics—Experiments 3. Science projects
ISBN 0-531-11193-8   LC 94-26877
Companion volume to Engineering projects for young
scientists (1987)
Projects include "the design of a rocking chair, a
windmill, a passive solar house, a wave energy genera-
tor, a recycling robot, a windspeed indicator, a simple
logic circuit, and other devices." Publisher's note
Includes bibliographical references

Magill's survey of science, applied science series;
edited by Frank N. Magill; consulting editor,
Martha Riherd Weller. Salem Press 1993 6v il
set $475   **620**
1. Engineering 2. Science
ISBN 0-89356-705-1   LC 92-35688
"This set's 382 articles cover the applied sciences,
from aerospace to zone refining. The largest number of
articles deal with engineering and materials science. . . .
The average article contains an introductory apparatus
with key definitions and a brief statement of the topic's
importance. The text then proceeds in three parts:
overview, uses of the technology, and context." Am Ref
Books Annu, 1994

621.36   Applied optics and paraphotic engineering

Billings, Charlene W., 1941-
Lasers; the new technology of light. Facts on
File 1992 118p il (Facts on File science
sourcebooks) lib bdg $17.95   **621.36**
1. Lasers
ISBN 0-8160-2630-0   LC 92-7324
Explains what lasers are and how they work and ex-
amines their various uses in such fields as medicine, the
military, industry, research, and communications
Includes glossary and bibliography

621.38   Electronics and communications engineering

Grob, Bernard
Basic electronics. McGraw-Hill $54.69   **621.38**
1. Electricity 2. Electronics
First published 1959. (7th edition 1992) Periodically
revised
An introductory text on the fundamentals of electricity
and electronics for technicians in radio, television, and
industrial electronics
Includes bibliography

621.381 Electronics

Turner, Rufus P.

The illustrated dictionary of electronics; by Rufus P. Turner and Stan Gibilisco. TAB Bks. il pa $39.95   **621.381**

1. Electronics—Dictionaries

First published 1980. (7th edition 1997) Periodically revised

This work "deals with electronics in the broadest sense, covering standard terminology as well as jargon and related trade terms. There are 27,000 entries in all. Definitions are concise, cross-referenced, and illustrated with line drawings." Nichols. Guide to Ref Books for Sch Media Cent. 4th edition

621.382 Communications engineering

Lampton, Christopher

Telecommunications: from telegraphs to modems. Watts 1991 144p il $22   **621.382**

1. Telecommunication

ISBN 0-531-12527-0   LC 90-48230

"A Venture book"

"Part I, about three quarters of the book, outlines analog telecommunication systems through wire and space. It introduces the nature and modulation of waves, and chapters follow on the history and development of the telegraph, telephone, radio, and television. . . . Part II examines digital communication and discusses digital encoding, the binary system, and digital information processing. Applications such as digital sound and compact disks are treated, and computer telecommunication is presented." Sci Books Films

Includes glossary and bibliography

Pierce, John Robinson, 1910-

Signals; the science of telecommunications; [by] John R. Pierce, A. Michael Noll. Scientific Am. Lib. 1990 247p il $32.95   **621.382**

1. Telecommunication

ISBN 0-7167-5026-0   LC 89-70207

First published 1981 by W. H. Freeman

This book attempts to show how "researchers and inventors have transformed the laws of physics into the technology of telecommunications—from Alexander Graham Bell's first attempts at sending sound waves of speech to NASA's beaming of signals to Voyager." Publisher's note

"It is the purposeful context and the engineer's air of tempered optimism and cheerful goodwill that make the technical discussion so readable." Sci Am

Includes bibliography

621.3841 Amateur (Ham) radio

The **ARRL** handbook for the radio amateur. American Radio Relay League il pa $38
                                                621.3841

1. Radio—Handbooks, manuals, etc. 2. Amateur radio stations—Handbooks, manuals, etc.

Annual. Began publication 1926. Editions 1 through 61 published with title: The Radio amateur's handbook

"The handbook offers most of the instruction and information needed to begin and enjoy ham-radio activity. . . . This is both authoritative and comprehensive." Wynar. Guide to Ref Books for Sch Media Cent. 3d edition

621.8 Machine engineering

Machines & inventions. Time-Life Bks. 1993 151p il (Understanding science & nature) $18.95
                                                   621.8

1. Machinery 2. Inventions

                                              LC 92-35710

"This book uses a question-and-answer format to introduce various inventions. Each two-page spread explains one device with a brief text, several full-color illustrations and/or diagrams, and explanatory captions. . . . After a chapter on historic inventions . . . the rest of the book concerns aspects of modern machines and equipment, such as smart cards, fax machines, escalators, vending machines, synthesizers, air conditioners, compact disks, mechanical hearts, faucets, CAT scanners, and sewing machines. The up-to-date information will make this a useful resource for many libraries." Booklist

623.4 Ordnance

Rhodes, Richard

Dark sun; the making of the hydrogen bomb. Simon & Schuster 1995 731p il $32.50; pa $16
                                                   623.4

1. Hydrogen bomb

ISBN 0-684-80400-X; 0-684-82414-0 (pa)

                                              LC 95-11070

This is a "chronicle of the rivalry between the U.S. and the U.S.S.R. to invent, build, test and stockpile hydrogen bombs. . . . Rhodes places the story of the bomb's development in the context of politics, science, technical hurdles and espionage. . . . He also brings in the case of convicted atomic spies Julius and Ethel Rosenberg." Publ Wkly

"This meticulously documented treatise presents a gripping story." Libr J

The making of the atomic bomb. Simon & Schuster 1986 886p il hardcover o.p. paperback available $16   **623.4**

1. Atomic bomb

ISBN 0-684-81378-5 (pa)   LC 86-15445

This book chronicles the development of the bomb "from the birth of modern physics in the late 19th century to the first tests of hydrogen bombs, by the United States in 1954 and the Soviet Union in 1955." Sci-

Rhodes, Richard—*Continued*
ence

"The book provides portraits of the many players from Szilard and Einstein to Oppenheimer. . . . The book is heavily documented and includes a 13-page bibliography. This is a definitive work, well written, with a gripping story. It is not an easy book to read, but is well worth the effort." Libr J

Weapons; an international encyclopedia from 5000 B.C. to 2000 A.D; [by] the Diagram Group. St. Martin's Press 1990 336p il $29.95; pa $18.95
623.4

1. Weapons—History
ISBN 0-312-03951-4; 0-312-03950-6 (pa)
LC 90-28498

First published 1980
This "is a visual display of combat weapons of every century and culture. It is not, however, arranged alphabetically or chronologically. Instead, chapters are ordered by function. . . . The historical and regional indexes will be useful to readers who want to focus on weapons of a particular time or place. . . . The quality of illustrations is what distinguishes Diagram Group publications, and these are up to the usual standards. More than 2,500 black-and-white drawings are included." Booklist

Includes bibliography

624   Civil engineering

Brown, David J., 1946-
Bridges. Macmillan 1993 176p il maps $30
624

1. Bridges—Design and construction
ISBN 0-02-517455-X
LC 93-9747

Illustrated with photographs, construction diagrams, and historical drawings and engravings, this book presents profiles of more than one hundred bridges, organized chronologically from ancient times to the twenty-first century. Each account includes the bridge's location, date of construction, designer, materials, dimensions, and the story behind its creation
Includes glossary and bibliography

Macaulay, David, 1946-
Underground. Houghton Mifflin 1976 109p il $16.95; pa $8.95
624

1. Civil engineering 2. Building 3. Public utilities
ISBN 0-395-24739-X; 0-395-34065-9 (pa)

In this "examination of the intricate support systems that lie beneath the street levels of our cities, Macaulay explains the ways in which foundations for buildings are laid or reinforced, and how the various utilities or transportation services are constructed." Bull Cent Child Books

Includes glossary

Petroski, Henry
Engineers of dreams; great bridge builders and the spanning of America. Knopf 1995 479p il $30; pa $15
624

1. Bridges 2. Civil engineering
ISBN 0-679-43939-0; 0-679-76021-0 (pa)
LC 94-48893

Focusing on the men who designed them, "Petroski depicts the building of several famous American bridges—New York's George Washington, St. Louis's Eads, and Michigan's Mackinaw, among others." Libr J
"An exhilarating saga of ingenuity and sheer determination, this chronicle of the great era of American bridge building intersects with the time of technological innovation, the transformation of the U.S. into an industrial power and the birth of modern civil engineering." Publ Wkly

Includes bibliographical references

624.1   Structural engineering and underground construction

Morgan, Sally
Structures; [by] Sally and Adrian Morgan. Facts on File 1993 48p il (Designs in science) $14.95
624.1

1. Structural engineering
ISBN 0-8160-2983-0
LC 93-20164

Examines a variety of manufactured structures, from skyscrapers to airplanes, and discusses how they imitate natural structures like eggs and seed pods in protecting and transporting living things
This "includes experiments, questions, interesting facts, diagrams and color photos. . . . [It] will provide a wealth of information and would be an excellent addition to middle and high school libraries." Book Rep
Includes glossary

625.1   Railroads

Schleicher, Robert H.
The HO model railroading handbook; [by] Robert Schleicher. rev ed. Chilton 1992 227p il pa $17.95
625.1

1. Railroads—Models
ISBN 0-8019-8346-0
LC 92-53147

First published 1979 with title: Tyco model railroad manual
This illustrated guide provides step-by-step instructions on basic layout planning; tools and techniques; trackwork, switches, wiring and finishing touches of scenery, vehicles and people

625.2   Railroad rolling stock

Foster, Gerald L., 1936-
A field guide to trains of North America. Houghton Mifflin 1996 146p il pa $14.95   **625.2**

1. Railroads
ISBN 0-395-70112-0
LC 95-44168

This book describes and illustrates American railroad cars, including 150 types of locomotive, and lists 840

Foster, Gerald L., 1936—Continued
American railroads
Includes bibliographical references

627 Hydraulic engineering

Dunar, Andrew J.
Building Hoover Dam; an oral history of the Great Depression; [by] Andrew J. Dunar, Dennis McBride. Twayne Pubs. 1993 350p il (Twayne's oral history series) $27.95; pa $15.95 **627**
1. Hoover Dam (Ariz. and Nev.)
ISBN 0-8057-9110-8; 0-8057-9133-7 (pa)
LC 92-44170
"Dunar and McBride have compiled a fascinating oral history of the construction of the Hoover Dam from 1931 to 1935. Based on the recollections of a broad spectrum of individuals involved in this unprecedented undertaking . . . this loosely woven narrative provides an intimate portrait of an amazing Depression-era project. Each individual offers a unique, firsthand perspective on an otherwise well-documented historical event." Booklist
Includes bibliographical references

629.04 Transportation engineering

Wilson, Anthony, 1939-
Dorling Kindersley visual timeline of transportation. Dorling Kindersley 1995 48p il $16.95 **629.04**
1. Transportation
ISBN 1-56458-880-7
LC 94-48714
"From transportation on land and water in 10,000 B.C. to future trends, [the author] documents innovations and milestones throughout the world . . . as well as related technological developments . . . and advances in scientific knowledge. The book is a browser's delight, but there's enough solid information for reports." Booklist

629.13 Aeronautics

Baker, David, 1944-
Flight and flying; a chronology. Facts on File 1993 549p il $65 **629.13**
1. Aeronautics—History
ISBN 0-8160-1854-5
LC 92-31491
"In addition to covering some 90 years of documented events of flying, up to 1992, [this work] covers the preflying era—back to 850 B.C.—when men tried to fly using kites, balloons, and dirigibles. Close to 7,000 entries emphasize World Wars I and II and the expansion of civil aviation in the 1920s and 1930s. . . . Coverage is comprehensive for historic aviators and inventors; commercial and military aircraft; aircraft manufacturers; and specifications for all aircraft mentioned as an entry. . . . With the enormous amount of information contained in this chronology, it is a miniencyclopedia on aircraft and flying." Booklist

Bilstein, Roger E.
Flight in America: from the Wrights to the astronauts. rev ed. Johns Hopkins Univ. Press 1994 386p il $50; pa $16.95 **629.13**
1. Aeronautics—History 2. Astronautics—United States
ISBN 0-8018-4827-X; 0-8018-4828-8 (pa)
LC 93-36027
First published 1984 with title: Flight in America, 1900-1983
This is an "historical treatise of significant events within various interrelated areas of aviation, aeronautics, and aerospace from 1918 to 1993. Each of the chapters, spanning about a decade, provides a comprehensive analysis of events occurring at the time within the military, general and commercial aviation, and aerospace sectors of the U.S. economy in the context of similar developments throughout the world." Sci Books Films
Includes bibliographical references

Earhart, Amelia, 1898-1937
Last flight; arranged by George Palmer Putnam; foreword by Walter J. Boyne. Orion Bks. (NY) 1988 c1937 135p il pa $9.95 **629.13**
1. Aeronautics—Flights
ISBN 0-517-56794-6
LC 87-7291
Also available in paperback from Crown
A reissue of the title first published 1937 by Harcourt Brace
"Earhart's account of the world flight on which she disappeared describes the five continents she saw and conveys her strongly feminist views, her flying skill, and the exhilaration of her 'shining adventure.'" Booklist

Hallion, Richard
Test pilots; the frontiersmen of flight. rev ed. Smithsonian Institution Press 1988 347p il pa $19.95 **629.13**
1. Aeronautics—History 2. Air pilots
ISBN 0-87474-549-7
LC 87-28846
First published 1981 by Doubleday
This book "provides the complete story of the men and women who were pioneers in flight. . . . A photo essay including rare photographs and interviews with the history-makers themselves make this book especially vivid." Univ Press Books for Second Sch Libr
Includes bibliography

Lindbergh, Charles, 1902-1974
The Spirit of St. Louis. Scribner 1975 c1953 513p lib bdg $60 **629.13**
1. Aeronautics—Flights 2. Spirit of St. Louis (Airplane)
ISBN 0-684-14421-2
Also available from Buccaneer Bks.
"Hudson River editions"
First published 1953
This is an account of the first solo transatlantic flight from New York to Paris, as well as a detailed description of the preparation for the flight which in turn mirrors aviation of the 1920's

Lopez, Donald S., 1923-
Aviation; a Smithsonian guide. Macmillan 1995
256p il $24.95; pa $18   **629.13**
1. Aeronautics—History
ISBN 0-02-860006-1; 0-02-860041-X (pa)
           LC 94-32992
"A Ligature book"
This history of world aviation contains more than 350
full-color photographs and illustrations of airplanes,
equipment, people and events. Includes a foldout timeline
Includes bibliographical references

Saint-Exupéry, Antoine de, 1900-1944
Wind, sand, and stars; translated from the
French by Lewis Galantière. Harcourt Brace
Jovanovich 1992 229p $15.95; pa $8   **629.13**
1. Aeronautics—Flights
ISBN 0-15-197087-4; 0-15-697090-2 (pa)
           LC 91-45986
"An HBJ modern classic"
First published 1940 by Reynal & Hitchcock
Philosophical essays on flights and fliers, containing
the elements of an autobiography of the French aviator-
author

Scott, Phil, 1961-
The shoulders of giants; a history of human
flight to 1919. Addison-Wesley 1995 337p il $24
           629.13
1. Aeronautics—History
ISBN 0-201-62722-1   LC 94-45977
"Scott chronicles . . . the endeavors of numerous avi-
ation pioneers, including Jean-Marie Le Bris and the
Wright brothers." Booklist
Includes bibliographical references

Wright, Orville, 1871-1948
How we invented the airplane; an illustrated
history; edited with an introduction and
commentary by Fred C. Kelly; additional text by
Alan Weissman. Dover Publs. 1988 c1953 87p il
pa $8.95   **629.13**
1. Wright, Wilbur, 1867-1912 2. Airplanes
ISBN 0-486-25662-6   LC 87-33037
Also available in hardcover from P. Smith
First published 1953 by D. McKay
This "account by the two inventors . . . covers experiments, discovery of aeronautical principles, construction
of planes and motors, first flights, much more. Also included is a later account written by both brothers." Publisher's note
Includes bibliography

629.133   Aircraft types

Dick, Harold G.
The golden age of the great passenger airships,
Graf Zeppelin & Hindenburg; [by] Harold G.
Dick, Douglas H. Robinson. Smithsonian
Institution Press 1985 226p il hardcover o.p.
paperback available $24.95   **629.133**
1. Graf Zeppelin (Airship) 2. Hindenburg (Airship)
ISBN 0-56098-219-5 (pa)   LC 84-600298
This "account of the design, construction, and opera-
tion of these two giant airships is based on the papers
and remembrances of coauthor Harold Dick, an
American who worked as a engineer at the Zeppelin
Company in Germany and who served as a crew member
on both the *Graf Zeppelin* and *Hindenburg*." Booklist
Includes glossary and bibliographical references

Jane's all the world's aircraft. Jane's Information
Group il $275   **629.133**
1. Aeronautics
ISSN 0075-3017
Also available CD-ROM version
Annual. First published 1909
This reference offers illustrations, descriptions and
specifications of all the aircraft of various countries of
the world

629.222   Passenger automobiles

Automotive encyclopedia. Goodheart-Willcox il
$45.80   **629.222**
1. Automobiles—Handbooks, manuals, etc.
Biennial. First published 1954 under the editorship of
W. K. Toboldt, with title: Motor Service's New automo-
tive encyclopedia. Supersedes: Dyke's Automobile and
gasoline engine encyclopedia. Title and editors vary
"Textbook on basic principles of automotive design,
construction, operation, maintenance, and repair; covers
American models and some foreign cars." N Y Public
Libr. Book of How & Where to Look It Up

Fariello, Sal
The people's car book; the one essential
handbook for people who don't trust mechanics,
car salesmen, or car manufacturers. St. Martin's
Press 1993 c1992 250p il $15.95   **629.222**
1. Automobiles—Maintenance and repair 2. Consumer education
ISBN 0-312-08278-9   LC 92-26608
"A Thomas Dunne book"
This is a "guide on what consumers should watch for
when they shop. Written for lay readers, the text gives
guidance on buying and leasing, preventive maintenance,
and repair. It stresses common sense and understanding,
pointing out that too much trust in a salesperson or mechanic can result in a ripoff. This book will help the
reader become an informed car consumer. Highly recommended for public and school libraries." Libr J

Willson, Quentin

The ultimate classic car book; [by] Quentin Willson with David Selby. Dorling Kindersley 1995 224p il $29.95   **629.222**

1. Automobiles

ISBN 0-7894-0159-2   LC 95-11903

"An introduction covers what the term 'classic car' means, goes on to discuss such models by decade, and has a section on the purchase of such a vehicle. One-paragraph profiles of innovators such as Andre Citrone, Ferdinand Porsche, and Lee Iacocca are included. But the drawing card here is the cars. There are more than 90 of them, all displayed in splendid full-color photographs." SLJ

629.227   Cycles

Ballantine, Richard

Richards' ultimate bicycle book; [by] Richard Ballantine, Richard Grant; photography by Philip Gatward. Dorling Kindersley 1992 192p il $29.95   **629.227**

1. Bicycles 2. Cycling

ISBN 1-56458-036-9   LC 91-31540

Revised edition of Richard's new bicycle book (1987)

"The book begins with a glimpse at the bicycle's evolution, from its almost forgotten invention by da Vinci in 1490, and then on to an overview of advances in materials and technology. Most of the book is devoted to vehicle types; mountain, racing, touring, and everyday bicycles are examined in terms of construction and competitiveness, supported with advice on exercise, among other topics." Booklist

Cuthbertson, Tom

Cuthbertson's all-in-one bike repair manual; illustrated by Rick Morrall. Ten Speed Press 1996 228p il pa $11.95   **629.227**

1. Bicycles—Maintenance and repair

ISBN 0-89815-800-1   LC 95-47828

Illustrated step-by-step instructions for repair and maintenance of cruiser, road, and mountain bikes. New technologies and tools are discussed

Wilson, Hugo

The encyclopedia of the motorcycle; photography by Dave King. Dorling Kindersley 1995 320p il maps $39.95   **629.227**

1. Motorcycles

ISBN 0-7894-0150-9   LC 95-47844

"This is primarily a visual reference of approximately 400 noteworthy or memorable international motorcycle makes, ranging from the earliest models to modern exotic specialty machines. . . . Companion text, though sparse, gives a bit of each model's history and its significant or innovative features. . . . All this is augmented by an exhaustive annotated directory of all motorcycles known to have been manufactured worldwide; more than 3000 makes are attributed here." Libr J

For a fuller review see: Booklist, Nov. 15, 1995

The ultimate motorcycle book; photography by Dave King. Dorling Kindersley 1993 192p il $29.95   **629.227**

1. Motorcycles

ISBN 1-56458-303-1   LC 93-21884

"Part one covers the history and development of the motorcycle, while the second and largest section deals with all the best-known makes and models from all over the world. Motorcycle sport is covered in part three, while part four deals with technical aspects from engines to electrical instruments to proper riding attire. Each page is illustrated with full-color photos that are labeled and accompanied by explanatory text. This book will be popular among high school students, especially boys." Book Rep

629.28   Motor land vehicles and cycles—Tests, driving, maintenance, repairs

Bennett, James S.

The complete motorcycle book; a consumer's guide; [by] James Bennett. Facts on File 1995 228p il $25.95; pa $14.95   **629.28**

1. Motorcycles

ISBN 0-8160-2899-0; 0-8160-3181-9 (pa)

    LC 94-20012

The author provides "information on many aspects of selecting and maintaining a motorcycle, along with a solid section discussing riding safely." Booklist

"Thorough and well written, this book should appeal to beginning riders." Libr J

Bicycling magazine's complete guide to bicycle maintenance and repair; including road bikes and mountain bikes; by the editors of Bicycling and Mountain bike magazines. new rev updated ed. Rodale Press 1994 324p il $24.95; pa $16.95   **629.28**

1. Bicycles—Maintenance and repair

ISBN 0-87596-218-1; 0-87596-207-6 (pa)

    LC 94-8380

First published 1986

This volume includes "information on suspension forks, cassette hubs, index shifters, and clipless pedals. . . . Each chapter opens with an exploded diagram of the part of the bike being discussed, and step-by-step diagrams and photos show how to repair and maintain all of the parts of the bicycle. This guide also explains gearing, how to set up a home repair station, and what tools to buy." Publisher's note

Includes glossary

Chilton's auto repair manual. Chilton il $28.95

    629.28

1. Automobiles—Maintenance and repair

First published 1953 with title: Chilton's automobile repair manual. (1993-1997 edition) Frequently revised

"Covers all mass-produced American cars of the past six or seven years plus the current year. Illustrated; includes charts to help diagnose problems. Useful for both novices and experts." N Y Public Libr. Book of How & Where to Look It Up

Plas, Rob van der, 1938-
The bicycle repair book; the new complete manual of bicycle care; illustrated by the author. 2nd fully updated ed. Bicycle Bks. 1993 192p il pa $9.95   **629.28**
1. Bicycles—Maintenance and repair
ISBN 0-933201-55-9   LC 92-83822
First published 1985
Among the topics covered are: selecting tools; preventative maintenance; adjusting brakes, gears, and bearings; wheel building and spoke replacement, and troubleshooting

Treganowan, Lucille
Lucille's car care; everything you need to know from under the hood—by America's most trusted mechanic; [by] Lucille Treganowan, with Gina Catanzarite. Hyperion 1996 257p il $19.95
629.28
1. Automobiles—Maintenance and repair 2. Consumer protection
ISBN 0-7868-6201-7   LC 95-46041
This book "shows how to make minor repairs, prevent large problems through routine maintenance, buy and sell a car, and more. . . . The book will appeal to those who want to know more about how their automobiles work but don't want scientific or overly mechanical explanations." Libr J

629.4   Astronautics

Baker, David, 1944-
Spaceflight and rocketry: a chronology. Facts on File 1996 528p il $65   **629.4**
1. Astronautics 2. Rocketry
ISBN 0-8160-1853-7   LC 95-41843
This chronology examines events "in the development of rocketry and spaceflight and includes rockets designed for peaceful pursuits such as Earth imaging, telecommunications and astronomical observation, as well as those used for military ends such as ballistic missiles and the Strategic Defense Initiative ('Star Wars') program." Publisher's note
Includes glossary

The **First** 25 years in space; a symposium; edited by Allan A. Needell. Smithsonian Institution Press 1983 152p il hardcover o.p. paperback available $12.95   **629.4**
1. Astronautics 2. Outer space—Exploration
ISBN 0-87474-713-9 (pa)   LC 83-600210
A record of the 1982 symposium sponsored by the National Air and Space Museum and the National Academy of Sciences evaluating twenty-five years of space activity since Sputnik I

Gibson, Roy
Space. Oxford Univ. Press 1992 153p il (Science, technology, and society series) $37.50
629.4
1. Astronautics 2. Outer space—Exploration
ISBN 0-19-858343-5   LC 91-43590
"Written for nonspecialists, the book surveys the history of space flight and considers manned missions,

space science, and the uses of different spacecraft." Univ Press Books for Public and Second Sch Libr

Herbst, Judith
Star crossing; how to get around in the universe. Atheneum Pubs. 1993 187p il $16.95   **629.4**
1. Outer space—Exploration 2. Interplanetary voyages
ISBN 0-789-31523-6   LC 92-8475
The author provides the reader with "explanations about the difficulties encountered in space travel in general and the developments in the field specifically. With references from 'Star Trek' as well as Einstein, Goddard, and others, Herbst gives her readers details that make sense; she takes scientific facts and changes them into everyday facts. And she accomplishes her task in straightforward, easy-to-read prose that often takes the form of what almost sound like science fiction short stories." Voice Youth Advocates
Includes bibliography

Lee, Wayne
To rise from earth; an easy-to-understand guide to space flight. Facts on File 1995 309p il $35
629.4
1. Astronautics 2. Space flight
ISBN 0-8160-3353-6   LC 95-38941
Produced by the To Rise From Earth Project in collaboration with the Flat Satellite Society
"Lee examines 'machines that make spaceflight possible' in an illustrated (black-and-white only), large format volume that introduces the principles of rocket propulsion and surveys space travel. An excellent resource for students and space fans." Booklist

Man in space; an illustrated history of space flight; edited by H. J. P. Arnold; foreword by Eugene A. Cernan. Smithmark Pubs. 1993 240p il $29.98   **629.4**
1. Space flight 2. Astronautics
ISBN 0-8317-4491-X
This illustrated overview of man's exploration of space highlights "major events, and interweaves into the narrative important background themes—the rivalry between the superpowers in the '60s and '70s; the rise of other space powers, such as China, Europe, and Japan; and the increasing commercialization of space activities which is underscored by the irony of the Russian Republic now offering its once-secret wares openly for hire on the international market." Publisher's note

Neal, Valerie
Spaceflight; a Smithsonian guide; [by] Valerie Neal, Cathleen S. Lewis, Frank H. Winter. Macmillan 1995 256p il $24.95; pa $18   **629.4**
1. Astronautics 2. Outer space—Exploration
ISBN 0-02-860007-X; 0-02-860040-1 (pa)
LC 94-23448
"A Ligature book"
An illustrated history of spacecraft design and engineering. Pioneers such as Von Braun and Goddard are discussed and summaries are provided for historic missions beginning with Sputnik
Includes bibliographical references

Space exploration: opposing viewpoints; Charles P. Cozic, book editor. Greenhaven Press 1992 192p lib bdg $19.95; pa $11.95   **629.4**
1. United States. National Aeronautics and Space Administration 2. Astronautics 3. Outer space—Exploration
ISBN 0-89908-197-5 (lib bdg); 0-89908-172-X (pa)
   LC 92-8149
"Opposing viewpoint series"
Debates such issues as the proper goals of space exploration, which programs should be pursued, the elimination of NASA, and the appropriateness of using space for warfare
Includes bibliographical references

Where next, Columbus? the future of space exploration; edited by Valerie Neal. Oxford Univ. Press 1994 231p il map $35   **629.4**
1. Outer space—Exploration
ISBN 0-19-509277-5   LC 94-11451
Stephen Jay Gould, Carl Sagan, Timothy Ferris and Harrison Schmitt are among the experts contributing essays to this illustrated survey of space exploration
Includes bibliographical references

629.45   Manned space flight

Jensen, Claus, 1949-
No downlink; a dramatic narrative about the Challenger accident and our time; translated by Barbara Haveland. Farrar, Straus & Giroux 1996 397p il $24   **629.45**
1. Challenger (Spacecraft) 2. Astronautics—United States 3. Aerospace industries
ISBN 0-374-12036-6   LC 95-33518
"On Jan. 28, 1986, the space shuttle Challenger exploded 73 seconds into its 10th flight. All seven crew members perished, including the teacher Christa McAuliffe. . . . [This book focuses] on the accident and its causes." N Y Times Book Rev
The crew members' "lives at the collision point between technology and human foible compel this narrative into page-turning status, which ought to induct it into the club of best-written general narratives about the space program." Booklist
Includes bibliographical references

Lovell, Jim
Lost moon: the perilous voyage of Apollo 13; [by] Jim Lovell & Jeffrey Kluger. Houghton Mifflin 1994 378p il $22.95   **629.45**
1. Apollo 13 (Spacecraft) 2. Space flight to the moon
ISBN 0-395-67029-2   LC 94-28052
"Launched in April 1970 and manned by Lovell, Jack Swigert and Jack Haise, Apollo 13 was scheduled to orbit the moon while Lovell and Haise descended to its surface. En route, though, a cyogenic tank exploded, causing a loss of oxygen and power in the command module. . . . What unfolds is a story of courage as the astronauts and the personnel at Mission Control in Houston labored to return the spacecraft to Earth." Publ Wkly
"Lovell and Kluger document every white-knuckle

phase of this near disaster, balancing fascinating technological detail with more, pardon the pun, down-to-earth concerns, such as how Marilyn Lovell kept her composure during the seemingly endless ordeal." Booklist

Shepard, Alan B., Jr.
Moon shot; the inside story of America's race to the moon; by Alan Shepard and Deke Slayton with Jay Barbree and Howard Benedict; introduction by Neil Armstrong. Turner Pub. (Atlanta) 1994 383p il $21.95   **629.45**
1. Apollo project 2. Space flight to the moon
ISBN 1-878685-54-6   LC 94-3027
"A firsthand account of the space program's early days. The narrative is at its best when it focuses on the astronauts' flight experiences—Shepard's brief Mercury flight, his lunar landing mission ten years later, and Slayton's long-delayed trip into space aboard the last Apollo mission in 1975." Libr J
"Even readers cool to space exploration will be caught up in an emotional roller-coaster of a narrative sprinkled with revelations." Publ Wkly

Vaughan, Diane
The Challenger launch decision; risky technology, culture, and deviance at NASA. University of Chicago Press 1996 575p il $24.95   **629.45**
1. Challenger (Spacecraft) 2. United States. National Aeronautics and Space Administration 3. Aerospace industries
ISBN 0-226-85175-3   LC 95-39858
In this look at the Challenger tragedy the author "finds the traditional explanation of the accident—'amorally calculating managers intentionally violating rules'—to be profoundly unsatisfactory. Why, she asks, would they knowingly indulge such a risk when the future of the space program, to say nothing of the lives of the astronauts, hung in the balance? . . . She seeks the answer in . . . sociological analysis of NASA culture." N Y Times Book Rev
"Fascinating reading for teens hooked on the space program as well as for those who remember the Challenger disaster." Booklist
Includes bibliographical references

Wolfe, Tom
The right stuff. Farrar, Straus & Giroux 1983 463p $30   **629.45**
1. Astronauts 2. Astronautics—United States
ISBN 0-374-25033-2   LC 84-162805
Also available in paperback from Bantam Bks.
A reissue of the title first published 1979
This is a "history of the early years of the space program. Starting with an account of the lives of military pilots [the book progresses] through the selection of the first seven astronauts, their training, and the Mercury flights." Libr J

629.8　Automatic control engineering

Heiserman, David L., 1940-
Build your own working robot; the second generation. [rev ed] TAB Bks. 1987 130p il $18.95　　**629.8**
1. Robotics
ISBN 0-8306-1181-9　　LC 86-30127
First published 1976
"The author supplies . . . construction and testing hints and includes everything from plans, wiring diagrams, and logic circuits to detailed descriptions of the drive/steer system, power supply and clock circuits, and the operator's control panel as well as all the schematic diagrams, line drawings and tables, and parts lists needed." Publisher's note

The **McGraw-Hill** illustrated encyclopedia of robotics & artificial intelligence; Stan Gibilisco, editor in chief. McGraw-Hill 1994 420p il $55.75; pa $24.95　　**629.8**
1. Robotics—Dictionaries 2. Artificial intelligence—Dictionaries
ISBN 0-07-023613-5; 0-07-023614-3 (pa)
LC 94-14309

In this encyclopedia "more than 500 terms, concepts, and important people and corporations in AI and robotics are arranged alphabetically. Each is clearly defined in entries ranging in length from one to two paragraphs to more than two pages. . . . The editor makes liberal use of cross-references to link concepts together. An index provides additional access." Booklist

Thro, Ellen
Robotics; the marriage of computers and machines. Facts on File 1993 119p il (Facts on File science sourcebooks) lib bdg $17.95　　**629.8**
1. Robotics 2. Robots
ISBN 0-8160-2628-9　　LC 92-16308
Introduces the science of robotics, discussing the nature of artificial intelligence, the history of robotics, the different kinds of robots, and their uses
Includes glossary and bibliography

630.9　Agriculture—Historical and geographic treatment

Rhodes, Richard
Farm: a year in the life of an American farmer; illustrations by Bill Greer. Simon & Schuster 1989 336p il o.p.　　**630.9**
1. Agriculture—United States 2. Farm life
LC 89-34944
The author "tells the story of life on a typical American family farm. Tom and Sally Bauer and their three children live in Crevecoeur County in central Missouri. Through Rhodes the reader gets to know each family member personally and to share the hard work and joy of living close to the land. . . . Rhodes does a masterful job of relating, for today's largely urban population, one farmer's story." Libr J

635　Garden crops (Horticulture)

The **American** Horticultural Society encyclopedia of gardening; editor-in-chief, Christopher Brickell, editor-in-chief, American Horticultural Society, Elvin McDonald, consulting editor, Trevor Cole. Dorling Kindersley 1993 648p il $59.95　　**635**
1. Gardening—Dictionaries
ISBN 1-56458-291-4　　LC 93-3042
"Originally a British publication, this beautifully illustrated encyclopedia . . . has been thoroughly revised for the American gardener. The book covers all aspects of gardening including techniques, plants, and maintenance for indoor and outdoor plants. It also discusses equipping the garden, the garden environment, and plant problems. An outstanding feature of the book is the 3,000-plus color photos that illustrate clearly written instructions and make gardening procedures easy to follow." Am Libr

Better Homes and Gardens new garden book. 4th ed. Meredith Corp. 1990 384p il $29.95; pa $16.95　　**635**
1. Gardening
ISBN 0-696-00042-3; 0-696-02557-4 (pa)
LC 89-63159
First published 1951 with title: Better Homes and Gardens garden book
"The 400 color photographs and 115 drawings add more than just spice to the detailed plant profiles. There are chapters on gardening basics (climate, soil, fertilizers, watering, compost, mulches, and tools), landscaping, special gardens, and houseplants. An essential one-volume library addition." Booklist

Bridwell, Raymond
Hydroponic gardening; the magic of modern hydroponics for the home gardener. new ed. Woodbridge Press 1989 216p il pa $12.95　　**635**
1. Hydroponics
ISBN 0-88007-176-1　　LC 90-216377
First published 1972
Cover subtitle: How to grow vital, healthful food without soil and insect problems, in nutritionally balanced solutions
Instructions on "modern, soilless, home food growing, showing you how to prepare growing beds, moisten them with nutritionally balanced solutions, and harvest abundant crops." Publisher's note

Denckla, Tanya
The organic gardener's home reference; a plant-by-plant guide to growing fresh, healthy food. Storey Communications 1994 273p il $29.95; pa $19.95　　**635**
1. Organic gardening
ISBN 0-88266-840-4; 0-88266-839-0 (pa)
LC 93-22835
"A Garden Way Publishing book"
First published 1991 with title: Gardening at a glance
This work "covers vegetables, herbs, fruits and nuts, and pest and disease control. The book has a good intro-

Denckla, Tanya—*Continued*
duction on garden stewardship, followed by chapters on vegetables, fruits and nuts, herbs, macro- and microdestructive agents with organic remedies, and allies and companions. For those who want to know about an edible plant, the book describes growth conditions, harvesting, storage requirements, growing tips, and selected varieties." Recomm Ref Books for Small & Medium-sized Libr & Media Cent, 1996
Includes bibliographical references

Rodale's all-new encyclopedia of organic gardening; the indispensable resource for every gardener; edited by Fern Marshall Bradley and Barbara W. Ellis. Rodale Press 1992 690p il $29.95; pa $19.95   **635**
1. Organic gardening
ISBN 0-87857-999-0; 0-87596-599-7 (pa)
   LC 91-32088
First published 1959 with title: Rodale's encyclopedia of organic gardening
"Entries are cross referenced and include further reading lists, related organizations, and key words. Common and botanical names are listed, and while food plants are entered under their common names, ornamentals and herbs are entered under their botanical names. This is an important, complete, well-arranged, and attractive reference tool." Libr J

Rodale's illustrated encyclopedia of herbs; Claire Kowalchik & William H. Hylton, editors; writers: Anna Carr [et al.] Rodale Press 1987 545p il $26.95   **635**
1. Herbs 2. Medical botany
ISBN 0-87857-699-1   LC 87-16019
Provides "the history, uses, and cultivation of over 100 herbs, plus information on making teas, lotions, scents, and dyes. Other sections include herbs as houseplants, the history and botany of herbs, and a particularly valuable chapter on the dangers of herbs. The book is attractive and well illustrated." Libr J
Includes bibliography

635.9   Flowers and ornamental plants

The **American** Horticultural Society encyclopedia of garden plants; editor-in-chief, Christopher Brickell; horticultural consultant, John Elsing. Macmillan 1989 608p il $59.95   **635.9**
1. Ornamental plants
ISBN 0-02-557920-7   LC 89-32155
New edition in preparation
"This encyclopedia covers over 8000 garden plants suitable for English gardening. The Plant Catalog section of the book includes 4000 color photos to aid in identification. This section is arranged by size, season of interest, and color of foliage or flower." Libr J

Chiusoli, Alessandro
Simon & Schuster's guide to houseplants; [by] Alessandro Chiusoli and Maria Luisa Boriani; photographs by Enzo Arnone, illustrations by Vittorio Salarolo; U.S. editor, Stanley Schuler. Simon & Schuster 1986 319p il hardcover o.p. paperback available $14   **635.9**
1. House plants
ISBN 0-671-63131-4 (pa)   LC 86-22018
This book "covers feeding, pruning, repotting, propagating, and dealing with pests and diseases. Each of the 243 plants discussed is portrayed via a color photograph printed on slick, glossy paper." Booklist

Hodgson, Larry
All about houseplants; created and designed by the editorial staff of Ortho Books; editor, Marianne Lipanovich; writers, Larry Hodgson, Susan M. Lammers. Ortho Bks. 1994 112p il $14.95; pa $9.95   **635.9**
1. House plants 2. Indoor gardening
ISBN 0-89721-348-3; 0-89721-264-9 (pa)
   LC 93-86235
Replaces 1982 edition written by Susan M. Lammers
Contains information on plant physiology, growth, soil mixes, containers, potting techniques and decorating with plants. Illustrated with color photographs

Moggi, Guido
Simon and Schuster's guide to garden flowers; by Guido Moggi and Luciano Giugnolini; U.S. editor, Stanley Schuler. Simon & Schuster 1983 511p il maps hardcover o.p. paperback available $15   **635.9**
1. Flower gardening
ISBN 0-671-46678-X (pa)   LC 82-19678
This guide provides information on "individual flowers, cultivation, climatic suitability, food requirements, history and origin of the plants, and other small tidbits of information." Malinowsky. Best Sci & Technol Ref Books for Young People
Includes glossary and bibliography

Wright, Michael, 1941-
The complete handbook of garden plants; [by] Michael Wright, assisted by Sue Minter and Brian Carter. Facts on File 1984 544p il map $24.95
   635.9
1. Ornamental plants
ISBN 0-87196-632-8   LC 83-14133
"This comprehensive handbook covers outdoor garden plants, excluding fruits and vegetables. Over 9,000 species are detailed, with the entries arranged by plant type. . . . Within each described type, the plants are listed in alphabetical order by botanical name, with information on sizes of the plants, leaf sizes, color descriptions of varieties, hardiness and soil needs, how and when to propagate, pruning, and the best varieties of each species." Malinowsky. Best Sci & Technol Ref Books for Young People

636.089 Veterinary sciences. Veterinary medicine

McCormack, John
Fields and pastures new; my first year as a country vet. Crown 1995 265p $23   **636.089**
1. Veterinarians
ISBN 0-517-59686-5   LC 95-21288
Also available G.K. Hall large print edition and in paperback from Fawcett Bks.
"McCormack describes his first year in Choctaw County, Alabama, as a country veterinarian in the 1960s." Book Rep
"Love of family, townspeople, and their animals shines through this readable, lively book by an author with a good ear for dialogue and a fine sense of place." SLJ

636.1 Horses and related animals

The **Complete** horse book; edited by Elwyn Hartley Edwards & Candida Geddes. Trafalgar Sq. 1988 c1987 344p il hardcover o.p. paperback available $22.95   **636.1**
1. Horses
ISBN 0-943955-41-6 (pa)   LC 87-50763
First published 1982 by Larousse with title: The complete book of the horse; this edition first published 1987 in the United Kingdom
"Separate articles by specialists provide comprehensive coverage of such topics as the physiological and cultural history of the horse, the development of specific breeds around the world, and the horse's anatomy and health. Practical information is also included on keeping and housing horses, breeding, training and riding, and participating in competitions. . . . Hard to beat as a general source of information on horses." Booklist

Edwards, Elwyn Hartley
The encyclopedia of the horse; photographs by Bob Langrish, Kit Houghton; foreword by Sharon Ralls Lemon. Dorling Kindersley 1994 400p il maps $39.95   **636.1**
1. Horses
ISBN 1-56458-614-6   LC 94-644
"Over 150 breeds of horses and ponies are featured in this work. . . . Arranged chronologically, chapters trace the horse from its evolution and early use to classical riding, its influence in different areas of the world, and the horse at work, in sports, and in war. Within each chapter are highlighted breeds associated with the period, geographic area, or activity." Am Libr
For a fuller review see: Booklist, Dec. 1, 1994

Horses; photographs by Bob Langrish. Dorling Kindersley 1993 256p il (Eyewitness handbooks) $29.95; pa $17.95   **636.1**
1. Horses
ISBN 1-56458-180-2; 1-56458-177-2 (pa)
                                       LC 92-53469
Illustrated with full-color photographs, this guide begins with a general overview of horses and then presents the histories and characteristics of various breeds

Morris, Desmond
Horsewatching. Crown 1989 c1988 150p il $15   **636.1**
1. Horses
ISBN 0-517-57267-2   LC 88-34019
First published 1988 in the United Kingdom
"Morris answers many questions about the anatomy, history, traditions, physiology, and interrelationships of horses. The inquiries on how a horse sleeps, eats, sees, hears, and mates give way to more complex questions that are just as succinctly answered in a page or two. . . . An intriguing browsing item and reference that will have wide appeal." Booklist

Vogel, Colin
The complete horse care manual. Dorling Kindersley 1995 192p il $24.95   **636.1**
1. Horses
ISBN 0-7894-0170-3   LC 95-6744
Among the topics discussed in this illustrated manual are: feeding, grooming and exercising; stabling; handling; fitting bits, bridles, and other pieces of tack; recognizing and treating the symptoms of common equine illnesses
Includes glossary

636.6 Birds other than poultry

Gerstenfeld, Sheldon L., 1943-
The bird care book; all you need to know to keep your bird healthy and happy. rev & updated ed. Addison-Wesley 1989 xxi, 229p il pa $15   **636.6**
1. Birds
ISBN 0-201-09559-9   LC 88-19290
First published 1981
This book offers suggestions on choosing, caring and feeding of cage birds and wild birds
Includes bibliography

636.7 Dogs

American Kennel Club
The complete dog book. Howell Bk. House il $27.50   **636.7**
1. Dogs
First published 1935. (18th edition 1992) Frequently revised
"The official guide to 124 AKC registered breeds and their history, appearance, selection, training, care and feeding, and first aid. Some color plates." N Y Public Libr. Ref Books for Child Collect. 2d edition

American Kennel Club dog care and training; [by] the American Kennel Club. Howell Bk. House 1991 214p il pa $11.50   **636.7**
1. Dogs
ISBN 0-87605-405-X   LC 91-8404
This book "describes the dog's basic needs and the owner's responsibilities. The message is clear: people who cannot fulfill these obligations should not buy a dog. Topics discussed include: 'think' before buying, care, showing, training, breeding, and illness." Libr J
Includes glossary and bibliography

Caras, Roger A.
A dog is listening; the way some of our closest friends view us. Summit Bks. 1992 239p il hardcover o.p. paperback available $12   **636.7**
1. Dogs
ISBN 0-671-79726-3 (pa)   LC 91-40649
The author "provides basic scientific facts about dog anatomy and sensual skills. Adding details of experiences with and observations of dogs he has known and loved, Caras then uses his findings and ideas to explain canine demeanor and evolution. . . . Caras's opinions and stories provide friendly, comfortable reading that will make this popular with dog lovers. Its particular value as a well-written, lay introduction to canine abilities also makes it a useful supplement in more authoritative animal behavior collections." Libr J

Fogle, Bruce
ASPCA complete dog training manual; training sequences by Patricia Holden White; foreword by Roger Caras. Dorling Kindersley 1994 128p il $22.95   **636.7**
1. Dogs—Training
ISBN 1-56458-487-9   LC 93-28352
This work ranges "from a general discussion of canine mentality and temperament to detailed instructions for beginning and advanced training. Fogle's message is that kind, patient, and consistent teaching results in a well-trained, safe, and happy dog. The text is clearly worded, and the instructions are easy to follow." SLJ

The encyclopedia of the dog; special photography by Tracy Morgan. Dorling Kindersley 1995 312p il $39.95   **636.7**
1. Dogs—Dictionaries
ISBN 0-7894-0149-5   LC 95-6745
This volume "covers more than 400 breeds. It includes up to a page of infobites on each breed, as well as discussion of canine evolution; anatomy and health; communication; grooming; and the dog in art, literature, film, sports, folklore, and religion." SLJ
For a fuller review see: Booklist, Oct. 1, 1995

Know your dog; an owner's guide to dog behavior; photography by David Ward; additional photography by Jane Burton. Dorling Kindersley 1992 128p il $22.95   **636.7**
1. Dogs
ISBN 1-56458-080-6   LC 92-4497
The author "offers a sort of canine psychology here. His premise is that in order to give the best care possible to your dog, and to have the best possible relationship with it, you need to know what various gestures, expressions, and postures mean. . . . Fogle's book is copiously illustrated in color, presenting a dog posed in the particular expressive behavior. . . . This is not a training or breed-identification book, but it will teach you the meaning of every doggy mood." Booklist

Herriot, James
James Herriot's dog stories. St. Martin's Press 1986 xxxiii, 426p il $19.95; pa $6.99   **636.7**
1. Veterinary medicine 2. Dogs
ISBN 0-312-43968-7; 0-312-92558-1 (pa)
LC 86-6637
In this collection of stories, Herriot "illustrates the various reactions of the dogs to the vet who treats them, thus providing the psychological side of animal doctoring. Especially interesting and enlightening are the descriptions of treatments given in the '30s as compared to what research has put into the hands of today's vet." SLJ

The **International** encyclopedia of dogs; edited by Anne Rogers Clark and Andrew H. Brace; with special contributions by Renee Sporre-Willes. Howell Bk. House 1995 496p il $49.95   **636.7**
1. Dogs—Dictionaries
ISBN 0-87605-624-9   LC 95-30193
"Introductory material covers selecting a dog, health and general care and feeding, breeding, development and training, and competition. This is followed by the breed entries [for over 300 breeds] containing information on origin and development, temperament, health, special care and training, adaptability, and standards. A beautiful color photograph accompanies each entry." Booklist
Includes glossary and bibliography

The **Reader's** Digest illustrated book of dogs. 2nd rev ed. Reader's Digest Assn. 1994 384p il $27
636.7
1. Dogs
ISBN 0-88850-205-2
First published 1982
Edited by Patricia Sylvester
Among the topics covered are: identifying dogs, pure breds, care and feeding, canine psychology, socialization, training and kennel clubs

Taylor, David, 1934-
The ultimate dog book; consulting editor, Connie Vanacore; commissioned photography by Dave King, Jane Burton. Simon & Schuster 1990 240p il $29.95   **636.7**
1. Dogs
ISBN 0-671-70988-7   LC 90-32242
"A Dorling Kindersley book"
"After a general introduction to dog origins, anatomy, and behavior, the most popular breeds . . . receive luscious double-page spreads. Each representative breed . . . is reproduced in a large, vibrantly colored photograph, while smaller illustrations embellish the information on the canine's history, temperament, and physical characteristics. The concluding chapters address dog care, maintenance, and breeding. Highly recommended for browsing and reference." Booklist

Thomas, Elizabeth Marshall, 1931-
The hidden life of dogs. Houghton Mifflin 1993 xxi, 148p il $18.95   **636.7**
1. Dogs—Psychology
ISBN 0-395-66958-8   LC 93-18289
Also available G.K. Hall large print edition and in paperback from Pocket Bks.

Thomas, Elizabeth Marshall, 1931——_Continued_
"A Peter Davison book"

In this book about animal behavior the author's "intention is to find out, by observing her own animals, what it is that dogs 'want'. The dogs were free to make their own decisions; Thomas fed them, sheltered them, and provided medical care, but otherwise didn't train them or direct their activities." Libr J

The author's "writing is so good not only because of her sense of language but also because of the quality of her observations. . . . A splendid book." Natl Rev

Includes bibliographical references

636.8 Cats

Fogle, Bruce
Know your cat; an owner's guide to cat behavior; photography by Jane Burton. Dorling Kindersley 1991 128p il $22.95   **636.8**
1. Cats
ISBN 1-879431-04-1   LC 91-60145

"Fogle loads his explanation of cat instincts and insights with more than 350 full-color photographs. First is his description of personality, defensive and offensive postures, the 16 talking sounds, territories, and patrols. Relationships follow, then a pictorial sequence of mating, birth, kittenhood, and adulthood." Booklist

Gebhardt, Richard H.
The complete cat book. Howell Bk. House 1991 224p il $19.95   **636.8**
1. Cats
ISBN 0-87605-919-1   LC 91-13279

This book "begins with brief chapters on the history of the cat and its domestication, and on the anatomical design and function of cats, including muscle structure and diagrams of skeletons. These are followed by an alphabetical set of entries on the breeds. . . . While this book is of primary interest to the breeder/competitor, it will also be a very useful reference tool for identification purposes for elementary, junior high, and high school students." SLJ

Includes bibliographical references

Gerstenfeld, Sheldon L., 1943-
The cat care book; all you need to know to keep your cat healthy and happy. rev & updated ed. Addison-Wesley 1989 xx, 280p il pa $15   **636.8**
1. Cats
ISBN 0-201-09569-6   LC 88-39579

First published 1979 with title: Taking care of your cat

This book offers suggestions on how to choose the proper breed and then discusses specific areas of cat care and breeding

Includes bibliography

Taylor, David, 1934-
The ultimate cat book; Daphne Negus, consulting editor; commissioned photography by Dave King, Jane Burton. Simon & Schuster 1989 192p il $29.95   **636.8**
1. Cats
ISBN 0-671-68649-6   LC 89-6097

"A Dorling Kindersley book"

"The guide covers not only the origins and specifics of each breed but provides technical information on health, behavior, and reproduction, and advice on showing and traveling. The 750 excellent color photographs and beautiful layout make this a standout." Libr J

638 Insect culture

Melzer, Werner, 1927-
Beekeeping; with color photos by outstanding animal and nature photographers, and drawings by Walter Berghoff; advisory editor, Matthew M. Vriends. Barron's Educ. Ser. 1989 70p il pa $6.95   **638**
1. Bees
ISBN 0-8120-4089-9   LC 88-8053

"A practical guide for the novice beekeeper: buying bees, management, rearing, honey production: special section, the beekeeper's yearly work cycle." Title page

This book is "business-oriented, with ample though succinct coverage of the investments in equipment and time the insects require. . . . The colorplates and many drawings provide apt illustration." Booklist

Includes glossary

639.3 Fish culture

Mattison, Christopher
The care of reptiles and amphibians in captivity. 3rd rev ed. Blandford Press; distributed by Sterling 1992 317p il pa $17.95   **639.3**
1. Reptiles 2. Amphibians
ISBN 0-7137-2338-6   LC 93-114518

First published 1982

"Mattison authoritatively addresses care, health, and breeding of captive reptiles and amphibians. More than half of his book is devoted to descriptions and care requirements of various species of salamanders, newts, frogs, toads, lizards, turtles, tortoises, and snakes. Black-and-white photos are supplemented by a 16-page color insert." Libr J

Mills, Dick
Aquarium fish; photography by Jerry Young. Dorling Kindersley 1993 304p il (Eyewitness handbooks) $29.95; pa $17.95   **639.3**
1. Fishes 2. Aquariums
ISBN 1-56458-294-9; 1-56458-293-0 (pa)
     LC 93-3155

This illustrated "guide provides general information on the choice and care of fish, natural habitats, required aquarium conditions, and specific details on freshwater

Mills, Dick—*Continued*

and marine tropical and coldwater fishes. Data for each species include family, common name, maximum adult size, physical characteristics of species, habitat, range, geographical distribution, peculiarites of species, alternative names, and a small, attractive photograph showing the male of the species." Libr J

"Although novice fishkeepers won't find enough in this handy book to answer all their questions, those looking for a fish identification guide will find the color photos and the brief information exceptionally useful." Booklist

Quinn, John R.

The fascinating fresh water fish book; how to catch, keep, and observe your own native fish. Wiley 1994 122p il pa $10.95 **639.3**

1. Fishes 2. Aquariums

ISBN 0-471-58601-3   LC 93-31691

This book "introduces young readers to aquarium maintenance of North American freshwater fishes and other selected freshwater organisms. The directions and advice provided are accurate and designed to prevent disastrous mistakes commonly made by beginning aquarists. . . . A list of important public aquaria in the United States and Canada is presented." Sci Books Films

Includes glossary

Scott, Peter W.

The complete aquarium; photography by Jane Burton and Kim Taylor. Knopf 1991 192p il o.p.; DK Pub. paperback available $16.95 **639.3**

1. Aquariums

ISBN 0-7894-0013-8 (pa)   LC 90-52912

"This is a step-by-step guide to building and maintaining a freshwater or marine aquarium and includes a section on the feeding, breeding, and health care of aquarium fish. . . . The main portion of the book is devoted to the setting up of 16 authentic and complete aquariums representing all areas of the world from Asia to the Carribbean. . . . Throughout this comprehensive book are over 400 color photographs, drawings and diagrams to guide the aquarium enthusiast through every aspect of creating the Complete Aquarium." BAYA Book Rev

Includes glossary

639.9 Conservation of biological resources

Animal kingdoms; wildlife sanctuaries of the world; prepared by the Book Division, National Geographic Society. National Geographic Soc. 1995 200p il $16 **639.9**

1. Wildlife refuges 2. National parks and reserves

ISBN 0-7922-2734-4   LC 95-11922

This volume contains "a retrospective of outstanding wildlife reserves both near and far, great and small, as seen through the eyes of . . . photographers and writers." Publisher's note

640 Home economics and family living

Santamaria, Peggy

High performance through self-management. Rosen Pub. Group 1996 64p il (Learning-a-living library) lib bdg $15.95 **640**

1. Time management 2. Life skills

ISBN 0-8239-2208-1   LC 95-38830

"After explaining the necessity and inherent worth of *Self-Management* in sucessful, satisfying lives, Santamaria shows how the principle can be developed at school, in the work place, in extra-curricular athletic pursuit, and in volunteer activities." SLJ

Includes glossary and bibliography

641 Food and drink

Livingston, A. D., 1932-

Edible plants and animals; unusual foods from aardvark to zamia; [by] A.D. Livingston and Helen Livingston. Facts on File 1993 292p il $25.95 **641**

1. Animal food 2. Edible plants

ISBN 0-8160-2744-7   LC 92-41501

This is a guide to unusual foods from different cultures and time periods. The 500 entries are "divided between edible animals and edible plants. . . . Entries include scientific and common names, uses, geographic distribution, toxic portions, and sometimes directions for preparation, nutritional values, and bibliographic citations." Booklist

Trager, James

The food chronology; a food lover's compendium of events and anecdotes from prehistory to the present. Holt & Co. 1995 783p il (Henry Holt reference book) $40 **641**

1. Food

ISBN 0-8050-3389-0   LC 95-6710

This chronology "contains over 20 categories, from political events and economics to the arts and humanities, each easily identified by a corresponding symbol. The book begins at one million B.C. with the emergence of the omnivorous *Homo erectus* and concludes with big business and environmental concerns of 1995. In between are centuries and individual years, full of more than 13,000 entries recording progress, regress, fads, milestones, and trivia." Libr J

For a fuller review see: Booklist, Jan. 1996

641.03 Food and drink— Encyclopedias and dictionaries

Claiborne, Craig

Craig Claiborne's The New York Times food encyclopedia. Wings Bks. 1994 496p il $14.99 **641.03**

1. Food—Dictionaries

ISBN 0-517-11906-4   LC 94-10846

A reprint of the title first published 1985 by Times Bks.

Claiborne, Craig—*Continued*
"Claiborne discusses, among many topics, the role of chicken feet in the making of broth, a recipe for cooking bluefish in a dishwasher . . ., how to preserve curry powder, and the origins of some popular dishes as well as their names." N Y Times Book Rev
"From the basics to the exotic, this volume will make a handy companion for serious cooks or for those who just want to browse." Booklist
Includes bibliographical references

641.1   Applied nutrition

Brody, Jane E.
Jane Brody's nutrition book; a lifetime guide to good eating for better health and weight control; by the personal health columnist of The New York Times. Norton 1981 xx, 552p il $29.95
                                                            641.1
1. Nutrition 2. Diet
ISBN 0-393-01429-0   LC 80-25117
Also available in paperback from Bantam Bks.
This nutrition guide for the layperson covers the basics in addition to popular concerns such as cholesterol, fiber, sugar and additives. Some recipes are included

Salter, Charles A., 1947-
Food risks and controversies; minimizing the dangers in your diet. Millbrook Press 1993 110p lib bdg $16.40   **641.1**
1. Food 2. Nutrition
ISBN 1-56294-259-X   LC 92-37442
"A Teen nutrition book"
Introduces the health hazards associated with food, examining such topics as manmade and natural toxins, food additives, and pesticides, and discusses how to eat safely and wisely
Includes bibliography

641.3   Food

Tannahill, Reay
Food in history. new, fully rev and updated ed. Crown 1989 c1988 424p il hardcover o.p. paperback available $16   **641.3**
1. Food—History 2. Dining
ISBN 0-517-88404-6 (pa)   LC 89-671
First published 1973 by Stein & Day; this edition first published 1988 in the United Kingdom
"A world history of food from prehistoric times to today, this book also traces the way in which food has influenced the entire course of human development." Publisher's note
Includes bibliography

641.5   Cooking

Albyn, Carole Lisa, 1955-
The multicultural cookbook for students; by Carole Lisa Albyn and Lois Sinaiko Webb. Oryx Press 1993 xxii, 287p maps pa $25.95   **641.5**
1. Cooking
ISBN 0-89774-735-6   LC 92-41634
Presents a collection of recipes from over 120 countries and briefly discusses the culture and culinary habits of each country

American Heart Association cookbook. Times Bks. $25   **641.5**
1. Cooking 2. Low-cholesterol diet
Also available in large print for $29.95 and in paperback for $6.99
First published 1973. (5th edition 1991) Periodically revised
This cookbook includes over 600 recipes from appetizers, spreads and snacks to desserts and breakfast dishes. Appendix gives tips for dining out and menus for holidays and special occasions
"No more comprehensive guide to the healthy eating suited to the 1990s is available." Booklist

Axcell, Claudia, 1946-
Simple foods for the pack; by Claudia Axcell, Diana Cooke, and Vikki Kinmont; illustrated by Bob Kinmont. rev ed. Sierra Club Bks. 1986 256p il pa $9   **641.5**
1. Outdoor cooking 2. Backpacking
ISBN 0-87156-757-1   LC 85-22076
First published 1976 under the authorship of Vikki Kinmont & Claudia Axcell
A collection of recipes and food suggestions for the outdoorsman
Includes bibliography

✓ **Bayless, Rick**
Authentic Mexican; regional cooking from the heart of Mexico; [by] Rick Bayless with Deann Groen Bayless; illustrations by John Sandford. Morrow 1987 384p il $27.50   **641.5**
1. Mexican cooking
ISBN 0-688-04394-1   LC 86-12706
"A wealth of cultural/culinary lore plus well-laid-out, easy-to-follow recipes replete with 'cook's notes' makes this an ideal resource for teens studying or interested in international cuisine." Booklist
Includes bibliography

Berry, Mary, 1935-
Classic home cooking; by Mary Berry and Marlena Spieler. Dorling Kindersley 1995 512p il $39.95   **641.5**
1. Cooking
ISBN 0-7894-0153-3   LC 95-2198
In addition to the 1,000 recipes this illustrated volume's "know-how section spotlights certain techniques and provides general instructions for microwaving, freezing, and storage. Streamlining dishes for time and convenience is also discussed." Booklist

Better Homes and Gardens new cook book. Meredith Corp. loose-leaf $25.95; pa $15.95
641.5

1. Cooking

First published 1930 with title: My Better Homes and Gardens cook book.(11th edition 1996) Periodically revised

"A standard cookbook . . . with staple recipes and types of cooking." N Y Public Libr. Book of How & Where to Look It Up

Child, Julia

The way to cook; photographs by Brian Leatart and Jim Scherer; food designer, Rosemary Manell. Knopf 1989 511p il $65
641.5

1. Cooking

ISBN 0-394-53264-3   LC 88-45838

"With her sensible-as-always approach to food, Child has produced a comprehensive cooking bible, filled with stunning photographs and practical illustrations, that will aid the novice, inspire the gourmet. . . . A masterwork from a master chef." Libr J

Chin, Leeann

Betty Crocker's new Chinese cookbook; recipes by Leeann Chin. Prentice-Hall 1990 138p il $16
641.5

1. Chinese cooking

ISBN 0-13-083254-5   LC 89-16053

First published 1981 with title: Betty Crocker's Chinese cookbook

This is a collection of recipes for Chinese foods for the typical American kitchen. "With easy-to-obtain ingredients, an overview of cooking methods, including cutting and use of utensils, and an ingredient glossary, basic cooking skills are reinforced." Booklist

Cooking A to Z; the complete culinary reference source; Jane Horn, editor/writer; Janet Fletcher, contributing writer; Annette Gooch, general editor. New and rev ed. Cole Group 1997 655p pa $29.95
641.5

1. Cooking

ISBN 1-56426-577-3   LC 95-16390

First published 1988 by Ortho Bks.

In addition to the more than 600 recipes this book contains entries that define cooking terms and describe cooking techniques

"Any high school library should have this well-organized and beautifully illustrated work." Nichols. Guide to Ref Books for Sch Media Cent. 4th edition

Crocker, Betty

Betty Crocker's cookbook. Prentice-Hall il $25
641.5

1. Cooking

First published with this title 1969 by Golden Press. (8th edition 1996 Betty Crocker's new cookbook) Periodically revised

"This book gives easily readable and understandable recipes. Also has a glossary of cooking terms in back, as well as nutritional guidelines and 'special helps.'" N Y Public Libr. Book of How & Where to Look It Up

Betty Crocker's new international cookbook. rev ed. Prentice-Hall 1994 376p il $19
641.5

1. Cooking

ISBN 0-671-88763-7   LC 96-137110

First published 1980 with title: Betty Crocker's international cookbook

This illustrated cookbook includes 450 recipes culled from over 50 countries. Includes a glossary of foreign ingredients and terms and a regional index

Farmer, Fannie Merritt, 1857-1915

The Fannie Farmer cookbook. Knopf il $30
641.5

1. Cooking

First published 1896. (1996 edition) Periodically revised. Recent editions edited by Marion Cunningham

This standard cookbook focuses on the selection, preparation, and serving of a wide variety of foods

The **Good** Housekeeping illustrated microwave cookbook; edited by Joyce A. Kenneally. Hearst Bks. 1990 400p il $25
641.5

1. Microwave cooking

ISBN 0-688-08473-7   LC 89-84254

"A Dorling Kindersley book"

"Each entry is accompanied by a brief description of the dish, a page reference, and a photograph of the finished product. Recipes with illustrated, step-by-step instructions and nutritional analyses make up the main body of the text. Well written and attractive." Booklist

Karoff, Barbara, 1929-

South American cooking; foods and feasts from the New World; illustrated by Earl Thollander. Aris Bks. 1989 xxi, 229p il hardcover o.p. paperback available $12.45
641.5

1. Latin American cooking 2. Menus

ISBN 0-201-55094-6 (pa)   LC 89-362

"Ten major countries are featured—all with menus that can be planned by season. Beans, squash, and corn are emphasized, and most other ingredients are just as easy to obtain. Main dishes constitute most of the 150 recipes." Booklist

Includes glossary and bibliography

Microwave cooking; contributing editor, Sarah Brown. Reader's Digest Assn. 1990 223p il pa $16
641.5

1. Microwave cooking

ISBN 0-89577-348-1   LC 89-70347

"RD home handbooks"

"Containing basic information on the care and use of microwave ovens as well as a variety of recipes, this will be helpful for those unfamiliar with microwave cookery." Booklist

The **New** Good Housekeeping cookbook; edited by Mildred Ying; with the assistance of Susan Deborah Goldsmith and Ellen H. Connelly. Hearst Bks. 1986 825p il $23
641.5

1. Cooking 2. Menus

ISBN 0-688-03897-2   LC 86-81549

Variant title: The Good Housekeeping cookbook

The New Good Housekeeping cookbook—*Continued*

This volume "goes a step beyond the fundamentals by adding a chapter on microwave cooking. Every 'Good Housekeeping' recipe tells not only how many servings it yields, but also how many calories are in each serving. Each chapter begins with an explanation of basic techniques for cooking the foods it focuses on . . . and progresses to more sophisticated treatments of that fundamental fare." Wilson Libr Bull

Rombauer, Irma von Starkloff, 1877-1962

Joy of cooking; [by] Irma S. Rombauer, Marion Rombauer Becker; illustrated by Ginnie Hofmann and Ikki Matsumoto. Macmillan il $25.50   **641.5**
1. Cooking
Also available in paperback from New Am Lib.
First published 1931. (1985 edition) Periodically revised
"All-purpose cookbook for informal and formal use with American and foreign recipes. Includes menu planning suggestions, nutrition, basic information on foods, basic cooking terminology, and methods of preparation." N Y Public Libr. Book of How & Where to Look It Up

Smith, Jeff

The Frugal Gourmet on our immigrant ancestors; recipes you should have gotten from your grandmother; Craig Wollam, culinary assistant; Chris Cart, illustrator; Terrin Haley, D. C. Smith, research assistants. Morrow 1990 539p il maps $22   **641.5**
1. Cooking
ISBN 0-688-07590-8   LC 90-48368
"Smith shares with readers recipes of immigrants who are often overlooked—Basques, Ethiopians, Jamaicans, Latvians, Scottish, Saudi Arabians, and many more. Each chapter begins with an illustration of the people, a map, and a few pages of introduction, including history and food customs. The recipes are clearly written and easy to follow. Hints and equipment lists are thorough. A cookbook bibliography, immigrant history bibliography, source list for unusual ingredients, and an index complete the package." SLJ

Weight Watchers healthy life-style cookbook; over 250 recipes based on the Personal Choice Program; set design and photography by Gus Francisco. NAL/Dutton 1991 358p il hardcover o.p. paperback available $12.95   **641.5**
1. Cooking 2. Reducing
ISBN 0-452-26755-2 (pa)   LC 90-13817
This cookbook features recipes "using a wide variety of foods. . . . Up-to-date nutritional information includes analysis of calories, protein, fat, carbohydrates, calcium, sodium, cholesterol and dietary fiber." Booklist
Includes glossary

643   Housing and household equipment

How things work in your home (and what to do when they don't); by the editors of Time-Life Books. 2nd ed. Holt & Co. 1985 368p il hardcover o.p. paperback available $19.95   **643**
1. Houses—Maintenance and repair 2. Plumbing—Repairing 3. Household equipment and supplies—Maintenance and repair
ISBN 0-8050-0126-3 (pa)   LC 84-28988
First published 1975 by Time-Life Books
This volume discusses the home toolkit, plumbing, electrical wiring, small and large appliances, heating systems, air conditioners and outdoor repairs
Includes bibliography

Plante, Ellen M.

The American kitchen, 1700 to the present; from hearth to highrise. Facts on File 1995 340p il $27.95   **643**
1. Kitchens 2. Cooking 3. United States—Social life and customs
ISBN 0-8160-3038-3   LC 94-33235
This is a "history of the evolution of the focal point of the American home, beginning with the colonial kitchen and traveling to the present. Plante gives readers not only a clear view of how the room has changed, but also of how the family itself has changed. The illustrations and reproductions of advertisements make visualizing the text interesting and easy. The 'Household Hints and Recipes' are outstanding, each worthy of the era they reflect." SLJ
Includes glossary and bibliography

646.2   Sewing and related operations

Reader's Digest complete guide to sewing. rev ed. Reader's Digest Assn. 1995 432p il $30   **646.2**
ISBN 0-88850-247-8
First published 1976
Editor: Sandy Shepherd
This illustrated guide begins with an overview of basic equipment and techniques. A discussion of patterns and fabrics is included. The bulk of the book provides step-by-step instructions for making clothes and home furnishings
"This is a great source for sound sewing basics." Libr J

646.7 Management of personal and family living. Grooming

✓ **Mathis, Darlene**

Women of color; the multicultural guide to fashion and beauty; foreword by Carole Jackson. Ballantine Bks. 1994 190p il $23   **646.7**
1. Personal grooming 2. African American women— Health and hygiene
ISBN 0-345-38929-8   LC 94-15715
"Although directed predominantly to working women, the accessible fashion advice Mathis supplies may attract teens concerned about personal image." Booklist

Scheman, Andrew J.

Cosmetics buying guide; [by] Andrew J. Scheman, David L. Severson. Consumer Repts. Bks. 1993 322p pa $14.95   **646.7**
1. Skin—Care and hygiene 2. Cosmetics 3. Consumer education
ISBN 0-89043-581-2   LC 93-11552
This "book details the basic components of different types of [cosmetic preparations], describing what each can and cannot do. Information about the few consumer protection laws that apply to cosmetics and about the industry's self-regulation are also included. The bulk of the book consists of detailed charts, grouped by product type, which compare the ingredients in each manufacturer's version of the product. Packing a lot of information into a small volume, this guide will be useful to consumers, students, and reference librarians." Libr J
Includes bibliographical references

647.9 Multiple dwellings for transients, eating and drinking places

Hostelling North America. American Youth Hostels maps pa $6.95   **647.9**
1. Youth hostels—Directories
First published 1934. Title varies
An annual directory of the youth hostels in the United States and Canada, published by American Youth Hostels and Canadian Hostelling Association

649 Child rearing

Barkin, Carol, 1944-

The new complete babysitter's handbook; by Carol Barkin & Elizabeth James; illustrated by Martha Weston. Clarion Bks. 1995 164p il $16.95; pa $7.95   **649**
1. Babysitting
ISBN 0-395-66557-4; 0-395-66558-2 (pa)
    LC 93-39345
First published 1980 by Simon & Schuster with title: The complete babysitter's handbook
This guide to babysitting covers such topics as finding jobs, acting professional, playing with and caring for babies and toddlers, first aid and what to do in an emergency

✓ **Dixon, Barbara M.**

Good health for African-American kids; [by] Barbara M. Dixon, with Josleen Wilson; foreword by Melvin E. Jenkins; preface by Keith C. Ferdinand. Crown Trade Paperbacks 1996 xxiii, 423p pa $18   **649**
1. African American children 2. Children—Health and hygiene
ISBN 0-517-88269-8   LC 95-34601
This work "begins with instructions for charting a family health tree to identify such genetic risk factors for heart disease as diabetes and hypertension. Advice on prenatal care is followed by that for infant, child and adolescent care. Focusing on disease prevention, Dixon includes ample advice on nutrition—including a few recipes. . . . An extensive directory of resources adds to the book's usefulness." Publ Wkly

Lindsay, Jeanne Warren

The challenge of toddlers; parenting your child from one to three. Morning Glory Press 1991 191p il $15.95; pa $9.95   **649**
1. Child rearing 2. Teenage mothers 3. Teenage fathers
ISBN 0-930934-59-8; 0-930934-58-X (pa)
    LC 91-30316
At head of title: Teens parenting
This "guide continues in the same format, style, and approach as the volume on infants [entered below], with advice, discussion, comments, options, and photographs about such issues as toddlers' independence, toilet training, active play, language development, fussiness with food, messiness, rest and sleep routines, extended families, and health and safety. Advice is also given on family planning, counseling, job seeking, further education, and financial planning. This easy-to-read book is recommended highly to a wide cultural and geographical young adult audience." Sci Books Films
Includes bibliography

Teen dads; rights, responsibilities and joys; photographs by David Crawford. Morning Glory Press 1993 191p il $15.95; pa $9.95   **649**
1. Teenage fathers 2. Child rearing 3. Parenting
ISBN 0-930934-77-6; 0-930934-78-4 (pa)
    LC 93-4450
A guide for teenage fathers who want to develop their parenting skills, with an emphasis on dealing with children from birth to the age of three
"The encouraging tone and informality of the text make the information easy to assimilate, and the inclusion of comments from teen dads will bring readers closer into the fatherhood fold. . . . Turn to this book for the practicalities and general good sense it contains." Booklist
Includes bibliography

Your baby's first year; a how-to-parent book especially for teenage parents. Morning Glory Press 1991 191p il $15.95; pa $9.95   **649**
1. Child rearing 2. Teenage mothers 3. Teenage fathers
ISBN 0-930934-53-9; 0-930934-52-0 (pa)
    LC 91-21513
At head of title: Teens parenting

Lindsay, Jeanne Warren—*Continued*

The author "covers a variety of topics, including feeding the baby, accident-proofing the home as well as the benefits of taking time to play with the baby. She also discusses problems which face young parents such as living with interfering relatives, the relationship with the baby's father, and the importance of finishing school." Voice Youth Advocates

"This invaluable book offers choices, as well as direction and guidance, to teen parents in a nonjudgmental and nonthreatening way. . . . The easy vocabulary, nonsexist language, honest comments, and helpful suggestions make this guidebook appropriate for a wide range of junior and senior high audiences." Sci Books Films

Includes bibliography

Stoppard, Miriam

Complete baby and child care. Dorling Kindersley 1995 351p il $29.95   **649**

1. Child care 2. Infants—Care 3. Child development

ISBN 1-56458-850-5   LC 94-26720

"This illustrated volume covers the basics of caring for children during the first five years of life. Practical advice on behavior, clothing, choosing nursery equipment and supplies, and traveling with children make this book very useful. The illustrations showing how to bathe an infant, positions for breastfeeding, methods of expressing breast milk, and first aid are outstanding. . . . A fine addition to parenting collections." Libr J

650.14   Success in obtaining jobs and promotions

Bloch, Deborah Perlmutter

How to write a winning resume. new ed. VGM Career Horizons 1994 146p pa $6.95   **650.14**

1. Résumés (Employment)

ISBN 0-8442-4172-5   LC 93-14223

First published 1985

The author addresses the writing and physical preparation of resumes as well as their distribution. Special issues facing new workers, re-entering workers, and career changers are explored. Appendices provide job descriptions and sources of job leads

Includes bibliographical references

Fry, Ronald W.

Your first resume; the essential, comprehensive guide for anyone entering or reentering the job market. Career Press il pa $9.99   **650.14**

1. Résumés (Employment)

First published 1988. (4th edition 1996) Periodically revised

A step-by-step guide for preparing a successful résumé. Numerous examples accompany the text

Résumés that get jobs. Macmillan pa $9.95

    650.14

1. Résumés (Employment) 2. Applications for positions

First published 1963 under the editorship of Edward C. Gruber. (8th edition 1996) Periodically revised

Current edition by Jean Reed and Ray Potter

This guide for job-seekers covers job-hunting, interview conduct and focuses on resume writing skills with sample resumes included for a wide variety of positions in various fields

651.3   Office management

Lindsell-Roberts, Sheryl

The secretary's quick reference handbook. 3rd ed. Prentice-Hall 1992 282p il pa $8   **651.3**

1. Secretaries—Handbooks, manuals, etc. 2. Office practice—Handbooks, manuals, etc.

ISBN 0-13-799396-X   LC 91-45320

"An Arco book"

First published 1983

This guide covers the basics of business English, letter writing techniques, and office practice and procedure

Merriam-Webster's secretarial handbook. 3rd ed. Merriam-Webster 1993 590p $15.95   **651.3**

1. Secretaries—Handbooks, manuals, etc. 2. Office practice—Handbooks, manuals, etc.

ISBN 0-87779-236-4   LC 93-10632

First published 1976 with title: Webster's secretarial handbook

Covers various aspects of the business office, including using computers, word processors and other machines; grammar and word usage; and business etiquette

The **Professional** secretary's handbook. 3rd ed. Houghton Mifflin 1995 578p il $18.95   **651.3**

1. Secretaries—Handbooks, manuals, etc. 2. Office practice—Handbooks, manuals, etc.

ISBN 0-395-69621-6   LC 95-12835

First published 1984

This handbook covers various aspects of office management including telecommunications, planning and conducting meetings, accounting and business law, English grammar, usage, and punctuation, editing, proofreading, and filing business documents, and career management

651.7   Business communication. Creation and transmission of records

Geffner, Andrea B.

How to write better business letters. 2nd ed. Barron's Educ. Ser. 1995 144p il pa $10.95

    651.7

1. Business letters

ISBN 0-8120-3643-3   LC 94-33883

First published 1982

This manual contains tips and techniques for commercial correspondence dealing with requests, replies, credit and collection, claims and adjustments, sales and public relations. In-house correspondence and business reports are also discussed

Includes glossary

652 Processes of written communication

Wrixon, Fred B.
Codes and ciphers. Prentice Hall General Ref. 1992 260p il pa $18   **652**
1. Cryptography 2. Ciphers
ISBN 0-13-277047-4   LC 91-42848
This work "includes entries for people, events, decoding equipment, titles of codes, names of ciphers, and general terminology of the field. . . . The codes discussed range from secret ones used by military and diplomatic personnel to the nonsecret codes used in science and industry (genetic code, bankcard code, etc.)." Booklist

653 Shorthand

Gregg shorthand dictionary; [by] John Robert Gregg [et al.] McGraw-Hill $24.95; pa $14.95   **653**
1. Shorthand
First published 1963. Periodically revised
Available in various editions and bindings
A compilation of shorthand outlines of words, names and frequently used phrases
"An excellent reference for stenographic students." Wynar. Guide to Ref Books for Sch Media Cent. 2d edition [review of 1963 edition]

658.1 Business organization and finance

Mariotti, Steve
The young entrepreneur's guide to starting and running a business; [by] Steve Mariotti with Tony Towle and Debra DeSalvo. Times Business 1996 322p il pa $15   **658.1**
1. Small business 2. Youth—Employment
ISBN 0-8129-2627-7   LC 95-42846
"Mariotti discusses the characteristics of the entrepreneur, selecting the business, financing, maintaining financial records, market research, advertising, and writing a business plan. Throughout, he provides numerous case studies of success stories." Libr J
"An excellent introduction for someone wanting to start a business. . . . School groups interested in raising money and teens tired of baby-sitting or working in retail stores will find this full of other earning options." Booklist
Includes bibliographical references

659.1 Advertising

Frisch, Carlienne, 1944-
Hearing the pitch; evaluating all kinds of advertising. Rosen Pub. Group 1994 48p il (Lifeskills library) lib bdg $14.95   **659.1**
1. Advertising
ISBN 0-8239-1694-4   LC 93-46200
This "explains advertising and its formats, examining the various devices used to influence people. . . . Good

examples are given, the writing is clear. . . . Black-and-white and full-color photos illustrate many points effectively and add interest." SLJ
Includes glossary and bibliography

Gay, Kathlyn
Caution! this may be an advertisement; a teen guide to advertising. Watts 1992 144p il lib bdg $22.70   **659.1**
1. Advertising
ISBN 0-531-11039-7   LC 91-38159
"In a mixture of history, reportage, and advice, Gay offers consumers an intelligent and informative guide to advertising. Opting for breadth rather than depth, the book touches on topics such as marketing research, packaging as promotion, image creation, and public service advertising." Bull Cent Child Books
Includes bibliographical references

Gross, Michael, 1948-
Model; the ugly business of beautiful women. Morrow 1995 524p il $25   **659.1**
1. Fashion models
ISBN 0-688-12659-6   LC 94-34610
Also available in paperback from Warner Bks.
In this "exposé of the modeling industry, . . . Gross examines the transformation of fashion modeling from the rise of the first modeling agencies in the 1920s to today's opulent and international scene. With equal interest in the business of modeling and its sordid underbelly, Gross stitches together detailed portraits of the industry's major players." Publ Wkly

660 Chemical engineering

Bains, William
Biotechnology from A to Z. Oxford Univ. Press 1993 358p il pa $19.95   **660**
1. Biotechnology—Dictionaries
ISBN 0-19-963334-7   LC 93-215815
This is a "glossary of about 280 terms designed to give the nonexpert an . . . insight into the meaning of biotechnology's fundamental concepts and jargon." Sci Books Films
"The delightful thing about the book is that everything is set in context. . . . A wonderfully lucid guide to an exciting but blindingly complex industry." New Sci

Steinberg, Mark L.
The Facts on File dictionary of biotechnology and genetic engineering; [by] Mark L. Steinberg, Sharon D. Cosloy. Facts on File 1994 197p il $27.95   **660**
1. Biotechnology—Dictionaries 2. Genetic engineering—Dictionaries
ISBN 0-8160-1250-4   LC 93-25337
"Containing some 1,600 entries and more than 70 illustrations to clarify them, this reference will be useful for everyone from students through professionals in genetics or biotechnology." Book Rep

Thro, Ellen
Genetic engineering; shaping the material of life. Facts on File 1993 121p il (Facts on File science sourcebooks) lib bdg $17.95 **660**
1. Genetic engineering
ISBN 0-8160-2629-7 LC 92-17256
Defines and traces the history of genetic engineering and describes its uses in medicine, agriculture, and business
Includes glossary and bibliography

664 Food technology

Winter, Ruth, 1930-
A consumer's dictionary of food additives. updated 4th ed. Crown Trade Paperbacks 1994 425p pa $15 **664**
1. Food additives—Dictionaries
ISBN 0-517-88195-0 LC 94-27332
First published 1972
This volume lists 8,000 food additives and explains food labels that are required on all processed food products
"Recommended for all who want to make informed choices leading to a healthier diet, the book aids in understanding the descriptions and effects of chemicals in packaged foods, and the regulations governing their use." Am Ref Books Annu, 1996

670 Manufacturing

How products are made; an illustrated guide to product manufacturing; Neil Schlager, editor. v1. Gale Res. 1994 524p il $75 **670**
1. Commercial products
ISBN 0-8103-8907-X
This volume, "which launches a series on the manufacturing processes of products from foods to cosmetics to electronics to vehicles, details the manufacture of 101 randomly selected items. The products covered here are a curious mix, including automobiles, blue jeans, chewing gum, jet engines, microwave ovens, pantyhose, salsa, stainless steel, tortilla chips, and zippers. Ranging from four to seven pages, each entry includes the product's description, history, design, manufacturing process, raw materials, by-products, future uses, and a bibliography. The text is nontechnical, and the illustrations are clear, making this book appropriate for YAs as well as adult lay readers." Libr J

Welsh, Heidi J.
Animal testing and consumer products. Investor Responsibility Res. Center 1990 167p pa $25 **670**
1. Animal experimentation 2. Product safety 3. Commercial products
ISBN 0-931935-39-2 LC 89-82428
"This report examines the animal protection movement and provides detailed company profiles of nine firms that have received shareholder resolutions on animal testing. It includes an analysis of animal use data reported to the U.S. Department of Agriculture by corporations and noncommercial research and testing facilities around the country. It also examines federal regulations on consumer product testing and discusses the emerging alternatives to animal use." Publisher's note
Includes bibliography

674 Lumber processing, wood products, cork

The **Encyclopedia** of wood; a tree-by-tree guide to the world's most versatile resource; foreword by John Makepeace; general editor, Aidan Walker. Facts on File 1989 192p il maps $29.95 **674**
1. Wood
ISBN 0-8160-2159-7 LC 89-33439
This book describes the properties, appearance, geographic distribution, and uses of seventy-five types of wood, and discusses trees, forest types, and logging procedures
"This *Encyclopedia* would be excellent for school and public libraries and as a supplemental source in academic libraries, especially for its outstanding illustrations." Booklist

684 Furnishings and home workshops

Cliffe, Roger W.
Woodworker's handbook. Sterling 1990 486p il pa $24.95 **684**
1. Woodwork
ISBN 0-8069-7238-6 LC 89-22019
First published 1981 with title: Woodworking, principles and practices
An illustrated step-by-step guide to the design and construction of 25 woodworking projects
Includes glossary

The **Complete** woodworker; edited by Bernard E. Jones. new ed. Ten Speed Press 1980 408p il (Cassell's handcraft library) $16.95; pa $9.95 **684**
1. Woodwork
ISBN 0-89815-034-5; 0-89815-022-1 (pa) LC 80-634
First published 1917 by Cassell
Provides a variety of woodworking projects which require hand tools only

Jackson, Albert, 1943-
The complete manual of woodworking; [by] Albert Jackson, David Day and Simon Jennings. Knopf 1989 320p il maps $40 **684**
1. Woodwork
ISBN 0-394-56488-X LC 89-45263
Among the topics the authors cover are choosing materials, maintenance of hand and power tools, sawing, joining, gluing and clamping, waxing, and finishing. Numerous illustrations accompany the text

Woodworker's 30 best projects; [by] the editors of Woodworker magazine. TAB Bks. 1988 212p il $23.95; pa $14.95 **684**
1. Woodwork
ISBN 0-8306-0421-9; 0-8306-9321-1 (pa)
LC 88-15688
The editors "focus on fine furniture in their selection of articles. . . . Several simpler items are also presented. Among the more unusual projects are a pool table and a gossip bench. Drawings, materials lists, and photographs are supplied for each item." Booklist

686.2 Printing

Madama, John
Desktop publishing; the art of communication. Lerner Publs. 1993 64p il (Media workshop) lib bdg $14.95 **686.2**
1. Desktop publishing
ISBN 0-8225-2303-5
LC 91-46314
Explains the desktop publishing process including computer basics, necessary writing and research skills, working with illustrations and photographs, typography, design, layout, production, and printing
"The attractive design is consistent with the content; the writing is lucid and readable. A solid introduction to a timely topic." SLJ
Includes glossary

690 Buildings

Macaulay, David, 1946-
Mill. Houghton Mifflin 1983 128p il $17.95; pa $8.95 **690**
1. Mills 2. Textile industry—History
ISBN 0-395-34830-7; 0-395-52019-3 (pa)
LC 83-10652
This is an "account of the development of four fictional 19th-Century Rhode Island cotton mills. In explaining the construction and operation of a simple water-wheel powered wooden mill, as well as the more complex stone, turbine and steam mills to follow, the author also describes the rise and decline of New England's textile industry." SLJ

Unbuilding. Houghton Mifflin 1980 78p il $16.95; pa $6.95 **690**
1. Empire State Building (New York, N.Y.) 2. Building 3. Skyscrapers
ISBN 0-395-29457-6; 0-395-45360-7 (pa)
LC 80-15491
This fictional account of the dismantling and removal of the Empire State Building describes the structure of a skyscraper and explains how such an edifice would be demolished
"Save for the fact that one particularly stunning double-page spread is marred by tight binding, the book is a joy: accurate, informative, handsome, and eminently readable." Bull Cent Child Books

700 THE ARTS

Creative fire; by the editors of Time-Life Books. Time-Life Bks. 1994 256p il (African Americans: voices of triumph) $29.95 **700**
1. African American arts
LC 93-31616
This book "begins with a look at the creative arts in ancient Africa, and then traces the development of filmmaking, music, writing, and the visual arts from their beginnings here in America to the present time. Excellent-quality fine-art reproductions appear throughout. What sets this book apart, however, is the scope and variety of the full-color and black-and-white archival photographs. . . . This treatment makes the subject accessible to a wide range of readers." SLJ
Includes bibliographical references

Dictionary of the arts. Facts on File 1994 564p $29.95 **700**
1. Arts—Dictionaries 2. Artists—Dictionaries
ISBN 0-8160-3205-X
LC 94-16276
A "one-volume reference that includes 6,000 alphabetically arranged entries on architecture, cinema, literature, craft and design, dance, fashion, music, mythology, painting, photography, sculpture, and theater. . . . Students will find quick, cross-referenced, and user-friendly info on such topics as detective fiction, leprechauns, Priam, Abba, Calvin Klein, Snow White, synthesizers, and Dickens, plus 1,000 quotations. A basic reference tool." SLJ

Haskins, James, 1941-
The Harlem Renaissance. Millbrook Press 1996 192p lib bdg $21.90 **700**
1. Harlem Renaissance 2. African American arts
ISBN 1-56294-565-3
LC 96-4608
This introduction to the Harlem Renaissance discusses "the music, art, and literature that were produced by African Americans in that time and place. Notables such as Duke Ellington, Zora Neale Hurston, Ethel Waters, Langston Hughes, Bill Robinson, Aaron Douglas, and Augusta Savage are included." SLJ
This "is a beautiful piece of bookmaking that is filled with photographs and portraits. The extensive source notes and a bibliography that includes books for adults and youngsters makes this a book that will appeal to adults as well as teens." Child Book Rev Serv

Ochoa, George
The timeline book of the arts; [by] George Ochoa and Melinda Corey. Ballantine Bks. 1995 402p il pa $12 **700**
1. Arts—History
ISBN 0-345-38264-1
LC 94-96512
"A Stonesong Press book"
A year-by year listing of events in such areas as architecture, the decorative and graphic arts, dance, drama, film, radio and television
Includes bibliographical references

Oxford illustrated encyclopedia of the arts;
volume editor, John Julius Norwich. Oxford
Univ. Press 1990 499p il $52.25   **700**
1. Arts—Dictionaries
ISBN 0-19-869137-8   LC 89-71125
This work "covers music, literature, drama, painting,
sculpture, architecture, cinema, and decorative and applied arts. Entries of one to three paragraphs survey the
major works, performances, and so forth, of architects,
writers, composers, performers, and other artists. Technique or style and country or period are provided. The
volume includes modern individuals in the arts (e.g.,
Margaret Atwood, Steven Spielberg, Luciano Pavarotti)
as well as famous artists of the past." Nichols. Guide to
Ref Books for Sch Media Cent. 4th edition

Rovin, Jeff
Adventure heroes; legendary characters from
Odysseus to James Bond. Facts on File 1994 314p
il $35; pa $19.95   **700**
1. Characters and characteristics in literature—Dictionaries 2. Heroes and heroines—Dictionaries
ISBN 0-8160-2881-8; 0-8160-2886-9 (pa)
LC 93-46603
"Charlie Chan, Modesty Blaise, Jonny Quest, and
Beowulf are just some of the more than 500 characters
listed here along with the works in which they appeared.
Rovin . . . has drawn entries from the realms of comic
books, comic strips, folklore, literature, mythology, motion pictures, opera, radio, television, video, and computer games. For each character or show he offers date and
place of first appearance, a biography, and comments
that are chock full of interesting information. . . . A
good ready reference for popular culture collections."
Libr J

701 Philosophy and theory

Canaday, John Edwin, 1907-1985
What is art? an introduction to painting,
sculpture, and architecture; [by] John Canaday.
Knopf 1980 386p il o.p.   **701**
1. Art 2. Art appreciation
LC 79-23256
A John L. Hochmann book
"Updated and expanded from 'The Metropolitan Semi-
nars in Art,' Canaday's series of 12 monographs on the
appreciation of painting that was published by the Metropolitan Museum of Art in 1958, this book discusses . . .
historical, stylistic, and technical categories of art."
Christ Sci Monit
"Of the 450 photos, 150 are well-reproduced color. Of
special interest are descriptions of such techniques as egg
tempera, fresco painting, etc. The glossary is a
comprehensive delight." Libr J

Yenawine, Philip
Key art terms for beginners. Abrams 1995 160p
il $24.95   **701**
1. Art appreciation
ISBN 0-8109-1225-2   LC 94-26911
In this illustrated introduction to art appreciation, the
author "divides the discussion into three main parts. The

longest chapter covers the periods and schools of art history from 'Aboriginal' to 'Western.' A shorter section on
mediums and materials ranges from 'Acrylics' to 'Weld-
ing.' A third section introduces the vocabulary of analysis and criticism. . . . The volume is filled with wonderful black-and-white and full-color photographs and reproductions." SLJ
Includes bibliographical references

702.5 Art—Directories

Artist's & graphic designer's market. Writer's
Digest Bks. il pa $24.99   **702.5**
1. Art—Marketing—Directories
ISSN 1075-0894
Annual. First published 1974 with title: Artist's market
"Listings of places where art can be sold and exhibited include brokers, studios, agencies, magazines, galleries, and art fairs. Each listing covers who to contact
and where, how much they pay, and additional information such as shipping requirements, preparing a portfolio,
etc." Ref Sources for Small & Medium-sized Libr. 5th
edition

702.8 Art—Technique, procedures, apparatus, equipment, materials

Spandorfer, Merle, 1934-
Making art safely; alternative methods and
materials in drawing, painting, printmaking,
graphic design, and photography; [by] Merle
Spandorfer, Deborah Curtiss, Jack Snyder. Van
Nostrand Reinhold 1993 255p il $44.95; pa $29.95
     702.8
1. Artists' materials—Safety measures
ISBN 0-442-23489-9; 0-442-02131-3 (pa)
LC 92-4841
A discussion "of the many hazards associated with art
materials and how to avoid physical risk. The book begins with an overview of the physical states of art materials; how toxins enter the body; reactions to toxic substances; and the most common hazards in art materials.
Chapter 2 provides a selection of information resources
. . . and background information on nontoxic art materials; labelling of art materials; and educational health and
safety programs for art studios, schools, and work places.
Then follow chapters on basic precautions for safety."
Choice
Includes bibliographical references

703 Art—Encyclopedias and dictionaries

International dictionary of art and artists; with a
foreword by Cecil Gould; editor, James Vinson.
St. James Press 1990 2v il set $300   **703**
1. Art—Dictionaries 2. Artists—Dictionaries
ISBN 1-55862-055-9   LC 91-186208
Volumes also available separately for $160
Contents: v1 Artists; v2 Art

International dictionary of art and artists—*Continued*

"This two-volume work presents an interesting overview of the history of art. The *Artists* volume is an alphabetical arrangement of the most significant artists from the 13th to the 20th centuries. . . . *Art* has a chronological arrangement of 500 works of art from Cimabue to Hockney. . . . While color reproductions would have enhanced the visual quality of these volumes, the black-and-white reproductions are of high quality." Libr J

The Oxford companion to art; edited by Harold Osborne. Oxford Univ. Press 1970 1277p il $55
703
1. Art—Dictionaries 2. Artists—Dictionaries
ISBN 0-19-866107-X
"Articles of varying lengths on the visual arts designed for the nonspecialist. Handicrafts and the practical arts are not included. Most articles have a coded reference to the bibliography, which numbers about 3000 items. Numerous cross-references." Ref Sources for Small & Medium-sized Libr. 5th edition

The Oxford dictionary of art; edited by Ian Chilvers and Harold Osborne; consultant editor, Dennis Farr. Oxford Univ. Press 1988 548p $52.25; pa $17.95
703
1. Art—Dictionaries 2. Artists—Dictionaries
ISBN 0-19-866133-9; 0-19-280022-1 (pa)
LC 88-5138
"This comprehensive guide to art describes the significance of individual artists in two or three paragraphs of succinct and well-considered assessment. Coverage of important institutions, art historians, and contemporary art terms is a particular boon. Non-Western art, architecture, pictures, and bibliographies are not included." Ref Sources for Small & Medium-sized Libr. 5th edition

704.9 Iconography

Carr-Gomm, Sarah
Dictionary of symbols in Western art. Facts on File 1995 240p il $24.95; pa $14.95
704.9
1. Art—Dictionaries 2. Symbolism—Dictionaries
ISBN 0-8160-3301-3; 0-8160-3326-9 (pa)
LC 95-17577
This dictionary focuses on "the meaning of symbols in Western art. Visual themes, religious and mythological, that occur in figurative paintings and sculpture from the late Middle Ages to the nineteenth century are covered alphabetically. . . . Interspersed alphabetically are feature panels on the treatment in art of major themes (the ages of man, the nude, virtues). See also references and footnotes are printed in the margins." Booklist

Hall, James, 1918-
Dictionary of subject and symbols in art; introduction by Kenneth Clark. rev ed. Harper & Row 1979 c1974 xxix, 349p il hardcover o.p. paperback available $16
704.9
1. Symbolism—Dictionaries 2. Art—Dictionaries
ISBN 0-06-430100-1 (pa)
LC 79-116436
"Icon editions"

First published 1974
This book seeks "to help the museum-goer and student identify and understand the subject matter of Western art, using subjects from the Old and New Testaments, the Christian saints and symbols, and classical mythology and literature . . . [as well as] historical episodes, figures and devices of moral allegory, themes of romantic epic poetry, and popular genre representations of Northern European art." Choice
Includes bibliography

McElroy, Guy C., d. 1990
Facing history; the black image in American art, 1710-1940; with an essay by Henry Louis Gates, Jr., and contributions by Janet Levine, Francis Martin, Jr., and Claudia Vess; edited by Christopher C. French. Bedford Arts Pubs. 1990 xlix, 140p il $50; pa $24.95
704.9
1. African Americans in art 2. American art
ISBN 0-938491-39-3; 0-938491-38-5 (pa)
LC 89-18007
Catalogue of an exhibition held at Corcoran Gallery of Art, January 13-March 25, 1990, and Brooklyn Museum, April 20-June 25, 1990
This work combines "essays on social history with stunning reproductions of visual images. . . . [It] examines the changes in the way blacks have been depicted—from slave and comic grotesque to worker, hero, and symbol of urban life—in works by American artists of all races." Booklist
Includes bibliographical references

708 Art—Galleries, museums private collections

Hibbard, Howard, 1928-1984
The Metropolitan Museum of Art. Harper & Row 1980 592p il
708
1. Metropolitan Museum of Art (New York, N.Y.) 2. Art
LC 80-7588
Available from Random House Value Pub. $29.99 (ISBN 0-517-61201-1)
"Less a history of the museum than a survey of its wide-ranging riches [this book] reviews the museum's holdings in chapters arranged by period of art history. . . . The superb illustrations (605 color, 442 black and white) are the splendor of the volume." Booklist
Includes bibliography

National Museum of American Art. Little, Brown 1995 279p il $40
708
1. American art
ISBN 0-8212-2216-3
LC 94-37723
Also available in paperback from the National Museum of American Art; for information about the CD-ROM version contact the Museum
"This catalog offers a rich visual sample of this collection, ranging from colonial to contemporary. It is divided into nine thematic sections. . . . Supplementing the 375 lush illustrations, very readable texts were culled from exhibition catalogs, critics commentaries, anecdotes, and many times the artist's own words, to provide a solid context for the works featured." Libr J
Includes bibliographical references

Walker, John, 1906-1995
National Gallery of Art, Washington; foreword by J. Carter Brown. new and rev ed. Abrams 1995 696p il $34.98   **708**
1. National Gallery of Art (U.S.)
ISBN 0-8109-8148-3   LC 95-1028
First published 1964
An illustrated look at the development of the gallery's collection and its benefactors. Arranged chronologically and then by country, reproductions are accompanied by a brief history, and entries include artist, title, date, material, size and donor's name

709   Art—Historical and geographic treatment

Clark, Kenneth, 1903-1983
Civilisation; a personal view. Harper & Row 1970 c1969 359p il o.p.   **709**
1. Art—History 2. Western civilization
First published 1969 in the United Kingdom
"The text traces the emergence of human values during crucial periods of man's history from the seventh century. . . . Clark's interpretations of representative paintings, sculpture, architectural masterpieces, and such small pieces as reliquaries and manuscripts afford an urbane review of archetypes of the past." Booklist

Cole, Bruce, 1938-
Art of the Western world; from ancient Greece to post-modernism; by Bruce Cole and Adelheid Gealt; with an introduction by Michael Wood. Summit Bks. 1989 xx, 345p il hardcover o.p. paperback available $18   **709**
1. Art—History
ISBN 0-671-74728-2 (pa)   LC 89-4311
"A companion volume to the PBS television series of the same title, this compact survey of Western art history is a . . . recapitulation of the conventional high art canon. Written on a level suitable for high school students and general readers, the volume includes good reproductions of one or two of the best known works by famous masters of painting, sculpture, and architecture." Libr J

Gardner's art through the ages. Harcourt Brace & Co. il maps $75; pa $54.50   **709**
1. Art—History
First published 1926 under the authorship of Helen Gardner. (10th edition 1996 revised by Richard G. Tansey and Fred S. Kleiner). Periodically revised
This book surveys world art from prehistoric times to the present day. Painting, sculpture, architecture and some decorative arts are considered. Although the focus is on European art, there are also chapters on ancient Near Eastern, Asian, pre-Columbian, American Indian, African and Oceanic art

Gombrich, E. H. (Ernst Hans), 1909-
The story of art. Prentice-Hall il pa $55   **709**
1. Art—History
Also available in hardcover and in paperback from Phaidon Press

First published 1950 by Phaidon Press. (16th edition 1995) Periodically revised
This survey of art examines artistic achievements in historical context to consider how prevailing social, political, and economic factors may have influenced the succession and popularity of certain artistic styles
Includes glossary and bibliography

Hartt, Frederick, 1914-1991
Art; a history of painting, sculpture, architecture. Prentice-Hall; Abrams il set $67; v1 $56; v2 $48   **709**
1. Art—History
First published 1976. (4th edition 1993) Periodically revised
An illustrated chronological history of art from prehistory to the contemporary period. Timelines link the political history, religions, literature, science and technology, with the painting, sculpture and architecture of each era

Janson, H. W. (Horst Woldemar), 1913-1982
History of art. 5th ed, revised and expanded by Anthony F. Janson. Abrams 1995 960p il maps $60   **709**
1. Art—History
ISBN 0-8109-3421-3   LC 94-14001
Also available in a two-volume paperback edition from Prentice-Hall; Fourth edition of History of art for young people, is also available
First published 1962
A history of art from prehistoric cave paintings to video art. While the focus is primarily on Western art, brief discussions of Oriental, Near Eastern, Islamic, African and Latin American arts are included
Includes bibliographical references

Stokstad, Marilyn, 1929-
Art history; [by] Marilyn Stokstad, with the collaboration of Marion Spears Grayson, and with chapters by Stephen Addiss [et al.] Abrams 1995 various paging il $60   **709**
1. Art—History
ISBN 0-8109-1960-5   LC 95-13402
Also available from Prentice Hall in a two volume paperback edition
This is a "global history of art from prehistoric times to the present. . . . The 1625 stunning illustrations (761 in color) are unrivaled. . . . Time lines chart parallel developments across cultures and civilizations; inserts spotlight literary and intellectual trends and artists' techniques." Publ Wkly
Includes bibliographical references

709.02   Art—500-1499

Cole, Alison
The Renaissance. Dorling Kindersley 1994 64p il (Eyewitness art) $16.95   **709.02**
1. Renaissance art
ISBN 1-56458-493-3   LC 93-21264
A guide to the art of Northern Europe and Italy from the 14th to the 16th century. Color photographs of paint-

Cole, Alison—*Continued*

ings, sculpture and architecture representative of the period include the works of Giotto, Leonardo, Dürer, Titian, Raphael and Michelangelo. Features include detailed close-ups, diagrams and charts
Includes glossary

Snyder, James

Medieval art; painting - sculpture - architecture, 4th-14th century. Abrams 1989 511p il maps $60
709.02
1. Medieval art 2. Christian art and symbolism 3. Medieval architecture
ISBN 0-8109-1532-4   LC 88-10394
Also available from Prentice-Hall
"Church architecture and decoration receive the bulk of Snyder's attention, with manuscript illumination and sumptuary and secular arts presented rather briefly. The volume is well illustrated, though chiefly in black-and-white photographs." Libr J
Includes bibliographical references

709.04   Art—1900-1999

Arnason, H. Harvard

History of modern art: painting, sculpture, architecture. 3rd ed, rev and updated by Daniel Wheeler. Abrams 1986 744p il $60   **709.04**
1. Modern art—1800-1899 (19th century) 2. Modern art—1900-1999 (20th century)
ISBN 0-8109-1097-7   LC 86-3411
Also available from Prentice-Hall
First published 1969
Chronologically arranged, with biographical sketches of individual artists
"Arnason attempts to keep abreast of every major development, school, and idiosyncratic individual who may figure in the history of art in our time. The past history of the modern movement from the late nineteenth century on is also adroitly presented. A wealth of illustrations . . . convey the visions of these artists." Booklist
Includes bibliography

Arwas, Victor

Art deco. rev ed. Abrams 1992 316p $75
709.04
1. Art deco
ISBN 0-8109-1926-5   LC 93-102875
First published 1980
The author "traces Art Deco's flowering in furniture, metal, silver, jewelry, enamel, lacquer, figurines, bronzes, sculpture, painting, posters, graphics, book illustrations, bookbinding, glass and ceramics. The extraordinary objects shown in 437 plates (340 in color) are among the finest Art Deco creations ever made." Publ Wkly

Encyclopedia of art deco; edited by Alastair Duncan. Dutton 1988 192p il o.p.   **709.04**
1. Art deco
LC 89-206285
In individual chapters, contributors to this volume discuss Art Deco architecture; sculpture; furniture and inte-

rior decoration; lighting; paintings, graphics and book-binding; glass; ceramics; metalwork; jewelry and accessories; and textiles. Biographical entries on the artists and designers of the Art Deco style appear along the lower portion of the pages throughout the book
"An exhilarating overview of cross-pollination in the decorative arts." N Y Times Book Rev
Includes bibliography

Livingstone, Marco

Pop art: a continuing history. Abrams 1990 271p il $60   **709.04**
1. Pop art
ISBN 0-8109-3707-7   LC 90-99
With 300 color plates this volume chronicles the work of 130 artists of the Pop Art movement, including Jasper Johns, Robert Rauschenberg, Andy Warhol, and Roy Lichtenstein
"Livingstone's selection revitalizes and broadens the definition of pop art. His commentary is learned and resourceful . . . an eye-opening volume of art at its feistiest." Booklist
Includes bibliography

Lucie-Smith, Edward, 1933-

Art today. Phaidon Press 1995 511p il $69.95
709.04
1. Modern art—1900-1999 (20th century)
ISBN 0-7148-3201-4
This "survey attempts to essay the scope and aims of the art of the world over the past 30 years. . . . As well as such well-trod ground as Pop Art, Lucie-Smith covers Conceptual Art, Installation Art, and Neo-Expressionism. He also covers a broad geographic range, including artists and works from the former Soviet Union, Africa, the Far East, and Latin America. Chapters are also included on 'Racial Minorities' and 'Feminist and Gay' art. Clearly written and with copious illustrations, the book offers brief biographies of all artists mentioned, a chronology, and bibliography." Libr J

Making their mark; women artists move into the mainstream, 1970-85; Randy Rosen, Catherine C. Brawer [compilers] Abbeville Press 1988 300p il $59.95; pa $29.95   **709.04**
1. Women artists 2. Modern art—1900-1999 (20th century)
ISBN 0-89659-958-2; 1-55859-161-3 (pa)
LC 88-22261
Catalog of an exhibition held at the Cincinnati Art Museum and other museums
This "volume celebrates and documents the art made by 87 contemporary American women artists. . . . While the heart of the book is the almost 200 illustrations, 70 in color, the essays, written by critics and art historians . . . place the work in a social and historical context." Booklist
Includes bibliography

Moszynska, Anna
Abstract art. Thames & Hudson 1990 240p il (World of art) pa $14.95   **709.04**
1. Abstract art
ISBN 0-500-20237-0   LC 88-51347
"The author explains both the general philosophy of abstractionism and the approaches of many individual artists to the form. Paintings and sculptures are featured, as are examples of graphic design and architecture." Booklist

The **Oxford** companion to twentieth-century art; edited by Harold Osborne. Oxford Univ. Press 1981 656p il o.p.   **709.04**
1. Modern art—1900-1999 (20th century)—Dictionaries 2. Artists
LC 82-126560
This book "sketches the careers of hundreds of artists who have done their most significant work between 1900 and 1975. International in scope, it includes articles on movements and on the state of art during the twentieth century in various countries and regions." Wilson Libr Bull
Includes bibliography

709.38   Ancient Greek art

The **Oxford** history of classical art; edited by John Boardman. Oxford Univ. Press 1993 406p il maps $55   **709.38**
1. Roman art 2. Greek art
ISBN 0-19-814386-9   LC 93-6825
An "overview of Greek and Roman art, ranging from the 8th century B.C.E. to the late Roman Empire. Each chapter includes a historical and social commentary on the changing styles as well as on the artists and their patrons. Hundreds of plates, with well-documented explanations, support the narrative essays and highlight the phenomenal growth and dissemination of classical art worldwide. An excellent reference source." SLJ
Includes bibliographical references

709.45   Italian art

Cooper, Tracy Elizabeth
Renaissance; [by] Tracy E. Cooper. Abbeville Press 1995 95p il map $12.95   **709.45**
1. Renaissance art 2. Italian art
ISBN 0-7892-0023-6   LC 95-20978
"Abbeville stylebooks"
An overview of Renaissance architecture and design. "The insides and outsides of buildings and furnishings of palaces and apartments, villas and farmhouses, public buildings, churches, gardens, theaters, piazzas, and the ideal city are all given attention. The double-page format includes many well-annotated photographs and reproductions." SLJ
Includes bibliographical references

Hirst, Michael
Michelangelo and his drawings. Yale Univ. Press 1988 132p il hardcover o.p. paperback available $28   **709.45**
1. Michelangelo Buonarroti, 1475-1564
ISBN 0-300-04796-7 (pa)   LC 88-50431
The text of this book "is organized by type of drawing: initial sketches, life studies, compositional drawings, architectural designs, and finished drawings used as gifts. It is followed by a thematically arranged index of drawings and a section of . . . plates." Libr J
"An informative, insightful, and eminently readable book. . . . This is an important contribution to Michelangelo scholarship." Choice

Labella, Vincenzo
A season of giants: Michelangelo, Leonardo, Raphael, 1492-1508; special photography by John McWilliams. Little, Brown 1990 240p il $45   **709.45**
1. Italian art 2. Renaissance art
ISBN 0-316-85646-0   LC 90-6252
"Published in conjunction with a . . . cable television series, this lavishly illustrated study of the three leading Italian Renaissance artists examines each individual's creative development and impact on his contemporaries. A well-detailed account that will interest browsers as well as history and art students." Booklist

Murray, Linda
Michelangelo; his life, work and times. Thames & Hudson 1984 240p il $19.95; pa $14.95   **709.45**
1. Michelangelo Buonarroti, 1475-1564
ISBN 0-500-18175-6; 0-500-20174-9 (pa)
LC 84-184090
First published 1980 by Oxford Univ. Press
"This fairly short, reliable introduction to Michelangelo's art and architecture [is] aimed at a broad, nonscholarly audience. . . . Murray is good on the political and economic background, and on the art itself." Choice
Includes bibliographical references

709.51   Chinese art

Tregear, Mary
Chinese art. rev ed. Thames & Hudson 1997 216p il maps (World of art) pa $14.95   **709.51**
1. Chinese art
ISBN 0-500-20299-0
First published 1980 by Oxford Univ. Press
An introduction to major decorative, ceremonial, figurative and narrative aspects of Chinese art. Coverage ranges from works of Neolithic groups and the bronzes of the Shang dynasty to Buddhist sculpture, ceramics, garden design and architecture. Emphasis is also placed on the interaction of poetry, painting and calligraphy
Includes bibliographical references

709.52 Japanese art

Elisseeff, Danielle
Art of Japan; [by] Danielle and Vadime Elisseeff; translated from the French by I. Mark Paris. Abrams 1985 622p il maps $175   **709.52**
1. Japanese art
ISBN 0-8109-0642-2   LC 84-14627
Original French edition, 1980
The authors "take individual media (ceramics, architecture) or ideas (literature into art, nature) and discuss Japanese artists' use and treatment of each. . . . This nontraditional approach is quite thought-provoking and enables the reader better to understand Japanese art as a whole. . . . [The plates] (176 magnificent color, 361 clear black-and-white) provide a wealth of study material." Libr J
Includes bibliography

709.6 African art

Drewal, Henry John
Yoruba; nine centuries of African art and thought; [by] Henry John Drewal and John Pemberton, 3rd with Rowland Abiodun; edited by Allen Wardwell. Abrams; Center for African Art 1990 256p il maps $65; pa $38   **709.6**
1. African art 2. Yoruba (African people)
ISBN 0-8109-1794-7; 0-945802-04-8 (pa)
   LC 89-22182
"Tracing Yoruba civilization from the twelfth through the twentieth centuries, the authors examine the Yoruba impetus for artistic creation, the history of their various kingdoms and empires as illustrated in their artwork, and the survival of traditional arts in modern Yoruba society." Booklist
This work "combines immaculate visual documentation of Yoruba art with the highest standards of scholarship." Times Lit Suppl
Includes glossary and bibliography

Willett, Frank
African art; an introduction; Frank Willett. rev ed. Thames & Hudson 1993 288p il maps (World of art) $14.95   **709.6**
1. African art
ISBN 0-500-20267-2   LC 93-60124
First published 1971 by Praeger Pubs.
A study of the art of the Yoruba, Bantu and other African peoples and its aesthetic impact on the development of twentieth-century western art
Includes bibliographical references

709.73 American art

Baigell, Matthew
Dictionary of American art. Harper & Row 1979 390p hardcover o.p. paperback available $17
   709.73
1. American art—Dictionaries 2. Artists, American
ISBN 0-06-430078-1 (pa)   LC 78-24824
"Icon editions"

"The encyclopedic dictionary covers the full range of visual arts (painters, graphic artists, sculptors, photographers) in the United States from colonial times through the 1970s. The 650 alphabetically arranged articles consist mainly of biographical profiles, but also include 69 articles on themes and movements." Wynar. Guide to Ref Books for Sch Media Cent. 3d edition

Bearden, Romare, 1914-1988
A history of African-American artists; from 1792 to the present; [by] Romare Bearden & Harry Henderson. Pantheon Bks. 1992 541p il $65
   709.73
1. African American artists 2. American art
ISBN 0-394-57016-2   LC 89-42782
"Opening in the 18th century with Joshua Johnston, the authors go on to examine the work of Robert S. Duncanson, Henry O. Tanner, Aaron Douglas, Edmonia Lewis, Jacob Lawrence, Auguste Savage, Ellis Wilson, Archibald Motley, Alma Thomas, and others born before 1925. Their lives and careers, which often involved overcoming racial barriers, are portrayed against the backdrop of artistic, social, and political events; black Renaissance and Depression artists receive the most attention." Libr J
"Richly illustrated and written with resounding empathy and pride, this is a major contribution to the literature on African American history and to the annals of American art." Booklist

Creation's journey; Native American identity and belief; edited by Tom Hill and Richard W. Hill, Sr. Smithsonian Institution Press 1994 255p il $60   **709.73**
1. National Museum of the American Indian (U.S.)
2. Indians of North America—Art
ISBN 1-56098-453-8   LC 94-4757
Published in conjunction with an exhibition held at the National Museum of the American Indian, New York City, October 1994-February 1997
This "volume links stories, anecdotes, descriptions of rituals, and spiritual beliefs to specific art objects, including an Osage cradleboard and a Winnebago bandolier bag. In each essay, the connection between spirituality and the making of art is articulated; each pattern, image, and symbol is shown to be an expression of dreams, visions, and beliefs." Booklist
Includes bibliographical references

Furst, Peter T.
North American Indian art; [by] Peter Furst, Jill Leslie Furst. Rizzoli Int. Publs. 1982 236p il hardcover o.p. paperback available $35   **709.73**
1. Indians of North America—Art
ISBN 0-8478-0572-7 (pa)   LC 82-40343
"An Art Press book"
This book "explores the integration of form and function in the visual arts of six major tribal areas: the Southwest, California, the Pacific Northwest, Eskimo culture in Alaska and Canada, the Plains, and the Eastern Woodlands." SLJ
"The text is well written as well as highly informative, while the illustrations, largely in color, show superb pieces." Atl Mon
Includes bibliography

Harlem Renaissance: art of black America; introduction by Mary Schmidt Campbell; essays by David Driskell, David Levering Lewis, and Deborah Willis Ryan. Studio Mus. in Harlem; Abrams 1987 200p il hardcover o.p. paperback available $14.98   **709.73**
1. African American artists 2. American art
ISBN 0-8109-8128-9 (pa)   LC 86-17229
This book "features four black artists: the sculptor Meta Warrick Fuller and the painters Aaron Douglas, Palmer Hayden and William H. Johnson. Also included are photographs . . . by James Van Der Zee." N Y Times Book Rev
"An eye-catching and eye-opening introduction to the black intelligensia who created the Harlem Renaissance of 1919-1930. . . . Black-and-white figures and color plates are plentiful and of fine quality." Choice
Includes bibliography

Henkes, Robert
The art of black American women; works of twenty-four artists of the twentieth century. McFarland & Co. 1993 274p il $39.95   **709.73**
1. African American artists 2. Women artists 3. Artists, American 4. American art
ISBN 0-89950-818-9   LC 92-50955
Artists represented include "Lois Mailou Jones, Vivian Browne, Jewel Simon, Faith Ringgold, Clementine Hunter, and Adell Westbrook. Typically, entries are 8-10 pages in length, accompanied by 6-8 black-and-white illustrations of artwork. Rather than biographical notes, the text is a discussion of the nature and vision of the artist, followed by listings of career highlights, education, awards, selected and solo exhibitions, and a bibliography. . . . This is a worthy contribution to the literature of a group of largely overlooked artists." Booklist

McLanathan, Richard B. K.
Art in America; a brief history. Harcourt Brace Jovanovich 1973 216p il (Harbrace history of art) hardcover o.p. paperback available $23.25   **709.73**
1. American art—History
ISBN 0-15-503466-9 (pa)
The author "begins with the Colonial period and describes briefly the architecture, painting, and sculpture for six chronological periods ending with the twentieth century. Generously illustrated in color and black and white." Booklist
Includes bibliography

The **Spirit** within; Northwest Coast native art from the John H. Hauberg collection. Rizzoli Int. Publs.; Seattle Art Mus. 1995 303p il maps $75; pa $35   **709.73**
1. Indians of North America—Art
ISBN 0-8478-1847-0; 0-932216-45-5 (pa)
    LC 94-69971
"Full-color plates and accompanying writings by Native authors provide insight into the function of the objects as well as the traditions of the Kwakwaka'wakw, Makah, Tlingit, Nuuchah-nulth, and Haida cultures. . . . Most valuable of all are the documentary photographs that show the artifacts in their original context. . . . An excellent resource, and an unusual treat." SLJ
Includes bibliographical references

709.8   Latin American art

Latin American artists of the twentieth century; edited by Waldo Rasmussen with Fatima Bercht and Elizabeth Ferrer. Museum of Modern Art 1993 424p il $65   **709.8**
1. Latin American art
ISBN 0-87070-431-1   LC 93-78095
Also available in hardcover from Abrams
Published in association with an exhibition held at the Museum of Modern Art, New York City, June 6-September 7, 1993
"The text is made up of thirteen essays by art historians such as Dore Ashton, Fatima Bercht, and Elizabeth Ferrer who illuminate various styles of twentieth century Latin American art and the work of individual artists, including muralists Orozco and Rivera. . . . The 357 plates (194 in color) display the work of more than 100 sculptors and painters that, taken together, effectively define modern art. . . . A biographical directory provides brief profiles of each artist. An invaluable and grand production." Booklist
Includes bibliographical references

711   Area planning

Macaulay, David, 1946-
City: a story of Roman planning and construction. Houghton Mifflin 1974 112p il $16.95; pa $7.95   **711**
1. City planning—Rome 2. Civil engineering 3. Roman architecture
ISBN 0-395-19492-X; 0-395-34922-2 (pa)
    LC 74-4280
"By following the inception, construction, and development of an imaginary Roman city, the account traces the evolution of Verbonia from the selection of its site under religious auspices in 26 B.C. to its completion in 100 A.D." Horn Book
Includes glossary

720   Architecture

Bennett, David, 1948-
Skyscrapers; form & function; James R. Steinkamp, principal photographer. Simon & Schuster 1995 120p il $35   **720**
1. Skyscrapers
ISBN 0-684-80318-6   LC 95-1018
"A Marshall edition"
"Photographs and other illustrations (some in multiple-page pull-out sections) dominate an introduction to skyscraper history, design, and function that introduces notable buildings, architects, and plans." Booklist
Includes bibliographical references

Macaulay, David, 1946-
Great moments in architecture. Houghton
Mifflin 1978 unp il $22.95; pa $13.95   **720**
1. Architecture—Cartoons and caricatures
ISBN 0-395-25500-7; 0-395-26711-0 (pa)
LC 77-15490
The author spoofs architecture and architects of the
past, present and future. Included are L'Arc de Defeat
(an inverted Arc de Triomphe), the excavated ruins of a
fast food restaurant, the plans for the Tower of Pisa on
a leaning drafting table, and the disastrous meeting of the
Greater and Lesser Walls of China
"An elaborately produced, whimsically conceived portfolio of architectural absurdities." Horn Book

720.3   Architecture—Encyclopedias and dictionaries

Ching, Frank, 1943-
A visual dictionary of architecture; [by] Francis
D. K. Ching. Van Nostrand Reinhold 1995 319p
il $42.95; pa $29.95   **720.3**
1. Architecture—Dictionaries
ISBN 0-442-00904-6; 0-442-02462-2 (pa)
LC 95-1476
This volume arranges some "5,000 entries thematically
under 68 concepts covering architectural design, history,
and technology. The topics, which are treated alphabetically, include building types (church, house, theater), sections (door, roof, stair), features (arch, column, vault),
and materials (brick, paint, wood). Terms are logically
clustered on oversize pages and defined with both line
drawings and text, usually 20 to 100 words." Booklist

Dictionary of architecture & construction; edited
by Cyril M. Harris. 2nd ed. McGraw-Hill 1993
924p il $65   **720.3**
1. Architecture—Dictionaries 2. Building—Dictionaries
ISBN 0-07-026888-6   LC 92-43562
First published 1975
"An essential source for architecture, including terms
for building conservation, building trades, materials,
products, equipment, and styles. This edition adds 2,300
new terms and updates previous definitions; it reflects
new developments in building systems. Contains some
2,000 line drawings." Guide to Ref Books. 11th edition

Fleming, John, 1919-
The Penguin dictionary of architecture; [by]
John Fleming, Hugh Honour, Nikolaus Pevsner;
drawings by David Etherton. 4th ed. Penguin Bks.
1991 497p il $13.95   **720.3**
1. Architecture—Dictionaries
ISBN 0-14-051241-1
First published 1966
Includes entries on individual architects, architectural
terms, building materials, ornamentation, styles and
movements, and types of building

720.9   Architecture—Historical and geographic treatment

Trachtenberg, Marvin
Architecture, from prehistory to post-modernism;
the western tradition; [by] Marvin Trachtenberg,
Isabelle Hyman. Abrams 1986 606p il $60   **720.9**
1. Architecture—History
ISBN 0-8109-1077-2   LC 85-7369
Also available in hardcover from Prentice-Hall
This work "emphasizes three aspects of building: as
engineering technology, as functional shelter, and as visual art. . . . An opening portfolio of 74 colorplates surveys the entire spectrum of building history, while the
numerous text illustrations are reproduced in excellent
black and white." Booklist
Includes glossary and bibliography

Watkin, David, 1941-
A history of Western architecture. Thames &
Hudson 1986 591p il hardcover o.p. paperback
available $24.95   **720.9**
1. Architecture—History
ISBN 0-500-27425-8 (pa)
This study focuses on the development of architecture
in Europe and the United States
"Watkin's book is beautifully illustrated and engaging-
ly written." Choice

720.973   Architecture—United States

Nash, Eric Peter
Frank Lloyd Wright; force of nature. Smithmark
Pubs. 1996 80p il $10.98   **720.973**
1. Wright, Frank Lloyd, 1867-1959 2. American ar-
chitecture
ISBN 0-8317-8086-X
In this illustrated introduction to the work of the
American architect "Nash does an excellent job of expli-
cating Wright's tremendously influential architectural in-
novations." Booklist

Wright, Frank Lloyd, 1867-1959
Frank Lloyd Wright: writings and buildings;
selected by Edgar Kaufmann and Ben Raeburn.
Horizon Press 1960 346p il map o.p.   **720.973**
1. American architecture
Partially analyzed in Essay and general literature index
"A representative selection of the American architect's
writings on such topics as prairie architecture, the nature
of materials, the young man in architecture, style and the
grammar of architecture. Generously illustrated with photographs, plans, perspective drawings, and sketches of a
number of buildings spanning the architect's long career." Booklist

722   Architecture from earliest times to ca. 300

Brown, Frank E., 1908-1988

Roman architecture. Braziller 1961 125p il (Great ages of world architecture) pa $10.95   **722**

1. Roman architecture
ISBN 0-8076-0331-7

This volume contains a preliminary essay followed by about 100 photographs with brief identification. It begins with an eighth century B.C. primitive hut and ends with the Church of the Hagia Sophia, sixth century A.D.

Includes bibliography

Scranton, Robert L.

Greek architecture. Braziller 1962 128p il (Great ages of world architecture) pa $11.95   **722**

1. Greek architecture
ISBN 0-8076-0337-6

This volume "concentrates on the development of the Greek temple, the ideal of Greek architecture, from Minoan residential fabrics. [Mr. Scranton] concludes with the stoa as the perfect representation of the Hellenistic period." Libr J

Includes glossary and bibliography

723   Architecture from ca. 300 to 1399

Branner, Robert

Gothic architecture. Braziller 1961 125p il (Great ages of world architecture) pa $10.95   **723**

1. Gothic architecture
ISBN 0-8076-0332-5

An illustrated introduction to the architectural style predominant in Western Europe from the twelfth through the fourteenth century

Includes bibliography

726   Buildings for religious and related purposes

Macaulay, David, 1946-

Cathedral: the story of its construction. Houghton Mifflin 1973 77p il $16.95; pa $7.95   **726**

1. Cathedrals 2. Gothic architecture
ISBN 0-395-17513-5; 0-395-31668-5 (pa)

LC 73-6634

This is a description, illustrated with black-and-white line drawings, of the construction of an imagined representative Gothic cathedral "in southern France from its conception in 1252 to its completion in 1338. The spirit that motivated the people, the tools and materials they used, the steps and methods of constructions, all receive . . . attention." Booklist

Includes glossary

Pyramid. Houghton Mifflin 1975 80p il $16.95; pa $7.95   **726**

1. Pyramids 2. Egypt—Civilization
ISBN 0-395-21407-6; 0-395-32121-2 (pa)

LC 75-9964

The construction of a pyramid in 25th century B.C. Egypt is described. "Information about selection of the site, drawing of the plans, calculating compass directions, clearing and leveling the ground, and quarrying and hauling the tremendous blocks of granite and limestone is conveyed as much by pictures as by text." Horn Book

Includes glossary

Weeks, John

The pyramids. Lerner Publs. 1977 c1971 51p il maps pa $9.95   **726**

1. Pyramids 2. Egypt—Civilization
ISBN 0-521-07240-9

"A Cambridge topic book"

First published 1971 in the United Kingdom

Published in cooperation with Cambridge University Press

A discussion of the construction and function of pyramids in ancient Egypt describing their planning, the quarrying, cutting and transporting of the stone, the building procedures and the workmen involved

728   Residential and related buildings

McAlester, Virginia, 1943-

A field guide to American houses; by Virginia and Lee McAlester; with drawings by Lauren Jarrett, and model house drawings by John Rodriquez-Arnaiz. Knopf 1984 525p il $35; pa $21.95   **728**

1. Domestic architecture 2. American architecture
ISBN 0-394-51032-1; 0-394-73969-8 (pa)

LC 82-48740

A guide to the "numerous architectural styles of American single-family houses. Houses featured range from 17th-century Georgians to Neoeclectics of the late 1970s, with more than 1200 drawings and photographs and brief histories and notable architects of each style." Libr J

Includes bibliography

Nabokov, Peter

Native American architecture; [by] Peter Nabokov, Robert Easton. Oxford Univ. Press 1989 431p il $50; pa $29.95   **728**

1. Indians of North America—Architecture
ISBN 0-19-503781-2; 0-19-506665-0 (pa)

LC 88-9944

This volume examines "the buildings and settlements created by American Indians from prehistoric times to the present." N Y Times Book Rev

"A rich, wide-ranging depiction of American Indian culture, belief, and history. . . . [The] scholarly, well-written text is complemented by a remarkable selection of photographs, drawings, and paintings." Nat Hist

Includes bibliography

728.8 Large and elaborate private dwellings

Macaulay, David, 1946-
Castle. Houghton Mifflin 1977 74p il $16.95; pa
$7.95 **728.8**
1. Castles 2. Fortification
ISBN 0-395-25784-0; 0-395-32920-5 (pa)
LC 77-7159
Macaulay depicts "the history of an imaginary thir-teenth-century castle—built to subdue the Welsh hordes—from the age of construction to the age of ne-glect, when the town of Aberwyfern no longer needs a fortified stronghold." Economist
Includes glossary

735 Sculpture from 1400

Read, Sir Herbert Edward, 1893-1968
A concise history of modern sculpture. Praeger Pubs. 1964 310p il (Praeger world of art series) o.p.; Thames & Hudson paperback available $14.95 **735**
1. Modern sculpture—1900-1999 (20th century)
ISBN 0-500-20014-9 (pa)
Companion volume to the author's A concise history of modern painting, entered in class 759.06
"A chronological survey, beginning with Rodin, of modern sculptors and their work. . . . [The author] con-centrates his attention on those who introduced or influ-enced stylistic movements such as cubism, constructiv-ism, futurism, and surrealism." Booklist

736 Carving and carvings. Paper cutting and folding

Aytüre-Scheele, Zülal
Beautiful origami. Sterling 1990 80p il $24.95; pa $12.95 **736**
1. Origami
ISBN 0-8069-7381-1; 0-8069-7382-X (pa)
LC 90-9735
The author presents folding instructions for thirty-three origami projects based on real and imaginary plants and animals

Jackson, Paul
The encyclopedia of origami & papercraft. Running Press 1991 192p il $24.95 **736**
1. Origami
ISBN 1-561-38063-6 LC 91-52902
"From a single folded form to sophisticated sculptures using papier-mâché, paper pulp, and casting, this com-pendium provides technical know-how and a good overview of three-dimensional paper art. . . . Step-by-step color photos indicate all phases of papermaking pro-cesses and equipment." Booklist

737.4 Coins

Cribb, Joe
The coin atlas; the world of coinage from its origins to the present day; [by] Joe Cribb, Barrie Cook, Ian Carradice; cartography by John Flower, with an introduction by the American Numismatic Association. Facts on File 1990 337p il maps $40 **737.4**
1. Coins
ISBN 0-8160-2097-3 LC 89-1353
This book "traces the almost 3000-year history and evolution of coinage in 200 modern nations. Selected coins from each country are described, along with signif-icant political or commercial events which influenced the creation of the nation's currency." Libr J

A **Guide** book of United States coins; by R. S. Yeoman; edited by Kenneth Bressett. Western il $10.95; pa $7.95 **737.4**
1. Coins
Annual. First published 1946 by Whitman
At head of title: Official red book of United States coins
This guide, "known as the 'Red Book,' is an outstand-ing reference on U.S. coins designed for use in identify-ing and grading coins. All issues from 1616 to the present are covered. The guide provides historical data, statistics, values, and detailed photographs for each coin. Additional sections deal with specialties such as Civil War and Hard Times tokens, misstruck coins, and uncirculated and proof sets. Prices provided are based on dealer averages." Nichols. Guide to Ref Books for Sch Media Cent. 4th edition

Krause, Chester L.
Standard catalog of world coins; by Chester L. Krause and Clifford Mishler. Krause Publs. pa $49.95 **737.4**
1. Coins
Also available Standard catalog of world coins, 19th century
First published 1972. (25th edition 1988) Frequently revised
This illustrated volume currently covers coins from throughout the world minted 1901-present. Prices are provided for each coin in up to four grades of preserva-tion. Includes commemorative issues

738 Ceramic arts

Levin, Elaine
The history of American ceramics, 1607 to the present; from pipkins and bean pots to contemporary forms. Abrams 1988 351p il o.p. **738**
1. American pottery
LC 88-3332
"Levin covers the history, traditions, and innovations in American ceramics. . . . Many excellent color and black-and-white illustrations supplement Levin's text, which examines both handmade, single examples and mass-produced items." Booklist
Includes bibliography

738.1   Ceramic arts—Techniques, equipment, materials

Nelson, Glenn C.
Ceramics; a potter's handbook. Harcourt Brace College Pubs. pa $45.75   **738.1**
1. Pottery
First published 1960. (5th edition 1984) Periodically revised
This manual for beginner to advanced potters presents forming and decorating techniques, body and glaze recipes, and sources for raw materials and equipment
Includes glossary and bibliography

Wensley, Doug
Pottery; a manual of techniques. Crowood, Press; distributed by Trafalgar Sq. 1991 192p il hardcover o.p. paperback available $29.95   **738.1**
1. Pottery
ISBN 1-85223-717-1 (pa)
Includes "step-by-step photographs of hand-building and wheel-throwing techniques. Black-and-white line drawings further describe the pottery-making process. . . . An eight-page color portfolio contains handsome examples of earthenware, stoneware, and porcelain vessels. This is a commendable primer for the beginner." Booklist

741.2   Drawing—Techniques, equipment, materials

Edwards, Betty
Drawing on the right side of the brain; a course in enhancing creativity and artistic confidence. rev ed. Tarcher, J.P. 1989 254p il $23.95; pa $14.95   **741.2**
1. Drawing 2. Creative ability
ISBN 0-87477-523-X; 0-87477-513-2 (pa)
LC 89-4561
First published 1979
This book describes the author's technique for teaching people how to draw more accurately and creatively by developing the capabilities of the brain's right side, which, according to "split-brain" research, controls the visual and perceptual functions
Includes bibliographical references

Harrison, Hazel
Pastel school. Reader's Digest Assn. 1996 176p il (Reader's Digest learn-as-you-go guides) $21   **741.2**
1. Pastel drawing
ISBN 0-89577-849-1   LC 95-33556
This work "describes the different types of pastels available, offers advice on putting together a starter palette and adding colors suitable to specific subjects, and presents simple exercises for exploring how various colors appear on papers of different tones and textures." Publisher's note

Smith, Stan
Drawing: the complete course. Reader's Digest Assn. 1994 160p il $25   **741.2**
1. Drawing
ISBN 0-89577-620-0   LC 94-12077
"Smith takes the student through the basics of materials, drawing fundamentals, simple projects, and advanced techniques. . . . Hundreds of books are available on this topic, but there are few general works of this quality for the beginner. Highly recommended." Libr J

741.5   Cartoons, caricatures, comics

The **Art** of Mickey Mouse; edited by Craig Yoe and Janet Morra-Yoe; introduction by John Updike. Hyperion Press (Westport) 1991 unp il $35; pa $19.95   **741.5**
1. Mickey Mouse (Cartoon character)
ISBN 1-56282-994-7; 1-56282-744-8 (pa)
LC 91-23545
"Paintings, watercolors, collages, drawings, photographs, sculpture, tapestry—the media used vary as much as the representations of Mickey. Artists include Andy Warhol, Charles Schultz, Maurice Sendak, R. Crumb, Peter Max, and William Steig. A drawing of Mickey by longtime fan Michael Jackson is also featured." Libr J

Daniels, Les, 1943-
Marvel; five fabulous decades of the world's greatest comics; introduction by Stan Lee. Abrams 1991 287p il $49.50; pa $24.95   **741.5**
1. Marvel comics (New York, N.Y.) 2. Comic books, strips, etc.
ISBN 0-8109-3821-9; 0-8109-2566-4 (pa)
LC 91-8783
"Daniels' behind-the-scenes look at the development of Marvel, his profiles of the line's foremost heroes and villains, and biographies of leading writers and artists will entice . . . young fans. . . . But the book's strongest appeal lies in the generous samplings of artwork spread throughout." Booklist

The **Encyclopedia** of American comics; edited by Ron Goulart. Facts on File 1990 408p il o.p.   **741.5**
1. Comic books, strips, etc.
LC 90-2974
This "guide focuses on comic heroes and villains; the creators, artists, and writers of comic strips and comic books; and the publishers and syndicates of the comics industry. The more than 1,000 entries are arranged in dictionary form." SLJ

Fleming, Robert Loren
The big book of urban legends; adapted from the works of Jan Harold Brunvand; by Robert Loren Fleming and Robert F. Boyd, Jr. Paradox Press 1994 223p il $12.95   **741.5**
1. Comic books, strips, etc. 2. Folklore—United States
ISBN 1-56389-165-4   LC 95-108717
This work is a "collection of some 200 [tales] told in comic strip format by a stunning variety of artists drawn from the comics mainstream . . . underground . . . and everywhere in between." Booklist

Gerberg, Mort

Cartooning; the art and the business. Morrow 1989 272p il pa $15   **741.5**

1. Cartoons and caricatures

ISBN 1-55710-017-9   LC 88-27544

First published 1983 by Arbor House with title: The Arbor House book of cartooning

This "guide thoroughly explains the creative techniques of drawing cartoons and explores the use of these illustrations in comic books, editorials, television, greeting cards, and children's books. Gerberg also covers the marketing of the cartoonist's work. . . . Illustrated with the work of such major cartoonists as Charles Addams, Gahan Wilson, and Mort Walker." Booklist

Includes bibliography

Goulart, Ron, 1933-

The comic book reader's companion; an A-to-Z guide to everyone's favorite art form. HarperCollins Pubs. 1993 191p il hardcover o.p. paperback available $15   **741.5**

1. Comic books, strips, etc.

ISBN 0-06-273117-3 (pa)   LC 92-18795

This book's "alphabetical essays cover specific characters—mostly superheroes but also cowboys, jungle queens, and funny animals—and leading titles from *Action Comics* to *Zip Comics*. . . . [There] are some 100 black-and-white illustrations." Booklist

Includes bibliographical references

The funnies; 100 years of American comic strips. Adams Pub. 1995 248p il pa $15.95 **741.5**

1. Comic books, strips, etc.

ISBN 1-55850-539-3   LC 95-21029

An illustrated look at the evolution of the comic strip beginning with The Yellow Kid, Little Nemo, and Mutt & Jeff and continuing through Krazy Kat, Dick Tracy, and Mary Worth to the success of Calvin & Hobbes. The author explores how the comics reflected social concerns and influenced public opinion

Includes bibliographical references

Harvey, Robert C.

The art of the comic book; an aesthetic history. University Press of Miss. 1996 288p il (Studies in popular culture) $45; pa $22   **741.5**

1. Comic books, strips, etc. 2. Popular culture—United States

ISBN 0-87805-757-9; 0-87805-758-7 (pa)

    LC 95-377

Harvey "attempts to situate the comic book in terms of its evolution from the comic strip to the world of publishing as a whole. . . . [He describes the] change brought upon comics by the institution of the Comics Code in 1954, which put horror and detective stories out of business and ushered in the primacy of superheroes. He also [examines] . . . the art itself, focusing on the development of the vocabulary of panel, layout, story, and style, and the relationship between writer and artist during various stages of comic book history. In addition, he . . . [discusses Will Eisner], Gil Kane, Frank Miller, and Robert Crumb." Libr J

Includes bibliograhical references

Larson, Gary

The far side. Andrews & McMeel 1982 unp il pa $7.95   **741.5**

1. Comic books, strips, etc.

ISBN 0-8362-1200-2   LC 82-72418

A collection of Larson's Far side cartoons

The prehistory of the Far side; a 10th anniversary exhibit. Andrews & McMeel 1989 288p il $19.95; pa $12.95   **741.5**

1. Comic books, strips, etc.

ISBN 0-8362-1861-2; 0-8362-1851-5 (pa)

    LC 89-84813

Retrospective of Larson's work that includes childhood drawings, and stories that evolved into Far side cartoons

McCloud, Scott

Understanding comics; the invisible art. Kitchen Sink Press 1993 215p il hardcover o.p. paperback available $19.95   **741.5**

1. Comic books, strips, etc.

ISBN 0-87816-243-7 (pa)   LC 93-30085

Cover title

The author "traces the 3,000-year history (from Egyptian paintings on) of telling stories through pictures; describes the language of comics—its 'grammar' and 'vocabulary'; explains the use of different types of images ranging from ironic to realistic; depicts how artists convey movement and the passage of time and use various symbols as shorthand; and [seeks to demonstrate] the expressive emotional qualities of different drawing styles." Booklist

Includes bibliographical references

Reidelbach, Maria

Completely Mad; a history of the comic book and magazine. Little, Brown 1991 208p il $50; pa $24.95   **741.5**

1. Mad (Periodical) 2. Comic books, strips, etc. 3. American wit and humor

ISBN 0-316-73890-5; 0-316-73891-3 (pa)

    LC 90-26439

"Reidelbach examines the different things *Mad* has done, and been accused of doing, and the tremendous influence it has had on the field of satire and the American consciousness. The book is profusely illustrated, well researched, and has numerous sidebars profiling the many *Mad* contributors over the years." Libr J

Includes bibliographical references

Ross, Al, 1911-

Cartooning fundamentals. Stravon Educ. Press 1977 192p il o.p.   **741.5**

1. Cartoons and caricatures

    LC 77-1201

"Reproducing more than 100 of his own cartoons and sketches to illustrate his points, Ross hammers away at what he feels are the true fundamentals of his craft. . . . He is a great believer in 'doodling' . . . and he devotes a chapter to the subject. As for drawing, he . . . emphasizes the study of the anatomy, the rhythms of the human body in action, the uses of comic exaggeration." Publ Wkly

Solomon, Charles
The Disney that never was. Hyperion 1995 224p
$40   **741.5**
1. Walt Disney Company 2. Animated films
ISBN 0-7868-6037-5   LC 95-3053
This work "documents dozens of film projects that
were abandoned in various stages of completion. They
range from shorts featuring Mickey, Donald, and Goofy,
to wartime propaganda films, to follow-ups to Fantasia
that were jettisoned after that feature's initial critical and
box-office failure. . . . Nearly every project discussed is
accompanied by concept art, animation drawings, and
other illustrations." Booklist
Includes bibliographical references

Thomas, Bob, 1922-
Disney's art of animation; from Mickey Mouse
to Beauty and the Beast. Hyperion 1991 208p il
$39.95; pa $19.95   **741.5**
1. Walt Disney Company 2. Animated films
ISBN 1-56282-997-1; 1-56282-899-1 (pa)
                                        LC 91-22562
"A Welcome book"
Using the history of the Disney studios as a model,
the author touches "on all aspects of making animated
films, including conceptualization, scripting,
storyboarding, artwork, character development, production, direction, acting, music, layout, animation, and special effects. . . . Highly recommended for general collections." Libr J

Trudeau, G. B. (Garry B.), 1948-
The Doonesbury chronicles; with an introduction
by Gary Wills. Holt, Rinehart & Winston 1975
unp il   **741.5**
1. Comic books, strips, etc.
Available in paperback from Holt & Co. and Harcourt
Brace College Pubs.
A collection of over 500 examples from the
Doonesbury comic strip published between the late
1960's and the mid-1970's

Watterson, Bill
The Calvin and Hobbes tenth anniversary book.
Andrews & McMeel 1995 208p il $19.95; pa
$14.95   **741.5**
1. Comic books, strips, etc.
ISBN 0-8362-0440-9; 0-8362-0438-7 (pa)
                                        LC 95-77563
A representative sampling of the popular comic strip
with commentary by the artist

741.6   Graphic design, illustration and commercial art

Barnicoat, John, 1924-
A concise history of posters: 1870-1970.
Abrams 1972 288p il o.p.; Thames & Hudson
paperback available $14.95   **741.6**
1. Posters—History
ISBN 0-500-20118-8 (pa)
"A survey of the poster art of the past century. . . .
Both text and illustration cover the subject on an interna-

tional scale, with expanded coverage of works from major periods such as Art Nouveau and Surrealism, as well
as political and war posters." Libr J

743   Drawing and drawings by subject

Gordon, Louise
How to draw the human figure; an anatomical
approach. Viking 1979 144p il o.p.; Penguin Bks.
paperback available $15.95   **743**
1. Artistic anatomy 2. Figure drawing
ISBN 0-14-046477-8 (pa)   LC 78-12863
"A Studio book"
In this drawing instruction book "clearly drawn figures
are usually combined with a diagram of the underlying
structure and all bones and muscles are named, their
functions discussed." SLJ
Includes glossary

Graves, Douglas R.
Drawing portraits. Watson-Guptill 1974 159p il
hardcover o.p. paperback available $14.95   **743**
1. Drawing 2. Artistic anatomy
ISBN 0-8230-1431-2 (pa)
The author discusses "the art and craft of portraiture
from beginning to end—seeing and drawing the anatomy
of the head and hands, posing and lighting the sitter,
conveying the weight, texture, and drape of the sitter's
clothing, composing the portrait (individual as well as
group), and dealing with such auxiliary problems as the
relationship between the artist and his sitter." Introduction
Includes bibliography

745   Decorative arts

Kauffman, Henry J., 1908-
Pennsylvania Dutch American folk art. [rev and
enl ed] Dover Publs. 1964 146p il map   **745**
1. Pennsylvania Dutch folk art 2. Decorative arts—
Pennsylvania
Available in paperback from Olde Springfield Shoppe
First published 1946 by American Studio Books
This book seeks to bring together a representative collection of illustrated material as both a record of the folk
art created by the Pennsylvania Dutch and a source of
further inspiration to present day American design and
decoration. It contains 279 photographs and 28 drawings,
accompanied by descriptive text
Includes bibliography

745.4   Pure and applied design and decoration

Pile, John F.
Dictionary of 20th-century design; [by] John
Pile. Facts on File 1990 312p il $35   **745.4**
1. Design—Dictionaries
ISBN 0-8160-1811-1   LC 89-77863
Also available in paperback from Da Capo Press

Pile, John F.—*Continued*
"A Roundtable Press book"
International in scope, this work focuses on product, industrial, graphic, interior, exhibition, typographic, and advertising design. There are more than 1,000 alphabetically arranged entries covering such topics as styles, designers, critics, design schools, and manufacturers

745.54   Paper handicrafts

Bawden, Juliet
The art and craft of papier mâché; photography by Peter Marshall. Grove Weidenfeld 1990 144p il o.p.; Chronicle Bks. paperback available $17.95
745.54
1. Paper crafts
ISBN 0-8118-0805-X (pa)   LC 89-23644
"Color photographs are coupled with step-by-step diagrams in this beautiful book that not only demonstrates dozens of papier mâché craft projects, but also introduces the artistic work of professionals as inspiration and art resource. A brief history of papier mâché . . . enhances the wide-ranging projects." SLJ
Includes glossary

745.58   Handicrafts from beads, found and other objects

Taylor, Carol, 1943-
Creative bead jewelry; weaving, looming, stringing, wiring, making beads. Sterling 1995 144p il pa $18.95
745.58
1. Beadwork 2. Jewelry
ISBN 0-8069-1306-1   LC 95-4595
The author provides information and gives guidance on many projects introducing different methods and designs. Color photographs and black-and-white illustrations are included

745.594   Decorative objects

Innes, Miranda
Jewelry; photography by Clive Streeter. DK Pub. 1996 96p il (Crafts library) pa $14.95
745.594
1. Jewelry
ISBN 0-7894-0433-8   LC 95-52791
The author "provides detailed instructions for making brooches, bangles, necklaces, earrings, and hat pins. Divided into three sections, paper jewelry, bead and glass jewelry, and wood and metal jewelry, the book includes thorough instructions and color photographs." Voice Youth Advocates

745.6   Calligraphy, illumination, heraldic design

Biegeleisen, J. I. (Jacob Israel), 1910-
The ABC of lettering. 5th ed. Harper & Row 1976 255p il o.p.; ST Publs. paperback available $10   **745.6**
1. Lettering
ISBN 0-911380-72-8 (pa)
First published 1940
"These lessons for the beginner in lettering seem unusually complete and detailed; they give careful instructions on strokes with exercises, and information about materials." Booklist

Goffe, Gaynor
Calligraphy school; [by] Gaynor Goffe & Anna Ravenscroft. Reader's Digest Assn. 1994 176p il (Reader's Digest learn-as-you-go guides) $21
745.6
1. Calligraphy
ISBN 0-89577-524-7   LC 94-2628
The authors "explore all the how-to's of calligraphy, from selecting appropriate materials to sewing a manuscript cover. Samples abound. . . . The progression from working simple letterforms to mastering cursive (or flowing) italic and versals (elaborately penned capital letters) is well thought out, enabling beginners to feel a sense of accomplishment at every step." Booklist

Harris, David, 1929-
The art of calligraphy. Dorling Kindersley 1995 128p il $24.95   **745.6**
1. Calligraphy
ISBN 1-56458-849-1   LC 94-26722
An "introduction to a wide variety of written scripts used from Roman times to modern days. The detailed, practical instructions for 26 styles focus on step-by-step, clear visuals, as well as on the proper equipment—brushes, pens, pencils, paper, and ink. A brief history with examples from calligraphic masters introduces each style." SLJ

Marsh, Don, 1957-
Calligraphy. North Light Bks. 1996 128p (First steps series) $16.99   **745.6**
1. Calligraphy
ISBN 0-89134-666-X   LC 96-4014
This guide to calligraphy is aimed at the beginner and includes various projects such as greeting cards and invitations
"Excellent for secondary school age and above." Libr J
Includes bibliographical references

Wilson, Elizabeth B.
Bibles and bestiaries; a guide to illuminated manuscripts. Farrar, Straus & Giroux 1994 64p il $25   **745.6**
1. Bible—Pictorial works 2. Illumination of books and manuscripts
ISBN 0-374-30685-0   LC 94-6687
"Using examples of illuminated manuscripts from the Pierpont Morgan Library as illustrations, Wilson describes how a book was crafted in the Middle Ages. . . . A beautiful adjunct to studies of the Middle Ages, the volume is as elegant and special as its subject." Booklist
Includes glossary and bibliographical references

746 Textile arts and handicrafts

Farris, Lynne
Sewing fun stuff! soft sculpture shortcuts; illustrations by Barbara Abrelat. Sterling 1996 c1995 160p il (Great sewing projects series) $24.95   **746**
1. Sewing
ISBN 0-8069-6164-3   LC 95-47447
First published 1995 by Sewing Information Resources
The author provides technical details on patterns and designs covering a wide range of subjects, including Kermit-like frogs

746.1 Yarn preparation and weaving

Hecht, Ann
The art of the loom; weaving, spinning, and dyeing across the world. Rizzoli Int. Publs. 1990 208p il $35   **746.1**
1. Weaving 2. Spinning 3. Dyes and dyeing
ISBN 0-8478-1147-6   LC 89-61382
"Following a full explanation of the basic principles of weaving, spinning, and dyeing, Hecht focuses on eight areas of the world where outstanding examples of age-old methods of these three interrelated crafts are still practiced today. Visually exceptional . . . as well as informatively superb, her book takes the reader to the American Southwest, the Middle East, West Africa, Indonesia, Japan, Nepal, Guatemala, and Peru." Booklist
Includes bibliography

746.4 Needle- and handwork

Reader's Digest complete guide to needlework. Reader's Digest Assn. 1979 504p il $28 **746.4**
1. Needlework
ISBN 0-89577-059-8   LC 78-71704
Editor: Virginia Colton
A guide to ten different needle crafts, "containing the ABCs, stitches, and techniques anyone would need to start—and finish—a particular crafts project. All aspects of the major forms of needlecraft are covered, from appliqué to rugmaking." Booklist

746.43 Knitting, crocheting, tatting

Hiatt, June
The principles of knitting. Simon & Schuster 1988 571p il $35   **746.43**
1. Knitting
ISBN 0-671-55233-3   LC 87-37665
"This is a comprehensive handbook for the knitter who wants to know the 'whys' as well as the 'hows' of hand-knitted fabric construction. Included are chapters on stitch formation, fabric construction, pattern design, project planning, and decorative work (e.g., multi-color knitting, inlay, and needlework embellishment). Superior organizations, layout, indexing, and the numerous illustrations add to the value of this work as a basic knitting reference." Libr J

746.46 Patchwork and quilting

Florence, Judy
A collection of favorite quilts; narratives, directions & patterns for 15 quilts. American Quilter's Soc. 1990 136p il pa $18.95   **746.46**
1. Quilting
ISBN 0-89145-961-8   LC 91-137433
Among the quilt patterns presented in this guide are classics, such as Sunbonnet Sue, Rose of Sharon, Lone Star, and Nine-Patch, and less familiar patterns, such as My Stars! and Arabic Lattice
Includes bibliographical references

746.6 Textile printing, painting, dyeing

Innes, Miranda
Fabric painting; photography by Clive Streeter. DK Pub. 1996 96p il (Crafts library) pa $14.95   **746.6**
1. Textile painting
ISBN 0-7894-0434-6   LC 95-42183
The author "explains the basic techniques of fabric painting, dyeing, printing and batik, and provides instructions for clothing and home decorating projects such as a dyed silk scarf, silk screen t-shirts, stenciled pillows, a potato print tablecloth and dyed ties." Voice Youth Advocates

750 Painting and paintings

Cumming, Robert, 1943-
Annotated art. Dorling Kindersley 1995 104p il $22.95   **750**
1. Art appreciation
ISBN 1-56458-848-3   LC 94-31843
"An exploration of some of the world's great paintings, ranging from the works of 14th-century Giotto through the Renaissance and Baroque periods to Neo-

Cumming, Robert, 1943— *Continued*

Classicists and Romantics, on to the Impressionists and Cubists up to Picasso. Cumming describes and decodes each of 45 paintings by graphic commentary using six guidelines: the subject, the technique, the symbolism, space and light, historical style, and personal interpretation." SLJ

Includes glossary

Frankel, David

Masterpieces: the best-loved paintings from America's museums. Simon & Schuster 1995 160p $35   **750**

1. Painting 2. Art museums

ISBN 0-684-80197-3   LC 95-939

Frankel persuaded "directors of 33 American museums to nominate the painting they believe is the most popular, or what one might call the signature work, in their galleries. . . . Each selection is accompanied by a fold-out page that includes everything from data about the museum to the artist and the artist's technique. Subject and small insert pictures help the reader identify nuances." Christ Century

751 Painting—Techniques, procedures, apparatus, equipment, materials

The **DK** art school series. Dorling Kindersley 1993-1995 12v il ea $16.95   **751**

1. Painting—Technique

Titles published in 1993: An introduction to acrylics, by R. Smith; An introduction to oil painting, by R. Smith; An introduction to pastels, by M. Wright; An introduction to watercolor, by R. Smith; Watercolor color, by R. Smith; Watercolor landscape, by R. Smith

Titles published in 1994: Drawing figures, by R. Smith; An introduction to drawing, by J. Horton; Oil painting portraits, by R. Smith; Watercolor still life, by L. E. Lloyd

Titles published in 1995: An introduction to mixed media, by M. Wright; An introduction to perspective, by R. Smith

"Each book begins with a very brief history of the medium specific to that volume. The best uses for each medium are introduced along with choices of tools, brushes, papers and canvas. Little prior knowledge is assumed; the reader is taken step-by-step through the techniques possible for each medium. . . . Each book is lavishly illustrated. A few photos are used, but the dominant look is that of the medium being discussed. . . . Examples of well-known art in each medium are also included. This series would serve as a good introduction that would not overwhelm beginners." Book Rep

751.42 Watercolor painting

Clarke, Michael, 1952-

Watercolor. Dorling Kindersley 1993 64p il (Eyewitness art) $16.95   **751.42**

1. Watercolor painting

ISBN 1-56458-174-8   LC 92-54547

"Providing a quick overview of the medium, this book . . . is adorned with photographic reproductions of some

of the world's finest paintings. Short paragraphs and blurbs provide quick points of reference for browsers. Because of its broad appeal, this volume will be quite useful to teachers, and should be included in basic art collections." SLJ

Harrison, Hazel

The encyclopedia of watercolor techniques. Running Press 1990 192p il $24.95   **751.42**

1. Watercolor painting—Technique

ISBN 0-89471-893-2   LC 91-155332

"A Quarto book"

This presentation of water-based paint techniques "includes gouache and acrylic paints as well as the more traditional transparents. . . . The first half of the book goes over approximately 40 techniques. Full-color illustrations show the techniques alone and in finished works. . . . The second section covers themes. . . . This useful volume provides options and splendid examples." Booklist

Smith, Ray Campbell, 1916-

The art of watercolor; a guide to the skills and techniques. Reader's Digest Assn. 1995 128p il $24   **751.42**

1. Watercolor painting—Technique

ISBN 0-89577-654-5   LC 94-35426

Separate chapters cover materials, color theory, perspective, composition, choosing and developing a subject, washes, and other techniques. Each chapter includes a suggested exercise and step-by-step demonstrations are spread throughout the book

Wiegardt, Eric

Watercolor free & easy. North Light Bks. 1996 120p il $27.99   **751.42**

1. Watercolor painting—Technique

ISBN 0-89134-613-9   LC 95-35787

An illustrated guide to utilizing the variety of vibrant colors available to the watercolorist with an intuitive painting style

751.45 Oil painting

Strisik, Paul, 1918-

Capturing light in oils. North Light Bks. 1995 135p il $27.99   **751.45**

1. Painting—Technique

ISBN 0-89134-592-2   LC 94-30895

The author explains techniques, discusses materials, methods, surfaces, conceptions and composition as well as the mechanical aspects of painting

"This colorful and factual guide will be helpful for beginning painters; browsers will enjoy the 150 color illustrations of impressionist landscapes." Book Rep

759.01 Painting of nonliterate peoples, and earliest times to 499

Chauvet, Jean-Marie

Dawn of art; the Chauvet Cave: the oldest known paintings in the world; [by] Jean-Marie Chauvet, Eliette Brunel Deschamps, and Christian Hillaire; epilogue by Jean Clottes; foreword by Paul G. Bahn. Abrams 1996 135p il map $39.95
759.01

1. Cave drawings 2. Prehistoric art
ISBN 0-8109-3232-6 LC 95-47571

"Chauvet, a French cave of astonishing size and singular in its revelation of Paleolithic art, was discovered late in December 1995. The cave's three discoverers here chronicle that discovery from the first day on, in a first-person account of their shared adventure as they journeyed through this underground wonder-world. Their description is subjective, painted in tones of excitement and amazement, and the reader feels the wondrous quality that the trio felt when they realized that they were the first to enter this cathedral-cavern in 20,000 years. . . . Beautifully illustrated by full color photographs." Choice

Includes bibliographical references

759.05 Painting—1800-1899

Welton, Jude, 1955-

Impressionism. Dorling Kindersley 1993 64p il maps (Eyewitness art) $16.95 **759.05**

1. Impressionism (Art) 2. French painting
ISBN 1-56458-173-X LC 92-54545

This visual introduction to the impressionist movement features full-color artworks, details of paintings, and photographs of artists' materials, equipment, and studios

This book is "eye-catching, informative, and priced nicely for high school collections." Booklist

Wiggins, Colin

Post-impressionism. Dorling Kindersley 1993 64p il (Eyewitness art) $16.95 **759.05**

1. Postimpressionism (Art) 2. French painting
ISBN 1-56458-334-1 LC 93-7615

"Wiggins interweaves biography and artistic analysis to provide an understanding of the Post-Impressionists and their works. Alongside the text are excellent reproductions of many of the great masterpieces of the era. In addition, specially selected works, which represent key developments or techniques, are examined in depth. . . . This volume is a simple, easy to understand introduction for aspiring young art students." Voice Youth Advocates

759.06 Painting—1900-1999

Read, Sir Herbert Edward, 1893-1968

A concise history of modern painting; preface by Benedict Read; additional material by Caroline Tisdall and William Feaver. enl and updated 3rd ed. Praeger Pubs. 1975 c1974 392p il (Praeger world of art series) o.p.; Thames & Hudson paperback available $14.95 **759.06**

1. Modern painting—1900-1999 (20th century)
ISBN 0-500-20141-2 (pa)

Companion volume to the author's A concise history of modern sculpture, entered in class 735

First published 1959; this edition first published 1974 in the United Kingdom

The author traces the development of modern painting, beginning with Cezanne. He covers cubism, futurism, surrealism, dadaism, constructivism and abstract expressionism, and the leading artists of these movements. A final chapter discusses the developments of the 1960's and 1970's

Includes bibliography

759.13 American painting

Berkow, Ita G.

Edward Hopper; an American master. Smithmark Pubs. 1996 80p il $10.98 **759.13**

1. Hopper, Edward, 1882-1967
ISBN 0-8317-8087-8

In this illustrated introduction to the American artist "Berkow mixes biography with psychology to analyze the sensuality and poignant psychology of Hopper's moody paintings." Booklist

Eldredge, Charles C.

Georgia O'Keeffe. Abrams 1991 160p il (Library of American art) $45 **759.13**

1. O'Keeffe, Georgia, 1887-1986
ISBN 0-8109-3657-7 LC 90-48459

Numerous reproductions, many in color, "chart the course of O'Keeffe's lengthy career, while Eldredge's accessible text discusses her artistic themes and stylistic subtleties. A beautiful retrospective." Booklist

Includes bibliographical references

Feelings, Tom, 1933-

The middle passage; white ships/black cargo; introduction by John Henrik Clarke. Dial Bks. 1995 unp il map $45 **759.13**

1. Blacks in art 2. Slavery—Pictorial works
ISBN 0-8037-1804-7 LC 95-13866

"Consisting entirely of Feeling's uncaptioned black-and white illustrations, this . . . picture book chronicles the inhumane conditions endured by enslaved Africans during 'four centuries of the slave trade.'" Booklist

"A book for careful study and discussion, both at home and in the classroom." N Y Times Book Rev

Includes bibliographical references

Hopper, Edward, 1882-1967

Edward Hopper: the art and the artist; [by] Gail Levin. Norton 1982 299p il $50; pa $35 **759.13**
ISBN 0-393-01374-X; 0-393-00082-6 (pa)

LC 79-27958

Published in association with the Whitney Museum of American Art

This "introduction to the paintings and drawings of the American realist stems from a [1981] exhibition at New York City's Whitney Museum. Curator Levin traces Hopper's development as an artist and illustrates the painter's characteristic themes in a lengthy introductory essay. Following this text is a large section of plates, in color and black and white." Booklist

Includes bibliography

Ketchum, William C., 1931-

Grandma Moses; an American original; [by] William C. Ketchum, Jr. Smithmark Pubs. 1996 80p il $10.98 **759.13**
1. Moses, Grandma, 1860-1961
ISBN 0-8317-8085-1

This is an introduction to the works of the American artist known for her paintings of rural life in the late 19th century. Illustrated with color reproductions

Lucie-Smith, Edward, 1933-

American realism. Abrams 1994 240p il $49.50 **759.13**
1. Realism in art 2. American painting
ISBN 0-8109-1941-9   LC 93-48535

This volume "traces the changes in American Realism, from the early pioneer days through the times of social realism to the contemporary scene." Booklist

"An interesting overview that covers much of what is familiar within a slightly different context and point of view." Libr J

Includes bibliographical references

Novak, Barbara

American painting of the nineteenth century; realism, idealism, and the American experience. 2nd ed. Harper & Row 1979 350p il pa $23 **759.13**
1. American painting 2. Modern painting—1800-1899 (19th century)
ISBN 0-06-430099-4   LC 79-2093
"Icon editions"

First published 1969 by Praeger

Following the introduction in which "she introduces Copley and the American tradition [the author] continues with a chapter on each of 12 representative American painters, Washington Allston, Thomas Cole, Asher Durand, Frederick Church and Albert Bierstadt, Fitz Hugh Lane, Martin J. Heade, William Mount, George Caleb Bingham, Winslow Homer, Thomas Eakins, Albert Ryder, William Harnett." Best Sellers

Includes bibliography

Yaeger, Bert D.

The Hudson River school; American landscape artists. Smithmark Pubs. 1996 80p il $10.98 **759.13**
1. American painting 2. Landscape painting
ISBN 0-8317-8084-3

"Yaeger's examination of the work of the first thoroughly American school of landscape painters includes the expected: Thomas Cole and Frederic Edwin Church, as well as some highly original followers, such as the luminist Martin Johnson Heade, Albert Bierstadt, and that master of subtleties, George Inness." Booklist

759.4 French painting

Courthion, Pierre

Edouard Manet. Abrams 1984 128p il $22.95 **759.4**
1. Manet, Édouard, 1832-1883
ISBN 0-8109-1318-6

Concise edition of the author's Manet, originally published 1959

The author discusses Manet's technique and choice of subjects, his rejection by the establishment, and the influences of other artists, writers, and society on his work

Georges Seurat. Abrams 1988 129p il $22.95 **759.4**
1. Seurat, Georges Pierre, 1859-1891
ISBN 0-8109-1519-7

Concise edition of the author's Georges Seurat, originally published 1968

This volume features a biographical essay, followed by an annotated portfolio of 40 full-page color plates. A selected bibliography is also included

Degas, Edgar, 1834-1917

Degas by Degas; edited by Rachel Barnes. Knopf 1990 80p il (Artists by themselves) $16.95 **759.4**
ISBN 0-394-58907-6   LC 90-52730

Color reproductions of Edgar Degas' paintings are accompanied by excerpts from the artist's writings. Includes a biographical introduction and chronology

"It is somewhat paradoxical that although Degas believed that paintings are not for talking about, his prose and poetic images duplicate those upon his canvases. . . . [This is] well worth acquiring for large public library collections and those serving YAs." Libr J

Gowing, Sir Lawrence, 1918-1991

Matisse. Oxford Univ. Press 1979 216p il (World of art) **759.4**
1. Matisse, Henri

LC 79-87876

Hardcover and paperback editions available from Thames & Hudson

This introduction to Matisse's art "is literate, informed, and discerning. . . . The illustrations are numerous and well selected." Choice

Includes bibliography

Howard, Michael, 1954-
Gauguin. Dorling Kindersley 1992 64p il
(Eyewitness art) $16.95   **759.4**
1. Gauguin, Paul, 1848-1903
ISBN 1-56458-066-0   LC 92-7067
An introduction to Gauguin's life and work. Discussions of his materials and techniques are juxtaposed with commentary on specific works which are reproduced in full color
Includes glossary

Lucie-Smith, Edward, 1933-
Toulouse-Lautrec. rev and enl ed. Phaidon Press 1983 31p il o.p.; Chronicle Bks. paperback available $14.95   **759.4**
1. Toulouse-Lautrec, Henri de, 1864-1901
ISBN 0-7148-2761-4 (pa)
First published 1977
"The introductory overview of the artist's life is followed by 48 chronologically arranged color plates and concise, paragraph-length analyses of individual works. . . . An intelligently written and well-illustrated survey." Choice

Pach, Walter, 1883-1958
Pierre Auguste Renoir; introduction by Walter Pach. Abrams 1983 126p il $22.95   **759.4**
1. Renoir, Auguste, 1841-1919
ISBN 0-8109-1593-6   LC 82-20785
Concise edition of the author's Pierre Auguste Renoir, originally published 1964
Forty color plates accompany a descriptive commentary on the work of a leading impressionist painter

Renoir, Auguste, 1841-1919
Renoir by Renoir; edited by Rachel Barnes. Knopf 1990 80p il (Artists by themselves) $16.95   **759.4**
ISBN 0-394-58908-4   LC 90-52731
"A selection of Renoir's works are accompanied by quotes from the author collected from his letters, writings and conversations. The quotes add a personal dimension to the art. There is a brief introductory essay, and a chronology. This small format book is attractive, and a charming introduction to the artist." BAYA Book Rev

759.5   Italian painting

Hartt, Frederick, 1914-1991
Michelangelo. Abrams 1984 128p il $22.95   **759.5**
1. Michelangelo Buonarroti, 1475-1564
ISBN 0-8109-1335-6
Concise edition of the author's Michelangelo, originally published 1964
At head of title: Michelangelo Buonarroti
The forty colorplates in this book include broad views and close details of Michelangelo's frescoes in the Sistine Chapel and of his other paintings

Wasserman, Jack, 1921-
Leonardo; text by Jack Wasserman. Abrams 1984 128p il $22.95   **759.5**
1. Leonardo, da Vinci, 1452-1519
ISBN 0-8109-1285-6
Concise edition of the author's Leonardo, originally published 1975
At head of title: Leonardo da Vinci
"Included here . . . are such masterpieces as the 'Mona Lisa' and the 'Last Supper,' and all the paintings known to be fully or in part by Leonardo's hand. A special section features his incomparably original drawings, including material from his famous notebooks." Publisher's note

759.6   Spanish painting

Chevalier, Denys
Picasso; the blue and rose periods. Crown 1991 96p il (Crown art library) $18   **759.6**
1. Picasso, Pablo, 1881-1973
ISBN 0-517-00904-8   LC 90-55848
Translated from the French
This book discusses the life and art of Picasso during the blue period, 1901-1904, and the rose period, 1905-1906, when he was in his twenties. It includes color reproductions of his paintings from museums and private collections
Includes bibliographical references

Domínguez Ortiz, Antonio
Velázquez; [by] Antonio Domínguez Ortiz, Alfonso E. Pérez Sánchez, Julián Gállego. Metropolitan Mus. of Art 1989 286p il $45; pa $19.95   **759.6**
1. Velázquez, Diego, 1599-1660
ISBN 0-87099-554-5; 0-87099-555-3 (pa)
    LC 89-12670
The catalog for an "exhibition at the Metropolitan Museum of Art, this volume is a stunning presentation of Velázquez' career and masterworks. The contributing authors expertly explain just what psychic and technical skill the Spanish artist put into his paintings, while also describing the social and political world in which Velázquez lived and worked." Booklist
Includes bibliography

Gudiol, José, 1904-1985
Goya. Abrams 1985 128p il $22.95   **759.6**
1. Goya, Francisco, 1746-1828
ISBN 0-8109-0992-8
Concise edition of the author's Goya, originally published 1964
At head of title: Francisco de Goya y Lucientes
The author "explores Goya's complex character and the technique of his art. . . . Forty colorplates with detailed analytical commentaries and a selection on Goya's prints are included." Publisher's note

Jaffe, Hans Ludwig C., 1915-1985
Pablo Picasso. Abrams 1983 126p il $22.95; pa $19.98 **759.6**
1. Picasso, Pablo, 1881-1973
ISBN 0-8109-1480-8; 0-8109-8142-4 (pa)
Concise edition of the author's Pablo Picasso, originally published 1964
A portrayal of one of the century's most complex and influential artists. Accompanied by 105 illustrations including 40 color plates from the artist's different periods

759.7 Russian painting

Chagall, Marc, 1887-1985
Chagall; general editor, José Maria Faerna; translated from the Spanish by Elsa Haas. Abrams 1995 64p il (Great modern masters) pa $11.98
759.7
ISBN 0-8109-4677-7   LC 95-232338
This volume "presents a crisp and enlightening profile of the artist and analysis of his distinctive style, aesthetics, technique, and place in art history. Here readers learn the story behind Chagall's lyrical and mythic compositions, paintings that celebrate rural Jewish life in Eastern Europe." Booklist

759.9492 Dutch painting

Bernard, Bruce
Van Gogh. Dorling Kindersley 1992 64p il (Eyewitness art) $16.95   **759.9492**
1. Gogh, Vincent van, 1853-1890
ISBN 1-56458-069-5   LC 92-7061
This "volume combines concise biographical material with brilliant color illustrations identified by detailed captions to convey [Van Gogh's life style], influences, creative output, and unique accomplishments. . . . A brief chronology, the locations of the works presented, and a glossary conclude [the] volume." Libr J

McQuillan, Melissa
Van Gogh. Thames & Hudson 1989 216p il (World of art) pa $14.95   **759.9492**
1. Gogh, Vincent van, 1853-1890
ISBN 0-500-20232-X   LC 88-50234
"McQuillan looks at van Gogh within the context of the artist's own period and finds some stimulating new ideas to investigate. . . . Small black-and-white reproductions and a limited number of colorplates illustrate the volume." Booklist
Includes bibliography

Schapiro, Meyer, 1904-1996
Vincent Van Gogh. Abrams 1983 128p il $22.95; pa $19.98   **759.9492**
1. Gogh, Vincent van, 1853-1890
ISBN 0-8109-1733-5; 0-8109-8117-3 (pa)
Concise edition of the author's Van Gogh, originally published 1969

"Schapiro traces the painter's developing technique, as well as his travels in France and Belgium, his stormy relations with painter Paul Gauguin, and his periods of confinement in a hospital and an asylum. . . . Quotations from Van Gogh's letters to his beloved brother Theo, reflections on his own approaching death, and his portraits of friends as well as of himself further our understanding of this tormented genius." Publisher's note

759.9493 Belgian painting

Stechow, Wolfgang, 1896-1974
Pieter Bruegel the Elder; text by Wolfgang Stechow. Abrams 1990 127p il (Masters of art) $22.95   **759.9493**
1. Brueghel, Pieter, the Elder, 1522?-1569
ISBN 0-8109-3103-6   LC 89-35780
First published 1970
The author "describes the art of this complex personality and comments in detail on the 40 . . . full-color plates. His introductory text [explores] . . . the variety and originality of Brueghel's subject matter, the depth of his beliefs, the moralizing attitudes displayed in many of his scenes, the subtlety of his compositions, and the radiance of his color palette." Publisher's note

760 Graphic arts. Printmaking and prints

Ayres, Julia
Printmaking techniques. Watson-Guptill 1993 160p il $35   **760**
1. Prints
ISBN 0-8230-4399-1   LC 92-43352
This is a guide to "identifying and understanding various printmaking procedures, tools, and materials. . . . [Ayres] explains the differences between relief, intaglio, and lithographic printing techniques, as well as screen printing, collagraphs, offset, and computer-generated printing." Booklist
"The author presents sufficient information to allow an aspiring printmaker to sort out the characteristics of different techniques and to begin working in one of the media." Libr J

760.2 Printmaking and prints—Miscellany

Ross, John, 1921-
The complete printmaker; techniques, traditions, innovations; [by] John Ross, Clare Romano, Tim Ross; edited and produced by Roundtable Press. rev & expanded ed. Free Press 1990 352p il $49.95; pa $35   **760.2**
1. Prints
ISBN 0-02-927371-4; 0-02-927372-2 (pa)
LC 89-11900
First published 1972
This introduction to printmaking covers innovative techniques such as computer-generated prints and copier art as well as relief prints, intaglio prints, screenprints, lithography, and other traditional methods

769 Prints

Escher, M. C. (Maurits Cornelis), 1898-1972
The world of M. C. Escher. Abrams 1972 59p
il o.p.; New Am. Lib. paperback available $9.95
                                                                769

ISBN 0-451-79961-5 (pa)
Edited by J. L. Locher
A "catalog of the graphic work of [the] Dutch mathe-
matician-artist. . . . [The book opens with five] essays
on the meanings and execution of his works, including
one by the master himself; but the greater portion of the
work is composed of close to 300 illustrations depicting
the . . . world Escher created graphically." Libr J

769.5 Forms of prints

Friedberg, Robert, 1912-
Paper money of the United States; a complete
illustrated guide with valuations. Coin & Currency
Inst. il $24.50   **769.5**
1. Paper money
First published 1953. (14th edition 1995) Periodically
revised
A guide to paper money of the United States from
1861 to the present. Contains descriptions, valuations,
and illustrations of notes, fractional currency, and certifi-
cates

769.56 Postage stamps

Davidson, Charles
Stamping our history; the story of the United
States portrayed on its postage stamps; by Charles
Davidson and Lincoln Diamant. Carol Pub. Group
1990 253p il $49.95; pa $24.95   **769.56**
1. Postage stamps 2. United States—History—Miscellanea
ISBN 0-8184-0532-5; 0-8065-1691-7 (pa)
                                                LC 90-38791
"A Lyle Stuart book"
"Davidson and Diamant have looked at a century of
stamps, from 1875 to 1975, in terms of the historical
events or individuals that inspired their making. As interesting as the history the stamps commemorate are the
myths that they perpetuate (such as Betsy Ross sewing
the first flag). The book is packed with color and black-
and-white illustrations; some are full-page, others are
stamp-size." Booklist

Scott's specialized catalogue of United States
stamps. Scott Pub. Co. (Sidney) il pa $35
                                                769.56
1. Postage stamps—Catalogs
Annual. First published 1923. Title and publisher's
name vary
This volume "lists a wide variety of different groups
of U.S. stamps such as air post envelopes, first day covers, postal cards, revenue stamps, savings stamps, and
telegraph stamps. Listings are in the form used in Scott's
Standard Catalogue. The 'Information for Collector' section is much more extensive and detailed." Wynar. Guide
to Ref Books for Sch Media Cent. 3d edition

Scott's standard postage stamp catalogue. Scott
Pub. Co. (Sidney) 6v il pa ea $35   **769.56**
1. Postage stamps—Catalogs
Annual. First published 1868. Title, publisher's name
and number of volumes vary
"Provides descriptions, photographs (where possible),
and monetary values for all known world stamps, past
and present." N Y Public Libr. Book of How & Where
to Look It Up

770 Photography and photographs

Shoot!; everything you ever wanted to know about
35mm photography; edited by Liz Harvey.
AMPHOTO 1993 256p il $29.95   **770**
1. Photography
ISBN 0-8174-5869-7   LC 92-39858
This handbook includes "chapters on framing, depth
of field manipulation, and use of light. . . . Although the
text provides solid instruction in black-and-white processing, color photography is the dominant concern here."
Libr J

770.1 Photography—Philosophy and theory

Goldberg, Vicki
The power of photography; how photographs
changed our lives. Abbeville Press 1991 279p
$39.95; pa $17.50   **770.1**
1. Photography
ISBN 1-55859-039-0; 1-55859-467-1 (pa)
                                                LC 91-3116
This study of photography "traces the medium from
its beginnings with the French daguerreotype of the
1840s to the powerful social tool and all-pervasive 'eye'
[the author considers] it has become." SLJ
Includes bibliographical references

Ritchin, Fred
In our own image; the coming revolution in
photography: how computer technology is
changing our view of the world. Aperture 1990
192p il $35; pa $15.95   **770.1**
1. Photography—Data processing
ISBN 0-89381-398-2; 0-89381-399-0 (pa)
                                                LC 90-80727
An examination of computer graphics technology,
which makes it easy to manipulate the photographic image, and its implications for photography, especially
photojournalism
The author "makes it clear that the ethical and esthetic
issues involved affect all of us. If we can no longer rely
on photography as our witness of time and place, he
writes, then what we perceive as reality is suddenly mal-
leable. . . . Mr. Ritchin brings to his discussion a passionate interest in the social role of photography." N Y
Times Book Rev
Includes bibliography

770.2 Photography—Miscellany

The Focal encyclopedia of photography; edited by Leslie Stroebel and Richard Zakia. 3rd ed. Focal Press 1993 914p il $125; pa $49.95   **770.2**
1. Photography—Dictionaries
ISBN 0-240-80059-1; 0-240-51417-3 (pa)
LC 92-44267
First published 1956
"A combination dictionary and encyclopedia, bringing together definitions of terms and articles on the history, techniques, art, and application of photography. . . . Excludes motion picture photography, video, and electronic still photography." Guide to Ref Books. 11th edition

Hedgecoe, John
John Hedgecoe's new book of photography. Dorling Kindersley 1994 264p il $29.95   **770.2**
1. Photography—Handbooks, manuals, etc.
ISBN 1-56458-508-5   LC 93-28346
Replaces The book of photography published 1984 by Knopf
"Generously illustrated with color and black-and-white photographs, this large-format book provides a broad overview of photography for amateurs and professionals alike. Beginning with a review of the camera itself and ending with a discussion on studio and darkroom equipment, this book is laden with good, practical advice for taking better portraits, still lifes, and landscapes." Libr J
Includes glossary

770.25 Photography—Directories

Photographer's market. Writer's Digest Bks. il $23.99   **770.25**
1. Photography—Marketing—Directories
ISSN 0147-247X
Annual. Originally published as part of Artist's and photographer's market, 1977. First published separately 1978
"Includes directories of many types of business firms (e.g., advertising agencies, galleries, book and periodical publishers, record companies) with their photographic requirements and name of contact person. Data on contests, foundations and grants, workshops, plus feature articles on the profession and the business of freelancing." Guide to Ref Books. 11th edition

770.9 Photography—Historical and geographic treatment

Newhall, Beaumont, 1908-1993
The history of photography; from 1839 to the present day. completely rev and enl ed. Museum of Modern Art 1982 319p il hardcover o.p. paperback available $32.50   **770.9**
1. Photography—History
ISBN 0-87070-381-1 (pa)   LC 82-81430
First published 1949
An illustrated history of photography focusing on important innovators and master photographers
Includes bibliography

771 Photography—Techniques, equipment, materials

Hedgecoe, John
John Hedgecoe's complete guide to black & white photography and darkroom techniques. Sterling 1994 160p il hardcover o.p. paperback available $19.95   **771**
1. Photography
ISBN 0-8069-0886-6 (pa)   LC 94-16839
This beginner's guide to black and white photography discusses principles of basic composition; subject areas, such as still lifes, portraits and landscapes; setting up a home darkroom; processing film and printing pictures; and advanced techniques, such as solarization

Langford, Michael John, 1933-
Photography. Dorling Kindersley 1995 72p il pa $6.95   **771**
1. Photography—Handbooks, manuals, etc.
ISBN 0-7894-0174-6
At head of title: 101 essential tips
This work covers camera choice, use and accessories. Suggestions on how to better compose and expose photographs are included

778.59 Television photography

Lewis, Roland
Video. Dorling Kindersley 1995 72p il pa $6.95   **778.59**
1. Video recording—Handbooks, manuals, etc.
ISBN 0-7894-0183-5
At head of title: 101 essential tips
In this guide "colored photographs accompany text explaining equipment, techniques, composition, lighting, editing, audio, and so forth. Additional tips are provided for shooting weddings, vacations, sporting events, and animals." Voice Youth Advocates

Stavros, Michael
Camcorder tricks & special effects; over 40 fun, easy tricks anyone can do! Amherst Media 1995 128p il $12.95   **778.59**
1. Camcorders
ISBN 0-936262-26-5   LC 94-71929
This illustrated book contains step-by-step instructions using a camcorder and simple props that allow you to simulate effects used by professionals
Includes glossary

778.7 Photography under specific conditions

Frink, Stephen
Wonders of the reef; diving with a camera; text and photographs by Stephen Frink. Abrams 1996 160p il $39.95   **778.7**
1. Underwater photography
ISBN 0-8109-3785-9   LC 95-34173
"The book first describes various reefs in the Caribbean, the Pacific, the Red Sea, and elsewhere around the world that offer the best photo opportunities. Useful chapters on underwater lighting, photo techniques, and various cameras, such as the Nikonos, follow. The appendixes include a list of suppliers of underwater equipment and helpful information for those who wish to sell their photographs to advertising agencies and publishers." Libr J

778.8 Special effects and trick photography

Zuckerman, Jim
Outstanding special effects photography on a limited budget. Writer's Digest Bks. 1993 135p il pa $24.95   **778.8**
1. Photography
ISBN 0-89879-553-2   LC 93-17148
The author "shows how techniques like hand-coloring, negative sandwiching, and masking can be used to illustrate a concept. Sample photos contain captions that explain, step by step, how an effect was produced. This text provides a functional yet fun how-to of photographic manipulation." Libr J

779 Photographs

Adams, Ansel, 1902-1984
Ansel Adams; [edited by] Richard Wrigley. Smithmark Pubs. 1992 43p il $7.98   **779**
1. Artistic photography
ISBN 0-8317-0518-3
Cover title: Ansel Adams: images of the American West
"A major feature of this collection of over 30 of the artist's landscape photographs is Wrigley's introduction. In it, he draws parallels between the development of his subject's artistry and that of American photography during the 60 years he worked, beginning in the 1920s when this country became more conscious of the need to preserve the pristine wilderness. . . . Most of the photographs present Adams' view of the American West; six of them study the Navajo as they fit into the Southwestern shadows and light patterns for which he has been long acclaimed." SLJ

The portfolios of Ansel Adams; introduction by John Szarkowski. New York Graphic Soc. 1977 124p il $40   **779**
1. Artistic photography
ISBN 0-8212-0723-7   LC 77-71628
"The seven Adams photographic portfolios produced in limited editions . . . are herein assembled into one volume. With few exceptions the 85 examples of his unique lensmanship are the stark black-and-white landscapes of the western U.S. for which he is renowned." Booklist

The **African** Americans; edited by Charles M. Collins and David Cohen; text by Cheryl Everette, Susan Wels, and Evelyn C. White. Viking Studio Bks. 1993 240p il $45   **779**
1. African Americans—Pictorial works
ISBN 0-670-84982-0   LC 93-1574
Color photographs portray Afro-American "educators, politicians, preachers, and numerous other figures, offering brief biographies detailing their claims to fame. With both contemporary and historical profiles, this volume includes ordinary people who have made significant contributions to society interspersed with well-known artists, filmmakers, movie stars, and authors." Libr J
Includes bibliographical references

American photography, 1890-1965, from the Museum of Modern Art, New York; [edited by] Peter Galassi; with an essay by Luc Sante. Museum of Modern Art 1995 256p il $60   **779**
1. Museum of Modern Art (New York, N.Y.) 2. Artistic photography
ISBN 0-8109-6143-1   LC 94-73385
This volume presents over 180 photographs from their collection dating from the 1880s to the 1960s
Galassi has "used his knowledge of the museum's collection to create a simultaneously seductive and contentious history of the evolution of photography in the United States." N Y Times Book Rev
Includes bibliographical references

Bendavid-Val, Leah
National Geographic, the photographs. National Geographic Soc. 1994 336p il $50; pa $46.95   **779**
1. Photojournalism 2. Documentary photography
ISBN 0-87044-986-9; 0-87044-987-7 (pa)
    LC 94-29971
A collection of photographs from National Geographic magazine, grouped into six chapters: Then and now; Faraway places; In the wild; Underwater; The sciences; In the U.S.A. The accompanying text presents the stories behind many of the images, including photographers' accounts of adventures in the field

Edwards, Harvey
The art of dance; foreword by Bruce Marks. Little, Brown 1989 144p il $35   **779**
1. Artistic photography 2. Dancing—Pictorial works
ISBN 0-8212-1734-8   LC 89-43017
"A Bulfinch Press book"
"Edwards takes his viewer from practice hall to performance in a series of shots that captures the emotional and physical ardor of the dancers at work, at rest, and onstage. These informal photographs are supplemented by a selection of more formally posed dance portraits." Booklist

Evans, Walker, 1903-1975

Walker Evans: the Getty Museum collection; [compiled by] Judith Keller. Getty Mus. 1995 xxii, 410p il $95   **779**
1. J. Paul Getty Museum 2. Artistic photography
ISBN 0-89236-317-7   LC 95-1592
"Walker Evans (1903-75), whose career spanned five decades, from the 1920s to the early 1970s, was arguably the most influential 20th-century American photographer. . . . This catalog of the Getty's collection of Evans's work is the most complete, most scholarly, and most useful to date, reproducing nearly 1200 images." Libr J
Includes bibliographical references

✓ Frankel, Godfrey, 1912-

In the alleys; kids in the shadow of the Capitol; photographs by Godfrey Frankel; text by Laura Goldstein; foreword by Gordon Parks. Smithsonian Institution Press 1995 104p il $55; pa $24.95   **779**
1. African American children—Pictorial works 2. Washington (D.C.)—Social conditions—Pictorial works
ISBN 1-56098-536-4; 1-56098-663-8 (pa)
    LC 95-14993
This is a collection of photographs taken by Frankel in the slums of southwest Washington, D.C., in 1943-44. "Living conditions were deplorable, yet according to former residents quoted in this book, the southwest alleys resembled a small Southern town in which everybody looked after one another, and these images accordingly resound with heartwarming vitality as well as appalling poverty." Booklist
Includes bibliographical references

Lange, Dorothea, 1895-1965

The photographs of Dorothea Lange; [by] Keith F. Davis with contributions by Kelle A. Botkin. Abrams 1995 132p il $35   **779**
1. Documentary photography
ISBN 0-8109-6315-9   LC 95-79156
Published by Hallmark Cards in association with H.N. Abrams
Published to accompany a traveling exhibition, this collection ranges from Depression era images to photographs of family and everyday life in distant lands
Includes bibliographical references

Lewinski, Jorge, 1921-

The camera at war; a history of war photography from 1848 to the present day. Simon & Schuster 1980 240p il o.p.   **779**
1. Photojournalism 2. War—Pictorial works
    LC 79-17021
This "survey of the history and practice of combat photography features more than 300 photographs. . . . [Photographers discussed include] Bourke-White, Brady, Capa, Faas, Fenton, Mydans, Smith, and other photojournalists on both sides of major conflicts from the Crimea to Southeast Asia." Libr J

Life laughs last; 200 more classic photos from the famous back page of America's favorite magazine; [edited] by Philip B. Kunhardt, Jr. Simon & Schuster 1989 223p il hardcover o.p. paperback available $14   **779**
1. Photojournalism
ISBN 0-671-68797-2 (pa)   LC 89-104107
"This sequel to 'Life Smiles Back' (1987) offers more smile-raising photos from the picture magazine's last page. A snowsuited tot hanging on a coathook and a worried-looking pooch in the vet's waiting room are typical of the subjects." Booklist

Life: the '60s; edited by Doris C. O'Neil; introduction by Tom Brokaw; commentary by John Neary. Little, Brown 1989 236p il $35   **779**
1. United States—History—1961-1974—Pictorial works 2. Photojournalism
ISBN 0-8212-1752-6   LC 89-7964
"A Bulfinch Press book"
A selection "of photographs from the archives of 'Life.' . . . Particularly in its condensation of events, this selection of 250 captioned photographs is rather haunting. . . . Readers will recognize a number of the more familiar photographs . . . which have become cultural icons representing the 1960s. A good summary of the decade." Libr J

Life: the first 50 years, 1936-1986. Little, Brown 1986 319p il o.p.   **779**
1. Photojournalism
    LC 86-2842
Editor: Philip B. Kunhardt, Jr.
"Black-and-white and color photos from 'Life's' pages are chronologically arranged. . . . A visual feast that will provide plenty of enjoyment at any browsing moment." Booklist

✓ Myers, Walter Dean, 1937-

One more river to cross; an African American photograph album. Harcourt Brace & Co. 1995 166p il $40   **779**
1. African Americans—Pictorial works
ISBN 0-15-100191-X   LC 95-3839
"This collection of period photography documents the African-American struggle from captivity to freedom." Book Rep
"This oversized, superbly produced album is dramatic, with spare, almost poetic narration by Myers. . . . Although there are some photos of well-known individuals, the strength of this book is the pictures of ordinary people, engaged in the everyday tasks and enjoyments of life. . . . In his introduction, Myers tells us he has set out to show the fullness of black life, not to portray African American people as simply victims. And in this, he amply succeeds." Voice Youth Advocates

Photographs that changed the world; the camera as witness, the photograph as evidence; [compiled by] Lorraine Monk. Doubleday 1989 51p il o.p.   **779**
1. Artistic photography
    LC 88-33595
"Most of the 51 photographs are in black and white, with several in color. The author has chosen these photo-

Photographs that changed the world—*Continued*
graphs because of the information they reveal about the
world, and how the world has changed because of them.
. . . Each photo is accompanied by a page of text, explaining the situation in the world and what makes this
particular image so special. The quality of reproduction
is excellent. . . . Each story is complete in itself, and
each photograph a testimony to its photographer." Voice
Youth Advocates

780   Music

Marsalis, Wynton
    Marsalis on music. Norton 1995 171p il music
$29.95   **780**
    1. Music
    ISBN 0-393-03881-5   LC 95-4470
    This book "is designed to show how basic elements of
music are shared by different musical styles. Chapters
are divided into rhythm, form, wind bands and jazz
bands, and practice. Musical examples are provided on
an accompanying audio CD. . . . Also included are biographical sketches of composers featured in the book."
Libr J
    "An outstanding companion to a PBS series. . . . A
superb resource for students and for other readers."
Booklist
    Includes glossary

Spence, Keith
    The young people's book of music; consultant,
Hugo Cole. Millbrook Press 1995 144p il lib bdg
$19.90; pa $14.95   **780**
    1. Music—History and criticism
    ISBN 1-56294-605-6 (lib bdg); 1-56294-784-2 (pa)
                                     LC 94-36699
    First published 1993 in the United Kingdom with title:
Watts book of music
    The "author attempts to present the types of music,
families of instruments, the history of music and a few
major composers, all in two-page spreads which are
packed with text and boxed photos and diagrams. It is
truly a concise encyclopedia of music and musicians.
The reading level of the text is demanding, although the
captions of the photos and diagrams are easier. A useful
reference tool for music studies of all kinds." Child Book
Rev Serv
    Includes glossary and bibliographical references

Wilson, Lee, 1951-
    Making it in the music business; a business and
legal guide for songwriters and performers.
Penguin Bks. 1995 278p pa $12.95   **780**
    1. Music industry 2. Copyright—Music 3. Music—
Law and legislation
    ISBN 0-452-26848-6   LC 94-30368
    "A Plume book"
    A "handbook that outlines all the information a fledg-
ling musician or songwriter needs to know, from basic
copyright law to how to get a legitimate agent or booking manager. There's even a chapter on how to organize
a rock band. . . . Wilson writes in a friendly, clever

style that acknowledges the 'rigmarole' of the legal system while using the necessary arrows to direct even the
novice musician to the road to success." Booklist
    Includes bibliographical references

780.2   Music—Miscellany

Lax, Roger
    The great song thesaurus; [by] Roger Lax,
Frederick Smith. 2nd ed updated & expanded.
Oxford Univ. Press 1989 774p $85   **780.2**
    1. Popular music
    ISBN 0-19-505408-3   LC 88-31267
    First published 1984
    "A compendium of various lists (e.g., a chronology of
'greatest' songs from the 16th century to the present;
award winners; lyricists and composers with titles of
their songs), the most extensive being of song titles (with
a separate section for British titles). The 'thesaurus' aspect of the work is provided by section IX, Thesaurus of
song titles by subject, key word, and category, which
permits finding the full title, date, and composer of a
song of which only a portion of the title or the subject
is known." Guide to Ref Books. 11th edition

    The **Rolling** Stone album guide; completely new
    reviews: every essential album, every essential
    artist; edited by Anthony DeCurtis and James
    Henke with Holly George-Warren; reviewers,
    Mark Coleman [et al.] Random House 1992
    838p pa $20   **780.2**
    1. Popular music—Discography 2. Sound record-
ings—Reviews
    ISBN 0-679-73729-4   LC 92-50156
    Replaces The Rolling Stone record guide (1980) and
The New Rolling Stone record guide (1983)
    Rock, soul, country, pop, rap, blues, jazz, folk and
gospel, albums are reviewed with the emphasis on popular rock releases. Arrangement is alphabetical by artist
and a rating system indicates the relative importance of
each record

780.3   Music—Encyclopedias and dictionaries

Ammer, Christine
    The HarperCollins dictionary of music. 3rd ed.
HarperPerennial 1995 512p il pa $18   **780.3**
    1. Music—Dictionaries
    ISBN 0-06-461049-7   LC 94-28689
    First published 1972 with title: Harper's dictionary of
music
    This work contains entries for the most commonly
used musical terms as well as material on musical history
and practice. Pronunciation is provided for names and
foreign terms. The text is accompanied by numerous pictures and musical illustrations

Kennedy, Michael, 1926-

The Oxford dictionary of music; associate editor, Joyce Bourne. 2nd ed. Oxford Univ. Press 1994 985p $39.95   **780.3**
1. Music—Dictionaries 2. Musicians—Dictionaries
ISBN 0-19-869162-9   LC 94-4539
First published 1985
This reference contains over 12,500 entries for: composers; performers and conductors; musical terms and forms; instruments; concert halls and opera houses; major musical publishers, producers and stage designers
This is a "comprehensive and useful resource for accurate and concise definitions and biographical sketches." Choice

The **New** Grove dictionary of music and musicians; edited by Stanley Sadie. Macmillan; Grove's Dictionaries of Music 1980 20v il music $1150; pa $550   **780.3**
1. Music—Dictionaries 2. Musicians—Dictionaries
ISBN 0-333-23111-2; 1-56159-174-2 (pa)
                                      LC 79-26207
Supersedes Grove's dictionary of music and musicians
"International in scope and highly comprehensive, this monumental work has become the foremost English-language music reference source. 'The New Grove,' 97 percent original, is clear and convenient, includes over three thousand illustrations, and contains an abundance of fascinating articles on all aspects of music. The outstanding bibliographies, detailed lists of composers' works, and overall high literary quality make this encyclopedia indispensable for scholars, students, and amateurs." RQ

The **New** Harvard dictionary of music; edited by Don Michael Randel. Belknap Press 1986 942p il lib bdg $39.95   **780.3**
1. Music—Dictionaries
ISBN 0-674-61525-5   LC 86-4780
First published 1944 with title: Harvard dictionary of music, by Willi Apel
"With the assistance of 70 scholars, Randel has assembled some 6,000 articles dealing primarily with Western music, but giving considerable attention to non-Western cultures. A number of essays on American popular music are included. There are no biographical entries. 'New Harvard's' strength is in musicological topics: music history, theory, and instruments." Choice

The **New** Oxford companion to music; general editor: Denis Arnold. Oxford Univ. Press 1983 2v il music set $150   **780.3**
1. Music—Dictionaries 2. Musicians—Dictionaries
ISBN 0-19-311316-3
Based on The Oxford companion to music, by Percy A. Scholes
"Articles, often many pages in length, concern the people who make music (mainly composers, including living persons), their careers and achievements; the musical environment or history of music in individual countries or geographic areas; and the music itself—individual works, instruments, forms, scales and modal patterns, music theory, etc." Guide to Ref Books. 11th edition

Roche, Jerome

A dictionary of early music; from the troubadours to Monteverdi; by Jerome & Elizabeth Roche. Oxford Univ. Press 1981 208p il $31.25
                                      780.3
1. Music—Dictionaries 2. Composers—Dictionaries
ISBN 0-19-520255-4   LC 81-82688
Approximately 1,000 entries dealing with medieval, Renaissance and early baroque music. In addition to entries devoted to composers are terms, types of music, instruments and cross-references. Printed editions of music are cited
"The explanations are necessarily brief, as are the biographical sketches . . . but they're clear, and carefully done. Recommended especially for collections with limited resources for music." Libr J

780.89   Music of racial, ethnic, national groups

Brooks, Tilford

America's black musical heritage. Prentice-Hall 1984 336p il music hardcover o.p. paperback available $53   **780.89**
1. African American music—History and criticism 2. African American musicians
ISBN 0-13-024307-8 (pa)   LC 83-11184
"In five chapters—Black Music and Its Roots, Black Music Forms Before 1900, Black Music Forms After 1900, The Black Musician in American Society, and American Black Composers in the European Tradition—Brooks offers a survey of his topic that is written well and concisely." Choice
Includes bibliography

✓ **Floyd, Samuel A.**

The power of black music; interpreting its history from Africa to the United States; [by] Samuel A. Floyd, Jr. Oxford Univ. Press 1995 316p il $30; pa $14.95   **780.89**
1. African American music—History and criticism
ISBN 0-19-508235-4; 0-19-510975-9 (pa)
                                      LC 94-21
The range of genres the author discusses includes "slaves' ring shouts, turn-of-the-century cotillion dances, jazz, R & B, etc. . . . Complementing the discourse are plenty of musical examples. Academics, critics, scholars, and fans alike stand to gain much from carefully reading this impressive work." Booklist
Includes bibliographical references, discography and filmography

✓ **Haskins, James, 1941-**

Black music in America; a history through its people; illustrated with photographs. Crowell 1987 198p il lib bdg $15.89   **780.89**
1. African American music—History and criticism 2. African American musicians
ISBN 0-690-04462-3   LC 85-47885
"Haskins traces the dual developments of black musicians who performed in white classical styles and black

Haskins, James, 1941——*Continued*
creators of spirituals, ragtime, blues, jazz, gospel, and soul music. The text alternates between passages giving historical perspective and biographical sketches of great musicians, from Elizabeth Taylor Greenfield, a successful operatic soprano in the 1850s, to Wynton Marsalis." Bull Cent Child Books
"This is one music history book that won't be judged boring by teens, and it certainly is one that belongs in every school and public library." Child Book Rev Serv

Oliver, Paul, 1927-
The new Grove gospel, blues and jazz; with spirituals and ragtime; [by] Paul Oliver, Max Harrison, William Bolcom. Norton 1988 395p il hardcover o.p. paperback available $16.95   **780.89**
1. Gospel music 2. Jazz music 3. Blues music
ISBN 0-393-30100-1 (pa)   LC 88-128521
Part of this material was first published in: The New Grove dictionary of music and musicians
"Blues authority Oliver contributes chapters on spirituals, blues, and gospel; pianist-composer-scholar William Bolcom covers ragtime; and British critic Max Harrison tackles jazz. They thoroughly yet succinctly chronicle and describe their subjects, producing all but ideal primers and starting points for serious study." Booklist
Includes bibliography

Southern, Eileen
The music of black Americans; a history. 3rd ed. Norton 1997 xxii, 678p il music $35; pa $26.95   **780.89**
1. African American music—History and criticism 2. African American musicians
ISBN 0-393-03843-2; 0-393-97141-4 (pa)
LC 96-28811
First published 1971
A chronological survey of African American music in the United States tracing black music from its origin in Africa through colonial America and up to the present
Includes bibliography and discography

780.9   Music—Historical and geographical treatment

Baker, Richard, 1925-
Richard Baker's companion to music; a personal A-Z guide to classical music. Parkwest Publs. 1994 208p $27.95   **780.9**
1. Music—Dictionaries
ISBN 0-563-36414-9
"Intended for the layperson interested in classical music, the . . . entries, which cover from Palestrina to the 1990's, include composers, soloists, orchestras, concert halls, famour compositions, musical forms, and instruments. Most entries are 6-10 lines in length, although broad subjects (*Choral Music, Jazz,* the *Proms*) receive a two-page spread." Booklist

Grout, Donald Jay, 1902-1987
A history of western music; [by] Donald Jay Grout, Claude V. Palisca. Norton il $49.95   **780.9**
1. Music—History and criticism
First published 1960. (5th edition 1996) Periodically revised
The authors survey the course of Western music from the ancient world to modern atonalism and dodecaphony. They cover vocal and instrumental forms, notation, performance, music-printing, the development of instruments, and biographical information on composers
Includes bibliographical references

Slonimsky, Nicolas, 1894-1995
Music since 1900. Schirmer Bks. $125   **780.9**
1. Music—History and criticism
First published 1937. (5th edition 1994) Periodically revised
"A chronology of musical events (with commentary on the events listed) makes up the bulk of the volume." Guide to Ref Books. 11th edition

Stanley, John
Classical music; an introduction to classical music through the great composers & their masterworks; foreword by Sir Georg Solti. Reader's Digest Assn. 1994 264p il $35   **780.9**
1. Music—History and criticism 2. Music appreciation 3. Composers
ISBN 0-89577-606-5   LC 94-1931
This is an "illustrated chronology of Western composers from 1600 to 1994. The year-by-year summary is subdivided into musical 'year clusters,' which give form to the events. . . . Each chapter includes a lengthy introduction to the events and music of the period, but the meat of the text is biographical sketches of the important composers of the age. Each composer's biography notes a recording of a representative piece of music, with the publisher, order number, cast, and summary critique from a *Gramaphone* review." Booklist

780.973   Music—United States

The New Grove dictionary of American music; edited by H. Wiley Hitchcock and Stanley Sadie; editorial coordinator Susan Feder. Grove's Dictionaries of Music 1986 4v il set $725   **780.973**
1. American music—Dictionaries
ISBN 0-943818-36-2   LC 86-404
"Includes names and terms germane to the musical tradition of the U.S. Expands articles from *The new Grove dictionary of music and musicians* where appropriate, but adds many more on art music, varieties of popular music, the political and patriotic repertories, specifically American genres, music of the present day, etc. Standard music topics are treated in the American context. Signed articles, many with bibliographies, lists of works, and discographies." Guide to Ref Books. 11th edition

781.1 Music—Aesthetics, appreciation, taste

Copland, Aaron, 1900-1990
What to listen for in music; with an introduction by William Schuman. McGraw-Hill 1988 xxiv, 307p music o.p.; New Am. Lib. paperback available $5.99   **781.1**
1. Music appreciation
ISBN 0-451-62735-0 (pa)   LC 87-27569
First published 1939. This is a reissue of the revised edition published 1957
In this book, based on a series of lectures delivered at the New School for Social Research in New York City, Copland discusses listening, inspiration, the four elements of music, tone color, and the orchestra

781.4 Techniques of music

Evans, Roger
How to read music; for singing, guitar, piano, organ, and most instruments. Crown 1979 c1978 112p music hardcover o.p. paperback available $10   **781.4**
1. Music—Study and teaching 2. Musical notation
ISBN 0-517-88438-0 (pa)   LC 79-20844
First published 1978 in the United Kingdom
An introduction to "music notation and score reading for an individual interested in learning and mature enough to follow directions. Some ability to play an instrument is useful but not mandatory. Examples are given showing both a piano keyboard and a guitar tablature." Voice Youth Advocates
"Fundamental musical concepts are presented here in a well-planned, logical order. . . . Evans has done a good job overall and has included a very useful directory of musical signs, note directory, and a brief musical dictionary." SLJ

781.6 Traditions of music. Classical music

Gammond, Peter
The Harmony illustrated encyclopedia of classical music; an essential guide to the world's finest music. [2nd ed] Harmony Bks. 1989 c1988 224p il pa $20   **781.6**
1. Music—History and criticism
ISBN 0-517-57094-7   LC 88-23750
"A Salamander book"
First published 1978 under the authorship of Lionel Salter with title: The illustrated encyclopedia of classical music. This edition first published in the United Kingdom with title: The Encyclopedia of classical music
This reference work is divided into the following categories: The orchestra; The opera; The composer; Chamber music; Musical instruments; Choral & vocal music; Medieval & renaissance music; Reading & using music; Recorded music

Rushton, Julian
Classical music; a concise history from Gluck to Beethoven; with 50 illustrations. Thames & Hudson 1986 192p il (World of art) pa $14.95
                                                781.6
1. Music—History and criticism
ISBN 0-500-20210-9   LC 86-50223
In this book the author "traces the gradual shift away from religious to secular music that took place during the late 1700s, and he discusses in detail the expansion of orchestras, which saw the introduction of cellos in the 1770s and clarinets in the 1790s. The development of new music forms is also analyzed, especially the sonata as pioneered by Scarlatti. . . . [A] short yet remarkably detailed work." Booklist
Includes bibliography

Swafford, Jan
The Vintage guide to classical music. Vintage Bks. 1992 xxi, 597p il pa $17   **781.6**
1. Music—History and criticism
ISBN 0-679-72805-8   LC 91-50217
This guide contains "chronologically arranged essays on nearly 100 composers, from Guillaume de Machaut (ca. 1300-1377) to Aaron Copland (1900-1990), that combine biography with detailed analyses of the major works while assessing their role in the social, cultural, and political climate of their times." Publisher's note
Includes glossary and bibliography

781.64 Western popular music

Gammond, Peter
The Oxford companion to popular music. Oxford Univ. Press 1991 739p $52.25; pa $19.95
                                                781.64
1. Popular music—Dictionaries
ISBN 0-19-311323-6; 0-19-280004-3 (pa)
                                LC 90-14209
"Aims to cover 'all music that would not normally be found in a reference book on "classical" or "serious music" . . . and the essential elements and personalities concerned with popular song of all periods.'"—*Introd.*
Dictionary arrangement of entries covers roughly 1850-1985, with emphasis on the English-speaking world. Many entries are lengthy, and some have bibliographies. Indexes: people and groups; shows and films; songs and albums." Guide to Ref Books. 11th edition

The **Guinness** encyclopedia of popular music; edited by Colin Larkin. 2nd ed. Stockton Press 1995 6v set $495   **781.64**
1. Popular music—Dictionaries
ISBN 1-56159-176-9
First published 1992 in four volumes by New England Pub.
This work gives comprehensive coverage to all forms of twentieth-century popular music, including pop, rock, heavy metal, country, R&B, rap, reggae, jazz, blues, ragtime, big band, Latin, folk and gospel with over 40,000 entries in all. Most entries are biographical on individual and musical groups and the arrangement is strictly alphabetical
For a review see: Booklist, April 15, 1996

√ **Jones, K. Maurice**

Say it loud! the story of rap music. Millbrook Press 1994 128p il $19.90; pa $12.95   **781.64**

1. Rap music

ISBN 1-56294-386-3; 1-56294-724-9 (pa)

LC 93-1939

A survey of rap music tracing "its origins back to the oratory tradition of the *griots* of West African societies. . . . Quotes and the use of lyrics (fully documented) by a variety of rappers and other recording artists effectively enhance and expand the discussion." SLJ

Includes glossary, discography and bibliography

Off the record; an oral history of popular music; [stories told to] Joe Smith; edited by Mitchell Fink. Warner Bks. 1988 429p il hardcover o.p. paperback available $14.95   **781.64**

1. Popular music 2. Musicians, American

ISBN 0-446-39090-9 (pa)

LC 88-24068

The author "interviewed some 200 greats or near-greats in the field, spanning the period from the 1950s to the present. Editor Mitchell Fink then pared the material down into brief, several-pages-each recollections, in which the interviewees detail career beginnings, memorable experiences, or the development of their musical styles." Booklist

"The sheer scope of the book is astounding. Nearly all the heavy hitters are here, from Lionel Hampton and Buddy Rich to Sting and George Michael. . . . Virtually all types of popular music are represented: jazz, rhythm & blues, folk, country-western, light pop and heavy metal." Publ Wkly

Press, David Paul, 1949-

A multicultural portrait of America's music; by David P. Press. Marshall Cavendish 1994 80p il (Perspectives) lib bdg $19.95   **781.64**

1. Popular music

ISBN 1-85435-666-6

LC 93-48847

This book covers the various forms of American popular music, including Native American traditional music, Cajun and zydeco, country, blues, ragtime, jazz, rock 'n' roll, doo-wop, R & B, soul and rap. Many individual artists are featured

Includes glossary and bibliography

Rose, Tricia

Black noise; rap music and black culture in contemporary America. Wesleyan Univ. Press 1994 237p il (Music culture) hardcover o.p. paperback available $15.95   **781.64**

1. Rap music

ISBN 0-8195-6275-0 (pa)

LC 93-41386

The author "traces rap's sonic history . . . and gives substantial information about the innovative rhythmic manipulations made possible by the techniques of sampling. She also makes clear the connections between rap's beginnings and the political turmoils that afflicted black and Latino urban neighborhoods throughout the 1970s and 1980s. . . . Fans, scholars, and detractors alike stand to learn a great deal by studying Rose's commendable treatise." Booklist

Includes bibliographical references

781.642   Country music

Bufwack, Mary A.

Finding her voice; the saga of women in country music; by Mary A. Bufwack and Robert K. Oermann. Crown 1993 594p il o.p.; Holt & Co. paperback available $18.95   **781.642**

1. Country music 2. Women musicians

ISBN 0-8050-4265-2 (pa)

LC 92-44269

This "study of ordinary, working-class women and their music . . . also functions as a social, political, and economic report that covers such topics as 19th-century showgirls, radio, protest songs, World War II, honky-tonks, Southern gospel music, rockabilly, bluegrass, and more. The text is well written, clearly organized, and accompanied by photographs. . . . The book's extensive bibliography justifies purchase in and of itself." Libr J

The **Comprehensive** country music encyclopedia; from the editors of Country music magazine. Times Bks. 1994 449p il $25   **781.642**

1. Country music

ISBN 0-8129-2247-6

LC 94-78321

"A Country Music Magazine Press book"

"Written in a style reminiscent of popular magazines, this . . . encyclopedia ranges from Roy Acuff to Zydeco. Biographical sketches of old-timers, seasoned favorites, the lesser known, and glitzy newcomers dominate the pages. . . . Among performers rating full-page write-ups are Dolly Parton, Minnie Pearl, George Jones, Emmylou Harris, Tennessee Ernie Ford, and Johnny Cash." Libr J

For a fuller review see: Booklist, Feb. 1, 1995

The **Illustrated** history of country music; from the editors of Country Music magazine; edited by Patrick Carr. Times Bks. 1995 564p il pa $25   **781.642**

1. Country music

ISBN 0-8129-2455-X

LC 95-1468

"A Country Music Magazine Press book"

This history of country music traces "the development of the genre from the Carter Family to Dolly Parton to Garth Brooks. A total of 650 photographs accompany the stories of the music and the musicians who went from the front porch to the stage of the Grand Ole Opry. Performers' anecdotes complement the . . . study of the structure, style, and content of this distinctively American art form." Publisher's note

Oermann, Robert K.

America's music; the roots of country; by Robert Oermann. Turner Pub. (Atlanta) 1996 240p il pa $24.95   **781.642**

1. Country music

ISBN 1-57036-228-9

LC 95-42484

This collection of reminiscences and musings by country's stars includes profiles highlighting each personality's home area, significance, popular songs, influences, and honors

781.643   Blues music

Awmiller, Craig
This house on fire; the story of the blues. Watts 1996 160p il (African-American experience) $22; pa $8   **781.643**
1. Blues music
ISBN 0-531-11253-5; 0-531-15797-0 (pa)
LC 96-10290
In this musical history the author portrays "such early blues greats as Blind Lemon Jefferson, Ma Rainey, and Robert Johnson. He follows the blues from the Mississippi Delta to Chicago, where the urban blues style was perfected, and goes on to today, giving strong emphasis to the blues influence on 1960s pop music along the way." Booklist
Includes bibliographical references and discography

Davis, Francis
The history of the blues. Hyperion 1995 309p il $24.95; pa $14.95   **781.643**
1. Blues music
ISBN 0-7868-6052-9; 0-7868-8124-0 (pa)
LC 94-23370
"Developed as a companion to a PBS series, this is a comprehensive examination and interpretive history of a musical form and its legendary artists. The inclusion of a timeline, a discography, and a bibliography help make the well-documented work a recommended purchase for most music collections." Booklist

Lomax, Alan, 1915-
The land where the blues began. Pantheon Bks. 1993 539p il $25   **781.643**
1. Blues music 2. African Americans—Mississippi
ISBN 0-679-40424-4   LC 91-52627
Also available in paperback from Dell
This is an account of the folklorist and musicologist's travels in the Mississippi Delta in the 1940s as he recorded the work of African American blues musicians
"If it were a novel, Alan Lomax's long-awaited account of his adventures in the Mississippi Delta would be called 'sprawling' and a 'must read.' . . . It is as delightful and hard to put down as any fictional epic." Booklist
Includes bibliographical references

Nothing but the blues; the music and the musicians; [edited by] Lawrence Cohn. Abbeville Press 1993 432p il $45; pa $7.95   **781.643**
1. Blues music
ISBN 1-55859-271-7; 1-55859-829-4 (pa)
LC 93-2791
Also available CD-ROM version
This "illustrated compilation of articles by 10 notable writers examines the origins of blues and the music's various styles and artists, including women." Booklist
Includes discography and bibliography

781.644   Soul music

Hirshey, Gerri
Nowhere to run; the story of soul music. Da Capo Press 1994 384p il pa $14.95   **781.644**
1. Soul music
ISBN 0-306-80581-2   LC 94-15454
First published 1984 by Times Bks.
"This richly detailed book tells the story of soul music largely through anecdotes and through interviews with James Brown, Aretha Franklin, Diana Ross, Michael Jackson, Ahmet Ertegun and many others." Publ Wkly

781.65   Jazz music

Feather, Leonard
The encyclopedia of jazz; appreciations by Duke Ellington, Benny Goodman, and John Hammond. Da Capo Press 1984 527p il music pa $24.95
781.65
1. Jazz music—Dictionaries 2. Jazz musicians
ISBN 0-306-80214-7   LC 83-26164
Companion volumes available: The encyclopedia of jazz in the sixties pa $16.95 (ISBN 0-306-80263-5); The encyclopedia of jazz in the seventies pa $17.95 (ISBN 0-306-80290-2)
First published 1955 by Horizon Press. This is a reissue of the 1960 revised and enlarged edition
"Contains biographical sketches of more than 2,000 jazz musicians, with a guide to their recordings, history of jazz on records, recommended jazz records, bibliography, and discography." Guide to Ref Books. 11th edition

Friedwald, Will, 1961-
Jazz singing; America's great voices from Bessie Smith to bebop and beyond. Scribner 1990 477p il hardcover o.p. paperback available $15
781.65
1. Jazz music 2. Singers
ISBN 0-02-080131-9 (pa)   LC 89-28172
"Starting with blues singers who laid the foundations for jazz-oriented popular singing, the author follows the development of this vocal style from Bing Crosby and Louis Armstrong through a host of performers." Publ Wkly
"This magisterial, lively, catholic, enthusiastic overview of jazz and jazz-influenced pop singers couldn't be more welcome. Nor could it be more fascinating. . . . This is an absolutely essential book for anybody who cares in the slightest about adult popular music." Booklist
Includes discography

Hentoff, Nat
Listen to the stories; Nat Hentoff on jazz and country music. HarperCollins Pubs. 1995 220p $23; pa $12   **781.65**
1. Jazz music 2. Country music
ISBN 0-06-019047-7; 0-06-092712-7 (pa)
LC 95-1395
This collection of pieces from Hentoff's column in the Wall Street Journal "presents a combination of recollec-

Hentoff, Nat—*Continued*
tions and personal profiles introducing legendary artists such as Billie Holiday and Duke Ellington as well as contemporary musicians such as 'jazz player' Wynton Marsalis." Booklist

"The pieces are short, mostly between three and five pages, but Hentoff always manages to make his point and to pique our interest in the music." Libr J

Includes bibliographical references

Jazz milestones; a pictorial chronicle of jazz, 1900-1990; compiled by Ken Vail. Omnigraphics 1996 c1993 176p il maps $45
781.65
1. Jazz music
ISBN 0-9522287-0-X
First published 1993 in the United Kingdom
This year-by-year chronology lists "significant events, births and deaths of musicians, any films or books about jazz, and important compositions and recordings." Booklist

Includes bibliographies

The **New** Grove dictionary of jazz; edited by Barry Kernfeld. St. Martin's Press 1994 xxxii, 1358p il $50
781.65
1. Jazz music
ISBN 0-312-11357-9   LC 94-12667
Revised edition of the title First published 1988 in two volumes

Includes articles on individuals, groups, topics and terms, instruments, record companies and labels. Includes bibliographies and selected discographies

Seymour, Gene
Jazz, the great American art. Watts 1995 176p il (African-American experience) lib bdg $22.70; pa $8
781.65
1. Jazz music 2. African American music
ISBN 0-531-11218-7 (lib bdg); 0-531-15793-8 (pa)
LC 95-4693
A history of jazz, from its roots in blues, ragtime, and swing to its various contemporary manifestations, discussing the major performers and the music's reflection of the experiences of African Americans

Includes bibliography and discography

781.66 Rock music

Bego, Mark
The rock & roll almanac. Macmillan 1996 308p il (Macmillan reference books) pa $12.95 **781.66**
1. Rock music
ISBN 0-02-860432-6   LC 95-38561
"The almanac covers a wide array of topics from chronologies, awards, and Hall of Famers to the more unusual, such as songs about disasters, rock star makeup, prestardom jobs, and lists of star or group names by theme (animals, numbers, etc.)." Booklist

The **Harmony** illustrated encyclopedia of rock; consultant editor, Mike Clifford. Harmony Bks. il pa $19   **781.66**
1. Rock music—Dictionaries 2. Rock musicians
First edition compiled and written by Nick Logan and Bob Woffinden published 1976 in the United Kingdom with title: The Illustrated New Musical Express encyclopedia of rock. First United States edition published 1977 with title: The Illustrated encyclopedia of rock. (7th ed 1992) Periodically revised

"Over 700 colorfully illustrated entries profile established British and American artists, giving background information, career highlights, and discographies of outstanding recordings. Illustrations are of individuals, groups, and album covers." Nichols. Guide to Ref Books for Sch Media Cent. 4th edition

Hertsgaard, Mark, 1956-
A day in the life; the music and artistry of the Beatles. Delacorte Press 1995 434p il $23.95; pa $13.95   **781.66**
1. Beatles
ISBN 0-385-31377-2; 0-385-31517-1 (pa)
LC 94-37709
"Hertsgaard offers an in-depth look at the popularity of the Beatles, their songs, and the art of their music. A good selection for the music shelf, with extensive documentation and a useful bibliography." Booklist

Includes discography

MacDonald, Ian
Revolution in the head; the Beatles' records and the sixties. Holt & Co. 1994 373p $25; pa $14.95
781.66
1. Beatles
ISBN 0-8050-2780-7; 0-8050-4245-8 (pa)
LC 94-20276
"The bulk of the book consists of musical analyses of each of the Beatles 186 songs, arranged chronologically. Entries include writer and performer credits, recording and release dates, historical background, and musical analysis. . . . A 34-page introductory essay attempts to evaluate the music of the Beatles against the social and cultural contexts of the 1960s." Choice

"Even if your Beatles shelf is groaning, MacDonald's work will be a useful addition." Booklist

Includes bibliographical references

The **New** Rolling Stone encyclopedia of rock & roll; edited by Patricia Romanowski and Holly George-Warren; consulting editor, Jon Pareles. completely rev and updated. Fireside Bks. 1995 1120p il pa $25   **781.66**
1. Rock music—Dictionaries
ISBN 0-684-81044-1   LC 95-35045
"A Rolling Stone Press book"
First published 1983 with title: The Rolling Stone encyclopedia of rock & roll

This volume includes 2200 "entries describing rock figures from the famous to the all but forgotten. A typical entry for a band gives the year and date the group formed, the members and their birth dates and places, their instruments, and a discography followed by an es-

The New Rolling Stone encyclopedia of rock & roll—*Continued*

say. The essays range from 100 words (Mungo Jerry) to four-plus pages (Elvis) and deal noncritically with the artists' work, history, and influence." Libr J

Nite, Norm N.

Rock on almanac; the first four decades of rock 'n' roll: a chronology. 2nd ed. HarperPerennial 1992 581p il pa $20   **781.66**

1. Rock music
ISBN 0-06-273157-2   LC 92-52544
First published 1989

"Compendium of information on rock from the 1940s through 1992. For each year, includes news and music highlights, artists and groups who debuted, monthly listing of popular songs in alphabetical order, top ten singles and albums, Grammy winners, Rock and Roll Hall of Fame inductions (beginning 1986), brief biographical facts on performers, rock movies, and motion picture Academy Awards." Guide to Ref Books. 11th edition
Includes discographies

Powell, Stephanie

Hit me with music; how to start, manage, record, and perform with your own rock band. Millbrook Press 1995 142p il lib bdg $16.40
781.66

1. Rock music 2. Music industry
ISBN 1-56294-653-6   LC 95-1965

In this guide to forming a rock band, "Powell covers everything from finding players; buying equipment; and writing songs to booking gigs; making recordings; and dealing with drugs, alcohol, and sex." SLJ

This is "a really good source for young rock musicians. Powell combines hard facts, practical tips, realistic advice, and encouragement in a readable, well-organized guide." Booklist
Includes bibliography

Reisfeld, Randi

This is the sound; the best of alternative rock. Aladdin Paperbacks 1996 144p il pa $7.99
781.66

1. Rock music
ISBN 0-689-80670-1   LC 95-43927

Identifies today's top alternative bands, observes what they're saying, and points out how they're affecting the present generation

"From the busy MTV-like cover cartoons to the Internettish typeface to the breathless and occasionally raunchy fan-mag prose, this breezily written paperback about nine of the most influential groups in alternative rock will lure teens." Bull Cent Child Books
Includes discographies

The **Rolling** Stone illustrated history of rock & roll; the definitive history of the most important artists and their music; edited by Anthony DeCurtis and James Henke with Holly George-Warren; original editor: Jim Miller. 3rd ed. Random House 1992 710p il pa $25.95
781.66

1. Rock music
ISBN 0-679-73728-6   LC 92-6339
First published 1976

This volume presents biographical information; definitions of rock styles and terms; and select discographies

"The essays are lucid, fun to read, and, for the most part, respectful toward the subjects. . . . With photos complementing the text, readers will dip into any part of this book and be hooked. Highly recommended as a historical view of the enduring aspects of rock music." Voice Youth Advocates

782.25   Sacred songs

We'll understand it better by and by; pioneering African American gospel composers; edited by Bernice Johnson Reagon. Smithsonian Institution Press 1992 384p il music hardcover o.p. paperback available $24.95   **782.25**

1. Gospel music 2. African American musicians 3. Composers
ISBN 1-56098-167-9 (pa)   LC 91-37954

"Reagon and her contributors explore every aspect of gospel's history, spiritual significance, and influence on secular music, but the primary focus is on individuals. The lives and achievements of six pioneering gospel music composers are examined in detail. . . . A splendidly comprehensive and invaluable history." Booklist
Includes discography and bibliography

782.42   Songs

Best loved songs of the American people; [edited by] Denes Agay; illustrated by Reisie Lonette. Doubleday 1975 403p il o.p.   **782.42**

1. American songs 2. Popular music

A collection of songs from Colonial times to the 1960s ranging from folk songs to Broadway tunes. Simple piano arrangements are included

Furia, Philip, 1943-

The poets of Tin Pan Alley; a history of America's great lyricists. Oxford Univ. Press 1990 322p $26; pa $12.95   **782.42**

1. Lyricists 2. Popular music 3. American songs
ISBN 0-19-506408-9; 0-19-507473-4 (pa)

LC 90-35937

This work examines "lyrics from stage and movie musicals and the work of ten lyricists: Irving Berlin, Lorenz Hart, Ira Gershwin, Cole Porter, Oscar Hammerstein, Howard Dietz, Yip Harburg, Dorothy Fields, Leo Robin, and Johnny Mercer. . . . Although primarily a record of one aspect of show business, the book is a good history of American popular culture." Choice
Includes bibliographical references

Lives of the great songs; edited by Tim de Lisle.
Pavilion Bks. 1994 148p il pa $24.95   **782.42**
1. Popular music 2. Songs
ISBN 1-85793-374-5

This work "Celebrates 35 exceptional popular songs,
and although its contents represent a series from the British newspaper, the *Independent*, its orientation is distinctly American. The songs covered range from mainstream
standards like 'My Funny Valentine' and 'How Long
Has This Been Going On?'; through country ('I Fall to
Pieces'), rock ('Satisfaction'), and AOR ('Bridge over
Troubled Waters'). . . . A collection bound to appeal to
music lovers who appreciate the entire spectrum of popular music." Booklist

Lomax, Alan, 1915-
The folk songs of North America in the English
language. Doubleday 1960 xxx, 623p il o.p.
   782.42

1. Folk songs—United States
"Dolphin books"
"Melodies and guitar chords transcribed by Peggy
Seeger; with one hundred piano arrangements by Matyas
Seiber and Don Banks. Illustrated by Michael Leonard;
editorial assistant: Shirley Collins." Title page
Includes words, music, and origins of over 300
American folk songs including ballads, work songs and
spirituals as well as a book list, guitar guide and a dis-
cography

National anthems of the world; edited by W.L.
Reed and M.J. Bristow. Blandford Press;
distributed by Sterling music $90   **782.42**
1. National songs
First published 1943 in the United Kingdom with title:
National anthems of the United Nations and France. (9th
edition 1997) Periodically revised
This volume contains national anthems of some 175
nations, including melody and accompaniment. Words
are presented in the native language with transliteration
provided where necessary. English translations follow.
Brief historical notes on the adoption of each anthem are
included and the book concludes with a list of national
holidays

Songwriter's market. Writer's Digest Bks. $21.99
   782.42
1. Popular music—Writing and publishing
ISSN 0161-5971
Annual. First published 1978
The main section of this guide consists of listings of
music publishers, record companies, producers, managers,
booking agents, and firms interested in original music.
Also included are articles which present an overview of
the songwriting field, and listings of resources such as
organizations, workshops, and contests

784   Instruments and instrumental ensembles and their music

Previn, André, 1929-
André Previn's guide to the orchestra; with
chapters on the voice, keyboards, mechanical, and
electronic instruments; edited by André Previn.
Putnam 1983 192p il o.p.   **784**
1. Orchestra 2. Musical instruments 3. Singing
      LC 83-4587
This volume "covers all kinds of music from the medieval period through classical to electronic instruments
to jazz to rock. There are chapters on string, woodwind,
brass, percussion, and keyboard instruments with sections
on terms attached. There is also a chapter on voice and
one on composing, performing and recording. A fascinating look at what makes all the sounds we enjoy and an
invaluable reference for music and history." Voice Youth
Advocates

784.19   Musical instruments

Musical instruments of the world; an illustrated
encyclopedia; [by] the Diagram Group. Facts on
File 1978 c1976 320p il $37.50; pa $19.95
   784.19

1. Musical instruments—Dictionaries
ISBN 0-87196-320-5; 0-8160-1309-8 (pa)
First published 1976 by Paddington Press
Covers "musical instruments from all periods and
places. With more than 4000 drawings and diagrams, this
work provides historical information and details on the
workings of instruments." Ref Sources for Small & Medium-sized Libr. 5th edition

784.2   Symphony orchestra

Steinberg, Michael
The symphony; a listener's guide. Oxford Univ.
Press 1995 678p music $35   **784.2**
1. Symphony 2. Music appreciation 3. Composers
ISBN 0-19-506177-2   LC 95-5568
"Steinberg describes 36 composers and, movement by
movement, 118 symphonies, including all the standard
repertory . . . as well as a few by less well known composers such as Gorecki, Harbison, Martinu, and Sessions.
The writing varies from formal and factual to chatty,
with candid asides and stories relevant to the composer,
the composition, or an important performance." Libr J
Includes bibliographical references

784.8   Wind band

Bailey, Wayne, 1955-
  The complete marching band resource manual; techniques and materials for teaching, drill design, and music arranging; percussion chapter by Thomas Caneva. University of Pa. Press 1994 various paging il spiral bdg $29.95   **784.8**
  1. Bands (Music)
  ISBN 0-8122-1508-7   LC 94-7036
  This guidebook for band directors features drill charts and instrumental arrangements

787.87   Guitar

Bacon, Tony
  The ultimate guitar book; [by] Tony Bacon & Paul Day. Knopf 1991 192p il $40   **787.87**
  1. Guitars
  ISBN 0-394-58955-6   LC 91-52714
  This is a "chronological history of the guitar, beginning with an example from 1552 and continuing through current times. Covering acoustic, electrical, and bass guitars, including all the big-name manufacturers such as Fender, Gibson, Martin, and Stratocaster, this informative and beautifully illustrated work will have wide appeal." SLJ
  Includes glossary

Chapman, Richard
  The complete guitarist. Dorling Kindersley 1993 192p il $29.95; pa $19.95   **787.87**
  1. Guitars
  ISBN 1-56458-181-0; 1-56458-411-8 (pa)
          LC 92-56493
  This work ranges "from fundamentals such as tuning, scales, chords, picking, and strumming, to advanced techniques of various styles such as rock, blues, and jazz. . . . [It also] includes discussions on such topics as sound and amplification, choosing a guitar, studio and home recording, plus care and maintenance of the instrument. An appealing book in the style of the 'Eyewitness' series, this should be both popular with and useful to students." SLJ

Denyer, Ralph
  The guitar handbook. [rev ed] Knopf 1992 256p il pa $25   **787.87**
  1. Guitars
  ISBN 0-679-74275-1   LC 92-53164
  "A Dorling Kindersley book"
  First published 1982
  Contains a learning program covering the range of guitar techniques from simple chords to improvised lead solos, profiles of famous and influential guitarists, an illustrated chord dictionary, chapters on guitar customizing and recording techniques, and sections on a variety of acoustic and electric guitars, amplification, special effects and stage sound systems

790.1   Recreational activities

Crisfield, Deborah
  Pick-up games; the rules, the players, the equipment; [by] D.W. Crisfield. Facts on File 1993 192p il lib bdg $27.95; pa $12.95   **790.1**
  1. Games 2. Sports
  ISBN 0-8160-2700-5 (lib bdg); 0-8160-3069-3 (pa)
          LC 92-16296
  "A Mountain lion book"
  "The book is arranged alphabetically by 15 sports (badminton, baseball, basketball, etc.). The fifteenth category is a general one that lists games that are simply 'a lot of fun to play.' Here are listed such classics as Capture the Flag, Kick the Can, and Manhunt. . . . Although several good game books are available, few are as clear and concise as *Pick-up Games*." Booklist
  Includes glossary and bibliography

791   Public performances

The New York Public Library performing arts desk reference. Macmillan 1994 424p il $35   **791**
  1. Performing arts—Dictionaries
  ISBN 0-671-79912-6   LC 94-22673
  "A Stonesong Press book"
  This work "covers the historical and contemporary worlds of dance, theater, and music with an international scope. It provides addresses of organizations, short biographies, definitions of technical terms, and lists of events of interest." Libr J

791.06   Public performances— Organizations and management. Amusement parks

Koenig, David
  Mouse tales; a behind-the-ears look at Disneyland; foreword by Art Linkletter. Bonaventure Press 1994 239p il $25.95; pa $13.95   **791.06**
  1. Disneyland (Anaheim, Calif.)
  ISBN 0-9640605-5-8; 0-9640605-6-6 (pa)
          LC 94-70439
  Koenig describes "Walt Disney's plan and the goals for his amusement park; the behind-the-scenes mechanisms of the attractions; the selection, training, and expectations of the employees; the persona of the Disney characters; profiles of guests; . . . [the] accidents that have occurred and the lawsuits that ensued; and the spinoffs throughout the world." Libr J
  "A valuable addition to popular culture literature and to Disneyana." Booklist

791.3   Circuses

Culhane, John
The American circus: an illustrated history. Holt & Co. 1990 xxii, 504p il hardcover o.p. paperback available $19.95   **791.3**
1. Circus
ISBN 0-8050-1647-3 (pa)   LC 89-2182
This book covers the circus from its antecedents in the European equestrian shows first staged in the United States in 1785 to the lavish spectacles of the present
The author "has written an engaging and well-researched history of the American circus. It is sure to be a valuable reference source as well as entertaining reading." Libr J
Includes bibliography

791.43   Motion pictures

The **Actor's** book of movie monologues; edited by Marisa Smith and Amy Schewel. Penguin Bks. 1986 xxx, 240p pa $12.95   **791.43**
1. Motion pictures 2. Monologues
ISBN 0-14-009475-X   LC 86-8093
"Although designed as a sourcebook for aspiring thespians who need material for auditions, this collection of famous movie monologues makes great browsing for all film buffs. . . . Featuring memorable speeches from more than 80 films, the text is arranged chronologically." Booklist

Adamson, Joe
Groucho, Harpo, Chico and sometimes Zeppo; a history of the Marx Brothers and a satire on the rest of the world. Simon & Schuster 1973 464p il o.p.   **791.43**
1. Marx Brothers 2. Motion pictures
"A thoroughly researched, thoroughly entertaining survey of the Marx brothers as individuals and as an almost mythical unit. Adamson has included dozens of stills and provided an index, notes, and bibliography, all useful." Choice

Basinger, Jeanine
American cinema; one-hundred-years of filmmaking. Rizzoli Int. Publs. 1994 300p $50   **791.43**
1. Motion pictures—History and criticism
ISBN 0-8478-1814-4   LC 94-12263
This companion volume to a PBS series "surveys both the film-factory world of the long-deceased studio system and today's independent productions. The text, which not only follows the history of film but dabbles in its sociology and psychology as well, is buttressed with 300 photographs." Libr J
Includes bibliographical references

Brown, Gene
Movie time; a chronology of Hollywood and the movie industry from its beginnings to the present; Mary Ann Lynch, photo editor. Macmillan 1995 450p il pa $19.95   **791.43**
1. Motion pictures—History and criticism 2. Motion picture industry
ISBN 0-02-860429-6   LC 95-9091
This is a year-by-year presentation of notable events and personalities associated with the Hollywood film industry
Includes bibliographical references

Chronicle of the cinema. Dorling Kindersley 1995 920p il $59.95   **791.43**
1. Motion pictures—History and criticism
ISBN 0-7894-0123-1
Editor in chief, Robyn Karney
This is an "overview of cinema's first 100 years. Over 3000 posters, portraits, and stills illustrate countless film facts, developments, and highlights in a clear, year-by-year format. Concise and easily accessible lists combine with captivating reviews to entice readers to roam throughout this volume." SLJ
For a fuller review see: Booklist, Oct. 1, 1995

✓ **George, Nelson**
Blackface; reflections on African Americans and the movies. HarperCollins Pubs. 1994 224p il $22; pa $12   **791.43**
1. African Americans in motion pictures
ISBN 0-06-017120-0; 0-06-092658-9 (pa)   LC 94-10686
Also available in hardcover from Borgo Press
The author's "recollection of his involvement with cinema, containing a time line of African American film milestones from the past three decades, can function both as a memoir and as an assessment of African American films. Worthwhile for both film and black studies students." Booklist

✓ **Hilger, Michael, 1940-**
From savage to nobleman; images of Native Americans in film. Scarecrow Press 1995 296p $54.50   **791.43**
1. Indians in motion pictures
ISBN 0-8108-2978-9   LC 94-42057
"Hilger traces the portrayal of Native Americans, from the silents and early sound films through films of each decade, covering over 800 films. An introduction discusses the traditional images of the Noble Red Man and Savage. The final chapter discusses new images based on tribal identities in recent films." Publisher's note
"A welcome addition to the film literature, libraries may want to use this book as a selection tool for their video collections." Booklist
Includes bibliographical references

Kerr, Walter, 1913-1996
The silent clowns. Knopf 1975 372p il $20   **791.43**
1. Motion pictures—History and criticism 2. Comedians
ISBN 0-394-46907-0
Also available in paperback from Da Capo Press

Kerr, Walter, 1913-1996—*Continued*
"A book about the great and near-great comic artists who carried the language of the silent screen to its peak of eloquence . . . and about the roots and reaches of the form itself." N Y Times Book Rev

Life goes to the movies. Time-Life Bks. 1975 305p il o.p.; Random House Value Pub. paperback available $19.99   **791.43**
1. Motion pictures—Pictorial works
ISBN 0-517-62585-7 (pa)
This volume contains some 750 selections from Life's files which portray the stars, the starlets, the movies, the studios, behind the scenes, the Academy Awards and the art that the magazine brought to its photographic coverage of movie-making

Maltin, Leonard
Leonard Maltin's movie and video guide. New Am. Lib. pa $19.95   **791.43**
1. Motion pictures 2. Videotapes
Annual. First published 1969 with title: TV movies. Title varies
Contains summaries of films and made-for-television movies playing on both commercial and pay-TV. Films currently available on video cassette are identified

Mast, Gerald, 1940-1988
A short history of the movies. Macmillan il pa $45   **791.43**
1. Motion pictures—History and criticism
First published 1971 by Pegasus Press. (6th edition 1996 edited by Bruce F. Kawin) Periodically revised
The author traces the history of motion pictures from their birth to the present day. Among the topics discussed are the coming of sound, the studio system and the cinemas of various countries including Russia, France and Germany. D. W. Griffith, Mack Sennet and Charlie Chaplin are among the personalities covered
Includes bibliography

Osborne, Robert A.
65 years of the Oscar; the official history of the Academy Awards; [by] Robert Osborne. 2nd ed. Abbeville Press 1994 352p il $65   **791.43**
1. Academy Awards (Motion pictures)
ISBN 1-55859-715-8   LC 94-198157
First published 1989 with title: 60 years of the Oscar
This volume "is organized around decade-length segments of the Motion Picture Academy's history. Each segment opens with a reckoning of the academy's activities followed by a year-by-year roundup of the Oscar ceremonies. All the nominees, plus the technical and special award winners, are listed. Photos abound, many in color." Libr J

Past imperfect; history according to the movies; general editor, Mark C. Carnes; edited by Ted Mico, John Miller-Monzon, and David Rubel. Holt & Co. 1995 304p il (Henry Holt reference book) $30; pa $17.95   **791.43**
1. Motion pictures—History and criticism
ISBN 0-8050-3759-4; 0-8050-3760-8 (pa)
    LC 95-354
"A Society of American Historians book"

"The editors have gathered four- to six-page essays that provide insightful comparisons of 60 films on historic subjects with historians' views of the subjects. Essays are written by qualified experts including Gore Vidal, Antonia Fraser and Arthur Schlesinger, Jr. The arrangement is chronological according to the subject. . . . Excellent for reports as well as for browsing." Book Rep

Phillips, Gene D.
Alfred Hitchcock. Twayne Pubs. 1984 211p il (Twayne's filmmakers series) $22.95; pa $14.95   **791.43**
1. Hitchcock, Alfred, 1899-1980 2. Motion pictures
ISBN 0-8057-9293-7; 0-8057-9301-1 (pa)
    LC 83-22786
"Hitchcock was a consummate craftsman who maintained control over every aspect of his films from story to costuming to lighting to scoring. Gene D. Philips . . . makes all this clear in an excellent little book on the work of a man who believed that film was 'life with the dull bits removed.'" Choice
Includes bibliography and filmography

Robinson, David, 1930-
From peep show to palace; the birth of American film; foreword by Martin Scorsese. Columbia Univ. Press 1995 213p il $29.50
    791.43
1. Motion pictures—History and criticism 2. Motion picture industry
ISBN 0-231-10338-7   LC 95-19014
This examination of the early cinema describes slide projecting devices of the 19th century, Thomas Edison's kinetoscope of 1891, the Lumiére brothers' film projector of 1895, and the early films of D. W. Griffith
Includes bibliographical references

Schneider, Steve
That's all folks! the art of Warner Bros. animation; foreword by Ray Bradbury. Holt & Co. 1988 252p il $39.95; pa $19.95   **791.43**
1. Warner Bros. Cartoons 2. Animated films
ISBN 0-8050-0889-6; 0-8050-1485-3 (pa)
    LC 88-81823
"A Donald Hutter book"
The first section of this book "chronicles Warner's growth and development over four decades, while the second part, 'The Stars,' contains short treatments of the major characters and their unique personalties." Libr J
This book is "more than a chronicle of the studio's creative eras under the direction of animators like Friz Freleng, Tex Avery, Bob Clampett and Chuck Jones; it is also something of a treatise on animation. And best of all, this volume is a compendium of classic Warner artwork." N Y Times Book Rev

Scott, Elaine, 1940-
Movie magic; behind the scenes with special effects. Morrow Junior Bks. 1995 95p il $16
    791.43
1. Cinematography
ISBN 0-688-12477-1   LC 95-2166
The author contracts old and new special effects techniques, discusses the influence computers have had on

Scott, Elaine, 1940——_Continued_
the film industry, and describes how such tools as
mattes, models, and special makeups are used today

Shale, Richard, 1947-
The Academy Awards index; the complete
categorical and chronological record; compiled
with an introduction by Richard Shale; foreword
by Robert Wise. Greenwood Press 1993 785p il
$79.50   **791.43**
1. Academy Awards (Motion pictures)
ISBN 0-313-27738-9   LC 92-40226
"Beginning with a brief history of the Academy of
Motion Picture Arts and Sciences, part 1 lists nominees
and winners of annual awards by category. . . . Part 2
is a chronological list of Academy Awards. Each year's
listings include the date and location of the awards cere-
mony and (except for the first year) the date the nominations were announced." Booklist

Sklar, Robert
Film; an international history of the medium.
Abrams 1993 560p il $49.50   **791.43**
1. Motion pictures—History and criticism
ISBN 0-8109-3321-7   LC 93-12279
Also available in paperback from Prentice-Hall
The author discusses "the early history of cinema, the
rise of the Hollywood monolith, art films, documentaries,
animation and experimental filmmaking. Both richly entertaining and intellectually stimulating, this survey will
serve as a basic sourcebook for film aficionados, students, casual moviegoers and historians." Publ Wkly

Smith, Julian, 1937-
Chaplin. Twayne Pubs. 1984 161p il (Twayne's
filmmakers series) $20.95; pa $14.95   **791.43**
1. Chaplin, Charlie, 1889-1977 2. Motion pictures
ISBN 0-8057-9294-5; 0-8057-9302-X (pa)
                    LC 83-22772
The author devotes "more time and space than usual
to the last three films Chaplin made in the US, 'The
Great Dictator,' 'Monsieur Verdoux,' and 'Limelight.'
Smith is persuasive if not thoroughly convincing in his
attempt to enhance the stature of these three films. He is
also very helpful as he places Chaplin in the development of the motion picture." Choice
Includes bibliography

Taub, Eric
Gaffers, grips, and best boys. rev ed. St.
Martin's Press 1994 276p il pa $12.95   **791.43**
1. Cinematography—Biography 2. Motion pictures—
Biography
ISBN 0-312-11276-9   LC 94-28113
First published 1987
The author "draws on interviews with contemporary
filmmakers—from director to camera operator and sound
mixer—to give an insider's look at who does what in the
making of a motion picture." Booklist

791.4303   Motion pictures— Encyclopedias and dictionaries

Konigsberg, Ira
The complete film dictionary. New Am. Lib.
1987 420p il hardcover o.p. paperback available
$18.95   **791.4303**
1. Motion pictures—Dictionaries
ISBN 0-452-00980-4 (pa)   LC 87-5747
"An excellent source for high schools, this dictionary
covers all aspects of the film industry—technology, production, distribution, economics, history, and criticism.
Over 3,500 clear, easy-to-understand entries also address
the artistic approach to film making by genre: fictional,
documentary, and experimental. Line drawings and mo-
tion-picture stills complement the text." Nichols. Guide
to Ref Books for Sch Media Cent. 4th edition

791.44   Radio

Lackmann, Ronald W.
Same time—same station; an A-Z guide to radio
from Jack Benny to Howard Stern; [by] Ron
Lackmann. Facts on File 1995 370p il $45
                           791.44
1. Radio programs
ISBN 0-8160-2862-1   LC 95-5662
A "look at the history of radio, both as a source of
entertainment and of news. Lackman gives synopsis of
hundreds of the old favorite shows, from the 1920s on,
with airtimes, short biographies of relevant personalities
and network figures, and excellent descriptions of radio
genres such as the popular mysteries and soap operas.
. . . The black-and-white photographs aptly create a feeling for the times." SLJ
For a fuller review see: Booklist, Feb. 15, 1996

791.45   Television

Day, Nancy
Sensational TV; trash or journalism? Enslow
Pubs. 1996 112p il (Issues in focus) lib bdg
$18.95   **791.45**
1. Broadcast journalism 2. Talk shows 3. Television
programs
ISBN 0-89490-733-6   LC 95-35675
Questions whether the mass media, especially television, present an accurate representation of the news or
whether it is more concerned with the sensational story
"The book is clearly intended to stimulate debate and
discussion. . . . Used by a creative and principled teacher, the book could be very useful in helping young minds
experience the joy of engaging issues having to do with
our society." Sci Books Films
Includes bibliographical references

Gerrold, David, 1944-

The world of Star Trek; written by David Gerrold in association with Starlog Magazine. rev ed. Bluejay Bks. 1984 xx, 209p il o.p.   **791.45**
1. Star trek (Television program) 2. Star trek (Motion picture)

First published 1973   LC 84-9205

The author follows the history of Star Trek from its beginning as a television series through the first three motion pictures

"The book, clearly a labor of love, is a bit short on critical insights, a fact that may not please serious students of popular culture. However, . . . most ST fans will enjoy this effort by a man who clearly loves their favorite show." Booklist

Koppel, Ted

Nightline; history in the making and the making of television; [by] Ted Koppel and Kyle Gibson. Times Bks. 1996 477p il $25   **791.45**
1. Nightline (Television program)
ISBN 0-8129-2478-9   LC 95-53838

Gibson "supplies the narrative here; Koppel's off-camera 'voice' appears in a long chapter on conducting live TV interviews and in the introduction and 'final thoughts.' But the *on*-camera words of Koppel and his *Nightline* guests pervade this retrospective: chapters full of excerpts from transcripts explain how and why *Nightline* got on the air and how it works, discuss the technological and stylistic innovations that have allowed the show to expand its journalistic envelope, and examine big stories where *Nightline* broke new ground." Booklist

Kurtz, Howard, 1953-

Hot air; all talk, all the time. Times Bks. 1996 407p $25   **791.45**
1. Talk shows
ISBN 0-8129-2624-2   LC 96-119318

This is an examination of American television and radio talk shows and their hosts. "Talk shows, [the author] writes, have become 'a powerful vehicle that trumpets the most extreme and polarizing views, that panders to sensationalism, that spreads innuendo and misinformation with stunning efficiency." N Y Times Book Rev

McGrath, Tom

MTV: the making of a revolution. Running Press 1996 208p il $22.95   **791.45**
1. MTV Networks Inc. 2. Music videos
ISBN 1-56138-703-7   LC 95-70676

The author "examines the cable channel that changed TV, pop music, and movies alike as it rose from an experiment in narrow-casting to a multimillion-dollar business alleged to be capable of making or breaking music acts. . . . Ultimately, this is the story of the war for MTV's corporate soul as told through the travails of its creators." Booklist

Reeves-Stevens, Judith

The art of Star Trek; by Judith & Garfield Reeves-Stevens; introduction by Herman Zimmerman. Pocket Bks. 1995 295p il $50
791.45
1. Star trek (Television program) 2. Star trek (Motion picture)
ISBN 0-671-89804-3   LC 95-231670

The work represented in this collection ranges from sketches, paintings and animation to sets, costumes and alien make-up. Covers all incarnations of Star Trek from the original series through Voyager

Shatner, William, 1931-

Star trek memories; [by] William Shatner with Chris Kreski. HarperCollins Pubs. 1993 306p il $22; pa $6.99   **791.45**
1. Star trek (Television program)
ISBN 0-06-017734-9; 0-06-109235-5 (pa)
LC 92-56233

"Captain Kirk revisits all those years spent on the *Star Trek* set—both in the TV studio and for the various movies." Libr J

"YA trekkers, particularly those into reruns of the original 'Star Trek' shows, will relish Shatner's chatty trip down memory lane." Booklist

Solow, Herbert

Inside Star trek; [by] Herbert F. Solow and Robert H. Justman. Pocket Bks. 1996 xx, 458p il $30   **791.45**
1. Star trek (Television program)
ISBN 0-671-89628-8

The authors, both members of the production staff, offer behind-the-scenes glimpses of the classic television program

Thompson, Robert J., 1959-

Television's second golden age; from Hill Street blues to ER: Hill Street blues, St. Elsewhere, Cagney & Lacey, Moonlighting, L.A. law, Thirtysomething, China Beach, Twin peaks, Northern exposure, Picket fences, with brief reflections on Homicide, NYPD blue, Chicago hope, and other quality dramas. Continuum 1995 220p il $27.50   **791.45**
1. Television programs
ISBN 0-8264-0901-6   LC 96-4675

A multidisciplinary examination of television drama over the past 15 years. The economic factors influencing the development of quality programming are explored
Includes bibliographical references

791.6 Pageantry

French, Stephanie Breaux, 1969-

The cheerleading book. Contemporary Bks. 1995 119p il pa $14.95   **791.6**
1. Cheerleading
ISBN 0-8092-3411-4   LC 94-47134

This "activity book includes: The history of cheerleading; The importance of warming up; Cheers—

French, Stephanie Breaux, 1969——_Continued_
with hand and leg motions; Sidelines—or cheering routines; Jumps—the most difficult [and fun] aspect of cheerleading." Publisher's note

Kuch, K. D. (Kathy Diane)
The cheerleaders almanac; illustrated by J.J. Smith-Moore; endorsed by National Cheerleaders Association. Bullseye Bks. 1996 80p il pa $4.99
791.6
1. Cheerleading
ISBN 0-679-87763-0　　　　LC 95-36533
Explains how to survive cheerleading tryouts and perform amazing stunts. Includes information on the latest trends and quotes from cheerleaders across the country

792　Stage presentations

Bordman, Gerald Martin
American theatre: a chronicle of comedy and drama, 1930-1969; [by] Gerald Bordman. Oxford Univ. Press 1996 472p $60　　　　**792**
1. Theater—United States 2. American drama—History and criticism
ISBN 0-19-509079-9　　　　LC 96-17572
Also available previous volumes in series covering 1869-1914 $95 (ISBN 0-19-503764-2); 1914-1930 $49.95 (ISBN 0-19-509078-0)
This is a season-by-season chronicle of the American theater. Printed in double columns with bold-faced play titles and names of figures, the text traces all New York productions with details of plot, critical reaction, and performance history
"Although this is a valuable reference work, reflecting an exhaustive knowledge of the theater, the vivid prose and memorable images also make it a joy to read. The reference value is enhanced by indexes to play titles, people, sources, and organizations." Choice

Corson, Richard
Stage makeup. Prentice-Hall il $75　　　　**792**
1. Theatrical makeup
First published 1942 by Appleton. (8th edition 1990) Periodically revised
The author discusses the art and technique of theatrical makeup, covering such topics as facial anatomy, various methods for applying greasepaint and other makeup, and the use of beards, wigs, and prosthetic pieces

Franks, Don, 1945-
Entertainment awards; a music, cinema, theatre and broadcasting reference, 1928 through 1993. McFarland & Co. 1996 536p $75　　　　**792**
1. Awards
ISBN 0-7864-0031-5　　　　LC 94-24192
Replaces the author's Tony, Grammy, Emmy, Country, published 1986
This book lists the winners of 13 major awards in the fields of music, film, theater and TV programming
For a review see: Booklist, Sept. 15, 1996

Gillette, J. Michael
Theatrical design and production; an introduction to scene design and construction, lighting, sound, costume, and makeup. 3rd ed. Mayfield 1997 573p il $44.95　　　　**792**
1. Theaters—Stage setting and scenery
ISBN 1-55934-701-5　　　　LC 96-21642
First published 1987
"Gillette presents a detailed, fully illustrated guide to theater craft. Stage equipment, tools and materials for building a set, techniques of scene painting, key considerations of lighting, multimedia projectors, theory and practice of costume design and makeup—all of this and more is covered in a readable text." Booklist
Includes bibliographical references

James, Thurston, 1933-
The what, where, when of theater props; an illustrated chronology from arrowheads to video games. Betterway Bks. 1992 222p il $29.95; pa $19.95　　　　**792**
1. Theaters—Stage setting and scenery
ISBN 1-55870-258-X; 1-55870-257-1 (pa)
LC 92-14963
"Essentially a dictionary, this book is an illustrated guide designed to provide historical and cultural reference for the theatrical properties master in identifying both common and obscure items required by many plays." Choice
"Even though the book was written as an aid to theater students and teachers, its clear illustrations, concise text, chronology within subject area, index, and emphasis on period detail make it a valuable tool for history students as well." SLJ

Matson, Katinka
The working actor; a guide to the profession; [by] Katinka Matson and Judith Katz. rev ed. Penguin Bks. 1993 189p pa $12　　　　**792**
1. Acting
ISBN 0-14-014433-1　　　　LC 93-12324
First published 1976 by Viking
In the first chapter of this guide actors B.D. Wong, Ally Sheedy, Jason Alexander, James McDaniel, and Jane Adams discuss their careers. The following chapters cover training; where the work is; trying out; agents and managers; tools of the profession; and union membership. Quotes from additional actors, directors, agents and others appear throughout. Also included are annotated listings of places to study and addresses of organizations to contact about auditions

O'Donnol, Shirley Miles, 1915-
American costume, 1915-1970; a source book for the stage costumer. Indiana Univ. Press 1982 270p il $39.95; pa $19.95　　　　**792**
1. Costume—History
ISBN 0-253-30589-6; 0-253-20543-3 (pa)
LC 81-48390
"Arrangement is by seven style periods within the time sequence 1915 to 1970. Within each division, O'Donnol provides textual descriptions (augmented by

O'Donnol, Shirley Miles, 1915——*Continued*
photographs and drawings) of typical sorts of period clothing, including evening wear, sportswear, sleepwear, coats, and even accessories and hairstyles. Suggestions are made for adopting each period's fundamental style to the stage." Booklist
Includes bibliography

Parker, W. Oren (Wilford Oren)
Scene design and stage lighting; [by] W. Oren Parker, R. Craig Wolf. Harcourt Brace & Co. il $46.75   **792**
1. Theaters—Stage setting and scenery 2. Stage lighting
First published 1963. (7th edition 1996) Periodically revised
An illustrated introduction to the technical aspects of stage settings and properties from design to construction. The pivotal role of lighting to the success of a production is emphasized. The latest developments in supplies and equipment are presented

Poisson, Camille L., 1948-
Theater and the adolescent actor; building a successful school program. Archon Bks. 1994 228p il $29.50   **792**
1. Drama in education 2. Theater—Production and direction 3. Acting
ISBN 0-208-02380-1   LC 93-36406
"This manual includes acting exercises for the body, mind, and imagination; lists of common materials needed for each lesson, sample charts, diagrams, forms and worksheets; as well as a running commentary to guide the teacher through the lesson plans." Publisher's note
The author's "specifics on musical selections and production will prove especially helpful. She also supplies annotated lists of plays for each age group, along with instructions on building a flat." Booklist
Includes glossary and bibliography

Theatre world. Applause Theatre Bk. Pubs. il
792
1. Theater—United States
Apply to publisher for available volumes and prices
Annual. Started publication with the 1944/45 season
Editor: 1944/45-1962/63, Daniel Blum; 1964/65-date, John Willis
A "survey of the American theater, with many illustrations. Emphasis is on Broadway productions, but attention is given to off-Broadway, regional theater, and touring companies. Lists casts, dates of opening and closing, etc., but gives no critical comment. Includes biographical sketches of outstanding players, producers, directors, designers, etc. Obituaries." Sheehy. Guide to Ref Books. 10th edition

Whelan, Jeremy
The ABC's of acting; (the art, business & craft); edited by Tom Wiecks. Grey Heron Bks. 1990 137p il pa $10.95   **792**
1. Acting
ISBN 0-935566-26-0   LC 89-091818
The author "addresses such topics as preparing the voice and body, creating emotions, interpreting the script, using objects, and rehearsing. The book also makes clear and useful distinctions between acting for the camera and acting on stage. . . . Through this book, beginners will be well on the way to understanding how to develop a character." SLJ

792.03   Theater—Encyclopedias and dictionaries

Bordman, Gerald Martin
The concise Oxford companion to American theatre. Oxford Univ. Press 1987 451p hardcover o.p. paperback available $13.95   **792.03**
1. Theater—United States—Dictionaries 2. American drama—Dictionaries
ISBN 0-19-506327-9 (pa)   LC 86-33294
An abridgment of The Oxford companion to American theatre, 1984 edition
This version contains "approximately 2,000 entries. . . . It appears that individual entries have not been shortened, but that approximately 40 percent of the parent volume's entries have been deleted altogether." Booklist

The Oxford companion to American theatre; [by] Gerald Bordman. 2nd ed. Oxford Univ. Press 1992 735p $60   **792.03**
1. Theater—United States—Dictionaries 2. American drama—Dictionaries
ISBN 0-19-507246-4
First published 1984
"In addition to entries for actors, directors, playwrights, theater companies, etc., and a few selected topics (e.g., censorship), about half the space is allotted to individual plays or musicals of merit or popularity. Some foreign works are also included, as are a number of non-American figures whose careers had an impact on theatre in the U.S. Emphasis is on Broadway and the New York stage." Guide to Ref Books. 11th edition

Cambridge guide to American theatre; edited by Don B. Wilmeth and Tice L. Miller. Cambridge Univ. Press 1993 547p il $54.95; pa $24.95
792.03
1. Theater—United States—Dictionaries 2. American drama—Dictionaries
ISBN 0-521-40134-8; 0-521-56444-1 (pa)
LC 92-35030
Based on The Cambridge guide to world theatre
This guide "offers brief, alphabetically arranged essays on American theatrical figures—actors, playwrights, producers, directors, designers—plays, and major theatres from the art form's origins in native American rituals to the present. . . . Wonderfully compact, well written and generously illustrated, this is recommended for most libraries." Libr J

The **Cambridge** guide to world theatre; edited by Martin Banham; editorial advisory board, James Brandon [et al.] Cambridge Univ. Press 1988 1104p il $80; pa $27.95   **792.03**
1. Theater—Dictionaries
ISBN 0-521-26595-9; 0-521-42903-X (pa)
LC 88-25804
This work "contains signed, alphabetically arranged articles on theatrical history and tradition for countries and cultures throughout the world. Everything from Shakespearean performers, Greek drama, and Broadway musicals to mime, jugglers, actors, directors, playwrights, designers, censorship, and criticism is covered. Cross-references connect related articles, and over 500 black-and-white illustrations support the volume." Nichols. Guide to Ref Books for Sch Media Cent. 4th edition
Includes bibliographies

The **Facts** on File dictionary of the theatre; edited by William Packard, David Pickering, Charlotte Savidge. Facts on File 1988 556p $35; pa $15.95   **792.03**
1. Theater—Dictionaries
ISBN 0-8160-1841-3; 0-8160-1945-2 (pa)
LC 88-28379
An alphabetical arrangement of entries on plays, playwrights, actors and their roles, critics, awards, and biographies of theatrical luminaries

The **Oxford** companion to the theatre; edited by Phyllis Hartnoll. 4th ed. Oxford Univ. Press 1983 934p il $60   **792.03**
1. Theater—Dictionaries
ISBN 0-19-211546-4
Also available in a concise edition for $45 (ISBN 0-19-866136-3); pa $10.95 (ISBN 0-19-281102-9)
First published 1951
"Offers definitions of terms, sketches of theater personalities of all periods, articles on specific theater companies and buildings, and historical profiles of theater in individual countries and cities. Scope is international, although emphasis is on British and American theater." Guide to Ref Books. 11th edition

792.09 Theater—Historical and geographic treatment

Brockett, Oscar Gross, 1923-
History of the theatre. Allyn & Bacon il $77.25
792.09
1. Theater—History 2. Drama—History and criticism
First published 1968. (7th edition 1995) Periodically revised
This work traces the development of the theater from primitive times to the present, with an emphasis on European theater

Henderson, Mary C.
Theater in America; 250 years of plays, players, and productions. New, updated ed. Abrams 1996 352p il $60   **792.09**
1. Theater—United States—History
ISBN 0-8109-3884-7   LC 95-38148
First published 1986

This illustrated popular history of U.S. theater "is unique in separately chronicling each profession's participants—producers, directors, designers, actors, and even architects, so that the reader easily can trace the development of each through time. . . . The distinctive layout and the many quality illustrations will make this a valuable addition to theater collections." Libr J
Includes bibliographical references

Hodges, C. Walter (Cyril Walter), 1909-
The Globe restored; a study of the Elizabethan theatre. Coward-McCann 1954 c1953 199p il maps o.p.; Native Am. Bk. Pubs. reprint available $59; pa $39   **792.09**
1. Shakespeare, William, 1564-1616—Stage history 2. Globe Theatre (London, England) 3. Theater—Great Britain—History
ISBN 1-878592-01-7; 1-878592-00-9 (pa)
Also available in hardcover from Somerset Pubs.
First published 1953 in the United Kingdom
An illustrated study of the theater, and especially the Globe, during Shakespeare's time. The book is based on research in England and America

The **Oxford** illustrated history of theatre; edited by John Russell Brown. Oxford Univ. Press 1995 582p il $49.95   **792.09**
1. Theater—History
ISBN 0-19-212997-X   LC 95-231683
Covering theatre history from the ancient Greeks to the 1990s, this "resource provides a wide variety of information from basic theatre chronology to detailed analyses of several well-known and important plays and playwrights. . . . The emphasis is on European and Western theatre, but a chapter provides a concise summary on Southern and Eastern Asian theatre." SLJ
Includes bibliographical references

792.5 Opera

Cross, Milton
The new Milton Cross' complete stories of the great operas. rev and enl ed, edited by Karl Kohrs. Doubleday 1955 688p o.p.   **792.5**
1. Opera—Stories, plots, etc.
First published 1947 with title: Milton Cross' complete stories of the great operas
This reference work describes over seventy famous operas, giving a plot synopsis and important arias. Also includes a short history of the development of the opera as a musical form and ballet as a traditional part of opera production
Includes bibliographies

The new Milton Cross' more stories of the great operas; by Milton Cross and Karl Kohrs. Revised and expanded by Karl Kohrs. Doubleday 1980 802p o.p.   **792.5**
1. Opera—Stories, plots, etc.
First published 1971 with title: Milton Cross' more stories of the great operas
This book describes 69 additional operas
Includes glossary and bibliography

Freeman, John W.

The Metropolitan Opera stories of the great operas. Metropolitan Opera Guild 1984-1996 2v v1 $24.95; v2 $35 **792.5**

1. Opera—Stories, plots, etc.

ISBN 0-393-01888-1 (v1); 0-393-04051-8 (v2)

Volume one contains the plots of 150 of the world's most popular operas including biographies of each of the 72 composers represented together with historical background information relevant to each work. Volume two includes 125 additional plot summaries covering less known works from the early operas of Monteverdi to that of contemporary composers, such as John Adams

Lazarus, John

The opera handbook. Hall, G.K. & Co. 1990 c1987 242p il (Performing arts) $30; pa $15.95 **792.5**

1. Opera—Stories, plots, etc.

ISBN 0-8161-9094-1; 0-8161-1827-2 (pa)

LC 89-77758

First published 1987 in the United Kingdom

This work "contains 200 opera plots selected according to number of performances given by major opera houses in the 1980s. . . . It presents concise historical backgrounds, premiere dates, plot summaries, overviews of each work emphasizing its relationship with other operas of similar theme, plot, or characterization, discography, and bibliography. It also includes a glossary of opera terms [and] biographical sketches of contemporary artists." Libr J

The **Oxford** illustrated history of opera; edited by Roger Parker. Oxford Univ. Press 1994 541p il $49.95 **792.5**

1. Opera

ISBN 0-19-816282-0

LC 93-24898

This "is a collection of essays presenting a chronological account of major and even minor movements and composers and works in the history of opera from its inception in Florence in the mid-1590s. . . . There's lots of well-presented information here." Booklist

Includes bibliographical references

The **Viking** opera guide; edited by Amanda Holden with Nicholas Kenyon and Stephen Walsh; consultant editor, Rodney Milnes; recordings consultant, Alan Blyth; with a preface by Sir Colin Davis. Viking 1993 [i.e. 1994] xxii, 1305p il $69.95 **792.5**

1. Opera—Stories, plots, etc.

ISBN 0-670-81292-7

LC 94-143500

Also available CD-ROM version

This guide covers "843 composers and 1,587 operas. . . . An outline of each composer's career and overall contribution is followed by details of each opera—including date of composition, premieres, cast lists, orchestration, plot synopsis, background, and musical highlights, plus recording and edition information." Publisher's note

792.6 Musical plays

Bordman, Gerald Martin

American musical theatre; a chronicle; [by] Gerald Bordman. 2nd ed. Oxford Univ. Press 1992 821p $62.50 **792.6**

1. Musicals

ISBN 0-19-507242-1

First published 1978

This "chronology traces the musical from its origins through the 1989-90 season, providing a delightful mix of history, criticism and theatrical lore." Libr J

Lerner, Alan Jay, 1918-1986

The musical theatre; a celebration. McGraw-Hill 1986 240p il o.p.; Da Capo Press paperback available $16.95 **792.6**

1. Musicals

ISBN 0-306-80364-X (pa)

LC 86-18499

This "history of the musical theater employs a chronological approach beginning with 19th-century European antecedents (Offenbach, Strauss, Gilbert and Sullivan) and continuing to 1985." Choice

"This fine last offering by one of Broadway's giants is recommended for most libraries and for all fans of musical comedy." Libr J

Includes bibliography

Lynch, Richard Chigley, 1932-

Musicals! a complete selection guide for local productions. 2nd ed. American Lib. Assn. 1994 404p pa $40 **792.6**

1. Musicals—Directories

ISBN 0-8389-0627-3

LC 93-27387

First published 1984

This work "contains information about 500 musicals . . . available for production by community theaters and schools. Listed alphabetically by title, each entry includes date of original production, playwright, composer, lyricist, plot summary, licensing agent and music publisher, recordings and librettos available . . ., and cast. . . . Indexes are by composer, lyricist, and librettist and by song title. The plot summaries are the most useful and interesting aspect of the book." Booklist

792.7 Variety shows

Cooper, Ralph

Amateur night at the Apollo; Ralph Cooper presents five decades of great entertainment; [by] Ralph Cooper with Steve Dougherty. Harper & Row 1990 260p il o.p. **792.7**

1. Apollo Theatre (New York, N.Y.) 2. African American entertainers 3. Harlem (New York, N.Y.)

LC 89-46522

This book includes "photographs and anecdotes about the astounding parade of performers who have crossed the Apollo stage, from Ella Fitzgerald and Pearl Bailey to Dionne Warwick and Luther Vandross. Along the way Mr. Cooper provides a thumbnail social history of Harlem and its night life over the last half century." N Y Times Book Rev

792.8   Ballet and modern dance

Dufort, Antony
   Ballet steps; practice to performance. rev & expanded ed. Potter 1990 160p il $18   **792.8**
   1. Ballet
   ISBN 0-517-57770-4   LC 89-37078
   First published 1985
   This work "describes and demonstrates (through handsome pencil sketches based on photographs) the major steps and movements of ballet. . . . A wonderful introduction to the movements of ballet for enthusiasts as well as for young dancers." Booklist
   Includes glossary and bibliographical references

Garfunkel, Trudy
   On wings of joy; the story of ballet from the 16th century to today; written by Trudy Garfunkel. Little, Brown 1994 194p il $18.95   **792.8**
   1. Ballet—History
   ISBN 0-316-30412-3   LC 93-41526
   After presenting "a little background on primitive, ancient, and medieval dance history, [the author] uses a storytelling approach to relate the lives and contributions of those who were influential in the development of ballet over the last 400 years." Voice Youth Advocates
   "The author does an excellent job of weaving historical events into her discussion of the dancers and their art. . . . A very readable, enjoyable book for young adults interested in music and dance." Booklist
   Includes glossary and bibliography

Haskins, James, 1941-
   Black dance in America; a history through its people. Crowell 1990 232p il o.p.   **792.8**
   1. African American dancers
                LC 89-35529
   The author "begins with the practice of 'dancing the slaves' on the ships coming from Africa; traces the origins of popular dances like the cakewalk, Charleston, tap, and modern dance; and introduces the reader to a host of interesting black dancers who fought through the multiple layers of prejudice in this country to pursue their dreams. . . . Haskins' writing is pleasant and will be easily absorbed by a wide-ranging audience." Voice Youth Advocates
   Includes bibliography

Long, Richard A., 1927-
   The black tradition in American modern dance; photographs selected and annotated by Joe Nash. Rizzoli Int. Publs. 1989 192p il $29.95   **792.8**
   1. Dancing—History 2. African American dancers
   ISBN 0-8478-1092-5   LC 89-31739
   A look at Afro-American dance influences and traditions. Pearl Primus, Katherine Dunham and Alvin Ailey are among those profiled
   Includes bibliographical references

Mitchell, Jack
   Alvin Ailey American Dance Theater: Jack Mitchell photographs; foreword by Judith Jamison; introduction by Richard Philp. Andrews & McMeel 1993 129p il $29.95; pa $19.95   **792.8**
   1. Alvin Ailey American Dance Theater 2. Dancing—Pictorial works
   ISBN 0-8362-4509-1; 0-8362-4508-3 (pa)
                LC 93-13582
   "A Donna Martin book"
   This collection of black-and-white photographs traces the work of choreographer Alvin Ailey over a thirty-year period, arranged chronologically from 1961 to 1993
   "Mitchell has done us all a great service by preserving these otherwise ephemeral creations." Booklist

Warren, Gretchen
   Classical ballet technique; [by] Gretchen Ward Warren; photographs by Susan Cook. University of S. Fla. Press 1989 395p il $85; pa $39.95   **792.8**
   1. Ballet
   ISBN 0-8130-0895-6; 0-8130-0945-6 (pa)
                LC 89-31141
   Text and numerous photographs explain the correct execution of ballet steps
   "General material on basic concepts, body structure and proportion, and ballet class proceed this extraordinary manual and guide." Booklist
   Includes glossary and bibliography

792.803   Ballet and modern dance— Encyclopedias and dictionaries

Koegler, Horst
   The concise Oxford dictionary of ballet. 2nd ed. Oxford Univ. Press 1982 459p il o.p.   **792.803**
   1. Ballet—Dictionaries
                LC 82-237993
   Original German edition, 1972. First published in the United States 1977 as an English adaptation
   Over 5,000 entries discuss: ballet history, theaters, dancers, choreographers, composers, schools and companies, and terms

792.9   Stage productions

Shakespeare: an illustrated stage history; edited by Jonathan Bate and Russell Jackson. Oxford Univ. Press 1996 253p il $39.95   **792.9**
   1. Shakespeare, William, 1564-1616—Dramatic production
   ISBN 0-19-812372-8   LC 95-12059
   "Twelve chapters describe the history of Shakespeare on the stage from various perspectives: archaeological (discussions of recent finds), historical (stories of actor-managers, directors, and companies), and personal (Judi Dench's discussion of her career playing Shakespeare), to name a few." Libr J
   "This beautifully illustrated volume . . . does fairly exhaustively recount the how of Shakespeare's rise from being one of many Elizabethans scribbling plays during a culturally fertile time to overwhelming preeminence in the theatrical canon." Booklist
   Includes bibliographical references

793.7 Games not characterized by action

Gardner, Martin, 1914-
Knotted doughnuts and other mathematical entertainments. Freeman, W.H. 1986 278p il pa $12.95   **793.7**
1. Mathematical recreations
ISBN 0-7167-1799-9   LC 85-31134
This volume contains "challenging games, puzzles, paradoxes, and brainteasers. . . . Gardner presents both age-old games and recently invented ones, all with clear instructions, background on game history, and a general sense of fun. Answers are included for each conundrum." Booklist
Includes bibliographies

Heafford, Philip Ernest
Great book of math puzzles; [by] Philip Heafford. Sterling 1993 96p il pa $5.95   **793.7**
1. Mathematical recreations
ISBN 0-8069-8814-2   LC 93-25890
An abridged edition of the author's The math entertainer, published 1959 by Emerson Bks.
Over 200 mathematical teasers grouped in thirty "quizzes," with answers provided at the end
"This puzzle book can challenge even the most skilled mathematician. . . . Students who are bored with working problem after problem from the traditional textbook will find the 'Great Book of Math Puzzles' challenging and refreshing." Voice Youth Advocates

Tahan, Malba, 1895-
The man who counted; a collection of mathematical adventures; illustrated by Patricia Reid Baquero & translated by Leslie Clark and Alastair Reid. Norton 1993 244p il hardcover o.p. paperback available $14.95   **793.7**
1. Mathematical recreations
ISBN 0-393-30934-7 (pa)   LC 92-18822
"First published in Brazil in 1949 by the mathematician Julio de Melo e Sousa (Tahan is the imaginary Arab author he claimed to have translated), [this book] is a series of . . . 'Arabian Nights'-style tales, with each story built around a classic mathematical puzzle." Libr J
"This small book is a joy. . . . These are beautifully expressive tales that find mathematical puzzles and numerical intrigue in human situations and speak not just of solving the problems but of the needs we all have for friendship, love, and beauty." Booklist

793.73 Puzzles and puzzle games

Eckler, A. Ross (Albert Ross), 1927-
Making the alphabet dance; recreational word play; by Ross Eckler. St. Martin's Press 1996 xx, 279p $23.95   **793.73**
1. Word games
ISBN 0-312-14032-0   LC 95-25472
This work "includes explanations of acrostics, palindromes, anagrams, word squares, and word worms [with]

pages of examples of each type of word play. . . . Anyone who writes, does crossword puzzles, or plays Scrabble will find this book a gem." Libr J

793.8 Magic and related activities

Blackstone, Harry, 1885-1965
The Blackstone book of magic & illusion; [by] Harry Blackstone, Jr., with Charles and Regina Reynolds; foreword by Ray Bradbury; magic effects illustrated by Eric Mason. Newmarket Press 1985 230p il hardcover o.p. paperback available $19.95   **793.8**
1. Magic tricks
ISBN 1-55704-177-6 (pa)   LC 84-29486
The author "provides a history of magic and the art of illusion, with biographies of some of the pros and an indepth description of the Great Blackstone's career." Publ Wkly
Includes bibliography

Finnigan, Dave
The complete juggler; illustrated by Bruce Edwards; with special contributions by Todd Strong; technical consultant, Allan Jacobs. 2nd ed. Jugglebug 1991 574p il lib bdg $19.95; pa $14.95   **793.8**
1. Juggling
ISBN 0-9615521-1-5 (lib bdg); 0-9615521-0-7 (pa)
                                     LC 91-61138
First published 1987 by Vintage Bks.
A step-by-step approach to various juggling routines. Includes information about equipment, performing, and business aspects

Severn, Bill
Bill Severn's best magic; 50 top tricks to entertain and amaze your friends on all occasions; illustrated by Timothy Wenk. Stackpole Bks. 1990 210p il $14.95   **793.8**
1. Magic tricks
ISBN 0-8117-2229-5   LC 89-11569
"Instructions for performing more than 50 simple magic tricks using cards, paper, and coins, etc., are presented in a logically structured manual that will be a good starting point for teens who want to learn magic without investing heavily in props and equipment." Booklist

794 Indoor games of skill

The World of games; their origin and history, how to play them, and how to make them; [by] Jack Botermans [et al.] Facts on File 1989 240p il o.p.   **794**
1. Games
                                     LC 89-31359
"More than 150 board games, dice games, card games, domino games, and activity games are featured in this

The World of games—*Continued*

[book]." Libr J

"The value of this book is in its historical and cross-cultural information (e.g., native American games) and its handsome illustrations." Booklist

Includes bibliography

794.1   Chess

Fischer, Bobby, 1943-

Bobby Fischer teaches chess; by Bobby Fischer, Stuart Margulies, Donn Mosenfelder. Basic Systems, Inc. 1966 334p il o.p.; Bantam Bks. paperback available $6.99   **794.1**

1. Chess

ISBN 0-553-26315-3 (pa)

In this book the authors give specific advice and hints aimed at both the beginning and advanced player. Each step-by-step lesson is fully illustrated

Hooper, David, 1915-

The Oxford companion to chess; [by] David Hooper and Kenneth Whyld. 2nd ed. Oxford Univ. Press 1992 483p il $45; pa $22.50   **794.1**

1. Chess

ISBN 0-19-866164-9; 0-19-280049-3 (pa)

LC 92-9619

First published 1984

This survey provides historical and technical information, including biographies of celebrated players, descriptions of openings and strategies, explanations of terms, and descriptions of ancient and modern variants of chess

United States Chess Federation

U.S. Chess Federation's official rules of chess; compiled and sanctioned by the U.S. Chess Federation; edited by Bill Goichberg, Carol Jarecki, Ira Lee Riddle. 4th ed. McKay, D. 1994 xxix, 370p il pa $16   **794.1**

1. Chess

ISBN 0-8129-2217-4   LC 92-40961

"This book, effective 1/1/94, supersedes the Official Rules of Chess First Edition 1974, Second Edition 1978, edited by Martin E. Morrison, and Third Edition 1987, edited by Tim Redman." Title page

In addition to the USCF rules, tournament regulations, equipment standards, code of ethics, and rating system, this handbook also includes tips to winning chess, how to read and write chess notation, and a listing of world and national champions

794.7   Indoor ball games

Mizerak, Steve, 1944-

Steve Mizerak's complete book of pool; [by] Steve Mizerak with Michael E. Panozzo. Contemporary Bks. 1990 195p il pa $14.95   **794.7**

1. Pool (Game)

ISBN 0-8092-4255-9   LC 90-39589

The author presents information and practical advice on various aspects of the game of pool. Topics covered

include history, game rules, strategy, technique, practice drills, and equipment

Includes glossary

795.4   Card games

Goren, Charles Henry, 1901-1991

Goren's new bridge complete; [by] Chas H. Goren. rev ed. Doubleday 1985 705p il $29.95   **795.4**

1. Bridge (Game)

ISBN 0-385-23324-8   LC 85-10344

First published 1951 with title: Contract bridge complete

Explanations of basic bridge for beginners as well as data on tournament-winning techniques for advanced players

Hugard, Jean, 1872-1959

Encyclopedia of card tricks; revised and edited by Jean Hugard, associate editor, John J. Crimmins, Jr.; illustrations by Nelson Hahne. Dover Publs. 1974 402p il pa $8.95   **795.4**

1. Card tricks

ISBN 0-486-21252-1

Revised edition of the Encyclopedia of self working card tricks by G. G. Gravatt

Explains how to perform over 600 card tricks

796   Athletic and outdoor sports and games

American women in sport, 1887-1987; a 100-year chronology; compiled by Ruth M. Sparhawk [et al.] Scarecrow Press 1989 149p il $29.50   **796**

1. Women athletes 2. Sports—History

ISBN 0-8108-2205-9   LC 89-6150

The main section of this "chronology is a year-by-year listing of accomplishments made by women in amateur and professional sports. This chronology can be accessed by a subject index to over 70 sports or by an extensive name index. There is also an unannotated bibliography." Voice Youth Advocates

The **Best** American sports writing. Houghton Mifflin $24.95; pa $12.95   **796**

1. Sports

ISSN 1056-8034

Annual. First published 1991. Editors vary

With selections culled from 350 American and Canadian newspapers, this series covers a wide range of sports and sports figures of interest to both the general reader and the die-hard sports fan

Encyclopedia of world sport; from ancient times to the present; David Levinson and Karen Christensen, editors. ABC-CLIO 1996 3v il lib bdg set $225   **796**

1. Sports—Dictionaries

ISBN 0-87436-819-7   LC 96-45437

This encyclopedia covering approximately 300 sports "describes and defines the role sport plays in preserving

Encyclopedia of world sport—*Continued*
local traditions, explores legal and medical concerns, and examines the politics and business of modern sport." Libr J

"Among the many strengths of this work are the cultural and social views it provides. . . . Interesting photographs and fascinating sidebars enhance this comprehensive work." Am Libr

Includes bibliographical references

Fox, Stephen R. (Stephen Russell)
Big leagues; professional baseball, football, and basketball in national memory; [by] Stephen Fox. Morrow 1994 522p il $25 **796**
1. Baseball 2. Football 3. Basketball
ISBN 0-688-09300-0 LC 94-6155
The author "capsulizes each sport's history, citing the input of fans and the arrival and acceptance of black athletes. He salutes baseball's New York Yankees, football's Green Bay Packers, and basketball's Boston Celtics as the all-time biggest winners. Concluding with his view of today's big money and drug problems, Fox gives an appealing story that any sports collection will find useful." Libr J

The **Guinness** book of sports records. Facts on File il $24.95; pa $13.95 **796**
1. Sports
ISSN 1054-4178
Annual. First published 1972 with title: Guinness sports record book. Variant title: Guinness book of sports records, winners & champions
Taken in part from the Guinness book of records, entered in class 032.02
This compilation presents records set in over seventy sports, from archery to yachting. Entries are arranged alphabetically by sport and include a brief history of the sport

Hickok, Ralph
The encyclopedia of North American sports history. Facts on File 1991 516p il $55 **796**
1. Sports—Dictionaries
ISBN 0-8160-2096-5 LC 91-6667
"This reference focuses on the evolution of sports, sports government, administration, and other issues of interest pertaining to sports in North America. Entries are arranged alphabetically and vary in length from 25 to 3000 words. The contents are divided into several broad categories ranging from history, biography, and key events to awards, cities, stadiums, and organizations." Libr J

Men in sports; great sports stories of all time from the Greek Olympic games to the American World Series; edited and with an introduction by Brandt Aymar. Crown 1994 499p $25; pa $16 **796**
1. Sports
ISBN 0-517-59544-3; 0-517-88395-3 (pa)
LC 93-19818
A "collection of nearly fifty sporting entries. Arranged alphabetically, the anthology includes fiction, nonfiction, sports reporting, and excerpts from longer works." Voice Youth Advocates

Nelson, Mariah Burton
Are we winning yet? how women are changing sports and sports are changing women. Random House 1991 238p $19.50 **796**
1. Women athletes 2. Sports 3. Sex discrimination
ISBN 0-394-57576-8 LC 90-42698
"Using interviews with well-known individuals to personalize her subject, a former Stanford University basketball player discusses a variety of issues facing women athletes—among them, stereotypes, gender roles, and sports ethics. An important and timely discussion." Booklist
Includes bibliographical references

Newton at the bat; the science in sports; edited by Eric W. Schrier and William F. Allman. rev ed. Scribner 1984 178p il hardcover o.p. paperback available $9.95 **796**
1. Sports 2. Force and energy
ISBN 0-684-18820-1 (pa) LC 84-1299
An examination of the roles played by physics, physiology, aerodynamics, and technology in athletics and physical activity

Rules of the game; the complete illustrated encyclopedia of all the sports of the world. [rev ed] St. Martin's Press 1990 320p il $24.95
796
1. Sports
ISBN 0-312-04574-3 LC 90-37196
First published 1974 with title: The rule book
This volume covers 150 sports "grouped under 13 headings such as water, court, team, wheels, and air. Each article contains a detailed discussion of major objectives, playing area and equipment, rules, timing and scoring, and participants and officials." Booklist

Sherrow, Victoria
Encyclopedia of women and sports. ABC-CLIO 1996 xxii, 382p il $65 **796**
1. Women athletes—Dictionaries 2. Sports—Dictionaries
ISBN 0-87436-826-X LC 96-19600
"More than 600 alphabetically organized entries highlight key individuals who have participated in or advanced the cause of women in sports and include related topics, such as sexual and racial discrimination, tournaments, organizations, leagues, awards, health issues, segregation, sport history, scholarships, and officiating. The volume not only records athletic achievements but chronicles other accomplishments as well. . . . [It] underscores the progress women have made not only as athletes but as coaches, officials, teachers, administrators, sportscasters, sportswriters, and women's rights advocates. Current as of the 1996 Summer Olympic Games, entries are concise, interesting, and readable." Am Ref Books Annu, 1997

Sports, everyone! recreation and sports for the physically challenged of all ages. Conway Greene 1995 247p pa $16.95 **796**
1. Sports for the handicapped
ISBN 1-884669-10-7
The first part of this book presents personal narratives, "each written by a disabled person or someone involved

Sports, everyone!—*Continued*
with the disabled. The second part of the book is a directory of organizations, services, and funding sources for those disabled interested in participating in sports. . . . A state-by-state guide offers information on locating assistive technology. Information is included about the Americans with Disabilities Act, and an index of associations, camps, and schools is followed by an index of sports activities. This excellent handbook belongs in all school and public library collections." Booklist

Sports in America; paradise lost? editor, Oliver Trager. Facts on File 1990 211p il $29.95
796
1. Sports
ISBN 0-8160-2412-X   LC 89-49285
"An Editorials on file book"
A collection of editorials and cartoons about sports in America. Topics including scandals involving drugs, gambling, steroids, players strikes, and racism

Sports in America: opposing viewpoints; William Dudley, book editor. Greenhaven Press 1994 263p lib bdg $19.95; pa $11.95   **796**
1. Sports
ISBN 1-56510-105-7 (lib bdg); 1-56510-104-9 (pa)
LC 93-30961
"Opposing viewpoints series"
Presents opposing viewpoints on various aspects of American sports, including the effects on youth, reform of college and professional sports, discrimination against minorities, sexism and homophobia, and the use of steroids
Includes bibliography

Weiss, Ann E., 1943-
Money games; the business of sports. Houghton Mifflin 1993 186p $14.95   **796**
1. Sports
ISBN 0-395-57444-7   LC 92-25002
A "look at the impact of money, both legal and illegal, on sports. The information is arranged chronologically, following the historical development of the professional leagues." Horn Book
"An extensive bibliography of sources rounds out an informative and occasionally provocative book." Booklist

796.09   Sports—Historical and geographic treatment

Macy, Sue, 1954-
Winning ways; a photohistory of American women in sports. Holt & Co. 1996 217p il $15.95
796.09
1. Sports 2. Women athletes
ISBN 0-8050-4147-8   LC 95-44969
"Black-and-white photographs and reproductions and an engaging text document the changes in the women's sports world over the past 150 years. . . . This well-documented, readable photohistory is excellent for reports or for leisure reading." SLJ
For a fuller review see: Booklist, Aug. 1996
Includes bibliographical references

796.2   Active games requiring equipment

Werner, Doug, 1950-
In-line skater's start-up; a beginner's guide to in-line skating and roller hockey. Tracks Pub. 1995 159p il (Start-up sports) pa $9.95   **796.2**
1. In-line skating
ISBN 1-884654-04-5   LC 95-60153
This work discusses the various techniques and equipment required for both skating and hockey. This illustrated guide also provides safety tips

796.323   Basketball

Bird, Larry
Bird on basketball; how-to strategies from the great Celtics champion; [by] Larry Bird with John Bischoff. rev ed. Addison-Wesley 1986 119p il pa $13   **796.323**
1. Basketball
ISBN 0-201-14209-0   LC 86-22209
First published 1983 by Phoenix Projects with title: Larry Bird's Basketball Birdwise
The basketball star gives instructions on the game's basics
"An excellent choice for most collections."
Includes glossary

Blais, Madeleine, 1947-
In these girls, hope is a muscle. Atlantic Monthly Press 1995 263p $21   **796.323**
1. Cathedral High School (Springfield, Mass.) 2. Basketball
ISBN 0-87113-572-8   LC 94-30394
Also available in paperback from Warner Bks.
"Weaving accounts of players' personal histories with reportage on their on-court performances, Madeleine Blais recounts the dramatic 1992-93 season of the Lady Hurricanes of Amherst (Mass.) Regional High School." N Y Times Book Rev
"Alternately funny, exciting and moving, the book should be enjoyed not only by girls and women who have played sports but also those who wanted to but let themselves be discouraged." Publ Wkly

Douchant, Mike, 1951-
Encyclopedia of college basketball; foreword, Hoop heaven, by Dick Vitale. Gale Res. 1995 615p il maps $42.95; pa $19.95   **796.323**
1. Basketball 2. College sports
ISBN 0-8103-9640-8; 0-8103-9483-9 (pa)
LC 94-35209
This volume contains "historical facts, statistics, and trivia in addition to coach, player, and team profiles. . . . Features include coverage of women's basketball, school directories, conference breakdowns, plus detailed statistics on the NCAA tournament from 1938 to the present." Libr J
"An excellent reference work." Booklist
Includes bibliographical references

Frey, Darcy
The last shot; city streets, basketball dreams. Houghton Mifflin 1994 230p $19.95 **796.323**
1. Abraham Lincoln High School (New York, N.Y.) 2. Basketball 3. School sports
ISBN 0-395-59770-6   LC 94-31545
Also available in paperback from Simon & Schuster
"For many adolescents on Coney Island, basketball is their only escape from the urban hell of poverty, crime, and drugs. *The Last Shot* chronicles a group of teenagers playing for one of the best teams in New York, the Abraham Lincoln Secondary School Railsplitters." Libr J
"Frey offers devastating anecdotes about dishonest college recruiters and about the NCAA. This excellent book is not only about basketball but about realizing a dream." Publ Wkly

Joravsky, Ben
Hoop dreams; a true story of hardship and triumph; introduction by Charles Barkley. Turner Pub. (Atlanta) 1995 301p il $22.95 **796.323**
1. Basketball 2. Chicago (Ill.)—Social conditions
ISBN 1-570-36153-3   LC 94-46398
Also available in paperback from HarperCollins Pubs.
"Based on the documentary film of the same name, this book . . . looks at the dream of ghetto youths to play in the NBA." Publ Wkly

Lieberman-Cline, Nancy, 1958-
Basketball for women; becoming a complete player; [by] Nancy Lieberman-Cline [and] Robin Roberts with Kevin Warneke. Human Kinetics 1996 283p il pa $16.95 **796.323**
1. Basketball 2. Women athletes
ISBN 0-87322-610-0   LC 95-17945
The author "begins with a history of the game dating back to the first official women's basketball game at Smith College in 1893. From there she discusses not only the dedication it takes to be a true player, but also basketball's position in her, and hopefully the reader's priorities. . . . Next she suggests the building of the plan, mentally and physically, to begin the ascent to the next level of playing. The following seven chapters are devoted to . . . drill techniques." Voice Youth Advocates
Includes bibliographical references

Mikes, Jay, 1953-
Basketball fundamentals; a complete mental training guide. Leisure Press 1987 258p il $21; pa $17.95 **796.323**
1. Basketball
ISBN 0-88011-281-6; 0-88011-442-8 (pa)
          LC 86-19133
This guide provides coaches and players with information and advice on the psychology of basketball. Chapter topics include training, shooting, free throws and rebounding
Includes bibliography

Miller, Faye Young
Winning basketball for girls; [by] Faye Young Miller and Wayne Coffey. new ed. Facts on File 1992 138p il $19.95; pa $11.95 **796.323**
1. Basketball
ISBN 0-8160-2769-2; 0-8160-2776-5 (pa)
          LC 91-36937
First published 1984
This volume covers "conditioning, footwork, rules, offensive and defensive moves, and drills for a multitude of skills intended to help young women improve their game. . . . Over 120 black-and-white photographs and diagrams are scattered throughout the manual." Libr J
Includes glossary

The **Official** NBA basketball encyclopedia; foreword by Julius Erving; introduction by David J. Stern; edited by Alex Sachare. 2nd ed. Villard Bks. 1994 842p il $39.95 **796.323**
1. Basketball
ISBN 0-679-43293-0   LC 94-11858
First published 1989
"Covers history, Hall of Fame, all-time records, all-star games, and official NBA rules. Includes complete statistical profile of every player who has ever appeared in the NBA. Illustrated with photographs; indexed." NY Public Libr Book of How & Where to Look It Up

St. Martin, Ted
The art of shooting baskets; from the free throw to the slam dunk; [by] Ted St. Martin with Frank Frangie. Contemporary Bks. 1992 xxiv, 118p il pa $11.95 **796.323**
1. Basketball
ISBN 0-8092-4009-2   LC 92-20264
Photographs and illustrations accompany advice on how to improve basketball shooting techniques

796.332 American football

Harrington, Denis J., 1932-
The Pro Football Hall of Fame; players, coaches, team owners, and league officials, 1969-1991. McFarland & Co. 1991 354p il lib bdg $35 **796.332**
1. Pro Football Hall of Fame 2. Football
ISBN 0-89950-550-3   LC 91-52636
The author "first offers a brief history of professional football and the NFL. Then, position by position, he profiles the Hall's members. He provides basic career statistics and information such as rushing yardage and years selected to the Pro Bowl as well as a text that incorporates career highlights with anecdotes." Booklist
"This book is a fine reference work for those wishing biographical and historical information on the people who have had a lasting impact on professional football." Voice Youth Advocates

Jarrett, William S.
Timetables of sports history, football. Facts on
File 1989 82p il $17.95   **796.332**
1. Football
ISBN 0-8160-1919-3   LC 89-30418
A chronological survey of college and professional
football from the mid-nineteenth century to the present
Includes bibliography

Neft, David S.
The sports encyclopedia: pro football; by David
S. Neft and Richard M. Cohen. St. Martin's Press
pa $21.99   **796.332**
1. Football
First published 1976 by Grosset & Dunlap. (13th edition 1995) Periodically revised
Covers pro football from 1960 to the present and contains team rosters, scores, statistical data on individual
players, and Super Bowls

Simms, Phil, 1955-
Phil Simms on passing; fundamentals on
throwing the football; by Phil Simms with Rick
Meier. Morrow 1996 205p il $25   **796.332**
1. Football
ISBN 0-688-14100-5   LC 96-12904
"This book breaks down the act of passing a football
into all its facets. . . . Simms details the basics of the
stance, the snap, the drop-back, the grip, and throwing
the football. He includes recommended drills, exercises,
and routines to practice these basics and the text is augmented by numerous photos and illustrations that demonstrate good and bad form" Libr J

Wilkinson, Bud, 1916-1994
Sports illustrated football: winning defense;
illustrations by Robert Handville. rev ed. Sports
Illustrated 1993 175p il pa $10.95   **796.332**
1. Football
ISBN 1-568-00003-0   LC 93-28164
"Sports illustrated winner's circle books"
First published 1973 by Lippincott
The author analyzes basic team and individual defen-
sive strategies and techniques, using diagrams, drawings
and photographs

Sports illustrated football: winning offense;
illustrations by Robert Handville. rev ed. Sports
Illustrated 1994 205p il pa $11.95   **796.332**
1. Football
ISBN 1-568-00002-2   LC 94-2070
"Sports illustrated winner's circle books"
First published 1972 by Lippincott
The author analyzes basic team and individual offen-
sive strategies and techniques, using diagrams, drawings
and photographs

796.334   Soccer

Bauer, Gerhard, 1940-
Soccer techniques, tactics & teamwork;
introduction by Franz Beckenbauer. Sterling 1993
159p il pa $14.95   **796.334**
1. Soccer
ISBN 0-8069-8730-8   LC 92-44087
Also available in hardcover from Borgo Press
The author "supplies extensive explanation of the theories of soccer, with easy-to-use diagrams and charts.
Frame-by-frame photographs display the correct form and
style to be used in the numerous exercises and drills described in the text. Both novices and advanced players
will benefit from the techniques covered here, and the
step-by-step instructions are a model of clarity." Booklist

Gardner, Paul, 1930-
The simplest game; the intelligent fan's guide to
the world of soccer; with a foreword by Pelé. [3rd
ed] Macmillan 1996 xxiv, 360p il $14.95
            796.334
1. Soccer
ISBN 0-02-860401-6   LC 96-16777
First published 1976 by Little, Brown
The author provides historical background on the
game's origin, he analyzes World Cup competitions and
offers facts, figures, rules and anecdotes on the sport

Herbst, Dan
Sports illustrated soccer; the complete player;
photography by Heinz Kluetmeier. new ed. Sports
Illustrated 1994 192p il pa $10.95   **796.334**
1. Soccer
ISBN 1-56800-005-7   LC 93-28166
"Sports illustrated winner's circle books"
First published 1984 by Harper & Row
This book presents basic ball skills, offensive strate-
gies, defense, goalkeeping, plays, drills and coaching tips
Includes glossary

Rosenthal, Gary
Soccer skills and drills. rev & updated [ed]
Simon & Schuster 1994 262p il $14   **796.334**
1. Soccer
ISBN 0-02-036435-0   LC 93-32462
"A Fireside book"
First published 1984 by Scribner
An introduction to basic soccer skills that includes
practice drills, official game rules, and explanations of
soccer terminology

796.34   Racket games

Boga, Steve, 1947-
Badminton; [by] Steven Boga. Stackpole Bks.
1996 100p il pa $10   **796.34**
1. Badminton (Game)
ISBN 0-8117-2487-5   LC 95-22434
This volume begins with "a brief history of the sport
as well as the rules and the court dimensions. Also at-

Boga, Steve, 1947—*Continued*
tended to are equipment selection and such basics as racket grip, positioning, footwork, and shotmaking. Singles, doubles, and mixed-doubles are presented in terms of both rules and strategy. . . . A glossary and national list of badminton clubs and organizations are appended. If you need a badminton how-to, this is the one to buy." Booklist

Turner, Edward T.
Winning racquetball; skills, drills, and strategies; [by] Ed Turner, Woody Clouse. Human Kinetics 1996 277p il pa $16.95   **796.34**
1. Racquetball
ISBN 0-87322-721-2   LC 95-13029
A revised edition of Skills & strategies for winning racquetball, by Ed Turner and Marty Hogan, published 1988 by Leisure Press
This guide to racquetball "provides tips for both the seasoned recreational player and the novice. [The authors] examine everything from equipment to match strategy in straightforward, conversational language augmented by more than 140 photos and line drawings." Booklist
Includes glossary and bibliography

Urick, Dave
Sports illustrated lacrosse; fundamentals for winning; photography by Heinz Kluetmeier. [rev ed] Sports Illustrated 1991 255p il pa $12.95
796.34
1. Lacrosse
ISBN 1-56800-071-5
"Sports illustrated winner's circle books"
First published 1988
An introduction to the game of lacrosse providing information about equipment rules, skills, strategy, and training

796.342 Tennis

Douglas, Paul
The handbook of tennis; foreword by John McEnroe. rev & updated ed. Knopf 1992 288p il $24   **796.342**
1. Tennis
ISBN 0-679-74062-7   LC 91-58566
"A Dorling Kindersley book"
First published 1982
This work gives instruction from beginning strokes to advanced level techniques. Fitness exercises, injuries and their treatment, and information on the construction of balls, rackets and courts are covered

Tennis. Dorling Kindersley 1995 72p il pa $6.95
796.342
1. Tennis
ISBN 0-7894-0182-7
At head of title: 101 essential tips
Aspects covered include strokes, positions, playing surfaces, dress and equipment
"This is a good text for those just picking up the sport, as well as for those seasoned players who want to brush up on their game or improve their strategy." Voice Youth Advocates

MacCurdy, Doug
Sports illustrated tennis; strokes for success! by Doug MacCurdy and Shawn Tully; illustrations by Robert Handville. [rev ed] Sports Illustrated 1994 156p il pa $12.95   **796.342**
1. Tennis
ISBN 1-56800-006-5   LC 94-2072
Also available in paperback from New Am. Lib./Dutton
"Sports illustrated winner's circle books"
First published 1980 by Lippincott
This introduction to tennis includes illustrations and text covering such topics as rules, equipment, racket technique, and competitions

796.352 Golf

Ballingall, Peter
Golf. Dorling Kindersley 1995 72p il pa $6.95
796.352
1. Golf
ISBN 0-7894-0172-X
At head of title: 101 essential tips
Aspects covered include clothing, equipment, club grips, stance, swing control, and rules

Campbell, Malcolm, 1944-
Ultimate golf techniques; contributor, Steve Newell; special photography, Dave Cannon. DK Pub. 1996 216p il $34.95   **796.352**
1. Golf
ISBN 0-7894-0442-7   LC 95-44327
Text and numerous illustrations present the basic techniques of the golf swing
"The effective mix of jump-off-the-page graphics and straightforward captions takes golf instruction into the realm of visual learning, where it naturally belongs." Booklist

Feinstein, John
A good walk spoiled; days and nights on the PGA tour. Little, Brown 1995 xx, 475p il $23.95; pa $13.95   **796.352**
1. PGA Tour Inc. 2. Golf
ISBN 0-316-27720-7; 0-316-27737-1 (pa)
LC 94-49552
Along with "profiles of the game's big names—Norman, Price, Watson—Feinstein's sojourn through the 1994 PGA tour also offers remarkable glimpses of the marginal players who struggle to first qualify for the tour and then maintain their tenuous places on it. . . . Golfers of all ages simply won't be able to put this book down." Booklist

Golf rules in pictures; illustrated by George Kraynack. new & rev ed, revised and updated by Michael Brown. Putnam Pub. Group 1993 84p il pa $10   **796.352**
1. Golf
ISBN 0-399-51799-5   LC 92-39631
"A Perigee book"
First published 1962 by Grosset & Dunlap

Golf rules in pictures—*Continued*

An official publication of the United States Golf Association

In addition to discussing the rules of golf, this guide covers playing etiquette and provides definitions for key terms. Illustrated with line drawings

Golf, the greatest game; by the United States Golf Association. HarperCollins Pubs. 1994 271p il $60   **796.352**
1. Golf
ISBN 0-06-017135-9   LC 94-8857

Published in conjunction with a TV documentary of the same title. Almost 400 photographs, 150 in color, accompany discussions of golf history, course architecture and the financial aspects of the sport

Mulvoy, Mark

Sports illustrated golf; play like a pro; photography by Heinz Kluetmeier. [rev ed] Sports Illustrated 1993 156p il pa $12.95   **796.352**
1. Golf
ISBN 1-56800-007-3

"Sports illustrated winner's circle books"

First published 1983 by Harper & Row

An illustrated look at golfing basics. Equipment and conditioning are discussed and step-by-step instructions on the golf swing and putting are included

Whitworth, Kathy, 1939-

Golf for women; [by] Kathy Whitworth with Rhonda Glenn. St. Martin's Press 1990 176p il $19.95; pa $13.95   **796.352**
1. Golf
ISBN 0-312-04013-X; 0-312-06984-7 (pa)
    LC 89-78002

"This guide covers grip, stance, body alignment, putting fundamentals, trouble shots, and golf-course strategy." Booklist

"A splendidly written, detailed, well-illustrated book." Libr J

796.357   Baseball

Adair, Robert Kemp

The physics of baseball. 2nd ed rev updated & enl. HarperPerennial 1994 142p il pa $11
    796.357
1. Physics 2. Baseball 3. Force and energy
ISBN 0-06-095047-1   LC 94-137035
First published 1990

A look at how some physical principles are applied to the game of baseball. Pitching, batting and the properties of bats are discussed

Asinof, Eliot, 1919-

Eight men out; the Black Sox and the 1919 world series. Holt & Co. 1963 302p il hardcover o.p. paperback available $12.95   **796.357**
1. Baseball
ISBN 0-8050-0346-0 (pa)
Also available in hardcover from Holtzman Press

"An Owl book"

The author has reconstructed the story of the Chicago White Sox baseball scandal, and describes the 1921 trial of the eight players who had arranged with gamblers to throw the 1919 World Series to Cincinnati

Baseball; four decades of Sports illustrated's finest writing on America's favorite pastime. Oxmoor House 1993 286p $17.99   **796.357**
1. Baseball
ISBN 0-8487-1147-5

This volume "brings together 30 of the magazine's finest articles through the years. The selections are arranged within eight general themes—'Spring,' 'Summer,' 'Fall,' 'Players,' 'Management,' 'Milestones,' 'They also serve,' and 'The Game.' . . . An essential purchase for any good sports collection." Booklist

The **Baseball** anthology; 125 years of stories, poems, articles, interviews, photographs, drawings, cartoons, and other memorabilia; general editor, Joseph Wallace; foreword by Sparky Anderson. Abrams 1994 296p il $45
    796.357
1. Baseball
ISBN 0-8109-3135-4   LC 94-5499

"Organized chronologically, the book combines a photo history of the game with a running narrative composed largely of excerpts from a wealth of well-known baseball writers. . . . The pictures are delightful, both for their excellent reproduction and for their content." Booklist

The **Baseball** encyclopedia; the complete and official record of major league baseball. Macmillan $59.95   **796.357**
1. Baseball—Statistics
Also available CD-ROM version

First published 1969. (10th edition 1996) Periodically revised. Editors vary

"Covers everything about Major League baseball, including awards and special achievements, all-time leaders, teams, players, home/road performance, championships, and major changes in playing and scoring rule, back to 1876." N Y Public Libr. Book of How & Where to Look It Up

Chadwick, Bruce

When the game was black and white; the illustrated history of the Negro leagues. Abbeville Press 1992 191p il $24.95   **796.357**
1. Baseball 2. African American athletes
ISBN 1-55859-372-1   LC 92-13673

A " survey of segregated baseball. Topics covered include barnstorming, Latin American ball, and games against white major leaguers. In addition to extremely rare photographs of ball players, including some from Satchel Paige's own scrapbook, there are examples of rare Negro Leagues memorabilia. . . . Highly recommended." Choice

Curran, William, 1921-
Strikeout; a celebration of the art of pitching.
Crown 1995 244p il $23   **796.357**
   1. Baseball
   ISBN 0-517-58841-2   LC 94-3605
The author "traces the development of pitching from baseball's earliest days, charting the ebb and flow of the pitcher's dominance. Curran doesn't simply point out the different eras (Dead Ball era, Babe Ruth era, etc.), he examines the developments that triggered them. . . . Amid all this evolutionary data, Curran sprinkles plenty of fascinating anecdotes about the pitchers themselves." Booklist

Dickson, Paul
The joy of keeping score; how scoring the game has influenced and enhanced the history of baseball. Walker & Co. 1996 117p il $17.95
    796.357
   1. Baseball
   ISBN 0-8027-1307-6   LC 96-11206
Also available in paperback from Harcourt Brace & Co.
The author "teaches the rudiments of scoring, including how the players are numbered, some of the obvious symbols (e.g., SB is a Stolen Base) and some of the less obvious. . . . He explains the nuances of scoring a ball game and how to read a box score, and profiles some of the celebrities who like to score games." Publ Wkly
"Baseball fans young and old are certain to enjoy this book." Booklist
Includes bibliographical references

The Worth book of softball; a celebration of America's true national pastime; photographs by Russell Mott. Facts on File 1994 276p il $22.95
    796.357
   1. Softball
   ISBN 0-8160-2897-4   LC 93-19312
This book "gives a detailed account of the history of the game, including legendary softball players. Rules of play are also included." Book Rep
Includes glossary and bibliographical references

Fimrite, Ron
The World Series; a history of baseball's fall classic. Oxmoor House 1993 224p il $40
    796.357
   1. World series (Baseball)
   ISBN 0-8487-1155-6
This book offers an "overview of the sporting world's premier event—the World Series. Fimrite's colorful narration gives the reader a feel for the dynamics of some of the greatest series ever played. . . . A marvelous tribute in words and pictures to what makes the World Series special." Booklist

Gilbert, Thomas W.
Baseball and the color line; by Tom Gilbert. Watts 1995 176p il (African-American experience) lib bdg $22.70; pa $9   **796.357**
   1. African American athletes 2. Baseball
   ISBN 0-531-11206-3 (lib bdg); 0-531-15747-4 (pa)
           LC 94-23935
"Over half the text is devoted to looking at the game in the late 19th century when a number of blacks made appearances in the various professional leagues, before the color line was totally enforced. . . . Gilbert gives scant attention to the Negro Leagues, concentrating on the efforts of those who tried to integrate the all-white professional leagues. Major players and other figures in this effort, and those who fought integration, are featured throughout the text. The author also ties prejudice in baseball to that found in American society at the time." SLJ
Includes bibliographical references

Superstars and monopoly wars; nineteenth-century major-league baseball; [by] Thomas Gilbert. Watts 1995 159p il (American game) lib bdg $22.70   **796.357**
   1. Baseball
   ISBN 0-531-11247-0   LC 95-31413
Discusses the growth of baseball in the nineteenth century from its enjoyment as a casual game to its commercialization
Includes bibliographical references

Gregorich, Barbara
Women at play; the story of women in baseball. Harcourt Brace & Co. 1993 214p il pa $14.95
    796.357
   1. All-American Girls Professional Baseball League 2. Baseball 3. Women athletes
   ISBN 0-15-698297-8   LC 93-16223
"A Harvest original"
In this history of women's professional baseball the author "focuses on personalities and teams, and tells stories from newspaper accounts and teammates' reminiscences. Women loving baseball and struggling to leap men's roadblocks are this attractive and unique book's themes." Libr J

Gutman, Dan
Baseball's greatest games. Viking 1994 212p il $14.99; pa $4.99   **796.357**
   1. Baseball
   ISBN 0-670-84604-X; 0-14-037933-9 (pa)
           LC 93-31504
"Gutman introduces young fans to nine of the greatest baseball games ever played, starting in 1886 and ending in 1988. Rather than going into batter-by-batter detail, he summarizes most of each game, then zeros in on moments of *tension*, the quality that Gutman defines a great game." Booklist
"This book is a lot of fun to read, Gutman's descriptions of the games don't get bogged down in too many details, and he has an old-fashioned, snappy, sportswriter's style that's just right for this type of presentation." SLJ
Includes bibliography

Gutman, Dan—*Continued*

The way baseball works; introduced by Tim McCarver; text by Dan Gutman. Simon & Schuster 1996 215p il $30   **796.357**
1. Baseball
ISBN 0-684-81606-7   LC 96-7289
"A Byron Preiss/Richard Ballantine book"
"Produced in conjuction with the National Baseball Hall of Fame"
"Including a wealth of diagrams and information on a wide range of baseball-related topics—from gloves to batting technique—this will be a popular item among the sport's fans." Booklist
Includes bibliographical references

Halberstam, David, 1934-

Summer of '49. Morrow 1989 304p il o.p.; Avon Bks. paperback available $10   **796.357**
1. New York Yankees (Baseball team) 2. Boston Red Sox (Baseball team)
ISBN 0-380-72146-5 (pa)   LC 89-2886
"This book is ostensibly about the pennant race between the Yankees and Red Sox [in 1949] and the 'rivalry' between Joe DiMaggio and Ted Williams. . . . It is a study of all the elements and personalities that influenced baseball that year and beyond. Halberstam brings them together in such an enjoyable, interesting, and informative manner that a reader needn't be a baseball fan to appreciate the book." Libr J

Hemphill, Paul, 1936-

The heart of the game; the education of a minor league ballplayer. Simon & Schuster 1996 284p $23   **796.357**
1. Malloy, Marty 2. Baseball
ISBN 0-684-81172-3   LC 95-40225
This book chronicles the life of Marty Malloy from his boyhood in "northern Florida, through high school and two years junior-college ball, through his signing with the Atlanta organization in 1992, and through his first four years in minor-league ball." Christ Sci Monit
The author a former minor-leaguer, "relives his own illusions of grandeur in an evocative account of the summer game as it's played in rickety ball parks far from big-league glamour." Booklist

Honig, Donald

Baseball: the illustrated history of America's game. Crown 1990 340p il $45   **796.357**
1. Baseball
ISBN 0-517-57295-8   LC 89-1223
The author chronicles baseball from its beginnings in 1839 up to the year 1988. For baseball's modern era, which began in 1901, he provides a year-by-year narrative of the highlights of each season. Included are more than 1,100 photographs

Kahn, Roger

The boys of summer. Harper & Row 1972 xxii, 442p il o.p.; Perennial Lib. paperback available $14   **796.357**
1. Brooklyn Dodgers (Baseball team) 2. Baseball
ISBN 0-06-091416-5 (pa)
Also available in hardcover from Buccaneer Bks.

The author describes attending Brooklyn Dodger games as a boy, covering Dodger games as a reporter for the Herald Tribune, and traveling throughout the country to speak with former Dodgers after the team left New York

Kindall, Jerry

Sports illustrated baseball; play the winning way; photography by Heinz Kluetmeier; illustrations by Don Tonry. new ed. Sports Illustrated 1993 256p il pa $12.95   **796.357**
1. Baseball
ISBN 1-56800-000-6
"Sports illustrated winner's circle books"
First published 1983 by Harper & Row
An illustrated overview of offensive and defensive baseball strategy. Includes tips on hitting, running, fielding, pitching and throwing. Equipment is discussed

Neft, David S.

The sports encyclopedia: baseball; [by] David S. Neft, Richard M. Cohen. St. Martin's Press pa $19.99   **796.357**
1. Baseball—Statistics
First published 1974 by Grosset & Dunlap. (1996 edition) Periodically revised
Covers baseball from 1876 to the present and contains team statistics, alphabetical registers of batters and pitchers, and summaries of each season

Reichler, Joseph L., 1915-1988

The great all-time baseball record book; revised and updated by Ken Samelson. Macmillan 1993 xxv, 592p $25   **796.357**
1. Baseball—Statistics
ISBN 0-02-603101-9   LC 91-38197
First published 1981
This volume is arranged in "four broad categories (individual batting records, individual pitching records, rookie records, and team records) . . . subarranged into a series of logical groupings (e.g., pinch hits), and within each subcategory, into a series of individual records (e.g., most career pinch hits). In all, records in some 475 categories are provided that cover virtually every individual and team record of interest." Am Ref Books Annu, 1994

Seaver, Tom

Great moments in baseball; by Tom Seaver with Marty Appel. Carol Pub. Group 1992 339p il $19.95   **796.357**
1. Baseball
ISBN 1-55972-095-6   LC 91-30596
Also available in paperback from Citadel Press
"A Birch Lane Press book"
Seaver "has compiled his choice of 50 spectacular events in major league baseball since 1903, when the fledgling American League met the National League in the first World Series. They include accounts of Walter Johnson's only World Series, Babe Ruth's called-shot home run, Joe DiMaggio's hitting streak, [and] Willie Mays's celebrated over-the-shoulder catch. . . . 'Great Moments in Baseball' is for addicts who yearn for more than computerized statistical tables." N Y Times Book Rev
Includes bibliographical references

Smith, Curt

The storytellers; from Mel Allen to Bob Costas: sixty years of baseball tales from the broadcast booth. Macmillan 1995 278p il $22.95 **796.357**

1. Baseball 2. Radio broadcasting

ISBN 0-02-860411-3 LC 95-9210

This volume presents the careers and memories of over sixty baseball announcers including Ernie Harwell, Lindsey Nelson, and Vin Scully

Williams, Ted, 1918-

The science of hitting; by Ted Williams and John Underwood. rev and updated ed. Simon & Schuster 1986 88p il pa $10.95 **796.357**

1. Baseball

ISBN 0-671-62103-3 LC 85-31203

"A Fireside book"

First published 1971

One of baseball's most successful hitters discusses his batting technique

796.42 Track and field

Higdon, Hal

Boston; a century of running: celebrating the 100th anniversary of the Boston Athletic Association Marathon. Rodale Press 1995 242p il $40 **796.42**

1. Boston Marathon

ISBN 0-87596-283-1 LC 95-4112

"In an illustrated 100-year retrospective, Higdon tracks the history of the premier marathon and highlights various runners, including champions and back-of-the-packers." Booklist

This is "an absorbing history, with 200-plus photos and dozens of sidebars." Publ Wkly

Includes bibliography

Marathon; the ultimate training and racing guide. Rodale Press 1993 207p pa $15.95 **796.42**

1. Running

ISBN 0-87596-159-2 LC 92-41569

The author "outlines a variety of programs, distilled from many sources, to help individuals compete successfully—or, short of that, at least *complete* the race. Higdon begins with a chapter for the overweight and sedentary. . . . There are also chapters on basic marathon training, more sophisticated methods for more accomplished runners, and race strategy. All in all, this is a competent, well-organized guide for runners of all levels." Booklist

Rosen, Mel

Sports illustrated track: championship running; by Mel Rosen and Karen Rosen; photography by Heinz Kluetmeier. new ed. Sports Illustrated 1994 173p il pa $12.95 **796.42**

1. Running

ISBN 1-56800-008-1 LC 94-2071

"Sports illustrated winner's circle books"

First published 1983 by Harper & Row

An introduction to competitive running, emphasizing training techniques and strategies for winning

Sandrock, Michael, 1958-

Running with the legends. Human Kinetics 1996 575p il pa $19.95 **796.42**

1. Athletes

ISBN 0-87322-493-0 LC 96-3790

The author "offers brief biographies of 21 of the best distance runners of the modern era, ranging from Emil Zapotek, the four-time Olympic gold-medal winner who set 18 world records in the late 1940s and early 1950s, to Uta Pippig, the East German defector who has recently dominated the women's marathon circuit." Booklist

This book provides "not only fascinating insights into how these athletes live, train, and run but also much-needed updates of our historical and political perspectives on running." Libr J

796.44 Sports gymnastics

Ryan, Joan

Little girls in pretty boxes; the making and breaking of elite gymnasts and figure skaters. Doubleday 1995 243p il $22.95 **796.44**

1. Gymnastics 2. Ice skating 3. Women athletes

ISBN 0-385-47790-2 LC 94-43317

Also available in paperback from Warner Bks.

"In an attempt to focus attention on the high price paid through pain, pressure, and humiliation to become an Olympic champion, Ryan has researched the stories behind some of the young female superstar gymnasts and figure skaters. The extraordinary cost to these young women in body, mind, and spirit is dramatized through the intense subculture dominated by gyms, trainers, parents, and sports officials who press for excellence and success without regard to the health and well-being of those involved. . . . A book to be pondered by coaches, parents, and young people." SLJ

796.48 Olympic games

Buchanan, Ian

Historical dictionary of the Olympic movement; by Ian Buchanan and Bill Mallon. Scarecrow Press 1995 lxxv, 247p il $44.50 **796.48**

1. Olympic games

ISBN 0-8108-3062-0 LC 95-22858

This work "includes a chronology of the Olympic movement, . . . entries on each Olympiad since 1896, and a dictionary that includes people (mostly athletes), countries, organizations, individual sports, and controversies (e.g., Sex Testing, Doping). Each entry provides a three-letter country, sport, or committee identifier as well as birth and death dates for people, along with 50- to 500-word essays." Booklist

Chronicle of the Olympics, 1896-1996. DK Pub. 1996 312p il $29.95 **796.48**

1. Olympic games

ISBN 0-7894-0608-X LC 95-52774

Original German edition, 1995

This chronology "begins with the first modern Olympics in 1896 and charts the story of the Olympic move-

Chronicle of the Olympics, 1896-1996—*Continued*

ment in words and photographs up to Atlanta in 1996.
. . . At the end of the volume, tables of statistics are
provided for each Olympiad with a list of gold, silver,
and bronze winners, plus a list of outstanding athletes,
and a table of countries' medals." Booklist

Guttmann, Allen

The Olympics, a history of the modern games.
University of Ill. Press 1992 191p il (Illinois
history of sport) $24.95; pa $12.95   **796.48**
1. Olympic games
ISBN 0-252-01701-3; 0-252-06396-1 (pa)
LC 91-32631
"The author's premise is that politics have been at the
foundation of modern Olympics from its inception in
Athens (1896) to Seoul (1988). Gold, silver, and bronze
medals have shared the victory stand with nationalism,
and have even been tarnished by arrogance, protests, terrorists, and boycotts. Although the text emphasizes the
political and socioeconomic climate of the Olympics, it
also contains memorable accounts of athletic competition." Libr J
Includes bibliographical references

Wallechinsky, David, 1948-

Sports illustrated presents the complete book of
the Summer Olympics. 1996 ed. Little, Brown
1996 xxx, 840p il $29.95; pa $15.95   **796.48**
1. Olympic games
ISBN 0-316-92093-2; 0-316-92094-0 (pa)
LC 95-46267
Replaces The complete book of the Olympics
Cover title: The complete book of the Summer Olympics
This volume includes "results, statistics, pictures, stories, and lore about every past summer Olympics, plus
complete information on rules and scoring for every
1996 event." Publisher's note

796.5   Outdoor life

Berger, Karen, 1959-

Hiking & backpacking; a complete guide;
introduction by John Viehman. Norton 1995 224p
il (Trailside series guide) flexible bdg $17.95
    796.5
1. Hiking 2. Backpacking
ISBN 0-393-31334-4   LC 95-5528
This companion volume to a public television series
includes sections on where to hike; conditioning; what to
wear; what to carry; food; minimum-impact camping;
safety and first aid; wildlife; maps and compasses; sharing the adventure with others; and winter camping
Includes bibliographical references

Climbing: the complete reference; compiled by
Greg Child. Facts on File 1995 264p il maps
$40; pa $19.95   **796.5**
1. Mountaineering—Dictionaries
ISBN 0-8160-2692-0; 0-8160-3653-5 (pa)
LC 94-33254
This is a "reference of North American and interna-
tional mountaineering and rock climbing. Not a hand-

book or how-to manual but essentially an encyclopedia,
this comprehensive book offers more than 1000 alphabetically arranged entries featuring biographies, notable des-
tinations, definitions, equipment, and recommended readings. The text is augmented by photographs, line drawings, maps, tables, and two appendixes on mountain and
glacier formations and standard symbols and abbreviations." Libr J
For a fuller review see: Booklist, Feb. 1, 1996

McManners, Hugh

The backpacker's handbook. Dorling Kindersley
1995 160p il maps flexible bdg $14.95   **796.5**
1. Backpacking
ISBN 1-56458-852-1   LC 94-32042
"The book is divided into five areas: getting started,
equipment and techniques, moving on the trail, camping
in the wild, and dealing with emergencies. . . . An essential how-to for backpackers." Libr J

Paulsen, Gary

Woodsong. Bradbury Press 1990 132p map lib
bdg $16   **796.5**
1. Sled dog racing 2. Outdoor life 3. Minnesota
ISBN 0-02-770221-9   LC 89-70835
Also available in paperback from Puffin Bks.
For the author and his family, life in northern Minnesota is a wild experience involving wolves, deer, and the
sled dogs that make their way of life possible. Includes
an account of Paulsen's first Iditarod, a dogsled race
across Alaska
"The book is packed with vignettes that range among
various shades of terror and lyrical beauty." Voice Youth
Advocates

Randall, Glenn, 1957-

The modern backpacker's handbook. Lyons &
Burford 1994 192p il pa $14.95   **796.5**
1. Backpacking
ISBN 1-55821-248-5   LC 93-37444
"Randall begins with advice on underclothing and appropriate fabrics for outerwear, and proceeds to packs,
sleeping bags, tents, stoves, and food. He tells how to
pack and use this gear on the trail and offers tips on
finding routes, trail etiquette, and safety. His straightforward recital of possible hazards should be a great help
to all backpackers." Booklist

Taylor, Michael R.

Cave passages; roaming the underground
wilderness. Scribner 1996 285p il $23   **796.5**
1. Caves
ISBN 0-684-81854-X   LC 95-26266
The author "introduces us to some unique personalities
and escapades, including 'squeezes' through places with
names like Agony, Criso Creak, and the Grim Crawl of
Death. He leads us through caves in Florida, Wyoming,
Jamaica, and China, among other places. He even gets us
safely through the old Croton Aqueduct in the Bronx.
Safety cautions and advice on how to join a caving
group are included." Libr J

796.6 Cycling and related activities

Clark, Jim
Mountain biking the national parks; off-road cycling adventures in America's national parks. Bicycle Bks. 1996 208p il maps pa $12.95 **796.6**
1. National parks and reserves—United States
2. Mountain bikes 3. Bicycle touring
ISBN 0-933201-69-9   LC 95-76297
"Organized into six geographic regions of the country, the book begins with a short introduction to familiarize you with each park in that region. Each of the rides is then fully detailed with a map and narrative presenting special points of interest." Publisher's note
Includes bibliography

King, Dave, 1955-
The mountain bike experience; a complete introduction to the joys of off-road riding; [by] Dave King and Michael Kaminer. Holt & Co. 1996 204p il pa $16.95   **796.6**
1. Mountain bikes
ISBN 0-8050-3723-3   LC 95-37734
"An Owl book"
The authors "cover everything from mountain bike techniques to nutrition and training." Booklist
Includes bibliographical references

Matheny, Fred, 1945-
Bicycling magazine's complete guide to riding and racing techniques. Rodale Press 1989 245p il $19.95; pa $14.95   **796.6**
1. Bicycle racing
ISBN 0-87857-804-8; 0-87857-805-6 (pa)
     LC 88-31654
"Matheny guides the beginning cyclist through some basic techniques and strategies for both riding and racing before advancing to requirements of specific forms of competition. Time trials, distance events, and off-road cycling are all covered, with more general advice on endurance and speed training." Booklist

Oliver, Peter
Bicycling; touring and mountain bike basics; introduction by John Viehman. Norton 1995 192p il (Trailside series guide) flexible bdg $17.95
     796.6
1. Mountain bikes 2. Bicycle touring
ISBN 0-393-31337-9   LC 95-5526
This illustrated guide to mountain bike touring covers equipment, clothing, safety, riding techniques, fitness, and bike maintenance, and lists organizations, mail-order sources, and information sources

796.7 Driving motor vehicles

Taylor, Rich, 1946-
Indy; seventy-five years of auto racing's greatest spectacle; foreword by A.J. Foyt, Jr. St. Martin's Press 1991 287p il $39.95   **796.7**
1. Automobile racing
ISBN 0-312-05447-5   LC 90-48934
"Auto racing enthusiasts will relish Taylor's overview, which includes highlights of auto racing history in general as well as a comprehensive view of racing at the Indianapolis Motor Speedway, site of the famous Indy 500." Booklist

796.8 Combat sports

Corcoran, John, 1948-
The martial arts sourcebook. HarperPerennial 1994 434p il pa $18   **796.8**
1. Martial arts
ISBN 0-06-273259-5   LC 93-46842
Replaces the author's The original martial arts encyclopedia
This "volume is divided into five parts: part 1 consists of the various styles and practices of the martial arts around the world; part 2 lists famous martial artists, members in the halls of fame and other awards, and birth and death dates of various personalities. Part 3 is the major section of the book and includes the champions of the martial arts, with competition results. . . . Parts 4 and 5 provide information on films and videos on the martial arts and a business directory and sources for martial arts associations, which is worldwide in scope." Booklist

796.9 Ice and snow sports

Stark, Peter
Winter adventure; a complete guide to winter sports; by Peter Stark and Steven M. Krauzer. Norton 1995 224p il (Trailside series guide) flexible bdg $17.95   **796.9**
1. Winter sports
ISBN 0-393-31400-6   LC 95-34646
This guide to winter sports covers sledding, snowshoeing, dogsledding and skijoring, snowboarding, games such as cross-country tag and hare and hounds, the nature of snow and ice, ice skating, iceboating, ice climbing, curling and barrel jumping, winter camping, walking on snow and ice, dressing for winter, and winter safety. It lists organizations, mail-order sources, and information sources

796.91 Ice skating

Brennan, Christine
Inside edge; a revealing journey into the secret world of figure skating. Scribner 1996 319p il $23
     796.91
1. Ice skating
ISBN 0-684-80167-1   LC 95-45697
Also available in paperback from Doubleday

Brennan, Christine—*Continued*
"A Lisa Drew book"
"Profiling the top-ranked skaters, this book focuses on the 1994-95 season." N Y Times Book Rev

796.93   Skiing

Cazeneuve, Brian
Cross-country skiing; a complete guide; illustrations by Ron Hildebrand. Norton 1995 192p il (Trailside series guide) flexible bdg $17.95
                                                                796.93
1. Skiing
ISBN 0-393-31335-2   LC 95-5529
This illustrated guide to cross-country skiing covers equipment, techniques, backcountry skiing, clothing, safety, and fitness, and lists organizations, mail-order sources, and information sources

Gamma, Karl
The handbook of skiing. rev & updated ed. Knopf 1992 320p il maps pa $21   796.93
1. Skiing
ISBN 0-679-74316-2   LC 92-53050
First published 1981
Illustrated with drawings, diagrams and photographs, this book offers tips on practicing, training, competition, equipment and developing style

796.962   Ice hockey

Falla, Jack
Sports illustrated hockey; learn to play the modern way. Sports Illustrated 1994 219p il pa $14.95   796.962
1. Hockey
ISBN 1-568-00004-9   LC 93-28165
"Sports illustrated winner's circle books"
First published 1987
This illustrated introduction to the sport presents information on equipment, strategy, goalkeeping, team play, training and conditioning

796.98   Winter Olympic games

Wallechinsky, David, 1948-
The complete book of the Winter Olympics. 1994 ed. Little, Brown 1993 xx, 205p il hardcover o.p. paperback available $8.95   796.98
1. Olympic games
ISBN 0-316-92080-0 (pa)   LC 93-17631
This volume presents final results of Winter Olympic games since 1908. The volume includes facts, stories and profiles

797.1   Boating

Conner, Dennis
Learn to sail; [by] Dennis Conner and Michael Levitt; illustrations by Chris Lloyd. St. Martin's Press 1994 240p il $22.95   797.1
1. Sailing
ISBN 0-312-11020-0   LC 94-2611
In this beginner's guide "Conner recommends boats on which to learn, defines sailing etiquette, offers weather analysis, and discusses sailing under adverse conditions and coping with emergencies. . . . This is an excellent introduction to the principles of the sport." Booklist
Includes bibliographical references

Harrison, David, 1938-
Canoeing; the complete guide to equipment and technique. Stackpole Bks. 1996 190p il $15.95
                                                                797.1
1. Canoes and canoeing
ISBN 0-8117-2426-3   LC 95-44934
First published 1981 by Harper & Row with title: Sports illustrated canoeing
This introduction to canoeing covers equipment, paddling technique, competitions, and more

Krauzer, Steven M.
Kayaking; whitewater and touring basics; introduction by John Viehman; illustrations by Ron Hildebrand. Norton 1995 192p il (Trailside series guide) flexible bdg $17.95   797.1
1. Canoes and canoeing
ISBN 0-393-31336-0   LC 95-5527
This illustrated guide to kayaking covers equipment, techniques, and safety and lists organizations, mail-order sources, and information sources

797.3   Other aquatic sports

Duane, Daniel, 1967-
Caught inside; a surfer's year on the California coast. North Point Press 1996 239p $21   797.3
1. Surfing
ISBN 0-86547-494-X   LC 95-25704
"Duane recounts his adventures surfing California's coastline, liberally interspersing his narrative with anecdotes of natural history (whale sightings and encounters with sharks), colorful portraits of companions and strangers, and the mundane aspects of making a surfboard." Booklist

798 Equestrian sports and animal racing

Paulsen, Gary
Winterdance; the fine madness of running the Iditarod. Harcourt Brace & Co. 1994 256p il $21.95; pa $12   **798**
1. Iditarod Trail Sled Dog Race, Alaska
ISBN 0-15-126227-6; 0-15-600145-4 (pa)
LC 93-42096
"This book is primarily an account of Paulsen's first Iditarod and its frequent life-threatening disasters. . . . However, the book is more than a tabulation of tribulations; it is a meditation on the extraordinary attraction this race holds for some men and women." Libr J

Schultz, Jeff
Iditarod; the great race to Nome; photography by Jeff Schultz; text by Bill Sherwonit; foreword by Joe Redington, Sr.; preface by Susan Butcher. Alaska Northwest Bks. 1991 144p il maps pa $19.95   **798**
1. Iditarod Trail Sled Dog Race, Alaska
ISBN 0-88240-411-3   LC 91-12909
This volume "gives a brief history of the Iditarod Trail, famous for the 1925 diphtheria serum run to Nome, and then describes the race route with highlights of the hazards facing participants and some of the exciting race finishes." Libr J
Includes bibliographical references

799 Fishing, hunting, shooting

Paulsen, Gary
Father water, Mother woods; essays on fishing and hunting in the North Woods; with illustrations by Ruth Wright Paulsen. Delacorte Press 1994 159p il $16.95   **799**
1. Hunting 2. Fishing
ISBN 0-385-32053-1   LC 94-2737
Also available in paperback from Bantam Doubleday Dell Bks. for Young Readers
"This collection of autobiographical essays, identifies [Paulsen's] youthful experiences in the woods and rivers of northern Minnesota. . . . Throughout it all, descriptions of light and water, of fish and wildlife, kindle in the reader a measure of the author's own complex respect for nature." Publ Wkly

799.1 Fishing

Mason, Bill, 1929-
Sports illustrated fly fishing; learn from a master. [rev ed] Sports Illustrated 1994 255p il pa $14.95   **799.1**
1. Fishing
ISBN 1-56800-033-2
"Sports illustrated winner's circle books"
First published 1988

An illustrated introduction to the sport of fly fishing. Emphasis is placed on equipment and technique

Merwin, John
Fly fishing; a Trailside guide; illustrations by Ron Hildebrand. Norton 1996 192p il (Trailside series guide) flexible bdg $17.95   **799.1**
1. Fly casting
ISBN 0-393-31476-6   LC 96-2141
This illustrated guide to fly fishing covers equipment, tying knots, types of flies, fly casting techniques for different types of fish, and lists organizations, schools, mail-order sources, and information sources
Include bibliographical references

800 LITERATURE AND RHETORIC

803 Literature—Encyclopedias and dictionaries

Abrams, M. H. (Meyer Howard), 1912-
A glossary of literary terms. Harcourt Brace & Co. pa $25   **803**
1. Literature—Dictionaries
First published 1957. (6th edition, 1993) Periodically revised
In a series of essays, the author discusses literary terms and definitions ranging from the traditional to the avant-garde. Subsidiary terms are included under major or generic terms

Beckson, Karl E., 1926-
Literary terms; a dictionary; [by] Karl Beckson and Arthur Ganz. 3rd ed rev & enl. Noonday Press 1989 308p pa $10.95   **803**
1. Literature—Dictionaries
ISBN 0-374-52177-8   LC 88-34368
First published 1960 with title: A reader's guide to literary terms
"This dictionary defines terms, concepts, and theories concerning various aspects of literary history and criticism. Alphabetically arranged terms are clearly and concisely defined with frequent illustrative quotations/excerpts from literature. Sources for further reading are given." Nichols. Guide to Ref Books for Sch Media Cent. 4th edition

Benet's reader's encyclopedia. HarperCollins Pubs. 1996 $50   **803**
1. Literature—Dictionaries
LC 96-217151
First published 1948 under the editorship of William Rose Benet. (4th edition 1996). Periodically revised
Current editor: Bruce Murphy
This encyclopedia contains over 10,000 entries and covers world literature from early times to the present. Includes entries on authors, literary movements, principal characters, plot synopses, terms, awards, myths and legends, etc.

Brewer's dictionary of phrase and fable. Harper & Row $45
803
1. Literature—Dictionaries 2. Allusions
First published 1870. (15th edition 1995) Periodically revised
Current editor: Ivor H. Evans
"Over 15,000 brief entries give the meanings and origins of a broad range of terms, expressions, and names of real, fictitious and mythical characters from world history, science, the arts and literature." N Y Public Libr. Ref Books for Child Collect. 2d edition

Columbia dictionary of modern European literature; Jean-Albert Bédé and William B. Edgerton, general editors. 2d ed fully rev and enl. Columbia Univ. Press 1980 895p $195
803
1. Literature—Dictionaries 2. Authors, European—Dictionaries
ISBN 0-231-03717-1   LC 80-17082
First published 1947
"Contains signed articles by some 500 contributors on over 1,800 authors who write (or wrote) in European languages other than English from the late 19th century to the present. General articles on individual literatures are also included." Choice

The **Concise** Oxford dictionary of literary terms; [compiled by] Chris Baldick. Oxford Univ. Press 1990 246p $24; pa $9.95
803
1. Literature—Dictionaries 2. English language—Terms and phrases
ISBN 0-19-811733-7; 0-19-282893-2 (pa)
LC 89-71330
"This work defines more than 1,000 literary terms, old and new, often omitted or not clearly defined in general dictionaries. Most terms are drawn from English, but frequently used foreign words and phrases are included. Those looking for the meaning of 'purple patches' or 'beat writers' will find those definitions and more, often with a touch of humor. Frequent illustrative examples are provided. Recommended for high schools." Nichols. Guide to Ref Books for Sch Media Cent. 4th edition

Cuddon, J. A. (John Anthony), 1928-
A dictionary of literary terms and literary theory. 3rd ed. Blackwell Ref. 1991 1051p hardcover o.p.; Penguin Bks. paperback available $15.95
803
1. Literature—Dictionaries
ISBN 0-14-051227-6 (pa)   LC 90-49943
First published 1977 by Doubleday with title: A dictionary of literary terms
"Comprehensive dictionary covering all literatures and time periods with basic definitions as currently used. Categories include technical terms, forms, genres, groups, movements, -isms, character types, phrases, motifs or themes, concepts, objects, and styles. Entries often indicate origin and cite examples. Numerous *see* and *see also* references." Guide to Ref Books. 11th edition

Cyclopedia of literary characters II; edited by Frank N. Magill. Salem Press 1990 4v set $300
803
1. Literature—Stories, plots, etc. 2. Literature—Dictionaries 3. Characters and characteristics in literature
ISBN 0-89356-517-2   LC 90-8550
Companion to Cyclopedia of literary characters (1963, o.p.)
New edition in preparation
"This set covers some 5,000 characters in 1,437 works. . . . Arranged alphabetically by title, characters for each work are listed in order of importance. Central characters are described more fully, and pronunciations for names are provided when necessary. Indexed by title, author, and character. . . . The set enables the reader to become familiar with personalities from important works or to identify the books in which specific characters appear." Nichols. Guide to Ref Books for Sch Media Cent. 4th edition

Encyclopedia of world literature in the 20th century; based on the first edition edited by Wolfgang Bernard Fleischmann; Leonard S. Klein, general editor. rev ed. Ungar; distributed by Gale Res. 1981-1993 5v il set $600   **803**
1. Literature—Dictionaries   2. Literature—Bio-bibliography
ISBN 0-8103-9619-X   LC 81-3357
First four volumes originally published 1967-1975
Volume 5 supplement and index, edited by Steven R. Serafin, published by Continuum. Available separately for $150 (ISBN 0-8264-0571-1)
"This multivolume encyclopedia provides extensive up-to-date coverage on international developments in twentieth-century literature. While emphasis is given to writers of Europe and North America, this work also represents one of the most valuable sources of information on national literatures, including Third World countries." Ref Sources for Small & Medium-sized Libr. 5th edition

Harmon, William, 1938-
A handbook to literature; [by] William Harmon, C. Hugh Holman; based on the original edition by William Flint Thrall and Addison Hibbard. Prentice-Hall pa $30
803
1. English literature—Dictionaries 2. American literature—Dictionaries
ISBN 0-13-234782-2
First published 1936 by Doubleday under the authorship of William Flint Thrall and Addison Hibbard. (7th edition 1995) Periodically revised
This work provides "explanations of terms, concepts, schools, and movements in literature. Alphabetical arrangement with numerous cross-references as well as bibliographic references for some entries." Guide to Ref Books. 11th edition

Larousse dictionary of writers; editor, Rosemary Goring. Larousse (London); distributed by Larousse Kingfisher Chambers 1994 1070p $40; pa $18.95 **803**
1. Literature—Bio-bibliography 2. Authors—Dictionaries
ISBN 0-7523-0006-7; 0-7523-0039-3 (pa)
LC 94-75741
This "is a broad survey of more than 6,000 authors 'from all periods and all countries.' While the editor admits to a British and American bias, a successful attempt has been made to include authors from numerous nations. . . . Entries are arranged by name, followed by year of birth and death in parentheses and the briefest of biographical sketches. These sketches usually include mention of works that might be considered representative." Booklist

Lass, Abraham Harold, 1907-
The Facts on File dictionary of classical, biblical, and literary allusions; [by] Abraham H. Lass, David Kiremidjian, Ruth M. Goldstein. Facts on File 1987 240p $21.95 **803**
1. Literature—Dictionaries 2. Allusions
ISBN 0-8160-1267-9
LC 86-24366
This dictionary has an "alphabetical rather than classified approach. Its classical heroes and gods, biblical persons and quotations, and literary references drawn mainly from Shakespeare's plays and from nineteenth-century novels are commonly encountered allusions derived from 'the Judeo-Christian and European literary and cultural traditions' (introduction). . . . Entries note the sources of the allusions and succinctly explain their original and current significance. Cross-references guide users from key words and phrases to entries." Am Ref Books Annu, 1988

Merriam-Webster's encyclopedia of literature. Merriam-Webster 1995 1236p il $39.95 **803**
1. Literature—Dictionaries
ISBN 0-87779-042-6
LC 94-42741
This work "offers entries on authors, characters, mythological and folkloric figures, scholars, critics, literary styles, movements, terms, landmarks, prizes, and journals. It also has a pronunciation guide for most entries and many photos and illustrations." Libr J
For a fuller review see: Booklist, July, 1995

Pringle, David
Imaginary people; a who's who of fictional characters from the eighteenth century to the present day. 2nd ed. Scolar Press 1996 296p $49.95 **803**
1. Characters and characteristics in literature—Dictionaries
ISBN 1-85928-162-1
LC 95-43986
First published 1988 by World Almanac Pub.
A dictionary of over 1400 fictional characters from over two-and-a-half centuries of stories, novels, films, songs, opera, television series, and comic strips. Each entry includes a brief outline of the character's creation and appearance in various sequels and adaptions in other media. An index of creators is included
Includes bibliographical references

808 Rhetoric

Bender, Sheila
Writing personal essays; how to shape your life experiences for the page. Writer's Digest Bks. 1995 233p il $17.99 **808**
1. Authorship 2. Rhetoric 3. Essay
ISBN 0-89879-665-2
LC 95-2755
The author uses "classroom-tested methods to help professional and amateur authors master eight classic essay structures, including description, definition, narration, and persuasion." Booklist
Includes bibliographical references

The **Chicago** manual of style. University of Chicago Press il $40 **808**
1. Authorship—Handbooks, manuals, etc. 2. Publishers and publishing 3. English language—Usage
First published 1906 with title: A manual of style. (14th edition 1993) Frequently reprinted with minor revisions
"This style manual has become recognized as a reliable standard for writers and editors preparing manuscripts for publication. Major sections cover bookmaking, style, and production and printing." N Y Public Libr. Book of How & Where to Look It Up

Dalton, Rick
The student's guide to good writing; building writing skills for success in college; [by] Rick Dalton and Marianne Dalton. College Entrance Examination Bd. 1990 166p pa $9.95 **808**
1. Creative writing
ISBN 0-87447-353-5
LC 89-85765
"The authors use anecdotes from college students about writing, excerpts from student writing, and a question and answer chapter from students to students. The information about the writing process is clear and a chapter on using word processors is a contemporary addition to a familiar topic." Voice Youth Advocates
Includes bibliography

Everhart, Nancy
How to write a term paper. 2nd ed. Watts 1994 142p il (Speak out, write on!) lib bdg $22.70 **808**
1. Report writing 2. Research
ISBN 0-531-11200-4
LC 94-29385
First published 1987 with title: So you have to write a term paper!
Describes the steps in writing a term paper, including choosing a topic, doing research, writing an outline, taking notes, doing a rough draft, and editing the final paper
Includes bibliographical references

Gibaldi, Joseph, 1942-
MLA handbook for writers of research papers. 4th ed. Modern Lang. Assn. of Am. 1995 293p il pa $12.50 **808**
1. Report writing
ISBN 0-87352-565-5
LC 94-38577
First published 1977 with title: MLA handbook for writers of research papers, theses, and dissertations

Gibaldi, Joseph, 1942-—*Continued*
This manual discusses research strategies, formatting, documenting sources, writing basics and utilizing electronic sources

Gutkind, Lee
Creative nonfiction; how to live it and write it. Chicago Review Press 1996 168p il $14.95   **808**
1. Authorship 2. English language—Composition and exercises
ISBN 1-55652-266-5   LC 96-1448
"A Ziggurat book for talented beginner"
The author has "concisely packaged a creative-writing course in a book, using readings from experts in the field and assignments from his university writing class. He considers topics such as ethics, shadowing, schedules, cinematic techniques, and frame or story structure. Twenty exercises, which require letter writing, journal keeping, essay writing, and revision, turn the reader into a class member sans grade." Libr J

Henderson, Kathy
The market guide for young writers; where and how to sell what you write. Writer's Digest Bks. pa $16.99   **808**
1. Authorship—Handbooks, manuals, etc.
First published 1986 by Savage Pub. (5th edition 1996) Periodically revised
Provides publishing information for the young writer including tips on preparing a manuscript, profiles of published young writers, opportunities online, and market and contest listings
Includes bibliographical references

Inventing the truth; the art and craft of memoir; [by] Russell Baker [et al.]; edited with an introduction by William Zinsser. rev & expanded 2nd ed. Houghton Mifflin 1995 202p pa $10.95   **808**
1. Authors, American
ISBN 0-395-73101-1   LC 95-17169
First published 1987
Russell Baker, Annie Dillard, Alfred Kazin, Toni Morrison, Eileen Simpson, Ian Frazier, Henry Louis Gates, Jill Ker Conway discuss what writing a memoir means to them
Includes bibliography

Karls, John B.
The writer's handbook; reviewer/consultants, John B. Karls, Ronald Szymanski. 2nd ed. National Textbook 1990 255p il $15.95; pa $9.95   **808**
1. Rhetoric 2. Authorship—Handbooks, manuals, etc.
ISBN 0-8442-5375-8; 0-8442-5372-3 (pa)
       LC 89-61659
This guide to writing skills covers grammar, punctuation, style, usage and spelling. A chapter is devoted to business writing

Kronenwetter, Michael
How to write a news article. Watts 1995 144p il (Speak out, write on!) lib bdg $22.70   **808**
1. Journalism 2. Authorship
ISBN 0-531-11238-1   LC 95-8527
Discusses basic aspects of news journalism, including judging what is newsworthy, gathering information, journalistic ethics and bias, and shaping a story
Includes bibliography

Li, Xia, 1964-
Electronic styles; a handbook for citing electronic information; [by] Xia Li and Nancy B. Crane. 2nd ed. Information Today 1996 213p pa $19.99   **808**
1. Bibliography 2. Information systems
ISBN 1-57387-027-7   LC 96-25799
First published 1993
The author presents standardized citation formats for electronic documents in both APA and MLA style. The guide shows how to cite full text information files, e-mail, bulletin board systems, Internet-accessible electronic journals, bibliography databases, commercial online documents and World Wide Web resources
Includes bibliographical references

Merriam-Webster's standard American style manual. Merriam-Webster 1994 480p $17.95
       808
1. Authorship—Handbooks, manuals, etc. 2. English language—Usage
ISBN 0-87779-133-3   LC 94-25362
First published 1985 with title: Webster's standard American style manual
This volume focuses on the basic elements of style: punctuation, capitalization, italicization, hyphenation, plurals, possessives, compounds, the treatment of numbers and abbreviations, bibliographical and footnoting forms. Relevant conventions, variations and exceptions are given

Mungo, Raymond, 1946-
Your autobiography; more than 300 questions to help you write your personal history; [by] Ray Mungo. Collier Bks. 1994 100p pa $8.95   **808**
1. Authorship 2. Biography as a literary form
ISBN 0-02-029545-6   LC 93-31918
"Mungo leads readers through the process of writing an autobiography in a handy guide filled with questions designed to stimulate recollection. Useful for student assignments." Booklist

The **New** York Public Library writer's guide to style and usage. HarperCollins Pubs. 1994 838p il $35   **808**
1. Authorship—Handbooks, manuals, etc. 2. English language—Usage
ISBN 0-06-270064-2   LC 93-33255
"A Stonesong Press book"
In five parts, this "guide covers (1) current English usage, with special attention given to bias-free language and commonly misused or confused words; (2) grammar, with an emphasis on controversial issues and with . . . illustrated examples; (3) style, including lists of common

The New York Public Library writer's guide to style and usage—*Continued*

abbreviations and a chapter on special characters in 19 different languages; (4) assembling and checking the manuscript, including a discussion of copyright and instructions for indexing; and (5) physical preparation of the manuscript. Information regarding computer-aided writing and production is [included]." Booklist

Includes bibliographical references

O'Connor, Stephen, 1952-
Will my name be shouted out? reaching inner city students through the power of writing. Simon & Schuster 1996 382p $23.50   **808**
1. English language—Study and teaching 2. Junior high schools 3. Education—Social aspects 4. Creative writing
ISBN 0-684-81186-3   LC 95-26536
"Can literature help inner-city kids cope with despair and violence? O'Connor assumed so until he began teaching creative writing at a New York City junior high school. Then the reality of his students' besieged lives—severe poverty, neglect, abuse, drug addiction, shootings, malnutrition, homelessness—seriously challenged his long-cherished ideals." Booklist
The author "weaves his youngsters' essays and poems into plays that they perform for the rest of the school. The ordeals of casting and rehearsing the plays—not to mention persuading the student actors to show up—provide much of the book's dramatic impact." N Y Times Book Rev

Plotnik, Arthur, 1937-
The elements of expression; putting thoughts into words. Holt & Co. 1996 225p $20   **808**
1. Rhetoric
ISBN 0-8050-3773-X   LC 95-42933
The author provides numerous examples of how to utilize the English language to write or speak forcefully and effectively
"As a book on language should be, it is well written, but it is also humorous, thought-provoking, and right on the mark." Libr J
Includes bibliography

Roberts, Edgar V.
Writing themes about literature. Prentice-Hall $21.75   **808**
1. Rhetoric 2. Literature—Study and teaching
First published 1964. (8th edition 1995) Periodically revised
This book presents a number of analytical approaches important to the study and assimilation of works of literature

Schiwy, Marlene A.
A voice of her own; women and the journal writing journey. Simon & Schuster 1996 380p pa $14   **808**
1. Diaries
ISBN 0-684-80342-9   LC 96-5325
"A Fireside book"

The author considers various aspects "of journal keeping, from how and why keeping a journal can make life more meaningful to various types of journals and writing styles. She offers advice about choosing blank books, keeping a journal private, and deciding when to reread old journals. Schiwy also delves into the history of women diarists and discusses the many reasons women keep diaries at different stages of life." Booklist

Includes bibliographical references

Strunk, William, 1869-1946
The elements of style; by William Strunk, Jr.; with revisions, an introduction, and a chapter on writing by E. B. White. 3d ed. Macmillan 1979 85p $10.95; pa $5.95   **808**
1. Rhetoric
ISBN 0-02-418190-0; 0-02-418200-1 (pa)
        LC 78-18444
First appeared 1918, privately printed; first trade edition published 1920 by Harcourt Brace & Co.
"This small volume, revised by award-winning children's writer and essayist White, is a valuable addition to any library. It is prescriptive, conservative, and humorous; in sum, it is the best book available on how to write English prose. Rules of good usage are stated, followed by incorrect and correct examples." Nichols Guide to Ref Books for Sch Media Cent. 4th edition

Turabian, Kate L., 1893-1987
A manual for writers of term papers, theses, and dissertations. University of Chicago Press (Chicago guides to writing, editing, and publishing) $27.50; pa $12.95   **808**
1. Report writing 2. Dissertations
First published 1937 with title: A manual for writers of dissertations. (6th edition 1996) Periodically revised
Designed to serve as a guide to suitable style in the presentation of formal papers—term papers, reports, articles, theses, dissertations—both in scientific and in non-scientific fields
"A standard publication, well-organized and widely used." Guide to Ref Books. 11th edition

Winkler, Anthony C.
Writing the research paper; a handbook with both the MLA and APA documentation styles; [by] Anthony C. Winkler, Jo Ray McCuen. 4th ed. Harcourt Brace College Pubs. 1994 354p il $16.75   **808**
1. Report writing 2. Research
ISBN 0-15-500166-3   LC 92-76185
First published 1979
Among the topics covered are: choosing a topic; libraries and background sources; outlining; rough drafts; documentation; punctuation, mechanics, and spelling. A sample student paper is included
Includes bibliographical references

The Writer's digest guide to good writing; edited by Thomas Clark [et al.] Writer's Digest Bks. 1994 338p $18.95   **808**
1. Authorship
ISBN 0-89879-640-7   LC 93-43554
This collection of articles culled from issues of Writer's Digest magazine contains "essays on how to write

The Writer's digest guide to good writing—
Continued

with simplicity, plot and pace a story, build suspense, create characters, and tackle certain genres, including mysteries, horror, romance, and various forms of nonfiction. The selections are organized by decades and include essays by Erle Stanley Gardner, Irving Wallace, Louis L'Amour [and] Allen Ginsberg." Booklist

The **Writer's** handbook. Writer $29.95　　**808**
1. Authorship—Handbooks, manuals, etc. 2. Publishers and publishing
ISSN 0084-2710

Annual. First published 1936. Current editor Sylvia Burack

"Articles on writing and manuscript preparation make up much of each annual. The main part of the book is a market guide, mainly to the periodical field but including radio, television, and book publishing as well. For each publisher the entry provides name, address, editor, editorial requirements, type of material sought, payment rate, and other useful information. . . . This work is far more than a directory of publishers. Its articles on how to write for specific markets make it a first choice of publications of its kind." Nichols. Guide to Ref Books for Sch Media Cent. 4th edition

The **Writer's** market. Writer's Digest Bks. $26.95
808
1. Authorship—Handbooks, manuals, etc. 2. Publishers and publishing
ISSN 0084-2729

Annual. First published 1926

"This guide to markets for prospective writers covers over 4,000 outlets from book and magazine publishers to script producers and greeting card companies. Each entry offers name and address, type of material sought, editorial needs, submission requirements, payment rates, and other useful data." Nichols. Guide to Ref Books for Sch Media Cent. 4th edition

Zinsser, William Knowlton
On writing well; an informal guide to writing nonfiction. HarperPerennial $27.50　　**808**
1. Rhetoric 2. Authorship
First published 1976. (5th edition 1994) Periodically revised

Among the topics discussed are: style, usage, clutter, imprecision and organization
Includes bibliographical references

808.06　Writing children's literature

Peck, Richard, 1934-
Love and death at the mall; teaching and writing for the literate young. Delacorte Press 1994 161p $16.95　　**808.06**
1. Authorship 2. Books and reading 3. Young adults' literature—Technique
ISBN 0-385-31173-7　　　　　　　　　LC 93-3933

The author "examines the creative process, literature that young adults . . . respond to, and how life is chang-

ing for parents and teachers in an era when young people are looking for alternative power sources. He touches the bases on conformity, the looming issue of censorship, and mall culture." Publisher's note
Includes bibliographical references

808.1　Rhetoric of poetry

Aristotle, 384-322 B.C.
Poetics　　　　　　　　　　　　　　　**808.1**
1. Poetics 2. Aesthetics
Hardcover and paperback editions available from various publishers

In this basic work of literary criticism, Aristotle discusses the fundamental principles of poetry and its various forms, emphasizing tragedy and the epic

Bugeja, Michael J.
The art and craft of poetry. Writer's Digest Bks. 1994 339p $19.95　　**808.1**
1. Poetics
ISBN 0-89879-633-4　　　　　　　　LC 93-38192

The author begins this handbook for aspiring poets by describing "how keeping a journal helps poets focus their observations, contemplations, and discoveries. Bugeja goes on to describe various genres of poetry, the elements of poems, styles such as narrative and lyric poetry, and forms such as the sonnet, villanelle, and sestina. His explanations are lucid, his examples illuminating, and his suggested exercises useful and geared to different levels of proficiency." Booklist

Deutsch, Babette, 1895-1982
Poetry handbook: a dictionary of terms. 4th ed. Funk & Wagnalls 1974 203p o.p.; HarperCollins Pubs. paperback available $13　　**808.1**
1. Poetics 2. Poetry—Terminology
ISBN 0-06-463548-1 (pa)
First published 1957

"The craft of verse described in dictionary form. Terms and techniques are defined and illustrated." N Y Public Libr. Ref Books for Child Collect. 2d edition

Drury, John
The poetry dictionary; foreword by Dana Gioia. Story Press (Cincinnati) 1995 324p $18.99　**808.1**
1. Poetry—Dictionaries 2. Poetics
ISBN 1-884910-04-1　　　　　　　　LC 95-4816

"Spanning the centuries from ode to rap, *The Poetry Dictionary* contains 284 entries that define movements and schools of poetry, forms of verse, rhyme and stress patterns, and poetic devices. Entries range in length from a paragraph for *canto* to more than seven pages for *sonnet*." Booklist

Higginson, William J., 1938-
The haiku handbook; how to write, share, and teach haiku; [by] William J. Higginson with Penny Harter. McGraw-Hill 1985 331p o.p.; Kodansha Am. paperback available $12　　**808.1**
1. Haiku
ISBN 4-770-01430-9 (pa)　　　　　　LC 84-17174

The author "surveys the original and related forms (renga, haibun, senryu), inventors and developers (Basho,

Higginson, William J., 1938——_Continued_

Buson, Issa, Shiki), and the numerous variations that later authors, especially in other languages, have wrought on haiku's simple principles. He discusses the many uses—artistic, personal, psychological—that the mode can serve, encouraging the reader all along the way to use the form, to experiment, and thus to express thoughts and feelings. . . . An extensive reference section gives word lists, a glossary, and good bibliographies." Booklist

Jerome, Judson

The poet's handbook. Writer's Digest Bks. 1980 224p hardcover o.p. paperback available $14.99

808.1

1. Poetics

ISBN 0-89879-219-3 (pa)   LC 80-17270

"This is not the usual alphabetized handbook. It gives a brief but scholarly background of the poet's place in early times and later history and moves on to discuss in individual chapters the craft of poetry: syllable-counting, meter, rhyme, free verse, the rhythms of the English language, and so on. It is more personal than one usually finds such a book to be, and it presents almost everything a beginning poet, as well as one who has mastered the craft, should know." Choice

Kowit, Steve

In the palm of your hand; a poet's portable workshop: a lively and illuminating guide for the practicing poet. Tilbury House 1995 274p il $12.95

808.1

1. Poetics

ISBN 0-88448-149-2   LC 94-48087

"Kowit covers a lot of technical material on metrical variations and line breaks and sound, and he balances it by attending to the sources of poetry in dream and emotion, in longing and loss. Although likely to find its largest audience among aspiring poets, Kowit's effort is substantial enough to be of use to more practiced poets and to poetry readers, too." Booklist

Includes bibliographical references

Oliver, Mary, 1935-

A poetry handbook. Harcourt Brace & Co. 1994 130p pa $11

808.1

1. Poetics

ISBN 0-15-672400-6   LC 93-49676

"A Harvest original"

A "handbook for young poets on the formal aspects and structure of poetry. Oliver excels at explaining the sound and sense of poetry—from scansion to imagery, diction to voice. . . . Sage advice is given in an entire chapter dedicated to revision, wherein Oliver urges poets to consider their first draft 'an unfinished piece of work' that can be polished and improved later. Written in a pleasant and lucid style, this book is a wonderful resource." Libr J

Packard, William

The poet's dictionary; a handbook of prosody and poetic devices. Harper & Row 1989 212p $25; pa $13

808.1

1. Poetics 2. Versification

ISBN 0-06-016130-2; 0-06-272045-7 (pa)

LC 88-45899

This "dictionary gives succinct definitions enhanced by some historical and other explanatory notes, always followed by examples from familiar sources. . . . Reliability and authenticity are hallmarks of this dictionary." Choice

Includes bibliographical references

Poet's market. Writer's Digest Bks. $22.99 **808.1**

ISSN 0883-5470

Annual. First published 1989

"Useful for those aspiring to publish their poems in literary journals and magazines. . . . Entries include a brief journal profile, submission requirements, and contact information. Offers advice to beginning poets on getting published, brief articles by working poets/editors, grant information, contests and awards, poetry readings, writing colonies, organizations and publications useful to poets. Indexes for chapbook publishers, publishers by subject, publishers by state, and a general index." Guide to Ref Books. 11th edition

Wallace, Robert, 1932-

Writing poems; [by] Robert Wallace, Michelle Boisseau. 4th ed. HarperCollins Pubs.; distributed by Addison Wesley Longman 1996 xxi, 410p pa $29.59

808.1

1. Poetics

ISBN 0-673-99013-3   LC 95-3563

The authors address topics ranging from discussions of verse forms to the technicalities of submitting a poem for publication

Includes bibliographical references

808.2   Rhetoric of drama

Catron, Louis E.

The elements of playwriting. Macmillan 1993 220p hardcover o.p. paperback available $9.95

808.2

1. Drama—Technique

ISBN 0-02-069291-9 (pa)   LC 92-31037

The author discusses "plot, dialogue, and character development, along with practical guidelines on working with actors and directors, getting produced and published, and finding an agent." Publisher's note

808.3   Rhetoric of fiction

Conrad, Barnaby, 1922-

The complete guide to writing fiction; [by] Barnaby Conrad and the staff of the Santa Barbara Writers' Conference. Writer's Digest Bks. 1990 309p $18.95

808.3

1. Fiction—Technique

ISBN 0-89879-395-5   LC 90-12287

"Keynote editorials, gleaned from speeches given at the annual Santa Barbara Writers' Conference, are writ-

Conrad, Barnaby, 1922——_Continued_
ten by a range of authors, including Danielle Steel, Ray
Bradbury, Eudora Welty, and Alice Adams. This nicely
organized tutorial on crafting the major elements of a
novel features further significant suggestions on revising
a manuscript, selling short stories, hiring an agent, marketing the manuscript, and handling rejection." Booklist

Gardner, John, 1933-1982
The art of fiction; notes on craft for young
writers. Knopf 1984 224p $17.95; pa $10　**808.3**
1. Fiction—Technique
ISBN 0-394-50469-0; 0-679-73403-1 (pa)
　　　　　　　　　　　　　　　　　LC 83-47850
"This essay distills the late Gardner's ripest thoughts
about what fiction is and how to go about learning to
write it. The initial section deals with 'literary-aesthetic
theory,' the second with 'the fictional process.' . . . The
book concludes with two sets of exercises, one for class
use and one for individual use. Recommended for any
young writer or writing class, and for all readers who
care about the craft of fiction." Booklist

Henry, Laurie
The fiction dictionary. Story Press (Cincinnati)
1995 324p $18.99　　　　　　　　　　**808.3**
1. Fiction—Technique 2. Fiction—Dictionaries
ISBN 1-884910-05-X　　　　　　LC 95-4269
Henry provides "definitions of 345 terms relating to
fiction, including genres, narrative devices, elements of
fictional works, and critical theories. In addition to citing
examples of works that illustrate a term, she frequently
supplements her explanations with brief excerpts from
novels and short stories." Booklist

Roth, Martin, 1924-
The writer's complete crime reference book. rev
ed. Writer's Digest Bks. 1993 287p il $19.95
　　　　　　　　　　　　　　　　　808.3
1. Mystery fiction—Technique 2. Crime
ISBN 0-89879-564-8　　　　　　LC 93-2889
First published 1990
"Chapters on crime, criminals, cops, investigations,
courts, prisons, and language offer tips to writers who
want their stories to be realistic but who cannot do the
primary research themselves. Specialized vocabulary,
including the latest crime-related slang, is presented and
most sections have lists for further reading." SLJ

Swain, Dwight V.
Creating characters; how to build story people.
Writer's Digest Bks. 1990 195p hardcover o.p.
paperback available $14.99　　　　　**808.3**
1. Fiction—Technique 2. Characters and characteristics in literature
ISBN 0-89879-662-8 (pa)　　　　LC 90-39640
"Swain talks to his readers in a conversational tone,
suggesting techniques, giving examples to illuminate his
points, and offering activities for sharpening character
development skills. This is a book for those already committed to writing fiction and who want to think about the
craft of writing." SLJ
Includes bibliographical references

808.5　Rhetoric of speech

Latrobe, Kathy Howard
Readers theatre for young adults; scripts and
script development; [by] Kathy Howard Latrobe,
Mildred Knight Laughlin. Teacher Ideas Press
1989 130p pa $20　　　　　　　　**808.5**
1. Drama—Collections 2. Drama in education
ISBN 0-87287-743-4　　　　　　LC 89-4552
Presents plays adapted from sixteen literary classics
and includes scenes from novels with suggestions for
adapting them into scripts
Includes bibliography

Leeds, Dorothy
Powerspeak; the complete guide to persuasive
public speaking and presenting. Prentice Hall Press
1988 xxii, 211p o.p.; Berkley Bks. paperback
available $5.50　　　　　　　　　**808.5**
1. Public speaking
ISBN 0-425-12489-4 (pa)　　　　LC 88-45006
The author "approaches the fears and obstacles facing
public speakers in an easy-to-understand treatment that
neither condescends to her audience nor makes light of
the subject. Practical, time-tested suggestions for improving the art of speech-making are provided throughout,
from preparation to presentation. A fine guide on a perennial topic that will boost confidence in even the most
experienced speakers." Booklist
Includes bibliography

Ryan, Margaret, 1950-
How to give a speech. rev ed. Watts 1994 143p
il (Speak out, write on!) lib bdg $22.70; pa $7.95
　　　　　　　　　　　　　　　　　808.5
1. Public speaking
ISBN 0-531-11199-7; 0-531-15804-7 (pa)
　　　　　　　　　　　　　　　　　LC 94-28074
First published 1987 with title: So you have to give
a speech!
The author provides an introduction to "speechmaking,
from how to choose a topic and research it, to how to
write and effectively deliver the speech—conquering
stagefright and other obstacles along the way. She offers
tips on assessing the audience, writing outlines and
drafts, practicing the delivery, using humor and visuals,
developing a style, and other techniques." Publisher's
note
Includes bibliographical references

808.53　Debating and public discussion

Dunbar, Robert E., 1926-
How to debate. rev ed. Watts 1994 128p il
(Speak out, write on!) lib bdg $22.70　　**808.53**
1. Debates and debating
ISBN 0-531-11122-9　　　　　　LC 93-11959
First published 1987

Dunbar, Robert E., 1926——*Continued*

"After a brief discussion of the history of debate, the book moves to a very detailed description of how debates are judged and how to prepare for successful competition. The analysis of successful debating is quite good, with a great deal of attention given to logical thinking and illustrated with examples from Abraham Lincoln to the participants in the 1992 presidential race." Voice Youth Advocates

Includes glossary and bibliography

808.8 Literature—Collections

Bearing witness: stories of the Holocaust; selected by Hazel Rochman and Darlene Z. McCampbell. Orchard Bks. 1995 135p il map $15.95; lib bdg $15.99   **808.8**

1. Holocaust, 1933-1945 2. Literature—Collections
ISBN 0-531-09488-X; 0-531-08788-3 (lib bdg)

LC 95-13352

A "selection of prose about aspects of the Holocaust by writers for adults who were themselves witnesses or brought the stories of participants to public attention, including Primo Levi, Art Spiegelman and Carl Friedman." N Y Times Book Rev

"The editors have included their personal connections to the Holocaust in their introduction. A bibliography of books at the end of the anthology is annotated and will serve as a helpful reference for young adult readers." Voice Youth Advocates

Border crossings: emigration and exile. Rosen Pub. Group 1992 170p il maps (Icarus world issues series) lib bdg $16.95; pa $8.95   **808.8**

1. Literature—Collections 2. Immigration and emigration
ISBN 0-8239-1364-3 (lib bdg); 0-8239-1365-1 (pa)

LC 92-5629

"These writings are a cross section of fiction, nonfiction and photography. . . . Each entry is preceded by a black and white map showing the country or geographical location of the story. There is also a brief biographical sketch and a picture of the author. These stories are set in widely diverse locales, from the United States to Europe, Asia and Africa." Voice Youth Advocates

"Teachers in various disciplines will appreciate the simple maps introducing each entry, and will be able to make good use of this volume." Booklist

Includes glossary and bibliography

Coming of age; the art of growing up; series editors, Roger Rosen and Patra McSharry Sevastiades. Rosen Pub. Group 1994 178p il (Icarus world issues series) lib bdg $16.95; pa $8.95   **808.8**

1. Literature—Collections 2. Youth
ISBN 0-8239-1805-X (lib bdg); 0-8239-1806-8 (pa)

LC 94-27347

"The 12 stories and essays in this collection (8 fiction, 4 nonfiction) reflect experiences of young people around the world as they enter adulthood. The authors and protagonists represent a broad cross-section of countries and cultures, in peace and at war." SLJ

"There is not a weak entry in this compassionate, thought-provoking, multicultural anthology." Booklist

Includes glossary and bibliography

Daughters of Africa; an international anthology of words and writings by women of African descent: from the ancient Egyptian to the present; edited and with an introduction by Margaret Busby. Pantheon Bks. 1992 li, 1089p o.p.; Ballantine Bks. paperback available $19.95   **808.8**

1. Literature—Collections 2. Black authors 3. Women authors
ISBN 0-345-38268-4 (pa)   LC 92-54116

A "comprehensive collection of writings by over 200 women. . . . An immense range of genres, countries of origin, and styles spans four centuries, seeking to reclaim for women of African descent a firm place in literature. Poetry, memoirs, songs, short stories, and oral histories weave rich, diverse tapestries. Coherently arranged by date of each author's birth, the pieces testify to the individuality of each voice. . . . An extensive scholarly bibliography further enhances the anthology's value." SLJ

Fantastic worlds; myths, tales, and stories; edited and with commentaries by Eric S. Rabkin. Oxford Univ. Press 1979 478p il hardcover o.p. paperback available $14.95   **808.8**

1. Fantasy fiction 2. Literature—Collections
ISBN 0-19-502541-5 (pa)   LC 78-11482

Included in this critical anthology of fantastic tales are "stories and snippets from Genesis, Greek myth, Br'er Rabbit, fairy tales, Carroll and Thurber, Lovecraft and Le Fanu, Bierce and William Morris, Hawthorne and Kafka [among others]." N Y Rev Books

Includes bibliography

Growing up gay; an anthology for young people; edited by Bennett L. Singer. New Press (NY) 1993 317p $21.95; pa $9.95   **808.8**

1. Literature—Collections 2. Homosexuality
ISBN 1-56584-102-6; 1-56584-103-4 (pa)

Paperback edition has title: Growing up gay/growing up lesbian

"Culled from the writings of 56 authors, this book offers a message to gay and lesbian youth that they are not alone. The material here ranges from fiction by James Baldwin, Rita Mae Brown, and David Leavitt to autobiographical essays by Audre Lord, Quentin Crisp, and Martina Navratilova. The book is arranged into categories that encompass self-discovery, relationships, family, and 'facing the world.' . . . Essential for all high school/college libraries and highly recommended for all public libraries." Libr J

Masterplots; 1,801 plot stories and critical evaluations of the world's finest literature; edited by Frank N. Magill; story editor, revised edition, Dayton Kohler. rev 2nd ed, consulting editor, Laurence W. Mazzeno. Salem Press 1996 12v set $600   **808.8**

1. Literature—Stories, plots, etc. 2. Literature—History and criticism
ISBN 0-89356-084-7   LC 96-23382

First published 1976

"Entries are arranged alphabetically by title, with the type of work, author, type and time of plot, locale, first publication date, and principal characters listed. A plot

Masterplots—*Continued*

synopsis is followed by a critical essay and a brief bibliography. Each entry is three to four pages in length. The four indexes included are by chronological date, by geographic locale, by title, and by author. The title *Masterplots* does not convey the depth of information contained in the 12 volumes. The titles treated range chronologically from antiquity to the early 1990s, with the major emphasis on literature of the nineteenth and twentieth centuries. While the majority of the entries are British, European, and United States fiction, the work also encompasses drama, works or collections of poetry, and nonfiction." Am Ref Books Annu, 1997

The **Oxford** book of money; edited by Kevin Jackson. Oxford Univ. Press 1995 479p $30; pa $14.95 **808.8**
1. Literature—Collections 2. Money
ISBN 0-19-214200-3; 0-19-282510-0 (pa)
LC 94-20563
"Rather than offering a history of money, the entries illustrate what writers have said about money and why they consider money important. Within ten sections, entries from Greek and Latin classics, the Bible, and English literature through to modern times illustrate various aspects of economics, personal finance, the stock exchange, and monetary reform. The anthology includes works of visionaries, film directors, philosophers, poets, theologians, and statesmen." Libr J

Read all about it! great read-aloud stories, poems, and newspaper pieces for preteens and teens; edited by Jim Trelease. Penguin Bks. 1993 489p il pa $11.95 **808.8**
1. Young adults' literature 2. Literature—Collections 3. Authors
ISBN 0-14-014655-5
LC 93-21781
This is a collection of 52 selections of fiction, poetry, and nonfiction from newspapers, magazines, and books by such authors as Cynthia Rylant, Jerry Spinelli, Howard Pyle, Rudyard Kipling, Robert W. Service, Maya Angelou, Moss Hart, Pete Hamill, and Leon Garfield. Includes biographical informaton about the authors

The **Sierra** Club desert reader; a literary companion; edited by Gregory McNamee. Sierra Club Bks. 1995 xxiv, 307p pa $16 **808.8**
1. Literature—Collections 2. Deserts
ISBN 0-87156-426-2
LC 95-5603
This is an anthology of fiction, poetry, folklore, natural history, and travel commentary about deserts of the world. It includes writings by Charles Darwin, Captain James Cook, Marco Polo, Edgar Allan Poe, Mark Twain, Antoine de Saint-Exupery, Edith Wharton, and many others
Includes bibliographical references

Teenage soldiers, adult wars. Rosen Pub. Group 1991 170p il (Icarus world issues series) $16.95; pa $8.95 **808.8**
1. Literature—Collections 2. War
ISBN 0-8239-1304-X; 0-8239-1305-8 (pa)
LC 90-26638
A collection of fictional and non-fictional stories and essays dealing with war and its effects on the young

"The scope is worldwide—Africa, Poland, China, Lebanon—with selections ranging from a Pulitzer Prize-winning photographer's record of travels through Nicaragua to an excerpt from a . . . Hebrew novel focusing on a young Israeli soldier on patrol in hostile territory." Booklist
Includes bibliographical references

808.81 Poetry—Collections

Ain't I a woman! a book of women's poetry from around the world; edited by Illona Linthwaite. Bedrick Bks. 1988 136p hardcover o.p. paperback available $7.95 **808.81**
1. Poetry—Women authors—Collections
ISBN 0-87226-209-X (pa)
LC 87-35577
"The poems range from ancient Greek lyrics to contemporary Jamaican 'Dub,' with emphasis on Commonwealth writers. . . . The editor's arrangement of the poems to tell the story of a woman's life from childhood through death provides a compelling framework." Booklist

Animal poems; selected and edited by John Hollander. Knopf 1994 256p (Everyman's library pocket poets) $10.95 **808.81**
1. Animals—Poetry 2. Poetry—Collections
ISBN 0-679-43631-6
This anthology focuses on the poetic treatment of animals from various traditions

A **Book** of love poetry; edited and with an introduction by Jon Stallworthy. Oxford Univ. Press 1974 c1973 393p $30; pa $13.95 **808.81**
1. Love poetry 2. Poetry—Collections
ISBN 0-19-519774-9; 0-19-504232-8 (pa)
First published 1973 in the United Kingdom with title: The Penguin book of love poetry
A collection of poems written during the past 2000 years arranged thematically from young love to the "long look back" of the aged
Includes indexes of poets, translators, titles and first lines

A **Book** of women poets from antiquity to now; edited by Aliki Barnstone & Willis Barnstone. rev ed. Schocken Bks. 1992 xxiv, 822p pa $20 **808.81**
1. Poetry—Women authors—Collections
ISBN 0-8052-0997-2
LC 91-52701
First published 1980
An anthology of representative work by women poets of various literary traditions

City lights pocket poets anthology; edited by Lawrence Ferlinghetti. City Lights Bks. 1995 259p $18.95 **808.81**
1. Poetry—Collections
ISBN 0-87286-311-5
LC 95-31608
"Drawing from the 52 volumes published in the Pocket Poets series since 1956, this selection provides a handy sampler of many of the prominent avant-garde and leftist poets of the post-WW II era. . . . The series' extensive international scope is highlighted in poems culled from German, Russian, Italian, Dutch, Nicaraguan and Spanish poets." Publ Wkly

The **Columbia** Granger's index to poetry; indexing anthologies published through June 30, 1993. 10th ed, completely rev, edited by Edith P. Hazen. Columbia Univ. Press 1994 2150p $225
808.81
1. Poetry—Indexes
ISBN 0-231-08408-0   LC 93-38761
Also available as part of Columbia Granger's world of poetry on CD-ROM

First edition, edited by Edith Granger, published 1904 by A. C. McClurg with title: Index to poetry and recitations. Fifth through eighth editions have title Granger's index to poetry

This work is organized into title and first line index, author index, subject index and a list of anthologies with their symbols. Coverage includes poetry translated into English

Holocaust poetry; edited by Hilda Schiff. St. Martin's Press 1995 234p $20; pa $12 **808.81**
1. Holocaust, 1933-1945—Poetry 2. Poetry—Collections
ISBN 0-312-13086-4; 0-312-14357-5 (pa)
    LC 95-2708
"In English and in translation from many languages, more than 80 poets—including Wiesel, Fink, Brecht, Yevtushenko, Auden, and Sachs—give voice to what seems unspeakable. Schiff points out that compelling historical accounts document the facts and numbers, but a poem, like a story, makes us imagine how it felt for one person. These poems are stark and deceptively simple." Booklist

I feel a little jumpy around you; a book of her poems & his poems collected in pairs; [by] Naomi Shihab Nye and Paul B. Janeczko. Simon & Schuster Bks. for Young Readers 1996 256p $17 **808.81**
1. Poetry—Collections
ISBN 0-689-80518-7   LC 95-44904
A collection of poems, by male and female authors, presented in pairings that offer insight into how men and women look at the world, both separately and together
"Though the gender counterpoint really plays little part in the juxtaposition, the pairings are piquant and provide a manageable way to start talking about a very large collection of poetry. An engaging marginal dialogue, taken from Nye's and Janeczko's collaborative fax correspondence, appears alongside the appendix and permits a revealing peek behind the scences. Highly readable notes from contributors are included, as is an index of poems and a gender-segregated index of poets." Bull Cent Child Books

Kline, Victoria
Last lines; an index to the last lines of poetry; [by] Victoria K. Kline. Facts on File 1990 2v set $145 **808.81**
1. Poetry—Indexes
ISBN 0-8160-1265-2   LC 88-30948
This index "seeks to assist the reader in identifying and locating 171,000 poems by last line. The poetry covered was written in English or translated into English and includes Egyptian verse of 2600 B.C. to contemporary poetry. Indexed are 497 anthologies published between 1900 and 1987." Booklist

Love poems. Knopf 1993 256p (Everyman's library pocket poets) $10.95 **808.81**
1. Love poetry 2. Poetry—Collections
ISBN 0-679-42906-9   LC 93-11427
Among the poets included are Robert Graves, W. B. Yeats, Pablo Neruda, Boris Pasternak, William Carlos Williams, Anna Akhmatova, Robert Browning and Christina Rossetti. An index of first lines is appended

The **Oxford** book of war poetry; chosen and edited by John Stallworthy. Oxford Univ. Press 1984 xxxi, 358p $29.95 **808.81**
1. War poetry 2. Poetry—Collections
ISBN 0-19-214125-2   LC 83-19303
"This comprehensive anthology focuses on poetic treatment of warfare ranging from the battlefields of ancient history to the conflicts in Vietnam, Northern Ireland, and El Salvador." Univ Press Books for Second Sch Libr
This collection "reminds one of the large numbers and great variety of war poems from many centuries that are very good poems. Mr. Stallworthy's selections include most of the best, at least the best in English." N Y Times Book Rev
Includes bibliography

Pierced by a ray of sun; poems about the times we feel alone; selected by Ruth Gordon. HarperCollins Pubs. 1995 105p $16; lib bdg $15.89 **808.81**
1. Poetry—Collections
ISBN 0-06-023613-2; 0-06-023614-0 (lib bdg)
    LC 94-3757
"Gordon has gathered poems reflecting that feeling of alienation that crosses all cultures and time periods. The collection includes a wide array of poetry from anonymous poets and from renowned Western poets such as Keats and Yeats, as well as translations of poems from around the globe." Book Rep
"Poetry, with its tendency towards private observation, is peculiarly suited to this theme, and young adults, who are struggling to find their place in the world, will find it particularly relevant, especially when they encounter it in such a fine poetic assortment." Bull Cent Child Books

Poems for the millennium; the University of California book of modern and postmodern poetry; edited by Jerome Rothenberg and Pierre Joris. v1: From fin de siécle to negritude. University of Calif. Press 1995 xxviii, 811p il $60; pa $24.95 **808.81**
1. Poetry—Collections
ISBN 0-520-07225-1; 0-520-07227-8 (pa)
    LC 93-49839
"A Centennial book"
This is the first of a projected two-volume anthology of twentieth-century world poetry. It covers the period from 1890 to 1945. "Beginning with a section of forerunners (e.g., Rimbaud, Whitman), Rothenberg and Joris concentrate on futurism, dada, expressionism, negritude, and objectivism, but they also present three 'galleries' of poets unconfined by any movement." Booklist
"Commentaries, many on individual poets—C. P. Cavafy, Gertrude Stein, William Carlos Williams, Osip Mandelstam and Pablo Neruda among them—and often

Poems for the millennium—*Continued*
in the poets' own words, give context to the unwieldy
mass of these poems, many difficult to find in English."
Publ Wkly

Stopping for death; poems of death and loss;
edited by Carol Ann Duffy; illustrated by Trisha
Rafferty. Holt & Co. 1996 134p il $14.95
808.81

1. Death—Poetry 2. Poetry—Collections
ISBN 0-8050-4717-4   LC 95-52423

A collection of poems about death, loss, and mourning
written by poets from all over the world including Janet
Frame, Alice Walker, and Seamus Heaney
"The collection is not all grim; there are evocatons of
paradise, hope, and memory here. Duffy's anthology addresses an often-avoided subject in a conscientious way,
and readers will gain from it a healthy understanding of
the ways to deal with and move on from loss." SLJ

This same sky; a collection of poems from around
the world; selected by Naomi Shihab Nye. Four
Winds Press 1992 212p il $17   **808.81**
1. Poetry—Collections
ISBN 0-02-768440-7   LC 92-11617

Also available in paperback from Aladdin Bks.

A poetry anthology in which 129 poets from sixty-
eight different countries celebrate the natural world and
its human and animal inhabitants
"Notes on the contributors, a map, suggestions for further reading, an index to countries, and an index to poets
are appended, adding additional luster to a book which
should prove invaluable for intercultural education as
well as for pure pleasure." Horn Book

A Time to talk; poems of friendship; selected by
Myra Cohn Livingston. Margaret K. McElderry
Bks. 1992 115p $13.95   **808.81**
1. Friendship—Poetry 2. Poetry—Collections
ISBN 0-689-50558-2   LC 91-42234

A collection of poems about friendship, by poets ranging from ancient China to the present
"A variety of poetic forms are represented including
a concrete poem by Lillian Morrison. The breadth of the
collection is excellent. Since the popularity of the theme
will assure continual use, readers will be exposed to a
richly diverse assortment of poets and their works."
Voice Youth Advocates

808.82   Drama—Collections

24 favorite one-act plays; edited by Bennett Cerf
and Van H. Cartmell. Doubleday 1958 455p pa
$12.95   **808.82**
1. Drama—Collections 2. One act plays
ISBN 0-385-06617-1

A wide assortment of one-act plays includes comedies,
tragedies, new and old, Irish, American, Russian, English, and Austrian. Includes the work of such playwrights
as Eugene O'Neill, Noel Coward, George S. Kaufman,
William Inge, and Dorothy Parker
"A good collection showing the variety of form and
subject used by modern masters of the short play." Good
Read

100 great monologues from the neo-classical
theatre; edited by Jocelyn A. Beard. Smith &
Kraus 1994 157p (Monologue audition series)
$9.95   **808.82**
1. Monologues 2. Acting
ISBN 1-88039-960-1   LC 94-33114

"Among the neoclassical soliloquies chosen for inclusion are excerpts from the works of Congreve, Dryden,
and Comielle. Molière is perhaps the most prominently
featured of all the assembled playwrights. Dramatic plays
such as Racine's *Phedre* are drawn upon to provide some
very potent material, while more comic passages are contained in Sheridan's splendid *The Rivals*." Booklist

The Actor's book of scenes from new plays;
edited by Eric Lane and Nina Shengold.
Penguin Bks. 1988 424p pa $11.95   **808.82**
1. Drama—Collections 2. Acting
ISBN 0-14-010487-9   LC 87-33389

"A Smith and Kraus Inc. book"
A collection of two-character scenes by contemporary
dramatists for classroom and audition use

The Best men's stage monologues of [date]; edited
by Jocelyn A. Beard. Smith & Kraus pa $11.95
808.82

1. Monologues 2. Acting
ISSN 1067-134X
Annual. First published 1991 for the 1990 theater sea-
son

This title and The Best women's stage monologues,
entered below, provide monologues with "a great range
of character choices involved in a wide variety of modern settings. Actors can also pick their audition pieces
from such contemporary issues as ethnicity, sexual orientation, and codependency. The one- to two-page selections were all chosen plays produced during the 1993
theatrical season. . . . These two titles provide unique alternatives to standard audition pieces and should have a
place in public, university, and . . . high-school libraries." Booklist [review of 1993 edition]

The Best plays of [date]: The Otis Guernsey/Burns
Mantle theater yearbook; edited by Otis L.
Guernsey, Jr. and Jeffrey Sweet; illustrated with
photographs and with drawings by Hirschfeld.
Limelight Eds. $47.50   **808.82**
1. Drama—Collections 2. Theater—United States
ISSN 1071-6971
Annual. First published 1920. Variant titles: The
Burns Mantle theater yearbook; The Applause/best plays
theater yearbook

Some back volumes published by Dodd, Mead available from Applause Theatre Bk. Pubs.; reprints of older
annuals available from Ayer; for full information on
availability and price contact publishers

The yearbook gives listings of casts and technical personnel for on- and off-Broadway productions, a summary
of the season, synopses and lengthy extracts of dialogue
from the best plays, and facts and figures on the New
York and regional theater

The **Best** women's stage monologues of [date]; edited by Jocelyn A. Beard. Smith & Kraus pa $11.95 **808.82**
1. Monologues 2. Acting
ISSN 1067-134X
Annual. First published 1991 for the 1990 theater season

The **Book** of monologues for aspiring actors; [edited by] Marsh Cassady. NTC Pub. Group 1995 212p il pa $16.95 **808.82**
1. Monologues 2. Acting
ISBN 0-8442-5771-0 LC 94-66239
"The selections range from the classical Greeks to Sam Shepard and Oscar Wilde; they give YA's the opportunity to develop characters of like ages in many different settings. Several questions to probe the actors' imaginations appear at the end of each monologue." SLJ

Cassady, Marsh, 1936-
The book of scenes for aspiring actors. NTC Pub. Group 1995 202p il pa $16.95 **808.82**
1. Acting 2. Drama—Collections
ISBN 0-8442-5769-9 LC 94-66240
"A collection of scripts for characters between the ages of 12-21. An introductory chapter analyzes the scene and the characters and gives information for both directors and actors on diagraming the set and blocking the action. . . . The selections come from Shakespeare, Jean Anouilh, and Maxwell Anderson and range in diversity from William Gillette's *Secret Service* to Brandon Thomas's *Charley's Aunt* and Arthur Laurents's *West Side Story*." Libr J

Great scenes for young actors from the stage; Craig Slaight, Jack Sharrar, editors. Smith & Kraus 1991 256p pa $11.95 **808.82**
1. Drama—Collections 2. Acting
ISBN 0-9622722-6-4
A "collection of 45 scenes from classic and contemporary plays that 'reflect life's experience through the eyes of the young.' The selections, graded according to ability level, include a broad range of roles for men, women, and groups. Providing a brief synopsis of each play along with special notes, this concise introduction to dramatic literature is an essential sourcebook for student actors and teachers." Booklist

Multicultural monologues for young actors; Craig Slaight and Jack Sharrar, editors. Smith & Kraus 1995 94p (Young actor series) pa $11.95 **808.82**
1. Monologues 2. Acting
ISBN 1-88039-947-4 LC 94-44188
Lorraine Hansberry, Danitra Vance, Miguel Piñero, and Amiri Baraka are among the authors represented in this collection of monologues on multicultural themes
"Absolutely *every* drama student in high school will be interested in this collection of monologues. . . . However—be forewarned—there are sex, drugs, and profanity in many of the excerpts." Voice Youth Advocates

Multicultural scenes for young actors; Craig Slaight and Jack Sharrar, editors. Smith & Kraus 1995 237p (Young actor series) pa $11.95 **808.82**
1. Drama—Collections 2. Acting
ISBN 1-880399-48-2 LC 94-44187
This collection "is organized according to cast requirements, and each of the cuttings from over 40 plays is preceded by source notes and a brief plot summary. Information regarding performance rights is appended. Although a few of the plays have been included in standard compilations, the multicultural theme makes this collection unique." SLJ

Play index. Wilson, H.W. 1953-1992 8v **808.82**
1. Drama—Indexes
ISSN 0554-3037
First volume published 1953, covering the years 1949-1952, and edited by Dorothy Herbert West and Dorothy Margaret Peake $48. Additional volumes: 1953-1960 $48 edited by Estelle A. Fidell and Dorothy Margaret Peake; 1961-1967 $48 edited by Estelle A. Fidell; 1968-1972 $48 edited by Estelle A. Fidell; 1973-1977 $48 edited by Estelle A. Fidell; 1978-1982 $48 edited by Juliette Yaakov; 1983-1987 $58 edited by Juliette Yaakov and John Greenfieldt; 1988-1992 $80 edited by Juliette Yaakov and John Greenfieldt
Play index indexes plays in collections and single plays; one-act and full-length plays; radio, television, and Broadway plays; plays for amateur production; plays for children, young adults, and adults. It is divided into four parts. Part I is an author, title, and subject index; the author or main entry includes the title of the play, brief synopsis of the plot, number of acts and scenes, size of cast, number of sets, and bibliographic information. Part II is a list of collections indexed, and Part III, a cast analysis, lists plays by the type of cast and number of players required. Part IV is a directory of publishers and distributors
"This index is an excellent source for locating published plays." Nichols. Guide to Ref Books for Sch Media Cent. 4th edition

The **Scenebook** for actors; great monologs & dialogs from contemporary & classical theatre; edited by Norman A. Bert. Meriwether 1990 246p pa $14.95 **808.82**
1. Drama—Collections 2. Acting
ISBN 0-916260-65-8 LC 90-52983
A collection of scenes, monologues and dialogues from scripts produced after 1975. Selections are for characters aged 18 to 30 and several are written for Afro-American and Hispanic actors
Includes bibliographical references

Scenes from classic plays, 468 B.C. to 1970 A.D.; Jocelyn A. Beard, editor. Smith & Kraus 1993 310p pa $11.95 **808.82**
1. Drama—Collections 2. Acting
ISBN 1-880399-36-9 LC 93-33010
"Arranged chronologically, the selected scenes average three pages in length and involve two to three characters. A one-line description of the setting and of each character is given, as well as a one- to two-sentence synopsis of what is occurring at the opening of the scene. This book must be commended for such a well-balanced representation of time-honored classics." Booklist

Thirty famous one-act plays; ed. by Bennett Cerf and Van H. Cartmell; with an introduction by Richard Watts, Jr. Modern Lib. 1949 c1943 xxii, 617p $16　　　　　　　**808.82**
ISBN 0-394-60473-3　　　　　　　LC 49-9032
"Modern Library giant"

A reprint of a book first published 1943 by Garden City Publishing Company

This anthology, with biographical sketches, ranges from plays by Anatole France and Strindberg through Schnitzler, O'Neill, Kaufman, Coward to Saroyan and Irwin Shaw

808.83　Fiction—Collections

Short story index. Wilson, H.W. $95 per year
　　　　　　　　　　　　　　　　808.83
1. Short stories—Indexes
ISSN 0360-9774
　　　　　　　　　　　　　　LC 75-649762
Also available: Short story index: collections indexed 1900-1978 $45 (ISBN 0-8242-0643-6)

Basic volume edited by Dorothy E. Cook and Isabel S. Monro published 1953 $55 (ISBN 0-8242-0384-4); Supplementary volumes: 1950-1954 edited by Dorothy E. Cook and Estelle A. Fidell $65 (ISBN 0-8242-0385-2); 1955-1958 edited by Estelle A. Fidell and Esther V. Flory $65 (ISBN 0-8242-0386-0); 1959-1963 edited by Estelle A. Fidell $65 (ISBN 0-8242-0387-9); 1964-1968 edited by Estelle A. Fidell $65 (ISBN 0-8242-0399-2); 1969-1973 edited by Estelle A. Fidell $65 (ISBN 0-8242-0497-2); 1974-1978 edited by Gary L. Bogart $95; 1979-1983 edited by Juliette Yaakov $105; 1984-1988 edited by Juliette Yaakov $135; 1989-1993 edited by John Greenfieldt and Juliette Yaakov $135. Beginning 1974 issued annually with five-year cumulations

This index offers a single-alphabet listing of stories by author, title and subject. The List of collections indexed provides full bibliographic information. Includes a Directory of periodicals and a Directory of publishers and distributors

"An invaluable access to short stories in collections." A L A. Ref Sources for Small & Medium-sized Libr. 5th edition

808.85　Speeches—Collections

Lend me your ears; great speeches in history; selected and introduced by William Safire. rev and expanded ed. Norton 1997 1,055p $39.95
　　　　　　　　　　　　　　　　808.85
1. Speeches
ISBN 0-393-04005-4　　　　　　LC 96-43423
First published 1992

Pope Urban II, Bobe Dole, Cicero, Jesus, Boris Yeltsin, Richard Nixon and Colin Powell are among the orators represented in this anthology of over 200 speeches grouped chronologically into thematic categories

The **Penguin** book of twentieth-century speeches; edited by Brian MacArthur. Viking 1993 xxiv, 488p $35; pa $13.95　　　　　　**808.85**
1. Speeches
ISBN 0-670-83126-3; 0-14-023234-6 (pa)
　　　　　　　　　　　　　　　LC 94-4040
First published 1992 in the United Kingdom

"Nelson Mandela, Winston Churchill, Emmeline Pankhurst, Martin Luther King, Jr., and Adolf Hitler are among the more than 140 famous speakers whose words are collected in this anthology that teens will use for reference and for browsing." Booklist

808.87　Satire and humor—Collections

The **Penguin** book of women's humor; edited with an introduction by Regina Barreca. Penguin Bks. 1995 xxxviii, 657p pa $15.95　　　**808.87**
1. Wit and humor 2. Women—Humor
ISBN 0-14-017294-7　　　　　　LC 95-9009
Contributors to this anthology range "from Aphra Behn to Elayne Boosler, from Erma Bombeck to Roz Chast and Nicole Hollander (yes, cartoonists are represented too). . . . Selections range from one-liners to longer excerpts from books. Most of these examples are just long enough to pique the reader's interest to seek out the source volume." Libr J

808.88　Collections of miscellaneous writings

✓ **American** Indian quotations; compiled and edited by Howard J. Langer. Greenwood Press 1996 260p il $49.95　　　　　　　　**808.88**
1. Indians of North America—Quotations
ISBN 0-313-29121-7　　　　　　LC 95-33151
"This volume offers 800 quotations covering more than four centuries of American life. Arranged chronologically, the quotations include the words of warriors, poets, politicians, doctors, lawyers, athletes, and others. . . . The book provides brief biographical information about those quoted, including both historical and contemporary figures, and cross-references the material through subject, author, and tribal indexes." Publisher's note

For a review see: Booklist, Nov. 15, 1996

Andrews, Robert, 1957-
The Columbia dictionary of quotations. Columbia Univ. Press 1993 1092p $34.95 **808.88**
1. Quotations
ISBN 0-231-07194-9　　　　　　LC 93-27305
Also available on CD-ROM as part of Microsoft bookshelf

"Focuses on quotations chosen for their appropriateness to contemporary life, featuring established writers as well as lesser-known figures, and groups underrepresented in other quotation collections (women, minorities, homosexuals and lesbians, etc.). . . . Identifies authors together with birth and death dates, and exact sources, often adding brief notes to provide context. The 'Index of sources' lists authors and the subjects under which their quotations are entered." Guide to Ref Books 11th edition

Bartlett, John, 1820-1905
Familiar quotations. Little, Brown $40   **808.88**
1. Quotations
Also available CD-ROM version
First published 1855. (16th edition 1992) Periodically revised. Editors vary
"Arranged chronologically by author, with exact references. Includes many interesting footnotes, tracing history or usage of analogous thoughts, the circumstances under which a particular remark was made, etc. Author and keyword indexes. One of the best books of quotations with a long history." Guide to Ref Books. 11th edition

Brallier, Jess M.
Presidential wit and wisdom; maxims, mottos, sound bites, speeches, and asides: memorable quotes from America's presidents; [by] Jess M. Brallier and Sally C. Chabert. Penguin Bks. 1996 270p pa $12.95   **808.88**
1. Presidents—United States—Quotations
ISBN 0-14-023904-9   LC 95-23184
Organized by president and indexed by subject, this is a compilation of memorable statements by the forty-two men who have served in the nation's highest office. Contains brief biographies and highlights of each administration

The **Columbia** Granger's dictionary of poetry quotations; edited by Edith P. Hazen. Columbia Univ. Press 1992 1132p $99   **808.88**
1. Quotations
ISBN 0-231-07546-4   LC 91-42240
This work contains the "most memorable lines written by the greatest poets of English. Quotations are organized alphabetically by poet, and coded so one can find full text in hundreds of current anthologies. With keyword and subject indexing." Univ Press Books for Public and Second Sch Libr

The **Concise** Oxford dictionary of quotations; edited by Angela Partington. 3rd ed. Oxford Univ. Press 1994 581p pa $9.95   **808.88**
1. Quotations
ISBN 0-19-280026-4   LC 95-103397
First published 1964 as a shortened version of the second edition of The Oxford Dictionary of quotations. This third concise edition is based on the fourth edition of the latter work, entered below
Collected here are quotations by authors from around the world ranging in time from the 8th century BC to the 1980's. Arrangement is alphabetical by the names of authors with sections such as Anonymous, Ballads, The Bible, the Mass in Latin, etc. included in the alphabetical order. Foreign quotations are given in the original language followed by the English translation. Indexed by key words

The **Dictionary** of war quotations; compiled and edited by Justin Wintle. Free Press 1989 506p $35   **808.88**
1. War—Quotations
ISBN 0-02-935411-0   LC 89-16818
The editor has "assembled over 4000 quotations offering a history of attitudes as well as behavior. Ranging

from paragraphs to aphorisms, they present war's enduring mix of fascination and horror. The *Dictionary* is organized in three sections. Part I deals with the general nature of war. Part II comments on wars and battles from the Stone Age to the Falklands, with no significant omissions. Part III features personalities." Libr J
Includes bibliographical references

✓ **Heart** full of grace; a thousand years of black wisdom; edited by Venice Johnson. Simon & Schuster 1995 unp $21; pa $12   **808.88**
1. African Americans—Quotations 2. Blacks—Quotations
ISBN 0-684-81428-5; 0-684-82542-2 (pa)
LC 95-38106
"This is a diverse anthology of quotations, from the sayings of Martin Luther King and Langston Hughes to political speeches and African proverbs." Libr J

Magill, Frank Northen, 1907-
Magill's quotations in context; by Frank N. Magill; associate editor, Tench Francis Tilghman: [1st-2nd ser] Salem Press 1965-1969 4v ser I o.p.; ser II 2v set $75   **808.88**
1. Quotations
ISBN 0-89356-136-3
This work, issued in two series contains over 1500 quotations in each series taken "from the classics, poetry, drama, fiction, and nonfiction. Entries, arranged alphabetically by keyword, provide pertinent information as to who said what, when, where, and why. The quotation is reprinted in context or with commentary of about 200 words. While the number of quotations is limited, the real value lies in the background information and special aids for interpretation. These features give the works educational value beyond that of typical quotation dictionaries." Wynar. Guide to Ref Books for Sch Media Cent. 3d edition

✓ **My** soul looks back, 'less I forget; a collection of quotations by people of color; Dorothy Winbush Riley, editor. HarperCollins Pubs. 1993 498p $27.50; pa $14   **808.88**
1. Quotations 2. Blacks—Quotations
ISBN 0-06-270086-3; 0-06-272057-0 (pa)
LC 92-25754
First published privately in 1991 by Winbush Pub. Co.
"Included are over 7000 quotes from 700 speakers that range from such early historical figures as Aesop and Amenemope to familiar contemporaries like Colin Powell and Clarence Thomas. Quotes are chronological within 450 alphabetically arranged topics. An index by speaker, contents by topics, and comprehensive bibliography of 400 sources used for this solidly researched work add to its usefulness." Libr J

The **New** York Public Library book of twentieth-century American quotations; edited by Stephen Donadio [et al.] Warner Bks. 1992 622p $24.95   **808.88**
1. Quotations
ISBN 0-446-51639-2   LC 91-50395
"A Stonesong Press book"

The New York Public Library book of twentieth-century American quotations—*Continued*

"A collection of quotations limited exclusively to 20th century Americans, arranged by thematic categories such as Dreams and ideals, Popular culture, Religion and spirituality, and Social issues, all subdivided. Emphasizes diversity of persons, comments, and points of view—scholarly statement to colloquial quip—in their historical context." Guide to Ref Books. 11th edition

The Oxford book of humorous quotations; edited by Ned Sherrin. Oxford Univ. Press 1995 543p $39.95; pa $14.95   **808.88**

1. Quotations 2. Wit and humor
ISBN 0-19-214244-5; 0-19-280045-0 (pa)
                                              LC 94-37211
A compilation of nearly 5,000 quotations arranged in themes. Shakespeare, Austen, Groucho Marx, Monty Python and Roseanne are among humorists and pundits represented. Includes author and key word indexes

The Oxford dictionary of modern quotations; edited by Tony Augarde. Oxford Univ. Press 1991 371p $29.95; pa $13.95   **808.88**

1. Quotations
ISBN 0-19-866141-X; 0-19-283086-4 (pa)
                                              LC 90-26588
This "collection of 5,000 quotations is arranged alphabetically by personal name. . . . To qualify as 'modern,' persons quoted had to have lived past 1900." Booklist

The Oxford dictionary of quotations; edited by Angela Partington. 4th ed. Oxford Univ. Press 1992 1061p $39.95   **808.88**

1. Quotations
ISBN 0-19-866185-1
Also available revised 4th edition $39.95 (ISBN 0-19-860058-5)
First published 1941
"Some 17,500 quotations are arranged in one alphabetical sequence of 2,500 English and foreign authors, the Bible, the Book of Common Prayer, and anonymous works. Most quotations from foreign literatures are given both in their original language as well as in an English translation. Exact bibliographical references are provided for known printed sources. Indexed by keyword." Guide to Ref Books. 11th edition

Tripp, Rhoda Thomas

The international thesaurus of quotations; compiled by Rhoda Thomas Tripp. Crowell 1970 1088p o.p.; HarperCollins Pubs. paperback available $25   **808.88**

1. Quotations
ISBN 0-06-091382-7 (pa)
"A Crowell reference book"
Arranged alphabetically by categories of meaning with cross-references to related subject categories, this thesaurus contains 16,000 sayings, with more than 6,000 from this century, the rest chosen for their relevance to today's concerns

The Whole world book of quotations; wisdom from women and men around the globe throughout the centuries; compiled and edited by Kathryn Petras and Ross Petras. Addison-Wesley 1995 476p $25   **808.88**

1. Quotations
ISBN 0-201-62258-0   LC 94-12465
"Including '3,000 overlooked quotations from Abigail Adams to Zoroaster,' this . . . reference source of quotations focuses on the thoughts of non-Westerners, non-whites, and women. . . . The volume is arranged alphabetically by general category (from 'Ability' to 'Zen') and includes between 5 and 20 quotations listed in chronological order. For the most part, the quotations are short. Each is followed by the individual's name, dates, and specific context or source of the quotation." Recommended Ref Books for Small & Medium-sized Libr & Media Cent, 1995

Includes bibliographical references

809 Literary history and criticism

Brown, Jean E., 1945-
Teaching young adult literature; sharing the connection; [by] Jean E. Brown, Elaine C. Stephens. Wadsworth Pub. Co. 1995 320p il $20.50   **809**

1. Young adults' literature—Study and teaching 2. Youth—Books and reading
ISBN 0-534-19938-0   LC 94-35183
This work combines "theory and practical ideas for enhancing the study of an important genre for adolescents. . . . The authors challenge teachers to expand their own reading repertoires, combining traditional and non-traditional works. Particularly helpful are sections detailing developmental tasks for YAs and applying those tasks to specific characters in YA literature. Also useful are in-depth interviews with YA authors, suggestions for 'bridging' potential connections between a YA work and other literature, and numerous effective pedagogical strategies for the classroom." Voice Youth Advocates

Includes bibliographical references

Calendar of literary facts; a daily and yearly guide to noteworthy events in world literature from 1450 to the present; Samuel J. Rogal, editor. Gale Res. 1991 877p $65   **809**

1. Literature—Chronology
ISBN 0-8103-2943-3   LC 90-14039
This is a chronology of "international authors, publications, and literary events. Following a list of sources from which the information has been taken, the Calendar is divided into a 'Day-by-Day Calendar,' a 'Year-by-Year Calendar, 1450-1989,' and an index." Booklist

Includes bibliographical references

Contemporary literary criticism. Gale Res.   **809**

1. Literature—History and criticism
ISSN 0091-3421
Irregular. Started publication in 1973
Volumes 1 to 97, 1973-1997, available at $134 each

Contemporary literary criticism—*Continued*

"Excerpts from criticism of the works of today's novelists, poets, playwrights, short story writers, scriptwriters, and other creative writers." Title page

"This multivolume, ongoing series offers significant passages from contemporary criticism on authors who are now living or who have died since December 31, 1959. . . . Brief author sketches are followed by critical excerpts, presented in chronological order. The number of authors covered in each volume has varied over the years, but recent volumes provide criticism on some forty to sixty literary figures." A L A Ref Sources for Small & Medium-sized Libr. 5th edition

Harris, Laurie Lanzen

Characters in 20th-century literature. Gale Res. 1990 480p $54   809
1. Literature—History and criticism 2. Characters and characteristics in literature
ISBN 0-8103-1847-4   LC 89-25709

"Descriptions of over 2,000 characters, drawn from 250 of the twentieth century's major novelists, dramatists, and short story writers, are included. . . . The book is arranged alphabetically by author. . . . The essay on each work contains a brief plot synopsis as well as commentary on thematic and stylistic aspects of the work and the way in which the characters illustrate the central themes and aesthetics of the author." Preface

Herz, Sarah K.

From Hinton to Hamlet; building bridges between young adult literature and the classics; [by] Sarah K. Herz with Donald R. Gallo. Greenwood Press 1996 127p $29.95   809
1. Young adults' literature—Study and teaching 2. Youth—Books and reading
ISBN 0-313-28636-1   LC 95-38657

"Connecting the best YA literature and the classics, this . . . practical guide challenges condescending stereotypes about YA literature and shows how it can be used in the English classroom, across the curriculum, and in the library to open students to the pleasure of reading, at least as an entry or bridge to more complex literature. The largest section of the book discusses using great YA novels with 10 commonly taught classics." Booklist

"Educators looking for some advice on this kind of curriculum and librarians looking to assist and encourage them will find this a useful volume." Bull Cent Child Books

Includes bibliographical references

Highet, Gilbert, 1906-1978

The classical tradition; Greek and Roman influences on Western literature. Oxford Univ. Press 1949 xxxviii, 764p hardcover o.p. paperback available $17.95   809
1. Literature—History and criticism 2. Comparative literature 3. Classical literature
ISBN 0-19-500206-7 (pa)
Analyzed in Essay and general literature index

"The twenty-four chapters fall into four main sections. The first takes in the Dark and Middle Ages—Anglo-Saxon poetry and prose, French epic and romance, Dante, Petrarch, Boccaccio, Chaucer. The second section comprises eight chapters on the Renaissance—drama, epic, pastoral and romance, lyric, the literature of translation, Rabelais, Montaigne. . . . [The] third section [is] 'The Baroque Age.' . . . After baroque, we come to our fourth and last section, the romantic, or . . . the revolutionary period 'and afterwards.'" Spectator

Includes bibliography

Howes, Kelly King

Characters in 19th-century literature. Gale Res. 1993 597p $54   809
1. Literature—History and criticism 2. Characters and characteristics in literature
ISBN 0-8103-8398-5   LC 92-75005

This reference work "provides brief plot summations and detailed character analyses for approximately 200 novels, plays, and short stories by 100 nineteenth-century writers who are currently studied in U.S. classrooms. . . . The book is arranged alphabetically by author and provides the individual's dates, nationality, and principal genres. Then the various works are considered in individual essays that analyze how the characters develop the author's themes." Booklist

"This volume will be of much use to students and teachers and just might entice some readers into books they might otherwise ignore." Voice Youth Advocates

Magill's survey of world literature; edited by Frank N. Magill. Marshall Cavendish 1992 6v il $389.95   809
1. Literature—History and criticism 2. Literature—Bio-bibliography
ISBN 1-85435-482-5   LC 92-11198

Companion set: Magill's survey of American literature, entered in class 810.9

Also available two-volume supplement published 1996 $124.95 (ISBN 0-7614-0104-0)

"The 215 alphabetical author entries date from antiquity to the late 20th century and include the gamut of genres. The major emphasis is on European writers, especially the British, with representation of English-language writers from non-European countries; Latin American authors and a smattering of authors from classical Eastern culture are also represented. . . . Each entry begins with a statement of the author's major achievement, followed by a biographical treatment and a critical summary of major works." Libr J

Includes bibliographical references

Masterpieces of women's literature; edited by Frank N. Magill. HarperCollins Pubs. 1996 594p $50   809
1. Literature—Women authors—History and criticism
ISBN 0-06-270138-X   LC 95-26601

This collection of 175 articles "emphasizes women's history and experience, feminist theory, and women's issues as it examines some of the most important works of fiction and nonfiction authored by women. The scope is broad—from ancient Greece to the late twentieth century, and from fourteen countries. In choosing works to be analyzed in this volume, an attempt was made to cover a relatively broad spectrum of women's literature by genre and by race, nationality, ethnicity, sexual orientation, and time period." Preface

Masterpieces of world literature; edited by Frank N. Magill. Harper & Row 1989 957p $50 **809**
1. Literature—History and criticism
ISBN 0-06-016144-2   LC 89-45052
"High school libraries unable to purchase the more extensive critical surveys by Magill or the *Cyclopedia of Literary Characters* may wish to consider this volume. The work, arranged alphabetically by title, contains plot summaries, character portrayals, and critical evaluations of 270 classics of world literature (novels, plays, stories, poems, and essays), all reprints from other Magill guides." Nichols. Guide to Ref Books for Sch Media Cent. 4th edition

✓ **Modern** black writers; compiled and edited by Michael Popkin. Ungar 1978-1995 2v (Library of literary criticism) v1 $65; v2 $95   **809**
1. American literature—African American authors—History and criticism 2. West Indian literature—History and criticism 3. African literature—History and criticism
ISBN 0-8044-3258-9 (v1); 0-8264-0688-2 (v2)
LC 76-15656
Volume two: Supplement edited by Steven R. Serafin published by Continuum
These volumes offer "excerpts of criticism dealing with major black poets, dramatists, and novelists from Africa, the Caribbean, and the U.S. . . . The organization is excellent." Choice
Includes bibliographical references

✓ The **Schomburg** Center guide to black literature from the eighteenth century to the present; Roger M. Valade III, editor, with Denise Kasinec. Gale Res. 1996 xxvi, 545p il $75
809
1. Literature—Bio-bibliography 2. Black authors—Dictionaries 3. Blacks in literature
ISBN 0-7876-0289-2   LC 95-36733
This is a "one-stop guide and ready reference to authors, works, characters, themes, and topics related to black literature. The scope includes both fiction and nonfiction writing from African American authors and international authors whose works have been translated into English. In a dictionary format, it includes biographical entries as well as separate entries for many individual novels, collections of poems, characters, and screenplays. . . . While the scope is defined as from the eighteenth century to the present, the majority of the entries and fuller treatment are given to late-twentieth-century figures." Booklist

809.2   Drama—History and criticism

Esslin, Martin
The theatre of the absurd. 3rd ed rev & enl. Penguin Bks. 1983 c1980 480p pa $13.95   **809.2**
1. Drama—History and criticism
ISBN 0-14-013728-9   LC 81-169374
First published 1961 by Anchor Bks. This edition first published 1980 in the United Kingdom

"This is a book on a development in the contemporary theatre: the type of drama associated with the names of Samuel Beckett, Eugène Ionesco, Arthur Adamov, Jean Genet, and a number of other avant-garde writers in France, Britain, Italy, Spain, Germany, the United States, and elsewhere." Preface
Includes bibliography

Masterplots II, drama series; edited by Frank N. Magill. Salem Press 1990 4v set $365   **809.2**
1. Drama—Stories, plots, etc. 2. Drama—History and criticism
ISBN 0-89356-491-5   LC 89-10989
This "set includes 327 works by 148 playwrights. . . . The selection of plays spans the spectrum from seminal works from the early years of the century to recent Broadway hits and is representative of the wide range of styles, themes, and dramatic techniques that characterize twentieth-century drama. About 70 of the plays treated in the set have been translated into English from other languages. . . . The present set contains the same strengths and weaknesses typically found in the various Masterplots series." Booklist

McGraw-Hill encyclopedia of world drama; an international reference work in 5 volumes; Stanley Hochman, editor in chief. [2nd ed] McGraw-Hill 1983 c1984 5v il set $430 **809.2**
1. Drama—Dictionaries 2. Drama—Bio-bibliography
ISBN 0-07-079169-4   LC 83-9919
First published 1972
"A majority of the entries emphasize playwrights and their contributions, with the remaining entries devoted to surveys of the world's dramatic literature, major dramatic genres, important theater groups and companies, and other subjects. The encyclopedia, international in scope and comprehensive in its level of treatment, will meet the needs of critics and theater buffs, as well as historians, educators, and performing artists. More than twenty-five hundred illustrations add dimension and depth to this multi-volume set." RQ

809.3   Fiction—History and criticism

Clute, John
Science fiction; the illustrated encyclopedia. Dorling Kindersley 1995 312p il $39.95   **809.3**
1. Science fiction—Dictionaries 2. Science fiction films
ISBN 0-7894-0185-1   LC 95-8083
"Arranged primarily by decade within each of eight chapters, the book covers visions of the future (accurate and off the mark); themes in history; influential magazines (from early pulp to the present); major authors (there are sketches of over 100 writers, photographs, signatures, and chronological bibliographies of major works); classic titles; graphic works; and genre films and international television." SLJ
For a fuller review see: Booklist, Jan. 15, 1996

Critical survey of short fiction; edited by Frank N. Magill. rev ed. Salem Press 1993 7v set $425
809.3
1. Short stories—History and criticism 2. Short stories—Bio-bibliography
ISBN 0-89356-843-0   LC 92-41950
First published 1981

"This work consists mainly of two sections. The article section, which is arranged alphabetically by author, contains biographical information about the author, a bibliography of works about that person, and a list of the individual's principal short fiction and other literary forms and major works. . . . The second section is a collection of 12 essays that discuss the development of the short story from antiquity to modern times." Am Ref Books Annu, 1994

DeAndrea, William L.
Encyclopedia mysteriosa; a comprehensive guide to the art of detection in print, film, radio, and television. Prentice Hall General Ref. 1994 405p il $27.50
809.3
1. Mystery fiction—Dictionaries 2. Detectives in mass media—Dictionaries
ISBN 0-671-85025-3   LC 94-2075

This work "covers mystery writers, actors, characters, novels, films, and TV and radio shows in a single A-to-Z arrangement. . . . Completeing the work are lists of mystery bookstores in the U.S., Canada, and England; organizations and awards; mystery magazines; and a mystery-related glossary." Booklist

The **Encyclopedia** of science fiction; edited by John Clute and Peter Nicholls; contributing editor, Brian Stableford; technical editor, John Grant. [2nd ed] St. Martin's Press 1993 xxxvi, 1370p il $75; pa $29.95
809.3
1. Science fiction—Dictionaries
ISBN 0-312-09618-6; 0-312-13486-X (pa)
LC 92-47048
First published 1979 with title: The Science fiction encyclopedia

"Signed entries, contributed by science fiction specialists, cover numerous aspects of the genre, including authors, themes, terminology, films, television, magazines, comics, illustrators, book publishers, original anthologies, awards. Extensive cross-references." Guide to Ref Books. 11th edition

Hooper, Brad
Short story writers and their work; a guide to the best. 2nd ed. American Lib. Assn. 1992 70p pa $16
809.3
1. Short stories—History and criticism
ISBN 0-8389-0587-0   LC 92-11944
First published 1988

"Brief, biographical essays focus on more than 100 contemporary and classic writers from various ethnic groups and both genders. . . . Author entries describe writing style, subject matter, settings, common themes, and critical opinions of the author's work. Citations are given to examples of the writer's best work." Publisher's note

Masterplots II, short story series; edited by Frank N. Magill. Salem Press 1986 6v set $425
809.3
1. Short stories—History and criticism 2. Fiction—History and criticism
ISBN 0-89356-461-3   LC 86-22025

Contains over 700 interpretative essays on noteworthy authors and short stories from around the world. Each entry provides the author's name, dates, the type and time of the story's plot, the setting, date of first publication and a list of major characters. Themes, style and technique are also discussed

May, Charles E. (Charles Edward), 1941-
The short story; the reality of artifice. Twayne Pubs. 1995 xx, 160p (Studies in literary themes and genres) $23.95; pa $14.95   **809.3**
1. Short stories—History and criticism
ISBN 0-8057-0953-3; 0-8057-9238-4 (pa)
LC 94-32325

"This book identifies the basic conventions of major short stories from Hawthorne and Poe to Ozick and Carver and discusses . . . the literary styles and forms unique to the genre." Publisher's note

Modern mystery writers; edited and with an introduction by Harold Bloom. Chelsea House 1995 201p (Writers of English: lives and works) $29.95; pa $14.95   **809.3**
1. Mystery fiction—History and criticism 2. Mystery fiction—Bio-bibliography
ISBN 0-7910-2375-3; 0-7910-2376-1 (pa)
LC 94-5888

John Dickson Carr, Ngaio Marsh, Margaret Millar, and Rex Stout are among the thirteen writers examined in this study of mystery and detective fiction from the 1930s to the 1960s. Each profile includes biographical information, critical extracts and a bibliography

Readers' guide to twentieth-century science fiction; compiled and edited by Marilyn P. Fletcher; James L. Thorson, consulting editor. American Lib. Assn. 1989 673p $30   **809.3**
1. Science fiction—History and criticism 2. Science fiction—Bio-bibliography
ISBN 0-8389-0504-8   LC 88-7815

This volume "presents 120 biographical and critical essays of science fiction authors in an alphabetical arrangement. Authors were included on the strength of their contribution to the field of science fiction. . . . Each entry includes life and works, themes and styles, plot summaries of major works (limited to six works), and biographical/bibliographical works." Wilson Libr Bull

Reference guide to short fiction; editor, Noelle Watson. St. James Press 1994 xxxii, 1052p $140
809.3
1. Short stories—History and criticism 2. Short stories—Bio-bibliography
ISBN 1-55862-334-5   LC 93-33650

Covering short story authors of the 19th and 20th centuries, this work "is divided into two parts: the first covers more than 300 authors and includes a biography, bib-

Reference guide to short fiction—*Continued*
liography, and essay on each author. The second covers selected short stories, offering not only a plot summary but a critical interpretation as well. . . . An essential purchase for all libraries" Libr J

Science fiction, fantasy, and horror writers; [edited by] Marie J. MacNee. U.X.L 1995 2v il set $43
809.3
1. Science fiction—Bio-bibliography 2. Fantasy fiction—Bio-bibliography 3. Horror fiction—Bio-bibliography 4. Authors—Dictionaries
ISBN 0-8103-9865-6　　　LC 94-32459
"In this two-volume set, classic authors such as Jules Verne and Mary Shelley rub elbows with newcomers such as Christopher Pike and R.L. Stine. The 80 biographical entries run three to six pages each. . . . The entries include discussions of the author's major or critically acclaimed works. B&W photos of the authors and stills from motion pictures enhance the text. Best Bets, a chronological listing of some of an author's best works, and Real Life, a list of movie adaptations, are extra bonuses." Book Rep

Science fiction writers; critical studies of the major authors from the early nineteenth century to the present day; E.F. Bleiler, editor. Scribner 1982 623p $100　　　**809.3**
1. Science fiction—History and criticism 2. Science fiction—Bio-bibliography
ISBN 0-684-16740-9　　　LC 81-51032
This book contains "essays on seventy-two American and British and three European authors of the nineteenth and twentieth centuries. Articles . . . have been written by science fiction authorities. . . . With its inclusion of pioneering nineteenth-century authors, [it] gives a desirable fullness to science fiction reference literature." Wilson Libr Bull

Science fiction writers of the golden age; edited and with an introduction by Harold Bloom. Chelsea House 1995 203p (Writers of English: lives and works) $24.95; pa $12.95　　　**809.3**
1. Science fiction—History and criticism 2. Science fiction—Bio-bibliography
ISBN 0-7910-2199-8; 0-7910-2198-X (pa)
　　　LC 94-4322
Isaac Asimov, James Blish, Fritz Leiber and Theodore Sturgeon are among the thirteen science fiction writers profiled in this volume. Biographical, critical, and bibliographical information is provided for each author

St. James guide to fantasy writers; editor, David Pringle. St. James Press 1996 711p (St. James guide to writers series) $95　　　**809.3**
1. Fantasy fiction—Bio-bibliography 2. Fantasy fiction—History and criticism
ISBN 1-55862-205-5　　　LC 95-48783
This volume "offers an A-to-Z compendium of major fantasy writers. Each entry consists of a brief biography, a complete list of published works, a signed critical essay, and comments from some living authors on their work." Libr J
For a fuller review see: Booklist, May 1, 1996

810.3　American literature—
Encyclopedias and dictionaries

Benét's reader's encyclopedia of American literature; edited by George Perkins, Barbara Perkins, and Phillip Leininger. HarperCollins Pubs. 1991 1176p $45　　　**810.3**
1. American literature—Dictionaries
ISBN 0-06-270027-8　　　LC 91-55001
"Portions of this book appeared in a somewhat modified form in The reader's encyclopedia of American literature, published by T. Y. Crowell in 1962, and in Benét's reader's encyclopedia, third edition, published by Harper & Row in 1987" Verso of title page
This work "covers the literary movements, genres of fiction and nonfiction, and social, political, and religious influences on literature throughout North and South America." Libr J

Dictionary of American literary characters; edited by Benjamin Franklin V; associate editors, Gary Greer and Judith Haig. Facts on File 1990 542p $65　　　**810.3**
1. American literature—Dictionaries 2. Characters and characteristics in literature
ISBN 0-8160-1917-7　　　LC 89-25820
"A Bruccoli Clark Layman book"
"Covering the years between 1789 and 1980, this . . . volume lists alphabetically more than 11,000 American literary characters taken from significant popular novels as well as from the works of the major authors. Entries are brief (approximately 20 words) and meticulously objective. . . . A three-level index lists the authors represented, their novels, and the characters themselves." Libr J

The **Oxford** companion to American literature. Oxford Univ. Press $49.95　　　**810.3**
1. American literature—Dictionaries 2. American literature—Bio-bibliography
First published 1941. (6th edition 1995) Periodically revised
In addiiton to over 2000 entries for individual authors and more than 1,100 for important works this reference includes entries for literary movements, awards, magazines, printers, book collectors and newspapers. A chronological index of literary and social history is appended

810.8　American literature—
Collections

African-American voices; edited and with introductions and notes by Michele Stepto. Millbrook Press 1995 159p il (Writers of America) $17.40　　　**810.8**
1. American literature—African American authors—Collections
ISBN 1-56294-474-6　　　LC 94-16081
"Stepto examines African American literature in light of four symbols of connection—the circle, the veil, water, and song. To illustrate these links, works by writers as diverse as Frederick Douglass, Toni Morrison, Paul Laurence Dunbar, Rita Dove, Ralph Ellison, W.E.B. Du-

African-American voices—*Continued*
Bois, Ernest Gaines, Andrea Lee, Langston Hughes, Richard Wright, Jamaica Kincaid, Gwendolyn Brooks, and others are excerpted. . . . Students and teachers alike will find the book enlightening, and the index, meticulous acknowledgments, and list for further reading make it easy to use." SLJ

American dragons: twenty-five Asian American voices; edited by Laurence Yep. HarperCollins Pubs. 1993 237p $16; lib bdg $15.89; pa $4.95
810.8
1. American literature—Asian American authors—Collections
ISBN 0-06-021494-5; 0-06-021495-3 (lib bdg); 0-06-440603-2 (pa)   LC 92-28489
These "short stories, poems, and other selections are written by a cross section of Asian Americans, with roots in China, Vietnam, Japan, Korea, Tibet, and Thailand. The book is organized by theme, covering such issues of interest to adolescents as identity, family relationships, generational and cultural conflicts, and love." Horn Book
"A kaleidoscopic, occasionally brilliant, illumination of the Asian-American experience." SLJ
Includes bibliography

American Indian voices; edited and with introductions and notes by Karen D. Harvey; consultant: Lisa Harjo. Millbrook Press 1995 144p il (Writers of America) $17.40   **810.8**
1. American literature—American Indian authors—Collections
ISBN 1-56294-382-0   LC 94-21418
"This anthology is divided into four sections—beliefs, traditions, change, and survival—each of which is prefaced with an introduction explaining what its broad theme means. . . . But those categories are by no means exclusive; indeed, the arrangements of modern poetry, speeches, prayers, short stories, and autobiographical essays within each chapter convey the timelessness of Native beliefs and traditions as well as the fluidity of change and survival." SLJ
Includes bibliography

Circle of women: an anthology of contemporary Western women writers; edited by Kim Barnes and Mary Clearman Blew. Penguin Bks. 1994 400p pa $11.95   **810.8**
1. American literature—Women authors—Collections
ISBN 0-14-023524-8   LC 94-10705
"The editors have selected short stories, poems, essays, and excerpts from novels that present women's perceptions of the American Rocky Mountain West. These pieces, by writers as diverse as Tess Gallagher, Pam Houston, Gretel Ehrlich, and Deidre McNamer, are powerful, moving, and uniquely expressed." Libr J

Crossing the danger water; three hundred years of African-American writing; edited and with an introduction by Deirdre Mullane. Anchor Bks. (NY) 1993 xxii, 769p $16.95   **810.8**
1. American literature—African American authors—Collections
ISBN 0-385-42243-1   LC 93-17194
This anthology "includes fiction, autobiography, poetry, songs, and letters by such writers as Frederick Doug-

lass, Sojourner Truth, W.E.B. Du Bois, Zora Neale Hurston, and Richard Wright. Many topics are covered, from slavery, education, the Civil War, Reconstruction, and political issues to spirituals, songs of the Civil Rights movement, and rap music." Libr J
"Besides its curriculum use, the book will introduce YAs to landmarks of history and literature." Booklist
Includes bibliographical references

Daughters of the fifth sun; a collection of Latina fiction and poetry; Bryce Milligan, Mary Guerrero Milligan, and Angela de Hoyos, editors. Riverhead Bks. 1995 283p $23.95
810.8
1. American literature—Hispanic American authors—Collections
ISBN 1-57322-009-4   LC 95-19641
This anthology of Latina poetry and fiction includes contributions by Sandra Cisneros, Cherríe Moraga, Alma Luz Villanueva, Enedina Cásarez Vásquez, and Ana Castillo

Grand mothers: poems, reminiscences, and short stories about the keepers of our traditions; edited by Nikki Giovanni. Holt & Co. 1994 xxi, 168p $15.95   **810.8**
1. Grandmothers 2. American literature—Women authors—Collections
ISBN 0-8050-2766-1   LC 94-6144
"This anthology brings together writings about grandmothers. . . . Though the topic of grandmothers might be expected to bring out a certain sentimentality, the writers cut through the clichés to the basic human needs that grandmothers fill and the fundamental questions their lives and their memories raise in those who know them, remember them, or pass down their stories. Varied in quality, but still a unique collection of writings." Booklist

Growing up Asian American; an anthology; edited and with an introduction by Maria Hong; afterword by Stephen H. Sumida. Morrow 1993 416p $23   **810.8**
1. American literature—Asian American authors—Collections
ISBN 0-688-11266-8   LC 93-14033
Also available in paperback from Avon Bks.
"Divided into three sections—First Memories, Beginnings of Identity, and Growing Up—this anthology of heartfelt essays, memoirs, and fictional writings by and about Asian Americans is suggested . . . for collections where there is a demand for Asian American literature." Booklist
Includes bibliographical references

Growing up Chicana/o; an anthology; edited and with an introduction by Tiffany Ana López; foreword by Rudolfo Anaya. Morrow 1993 272p $20   **810.8**
1. American literature—Mexican American authors—Collections
ISBN 0-688-11467-9   LC 93-28195
Also available in paperback from Avon Bks.

Growing up Chicana/o—*Continued*

"Twenty leading Mexican American authors write about childhood in a splendid anthology that belongs in every YA collection. . . . Teens will discover themselves in these stories about family and leaving home and friends and falling in love." Booklist

Growing up Latino; memoirs and stories; edited with an introduction by Harold Augenbraum and Ilan Stavans; foreword by Ilan Stavans. Houghton Mifflin 1993 xxix, 344p hardcover o.p. paperback available $13.95   810.8

1. American literature—Hispanic American authors—Collections

ISBN 0-395-66124-2 (pa)   LC 92-32624

"A Marc Jaffe book"

A collection of short stories and excerpts from novels and memoirs written by twenty-five Latino authors. Among the contributors are Julia Alvarez, Oscar Hijuelos, Denise Chávez, Rolando Hinojosa, and Sandra Cisneros

Includes bibliographical references

Growing up Native American; an anthology; edited with an introduction by Patricia Riley; foreword by Ines Hernandez. Morrow 1993 333p $23   810.8

1. American literature—American Indian authors—Collections

ISBN 0-688-11850-X   LC 92-46484

Also available in paperback from Avon Bks.

"Essays, short stories, and excerpts from novels and biographies are collected in this anthology, which contains the work of 22 Native American writers, both historic and contemporary, female and male, representing a variety of tribal groups and geographical areas." Book Rep

"An excellent choice for high school English classes and good popular reading for YA and general adult readers." Libr J

Here is my kingdom; Hispanic-American literature and art for young people; edited by Charles Sullivan; foreword by Luis R. Cancel. Abrams 1994 119p il $24.95   810.8

1. American literature—Hispanic American authors—Collections 2. Hispanic American art

ISBN 0-8109-3422-1   LC 93-37412

The editor "combines poetry and short prose works with art to introduce young people to selected aspects of various Hispanic cultures. More than 118 writers and artists from countries such as Mexico, Puerto Rico, Cuba, Peru and Chile are represented. A wide spectrum of history is covered, from early explorers to contemporary issues such as the Vietnam War. The works of art, reproduced in color and b&w, are skillfully combined with thematically related text." Book Rep

Infinite divisions: an anthology of Chicana literature; [edited by] Tey Diana Rebolledo, Eliana S. Rivero. University of Ariz. Press 1993 xxii, 393p il hardcover o.p. paperback available $21.50   810.8

1. American literature—Mexican American authors—Collections 2. American literature—Women authors—Collections

ISBN 0-8165-1384-8 (pa)   LC 92-45101

"This collection, which includes 178 texts by 56 women, is organized historically and thematically. The first chapter includes early narratives from both oral and written traditions. Later chapters focus on personal identity, relationships within the community, and archetypes and myths. Authors include Gloria Anzaldúa, Denise Chavez, Sandra Cisneros, Margarita Cota Cárdenas, Pat Mora, and Antonia Quantana Pigno. Introductory essays set the tone for each new chapter, and extensive footnotes are included. Texts originally in Spanish are presented in both Spanish and English." Libr J

Includes bibliography

Jump up and say! a collection of black storytelling; [edited by] Linda Goss and Clay Goss. Simon & Schuster 1995 301p il $25; pa $13   810.8

1. American literature—African American authors—Collections

ISBN 0-684-81090-5; 0-684-81001-8 (pa)

                LC 95-22008

"A Touchstone book"

This collection "is divided into eight sections: moral tales, tales on freedom, family and friends, rhythm talking, humorous tales, songs and poems, ghost tales, and superstitions." Booklist

Includes bibliographical references

Latina: women's voices from the borderlands; edited by Lillian Castillo-Speed. Simon & Schuster 1995 284p $25; pa $13   810.8

1. American literature—Hispanic American authors—Collections 2. American literature—Women authors—Collections

ISBN 0-684-80381-X; 0-684-80240-6 (pa)

                LC 95-10397

"A Touchstone book"

This anthology contains short stories, novel excerpts, personal essays, memoirs and political writings by thirty-one Latina writers. Sandra Cisneros, Julia Alvarez, Judith Ortiz Cofer and Christina Garcia are among the contributors

Latino voices; edited by Frances R. Aparicio. Millbrook Press 1994 143p il (Writers of America) $17.40   810.8

1. American literature—Hispanic American authors—Collections

ISBN 1-56294-388-X   LC 93-42893

An anthology of Latino fiction, poetry, biography, and other writings which describe the experiences of Hispanic Americans

This book "is an excellent way to help youngsters understand another culture or begin to make sense of living in two cultures. The book will enhance bi-cultural education, stimulate discussions, and help students learn what it means to be an American." Child Book Rev Serv

Includes bibliography

Modern American memoirs; selected and edited by Annie Dillard and Cort Conley. HarperCollins Pubs. 1995 449p $27.50 **810.8**
1. American literature—Collections 2. Authors, American
ISBN 0-06-017040-9   LC 95-30755

The editors "have collected excerpts from the memoirs of 35 20th-century American authors. The selections represent the best in autobiographical writing published between 1917 and 1992. Included are nine women and 26 men, both black and white, some better known than others, all distinguished writers and wonderful storytellers. . . . The editors precede each entry with a biographical and contextual note. There's an opening essay on the art of the memoirist and an afterword listing additional classics in the genre." Libr J

The **Oxford** book of women's writing in the United States; edited by Linda Wagner-Martin, Cathy N. Davidson. Oxford Univ. Press 1995 596p $30   **810.8**
1. American literature—Women authors—Collections
ISBN 0-19-508706-2   LC 95-1499

This anthology provides "samples of the public and private work of 99 women of diverse racial and ethnic backgrounds who write in English and were born in or have lived in the United States over the past four centuries. They include short fiction (almost half of the book), poems, essays, plays, and speeches but have also gone beyond traditional genre categories to include performance pieces, erotica, diaries, letters, and recipes." Libr J

The **Portable** Harlem Renaissance reader; edited and with an introduction by David Levering Lewis. Viking 1994 xlvii, 766p hardcover o.p. paperback available $14.95   **810.8**
1. American literature—African American authors—Collections 2. Harlem Renaissance
ISBN 0-14-017036-7 (pa)   LC 93-30233

"General categories include essay, memoir, fiction, poetry, and drama; specific writers include such expected names as Langston Hughes, Zora Neale Hurston, and Claude McKay, but lesser-known names are also represented. There is anger in these pages and also frustration, pride, pain, and elation, but above all there is incredible talent. Reading the collection straight through would be a wonderful education, but most readers will dip in here and there, and that is edifying, too." Booklist

Rising voices; writings of young Native Americans; selected by Arlene B. Hirschfelder and Beverly R. Singer. Scribner 1992 115p $13.95   **810.8**
1. American literature—American Indian authors—Collections 2. Indians of North America 3. Children's writings
ISBN 0-684-19207-1   LC 91-32083

Also available in paperback from Ivy Bks.

A collection of poems and essays in which young Native Americans speak of their identity, their families and communities, rituals, and the harsh realities of their lives

"These 'rising voices' speak eloquently in this important collection. . . . Some pieces are over 100 years old; some are quite current. Some were written by elementary school students, and others by high schoolers. All are poignant and haunting." Voice Youth Advocates

Sister to sister; women write about the unbreakable bond; edited by Patricia Foster. Doubleday 1995 354p $12.95; pa $12.95 **810.8**
1. American literature—Women authors—Collections
ISBN 0-385-47129-7; 0-385-47129-7 (pa)
LC 95-10486

"Contributors to this volume include bell hooks, Robin Behn, Letty Cottin Pogrebin, and Joy Williams. The essays, while all centering on the themes of sisterly relationships, run the literary gamut. Fanciful fiction pieces are included, as are straightforward autobiographical anecdotes and a couple of critical essays. Any library with a demand for contemporary women's literature should have this collection." Libr J

Where coyotes howl and wind blows free; growing up in the West; edited by Alexandra R. Haslam and Gerald W. Haslam. University of Nev. Press 1995 201p $18.50   **810.8**
1. American literature—Collections 2. West (U.S.)
ISBN 0-87417-255-1   LC 94-38567

A collection of stories, folktales, legends, memoirs, and essays set in the American West. Among the contributors are: Rudolfo Anaya, Hisaye Yamamoto, Gary Soto, Wanda Coleman, Cyra McFadden, Maxine Hong Kingston and Zilpha Keatley Snyder

"The unifying theme for these 35 selections is that all the authors grew up in the American West and are writing to relate some aspect of that experience. . . . The editors chose well, providing for variety of style as well as diversity of viewpoint. This would be a wonderful tool for any unit with a multicultural bent." Booklist

Includes bibliographical references

810.9   American literature—History and criticism

African-American voices in young adult literature; tradition, transition, transformation; edited by Karen Patricia Smith. Scarecrow Press 1994 xxxv, 405p $45   **810.9**
1. Young adults' literature 2. African Americans in literature
ISBN 0-8108-2907-X   LC 94-13800

"Citing a need for professional reading about African-American young adult narratives, the editor of this collection of fourteen original essays has gathered writings which make audible diverse voices within a dynamic literature. . . . The book, anxious to hear from both established and new voices, includes examinations of frequently recognized African-American authors—Virginia Hamilton, Mildred Taylor, and Walter Dean Myers, for instance—as well as writers with growing reputations, such as Angela Johnson." Voice Youth Advocates

Includes bibliographical references

American diversity, American identity; the lives and works of 145 writers who define the American experience; John K. Roth, editor. Holt & Co. 1995 709p (Henry Holt reference book) $45 **810.9**
1. American literature—History and criticism 2. Multiculturalism in literature 3. United States—Intellectual life
ISBN 0-8050-3430-7 LC 94-38425
"The text encompasses, '145 writers who define the American experience.' Each entry has a list of the author's works, a biography, an overview of literary style, and analysis of the writing." Book Rep
For a fuller review see: Booklist, Nov. 15, 1995
Includes bibliographical references

American literary almanac; from 1608 to the present: an original compendium of facts and anecdotes about literary life in the United States of America; edited by Karen L. Rood. Facts on File 1988 427p il $35; pa 19.95 **810.9**
1. American literature—History and criticism 2. United States—Intellectual life
ISBN 0-8160-1245-8; 0-8160-1575-9 (pa)
LC 88-3689
"A Bruccoli Clark Layman book"
This volume contains "entries on eccentric writers, literary hoaxes, minorities in literature, famous feuds, relations with publishers, nasty reviews, and parting words and epitaphs. Unfortunately, the book is marred by obvious errors in dates and by lines transposed, omitted, or unevenly spaced. Still, it is delightful for browsing, and a fine source of information for students and teachers alike." Booklist
Includes bibliography

American nature writers; John Elder, editor. Scribner 1996 2v il set $220 **810.9**
1. American literature—History and criticism 2. American literature—Bio-bibliography 3. Nature in literature
ISBN 0-684-19692-1 LC 96-31237
Contents: v1 Edward Abbey to John McPhee; v2 Peter Matthiessen to Western geologists and explorers
"This work presents critical biographical essays on 70 American nature writers who have contributed or are contributing to the genre. Although the biographies reach back to individuals popular in the 18th and 19th centuries (e.g., William Bartram, Henry David Thoreau, John Burroughs, Susan Fenimore Cooper, Gene Stratton Porter), more than a third cover contemporary authors. . . . Twelve other essays treating African and Native Americans and nature writing, contemporary ecofiction and nature poetry, and the literatures of mountaineering, geology, and birdwatching [are included]." Choice
For a fuller review see: Booklist, Feb. 1, 1997
Includes bibliographical references

American women writers; a critical reference guide from colonial times to the present; editor, Lina Mainiero; associate editor, Langdon Lynne Faust. Ungar 1979-1982 4v o.p. **810.9**
1. American literature—History and criticism 2. Women authors 3. American literature—Bio-bibliography
Volume 5: Supplement published 1994 by Continuum available $95 (ISBN 0-8264-06033)
"Offers biobibliographical essays (with some critical comment) on a wide range of American women writers of all periods. Articles are signed by the contributors and carry lists of works by and about the authors treated. Aims to include all women writers of established literary reputation." Guide to Ref Books. 11th edition

Black American poets and dramatists before the Harlem Renaissance; edited and with an introduction by Harold Bloom. Chelsea House 1994 145p (Writers of English: lives and works) $24.95; pa $12.95 **810.9**
1. American literature—African American authors—Bio-bibliography 2. American literature—African American authors—History and criticism
ISBN 0-7910-2205-6; 0-7910-2230-7 (pa)
LC 93-8344
Also available companion volume Black American poets and dramatists of the Harlem Renaissance
Paul Laurence Dunbar, Phillis Wheatley and James Weldon Johnson are among the eleven black American poets and dramatists profiled. A biographical sketch, a selection of critical extracts and a bibliography are provided for each author

Black American prose writers before the Harlem Renaissance; edited and with an introduction by Harold Bloom. Chelsea House 1994 159p (Writers of English: lives and works) $24.95; pa $12.95 **810.9**
1. American literature—African American authors—Bio-bibliography 2. American literature—African American authors—History and criticism
ISBN 0-7910-2202-1; 0-7910-2227-7 (pa)
LC 93-13022
Among the black American prose writers covered in this volume are Charles W. Chesnutt, W. E. B. DuBois, Pauline E. Hopkins and James Weldon Johnson
"This is a valuable resource for students of black history. Each entry comprises a brief biography and excerpts from literary criticism from the author's own era to the present, and it is these criticisms that illuminate the bare bones of the biographies." Voice Youth Advocates

Black American prose writers of the Harlem Renaissance; edited and with an introduction by Harold Bloom. Chelsea House 1994 174p (Writers of English: lives and works) $24.95; pa $12.95 **810.9**

1. American literature—African American authors—Bio-bibliography 2. American literature—African American authors—History and criticism 3. Harlem Renaissance

ISBN 0-7910-2203-X; 0-7910-2228-5 (pa)

LC 93-17979

Langston Hughes, Countee Cullen and Nella Larsen are among the thirteen black American prose writers profiled. Biographical information, a selection of critical extracts and a bibliography are provided for each author

The **Cambridge** history of American literature; general editor, Sacvan Bercovitch; associate editor, Cyrus R.K. Patell. Cambridge Univ. Press 1994-1996 3v **810.9**

1. American literature—History and criticism

LC 92-42479

First three volumes of a projected eight volume set

Contents: v1 1590-1820 $69.95, pa $27.95 (ISBN 0-521-30105-X; 0-521-58571-6); v2 Prose writing 1820-1865 $74.95 (ISBN 0-521-30106-8); v8 Poetry and criticism, 1940-1995 (ISBN 0-521-49733-7)

Scholars contribute essays assessing major authors, movements and trends in the development of American literature

Carroll, Rebecca

I know what the red clay looks like; the voice and vision of black American women writers. Crown Trade Paperbacks 1994 246p il $22.50; pa $12 **810.9**

1. American literature—African American authors—History and criticism 2. Women authors 3. African Americans in literature

ISBN 0-517-59638-5; 0-517-88261-2 (pa)

LC 94-8342

"In this collection, writer and free-lance editor Carroll conducts interviews with eight of the most famous African American women writers (e.g., Rita Dove, Gloria Naylor, Nikki Giovanni) as well as seven lesser-knowns (Lorene Cary, Barbara Neely, Davida Adedjouma), who praise the noted black women writers preceding them." Libr J

Censored books; critical viewpoints; edited by Nicholas J. Karolides, Lee Burress, John M. Kean. Scarecrow Press 1993 xxvi, 498p $49.50 **810.9**

1. American literature—History and criticism 2. Censorship

ISBN 0-8108-2667-4

LC 93-349

"This collection of essays includes both broad statements against censorship and articles defending individual books that have been relentlessly challenged during the past 50 years." Booklist

Includes bibliographical references

Contemporary black American poets and dramatists; edited and with an introduction by Harold Bloom. Chelsea House 1995 200p (Writers of English: lives and works) $29.95; pa $14.95 **810.9**

1. American literature—African American authors—History and criticism 2. American literature—African American authors—Bio-bibliography

ISBN 0-7910-2213-7; 0-7910-2238-2 (pa)

LC 94-5885

Ed Bullins, Thylias Moss, Ishmael Reed, and Ntozake Shange are among the fourteen black American writers profiled. Biographical information, a selection of critical extracts and a bibliography are provided for each author

Davis, Cynthia J., 1964-

Women writers in the United States; a timeline of literary, cultural, and social history; [by] Cynthia Davis and Kathryn West. Oxford Univ. Press 1996 488p $45 **810.9**

1. American literature—Women authors 2. American literature—Chronology 3. Women—United States

ISBN 0-19-509053-5

LC 95-31815

In a timeline format, the authors "present information on the full spectrum of women's writing—including fiction, poetry, biography, political manifestos, essays, advice columns, and cookbooks, alongside a chronology of developments in social and cultural history that are especially pertinent to women's lives." Publisher's note

For a review see: Booklist, Sept. 1, 1996

Drew, Bernard A. (Bernard Alger), 1950-

The 100 most popular young adult authors; biographical sketches and bibliographies. Libraries Unlimited 1996 xxx, 547p $55 **810.9**

1. Young adults' literature—Bio-bibliography

ISBN 1-56308-319-1

LC 95-41913

Each of the profiles "has a complete list of the writer's works (with year of publication and one-line synopsis of the plot), critical comments from a variety of sources, and suggestions for further reading. The book focuses on individuals writing in the '90s, but also includes 12 classic authors (e.g., Mark Twain, Louisa May Alcott, J.R.R. Tolkien). . . . It also covers some authors known primarily for adult literature (e.g., Stephen King) and some who write mainly for middle readers but are also popular among young adults (e.g., Betsy Byars)." Publisher's note

For a review see: Booklist, Oct. 1, 1996

Ehrlich, Eugene H.

The Oxford illustrated literary guide to the United States; [by] Eugene Ehrlich and Gorton Carruth. Oxford Univ. Press 1982 464p il $45 **810.9**

1. Literary landmarks—United States 2. United States—Description

ISBN 0-19-503186-5

LC 82-8034

"A Hudson Group book"

"Beginning in New England and progressing westward through five regions, the guide describes the literary associations of 1,527 authors in 1,586 towns in all fifty

Ehrlich, Eugene H.—*Continued*

states. Within regional sections, states are arranged geographically in a roughly East-to-West fashion, and towns are listed alphabetically within state sections. Numerous photographs of houses, writers, and monuments and marginal quotations from literary works animate descriptions of the places." Wilson Libr Bull

Magill's survey of American literature; edited by Frank N. Magill. Marshall Cavendish 1991 6v il set $389.95   **810.9**
1. American literature—History and criticism 2. American literature—Bio-bibliography
ISBN 1-85435-437-X   LC 91-28113
Companion set: Magill's survey of world literature, entered in class 809
Also available two-volume supplement published 1996 $124.95 (ISBN 1-85435-734-4)
This set presents coverage of 190 American writers from the seventeenth century to the present
"No one can accuse Magill of elitism, for he combines alphabetically into this manageably sized set both the time-tested and the currently trendy authors of American literature. Nor can he be accused of ignoring women, for 46 of the 190 entries are women. . . . Current black, Hispanic, and Native American writers are well represented." Libr J

Major modern black American writers; edited and with an introduction by Harold Bloom. Chelsea House 1995 196p (Writers of English: lives and works) $29.95; pa $14.95   **810.9**
1. American literature—African American authors—History and criticism 2. American literature—African American authors—Bio-bibliography
ISBN 0-7910-2219-6; 0-7910-2244-7 (pa)
     LC 94-4336
Maya Angelou, James Baldwin, Amiri Baraka, Gwendolyn Brooks, Ralph Ellison, Lorraine Hansberry, and Alice Walker are among the twelve writers covered in this volume

Masterpieces of African-American literature; edited by Frank N. Magill. HarperCollins Pubs. 1992 593p $45   **810.9**
1. American literature—African American authors—Dictionaries 2. African Americans in literature
ISBN 0-06-270066-9   LC 92-52542
This work "includes articles on 149 titles in African American literature from various genres. Some 91 authors are represented, 37 of whom are women. Entries, which are generally well written and informative, include sections on the principal characters, plot, analysis, and the critical context. Descriptions of the standard works, including a number of young adult titles, are presented. . . . This is an essential purchase that provides material not always easily available elsewhere." Libr J

Masterpieces of American literature; edited by Frank N. Magill. HarperCollins Pubs. 1993 626p $40   **810.9**
1. American literature—History and criticism
ISBN 0-06-270072-3   LC 93-15940
"Magill here provides brief plot summaries of over 200 great works of fiction and poetry. Each entry includes basic information, a plot summary, and a critical evaluation. Entries include the standard classics from colonial times to the present day." Libr J

Modern American women writers; Elaine Showalter, consulting editor; Lea Baechler, A. Walton Litz, general editors. Scribner 1991 xxii, 583p $100   **810.9**
1. American literature—Women authors 2. American literature—Bio-bibliography
ISBN 0-684-19057-5   LC 90-52917
"This work focuses on 41 representative American women who have published since 1870. Among those included are Anne Tyler, Alice Walker, and Emily Dickinson. The essays, ranging from 8 to 22 pages, emphasize the social and historical environment in which each wrote." Nichols. Guide to Ref Books for Sch Media Cent. 4th edition
Includes bibliographical references

Native North American literature; biographical and critical information on native writers and orators from the United States and Canada from historical times to the present; Janet Witalec, editor; Jeffery Chapman, Christopher Giroux, associate editors. Gale Res. 1994 xlv, 706p il maps $99   **810.9**
1. American literature—American Indian authors—Bibliography 2. Canadian literature—Canadian Indian authors—Bio-bibliography
ISBN 0-8103-9898-2   LC 94-32397
"Representing tribal cultures from Canada and the U.S., the 78 individuals included range from well-known historical figures such as Chief Joseph, Sitting Bull, and Tecumseh to such noted contemporary writers as Louise Erdrich, N. Scott Momaday, and James Welch. . . . The entries themselves appear within two major sections, with part 1 devoted to oral literature (subdivided into oral autobiography and oratory) and part 2 focusing on written literature. Each entry consists of a brief overview of the writer's life and career; a list of major writings; lengthy excerpts from book reviews, critical commentary, interviews, etc.; and a bibliography of secondary sources." Booklist

Otfinoski, Steven, 1949-
Nineteenth-century writers. Facts on File 1991 122p il (American profiles) $17.95   **810.9**
1. American literature—History and criticism 2. Authors, American
ISBN 0-8160-2486-3   LC 90-20107
Contains profiles of ten nineteenth-century American literary giants, from Washington Irving to Stephen Crane, and assesses their work and its significance for American life and culture
Includes bibliographical references

The **Oxford** companion to women's writing in the United States; editors in chief, Cathy N. Davidson, Linda Wagner-Martin; editors, Elizabeth Ammons [et al.] Oxford Univ. Press 1995 xxx, 1021p $55   **810.9**
1. American literature—Women authors—Dictionaries 2. American literature—Women authors—Bio-bibliography
ISBN 0-19-506608-1   LC 94-26359
This "publication consists of over 800 entries that span four centuries of American women's writing. Full biographies and brief bibliographies detail the lives of women from all ethnic groups and regions of the country, including authors as diverse as Willa Cather and Rita Dove. Women who are not known chiefly as writers are also included, i.e., Rachel Carson, Margaret Mead, and Susan B. Anthony. Entries also include literary styles (French feminism), objects (journals and diaries), and institutions (libraries) central to women's writing. All essays are signed, and many contributors are famous in their own right, Susan Faludi and Deborah Tannen among them." Libr J
For a fuller review see: Booklist, Jan. 15, 1995

Russell, Sandi
Render me my song; African American women writers from slavery to the present. St. Martin's Press 1991 227p hardcover o.p. paperback available $9.95   **810.9**
1. American literature—African American authors—History and criticism 2. Women authors 3. African Americans in literature
ISBN 0-312-07074-8 (pa)   LC 90-49209
"From Lucy Terry's earliest recorded rhyme in 1746, to Ntozake Shange's novels of the 1980s, Russell surveys the development of black women's literary traditions in America." Booklist

811   American poetry

Adoff, Arnold, 1935-
Slow dance heartbreak blues; with artwork by William Cotton. Lothrop, Lee & Shepard Bks. 1995 unp il $14   **811**
ISBN 0-688-10569-6   LC 94-48242
"The author captures the concerns that are uniquely part of the early teen years: the agonies of first love, drugs, physical appearance, playing ball. . . . Most young teens will find portions of themselves in Adoff's poetry and will enjoy his writing." Book Rep

Aiken, Conrad, 1889-1973
Collected poems. 2nd ed. Oxford Univ. Press 1970 1049p $45   **811**
ISBN 0-19-501258-5
First published 1953
This volume contains all of the poet's published verse written since 1953 and the verse he chose to preserve from more than five decades of previously published work. The arrangement is chronological
The "work of one of the masters of our time, a poet who can charm, surprise, enlighten, or terrify, varying but never losing a harpsichordist's elegance of touch." Atl Mon

Angelou, Maya
The complete collected poems of Maya Angelou. Random House 1994 273p $23   **811**
ISBN 0-679-42895-X   LC 94-14501
This volume contains all of Angelou's published poems including her inaugural poem On the pulse of morning

Baldwin, James, 1924-1987
Jimmy's blues; selected poems. St. Martin's Press 1985 75p $11.95; pa $9.95   **811**
ISBN 0-312-44247-5; 0-312-05104-2 (pa)
                                      LC 85-25185
The first published collection of poetry from the author of If Beale Street could talk, Another country and The fire next time

Benét, Stephen Vincent, 1898-1943
John Brown's body   **811**
1. Brown, John, 1800-1859—Poetry 2. United States—History—Poetry
Hardcover and paperback editions available from various publishers
First published 1928 by Doubleday, Doran
"An epic poem by Stephen Vincent Benét. A narrative of the Civil War, it opens with a prelude on the introduction of slavery, which is followed by a description of John Brown and his raid on Harpers Ferry. The poem, which considers both sides of the conflict with sympathy, includes sketches of famous participants, battles, the hardships of those on the home front, etc." Reader's Ency. 4th edition

Benvenuto, Richard
Amy Lowell. Twayne Pubs. 1985 163p (Twayne's United States authors series) lib bdg $22.95   **811**
1. Lowell, Amy, 1874-1925
ISBN 0-8057-7436-X   LC 85-5433
An assessment of the life, work, and influence of one of America's leading imagist poets
Includes bibliography

Bishop, Elizabeth, 1911-1979
The complete poems, 1927-1979. Farrar, Straus & Giroux 1983 287p hardcover o.p. paperback available $13   **811**
ISBN 0-374-51817-3 (pa)   LC 82-21119
Supersedes the author's Complete poems, published 1969
This volume contains poems from four collections: North & South (1946); A cold spring (1955, winner of Pulitzer prize); Questions of travel (1965); and Geography III (1977). Also included are translations, uncollected poems, and sections entitled "Poems written in youth" and "Occasional poems"
Bishop's "reputation is founded on perhaps 25 poems. . . . Altogether that looks like a modest achievement until one considers that most of the larger poetic reputations of the past century have been founded on similar evidence. The difference is that Bishop's masterpieces stand in a higher ratio to her work as a whole." N Y Times Book Rev

Brooks, Gwendolyn
Selected poems. Harper & Row 1963 127p hardcover o.p. paperback available $11   **811**
> ISBN 0-06-090989-7 (pa)

"The subject of this poetry is the lives of African American residents of Northern urban ghettos, particularly women, and Brooks has been praised for her depiction of that experience in forms ranging from terza rima to blues meter." Benet's Reader's Ency of Am Lit

Ciardi, John, 1916-1986
Echoes; poems left behind. University of Ark. Press 1989 65p hardcover o.p. paperback available $8.95   **811**
> ISBN 1-55728-063-0 (pa)   LC 88-21927

"Ciardi's fourth posthumous volume in the three years since his death—collects 45 previously unknown, unpublished poems found among his manuscripts. Those familiar with his poetry will discover no surprises here—just the same sure-footedness of line, mastery of form, and acuteness that allowed him to render both natural and remembered landscapes with painterly precision." Libr J

Clifton, Lucille, 1936-
Quilting; poems, 1987-1990. BOA Eds. 1991 89p (American poets continuum series) pa $10   **811**
> ISBN 0-918526-81-7   LC 91-70845

"The past, for Clifton, is always present, and its silences speak out; the unnamed graves of women in a slave cemetery, Eve's version of Eden, the unrecorded saga of childhood. This is a carefully wrought book in which the stories, the vignettes, and the documentation of the lives of martyred heroes or of brave friends and neighbors fall together with the rightness of proverbs." Christ Sci Monit

Crane, Stephen, 1871-1900
The complete poems of Stephen Crane; edited and with an introduction by Joseph Katz. Cornell Univ. Press 1972 xxxvii, 154p pa $13.95   **811**
> ISBN 0-8014-9130-4

This collection of 134 poems, arranged in chronological order, includes poems from the two collections printed during Crane's lifetime: The black riders and other lines (1895) and War is kind (1899), as well as poems which he contributed to periodicals and those surviving in verifiable holographs or typescripts

"Crane's experimental free verse heralded and somewhat influenced the imagist movement of Ezra Pound and Amy Lowell." Herzberg. Reader's Ency of Am Lit
Includes bibliographical references

Cummings, E. E. (Edward Estlin), 1894-1962
Complete poems, 1904-1962; containing all the published poetry; edited by George J. Firmage. rev corr & expanded ed. Norton 1994 xxxii, 1102p $50   **811**
> ISBN 0-87140-152-5   LC 91-29158

Expanded version of Complete poems, 1913-1962 (1972)

"This volume has been prepared directly from the poet's original manuscripts, preserving the original typography and format. It includes all the previously published works, from *Tulips* (1922) to *Etcetera* (1983), as well as 36 uncollected poems that originally appeared in little magazines or anthologies." Libr J

Dickey, James
The whole motion; collected poems, 1949-1992. Wesleyan Univ. Press 1992 477p (Wesleyan poetry) $29.95; pa $19.95   **811**
> ISBN 0-8195-2202-3; 0-8195-1218-4 (pa)
>   LC 91-50811

"A definitive retrospective of an American poet known for his experimental and probing approach. . . . This robust collection embraces more than 200 poems from over a dozen books, including his first, *Into the Stone*,

Dickinson, Emily, 1830-1886
The complete poems of Emily Dickinson; edited by Thomas H. Johnson. Little, Brown 1960 770p $29.95; pa $16.95   **811**
> ISBN 0-316-18414-4; 0-316-18413-6 (pa)

A chronological arrangement of all known Dickinson poems and fragments

Final harvest; Emily Dickinson's poems; selection and introduction by Thomas H. Johnson. Little, Brown 1961 331p $27.95; pa $13.95   **811**
> ISBN 0-316-18416-0; 0-316-18415-2 (pa)

A selection of 575 poems from: The complete poems of Emily Dickinson, entered above. The editor's aim has been to allow the reader to realize the full scope and diversity of the poet's work

New poems of Emily Dickinson; edited by William H. Shurr with Anna Dunlap & Emily Grey Shurr. University of N.C. Press 1993 125p $19.95; pa $10.95   **811**
> ISBN 0-8078-2115-2; 0-8078-4416-0 (pa)
>   LC 93-20353

This volume increases Dickinson's "body of work by 498 selections. Shurr has accomplished this by combining three volumes of the poet's letters and identifying epigrams, riddles, and various longer lyrical pieces within the prose. These will both challenge and delight serious readers, for wit, unusual rhythms, and musical rhymes predominate." SLJ

Includes bibliography

The selected poems of Emily Dickinson. Modern Lib. 1996 295p $14.50   **811**
> ISBN 0-679-60201-1

This "edition presents the more than four hundred poems that were published between Dickinson's death and 1900. They express her concepts of life and death, of love and nature, and of what Henry James called 'the landscape of the soul.'" Publisher's note

Dillard, Annie

Mornings like this; found poems. HarperCollins Pubs. 1995 75p $20; pa $10   **811**

ISBN 0-06-017155-3; 0-06-092725-9 (pa)

LC 95-8675

"What Dillard has done is construct poems out of 'bits of broken text'; that is, she's lifted sentences and used them to create original poems on her own themes. So these are language collages, meticulous and surprisingly effective. Dillard found gems embedded in such unlikely and obscure sources as a boys' project manual, nineteenth-century scientific texts, and memoirs, and she has turned them into poems of wonderful resonance, some very moving, others quite funny." Booklist

Dove, Rita

Mother love; poems. Norton 1995 77p $17.95; pa $10   **811**

ISBN 0-393-03808-4; 0-393-31444-8 (pa)

LC 95-5394

"Most poems included here are autobiographical. Dove writes of childhood bullies, rock songs crooned in the driveway, and, in the long poem, 'Persephone in Hell,' a stay in Paris over 20 years ago. Her language is simple and clear." Libr J

Selected poems. Vintage Bks. 1993 xxvi, 210p $25; pa $12   **811**

ISBN 0-679-43083-0; 0-679-75080-0 (pa)

LC 93-26112

"This volume places three previous collections under one cover. . . . The selection begins with *The Yellow House on the Corner,* Dove's first book, most notable for its poems derived from slave narratives. *Museum,* her second book, offers a potpourri of work that ranges over several continents and many millenia; Dove's tirelessly exact language illuminates the lives of saints, contemporary lifestyles, and Greek myths. Finally, the Pulitzer Prize-winning *Thomas and Beulah* offers slices of African American life from the early part of the century." Booklist

Eliot, T. S. (Thomas Stearns), 1888-1965

Collected poems, 1909-1962. Harcourt Brace Jovanovich 1963 221p $20   **811**

ISBN 0-15-118978-1

This volume contains the complete text of Collected poems, 1909-1935, the Four quartets, and several other poems accompanied by brief prefatory notes

The waste land, and other poems. Harcourt Brace Jovanovich 1955 c1934 88p pa $7   **811**

ISBN 0-15-694877-X

Also available in hardcover from Buccaneer Bks.

"A Harvest book"

In addition to Eliot's long poem of despair this volume contains a representative selection of his best known shorter works

Emerson, Ralph Waldo, 1803-1882

Collected poems & translations. Library of Am. 1994 637p $35   **811**

ISBN 0-940450-28-3   LC 93-40245

Contains Emerson's published poetry, plus selections of his unpublished poetry from journals and notebooks, and some of his translations of poetry from other languages, notably Dante's La vita nuova

Emily Dickinson: a collection of critical essays. Prentice-Hall 1963 182p $12.95   **811**

1. Dickinson, Emily, 1830-1886

ISBN 0-13-208785-5

"A Spectrum book. Twentieth century views"

Edited by Richard B. Sewall

Sixteen analytical essays previously published in journals and books. Among the contributors are Conrad Aiken, John Crowe Ransom, Louise Bogan, and Archibald MacLeish

Ferlazzo, Paul J.

Emily Dickinson. Twayne Pubs. 1976 168p (Twayne's United States authors series) lib bdg $21.95   **811**

1. Dickinson, Emily, 1830-1886

ISBN 0-8057-7180-8

Also available in paperback from Macmillan

"After opening with a chapter comparing the 'myth of Emily' with the known facts of her life, Ferlazzo presents five thematic chapters (e.g., on love, death, nature) in which analyses of poems (including many of her major ones) related to these subjects are provided." Libr J

"Chapter notes, bibliography, and index are in keeping with the solid excellence of this little book." Choice

Ferlinghetti, Lawrence

These are my rivers; new & selected poems, 1955-1993. New Directions 1993 308p il $22.95; pa $12.95   **811**

ISBN 0-8112-1252-1; 0-8112-1273-4 (pa)

LC 93-10383

"Reading this hefty selection from 12 previous volumes, plus 50 pages of new poems, we realize how accurately the poet described himself in 1979: a man who 'thinks he's Dylan Thomas and Bob Dylan rolled together with Charlie Chaplin thrown in.' . . . His style is recognizable throughout—phlegmatic poems running several pages, often lacking stanza breaks, with short lines at the left margin or moving across the page as hand follows eye." Libr J

Fowler, Virginia C., 1948-

Nikki Giovanni. Twayne Pubs. 1992 192p (Twayne's United States authors series) $21.95   **811**

1. Giovanni, Nikki

ISBN 0-8057-3983-1   LC 92-16731

This introduction to the black poet assesses her work in political, sociological and biographical terms. An interview with Giovanni is included

"The full bibliography contains helpful annotations. This clear introduction provides a base for further study of Giovanni's work." Libr J

Frost, Robert, 1874-1963
The poetry of Robert Frost; edited by Edward Connery Lathem. Holt & Co. 1969 607p hardcover o.p. paperback available $15.95   811
ISBN 0-8050-0501-3 (pa)
"A one-volume edition of Frost's eleven volumes of poetry and two short blank-verse plays. The collection ranges in time from A Boy's Will (1913) to In the Clearing (1962). . . . [There is] an appendix of bibliographical and textual notes for each of the poems." Nation

Frye, Northrop
T.S. Eliot; an introduction. University of Chicago Press 1981 109p pa $9.95   811
1. Eliot, T. S. (Thomas Stearns), 1888-1965
ISBN 0-226-26649-4   LC 80-29344
First published 1963 by Grove Press
This brief introduction to Eliot's achievement as a man of letters deals with his literary theory and practice, discussing his major poetical works and referring also to his dramatic works and essays. Eliot's use of symbols and archetypes is discussed
Includes bibliography

Gerber, Philip L.
Robert Frost. rev ed. Twayne Pubs. 1982 203p (Twayne's United States authors series) lib bdg $21.95   811
1. Frost, Robert, 1874-1963
ISBN 0-8057-7348-7   LC 81-6976
First published 1966
This book reviews Frost's life and career with principal emphasis on his craftsmanship, poetic theories, and major themes
Includes bibliography

Gibran, Kahlil, 1883-1931
The Prophet. Knopf 1923 107p il $15   811
ISBN 0-394-40428-9
Also available pocket library editions
A collection of poems by the mystical writer/artist, who was born in Lebanon and died in the United States, in which the prophet Almustafa deals with fundamental aspects of human life such as love, friendship, good and evil, self-knowledge, passion and reason, joy and sorrow, freedom, work, marriage and children, prayer and death

Ginsberg, Allen, 1926-1997
Collected poems, 1947-1980. Harper & Row 1984 xxi, 837p il hardcover o.p. paperback available $22.50   811
ISBN 0-06-091494-7 (pa)   LC 84-47573
"A complete collection of the poetry of the most celebrated Beat, gathered from the many small-press volumes and magazines in which they have appeared, with sometimes extraordinary notes by the poet." N Y Times Book Rev
Includes title, first line, and proper name indexes

Cosmopolitan greetings; poems, 1986-1992. HarperCollins Pubs. 1994 118p $20; pa $12   811
ISBN 0-06-016770-X; 0-06-092623-6 (pa)
                                LC 93-43627
This collection is "suffused with a range of emotional colors that gives Ginsberg's work an added depth, a rest-

less energy and ultimately an elegiac tone. Writing from China, Warsaw, Nicaragua and New York City, the poet makes strong statements on two of his favorite subjects, politics . . . and sexuality." Publ Wkly

Giovanni, Nikki
The selected poems of Nikki Giovanni (1968-1995). Morrow 1996 224p $20   811
ISBN 0-688-14047-5   LC 95-31646
"Writing as an African American and as a woman, Giovanni speaks with powerful music about politics, love, feminism, and family; this collection will move many teens." Booklist

Hall, Donald, 1928-
Old and new poems. Ticknor & Fields 1990 244p hardcover o.p. paperback available $14.95
                                811
ISBN 0-89919-954-2 (pa)   LC 90-31087
This collection "gathers a generous selection of the work from 1947 to the present. Mr. Hall, as this collection makes clear, has improved with the years. . . . In the triumphant work of his maturity, in a burly line not strictly metrical but full-blown in its sonority, Mr. Hall celebrates with grieving joy the transmutation of matter into energy and the consumption of life by death, death seen as the unrefusable essence of life itself. . . . This is poetry that marches in a stately order; classical in its dignity and perfectly readable, it argues the mystical union of dark and light, death and life." N Y Times Book Rev

Harjo, Joy, 1951-
The woman who fell from the sky; poems. Norton 1994 69p $21; pa $10   811
ISBN 0-393-03715-0; 0-393-31362-X (pa)
                                LC 96-23014
Hardcover edition includes audiocassette of Harjo performing her work
"Harjo sets 25 prayer-like prose poems in a spooky land of myth . . . depicting an ongoing moral 'war' between forces of creation (northern lights, wolves) vs. destruction (alcoholism, Vietnam). Like contemporary Jobs, the people in these pieces search for an intelligible response to 'the wreck of culture,' their efforts symbolizing the impact of alienation on the psyche." Libr J

Hughes, Langston, 1902-1967
The collected poems of Langston Hughes; Arnold Rampersad, editor; David Roessel, associate editor. Knopf 1994 708p $30   811
1. African Americans—Poetry
ISBN 0-679-42631-0   LC 94-14509
"The editors have attempted to collect every poem (860 in all) published by the writer in his lifetime, and have also provided a brief but informative introduction, a detailed chronology and extensive textual notes that include the original date and place of publication for each poem. . . . Although Hughes is best known for his poems celebrating African American life, he was also a passionately political poet." Publ Wkly

James Dickey; edited and with an introduction by
Harold Bloom. Chelsea House 1987 168p
(Modern critical views) $29.95   **811**
1. Dickey, James
ISBN 1-55546-272-3   LC 86-34321
Among the contributors to this critical overview of
Dickey's work are Joyce Carol Oates, Robert Penn War-
ren and Linda Wagner
Includes bibliography

Jarrell, Randall, 1914-1965
The complete poems. Farrar, Straus & Giroux
1969 507p $45; pa $16   **811**
ISBN 0-374-12716-6; 0-374-51305-8 (pa)
Collected here are the entire contents of three published volumes: Selected poems (1955), The woman at
the Washington Zoo (1960), and The Lost World (1965)
plus poems published from 1934 to 1964 but never collected and some never before published

Johnson, James Weldon, 1871-1938
God's trombones: seven Negro sermons in
verse; drawings by Aaron Douglas, lettering by C.
B. Falls. Viking 1927 56p il o.p.; Penguin Bks.
paperback available $7.95   **811**
ISBN 0-14-018403-1 (pa)
Seven sermons in verse inspired by memories of sermons by black preachers heard by Mr. Johnson in childhood. His themes are similar and the poems are written
after the manner of the sermons, but not in dialect

Kennedy, Richard S., 1920-
E.E. Cummings revisited. Twayne Pubs. 1993
155p il (Twayne's United States authors series)
$22.95   **811**
1. Cummings, E. E. (Edward Estlin), 1894-1962
ISBN 0-8057-3995-5   LC 93-4853
"In nine chapters tracing Cummings' development as
a writer, Kennedy defines his subject's primary styles
and their sources in naturalism, cubism, expressionism,
surrealism, and other manifestations in the visual arts."
Publisher's note
Includes bibliography

Kerouac, Jack, 1922-1969
Pomes all sizes; introduction by Allen Ginsberg.
City Lights Bks. 1992 175p pa $10.95   **811**
ISBN 0-87286-269-0   LC 92-1204
"This book, which Kerouac prepared for publication
before his death in 1969, collects poems written between
1954 and 1965. Most are playful—comments about
friends, variations on the sounds of words. Yet a few extremely sensitive longer pieces appear, including
'Caritas,' in which the poet runs after a barefoot beggar
boy to give him money for shoes and then begins to
doubt the boy's veracity. Other intriguing poems reflect
the poet's religious concerns of the moment, running the
gamut of Eastern and Western religions." Libr J

Kunitz, Stanley, 1905-
Passing through; the later poems, new and
selected. Norton 1995 175p $18.95   **811**
ISBN 0-393-03870-X   LC 95-2651
This volume "includes works from three collections
published since 1971 as well as nine poems written since
1985. Such longevity has been most kind to Kunitz, who
writes in 'The Round': 'I can scarcely wait til tomor-
row/when a new life begines for me,/as it does each
day,/as it does each day.' And it is this enthusiasm for
knowing what's next—mingled with the equally strong
drive back through memory and regret—that generates
the very particular force and unencumbered immediacy
of Kunitz's poems." Libr J

Levertov, Denise, 1923-
Sands of the well. New Directions 1996 136p
$20.95   **811**
ISBN 0-8112-1316-1   LC 96-4324
"The outstanding sections in Levertov's eighteenth
collection are 'Sojourns in the Parallel World' and 'Close
to a Lake,' which contain, respectively, poems about nature and religious poems. . . . In other sections are poems about music, spring, memory, and political protest;
all are technically marvelous, for Levertov remains the
best free verse poet writing in English" Booklist

Levine, Philip, 1928-
New selected poems. Knopf 1991 292p
hardcover o.p. paperback available $15   **811**
ISBN 0-679-74056-2 (pa)   LC 90-53422
This selection contains poems Levine chose for his
earlier Selected poems (1984), plus 15 new works
"This is a monumental work that somehow remains
wonderfully accessible, largely because Levine has chosen pieces carefully, favoring shorter works and poems
that address his staple themes of family (like 'Uncle' and
'My Son and I') and childhood ('Coming Home'). Many
of the poems are powerfully imagistic." Libr J

Lowell, Robert, 1917-1977
Selected poems. rev ed. Farrar, Straus & Giroux
1977 255p hardcover o.p. paperback available $14
                                      811
ISBN 0-374-51400-3 (pa)   LC 78-104855
First published 1976
A selection of over 200 poems tracing the develop-
ment of one of the premier confessional poets of his gen-
eration

MacLeish, Archibald, 1892-1982
Collected poems, 1917-1982; with a prefatory
note to the newly collected poems by Richard B.
McAdoo. Houghton Mifflin 1985 524p hardcover
o.p. paperback available $16.95   **811**
ISBN 0-395-39569-0 (pa)   LC 85-14392
Collects all the known poetry of the author/public servant. As an expatriate in Paris his early work was heavily influenced by Pound and Eliot. After returning to the
States his verse concerned itself more with America's
political, social, and cultural heritage

Masters, Edgar Lee, 1868-1950
Spoon River anthology   **811**

Hardcover and paperback editions available from various publishers
First published 1915 by Macmillan
"The men and women of Spoon River narrate their own biographies from the cemetery where they lie buried. Realistic and sometimes cynical, these free-verse monologues often contradict the pious and optimistic epitaphs written on the gravestones." Reader's Ency. 4th edition

Merriam, Eve, 1916-1992
The inner city Mother Goose; illustrated by David Diaz; introduction by Nikki Giovanni. Simon & Schuster Bks. for Young Readers 1996 70p $16   **811**
1. Mother Goose—Parodies, imitations, etc 2. City life—Poetry
ISBN 0-689-80677-9   LC 95-22553
A revised and newly illustrated edition of the title first published 1969
Poems inspired by traditional nursery rhymes depict the grim reality of inner city life, including such topics as crime, drug abuse, unemployment, and inadequate housing

Merrill, James
Selected poems, 1946-1985. Knopf 1992 339p $25; pa $15   **811**
ISBN 0-679-41082-1; 0-679-74731-1 (pa)
LC 91-58622
"By relying on exaggeratedly artificial forms, mixing different stanzaic patterns with blank verse and even prose, cultivating a composite tone, and referring to the writing process within his work, Merrill has continued to resist and interrupt any illusions of unmediated speech. Whatever his ostensible subject, the poet is always placed at the scene of writing, choosing his words, revising, and commenting on what he is doing." Benet's Reader's Ency of Am Lit

Millay, Edna St. Vincent, 1892-1950
Collected poems; edited by Norma Millay. Harper & Row 1956 xxi, 738p hardcover o.p. paperback available $22.50   **811**
ISBN 0-06-090889-0 (pa)
Also available in hardcover from Buccaneer Bks.
The poems in this collection "are divided into two separate sections of lyrics and sonnets, arranged chronologically and printed in groups under the titles of the original volumes, ranging from 'Renascence' of 1917 to 'Mine the harvest,' published in 1954, four years after the poet's death." Booklist

Miller, James Edwin, 1920-
Walt Whitman; [by] James E. Miller, Jr. Twayne Pubs. 1962 188p (Twayne's United States authors series) $22.95   **811**
1. Whitman, Walt, 1819-1892
ISBN 0-8057-7600-1
"A critical essay on Whitman which studies first his views of himself and the major events of his life as relat-

ed to his poetry. Subsequently the structure, language, recurring images, and democratic tone of his poetry are reviewed. Finally considered are the sexuality and mysticism that infused his work. A chronology precedes the text while notes and bibliography follow." Booklist

Moore, Marianne, 1887-1972
The complete poems of Marianne Moore. Macmillan; Viking 1981 305p hardcover o.p. paperback available $9.95   **811**
ISBN 0-14-058601-6 (pa)   LC 80-13586
This "definitive edition of 'The Complete Poems' was prepared by Clive Driver and presents all of Moore's final emendations and cuts, punctuation, hyphens, line arrangements, and revised notes (all critical components of her poetry). It also includes five poems Moore wrote between the publication of the 1967 edition and the time of her death." Libr J

Nash, Ogden, 1902-1971
I wouldn't have missed it: selected poems of Ogden Nash; selected by Linell Smith and Isabel Eberstadt; introduction by Archibald MacLeish. Little, Brown 1975 xxiii, 407p il $29.95   **811**
ISBN 0-316-59830-5
This "is a collection of poems by Ogden Nash covering a period of more than forty years, from his early days at the 'New Yorker' until his death in 1971. The collection of more than four hundred poems was selected by his daughters. Interspersed throughout the book are sixteen line drawings by Nash, very much in the Thurber style. The book also contains a useful double index of poems by first and last lines." Best Sellers

Nemerov, Howard
Trying conclusions; new and selected poems, 1961-1991. University of Chicago Press 1991 161p $18.95   **811**
ISBN 0-226-57263-3   LC 91-3217
This is a selection of work from Nemerov's "seven previous volumes, plus a last section of 23 new poems." Christ Sci Monit
"By and large a formalist in style, [Nemerov] nevertheless interpolated a truly American diction and easygoing wit reminiscent of Mark Twain and Will Rogers. Something of a fatalist . . . Nemerov stood undeceived but not smug, wondering at our 'many destinies.'" Libr J

Oliver, Mary, 1935-
New and selected poems. Beacon Press 1992 255p $27.50; pa $16   **811**
ISBN 0-8070-6818-7; 0-8070-6819-5 (pa)
LC 92-7767
This collection "joins together poems written over 30 years. One of the astonishing aspects of Oliver's work is the consistency of tone over this long period. What changes is an increased focus on nature and an increased precision with language that has made her one of the very best poets." N Y Times Book Rev

Plath, Sylvia

The collected poems; edited by Ted Hughes. Harper & Row 1981 351p hardcover o.p. paperback available $17   **811**

ISBN 0-06-090900-5 (pa)

The collection contains "all the poems Plath wrote, published and unpublished, from 1956 to 1963, as well as a sample of her early work." Publ Wkly

"Although her best poems deal with suffering and death, others are exhilarating and affectionate, and her tone is frequently witty as well as disturbing." Drabble. Concise Oxford Companion to Engl Lit

Crossing the water; transitional poems. Harper & Row 1971 56p hardcover o.p. paperback available $10   **811**

ISBN 0-06-090789-4 (pa)

This posthumous collection of poems written in 1960 and 1961 evidences "Plath's preoccupation with death [which] is conveyed in obsessive use of the word black to connote despair and in other metaphors. . . . Desperate funnels of words, structured in strength and discipline, allude to nature, people, time and painful experiences of living." Booklist

Poe, Edgar Allan, 1809-1849

Poems; edited by Thomas Olive Mabbott. Harvard Univ. Press 1969 xxx, 627p il (Collected works of Edgar Allan Poe v1) $51.95   **811**

ISBN 0-674-13935-6

"Belknap Press"

"The editor has included complete versions of all the variants, and he has also included a considerable number of poems that have been attributed to Poe, with . . . editorial comment. He has also included . . . biographical and critical material that might throw light on the poems." Va Q Rev

Includes bibliography

Pound, Ezra, 1885-1972

Selected poems. new ed. New Directions 1957 184p pa $8.95   **811**

ISBN 0-8112-0162-7

First published 1949

This "provides a good sampling of the Pound who wrote 'A Virginal,' the latter-day Renaissance poet, as well as the reincarnate Li Po and the other 'personae' that Ezra wore during the years he spent absorbing the styles (and not the political thinking) of other centuries." Saturday Rev

Rexroth, Kenneth, 1905-1982

Selected poems; edited with an introduction by Bradford Morrow. New Directions 1984 152p hardcover o.p. paperback available $9.95   **811**

ISBN 0-8112-0917-2 (pa)   LC 84-9972

"This selection retrieves the immensely talented teenager of the early '20s and all the other steps toward the authoritative aged poet of the '70s. We see from Morrow's choices the shape of a career, at once distinctive from, but also exemplary of, the grand sweep of American modernism, which Rexroth very obviously helped—along with Pound and Eliot, Williams and Stevens—to create. Morrow's useful notes illuminate the more arcane allusions." Choice

Rich, Adrienne

Collected early poems, 1950-1970. Norton 1993 xxi, 435p $27.50   **811**

ISBN 0-393-03418-6   LC 92-13150

This collection contains all of the work included in Rich's first six books, and a few previously uncollected pieces

"In her early work, Rich demonstrates a rare mastery of formal verse, and explores art as a haven in a world of menacing change and a means to understand and control emotional experience." Reader's Ency. 4th edition

The fact of a doorframe; poems selected and new, 1950-1984. Norton 1984 341p pa $10.95   **811**

ISBN 0-393-30204-0   LC 84-6107

This collection "is a selection from nine previous books, with an additional number of uncollected and more recent poems." Foreword

"Rich's great virtue is her long struggle for authenticity. . . . She will be remembered in literary history as one of the first American women to claim a public voice in lyric." New Repub

Robert Frost: a collection of critical essays. Prentice-Hall 1962 205p $12.95   **811**

1. Frost, Robert, 1874-1963

ISBN 0-13-331512-6

Analyzed in Essay and general literature index

"A Spectrum book. Twentieth century views"

Edited by James M. Cox

"These eleven critical views appraising the poet's work range from high praise to severe judgment." Chicago. Public Libr

Roethke, Theodore, 1908-1963

The collected poems of Theodore Roethke. Doubleday 1966 279p hardcover o.p. paperback available $12.95   **811**

ISBN 0-385-08601-6 (pa)

Roethke's "refreshingly original rhythms are keenly articulated and often hypnotic. Although his work is uneven and he sometimes gives way to self-indulgence or to surprising naiveté, many of his best poems recreate disconcertingly intense psychic or mystical experience. He also had a flair for the seductively lyrical and the brashly irreverent. He ranks as one of the best poets of the first postmodern generation." Benet's Reader's Ency of Am Lit

Rylant, Cynthia

Something permanent; photographs by Walker Evans; poetry by Cynthia Rylant. Harcourt Brace & Co. 1994 61p il $16.95   **811**

ISBN 0-15-277090-9   LC 93-3861

"Nearly 60 years ago, Walker Evans and James Agee documented the lives of poor Southern sharecroppers. Their efforts resulted in a devastating, legendary account of the Depression, *Let Us Now Praise Famous Men* [entered in class 976.1]. Here, Rylant pairs Evans's photographs with 29 short, lyrical poems." SLJ

"For students in junior high and high school, the juxtaposition of Evans' photos and Rylant's poems will demonstrate how emotions can be rooted in objects and how, to dig them out, you need to use strong, sturdy words." Booklist

Sandburg, Carl, 1878-1967

The complete poems of Carl Sandburg. rev and expanded ed. Harcourt Brace Jovanovich 1970 xxxi, 797p $29.95   **811**
  ISBN 0-15-120773-9
  First published 1950
  Introduction by Archibald MacLeish
  A collection of seven of the author's books: Chicago poems, 1916; Cornhuskers, 1918; Smoke and steel, 1920; Slabs of the sunburnt West, 1922; Good morning, America, 1925; The people, yes, 1936; Honey and salt, 1963
  "Known for his free verse, written under the influence of Walt Whitman and celebrating industrial and agricultural America, American geography and landscape, figures in American history, and the American common people, [Sandburg] frequently makes use of contemporary American slang and colloquialisms." Herzberg. Reader's Ency of Am Lit

Selected poems; edited by George Hendrick and Willene Hendrick. Harcourt Brace & Co. 1996 xxix, 285p pa $15   **811**
  ISBN 0-15-600396-1   LC 95-50686
  "A Harvest original"
  "With a preface that puts the poet and his work in perspective, this 'one-volume edition of Sandburg's best and most characteristic poetry' is ideal for student and poetry enthusiast alike." Booklist
  Includes bibliographical references

Sexton, Anne

The complete poems; with a foreword by Maxine Kumin. Houghton Mifflin 1981 xxiv, 622p $35; pa $15.95   **811**
  ISBN 0-395-29475-4; 0-395-32935-3 (pa)
                                            LC 81-2482
  "This collection contains all the poems in the eight volumes published in Sexton's lifetime, the two published after her death, and seven poems never before in print." Libr J
  "Even before her death in 1974, Sexton's work was the subject of critical controversy, often dismissed as mere confessionalism. But, as Maxine Kumin observes in an insightful introductory essay, Sexton 'delineated the problematic position of women—the neurotic reality of the time' and in so doing 'earned her place in the canon.'" Choice

Shapiro, Karl Jay, 1913-

New & selected poems, 1940-1986; [by] Karl Shapiro. University of Chicago Press 1987 103p pa $9.95   **811**
  ISBN 0-226-75033-7   LC 87-10790
  This volume includes poems published since the appearance of Collected poems, 1940-1978, o.p. They are accompanied by the poet's own selections from each period of his career
  Shapiro "finds cause for personal celebration in the most quotidian occurrences; yet he is equally adept at probing more public subjects. . . . It would have been helpful if the poems had been dated and/or had included an indication of which book they were selected from; but despite that shortcoming, readers will find these 'Selected Poems' a treasure." Libr J

Smith, William Jay, 1918-

Collected poems, 1939-1989. Scribner 1990 254p $24.95   **811**
  ISBN 0-684-19167-9   LC 90-40760
  "Smith has had a lifelong love affair with the lyric. Unabashedly musical, he grounds the reader in a memorable detail: a willow in winter is 'a frozen harp,' a tulip 'a slender goblet wreathed in flame.' Smith's formal, witty style lends itself to the all-but-forgotten arts of light and occasional verse. But the themes of love and mortality are ever-present and reach fruition in the moving later poems." Libr J

Snodgrass, W. D. (William De Witt), 1926-

Selected poems, 1957-1987. Soho Press 1987 270p $19.95   **811**
  ISBN 0-939149-04-4   LC 87-9463
  "These selected poems reveal an important American poet's impressive array of dramatic powers. Selections from 'Heart's Needle' (his Pulitzer Prize-winning volume), small press poems, and excerpts from the intriguing 'Fuehrer Bunker'—dramatic monologues from the top members of Hitler's Third Reich—are included." Libr J

Snyder, Gary

No nature; new and selected poems. Pantheon Bks. 1992 390p $25; pa $14   **811**
  ISBN 0-679-41385-5; 0-679-74252-2 (pa)
                                            LC 92-54110
  This is a "selection of the best of Snyder's career, spanning from Riprap (1959), published at the time of his involvement with the Beatniks and the San Francisco Renaissance, to a previously unpublished group of sixteen poems entitled 'No Nature.'" Libr J
  "There is an understated majesty about the ease with which Mr. Snyder puts the present into perspective." N Y Times Book Rev

Soto, Gary

New and selected poems. Chronicle Bks. 1995 177p $22.95; pa $12.95   **811**
  ISBN 0-8118-0758-4; 0-8118-0761-4 (pa)
                                            LC 94-27081
  "In one of his more striking poems, Soto stares longingly at the unkempt lot in the California slum where his family's house used to be. Elsewhere, a Mexican American simply jogs and laughs after he has been ushered out the back door when immigration officials show up at his workplace. With rare lyricism, gentleness, and a touch of humor, Soto covers the ground that leads many highly touted poets to erupt in pulsating anger. Soto has it all—the learned craft, the intrinsic abilities with language, a fascinating autobiography, and the storyteller's ability to manipulate memories into folklore." Libr J

Stevens, Wallace, 1879-1955

The collected poems of Wallace Stevens. Knopf 1954 534p $40   **811**
  ISBN 0-394-40330-4
  Steven's "poems range from descriptive and dramatic lyrics to meditative and discursive discourse, but all

Stevens, Wallace, 1879-1955—*Continued*
show a deep engagement in experience and in art. His musical verse, rich in tropic imagery but precise and intense in statement, is marked by concern with means of knowledge, with the contrast between reality and appearance, and the emphasis upon imagination as giving an aesthetic insight and order to life." Oxford Companion to Am Lit. 6th edition

Swenson, May, 1919-1989
Nature; poems old and new. Houghton Mifflin 1994 xxiii, 240p $29.95; pa $17.95 **811**
ISBN 0-395-69463-9; 0-395-69462-0 (pa)
LC 93-45642
This collection of Swenson's poetry "brings together poems from several earlier books, as well as poems published only in magazines, and introduces us to nine splendid poems published here for the first time. This collection . . . is brought together with special attention to poems describing the environment; poems of tides and the sea, of birds and gardens, of moods and seasons, of self and others. . . . This is a collection to be treasured; it belongs in all libraries with even a modest selection of poetry." Libr J

Updike, John
Collected poems, 1953-1993. Knopf 1993 xxiv, 387p il $30 **811**
ISBN 0-679-42221-8 LC 92-28957
"From the outset Updike's poems are crisp and exact. There is a mock humbleness, ready wit, and divine concreteness to his subjects, an unrelenting curiosity behind his descriptions, and a prodding tension between the tactile and the abstract. . . . From the cocky exuberance of 'Midpoint,' a 1968 autobiographical cycle, to the wry, tender mischief of poems about domesticity, marriage, and aging, Updike's thrill over the unending discovery of poetry inspires images and metaphors of time-stopping perfection as well as humor rich in grace and knowingness." Booklist
Includes bibliographical references

Walcott, Derek
Collected poems, 1948-1984. Farrar, Straus & Giroux 1986 515p $30; pa $15.95 **811**
ISBN 0-374-12626-7; 0-374-52025-9 (pa)
LC 85-20688
"It is difficult to think of a poet in our century who—without ever betraying his native sources—has so organically assimilated the evolution of English literature from the Renaissance to the present, who has absorbed the Classical and Judeo-Christian past, and who has mined the history of Western painting as Walcott has. Throughout his entire body of work he has managed to hold in balance his passionate moral concerns with the ideal of art." Poetry
Includes bibliography

Omeros. Farrar, Straus & Giroux 1990 325p $30; pa $12 **811**
ISBN 0-374-22591-5; 0-374-52350-9 (pa)
LC 90-33592
This epic poem "follows the wanderings of a present-day Odysseus and the inconsolable sufferings of those who are displaced and traveling with trepidation toward their homes. Written in seven circling books and . . . tercets, the poem illuminates the classical past and its motifs through an extraordinary cast of contemporary characters from the island of Santa Lucia." Publ Wkly
"No poet rivals Mr. Walcott in humor, emotional depth, lavish inventiveness in language or in the ability to express the thoughts of his characters and compel the reader to follow the swift mutations of ideas and images in their minds. This wonderful story moves in a spiral, replicating human thought." N Y Times Book Rev

Walker, Alice, 1944-
Her blue body everything we know; earthling poems, 1965-1990, complete. Harcourt Brace Jovanovich 1991 463p $24.95; pa $14.95 **811**
ISBN 0-15-140040-7; 0-15-640093-6 (pa)
LC 90-5160
In this volume of Walker's "complete earlier work, joined to new, previously uncollected poems, we see a quarter century of impressive artistic development." Booklist

Warren, Robert Penn, 1905-1989
Being here: poetry, 1977-1980. Random House 1980 108p $10.95; pa $4.95 **811**
ISBN 0-394-51304-5; 0-394-73935-3 (pa)
LC 80-11520
This volume "marks an interesting return by this most gifted of major American poetic voices to more traditional forms—forms rather resembling those with which Warren began decades ago—embodying, still, the discoveries about the need for telling concrete imagery the poet has made in the lengthy interim." Choice

New and selected poems, 1923-1985. Random House 1985 322p hardcover o.p. paperback available $20 **811**
ISBN 0-394-73848-9 (pa) LC 84-45755
"The newly collected poems, 1980-84, are grouped under the apt rubric 'Altitudes and Extensions,' for the poet here takes the long and high view of his personal history, beliefs, and perennial themes. . . . The rest of the volume presents strong poems from 11 previous books, in reverse chronological order. Forward to back, these display a consistency of vision and rhythmic poise that help explain how, after such prolific labors, the poet can still be going strong." Booklist

Whitman, Walt, 1819-1892
Leaves of grass **811**

Hardcover and paperback editions available from various publishers
First published 1855
"The book, radical in form and content, takes its title from the themes of fertility, universality, and cyclical life. . . . As he revised and added to the original edition, Whitman arranged the poems in a significant autobiographical order." Reader's Ency. 4th edition

Williams, William Carlos, 1883-1963
The collected poems of William Carlos Williams. New Directions 1986-1988 2v   **811**

Contents: v1 1909-1939; edited by A. Walton Litz and Christopher MacGowan $35, pa $21.95 (ISBN 0-8112-0999-7; 0-8112-1187-8); v2 1939-1962; edited by Christopher MacGowan $37, pa $21.95 (ISBN 0-8112-1063-4; 0-8112-1188-6)

"Williams's poetry is firmly rooted in the commonplace detail of everyday American life. He conceived of the poem as an object: a record of direct experience that deals with the local and the particular. He abandoned conventional rhyme and meter in an effort to reduce the barrier between the reader and his consciousness of his immediate surroundings. . . . Williams's original approach to poetry, his insistence on the importance of the ordinary, and his successful attempts at making his verse as 'tactile' as the spoken word had a far-reaching effect on American poetry." Reader's Ency. 4th edition

811.008   American poetry— Collections

American poetry: the nineteenth century; edited by John Hollander. Library of Am. 1993 2v set $70   **811.008**
1. American poetry—Collections
ISBN 1-883011-00-0   LC 93-10702
Also available CD-ROM version

Contents v1 Freneau to Whitman; v2 Melville to Stickney; American Indian poetry; Folk songs and spirituals

An anthology of more than 1,000 poems by nearly 150 poets. Arrangement is chronological by poet's date of birth. Biographical sketches of the poets, a chronology of significant events from 1800 to 1900, and an essay on textual selection are included

Hollander has compiled "a selection of nineteenth-century American verse so wonderfully catholic that it not just augments but supersedes every other similar collection." Booklist

Beat voices; an anthology of beat poetry; edited by David Kherdian. Holt & Co. 1995 144p $14.95   **811.008**
1. American poetry—Collections
ISBN 0-8050-3315-7   LC 94-36106

A collection of American poetry by and about the beat generation, written by such poets as Gregory Corso, Jack Kerouac, Diane di Prima, and Allen Ginsberg

"The lines are harsh, speaking of abuse, drugs, sex, and carnage amid hope and dreams. The words are oft confusing, sometimes seemingly random, but always flailing against that brick wall of convention. With an open mind and ear, readers can gather a pretty good sense of the thoughts and lives of these confused, mighty, and eloquent writers. Brief bios offer a fleeting additional glimpse." SLJ

Includes bibliographical references

Black sister; poetry by black American women, 1746-1980; edited with an introduction by Erlene Stetson. Indiana Univ. Press 1981 xxiv, 312p $29.95; pa $13.95   **811.008**
1. American poetry—African American authors—Collections 2. American poetry—Women authors—Collections
ISBN 0-253-30512-8; 0-253-20268-X (pa)
     LC 80-8847

"This anthology of black American women poets could amplify the reading lists of courses in black women's literature, Afro-American literature, and women's poetry because it includes both the lesser-known works of familiar poets (Wheatley, Harper, Brooks, Giovanni, Evans), and poems by several less widely read poets ('Ada,' Piper, Hall-Evans)." Choice

Includes bibliography

The **Columbia** anthology of American poetry; edited by Jay Parini. Columbia Univ. Press 1995 757p $29.95   **811.008**
1. American poetry—Collections
ISBN 0-231-08122-7   LC 94-32423

"Ranging from Anne Bradstreet to Louise Glück, editor Parini aims to represent 'the main schools of poetry that have co-existed in the United States . . . in proportion to their influence,' including more poetry by women and minorities 'than one generally finds' in older anthologies." Libr J

The **Columbia** book of Civil War poetry; Richard Marius, editor; Keith W. Frome, associate editor. Columbia Univ. Press 1994 xxxvi, 543p il $24.95   **811.008**
1. American poetry—Collections 2. United States—History—1861-1865, Civil War—Poetry
ISBN 0-231-10002-7   LC 94-6481

"Bret Harte, Walt Whitman, and Robert Frost are but three of the many writers whose poems about the Civil War fill this noteworthy collection. Of value to literature and history student alike." Booklist

Cool salsa; bilingual poems on growing up Latino in the United States; edited by Lori M. Carlson; introduction by Oscar Hijuelos. Holt & Co. 1994 xx, 123p il $14.95   **811.008**
1. American poetry—Hispanic American authors—Collections 2. Bilingual books—English-Spanish
ISBN 0-8050-3135-9   LC 93-45798
Also available in paperback from Fawcett Bks.

"This collection presents poems by 29 Mexican-American, Cuban-American, Puerto Rican, and other Central and South American poets, including Sandra Cisneros, Luis J. Rodriguez, Pat Mora, Gary Soto, Ana Castillo, Oscar Hijuelos, Ed J. Vega, Judith Ortiz-Cofer, and other Latino writers both contemporary and historical. Brief biographical notes on the authors are provided. All the poems deal with experiences of teenagers." Book Rep

Drive, they said; poems about Americans and their cars; edited by Kurt Brown. Milkweed Eds. 1994 xxiii, 326p $14.95 **811.008**
1. Automobiles—Poetry 2. American poetry—Collections
ISBN 0-915943-90-5 LC 93-33856
"Poems about Americans and their cars—the technology, the road, and the metaphor—will grab even those teens who think poetry is not for them." Booklist

Eight American poets; an anthology: Theodore Roethke, Elizabeth Bishop, Robert Lowell, John Berryman, Anne Sexton, Sylvia Plath, Allen Ginsberg, James Merrill; edited by Joel Conarroe. Random House 1994 xxiv, 306p il hardcover o.p. paperback available $13 **811.008**
1. American poetry—Collections
ISBN 0-679-77643-5 (pa) LC 94-10186
This anthology contains representative work by eight 20th century American confessional poets

✓ **Every** shut eye ain't asleep; an anthology of poetry by African Americans since 1945; edited by Michael Harper and Anthony Walton. Little, Brown 1994 327p $27.95 **811.008**
1. American poetry—African American authors—Collections
ISBN 0-316-34712-4 LC 93-10788
"Using Robert Hayden and Gwendolyn Brooks's poetry as 'emblematic' successes, this anthology selects 35 African American poets (spanning three generations) who were born between 1913 and 1962 and came of age after 1945. Besides the well-known Imamu Baraka, Lucille Clifton, Rita Dove, and Etheridge Knight, the editors feature little-known or younger poets like Elizabeth Alexander, Gerald Barrax, Jayne Cortez, and Dolores Kendrick." Libr J

✓ **Harper's** anthology of 20th century Native American poetry; edited by Duane Niatum. Harper & Row 1988 xxxii, 396p $28; pa $19 **811.008**
1. American poetry—American Indian authors—Collections
ISBN 0-06-250665-X; 0-06-250666-8 (pa) LC 86-45023
This collection "contains the work of 36 native American poets, with hearty selections from each. Among the 36 are poets near the mainstream (Scott Momaday, James Welch, Louise Erdrich); those in academe (Gerald Vizenor, Linda Hogan, Jim Barnes; those writing in the tribal oral tradition (Barney Bush, Peter Blue Cloud, Wendy Rose); and those working in a modernist voice (Gladys Cardiff, Paula Gunn Allen). This book belongs in every collection that claims to represent the multiple voices of American literature today." Booklist
Includes bibliography

✓ **I** am the darker brother; an anthology of modern poems by Negro Americans; drawings by Benny Andrews; foreword by Charlemae Rollins. Macmillan 1968 128p il hardcover o.p. paperback available $4.95 **811.008**
1. American poetry—African American authors—Collections
ISBN 0-02-041120-0 (pa)
Edited by: Arnold Adoff
"A most interesting anthology, with many contributions from such well-known poets as Brooks, Dunbar, Hayden, Hughes, and McKay, and a broad representation of selections from the work of some two dozen other modern authors." Bull Cent Child Books

✓ **In** search of color everywhere; a collection of African-American poetry; edited by E. Ethelbert Miller; illustrated by Terrance Cummings. Stewart, Tabori & Chang 1994 255p il $24.95 **811.008**
1. American poetry—African American authors—Collections
ISBN 1-55670-339-2 LC 94-4395
This "anthology gathers a generous range of work, from anonymous spirituals to Langston Hughes's classic 'Mother to Son.' It also includes poetry by Pulitzer Prize-winning Yusef Komunyakaa, Poet Laureate Rita Dove, Lucille Clifton, June Jordan, the gifted young Elizabeth Alexander and many others. The editorial choices are imaginative, and not all of the writers will be immediately or widely familiar—a boon for any reader looking to make discoveries." Publ Wkly
Includes bibliographical references

Letters to America; contemporary American poetry on race; edited by Jim Daniels. Wayne State Univ. Press 1995 230p pa $19.95 **811.008**
1. American poetry—Collections 2. United States—Race relations—Poetry
ISBN 0-8143-2542-4 LC 95-19996
This volume collects "the probings of several dozen American poets on their nation's nightmare. . . . If a large proportion of the poets selected are black, Indian, Chicano, or Asian, that is unsurprising, for they are the ones upon whom the subject thrusts itself most insistently." Booklist

Lights, camera, poetry! American movie poems the first hundred years; edited by Jason Shinder. Harcourt Brace & Co. 1996 190p pa $14 **811.008**
1. Motion pictures—Poetry 2. American poetry—Collections
ISBN 0-15-600115-2 LC 95-45538
"A Harvest original"
This anthology contains "more than 100 poems about the movies written by American poets from Robert Frost and Carl Sandburg to Patricia Smith and Michael Warr. Arranged chronologically, these poems express everything from rapture to affection, bemusement, melancholy, irony, and outrage over racial stereotyping." Booklist

Men of our time; an anthology of male poetry in contemporary America; edited by Fred Moramarco and Al Zolynas. University of Ga. Press 1992 xxxvii, 408p $45; pa $19.95

811.008

1. American poetry—Collections
ISBN 0-8203-1404-8; 0-8203-1430-7 (pa)

LC 91-31462

"Featuring 257 poems from more than 170 poets, this collection affirms both the diversity and commonality of male experience in the U.S. today. Unapologetically grounded in a distinctly male ethos or imagination, the poems also embrace and celebrate the multicultural tenor of American life through their mix of ethnic and racial perspectives." Univ Press Books for Public and Second Sch Libr

The Music of what happens; poems that tell stories; selected by Paul B. Janeczko. Orchard Bks. 1988 188p $17.95; lib bdg $18.99

811.008

1. American poetry—Collections
ISBN 0-531-05757-7; 0-531-08357-8 (lib bdg)

LC 87-30791

Among the poets included in this collection of narrative verse are: Ann Stafford, Paul Zimmer, Norman Dubie, Erika Mumford and Robert Morgan

"Janeczko has played these poems like a piano, combining themes, tones, and even sounds for a true composition that will take young readers beyond the usual dose of Henry Wadsworth Longfellow or Rudyard Kipling." Bull Cent Child Books

The New Oxford book of American verse; chosen and edited by Richard Ellmann. Oxford Univ. Press 1976 liv, 1076p $45   **811.008**

1. American poetry—Collections
ISBN 0-19-502058-8

Replaces The Oxford book of American verse, edited by F. D. Matthiessen (1950)

"This volume begins with Anne Bradstreet, who died in 1672, and ends with Imamu Amiri Baraka (LeRoy Jones), born in 1934. . . . A few ballads and folk songs, and one hymn, are . . . included. Most of the poets are represented with some amplitude so as to give a sense of their range and variety." Introduction

No more masks! an anthology of twentieth-century American women poets, newly revised and expanded; edited with an introduction by Florence Howe. HarperPerennial 1993 lxvi, 488p pa $16   **811.008**

1. American poetry—Women authors—Collections
ISBN 0-06-096517-7   LC 92-54843

First published 1973 by Anchor Press

"Howe divides the volume into three chronological sectors from 1875-1992. . . . This collection representing 104 poets in nearly 400 poems is tied together by a common search for justice through the elimination of violence. Brief biographical data is provided in a supplementary section." SLJ

The Open boat; poems from Asian America; edited and with an introduction by Garrett Hongo. Anchor Bks./Doubleday 1993 xlii, 304p il pa $12.95   **811.008**

1. American poetry—Asian American authors—Collections
ISBN 0-385-42338-1   LC 92-11089

An "anthology of poems by 31 Asian American writers. . . . Most of these poets were born in America, but grew up listening to their grandparents and parents tell stories about life in China, Vietnam, India, Japan, Indonesia, Laos, Thailand, and the Philippines. Their precise and dramatic poems are about food, family, light, music, cruelty, unexpected glory, and the layering of cultural outlooks and conflicts." Booklist

The Oxford book of American light verse; chosen and edited by William Harmon. Oxford Univ. Press 1979 l, 540p $36.50   **811.008**

1. American poetry—Collections 2. Humorous poetry
ISBN 0-19-502509-1   LC 78-12356

A companion volume to: The New Oxford book of English light verse, entered in class 821.008

"Light verse may be humorous, or ribald or witty, or satirical, or some combination of those qualities and others. Ogden Nash wrote it, of course, but so, on occasion, did such poets as Nemerov, Corso, and Whitman. . . . [Included are] such well-known poems as 'Yankee Doodle,' 'A visit from St. Nicholas,' 'Paul Revere's Ride,' 'Ten Little Indians'; lyrics by such figures as Stephen Foster, Cole Porter, and Stephen Sondheim; and a wide assortment of satires, puns, and yarns. It is light and it is fun." Libr J

Paper dance; 55 Latino poets; edited by Victor Hernández Cruz, Leroy V. Quintana, and Virgil Suarez. Persea Bks. 1995 242p $14   **811.008**

1. American poetry—Hispanic American authors—Collections 2. Hispanic Americans—Poetry
ISBN 0-89255-201-8   LC 94-15586

"This collection of poetry attests to the richness of culture in the Hispanic diaspora in the U.S., and includes well-known writers such as Julia Alvarez, Luis J. Rodriguez, and Lucha Corpi, to name a few. . . . The poets' themes are as varied as they are intriguing. Ranging in scope from contemplations on race and ethnicity to love and death, they demand that readers pay attention to vital threads in the fabric of the American literary tapestry." SLJ

Pocket poems; selected for a journey by Paul B. Janeczko. Bradbury Press 1985 138p pa $13.95

811.008

1. American poetry—Collections
ISBN 0-02-747820-3   LC 84-21537

"In a pocket-size anthology of 120 short modern poems, Janeczko . . . draws young adults to the pleasure and power of poetry rooted in the familiar. The subjects from a daily, contemporary world include food, flowers, cars, travel, pets, love, friendship, family, and the threat of war. The 80 poets include the famous, such as Angelou, Stafford, and Zimmer, as well as some new voices." Booklist

The **Poetry** of black America; anthology of the 20th century; introduction by Gwendolyn Brooks. Harper & Row 1973 xxxi, 552p $25.95; lib bdg $24.89 **811.008**
1. American poetry—African American authors—Collections
ISBN 0-06-020089-8; 0-06-020090-1 (lib bdg)
"This collection of over 600 poems by black Americans traces the development of black consciousness from the beginning realization of self-identity at the turn of the century through the Harlem renaissance to the racial and cultural upheavals of today. Among the 145 authors are those well-known from the earlier years (James Weldon Johnson, Paul Laurence Dunbar, and Langston Hughes) and from today (Gwendolyn Brooks, Sonia Sanchez, Don Lee, and Nikki Giovanni). . . . Biographical sketches are provided at the end along with an author, title, first line index." Booklist

Poetspeak: in their work, about their work; a selection by Paul B. Janeczko. Bradbury Press 1983 238p il o.p.; Collier Bks. paperback available $9.95 **811.008**
1. American poetry—Collections
ISBN 0-02-043850-8 (pa) LC 83-2715
"In an anthology that includes the work of sixty contemporary poets, Janeczko includes comments by the poets about themselves, their writing, and at times about the particular poem that precedes the comment. The contributors include such well-known writers as William Dickey, Nikki Giovanni, X. J. Kennedy, Howard Nemerov, Joyce Carol Oates, and John Updike, as well as others, and many poets, who are less well-known. The book has variety in mood, style, theme, and subject, and the poems reflect many of the interests of adolescents." Bull Cent Child Books

Postmodern American poetry; a Norton anthology; edited by Paul Hoover. Norton 1994 xxxix, 701p pa $24.95 **811.008**
1. American poetry—Collections
ISBN 0-393-31090-6 LC 93-22753
Hoover "brings together more than 100 writers from the 1950s and since—Olson, Duncan, O'Hara, Ginsberg, Corso, Dorn, Major, Ashbery, Guest—whose adventures with the language renew it for far more than a readymade membership." Publ Wkly

Reflections on a gift of watermelon pickle—and other modern verse; [compiled by] Stephen Dunning, Edward Lueders, Hugh Smith. Lothrop, Lee & Shepard Bks. 1967 c1966 139p il $18; lib bdg $15.93 **811.008**
1. American poetry—Collections
ISBN 0-688-41231-9; 0-688-51231-3 (lib bdg)
First published 1966 by Scott, Foresman in a text edition
"Although some of the [114] selections are by recognized modern writers, many are by minor or unknown poets, and few will be familiar to the reader. Nearly all are fresh in approach and contemporary in expression. . . . Striking photographs complementing or illuminating many of the poems enhance the attractiveness of the volume." Booklist

Shimmy shimmy shimmy like my sister Kate; looking at the Harlem Renaissance through poems; [edited by] Nikki Giovanni. Holt & Co. 1995 186p $16.95 **811.008**
1. American poetry—African American authors—Collections 2. Harlem Renaissance
ISBN 0-8050-3494-3 LC 95-38617
This anthology includes poems by such authors as Paul Laurence Dunbar, Langston Hughes, Countee Cullen, Gwendolyn Brooks, and Amiri Baraka. Commentary and a discussion of the development of African American arts known as the Harlem Renaissance is provided by editor Giovanni
Includes bibliographical references

Singing America; selected with an introduction by Neil Philip; illustrated by Michael McCurdy. Viking 1995 160p il $19.99 **811.008**
1. American poetry—Collections
ISBN 0-670-86150-2
This "collection of poems includes traditional songs and poetry from the eighteenth century through the twentieth century. . . . The voices of poetry represent Native Americans, African Americans, Asian Americans, Hispanic Americans, and European immigrants." Voice Youth Advocates
"McCurdy's bold, beautiful woodcuts, many depicting people at work, extend the energy and individuality of the words." Booklist

Six American poets; an anthology; edited by Joel Connaroe. Random House 1991 xxxiv, 281p il $27.50; pa $13 **811.008**
1. American poetry—Collections
ISBN 0-679-40689-1; 0-679-74525-4 (pa)
LC 91-15375
This anthology contains 247 representative poems by Walt Whitman, Emily Dickinson, Wallace Stevens, William Carlos Williams, Robert Frost and Langston Hughes

Sweet nothings; an anthology of rock and roll in American poetry; edited, with an introduction, by Jim Elledge. Indiana Univ. Press 1994 283p $29.95; pa $15.95 **811.008**
1. American poetry—Collections 2. Rock music—Poetry
ISBN 0-253-31936-6; 0-253-20864-5 (pa)
LC 93-11795
In this anthology the editor "explores the influence that rock 'n' roll has had on American poets who came of age to the sexy and defiant beat of Otis Redding, Buddy Holly, Aretha Franklin, Bob Dylan, and the Rolling Stones. Elledge's introduction provides a peppy . . . overview of the rise of rock 'n' roll and a sensitive assessment of how rock has shaped poetry both overtly and subtly. His theories are well supported by the poems themselves." Booklist
Includes bibliographical references

Unsettling America; an anthology of contemporary multicultural poetry; edited by Maria Mazziotti Gillan and Jennifer Gillan. Penguin Bks. 1994 xxv, 406p hardcover o.p. paperback available $14.95   **811.008**
1. American poetry—Collections
ISBN 0-14-023778-X (pa)   LC 94-722
This "anthology provides exposure to poets, emerging and established—Louis Simpson, Rita Dove, Luis Rodriguez—who write directly from the immigrant, ethnic and/or religious experience. . . . This collection is a must for anyone seeking an inclusive, unwincing catalogue of the American experience." Publ Wkly

The **Vintage** book of contemporary American poetry; edited and with an introduction by J.D. McClatchy. Vintage Bks. 1990 xxx, 560p pa $16   **811.008**
1. American poetry—Collections
ISBN 0-679-72858-9   LC 90-12246
"With selections from 65 poets writing over the last 40 years, and with brief notes on their lives and work, this anthology will introduce YAs to much of the best modern poetry." Booklist
Includes bibliographical references

Visions of war, dreams of peace; writings of women in the Vietnam War; edited by Lynda Van Devanter and Joan A. Furey. Warner Bks. 1991 214p pa $9.95   **811.008**
1. Vietnam War, 1961-1975—Poetry—Collections 2. American poetry—Women authors—Collections
ISBN 0-446-39251-0   LC 90-23284
This anthology collects poetry about the Vietnam War as experienced by women who served and those who remained stateside while their husbands, brothers and fathers fought

Walk on the wild side; urban American poetry since 1975; edited by Nicholas Christopher. Collier Bks. 1993 230p $27.50; pa $12
                                                   811.008
1. American poetry—Collections
ISBN 0-02-042725-5; 0-684-19623-9 (pa)
                                          LC 93-29443
The editor has "selected 120 evocative poems by such radiant poets as Diane Ackerman, Amy Clampitt, Jessica Hagedorn, Edward Hirsch, Garrett Hongo, Mark Jarman, Joseph Lawrence, Philip Levine, and Carol Muske to demonstrate the 'infinite range of subject matter' generated by an urban perspective and urban settings. . . . This is an incandescent and powerful volume." Booklist

Wherever home begins; 100 contemporary poems; selected by Paul B. Janeczko. Orchard Bks. 1995 114p $15.95; lib bdg $15.99   **811.008**
1. American poetry—Collections
ISBN 0-531-09481-2; 0-531-08781-6 (lib bdg)
                                          LC 94-48740
"A Richard Jackson book"
"This collection of thoughtful unrhymed poems reflects the myriad places people call home from the sleepy, rural towns to the noisy, city streets. . . . The volume contains poems by familiar writers including Gary Soto, George Ella Lyon, Ronald Koertge, X.J. Kennedy, and Naomi Shihab Nye." Voice Youth Advocates

811.009   American poetry—History and criticism

Breslin, James E. B., 1935-1996
From modern to contemporary; American poetry, 1945-1965. University of Chicago Press 1984 272p hardcover o.p. paperback available $9.95   **811.009**
1. Ginsberg, Allen, 1926-1997. Howl 2. American poetry—History and criticism
ISBN 0-226-07409-9 (pa)   LC 83-17869
Analyzed in Essay and general literature index
In this assessment of postwar American poetry the author examines the work of Richard Wilbur, Adrienne Rich, Charles Olson, Allen Ginsberg, Robert Lowell, Denise Levertov, James Wright and Frank O'Hara
"The writing is clear, detailed but never cumbersome. This is literary history at its best." Libr J

The **Columbia** history of American poetry; Jay Parini, editor; Brett C. Millier, associate editor. Columbia Univ. Press 1993 xxxi, 894p $59.95
                                                   811.009
1. American poetry—History and criticism
ISBN 0-231-07836-6   LC 92-29399
"These 31 essays by various experts in the field interrogate, dismantle, and ultimately reassemble the history of poetry in the United States, from the work of the slave George Moses Horton . . . to the writings of Beat, Black Arts, and Marxist-oriented Language Poets of today. The great figures of the past—Whitman, Poe, Eliot, and so on—still loom, yet each time we are made to see them in some new way. . . . An essential volume that shows how poetry intersects with our lives and vice versa." Libr J
Includes bibliographical references

Shucard, Alan, 1935-
American poetry; the Puritans through Walt Whitman. Twayne Pubs. 1988 207p (Twayne's critical history of poetry series, American literature) $33.50   **811.009**
1. American poetry—History and criticism
ISBN 0-8057-8450-0   LC 88-1524
Also available in paperback from University of Mass. Press
This is "the first in a three-volume critical history of American poetry. . . . [It] provides a comprehensive, informative, and reliable account of an emergent national poetry, allotting the most space to the major figures—Melville, Poe, Emerson, Whitman. . . . Shucard has produced a literary history that has broad appeal." Choice
Includes bibliography

Modern American poetry, 1865-1950; [by] Alan Shucard, Fred Moramarco, William Sullivan. Twayne Pubs. 1989 285p (Twayne's critical history of poetry series, American literature) $26.75   **811.009**
1. American poetry—History and criticism
ISBN 0-8057-8451-9   LC 89-30570
Also available in paperback from University of Mass. Press

Shucard, Alan, 1935—_Continued_
This volume "opens with an investigation into Emily Dickinson's verse and closes with a chapter on the fugitive and objectivist schools of poetry. On the pages between, the authors cover the expected luminaries—Frost, Moore, Eliot, Pound, Stevens, Williams—and the more important and widely recognized literary movements. Students or general readers needing a quick overview of the period and its important works will find this volume indispensable." Booklist
Includes bibliography

Voices & visions; the poet in America; edited by Helen Vendler. Random House 1987 xxx, 528p il $29.95 **811.009**
1. American poetry—History and criticism
ISBN 0-394-53520-0 LC 86-40154
Analyzed in Essay and general literature index
In this companion volume to the PBS television series, "each of the 13 poets (Whitman, Dickinson, Frost, Stevens, Williams, Pound, Moore, Eliot, Crane, Hughes, Bishop, Lowell, and Plath) is covered in an essay written by a leading critic (Richard Poirier on Frost, Hugh Kenner on Pound, Vendler herself on Stevens, etc.). Like the series, the text scants biography in favor of close reading, focusing on poems rather than poets. As such, however, it provides solid critical overviews of these 13 important poets." Booklist

812 American drama

Albee, Edward, 1928-
Three tall women; a play in two acts. Dutton 1995 c1994 110p $17.95; pa $9.95 **812**
ISBN 0-525-93960-1; 0-452-27400-1 (pa)
LC 94-23234
Also available in paperback from Dramatists Play Service
Awarded the Pulitzer prize, 1994
Characters: 1 man, 3 women. 2 acts. First produced at Vienna's English Theatre, Vienna, Austria, June 14, 1991
This drama "begins as a naturalistic conversation among three women (identified as A, B, and C) from successive generations who meet in a hospital room. Each is undergoing a change from one life phase to another, and each faces her travails and disappointments with lots of Albee's trademark bitter wit. In the second act, however, the three women become representatives of the same person at different ages (26, 52, late 80s), and their bickering talk becomes a touching internal colloquy about life, love, and the inevitability of loss." Booklist

Who's afraid of Virginia Woolf? a play. Atheneum Pubs. 1962 242p hardcover o.p. paperback available $9 **812**
ISBN 0-689-70565-4 (pa)
Characters: 2 men, 2 women. 3 acts, 1 setting. First produced at the Billy Rose Theatre, New York City, October 13, 1962
Albee's drama "presents an all-night drinking bout of a middle-aged professor and his wife, joined by a vacuous instructor and his silly wife, in which through horrid verbal torturing of one another they eventually achieve catharsis by exorcising their fixation about a nonexistent son, which the older couple had created to sustain themselves." Oxford Companion to Am Lit. 6th edition

Arthur Miller; edited and with an introduction by Harold Bloom. Chelsea House 1987 164p (Modern critical views) $29.95 **812**
1. Miller, Arthur, 1915-
ISBN 0-87754-711-4 LC 86-29962
A collection of critical essays focusing on Death of a salesman, The crucible and A view from the bridge
Includes bibliography

Carpenter, Frederic Ives, 1903-1991
Eugene O'Neill; by Frederic I. Carpenter. rev ed. Twayne Pubs. 1979 192p (Twayne's United States authors series) $21.95 **812**
1. O'Neill, Eugene, 1888-1953
ISBN 0-8057-7267-7 LC 78-11672
First published 1964
Following a discussion of the relationship between O'Neill's life and his plays, the author describes and criticizes the major plays individually, and concludes with an overview of O'Neill's critical standing
Includes bibliography

DeRose, David J.
Sam Shepard. Twayne Pubs. 1992 171p il (Twayne's United States authors series) $22.95 **812**
1. Shepard, Sam, 1943-
ISBN 0-8057-3964-5 LC 92-13511
The author "analyzes Shepard's plays in light of his theatrical as well as thematic intentions. . . . Supported by evidence gleaned from stage directions, visual imagery, and physical staging, DeRose's readings of Shepard's plays are balanced and perceptive. A good general introduction to Shepard and his work." Libr J
Includes bibliographical references

Edward Albee; edited and with an introduction by Harold Bloom. Chelsea House 1987 181p (Modern critical views) $24.95 **812**
1. Albee, Edward, 1928-
ISBN 0-87754-707-6 LC 86-29943
Ronald Hayman, Gerald Weales, and Anthony Hopkins are among the authors who assess Albee's contributions to the theater
Includes bibliography

Falk, Signi Lenea
Tennessee Williams; by Signi Falk. 2nd ed. Twayne Pubs. 1978 194p (Twayne's United States authors series) lib bdg $21.95 **812**
1. Williams, Tennessee, 1911-1983
ISBN 0-8057-7202-2 LC 77-16575
First published 1962
This study examines Williams' theatrical work with particular emphasis on his characters and his position among other Southern writers
Includes bibliography

Floyd, Virginia

The plays of Eugene O'Neill; a new assessment. Ungar 1985 xxvi, 605p il (Literature and life series) hardcover o.p. paperback available $15.95   **812**

1. O'Neill, Eugene, 1888-1953
ISBN 0-8044-6153-8 (pa)   LC 84-8874

The dramatist's entire canon is treated chronologically, with Floyd analyzing O'Neill's major themes and artistic goals, and drawing parallels between his tormented life and his plays

Includes bibliography

Foote, Horton

The young man from Atlanta. Dutton 1995 110p il $19.95; pa $9.95   **812**

ISBN 0-525-94114-2; 0-452-27633-0 (pa)

Also available in paperback from Dramatists Play Service

Awarded the Pulitzer Prize, 1995

Characters: 5 men, 4 women. 6 scenes. First produced by Signature Theatre Company, New York City, January 27, 1995

"The implication is strong that [the title character] was the lover of Will and Lily Dale Kidder's son Bill. He's a needy young man who extracted from Bill thousands of the dollars Will sent him while he floundered about after World War II service. Even after Bill's suicide, which has devastated Will, the young man has importuned Bill's parents, successfully persuading Lily Dale to give him, unbeknownst to Will, half her savings. Now he's back on the Kidders' doorstep in Houston in 1950." Booklist

Fuller, Charles

A soldier's play; a play. Hill & Wang 1982 c1981 100p   **812**

1. African American soldiers—Drama
LC 82-15395

Available from Samuel French

Awarded the Pulitzer Prize, 1982

"A Mermaid dramabook"

Characters: 12 men. 2 acts. First produced at Theater Four, New York City, November 20, 1981

Racial tensions erupt as murder investigation is being conducted in Southern army camp during World War II

Gibson, William, 1914-

The miracle worker; a play for television. Knopf 1957 131p $20   **812**

1. Keller, Helen, 1880-1968—Drama 2. Sullivan, Anne, 1866-1936—Drama
ISBN 0-394-40630-3

Also available in paperback from Bantam Bks.

"A dramatization of the miracle wrought by Annie Sullivan, the young teacher of Helen Keller, encompasses the first year of their long association and reaches its climax when after months of patient effort Helen speaks her first word." Booklist

"The present text is meant for reading, and differs from the telecast version in that I have restored some passages that read better than they play and others omitted in performance for simple lack of time." Author's note

Goodrich, Frances, 1891-1984

The diary of Anne Frank; dramatized by Frances Goodrich and Albert Hackett; based upon the book, Anne Frank: diary of a young girl; with a foreword by Brooks Atkinson. Random House 1956 174p il $16   **812**

1. Netherlands—History—1940-1945, German occupation—Drama 2. World War, 1939-1945—Jews—Drama 3. Jews—Netherlands—Drama
ISBN 0-394-40564-1

Awarded the Pulitzer Prize and the New York Drama Critics Circle Award for 1956

Characters: 5 men, 5 women. 2 acts 1 setting. First produced at the Cort Theatre, New York City, October 5, 1955

Dramatization of Anne Frank: diary of a young girl, entered in class 92. Portrays ultimately unsuccessful attempt of Jewish family to remain hidden during the German occupation of Holland

Gurney, A. R. (Albert Ramsdell), 1930-

Love letters and two other plays: The golden age, and What I did last summer; with an introduction by the playwright. Penguin Bks. 1990 209p pa $10.95   **812**

ISBN 0-452-26501-0   LC 90-34177

"A Plume book"

Love letters dramatizes the 30-year epistolary "exchange between an upper-class man and an upper-upper-class woman. . . . *The Golden Age* is an updated, romantic-comic variation upon Henry James' *Aspern Papers*

Hansberry, Lorraine, 1930-1965

A raisin in the sun. Modern Lib. 1995 xxvi, 135p $12.50   **812**

1. African Americans—Drama
ISBN 0-679-60172-4   LC 95-16074

Also available in paperback from Plume Bks.

Awarded the New York Drama Critics Circle Award for the 1958-1959 season

First published 1959

Characters: 8 men, 3 women. 6 scenes in 3 acts. First produced at the Ethel Barrymore Theatre, New York City, March 11, 1959

"Hansberry's drama focuses on the Youngers, a 1950s African-American working-class family in Chicago striving to realize their individual dreams of prosperity and education, and their collective dream of a better life. It was the first play by an African-American woman to be produced on Broaday." Reader's Ency. 4th edition

Henley, Beth

Crimes of the heart; a play. Viking 1982 125p hardcover o.p. paperback available $7.95   **812**

ISBN 0-14-048212-1 (pa)   LC 81-24026

Awarded the Pulitzer Prize and the Drama Critics Circle Award, 1981

Characters: 2 men, 4 women. 3 acts. 1 interior. First produced at Actors Theatre of Louisville in February 1979

Set in Hazelhurst, Mississippi five years after Hurri-

Henley, Beth—*Continued*
cane Camille, this comedy-drama explores the lives of three young sisters as they gather to await news of the family patriarch, their grandfather, who is near death in the local hospital

Inge, William, 1913-1973
4 plays. Grove Press 1979 c1958 304p pa $12
812
ISBN 0-8021-3209-X   LC 78-73032
The author was awarded the Pulitzer Prize, 1953, for Picnic
"A Black cat book"
First published 1958 by Random House
Contents: Come back, Little Sheba; Picnic; Bus stop; The dark at the top of the stairs

Kushner, Tony
Angels in America; a gay fantasia on national themes. Theatre Communications Group 1993-1994 2v pa ea $10.95 **812**
1. Cohn, Roy, 1927-1986—Drama
LC 92-44011
Also available in a one-volume edition for $35, pa $21.95 (ISBN 1-55936-107-7; 1-55936-098-4)
Contents: Part one: Millennium approaches (ISBN 1-55936-061-5); Part two: Perestroika (ISBN 1-55936-073-9)
Millennium approaches first presented at the Eureka Theatre Company, San Francisco, May 1991. Perestroika first presented at the Mark Taper Forum, Los Angeles, November 1992
A look at the political, sexual and religious aspects of contemporary American life set against the AIDS epidemic and the life of Roy Cohn

Lawrence, Jerome, 1915-
The selected plays of Jerome Lawrence and Robert E. Lee; edited by Alan Woods; foreword by Norman Cousins. Ohio State Univ. Press 1995 579p il $39.50 **812**
ISBN 0-8142-0646-8   LC 94-15894
Contents: Inherit the wind; Auntie Mame; The gang's all here; Only in America; A call on Kuprin; Diamond orchid (original version of Sparks fly upward); The night Thoreau spent in jail; First Monday in October
"Of particular value are the lengthy general introduction by editor Woods and more specific introductions to each play. Woods intelligently discusses the Lawrence/Lee collaboration and their plays, contributions, and 'place' in the theatrical world of the 1950s, 1960s, and 1970s. Also of special note are the prefaces by Lawrence and Lee themselves as well as the cast lists and production information that accompany each play." Libr J

Includes bibliographical references

Lerner, Alan Jay, 1918-1986
Camelot; a new musical; book and lyrics by Alan Jay Lerner; music by Frederick Loewe. Random House 1961 115p il $13.95 **812**
1. Arthur, King—Drama
ISBN 0-394-40521-8
Characters: 14 men, 5 women, extras. 19 scenes in 2 acts. First produced at the Majestic Theatre, New York

City, December 3, 1960
"Based on The once and future king, by T. H. White." Title page
A musical recreation of the Arthurian legend from the marriage of Arthur and Guenevere to the wars following Lancelot and Guenevere's defections

Lindsay, Howard, 1889-1968
The sound of music; a new musical play; music by Richard Rodgers; lyrics by Oscar Hammerstein II; book by Howard Lindsay and Russel Crouse. Random House 1960 141p il $12.95 **812**
1. Trapp family—Drama
ISBN 0-394-40724-5
"(Suggested by the Trapp family singers by Maria Augusta Trapp)." Title Page
Characters: 8 men, 13 women, 1 boy, 2 girls. 2 acts, 20 scenes. First produced at the Lunt-Fontanne Theatre, New York City, on November 16, 1959
This musical "tells the story of Maria Rainer, a young postulant in Austria who leaves the convent to make a final decision regarding her future. As governess to Captain von Trapp's motherless children she begins a new life that leads to her marriage with the captain. The family's escape from Nazi soldiers ends a play filled with exuberant lyrics and warm sentiment." Booklist

Mamet, David
Glengarry Glen Ross; a play. Grove Press 1984 108p pa $10 **812**
ISBN 0-8021-3091-7   LC 83-49380
Awarded the Pulitzer Prize, 1984
Characters: 7 men. 2 acts, 4 scenes. First produced at The Cottlesoe Theatre, London, England, September 21, 1983
Comedy about sharp dealings of small-time, cutthroat real estate salesmen

McCullers, Carson, 1917-1967
The member of the wedding; a play. New Directions 1951 118p pa $7.95 **812**
ISBN 0-8112-0093-0
Awarded the New York Drama Critics Circle Award for 1950
Characters: 6 men, 7 women. 3 acts with 3 scenes in the last act. First produced at the Empire Theatre, New York City, January 3, 1950
Based on her novel of the same title, McCullers "with great sensitivity presents the feelings of a 12-year-old girl on the occasion of her brother's impending wedding." Oxford Companion to Am Lit. 6th edition

McNally, Terrence, 1939-
15 short plays. Smith & Kraus 1994 373p (Contemporary playwrights series) pa $20.25 **812**
ISBN 1-880399-34-2   LC 94-10070
"By providing a sampling of McNally's plays from the late 1960s to the early 1990s, the entire span of his career, this volume allows a great deal of insight into the range and depth of his development as he courses his way through some of the social, political, and sexual forces that have shaped the American temperament. . . . This is a splendid collection and these plays cut to the emotional bone." Voice Youth Advocates

Medoff, Mark Howard

Children of a lesser god; a play in two acts; by Mark Medoff. White, J.T. 1981 xxii, 91p   **812**

1. Deaf—Drama

                LC 80-24379

Available in paperback from Dramatists Play Service

Characters: 3 men, 4 women. 2 acts. First produced at the Longacre Theatre, New York City, March 30, 1980

"The sensitive drama of the love and growth of James Leeds, a speech teacher at a state school for the deaf, and Sarah Norman, one of his students, may lack some impact in reading since the effect of Sarah's isolation and skilled signing is lost, but Medoff's story remains a powerful, valuable one." Booklist

Miller, Arthur, 1915-

The crucible; a play in four acts. Viking 1953 145p hardcover o.p. paperback available $7.95

                               812

1. Witchcraft—Drama 2. Salem (Mass.)—Drama

ISBN 0-14-018964-5 (pa)

Characters: 11 men, 10 women. First produced at the Martin Beck Theatre in New York City, January 22, 1953

A play based on the Salem witchcraft trials of 1692. It deals particularly with the hounding to death of the nonconformist John Proctor

Death of a salesman; certain private conversations in two acts and a requiem. Viking 1949 139p o.p.; Penguin Bks. paperback available $7.95   **812**

ISBN 0-14-048134-6 (pa)

Also available in hardcover from Amereon

Winner of the New York Drama Critics Circle Award and the Pulitzer Prize, 1949

Characters: 8 men, 5 women. First produced at the Morosco Theatre, New York City, February 10, 1949

"The tragedy of a typical American—a salesman who at the age of sixty-three is faced with what he cannot face: defeat and disillusionment. It is a bitter and moving experience of groping for values and for material success." Wis Libr Bull

The portable Arthur Miller; original introduction by Harold Clurman. rev ed, edited, with an introduction, by Christopher Bigsby. Penguin Bks. 1995 xli, 575p pa $14.95   **812**

ISBN 0-14-024709-2   LC 95-9485

Replaces the edition published 1971 under the editorship of Harold Clurman

This volume contains the complete texts of Death of a salesman, The crucible, After the fall, The American clock, The last Yankee, and Broken glass. An excerpt from a radio play thought lost for years and two very brief selections from the memoir Timebends are also included

Includes bibliography

The price; a play. Viking 1968 116p hardcover o.p. paperback available $7.95   **812**

ISBN 0-14-048194-X (pa)

Characters: 3 men, 1 woman. 2 acts, 1 setting. First produced at the Morosco Theatre, New York City, Feb-

ruary 7, 1968

A "play about two estranged brothers who meet after [many] years to dispose of their parents' furniture. One sacrificed a science career and became a policeman to support their father during the depression while the other studied to become a surgeon. Questions of self-sacrifice, self-interest, responsibility, and illusions are explored but left for the reader to resolve." Wis Libr Bull

Moss, Leonard, 1931-

Arthur Miller. rev ed. Twayne Pubs. 1980 182p il (Twayne's United States authors series) lib bdg $23.50   **812**

1. Miller, Arthur, 1915-

ISBN 0-8057-7311-8   LC 79-25071

First published 1967

The author provides critical readings of Miller's plays up to The creation of the world and other business (1973). A 1970 interview with Miller is included

Includes bibliography

O'Neill, Eugene, 1888-1953

Complete plays. Library of Am. 1988 3v ea $35

                                 812

ISBN 0-940450-48-8   LC 88-50685

Selected and with notes by Travis Bogard

Contents: [v1] 1913-1920; [v2] 1920-1931; [v3] 1932-1943

The iceman cometh; a play. Vintage Bks. 1946 260p pa $9   **812**

ISBN 0-394-70018-X

Characters: 16 men, 3 women. First produced at the Martin Beck Theatre, New York City, October 9, 1946

Thoughts and actions of a group of derelicts, habitués of a cheap New York saloon. The time is 1912

Long day's journey into night. Yale Univ. Press 1956 c1955 176p $18.50; pa $9   **812**

ISBN 0-300-00807-4; 0-300-00176-2 (pa)

Also available in hardcover from Amereon

Awarded the Pulitzer Prize, 1957

Characters: 3 men, 2 women. 4 acts, 5 scenes. First produced in Stockholm, Sweden, February, 1956

"Among the papers Eugene O'Neill left when he died in 1953 was the manuscript of an autobiography. Not an autobiography in the usual sense, however. For 'Long Day's Journey Into Night' is in the form of a play—a true O'Neill tragedy, set in 1912 in the summer home of a theatrical family that is isolated from the community by a kind of ingrown misery and a sense of doom." N Y Times Book Rev

Nine plays; by Eugene O'Neill, selected by the author. Modern Lib. 1993 829p $20   **812**

ISBN 0-679-60028-0   LC 92-27149

First published 1932 by Liveright; first Modern Library edition 1941

Contents: The Emperor Jones; The hairy ape; All God's chillun got wings; Desire under the elms; Marco Millions; The Great god Brown; Lazarus laughed; Strange interlude; Mourning becomes Electra

Shange, Ntozake

For colored girls who have considered suicide/when the rainbow is enuf; a choreopoem. Macmillan 1977 64p hardcover o.p. paperback available $5.95   **812**
1. African American women—Drama
ISBN 0-02-024891-1 (pa)   LC 77-3034
Choreopoem performed by seven women exploring the joys and sorrows of being black and being a woman

Shepard, Sam, 1943-

A lie of the mind; a play in three acts; [and] The war in heaven: angel's monologue, by Joseph Chaikin and Sam Shepard. New Am. Lib. 1987 155p hardcover o.p. paperback available $6.95   **812**
ISBN 0-452-25869-3 (pa)   LC 86-21884
Cast of characters for A lie of the mind: 4 men, 4 women. 3 acts, 14 scenes. First produced at the Promenade Theater, New York City, December 5, 1985
In A lie of the mind violence underlies the destinies of two families, linked by marriage, but kept apart by jealousy and distrust. The war in heaven is a poetic monologue by an angel

Simon, Neil

Biloxi blues. Random House 1986 101p $11.95
812
ISBN 0-394-55139-7   LC 85-24173
Characters: 6 men, 2 women. 2 acts, 17 scenes. First produced at the Ahmanson Theatre, Los Angeles, December 8, 1984
Second play in Simon's semi-autobiographical trilogy. Comedy/drama set in basic training camp in Biloxi, Mississippi in the year 1943. Young recruit encounters army life, discipline and shades of anti-semitism

Brighton Beach memoirs. Random House 1984 130p $14.95   **812**
ISBN 0-394-53739-4   LC 83-21216
Also available in paperback from New Am. Lib.
Awarded the New York Drama Critics Circle Award, 1983
Characters: 3 men, 4 women. 2 acts, 1 setting. First produced at the Ahmanson Theatre, Los Angeles, March 27, 1983
First play in author's semi-autobiographical trilogy about growing up in Depression era Brooklyn

Broadway bound. Random House 1987 118p $13.95   **812**
ISBN 0-394-56395-6   LC 87-42653
Also available in paperback from New Am. Lib.
Characters: 4 men, 2 women. 2 acts, 1 interior. First produced at the Broadhurst Theatre, New York City, December 4, 1986
Third play in the author's semi-autobiographical trilogy deals with brothers pursuing radio-comedy career amidst family upheavals

The collected plays of Neil Simon; with an introduction by Neil Simon. v2-3. Random House 1979-1991 2v v2 $29.95, v3 $34.50   **812**
ISBN 0-394-50770-3 (v2); 0-679-40889-4 (v3)
Volume 2 also available in paperback from New Am. Lib.
Volume 1 entered below with title The comedy of Neil Simon
Contents v2: Little me; The gingerbread lady; The prisoner of Second Avenue; The Sunshine Boys; The good doctor; God's favorite; California suite; Chaper two; v3: Sweet Charity; They're playing our song; I ought to be in pictures; Fools; The odd couple (female version); Brighton Beach memoirs; Biloxi blues; Broadway bound

The comedy of Neil Simon; with an introduction by Neil Simon. Random House 1971 657p $25   **812**
ISBN 0-394-47364-7
Contents: Come blow your horn; Barefoot in the park; The odd couple; The star-spangled girl; Promises, promises; Plaza suite: Visitor from Mamaroneck; Plaza suite: Visitor from Hollywood; Plaza suite: Visitor from Forest Hills; Last of the red hot lovers

Lost in Yonkers. Random House 1991 120p $16.50   **812**
ISBN 0-679-40890-8   LC 91-53112
Also available in paperback from New Am. Lib.
Awarded the Pulitzer Prize, 1991
Characters: 4 men, 3 women. 2 acts. First presented at the Stevens Center for the Performing Arts, Winston-Salem, December 31, 1990
This play, "set in 1940s New York, is a sad-funny portrait of a dysfunctional family, headed by a woman who provided for her children but never showed them love." Booklist

Vonnegut, Kurt, 1922-

Happy Birthday, Wanda June; a play; by Kurt Vonnegut, Jr. Delacorte Press 1971 199p il hardcover o.p. paperback available $11.95   **812**
1. Homer—Parodies, travesties, etc.
ISBN 0-385-28386-5 (pa)
"A Seymour Lawrence book"
Characters: 5 men, 3 women, 1 boy, 1 girl. 3 acts, 12 scenes. First produced at the Theatre de Lys, New York City, October 7, 1970
A satirical retelling of the story of Ulysses' homecoming. After eight years absence, Harold Ryan, a legendary hunter, returns home to his wife Penelope who is engaged to marry someone else

Wasserman, Dale, 1917-

Man of La Mancha; a musical play; lyrics by Joe Darion; music by Mitch Leigh. Random House 1966 82p il hardcover o.p. paperback available $9.95   **812**
ISBN 0-394-40619-2 (pa)
Winner of the New York Drama Critics Circle award "Best Musical 1966"

Wasserman, Dale, 1917——_Continued_

Characters: 14 men, 5 women, extras. First produced at the ANTA Washington Square Theatre, New York City, November 22, 1965

This musical play-adaptation of Don Quixote is built around Cervantes' defense, when imprisoned and held for inquisition. He arranges a mock trial performance to present his case

Wasserstein, Wendy

The Heidi chronicles and other plays. Harcourt Brace Jovanovich 1990 249p $17.95   **812**

ISBN 0-15-139985-9   LC 89-28114

Also available in paperback from Vintage Bks.

Contents: Uncommon women and others; Isn't it romantic; The Heidi chronicles

Wilder, Thornton, 1897-1975

Our town; a play in three acts. Coward-McCann 1938 128p o.p.; HarperCollins Pubs. paperback available $6   **812**

ISBN 0-06-080779-2 (pa)

Awarded the Pulitzer Prize, 1938

Characters: Large mixed cast. First produced at McCarter's Theatre, Princeton, N.J., January 22, 1938

"Presented without scenery of any kind, utilizing a narrator and loose episodic form, adventurous and imaginative in style, this unique play . . . is one of the most distinguished in the modern repertoire. It deals with the simplest and most touching aspects of life in a small town. A stage manager casually introduces the characters, and his narration bridges the gap between the audience and the play's action. At times he also enters the scene and becomes part of the play. The play's action centers around the life of the Webb family and the Gibbs family, their neighbors. George Gibbs and Emily Webb fall in love and marry, and she dies while the life of the town continues to move about them." Benet's Reader's Ency of Am Lit

Three plays: Our town, The skin of our teeth, The matchmaker; with a preface. Harper & Row 1957 401p hardcover o.p. paperback available $14   **812**

ISBN 0-06-091293-6 (pa)

Wilder was awarded the Pulitzer Prize, 1938 for Our town, and 1943 for The skin of our teeth

A collection of three titles first copyrighted 1938, 1942, and 1955 respectively. An earlier version of: The matchmaker, was first copyrighted 1939 with title: The merchant of Yonkers

Our town is entered separately. The skin of our teeth is an allegorical fantasy about man's struggle to survive. The matchmaker is a romantic farce set in the 1880's

Williams, Tennessee, 1911-1983

Cat on a hot tin roof. New Directions 1975 173p pa $9.95   **812**

ISBN 0-8112-0567-3

Also available in paperback from New Am. Lib.

Awarded the 1955 Pulitzer Prize and the New York Drama Critics Circle Award

First published 1955; the 1975 edition is based on the American Shakespeare Theatre (Stratford, Connecticut) revival which contains a completely rewritten third act

Characters: 6 men, 5 women, 2 boys, 2 girls. 3 acts, interior. First produced by the Playwright's Company at the Morosco Theatre, New York City, March 24, 1955

A dying Mississippi Delta plantation owner's sons and their wives struggle for control of his estate

"The play became notorious for its treatment of homosexuality, which is never directly presented, but is depicted in a way that took contemporary audiences by surprise." Oxford Companion to 20th Cent Lit in Engl

The glass menagerie; a play. New Directions 1949 c1945 124p pa $5.95   **812**

ISBN 0-8112-0220-8

Awarded the New York Drama Critics Circle Award, 1945

"The New classics"

A reprint of the edition first published 1945 by Random House, with the addition of a brief essay entitled: "The catastrophe of success"

Characters: 2 men, 2 women. 2 parts. One set of scenery. First produced at the Civic Theatre, Chicago, December 26, 1944

"A poignant and painful family drama set in St. Louis, in which a frigid and frustrated mother's dreams of her glamorous past as a Southern belle conflict with the grimness of her reduced circumstances, as she persuades her rebellious son Tom to provide a 'gentleman caller' for her crippled daughter, Laura." Oxford Companion to Engl Lit. 5th edition

A streetcar named Desire. New Directions 1980 c1947 179p $8.95   **812**

ISBN 0-8112-0765-X

Awarded the Pulitzer Prize, 1948

First published 1947

Characters: 6 women, 7 men. 11 scenes. First produced at the Barrymore Theatre, New York City, December 3, 1947

"A study of sexual frustration, violence, and aberration, set in New Orleans, in which Blanche Dubois' fantasies of refinement and grandeur are brutally destroyed by her brother-in-law, Stanley Kowalski, whose animal nature fascinates and repels her." Oxford Companion to Engl Lit. 5th edition

Wilson, August

Fences; a play; introduction by Lloyd Richards. New Am. Lib. 1986 101p pa $8.95   **812**

1. African Americans—Drama

ISBN 0-452-26401-4   LC 86-5264

Awarded the Pulitzer Prize, 1987

"A Plume book"

Characters: 5 men, 1 woman, 1 girl. 2 acts, 9 scenes. First produced at the Yale Repertory Theater, New Haven, Connecticut, April 30, 1985

Family drama about black experience in America. 1960's spirit of liberation alienates hard working father from wife and son

Joe Turner's come and gone; a play in two acts. New Am. Lib. 1988 94p pa $8.95   **812**

1. African Americans—Drama

ISBN 0-452-26009-4   LC 88-1660

"A Plume book"

Wilson, August—*Continued*

Characters: 6 men, 5 women. 2 acts 10 scenes. 1 setting. First produced at the Yale Repertory Theatre, New Haven, Connecticut, April 29, 1986

This realistic drama looks at life in a Pittsburgh boarding house for blacks in 1911

The piano lesson. New Am. Lib. 1990 108p hardcover o.p. paperback available $8.95   **812**

1. African Americans—Drama

ISBN 0-452-26534-7 (pa)   LC 90-38734

Awarded the Pulitzer Prize and the New York Drama Critics Circle Award, 1990

Characters: 5 men, 3 women. 2 acts, 7 scenes. First produced at the Yale Repertory Theatre, New Haven, November 26, 1987

Drama set in 1936 Pittsburgh chronicles black experience in America. Family conflict arises over heirloom piano

Two trains running. Dutton 1992 110p o.p.; New Am. Lib. paperback available $8.95   **812**

1. African Americans—Drama

ISBN 0-452-26929-6 (pa)   LC 92-21760

Characters: 6 men, 1 woman. 2 acts, 8 scenes. First produced at the Yale Repertory Theatre, New Haven, March 27, 1990

Drama set in Pittsburgh luncheonette about the black experience in 1960s America

Zindel, Paul

The effect of gamma rays on man-in-the moon marigolds; a drama in two acts; drawings by Dong Kingman. Harper & Row 1971 108p il $18   **812**

ISBN 0-06-026829-8

Also available in paperback from Bantam Bks.

Awarded the Pulitzer Prize, 1971, and the 1969-70 New York Drama Critics Circle Award

Characters: 5 women. First produced at the Mercer-O'Casey Theatre, New York City, April 7, 1970

In this play about a widow and her two teenage daughters, "the mother is embittered by a life of disappointments and shattered dreams. . . . One daughter is beyond hope, jealous and vindictive . . . and subject to convulsive seizures. The other, having been inspired by a science teacher, wins a prize for her experiment on marigolds and discovers there are galaxies out beyond her harsh world." Choice

812.008   American drama— Collections

9 plays by black women; edited and with an introduction by Margaret B. Wilkerson. New Am. Lib. 1986 xxv, 508p pa $6.99   **812.008**

1. American drama—African American authors—Collections 2. American drama—Women authors—Collections

ISBN 0-451-62820-9   LC 86-60744

"A Mentor book"

Contents: A black woman speaks, by B. Richards; Toussaint, by L. Hansberry; Wedding band, by A. Childress; The tapestry, by A. De Veaux; Unfinished women cry in no man's land while a bird dies in a gilded cage, by A. Rahman; Spell #7, by N. Shange; The brothers, by K. Collins; Paper dolls, by E. Jackson; Brown silk and magenta sunsets, by P. J. Gibson

Includes bibliography

Best American plays: 3rd series—1945-1951; edited with an introduction by John Gassner. Crown 1952 xxviii, 707p $35   **812.008**

1. American drama—Collections

ISBN 0-517-50950-4

First series has title: Twenty best plays of the modern American Theatre. Second series has title: Best plays of the modern American theatre, both entered below

This collection "includes Arthur Miller's 'Death of a Salesman,' Tennessee Williams' 'A Streetcar Named Desire,' William Inge's 'Come Back, Little Sheba' and 14 others." Publ Wkly

Best American plays: 4th series—1951-1957; edited with an introduction by John Gassner. Crown 1958 xxii, 648p $35   **812.008**

1. American drama—Collections

ISBN 0-517-50436-7

"Contains the complete reading texts of 17 plays which were . . . successful stage productions. An introductory essay by the editor assesses trends and achievements in the American theater during the period covered. Each play is prefaced by a brief introduction." Booklist

Includes a supplementary list of plays and a bibliography

Best American plays: 5th series—1957-1963; edited with an introduction and prefaces to the plays by John Gassner. Crown 1963 xxiv, 678p o.p.   **812.008**

1. American drama—Collections

The editor's brief evaluation "of American drama introduces complete texts of 17 plays. . . . Selected lists of Broadway and off-Broadway plays during the period are included." Booklist

Best American plays: 6th series—1963-1967; edited by John Gassner and Clive Barnes. Crown 1971 594p $35   **812.008**

1. American drama—Collections

ISBN 0-517-50951-2

An anthology of seventeen plays, produced on and off Broadway. Among the plays included are Tiny Alice, Hogan's goat, The Fantasticks, and Fiddler on the roof

Best American plays: 7th series—1967-1973; edited with an introduction by Clive Barnes. Crown 1975 585p $35   **812.008**

1. American drama—Collections

ISBN 0-517-51387-0

Includes nineteen American plays which have been produced on Broadway and off-Broadway. Among them are Jules Feiffer's 'Little Murders,' Lonne Elder's 'Ceremonies in Dark Old Men,' and Arthur Miller's 'The Price'

Best American plays: 8th series—1974-1982; edited by Clive Barnes; introduction and biographies of Neil Simon, Tennessee Williams, Lanford Wilson, and David Rabe by Clive Barnes; other biographies by Lori Weinless. Crown 1983 548p o.p.   **812.008**
1. American drama—Collections

This anthology contains seventeen plays; playwrights represented include Ntozake Shange, Jason Miller, Sam Shepard, David Mamet, Michael Weller and Arthur Kopit

Best American plays: 9th series—1983-1992; edited by Clive Barnes; introduction by Clive Barnes; biographical introductions by Lori Weinless. Crown 1993 526p $40   **812.008**
1. American drama—Collections
ISBN 0-517-57452-7

This collection includes Tina Howe's Painting Churches, Lanford Wilson's Burn this, Alfred Uhry's Driving Miss Daisy, and 13 other plays

Best American screenplays; complete screenplays; edited by Sam Thomas; foreword by Frank Capra. Crown 1986-1990 2v   **812.008**
1. Motion picture plays

First series o.p.; Second series $35 (ISBN 0-517-57463-2)

Collects final versions of screenplays produced over a 50-year period, 1930-1980. Brief biographies of the screenwriter precede each screenplay

Best plays of the early American theatre; from the beginning to 1916; edited with introductions by John Gassner in association with Mollie Gassner. Crown 1967 xlviii, 716p o.p. **812.008**
1. American drama—Collections

Among the sixteen plays included in this collection are Salvation Nell, The octoroon, The Count of Monte Cristo, Uncle Tom's cabin, The scarecrow, The great divide, and The witching hour

Includes bibliography

Best plays of the modern American theatre: 2nd series; edited with an introduction by John Gassner. Crown 1947 xxx, 776p o.p.   **812.008**
1. American drama—Collections

The first of this series, entered below, has title: Twenty best plays of the modern American theatre. Succeeding volumes of the series entered above, with title: Best American plays

The editor "surveys the plays that represent the theater of the turbulent period of 1939-1945. . . . He analyzes the effects of the war, and presents . . . [complete texts of 17] plays as his choices for the best." Cleveland Public Libr

Includes bibliography

The **Big** book of large-cast plays; 27 one-act plays for young actors; edited by Sylvia E. Kamerman. Plays 1994 351p $18.95   **812.008**
1. One act plays
ISBN 0-8238-0302-3   LC 94-32725

"The selections are arranged into four sections: 'Junior and Senior High,' 'Middle and Lower Grades,' 'Curtain Raisers,' and 'A Special Christmas Program.' Some of the plays are based on folk or fairy tales. Some allude to American history. Still others have particular seasonal appeal within the school year calendar, and many are humorous. Each play includes production notes." Booklist

Black theatre USA; plays by African Americans, 1847 to today; edited by James V. Hatch, Ted Shine. rev and expanded ed. Free Press 1996 916p $60   **812.008**
1. American drama—African American authors—Collections
ISBN 0-684-82306-3   LC 95-40329

Also available two volume paperback edition ea $20 v1 The early period, 1847-1938 (0-684-82308-X); v2 The recent period, 1935-today (0-684-82307-1)

First published 1974

Among the plays are: Star of Ethiopia, by W. E. B. Du Bois; A soldier's play, by C. Fuller; Sally's rape, by R. McCauley; Contribution, by T. Shine; Fires in the mirror, by A. D. Smith

Includes bibliography

Center stage; one-act plays for teenage readers and actors; edited by Donald R. Gallo. Harper & Row 1990 361p hardcover o.p. paperback available $5.95   **812.008**
1. One act plays
ISBN 0-06-447078-4 (pa)   LC 90-4050

This collection of ten "plays are appropriate for individual reading, but equally well suited for performance. Some are serious, some comic. Robin Brancato creates a gang verbal warfare in 'War of the Words,' wherein one gang speaks in monosyllables and cliches, the other in iambic pentameter; Walter Dean Myers, in a good versus possible evil drama, creates a metaphor for freedom in 'Cages.' Other equally provocative plays have been written by Susan Beth Pfeffer, Dallin Malmgren, Jean Davies Okimoto, Sandy Asher, and Lensey Namioka. *Center Stage*

Garner, Joan
Stagings; short scripts for middle and high school students; written and illustrated by Joan Garner. Teacher Ideas Press 1995 233p il pa $27   **812.008**
1. Acting 2. One act plays
ISBN 1-56308-343-4   LC 95-19013

"This book presents nine science fiction and fantasy one-act plays for young people to perform. . . . Each script begins with a thorough description of characters and costumes, followed by a scene design, set description and a props list. Other notes describe how a teacher could use the play in the classroom and specifically discuss the best staging possibilities for the script." Book Rep

Great monologues for young actors; Craig Slaight, Jack Sharrar, editors. Smith & Kraus 1992 xx, 186p pa $11.95   **812.008**
1. Monologues 2. Acting
ISBN 1-880399-03-2

"Audition length cuts for men and women have been made from contemporary works, classic plays, and litera-

Great monologues for young actors—*Continued*
ture. Each is accompanied by a brief synopsis so an actor will have some idea of what's happening before and after the scene, and dialogue from other characters is left in, enclosed by parentheses, so that the piece flows as a whole. Selections are varied with a nice choice of both humor and drama." Voice Youth Advocates

Kehret, Peg
Encore! more winning monologs for young actors: 63 more honest-to-life monologs for teenage boys and girls. Meriwether 1988 176p pa $12.95   **812.008**
1. Acting 2. Monologues
ISBN 0-916260-54-2   LC 88-42541
Also available: Winning monologs for young actors pa $12.95 (ISBN 0-916260-38-0)
A collection of monologs for use in junior high and high school drama classes

Monologues for young actors; [edited by] Lorraine Cohen. Avon Bks. 1994 198p pa $4.99
                                       812.008
1. Monologues 2. Acting
ISBN 0-380-76187-4   LC 94-94067
This "collection of monologues, compiled specifically for young actors, contains an audition piece for even the hard to please performer. Whether students are looking for comedy, tragedy, or something in between, this has what they need. It even includes monologues written specifically for young African American actors. All audition pieces in this excellent source are from celebrated contemporary or classical plays." Voice Youth Advocates

The **Most** popular plays of the American theatre; ten of Broadway's longest-running plays; edited with an introduction and notes by Stanley Richards. Scarborough House 1979 703p il $24.95   **812.008**
1. American drama—Collections
ISBN 0-8128-2682-5   LC 79-65112
"Ranging from melodramatic thrillers to contemporary comedies, these dramas are sure to appeal to popular tastes and amateur theatrical groups. Included are the complete texts of 'Life with Father; Tobacco Road; Abie's Irish Rose; Harvey; Mary, Mary; Barefoot in the Park; Arsenic and Old Lace; Same Time, Next Year; Angel Street; and Cactus Flower.'" Booklist

Play it again! more one-act plays for acting students; [compiled] by Norman A. Bert & Deb Bert. Meriwether 1993 280p il pa $14.95
                                       812.008
1. Acting 2. One act plays
ISBN 0-916260-97-6   LC 93-312
Also available: One-act plays for acting students pa $14.95 (ISBN 0-916260-47-X)
This collection of twenty-five one-act plays includes scripts for two actors, scripts for three actors, and monologs
Includes bibliography

Ten out of ten; ten winning plays selected from the Young Playwrights Festival, 1982-1991, produced by the Foundation of the Dramatists Guild; edited by Wendy Lamb; preface by Wendy Wasserstein; introduction by Nancy Quinn. Delacorte Press 1992 296p hardcover o.p. paperback available $4.99   **812.008**
1. American drama—Collections 2. One act plays 3. Children's writings
ISBN 0-440-21914-0 (pa)   LC 92-7944
"This presents nine plays highlighted in previous anthologies and one, 'I'm Not Stupid' by David Rodriguez, from the 1991 Festival, which appears in print here for the first time." Booklist
"That this volume is the 'The best of the best' should imply that the collection is superlative, and it is. Quinn refers to the collection as 'a multigenerational multicultural resource' and that is true as well. Some readers may blanch at the language, some at the ideas expressed, many will become uncomfortable while reading, but all should be impressed with what is being said." Voice Youth Advocates

Twenty best plays of the modern American theatre; edited with an introduction by John Gassner. Crown 1939 xxii, 874p o.p.   **812.008**
1. American drama—Collections
This is the first volume in the series of Best American plays. The second is entered above under title: Best plays of the modern American theater
Complete texts of 20 successful plays
Includes a supplementary list of plays and a bibliography

813.009   American fiction—History and criticism

Abramson, Edward A.
Bernard Malamud revisited. Twayne Pubs. 1993 162p (Twayne's United States authors series) $23.95   **813.009**
1. Malamud, Bernard, 1914-1986
ISBN 0-8057-7641-9   LC 92-27568
"Abramson strives to provide a comprehensive study of Malamud's work, including the posthumous 1969 publication, The People and Uncollected Stories. . . . Approaching the works chronologically, Abramson skillfully examines Malamud's major themes and stylistic techniques, arguing convincingly that Malamud's pervasive interest in morality and allegory places him in the central American tradition of Hawthorne, Melville, James, and Faulkner." Choice
Includes bibliographical references

Chaim Potok. Twayne Pubs. 1986 159p (Twayne's United States authors series) lib bdg $20.95   **813.009**
1. Potok, Chaim, 1929-
ISBN 0-8057-7463-7   LC 86-3139
"Abramson sufficiently orients the reader to the Jewish background against which each book is set before dealing with elements of the work itself. . . . The author

Abramson, Edward A.—*Continued*
highlights Potok's strengths, but he does provide a balanced critical view, admitting to and discussing certain stylistic weaknesses. The book serves as a good explanation of why Potok's books 'have caught on more with people than with critics.' The annotated bibliography of secondary sources is helpful." Choice

Ahab; edited and with an introduction by Harold Bloom. Chelsea House 1991 247p (Major literary characters) $34.95   **813.009**
1. Melville, Herman, 1819-1891. Moby Dick; or, The whale
ISBN 0-7910-0933-5   LC 90-40960
Scholars discuss the Pequod's vengeful Captain Ahab from Melville's symbolic novel of good and evil
Includes bibliographical references

Alice Walker: critical perspectives past and present; edited by Henry Louis Gates, Jr., and K.A. Appiah. Amistad Press 1993 368p (Amistad literary series) $24.95; pa $14.95
                                         813.009
1. Walker, Alice, 1944-
ISBN 1-56743-013-9; 1-56743-026-0 (pa)
                                        LC 92-45754
This volume brings together reviews of the author's work from such sources as the New Yorker, Saturday Review, and The New York Times Book Review; sixteen essays on her short stories, poems, essays, and novels; and two interviews with Walker
Includes bibliography

The **American** short story, 1900-1945/1945-1980; a critical history. Twayne Pubs. 1983-1984 2v (Twayne's critical history of the short story)
                                         813.009
1. Short stories—History and criticism 2. American fiction—History and criticism
Contents: Volume 1900-1945, edited by Philip Stevick lib bdg $23.95 (ISBN 0-8057-9353-4); 1945-1980 volume edited by Gordon Weaver lib bdg $23.95 (ISBN 0-8057-9350-X)
The influence of social, cultural and historical events is examined and the experimental and innovative stories of the post-war period are analyzed
This "is an excellent guide for student and scholar alike. . . . A notable aspect of the work is the adequate coverage given to the contributions of black and women writers." Choice [review of 1945-1980 edition]
Includes bibliography

Baker, Carlos, 1909-1987
Hemingway: the writer as artist. [4th ed] Princeton Univ. Press 1972 xx, 438p hardcover o.p. paperback available $19.95   **813.009**
1. Hemingway, Ernest, 1899-1961
ISBN 0-691-01305-5 (pa)
First published 1952
Following a discussion of Hemingway's expatriation and his aesthetic principles, Baker analyzes both the fiction and nonfiction focusing on their texture, structure and symbolism. An annotated checklist of Hemingway's poetry, prose, and journalism is included

Bakish, David
Richard Wright. Ungar 1973 114p (Modern literature monographs) o.p.   **813.009**
1. Wright, Richard, 1908-1960
"The study weighs the impact of Wright's political concepts and personal experiences as dominant factors in the formulation of his writing style and through synopses of both familiar and less-known works shows Wright's critical importance as a black author." Booklist

Baym, Nina
The scarlet letter; a reading. Twayne Pubs. 1986 xxix, 116p (Twayne's masterwork studies) $23.95; pa $13.95   **813.009**
1. Hawthorne, Nathaniel, 1804-1864. Scarlet letter
ISBN 0-8057-7957-4; 0-8057-8001-7 (pa)
                                        LC 86-9774
This study covers the "major aspects of author, text, and critical history, raising a variety of thought-provoking questions about the reader's experience with the story. It will no doubt prove the starting point for study of 'The Scarlet Letter' for a whole new generation of readers." Choice
Includes bibliography

Bishop, Rudine Sims, 1937-
Presenting Walter Dean Myers. Twayne Pubs. 1990 123p il (Twayne's young adult authors series) $20.95   **813.009**
1. Myers, Walter Dean, 1937-
ISBN 0-8057-8214-1   LC 90-38062
An "introduction to the life and works of a prolific and popular spokesman for young African Americans. . . . Bishop has selected fourteen from among his thirty-one books for children and young adults for balanced, thoughtful analysis." Horn Book
Includes bibliographical references

Black American women fiction writers; edited and with an introduction by Harold Bloom. Chelsea House 1995 220p (Writers of English: lives and works) $29.95; pa $14.95   **813.009**
1. African American authors—Bio-bibliography
2. American fiction—History and criticism
3. American fiction—Women authors—Bio-bibliography
ISBN 0-7910-2208-0; 0-7910-2233-1 (pa)
                                        LC 94-5887
This volume provides biographical, critical and bibliographical information on fifteen African American women fiction writers. Among the authors covered are Maya Angelou, Zora Neale Hurston, Paule Marshall, Toni Morrison, and Gloria Naylor

Brooks, Cleanth, 1906-1994
William Faulkner; the Yoknapatawpha country. Yale Univ. Press 1963 499p o.p.; Louisiana State Univ. Press paperback available $16.95 **813.009**
1. Faulkner, William, 1897-1962
ISBN 0-8071-1601-7 (pa)
"Introductory chapters contrast Faulkner with various other regional writers, comment on the social structure in

Brooks, Cleanth, 1906-1994—*Continued*
his novels, and discuss his poetic treatment of nature. 'Sanctuary,' 'Light in August,' 'The sound and the fury,' 'Absalom, Absalom!' and other works are analyzed in remaining chapters. Genealogies and a character index are included." Booklist

Includes bibliographical references

Bryant, Hallman Bell, 1936-
A separate peace; the war within. Twayne Pubs. 1990 130p il (Twayne's masterwork studies) $23.95; pa $12.95   **813.009**
1. Knowles, John, 1926- Separate peace
ISBN 0-8057-8087-4; 0-8057-8131-5 (pa)
                                             LC 89-26817
"The initial biographical chronology and brief chapters on historical context and critical reception are followed by a more lengthy 'reading,' or chapter-by-chapter critical analysis. Bryant explains what to look for so readers can better understand Knowles's admirable use of language, symbols, allusion, characterization, setting, overall structure, and so on. . . . Recommended for all senior high level collections." Voice Youth Advocates

Includes bibliographical references

Cady, Edwin Harrison, 1917-
Stephen Crane; by Edwin H. Cady. rev ed. Twayne Pubs. 1980 175p (Twayne's United States authors series) lib bdg $22.95   **813.009**
1. Crane, Stephen, 1871-1900
ISBN 0-8057-7299-5   LC 79-26608
First published 1962
The author examines Crane's life and work. He feels that most biographers and/or critics have neglected or misemphasized aspects of Crane's life pertinent to an understanding of his writings. He summarizes the principal modes of Crane criticism with reference to this revised point of view

Includes bibliography

Campbell, Patricia J., 1930-
Presenting Robert Cormier. updated ed. Twayne Pubs. 1989 152p (Twayne's young adult authors series) lib bdg $20.95   **813.009**
1. Cormier, Robert
ISBN 0-8057-8212-5   LC 89-33707
First published 1985
This is a discussion of the life and work of the author of such books as Now and at the hour, Take me where the good times are, and Fade

Includes bibliography

Carson McCullers; edited and with an introduction by Harold Bloom. Chelsea House 1986 159p (Modern critical views) $29.95   **813.009**
1. McCullers, Carson, 1917-1967
ISBN 0-87754-630-4   LC 86-9718
Scholars evaluate the author of The ballad of the sad cafe, The heart is a lonely hunter, Reflections in a golden eye and The member of the wedding

Includes bibliography

Cart, Michael
Presenting Robert Lipsyte. Twayne Pubs. 1995 163p il (Twayne's young adult authors series) $20.95   **813.009**
1. Lipsyte, Robert
ISBN 0-8057-4151-8   LC 94-44520
This profile "of Lipsyte, which is based on personal interviews as well as an analysis of his works, considers both the man and his writings for young adults." Booklist

Includes bibliography

Contemporary black American fiction writers; edited and with an introduction by Harold Bloom. Chelsea House 1995 184p (Writers of English: lives and works) $29.95; pa $14.95
                                             813.009
1. African American authors—Bio-bibliography
2. American fiction—History and criticism
ISBN 0-7910-2212-9; 0-7910-2237-4 (pa)
                                             LC 94-5883
Among the twelve writers profiled in this volume are Toni Cade Bambara, Ernest J. Gaines, Alex Haley, Terry McMillan, Toni Morrison, and Ishmael Reed. A biographical sketch, a selection of critical extracts and a bibliography are provided for each author

Critical essays on Eudora Welty; [edited by] W. Craig Turner, Lee Emling Harding. Hall, G.K. & Co. 1989 314p il (Critical essays on American literature) $47   **813.009**
1. Welty, Eudora, 1909-
ISBN 0-8161-8888-2   LC 88-24737
"After providing an introduction that gives a succinct survey of Welty criticism and scholarship to date, Turner and Harding present a sample of this commentary in 28 pieces ranging from brief periodical reviews (several of them hostile) to in-depth analyses of individual works to thoughtful retrospective essays. There are two to four articles on each of Welty's nine books of fiction. This book should be another most useful reference for students and scholars seeking an overall perspective on Welty's highly distinguished body of fiction." Choice

Includes bibliographies

Critical essays on F. Scott Fitzgerald's Tender is the night; [edited by] Milton R. Stern. Hall, G.K. & Co. 1986 280p (Critical essays on American literature) $47   **813.009**
1. Fitzgerald, F. Scott (Francis Scott), 1896-1940. Tender is the night
ISBN 0-8161-8444-5   LC 85-17601
"Fitzgerald was far from satisfied with the version of 'Tender is the night' published in 1934, and he kept reworking it until he died, ultimately producing a 'final' version with radically altered chronology that was published in 1951 and promptly forgotten. . . . The essays and reviews gathered here are arranged by decade, giving a thorough overview of the novel's original reception and subsequent re-evaluations." Booklist

Includes bibliographies

Critical essays on Henry James: the early novels; [edited by] James W. Gargano. Hall, G.K. & Co. 1987 207p (Critical essays on American literature) $47 **813.009**
1. James, Henry, 1843-1916
ISBN 0-8161-8876-9 LC 87-226
Scholars offer critical assessments of the early novels of the influential American author
Includes bibliographies

Critical essays on Henry James: the late novels; [edited by] James W. Gargano. Hall, G.K. & Co. 1987 212p (Critical essays on American literature) $47 **813.009**
1. James, Henry, 1843-1916
ISBN 0-8161-8877-7 LC 86-25686
Among the novels discussed by literary critics in this collection of essays are The wings of the dove, The ambassadors, and The golden bowl
Includes bibliographies

Critical essays on Steinbeck's The grapes of wrath; [edited by] John Ditsky. Hall, G.K. & Co. 1989 168p il (Critical essays on American literature) $47 **813.009**
1. Steinbeck, John, 1902-1968. Grapes of wrath
ISBN 0-8161-8887-4 LC 88-24736
This volume presents selections from 50 years of critical response to Steinbeck's classic novel
Includes bibliographies

Critical essays on Stephen Crane's The red badge of courage; [edited by] Donald Pizer. Hall, G.K. & Co. 1990 269p (Critical essays on American literature) $47 **813.009**
1. Crane, Stephen, 1871-1900. Red badge of courage
ISBN 0-8161-8898-X LC 90-30087
This collection of essays on Crane's classic Civil War novel contains both early reviews and modern scholarship. Among the contributors are William Dean Howells, Harold Frederic, James Nagel and Jean Cazemajou
Includes bibliographies

Daly, Jay
Presenting S. E. Hinton. updated ed. Twayne Pubs. 1989 148p (Twayne's young adult authors series) lib bdg $20.95 **813.009**
1. Hinton, S. E.
ISBN 0-8057-8211-7 LC 89-32347
First published 1987
An introductory look at the life and work of the author of The outsiders, Tex, and Rumble fish
Includes bibliography

Detweiler, Robert
John Updike. rev ed. Twayne Pubs. 1984 200p (Twayne's United States authors series) $20.95 **813.009**
1. Updike, John
ISBN 0-8057-7422-X LC 83-18472
First published 1972
A critical look at Updike's fiction through the early 1980s
Includes bibliography

Doyle, Paul A., 1925-
Pearl S. Buck. rev ed. Twayne Pubs. 1980 179p (Twayne's United States authors series) $22.95 **813.009**
1. Buck, Pearl S. (Pearl Sydenstricker), 1892-1973
ISBN 0-8057-7325-8 LC 80-24376
First published 1965
This study examines Buck's thematic interests, plots, arguments, characterization, and style
Includes bibliography

Dutton, Robert R.
Saul Bellow. rev ed. Twayne Pubs. 1982 212p (Twayne's United States authors series) $22.95 **813.009**
1. Bellow, Saul
ISBN 0-8057-7353-3 LC 81-6977
First published 1971
This study of Bellow attempts to show the symbolism and romantic irony present in his novels
Includes bibliography

Eble, Kenneth Eugene
F. Scott Fitzgerald; by Kenneth Eble. rev ed. Twayne Pubs. 1977 187p (Twayne's United States authors series) $21.95 **813.009**
1. Fitzgerald, F. Scott (Francis Scott), 1896-1940
ISBN 0-8057-7183-2 LC 77-429
Also available in paperback from Macmillan
First published 1963
This assessment of Fitzgerald's oeuvre places particular emphasis on his achievement in the short story format
Includes bibliography

Evans, Elizabeth, 1935-
Anne Tyler. Twayne Pubs. 1993 173p (Twayne's United States authors series) $21.95 **813.009**
1. Tyler, Anne, 1941-
ISBN 0-8057-3985-8 LC 92-44339
After a brief biographical section the author assesses Tyler's short stories, nonfiction and novels. Emphasis is placed on Tyler's handling of domestic themes
Includes bibliography

Forman, Jack Jacob
Presenting Paul Zindel. Twayne Pubs. 1988 120p il (Twayne's young adult authors series) $21.95 **813.009**
1. Zindel, Paul
ISBN 0-8057-8206-0 LC 88-513
"After summarizing the plot of each novel and outlining its critical reception, Forman devotes several chapters to Zindel's treatment of teen alienation, parent figures, sex roles, etc." Booklist
Includes bibliography

French, Warren G., 1922-
J.D. Salinger, revisited; by Warren French. Twayne Pubs. 1988 147p (Twayne's United States authors series) $21.95 **813.009**
1. Salinger, J. D. (Jerome David), 1919-
ISBN 0-8057-7522-6 LC 88-4851
Also available in paperback from Macmillan

French, Warren G., 1922——_Continued_
First published 1976

"Summarizing contemporary critical thought while advancing his own reading of Salinger's work, French raises a number of fascinating points: how Mark David Chapman's misreading of *Catcher in the Rye* contributed to his decision to assassinate John Lennon; how Holden Caulfield was, in many ways, 'a prescient portrait of an attempt to create a counterculture'; and how Salinger's obsession with Hinduism has not only led to his refusal to publish, but has also caused him to lose touch with the general reader." Booklist
Includes bibliographies

Jack Kerouac; [by] Warren French. Twayne Pubs. 1986 xx, 147p (Twayne's United States authors series) lib bdg $21.95   **813.009**
1. Kerouac, Jack, 1922-1969
ISBN 0-8057-7467-X   LC 86-4817

The author "believes that Kerouac is worth taking seriously, not so much for the oft-misread beat bible 'On the Road' as for the various works constituting the 'Duluoz Legend' (in particular, 'Big Sur'), all of which build on the legend Kerouac tried to create for himself and all of which reveal, in one way or another, his agonizing internal conflicts. A thoughtful, intelligent effort to revise the critical thinking on Kerouac." Booklist
Includes bibliography

Friedman, Lenemaja
Shirley Jackson. Twayne Pubs. 1975 182p (Twayne's United States authors series) $21.95
813.009
1. Jackson, Shirley, 1919-1965
ISBN 0-8057-0402-7

"Five chapters treating, respectively, the short stories, the first novel, two psychological novels, three novels of 'setting,' and the family chronicles are framed by a preface, a chronology and a 'life and times of' at the beginning and an 'overview,' notes, an annotated bibliography, and index at the end." Choice

Gallo, Donald R.
Presenting Richard Peck. Twayne Pubs. 1989 154p (Twayne's young adult authors series) $21.95
813.009
1. Peck, Richard, 1934-
ISBN 0-8057-8209-5   LC 89-32346

Discusses the life and work of Richard Peck, examining his essays, poetry, and novels for children, young adults, and adults

The author "provides background on Peck's career, but he lets his subject do most of the talking, smoothly interweaving Peck's remarks throughout the text." Booklist
Includes bibliography

Gatsby; edited and with an introduction by Harold Bloom. Chelsea House 1991 211p (Major literary characters) $34.95   **813.009**
1. Fitzgerald, F. Scott (Francis Scott), 1896-1940. Great Gatsby
ISBN 0-7910-0958-0   LC 90-2041

Various scholars analyze the title character of Fitzgerald's classic portrait of false glamor and cultural aridity
Includes bibliographical references

Gerber, Philip L.
Willa Cather. rev ed. Twayne Pubs.; Prentice-Hall Int. 1995 152p il $22.95   **813.009**
1. Cather, Willa, 1873-1947
ISBN 0-8057-4035-X   LC 94-45354
First published 1975

A survey of the major concerns of Cather's fiction as they developed out of her life experiences. In addition to examining the major novels and short stories the author also explores Cather's underlying aesthetic principles
Includes bibliographical references

Gladstein, Mimi Reisel
The Ayn Rand companion. Greenwood Press 1984 130p lib bdg $35; pa $12.95   **813.009**
1. Rand, Ayn, 1905-1982
ISBN 0-313-22079-4 (lib bdg); 0-313-25737-X (pa)
LC 84-540

"This guide to Rand's work emphasizes plot and characters; while recognizing the philosophy, Gladstein does not overemphasize it. There is a detailed summary for each work of fiction or drama and an exhaustive listing by role of all the characters in these works. . . . There is a chapter devoted to the nonfiction and there is biographic material." Choice
Includes bibliography

Grebstein, Sheldon Norman
Sinclair Lewis. Twayne Pubs. 1962 192p (Twayne's United States authors series) $21.95
813.009
1. Lewis, Sinclair, 1885-1951
ISBN 0-8057-0448-5
Also available in paperback from New College & Univ. Press

A "study of Lewis' life, career, and ambivalent attitudes toward American conditions. . . . Starts with a 'psychograph' of the writer and then presents in chronological order each of the novels, stressing particularly those written from 1920-1929—the works upon which Grebstein feels Lewis' reputation will rest—as the conscience of his generation." Booklist
Includes bibliography

Harter, Carol C.
E. L. Doctorow; [by] Carol C. Harter and James R. Thompson. Twayne Pubs. 1990 143p (Twayne's United States authors series) $21.95
813.009
1. Doctorow, E. L., 1931-
ISBN 0-8057-7604-4   LC 89-24630

A volume of critical essays on Ragtime, Billy Bathgate, Loon Lake, and other novels and short stories
Includes bibliographical references

Hendrick, Willene, 1928-
Katherine Anne Porter; by Willene Hendrick and George Hendrick. rev ed. Twayne Pubs. 1988 160p (Twayne's United States authors series) $21.95   **813.009**
1. Porter, Katherine Anne, 1890-1980
ISBN 0-8057-7513-7   LC 87-21246
First published 1965

Hendrick, Willene, 1928-—*Continued*
The author analyzes Porter's essays as well as her fiction. While primarily an examination of the short stories, this book offers an account of the mixed critical reception of Ship of fools, Porter's only novel
Includes bibliography

Henry James's Daisy Miller, The turn of the screw, and other tales; edited and with an introduction by Harold Bloom. Chelsea House 1987 148p (Modern critical interpretations) $34.95   **813.009**
1. James, Henry, 1843-1916
ISBN 1-55546-007-0   LC 87-5215
A collection of eight critical essays on the major novellas of James including The Aspern papers, Daisy Miller, and The turn of the screw
Includes bibliography

Hester Prynne; edited and with an introduction by Harold Bloom. Chelsea House 1990 200p (Major literary characters) $34.95   **813.009**
1. Hawthorne, Nathaniel, 1804-1864. Scarlet letter
ISBN 0-7910-0945-9   LC 89-23855
Critical essays discuss the central character of Hawthorne's classic examination of the effects of sin in a closed society
Includes bibliographical references

Hettinga, Donald R.
Presenting Madeleine L'Engle. Twayne Pubs. 1993 171p (Twayne's young adult authors series) $21.95   **813.009**
1. L'Engle, Madeleine, 1918-
ISBN 0-8057-8222-2   LC 93-9188
Following a quick overview of L'Engle's life the author discusses the characters and themes of her major novels. Hettinga stresses the influence of L'Engle's Christian faith on her work
Includes bibliography

Hillway, Tyrus
Herman Melville. rev ed. Twayne Pubs. 1979 177p (Twayne's United States authors series) $21.95   **813.009**
1. Melville, Herman, 1819-1891
ISBN 0-8057-7256-1   LC 78-11937
First published 1963
An introductory look at the plots, characters, and dominant themes of Melville's works, beginning with Typee (1846)
Includes bibliography

Hoffman, Frederick J., 1909-1967
William Faulkner. 2nd ed rev. Twayne Pubs. 1966 160p (Twayne's United States authors series) $21.95   **813.009**
1. Faulkner, William, 1897-1962
ISBN 0-8057-0244-X
First published 1961
Following a survey of the dominant themes and patterns of Faulkner's work as a whole, the author then discusses each of the novels
Includes bibliography

Holden Caulfield; edited and with an introduction by Harold Bloom. Chelsea House 1990 182p (Major literary characters) $34.95   **813.009**
1. Salinger, J. D. (Jerome David), 1919- Catcher in the rye
ISBN 0-7910-0953-X   LC 90-1678
Contributors discuss Salinger's adolescent protagonist of The catcher in the rye
Includes bibliographical references

Hughes, R. S., 1948-
John Steinbeck; a study of the short fiction. Twayne Pubs. 1988 218p il (Twayne's studies in short fiction) $23.95   **813.009**
1. Steinbeck, John, 1902-1968
ISBN 0-8057-8302-4   LC 88-19967
"Underscored with the sentiment that Steinbeck's stories are equal if not superior to his more famous novels, Hughes' examination falls into three parts. Part 1 is a critical analysis, story by story. . . . Part 2 is a collection of statements by Steinbeck himself about the writing of short stories. Part 3 brings together a handful of critical essays about Steinbeck." Booklist
Includes bibliography

J.D. Salinger; edited and with an introduction by Harold Bloom. Chelsea House 1987 147p (Modern critical views) $29.95   **813.009**
1. Salinger, J. D. (Jerome David), 1919-
ISBN 0-87754-716-5   LC 86-29941
This collection of nine essays provides a view of Salinger's critical reception. Among the contributors are Alfred Kazin, David Galloway and Gerald Rosen
Includes bibliography

John Steinbeck; edited and with an introduction by Harold Bloom. Chelsea House 1987 172p (Modern critical views) $29.95   **813.009**
1. Steinbeck, John, 1902-1968
ISBN 0-87754-635-5   LC 86-29958
A selection of criticism, arranged in chronological order of publication, devoted to the fiction of John Steinbeck
Includes bibliography

John Updike; edited and with an introduction by Harold Bloom. Chelsea House 1987 172p (Modern critical views) $29.95   **813.009**
1. Updike, John
ISBN 0-87754-717-3   LC 86-29971
Critical interpretations of Updike's fiction from the Rabbit and Bech novels to The coup. Contributors include Joyce Carol Oates, Tony Tanner and Cynthia Ozick
Includes bibliography

Johnson, Claudia D.
Understanding The scarlet letter; a student casebook to issues, sources, and documents. Greenwood Press 1995 228p $35   **813.009**
1. Hawthorne, Nathaniel, 1804-1864. Scarlet letter
ISBN 0-313-29328-7   LC 94-39083
The author examines the sources, themes, characters, symbols and style of Hawthorne's classic. Secondary lit-

Johnson, Claudia D.—*Continued*
erature is examined
Includes bibliographical references

Johnson-Feelings, Dianne
Presenting Laurence Yep. Twayne Pubs. 1995
137p (Twayne's young adult authors series) $22.95

813.009
1. Yep, Laurence
ISBN 0-8057-8201-X   LC 95-10307
"This biocritical study draws on Yep's autobiography, *The Lost Garden* (1991), and on interviews with Yep and his editors, and then combines the personal material with a detailed discussion of his work. Whether Johnson-Feelings is talking about Yep's picture books, folklore, science fiction, historical fiction, or contemporary realism, she writes with subtlety about Yep's identity as an English-speaking Chinese American artist." Booklist
Includes bibliography

Kies, Cosette N., 1936-
Presenting Lois Duncan. Twayne Pubs. 1993
139p il (Twayne's young adult authors series) $21.95

813.009
1. Duncan, Lois, 1934-
ISBN 0-8057-8221-4   LC 93-36336
In addition to analyses of Duncan's young adult novels, a chapter is devoted to Who killed my daughter, the author's account of the unsolved murder of her daughter in 1989
Includes bibliography

Presenting young adult horror fiction; [by] Cosette Kies. Twayne Pubs. 1992 203p (Twayne's young adult authors series) $21.95   **813.009**
1. Horror fiction—History and criticism 2. American fiction—History and criticism
ISBN 0-8057-8217-6   LC 91-27002
"A look at the history of the genre; an analysis of select elements (traditional Gothic, satanism, true crime, splatterpunk, and dark fantasy); criticism of popular authors (V. C. Andrews, Dean R. Koontz, John Saul, Robert R. McCammon, Anne Rice, Chelsea Quinn Yarbro, Robert Bloch, and Stephen King); and projections for the future are all here." SLJ

Klinkowitz, Jerome
Kurt Vonnegut. Methuen 1982 96p (Contemporary writers) pa $8.50   **813.009**
1. Vonnegut, Kurt, 1922-
ISBN 0-416-33480-6   LC 81-22558
In this "overview of Vonnegut's work, Klinkowitz [seeks to] describe the ties that bind Vonnegut's art to his experiences during the Depression, in WW II, as an advertising writer for GE, and as a commercial writer." Choice
"The author presents well-documented and scholarly arguments." SLJ
Includes bibliography

Kuehl, John Richard, 1928-
F. Scott Fitzgerald; a study of the short fiction; [by] John Kuehl. Twayne Pubs. 1991 200p il (Twayne's studies in short fiction) $23.95

813.009
1. Fitzgerald, F. Scott (Francis Scott), 1896-1940
ISBN 0-8057-8332-6   LC 90-48727
Kuehl "closely analyzes the works of short fiction that made F. Scott Fitzgerald, according to the author, one of the 'few modern American masters of the form.' The insights Kuehl shares with readers bring a richness and new dimension to our understanding of Fitzgerald's fiction and of the writer himself." Booklist
Includes bibliographical references

Labor, Earle, 1928-
Jack London; [by] Earle Labor and Jeanne Campbell Reesman. rev ed. Twayne Pubs. 1994 186p (Twayne's United States authors series) $21.95   **813.009**
1. London, Jack, 1876-1916
ISBN 0-8057-4033-3   LC 93-49825
First published 1974
The authors analyze several of London's novels and short stories and discuss their themes, characterization and style
Includes bibliographical references

Lundquist, James
Theodore Dreiser. Ungar 1974 150p (Modern literature monographs) $19.95   **813.009**
1. Dreiser, Theodore, 1871-1945
ISBN 0-8044-2563-9
"Lundquist's brief critical and biographical introduction . . . [attempts] to cover both life and major works and also to examine Dreiser's philosophy that shaped his writing." Choice
"Within his survey of the life and works of Dreiser, Lundquist manages to incorporate the most valuable insights of scholarly research and opinion. In a style that is both clear and interesting, he succeeds in making his points without scanting supporting illustration or critical opinion." Libr J
Includes bibliography

Magistrale, Tony
Stephen King; the second decade, Danse macabre to The dark half. Twayne Pubs. 1992 188p il (Twayne's United States authors series) $22.95   **813.009**
1. King, Stephen, 1947-
ISBN 0-8057-3957-2   LC 91-44424
"Magistrale has written this critique with clarity, simplicity, and obvious admiration for his subject. A book that could easily be read from cover to cover, it may also serve as a reference for students interested in King's more recent works." SLJ
Includes bibliography

Major characters in American fiction; general editors, Jack Salzman and Pamela Wilkinson; with Lucile Bruce, Janet Dean, Cybele Merrick, and the staff of the Columbia University Center for American Culture Studies. Holt & Co. 1994 952p (Henry Holt reference book) $60; pa $25
     813.009

1. Characters and characteristics in literature—Dictionaries 2. American fiction—Dictionaries
ISBN 0-8050-3060-3; 0-8050-4564-3 (pa)
     LC 94-11460

This work "covers close to 1600 names from books (not including plays) published between 1790 and 1991. Entries are arranged alphabetically and include brief bibliographical information and a five- to seven-paragraph biography. Three sections that cross list the characters in terms of author, title, and alternate name are also provided." Libr J
For a fuller review see: Booklist, Feb. 15, 1995

Mark Twain: a collection of critical essays. Prentice-Hall 1963 179p $12.95   **813.009**
1. Twain, Mark, 1835-1910
ISBN 0-13-933317-7
"A Spectrum book. Twentieth century views"
Edited by Henry Nash Smith
This collection of essays includes Van Wyck Brooks on Twain's humor, James M. Cox on A Connecticut Yankee, Kenneth Lynn on Roughing it, and Walter Blair on Tom Sawyer
Includes bibliography

Martin, Terence
Nathaniel Hawthorne. rev ed. Twayne Pubs. 1983 221p (Twayne's United States authors series) $21.95   **813.009**
1. Hawthorne, Nathaniel, 1804-1864
ISBN 0-8057-7384-3   LC 82-23419
First published 1965
A critical introduction to the nature and extent of Hawthorne's achievement in fiction, giving insight into his romances and tales
Includes bibliography

Mazzeno, Laurence W.
Herman Wouk. Twayne Pubs. 1994 132p (Twayne's United States authors series) $23.95
     813.009
1. Wouk, Herman, 1915-
ISBN 0-8057-3982-3   LC 93-29926
An examination of the life and work of the novelist best known for The Caine mutiny, Winds of war, and War and remembrance
Includes bibliography

McDowell, Margaret B.
Edith Wharton. Twayne Pubs. 1976 158p (Twayne's United States authors series) $21.95
     813.009
1. Wharton, Edith, 1862-1937
ISBN 0-8057-7618-4
"Extensive analysis of her post-1920 fiction from 'A Son at the Front' (1923) to 'A Backward Glance' (1934)

shows how Wharton continually developed and explored new genres, techniques, and subject materials." Libr J
Includes bibliography

McSweeney, Kerry, 1941-
Moby-Dick; Ishmael's mighty book. Twayne Pubs. 1986 131p (Twayne's masterwork studies) lib bdg $23.95; pa $13.95   **813.009**
1. Melville, Herman, 1819-1891. Moby-Dick; or, The whale
ISBN 0-8057-7954-X (lib bdg); 0-8057-8002-5 (pa)
     LC 86-4839

This study "focuses on the major themes and concepts of Melville's most widely studied novel. Also covered are such matters as the novel's historical context and its critical reception. Introduced by a chronology of Melville's life, the monograph concludes with lists of primary and, more important for the student, secondary sources." Booklist

✓ **Mikkelsen, Nina**
Virginia Hamilton. Twayne Pubs. 1994 169p il (Twayne's United States authors series) $22.95
     813.009
1. Hamilton, Virginia, 1936-
ISBN 0-8057-4010-4   LC 94-621
"The introductory chapters describe Hamilton's own childhood and the influence of her extended rural midwestern family on the 'nurturing of narrative.' Then Mikkelsen combines in-depth literary criticism of each of Hamilton's 30 books—grouped by genre and arranged in chronological order—with a general evaluation of her themes, techniques (including 'psychic realism and surrealistic setting'), and her crucial influence on other writers in the field." Booklist
Includes bibliographical references

Mogen, David, 1945-
Ray Bradbury. Twayne Pubs. 1986 186p (Twayne's United States authors series) lib bdg $21.95   **813.009**
1. Bradbury, Ray, 1920-
ISBN 0-8057-7464-5   LC 86-11972
"Mogen begins with an overview of Bradbury's personal and literary history. His major works are discussed and compared. The book, thus, is valuable both as a source for biographical material and as a collection of literary criticism of Bradbury's works." SLJ
Includes bibliography

Nilsen, Alleen Pace
Presenting M. E. Kerr; illustrated by Meg Kelleher. Twayne Pubs. 1986 142p il (Twayne's young adult authors series) lib bdg $21.95
     813.009
1. Kerr, M. E., 1927-
ISBN 0-8057-8202-8   LC 86-4297
This biographical and critical study of the young adult author discusses her 12 YA novels (with plot summaries), her use of humor and other devices to spotlight contemporary issues, and the autobiographical aspects of her work
Includes bibliography

Norris, Jerrie
Presenting Rosa Guy. Twayne Pubs. 1988 111p
(Twayne's young adult authors series) $21.95
813.009
1. Guy, Rosa
ISBN 0-8057-8207-9   LC 88-5369
Examines the life and works of the author, born in
Trinidad and raised in Harlem, of such young adult fic-
tion as Ruby and The friends
Includes bibliography

Nye, Jody Lynn, 1957-
The dragonlover's guide to Pern; [by] Jody
Lynn Nye, with Anne McCaffrey; illustrated by
Todd Cameron Hamilton; maps and additional
illustrations by James Clouse. Ballantine Bks. 1989
178p il maps hardcover o.p. paperback available
$14   **813.009**
1. McCaffrey, Anne
ISBN 0-345-37946-2 (pa)   LC 89-6715
"A Del Rey book"
An illustrated look at Anne McCaffrey's fictional
Pern, the science fiction world where humans and tele-
pathic dragons together fight the evil Thread
Includes bibliographical references

Ostrom, Hans A.
Langston Hughes; a study of the short fiction.
Twayne Pubs. 1993 125p (Twayne's studies in
short fiction) $23.95   **813.009**
1. Hughes, Langston, 1902-1967
ISBN 0-8057-8343-1   LC 93-18405
This book is divided into three sections. The first part
examines the author's collections The ways of white
folks, Laughing to keep from crying, and Something in
common, and his stories featuring the character Jesse B.
Simple. The second part contains comments from Hughes
about his work. Excerpts from reviews appear in the last
part
Includes bibliography

Phy, Allene Stuart
Presenting Norma Klein. Twayne Pubs. 1988
189p il (Twayne's young adult authors series)
$21.95   **813.009**
1. Klein, Norma, 1938-1989
ISBN 0-8057-8205-2   LC 88-514
"Leading off with a glimpse at Klein's personal background, Phy conveys a strong sense of the woman behind the books—devoted daughter; tough, outspoken
writer/crusader for honesty and realism in children's
books; mother; and feminist." Booklist
Includes bibliography

Pinsker, Sanford
The catcher in the rye; innocence under
pressure. Twayne Pubs. 1993 107p (Twayne's
masterwork studies) $23.95; pa $13.95   **813.009**
1. Salinger, J. D. (Jerome David), 1919- Catcher in
the rye
ISBN 0-8057-7978-7; 0-8057-8028-9 (pa)
     LC 92-31048
"Pinsker provides a chronology of J.D. Salinger's life
and works, sets 'The Catcher in the Rye' in its 1950s

historical context, and discusses its importance and critical reception. He then examines the story itself, quoting
and interpreting passages from the book and offering
comparisons and references to a varity of works." Voice
Youth Advocates
Includes bibliography

Potts, Stephen W., 1949-
Catch-22: antiheroic antinovel. Twayne Pubs.
1989 136p (Twayne's masterwork studies) $23.95;
pa $13.95   **813.009**
1. Heller, Joseph. Catch-22
ISBN 0-8057-7992-2; 0-8057-8041-6 (pa)
     LC 88-33277
"The first two chapters discuss the novel's historical
context and critical reception. The author then devotes
six chapters to a meticulous analysis of the book's structure, language, themes, and characters spending considerable time recounting the critical debate over the novel's
lack of a traditional chronological plot. In conclusion, he
argues that the work has lost none of its relevance."
Booklist
Includes bibliography

Ralph Ellison: a collection of critical essays;
edited by John Hersey. Prentice-Hall 1974 180p
$12.95   **813.009**
1. Ellison, Ralph. Invisible man
ISBN 0-13-274357-4
"A Spectrum book. Twentieth century views"
This collection brings together selections by critics
and authors such as Robert Penn Warren, Saul Bellow,
Irving Howe, and Tony Tanner. The essays focus primarily on Invisible Man, Ellison's symbolic, epic narrative
of a black man's maturation in white America
Includes bibliography

Readings on John Steinbeck; Clarice Swisher,
book editor. Greenhaven Press 1996 192p
(Greenhaven Press literary companion to
American authors) $19.95; pa $11.95   **813.009**
1. Steinbeck, John, 1902-1968
ISBN 1-565-10467-6; 1-565-10468-4 (pa)
     LC 95-51243
This volume of essays "includes several general critical selections, thus providing an overview of the author's
work followed by several entries on each of the following novels: The Red Pony, The Pearl, Of Mice and Men,
and The Grapes of Wrath." SLJ
Includes bibliographical references

Readings on Nathaniel Hawthorne; Clarice
Swisher, book editor. Greenhaven Press 1996
191p (Greenhaven Press literary companion to
American authors) $19.95; pa $11.95   **813.009**
1. Hawthorne, Nathaniel, 1804-1864
ISBN 1-565-10459-5; 1-565-10458-7 (pa)
     LC 95-43122
This volume "includes essays on the author's subject
matter and resources; discussions of short story and nov-
el literary techniques; and four essays on The Scarlet
Letter

Reed, Kenneth T.
Truman Capote. Twayne Pubs. 1981 145p
(Twayne's United States authors series) $22.95
                                                      813.009
1. Capote, Truman, 1924-1984
ISBN 0-8057-7321-5   LC 80-26056
This "overview of Capote's place in American letters
. . . begins with a condensed interpretive biographical
section, followed by somewhat more expansive literary
criticism of Capote's short fiction, novels, and reportage.
Capote's style, themes, characterizations, and influences
receive summary interpretation." Booklist
Includes bibliography

Reid, Suzanne Elizabeth
Presenting Cynthia Voigt. Twayne Pubs. 1995
133p il (Twayne's young adult authors series)
$21.95   **813.009**
1. Voigt, Cynthia
ISBN 0-8057-8219-2   LC 94-44197
This work "provides a brief biography and then
comprehensive, in-depth analysis of each of Voigt's novels. . . . Reid quotes from a range of critical reviews,
but her own literary analysis is almost entirely positive.
The focus is on interpretation, and she does a fine job of
identifying Voigt's dominant themes—the challenge to
traditional gender roles, the emphasis on work, etc.—in
a style that's both scholarly and stimulating." Booklist
Includes bibliography

Reino, Joseph
Stephen King; the first decade, Carrie to Pet
sematary. Twayne Pubs. 1988 162p (Twayne's
United States authors series) lib bdg $22.95
                                                      813.009
1. King, Stephen, 1947-
ISBN 0-8057-7512-9   LC 87-19247
The author analyzes King's major published work be-
tween 1973 and 1983. He argues that 'Salem's Lot is
King's most successful novel from this period
Includes bibliography

Reynolds, Michael S., 1937-
The sun also rises, a novel of the twenties.
Twayne Pubs. 1988 106p (Twayne's masterwork
studies) $23.95; pa $13.95   **813.009**
1. Hemingway, Ernest, 1899-1961. Sun also rises
ISBN 0-8057-7962-0; 0-8057-8015-7 (pa)
                                      LC 88-1309
The author's "treatment of the signs, motifs, and
themes in the story helps us to see the overall unity of
the novel which otherwise seems so loose and rambling
in its structure. Of particular interest is Reynolds' discussion of Hemingway's own conception of the novel, and
the changes it underwent from initial drafts to publication." Voice Youth Advocates
Includes bibliography

Richard Wright: critical perspectives past and
present; edited by Henry Louis Gates, Jr., and
K.A. Appiah. Amistad Press 1993 476p
(Amistad literary series) $24.95; pa $14.95
                                                      813.009
1. Wright, Richard, 1908-1960
ISBN 1-56743-014-7; 1-56743-027-9 (pa)
                                      LC 92-45757
A collection of critical writings which examine
Wright's fiction, nonfiction, and autobiographical works.
The volume begins with a selection of reviews, written
by such authors as Zora Neale Hurston, Clifton Fadiman,
Ralph Ellison, Sinclair Lewis and Irving Howe. The sec-
ond part consists of twenty-two present-day essays. Also
included are a chronology and a bibliography

Richard Wright's Native son; edited and with an
introduction by Harold Bloom. Chelsea House
1988 174p (Modern critical interpretations)
$29.95   **813.009**
1. Wright, Richard, 1908-1960. Native son
ISBN 1-55546-055-0   LC 87-30402
A collection of critical essays on Wright's classic portrayal of the black experience, arranged chronologically
in the order of their original publication
Includes bibliography

Rovit, Earl H.
Ernest Hemingway; [by] Earl Rovit, Gerry
Brenner. rev ed. Twayne Pubs. 1986 214p
(Twayne's United States authors series) $21.95
                                                      813.009
1. Hemingway, Ernest, 1899-1961
ISBN 0-8057-7455-6   LC 85-28916
First published 1963
Hemingway's work is presented through an analysis of
the Hemingway style, his characteristic employment of
narrational structures, recurrent themes, and the Heming-
way "code" as elements in his total achievement
Includes bibliography

Sinclair Lewis; edited and with an introduction by
Harold Bloom. Chelsea House 1987 144p
(Modern critical views) $24.95   **813.009**
1. Lewis, Sinclair, 1885-1951
ISBN 0-87754-628-2   LC 86-29912
A collection of ten critical essays on the novels of
Sinclair Lewis which examine their ironic, satiric and
moral dimensions
Includes bibliography

Skaggs, Peggy
Kate Chopin. Twayne Pubs. 1985 130p
(Twayne's United States authors series) $21.95
                                                      813.009
1. Chopin, Kate, 1851-1904
ISBN 0-8057-7439-4   LC 84-27977
The author "provides careful analyses of Chopin's two
volumes of published short stories ('Bayou Folks' and 'A
Night in Arcadie'), the stories of her unpublished vol-
ume, 'A Vocation and a Voice,' her uncollected short
stories, poems, and essays, as well as her two novels, 'At
Fault' and 'The Awakening.' A thorough critical study of
interest to both general readers and scholars." Booklist
Includes bibliography

Springer, Marlene
Ethan Frome; a nightmare of need. Twayne Pubs. 1993 130p il (Twayne's masterwork studies) $23.95; pa $13.95 **813.009**
1. Wharton, Edith, 1862-1937. Ethan Frome
ISBN 0-8057-9437-9; 0-8057-8586-8 (pa)
LC 92-42509
The first part of this work discusses the events in Wharton's personal life relevant to the writing of Ethan Frome, and the critical reception of the novel. The second part focuses on characterization, setting and symbolism
Includes bibliography

Stover, Leon E., 1929-
Robert A. Heinlein; by Leon Stover. Twayne Pubs. 1987 147p il (Twayne's United States authors series) lib bdg $21.95 **813.009**
1. Heinlein, Robert A. (Robert Anson), 1907-1988
ISBN 0-8057-7509-9 LC 87-14876
A critical introduction to the prolific science fiction author
Includes bibliography

Thomas Wolfe; edited and with an introduction by Harold Bloom. Chelsea House 1987 174p (Modern critical views) $24.95 **813.009**
1. Wolfe, Thomas, 1900-1938
ISBN 0-87754-638-X LC 86-29952
A collection of critical essays that examine the structure, themes and metaphors employed by Wolfe in his fiction. Morris Beja, Leo Gurko and David Herbert Donald are among the contributors
Includes bibliography

Toni Morrison: critical perspectives past and present; edited by Henry Louis Gates, Jr., and K.A. Appiah. Amistad Press 1993 448p (Amistad literary series) $24.95; pa $14.95
813.009
1. Morrison, Toni, 1931-
ISBN 1-56743-012-0; 1-56743-025-2 (pa)
LC 92-45755
This collection contains reviews of Morrison's six novels, written by Reynolds Price, John Irving, Margaret Atwood, Edna O'Brien, and others; fifteen essays which examine her themes and influences; and four interviews with Morrison. Also included is a chronology of her life and career
Includes bibliography

The **Tony** Hillerman companion; a comprehensive guide to his life and work; edited by Martin Greenberg. HarperCollins Pubs. 1994 375p il $25 **813.009**
1. Hillerman, Tony
ISBN 0-06-017034-4 LC 93-49507
"In addition to a Hillerman chronology listing highlights of the writer's life, the guide includes an interview with the author and a lengthy critical essay on his works. . . . The volume also contains a short, informative essay on Navajo culture, detailed listings and explanations of the Native American clans and characters featured in Hillerman's fiction, and excerpts from some of Hillerman's most popular works, both fiction and nonfiction." Booklist

Twentieth century interpretations of The great Gatsby; a collection of critical essays. Prentice-Hall 1968 119p $22.50 **813.009**
1. Fitzgerald, F. Scott (Francis Scott), 1896-1940. The great Gatsby
ISBN 0-13-363820-0
"A Spectrum book"
Edited by Ernest Lockridge
This volume, which ranges across forty years of criticism of this American classic, includes contributions by Marius Bewley, Thomas A. Hanzo, Edith Wharton, Lionel Trilling, and Fitzgerald himself
Includes bibliography

Wagenknecht, Edward, 1900-
The novels of Henry James. Ungar 1983 329p (Literature and life series) $19.95 **813.009**
1. James, Henry, 1843-1916
ISBN 0-8044-2959-6 LC 82-40280
"After introductory chapters on the life of Henry James and his theory of fiction, Wagenknecht describes and evaluates each novel, in chronological order, each work being considered both as an entity and in relationship to the author's total oeuvre." Publisher's note
Includes bibliography

The tales of Henry James. Ungar 1984 266p (Literature and life series) $19.95 **813.009**
1. James, Henry, 1843-1916
ISBN 0-8044-2957-X LC 84-34
In this "critical survey of every piece of prose literature James produced—except for the works James himself classified as novels—Wagenknecht analyzes, in chronological order, all of the stories collected in the definitive New York Edition, as well as those published in 'The Finer Grain.' Other stories are . . . discussed in an appendix, where they are arranged . . . in alphabetical order." Publisher's note
Includes bibliographical references

Wagner-Martin, Linda
The modern American novel, 1914-1945; a critical history. Twayne Pubs. 1989 163p (Twayne's critical history of the novel) $23.95; pa $9.95 **813.009**
1. American fiction—History and criticism
ISBN 0-8057-7851-9; 0-8057-7853-5 (pa)
LC 89-15515
The author "considers a wide array of authors, including famous ones (Willa Cather, Gertrude Stein, Ernest Hemingway, Frank Norris, William Faulkner, and James Agee) and lesser-knowns (Nella Larsen, Meridel Le Sueur, Martha Gellhorn, and Harry Brown)." Booklist
Includes bibliography

Wasserman, Loretta
Willa Cather: a study of the short fiction. Twayne Pubs. 1991 178p (Twayne's studies in short fiction) $23.95 **813.009**
1. Cather, Willa, 1873-1947
ISBN 0-8057-8330-X LC 90-5149
This overview "includes some of Cather's own comments about her writing. Divided into three segments en-

Wasserman, Loretta—*Continued*
titled 'The Short Fiction,' 'The Writer,' and 'The Critics,' this collection of articles offers varied perceptions of Cather's little-noticed work. . . . Students will appreciate Cather's views on the short story and its differences from the novel. Teachers will welcome the comprehensive consideration of the often underplayed efforts of this most American of authors." SLJ
Includes bibliography

Weidt, Maryann N.
Presenting Judy Blume. Twayne Pubs. 1990 148p il (Twayne's young adult authors series) $21.95   **813.009**
1. Blume, Judy
ISBN 0-8057-8208-7   LC 89-11193
The author "discusses Blume's life, career moves, relationships, and family. . . . An entire chapter is devoted to Blume's most controversial title to date, 'Forever'; other titles are grouped according to character, theme, or plot. 'Wifey' and 'Smart Women', Blume's adult novels are also included." Voice Youth Advocates
Includes bibliography

Wenke, John Paul
J.D. Salinger; a study of the short fiction; [by] John Wenke. Twayne Pubs. 1991 177p (Twayne studies in short fiction) $23.95   **813.009**
1. Salinger, J. D. (Jerome David), 1919-
ISBN 0-8057-8334-2   LC 91-11574
A critical analysis of the novelist's short story collection Nine stories and his early short fiction which originally appeared in the New Yorker, the Saturday Evening Post, and other publications
Includes bibliographical references

Winchell, Donna Haisty
Alice Walker. Twayne Pubs. 1992 152p (Twayne's United States authors series) $21.95   **813.009**
1. Walker, Alice, 1944-
ISBN 0-8057-7642-7   LC 91-45309
This study assesses Walker's entire body of work including her poetry and her novel The temple of my familiar (1989). The author combines biographical information with critical analysis to provide an overview of Walker's accomplishments
Includes bibliography

Writers of multicultural fiction for young adults; a bio-critical sourcebook; edited by M. Daphne Kutzer; Emmanuel S. Nelson, advisory editor. Greenwood Press 1996 487p $75   **813.009**
1. Young adults' literature—Bio-bibliography
2. American fiction—Bio-bibliography
3. Multiculturalism in literature
ISBN 0-313-29331-7   LC 95-502
"Included are entries for 51 writers. . . . Each entry provides biographical, critical, and bibliographical information, while a general bibliography of works on multicultural literature concludes the book." Publisher's note
Includes bibliographical references

Zora Neale Hurston: critical perspectives past and present; edited by Henry Louis Gates, Jr., and K.A. Appiah. Amistad Press 1993 330p (Amistad literary series) $24.95; pa $14.95   **813.009**
1. Hurston, Zora Neale, 1891-1960
ISBN 1-56743-015-5; 1-56743-028-7 (pa)
LC 92-45759
A collection of critical writings about Hurston's works. The first section contains reviews which first appeared in The New York Times Book Review and other publications between 1934 and 1948. The second section contains critical essays which were published between 1982 and 1992. A chronology and a bibliography are also included

814   American essays

Angelou, Maya
Wouldn't take nothing for my journey now. Random House 1993 141p $17   **814**
ISBN 0-679-42743-0   LC 93-5904
The author "shares her thoughts about humankind: how to respect others of different cultures, opinions, and values as taught by universal philosophies. . . . Angelou's prose is brisk, fluid, and entrancing. This work will provide a taste of wisdom to all who read it." Libr J

Baldwin, James, 1924-1987
The price of the ticket; collected nonfiction, 1948-1985. St. Martin's/Marek 1985 xx, 690p $29.95   **814**
ISBN 0-312-64306-3   LC 85-11733
"Classic Baldwin pieces are here—'Nobody Knows My Name,' 'Notes of a Native Son,' 'The Fire Next Time'—as well as little-known reviews, all of which demonstrate the stunning articulateness and passion that have prompted critics and the reading public alike to consider his voice, in both fiction and nonfiction, as one of extreme intelligibility in depicting black experiences and attitudes." Booklist

Buckley, William F. (William Frank), 1925-
Happy days were here again; reflections of a libertarian journalist; [by] William F. Buckley, Jr.; edited by Patricia Bozell. Random House 1993 xxii, 473p o.p.; Adams Pub. paperback available $12.95   **814**
ISBN 1-55850-471-0 (pa)   LC 93-16597
"In this collection of essays, columns, speeches, and magazine articles Buckley gleefully skewers misguided liberals, makes fun of (while defending) his propensity for using high-blown language, details his love of sailing and Bach, and writes glowingly of those he admires. . . . This volume is further proof that Buckley is a superb writer." Libr J

Giovanni, Nikki

Racism 101; foreword by Virginia C. Fowler. Morrow 1994 203p $20; pa $11   **814**

ISBN 0-688-04332-1; 0-688-14234-6 (pa)

LC 93-29602

This "group of essays varies in tone from breezy to vehement and covers a mind-tingling assortment of topics that all relate in one way or another to being a black American. . . . Giovanni is a shrewd observer and an exhilarating essayist." Booklist

Sacred cows—and other edibles. Morrow 1988 167p $12.95; pa $7.95   **814**

ISBN 0-688-04333-X; 0-688-08909-7 (pa)

LC 87-22045

In these essays, the author "expresses (and impresses with) her strong attitudes about poverty, stupidity, prejudice, ineffectual black leadership, insects, credit cards and other inducements to consumerism, female exploitation, TV commercials, ex-smokers, required seat-belting, men who walk a picket line against abortion, dumb sports announcers. She feels more positively about her teenage son, soap, being happy with what she has, *Little House on the Prairie* and the virtues of baseball." Publ Wkly

Hamill, Pete

Piecework; writings on men and women, fools and heroes, lost cities, vanished friends, small pleasures, large calamities, and how the weather was; foreword by Jimmy Breslin. Little, Brown 1996 432p $23.95   **814**

ISBN 0-316-34104-5   LC 95-4738

This is a collection of previously-published essays by the New York newspaper reporter and columnist

"These essays are opinionated, hard-hitting, passionate, and sometimes disturbing. Writing for magazines ranging from Esquire to Art & Antiques, Hamill's writings show readers the decay of New York and other cities, the violence and heartbreak of Lebanon and Nicaragua, and the unraveling of civil life in many parts of our society." Libr J

White, E. B. (Elwyn Brooks), 1899-1985

Essays of E. B. White. Harper & Row 1977 277p hardcover o.p. paperback available $13 **814**

ISBN 0-06-090662-6 (pa)   LC 77-7717

Also available in hardcover from Borgo Press

Analyzed in Essay and general literature index

Most of the essays first appeared in The New Yorker. "They range from a 1934 piece on the St. Nicholas Magazine 'League' and the distinguished writers who were members of it as children, to a 1975 report from Allen Cove, Maine, where White had retreated from the bedlam of the city." Publ Wkly

815.008   American speeches— Collections

Historic speeches of African Americans; introduced and selected by Warren J. Halliburton. Watts 1993 192p il (African-American experience) lib bdg $22.70; pa $6.95   **815.008**

1. African Americans—History 2. American speeches

ISBN 0-531-11034-6 (lib bdg); 0-531-15677-X (pa)

LC 92-39318

Presents speeches by various African American religious and political leaders from the days of slavery to the present, along with biographical information and historical background

"Kids will dip into this for personal reading, and for curriculum research; they'll also find stirring pieces to read aloud and think about. The detailed sources at the end of the book make it easy to find out more about the individuals and their ideas." Booklist

Hold fast your dreams; twenty commencement speeches; [compiled by] Carrie Boyko and Kimberly Colen. Scholastic 1996 230p il $10.95   **815.008**

1. American speeches

ISBN 0-590-50956-X   LC 95-36057

A collection of "baccalaureate speeches by 20 prominent Americans (some recently deceased). The speeches represent a multicultural, cross-section of individuals, both male and female. Wisdom and common sense is evident in the addresses of Cathy Guisewite, Billy Joel, and Robert Fulgham. Humor characterizes the advice of Neil Simon and Dr. Seuss. Others included are Jimmy Carter, Arthur Ashe, Wilma Mankiller, Marian Wright Edelman, and Colin Powell. Brief biographical sketches and photos precede each entry." SLJ

Representative American speeches. Wilson, H.W. (Reference shelf) pa $15   **815.008**

1. American speeches

Annual. First published 1937-1938

Current compiler: Owen Peterson

A compilation containing a selection of speeches of the year made by eminent men and women on major trends and events. Each speech is prefaced by a note about the speaker and the occasion. The appendix in each volume contains biographical notes

Voices of multicultural America; notable speeches delivered by African, Asian, Hispanic, and Native Americans, 1790-1995; Deborah Gillan Straub, editor. Gale Res. 1996 lii, 1372p il $95   **815.008**

1. American speeches 2. Ethnic groups

ISBN 0-8103-9378-6   LC 95-31473

This is a collection of "230 speeches by 130 persons. . . . The entries are arranged in one alphabet by name, each beginning with an approximately two-page biographical sketch. The historical context of the speech and the specific occasion provide perspective. Following the speech, which is usually presented in its entirety, a brief paragraph describes its aftermath. . . . The book represents a remarkably diverse range of political and social viewpoints." Booklist

Includes bibliographical references

817   American satire and humor

Macaulay, David, 1946-
Motel of the mysteries. Houghton Mifflin 1979
95p il hardcover o.p. paperback available $11.95
817

ISBN 0-395-28425-2 (pa)   LC 79-14860

In this satire the author pictures an amateur archeologist, who in the year 4022 stumbles upon an American motel which has been buried in 1985 in "a cataclysmic coincidence of previously unknown proportion [which] extinguished virtually all forms of life on the North American continent." The excavation of the motel and the ensuing explanations and interpretations of its human remains and artifacts provide a humorous satire of archeological finds and civilization, circa 1980

Marquis, Don, 1878-1937
The lives and times of Archy & Mehitabel; with pictures by George Herriman and an introduction by E. B. White. Doubleday 1950 xxiv, 477p il hardcover o.p. paperback available $8.95   **817**

ISBN 0-385-09478-7 (pa)

Also available in hardcover from Amereon and Buccaneer Bks.

An omnibus edition of three titles published separately: Archy and Mehitabel (1927); Archy's life of Mehitabel (1933); Archy does his part (1935)

"It takes something approaching genius to make a cockroach and an alley cat understandable and sympathetic characters, and that is what Mr. Marquis has done with the literary bug, Archy, and his friend, Mehitabel, whose motto is 'toujours gai' and who is forever the lady, no matter how undignified and even immoral, her conduct may appear at times." North Am Rev

Morsberger, Robert Eustis, 1929-
James Thurber; [by] Robert E. Morsberger. Twayne Pubs. 1964 224p (Twayne's United States authors series) $21.95   **817**

1. Thurber, James, 1894-1961

ISBN 0-8057-0728-X

A critical study of the American humorist, whose timorous husbands, aggressive wives, and amiable dogs make a strong statement about the human condition

Includes bibliography

Thurber, James, 1894-1961
The Thurber carnival; written and illustrated by James Thurber. Modern Lib. 1994 443p il $15.50
817

ISBN 0-679-60089-2   LC 93-29575

Also available in paperback from HarperCollins

First published 1945 by Harper

A Thurber omnibus containing stories mainly from: My world and welcome to it; Let your mind alone; The middle-aged man on the flying trapeze; My life and hard times; Fables for our time and famous poems illustrated; The owl in the attic; The seal in the bedroom; Men, women and dogs; The war between men and women

Twain, Mark, 1835-1910
The innocents abroad; or, The new Pilgrims progress, being some account of the steamship Quaker City's pleasure excursion to Europe and the Holy Land   **817**

1. Voyages and travels 2. Europe—Description
3. Middle East—Description

Paperback editions available from various publishers

First published 1869

"Humorous account of a voyage through the Mediterranean and travel in the bordering countries." Carnegie Libr of Pittsburgh

817.008   American satire and humor—Collections

Fireside treasury of new humor; edited by Al Sarrantonio. Simon & Schuster 1989 328p $22.95   **817.008**

1. American wit and humor 2. English wit and humor

ISBN 0-671-68380-2   LC 89-1599

Companion volume to Fireside treasury of humor (1987)

"A Fireside book"

This book "draws together many of today's bestselling humorists, as well as a few lesser-known yet talented writers. Among those represented here are Art Buchwald, Doug Kenney, Martin Mull, Jonathan Winters, Bob and Ray, Dave Barry, Garrison Keillor, Stephanie Brush, Tom Bodett, Fran Lebowitz, and Cynthia Heimel." Libr J

Russell Baker's book of American humor; edited by Russell Baker. Norton 1993 598p il $30
817.008

1. American wit and humor

ISBN 0-393-03592-1   LC 93-22733

"Two hundred years of American humor have gone into the making of this anthology. . . . In the lineup are many of the old pros—Mark Twain, Fred Allen, James Thurber—and several relative newcomers—Fran Lebowitz, Nora Ephron, P.J. O'Rourke, and Dave Barry. The selections are nicely assorted in substance and are arranged by theme rather than chronology." Libr J

Includes bibliographical references

818   American miscellany

Abbey, Edward, 1927-1989
The serpents of paradise; a reader; edited by John Macrae. Holt & Co. 1995 400p $25   **818**

ISBN 0-8050-3132-4   LC 94-44065

"A John Macrae book"

The editor has organized these "essays, travel pieces, and works of fiction to parallel events in Abbey's unusual life. Since everything Abbey wrote was autobiographical no matter what literary form it took, a biographical structure is the ideal context for a sampling of his work. His fiction is represented by excerpts from several of his novels, . . while his nonfiction, usually considered his strongest and most influential writing, is culled from many sources." Booklist

Includes bibliographical references

Amory, Cleveland

The cat and the curmudgeon; illustrations by Lisa Adams. Little, Brown 1990 295p il hardcover o.p. paperback available $10.95   **818**
ISBN 0-316-03745-1 (pa)   LC 90-6419
Also available G.K. Hall large print edition
"Amory pokes great fun at himself while heaping praise upon his beloved cat. Although most of the anecdotes are humorous, light reading, the section on cruelty to animals by individuals and institutions is serious. Students would find this chapter . . . useful for debates or reports, while the further adventures of this entertaining duo will please animal lovers." SLJ

The cat who came for Christmas; illustrations by Edith Allard. Little, Brown 1987 240p il $22.95   **818**
ISBN 0-316-03737-0   LC 87-3258
Also available in paperback from Penguin Bks.
This is the "story of a white cat rescued by Amory one Christmas Eve. Struggling to understand his feline friend, he becomes devoted to a degree that not everyone will understand. An animal rights activist, Amory shares his feelings about veterinarians, airlines, hotels, human and animal natures, and the complexities of modern life." Libr J

Baker, Russell, 1925-

There's a country in my cellar; the best of Russell Baker. Morrow 1990 432p o.p.; Avon Bks. paperback available $8.95   **818**
ISBN 0-380-71451-5 (pa)   LC 90-36699
"Baker has selected . . . 137 of 3800 or so of his 'Observer' columns, written for the [New York] Times between 1963 and 1989." Libr J

The Best of the West; an anthology of classic writing from the American West; edited by Tony Hillerman. HarperCollins Pubs. 1991 528p hardcover o.p. paperback available $16   **818**
1. West (U.S.) in literature
ISBN 0-06-092352-0 (pa)   LC 90-55930
This anthology's "nonfiction sources run from 500 B.C. to the late nineteenth century; fictional selections by Harte, Crane, Scarborough, Davis, Stegner, and Norris are included. . . . Hillerman's subject groupings (e.g., explorers, settlers, Navajos, Hispanics, cowboys, miners, women, travel, and the military) make sense, and his juxtapositions encourage a thoughtful response." Booklist

Bohner, Charles H., 1927-1995

Robert Penn Warren; by Charles Bohner. rev ed. Twayne Pubs. 1981 por (Twayne's United States authors series) $22.95   **818**
1. Warren, Robert Penn, 1905-1989
ISBN 0-8057-7345-2   LC 81-4269
Also available in paperback from New College & Univ. Press
First published 1964
The author's "study traces Warren's literary career, charts the development of his art, and analyzes the themes that have recurred throughout his poetry and prose for more than 40 years." Booklist
Includes bibliography

Bowden, Mary Weatherspoon

Washington Irving. Twayne Pubs. 1981 201p (Twayne's United States authors series) $21.95   **818**
1. Irving, Washington, 1783-1859
ISBN 0-8057-7314-2   LC 80-21364
This study incorporates biographical information with a critical discussion of Irving's essays, histories and biographies
Includes bibliography

Buranelli, Vincent

Edgar Allan Poe. 2nd ed. Twayne Pubs. 1977 166p (Twayne's United States authors series) $21.95   **818**
1. Poe, Edgar Allan, 1809-1849
ISBN 0-8057-7189-1   LC 77-7265
Also available in paperback from Macmillan
First published 1961
The author discusses the short stories, poetry and criticism as well as parts of Poe's life which had a direct bearing on his work
Includes bibliography

Cather, Willa, 1873-1947

Stories, poems, and other writings. Library of Am. 1992 1039p $35   **818**
ISBN 0-940450-71-2   LC 91-62294
This volume contains the novels Alexander's bridge (1912) and My mortal enemy (1926); the poetry collection April twilights, and other poems (1923); the essay collection Not under forty (1936); and the following short story collections: Youth and the bright Medusa (1920); Obscure destinies (1932); The old beauty, and others (1948); and uncollected stories from 1892-1929

Crane, Stephen, 1871-1900

Prose and poetry. Library of Am. 1984 1379p $35   **818**
ISBN 0-940450-17-8   LC 83-19908
Edited by J. C. Levenson
"Maggie: a girl of the streets; The red badge of courage; Stories, sketches, and journalism; Poetry." Title page
"This collection also includes both Crane's collections of epigrammatic free verses—'The Black Riders' and 'War is kind'—and selections from his uncollected poems." Publisher's note
Includes bibliographical references

Critical essays on Henry David Thoreau's Walden; [edited by] Joel Myerson. Hall, G.K. & Co. 1988 254p (Critical essays on American literature) $47   **818**
1. Thoreau, Henry David, 1817-1862. Walden
ISBN 0-8161-8885-8   LC 88-1818
Scholars discuss Thoreau's classic from both philosophical and literary perspectives
Includes bibliographies

Critical essays on Washington Irving; [edited by] Ralph M. Aderman. Hall, G.K. & Co. 1990 276p (Critical essays on American literature) $47   **818**
1. Irving, Washington, 1783-1859
ISBN 0-8161-8896-3   LC 90-35739
A collection of critical essays on Irving's essays, historical writings, biographies, tales, and humorous pieces
Includes bibliographical references

Crowder, Richard
Carl Sandburg. Twayne Pubs. 1964 176p (Twayne's United States authors series) $21.95
                                               818
1. Sandburg, Carl, 1878-1967
ISBN 0-8057-0648-8
"The object of this present book is five-fold: (1) to give the details of Sandburg's life that are relevant to his writing, (2) to summarize the prose and sample the verse content of his books; (3) to review the critics' reception of each major work; (4) to analyze the themes and the craftsmanship in each volume; and (5) to appraise Sandburg's achievement." Preface
Includes bibliography

Cullen, Countee, 1903-1946
My soul's high song; the collected writings of Countee Cullen, voice of the Harlem Renaissance; edited with an introduction by Gerald L. Early. Doubleday 1991 618p hardcover o.p. paperback available $14.95   **818**
ISBN 0-385-41295-9 (pa)   LC 90-40926
This compilation includes "an extensive selection of Cullen's poetry, his one novel (*One Way to Heaven,* 1932), his translation of the Greek tragedy *Medea,* as well as essays, travel pieces, and speeches. . . . Gerald Early's lengthy but trenchant introduction places Cullen in the context of black writing of the time and spells out his specialness." Booklist
Includes bibliography

Dillard, Annie
The Annie Dillard reader. HarperCollins Pubs. 1994 455p $25; pa $14   **818**
ISBN 0-06-017158-8; 0-06-092660-0 (pa)
                                       LC 94-19482
This reader includes Holy the firm; excerpts from Pilgrim at Tinker Creek, An American childhood, and Teaching a stone to talk; and a reworked version of her 1978 short story The living
"This selection of writings, chosen by Dillard herself, provides a perfect sampling of her incisive, versatile, and impeccable achievements." Booklist

Pilgrim at Tinker Creek. Harper & Row 1974 271p hardcover o.p. paperback available $13 **818**
1. Natural history—Virginia
ISBN 0-06-091545-5 (pa)
Starting with January, Dillard "records the seasons as they come and go at Tinker Creek in Virginia." Time
This work is "in an honored tradition of literature, not quite environmentalism and not the philosophy of sci-

ence, it is rather the refraction of natural philosophy through the prismatic conscience of art. Highly recommended for the general reader—any general reader, anywhere—who wishes to deepen his awareness of his yard of world and to reflect upon it more profoundly." Choice

Du Bois, W. E. B. (William Edward Burghardt), 1868-1963
Writings. Library of Am. 1986 1334p $35
                                               818
ISBN 0-940450-33-X   LC 86-10565
Edited by Nathan Huggins
Contents: The suppression of the African slave-trade; The souls of black folk; Dusk of dawn; Essays; Articles from The cirisis
Includes bibliography

Eliot, T. S. (Thomas Stearns), 1888-1965
The complete poems and plays, 1909-1950. Harcourt Brace Jovanovich 1952 392p $30   **818**
ISBN 0-15-121185-X
This book is made up of six individual titles formerly published separately: Collected poems (1909-1935); Four quartets; Old Possum's book of practical cats; Murder in the cathedral; Family reunion; Cocktail party

Emanuel, James A.
Langston Hughes. Twayne Pubs. 1967 192p (Twayne's United States authors series) $21.95
                                               818
1. Hughes, Langston, 1902-1967
ISBN 0-8053-0388-8
"The chapters have been arranged to present, first, a comprehensive biographical and literary survey of Hughes to 1960, in order to provide a broad understanding of the author's main achievements in all genres, and of events and individuals that helped to mold his purposes. Subsequent chapters resort to analysis in depth of the most revealing works." Preface

Emerson, Ralph Waldo, 1803-1882
Essays & lectures. Library of Am. 1983 1321p $30   **818**
ISBN 0-940450-15-1   LC 83-5447
Edited by Joel Porte
Contents: Nature; Addresses and lectures; Essays, first and second series; Representative men; English traits; The conduct of life; Uncollected prose
Includes bibliography

The portable Emerson. [rev ed], edited by Carl Bode in collaboration with Malcolm Cowley. Penguin Bks. 1981 xxxix, 670p pa $14.95   **818**
ISBN 0-14-015094-3   LC 81-4047
"The Viking portable library"
First published 1946 by Viking and analyzed in Essay and general literature index
The editors have provided the following selections: essays, including History, Self-reliance, The over-soul, Circles and The poet; The complete texts of Nature and English traits; biographical essays on Plato, Napoleon, Henry David Thoreau, Thomas Carlyle, and others as well as twenty-two poems
Includes bibliography

Fleming, Robert E. (Robert Edward), 1936-
James Weldon Johnson. Twayne Pubs. 1987 123p il (Twayne's United States authors series) lib bdg $22.95 **818**
1. Johnson, James Weldon, 1871-1938
ISBN 0-8057-7491-2 LC 86-31824
An examination of the life and works of the poet, novelist, and civil rights leader
Includes bibliography

Frost, Robert, 1874-1963
Collected poems, prose, & plays. Library of Am. 1995 1036p $35 **818**
ISBN 1-883011-06-X LC 94-43693
This volume contains "all of the plays, a generous selection of prose, all collected poems, and 94 uncollected poems, as well as 17 poems that were previously unpublished." Libr J

Gerber, John C.
Mark Twain. Twayne Pubs. 1988 176p (Twayne's United States authors series) $21.95 **818**
1. Twain, Mark, 1835-1910
ISBN 0-8057-7518-8 LC 87-28816
A critical assessment of the novelist, short-story writer and humorist
Includes bibliography

Henry David Thoreau; edited and with an introduction by Harold Bloom. Chelsea House 1987 276p (Modern critical views) $29.95 **818**
1. Thoreau, Henry David, 1817-1862
ISBN 0-87754-697-5 LC 86-31020
Stanley Cavell, Loren Eiseley and Walter Ben Michaels are among the contributors who discuss Thoreau's language, narrative technique and philosophy
Includes bibliography

Hughes, Langston, 1902-1967
The return of Simple; edited by Akiba Sullivan Harper; introduction by Arnold Rampersad. Hill & Wang 1994 xxii, 218p $20; pa $9.95 **818**
ISBN 0-8090-8676-X; 0-8090-1582-X (pa)
LC 93-45373
This collection brings together the "narrations of the fictional Jesse B. Semple, or 'Simple,' which first appeared in 1943 in [Hughes'] column in the *Chicago Defender*

Hurston, Zora Neale, 1891-1960
Folklore, memoirs, and other writings. Library of Am. 1995 1001p il $35 **818**
ISBN 0-940450-84-4 LC 94-21384
Companion volume to Novels and stories, entered in Fiction section
"This is the first time the unexpurgated version of Hurston's 1942 autobiography, *Dust Tracks on the Road*, is being published; sections deemed too provocative (dealing with politics, race, and sex) have been restored.

Mules and Men (1935) is a collection of African American folklore she gleaned on travels in the South, while *Tell My Horse* (1938) tenders her personal findings on African-based religion in Jamaica and Haiti. Additionally, 22 magazine and book articles with anthropological themes . . . that have never been gathered into book form are corralled here." Booklist

I love myself when I am laughing—and then again when I am looking mean and impressive; a Zora Neale Hurston reader; edited by Alice Walker; introduction by Mary Helen Washington. Feminist Press 1979 313p hardcover o.p. paperback available $14.95 **818**
ISBN 0-912670-66-5 (pa) LC 79-17582
This "anthology contains selections from Hurston's autobiographical works, collections of black American and West Indian folklore, essays, and fiction." Choice
Includes bibliographical references

Kerouac, Jack, 1922-1969
The portable Jack Kerouac; edited by Ann Charters. Viking 1995 xxv, 625p $27.95 **818**
ISBN 0-670-84957-X LC 94-20120
"Charters has chosen selections from each of Kerouac's 14 novels, which comprise a complex and evocative autobiographical series Kerouac called the Legend of Duluoz. . . . Charters has also included poetry from *San Francisco Blues* and *Book of Haikus*, as well as a group of essays that cover Kerouac's main passions and interests: writing, traveling, jazz, and Buddhism." Booklist
Includes bibliographical references

Langston Hughes: critical perspectives past and present; edited by Henry Louis Gates, Jr., and K.A. Appiah. Amistad Press 1993 255p (Amistad literary series) $24.95; pa $14.95 **818**
1. Hughes, Langston, 1902-1967
ISBN 1-56743-016-3; 1-56743-029-5 (pa)
LC 92-45756
A collection of critical writings about Hughes's poetry, novels, short stories and other works. The first part contains reviews by Countee Cullen, Richard Wright, James Baldwin, and others. The second part of the book consists of ten critical essays
Includes bibliography

London, Jack, 1876-1916
The portable Jack London; edited by Earle Labor. Penguin Bks. 1994 xxxvii, 563p pa $13.95 **818**
ISBN 0-14-017969-0 LC 93-38740
This volume contains selected short stories, the complete text of The call of the wild, personal letters, and a sampling of journalistic pieces
Includes bibliographical references

The **Mark** Twain encyclopedia; editors, J.R. LeMaster, James D. Wilson; editorial and research assistant, Christie Graves Hamric. Garland 1993 xxx, 848p (Garland reference library of the humanities) $95   **818**
1. Twain, Mark, 1835-1910
ISBN 0-8240-7212-X   LC 92-45662
This "reference guide consists of approximately 740 signed articles by noted authorities. The articles cover all aspects of Twain's life. . . . Each article includes a bibliography. There are a detailed chronology of Twain's life and a lengthy Clemens genealogy." Am Libr
"This carefully conceived, meticulously edited, and admirably executed compendium could serve as a model for encyclopedias on individual authors." Booklist

Rasmussen, R. Kent
Mark Twain A to Z; the essential reference to his life and writings; foreword by Thomas A. Tenney. Facts on File 1995 xxiv, 552p il maps $45   **818**
1. Twain, Mark, 1835-1910
ISBN 0-8160-2845-1   LC 94-39156
"The nearly 1,300 entries are devoted primarily to proper names relating to Twain, including titles of all of his major and many of his minor works; characters and fictional locales; his family, friends, and associates; places he lived or visited; publishers and illustrators of his works; and periodicals in which he published. . . . The most extensive entries are those devoted to Twain's more widely read works. Each of these provides an introduction to the work (including a word count), a chapter-by-chapter synopsis, and a publication history." Booklist
Includes bibliographical references

Steinbeck, John, 1902-1968
The grapes of wrath and other writings, 1936-1941. Library of Am. 1996 1067p $35 **818**
ISBN 1-883011-15-9   LC 96-3725
This volume contains the short story collection The long valley (1938) and the novel The grapes of wrath (entered in Fiction section). Also included is The log from the Sea of Cortez (1941) Steinbeck's narrative about marine research in the Gulf of California and The harvest gypsies, a series of newspaper articles on migrant labor that was published with title Their blood is strong (1938)

The portable Steinbeck; revised, selected and introduced by Pascal Covici, Jr. Viking 1971 xlii, 692p o.p.; Penguin Bks. paperback available $14.95   **818**
1. Short stories
ISBN 0-14-015002-1 (pa)
"The Viking portable library"
First published 1943 with title: Steinbeck
A collection of the author's works, mainly fiction, some complete, some excerpted
A sampling of the titles included are: The long valley; The Pastures of Heaven; Tortilla Flat; In dubious battle; Of Mice and men; The red pony; The grapes of wrath; Sea of Cortez; East of Eden; Travels with Charley in search of America; The language of awareness

Stephen Crane: a collection of critical essays. Prentice-Hall 1967 184p $12.95   **818**
1. Crane, Stephen, 1871-1900. The red badge of courage 2. Crane, Stephen, 1871-1900. Maggie: a girl of the streets 3. Crane, Stephen, 1871-1900
ISBN 0-13-188888-9
Analyzed in Essay and general literature index
"A Spectrum book. Twentieth century views"
Edited by Maurice Bassan
The essays in this book examine the structure and themes of Crane's prose and poetry, and provide psychological studies of the man
"A good collection of scholarly criticism for students and others familiar with the work of [this] American writer." Booklist
Includes bibliography

Thoreau, Henry David, 1817-1862
Walden   **818**

Hardcover and paperback editions available from various publishers
First published 1854
"Philosophy of life and observations of nature drawn from the author's solitary sojourn of two years in a cabin on Walden Pond near Concord, Massachusetts." Pratt Alcove

A week on the Concord and Merrimack rivers; Walden, or, Life in the woods; The Maine woods; Cape Cod. Library of Am. 1985 1114p il $30
                                            818
ISBN 0-940450-27-5   LC 85-5175
Edited by Robert F. Sayre
The first volume of a projected two volume set of Thoreau's work
"Politically the most conscious of the Transcendentalists, an acute observer of natural and social facts, Thoreau was an outstanding prose stylist." Reader's Ency. 4th edition
Includes bibliography

Thurber, James, 1894-1961
Writings and drawings. Library of Am. 1996 1004p il $35   **818**
1. American wit and humor
ISBN 1-883011-22-1   LC 96-5853
Edited by Garrison Keillor
Includes the complete texts of The seal in the bedroom (1932), the autobiography My life and hard times (1933); the anti-war parable The last flower (1939) and the children's tale The 13 clocks (1950)
"These stories, parodies, reminiscences, cartoons, and drawings present Thurber's unique and masterful take on work, psychotherapy, fantasizing, domesticity, and the battle between the sexes." Booklist

Twain, Mark, 1835-1910
Life on the Mississippi   **818**
1. Mississippi River valley
Hardcover and paperback editions available from various publishers
First published 1874

Twain, Mark, 1835-1910—*Continued*
Mark Twains's famous account of life on the Mississippi in the old steamboat days and his own experiences as a pilot
"Its historical sketches, its frequent passages of vivid description, and its humorous episodes combine to make [this] a masterpiece of the literature of the Middle West." Eng and Pope's What to Read

Roughing it   **818**
1. Hawaii—Description 2. West (U.S.)—Description
Hardcover and paperback editions available from various publishers
First published 1872
A humorous account of a trip across the plains to California and then to Hawaii in the early 1860's

Wharton, Edith, 1862-1937
Novellas and other writings. Library of Am. 1990 1137p il $35   **818**
ISBN 0-940450-53-4   LC 89-62930
This volume contains the following novelettes: Madame de Troyes (1907); Ethan Frome (1911); Summer (1917); The mother's recompense (1925). Old New York (1924) is a collection of four novelettes: False dawn; The old maid; The spark; New Year's day. Also included is the autobiographical A backward glance (1934)
Includes bibliographical references

White, E. B. (Elwyn Brooks), 1899-1985
Poems and sketches of E. B. White. Harper & Row 1981 217p o.p.   **818**
LC 81-47240
"In this companion to his 'Essays' (1977) [entered in class 814] and 'Letters' (1976) E. B. White offers us a . . . collection of sketches, parodies, stories, and poems. Many of the items have never been collected, and a few were previously unpublished." Libr J

Whitman, Walt, 1819-1892
Poetry and prose. Library of Am. 1996 1407p $16.95   **818**
ISBN 1-883011-35-3   LC 95-52466
"Library of America college editions"
Revised edition of: Complete poetry and collected prose (1982)
Contents: Leaves of grass (1855); Leaves of grass (1891-92); Supplementary poems; Complete prose works (1892); Supplementary prose

Wright, Richard, 1908-1960
Works. Library of Am. 1991 2v ea $35   **818**
1. African Americans—Fiction
ISBN 0-940450-66-6 (v1); 0-940450-67-4 (v2)
LC 91-60540
Contents: v1 Early works; v2 Later works
This set contains the complete novels Native son; The outsider (1953); and Lawd today! (1963); the story collection Uncle Tom's children; and the memoir Black boy

Yannella, Donald
Ralph Waldo Emerson. Twayne Pubs. 1982 147p (Twayne's United States authors series) $21.95   **818**
1. Emerson, Ralph Waldo, 1803-1882
ISBN 0-8057-7344-4   LC 81-20321
The author "provides an overview of Emerson's career, a chronological assessment of his essays and poems, biographical information, a discussion of transcendentalism as a cultural movement, an appraisal of Emerson's place in American literary history, and a bibliography of where to go for more information." Booklist

820.3 English literature— Encyclopedias and dictionaries

The **Cambridge** guide to literature in English; [edited by] Ian Ousby; foreword by Doris Lessing. new ed. Cambridge Univ. Press 1993 1054p il $49.95   **820.3**
1. English literature—Dictionaries 2. English literature—Bio-bibliography 3. American literature—Dictionaries 4. American literature—Bio-bibliography
ISBN 0-521-44086-6   LC 93-7941
First published 1988
"A handbook to the literature in English produced by all English speaking cultures. . . . Includes entries for authors, major individual works, and genres, movements, groups, critical concepts, etc. Attempts to be very current and includes a number of living authors. Also has black-and-white illustrations." Guide to Ref Books. 11th edition

Dictionary of British literary characters; edited by John R. Greenfield; associate editor, David Brailow, with the assistance of Arlyn Bruccoli. Facts on File 1993 2v set $115   **820.3**
1. English fiction—Dictionaries 2. Characters and characteristics in literature
ISBN 0-8160-2178-3   LC 90-3998
"A Bruccoli Clark Layman book"
Contents: v1 18th- and 19th-century novels; v2 20th century novels
Each volume covers the major and minor characters of some 500 novels published during the period indicated. Arranged alphabetically by characters' names, each entry identifies the work in which the character appeared, the character's role in the novel, and the character's significance to the plot

Dictionary of fictional characters. Completely rev ed, [by] Martin Seymour-Smith. Writer 1992 c1991 598p $18.95   **820.3**
1. English literature—Dictionaries 2. American literature—Dictionaries 3. Characters and characteristics in literature
ISBN 0-87116-166-4   LC 92-5025
First published 1963 under the authorship of William Freeman
This work identifies characters from English and American novels, short stories, poems, plays, and operas. The main section arranges entries alphabetically by name of character giving for each the entrant's relationship to main characters in the work, the title of the work, publication date, and author

The **Oxford** companion to English literature; edited by Margaret Drabble. Oxford Univ. Press $55   **820.3**
1. English literature—Dictionaries 2. English literature—Bio-bibliography 3. American literature—Dictionaries 4. American literature—Bio-bibliography
ISBN 0-19-866221-1
Also available in a concise edition pa $14.95
First published 1932 under the editorship of Sir Paul Harvey. (revised 5th edition 1995) Periodically revised
Includes entries for literary authors, works, critics, movements, terminology, fictional characters, significant non literary figures and important periodicals. A literary chronology is appended

The **Oxford** companion to twentieth-century literature in English; edited by Jenny Stringer; with an introduction by John Sutherland. Oxford Univ. Press 1996 xxi, 751p $45   **820.3**
1. English literature—Dictionaries 2. English literature—Bio-bibliography 3. American literature—Dictionaries 4. American literature—Bio-bibliography 5. Commonwealth of Nations literature (English)—Dictionaries
ISBN 0-19-212271-1   LC 96-26699
"The 3,000 entries in this compilation cover English-language writers and writing from Africa, Asia, Australia, the Caribbean, New Zealand, Canada, the U.S., the United Kingdom, and Ireland. Author entries, which number approximately 2,400, are devoted primarily to novelists, playwrights, and poets, but nonfiction writers are also represented. . . . Of the remaining entries, 400 treat significant works, while the rest pertain to literary groups, movements, or genre, periodicals, and critical concepts." Booklist

Reference guide to English literature. 2nd ed, editor, D.L. Kirkpatrick. St. James Press 1991 3v set $295   **820.3**
1. English literature—Bio-bibliography 2. English literature—History and criticism 3. Authors, English—Dictionaries
ISBN 1-55862-080-X   LC 91-61857
First published 1985 in eight volumes with title: St. James reference guide to English literature
"This set excludes 20th-century American authors and focuses on English-language writers of Great Britain, Ireland, Canada, Australia, New Zealand, Africa, Asia, and the Caribbean. Includes introductory essays and suggested readings for periods and genres. Entries for 894 individual authors include brief biographical data, a list of publications, a bibliography of book-length critical studies . . . and a succinct critical essay." Guide to Ref Books. 11th edition

820.8   English literature— Collections

British women writers; an anthology from the fourteenth century to the present; edited by Dale Spender and Janet Todd. Bedrick Bks. 1990 c1989 925p $39.95; pa $19.95   **820.8**
1. English literature—Women authors—Collections
ISBN 0-87226-326-6; 0-87226-216-2 (pa)
LC 89-6572
This chronologically arranged collection "brings together established literary figures and less familiar writers from the Middle Ages to the present day. . . . The anthology includes poems, plays, short stories, extracts from novels, diaries, letters, autobiography and journalism." Publisher's note
Includes bibliography

The **Irish**; a treasury of art and literature; edited by Leslie Conron Carola. Levin Assocs. 1993 368p il $75; pa $24.95   **820.8**
1. Irish literature—Collections 2. Irish art
ISBN 0-88363-393-0; 0-88363-701-4 (pa)
A "cultural survey of Ireland and the Irish from prehistory to the 20th century. Selections are drawn from over 100 previously published sources: books, journals, documents, letters, diaries, speeches, folk songs, and poems, including many delightful character sketches and excerpts from the works of Shaw, Synge, Yeats, Swift, Goldsmith, Sean O'Casey, and Eugene O'Neill. . . . Over 200 lavish illustrations, many from the National Gallery, complement the text nicely. . . . An effective introduction to the country, a visual joy, and delightful browsing, this is recommended for general collections." Libr J

The **Norton** anthology of literature by women; the traditions in English; [compiled by] Sandra M. Gilbert, Susan Gubar. 2nd ed. Norton 1996 xxxviii, 2452p pa $43.95   **820.8**
1. American literature—Women authors—Collections 2. English literature—Women authors—Collections
ISBN 0-393-96825-1   LC 96-5751
First published 1985
The editors provide representative selections of prose and poetry by women. Period introductions, biographical headnotes and bibliographies are provided

The **Oxford** anthology of English literature; general editors: Frank Kermode and John Hollander. Oxford Univ. Press 1973 6v in 2 il maps hardcover o.p. paperback available ea $32   **820.8**
1. English literature—Collections
ISBN 0-19-501657-2 (v1); 0-19-501658-0 (v2)
Each of the six parts collected here were published separately and are available in paperback at prices indicated below
Contents: v1 The Middle Ages through the eighteenth century: Medieval English literature, edited by J. B. Trapp $19.95 (ISBN 0-19-501624-6); The literature of Renaissance England, edited by John Hollander and Frank Kermode $19.95 (ISBN 0-19-501637-8); The Restoration and the eighteenth century, edited by Martin

The Oxford anthology of English literature—
Continued
Price $19.95 (ISBN 0-19-501614-9); v2 1800 to the present: Romantic poetry and prose, edited by Harold Bloom and Lionel Trilling $19.95 (ISBN 0-19-501615-7); Victorian prose and poetry, edited by Lionel Trilling and Harold Bloom $18.95 (ISBN 0-19-501616-5); Modern British literature, edited by Frank Kermode and John Hollander $19.95 (ISBN 0-19-501652-1)

820.9 English literature—History and criticism

Burrow, J. A. (John Anthony)
Medieval writers and their work; Middle English literature and its background, 1100-1500. Oxford Univ. Press 1982 148p hardcover o.p. paperback available $15.95   **820.9**
1. Medieval literature—History and criticism 2. English literature—History and criticism
ISBN 0-19-289122-7 (pa)   LC 81-16967
This book concentrates on "some of the chief differences which confront a reader of modern literature when he first approaches [Middle English writings:] differences in the notion of literature itself (Chapter 1), in the circumstances under which writings were produced and received (Chapter 2), in the types of writing produced (Chapter 3), and in the kinds of meaning to be found in them (Chapter 4). Chapters 1 and 5 also attempt to characterize the Middle English period in relation to earlier and later periods of English literature." Preface
Includes bibliography

The Feminist companion to literature in English; women writers from the Middle Ages to the present; [edited by] Virginia Blain, Patricia Clements, Isobel Grundy. Yale Univ. Press 1990 1231p $60   **820.9**
1. English literature—Women authors—Bio-bibliography 2. American literature—Women authors—Bio-bibliography
ISBN 0-300-04854-8   LC 90-70515
"Over 2,700 biographical entries, most of about 500 words, seek to set each writer in the context of her time and to intimate her relevance to us today." Am Libr

Larousse dictionary of literary characters; editor, Rosemary Goring. Larousse (London); distributed by Larousse Kingfisher Chambers 1994 849p $35; pa $17.95   **820.9**
1. Characters and characteristics in literature—Dictionaries
ISBN 0-7523-0001-6; 0-7523-0037-7 (pa)
                                           LC 94-75740
This dictionary contains over 6500 entries for major characters from novels, poems, and plays written in English. Each character's occupation, personality and role are discussed
For a review see: Booklist, Feb. 15, 1995

Modern British literature; compiled and edited by Ruth Z. Temple, Martin Tucker. Ungar 1966-1985 5v (Library of literary criticism) v1-4 op, v5 $75   **820.9**
1. English literature—History and criticism
ISBN v5 0-8044-3140-X
Contents: v 1 A-G; v2 H-P; v3 R-Z; v4 Supplement, compiled and edited by Martin Tucker and Rita Stein; v5 Second supplement, compiled and edited by Denis Lane and Rita Stein
"For each of the authors included, excerpts from criticism have been chosen to describe his qualities, define his status, indicate, if he is well known, something of his life and personality. . . . Excerpts have been selected, and are arranged in chronological order, to show the rise and sometimes fall of fame or favor." Introduction
The supplementary volume brings criticism up to date on approximately one-third of the authors entered in the 3 main volumes. The second supplementary volume brings criticism up to date covering the years 1975 onward. Each of the 5 volumes includes bibliographies and an index to critics

The New Moulton's library of literary criticism; general editor, Harold Bloom. Chelsea House 1985-1990 11v (Chelsea House library of literary criticism) set $770   **820.9**
1. Criticism 2. English literature—History and criticism 3. American literature—History and criticism
ISBN 0-87754-778-5
Individual volumes also available separately at $70 each
Replaces The Library of literary criticism of English and American authors (also known as Moulton's library of literary criticism) and The Library of literary criticism of English and American authors through the beginning of the twentieth century
"Provides excerpts from criticism written before the 20th century concerning 532 authors and anonymous works written from the 8th century up to 1904. Entries, which include biographies as well as critical information, are arranged chronologically by death date within each volume. Figures covered include nonliterary authors (e.g., Thomas Jefferson, Charles Darwin). Vol. II contains bibliographical references and author and critic indexes for the entire set." Guide to Ref Books. 11th edition

The Oxford companion to Irish literature; edited by Robert Welch, assistant editor, Bruce Stewart. Oxford Univ. Press 1996 xxv, 614p maps $49.95   **820.9**
1. Irish literature—Dictionaries 2. Irish literature—Bio-bibliography
ISBN 0-19-866158-4   LC 95-44943
Encompassing "Ireland's literary heritage from the bardic poets and Celtic sagas to twentieth-century authors like Brian Friel, Edna O'Brien, and Nuala Ní Dhomhnaill, the more than 2,000 unsigned entries cover writers, titles of major works, literary genres and motifs, folklore, mythology, periodicals, associations, and historical figures and events." Booklist

Sanders, Andrew
The short Oxford history of English literature. Oxford Univ. Press 1994 678p $39.95; pa $16.95
820.9

1. English literature—History and criticism
ISBN 0-19-811202-5; 0-19-811201-7 (pa)
LC 93-32330

Designed to replace Emile Legouis's A short history of English literature (1934), Sanders's "book has ten major chapters covering Old English, medieval, Renaissance, Shakespearean, 17th-and-18th-century, Romantic, Victorian, Modern, and postwar literature. Innovative essays include 'Women's Writing in the Restoration' and 'The New Morality,' which examines the 1970s and 1980s." Libr J
Includes bibliographical references

821 English poetry

Auden, W. H. (Wystan Hugh), 1907-1973
Auden; poems; selected by Edward Mendelson. Knopf 1995 256p (Everyman's library pocket poets) $10.95
821
ISBN 0-679-44367-3
A representative selection of lyrics that span the influential poet's career

Collected poems; edited by Edward Mendelson. Vintage Bks. 1991 xxvii, 926p pa $22.50
821
ISBN 0-679-73197-0
LC 91-158031
Originally published in hardcover in different form by Random House in 1976
A compilation of all the poems Auden wished to preserve, in his final revisions. Previous collected editions and later shorter poems are included. There is also an absurdist play written 1928: Paid on both sides

Bentman, Raymond
Robert Burns. Twayne Pubs. 1987 155p (Twayne's English authors series) lib bdg $22.95
821

1. Burns, Robert, 1759-1796
ISBN 0-8057-6952-8
LC 87-8554
A critical introduction to the renowned 18th century Scottish poet and songwriter
Includes bibliography

Blake, William, 1757-1827
Poems. Knopf 1994 283p (Everyman's library pocket poets) $10.95
821
ISBN 0-679-43633-2
A collection of representative and epic poems by the visionary Romantic poet, painter and engraver

Brontë, Emily, 1818-1848
Brontë: poems. Knopf 1996 255p (Everyman's library pocket poets) $12.50
821
ISBN 0-679-44725-3
A representative selection of Brontë's poetical output including many of her mythical works

No coward soul is mine; poems. Odessa 1993 172p il lib bdg $21.95
821
ISBN 0-9634340-0-4
LC 93-239756
A representative selection of Brontë's poetic work. "Included are 33 Gondal poems, based on the imaginary Kingdom of Gondal invented by Emily and Anne Brontë. . . . This collection is recommended for libraries that have little of Brontë's poetry." Libr J

Browning, Elizabeth Barrett, 1806-1861
The poetical works of Elizabeth Barrett Browning; with a new introduction by Ruth M. Adams. Houghton Mifflin 1974 xxii, 548p o.p.
821

"Cambridge editions"
First published 1900 with title: The complete poetical works of Elizabeth Barrett Browning
This collection "does not carry a full biographical sketch of Elizabeth Barrett Browning. . . . Rather the Introduction identifies that part of the poetry which has proved of lasting value or interest, considers two major achievements, 'Sonnets from the Portuguese' and 'Aurora Leigh,' and estimates the place that Elizabeth Barrett Browning may be expected to claim in a reader's attention and in poetic evaluation." Editor's note
Includes indexes of first lines and titles

Sonnets from the Portuguese
821

Hardcover and paperback editions available from various publishers
A series of sonnets which "were written during a period of seven years and are considered by some scholars to have been inspired by her love for her husband [poet Robert Browning]." New Cent Handb of Engl Lit

Browning, Robert, 1812-1889
The poetical works of Robert Browning; with a new introduction by G. Robert Stange. Houghton Mifflin 1974 1032p o.p.
821

"Cambridge editions"
Based on the 1895 Cambridge edition, The complete poetic and dramatic works of Robert Browning, this book also contains a chronology of Browning's life, notes, index of first lines, and an essay on Shelley

Robert Browning's poetry; authoritative texts, criticism; selected and edited by James F. Loucks. Norton 1980 c1979 604p hardcover o.p. paperback available $17.95
821
ISBN 0-393-09092-2 (pa)
LC 79-10295
"A Norton critical edition"
"Editor Loucks has chosen wisely from Browning's prodigious output (filling 12 volumes in the 'complete' edition), with selections covering the early 'experimental phase' as well as the interesting, though less studied, years of 'later achievement,' but with a greater part of his emphasis upon the poet's middle and major period (1855-69)." Booklist
Includes bibliography

Burns, Robert, 1759-1796
The poetical works of Burns; edited by Raymond Bentman. Houghton Mifflin 1974 xxxii, 414p $40 **821**

ISBN 0-395-18486-X
"Cambridge editions"
First published 1897 with title: Complete poetical works of Robert Burns
"The greatest of Scottish lyrical poets and song writers. He wrote mainly in dialect. His poems show warm passions and sympathies, and an intense love for man and nature." Pratt Alcove

Byron, George Gordon Byron, 6th Baron, 1788-1824
Byron; poems. Knopf 1994 288p (Everyman's library pocket poets) $10.95 **821**
ISBN 0-679-43630-8
A selection of lyric and dramatic poetry by the English Romantic poet and satirist

Carey, John, 1934-
John Donne, life, mind, and art. new ed. Faber & Faber 1990 303p pa $9.95 **821**
1. Donne, John, 1572-1631
ISBN 0-571-14337-7   LC 90-197663
First published 1981 by Oxford Univ. Press
This examination of Donne's achievement focuses on how his beliefs about the physical and organic world are reflected in his work
Includes bibliographical references

Chaucer, Geoffrey, d. 1400
The Canterbury tales   **821**

Hardcover and paperback editions available from various publishers
"A collection of twenty-four stories, all but two of which are in verse, written by Geoffrey Chaucer mainly between 1386 and his death in 1400. The stories are supposed to be related by members of a company of thirty-one pilgrims (including the poet himself) who are on their way to the shrine of St. Thomas at Canterbury. The prologue which tells of their assembly at the Tabard Inn in Southwark and their arrangement that each shall tell two stories on the way to Canterbury and two on the return journey, is a remarkable picture of English social life in the fourteenth century, inasmuch as every class is represented from the gentlefolks to the peasantry." Keller. Reader's Dig of Books

The portable Chaucer; selected, translated and edited by Theodore Morrison. rev ed. Viking 1975 611p o.p.; Penguin Bks. paperback available $14.95 **821**
ISBN 0-14-015081-1 (pa)
"The Viking portable library"
First published 1949
Contains selections from The Canterbury tales, The book of the duchess and The bird's parliament. The complete text of Troilus and Cressida is included as is selected verse
Includes bibliography

Critical essays on John Keats; [edited by] Hermione de Almeida. Hall, G.K. & Co. 1990 365p (Critical essays on British literature) $47 **821**

1. Keats, John, 1795-1821
ISBN 0-8161-8851-3   LC 89-71719
Scholars assess the achievement of the influential romantic poet and focus on such works as Ode on a Grecian urn, The eve of St. Agnes, and The fall of Hyperion
Includes bibliographical references

Critical essays on W.B. Yeats; [edited by] Richard J. Finneran. Hall, G.K. & Co. 1986 258p (Critical essays on modern British literature) $47 **821**
1. Yeats, W. B. (William Butler), 1865-1939
ISBN 0-8161-8758-4   LC 85-30207
"The volume is composed of essays by 14 leading Yeats scholars. . . . The text is supplemented by an annotated bibliography of earlier collections and a review of book-length studies on Yeats in general or his poetry, but (unfortunately) not his plays." Booklist

Critical essays on William Wordsworth; [edited by] George H. Gilpin. Hall, G.K. & Co. 1990 362p (Critical essays on British literature) $47 **821**

1. Wordsworth, William, 1770-1850
ISBN 0-8161-8774-6   LC 89-71694
Contributors analyze Wordsworth's work, critical theories and influence
Includes bibliographical references

De la Mare, Walter, 1873-1956
The collected poems of Walter de la Mare. Faber & Faber 1979 467p hardcover o.p. paperback available $19.95 **821**
ISBN 0-571-11382-6 (pa)   LC 79-670359
"A chronological arrangement of the enduring poems of de la Mare, excluding his poems for children . . . this definitive volume contains 598 pieces, including two long poems that had been published separately—'The traveler' (1945) and 'Winged Chariot' (1970). . . . This single volume encompasses all the poems that de la Mare wished to be remembered by; no poems are included from uncollected or unpublished works." Choice

Donne, John, 1572-1631
The complete English poems. Knopf 1991 569p $20 **821**
ISBN 0-679-40558-5   LC 91-52975
"Everyman's library"
A reissue of the 1985 Dent edition
Compiled by C. A. Patrides
A collection based primarily on early printed editions, with notes, variant readings, poems attributed to Donne, a bibliography, and title and first line indices
Includes bibliographical references

Gawain and the Grene Knight
Sir Gawain and the Green Knight   **821**

Hardcover and paperback editions available from various publishers

Gawain and the Grene Knight—*Continued*

"Combining a complex stanza-form with regular alliteration [Sir Gawain and the Green Knight] is a consciously literary poem written for a sophisticated audience. . . . It is best approached as an example of chivalric romance, whose theme is the knightly quest for perfection and self-knowledge, here illustrated in the testing of Gawain's courage through the 'Beheading Game' proposed by the mysterious Green Knight, and of his courtesy and chastity by the Lady of the castle. The poet combines humour and a light touch with a powerful evocation of the grotesque and savage." Penguin Companion to Engl Lit

Hallissy, Margaret

A companion to Chaucer's Canterbury tales. Greenwood Press 1995 333p il $49.95   **821**

1. Chaucer, Geoffrey, d. 1400. Canterbury tales

ISBN 0-313-29189-6   LC 95-16017

This work is "designed specifically for first-time readers. . . . It provides students with simple interpretations and amplifications and makes their journey through this great unfinished work enjoyable and rewarding. Particularly helpful are the opening sections on Chaucer's world and language. There are essays of explanation as well on each of the major tales." SLJ

Includes bibliographical references

Hardy, Thomas, 1840-1928

Poems. Knopf 1995 254p (Everyman's library pocket poets) $10.95   **821**

ISBN 0-679-44368-1

A representative selection of the English author's verse. An index of first lines is included

Heaney, Seamus

Selected poems, 1966-1987. Farrar, Straus & Giroux 1990 273p $30; pa $15   **821**

ISBN 0-374-25868-6; 0-374-52280-4 (pa)

This collection "offers an ample selection of some of the best work by one of our finest contemporary poets. . . . Readers will savor the author's rich Irish-English vocabulary, the sinuous power of his line, and his distinctive music." Libr J

Station Island. Farrar, Straus & Giroux 1985 123p $20; pa $12   **821**

ISBN 0-374-26978-5; 0-374-51935-8 (pa)

LC 84-21067

"The collection contains a wide range of material amounting to a thorough survey of all [Heaney's] principal concerns; the twelve poems of 'Station Island' involve him in an ordeal of confronting his origins and obligations, repeatedly through dramatically imagined encounters with the dead, who include the ghosts of Kavanagh and James Joyce. The book concludes with a new assertion of artistic freedom." Oxford Companion to 20th Cent Lit in Engl

The **Heinemann** book of African poetry in English; selected by Adewale Maja-Pearce. Heinemann Educ. Bks. 1990 224p pa $10.95

821

1. African poetry—Collections

ISBN 0-435-91323-9

This anthology of African poetry written in English "covers thirty years and contains 130 poems, grouped by author in chronological order of the authors' births (none later than 1961), with the intention of demonstrating the development of a tradition." New Statesman Soc

Includes bibliography

Hirst, Wolf Z.

John Keats. Twayne Pubs. 1981 194p il (Twayne's English authors series) $22.95   **821**

1. Keats, John, 1795-1821

ISBN 0-8057-6821-1   LC 81-1938

A look at the life, philosophy, and poetics of the influential romantic

Includes bibliography

Hopkins, Gerard Manley, 1844-1889

The poems of Gerard Manley Hopkins. 4th ed. Oxford Univ. Press 1967 lxvi, 362p $39.95; pa $19.95   **821**

ISBN 0-19-500164-8; 0-19-281094-4 (pa)

First published 1918 in the United Kingdom; 1948 in the United States

"Based on the first edition of 1918 and enlarged to incorporate all known poems and fragments; edited with additional notes, a foreword on the revised text, and a new biographical and critical introduction by W. H. Gardner and N. H. Mackenzie." Title page

This book brings together all the poems, including the early verses first published in the poet's "Journals and Papers" (1959), the remainder of his Latin verse together with translations into English of all the Latin poems which are entirely original compositions

Housman, A. E. (Alfred Edward), 1859-1936

The collected poems of A. E. Housman. Holt & Co. 1965 254p o.p.   **821**

Available in hardcover from Amereon and Buccaneer Bks.

This anthology "constitutes the authorized canon of A. E. Housman's verse as established in 1939." Note on the text

This collection includes A Shropshire lad (1896), Last poems (1922), and More poems (1936)

Includes indexes of titles and first lines

Hughes, Ted, 1930-

New selected poems. Harper & Row 1982 242p hardcover o.p. paperback available $17   **821**

ISBN 0-06-090925-0 (pa)   LC 80-8207

"Nearly half of this book is a reprint of Hughes' 'Selected Poems, 1957-1967' [o.p.]; the rest is drawn from his brilliant fourth collection, 'Crow' and from five other books published in the past decade—more than 150 pieces all together, but no new, previously unpublished poems." Libr J

John Dryden; edited and with an introduction by Harold Bloom. Chelsea House 1987 234p (Modern critical views) $29.95 **821**
1. Dryden, John, 1631-1700
ISBN 1-55546-277-4   LC 86-34306

A collection of twelve critical essays on the work of Dryden, arranged in chronological order of original publication

Includes bibliography

Keats, John, 1795-1821
Poems. Knopf 1994 253p (Everyman's library pocket poets) $10.95 **821**
ISBN 0-679-43319-8   LC 94-2495

A representative collection by the influential English romantic

Poetical works; edited by H. W. Garrod. Oxford Univ. Press 1956 xxviii, 477p (Oxford standard authors) hardcover o.p. paperback available $19.95 **821**

ISBN 0-19-281067-7 (pa)

"Keats wrote a surprisingly large body of poetry before his early death, and practically all the finished poems of the 1818-19 group are the work of a mature poet, and a few of them, such as the magnificent 'To Autumn,' are among the finest examples of English lyric poetry." Reader's Ency. 4th edition

Kipling, Rudyard, 1865-1936
Complete verse; definitive edition. Doubleday 1989 c1940 850p hardcover o.p. paperback available $17.95 **821**
ISBN 0-385-26089-X (pa)   LC 88-7364

Replaces Rudyard Kipling's verse: definitive edition, published 1940

This edition includes all of Kipling's published poetry and, in addition, more than 20 poems which have not previously appeared in the inclusive edition of his verse
Includes index to first lines

Milton, John, 1608-1674
Complete poetical works; edited by Douglas Bush. Houghton Mifflin 1965 xxxiii, 570p hardcover o.p. paperback available $8.95 **821**
ISBN 0-395-07493-2 (pa)

"Cambridge editions"

"Every form that Milton attempted—the masque, the elegy, the sonnet, the long epic, the short epic, the verse drama—seemingly achieved its potentiality at his hands. And distinguishable as Milton's various periods might be from each other, each is unmistakably 'Miltonic,' an epithet suggesting a standard of poetic power and intellect never since challenged." Coll & Adult Read List

Payne, Robert O.
Geoffrey Chaucer. 2nd ed. Twayne Pubs. 1986 153p il (Twayne's English authors series) lib bdg $22.95 **821**
1. Chaucer, Geoffrey, d. 1400
ISBN 0-8057-6908-0   LC 85-16368
First published 1964

The author discusses "Chaucer's poetry in its own right and for its own artistic values, but also as it developed from the context of late medieval European literary traditions and practices, with which Chaucer was widely and deeply acquainted." Preface
Includes bibliography

Peterson, Richard F.
William Butler Yeats. Twayne Pubs. 1982 228p (Twayne's English authors series) $22.95 **821**
1. Yeats, W. B. (William Butler), 1865-1939
ISBN 0-8057-6815-7   LC 81-7025

"Peterson often devotes a paragraph or even a page to a single poem, and a page or two to a single play; if his comments are unsurprising they are, nevertheless, well informed, at least, and his notes direct the reader to more detailed studies." Choice
Includes bibliography

Rossetti, Christina Georgina, 1830-1894
Poems. Knopf 1993 256p (Everyman's library pocket poets) $10.95 **821**
ISBN 0-679-42908-5   LC 93-14362

The poems in this collection are grouped under the following headings: Lyric poems, Dramatic and narrative poems, Rhymes and riddles, Sonnet sequences, Prayers and meditations. An index of first lines is included

Shakespeare, William, 1564-1616
Poems. Knopf 1994 252p (Everyman's library pocket poets) $10.95 **821**
ISBN 0-679-43320-1   LC 94-2494

A representative selection of Shakespeare's verse

Sonnets   **821**

Hardcover and paperback editions available from various publishers

A series of 154 sonnets. "Probably composed between 1593 and 1601, they are written in the form of three quatrains and a couplet that has come to be known as Shakespearean. Influenced by, and often reacting against, the popular sonnet sequences of the time, notably Sir Philip Sidney's 'Astrophel and Stella', Shakespeare's sonnets are among the finest examples of their kind." Reader's Ency. 4th edition

Shelley, Percy Bysshe, 1792-1822
The complete poems of Percy Bysshe Shelley; with notes by Mary Shelley. Modern Lib. 1994 xxv, 914p $20 **821**
ISBN 0-679-60111-2   LC 94-3320

This volume collects Shelley's political epics, hymns, satires, odes, elegies, lyrical dramas and verse epistles

Tennyson, Alfred Tennyson, Baron, 1809-1892
The Lady of Shalott; illustrated by Charles Keeping. Oxford Univ. Press 1986 unp il $16; pa $9 **821**
ISBN 0-19-276057-2; 0-19-272211-5 (pa)

"In a large-size picture book for older readers, Keeping's sweepingly dramatic black-and-white drawings il-

Tennyson, Alfred Tennyson, Baron, 1809-1892—*Continued*

lustrate Tennyson's famous Arthurian poem of longing and mystery about the beautiful doomed lady locked up in a castle." Booklist

The poetical works of Tennyson; edited by G. Robert Strange. Houghton Mifflin 1974 xx, 706p o.p.   **821**

"Cambridge editions"

First published 1898 with title: The poetic and dramatic works of Alfred, Lord Tennyson

"Tennyson has made the widest appeal of any English poet of the nineteenth century. His verse is graceful, romantic, elegant, of great pictorial beauty, and imbued with deep religious feeling. Tennyson's poetry perfectly mirrored the spirit of his era in England." Pratt Alcove

Tennyson; a selected edition, incorporating the Trinity College manuscripts; edited by Christopher Ricks. University of Calif. Press 1989 xxxi, 1032p $58; pa $18.95   **821**

ISBN 0-520-06588-3; 0-520-06666-9 (pa)
LC 88-40556

Included in this annotated selection of the Victorian poet's work are the complete texts of The princess, In memoriam, Maud, and Idylls of the King

Thomas, Dylan, 1914-1953

The collected poems of Dylan Thomas. New Directions 1953 203p hardcover o.p. paperback available $10.95   **821**

ISBN 0-8112-0205-4 (pa)

"The prologue in verse, written for this collected edition of my poems, is intended as an address to my readers, the strangers. This book contains most of the poems I have written, and all, up to the present year, that I wish to preserve. Some of them I have revised a little." Preface

The poems of Dylan Thomas; edited with an introduction and notes by Daniel Jones. New Directions 1971 291p $19.95   **821**

ISBN 0-8112-0398-0

"To the 90 poems Thomas published in Collected Poems, 1934-1952 Jones has added 102 and placed the total, as far as he could determine, in the chronological order of their composition. Some of the poems were still in manuscript form when Thomas died; others had been published in periodicals and anthologies. In an appendix, Jones offers Thomas' early poems—including one written when the poet was 12." Libr J

Includes bibliographical references

Warnke, Frank J., 1925-1988

John Donne. Twayne Pubs. 1987 143p (Twayne's English authors series) lib bdg $22.95   **821**

1. Donne, John, 1572-1631
ISBN 0-8057-6941-2   LC 86-27096

The author "provides a clear, thorough overview of Donne's life, career, and environment (the Baroque Era

in Europe and England); a perceptive analysis of his writings (juvenilia, satires, early elegies, songs and sonnets, mid-period poetry and prose, sermons, devotions, divine poems); and an evaluation of his reputation and influence as no longer central in the post-modernist era but nevertheless as the greatest of English love poets and preachers." Libr J

Includes bibliography

Wordsworth, William, 1770-1850

Poems. Knopf 1995 256p (Everyman's library pocket poets) $10.95   **821**

ISBN 0-679-44369-X

A selection of work representative of the prominent Romantic's poetic legacy

Poetical works; with introductions and notes; edited by Thomas Hutchinson. new ed, revised by Ernest de Sélincourt. Oxford Univ. Press 1950 xxx, 779p (Oxford standard authors) hardcover o.p. paperback available $19.95   **821**

ISBN 0-19-281052-9 (pa)

Variant title: The complete poetical works of William Wordsworth

"One of England's greatest poets, who revealed the extraordinary beauty and significance of simple people and things." Good Read

Wright, George Thaddeus

W.H. Auden; by George T. Wright. rev ed. Twayne Pubs. 1981 c1969 232p (Twayne's United States authors series) $22.95   **821**

1. Auden, W. H. (Wystan Hugh), 1907-1973
ISBN 0-8057-7346-0   LC 81-4153
First published 1969

The author portrays the Anglo-American writer Auden as a consistent, serious, developing poet who sought a poetry which avoids vague Romantic symbolism and self-concern while achieving impressiveness and scope

Includes bibliography

Yeats, W. B. (William Butler), 1865-1939

The poems; edited by Richard J. Finneran. rev ed. Macmillan 1989 xxviii, 751p $35   **821**

ISBN 0-02-632701-5   LC 88-13700
First published 1983

This edition of the Nobel Laureate's verse contains texts of all the poems Yeats is known to have written. The editor has restored Yeat's rhetorical punctuation and provides textual notes

Under the moon; the unpublished early poetry; edited by George Bornstein. Scribner 1995 128p $22   **821**

ISBN 0-684-80254-6   LC 95-8445

This collection contains 38 previously unpublished poems written between the poet's late teens and early twenties. An introduction places the poems in their literary and biographical contexts

"Here is the fulfillment of a literary scholar's dream—previously unknown poems by one of the masters. . . . A vital source for understanding a great poet's later glories." Booklist

821.008 English poetry—Collections

Chapters into verse; poetry in English inspired by the Bible; assembled and edited by Robert Atwan & Laurance Wieder. Oxford Univ. Press 1993 2v set $50 **821.008**
1. Religious poetry—Collections
ISBN 0-19-508493-4   LC 92-37206
Contents: v1 Genesis to Malachi; v2 Gospels to Revelation

"An anthology of poems from all eras, styles, and degree of reverence, which take as their major inspiration lines, verses, or chapters from the Bible. Arranged in Biblical order in two volumes . . . the poems are preceded by the appropriate chapters and verses (the King James version has been used throughout). Poets as wide-ranging as Emily Dickinson, Sylvia Plath, and Delmore Schwartz are interspersed with D.H. Lawrence and writers from the Harlem Renaissance." Libr J

Ciardi, John, 1916-1986
How does a poem mean? [by] John Ciardi, Miller Williams. 2nd ed. Houghton Mifflin 1975 xxiii, 408p hardcover o.p. paperback available $23.95 **821.008**
1. English poetry—Collections 2. American poetry—Collections 3. Poetry—History and criticism
ISBN 0-395-18605-6 (pa)
First published 1960
This volume discusses the value and nature of poetry, its kinds, structure and techniques through detailed analysis of individual poems from the medieval age down to the present

The **Columbia** anthology of British poetry; edited by Carl Woodring and James Shapiro. Columbia Univ. Press 1995 xxxi, 891p $29.95 **821.008**
1. English poetry—Collections
ISBN 0-231-10180-5   LC 94-46333
This anthology "contains major British poetry from Beowulf to the present day. Poets receive a short biographical introduction along with their poetry. . . . It includes more female poets than most comparable anthologies, and is conducive to browsing. Major poems such as Coleridge's 'Rime of the Ancient Mariner,' Britain's best-loved poems, and newly rediscovered poems are part of this collection." SLJ

The **Golden** treasury of the best songs & lyrical poems in the English language; selected and arranged by Francis Turner Palgrave; updated by John Press. 6th ed. Oxford Univ. Press 1994 701p $30; pa $15.95 **821.008**
1. English poetry—Collections
ISBN 0-19-254202-8; 0-19-282315-9 (pa)
     LC 94-655
First published 1861
This anthology of representative British poetry includes works ranging from Wyatt and Shakespeare to Larkin and Gunn
"Despite the countless anthologies emerging every year, Palgrave's is still the measuring stick, and Press's additions assure that it will remain so into the new millennium." Publ Wkly
Includes bibliographical references

The **Home** book of modern verse; an extension of The home book of verse; being a selection from American and English poetry of the twentieth century; compiled and arranged by Burton Egbert Stevenson. 2nd ed. Holt & Co. 1966 c1953 xlix, 1124p o.p. **821.008**
1. English poetry—Collections 2. American poetry—Collections
First published 1925
The poems in this collection are arranged by such subjects as: Poems of youth and age, Poems of love, Poems of nature, Familiar verse and poems humorous and satiric, Poems of patriotism, history and legend, Poems of sentiment and reflection, Poems of sorrow, death, and immortality

Life doesn't frighten me at all; poems; compiled by John Agard. Holt & Co. 1990 96p il $14.95 **821.008**
1. English poetry—Collections 2. American poetry—Collections
ISBN 0-8050-1237-0   LC 89-26766
This is a collection of poems by such authors as Maya Angelou, Gwendolyn Brooks, Bob Marley, Anne Sexton, and Dory Previn
"The textual diversity is matched by a format whose every page surprises a reader with varied typefaces, drawings, and decorations that are choreographed well enough not to become jarring. Notes on or by the writers are random but interesting. While the quality of the poems is uneven, the voices are fresh. Teenagers will find the book informal, approachable, even alluring." Bull Cent Child Books

The **Major** poets: English and American. 2nd ed, revised and edited by Gerrit Hubbard Roelofs. Harcourt Brace Jovanovich 1969 xxv, 581p pa $23.50 **821.008**
1. English poetry—Collections 2. American poetry—Collections
ISBN 0-15-554545-0
First published 1954 under the editorship of Charles Monroe Coffin
The poets in this anthology display the development of English poetry over a period of seven centuries
Includes bibliographic references and an index of authors, titles, and first lines

The **New** Oxford book of eighteenth century verse; chosen and edited by Roger Lonsdale. Oxford Univ. Press 1984 xlii, 870p $41.75 **821.008**
1. English poetry—Collections
ISBN 0-19-214122-8   LC 83-17477
Replaces The Oxford Book of eighteenth century verse, edited by David Nicol Smith (1926)
This anthology "will be welcome to anyone interested in the poetry of the period. The casual reader will find a goodly selection of the familiar . . . [and] a number of unfamiliar works, since about 25 percent of the inclusions are of such obscure writers as John Hawthorn, J. Wilde, and that most prolific of authors, Anonymous. One may question whether the space allowed these lesser lights might not have been given instead to better poets, but their inclusion does provide a fuller picture of the period than would a sampling limited to the Greats

The New Oxford book of eighteenth century verse—*Continued*

whose works are, moreover, readily available elsewhere. Indexed by first line and author, with brief biographical and historical notes." Libr J

The New Oxford book of English light verse; chosen by Kingsley Amis. Oxford Univ. Press 1978 xxxiv, 347p $35   **821.008**
1. English poetry—Collections 2. Humorous poetry
ISBN 0-19-211862-5

A companion volume to The Oxford Book of American light verse, entered in class 811.008

Replaces The Oxford Book of light verse, edited by W. H. Auden (1938)

This anthology of humorous poetry contains work by mostly British authors. Americans represented include: Bret Harte, Robert Frost, Peter De Vries and Phyllis McGinley

Includes author and first line indexes

The New Oxford book of English verse, 1250-1950; chosen and edited by Helen Gardner. Oxford Univ. Press 1972 974p $45   **821.008**
1. English poetry—Collections
ISBN 0-19-812136-9

Replaces The Oxford Book of English verse, 1250-1900, edited by Sir Arthur Quiller-Couch (1900)

This anthology covers seven centuries of verse and brings the terminal date down to 1950. It "covers the entire spectrum of English poetic genius. As well as private and personal poems, there are poems dealing with public events, historic occasions, religious, moral, and political convictions, satire, and . . . light verse." Publisher's note

Includes author and first line indexes

The New Oxford book of Irish verse; edited with translations by Thomas Kinsella. Oxford Univ. Press 1986 xxx, 423p hardcover o.p. paperback available $11.95   **821.008**
1. Irish poetry—Collections
ISBN 0-19-282643-3 (pa)   LC 85-21479

Replaces The Oxford Book of Irish verse, XVIIth century-XXth century, chosen by Donagh MacDonagh and Lennox Robinson (1958)

"This selection is divided into three parts. Book I opens with the earliest pre-Christian poetry in Old Irish and ends in the fourteenth century with the first Irish poetry in the English language. Book II covers the fourteenth to the eighteenth centuries and Book III the nineteenth and twentieth centuries." Publisher's note

The New Oxford book of seventeenth century verse; edited by Alastair Fowler. Oxford Univ. Press 1991 xlv, 831p $45   **821.008**
1. English poetry—Collections
ISBN 0-19-214164-3   LC 90-22290

Replaces The Oxford book of seventeenth century verse, edited by H. J. C. Grierson and G. Bullough (1934)

The editor has "tried to produce a 'representative' selection, which means more generous helpings of minor poets like Drayton, Cowley, Oldham and Strode; more

women; and the inclusion of 'marginal' figures. . . . Fortunately, the anthology is a critical as well as a scholarly achievement. Fowler's eye for what is good, or at least notable, about a poet's work seems more or less unfailing." London Rev Books

Includes bibliographical references

The New Oxford book of Victorian verse; edited by Christopher Ricks. Oxford Univ. Press 1987 xxxiv, 654p hardcover o.p. paperback available $14.95   **821.008**
1. English poetry—Collections
ISBN 0-19-282778-2 (pa)   LC 86-23701

Replaces The Oxford book of Victorian verse, edited by Sir Arthur Quiller-Couch (1912)

An anthology of 19th century English poetry. Among the poets prominently featured are: Clough, Morris, Arnold, the Decadents, Emily Brontë, Clare, Barnes, and Christina Rossetti

"While general collections should all add Ricks, those retaining [the Quiller-Couch edition] should dust him off and keep him available in order to represent fully Victorian verse and changing attitudes toward it." Libr J

Includes bibliography

The Norton anthology of modern poetry; edited by Richard Ellmann and Robert O'Clair. 2nd ed. Norton 1988 xlix, 1865p pa $39.95   **821.008**
1. English poetry—Collections 2. American poetry—Collections
ISBN 0-393-95636-9   LC 87-28310

First published 1973

An anthology of English and American verse from Whitman to the present day

Includes bibliography

The Norton anthology of poetry; [edited by] Margaret Ferguson, Mary Jo Salter, Jon Stallworthy. 4th ed. Norton 1996 lxxx, 1998p pa $39.95   **821.008**
1. English poetry—Collections 2. American poetry—Collections
ISBN 0-393-96820-0   LC 96-8035

Also available in a shorter version $36.95 (ISBN 0-393-96924-X)

First published 1970

An anthology of British and American poetry from before Chaucer to the present. The order is chronological with poets appearing according to dates of their birth. A glossary identifies technical terms of prosody. Indexed by poet, title, and first line

The Norton book of light verse; edited by Russell Baker; with the assistance of Kathleen Leland Baker. Norton 1986 447p $25   **821.008**
1. English poetry—Collections 2. American poetry—Collections 3. Humorous poetry
ISBN 0-393-02366-4   LC 86-18172

Arranged by subject, this anthology presents some four hundred British and American light verse selections. The poems date from the sixteenth-century to the present

The Oxford book of ballads; selected and edited by James Kinsley. Oxford Univ. Press 1969 711p o.p.   **821.008**
1. English ballads 2. Scottish ballads
Available from Somerset Pubs.

The Oxford book of ballads—*Continued*

Replaces The Oxford Book of ballads, compiled by Sir Arthur Quiller-Couch (1910)

This volume "contains for the most part, ballads from the Child canon. Texts of the 150 ballads are, however, based on single rather than composite versions and aim less for poetic quality than for closeness to oral tradition. Grouping is by relation in theme or mood without a formal subject arrangement and the compiler has included musical airs for more than 80 of the ballads. Sources for both poetry and music are indicated in the notes; title index." Booklist

The Oxford book of narrative verse; chosen and edited by Iona and Peter Opie. Oxford Univ. Press 1983 407p $35; pa $12.95 **821.008**
1. English poetry—Collections 2. American poetry—Collections
ISBN 0-19-214131-7; 0-19-282243-8 (pa)
LC 82-22494

This collection of poetry "includes fairy-tales, and folk-stories, broadsides and ballads, adventure and romance, passion and parody." Economist

This is an "anthology predictably freighted with English poets (34 of the 46 selections) but none the worse for that. 'This book,' says the Opies, 'pretends to be nothing more than a story book.' It is nothing less, and leaves you wondering where this admirable kind of verse has gone." Libr J

The Oxford book of nineteenth-century English verse; chosen by John Hayward. Oxford Univ. Press 1964 xxxv, 969p o.p. **821.008**
1. English poetry—Collections

This single volume work includes material first published in "The Oxford Book of English verse of the romantic period" (1928) and "The Oxford Book of Victorian Verse" (1912)

In this anthology, "Victorian verse is more fully represented by the use of longer poems and by substantial extracts from poems. Some 600 poems and extracts by 85 poets have been selected in the light of current taste and critical opinion. . . . Arranged chronologically by birth date of the poet, and with first line and author indexes." Wilson Libr Bull

The Oxford book of twentieth-century English verse; chosen by Philip Larkin. Oxford Univ. Press 1973 1,641p $35 **821.008**
1. English poetry—Collections
ISBN 0-19-812137-7

This anthology of more than 600 poems by more than 200 twentieth-century British writers includes works by John Masefield, T. S. Eliot, W. B. Yeats, W. H. Auden, Dylan Thomas and Alan Sillitoe

"A strong vein of neo-Georgianism runs throughout the book, resulting in a clear partiality for work that is explicitly, even documentarily, English in locale, for poems that are narrative or anecdotal, for neat, well-populated fables and for moralistic ruminations." New Statesman

Includes author and first line indexes

The Penguin book of Irish verse; introduced and edited by Brendan Kennelly. 2nd ed. Penguin Bks. 1981 470p pa $12.95 **821.008**
1. Irish poetry—Collections
ISBN 0-14-058526-5
First published 1970

"Most of Kennelly's selections are virtually unknown to the general reader and, indeed, many are almost unavailable. . . . And, perhaps wisely, he has relegated major authors, especially Yeats, to but brief examples, since they are easy to come by." Publ Wkly

Includes indexes of titles and first line

Poetry of the world wars; edited by Michael Foss. Bedrick Bks. 1990 192p il $18.95 **821.008**
1. World War, 1939-1945—Poetry—Collections
2. World War, 1914-1918—Poetry—Collections
3. War poetry
ISBN 0-87226-336-3
LC 89-18570

"Beginning with Thomas Hardy's 'Men Who March Away' and concluding with Edwin Muir's 'The Child Dying,' editor Foss presents a wide array of poems dealing with the two world wars—and the years of disillusionment and healing that lay between. Of the 65 poets whose works—some 181 poems in all—are included, most are British, all are men, and except in a few cases, all are well known and highly regarded." Booklist

Poetry out loud; edited by Robert Alden Rubin; with an introduction by James Earl Jones. Algonquin Bks. 1993 215p il hardcover o.p. paperback available $9.95 **821.008**
1. English poetry—Collections 2. American poetry—Collections
ISBN 1-56512-122-8 (pa)
LC 93-3946

An anthology of over 100 poems specifically chosen for reading aloud

Includes bibliographical references

The Top 500 poems; edited by William Harmon. Columbia Univ. Press 1992 xxx, 1132p $29.95 **821.008**
1. English poetry—Collections 2. American poetry—Collections
ISBN 0-231-08028-X
LC 91-42239

"Harmon devises an interesting method (collecting the 500 most anthologized shorter English and American poems as indexed in the *Columbia Granger's Index to Poetry,*

Understanding poetry; [edited by] Cleanth Brooks, Robert Penn Warren. 4th ed. Holt, Rinehart & Winston; distributed by Harcourt Brace College Pubs. 1976 xxii, 602p pa $28 **821.008**
1. English poetry—Collections 2. American poetry—Collections 3. Poetry—History and criticism
ISBN 0-03-076980-9
First published 1938

This volume explores the meaning and structure of poetry with discussions of the nuances of theme, dramatic structure and metrics. Approximately 350 English and American poems ranging from the 16th century to the present are included in this collection

821.009 English poetry—History and criticism

The **Columbia** history of British poetry; Carl Woodring, editor; James Shapiro, associate editor. Columbia Univ. Press 1993 732p $59.95   **821.009**
1. English poetry—History and criticism
ISBN 0-231-07838-2   LC 93-18226
David Daiches, Jerome McGann, Calvin Bedient and Margaret Anne Doody are among the contributors to this "overview of British poetry. The 26 essays succeed in placing the rich poetry of the British Isles in a historical perspective that takes into account the theological, economical, cultural, and aesthetic influences of each major period." Libr J

The **Oxford** companion to twentieth-century poetry in English; edited by Ian Hamilton. Oxford Univ. Press 1994 602p $45   **821.009**
1. English poetry—Dictionaries 2. English poetry—Bio-bibliography 3. American poetry—Dictionaries
ISBN 0-19-866147-9   LC 93-1436
"More accurately described as a companion to poets than a companion to poetry—though it does include such entries as 'deep image,' 'Georgian poetry,' and 'The Hudson Review'—this reference focuses on some 1500 20th-century poets from all around the world who write in English. . . . The work offers signed entries by poet-critics, including brief biographical sketches, overviews of themes, commentaries on style, general critical evaluations, and brief primary and secondary bibliographies. The articles are objective yet sympathetic to each poet's intent, with no particular critical perspective obscuring the issue." Libr J

822 English drama

Behan, Brendan, 1923-1964
The complete plays; introduced by Alan Simpson; with a bibliography by E. H. Mikhail. Grove Weidenfeld 1978 384p pa $14   **822**
ISBN 0-8021-3070-4   LC 78-53931
"An Evergreen book"
First published 1978
Contents: The quare fellow; The hostage; Richard's cork leg; Moving out; A garden party; The big house
Includes bibliography

Besier, Rudolf, 1878-1942
The Barretts of Wimpole Street; a comedy in five acts. Little, Brown 1930 165p   **822**
1. Browning, Elizabeth Barrett, 1806-1861—Drama 2. Browning, Robert, 1812-1889—Drama
Available in paperback from Dramatists Play Service
Characters: 13 men, 4 women. One setting. First produced in England at the Malvern Festival, August 20, 1930
"The long-famous courtship and elopement of Elizabeth Barrett and Robert Browning furnish the theme for this drama. . . . The author has followed the known facts faithfully and yet has succeeded in creating a play which is of commanding interest in itself." Carnegie Libr. of Pittsburgh

Bolt, Robert
A man for all seasons; a play in two acts. Random House 1962 xxv, 163p il hardcover o.p. paperback available $8   **822**
1. More, Sir Thomas, Saint, 1478-1535—Drama 2. Great Britain—History—1485-1603, Tudors—Drama
ISBN 0-679-72822-8 (pa)
Characters: 11 men, 2 women. 1 setting. First produced in the United States at the ANTA Theatre, New York City, November 22, 1961
A play set in sixteenth century England about Sir Thomas More, a devout Catholic, and his conflict with Henry VIII

Burgess, Anthony, 1917-1993
Cyrano de Bergerac; by Edmond Rostand; translated and adapted for the modern stage by Anthony Burgess. Knopf 1971 174p $16.95; pa $11   **822**
ISBN 0-394-47239-X; 0-679-73413-9 (pa)
Also available in paperback from Applause Theatre Bk. Pubs.
This version was commissioned for production at the Tyrone Guthrie Theater in Minneapolis. It is newly adapted and translated from the French play originally produced in 1897. Cyrano, the hero, a Gascon poet and swordsman notorious for his long nose, is in love with Roxana

Fugard, Athol
"Master Harold"—and the boys. Knopf 1982 60p o.p.; Penguin Bks. paperback available $7.95   **822**
1. South Africa—Race relations—Drama
ISBN 0-14-048187-7 (pa)   LC 82-48027
Characters: 3 men. 1 act. 1 interior. First produced at the Yale Repertory theatre, New Haven, Connecticut, 1982
This play, "based on Fugard's experiences as a teenager in Port Elizabeth, concerns a boy whose problematic relationship with his father leads him to ill-treat his two family servants." Oxford Companion to 20th Cent Lit in Engl

Pinter, Harold, 1930-
The birthday party, and The room; two plays. Grove Press 1961 120p il pa $8.95   **822**
ISBN 0-8021-5114-0
An Evergreen original
The birthday party, first performed in 1958 and published in 1959, portrays the mental destruction of a young pianist living obscurely in an English seaside town. In The room, first produced in 1957, an elderly couple seems about to be evicted from their boarding house

Pomerance, Bernard

The Elephant Man; a play. Grove Press 1979 71p hardcover o.p. paperback available $8.95

822

1. Merrick, Joseph Carey, 1862 or 3-1890—Drama 2. Physically handicapped—Drama
ISBN 0-8021-3041-0 (pa)   LC 79-7792
Characters: 5 men, 2 women. 21 scenes. First produced at the Hampstead Theatre, London, 1977
Play based on the life of John [i.e. Joseph Carey] Merrick who from birth was so grotesquely deformed that he became known as the Elephant Man. Merrick was exhibited as a freak until a London surgeon found him permanent residence in a hospital where he became a favorite of aristocracy and literati

Rusinko, Susan

Tom Stoppard. Twayne Pubs. 1986 164p (Twayne's English authors series) $22.95   **822**
1. Stoppard, Tom
ISBN 0-8057-6909-9   LC 85-17589
The author examines Stoppard's various writings—stage dramas; television, radio and screen plays; stage adaptations—and analyzes his position in contemporary British theater
Includes bibliography

Shaffer, Peter

Equus. Atheneum Pubs. 1974 211p o.p.; Penguin Bks. paperback available $7.95   **822**
ISBN 0-14-048185-0 (pa)
Characters: 5 men, 4 women. 1 act, 35 scenes. 1 setting. First produced by the National Theater, London, July 26, 1973
Drama about "a jolting confrontation between a psychiatrist and a 17-year-old boy who has blinded six horses from the stable where he is employed. As the probe into the boy's attitudes and behavior deepens, this criminal act is revealed to have been a result of his notions of a sexual/religious spirit in horses." Booklist

Peter Shaffer's Amadeus. Harper & Row 1981 97p music hardcover o.p. paperback available $11
822
1. Mozart, Wolfgang Amadeus, 1756-1791—Drama 2. Salieri, Antonio, 1750-1825—Drama
ISBN 0-06-090783-5 (pa)   LC 79-3415
A revised version of the title first published 1980 in the United Kingdom
Characters: 9 men, 1 woman, extras. 2 acts. First produced at the National Theater of Great Britain, November 1979
Explores relationship between Austrian court composer Antonio Salieri and the divinely gifted young Wolfgang Amadeus Mozart

Shaw, Bernard, 1856-1950

The portable Bernard Shaw; edited with an introduction and notes by Stanley Weintraub. Viking 1977 698p o.p.; Penguin Bks. paperback available $14.95   **822**
ISBN 0-14-015090-0 (pa)   LC 77-7457
This volume includes the complete texts of the following plays: The Devil's disciple, Pygmalion, Heartbreak

house and Shakes versus Shav. Also included: In the beginning (pt. 1 of Back to Methuselah); Don Juan in Hell (from Man and superman) as well as the prose work The adventures of the black girl in her search for God, and miscellaneous reviews, articles and letters

Sheridan, Richard Brinsley Butler, 1751-1816

The rivals   **822**

Available from Amereon and in paperback from Norton and Oxford Univ. Press
In this satirical comedy, first presented in 1775, two gentlemen woo Lydia Languish, a young woman with highly romantic ideas concerning love whose fortune will be forfeited if she marries without the consent of her aunt. The aunt, Mrs. Malaprop, has become famous for her eccentric use of the English language

Stoppard, Tom

Rosencrantz and Guildenstern are dead. Grove Press 1967 126p hardcover o.p. paperback available $8.95   **822**
1. Shakespeare, William, 1564-1616—Parodies, travesties, etc.
ISBN 0-8021-3275-8 (pa)
Characters: 13 men, 2 women, extras. First produced in this form April 11, 1967 in London
This play "took the theatre world on both sides of the Atlantic by storm. The originality of the idea which put Hamlet's two insignificant friends centerstage was matched by the brilliance of the dialogue between these bewildered nonentities." Reader's Ency. 4th edition

Thomas, Dylan, 1914-1953

Under milk wood; a play for voices. New Directions 1954 107p music pa $6.95   **822**
ISBN 0-8112-0209-7
"A radio play for voices. Written in poetic, inventive prose, this play is full of humor, a joyful sense of the goodness of life and love, and a strong Welsh flavor. It is an impression of a spring day in the lives of the people of Llareggub, a Welsh village situated under Milk Wood. It has no plot, but a wealth of characters who dream aloud, converse with one another, and speak in choruses of alternating voices." Reader's Ency. 4th edition

Wilde, Oscar, 1854-1900

The importance of being Earnest   **822**

Hardcover and paperback editions available from various publishers
First published 1899 in the United Kingdom
Drawing room comedy exposing quirks and foibles of Victorian society with plot revolving around amorous pursuits of two men who face social obstacles when they woo young ladies of quality

822.008   English drama—Collections

100 great monologues from the Renaissance
theatre; edited by Jocelyn A. Beard. Smith &
Kraus 1994 186p pa $9.95   **822.008**
1. Monologues 2. Acting
ISBN 1-880399-59-8   LC 94-19393

A collection of monologues for men and women selected to represent the range of English Renaissance
stage roles

822.009   English drama—History and criticism

Cleopatra; edited and with an introduction by
Harold Bloom. Chelsea House 1990 269p
(Major literary characters) $34.95   **822.009**
1. Cleopatra, Queen of Egypt, d. 30 B.C. 2. Shakespeare, William, 1564-1616. Antony and Cleopatra
3. Shaw, Bernard, 1856-1950. Caesar and Cleopatra
4. Dryden, John, 1631-1700. All for love
ISBN 0-7910-0915-7   LC 89-29607

Contributors discuss how Cleopatra has been portrayed
in works of Horace, Shakespeare, Dryden, Shaw,
Corneille, Pushkin and Wilder

Includes bibliographical references

Critical survey of drama; edited by Frank N.
Magill. rev ed. Salem Press 1994 7v set $425
    822.009
1. English drama—History and criticism 2. American
drama—History and criticism 3. English drama—Bio-
bibliography 4. American drama—Bio-bibliography
ISBN 0-89356-851-1   LC 93-41618

First published 1985 with title: Critical survey of drama, English language series

"The first six volumes feature 240 articles on individual dramatists, alphabetically arranged by last name. . . .
The individual presentations begin with a listing of the
playwright's principal dramas, followed by a list of other
literary forms, if applicable. A biography is followed by
a literary analysis including summaries of major plays
and discussions of major themes. . . . Volume 7 contains
21 essays giving an overview of the development of
English language drama." Book Rep

Dietrich, Richard F., 1936-
British drama, 1890 to 1950; a critical history.
Twayne Pubs. 1989 308p il (Twayne's critical
history of British drama) $25.95   **822.009**
1. English drama—History and criticism
ISBN 0-8057-8951-0   LC 88-37964

"Dietrich provides useful information on the various
dramatic movements leading up to the 'triumph' of the
'New Drama.' The bulk of his book is a discussion of
individual authors, with Shaw the dominant figure. . . .
[The volume provides] biographical information, discussions of selected plays, and a brief assessment of each
author's contribution to modern drama." Libr J

Includes bibliography

Rusinko, Susan
British drama, 1950 to the present; a critical
history. Twayne Pubs. 1989 257p il (Twayne's
critical history of British drama) $25.95   **822.009**
1. English drama—History and criticism
ISBN 0-8057-8957-9   LC 88-37951

The author "furnishes a brief introduction before
launching into separate chapters on Beckett, Osborne,
Pinter, and Stoppard. Some three dozen lesser figures are
grouped into categories and discussed briefly in the second part of the book. . . . [A] useful [survey] for students and general readers seeking an overview of modern
drama or a brief introduction to a specific playwright."
Libr J

Includes bibliography

822.3   William Shakespeare

Bieman, Elizabeth
William Shakespeare: the romances. Twayne
Pubs. 1990 151p (Twayne's English authors series)
$23.95   **822.3**
1. Shakespeare, William, 1564-1616—Criticism, inter-
pretation, etc.
ISBN 0-8057-6995-1   LC 89-26857

An examination of the themes and techniques used in
Pericles, Cymbeline, The winter's tale and The tempest

Includes bibliographical references

Boyce, Charles
Shakespeare A to Z; the essential reference to
his plays, his poems, his life and times, and more;
David White, editorial consultant; foreword by
Terry Hands. Facts on File 1990 742p il $45
    822.3
1. Shakespeare, William, 1564-1616—Dictionaries
ISBN 0-8160-1805-7   LC 90-31239
Also available in paperback from Dell
"A Roundtable Press book"

This book has "synopses of all of Shakespeare's plays
by act and scene; sketches of all of his characters, as
well as the historic personages on whom some of them
were based; biographies of his contemporaries in the
Elizabethan theater; portraits of many of the actors who
achieved fame in his plays; and mentions of many modern theatrical works that have been influenced by him.
One can also find definitions of literary and theatrical
terms relevant to his work, along with descriptions of the
places that figured so prominently in Shakespeare's
plays. The book is truly a treasure trove of information
for students of Shakespeare." SLJ

Includes bibliographical references

Chute, Marchette Gaylord, 1909-1994
Shakespeare of London; [by] Marchette Chute.
Dutton 1949 397p o.p.   **822.3**
1. Shakespeare, William, 1564-1616—Biography

"Retelling of Shakespeare's life, reconstructed from
documentary evidence and a sound knowledge of Shakespeare's England. . . . The author's Shakespeare is a
young man of talent, who made good at a congenial oc-

Chute, Marchette Gaylord, 1909-1994—*Continued*

cupation at a time when the political and cultural atmosphere was conducive to the development of literary and dramatic talent." Booklist

Includes bibliography

Dawson, Anthony B.

Watching Shakespeare: a playgoers' guide. St. Martin's Press 1988 260p il $30   **822.3**

1. Shakespeare, William, 1564-1616

ISBN 0-312-01563-1   LC 87-24166

This guide provides the reader with synopses and stage history of each of Shakespeare's plays

Includes bibliography

Garfield, Leon, 1921-1996

Shakespeare stories [I]-II; illustrated by Michael Foreman. Houghton Mifflin 1991-1995 c1985-c1994 2v il ea $24.95   **822.3**

1. Shakespeare, William, 1564-1616—Adaptations

ISBN 0-395-56397-6; 0-395-70893-1

Original volume first published 1985 by Schocken Bks.

In these volumes Garfield has rewritten twenty-one of Shakespeare's plays in narrative form, retaining much of the original language

Hillman, Richard, 1949-

William Shakespeare: the problem plays. Twayne Pubs. 1993 185p (Twayne's English authors series) $23.95   **822.3**

1. Shakespeare, William, 1564-1616—Criticism, interpretation, etc.

ISBN 0-8057-7035-6   LC 92-30216

A critical examination of All's well that ends well, Troilus and Cressida and Measure for measure

Includes bibliographical references

Jorgensen, Paul A.

William Shakespeare: the tragedies. Twayne Pubs. 1985 164p il (Twayne's English authors series) $23.95   **822.3**

1. Shakespeare, William, 1564-1616—Criticism, interpretation, etc.

ISBN 0-8057-6906-4   LC 85-8587

"This comprehensible analysis of Shakespeare's 10 authentic tragedies, each given separate treatment, is suitable supplementary material for advanced English literature students." Booklist

Includes bibliography

Levi, Peter, 1931-

The life and times of William Shakespeare. Holt & Co. 1989 c1988 xxiii, 392p il maps $29.95; pa $14.95   **822.3**

1. Shakespeare, William, 1564-1616—Biography

ISBN 0-8050-1199-4; 0-8050-1552-3 (pa)

                    LC 89-30501

First published 1988 in the United Kingdom

The author "offers information about Shakespeare's background and parentage, the Stratford and London that he knew, events that shaped his experience, and the actors, managers and writers with whom he associated. But most of the facts relate to the times." Publ Wkly

"Textual interpretation is kept to a minimum. . . . [The author's] balanced style is both informative and accessible." Libr J

Includes bibliography

Macbeth; edited and with an introduction by Harold Bloom. Chelsea House 1991 259p (Major literary characters) $34.95   **822.3**

1. Shakespeare, William, 1564-1616. Macbeth 2. Macbeth, King of Scotland, d. 1057

ISBN 0-7910-0923-8   LC 90-2459

Contributors examine how Shakespeare incorporated the historical Macbeth into one of his best known dramas

Includes bibliographical references

Onions, Charles Talbut, 1873-1965

A Shakespeare glossary. 3rd ed, enlarged and revised throughout by Robert D. Eagleson. Oxford Univ. Press 1986 326p hardcover o.p. paperback available $17.95   **822.3**

1. Shakespeare, William, 1564-1616—Dictionaries

ISBN 0-19-812521-6 (pa)   LC 84-7912

First published 1911

This dictionary of Shakespearean language concentrates on words whose connotations might be unfamiliar to the contemporary reader. Dialect forms, idioms, and colloquial phrases are emphasized

Includes bibliography

Readings on the tragedies of William Shakespeare; Clarice Swisher, book editor. Greenhaven Press 1996 214p (Greenhaven Press literary companion to British authors) lib bdg $19.95; pa $11.95   **822.3**

1. Shakespeare, William, 1564-1616—Criticism, interpretation, etc.

ISBN 1-56510-467-6 (lib bdg); 1-56510-466-8 (pa)

                    LC 96-1292

This volume contains "twenty-four critical essays that span the time period from 1811 to 1995. The essays are authored by prominent historical figures such as Charles Lamb, Samuel Taylor Coleridge, and William Hazlitt, as well as by several noted modern critics, including A.C. Bradley, Northrop Frye, and Caroline F.E. Spurgeon. Six major tragedies are discussed: *Romeo and Juliet, Julius Caesar, Hamlet, Othello, Macbeth*, and *King Lear*." Publisher's note

Rowse, A. L. (Alfred Leslie), 1903-

Shakespeare the man. rev ed. St. Martin's Press 1989 c1988 253p il pa $13.95   **822.3**

1. Shakespeare, William, 1564-1616—Biography 2. Shakespeare, William, 1564-1616—Criticism, interpretation, etc.

ISBN 0-312-03425-3   LC 89-33020

First published 1973 by Harper & Row; this edition first published 1988 in the United Kingdom

An exploration of Shakespeare's life, works and times with particular emphasis on the identity of the Dark Lady of the sonnets

Includes bibliographical references

Saccio, Peter

Shakespeare's English kings; history, chronicle, and drama. Oxford Univ. Press 1977 268p il hardcover o.p. paperback available $10.95   **822.3**

1. Shakespeare, William, 1564-1616—Criticism, interpretation, etc. 2. Great Britain—History 3. Great Britain—Kings, queens, rulers, etc.

ISBN 0-19-502156-8 (pa)   LC 76-42676

"Intended to provide background for the general reader and play-goer, this book provides modernized accounts of English history of Shakespeare's 10 history plays, including 'Henry VIII.' It also carefully outlines the Tudor historians' perspectives on these reigns, as well as where Shakespeare deviated from his sources." Choice

Includes bibliography

Schoenbaum, Samuel, 1927-1996

William Shakespeare: a compact documentary life. rev ed, with a new postscript. Oxford Univ. Press 1987 xx, 384p il pa $16.95   **822.3**

1. Shakespeare, William, 1564-1616—Biography

ISBN 0-19-505161-0   LC 87-1729

First published 1977

This is an abridgment of the author's William Shakespeare: a documentary life (1975)

Those "who want a brief, readable, but scrupulously detailed and scrupulously accurate account of Shakespeare's life will have to use this book." Choice

Includes bibliographical references

Shakespeare, William, 1564-1616

The complete works of William Shakespeare

                    822.3

Hardcover and paperback editions available from various publishers

For a comparison of most of the editions of Shakespeare see: The Reader's Advisor

The essential Shakespeare; selected and with an introduction by Ted Hughes. Ecco Press 1991 230p (Essential poets) hardcover o.p. paperback available $8   **822.3**

ISBN 0-88001-314-1 (pa)   LC 91-17522

Ted Hughes has selected a "combination of sonnets, songs, speeches, and poetry that best illustrate the incredible breadth of Shakespeare's genius. In his introduction, Hughes explores the origins of Shakespeare's language." Publisher's note

An Oxford anthology of Shakespeare; selected and introduced by Stanley Wells. Oxford Univ. Press 1987 xx, 396p $24.95; pa $9.95   **822.3**

ISBN 0-19-812935-1; 0-19-282240-3 (pa)

                   LC 87-5788

"Shakespearean scholar Wells has gleaned from Shakespeare's 43 plays and 14 of his sonnets a collection of poems and passages whose strengths lie in their artistic, rhetorical, and literary value rather than their dramatic qualities. Organized under 13 headings, the passages could supplement a study of Shakespeare or could be used for private readings. . . . An excellent source because truly readable pieces have been chosen." Libr J

Shakespeare for students; Mark W. Scott, editor; Joseph C. Tardiff, associate editor; advisors, Kathy Lee Martin, Gladys V. Veidemanis. Gale Res. 1992 529p il $65   **822.3**

1. Shakespeare, William, 1564-1616—Criticism, interpretation, etc.

ISBN 0-8103-8247-4   LC 92-1148

Also available CD-ROM version

"Critical interpretations of As you like it, Hamlet, Julius Caesar, Macbeth, The merchant of Venice, A midsummer night's dream, Othello, and Romeo and Juliet." Title page

For each play this volume provides a look at "Shakespeare's sources, a plot synopsis . . . character sketches, and an initial treatment of the major critical issues surrounding the play." Voice Youth Advocates

Includes bibliographical references

Shewmaker, Eugene F.

Shakespeare's language; a glossary of unfamiliar words in Shakespeare's plays & poems. Facts on File 1996 515p $50   **822.3**

1. Shakespeare, William, 1564-1616—Dictionaries

ISBN 0-8160-3276-9   LC 95-12778

Shewmaker defines "over 15,000 words found in Shakespeare's plays and poetry. Every entry includes an in-context quotation showing how the word or phrase was used by Shakespeare." Libr J

Includes bibliographical references

Spurgeon, Caroline F. E., 1869-1942

Shakespeare's imagery and what it tells us; with charts and illustrations. Cambridge Univ. Press 1935 408p il hardcover o.p. paperback available $29.95   **822.3**

1. Shakespeare, William, 1564-1616—Technique 2. Shakespeare, William, 1564-1616—Criticism, interpretation, etc.

ISBN 0-521-09258-2 (pa)

"A scholarly study of Shakespeare's use of images and of his personality and thought as they may be deduced from his imagery." Booklist

"A distinctive contribution to Shakespeare's criticism, bold and original in idea, scrupulous and exhaustive in method, and of all things, readable as a detective story." N Y Times Book Rev

Vaughn, Jack A., 1935-

Shakespeare's comedies. Ungar 1980 249p il (World dramatists series) hardcover o.p. paperback available $6.95   **822.3**

1. Shakespeare, William, 1564-1616—Criticism, interpretation, etc.

ISBN 0-8044-6947-4 (pa)   LC 79-48080

In his discussion of 17 Shakespearean comedies, the author provides "information about each play's plot, history, contemporary stagecraft, and place in the comic tradition." Booklist

Includes bibliography

823.009 English fiction—History and criticism

1984 revisited; totalitarianism in our century; edited by Irving Howe. Harper & Row 1983 276p o.p.   **823.009**
1. Orwell, George, 1903-1950. Nineteen eighty-four 2. Totalitarianism

LC 82-48668

Analyzed in Essay and general literature index
"Irving Howe and 12 other authors and thinkers here consider Orwell's work, its accuracy as prediction or warning, and whether Orwell's concerns ought still to be our own." Booklist

Baker, James R., 1925-
Critical essays on William Golding. Hall, G.K. & Co. 1988 197p (Critical essays on British literature) $47   **823.009**
1. Golding, William, 1911-1993
ISBN 0-8161-8764-9   LC 87-33312
The author examines the moral and philosophical aspects in the work of the British Nobel laureate
Includes bibliographical references

Baldwin, Dean R., 1942-
Virginia Woolf: a study of the short fiction. Twayne Pubs. 1989 157p (Twayne's studies in short fiction) $23.95   **823.009**
1. Woolf, Virginia, 1882-1941
ISBN 0-8057-8314-8   LC 88-34765
A "critical book devoted to Woolf's short stories. . . . Baldwin's choice of a chronological, biographical approach makes this study a good choice for the nonspecialist reader. The inclusion of several of Woolf's own essayistic statements on the craft of fiction, as well as a selection of comments by other critics (including Katherine Mansfield) increases both the book's scholarly value and its interest for the novice." Booklist
Includes bibliography

Berg, Maggie
Jane Eyre; portrait of a life. Twayne Pubs. 1987 134p (Twayne's masterwork studies) lib bdg $23.95; pa $13.95   **823.009**
1. Brontë, Charlotte, 1816-1855. Jane Eyre
ISBN 0-8057-7955-8 (lib bdg); 0-8057-8010-6 (pa)
LC 87-14877
The author considers Brontë's novel as a self-portrait of a female artist, focusing on Jane Eyre as protagonist and narrator
Includes bibliography

Blom, Margaret Howard
Charlotte Brontë. Twayne Pubs. 1977 176p (Twayne's English authors series) $21.95 **823.009**
1. Brontë, Charlotte, 1816-1855
ISBN 0-8057-6673-1   LC 76-42225
The author "follows the series format—chronology, biography, criticism, notes, annotated bibliography. There

are no radical interpretations or flights of fancy. Especially noteworthy is the chapter on Charlotte's early unpublished writings. Blom succeeds admirably in following the contorted paths of this early writing and making sense of it." Libr J

Brunsdale, Mitzi
James Joyce; a study of the short fiction; [by] Mitzi M. Brunsdale. Twayne Pubs. 1993 xxv, 264p il (Twayne's studies in short fiction) $23.95
823.009
1. Joyce, James, 1882-1941
ISBN 0-8057-0854-5   LC 92-39802
A critical examination of the characters, plots, symbolism and themes of Joyce's shorter fiction
Includes bibliographical references

Bunson, Matthew
Encyclopedia Sherlockiana; an A-to-Z guide to the world of the great detective; [by] Matthew E. Bunson. Macmillan 1994 326p il $25 **823.009**
1. Doyle, Sir Arthur Conan, 1859-1930 2. Holmes, Sherlock (Fictitious character)
ISBN 0-671-79826-X   LC 94-10714
This volume includes synopses of all the stories and novels; entries on cases and characters; a history of Holmes on stage and screen; a profile of Arthur Conan Doyle; and a listing of Sherlock Holmes societies. More than 100 black-and-white illustrations of movie stills, London sites, maps, diagrams, and original drawings from the Strand complement the text
Includes bibliographical references

Burt, Forrest D., 1939-
W. Somerset Maugham. Twayne Pubs. 1985 157p (Twayne's English authors series) $23.95
823.009
1. Maugham, W. Somerset (William Somerset), 1874-1965
ISBN 0-8057-6885-8   LC 84-25288
An examination of the life and work of the author of The razor's edge, The moon and sixpence and Of human bondage. An assessment of Maugham's short stories is also included
Includes bibliography

Chance, Jane, 1945-
The lord of the rings; the mythology of power. Twayne Pubs. 1992 130p il (Twayne's masterwork studies) $23.95; pa $13.95   **823.009**
1. Tolkien, J. R. R. (John Ronald Reuel), 1892-1973. Lord of the rings
ISBN 0-8057-9441-7; 0-8057-8571-X (pa)
LC 92-1402
Chance "interprets the layers of meaning in various volumes of 'The Lord of the Rings' as they relate to the 20th century. . . . She concentrates mostly on the specific themes of power, language, and politics. . . . The author has taken a complex and convoluted masterpiece and dissected it in a clear and concise style." SLJ
Includes bibliographical references

Costa, Richard Hauer

H.G. Wells. rev ed. Twayne Pubs. 1985 177p
(Twayne's English authors series) $22.95 **823.009**
1. Wells, H. G. (Herbert George), 1866-1946
ISBN 0-8057-6887-4   LC 84-25305
First published 1967
A study of the wide variety of Wells's literary output,
the criticism it has engendered, and its influence
Includes bibliography

Cox, Don Richard

Arthur Conan Doyle. Ungar 1985 251p
(Literature and life series) $19.95   **823.009**
1. Doyle, Sir Arthur Conan, 1859-1930
ISBN 0-8044-2146-3   LC 84-28050
This introduction to the life and work of the creator
of Sherlock Holmes includes discussions of his historical
fiction, adventure stories, science fiction and fantasies,
scientific monographs and political pamphlets
Includes bibliography

Crabbe, Katharyn W., 1945-

J.R.R. Tolkien. rev and expanded ed. Ungar
1988 233p (Literature and life, British writers)
hardcover o.p. paperback available $9.95 **823.009**
1. Tolkien, J. R. R. (John Ronald Reuel), 1892-1973
ISBN 0-8044-6106-6 (pa)   LC 87-5931
First published 1981
The author examines the themes of good, evil and
moral courage in the Middle-Earth fantasies. Tolkien's
scholarly writings are also examined
Includes bibliography

Critical essays on James Joyce; [edited by]
Bernard Benstock. Hall, G.K. & Co. 1985 236p
(Critical essays on modern British literature) $47
      823.009
1. Joyce, James, 1882-1941
ISBN 0-8161-8751-7   LC 84-12987
A collection of 19 critical essays that analyze the
work and influence of Joyce
Includes bibliography

Critical essays on Nadine Gordimer; [edited by]
Rowland Smith. Hall, G.K. & Co. 1990 226p
(Critical essays on world literature) $47
      823.009
1. Gordimer, Nadine, 1923-
ISBN 0-8161-8847-5   LC 90-31945
Critics examine the novels and short stories of the
South African Nobel laureate
Includes bibliographical references

Critical essays on Thomas Hardy; the novels;
[edited by] Dale Kramer with the assistance of
Nancy Marck. Hall, G.K. & Co. 1990 259p
(Critical essays on British literature) $47
      823.009
1. Hardy, Thomas, 1840-1928
ISBN 0-8161-8850-5   LC 90-30431
Critics provide new readings of such works as: Far
from the madding crowd, The mayor of Casterbridge,
Tess of the D'Urbervilles, The return of the native, and
Jude the obscure

D.H. Lawrence's Sons and lovers; edited and with
an introduction by Harold Bloom. Chelsea
House 1988 170p (Modern critical
interpretations) $24.95   **823.009**
1. Lawrence, D. H. (David Herbert), 1885-1930. Sons
and lovers
ISBN 1-55546-024-0   LC 87-17831
Contributors offer critical assessments of Lawrence's
classic evocation of working-class life
Includes bibliography

Daniel Defoe; edited and with an introduction by
Harold Bloom. Chelsea House 1987 234p
(Modern critical views) $34.95   **823.009**
1. Defoe, Daniel, 1661?-1731
ISBN 1-55546-284-7   LC 87-6346
A collection of thirteen critical essays on Defoe and
his works arranged in chronological order of publication.
Particular emphasis is placed on his novels Robinson
Crusoe and Moll Flanders
Includes bibliography

De Vitis, A. A.

Graham Greene. rev ed. Twayne Pubs. 1986
218p (Twayne's English authors series) $23.95
      823.009
1. Greene, Graham, 1904-1991
ISBN 0-8057-6911-0   LC 85-17612
First published 1964
The author focuses primarily on Greene's fiction from
the early The man within and Brighton Rock to Monsig-
nor Quixote and The tenth man. Also discussed are pertinent biographical facts that may effect an understanding
of the work, and Greene's journalistic contributions,
including his film reviews
Includes bibliography

Ermarth, Elizabeth, 1939-

George Eliot; [by] Elizabeth Deeds Ermarth.
Twayne Pubs. 1985 163p (Twayne's English
authors series) $22.95   **823.009**
1. Eliot, George, 1819-1880
ISBN 0-8057-6910-2   LC 85-8603
"In the biographical sketch that opens the book, and
in the following chapter devoted to Eliot's translations
and essays, Ermarth tallies the influences that contributed
to the novelist's intellectual development. . . . Ermarth
is consistently successful in locating the central issues of
each of the novels and in relating them in turn to Eliot's
own system of moral and philosophical belief." Booklist
Includes bibliography

Fargnoli, A. Nicholas

James Joyce A to Z; the essential reference to
the life and work; [by] A. Nicholas Fargnoli and
Michael Patrick Gillespie. Facts on File 1995 304p
$45   **823.009**
1. Joyce, James, 1882-1941
ISBN 0-8160-2904-0   LC 94-34660
Also available in paperback from Oxford Univ. Press

Fargnoli, A. Nicholas—*Continued*
The main portion of this compendium "is an A-Z listing of all things Joyce, from 'Abbey Theatre' to 'Works in Progress,' and most things in between. The several appendixes that follow offer a marvelous list of Joycean arcanum, including a time line from *Ulysses*, the text of Judge Woolsey's 1993 decision to lift the ban on the book in the United States, and a working outline of *Finnigans Wake*. Overall, this is a delightful and helpful volume." Libr J
Includes bibliographical references

Fonstad, Karen Wynn
The atlas of Middle-earth. [rev ed] Houghton Mifflin 1981 208p il maps pa $19.95   **823.009**
1. Tolkien, J. R. R. (John Ronald Reuel), 1892-1973
ISBN 0-395-53516-6   LC 80-22132
First published 1981
A guide to the journeys, lands, peoples, and history of Tolkien's imaginary kingdom
Includes bibliography

Friedman, Lawrence S.
William Golding. Continuum 1993 191p (Literature and life, British writers) $19.95
823.009
1. Golding, William, 1911-1993
ISBN 0-8264-0564-9   LC 91-41115
"A Frederick Ungar book"
"A concise biographical and critical introduction to Golding. A chronology, critiques of writings, bibliography, and an index are part of this book that is easy to read and understand. It will spark readers' interest in the author, his writings, and his place in literary history." SLJ

George Orwell's 1984; edited and with an introduction by Harold Bloom. Chelsea House 1987 135p $29.95   **823.009**
1. Orwell, George, 1903-1950. Nineteen eighty-four
ISBN 1-55546-026-7   LC 86-21577
A collection of essays providing international appraisal and interpretation of Orwell's apocalyptic novel
Includes bibliography

Gillon, Adam, 1921-
Joseph Conrad. Twayne Pubs. 1982 210p (Twayne's English authors series) $24.95 **823.009**
1. Conrad, Joseph, 1857-1924
ISBN 0-8057-6820-3   LC 81-13301
This work "ranges over every essential aspect of the writer's life and work. . . . The scope is admirable: the literary heritage (such as Shakespeare's influence on Conrad, for example), the major themes of the fiction, the references to the abiding critical evaluations of others, and the aim to isolate key motifs of both life and work." Choice
Includes bibliography

Horror: the 100 best books; edited by Stephen Jones and Kim Newman. Carroll & Graf Pubs. 1988 254p $15.95; pa $8.95   **823.009**
1. Horror fiction—History and criticism 2. Books and reading—Best books
ISBN 0-88184-417-9; 0-88184-594-9 (pa)
                                     LC 88-7351
"Each of 100 writers and editors of horror fiction plugs his or her own favorite book in the genre. Chronologically, the resulting '100 Best' span from 1592 and Marlowe's play, 'Doctor Faustus,' to a novel and a short-story collection both published in 1987. Genre classics such as 'Frankenstein,' 'Dracula,' and 'Dr. Jekyll and Mr. Hyde' are expectably honored, as are contemporary titles by King, Barker, Strieber, Straub, et al., and works by many of Edwardian England's and mid-twentieth-century America's horror specialists." Booklist

Hussey, Mark, 1956-
Virginia Woolf A-Z; a comprehensive reference for students, teachers, and common readers to her life, work, and critical reception. Facts on File 1995 452p il $50   **823.009**
1. Woolf, Virginia, 1882-1941
ISBN 0-8160-3020-0   LC 94-36500
Also available in paperback from Oxford Univ. Press
This work provides synopses and publishing histories of works; discussions of intellectual and literary influences on Woolf; biographical entries on important people in her life, including family and friends; and an overview of the critical reception to her work
Includes bibliographical references

Jaffe, Jacqueline A.
Arthur Conan Doyle. Twayne Pubs. 1987 148p (Twayne's English authors series) lib bdg $22.95
823.009
1. Doyle, Sir Arthur Conan, 1859-1930
ISBN 0-8057-6954-4   LC 87-8421
"Jaffe organizes Doyle's diverse canon by genre and discusses it in the context of the late 19th century romantic revival. Devoting two chapters to the Holmes novels and stories, she shows Doyle fusing romantic assumptions with rationalist certainties, to create a uniquely popular hero: the knight-errant as master detective. Jaffe promotes renewed attention for Doyle's historical novels and scientific romances." Publisher's note
Includes bibliography

John le Carré; edited and with an introduction by Harold Bloom. Chelsea House 1987 180p (Modern critical views) $24.95   **823.009**
1. Le Carré, John, 1931-
ISBN 0-87754-703-3   LC 86-31026
A selection of critical essays, arranged in chronological order of publication, devoted to the fiction of John le Carré
Includes bibliography

Keating, H. R. F. (Henry Reymond Fitzwalter), 1926-
Crime and mystery: the 100 best books. Carroll & Graf Pubs. 1987 219p $15.95; pa $8.95
823.009
1. Mystery fiction—Bibliography 2. Books and reading—Best books
ISBN 0-88184-345-8; 0-88184-441-1 (pa)
LC 87-17377
A "collection of essays reflecting one writer's ideas about what constitutes the best in crime and mystery fiction. The two-page essays extend from Poe's *Tales of Mystery and Imagination* through P.D. James's *A Taste for Death*, forming a sort of history of the genre. Each essay contains a synopsis of the plot or theme, a critical assessment, and a list of first and recent editions. Keating, a prolific mystery writer, seems an ideal choice to compile such a work, and his wit and intelligence make these essays as much fun as they are informative." Libr J

Kelly, Richard Michael, 1937-
Daphne du Maurier. Twayne Pubs. 1987 156p (Twayne's English authors series) lib bdg $22.95
823.009
1. Du Maurier, Dame Daphne, 1907-1989
ISBN 0-8057-6931-5
LC 86-12113
Following a brief biographical introduction the author assesses the style, characterizations, and symbolism of the English mystery writer
Includes bibliography

Knapp, Bettina Liebowitz, 1926-
The Brontës; Branwell, Anne, Emily, Charlotte; [by] Bettina L. Knapp. Continuum 1991 204p (Literature and life, British writers) $19.95
823.009
1. Brontë family
ISBN 0-8264-0514-2
LC 90-2554
"A Frederick Ungar book"
"Knapp's overriding concern is to reach a firm understanding of why the writings of a rather reclusive and eccentric Victorian family have intrigued and moved contemporary American readers; that is, she locates and describes the Brontës' universal appeal. While scholars will turn to this book for its obvious research value, lay readers will be fascinated by its biographical details, especially concerning the two lesser-known Brontës, Anne (author of the worthy feminist novel *Agnes Grey*) and Branwell (dead at age 31 from drugs and drink)." Booklist
Includes bibliographical references

Lowe-Evans, Mary
Frankenstein; Mary Shelley's wedding guest. Twayne Pubs. 1993 98p (Twayne's masterwork studies) $23.95; pa $13.95
823.009
1. Shelley, Mary Wollstonecraft, 1797-1851. Frankenstein
ISBN 0-8057-8376-8; 0-8057-8597-3 (pa)
LC 92-41553
A historicist reading of Shelley's classic novel about the conflict between Romantic ideals and Victorian reality. Shelley's views on marriage are examined in depth
Includes bibliography

Mellor, Anne Kostelanetz
Mary Shelley, her life, her fiction, her monsters. Methuen 1988 xx, 275p il $35; pa $14.95
823.009
1. Shelley, Mary Wollstonecraft, 1797-1851
ISBN 0-415-02591-5; 0-415-90147-2 (pa)
LC 87-31249
The author "blends biography and informed criticism here to give a feminist reevaluation of Mary Shelley and her fiction, especially *Frankenstein*. . . . Mellor's book is clearly written and forcefully argued." Choice
Includes bibliography

Moler, Kenneth L.
Pride and prejudice; a study in artistic economy. Twayne Pubs. 1989 110p (Twayne's masterwork studies) $23.95; pa $13.95
823.009
1. Austen, Jane, 1775-1817. Pride and prejudice
ISBN 0-8057-7983-3; 0-8057-8032-7 (pa)
LC 88-16335
The author takes a critical look at the language, themes and style of Austen's masterful portrayal of class prejudice and false pride
Includes bibliography

Nelson, Harland S.
Charles Dickens. Twayne Pubs. 1981 266p (Twayne's English authors series) $21.95 **823.009**
1. Dickens, Charles, 1812-1870
ISBN 0-8057-6805-X
LC 81-5050
This study of Dickens' work focuses primarily on: The posthumous papers of the Pickwick Club, David Copperfield, Bleak House, Great expectations, and Oliver Twist
Includes bibliography

A **Reader's** guide to the twentieth-century novel; editor, Peter Parker; consultant editor, Frank Kermode. Oxford Univ. Press 1995 xxx, 748p $40
823.009
1. English fiction—History and criticism 2. American fiction—History and criticism
ISBN 0-19-521153-7
LC 94-43056
First published 1994 in the United Kingdom with title: The Reader's companion to the twentieth-century novel
"This compilation provides critical plot summaries for some 750 novels written in English between 1900 and 1993, with 60 percent published since 1945. Its focus is 'literary,' so only a few representative genre works are included, e.g., Raymond Chandler's *Farewell, My Lovely*. The unsigned entries are arranged chronologically, and no bibliographies are included." Libr J

Rogers, Deborah Webster
J.R.R. Tolkien; by Deborah Webster Rogers and Ivor A. Rogers. Twayne Pubs. 1980 164p (Twayne's English authors series) $22.95 **823.009**
1. Tolkien, J. R. R. (John Ronald Reuel), 1892-1973
ISBN 0-8057-6796-7
LC 80-11518
The authors analyze the connection between Tolkien's philological background and his place in the development of fantasy literature
Includes bibliography

Thornton, Weldon

D.H. Lawrence; a study of the short fiction. Twayne Pubs. 1993 174p (Twayne's studies in short fiction) $23.95 **823.009**

1. Lawrence, D. H. (David Herbert), 1885-1930
ISBN 0-8057-0862-6   LC 93-25540

This study of Lawrence's short stories is divided into three parts. Part one, The short fiction, examines nine separate stories. Part two, The writer, includes excerpts from Lawrence's essays, letters and other writings in which he discusses his own short stories and those of others. The last part, The critics, contains excerpts from critical essays

Includes bibliography

Wagoner, Mary

Agatha Christie. Twayne Pubs. 1986 162p (Twayne's English authors series) $22.95 **823.009**

1. Christie, Agatha, 1890-1976
ISBN 0-8057-6938-2   LC 86-10004

"Dispensing quickly with the details of Christie's long, fairly uneventful, and already much-discussed life, Wagoner concentrates on Christie's extensive body of work. Along with synopses of the whodunits, the spy stories, and the romance thrillers . . . Wagoner offers perceptive critical commentary." Booklist

Includes bibliography

West, Mark I.

Roald Dahl. Twayne Pubs. 1992 148p (Twayne's English authors series) $22.95 **823.009**

1. Dahl, Roald
ISBN 0-8057-7019-4   LC 91-33737

A critical examination of Dahl's entire canon, with emphasis on the children's fiction. The text incorporates biographical information as well as quotes from an interview with the author

Includes bibliographical references

824 English essays

The **Oxford** book of essays; chosen and edited by John Gross. Oxford Univ. Press 1991 xxiii, 680p $30; pa $17.95 **824**

ISBN 0-19-214185-6; 0-19-282970-X (pa)
LC 90-34948

"The collection begins in the 17th century with Sir Francis Bacon moralizing on truth and ends with a scathing review of a Judith Krantz best seller by Clive James. In between there is something for just about everyone, e.g., Boswell on war, Thoreau on moonlight, Banham on potato chips. Literary, theological, sociological, political, and humorous essays are included." Libr J

Includes bibliographical references

828 English miscellany

Blake, William, 1757-1827

The complete poetry and prose of William Blake; edited by David V. Erdman; commentary by Harold Bloom. newly rev ed. University of Calif. Press 1982 xxvi, 990p $47.50 **828**

ISBN 0-520-04473-8   LC 81-40323

First published 1965 with title: Poetry and prose of William Blake

This collection contains the complete poetry and prose of Blake, including his letters, as well as critical commentary

The portable Blake; selected and arranged with an introduction by Alfred Kazin. Viking 1946 713p il o.p.; Penguin Bks. paperback available $14.95 **828**

ISBN 0-14-015026-9 (pa)

"The Viking portable library"

A "generous selection of verse, prose, letters, and essays. Blake is shown as an artist and poet against all institutions but ever seeking unity (though his was the mystic's quest) while hunting for realism and naturalism." Cincinnati Public Libr

Includes bibliography

William Blake; edited by Michael Mason. Oxford Univ. Press 1988 xxv, 601p hardcover o.p. paperback available $22 **828**

ISBN 0-19-282001-X (pa)   LC 87-22104

"Organized by genre and subject . . . the anthology includes nearly all of Blake's poetry and prose works and some of his letters. The epic narratives *Milton* and *Jerusalem* are reproduced in full, and an index of Blakean names and motifs is included." Publisher's note

Includes bibliography

Christopher, Joe R.

C. S. Lewis. Twayne Pubs. 1987 150p (Twayne's English authors series) $21.95 **828**

1. Lewis, C. S. (Clive Staples), 1898-1963
ISBN 0-8057-6944-7   LC 86-25757

A critical introduction to the English literary critic, moral theorist, and author of children's books

Includes bibliography

Coleridge, Samuel Taylor, 1772-1834

The portable Coleridge; edited and with an introduction by I. A. Richards. Viking 1950 630p o.p.; Penguin Bks. paperback available $13.95 **828**

ISBN 0-14-015048-X (pa)

"The Viking portable library"

Includes: The rime of the ancient mariner (1875); Christabel; Kubla Khan; and most of the shorter poems; ample representation of the "Biographia literaria," generous selections from the other literary criticism, political essays, notebooks, and letters; also a lengthy biographical introduction

Includes bibliography

Conrad, Joseph, 1857-1924
The portable Conrad; edited and with an introduction and notes by Morton Dauwen Zabel. rev ed, [edited] by Frederick R. Karl. Viking 1969 762p o.p.; Penguin Bks. paperback available $14.95   **828**
ISBN 0-14-015033-1 (pa)
"The Viking portable library"
First published 1947
Contains two novels: The Nigger of the Narcissus and Typhoon; three long stories; six shorter stories; and a selection from Conrad's prefaces, letters and autobiographical writings
Includes bibliography

Donne, John, 1572-1631
The complete poetry and selected prose of John Donne; edited, with an introduction by Charles M. Coffin. Modern Lib. 1994 xlv, 594p $18.50   **828**
ISBN 0-679-60102-3   LC 94-4354
This volume contains Donne's love poetry, satires, epigrams, verse letters and holy sonnets. Also includes selected prose and a sampling of private letters

Greene, Graham, 1904-1991
The portable Graham Greene; edited with an introduction by Philip Stratford. updated & rev ed. Penguin Bks. 1994 xxvii, 527p pa $13.95   **828**
ISBN 0-14-023359-8   LC 93-49078
First published 1973
"Includes the complete novels The Heart of the Matter and The Third Man, along with excerpts from ten other novels, short stories, selections from Greene's memoirs and travel writings, and essays on English and American literature." Publisher's note

Hammond, J. R. (John R.), 1933-
A George Orwell companion; a guide to the novels, documentaries and essays. St. Martin's Press 1982 278p il $29.95   **828**
1. Orwell, George, 1903-1950
ISBN 0-312-32452-9   LC 82-875
The author's "synopses discover Orwell's main arguments and their place in his development even as they mark distinguishing characteristics of style. Such features as the 'George Orwell Dictionary' (an arrangement of Orwell's books, essays, and poems with apt commentary), the 'Key to the Characters and Locations,' and the appendix, which lists film versions and gives an example of Orwell's method of composition, are most helpful to any inquirer after a particular. . . . Footnotes, select bibliography, and index complete this useful work." Choice

Harrison, James, 1927-
Rudyard Kipling. Twayne Pubs. 1982 173p (Twayne's English authors series) $22.95   **828**
1. Kipling, Rudyard, 1865-1936
ISBN 0-8057-6825-4   LC 82-1999
This critical study of the English poet, short story writer and journalist incorporates biographical information
Includes bibliography

Kelly, Richard Michael, 1937-
Lewis Carroll; [by] Richard Kelly. rev ed. Twayne Pubs. 1990 190p il (Twayne's English authors series) lib bdg $22.95   **828**
1. Carroll, Lewis, 1832-1898
ISBN 0-8057-6988-9   LC 89-36943
First published 1977
The author presents overviews of Carroll's literary writings with particular emphasis on the Alice books and The hunting of the snark
Includes bibliography

Kipling, Rudyard, 1865-1936
The portable Kipling; edited and with an introduction by Irving Howe. Viking 1982 xlii, 687p o.p.; Penguin Bks. paperback available $14.95   **828**
ISBN 0-14-015097-8 (pa)   LC 81-52466
"The Viking portable library"
This volume collects short stories and verse. Included are about 50 poems. "The twenty-eight stories included give about equal weight to 'Stories of India' and 'Soldiers' Tales' and analyses of the effects of world war on disappointed idealists and activists." Christ Sci Monit

Lawrence, D. H. (David Herbert), 1885-1930
The portable D. H. Lawrence; edited and with an introduction by Diana Trilling. Viking 1947 692p hardcover o.p. paperback available $14.95   **828**
ISBN 0-14-015028-5 (pa)
Partially analyzed in Essay and general literature index
"The Viking portable library"
This volume contains eight short stories or novelettes: The Prussian officer; Tickets, please; The blind man; Two blue birds; The lovely lady; The rockinghorse winner; The princess; The fox; excerpts from The rainbow, and Women in Love; a dozen poems; travel sketches; letters; and a number of essays and critical writings

Lewis, C. S. (Clive Staples), 1898-1963
The essential C. S. Lewis; edited and with an introduction by Lyle W. Dorsett. Macmillan 1988 536p hardcover o.p. paperback available $14   **828**
ISBN 0-02-019550-8 (pa)   LC 88-11882
This work "includes a brief autobiographical sketch, a smattering of letters, and selections from each of the literary categories the versatile Lewis adopted: children's fiction, adult fiction, religion and morality, poetry, philosophy, and literary history and criticism. Arrangement is by genre, and each chapter is preceded by a brief introduction. The entire texts of two novels, The Lion, the Witch and the Wardrobe and Perelandra, are included." Booklist
Includes bibliography

Mayle, Peter
A dog's life; with drawings by Edward Koren. Knopf 1995 192p il $20; pa $11   **828**
1. Dogs 2. Provence (France)—Social life and customs
ISBN 0-679-44122-0; 0-679-26267-1 (pa)
    LC 94-42590
Also available Thorndike Press large print edition

Mayle, Peter—*Continued*

"Both canine 'memoir' and cautionary tale, this sprightly account of the further adventures of Boy, Mayle's real-life dog introduced in *Toujours Provence* (1991) is a gem of its kind. As animated by Mayle, Boy is a clever chap given to literary allusions, urbane observations and stinging bon mots." Publ Wkly

Milton, John, 1608-1674

The portable Milton; edited and with an introduction by Douglas Bush. Viking 1949 693p o.p.; Penguin Bks. paperback available $14.95
828

ISBN 0-14-015044-7 (pa)
"The Viking portable library"
A selection of the early poems and sonnets; "Areopagitica" complete; lengthy selections from the other chief prose works; and the three major poems, "Paradise lost," "Paradise regained," and "Samson Agonistes," complete
Includes glossary and bibliography

The **Oxford** book of literary anecdotes; edited by James Sutherland. Oxford Univ. Press 1975 382p hardcover o.p. paperback available $8.95
828

1. English literature—Anecdotes 2. Authors, English—Anecdotes
ISBN 0-19-281936-4 (pa)
"Clarendon Press"
This is a collection of some four hundred anecdotes by and about British literary figures from the seventh-century poet Caedmon down to P. G. Wodehouse and Dylan Thomas
The editor "quotes original sources—memoirs, letters, diaries, early biographies—and his book is more than a succession of quips and repartees. His criteria are elastic enough to include material we might not ordinarily think of as anecdotes." Newsweek
Includes bibliographical references

Saposnik, Irving S.

Robert Louis Stevenson. Twayne Pubs. 1974 164p (Twayne's English authors series) $22.95
828

1. Stevenson, Robert Louis, 1850-1894
ISBN 0-8057-1517-7
This study of Stevenson's work includes "chapters on Stevenson's lesser known accomplishments in such genres as drama and the essays [as well as] . . . reassessments of the more widely read works. . . . Also, the plentiful biographical material which appears here, both in an introductory sketch and in conjunction with the critical comments, goes a long way toward correcting many of the popular misconceptions about Stevenson's life." Libr J
Includes bibliography

Thomas, Dylan, 1914-1953

A child's Christmas in Wales
828

1. Christmas—Wales
Hardcover and paperback editions available from various publishers

First published 1954 by New Directions
A portrait of Christmas Day in a small Welsh town and of the author's childhood there
For any season of the year "the language is enchanting and the poetry shines with an unearthly radiance." N Y Times Book Rev

Tolkien, J. R. R. (John Ronald Reuel), 1892-1973

Poems and stories; illustrated by Pauline Baynes. Houghton Mifflin 1994 c1980 342p il $24.95
828
ISBN 0-395-68999-6   LC 93-42619
First published 1980 in the United Kingdom
This volume includes The adventures of Tom Bombadil, a collection of songs and verses; the dramatic poem, The homecoming of Beorhtnoth Beorhthelm's son; an essay: On fairy stories; and three stories: Leaf by Niggle; Farmer Giles of Ham; and Smith of Wootton Major

Wilde, Oscar, 1854-1900

The portable Oscar Wilde; selected and edited by Richard Aldington and Stanley Weintraub. rev ed. Viking 1981 741p o.p.; Penguin Bks. paperback available $14.95
828
ISBN 0-14-015093-5 (pa)   LC 80-39827
"The Viking portable library"
First published 1946
This volume contains The critic as artist, The picture of Dorian Gray, Salomé, The importance of being Earnest, De profundis, and selected poems, reviews, letters and phrases from other works

Woolf, Virginia, 1882-1941

The Virginia Woolf reader; edited by Mitchell A. Leaska. Harcourt Brace Jovanovich 1984 371p hardcover o.p. paperback available $12.95
828
ISBN 0-15-693590-2 (pa)   LC 84-4478
"A Harvest book"
Excerpts from Woolf's "novels form less than 20 percent of a reader whose selections of short stories, essays, letters, and diary entries are excellent. This collection will be useful to those already familiar with Woolf's novels and seeking an introductory selection of her other writings." Libr J

829 Old English (Anglo-Saxon)

Beowulf

Beowulf
829

Hardcover and paperback editions available from various publishers
This epic of a dragon-slaying hero "is the earliest extant written composition of such length in English, and indeed in all Teutonic literature. Its content was based on Norse legends merged with historical events of the early sixth century in Denmark; this oral tradition was carried to England by Danish invaders of the mid-sixth century, fused with the Christianity they absorbed there, and finally written down by a single but unknown poet." Reader's Ency

Beowulf; edited and with an introduction by
Harold Bloom. Chelsea House 1987 144p
(Modern critical interpretations) $29.95   **829**
ISBN 0-87754-904-4   LC 87-8093
A collection of critical essays on the Old English epic
poem
Includes bibliography

Clark, George, 1932-
Beowulf. Twayne Pubs. 1990 170p (Twayne's
English authors series) $23.95   **829**
1. Beowulf
ISBN 0-8057-6996-X   LC 89-77340
A critical reading of the Old English alliterative verse
epic
Includes bibliographical references

830.3   German literature— Encyclopedias and dictionaries

Garland, Henry B. (Henry Burnand)
The Oxford companion to German literature; by
Henry and Mary Garland. 2nd ed. Oxford Univ.
Press 1986 1020p $55   **830.3**
1. German literature—Dictionaries 2. German literature—Bio-bibliography
ISBN 0-19-866139-8   LC 85-25962
First published 1976
Entries include biographies, synopses of important
works, literary terms and movements, historical events
and figures, and material relevant to the social and intellectual background of German literature from the earliest
records to the present

831   German poetry

Rilke, Rainer Maria, 1875-1926
Selected poems of Rainer Maria Rilke; a
translation from the German and commentary by
Robert Bly. Harper & Row 1981 224p hardcover
o.p. paperback available $14   **831**
ISBN 0-06-090727-4 (pa)   LC 78-2114
A bilingual edition of the German poet's verse select-
ed from A Book for the Hours of Prayer, The Book of
Pictures, New Poems, The Uncollected and Occasional
Poems, and Sonnets to Orpheus. The translator also in-
cludes five introductory essays
"Bly's comments make us see Rilke's work in relation
to events of the poet's life and to creative inner tensions
within certain periods. They also afford an awareness of
Rilke's specific inwardness, a sensibility and disposition
of soul very different from that of any American poet."
Libr J

831.008   German poetry— Collections

German poetry, 1910-1975; an anthology;
translated and edited by Michael Hamburger.
Persea Bks. 1976 xxxiii, 533p o.p.   **831.008**
1. German poetry—Collections
Replaces: Modern German poetry, 1910-1960

"The reader can follow German poetry from Expressionism through Modern Realism to contemporary
imaginism and neo-realism. There are well-known names
here, Else Lasker-Schiller, Franz Werfel, Bertolt Brecht,
Nelly Sachs, and Günter Grass. More important still is
the inclusion of lesser-known but excellent poets."
Choice

832   German drama

Brecht, Bertolt, 1898-1956
Galileo; English version by Charles Laughton;
edited and with an introduction by Eric Bentley.
Grove Weidenfeld 1991 155p pa $6.95   **832**
1. Galilei, Galileo, 1564-1642—Drama
ISBN 0-8021-3059-3   LC 91-22966
"An Evergreen book"
Written 1938-39, first performed 1943
"The play concerns Galileo Galilei's conflict with the
church over the application of the Copernican system,
which the church viewed as anathema. Brecht deliberately portrays Galileo as a self-serving and decidedly unhe-
roic character, willing to compromise his principles in
the face of pressure." Reader's Ency. 4th edition

Two plays; revised English versions by Eric
Bentley. New Am. Lib. 1983 236p pa $4.95   **832**
ISBN 0-452-00857-3   LC 82-61769
This volume contains two of Brecht's parable plays:
The good woman of Setzuan, deals with the conflict of
good and evil as seen in the life of a poor virtuous wom-
an; The Caucasian chalk circle, based on the Chinese
drama The circle of chalk, explores the rights of a bio-
logical mother versus those of a foster mother
Includes bibliography

833.009   German fiction—History and criticism

Critical essays on Franz Kafka; [edited by] Ruth
V. Gross. Hall, G.K. & Co. 1990 281p (Critical
essays on world literature) $47   **833.009**
1. Kafka, Franz, 1883-1924
ISBN 0-8161-8848-3   LC 90-4411
Contributors assess the artistic achievement and continuing influence of the Czech author of novels, stories,
parables and sketches
Includes bibliographical references

Field, George Wallis
Hermann Hesse. Twayne Pubs. 1970 198p
(Twayne's world authors series) $23.95   **833.009**
1. Hesse, Hermann, 1877-1962
ISBN 0-8057-2424-9
In addition to coverage of Hesse's life and works the
author also assesses the state of Hesse criticism
Includes bibliography

Firda, Richard Arthur, 1931-
All quiet on the western front; literary analysis and cultural context. Twayne Pubs. 1993 149p (Twayne's masterwork studies) $23.95; pa $13.95
833.009
1. Remarque, Erich Maria, 1898-1970. All quiet on the western front
ISBN 0-8057-8386-5; 0-8057-8387-3 (pa)
LC 93-3872
This examination and interpretation of Remarque's antiwar classic discusses its autobiographical elements, its style and characterization, and its two sequels
Includes bibliography

Franz Kafka's The metamorphosis; edited and with an introduction by Harold Bloom. Chelsea House 1988 149p (Modern critical interpretations) $29.95
833.009
1. Kafka, Franz, 1883-1924. The metamorphosis
ISBN 1-55546-070-4
LC 87-17827
Martin Greenberg, Stanley Corngold and Evelyn Torton Beck are among the contributors to this collection of critical assessments of Kafka's classic
Includes bibliography

Franz Kafka's The trial; edited and with an introduction by Harold Bloom. Chelsea House 1987 142p (Modern critical interpretations) $24.95
833.009
1. Kafka, Franz, 1883-1924. The trial
ISBN 1-55546-071-2
LC 87-9360
A selection of modern critical interpretations of Franz Kafka's novel
Includes bibliography

Spann, Meno
Franz Kafka. Twayne Pubs. 1976 205p il (Twayne's world authors series) $22.95   **833.009**
1. Kafka, Franz, 1883-1924
ISBN 0-8057-6182-9
"Quotations from the broad range of Kafka's criticism (often paradoxical) are well integrated into the analysis. Spann offers as the basic inspiration for Kafka's works the author's problematic existence and describes his genre as 'inner' biography which uses different metaphors and 'abstractions not revealed.' An interesting addition to any collection of Kafka criticism." Libr J
Includes bibliography

839   Other Germanic literatures

Alexander, Edward, 1936-
Isaac Bashevis Singer. Twayne Pubs. 1980 161p (Twayne's world authors series) $22.95   **839**
1. Singer, Isaac Bashevis, 1904-1991
ISBN 0-8057-6424-0
LC 79-21272
While analyzing the novels, short stories and memoirs, Alexander assesses Singer's place in European and world literary history
Includes bibliography

Isaac Bashevis Singer: a study of the short fiction. Twayne Pubs. 1990 147p (Twayne's studies in short fiction) $23.95   **839**
1. Singer, Isaac Bashevis, 1904-1991
ISBN 0-8057-8329-6
LC 90-37724
This critical study of Singer's short stories also includes an interview with the Nobel laureate
Includes bibliographical references

839.3   Dutch, Flemish, Afrikaans literatures

Frank, Anne, 1929-1945
Anne Frank's Tales from the secret annex; with translations by Ralph Manheim and Michel Mok. Doubleday 1984 c1983 136p o.p.; Bantam Bks. paperback available $3.99   **839.3**
ISBN 0-553-56983-X (pa)
LC 82-45871
Original Dutch edition copyrighted 1949. First English translation published 1960 in the United Kingdom with title: Tales from the house behind
This volume presents all of Anne Frank's existing stories, sketches and drafts as well as her personal reminiscences and essays
"The bulk of the collection is on the sober side: tales of poor or solitary young girls, and earnest pleas for understanding and charity among people. Less likely to appeal to the cynical reader, these stories display Anne Frank's best talent: a narrative, neither pretentious nor dull, that is without match for both the compelling message and the elusive sentiment." Best Sellers

The works of Anne Frank; introduction by Ann Birstein and Alfred Kazin; drawings by Peter Spier. Greenwood Press 1973 c1959 332p il $55
839.3
1. World War, 1939-1945—Jews 2. Netherlands—History—1940-1945, German occupation 3. Jews—Netherlands
ISBN 0-8371-7206-3
Reprint of the title first published 1959 by Doubleday
Collected here are the contents of two notebooks. One notebook contained Anne Frank's now famous "Diary," originally published in 1952, and entered separately in class 92. In the other notebook were Anne's personal reminiscences, stories, fairy tales, formal essays, and attempts at "adult" fiction

839.8   Danish and Norwegian literatures

Ibsen, Henrik, 1828-1906
The complete major prose plays; translated and introduced by Rolf Fjelde. Farrar, Straus & Giroux 1978 1143p o.p.; New Am. Lib. paperback available $21.95   **839.8**
ISBN 0-452-26205-4 (pa)
LC 77-28349
Contents: Pillars of society; A doll's house; Ghosts; An enemy of the people; The wild duck; Rosmersholm; The lady from the sea; Hedda Gabler; The master builder; Little Eyolf; John Gabriel Borkman; When we dead awaken
Includes bibliography

Ibsen, Henrik, 1828-1906—*Continued*

Ibsen: four major plays; translated by Rick
Davis and Brian Johnston. Smith & Kraus 1995
286p (Great translations for actors) pa $19.95
839.8

ISBN 1-880399-67-9   LC 95-13632

Contents: A doll house; Ghosts; An enemy of the people; Hedda Gabler

"All four of these versions have been 'production-
tested,' which shows in their graceful and believable dialogue and their sheer theatricality. Davis and Johnston
have unlocked the power in Ibsen's works and made it
clear why Ibsen was once *the* playwright for firebrands,
Fabians, and other progressives throughout the world."
Booklist

840.3 French literature—
Encyclopedias and dictionaries

The New Oxford companion to literature in
French; edited by Peter France. Oxford Univ.
Press 1995 li, 865p maps $55   **840.3**
1. French literature—Dictionaries 2. French litera-
ture—Bio-bibliography
ISBN 0-19-866125-8   LC 95-225097

First published 1959 with title: The Oxford companion
to French literature

"This work views literature from the perspective of its
greater cultural context. Accordingly, topics discussed go
beyond the poets, novelists, and dramatists of the traditional French canon, and include philosophy, science, art,
history, linguistics, and cinema. Even strip cartoons and
pamphlets are treated. . . . The more than 3,000 entries
are written by approximately 130 international experts. In
addition to brief entries, there are long articles on general
topics, such as Québec, feminism, Occitan literature, and
the history of the French language." Am Ref Books
Annu, 1996

For a fuller review see: Booklist, Sept. 1, 1995

840.9 French literature—History
and criticism

A New history of French literature; edited by
Denis Hollier with R. Howard Bloch [et al.]
Harvard Univ. Press 1989 xxv, 1150p il maps
lib bdg $62.50; pa $29.95   **840.9**
1. French literature—History and criticism
ISBN 0-674-61565-4 (lib bdg); 0-674-61566-2 (pa)
LC 88-27027

"Using an episodic approach, Hollier . . . has put together a cast of 164 mostly American scholars who
present original and outstanding overviews of the key
topics and themes of French literature from the Stras-
bourg Oaths of 842 through 1983. Essays are introduced
by a date and chronologically arranged. Their focus includes genres, major literary movements, the role of
women, as well as lengthy survey articles." Libr J

Includes bibliographies

841 French poetry

La Fontaine, Jean de, 1621-1695
Fifty fables of La Fontaine; translated by
Norman R. Shapiro; with illustrations by Alan
James Robinson. University of Ill. Press 1988
119p il $29.95   **841**
1. Fables
ISBN 0-252-01513-4   LC 87-28750

"With English and French on facing pages, these close
translations will be especially useful to advanced readers
of French." Booklist

Rimbaud, Arthur, 1854-1891
Poems. Knopf 1994 288p (Everyman's library
pocket poets) $10.95   **841**
ISBN 0-679-43321-X   LC 94-2496

A collection of work by the French Symbolist known
for his daring images and pioneering prose poems

841.008 French poetry—Collections

The Random House book of twentieth-century
French poetry; with translations by American
and British poets; edited by Paul Auster.
Random House 1982 xlix, 635p hardcover o.p.
paperback available $26   **841.008**
1. French poetry—Collections
ISBN 0-394-71748-1 (pa)   LC 82-280

This bilingual edition collects the verse of forty-eight
poets as translated by eighty-four poets. The volume
opens with a section of poems by Guillaume Apollinaire
and closes with a group of poems by Philippe Denis. The
original and translation appear on facing pages

"This excellent anthology undertakes a double task: to
provide a comprehensive view of French poetry in the
twentieth century and to show, in the range of translators
it offers, the influences of that poetry on American and
British poets. . . . Paul Auster has done an excellent job
of matching poets and translators." Nation

Includes bibliographical references

842 French drama

Beckett, Samuel, 1906-1989
Waiting for Godot; tragicomedy in 2 acts. Grove
Press 1954 60p il hardcover o.p. paperback
available $8.95   **842**
ISBN 0-8021-3034-8 (pa)

Translated from the French by the author

A play originally written in French, by an Irish writer.
The play was first produced in Paris during the winter of
1952

"There are strong biblical references throughout, but
Beckett's powerful and symbolic portrayal of the human
condition as one of ignorance, delusion, paralysis, and
intermittent flashes of human sympathy, hope, and wit
has been subjected to many varying interpretations. The
theatrical vitality and versatility of the play have been
demonstrated by performances throughout the world."
Oxford Companion to Engl Lit. 5th edition

Genet, Jean, 1910-1986

The maids [and] Deathwatch; two plays; with an introduction by Jean-Paul Sartre; translated from the French by Bernard Frechtman. Grove Press 1954 166p hardcover o.p. paperback available $9.95 **842**

ISBN 0-8021-5056-X (pa)

Deathwatch, a one-act play written 1947 and first produced 1949 "deals with an insignificant criminal who tries to assume the highly desirable and prestigious role of murderer. . . . In 'The Maids (Les bonnes),' produced in 1947, . . . two servant girls have created an elaborate ritual in which they impersonate their mistress and finally murder her symbolically." McGraw-Hill Ency of World Drama

Ionesco, Eugène

Four plays; translated by Donald M. Allen. Grove Press 1958 160p pa $9.95 **842**

ISBN 0-8021-3079-8

Original French edition, 1954

Contents: The bald soprano; The lesson; Jack; or, The submission; The chairs

The bald soprano is a comedy satirizing English middle class life, while Jack, concerns a sulky young man who disappoints his family by refusing to marry the girl of their choice. An avant-garde drama, The chairs focuses on an old couple who receives many imaginary guests. The murder of a young student by his elderly teacher ends a bizarre lesson in The lesson

Rhinoceros, and other plays; translated by Derek Prouse. Grove Press 1960 141p pa $10 **842**

ISBN 0-8021-3098-4

Also available in hardcover from P. Smith

"An Evergreen book"

Contents: Rhinoceros; The future is in eggs; The leader

Three satirical comedies by a leading dramatist of the "theater of the absurd." In Rhinoceros, one man resists the pressure to conform as everyone about him accepts their transformation into rhinoceroses and he finds himself socially isolated. In The future is in eggs, a couple must produce eggs destined to become intellectuals. The leader is a satire on the mass adulation of political figures in which the leader turns out to be a headless figure

Samuel Beckett's Waiting for Godot; edited and with an introduction by Harold Bloom. Chelsea House 1987 131p (Modern critical interpretations) $34.95 **842**

1. Beckett, Samuel, 1906-1989. Waiting for Godot
ISBN 1-55546-058-5 LC 86-34301

Critical interpretations of Beckett's classic tragicomedy illustrating the apparent meaninglessness of life

Includes bibliography

Sartre, Jean Paul, 1905-1980

No exit, and three other plays. Vintage Bks. 1989 275p pa $11 **842**

ISBN 0-679-72516-4 LC 89-40097

Contents: No exit; The flies; Dirty hands; The respectful prostitute

"Sartre rejected psychological theatre, defining his as a 'theatre of situations' in which characters are defined not by their psychological states, but by their choices and actions. Sartre's existentialism posits a world of interpersonal relations in which each person struggles to control the other." Cambrige Guide to Theatre

843.009 French fiction—History and criticism

Buck, Stratton

Gustave Flaubert. Twayne Pubs. 1966 153p (Twayne's world authors series) $22.95 **843.009**

1. Flaubert, Gustave, 1821-1880
ISBN 0-8057-2312-9

The author has attempted "to discover the evolution and composition of Flaubert's novels, to describe the nature and the content of each, and to offer an estimate of its artistic importance." Libr J

Includes bibliography

Gans, Eric, 1941-

Madame Bovary; the end of romance. Twayne Pubs. 1989 138p $23.95; pa $13.95 **843.009**

1. Flaubert, Gustave, 1821-1880. Madame Bovary
ISBN 0-8057-7984-1; 0-8057-8033-5 (pa)

LC 88-24155

The author considers Flaubert's detailed look at an ordinary woman and her problems a major step in the development of the novel

Includes bibliography

844 French essays

Camus, Albert, 1913-1960

The myth of Sisyphus, and other essays; translated from the French by Justin O'Brien. Knopf 1955 212p o.p.; Vintage Bks. paperback available $11 **844**

ISBN 0-679-73373-6 (pa)

Analyzed in Essay and general literature index

Personal reflections on the meaning of life and the philosophical questions surrounding suicide

848 French miscellany

Ben-Zvi, Linda

Samuel Beckett. Twayne Pubs. 1986 230p (Twayne's English authors series) $22.95 **848**

1. Beckett, Samuel, 1906-1989
ISBN 0-8057-6912-9 LC 85-31828

A critical introduction to the Irish-born French novelist, dramatist, and poet best known for his comically pessimistic portraits of the human condition

Includes bibliography

Brosman, Catharine Savage, 1934-
Jean-Paul Sartre. Twayne Pubs. 1983 146p
(Twayne's world authors series) $23.95   **848**
1. Sartre, Jean Paul, 1905-1980
ISBN 0-8057-6544-1   LC 83-4382
An "analysis of Sartre's major and minor philosophical works and of almost all the literary and critical works
as well." Choice
"Throughout the book, the author shows tact and discrimination in judging Sartre's tangled political history
and in relating his involvements with the world of events
to the stresses in his work." Booklist
Includes bibliography

Jean-Jacques Rousseau; edited and with an
introduction by Harold Bloom. Chelsea House
1988 311p (Modern critical views) $34.95 **848**
1. Rousseau, Jean-Jacques, 1712-1778
ISBN 1-55546-296-0   LC 87-11796
A selection of critical essays, arranged in chronological order of publication, devoted to the works of the
eighteenth-century French author and philosopher
Includes bibliography

Rhein, Phillip H.
Albert Camus. rev ed. Twayne Pubs. 1989 144p
il (Twayne's world authors series) $23.95   **848**
1. Camus, Albert, 1913-1960
ISBN 0-8057-8253-2   LC 89-31097
First published 1969
This study analyzes the evolution of Camus' art and
philosophy through discussion of his novels, plays and
essays
Includes bibliography

Richter, Peyton E.
Voltaire; by Peyton Richter and Ilona Ricardo.
Twayne Pubs. 1980 192p (Twayne's world authors
series) $22.95   **848**
1. Voltaire, 1694-1778
ISBN 0-8057-6425-9   LC 79-24985
The authors "explore central aspects of [Voltaire's]
work and nature in an excellent introduction to his art,
life, and influence on both French and European
thought." Booklist
Includes bibliography

Robinson, Joy D. Marie
Antoine de Saint-Exupéry. Twayne Pubs. 1984
179p (Twayne's world authors series) $23.95
   848
1. Saint-Exupéry, Antoine de, 1900-1944
ISBN 0-8057-6552-2   LC 84-10769
Biographical and critical assessments of the French
aviator-author. The classic The little prince is examined
in depth
Includes bibliography

Voltaire, 1694-1778
Candide, and other writings; edited with an
introduction by Haskell M. Block. Modern Lib.
1985 c1956 576p pa $7.95   **848**
ISBN 0-394-60522-5
A reissue of the title first published 1956 by Random
House; copyright renewed 1984
This volume includes the complete text of Candide,
plus writings on poetry, literature, philosophy, and a
number of dialogues and shorter pieces

The portable Voltaire; edited, and with an
introduction by Ben Ray Redmen. Viking 1949
569p o.p.; Penguin Bks. paperback available
$14.95   **848**
ISBN 0-14-015041-2 (pa)
"The Viking portable library"
The selections from Voltaire's works include:
Candide, part one; Three stories: Zadig, Micromegas, and
Story of a good Brahmin; Letters, and selections from
the Philosophical Dictionary and other works. The edi-
tor's introduction gives a biographical sketch of Voltaire

851   Italian poetry

Dante Alighieri, 1265-1321
The portable Dante; translated, edited, and with
an introduction and notes by Mark Musa. Penguin
Bks. 1995 xliii, 654p pa $12.50   **851**
ISBN 0-14-023114-5   LC 94-15988
First published 1947
Contains complete verse translations of The Divine
comedy and La vita nuova
Includes bibliographical references

Levi, Primo, 1919-1987
The collected poems of Primo Levi; translated
by Ruth Feldman and Brian Swann. Faber & Faber
1988 78p hardcover o.p. paperback available $8.95
   851
ISBN 0-571-15256-2 (pa)   LC 88-3847
"Written both during the war and after, the poems,
whether they consider the natural world of stars, glaciers,
or snails; the everyday life of Mondays, chess, and
bridges; or more metaphysical concerns, are infused with
the vision and ineluctable memory of the horrors that he
and so many others experienced. . . . His sparse, finely
tuned lines are beautifully translated." Libr J

852   Italian drama

Pirandello, Luigi, 1867-1936
Naked masks; five plays; edited by Eric
Bentley. Dutton 1952 xxvii, 386p hardcover o.p.
paperback available $7.95   **852**
ISBN 0-525-48319-5 (pa)
Contents: Liolà; It is so! (If you think so); Henry IV;
Six characters in search of an author; Each in his own
way

860.3 Spanish literature— Encyclopedias and dictionaries

Dictionary of Mexican literature; edited by Eladio Cortés. Greenwood Press 1992 xliii, 768p $95

860.3

1. Mexican literature—Dictionaries
ISBN 0-313-26271-3   LC 91-10529

This volume contains "500 entries covering the most important writers, literary schools, and cultural movements in Mexican literary history. The 41 contributors include American, Mexican, and Hispanic scholars with assistance from some of the authors themselves." Libr J

The **Oxford** companion to Spanish literature; edited by Philip Ward. Oxford Univ. Press 1978 629p o.p.   **860.3**

1. Spanish literature—Dictionaries 2. Spanish literature—Bio-bibliography

LC 78-325227

This book "covers literature written in the languages of Spain (Castilian, Catalan, Basque, Galician) from Roman times to 1977. Central and South America are covered as well as peninsular Spain. The bulk of the entries—which range from a paragraph to a page—are for authors and specific works, but there are also some for movements, groups, styles, and terms related to literature." Wilson Libr Bull

"This is an indispensable sourcebook." Choice

860.8 Spanish literature— Collections

The **Tree** is older than you are; a bilingual gathering of poems & stories from Mexico with paintings by Mexican artists; selected by Naomi Shihab Nye. Simon & Schuster Bks. for Young Readers 1995 111p il $19.95   **860.8**

1. Mexican literature—Collections 2. Bilingual books—English-Spanish
ISBN 0-689-80297-8   LC 95-1565

"This bilingual anthology of poems, stories, and paintings by Mexican writers and artists brims over with a sense of wonder and playful exuberance, its themes as varied and inventive as a child's imagination." Voice Youth Advocates

860.9 Spanish literature—History and criticism

Hispanic literature criticism; Jelena Krstovic, editor. Gale Res. 1994 2v il set $190   **860.9**

1. Latin American literature—History and criticism 2. Spanish literature—History and criticism 3. American literature—Hispanic American authors—History and criticism 4. Authors, Latin American
ISBN 0-8103-9145-7   LC 94-76177

Contents: v1 Allende to Jimenez; v2 Lorca to Zamora

This reference work "focuses on the major literary figures of the Spanish- and Portuguese-speaking world. It offers a brief biographical sketch, a list of principal works, numerous critical essays, and a short bibliography of additional articles about 71 prominent authors from Spain, Portugal, Latin America, and Latino United States." Libr J

Masterpieces of Latino literature; edited by Frank N. Magill. HarperCollins Pubs. 1994 655p $45   **860.9**

1. Latin American literature—History and criticism 2. American literature—Hispanic American authors—History and criticism
ISBN 0-06-270106-1   LC 94-8803

This reference "covers works by 105 authors of Latino heritage from South, Central, and North America, from the seventeenth century to the present. . . . Entries are arranged alphabetically, by title for individual works, and by genre in the case of essays covering all the work of a particular type by an author, such as 'The Essays of Jorge Luis Borges' and 'The Poetry of Gary Soto.' There are 140 entries on individual titles, and 33 entries on genres." Booklist

861 Spanish poetry

Cid, ca. 1043-1099
The poem of the Cid   **861**

Paperback editions available from various publishers

"The poem is based on the exploits of Rodrigo or Ruy Díaz de Bivar (c.1043-1099), who was known as 'el Cid.' . . . Similar in form to the 'Chanson de Roland,' the poem is notable for its simplicity and directness and for its exact, picturesque detail. Despite the inclusion of much legendary material, the figure of the Cid, who is depicted as the model Castillian warrior, is not idealized to an extravagant degree." Reader's Ency. 4th edition

Neruda, Pablo, 1904-1973
Late and posthumous poems, 1968-1974; introduction by Manuel Duran; edited and translated by Ben Belitt. Grove Press 1988 239p hardcover o.p. paperback available $11.95   **861**
ISBN 0-8021-3145-X (pa)   LC 88-11290

"With the exception of the darker surrealism of the 1930s, Nobel Prize-winning poet Neruda's work was consistently life-affirming, even to his last days. Translated by Belitt, no stranger to Neruda, the 'late and posthumous poems' display an exhilarating variety. These poems attest to Neruda's warmth, profundity, and humility." Libr J

Selected odes of Pablo Neruda; translated, with an introduction by Margaret Sayers Peden. University of Calif. Press 1990 375p (Latin American literature and culture) hardcover o.p. paperback available $13.95   **861**
ISBN 0-520-07172-7 (pa)   LC 90-10707

"With the Spanish text and the English translation on facing pages, the beautiful odes of the great Chilean poet pay tribute to simple things in simple words, from bicycles and birds to his suit." Booklist

Neruda, Pablo, 1904-1973—*Continued*

Twenty love poems and a song of despair; translated by W. S. Merwin. Penguin Bks. 1978 68p (Penguin poets) pa $8.95　　　**861**
ISBN 0-14-018648-4　　　LC 76-29006

Original Spanish edition 1924; this translation first published 1971 by Grossman Pubs.

This bilingual collection presents a series of poems that contains "sea and nature imagery that associates woman with the productive forces of Mother Earth." Choice

Includes bibliography

Paz, Octavio, 1914-

The collected poems of Octavio Paz, 1957-1987; edited & translated by Eliot Weinberger; with additional translations by Elizabeth Bishop [et al.] New Directions 1987 669p il $37.50; pa $21
　　　861

ISBN 0-8112-1037-5; 0-8112-1173-8 (pa)
　　　LC 87-23989

"Dense, weighty, and miraculous, this bilingual edition compresses into one volume all the poems published in book form since 1957. Nearly 200 poems, some newly translated, many new to an English-language edition, conclusively demonstrate Paz's power." Libr J

Includes bibliography

Selected poems; edited by Eliot Weinberger; translated from the Spanish by G. Aroul [et al.] New Directions 1984 147p hardcover o.p. paperback available $9.95　　　**861**
ISBN 0-8112-0899-0 (pa)　　　LC 84-9856

"The 67 well-chosen selections show Paz in his several phases and guises—in lyrics and prose poems, in long, free-form pieces and short, impressionistic works—a range of styles representing the best modes of East and West as practiced South over the last half-century. Many of the translations are by his peers (Elizabeth Bishop, Mark Strand, W. C. Williams)." Booklist

863.009　Spanish fiction—History and criticism

Durán, Manuel, 1925-

Cervantes. Twayne Pubs. 1974 189p (Twayne's world authors series) $22.95　　　**863.009**
1. Cervantes Saavedra, Miguel de, 1547-1616
ISBN 0-8057-2206-8

"In addition to supplying chapters of a historical and biographical nature, Durán studies Cervantes as poet, playwright, short story writer, and novelist; provides plot summaries and pertinent quotes; and includes other critics' views." Libr J

Includes bibliography

The **Latin** American short story; a critical history; Margaret Sayers Peden, editor. Twayne Pubs. 1983 160p (Twayne's critical history of the short story) $23.95　　　**863.009**
1. Latin American literature—History and criticism
2. Short stories—History and criticism
ISBN 0-8057-9351-8　　　LC 83-20

A study of the short story "form in all countries of Latin America, both Spanish- and Portuguese-speaking from colonial origins to the present. . . . Essays in this book are arranged chronologically; within each piece, individual writers are grouped by the trends and movements they represent." Booklist

Includes bibliography

Lindstrom, Naomi, 1950-

Jorge Luis Borges; a study of the short fiction. Twayne Pubs. 1990 174p (Twayne's studies in short fiction) $23.95　　　**863.009**
1. Borges, Jorge Luis, 1899-1986
ISBN 0-8057-8327-X　　　LC 90-4155

A critical reading of Borges' short fiction which blends myth, fantasy, symbolism, and erudition

Includes bibliographical references

Wood, Michael, 1936-

Gabriel García Márquez: One hundred years of solitude. Cambridge Univ. Press 1990 116p (Landmarks of world literature) $29.95; pa $10.95
　　　863.009

1. García Márquez, Gabriel, 1928- One hundred years of solitude
ISBN 0-521-32823-3; 0-521-31692-8 (pa)
　　　LC 89-22332

A critical examination of the Nobel laureate's fictional portrayal of social, economic and political evil in Latin America

Includes bibliographical references

870.8　Latin literature—Collections

The **Portable** Roman reader; edited, and with an introduction by Basil Davenport. Viking 1951 656p o.p.; Penguin Bks. paperback available $13.95　　　**870.8**
1. Latin literature—Collections
ISBN 0-14-015056-0 (pa)

This anthology includes selections from Plautus, Terence, Caesar, Virgil, Seneca, Juvenal as well as complete plays by Plautus and Terence and the anonymous poem Vigil of Venus

870.9　Latin literature—History and criticism

Hamilton, Edith, 1867-1963

The Roman way. Norton 1932 281p hardcover o.p. paperback available $8.95　　　**870.9**
1. Latin literature—History and criticism 2. Rome—Civilization
ISBN 0-393-31078-7 (pa)

Also available in hardcover from Buccaneer Bks.

Hamilton, Edith, 1867-1963—*Continued*

Companion volume to The Greek way, class 880.9

An interpretation of Roman life from the descriptions in the works of great writers from Plautus and Terence to Virgil and Juvenal

873 Latin epic poetry and fiction

Gransden, K. W.

Virgil, the Aeneid. Cambridge Univ. Press 1990 118p (Landmarks of world literature) $29.95; pa $10.95 **873**

1. Virgil. Aeneid

ISBN 0-521-32329-0; 0-521-31157-8 (pa)

LC 89-22273

A critical reassessment of Virgil's masterpiece and its influence on world literature

Ovid, 43 B.C.-17 or 18

Metamorphoses **873**

Hardcover and paperback editions available from various publishers

"A series of tales in Latin verse. . . . Dealing with mythological, legendary, and historical figures, they are written in hexameters, in fifteen books, beginning with the creation of the world and ending with the deification of Caesar and the reign of Augustus." Reader's Ency. 4th edition

Virgil

The Aeneid of Virgil **873**

Hardcover and paperback editions available from various publishers

"The Aeneid is in twelve books: the first six in imitation of the Odyssey; the last six, of the Iliad. The Trojan hero is led to Italy, where he is to be the father of a race and of an empire supreme among nations. On his way thither he tarries at Carthage, whose queen, Dido, loves him as with the first love of a virgin. To her he tells the story of Troy. For love of him she slays herself when the gods lead him from her shores. Arrived in Italy he seeks the underworld, under the protection of the Sibyl of Cumæ. He emerges thence to overcome his enemies." Keller. Reader's Dig of Books

880.3 Classical Greek literature—Encyclopedias and dictionaries

The **Oxford** companion to classical literature; edited by M. C. Howatson. 2nd ed. Oxford Univ. Press 1989 615p il maps $55 **880.3**

1. Classical literature—Dictionaries

ISBN 0-19-866121-5 LC 88-27330

First published 1937 under the editorship of Sir Paul Harvey

This work "covers classical literature from the appearance of the Greeks, around 2200 B.C., to the close of the Athenian philosophy schools in A.D. 529. It includes ar-

ticles on authors, major works, historical notables, mythological figures, and topics of literary significance. Short summaries of major works, chronologies, charts, and maps are special features." Nichols. Guide to Ref Books for Sch Media Cent. 4th edition

880.8 Classical Greek literature—Collections

The **Norton** book of classical literature; edited by Bernard Knox. Norton 1993 866p $29.95

880.8

1. Greek literature—Collections 2. Latin literature—Collections

ISBN 0-393-03426-7 LC 92-10378

"A comprehensive volume of more than 300 pieces of classical literature, primarily Greek but also some Roman." Booklist

The **Portable** Greek reader; edited, and with an introduction by W. H. Auden. Viking 1948 726p o.p.; Penguin Bks. paperback available $14.95

880.8

1. Greek literature—Collections

ISBN 0-14-015039-0 (pa)

"Selections from representative Greek writers, from Homer to Galen, aimed at providing the reader with an introduction to all facets of Greek culture, rather than to its literature alone. Mr. Auden's preface deals chiefly with the various Greek concepts of the hero, in comparison with our own, and points up the immense differences between the two civilizations." New Yorker

880.9 Classical Greek literature—History and criticism

Ancient Greek literature; K. J. Dove, editor [et al.] Oxford Univ. Press 1980 186p maps hardcover o.p. paperback available $16.95 **880.9**

1. Greek literature—History and criticism

ISBN 0-19-289124-3 (pa) LC 80-507991

Analyzed in Essay and general literature index

An historical survey of Greek literature from 700 B.C. to 500 A.D. with chapters on Homeric and Hesiodic poetry, tragedy, comedy, classical science and philosophy, classical oratory and the classical historian

Includes bibliography

Hamilton, Edith, 1867-1963

The echo of Greece. Norton 1957 224p hardcover o.p. paperback available $9.95 **880.9**

1. Greek literature—History and criticism 2. Greek civilization

ISBN 0-393-00231-4 (pa)

An interpretive essay on the Greek way of life during the fourth century B.C. It deals particularly with the political philosophies of Greek teachers and leaders—Isocrates, Plato, Aristotle, Demosthenes, and Alexander the Great

Hamilton, Edith, 1867-1963—*Continued*
The Greek way. Norton 1943 347p hardcover
o.p. paperback available $8.95   **880.9**
1. Greek literature—History and criticism 2. Greek
civilization
ISBN 0-393-00230-6 (pa)
Also available in hardcover from Amereon and Bucca-
neer Bks.
Companion volume to The Roman way, class 870.9
First published 1930. Variant title: The great age of
Greek literature
An account of writers and literary forms of the Peri-
clean Age including discussions of Pindar, Aristophanes,
Aeschylus, tragedy, Greek religion and philosophy

881.008   Classical Greek poetry— Collections

The **Oxford** book of classical verse in translation;
edited by Adrian Poole and Jeremy Maule.
Oxford Univ. Press 1995 xlix, 606p $29.95
    881.008
1. Classical poetry—Collections
ISBN 0-19-214209-7   LC 95-8871
A "collection of classical verse from Homer to Boethi-
us. Translations, modern and older, are brought together
in a rich blending of Greek and Latin writings. Some of
the greatest poets in the English language—Dryden,
Pope, Tennyson, Poe, Byron, Yeats, Browning, House-
man, Wilde, Shelley, and Pound are among the translators. They emphasize the debt English poetry owes to the
classics. An amazing and interesting body of work and
one that should be part of any high school collection."
SLJ

882   Classical Greek dramatic poetry and drama

Scodel, Ruth
Sophocles. Twayne Pubs. 1984 155p (Twayne's
world authors series) $23.95   **882**
1. Sophocles
ISBN 0-8057-6578-6   LC 83-26563
A critical assessment of the classical Greek dramatist.
Works discussed include Antigone, Oedipus the King,
and Electra
Includes bibliography

Sophocles
Antigone   **882**

Hardcover and paperback editions available from various publishers
"One of the earliest extant tragedies of Sophocles. After the defeat of the expedition of The Seven Against
Thebes, Creon, now king, decrees that the body of Poly-
nices shall be unburied, in defiance of the rites due the
dead. Antigone, Oedipus' daughter, gives her brother a
token burial and, though she is affianced to his son
Haemon, Creon condemns her to be buried alive. Warned
by Tiersias, he regrets his act too late; Antigone and
Haemon kill themselves, and Creon's wife, Eurydice
does the same on hearing the news." Reader's Ency. 4th
edition

Electra, Antigone, Philoctetes; translated by
Kenneth McLeish. Cambridge Univ. Press 1979
160p (Translations from Greek and Roman
authors) pa $12.95   **882**
ISBN 0-521-22010-6   LC 78-51679
A collection of three classical Greek tragedies based
on legendary themes. In the first, Agamemnon's daughter, Electra, and her brother, Orestes, slay their mother
and her paramour to avenge the murder of their father.
Antigone is entered separately above. In the third play,
the wily Odysseus and the honest Neoptolemus, the son
of the hero Achilles, are sent on a mission to secure the
assistance of the archer Philoctetes in the siege of Troy.
Philoctetes, who had been abandoned by his fellow
Greeks on an island, resists their entreaties
Includes bibliography

Oedipus the King   **882**

Hardcover and paperback editions available from various publishers
This classical tragedy deals with the fulfillment of a
prophecy as it is revealed that Oedipus has unwittingly
killed his father, married his mother and brought the
plague to Thebes. He blinds himself in horror and becomes an outcast

882.008   Classical Greek dramatic poetry and drama—Collections

The **Actor's** book of classical monologues;
collected and introduced by Stefan Rudnicki.
Penguin Bks. 1988 314p pa $11.95   **882.008**
1. Greek drama—Collections 2. Acting 3. Monologues
ISBN 0-14-010676-6   LC 88-1378
A collection of short monologues culled from Greek
classical drama

Four Greek plays; edited by Dudley Fitts.
Harcourt Brace & Co. 1960 310p pa $8.95
    882.008
1. Greek drama—Collections
ISBN 0-15-632777-5
Also available in hardcover from Amereon
Contents: The Agamemnon of Aeschylus; The Oedi-
pus Rex of Sophocles; The Alcestis of Euripides; The
birds of Aristophanes

Seven famous Greek plays; edited, with
introductions by Whitney J. Oates and Eugene
O'Neill, Jr. Modern Lib. 1950 xxv, 446p o.p.;
Random House paperback available $9 **882.008**
1. Greek drama—Collections
ISBN 0-394-70125-9 (pa)
Contents: Prometheus bound and Agamemnon by Aes-
chylus; Oedipus the king and Antigone by Sophocles;
Alcestis and Medea by Euripides; The frogs by Aristoph-
anes
Includes bibliography

883 Classical Greek epic poetry and fiction

Homer
The Iliad   883
1. Trojan War—Poetry
Hardcover and paperback editions available from various publishers
A "Greek epic poem (9th century B.C.?) attributed to Homer. In twenty-four books of dactylic hexameter verse, it details the events of the few days near the end of the Trojan War, focusing on the withdrawal of Achilles from the contest and the disastrous effects of this act on the Greek campaign." Reader's Ency. 4th edition

The Odyssey   883

Hardcover and paperback editions available from various publishers
"An epic poem in Greek hexameters. . . . The 'Odyssey' is a sequel to the 'Iliad' and narrates the ten years' adventures of Ulysses during his return journey from Troy to his own kingdom, the island of Ithaca." Keller. Reader's Dig of Books

Willcock, Malcolm M.
A companion to the Iliad; based on the translation by Richmond Lattimore. University of Chicago Press 1976 293p il maps hardcover o.p. paperback available $10.95   883
1. Homer—Iliad—Concordances
ISBN 0-226-89855-5 (pa)
"The notes here are directed mostly toward the explanation of words, expressions, and allusions in the text; but they also include summaries of books and sections, and assistance toward the appreciation of Homer's broader composition, by drawing attention to the implications of the narrative and the very effective characterization of the major heroes." Preface
Includes bibliography

888 Classical Greek miscellany

Aristotle, 384-322 B.C.
The basic works of Aristotle; edited, and with an introduction by Richard McKeon. Random House 1941 xxxix, 1487p $40   888
ISBN 0-394-41610-4
Follows the Oxford translation of 1931
Contains entire texts of the following: Physica; De generatione et corruptione; De anima; Parva naturalia; Metaphysica; Ethica Nicomachea; Politica; De poetica
Some chapters have been omitted from the following included works: Organon; De caelo; Historia animalium; De partibus animalium; De generatione animalium; Rhetorica
Includes bibliography

Plato
The Republic   888
1. Utopias 2. Political science
Hardcover and paperback editions available from various publishers

In this section of the celebrated Dialogues in which Socrates is represented as interlocutor, Plato develops his views of the ideal state. "Political thought in Europe has been more or less consciously influenced by the Republic for twenty-three centuries." Dickinson. Best Books Ser

891 East-Indo European literatures

Mahābhārata
Mahābhārata   891

Hardcover and paperback editions available from various publishers
"One of the two great epic poems of ancient India (the other being the 'Rāmāyana'), about eight times as long as the 'Iliad' and 'Odyssey' together. It is a great compendium, added to as late as AD 600, although it had very nearly acquired its present form by the 4th century. Covering an enormous range of topics, the *Mahābhārata*, with its famous interpolation, the 'Bhagavadgītā', has as its central theme the great war between the sons of two royal brothers, in a struggle for succession." Reader's Ency. 4th edition

Mahābhārata. Bhagavadgītā
The Bhagavad Gita   891

Hardcover and paperback editions available from various publishers
"An eighteen-part discussion between the god Krishna, an avatar of Vishnu appearing as a charioteer, and Arjuna, a warrior about to enter battle, on the nature and meaning of life. Sometimes called the New Testament of Hinduism, it is an interpolation in the great Hindu epic the Mahābhārata." Reader's Ency. 4th edition

Omar Khayyam
Rubáiyát of Omar Khayyám   891

Hardcover and paperback editions available from various publishers
"The Rubáiyát' (Quatrains) of Omar the Tentmaker, of Persia, is composed of a series of stanzas forming 'a medley of love and tavern songs, tinged with Sufi mysticism, and with the melancholy of Eastern fatalism.'" Dickinson. Best Books Ser

891.7 Russian literature

Chekhov, Anton Pavlovich, 1860-1904
Anton Chekhov's plays—backgrounds, criticism; translated and edited by Eugene K. Bristow. Norton 1978 c1977 xxxii, 412p il hardcover o.p. paperback available $12.95   891.7
ISBN 0-393-09163-5 (pa)
"A Norton critical edition"
"The sea gull; Uncle Vanya; The three sisters; The cherry orchard." Title page
"What makes this collection of particular value is the addition of critical essays (some 200 pages) on a wide variety of Chekhov's theatrical technique and related essays." Choice

Fyodor Dostoevsky; edited and with an introduction by Harold Bloom. Chelsea House 1989 295p (Modern critical views) $34.95
891.7

1. Dostoyevsky, Fyodor, 1821-1881
ISBN 1-55546-294-4   LC 87-15766
Scholars explore Dostoevsky's religious and philosophical views as well as his aesthetics
Includes bibliography

Handbook of Russian literature; edited by Victor Terras. Yale Univ. Press 1985 558p hardcover o.p. paperback available $26   **891.7**
1. Russian literature—Dictionaries
ISBN 0-300-04868-8 (pa)   LC 84-11871
"The volume includes entries on authors, genres, literary movements, and period studies, together with reviews of notable journals. The lengthiest entries run to more than 6,000 words, and the shortest have been kept to a single paragraph." Booklist
"A valuable resource for students, scholars, and general readers." Libr J
Includes bibliography

Kirk, Irina
Anton Chekhov. Twayne Pubs. 1981 165p (Twayne's world authors series) $23.95   **891.7**
1. Chekhov, Anton Pavlovich, 1860-1904
ISBN 0-8057-6410-0   LC 80-19110
This introduction to Chekhov's life and works examines and analyzes the Russian author's plays and short stories, placing them in the context of world literature
Includes bibliography

Leatherbarrow, William J.
Fedor Dostoevsky. Twayne Pubs. 1981 185p (Twayne's world authors series) $23.95   **891.7**
1. Dostoyevsky, Fyodor, 1821-1881
ISBN 0-8057-6480-1   LC 80-28318
The author "provides an introduction to the great nineteenth-century novelist, written with the student and the general reader in mind. Basing his interpretations on close reading of the texts, Leatherbarrow analyzes Dostoevski's religious and philosophical views while addressing such topics as aesthetics and point of view." Booklist
Includes bibliography

Pasternak, Boris Leonidovich, 1890-1960
Selected poems; translated from the Russian by Jon Stallworthy and Peter France. Norton 1982 160p o.p.; Penguin Bks. paperback available $9.95
891.7
ISBN 0-14-018466-X (pa)   LC 83-8334
A representative collection of the Nobel Prize winning author's poetic output spanning his career
The editors' "selection includes poems from all periods of the poet's life, and with its introduction and notes forms a guide to his work that so far is the best readers of English have at their disposal." Times Lit Suppl

The **Portable** nineteenth-century Russian reader; edited by George Gibian. Penguin Bks. 1993 xxii, 641p pa $13.95   **891.7**
1. Russian literature—Collections
ISBN 0-14-015103-6   LC 92-39863
This collection includes Pushkin's poem 'The Bronze Horseman'; Gogol's 'The Overcoat'; Turgenev's 'First Love'; Chekhov's 'Uncle Vanya'; Tolstoy's 'The Death of Ivan Ilych'; and 'The Grand Inquisitor' episode from Dostoyevsky's 'The Brothers Karamazov'; plus poetry, plays, short stories, novel excerpts, and essays by such writers as Griboyedov, Pavlova, Herzen, Goncharov, Saltykov-Shchedrin, and Maksim Gorky

The **Portable** twentieth-century Russian reader; edited with an introduction and notes, by Clarence Brown. rev & updated ed. Penguin Bks. 1993 615p pa $14.95   **891.7**
1. Russian literature—Collections
ISBN 0-14-015107-9   LC 84-19113
First published 1985
This collection "includes stories by Chekhov, Gorky, Bunin, Zamyatin, Babel, Nabokov, Solzhenitsyn, and Voinovich; excerpts from Andrei Bely's *Petersburg*, Mikhail Bulgakov's *The Master and Margarita*, Boris Pasternak's *Dr. Zhivago*, and Sasha Sokolov's *A School for Fools*, as well as the complete text of Yuri Olesha's 1927 masterpiece *Envy*; and poetry by Alexander Blok, Anna Akhmatova, and Osip Mandelstam." Publisher's note

Rowe, William Woodin
Leo Tolstoy; by William W. Rowe. Twayne Pubs. 1986 143p (Twayne's world authors series) lib bdg $23.95   **891.7**
1. Tolstoy, Leo, graf, 1828-1910
ISBN 0-8057-6623-5   LC 85-22013
"The volume opens with a chronology and biography, which relate the key episodes of Tolstoy's life to persistent themes found throughout his work. Thereafter, Tolstoy's novels are discussed in chronological order, and chapters are allotted to the principal short stories and novellas. . . . The volume is altogether an excellent introduction to both the novelist and his work." Booklist
Includes bibliography

Tolstoy, Leo, graf, 1828-1910
The portable Tolstoy; selected and with a critical introduction, biographical summary, and bibliography by John Bayley. Viking 1978 888p o.p.; Penguin Bks. paperback available $15.95
891.7
ISBN 0-14-015091-9 (pa)   LC 78-6784
This anthology contains the complete text of the play The power of darkness, the novelette The Kreutzer sonata, ten short stories and philosophical, religious, social and critical writings including essays from What is art?

Yevtushenko, Yevgeny Aleksandrovich, 1933-
The collected poems, 1952-1990; [by] Yevgeny Yevtushenko; edited by Albert C. Todd with the author and James Ragan. Holt & Co. 1990 659p hardcover o.p. paperback available $18.95   **891.7**
ISBN 0-8050-2378-X (pa)   LC 90-44794
"A John Macrae book"

Yevtushenko, Yevgeny Aleksandrovich, 1933— *Continued*

"Based on Yevtushenko's own selections from the complete six-volume Russian edition, this collection is fluently translated by many distinguished poets, among them Richard Wilbur, Stanley Kunitz, and D.M. Thomas. Helpful textual annotations explain the many geographical and historical references, making the poems more accessible to the general reader." Libr J

892 Afro-Asiatic literatures. Semitic literatures

Modern poetry of the Arab world; translated and edited by Abdullah al-Udhari. Penguin Bks. 1986 154p o.p. **892**
1. Arabic poetry—Collections

LC 87-101701

This is an anthology of twentieth-century Arabic poetry in English translation. The poems are divided into four sections: Taf'ila Movement (Iraqi School): 1947-57; Majallat Shi'r Movement (Syrian School): 1957-67; Huzairan Experience: 1967-82; and Beirut Experience: 1982-. The table of contents includes biographical notes on the poets

"Modes range from brief lyrics to elaborate and extended forms of many stanzas. Even in translation, most of these poems survived as artful, elegant, and eloquent." Christ Sci Monit

895.1 Chinese literature

Lin, Julia C.

Modern Chinese poetry; an introduction. University of Wash. Press 1972 264p (Publications on Asia of the Institute for Comparative and Foreign Area Studies) hardcover o.p. paperback available $10 **895.1**
1. Chinese poetry—Collections
ISBN 0-295-95281-4 (pa)

"Poetry expressive of a break from traditional forms is discussed in a study of Chinese poems written since 1919 and in criticism of the themes, style, and contributions of major modern Chinese poets. . . . The poetry is analyzed in chronologically divided sections which cover traditional forms before 1917; poems by pioneers, formalists, and symbolists who wrote during the following 20 years; 'Proletarian' poetry from the World War II era; and poems written after 1949." Booklist

Includes bibliography

One hundred poems from the Chinese; [edited and translated] by Kenneth Rexroth. New Directions 1956 159p hardcover o.p. paperback available $8.95 **895.1**
1. Chinese poetry—Collections
ISBN 0-8112-0180-5 (pa)

"Nine poets, who lived centuries ago, speak with the poignancy of understatement of unchanging things; the brevity of life, the richness of friendship, the beauties of nature, the inevitability of old age and death." Booklist

Includes bibliography

895.6 Japanese literature

Anthology of Japanese literature from the earliest era to the mid-nineteenth century; edited by Donald Keene. Grove Press 1955 442p il pa $13.95 **895.6**
1. Japanese literature—Collections
ISBN 0-8021-5058-6

"UNESCO Collection of representative works: Japanese series"

"Covers the period from 712 A.D., when 'Record of Ancient Matters,' the earliest surviving Japanese book, was completed to about 1850. . . . The selections here include self-contained episodes from plays and novels (among them the classic 'The Tale of Genji'), fairy tales, short stories, and personal reminiscences, and numerous . . . poems." New Yorker

The **Classic** Noh theatre of Japan; [edited and translated] by Ezra Pound and Ernest Fenollosa. New Directions 1959 163p pa $10.95 **895.6**
1. Nō plays
ISBN 0-8112-0152-X

A collection of classical Japanese No verse dramas, dealing with various aspects of social life and incorporating folklore

From the country of eight islands; an anthology of Japanese poetry; edited and translated by Hiroaki Sato and Burton Watson; with an introduction by Thomas Rimer; associate editor, Robert Fagan. University of Wash. Press 1981 xliv, 652p o.p.; Columbia Univ. Press paperback available $19 **895.6**
1. Japanese poetry—Collections
ISBN 0-231-06395-4 (pa)   LC 80-39506

This anthology ranges "from the Kojiki (Record of Ancient Matters) . . . to a nineteenth-century transcript of a cycle of rice-planting songs, and from Kakinomoto no Hitimaro, [a] writer of elegies, who lived in the sixth century, to such recent poets as Tomioka Taeko. . . . Also included are Fujiwara no Teika's anthology of one hundred three 'tanka,' a no play, six sequences of 'renga' or linked verse, the 'frog matches' in which Bashō participated, and some longer modern poems rendered in full." Publisher's note

Includes bibliography

Katō, Shūichi, 1919-

A history of Japanese literature; translated by David Chibbett; foreword by Ronald Dore. Kodansha Am. 1979-1983 3v v1 pa $10, v2-3 pa ea $8.95 **895.6**
1. Japanese literature—History and criticism
LC 77-75967

Volumes 2-3 translated by Don Sanderson

Contents: v1 The first thousand years (ISBN 0-87011-491-3); v2 The years of isolation (ISBN 4-7700-1546-1); v3 The modern years (ISBN 4-7700-1547-X)

"Discussion of texts is complemented by frequent quotations and expert re-creations of the social and cultural milieu from which the literature emerged. A great deal of information is conveyed in the most painless way—a laudable achievement." Libr J

Includes bibliographies

One hundred poems from the Japanese; [edited and translated] by Kenneth Rexroth. New Directions 1956 143p hardcover o.p. paperback available $7.95   **895.6**
1. Japanese poetry—Collections
ISBN 0-8112-0181-3 (pa)

A bilingual collection of poems drawn chiefly from the traditional Manyōshu, Kokinshū, and Hyakunin Isshu collections and also containing examples of haiku and other later forms. The translator's introduction provides background information on the history and nature of Japanese poetry

Includes bibliography

One man's moon; 50 haiku; by Bashō [et al.]; versions by Cid Corman. Gnomon Press 1984 50p pa $7.50   **895.6**
1. Haiku
ISBN 0-917788-26-5

Poet/translator Corman offers his versions of haiku by some of its most adept practitioners

895.7   Korean literature

Anthology of contemporary Korean poetry; [selected and translated by] Koh Chang-soo. Seoul Int. Pub. House; distributed by Tuttle 1987 130p o.p.   **895.7**
1. Korean poetry
First volume of a representative collection of 20th century Korean poetry

896   African literatures

African literatures in the 20th century; a guide; edited by Leonard S. Klein. Ungar 1986 245p pa $12.95   **896**
1. African literature—History and criticism
ISBN 0-8044-6362-X   LC 85-24579

"The articles on Africa from Ungar's 1981-84 'Encyclopedia of World Literature in the 20th Century' [entered in class 803] have been reproduced here in a handy one-volume paperback. There is a brief essay on 'Negritude,' but otherwise, the articles—many by experts in the field, such as Bernth Lindfors—are arranged alphabetically by country. In each case, there is a survey of the literature in the country's major languages and a bibliography; where applicable there also are articles on individual major writers, black and white, with bibliographies. Sure to be in demand in most public and high school libraries." Booklist

Heinemann book of African women's poetry; edited by Stella Chipasula and Frank Chipasula. Heinemann Educ. Bks. 1995 230p pa $10.95   **896**
1. African poetry—Collections 2. Women poets
ISBN 0-435-90680-1

The editors "have selected work by women poets from 18 African countries, from Algeria to Senegal, Mauritius, and Zimbabwe. This broad geographical and cultural spectrum highlights Africa's considerable diversity while, simultaneously, affirming the shared experiences and perspectives of African women writers." Booklist

The **Heritage** of African poetry; an anthology of oral & written poetry; edited with an introduction and notes by Isidore Okpewho. Longman 1985 279p il pa $24.95   **896**
1. African poetry—Collections
ISBN 0-582-72704-9   LC 84-19360

"Okpewho gives brief but lucid accounts of major eras of African history—precolonial, colonial, early independence—and their effects on native poets, emphasizing in particular the lasting influence of oral tradition upon modern and contemporary African writers. . . . He then presents 100 poems. . . . Extensive notes, brief biographies, and an index of first lines." Booklist

The **Penguin** book of modern African poetry; edited by Gerald Moore and Ulli Beier. 3rd ed. Penguin Bks. 1988 315p pa $12.95   **896**
1. African poetry—Collections
ISBN 0-14-058573-7

First published 1963 in the United Kingdom with title: Modern poetry from Africa

"To convey a sense of national traditions within the broader poetic tradition of each European language, the poems are organized by country; to give a sense of the increasing sophistication within each country's tradition, the poets are organized by age, from oldest to youngest." N Y Times Book Rev

Poems of black Africa; edited and with an introduction by Wole Soyinka. Hill & Wang 1975 378p o.p.   **896**
1. African poetry—Collections

This anthology covers "all of tropical Africa—the English, the French and the Portuguese language areas [and] includes a good number of traditional songs translated from the vernacular languages." New Repub

897   North American native literatures

Coltelli, Laura, 1941-
Winged words: American Indian writers speak; [reported by] Laura Coltelli. University of Neb. Press 1990 211p il (American Indian lives) hardcover o.p. paperback available $9.95   **897**
1. American literature—American Indian authors
ISBN 0-8032-6351-1 (pa)   LC 89-39323

A compilation of interviews with Louise Erdrich, N. Scott Momaday, James Welch and eight other native American writers

"Coltelli's questions probe the writers' sources of inspiration, methods of composition, and perceptions of their own and their works' relationship to tribal culture, among other broad areas. But it's the questions Coltelli has tailored to each individual that hit pay dirt and result in some illuminating moments." Booklist

Includes bibliographical references

Coming to light; contemporary translations of the native literatures of North America; edited and with an introduction by Brian Swann. Random House 1994 801p hardcover o.p. paperback available $17 **897**
1. Indians of North America—Literature 2. American literature—American Indian authors—Collections
ISBN 0-679-74358-8 (pa) LC 94-13457
"Swann has gathered intact texts from storytellers, singers, and orators. Arranged by region and tribe, each set of translations is prefaced by a lengthy introduction by the translator that sets the stories in context. The focus varies, depending on whether the translator is a linguist, anthropologist, or educator and whether he or she is a Native speaker, of which a fair number are. This wide-ranging collection goes far toward achieving Swann's goal of presenting a collection of reliable translations placed in their cultural and historical environments." Libr J
Includes bibliographical references

Dancing on the rim of the world; an anthology of contemporary Northwest Native American writing; edited by Andrea Lerner. University of Ariz. Press 1990 266p il (Sun tracks) $37.50; pa $18.95 **897**
1. Indians of North America—Literature 2. American literature—American Indian authors—Collections
ISBN 0-8165-1097-0; 0-8165-1215-9 (pa)
LC 90-11006
"The emphasis is on poetry in a choice, evocative anthology of contemporary Northwest native American poetry and short prose by 34 writers, both established and emerging, whose work will be appreciated by poetry lovers in general as well as those interested in native American writing." Booklist
Includes bibliographical references

Day, A. Grove (Arthur Grove), 1904-
The sky clears: poetry of the American Indians. Greenwood Press 1983 c1951 204p $59.75 **897**
1. American poetry—American Indian authors—Collections
ISBN 0-313-23883-9 LC 83-1576
A reissue of the title first published 1951 by Macmillan
Some 200 examples of American Indian songs and chants have been assembled by the editor. The translations have been studied as contributions to American literature. The introductory material to the poems provides a review of the form and content of this poetry
Includes bibliography

Dictionary of Native American literature; Andrew Wiget, editor. Garland 1994 598p (Garland reference library of the humanities) $95 **897**
1. American literature—American Indian authors 2. Indians of North America—Literature
ISBN 0-8153-1560-0 LC 94-3811
Wiget "offers 73 essays, written by experts and arranged by subject and by period in three parts. The first, 'Native American Oral Literatures,' has an overview by Wiget and nine chapters on the oral literature of different geographic areas of Native America, followed by chap-

ters on themes such as oratory, the trickster, dreams and songs, and revitalization movements. The second section, 'The Historical Emergence of Native American Writing,' with an introduction by Ruoff, is followed by chapters on topics such as federal Indian policy, autobiography, women's autobiography, and humor, as a backdrop to descriptions of the major native writers of the period. The third section, 'A Native American Renaissance: 1967 to the Present,' presents an overview by Joseph Bruchac followed by chapters on critical responses to Native American literature, teaching American Indian literature, the literature of Canada, fiction, theater, and Indians in Anglo-American literature." Choice
Includes bibliographical references

Returning the gift; poetry and prose from the first North American Native Writers Festival; Joseph Bruchac, editor, with the support of the Association for the Study of American Indian Literatures. University of Ariz. Press 1994 xxix, 369p (Sun tracks) $45; pa $19.95 **897**
1. Indians of North America—Literature 2. American literature—American Indian authors—Collections
ISBN 0-8165-1376-7; 0-8165-1486-0 (pa)
LC 94-4845
An "anthology of poetry and prose from the recent North American Native Writers' Festival, this provides a rich introduction to the diversity of contemporary Native writing in Canada and the U.S." Booklist

900 GEOGRAPHY AND HISTORY

901 History—Philosophy and theory

Durant, William James, 1885-1981
The lessons of history; by Will and Ariel Durant. Simon & Schuster 1968 117p $17.95 **901**
1. History—Philosophy
ISBN 0-671-41333-3
A series of essays about the nature, the conduct and the prospects of man, seeking in the great lives, the great ideas, the great events of the past for the meaning of man's long journey through war, conquest and creation
Includes bibliography

902 History—Miscellany. Chronologies

Carruth, Gorton
The encyclopedia of world facts and dates. HarperCollins Pubs. 1993 1310p $55 **902**
1. Historical chronology
ISBN 0-06-270012-X LC 89-46521
Companion volume to The encyclopedia of American facts and dates, entered in class 973.02
"A Hudson Group book"

Carruth, Gorton—*Continued*

This volume contains "brief descriptions of events ranging from pre-human history (18 billion years before present time) to the end of 1992. The work is arranged chronologically, providing information for each period in standardized subject areas (demographics, disasters, politics, religion, science, society, arts, sports, etc.)." Choice

Chronicle of the world. DK Pub. 1996 1175p il maps $59.95 **902**

1. Historical chronology

ISBN 0-7894-1201-2   LC 96-14225

Editor in chief, Derek Mercer; editor, Jerome Burne

In this work "a broad spectrum of social, political, technological, and natural events from 3.5 million B.C. through A.D. 1995 are arranged chronologically in a column for each year. Major events are described as if written by a modern journalist reporting a contemporary happening. . . . This approach necessitates a lengthy index alphabetized by topic, followed by chronologically arranged events. The accounts are straightforward, objective, and enlivened by two to five (mostly color) illustrations and photos on each large page." Libr J

The **Chronology** of world history; [by] H. E. L. Mellersh [et al.] compact ed. ABC-CLIO 1995 516p $49.50 **902**

1. Historical chronology

ISBN 0-87436-866-9

A single-volume abridgement of the Chronologies of world history, originally published as four separate volumes

"This book covers world-wide events in several categories that happened between 10,000 BC-AD 1994. The material is organized by date and then by themed headings such as Politics, Government, Law and Economy; Humanities; Art; Music; Literature; Everyday Life; Sport and Recreation; Science, Technology, and Discovery; Media; and Statistics. . . . A very comprehensive index makes items easy to find." Voice Youth Advocates

DeFord, Miriam Allen, 1888-1975

Who was when? a dictionary of contemporaries; [by] Miriam Allen De Ford and Joan S. Jackson. 3rd ed. Wilson, H.W. 1976 unp $53 **902**

1. Historical chronology

ISBN 0-8242-0532-4

First published 1940

"Covering the period from 500 B.C. to A.D. 1974, the chronology gives quick access to the birth and death dates of 10,000 influential persons, their major area of importance, and contemporaries. Information is arranged in 11 columns; the first lists years, the others represent 10 broad fields of activity covering political, cultural, and religious life." Wynar. Guide to Ref Books for Sch Media Cent. 3d edition

Stewart, Robert, 1941-

The illustrated almanac of historical facts; from the dawn of the Christian Era to the New World Order. Prentice-Hall 1992 320p il maps hardcover o.p. paperback available $23 **902**

1. Historical chronology

ISBN 0-671-89266-5 (pa)   LC 91-66999

"A chronology of selected events in world history from A.D. 9 to 1990, with entries of 120 to 150 words

each. The emphasis is on political events, but many scientific and technological breakthroughs are covered. Non-Western people and events are extensively included, but most of the entries concern western history." SLJ

"Many years have no event listed, and it is the rare year that has more than one. However, it will be useful for browsing and will help readers gain a sense of major events that may be lost in the detail of other chronologies." Booklist

The **Timetables** of American history; Laurence Urdang, editor; with an introduction by Henry Steele Commager; and a new foreword by Arthur Schlesinger, Jr. updated ed. Simon & Schuster 1996 516p il pa $21 **902**

1. Historical chronology

ISBN 0-684-81420-X   LC 96-18446

"A Touchstone book"

First published 1982

Presents information chronologically in tabular form. Each double-page spread has columns for history and politics, the arts, science and technology, and miscellaneous

Wetterau, Bruce

The New York Public Library book of chronologies. Prentice-Hall 1990 634p o.p.; Macmillan paperback available $16 **902**

1. Historical chronology

ISBN 0-671-89265-7 (pa)   LC 90-46768

"A Stonesong Press book"

This book contains "250 separate chronologies, each covering an area of history or culture, organized under 14 topics. Within each chapter numerous lists trace subjects that relate to the major one." Libr J

903 History—Encyclopedias and dictionaries

Cook, Chris, 1945-

Dictionary of historical terms. 2nd ed. Bedrick Bks. 1990 c1989 350p $34.95; pa $14.95 **903**

1. History—Dictionaries

ISBN 0-87226-331-2; 0-87226-241-3 (pa)

LC 89-14934

First published 1983

This reference work "covers political, religious, and social terms, but not people, wars, or battles. . . . The alphabetically arranged entries range from a brief sentence to more than 500 words. The origin and translation of foreign terms appear in parentheses immediately following the terms. . . . A wealth of valuable information." Booklist

The **Hutchinson** dictionary of world history. ABC-CLIO 1994 c1993 699p maps $49.50

903

1. World history—Dictionaries

ISBN 0-87436-765-4

First published 1993 in the United Kingdom

The Hutchinson dictionary of world history—
Continued

"Alphabetically arranged entries here include cities, countries, major civilizations, events, and historical and religious figures, with cross references provided. There are eight topical appendixes and an extensive 'world chronology,' and clearly presented maps enrich the entries." Libr J

Kohn, George C.

Dictionary of historic documents; introduction by Leonard Latkovski. Facts on File 1990 408p $45 **903**

1. History—Sources—Dictionaries
ISBN 0-8160-1978-9   LC 90-42305

"This publication provides brief descriptions in alphabetical order of . . . influential public documents and other written records of historical significance. The *Dictionary* is international in scope and covers all time periods." Booklist

"There is little fault to be found with this excellent volume. . . . Given the restrictions of describing the who, what, when, and why for each entry, the writing is still crisp and varied. . . . For its concise yet satisfying definitions and comprehensive scope in treating an occasionally overwhelming subject, this book represents ready reference at its best." Libr J

Kurian, George Thomas

Encyclopedia of the First World. Facts on File 1990 2v il maps $145 **903**

1. Geography—Dictionaries
ISBN 0-8160-1233-4   LC 89-11649
Companion volume Encyclopedia of the Second World available for $95 (ISBN 0-8160-1232-6)

"This reference [work] defines First World countries as 'advanced, developed, industrial, or post industrial,' and non-Communist. These include Western Europe, North America, Australia, New Zealand, and Japan." Libr J

Encyclopedia of the Third World. Facts on File 3v il maps set $225 **903**

1. Developing countries—Dictionaries
First published 1978 as a two volume set. (4th edition 1992) Periodically revised

"Basic facts, location, weather, population, ethnicity, and language are given for nations of the Third World. Political, economic, educational, military, legal, cultural, and social information is supplied. . . . Comprehensive, well organized, and convenient, set in large type, with an introduction of relevant international organizations, several valuable appendixes, and a good index, this tool will meet the demands placed on libraries for current Third World data." Ref Sources for Small & Medium-sized Libr. 5th edition

Larousse dictionary of world history; consultant editor, Bruce P. Lenman. Larousse (London); distributed by Larousse Kingfisher Chambers 1994 996p maps $40; pa $18.95 **903**

1. History—Dictionaries
ISBN 0-7523-5001-3; 0-7523-5008-0 (pa)
                                 LC 93-72902
Published 1993 in the United Kingdom with title: Chambers dictionary of world history

"In one alphabetical arrangement, the 7,500 entries in this new dictionary cover world political, military, and diplomatic history from earliest times until 1992. . . . People, movements, and events are defined in entries ranging in length from one sentence to one page." Choice

Townson, Duncan

The new Penguin dictionary of modern history, 1789-1945. Penguin Bks. 1994 941p pa $13.95 **903**

1. Modern history—Dictionaries
ISBN 0-14-051274-8   LC 94-240542
Replaces The Penguin dictionary of modern history, 1789-1945, second edition by Alan Palmer (1983)

This is a dictionary of primarily political and economic history, covering the period beginning with the French Revolution and ending with the Second World War. Entries are arranged alphabetically and include wars, upheavals, political movements, military leaders, heads of state, economists, industrialists, politicians, social reformers, and more

904   Collected accounts of events

Davis, Lee Allyn

Natural disasters; from the Black Plague to the eruption of Mt. Pinatubo. Facts on File 1992 321p il $40 **904**

1. Natural disasters
ISBN 0-8160-2034-5   LC 91-38395
A worldwide survey of natural disasters throughout history. Over 500 alphabetical entries, organized by disaster type, cover a range of events, including: earthquakes, floods, typhoons, snowstorms, hurricanes, and tornadoes

Includes bibliographical references

Eggenberger, David

An encyclopedia of battles; accounts of over 1,560 battles from 1479 B.C. to the present. Dover Publs. 1985 533p il maps pa $14.95 **904**

1. Battles—Dictionaries
ISBN 0-486-24913-1   LC 85-6817
First published 1967 with title: A dictionary of battles

"Maps by Donald T. Pitcher"

Arranged alphabetically, the entry for each battle contains information on the strategic situation, military commanders, opposing forces employed, casualties suffered, tactics used, and impact on the larger conflict

Includes bibliography

Great disasters; dramatic true stories of nature's awesome powers. Reader's Digest Assn. 1989 320p il maps $30 **904**

1. Natural disasters
ISBN 0-89577-321-X   LC 88-26504

"Natural calamities—from the death of the dinosaurs and the eruption of Vesuvius to the Chicago Fire, the Armenian earthquake, and the threat of global warming—are discussed in a profusely illustrated account." Booklist

"This is a well-produced volume. . . . The text is crisp, the photos attractive and relevant, the diagrams clear and informative." Libr J

Raging forces: earth in upheaval; prepared by the Book Division, National Geographic Society. National Geographic Soc. 1995 200p il $16
904
1. Natural disasters
LC 95-36295
This book describes, with text and numerous color illustrations, a variety of natural disasters around the world, including earthquakes, tornadoes, volcanic eruptions, and floods

907 History—Education and related topics

Tuchman, Barbara Wertheim
Practicing history; selected essays; by Barbara W. Tuchman. Knopf 1981 306p $16.50 **907**
1. Historiography 2. Modern history
ISBN 0-394-52086-6 LC 81-47509
Also available in paperback from Ballantine Bks.
A collection of essays on the nature, methodology and writing of history

909 World history. Civilization

Eban, Abba, 1915-
My people: the story of the Jews. Random House 1968 534p il hardcover o.p. paperback available $14.95 **909**
1. Jews—History 2. Israel—History
ISBN 0-394-72759-2 (pa)
Following a broad outline of Jewish history the author looks at the modern state of Israel, its place in world affairs, and its relations with its neighbors

Encyclopedia of Jewish history; events and eras of the Jewish people. Facts on File 1986 287p il maps $40 **909**
1. Jews—History—Dictionaries
ISBN 0-8160-1220-2 LC 85-23941
This volume "traces Jewish history from ancient times through the origins of Zionism, the Holocaust, and the rise of modern Israel. . . . Leanly written and informative." Booklist

Everyday life through the ages. Reader's Digest Assn. 1992 384p il maps $35 **909**
1. Civilization—History
ISBN 0-276-42035-7
Editor: Michael Worth Davison
"Social history—30,000 years of it—is compiled into this . . . chronology. Beginning with the Stone Age and concluding with the 20th century, it includes the rituals of food and drink, fads and fashions, sports, courtship and marriage, crime and punishment, weapons, death and burial. In short, it offers collages of world cultures. More than 900 artists' renderings and photographs of everyday objects bring ancient civilizations to life." SLJ

Fargues, Philippe
The atlas of the Arab world; [by] Philippe Fargues & Rafic Boustani. Facts on File 1991 144p il maps $50 **909**
1. Arab countries
ISBN 0-8160-2346-8 LC 89-675447
"A wealth of information presented in colorful maps, graphs, diagrams, and charts. Arranged by broad cultural topics such as ethnic groups and religions, society, cities, oil and industry, facts not readily available in standard resources are presented and compared. . . . This timely, useful, eye-catching resource should be carefully considered." SLJ

Fernández-Armesto, Felipe
Millennium; a history of the last thousand years. Scribner 1995 816p $35; pa $18 **909**
1. World history
ISBN 0-684-80361-5; 0-684-82536-8 (pa)
LC 95-18899
"Surveying the last 1000 years of human history, Fernández-Armesto . . . deals with Islamic countries, China, Africa, and South America, as well as Western civilization and the recent rise of various Pacific nations. Writing in an authoritative yet not dry or academic style, he recounts the rise and decline of major civilizations. His use of the revealing historical detail . . . enlivens the tome and adds to the reader's depth of understanding." Libr J
Includes bibliographical references

Heyman, Neil M.
Western civilization; a critical guide to documentary films. Greenwood Press 1996 244p $59.95 **909**
1. Western civilization—Filmography 2. Documentary films—Reviews
ISBN 0-313-28438-5 LC 95-35676
"Critical reviews of 173 documentaries suitable for use in Western Civilization courses are arranged in chronological order here. Each entry includes length, year of production, color or black-and-white designation, producer or distributor, and name of the series of which the individual film may be a part. A letter grade is assigned to each film that reflects the author's assessment of its relative worth for classroom use." Booklist
Includes bibliographical references

Hitti, Philip Khuri, 1886-1978
History of the Arabs, from the earliest times to the present; [by] Philip K. Hitti. 10th ed. St. Martin's Press 1970 xxiv, 822p il maps pa $42.65 **909**
1. Arabs—History 2. Arab civilization
ISBN 0-312-37520-4
First published 1937
A comprehensive history from the pre-Islamic age to the end of the Mamluk rule with sections on the Arabs in Europe
"Professor Hitti's wonderful work remains a standard authoritative book in English on the ancient and later history of the Arab world." Libr J
Includes bibliographical references

The **Illustrated** atlas of Jewish civilization; 4,000 years of Jewish history; consulting editor, Martin Gilbert. Macmillan 1990 224p il maps $40 **909**
1. Jews—History—Maps
ISBN 0-02-543415-2   LC 90-675150
"A Quarto book"
"This visual overview of Jewish history is a successful blend of beautiful cartography, arresting illustrations, and informative text covering the entire range of the Jewish historical experience from patriarchal times to the present. . . . Artistic and cultural developments are treated as well as political and social events." Libr J

James, Lawrence
The rise and fall of the British Empire. St. Martin's Press 1995 704p il $35   **909**
1. Great Britain—Colonies—History 2. Commonwealth countries—History
ISBN 0-312-14039-8   LC 95-38774
First published 1994 in the United Kingdom
The author "surveys the major periods and events in Britain's rise and decline as a global power without attempting to be the definitive study of any one of those periods or events. . . . James' focus rests primarily on individuals—those who built the British Empire, those who maintained it, and those who, when it came time, eased it out of existence." Booklist

The **March** of Islam: timeframe AD 600-800; by the editors of Time-Life Books. Time-Life Bks. 1988 176p il maps $25.93   **909**
1. Islam 2. Middle Ages—History
LC 87-33584
This book follows the spread of Islam and Islamic culture in Arabia, Byzantium, Europe, India, Southeast Asia, China, and Japan during the years 600 to 800 AD
Includes bibliography

Rachlin, Harvey, 1951-
Lucy's bones, sacred stones, & Einstein's brain; the remarkable stories behind the great objects and artifacts of history, from antiquity to the modern era. Holt & Co. 1996 402p il (Henry Holt reference book) $27.50   **909**
1. History—Miscellanea 2. Antiquities
ISBN 0-8050-3964-3   LC 95-19935
"The Shroud of Turin, George Washington's false teeth, King Tutankhamen's royal burial treasures . . . are among the artifacts and relics spotlighted in this entertaining and enlightening survey. Organized in rough chronological order . . . the 50-plus objects make up a pageant of human aspiration, achievement, obsession and belief." Publ Wkly
Includes bibliographical references

Roberts, J. M. (John Morris), 1928-
History of the world. Oxford Univ. Press 1993 952p il maps $45   **909**
1. World history
ISBN 0-19-521043-3   LC 93-14431
"Roberts begins with a discussion of the prehuman past and continues up until mid-1990. The text is divided into eight 'books,' each of which is organized around a central focus and begins with a brief overview. These books are then subdivided into shorter chapters." SLJ

Somerset Fry, Plantagenet, 1931-
The Dorling Kindersley history of the world. Dorling Kindersley 1994 384p il maps $39.95   **909**
1. World history
ISBN 1-56458-244-2   LC 94-4856
"This book is a pictorial history of the world from 500 million years ago to 1993. . . . The material is presented in topical and chronological units subdivided into regions, i.e., Europe, North America, etc. Within each region and period, selections of events or people are listed as important or representative. Most are covered with a brief text . . . and accompanied by a color photograph or illustration. . . . This book with its excellent illustrations and broad survey approach will fascinate both the youthful reader and the curious general reader." Sci Books Films
Includes glossary

Toynbee, Arnold, 1852-1883
A study of history; abridgment of volumes I-X; by D. C. Somervell. Oxford Univ. Press 1946-1957 2v ea pa $16.95   **909**
1. Civilization—History 2. History—Philosophy
Contents: v1 Abridgement of volumes I-VI (ISBN 0-19-505080-0); v2 Abridgement of volumes VII-X (ISBN 0-19-505081-9)
An abridgment of Toynbee's 10 volume study on the rise and fall of civilizations. The editor has followed the pattern of the original work and has added a final chapter on how this book came to be written and a summary of the ten volumes

909.07 World history — ca. 500-1450/1500

Fury of the Northmen: timeframe AD 800-1000; by the editors of Time-Life Books. Time-Life Bks. 1988 176p il maps $25.93   **909.07**
1. Vikings 2. Middle Ages—History
LC 87-33585
This book examines the Viking era from 800-1000 AD to include discussion of culture, trade routes, invasions, religion, and the discovery of the new world. Also includes coverage of the history and cultural developments in Byzantium, Japan, and the Americas during the same timeframe
Includes bibliography

Harpur, James
Revelations, the Medieval world; Elizabeth Hallam, consultant. Holt & Co. 1995 119p il (Henry Holt reference book) $35   **909.07**
1. Middle Ages—History
ISBN 0-8050-4140-0   LC 95-970
This illustrated look at medieval life focuses on five representative spheres of society: the castle, the cathedral, the town, the monastery, and the battlefield
"Highly readable and a work of art." SLJ
Includes bibliography

The **Middle** Ages; William Chester Jordan, editor in chief for the American Council of Learned Societies. Scribner 1996 4v il maps set $350
909.07
1. Middle Ages—Dictionaries
ISBN 0-684-19773-1   LC 95-49597
Based on the 13-volume Dictionary of the Middle Ages (1982) this "four-volume set has been scaled down and simplified for young people. Organized in an easy-to-use A-to-Z format and covering more than 700 topics, this resource focuses on the Byzantine and Muslim worlds, as well as all of Europe. Shorter, half-page articles treat specific aspects of medieval life, describing people, places, literary works, and historic events. Longer, thematic articles address broader topics—'Chivalry,' 'Family,' 'Law,' and 'Science.'" SLJ

The **Oxford** illustrated history of the Crusades; edited by Jonathan Riley-Smith. Oxford Univ. Press 1995 436p il maps $49.95   **909.07**
1. Crusades
ISBN 0-19-820435-3   LC 94-24229
Scholars discuss the religious, economic, and military aspects of the Crusades
"In a collaborative volume that freely calls on work beyond that of the writers themselves in attempting a synthesis of current opinion, the contributors promote an impressively coherent vision." Times Lit Suppl
Includes bibliography

Runciman, Sir Steven, 1903-
A history of the Crusades. Cambridge Univ. Press 1951-1954 3v il maps set $115; pa set $49.95   **909.07**
1. Crusades 2. Church history—600-1500, Middle Ages 3. Middle Ages—History
ISBN 0-521-20554-9; 0-521-35997-X (pa)
Volumes also available separately in hardcover and paperback
Contents: v1 The First Crusade and the foundation of the Kingdom of Jerusalem; v2 The Kingdom of Jerusalem and the Frankish East, 1100-1187; v3 The Kingdom of Acre and the later Crusades
Includes bibliographies

909.08   Modern history, 1450/1500-

The **Encyclopedia** of revolutions and revolutionaries; from anarchism to Zhou Enlai; [editor-in-chief] Martin van Creveld. Facts on File 1996 494p il $75   **909.08**
1. World politics—Dictionaries 2. Revolutions—Dictionaries
ISBN 0-8160-3236-X   LC 95-44502
This volume contains descriptions of various types of revolution and resistance; historical articles recounting rebellions and revolutions from ancient times to the contemporary world; biographical accounts of revolutionaries
For a review see: Booklist, May 15, 1996

The **New** Cambridge modern history. Cambridge Univ. Press 1957-1979 14v apply to publisher for price   **909.08**
1. Modern history
This 14-volume set replaces The Cambridge Modern history, first published 1902-1912 by Macmillan in thirteen volumes
Contents: v1 The Renaissance, 1493-1520; v2 The Reformation, 1520-1559; v3 The Counter-Reformation and the price of revolution, 1559-1610; v4 The decline of Spain and the Thirty-Years' War, 1609-48/59; v5 The ascendency of France, 1648-88; v6 The rise of Great Britain and Russia, 1688-1715/25; v7 The old regime, 1713-63; v8 The American and French revolutions, 1763-93; v9 War and peace in an age of upheaval, 1793-1830; v10 The zenith of European power, 1830-70; v11 Material progress and world-wide problems, 1870-1898; v12 The shifting balance of world forces, 1893-1945. Originally titled: The era of violence; v13 Companion volume; v14 Atlas (o.p.)
"The most important general modern history, useful for reference purposes because of its high authority." Sheehy. Guide to Ref Books. 10th edition

Tuchman, Barbara Wertheim
The march of folly; from Troy to Vietnam; [by] Barbara W. Tuchman. Knopf 1984 447p il o.p.; Ballantine Bks. paperback available $15   **909.08**
1. Modern history
ISBN 0-345-30827-9 (pa)   LC 83-22206
The author analyzes examples of governmental bumbling including the Trojan horse, the U.S. involvement in Vietnam, and the British loss of the American colonies
Includes bibliography

909.81   World history—19th century, 1800-1899

Stearns, Peter N.
The ABC-CLIO world history companion to the industrial revolution; [by] Peter N. Stearns, John H. Hinshaw. ABC-CLIO 1996 328p $60   **909.81**
1. Modern history—1800-1899 (19th century) 2. Industrial revolution 3. Economic conditions
ISBN 0-87436-824-3   LC 96-19326
This is a "guide to historical events, trends, people, legislation, processes, and the effects of the revolution from the 18th century to the present. Entries on topics such as cartels, five-year plans, Luddites, and South Korea are offered in a brief and readable format. Biographical entries range from the famous (Henry Ford, Joseph Stalin) to the not-so-famous (Sergei Witte, William Cockerill)." Libr J
For a fuller review see: Booklist, Sept. 1, 1996

909.82 World history—20th century, 1900-1999

Arms, Thomas S.

Encyclopedia of the Cold War. Facts on File 1994 628p il $70 **909.82**

1. Cold War—Dictionaries
ISBN 0-8160-1975-4   LC 90-26899

This reference work on the Cold War includes "every event, place, and person associated with that period's long history. Alphabetically arranged entries range in length from 500 to 1500 words, depending on the significance of the subject. . . . This very important reference work is highly recommended for all libraries." Libr J

Brownstone, David M.

Timelines of the twentieth century; a chronology of over 7,500 key events, discoveries, and people that shaped our century; [by] David Brownstone and Irene Franck. Little, Brown 1996 506p $29.95; pa $19.95 **909.82**

1. Modern history—1900-1999 (20th century)
ISBN 0-316-11406-5; 0-316-11501-0 (pa)
    LC 95-35200

In this chronology "events are placed within four broad categories: politics and war; science, technology, and medicine; arts and literature; and social, economic, and everyday life. The arts section is primarily a list of the births and deaths (without dates) of famous people, with books, movies, and plays added. Most entries consist of one- or two-sentence statements of fact." Libr J

Chronicle of the 20th century. Dorling Kindersley 1995 1484p il maps $69.95 **909.82**

1. Modern history—1900-1999 (20th century)
ISBN 0-7894-0332-3

Also available CD-ROM version

First published 1987 by Chronicle Publs.

Editor in chief, Clifton Daniel; created and produced by Jacques Legrand

"Brief newspaperlike articles of social, political, and cultural events surround monthly chronologies and present a concise picture of the events and the way of life at the time. The present edition copies the original through 1987 and moves forward through May 21, 1995. The photographs, usually in color, and maps draw attention to the articles and present additional information. . . . A great resource and a fun, educational choice for browsing." SLJ

Cook, Chris, 1945-

The Facts on File world political almanac; compiled by Chris Cook. 3rd ed. Facts on File 1995 536p $45 **909.82**

1. World politics
ISBN 0-8160-2838-9   LC 94-5920

First published 1989

Facts and figures about post World War II national and international politics. Topics covered include: heads of state; legislatures and constitutions; treaties and alliances; population and urbanization trends; the nuclear era; terrorism

Great events. Salem Press 1992 10v il (Twentieth century) set $250 **909.82**

1. Modern history—1900-1999 (20th century)
ISBN 0-89356-796-5   LC 92-28671

"A Magill book"

Surveys significant events in the history of civil rights, military conflicts, economics, international relations, legislation, and social reform in the twentieth century

This "is tailor-made for students from grade 6 through high school. The information is concise and accurately presented in an interesting manner. Students will find it a good starting place for identification of historical and international topics." Booklist

Leonard, Thomas M., 1937-

Day by day: the seventies; by Thomas Leonard, Cynthia Crippen, and Marc Aronson. Facts on File 1988 2v il set $195 **909.82**

1. Modern history—1900-1999 (20th century)
ISBN 0-8160-1020-X   LC 83-11520

This title "will be useful in public, high school, and college libraries needing a summary of events of the decade that brought us the end of U.S. military involvement in Vietnam, the resignation of a president, and the world's first test-tube baby." Booklist

Meltzer, Ellen

Day by day: the eighties; [by] Ellen Meltzer and Marc Aronson. Facts on File 1995 2v il set $195 **909.82**

1. Modern history—1900-1999 (20th century)
ISBN 0-8160-1592-9   LC 94-26632

Entries addressing politics, economics, culture and recreation are presented in chronological order

Parker, Thomas, 1947-

Day by day: the sixties; by Thomas Parker and Douglas Nelson. Facts on File 1983 2v il set $195 **909.82**

1. Modern history—1900-1999 (20th century)
ISBN 0-87196-648-4   LC 80-22432

This volume traces events of the 1960s in a day by day chronological order

Shafritz, Jay M.

The dictionary of 20th-century world politics; [by] Jay M. Shafritz, Phil Williams, Ronald S. Calinger. Holt & Co. 1993 756p il (Henry Holt reference book) $60 **909.82**

1. Modern history—1900-1999 (20th century)—Dictionaries 2. Political science—Dictionaries
ISBN 0-8050-1976-6   LC 93-15204

This "title provides brief information on more than 5000 topics—events, people, and ideas—that have had an impact on world politics since 1900. The entries range from one paragraph to half a page in length and are often supplemented by chronologies, quotations, or excerpts. Recent events are well covered." Libr J

Tuchman, Barbara Wertheim
The proud tower; a portrait of the world before
the war, 1890-1914; [by] Barbara W. Tuchman.
Macmillan 1966 528p il o.p.; Ballantine Bks.
paperback available $14   **909.82**
1. Modern history—1900-1999 (20th century)
2. Modern history—1800-1899 (19th century) 3. Europe—Social conditions 4. United States—Social conditions
ISBN 0-345-40501-3 (pa)
The author describes pre-war social conditions in the
U.S., France, England and Germany
Includes bibliographical references

910   Geography and travel

Bryan, C. D. B. (Courtlandt Dixon Barnes)
The National Geographic Society: 100 years of
adventure and discovery. Abrams 1987 484p il
$55; pa $29.98   **910**
1. National Geographic Society (U.S.)
ISBN 0-8109-1376-3; 0-8109-8135-1 (pa)
                                          LC 87-1397
"Magnificent photographs complement the text in telling the story of the institution; its leaders, and its journal, *National Geographic*. Bryan also addresses the issue
of the *National Geographic's* coverage of conflicts and
wars. . . . Bryan has done an admirable job of presenting such a wealth of material." Libr J
Includes bibliography

Great rivers of the world. National Geographic
Soc. 1984 448p il maps $40   **910**
1. Rivers
ISBN 0-87044-537-5   LC 84-1163
Essays accompanied by full-color photographs and
maps describe life along the major rivers of the world

Into the unknown; the story of exploration.
National Geographic Soc. 1987 336p il maps
$39.95   **910**
1. Exploration 2. Explorers
ISBN 0-87044-695-9   LC 87-5525
An account of famous men and women who explored
various parts of the New World, including Lewis and
Clark, Cousteau, Marco Polo, and Mary Kingsley

National geographic index, 1888-1988. National
Geographic Soc. 1989 1215p il maps $29.95
                                              910
1. National geographic (Periodical)—Indexes 2. Geography—Periodicals—Indexes
ISBN 0-87044-764-5   LC 88-33086
Also available volume covering 1989-1993 pa $10 and
indexes covering 1994, 1995 and 1996 pa each $6
This index to National Geographic magazine "indexes
some 7,000 articles published in the 1,148 issues of the
magazine over the last 100 years. Articles may be located by subject, title, author, or photographer." Booklist

Nature's wonderlands: national parks of the
world. National Geographic Soc. 1989 304p il
maps $29.95   **910**
1. National parks and reserves
ISBN 0-87044-766-1   LC 89-3292
"A tour of the world's national parks supplies a global
view of wilderness treasures through *National Geographic*

910.2   Geography—Miscellany. Travel guides

Davis, Kenneth C.
Don't know much about geography; everything
you need to know about the world but never
learned. Morrow 1992 384p il maps $23   **910.2**
1. Geography 2. Questions and answers
ISBN 0-688-10332-4   LC 92-19142
Also available in paperback from Avon Bks.
The author's "survey of geography is intricately tied
to world history and interspersed with passages from
great historians, explorers, and travel writers. Questions
open each chapter and are answered at the end following
a neat chronology of the information covered. Davis succeeds admirably in his goal of showing that geography
is not a 'dusty mystery, but an exciting art as well as a
useful science.'" Booklist
Includes bibliographical references

Fodor's travel guides. Fodor's Travel Publs. prices
vary   **910.2**

Formerly: Fodor's modern guides, published by Mc-
Kay
Revised annually, "Fodor's offers more than [400]
guides to the world's nations, regions, and cities—from
Acapulco to Williamsburg. The books give details on
how to get to all these places and where to stay, where
to eat, and what to see once you get there." N Y Public
Libr. Book of How & Where to Look It Up

Michelin guides. Michelin Tire Corp. prices vary
                                             910.2

The Michelin Red guides issued annually deal primarily with accomodations and restaurants, garages and service stations. Text is in French, English, Italian and German. The Michelin Green guides are mainly concerned
with sightseeing, places of interest and suggested itiner-
aries and routes

910.3   Geography—Dictionaries, encyclopedias, gazetteers

Cities of the world. Gale Res. 4v il maps set $299
                                             910.3
1. Cities and towns
ISSN 0889-2741
First published 1982. (4th edition 1993) Periodically
revised
"A compilation of current information on cultural,
geographical, and political conditions in the countries and
cities of six continents, based on the Department of
State's 'Post reports.'" Title page of 1993 edition

Cities of the world—*Continued*

Contents v1 Africa; v2 The Western Hemisphere (exclusive of the United States); v3 Europe and the Mediterranean Middle East; v4 Asia, the Pacific, and the Asiatic Middle East, cumulative index

Countries of the world and their leaders yearbook.
Gale Res. 2v il maps $205 **910.3**
1. Geography 2. Politicians 3. Political science
ISSN 0196-2809

First published 1974 with title: Countries of the world; issued annually since 1980 with slight variations in title. Supplementary volume published at mid-year available at $90

A compilation of U.S. Department of State Background Notes and other government reports, this two-volume yearbook offers geographical, social, political, and economic data on about 170 nations. In addition, it provides information on: overseas business services from the Departments of State and Commerce, U.S. embassies and consulates, travel warnings, world health, and climate

Encyclopedia of world geography. Marshall
Cavendish 1994 24v set $499.95 **910.3**
1. Geography—Dictionaries
ISBN 1-85435-631-3 LC 93-24969

"Each of the first 23 volumes focuses on a specific geographic area in the world, offering profiles for each country, followed by thematic profiles for the region as a whole and a brief glossary, index, and bibliography. The country profiles focus on environment, society, economy, and history; the regional profiles include physical geography, habitats, animal and plant life, agriculture, industry, cultures, cities, government, and environmental issues. . . . While this work is most appropriate for secondary-school students and public library patrons, its brief survey articles will be helpful for beginning college students." Libr J

Exploring your world; the adventure of
geography. rev. National Geographic Soc. 1993
608p il maps $40 **910.3**
1. Geography—Dictionaries
ISBN 0-87044-726-2 LC 93-1849
First published 1989

"A one-volume encyclopedia of geography covering subjects from agriculture through international organization to zone. . . . This book is very attractive, with its glossy pages and many photographs, and provides valuable information on the physical, human, and political geography of the world." Am Ref Books Annu, 1995

Lands and peoples. Grolier 6v il maps lib bdg set
$259 **910.3**
1. Geography—Dictionaries 2. World history—Dictionaries 3. Civilization—Dictionaries
Biennial. First published 1929-1930

Contents: v1 Africa; v2 Asia, Australia, New Zealand, Oceania; v3-4 Europe; v5 North America; v6 Central and South America, Antarctica, Facts and figures, Selected readings, Index

"The uniform format for each country provides basic data, color maps and photos, and an article about the people, land, economy, and history. . . . The editors

state that 'the basic principle' of their editorial policy 'is presentation of fact, not opinion.' Articles are generally objective; however, controversial issues are often avoided." Wynar. Guide to Ref Books for Sch Media Cent. 3d edition

The **Oxford** dictionary of the world; [edited by]
David Munro. Oxford Univ. Press 1995 686p il
maps $39.95 **910.3**
1. Gazetteers
ISBN 0-19-866184-3 LC 95-22546

This gazetteer's "A-to-Z entries identify and describe inhabited places, physical features such as named rivers and mountains, and major political entities such as nations, autonomous republics or regions, and provinces. They also define elements of the physical landscape and social and political phenomena associated with places." Booklist

Reader's Digest natural wonders of the world.
Reader's Digest Assn. 1980 463p il $27 **910.3**
1. Natural monuments—Dictionaries
ISBN 0-89577-087-3 LC 80-50353

Editors: Richard L. Scheffel and Susan J. Wernert; writers: Oliver E. Allen and others

This book explains "the processes that have shaped some 500 natural phenomena all over the world. The encyclopedic format, clear diagrams, and well-chosen, often spectacular photographs explain everything from sulfur springs to natural bridges." Libr J

The **Statesman's** year-book world gazetteer;
[edited by] John Paxton. 4th ed. St. Martin's
Press 1991 693p $49.95 **910.3**
1. Gazetteers
ISBN 0-312-05597-8

First published 1975 in the United Kingdom

"Intended as a companion to *The statesman's yearbook*

Webster's new geographical dictionary.
Merriam-Webster il maps $24.95 **910.3**
1. Geography—Dictionaries 2. Gazetteers

First published 1949 with title: Webster's geographical dictionary. Periodically revised

"Concise and easy-to-read gazetteer, listing both ancient and modern place names. Most entries include pronunciation, brief description, population and brief history. Includes numerous charts and lists, some maps and a list of geographical terms from other languages." N Y Public Libr. Ref Books for Child Collect. 2d edition

The **World** factbook; [produced by] Central
Intelligence Agency. Brassey's pa $32.95 **910.3**
ISSN 0277-1527

Available CD-ROM version

Annual. First published 1981

Gale reprints this annual in smaller format without the regional maps as: Handbook of the nations

"For each country of the world (in alphabetical order), provides brief data on geography, people, government, economy, membership in international intergovernmental organizations, communications, and defense forces. Small maps of each country; regional maps in color. Includes introductory notes, definitions, and abbreviations." Guide to Ref Books. 11th edition

World geographical encyclopedia. McGraw-Hill
1995 5v set $555.75   **910.3**
1. Geography—Dictionaries
ISBN 0-07-911496-2   LC 94-29086
Also available CD-ROM version, GeoNavigator
Sybil P. Parker, editor
Contents: v1 Africa; v2 Americas; v3 Asia; v4 Europe; v5 Oceania, Polar regions, general geography
"This major encyclopedia was originally published
[1994] in Italy. . . . The first volume, covering Africa,
is arranged with an introduction and an overview of the
continent as a whole, including natural environment, geological structure and relief, climate, hydrography, flora
and fauna, population, economic summary, and history
and culture. Then the various parts of the continent are
considered, region by region, with information about the
countries within the region. . . . The format used in the
African volume is followed in the other volumes." Am
Ref Books Annu, 1996

Worldmark encyclopedia of the nations. Gale
Res.; distributed by Wiley 5v il maps set $450
     910.3
1. Geography—Dictionaries 2. World history—Dictionaries 3. World politics—Dictionaries
First published 1960 by Worldmark Press. (8th edition
1995) Periodically revised
The first volume of this set is devoted to the United
Nations, covering its structure, history, organization and
agencies. The remaining volumes, divided by geographic
area, consist of alphabetically arranged profiles of some
200 countries
For a review see: Booklist, April 1, 1995

910.4   Accounts of travel. Seafaring life. Buried treasure

Ballard, Robert D.
The discovery of the Titanic; [by] Robert D.
Ballard, with Rick Archbold; introduction by
Walter Lord; illustrations of the Titanic by Ken
Marschall. new & updated [ed] Madison Press
Bks. 1995 287, liiip il pa $12.99   **910.4**
1. Titanic (Steamship) 2. Shipwrecks 3. Underwater
exploration
ISBN 0-446-67174-6   LC 95-226990
"A Warner/Madison Press book"
First published 1987 by Warner Bks.
An account of the discovery and exploration of the
sunken ocean liner by the leader of the joint
French/American expedition

Callahan, Steven
Adrift; seventy-six days lost at sea; illustrated
by the author. Houghton Mifflin 1986 234p il o.p.;
Ballantine Bks. paperback available $11   **910.4**
1. Napoleon Solo (Yacht) 2. Survival after airplane
accidents, shipwrecks, etc. 3. Shipwrecks
ISBN 0-345-41015-7 (pa)   LC 85-14433
In 1983, the author "was west of the Canary Islands
on a solo Atlantic crossing when his small sloop was

sunk by what he thinks was a whale. All the life-threatening dangers are here—thirst, hunger, the battle
against the relentless rays of the sun, numbing cold, belligerent seas, sharks and the ever-present specter of death
by exhaustion or by drowning." N Y Times Book Rev

Dana, Richard Henry, 1815-1882
Two years before the mast   **910.4**
1. Seafaring life 2. Voyages and travels
Hardcover and paperback editions available from various publishers
First published anonymously in 1840
The author "shipped out of Boston in 1834 on the
Pilgrim and sailed around the Horn to California on a
hide-trading expedition. The book is based on the journal
he kept during the voyage. Horrified by the brutal captain's mistreatment of the sailors, and shocked by their
lack of legal redress, Dana wrote with a burning indignation that did much to rouse the public to the mariners'
plight." Benet's Reader's Ency of Am Lit

Graham, Robin Lee
Dove; [by] Robin Lee Graham with Derek L. T.
Gill. Harper & Row 1972 199p il hardcover o.p.
paperback available $11   **910.4**
1. Dove (Sloop) 2. Voyages around the world 3. Seafaring life
ISBN 0-06-092047-5 (pa)
Also available in hardcover from Borgo Press
"A Cass Canfield book"
"Setting sail aboard the 24-foot sloop 'Dove' in July
1965 at the age of sixteen Graham embarked on a five-year solo voyage around the world. The first-person narrative, which includes excerpts from Graham's tape-recorded diary, records not only his sailing experiences
and impressions of lands and peoples along the way but
his love affair with Patti Ratterree." Booklist

Heyer, Paul, 1946-
Titanic legacy; disaster as media event and
myth. Praeger Pubs. 1995 175p il $39.95   **910.4**
1. Titanic (Steamship) 2. Shipwrecks
ISBN 0-275-95352-1   LC 95-22016
Heyer "terms the *Titanic* disaster the century's first
collective nightmare. . . . The book's four parts examine
the situation that brought mammoth liners into being; the
way the disaster dramatized the potential and limitations
of Marconi's wireless telegraph and how the sinking hastened the passage of new regulations governing the medium's operation; press coverage of the biggest single-event news stories of this century . . . and how the
event influenced the fortunes of *The New York Times*,
and the representation of the *Titanic* in popular culture
since 1912." Choice
Includes bibliographical references

Heyerdahl, Thor
Kon-Tiki: across the Pacific by raft; translated by F.H. Lyon. Rand McNally 1950 304p il o.p.; Simon & Schuster paperback available $5.99
910.4
1. Kon-Tiki Expedition (1947) 2. Pacific Ocean 3. Ethnology—Polynesia
ISBN 0-671-72652-8 (pa)
Also available in hardcover from Amereon and Buccaneer Bks.
Original Norwegian edition, 1948
The "story of the six men who crossed the Pacific from Peru to the Polynesians on a primitive balsa-log raft such as Peruvian natives of the fifth century used, to prove that it was possible that the legendary race that came to Easter Island and the Polynesians could have come from Peru." Wis Libr Bull

Lord, Walter, 1917-
The night lives on. Morrow 1986 272p il
910.4
1. Titanic (Steamship) 2. Shipwrecks
LC 86-5182
Available in hardcover from Amereon
Further thoughts about the steamship disaster prompted by the 1985 discovery and filming of the wreckage

A night to remember. Holt & Co. 1955 209p il
910.4
1. Titanic (Steamship) 2. Shipwrecks
ISBN 0-8050-1733-X
Available in hardcover from Buccaneer Bks. and in paperback from Bantam Bks.
A detailed account of "the tragic drama of that terrible night—April 4, 1912—when the 'Titanic,' the unsinkable ship, struck an iceberg and went down in the icy waters of the Atlantic." Libr J

Lost treasure; by the editors of Time-Life Books. Time-Life Bks. 1991 143p il (Library of curious and unusual facts) $17.27
910.4
1. Buried treasure
LC 90-20110
Numerous illustrations accompany a text that discusses ancient treasures such as King Tut's tomb, sunken Spanish ships, piracy, and gold and diamond mining
Includes bibliography

Marley, David F.
Pirates and privateers of the Americas. ABC-CLIO 1994 458p il maps $62.50
910.4
1. Pirates 2. Privateering
ISBN 0-87436-751-4
LC 94-31348
This work consists of alphabetically arranged entries "focusing mainly on Caribbean pirates of the 1600s. . . . Marley has articles on people, places, and terms such as *pieces of eight*, *Spanish Main*, and *dubloon*. His articles on pirates consist primarily of factual accounts of raids, campaigns, and battles." Booklist
Includes bibliographical references

The **Oxford** book of exploration; selected by Robin Hanbury-Tenison. Oxford Univ. Press 1993 530p $35; pa $14.95
910.4
1. Exploration 2. Voyages and travels
ISBN 0-19-214208-9; 0-19-282396-5 (pa)
LC 93-10770
"A sampler of some of the best of the vast literature of exploration from around the world. It consists of carefully selected brief excerpts from the writings of Chinese foot and camel travelers of c.300 A.D. to 20th-century explorers on polar expeditions by balloon and airplane. Each excerpt is accompanied by a brief description of the expedition and a reference to the complete source of the excerpt. . . . Suitable for both young adult and adult readers and a worthwhile addition to all libraries." Libr J

Pickford, Nigel
The atlas of shipwrecks & treasure; the history, location, and treasures of ships lost at sea. Dorling Kindersley 1994 200p il maps $29.95
910.4
1. Buried treasure 2. Shipwrecks
ISBN 1-56458-599-9
LC 93-48856
The author "chronicles shipwrecks from the Bronze Age to the Vikings, then moves on to Chinese junks, the Levantine trade, the Portuguese and Spanish plate fleets, pirates, gold rush paddle-steamers, and, finally, to the *Titanic* and other modern ships. To be included, wrecks must have been laden with treasure. Colorful maps detail the historical trade routes and pinpoint the wrecks." Libr J
"Recommended as a seaworthy addition to public, academic, and elementary and secondary school libraries for both reference and browsing." Booklist

Read, Piers Paul, 1941-
Alive; the story of the Andes survivors. Lippincott 1974 352p il maps o.p.; Avon Bks. paperback available $6.50
910.4
1. Survival after airplane accidents, shipwrecks, etc. 2. Andes
ISBN 0-380-00321-X (pa)
The author describes the extraordinary hardships endured by the survivors of a horrific plane crash in the Andes

Ritchie, David, 1952-
Shipwrecks; an encyclopedia of the world's worst disasters at sea. Facts on File 1996 292p il $40
910.4
1. Shipwrecks—Dictionaries
ISBN 0-8160-3163-0
LC 95-15664
In this volume the author "lists several hundred shipwrecks alphabetically by ship name; vessels named after people are in last name order. The greatest number of wrecks he includes date from the middle 1800s to the 1940s. Specifically excluded are ships sunk during combat. Some wrecks are given page-long coverage and contain many colorful anecdotes. . . . Ritchie gives good, balanced accounts of such controversial wrecks as the *Mary Celeste*, *SS Waratah*, *Lusitania*, and *Titanic*." Libr J

Robertson, Dougal

Survive the savage sea. Praeger Pubs. 1973 269p il o.p.; Sheridan House paperback available $14.95   **910.4**

1. Survival after airplane accidents, shipwrecks, etc.

ISBN 0-924486-73-2 (pa)

An account of how the Robertson family survived for 38 days in a rubber raft in the middle of the Pacific Ocean

Rogoziński, Jan

Pirates! brigands, buccaneers, and privateers in fact, fiction, and legend. Facts on File 1995 398p il $50; pa $19.95   **910.4**

1. Pirates

ISBN 0-8160-2761-7; 0-8160-2773-0 (pa)

LC 94-12717

Entries in this work cover "actual and fictional pirates since the fourth century B.C., movies, operas, and fiction about pirates, nautical slang, and terminology. There is an emphasis throughout on differentiating pirate myth from fact. Narratives range from a few lines to detailed profiles of several pages. . . . Rogozinski's treatment should have [broad] appeal given its worldwide coverage and inclusion of films and novels from which much of our familiarity with pirate history and lore is derived." Libr J

Includes bibliographical references

911   Historical geography

Atlas of American history. 2nd rev ed. Scribner 1985 c1984 306p maps lib bdg $75   **911**

1. United States—Historical geography—Maps

ISBN 0-684-18411-7   LC 84-675413

First published 1943 under the editorship of James Truslow Adams

"Development of the United States illustrated by maps. Provides coverage through the Vietnam War. Includes some demographic maps. Indexed." N Y Public Libr. Book of How & Where to Look It Up

Atlas of classical history; edited by Richard J.A. Talbert. Macmillan 1985 217p il maps o.p.; Routledge paperback available $19.95   **911**

1. Historical atlases

ISBN 0-415-03463-9 (pa)   LC 85-675113

"Covers Greek and Roman history from Troy and Knossos to the Roman Empire in 314 CE. The black-and-white maps, though small, are very clear. Many city maps. The text is brief, in many cases good mainly for identification, a skeletal history, or verification of a few key dates." Guide to Ref Books. 11th edition

Includes bibliography

Beck, Warren A.

Historical atlas of the American West; by Warren A. Beck and Ynez D. Haase. University of Okla. Press 1989 xlii, 78p maps hardcover o.p. paperback available $21.95   **911**

1. West (U.S.)—Historical geography—Maps 2. Historical atlases

ISBN 0-8061-2456-3 (pa)   LC 88-40540

"Defining the West as that part of the United States lying west of the 100th meridian, Beck and Haase pro-

vide a cartographic survey of the history of the region. In addition to maps illustrating such standard themes as natural resources, exploration and travel routes, the growth of the transportation network, and Indian tribal lands, the authors have included detailed maps on such topics as the Spanish-Mexican land grants and the Mt. St. Helens's eruption. . . . This atlas is an essential purchase for most libraries." Libr J

Includes bibliography

Ferrell, Robert H.

Atlas of American history; [by] Robert H. Ferrell, Richard Natkiel. rev and updated. Facts on File 1995 192p il maps $29.95   **911**

1. United States—Historical geography—Maps

ISBN 0-8160-3441-9   LC 95-24122

First published 1987

This work incorporates 250 maps and charts along with archival photographs, drawings and paintings to cover American history from Columbus' voyages up to the conflicts of 1995. Geography, politics, economics and social conditions are surveyed but the emphasis is primarily on warfare, both foreign and domestic

Gilbert, Martin, 1936-

Atlas of British history. 2nd ed. Oxford Univ. Press 1993 144p maps $19.95; pa $9.95   **911**

1. Great Britain—Historical geography—Maps

ISBN 0-19-521040-9; 0-19-521060-3 (pa)

LC 93-21922

First published 1968 in the United Kingdom with title: British history atlas; first United States edition published 1969 by Macmillan

"The 144 maps listed at the beginning of the work range from the Celts in 50 B.C. to the amount of public spending in the 1993-94 British government budget. They reflect both Great Britain's presence around the globe (maps of the Empire and the Commonwealth) and the important role war has played in its history. . . . The maps are simply drawn in black and white and make effective use of shading, bold or broken lines, and a variety of clearly described symbols." Booklist

Atlas of Russian history. 2nd ed. Oxford Univ. Press 1993 various paging maps $19.95; pa $13.95   **911**

1. Russia—Historical geography—Maps 2. Soviet Union—Historical geography—Maps

ISBN 0-19-521041-7; 0-19-521061-1 (pa)

LC 93-21920

First published 1972 by Macmillan with title: Russian history atlas

This atlas includes the following topics: "'Ancient and Early Modern Russia,' 'The Soviet Union' [and] 'The End of the Soviet Union.' . . . Russia's role in the history of Europe and the Middle and Far East is depicted, as well as economic and human rights matters." Booklist

Historical atlas of the United States. rev ed. National Geographic Soc. 1993 289p il maps $100   **911**

1. United States—Historical geography—Maps

ISBN 0-87044-970-2   LC 93-32201

First published 1988

Historical atlas of the United States—*Continued*
This oversize volume contains maps, timelines, historical charts, photographs and other illustrations. It is divided into six thematic sections covering the land, people, boundaries, economy, networks of transportation, and communities, alternating with five chronological chapters that highlight changes from 1400 to the 1990s

Historical maps on file. Facts on File 1984 various paging maps $155   **911**
1. Historical atlases
ISBN 0-87196-708-1   LC 82-675379
Maps copyrighted by Martin Greenwald Associates; text copyrighted by Facts on File
A looseleaf collection of approximately 300 black-and-white maps arranged by continent. A section on ancient civilizations is included

Matthew, Donald, 1930-
Atlas of medieval Europe. Facts on File 1983 240p il maps $45   **911**
1. Europe—Historical geography—Maps 2. Historical atlases 3. Medieval civilization
ISBN 0-87196-133-4   LC 82-675303
"An Equinox book"
An "illustrated history of European culture and politics from the decline of the Roman Empire to the fifteenth-century discovery of the New World." Booklist
"This richly illustrated and absorbing text and the clear, informative maps are coordinated well. Both gazetteer and index are thorough and accurate." Wilson Libr Bull
Includes bibliography

Riley-Smith, Jonathan
The atlas of the Crusades. Facts on File 1991 c1990 192p il maps $40   **911**
1. Crusades—Maps 2. Historical atlases
ISBN 0-8160-2186-4   LC 90-33846
This atlas covers "crusading theatres in the Iberian Peninsula and the Baltic as well as the eastern Mediterranean, and generously extending the span of the crusading era into the 16th (Lepanto, Spanish Armada) and 17th (Siege of Vienna) centuries." Economist
Includes glossary and bibliographical references

The **Settling** of North America; the atlas of the great migrations into North America from the Ice Age to present; edited by Helen Hornbeck Tanner; associate editors, Janice Reef [et al.] Macmillan 1995 208p il maps $39.95   **911**
1. Immigration and emigration 2. North America—History—Maps
ISBN 0-02-616272-5   LC 95-37756
"This historical atlas focuses on the U.S. and Canada. Arrangement is chronological, with seven sections covering prehistoric times to 1950-55; the final section looks at aspects of the present. An illustrated introduction prefaces each of the first seven sections; a time line follows, with parallel columns for North America, Central and South America, and the rest of the world. Then double-page spreads present thematic maps (several per spread), text, and illustrations. . . . Libraries with interests in im-

migration, cultural diversity, genealogy, geography, and/or social history should consider purchase to complement their atlas collection. The physical attractiveness and broad intellectual sweep of *The Settling of North America*

The **Times** atlas of European history; editorial direction: Thomas Cussans [et al.]; maps prepared by Bartholomew, Edinburgh. HarperCollins Pubs. 1994 206p maps $40   **911**
1. Europe—Historical geography—Maps
ISBN 0-06-270101-0   LC 95-106731
"This atlas is above all a political portrayal of European history from 900 B.C. to 1994, tracing its development from the rise of the first states . . . to the breakup of the USSR. . . . Brief textual interpretations accompany the effective and visually appealing maps." Libr J

The **Times** atlas of the Second World War; edited by John Keegan. Harper & Row 1989 254p il maps   **911**
1. World War, 1939-1945—Maps 2. Historical atlases
                                      LC 89-45070
Available from Random House Value Pub.
"Covers the war in maps, charts, photographs, and brief essays, beginning with Europe after the First World War and continuing through 1945. The arrangement is roughly chronological, then area by area. Besides military aspects, sections for The world war economies, The casualties, Resistance in Eastern Europe." Guide to Ref Books. 11th edition
Includes glossary and bibliography

The **Times** atlas of world exploration; 3,000 years of exploring, explorers, and mapmaking; edited by Felipe Fernández-Armesto; consultant editors, Kirti Chaudhuri [et al.] HarperCollins Pubs. 1991 unp il maps $75   **911**
1. Exploration—Atlases 2. Explorers
ISBN 0-06-270032-4   LC 91-55000
Over 130 full-color maps trace the history of exploration from China in 1700 B.C. to current satellite projects. The maps are arranged by region

The **Times** atlas of world history; edited by Geoffrey Barraclough. 4th ed, edited by Geoffrey Parker. Hammond 1993 360p il maps $95   **911**
1. Historical atlases
ISBN 0-7230-0534-6   LC 93-23944
First published 1978
"Plates, with accompanying text by contributing scholars, are grouped in seven main sections: (1) The world of early man; (2) The first civilisations; (3) The classical civilisations of Eurasia; (4) The world of divided regions; (5) The world of the emerging West; (6) The age of European dominance; (7) The age of global civilisation." Guide to Ref Books. 11th edition

United States history atlas. Hammond il maps pa $9.95   **911**
1. United States—Historical geography—Maps
First published 1968. Periodically revised. Title varies. Variant title: Atlas of United States history
Includes more than sixty maps, graphs, and diagrams depicting the economic, social, political, demographic, and ecological factors that have molded American history

912   Atlases. Maps

Africa on file. Facts on File 1995 various paging
il maps $255   **912**
1. Africa—Maps
ISBN 0-8160-3288-2   LC 95-23088
This looseleaf compilation of black-and-white maps,
graphs and charts "highlights 52 African countries,
emphazing in more detail 6 major countries: Kenya, Tanzania, South Africa, Sudan, Nigeria, and Uganda." Am
Ref Books Annu, 1996

Atlas of the British Empire. Facts on File 1989
256p il maps $40   **912**
1. Great Britain—Colonies—Maps
ISBN 0-8160-1995-9   LC 89-214508
Editor: C. A. Bayly
This work "contains 39 specially commissioned maps
and more than 200 photographs. . . . The book is arranged in five sections that describe the expansion and
decline of the British Empire. . . . A helpful resource for
those seeking information concerning the Empire and its
impact on social, political, and economic history." Booklist

Atlas of the Third World; edited by George
Kurian. 2nd ed. Facts on File 1992 384p il maps
$125   **912**
1. Developing countries
ISBN 0-8160-1930-4   LC 88-675259
Companion to Encyclopedia of the Third World
First published 1983
"Uses two-color maps, charts, and graphs to illustrate
social, economic, and political indicators for the Third
World as a whole and for individual countries. In two
sections: pt. 1 has thematic profiles for the Third World
in 11 categories (e.g., political divisions, industry, environment); pt. 2 is comprised of alphabetically-arranged
country profiles." Guide to Ref Books. 11th edition

The **Dorling** Kindersley world reference atlas. 2nd
ed. DK Pub. 1996 731p il maps $49.95   **912**
1. Atlases
ISBN 0-7894-1085-0
First published 1994
This atlas is "arranged in four sections: The World
Today, The Nations of the World, Global Issues, and In-
dex-Gazetteer. The world's 192 independent nations are
individually surveyed and mapped in detail, with inclusion of overseas territories and dependencies a feature of
special note. Each nation is analyzed by at least 20
criteria: summary overview, maps, climate, communications, tourism, people, politics, world affairs, aid, defense, economy, resources, ecology, media, education,
crime, health, wealth, historical chronology, and world
ranking." Libr J

Encyclopedic world atlas. Oxford Univ. Press
1994 264p il maps $39.95   **912**
1. Atlases 2. Encyclopedias and dictionaries
ISBN 0-19-521090-5   LC 94-16312
Cartography by George Philip & Son
"With only minor changes, the publisher has taken the
thematic geographical maps as well as the physical and
political maps of the continents from its *Oxford Concise*

Atlas of the World (1994) and added country-by-country
coverage with informative text entries." Libr J
For a fuller review see: Booklist, March 1, 1995

Geography on file. Facts on File various paging
il maps loose-leaf $183.50   **912**
1. Atlases 2. Geography
Annual updates available for $40
First published 1991. Periodically revised
A collection of more than 250 maps, graphs, and statistical charts on both human and physical geography.
Topics covered include demographic shifts, economic
growth, language distribution, and political institutions

Goode's world atlas. Rand McNally il maps
$34.95   **912**
1. Atlases
First published 1922 with title: Goode's school atlas.
(19th edition 1994) Periodically revised
"Physical, political and economic atlas arranged by
continent and region. Includes metropolitan area maps
and much statistical data. Number of thematic maps has
been increased. Standard atlas." N Y Public Libr. Ref
Books for Child Collect. 2d edition

Maps on file. Facts on File 2v maps loose-leaf
$185   **912**
1. Atlases
ISSN 0275-8083
Annual updates available for $40
First published 1981. Frequently revised
Maps copyrighted by Martin Greenwald Associates
A collection of approximately 500 black-and-white
maps covering countries, every U.S. state, Canadian
provinces, oceans, and continents

National Geographic atlas of the world. National
Geographic Soc. il maps $100   **912**

First published 1963. (6th edition, 2nd rev. 1995) Periodically revised
"Well balanced in coverage between the U.S. and the
rest of the world, with maps by area rather than by state
or country. While some maps have a crowded appearance, they are legible and generally up-to-date. Includes
a fold-out map of the world using the recently adopted
Robinson projection, and a number of spacecraft images
of the earth and the planets. Indexes more than 150,000
place names." Guide to Ref Books. 11th edition

The **New** international atlas; Der neue
internationale atlas = El nuevo atlas
internacional = Le nouvel atlas international = O
nôvo atlas internacional. 25th anniversary ed.
Rand McNally 1994 various paging il maps
$150   **912**
1. Atlases
ISBN 0-528-83693-5   LC 94-15784
First published 1969 with title: The International atlas
Text in English, French, German, Portuguese and
Spanish
"Map sequences follow from world to metropolitan
maps; individual map layouts depict geographic and eco-
nomic regions rather than individual countries. Conclud-

The New international atlas—*Continued*
ing portion of the atlas offers a series of thematic maps, glossary, tables of geographic changes, population of cities and towns, and an index of 160,000 names. Maps are exceptionally clear and easy to interpret." Guide to Ref Books. 11th edition

The New York Times atlas of the world. new family ed. Times Bks. 1992 156p il maps $37.50   **912**
1. Atlases
ISBN 0-8129-2075-9   LC 92-53666
First published 1972 in the United Kingdom with title: The Times concise atlas of the world. Adapted from the Times atlas of the world, comprehensive edition
"An introductory section includes information about states and territories and lists of geographic comparisons. Beautiful, full-color maps, city plans, views of the solar system, and many other features come together to provide a first-rate atlas." SLJ

Rand McNally cosmopolitan world atlas. Rand McNally il maps $70   **912**
1. Atlases
First published 1949. (1996 edition) Frequently revised. Title varies
This atlas contains large-scale maps of continents, countries, states and provinces. Features included are thematic maps on two-page spreads, case study maps, photographs and diagrams

Stefoff, Rebecca, 1951-
The young Oxford companion to maps and mapmaking. Oxford Univ. Press 1995 303p il maps $40   **912**
1. Maps—Dictionaries 2. Map drawing—Dictionaries 3. Exploration—Dictionaries
ISBN 0-19-508042-4   LC 94-7900
"Encyclopedic in format, a diversity of terms can be searched alphabetically: 'Mid-Ocean Ridge,' 'Ptolemy,' 'Treasure Maps,' 'Lewis and Clark Expedition,' major regions of the world with the subtopic 'Mapping of' and, . . . the names of many explorers. Each entry is followed by a succinct but meaty article, just the right length, in fact, to appeal to student researchers. The abundant illustrations include elaborate ancient maps, portraits of explorers, a computer-processed map, and photographs of elegant, historic items." Voice Youth Advocates
For a fuller review see: Booklist, May 1, 1995

The Times atlas of the world. comprehensive ed. Times Bks. il maps $175   **912**
1. Atlases
First published 1967. (9th edition 1992) Periodically revised
"Offers 47 pages of prefatory information; graphic size comparisons of continents, oceans, river drainage basins, islands, and inland water bodies; eight pages of world thematic mapping; and an index that includes more than 210,000 place names and continues to provide latitude and longitude coordinates." Guide to Ref Books. 11th edition

915   Geography of and travel in Asia

Polo, Marco, 1254-1323?
The travels of Marco Polo   **915**
1. Asia—Description 2. Voyages and travels
Hardcover and paperback editions available from various publishers
An autobiographical account of Marco Polo's thirteenth century travels in Asia

915.1   Geography of travel in China and adjacent areas

Jenkins, Peter, 1951-
Across China. Morrow 1986 351p il maps o.p.; Fawcett Bks. paperback available $5.95   **915.1**
1. China—Description
ISBN 0-449-21456-7 (pa)   LC 86-21646
"A William Morrow/Sweet Springs Press book"
"In chronological sequence Jenkins writes three different types of narrative. The first, set at his Tennessee home, recounts the origins of his China trip. Another follows the 1984 American expedition to Mt. Everest via the unclimbed north slope in Tibet. A third narrative shifts Jenkins's own travel to the grasslands of Inner Mongolia and the south China coast at Fuzhou." Libr J
Includes bibliography

Journey into China. National Geographic Soc. 1982 518p il maps lib bdg $23.95   **915.1**
1. China—Description
ISBN 0-87044-461-1   LC 82-14132
"With chapters organized by region of China and contributed by several writers, [this book] covers both familiar areas and regions seldom visited by Westerners. The focus is on the diverse landscape and the people, with unusual attention to China's ethnic minorities." Libr J
Includes bibliography

Salzman, Mark
Iron & silk. Random House 1987 c1986 211p $17.95; pa $11   **915.1**
1. China—Description 2. Martial arts
ISBN 0-394-55156-7; 0-394-75511-1 (pa)
                                                            LC 86-11846
The author tells of his two years teaching English to medical students in China's Hunan Province following his graduation from Yale University in 1982
This book is "not so much a treatise on modern Chinese mores as a series of telling vignettes. . . . [The author] describes his encounter with Pan Qingfu, the country's foremost master of wushu, the traditional Chinese martial art." Time

917   Geography of and travel in North America

National parks of North America; Canada, United States, Mexico; prepared by the Book Division, National Geographic Society. National Geographic Soc. 1995 336p il maps $40   **917**
1. National parks and reserves—North America
ISBN 0-7922-2954-1   LC 95-10989
Contains profiles of more than 130 wild parklands in the U.S., Canada and Mexico. Over 330 color photographs, diagrams and maps illustrate the text. Sidebars feature natural, historical and cultural highlights of the major parks

917.3   Geography of and travel in the United States

America's historic places; an illustrated guide to our country's past. Reader's Digest Assn. 1988 352p il maps $29.95   **917.3**
1. Historic sites 2. United States—Description 3. United States—Local history
ISBN 0-89577-265-5   LC 87-4757
"Listed under 5 regional headings are 500 historic sites arranged alphabetically by state within each area—famous American homes, museum villages, forts, battlefields, government buildings, historic districts, churches, ghost towns, and engineering wonders. Natural wonders, such as the Grand Canyon and Niagara Falls, are excluded. Each site is briefly described and located on a regional map. The volume is profusely illustrated with color photographs for almost every site." Nichols. Guide to Ref Books for Sch Media Cent. 4th edition

The **Cambridge** gazetteer of the United States and Canada; a dictionary of places; edited by Archie Hobson. Cambridge Univ. Press 1995 743p maps $49.95   **917.3**
1. United States—Gazetteers 2. Canada—Gazetteers
ISBN 0-521-41579-9   LC 95-8898
The over 12,000 listings for places in the U.S. and Canada include entries for municipalities, states, countries, geographical features, notable neighborhoods, regional names, and a few legendary places. Includes definitions of about 170 geographical terms
For a review see: Booklist, Nov. 1, 1995

Cantor, George, 1941-
North American Indian landmarks; a traveler's guide; foreword by Suzan Shown Harjo. Gale Res. 1993 liv, 409p il maps $45; pa $17.95   **917.3**
1. Historic sites 2. Indians of North America 3. United States—Local history 4. United States—Description
ISBN 0-8103-8916-9; 0-8103-9132-5 (pa)
        LC 93-12931
"This geographically arranged guide provides information on more than 340 sites in the U.S. and Canada. Included are entries for monuments, museums, parks, battlefields, reservations, and places of birth and burial. Brief narratives outline the history and importance of each site, and information is included about location, hours, fees, and telephone numbers." Booklist
"Well organized, clear, and succinct, interested travelers . . . will find a wealth of information in this volume." Voice Youth Advocates
Includes glossary and bibliography

Curtis, Nancy C.
Black heritage sites; an African American odyssey and finder's guide. American Lib. Assn. 1996 677p il $70   **917.3**
1. Historic sites 2. African Americans—History
ISBN 0-8389-0643-5   LC 95-5788
This "guide locates significant places in African-American history and supplies . . . recent addresses, phone numbers, and visitors' information. . . . Organized by region, a historical essay introduces each section, presenting the culture and history in that area." Publisher's note
For a review see: Booklist, Oct. 1, 1996

Heat Moon, William Least
Blue highways; a journey into America; photographs by the author. Little, Brown 1983 c1982 421p il o.p.; Houghton Mifflin paperback available $12.95   **917.3**
1. United States—Description
ISBN 0-395-58568-6 (pa)   LC 82-14942
Also available in paperback from Houghton Mifflin
"An Atlantic Monthly Press book"
An account of the author's journey across the U.S. in a van taking only secondary roads

Historic places. Reader's Digest Assn. 1993 144p il maps (Explore America) lib bdg $16.98
        917.3
1. Historic sites 2. United States—Local history 3. United States—Description
ISBN 0-89577-506-9   LC 93-21872
This guidebook devotes a chapter each to the following historic sites: St. Augustine, Fla.; Plimoth Plantation, Mass.; Mackinac Island, Mich.; Williamsburg, Va.; Boston; Philadelphia; the California mission towns; New Salem, Ill.; Charleston, S.C.; and Virginia City, Mont. Each of these sites represents a particular period in United States history. A separate Gazetteer section presents brief information about an additional twenty-five sites in sixteen states

Jenkins, Peter, 1951-
A walk across America. Morrow 1979 288p il maps o.p.; Fawcett Bks. paperback available $6.99
        917.3
1. United States—Description
ISBN 0-449-20455-3 (pa)   LC 78-10320
Also available in paperback from Fawcett Bks.
This book chronicles the author's journey with his dog from New York to the Gulf of Mexico

Jenkins, Peter, 1951—_Continued_
The walk west; a walk across America 2; by
Peter and Barbara Jenkins. Morrow 1981 349p il
maps o.p.   **917.3**
 1. United States—Description
                                       LC 81-11177
The authors describe their 3 year, 2,000 mile walk
from New Orleans to Oregon

Lawliss, Chuck
The early American sourcebook; a traveler's
guide. Crown Trade Paperbacks 1996 310p il maps
pa $20   **917.3**
 1. Historic sites 2. United States—Description
ISBN 0-517-88391-0   LC 96-4302
The author "provides a handbook of sources of historic interest for states east of the Mississippi. By 'early
American,' he means from the first settlements to the beginning of the Civil War. By 'sources' he means primarily buildings of historic interest. . . . Occasionally, nearby accommodations are listed if they are of historic interest, usually of the bed-and-breakfast type. This is a
handy guide for the traveler interested in historic houses
and sites." Libr J

Little, Charles E.
Discover America; the Smithsonian book of the
national parks; photographs by David Muench.
Smithsonian Bks. 1995 224p il maps $34.95
                                             917.3
 1. National parks and reserves—United States
ISBN 0-89599-050-4   LC 95-33596
Photographs accompany a text that "concentrates on
those parks that highlight the natural, historic, social, and
political milestones of America." Libr J

National parks. Reader's Digest Assn. 1993 144p
il maps (Explore America) $16.98   **917.3**
 1. National parks and reserves—United States
ISBN 0-89577-447-X   LC 92-35785
Full color illustrations accompany texts surveying the
following national parks: Acadia, Great Smoky Mountains, Everglades, Big Bend, Grand Canyon, Yellowstone, Yosemite, Olympic, Denali and Hawaii Volcanoes.
Nearby sites and attractions are mentioned

Our national parks; America's spectacular
wilderness heritage. updated ed. Reader's Digest
Assn. 1989 352p il maps $30   **917.3**
 1. National parks and reserves—United States
ISBN 0-89577-336-8   LC 89-33561
First published 1985
"A general visitors' guide and history is followed by
individual chapters on each park, arranged alphabetically.
. . . The focus is on plants, wildlife, and geology, and
there is a detailed map of each park." Booklist
"The photographs are uniformly excellent, and the
maps clearly show the locations, boundaries, and impor-
tant and interesting sites." Libr J

Parks directory of the United States; Darren L.
Smith, editor. Omnigraphics maps $145   **917.3**
 1. Parks—United States 2. Historic sites
First published 1992. Frequently revised

"A guide to more than 4,700 national and state parks,
recreation areas, historic sites, battlefields, monuments,
forests, preserves, memorials, seashores, trails, urban
parks, wildlife refuges, and other designated recreation
areas in the United States administered by national and
state park agencies." Title page

917.4 Geography of and travel in New England

Durham, Michael S., 1935-
The Mid-Atlantic States; text by Michael S.
Durham; special photography by Michael Melford;
editorial director, Roger G. Kennedy. Stewart,
Tabori & Chang 1989 495p il (Smithsonian guide
to historic America) hardcover o.p. paperback
available $18.95   **917.4**
 1. Historic sites 2. Atlantic States—Description
ISBN 1-55670-050-4 (pa)   LC 88-16001
This guide to important landmarks and sites in New
York, New Jersey, and Pennsylvania provides addresses,
hours, fees, and phone numbers, as well as a brief history of the Mid-Atlantic region

New England, land of scenic splendor; prepared by
the Special Publications Division, National
Geographic Society. National Geographic Soc.
1989 199p il $16; lib bdg $12.95   **917.4**
 1. New England—Description
ISBN 0-87044-715-7; 0-87044-720-3 (lib bdg)
                                       LC 89-12127
Numerous full color photographs accompany a text
that explores the natural beauty of the New England
states throughout the year
Includes bibliography

917.8 Geography of and travel in Western United States

Fishbein, Seymour L.
Yellowstone country; the enduring wonder;
photographed by Raymond Gehman; prepared by
the Special Publications Division, National
Geographic Society. National Geographic Soc.
1989 193p il maps $16; lib bdg $12.95   **917.8**
 1. Yellowstone National Park
ISBN 0-87044-713-0; 0-87044-718-1 (lib bdg)
                                       LC 89-3353
The author/photographer team explore both Yellowstone and Grand Teton National Parks, offering a look at
each park's history, ecosystems and present ecological
concerns
Includes bibliography

917.9 Geography of and travel in Great Basin and Pacific Coast states

Brower, Kenneth, 1944-
Yosemite; an American treasure; prepared by the Special Publications Division. National Geographic Soc. 1990 199p il map $12.95 **917.9**
1. Yosemite National Park (Calif.)
ISBN 0-87044-789-0   LC 90-5655
Text and photographs "chronicle how rivers of ice shaped the valley and relate the saga of Yosemite—from the time it was the secret refuge of the Ahwahneechee Indians through its first one hundred years as a national park. . . . Brower details the captivating variety of Yosemite's plants and animals. He portrays, too, the people." Publisher's note
Includes bibliographical references

920 Biography

Books of biography are arranged as follows: 1. Biographical collections (920) 2. Biographies of individuals alphabetically by name of biographee (92)

Aaseng, Nathan, 1953-
Athletes. Facts on File 1995 xxv, 118p il (American Indian lives) $17.95   **920**
1. Athletes 2. Indians of North America—Biography
ISBN 0-8160-3019-7   LC 94-12469
The author profiles a number of Native American athletes, including Jim Thorpe, Olympic track star Billy Mills, and baseball stars Harley Bender, John Meyers and Allie Reynolds
This book is "written in crisp sports journalistic style. . . . A welcome addition to Native American, biography, and sports collections." Booklist
Includes bibliographical references

Great Justices of the Supreme Court. Oliver Press 1992 160p il (Profiles) lib bdg $16.95 **920**
1. United States. Supreme Court 2. Judges
ISBN 1-881508-01-3   LC 92-18443
Profiles eight notable justices of the United States Supreme Court and landmark cases in which each was involved: John Marshall, Roger Taney, John Harlan, Oliver Wendell Holmes, Louis Brandeis, Charles Evans Hughes, Hugo Black, Earl Warren
"In addition to its biographical value, this attractive, well-written book can also be used as a source for information on such cases as 'Brown v. The Board of Education of Topeka,' 'Dennis v. United States,' 'Gideon v. Wainwright,' and the Dred Scott Decision. Early civil rights cases are examined and related to current issues." SLJ
Includes bibliography

Twentieth-century inventors. Facts on File 1991 132p il (American profiles) lib bdg $17.95   **920**
1. Inventors
ISBN 0-8160-2485-5   LC 90-46547
Provides accounts of ten significant twentieth-century inventions and the people behind them, including the Wright brothers and their airplane, Robert Goddard and his rocket, and Gordon Gould and his laser
"The 10-to-12 page chapter entries are informative, well-balanced, and clearly written." SLJ
Includes bibliographies

Abdul-Jabbar, Kareem, 1947-
Black profiles in courage; a legacy of African American achievement; [by] Kareem Abdul-Jabbar and Alan Steinberg; foreword by Henry Louis Gates, Jr. Morrow 1996 xxiv, 232p il $22   **920**
1. African Americans—Biography
ISBN 0-688-13097-6   LC 96-26245
This book "profiles the historical achievements of 11 historical black figures from Estevanico de Dorantes to Rosa Parks." Libr J
The authors have provided "interesting and nuanced accounts of heroic African Americans whose accomplishments changed U.S. history. . . . Although Abdul-Jabbar is highly critical of past and present racism in the U.S., he gives credit to the abolitionist movement and leaders such as William Lloyd Garrison for their efforts toward ending slavery." Publ Wkly
Includes bibliographical references

Acker, Ally
Reel women; pioneers of the cinema, 1896 to the present; foreword by Judith Crist; afterword by Marc Wanamaker. Continuum 1991 xxvi, 374p il hardcover o.p. paperback available $18.95   **920**
1. Women in the motion picture industry 2. Motion picture industry
ISBN 0-8264-0579-7 (pa)   LC 90-43743
"A Frederick Ungar book"
This volume profiles "more than 120 women directors, writers, producers, editors, stuntpersons, etc., who worked or are working in the U.S. film industry. . . . Each entry includes a biographical sketch . . . and filmographies. . . . Acker wisely avoids any critical analyses of her subjects' films, and should be commended for her accuracy." Libr J
Includes bibliographical references

Almanac of American presidents; from 1789 to the present: an original compendium of facts and anecdotes about politics and the presidency in the United States of America; edited by Thomas L. Connelly and Michael D. Senecal. Facts on File 1991 485p il $45   **920**
1. Presidents—United States
ISBN 0-8160-2219-4   LC 91-18895
"A Manly, Inc. book"
This reference covers "41 presidents including their families; first ladies; children and other relatives; education; elections, including split-ticket campaigns; close races, contested elections, campaign slogans and songs; personal, political and financial scandals; careers—military, congressional, offices, and odd jobs they held; famous last words [and] where they are buried." Publisher's note
Includes bibliographical references

American first ladies; their lives and their legacy; edited by Lewis L. Gould. Garland 1996 xx, 686p il $95   **920**
1. Presidents—United States—Spouses
ISBN 0-8153-1479-5   LC 95-45052
A "biographical resource that presents personality traits, health issues, friends, habits, and quotations about the First Ladies, from Martha Washington to Hillary Clinton. An extensive list of sources for more information is included for each entry." SLJ
This "features excellent scholarship, exhaustive research, extensive bibliographies, index, appendixes and enormous detail. . . . A definitive work on American first ladies." Book Rep

✓ **Archer, Jules**
They had a dream; the civil rights struggle from Frederick Douglass to Marcus Garvey to Martin Luther King and Malcolm X. Viking 1993 258p il (Epoch biographies) $16.99; pa $5.99   **920**
1. African Americans—Biography 2. African Americans—Civil rights
ISBN 0-670-84494-2; 0-14-034954-5 (pa)
   LC 92-40071
Traces the progression of the civil rights movement and its effect on history through biographical sketches of four prominent and influential African Americans
"This discussion of the contributions of four pivotal civil rights activists is balanced and substantive, and the conclusion, which touches on Anita Hill and Clarence Thomas, Sister Souljah and Bill Clinton, is not only timely but persuasive." Publ Wkly
Includes bibliography

Barker, Juliet R. V.
The Brontës; [by] Juliet Barker. St. Martin's Press 1995 1003p il $35; pa $24.95   **920**
1. Brontë family
ISBN 0-312-13445-2; 0-312-14555-1 (pa)
   LC 95-22806
"A Thomas Dunne book"
This is a biography of Patrick Brontë and his children Charlotte, Emily, Anne, and Branwell
This is a "monumental book: patient, thoughtful, sustained and bound to become indispensable. We are given new manuscripts and obscure texts, a wealth of information from local newspapers about Haworth's everyday life, and constant reminder of the wider historical context against and within which the sisters' work is set." Times Lit Suppl
Includes bibliography

✓ **Bearing** witness: selections from African-American autobiography in the twentieth century; edited by Henry Louis Gates, Jr. Pantheon Bks. 1991 385p il pa $16   **920**
1. African Americans—Biography
ISBN 0-679-73520-8   LC 90-52538
"Gates has brought together excerpts from 28 African-American autobiographies. These statements represent both men and women and include the memories of scholars, politicians, creative writers, and journalists." Voice Youth Advocates
"Highly recommended as an introduction to black studies; especially useful in schools." BAYA Book Rev

Bell, Eric Temple, 1883-1960
Men of mathematics; [by] E. T. Bell. Simon & Schuster 1937 xxi, 592p il hardcover o.p. paperback available $14.95   **920**
1. Mathematicians
ISBN 0-671-62818-6 (pa)
Analyzed in Essay and general literature index
This volume looks at the lives and contributions of 35 pioneers of modern mathematics

Biography index; a cumulative index to biographical material in books and magazines. Wilson, H.W. annual subscription $190   **920**
1. Biography—Indexes 2. Biography—Bibliography
ISSN 0006-3053
Also available CD-ROM version
First issued September 1946
Published quarterly, November, February, May, and August, with bound annual and permanent two-year cumulations. Permanent volumes $175 each
"'Biography Index' is a dependable and time-tested source that is basic in reference collections. It will serve many needs and holds a positive place in the vast area of biographical research." Am Ref Books Annu, 1982

✓ **Black** leaders of the nineteenth century; edited by Leon Litwack and August Meier. University of Ill. Press 1988 344p il (Blacks in the new world) $41.75; pa $13.95   **920**
1. African Americans—Biography
ISBN 0-252-01506-1; 0-252-06213-2 (pa)
   LC 87-19439
"Including individual essays on the famous, such as Frederick Douglass and Harriet Tubman, as well as a general discussion of black Reconstructionist leaders at the grass roots, this scholarly collection provides in-depth information." Booklist
Includes bibliography

✓ **Black** leaders of the twentieth century; edited by John Hope Franklin and August Meier. University of Ill. Press 1982 372p il (Blacks in the new world) $29.95; pa $13.95   **920**
1. African Americans—Biography
ISBN 0-252-00870-7; 0-252-00939-8 (pa)
   LC 81-11454
This companion volume to the title entered above includes profiles of W. E. B. DuBois, Marcus Garvey, Whitney Young, Jr. and Malcolm X
Includes bibliographies

Bolton, Jonathan
Scholars, writers, and professionals; [by] Jonathan W. Bolton and Claire M. Wilson. Facts on File 1994 146p il (American Indian lives) $17.95   **920**
1. Indians of North America—Biography
ISBN 0-8160-2896-6   LC 93-31683
This "begins with a comprehensive essay and then continues with biographical profiles. Bolton and Wilson do a good job of gathering various subjects, which include everyone from Sequoyah, who invented the Cherokee syllabary, to authors Michael Dorris and Louise Erdrich. The writing is dry at times, but there is plenty here for young people on the assignment trail." Booklist
Includes bibliography

Brodie, James Michael, 1957-
Created equal; the lives and ideas of black American innovators. Morrow 1993 208p il $20; pa $12   **920**
1. African Americans—Biography 2. African American inventors 3. Scientists
ISBN 0-688-11536-5; 0-688-13790-3 (pa)
LC 92-40979
Daniel Hall Williams, Matthew Henson and Michael Crostin are among the more than 60 African American scientists and inventors profiled
"This book makes informative reading and a valuable research source for any library." Booklist

Character above all; ten presidents from FDR to George Bush; edited by Robert A. Wilson. Simon & Schuster 1996 256p $23; pa $12   **920**
1. Presidents—United States 2. United States—Politics and government—1900-1999 (20th century)
ISBN 0-684-81411-0; 0-684-82709-3 (pa)
LC 95-44827
This is a collection of essays that aims to explore the character of ten modern presidents
"The authors of these essays are all historians who have written impressive biographies of presidents. . . . Every essayist abounds with arch style and cogent insights." Booklist

Cloulas, Ivan
The Borgias; translated by Gilda Roberts. Watts 1989 388p o.p.   **920**
1. Borgia family 2. Italy—History
LC 88-34560
Original French edition, 1987
This collective biography of Rodrigo, Lucretia, Cesare, and Francis Borgia "succeeds in placing the Borgias within the broader perspective of Renaissance politics, religion, and ordinary dynastic ambition. Known fact is separated from legend, as the author weaves together, over two centuries, a complex group portrait. . . . A balanced narrative likely to become the standard work." Libr J
Includes bibliographies

Contemporary heroes and heroines; Ray B. Browne, editor; in association with Glenn J. Browne and Kevin O. Browne. Gale Res. 1990-1992 2v il ea $63   **920**
1. Heroes and heroines
ISBN 0-8103-4860-8 (bk1); 0-8103-8336-5 (bk2)
LC 90-132617
Book 2 edited by Deborah Gillan Straub
Each volume presents brief profiles of more than 150 contemporary men and women from all walks of life whose activities reflect heroic traits. Following vital statistics in each entry the profiled person's motivations, ambitions and accomplishments are outlined

Curtis, Robert H.
Great lives: medicine. Scribner 1993 326p il $23   **920**
1. Physicians 2. Scientists
ISBN 0-684-19321-3   LC 92-5387
"A history of medicine, from its crude and often barbaric beginnings to modern times, is presented through

the brief biographies of scientists and doctors who advanced the field to what it is today. . . . Individually, the biographical sketches are presented in a lively manner, written in an easy-to-read style, with each discussing the subject's childhood, personal life, and contributions to medical science." SLJ
Includes bibliographical references

Dash, Joan
The triumph of discovery: women scientists who won the Nobel Prize. Messner 1991 148p il hardcover o.p. paperback available $8.95   **920**
1. Nobel Prizes 2. Women scientists
ISBN 0-671-69333-6 (pa)   LC 90-39308
Examines the lives of Barbara McClintock, Maria Mayer, Rosalyn Yalow, and Rita Levi-Montalcini, women scientists who won the Nobel Prize against extraordinary odds, in different fields and under different circumstances
Includes bibliography

Davis, Michael D., 1939-
Black American women in Olympic track and field; a complete illustrated reference. McFarland & Co. 1992 170p il lib bdg $27.50   **920**
1. Women athletes 2. African American athletes 3. Olympic games
ISBN 0-89950-692-5   LC 91-50946
"Following a short introduction is an 'Olympic Checklist,' a seven-page summary of the participation of black American women from the 1932 through the 1988 games. The rest of the book is an alphabetically arranged biographical dictionary. Entries vary from 2 lines to 20 pages on Wilma Rudolph. Twenty of the more than 90 entries are based on first-person interviews. The interviews are particularly enlightening, not only for information about training and competition, but for the light they shed on race relations." Booklist

De Kruif, Paul, 1890-1971
Microbe hunters. Harcourt Brace Jovanovich 1966 c1926 337p il pa $13   **920**
1. Bacteriologists
ISBN 0-15-659413-7
"A Harvest/HBJ book"
First published 1926 and analyzed in Essay and general literature index
Contents: Leeuwenhoek; Spallanzani; Pasteur; Koch; Roux and Behring; Metchnikoff; Theobald Smith; Bruce; Ross vs. Grassi; Walter Reed; Paul Ehrlich
"A series of biographical sketches involving epoch making scientific discoveries, it is as discerning in its studies of temperament as it is accurate in its information on research." Saturday Rev

Deffaa, Chip, 1951-
Voices of the Jazz Age; profiles of eight vintage jazzmen. University of Ill. Press 1990 255p il (Music in American life) $29.95   **920**
1. Jazz musicians
ISBN 0-252-01681-5   LC 89-5242
"These eight essays help document the development of jazz in its infancy by profiling jazzmen who came up in

Deffaa, Chip, 1951——*Continued*
the 1920s, including saxophonist Bud Freeman and trumpeter Jimmy McPartland of the Austin High Gang, and trumpeters Bix Beiderbecke and Jabbo Smith. Pioneering big band leader Sam Wooding, saxophonist Benny Waters, tuba player Joe Tarto, and drummer Freddie Moore also tell colorful stories." Libr J

"The author presents an excellent synthesis of the interview material in a highly readable form." Choice

Includes bibliographical references and discography

✓ **Distinguished** African American scientists of the 20th century; [by] James H. Kessler [et al.]; with Sigrid Berge, portrait artist, and Alyce Neukirk, computer graphics artist. Oryx Press 1996 382p il $59.95 **920**
1. Scientists 2. African Americans—Biography
ISBN 0-89774-955-3 LC 95-43880

"One hundred famous and not-so-famous African American scientists (both living and dead) are covered in this biographical reference. . . . Men and women accomplished in anthropology, biology, chemistry, engineering, geology, mathematics, medicine, and physics are included. Those profiled include lesser-known scientists such as Christine Darden (an engineer with NASA) as well as the better known, e.g., George Washington Carver." Libr J

For a fuller review see: Booklist, Feb. 15, 1996

Includes bibliographical references

Faber, Doris, 1924-
Love & rivalry; three exceptional pairs of sisters. Viking 1983 200p il o.p. **920**
1. Stowe, Harriet Beecher, 1811-1896 2. Cushman, Charlotte, 1816-1876 3. Dickinson, Emily, 1830-1886
LC 83-6566

The author "explores the relationships between three famous women of the nineteenth century and their less well known sisters. The three pairs are Catherine Beecher and Harriet Beecher Stowe, Charlotte Cushman and Susan Cushman Muspratt, and Emily and Lavinia Dickinson." Bull Cent Child Books

Includes bibliography

Felder, Deborah G.
The 100 most influential women of all time; a ranking past and present. Carol Pub. Group 1996 374p il $24.95 **920**
1. Women—Biography
ISBN 0-8065-1726-3 LC 95-19222
"A Citadel Press book"

The author profiles and ranks 100 women of influence from various fields of endeavor

"This is an irresistible book by nature of its accessible format and gutsy ranking of important people. . . . Felder's succinct profile of each notable woman is quite passionate and surprisingly full of information." Booklist

Includes bibliographical references

Fraser, Rebecca
The Brontës; Charlotte Brontë and her family. Crown 1988 543p il o.p.; Fawcett Bks. paperback available $14 **920**
1. Brontë family 2. Authors, English 3. Women authors
ISBN 0-449-90465-2 (pa) LC 88-29918

This "biography sets Charlotte Brontë in her rightful place as the central figure in a remarkable and gifted family. Fraser gives a full account of the parents, home, teachers, publishers, friends, fellow writers and finally the husband of the woman who chose the masculine *nom-de-plume* 'Currer Bell.' The writings of Emily ('Ellis Bell') and Anne ('Action') are described and evaluated, as are the unpublished effusions of their wastrel brother Branwell." Publ Wkly

Includes bibliography

Going where I'm coming from; memoirs of American youth; edited by Anne Mazer. Persea Bks. 1995 166p $15.95; pa $6.95 **920**
1. Authors, American
ISBN 0-89255-205-0; 0-89255-206-9 (pa)
LC 94-15595

"Containing selections from such adult and children's writers as Naomi Shabib Nye, Gary Soto, and Susan Power, this book puts establishing identity and experiencing life as a young person into a multicultural perspective. Most of the writers recall things from their growing up—incidents that speak about intergenerational ties, prejudice, or the immigrant experience. Their stories are poignant and perceptive." Booklist

Gombar, Christina
Great women writers, 1900-1950. Facts on File 1996 168p il (American profiles) $17.95 **920**
1. Women authors 2. Authors, American
ISBN 0-8160-3060-X LC 95-43305

This volume profiles the life and work of Edith Wharton, Willa Cather, Gertrude Stein, Katherine Anne Porter, Zora Neale Hurston, Pearl Buck, Eudora Welty and Flannery O'Connor

Includes bibliographical references

✓ **Great** slave narratives; selected and introduced by Arna Bontemps. Beacon Press 1969 331p pa $17.75 **920**
1. Slavery—United States 2. African Americans—Biography
ISBN 0-8070-5473-9

This volume includes: The life of Olaudah Equiano; The fugitive blacksmith; and Running a thousand miles for freedom

✓ **Haley, Alex**
Roots. Doubleday 1976 587p $25 **920**
1. Haley family 2. Kinte family
ISBN 0-385-03787-2
Also available in paperback from Dell

This book details Haley's "search for the genealogical history of his family. He describes his trip to Gambia, the African homeland of his ancestors, and recounts the lives of his forebears." Benet's Reader's Ency of Am Lit

Heller, Nancy G.

Women artists; an illustrated history. Abbeville Press 1987 244p il hardcover o.p. paperback available $35   **920**

1. Women artists

ISBN 1-55859-211-3 (pa)   LC 87-904

"Organized in six chapters by century, the survey provides brief biographical information, some critical analysis and context, and at least one color plate of the work of 125 women artists who lived and worked in Europe or North America between the 16th Century and the 1980s. . . . An excellent resource for students." SLJ

Includes bibliography

Henderson, Harry, 1951-

Modern mathematicians. Facts on File 1996 139p il (Global profiles) $17.95   **920**

1. Mathematicians

ISBN 0-8160-3235-1   LC 95-18363

This book "includes thirteen brief biographies of men and women who, through achievements in the field of mathematics, advanced modern science. . . . The biographies are arranged chronologically. . . . The coverage of women scientists and the demonstrations of how discoveries in the fields of logic, algebra, and chaos have led to a greater understanding in other scientific fields make this book a valuable resource." Voice Youth Advocates

Includes bibliographical references

√ Henkes, Robert

Native American painters of the twentieth century; the works of 61 artists. McFarland & Co. 1995 219p il lib bdg $38.50   **920**

1. Artists, American 2. Indians of North America—Art

ISBN 0-7864-0092-7   LC 95-16637

"Biographical information is provided about each of the sixty-one artists, along with critical assessments of the artist's work, the artist's own comments about the paintings and techniques, along with black and white examples of each artist's work. Entries include major painters recognized as Native American such as Yeffe Kimball, King Kuka, George Longfish, George Morrison, Annie Nash and Joe Baker." Voice Youth Advocates

Includes bibliographical references

Herstory; women who changed the world; edited by Ruth Ashby and Dobrorah Gore Ohrn; introduction by Gloria Steinem. Viking 1995 304p il $19.95   **920**

1. Women—Biography

ISBN 0-670-85434-4   LC 94-61492

"A Byron Preiss book"

"Here are 120 biographical sketches of women from around the world, from ancient times to the present, ranging from Queen Hatshepsut to Rigoberta Menchú. Helpful introductory material, bibliography and indexes. A great book for browsing." N Y Times Book Rev

For a fuller review see: Booklist, Oct. 1, 1995

Herzog, Brad

The sports 100; the one hundred most important people in American sports history. Macmillan 1995 418p il pa $16.95   **920**

1. Athletes 2. Sports

ISBN 0-02-860402-4   LC 95-40968

This work profiles 100 athletes and others involved in sports, including coaches, sportscasters, sports executives, promoters and financiers

Includes bibliographical references

The Jazz musician; edited by Tony Scherman and Mark Rowland. St. Martin's Press 1994 261p il $22.95; pa $12.95   **920**

1. Jazz musicians

ISBN 0-312-09499-X; 0-312-09500-7 (pa)

     LC 93-10638

Also available: The Rock musician, edited by Tony Scherman $22.95, pa $12.95 (ISBN 0-312-09501-5; 0-312-09502-3)

"Drawing interviews and profiles from the first 15 years of *Musician Magazine*, Scherman and Rowland attempt to figure out what make legendary jazz artists such as Miles Davis, John Coltrane, and Dizzy Gillespie tick." Booklist

Kane, Joseph Nathan, 1899-

Facts about the presidents; a compilation of biographical and historical information. 6th ed. Wilson, H.W. 1993 433p il $55   **920**

1. Presidents—United States

ISBN 0-8242-0845-5   LC 93-9207

First published 1959

The main part of this work provides an individual chapter on each President, from Washington through Clinton, presenting such information as family, education, election, Vice President, main events and accomplishments of his administration, and First Lady. Part two contains tables and lists presenting comparative data on all the Presidents

Kennedy, John F. (John Fitzgerald), 1917-1963

Profiles in courage; special foreword by Robert F. Kennedy. Commemorative ed. Perennial Lib. 1988 c1964 282p pa $7   **920**

1. Politicians—United States 2. Courage

ISBN 0-06-080698-2

Also available G.K. Hall large print edition

First published 1956 by Harper & Brothers

This series of profiles of Americans who took courageous stands at crucial moments in public life includes John Quincy Adams, Daniel Webster, Thomas Hart Benton, Sam Houston, Edmund G. Ross, Lucius Q. C. Lamar, George Norris, Robert A. Taft and others

Includes bibliography

√ Leadership; by the editors of Time-Life Books. Time-Life Bks. 1994 256p il (African Americans: voices of triumph) $29.95   **920**

1. African Americans—Biography

     LC 93-21147

This volume "discusses African-Americans who have excelled in science, business, religion, education, and politics. It is immensely informative, well organized, and clearly written." SLJ

Includes bibliographical references

Lipsyte, Robert

Idols of the game; a sporting history of the American century; by Robert Lipsyte and Peter Levine. Turner Pub. (Atlanta) 1995 368p il $23.95

920

1. Athletes 2. Sports

ISBN 1-57036-154-1   LC 95-18929

In this companion to a TBS television series, "sixteen American sports heroes from the past 100 years—from John L. Sullivan to Martina Navratilova—are profiled in light of what their public personas and private realities tell us about American culture. The vibrant writing covers such issues as gender, race, marketing and commercialism, political opportunism and hypocrisy, and the role of the media. This work rises above the sports genre and is highly recommended for all libraries." Libr J

Includes bibliographical references

Lucas, Eileen

Naturalists,   conservationists,   and environmentalists. Facts on File 1994 150p il (American profiles) $16.95   **920**

1. Naturalists 2. Environmentalists

ISBN 0-8160-2919-9   LC 93-46070

This presents biographies of naturalists, conservationists, and people involved in the environmental movements. The subjects are John James Audubon, John Muir, Rachel Carson, "George Perkins Marsh, Aldo Leopold, Olaus and Margaret Murie, Marjory Stoneman Douglas, David Brower and Gaylor Nelson." Appraisal

Includes bibliography

McGrayne, Sharon Bertsch

Nobel Prize women in science; their lives, struggles, and momentous discoveries. Carol Pub. Group 1993 419p il $26.95   **920**

1. Women scientists 2. Nobel Prizes

ISBN 1-55972-146-4   LC 92-21131

"A Birch Lane Press book"

"The 14 women whose stories are featured overcame tremendous difficulties and hardships in order to pursue a life of the mind within the scientific community. Written in accessible language, free of esoteric jargon, Bertsch's narrative captures the excitement involved in the pursuit of ground-breaking research and the passionate dedication that leads to discovery." Booklist

Includes bibliographical references

Meadows, A. J. (Arthur Jack)

The great scientists; [by] Jack Meadows. Oxford Univ. Press 1987 248p il $41.75; pa $23.95 **920**

1. Scientists 2. Science—History

ISBN 0-19-520620-7; 0-19-520815-3 (pa)

LC 87-18567

"The 12 scientists portrayed are Aristotle, Galileo Galilei, William Harvey, Isaac Newton, Antoine Lavoisier, Alexander van Humboldt, Michael Faraday, Charles Darwin, Louis Pasteur, Marie Curie, Sigmund Freud, and Albert Einstein. . . . *The Great Scientists* also includes capsule summaries of the achievements of more than 300 other scientists . . . as well as more than 2000 pivotal dates in history." Sci Teach

Includes glossary and bibliography

The **Mighty** chieftains; by the editors of Time-Life Books. Time-Life Bks. 1993 184p il maps (American Indians) $19.95   **920**

1. Indians of North America—Biography

LC 93-22395

This collection of Native American profiles "explains why these individuals became prominent among their respective peoples. . . . A useful and detailed reference for all libraries, especially for reports." SLJ

Includes bibliographical references

Montgomery, Sy

Walking with the great apes; Jane Goodall, Dian Fossey, Biruté Galdikas. Houghton Mifflin 1991 280p il hardcover o.p. paperback available $13.95

920

1. Goodall, Jane, 1934- 2. Fossey, Dian 3. Galdikas, Biruté 4. Women scientists

ISBN 0-395-61156-3 (pa)   LC 90-48043

"A Peter Davison book"

A "group biography of the three women recruited by Louis Leakey to study the great apes in their natural habitats." Libr J

"This is an exciting book. Montgomery provides an outstanding, popularized synthesis. . . . The author also conveys a fine sense of the diverse personalities of the three." Booklist

Includes bibliographical references

Morell, Virginia

Ancestral passions; the Leakey family and the quest for humankind's beginnings. Simon & Schuster 1995 638p il $30; pa $16   **920**

1. Leakey, Louis Seymour Bazett, 1903-1972 2. Leakey, Mary D., 1913-1996 3. Leakey, Richard E., 1944- 4. Anthropologists 5. Human origins

ISBN 0-684-80192-2; 0-684-82470-1 (pa)

LC 95-14306

"The Leakey family, now in its third generation of hunting hominid fossils in East Africa, is the subject of this exquisitely written biography about the search for the beginnings of humankind. . . . With access to volumes of personal and professional papers and extensive interviews with Mary, Richard, and Meave Leakey, as well as many others who played a role in the story of human origins, Virginia Morell has allowed the reader to gain unparalleled insight into the oftentimes complex lives of the world's 'first family of human evolution.'" Sci Books Films

Includes bibliographical references

My folks don't want me to talk about slavery; twenty-one oral histories of former North Carolina slaves; edited by Belinda Hurmence. Blair 1984 103p hardcover o.p. paperback available $5.95   **920**

1. Slavery—United States 2. African Americans—Biography

ISBN 0-89587-039-8 (pa)   LC 84-16891

The narratives presented here were part of a Federal Writers' project during which some 2,000 former slaves were interviewed during the 1930s

A "unique glimpse of slavery viewed from the less

My folks don't want me to talk about slavery—
Continued
well-recorded side, the side of the subjugated." Sci
Books Films
Includes bibliography

Nash, Jay Robert
Bloodletters and badmen; a narrative
encyclopedia of American criminals from the
Pilgrims to the present. completely rev updated &
expanded [ed] Evans & Co. 1995 698p il pa
$19.95   **920**
1. Criminals
ISBN 0-87131-777-X   LC 94-49585
First published 1973 by Lippincott
Among the notorious Americans profiled are Charles
Whitman, David Berkowitz, Charlie Starkweather, Rich-
ard Speck, Lee Harvey Oswald, Al Capone, Dutch
Schultz, Bonnie Parker, Clyde Barrow, Frank and Jesse
James, and the Wild Bunch
Includes bibliographical references

Nichols, Janet, 1952-
American music makers; an introduction to
American composers. Walker & Co. 1990 232p il
$19.95; lib bdg $19.85   **920**
1. Composers, American 2. American music—History
and criticism
ISBN 0-8027-6957-8; 0-8027-6958-6 (lib bdg)
                                            LC 90-11924
"This is a collective biography of ten American composers: Louis Gottschalk, Edward MacDowell, Charles
Ives, Henry Cowell, Ruth Seeger, George Gershwin, Milton Babbitt, George Crumb, Steve Reich, and Philip
Glass. It is also a history of American music from Gottschalk, who lived during the mid-1800s . . . to Glass,
who was born in 1937." Voice Youth Advocates
"More than a mere collection of facts, the book explores the relationships between composers' works and
their times. . . . Concepts such as total serialism, twelve-
tone music, and minimalism are clearly explained. . . .
An excellent resource for reports." SLJ
Includes glossary, bibliography, and discography

The **Norton** book of interviews; an anthology
from 1859 to the present day; edited with an
introduction by Christopher Silvester; preface by
Gay Talese. Norton 1996 xxi, 626p $30   **920**
ISBN 0-393-03876-9   LC 95-5791
First published 1993 in the United Kingdom with title:
The Penguin book of interviews
"This wide-ranging anthology includes conversations
with prominent literary figures, individuals who have
achieved greatness in other realms, and, in a few instances, characters distinguished by conduct deemed dis-
reputable. A long-ago discussion between Horace Greeley and Brigham Young (purported to be the earliest example of the interview format) is followed by more recent question-and-answer sessions with such notables as
Hitler, Stalin, Hoffa, Monroe, and Nabokov." Booklist
Includes bibliography

The **Norton** book of women's lives; edited by
Phyllis Rose. Norton 1993 826p $30   **920**
1. Women—Biography
ISBN 0-393-03532-8   LC 92-40015
The editor "has selected excerpts from the autobiographies, memoirs, or journals of 61 twentieth-century wom-
en. . . . Rose has focussed primarily on women writers,
but she has also included women from other walks of
life who took the time to record their life story." Booklist
"Because of the breadth and richness of these 61 selections, which demonstrate the evolution of women's
autobiographical writing, this anthology is destined to become a classic." Libr J
Includes bibliographical references

Oleksy, Walter G., 1930-
Military leaders of World War II; [by] Walter
Oleksy. Facts on File 1994 154p il (American
profiles) $17.95   **920**
1. World War, 1939-1945—Biography 2. United
States—Armed Forces—Biography
ISBN 0-8160-3008-1   LC 93-33641
The author "profiles 10 outstanding leaders of World
War II, among them Nimitz, MacArthur, Eisenhower,
Bradley, LeMay, and Patton. Each biography provides a
glimpse of the subject's civilian life prior to the war as
well as his wartime and postwar life." Booklist
"Oleksy's crisp, no-nonsense, understated prose is
consistent with his subject matter. . . . What sets this
work apart from others—besides the writing—is the very
detailed index." SLJ
Includes bibliographical references

Opfell, Olga S.
Queens, empresses, grand duchesses, and
regents; women rulers of Europe, A.D. 1328-1989.
McFarland & Co. 1989 282p il lib bdg $37.50
                                            920
1. Kings, queens, rulers, etc. 2. Europe—History
3. Princes and princesses 4. Women—Biography
ISBN 0-89950-385-3   LC 88-43484
"This is a collection of 39 vignettes of European
women rulers. . . . It is arranged chronologically. . . .
The book successfully provides a feeling of the rulers'
triumphs, tragedies, jealousies, and romances with an ob-
jectively written and often colorful, lively style that is
aimed at both popular and serious readers. The focus is
more on rulers' lives, their families, and how contemporaries viewed them than on the events that surrounded
them." Libr J
Includes bibliography

Women prime ministers and presidents.
McFarland & Co. 1993 237p il lib bdg $35   **920**
1. Heads of state 2. Women—Biography
ISBN 0-89950-790-5   LC 92-56675
"This book contains up-to-date profiles of all women
heads of government to the date of publication. The entries are in chronological order. Each gives biographical
information and the history and politics of the woman's
country during her lifetime. . . . This is an essential purchase for women's studies collections." Voice Youth Advocates
Includes bibliographical references

Osen, Lynn M.

Women in mathematics. MIT Press 1974 185p il hardcover o.p. paperback available $13.95 **920**
1. Women mathematicians

ISBN 0-262-65009-6 (pa)

This collection contains sketches of famous female mathematicians from the fifth to twentieth centuries

Includes bibliographical references

The Presidents: a reference history; Henry F. Graff, editor. 2nd ed. Scribner 1996 811p il $105 **920**
1. Presidents—United States 2. United States—Politics and government

ISBN 0-684-80471-9   LC 96-1730

First published 1984

This work offers a chronological history of the presidency through Bill Clinton. Contributors provide an interpretive essay on each president that examines the events and developments of each administration, and the impact of the man and his policies. An appended essay assesses the role of the First Lady. Annotated bibliographies accompany each essay

For a review see: Booklist, Sept. 1, 1996

Includes bibliographical references

✓ **Rake, Alan**

100 great Africans. Scarecrow Press 1994 431p maps $59.50 **920**
1. Africa—Biography

ISBN 0-8108-2929-0   LC 94-25934

This "work covers all areas and time periods of Africa, from Queen Hatshepsut of ancient Egypt to Nelson Mandela, and is divided into ten general categories (e.g., those who resisted the imposition of colonialism.)" Libr J

For a fuller review see: Booklist, March 1, 1995

Ritter, Lawrence S.

The glory of their times; the story of the early days of baseball told by the men who played it. new enl ed. Morrow 1984 360p il hardcover o.p. paperback available $10 **920**
1. Baseball—Biography

ISBN 0-688-11273-0 (pa)   LC 84-221549

First published 1966 by Macmillan

A collection of 26 oral histories of baseball's early days by veteran players

See, Lisa

On Gold Mountain. St. Martin's Press 1995 394p il maps $24.95 **920**
1. Seay family 2. Chinese Americans

ISBN 0-312-11997-6   LC 95-12610

Also available in paperback from Vintage Bks.

"See's chronicle melds together the life stories of her Chinese and American ancestors, beginning with a great-great-grandfather's journey from China to San Francisco. . . . Her tale is most specific in its descriptions of the hardships and discrimination endured for decades by large numbers of Chinese immigrants." Booklist

"Facing the nimble shell game her family plays with its history, Ms. See has done a gallant and fair-minded job of fashioning anecdote, fable and fact into an engaging account." N Y Times Book Rev

The **Smithsonian** book of the First Ladies; their lives, times, and issues; Edith P. Mayo, general editor; foreword by Hillary Rodham Clinton. Holt & Co. 1996 302p il $24.95 **920**
1. Presidents—United States—Spouses

ISBN 0-8050-1751-8   LC 94-6147

This "book gives a brief account of the life and White House doings of first ladies from Martha Washington to Hillary Rodham Clinton; it also mentions White House hostesses who were not presidential wives (such as James Buchanan's niece) and gives a quick précis of those women who didn't live long enough to see their husbands attain the highest office in the land." Bull Cent Child Books

"Well illustrated and punctuated with tidbits of useful information, this is both an excellent reference book for studying America's First Ladies and an informative look at women's history." Voice Youth Advocates

Includes bibliography

Sonneborn, Liz

Performers. Facts on File 1995 112p il (American Indian lives) $17.95 **920**
1. Entertainers 2. Indians of North America—Biography

ISBN 0-8160-3045-6   LC 94-25587

This volume "profiles eight talented individuals of Native American ancestry noted for their contributions to the performing arts from the late 1800s to the present. . . . Proudly presenting the experiences and diversity of these individuals, *Performers* clearly shows how little has changed for Native American entertainers, particularly in the movie industry." Booklist

Includes bibliography

Stefoff, Rebecca, 1951-

Women pioneers. Facts on File 1995 126p il (American profiles) $17.95 **920**
1. Frontier and pioneer life—West (U.S.) 2. Women—West (U.S.)

ISBN 0-8160-3134-7   LC 95-13552

The author presents "nine stories of pioneer women and their courage, ingenuity, and triumph. Based on primary sources, the accounts are delivered in a narrative style that enhances readability without sacrificing detail or accuracy. A variety of figures are represented, from Rebecca Burlend, raised in England; to Clara Brown, born a slave in Virginia; to Polly Bemis, born in China." SLJ

Includes bibliographical references

Strachey, Lytton, 1880-1932

Eminent Victorians; Cardinal Manning, Florence Nightingale, Dr. Arnold, General Gordon **920**
1. Great Britain—Biography

Hardcover and paperback editions available from various publishers

First published 1918 by Putnam and analyzed in Essay and general literature index

"A collection of four biographical essays . . . Strachey's wit, iconoclasm, satiric edge, and narrative powers captured a large readership." Concise Oxford Companion to Engl Lit

Includes bibliographies

Terkel, Studs, 1912-

Giants of jazz. rev ed, revised and updated by Studs Terkel, with Milly Hawk Daniel. Crowell 1975 210p il   **920**

1. Jazz musicians 2. African American musicians

Available in hardcover from Amereon

First published 1957

This book discusses the lives and music of thirteen jazz musicians including Louis Armstrong, Bessie Smith, Duke Ellington, Benny Goodman, Woody Herman and Dizzy Gillespie

"The subjects were chosen either for their influence or their mastery of a particular instrument or style; the writing is informed and informal. An excellent divided discography and an index are appended." Bull Cent Child Books

Truman, Margaret, 1924-

First ladies. Random House 1995 368p il $25   **920**

1. Presidents—United States—Spouses

ISBN 0-679-43439-9   LC 95-9713

Also available in paperback from Fawcett Bks.

"Truman's look at the nation's first ladies features capsule accounts of a selective number of women who have shared the White House with their husbands. She includes the obvious subjects such as Martha Washington, Dolley Madison, Mary Todd Lincoln, Eleanor Roosevelt and all the modern presidents' wives, along with lesser-known first ladies [such] as Julia Grant and Julia Tyler." Publ Wkly

"Written in a chatty, gossipy, easy-to-read style, the book offers thumbnail sketches that are insightful, amusing, factual, personal, and sometimes colored by [the author's] own experiences in the White House." SLJ

Unger, Harlow G., 1931-

Teachers and educators. Facts on File 1994 126p il (American profiles) $17.95   **920**

1. Teachers 2. Educators

ISBN 0-8160-2990-3   LC 94-8628

This "collection contains eight snapshot synopses about notable nineteenth century educational leaders. Catharine Beecher, Horace Mann, W.E.B. DuBois, and Emma Willard are among those included. . . . The biographies are detailed, and Unger links personal facts with political and historical events so students will easily become familiar with the educators." Voice Youth Advocates

Includes bibliographical references

Untermeyer, Louis, 1885-1977

Lives of the poets; the story of one thousand years of English and American poetry. Simon & Schuster 1959 757p o.p.   **920**

1. Poets, English 2. Poets, American 3. American poetry—History and criticism 4. English poetry—History and criticism

Includes biographies of: Blake, Elizabeth and Robert Browning, Burns, Byron, Coleridge, Dickinson, Donne, Dryden, Hopkins, Keats, Milton, Pope, Shakespeare, Shelley, Southey, Whitman, Wordsworth

Wakin, Edward

Contemporary political leaders of the Middle East. Facts on File 1996 142p il map (Global profiles) $17.95   **920**

1. Heads of state 2. Middle East—Politics and government

ISBN 0-8160-3154-1   LC 95-18814

Profiles eight Arab and Israeli leaders who have been instrumental in shaping the history of the Middle East

"Wakin is careful to set each biography in the context of the region. He tells both sides, or in some cases many sides, of the same story, using quotes by others to place the leaders in the larger world arena. The text is interesting, carefully organized, and gives enough detail without becoming overwhelming." SLJ

Walker, Paul Robert

Great figures of the Wild West. Facts on File 1992 125p il map (American profiles) lib bdg $20   **920**

1. Frontier and pioneer life—West (U.S.)

ISBN 0-8160-2576-2   LC 91-9744

Profiles eight people who helped shape the popular image of the Wild West: Sitting Bull, Buffalo Bill, Jesse James, Wyatt Earp, Billy the Kid, Geronimo, Belle Starr, and Judge Roy Bean

"This is a useful collection. The biographical sketches are better researched than usual." SLJ

Includes bibliography

Weir, Alison

The children of Henry VIII. Ballantine Bks. 1996 385p il $25   **920**

1. Great Britain—History—1485-1603, Tudors

ISBN 0-345-39118-7   LC 96-14849

Published in the United Kingdom with title: Children of England

This "book covers the lives of Henry's children Mary Tudor and Edward VI, but it only takes Elizabeth up to her accession, and it also includes the entire short life of Jane Grey, the granddaughter of Henry's sister Mary. When Henry died in 1547, he left a country embroiled in several social problems brought about by the enclosure of common lands, the high cost of his European wars, and the closure of monasteries. How his heirs dealt with these problems, along with their relationships, makes interesting reading." Libr J

Includes bibliographical references

Whitney, David C., 1921-

The American presidents. Reader's Digest Assn. il pa $15.95   **920**

1. Presidents—United States

First published 1967 by Doubleday. (8th edition 1996) Periodically revised

This volume contains biographical sketches of all United States presidents from Washington through Clinton. . . . Articles and tables on First Ladies, Vice Presidents, elections, historical sites, and what presidents have said about their office, are included

Written by herself; an anthology; edited and with an introduction by Jill Ker Conway. Vintage Bks. 1992-1996 2v v1 pa $15, v2 pa $16 **920**
1. Women—United States—Biography

LC 92-50081

Volume 3 in preparation

Contents: [v1] Autobiographies of American women (ISBN 0-679-73633-6; v2 Women's memoirs from Britain, Africa, Asia, and the United States (ISBN 0-679-75109-2)

"Marian Anderson, Cecilia Payne Gaposchkin, Maxine Hong Kingston, and Gloria Steinem are among the 25 women whose writings have been gathered in [the first] volume. Autobiographical in nature, the entries deal with their personal lives, their work, their hopes and dreams, their failures and successes." SLJ

Among the contributors to volume 2 are Isak Dinesen, Vera Brittain, Vivian Gornick, and Shudha Mazumdar

Includes bibliography

Yount, Lisa
Contemporary women scientists. Facts on File 1994 124p il (American profiles) lib bdg $17.95 **920**
1. Women scientists
ISBN 0-8160-2895-8   LC 93-26821

An introduction to the life and work of 10 women prominent in the natural sciences. "Each chapter teaches some of the science relevant to that woman's career and contributions in an exceptionally clear way, defining terms and giving enough background so that the content is understandable to those with little scientific background." Sci Books Films

Includes bibliography

Women aviators. Facts on File 1995 144p il (American profiles) $17.95 **920**
1. Women air pilots
ISBN 0-8160-3062-6   LC 94-23134

"Yount devotes 11 lengthy chapters to prominent female aviators. . . . The book [makes] clear the determination required, then and now, for a woman to achieve in aviation and aeronautics. The many different examples of how that determination proved successful are the book's strength." Booklist

Includes bibliographical references

920.003 Biographical reference works

Abrams, Irwin
The Nobel Peace Prize and the laureates; an illustrated biographical history, 1901-1987. Hall, G.K. & Co. 1988 269p $60 **920.003**
1. Nobel Prizes 2. Biography—Dictionaries
ISBN 0-8161-8609-X   LC 88-16313

This "volume contains biographies of the 87 famous and not-so-famous individuals who have been recipients of the prize from 1901 to 1987, and also discusses each prize period separately, providing an overview of the social, political, and historical decision-making environment that influenced the selection choice." Libr J

African-American sports greats; a biographical dictionary; edited by David L. Porter. Greenwood Press 1995 429p il $59.95 **920.003**
1. African American athletes—Dictionaries
ISBN 0-313-28987-5   LC 95-7189

This work lists 166 athletes representing 11 sports. "Baseball, football, and basketball players account for more than half the entries. Entries are arranged under the current name of the athlete, which leaves married women at a disadvantage because many made their mark in the sports world under their maiden names. The index, however, provides cross references. The preface clearly states the selection criteria, and each signed entry includes a bibliography." Libr J

For a fuller review see: Booklist, Nov. 15, 1995

American authors, 1600-1900; a biographical dictionary of American literature; edited by Stanley J. Kunitz and Howard Haycraft. Wilson, H.W. 1938 846p il (Authors series) $76
920.003
1. Authors, American—Dictionaries 2. American literature—Bio-bibliography
ISBN 0-8242-0001-2

"Complete in one volume with 1300 biographies and 400 portraits." Title page

"This volume contains biographies of 1,300 authors who contributed to the development of American literature, from the founding of Jamestown (1607) to the end of the nineteenth century. Each essay describes the author's life, discusses past and present significance, and evaluates principal works." Nichols. Guide to Ref Books for Sch Media Cent. 4th edition

American cultural leaders; from colonial times to the present; [by] Justin Harmon [et al.]; editors, Amy Lewis, Paula McGuire; consulting editors, Robert J. Clark [et al.] ABC-CLIO 1993 550p il (Biographies of American leaders) $65
920.003
1. American arts—Biography—Dictionaries
ISBN 0-87436-673-9   LC 93-36284

"The 360 profiles fall into six fields: art, dance, film, literature, music and theater. These are highly readable biographies about 400 to 1,000 words in length. Arranged alphabetically by name, profiles include such diverse personalities as Walt Disney, Alvin Ailey, Georgia O'Keeffe, and Stephen Crane. . . . A valuable addition to the reference collection. Highly recommended." Voice Youth Advocates

American men & women of science; a biographical directory of today's leaders in physical, biological and related sciences. Bowker 8v set $850 **920.003**
1. Scientists—Dictionaries
ISSN 0192-8570

Also available CD-ROM version

Irregular. First published 1906 by Science Press with title: American men of science. Some editions were divided into two sections: Physical and biological sciences and Social sciences (19th edition 1995-96)

"Provides brief biographical sketches of . . . scientists active in all natural science fields in the United States

American men & women of science—*Continued*
and Canada. Arranged alphabetically, with discipline index." Ref Sources for Small & Medium-sized Libr. 5th edition

American reformers; an H. W. Wilson biographical dictionary; editor, Alden Whitman. Wilson, H.W. 1985 xx, 930p il $89   **920.003**
1. Reformers 2. United States—Biography—Dictionaries
ISBN 0-8242-0705-X   LC 85-636
This volume offers biographies of 508 men and women who were the principal architects of reform in America, from the seventeenth century to modern times
"An imposing panel of historians contributed to the work and all major reform areas are covered, including abolition and civil rights, health, labor, temperance, and women's rights. The work is technically faultless. . . . An excellent and useful addition to any general reference collection." Choice

American writers; a collection of literary biographies; Leonard Unger, editor in chief. Scribner 1974-1991 4v + supplement I-III (in 6v) set $800   **920.003**
1. Authors, American—Dictionaries 2. American literature—Bio-bibliography 3. American literature—History and criticism
ISBN 0-684-19594-1
Also available CD-ROM version
Supplement four published 1996 available $199 (ISBN 0-684-19785-5)
Contents: v1 Henry Adams to T. S. Eliot; v2 Ralph Waldo Emerson to Carson McCullers; v3 Archibald MacLeish to George Santayana; v4 Isaac Bashevis Singer to Richard Wright; supplement I pt 1 Jane Addams to Sidney Lanier; supplement I pt2 Vachel Lindsay to Elinor Wylie; supplement II pt 1 W. H. Auden to O'Henry; supplement II pt2 Robinson Jeffers to Yvor Winters; supplement III pt 1 John Ashbery to Walker Percy; supplement III pt2 Philip Roth to Louis Zukofsky and cumulative index to volumes 1-4 and supplements I, II and III
"Signed essays on the life and works of selected American authors; selective bibliographies by and about each author. The basic set (1974. 4 v.) contains 97 essays originally published in the University of Minnesota pamphlets on American writers series; some have been revised and updated. Each of the 2-v. supplements covers 29 writers not included in the parent series; the supplements give greater attention to women and minorities." Guide to Ref Books. 11th edition

Authors & artists for young adults. Gale Res. il ea $75   **920.003**
1. Authors—Dictionaries 2. Artists—Dictionaries 3. Literature—Bio-bibliography
ISSN 1040-5682
Semi-annual. First published 1988
Editors vary
"Each volume contains 20-25 entries offering personal, behind-the-scenes information, . . . sidelights, portraits, movie stills, bibliographies, cumulative index and much more. Its international scope ranges from contemporary to classic, fantasy to nonfiction." Publisher's note

Axelrod, Alan, 1952-
Dictators and tyrants; absolute rulers and would-be rulers in world history; [by] Alan Axelrod and Charles Phillips. Facts on File 1995 340p il $45   **920.003**
1. Dictators—Dictionaries
ISBN 0-8160-2866-4   LC 94-6200
"Over 500 brief, informative entries detail the lives, campaigns and intrigues of kings and tyrants alike, spanning in time from the earliest pharoahs to modern-day dictators such as Khomeini, Hussein, and Ceausescu. The writing is brisk and clear, and the text is complemented by black-and-white illustrations, paintings, and photographs." SLJ

The environmentalists; a biographical dictionary from the 17th century to the present; [by] Alan Axelrod and Charles Phillips. Facts on File 1993 258p il $45   **920.003**
1. Naturalists 2. Environmentalists
ISBN 0-8160-2715-3   LC 92-38773
"An alphabetical compendium of 600 individuals, private agencies, and governmental organizations that have been influential in the development of ecology. The focus is primarily American, though some international listings are included. . . . The occupations of the individuals vary as much as their interests in and impact on—positive or negative—the environment." SLJ
"This work is unique in scope and content. There are many directories of environmental organizations but none that provide both historical and current biographical information on a wide range of individuals." Booklist

Baker's biographical dictionary of musicians. Schirmer Bks. $125   **920.003**
1. Music—Bio-bibliography 2. Musicians—Dictionaries
First published 1900 under the authorship of Theodore Baker (8th edition edited by Nicolas Slonimsky 1992). Periodically revised
"Brief articles about composers, performers, critics, conductors, and teachers arranged alphabetically under surname with pronunciation." Ref Sources for Small & Medium-sized Libr. 5th edition
Includes bibliographies

Bentley, James, 1937-
A calendar of saints: the lives of the principal saints of the Christian year. Facts on File 1986 256p il $29.95   **920.003**
1. Christian saints—Dictionaries
ISBN 0-8160-1682-8   LC 86-19626
"Brief, chronologically arranged biographies. Includes one saint for each calendar day. Profusely illustrated with reproductions from various periods of religious art." N Y Public Libr. Ref Books for Child Collect. 2d edition

A **Biographical** dictionary of artists; general editor, Sir Lawrence Gowing. rev ed. Facts on File 1995 784p il $50   **920.003**
1. Artists—Dictionaries
ISBN 0-8160-3252-1   LC 94-38801
"An Andromeda book"
First published 1983 by Prentice-Hall as volume two of the Encyclopedia of visual art

A Biographical dictionary of artists—*Continued*

"Although concentrating on classic Western artists, this heavily illustrated collection of 1340 entries includes non-Western figures both ancient and modern. Concise biographical sketches summarize the individuals' styles and important works, assess their contributions to the arts, and provide basic biographical data. YAs will gain insight into the greats and near-greats . . . from the ancient Japanese to Western pop artists." SLJ

For a fuller review see: Booklist, Jan. 1-15, 1996

The **Biographical** dictionary of scientists; consultant editor, Roy Porter. 2nd ed. Oxford Univ. Press 1994 lvii, 891p il maps $99

920.003

1. Scientists—Dictionaries
ISBN 0-19-521083-2   LC 94-10982

First published 1983-1985 in the United Kingdom; first United States edition edited by David Abbott published 1984-1986 by Bedrick Bks.

"This comprehensive biographical dictionary includes over 1,200 entries on noted scientists through the ages. As a convenient source of key information, this reference will be indispensable for students and science enthusiasts." Univ Press Books for Public and Second Sch Libr

Includes glossary

✓ **Black** writers; a selection of sketches from Contemporary authors; Sharon Malinowski, editor. 2nd ed. Gale Res. 1994 721p $89

920.003

1. African American authors—Bio-bibliography 2. Black authors—Bio-bibliography
ISBN 0-8103-7788-8

First published 1989 under the editorship of Linda Metzger

This work presents profiles of more than 400 twentieth-century African American, Caribbean and African authors, selected from the publisher's on-going series Contemporary authors. In addition to novelists, poets, short story writers, dramatists and journalists, social and political activists are also included

British authors before 1800; a biographical dictionary; edited by Stanley J. Kunitz and Howard Haycraft; complete in one volume with 650 biographies and 220 portraits. Wilson, H.W. 1952 584p il (Authors series) $64   **920.003**

1. Authors, English—Dictionaries 2. English literature—Bio-bibliography
ISBN 0-8242-0006-3

"Short biographical essays on principal and marginal figures in British literature. Bibliographies appended to essays." N Y Public Libr. Book of How & Where to Look It Up

British authors of the nineteenth century; edited by Stanley J. Kunitz; associate editor: Howard Haycraft; complete in one volume with 1000 biographies and 350 portraits. Wilson, H.W. 1936 677p il (Authors series) $68   **920.003**

1. Authors, English—Dictionaries 2. English literature—Bio-bibliography
ISBN 0-8242-0007-1

"More than a thousand authors of the British Empire (including Canada, Australia, South Africa, and New Zealand) are represented by sketches varying in length from approximately 100 to 2500 words, roughly proportionate to the importance of the subjects." Preface

British writers; edited under the auspices of the British Council; Ian Scott-Kilvert, general editor. Scribner 1979-1992 7v + supplement I-II set $800   **920.003**

1. Authors, English—Dictionaries 2. English literature—Bio-bibliography 3. English literature—History and criticism
ISBN 0-684-19593-3

Also available CD-ROM version

Supplement three published 1995 available $110 (ISBN 0-684-19714-6)

Contents: v1 William Langland to the English Bible; v2 Thomas Middleton to George Farquhar; v3 Daniel Defoe to the Gothic novel; v4 William Wordsworth to Robert Browning; v5 Elizabeth Gaskell to Francis Thompson; v6 Thomas Hardy to Wilfred Owen; v7 Sean O'Casey to poets of World War II; Supplement I Graham Greene to Tom Stoppard; Supplement II Kingsley Amis to J.R.R. Tolkien

"This work presents articles by distinguished contributors on major British writers from the fourteenth century to the present. . . . The biographical sketch that opens each entry is followed by a survey of the author's principal works, a critical evaluation, and an updated bibliography." Ref Sources for Small & Medium-sized Libr. 5th edition

Butler, Alban, 1711-1773

Butler's lives of the saints; complete edition; edited, revised and supplemented by Herbert Thurston and Donald Attwater. Christian Classics 1956 4v $140; pa $95   **920.003**

1. Saints—Dictionaries
ISBN 0-87061-045-7; 0-87061-137-2 (pa)

Also available in a concise edition, revised and updated 1991, edited by Michael Walsh, in paperback from HarperSanFrancisco

A reprint of the four volume set published 1956 by Kenedy

New edition of a work first published 1756-1759. The calendar arrangement is retained, but the number of entries has almost doubled and many of the entries have been rewritten in whole or part

"The biographies of the saints and beati are arranged by their feast days with each of the four volumes containing three months. . . . Each volume has a table of contents arranged by the days of the month with a list of the feasts for each day." Booklist

The **Cambridge** dictionary of American biography; edited by John S. Bowman. Cambridge Univ. Press 1995 903p $44.95

920.003

1. United States—Biography—Dictionaries
ISBN 0-521-40258-1   LC 94-5057

This biographical dictionary contains "entries on 9000 individuals from political, military, social, cultural, and economic realms as well as from popular culture." Libr J

For a fuller review see: Booklist, Aug. 1995

Composers since 1900; a biographical and critical guide; compiled and edited by David Ewen. Wilson, H.W. 1969 639p il $69   **920.003**
1. Composers—Dictionaries   2. Music—Bio-bibliography
ISBN 0-8242-0400-X

First supplement published 1981 available for $49 (ISBN 0-8242-0664-9)

Replaces Composers of today, American composers today, and European composers today, originally published 1934, 1949 and 1954, respectively

This work contains biographical sketches of 220 principal composers of the twentieth century. Included among traditionalists, innovators, eclectics, and romanticists are the avant-garde. The first supplement includes 47 additional composers and updated information on 172 composers from the base volume

Contemporary authors. Gale Res. apply to publisher for price and availability   **920.003**
1. Authors—Dictionaries   2. Literature—Bio-bibliography
ISSN 0010-7468

Also available CD-ROM version

Started publication 1962. Frequency varies. Indexes cumulate at frequent intervals. Editors vary

"A bio-bibliographical guide to current writers in fiction, general nonfiction, poetry, journalism, drama, motion pictures, television, and other fields." Title page

"Related title Contemporary authors new revision series, is a separate set that updates sketches from the 'original series.' Both series are recommended." Nichols. Guide to Ref Books for Sch Media Cent. 4th edition

"Published to give an up-to-date source of biographical information on current authors in many fields—humanities, social sciences, and sciences—and from many countries. Sketches attempt to give, as pertinent: personal facts (including names of parents, children, etc.), career, writings (as complete a bibliography as possible), work in progress, sidelights, and occasional biographical sources." Guide to Ref Books. 11th edition

Contemporary dramatists. St. James Press $140   **920.003**

First published 1972 by St. Martin's Press. (5th edition 1993) Periodically revised

"Biographies, published work, and critical essays on living dramatists, with supplements for screen, radio, and television writers, musical librettists, and theater groups." N Y Public Libr. Book of How & Where to Look It Up

Contemporary musicians; profiles of the people in music. Gale Res.   **920.003**
1. Musicians—Dictionaries
ISSN 1044-2197

Apply to publisher for price and availability

Biannual. First published 1989. Editors vary

Each volume provides "information on 80 to 100 musical artists from all the genres that form the broad spectrum of contemporary music . . . as well as selected classical artists who have achieved 'crossover' success with the general public." Introduction

Contemporary novelists. St. James Press $140   **920.003**
1. Novelists, English—Dictionaries 2. Novelists, American—Dictionaries 3. English fiction—Bio-bibliography 4. American fiction—Bio-bibliography

First published 1972 by St. Martin's Press. (6th edition 1996) Periodically revised. Editors vary

Contains bio-critical information on English-language novelists from around the world. Each entry lists essential biographical data; publications according to genre; a brief bibliography of secondary sources; the location of the author's manuscript collection; and a short critical essay on the novels

Contemporary poets. St. James Press $160   **920.003**
1. Poets, English—Dictionaries 2. Poets, American—Dictionaries 3. English poetry—Bio-bibliography 4. American poetry—Bio-bibliography

First published 1970 with title: Contemporary poets of the English language. (6th edition 1996) Periodically revised. Editors vary

"A biographical handbook of contemporary poets, arranged alphabetically. Entries consist of a short biography, full bibliography, comments by some of the poets, and a signed critical essay." Ref Sources for Small & Medium-sized Libr. 5th edition

Contemporary world writers; preface, Susan Bassnett; editor, Tracy Chevalier. 2nd ed. St. James Press 1993 686p $140   **920.003**
1. Authors—Dictionaries   2. Literature—Bio-bibliography
ISBN 1-55862-200-4   LC 93-5352

First published 1984 by St. Martin's Press with title: Contemporary foreign language writers

"A biobibliography of approximately 340 living authors from 60 countries, whose works have been translated in whole or in part into English. For each writer, a biographical sketch is followed by a bibliography of works (with translated English language titles or publications), a section of secondary studies in English if available, and a signed critical essay reviewing the author's work." Guide to Ref Books. 11th edition

Current biography: cumulated index, 1940-1995. Wilson, H.W. 1996 137p $27   **920.003**
1. Biography—Periodicals—Indexes
ISBN 0-8242-0892-7

"Providing access to more than 14,000 biographies from 55 years of coverage, this index lists the subjects of all the articles, updates, and obituaries that have appeared in Current Biography since January 1940. Includes cross-references from name variants and pseudonyms." Publisher's note

Current biography yearbook. Wilson, H.W. il $69   **920.003**
1. Biography—Periodicals
ISSN 0084-9499

Also available CD-ROM version

Annual. First published 1940 with title: Current biography

Also issued monthly except December at a subscription price of $69 per year (ISSN 0011-3344)

Current biography yearbook—*Continued*

"Biographies of prominent people written in lively, popular prose. Emphasis is on entertainers, star athletes, politicians, and other celebrities. Series is cumulative, with biographies revised and updated occasionally. Each volume has seven-year index." NY Public Libr. Book of How & Where to Look It Up

Dictionary of American biography. Scribner 1946 c1927-c1936 10v + supplement 1-10 in 8v + comprehensive index set $1750   **920.003**

1. United States—Biography—Dictionaries
ISBN 0-684-80540-5

Also available CD-ROM version

First published 1928-1936 as 20 volume set plus index. Supplements 1-10 covering 1931-1980 published 1944-1995. Comprehensive index complete through supplement ten published 1996

Set and first eight supplements published under the auspices of the American Council of Learned Societies
Editors vary

"The scholarly American biographical dictionary designed on the lines of the English 'Dictionary of national biography' . . . with signed articles and bibliographies. . . . More than 13,600 biographies in the basic set. Does not include living persons." Guide to Ref Books. 11th edition

✓ **Dictionary** of Hispanic biography; Joseph C. Tardiff & L. Mpho Mabunda, editors; foreword by Rudolfo Anaya. Gale Res. 1996 xxv, 1011p il $120   **920.003**

1. Hispanic Americans—Dictionaries 2. Spain—Biography—Dictionaries 3. Latin America—Biography—Dictionaries
ISBN 0-8103-8302-0   LC 95-38261

"Ranging from the 'period of discovery' to the present (70 percent of the entries are from the contemporary period), this work covers some 471 notable Hispanics of Spain, Spanish America, and the United States. Virtually all vocations are represented." Libr J

For a fuller review see: Booklist, March 15, 1996

The **Dictionary** of national biography: the concise dictionary. Oxford Univ. Press 1953-1982 2v pt. 2 $45   **920.003**

1. Great Britain—Biography—Dictionaries 2. Great Britain—Bio-bibliography

Half title: The concise dictionary of national biography

Contents: pt. 1 From the beginnings to 1900; Being an epitome of the main work and its supplement op; pt. 2 1901-1970 (ISBN 0-19-865303-4)

"Alphabetically arranged, it lists signed articles on deceased noteworthy persons who lived in the British Isles and the colonies." Peterson. Ref Books for Elem & Jr High Sch Libr. 2d edition

"'The concise dictionary' serves a double purpose, i.e., it is both an index [to the work originally published 1885-1901 in sixty-six volumes and reissued 1908-1909 in twenty-two volumes, and to its supplements published up to 1959] and also an independent biographical dictionary." Guide to Ref Books. 11th edition

Dictionary of scientific biography; Charles Coulston Gillispie, editor in chief. Scribner 1981 16v in 8 set $1400   **920.003**
ISBN 0-684-16962-2

Also available Volumes 17-18 designated Supplement II published 1990 set $190 (ISBN 0-684-18294-7)

This is a reprint of the title published 1970-1980 in 16 volumes, now bound in double volumes, retaining original numbering on spine. Volumes 15-16 are Supplement I and Index

Published under the auspices of the American Council of Learned Societies

This "biographical dictionary covers over forty-five hundred people ranging from Einstein, Newton, and Pasteur to Marx, Columbus, and Abailard. Its focus is on the biographee's place in the history of science, rather than on his or her life story. The signed entries run from part of a page to many pages and include excellent bibliographies." RQ

A **Dictionary** of twentieth-century world biography; consultant editor, Asa Briggs. rev ed. Oxford Univ. Press 1992 615p $31.25 **920.003**

1. Biography—Dictionaries
ISBN 0-19-211679-7   LC 91-27696

First published 1985 in the United Kingdom with title: Longman dictionary of 20th century biography

"This work provides brief biographies of 1,750 people considered important in recent history. . . . While some current people, such as Michael Jackson, are included, the majority of the biographees are deceased. Entries are arranged in a single alphabetical sequence, and their length ranges from a single paragraph to a full page for Winston Churchill. Year of birth (and death, when appropriate) is given after the name, followed by a brief characterization." Booklist

European authors, 1000-1900; a biographical dictionary of European literature; edited by Stanley J. Kunitz and Vineta Colby; complete in one volume with 967 biographies and 309 portraits. Wilson, H.W. 1967 1016p il (Authors series) $77   **920.003**

1. Authors, European—Dictionaries 2. Literature—Bio-bibliography
ISBN 0-8242-0013-6

Includes continental European writers born after the year 1000 and dead before 1925. Nearly a thousand major and minor contributors to thirty-one different literatures are discussed

"These biographies provide quick, satisfactory introductions to a staggering variety of authors and literatures." Choice

Includes bibliographies

Explorers and discoverers of the world; edited by Daniel B. Baker. Gale Res. 1993 xli, 637p il maps $81   **920.003**

1. Explorers—Dictionaries
ISBN 0-8103-5421-7   LC 92-055094

"Exploration and discovery are conceived in the broadest sense in this work, encompassing all chronological periods with articles on aviators, mountaineers, underwater and space explorers as well as those who promoted exploration. Lesser known individuals, including women and non-Europeans, make up the 320 biographical profiles." Libr J

Flores, Angel, 1900-1992
Spanish American authors; the twentieth century. Wilson, H.W. 1992 915p $100   **920.003**
1. Authors, Latin American—Dictionaries 2. Latin American literature—Bio-bibliography
ISBN 0-8242-0806-4   LC 92-7591
"A monumental and distinguished work covering more than 330 novelists and poets from Central and South America, Puerto Rico, and the Caribbean, some appearing for the first time in a reference source. Essential in any library supporting study of Latin America. . . . For each writer, provides biographical information, critical analysis and summaries of criticism, and a bibliography of primary and secondary works, excluding dissertations." Guide to Ref Books. 11th edition

Grant, Michael, 1914-
Greek and Latin authors, 800 B.C.-A.D. 1000; a biographical dictionary. Wilson, H.W. 1980 490p il (Authors series) $68   **920.003**
1. Authors, Greek—Dictionaries 2. Authors, Latin—Dictionaries 3. Classical literature—Bio-bibliography
ISBN 0-8242-0640-1   LC 79-27446
Covers more than 370 classical authors. Each entry includes "the pronunciation of the author's name, biographical background, an overview of major works with critical commentary on the nature and quality of those works, and, where relevant, a brief discussion of the influence of the author's works on later literature." Ref Sources for Small & Medium-sized Libr. 5th edition

Great composers, 1300-1900; a biographical and critical guide; compiled and edited by David Ewen. Wilson, H.W. 1966 429p il $62
      920.003
1. Composers—Dictionaries   2. Music—Bio-bibliography
ISBN 0-8242-0018-7
Companion volume to Composers since 1900, entered above
"Complete and detailed biographical, historical and critical information on about 200 composers of the past plus listings of their principal works and bibliographies. Most have portraits." N Y Public Libr. Ref Books for Child Collect. 2d edition

Great lives from history, American women series; edited by Frank N. Magill. Salem Press 1995 5v set $365   **920.003**
1. Women—United States—Biography 2. United States—Biography—Dictionaries
ISBN 0-89356-892-9   LC 94-38308
"The five volumes contain 408 signed articles that highlight the achievements of women who have had 'distinct impact on North American society and culture.' Readability and quick access to information are enhanced by the clear format of each article. . . . The set spans a variety of fields . . . and includes both famous and lesser-known figures, born as early as 1591 (Anne Hutchinson) and as late as 1971 (Kristi Yamaguchi)." Choice
For a fuller review see: Booklist, Aug. 1995

Great women writers; the lives and works of 135 of the world's most important women writers, from antiquity to the present; Frank N. Magill, editor; introduction by Rosemary Canfield Reisman. Holt & Co. 1994 611p (Henry Holt reference book) $40   **920.003**
1. Literature—Bio-bibliography 2. Women authors—Dictionaries
ISBN 0-8050-2932-X   LC 93-47648
This volume "covers women writers from antiquity to the present. Poets, playwrights, and fiction authors are included. Of the 135 authors, 71 are American (11 African American) and the majority of the remainder are European. . . . The author's birth and (when appropriate) death dates are followed by a list of principal works, a . . . summary of achievements, biographical information, and critical analysis of her work." Booklist
"This excellent book provides biographical and critical information, written in an easy-to-read style." SLJ

Hickok, Ralph
A who's who of sports champions; their stories and records. Houghton Mifflin 1995 904p hardcover o.p. paperback available $19.95
      920.003
1. Athletes—Dictionaries
ISBN 0-395-73312-X (pa)   LC 94-49144
"This book provides biographical information for 2200 American and Canadian individuals representing over 50 competitive sports. Olympic gold medalists, members of major sports Halls of Fame, and individuals responsible for major innovations in their sport are included. . . . The major professional and college sports receive the best coverage, and entries are written with an emphasis on the subjects' connections to their sports." Libr J
For a fuller review see: Booklist, July 1995

✓ **Hispanic** writers; a selection of sketches from Contemporary authors; Bryan Ryan, editor. Gale Res. 1991 xxvi, 514p $95   **920.003**
1. Authors, Latin American—Bio-bibliography
ISBN 0-8103-7688-1   LC 90-83635
This volume "includes over 400 biographical sketches. The majority are from the United States, although Mexico, Argentina, and Spain are represented. While 40 percent of the entries come from previously published *Contemporary Authors'* [entered above] volumes, over 250 are new." SLJ

Index to the Wilson authors series. rev 1997 [ed] Wilson, H.W. 1997 135p $27   **920.003**
1. Authors—Dictionaries—Indexes
ISBN 0-8242-0900-1   LC 96-48600
"Biographical dictionaries in the Wilson authors series; Greek and Latin authors, 800 B.C.-A.D. 1000; European authors, 1000-1900; British authors before 1800; British authors of the nineteenth century; American authors, 1600-1900; Twentieth century authors; Twentieth century authors: first supplement; World authors, 1900-1950; World authors, 1950-1970; World authors, 1970-1975; World authors, 1975-1980; World authors, 1980-1985; World authors, 1985-1990; Spanish American authors: the twentieth century; The junior book of authors; More junior authors; Third book of junior authors;

Index to the Wilson authors series—*Continued*
Fourth book of junior authors and illustrators; Fifth book of junior authors and illustrators; Sixth book of junior authors and illustrators; Seventh book of junior authors and illustrators." Title page

Larousse biographical dictionary; general editor, Magnus Magnusson: assistant editor, Rosemary Goring. Larousse (London); distributed by Larousse Kingfisher Chambers 1994 1604p hardcover o.p. paperback available $29.95

920.003

1. Biography—Dictionaries
ISBN 0-7523-5003-X (pa)   LC 93-072901
Previously published 1990 as: Cambridge biographical dictionary

"The 19,000 entries . . . are arranged two columns per page with the name in boldface. Names of individuals mentioned within a biography are also in bold if they have their own entries. Biographies range from 20 to approximately 2,500 words (Shakespeare)." Booklist

"As a single-volume, worldwide, all-period biographical dictionary this has no peers." Libr J

Levine, Michael, 1954-
The address book; how to reach anyone who is anyone. Berkley Pub. Group pa $12   **920.003**
1. United States—Directories 2. Celebrities—Directories

First published 1980 with title: How to reach anyone who's anyone. (8th edition 1997) Frequently revised

"Levine supplies the mailing addresses of famous people and organizations. . . . The author includes professional tricks for getting letters answered, some no-no's for celebrity correspondence, and a sample complaint letter." Booklist

The **Lincoln** library of sports champions. 6th ed. Frontier Press (Columbus) 1993 14v il set $495

920.003

1. Athletes
ISBN 0-912168-14-5   LC 92-75323
First published 1975
Presents brief, alphabetically arranged biographies of nearly 300 great sports personalities, past and present, from around the world. Features a table of contents arranged by sport and a supplementary reading list

Merriam-Webster's biographical dictionary.
Merriam-Webster 1995 1170p $27.95   **920.003**
1. Biography—Dictionaries
Replaces Webster's new biographical dictionary
This work "chronicles the lives of more than 34,000 celebrated, important, and notorious men and women from all parts of the world, all eras, and all fields of endeavor. . . . [Arranged alphabetically, the] entries provide birth and death dates, nationality or ethnic origin, pronunciations, pseudonyms, variant spellings, pertinent information about the individual's career, and more." Publisher's note

Musicians since 1900; performers in concert and opera; compiled and edited by David Ewen. Wilson, H.W. 1978 974p il $82   **920.003**
1. Musicians—Dictionaries   2. Music—Bio-bibliography 3. Opera—Bio-bibliography
ISBN 0-8242-0565-0   LC 78-12727
"Replaces 'Living musicians' and its supplement (1940-57). Gives 'detailed biographical, critical and personal information about 432 of the most distinguished performing musicians in concert and opera since 1900.'—*Introd.* . . . A few bibliographical references are given at the end of each biography; a classified list of musicians concludes the volume." Sheehy. Guide to Ref Books. 10th edition

Nobel Prize winners; an H.W. Wilson biographical dictionary; editor, Tyler Wasson; consultants, Gert H. Brieger [et al.] Wilson, H.W. 1987 xxxiv, 1165p $90   **920.003**
1. Nobel Prizes 2. Biography—Dictionaries
ISBN 0-8242-0756-4   LC 87-16468
Also available 1987-1991 supplement $35 (ISBN 0-8242-0834-X) and 1992-1996 supplement $35 (ISBN 0-8242-0906-0)
"Contains 'profiles of all 566 men, women, and institutions that have received the Nobel Prize between 1901 and 1986.'—*Pref.* The two- to three-page essays, which have a photograph of the recipient, include a list of selected writings and a brief bibliography of secondary sources." Guide to Ref Books. 11th edition

North American women artists of the twentieth century; a biographical dictionary; edited by Jules Heller and Nancy G. Heller. Garland 1995 xxii, 612p il (Garland reference library of the humanities) $125; pa $29.95   **920.003**
1. Women artists—Dictionaries
ISBN 0-8240-6049-0; 0-8153-2584-3 (pa)
     LC 94-49710
This is a "guide to more than 1500 Canadian, Mexican, and United States women artists born between 1850 and 1960. Artists are listed alphabetically, and each artist . . . is briefly treated in several paragraphs that end with bibliographical citations, often to important journal articles. More than 100 illustrations provide a small sampling of their work. . . . An essential acquisition for all art reference libraries." Libr J
For a fuller review see: Booklist, Oct. 15, 1995

Notable American women, 1607-1950; a biographical dictionary; Edward T. James, editor; Janet Wilson James, associate editor; Paul S. Boyer, assistant editor. Harvard Univ. Press 1971 3v hardcover o.p. paperback available set $50   **920.003**
1. Women—United States—Biography 2. United States—Biography—Dictionaries
ISBN 0-674-62734-2 (pa)
1,359 American "women—art patrons, astronomers, Indian captives, circus performers, entrepreneurs, inventors, philosophers—are treated in well written articles which range from 400 to 7,000 words. . . . Each article is followed by bibliographical references." Choice

Notable American women: the modern period; a biographical dictionary; edited by Barbara Sicherman [et al.] Harvard Univ. Press 1980 xxii, 773p hardcover o.p. paperback available $32   **920.003**

1. Women—United States—Biography 2. United States—Biography—Dictionaries

ISBN 0-674-62733-4 (pa)   LC 80-18402

This companion volume to the title entered above adds 442 biographies and extends coverage to women who died between 1951 and 1975

Notable Asian Americans; Helen Zia and Susan B. Gall, editors; foreword by George Takei. Gale Res. 1995 xxxviii, 468p il $75   **920.003**

1. Asian Americans—Biography—Dictionaries

ISBN 0-8103-9623-8   LC 94-33638

This volume "features 250 role models, most of whom are contemporary. Coverage includes Asian Indians, those from Southeast Asia and the Far East, Pacific Islanders, and Hawaiians. The largest number of biographees are of Chinese or Japanese descent. Typical entrants include Judge Ito, author Deepak Chopra, cellist Yo Yo Ma, actor Bruce Lee, comedian Margaret Cho, and sculptor Isamu Noguchi. . . . Accessible to highschoolers and up, *Notable Asian Americans* is an interesting place to start reading about these personalities." Booklist

Notable black American women [bk I-II]; Jessie Carney Smith, editor. Gale Res. 1992-1995 2v il ea $80   **920.003**

1. African American women—Dictionaries 2. United States—Biography—Dictionaries

ISBN 0-8103-4749-0 (bk I); 0-8103-9177-5 (bk II)   LC 91-35074

"This biographical encyclopedia documents the achievements of 500 African-American women who have made significant contributions to American culture from the colonial era to the present. . . . Subjects include women active in all fields of endeavor, from education, science, and the arts, to business, law and politics. . . . Authoritative and entertaining at the same time, these sketches are appropriate for high school and college students as well as the general reader." Am Libr [review of first volume]

Notable Hispanic American women; Diane Telgen and Jim Kamp, editors; foreword by Graciela Beecher. Gale Res. 1993 xxxvii, 448p il $65   **920.003**

1. Women—United States—Biography 2. Hispanic Americans—Dictionaries

ISBN 0-8103-7578-8   LC 92-42483

This work covers "nearly 300 notable Hispanic American women. Alphabetically arranged by surname, the volume features both historical and contemporary women representing a broad range of professions." Libr J

Notable native Americans; Sharon Malinowski, editor; George H.J. Abrams, consulting editor and author of foreword. Gale Res. 1995 xliv, 492p il $75   **920.003**

1. Indians of North America—Biography—Dictionaries

ISBN 0-8103-9638-6   LC 94-36202

This is a "compilation of biographical and bibliographical information on more than two hundred and sixty-five notable Native North American men and women throughout history, from all fields of endeavor. . . . Approximately thirty percent of the entries focus on historical figures and seventy percent on contemporary or twentieth-century individuals. Signed narrative essays, ranging from one to three pages in length, include Indian names and their English translations as well as name variants." Preface

Notable twentieth century scientists; Emily J. McMurray, editor; Jane Kelly Kosek and Roger M. Valade III, associate editors. Gale Res. 1995 4v il set $295   **920.003**

1. Scientists—Dictionaries 2. Engineers—Dictionaries

ISBN 0-8103-9181-3   LC 94-5263

This "reference details the lives and work of 1300 scientists from this century. The editor has included 225 women scientists and 150 minority scientists. Each entry begins with the individual's vital statistics, followed by a 400- to 2500-word essay that includes a detailed description of the scientist and his or her work. The essay is followed by a selected bibliography of the scientist's publications and a list of secondary sources on him or her." Libr J

For a fuller review see: Booklist, Feb. 1, 1995

Prominent women of the 20th century; edited by Peggy Saari. U.X.L 1995 4v il lib bdg set $115   **920.003**

1. Women—Biography—Dictionaries

ISBN 0-7876-0646-4   LC 95-41363

This "set presents 200 biographies of women 'whose achievements have made a significant and lasting imprint on life in the twentieth century.' . . . Profiles range in length from five to eight pages. Each give date of birth and the reason for inclusion. Almost all include a photograph of the biographee. A brief quotation in the margin indicates the woman's philosophy." Booklist

These profiles "are presented in a readable and lively manner. What makes this set especially valuable, however, is that a Fields of Endeavor index (from art and design to writing) and a Nationality/Ethnicity index (African American to Yugoslavian) open each volume." SLJ

Includes bibliographical references

Purcell, L. Edward

Who was who in the American revolution. Facts on File 1993 548p il $60   **920.003**

1. United States—History—1775-1783, Revolution—Biography

ISBN 0-8160-2107-4   LC 92-19831

A collection of brief "biographical sketches covering the well-known (Washington, George III, etc.), the lesser known, and the unknown soldiers, politicians, and civilians. Most entries include bibliographies." Libr J

Read, Phyllis J.

The book of women's firsts; break-through achievements of almost 1000 American women; [by] Phyllis J. Read, Bernard L. Witlieb. Random House 1992 511p il hardcover o.p. paperback available $16   **920.003**

1. Women—United States—Biography

ISBN 0-679-74280-8 (pa)   LC 92-16872

"A biographical dictionary of 1000 American women who were the first to achieve in fields previously restricted to men. Their accomplishments range from the serious to the frivolous and often include the outrageous. The information is brief, intended to serve as inspiration or as a springboard for further research. . . . Useful to support gender-awareness curriculums and an excellent resource for Women's History Month." SLJ

Roses, Lorraine Elena, 1943-

Harlem Renaissance and beyond: literary biographies of 100 black women writers, 1900-1945; [by] Lorraine Elena Roses, Ruth Elizabeth Randolph. Hall, G.K. & Co. 1989 413p il $50   **920.003**

1. African American authors—Dictionaries 2. Women authors—Dictionaries 3. American literature—African American authors—Bio-bibliography

ISBN 0-8161-8926-9   LC 89-38731

"Included are the major figures, such as Zora Neale Hurston, as well as many writers who have published only two or three pieces but whose work deserves attention. These short sketches, augmented by bibliographical listings and critical commentary, should provide the impetus for further interest and investigation into long-neglected works. A valuable reference tool." Libr J

Sandoval, Annette

The directory of saints; a concise guide to patron saints. Dutton 1996 309p il $18.95

920.003

1. Christian saints—Dictionaries

ISBN 0-525-94154-1   LC 95-44252

Sandoval offers a "compilation of several hundred saints listed alphabetically by patron subject (places, conditions, and occupations). Her introduction gives a simple overview of the saint-making process today. . . . She includes modern saints in her listing, but the majority date from the early centuries to the Middle Ages; some patronage areas have more than one saint assigned." Libr J

Includes bibliographical references

Sifakis, Stewart

Who was who in the Civil War. Facts on File 1988 766p il hardcover o.p. paperback available $41   **920.003**

1. United States—History—1861-1865, Civil War—Biography

ISBN 0-8160-2202-X (pa)   LC 84-1596

"Sifakis provides a readable, useful biographical dictionary of over 2500 individuals. He includes sketches of all officers attaining the rank of general, and accounts of the principal political, social, and naval figures." Libr J

The **Supreme** Court justices; illustrated biographies, 1789-1993; edited by Clare Cushman; foreword by William H. Rehnquist. Congressional Quarterly 1993 xxi, 576p il $48.95; pa $33.95   **920.003**

1. United States. Supreme Court 2. Judges

ISBN 0-87187-723-6; 0-87187-773-2 (pa)

LC 93-1446

This "collection of biographies of the 106 Supreme Court justices through Clarence Thomas has been compiled at the request of the Supreme Court Historical Society. . . . It presents the reason for their appointment, their educational and professional background, and how these might have impacted their judicial decisions." Am Libr

Twentieth-century author biographies master index; edited by Barbara McNeil. Gale Res. 1984 519p (Gale biographical index series) $69; pa $39   **920.003**

1. Authors—Dictionaries—Indexes

ISBN 0-8103-2095-9; 0-8103-2096-7 (pa)

LC 84-10349

"A consolidated index to more than 170,000 biographical sketches concerning modern day authors as they appear in a selection of the principal biographical dictionaries devoted to authors, poets, journalists, and other literary figures." Title page

Derived in part from the publisher's Author biographies master index (second edition, 1983) "this index includes . . . citations to an estimated 90,000 persons. . . . For persons needing access to sketches of modern authors in a wide array of biographical sources, this index will be most useful." Booklist

Twentieth-century young adult writers; with an introductory essay by Robert Cormier; editor, Laura Standley Berger. St. James Press 1994 xxiii, 830p $132   **920.003**

1. Authors—Dictionaries 2. Young adults' literature—Bio-bibliography

ISBN 1-55862-202-0   LC 93-42870

"Covering 406 novelists, poets, and dramatists whose works appeal to readers ages 11-19, this . . . compilation also treats a large number of authors who write for an adult audience but whose works have found a following among younger readers. Thus, its entrants include such figures as Joseph Heller, Stephen King, William Golding, Terry McMillan, and Amy Tan." Booklist

Waldman, Carl

Who was who in Native American history; Indians and non-Indians from early contacts through 1900. Facts on File 1990 410p il $50   **920.003**

1. Indians of North America—Biography—Dictionaries

ISBN 0-8160-1797-2   LC 89-35088

"Approximately 1,000 brief biographical sketches are provided for Indians and non-Indians; coverage is split evenly between the two groups. There is no index, but cross-references are used throughout the descriptions. The appendix contains a listing of Native Americans by tribes and a listing of non-Indians by major categories." Booklist

Waldrup, Carole Chandler, 1925-
The vice presidents; biographies of the 45 men who have held the second highest office in the United States. McFarland & Co. 1996 271p il $35
                920.003
1. Vice-presidents—United States—Biography
ISBN 0-7864-0179-6   LC 96-30538
This work "presents biographical portraits of the 45 individuals who have theoretically been 'a heartbeat from the presidency.' These portraits are presented in chronological order of service, from John Adams to Albert Gore Jr." Am Ref Books Annu, 1997
"Well-written with clear, precise language and vocabulary, this informative book will be useful in either the reference section or with the collective biographies. The format, compact biographies of six to seven pages, provides excellent accessibility for students. The author manages to present not only the key facts of each man's life, but to offer interesting insights and information." Book Rep
Includes bibliographical references

Who was who in America; a companion biographical reference work to Who's who in America. Marquis Who's Who 1942-1996 11v ea $90   **920.003**
1. United States—Biography—Dictionaries
Also available index volume to v1-11 and historical volume $45 (ISBN 0-8379-0226-6)
Contents: v1 1897-1942 (ISBN 0-8379-0201-0); v2 1943-1950 (ISBN 0-8379-0206-1); v3 1951-1960 (ISBN 0-8379-0203-7); v4 1961-1968 (ISBN 0-8379-0204-5); v5 1969-1973 (ISBN 0-8379-0205-3); v6 1974-1976 (ISBN 0-8379-0207-X); v7 1977-1981 (ISBN 0-8379-0210-X); v8 1982-1985 (ISBN 0-8379-0214-2); v9 1985-1989 (ISBN 0-8379-0217-7); v10 1989-1993 (ISBN 0-8379-0220-7); v11 1993-1996 (ISBN 0-8379-0225-8)
"Includes sketches removed from 'Who's who in America' because of death of the biographee; date of death and, often, interment location is added. With the 'Historical volume' [listed below] these volumes form a series entitled 'Who's who in American history.'" Guide to Ref Books. 11th edition

Who was who in America: historical volume, 1607-1896; a component volume of Who's who in American history. rev ed 1967. Marquis Who's Who 1967 689p $90   **920.003**
1. United States—Biography—Dictionaries
ISBN 0-8379-0200-2
First published 1963
"A compilation of sketches of individuals, both of the United States of America and other countries, who have made contribution to, or whose activity was in some manner related to, the history of the United States, from the founding of Jamestown Colony to the year of continuation by 'Vol 1 of Who was who' [entered above]." Title page

Who's who among African Americans. Gale Res. $140   **920.003**
1. African Americans—Biography—Dictionaries
First published 1976 with title: Who's who among black Americans by Educational Communications. Biennial schedule after 5th edition

"Short entries focusing on career achievements and positions. Indexes list entries by place of birth and profession." N Y Public Libr. Book of How & Where to Look It Up

World artists, 1950-1980; an H.W. Wilson biographical dictionary; [edited] by Claude Marks. Wilson, H.W. 1984 912p il $83
                920.003
1. Artists—Dictionaries
ISBN 0-8242-0707-6   LC 84-13152
"The 312 painters, sculptors, and graphic artists in this biographical dictionary were selected from the outstanding artistic figures in the US, Europe, and Latin America. . . . The biographical information includes family, working background, and aesthetic beliefs. There are many quotations from the artist and from critics. Also included is a list of significant collections and a bibliography." Choice

World artists, 1980-1990; an H.W. Wilson biographical dictionary; edited by Claude Marks. Wilson, H.W. 1991 413p il $58   **920.003**
1. Artists—Dictionaries
ISBN 0-8242-0802-1   LC 91-13183
This volume contains brief biographies of 118 artists from around the world who have been influential in the decade of the 1980's

World authors, 1900-1950; editors, Martin Seymour-Smith and Andrew Kimmens. Wilson, H.W. 1996 4v il (Authors series) set $395
                920.003
1. Authors—Dictionaries
ISBN 0-8242-0899-4   LC 96-16380
Replaces Twentieth century authors (1942) and its First supplement (1955)
Contents: v1 Abbot-Doyle; v2 Dreiser-Ledwidge; v3 Lee-Saintsbury; v4 Saki-Zweig
Provides almost 2700 articles on twentieth-century authors from all over the world who wrote in English or whose works are available in English translation

World authors, 1950-1970; a companion volume to Twentieth century authors; edited by John Wakeman; editorial consultant: Stanley J. Kunitz. Wilson, H.W. 1975 1594p il (Authors series) $95   **920.003**
1. Authors—Dictionaries   2. Literature—Bio-bibliography
ISBN 0-8242-0419-0
This volume includes 959 "authors who came into prominence between 1950 and 1970. . . . Authors were chosen for literary importance or outstanding popularity." Wilson Libr Bull

World authors, 1970-1975; editor, John Wakeman; editorial consultant, Stanley J. Kunitz. Wilson, H.W. 1980 894p il (Authors series) $85
                920.003
1. Authors—Dictionaries   2. Literature—Bio-bibliography
ISBN 0-8242-0641-X   LC 79-21874
This volume provides biographical or autobiographical sketches for 348 of the most influential and popular men and women of letters who have come into prominence between 1970 and 1975

World authors, 1975-1980; editor, Vineta Colby. Wilson, H.W. 1985 829p il (Authors series) $85
920.003
1. Authors—Dictionaries   2. Literature—Bio-bibliography
ISBN 0-8242-0715-7   LC 85-10045
This work profiles the lives and works of 379 writers

World authors, 1980-1985; editor, Vineta Colby. Wilson, H.W. 1990 938p il (Authors series) $85
920.003
1. Authors—Dictionaries   2. Literature—Bio-bibliography
ISBN 0-8242-0797-1   LC 90-49782
This volume covers 320 contemporary writers
Includes bibliographical references

World authors, 1985-1990; a volume in the Wilson authors series; editor, Vineta Colby. Wilson, H.W. 1995 970p il (Authors series) $85
920.003
1. Authors—Dictionaries   2. Literature—Bio-bibliography
ISBN 0-8242-0875-7   LC 95-41656
This volume covers 345 novelists, playwrights, poets, and other authors who have risen to prominence in the late 1980s

World film directors; editor, John Wakeman. Wilson, H.W. 1987-1988 2v il ea $90 **920.003**
1. Motion picture producers and directors—Dictionaries
Contents: v1 1890-1945 (ISBN 0-8242-0757-2); v2 1945-1985 (ISBN 0-8242-0763-7)
"Four hundred and nineteen directors, about evenly divided between the two volumes, are discussed in 1500- to 8000-word essays. Each entry summarizes and appraises the director's life and career. . . . A complete filmography and list of suggested futher reading also follows each entry. This reference's strength lies in its easy-to-use alphabetical arrangement and in the depth of information given." SLJ

Writers for young adults: biographies master index; Joyce Nakamura, editor. 3rd ed. Gale Res. 1989 lxix, 183p $92   **920.003**
1. Authors—Dictionaries—Indexes
ISBN 0-8103-1833-4   LC 89-113547
First published 1979 under the editorship of Adele Sarkissian
"An index to sources of biographical information about novelists, poets, playwrights, nonfiction writers, songwriters and lyricists, television and screenwriters who are of interest to high school students and to teachers, librarians, and researchers interested in high school reading materials." Title page
New edition in preparation
This index "leads to sources of information about 16,000 writers of interest to students in grades 7-12 in almost 600 biographical dictionaries." Booklist

92   Individual biography

Lives of individuals are arranged alphabetically under the name of the person written about. Some subject headings have been added to aid in curriculum work.

Aaron, Hank, 1934-
Aaron, Hank. I had a hammer: the Hank Aaron story; [by] Henry Aaron with Lonnie Wheeler. HarperCollins Pubs. 1991 333p il hardcover o.p. paperback available $5.99   **92**
1. Baseball—Biography 2. African American athletes
ISBN 0-06-109956-2 (pa)   LC 90-55521
This biography traces "Aaron's incredible career—which saw him, from 1954 to 1976, break Babe Ruth's all-time home run record, win the Most Valuable Player Award, and appear in many All-Star games, two World Series, and one League Championship Series." Booklist

Adams, Abigail, 1744-1818
Bober, Natalie. Abigail Adams; witness to a revolution; [by] Natalie S. Bober. Atheneum Bks. for Young Readers 1995 248p il maps $17   **92**
1. Presidents—United States—Spouses
ISBN 0-689-31760-3   LC 94-19259
"By interweaving excerpts from Adams's correspondence into a coherent biography, Bober creates a vibrant, three-dimensional portrait of a fascinating person whose comments on women's place have reverberated throughout history. This scholarly, thoroughly documented study will appeal to more mature readers, but it is more formidable in appearance than in presentation. Black-and-white reproductions are included." Horn Book Guide
Includes bibliography

Adams, Ansel, 1902-1984
Adams, Ansel. Ansel Adams, an autobiography; [by] Ansel Adams with Mary Street Alinder. Little, Brown 1985 400p il $65; pa $13.95   **92**
1. Photographers
ISBN 0-8212-1596-5; 0-8212-2241-4 (pa)
LC 85-8135
"A New York Graphic Society book"
The American photographer's "autobiography moves from family reminiscences to his experiences with Edward Weston, Paul Strand, Dorothea Lange, the Newhalls, Georgia O'Keeffe, Stieglitz, and Steichen, giving Adams's perspective on developments in the visual arts." Libr J
"Consisting of an almost perfect mix of interacting text and images, including some unexpected candid snapshops of Adams himself, this work is an outstanding document of 20th-century American photography." Choice
Includes bibliography

Adams, Henry, 1838-1918
Adams, Henry. The education of Henry Adams
92
Hardcover and paperback editions available from various publishers

Adams, Henry, 1838-1918—*Continued*

"Autobiographical work . . . that was privately printed in 1906 and published in 1918. Considered to be one of the most distinguished examples of the genre, the *Education* combines autobiography, bildungsroman, and critical evaluation of an age." Merriam Webster's Ency of Lit

Addams, Jane, 1860-1935

Addams, Jane. Twenty years at Hull-House

92

1. Hull House (Chicago, Ill.) 2. Chicago (Ill.)—Social conditions

Hardcover and paperback editions available from various publishers

First published 1910 by Macmillan

"This classic of the reform era is actually an autobiography of the woman who practically founded social service work in this country. . . . It tells her life story, but the greater part of it is devoted to the setting up of Chicago's Hull House, the first settlement house in the United States." Guide to Read in Am Hist

Alcott, Louisa May, 1832-1888

Alcott, Louisa May. The selected letters of Louisa May Alcott; with an introduction by Madeleine B. Stern; editors, Joel Myerson and Daniel Shealy; associate editor, Madeleine B. Stern. Little, Brown 1987 lvi, 352p il o.p.; University of Ga. Press paperback available $19.95

92

1. Authors, American 2. Women authors

ISBN 0-8203-1740-3 (pa)   LC 86-27334

This volume contains "a wealth of colorful, determined, cranky, humorous, affectionate correspondence, salted with Yankee colloquialisms. The recipients range from eminent people like Lucy Stone, Ralph Waldo Emerson and publisher Thomas Niles to friends of the Alcott and May families. A large part of the correspondence is about her books. . . . The voice of the writer and woman is palpable throughout, insistent and appealing." Publ Wkly

Includes bibliography

Anderson, William T. The world of Louisa May Alcott; a first-time glimpse into the life and times of Louisa May Alcott, author of "Little Women"; [by] William Anderson; with photographs by David Wade. HarperPerennial 1995 120p il maps pa $22.50

92

1. Authors, American 2. Women authors

ISBN 0-06-095156-7   LC 95-24373

This is a visual presentation of the life of Louisa May Alcott, illustrated with many photographs of the Alcott family, their various homes, their famous friends (Thoreau, Emerson and Hawthorne), and Louisa's travels in Europe. Also included are maps, period engravings, illustrations from several of Louisa's books, and artwork by her sister May

Alexander, the Great, 356-323 B.C.

Arrian. Alexander the Great; selections from Arrian; [translated by] J. G. Lloyd. Cambridge Univ. Press 1981 104p il maps (Translations from Greek and Roman authors) pa $11.50

92

1. Greece—History 2. Kings, queens, rulers, etc.

ISBN 0-521-28195-4   LC 81-9453

Born over four hundred years after the death of Alexander the Great, Arrian served in the Roman army and devoted his life's work to the study of Alexander's empire, a section of which he governed under the auspices of Rome. Here are selections from his history which focus primarily on Alexander's military campaigns

"This book may seem to be a military account, but first and foremost it is the story of a man." Introduction

Includes bibliography

Alexandra, Empress, consort of Nicholas II, Emperor of Russia, 1872-1918

Massie, Robert K. Nicholas and Alexandra. See entry under Nicholas II, Emperor of Russia, 1868-1918

√ **Ali, Muhammad, 1942-**

Hauser, Thomas. Muhammad Ali; his life and times. Simon & Schuster 1991 544p il hardcover o.p. paperback available $15

92

1. Boxing—Biography 2. African American athletes

ISBN 0-671-77971-0 (pa)   LC 91-10395

In this biography the author quotes the recollections of more than 200 acquaintances, friends, enemies, associates, relations, opponents, and observers of the American boxer

Includes bibliographical references

Lipsyte, Robert. Free to be Muhammad Ali. Harper & Row 1978 124p lib bdg $14.89   92

1. Boxing—Biography 2. African American athletes

ISBN 0-06-023902-6   LC 77-25640

"An Ursula Nordstrom book"

"Lipsyte presents a warm and personal look at the Champ. Facing head-on the controversies that have attended Ali's tumultuous career, the author offers insightful background material on the climate of boxing in the 1960s and on the civil unrest and growing disturbance over the Vietnam war—issues on which Ali took definite and, at the time, unpopular stands." Booklist

Allende, Isabel

Allende, Isabel. Paula; translated from the Spanish by Margaret Sayers Peden. HarperCollins Pubs. 1995 330p $24; pa $12.50   92

1. Allende family 2. Authors, Latin American 3. Women authors

ISBN 0-06-017253-3; 0-06-092721-6 (pa)

LC 95-2452

Also available G.K. Hall large print edition

Allende "interweaves the story of her own life with the slow dying of her 28-year-old daughter, Paula." Publ Wkly

This "is a deeply affecting tale, written in the rich, luminous prose typical of Allende's novels, that investigates the sources of her writing as it paints a vivid portrait of Chile." Libr J

Anderson, Marian, 1897-1993
Patterson, Charles. Marian Anderson. Watts 1988 159p il (Impact biography) lib bdg $22.70
92
1. African American singers 2. African American women
ISBN 0-531-10568-7   LC 88-10695
A biography of the opera and concert singer who, among other achievements, was the first black soloist to perform with the Metropolitan Opera Company in 1955
Includes bibliography

Anderson, Terry
Anderson, Terry. Den of lions; memoirs of seven years; [by] Terry A. Anderson. Crown 1993 356p il $25   92
1. Hostages
ISBN 0-517-59301-7   LC 93-19802
Also available G.K. Hall large print edition and in paperback from Ballantine Bks.
An "account of Anderson's confinement from 1985-1991 at the hands of Shiite Muslims in Lebanon. He gives a clear outline of the political and religious situation there in the 1980s, the Iran-Contra affair, and the role of the UN in negotiating his release. Anderson is a shrewd observer and offers a candid and detailed description of how he and his fellow hostages survived brutal physical mistreatment and fought psychological deterioration. Any young person interested in current affairs, the Middle East, or journalism will find his book compelling reading." SLJ

Angelou, Maya
Angelou, Maya. I know why the caged bird sings. Random House 1970 c1969 281p $20   92
1. African American authors 2. Women authors
ISBN 0-394-42986-9
Also available in paperback from Bantam Bks.
The first volume in the author's autobiographical series covers her childhood and adolescence in rural Arkansas, St. Louis, and San Francisco
"Angelou is a skillful writer; her language ranges from beautifully lyrical prose to earthy metaphor, and her descriptions have power and sensitivity." Libr J
Followed by Gather together in my name (1974); Singin' and swingin' and gettin' merry like Christmas (1976); The heart of a woman (1981); All God's children need traveling shoes (1986)

Anthony, Susan B., 1820-1906
Barry, Kathleen. Susan B. Anthony: a biography of a singular feminist. New York Univ. Press 1988 426p il $40   92
1. Feminism
ISBN 0-8147-1105-7   LC 88-1228
The author explores "the 'subjectivity' of Anthony and the transformation of her political consciousness. . . . Although the text occasionally suffers from polemics, adulation, and novelistic twists, Barry is to be praised for her prodigious research and for her success in placing Anthony, as a major historical actor, in her own social-historical milieu." Choice
Includes bibliography

Armstrong, Louis, 1900-1971
Brown, Sandford. Louis Armstrong. Watts 1993 124p il (Impact biography) lib bdg $21.20; pa $6.95   92
1. Jazz musicians 2. African American musicians
ISBN 0-531-13028-2 (lib bdg); 0-531-15680-X (pa)
LC 92-43192
Examines the personal life and musical career of the famous jazz trumpeter and singer known as Satchmo
"Besides providing a precise biography, Brown reviews the history of American jazz as a background for the life of Louis Armstrong. The author's objectivity, difficult for an enthusiastic biographer to maintain, adds to the book's quality." Booklist
Includes glossary and bibliography

Collier, James Lincoln. Louis Armstrong: an American success story. Macmillan 1985 165p il hardcover o.p. paperback available $5.95   92
1. Jazz musicians 2. African American musicians
ISBN 0-02-042555-4 (pa)   LC 84-42982
"Evokes Armstrong's life as a poverty-stricken boy from a broken home in New Orleans, a poor, struggling black musician in the South, and one of the outstanding jazz musicians of all time. An intriguing, absorbing portrait that reveals musical genius that could not be denied in an artist who never had a music lesson. Information about recordings is combined with a short annotated bibliography." Soc Educ

Arnold, Benedict, 1741-1801
Brandt, Clare. The man in the mirror: a life of Benedict Arnold. Random House 1994 xxii, 360p il maps $25   92
1. Generals 2. United States—History—1775-1783, Revolution
ISBN 0-679-40106-7   LC 92-45118
This "biography of famous American traitor Benedict Arnold presents the man not only as a brilliant soldier, but also as an individual plagued with personal and social insecurities." Booklist
This book "is an absorbing contribution to our understanding of the period, and it also provides a convincing analysis of the psychological motives for betrayal." N Y Times Book Rev
Includes bibliography

Arthur, King
Ashe, Geoffrey. The discovery of King Arthur; [by] Geoffrey Ashe in association with Debrett's Peerage. Anchor Press/Doubleday 1985 226p il o.p.; Holt & Co. paperback available $12.95   92
1. Geoffrey, of Monmouth, Bishop of St. Asaph, 1100?-1154. Historia Britonum 2. Great Britain—Kings, queens, rulers, etc. 3. Great Britain—History—0-1066
ISBN 0-8050-0115-8 (pa)   LC 83-45168
The author explores archeological findings that support the theory that Arthur was a real leader in the 5th century. Arthurian themes in literature and art are also examined
Includes bibliography

Ashe, Arthur

Ashe, Arthur. Days of grace; a memoir; by Arthur Ashe and Arnold Rampersad. Knopf 1993 317p il $24   **92**

1. Tennis—Biography 2. African American athletes
ISBN 0-679-42396-6   LC 92-54919
Also available G.K. Hall large print edition and in paperback from Ballantine Bks.

Ashe discusses "the issues of greatest import to him: family, education, religion, athletics, health, politics, and social injustice. . . . The bulk of the work centers on his life after retirement from tennis . . . and his championing of various causes, including the fight against AIDS. In anticipation of his passing, he closes with an open letter to his daughter, Camera." Libr J

"This is a truly gripping book. It's gripping, it's moving, it's admirable; and what makes it so is Ashe's capacity for evaluating himself and the world with intelligence and honor." N Y Times Book Rev

Austen, Jane, 1775-1817

Fergus, Jan S. Jane Austen; a literary life; [by] Jan Fergus. St. Martin's Press 1991 201p hardcover o.p. paperback available $15.95   **92**

1. Authors, English 2. Women authors
ISBN 0-312-12190-3 (pa)   LC 90-47976
The author "analyzes the brilliance of Austen's social satire and literary parody, her narrative technique, and the material conditions of her authorship. She also pulls together the information of many other sources to create a picture of what it meant to be a woman writer in England in the late eighteenth and early nineteenth centuries." Women's Rev Books

"There is a generous amount of hard data . . . but the handling of more abstract topics, such as Austen's tone, her sense of style and her predilections in choosing topics and themes is especially adroit. . . . Researchers will appreciate the extensive notes and ample index." Choice

Tucker, George Holbert. Jane Austen the woman; some biographical insights; foreword by John McAleer. St. Martin's Press 1994 268p il $23.95; pa $13.95   **92**

1. Authors, English 2. Women authors
ISBN 0-312-12049-4; 0-312-12688-3 (pa)
                                       LC 93-35954
The author argues "that Austen was a lively and witty woman who participated fully in the English social life she wrote about. Her romances and friendships, the trips she took throughout England and her enjoyment of dancing, music and theater are described." Publ Wkly

This "is a well-written and well-researched study. Quite deliberately, this is not a critical biography; there is little discussion of the works themselves." Choice

Includes bibliographical references

Baek, Hongyong, 1912-

Lee, Helie. Still life with rice; a young American woman discovers the life and legacy of her Korean grandmother. Scribner 1996 320p $24
                                       92

1. Korean Americans
ISBN 0-684-80270-8   LC 95-41921
"Lee traveled from California to Korea to recapture the life of her grandmother. Hongyong Baek (b. 1912) grew up in northern Korea, the daughter of wealthy parents, and at 22 entered into an arranged marriage. . . . Drawing on interviews with her grandmother and writing in her voice, Lee . . . describes the aftermath of the Japanese occupation of Korea, which forced Baek, her husband (with whom she ultimately fell in love) and their children to flee to China in 1939, where they supported themselves by selling opium. After they returned to Korea, the 1950s' civil war caused them extreme hardship. . . . Baek emigrated to the U.S. in 1972." Publ Wkly

"Written with great narrative power and attention to detail, a testament to the will to survive." Booklist

Baker, Russell, 1925-

Baker, Russell. The good times. Morrow 1989 351p il $19.95   **92**

1. Journalists
ISBN 0-688-06170-2   LC 89-46
Also available G.K. Hall large print edition and in paperback from New Am. Lib.

"A Thomas Congdon book"

"This is a sequel to Baker's Pulitzer Prize-winning 'Growing up' [entered below]. Here, he recounts the mischances and lucky breaks that have guided his journalism career." Libr J

"'The Good Times' is a superb autobiography, wonderfully told, often hilarious, always intelligent and unsparing." N Y Times Book Rev

Baker, Russell. Growing up. Congdon & Weed 1982 278p il o.p.; New Am. Lib. paperback available $8.95   **92**

1. Journalists
ISBN 0-452-25275-X (pa)   LC 82-12534
This book "recounts the first 24 years of [Baker's] life as the son of an independent and deep-rooted Virginian family. . . . Here is a modest book, a modest autobiographical story. . . . It ought to be put before every young American to see what can be done with the great language of a nation." Natl Rev

Balanchine, George, 1904-1983

Taper, Bernard. Balanchine; a biography. Times Bks. 1984 438p il o.p.; University of Calif. Press paperback available $15.95   **92**

1. Ballet 2. Choreographers
ISBN 0-520-20639-8 (pa)   LC 84-40107
This biography was first published 1963 by Harper; a second edition published by Macmillan appeared in 1974. This edition includes material about the last years of Balanchine's life

"The book is gracefully written and admirably detailed. . . . As Mr. Taper sensitively reveals, Balanchine's ballets were remarkable for their clarity, but Balanchine himself was always an enigma." N Y Times Book Rev

Baldwin, James, 1924-1987

Baldwin, James. Conversations with James Baldwin; edited by Fred L. Standley and Louis H. Pratt. University Press of Miss. 1989 297p (Literary conversations series) $39.50; pa $15.95
92

1. Authors, American 2. African American authors
ISBN 0-87805-388-3; 0-87805-389-1 (pa)
LC 88-36560

"During the sixties, seventies, and eighties, Baldwin participated in more than fifty situations having the format of interview, conversation, discussion or dialogue. . . . The twenty-seven pieces selected for this collection range from 1961 after his fourth book, 'Nobody Knows My Name,' to just prior to his death in a last formal conversation with poet Quincy Troupe." Introduction

Kenan, Randall. James Baldwin; Martin B. Duberman, general editor. Chelsea House 1994 143p il (Lives of notable gay men and lesbians) lib bdg $19.95; pa $9.95
92

1. Authors, American 2. African American authors
ISBN 0-7910-2301-X (lib bdg); 0-7910-2876-3 (pa)
LC 93-22776

Describes the life of the writer James Baldwin, focusing on his experiences as an African-American civil rights worker and as a gay man

"The book will be welcome in collections serving students, both for Black History Month assignments and for literature classes." Booklist

Includes bibliography

Leeming, David Adams. James Baldwin; a biography; [by] David Leeming. Knopf 1994 442p il $25
92

1. Authors, American 2. African American authors
ISBN 0-394-57708-6
LC 93-30847

Also available in paperback from Holt & Co.

The author "draws on interviews with Baldwin to illuminate the writer's difficulty in accepting his homosexuality, his attempted suicide in Paris in 1956, the strong autobiographical component in his fiction, his uneasy association with the Black Panthers and his formative relationship with his unloving stepfather." Publ Wkly

This "is the most revealing and subjectively penetrating assessment of Baldwin's life yet published." N Y Times Book Rev

Includes bibliographical references

Barnum, P. T. (Phineas Taylor), 1810-1891

Kunhardt, Philip B. P.T. Barnum; America's greatest showman; by Philip B. Kunhardt, Jr., Philip B. Kunhardt III, Peter W. Kunhardt. Knopf 1995 358p il $45
92

1. Circus
ISBN 0-679-43574-3
LC 94-42597

Published in conjunction with Discovery Channel's documentary of same name

"The authors present a straightforward, chronological life of the American businessman who had a boundless talent for predicting and manipulating the public's curiosity. . . . They have compiled a vast amount of photographic and printed ephemera, much of it extremely rare, that will attract many casual readers and bring new revelations to Barnum enthusiasts." Libr J

Includes bibliographical references

Barton, Clara, 1821-1912

Oates, Stephen B. A woman of valor: Clara Barton and the Civil War. Free Press 1994 527p il map $27.95; pa $14
92

1. United States—History—1861-1865, Civil War
ISBN 0-02-923405-0; 0-02-874012-2 (pa)
LC 93-38830

The author "uses both primary and secondary sources in addressing the Civil War career of Clara Barton. . . . An 'angel of the battlefield' who succored the wounded while under fire, Barton also raised funds and supplies through a network of women's support groups, while challenging the conventional belief that nursing was inappropriate for respectable women." Publ Wkly

"This is a carefully written and researched work that brings to life both the Civil War and a period of Barton's life that was to affect her forever." Libr J

Includes bibliographical references

Basie, Count, 1904-1984

Basie, Count. Good morning blues: the autobiography of Count Basie; as told to Albert Murray. Random House 1985 399p il o.p.; Da Capo Press paperback available $15.95
92

1. Jazz musicians 2. African American musicians
ISBN 0-306-80609-6 (pa)
LC 85-2439

"Basie pays tribute to his colleagues and managers (and to John Hammond for 'discovering' him), but does not hesitate to discuss their weaknesses and shortcomings; his language is direct and earthy. Although some of the book reads more like a catalogue or itinerary than an autobiography, it will have strong appeal for jazz buffs and fans of the late bandleader." Publ Wkly

Bauer, Marion Dane, 1938-

Bauer, Marion Dane. A writer's story; from life to fiction. Clarion Bks. 1995 134p $14.95; pa $6.95
92

1. Authors, American 2. Women authors
ISBN 0-395-72094-X; 0-395-75053-9 (pa)
LC 94-48800

"Drawing on her own experiences, the novelist examines the origins of inspiration and the subconscious drives that compel authors to write. She points out that many components of fiction—characters, settings, plot details—need not be autobiographical, yet the text does suggest that a story's meaning is directly linked to the unique experiences of its creator. . . . Bauer provides invaluable information for both writers and readers of fiction." Publ Wkly

Biko, Stephen, 1946-1977

Woods, Donald. Biko. rev and updated ed. Holt & Co. 1987 418p il hardcover o.p. paperback available $13.95
92

1. South Africa—Race relations
ISBN 0-8050-1899-9 (pa)
LC 87-11862

Also available in hardcover from P. Smith

First published 1978 by Paddington Press

"The material includes a history of South Africa. . . . From his short 30 years, little biographical material about Steve Biko can be presented, but Woods, Biko's close friend, is able to give details and lengthy descriptions of the philosophy and program of the great Bantu leader." Voice Youth Advocates

Bird, Larry

Bird, Larry. Drive: the story of my life; by Larry Bird with Bob Ryan; foreword by Magic Johnson. Doubleday 1989 259p il o.p.; Bantam Bks. paperback available $6.50   **92**

1. Basketball—Biography
ISBN 0-553-28758-3 (pa)   LC 89-37228

"Presented as a memoir about 'overcoming obstacles,' the discussions of the events that shaped Bird's life, including his parents' divorce and father's suicide . . . serve as mere asides to innocuous, though entertaining basketball anecdotes." Publ Wkly

Black Elk, 1863-1950

Black Elk. Black Elk speaks; being the life story of a holy man of the Oglala Sioux; as told through John G. Neihardt (Flaming Rainbow); introduction by Vine Deloria, Jr.; illustrated with drawings by Standing Bear and a portfolio of photographs. University of Neb. Press 1979 299p il $25; pa $9.95   **92**

1. Oglala Indians
ISBN 0-8032-3301-9; 0-8032-8359-8 (pa)
LC 79-12367

A reprint of the title first published 1932 by Morrow
The Indian whose life story this is, was born in 1863. He was a famous warrior and hunter in his youth, and became a practicing medicine man among his people. Of him Neihardt says, "As an indubitable seer, he seemed to represent the consciousness of the Plains Indian more fully than any other I had ever known."

This "is about as near as you can get to seeing life and death, war and religion, through an Indian's eyes." Outlook

Blake, William, 1757-1827

Ackroyd, Peter. Blake. Knopf 1996 399p il $35
92

1. Poets, English 2. Artists, British
ISBN 0-679-40967-X   LC 96-75018
First published 1995 in the United Kingdom
Ackroyd explores "Blake's childhood, education, training as an artist, marriage, and interior spiritual terrain. Moreover, he offers adept insights into Blake's influences and work, art and poetry." Booklist

"Combining meticulous scholarship with uncanny psychological insight, this marvelously illustrated biography (with color and b&w plates of Blake's paintings, drawings and engravings) presents him as a prescient social critic who, long before Freud, saw warfare as a form of repressed sexuality, and whose prophetic epic poems offer a cogent vision of humanity's spiritual renewal." Publ Wkly

Includes bibliographical references

Blanc, Mel, 1908-1989

Blanc, Mel. That's not all folks; [by] Mel Blanc and Philip Bashe. Warner Bks. 1988 275p il o.p.
92
LC 88-14724

"In his autobiography Blanc takes us behind the scenes not only of his years working with animators at (of course) Warner Brothers . . . where he did . . . the voices for a host of cartoon stars Daffy Duck, Sylvester the Cat, Porky Pig, Yosemite Sam, etc. but also the days working on The Jack Benny Show. . . . No fan of Blanc's many cartoon characters or of Jack Benny can fail to enjoy this." West Coast Rev Books

Bly, Nellie, 1867-1922

Kroeger, Brooke. Nellie Bly; daredevil, reporter, feminist. Times Bks. 1994 xxi, 631p il hardcover o.p. paperback available $16   **92**

1. Women journalists
ISBN 0-8129-2525-4 (pa)   LC 93-30656

"Kroeger goes beyond the well-known stories about Bly, documenting her reporting career and her life as an industrialist. This is a remarkable biography of an extraordinary woman that should be added to most library collections." Libr J

Includes bibliography

Boone, Daniel, 1734-1820

Faragher, John Mack. Daniel Boone; the life and legend of an American pioneer. Holt & Co. 1992 429p il maps $27.50; pa $14.95   **92**

1. Frontier and pioneer life
ISBN 0-8050-1603-1; 0-8050-3007-7 (pa)
LC 92-21873

"The popular image of Daniel Boone is that of an unlettered backwoodsman, skilled hunter and Indian fighter. But evidence argues that he was reasonably well educated for his time and place, that he was a landowner, businessman and a respected leader of frontier society. Faragher . . . has sifted through folklore and fact to reconstruct a realistic portrait of Boone and the expanding frontier." Publ Wkly

Includes bibliographical references

Bourke-White, Margaret, 1904-1971

Bourke-White, Margaret. Portrait of myself. Simon & Schuster 1963 383p il o.p.   **92**

1. Women photographers
Autobiographical account of Miss Bourke-White's career in commercial photography, her two unsuccessful marriages, and her fight with Parkinsonism

"Some of her finest photographs (none of them violent) adorn this book, and if Maggie cannot always find words to equal the pictures in eloquence and perception, her story is most exciting in simple, straightforward prose." N Y Times Book Rev

Bradley, Bill

Bradley, Bill. Time present, time past; a memoir. Knopf 1996 442p il maps $26; pa $13
92

ISBN 0-679-44488-2; 0-679-76815-7 (pa)
LC 96-105111
Also available Thorndike Press large print edition

"Bradley examines many of the current issues confronting America, from the perspectives of his early upbringing in small-town Missouri, his experiences as a Rhodes scholar at Oxford and as a professional basketball star, and his 17 years as a U.S. Senator from New Jersey." Libr J

This book "is highly readable, thought provoking, and refreshingly honest." Booklist

Bradley, Omar Nelson, 1893-1981
Bradley, Omar Nelson. A general's life; an autobiography; by Omar N. Bradley and Clay Blair. Simon & Schuster 1983 752p il o.p.; TAB Bks. reprint available $19.95 **92**
1. Generals
ISBN 0-8306-3312-X LC 82-19404
Also available in hardcover from Buccaneer Bks.
"Written in the first person by collaborator Blair and not completed until after Bradley's death (1981), this 'joint autobiography' is actually better described as a fluent and historically sound 'authorized' biography. . . . Blair's prose is readable . . . and his research impeccable." Libr J
Includes bibliographical references

Brave Bird, Mary
Brave Bird, Mary. Lakota woman; by Mary Crow Dog and Richard Erdoes. Grove Weidenfeld 1990 263p il o.p.; HarperCollins Pubs. paperback available $13 **92**
1. Dakota Indians
ISBN 0-06-097389-7 (pa) LC 89-24862
"Born in 1955 and raised in poverty on the Rosebud Reservation, Mary Crow Dog escaped an oppressive Catholic boarding school but fell into a marginal life of urban shoplifting and barhopping. A 1971 encounter with AIM (the American Indian Movement), participation in the 1972 Trail of Broken Treaties march on Washington, and giving birth to her first child while under fire at the 1973 siege of Wounded Knee radicalized her." Libr J
"The story of Mary Crow Dog's coming of age in the Indian civil rights movement is simply told—and, at times, simply horrifying." N Y Times Book Rev

Brontë, Charlotte, 1816-1855
Gordon, Lyndall. Charlotte Brontë; a passionate life. Norton 1995 418p il $27.50; pa $17 **92**
1. Authors, English 2. Women authors
ISBN 0-393-03722-3; 0-393-31448-0 (pa)
First published 1994 in the United Kingdom
The author "dismantles once and for all the image of Charlotte Brontë as a figure of pathos and presents, instead, a courageous survivor, a determined writer, and a woman of volcanic emotion. . . . Gordon, as skilled at literary analysis as at chronicling a life, approaches Brontë's tragic and enduringly relevant story from several angles, carefully identifying all the autobiographical elements of her novels and contrasting her commitment to writing and her independent spirit to her era's strict and pitiless code of behavior for women." Booklist
Includes bibliography

Brooks, Gwendolyn
Kent, George E. A life of Gwendolyn Brooks. University Press of Ky. 1990 287p hardcover o.p. paperback available $19.95 **92**
1. Poets, American 2. African American authors 3. Women poets
ISBN 0-8131-0827-6 (pa) LC 89-31738
This is a "biography of the Pulitzer Prize-winning poet. Kent carefully chronicles Brooks's aesthetic and political development in relation to familial and literary influence, the Chicago arts community, and the civil rights and black nationalist movements. . . . Her achievements as a critic, teacher, speaker, philanthropist, and activist are also emphasized." Libr J
"No attempt has been made to cover Brooks' career after 1978. . . . Otherwise, this is a complete, informed, and sympathetic portrayal of Brooks as a personality and writer." Booklist
Includes bibliography

Brown, Claude, 1937-
Brown, Claude. Manchild in the promised land. Macmillan 1965 415p o.p.; New Am. Lib. paperback available $6.99 **92**
1. African Americans—Biography 2. Harlem (New York, N.Y.)—Social conditions
ISBN 0-451-16827-5 (pa)
This is "the autobiography of a young black man raised in Harlem. [It is] a realistic description of life in the ghetto. . . . The core of the book concerns the 'plague' of heroin addiction that swept through Harlem in the 1950s taking the lives of many of Brown's contemporaries." Publ Wkly

Brown, James
Brown, James. James Brown, the godfather of soul; [by] James Brown, with Bruce Tucker. Macmillan 1986 336p il o.p.; Thunder's Mouth Press paperback available $13.95 **92**
1. African American singers 2. Soul music
ISBN 1-56025-115-8 (pa) LC 86-12715
Brown's musical "style defines the genre called soul. He has chronicled his life, from his birth in 1933 through a troubled youth, prison, and the ups and downs of a spiraling career." Libr J
This "is a solid, informative autobiography, and fans will welcome its vast discography." N Y Times Book Rev

Browning, Elizabeth Barrett, 1806-1861
Markus, Julia. Dared and done: the marriage of Elizabeth Barrett and Robert Browning. See entry under Browning, Robert, 1812-1889

Browning, Robert, 1812-1889
Markus, Julia. Dared and done: the marriage of Elizabeth Barrett and Robert Browning. Knopf 1995 382p il $30 **92**
1. Browning, Elizabeth Barrett, 1806-1861 2. Poets, English
ISBN 0-679-41602-1 LC 94-11573
This work presents an "analysis of the courtship and marriage of two well-known English poets, which presents their relationship as reflected in their work. . . . Quoting heavily from their poetry and Barrett's correspondence, Markus shows the richness that love brought into the couple's life together." SLJ
Includes bibliography

Bryan, William Jennings, 1860-1925

Ashby, LeRoy. William Jennings Bryan; champion of democracy. Twayne Pubs. 1987 245p il (Twayne's twentieth-century American biography series) lib bdg $30   92

1. United States—Politics and government
ISBN 0-8057-7760-1   LC 87-8407

This biography of the politician, lecturer, and lawyer is "thoughtful and well-balanced. . . . For a generation who know Bryan only in terms of the Scopes trial, if at all, this biography is a richly deserved, lively rendering of an important American hero. It is highly readable and enjoyable." SLJ

Includes bibliography

Bunche, Ralph J. (Ralph Johnson), 1904-1971

Urquhart, Brian E. Ralph Bunche; an American life; [by] Brian Urquhart. Norton 1993 496p il maps $27.50   92

1. African Americans—Biography
ISBN 0-393-03527-1   LC 92-46564

The author "describes Bunche's itinerant childhood, academic background, teaching and research, OSS service in World War II, significant contributions at the Dumbarton Oaks Conference of Allied leaders, and troubleshooting and mediation on behalf of the UN throughout the Middle East, Africa, and Asia. . . . Urquhart has made a fascinating narrative of the accomplishments of an American-born international diplomat." Booklist

Includes bibliographical references

Burch, Jennings Michael

Burch, Jennings Michael. They cage the animals at night. New Am. Lib. 1984 293p hardcover o.p. paperback available $4.99   92

1. Children—Institutional care 2. Foster home care
ISBN 0-451-15941-1 (pa)   LC 84-6809

"One of six sons from a broken home in New York City, Burch was shifted in and out of private and municipal children's shelters and foster homes for several years as his sickly mother tried—and failed—to cope with her overwhelming responsibilities. This is a recreation of those 1950s years." Publ Wkly

"The author articulates well his childhood feelings of helplessness and fear. . . . Gripping and readable, this will keep teenagers involved from start to finish." SLJ

Bush, Barbara, 1925-

Kilian, Pamela. Barbara Bush; a biography. St. Martin's Press 1992 245p il hardcover o.p. paperback available $4.99   92

1. Bush, George, 1924- 2. Presidents—United States—Spouses
ISBN 0-312-92892-0 (pa)   LC 92-3363

Also available Thorndike Press large print edition

"A Thomas Dunne book"

"This is a straightforward biography of the popular First Lady. . . . Throughout, her honesty and humor come across, making this a nice addition to all popular biography collections." Libr J

Includes bibliographical references

Campanella, Roy, 1921-1993

Macht, Norman L. (Norman Lee). Roy Campanella; baseball star. Chelsea House 1996 111p il (Great achievers: lives of the physically challenged) lib bdg $19.95   92

1. Brooklyn Dodgers (Baseball team) 2. Baseball—Biography
ISBN 0-7910-2083-5   LC 95-15355

A biography of Roy Campanella, the award-winning catcher whose baseball career was cut short by an accident which left him partially paralyzed

Includes bibliographical references

Capote, Truman, 1924-1984

Capote, Truman. One Christmas. Random House 1994 c1983 41p $15   92

1. Christmas
ISBN 0-679-44346-0

A reissue of the title first published 1983

"Capote's recollection of the Christmas he spent with his father in New Orleans when he was six years old." Booklist

"Capote manages to recapture the feelings of the experience: his homesickness, his amazement at his father's lavish and unusual life style, and the abrupt yet bittersweet way in which his little boy's belief in Santa Claus ends." Christ Sci Monit

Clarke, Gerald. Capote; a biography. Simon & Schuster 1988 631p il $18.45   92

1. Authors, American
ISBN 0-671-22811-0   LC 88-3144

Also available in paperback from Ballantine Bks.

This biography "tackles the writer's whole life and attempts an incisive psychological investigation of what made Capote tick as man and artist." Booklist

"In this work of prodigious research gracefully presented, Mr. Clarke, who had his subject's confidence during the last years, gives Capote what the writer himself, in a last grand, gutsy gesture, declared he wanted: a book in which nothing, nothing at all, was left out." N Y Times Book Rev

Includes bibliography

Carnegie, Andrew, 1835-1919

Wall, Joseph Frazier. Andrew Carnegie. University of Pittsburgh Press 1989 1137p il $49.95; pa $22.50   92

1. Capitalists and financiers
ISBN 0-8229-3828-6; 0-8229-5904-6 (pa)
                                       LC 88-38160

A reissue of the title first published 1970 by Oxford University Press

This biography follows Carnegie from his boyhood in Scotland through his emigration to America, his rise in the business world, and his early ventures in oil, railroads, telegraphy, and the iron and steel industries

Includes bibliography

Carroll, James

Carroll, James. An American requiem; God, my father, and the war that came between us. Houghton Mifflin 1996 279p il $23.95 **92**
1. Authors, American
ISBN 0-395-77926-X LC 95-52125
"The author's father studied to be a priest but quit before taking his vows, married, and eventually became a leader of the military-intelligence community during the Vietnam War. James Carroll went his father one better: he was ordained, then devoted his career as a priest to resisting the war. But he, too, resigned the priesthood and married. . . . Told with integrity and style, this is a moving account of the generational strains of the Vietnam era, and the timeless agonies of fathers and sons." New Yorker

Carroll, Lewis, 1832-1898

Cohen, Morton Norton. Lewis Carroll; a biography; by Morton N. Cohen. Knopf 1995 xxiii, 577p il $35; pa $17 **92**
1. Authors, English
ISBN 0-679-42298-6; 0-679-74562-9 (pa)
LC 95-2663
Cohen begins by "tracing Dodgson's early years up through his most productive decade, the 1860s, . . . then retraces his steps in order to examine Dodgson's achievements and personality." Booklist
"Delightfully illustrated with photographs and Carroll's drawings woven throughout, this extraordinary, meticulous biography gives us a sharper and deeper picture of Carroll than any before, presenting a many-sided man." Publ Wkly

Carson, Kit, 1809-1868

Carson, Kit. Kit Carson's autobiography; edited by Milo Milton Quaife. Donnelley 1935 xxxii, 192p o.p.; University of Neb. Press paperback available $9 **92**
1. Frontier and pioneer life—West (U.S.)
ISBN 0-8032-5031-2 (pa)
First published 1926 with title: Kit Carson's own story of his life, as dictated to Col. and Mrs. D. C. Peters about 1856-57
An account of Kit Carson's life as a trapper, Indian fighter, guide, and buffalo hunter up until the fall of 1856. It includes accounts of a trapping expedition to California (1829-1831), three expeditions with Frémont (1842-1845), exploits in the Mexican War, and service as an Indian agent in New Mexico

Carson, Rachel, 1907-1964

Carson, Rachel. Always, Rachel; the letters of Rachel Carson and Dorothy Freeman, 1952-1964; edited by Martha Freeman. Beacon Press 1994 xxx, 567p il (Concord library) $35; pa $18 **92**
1. Freeman, Dorothy, 1898-1978 2. Women scientists
ISBN 0-8070-7010-6; 0-8070-7011-4 (pa)
LC 94-25849
This is a collection of some 750 letters exchanged between Carson and her summer neighbor and beloved friend, Dorothy Freeman

"To read this collection is like eavesdropping on an extended conversation that mixes the mundane events of the two women's family lives with details of Carson's research and writing and, later, her breast cancer." Publ Wkly
Includes bibliographical references

Hynes, H. Patricia. The recurring silent spring. Pergamon Press 1989 227p (Athene series) $30; pa $14.95 **92**
1. Women scientists
ISBN 0-08-037117-5; 0-08-037116-7 (pa)
LC 88-29049
Also available in paperback from Teachers College Press
"Hynes reexamines the life and work of Rachel Carson, . . . maintaining that Carson wrote in part in refutation of the view, long held by professional men, that women had 'lesser mental ability and stamina to do science.' Hynes contends that . . . Carson's Silent Spring [entered in class 363.7] continues to serve 'as a fundamental text on evolution—neither outdated nor inaccurate.'" Choice
Includes bibliographical references

Carver, George Washington, 1864?-1943

McMurry, Linda O. George Washington Carver; scientist and symbol. Oxford Univ. Press 1981 367p il hardcover o.p. paperback available $13.95 **92**
1. Scientists 2. African Americans—Biography
ISBN 0-19-503205-5 (pa) LC 81-4896
"Calling Carver 'one of the best-known, and least understood, blacks who ever lived,' McMurry strips the 'Peanut Man' of myth and lays bare the reality of a man caught in complexity, contradiction, and paradox. According to the author, Carver's talents, the racial climate of his times, and his sense of racial responsibility trapped him in the role of a folk hero . . . [and] this role obscured Carver's real contributions and legacy." Libr J
Includes bibliographical references

Cary, Lorene

Cary, Lorene. Black ice. Knopf 1991 237p $24; pa $10 **92**
1. St. Paul's School (Concord, N.H.) 2. African American women
ISBN 0-394-57465-6; 0-679-73745-6 (pa)
LC 90-52988
"In the early 1970's, an Eastern prep school recruiting minority students opened its doors to Cary, then a 15-year-old Philadelphia high school girl. These affecting recollections explore her experiences—interactions with teachers, an affair with another student, friendships, and problems with prejudice—as well as her struggle to determine her own black identity." Booklist

Casals, Pablo, 1876-1973

Baldock, Robert. Pablo Casals. Northeastern Univ. Press 1993 334p il $35.50 **92**
1. Musicians
ISBN 1-55553-176-8 LC 93-10115
"Baldock documents the life and musical career of the acclaimed cellist, conductor, and performer Pablo Casals,

Casals, Pablo, 1876-1973—*Continued*
who in 1894 at age 18, was considered the 'most outstanding musical talent in Spain.' A well-researched biography." Booklist
Includes bibliography and discography

Cassatt, Mary, 1844-1926
Mathews, Nancy Mowll. Mary Cassatt; a life. Villard Bks. 1994 383p il $28   **92**
1. Artists, American 2. Women artists
ISBN 0-394-58497-X   LC 93-22148
"Mathews presents the little-known facts of Cassatt's very private life and answers the question: Why did Cassatt, single and childless, choose to make motherhood her 'signature theme'?" Publ Wkly
This "is an evenly written, well-documented, and sympathetic—but not patronizing—biography that should be acquired by most libraries." Libr J

Castro, Fidel, 1927-
Beyer, Don E. Castro! Watts 1993 144p il (Impact biography) lib bdg $22.70   **92**
1. Cuba—Politics and government
ISBN 0-531-13027-4   LC 92-34534
This biography focuses on the Cuban leader's early life, his embrace of revolutionary politics and his rise to power
"The strength of the book is the detailed information presented on the revolution and Castro's rise to total control; unfortunately, the author glosses over the years after the Revolution." Voice Youth Advocates
Includes bibliography

Geyer, Georgie Anne. Guerrilla prince: the untold story of Fidel Castro. 2nd rev ed. Andrews & McMeel 1993 xxi, 458p il pa $12.95   **92**
1. Cuba—Politics and government
ISBN 0-8362-8017-2   LC 93-233091
This biography "focuses on Castro's personality, on his personal rather than policy motivations, and offers a detailed psychological portrait. . . . The reader is left with a persuasive picture of a paranoid, erratic megalomaniac, whose personal life is a microcosm of his public behavior." Libr J
Includes bibliographical references

Cather, Willa, 1873-1947
Keene, Ann T. Willa Cather. Messner 1994 156p il (Classic American writers) $15   **92**
1. Authors, American 2. Women authors
ISBN 0-671-86760-1   LC 93-45743
"Keene's biography traces Cather's roots from her childhood in Virginia's Shenandoah Valley in the 1870s through her family's move to Nebraska, her college years, and her careers as journalist, editor, and high-school teacher. Cather was nearly 40 before she began to publish the fiction for which she is so noted, and her life as a writer is well chronicled. . . . Chapter notes, a chronology, and a list for further reading that includes works by and about Cather are appended." Booklist

Lee, Hermione. Willa Cather; double lives. Pantheon Bks. 1989 410p il hardcover o.p. paperback available $15   **92**
1. Authors, American 2. Women authors
ISBN 0-679-73649-2 (pa)   LC 89-43233
"This interpretive biography . . . examines the relationship between Cather's work and her personal life." Booklist
The author's "discussion of Cather's 12 novels and numerous stories is so absorbing that it provokes a rereading of the work, which makes it a valuable critical study." N Y Times Book Rev
Includes bibliography

Catherine II, the Great, Empress of Russia, 1729-1796
Alexander, John T. Catherine the Great; life and legend. Oxford Univ. Press 1989 418p il maps $31.25; pa $15.95   **92**
1. Russia—Kings, queens, rulers, etc. 2. Russia—History
ISBN 0-19-505236-6; 0-19-506162-4 (pa)
                     LC 88-10122
"Catherine was born an obscure German princess; she married into the imperial Russian line, to a grandson of Peter the Great. She usurped the throne from her husband and for 34 years ruled in his place. Alexander chronicles and analyzes her long reign. . . . This is a work of impeccable scholarship and prose; Alexander fathoms his subject completely, and he writes a most compelling narrative." Booklist
Includes bibliography

Cézanne, Paul, 1839-1906
Rewald, John. Cézanne; a biography. Abrams 1986 288p il $75   **92**
1. Artists, French
ISBN 0-8109-0775-5   LC 86-1017
This biography of the French painter is a revised and expanded version of the author's 1936 Sorbonne doctoral dissertation. An English translation was published in 1948 by Simon & Schuster under the title: Paul Cézanne: a biography
"The artist's character is revealed in his own words and in those of his friends . . . making Cézanne accessible in a way simple narrative cannot. Adding greatly to our understanding of Cézanne's development as a painter are the 270 illustrations." Libr J
Includes bibliography

Chagall, Marc, 1887-1985
Kagan, Andrew. Marc Chagall. Abbeville Press 1989 128p il (Modern masters series) $32.95; pa $22.95   **92**
1. Artists
ISBN 0-89659-932-9; 0-89659-935-3 (pa)
                     LC 89-6693
This illustrated biography of the Russian Jewish artist explores his paintings, graphics, mosaics, tapestries, and stained glass works. A biochronology and a selected exhibitions list are appended
Includes bibliography

Chambers, Veronica

Chambers, Veronica. Mama's girl. Riverhead Bks. 1996 194p $22.95   92

1. African American women

ISBN 1-57322-030-2   LC 95-53765

"In this troubling testament to grit and mother love, Chambers, a former *Times* editor, sets down in telling detail the harsh balance of power in her black immigrant family. While the story of her own achievement under grim, often violent circumstances is extraordinary, the reader is left feeling particularly grateful for the author's compassion. Her portrait of her Panamanian mother, Cecilia—proud, protective, angry, and in need—is one of the finest and most evenhanded in the genre in recent years." New Yorker

Chaplin, Charlie, 1889-1977

Milton, Joyce. Tramp: the life of Charlie Chaplin. HarperCollins Pubs. 1996 578p il $32
          92

1. Actors

ISBN 0-06-017052-2   LC 95-48438

The author "shows how Chaplin, brought up in London's East End culture, was instilled with a class consciousness that later resonated in his Communist sympathies and his creation of the lumpenproletariat icon of the 'Little Guy'—the celluloid role he could never eclipse." Libr J

"Milton presents a well-researched, evenhanded portrait of a troubled entertainment genius." Publ Wkly

Includes bibliographical references

Charles II, King of Great Britain, 1630-1685

Fraser, Antonia. Royal Charles: Charles II and the Restoration. Knopf 1979 524p il o.p.   92

1. Great Britain—Kings, queens, rulers, etc. 2. Great Britain—History—1603-1714, Stuarts

          LC 79-2208

In this biography "Antonia Fraser's greatest achievement is her dissection and reconstruction of the king's political and personal character. . . . The best pages . . . are those which deal with the period of civil war and exile. . . . In general Antonia Fraser's judgments are sound, her details are accurate, and she is superbly convincing on . . . her subject's personality." Economist

Includes bibliography

Chase, Clifford

Chase, Clifford. The hurry-up song; a memoir of losing my brother. HarperSanFrancisco 1995 220p il $20; pa $10   92

1. Chase, Ken, 1952?-1989 2. AIDS (Disease) 3. Gay men

ISBN 0-06-251019-3; 0-06-251020-7 (pa)

          LC 94-30209

"In an affecting memoir that recalls his older brother's death from AIDS at age 37, Chase delves into family history and relationships while expressing frustration with his brother, who grew more distant and confused as his illness progressed." Booklist

Chavez, Cesar, 1927-1993

Griswold del Castillo, Richard. César Chávez; a triumph of spirit; by Richard Griswold del Castillo and Richard A. Garcia. University of Okla. Press 1995 206p il (Oklahoma western biographies) $19.95   92

1. Migrant labor 2. Mexican Americans

ISBN 0-8061-2758-9   LC 95-15230

"In this biography of the embattled farm labor organizer, del Castillo . . . focuses on Chávez's formation, growth, and development as a leader in the movement to unionize farm workers in the Southwest. . . . Del Castillo's account is balanced, highly readable, and engaging." Libr J

Includes bibliographical references

Chekhov, Anton Pavlovich, 1860-1904

Pritchett, V. S. (Victor Sawdon). Chekhov; a spirit set free. Random House 1988 235p $17.95
          92

1. Authors, Russian

ISBN 0-394-54650-4   LC 87-43213

This is a biographical study of the Russian writer and an analysis of his work

"Chekhov's originality and artistry take on new vitality in part because Pritchett's English imagination harmonizes with the Russian's." Choice

Christie, Agatha, 1890-1976

Gill, Gillian. Agatha Christie; the woman and her mysteries. Free Press 1990 243p il hardcover o.p. paperback available $12.95   92

1. Authors, English 2. Women authors

ISBN 0-02-911703-8 (pa)   LC 90-38545

Also available G.K. Hall large print edition

An "unraveling of the mystique of the world's most famous female mystery writer. . . . By examining her novels closely and comparing them to events in Christie's own life, Gill sheds new light on the woman and the writer. Although Gill's treatment is scholarly and her vocabulary challenging, students of fiction writing and admirers of Christie's work will welcome Gill's insights." SLJ

Includes bibliographical references

Cleary, Beverly

Cleary, Beverly. My own two feet. Morrow Junior Bks. 1995 261p il $15   92

1. Authors, American 2. Women authors

ISBN 0-688-14267-2   LC 95-1764

Also available in paperback from Avon Bks.

"This second installment of the Newbery Medalist's autobiography (after A Girl from Yamhill) begins during the '30s, with the young Cleary leaving her home state of Oregon to attend junior college in California. The volume ends in 1949, with Morrow's acceptance of Cleary's first novel, the now-classic *Henry Huggins*." Publ Wkly

"Cleary recalls the past with humor, affection, and insight. Those who have always admired her books will, after reading this memoir, have an even greater admiration for the author." Horn Book

Clinton, Bill, 1946-

Maraniss, David. First in his class: a biography of Bill Clinton. Simon & Schuster 1995 512p il $25; pa $14 **92**

1. Presidents—United States
ISBN 0-671-87109-9; 0-684-81890-6 (pa)
LC 94-48245

The author "offers a heavily documented (nearly 400 interviews), unauthorized biography that ends with Clinton's announcement for the presidency. Maraniss writes, 'My goal was for this book to be neither pathography nor hagiography, but a fair-minded examination of a complicated human being and the forces that shaped him and his generation.' He has achieved his goal. . . . All in all, *First in His Class* is solid journalism that thoughtfully evokes the tumultuous times—desegregation, assassinations, Vietnam—that shaped Clinton." Booklist

Includes bibliographical references

Cochise, Apache Chief, d. 1874

Sweeney, Edwin R. (Edwin Russell). Cochise, Chiricahua Apache chief. University of Okla. Press 1991 xxiii, 501p il maps (Civilization of the American Indian series) hardcover o.p. paperback available $17.95 **92**

1. Apache Indians
ISBN 0-8061-2606-X (pa)
LC 90-50699

The author traces Cochise's "rise to leadership of his Apache band, his . . . skirmishes with the military and others in both the United States and Mexico, and his successful negotiations for a reservation in the homeland of his peoples." Libr J

"An insightful, and exciting work that ranks with the best efforts of ethnohistory. . . . This book is the definitive life story of history's most important Apache chief and restores him to his proper preeminent role in the region's history." Choice

Includes bibliography

Cole, Nat King, 1919?-1965

Gourse, Leslie. Unforgettable: the life and mystique of Nat King Cole. St. Martin's Press 1991 309p il hardcover o.p. paperback available $12.95 **92**

1. African American singers
ISBN 0-312-07877-3 (pa)
LC 90-27409

This biography looks at "Cole's Chicago childhood, musical roots, early successes, marriages, growing fame, near-disastrous run-in with the IRS, and early death from lung cancer." Booklist

Includes discography and bibliography

Columbus, Christopher

Meltzer, Milton. Columbus and the world around him. Watts 1990 192p il maps lib bdg $22 **92**

1. Explorers 2. America—Exploration
ISBN 0-531-10899-6 (lib bdg)
LC 89-24764

Describes the voyages of Columbus, the terrible impact of the Spaniards on the Indians, and the ultimate cultural influence of the Native Americans on their white conquerors

"Meltzer excels in a candid and graphic exposé of the Spaniards' behaviors and attitudes, including enormous cruelty and greed. . . . This thought-provoking book includes handsome and profuse reproductions of historical maps, artwork, manuscripts, and letters." Booklist

Includes bibliographical references

Conrad, Joseph, 1857-1924

Reilly, Jim. Joseph Conrad. Rourke 1990 110p il maps (Life and works) lib bdg $19.94 **92**

1. Authors, English
ISBN 0-86593-021-X
LC 89-77070

Briefly surveys the life of Joseph Conrad and analyzes in depth some of his major works

Includes glossary and bibliographical references

Conway, Jill K., 1934-

Conway, Jill K. The road from Coorain; [by] Jill Ker Conway. Knopf 1989 238p il $25; pa $11 **92**

1. Australia
ISBN 0-394-57456-7; 0-679-72436-2 (pa)
LC 88-25932

Also available G.K. Hall large print edition

This is a memoir by "the historian and former president of Smith College, who grew up on a sheep station in the western grasslands of New South Wales, Australia." N Y Times Book Rev

The author's "inspiring story is told with rich, vivid details. . . . For teenage readers, the chapters on her life in the outback . . . will be especially riveting. . . . The later chapters covering her life in Sydney, family struggles, and university studies will be both challenging and intellectually rewarding." Voice Youth Advocates

Copland, Aaron, 1900-1990

Copland, Aaron. Copland, since 1943; by Aaron Copland and Vivian Perlis. St. Martin's Press 1989 463p il hardcover o.p. paperback available $14.95 **92**

1. Composers, American
ISBN 0-312-05066-6 (pa)
LC 89-34847

First volume of autobiography covering the years 1900 through 1942, published 1984 available pa $12.95 (ISBN 0-312-01149-0)

"This second volume of the well-known Copland-Perlis collaboration is essentially an autobiography interspersed with historical narrative and reminiscences by Copland's associates. Perlis, ever the diligent historian, provides copious documents and footnotes. . . . Scholars and lay readers alike will find this an indispensable source of Copland lore." Libr J

Includes bibliography

Cormier, Robert

Cormier, Robert. I have words to spend; reflections of a small town editor; edited and with a preface by Constance Senay Cormier. Delacorte Press 1991 209p hardcover o.p. paperback available $9.95 **92**

1. Authors, American
ISBN 0-385-31204-0 (pa)
LC 90-44878

A collection of biographical essays by the author of several popular young adult novels

Cormier, Robert—*Continued*

This work "will be enjoyed by all who value what Cormier has to say." Quill Quire

Cortés, Hernán, 1485-1547

Marks, Richard Lee. Cortés; the great adventurer and the fate of Aztec Mexico. Knopf 1993 347p il maps $27.50   92

1. Explorers 2. Mexico—History

ISBN 0-679-40609-3   LC 92-37170

"Cortés's early life in Spain and Cuba is recounted briefly, along with his postconquest triumphs and tribulations, but most of the tale is a battle-by-battle account of the invasion of Mexico in 1519-21. . . . This work will appeal to adventure fans and scholars of Mexican history; recommended for public and high school libraries." Libr J

Includes bibliography

Craven, Margaret

Craven, Margaret. Again calls the owl; illustrated by Joan Miller. Putnam 1980 120p il o.p.; Dell paperback available $5.50   92

1. Authors, American 2. Women authors

ISBN 0-440-30074-6 (pa)   LC 79-22388

"The author sketches the highlights of her life leading up to the writing of her first novel [I heard the owl call my name, entered in Fiction section]. . . . She recalls her childhood on Puget Sound, Washington; her student days at Stanford; and the people, . . . who encouraged her in her career as an editorial columnist and a short-story writer." Horn Book

"This engaging, spare account of a writer's development is refreshingly short and witty." Publ Wkly

✓ Crazy Horse, Sioux Chief, ca. 1842-1877

Goldman, Martin S. Crazy Horse; war chief of the Oglala Sioux. Watts 1996 208p il maps (American Indian experience) lib bdg $22   92

1. Oglala Indians

ISBN 0-531-11258-6   LC 95-26412

A biography of the Sioux leader set against the history of the Indian wars, with a full account of the Battle of the Little Bighorn

Includes bibliographical references

Cromwell, Oliver, 1599-1658

Fraser, Antonia. Cromwell, the Lord Protector. Knopf 1973 xx, 774p il maps o.p.; Smithmark Pubs. reprint available $14.98   92

1. Great Britain—History—1642-1660, Civil War and Commonwealth

ISBN 0-8317-5641-1

Published in the United Kingdom with title: Cromwell: our chief of men

This book presents a portrait of the 17th-century genius, who in roles of legislator, soldier, and ruler dominated Britain during and after the Great Civil War

The author has "presented her findings in a smooth-flowing narrative which is a pleasure to read. . . . To some extent the book lacks historical background and depth. But as a portrait of a man it is a genuine work of art: complete, subtle, understanding and convincing." New Statesman

Includes bibliography

Cummings, E. E. (Edward Estlin), 1894-1962

Berry, S. L. E.E. Cummings; text by S. L. Berry; artwork by Stasys Eidrigevicius. Creative Educ. 1994 45p il (Voices in poetry) lib bdg $16.95   92

1. Poets, American

ISBN 0-88682-611-X   LC 93-743

A biography of the twentieth-century American writer whose poetry combined artistic composition with word play and traditional rhyme and meter. Includes examples of his work

"E.E. Cummings is one of the most visual and most inviting of American poets, and this biography-*cum*-moodpiece makes for an evocative introduction. . . . This isn't a substitute for a traditional biography, but kids better able to look than to listen may find it an intriguing opening into poetry." Bull Cent Child Books

Includes bibliography

Curie, Marie, 1867-1934

Pasachoff, Naomi E. Marie Curie and the science of radioactivity; [by] Naomi Pasachoff. Oxford Univ. Press 1996 109p il (Oxford portraits in science) lib bdg $20   92

1. Chemists 2. Women scientists

ISBN 0-19-509214-7   LC 95-13639

"The book discusses the lack of recognition accorded the Curies by the French scientific community, the personal attacks Curie experienced because of her friendship with Paul Langevin, and professional criticisms of her work. Boxed sections provide related information on such topics as radioactivity, radon, and Mendeleyev's organization of the periodic table." Booklist

"This is a thorough biography, particularly useful for reports." SLJ

Includes bibliography

Quinn, Susan. Marie Curie; a life. Simon & Schuster 1995 509p il $30   92

1. Women scientists

ISBN 0-671-67542-7   LC 94-43517

This is a biography of the Polish-born scientist who was twice the recipient of the Nobel Prize for her work with radium

"A well-written, evenhanded story of dedication, disappointment, tragedy, and extraordinary achievement." Booklist

Includes bibliography

Custer, George Armstrong, 1839-1876

Barnett, Louise K. Touched by fire: the life, death, and mythic afterlife of George Armstrong Custer; [by] Louise Barnett. Holt & Co. 1996 540p il $30   92

1. Generals

ISBN 0-8050-3720-9   LC 95-43995

The author "after briefly sketching Custer's life up to 1866, examines his relationship with his wife, Libbie, and shows us a man who was more interested in the natural environment of the Plains than in the men under his command. Barnett also examines Libbie's role in creating the Custer legend." Libr J

"An exemplary exploration of the literary concept of the hero, in social and historical contexts." Booklist

Includes bibliographical references

Custer, George Armstrong, 1839-1876—*Continued*

Wert, Jeffry D. Custer; the controversial life of George Armstrong Custer. Simon & Schuster 1996 462p il maps $27.50   **92**
1. Generals
ISBN 0-684-81043-3   LC 96-7290
"Focusing on Custer's Civil War actions, Wert methodically examines a man often considered an enigma in American history. Clear writing and excellent use of primary source materials demonstrate how history should be written." Booklist
Includes bibliographical references

Dahl, Roald
Dahl, Roald. Boy: tales of childhood. Farrar, Straus & Giroux 1984 160p il $16   **92**
1. Authors, English
ISBN 0-374-37374-4   LC 84-48462
Also available in paperback from Penguin Bks.
"In these memoirs, Dahl reminisces about growing up in a large Norwegian family living in Wales during the 1920s and 1930s. The text is illustrated with sketches, old photographs and excerpts of letters he wrote as a boy." SLJ
"This should be of particular interest to Dahl's fans, but it should also appeal to anyone who likes writing that is direct, candid, and free-flowing." Bull Cent Child Books

Dahl, Roald. Going solo. Farrar, Straus & Giroux 1986 207p il $14.95   **92**
1. Authors, English 2. World War, 1939-1945—Personal narratives
ISBN 0-374-16503-3   LC 86-12022
Also available in paperback from Penguin Bks.
Continuing his autobiography, the author presents his impressions of Tanzania, where he worked for the Shell Oil Company prior to World War II, and describes his later experiences as a RAF fighter pilot
"A brief, masterly remembrance of the gifts of youth and good luck." Time

Dalai Lama XIV, 1935-
Dalai Lama XIV. Freedom in exile; the autobiography of the Dalai Lama. HarperCollins Pubs. 1990 288p il maps hardcover o.p. paperback available $13   **92**
1. Buddhism 2. Tibet (China)
ISBN 0-06-098701-4 (pa)   LC 89-46523
"A Cornelia & Michael Bessie book"
"The Dalai Lama's story is, in part, a chapter in the 2,500-year history of Buddhism as well as a testament to the 'mendacity and barbarity' of Communist China. He shares the details of his amazing life, a glimpse at some of the mysteries of Tibetan Buddhism, and his unshakable belief in the basic good of humanity." Booklist

Darwin, Charles, 1809-1882
Bowlby, John. Charles Darwin; a new life. Norton 1991 511p il maps hardcover o.p. paperback available $14.95   **92**
1. Naturalists
ISBN 0-393-30930-4 (pa)   LC 90-7484
"Charles Darwin and his theories have remained controversial for more than a century after his death. One debate that has occupied scholars is the source of Darwin's chronic ill health. Bowlby, . . . zooms in on this issue, using it as a key to Darwin's astonishingly prolific life." Booklist
Includes bibliographical references

Milner, Richard. Charles Darwin; evolution of a naturalist. Facts on File 1994 158p il (Makers of modern science) lib bdg $17.95   **92**
1. Naturalists
ISBN 0-8160-2557-6   LC 92-37792
This volume "reviews Charles Darwin's development as a biologist-naturalist from his childhood through the voyage of the *Beagle* and subsequently to his eminence as a naturalist-philosopher-evolutionist. The text clearly shows, systematically and step by step, how Darwin observed, developed, questioned, sought answers, hypothesized, and finally unified concepts in his *Origin of Species*

White, Michael. Darwin; a life in science; [by] Michael White and John Gribbin. Dutton 1995 322p $24.95   **92**
1. Naturalists
ISBN 0-525-94002-2   LC 95-24567
"In alternating chapters, journalist White chronicles Darwin's personal life and scientist Gribbin covers his scientific career. The sections tracing development of concepts concerning evolution and related religious ideas are well done. . . . The broad strokes of personal history and cultural background are enlightening." Publ Wkly
Includes bibliography

De Mille, Agnes
De Mille, Agnes. Dance to the piper; new preface by Cynthia Gregory. Da Capo Press 1980 c1952 342p il (Da Capo series in dance) $49.50
92
1. Dancers 2. Choreographers
ISBN 0-306-79615-5   LC 79-28689
A reprint of the title first published 1952 by Little, Brown
Autobiography of the American ballerina and choreographer who created Rodeo and the ballets in Carousel and Oklahoma. Among the famous persons who appear in the book is her uncle, Cecil B. De Mille
This book "is considerably more than the success story of a poor little rich girl. It is a witty, civilized account of an age of revolution in the dance by one of the spunkiest of the revolutionaries." Time

Degas, Edgar, 1834-1917
Meyer, Susan E. Edgar Degas. Abrams 1994 92p il (First impressions) $19.95   **92**
1. Artists, French
ISBN 0-8109-3220-2   LC 94-8420
"The many contradictions in Degas's life, including the contrasts between his artistic theories and that of the

Degas, Edgar, 1834-1917—*Continued*

Impressionists with whom his name is associated, serve as the unifying theme of a solid, handsomely designed biography . . . which sets his major works in the context of the social and political milieu of the late nineteenth century." Horn Book

Delany, Bessie

Delany, Sadie. Having our say. See entry under Delany, Sadie

Delany, Sadie

Delany, Sadie. Having our say; the Delany sisters' first 100 years; [by] Sarah and A. Elizabeth Delany; with Amy Hill Hearth. Kodansha Int./USA 1993 210p il $20   **92**
1. Delany, Bessie 2. Delany family 3. African American women 4. United States—Race relations
ISBN 1-56836-010-X   LC 93-23890
Also available G.K. Hall large print edition and in paperback from Dell
"The Delany sisters' story is a collective meditation on American life since Sadie's birth in 1889 and Bessie's in 1891 in Raleigh, North Carolina. . . . The sisters migrated to New York City's Harlem in the 1910s and in the 1950s to the suburb of Mt. Vernon, New York. The assertive Bessie battled racism and sexism as the only black female member of her Columbia University Dental School class in the 1920s. The more reticent Sadie became the first black domestic science teacher in the New York City high schools." Libr J
"The combination of the two voices, beautifully blended by Ms. Hearth, evokes an epic history, often cruel and brutal, but always deeply humane in their spirited telling of it." N Y Times Book Rev

Dickens, Charles, 1812-1870

Kaplan, Fred. Dickens; a biography. Morrow 1988 607p il o.p.; Avon Bks. paperback available $12.95   **92**
1. Authors, English
ISBN 0-380-70896-5 (pa)   LC 88-12859
"In tracing Dickens's career from 'boy prodigy' to grizzled Victorian giant of letters . . . Kaplan covers his roles as journalist, novelist, social reformer and businessman." Publ Wkly
"Kaplan has synthesized the vast amount of biodata into a coherent account of Dickens's public and private selves. . . . Important to Dickens scholars while accessible to the general public." Libr J
Includes bibliography

Martin, Christopher. Charles Dickens. Rourke 1990 112p il (Life and works) lib bdg $19.94
          92
1. Authors, English
ISBN 0-86593-016-3   LC 89-28320
Explores the life and work of the nineteenth-century English novelist
Includes glossary and bibliographical references

Smith, Grahame. Charles Dickens; a literary life. St. Martin's Press 1996 190p (Literary lives) $29.95   **92**
1. Authors, English
ISBN 0-312-12919-X   LC 95-31652
Smith "concentrates on Dickens as a professional writer, describing and analyzing the literary contexts that surrounded Dickens as he was writing his novels. . . . [The author] succeeds in contextualizing Dickens's career as a professional writer; his discussions of Dickens's efforts in every realm of publishing and his interest in the economic, social, and religious issues of his time are admirable." Choice
Includes bibliographical references

Dickinson, Emily, 1830-1886

Longsworth, Polly. The world of Emily Dickinson. Norton 1990 136p il maps $35   **92**
1. Poets, American 2. Women poets
ISBN 0-393-02892-5   LC 90-31672
Drawings, maps, and photographs illustrate the home, friends, landscape and influence of the nineteenth-century American poet

Wolff, Cynthia Griffin. Emily Dickinson. Knopf 1986 641p il $25   **92**
1. Poets, American 2. Women poets
ISBN 0-394-54418-8   LC 86-15192
Also available in paperback from Addison-Wesley
This biography of the New England poet focuses on her life in relation to her literary work. The biographer maintains that "early stresses became the source of the anxiety, terror, doubt, mistrust, grief and rage that pervade Dickinson's poetry." N Y Times Book Rev
"The rich interweaving of times, life, mind, and letters makes this a formidable addition to the canon of enduring Dickinson studies." Libr J
Includes bibliography

Dillard, Annie

Dillard, Annie. An American childhood. Harper & Row 1987 255p hardcover o.p. paperback available $13   **92**
1. Authors, American 2. Women authors
ISBN 0-06-091518-8 (pa)   LC 87-45042
In this autobiography, the author of Pilgrim at Tinker Creek (entered in class 818) presents an account of her life from her childhood in Pittsburgh until her entrance into college
"Dillard fans will especially appreciate the insight she offers into her early consciousness and development, while others will enjoy this picture of growing up in the 1950s or simply the humor and sensitivity of the writing." Libr J

DiMaggio, Joe

Stout, Glenn. DiMaggio; an illustrated life; edited by Dick Johnson; text by Glenn Stout. Walker & Co. 1995 272p il $29.95   **92**
1. Baseball—Biography
ISBN 0-8027-1311-4   LC 95-31775
"Biographical segments discuss the subject's life off the playing field, and essays are devoted to his impact on

DiMaggio, Joe—*Continued*

the game. . . . The numerous black-and-white photographs and large bold print will immediately catch readers' attention. The interesting writing style is succinct and to the point." SLJ

Includes bibliographical references

Disney, Walt, 1901-1966

Schickel, Richard. The Disney version; the life, times, art, and commerce of Walt Disney. 3rd ed. Dee, I.R. 1997 384p pa $14.95   **92**

1. Walt Disney Company 2. Motion pictures—Biography

ISBN 1-56663-158-0   LC 96-52429

"Elephant paperbacks"

First published 1968 by Simon & Schuster

The author "takes us from Disney's wandering youth through the desperate gamble of opening his own animation studio, his daring decision to crash Hollywood, the sudden, inspired invention of Mickey Mouse on a transcontinental train ride—and on to the creation of a multimillion-dollar international entertainment empire." Publisher's note

Includes bibliographical references

Douglass, Frederick, 1817?-1895

Douglass, Frederick. Autobiographies. Library of Am. 1994 1126p $35; pa $13.95   **92**

1. Abolitionists 2. African Americans—Biography

ISBN 0-940450-79-8; 1-883011-30-2 (pa)

LC 93-24168

Contents: Narrative of the life of Frederick Douglass, an American slave; My Bondage and my freedom; Life and times of Frederick Douglass

"This one volume containing Douglass's seminal works is highly recommended for black history collections." Libr J

Includes bibliographical references

Douglass, Frederick. The life and times of Frederick Douglass; his early life as a slave, his escape from bondage, and his complete history; written by himself   **92**

1. Abolitionists 2. African Americans—Biography

Hardcover and paperback editions available from various publishers

Reprinted from the revised edition of My bondage and my freedom, published 1892

"The first section pictures several different ways slavery was practiced. . . . The second section deals with the rise and development of the abolitionist cause and Douglass' experiences in England. The last section emphasizes politics and Douglass' relationships with and opinions of Presidents Lincoln, Johnson, Hayes, Grant, Garfield, and Cleveland." Stanford. Black Lit for Sch Stud

Huggins, Nathan Irvin. Slave and citizen: the life of Frederick Douglass; edited by Oscar Handlin. Little, Brown 1980 194p (Library of American biography) o.p.; Scott, Foresman paperback available $16   **92**

1. Abolitionists 2. African Americans—Biography

ISBN 0-673-39342-9 (pa)   LC 79-89336

"Huggins has written the preeminent biography of the preeminent black man of the 19th Century. . . . This in-

telligent, insightful, and even angry, book offers an excellent introduction to Douglass, black life, and the snarls of race relations in the last century." Libr J

Includes bibliographical references

McFeely, William S. Frederick Douglass. Norton 1991 465p il map $24.95; pa $12.95   **92**

1. Abolitionists 2. African Americans—Biography

ISBN 0-393-02823-2; 0-393-31376-X (pa)

LC 89-36517

This "biography of Frederick Douglass supplies a welcome portrait of the slave-turned-abolitionist-orator and a careful reconsideration of his ideas and writings." Booklist

Includes bibliographical references

Doyle, Sir Arthur Conan, 1859-1930

Symons, Julian. Conan Doyle: portrait of an artist. Mysterious Press 1987 c1979 137p il hardcover o.p. paperback available $9.95   **92**

1. Authors, English

ISBN 0-89296-926-1 (pa)   LC 87-20432

First published 1979 in the United Kingdom

Symons "writes knowledgeably and empathetically about the prolific Victorian doctor turned author. . . . The book contains perceptive comments on the Holmesian adventures and other literary works that Doyle considered superior to the detecting tales that made him enduringly famous." Publ Wkly

Includes bibliography

Drake, Sir Francis, 1540?-1596

Cummins, John G. (John George). Francis Drake; the lives of a hero; [by] John Cummins. St. Martin's Press 1995 348p il maps $29.95   **92**

1. Explorers

ISBN 0-312-15811-4   LC 95-43509

"The author reexamines the myth of Francis Drake the Elizabethan adventurer in order to present a truly balanced chronicle of Francis Drake the man. . . . As Cummins recounts Drake's humble origins and meteoric rise, a full-bodied portrait of a brilliant but flawed hero emerges. Fueled by a dazzling combination of luck, talent, and ambition, Drake parlayed a successful career as a navigator and a profiteer into a formidable legend that has survived centuries of scrutiny." Booklist

Includes bibliographical references

Du Bois, W. E. B. (William Edward Burghardt), 1868-1963

Du Bois, W. E. B. (William Edward Burghardt). The autobiography of W. E. B. DuBois; a soliloquy on viewing my life from the last decade of its first century. International Pubs. (NY) 1968 448p il $19; pa $10.95   **92**

1. African Americans—Biography

ISBN 0-7178-0235-3; 0-7178-0234-5 (pa)

Edited by Herbert Aptheker

Completed in 1960 when Du Bois was past ninety, the black leader gives an account of his life

"What is especially unique about the Autobiography . . . is the insight it offers into his personality. . . . The

Du Bois, W. E. B. (William Edward Burghardt), 1868-1963—*Continued*
other fresh contribution made by the Autobiography is its synthesis of Du Bois's activities and thought." Saturday Rev
Includes bibliography

Lewis, David Levering. W.E.B. DuBois; biography of a race, 1868-1919. Holt & Co. 1993 735p il $35; pa $17.95   **92**
1. African Americans—Biography 2. African Americans—Civil rights
ISBN 0-8050-2621-5; 0-8050-3568-0 (pa)
LC 93-16617
In this first volume of a projected two-volume set, "the first 50 years of DuBois's life are detailed, not only on a personal level but also in the context of American history. This exhaustive study includes an in-depth analysis of the civil rights movement of the 19th and early 20th centuries. . . . A magnificent resource." SLJ
Includes bibliographical references

Marable, Manning. W.E.B. DuBois, black radical democrat. Twayne Pubs. 1986 285p il (Twayne's twentieth-century American biography series) lib bdg $28.95   **92**
1. African Americans—Biography
ISBN 0-8057-7750-4   LC 86-14881
The author examines "the body of Du Bois' social thought in all its branches, from segregation to Christianity, from colonialism to communism. What emerges is the common thread running through all Du Bois' work." Booklist
"A valuable and useful study." Libr J
Includes bibliography

McKissack, Patricia C. W.E.B. DuBois; [by] Patricia and Fredrick McKissack. Watts 1990 143p il (Impact biography) lib bdg $21.20   **92**
1. African Americans—Biography
ISBN 0-531-10939-9   LC 90-37823
"This is a biography that emphasizes [Du Bois'] dedication, determination, disappointment, and triumph in the continuing struggle for worldwide human rights." Voice Youth Advocates
"A revealing book . . . that should entice readers to seek more information about this complex man." SLJ
Includes bibliography

Duncan, Isadora, 1878-1927
Life into art: Isadora Duncan and her world; edited by Dorée Duncan, Carol Pratl, and Cynthia Splatt; foreword by Agnes de Mille; text by Cynthia Splatt. Norton 1993 199p il $40   **92**
1. Dancers
ISBN 0-393-03507-7   LC 93-1737
The "text spans Duncan's life and career, including her childhood and early years as a dancer, her attempts at establishing a school, the tragic loss of her children, her later years, and her untimely death. . . . Although words and still pictures can never fully capture the art that is dance, this rich and detailed book comes very close." Libr J

Duncan, Lois, 1934-
Duncan, Lois. Chapters: my growth as a writer. Little, Brown 1982 263p o.p.   **92**
1. Authors, American 2. Women authors
LC 81-19339
"Lois Duncan began writing and submitting short stories when she was ten, received her first check when she was thirteen, and continued as a magazine writer for many years before she turned to book-length novels. In this . . . [autobiography, she includes] examples of her stories and [attempts to] show how she used material and people from her real life experiences." Bull Cent Child Books

Earhart, Amelia, 1898-1937
Lovell, Mary S. The sound of wings: the life of Amelia Earhart. St. Martin's Press 1989 xxv, 420p il hardcover o.p. paperback available $17.95   **92**
1. Women air pilots
ISBN 0-312-05160-3 (pa)   LC 89-34935
This biography concentrates on Earhart's "personality and character and the relationships with family and friends as they contributed to her accomplishments. . . . The book also contains excerpts from *Last Flight*, Earhart's reworked logbook and notes on the fateful 1937 flight." Libr J
Includes bibliographical references

Rich, Doris L. Amelia Earhart; a biography. Smithsonian Institution Press 1989 321p il $27.50; pa $14.95   **92**
1. Women air pilots
ISBN 0-87474-836-4; 1-56098-725-1 (pa)
LC 89-32181
"Rich emphasizes Earhart's flying career and the stories and personalities behind her accomplishments. It is a scholarly account of her life, highlighting her goals, enthusiasm, and competitive pioneer spirit." Libr J
A "fast-paced, richly detailed biography." Publ Wkly
Includes bibliography

Edison, Thomas A. (Thomas Alva), 1847-1931
Adair, Gene. Thomas Alva Edison; inventing the electric age. Oxford Univ. Press 1996 141p il (Oxford portraits in science) $20   **92**
1. Inventors
ISBN 0-19-508799-2   LC 95-37499
Details the life and work of Thomas Edison, who developed the electric light bulb and over 1000 patents for other inventions and innovations
Edison's "life reads like the adventure it was and will delight pleasure readers and information seekers alike. Adair carefully explains the scientific principles on which Edison based his work and devotes sidebars to particular inventions. Black-and-white photos and many of Edison's sketches and patent drawings enhance the text." Booklist
Includes bibliography

Einstein, Albert, 1879-1955

Brian, Denis. Einstein; a life. Wiley 1996 509p $30 **92**
1. Physicists
ISBN 0-471-11459-6 LC 95-12075
In this "anecdotal look at the scientist, the author begins with Einstein's childhood and youth in Germany and Switzerland. He proceeds to chronologically trace the personal life, education and career of this remarkably multifaceted, gifted scholar, scientist, musician, teacher, husband, father and friend, and his attempts to pursue a relatively normal personal life and scientific career, under the intense scrutiny of world and academic powers and an awed and admiring public." Book Rep
Includes bibliographical references

Goldberg, Jacob. Albert Einstein. Watts 1996 128p il (Impact biography) lib bdg $22.70 **92**
1. Physicists
ISBN 0-531-11251-9 LC 95-48768
Describes the life and work of the scientist whose theory of relativity revolutionized scientific thinking
"Goldberg's well-written summary of biographical information provides a well-organized and quite readable account of Einstein's life story." Booklist
Includes glossary and bibliography

Hoffmann, Banesh. Albert Einstein, creator and rebel; [by] Banesh Hoffmann with the collaboration of Helen Dukas. Viking 1972 272p il o.p.; New Am. Lib. paperback available $12.95 **92**
1. Physicists
ISBN 0-452-26193-7 (pa)
An "account of Einstein's life and personality. The hallmark of this book however, is its technical exposition on Einstein's theories and the way he developed them. . . . It is rare to find such technical competence accompanying a good biography." Sci Books

Eisenhower, Dwight D. (Dwight David), 1890-1969

Ambrose, Stephen E. Eisenhower; soldier and president. Simon & Schuster 1990 635p il hardcover o.p. paperback available $16 **92**
1. Presidents—United States 2. Generals
ISBN 0-671-74758-4 (pa) LC 90-9701
Condensed version of a two volume work published 1983-1984
"Tracing Eisenhower's family background, education, military and political careers, and influence as elder statesman, the author chronicles Eisenhower's triumphs and failures and at the same time provides a vivid picture of the off-duty Ike. . . . This is the definitive one-volume biography of Eisenhower." Publ Wkly
Includes bibliographical references

Elizabeth I, Queen of England, 1533-1603

Somerset, Anne. Elizabeth I. Knopf 1991 636p il hardcover o.p.; St. Martin's Press paperback available $15.95 **92**
1. Great Britain—History—1485-1603, Tudors
ISBN 0-312-08183-9 (pa) LC 91-52731
The author "offers some fresh thinking about various factors and actions of Elizabeth, queen and woman,

including the influence on her sense of identity played by the execution and infamy of her mother, Anne Boleyn, and, toward the end of her reign, her refusal to name a successor." Booklist
The author "painstakingly reconstructs the world of the late 16th century. The research behind her portrayal of Elizabeth is prodigious, and her attention to particulars is unfailing." N Y Times Book Rev
Includes bibliographical references

Elizabeth II, Queen of Great Britain, 1926-

Bradford, Sarah. Elizabeth; a biography of Britain's Queen. Farrar, Straus & Giroux 1996 564p il $30 **92**
1. Great Britain—Kings, queens, rulers, etc.
ISBN 0-374-14749-3 LC 95-47619
In this biography "the author offers both inside knowledge and a keen assessment of the real nature not only of the main subject herself but also of her mother and her father, the late George VI and the beloved Queen mother; her sister, unhappy Princess Margaret; and (in the face of the queen's emphasis on being a conscientious sovereign rather than a dedicated mother) her four children. This . . . will remain the best word on the queen for some time to come." Booklist
Includes bibliographical references

Longford, Elizabeth Harman Pakenham, Countess of. The Queen: the life of Elizabeth II; [by] Elizabeth Longford. Knopf 1983 415p il o.p. **92**
1. Great Britain—Kings, queens, rulers, etc. 2. Great Britain—History—1900-1999 (20th century) LC 83-48115
"The book begins with Elizabeth's birth in 1926 and describes her and her sister, Princess Margaret (four years younger), growing up happily. . . . Longford describes the excitement and sorrows thereafter: Elizabeth's marriage to Philip, the death of her father, the years following her coronation." Publ Wkly
Includes bibliography

Ellington, Duke, 1899-1974

✓ Collier, James Lincoln. Duke Ellington. Oxford Univ. Press 1987 340p il $31.25 **92**
1. Jazz musicians 2. African American musicians
ISBN 0-19-503770-7 LC 86-33309
This book, "which includes minibiographies of Ellington's sidemen and detailed musical discussions of individual recordings, is a . . . reflective look at Ellington's career and recordings. The greater part is devoted to Ellington's salad days as a bandleader from the 1920s to the 1940s." Libr J
Includes discography

✓ Ellington, Duke. Music is my mistress; by Edward Kennedy Ellington. Doubleday 1973 522p il o.p.; Da Capo Press paperback available $15.95 **92**
1. Jazz musicians 2. African American musicians
ISBN 0-306-80033-0 (pa)
"After a prologue there are eight acts unfolding in chronological order—all dealing with Duke Ellington's

Ellington, Duke, 1899-1974—*Continued*

life. . . . The book is complete with abundant pictures of family, friends, and influential people the composer-bandleader-pianist has met and played with." Best Sellers

Includes bibliography and discography

Farrakhan, Louis

Magida, Arthur J. Prophet of rage: a life of Louis Farrakhan and his nation. Basic Bks. 1996 xxiii, 264p il $25   92

1. African Americans—Biography

ISBN 0-465-06436-1   LC 96-2767

This is a "biography of controversial Nation of Islam leader Louis Farrakhan. . . . Magida details Farrakhan's public record, heated conflicts with the Jewish community, and political positions that were often contrary to those of such Civil Rights leaders as Martin Luther King Jr." Libr J

"Hardly the last word on either Farrakhan, who finally seems a figure motivated primarily by love of notoriety, or the Nation of Islam, Magida's effort is still good enough as a first take on both." Booklist

Includes bibliographical references

Fermi, Enrico, 1901-1954

Gottfried, Ted. Enrico Fermi, pioneer of the atomic age. Facts on File 1992 138p il (Makers of modern science) lib bdg $17.95   92

1. Physicists

ISBN 0-8160-2623-8   LC 92-14683

Describes the life and work of the Nobel prize-winning physicist known for his research in the area of nuclear energy

This is "excellent. . . . Gottfried is adept at explaining complex principles of physics and the political background in Italy that eventually led Fermi to America and his work on the atomic bomb." SLJ

Includes glossary and bibliography

Filipovic, Zlata

Filipovic, Zlata. Zlata's diary; a child's life in Sarajevo; with an introduction by Janine Di Giovanni; translated with notes by Christina Pribichevich-Zorić. Viking 1994 200p il hardcover o.p. paperback available $7.95   92

1. Sarajevo (Bosnia and Hercegovina)

ISBN 0-14-024205-8 (pa)   LC 94-165459

"In September 1991, at the beginning of a new school year and while war was already as close as Croatia, Filipovic, a ten-year-old girl in Sarajevo began keeping a diary about her school friends, her classes, and her after-school activities. The following spring that childhood world disappeared when the war moved to Sarajevo." Libr J

"Filipovic's diary personalizes the tragedy in war-torn Sarajevo. A must for YA collections." Booklist

Fitzgerald, Ella

Wyman, Carolyn. Ella Fitzgerald; jazz singer supreme. Watts 1993 128p il (Impact biography) lib bdg $22.70; pa $6.95   92

1. African American singers 2. African American women

ISBN 0-531-13031-2 (lib bdg); 0-531-15679-6 (pa)   LC 92-41969

This biography chronicles the personal life and singing career of the well-known jazz artist and discusses her impact on contemporary music

"Including source notes, a discography, and a bibliography, the book will be a good reference source." Booklist

Fitzgerald, F. Scott (Francis Scott), 1896-1940

Fitzgerald, F. Scott (Francis Scott). A life in letters; edited by Matthew J. Bruccoli; with the assistance of Judith S. Baughman. Scribner 1994 xxiii, 503p $30; pa $16   92

1. Authors, American

ISBN 0-684-19570-4; 0-684-80153-1 (pa)   LC 93-31011

"Early letters to his editor, Maxwell Perkins, and friends, Edmund Wilson and Ernest Hemingway, document Fitzgerald's devotion to craft, exemplified by *The Great Gatsby* (1925), as well as the novelist's ever-present financial problems. . . . Letters to his wife, Zelda—when she was hospitalized for mental illness—detail the destruction of their marriage." Publ Wkly

"Essential reading for a full understanding of Fitzgerald as an artist and a man." Libr J

Flaubert, Gustave, 1821-1880

Lottman, Herbert R. Flaubert; a biography. Little, Brown 1989 396p il $24.95   92

1. Authors, French

ISBN 0-316-53342-4   LC 88-21919

Also available in paperback from Fromm Int.

"Lottman regards Flaubert as a master of his craft and as perhaps the first truly modern author. Instead of depending on opinions on Flaubert's habits and talent, the biographer has researched his subject in many original documents. . . . The reassessment made possible by this method corrects some previous misconceptions and redefines the impressive acclaim that Flaubert has already been accorded." Booklist

Includes bibliography

Ford, Gerald R., 1913-

Cannon, James M. Time and chance: Gerald Ford's appointment with history. HarperCollins Pubs. 1993 496p il $25   92

1. Presidents—United States 2. United States—Politics and government—1961-1974 3. United States—Politics and government—1974-1989

ISBN 0-06-016539-1   LC 92-53362

An "account of the political and personal style of Gerald R. Ford. . . . Early chapters examine his difficult childhood prior to his mother's marriage to Gerald R. Ford, whose name he later adopted. While aficianados of political biography will enjoy the chapters detailing the

Ford, Gerald R., 1913——*Continued*

young Representative Ford's climb up the House ladder, the real contribution of this work comes in the second half when Cannon details the agony of the new vice president Ford . . . as he watches his old friend and political colleague Richard Nixon destroy his presidency. Riveting and insight-filled, this book is highly recommended for all collections." Libr J

Includes bibliographical references

Foreman, George

Foreman, George. By George; the autobiography of George Foreman; [by] George Foreman and Joel Engel. Villard Bks. 1995 262p il $23   92
1. Boxing—Biography 2. African American athletes
ISBN 0-679-44394-0   LC 95-7693
The "world heavyweight boxing champ pulls no punches in this account of his life." Libr J

Fossey, Dian

Mowat, Farley. Woman in the mists: the story of Dian Fossey and the mountain gorillas of Africa. Warner Bks. 1987 380p il hardcover o.p. paperback available $11.99   92
1. Gorillas
ISBN 0-446-38720-7 (pa)   LC 87-40166
Ethologist Fossey studied mountain gorillas in Rwanda, Africa, for nineteen years until her murder in December, 1985. Mowat uses Fossey's diaries and personal archives in this biography
"YAs will identify with Fossey's vision, idealism, and vigor and, thanks to Mowat's skill as a writer, feel the loss of an intimate friend." SLJ

Francis, of Assisi, Saint, 1182-1226

Green, Julien. God's fool: the life and times of Francis of Assisi; translated by Peter Heinegg. Harper & Row 1985 273p hardcover o.p. paperback available $13   92
1. Christian saints
ISBN 0-06-063464-2 (pa)   LC 84-48771
Original French edition, 1983
An "account of the life of Francesco Bernardone, the riotous, reveling son of a silk merchant, who underwent a dramatic, God-inspired personal transformation, eventually becoming known to the world as the beloved saint of Assisi. Green has woven a thick fabric of history into his tale. . . . A remarkable and absorbing profile." Booklist

Frank, Anne, 1929-1945

Frank, Anne. The diary of a young girl; translated from the Dutch by B. M. Mooyaart-Doubleday   92
1. World War, 1939-1945—Jews 2. Netherlands—History—1940-1945, German occupation 3. Jews—Netherlands
Available in various bindings and editions including Spanish language edition
This is the diary of a "German-Jewish girl who hid from the Nazis with her parents, their friends, and some other fugitives in an Amsterdam warehouse from 1942 to 1944. Her diary, covering the years of hiding, was found by friends and published as *Het achterhus* (1947); it was later published in English as *The Diary of a Young Girl* (1952). . . . Written with humor as well as insight, it shows a growing girl with all the preoccupations of adolescence and first love. The diary ends three days before the Franks and their group were discovered by the Nazis." Reader's Ency. 4th edition

Frank, Anne. The diary of a young girl: the definitive edition; edited by Otto H. Frank and Mirjam Pressler; translated by Susan Massotty. Doubleday 1995 340p il $25; pa $12.95   92
1. World War, 1939-1945—Jews 2. Netherlands—History—1940-1945, German occupation 3. Jews—Netherlands
ISBN 0-385-47378-8; 0-385-48033-4 (pa)
LC 94-41379
Also available G.K. Hall large print edition
"This new translation of Frank's famous diary includes material about her emerging sexuality and her relationship with her mother that was originally excised by Frank's father, the only family member to survive the Holocaust." Libr J

Franklin, Aretha

Gourse, Leslie. Aretha Franklin; Lady Soul. Watts 1995 160p il (Impact biography) lib bdg $22.70; pa $8   92
1. African American singers 2. African American women
ISBN 0-531-13037-1 (lib bdg); 0-531-15750-4 (pa)
LC 94-29074
"Gourse chronicles the personal life and musical development of the multidimensional singer, whose voice and music have been influenced by blues, gospel, soul, and jazz. . . . This detailed and well-written book meets a need for solid biographies of famous African American women." SLJ
Includes discography, filmography, and bibliography

Franklin, Benjamin, 1706-1790

Franklin, Benjamin. The autobiography of Benjamin Franklin   92
Hardcover and paperback editions available from various publishers
"Franklin's account of his life, written for his son William. . . . During the Revolutionary War, the manuscript was put aside. . . . Franklin later more than doubled the length . . . but still took the story only to 1757-1759, ending before the period of his greatest public service. Still, the book remains the first undisputed classic of American literature and one of the most interesting autobiographies in English." Benet's Reader's Ency of Am Lit

Frazier, Joe

Frazier, Joe. Smokin' Joe; the autobiography of a heavyweight champion of the world, Smokin' Joe Frazier; [by] Joe Frazier with Phil Berger. Macmillan 1996 213p il $23.95 **92**
1. Boxing—Biography 2. African American athletes
ISBN 0-02-860847-X LC 96-4067
This biography of the heavyweight boxing champion covers his rise to fame with emphasis on his rivalry with boxer Muhammad Ali
Frazier retells his "story in colorful and pungent detail." N Y Times Book Rev

Freeman, Dorothy, 1898-1978

Carson, Rachel. Always, Rachel. See entry under Carson, Rachel, 1907-1964

Freeman, Joseph, 1915-

Freeman, Joseph. Job; the story of a Holocaust survivor. Praeger Pubs. 1996 130p maps $19.95; pa $9.95 **92**
1. Jews—Poland 2. Holocaust, 1933-1945—Personal narratives
ISBN 0-275-95586-9; 1-55778-738-7 (pa)
LC 96-3627
"Early in 1941 the Freeman family was forced to move into a ghetto. In August 1942, Nazis attacked the ghetto, killing many of the Jews. The author's mother, father, brother, and sister were sent to their deaths. Freeman was taken to work in a leather goods factory; later, he was forced to join other Jews on a three-week march to Auschwitz, and he was shifted to other camps until he was rescued by U.S. Army troops. Freeman ends with his subsequent marriage to another survivor, their immigration to and life in America, and his meeting with the American soldier who had liberated him 40 years earlier." Booklist
Includes bibliographical references

Freud, Sigmund, 1856-1939

Gay, Peter. Freud; a life for our time. Norton 1988 xx, 810p il $30 **92**
1. Psychiatrists
ISBN 0-393-02517-9 LC 87-20454
Also available in paperback from Anchor Bks. (NY)
This biography provides an "updating of our knowledge of the life of the founder of psychoanalysis . . . and it also delineates the continuing impact of Freud's thought on modern endeavors in a number of fields." Sci Books Films
"The book is beautifully written. Gay's approach is to try to understand Freud and his alliances and environment rather than to worship or challenge him." Choice
Includes bibliography

Frost, Robert, 1874-1963

Bober, Natalie. A restless spirit: the story of Robert Frost; by Natalie S. Bober. rev & expanded ed. Holt & Co. 1991 197p il $19.95 **92**
1. Poets, American
ISBN 0-8050-1672-4 LC 91-13970
First published 1981 by Atheneum Pubs.

A biography of the famous American poet, detailing the events of his frequently unhappy life, his love for his wife and children, and the way all of this was woven into his poetry
Includes bibliography

Meyers, Jeffrey. Robert Frost; a biography. Houghton Mifflin 1996 424p il $30 **92**
1. Poets, American
ISBN 0-395-72809-6 LC 95-45647
"A Peter Davison book"
In this biography Meyers contends "that Frost lived his life for and through poetry and that poetry prompted many of his life responses to events ranging from the seduction of his wife to the death of his children." Libr J
"The author provides new facts, useful sketches of the many people Frost dealt with, a sympathetic but not idolatrous view of Frost's character and actions, and an astute if sometimes overanalytical interpretation of his poetry." Atl Mon
Includes bibliography

Fulton, Arabella, 1844-1934

Fulton, Arabella. A pioneer woman's memoir; based on the journal of Arabella Clemens Fulton; [edited by] Judith E. Greenberg and Helen Carey McKeever. Watts 1995 160p il map (In their own words) lib bdg $22.70 **92**
1. Frontier and pioneer life—West (U.S.) 2. West (U.S.)—History
ISBN 0-531-11211-X LC 94-48043
"In 1864, Arabella Clemens Fulton left Missouri to follow the Oregon Trail with her sisters and their husbands. This edited version of her memoir is both insightful and entertaining. Each chapter begins with introductory remarks by the editors, then continues Arabella's story, beginning with the time she left on the wagon train until the end of her life." Book Rep
Includes bibliography

Gaines, Ernest J., 1933-

Gaines, Ernest J. Conversations with Ernest Gaines; edited by John Lowe. University Press of Miss. 1995 335p il (Literary conversations series) $39.50; pa $15.95 **92**
1. Authors, American 2. African American authors
ISBN 0-87805-782-X; 0-87805-783-8 (pa)
LC 95-13838
This is a collection of interviews given by the African American author between 1969 and 1994

Galilei, Galileo, 1564-1642

Reston, James, Jr. Galileo; a life. HarperCollins Pubs. 1994 319p il hardcover o.p. paperback available $13.50 **92**
ISBN 0-06-092607-4 (pa) LC 93-29221
The author "delineates the personal and institutional storms that Galileo endured and seemed unerringly to seek out. He collided with church authorities in Rome, his peers and a succession of patrons. Reston scants both science and 17th-century theology in setting the stage for the general reader, but he recreates the era with immediacy by mining Galileo's journals and letters for dialogue." Publ Wkly
Includes bibliographical references

Gallaudet, T. H. (Thomas Hopkins), 1787-1851
Neimark, Anne E. A deaf child listened:
Thomas Gallaudet, pioneer in American education.
Morrow 1983 116p $15   92
1. Deaf—Education
ISBN 0-688-01719-3   LC 82-23942
This biography of the man who established the first
school for the deaf in the United States "is both a record
of Gallaudet's life and his battles on behalf of deaf chil-
dren." Bull Cent Child Books
The author presents "a thorough sketch of the man,
personally and professionally. She does not end the book
with Gallaudet's death, but with the progress deaf education has made . . . including a synopsis of Gallaudet
College. A well-researched, readable book." SLJ
Includes bibliography

Gandhi, Mahatma, 1869-1948
Gandhi, Mahatma. All men are brothers; life
and thoughts of Mahatma Gandhi as told in his
own words. Unesco Press 1958 196p il o.p.;
Continuum paperback available $11.95   92
1. India—Politics and government
ISBN 0-8264-0003-5 (pa)
"Excerpts from Gandhi's own writings and speeches
form a partial autobiography of the Mahatma. The stress
is on his moral, spiritual, and political experiments rather
than on personal matters, although these are sometimes
briefly mentioned." Booklist

García Márquez, Gabriel, 1928-
Bell-Villada, Gene H. García Márquez; the man
and his work. University of N.C. Press 1990 247p
maps hardcover o.p. paperback available $17.95
                                                        92
1. Authors, Colombian
ISBN 0-8078-4264-8 (pa)   LC 89-16474
A look at the life and work of the Colombian Nobel
laureate
"Throughout the book, the looming presence of *One
Hundred Years of Solitude* and the multiplicity of symbols, imagery, and allusions to other literature can be
found." SLJ
Includes bibliography

Garibaldi, Giuseppe, 1807-1882
Mack Smith, Denis. Garibaldi. Knopf 1956 207p
(Great lives in brief series) o.p.; Greenwood Press
reprint available lib bdg $55   92
1. Italy—History—1815-1914
ISBN 0-313-23618-6 (lib bdg)
A compact biography of Garibaldi, the hero of Italian
independence
"Smith has succeeded in capturing the essence of Gar-
ibaldi's colorful life. Highly readable and informative."
Libr J
Includes bibliography

Garvey, Marcus, 1887-1940
Cronon, E. David (Edmund David). Black
Moses; the story of Marcus Garvey and the
Universal Negro Improvement Association;
foreword by John Hope Franklin. University of
Wis. Press 1955 xxiii, 278p il hardcover o.p.
paperback available $12.95   92
1. Universal Negro Improvement Association
2. African Americans—Biography
ISBN 0-299-01214-X (pa)
The author traces the life of the Jamaica-born black
leader and his rise to fame in the 1920's
"What results from [this] examination of a wide range
of materials . . . is a vivid, detailed and sound portrait
of a man and his dreams." Polit Sci Q

Gauguin, Paul, 1848-1903
Greenfeld, Howard. Paul Gauguin. Abrams 1993
92p il (First impressions) $19.95   92
1. Artists, French
ISBN 0-8109-3376-4   LC 93-9454
Examines the life and work of the nineteenth-century
post-Impressionist painter known for his use of bright
colors and his depiction of South Seas scenes
This is "written in a conversational tone that will hold
readers' interest. . . . The format is an open and inviting
one, and the numerous full-color reproductions are of excellent quality. Engaging and informative." SLJ

Gehrig, Lou, 1903-1941
Robinson, Ray. Iron horse: Lou Gehrig in his
time. Norton 1990 300p il $22.50   92
1. Baseball—Biography
ISBN 0-393-02857-7   LC 89-29272
Also available Thorndike Press large print edition and
in paperback from HarperCollins Pubs.
"Playing in the considerable shadow of Babe Ruth,
Lou Gehrig's accomplishments as baseball's 'Iron Horse'
include a legendary record of 2,130 consecutive games
played. . . . Robinson's narrative not only traces
Gehrig's life and career but also provides an insightful
look at baseball in the 1920s and the Depression years."
Libr J

Geronimo, Apache Chief, 1829-1909
Debo, Angie. Geronimo; the man, his time, his
place. University of Okla. Press 1976 xx, 480p il
(Civilization of the American Indian series)
hardcover o.p. paperback available $18.95   92
1. Apache Indians
ISBN 0-8061-1828-8 (pa)   LC 76-13858
The author "interviewed people who knew Geronimo,
who fought with him and lived with him in captivity.
She has written a colorful narrative of revenge and raids,
of escape, pursuit and surrender. . . . Her portrait of Geronimo the old celebrity is touching, and a tribute to an
exceptional leader." Publ Wkly
Includes bibliography

Gibson, Josh, 1911-1947

Ribowsky, Mark. The power and the darkness: the life of Josh Gibson in the shadows of the game. Simon & Schuster 1996 319p il $23   **92**
1. Baseball—Biography 2. African American athletes
ISBN 0-684-80402-6   LC 96-292

"Hall-of-Famer Gibson (1911-1947) was to black baseball what Babe Ruth was to white baseball: a prolific home run hitter who also hit for average. He was a victim of the game's color bar and died just three months before Jackie Robinson broke it. . . . His personal life was darkened by the death of his wife in childbirth, and although he later had a longtime common-law wife, Ribowski raises the question of whether Gibson ever had a happy domestic life." Publ Wkly

"A compelling examination of a fascinating, tragic life." Booklist

Gilbreth, Frank Bunker, 1868-1924

Gilbreth, Frank B. (Frank Bunker). Cheaper by the dozen; [by] Frank B. Gilbreth, Jr. and Ernestine Gilbreth Carey; drawings by Vasiliu. [updated ed] Crowell 1963 245p il o.p.; Bantam Bks. paperback available $5.50   **92**
1. Gilbreth family
ISBN 0-553-27250-0 (pa)

Also available in hardcover from Amereon and Buccaneer Bks.

First published 1948

This biographical portrait of family life highlights the reminiscences of the twelve Gilbreth children and their adventures with their father, whose time and efficiency studies were applied to domestic life

Giovanni, Nikki

Giovanni, Nikki. Conversations with Nikki Giovanni; edited by Virginia C. Fowler. University Press of Miss. 1992 xxii, 220p il (Literary conversations series) hardcover o.p. paperback available $15.95   **92**
1. African American authors 2. Women poets
ISBN 0-87805-587-8 (pa)   LC 92-28484

This collection of interviews with poet Nikki Giovanni spans 20 years and traces "the evolution of Giovanni's art and outlook. . . . Fowler's introduction and chronology summarize Giovanni's often paradoxical career and highlight recurring themes that emerge in the poet's interviews." Booklist

Goddard, Robert Hutchings, 1882-1945

Coil, Suzanne M. Robert Hutchings Goddard; pioneer of rocketry and space flight. Facts on File 1992 134p il (Makers of modern science) lib bdg $17.95   **92**
1. Physicists
ISBN 0-8160-2591-6   LC 91-47503

Discusses the life and achievements of a pioneer in the fields of rocketry and space flight
Includes bibliographical references

Goldwater, Barry M. (Barry Morris), 1909-

Goldwater, Barry M. (Barry Morris). Goldwater; by Barry M. Goldwater with Jack Casserly. Doubleday 1988 414p il o.p.; St. Martin's Press paperback available $5.95   **92**
1. United States—Politics and government—1900-1999 (20th century)
ISBN 0-312-92000-8 (pa)   LC 87-38136

"In this memoir, Goldwater focuses primarily on his political career and his role in helping the conservative arm of the Republican Party gain . . . legitimacy and power. In addition to his discussion of the 1964 presidential race . . . he provides chapters on Vietnam, Nixon, Watergate, and Reagan." Libr J

Gooden, Dwight

Klapisch, Bob. High and tight: the rise and fall of Dwight Gooden and Darryl Strawberry. Villard Bks. 1996 228p il $22   **92**
1. Strawberry, Darryl 2. Baseball—Biography 3. African American athletes
ISBN 0-679-44899-3   LC 96-10532

"Dwight Gooden and Darryl Strawberry were baseball superstars. . . . They had trouble with alcohol and other drugs. Both fell afoul of the law, were suspended from Major League Baseball, and eventually scraped bottom when they could not rehabilitate themselves. At the book's end, both men are trying to stay clean and come back to baseball." Book Rep

Goodman, Benny, 1909-1986

Collier, James Lincoln. Benny Goodman and the Swing Era. Oxford Univ. Press 1989 404p il $36.50; pa $10.95   **92**
1. Jazz musicians
ISBN 0-19-505278-1; 0-19-506776-2 (pa)
LC 89-16030

Collier "recreates a colorful popular music world of the 1920s and 1930s, as he chronicles the rise and success of Goodman and his band against the social milieu and popular music of the time. The author captures the musician's elusive personality as well as analyzes dozens of Goodman's significant recordings." Univ Press Books for Public Libr
Includes bibliography

Goya, Francisco, 1746-1828

Waldron, Ann. Francisco Goya. Abrams 1992 92p il (First impressions) $19.95   **92**
1. Artists, Spanish
ISBN 0-8109-3368-3   LC 92-7086

A biography of the Spanish painter, a forerunner of the impressionist movement, who was noted for his royal portraits, his drawings of the horrors of war, and his politically and socially satirical etchings

"Well-spaced text and fine art reproduction, complement the smooth, professionalism of the writing. . . . The biography is a fine introduction to one of the greatest and most interesting painters of Europe." SLJ

Graham, Martha

Graham, Martha. Blood memory. Doubleday 1991 279p il o.p.; Washington Sq. Press paperback available $12   **92**

1. Choreographers 2. Dancers
ISBN 0-671-78217-7 (pa)   LC 91-15444

"In her memoir, the legendary Graham, the leading exponent of contemporary dance, speaks of her remarkable life. She recounts her early apprenticeship with the Denishawn School, her stint as 'Art' in the Greenwich Village Follies, and the struggle to form and maintain her own company." Libr J

"Five months after her death in April [1991] at the age of 96, Martha Graham has given the world a masterly, buoyant legacy of her life and her art. Like her dances, her book 'Blood Memory' explores life inside out and in many roles and guises." N Y Times Book Rev

Grant, Ulysses S. (Ulysses Simpson), 1822-1885

Catton, Bruce. Grant moves south; with maps by Samuel H. Bryant. Little, Brown 1960 564p maps $27.95; pa $16.95   **92**

1. United States—History—1861-1865, Civil War—Campaigns 2. Presidents—United States 3. Generals
ISBN 0-316-13207-1; 0-316-13244-6 (pa)

"Grant's development as a man and leader is brilliantly shown in this reconstruction of his Mississippi campaign." Booklist
Includes bibliography

Catton, Bruce. Grant takes command; with maps by Samuel H. Bryant. Little, Brown 1969 556p maps hardcover o.p. paperback available $15.95   **92**

1. United States—History—1861-1865, Civil War—Campaigns 2. Presidents—United States 3. Generals
ISBN 0-316-13240-3 (pa)

This sequel to Grant moves South, entered above, "takes up Ulysses S. Grant's career just after his capture of Vicksburg in 1863. . . . It carries the action right up to Richmond and Lee's surrender at Appomattox." Publ Wkly
Includes bibliography

Smith, Gene. Lee and Grant. See entry under Lee, Robert E. (Robert Edward), 1807-1870

Graves, Robert, 1895-1985

Graves, Robert. Goodbye to all that. new ed, revised with a prologue and an epilogue. Doubleday 1957 347p pa $12   **92**

1. World War, 1914-1918—Personal narratives
ISBN 0-385-09330-6
Also available in hardcover from P. Smith
"Doubleday Anchor books"
First published 1929 in the United Kingdom

The author "calls his book an autobiography, and sets his war experiences in between descriptions of his schooldays (just before the war) and of his subsequent adventures since 1918 in the literary world." New Statesman

Griffith, D. W. (David Wark), 1875-1948

Schickel, Richard. D.W. Griffith; an American life. Limelight Eds. 1996 672p il pa $22.50   **92**

1. Motion picture producers and directors
ISBN 0-87910-080-X   LC 96-11304
First published 1984 by Simon & Schuster

The author traces "Griffith's career from his reluctant entry into films in 1908 to his involuntary idleness after 1931." Libr J

"This memorable biography is a beautifully written and boldly assertive analysis of what Griffith wrought." Booklist
Includes bibliographical references

Gunther, John, 1929-1947

Gunther, John. Death be not proud; a memoir. Harper & Row 1949 261p il hardcover o.p. paperback available $7   **92**

ISBN 0-06-080973-6 (pa)
Also available in hardcover from Borgo Press

A memoir of John Gunther's seventeen-year-old son, who died after a series of operations for a brain tumor. Not only a tribute to a remarkable boy but an account of a brave fight against disease

Guthrie, Woody, 1912-1967

Guthrie, Woody. Bound for glory; illustrated with sketches by the author. Dutton 1943 428p il o.p.; New Am. Lib. paperback available $13.95   **92**

1. Musicians
ISBN 0-452-26445-6 (pa)
Also available in hardcover from P. Smith

"Here Woody Guthrie tells his own story, painting vivid pictures of the people he met and the experiences he shared with them. . . . In Guthrie's recollections of his boxcar travels, we hear the music of one of America's best-loved folk poets." Books for You

✓ Hamer, Fannie Lou Townsend, 1917-1977

Mills, Kay. This little light of mine: the life of Fannie Lou Hamer. Dutton 1993 390p il map hardcover o.p. paperback available $13.95   **92**

1. African American women 2. African Americans—Civil rights
ISBN 0-452-27052-9 (pa)   LC 92-19713

"The daughter and wife of poor Mississippi sharecroppers, Hamer was 'converted' to the Civil Rights movement after attending a mass voter-registration meeting in 1962. For the next 15 years, she was in the forefront of major struggles in Mississippi involving voter registration and economic and educational rights for its black citizens." Libr J

"In making sure we see Fannie Lou Hamer in full, Kay Mills has done more than render a biography that is true to its subject. She has provided a history that helps us to understand the choices made by so many black men and women of Hamer's generation." N Y Times Book Rev
Includes bibliographical references

✓ **Hansberry, Lorraine, 1930-1965**

Hansberry, Lorraine. To be young, gifted and black; Lorraine Hansberry in her own words; adapted by Robert Nemiroff; with original drawings and art by Miss Hansberry; and an introduction by James Baldwin. Prentice-Hall 1969 xxii, 266p il   **92**

1. African American authors 2. Women authors

Available in paperback from Random House and New Am. Lib.

Work on this book and on the script for the play of the same title, which was presented at New York's Cherry Lane Theatre in 1969, "proceeded concurrently, each drawing upon the experiences and creative discoveries of the other, but ultimately diverging quite drastically." Postscript

Hart, Moss, 1904-1961

Hart, Moss. Act one: an autobiography. Random House 1959 444p o.p.; St. Martin's Press paperback available $14.95   **92**

1. Theater—United States

ISBN 0-312-03272-2 (pa)

Also available in hardcover from Buccaneer Bks.

"A hilarious account of the playwright's youth and first experiences in the theater. . . . The writer displays the same comic and satiric gifts that mark his later Broadway triumphs. A candid personal history and an affectionate backward glance at the theater of the 1930's." Booklist

Hawking, S. W. (Stephen W.)

McDaniel, Melissa. Stephen Hawking; revolutionary physicist. Chelsea House 1994 111p il (Great achievers: lives of the physically challenged) lib bdg $18.95   **92**

1. Physicists 2. Physically handicapped

ISBN 0-7910-2078-9   LC 93-4832

"Hawking, who suffers from amyotrophic lateral sclerosis (Lou Gehrig's disease), is one of the century's great scientific theorists. [His] physical challenges are neither over- nor underemphasized in the clearly written, well-rounded, and inspiring [biography]." Horn Book Guide

Includes bibliography

Hawthorne, Nathaniel, 1804-1864

Miller, Edwin Haviland. Salem is my dwelling place: a life of Nathaniel Hawthorne. University of Iowa Press 1991 596p il $37.95; pa $18.95   **92**

1. Authors, American

ISBN 0-87745-332-2; 0-87745-381-0 (pa)

LC 91-14543

This is a biography of the 19th century American novelist

"Psychologically probing (but free of all jargon), Miller's elegantly written study gives us a fresh, sympathetic picture of an immensely complex, repressed man. . . . A masterful work, wholly satisfying." Libr J

Includes bibliographical references

Hayslip, Le Ly

Hayslip, Le Ly. When heaven and earth changed places: a Vietnamese woman's journey from war to peace; [by] Le Ly Hayslip with Jay Wurts. Doubleday 1989 368p o.p.; New Am. Lib. paperback available $12.95   **92**

1. Vietnam War, 1961-1975—Personal narratives

ISBN 0-452-27168-1 (pa)   LC 88-33542

"Hayslip was born a Vietnamese peasant in 1949; little more than 20 years later she left for the United States with an American husband. Her early years were spent as a Viet Cong courier and lookout; a black marketeer; an unwed mother; a bar girl; a hospital aide. . . . She was tortured by the South Vietnamese army, raped by Viet Cong, and harassed by Americans. This story is juxtaposed with the tale of her . . . return to Vietnam in 1986." Libr J

"The book is a searing and human account of Vietnam's destruction and self-destruction. Lucidly, sometimes even lyrically, Ms. Hayslip paints an intensely intimate portrait." N Y Times Book Rev

Hearst, William Randolph, 1863-1951

Swanberg, W. A. Citizen Hearst: a biography of William Randolph Hearst. Scribner 1961 555p il hardcover o.p. paperback available $7.95   **92**

1. Journalists 2. Publishers and publishing

ISBN 0-684-17147-3 (pa)

In this book the author examines every side of his subject: Hearst the millionaire, the newspaper tycoon, the politician, the kingmaker; his influence on the Spanish-American War, his sumptuous life at San Simeon, and his art collecting

Includes bibliography

Hellman, Lillian, 1906-1984

Hellman, Lillian. Three; with new commentaries by the author; introduction by Richard Poirier. Little, Brown 1979 xxv, 726p il $19.95   **92**

1. Dramatists, American 2. Women authors

ISBN 0-316-35514-3   LC 79-108376

Contains the playwright's trio of personal memoirs, all published separately. An unfinished woman (1969) describes her entry into the New York world of publishing and celebrities, including Dashiell Hammett, her lover for 30 years. Pentimento (1973) portrays persons in her New Orleans past, her friend Julia who became a Nazi victim, Dashiell Hammett, and experiences in the theater. Scoundrel time (1976) recalls the witch-hunting days of the 1950's, particularly the author's appearance in 1952 before the House Un-American Activities Committee where she refused to incriminate her writing and acting acquaintances

Hemingway, Ernest, 1899-1961

Hemingway, Ernest. A moveable feast. Scribner 1964 211p il $35; pa $10   **92**

1. Authors, American 2. Paris (France)—Description

ISBN 0-684-17340-9; 0-684-82499-X (pa)

A posthumously published collection of sketches, which Hemingway said might be regarded as fiction, about the author's early life in Paris during the 1920's. In addition to picturing the Parisian scene, Hemingway portrays Gertrude Stein, Ezra Pound, Ford Madox Ford, and others

Hemingway, Ernest, 1899-1961—*Continued*

Lyttle, Richard B. Ernest Hemingway; the life and the legend. Atheneum Pubs. 1992 212p il maps $15.95   **92**

1. Authors, American
ISBN 0-689-31670-4   LC 91-11218

"Lyttle thoroughly sequences the complex life of Hemingway all the way to its tragic demise. It is evident that Hemingway was a multi-faceted man and this biography touches on his career as a reporter, his experience as an outdoors man, his talent as a war correspondent, and his fame as a writer of novels and short stories." Voice Youth Advocates

Includes bibliographical references

Hendrix, Jimi

Hopkins, Jerry. Hit and run: the Jimi Hendrix story; with a discography by Ken Matesich and Dave Armstrong. Perigee Bks. 1983 336p il o.p.   **92**

1. Rock musicians 2. African American musicians
LC 82-5284

This "anecdotal account . . . briefly covers the rock superstar's short, spectacular, and notorious career." Libr J

"Whether you are a Hendrix fan or not, the book offers a reminiscent trek through the music scene of the sixties and a behind-the-scenes peek at the groupies and rivalries and relationships that permeated the times." Best Sellers

Herriot, James

Herriot, James. All creatures great and small. 20th anniversary ed. St. Martin's Press 1992 442p $18.95   **92**

1. Veterinarians
ISBN 0-312-08498-6   LC 92-18975

Also available in paperback from Bantam Bks.
First published 1972

The first volume of Herriot's autobiographical account of the practice of veterinary medicine in Yorkshire, England in the 1930s

Herriot, James. All things bright and beautiful. St. Martin's Press 1974 378p $18.95   **92**

1. Veterinarians
ISBN 0-312-02030-9

Also available in paperback from Bantam Bks.

A continuation of Herriot's reminiscences of pre-World War II Yorkshire

Herriot, James. All things wise and wonderful. St. Martin's Press 1977 432p $18.95   **92**

1. Veterinarians
ISBN 0-312-02031-7   LC 77-76640

Also available in paperback from Bantam Bks.

This installment of Herriot's memoirs focuses on his RAF service during the war

Herriot, James. The Lord God made them all. St. Martin's Press 1981 373p $17.95   **92**

1. Veterinarians
ISBN 0-312-49834-9   LC 80-29097

Also available G.K. Hall large print edition and in paperback from Bantam Bks.

The concluding volume deals with post-war changes in veterinary medicine and Herriot's trips to Russia and Turkey

Heyerdahl, Thor

Heyerdahl, Thor. Green was the earth on the seventh day. Random House 1996 308p il maps $27.50   **92**

1. Explorers
ISBN 0-679-44093-3   LC 95-24989

"Well-known adventurer and naturalist, Heyerdahl first journeyed to Polynesia as a newly married young man. His memoir is a fascinating account of that inaugural trip and the life he and his wife, Liv, shared in their tropical paradise." Booklist

Hickok, Wild Bill, 1837-1876

Rosa, Joseph G. Wild Bill Hickok; the man and his myth. University Press of Kan. 1996 xxiv, 276p $24.95   **92**

1. Frontier and pioneer life—West (U.S.)
ISBN 0-7006-0773-0   LC 95-54015

"Rosa delves for the man behind the myth in his examination of the highly controversial historical character. . . . The author also examines how Hickok was overtaken by his own legend, the deliberate lies that vested him with the reputation of a mankiller, and the initiation and perpetuation of myths in the 19th century frontier." Ref Research Book News

Includes bibliographical references

Himmler, Heinrich, 1900-1945

Breitman, Richard. The architect of genocide: Himmler and the final solution. Knopf 1991 335p $23   **92**

1. National socialism 2. Germany—Politics and government—1933-1945 3. Holocaust, 1933-1945
ISBN 0-394-56841-9   LC 90-52956

Also available in paperback from University Press of New England

The author "focuses on Himmler's role in the decision making of the final solution, on how Himmler and the SS gained control of Nazi Germany's Jewish policy, and on other related World War II activities." Booklist

"This engrossing, detailed study constitutes a powerful refutation of revisionist scholars who claim that Hitler did not plan the Final Solution in advance but instead improvised it out of either military or political frustration." Publ Wkly

Includes bibliographical references

Hirohito, Emperor of Japan, 1901-1989

Behr, Edward. Hirohito; behind the myth. Villard Bks. 1989 xxvi, 437p il $22.50   **92**

1. Japan—Kings, queens, rulers, etc.
ISBN 0-394-58072-9   LC 89-5677

The author "presents a well-researched (though in English-language sources only) study that provides a fascinating and probing look at the life of the 20th century's longest-reigning monarch." Libr J

Includes bibliography

Hitler, Adolf, 1889-1945

Hitler, Adolf. Mein Kampf; translated by Ralph Manheim. Houghton Mifflin 1943 xxi, 694p $27.50; pa $18   **92**
1. National socialism 2. Germany—Politics and government—1918-1933
ISBN 0-395-07801-6; 0-395-08362-1 (pa)
"Hitler's steady rise to power was interrupted only by the Beer Hall Putsch (1923), an unsuccessful attempt to overthrow the Weimar Republic. . . . During the nine months of imprisonment that followed he wrote 'Mein Kampf' (1924; tr. 'My struggle,' 1940). This book contained autobiographical and reflective passages, rife with hysterical anti-Semitism and paranoia, as well as the program he intended to implement; for the West it was a warning that went unheeded." Reader's Ency. 3d edition

Toland, John. Adolf Hitler. Doubleday 1976 xx, 1035p il maps hardcover o.p. paperback available $19.95   **92**
1. Dictators 2. Germany—Politics and government—1933-1945 3. National socialism
ISBN 0-385-42053-6 (pa)   LC 74-25126
This biography is based on more than 250 interviews with people acquainted with Hitler and materials from U.S. and British archives
"In the course of detailed and painstaking investigations [Toland] has disposed of a number of myths." N Y Times Book Rev
Includes glossary and bibliography

Hockenberry, John

Hockenberry, John. Moving violations; war zones, wheelchairs, and declarations of independence. Hyperion 1995 367p $24.95; pa $14.95   **92**
1. Journalists 2. Physically handicapped
ISBN 0-7868-6078-2; 0-7868-8162-3 (pa)
    LC 94-37190
"Correspondent Hockenberry covered the war in the Middle East in a wheelchair, but that's only one of the many triumphs in a life steeped in adversity. Hockenberry describes his struggles to live a full life in spite of his paraplegia in this frank and searing memoir." Booklist

✓ Holiday, Billie, 1915-1959

De Veaux, Alexis. Don't explain: a song of Billie Holiday. Harper & Row 1980 151p il o.p.; Writers & Readers Pub. paperback available $7.95   **92**
1. African American singers 2. African American women
ISBN 0-86316-132-4 (pa)   LC 78-19471
Presents a prose poem recounting the life of the American jazz singer affectionately known as Lady Day
"This rhythmically phrased ode to Lady Day both involves and moves the reader as it follows the vicissitudes of her career, her relationships, and her struggle with heroin. . . . It also affords a telling portrait of what it was like to be talented and black in America in the 1930s, '40s, and '50s. A very special book for perceptive readers, especially those attuned to jazz and/or poetry." Booklist
Includes bibliography and discography

Gourse, Leslie. Billie Holiday; the tragedy and triumph of Lady Day. Watts 1995 127p il (Impact biography) lib bdg $22.70; pa $8   **92**
1. African American singers 2. African American women
ISBN 0-531-11248-9 (lib bdg); 0-531-15753-9 (pa)
    LC 95-17462
Relates the story of the African American woman who, despite a turbulent life, became one of the most famous singers in the history of jazz
Includes discography and bibliographical references

✓ Holiday, Billie. Lady sings the blues; by Billie Holiday with William Dufty. Doubleday 1956 250p o.p.; Penguin Bks. paperback available $10.95   **92**
1. African American singers 2. African American women
ISBN 0-14-006762-0 (pa)
"A hard, bitter and unsentimental book, written with brutal honesty and having much to say not only about Billie Holiday, the person, but about what it means to be poor and black in America." N Y Her Trib Books

Holmes, Oliver Wendell, 1841-1935

Aichele, Gary Jan. Oliver Wendell Holmes, Jr.—soldier, scholar, judge; [by] Gary J. Aichele. Twayne Pubs. 1989 212p il (Twayne's twentieth-century American biography series) lib bdg $30; pa $12.95   **92**
1. United States. Supreme Court 2. Judges
ISBN 0-8057-7766-0 (lib bdg); 0-8057-7784-9 (pa)
    LC 88-24750
"This well-researched biography of U.S. Supreme Court Justice Holmes views the judge's Yankee roots as well as the lengthy judicial career that earned him the nickname 'great dissenter.'" Booklist
Includes bibliography

Homer, Winslow, 1836-1910

Cikovsky, Nicolai, Jr. Winslow Homer. Abrams 1990 156p il (Library of American art) $45   **92**
1. Artists, American
ISBN 0-8109-1193-0   LC 89-17839
Published in association with the National Museum of American Art, Smithsonian Institution
The author attempts "to discern how the meaning and form of Homer's art were shaped by the cultural, social, and political life of the time." Choice
Includes bibliographical references

Hooks, Bell

Hooks, Bell. Bone black: memories of girlhood. Holt & Co. 1996 183p $20   **92**
1. African American women 2. Feminism
ISBN 0-8050-4145-1   LC 96-7308
This autobiographical work "presents 61 snapshot vignettes of two-to-three pages in length of the author growing up in a southern town as an African-American rebel in a family of six girls and one boy. Memories flow chronologically and reveal Hooks's growing awareness of the world around her and her role in it. She fits

Hooks, Bell—*Continued*

these experiences, dreams, and fantasies together to help explain how she came to be the writer and woman she is today . . . . A unique autobiography of a contemporary African-American woman that should find a place in all collections." SLJ

Hopper, Edward, 1882-1967

Hobbs, Robert Carleton. Edward Hopper; [by] Robert Hobbs. Abrams 1987 158p il (Library of American art) $45   **92**

1. Artists, American
ISBN 0-8109-1162-0   LC 86-32276
"A Times Mirror book"
Published in association with the National Museum of American Art, Smithsonian Institution

The author's "treatment of the arguably most popular twentieth-century U.S. artist is almost exclusively critical. . . . It is a commonplace that Hopper is the visual poet of alienation. Hobbs lets this perception stand." Booklist

"Hobbs's discussions are thought-provoking and perceptive. . . . A beautifully produced introductory study with fine reproductions." Choice

Includes bibliography

Horne, Lena

Haskins, James. Lena: a personal and professional biography of Lena Horne; [by] James Haskins with Kathleen Benson. Stein & Day 1984 226p il o.p.; Scarborough House paperback available $10.95   **92**

1. African American singers 2. African American women
ISBN 0-8128-8524-4 (pa)   LC 81-48456
"Lena Horne first came to national prominence in the 1940s . . . as a singer and actress. . . . This biography is a straightforward, balanced, and well-researched account of her life. It wisely skirts extreme depths of psychological interpretation." Libr J

Houdini, Harry, 1874-1926

Brandon, Ruth. The life and many deaths of Harry Houdini. Random House 1994 355p il $25   **92**

1. Magicians
ISBN 0-679-42437-7   LC 94-4080
Also available in paperback from Kodansha Am.

The author provides a psychological "portrait of the great and enigmatic escape artist Harry Houdini. She not only reveals Houdini's impressive technical secrets but also identifies the sources of his unabashed melodramatics and puzzling innocence. . . . Houdini was one of the most compelling 'idols of popular culture' in the early years of this mass-appeal century, and he still works his magic through the medium of Brandon's bold and magnetic interpretation." Booklist

Includes bibliographical references

Hoyle, Mark, 1972-1986

Hoyle, Jay. Mark; how a boy's courage in facing AIDS inspired a town and the town's compassion lit up a nation. Langford Bks. 1988 280p il $18.95   **92**

1. AIDS (Disease)
ISBN 0-912083-30-1   LC 88-15466
This is the story of "the author's hemophiliac son Mark who contracted AIDS from a blood transfusion. . . . The family's and Mark's ordeal is . . . noteworthy not only because he was the first child with AIDS knowingly allowed to attend public school but also because the community of Swansea, Mass., ultimately rallied behind the junior-high-school student instead of banishing him." Publ Wkly

Hubble, Edwin Powell, 1889-1953

Christianson, Gale E. Edwin Hubble: mariner of the nebulae. Farrar, Straus & Giroux 1995 420p il $27.50   **92**

1. Astronomers
ISBN 0-374-14660-8   LC 94-45995
Also available in paperback from University of Chicago Press

This is a biography of "the first astronomer to offer observational evidence supporting the theory of an expanding universe." Booklist

"Christianson's work is a pleasure to read. Jargon-free and requiring no mathematics, it reads more like a novel than a biography and reveals the man behind the scientist." Libr J

Includes bibliographical references

Hughes, Langston, 1902-1967

Hughes, Langston. The big sea: an autobiography. Knopf 1940 335p o.p.; Hill & Wang paperback available $14   **92**

1. Poets, American 2. African American authors
ISBN 0-8090-1549-8 (pa)
This volume recounts the black poet, novelist and playwright's life up to the age of twenty-seven

Hughes, Langston. I wonder as I wander; an autobiographical journey. Rinehart 1956 405p o.p.; Hill & Wang reprint available $14.95   **92**

1. Poets, American 2. African American authors
ISBN 0-8090-1550-1
In this continuation of his autobiography Hughes recalls incidents that occurred at various poetry readings as well as his travels to Russia, Spain, China and Japan

Rampersad, Arnold. The life of Langston Hughes. Oxford Univ. Press 1986-1988 2v il v1 $39.95, pa $15.95; v2 $41.75, pa $17.95   **92**

1. Poets, American 2. African American authors
      LC 86-2565
Contents: v1 1902-1941: I, too, sing America (ISBN 0-19-504011-2; 0-19-505426-1); v2 1941-1967: I dream a world (ISBN 0-19-504519-X; 0-19-506169-1)

"Rampersad is an unsparing but sympathetic analyst of Hughes's life and work; he has written an absorbing critical biography that is also a deft social history of black America in the 20th century." Publ Wkly

Includes bibliographical references

Hurston, Zora Neale, 1891-1960

Hemenway, Robert E. Zora Neale Hurston; a literary biography; with a foreword by Alice Walker. University of Ill. Press 1977 xxvi, 371p il hardcover o.p. paperback available $12.50   92

1. African American authors 2. Women authors
   ISBN 0-252-00807-3 (pa)   LC 77-9605

This biography includes "summaries and analyses of all Hurston's extant work, both published and unpublished. . . . [The author] offers also much matter for speculation on the nature of the creative process in the unique case of Zora Hurston." New Repub
   Includes bibliography

Hurston, Zora Neale. Dust tracks on a road; with a new foreword by Maya Angelou. HarperCollins Pubs. 1991 277p $22.50; pa $13.50   92

1. African American authors 2. Women authors
   ISBN 0-06-016726-2; 0-06-092168-4 (pa)
   LC 90-55501

First published 1942 by Lippincott

The author describes her wanderings in and out of schools and jobs as a young girl, finishing her course work at Barnard, and beginning her life's work
   Includes bibliography

Lyons, Mary E. Sorrow's kitchen: the life and folklore of Zora Neale Hurston. Scribner 1990 144p il $15; pa $6.95   92

1. African American authors 2. Women authors
   ISBN 0-684-19198-9; 0-02-044445-1 (pa)
   LC 90-8058

This biography details "Hurston's migration from Florida to Baltimore, Washington, D.C., and finally Harlem as well as her travels through the West Indies to collect folklore. The text contains eleven excerpts from Hurston's books. . . . Lyons has created a prime example of biography—fascinating, enlightening, stimulating, and satisfying." Horn Book
   Includes bibliographical references

Hussein, Şaddām

Stefoff, Rebecca. Saddam Hussein; absolute ruler of Iraq. Millbrook Press 1995 128p il lib bdg $16.40   92

1. Iraq—Politics and government
   ISBN 1-56294-475-4   LC 94-16982

"Grounded in the complex history of the Middle East, Stefoff's biography of Iraq's infamous leader is intricately interwoven with the events that have given rise to Saddam Hussein's reputation. . . . Stefoff carefully links the country's last two wars and domestic and foreign policy to the dictator's ambitions. This well-written biography makes edifying, if uneasy, reading." Booklist
   Includes bibliographical references

Ireland, Patricia

Ireland, Patricia. What women want. Dutton 1996 323p il $24.95   92

1. Feminism
   ISBN 0-525-93857-5   LC 96-5490

"A former airline stewardess, then a law partner, National Organization for Women president Ireland sketches her personal journey in the women's movement against the broader background of the social and political conditions of women in contemporary America." Libr J

"Based on an exploration of her own road to feminism, the often controversial Ireland endeavors not to provide a single answer to Freud's generic question but to urge individual women to ask, What do I want? and then take both personal and collective action to achieve their goals." Booklist

Jackson, Andrew, 1767-1845

Meltzer, Milton. Andrew Jackson and his America. Watts 1993 207p il maps lib bdg $23.43   92

1. Presidents—United States 2. United States—Politics and government—1815-1861
   ISBN 0-531-11157-1   LC 93-3947

"Jackson's life is covered from his birth, poor beginnings and numerous scuffles, through his apprenticeship in the study of law, to his political career. The author tries to show Jackson in the context of his time." Book Rep

"Besides providing the young adult reader with an enjoyable biography, the author has succeeded in creating a critical survey of Jackson's life that is useful and credible as a piece of historical research." Voice Youth Advocates
   Includes bibliographical references

Jackson, Jesse L., 1941-

Frady, Marshall. Jesse: the life and pilgrimage of Jesse Jackson. Random House 1996 552p $28.50   92

1. African Americans—Biography
   ISBN 0-394-57586-5   LC 95-43668

This biography "makes extensive use of numerous interviews and conversations that the author had with Jackson, his family, and many of his associates. The book offers valuable insights into Jackson's difficult childhood and its effect on his personality; his relationship with Martin Luther King; and his two presidential campaigns." Libr J
   Includes bibliography

Haskins, James. I am somebody! a biography of Jesse Jackson. Enslow Pubs. 1992 112p il lib bdg $18.95   92

1. African Americans—Biography
   ISBN 0-89490-240-7   LC 91-34079

Presents the life, accomplishments, and goals of the civil rights activist and politician Jesse Jackson, from his childhood in North Carolina through his years in Chicago and Washington, D.C

"Haskins presents both the public and private Jackson as a man with flaws but a dynamic and charismatic leader in spite of them. The index and extensive bibliography make this a good starting place for those doing reports." Booklist

Jackson, Stonewall, 1824-1863
Farwell, Byron. Stonewall: a biography of General Thomas J. Jackson. Norton 1992 560p il maps hardcover o.p. paperback available $15.95
      92
1. Generals 2. United States—History—1861-1865, Civil War
ISBN 0-393-31086-8 (pa)   LC 91-44988
"Farwell reinterprets the South's most legendary soldier in this respectful but thoroughly debunking biography. . . . In his efforts to establish the facts of Jackson's life and career, he concludes that most of the Jackson legends, including his fabled eccentricities, lack factual basis." Libr J
Includes bibliographical references

James, Daniel, 1920-1978
Phelps, J. Alfred. Chappie; America's first Black four-star general: the life and times of Daniel James, Jr. Presidio Press 1991 366p il maps hardcover o.p. paperback available $9.95   **92**
1. Generals 2. African Americans—Biography
ISBN 0-89141-464-9 (pa)   LC 90-43537
"'Chappie' James (1920-1978) became one of the legendary Tuskegee Airmen during World War II, took part in the struggle of black officers for racial equality in the Army Air Corps, flew combat missions in Korea and Vietnam, served as Air Force PR chief during the height of the anti-war protests, and concluded a brilliant career as a four-star general. . . . [An] inspiring biography of an American hero." Publ Wkly
Includes bibliography

Jefferson, Thomas, 1743-1826
Bober, Natalie. Thomas Jefferson: man on a mountain; by Natalie S. Bober. Atheneum Pubs. 1988 274p il hardcover o.p. paperback available $6.95   **92**
1. Presidents—United States
ISBN 0-02-041797-7 (pa)   LC 87-37462
The life of the author of the Declaration of Independence and third president of the United States who was also a noted inventor, architect, farmer, statesman, and educator
"The information in the book is presented in an interesting fashion; the narrative style is easy to absorb; the characters, in this case real people, come to life in a way that rarely happens in average biographies; and the role the man—not the name—played in our nation's history and in the world's history comes to life before us." Voice Youth Advocates
Includes bibliography

Brodie, Fawn McKay. Thomas Jefferson; an intimate history; [by] Fawn M. Brodie. Norton 1974 591p il o.p.; Bantam Bks. paperback available $7.99   **92**
1. Presidents—United States
ISBN 0-553-27335-3 (pa)
"Emphasis on Jefferson's personality, the private thoughts and experiences which influenced his political evolution and in turn shaped the course of history, marks a compelling psychological biography." Booklist
Includes bibliography

McLaughlin, Jack. Jefferson and Monticello; the biography of a builder. Holt & Co. 1988 481p il hardcover o.p. paperback available $15.95   **92**
1. Presidents—United States
ISBN 0-8050-1463-2   LC 87-23664
In this work the author focuses on the domestic life of the third U.S. President, and his near lifetime involvement with the building of his home, Monticello
"McLaughlin's book is that rare combination: a scholarly but immensely readable work that provides new insights into Jefferson's personality through a detailed examination of his home." Libr J
Includes bibliography

Meltzer, Milton. Thomas Jefferson; the revolutionary aristocrat. Watts 1991 255p il maps lib bdg $15.90   **92**
1. Presidents—United States
ISBN 0-531-11069-9   LC 91-15943
An "examination of Jefferson's brilliant and complex life, detailing his successes and failures. Meltzer writes with his usual lively style and clarity and provides plenty of historical background and detail." SLJ
Includes bibliography

Randall, Willard Sterne. Thomas Jefferson; a life. Holt & Co. 1993 708p $35   **92**
1. Presidents—United States
ISBN 0-8050-1577-9   LC 93-2057
"A John Macrae book"
This biography focuses on Jefferson's "youthful lawyering on the frontier, his political eclipse as Virginia's ineffectual war governor, and his ambassadorship to France." Booklist
"Randall's substantial, balanced biography will be valuable for general readers who seek a one-volume work on one of the leading Founding Fathers." Libr J
Includes bibliographical references

Jewett, Sarah Orne, 1849-1909
Blanchard, Paula. Sarah Orne Jewett; her world and her work. Addison-Wesley 1994 397p il (Radcliffe biography series) $27.50; pa $15   **92**
1. Authors, American 2. Women authors
ISBN 0-201-51810-4; 0-201-48934-1 (pa)
     LC 94-7696
"A Merloyd Lawrence book"
This biography focuses on the "influences that most shaped Jewett's literary art. Deeply rooted in the stern, rocky soil of Maine, Jewett nonetheless knew and responded to the work of European masters, including Flaubert and Turgenev. By probing the social significance of such works as *A Country Doctor* and *A Marsh Island,* Blanchard enriches an already large body of feminist scholarship on Jewett." Booklist
Includes bibliographical references

Joan, of Arc, Saint, 1412-1431
Brooks, Polly Schoyer. Beyond the myth: the story of Joan of Arc. Lippincott 1990 176p il maps lib bdg $15.89   **92**
1. Christian saints 2. France—History—1328-1589, House of Valois
ISBN 0-397-32423-5   LC 89-37327
Places the life of the fifteenth-century girl who has become a French national symbol within the social, reli-

Joan, of Arc, Saint, 1412-1431—*Continued*
gious, and political context of her time
This "scholarly, well-written biography of France's great heroine . . . is thorough, interesting, and full of detail. . . . Brooks writes for serious readers, and her book, although challenging, is richly rewarding." SLJ
Includes bibliography

Johnson, Earvin, 1959-
Johnson, Earvin. My life; [by] Earvin "Magic" Johnson with William Novak. Random House 1992 329p il o.p.; Fawcett Bks. paperback available $5.99   92
1. Basketball—Biography 2. African American athletes
ISBN 0-449-22254-3 (pa)   LC 92-53637
"In this autobiography, Johnson recounts his life, culminating with his now well-known participation as a member of the 'Dream Team' at the Barcelona Olympics." Libr J
"Basketball superstar Johnson's straight talk on AIDS gives his autobiography its thrust and power. . . . Fans will enjoy his replays of key games and seasons, as well as his frank impressions of his former Los Angeles Lakers teammates, coach Pat Riley, the Boston Celtics' Larry Bird and other players." Publ Wkly

Johnson, Lyndon B. (Lyndon Baines), 1908-1973
Eskow, Dennis. Lyndon Baines Johnson. Watts 1993 160p il (Impact biography) lib bdg $22.70
                                                            92
1. Presidents—United States
ISBN 0-531-13019-3   LC 92-43687
"In this biography, which begins with Johnson's birth in the hill country of Texas and follows him to the White House and back to Texas for his final days, Eskow presents LBJ as 'a consummate politician, a man who lived to make the political system work in his favor.' . . . By and large, the account is sympathetic, but Eskow does a good job of raising ethical questions, separating rumor from fact, and pointing out contradictions in the source material." Booklist
Includes bibliographical references

Goodwin, Doris Kearns. Lyndon Johnson and the American dream; [by] Doris Kearns. Harper & Row 1976 432p o.p.; St. Martin's Press paperback available $15.95   92
1. Presidents—United States
ISBN 0-312-06027-0 (pa)   LC 75-42831
"Confidante of Lyndon Johnson during the last five years of his life, Kearns cuts through the public figure to reveal much of the real man. A fascinating biography for older readers, especially those with a political bent." Booklist
Includes bibliographical references

Johnson, Samuel, 1709-1784
Boswell, James. The life of Samuel Johnson
                                                            92
1. Authors, English
Hardcover and paperback editions available from various publishers

First published 1791
Variant title: The life of Johnson
"The most famous biography in the English language. It is an intimate and minute delineation of the great lexicographer's life, character and person, enlivened with small-talk, gossip and bits of familiar correspondence. It is also an admirable portrayal of the society of which Johnson was the outstanding figure." Pratt Alcove

Jones, James Earl
Jones, James Earl. James Earl Jones: voices and silences; [by] James Earl Jones and Penelope Niven. Scribner 1993 xxii, 394p il $24; pa $14
                                                            92
1. African American actors
ISBN 0-684-19513-5; 0-671-89945-7 (pa)
                                    LC 93-19021
"Black history comes alive when Jones speculates about his forebears, African, Irish, and Choctaw Indian. Theater anecdotes abound, as do serious and superficial discussions of acting methods. His research for the role of Othello is impressive. He becomes a bit didactic at times, e.g., on the subject of censorship. Chapters about Howard Sackler's *The Great White Hope* (1968) and August Wilson's *Fences* (1986) are very good." Choice

Jones, John Paul, 1747-1792
Morison, Samuel Eliot. John Paul Jones; a sailor's biography; with an introduction by James C. Bradford; charts and diagrams by Erwin Raisz. Naval Inst. Press 1989 xxvi, 537p il (Classics of naval literature) $32.95   92
1. United States—Naval history
ISBN 0-87021-323-7   LC 89-13423
Also available in paperback from Northeastern Univ. Press
A reissue with a new introduction of the title first published 1959 by Little, Brown
This "documented chronicle of the American sea captain's life . . . is particularly concerned with his ability as a seaman and with the naval engagements in which he took part." Booklist
"Morison has destroyed the myth of John Paul Jones but has left us a more human, more understandable character." Best Sellers
Includes bibliographical references

Joplin, Scott, 1868-1917
Haskins, James. Scott Joplin; [by] James Haskins with Kathleen Benson. Doubleday 1978 248p il o.p.; Scarborough House paperback available $6.95   92
1. Composers, American 2. African American musicians
ISBN 0-8128-6066-7 (pa)   LC 76-50768
This is a biography of the black ragtime composer. "Haskins evokes the era, the music and the man, showing how . . . Joplin created an astonishing number of innovative, delightful 'rags' (and opera) that were never to receive anything approaching full appreciation until our own time." Publ Wkly
"'Authoritative' is the word for Haskins' solid, sober,

Joplin, Scott, 1868-1917—*Continued*
and informative biography. . . . The work possesses a
dignity and depth worthy of the tragic talent it describes." Libr J
Includes bibliography

✓ Otfinoski, Steven. Scott Joplin; a life in ragtime.
Watts 1995 143p il (Impact biography) lib bdg
$22.70   **92**
1. Composers, American 2. African American musi-
cians
ISBN 0-531-11244-6   LC 95-8526
The story of one of America's most famous compos-
ers of ragtime music
Includes discography and bibliographical references

Jordan, Michael
Krugel, Mitchell. Jordan; the man, his words,
his life. St. Martin's Press 1994 277p il $21.95; pa
$5.99   **92**
1. Basketball—Biography 2. African American ath-
letes
ISBN 0-312-11090-1; 0-312-95814-5 (pa)
                                     LC 94-459
"A Thomas Dunne book"
Chicago Bull great Jordan "provides a brief introduc-
tion to each chapter of *Hammond Times* reporter
Krugel's surprisingly candid and objective biography.
Krugel carefully examines Jordan's legendary
competitiveness, concluding that it is both the source of
Michael's athletic greatness and a kind of personal
curse." Booklist

✓ Smith, Sam. Second coming: the strange
odyssey of Michael Jordan—from courtside to
home plate and back again. HarperCollins Pubs.
1995 xxii, 281p il $23; pa $5.99   **92**
1. Basketball—Biography 2. African American athletes
ISBN 0-06-017502-8; 0-06-109455-2 (pa)
                                 LC 95-37153
This book details the professional career of the sports
superstar

Joseph, Nez Percé Chief, 1840-1904
Scott, Robert Alan. Chief Joseph and the Nez
Percés; [by] Robert A. Scott. Facts on File 1993
134p il maps (Makers of America) lib bdg $17.95
                                       92
1. Nez Percé Indians
ISBN 0-8160-2475-8   LC 92-15885
A biography of the nineteenth-century Nez Percé
chief, concentrating on his unending struggle to win
peace and equality for his people
Includes bibliographical references

Joyce, James, 1882-1941
Ellmann, Richard. James Joyce. new and rev ed.
Oxford Univ. Press 1982 887p il $52.25; pa $25
                                       92
1. Authors, Irish
ISBN 0-19-503103-2; 0-19-503381-7 (pa)
                                     LC 81-22455
First published 1959

This biography describes "Joyce's working methods,
views on life and literature, political opinions, familial
relationships and problems, and incessant struggle against
poverty and threatening blindness." Publ Wkly
This "is a vast undertaking and continuing achievement—massive, masterly, and definitive, rich in anecdote
and detail. It is also extremely readable; the easy, often
sympathetic style communicates gracefully not only facts
but analysis." Choice
Includes bibliographical references

Karr, Mary
Karr, Mary. The Liar's Club; a memoir. Viking
1995 320p il $22.95; pa $11.95   **92**
ISBN 0-670-85053-5; 0-14-017983-6 (pa)
                                     LC 94-41252
Poet "Karr and her older sister grew up in an east
Texas oil town where they learned to cope with their
mother's psychotic episodes, the ostracism by neighbors
and their father's frequent absences. Karr's happiest
times were the afternoons she spent at the 'Liars Club,'
where her father and a group of men drank and traded
boastful stories." Publ Wkly
"This barbed memoir of a close and calamitous family
from a Texas oil town moves with the same quickness
as its doubledged title. . . . The revelations continue to
the final page, with a misleading carelessness as seductive as any world-class liar's." New Yorker

Keller, Helen, 1880-1968
Keller, Helen. The story of my life. Doubleday
1954 382p il   **92**
1. Blind 2. Deaf
Available G.K. Hall large print edition, in hardcover
from Buccaneer Bks. and in paperback from various publishers
First published 1903
This biography of the inspirational Keller contains accounts of her home life and her relationship with her devoted teacher Anne Sullivan

Lash, Joseph P. Helen and teacher: the story of
Helen Keller and Anne Sullivan Macy. Delacorte
Press 1980 811p il (Radcliffe biography series)
o.p.; Addison-Wesley paperback available $6.95
                                       92
1. Sullivan, Anne, 1866-1936 2. Blind 3. Deaf
ISBN 0-201-69468-9 (pa)   LC 79-25599
"A Merloyd Lawrence book"
The author "tells the life stories of both Keller and the
educator who devoted her life to her, the woman Helen
referred to simply as 'Teacher.'" Ms
"This is a deeply absorbing portrait of two intertwined
lives whose meanings can't be understood separately." N
Y Times Book Rev
Includes bibliography

Nicholson, Lois. Helen Keller; humanitarian;
[by] Lois P. Nicholson. Chelsea House 1996 111p
il (Great achievers: lives of the physically
challenged) lib bdg $18.95   **92**
1. Blind 2. Deaf
ISBN 0-7910-2086-X   LC 94-37512
This biography emphasizes Keller's strong personality
traits which, with the guidance of her teacher, Anne Sul-

Keller, Helen, 1880-1968—*Continued*
livan, enabled her to succeed as a best-selling author, political activist, popular lecturer, and renowned humanitarian

Includes bibliography

Kennedy, John F. (John Fitzgerald), 1917-1963
Burner, David. John F. Kennedy and a new generation; edited by Oscar Handlin. Little, Brown 1988 189p (Library of American biography) o.p.; Scott, Foresman paperback available $16   **92**
1. Presidents—United States 2. United States—Politics and government—1961-1974
ISBN 0-673-39810-2 (pa)   LC 88-15595
"Though the author offers significant insight into how Kennedy's domineering father and privileged background strongly influenced the pragmatic nature of his politics, he does not entirely discount Kennedy's tremendous impact upon the ideals and expectations of a new generation of voters. This meditative analysis provides a welcome balance between increasingly extremist interpretations of Kennedy's career." Booklist
Includes bibliography

Life in Camelot; the Kennedy years; edited by Philip B. Kunhardt, Jr. Little, Brown 1988 319p il hardcover o.p. paperback available $19.95   **92**
1. Presidents—United States
ISBN 0-316-50602-8 (pa)   LC 88-3640
A pictorial look at both the public and private Kennedy during the years of his presidency

Lowe, Jacques. JFK remembered; with a foreword by Arthur Schlesinger, Jr. Random House 1993 191p il $37.50   **92**
1. Presidents—United States—Pictorial works
ISBN 0-679-42399-0   LC 93-4181
This album of photographs "is divided into images from the 1960 campaign and those of JFK exercising power. Black-bordered, black-and-white full-page spreads predominate. . . . Lowe's text identifies the pictured events, such as the West Virginia primary, the Democratic convention, JFK's first cabinet meeting, and his first foreign trip as president." Booklist

Manchester, William. One brief shining moment: remembering Kennedy. Little, Brown 1983 280p il hardcover o.p. paperback available $16.95   **92**
1. Presidents—United States 2. United States—Politics and government—1961-1974
ISBN 0-316-54511-2 (pa)   LC 83-17590
Some two hundred "photographs supplement the author's reminiscences and those of 150 members of the Kennedy entourage. Kennedy is presented as a dynamic president whose principal achievements were in the Nuclear Test Ban Treaty, civil rights, education, and health legislation." Libr J

Kenyatta, Jomo, ca. 1891-1978
Wepman, Dennis. Jomo Kenyatta. Chelsea House 1985 112p il (World leaders past & present) lib bdg $19.95   **92**
ISBN 0-87754-575-8   LC 84-28506
This volume covers the life of the first president of Kenya, who worked to develop the economy and unite

the country's diverse populations
Includes bibliography

Khanga, Yelena
Khanga, Yelena. Soul to soul; a black Russian American family, 1865-1992; [by] Yelena Khanga with Susan Jacoby. Norton 1992 317p il $22.95; pa $10.95   **92**
1. African Americans—Biography 2. Jews—Russia
ISBN 0-393-03404-6; 0-393-31155-4 (pa)
LC 92-7043
The author writes about her Jewish and African-American forebears in this memoir. Khanga is the "granddaughter of Oliver Golden and Bertha Bialek, American Communists who emigrated to the Soviet Union in 1931." Libr J
"The book has a conversational, easy-to-read tone as it takes the reader on an engaging odyssey." Christ Sci Monit

Kherdian, Veron, 1907-
Kherdian, David. The road from home; the story of an Armenian girl. Greenwillow Bks. 1979 238p il map $13.95; lib bdg $14.93; pa $4.95   **92**
1. Armenians—Turkey 2. Armenian massacres, 1915-1923
ISBN 0-688-80205-2; 0-688-84205-4 (lib bdg); 0-688-14425-X (pa)   LC 78-72511
The author presents a "biography of his mother's early life as a young Armenian girl. Veron Dumehjian was part of a prosperous Armenian family in Turkey, but the Armenian minority undergoes a holocaust when the Turkish government persecutes its Christian minorities. In 1915 Veron and her family are deported and, as refugees, live through hardships of disease, starvation, bombing, and fire until, at sixteen, Veron is able to go to America as a 'mail-order' bride." Babbling Bookworm

King, B. B.
Shirley, David. Everyday I sing the blues: the story of B.B. King. Watts 1995 127p il (Impact biography) lib bdg $22.70; pa $8   **92**
1. African American musicians
ISBN 0-531-11229-2 (lib bdg); 0-531-15752-0 (pa)
LC 95-16151
Traces the life of the influential African American blues musician, from his birth in the Mississippi Delta in 1925 to the present
Includes bibliographical references

King, Martin Luther, 1929-1968
Bennett, Lerone. What manner of man: a biography of Martin Luther King, Jr.; by Lerone Bennett, Jr.; with an introduction by Benjamin E. Mays. [3rd rev ed] Johnson 1968 251p il $19.95   **92**
1. African Americans—Biography 2. African Americans—Civil rights
ISBN 0-87485-027-4
First published 1964
The author recalls Martin Luther King from his childhood, education, accomplishments as a Baptist minister, his leadership in the black Civil Rights movement, his winning the 1964 Nobel Peace Prize to the tragic end of his life in 1968

King, Martin Luther, 1929-1968—*Continued*

Colaiaco, James A. Martin Luther King, Jr; apostle of militant nonviolence. St. Martin's Press 1988 238p hardcover o.p. paperback available $14.95   92

    1. African Americans—Biography 2. African Americans—Civil rights

    ISBN 0-312-08843-4 (pa)   LC 88-14900

"Colaiaco's book fills a very important place in the historiography of Martin Luther King Jr. It is a short, thorough work that touches all the main issues and themes, and puts them into the context of the times. The book can serve as supplemental reading on the Civil Rights Movement for high schools. . . . More than a fact-by-fact biography, Colaiaco's study reveals the ideological contradictions . . . underlying the events he describes." Choice

Includes bibliography

Garrow, David J. Bearing the cross: Martin Luther King, Jr., and the Southern Christian Leadership Conference. Morrow 1986 800p o.p.; Random House paperback available $18   92

    1. Southern Christian Leadership Conference 2. African Americans—Biography 3. African Americans—Civil rights

    ISBN 0-394-75623-1 (pa)   LC 86-8594

This book is a "study of King's participation in the civil rights revolution. It [seeks to] portray his interaction with the staff members of the major civil rights institutions and . . . [other participants] in that struggle." Christ Century

"Granting its limitations, Bearing the Cross is likely to remain for a long time the most informative life of Martin Luther King, Jr., and the most thorough study of the civil rights movement, or the large part of it in which King and the SCLC was active." N Y Rev Books

Includes bibliography

King, Coretta Scott. My life with Martin Luther King, Jr; introduction by Bernice, Dexter, Martin, and Yolanda King. rev ed. Holt & Co. 1993 335p il $17.95   92

    1. African Americans—Biography 2. African Americans—Civil rights

    ISBN 0-8050-2445-X   LC 92-23525

Also available in paperback from Puffin Bks.

First published 1969

An inside look at the life and work of the noted civil rights leader, from the viewpoint of his wife Coretta Scott King

"King's voice comes through clearly, as does her personality. At times, though, she sounds old-fashioned, particularly when she makes an appeal to today's teenagers. Her view of her husband is naturally an uncritical one, and it is but one perspective in a many-sided and often acrimonious debate." SLJ

Martin Luther King, Jr.: a documentary—Montgomery to Memphis; with an introduction by Coretta Scott King. Editor: Flip Schulke; associate editor: Bob Fitch; text by: Penelope McPhee. Norton 1976 224p il hardcover o.p. paperback available $15.95   92

    1. African Americans—Biography 2. African Americans—Civil rights

    ISBN 0-393-07492-7 (pa)

This photographic essay on the late civil-rights leader "emphasizes King's accomplishments and his philosophy of nonviolence. . . . An introduction by Coretta King and an appendix containing several of King's most famous speeches frame the body of the work." Libr J

Oates, Stephen B. Let the trumpet sound: the life of Martin Luther King, Jr. Harper & Row 1982 560p il hardcover o.p. paperback available $16.50   92

    1. African Americans—Biography 2. African Americans—Civil rights

    ISBN 0-06-091473-X (pa)   LC 81-48046

"Mr. Oates treats King's personality with insight and tact, but his focus, understandably, is on the public man. He is particularly successful in tracing the origins of King's ideas in his early upbringing and preparation for the ministry. . . . [The author] displays a remarkable understanding of King's individual role in the civil rights movement." N Y Times Book Rev

Includes bibliographical references

Schulke, Flip. King remembered; [by] Flip Schulke and Penelope McPhee; foreword by Jesse Jackson. Norton 1986 303p il $22.95   92

    1. African Americans—Biography 2. African Americans—Civil rights

    ISBN 0-393-02256-0   LC 85-22172

Also available in paperback from Pocket Bks.

"The authors survey King's life, underscoring his significance in civil rights in terms of what he stood for and his actual personal achievements. The text is an eloquent statement of his goodness and dynamism, yet the photographs speak with perhaps even more clarity and strength." Booklist

King, Stephen, 1947-

King, Stephen. Feast of fear; conversations with Stephen King; Tim Underwood and Chuck Miller, editors. Carroll & Graf Pubs. 1992 282p o.p.; Warner Bks. paperback available $9.99   92

    1. Authors, American

    ISBN 0-446-39505-6 (pa)   LC 92-6902

"Sprinkled with personal revelations, these interviews, a feast for fans, furnish a rare glimpse into King's private universe. Underwood and Miller . . . have cleverly stitched together 47 newspaper and magazine interviews, many published in obscure places, which follow the novelist chronologically from his years working in an industrial laundry to his phenomenal success and cozy family life in Bangor, Maine." Publ Wkly

Kingston, Maxine Hong

Kingston, Maxine Hong. The woman warrior; memoirs of a girlhood among ghosts. Knopf 1976 209p $24.95; pa $11   **92**
1. Chinese Americans
ISBN 0-394-40067-4; 0-679-72188-6 (pa)
LC 76-13674

The memoirs of a Chinese-American woman born during the 1940's in San Francisco to recent immigrants. Maxine Hong Kingston grew up haunted by two sets of ghosts. The first were ghosts of ancestral and legendary figures from Chinese village life handed down in cautionary tales by her mother. The second were the white-faced Americans who were considered ghosts by the Chinese of her parents' generation

The author's voice "is as fierce as a warrior's voice, and as eloquent as any artist's." N Y Times Book Rev

Kinmont, Jill

Valens, Evans G. The other side of the mountain: the story of Jill Kinmont; [by] E. G. Valens; photographs by Burk Uzzle and others. Perennial Lib. 1988 313p il pa $7   **92**
1. Skiing—Biography 2. Physically handicapped—Rehabilitation
ISBN 0-06-080948-5   LC 88-45124

First published 1966 in hardcover by Harper & Row with title: A long way up

"In 1955 when Jill Kinmont was 18 and a leading candidate for the U.S. Olympic ski team, she crashed while competing in the Snow Cup giant slalom in the mountains near Salt Lake City. The accident left her a quadriplegic, permanently paralyzed from the shoulders down. . . . The book sketches her rehabilitation, mental as well as physical and gives glimpses of her family and friends." Libr J

Kissinger, Henry, 1923-

Kissinger, Henry. Years of upheaval. Little, Brown 1982 xxi, 1283p il $29.95   **92**
1. United States—Foreign relations
ISBN 0-316-28591-9   LC 81-86320

Companion volume White House years (1979) o.p.

This volume covers the "unraveling of the Paris agreement, the continuation of triangular diplomacy with Peking and Moscow . . . the overthrow of Salvador Allende, the . . . October 1973 war in the Middle East, the first oil crisis, Kissinger's shuttle diplomacy, the beginning of the anti-détente campaign in the United States, Richard Nixon's . . . Middle East journal—and [Watergate]." N Y Rev Books

"Dr. Kissinger's account of these [years] is a literary and historical masterpiece that makes superb reading." Christ Sci Monit

Includes bibliographical references

Koehn, Ilse, 1929-1991

Koehn, Ilse. Mischling, second degree: my childhood in Nazi Germany; with a foreword by Harrison E. Salisbury. Greenwillow Bks. 1977 240p o.p.; Puffin Bks. paperback available $5.99   **92**
1. World War, 1939-1945—Jews 2. Germany—History—1933-1945 3. Jews—Germany
ISBN 0-14-034290-7 (pa)   LC 77-6189

This story "is told in retrospect by an author who did not know why her loving parents separated until after the war, when she learned that it had helped her and her mother avoid the consequences of the fact that her father had one Jewish parent. Liberals and intellectuals, the Koehns coped, as many did, with a government and a philosophy they detested. And Ilse, a young adolescent, was drafted into the Hitler Youth, forced to go through the motions of devotion." Bull Cent Child Books

Kuralt, Charles, 1934-1997

Kuralt, Charles. A life on the road. Putnam 1990 253p il o.p.; Ivy Bks. paperback available $6.99   **92**
1. Journalists 2. United States—Social life and customs
ISBN 0-8041-0869-2 (pa)   LC 90-39461

"Kuralt reviews his career in print journalism and as a reporter for the electronic media. He recalls his most unusual and memorable programs and interviewees." Publ Wkly

"The anecdotes from his motor-home days are priceless and fill nearly half the book. Kuralt is able to sum up a situation perfectly, imparting a strong visual image laced with wit." Booklist

L'Amour, Louis, 1908-1988

L'Amour, Louis. Education of a wandering man. Bantam Bks. 1989 232p il hardcover o.p. paperback available $5.99   **92**
1. Authors, American
ISBN 0-553-28652-8 (pa)   LC 89-14903

"These unfinished memoirs by the noted Western author possess a raw enthusiasm for life and for books that is too rarely encountered today. For most of the book, L'Amour recounts scattered anecdotes of his knockabout years as a sailor, prize fighter, silver miner, and longshoreman who ranged from New Orleans to Singapore with a book in his hip pocket." Libr J

Includes bibliography

Lange, Dorothea, 1895-1965

Dorothea Lange—a visual life; edited by Elizabeth Partridge. Smithsonian Institution Press 1994 168p il $55; pa $29.95   **92**
1. Women photographers
ISBN 1-56098-350-7; 1-56098-455-4 (pa)
LC 94-25869

This is a "collection of photos and insightful essays about the photographer whose work captured more than four decades of American history. . . . Interwoven with Lange's personal story are the photographic records of the '30s, '40s, and '50s so dramatically captured by her insightful choices." SLJ

Includes bibliographical references

Lawrence, T. E. (Thomas Edward), 1888-1935

Wolfe, Daniel. T.E. Lawrence. Chelsea House 1995 151p il map (Lives of notable gay men and lesbians) lib bdg $19.95; pa $9.95   **92**
1. World War, 1914-1918—Middle East
ISBN 0-7910-2324-9 (lib bdg); 0-7910-2891-7 (pa)
                   LC 94-27034

This look at the legendary Lawrence ranges from his adventures in the Middle East during World War I to his role in the Arab revolt against the Turks

"Wolfe takes care to distinguish between realities and myths, and plainly states when no such discernment is possible. The subject's personal history is presented in a forthright, objective manner." SLJ

Includes bibliography

Lee, Robert E. (Robert Edward), 1807-1870

Marrin, Albert. Virginia's general: Robert E. Lee and the Civil War. Atheneum Pubs. 1994 218p il maps $19.95   **92**
1. Generals 2. United States—History—1861-1865, Civil War
ISBN 0-689-31838-3   LC 94-13353

"Beginning with Lee's pivotal decision to refuse command of the U.S. Army, the book fills in the details of his childhood, education, marriage, and career, and then concentrates on the Civil War years. Quotations from Lee, his generals, and particularly his soldiers offer insight into the times." Booklist

Includes bibliographical references

Smith, Gene. Lee and Grant; a dual biography. McGraw-Hill 1984 412p il o.p.; New Am. Lib. paperback available $10.95   **92**
1. Grant, Ulysses S. (Ulysses Simpson), 1822-1885 2. Generals 3. Presidents—United States 4. United States—History—1861-1865, Civil War
ISBN 0-452-00773-9 (pa)   LC 83-25555

This "dual biography features alternating chapters that depict the ironic contrasts in the lives of two of the nineteenth century's most prominent personalities." Booklist

"The action rapidly shifts between the two protagonists at various points throughout their lives, a literary technique that Smith manages with nimbleness and aplomb. The result is a satisfying look at the early years of both men and a revealing run-through of the war itself." Libr J

Includes bibliography

Thomas, Emory M. Robert E. Lee; a biography. Norton 1995 472p il maps $30   **92**
1. Generals
ISBN 0-393-03730-4   LC 95-10522

"Civil War historian Thomas presents Lee as neither an icon nor a flawed figure, but rather as a man who made the best of his lot, whose comic vision of life ultimately shaped him into an individual who was both more and less than his legend." Publ Wkly

Includes bibliography

Lemieux, Mario

Klein, Jeff Z. Mario Lemieux, ice hockey star. Chelsea House 1995 111p il (Great achievers: lives of the physically challenged) lib bdg $18.95; pa $7.95   **92**
1. Pittsburgh Penguins (Hockey team) 2. Hockey—Biography 3. Cancer
ISBN 0-7910-2400-8 (lib bdg); 0-7910-2401-6 (pa)
                   LC 94-31522

This biography of the Pittsburgh Penguins center relates his battle against Hodgkin's disease

Includes bibliography

Leonardo, da Vinci, 1452-1519

Bramly, Serge. Leonardo; discovering the life of Leonardo da Vinci; translated by Siân Reynolds. HarperCollins Pubs. 1991 493p il o.p.; Penguin Bks. paperback available $18.95   **92**
1. Artists, Italian
ISBN 0-14-023175-7 (pa)   LC 90-56356
"An Edward Burlingame book"
Original French edition, 1988

"Bramly's book sheds light on the more personal aspects of Leonardo. . . . As he follows da Vinci's often frustrating career and ever-widening sphere of inquiries, inventions, and discoveries, he also patches together overlooked clues about his private life, causing us to marvel anew at Leonardo's fertile and versatile mind while acquiring a sharper image of Leonardo the man. A richly detailed, expansive, and thoroughly enjoyable portrait." Booklist

Includes bibliographical references

Lewis, C. S. (Clive Staples), 1898-1963

Wilson, A. N. (Andrew Norman). C.S. Lewis; a biography. Norton 1990 334p il $25   **92**
1. Authors, English
ISBN 0-393-02813-5   LC 89-27361

Also available in paperback from Fawcett Columbine

This biography "brings to light the most important episodes and aspects of Lewis' life: for instance, his curious and longstanding relationship with Janie ('Minto') Moore, his troubled friendship with J. R. R. Tolkien, his secret marriage to Joy Gresham, his conversion to Christianity, and his unending and increasingly subtle scrutiny of what it meant to be a Christian." Booklist

"The mixture presented in Wilson's biography of the life of learning, the college life at Magdalen where he taught, of domestic drama and bad temper, religion, and sex, is irresistible." N Y Rev Books

Includes bibliographical references

Lincoln, Abraham, 1809-1865

Donald, David Herbert. Lincoln. Simon & Schuster 1995 714p il maps $35; pa $17   **92**
1. Presidents—United States
ISBN 0-684-80846-3; 0-684-82535-X (pa)
                   LC 95-4782

This book "moves between Lincoln's private and public lives with a clarity that illuminates the connections between them. Donald negotiates the potential pitfalls for Lincoln biographers with surefooted grace: Lincoln's re-

Lincoln, Abraham, 1809-1865—*Continued*
lationship with his father; his romance with Ann Rutledge; his bouts of 'hypo,' which amounted at times almost to clinical depression; his marriage; his political ambition; his attitudes toward slavery and black people; his relations with radical Republicans during the Civil War; the mistakes and successes of his wartime leadership." Atl Mon
Includes bibliographical references

Handlin, Oscar. Abraham Lincoln and the Union; [by] Oscar and Lilian Handlin. Little, Brown 1980 204p il (Library of American biography) o.p.; Scott, Foresman paperback available $16   92
  1. Presidents—United States 2. United States—Politics and government—1815-1861
ISBN 0-673-39340-2 (pa)   LC 80-81259
"An Atlantic Monthly Press book"
This is a "character study of Abraham Lincoln which surveys his entire life but places the greatest emphasis on his early formative years. . . . The authors . . . outline his philosophical views in a clear, concise, and highly readable fashion." Choice
Includes bibliography

Kunhardt, Philip B. Lincoln; an illustrated biography; by Philip B. Kunhardt, Jr., Philip B. Kunhardt III, Peter W. Kunhardt; foreword by David Herbert Donald; contributing writer, Daniel Terris. Knopf 1992 415p il maps $50; pa $30
                                    92
  1. Presidents—United States
ISBN 0-679-40862-2; 0-679-75563-2 (pa)
                               LC 92-53043
"The photographs reproduced here, arrestingly arranged across oversize pages, were drawn from the archives of a major Lincoln repository, and the textual accompaniment borrows passages from A.L.'s own letters and speeches, as well as from diaries of his contemporaries. . . . Scholars and generalists alike will be absorbed by the splendid visual presentation." Booklist
Includes bibliography

Oates, Stephen B. Abraham Lincoln, the man behind the myths. Harper & Row 1984 224p hardcover o.p. paperback available $12.50   92
  1. Presidents—United States 2. United States—History—1861-1865, Civil War
ISBN 0-06-092472-1 (pa)   LC 83-48798
This book first suggests some myths about Lincoln and then includes chapters on his political development; "themes in his personal life; his abilities as a war leader, especially as emancipator; and the assassination. Oates also [presents a section on Mary Lincoln]." Libr J
"Oates re-creates the life and world of Abraham Lincoln with the skill of a master painter, using images and colors on a canvas. . . . [The author] succeeds in portraying both the facts and myths of history as essential to our understanding it." Christ Sci Monit
Includes bibliographical references

Oates, Stephen B. With malice toward none: the life of Abraham Lincoln. Harper & Row 1977 492p il hardcover o.p. paperback available $16
                                    92
  1. Presidents—United States
ISBN 0-06-092471-3 (pa)   LC 76-12058
The author wanted "to rescue Abraham Lincoln from the 'mists of legend.' Lincoln, he insists, was neither a superhuman prairie democrat nor a saintly Great Emancipator." Saturday Rev
Includes bibliographical references

Sandburg, Carl. Abraham Lincoln: The prairie years and The war years. illustrated ed. Harcourt Brace Jovanovich 1970 640p il maps hardcover o.p. paperback available $22   92
  1. Presidents—United States 2. Frontier and pioneer life 3. United States—History—1861-1865, Civil War
ISBN 0-15-602611-2 (pa)
First published 1954
A condensation of the two volumes of "The prairie years" (1926) and the four volumes of "The war years" (1939). The author has taken advantage of material made available since the original volumes were published to include in this edition of his lifetime study of Lincoln
"A biography that as a whole is superior to the longer life. This one volume has a form which the six lacked. It is a tighter and tidier book. It retains the superb qualities of the original work without the faults of the latter." Saturday Rev
Includes bibliographical references

Lindbergh, Anne Morrow, 1906-
Lindbergh, Anne Morrow. War within and without; diaries and letters of Anne Morrow Lindbergh, 1939-1944. Harcourt Brace Jovanovich 1980 xxxi, 471p il hardcover o.p. paperback available $14.95   92
ISBN 0-15-694703-X (pa)   LC 79-21614
"A Helen and Kurt Wolff book"
This is the final volume of the author's letters and diaries; previous volumes: Bring me a unicorn (1972); Hour of gold, hour of lead (1973); Locked rooms and open doors (1974) and The flower and the nettle (1976)
This volume "covers the prewar and war years, during which she and her celebrated husband took their stand against the Roosevelt administration and interventionist lobbies at home and abroad, to serve as spokesmen for the isolationist position. . . . [The volume also deals with such experiences as] having babies, engaging nurses and secretaries, finding suitable rental properties on Long Island, Martha's Vineyard, and so forth." Christ Sci Monit
Includes bibliographical references

Lindbergh, Anne Morrow, 1906—— *Continued*
Milton, Joyce. Loss of Eden: a biography of
Charles and Anne Morrow Lindbergh. See entry
under Lindbergh, Charles, 1902-1974

Lindbergh, Charles, 1902-1974
Denenberg, Barry. An American hero: the true
story of Charles A. Lindbergh. Scholastic 1996
255p il maps $16.95   **92**
  1. Air pilots
  ISBN 0-590-46923-1   LC 95-24628
Dividing "Lindbergh's life into two parts, 'Ascent'
and 'Descent,' Denenberg charts his subject's course
from childhood and adolescence through his historic
transatlantic flight and marriage to Anne Morrow." Bull
Cent Child Books
  "Denenberg delivers a fascinating, evenhanded, and
carefully researched examination of the aviator. . . .
Well-placed excerpts from Lindbergh's own writings and
from those of Anne Morrow Lindbergh effectively position the reader in the excitement of the moment." Booklist
  Includes bibliography

Lindbergh, Charles. "We"; with a foreword by
Myron T. Herrick; fully illustrated. Putnam 1927
318p il   **92**
  1. Air pilots 2. Aeronautics—Flights
Available in hardcover from Amereon and Buccaneer
Bks.
  "The famous flier's own story of his life, and his
transatlantic flight, together with his views on the future
of aviation." Subtitle

Milton, Joyce. Loss of Eden: a biography of
Charles and Anne Morrow Lindbergh.
HarperCollins Pubs. 1993 520p il hardcover o.p.
paperback available $17.50   **92**
  1. Lindbergh, Anne Morrow, 1906- 2. Air pilots
  ISBN 0-06-092482-9 (pa)   LC 92-53319
This dual biography "examines the events and circumstances that brought the couple fame: Charles's unprecedented nonstop solo airplane flight across the Atlantic in
1927; Anne's social prominence; the kidnapping and
murder of their son in 1932; their notorious role in the
isolationist movement during WW II; their literary
achievements; Charles's naïve respect for Hitler. At the
same time, Milton's superb research yields exceptionally
evocative period details." Publ Wkly
  Includes bibliographical references

Little Crow, Sioux Chief, d. 1863
Anderson, Gary Clayton. Little Crow,
spokesman for the Sioux. Minnesota Hist. Soc.
Press 1986 259p il hardcover o.p. paperback
available $10.95   **92**
  1. Dakota Indians
  ISBN 0-87351-196-4 (pa)   LC 86-795
  Little Crow is represented as "an accommodationist
Indian leader who, frustrated by increasing pressure from
white encroachments on Indian lands and consequent loss
of personal status among tribesmen, turned from accom-

modation to warfare." Am Hist Rev
  The author "weaves a fine narrative. He emphasizes
the importance of understanding the Dakota culture (especially social systems, leadership, and religion) and how
it interacted with government policy. This interethnic
study succeeds more in its presentation of the Indian side
than of the white." Choice
  Includes bibliography

Long, Huey Pierce, 1893-1935
LeVert, Suzanne. Huey Long; the Kingfish of
Louisiana. Facts on File 1995 134p il (Makers of
America) $17.95   **92**
  1. Politicians—United States
  ISBN 0-8160-2880-X   LC 94-19439
The book begins with "the assassination, then pro-
ceeds to analyze the key events in Long's life, putting
his beliefs and political contributions in the context of
the time in which he lived. . . . [A] factual, unbiased
look at the inner workings of government." Booklist
  Includes bibliographical references

Williams, T. Harry (Thomas Harry). Huey Long.
Knopf 1969 884, xxiip il $40; pa $21   **92**
  1. Politicians—United States
  ISBN 0-394-42954-0; 0-394-74790-9 (pa)
"Huey Long's enemies considered him to be a danger-
ous demagogue and radical while his loyal followers
looked upon him as the champion of the poor against the
power of the big corporations. . . . Professor T. Harry
Williams . . . interviewed almost 300 individuals who
knew Huey Long. He analyzed the development of
Long's personality from his early childhood days in the
northern parish of Winn to his career in the United
States Senate." Best Sellers
  Includes bibliographical references

Lost Bird, d. 1920
Flood, Renée S. Lost Bird of Wounded Knee;
spirit of the Lakota; [by] Renée Sansom Flood.
Scribner 1995 384p il $25   **92**
  1. Dakota Indians
  ISBN 0-684-19512-7   LC 95-7652
A "biography of one of the few Native American survivors of the massacre at Wounded Knee in 1890. . . .
Adopted by General Leonard Wright Colby, a corrupt
and unscrupulous army officer and attorney, and his
wife, prominent suffrage leader, Clara B. Colby, Lost
Bird was financially exploited and sexually abused by
the general and patronized by the well-meaning but misguided Mrs. Colby. Rejected by and alienated from two
cultures and traumatized by the nightmarish quality of
her rootless childhood, Lost Bird went on to face one
devastating misfortune after another during her brief and
bitter adulthood." Booklist
  Includes bibliographical references

Louis, Joe, 1914-1981
Barrow, Joe Louis. Joe Louis; 50 years an
American hero; by Joe Louis Barrow, Jr. &
Barbara Munder. McGraw-Hill 1988 270p il   **92**
  1. Boxing—Biography 2. African American athletes
                                            LC 88-9019
Available only in G.K. Hall large print edition

Louis, Joe, 1914-1981—*Continued*
This "biography is the result of Barrow's search for his father. He interviewed dozens of Louis' contemporaries, who fondly recall a warm, witty, and generous individual. . . . This intimate human saga of a son seeking to learn whatever he can concerning a father he barely knew offers a whole new perspective on Joe Louis as a man." Booklist
Includes bibliography

Mead, Chris. Champion: Joe Louis, black hero in white America. Scribner 1985 330p il o.p.; Robson/Parkwest Publs. paperback available $12.95   92
    1. Boxing—Biography 2. African American athletes
    ISBN 0-86051-848-5 (pa)   LC 85-14440
"Primarily through an analysis of press accounts, Mr. Mead traces the development of white attitudes toward Louis in particular and, by extension, blacks in general." N Y Times Book Rev
"In addition to perceptive social analysis, this study has plenty to say about boxing itself. Mead has a fine sense of the sport, and his accounts of Louis' ring triumphs are genuinely exciting. A superior sports biography." Booklist
Includes bibliography

Luce, Henry Robinson, 1898-1967
Baughman, James L. Henry R. Luce and the rise of the American news media. Twayne Pubs. 1987 264p il (Twayne's twentieth-century American biography series) hardcover o.p. paperback available $14.95   92
    1. Journalists 2. Publishers and publishing
    ISBN 0-8057-7755-5 (pa)   LC 87-14891
This biography of the founder of Time magazine "focuses on Luce's two-stage career. The first involved the new types of information media: the news-magazine, the business periodical, the photo weekly. The second involved Luce the public man, more concerned about presidential politics and world affairs. . . . Baughman presents a balanced picture of the man and of a golden age of journalism." Booklist
Includes bibliography

Lund, Eric
Lund, Doris Herold. Eric; [by] Doris Lund. Lippincott 1974 345p hardcover o.p. paperback available $6   92
    1. Leukemia—Personal narratives
    ISBN 0-06-080925-6 (pa)
An account, by his mother, of the "last four years in the life of Eric Lund, dead at 20 of leukemia, who faced both his life and his approaching death with courage and good humor." SLJ

Luther, Martin, 1483-1546
Bainton, Roland Herbert. Here I stand: a life of Martin Luther   92
    1. Europe—Church history 2. Reformation
Hardcover and paperback editions available from various publishers
First published 1950 by Abingdon-Cokesbury Press

This biography of Martin Luther interprets his work, writings, and lasting contributions. It recreates the spiritual setting of the sixteenth century and shows Luther's place within it

Lynn, Loretta
Lynn, Loretta. Loretta Lynn: coal miner's daughter; [by] Loretta Lynn with George Vecsey. Da Capo Press 1996 204p il pa $13.95   92
    1. Country musicians 2. Singers
    ISBN 0-306-80680-0   LC 95-46394
"A Bernard Geis Associates book"
First published 1976 by Regnery
The author "tells in her own words of her youth in Butcher Holler, Kentucky, her marriage at 14 to Doolittle 'Mooney' Lynn, being a grandmother at age 29, and her rise to country music's Best Female Vocalist. . . . The book seems an honest account of her career and marriage." Libr J

Mabry, Marcus
Mabry, Marcus. White bucks and black-eyed peas; coming of age black in white America. Scribner 1995 303p $23   92
    1. African Americans—Biography 2. United States—Race relations
    ISBN 0-684-19669-7   LC 95-16110
The author writes of "his path from the ghetto to a sometimes precarious place in the white mainstream. . . . Most of this book . . . concerns Mabry's rewarding but rocky times as a scholarship prep-school student at Lawrenceville (N.J.) and as an undergraduate at Stanford, plus his entrée into France and a budding career at Newsweek." Publ Wkly
"A penetrating, gracefully written dissection of life on the racial and generational cusp." Booklist

MacArthur, Douglas, 1880-1964
Manchester, William. American Caesar: Douglas MacArthur, 1880-1964. Little, Brown 1978 793p il maps $40   92
    1. Generals
    ISBN 0-316-54498-1   LC 78-8004
Also available in paperback from Dell
Manchester examines the life of the American general who was United Nations commander-in-chief in Korea
"William Manchester concentrates on MacArthur's character and personality and the reactions of others to him, giving only sketches of his battles." Harpers
Includes bibliography

Malcolm X, 1925-1965
Brown, Kevin. Malcolm X; his life and legacy. Millbrook Press 1995 112p il lib bdg $19.90; pa $9.95   92
    1. African Americans—Biography 2. Black Muslims
    ISBN 1-56294-500-9 (lib bdg); 1-56294-890-3 (pa)
                            LC 94-5381
"This biography provides the familiar aspects of Malcolm X's life as well as an excellent analysis of his political ideology. Brown combines a mature vocabulary

Malcolm X, 1925-1965—*Continued*

with precise writing to create an intelligently honed and not-too-worshipful portrait, presenting the history of the civil rights movement as the context for Malcolm's development." SLJ

Includes bibliographical references

Gallen, David. Malcolm X: as they knew him. Carroll & Graf Pubs. 1992 288p il $21.95; pa $11.95   92

1. African Americans—Biography 2. Black Muslims

ISBN 0-88184-851-4; 0-88184-850-6 (pa)

LC 92-6436

"The first section is a richly woven narrative—oral reminiscences by a variety of people who knew Malcolm intimately or professionally. Familiar (Maya Angelou, the late Alex Haley, Kenneth B. Clark, Mike Wallace) and unfamiliar names blend together in this testimony to Malcolm's prophetic and charismatic nature. . . . The second section of the book consists of seven interviews with Malcolm. . . . Part Three contains six reflective essays on Malcolm's role in African American history. Among the diverse views presented are those by Eldridge Cleaver, James Baldwin, and Robert Penn Warren." Libr J

Malcolm X. The autobiography of Malcolm X; with the assistance of Alex Haley; introduction by M. S. Handler; epilogue by Alex Haley; afterword by Ossie Davis. Ballantine Bks. 1992 500p $20; pa $12   92

1. African Americans—Biography 2. Black Muslims

ISBN 0-345-37975-6; 0-345-37671-4 (pa)

LC 92-52659

First published 1965 by Grove Press

Based on tape-recorded conversations with Alex Haley, this account of the life of the Black Muslim leader was completed shortly before his murder

Alex Haley "did his job with sensitivity and with devotion. . . . [The book] will have a permanent place in the literature of the Afro-American struggle." N Y Rev Books

Myers, Walter Dean. Malcolm X; by any means necessary; a biography. Scholastic 1993 210p il $13.95; pa $4.50   92

1. African Americans—Biography 2. Black Muslims

ISBN 0-590-46484-1; 0-590-48109-6 (pa)

LC 92-13480

"Myers organizes Malcolm X's life into four stages: his childhood; his adolescence; his period of working under Elijah Mohammad; and his life after breaking with the Nation of Islam. Throughout, his experiences and actions are presented in a broader social context." SLJ

"If you can choose only one book about Malcolm X this is the book of choice. . . . Myers respects his subject and his teenage audience." Voice Youth Advocates

Includes bibliography

Mandela, Nelson

Hoobler, Dorothy. Mandela; the man, the struggle, the triumph; by Dorothy & Thomas Hoobler. Watts 1992 142p il lib bdg $22.70   92

1. Mandela, Winnie 2. African National Congress 3. South Africa—Race relations

ISBN 0-531-11141-5   LC 91-36649

Updated edition of Nelson and Winnie Mandela, first published 1987

This biography "opens with Mandela's speech to the U.S. Congress in July 1990 and goes on to give a few paragraphs about the history of the Xhosa people. After a description of Mandela's ancestors' defeat by the whites, there is a section on the historical sources of the broader South African conflict. With the stage set, the narrative of his life within this system continues." SLJ

"The narrative is clean and objective in dealing [both] with Nelson Mandela and his [ex-]wife Winnie. The arrest and trial of Winnie Mandela, on charges of participating in the murder of two youths, are presented factually." Voice Youth Advocates

Includes bibliography

Mandela, Nelson. Long walk to freedom: the autobiography of Nelson Mandela. Little, Brown 1994 558p il $24.95   92

1. South Africa—Politics and government

ISBN 0-316-54585-6   LC 94-79980

This is an account of Nelson "Mandela's life from his 'country childhood' following his birth on July 18, 1918 to his inauguration as president of South Africa on May 10, 1994." Libr J

This book "provides important new evidence to the forty-year story of apartheid, as seen by its most formidable opponent. And there is enough candour to provide insights into the nature of leadership." Times Lit Suppl

Mandela, Nelson. Mandela; an illustrated autobiography. Little, Brown 1996 208p il map $29.95   92

1. South Africa—Race relations 2. South Africa—Politics and government

ISBN 0-316-55038-8   LC 96-77497

"This is an illustrated and abridged edition of Long walk to freedom: the autobiography of Nelson Mandela." Verso of title page

"The photos, from a variety of archives and journalistic sources, ably illustrate Mandela and, even more so, the South Africa around him." Libr J

Otfinoski, Steven. Nelson Mandela; the fight against apartheid. Millbrook Press 1992 128p il map lib bdg $16.40   92

1. African National Congress 2. South Africa—Race relations

ISBN 1-56294-067-8   LC 91-35031

The author profiles the life and career of the South African president. The book opens with a "description of Mandela's release from prison in 1990; the next chapter briefly recounts South Africa's history up to the decade in which [Mandela] was born and his boyhood until he leaves the reserve for Johannesburg. The remaining nine chapters discuss his growing political leadership, long imprisonment, and activities since his release." SLJ

Includes bibliography

Manet, Édouard, 1832-1883
Wright, Patricia. Manet. Dorling Kindersley
1993 64p il (Eyewitness art) $16.95   **92**
1. Artists, French
ISBN 1-56458-172-1   LC 92-54546
This visual introduction to the life and works of the
French painter includes many reproductions of his paint-
ings, photographs of his studio and tools, and close-up
details to show his technique
Includes glossary

Mantle, Mickey, 1931-1995
Schoor, Gene. The illustrated history of Mickey
Mantle. Carroll & Graf Pubs. 1996 213p il $28.95
                                                 92
1. Baseball—Biography
ISBN 0-7867-0305-9   LC 96-14981
The story of Mantle's "meteoric rise from the minors
to the majors, his eagerness to play even when badly injured and his legendary carouses with teammates Billy
Martin and Whitey Ford has been told many times, but
not in so prolifically illustrated a format. . . . The book
contains more than 200 photos, some in color, many of
them fine action shots." Publ Wkly

✓ **Mao Zedong, 1893-1976**
Stefoff, Rebecca. Mao Zedong; founder of the
People's Republic of China. Millbrook Press 1996
128p il lib bdg $16.40   **92**
1. China—History 2. Communism—China
ISBN 1-56294-531-9   LC 95-24662
"Mao Zedong's life and career are considered in seven
chapters. . . . Stefoff starts with the founding of the People's Republic of China, then switches to a more chronological order, . . . [discussing] the subject's youth and
development within the . . . framework of modern Chinese history." SLJ
"Readers get a clear sense of Mao's profound influence on Chinese (and world) history. Stefoff relates her
subject's life history and his later actions without being
pedantic or simplistic. The account is well documented
and includes many relevant, well-placed photographs."
Booklist
Includes bibliography

Markham, Beryl, 1902-1986
Lovell, Mary S. Straight on till morning: the
biography of Beryl Markham. St. Martin's Press
1987 xxiv, 408p il hardcover o.p. paperback
available $10.95   **92**
1. Women air pilots
ISBN 0-312-01895-9 (pa)   LC 87-16329
This is a life of the British aviatrix. "Raised in Kenya
alongside the sons of Nandi hunters, Markham was the
first person to fly west across the Atlantic solo." Libr J
Lovell does not "record only the high points of Beryl's life, nor does she eulogize her; rather, she gives the
whole picture of a woman. . . . Her biography provides
an enthralling study, not simply of a remarkable personality, but of a place, a period, and a culture." Wilson
Libr Bull
Includes bibliography

Marley, Bob
Talamon, Bruce. Bob Marley; spirit dancer; [by]
Bruce W. Talamon; text by Roger Steffens;
foreword by Timothy White. Norton 1994 128p il
$35; pa $17.95   **92**
1. Singers 2. Black musicians
ISBN 0-393-03686-3; 0-393-31200-3 (pa)
                                      LC 94-18321
This book consists mainly of Talamon's photographs
of the Jamaican reggae musician, with brief text by Steffens
"Tasteful and well done, Talamon's photographic essay stands in stark contrast to some of the raw, slapdash
products intended primarily to cash in on Marley's fame.
. . . A moving portrait of a great musician." Booklist

**Marshall, George C. (George Catlett), 1880-
1959**
Stoler, Mark A. George C. Marshall:
soldier-statesman of the American century. Twayne
Pubs. 1989 252p il (Twayne's twentieth-century
American biography series) lib bdg $30; pa $15.95
                                                 92
1. Generals
ISBN 0-8057-7768-7 (lib bdg); 0-8057-7785-7 (pa)
                                      LC 88-29474
"Stoler covers Marshall's long and distinguished career in as much detail as the scope of the volume allows,
with thorough research, clear writing, and balanced judgments. Marshall emerges as a man with his share of
flaws, but these are completely outweighed by his enormous gifts, particularly his leadership, organization, and
ability to understand both the uses and abuses of power."
Booklist
Includes bibliography

Marshall, John, 1755-1835
Stites, Francis N. John Marshall, defender of the
Constitution; edited by Oscar Handlin. Little,
Brown 1981 181p (Library of American
biography) o.p.; Scott, Foresman paperback
available $16   **92**
1. United States. Supreme Court 2. Judges
ISBN 0-673-39353-4 (pa)   LC 80-82014
A look at the man who served on the Supreme Court
for 34 years and his impact on American judicial history
Includes bibliographical references

Marshall, Thurgood
Davis, Michael D. Thurgood Marshall; warrior
at the bar, rebel on the bench; [by] Michael D.
Davis and Hunter R. Clark. Carol Pub. Group
1992 400p il $24.95; pa $16.95   **92**
1. United States. Supreme Court 2. African Americans—Biography 3. African Americans—Civil rights
ISBN 1-55972-133-2; 0-8065-1494-9 (pa)
                                      LC 92-26996
"A Birch Lane Press book"
This book "focuses on the professional life of the eloquent, hard-driven man who spearheaded the greatest legal victories for desegregation and civil rights for all

Marshall, Thurgood—*Continued*

people in this century. . . . As a guide to the legal struggles of this American leader, this book is written clearly and with obvious affection and admiration for Marshall." Booklist

Includes bibliographical references

Mathabane, Mark

Mathabane, Mark. Kaffir boy; the true story of a black youth's coming of age in apartheid South Africa. Macmillan 1986 354p il o.p.; New Am. Lib. paperback available $12.95   92

1. Blacks—Biography 2. South Africa—Race relations

ISBN 0-452-26471-5 (pa)   LC 86-53

"Born in the township of Alexandra in 1960, the author of this memoir experienced hunger, crime, and [segregation] . . . during his formative years. His mother and grandmother worked hard to enable him to finish school. . . . The narrative ends in 1978, as Mathabane takes up a U.S. tennis scholarship." Libr J

"Mathabane's account has a fierce physical and psychological authenticity. . . . The searing indictment of the apartheid system stems from personal experience and social observation." Booklist

Mathabane, Mark. Kaffir boy in America; an encounter with apartheid. Scribner 1989 303p il hardcover o.p. paperback available $10   92

1. Blacks—Biography 2. South Africa—Race relations 3. United States—Race relations

ISBN 0-02-034530-5 (pa)   LC 89-4199

In this sequel to the title entered above, Mathabane describes his life in the United States

Matisse, Henri

Gilot, Françoise. Matisse and Picasso; a friendship in art. Doubleday 1990 339p il hardcover o.p. paperback available $16   92

1. Picasso, Pablo, 1881-1973 2. Artists

ISBN 0-385-42241-5 (pa)   LC 90-34869

In Gilot's "memoir, Matisse, whom she greatly admired as kindred soul and fellow painter, seems to be the force holding together her roller-coaster relationship with Picasso. . . . Partly a valentine to a bygone Paris, her narrative also fills in the early years of Matisse and Picasso, with telling glimpses of Colette, Giacometti, Cocteau, Braque, Gertrude Stein, Juan Gris and many others. The book is charmingly illustrated with paintings, graphics and photographs." Publ Wkly

Herrera, Hayden. Matisse; a portrait. Harcourt Brace & Co. 1993 223p il $29.95; pa $16   92

1. Artists, French

ISBN 0-15-158183-5; 0-15-600204-3 (pa)

LC 92-31313

An "illustrated critical biography. The author demonstrates Matisse's progression from Fauvism to individual expression, illuminating some significant paintings along the way. She also explores the role of the artist's family in various creations. . . . Although she is breaking no new ground, comprehensive collections will want this book as a well-chosen window from which to observe the artist." Libr J

Mays, Willie, 1931-

Mays, Willie. Say hey: the autobiography of Willie Mays; [by] Willie Mays with Lou Sahadi. Simon & Schuster 1988 286p il hardcover o.p. paperback available $4.50   92

1. Baseball—Biography 2. African American athletes

ISBN 0-671-67836-1 (pa)   LC 88-6699

"A veteran of the Negro Leagues, where he played with his father in the late 1940s, Mays reached the majors in 1951 with the New York Giants. The 22-year career that followed is the stuff of baseball legend." Booklist

This "autobiography reveals Mays to be a fine man as well as someone who played baseball for the love of the game." Libr J

McCall, Nathan

McCall, Nathan. Makes me wanna holler; a young black man in America. Random House 1994 404p $23; pa $12   92

1. African Americans—Biography

ISBN 0-679-41268-9; 0-679-74070-8 (pa)

LC 93-30654

The author relates the "story of his rise from poverty to success as a journalist at the *Washington Post*. He uses graphic language, blunt descriptions, honest expression, introspection, and careful observation to describe his early years in Portsmouth, Virginia, as a young black male, the recipient of a 12-year prison sentence for armed robbery, whose life was dangerously out of control. Insensitivity, alienation, racial hatred, drugs (especially crack), guns, rape, robbery, the black American as an endangered species—McCall covers it all in a depressing yet spellbinding documentary." Libr J

McCandless, Christopher, 1968-1992

Krakauer, Jon. Into the wild. Villard Bks. 1996 207p maps $22   92

1. Alaska—Description

ISBN 0-679-42850-X   LC 95-20008

Also available in paperback from Anchor Bks. (NY)

"Christopher McCandless was a disaffected, idealistic young man who trekked into the Alaskan wilderness in search of transcendence and perished there. This narrative, which ponders his journey and inner life with sympathy and imagination, has YA appeal on many levels." Booklist

McCarthy, Joseph, 1908-1957

Reeves, Thomas C. The life and times of Joe McCarthy; a biography. Stein & Day 1982 819p il o.p.; Scarborough House paperback available $14.95   92

1. United States—Politics and government—1945-1953 2. United States—Politics and government—1953-1961

ISBN 0-8128-6200-7 (pa)   LC 79-3730

This "treatment of McCarthy's life and career . . . attempts to trace [his] activities, sorting and weighing the evidence on both sides of controversial issues. Reeves is critical of McCarthy, but is also critical of previous McCarthy critics, whom he accuses of McCarthyism."

McCarthy, Joseph, 1908-1957—*Continued*
Libr J

"About two-thirds of Mr. Reeves's jampacked pages are devoted to the Senator's . . . anti-Communist furies. . . . As the book reaches the period of the Army-McCarthy hearings, it takes on a compelling quality because of its very completeness." N Y Times Book Rev
Includes bibliography

McCourt, Frank

McCourt, Frank. Angela's ashes; a memoir. Scribner 1996 364p il $25   92
1. McCourt family 2. Irish Americans
ISBN 0-684-87435-0   LC 96-5335
"Frank McCourt, a teacher, grandfather and occasional actor, was born in New York City, but grew up in the Irish town of Limerick during the grim 1930's and 40's before he came back here as a teen-ager. His recollections of childhood are mournful and humorous, angry and forgiving." N Y Times Book Rev

Means, Russell, 1939-

Means, Russell. Where white men fear to tread; the autobiography of Russell Means; [by] Russell Means, with Marvin J. Wolf. St. Martin's Press 1995 573p il maps $26.95; pa $16.95   92
1. Oglala Indians
ISBN 0-312-13621-8; 0-312-14761-9 (pa)
                    LC 95-23289
American Indian activist Means "first came to worldwide media attention during the 1973 siege at Wounded Knee, South Dakota, and has rarely been out of the spotlight since. . . . This extremely readable and chatty autobiography gives an insider's eyewitness account of the events of Means's life, allowing non-Native readers some insight into the world of contemporary Native America with all of its strengths and weaknesses." Libr J

Meitner, Lise, 1878-1968

Sime, Ruth Lewin. Lise Meitner; a life in physics. University of Calif. Press 1996 526p il (California studies in the history of science) $34.95   92
1. Women scientists 2. Physicists
ISBN 0-520-08906-5   LC 95-35246
"A Centennial book"
"In addition to discovering the element protactinium, Lise Meitner's fame rests on experiments that led to the fissioning of uranium. But for multiple reasons—her own modesty, sexism in science, her flight from Germany in 1938—priority (and the Nobel Prize) went to her colleague Otto Hahn. Drawing from their correspondence, Sime reveals that Hahn had been initially stumped by what happened to the uranium he fired neutrons at; Meitner wrote back with the explanation. So, in effect, Sime has constructed here an admirable restorative of scientific credit." Booklist
Includes bibliography

Melville, Herman, 1819-1891

Stefoff, Rebecca. Herman Melville. Messner 1994 156p il (Classic American writers) lib bdg $15   92
1. Authors, American
ISBN 0-671-86771-7   LC 93-11751
"This biography recreates the excitement of Melville's early years and the depression in his later life when he is lacking money. American literature students will be interested in the relationship between Melville and Hawthorne. . . . Stefoff includes analysis of Melville's novels, short stories and poems as well as interesting details of his life. The biography is short enough to appeal to less proficient readers and to those who have read his works." Voice Youth Advocates
Includes bibliography

Michelangelo Buonarroti, 1475-1564

Hibbard, Howard. Michelangelo. Harper & Row 1974 347p il hardcover o.p. paperback available $18   92
1. Artists, Italian
ISBN 0-06-430148-6 (pa)
"Icon editions"
The author provides an introduction to Michelangelo's life and his achievements as sculptor, painter, and architect
"Every work is illustrated where it is discussed. . . . The reader is painlessly made to understand such complicated matters as the iconographical scheme of the Sistine ceiling." Natl Rev
Includes bibliography

Miller, Arthur, 1915-

Miller, Arthur. Timebends; a life. Grove Press 1987 614p il o.p.; Penguin Bks. paperback available $14.95   92
1. Dramatists, American
ISBN 0-14-024917-6 (pa)   LC 87-12074
"This beautifully written autobiography by the noted playwright draws us effortlessly into his life and times. Not strictly chronological in his narrative, Miller ranges widely, weaving together his writings and his life in the theater, his childhood and family, his political thinking, and his marriages into a rich, fluid whole." Libr J

Monet, Claude, 1840-1926

Waldron, Ann. Claude Monet. Abrams 1991 92p il (First impressions) $19.95   92
1. Artists, French 2. Impressionism (Art)
ISBN 0-8109-3620-8   LC 91-8602
Examines the life and work of Monet, describing his struggle for artistic recognition and providing examples of his paintings
"Lavishly illustrated with photographs and color reproductions, [this] readable introduction will interest art students and browsers." Booklist

Monroe, Marilyn, 1926-1962

Lefkowitz, Frances. Marilyn Monroe. Chelsea House 1995 127p il (Pop culture legends) lib bdg $19.95; pa $7.95   **92**
1. Actors
ISBN 0-7910-2342-7 (lib bdg); 0-7910-2367-2 (pa)
                                        LC 94-36335

An exploration of the private and professional life of the actress and pop culture icon. Illustrated with black-and-white photographs
Includes bibliography

More, Sir Thomas, Saint, 1478-1535

Kenny, Anthony John Patrick. Thomas More; [by] Anthony Kenny. Oxford Univ. Press 1983 111p (Past masters series) hardcover o.p. paperback available $7.95   **92**
1. Great Britain—History—1485-1603, Tudors
ISBN 0-19-287573-6 (pa)   LC 83-4209
This overview of More's life and times includes a close reading of Utopia and a discussion of his role as a staunch defender of Roman Catholicism
Includes bibliography

Morrison, Jim, 1943-1971

Jones, Dylan. Jim Morrison, dark star. Viking Studio Bks. 1991 191p il hardcover o.p. paperback available $19.95   **92**
1. Rock musicians
ISBN 0-14-016833-8 (pa)   LC 90-12885
In this biography of the controversial rock singer and songwriter "the journalist Dylan Jones charts the star's rise and fall and offers some fresh insights into his motivations and early influences." N Y Times Book Rev
Includes bibliographical references

Morrison, Toni, 1931-

Morrison, Toni. Conversations with Toni Morrison; edited by Danille Taylor-Guthrie. University Press of Miss. 1994 293p (Literary conversations series) $39.50; pa $15.95   **92**
1. Authors, American 2. Women authors 3. African American authors
ISBN 0-87805-691-2; 0-87805-692-0 (pa)
                                        LC 93-44738

This is a collection of interviews with and essays about the Nobel prize winning African American novelist from a variety of sources from 1974 to 1992

Mowat, Farley

Mowat, Farley. Born naked. Houghton Mifflin 1994 c1993 256p il maps $21.95; pa $10.95   **92**
1. Authors, Canadian
ISBN 0-395-68927-9; 0-395-73528-9 (pa)
                                        LC 93-23702

"A Peter Davison book"
First published 1993 in Canada
The "renowned naturalist and writer gives us a glimpse of his parents, his growing up in Canada, and the roots of his love for animals." Booklist
"There are no dull pages here; every man, woman, child, and animal mentioned even casually makes an impression. . . . Highly recommended to all those who like good writing." Libr J

Muir, John, 1838-1914

Wilkins, Thurman. John Muir; apostle of nature. University of Okla. Press 1995 xxvii, 302p il maps (Oklahoma western biographies) $24.95; pa $14.95   **92**
1. Naturalists
ISBN 0-8061-2712-0; 0-8061-2797-X (pa)
                                        LC 95-11426
"Wilkins follows Muir from his Scottish boyhood, clouded by a harsh, fundamentalist father, to an adolescence of arduous farmwork in Wisconsin to a lifelong career of exploration and study of wildernesses, particularly those of the western U.S., and vividly relates some of Muir's more perilous adventures on cliffside and snowfield. . . . An affectionate, uncluttered tale of an American folk hero." Booklist
Includes bibliographical references

Mussolini, Benito, 1883-1945

Hoyt, Edwin Palmer. Mussolini's empire; the rise and fall of the fascist vision; [by] Edwin P. Hoyt. Wiley 1994 298p $24.95   **92**
1. Dictators 2. Fascism—Italy 3. Italy—Politics and government
ISBN 0-471-59151-3   LC 93-11881
This work examines the career and personal life of the Italian dictator
"Hoyt sees Mussolini's failures as essentially political rather than moral. He glosses over the man's blatant cynicism, self-absorption, and inability to commit to anyone or anything beyond his personal aggrandizement. Still, Hoyt's unique psychological insights and his ability to place them into historical context make this a readable and valuable biography." Booklist
Includes bibliography

Newton, Sir Isaac, 1642-1727

Christianson, Gale E. In the presence of the creator: Isaac Newton and his times. Free Press 1984 623p il $29.95   **92**
1. Physicists 2. Mathematicians
ISBN 0-02-905190-8   LC 83-49211
This is an "account of the life of the 17th century genius whose basic discoveries—the three laws of motion, the existence of gravity, the mathematics of calculus and the nature of light—are the foundations of modern science." Publ Wkly
Includes bibliography

Ngor, Haing S.

Ngor, Haing S. A Cambodian odyssey; [by] Haing Ngor with Roger Warner. Macmillan 1987 478p il o.p.   **92**
1. Cambodia—History—1975-   LC 87-27355
An autobiographical account of a Phnom Penh physician's experiences from 1975 to 1979 while enslaved in Khmer Rouge work camps

Nicholas II, Emperor of Russia, 1868-1918

Massie, Robert K. Nicholas and Alexandra. Atheneum Pubs. 1967 584p il o.p.; Dell paperback available $7.99   **92**
1. Alexandra, Empress, consort of Nicholas II, Emperor of Russia, 1872-1918 2. Russia—Kings, queens, rulers, etc. 3. Russia—History
ISBN 0-440-36358-6 (pa)
This study provides an intimate account of the Romanov family and the coming of the Russian Revolution. Kerensky, Lenin and Rasputin are among the personalities profiled
This book, "solid with research, reads as lightly as a novel, as authoritatively as a textbook. Dialogue and lively description lend a sense of immediacy, but his notes, discreetly relegated to the back of the book, show how carefully he has avoided slipping into fiction." Christ Sci Monit
Includes bibliography

Nixon, Richard M. (Richard Milhous), 1913-1994

Aitken, Jonathan. Nixon, a life. Regnery Bks. 1993 633p il $28; pa $17.95   **92**
1. Presidents—United States 2. United States—Politics and government—1900-1999 (20th century)
ISBN 0-89526-489-7; 0-89526-720-9 (pa)
                                    LC 94-5671
The author "portrays former U.S. President Richard Nixon as a master geopolitical strategist who shifted the global balance of power in the West's favor through rapprochement with China and who achieved 'peace with honor' in Vietnam. Aitken views Nixon as 'an original and progressive domestic President.' . . . This biography draws on interviews with Nixon, his aides and family, and unique access to his private diaries and letters. Both critics and supporters will find . . . material to ponder." Publ Wkly
Includes bibliographical references

Nixon, Richard M. (Richard Milhous). In the arena: a memoir of victory, defeat, and renewal; [by] Richard Nixon. Simon & Schuster 1990 384p il hardcover o.p. paperback available $6.99   **92**
1. Presidents—United States
ISBN 0-671-72934-9 (pa)   LC 90-30013
"This volume serves as a kind of omnibus collection: Nixon on China, Nixon on glasnost, Nixon on the press, Nixon on philosophy of life, Nixon on campaigning, and so on." Booklist
"The memoir adds nothing new on Watergate. What it does is subtly round out our picture of a man." Christ Sci Monit

Nixon, Richard M. (Richard Milhous). RN: the memoirs of Richard Nixon; with a new introduction by President Nixon. Simon & Schuster 1990 1122p il pa $23   **92**
1. Presidents—United States
ISBN 0-671-70741-8   LC 90-31641
"A Touchstone book"
A reissue with a new introduction of the title first published 1978 by Grosset & Dunlap

Among the topics Nixon discusses are: his negotiations with the Soviets and Chinese, his conduct of the Vietnam War and his tendentious relationship with the press

Nostradamus, 1503-1566

Randi, James. The mask of Nostradamus. Scribner 1990 256p il o.p.; Prometheus Bks. paperback available $18.95   **92**
1. Prophecies (Occultism)
ISBN 0-87975-830-9 (pa)   LC 89-70189
A biographical study of "Michel de Notredame, better known as Nostradamus, the famous 16th-century French physician, astrologer and seer. Commentators claim that Nostradamus's cryptic verses accurately prophesied such events and personalities as Napoleon, Hitler, the French Revolution, the Great Fire of London and the invention of the Montgolfier balloon. Nonsense, argues Randi, and his meticulous readings of key quatrains make a potent case for his contention." Publ Wkly
Includes bibliography

O'Keeffe, Georgia, 1887-1986

Robinson, Roxana. Georgia O'Keeffe; a life. Harper & Row 1989 639p il hardcover o.p. paperback available $18   **92**
1. Artists, American 2. Women artists
ISBN 0-06-092000-9 (pa)   LC 89-45061
"An Edward Burlingame book"
"This biography, the first to draw on sources unavailable during O'Keeffe's lifetime—and the first to be granted her family's cooperation—offers a persuasive feminist analysis of the life and work of an iconic figure in American art. . . . [The author's] detailed, sensitive critique of O'Keeffe's work . . . alternates with an absorbing, intimate narrative of O'Keeffe's personal life." Publ Wkly
Includes bibliography

Olajuwon, Hakeem

Olajuwon, Hakeem. Living the dream; my life and basketball; [by] Hakeem Olajuwon, with Peter Knobler. Little, Brown 1996 300p il $22.95   **92**
1. Basketball—Biography 2. African American athletes
ISBN 0-316-09427-7   LC 95-81724
"Mr. Olajuwon recounts his childhood in Nigeria and the odd twists of fate that led him to play collegiate and professional basketball in the United States. . . . His refreshingly uncynical view of the sport is one of the most enjoyable aspects of his book. Although there are the requisite glimpses of other players and the N.B.A. life, the book is most moving when Mr. Olajuwon describes how he draws strength from his native culture and his Muslim faith." N Y Times Book Rev

Onassis, Jacqueline Kennedy

Heymann, C. David (Clemens David). A woman named Jackie: an intimate biography of Jacqueline Bouvier Kennedy Onassis. complete updated ed. Carol Pub. Group 1994 766p il $24.95; pa $17.95
92

1. Presidents—United States—Spouses
ISBN 1-55972-266-5; 1-55972-276-2 (pa)
LC 94-39215
"A Birch Lane Press book"
First published 1989 by L. Stuart
"In his attempt to unravel the personality of Jacqueline Kennedy Onassis, C. David Heymann . . . has painted a portrait of a good-looking woman of one-dimensional talents, intelligence, sensitivity and self-awareness, whose personality was dominated by three men: her father and her two husbands." N Y Times Book Rev
Includes bibliographical references

Orwell, George, 1903-1950

Flynn, Nigel. George Orwell. Rourke 1990 112p il (Life and works) lib bdg $19.94   **92**
1. Authors, English
ISBN 0-86593-018-X   LC 89-28359
Traces the life of the English author and social critic and provides critical interpretations of his controversial works
"The quotes in this literary biography are like booktalks, luring you to the original stories and essays." Booklist
Includes glossary and bibliographical references

Owens, Jesse, 1913-1980

Baker, William J. (William Joseph). Jesse Owens; an American life. Free Press 1986 289p il hardcover o.p. paperback available $14.95   **92**
1. African American athletes
ISBN 0-02-901760-2 (pa)   LC 86-4671
This biography of the gifted black track athlete intertwines the chronological story of Owens's life with the major political and social events of his time
Includes bibliography

Paine, Thomas, 1737-1809

Ayer, A. J. (Alfred Jules). Thomas Paine. Atheneum Pubs. 1988 195p il o.p.; University of Chicago Press paperback available $15.95   **92**
ISBN 0-226-03339-2 (pa)   LC 88-16622
"Tracing Paine's life from his birth in England to his emigration to America just before the Revolutionary War, Ayer considers the effect of Paine's pamphlet *Common Sense* upon that war. *Rights of Man* is then discussed in light of Burke's attacks upon the French Revolution and the thought of Hobbes, Locke, Hume, and Rousseau. The saga concludes with an account of the acrimony heaped upon Paine for his diatribes against Christian religious beliefs and his espousal of deism in *The Age of Reason*." Libr J
Includes bibliography

Parker, Quanah, Comanche Chief, 1854?-1911

Neeley, Bill. The last Comanche chief: the life and times of Quanah Parker. Wiley 1995 276p il maps $24.95; pa $16.95   **92**
1. Comanche Indians
ISBN 0-471-11722-6; 0-471-16076-8 (pa)
LC 94-38101
The author traces Parker's "life from youth to warrior chief to respected cattleman. He describes the last wars between the Comanches and settlers, the peyote ritual and pressures on Native Americans to conform to white society. . . . This is a fine portrait of the legendary chief and an illuminating glimpse into the history of the American West." Publ Wkly
Includes bibliographical references

Parks, Gordon

Parks, Gordon. A choice of weapons. Harper & Row 1966 274p o.p.; Minnesota Hist. Soc. Press paperback available $10.95   **92**
1. African Americans—Biography
ISBN 0-87351-202-2 (pa)
This autobiography traces Parks' early years from his days as busboy and musician to his assignment as photographer for the Farm Security Administration

Parks, Rosa, 1913-

Parks, Rosa. Quiet strength; the faith, the hope, and the heart of a woman who changed a nation; reflections by Rosa Parks with Gregory J. Reed. Zondervan 1994 93p il $12.99   **92**
1. African American women 2. African Americans—Civil rights
ISBN 0-310-50150-4   LC 94-46141
In 1955, "Rosa Parks was arrested for refusing to give up her seat on an Alabama bus to a white man. . . . [Here, she] talks about the principles and convictions that guided her throughout her life. . . . The afterword features a chronology of events in the life of Rosa Parks." MultiCult Rev
Includes bibliographical references

Patton, George S. (George Smith), 1885-1945

Blumenson, Martin. Patton, the man behind the legend, 1885-1945. Morrow 1985 320p il maps hardcover o.p. paperback available $15   **92**
1. Generals 2. World War, 1939-1945—Campaigns
ISBN 0-688-13795-4 (pa)   LC 85-15301
This biography of the World War II general uses quotes from Patton and his family
"At a glance, the book is deceptive. It appears to be a short popular biography written in a pleasing style, but it rests on a solid foundation of research." N Y Times Book Rev
Includes bibliography

Pauling, Linus C., 1901-1994

Hager, Thomas. Force of nature: the life of Linus Pauling. Simon & Schuster 1995 721p il $35   **92**
1. Chemists
ISBN 0-684-80909-5   LC 95-34072
The author "portrays Pauling as a man of insight and conscience and a major player in science, politics, and

Pauling, Linus C., 1901-1994—*Continued*
society throughout some extraordinary times. . . . Hager
does a superior job of fleshing out the details of Pauling's influences and motivations. He also interprets freely, especially in sections describing Pauling's political
convictions." Libr J
Includes bibliographical references

Perón, Eva, 1919-1952
Fraser, Nicholas. Eva Perón; [by] Nicholas
Fraser and Marysa Navarro. Norton 1981 c1980
192p il hardcover o.p. paperback available $11
                                                                    92
1. Argentina—Politics and government
ISBN 0-393-30238-5 (pa)   LC 80-29148
First published 1980 in the United Kingdom
This is an "excellent biographical analysis of Eva Pe-
rón, stressing her public life and public personality. The
book is extremely well researched, using the important
written material and many interviews by the authors.
There is a good bibliography and a footnote section."
Choice

Perón, Juan Domingo, 1895-1974
Page, Joseph A. Perón; a biography. Random
House 1983 594p il $25   92
1. Argentina—Politics and government
ISBN 0-394-52297-4   LC 82-40136
"This biography covers the political as well as the
personal aspects of Perón's life, including Perón's han-
dling of developments internally and internationally that
affected Argentina." Choice
Includes bibliography

**Peter I, the Great, Emperor of Russia, 1672-
1725**
Massie, Robert K. Peter the Great; his life and
world. Knopf 1980 909p il $40   92
1. Russia—Kings, queens, rulers, etc. 2. Russia—His-
tory
ISBN 0-394-50032-6   LC 80-7635
Also available in paperback from Ballantine Bks.
The author "explains Russia's foreign relations in the
late 1600's and early 1700's and the opening of Russia
to westernization. This is a sympathetic appraisal of Peter's accomplishments. . . . The lives of the aristocracy
are explored . . . and the changes wrought upon them
emphasized. This lengthy and informative book reads
like a novel full of romance and intrigue." Libr J
Includes bibliography

Picasso, Pablo, 1881-1973
Beardsley, John. Pablo Picasso. Abrams 1991
92p il (First impressions) $19.95   92
1. Artists, Spanish
ISBN 0-8109-3713-1   LC 91-7741
Examines the life and work of Picasso, discussing
how and why his art looks the way it does and how it
relates to the artist
This is a "readable and informative study. . . . This
book is as much a series of marvelous lessons in 'reading' art as it is a tribute to a unique artist." Horn Book

Gilot, Françoise. Matisse and Picasso. See entry
under Matisse, Henri

Piccolo, Brian, 1943-1970
Morris, Jeannie. Brian Piccolo; a short season.
special 25th anniversary ed. Bonus Bks. 1995
159p pa $12.95   92
1. Football—Biography 2. Cancer
ISBN 1-56625-024-2   LC 95-75028
First published 1971 by Rand McNally
"Brian Piccolo was a highly talented running back for
the Chicago Bears who lost his battle with cancer . . .
at the age of 26. This is the story of his outstanding athletic career from high school, through college, and on to
the pros. It is also the moving story of a devoted family
man who fought with confidence and courage the dread
disease that took his life." Libr J

Pirsig, Robert M.
Pirsig, Robert M. Zen and the art of motorcycle
maintenance; an inquiry into values. Morrow 1974
412p $22.95; pa $12.95   92
ISBN 0-688-00230-7; 0-688-05230-4 (pa)
A collection of the author's philosophical musings inspired by a motorcycle trip with his son

Plath, Sylvia
Plath, Sylvia. The journals of Sylvia Plath;
foreword by Ted Hughes; Ted Hughes, consulting
editor and Frances McCullough, editor. Dial Press
(NY) 1982 370p il o.p.; Ballantine Bks. paperback
available $5.95   92
1. Poets, American 2. Women poets
ISBN 0-345-35168-1 (pa)   LC 81-19435
These edited selections from Plath's journals cover the
period from July, 1950 (the summer before she entered
college) to December 1959 when she and her husband
Ted Hughes left for England

Pocahontas, d. 1617
Woodward, Grace Steele. Pocahontas. University
of Okla. Press 1969 227p il (Civilization of the
American Indian series) hardcover o.p. paperback
available $14.95   92
1. Powhatan Indians 2. United States—History—
1600-1775, Colonial period
ISBN 0-8061-1642-0 (pa)
This is the "story of the appealing daughter of Chief
Powhatan and her friendship with the colonists of the
Jamestown settlement. . . . Her marriage and brief life in
England are vividly re-created." Booklist
Includes bibliography

Poe, Edgar Allan, 1809-1849
Anderson, Madelyn Klein. Edgar Allan Poe; a
mystery. Watts 1993 158p il (Impact biography)
lib bdg $22.70   92
1. Authors, American
ISBN 0-531-13012-6   LC 92-43935
This biography traces "Poe's history from his childhood with his foster family, his mercurial relations with

Poe, Edgar Allan, 1809-1849—*Continued*
friends and enemies (particularly female friends and enemies), and his professional life as an editor and writer
for various periodicals." Bull Cent Child Books

The author "includes a useful chronology of composition and publication dates for all the poems and tales and
a rather unique bibliography in which she states 'not all
the books . . . are recommended.' She explains that
many are inaccessible for a variety of reasons and then
tells which are good for young readers." Voice Youth
Advocates

Porter, Katherine Anne, 1890-1980
Givner, Joan. Katherine Anne Porter; a life. rev
ed. University of Ga. Press 1991 576p il $45; pa
$19.95 **92**
1. Authors, American 2. Women authors
ISBN 0-8203-1348-3; 0-8203-1340-8 (pa)
LC 90-23496
"Brown thrasher books"
First published 1982 by Simon & Schuster
A biography of the American writer whose works in-
clude: Flowering Judas, Hacienda, Noon wine, Ship of
fools, and Pale horse, pale rider

"Givner has plumbed Porter's every year thoroughly
in this comprehensive and well-rounded study. . . . With
patience and understanding, she presents this woman as
the 'aristocratic first lady of American letters, linguist,
musician, femme fatale, and raconteur.'" Christ Sci
Monit [review of 1982 edition]
Includes bibliographical references

Powell, Colin L.
✓ Powell, Colin L. My American journey; [by]
Colin L. Powell, with Joseph E. Persico. Random
House 1995 643p il $25.95 **92**
1. Generals 2. African American soldiers
ISBN 0-679-43296-5 LC 95-17119
Also available large print edition for $25.95 (ISBN 0-
679-76511-5) and in paperback from Ballantine Bks.

"This is the 'story so far,' as General Powell tells it,
from the Bronx to Vietnam to the White House, from the
common to the regal. His account is one of . . . extremes, tales that span from peeling potatoes with the Soviet General Staff to conversing with the Queen of England." Libr J

This "is an endearing and well-written book. It will
make you like Colin Powell." N Y Times Book Rev

✓ Roth, David. Sacred honor: a biography of
Colin Powell. Zondervan 1993 256p il $19.99; pa
$10.99 **92**
1. Generals 2. African American soldiers
ISBN 0-310-60480-X; 0-310-20656-1 (pa)
LC 93-4644
This "biography presents the details of Powell's life,
from his birth and childhood in South Bronx, surrounded
by a loving Jamaican family, to the 'highest military job
in America.' . . . Throughout the book, his bravery, his
consideration for others, his self-discipline, his moral integrity is uppermost, with not one negative mentioned."
Book Rep

Presley, Elvis, 1935-1977
Geller, Larry. If I can dream; Elvis' own story;
[by] Larry Geller and Joel Spector with Patricia
Romanowski. Simon & Schuster 1989 331p il o.p.;
Avon Bks. paperback available $4.95 **92**
1. Singers 2. Rock musicians
ISBN 0-380-71042-0 (pa) LC 89-4231
"Geller, Presley's hairdresser, who describes himself
as a confidant and spiritual advisor to the late singer,
kept a diary that is the basis for this book. The biography is easily read, evenhanded, straightforward, unapolo-
getic, and seemingly unbiased. The material is treated
with care, thought, and cool reason." SLJ

Guralnick, Peter. Last train to Memphis: the rise
of Elvis Presley. Little, Brown 1994 560p il
$24.95; pa $14.95 **92**
1. Singers 2. Rock musicians
ISBN 0-316-33220-8; 0-316-33225-9 (pa)
LC 94-10763
The first of a projected two volume biography of the
rock pioneer

The author "depicts Elvis as a naive yet extremely talented boy whose dream of stardom came true, leaving
him a virtual prisoner of his own success. Realized
through scores of interviews and hours of in-depth research, Guralnick's Elvis is ignorant of worldly matters,
seemingly without artifice, but a quick study; he aims to
please, wants to be a good role model, and is genuinely
distressed when some find his gyrations vulgar, even
pornographic. . . . Taking pains to keep the story fresh
and flowing and refraining from foreshadowing and edi-
torializing, Guralnick lets the facts speak for themselves." Booklist
Includes bibliographical references

Pushkin, Aleksandr Sergeevich, 1799-1837
Edmonds, Robin. Pushkin; the man and his age.
St. Martin's Press 1995 303p il $27.95 **92**
1. Authors, Russian
ISBN 0-312-13593-9 LC 95-34753
First published 1994 in the United Kingdom
"Born to the nobility, Pushkin squandered much of his
money on cards. Politically liberal, he narrowly escaped
the wrath of the czar, who felt that it was Pushkin's
verse that contributed to the explosive sentiments behind
the ill-fated Decembrist revolt in 1825. Pushkin's most
productive years were spent in exile. The strength of Edmonds's biography is its literary analysis of the poems.
Quoting both from the original Russian and translations,
Edmonds puts the poems into the larger context of Pushkin's life and times." Libr J
Includes bibliographical references

Rabin, Yitzhak, 1922-1995
Ben Artzi-Pelossof, Noa. In the name of sorrow
and hope. Knopf 1996 181p il $21 **92**
1. Prime ministers—Israel 2. Israel—Politics and government
ISBN 0-679-45079-3 LC 96-143582
Also available large print edition (ISBN 0-679-
44245-6) $24

Rabin, Yitzhak, 1922-1995—Continued

"In this memoir of her grandfather and of the political climate that shaped his life and death, Ben Artzi-Pelossof shows that her funerary eloquence was no fluke; that she is, as much for her passion as for her lineage, a natural spokesperson for the sorrow and hope of a young generation of Israelis. The author presents family lore about Rabin, and her own memories—loving but not hagiographic—of the man, and speaks of the difficulty of growing up in a celebrated family." Publ Wkly

Radner, Gilda, 1946-1989

Radner, Gilda. It's always something. Simon & Schuster 1989 269p il $17   92
1. Cancer—Personal narratives
ISBN 0-671-68361-6   LC 89-6303
Also available in paperback from Avon Bks.
In this account of her struggle with ovarian cancer "the spirited star of 'Saturday Night Live' has laid out all the horrors of surgery and chemotherapy, but there are also lighter moments, like her 1984 marriage to the actor Gene Wilder. . . . 'It's Always Something' is compelling as testimony from the cancer wars by a courageous and much-loved entertainer." N Y Times Book Rev

Rand, Ayn, 1905-1982

Branden, Barbara. The passion of Ayn Rand. Doubleday 1986 442p il hardcover o.p. paperback available $15.95   92
1. Authors, American 2. Women authors
ISBN 0-385-24388-X (pa)   LC 85-20704
A critical look at the life and work of the influential novelist and conservative philosopher
Includes bibliography

Rasputin, Grigoriĭ Efimovich, 1871-1916

Fuhrmann, Joseph T. Rasputin; a life. Praeger Pubs. 1990 276p il $39.95   92
ISBN 0-275-93215-X   LC 89-3651
"The author distinguishes fact and probability from myth in the life of Grigory Rasputin, a Siberian peasant known as a profligate, religious leader, and faith healer. Fuhrmann documents how Rasputin's ability to aid the hemophiliac heir, Alexis, led to his power to influence Empress Alexandra and through her, Nicholas II, Russia's last tsar." Libr J
Includes bibliography

Rather, Dan

Rather, Dan. The camera never blinks twice; the further adventures of a television journalist; with Mickey Herskowitz. Morrow 1994 368p hardcover o.p. paperback available $10   92
1. Journalists 2. Broadcast journalism
ISBN 0-688-14350-4 (pa)   LC 94-12836
Companion volume to The camera never blinks (1977)
"Network news anchor Rather recalls numerous incidents in his career in a candid memoir, suggested for teens who enjoyed his earlier best-seller." Booklist

Rawlings, Marjorie Kinnan, 1896-1953

Silverthorne, Elizabeth. Marjorie Kinnan Rawlings; sojourner at Cross Creek. Overlook Press 1988 374p il $24.95; pa $14.95   92
1. Authors, American 2. Women authors
ISBN 0-87951-308-X; 0-87951-320-9 (pa)
LC 87-28589
A "biography of the author of The Yearling, South Moon Under, and Cross Creek. Tracing her childhood, her struggles as a young journalist in New York, and her discovery of the Florida wild, Silverthorne relates the life to the work, documenting Rawlings' often painful struggle to become the real artist she longed to be." Publisher's note
Includes bibliography

Reagan, Ronald, 1911-

Sullivan, George. Ronald Reagan. rev ed. Messner 1991 142p il lib bdg $14.98   92
1. Presidents—United States
ISBN 0-671-74537-9   LC 91-3744
First published 1985
Traces the life of the fortieth President, including his childhood, film career, and his years in state and national politics

Reiss, Johanna

Reiss, Johanna. The upstairs room. Crowell 1972 273p $15; pa $4.50   92
1. World War, 1939-1945—Jews 2. Netherlands—History—1940-1945, German occupation 3. Jews—Netherlands
ISBN 0-690-85127-8; 0-06-440370-X (pa)
"The author recalls her experiences as a Jewish child hiding from the Germans occupying her native Holland during World War II. . . . Ten-year-old Annie and her twenty-year-old sister Sini . . . are taken in by a Dutch farmer, his wife, and mother who hide the girls in an upstairs room of the farm house." Booklist
Followed by The journey back (1976)

Rembrandt Harmenszoon van Rijn, 1606-1669

Schwartz, Gary. Rembrandt. Abrams 1992 92p il (First impressions) $19.95   92
1. Artists, Dutch
ISBN 0-8109-3760-3   LC 91-26171
Surveys the life and work of the well-known seventeenth-century Dutch artist and discusses the reasons for the rise and fall of artists' reputations
The author "presents a Rembrandt with all the flaws and quirks he had, telling an engrossing story that even those who know something about the artist will find hard to put down. Cream-colored frames around each page make the book visually inviting." SLJ

Reno, Janet, 1938-

Anderson, Paul. Janet Reno; doing the right thing. Wiley 1994 328p il $22.95   92
ISBN 0-471-01858-9   LC 94-4262
The author "traces Reno's background as the daughter of two Miami journalists, her 'straight arrow' years as

Reno, Janet, 1938——_Continued_
one of a few women at Harvard Law School and her introduction to law and politics when she returned to Florida. He describes Reno's triumphs and traumas as Dade County prosecutor, her appointment by President Clinton in the wake of two failed nominations and her performance as head of the Justice Department, including the Branch Davidian disaster in Waco, Tex., her criticism of TV violence and her limited role in formulating Clinton's crime bill." Publ Wkly

Revere, Paul, 1735-1818
Forbes, Esther. Paul Revere & the world he lived in. Houghton Mifflin 1942 510p il hardcover o.p. paperback available $14.95　　　　**92**
1. Boston (Mass.)—History 2. United States—History—1775-1783, Revolution
ISBN 0-395-08370-2 (pa)
Also available in hardcover from P. Smith
This biography of the American patriot is also an examination of life in 18th century Boston
Includes bibliography

Ripken, Cal, Jr.
Rosenfeld, Harvey. Iron man: the Cal Ripken, Jr., story. St. Martin's Press 1995 276p il $22.95　　　　**92**
1. Baltimore Orioles (Baseball team) 2. Baseball—Biography
ISBN 0-312-13524-6　　　　LC 95-20250
The author traces the life and career of the Baltimore Orioles shortstop who broke Lou Gehrig's record for number of consecutive games played
Ripken "is a veritable paragon. But Rosenfeld keeps his objectivity about his subject and so is all the more convincing when he declares Ripken the best shortstop who ever played the game." Publ Wkly

Robeson, Paul, 1898-1976
Larsen, Rebecca. Paul Robeson, hero before his time. Watts 1989 158p il lib bdg $22.70　　　　**92**
1. African Americans—Biography
ISBN 0-531-10779-5　　　　LC 89-8880
"Larsen traces Robeson's achievements in a straightforward manner, from his days as valedictorian and All-American football player at Rutgers, through Columbia Law School, to the world's concert and drama stages, to the human rights arena." ALAN
Includes bibliography

Robinson, Jackie, 1919-1972
Robinson, Jackie. I never had it made; an autobiography; by Jackie Robinson as told to Alfred Duckett; foreword by Cornel West; introduction by Hank Aaron. Ecco Press 1995 xxii, 275p il $24; pa $13　　　　**92**
1. Baseball—Biography 2. African American athletes
ISBN 0-88001-419-9; 0-88001-544-6 (pa)
　　　　LC 94-45279
A reissue of the title first published 1972 by Putnam

This book "focuses on Robinson's political involvements after his career ended in 1956 and his friendships with such diverse characters as Martin Luther King, Malcolm X, William Buckley and Nelson Rockefeller." Publ Wkly
"Included are introductions by Hank Aaron and Cornel West that provide fresh perspectives on the significance of the legendary star's breaking of major league baseball's color barrier. With each retelling, it is clear that Robinson's story has become less a baseball story than a major cultural milestone in the nation's history." Libr J

Robinson, Sharon. Stealing home: an intimate family portrait by the daughter of Jackie Robinson. HarperCollins Pubs. 1996 213p il $24　　　　**92**
1. Baseball—Biography 2. African American athletes
ISBN 0-06-017191-X　　　　LC 96-3982
"The author, the daughter of baseball great Jackie Robinson, reveals what it is like to grow up in the shadow of a legend. Robinson is especially frank in addressing her family's personal problems." Libr J
"This poignant memoir offers a unique view of the human being behind the legend." Booklist

Rodin, Auguste, 1840-1917
Laurent, Monique. Rodin; translated by Emily Read. Holt & Co. 1990 160p il hardcover o.p. paperback available $19.95　　　　**92**
1. Artists, French
ISBN 0-8050-1363-6 (pa)　　　　LC 89-45937
This biography of the French sculptor is illustrated with photographs of his works in the Musée Rodin

Rogers, Will, 1879-1935
Yagoda, Ben. Will Rogers; a biography. Knopf 1993 409p il $27.50　　　　**92**
1. Entertainers
ISBN 0-394-58512-7　　　　LC 92-40177
Also available in paperback from HarperCollins Pubs.
This is a biography of "the rope-twirling vaudeville monologist, salty political commentator, silent film actor and New York Times columnist [who died in a plane crash in 1935]. . . . [This is] a resonant portrait imbued with Rogers's irreverent spirit, yet attuned to both the strengths and limitations of his commonsense, crackerbarrel world view." Publ Wkly
Includes bibliographical references

Roosevelt, Eleanor, 1884-1962
Cook, Blanche Wiesen. Eleanor Roosevelt. v1: 1884-1933. Viking 1992 587p il hardcover o.p. paperback available $14.95　　　　**92**
1. Presidents—United States—Spouses
ISBN 0-14-009460-1 (pa)　　　　LC 87-40632
This volume "spans the years from Eleanor's birth to her husband Franklin Delano's inauguration." Publisher's note
"A feminist biography that regards its subject not only as a mostly 19th-century woman who invented her own life with very little help, but also as a self-created political figure of considerable significance." N Y Times Book Rev
Includes bibliographical references

Roosevelt, Eleanor, 1884-1962—*Continued*

Goodwin, Doris Kearns. No ordinary time. See entry under Roosevelt, Franklin D. (Franklin Delano), 1882-1945

Lash, Joseph P. Eleanor and Franklin; the story of their relationship; based on Eleanor Roosevelt's private papers; foreword by Arthur M. Schlesinger, Jr.; introduction by Franklin D. Roosevelt, Jr. Norton 1971 765p il o.p.; Smithmark Pubs. reprint available $14.98 **92**
1. Roosevelt, Franklin D. (Franklin Delano), 1882-1945 2. Presidents—United States—Spouses
ISBN 0-8317-9402-X
Also available in paperback from New Am. Lib.
Focusing upon Mrs. Roosevelt's private and public life, the author gives insight into her childhood and reconstructs the relationship between the famous couple
Includes bibliographical references

Scharf, Lois. Eleanor Roosevelt; first lady of American liberalism. Twayne Pubs. 1987 202p il (Twayne's twentieth-century American biography series) lib bdg $26.95; pa $16.95 **92**
1. Presidents—United States—Spouses
ISBN 0-8057-7769-5 (lib bdg); 0-8057-7778-4 (pa)
LC 87-17725
"Scharf's book emphasizes breadth rather than depth, but it does an excellent job of encapsulating Roosevelt's life in a compassionate, questioning, and lively manner. . . . Recommended for those looking for a short, well-written biography that never veers into hagiography." Libr J
Includes bibliography

Roosevelt, Franklin D. (Franklin Delano), 1882-1945

Freidel, Frank Burt. Franklin D. Roosevelt: a rendezvous with destiny; by Frank Freidel. Little, Brown 1990 710p il $24.95; pa $19.95 **92**
1. Presidents—United States 2. United States—History—1933-1945
ISBN 0-316-29260-5; 0-316-29261-3 (pa)
LC 89-12580
In this biography "the many facets of FDR—son, student, husband, father, state senator, political appointee, polio victim, politician, governor, chief executive, commander-in-chief, world statesman—are revealed in turn, comprising a full accounting of the man and his works. . . . This is as fine a one-volume biography of the 32nd president as we are likely to get." Publ Wkly
Includes bibliographical references

Goodwin, Doris Kearns. No ordinary time; Franklin and Eleanor Roosevelt: the home front in World War II. Simon & Schuster 1994 759p il $30; pa $16 **92**
1. Roosevelt, Eleanor, 1884-1962 2. Presidents—United States 3. World War, 1939-1945—United States 4. United States—History—1933-1945
ISBN 0-671-64240-5; 0-684-80448-4 (pa)
LC 94-28565
"This is a nearly day-by-day account of the doings of Franklin and Eleanor Roosevelt during the Second World War. While Eleanor was championing the rights of female munitions workers and of Negroes in segregated Army barracks, her husband was making and breaking policy." New Yorker
Includes bibliographical references

Lash, Joseph P. Eleanor and Franklin. See entry under Roosevelt, Eleanor, 1884-1962

Nardo, Don. Franklin D. Roosevelt; U.S. President. Chelsea House 1996 111p il (Great achievers: lives of the physically challenged) lib bdg $18.95 **92**
1. Presidents—United States
ISBN 0-7910-2406-7
LC 94-37511
This biography of the United States President elected for four terms emphasizes that his paralysis caused by polio did not prevent him from achieving greatness
Includes bibliography

Roosevelt, Theodore, 1858-1919

Meltzer, Milton. Theodore Roosevelt and his America. Watts 1994 191p il lib bdg $25.80 **92**
1. Presidents—United States
ISBN 0-531-11192-X
LC 94-17369
"Both critical and appreciative, Meltzer's biography conveys a sense of the complexities and contradictions in the president who led his country during the tumultuous first years of the twentieth century. . . . There's no direct documentation, even for quotes, but a fine bibliographic note discusses TR's own writings, what various people have written about him, and how Meltzer's personal values must inevitably come into play in how he selects his material." Booklist

Roosevelt, Theodore. Theodore Roosevelt; an American mind: a selection from his writings; edited and introduced by Mario R. DiNunzio. St. Martin's Press 1994 359p il $24.95 **92**
1. Presidents—United States
ISBN 0-312-10352-2
LC 93-26611
Also available in paperback from Penguin Bks.
A collection of Theodore Roosevelt's "writings as rough rider, historian, president, and commentator. . . . [The editor] rounds out his selection with a thumbnail biography of Roosevelt and brief introductions to topical sections dealing with TR and politics, patriotism, the outdoor life, women, race, and the arts." Libr J

Rosenberg, Ethel, 1915-1953

Meeropol, Robert. We are your sons: the legacy of Ethel and Julius Rosenberg. See entry under Rosenberg, Julius, 1918-1953

Philipson, Ilene J. Ethel Rosenberg; beyond the myths; by Ilene Philipson. Watts 1988 390p o.p.; Rutgers Univ. Press paperback available $14.95 **92**
1. Trials (Espionage)
ISBN 0-8135-1917-9 (pa)
LC 87-31634
"Without attempting a definitive judgment on whether Ethel Rosenberg was a Communist spy or a martyr to

Rosenberg, Ethel, 1915-1953—*Continued*

political paranoia, Philipson aims for a deeper understanding of her subject's personality, beliefs, and actions. The book covers the many complex conflicts that made up Rosenberg's life and career." Booklist

This is "a fine psycho-historical study of a complex figure." BAYA Book Rev

Includes bibliography

Rosenberg, Julius, 1918-1953

Meeropol, Robert. We are your sons: the legacy of Ethel and Julius Rosenberg; written by their children Robert and Michael Meeropol. 2nd ed, with a foreword by Eric Foner. University of Ill. Press 1986 xxxiii, 470p il $34.95   **92**

1. Rosenberg, Ethel, 1915-1953 2. Trials (Espionage)
ISBN 0-252-01263-1   LC 85-30892

First published 1975 by Houghton Mifflin

Charged with conspiracy to commit espionage, Ethel and Julius Rosenberg were convicted in 1951 and executed in 1953. This volume presents their prison letters with a connecting narrative on the trial by their son Michael. His brother Robert continues, with an autobiographical account of the sons' lives after their parents' execution, revealing their involvement in New Left politics and their commitment to clearing their parents' names

Includes bibliography

Russell, Charles M. (Charles Marion), 1864-1926

Hassrick, Peter H. Charles M. Russell. Abrams 1989 155p il (Library of American art) $45   **92**

1. Artists, American
ISBN 0-8109-1571-5   LC 88-7391

A biographical and critical "study of the quintessential cowboy artist. . . . Hassrick describes Russell's career ably and verifies his reputation as a most appealing working-man artist via 52 resplendent colorplates and nearly as many black-and-white figures." Booklist

Includes bibliography

Taliaferro, John. Charles M. Russell; the life and legend of America's cowboy artist. Little, Brown 1996 318p il map $27.95   **92**

1. Artists, American
ISBN 0-316-83190-5   LC 95-45795

"In 1880, aged 16, Russell left home for Montana Territory to be a cowboy. For the next 15 years, he led a devil-may-care existence as a wrangler, drinking heavily, womanizing, pleading for credit. Journalist Taliaferro brings the artist and the frontier to life in this sparkling biography." Publ Wkly

Includes bibliographical references

Ruth, Babe, 1895-1948

Creamer, Robert W. Babe; the legend comes to life. Simon & Schuster 1974 443p il hardcover o.p. paperback available $12   **92**

1. Baseball—Biography
ISBN 0-671-76070-X (pa)

This biography covers Babe Ruth's personal life and his sports career

Sakharov, Andreĭ Dmitrievich, 1921-1989

Sakharov, Andreĭ Dmitrievich. Memoirs; [by] Andrei Sakharov; translated from the Russian by Richard Lourie. Knopf 1990 xxi, 773p il $29.95   **92**

1. Russia—History
ISBN 0-394-53740-8   LC 90-53068

The Soviet physicist and political dissident discusses his life and career up until 1986

"Virtually everyone . . . is likely to find the second half of the book unforgettable. It describes, blow by blow, Sakharov and [his wife Elena] Bonner's . . . battle for their personal as well as universal rights." New Leader

Includes bibliographical references

Salk, Jonas, 1914-1995

Sherrow, Victoria. Jonas Salk. Facts on File 1993 134p il (Makers of modern science) lib bdg $17.95   **92**

1. Scientists
ISBN 0-8160-2805-2   LC 92-32302

This "biography of the scientist credited with developing a successful polio vaccine begins with some history of the disease and then follows Salk through his schooling and into the scientific laboratory. Salk's years of research and laboratory work, described in some detail, are the subject of several chapters. The last section explains the Salk Institute's recent work in researching cancer and AIDS. . . . A readable, inspiring portrait of a hero in the field of medical research." Booklist

Includes glossary and bibliography

Salzman, Mark

Salzman, Mark. Lost in place; growing up absurd in suburbia. Random House 1995 273p $22; pa $12   **92**

1. Authors, American
ISBN 0-679-43945-5; 0-679-76778-9 (pa)
     LC 95-7847

In this "memoir about his 'existential angst' as a slightly off-center teenager, . . . writer Salzman . . . recalls his unconventional friends, frugal parents, and other memorable characters from his freewheeling, Connecticut youth." Booklist

"This very different journey through adolescence is a delight to read, and is one that many YAs will relate to and enjoy." SLJ

Sandburg, Carl, 1878-1967

Niven, Penelope. Carl Sandburg; a biography. Scribner 1991 843p il o.p.; University of Ill. Press paperback available $19.95   **92**

1. Authors, American
ISBN 0-252-02115-0 (pa)   LC 90-20664

"A Robert Stewart book"

The author presents Sandburg, the "son of immigrant Swedes in his roles as hobo, soldier, journalist, orator, socialist, biographer of Abraham Lincoln and poet." Publ Wkly

"Niven has done a notable job in humanizing Sandburg through the portrayal of his family life and in outlining some of his professional torments and struggles." Booklist

Includes bibliography

Sandburg, Carl, 1878-1967—_Continued_

Sandburg, Carl. Always the young strangers. Harcourt Brace & Co. 1953 445p hardcover o.p. paperback available $12.95   92
1. Authors, American
ISBN 0-15-604765-9 (pa)
This autobiography by the American poet is an "account of the circumstances and the people that moulded his formative years. Swedish parents in poor circumstances, a typical middle west small town, and a limited grade school education were the soil in which the great democratic poet has his roots." Ont Libr Rev

Sandburg, Carl. Ever the winds of chance; with an introduction by Margaret Sandburg and George Hendrick. University of Ill. Press 1983 172p il $19.95   92
1. Authors, American
ISBN 0-252-01089-2   LC 83-6997
Sandburg "never got around to completing the autobiography he began with . . . 'Always the Young Strangers' [entered above]. Toward a sequel, however, he did leave several pages of typescript—here tidied up by his daughter Margaret and George Hendrick—which cover his Lombard College days in Galesburg, Illinois, his classmates, and early (and brief) jobs as a salesman, copywriter, bum, and 'jailbird.'" Booklist

Sanger, Margaret, 1879-1966
Chesler, Ellen. Woman of valor: Margaret Sanger and the birth control movement in America. Simon & Schuster 1992 639p il o.p.; Anchor Bks. (NY) paperback available $14.95
                    92
1. Birth control
ISBN 0-385-46980-2 (pa)   LC 92-11496
"Chesler believes that Sanger's impact on women's lives has not been adequately appreciated or documented. This biography succeeds admirably in filling the gap with a . . . look at Sanger's private and public life. Interwoven in this account are discussions of the sweeping social and political developments of the 20th century. . . . This work is carefully documented and . . . is a major contribution to women's history." Libr J
Includes bibliographical references

Santiago, Esmeralda
Santiago, Esmeralda. When I was Puerto Rican. Addison-Wesley 1993 274p $20   92
1. Puerto Ricans—New York (N.Y.)
ISBN 0-201-58117-5   LC 93-24522
Also available in paperback from Vintage Bks.
"A Merloyd Lawrence book"
The author "tells of her childhood in Puerto Rico in the 1950s and of her family's move to New York when she was 13." Libr J
"At once heart-wrenching and remarkably inspirational, this lyrical account depicts rural life in Puerto Rico amid the hardships and tensions of everyday life and Santiago's awakening as a young woman, who, although startled by culture shock, valiantly confronted New York head-on. When in the epilogue Santiago refers to her studies at Harvard, it is both a stirring and poignant reminder of the capacities of the human spirit." Booklist
Includes glossary

Schwarzkopf, H. Norman
Cohen, Roger. In the eye of the storm: the life of General H. Norman Schwarzkopf; [by] Roger Cohen, Claudio Gatti. Farrar, Straus & Giroux 1991 342p il maps $19.95   92
1. Generals
ISBN 0-374-17708-2   LC 91-15581
Also available G.K. Hall large print edition and in paperback from Berkley Pub. Group
This biography of the U.S. general covers his life in the military, his family, and his role in the Persian Gulf War
"On the whole it is a rather serious and highly readable book that provides important insights into the general, especially into his origins, character and psychology." N Y Times Book Rev

Senesh, Hannah, 1921-1944
Atkinson, Linda. In kindling flame: the story of Hannah Senesh, 1921-1944. Lothrop, Lee & Shepard Bks. 1985 214p il hardcover o.p. paperback available $4.95   92
1. World War, 1939-1945—Underground movements
2. Jews—Hungary 3. Holocaust, 1933-1945
ISBN 0-688-11689-2 (pa)   LC 83-24392
"Hannah Senesh was a young Hungarian Jew who left the relative safety of Palestine to return to her homeland as a resistance fighter during World War II and the Nazi Holocaust. Atkinson brings her remarkable story to life by including in the narrative both passages from Hannah's own diary and quotes from her family and friends. Atkinson also incorporates general information about events of the Holocaust and the war into Hannah's story." Voice Youth Advocates
Includes bibliography

Senesh, Hannah. Hannah Senesh, her life & diary; introduction by Abba Eban. Schocken Bks. 1972 257p il hardcover o.p. paperback available $16   92
1. World War, 1939-1945—Underground movements
2. Jews—Hungary 3. Holocaust, 1933-1945
ISBN 0-8052-0410-5 (pa)
Original Hebrew edition, 1950; this translation first published 1971 in the United Kingdom
The diary, letters, and poems of the Hungarian-born Jew who was executed by the Nazis in 1944 at the age of 23

Seurat, Georges Pierre, 1859-1891
Rewald, John. Seurat; a biography. Abrams 1990 248p il $75; pa $34.98   92
1. Artists, French
ISBN 0-8109-3814-6; 0-8109-8124-6 (pa)
                    LC 90-30519
First English translation by Lionel Abel published 1943 by Wittenborn & Co. with title: Georges Seurat
"This new translation of Rewald's French text . . . includes an updated bibliography and a new series of illustrations to accompany the author's classic commentary on the French artist. All of Seurat's major works are reproduced in color, and many studies and sketches for these masterpieces are also presented in an exceptional sequence of illustrations." Booklist

Shaw, Robert Gould, 1837-1863

Burchard, Peter. "We'll stand by the Union": ✓ Robert Gould Shaw and the Black 54th Massachusetts Regiment. Facts on File 1993 132p il (Makers of America) $17.95   **92**

1. United States. Army. Massachusetts Infantry Regiment, 54th (1863-1865) 2. African American soldiers 3. United States—History—1861-1865, Civil War

ISBN 0-8160-2609-2   LC 92-37132

"The son of wealthy abolitionists, Shaw grew up in Boston, went to Harvard, traveled in Europe, and when war broke out, joined the Union army, and eventually was charged with training and leading Massachusetts' first black regiment. Although the book focuses mainly on Shaw, it includes a history of the regiment after his death and assesses the impact of black soldiers on the course of the war." Booklist

Includes bibliographical references

Shelley, Mary Wollstonecraft, 1797-1851

Sunstein, Emily W. Mary Shelley; romance and reality. Little, Brown 1989 478p il o.p.; Johns Hopkins Univ. Press paperback available $15.95
                                        92

1. Authors, English 2. Women authors

ISBN 0-8018-4218-2 (pa)   LC 88-12990

A "revisionist account of a woman who 'literally embodies the English Romantic movement'. . . . Sunstein provides substantial documentation of the breadth of Shelley's education and the extent of her writing. . . . Most rewarding, perhaps, are Sunstein's astute insights into Shelley's emotional life." Choice

Includes bibliography

Shelley, Percy Bysshe, 1792-1822

O'Neill, Michael. Percy Bysshe Shelley; a literary life. St. Martin's Press 1990 176p (Literary lives) $35   **92**

1. Poets, English

ISBN 0-312-03248-X   LC 89-34864

First published 1989 in the United Kingdom

This biography "offers an account of the poet in the light of 'the literary, sociopolitical and ideological conditions' of his day." Times Lit Suppl

Includes bibliography

Shyer, Christopher

Shyer, Marlene Fanta. Not like other boys— growing up gay; a mother and son look back; [by] Marlene Fanta Shyer and Christopher Shyer. Houghton Mifflin 1996 259p $21.95   **92**

ISBN 0-395-70939-3   LC 95-35698

This is a "memoir of the mother and her gay son, who came of age in the conservative climate of Larchmont, N.Y., in the 1960's and 70's. 'Not Like Other Boys' is a dual coming out that is as much about the sin of small-mindedness as it is about homosexuality. Marlene Fanta Shyer, the author of three novels and several children's books, and her son Christopher alternate chapters to recreate their simultaneous awareness of Chris's emerging sexual identity." N Y Times Book Rev

Sitting Bull, Dakota Chief, 1831-1890

Vestal, Stanley. Sitting Bull, champion of the Sioux; a biography. [new ed] University of Okla. Press 1969 c1957 xxi, 531p il (Civilization of the American Indian series) hardcover o.p. paperback available $16.95   **92**

1. Dakota Indians

ISBN 0-8061-2219-6 (pa)

First published 1932 by Houghton Mifflin

"A scholarly and well-documented story of a great Sioux chief (1834-1890), written in an interesting narrative style, uncluttered by long quotations from documents and eyewitness accounts. The book begins when the subject was a boy-volunteer called 'Slow' and ends with the great chief's death because he refused to be captured." Stensland. Lit By & About the Am Indian. 2d edition

Smith, Howard K., 1914-

Smith, Howard K. Events leading up to my death; the life of a twentieth century reporter. St. Martin's Press 1996 419p il map $24.95   **92**

1. Journalists

ISBN 0-312-13970-5   LC 95-40045

"A Thomas Dunne book"

Journalist Smith relates "stories about covering the Allied race across Europe; being CBS's voice in Berlin after the war; reporting on the Nuremburg trials; his relationship with Edward R. Murrow; and his easy transition to TV. He goes on to describe leaving CBS (over civil rights reporting) and working at ABC, covering JFK and LBJ and his run-ins with Richard Nixon." Publ Wkly

"Mr. Smith's account is honest and self-effacing, and his book has much to offer those who care about history, the news media and the world at large." N Y Times Book Rev

Soto, Hernando de, ca. 1500-1542

Duncan, David Ewing. Hernando de Soto; a savage quest in the Americas. Crown 1995 xxxvii, 570p il maps $40   **92**

1. Explorers 2. America—Exploration

ISBN 0-517-58222-8   LC 95-663

This is a "biography of the conquistador who from 1539 to his death in 1543 was 'the first European to penetrate deeply into the interior of our continent.'" Libr J

"Duncan's scholarship and documentation are impeccable, and his chronology unfolds like a superbly crafted novel." Booklist

Includes bibliographical references

Spielberg, Steven, 1947-

Sanello, Frank. Spielberg; the man, the movies, the mythology. Taylor Pub. Co. 1996 274p il $22.95   **92**

1. Motion picture producers and directors

ISBN 0-87833-911-6   LC 95-39329

In this biography of the filmmaker, Sanello "chronicles behind-the-scenes stories about the making of each Spielberg picture. He also looks at the director's marriages to actresses Amy Irving and Kate Capshaw. Although the author tends to psychoanalyze Spielberg over his emerging sense of Jewish identity and the making of *Schindler's List* (for which Spielberg won an Oscar for best director), this is a solid, fast-paced bio." Publ Wkly

Includes filmography

Springsteen, Bruce

Bruce Springsteen; the Rolling stone files: the ultimate compendium of interviews, articles, facts, and opinions from the files of Rolling stone; by the editors of Rolling stone; introduction by Parke Puterbaugh. Hyperion 1996 353p $12.95   **92**
1. Rock musicians
ISBN 0-7868-8153-4   LC 95-47362
"This book presents the life and career of Bruce Springsteen through a chronological arrangement of the many articles about him that have appeared in Rolling Stone magazine. It begins in 1973 with a brief blurb on him in the 'Random Notes' (read 'gossip') column and ends with a review of his latest album at the end of 1995." Libr J
Includes discography and videography

Stalin, Joseph, 1879-1953

Marrin, Albert. Stalin. Viking Kestrel 1988 244p il hardcover o.p. paperback available $5.99   **92**
1. Soviet Union—Politics and government 2. Dictators
ISBN 0-14-032605-7 (pa)   LC 88-17345
An account of the life of the man who shaped the Soviet Union, from pre-revolutionary Russia to its evolution as a superpower and the descent of the Iron Curtain
The author has "written a compelling historical perspective that is every bit as readable and fascinating as it is rich in fact. A selection of black-and-white photographs is included, as is an extensive bibliography." Booklist

Radzinsky, Edvard. Stalin; the first in-depth biography based on explosive new documents from Russia's secret archives; translated by H.T. Willetts. Doubleday 1996 607p il $30; pa $15.95   **92**
1. Soviet Union—Politics and government 2. Dictators
ISBN 0-385-47397-4; 0-385-47954-9 (pa)
    LC 95-4495
For this biography of the Soviet ruler the author "has examined mountains of rare archival sources and interviewed many who lived through decades of Stalinist (mis)rule. The result is the best general biography of Stalin to date. Radzinsky strips away layer after layer of myth, falsehood, and enigma to produce a riveting portrait of a man whose primary role model was Ivan the Terrible." Libr J
Includes bibliographical references

Stanton, Elizabeth Cady, 1815-1902

Banner, Lois W. Elizabeth Cady Stanton; a radical for woman's rights; edited by Oscar Handlin. Little, Brown 1980 189p il (Library of American biography) o.p.; Scott, Foresman paperback available $16   **92**
1. Feminism
ISBN 0-673-39319-4 (pa)   LC 79-2242
This biography of the nineteenth-century American feminist describes her upbringing, marriage, motherhood, and development as a leader
Includes bibliographical references

Cullen-DuPont, Kathryn. Elizabeth Cady Stanton and women's liberty. Facts on File 1992 133p il (Makers of America) lib bdg $17.95   **92**
1. Feminism
ISBN 0-8160-2413-8   LC 91-21781
A biography of one of the first leaders of the women's rights movement, whose work led to the adoption of the nineteenth amendment that ensured women's right to vote
"The presentation is superb, relying on original sources and written in a style that is both accessible to young readers and sophisticated enough to do justice to its subject matter. The text is supplemented by archival photographs and reproductions of Cady Stanton and her family that capture the character of the woman and her times." SLJ
Includes bibliography

Steffan, Joseph

Steffan, Joseph. Honor bound; a gay American fights for the right to serve his country. Villard Bks. 1992 245p il o.p.; Avon Bks. paperback available $10   **92**
1. United States Naval Academy 2. United States. Navy 3. Gay men—Civil rights
ISBN 0-380-71501-5 (pa)   LC 92-53654
"Discharged from the U.S. Naval Academy in 1987 for being a homosexual, Steffan filed suit a year later challenging the regulations that ban gays and lesbians from the armed services. In this memoir he narrates his discovery and affirmation of his sexual identity, then criticizes Annapolis for intolerance and inflexibility." Publ Wkly
This "is more than just a book about a young gay man who wants to serve his country in the U.S. Navy. It is an interesting, timely account of life in a military academy. . . . This is a book that should be available in all high school and public libraries." Libr J

Stein, Gertrude, 1874-1946

Stein, Gertrude. The autobiography of Alice B. Toklas. Modern Lib. 1993 342p $15.50; pa $11   **92**
1. Toklas, Alice B. 2. Authors, American 3. Women authors 4. Paris (France)—Intellectual life
ISBN 0-679-60081-7; 0-679-72463-X (pa)
    LC 93-15339
A reissue of the title first published 1933 by Harcourt Brace & Co.
"The book is really Stein's autobiography, presented as though written by her secretary, Alice Toklas. The book provoked a rejoinder from various Parisian artists and writers, *Testimony Against Gertrude Stein* (1935). . . . For the average reader, however, Stein's book holds much fascination in its views of Parisian life and personalities, and the whole is offered in a genuinely witty style." Benet's Reader's Ency of Am Lit

Steinbeck, John, 1902-1968

Benson, Jackson J. The true adventures of John Steinbeck, writer; a biography. Viking 1984 1116p il hardcover o.p. paperback available $19.95 **92**
1. Authors, American
ISBN 0-14-014417-X (pa)   LC 82-17534
The author "devotes surprisingly little time to critical analysis of Steinbeck's works, but he does do a thorough job of discussing their philosophical underpinnings. The book's emphasis, though, is on Steinbeck's lifetime struggle to be a writer; Benson captures vividly the agony of this admirably tough-minded yet chronically sentimental man's dedication to his craft." Booklist
Includes bibliography

Parini, Jay. John Steinbeck; a biography. Holt & Co. 1995 xxi, 535p il $30; pa $14.95   **92**
1. Authors, American
ISBN 0-8050-1673-2; 0-8050-4700-X (pa)
                                            LC 94-21893
First published 1994 in the United Kingdom
"Drawing heavily on correspondence and on interviews with Steinbeck's friends and others, Parini's energetic biography details the personal life (multiple marriages, bouts with depression) and professional accomplishments (the Nobel Prize for literature) of the acclaimed writer." Booklist
Includes bibliographical references

Reef, Catherine. John Steinbeck. Clarion Bks. 1996 163p il $17.95   **92**
1. Authors, American
ISBN 0-395-71278-5   LC 95-11500
"The book traces Steinbeck's life from his childhood in California, to his burgeoning writing career and his passion for social justice, to his worldwide recognition. Reef does an excellent job of synthesizing Steinbeck's work, his private life, and his politics and philosophy." Bull Cent Child Books
Includes bibliography

Steinbeck, John. Conversations with John Steinbeck; edited by Thomas Fensch. University Press of Miss. 1988 xxi, 116p (Literary conversations series) $39.50; pa $15.95   **92**
1. Authors, American
ISBN 0-87805-359-X; 0-87805-360-3 (pa)
                                            LC 88-17538
"This collection of Steinbeck's interviews allows him to speak on his own behalf in an illuminating expression of his intentions, goals, and achievements. From the beginning of his career through his last years the interviews reveal a fascinating, controversial, and captivating personality." Univ Press Books for Second Sch Libr
Includes bibliography

Steinem, Gloria

Heilbrun, Carolyn G. The education of a woman: the life of Gloria Steinem. Dial Press (NY) 1995 xxv, 451p il $24.95   **92**
1. Feminism
ISBN 0-385-31371-3   LC 95-19683
Also available in paperback from Ballantine Bks.

The author "offers a study of Steinem that takes into account both her feminine and feminist appeal." Libr J
"The portrait that results is nuanced and thoughtful. . . . Heilbrun's goal is at once to understand how Steinem became the woman she is, and what her life can teach us about childhood and family, self and society. Slow at the start, but Heilbrun soon captures readers' interest and imagination." Booklist
Includes bibliographical references

Stengel, Casey

Stengel, Casey. The gospel according to Casey; Casey Stengel's inimitable, instructional, historical baseball book; [compiled by] Ira Berkow and Jim Kaplan. St. Martin's Press 1992 172p il $18.95; pa $12.95   **92**
1. Baseball—Biography
ISBN 0-312-06922-7; 0-312-09301-2 (pa)
                                            LC 91-37842
"A Thomas Dunne book"
This book collects the baseball manager's comments on various aspects of the sport along with remembrances of Stengel from people who knew him
"Most of the material is presented in quote form, but while the format makes for breezy reading and there are some funny lines, the tone is often serious." Quill Quire
Includes bibliographical references

Stevenson, Robert Louis, 1850-1894

Bell, Ian. Dreams of exile: Robert Louis Stevenson: a biography. Holt & Co. 1993 xxiii, 296p hardcover o.p. paperback available $12.95
                                            92
1. Authors, English
ISBN 0-8050-3938-4 (pa)   LC 93-3792
"Stevenson's own life reads like an adventure tale: a bad beginning as an only child, sickly and coddled; a bohemian youth spent in Edinburgh and France; a long struggle against tuberculosis; marriage to an American woman ten years his senior; and travels through America, Europe, and the South Seas. . . . Bell has written a vivid and sensitive biography." Libr J
Includes bibliography

McLynn, F. J. Robert Louis Stevenson; a biography; [by] Frank McLynn. Random House 1994 567p il $30   **92**
1. Authors, English
ISBN 0-679-41284-0   LC 94-19704
First published 1993 in the United Kingdom
This "biography is propelled by the conviction that Stevenson (1850-1894) was not merely a writer of adventure yarns for boys but Scotland's greatest writer and a major influence on Conrad, Wilde and even Yeats. In lucid, erudite prose, McLynn . . . examines the forces that decisively shaped Stevenson's work." Publ Wkly
Includes bibliographical references

Stoker, Bram, 1847-1912

Belford, Barbara. Bram Stoker; a biography of the author of Dracula. Knopf 1996 381p il $30
92

1. Authors, English
ISBN 0-679-41832-6   LC 96-4632

Belford depicts Bram Stoker as "a charming but self-effacing figure overshadowed in his lifetime by his flamboyant employer, larger-than-life actor Henry Irving, then overshadowed after death by his greatest creation, Dracula." Booklist

"Valuable as both a biography of Stoker and a study of late 19th-century British theater, Belford's book provides interesting glimpses into the lives of playwrights such as George Bernard Shaw and Oscar Wilde." Libr J

Includes bibliography

Stowe, Harriet Beecher, 1811-1896

Coil, Suzanne M. Harriet Beecher Stowe. Watts 1993 173p il (Impact biography) lib bdg $20.57
92

1. Authors, American 2. Women authors 3. Abolitionists
ISBN 0-531-13006-1   LC 93-13710

A biography of the nineteenth-century author whose anti-slavery novel "Uncle Tom's Cabin" helped intensify the disagreement between North and South

"This is an excellent biography for any collection. Coil has gone beyond a mere recounting of the facts to paint an excellent picture of life in the United States in the middle of the 19th century." Voice Youth Advocates

Includes bibliography

Hedrick, Joan D. Harriet Beecher Stowe; a life. Oxford Univ. Press 1994 507p il $35; pa $15.95
92

1. Authors, American 2. Women authors 3. Abolitionists
ISBN 0-19-506639-1; 0-19-509639-8 (pa)
LC 93-16610

This biography "brings to life not just the complex and fascinating woman and writer but also the 19th-century America that shaped her and was in turn shaped by her. Hedrick manages to weave into this immensely readable biography a history teeming with the domestic detail of the famous Beecher clan, the settling of the West, and the impact of the Civil War and the abolition movement." Libr J

Includes bibliographical references

Strawberry, Darryl

Klapisch, Bob. High and tight: the rise and fall of Dwight Gooden and Darryl Strawberry. See entry under Gooden, Dwight

Sullivan, Anne, 1866-1936

Lash, Joseph P. Helen and teacher: the story of Helen Keller and Anne Sullivan Macy. See entry under Keller, Helen, 1880-1968

Tecumseh, Shawnee Chief, 1768-1813

Eckert, Allan W. A sorrow in our heart: the life of Tecumseh. Bantam Bks. 1992 862p maps hardcover o.p. paperback available $7.50   92
1. Shawnee Indians
ISBN 0-553-56174-X (pa)   LC 91-31858

This is a "narrative biography of Tecumseh, the remarkable Shawnee warrior and statesman who succeeded in organizing a group of disparate tribes into a cohesive confederacy of nations. . . . Eckert places his subject firmly within his proper social and historical context by providing a tremendous amount of meticulously researched and authenticated background information, including illuminating details of tribal life and Shawnee culture." Booklist

Includes bibliographical references

Edmunds, R. David (Russell David). Tecumseh and the quest for Indian leadership; edited by Oscar Handlin. Little, Brown 1984 246p il map o.p.; Scott, Foresman paperback available $16
92

1. Shawnee Indians 2. Indians of North America—Wars
ISBN 0-673-39336-4 (pa)   LC 83-19560

"Shawnee Indian leader Tecumseh and his brother, Prophet, almost succeeded in forging a strong and lasting nineteenth-century Indian nation. Edmunds' account of Tecumseh's growth from youth to warrior to leader provides a lively synopsis of this unique episode in American history." Booklist

Includes bibliography

Teresa, Mother, 1910-

Teresa, Mother. My life for the poor; [by] Mother Teresa of Calcutta; edited by José Luis González-Balado and Janet N. Playfoot. Harper & Row 1985 107p o.p.; Ballantine Bks. paperback available $5.99   92
1. Missionaries of Charity 2. Missions—India
ISBN 0-345-33780-8 (pa)   LC 85-42787

In this collection of Mother Teresa's own reflections the "editors have shaped her beliefs, her fears, and her joys into an intimate portrait, giving the reader a glimpse of the remarkable spirituality that is the essence of a truly inspirational life story." Booklist

Thatcher, Margaret

Thatcher, Margaret. The Downing Street years. HarperCollins Pubs. 1993 914p il o.p.; Smithmark Pubs. reprint available $5.98   **92**

1. Great Britain—Politics and government—1952-
ISBN 0-8317-5448-6   LC 93-239539

These political memoirs cover Thatcher's tenure as Britain's prime minister from 1979 to 1990

"Mrs. Thatcher's memoirs are essential for an understanding of her time because they capture all the qualities of her character and, inevitably, some of her defects as well. They are lucid, opinionated, self-assured, wide-ranging and indispensable." N Y Times Book Rev

Thatcher, Margaret. The path to power. HarperCollins Pubs. 1995 656p il hardcover o.p. paperback available $18   **92**

ISBN 0-06-092732-1 (pa)   LC 95-11176

In this volume the former British prime minister discusses her early years and her life since leaving office

Thoreau, Henry David, 1817-1862

Miller, Douglas T. Henry David Thoreau; a man for all seasons. Facts on File 1991 114p il maps (Makers of America) lib bdg $19   **92**

1. Authors, American
ISBN 0-8160-2478-2   LC 91-10787

Presents the life and philosophies of this country's premier idealist

"Miller presents a purposeful, determined portrait of the man whose unique life-style and great passion for the outdoors aroused suspicion and scorn among many of his contemporaries. . . . Miller provides an honest, if sympathetic, view of one of America's most remarkable personalities. . . . Young adults concerned with issues of ecology and peace will find much to admire in this voice from the past." Booklist

Includes bibliographical references

Tolkien, J. R. R. (John Ronald Reuel), 1892-1973

Hammond, Wayne G. J.R.R. Tolkien, artist & illustrator; [by] Wayne G. Hammond, Christina Scull. Houghton Mifflin 1995 207p il $40   **92**

1. Authors, English
ISBN 0-395-74816-X   LC 96-105237

Along with biographical material and text describing his artwork, this book reproduces more than 200 drawings, sketches and paintings Tolkien made throughout his life. Included are the "Father Christmas" letters to his children and images created in connection with The Hobbit and The Lord of the Rings

"The open and inviting format and the reproductions of his art make this a Tolkien lover's dream, and the insightful text will quickly capture attention as well." Booklist

Includes bibliography

Truman, Harry S., 1884-1972

Feinberg, Barbara Silberdick. Harry S. Truman. Watts 1994 144p il (Impact biography) lib bdg $21.20   **92**

1. Presidents—United States 2. United States—Politics and government—1945-1953
ISBN 0-531-13036-3   LC 93-30895

This is an exploration of the life and career of the thirty-third president. The end of World War II, the arrival of the atomic age, the Cold War, and the Korean War are some of the topics discussed in connection with his administration

Includes glossary and bibliography

McCullough, David G. Truman; [by] David McCullough. Simon & Schuster 1992 1117p il $30; pa $16   **92**

1. Presidents—United States
ISBN 0-671-45654-7; 0-671-86920-5 (pa)
    LC 92-5245

This biography of the 33rd president "not only conveys in rich detail Truman's accomplishments as a politician and statesman, but also reveals the character and personality of this constantly-surprising man—as schoolboy, farmer, soldier, merchant, county judge, senator, vice president and chief executive. The book relates how Truman overcame the stigma of business failure and debt . . . and acquired a reputation for honesty, reliability and common sense." Publ Wkly

Includes bibliographical references

Miller, Merle. Plain speaking: an oral biography of Harry S. Truman. Berkley Bks. 1974 448p hardcover o.p. paperback available $6.99   **92**

1. Presidents—United States 2. United States—Politics and government—1945-1953
ISBN 0-425-09499-5 (pa)

Parts of this book deal with the memories of people who knew the President before 1935, the year he first went to Washington as Senator from Missouri. Other parts deal with his Presidency and the period following it. The work is based on tapes Miller compiled from interviews with Truman and others in 1961-1962 in Independence, Missouri

Pemberton, William E. Harry S. Truman; fair dealer and cold warrior. Twayne Pubs. 1989 227p il (Twayne's twentieth-century American biography series) lib bdg $26.95; pa $15.95   **92**

1. Presidents—United States 2. United States—Politics and government—1945-1953
ISBN 0-8057-7767-9 (lib bdg); 0-8057-7783-0 (pa)
    LC 88-16534

The author "acknowledges the traits that have made Truman the darling of earlier biographers—simplicity, hard work, honesty, and compassion—but chides him for creating the imperial presidency, manipulating the U.S. people, and failing to champion social programs. . . . The final verdict—'competent but conventional'—is, like the rest of the book, plainspoken." Booklist

Includes bibliography

Truman, Harry S., 1884-1972—*Continued*

Truman, Harry S. The autobiography of Harry S. Truman; edited by Robert H. Ferrell. Colorado Associated Univ. Press 1980 153p il map hardcover o.p. paperback available $14.95   **92**
1. Presidents—United States
ISBN 0-87081-091-X (pa)   LC 80-66304
"At different times in his life, Truman recorded his recollections of past events. These accounts give one a flavor of the personality of the former President but refer more to his earlier life than his years in the White House." Choice
Includes bibliographical references

Truman, Margaret. Harry S. Truman. Morrow 1973 c1972 602p il o.p.; Avon Bks. paperback available $12.50   **92**
1. Presidents—United States 2. United States—Politics and government—1945-1953
ISBN 0-380-72112-0 (pa)
The daughter of the late president writes this portrait of her father from his early years to his retirement in Independence, Missouri

Truth, Sojourner, d. 1883
Ortiz, Victoria. Sojourner Truth, a self-made woman. Lippincott 1974 157p il lib bdg $13.89
92
1. African American women 2. Feminism 3. Abolitionists
ISBN 0-397-32134-1
The author "goes far beyond the well-known 'Ain't I a Woman?' speech to present evidence of this woman's understanding of people and institutions and her uncanny ability to transmit that understanding to others. . . . The fine writing style and insightful portrayal make this valuable for Black studies and women's rights collections." SLJ

Twain, Mark, 1835-1910
Meltzer, Milton. Mark Twain: a writer's life. Watts 1985 120p il lib bdg $25.80   **92**
1. Authors, American
ISBN 0-531-10072-3   LC 85-5108
This work surveys the life of Samuel Clemens, who grew up in Missouri, was a river pilot on the Mississippi, became a journalist, and achieved fame as a writer under the pen name Mark Twain
Includes bibliography

Twain, Mark. The autobiography of Mark Twain; as arranged and edited with an introduction and notes, by Charles Neider. Harper & Row 1959 xxvi, 388p il hardcover o.p. paperback available $13.50   **92**
1. Authors, American
ISBN 0-06-092025-4 (pa)
The editor "has arranged the selections in coordinated chronological order, ending with the death of Clemens' daughter Jean in December, 1909." Booklist

Two Trees, Joe
Kazimiroff, Theodore L. The last Algonquin. Walker & Co. 1982 xxv, 197p maps $18.95; pa $12.95   **92**
1. Algonquian Indians
ISBN 0-8027-0698-3; 0-8027-7517-9 (pa)
LC 81-69711
Kazimiroff recounts the lives of "his father and Joe Two Trees, 'the last Algonquin.' As a young boy growing up in the Bronx, Kazimiroff's father, in 1924, met Joe Two Trees who was then living 'off the land' on Hunter's Island, in the Pelham Bay area. A close friendship developed between the two, and the old man taught the boy the ways of the Algonquin. In the latter part of the book, Kazimiroff describes the earlier life of Joe Two Trees." Libr J
"Bittersweet and realistic, this book is an experience to be read breathlessly, as the reader is led into the soul of the Indian to understand his resilient strength in the face of hopelessness." Voice Youth Advocates

Tz'u-hsi, Empress dowager of China, 1835-1908
Seagrave, Sterling. Dragon lady; the life and legend of the last empress of China; by Sterling Seagrave with the collaboration of Peggy Seagrave. Knopf 1992 601p il maps hardcover o.p. paperback available $16   **92**
1. China—History
ISBN 0-679-73369-8 (pa)   LC 91-52712
This is a biography of the Empress Dowager. "As Regent for the young T'ung-chih and Kuang-hsu (her son and nephew), she ruled China almost continuously between 1861 and her death in 1908." Times Lit Suppl
"The last empress of China is conventionally portrayed as an evil, ruthless tyrant, a murderer and a depraved concubine. . . . Now along comes this superb, impeccably researched, absorbing biography-cum-history to explode the myth of the dragon empress." Publ Wkly
Includes bibliography

Updike, John
Updike, John. Conversations with John Updike; edited by James Plath. University Press of Miss. 1994 xxvi, 274p (Literary conversations series) $39.50; pa $15.95   **92**
1. Authors, American
ISBN 0-87805-699-8; 0-87805-700-5 (pa)
LC 93-44741
This is a "collection of 32 interviews given by the fiction writer and poet between 1959 and [1993]. . . . His intelligence, his views (not limited to literature but extended to life in general), and his articulateness come readily to the fore." Booklist
Includes bibliographical references

Victoria, Queen of Great Britain, 1819-1901
Strachey, Lytton. Queen Victoria. Harcourt Brace & Co. 1921 434p il hardcover o.p. paperback available $15   **92**
1. Great Britain—History—1800-1899 (19th century) 2. Great Britain—Kings, queens, rulers, etc.
ISBN 0-15-675696-X (pa)
Also available in paperback from Penguin Bks.

Victoria, Queen of Great Britain, 1819-1901—
Continued

"Harbrace modern classics"

A "presentation of Queen Victoria and her time, characterizations of Lord Melbourne, Palmerston, Gladstone and Disraeli, and a . . . portrait of the prince consort." Booklist

Includes bibliography

Vlad II, Dracul, Prince of Wallachia, 1431-1476

Florescu, Radu R. N. Dracula; prince of many faces, his life and his times; [by] Radu R. Florescu, Raymond T. McNally. Little, Brown 1989 xxii, 261p il maps hardcover o.p. paperback available $14.95   **92**

ISBN 0-316-28656-7 (pa)   LC 89-8164

This is a biography of the "fifteenth-century Romanian prince. The authors present him as a . . . national hero still revered for defending Romania from the Turks, yet also a psychopath who used his power indiscriminately to torture and murder thousands of his enemies and subjects." Libr J

This book "will probably be reckoned the last word on the real man behind the fictional vampire for many years to come." Booklist

Includes bibliographical references

Von Braun, Wernher, 1912-1977

Spangenburg, Ray. Wernher von Braun; space visionary and rocket engineer; [by] Ray Spangenburg and Diane K. Moser. Facts on File 1995 134p il (Makers of modern science) $17.95   **92**

1. Rocketry 2. Scientists
ISBN 0-8160-2924-5   LC 94-22520

"The story of rocket development is . . . integrated with the story of von Braun's life. . . . Varied sources of information, including oral histories and archival materials are interwoven with diagrams and photographs that aptly explain the accompanying text. Lucid explanations are provided for scientific concepts such as jet rocket propulsion. They are simple but not simplistic." Appraisal

Includes glossary and bibliographical references

Vonnegut, Kurt, 1922-

Vonnegut, Kurt. Conversations with Kurt Vonnegut; edited by William Rodney Allen. University Press of Miss. 1988 305p (Literary conversations series) hardcover o.p. paperback available $15.95   **92**

1. Authors, American
ISBN 0-87805-358-1 (pa)   LC 88-13968

"In the twenty years of interviews collected here . . . the reader can hear Vonnegut working through his various personae of science fiction writer, black humorist, pop culture guru, and elder statesman toward a truer definition of himself and his art." Univ Press Books for Second Sch Libr

Walker, Alice, 1944-

Walker, Alice. The same river twice; honoring the difficult: a meditation on life, spirit, art, and the making of the film The color purple, ten years later. Scribner 1996 302p il $24; pa $14   **92**

1. African American authors 2. Women authors
ISBN 0-684-81419-6; 0-671-00377-1 (pa)

LC 95-30056

This "book finds the Pulitzer Prize-winning author still grappling with criticism of the film version of her novel *The Color Purple*. . . . Walker's memoir pieces together assorted journal entries, magazine clippings, occasional photographs and even her original screenplay to form an intimate scrapbook of the period." Publ Wkly

Includes bibliographical references

Wallenberg, Raoul

Linnea, Sharon. Raoul Wallenberg: the man who stopped death. Jewish Publ. Soc. 1993 151p il $17.95; pa $9.95   **92**

1. Holocaust, 1933-1945 2. Jews—Hungary
ISBN 0-8276-0440-8; 0-8276-0448-3 (pa)

LC 93-12140

Traces the life of the Swedish diplomat who saved Hungarian Jews during World War II and then mysteriously disappeared after the Russians occupied Budapest

"Linnéa has a sound sense of her young audience. Her writing is lucid and vivid." Voice Youth Advocates

Waller, Fats, 1904-1943

Kirkeby, Ed. Ain't misbehavin': the story of Fats Waller; [by] Ed Kirkeby, in collaboraton with Duncan P. Schiedt and Sinclair Traill. Da Capo Press 1975 c1966 248p il hardcover o.p. paperback available $11.95   **92**

1. Jazz musicians 2. African American musicians
ISBN 0-306-80015-2 (pa)

First published 1966 by Dodd, Mead

A biography of the jazz pianist and composer who wrote "Honeysuckle Rose," "I've Got a Feelin' I'm Falling," and "Ain't Misbehavin'"

"In addition to the story of Fats Waller, . . . this book presents a fascinating picture of Harlem in the 1920's and the musicians who flourished at that time." Libr J

Includes discography

Warhol, Andy, 1928?-1987

Bourdon, David. Warhol. Abrams 1989 432p il $49.50; pa $24.95   **92**

1. Artists, American
ISBN 0-8109-1761-0; 0-8109-2634-2 (pa)

LC 89-436

"Woven into Bourdon's very readable text are keen observations and insight about the work and the artist. . . . He is unfailingly careful to present opposing viewpoints about controversial issues, yet his own perceptions are clearly articulated as an informative guide to the complexities of Warhol's complex career." Choice

Includes bibliography

Washington, Booker T., 1856-1915

Harlan, Louis R. Booker T. Washington: the making of a black leader, 1856-1901. Oxford Univ. Press 1972 379p hardcover o.p. paperback available $15.95   92
1. African American educators
ISBN 0-19-501915-6 (pa)
This book "covers Washington's life from his birth as a slave in western Virginia up to [the year 1901, when he dined] with Theodore Roosevelt at the White House, an event signifying white recognition of Washington as the chief spokesman for black interests in the period before World War I." Libr J
Includes bibliographical references

✓ Harlan, Louis R. Booker T. Washington: the wizard of Tuskegee, 1901-1915. Oxford Univ. Press 1983 548p il hardcover o.p. paperback available $16.95   92
1. Tuskegee Institute 2. African American educators
ISBN 0-19-504229-8 (pa)   LC 82-14547
This is the second and concluding volume of a life of the black educator and founder of Tuskegee Institute
"Having avoided the pitfalls of white guilt and black rage and the temptation to judge the past by standards of the present, Mr. Harlan deserves honors for his remarkable achievement." N Y Times Book Rev
Includes bibliographical references

Washington, Booker T. Up from slavery; an autobiography   92
1. Tuskegee Institute 2. African American educators
Hardcover and paperback editions available from various publishers
First published 1901
"The classic autobiography of the man who, though born in slavery, educated himself and went on to found Tuskegee Institute." N Y Public Libr

Washington, George, 1732-1799

Flexner, James Thomas. George Washington. Little, Brown 1965-1972 4v il ea $40   92
1. Presidents—United States 2. United States—History
Contents: [v1] The forge of experience (1732-1775) (ISBN 0-316-28597-8); [v2] George Washington in the American Revolution (1775-1783) (ISBN 0-316-28595-1); [v3] George Washington and the new nation (1783-1793) (ISBN 0-316-28600-1); [v4] Anguish and farewell (1793-1799) (ISBN 0-316-28602-8)
Includes bibliographies

Flexner, James Thomas. Washington, the indispensable man. Little, Brown 1974 423p il hardcover o.p. paperback available $16.95   92
1. Presidents—United States
ISBN 0-316-28616-8 (pa)
This study is based on the author's four volume biography, entered above
"This more popular account has been rewritten rather than patched together from the larger work." Libr J
Includes bibliography

Lewis, Thomas A. For king and country: the maturing of George Washington, 1748-1760. HarperCollins Pubs. 1993 296p map o.p.; Wiley paperback available $14.95   92
1. Presidents—United States 2. United States—History—1600-1775, Colonial period
ISBN 0-471-10465-5 (pa)   LC 92-53346
This "biography concentrates on the youth Washington spent as a surveyor, diplomat and soldier." N Y Times Book Rev
"Fired by ambition and hampered by snobbery, Washington seems very human in this account of his progress from social climber to acclaimed military leader. Lewis' readable style and his attention to Washington's late teen years make the book a good choice for YA collections." Booklist
Includes bibliographical references

Wells, H. G. (Herbert George), 1866-1946

Martin, Christopher. H.G. Wells. Rourke 1989 112p il (Life and works) lib bdg $19.94   92
1. Authors, English
ISBN 0-86592-297-7   LC 88-15650
First published 1988 in the United Kingdom
"Martin shows how Wells' novels of social criticism were based on his own early life of shabby genteel poverty and his dreary first career as a draper's assistant. Then the account turns to his enormously popular science fiction stories, with their themes of space invasion, time travel, catastrophe, and alien worlds. Finally, Martin discusses Wells' less successful Utopian fiction." Booklist
Includes glossary and bibliography

Welty, Eudora, 1909-

Welty, Eudora. More conversations with Eudora Welty; edited by Peggy Whitman Prenshaw. University Press of Miss. 1996 xxi, 304p (Literary conversations series) $39.50; pa $16.95   92
1. Authors, American 2. Women authors
ISBN 0-87805-864-8; 0-87805-865-6 (pa)
                                        LC 95-25720
Companion volume Conversations with Eudora Welty available pa $15.95 (ISBN 0-87805-206-2)
These interviews with the author cover the "years since 1983. The interviews set the record straight on certain issues—her parents, friends, writers, childhood—and bend it more on others, particularly interpretations of her writing." Booklist
Includes bibliographical references

Welty, Eudora. One writer's beginnings. Harvard Univ. Press 1984 104p il (William E. Massey, Sr. lectures in the history of American civilization) $15.95; pa $10   92
1. Authors, American 2. Women authors
ISBN 0-674-63925-1; 0-674-63927-8 (pa)
                                        LC 83-18638
A series of lectures in which the author reflects on her Southern heritage and her early artistic influences

Wharton, Edith, 1862-1937

Lewis, R. W. B. (Richard Warrington Baldwin). Edith Wharton; a biography. Harper & Row 1975 592p il o.p.; Fromm Int. paperback available $20 **92**

1. Authors, American 2. Women authors
ISBN 0-88064-020-0 (pa)

This is a "scholarly biography of the sometimes enigmatic but always fascinating Edith Wharton. Dr. Lewis is showing us Edith Wharton as a woman and as an author of first rank with the specific intent of asking us to understand her in relation to her age and to her contemporary artists. . . . Her development as a writer and as a person is documented thoroughly." Best Sellers

Includes bibliography

Worth, Richard. Edith Wharton. Messner 1994 154p il (Classic American writers) $15 **92**

1. Authors, American 2. Women authors
ISBN 0-671-86615-X LC 93-23207

"This book looks at how Wharton's life influenced her work and why she is still considered a great American writer. Beginning with a brief description of the monied society in which she grew up, Worth goes on to blend plots of Wharton's major works chronologically into the text." SLJ

Includes bibliographical references

Wheatley, Phillis, 1753-1784

Jensen, Marilyn. Phillis Wheatley; Negro slave of Mr. John Wheatley of Boston. Lion Bks. 1987 233p $21.95 **92**

1. Poets, American 2. African American authors 3. Women poets
ISBN 0-87460-326-9 LC 87-17135

This is a biography of the colonial slave who, after being purchased by John Wheatley at the age of seven and educated by his wife, became the first black poet in Colonial America

"The facts of Wheatley's life are adequately marshalled, the tone is seldom adulatory, and the author is candid about the limitations of a slave's life even in Massachusetts, even when she was as celebrated and articulate as Wheatley. Material about the Revolution is smoothly incorporated into a life story that is inherently dramatic." Bull Cent Child Books

Includes bibliography

Whistler, James McNeill, 1834-1903

Berman, Avis. James McNeill Whistler. Abrams 1993 92p il (First impressions) $19.95 **92**

1. Artists, American
ISBN 0-8109-3968-1 LC 93-9453

A biography of the nineteenth-century American artist who spent most of his life in Europe and is known for his flamboyant personality, as well as his innovative painting and printmaking techniques and famous portrait of his mother

This book is "filled with attractive black-and-white and color reproductions. . . . Berman's text . . . is chatty and readable, fleshing out the character of Whistler as well as describing in clear and concise terms his techniques and philosophies." Bull Cent Child Books

White, Ryan

White, Ryan. Ryan White: my own story; by Ryan White and Ann Marie Cunningham. Dial Bks. 1991 277p il $16.95; pa $5.99 **92**

1. AIDS (Disease)—Personal narratives
ISBN 0-8037-0977-3; 0-451-17322-8 (pa)
LC 90-21038

Ryan White describes how he got AIDS, engaged in a legal battle to return to school, and became a celebrity and spokesperson for issues concerning the deadly disease

The book contains "surprising snatches of humor and insight that lend dimension to the vulnerable young man whose positive outlook shines through so clearly. Not saccharine, not angry, not bitter, this unusual book, delivered without an ounce of self-pity, seems as honest as it is inspiring. It will touch both adults and teens." Booklist

White, Theodore H., 1915-1986

White, Theodore H. In search of history; a personal adventure. Harper & Row 1978 561p o.p.; Warner Bks. paperback available $7.95 **92**

1. Modern history—1900-1999 (20th century)
ISBN 0-446-34657-8 (pa) LC 78-2177

In this book White "looks back on the major events he has reported during his journalistic career—China just prior to and during World War II, the Marshall Plan, the 1960 presidential campaign, etc.—and attempts to place them in historical perspective. The work in some sense also constitutes an autobiography." Libr J

Whitman, Walt, 1819-1892

Reef, Catherine. Walt Whitman. Clarion Bks. 1995 148p il $16.95 **92**

1. Poets, American
ISBN 0-395-68705-5 LC 94-7405

"Here is a biography of Whitman that presents the life of the subject, the world in which he lived, and representative passages from his writings." Voice Youth Advocates

"This is not a biography for pleasure reading, but it could be a source for those interested in historical events of 19th century America. It also would be a good resource for students doing a critique of Whitman's work for an American literature course." Book Rep

Includes bibliography

Wiesel, Elie, 1928-

Wiesel, Elie. All rivers run to the sea; memoirs. Knopf 1995 432p il $30; pa $15 **92**

1. Authors, French 2. Jews—Biography 3. Holocaust, 1933-1945—Personal narratives
ISBN 0-679-43916-1; 0-8052-1028-8 (pa)
LC 95-17607

Also available Thorndike Press large print edition
Original French edition, 1994

Wiesel "begins with his boyhood in the Carpathian Mountains of Central Europe and his uprooting and transport by cattle car to the barbed wire infernos of Auschwitz and Buchenwald. Here Wiesel describes the horror of being among Jews bound for the death camps as the war was drawing to a close. . . . He describes in

Wiesel, Elie, 1928-—*Continued*
following chapters his schooling in postwar France, his decision to become a journalist, and his travels to Israel and throughout the world." Libr J

"Wiesel's immensely moving, unforgettable memoir has the searing intensity of his novels and autobiographical tales." Publ Wkly

Includes glossary

Wilder, Laura Ingalls, 1867-1957
Zochert, Donald. Laura: the life of Laura Ingalls Wilder. Regnery 1976 260p il o.p.; Avon Bks. paperback available $5.99 **92**
    1. Women authors 2. Frontier and pioneer life
    ISBN 0-380-01636-2 (pa)   LC 75-35002
This biography of the author of the "Little House" books describes her early life and offers insight into her works

Williams, Ted, 1918-
Linn, Edward. Hitter: the life and turmoils of Ted Williams; [by] Ed Linn. Harcourt Brace Jovanovich 1993 437p il $23.95; pa $12.95 **92**
    1. Boston Red Sox (Baseball team) 2. Baseball—Biography
    ISBN 0-15-193100-3; 0-15-600091-1 (pa)
         LC 92-41870
"Linn's book is not a typical game-by-game baseball biography, but a series of snapshots of Williams's career. The [author] . . . touches on the many high points, but does not neglect Williams's warts, including his constant battle with Boston baseball writers. The product of an unhappy childhood, Williams formed close friendships with the 'underdogs,' and gave unsparingly of himself to a charity for combatting cancer in children." Libr J

Williams, Tennessee, 1911-1983
Williams, Tennessee. Conversations with Tennessee Williams; edited by Albert J. Devlin. University Press of Miss. 1986 xx, 369p il (Literary conversations series) $32.50; pa $15.95 **92**
    1. Dramatists, American
    ISBN 0-87805-262-3; 0-87805-263-1 (pa)
         LC 86-9180
A collection of interviews with the playwright in which he discusses his literary output, lifestyle, illnesses, critics and contemporaries

Wilson, Woodrow, 1856-1924
Clements, Kendrick A. Woodrow Wilson; world statesman. Twayne Pubs. 1987 272p il (Twayne's twentieth-century American biography series) lib bdg $14.95 **92**
    1. Presidents—United States 2. United States—Foreign relations
    ISBN 0-8057-7756-3   LC 87-25390
"The book includes coverage of Wilson's youth, education, academic career, health, and involvement in state politics. Clements also treats Wilson's domestic programs as President, his Latin American and Asian policies, and his role as war leader and peacemaker." Choice

"A well documented and summarized history in which Clements gives the background for and the moral reasons on which Wilson based his decisions. This [is an] easily read and understood book." SLJ

Includes bibliography

Wolff, Tobias, 1945-
Wolff, Tobias. This boy's life: a memoir. Atlantic Monthly Press 1989 288p o.p.; HarperCollins Pubs. paperback available $12.50 **92**
    1. Authors, American
    ISBN 0-06-097277-7 (pa)   LC 88-17600
The novelist and short story writer "offers an engrossing and candid look into his childhood and adolescence in his first book of nonfiction. In unaffected prose he recreates scenes from his life that sparkle with the immediacy of narrative fiction. The result is an intriguingly guileless book, distinct from the usual reflective commentary of autobiography." Libr J

Wozniak, Stephen
Kendall, Martha E. Steve Wozniak; inventor of the Apple computer. Walker & Co. 1994 104p il $14.95; lib bdg $15.85 **92**
    1. Apple Computer Inc.
    ISBN 0-8027-8341-4; 0-8027-8342-2 (lib bdg)
         LC 94-38804
"The story of the whiz kid of the Silicon Valley who built a computer when he was 11 and developed the revolutionary Apple just 15 years later. Today, the man is a multimillionaire, volunteer computer teacher, and doting father. This biography, written with the cooperation of Wozniak and family, paints a positive picture of the electronics genius, although unflattering characteristics surface from time to time." SLJ

Includes glossary

Wright, Frank Lloyd, 1867-1959
Boulton, Alexander O. Frank Lloyd Wright, architect; an illustrated biography; introduction by Bruce Brooks Pfeiffer. Rizzoli Int. Publs. 1993 128p il $24.95 **92**
    1. Architects
    ISBN 0-8478-1683-4   LC 93-12188
The author "shows how Wright changed forever contemporary architecture with his radical approach to creating a uniquely American design for homes and buildings. . . . This is also an art book; interspersed throughout the spacious text are many fine reproductions of Wright's drawings and color photographs of his famous homes and buildings. His life story, including the scandal that surrounded his private life, is presented in a straightforward style." Booklist

Includes glossary and bibliographical references

Rubin, Susan Goldman. Frank Lloyd Wright. Abrams 1994 92p il (First impressions) $19.95 **92**
    1. Architects
    ISBN 0-8109-3974-6   LC 93-48523
"Rubin integrates Wright's life story with a detailed focus on his development as an architect and on his wide

Wright, Frank Lloyd, 1867-1959—*Continued*
and lasting influence." Booklist

"Lots of photographs and illustrations, many in full
color, provide a look at many interesting projects, including the only dog house Wright ever designed." SLJ

Wright, Richard, 1908-1960
Gayle, Addison. Richard Wright; ordeal of a
native son. Anchor Press/Doubleday 1980 342p
92
1. Authors, American 2. African American authors
LC 77-12854
Available from P. Smith

This biography of the black author was written with
access to "previously classified documents from the files
kept on Wright by the US government from the mid-
1930s until his death in 1960. . . . [These included] 187
bits and pieces from the FBI along with a handful of
sheets from the CIA and other government agencies."
New Repub

Includes glossary and bibliography

Wright, Richard. Black boy; a record of
childhood and youth. Harper & Row 1964 c1945
285p hardcover o.p. paperback available $7   92
1. Authors, American 2. African American authors
ISBN 0-06-081250-8 (pa)

Also available in hardcover from Buccaneer Bks.

A reissue of the title first published 1945 by World
Publishing Company

This autobiographical work concludes with Wright
"newly arrived in Chicago in 1927 as a fugitive from the
white South that never knew him. [It] relates his nomadic life in Tennessee, Arkansas, and Mississippi, abandoned by his father and with his mother working at me-
nial jobs or incapacitated by illness." Benet's Reader's
Ency of Am Lit

Wright, Richard. Conversations with Richard
Wright; edited by Keneth Kinnamon and Michel
Fabre. University Press of Miss. 1993 xxi, 253p il
(Literary conversations series) hardcover o.p.
paperback available $15.95   92
1. Authors, American 2. African American authors
ISBN 0-87805-633-5 (pa)   LC 93-13938

In this collection of interviews, "the author of *Native
Son*, *Black Boy*, and *Uncle Tom's Children* expounds on
topics not only of literature but of politics, race, and society." Booklist

Wyeth, Andrew, 1917-
Meryman, Richard. Andrew Wyeth. Abrams
1991 92p il (First impressions) $19.95   92
1. Artists, American
ISBN 0-8109-3956-8   LC 90-47605

The author "provides in-depth coverage of the painter's formative years. . . . The book contains a number
of black-and-white photographs and 28 full-color plates
that complement the text nicely. Although the book
presents paintings created as recently as 1988, the biography ends in the late 1940s. . . . This is a beautiful,
powerful book that stresses the significance of childhood." SLJ

Wyeth, Andrew. Andrew Wyeth, autobiography;
introduction by Thomas Hoving; with
commentaries by Andrew Wyeth. Little, Brown
1995 168p il $50; pa $29.95   92
1. Artists, American
ISBN 0-8212-2159-0; 0-8212-2217-1 (pa)
LC 94-48305

"A Bulfinch Press book"

Published in conjunction with a retrospective exhibit,
this book reproduces 137 paintings. "Each painting is accompanied by commentary from the artist that lends insight into his life and character. Several nude studies are
included." Booklist

Includes bibliographical references

Yamazaki, James N., 1916-
Yamazaki, James N. Children of the atomic
bomb; an American physician's memoir of
Nagasaki, Hiroshima, and the Marshall Islands;
[by] James N. Yamazaki with Louis B. Fleming.
Duke Univ. Press 1995 182p il maps
(Asia-Pacific) $16.95   92
1. Physicians 2. Atomic bomb victims 3. Japanese
Americans
ISBN 0-8223-1658-7   LC 95-6683

"An army surgeon who was captured at the Battle of
the Bulge, Yamazaki practiced pediatrics after the war.
In this . . . memoir, he recalls his enlistment in the official commission investigating the casualities inflicted by
the Nagasaki explosion." Booklist

The author "describes the incredible destruction of
lives and buildings, cooperation from Japanese officials
and health care personnel (doctors, nurses, midwives),
firsthand reports from survivors, and the medical studies
of pregnancies and short- and long-term effects on children. . . . This autobiography is unique in the history of
this genre." Choice

Includes bibliographical references

Yeager, Chuck, 1923-
Yeager, Chuck. Yeager; an autobiography; [by]
Chuck Yeager & Leo Janos. Bantam Bks. 1985
342p il hardcover o.p. paperback available $6.99
92
1. Air pilots
ISBN 0-553-25674-2 (pa)   LC 85-3959

Yeager "describes his early life in the hills of West
Virginia; his years as fighter pilot in World War II,
where he was shot down in occupied France and escaped
with the help of the French Resistance. . . . He tells his
story vividly and pulls no punches in describing the
events and the people who made history with him." SLJ

Yeltsin, Boris
Otfinoski, Steven. Boris Yeltsin and the rebirth
of Russia. Millbrook Press 1995 110p il lib bdg
$15.90   92
1. Russia (Republic)—Politics and government 2. Soviet Union—Politics and government
ISBN 1-56294-478-9   LC 94-20296

"Otfinoski traces the Russian leader's dogged determinism, his identification with the common people, and

Yeltsin, Boris—*Continued*
his improbable rise to power in spite of Gorbachev's machinations to quiet him." Booklist
"The story of communism's demise and the rise of a democratic Russia is told with clarity and verve. Oftinoski succeeds in making recent history and the clash of rival ideologies understandable. Yeltsin emerges as a very human hero." SLJ
Includes bibliographical references

Zaharias, Babe Didrikson, 1911-1956
Cayleff, Susan E. Babe: the life and legend of Babe Didrikson Zaharias. University of Ill. Press 1995 327p il (Women in American history) $29.95; pa $14.95   **92**
1. Women athletes
ISBN 0-252-01793-5; 0-252-06593-X (pa)
    LC 94-35584
The author "presents a feminist analysis of the life, sports career, and legacy of Mildred Ella 'Babe' Didrikson Zaharias. . . . Cayleff examines Babe's amateur athletic career from high school through the 1932 Olympics, as well as her professional and amateur golf accomplishments. . . . Although it will undoubtedly be controversial, *Babe* is a very important book about a unique and significant figure in US sports." Choice
Includes bibliographical references

929 Genealogy, names, insignia

Doane, Gilbert Harry, 1897-1984
Searching for your ancestors; the how and why of genealogy; [by] Gilbert H. Doane and James B. Bell. 6th ed. University of Minn. Press 1992 334p pa $17.95   **929**
1. Genealogy
ISBN 0-8166-1990-5   LC 91-32606
First published 1937
This guide shows how to "construct a family tree, trace elusive ancestors, discriminate between promising leads and false information, [and] use new computer research methods. . . . Also included is information on how to utilize the Family History Library in Salt Lake City and its Family Centers, the Library of Congress's Local History and Genealogy Room, the National Archives, and regional public library systems." Publisher's note
Includes bibliography

Fletcher, William P.
Recording your family history. Dodd, Mead 1986 313p o.p.; Ten Speed Press paperback available $14.95   **929**
1. Genealogy
ISBN 0-89815-324-7 (pa)   LC 86-13598
First published 1983 in mimeograph format with title: Talking your roots
"A guide to preserving oral history with videotape, audiotape, suggested topics and questions, interview techniques." Title page
"For librarians wishing to start an oral history program with young adults, this is the finest guide available because it updates other sources and includes videotape information." Voice Youth Advocates
Includes bibliography

Stryker-Rodda, Harriet
How to climb your family tree; genealogy for beginners. Lippincott 1977 144p o.p.; Genealogical paperback available $8.95   **929**
1. Genealogy
ISBN 0-8063-1006-5 (pa)   LC 77-24667
Also available G.K. Hall large print edition
"The book is divided into three sections. In the first, the author stresses the importance of compiling one's own autobiography and keeping personal records of the immediate family. Public records, such as church documents, cemetery records, deeds, mortgages, military records and the census are discussed in the second section. Part three warns against pitfalls for the beginner to avoid." Libr J
Includes bibliography

929.4 Personal names

Hanks, Patrick
A dictionary of first names; [by] Patrick Hanks and Flavia Hodges. Oxford Univ. Press 1990 xxxvi, 443p $39.95   **929.4**
1. Personal names
ISBN 0-19-211651-7   LC 90-7001
This is a "collection of 4,500 European and American first names. Entries give the ethnic roots of names and their meanings, if any. . . . Entries also list nicknames and variants in other languages." Booklist
Includes bibliographical references

Hook, J. N. (Julius Nicholas), 1913-
Family names; how our surnames came to America. Macmillan 1982 388p hardcover o.p.; paperback available $8.95   **929.4**
1. Personal names—United States
ISBN 0-02-080000-2 (pa)   LC 81-18646
"In separate chapters devoted to various nationalities, Hook discusses surnames, especially in relation to the development of the U.S." Booklist
Includes bibliography

Kolatch, Alfred J., 1916-
Dictionary of first names. 2nd ed. Perigee Bks. 1990 xxxii, 506p pa $12   **929.4**
1. Personal names
ISBN 0-399-51633-6   LC 90-7394
First published 1980 by J. David with title: The Jonathan David dictionary of first names
"Gives meaning and etymology, variant forms, contemporary examples, etc. Masculine and feminine names in separate alphabets." Sheehy. Guide to Ref Books. 10th edition [review of 1980 edition]
Includes bibliographical references

Robb, H. Amanda
Encyclopedia of American family names; [by] H. Amanda Robb and Andrew Chesler. HarperCollins Pubs. 1995 710p $46   **929.4**
1. Personal names—United States
ISBN 0-06-270075-8   LC 94-28719
"This book lists the 5,000 most common family names in the U.S. as reported by the Social Security Adminis-

Robb, H. Amanda—*Continued*
tration. Entries are listed alphabetically, with variant
forms in parentheses. Each notes the ranking on the SSA
list (Smith is number one), the number of people on the
SSA list with that name (3,376,494 Smiths), and the derivation of the name, including the country of origin and
a brief etymology. Many entries contain information
about famous bearers of that name. Any published genealogies are noted at the end of entries." Booklist
Includes bibliographical references

Room, Adrian
Cassell dictionary of proper names. Cassell;
distributed by Sterling 1994 xxix, 610p $24.95
                                   929.4
1. Names—Dictionaries
ISBN 0-304-34447-8   LC 94-231872
First published 1992 with title: Brewer's dictionary of
names
"Alphabetical entries cite sources and meanings of the
proper nouns used to identify places, first and last names,
literary characters, music, holidays, modern musical
groups, astronomy, sports teams, mythological places and
people, etc. Although there is no guide to pronunciation,
this is an ideal source for quick introductory research or
a fun browsing item for students interested in learning
about their own names." SLJ

Shankle, George Earlie
American nicknames; their origin and
significance. 2nd ed. Wilson, H.W. 1955 524p $44
                                   929.4
1. Nicknames 2. Personal names—United States
3. Geographic names—United States
ISBN 0-8242-0004-7
First published 1937
"Not limited to nicknames of persons, but includes
also those applied to places, institutions, or objects, arranged by real names with cross references from nicknames. Information under the real names includes some
explanation of the nicknames and their origin, and gives
references to sources of information in footnotes." Guide
to Ref Books. 11th edition

Stewart, George Rippey, 1895-1980
American given names; their origin and history
in the context of the English language; [by]
George R. Stewart. Oxford Univ. Press 1979 264p
$31.25; pa $8.95   **929.4**
1. Personal names—United States
ISBN 0-19-502465-6; 0-19-504040-6 (pa)
                                LC 78-17603
This "is a dictionary of more than 800 names, including slave names used on antebellum plantations. Each
entry gives derivation, meaning, [and] times of greatest
popularity." Libr J
Includes bibliographical references

Stewart, Julia
African names; names from the African
continent for children and adults. Carol Pub.
Group 1993 171p pa $10.95   **929.4**
1. Personal names
ISBN 0-8065-1386-1   LC 93-9441
"A Citadel Press book"

"This book consists of about 1000 names culled from
across Black Africa, although there is a slight emphasis
on Swahili names. It includes not only personal names,
but names of towns, lakes, ethnic groups, etc., useful in
formulating an African name for oneself. Each name is
accompanied by information about its pronunciation, origins, and meaning." Libr J

929.9   Flags

Sedeen, Margaret
Star-spangled banner; our nation and its flag;
prepared by the Book Division, National
Geographic Society. National Geographic Soc.
1993 232p il $37.50   **929.9**
1. Flags—United States
ISBN 0-87044-944-3   LC 93-15173
"Sections deal with the invention of this national symbol, its wartime and diplomatic uses, its appearance in
exploration of earth and space, and its role in everyday
American life." Libr J
"With enough history for student researchers and lots
of pictures for browsers, this attractive book about the
flag is recommended for most collections." Booklist

Shearer, Benjamin F.
State names, seals, flags, and symbols; a
historical guide; [by] Benjamin F. Shearer and
Barbara S. Shearer; illustrations by Jerrie Yehling
Smith. rev & expanded. Greenwood Press 1994
438p il $49.95   **929.9**
1. Geographic names—United States 2. Seals (Numismatics) 3. Flags—United States
ISBN 0-313-28862-3   LC 93-49552
First published 1987
"Chapters on mottoes, flowers, trees, birds, songs, holidays, and license plates are just a sampling of what is
covered, and the format is such that the concisely written
material can be found as expeditiously as possible. Even
though the book is touted predominantly as a reference
tool, the information provided makes fascinating and enlightening reading." Libr J
Includes bibliographical references

930   History of ancient world

The **Age** of god-kings: timeframe 3000-1500 BC;
by the editors of Time-Life Books. Time-Life
Bks. 1987 176p il maps $19.95   **930**
1. Ancient history
                                LC 87-10229
An account of the parallel rise of civilizations in Mesopotamia, Egypt, the Mediterranean, and Asia, between
3000 BC and 1500 BC. Includes discussion of connecting trade routes, influential kings and dynasties, development of written languages, building styles, industry and
religion
Includes bibliography

Barbarian tides: timeframe 1500-600 BC; by the editors of Time-Life Books. Time-Life Bks. 1987 175p il maps $19.95   **930**
1. Ancient history

LC 87-17961

Describes the historical events and the various civilizations that flourished throughout the world, with emphasis on the Mediterranean area, from 1500 to 600 B.C

Includes bibliography

Builders of the ancient world; marvels of engineering; prepared by the Special Publications Division, National Geographic Society. National Geographic Soc. 1986 199p il maps $12.95   **930**
1. Ancient civilization 2. Ancient architecture
ISBN 0-87044-585-5   LC 86-5278

"Ancient constructions that stand out as exceptional examples of engineering technology and enduring beauty are described in this panoramic study. One chapter each is devoted to ancient Greece and Rome, MesoAmerica, South America, India and Southeast Asia, and China. Each chapter is written by an archaeologist or historian." SLJ

Includes bibliography

The **Cambridge** ancient history. Cambridge Univ. Press 1970-1996 il maps apply to publisher for price   **930**
1. Ancient history

Original 12 volume set published 1923-1939 with 5 volumes of plates

Contents: v1, pt 1 Prolegomena and prehistory 3rd ed. 1970; v1, pt 2 Early history of the Middle East 3rd ed. 1971; v2, pt 1 History of the Middle East and the Aegean Region, ca. 1800-1380 B.C. 3rd ed. 1973; v2, pt 2 History of the Middle East and the Aegean Region, ca. 1380-1000 B.C. 3rd ed. 1975; v3, pt 1 The prehistory of the Balkans; the Middle East and the Aegean world, tenth to eighth centuries B.C. 2nd ed. 1982; v3, pt 2 The Assyrian and Babylonian Empires and other states of the Near East, from the eighth to the sixth centuries B.C. 2nd ed. 1992; v3, pt 3 The expansion of the Greek world, eighth to sixth centuries B.C. 2nd ed. 1982; v4 Persia, Greece and the Western Mediterranean, ca. 525 to 479 B.C. 2nd ed. 1988; v5 The Fifth Century B.C. 2nd ed. 1992; v6 The Fourth Century B.C. 2nd ed. 1994; v7, pt 1 The Hellenistic World 2nd ed. 1984; v7, pt 2 The rise of Rome to 220 B.C. 2nd ed. 1990; v8 Rome and the Mediterranean to 133 B.C. 2nd ed. 1990; v9 The last age of the Roman Republic, 146-43 B.C. 2nd ed. 1994; v10 The Augustan Empire, 43 B.C.-A.D. 69 2nd ed. 1996; v11 The imperial peace, A.D. 70-192; v12 The imperial crisis and recovery, A.D. 193-3244

Available volumes of plates illustrating v1-2, v3, v4, v5-6, v7 pt 1

"An excellent reference history. Each chapter has been written by a specialist, with full bibliographies at the end of each volume." Guide to Ref Books. 11th edition

Empires ascendant: timeframe 400 BC-AD 200; by the editors of Time-Life Books. Time-Life Bks. 1987 175p il maps $19.95   **930**
1. Ancient history 2. Ancient civilization

LC 87-18054

Traces major cultural and historical events in Greece, Rome, India, Parthia, and China from 400 BC to AD 200

Includes bibliography

Empires besieged: timeframe AD 200-600; by the editors of Time-Life Books. Time-Life Bks. 1988 175p il maps $19.95   **930**
1. Ancient history 2. Ancient civilization

LC 87-18104

Focusing primarily on the effects of major military campaigns between 200 and 600 AD, this volume discusses the history and culture of the Roman Empire, as well as that of influential civilizations throughout India, Persia, China, Southeast Asia, and the Americas

Includes bibliography

Mysteries of mankind; Earth's unexplained landmarks; prepared by the Book Division, National Geographic Society. National Geographic Soc. 1992 200p il $16   **930**
1. Megalithic monuments 2. Excavations (Archeology)
ISBN 0-87044-864-1   LC 92-22242

An illustrated look at "unexplained human-made landmarks of the world. The landmarks covered are located on most of the continents, thus giving a global perspective to the book. Each chapter addresses one or more landmarks and provides the reader with an overview of the feature(s). Topics such as the people and culture, history of the site, physical details of the landmark and surrounding area, past and current excavations, and past and current theories of why and how the landmark was built are presented." Sci Books Films

Includes bibliographical references

Smithsonian timelines of the ancient world; [editor-in-chief] Chris Scarre. Dorling Kindersley 1993 256p il maps $49.95   **930**
1. Historical chronology 2. Ancient history—Pictorial works 3. Middle Ages—History—Pictorial works
ISBN 1-56458-305-8   LC 93-18480

Published in the United Kingdom with title: Timelines of the ancient world

"Information is displayed across 18 broad time periods utilizing [a] . . . grid that allows the user to look up a specific time period and region and discover facts about food and environment, shelter, technology, art, and ritual, for a specific location and time. Each time period is illustrated with characteristic artifacts of each period and region." Am Libr

"This beautiful reference book . . . should be a part of reference sections in every public library and all school libraries." Booklist

A **Soaring** spirit: timeframe 600-400 BC; by the editors of Time-Life Books. Time-Life Bks. 1987 174p il maps $19.95   **930**
1. Ancient history

LC 87-18018

An account of major historical events and cultural developments which occurred in Persia, Greece, Europe

A Soaring spirit: timeframe 600-400 BC—*Continued*
and Asia between 600 BC and 400 BC. Includes discussion of such notables as Cyrus the Great, Darius I, Solon, Pericles, Buddha, Confucius, and others
Includes bibliography

Splendors of the past; lost cities of the ancient world; prepared by the Special Publications Division, National Geographic Society. National Geographic Soc. 1981 295p il maps $19.95
930
1. Extinct cities 2. Ancient civilization
ISBN 0-87044-358-5   LC 80-7827
This volume "focuses on the lost cities of seven ancient civilizations, among them those of Sumeria, Pompeii, Angkor, and the Hittite empire. The popularly written articles convey the meticulous labor involved in the cities' construction, provide a glimpse of ancient ways of life, and suggest the excitement of archaeological discovery." Booklist
Includes bibliography

Starr, Chester G., 1914-
A history of the ancient world. 4th ed. Oxford Univ. Press 1991 742p il maps $39.95   **930**
1. Ancient history
ISBN 0-19-506629-4   LC 90-34970
First published 1965
Incorporating recent archaeological and anthropological discoveries, the author surveys the changing economic and social structures of societies, from prehistory to the fifth century A.D. Egyptian, Assyrian, Chinese and Greek are among the civilizations discussed
Includes bibliographical references

930.1   Archaeology

Ceram, C. W., 1915-1972
Gods, graves, and scholars; the story of archaeology; translated from the German by E. B. Garside and Sophie Wilkins. 2nd rev and substantially enl ed. Knopf 1967 441p il maps hardcover o.p. paperback available $12   **930.1**
1. Archeology—History
ISBN 0-394-74319-9 (pa)
Original German edition, 1949; first English edition, 1951
"The story of Champollion and the reading of the Rosetta Stone, the decipherment of the inscriptions on the monument of Darius the Great, Leonard Woolley's famous excavations at Ur, and John Lloyd Stephens' discovery of the ruins of a great Mayan city are . . . told in this book." Doors to More Mature Read
Includes bibliography

Fagan, Brian M.
Time detectives; how archaeologists use technology to recapture the past; by Brian Fagan. Simon & Schuster 1995 288p il $24; pa $14
930.1
1. Archeology
ISBN 0-671-79385-3; 0-684-81828-0 (pa)
LC 94-32458
Describing thirteen archeological sites around the world, the author "explores how modern archeologists are using techniques like computer imaging, infrared photography and pollen analysis to reconstruct ancient cultures." Publ Wkly
"Stimulating and informative for lay reader and student alike, this is a wide ranging, well-researched and very readable book. It is also an illuminating account of how far archaeology has come during the 20th century." New Sci
Includes bibliographical references

Robbins, Lawrence H.
Stones, bones, and ancient cities; the greatest archaeological discoveries of all time. St. Martin's Press 1990 267p il $18.95   **930.1**
1. Antiquities 2. Archeology 3. Ancient civilization
ISBN 0-312-04431-3   LC 89-77948
The author "has compiled facts, theories, and personal experience into seven chapters exploring missing links to human ancestors, cave art, burial practices, the discovery of lost cities, underwater archaeology, archaeoastronomy (the study of 'ancient monuments of an astronomical nature'), and the origin of writing. . . . A fascinating, highly readable, and informative excursion into the richness of the past and the secrets it still holds." Booklist
Includes bibliography

931   China to 420 A.D.

China's buried kingdoms; by the editors of Time-Life Books. Time-Life Bks. 1993 168p il maps (Lost civilizations) $19.95   **931**
1. Excavations (Archeology)—China 2. China—Antiquities

LC 93-15068
A "presentation of the archaeological record of the Shang, Zhou, Qin, and Han dynasties. . . . [This] volume is impressively illustrated with color photographs, maps, drawings, and charts. Readers will be especially interested in the well-known terra cotta army of Qin Shihuangdi, China's first emperor, and the lesser-known tomb of Lady Xin of the Han Dynasty, remarkably well preserved more than two millenniums after her death. The text is informative, presenting much detail in a manner accessible to general readers." Libr J
Includes bibliography

932   Egypt to 640 A.D.

Aldred, Cyril, 1914-1991
The Egyptians. rev and enl ed. Thames & Hudson 1984 216p il maps hardcover o.p. paperback available $15.95   **932**
1. Egypt—History 2. Egypt—Antiquities
ISBN 0-500-27345-6 (pa)   LC 83-50637
First published 1961 in the United Kingdom
This study of the history and culture of ancient Egypt traces the various kingdoms and dynasties and examines the sites, cities and temples
Includes bibliography

Bunson, Margaret R.
The encyclopedia of ancient Egypt; [by] Margaret Bunson. Facts on File 1991 291p il maps $40   **932**
1. Egypt—Civilization—Dictionaries 2. Egypt—Antiquities—Dictionaries
ISBN 0-8160-2093-0   LC 89-27473
This work "consists of more than 1,500 alphabetically arranged entries covering Egypt from around 3200 B.C. to the fall of the New Kingdom in 1070 B.C. There are several broad entries such as *Egypt, Agriculture, and Religion*

David, A. Rosalie (Ann Rosalie)
Discovering ancient Egypt; [by] Rosalie David. Facts on File 1994 192p il $22.95   **932**
1. Egypt—Antiquities 2. Archeologists
ISBN 0-8160-3105-3   LC 93-38601
"In this guide to the explorers of Egyptian antiquities and their discoveries, David begins her survey of the discoverers with the classical writer Herodotus (484-430 B.C.) so that she is able to refer to many findings that were later pillaged and unavailable to more contemporary archaeologists. . . . This treasure trove for researchers concludes with a helpful summation of Egyptian history from the predynastic period (5000-3100 B.C.) to the Greco-Roman period (332 B.C.-A.D.641)." Booklist
Includes bibliographical references

Egypt: land of the pharaohs; by the editors of Time-Life Books. Time-Life Bks. 1992 168p il map (Lost civilizations) $19.95   **932**
1. Egypt—Antiquities 2. Egypt—Civilization
    LC 91-36255
An illustrated look at ancient Egypt focusing on mummies, the pyramids, the pharaohs, burial practices and the treasures of Tutankhamen
Includes bibliography

Hoffman, Michael A., 1944-
Egypt before the pharaohs; the prehistoric foundations of Egyptian civilization. rev and updated. University of Tex. Press 1991 xxi, 409p il pa $17.95   **932**
1. Egypt—Antiquities 2. Prehistoric man
ISBN 0-292-72073-4   LC 90-70161
First published 1979 by Knopf

This volume studies the cultural development of prehistoric Egyptian society
Includes bibliographical references

Mertz, Barbara, 1927-
Temples, tombs, and hieroglyphs; a popular history of ancient Egypt. rev ed. Bedrick Bks. 1990 335p il pa $15.95   **932**
1. Egypt—Antiquities 2. Egypt—Civilization
ISBN 0-87226-223-5   LC 89-17911
First published 1964 by Coward-McCann
This "is an informal study of Egyptology. The author . . . has included in her text not only straight archeological reporting, but an account of the methodologies employed by archeologists and the various controversies that have preoccupied figures in the field." Sci Books Films
Includes glossary and bibliographical references

Romer, John, 1941-
Ancient lives; daily life in Egypt of the pharaohs. Holt & Co. 1984 235p il maps hardcover o.p. paperback available $18.95   **932**
1. Egypt—Antiquities 2. Egypt—Civilization
ISBN 0-8050-1244-3 (pa)   LC 84-12908
Published in the United Kingdom with subtitle: The story of the pharaohs' tombmakers
"A lively reconstruction of the history of workers and their households in the Valley of the Kings 3000 years ago. Valuable for students of ancient history." SLJ
Includes bibliography

Taylor, John H.
Unwrapping a mummy; the life, death and embalming of Horemkenesi. University of Tex. Press 1996 111p il (Egyptian bookshelf) pa $18.95   **932**
1. Horemkenesi 2. Mummies 3. Egypt—Civilization
ISBN 0-292-78141-5   LC 95-61446
An exploration of ancient Egyptian civilization based on the study of the mummy of Horemkenesi. Customs surrounding death and the process of mummification are discussed in detail
Includes bibliographical references

933   Palestine to 70 A.D.

Shanks, Hershel
Jerusalem; an archaeological biography. Random House 1995 256p il maps $50   **933**
1. Excavations (Archeology)—Israel 2. Jerusalem—History 3. Jerusalem—Antiquities
ISBN 0-679-44526-9   LC 95-24404
This is an overview of the history and archeology of Jerusalem from the Chalcolithic period (around 3500 B.C.E.) to modern times
"With 200 color photographs and innumerable charts and black-and-white pictures, this introduction to the city . . . is a most enjoyable read. . . . The book will interest Christians, Moslems, and Arabs, as well as Jews, for each of whom Jerusalem has its own special meaning." Choice
Includes bibliographical references

934   India to 647 A.D.

Ancient India; land of mystery; by the editors of
Time-Life Books. Time-Life Bks. 1994 168p il
(Lost civilizations) $19.95   **934**
1. India—Antiquities 2. India—Civilization
LC 94-29622
Based on archaeological discoveries, this is an illus-
trated look at the ancient civilization that gave birth to
several of the world's major religions
Includes bibliography

935   Mesopotamia and Iranian Plateau to 637 A.D.

Mesopotamia: the mighty kings; by the editors of
Time-Life Books. Time-Life Bks. 1995 168p il
map (Lost civilizations) $19.95   **935**
1. Excavations (Archeology)—Iraq 2. Iraq—Antiquities
LC 94-24305
This "illustrated book spans the history and culture of
ancient Mesopotamia during the last two millennia
B.C.—from the rise of Hammurabi to the conquest of
Babylon in 539 B.C.—with emphasis on the archaeological evidence. The stories of the Babylonian and Assyrian
empires, along with the history of their excavation, are
told in well-written style, threaded through with quotations from ancient texts and data from excavators themselves." Libr J
Includes bibliography

Persians; masters of empire; by the editors of
Time-Life Books. Time-Life Bks. 1995 168p il
maps (Lost civilizations) $19.95   **935**
1. Iran—Antiquities
LC 95-13943
This illustrated volume, based on archaeological discoveries, explores the civilization that conquered much of
the ancient world
Includes bibliography

Roaf, Michael
Cultural atlas of Mesopotamia and the ancient
Near East. Facts on File 1990 238p il maps $45
       935
1. Iraq—Civilization 2. Middle East
ISBN 0-8160-2218-6   LC 90-3429
"An Equinox book"
This is a "study of the geography, history, archaeolo-
gy, and anthropology of Mesopotamia and the Near East.
. . . Special topics and archaeological sites are featured,
described, and illustrated. Some of the topics include the
origin of writing, ivory carving, and Mesopotamian war-
fare. . . . Excellent full-page maps and a wealth of full-
color illustrations add to the reference value." SLJ
Includes glossary and bibliographical references

936   Europe north and west of Italian peninsula to ca. 499 A.D.

Celts: Europe's people of iron; by the editors of
Time-Life Books. Time-Life Bks. 1994 168p il
maps (Lost civilizations) $19.95   **936**
1. Celts
LC 94-10175
Beginning with a discussion of Lindow man, an Iron
Age man found in a bog in England, this illustrated survey of the Celts goes on to describe Celtic finds in Austria, Switzerland, Germany, France and other parts of Europe. In addition to the archaeological evidence presented, the book also includes descriptions of the Celts by
their Greek and Roman contemporaries
Includes bibliography

Early Europe; mysteries in stone; by the editors of
Time-Life Books. Time-Life Bks. 1995 168p il
maps (Lost civilizations) $19.95   **936**
1. Prehistoric man 2. Megalithic monuments 3. Europe—Antiquities
LC 94-46002
This illustrated look at ancient European civilization
discusses Stonehenge and the 1991 discovery of the perfectly preserved body of a 5,999-year-old man
Includes bibliography

The **Oxford** illustrated prehistory of Europe;
edited by Barry Cunliffe. Oxford Univ. Press
1994 532p il $49.95   **936**
1. Prehistoric man 2. Europe—Antiquities
ISBN 0-19-814385-0   LC 93-49342
This covers the period "from the replacement of Nean-
derthals by, or their evolution into, modern humans
40,000 years ago to the fall of Rome. . . . To augment
the scholarship, there are many glossy, informative illustrations. The writers, all affiliated with British universities, examine self-contained subjects with a degree of accessibility that should appeal to all archaeological tastes."
Booklist
Includes bibliographical references

936.2   England to 410 A.D.

Chippindale, Christopher
Stonehenge complete. Cornell Univ. Press 1983
296p il maps hardcover o.p. paperback available
$24.95   **936.2**
1. Stonehenge (England) 2. Great Britain—Antiquities
ISBN 0-8014-9451-6 (pa)   LC 83-70803
"Chronologically arranged chapters begin with the ear-
liest-known mention of Stonehenge, in A.D. 1130, and
proceed up to the present day." Libr J
"This is a splendidly illustrated social history. Although the Neolithic and Bronze Ages are referred to, it
is the attitudes of medieval Stuart, Victorian and modern
times that most concern Mr. Chippindale." Times Lit
Suppl
Includes bibliography

Salway, Peter
The Oxford illustrated history of Roman Britain. Oxford Univ. Press 1993 563p il maps $49.95
936.2
1. Romans—Great Britain 2. Great Britain—History—0-1066 3. Great Britain—Antiquities
ISBN 0-19-822984-4   LC 93-12951
This "work begins with a short discussion of Britain before the first Roman invasion and ends with discussions on the influences of over 500 years of Roman rule on the British economy, religion, society, and daily life. The writing is clear, concise, and highly readable. The impressive illustrations (over 320 maps, drawings, photographs, and color plates) add significantly to the text." Libr J
Includes bibliographical references

937 Roman Empire

Adkins, Lesley
Handbook to life in ancient Rome; [by] Lesley Adkins and Roy A. Adkins. Facts on File 1994 404p il maps $40
937
1. Rome—Civilization 2. Rome—Social life and customs
ISBN 0-8160-2755-2   LC 93-11213
This work covers politics, military affairs, literature, religion, architecture, geography, and social life in ancient Rome from the 8th century B.C. to the 5th century A.D. Illustrated with site-specific photographs and line drawings

Bunson, Matthew
Encyclopedia of the Roman Empire. Facts on File 1994 494p il maps $50
937
1. Rome—History—Dictionaries
ISBN 0-8160-2135-X   LC 91-38036
This reference work provides information on the key places, people, events, and culture of Roman history, from the reign of Julius Caesar to the fall of the last Roman emperor in 476 A.D.
For a review see: Booklist, June 15, 1994

Cornell, T. J. (Tim J.)
Atlas of the Roman world; by Tim Cornell and John Matthews. Facts on File 1982 240p il maps $45
937
1. Rome—History 2. Rome—Civilization
ISBN 0-87196-652-2   LC 81-19591
"More than just an atlas, this is a concise and authoritative history of Rome from its beginnings in the eighth century B.C. to the death of Justinian in 565 A.D. . . . The more than 50 colorful maps relay information rarely collected elsewhere, such as the linguistic divisions of the Roman Empire." Booklist
Includes bibliography

Davis, William Stearns, 1877-1930
A day in old Rome; a picture of Roman life. Biblo & Tannen 1959 xxiv, 482p il maps $22
937
1. Rome—Social life and customs 2. Rome—Civilization
ISBN 0-8196-1206-5
A reprint of the title first published 1925 by Allyn
Depicts the daily life and customs of Roman civilization, including government, religion, games, courts and orators, country life, and occupations

Etruscans; Italy's lovers of life; by the editors of Time-Life Books. Time-Life Bks. 1995 168p il (Lost civilizations) $19.95
937
1. Etruscans
LC 94-43686
This illustrated volume deals "with Etruscan history and the rediscovery of the Etruscans, their economic and social life, the way they enjoyed their affluence, and, finally, their obscure religious practices and beliefs, all revealed and interpreted through archaeological excavations along with Greek and Roman accounts." Sci Books Films
Includes bibliography

Langguth, A. J., 1933-
A noise of war; Caesar, Pompey, Octavian and the struggle for Rome. Simon & Schuster 1994 384p il maps $25
937
1. Rome—History
ISBN 0-671-70829-5   LC 93-39196
This history "begins in 81 B.C. with the confrontation of Julius Caesar and the dictator Sulla and the emergence of Marcus Tullius Cicero. Langguth then proceeds, through a series of progressively graver crises and progressively closer approaches to one-man rule, to the emergence of Caesar as supreme power. . . . Caesar and Cicero are the focal figures in Langguth's version of that story, but a host of other memorable actors are vividly portrayed." Booklist
Includes bibliographical references

Pompeii; the vanished city; by the editors of Time-Life Books. Time-Life Bks. 1992 168p il (Lost civilizations) $19.95
937
1. Pompeii (Extinct city)
LC 92-1277
A heavily illustrated look at the social life and customs of Pompeii at the time of Vesuvius' eruption. The excavations at Herculaneum are also discussed
Includes bibliography

Rome: echoes of imperial glory; by the editors of Time-Life Books. Time-Life Bks. 1994 168p il (Lost civilizations) $19.95
937
1. Hadrian, Emperor of Rome, 76-138 2. Rome—Civilization 3. Rome—History
LC 93-37766
This book about ancient Roman civilization "highlights the importance of the forum as a center of politics and life, the career and personal life of the emperor Hadrian, colonial expansion, and the army as the instrument that actually forged and built the empire." SLJ
Includes bibliographical references

938   Greece to 323 A.D.

Civilization of the ancient Mediterranean: Greece and Rome; edited by Michael Grant and Rachel Kitzinger. Scribner 1988 3v il maps set $195
938
1. Greek civilization 2. Rome—Civilization
ISBN 0-684-17594-0   LC 87-23465
Companion to Civilizations of the ancient Near East, entered in class 939
This reference work contains "97 chapters by 88 authorities on everything from farming and cooking to taxes, warfare and divinities in Greece and Rome. . . . The bibliographies following each chapter are . . . comprehensive, the photographs and illustrations are as instructive as they are delightful and the maps are easy to read." N Y Times Book Rev

Durant, William James, 1885-1981
The life of Greece; [by] Will Durant. Simon & Schuster 1939 754p il (Story of civilization, pt2) $35
938
1. Greece—History 2. Greek civilization
ISBN 0-671-41800-9
Another title in series: Caesar and Christ available for $35 (ISBN 0-671-11500-6)
"Being a history of Greek civilization from the beginnings, and of civilization in the Near East from the death of Alexander, to the Roman conquest; with an introduction of the prehistoric culture of Crete." Title page
Includes glossary and bibliography

Grant, Michael, 1914-
The founders of the Western world; a history of Greece and Rome. Scribner 1991 352p maps $27.50
938
1. Greece—History 2. Rome—History
ISBN 0-684-19303-5   LC 90-23818
The author "begins with archaic Greece and the spread of its culture throughout the eastern Mediterranean . . . [and then discusses] the Persian wars, the resulting dominance of Athens, and the classical phase of Greek culture. Grant then covers Alexander's conquests and the spread of Hellenism. The . . . narrative then moves to the story of Rome, from the Etruscans and through republic, empire, and finally decline." Natl Rev
"A cornerstone acquisition for any and every library." Booklist
Includes bibliography

A social history of Greece and Rome. Scribner 1993 197p $20
938
1. Greece—History 2. Rome—History
ISBN 0-684-19309-4   LC 92-32690
The author discusses the "ancient Greece and Rome known to ordinary people. The status of women, citizens as well as slaves, and of freedmen and women are all focal points in his analysis of social structures. In addition, he examines the lives of foreigners within Greek and Roman cities and reconsiders the influence of Marxist social analysis on the field." Publisher's note
Includes bibliographical references

Greece: temples, tombs, & treasures; by the editors of Time-Life Books. Time-Life Bks. 1994 168p il (Lost civilizations) $19.95   **938**
1. Greek civilization 2. Greece—History
LC 93-43570
This book about ancient Greek civilization "provides views from the Bronze Age palace cultures to the classical period of city states to the eventual conquest by Rome." SLJ
Includes bibliographical references

Levi, Peter, 1931-
Atlas of the Greek world. Facts on File 1981 c1980 239p il maps (Historical atlas series) $45
938
1. Greece—Maps 2. Greek civilization 3. Greece—Antiquities
ISBN 0-87196-448-1   LC 81-122477
First published 1980 in the United Kingdom
"After a part on 'the land in context,' the material is arranged chronologically: the ages of Bronze, of tyranny, of Pericles, and of Alexander. A final part on 'the fate of Hellenism' deals with Greece's influence on later Western civilization." Libr J
"Highly recommended for high schools." Wynar. Guide to Ref Books for Sch Media Cent. 3d edition
Includes glossary and bibliography

Robinson, Cyril Edward, b. 1884
Everyday life in ancient Greece; [by] C. E. Robinson. Oxford Univ. Press 1933 159p il maps o.p.; Greenwood Press reprint available lib bdg $49.95
938
1. Greek civilization 2. Greece—Social life and customs
ISBN 0-8371-9078-9 (lib bdg)
The development of Greek society is traced from its origins to the end of the classical age. Special focus is on Athens and its economy, politics, art, religion and education

Sacks, David
Encyclopedia of the ancient Greek world. Facts on File 1995 306p il $45   **938**
1. Greece—History—Dictionaries
ISBN 0-8160-2323-9   LC 94-33229
Also available paperback edition with title: A dictionary of the ancient Greek world (ISBN 0-19-511206-7) $16.95
This "source features articles ranging from 100 to 3,000 words on all aspects of the Greek world. . . . The 525 articles are accompanied by line drawings that generally reproduce famous artwork. A bibliography and index conclude the work. Sacks covers almost every topic of interest, ranging from mythological figures (*Cassandra, Paris*), historical people (*Arion, Sappho*), events (*Peloponnesian War*—the longest entry in the work), and places (*Argos, Megara*) to general topics (*Clothing, Ships and Seafaring*)." Booklist

938.003 Classical dictionaries

Grant, Michael, 1914-
A guide to the ancient world; a dictionary of classical place names. Wilson, H.W. 1986 728p maps $68   **938.003**
1. Classical dictionaries 2. Mediterranean region—Gazetteers
ISBN 0-8242-0742-4   LC 86-15785
"About 700 places, primarily cities and towns of the ancient Greek, Etruscan, and Roman worlds, are described in entries that range from one-half to one page in length. 'Each entry includes data of a historical, geographical, archaeological and (where appropriate) artistic and mythological character.' Numerous cross-references. Introductory section of locator maps; extensive bibliography." Guide to Ref Books. 11th edition

The **Oxford** classical dictionary; edited by Simon Hornblower and Antony Spawforth. 3rd ed. Oxford Univ. Press 1996 liv, 1640p $90
     938.003
1. Classical dictionaries
ISBN 0-19-866172-X   LC 96-5352
First published 1949 under the editorship of M. Cary and others

"A scholarly dictionary, with signed articles, covering biography, literature, mythology, philosophy, religion, science, geography, etc. Most of the articles are brief, but there are some longer survey articles, e.g. Rome, music, scholarship, etc." Guide to Ref Books. 11th edition
For a review see: Booklist, May 1, 1997

Radice, Betty, 1912-1985
Who's who in the ancient world; a handbook to the survivors of the Greek and Roman classics; selected with an introduction by Betty Radice. rev. Penguin Bks. 1973 336p il maps pa $12.50
     938.003
1. Classical dictionaries 2. Greece—Biography 3. Rome—Biography
ISBN 0-14-051055-9
"Penguin reference books"
First published 1971 by Stein & Day
"An encyclopedia of persons and places from the ancient classical world. The entries are concise and, wherever possible, emphasize the later uses of the classical characters and places in the literature, theater, etc. of the Western world." Choice
Includes bibliography

939 Other parts of ancient world to ca. 640

Anatolia; cauldron of cultures; by the editors of Time-Life Books. Time-Life Bks. 1995 168p il maps (Lost civilizations) $19.95   **939**
1. Turkey—Civilization 2. Turkey—Antiquities
     LC 95-20268
"Chatal Hoyuk, in what is now south central Turkey, was excavated in the early 1960s and turned out to be one of the very first places that could be called a city. . . . Other archaeologists' efforts in Turkey have resulted in the discovery of the ancient empire of the Hittites, lost to history for centuries. These and several other little-known and understood civilizations are described. Numerous full-color photographs and illustrations add an extra dimension to the text." SLJ
Includes bibliography

Civilizations of the ancient Near East; Jack M. Sasson, editor in chief. Scribner 1995 4v il maps set $449   **939**
1. Middle East—Civilization
ISBN 0-684-19279-9   LC 95-1712
Companion to Civilization of the ancient Mediterranean: Greece and Rome, entered in class 938

This "work concentrates on the Near East, broadly defined to include a region from Northeast Africa to India, Pakistan, and Burma, with principal focus on the core areas of Egypt, Syro-Palestine, Mesopotamia, and Anatolia. The time span ranges from the third millennium B.C.E., when writing was invented, to 330 B.C.E., when Alexander triumphed over the Persian Empire. The 189 contributors from five continents and 16 countries include some of the world's finest scholars." Libr J
For a fuller review see: Booklist, April 15, 1996

Wondrous realms of the Aegean; by the editors of the Time-Life Books. Time-Life Bks. 1993 167p il maps (Lost civilizations) $19.95   **939**
1. Aegean Islands (Greece and Turkey)—Antiquities 2. Bronze Age
     LC 92-29449
An illustrated look at the Bronze Age civilizations of the Aegean region. Among the topics covered are the excavations of the Minoan palaces at Knossos and the archaeological search for the fabled city of Troy
Includes bibliography

940.1 Europe—Early history to 1453

Bunson, Matthew
The encyclopedia of the Middle Ages; [by] Matthew E. Bunson. Facts on File 1995 498p il maps $50   **940.1**
1. Middle Ages—Dictionaries
ISBN 0-8160-2456-1   LC 94-33232
"Bunson defines the Middle Ages as spanning the years 410 to 1492. Arranged alphabetically, the articles average five pages, with *See Also* references pointing readers to related subjects and mentions of topics with their own entries appearing in bold type. The articles are tersely factual, concentrating on names of people, places, and events; coverage is less satisfactory for social concepts or philosophies." Libr J
For a fuller review see: Booklist, Feb. 1, 1996

Cantor, Norman F.

Medieval lives; eight charismatic men and women of the Middle Ages. HarperCollins Pubs. 1994 197p hardcover o.p. paperback available $12
940.1

1. Medieval civilization 2. Middle Ages—History
ISBN 0-06-092579-5 (pa)   LC 93-37051

The author presents "portraits of five men and three women whose idealism exerted great influence during the medieval era, beginning with Helena Augusta (c.255-329), the mother of Constantine the Great, and ending with John Duke of Bedford (c.1389-1435), who was regent of France for Henry VI. Cantor creates vignettes in which his subjects engage in discourse with their contemporaries. . . . Although the author uses fictionalized conversations, his reconstructions rest on solid research and result in compelling depictions of important medieval thinkers." Publ Wkly

Includes bibliographical references

Durant, William James, 1885-1981

The age of faith; [by] Will Durant. Simon & Schuster 1950 1196p il (Story of civilization, pt4) $35
940.1

1. Medieval civilization 2. Middle Ages—History 3. Religion
ISBN 0-671-01200-2

"A history of medieval civilization—Christian, Islamic, and Judaic—from Constantine to Dante: A.D. 325-1300." Title page

Includes bibliography

The **Early** Middle Ages. Raintree Pubs. 1990 72p il maps (History of the world) $27.11   **940.1**

1. Middle Ages—History 2. Medieval civilization
ISBN 0-8172-3307-5   LC 90-8102

Surveys the history of Europe and the Middle East from the fall of the Roman Empire to the year 1000, with emphasis on the founding and spread of Islam and the rise and the fall of the Byzantine and Carolingian Empires

Includes glossary

Gies, Frances

The knight in history. Harper & Row 1984 255p il maps hardcover o.p. paperback available $13.50
940.1

1. Knights and knighthood 2. Middle Ages—History
ISBN 0-06-091413-0 (pa)   LC 84-47571

This book describes the rise and fall of the institution of knighthood and the influence of the medieval knight throughout history

Includes bibliography

Life in a medieval village; [by] Frances and Joseph Gies. Harper & Row 1990 257p il maps hardcover o.p. paperback available $13   **940.1**

1. Medieval civilization 2. Middle Ages—History
ISBN 0-06-092046-7 (pa)   LC 89-33759

"Elton, England, is the focal point of the authors' efforts to portray the everyday life and social structure of the High Middle Ages. After giving a brief summary of Elton's origins and development in the Roman and Anglo-Saxon periods, the book examines just how the residents lived and worked within the feudal structure at the beginning of the fourteenth century." Booklist

Includes glossary and bibliography

Gies, Joseph

Life in a medieval castle; [by] Joseph and Frances Gies. Crowell 1974 272p il o.p.; Harper & Row paperback available $13   **940.1**

1. Castles 2. Middle Ages—History
ISBN 0-06-090674-X (pa)

Using Chepstow Castle on the Welsh border as a model, the authors provide "descriptions of the medieval world where the castle was household, feudal center, and military target, and by concentrating on Anglo-Norman examples illustrate what existence was like as the dark ages began to brighten." Booklist

Includes glossary and bibliography

The **Late** Middle Ages. Raintree Pubs. 1990 71p il maps (History of the world) $27.11   **940.1**

1. Middle Ages—History 2. Medieval civilization
ISBN 0-8172-3308-3   LC 90-8098

Examines European life between the years 1000 and 1300 focusing on the growth of cities, the development of a money-based economy, and the emergence of a Europe newly unified by a shared religion and increased trade

Includes glossary

The **Middle** Ages; by Morris Bishop. American Heritage 1985 c1968 350p il (American Heritage library) pa $13.95   **940.1**

1. Middle Ages—History 2. Medieval civilization
ISBN 0-8281-0487-5   LC 85-23013

Also available in hardcover from P. Smith

First published 1968 with title: The Horizon book of the Middle Ages

This volume covers the period from the conversion of Constantine in 312 A.D. through the conclusion of the Hundred Years War in 1461

The **Middle** Ages: a concise encyclopaedia; general editor: H. R. Loyn. Thames & Hudson 1989 352p il maps hardcover o.p. paperback available $24.95   **940.1**

1. Middle Ages—Dictionaries 2. Medieval civilization
ISBN 0-500-27645-5 (pa)   LC 88-50254

"Covering the period from A.D. 400 to 1500, this . . . [volume] provides nearly 1,000 entries on people, places, customs, and concepts, from Scandinavia to the Middle East, including Islamic culture." Booklist

The **Oxford** illustrated history of medieval Europe; edited by George Holmes. Oxford Univ. Press 1988 398p il maps $49.95; pa $22.50   **940.1**

1. Europe—History—476-1492
ISBN 0-19-820073-0; 0-19-285220-5 (pa)

LC 87-11122

An "account of medieval Europe from the fall of Rome to the eve of the Reformation. This popular history, well-written by professional historians, is for the intelligent general reader. . . . Maps, charts, and illustrations deserve high praise. Highly recommended." Libr J

Includes bibliography

Vikings: raiders from the North; by the editors of Time-Life Books. Time-Life Bks. 1993 168p il maps (Lost civilizations) $19.95   **940.1**
1. Vikings

LC 93-14028

This is an illustrated history of the Norsemen
"To read this title is to alter forever mythical perceptions of Viking heroes. The clearly written text avoids romanticizing, yet presents an engrossing, if not glamorous, picture of the Viking era. Hence, while readers may be impressed by the artistic skill, bravery, and determination of Norsemen adventurers, they also see their undeniable brutality." SLJ

Includes bibliographical references

940.2   Europe—1453-

Durant, William James, 1885-1981
The age of Louis XIV; by Will and Ariel Durant. Simon & Schuster 1963 802p il (Story of civilization, pt8) $35   **940.2**
1. Europe—Civilization 2. Europe—History—1492-1789
ISBN 0-671-01215-0
"A history of European civilization in the period of Pascal, Molière, Cromwell, Milton, Peter the Great, Newton and Spinoza: 1648-1715." Title page
Includes bibliography

The age of Napoleon; by Will and Ariel Durant. Simon & Schuster 1975 xxi, 872p il (Story of civilization, pt11) $35   **940.2**
1. Napoleon I, Emperor of the French, 1769-1821 2. Europe—Civilization 3. Europe—History—1789-1900
ISBN 0-671-21988-X
"A history of European civilization from 1789-1815." Subtitle
This look at the social and political history of 1789-1815 Europe focuses on the influence of Napoleon
Includes bibliography

The age of reason begins; by Will and Ariel Durant. Simon & Schuster 1961 732p il (Story of civilization, pt7) $35   **940.2**
1. Europe—Civilization 2. Europe—History—1492-1789
ISBN 0-671-01320-3
"A history of European civilization in the period of Shakespeare, Bacon, Montaigne, Galileo, and Descartes: 1558-1648." Title page
Includes bibliography

The age of Voltaire; by Will and Ariel Durant. Simon & Schuster 1965 898p il (Story of civilization, pt9) $35   **940.2**
1. Voltaire, 1694-1778 2. Europe—Civilization 3. Europe—History—1492-1789
ISBN 0-671-01325-4
"A history of civilization in Western Europe from 1715 to 1756, with special emphasis on the conflict between religion and philosophy." Title page
Includes bibliography

The Reformation; [by] Will Durant. Simon & Schuster 1957 1025p il (Story of civilization, pt6) $35   **940.2**
1. Europe—Civilization 2. Reformation 3. Europe—History—476-1492 4. Europe—History—1492-1789
ISBN 0-671-61050-3
"A history of European civilization from Wyclif to Calvin: 1300-1564." Title page
Among the personalities discussed are: Charles V, Chaucer, Knox, Luther, Mary I, More, Rabelais and Wolsey
Includes bibliography

Rousseau and revolution; by Will and Ariel Durant. Simon & Schuster 1967 xx, 1091p il maps (Story of civilization, pt10) $35   **940.2**
1. Europe—Civilization 2. Europe—History—1492-1789 3. Eighteenth century
ISBN 0-671-63053-X
"A history of civilization in France, England, and Germany from 1756 and in the remainder of Europe from 1715 to 1789." Title page
There is "no popular history that is so encyclopedic in scope, so brightly readable in style." Saturday Rev
Includes bibliography

The **Oxford** illustrated history of modern Europe; edited by T. C. W. Blanning. Oxford Univ. Press 1996 362p il maps $45   **940.2**
1. Europe—History—1789-1900 2. Europe—History—1900-1999 (20th century)
ISBN 0-19-820374-8
This volume covers "politics, economics, warfare, class structure, art, and culture from the time of the revolution through 1995. Central themes include the idea that revolution against established order was possible, successful, and, once underway, perhaps unstoppable." Libr J

Includes bibliography

Taylor, A. J. P. (Alan John Percivale), 1906-1990
The struggle for mastery in Europe, 1848-1918. Oxford Univ. Press 1954 xxxvi, 683p maps (Oxford history of modern Europe) $65; pa $22   **940.2**
1. Europe—History—1789-1900
ISBN 0-19-822101-0; 0-19-881270-1 (pa)
A history of Europe that concentrates on the diplomatic causes of World War I
Includes bibliography

Wilson, Ellen Judy
Encyclopedia of the Enlightenment; Peter Hanns Reill, consulting editor; Ellen Judy Wilson, principal author. Facts on File 1996 485p il $50   **940.2**
1. Enlightenment 2. Philosophy 3. Europe—Intellectual life
ISBN 0-8160-2989-X   LC 95-11962
This work identifies and discusses the "key people, subject fields, terms, styles, works, and European loca-

Wilson, Ellen Judy—*Continued*
tions important in history from the late 1600s to 1800.
Americans such as Franklin, Jefferson, and Paine are included." SLJ
For a fuller review see: Booklist, May 1, 1996

940.3   World War I, 1914-1918

The **American** Heritage history of World War I;
by the editors of American Heritage; narrative
by S.L.A. Marshall; with a prologue by Edmund
Stillman; editor in charge, Alvin M. Josephy,
Jr.; managing editor, Joseph L. Gardner.
Bonanza Bks. 1982 384p il $19.99   **940.3**
1. World War, 1914-1918
ISBN 0-517-38555-4   LC 82-9617
First published 1964 by American Heritage
An analysis of the origins, course, and aftermath of
the First World War that incorporates historical and pictorial elements

Bosco, Peter I.
World War I; John Bowman, general editor.
Facts on File 1991 124p il maps (America at war)
$17.95   **940.3**
1. World War, 1914-1918—United States
ISBN 0-8160-2460-X   LC 90-49086
Tells why America abandoned its isolationism to participate in World War I, and its significance for America
"The text . . . is nicely balanced. Bosco concisely discusses all aspects of the war, from military logistics and
political maneuvering to the horrors of the battlefield."
SLJ
Includes bibliographical references

Gilbert, Martin, 1936-
The First World War; a complete history. Holt
& Co. 1994 xxiv, 615p il maps $35; pa $19.95
      940.3
1. World War, 1914-1918
ISBN 0-8050-1540-X; 0-8050-4734-4 (pa)
      LC 94-27268
This work "covers WW I on all major fronts—domestic, diplomatic, military—as well as such bloody preludes
as the Armenian massacre of 1915." Publ Wkly
"What Mr. Gilbert seeks to do, and frequently succeeds in doing, is to humanize, indeed to personalize,
World War I. His effort and accomplishment make this
a rewarding and significant book." N Y Times Book Rev
Includes bibliographical references

Jantzen, Steven, 1941-
Hooray for peace, hurrah for war; the United
States during World War I. Facts on File 1991
181p il (Library of American history) $17.95
      940.3
1. World War, 1914-1918—United States 2. United
States—Social conditions
ISBN 0-8160-2453-7   LC 90-13916
"Originally published in a different form by Alfred
Knopf Inc. c1971"

Traces the impact of World War I on American society, from the spirited organization of the "home front" to
the social conditions and contributions of poor immigrants, middle classes, and the wealthy
Includes bibliographical references

Kennedy, David M., 1941-
Over here; the First World War and American
society. Oxford Univ. Press 1980 404p hardcover
o.p. paperback available $13.95   **940.3**
1. World War, 1914-1918—United States 2. United
States—Social conditions
ISBN 0-19-503209-8 (pa)   LC 80-11753
"Kennedy has assembled a series of narrative essays
designed to explore those aspects of America's World
War experience that proved most formative in shaping
20th-Century U.S. society." Libr J
Includes bibliography

Marrin, Albert, 1936-
The Yanks are coming; the United States in the
First World War. Atheneum Pubs. 1986 248p il
maps $15.95   **940.3**
1. World War, 1914-1918
ISBN 0-689-31209-1   LC 86-3585
"Marrin describes America's role in World War I
from its belated entry in 1917 . . . through the war at
sea, in the air, and in the trenches, to the final hard-won
victory. He dramatically re-creates a routine flying mission in the first fragile fighter planes . . . and combines
such general accounts with details of particular battles
and military tactics, and with tales of individual daring
and endurance." Booklist
Includes bibliography

Pope, Stephen
The dictionary of the First World War; by
Stephen Pope and Elizabeth-Anne Wheal;
consultant editor, Keith Robbins; with original
maps by Brendan Eddison. St. Martin's Press 1996
xxviii, 561p maps $40   **940.3**
1. World War, 1914-1918—Dictionaries
ISBN 0-312-12931-9   LC 95-46288
The authors "use facts, narrative, and analysis in over
1200 dictionary entries to cover all areas of World War
I. The entries range in length from single-sentence definitions to several pages and present a comprehensive picture of the global aspect of the conflict." Libr J
For a fuller review see Booklist, Feb. 1, 1996

Stokesbury, James L.
A short history of World War I. Morrow 1981
348p maps hardcover o.p. paperback available $11
      940.3
1. World War, 1914-1918
ISBN 0-688-00129-7 (pa)   LC 80-22206
This chronologically arranged history of World War I
presents both the political and military perspectives
Includes bibliography

Tuchman, Barbara Wertheim

The guns of August; [by] Barbara W. Tuchman. anniversary ed. Macmillan 1988 c1962 511p il maps o.p.; Ballantine Bks. paperback available $14
940.3
1. World War, 1914-1918
ISBN 0-345-38623-X (pa)   LC 88-29330
A reissue with a new preface by the author of the title
First published 1962
A history of the negotiations that preceded World War I and the course of the war's first month
Includes bibliography

The Zimmermann telegram; [by] Barbara W. Tuchman. [new ed] Macmillan 1966 244p il hardcover o.p. paperback available $11   **940.3**
1. World War, 1914-1918—Causes
ISBN 0-02-054820-6 (pa)
Also available in paperback from Ballantine Bks.
First published 1958
The author discusses the German plan to induce Mexico to attack the U.S. during World War I
Includes bibliographical references

The **United** States in the First World War; an encyclopedia; editor, Anne Cipriano Venzon; consulting editor, Paul L. Miles. Garland 1995 xx, 830p maps (Garland reference library of the humanities) $95   **940.3**
1. World War, 1914-1918
ISBN 0-8240-7055-0   LC 95-1782
"Biography, economics, civil rights, women's issues, foreign relations, battles, armaments, and conferences are among the topics included. Arrangement is alphabetical, and most articles are brief—between one column and a page. . . . Most articles include brief bibliographies. There are six maps, but no other illustrations." Libr J
For a fuller review see: Booklist, Feb. 1, 1996

940.4 World War I, 1914-1918 (Military conduct of the war)

Lawrence, T. E. (Thomas Edward), 1888-1935

Seven pillars of wisdom; a triumph   **940.4**
1. World War, 1914-1918—Middle East 2. Arabs 3. Bedouins 4. Wahhabis
Hardcover and paperback editions available from various publishers
First published 1935 by Doubleday, Doran
A "largely autobiographical account of the Arab Revolt against the Turks during the First World War. . . . The book describes events between Lawrence's arrival in Jidda in October 1916 and the establishment of an Arab government in Damascus two years later. Episodic, vividly descriptive, accounts of the actions of the highly mobile campaign and the desert landscapes in which it took place form the essential substance of the work. Much controversy has surrounded the matter of Lawrence's accuracy as a military historian, which is considered to have been diminished by his desire to convey a heroic impression of the Arab people and himself." Oxford Companion to 20th Cent Lit in Engl

Weintraub, Stanley, 1929-

A stillness heard round the world; the end of the Great War: November, 1918. Dutton 1985 467p il o.p.; Oxford Univ. Press paperback available $11.95   **940.4**
1. World War, 1914-1918
ISBN 0-19-505208-0 (pa)   LC 85-6775
"A Truman Talley book"
A "history of the last days of the First World War. The logistics of armistice, the difficulty of disseminating accurate news, the problems of repatriating prisoners of war, and the heady mix of triumph and relief felt by the victors are here in ample detail." Publ Wkly
Includes bibliography

940.53 World War II, 1939-1945

Adler, David A., 1947-

We remember the Holocaust. Holt & Co. 1989 147p il $18.95; pa $9.95   **940.53**
1. Holocaust, 1933-1945—Personal narratives 2. World War, 1939-1945—Jews
ISBN 0-8050-0434-3; 0-8050-3715-2 (pa)
LC 87-21139
"Survivors of the Holocaust share their unique stories in an informative, moving account that serves to remind readers of the terrible effects of hatred." Soc Educ
Includes glossary and bibliography

And justice for all; an oral history of the Japanese American detention camps; [edited] by John Tateishi. Random House 1984 xxvii, 259p il map $18.95   **940.53**
1. Japanese Americans—Evacuation and relocation, 1942-1945 2. World War, 1939-1945—United States
ISBN 0-394-52955-3   LC 82-42823
"Recollections from 30 Japanese Americans who were placed in government detention camps following Japan's attack on Pearl Harbor lend valuable insight into this tragic event in U.S. history." Booklist

Armor, John

Manzanar; by John Armor and Peter Wright; commentary by John Hersey; photographs by Ansel Adams. Times Bks. 1988 xx, 167p il $27.50
940.53
1. Manzanar War Relocation Center 2. Japanese Americans—Evacuation and relocation, 1942-1945
ISBN 0-8129-1727-8   LC 88-40155
Armor, Wright, and Hersey describe the "relocation of Japanese Americans in World War II. Specific attention to Manzanar, the first camp, appears in the form of 100 photographs taken by Ansel Adams in 1943." Libr J
"A superbly done book by any definition, this will be useful for browsing, reports, booktalking, and discussions of Constitutional issues." Voice Youth Advocates

Art from the ashes; a Holocaust anthology; edited by Lawrence L. Langer. Oxford Univ. Press 1995 689p il $30; pa $19.95   **940.53**
1. Holocaust, 1933-1945—Personal narratives 2. Holocaust, 1933-1945 in literature
ISBN 0-19-507559-5; 0-19-507732-6 (pa)
                            LC 94-11446

This collection "includes both fiction and nonfiction, as well as drama and poetry. Among the nonfiction pieces are excerpts from the ghetto diaries of Abraham Lewin (Warsaw) and Avraham Tory (Kovno), an essay from Primo Levi's *The Drowned and the Saved,* and an essay from Elie Wiesel's *Legends of Our Time.*" Booklist
A "remarkable volume, perfectly suited for anyone studying the Holocaust. . . . Compared with [the] first-hand accounts, fiction could be, one would think, only a pallid version of reality. Yet the fiction Mr. Langer collects . . . highlights the reality of the Holocaust with stunning intensity." N Y Times Book Rev

Auschwitz; a history in photographs; compiled and edited by Teresa Świebocka; English edition prepared by Jonathan Webber and Connie Wilsack. Indiana Univ. Press 1993 295p il maps $75   **940.53**
1. Holocaust, 1933-1945—Pictorial works 2. Auschwitz (Poland: Concentration camp)—Pictorial works
ISBN 0-253-35581-8   LC 93-1083
Original Polish edition, 1990
"Published for the Auschwitz-Birkenau State Museum, Oświecim." Title page
"This book provides photographic documentation of the Holocaust and the suffering at Auschwitz. . . . The photographs, which come from a variety of sources, include official Nazi pictures, smuggled photographs by prisoners, aerial views, and liberation pictures. Chosen to show all aspects of the camp's history, the photographs provide visual evidence of what happened to the Jewish people. Essays and captions provide insightful information and history." Libr J
Includes bibliographical references

Ayer, Eleanor H.
Parallel journeys; [by] Eleanor H. Ayer with Helen Waterford and Alfons Heck. Atheneum Bks. for Young Readers 1995 244p il $15   **940.53**
1. Holocaust, 1933-1945 2. Germany—History—1933-1945 3. Jews—Germany
ISBN 0-689-31830-8   LC 94-23277
"Alternating chapters contrast the wartime experiences of two young Germans—Waterford, who was interned in a Nazi concentration camp, and Heck, a member of the Hitler Youth. The volume is composed mainly of excerpts from their published autobiographies, connected by Ayer's overall account of the era. A powerful and painful picture emerges, vividly describing life before, during, and, most impressively, after the Holocaust." Horn Book Guide
Includes bibliography

Berenbaum, Michael, 1945-
The world must know; the history of the Holocaust as told in the United States Holocaust Memorial Museum; Arnold Kramer, editor of photographs. Little, Brown 1993 240p il $40; pa $21.95   **940.53**
1. United States Holocaust Memorial Museum 2. Holocaust, 1933-1945
ISBN 0-316-09135-9; 0-316-09134-0 (pa)
                         LC 92-32813
This work was written to commemorate the opening of the U.S. Holocaust Memorial Museum in April 1993 on the fiftieth anniversary of the Warsaw Ghetto uprising. Berenbaum uses the museum's photographs and documents to "chronicle the Holocaust's four historical participants: the victims, the perpetrators, the bystanders, and the rescuers." Booklist
"Visually evocative and unsettling, the book, supplemented with a useful bibliography, is an excellent choice for those with little acquaintance of the subject or those needing a concise synopsis." Libr J

Boas, Jacob
We are witnesses; five diaries of teenagers who died in the Holocaust. Holt & Co. 1995 196p $15.95   **940.53**
1. Holocaust, 1933-1945—Personal narratives 2. World War, 1939-1945—Jews 3. Jews—Europe
ISBN 0-8050-3702-0   LC 94-43889
Also available in paperback from Scholastic
"Narrative accounts of five young Jews, including Anne Frank, whose diaries hold their observations and emotions, give immediacy to the horrors of the Holocaust. The text provides historical information and compares the experiences of the diarists, quoting liberally from the teenagers' writings. Although these condensed versions lack the impact of a complete diary, the cumulative effect of the five journals is overwhelming." Horn Book Guide
Includes bibliographical references

Brimner, Larry Dane
Voices from the camps; internment of Japanese Americans during World War II. Watts 1994 110p il lib bdg $22.70   **940.53**
1. Japanese Americans—Evacuation and relocation, 1942-1945 2. World War, 1939-1945—United States
ISBN 0-531-11179-2   LC 93-30201
This is "an account of the effect of American policy during World War II on Japanese Americans in California. The internment in prison camps is described through interviews with the survivors and their children." Publisher's note
"Brimner has done an effective job relating the various kinds of experiences that occurred as the Japanese Americans were forced to leave their homes and businesses, often selling them at a mere fraction of their worth, and journey to the various camps for their incarceration. . . . In addition, he has included a number of black and white photos that help to document the events." Voice Youth Advocates
Includes glossary and bibliography

Children in the Holocaust and World War II; their secret diaries; [compiled by] Laurel Holliday. Pocket Bks. 1995 xxi, 409p il map $20; pa $12
940.53
1. Holocaust, 1933-1945—Personal narratives 2. World War, 1939-1945—Children
ISBN 0-671-52054-7; 0-671-52055-5 (pa)
LC 95-3211
"Diary entries written by young people in ghettos, concentration camps, cities, and a Copenhagen prison camp offer . . . glimpses of life during World War II. Each selection is introduced by a brief biography that includes the author's name, country, age, family circumstances before and during the war, and concludes with circumstances of death or postwar life. Nine girls and 14 boys, Jews and gentiles, aged 10 to 18, are featured." SLJ

"This anthology is a haunting reminder of the impact of war on children. The powerful images will long be remembered." Voice Youth Advocates

Includes bibliographical references

Churchill, Sir Winston, 1874-1965
Closing the ring. Houghton Mifflin 1951 749p maps (Second World War, v5) hardcover o.p. paperback available $14.95
940.53
1. World War, 1939-1945 2. World War, 1939-1945—Great Britain
ISBN 0-395-41059-2 (pa)
"'Closing the Ring' sets forth the year of conflict from June 1943 to June 1944. Aided by the command of the oceans, the mastery of the U-boats, and our ever growing superiority in the air, the Western Allies were able to conquer Sicily and invade Italy, with the result that Mussolini was overthrown and the Italian nation came over to our side." Preface

The gathering storm. Houghton Mifflin 1948 784p maps (Second World War, v1) hardcover o.p. paperback available $16.95
940.53
1. World War, 1939-1945 2. World War, 1939-1945—Great Britain
ISBN 0-395-41055-X (pa)
The first volume of Churchill's monumental history of the Second World War describes the days between the false peace and Hitler's near-victory just before Dunkirk

The grand alliance. Houghton Mifflin 1950 903p maps (Second World War, v3) hardcover o.p. paperback available $14.95
940.53
1. World War, 1939-1945 2. World War, 1939-1945—Great Britain
ISBN 0-395-41057-6 (pa)
This volume begins with the German drive in the East, covers the War in Africa and describes the entrance into the war of Russia and, after Pearl Harbor, the United States

The great battles and leaders of the Second World War; an illustrated history; introduction by John Keegan. Houghton Mifflin 1995 328p il maps $40
940.53
1. World War, 1939-1945
ISBN 0-395-75516-6
LC 95-18483
"Accompanied by many photographs, these selections from Churchill's multi-volume *Second World War* give readers a personalized perspective on the wartime events and the military and political personalities involved in them." Booklist

The hinge of fate. Houghton Mifflin 1950 1000p maps (Second World War, v4) hardcover o.p. paperback available $14.95
940.53
1. World War, 1939-1945 2. World War, 1939-1945—Great Britain
ISBN 0-395-41058-4 (pa)
Describing events leading to the invasion of Sicily, warfare in Africa, the discouragingly slow job of reconquest in Europe, meetings with Roosevelt, and efforts at collaboration with Stalin, this volume covers the period from January 1942 to May 1943

Their finest hour. Houghton Mifflin 1949 751p maps (Second World War, v2) hardcover o.p. paperback available $14.95
940.53
1. World War, 1939-1945 2. World War, 1939-1945—Great Britain
ISBN 0-395-41056-8 (pa)
This volume starts with the problems confronting Churchill as he assumed the office of Prime Minister in 1940 and continues with accounts of the Battle of Britain, the Battle of France and Dunkirk

Triumph and tragedy. Houghton Mifflin 1953 800p maps (Second World War, v6) hardcover o.p. paperback available $14.95
940.53
1. World War, 1939-1945 2. World War, 1939-1945—Great Britain
ISBN 0-395-41060-6 (pa)
The concluding volume of Churchill's history of World War II begins with D-Day and covers campaigns leading to the defeat of Germany and Japan

Daniels, Roger
Prisoners without trial; Japanese Americans in World War II; consulting editor, Eric Foner. Hill & Wang 1993 146p il (Critical issue series) $22.95; pa $7.95
940.53
1. Japanese Americans—Evacuation and relocation, 1942-1945 2. World War, 1939-1945—United States
ISBN 0-8090-7897-X; 0-8090-1553-6 (pa)
LC 92-27144
An account of "the relocation of Japanese Americans during World War II, an injustice prompted not by military necessity but by political and racial motivations. The purpose of this volume is to tell the story in light of the redress legislation enacted in 1988." Libr J

Dawidowicz, Lucy S.
The war against the Jews, 1933-1945. 10th anniversary ed. Free Press 1986 c1975 xxxx, 466p maps o.p.; Bantam Bks. paperback available $15.95
940.53
1. Holocaust, 1933-1945 2. Jews—Europe
ISBN 0-553-34532-X (pa)
LC 86-6516
A reissue with new introduction and supplementary bibliography of the title first published 1975 by Holt, Rinehart & Winston
"One of the best histories of the mass murder of Jews in World War II. Argues for the centrality of anti-Semitism in Hitler's program." Reader's Adviser. 13th edition

Different voices; women and the Holocaust; edited and with introductions by Carol Rittner and John K. Roth. Paragon House 1993 435p il maps $26.95; pa $19.95   **940.53**
1. Holocaust, 1933-1945—Personal narratives 2. World War, 1939-1945—Women
ISBN 1-55778-503-1; 1-55778-504-X (pa)
                LC 92-28233
This "assortment of memoirs, essays, and reflections written by and about adult women who encountered the Holocaust through their own or their forbearers' experiences, will be a compelling, unusual addition to Holocaust collections." Booklist
Includes bibliographical references

Epstein, Helen, 1947-
Children of the Holocaust; conversations with sons and daughters of survivors. Putnam 1979 348p o.p.; Penguin Bks. paperback available $12.95   **940.53**
1. Holocaust, 1933-1945—Psychological aspects
ISBN 0-14-011284-7 (pa)   LC 78-23429
A series of interviews with the children of Holocaust survivors living in the U.S., Canada, South America, and Israel
Includes bibliographical references

Fox, Stephen C. (Stephen Carey)
The unknown internment; an oral history of the relocation of Italian Americans during World War II; [by] Stephen Fox. Twayne Pubs. 1990 223p il (Twayne's oral history series) lib bdg $25.95
                         940.53
1. World War, 1939-1945—United States 2. Italian Americans
ISBN 0-8057-9108-6   LC 89-78474
The author documents the forcible relocation of Italian Americans from the West Coast of the United States beginning in 1942
"These informative, often poignant interviews touch not only on the internment but also on many other aspects of Italian American life before World War II. Combined with historical data and Fox's insights into the panic behind the government's actions, they make a valuable addition to history collections." Booklist
Includes bibliographical references

Ganor, Solly, 1928-
Light one candle; a survivor's tale from Lithuania to Jerusalem. Kodansha Am. 1995 xxii, 353p $25   **940.53**
1. Holocaust, 1933-1945—Personal narratives 2. Jews—Lithuania
ISBN 1-56836-098-3   LC 95-20720
This "memoir offers a detailed account of the author's struggle to survive the German occupation of Lithuania amid the terrorizing, torture and liquidation of most of the inhabitants of the Kaunas ghetto during WW II. Ganor describes the diabolical way the Nazis turned gentile Lithuanians against Jews and, inside the ghetto itself, neighbor against neighbor. . . . This absorbing memoir, with its record of suffering and catharsis, is a valuable addition to Holocaust literature." Publ Wkly

Gies, Miep, 1909-
Anne Frank remembered; the story of the woman who helped to hide the Frank family; [by] Miep Gies with Alison Leslie Gold. Simon & Schuster 1987 252p il maps hardcover o.p. paperback available $10   **940.53**
1. Frank family 2. Netherlands—History—1940-1945, German occupation 3. Holocaust, 1933-1945
ISBN 0-671-66234-1 (pa)   LC 86-25991
"A memoir of the courageous Dutch woman who helped hide the Frank family, this book augments the Anne Frank story. Perceptive characterizations, with insight into life in Amsterdam during the Nazi occupation." SLJ

Gilbert, Martin, 1936-
The Holocaust; a history of the Jews of Europe during the Second World War. Holt & Co. 1986 c1985 959p il maps hardcover o.p. paperback available $18.95   **940.53**
1. Holocaust, 1933-1945
ISBN 0-8050-0348-7 (pa)   LC 85-5523
"Proceeding chronologically from Hitler's rise to power in 1933 to Germany's surrender and the liberation of the concentration camps, [the author] documents the countless horrors of this 'unprecedented explosion of evil over good,' drawing extensively on records and testimonies of those who survived (as well as some who eventually perished)." Booklist
Includes bibliography

Gill, Anton
The journey back from hell; an oral history: conversations with concentration camp survivors. Morrow 1989 c1988 494p il maps o.p.; Avon Bks. paperback available $10.95   **940.53**
1. Concentration camps 2. Holocaust, 1933-1945—Personal narratives
ISBN 0-380-70777-2 (pa)   LC 88-38663
First published 1988 in the United Kingdom
"Based on interviews with 120 people from 14 countries who lived through the horror of the German concentration camps. . . . [This work] records the experiences of German, Hungarian, Austrian, Czechoslovakian, and Polish Jews, as well as resistance fighters and political prisoners. In each interview a survivor describes prewar life, experiences in the camps and present-day existence." Publisher's note
Includes glossary and bibliography

Gold, Ruth Glasberg, 1930-
Ruth's journey; a survivor's memoir. University Press of Fla. 1996 293p il maps $34.95   **940.53**
1. Jews—Romania 2. Holocaust, 1933-1945—Personal narratives
ISBN 0-8130-1400-X   LC 95-6771
"With the onset of World War II, 11-year-old Ruth Glasberg changed from being a happy and prosperous child to becoming her family's lone survivor within a few months. As she grew and continued to survive in Nazi-controlled Europe, she began to believe the real punishment was to continue living. She describes exis-

Gold, Ruth Glasberg, 1930—*Continued*
tence in the concentration camps of Transnistria, rescue failures, and ultimately freedom in Palestine. She tells of how she felt as a child, and brings in what she, as an adult, now knows as truth regarding the events that overtook her young life. The author takes her story beyond the Holocaust, and includes her experiences in the newly formed nation of Israel. Family photographs appear throughout." SLJ
Includes bibliographical references

Goldhagen, Daniel
Hitler's willing executioners; ordinary Germans and the Holocaust. Knopf 1996 622p il maps $30; pa $16 **940.53**
1. Holocaust, 1933-1945 2. Germany—History—1933-1945 3. Antisemitism 4. National socialism
ISBN 0-679-44695-8; 0-679-77268-5 (pa)
LC 95-38591
The author "endeavors to show that the common apologia for the Germans—that Hitler 'brainwashed' them—is nonsense and that most Germans gave their active assent to genocide. An ordinary German commander, for example, might feel himself bound by a strict code of conduct yet not be at all averse to murdering Jews. The book ends with a detailed notes section and an appendix that explains the correct methodology for studying the Nazi period." Libr J

Historical atlas of the Holocaust. Macmillan; Prentice-Hall Int. 1996 252p maps $39.95
940.53
1. Holocaust, 1933-1945—Maps
ISBN 0-02-897451-4
LC 95-9354
This atlas depicts "Europe between 1933 and 1950. Compiled from archives around the world, the *Atlas* is based on extensive research into primary sources—such as period maps captured from the German army, survivor testimony, and aerial photographs taken by American, British, and German forces—illustrating the Nazi camp system that pervaded Europe. . . . In addition to maps of major cities and ghettos, the *Atlas* charts the destruction of synagogues during Kristallnacht; the routes of deportations and forced marches; and the location of Nazi pseudo-scientific experimental facilities." Publisher's note
For a review see: Booklist, May 1, 1996

Horn, Joseph, 1926-
Mark it with a stone. Barricade Bks. 1996 223p $20 **940.53**
1. Holocaust, 1933-1945—Personal narratives
2. Jews—Poland
ISBN 1-56980-068-5
LC 95-51075
This is an account of the author's experiences during the Holocaust. Born in Radom, Poland, Horn was twelve when the Germans occupied Poland. "His parents and sister were killed in Treblinka, and his two brothers and two uncles also perished. Horn survived Auschwitz and six other concentration camps before being sent to Bergen-Belsen." Booklist
"In this slim volume, Horn has written a heartrending account of his struggle to stay alive under the most horrific conditions. . . . Grim but compelling reading." Libr J

Keegan, John, 1934-
The Second World War. Viking 1990 c1989 608p il maps hardcover o.p. paperback available $19.95 **940.53**
1. World War, 1939-1945
ISBN 0-14-011341-X (pa)
LC 89-16682
First published 1989 in the United Kingdom
This military and strategic history contains sections covering the Eastern and Western fronts and the war in the Pacific
"Keegan accompanies his narrative with a series of set battlepieces, of strategic analyses, and of 'themes of war'. . . . [The book] is beautifully ordered and . . . a pleasure to read." New Statesman

Langer, Lawrence L.
Holocaust testimonies; the ruins of memory. Yale Univ. Press 1991 216p $35; pa $14 **940.53**
1. Holocaust, 1933-1945—Personal narratives
ISBN 0-300-04966-8; 0-300-05247-2 (pa)
LC 90-44768
This examination of the Holocaust is based on more than 300 interviews with survivors. The author analyzes the psychology behind these accounts as distinct forms of memory

Leitner, Isabella
Isabella; from Auschwitz to freedom; [by] Isabella Leitner and Irving A. Leitner. Anchor Bks. (NY) 1994 233p pa $12.95 **940.53**
1. Holocaust, 1933-1945—Personal narratives
2. Auschwitz (Poland: Concentration camp)
ISBN 0-385-47318-4
LC 93-47892
Merges and re-works the author's Fragments of Isabella (1978) and Saving the fragments (1985)
These are the author's "memoirs of Auschwitz and her emigration to the U.S." Publ Wkly

Levi, Primo, 1919-1987
The drowned and the saved; translated from the Italian by Raymond Rosenthal. Summit Bks. 1988 203p o.p.; Vintage Bks. paperback available $10 **940.53**
1. Holocaust, 1933-1945—Personal narratives
2. Auschwitz (Poland: Concentration camp)
ISBN 0-679-72186-X (pa)
LC 87-18052
Auschwitz survivor Levi, an Italian Jewish chemist from Turin, wrote this final contemplation of the Holocaust before his suicide in 1987
"If the unending tragedy of the Holocaust can ever be said to make sense, then it does so in these pages." New Yorker

Survival in Auschwitz; and, The reawakening; two memoirs; translated by Stuart Woolf. Summit Bks. 1986 c1985 397p map **940.53**
1. World War, 1939-1945—Personal narratives
2. Holocaust, 1933-1945—Personal narratives
3. Auschwitz (Poland: Concentration camp)
LC 85-27618
Both works available separately in paperback from Simon & Schuster

Levi, Primo, 1919-1987—*Continued*

Survival in Auschwitz originally published 1958 in Italy; first United States edition published 1959 by Orion Press with title: If this is a man. The reawakening originally published 1963 in Italy; first United States edition published 1965 by Little, Brown

This volume brings together two memoirs that tell of the Italian Jewish chemist's ten months as a concentration camp inmate and of his liberation and return journey home through the Soviet Union, Hungary and Romania

"These books are at one time powerful and understated, offered without a whisper of self-pity, even quite frequently with humor." America

Levine, Ellen

A fence away from freedom; Japanese-Americans and World War II. Putnam 1995 260p il map $17.95   **940.53**

1. Japanese Americans—Evacuation and relocation, 1942-1945 2. World War, 1939-1945—United States
ISBN 0-399-22638-9   LC 95-13357

This book "reveals little known facts about the internment of Japanese-Americans during World War II and its aftermath. Levine interviewed evacuees who were children and teenagers at the time and who were interned in all the states in which camps were established. She intersperses their stories with her narrative of the 'relocation.'" Book Rep

"This is an excellent source of information about a period of our history that is just beginning to be fully examined." SLJ

Includes bibliographical references

Lindwer, Willy

The last seven months of Anne Frank; translated from the Dutch by Alison Meersschaert. Pantheon Bks. 1991 204p il o.p.; Anchor Bks. (NY) paperback available $12   **940.53**

1. Frank, Anne, 1929-1945 2. Holocaust, 1933-1945—Personal narratives 3. Netherlands—History—1940-1945, German occupation
ISBN 0-385-42360-8 (pa)   LC 90-53437

"Six Dutch Jewish women who survived the concentration camps in the last months of the war bear witness to the kind of suffering that Anne Frank endured before she died." Booklist

Lyons, Michael J., 1930-

World War II: a short history; Michael J. Lyons. 2nd ed. Prentice-Hall 1994 368p il maps $22.05   **940.53**

1. World War, 1939-1945
ISBN 0-13-501156-6   LC 93-14685
First published 1989

The author explores the causes of World War II, the rise of fascism, the major battles, military compaigns, important personalities and the decision to use the atomic bomb

Includes bibliographical references

Mee, Charles L.

Meeting at Potsdam; by Charles L. Mee, Jr. Evans & Co. 1975 370p il o.p.; Franklin Sq. Press paperback available $14.95   **940.53**

1. Berlin Conference, 1945 2. World War, 1939-1945—Peace
ISBN 1-879957-50-7 (pa)

This is an account of the historic conference held in Potsdam in the summer of 1945 at which Stalin, Churchill, and Truman discussed post-World War II strategies

Includes bibliography

Meltzer, Milton, 1915-

Never to forget: the Jews of the Holocaust. Harper & Row 1976 217p maps lib bdg $15.89; pa $6.95   **940.53**

1. Holocaust, 1933-1945
ISBN 0-06-024175-6 (lib bdg); 0-06-446118-1 (pa)

"The mass murder of six million Jews by the Nazis during World War II is the subject of this compelling history. Interweaving background information, chilling statistics, individual accounts and newspaper reports, it provides an excellent introduction to its subject." Interracial Books Child Bull

Includes bibliography

Nomberg-Przytyk, Sara, 1915-

Auschwitz; true tales from a grotesque land; translated by Roslyn Hirsch; edited by Eli Pfefferkorn and David H. Hirsch. University of N.C. Press 1985 185p hardcover o.p. paperback available $13.95   **940.53**

1. Holocaust, 1933-1945 2. Auschwitz (Poland: Concentration camp)
ISBN 0-8078-4160-9 (pa)   LC 84-17386

"In 1943 Nomberg-Przytyk was shipped from Poland's Bialystok ghetto to the Stutthof concentration camp and then to Auschwitz. Here she became an attendant in the hospital of Dr. Josef Mengele—Auschwitz' infamous Angel of Death. The author gives a first-hand account of the cruel medical experiments that left nearly a half-million Jews dead." Booklist

Includes glossary and bibliography

Okihiro, Gary Y., 1945-

Whispered silences; Japanese Americans and World War II; photographs by Joan Myers. University of Wash. Press 1996 249p il $60; pa $29.95   **940.53**

1. Japanese Americans—Evacuation and relocation, 1942-1945
ISBN 0-295-97497-4; 0-295-97498-2 (pa)
     LC 95-21895

"A Samuel & Althea Stroum book"

This collaboration contains "stark images of the decaying remains of the World War II relocation camps in photographs taken since 1981 by noted photographer Myers. Okihiro's text combines personal memory, his family history, and personal accounts of many Japanese Americans from Hawaii and the West Coast, from the early years of immigration through the 1980's but focusing on the war years." Libr J

Includes bibliographical references

Overy, R. J. (Richard James), 1947-

The road to war; [by] Richard Overy with Andrew Wheatcroft. Random House 1989 364p il maps $24.95   **940.53**

1. World War, 1939-1945—Causes

ISBN 0-394-58260-8   LC 89-10435

"Overy presents the 1920s and 1930s as perceived by the major powers at the time without the benefit of hindsight. There are no 'pure knights' here preparing for the 'good war,' only paranoid politicians haunted by the effects of World War I, the Russian Revolution, and the Great Depression weaving alliances motivated by an all-pervading social Darwinism." Libr J

"The book is a concise, highly readable account of how WW II came about." Publ Wkly

Includes bibliography

Why the Allies won. Norton 1996 396p il maps $29.95   **940.53**

1. World War, 1939-1945 2. Strategy

ISBN 0-393-03925-0   LC 95-52444

"Eschewing the belief that the Allies won solely because of their prodigious production of weapons and equipment, Mr. Overy points out that in the early stages of the war, before the Allies were fully mobilized, the Axis countries held the production advantage, yet failed to achieve victory because Germany's management of supply logistics was far inferior to that of the Allies—frequently as a result of Hitler's wrongheaded interference. . . . Assiduously researched and concisely written, this is a highly perceptive study." N Y Times Book Rev

Includes bibliography

The **Oxford** companion to World War II; general editor, I.C.B. Dear; consultant editor, M.R.D. Foot. Oxford Univ. Press 1995 xxii, 1343p il maps $60   **940.53**

1. World War, 1939-1945—Dictionaries

ISBN 0-19-866225-4   LC 95-148182

"Nearly 1800 A-Z entries describe key political and military leaders, battles and campaigns, weapons and inventions, alliances and diplomatic efforts, and events and phenomena. . . . Enhanced by 3900 illustrations and maps, the volume boasts well over 100 contributors." Libr J

For a fuller review see: Booklist, Aug. 1995

The **Pictorial** history of the Holocaust; edited by Yitzhak Arad; designed by Hava Mordohovich; [photographs from] Yad Vashem, The Holocaust Martyrs' and Heroes' Remembrance Authority, Jerusalem. Macmillan 1990 396p il maps $100   **940.53**

1. Holocaust, 1933-1945—Pictorial works

ISBN 0-02-897011-X   LC 90-6044

"The more than 400 photographs provide an exceptional look at the unspeakable horror of the Holocaust." SLJ

Pyle, Ernie, 1900-1945

Ernie's war; the best of Ernie Pyle's World War II dispatches; edited with a biographical essay by David Nichols; foreword by Studs Terkel. Random House 1986 432p il $19.95   **940.53**

1. World War, 1939-1945

ISBN 0-394-54923-6   LC 85-18390

"Organized chronologically and following Pyle's path from Britain during the Blitz to North Africa, Sicily, Italy, France, and the Pacific, the text reveals vivid details about the day-to-day life of the infantry soldier as well as offering a unique view of the basics of warfare." Booklist

Includes bibliography

Rogasky, Barbara

Smoke and ashes: the story of the Holocaust. Holiday House 1988 187p il maps $19.95; pa $12.95   **940.53**

1. Holocaust, 1933-1945

ISBN 0-8234-0697-0; 0-8234-0878-7 (pa)

     LC 87-28617

The author "details the dark horror of Nazism—from the beginning pogroms the Nazis organized against German Jews to the setting up of concentration camps and death factories. . . . In clear and simple prose, she relates how the Jews lived and died in the camps . . . and how a small number of non-Jews helped them in their struggle. She concludes with an account of the Nuremburg Trials and the many instances of contemporary anti-Semitism that have outlived Hitler." SLJ

Includes bibliography

Smith, Page

Democracy on trial; the Japanese-American evacuation and relocation in World War II. Simon & Schuster 1995 476p $27.50   **940.53**

1. Japanese Americans—Evacuation and relocation, 1942-1945

ISBN 0-684-80354-2   LC 95-17957

"Smith describes how FDR's Executive Order 9066, issued eight weeks after Pearl Harbor, drastically affected the lives of some 120,000 Japanese Americans. Forcibly evacuated from their homes, deprived of their livelihood and property, they were moved into bleak internment camps for the duration of the war. Included in this monumental study is a review of the U.S.-Japanese relationship, the history of Japanese immigrants in America and the problem of divided loyalties on the part of those with dual citizenship." Publ Wkly

Includes bibliographical references

Spiegelman, Art

Maus; a survivor's tale. Pantheon Bks. 1996 2v in 1 il $35   **940.53**

1. Spiegelman, Vladek 2. Holocaust, 1933-1945

ISBN 0-679-40641-7   LC 96-32796

Also available CD-ROM version, The complete Maus A combined edition of Maus (1986) and Maus II (1991)

Contents: My father bleeds history; And here my troubles began

Spiegelman, Art—*Continued*

In this work "Spiegelman takes the comic book to a new level of seriousness, portraying Jews as mice and Nazis as cats. Depicting himself being told about the Holocaust by his Polish survivor father, Spiegelman not only explores the concentration-camp experience, but also the guilt, love, and anger between father and son." Rochman. Against borders

Steiner, Jean François, 1938-

Treblinka; preface by Simone de Beauvoir; translated from the French by Helen Weaver. Simon & Schuster 1967 415p o.p.; New Am. Lib. paperback available $13.95   **940.53**

1. Treblinka (Poland: Concentration camp) 2. Holocaust, 1933-1945

ISBN 0-451-01124-8 (pa)

Original French edition, 1966

This book "documents the incredible story of the death camp Treblinka, in which a handful of indomitable men planned and led an armed revolt against their SS masters." Chicago. Public Libr

Stokesbury, James L.

A short history of World War II. Morrow 1980 420p maps hardcover o.p. paperback available $12   **940.53**

1. World War, 1939-1945

ISBN 0-688-08587-3 (pa)   LC 79-20896

An overview of the military conduct of the War in both Europe and the Pacific

Includes bibliography

Terkel, Studs, 1912-

"The good war"; an oral history of World War Two. Pantheon Bks. 1984 589p o.p.; New Press (NY) paperback available $13   **940.53**

1. World War, 1939-1945—Personal narratives

ISBN 1-56584-343-6 (pa)   LC 84-42710

In a series of interviews Terkel depicts how WWII affected the lives of average Americans

Weatherford, Doris

American women and World War II. Facts on File 1990 338p il (History of women in America) $29.95   **940.53**

1. World War, 1939-1945—Women 2. Women—United States—History

ISBN 0-8160-2038-8   LC 89-71489

"The author provides information on the role of women in World War II, covering such topics as their jobs, their 'new' status, and their image in the eyes of their fellow citizens." Booklist

"This is a fascinating and immensely readable account." Libr J

Includes bibliographical references

Weglyn, Michi, 1926-

Years of infamy; the untold story of America's concentration camps. Morrow 1976 351p il map hardcover o.p. paperback available $15.45   **940.53**

1. Japanese Americans—Evacuation and relocation, 1942-1945 2. World War, 1939-1945—United States

ISBN 0-688-07996-2 (pa)

Also available in paperback from University of Wash. Press

A first-person account of the injustices experienced during the evacuation and relocation of Japanese Americans during World War II

Includes bibliography

Weinberg, Jeshajahu, 1918-

The Holocaust Museum in Washington; by Jeshajahu Weinberg and Rina Elieli. Rizzoli Int. Publs. 1995 200p il $45; pa $29.95   **940.53**

1. United States Holocaust Memorial Museum 2. Holocaust, 1933-1945

ISBN 0-8478-1906-X; 0-8478-1907-8 (pa)

     LC 95-1622

This illustrated volume "chronicles the story of the development of and meaning behind the museum. Weinberg and Elieli provide readers with insight into the plan and construction of the structure; the design and selection of materials for the permanent exhibits; and the architectural considerations that helped to create such a rich and meaningful experience for all who visit the memorial. The authors explore the building and exhibits as well as discuss the values and principles inherent in any Holocaust collection." SLJ

Wheal, Elizabeth-Anne

A dictionary of the Second World War; [by] Elizabeth-Anne Wheal, Stephen Pope and James Taylor. Bedrick Bks. 1990 541p il maps $39.95   **940.53**

1. World War, 1939-1945—Dictionaries

ISBN 0-87226-337-1   LC 90-312

"Some 1,600 alphabetically arranged articles, varying from a sentence to several pages, cover people, events, weapons, battles, and other aspects of the war and its era. Special features include chronologies for each of the 7 major military theaters and 37 campaign maps. Useful for browsing and quick reference." Nichols. Guide to Ref Books for Sch Media Cent. 4th edition

When they came to take my father—; voices of the Holocaust; photographs by Mark Seliger; edited by Leora Kahn & Rachel Hager; introduction by Robert Jay Lifton. Arcade Pub. 1996 175p il $35   **940.53**

1. Holocaust, 1933-1945—Personal narratives

ISBN 1-55970-305-9   LC 95-17852

"This photo essay is composed of 46 interviews with Holocaust survivors. Photographs and brief biographic information about each survivor accompany the text. The volume also contains a superb introduction by Robert J. Lifton as well as essays by such figures as Rabbi Arthur Hertzberg, Abraham Foxman, and Anne Roiphe. The interviews and the excellent photographs of the survivors bring to life the memories of this unspeakable time." Libr J

Women in the resistance and in the Holocaust; the voices of eyewitnesses; edited and with an introduction by Vera Laska; foreword by Simon Wiesenthal. Greenwood Press 1983 330p il (Contributions in women's studies) lib bdg $59.95 **940.53**
1. Holocaust, 1933-1945—Personal narratives 2. World War, 1939-1945—Underground movements 3. World War, 1939-1945—Personal narratives
ISBN 0-313-23457-4   LC 82-12018
The first two sections of this book deal with the Resistance and concentration camp life. A third section looks at survivors' attempts to re-enter society
Includes bibliography

Women of Theresienstadt; voices from a concentration camp; [edited by] Ruth Schwertfeger. Berg Pubs.; distributed by St. Martin's Press 1989 c1988 152p il $29.95 **940.53**
1. Holocaust, 1933-1945—Personal narratives 2. Terezin (Czechoslovakia: Concentration camp)
ISBN 0-85496-192-5   LC 88-29341
"This is an anthology of poems and memoirs of Theresienstadt inmates, with a history of the camp preceding the collection." Libr J
"These writings on children, loss, death and hope are powerful documents." N Y Times Book Rev
Includes bibliography

The **World** almanac of World War II; the complete and comprehensive documentary of World War II; edited by Peter Young. rev ed. World Almanac 1986 c1981 613p il hardcover o.p. paperback available $18.95 **940.53**
1. World War, 1939-1945 2. Historical chronology 3. World War, 1939-1945—Biography
ISBN 0-88687-712-1 (pa)   LC 86-196736
First published 1981 with title: The World almanac book of World War II
This book consists of a chronology (June 1939 through June 1950) and discussions of land, sea and air weapons. Approximately 350 biographies are also included

The **World** at arms: the Reader's Digest illustrated history of World War II. Reader's Digest Assn.; distributed by Random House 1989 480p il maps $29.95 **940.53**
1. World War, 1939-1945
ISBN 0-89577-333-3
"Detailed information about campaigns and individual battles is side by side with short boxed biographies of the commanders involved. Maps show troop movements during campaigns and battles and dioramas are included for decisive battles." Voice Youth Advocates
"There is a fine index and reference section. This would be an excellent reference tool for a school library." BAYA Book Rev

940.54 World War II, 1939-1945 (Military conduct of the war)

Alperovitz, Gar
The decision to use the atomic bomb and the architecture of an American myth; [by] Gar Alperovitz with the assistance of Sanho Tree [et al.] Knopf 1995 843p $32.50 **940.54**
1. World War, 1939-1945—United States 2. Hiroshima (Japan)—Bombardment, 1945 3. United States—Foreign relations
ISBN 0-679-44331-2   LC 95-8778
The author argues "that the nuclear bombing of Japan was unnecessary and that America bears a hefty responsibility for the cold war. . . . His main and probably most controversial contention is that certain documents pertaining to the decision were doctored, some by none other than Truman himself." Booklist
Includes bibliographical references

Ambrose, Stephen E.
D-Day, June 6, 1944; the climactic battle of World War II. Simon & Schuster 1994 655p il maps $30; pa $16 **940.54**
1. World War, 1939-1945—Campaigns—France 2. Normandy (France), Attack on, 1944
ISBN 0-671-88403-4; 0-671-88403-4 (pa)
    LC 93-40353
This is an account of the Allied invasion of Normandy in 1944. The author argues "that the invasion represented a triumph of the old United States Army, whose officers had transformed millions of civilians into a cohesive, highly trained and motivated mass army that, backed by a united nation, won with relative ease." Christ Sci Monit
"Long, detailed, immediate, and readable, this is for all those teens who can't get enough of World War II military drama." Booklist
Includes bibliographical references

Astor, Gerald, 1926-
Crisis in the Pacific; the battles for the Philippine Islands by the men who fought them—an oral history. Fine, D.I. 1996 478p il $27.95 **940.54**
1. World War, 1939-1945—Campaigns—Philippines 2. World War, 1939-1945—Personal narratives
ISBN 1-55611-484-2   LC 95-50032
This is a study of the "crucial Pacific campaign from the viewpoint of both the individual soldier and military leaders. Astor expresses opinions on many topics, such as Douglas MacArthur as a military leader, the American war plan for the Pacific, and Japanese policy toward POWs." Libr J
Includes bibliographical references

Beck, Earl R. (Earl Ray), 1916-
Under the bombs; the German home front,
1942-1945. University Press of Ky. 1986 252p il
$30   **940.54**
1. World War, 1939-1945—Germany 2. World War,
1939-1945—Aerial operations
ISBN 0-8131-1567-1   LC 85-24681
An "account of the Allied bombing of German cities
during the final three years of World War II." Booklist
The author "includes a well-chosen selection of German war humor and anecdotes. . . . A very readable introduction to the destructive consequences of total war."
Choice
Includes bibliography

Bernstein, Alison R., 1947-
American Indians and World War II; toward a
new era in Indian affairs. University of Okla. Press
1991 247p il $21.95   **940.54**
1. World War, 1939-1945 2. Indians of North Ameri-
ca—Government relations
ISBN 0-8061-2330-3   LC 90-50682
The author surveys the wartime experiences of Native
Americans and examines how the war affected subsequent Indian affairs. Bernstein argues "that the impact on
Indian affairs of World War II was more profound and
lasting than that of any other event or policy, including
Roosevelt's Indian New Deal and efforts under
Eisenhower to terminate federal responsibility for tribes."
Publisher's note
"This reference is the most comprehensive synthesis
available on Indian affairs during the 1940s. Information
on the difficulties that Indian people faced when they left
the reservation and tried to adjust to off-reservation life
and the effects of termination is limited. This synopsis of
Indian involvement during the war years will be invalu-
able to students of American Indian history." Kuipers.
Am Indian Ref & Resource Books for Child & Young
Adults. 2d edition
Includes bibliographical references

Boyne, Walter J., 1929-
Clash of Titans; World War II at sea. Simon &
Schuster 1995 381p il maps $27.50   **940.54**
1. World War, 1939-1945—Naval operations
ISBN 0-684-80196-5   LC 95-5432
Companion volume to Clash of wings (1994)
This volume covers "the great naval campaigns from
1939 to 1945. Boyne vividly depicts all the pivotal bat-
tles and skillfully analyzes each nation's naval tactics
and strategy as he explains how seapower shaped and
changed the course of the war." Libr J
Includes bibliographical references

Brickhill, Paul, 1916-1991
The great escape; introduction by George Harsh.
Norton 1950 264p il map o.p.   **940.54**
1. World War, 1939-1945—Prisoners and prisons
2. Escapes
Available G.K. Hall large print edition; in hardcover
from Amereon and Buccaneer Bks. and paperback from
Fawcett Bks.

"Exciting story behind the escape of nearly 100 British prisoners of war from Stalag Luft III in 1944. Over
600 prisoners worked secretly on this great venture for
a year digging 'Tom,' 'Dick' and 'Harry,' three tunnels."
Cincinnati Public Libr

Chandler, David, 1934-
Battles and battlescenes of World War Two;
[by] David G. Chandler. Macmillan 1989 160p il
maps $19.95   **940.54**
1. World War, 1939-1945—Campaigns 2. Battles
ISBN 0-02-897175-2   LC 89-12122
This book covers fifty-two battles of the Second
World War. "Each alphabetically arranged entry begins
with a table containing such . . . facts as date, location,
object, opposing sides, forces engaged, casualties, and result; a list of suggested readings completes each table."
Booklist
"The very readable text condenses a great deal of military history into an accessible format. This is an excellent ready reference." SLJ

Childers, Thomas
Wings of morning; the story of the last
American bomber shot down over Germany in
World War II. Addison-Wesley 1995 276p il $23;
pa $12   **940.54**
1. World War, 1939-1945—Aerial operations
ISBN 0-201-48310-6; 0-201-40722-1 (pa)
     LC 94-24296
"This outstanding remembrance, possibly the most
original title among this year's World War II anniversary
works, was reconstructed from the 'last American bomb-
er's' letters home." Booklist
Includes bibliographical references

Deighton, Len, 1929-
Blood, tears, and folly; an objective look at
World War II; with maps and drawings by Denis
Bishop. HarperCollins Pubs. 1993 653p il maps
$30   **940.54**
1. World War, 1939-1945
ISBN 0-06-017000-X
"Deighton explores and analyzes some of the myths
and realities of the war, the mistakes and the achieve-
ments, the ironies and failures—of intelligence, technolo-
gy, planning and policies—of both the Allied and the
Axis powers." Publisher's note
This "massive, but thoroughly accessible history of
World War II, will enrich high-school history collections
and be an excellent tool for research." Booklist
Includes bibliographical references

Duffy, James P., 1941-
Hitler slept late and other blunders that cost him
the war. Praeger Pubs. 1991 176p $35   **940.54**
1. Hitler, Adolf, 1889-1945 2. World War, 1939-
1945—Germany
ISBN 0-275-93667-8   LC 90-25350
This "examination of Hitler's military leadership and
strategies analyzes specific decisions that had great im-

Duffy, James P., 1941—Continued
pact on the outcome of World War II and refutes popular
beliefs of American military superiority. Military history
buffs and students will enjoy it as an insightful
overview." Booklist
Includes bibliographical references

Dunnigan, James F.
Victory at sea; World War II in the Pacific; [by]
James F. Dunnigan and Albert A. Nofi. Morrow
1995 612p $25; pa $16   **940.54**
1. World War, 1939-1945—Campaigns—Pacific
Ocean 2. World War, 1939-1945—Naval operations
ISBN 0-688-05290-8; 0-688-14947-2 (pa)
LC 94-41232
This "is a collection of hundreds of facts on the Pacific War divided into 11 chapters that cover the campaigns, ships, and aircraft of both sides. There is a biographical chapter, a gazeteer, and a chronology." Libr J

Gelb, Norman
Dunkirk: the complete story of the first step in
the defeat of Hitler. Morrow 1989 352p il
hardcover o.p. paperback available $12   **940.54**
1. Dunkerque (France), Battle of, 1940
ISBN 0-688-10737-0 (pa)   LC 89-32357
"The story of the dramatic rescue of the British army
under the guns of Hitler's panzers." Libr J
"What makes this book special is its swift and gripping narrative, which conveys the sense of movement
and calamity that accompanied the 10 days of fighting
and the events leading up to it." Booklist
Includes bibliography

Gilbert, Martin, 1936-
The day the war ended; May 8, 1945—victory
in Europe. Holt & Co. 1995 xxi, 473p il $30; pa
$16.95   **940.54**
1. World War, 1939-1945
ISBN 0-8050-3926-0; 0-8050-4735-2 (pa)
LC 94-45809
"Leaders and civilians, prisoners and spies, war-torn
peasants and soldiers from each side describe where they
were and what they were doing when news of the Allied
victory came." Libr J
Gilbert "has assembled a mosaic of reminiscences that
makes this volume both heartrending and informative."
New Yorker

Gruhzit-Hoyt, Olga, 1922-
They also served; American women in World
War II. Carol Pub. Group 1995 279p il $19.95
940.54
1. World War, 1939-1945—Women 2. Women in the
armed forces
ISBN 1-55972-280-0   LC 94-43921
"A Birch Lane Press book"
"Gruhzit-Hoyt has assembled over 30 firsthand accounts of American servicewomen and women who
served in civilian agencies during World War II. Appended are short biographies of nearly 40 more women.

Most sketches . . . describe rigorous basic training, service at home or abroad, obstacles or discrimination encountered, and the great pride and satisfaction these
women felt in having been a part of the war effort." Libr
J
Includes bibliographical references

Hersey, John, 1914-1993
Hiroshima; a new edition with a final chapter
written forty years after the explosion. Knopf 1985
196p il $25; pa $5.50   **940.54**
1. Hiroshima (Japan)—Bombardment, 1945 2. Atomic
bomb 3. World War, 1939-1945—Japan
ISBN 0-394-54844-2; 0-679-72103-7 (pa)
LC 85-40346
Also available G.K. Hall large print edition and from
Buccaneer Bks.
First published 1946
An account of the aftermath of the first atomic bomb
as reflected in the lives of six survivors

Hough, Richard Alexander, 1922-
The Battle of Britain; the greatest air battle of
World War II; [by] Richard Hough and Denis
Richards. Norton 1989 413p il maps hardcover
o.p. paperback available $17.95   **940.54**
1. Britain, Battle of, 1940
ISBN 0-393-30734-4 (pa)   LC 89-12697
The authors "analyze—in terms of men, materials, and
strategy—the strengths and weaknesses of the Royal Air
Force and the Luftwaffe, incorporating quotes from both
German and British airmen." Booklist
Includes bibliographical references

Hoyt, Edwin Palmer
The GI's war; the story of American soldiers in
Europe World War II; [by] Edwin P. Hoyt.
McGraw-Hill 1988 620p il maps o.p.; Da Capo
Press paperback available $16.95   **940.54**
1. World War, 1939-1945—Campaigns 2. Soldiers—
United States
ISBN 0-306-80448-4 (pa)   LC 87-29868
The author "uses simple, almost stark, stories to establish the matter-of-fact attitude of rank-and-file American
soldiers who fought the Germans. A reporter and foxhole-level narrator, he relies heavily on letters, tapes, and
interviews from junior officers and enlisted men who
served in the U.S. Army's combat arms in the European
theater." Libr J
Includes bibliography

Kaplan, Philip
Their finest hour: the Battle of Britain
remembered; [by] Philip Kaplan and Richard
Collier; introduction by Peter Townsend. Abbeville
Press 1989 224p il $29.98   **940.54**
1. Britain, Battle of, 1940
ISBN 1-55859-047-1   LC 89-6596
This volume "contains excellent photographs of the
airplanes and crews that took part in the battle and excerpts from diaries and other correspondence." Booklist
Includes bibliography

Leckie, Robert
Okinawa; the last battle of World War II.
Viking 1995 220p il $24.95; pa $13.95   **940.54**
1. World War, 1939-1945—Campaigns—Okinawa Island
ISBN 0-670-84716-X; 0-14-017389-7 (pa)
LC 94-39145
In this history of the Battle of Okinawa "Leckie supplies an accessible historical overview of a perplexing war tactic, the kamikaze attack." Booklist

Lifton, Betty Jean
A place called Hiroshima; text by Betty Jean Lifton; photographs by Eiko Hosoe. Kodansha Int./USA 1985 151p il hardcover o.p. paperback available $14.95   **940.54**
1. Hiroshima (Japan)—Bombardment, 1945 2. Atomic bomb
ISBN 0-87011-961-3 (pa)   LC 84-48127
Companion volume to Return to Hiroshima (1970)
The author and the photographer "show what has become of the city, some of the survivors of the bomb . . . and some of the victims' children and grandchildren, who themselves suffer the long-term effects of the bomb." Booklist

Lifton, Robert Jay, 1926-
Hiroshima in America; fifty years of denial; [by] Robert Jay Lifton & Greg Mitchell. Putnam 1995 425p il $27.50   **940.54**
1. Atomic bomb 2. Hiroshima (Japan)—Bombardment, 1945
ISBN 0-399-14072-7   LC 95-13734
Also available in paperback from Avon Bks.
"A Grosset/Putnam book"
Lifton and Mitchell examine "the reaction of the American people to the bombing of Hiroshima in 1945 and its domestic aftermath. The authors examine what they perceive to be a conspiracy by the government to mislead and suppress information about the actual bombing. Truman's decision to drop the bomb, and the birth and mismanagement of the beginning of the nuclear age." Libr J
Includes bibliographical references

Lord, Walter, 1917-
Day of infamy. Holt & Co. 1957 243p il maps o.p.   **940.54**
1. Pearl Harbor (Oahu, Hawaii), Attack on, 1941
Available in hardcover from Admiral Nimitz Foundation
Based on over 500 eyewitness reports, this book provides a minute-by-minute account of the Japanese attack on Pearl Harbor

Morin, Isobel V., 1928-
Days of judgment; the World War II war crimes trials. Millbrook Press 1995 144p il lib bdg $16.40   **940.54**
1. War crime trials 2. World War, 1939-1945—Atrocities
ISBN 1-56294-442-8   LC 94-11295
This book "consists of two sections: the first provides background information of the causes leading to World War II in Europe, the major defendants at the war crimes trials, and the highlights of the actual trial proceedings that dealt with German war criminals; the second portion of the book gives the same areas of information, but dealing with World War II in the Pacific and the Japanese." Book Rep
Includes bibliographical references

Mowat, Farley
And no birds sang. Little, Brown 1980 c1979 219p o.p.; Bantam Bks. paperback available $6.99   **940.54**
1. World War, 1939-1945—Personal narratives
ISBN 0-7704-2237-3 (pa)   LC 79-23231
Also available from Amereon
"An Atlantic Monthly Press book"
First published 1979 in Canada
Mowat "shares memories of his experiences as a young World War II Canadian soldier, recalling both his early heroic preconceptions of war and the devastating truth he came to understand." Booklist

Ooka, Shohei, 1909-1988
Taken captive; a Japanese POW's story; translated from the Japanese and edited by Wayne P. Lammers. Wiley 1996 330p il map $27.95   **940.54**
1. World War, 1939-1945—Personal narratives 2. Japanese prisoners of war
ISBN 0-471-14285-9   LC 95-35865
"Shohei, a 35-year-old literary critic, was drafted into the Japanese Imperial Army in early 1944. Following very basic training, he was stationed on the Japanese-occupied island of Mindoro to await the expected American landing in the Phillipines. Gripping details of life on the island end with its capture and the author's imprisonment on Leyte. Into his narrrative as a POW, he integrates details of Japanese culture and documents his interactions with the Japanese and the Americans with whom he and his fellow captives had most intimate contact." SLJ

Read, Anthony
The fall of Berlin; [by] Anthony Read and David Fisher. Norton 1993 513p il maps $29.95   **940.54**
1. Berlin, Battle of, 1945 2. World War, 1939-1945—Germany 3. Germany—History—1933-1945
ISBN 0-393-03472-0   LC 92-28641
Also available in paperback from Da Capo Press
A description of "the bombing of Berlin by the British and Americans and how the Russian Army fought its way toward and through Berlin in 1945. The authors intend no startling new interpretations or profound analysis. Instead, they offer vignettes, often based on diaries, to describe life in Berlin late in the war. They also retell the story of fanatical Nazi leaders and of the Wehrmacht's desperate efforts to defend the city. The result is a highly readable and, at the same time, sophisticated and reliable narrative history." Libr J
Includes bibliography

Reporting World War II. Library of Am. 1995 2v
set $70 **940.54**
1. World War, 1939-1945 2. Reporters and reporting
ISBN 1-883011-04-3 LC 94-45463
Contents: v1 American journalism, 1938-1944; v2
American journalism, 1944-1946
This "collection of some 200 entries by nearly 90
writers, drawn from newspapers, magazine articles,
broadcast transcripts and book excerpts, recalls WW II
campaigns and battles in all theaters but pays attention
to the home front as well. It begins with an excerpt from
William L. Shirer's *Berlin Diary* and ends with one from
John Hersey's *Hiroshima*. . . . This is a treasure trove
of war reporting, featuring writing of the highest order."
Publ Wkly

Rice, Earle
The Battle of Midway; by Earle Rice, Jr. Lucent
Bks. 1996 110p il (Battles of World War II) lib
bdg $19.95 **940.54**
1. Midway, Battle of, 1942
ISBN 1-56006-415-3 LC 95-12206
An account of the American victory over the Japanese
at Midway in June 1942. Sidebars, maps, diagrams and
photographs illustrate the text. Accounts from battle participants are included
Includes bibliographical references

Rogers, James T.
The secret war; espionage in World War II.
Facts on File 1991 112p il (World espionage)
$16.95 **940.54**
1. World War, 1939-1945—Secret service 2. Espionage
ISBN 0-8160-2395-6 LC 91-2724
The author maintains "that the British and Americans
were more successful at espionage, counter-espionage,
and deception than either the Germans or the Japanese.
It was the breaking of codes, he states, that helped Allied
commanders appear to be more perceptive and clever
than they really were. . . . Periodic black-and-white photos and a suggested reading list complete the coverage of
Roger's outstanding work." SLJ

Ross, Bill D.
Iwo Jima; legacy of valor. Vanguard Press 1985
376p il maps o.p.; Vintage Bks. paperback
available $14 **940.54**
1. Iwo Jima, Battle of, 1945
ISBN 0-394-74288-5 (pa) LC 84-15186
A day-by-day account of the 1945 Pacific battle between the Japanese and the U.S. Marines
Includes bibliography

Ryan, Cornelius
The last battle. Simon & Schuster 1966 571p il
maps hardcover o.p. paperback available $15.95
940.54
1. Berlin, Battle of, 1945
ISBN 0-684-80329-1 (pa)
This is the story of those three weeks in 1945 "in
which the city of Berlin, gutted, smoldering, terrorized,
yet still miraculously alive, was the focal point of millions of lives: the last obstacle of triumphant allies, the
last defense for the Germans, the last refuge for the Füh-
rer." Publisher's note
Includes bibliography

Salisbury, Harrison Evans, 1908-1993
The 900 days; the siege of Leningrad; [by]
Harrison E. Salisbury. Harper & Row 1969 635p
il maps o.p.; Da Capo Press paperback available
$16.95 **940.54**
1. St. Petersburg (Russia)—Siege, 1941-1944
ISBN 0-306-80253-8 (pa)
The author chronicles the siege of Leningrad, describes the suffering of its people and exposes the role
of Stalin's political police throughout the war

Smurthwaite, David
The Pacific war atlas. Facts on File 1995 unp il
maps $32.95; pa $15.95 **940.54**
1. World War, 1939-1945—Campaigns—Pacific
Ocean
ISBN 0-8160-3285-8; 0-8160-3286-6 (pa)
LC 95-12018
This volume's 75 multicolor maps and 50 contempo-
rary photographs illustrate "the evolution of U.S. strate-
gy, the Japanese strikes and invasions, the fall of the
Philippines, command areas, resource of the nations in-
volved, naval battles, air raids, civilian and military casu-
alties, and other information pertinent to the war in the
Pacific." Publisher's note

Takaki, Ronald T., 1939-
Hiroshima; why America dropped the atomic
bomb; [by] Ronald Takaki. Little, Brown 1995
193p il $19.95; pa $11.95 **940.54**
1. World War, 1939-1945—United States 2. Atomic
bomb 3. Hiroshima (Japan)—Bombardment, 1945
ISBN 0-316-83122-0; 0-316-83124-7 (pa)
LC 95-13546
This study of the bombings of Hiroshima and Nagasaki focuses on the psychological motivations of the
American decision-makers, especially Harry Truman
"Right or wrong, the study is a provocative addition
to the unresolved debate over the dropping of the atomic
bombs." Publ Wkly
Includes bibliographical references

Tomblin, Barbara
G.I. nightingales; the Army Nurse Corps in
World War II; [by] Barbara Brooks Tomblin.
University Press of Ky. 1996 254p il $29.95
940.54
1. United States. Army Nurse Corps
ISBN 0-8131-1951-0 LC 96-1018
This is "an account of the 80,000 army nurses who
served during World War II. These nurses participated in
every theater of the war; some died while on duty, and
many were decorated for their bravery. Along with their
deserving stories, the reader learns the history of women
nurses in the military." Libr J
Includes bibliography

Voss, Frederick

Reporting the war; the journalistic coverage of World War II; [by] Frederick S. Voss. Smithsonian Institution Press 1994 218p il $39.95; pa $24.95   **940.54**

1. World War, 1939-1945

ISBN 1-56098-349-3; 1-56098-348-5 (pa)

LC 93-36113

"The highlights of this companion volume to an . . . exhibit at the National Portrait Gallery are 121 photographs and illustrations, including such famous images as Joe Rosenthal's Pulitzer Prize-winning image of Iwo Jima and Margaret Bourke-White's picture of the liberation of the prisoners at Buchenwald. Also compelling are reprints of famous news stories and broadcasts by, among others, Ernie Pyle and Edward R. Murrow." Publ Wkly

Includes bibliographical references

Waller, John H.

The unseen war in Europe; espionage and conspiracy in the Second World War. Random House 1996 475p $35   **940.54**

1. World War, 1939-1945—Secret service 2. Espionage

ISBN 0-679-44826-8   LC 95-32723

An "account of the remarkably complex espionage network that flourished during the war. Although much of what Waller tells us has been known for years, he has pulled together a lot of disparate threads to create his story. By far the most interesting character portrayed here is of Adm. Wilhelm Canaris, head of German military intelligence, who endeavored throughout the war to assist the Allies wherever possible. Waller probes the voluminous sources that have come to light in recent years to profile Canaris, American counterpart Allen Dulles, and the cast of shadowy figures who slipped in and out of the espionage picture." Libr J

Includes bibliography

We're in this war too; World War II letters from American women in uniform; [edited by] Judy Barrett Litoff, David C. Smith. Oxford Univ. Press 1994 272p il $25   **940.54**

1. World War, 1939-1945—Personal narratives 2. Women soldiers

ISBN 0-19-507504-8   LC 93-36523

"Based on letters from women in the military, this comprehensive volume offers glimpses of what women encountered in the service (racism, for example) as well as evidence of the many important ways they participated in World War II. A must purchase for libraries needing primary-source material." Booklist

Includes bibliographical references

Winston, Keith, 1912-1970

Letters from a World War II GI; [edited] by Judith E. Greenberg and Helen Carey McKeever. Watts 1995 144p il map (In their own words) $22.70   **940.54**

1. World War, 1939-1945—Personal narratives

ISBN 0-531-11212-8   LC 94-46656

"Private Keith Winston's thoughtful, well-written letters to his wife provide an eye-opening account of what the average World War II GI went through. The letters date from Winston's participation in basic training in March of 1944 to his return to the States in December of 1945. Greenberg and McKeever insert explanations after some of the missives to let readers know what Winston was referring to when he wrote of C rations, victory gardens, etc." SLJ

Includes bibliographical references

940.55   Europe—1945-

Dornberg, John

Western Europe. Oryx Press 1996 290p il maps (International government & politics series) pa $34.95   **940.55**

1. Europe—History

ISBN 0-89774-943-X   LC 95-43046

"In the first section of this volume, Dornberg examines Western Europe as a whole, its complex cultural mix, and the development of the European Union. After discussing the mechanics of the Union's operation, he turns to some controversial issues in its member states. . . . The second part of the book [focuses] on individual countries." SLJ

Includes bibliographical references

941   British Isles

The Cambridge historical encyclopedia of Great Britain and Ireland; editor, Christopher Haigh. Cambridge Univ. Press 1985 392p il maps hardcover o.p. paperback available $29.95   **941**

1. Great Britain—History—Dictionaries

ISBN 0-521-39552-6 (pa)   LC 85-47568

"Broad chronological overview of seven themes ranging from government to culture. The essays on topics such as government and politics, warfare, society, the economy, and international relations are supported by short identification paragraphs in the margins. The time period covered extends from 100 B.C. to 1975. There is a biographical section with about 800 entries." Ref Sources for Small & Medium-sized Libr. 5th edition

Cannon, John, 1926-

The Oxford illustrated history of the British monarchy; [by] John Cannon and Ralph Griffiths. Oxford Univ. Press 1988 727p il $55   **941**

1. Great Britain—Kings, queens, rulers, etc. 2. Great Britain—Politics and government

ISBN 0-19-822786-8   LC 88-5172

"A dynastic account of the history, public and private, of the British monarchy. Augmented by many illustrations that show the visual magnificence that is part of the monarchy." N Y Public Libr. Book of How & Where to Look It Up

Includes bibliography

Churchill, Sir Winston, 1874-1965

A history of the English-speaking peoples. Dodd, Mead 1956-1958 4v maps   **941**

1. Great Britain—History

Available in hardcover from Buccaneer Bks.

Churchill, Sir Winston, 1874-1965—*Continued*
Contents: v1 The birth of Britain; v2 The new world; v3 The age of revolution; v4 The great democracies
A four volume history of the British Empire from the Roman invasions to the death of Queen Victoria, and of Britain's influence upon the other English-speaking peoples of the world

Johnson, Paul, 1928-
Castles of England, Scotland and Wales. Harper & Row 1989 215p il maps hardcover o.p. paperback available $25   **941**
1. Castles 2. Great Britain—Description
ISBN 0-06-092351-2 (pa)   LC 89-45046
First published 1978 in the United Kingdom with title: The National Trust book of British castles
"Johnson's survey of castle-building and restoration leads the reader through the architectural, military, and political history of England, Wales, and Scotland. . . . Johnson provides a fascinating tour, via excellent color photographs and sharp diagrams, of these surviving structures and their historical importance." Booklist
Includes glossary

The **Oxford** illustrated history of Britain; edited by Kenneth O. Morgan. Oxford Univ. Press 1984 640p il maps $49.95; pa $25   **941**
1. Great Britain—History
ISBN 0-19-822684-5; 0-19-285174-8 (pa)
          LC 83-21990
"2,000 years of British history as told by ten leading historians. Details how the past has shaped British character, patriotism, and ethnocentrism. Includes over 250 illustrations, chronologies, genealogies of monarchs, and a table of Prime Ministers." N Y Public Libr. Book of How & Where To Look It Up
Includes bibliography

941.08 British Isles—Period of Victoria and House of Windsor, 1837-

Bland, Celia
The mechanical age; the industrial revolution in England. Facts on File 1995 138p il maps (World history library) $17.95   **941.08**
1. Industrial revolution 2. Great Britain—Economic conditions
ISBN 0-8160-3139-8   LC 94-40971
Surveys the social and mechanical innovations of the Industrial Revolution in England and the reforms and imperialism that grew out of these changes
"A wealth of material on major events and personalities is delivered in an instructive, lively style that reveals the author's personal interest in her subject. . . . Detailed source chapter notes; chronology; extensive bibliography of historical sources and literature of the period." Booklist

The **Cambridge** illustrated history of the British Empire; edited by P.J. Marshall. Cambridge Univ. Press 1996 400p il maps $39.95   **941.08**
1. Great Britain—Colonies—History 2. Commonwealth countries—History 3. Imperialism
ISBN 0-521-43211-1   LC 95-14535
"This book examines the experience of colonialism in North America, India, Africa, Australia and the Caribbean, giving a brief history of the British imperial territories and looking at slavery, trade, religion, art, transportation, and the development of new ideas." Book Rep
Includes bibliographical references

941.081 British Isles—Reign of Victoria, 1837-1901

The **Encyclopedia** of the Victorian world; a reader's companion to the people, places, events, and everyday life of the Victorian era; Melinda Corey and George Ochoa, editors. Holt & Co. 1996 519p il (Henry Holt reference book) $50   **941.081**
1. Great Britain—History—1800-1899 (19th century) 2. Great Britain—Civilization
ISBN 0-8050-2622-3   LC 95-21077
"A Roundtable Press book"
The editors "adhere tightly to the constraints of Victoria's reign, 1837-1901. Their encyclopedia's focus is Western, but it cannot help but cover the world, as did the English presence at the time. Entries are strictly alphabetical, brief yet informative, and broad in scope, illuminating the great strides made in the arts, sciences, medicine, and philosophy in this dynamic era." Libr J
For a fuller review see: Booklist, Sept. 15, 1996

941.5 Ireland

Foster, R. F. (Robert Fitzroy), 1949-
Modern Ireland, 1600-1972. Allen Lane; distributed by Viking 1989 c1988 688p il maps $35; pa $15.95   **941.5**
1. Ireland—History
ISBN 0-7139-9010-4; 0-14-012510-8 (pa)
          LC 89-118698
First published 1988 in the United Kingdom
The author "charts the country's political, economic, and social evolution in his examination of just what and who were responsible for Ireland's problems over the centuries." Booklist
This "is late-20th-century history at its very best. . . . So many facts and so many insights are crammed into this book that it would not be an exaggeration to call it a minor masterpiece." N Y Times Book Rev
Includes bibliography

Lange, Dorothea, 1895-1965

Dorothea Lange's Ireland; text by Gerry Mullins; essay by Daniel Dixon; photographs from the collection of the Oakland Museum of California. Elliott & Clark Pub. 1996 120p il $29.95   **941.5**

1. Ireland—Pictorial works

ISBN 1-880216-35-3   LC 95-38835

Photographer Lange "spent six weeks in Ireland in 1954. This book of over 100 black-and-white photographs depicting the people and customs of Irish country life is the result of that trip. . . . Throughout, the reader gets a sense of the lifestyle, concerns, and humanity of her subjects. The essays are informative and put the photographs in the context of todays's Ireland." Libr J

Includes bibliographical references

Newman, Peter R.

A companion to Irish history, 1603-1921; from the submission of Tyrone to partition. Facts on File 1991 244p maps $27.95   **941.5**

1. Ireland—History—Dictionaries 2. Ireland—Biography—Dictionaries

ISBN 0-8160-2572-X   LC 91-23677

"Newman takes as his starting point the destruction of the native order after the defeat of Hugh O'Neill and Hugh O'Donnell at Kinsale (1601) and the subsequent confiscation of their lands in the northern province. His ending point is the signing of the Anglo-Irish Treaty in December 1921. . . . Entries are arranged in alphabetical order followed by appendixes listing administrators, a chronology, a bibliography, and six maps." Choice

"Providing objective treatment of a controversial subject, Newman's encyclopedia will help a wide variety of patrons." Libr J

The Oxford illustrated history of Ireland; edited by R.F. Foster. Oxford Univ. Press 1989 382p il maps $49.95; pa $22.50   **941.5**

1. Ireland—History

ISBN 0-19-822970-4; 0-19-285245-0 (pa)

    LC 89-16168

This illustrated history includes "six essays by Irish scholars, five covering chronological periods in Irish history and the sixth a . . . discussion of the interplay between Irish literature and history." Libr J

"A thoughtful and highly informative volume that manages to underscore the ancient and rooted aspects of Irish culture, even while it explores in depth the mobility and shifting of the Irish people into 'fractured and sometimes unexpected patterns.'" Booklist

Includes bibliographical references

Ranelagh, John

A short history of Ireland; [by] John O'Beirne Ranelagh. 2nd ed. Cambridge Univ. Press 1994 303p map $65; pa $22.95   **941.5**

1. Ireland—History

ISBN 0-521-47548-1; 0-521-46944-9 (pa)

    LC 95-168606

First published 1983

An overview of Irish history from the Viking invasions and the Tudor period to later struggles for national identity and independence. Ireland's literature and cultural traditions are explored

Includes bibliographical references

Woodham Smith, Cecil Blanche Fitz Gerald, 1896-1977

The great hunger: Ireland, 1845-1849; [by] Cecil Woodham Smith. Harper & Row 1962 510p il o.p.; Penguin Bks. paperback available $13.95

    941.5

1. Famines 2. Ireland—History 3. Ireland—Immigration and emigration

ISBN 0-14-014515-X (pa)

A history of the Irish potato famine of the 1840s, this book describes the effects of that disaster on Ireland, England, and North America

941.6   Ulster. Northern Ireland

Coogan, Tim Pat, 1935-

The troubles; Ireland's ordeal 1966-1995 and the search for peace. Roberts Rinehart Pubs. 1996 c1995 460p il maps $29.95   **941.6**

1. Northern Ireland—History

ISBN 1-57098-092-6

First published 1995 in the United Kingdom

In this political history the author "examines all parties to the struggle. . . . He reconstructs the past 30 years, from the 1969 marching and riots to the H-Block protests, the MacBride Principles, the Anglo-Irish agreement, and the recent paramilitary cease-fire. Coogan traces the current peace process, stalled by Great Britain's insistence that the IRA hand in its weapons, to the 1979 visit of Pope John Paul II." Libr J

Includes bibliography

Meyer, Carolyn

Voices of Northern Ireland; growing up in a troubled land. Harcourt Brace Jovanovich 1987 212p maps $15.95; pa $9.95   **941.6**

1. Northern Ireland—Social conditions 2. Northern Ireland—Description

ISBN 0-15-200635-4; 0-15-200638-9 (pa)

    LC 87-199

"Gulliver books"

This book is a "first hand account of the 'Troubles' in Northern Ireland that have made that country a political hotspot. For six weeks during the summer of 1986, [the author] traveled throughout the country's six counties while interviewing people from all walks of life, both Protestant and Catholic." Voice Youth Advocates

Includes bibliography

942.01   England—Early history to 1066

Campbell, James, 1935-

The Anglo-Saxons; [by] James Campbell, Eric John, Patrick Wormald; general editor, James Campbell; with contributions from P.V. Addyman [et al.] Cornell Univ. Press 1982 272p il o.p.; Penguin Bks. paperback available $24.95   **942.01**

1. Anglo-Saxons 2. Great Britain—History—0-1066

ISBN 0-14-014395-5 (pa)   LC 81-70710

"Cornell/Phaidon books"

Campbell, James, 1935—*Continued*
This volume offers a survey of the Anglo-Saxons "from Roman times to the end of the 11th century in terms of political history, daily life, intellectual development, and art." Libr J
Includes bibliography

Day, David, 1949-
The search for King Arthur; foreword by Terry Jones. Facts on File 1995 176p il $24.95 **942.01**
1. Arthur, King 2. Arthurian romances 3. Great Britain—History—0-1066
ISBN 0-8160-3370-6 LC 95-24119
The author "traces the historical roots of King Arthur to the fifth-century champion Artorius Dux Bellorum and then analyzes the social and political forces that turned him into one of the 'world's most popular heroes.' Day retells many key Arthurian legends, paying special attention to Merlin the Magician. . . . Day's illuminating and thoroughly enjoyable narrative is enchanced by more than 170 luscious full-color illustrations by such celebrated artists as Gustave Doré and Arthur Rackham as well as contemporary illustrator Alan Lee." Booklist

942.02 England—Norman period, 1066-1154

Howarth, David Armine, 1912-
1066: the year of the conquest; [by] David Howarth; illustrations to chapter headings by Gareth Floyd. Viking 1978 c1977 207p il hardcover o.p. paperback available $11.95 **942.02**
1. Great Britain—History—1066-1154, Norman period 2. Hastings (East Sussex, England), Battle of, 1066
ISBN 0-14-005850-8 (pa) LC 77-21694
First published 1977 in the United Kingdom
A history of the invasion of England by the Normans and William the Conqueror's victory at the Battle of Hastings
Includes bibliography

Lace, William W.
The Battle of Hastings. Lucent Bks. 1996 96p il maps (Battles of the Middle Ages) lib bdg $19.95 **942.02**
1. Hastings (East Sussex, England), Battle of, 1066 2. Great Britain—History—1066-1154, Norman period
ISBN 1-56006-416-1 LC 95-11711
An overview of William the Conqueror's pivotal victory at the Battle of Hastings in 1066. A chronology, maps and black-and-white illustrations supplement the text
Includes bibliographical references

942.03 England—Period of House of Plantagenet, 1154-1399

Singman, Jeffrey L.
Daily life in Chaucer's England; [by] Jeffrey L. Singman and Will McLean. Greenwood Press 1995 252p il (Greenwood Press daily life through history series) $45 **942.03**
1. Chaucer, Geoffrey, d. 1400—Contemporary England 2. Great Britain—History—1154-1399, Plantagenets
ISBN 0-313-29375-9 LC 95-7568
"Included are descriptions of the feudal system in the 1300s, the medieval calendar, homes (including manors, but not castles), clothing, armor, food and entertainment, with enough detail to actually recreate certain aspects of daily life. For instance, patterns are provided for selected clothing, sample recipes come with modern equivalents, and medieval songs include notations." Book Rep
For a fuller review see: Booklist, Jan. 1 & 15, 1996
Includes bibliographical references

942.04 England—Period of Houses of Lancaster and York, 1399-1485

Weir, Alison
The Wars of the Roses. Ballantine Bks. 1995 462p il hardcover o.p. paperback available $12.95 **942.04**
1. Great Britain—History—1455-1485, War of the Roses
ISBN 0-345-40433-5 (pa)
This is an account "of the first phase of the War of the Roses. Accepting the Tudor view that the conflict originated with Richard II's deposition, [the author] devotes half of the book to relations between Lancaster and York from 1399 to 1455. The second half deals with the period from the first Battle of St. Albans (1455) to the Battle of Tewkesbury (1471)." Libr J
"No history collection should do without this perfectly focused and beautifully unfolded account." Booklist

942.05 England—Tudor period, 1485-1603

Martin, Colin, 1939-
The Spanish Armada; [by] Colin Martin & Geoffrey Parker. Norton 1988 296p il hardcover o.p. paperback available $12.95 **942.05**
1. Spanish Armada, 1588
ISBN 0-393-30618-6 (pa) LC 89-102323
"A concise history describing the power struggles and political intrigues of Europe that led to the launching of the armada." Publ Wkly
Includes bibliographical references

Mattingly, Garrett, 1900-1962
The Armada. Houghton Mifflin 1988 c1959
443p il maps hardcover o.p. paperback available
$13.95   **942.05**
1. Spanish Armada, 1588
ISBN 0-395-08366-4 (pa)   LC 87-26210
A reissue of the title first published 1959; 1984 edition had title: The defeat of the Spanish Armada
This account of the defeat of the Spanish Armada by the British in 1588 describes in detail the "military measures and actions, the sentiments and passions of the public, political intrigue, and the motives and maneuvering of the royal figures involved, notably Elizabeth." Publ Wkly
Includes bibliographical references

McMurtry, Jo, 1937-
Understanding Shakespeare's England; a companion for the American reader. Archon Bks. 1989 254p il lib bdg $37.50   **942.05**
1. Shakespeare, William, 1564-1616—Contemporary England 2. Great Britain—History—1485-1603, Tudors
ISBN 0-208-02248-1   LC 89-32451
"This book provides information on such wide-ranging topics as degree and rank, money, life in London and the countryside, marriage customs and the role of women, witches and criminals, and even cuckoldry. Nearly every facet of Elizabethan life is explored in a straightforward and often amusing manner." Libr J
Includes bibliography

Singman, Jeffrey L.
Daily life in Elizabethan England. Greenwood Press 1995 227p il (Greenwood Press daily life through history series) $45   **942.05**
1. Great Britain—History—1485-1603, Tudors
ISBN 0-313-29335-X   LC 95-3807
"Following a brief history of the era, an overview chapter discusses the social structure, governmental organization, religious establishment, and economy of the period. Subsequent chapters outline the cycle of life, from birth to death, and the cycles of time, moving through the day, week, and year as experienced by the people of the era. . . . Appendixes give instructions for organizing a living-history event and list useful suppliers and contacts for such an event. Bibliographies include audiovisual material." Booklist

942.06   England—Stuart and Commonwealth periods, 1603-1714

Trevelyan, George Macaulay, 1876-1962
The English Revolution, 1688-1689. Holt & Co. 1939 c1938 281p o.p.; Oxford Univ. Press paperback available $7.95   **942.06**
1. Great Britain—History—1603-1714, Stuarts
ISBN 0-19-500263-6 (pa)
First published 1938 in the United Kingdom
This study covers not only the revolution itself but also the events of the reign of James II, which led up to it and the political changes which followed
Includes bibliography

942.1   London

Paterson, John, 1923-
Edwardians; London life and letters, 1901-1914.
Dee, I.R. 1996 330p il $27.50   **942.1**
1. London (England)—Intellectual life 2. Great Britain—History—1900-1999 (20th century)
ISBN 1-56663-101-7   LC 95-45742
This overview of Edwardian London focuses on what the major "writers said about each other and their books, publishers, agents, critics, and nonliterary friends. Paterson . . . deploys his riches of anecdotes and excerpts from letters, memoirs, and biographies in three sections. 'London Denied,' the shortest, focuses on the lure of the countryside for the urban dweller. 'London Deliver'd,' by far the longest section, details the metropolis's myriad attraction—politics, publishing, leisure, art, and the rich variety of Edwardian challenges to conventional views of sex, marriage, and social class. 'London Declined' locates evidence of disillusionment with the period's initial enthusiasms, such as liberal reforms, Fabianism, the Court Theatre, and Impressionism." Choice
Includes bibliographical references

943   Central Europe. Germany

Carr, William, 1921-
A history of Germany, 1815-1945. 2nd ed. St. Martin's Press 1979 414p maps $25   **943**
1. Germany—History
ISBN 0-312-37871-8   LC 79-20108
First published 1969
This history of Germany concentrates on the following: Bismarck's motives for the Franco-Prussian War; Bismarck's foreign policy, in particular with Russia; whether or not the war in 1914 was inevitable; reasons for the Nazi party victory; and the role of industrialists in helping Hitler come to power
Includes bibliographical references

Fulbrook, Mary, 1951-
A concise history of Germany. Cambridge Univ. Press 1991 c1990 263p il maps (Cambridge concise histories) $49.95; pa $14.95   **943**
1. Germany—History
ISBN 0-521-36283-0; 0-521-36836-7 (pa)
                         LC 90-32506
First published 1990 in the United Kingdom
This book examines German history, including reunification, in political, social and cultural contexts. Among major figures given particular emphasis are Martin Luther, Immanuel Kant and Adolf Hitler
"No particular ideological stance colors the presentation, and judicious references to the various interpretations of other historians balance the account. . . . This is a beginner's volume, a good one." Libr J
Includes bibliography

Spencer, William
Germany then and now. Watts 1994 160p il map lib bdg $22.70 **943**
1. Germany—History
ISBN 0-531-11137-7 LC 93-29444
This is an overview of 2,000 years of German history, from the Germanic tribes who defeated the Roman legions to the reunified nation of the present
Includes bibliography

943.086 Germany—Period of Third Reich, 1933-1945

Davidson, Eugene, 1902-
The unmaking of Adolf Hitler. University of Mo. Press 1996 519p $29.95 **943.086**
1. Hitler, Adolf, 1889-1945 2. National socialism 3. Germany—Politics and government—1933-1945
ISBN 0-8262-1045-7 LC 95-53092
"Davidson paraphrases the Hitler story from 1933 through 1939 in a narrative summary of the protagonist's speeches and conferences pertaining to his consolidation of power and campaign to overturn the Treaty of Versailles." Booklist
"The work provides a detailed account of diplomacy from the occupation of the Rhineland to the Czech crisis, Munich, and the outbreak of war . . . . Overall, a well-written, useful work." Choice
Includes bibliographical references

Gill, Anton
An honorable defeat; a history of the German resistance to Hitler, 1933-1945. Holt & Co. 1994 293p il maps $25; pa $14.95 **943.086**
1. Hitler, Adolf, 1889-1945 2. Germany—Politics and government—1933-1945
ISBN 0-8050-3514-1; 0-8050-3515-X (pa) LC 94-14833
The author provides an overview of the "individuals and groups who participated in the opposition to National Socialism in Germany, including those in the church and the Foreign Office, members of the Abwehr and of Hitler's general staff, Communists, Social Democrats, aristocrats, and students." Libr J
Includes bibliographical references

Heyes, Eileen
Children of the swastika; the Hitler Youth. Millbrook Press 1993 96p il map lib bdg $16.40 **943.086**
1. Hitler-Jugend 2. National socialism 3. Germany—History—1933-1945
ISBN 1-56294-237-9 LC 92-13204
Describes the Hitler Youth, the state-sponsored youth organization founded by the Nazi regime to train boys and girls ten and older to serve Hitler's government with unquestioning devotion
"Heyes captures in well-organized, concise, clear prose the insidiousness of the Third Reich's *Hitler Jugend*

Shirer, William L. (William Lawrence)
The rise and fall of the Third Reich; a history of Nazi Germany; with a new afterword by the author. Simon & Schuster 1990 1249p hardcover o.p. paperback available $18 **943.086**
1. Germany—History—1933-1945
ISBN 0-671-72868-7 (pa) LC 90-221762
Also available in hardcover from Buccaneer Bks.
"A Touchstone book"
First published 1960
This is a comprehensive, documented history of Germany from the beginning of the Nazi party in 1918 to the World War II defeat of Germany in 1945. Here is a detailed account of the events, and the leading figures of the Nazi era, especially Adolf Hitler
Includes bibliographical references

Speer, Albert, 1905-1981
Inside the Third Reich; memoirs; translated from the German by Richard and Clara Winston; introduction by Eugene Davidson. Macmillan 1970 xxiii, 596p il hardcover o.p. paperback available $16 **943.086**
1. Hitler, Adolf, 1889-1945 2. Germany—History—1933-1945 3. World War, 1939-1945—Germany
ISBN 0-02-037500-X (pa)
Also available in hardcover from Buccaneer Bks.
Original German edition, 1969
The author, Hitler's "architect and later his armaments minister, was in the dictator's inner circle for almost 12 years. . . . [After the war] Speer used the enforced leisure of his 20 prison years as a war criminal to plan and write these memoirs." Libr J
Includes bibliographical references

943.087 Germany—1945-

Hasselbach, Ingo
Fuhrer-Ex; memoirs of a former Neo-Nazi; by Ingo Hasselbach with Tom Reiss. Random House 1996 384p $24 **943.087**
1. Fascism—Germany 2. Germany—Politics and government—1990-
ISBN 0-679-43825-4 LC 95-31751
"Hasselbach recalls how he became attracted to the neo-Nazi movement while in prison, developed his personal ideology of hatred and violence and went on to establish East Germany's first neo-Nazi political party." Publ Wkly
This book "is especially valuable for its portraits of the various figures Mr. Hasselbach met in the movement. They range from pure psychopaths to convinced ideologues to elderly widows of Nazi officers. . . . More than simply the story of one tragically misguided hoodlum, it is, perhaps unintentionally, an insightful study of how and why young people are drawn to groups dedicated to the violent propagation of hatred." N Y Times Book Rev

943.8 Poland

Davies, Norman
Heart of Europe; a short history of Poland.
Oxford Univ. Press 1984 xxi, 511p il hardcover
o.p. paperback available $14.95   **943.8**
1. Poland—History
ISBN 0-19-285152-7 (pa)   LC 83-22003
The author uses a reverse chronological approach to
examine Poland during WW II and its aftermath, the Par-
titions, and the independent monarchies
Includes bibliographical references

Otfinoski, Steven, 1949-
Poland. Facts on File 1995 133p il maps
(Nations in transition) lib bdg $17.95   **943.8**
1. Poland—History
ISBN 0-8160-3063-4   LC 95-17252
Examines the history, politics, and culture of Poland,
with an emphasis on its transition from a communist to
a free nation
Includes bibliographical references

943.9 Hungary

Michener, James A. (James Albert), 1907-
The bridge at Andau. Random House 1957 270p
map o.p.; Fawcett Bks. paperback available $5.99
                                    943.9
1. Hungary—History—1956, Revolution 2. Hungarian
refugees
ISBN 0-449-21050-2 (pa)
"The heroism, horror and tragedy of the 1956 Hungarian revolt is revealed through interviews with many refugees [who crossed the bridge at Andau to freedom]."
Cleveland Public Libr

944 France and Monaco

Riché, Pierre
Daily life in the world of Charlemagne;
translated by Jo Ann McNamara. University of Pa.
Press 1978 336p il (Middle Ages) hardcover o.p.
paperback available $21.50   **944**
1. France—Civilization
ISBN 0-8122-1096-4 (pa)   LC 78-53330
Riché provides "glimpses of daily life in Frankish
Gaul taken from such primary sources as . . . monastic
annals, surveys of manorial holdings, accounts left by
pilgrims and merchants, and illustrations from manuscripts." Choice
Includes bibliographical references

Tuchman, Barbara Wertheim
A distant mirror; the calamitous 14th century;
[by] Barbara W. Tuchman. Knopf 1978 xx, 677p
il maps $45   **944**
1. Coucy, Enguerrand de, 1340-1397 2. France—History—1328-1589, House of Valois 3. Fourteenth
century 4. Medieval civilization
ISBN 0-394-40026-7   LC 78-5985
Also available in paperback from Ballantine Bks.

The author traces the history of the fourteenth century
by following the career of a "feudal lord, Enguerrand de
Coucy VII, the seigneur of some 150 towns and villages
in Picardy. He was born in 1340, and he died in captivity in 1397, having been made a prisoner by the Turks."
Time
Includes bibliography

944.04 France—Revolutionary period, 1789-1804

Bernier, Olivier
Words of fire, deeds of blood; the mob, the
monarchy, and the French Revolution. Little,
Brown 1989 452p il $21.95   **944.04**
1. France—History—1789-1799, Revolution
ISBN 0-316-09206-1   LC 88-35549
This "history of the French Revolution starts with the
storming of the Bastille in 1789 and ends with Marie
Antoinette's execution in 1793. . . . Though the vivid
narrative occasionally threatens to collapse into a royal-
family drama, Bernier ably works in the clash of personalities, political maneuvers, upheavals in daily life, the
friction between classes jockeying for power." Publ Wkly
Includes bibliography

Bosher, J. F. (John Francis)
The French Revolution. Norton 1988 lxi, 353p
maps (Revolutions in the modern world) hardcover
o.p. paperback available $11.25   **944.04**
1. France—History—1789-1799, Revolution
ISBN 0-393-95997-X (pa)   LC 87-31224
The author "emphasizes the background of the French
Revolution, focusing to an unusually large extent on the
years prior to [the] outbreak of the conflict in 1789. . . .
The book is somewhat unusual in that the author takes
a rather independent, evenhanded look at the forces
working in France to produce the upheaval. . . . Nicely
written, well organized, and thoroughly researched."
Choice
Includes bibliography

Doyle, William, 1942-
The Oxford history of the French Revolution.
Oxford Univ. Press 1989 466p il maps $35; pa
$14.95   **944.04**
1. France—History—1789-1799, Revolution 2. Europe—History—1789-1900
ISBN 0-19-822781-7; 0-19-285221-3 (pa)
                                    LC 88-37235
The author "addresses the social, economic, and political causes of the French Revolution. . . . The revolution's impact on Europe plays an important role in
Doyle's story. He assesses both the intellectual context
of the revolution and its effects on ordinary people, not
only in France but throughout the continent." Booklist
Includes bibliography

Hibbert, Christopher, 1924-
The days of the French Revolution. Morrow 1980 351p il maps hardcover o.p. paperback available $13.45   **944.04**
  1. France—History—1789-1799, Revolution
  ISBN 0-688-00746-5 (pa)   LC 80-19549
  Published in the United Kingdom with title: The French Revolution
  This narrative history of the French Revolution "covers all the main events from the convening of the Estates General in 1789 to Napoleon's 'coup d'état' 10 years later, with proper emphasis on the fall of the Bastille, the Declaration of the Rights of Man, the attempted flight and subsequent execution of the inept Louis XVI and his extravagant queen Marie Antoinette, and the Reign of Terror." Publ Wkly
  Includes glossary and bibliography

Kennedy, Emmet
A cultural history of the French Revolution. Yale Univ. Press 1989 xxviii, 463p il $50; pa $23   **944.04**
  1. France—History—1789-1799,   Revolution
  2. France—Civilization
  ISBN 0-300-04426-7; 0-300-05013-5 (pa)
                                              LC 88-39966
  The author explores the cultural and intellectual underpinnings of the Revolution and its effect on religion, art, music, literature and culture
  Includes bibliography

Kirchberger, Joe H.
The French Revolution and Napoleon; an eyewitness history. Facts on File 1989 xxiii, 376p il (Eyewitness history series) $45   **944.04**
  1. Napoleon I, Emperor of the French, 1769-1821
  2. France—History—1789-1799, Revolution
  ISBN 0-8160-2090-6   LC 89-12058
  "A lengthy preface summarizes differing theories of the Revolution, and each subsequent chapter contains an overview of events, a chronology, and eyewitness testimony. The latter consists of excerpts from letters, memoirs, speeches, and other documents in order to show the full spectrum of reactions by contemporaries. . . . This is a history of emotions rather than dry facts." Libr J
  Includes bibliography

Paxton, John, 1923-
Companion to the French Revolution. Facts on File 1988 231p il maps hardcover o.p. paperback available $12.95   **944.04**
  1. France—History—1789-1799, Revolution—Dictionaries
  ISBN 0-8160-1937-1 (pa)   LC 84-21489
  "This easy-to-use and comprehensive reference . . . is extremely reliable on definitions and dates." Libr J
  Includes bibliography

Rudé, George F. E., 1910-1993
The French Revolution; [by] George Rudé. Weidenfeld & Nicolson 1988 224p il hardcover o.p. paperback available $12.95   **944.04**
  1. France—History—1789-1799, Revolution
  ISBN 0-8021-3272-3 (pa)   LC 88-10707
  "An introductory survey of the views of various historians of the Revolution over the years, including Michelet, Tocqueville, Aulard, Jaurès, LeFebvre, Cobban, and Furet." Booklist
  Includes bibliography

Schama, Simon
Citizens: a chronicle of the French Revolution. Knopf 1989 xx, 948p il maps hardcover o.p. paperback available $22   **944.04**
  1. France—History—1789-1799, Revolution
  ISBN 0-679-72610-1 (pa)   LC 88-45320
  The author "offers a narrative in the form of a nineteenth-century chronicle that delves into the events and meaning of that momentous series of historical events." Booklist
  "This well-written, thoroughly documented book should be on every high-school library shelf." SLJ
  Includes bibliography

Tocqueville, Alexis de
The old régime and the French Revolution; translated by Stuart Gilbert. Doubleday 1955 300p hardcover o.p. paperback available $11   **944.04**
  1. France—History—1789-1799, Revolution
  ISBN 0-385-09260-1 (pa)
  Also available in hardcover from P. Smith
  Originally published in 1856 this is "still one of the most valuable works on the eighteenth century; deals almost exclusively with the old régime; based upon a wide study of documents, though unfortunately few references are given." Dutcher. Guide to Hist LIt

944.05 France—Period of First Empire, 1804-1815

Schom, Alan
One hundred days; Napoleon's road to Waterloo. Atheneum Pubs. 1992 398p il maps $28   **944.05**
  1. Napoleon I, Emperor of the French, 1769-1821
  2. Waterloo, Battle of, 1815
  ISBN 0-689-12097-4   LC 92-4249
  Also available in paperback from Oxford Univ. Press
  This is an account of "Napoleon's escape from Elba in February 1815 and his return . . . to France. Rallying the nation behind him, he mustered his army and marched off to meet Wellington at Waterloo. . . . This is a first-class reconstruction of Napoleon's final campaign." Publ Wkly
  Includes bibliography

944.08   France—1870-

French culture, 1900-1975; edited by Catharine
Savage Brosman; associate editors, Tom Conley
[et al.] Gale Res. 1995 xl, 449p il (Dictionary
of twentieth-century culture) $90   **944.08**
1. Popular culture—France 2. France—Civilization—
Dictionaries
ISBN 0-8103-8482-5   LC 94-44385
"A Manly, Inc. book"
This work contains "approximately 600 entries dealing
with high as well as popular culture. Each entry contains
a reference section that guides readers to additional reading. The entries include people, places, events, and institutions as well as intellectual and artistic movements.
Even things like the two world wars and the Algerian
war receive particular treatment—in terms of how they
affected or were affected by newspapers, literature, films,
and art." Libr J

944.081   France—Period of Third Republic, 1870-1945

Bredin, Jean-Denis
The affair; the case of Alfred Dreyfus; translated
from the French by Jeffrey Mehlman. Braziller
1986 628p il hardcover o.p. paperback available
$19.95   **944.081**
1. Dreyfus, Alfred, 1859-1935 2. Trials (Espionage)
3. Antisemitism 4. France—Politics and government—1815-1914
ISBN 0-8076-1175-1 (pa)   LC 85-22374
Original French edition, 1983
In his examination of the case, the author seeks to "set
the affair within the . . . currents of French history and
the rising tide of anti-Semitism." Choice
"That Bredin manages to be both passionate and exact
is his first outstanding virtue. He is admirably free of the
baroque conspiracy theories that sprout so luxuriantly on
both sides of this case." N Y Rev Books
Includes bibliography

945   Italian Peninsula and adjacent islands. Italy

Barzini, Luigi Giorgio, 1908-1984
The Italians; [by] Luigi Barzini. Atheneum
Pubs. 1964 352p maps hardcover o.p. paperback
available $13   **945**
1. Italian national characteristics 2. Italy—Civilization
ISBN 0-689-70540-9 (pa)
Also available in hardcover from P. Smith
"The Italians as they are and as foreigners think they
are . . . described by an Italian journalist whose probing
examination of national life and character does not over-
simplify a society webbed with contradiction and incon-
gruity." Booklist

Burckhardt, Jacob, 1818-1897
The civilization of the Renaissance in Italy
                                           945
1. Italy—Civilization 2. Renaissance
Hardcover and paperback editions available from various publishers
Original German edition published 1860 in Switzerland; this translation, by S.G.C. Middlemore, first published 1929
"The scope of the book is to discuss the Renaissance
in its various aspects, more specifically literary, social,
political and moral." Nation and Ath

Durant, William James, 1885-1981
The Renaissance; [by] Will Durant. Simon &
Schuster 1953 776p il (Story of civilization, pt5)
$35   **945**
1. Renaissance 2. Italy—Civilization 3. Italy—His-
tory—0-1559
ISBN 0-671-61600-5
"A history of civilization in Italy from 1304-1576
A.D." Title page
"A mosaic of biographical sketches interspersed with
lively passages on manners, morals, dress, food, festivals,
plagues, pastimes and artistic preferences among the Ital-
ian élite, during some eight generations." N Y Her Trib
Books
Includes bibliography

Hearder, Harry
Italy; a short history. Cambridge Univ. Press
1991 c1990 285p il maps $44.95; pa $15.95 **945**
1. Italy—History
ISBN 0-521-33073-4; 0-521-33719-4 (pa)
                                           LC 89-13991
First published 1990 in the United Kingdom
An "account of the principal developments in Italian
history from the Ice Age to the present day. . . .
Hearder's account centres on the main political developments, placed in their appropriate economic and social
context, and shows how these were related to the great
moments of artistic and cultural endeavour." Publisher's
note
Includes bibliography

Walker, Paul Robert
The Italian Renaissance. Facts on File 1995
150p il map (World history library) $17.95 **945**
1. Renaissance 2. Italy—Civilization
ISBN 0-8160-2942-3   LC 94-34605
This "book is an encyclopedia catalog of . . . cre-
ative, or at least politically notable, individuals. . . .
Chapters on the wealthy leaders and political history of
the major Italian city states are followed by chapters on
the most famous humanists, artists, and early scientists."
SLJ
Includes bibliographical references

946 Iberian Peninsula and adjacent islands. Spain

Crow, John Armstrong
Spain: the root and the flower; an interpretation of Spain and the Spanish people; [by] John A. Crow. 3rd ed expanded and updated. University of Calif. Press 1985 455p $50; pa $15.95 **946**
1. Spain—Civilization 2. Spanish national characteristics
ISBN 0-520-05123-8; 0-520-05133-5 (pa)
LC 84-8652
First published 1963 by Harper & Row
This "history of Spanish civilization features . . . coverage of the post-Franco period. The substance of Spanish culture—art, literature, architecture, and music—is emphasized here instead of straight politics. . . . This important study is written with fluidity, passion, and expertise." Booklist
Includes glossary and bibliography

Fuentes, Carlos, 1928-
The buried mirror; reflections on Spain and the New World. Houghton Mifflin 1992 399p il hardcover o.p. paperback available $29.95 **946**
1. Spain—Civilization 2. Latin America—Civilization
ISBN 0-395-67281-3 (pa)
LC 91-34312
The author "believes that a common cultural heritage can help the countries of Latin America transcend disunity and fragmentation. . . He . . . explores Spanish America's love-hate relationship with Spain and its search for an identity in its multicultural roots." Publ Wkly
"Every page in this lapidary essay offers profound insight into the Spanish American psyche." Libr J
Includes bibliographical references

Historical dictionary of modern Spain, 1700-1988; Robert W. Kern, editor-in-chief, Meredith D. Dodge, associate editor. Greenwood Press 1989 xxv, 697p il maps $95 **946**
1. Spain—History
ISBN 0-313-25971-2
LC 89-7471
This reference work "covers people, events, politics, and international relations. The alphabetically arranged articles, ranging from 1 to 15 or more pages, are well written and informative. Entries, which are written by scholars, include brief bibliographies and numerous cross-references." Nichols. Guide to Ref Books for Sch Media Cent. 4th edition

Kern, Robert W., 1934-
The regions of Spain; a reference guide to history and culture; photographs by Chuck Smith. Greenwood Press 1995 411p il maps $55 **946**
1. Spain—Civilization
ISBN 0-313-29224-8
LC 95-6481
"Each chapter deals with one of Spain's eighteen regions, begins with a brief description of regional characteristics, and then describes the provinces that fall into that region. The description of each province is much more detailed than the description of the region as a whole and is broken up into categories that offer information about topics such as history, economy, social life and customs, and fine arts." Voice Youth Advocates
Includes bibliographical references

Vincent, Mary
Cultural atlas of Spain and Portugal; [by] Mary Vincent and R.A. Stradling. Facts on File 1994 240p il maps $45 **946**
1. Spain 2. Portugal
ISBN 0-8160-3014-6
LC 94-31211
This volume explores the cultural history of the Iberian peninsula. "The text and maps are complemented by 240 beautiful color photographs that highlight many important historical and cultural events. These encompass features on art, palaces, buildings, artists, posters, food, and even Expo'92 in Seville. A chronology, dynastic chart, glossary, short bibliography, and gazetteer complete the volume." Am Ref Books Annu, 1996

947 Russia. Eastern Europe

The **Breakup** of communism; the Soviet Union and Eastern Europe; edited by Matthew A. Kraljic. Wilson, H.W. 1993 224p (Reference shelf, v65 no1) pa $15 **947**
1. Communism 2. Eastern Europe—Politics and government 3. Former Soviet republics 4. Russia (Republic)
ISBN 0-8242-0840-4
LC 92-42466
Articles in this compilation examine the Cold War and theories on why the Soviet system failed; changes that have occurred since the collapse of the Berlin Wall; problems and hardships created by economic reforms in Eastern Europe and the former Soviet republics; and the rise of the "new world order"
Includes bibliography

The **Cambridge** encyclopedia of Russia and the former Soviet Union; edited by Archie Brown, Michael Kaser and Gerald S. Smith; associate editor Patricia Brown. 2nd ed. Cambridge Univ. Press 1994 604p il maps $54.95 **947**
1. Russia—Dictionaries 2. Soviet Union—Dictionaries 3. Former Soviet republics—Dictionaries
ISBN 0-521-35593-1
LC 94-24668
First published 1982 with title: The Cambridge encyclopedia of Russia and the Soviet Union
This encyclopedia, organized "around broad topics like the country's peoples, history, cultural life, and physical environment, . . . emphasizes recent and contemporary issues, with a special focus on the Gorbachev era. A visual treat, it is enhanced by numerous illustrations, many of them in color." Libr J
For a fuller review see: Booklist, Feb. 15, 1995

Dornberg, John

Central and Eastern Europe. Oryx Press 1995
238p il maps (International government & politics
series) $27.50   **947**

1. Eastern Europe—History—1989- 2. Central Europe—History

ISBN 0-89774-942-1   LC 95-16582

"This book addresses the developments, changes, and
issues that have occurred in Central and Eastern Europe
since 1990 when the Cold War ended. . . . The first part
of the book examines the area's geography, diverse mixture of peoples and ethnic groups, and history. Also covered are the region's current political, economic, social,
and cultural developments, problems, and prospects.
Maps and photographs add interest and clarification of
borders. Part II treats each country separately, providing
a statistical profile and map for each one." SLJ

Includes bibliographical references

Duffy, James P., 1941-

Czars; Russia's rulers for more than one
thousand years; [by] James P. Duffy, Vincent L.
Ricci. Facts on File 1995 372p il maps $35   **947**

1. Russia—Kings, queens, rulers, etc.

ISBN 0-8160-2873-7   LC 94-44654

"A basic survey of Russian czardom from the legendary mists of the ninth century to the murder of Nicholas
II in 1918. . . . Though the authors offer little thematic
analysis, they present an interesting series of profiles replete with colorful anecdotes." Libr J

Includes bibliographical references

Great dates in Russian and Soviet history; general
editor, Francis Conte. Facts on File 1993 358p
maps $27.95   **947**

1. Russia—History 2. Soviet Union—History—Chronology

ISBN 0-8160-2687-4   LC 93-20364

"Beginning with a history of the Slavs before 979 and
continuing through the dissolution of the Soviet Union to
1992 and the CIS, each of the 34 chapters lists and explains the significance of individual dates and offers a
concise overview of the relevant time period. . . . A
very handy one-volume reference tool." SLJ

Paxton, John, 1923-

Encyclopedia of Russian history; from the
Christianization of Kiev to the break-up of the
U.S.S.R. ABC-CLIO 1993 483p maps $65   **947**

1. Russia—Dictionaries 2. Soviet Union—Dictionaries

ISBN 0-87436-690-9   LC 93-29564

First published 1983 with title: Companion to Russian
history

This volume includes more than 2,500 entries covering people, events, places and politics. Other features include a separate chronology and a section of maps

Riasanovsky, Nicholas Valentine, 1923-

A history of Russia; [by] Nicholas V.
Riasanovsky. 5th ed. Oxford Univ. Press 1993 xx,
711p il maps $42.25   **947**

1. Russia—History

ISBN 0-19-507462-9   LC 91-43254

First published 1963

This narrative history includes discussions of economics, social organization, religion, and culture

Includes bibliographical references

Russia and the independent states; edited by
Daniel C. Diller. Congressional Quarterly 1993
342p il maps $50.95; pa $32.95   **947**

1. Soviet Union—History 2. Russia—History 3. Eastern Europe—History

ISBN 0-87187-862-3; 0-87187-617-5 (pa)

     LC 92-33273

Replaces Congressional Quarterly's The Soviet Union

"Part 1 traces Russian and Soviet history (primarily
19th and 20th century) through the August 1991 coup
and Mikhail Gorbachev's subsequent resignation. . . .
Part 2 covers the new Commonwealth of Independent
States: its defenses, economy, and foreign relations. Part
3 profiles the newly independent republics individually."
Libr J

Stokes, Gale

The walls came tumbling down; the collapse of
communism in Eastern Europe. Oxford Univ. Press
1993 319p hardcover o.p. paperback available
$15.95   **947**

1. Communism 2. Eastern Europe—Politics and government

ISBN 0-19-506645-6 (pa)   LC 92-44862

The author "deals with all the formerly Communist
countries in Eastern Europe except Albania, and he
traces the history of the collapse of the Soviet-type regimes rather than concentrating . . . on their evolution
since the collapse." N Y Times Book Rev

This book "can be recommended as a coherent, well-
written history that defines its time frame well, provides
sound coverage, makes prudent judgments, and wears its
analysis lightly. . . . Stokes's overview traces the ebb
and flow of personalities and events in a manner that is
both accessible to lay readers and informative to scholars." Libr J

947.08   Russia since 1855

Massie, Robert K., 1929-

The Romanovs; the final chapter. Random
House 1995 308p il $25   **947.08**

1. Nicholas II, Emperor of Russia, 1868-1918
2. House of Romanov 3. Russia—Kings, queens, rulers, etc.

ISBN 0-394-58048-6   LC 95-4718

Also available in paperback from Ballantine Bks.

This book "is divided into three major parts. The first
segment—by far the most fascinating and original—focuses on the complex scientific process used in identifying the Romanovs' remains. . . . The second part concerns the various impostors who have claimed to be
members of the Russian imperial family. . . . [The] third
segment [is] a report on those Romanov émigrés—close
relatives of the Czar's—who survived the Bolsheviks'
persecution." N Y Times Book Rev

Includes bibliographical references

Pipes, Richard
A concise history of the Russian Revolution. Knopf 1995 431p il maps $30; pa $16 **947.08**
1. Russia—History
ISBN 0-679-42277-3; 0-679-74544-0 (pa)
LC 95-3127
A one volume condensation of the author's The Russian Revolution and Russia under the Bolshevik regime
"Forcefully showing why the 70-year-old Communist experiment failed [Pipes] provides the nonacademic reader with accurate historical events in a highly readable format." Libr J
Includes bibliographical references

947.084 Russia (Soviet Union)— 1917-1991

Medvedev, Roy Aleksandrovich, 1925-
Let history judge; the origins and consequences of Stalinism; [by] Roy Medvedev. rev and expanded ed, edited and translated by George Shriver. Columbia Univ. Press 1989 xxi, 903p $83.50; pa $24.50 **947.084**
1. Stalin, Joseph, 1879-1953 2. Soviet Union—Politics and government
ISBN 0-231-06350-4; 0-231-06351-2 (pa)
LC 89-758
Original Russian edition copyrighted 1967; first United States edition published 1972 by Knopf
"Never have Stalin's crimes against humanity been more forcefully or more thoroughly documented than in . . . [this book, which] distills firsthand testimonies of the mass arrests, torture, imprisonment and executions that befell millions of innocent Soviet citizens." Publ Wkly
Includes glossary and bibliographical references

The October Revolution; [by] Roy A. Medvedev; translated by George Saunders; foreword by Harrison E. Salisbury. Columbia Univ. Press 1979 240p il hardcover o.p. paperback available $19.50 **947.084**
1. Soviet Union—History—1917-1921, Revolution
ISBN 0-231-04591-3 (pa) LC 79-9854
The author discusses "from a Marxist point of view, the questions whether the October Revolution was inevitable, whether it was 'premature,' and at which point did it (in the author's opinion) go 'wrong.' . . . Though this is essentially a book of opinion and interpretation, not a meticulous history of events, it is at the same time a smooth, well-translated narrative and sufficiently documented." Choice
Includes glossary and bibliographical references

947.085 Russia (Soviet Union)— 1953-1991

Kort, Michael
Russia. Facts on File 1995 168p il maps (Nations in transition) lib bdg $17.95 **947.085**
1. Russia—History
ISBN 0-8160-3061-8 LC 95-12200
"Kort begins with the history of Russia from its beginnings through the Soviet period. He draws in readers by commenting on how events and policies affected ordinary people. However, the book's greatest strength may be in its clear explanations of the period of transition after 1991. . . . In chapters on politics and government, building a new economy, and daily life, the author uses concrete examples and quotes by Russians to enliven his account." SLJ
Includes bibliographical references

Medvedev, Roy Aleksandrovich, 1925-
Khrushchev: the years in power; [by] Roy A. Medvedev, Zhores A. Medvedev; translated by Andrew R. Durkin. Columbia Univ. Press 1976 198p il map $42 **947.085**
1. Khrushchev, Nikita Sergeevich, 1894-1971 2. Soviet Union—Politics and government
ISBN 0-231-03939-5
Also available in paperback from Norton
The authors, Soviet dissidents, "attempt to sketch the Krushchev era from their perspective inside Soviet society. They outline the issues surrounding Krushchev's rise to power and the failures of his domestic policies, primarily agricultural, that led to his political demise." Choice

947.086 Russia—1991-

Adelman, Deborah
The "children of perestroika" come of age; young people of Moscow talk about life in the new Russia. Sharpe, M.E. 1994 xxii, 194p il $41.95; pa $23.95 **947.086**
1. Youth—Russia (Republic) 2. Russia (Republic)—Social conditions
ISBN 1-56324-286-9; 1-56324-287-7 (pa)
LC 93-10936
In this "follow-up to The 'Children of Perestroika' (Sharpe, 1991), Adelman reflects the recent changes in the lives of the 11 teenagers she originally interviewed in 1989. . . . These updated interviews present a comprehensive look at the new Russia from a unique viewpoint, and result in a strikingly honest overview of youthful attitudes toward parents, gender stereotypes, marriage and family, religion, careers, political beliefs, and numerous other issues." SLJ
Includes glossary

The **Breakup** of the Soviet Union: opposing viewpoints; William Barbour, book editor; Carol Wekesser, book editor. Greenhaven Press 1994 264p lib bdg $19.95; pa $11.95 **947.086**
1. World politics—1965- 2. Soviet Union—History 3. Russia (Republic)
ISBN 1-56510-068-9 (lib bdg); 1-56510-067-0 (pa)
LC 93-1809
"Opposing viewpoints series"
A collection of articles debating issues related to the collapse of the former Soviet Union, the future of the region, and America's foreign policy there
This "will be a valuable tool for helping students to understand the issues and for encouraging discussion in a history, political science, or current events curriculum." Booklist
Includes bibliography

948 Scandinavia

Cultural atlas of the Viking world; [by] Colleen Batey [et al.]; edited by James Graham-Campbell. Facts on File 1994 240p il maps $45 **948**
1. Vikings
ISBN 0-8160-3004-9 LC 94-209950
"An Andromeda book"
"Using data gathered by scientists, the authors trace the emergence of Scandinavia from pre-Viking settlement through the development of the true Viking society, Viking expansion throughout Europe and finally the end of their era and the lasting marks they made on European culture. Excellent photography, interesting text, and a wealth of maps and supplemental information make this a fascinating book." Book Rep

949.7 Yugoslavia and Bulgaria

The **Black** book of Bosnia; the consequences of appeasement; by the writers and editors of The New republic; edited by Nader Mousavizadeh; afterword by Leon Wieseltier. Basic Bks. 1996 219p maps pa $10 **949.7**
1. Yugoslav War, 1991-
ISBN 0-465-09835-5 LC 95-50103
Contributors explore the political, social, and economic impact of the ethnically based conflict in the former Yugoslavia
Includes bibliographical references

Maass, Peter, 1960-
Love thy neighbor; a story of war. Knopf 1996 305p $25; pa $13 **949.7**
1. Yugoslav War, 1991- 2. Bosnia and Hercegovina
ISBN 0-679-44433-5; 0-679-76389-9 (pa)
LC 95-39250
This book on the Yugoslav war is based on Maass's experiences "in 1992-93 as the Washington Post's reporter in Bosnia." Booklist
"Maass was only in Bosnia for about a year, from 1992 to 1993, but he saw a great deal. And he displays extraordinary sensitivity to the ambiguities of his position." Nation
Includes bibliography

Malcolm, Noel
Bosnia; a short history. New York Univ. Press 1994 xxiv, 340p $26.95; pa $18.95 **949.7**
1. Yugoslavia—History 2. Bosnia and Hercegovina
ISBN 0-8147-5520-8; 0-8147-5561-5 (pa)
LC 94-11560
"To explain the origins of the current conflict in Bosnia, Malcolm reaches back to Turkish occupation, Austro-Hungarian rule, both world wars and the era of Stalinist oppression under Tito." Publ Wkly
"The author cogently dispels the myths of forcible conversion to Islam by the Ottomans. . . . Although Malcolm is least comfortable in dealing with the segment of Bosnia's history as a part of Yugoslavia, he makes the case that its subsequent destruction was an object of 'rational strategy' rather than religious hatred." Libr J
Includes bibliographical references

950 Asia. Orient. Far East

Cook, Chris, 1945-
The Facts on File Asian political almanac; compiled by Chris Cook. Facts on File 1994 264p il $39 **950**
1. Asia—Politics and government
ISBN 0-8160-2585-1 LC 93-26319
This volume presents "information on Asian politics and government during the half century since 1945. . . . Data is arranged in 11 sections—Asian constitutions, heads of state, political parties, elections, etc. Some sections are further subdivided topically." Choice
"Asian studies collections at the high-school level and above that need a digest of the most important political facts, names, and events of the past 50 years will need to consider this book." Booklist

Durant, William James, 1885-1981
Our Oriental heritage; [by] Will Durant. Simon & Schuster 1935 1049p il (Story of civilization, pt1) $35 **950**
1. Asian civilization
ISBN 0-671-54800-X
"Being a history of civilization in Egypt and the Near East to the death of Alexander, and in India, China and Japan from the beginning to our own day; with an introduction on the nature and foundations of civilization." Title page
Includes glossary and bibliography

Hinton, Harold C., 1924-1993
East Asia and the Western Pacific. Stryker-Post Publs. il maps (World today series) pa $11.50
950
1. East Asia 2. Southeast Asia 3. Islands of the Pacific
ISSN 0084-229X
Annual. First published 1968 with title: The Far East and Southwest Pacific. Variant title: The Far East and Western Pacific
Among the nations profiled in this survey are: Australia, Burma, Cambodia, China, the Philippines, Singapore, Thailand and Vietnam. Maps and illustrations accompany the discussions of each country's history, culture and economy

951 China and adjacent areas

The **Cambridge** encyclopedia of China; editor, Brian Hook; consultant editor, Denis Twitchett. 2nd ed. Cambridge Univ. Press 1991 502p il maps $69.95 **951**
1. China—Dictionaries
ISBN 0-521-35594-X   LC 91-18600
First published 1982

"'A source of information about all aspects of Chinese civilization, traditional and contemporary.'—*Pref.* A considerably revised and expanded edition, reflecting recent events in China. Almost a third of the volume is a dynasty-by-dynasty review of Chinese history. Subject index and bibliography; glossary of Chinese terms with pinyin and Wade-Giles transliteration, and Chinese characters." Guide to Ref Books. 11th edition

"A useful purchase, especially for smaller libraries." Libr J

China; ancient culture, modern land; general editor, Robert E. Murowchick. University of Okla. Press 1994 192p il maps (Cradles of civilization) $34.95 **951**
1. China—Civilization
ISBN 0-8061-2683-3   LC 94-13366

This volume outlines "the evolution of Chinese culture and history from antiquity to the modern era. . . . Individual chapters focus on the land, people, government, philosophers and statesmen, religion, language, and revolution. This well-illustrated volume provides a solid overview of a highly complex society rooted in ancient traditions. A splendid introductory study." Booklist
Includes bibliography

Fairbank, John King, 1907-1991
The great Chinese revolution: 1800-1985. Harper & Row 1986 396p maps hardcover o.p. paperback available $14 **951**
1. China—History
ISBN 0-06-039076-X (pa)   LC 86-665
"A Cornelia & Michael Bessie book"

Contents: Late imperial China: growth and change, 1800-1895; The transformation of the late imperial order, 1895-1911; The era of the first Chinese Republic, 1912-1949; The Chinese People's Republic, 1949-1985
"The book is never pedantic, but gathers together a lifetime of scholarship plus a true gift for presentation of complex issues and a fine eye for telling illustration." Libr J
Includes bibliography

Huang, Ray
China, a macro history. Sharpe, M.E. 1989 c1988 277p il maps $51.95; pa $19.95 **951**
1. China—History
ISBN 0-87332-452-8; 0-87332-728-4 (pa)
          LC 87-28898
"An East Gate book"
The author examines the broad sweep of Chinese political and social history while also making comparative references to the development of Western civilization

Spence, Jonathan D.
The search for modern China. Norton 1990 xxv, 876p il maps $32.95; pa $26.95 **951**
1. China—History
ISBN 0-393-02708-2; 0-393-30780-8 (pa)
          LC 89-9241
"Beginning with the decline of the Ming dynasty and ending with the Tiananmen Square massacre, Spence chronicles the cultural and social transformations of the country, concentrating on the many wars and rebellions." Booklist
Spence's "own sense of China's past is so vivid, his understanding so sure and his writer's skill so powerful that the reader apprehends distant events as if they were contemporary." New Statesman
Includes glossary and bibliography

951.05 China—Period of People's Republic, 1949-

Kort, Michael
China under communism. Millbrook Press 1995 c1994 175p il $17.40 **951.05**
1. China—History—1949- 2. Communism—China
ISBN 1-56294-450-9   LC 94-8312
"This overview of modern Chinese history opens with a two-chapter review of China's long civilization and an examination of the conditions that brought Mao and the communists to power. The rest of the book examines the communist government's policies, including Mao's grandiose plans, such as the Great Leap Forward and the Cultural Revolution, and the post-Mao leadership's strange dual policy of economic freedom and political repression, which has led to human rights abuses and public showdowns such as the one at Tiananmen Square. Kort is objective about his subject." Book Rep
Includes bibliographical references

Lord, Bette Bao
Legacies: a Chinese mosaic. Knopf 1990 245p $19.95 **951.05**
1. China—Social life and customs 2. China—Politics and government
ISBN 0-394-58325-6   LC 89-43452
Also available G.K. Hall large print edition and in paperback from Fawcett Bks.
The author lived in China from 1985 to 1989. Her book is based on interviews with Chinese people, including an actress, a teacher, a veteran of the Long March, an artist, a journalist, a peasant, an entrepreneur and a Communist Party cadre, who recount their experiences of persecution during the Cultural Revolution. The author also describes her own experiences and her family history
"A vivid and startling mosaic of the political struggles that foreshadowed the Tiananmen Square uprising." Time

Salisbury, Harrison Evans, 1908-1993

Tiananmen diary; thirteen days in June; [by] Harrison E. Salisbury. Little, Brown 1989 176p maps $18.95; pa $10.95 **951.05**
   1. China—History—1989, Tiananmen Square Incident
   2. College students—Political activity
   ISBN 0-316-80904-7; 0-316-80905-5 (pa)
                                        LC 89-85228

This is a day-by-day account of the author's experiences in China during the student democracy movement demonstrations in June 1989

The author's "political insights and informed theories provide the motivation and historical reference that were missing in the news media's extensive coverage of the Tiananmen Square massacre, while his intense and angry reactions make the events gripping and real." N Y Times Book Rev

Simmie, Scott

Tiananmen Square; [by] Scott Simmie and Bob Nixon. University of Wash. Press 1990 c1989 206p il maps pa $16.95 **951.05**
   1. China—History—1989, Tiananmen Square Incident
   2. College students—Political activity
   ISBN 0-295-96950-4   LC 90-103446
   First published 1989 in Canada

A look at events leading to the student pro-democracy demonstrations and the government's violent reaction

Terrill, Ross

China in our time; the epic saga of the People's Republic from the Communist victory to Tiananmen Square and beyond. Simon & Schuster 1992 366p il map $25 **951.05**
   1. China—History—1949-
   ISBN 0-671-68096-X   LC 92-7699

This is an account of political developments and social conditions in China since 1964. Terrill also writes about his experiences within the country and the changes in his perception of Communist rule

"An informal but fact-filled view of China's revolution and evolution." Booklist

Includes bibliographical references

Woodruff, John

China in search of its future; years of great reform, 1982-87; foreword by Michel Oksenberg. University of Wash. Press 1989 218p il maps $22.50 **951.05**
   1. China—History—1976- 2. China—Social conditions
   ISBN 0-295-96803-6   LC 88-29027
   Also available revised updated paperback edition from Carol Pub. Group

The author "begins with some history that takes China back to the turn of the century, but chapters deal mainly with topics such as the position of women, people in the countryside, politics in China, and student activism in the streets. It is excellent background material for anyone needing a basic understanding of a complex country that has undergone tremendous changes in its lifestyle." SLJ

Includes bibliography

951.9 Korea

Blair, Clay, 1925-

The forgotten war; America in Korea, 1950-1953. Times Bks. 1987 1136p il maps $29.95 **951.9**
   1. Korean War, 1950-1953
   ISBN 0-8129-1670-0   LC 87-40195
   Also available in paperback from Anchor Bks.

"Blair describes troop movements and tactics, analyzes decisions, and explores how the personalities and characters of the commanders . . . influenced the progress of the war." Publisher's note

This book "deserves an important place in the historiography of the Korean War." New Repub

Includes bibliography

Goulden, Joseph C.

Korea; the untold story of the war. Times Bks. 1982 xxvi, 690p il o.p.; McGraw-Hill paperback available $14.95 **951.9**
   1. Korean War, 1950-1953
   ISBN 0-07-023580-5 (pa)   LC 81-21262

The author's thesis is "that in the Korean War the West defeated a specific case of Communist aggression at a high cost, although it could not have changed the Soviet policy of aggression-by-proxy elsewhere without a direct confrontation with the Soviets." Booklist

This book "is as much a study of American leadership as of day-by-day events. Especially noteworthy is a superbly balanced study of General MacArthur's complex personality and his removal from command. Throughout, the author pays somewhat less attention to the battlefield itself." Libr J

Includes bibliographical references

Hastings, Max

The Korean War. Simon & Schuster 1987 391p il maps hardcover o.p. paperback available $14 **951.9**
   1. Korean War, 1950-1953
   ISBN 0-671-66834-X (pa)   LC 87-16547

The author covers the political and military background of the Korean War, and also discusses how it served as a prelude to the American involvement in the Vietnam War, 15 years later

This is a "readable, informative and sensible study." Booklist

Includes bibliography

Isserman, Maurice

The Korean War. Facts on File 1992 117p il maps (America at war) lib bdg $17.95 **951.9**
   1. Korean War, 1950-1953
   ISBN 0-8160-2688-2   LC 92-10201

Examines the political climate and military situation that led to the Korean War and discusses the key people and events involved in the conflict itself

This combines "a well-written and well-researched account of what some have termed America's 'forgotten war'. . . . The book is thought-provoking as well as informative and entertaining." SLJ

Includes bibliography

MacDonald, C. A.

Korea: the war before Vietnam; [by] Callum A. MacDonald. Free Press 1987 c1986 330p il maps $32.95 **951.9**

1. Korean War, 1950-1953

ISBN 0-02-919621-3 LC 86-22943

First published 1986 in the United Kingdom

This is an account of "how the Korean War started, how the U.S. became involved, what the high-level decisions were that determined the course of the fighting, why Truman dismissed MacArthur and why it took two years to negotiate a ceasefire." Publ Wkly

Includes bibliography

Stokesbury, James L.

A short history of the Korean War. Morrow 1988 276p maps hardcover o.p. paperback available $8.95 **951.9**

1. Korean War, 1950-1953

ISBN 0-688-09513-5 (pa) LC 88-5229

Stokesbury seeks to "trace the background of the Korean situation during the . . . years prior to July and August 1950. . . . [There is a discussion] of the first year of maneuvers and battles before and after the Chinese Communists intervened, and also of the . . . fighting from time to time during the two years of peace negotiations." Publisher's note

"Stokesbury's combination of scholarship, clear writing, balanced judgments, and wit has reached a new high. It would be hard to imagine better personality portraits or better coverage of the prisoner-of-war issue." Booklist

Includes bibliography

Summers, Harry G.

Korean War almanac; [by] Harry G. Summers, Jr. Facts on File 1990 288p il maps $27.95; pa $14.95 **951.9**

1. Korean War, 1950-1953

ISBN 0-8160-1737-9; 0-8160-2463-4 (pa)

LC 89-33560

"This reference book on the war contains an overview of the entire conflict, a chronology of events, and 375 articles on the people, battles, weapons, military units, and key concepts of the war." N Y Public Libr. Book of How & Where to Look It Up

Includes bibliography

Yi, Ki-baek, 1926-

A new history of Korea; [by] Ki-Baik Lee; translated by Edward W. Wagner with Edward J. Shultz. Harvard Univ. Press 1984 xxii, 474p il maps $25; pa $14.95 **951.9**

1. Korea—History

ISBN 0-674-61575-1; 0-674-61576-X (pa)

LC 83-246

Original Korean edition, 1961; this is a translation of the 1967 revised edition

"Published for the Harvard-Yenching Institute"

The author "incorporates integral social and cultural development into the history of events and also stresses the leadership elite and their role in Korean history." Booklist

Includes bibliography

952 Japan

The **Cambridge** encyclopedia of Japan; editors, Richard Bowring, Peter Kornicki. Cambridge Univ. Press 1993 400p il maps $59.95 **952**

1. Japan

ISBN 0-521-40352-9 LC 92-8167

This volume is divided "into eight categories: geography, history, language, thought and religion, arts and crafts, society, politics, and the economy. Each of these categories is further divided into 7-11 subjects that deal with numerous topics, such as the physical structure of the country, climate, education, family, judicial system, cinema, products, foreign policy, and important historical figures." Am Ref Books Annu, 1994

"More useful for the general reader than for specialists. Lavish use of color illustration." Guide to Ref Books. 11th edition

Dunn, Charles James

Everyday life in traditional Japan; [by] C. J. Dunn; drawings by Laurence Broderick. Putnam 1969 197p il map o.p.; Tuttle paperback available $12.95 **952**

1. Japan—Social life and customs 2. Japan—Civilization

ISBN 0-8048-1384-1 (pa)

"A description of Japanese life during the stable . . . reign of the Tokugawa shoguns [1600-1850]." Cincinnati Public Libr

Includes bibliography

Japan: an illustrated encyclopedia. Kodansha Am. 1993 2v il set $250 **952**

1. Japan—Dictionaries

ISBN 4-06-931098-3 LC 93-20512

Based on Kodansha encyclopedia of Japan published 1983 in nine volumes

This "work provides a comprehensive overview of Japanese society, culture, and history. With more than 11,000 entries ranging from 50 words to pictorial essays and long feature articles, an international group of scholars has focused on Japan's natural setting, history, economy, technology, and daily life. The entries are accompanied by hundreds of lavish color photos, illustrations, charts, and tables." Am Libr

Reischauer, Edwin O. (Edwin Oldfather), 1910-1990

Japan, tradition & transformation; [by] Edwin O. Reischauer, Albert M. Craig. rev ed. Houghton Mifflin 1989 352p il $35.56 **952**

1. Japan—History

ISBN 0-395-49696-9 LC 88-83734

First published 1978

This text on the history and culture of Japan examines the traditions of the Japanese people and analyzes the changes wrought by foreign influences

952.04   Japan—1945-

Ross, Stewart
The rise of Japan and the Pacific Rim. Raintree
Steck-Vaughn 1996 80p il maps (Causes and
consequences) lib bdg $25.69   **952.04**
   1. Japan—Economic conditions 2. Pacific rim—Economic conditions
   ISBN 0-8172-4054-3   LC 95-17257
Explains the sudden and rapid growth of the economies of Japan and the Pacific Rim countries occurring
after World War II and primarily since 1960. "Roles of
traditional aspects of the Asian nations, such as Confucianism and authoritarian government, as well as communism, are examined." Book Rep
Includes bibliographical references

953   Arabian Peninsula and adjacent areas

Theroux, Peter
Sandstorms: days and nights in Arabia. Norton
1990 281p hardcover o.p. paperback available
$10.95   **953**
   1. Arab countries—Description
   ISBN 0-393-30797-2 (pa)   LC 89-28609
The author "recounts his experiences in the Middle
East of the 1980s. The author went to Egypt to teach
English and wound up chronicling the disappearance of
Lebanon's Shia Iman Moussa Sadr. But *Sandstorms* is
the human side of an American in Arabia: swapping
dirty jokes, drinking till all hours in dirty cafés, reading
Saudi literature to try and touch the Arabian soul." Libr
J

954   South Asia. India

The **Cambridge** encyclopedia of India, Pakistan,
Bangladesh, Sri Lanka, Nepal, Bhutan, and the
Maldives; editor, Francis Robinson. Cambridge
Univ. Press 1989 520p il maps $69.95   **954**
   1. India—Dictionaries 2. South Asia—Dictionaries
   ISBN 0-521-33451-9   LC 88-26737
"A regional encyclopedia focusing on the history and
sociology of the area. Seventy contributors provide an in-
depth and comprehensive picture of South Asia and the
Indian subcontinent. Includes 75 maps, 69 tables, and dy-
nastic charts from 500 B.C. to the present." N Y Public
Libr. Book of How & Where to Look It Up

Wolpert, Stanley A., 1927-
A new history of India; [by] Stanley Wolpert.
Oxford Univ. Press il maps $45; pa $19.95   **954**
   1. India—History
First published 1977. (5th edition 1997) Periodically
revised
   A comprehensive survey of Indian history from its
early beginnings to the present. Includes discussion of
the assassination of Rajiv Gandhi; violence in Kashmir,
Punjab, and Assam; and the effects of rural development
Includes bibliographical references

954.03   India—Period of British rule, 1785-1947

Bayly, C. A. (Christopher Alan)
Indian society and the making of the British
Empire. Cambridge Univ. Press 1988 230p il maps
(New Cambridge history of India) $47.95; pa
$18.95   **954.03**
   1. India—History—1765-1947, British occupation
   ISBN 0-521-25092-7; 0-521-38650-0 (pa)
      LC 87-704
The author examines "aspects of the British East India
Company's commercial power in the period of Mogul
decline with a view toward understanding how economic
penetration first obtained Indian collaborators, then
changed Indian society, and ultimately gained political
power." Choice
"Bayly's richly complex text goes far to explain why
Indian society allowed this sequence of events to occur.
. . . Bayly brings out the fantastic complexity of Indian
societies." Hist Today
Includes glossary and bibliography

954.04   India—1947-1971

Collins, Larry, 1929-
Freedom at midnight; [by] Larry Collins and
Dominique Lapierre. Simon & Schuster 1975 572p
il maps o.p.; Avon Bks. paperback available $5.95
      954.04
   1. India—History
   ISBN 0-380-00693-6 (pa)
"The authors skillfully reconstruct the years during
which India gained independence and delineate the peo-
ple who played important roles in the dramatic event."
Booklist
Includes bibliography

955   Iran

Mackey, Sandra, 1937-
The Iranians; Persia, Islam, and the soul of a
nation; W. Scott Harrop, research assistant. Dutton
1996 xxii, 426p maps $26.95   **955**
   1. Iran—Politics and government
   ISBN 0-525-94005-7   LC 95-44135
The author presents "information on Iranian civilization from Cyrus the Great to the present. Throughout this
turbulent history of invasions and conquerors, the Persian
soul, with its foundations in the Zoroastrian concept of
justice overlaid with Shia Islam, has steadfastly endured.
Since many Westerners had little familiarity with Iran
until the overthrow of the Shah in 1979, this very readable book provides a perspective on what led up to those
events, what is happening in Iran today, and how the
current situation is likely to affect the future of Iran and
its relationship with the West." Libr J

956 Middle East

The **Cambridge** encyclopedia of the Middle East and North Africa; executive editor, Trevor Mostyn, advisory editor, Albert Hourani. Cambridge Univ. Press 1988 504p il maps $69.95 **956**
1. Middle East
ISBN 0-521-32190-5   LC 88-10866
"Offers an overview of various subject areas for the region: e.g., history, quick survey by major periods; culture, including religion, literature, arts, music, Islamic science, Islamic law; economics, with statistics as current as 1986. Pt. 5 is a survey of individual countries, Mauritania to Afghanistan to Somalia. The volume ends with 'peoples without a country,' e.g., Kurds, Armenians, Palestinians." Guide to Ref Books. 11th edition

Includes bibliographies

Cleveland, Ray L., 1929-
The Middle East and South Asia. Stryker-Post Publs. il maps (World today series) pa $11.50
     956
1. Middle East 2. South Asia
ISSN 0084-2311
Annual. First published 1967
This illustrated volume discusses the geography, history, culture, and economy of nations and territories in the region

Friedman, Thomas L.
From Beirut to Jerusalem. Farrar, Straus & Giroux 1991 c1990 541p il maps $25   **956**
1. Middle East—Politics and government 2. Jewish-Arab relations 3. Lebanon—History 4. Israel—Politics and government
ISBN 0-374-15895-9   LC 92-148666
Also available in paperback from Anchor Bks. (NY)
First published 1989
The author presents an account of the political situation in the Middle East as he witnessed it in his years as a reporter in Lebanon and Jerusalem
"When recounting his frequently harrowing experiences in that troubled region, Friedman can be absolutely riveting; similarly, his historical insights, his explanation of the root causes of the Arab-Israeli conflict, and his impressions of people and places in the Holy Land never fail to fascinate." Booklist

Herzog, Chaim, 1918-1997
The Arab-Israeli wars; war and peace in the Middle East. Random House 1982 392p il maps hardcover o.p. paperback available $16   **956**
1. Jewish-Arab relations
ISBN 0-394-71746-5 (pa)   LC 80-5291
This book traces "the Arab-Israeli wars and military conflicts from the 1948 War of Independence through the 1973 Yom Kippur War." Libr J
Includes bibliography

Hiro, Dilip
A dictionary of the Middle East. St. Martin's Press 1996 367p il map $30   **956**
1. Middle East—Dictionaries
ISBN 0-312-12554-2   LC 96-4395
"In more than 1,000 alphabetically arranged entries, varying in length from a few lines to a few pages, Hiro covers more than 150 personalities in politics, business, culture, and religion; places of religious and cultural significance; oil and other minerals; political and religious sects; economic infrastructure; and political and religious ideologies." Booklist
"Students of the Middle East at all levels will find this a useful source, and it is likely that even those with long exposure to the field will find some new insights here. Hiro's work is probably the best of the current guides to the politics of the area." Am Ref Books Annu, 1997

Lewis, Bernard
The Middle East; a brief history of the last 2,000 years. Scribner 1995 433p il $30   **956**
1. Middle East—History
ISBN 0-684-80712-2   LC 96-4384
"Lewis has chosen to accentuate the social, economic, and cultural changes that have occurred over 20 centuries. He ranges from seemingly trivial concerns (changes in dress and manners in an Arab coffeehouse) to earth-shaking events (the Mongol conquest of Mesopotamia) in painting a rich, varied, and fascinating portrait of a region that is steeped in traditionalism while often forced by geography and politics to accept change." Booklist
Includes bibliographical references

The **Middle** East. Congressional Quarterly il maps pa $43.95   **956**
1. Middle East—Politics and government 2. Jewish-Arab relations 3. United States—Foreign relations—Middle East 4. Middle East—Foreign relations—United States
First published 1974. (8th edition 1995) Periodically revised
Covers topics such as oil, Islam, the Arab-Israeli conflict, the Persian Gulf, and the arms trade in the Middle East. Also presents profiles of Middle Eastern nations and twentieth-century leaders and includes documents such as UN resolutions and peace treaties
"Recommended for most high school collections as a thorough source book." Booklist
Includes bibliography

The **Middle** East: opposing viewpoints; William Dudley, book editor. Greenhaven Press 1992 264p il map lib bdg $19.95; pa $11.95   **956**
1. Middle East
ISBN 0-89908-185-1 (lib bdg); 0-89908-160-6 (pa)
     LC 91-43280
"Opposing viewpoints series"
Replaces the edition published 1988 under the editorship of Janelle Rohr
Covers the history of Middle Eastern conflicts, outside intervention, Islamic fundamentalism and the Palestinian question
Includes bibliographical references

956.7   Iraq

Allen, Thomas B., 1929-
War in the Gulf; [by Thomas B. Allen, F. Clifton Berry, Norman Polmar] Turner Pub. (Atlanta) 1991 240p il maps $29.95; pa $19.95
       956.7

1. Persian Gulf War, 1991
ISBN 1-878685-00-7; 1-878685-01-5 (pa)
       LC 91-65803

At head of title: CNN
The authors "provide background on the war, detail its progress, discuss the international reaction to events, chart the use of the various forms of military hardware, and profile the key leaders involved. The clearly presented text does a good job of stating the facts and venturing opinions, but it's probably the photos—all well printed and very colorful—that will draw an audience." Booklist

Desert Storm; the war in the Persian Gulf; by the editors of Time magazine; edited by Otto Friedrich. Little, Brown 1991 232p il $19.95
       956.7

1. Persian Gulf War, 1991
ISBN 0-316-85100-0   LC 91-52896
"A Time book"
This volume assesses the actual military engagement, and the aftermath of the international coalition's defeat of Saddam Hussein

The **Gulf** war reader; history, documents, opinions; edited by Micah L. Sifry and Christopher Cerf. Times Bks. 1991 526p pa $17   **956.7**
1. Persian Gulf War, 1991
ISBN 0-8129-1947-5   LC 91-3205
"Examining the historical events that led to . . . conflict in the Gulf and Middle East, this anthology of selected articles documents the differing viewpoints of leading policymakers and journalists, among them George Bush, Saddam Hussein, William Safire, and Walter Cronkite. A concise overview and analysis for students of current events and Middle East politics." Booklist

Includes bibliographical references

Iraq; William Dudley & Stacey L. Tipp, book editors. Greenhaven Press 1991 256p (Current controversies) lib bdg $19.95; pa $11.95 **956.7**
1. Persian Gulf War, 1991
ISBN 0-89908-575-X (lib bdg); 0-89908-581-4 (pa)
       LC 91-30036

An anthology of articles debating issues surrounding the Persian Gulf War, including its effects on the United States and the Middle East, the justification of military action, the accuracy of the media coverage, and lessons learned from the war
"This is a valuable contribution to the literature on this subject, and could be used effectively in classrooms, as a library resource, and as a text for both student and adult study groups." SLJ

Includes bibliographical references

Summers, Harry G.
Persian Gulf War almanac; [by] Harry G. Summers, Jr. Facts on File 1995 301p il maps $35
       956.7

1. Persian Gulf War, 1991
ISBN 0-8160-2821-4   LC 94-28450
"Background to the conflict is provided in several essays that discuss the historical and geographic realities of the area. . . . A chronology with day-by-day entries starts on February, 19, 1990, with Iraq's additional reparations claims in the Iran-Iraq War, and ends with Iraq's surrender at the end of the ground war on March 5, 1991. The main body of the work is in dictionary arrangement and is illustrated with 20 maps and charts and 68 black-and-white photographs." Booklist

956.94   Palestine. Israel

Armstrong, Karen
Jerusalem; one city, three faiths. Knopf 1996 xxi, 471p il maps $30   **956.94**
1. Jerusalem—History
ISBN 0-679-43596-4   LC 96-75888
Armstrong's "overarching theme, that Jerusalem has been central to the experience and 'sacred geography' of Jews, Muslims and Christians and thus has led to deadly struggles for dominance, is a familiar one, yet she brings to her sweeping, profusely illustrated narrative a grasp of sociopolitical conditions seldom found in other books." Publ Wkly

Israel: opposing viewpoints; Charles P. Cozic, book editor. Greenhaven Press 1994 288p il maps lib bdg $19.95; pa $11.95   **956.94**
1. Israel 2. Zionism 3. Palestinian Arabs
ISBN 1-56510-133-2 (lib bdg); 1-56510-132-4 (pa)
       LC 93-30964

"Opposing viewpoints series"
Replaces the edition published 1984 under the editorship of Bob Anderson and Janelle Rohr
"This volume presents six chapters arranged in a debate format that focus on the history, current socioeconomic considerations, and global political effects of Arab-Israeli conflicts. It is a thorough collation of diverse opinions written by journalists, academics, and religious and political leaders." SLJ
Includes bibliography

Makovsky, David
Making peace with the PLO; the Rabin government's road to the Oslo Accord. Westview Press 1996 239p $53; pa $16.95   **956.94**
1. Jewish-Arab relations 2. Israel-Arab conflicts 3. Israel—Politics and government
ISBN 0-8133-2425-4; 0-8133-2426-2 (pa)
       LC 95-39631
"Published in cooperation with the Washington Institute for Near East Policy"
Makovksy presents an "account of the Arab-Israeli peace process from the Madrid Conference in October 1991 through the Israeli-PLO Declaration-of-Principles (DOP) signed on September 13, 1993. An epilogue

Makovsky, David—*Continued*
brings the chronology of the peace process up to the formal peace treaty signed between Jordan and Israel on October 26, 1994." Choice

This is a "thoroughly researched, well-written account. Rich in detail and filled with insights about Israeli politics, Mr. Makovsky's narrative takes readers behind the headlines and offers information unavailable elsewhere." N Y Times Book Rev
Includes bibliographical references

Ross, Stewart
The Arab-Israeli conflict. Raintree Steck-Vaughn 1996 80p il maps (Causes and consequences) lib bdg $25.26 **956.94**
1. Israel-Arab conflicts 2. Jewish-Arab relations
ISBN 0-8172-4051-9 LC 95-17097
"Ross traces the history of the Middle East's long, bitter discord and gives a somewhat critical appraisal of Britain's involvement in the creation of the state of Israel in 1948. The roles of the United States, Soviet Union, and United Nations in the Arab-Israeli conflict are explored, as is the Palestinian question. This concise look at this vital region goes a long way toward explaining the reasons for the continued hostility." SLJ
Includes bibliographical references

959 Southeast Asia

Southeast Asia: a past regained; by the editors of Time-Life Books. Time-Life Bks. 1995 168p il maps (Lost civilizations) $19.95 **959**
1. Southeast Asia—Civilization 2. Southeast Asia—Antiquities
LC 95-34501
This look at the ancient civilizations of Southeast Asia features illustrated essays on the discovery of the Angkor Wat complex and the efforts to preserve Java's Buddhist edifice of Borobodur
Includes bibliography

959.6 Cambodia

Criddle, Joan D.
To destroy you is no loss; the odyssey of a Cambodian family; [by] Joan D. Criddle and Teeda Butt Mam. Atlantic Monthly Press 1987 289p map o.p.; Doubleday paperback available $11.95 **959.6**
1. Cambodia—History—1975- 2. Cambodian refugees
ISBN 0-385-26628-6 (pa) LC 87-1396
"With the Khmer Rouge takeover in 1975, gently bred, 15-year-old Teeda and 15 members of her upper-class family were among millions driven from Phnom Penh into the countryside. . . . Before Teeda's family emigrated to America in 1980, they led a slavelike existence . . . a life of constant terror." Publ Wkly
"Mam's story, told to Criddle (who sponsored the family's emigration to the United States), reveals with simple sensitivity and insight another perspective of the nightmare. . . . A moving, difficult, important book." Libr J

959.704 Vietnam—1949-

America in Vietnam; a documentary history; edited with commentaries by William Appleman Williams [et al.] Anchor Press/Doubleday 1985 345p map o.p.; Norton paperback available $12.95 **959.704**
1. Vietnam War, 1961-1975
ISBN 0-393-30555-4 (pa) LC 84-9321
In this collection of original essays and documentary sources, historians try to explain the U.S.-Vietnamese War of 1963-75 within the greater context of two centuries of American involvement in Asia
Includes bibliography

Baker, Mark, 1950-
Nam; the Vietnam War in the words of the men and women who fought there. Morrow 1981 324p o.p.; Berkley Bks. paperback available $5.99 **959.704**
1. Vietnam War, 1961-1975—Personal narratives
ISBN 0-425-10144-4 (pa)
The author "has painstakingly interviewed close to one-hundred Vietnam veterans—officers, enlisted men, and military nurses—in his efforts to analyze the impact of the war on the personalities of those involved." Best Sellers
Includes glossary

Berman, Larry
Lyndon Johnson's war; the road to stalemate in Vietnam. Norton 1989 254p il maps hardcover o.p. paperback available $9.95 **959.704**
1. Johnson, Lyndon B. (Lyndon Baines), 1908-1973
2. Vietnam War, 1961-1975 3. United States—Politics and government—1961-1974
ISBN 0-393-30778-6 (pa) LC 88-25360
Companion volume Planning a tragedy (1982)
"A concise, revealing examination of American policy in Vietnam from late 1965 through March 1968. . . . The author neatly dissects the flawed decision-making process that led to a stalemate in the war. Both tragic hero and deceiver of the public, Johnson becomes the chief architect of US failure to 'win' the war." Choice

Bloods: an oral history of the Vietnam War by black veterans; [edited by] Wallace Terry. Random House 1984 311p il o.p.; Ballantine Bks. paperback available $5.95 **959.704**
1. Vietnam War, 1961-1975—Personal narratives
2. African American soldiers
ISBN 0-345-31197-3 (pa) LC 83-42775
Twenty black veterans relate their experiences in Vietnam and back home
This is "an intimate overview that often makes the reader stop, sit back, and think about this war that tore at America. . . . The accounts are moving, powerful and offer several views." Voice Youth Advocates
Includes bibliography

Dear America: letters home from Vietnam; edited by Bernard Edelman for the New York Vietnam Veterans Memorial Commission. Norton 1985 316p il maps $13.95   **959.704**
1. Vietnam War, 1961-1975—Personal narratives
ISBN 0-393-01998-5   LC 85-273
Also available in paperback from Pocket Bks.
"The letters have been intelligently organized to follow a typical tour of duty in Vietnam. . . . Readers will be struck by the variations in attitudes reflected in these letters of the combatants. . . . This is a wonderful book of raw data for the reader to sift through and interpret." Readings

Denenberg, Barry
Voices from Vietnam. Scholastic 1995 249p $16.95   **959.704**
1. Vietnam War, 1961-1975
ISBN 0-590-44267-8   LC 93-44886
"Tracing the history of the Vietnam War in chronological sequence, the volume contains personal narratives of those who were involved—from presidents and generals to soldiers, nurses, and Vietnamese citizens. The disparate voices speak with insight, passion, and occasional graphic language to create a picture of war gone wrong, in this extremely powerful book." Horn Book Guide
Includes glossary and bibliography

Encyclopedia of the Vietnam War; editor in chief, Stanley I. Kutler. Scribner 1996 xxxiv, 711p il maps $99   **959.704**
1. Vietnam War, 1961-1975
ISBN 0-13-276932-8   LC 95-20940
This "work brings together the political, military, diplomatic, and cultural aspects of the war, with the most detailed focus on America's involvement. Many articles trace the historical background of Southeast Asia and the war's impact on the region and the wider world. . . . A chronology outlines Vietnam's early history, the French colonial era, growing U.S. intervention, full-scale war, and the aftermath, concluding with U.S. recognition in 1995." Booklist

Engelmann, Larry
Tears before the rain; an oral history of the last days of South Vietnam. Oxford Univ. Press 1990 375p il $22.95   **959.704**
1. Vietnam War, 1961-1975—Personal narratives
ISBN 0-19-505386-9   LC 89-26629
This book presents interviews with Americans and Vietnamese "about their experiences during the last days of the fall of Saigon in 1975." N Y Rev Books
"The book's only weakness is that it slights the American antiwar perspective. Otherwise, this is a very strong collection of interviews." Choice
Includes glossary

Everything we had; an oral history of the Vietnam War; by thirty-three American soldiers who fought it; [edited by] Al Santoli. Random House 1981 265p il o.p.; Ballantine Bks. paperback available $6.99   **959.704**
1. Vietnam War, 1961-1975 2. Veterans
ISBN 0-345-32279-7 (pa)   LC 80-5309
Interviews with 33 veterans assess the impact the Vietnam War has had on their lives
Includes glossary

FitzGerald, Frances, 1940-
Fire in the lake; the Vietnamese and the Americans in Vietnam. Little, Brown 1972 491p maps o.p.; Random House paperback available $15   **959.704**
1. Vietnam War, 1961-1975 2. Vietnam—Politics and government
ISBN 0-679-72394-3 (pa)
"An Atlantic Monthly Press book"
This book looks at the effects American intervention had on the Vietnamese social and intellectual landscape
Includes bibliography

Hendrickson, Paul
The living and the dead; Robert McNamara and five lives of a lost war. Knopf 1996 427p il $30   **959.704**
1. McNamara, Robert S., 1916- 2. Vietnam War, 1961-1975
ISBN 0-679-42761-9   LC 96-7445
In this look at the Vietnam War, the author "probes the histories of several men and women whose lives were irreversibly altered by the war: an Army nurse, a Quaker protester who immolated himself outside the Pentagon, a Marine helicopter gunner, and a Vietnamese politician. But the main exhibit here is the life and conscience of Robert McNamara." New Yorker
"Exhaustively researched, probing, important contribution to the annals of American history." Publ Wkly
Includes bibliographical references

Isserman, Maurice
The Vietnam War. Facts on File 1992 133p il maps (America at war) $17.95   **959.704**
1. Vietnam War, 1961-1975
ISBN 0-8160-2375-1   LC 91-21498
Discusses the historical and political background, military strategies, and battles of the Vietnam War
This book is "clear and well organized, covering both military and political history in chronological order. Isserman is objective about the war, showing readers how and why the U.S. became increasingly entangled in a situation it would not and eventually could not win." SLJ
Includes bibliographical references

Karnow, Stanley
Vietnam; a history. 2nd rev & updated ed. Penguin Bks. 1997 768p il maps pa $17.95   **959.704**
1. Vietnam War, 1961-1975 2. Vietnam—History
ISBN 0-14-026547-3
First published 1983

Karnow, Stanley—*Continued*

A summation "of over two centuries of conflict in Indochina. Chronicling a tragic history, Karnow presents a balanced and sympathetic view of Vietnamese aspirations and the mishaps that led to American involvement in a 'war nobody won.'" Voice Youth Advocates [review of 1983 edition]

Includes bibliographical references

Kovic, Ron

Born on the Fourth of July. McGraw-Hill 1976 208p o.p.; Pocket Bks. paperback available $5.50
                                                                                          959.704
1. Vietnam War, 1961-1975—Personal narratives
ISBN 0-671-73914-X (pa)

The autobiography of a young marine who was physically and emotionally scarred by his experience in Vietnam

Marrin, Albert, 1936-

America and Vietnam; the elephant and the tiger. Viking 1992 277p il maps $16   959.704
1. Vietnam War, 1961-1975
ISBN 0-670-84063-7   LC 91-28795

Examines the political history, military events, social impact, and long-term effects of the Vietnam War

"The prose is often pungent as brutal events are described. As he moves along in his account, Marrin occasionally interjects anecdotal material from his own experiences with individuals who fought in the war; these anecdotes do not intrude on his objective account but nicely suggest personal experience with his subject. The book explores the profound effects of the war on both countries." Horn Book

Mason, Robert, 1942-

Chickenhawk. Viking 1983 339p il map hardcover o.p. paperback available $11.95
                                                                                          959.704
1. Vietnam War, 1961-1975—Personal narratives
2. Vietnam War, 1961-1975—Aerial operations
ISBN 0-14-007218-7 (pa)   LC 82-42737

Companion volume Chickenhawk: back in the world available pa $10.95 (ISBN 0-14-015876-6)

This book describes Mason's experiences as an Army helicopter pilot in Vietnam

The author's "prose, low-keyed and carefully unemotional, lets the facts of misjudgment, destruction, mutilation, and death make their own cumulative and devastating effect. His report is exciting, and moving, and the ending is a bitter shock." Atl Mon

✓**Palmer, Laura**

Shrapnel in the heart; letters and remembrances from the Vietnam Veterans Memorial. Random House 1987 xx, 243p il $17.95; pa $11   959.704
1. Vietnam Veterans Memorial (Washington, D.C.)
2. Vietnam War, 1961-1975—Personal narratives
ISBN 0-394-56027-2; 0-394-75988-5 (pa)
                                                         LC 87-42652

"A collection of letters and poems that have been left at the Vietnam Veterans Memorial, with background information on the deceased and the bereaved writers." Booklist

Safer, Morley

Flashbacks: on returning to Vietnam. Random House 1990 206p $18.95   959.704
1. Vietnam—Description 2. Vietnam War, 1961-1975—Personal narratives
ISBN 0-394-58374-4   LC 89-24242

Also available in paperback from St. Martin's Press

"In 1965 Morley Safer accompanied a force of U.S. Marines on a search-and-destroy mission to the hamlet of Cam Ne. It was mostly destroy. The footage of troops burning peasant huts was seen by millions on the CBS News. It was an era of 'tragic foolishness,' says Safer in Flashbacks, an artful contrast of past and present that recalls a time when the typewriter, not the portable hair dryer, was the essential tool of the TV journalist." Time

Smith, Winnie

American daughter gone to war; on the front lines with an Army nurse in Vietnam. Morrow 1992 352p il $22   959.704
1. Vietnam War, 1961-1975—Personal narratives
ISBN 0-688-11188-2   LC 91-32138

Also available in paperback from Pocket Bks.

"A former member of the Army Nurse Corps who served in Vietnam recalls not only her tour of duty, but also her difficult adjustment to civilian life." Booklist

"An excellent picture of both the medical role in the war and war's cruel effect on the healers." Libr J

Summers, Harry G.

Historical atlas of the Vietnam War; [by] Harry G. Summers, Jr.; introduction and epilogue by Stanley Karnow. Houghton Mifflin 1995 224p il maps $39.95   959.704
1. Vietnam War, 1961-1975 2. Vietnam—Politics and government
ISBN 0-395-72223-3   LC 95-22200

The author begins by reviewing Vietnam's geography, culture, and military and diplomatic history over the past century. The roles of China and France in the region are described along with the evolution of United States involvement

"The details in the 100 four-color maps, the 100 pertinent photos, the effective use of quotations, and an index of places and names make this book an excellent addition for high-school, public, and academic libraries." Booklist

✓Vietnam War almanac; [by] Harry G. Summers, Jr. Facts on File 1985 414p il $27.95; pa $14.95
                                                                                          959.704
1. Vietnam War, 1961-1975
ISBN 0-8160-1017-X; 0-8160-1813-8 (pa)
                                                         LC 83-14054

"Provides a clear, accessible, and objective look at the conflict that shaped a generation. Includes an introductory history of the country and a description of the physical and historical conditions that shaped American policy there; a chronology of events, both in Vietnam and in the United States; and 500 articles." N Y Public Libr. Book of How & Where to Look It Up

The **Vietnam** war: opposing viewpoints; William
Dudley & David Bender, book editors. 2nd ed,
rev. Greenhaven Press 1990 240p il map lib bdg
$19.95; pa $11.95   **959.704**
1. Vietnam War, 1961-1975
ISBN 0-89908-478-8 (lib bdg); 0-89908-453-2 (pa)
                                                    LC 90-39794
"Opposing viewpoints series"
Replaces the edition published 1984 under the
editorship of David L. Bender
Presents opposing viewpoints on various aspects of the
Vietnam War, including the reasons for American involvement, the failure of United States policy there, and
the effects on veterans
"The editors have taken care to include a balance of
opinion. Political cartoons illustrate the text, which contains . . . curriculum-related activities and excellent bibliographies." Booklist

Wormser, Richard, 1933-
Three faces of Vietnam; [by] Richard L.
Wormser. Watts 1993 157p il lib bdg $19.86
                                                    959.704
1. Vietnam War, 1961-1975
ISBN 0-531-11142-3   LC 93-11099
This book examines the Vietnam War from the perspectives of antiwar protesters, the Vietnamese people,
and the American soldiers who fought in the war
"The tone of the book never becomes dry, and facts
about the conflict are always focused or exemplified
through the often terrible personal experiences of individuals, making this a strong complement to more straightforward chronologies." Bull Cent Child Books
Includes bibliography

959.9   Philippines

Karnow, Stanley
In our image; America's empire in the
Philippines. Random House 1989 494p il maps
$24.95   **959.9**
1. Philippines—History
ISBN 0-394-54975-9   LC 88-42676
Also available in paperback from Foreign Policy Assn.
A history of American involvement in the Philippines
from 1898 to the present
The author's "treatment of the indecisiveness of Presi-
dent McKinley over the issue of empire and of the ego-
tistical General MacArthur make the work a definite purchase for libraries. . . . Those who love swashbuckling
history will enjoy this work." Libr J
Includes bibliographical references

960   Africa

Africa; edited by Phyllis M. Martin and Patrick
O'Meara; maps and charts by Cathryn L.
Lombardi and John M. Hollingsworth. 3rd ed.
Indiana Univ. Press 1995 448p il maps $39.95;
pa $18.75   **960**
1. Africa
ISBN 0-253-32916-7; 0-253-20984-6 (pa)
                                                    LC 95-5772
First published 1977

This collection of essays covers African history, politics, colonial heritage, economics, fine arts, literature,
popular culture, music, sociology, and law. A bibliographic essay concludes the volume

Africa: opposing viewpoints; Carol Wekesser,
book editor; Christina Pierce, assistant editor.
Greenhaven Press 1992 240p il $19.95; pa
$11.95   **960**
1. Africa
ISBN 0-89908-186-X; 0-89908-161-4 (pa)
                                                    LC 91-42292
"Opposing viewpoints series"
Replaces Problems of Africa: opposing viewpoints,
published 1986 under the editorship of Janelle Rohr
This book offers various views on the effects of colo-
nialism, famine, Western aid to African nations, and
apartheid
Includes bibliographical references

Africa's glorious legacy; by the editors of
Time-Life Books. Time-Life Bks. 1994 168p il
maps (Lost civilizations) $18.95   **960**
1. Excavations (Archeology)—Africa 2. Africa—An-
tiquities 3. African civilization
                                                    LC 94-916
Using archeological evidence, this book explores civi-
lizations from Africa's past, including ancient Nubia; the
Kingdoms of Ghana, Mali and Benin; and peoples of
Great Zimbabwe
Includes biblographical references

Davidson, Basil, 1914-
Africa in history; themes and outlines. rev and
expanded ed. Collier Bks. 1991 425p o.p.; Simon
& Schuster paperback available $16   **960**
1. Africa—History
ISBN 0-684-82667-4 (pa)   LC 90-23905
First published 1966 with title: Africa: history of a
continent
Among the topics discussed are Africa's diverse re-
gional differences, apartheid, the rise of Islam, tribal mo-
res, slavery and colonization
Includes bibliographical references

The lost cities of Africa. rev ed. Little, Brown
1970 xxiii, 366p il maps hardcover o.p. paperback
available $14.95   **960**
1. Africa—Antiquities 2. African civilization
ISBN 0-316-17431-9 (pa)
"An Atlantic Monthly Press book"
First published 1959
"This book is about Africa and Africans south of the
Sahara Desert, during the fifteen hundred years or so before the colonial period began. Its aim is to present in
outline what is now known and what it now seems reasonable to believe about some leading aspects and
achievements of African life and civilization during that
time." p xx
Includes bibliography

✓ **Dostert, Pierre Etienne**
Africa. Stryker-Post Publs. il maps (World today series) pa $11.50   **960**
1. Africa
ISSN 0084-2281
Annual. First published 1966
Surveys the history, politics, culture and economy of the countries of Africa

Fage, J. D. (John Donnelly)
A history of Africa. 3rd ed. Routledge 1995 595p il pa $24.95   **960**
1. Africa—History
ISBN 0-415-12721-1   LC 95-5789
First published 1978
A narrative history of the continent from prehistoric times to the 1994 South African elections. The author explores the effect on Africa of the collapse of the Soviet Union and the ending of the Cold War, the rise of Islamic fundamentalism, famine, postcolonialism, tribal conflict, foreign debt and warfare
Includes bibliographical references

✓ **Jones, Constance, 1961-**
Africa, 1500-1900. Facts on File 1993 140p il maps (World history library) $17.95   **960**
1. Africa—History
ISBN 0-8160-2774-9   LC 92-22677
Examines the history of Africa from the sixteenth through the nineteenth century, discussing such topics as the different cultures that have existed on the continent, the importance of Islam, European colonization, and the slave trade
"Clear, uncluttered black-and-white maps and historical photographs are interspersed throughout. The book is nicely laid out, with lots of boldface type to break up the text. There is an excellent chronology, and the list for further reading includes both fiction and nonfiction titles." SLJ

✓ **Wepman, Dennis**
Africa: the struggle for independence. Facts on File 1993 151p il maps (World history library) $17.95   **960**
1. Africa—History
ISBN 0-8160-2820-6   LC 93-20020
"Acknowledging the historic traditions of early Africa, Wepman focuses on the cruel and arbitrary division of the continent by European countries, and the struggle of various African regions against colonial rule. The style is accessible, and the approach is never simplistic." Booklist
Includes bibliographical references

962   Egypt and Sudan

Moorehead, Alan, 1910-1983
The Blue Nile. rev ed. Harper & Row 1972 336p il maps   **962**
1. Nile River 2. Africa—History 3. Africa—Exploration 4. Explorers
Available in hardcover from Amereon

First published 1962
This book "deals with events from 1798 to 1869 on the Blue Nile and the main stream that descends from Ethiopia through the Sudan and Egypt to the sea. Thus it complements 'The White Nile,' which is concerned with the years between 1856 and 1900, and completes my study of the history of the river in the nineteenth century." Author's note
Includes bibliography

967   Central Africa and offshore islands

Davidson, Basil, 1914-
The African slave trade. rev and expanded ed. Little, Brown 1980 304p il maps hardcover o.p. paperback available $12.95   **967**
1. Central Africa—History 2. Slave trade
ISBN 0-316-17438-6 (pa)   LC 81-65588
"An Atlantic Monthly Press book"
First published 1961 with title: Black mother
An account of the slave trade and its impact on West African society
Includes bibliography

The search for Africa; history, culture, politics. Times Bks. 1994 373p $25; pa $14   **967**
1. Sub-Saharan Africa—Politics and government
2. South Africa—Politics and government
ISBN 0-8129-2278-6; 0-8129-2527-0 (pa)
          LC 93-28690
A compilation of articles "written between the 1950s and the early 1990s. The essays deal with the corruption of racist colonialism, the liberation movements across the continent, the struggle against apartheid, and the failures of contemporary African political states. As these essays make clear throughout, Davidson has remained hopeful for Africa." Libr J
Includes bibliographical references

967.62   Kenya

Dinesen, Isak, 1885-1962
Out of Africa and Shadows on the grass. Vintage Bks. 1989 462p pa $13   **967.62**
1. Kenya
ISBN 0-679-72475-3   LC 89-40144
A combined edition of two titles first published 1938 and 1960 respectively
Out of Africa records the experiences and observations of the author's years on a farm in Kenya. Much of the book centers on the manners and customs of the natives and their outlook on life. Shadows on the grass consists of four short essays which present the author's recollections of her servants in Africa

968 Southern Africa. Republic of South Africa

Illustrated history of South Africa; the real story. expanded 3rd ed completely updated. Reader's Digest Assn. 1994 559p il maps $30   **968**
1. South Africa—History
ISBN 0-947008-90-X
First published 1988 in South Africa; first United States edition 1989
At head of title: Reader's Digest
This history of South Africa covers early civilizations, the impact of European settlement on the native population, the economics of the diamond and gold trades, conflicting goals of Africans, Afrikaners, and the British, and significant events of the 20th century including the growth of Afrikaner nationalism, and the end of apartheid

Sparks, Allister
The mind of South Africa. Knopf 1990 424p o.p.   **968**
1. South Africa—Race relations
LC 89-45890
"An eminent liberal Johannesburg journalist looks at his country from the earliest times when blacks first came there through the present seething confrontation between the 'neo-apartheid' government and the forces of resistance. Sparks synthesizes individual experience and global politics, past and present." Booklist
Includes bibliography

Thompson, Leonard Monteath
A history of South Africa; [by] Leonard Thompson. rev ed. Yale Univ. Press 1995 xx, 332p il maps $40; pa $17   **968**
1. South Africa—History
ISBN 0-300-06542-6; 0-300-06543-4 (pa)
LC 95-32729
First published 1990
This "exploration of South Africa's history—from the earliest known human settlement of the region to the present—focuses primarily on the experiences of its black inhabitants, rather than on those of its white minority." Publisher's note
Includes bibliographical references

968.04 Southern Africa—1814-1910

Pakenham, Thomas, 1933-
The Boer War. illustrated ed. Random House 1994 c1993 304p il maps $40   **968.04**
1. South African War, 1899-1902
ISBN 0-679-43047-4   LC 93-26234
An illustrated abridged edition of the title published 1979; this edition first published 1993 in the United Kingdom
This history of the Boer War, fought 1899-1902 in South Africa, is based on primary source material including private papers, letters, and diaries of officers and enlisted men. The author also interviewed 52 elderly veterans

968.06 Republic of South Africa, 1961-

Biko, Stephen, 1946-1977
I write what I like; [by] Steve Biko; a selection of his writings edited with a personal memoir by Aelred Stubbs. Harper & Row 1979 c1978 216p o.p.; LPC/InBook paperback available $14.95
968.06
1. South Africa—Race relations 2. South Africa—Politics and government
ISBN 0-906097-49-5 (pa)   LC 78-19499
First published 1978 in the United Kingdom
"This selection of writings by the South African black leader who died in custody . . . contains letters, addresses, conference papers and articles written for the newsletter of the South African Student's Organization." Publ Wkly
"Readers will find [Biko's] essential humaneness, intelligence, and lack of malice as impressive as his eloquence and compelling arguments." Libr J

Bradley, Catherine
The end of apartheid. Raintree Steck-Vaughn 1996 79p il maps (Causes and consequences) lib bdg $25.69   **968.06**
1. Apartheid 2. South Africa—Race relations
ISBN 0-8172-4055-1   LC 95-17669
Traces the origins of apartheid, the struggle against it, and the changes in South African society that brought about its end
Includes bibliographical references

Finnegan, William
Crossing the line; a year in the land of apartheid. Harper & Row 1986 418p il maps o.p.; University of Calif. Press paperback available $13
968.06
1. South Africa—Race relations 2. High schools—South Africa 3. Discrimination in education
ISBN 0-520-08872-7 (pa)   LC 85-45633
The author, an American school teacher, recalls his experiences in the segregated black schools of South Africa

Malan, Rian
My traitor's heart; a South African exile returns to face his country, his tribe, and his conscience. Atlantic Monthly Press 1990 349p o.p.; Vintage Bks. paperback available $14   **968.06**
1. South Africa—Race relations 2. South Africa—Social conditions
ISBN 0-679-73215-2 (pa)   LC 89-15169
"A Morgan Entrekin book"
This is an "account of an Afrikaner's life in apartheid South Africa. . . . [Malan] left South Africa in 1977, in part to avoid military service, and returned eight years later. This book reports his observations of violent death in the land." Libr J
The author's "informal style shows a reporter's awareness of human story and social issue, a novelist's sense of character and scene, a participant's anguish. The reader is profoundly moved." Booklist

Mandela, Nelson

Nelson Mandela speaks; forging a democratic nonracial South Africa. Pathfinder Press 1993 296p il map lib bdg $50; pa $18.95 **968.06**
1. African National Congress 2. South Africa—Politics and government 3. Apartheid
ISBN 0-87348-775-3 (lib bdg); 0-87348-774-5 (pa)
LC 93-85689
In this volume "the South African leader's significant speeches, letters, and interviews from the period since his February 1990 release from prison are brought together. . . . [The editor] provides a useful glossary and chronology of the 1990-93 period, and supplies a brief introduction to each entry." Booklist

Sparks, Allister

Tomorrow is another country; the inside story of South Africa's road to change. Hill & Wang 1995 254p il $22 **968.06**
1. South Africa—Politics and government 2. South Africa—Race relations
ISBN 0-8090-9405-3 LC 94-79508
Also available in paperback from University of Chicago Press
This is an account "of South Africa's political transformation from the mid-1980s to the elections of April 1994. . . . [Much of the book] is devoted to the details of the secret negotiations that went on for five years before the 1990 release of Nelson Mandela from prison." Libr J
The author "has written a gripping, fast-paced, authoritative account. . . . Like John Reed's classic 'Ten Days That Shook the World,' Mr. Sparks's book is the work of a fine reporter who was in the right place at the right time." N Y Times Book Rev
Includes bibliographical references

Tutu, Desmond

The words of Desmond Tutu; selected by Naomi Tutu. Newmarket Press 1989 109p il $12.95; pa $7.95 **968.06**
1. South Africa—Race relations
ISBN 1-55704-038-9; 1-55704-215-2 (pa)
LC 88-34567
"This title contains quotations selected by Tutu's daughter Naomi, ranging in length from one sentence to one page. . . . The selections are separated into the topical categories of Apartheid, Faith and Responsibility, Nonviolence and Violence, Family, The Community—Black and White, and Toward a New South Africa." Voice Youth Advocates
Includes bibliographical references

968.91 Zimbabwe

Lessing, Doris May, 1919-

African laughter; four visits to Zimbabwe; [by] Doris Lessing. HarperCollins Pubs. 1992 442p hardcover o.p. paperback available $13 **968.91**
1. Zimbabwe
ISBN 0-06-092433-0 (pa) LC 92-52590
"After the wars fought by black nationalists for the liberation of Rhodesia ended in 1980 and the nation of Zimbabwe came into being, Lessing was able to return to the homeland that had officially exiled her 25 years earlier because of her opposition to the white government. The distinguished novelist . . . details four trips she made to Zimbabwe in 1982, 1988, 1989, and 1992 in a series of haunting vignettes dealing with facets of life there." Publ Wkly

970 North America

Morgan, Ted, 1932-

Wilderness at dawn; the settling of the North American continent. Simon & Schuster 1993 541p il maps hardcover o.p. paperback available $15 **970**
1. North America—History 2. United States—History—1600-1775, Colonial period 3. Canada—History—0-1763 (New France)
ISBN 0-671-88237-6 (pa) LC 93-2628
The author discusses "movements of people into what is today the US, from the arrival of the earliest hunters approximately 15,000 years ago to the colonists of the late 18th century." Choice
Morgan "tells a good story, emphasizing the ordinary people who did the actual settlement. . . . A useful survey of the colonial frontier." Libr J
Includes bibliographical references

970.004 North American native peoples

Acatos, Sylvio

Pueblos; prehistoric Indian cultures of the Southwest; Maximilien Bruggmann, photographs; Sylvio Acatos, text; translated by Barbara Fritzemeier; Wolfgang Lindig, foreword. Facts on File 1990 240p il maps $45 **970.004**
1. Pueblo Indians 2. Southwestern States—Antiquities
ISBN 0-8160-2437-5 LC 89-49601
"The text offers an archaeological investigation of prehistoric civilization in Utah, Colorado, Arizona, and New Mexico. The approach is thematic, with chapters concentrating on architecture, daily life, pottery, and social and religious traditions rounding out strictly historical discussions." Booklist
Includes bibliographical references

Algonquians of the East Coast; by the editors of Time-Life Books. Time-Life Bks. 1995 175p il maps (American Indians) $19.95 **970.004**
1. Algonquian Indians

LC 95-35037
This book describes the history and customs of "the Abanaki, Micmacs, Penobscot, Pequots and Narragansetts of New England; Lenni Lenape of Delaware; Powhattans of Virginia and Lumbee of North Carolina." Publisher's note
Includes bibliographical references

America's fascinating Indian heritage. Reader's Digest Assn. 1990 c1978 416p il maps $30

        970.004

1. Indians of North America
ISBN 0-89577-372-4
First published 1978
At head of title: Reader's Digest

Discusses the "customs, history, and art of every major tribe in North America. Laid out regionally and chronologically, it is an ideal reference. The maps, drawings, and diagrams bring the well-written text to life." SLJ

Bancroft-Hunt, Norman

The Indians of the Great Plains; photographs by Werner Forman. Bedrick Bks. 1989 c1981 128p il map (Echoes of the ancient world) o.p.; University of Okla. Press paperback available $22.95

        970.004

1. Indians of North America—Great Plains
ISBN 0-8061-2465-2 (pa)   LC 88-7676
First published 1981 in the United Kingdom

Photographs of indigenous artwork and the country in which these tribes lived illustrate this introduction to the history and culture of the various Great Plains tribes
Includes bibliography

Bierhorst, John

The way of the earth; Native America and the environment. Morrow 1994 329p il $15   **970.004**

1. Indians—Folklore 2. Ecology 3. Nature
ISBN 0-688-11560-8   LC 93-28971

"Bierhorst looks at how various Native peoples transmit environmental wisdom and knowledge through their myths, stories, parables, and proverbs. Broadly divided into five parts covering personality, kinship, restraint, death, and renewal, the author ranges up and down the Americas drawing parallels from the traditions of numerous cultures." SLJ

"A synthesis of rare integrity, this will prove valuable for research, reference, informational browsing." Bull Cent Child Books

Includes bibliography

Bordewich, Fergus M.

Killing the white man's Indian; the reinvention of Native Americans at the end of the 20th century. Doubleday 1996 400p $27.50; pa $14

        970.004

1. Indians of North America
ISBN 0-385-42035-8; 0-385-42036-6 (pa)

        LC 95-23069

In separate chapters the author examines "historic Indian-white relations, modern Indian identity, the revival of tribal authority, Indians and environmentalism, conflicts between reinvigorated Indian property rights and archaeological research, new Indian claims to lands said to be sacred, Indian alcoholism, the reservation-based system of Indian colleges, and the promise and perils of growing economic and political cooperation with the world beyond the reservation." Booklist

Brooks, Drex

Sweet medicine; sites of Indian massacres, battlefields, and treaties; photographs by Drex Brooks; essay by Patricia Nelson Limerick; foreword by James Welch. University of N.M. Press 1995 163p il $50   **970.004**

1. Indians of North America—Wars
ISBN 0-8263-1538-0   LC 94-6689

For this book, Brooks located and photographed the sites of wars between Indians and whites. "Arranged chronologically by event, the 'story' begins with Plymouth Rock (1620) and ends with a little-known 1898 Minnesota skirmish. . . . An intriguing essay by historian Limerick challenges the reader to look beyond the elements of battle, to appreciate the very human concerns of combatants on both sides, and to view both Indians and whites as full participants in our nation's history." Libr J

Includes bibliographical references

Brown, Dee Alexander

Bury my heart at Wounded Knee; an Indian history of the American West. Holt & Co. 1970 487p il $27.50; pa $14.95   **970.004**

1. Indians of North America—West (U.S.) 2. West (U.S.)—History 3. Indians of North America—Wars
ISBN 0-8050-1045-9; 0-8050-1730-5 (pa)

This is an account of the experience of the American Indian during the white man's expansion westward

"A gripping chronicle of 30 years of conflict between Native Americans and whites." Rochman. Against borders

Includes bibliography

The **Buffalo** hunters; by the editors of Time-Life Books. Time-Life Bks. 1993 192p il (American Indians) $18.95   **970.004**

1. Indians of North America—Great Plains 2. Bison

        LC 92-39726

An illustrated look at the nomadic lifestyle centered on buffalo hunts that developed among the tribes of the western Plains

Includes bibliographical references

Chroniclers of Indian life; by the editors of Time-Life Books; with text by Stephen G. Hyslop. Time-Life Bks. 1996 192p (American Indians) $18.95   **970.004**

1. Indians of North America

        LC 95-45627

This illustrated look at various Native American cultures includes accounts of explorers, missionaries, captives, ethnographers, artists, and Indian chroniclers themselves

Includes bibliographical references

Chronology of Native North American history; from Pre-Columbian times to the present; Duane Champagne, editor. Gale Res. 1994 lxxv, 574p il maps $59.95   **970.004**

1. Indians of North America
ISBN 0-8103-9195-3   LC 94-18455

"The book opens with brief chronologies of two dozen tribes, noting relocations, establishment of tribal govern-

Chronology of Native North American history—
Continued

ment, etc. The lengthy introduction is an in-depth history of Native American peoples. . . . The chronology is in three parts: 50,000 B.C.—A.D. 1492, 1500-1959, and 1960-1994. Events are listed sequentially; there are no subdivisions for arts, politics, etc. Each section is handsomely supplied with pictures, photographs, and maps. At the end of the chronology are brief biographies of American Indian orators and summaries of important historical documents and legal cases." Booklist

Cordell, Linda S.

Ancient Pueblo peoples. Smithsonian Bks. 1995 c1994 176p il (Exploring the ancient world) $19.95   **970.004**
1. Pueblo Indians 2. Southwestern States—Antiquities
ISBN 0-89599-038-5   LC 94-2308
The author explores the archaeological links between the prehistoric Mogollon and Anasazi cultures and the various Pueblo peoples of today
Includes bibliographical references

Crow Dog, Leonard, 1942-

Crow Dog; four generations of Sioux medicine men; [by] Leonard Crow Dog and Richard Erdoes. HarperCollins Pubs. 1995 243p il $25; pa $13
                                                    970.004
1. American Indian Movement 2. Dakota Indians
ISBN 0-06-016861-7; 0-06-092682-1 (pa)
                                        LC 94-40695
Erdoes has recorded Leonard Crow Dog's oral narrative of the history of his family and his people, the Lakota. Mr. Crow Dog discusses "the generations of his family who have carried the name Crow Dog since the American government told them it would be their family name. . . . He tells of his involvement as the spiritual leader of the American Indian Movement and the occupation of Wounded Knee in the early 1970's." Booklist
"Through the experiences of this family of great medicine men, readers are taken on an intimate journey through 120 years of Lakota history. Events that will already be familiar to some readers are recounted within a moving spiritual framework." Libr J

Cycles of life; by the editors of Time-Life Books. Time-Life Bks. 1994 176p il (American Indians) $18.95   **970.004**
1. Indians of North America—Social life and customs
                                        LC 93-27327
"Concentrating on growing up, rites of passage (especially puberty ceremonies and courtship and marriage), and spiritual beliefs and religion, the editors have created a kaleidoscopic yet focused tour through Indian America both past and present. Although the emphasis leans towards the peoples west of the Mississippi, examples from eastern tribes are provided as well." SLJ
Includes bibliographical references

Debo, Angie, 1890-1988

A history of the Indians of the United States. University of Okla. Press 1970 386p il maps (Civilization of the American Indian series) hardcover o.p. paperback available $17.95
                                                    970.004
1. Indians of North America
ISBN 0-8061-1888-1 (pa)
This historical survey of the Indians of North America, including the Eskimos and Aleuts of Alaska, discusses the first meetings with European explorers, their dispossession by colonial expansion, and their relations with the new American republic
Includes bibliography

Deloria, Vine

American Indians, American justice; by Vine Deloria, Jr. and Clifford M. Lytle. University of Tex. Press 1983 262p hardcover o.p. paperback available $12.95   **970.004**
1. Indians of North America—Government relations
2. Courts—United States
ISBN 0-292-73834-X (pa)   LC 83-6975
The authors "trace the history of the federal government's involvement in the legal affairs of American Indians from the first treaties to the present. The federal court system is contrasted with the evolution of tribal forms of government and tribal court systems." Libr J
Includes bibliography

Custer died for your sins; an Indian manifesto; by Vine Deloria, Jr. Macmillan 1969 279p o.p.; University of Okla. Press paperback available $14.95   **970.004**
1. Indians of North America
ISBN 0-8061-2129-7 (pa)
The author examines how anthropologists, missionaries, and government agencies have mistreated American Indians

Dictionary of daily life of Indians of the Americas. American Indian Pubs. 1981 2v il lib bdg set $195   **970.004**
1. Indians—Dictionaries
ISBN 0-937862-26-6   LC 82-1761
New edition in preparation
This "dictionary offers a scholarly approach to the study of American Indian culture. The entries are arranged alphabetically. . . . Information covers the cultural periods before the arrival of Columbus, the changes during the period of European intervention in Indian lifeways, as well as the present status of Inuit and Indian people of the North American continent, including Latin America." Kuipers. Am Indian Ref Books for Child & Young Adults

Encyclopedia of North American Indians; Frederick E. Hoxie, editor. Houghton Mifflin 1996 756p il maps $45   **970.004**
1. Indians of North America—Dictionaries
ISBN 0-395-66921-9   LC 96-21411
"More than 260 authorities, many of whom are Indian, contributed to this single-volume work. It includes four

Encyclopedia of North American Indians—*Continued*

types of entries: descriptions of tribes; biographical sketches selected to provide regional representation; overview interpretive essays on cultural and historical topics; and definitions for often misunderstood terms." Libr J

The **First** Americans; by the editors of Time-Life Books. Time-Life Bks. 1992 183p il maps (American Indians) $18.95   **970.004**
1. Indians of North America
                LC 92-6548

An illustrated look at Native American social customs, crafts, religion and culture
Includes bibliography

The **First** Americans series. Facts on File 1991-1992 8v il maps ea $21.95   **970.004**
1. Indians of North America
Contents: California Indians, by C. L. Keyworth; Indians of the Arctic and Subarctic, by P. Younkin; Indians of the Northeast, by C. G. Calloway; Indians of the Pacific Northwest, by K. Liptak; Indians of the Plains, by E. K. Andrews; Indians of the Plateau and Great Basin, by V. Sherrow; Indians of the Southeast, by R. E. Mancini; Indians of the Southwest, by K. Liptak

"Each of the eight volumes in [this] series focuses on the major North American tribes in one region. . . . Describing the social, political, and religious life of major tribes . . . each volume has four chapters, concluding with eight-page photo-essays in color. . . . These books offer a manageable overview . . . while emphasizing the uniqueness of each tribe." Booklist

Francis, Lee
Native time: an historical time line of native America. St. Martin's Press 1996 356p il map $35
                        970.004
1. Indians of North America
ISBN 0-312-13129-1   LC 95-8027
This "volume traces a year-by-year history of Native Americans in four categories: history, law, and politics; literature, art, legend, and stories; heroes, leaders, and victims; and elder wisdom, philosophy, and songs. The time line begins in the year 200,000 B.C.E., when Native American civilizations flourished prior to the arrival of Columbus, and ends up almost in the present day. . . . This highly illustrated volume is useful as a handy ready-reference guide." Libr J
Includes bibliographical references

From the heart; voices of the American Indian; edited and with narrative by Lee Miller. Knopf 1995 405p il $24; pa $14   **970.004**
1. Indians of North America
ISBN 0-679-43549-2; 0-679-76891-2 (pa)
                LC 94-28492

An anthology of excerpts from speeches by Native Americans from the 16th to the 19th centuries
"Arranged by region and chronology, these extraordinarily moving extracts are placed into appropriate historical context by Miller's descriptive narrative. In addition, pertinent quotations of non-Indian witnesses are also included. A haunting and eloquent anthology." Booklist
Includes bibliographical references

Gerber, Peter R.
Indians of the Northwest coast; photographs by Maximilien Bruggmann; text by Peter R. Gerber; translated by Barbara Fitzmeier. Facts on File 1989 232p il $45   **970.004**
1. Indians of North America—Northwest Coast of North America
ISBN 0-8160-2028-0   LC 89-1330
The author "incorporates the history of the peoples of the Northwest Coast and their extraordinary artifacts into a portrait of the present. . . . Throughout his text, he puts artifacts in the context of kinship systems, class structure, religious practices, and historical development." Christ Sci Monit
Includes bibliography

Gilbert, Joan
The Trail of Tears across Missouri. University of Mo. Press 1996 122p il map (Missouri heritage readers series) pa $9.95   **970.004**
1. Cherokee Indians
ISBN 0-8262-1063-5   LC 96-10232
"Gilbert retells the tragic story of the removal of the Cherokees from their established homes in the southeastern United States to the Indian Territory that is now Oklahoma. . . . This title would be an excellent addition to both school and public libraries with an interest in Native American or Midwest cultural history." Libr J
Includes bibliographical references

Goetzmann, William H.
The first Americans; photographs from the Library of Congress; text by William H. Geotzmann. Starwood Pub. 1991 144p il (Library of Congress classics) $34.95   **970.004**
1. Indians of North America—Pictorial works
ISBN 0-912347-96-1   LC 91-12662
"This volume demonstrates that melodramatic images created by commercial photographers of the late 19th and early 20th centuries perpetuated fallacies about Native Americans. Goetzmann . . . selects photos of 'real Indians' and costumed actors, and explains how professional photographers and artists interpreted Native American culture according to classical and romantic ideals. The work of Edward S. Curtis, who attempted to document the tribal way of life, is well represented here." Publ Wkly
Includes bibliographical references

Gravelle, Karen
Soaring spirits; conversations with Native American teens. Watts 1995 128p il maps (American Indian experience) lib bdg $22
                        970.004
1. Indians of North America 2. Youth
ISBN 0-531-11221-7   LC 95-6822
In this book "about growing up Native American today, teenagers from the Mohawk, Anishnabe, Quinault, Shinnecock, Cherokee, and Pueblo peoples speak about themselves. Gravelle interviewed and photographed 17 young people on Indian reservations across the country. They speak candidly in many voices about family,

Gravelle, Karen—_Continued_
school, community, dating, religion, sports, work, etc.
. . . Teens everywhere will recognize the conflict in living between two cultures." Booklist
Includes bibliographical references

Griffin-Pierce, Trudy
The encyclopedia of Native America. Viking
1995 192p il $25 **970.004**
1. Indians of North America
ISBN 0-670-85104-3 LC 94-61491
"Each chapter covers a specific geographical area of
the United States, such as The Great Plains or the Southwest, and the tribes that resided there. Topics include
languages of tribes with a map showing where each language group lived, descriptions of each tribe and its way
of life, and European contact with the tribes and the results. Along with historical information about the tribes,
Griffin-Pierce has included information on the present-day status of Native Americans." Booklist

Handbook of North American Indians; William C.
Sturtevant, general editor. Smithsonian
Institution Press 1978- il maps prices vary per
volume **970.004**
1. Indians of North America
LC 77-17162
Also available in hardcover from U.S. Government
Printing Office, Superintendent of Documents
Volumes available are: v4 History of Indian-white relations; Wilcomb E. Washburn, volume editor $51 (ISBN
0-87474-184-X); v5 Arctic; David Damas, volume editor
$52 (ISBN 0-87474-185-8); v6 Subarctic; June Helm,
volume editor $51 (ISBN 0-87474-186-6); v7 Northwest
coast; Wayne Suttles, volume editor $51 (ISBN 0-87474-
187-4); v8 California; Robert F. Heizer, volume editor
$51 (ISBN 0-87474-188-2); v9-10 Southwest; Alfonso
Ortiz, volume editor v9 $49, v10 $52 (ISBN 0-87474-
189-0; 0-87474-190-4); v11 Great Basin; Warren L.
D'Azevedo, volume editor $52 (ISBN 0-87474-191-2);
v15 Northeast; Bruce G. Trigger, volume editor $53
(ISBN 0-87474-195-5); v17 Languages; Ives Goddard,
volume editor $74 (ISBN 0-87474-197-1)
"This projected twenty-one volume set . . . gives an
encyclopedic summary of current historical-cultural
knowledge of North American Indians. Extensively researched, readable essays are accompanied by illustrations, maps, and bibliographies." Ref Sources for Small
& Medium-sized Libr. 5th edition
Includes bibliographies

Hirschfelder, Arlene B.
The Native American almanac; a portrait of
Native America today; [by] Arlene Hirschfelder,
Martha Kreipe de Montaño. Prentice Hall General
Ref. 1993 341p il maps $25 **970.004**
1. Indians of North America
ISBN 0-671-85012-1 LC 93-1057
This almanac contains "15 chapters covering demographics, law, treaties, relations with the federal government, tribal government, language, education, religion,
games and sports, media, and an extensive bibliography.
Also included are lists of tribes, reservations, treaties, as
well as a chronology. . . . An unusual, informative reference work." Libr J

Hoig, Stan
Night of the cruel moon; Cherokee removal and
the Trail of Tears. Facts on File 1996 138p il
(Library of American Indian history) $17.95; pa
$9.95 **970.004**
1. Cherokee Indians
ISBN 0-8160-3307-2; 0-8160-3491-5 (pa)
LC 95-22039
A narrative history of the removal by white Americans
of the Cherokee peoples from their eastern homeland to
the Indian territory now known as Oklahoma
"The narrative, packed with details and well-documented information, is not a personalized account
but a very factual record of the events that occurred.
. . . Hoig clearly shows the complexity of the situation."
Booklist
Includes bibliography

Houston, James A., 1921-
Confessions of an igloo dweller; [by] James
Houston. Houghton Mifflin 1996 c1995 320p il
$24.95 **970.004**
1. Inuit
ISBN 0-395-78890-0 LC 96-1852
"A Peter Davison book"
The author "recounts his experiences living in Canada's northernmost reaches from 1948 to 1962. . . . He
brings intensely alive the look and smell and feel of the
region while providing a portrait of himself and his family. Houston includes a large number of his own black-and-white sketches to add grace to a charming book."
Libr J

Hunters of the northern forests; by the editors of
Time-Life Books. Time-Life Bks. 1995 184p il
(American Indians) $18.95 **970.004**
1. Indians of North America
LC 95-5374
Describes in text and illustrations the history, customs,
mythology, and social institutions of the Montagnais,
Chipewyans, Cree, Koyukon and other native peoples of
Alaska and Canada
Includes bibliographical references

The Indians of California; by the editors of
Time-Life Books. Time-Life Bks. 1994 192p il
(American Indians) $18.95 **970.004**
1. Indians of North America—California
LC 94-4835
Text and numerous illustrations examine the impact of
the Spanish mission system and the gold rush on California's native culture
"This excellent book offers something for nearly every
level of reader, and its exquisite photographs warrant
sufficient reason to recommend it for both educational
and general audiences." Sci Books Films
Includes bibliographical references

Josephy, Alvin M., 1915-
500 nations; an illustrated history of North
American Indians; based on a documentary
filmscript by Jack Leustig [et al.]; with
contributions by John M.D. Pohl. Knopf 1994
468p il maps $50   **970.004**
1. Indians of North America
ISBN 0-679-42930-1   LC 94-29695
A "chronological overview of the history of North
American Indians from the ancient legends of the peoples' origins to the problems faced during the Western
expansion to the present. . . . The narrative is brought
to life by excerpts from journals and diaries as well as
through contemporary interviews. The book is beautifully
and colorfully illustrated with 485 paintings, drawings,
prints, historical photographs, and artifacts." SLJ
Includes bibliographical references

Mather, Christine
Native America; arts, traditions, and
celebrations; photographs by Jack Parsons; design
by Paul Hardy. Potter 1990 240p il $40   **970.004**
1. Indians of North America—Social life and customs
2. Indians of North America—Art
ISBN 0-517-57436-5   LC 90-7059
An illustrated look at the various arts of Native Americans

Native America in the twentieth century; an
encyclopedia; edited by Mary B. Davis; assistant
editors, Joan Berman, Mary E. Graham, Lisa A.
Mitten. Garland 1994 xxxvii, 787p il maps
(Garland reference library of social science)
$105.75; pa $24.95   **970.004**
1. Indians of North America—Dictionaries
ISBN 0-8240-4846-6; 0-8153-2583-5 (pa)
       LC 94-768
This volume offers "tribal-specific information on the
art, daily life, economic development, and religion of
20th-century American Indians and Alaskan Natives and
the government policy that affects them." Libr J
"This is an easy-to-use reference work. It is an excellent source for hard-to-find information about lesser-
known tribes." Booklist

√ The **Native** American experience; editor, Lelia
Wardwell. Facts on File 1991 various paging il
(American historical images on file) $155
       970.004
1. Indians of North America—Pictorial works
ISBN 0-8160-2228-3   LC 90-37369
A looseleaf collection of 288 images depicting impor-
tant people and events in Native American history and
culture

The **Native** Americans; an illustrated history;
introduction by Alvin M. Josephy, Jr.; text by
David Hurst Thomas [et al.]; edited by Betty
Ballantine, Ian Ballantine. Turner Pub. (Atlanta)
1993 479p $50; pa $29.95   **970.004**
1. Indians of North America
ISBN 1-878685-42-2; 0-57036-239-4 (pa)
       LC 93-29900
Blending "essays by historians and anthropologists
with 449 color and duotone illustrations, this compelling

history re-creates life as it was experienced by North
America's original inhabitants. Though written for the
general reader, the book is informed by the latest scholarship. . . . A remarkable kaleidoscopic sourcebook."
Publ Wkly

Native Americans information directory; Julia C.
Furtaw, editor; Kimberly Burton Faulkner,
associate editor. Gale Res. 1993 371p $85
       970.004
1. Indians of North America—Directories
ISBN 0-8103-8854-5
"A guide to organizations, agencies, institutions, programs, publications, services, and other resources concerned with the indigenous peoples of the United States
and Canada, including: American Indians, Alaska natives,
native Hawaiians, aboriginal Canadians." Title page
This "directory is divided into five parts. Each of the
first four parts covers a specific group . . . and includes
descriptive entries on tribal communities. . . . Its arrangement by native American group makes locating specific information extremely efficient. Also, it is one of
the few sources that lists grant and scholarship opportunities specifically for native Americans." Booklist

√ The **Native** North American almanac; edited by
Duane Champagne. Gale Res. 1994 1275p il
maps $95   **970.004**
1. Indians of North America
ISBN 0-8103-8865-0
Also available two volume junior version from
U.X.L./Gale Res.
Also available abridged version entitled Native Ameri-
ca: portrait of a people from Visible Ink $18.95 (ISBN
0-8103-9452-9)
This work covers "such topics as culture areas, reli-
gion, arts, health, education, economy, languages, and
legislation, plus a chronology from 11,000 B.C. through
the early 1990s and biographies of prominent Native
North Americans. The latter part of each chapter covers
Canadian aboriginals." Libr J

Paths of life; American Indians of the Southwest
and northern Mexico; edited by Thomas E.
Sheridan & Nancy J. Parezo. University of Ariz.
Press 1996 xxxiii, 298p il maps $45; pa $17.95
       970.004
1. Indians of North America—Southwestern States
2. Indians of Mexico
ISBN 0-8165-1549-2; 0-8165-1466-6 (pa)
       LC 95-32531
Analyzed in Essay and general literature Index
"This book surveys the history and culture of ten Indian groups in Arizona and northern Mexico. Chapters on
the Navajo, Yaqui, Apache, Pais, O'odham, Tarahumara,
Southern Paiute, Seri, River Yuman, and Hopi are included. . . . Historical accounts of each tribe are enhanced with descriptions of their religion and philosophy
to produce accurate and culturally sensitive portraits.
Many excellent illustrations accompany the text." Libr J
Includes bibliographical references

People of the western range; by the editors of Time-Life Books. Time-Life Bks. 1995 192p il (American Indians) $18.95 **970.004**

1. Indians of North America—West (U.S.)

LC 94-43685

This book provides a "summary of the culture and history of the Native American people who lived in the Great Basin and Plateau regions between the Rocky and Pacific coast mountain ranges. It is richly illustrated and has good sections on special topics and recent events." Sci Books Films

Includes bibliographical references

The **Plains** Indians of the twentieth century; edited and with an introduction by Peter Iverson. University of Okla. Press 1985 277p il maps hardcover o.p. paperback available $14.95

970.004

1. Indians of North America—Great Plains 2. Indians of North America—Government relations

ISBN 0-8061-1959-4 (pa)   LC 85-40475

A collection of essays focusing on "issues concerning Indian reservations and land rights (e.g., water rights, territorial control). The lives of the various tribal members are also examined. . . . A sound and valuable contribution to native American history." Booklist

Includes bibliographical references

Realm of the Iroquois; by the editors of Time-Life Books. Time-Life Bks. 1993 176p il maps (American Indians) $18.95 **970.004**

1. Iroquois Indians

LC 92-39727

This book "focuses on the key role of the Iroquois in the struggle between the French and the English for control of North America before the American Revolution. . . . Iroquois history and activities since the Civil War are briefly touched on in a few concluding pages." SLJ

"The text is well written and informative, but the extensive use of reproduced maps, b&w and color photos, and other visual representations is the most valuable aspect of the book." Book Rep

Includes bibliography

Reference encyclopedia of the American Indian; edited by Barry T. Klein. Todd Publs. $125; pa $75 **970.004**

1. Indians of North America—Dictionaries

First published 1967 by B. Klein. (6th edition 1993). Periodically revised

"This volume is actually a multipurpose resource: encyclopedia, directory, bibliography, and biographical source. . . . The consolidation and incorporation of a variety of resources on Native Americans here make this a very useful reference volume." Booklist

The **Reservations**; by the editors of Time-Life Books. Time-Life Bks. 1995 192p il maps (American Indians) $18.95 **970.004**

1. Indians of North America—Reservations 2. Indians of North America—Government relations

LC 95-4967

"Chronicles the social and political experiences of various tribes, from the mid-1800's to World War II, as the Indians were forced off their lands and made to submit to alien ways of life on reservations." Publisher's note

Includes bibliographical references

Roberts, David, 1943-

In search of the old ones; exploring the Anasazi world of the Southwest. Simon & Schuster 1996 271p il map $24; pa $12 **970.004**

1. Pueblo Indians 2. Southwestern States—Antiquities

ISBN 0-684-81078-6; 0-684-83212-7 (pa)

LC 95-46218

Roberts "chronicles the search for clues to the mystery of the Anasazi's abandonment of their extraordinary cliff dwellings some 700 years ago. Roberts blends accounts of his hiking adventures in the glorious canyon country of the Southwest with a chronicle of Anglos of the nineteenth century who shared his passion for studying the elusive Anasazi, especially the cowboy-archaeologist Richard Wetherell. Then, as he compares the discoveries of Wetherell and his peers with more recent revelations, Roberts considers the complex ethical questions raised by the inevitably intrusive work of archaeologists and anthropologists." Booklist

Includes bibliographical references

The **Smithsonian** book of North American Indians; before the coming of the Europeans; by Philip Kopper and the editors of Smithsonian Books. Smithsonian Bks. 1986 288p il $39.95

970.004

1. Indians of North America 2. North America—Antiquities

ISBN 0-89599-018-0   LC 86-20239

Also available from Abrams

This "book attempts to reconstruct the picture of those people's lives, religious customs, hunting tools, artistic achievements, and architecture. Arranged by geographical location, the text examines the cultures of the Arctic, North America, and Central America." Booklist

Through Indian eyes; the untold story of Native American peoples. Reader's Digest Assn. 1995 400p il $40 **970.004**

1. Indians of North America

ISBN 0-89577-819-X   LC 95-34273

This volume explores the daily experience and worldviews of Native Americans as expressed in art, myths, religion, rituals, customs and architecture. Illustrated with photographs, paintings, drawings, maps and archival material. A chronology of Indian-white relations is included

"This is both a basic sourcebook and a magnificent visual repository." Publ Wkly

Includes bibliography

Tribes of the southern Plains; by the editors of Time-Life Books. Time-Life Bks. 1995 184p il maps (American Indians) $18.95 **970.004**

1. Indians of North America—Great Plains 2. Indians of North America—Southwestern States

LC 95-8790

Describes in text and illustrations the cultures of the Comanche, Pawnee, and other American Indian tribes of the southern Great Plains

Includes bibliographical references

Tribes of the southern woodlands; by the editors of Time-Life Books. Time-Life Bks. 1994 176p il (American Indians) $18.95   **970.004**
   1. Indians of North America—Southern States
                    LC 93-40640

An illustrated look at Indian societies that settled the river valleys of the American southeast
   Includes bibliographical references

Viola, Herman J.
   After Columbus; the Smithsonian chronicle of the North American Indians. Smithsonian Bks.; Orion Bks. (NY) 1990 288p il maps hardcover o.p. paperback available $24.95   **970.004**
   1. Indians of North America
   ISBN 0-89599-028-8 (pa)   LC 90-9990
   The author has drawn upon Native American oral history, archaeological records, and the resources of the Smithsonian Institution to present approximately 500 years of North American Indian history. The volume is heavily illustrated with photographs of artifacts, portraits, historical paintings, and maps

Vogel, Virgil J.
   American Indian medicine. University of Okla. Press 1970 xx, 583p il (Civilization of the American Indian series) hardcover o.p. paperback available $24.95   **970.004**
   1. Indians of North America—Medicine
   ISBN 0-8061-2293-5 (pa)
   Covers "Indian theories of disease; early white doctors' and frontiersmen's observations in different parts of the country and among different tribes; Indians' influence on folk, fake, and patent medicine; Indian therapeutic methods in drug and drugless therapy, treatment of injuries, obstetrics, pediatrics, dentistry, diet, etc." Libr J
   Includes bibliography

Waldman, Carl
   Atlas of the North American Indian; maps and illustrations by Molly Braun. Facts on File 1985 276p il maps $35; pa $18.95   **970.004**
   1. Indians of North America
   ISBN 0-87196-850-9; 0-8160-2136-8 (pa)
                    LC 83-9020
   "Details the migration of prehistoric tribes to North America from Asia. A unique section on 'Lifeways' provides information on all socioeconomic and religious aspects of Native American cultures, both pre- and post-contact with European Americans. Covers the Indian Wars, the Land Cessions, and contemporary Native American conditions." N Y Public Libr. Book of How & Where to Look It Up
   Includes bibliography

   Encyclopedia of Native American tribes; illustrations by Molly Braun. Facts on File 1988 293p il $45   **970.004**
   1. Indians of North America—Dictionaries
   ISBN 0-8160-1421-3   LC 86-29066
   "Discusses more than 150 tribes of North America and gives summaries of the historic record including loca-

tions, migrations, languages, war, culture, contact with Europeans, and present conditions." N Y Public Libr. Book of How & Where to Look It Up
   Includes glossary and bibliography

   Word dance; the language of native American culture; pen-and-ink drawings by Molly Braun. Facts on File 1994 290p il $27.95; pa $15.95
                   970.004
   1. Indians of North America—Dictionaries
   ISBN 0-8160-2834-6; 0-8160-3494-X (pa)
                    LC 94-10311
   This work "consists of 270 pages of terms listed in alphabetical order, each with a brief definition of varying length. The terms, ranging from 'Abenaki' to 'Zuni,' include individuals, groups, objects, activities, events, foods, aspects of the environment, and some anthropological expressions—e.g., 'affinal,' 'cognate,' 'ethnocentric,' and 'excavation.' Alternate spellings as well as synonyms and some acronyms are given." Choice
   For a fuller review see: Booklist, Feb. 1, 1995
   Includes bibliography

War for the plains; by the editors of Time-Life Books. Time-Life Bks. 1994 192p il (American Indians) $18.95   **970.004**
   1. Indians of North America—Great Plains 2. Indians of North America—Wars
                    LC 93-23449
   "Part One focuses upon the 1862 Dakota uprising in Minnesota, and Part Three emphasizes the 1876 battle at Little Bighorn in Montana. Part Two covers events in and around Colorado, Kansas, and Nebraska between the decades of the sixties and seventies. The narrative is a straightforward historical account. . . . The book is a much more balanced history than earlier works written by white scholars." Sci Books Films
   Includes bibliographical references

The Way of the warrior; by the editors of Time-Life Books. Time-Life Bks. 1993 184p il (American Indians) $18.95   **970.004**
   1. Indians of North America—Wars
                    LC 92-22261

An illustrated look at Indian weaponry, fighting tactics and tribe-against-tribe conflicts
   Includes bibliographical references

Winds of renewal; by the editors of Time-Life Books. Time-Life Bks. 1996 176p il (American Indians) $18.95   **970.004**
   1. Indians of North America
                    LC 95-37240
   "From mid-century to present, covers American Indian Movement (1961-1975) struggles over land rights and self-determination and other contemporary issues." Publisher's note
   Includes bibliographical references

The Woman's way; by the editors of Time-Life Books. Time-Life Bks. 1995 184p il (American Indians) $18.95   **970.004**
   1. Indians of North America—Women
                    LC 94-38432
   "In the first chapter, the editors illustrate some of the misconceptions still held about Native American women.

The Woman's way—*Continued*

. . . The second chapter portrays Native American women as interpreters, advisers, and 'bridges' between their world and that of European settlers; it focuses on the lives of three influential women and illustrates the complex historical role that they held. The final section of the book shows how Native American women preserved indigenous ways and adhered to tribal customs, and have continued to do so. The book is generously illustrated." Sci Books Films

Includes bibliography

Wright, Ronald

Stolen continents; the Americas through Indian eyes since 1492. Houghton Mifflin 1992 424p il maps $22.95; pa $12.70   **970.004**

1. Indians 2. America—Exploration
ISBN 0-395-56500-6; 0-395-65975-2 (pa)
     LC 91-36202

"A Peter Davison book"

The author "views the past 500 years from the native American perspective by drawing on long-neglected post-Columbian documents. Maintaining a five-track narrative, he follows the history of the distinct groups that survived the European invasion: the Aztecs of Mexico, The Maya of Guatemala and Yucatan, the Incas of Peru, and the Cherokees and Iroquois of North America. . . . Compelling, important, and well told." Booklist

Includes bibliography

970.01   North America—Early history to 1599

America in 1492; the world of the Indian peoples before the arrival of Columbus; edited and with an introduction by Alvin Josephy, Jr.; developed by Frederick E. Hoxie. Knopf 1992 477p il maps hardcover o.p. paperback available $18
     970.01

1. Indians—History 2. Indians—Antiquities 3. America—Exploration 4. America—Antiquities
ISBN 0-679-74337-5 (pa)   LC 90-26222

These essays depict "the diverse lives of the approximately 75 million people living in the Americas around the turn of the fifteenth century. Geography guides the first section. . . . Another section focuses on languages, spiritual beliefs and customs, art, and 'systems of knowledge.'" Booklist

"Although 'America in 1492' is very scholarly, it is filled with a variety of interesting and fascinating information which is presented in a readable format. . . . Every senior high library should add this book to its collection." Voice Youth Advocates

Includes bibliographical references

Christopher Columbus and his legacy: opposing viewpoints; Mary Ellen Jones, editor. Greenhaven Press 1992 309p (American history series) lib bdg $19.95; pa $11.95   **970.01**
1. Columbus, Christopher 2. America—Exploration
ISBN 0-89908-196-7 (lib bdg); 0-89908-171-1 (pa)
     LC 92-18160

"Opposing viewpoints series"

Articles present opposing viewpoints on such Columbus-related issues as the motives of the conquistadors, treatment of the Indians, and twentieth-century views of Columbus

"An antidote to any form of political correctness, this book is recommended for its lively, scholarly approach to the subject." Booklist

Includes bibliographical references

Coe, Michael D.

Atlas of ancient America; by Michael Coe, Dean Snow, and Elizabeth Benson. Facts on File 1986 240p il maps $45   **970.01**
1. Indians—Antiquities 2. America—Antiquities
ISBN 0-8160-1199-0   LC 84-25999

"This color-illustrated atlas explores the culture and behavior of ancient North, South, and Meso-American peoples. After a general discussion of the distribution, languages, and environment of the American cultures, the . . . text offers a survey of the major Indian groups, including Hopi, Iroquois, Maya, Aztec, Nacza, and Inca." Booklist

"Excellent for student research, fun for browsing." SLJ

Includes bibliography

Faber, Harold

The discoverers of America. Scribner 1992 290p maps $17.95   **970.01**
1. Explorers 2. America—Exploration
ISBN 0-684-19217-9   LC 91-17001

Chronicles the discoverers of America, from the Native Americans believed to have crossed the Bering Strait after the last Ice Age, through the Vikings and the major European explorers, concluding with Bering's discovery of Alaska and Cook's voyage to Hawaii

"Explorers from Leif Ericson to James Cook are engagingly presented as 'real' personalities. Especially revealing are the politics surrounding the granting of their explorations by benefactors. Chronology, index, and bibliography accompany a mature textual reading level." BAYA Book Rev

Jones, Constance, 1961-

The European conquest of North America. Facts on File 1995 152p il maps (World history library) $17.95   **970.01**
1. Indians of North America 2. North America—History
ISBN 0-8160-3041-3   LC 94-12470

"This title covers the European conquest and settlement of North America, the resulting conflicts that arose between the colonizing nations and the indigenous peoples of the continent, and the effects of the conquest on those peoples. . . . There is an abundance of factual material, and the excellent chronology, index, and bibliography make this a useful source for student research." Voice Youth Advocates

MacLeish, William H., 1928-

The day before America; illustrated by Will Bryant. Houghton Mifflin 1994 277p il hardcover o.p. paperback available $11.95   **970.01**

1. Indians of North America 2. Natural history—North America 3. Human ecology

ISBN 0-395-74014-2 (pa)   LC 94-9504

"A Richard Todd book"

"MacLeish charts the ecological devastation and societal upheaval wrought by Spanish, French, English and Dutch colonizers of the New World. Drawing on interviews with ecologists, archeologists, prehistorians and anthropologists, as well as his own travels, he . . . evokes the lush pre-Columbian Americas." Publ Wkly

"A storyteller with a penchant for history, MacLeish weaves a spellbinding tale about human life and environmental change in North America. . . . This unique and engaging essay will be of interest to the general reader." Libr J

Includes bibliographical references

Mysteries of the ancient Americas; the new world before Columbus. Reader's Digest Assn. 1986 320p il maps $29.95   **970.01**

1. Indians—Antiquities 2. America—Exploration 3. America—Antiquities

ISBN 0-89577-183-7   LC 84-15038

At head of title: Reader's Digest

"This book focuses on some puzzles—who 'discovered' America, how and when the first settlers came, who built the New World pyramids, and Lost Cities—that have intrigued historians, archaeologists, and laymen over the centuries. Each section contains various theories of explanation. . . . This attractive volume will be useful for reports." SLJ

Includes bibliography

The **Search** for El Dorado; by the editors of Time-Life Books. Time-Life Bks. 1994 168p il (Lost civilizations) $18.95   **970.01**

1. America—Exploration 2. Indians of South America—Antiquities

LC 94-17846

An examination of the "ancient peoples and legends associated with the so-called gold cultures of Panama, Colombia, Venezuela, Ecuador, and Peru." Sci Books Films

"This well-organized study of South American Indian cultures is an effective blend of history and legend—further enhanced by a remarkable collection of photographs of artifacts, ruins, and excavations, plus 16th-century engravings depicting scenes from expeditions and facets of the El Dorado legend." SLJ

Includes bibliography

Stuart, Gene S., 1930-1993

America's ancient cities; photographed by Richard Alexander Cooke III; paintings by H. Tom Hall; prepared by the Special Publications Division, National Geographic Society. National Geographic Soc. 1988 199p il $16   **970.01**

1. Indians—Antiquities 2. Extinct cities 3. North America—Antiquities 4. Central America—Antiquities 5. Mexico—Antiquities

ISBN 0-87044-627-4   LC 87-34851

Numerous color photographs illustrate this look at ancient cities in North America, Central America and Mexico. The political and social history of the Indian inhabitants is discussed

Includes bibliography

971   Canada

Canada; edited by Mel Watkins. Facts on File 1993 701p maps (Handbooks to the modern world) $60   **971**

1. Canada

ISBN 0-8160-1831-6   LC 91-45584

"Survey articles by scholars and researchers (many Canadian) are grouped in five areas: Provinces and territories, History, Politics, Economy, Social Affairs. Maps; tables in Comparative statistics section. Suggestions for further reading at end of each article. Topical index." Guide to Ref Books. 11th edition

Canada's incredible coasts; prepared by the Book Division. National Geographic Soc. 1991 199p il maps $16   **971**

1. Canada—Description 2. Natural history—Canada

ISBN 0-87044-829-3   LC 91-19420

This book provides a pictorial description of life in Canada along the Arctic, Atlantic, and Pacific Coasts as well as the Gulf of St. Lawrence and the Baffin Bay region

Weihs, Jean Riddle

Facts about Canada, its provinces and territories; [by] Jean Weihs; illustrations by Cameron Riddle. Wilson, H.W. 1995 246p il maps $35   **971**

1. Canada

ISBN 0-8242-0864-1   LC 94-23275

This book presents "information about each province and territory, including population, government, and climate. A description of flags, coats of arms, and holidays begins each chapter. Also included are geography and climate, parks and historic sites, demography, government and politics, financial and economic information, history, culture and education, motor vehicle use statistics, trivia about the 'first, biggest and best,' information sources and a selected bibliography. Weihs provides very current information and has clearly researched her topic extensively." Voice Youth Advocates

For a fuller review see: Booklist, Nov. 1, 1995

972   Middle America. Mexico

Bunson, Margaret R.
Encyclopedia of ancient Mesoamerica; [by] Margaret R. Bunson and Stephen M. Bunson. Facts on File 1996 322p il $45   **972**
1. Indians of Mexico—Dictionaries 2. Indians of Central America—Dictionaries 3. Mexico—Antiquities—Dictionaries 4. Central America—Antiquities—Dictionaries
ISBN 0-8160-2402-2   LC 95-13085
This work "covers the people, places, and events of the region from the rise of early cultures at the end of the last Ice Age, circa 11,000 BC, to the demise of the Aztecs after the Spanish conquest in the 1500s. It explores such civilizations as the Aztecs, Olmecs, Zapotecs, Tehtihuacans, and the Mayans. Coverage includes essays on such topics as art and architecture, social life, belief systems, and the military; entries on rulers, sites, and events of note; a general chronology as well as individual empire timelines; more than 100 black-and-white drawings." Publisher's note

Coe, Michael D.
Mexico; from the Olmecs to the Aztecs. 4th ed fully rev & expanded. Thames & Hudson 1994 215p il (Ancient peoples and places) pa $15.95
    972
1. Indians of Mexico 2. Mexico—History 3. Mexico—Antiquities
ISBN 0-500-27722-2   LC 93-60419
First published 1962 by Praeger
This study looks at the cultural achievements of the pre-Columbian peoples of Mexico in their geographical and climatic context
Includes bibliographical references

The **Magnificent** Maya; by the editors of Time-Life Books. Time-Life Bks. 1993 168p il (Lost civilizations) $18.95   **972**
1. Mayas
    LC 92-39965
An illustrated survey of Mayan society, culture, government and religion
Includes bibliographical references

Meyer, Carolyn
The mystery of the ancient Maya; [by] Carolyn Meyer and Charles Gallenkamp. rev ed. Margaret K. McElderry Bks. 1995 159p $15   **972**
1. Mayas
ISBN 0-689-50619-8   LC 94-18274
First published 1985
This overview of Mayan culture examines the discovery of ancient ruins in the mid-1800s and follows modern scientists and archaeologists as they seek an explanation for the civilization's abrupt end
Includes glossary

Meyer, Michael C.
The course of Mexican history; [by] Michael C. Meyer, William L. Sherman. Oxford Univ. Press $26.50   **972**
1. Mexico—History
ISBN 0-19-508980-4
First published 1979. (5th edition 1995) Periodically revised
A chronologically arranged survey of the political, economic, social, and cultural history of Mexico, ranging from the pre-Columbian period to the present

The **Route** of the Mayas. Knopf 1995 424p il maps pa $25   **972**
1. Mayas 2. Mexico—Antiquities 3. Central America—Antiquities
ISBN 0-679-75569-1   LC 95-1871
"Knopf guides"
"An illustrated guide to historical and contemporary Mayan life and culture in Mexico and Central America. It covers every aspect of the civilization from food cultivation and preparation to religion, urban development, and architecture. The book contains hard-to-find information on family life, textiles, and natural life plus excerpts from traveler's journals ranging in time from 1500-1970." SLJ
"This book looks like a travel book but it has so much useful information that it can double for a reference work on the Mayan culture." Voice Youth Advocates
Includes bibliographical references

Stuart, Gene S., 1930-1993
Lost kingdoms of the Maya; by Gene S. Stuart and George E. Stuart; prepared by the Book Division of the National Geographic Society. National Geographic Soc. 1993 248p il map $34.95   **972**
1. Mayas 2. Central America—Antiquities 3. Mexico—Antiquities
ISBN 0-87044-928-1   LC 92-40803
"Interspersed among the historical and factual accounts are short sections highlighting areas of special interest including castes, trade, calendar, writing, religion and rituals, buildings, the arts, royal society, warfare, and myths. For the sociologist, the book also includes discussion and photos of the people and how they live today." Book Rep
Includes bibliographical references

Suchlicki, Jaime
Mexico; from Montezuma to NAFTA, Chiapas, and beyond. Brassey's 1996 227p il map $21.95
    972
1. Mexico—History
ISBN 1-57488-031-4   LC 95-20060
The author provides a "historical narrative of Mexico from the time of the conquest through the Zedillo administration. Although the book focuses primarily on the period between 1500 and 1970, Suchlicki argues that many of the variables in the present crises can be found in Mexico's historical experience." Libr J
Includes bibliographical references

Townsend, Richard F.
The Aztecs. Thames & Hudson 1992 224p il
(Ancient peoples and places) hardcover o.p.
paperback available $15.95   **972**
1. Aztecs
ISBN 0-500-27720-6 (pa)
"In addition to analyzing the advancement and eventual dissolution of the extensive Aztec empire, the author
also provides a fascinating record of the minutiae of daily life. . . . A compact introduction to the historical and
sociological evolution of a prominent Meso-American
civilization." Booklist
Includes bibliography

972.08   Mexico since 1867

Lewis, Oscar, 1914-1970
The children of Sánchez; autobiography of a
Mexican family. Random House 1961 xxxi, 499p
hardcover o.p. paperback available $16   **972.08**
1. Mexico City (Mexico)—Social conditions
2. Poor—Mexico City (Mexico) 3. Family
ISBN 0-394-70280-8 (pa)
"First-person autobiographical narratives by the members of a poor family in Mexico City. One by one, the
father and his four grown children told the anthropologist
author their stories of fights, sex, struggles for jobs, bit-
terness, hate, sickness, death, and only a little happiness." Publ Wkly
"Oscar Lewis has made something brilliant and of singular significance, a work of such unique concentration
and sympathy." N Y Times Book Rev

972.87   Panama

McCullough, David G., 1933-
The path between the seas; the creation of the
Panama Canal, 1870-1914; [by] David
McCullough. Simon & Schuster 1977 698p il
maps hardcover o.p. paperback available $14.95
                                              972.87
1. Panama Canal
ISBN 0-671-24409-4 (pa)   LC 76-57967
This is a "history of the canal project, beginning with
de Lesseps' bold and ultimately disastrous investment
and ending with the triumph of American enterprise in
1914." Libr J
"Not only is this a well-told story of the building of
the Panama Canal but it also supplies welcome background for the . . . debate on the canal's role in inter-
American relations." Booklist
Includes bibliography

972.9   West Indies and Bermuda

Rogoziński, Jan
A brief history of the Caribbean; from the
Arawak and the Carib to the present. Facts on File
1992 324p il maps $29.95   **972.9**
1. West Indies—History
ISBN 0-8160-2451-0   LC 91-860
Also available in paperback from New Am. Lib

This historical overview "covers Spanish rule, the
northern European influence, the sugar empire, independence, and post-World War I development. Textual clarity, access to straightforward tables covering primarily demographic information, and various statistics will prove
useful to the reader looking for a ready reference
source." Libr J
Includes bibliographical references

972.91   Cuba

Kufeld, Adam
Cuba; introduction by Tom Miller. Norton 1994
128p il hardcover o.p. paperback available $19.95
                                              972.91
1. Cuba—Pictorial works
ISBN 0-393-31023-X (pa)   LC 94-11756
This volume documents life in contemporary Cuba
with over 100 full-color photographs

Persons, Albert C., 1915-
Bay of Pigs; a firsthand account of the mission
by a U.S. pilot in support of the Cuban invasion
force in 1961; with a foreword by Joseph L.
Shannon. McFarland & Co. 1990 162p maps pa
$22.95   **972.91**
1. United States. Central Intelligence Agency
2. Cuba—History—1961, Invasion
ISBN 0-89950-483-3   LC 89-13566
"This personal recollection of a CIA 'contract' pilot is
an involving and earnest account of one man's activities
in the days before and during the disastrous adventure.
. . . His views of fellow pilots, military and CIA leaders, and the few Cubans he knew lend valuable insight
into the way covert operations come about and grow to
reality." Libr J
Includes bibliographical references

972.95   Puerto Rico

Abodaher, David J.
Puerto Rico: America's 51st state? Watts 1993
95p il maps lib bdg $22.70   **972.95**
1. Puerto Rico
ISBN 0-531-13024-X   LC 92-39474
"An Impact book"
Surveys the history of the island nation of Puerto
Rico, from its colonization by Spain through its time un-
der American control to debate over statehood and inde-
pendence
"This book is recommended highly on the basis of its
introduction to Puerto Rico and its value for stimulating
discussion of the central issue." Sci Books Films
Includes bibliography

973 United States

100 key documents in American democracy; edited by Peter B. Levy; foreword by William E. Leuchtenburg. Greenwood Press 1994 502p il $59.95 **973**
1. United States—History—Sources
ISBN 0-313-28424-5   LC 93-1137
"The work is arranged chronologically within sections, such as 'The Early Republic' and 'The Progressive Era.' Beginning with Powhatan's call for peace in his 1609 'Letter to John Smith' and concluding with Jesse Jackson's moving speech at the 1988 Democratic National Convention. . . . Each piece is prefaced by a short chronology that sets the historical context and a commentary on the document that often refers to other writings in the book. Shorter documents are reprinted in their entirety, while longer ones have been edited." Booklist

Album of American history. Scribner 1981 6v in 3 il set $295 + supplementary volume **973**
1. United States—History—Pictorial works 2. United States—Social life and customs—Pictorial works
ISBN 0-684-16848-0   LC 80-26075
Volumes 1-4 and an index volume, first published between 1944-1949 and edited by James Truslow Adams. Volume 5, published 1960, and volume 6 with general index, first published 1961, were edited by Joseph G. E. Hopkins. This is a reissue in three volumes of the six volume set published 1969
Supplementary volume 1968-1982, published 1985 $75 (ISBN 0-684-17440-5)
Contents: v1 Colonial period; v2 1783-1853; v3 1853-1893; v4 End of an era; v5 1917-1953; v6 1953-1968; General index
This "is a pictorial chronicle of American history and life from 1783 to 1968. The set contains over 6,300 reproductions representative of a wide variety of contemporary illustration printed from new plates. The 'Supplement' presents 300 photos organized in 10 chapters that cover the presidency, Vietnam, social consciousness, business, ecology, architecture, and daily life. A brief introduction opens each chapter, and captions accompany the black-and-white pictures." Wynar. Guide to Ref Books for Sch Media Cent. 3d edition

The **Annals** of America. Encyclopaedia Britannica 1968-1986 24v il maps set $395 **973**
1. United States—History—Sources
ISBN 0-87827-199-6
Each volume has a distinctive title
This work "is a chronological record of American life, events, and thought. . . . It is a comprehensive general compendium of source material containing laws, speeches, stories, transcriptions of dialogues, on-the-scene reports, reminiscences, and other primary sources." Wynar. Guide to Ref Books for Sch Media Cent. 3d edition

Basic documents in American history; [edited by] Richard B. Morris. Krieger 1980 c1965 193p pa $11.50 **973**
1. United States—History—Sources
ISBN 0-89874-202-1   LC 80-12822
First published 1956. This is a reprint of the edition published 1965 by Van Nostrand

"A collection of documents, with brief analysis and evaluation for each selection, covering from 1620 to the 1960s." Wynar. Guide to Ref Books for Sch Media Cent. 3d edition

Boorstin, Daniel J. (Daniel Joseph), 1914-
The Americans: The democratic experience. Random House 1973 717p hardcover o.p. paperback available $16 **973**
1. United States—Civilization 2. United States—Social conditions 3. United States—Economic conditions
ISBN 0-394-71011-8 (pa)
Concluding volume of the author's trilogy which began with The Americans: The colonial experience, entered in class 973.2 and continued with The Americans: The national experience, entered below
This volume is concerned with the democratization of the national character over the past hundred years and the growth of technology
Includes bibliographical references

The **Americans**: The national experience. Random House 1965 517p $35; pa $15 **973**
1. United States—Civilization 2. American national characteristics 3. United States—Intellectual life
ISBN 0-394-41453-5; 0-394-70358-8 (pa)
This is the second volume of the author's trilogy
A cultural interpretation of American history, this book traces "the roots of contemporary American life to the years between the Revolution and the Civil War." Booklist
Includes bibliographical references

Davis, Kenneth C.
Don't know much about history; everything you need to know about American history but never learned. Crown 1990 462p $24.95 **973**
1. United States—History
ISBN 0-517-57706-2   LC 89-25215
Also available in paperback from Avon Bks.
This book "is organized in chronological order from the beginning of American history to the Reagan presidency. The chapters contain questions and answers and excerpts from speeches and related writings of the time." SLJ
"Well written, with a dry humor, this is an interesting history lesson, as well as a reference tool." Voice Youth Advocates
Includes bibliographical references

Discovering America's past; customs, legends, history & lore of our great nation. Reader's Digest Assn. 1993 400p il $32.95 **973**
1. United States—History 2. United States—Social life and customs
ISBN 0-89577-520-4   LC 93-3508
"Chapters are devoted to a variety of topics, including the family, food and drink, leisure, education, business and industry, the Wild West, and country and city life. Brimming with an abundance of priceless vintage photographs, paintings, and engravings, this fascinating cultural potpourri is an ideal browsing item." Booklist

Facts about the states; editors, Joseph Nathan
Kane, Janet Podell, Steven Anzovin. 2nd ed.
Wilson, H.W. 1994 c1993 624p il $60   **973**
1. United States—Local history 2. State governments
ISBN 0-8242-0849-8   LC 93-30328
First published 1989
Provides geographic, demographic, economic, political,
and cultural facts about the fifty states, Puerto Rico, and
the District of Columbia. Part I presents state entries in
alphabetical order. Part II provides comparative tables
that rank states in categories such as population, geography, education, and finance

Garraty, John Arthur, 1920-
1,001 things everyone should know about
American history; [by] John A. Garraty.
Doubleday 1989 207p il hardcover o.p. paperback
available $12   **973**
1. United States—History
ISBN 0-385-42577-5 (pa)   LC 88-14446
"Interesting facts about American history are found in
this volume, which is arranged in eight thematic areas.
The 1,001 entries concern people, places, music, books,
songs, events, and much more." Nichols. Guide to Ref
Books for Sch Media Cent. 4th edition

Harvard guide to American history; Frank
Freidel, editor, with the assistance of Richard K.
Showman. rev ed. Harvard Univ. Press 1974 2v
o.p. one-volume paperback available $26.50
    973
1. United States—Historiography 2. United States—
History—Bibliography
ISBN 0-674-37555-6 (pa)
"Belknap Press"
First published 1954 in one volume under the
editorship of Oscar Handlin
A manual for the general reader on the source materi-
als in American history through June 1970
"The basic reference bibliography for American his-
tory. A selective listing covering the whole range of
American history, and including citations to both book
and periodical materials." Guide to Ref Books. 11th edi-
tion

Images of America: a panorama of history in
photographs. Smithsonian Bks. 1989 255p il
$47.50   **973**
1. United States—History—Pictorial works
ISBN 0-89599-023-7   LC 89-11322
"Nostalgia is the essence of *Images of America*, a
compendium of photos owned by the Smithsonian Institution and chosen for their historical rather than artistic
value. . . . Whether good or indifferent aesthetically,
they are collectively proffered as a national family album
meant to stir pride for the national record. . . . A real
crowd-pleaser of a book." Booklist

Invisible America; unearthing our hidden history;
[editors], Mark P. Leone, Neil Asher Silberman.
Holt & Co. 1995 287p il maps (Henry Holt
reference book) $35   **973**
1. Popular culture—United States 2. United States—
Social life and customs
ISBN 0-8050-3525-7   LC 95-31067
The editors "use artifacts of everyday life to tell forgotten stories of America's past. Their work tries to do
this by breaking the past into five periods of history
(1492-1607, 1607-1780, etc.) and devoting two-page articles to various areas of interest in each era." Libr J

Keegan, John, 1934-
Fields of battle; the wars for North America.
Knopf 1996 c1995 348p il maps $30; pa $15
    973
1. North America—Military history
ISBN 0-679-42413-X; 0-679-74664-1 (pa)
      LC 96-154385
First published 1995 in the United Kingdom with title
Warpaths: travels of a military historian in North Ameri-
ca
The author "demonstrates how North America's geog-
raphy has influenced its history: how its mountain chains
and river systems have determined where people fought,
and fought repeatedly. For example, the defenses that
Cornwallis built at Yorktown to deter American forces
were improved and reused by the Confederates almost a
century later. Keegan's tour of the continent skips the
Mexican War, and his book is atypically discursive. For
Americans, the charm is the familiarity of its sites—
Brooklyn, Pittsburgh, Laramie, and other home towns."
New Yorker

Langdon, William Chauncy, 1871-1947
Everyday things in American life, 1776-1876.
Scribner 1941 398p il map   **973**
1. United States—Social life and customs
ISBN 0-684-17416-2
Available in hardcover from Reprint Services Corp.
Companion volume to Everyday things in American
life, 1607-1776, entered in class 973.2
The emphasis in this book "is on expansion, with
chapters on Roads and turnpikes, Covered bridges, River
transportation, The passing of canals, The development
of steam. Other chapters treat of home life upstairs and
down, clothes and their materials, and the improvements
in farm machinery, all illustrated with well chosen pictures." Wis Libr Bull
Includes bibliography

Lind, Michael, 1962-
The next American nation; the new nationalism
and the fourth American revolution. Free Press
1995 436p $25; pa $15   **973**
1. United States—Civilization 2. Nationalism
3. Multiculturalism
ISBN 0-02-919103-3; 0-684-82503-1 (pa)
      LC 95-13621
The author "proposes a new transracial coalition politics that dismantles 'white overclass' domination, recon-

Lind, Michael, 1962——*Continued*
structs the American class system toward a post-racist, social-democratic republic, and blends races and cultures into a 'trans-American melting pot.' . . . Lind, not a professional historian, makes historical arguments from which some historians will dissent; they may find his depiction of America's first two republics overdrawn. But this book is about change and the American politics of identity and whether an emerging multiracial middle-class majority can find a politics that will renew the nation's democratic promise." Choice

Includes bibliographical references

Morison, Samuel Eliot, 1887-1976
The growth of the American Republic; [by] Samuel Eliot Morison, Henry Steele Commager, and William E. Leuchtenburg. 7th ed. Oxford Univ. Press 1980 2v il maps ea $40   973
1. United States—History
ISBN 0-19-502593-8 (v1); 0-19-502594-6 (v2)
       LC 79-52432
First published 1930 in a single volume
A history of the United States that deals with military, political, economic, social, literary and spiritual aspects of the nation's development
"A good general history, well-written." Sheehy. Guide to Ref Books. 10th edition

Moss, Joyce, 1951-
Profiles in American history; significant events and the people who shaped them; [by] Joyce Moss and George Wilson. U.X.L 1994 8v il maps set $250   973
1. United States—History 2. United States—Biography
ISBN 0-8103-9207-0
v1 Exploration to Revolution; v2 Constitutional convention to the War of 1812; v3 Indian removal to the antislavery movement; v4 Westward movement to the Civil War; v5 Reconstruction to the Spanish-American War; v6 Immigration to women's rights and roles; v7 Great Depression to the Cuban Missile Crisis; v8 Civil rights movement to the present
"Each volume encompasses a specific time period, focusing on 5 to 7 events and 20 people who helped shape those events. The intent of the series is to expose middle-school and high-school readers to the diversity of personalities who left their mark on America. . . . While biographical information on most of the subjects is available elsewhere, the vocabulary, simple explanation of events, and obvious interrelation of people and events make this a good source for middle-school libraries or high schools needing material for lower-level students." Booklist

Opposing viewpoints in American history; William Dudley, book editor. Greenhaven Press 1996 2v ea lib bdg $29.95; pa $15.95   973
1. United States—History—Sources
       LC 95-33446
Contents: v1: From colonial times to Reconstruction (ISBN 1-56510-348-3; 1-56510-347-5); v2: From Reconstruction to the present (ISBN 1-56510-350-5; 1-56510-349-1)

This "title takes 82 episodes/issues in U.S. history—from the early colonial period to 1992—and presents alternative primary source commentary on each. . . . Each pair of readings begins with a well-written introduction that gives important background facts and ends with an up-to-date bibliography of further sources. . . . An important addition to primary source material in U.S. history collections." Booklist

Pageant of America; a pictorial history of the United States; edited by Ralph Henry Gabriel and others. independence ed. Yale Univ. Press 1925-1929 15v il maps   973
1. United States—History—Pictorial works
Some volumes available from Reprint Services Corp.
Contents: v1 Adventures in the wilderness, by C. Wissler; v2 Lure of the frontier, by R. H. Gabriel; v3 Toilers of land and sea, by R. H. Gabriel; v4 March of commerce, by M. Keir; v5 Epic of industry, by M. Keir; v6 Winning of freedom, by W. Wood; v7 In defense of liberty, by W. Wood; v8 Builders of the republic, by F. A. Ogg; v9 Makers of a new nation, by J. S. Bassett; v10 American idealism, by L. A. Weigle; v11 American spirit in letters, by S. T. Williams; v12 American spirit in art, by F. J. Mather; v13 American spirit in architecture, by T. F. Hamlin; v14 The American stage, by O. S. Coad ; v15 Annals of American sport, by J. A. Krout
Provides a "pictorial record of the history of the United States. . . . Included in the collection are reproductions of art works and documents, portraits, photos, maps, and cartoons." Wynar. Guide to Ref Books for Sch Media Cent. 2d edition

Savage, William W.
The cowboy hero; his image in American history & culture; by William W. Savage, Jr. University of Okla. Press 1979 179p il hardcover o.p. paperback available $14.95   973
1. Cowhands
ISBN 0-8061-1920-9 (pa)   LC 79-4730
The author's "research extends into all facets of Western history with emphasis on the popular glorification of the cowboy in books, movies, radio, and television. . . . Savage . . . appears to have a real affection for his subject." Libr J
Includes bibliography

Schlesinger, Arthur M., 1917-
The disuniting of America. Norton 1992 160p $15.95; pa $7.95   973
1. Multiculturalism 2. Multicultural education 3. United States—Historiography 4. United States—Civilization
ISBN 0-393-03380-5; 0-393-30987-8 (pa)
       LC 91-38884
"This book examines the contemporary controversy regarding the teaching of history and its ramifications for a multiethnic society. The author argues that the critical traditions of scholarship based on diversity, dissent, and close scrutiny of broad claims must not be abandoned. . . . [He contends] that schools and colleges must not degrade history by allowing its contents to be dictated by pressure groups, whether political, economic, religious, or ethnic." N Y Rev Books
This is "a sane and temperate book." N Y Times Book Rev

Scott, John Anthony, 1916-
The Facts on File history of the American people. Facts on File 1990 213p il maps music $27.95   **973**
1. United States—History
ISBN 0-8160-1739-5   LC 89-28285
The author "recounts the history of the U.S. from the 'Wanderers and Settlers' of the age of the Amerindians to the present-day." SLJ
"Readers will find most of the normal historical events such as colonization, settlement, war, and presidential elections. Beyond this, the author stresses events he feels have shaped and added to the personal freedom of Americans. . . . This social history will make a valuable research tool." Voice Youth Advocates
Includes bibliography

The story of America; a National Geographic picture atlas. rev ed. National Geographic Soc.; distributed by Random House 1993 324p il maps $25   **973**
1. United States—History
ISBN 0-87044-887-0   LC 92-13800
First published 1984
Chronicles the history of the United States from its beginning before 1630 to the present day

Steinbeck, John, 1902-1968
Travels with Charley; in search of America. Viking 1962 246p hardcover o.p. paperback available $10.95   **973**
1. United States—Civilization 2. United States—Description
ISBN 0-14-018741-3 (pa)
The Nobel laureate recounts his impressions and observations of America gathered during a trip through forty states in the company of his French poodle Charley

973.02 United States—History—Miscellany. Chronologies

Carruth, Gorton
The encyclopedia of American facts and dates. HarperCollins Pubs. $45   **973.02**
1. United States—History—Chronology 2. Historical chronology
Also available from New Am Lib. in a paperback abridged edition with title: What happened when
First published 1956 by Crowell. (10th edition 1997)
Periodically revised
Entries that deal with a variety of topics are chronologically arranged in parallel columns to show concurrent events in American life, from around 1000 A.D. to the present

Chronicle of America. Dorling Kindersley 1995 1008p il maps $59.95   **973.02**
1. United States—History—Chronology 2. Historical chronology
ISBN 0-7894-0124-X
Editorial director: Clifton Daniel; editor-in-chief, John W. Kirshon

"Book documents the history of the American nation from the arrival of Asian tribes (40,000-8000 B.C.) to the April 1995 Oklahoma City bombing. Annual listings of significant political, social, and cultural events are arranged in eight chapters, each with a brief essay outlining the time period covered." Libr J

Corey, Melinda
American history; the New York Public Library book of answers; [by] Melinda Corey and George Ochoa. Simon & Schuster 1993 240p pa $11
                                              973.02
1. United States—History—Miscellanea
ISBN 0-671-79634-8   LC 93-26736
"A Stonesong Press book. A Fireside book"
This work presents some nine hundred questions and their answers, arranged under thirty-two headings, such as African-American history, Coming to America, Economic history, Fine arts and letters, Landmarks and symbols, Native American history, Popular culture, Statistics, and Women's history

Great dates in United States history; general editor, Andrè Kaspi. Facts on File 1994 266p maps $27.95   **973.02**
1. United States—History—Chronology
ISBN 0-8160-2592-4   LC 93-42889
"This chronological approach to the American experience consists of 20 chapters, each of which opens with a brief synopsis of the era followed by key dates organized by categories such as politics and institutions, foreign affairs, economy and society, and civilization and culture. Each chapter also includes appropriate tables and maps. . . . This book will be valuable for those interested in a quick review of United States history, particulary young adults studying for a test." Book Rep

Smith, Ronald D., 1935-
Fascinating people and astounding events from American history; [by] Ronald D. Smith, William L. Richter. ABC-CLIO 1993 274p $40   **973.02**
1. United States—History—Miscellanea
ISBN 0-87436-693-3   LC 93-23532
This "is an American history book whose purpose seems to be providing information which tantalizes the curiosity of its readers, and gives enough facts about different incidents and people in order to make students want to find out more. . . . The book's strengths include its systematic, timewise organization through history, a readable, story-like style which will appeal to teenagers, and an accurate index." Voice Youth Advocates

973.03 United States—History—Encyclopedias and dictionaries

Dictionary of American history. rev ed. Scribner 1976 8v set $700   **973.03**
1. United States—History—Dictionaries
ISBN 0-684-13856-5
First published 1940
"The set contains readable articles that explain the concepts, events, and places of American history. It covers political, economic, social, industrial, and cultural history. It does not include biographical sketches." Ref Sources for Small & Medium-sized Libr. 5th edition

Dictionary of American history, Supplement; Robert H. Ferrell and Joan Hoff, senior editors. Scribner 1996 2v set $200   **973.03**
1. United States—History—Dictionaries
ISBN 0-684-19579-8   LC 96-7844
Contents: pt. 1. AARP-Lyme disease; pt. 2. Mac-Arthur Foundation-Zoology

These supplementary volumes update and expand the original work. The two "volumes 'contain 757 entries . . . of these, 469 are completely new,' with the rest replacing or updating entries in the original set. . . . Cross-references to the other articles in the main set and elsewhere in the supplement are given at the end of entries." Booklist

Includes bibliographical references

Encyclopedia of the United States in the twentieth century; Stanley I. Kutler, editor in chief; Robert Dallek, David A. Hollinger, Thomas K. McCraw, associate editors; Judith Kirkwood, assistant editor. Scribner 1996 4v il maps set $385   **973.03**
1. United States—Civilization 2. United States—History—1900-1999 (20th century) 3. Popular culture—United States
ISBN 0-13-210535-7   LC 95-22696
Kutler "has produced a masterly edited publication that captures the essence of many political, social, cultural, and technological developments and trends that have occurred in the US during this century. In six broad topical sections ('The American People'; 'Politics'; 'Global America'; 'Science, Technology, and Medicine'; 'The Economy'; and 'Culture'), 80 prominent academic historians provide 74 interpretative essays based on current scholarship that analyze major topics and themes of the century." Choice

For a fuller review see: Booklist, March 1, 1996

The **Reader's** companion to American history; Eric Foner and John A. Garraty, editors; sponsored by the Society of American Historians. Houghton Mifflin 1991 xxii, 1226p $35   **973.03**
1. United States—History—Dictionaries
ISBN 0-395-51372-3   LC 91-19508
"The nearly 1000 entries, ranging from concise explanations to multipage essays, are all equally well written, crisp, and entertaining. Most entries are signed by the nearly 400 contributors, many of whom are acknowledged experts in their fields. . . . Brief bibliographies and thorough 'See also' references to related articles follow each entry. The accustomed bow to American popular culture is included, with Sinatra and Astaire rubbing elbows with Jefferson and King." Libr J

Worldmark encyclopedia of the States. 3rd ed. Gale Res. 1995 758p maps $135   **973.03**
1. United States—Dictionaries
ISBN 0-8103-9877-X   LC 94-38557
First published 1981 by Harper & Row
"Comprehensive examination of each state within the framework of 50 standard subject headings. Includes economic policy, energy and power, resources, education, the press, famous persons, etc." N Y Public Libr. Ref Books for Child Collect. 2d edition

Yanak, Ted
The great American history fact-finder; [by] Ted Yanak and Pam Cornelison; with a foreword by Norman Y. Mineta. Houghton Mifflin 1993 496p il maps hardcover o.p. paperback available $14.95
                    973.03
1. United States—History—Dictionaries
ISBN 0-395-61715-4 (pa)   LC 92-37245
A dictionary of people, places and events of importance to American politics, economics, social trends and popular culture
"Fun for browsers and useful for students needing quick facts." Booklist

973.05   United States—History—Serial publications

American Heritage. American Heritage $32 per year   **973.05**
1. United States—History—Periodicals 2. United States—Civilization
ISSN 0002-8738
Eight issues a year. First published 1947. Sponsored by the Society of American Historians
"All aspects of the American experience, whether monumental or of marginal importance, are the focus of this highly successful and popular magazine. . . . The very readable articles are of varying length. The numerous photographs and other illustrations result in a very handsome effect. Both the quality of this lively publication and its wide appeal make it a standard selection for most American libraries." Katz. Mag for Libr. 8th edition

973.1   United States—Early history to 1607

Morison, Samuel Eliot, 1887-1976
The European discovery of America. Oxford Univ. Press 1971-1974 2v il maps   **973.1**
1. America—Exploration 2. Voyages and travels 3. Explorers
Contents: v1 The northern voyages, A.D.500-1600 pa $19.95 (ISBN 0-19-508271-0); v2 The southern voyages, A.D.1492-1616 $39.95 (ISBN 0-19-501823-9; pa $19.95 ISBN 0-19-508272-9)
Includes bibliographical references

973.2   United States—Colonial period, 1607-1775

Andrews, Charles McLean, 1863-1943
The colonial background of the American Revolution; four essays in American colonial history; [by] Charles M. Andrews. rev ed. Yale Univ. Press 1931 220p hardcover o.p. paperback available $15   **973.2**
1. United States—History—1600-1775, Colonial period 2. United States—History—1775-1783, Revolution 3. Great Britain—Colonies—United States
ISBN 0-300-00004-9 (pa)
First published 1924

Andrews, Charles McLean, 1863-1943—*Continued*

"A balanced study of Colonial conditions and British policy which led to the Revolution. The author feels the British did not understand the stage of development that the colonies had reached and therefore tried to apply ill-advised solutions." Guide to Read in Am Hist

Boorstin, Daniel J. (Daniel Joseph), 1914-

The Americans: The colonial experience. Random House 1958 434p $40; pa $13   **973.2**
1. United States—Civilization 2. United States—History—1600-1775, Colonial period 3. American national characteristics 4. United States—Intellectual life
ISBN 0-394-41506-X; 0-394-70513-0 (pa)
The first volume of the author's trilogy entitled: The Americans

"This study of colonial America attempts to show that it was not merely an offshoot of the mother country, but a new civilization. . . . The author centers his highly informative work on colonial education, the special qualities of American speech, and the growth of a distinct culture." Booklist
Includes bibliography
Followed by: The Americans: The national experience, entered in class 973

Daily life in colonial America. Reader's Digest Assn. 1993 144p il maps (Journeys into the past) $18.98   **973.2**
1. United States—Social life and customs—1600-1775, Colonial period
ISBN 0-89577-497-6   LC 93-2719
This volume examines colonial social, cultural, religious, domestic and intellectual life

Fisher, Sydney George, 1856-1927

The Quaker colonies; a chronicle of the proprietors of the Delaware; by Sydney G. Fisher. Yale Univ. Press 1919 244p il map (Chronicles of America series, v8)   **973.2**
1. Pennsylvania—History 2. New Jersey—History 3. Delaware—History 4. Society of Friends
Available in hardcover from Reprint Services Corp.
"Abraham Lincoln edition"
Contents: Birth of Pennsylvania; Penn sails for the Delaware; Life in Philadelphia; Types of the population; Troubles of Penn and his sons; French and Indian War; Decline of Quaker government; Beginning of New Jersey; Planters and traders of southern Jersey; Scotch covenanters and others in east Jersey; United Jerseys; Little Delaware; English conquest; Bibliography

Hawke, David Freeman

Everyday life in early America. Harper & Row 1988 195p il (Everyday life in America) hardcover o.p. paperback available $13   **973.2**
1. United States—History—1600-1775, Colonial period 2. United States—Social life and customs
ISBN 0-06-091251-0 (pa)   LC 87-17667
Also available in hardcover from Borgo Press

The author "provides enlightening and colorful descriptions of early Colonial Americans and debunks many widely held assumptions about 17th century settlers. . . . This book is informative but could have been more deeply researched." Publ Wkly
Includes bibliography

Hofstadter, Richard, 1916-1970

America at 1750; a social portrait. Knopf 1971 293p hardcover o.p. paperback available $9   **973.2**
1. United States—History—1600-1775, Colonial period 2. United States—Social conditions
ISBN 0-394-71795-3 (pa)
"Using primarily secondary accounts, Hofstadter examines the ethnic composition of the colonies in 1750; traces the development of white servitude, the slave trade, and the slave system; sketches briefly the middle-class framework of early America; and dissects the colonial religious paradigm and the impact of the Great Awakening." Choice
Includes bibliographical references

Langdon, William Chauncy, 1871-1947

Everyday things in American life, 1607-1776. Scribner 1937 xx, 353p il map   **973.2**
1. United States—Social life and customs—1600-1775, Colonial period
Available in hardcover from Reprint Services Corp.
Companion volume to Everyday things in American life, 1776-1876, entered in class 973
"How the early colonists lived, what they ate, what they worked at, how they travelled, all helped out with a variety of illustrative material." New Yorker
Includes bibliography

Reich, Jerome R.

Colonial America. 3rd ed. Prentice-Hall 1994 332p il maps pa $22.95   **973.2**
1. United States—History—1600-1775, Colonial period
ISBN 0-13-088808-7   LC 92-46073
First published 1984
This book takes readers "from Norse explorations to the events leading up to the Declaration of Independence. Included are glimpses of life in the colonies, colonial government and administration, and a bit of Amerindian history." Hist Rev New Books [review of 1984 edition]
Includes bibliographical references

Scott, John Anthony, 1916-

Settlers on the Eastern Shore; the British colonies in North America, 1607-1750; illustrated with contemporary prints and photographs. Facts on File 1991 133p il maps music (Library of American history) $17.95   **973.2**
1. United States—History—1600-1775, Colonial period
ISBN 0-8160-2327-1   LC 90-13860
First published 1967 by Knopf in a different form
A "view of British colonial America that utilizes primary sources such as diaries, letters, and other accounts

Scott, John Anthony, 1916— *Continued*
to show how the settlers felt about their new home and
what life was actually like. . . . [A] strength here is the
inclusion of material about groups such as Native Americans, indentured servants, and slaves." SLJ
Includes bibliographical references

Washburne, Carolyn Kott, 1944-
A multicultural portrait of colonial life. Marshall
Cavendish 1994 80p il (Perspectives) lib bdg
$19.95   **973.2**
1. Minorities 2. United States—History—1600-1775,
Colonial period 3. United States—Social life and customs—1600-1775, Colonial period
ISBN 1-85435-657-7   LC 93-10320
"Washburne examines the influences of African Americans, women, and Native Americans on U.S. colonial
life. Individuals such as Abigail Adams, Mary Katherine
Goddard, James Forten, Pontiac, and Phillis Wheatley are
briefly profiled and placed in a historical context. Each
group's form of governance; work, trade, and manufacturing; home and family life; alliances and conflicts; and
enduring legacies are related. . . . An attractive resource." SLJ
Includes glossary and bibliography

Wolf, Stephanie Grauman
As various as their land; the everyday lives of
eighteenth-century Americans. HarperCollins Pubs.
1993 305p il maps (Everyday life in America)
hardcover o.p. paperback available $13.50   **973.2**
1. United States—Social life and customs—1600-
1775, Colonial period
ISBN 0-06-092537-X (pa)   LC 92-54754
The author examines the "diversity of experience that
marked America's people in the 100 or so years preceding nationhood. Wolf's main concern is with immigrant
cultures and their transfer to, and transformation of, the
soil of New England, the Middle Atlantic region, and the
American South." Libr J
"An excellent overview of the foundation of our society's successes and failures." Booklist
Includes bibliography

973.3 United States—Periods of Revolution and Confederation, 1775-1789

The **American** Revolution: opposing viewpoints;
William Dudley, book editor. Greenhaven Press
1992 287p il (American history series) lib bdg
$19.95; pa $11.95   **973.3**
1. United States—History—1775-1783, Revolution
ISBN 1-56510-011-5 (lib bdg); 1-56510-010-7 (pa)
                                              LC 92-21795
"Opposing viewpoints series"
A collection of papers exploring the causes, conduct
and participants of the American Revolution
Includes bibliographical references

Draper, Theodore, 1912-
A struggle for power; the American Revolution.
Times Bks. 1996 544p $35; pa $17   **973.3**
1. United States—History—1775-1783, Revolution
ISBN 0-8129-2575-0; 0-679-77642-7 (pa)
                                              LC 95-11605
The author "maintains that the Revolution was really
a power struggle spawned by the British system of char-
tering colonies, which placed fiscal control of public
funds with the colonial assemblies." Libr J
This is an "elegantly written, masterful study. . . .
Drawing freely on period pamphlets, letters, petitions,
travelogues and assembly minutes, [the author] vividly
evokes the populist discontent, intellectual gymnastics
and mob violence that led to revolution." Publ Wkly
Includes bibliographical references

The **Encyclopedia** of colonial and revolutionary
America; general editor, John Mack Faragher.
Facts on File 1990 484p il maps $50   **973.3**
1. United States—History—1600-1775, Colonial period—Dictionaries 2. United States—History—1775-
1783, Revolution—Dictionaries
ISBN 0-8160-1744-1   LC 88-26049
Also available in paperback from Da Capo Press
This "reference provides brief explanations of the role
events, places, persons, and institutions played throughout the North American continent from the voyages of
Columbus through nationhood under the Articles of Con-
federation." Wilson Libr Bull

Hibbert, Christopher, 1924-
Redcoats & Rebels; the American Revolution
through British eyes. Norton 1990 375p il maps
o.p.; Avon Bks. paperback available $13.50
                                              973.3
1. United States—History—1775-1783, Revolution
ISBN 0-380-71544-9 (pa)   LC 90-31753
"Beginning with the Stamp Act of 1765, which the
British saw as not only perfectly legal but also morally
defensible . . . the author interprets the War for Independence as viewed by the mother country: more a dirty
insurrection than the sacred pursuit of liberty." Booklist
"By providing the often overlooked side of an important and commonly told story, this book offers new insights and pleasurable reading." SLJ

Leckie, Robert
George Washington's war; the saga of the
American Revolution. HarperCollins Pubs. 1992
672p maps hardcover o.p. paperback available
$17.50   **973.3**
1. United States—History—1775-1783, Revolution
ISBN 0-06-092215-X (pa)   LC 92-52607
"Tracing the causes and events leading to the
American Revolution, Leckie's insightful analysis of ma-
jor political and military leaders, key battles, and foreign
alliances offers a unique perspective for history students
and teachers." Booklist
Includes bibliographical references

Marrin, Albert, 1936-
The war for independence; the story of the American Revolution. Atheneum Pubs. 1988 276p il maps $19   **973.3**
   1. United States—History—1775-1783, Revolution
   ISBN 0-689-31390-X   LC 87-13711
This is an account of events in American history from the end of the French and Indian Wars to the battle of Yorktown
"Profusely illustrated by prints, paintings, and maps, the text is notable both for its style and its depth." Bull Cent Child Books
Includes bibliography

Morgan, Edmund Sears
The birth of the Republic, 1763-89. 3rd ed. University of Chicago Press 1992 206p (Chicago history of American civilization) $33; pa $9.95
973.3
   1. United States—History—1775-1783, Revolution
   2. United States—History—1783-1809
   ISBN 0-226-53756-0; 0-226-53757-9 (pa)
LC 92-8871
First published 1956
A brief study of the American revolutionary period from 1763 to 1789
Includes bibliographical references

Purvis, Thomas L., 1949-
Revolutionary America, 1763-1800. Facts on File 1995 383p il maps (Almanacs of American life) $75   **973.3**
   1. United States—History—1775-1783, Revolution
   2. United States—Social life and customs
   ISBN 0-8160-2528-2   LC 93-38382
"Arranged thematically, sections such as 'Climate,' 'Economy,' 'Population,' 'Health,' 'Religion,' 'Architecture,' and 'Education' provide statistical charts, graphs, and other data to show what life was like in the various parts of the country. . . . The text, covering perhaps a third of the book, explains and elaborates on the tabular information, pulling everything together in a relevant, interesting manner." SLJ
For a fuller review see: Booklist, Oct. 1, 1995
Includes bibliographical references

Stokesbury, James L.
A short history of the American Revolution. Morrow 1991 304p maps hardcover o.p. paperback available $10   **973.3**
   1. United States—History—1775-1783, Revolution
   ISBN 0-688-12304-X (pa)   LC 90-29108
"Stokesbury's concise retelling of the war is spiced with his own insights and explanations. . . . This is shorter history at its best: informative, lively, and fun to read, yet thoughtful and erudite." Libr J
Includes bibliographical references

Tuchman, Barbara Wertheim
The first salute; a view of the American Revolution; [by] Barbara W. Tuchman. Knopf 1988 347p il maps $22.95   **973.3**
   1. United States—History—1775-1783, Revolution
   ISBN 0-394-55333-0   LC 88-45216
Also available Thorndike Press large print edition and in paperback from Ballantine Bks.
"'The first salute' accorded to the striped flag of the thirteen States was given by a Dutch colony, St. Eustatius, in November, 1776. The subject of this study is the contribution of the Dutch and the French, to the independence of the United States." West Coast Rev Books
"The book is a tightly woven narrative, ingeniously structured. It is not a blow-by-blow account of the conflict; familiarity with issues and events is assumed. Instead, Tuchman takes a specific incident and through it elucidates the course and outcome of the war." Christ Sci Monit
Includes bibliography

Wood, W. J. (William J.), 1917-
Battles of the Revolutionary War, 1775-1781; with an introduction by John S.D. Eisenhower. Algonquin Bks. 1990 xxxii, 315p il maps (Major battles and campaigns) $24.95   **973.3**
   1. United States—History—1775-1783, Revolution—Campaigns
   ISBN 0-945575-03-3   LC 89-18463
"Wood focuses on 10 major battles and campaigns of the American Revolution that have unique military qualities. Maps and new insights about the leadership of both armies make this a worthy addition to military history collections." Booklist
Includes bibliographical references

The **World** almanac of the American Revolution; edited by L. Edward Purcell and David F. Burg. World Almanac 1992 386p il pa $18.95 **973.3**
   1. United States—History—1775-1783, Revolution
   ISBN 0-88687-574-9   LC 91-32057
A chronological examination of the events of the American Revolution and its aftermath, describing political and military actions. A separate section provides biographical information on important figures. Beginning with 1775, a one-page summary begins each year's events. Interspersed in the chronology are essays on special topics
Includes bibliographical references

973.4 United States—Constitutional period, 1789-1809

Cunliffe, Marcus, 1922-1990
The nation takes shape, 1789-1837. University of Chicago Press 1959 222p il (Chicago history of American civilization) hardcover o.p. paperback available $14.95   **973.4**
   1. United States—History—1783-1865
   ISBN 0-226-12667-6 (pa)
The author gives us a "commentary on the men and events which set the pattern for later American growth.

Cunliffe, Marcus, 1922-1990—*Continued*
Not confined to political history, the book ranges to such topics as 'The West,' 'Commerce and Industry,' 'Nationalism and Sectionalism,' 'Conservatism and Democracy,' and 'The American Character.'" Libr J
Includes bibliography

Lavender, David Sievert, 1910-
The way to the Western sea; Lewis and Clark across the continent; [by] David Lavender. Harper & Row 1988 444p il maps o.p.; Anchor Bks. (NY) paperback available $14   **973.4**
   1. Lewis, Meriwether, 1774-1809 2. Clark, William, 1770-1838 3. Lewis and Clark Expedition (1804-1806)
   ISBN 0-385-41155-3 (pa)   LC 88-45040
"An intimate account of the cross-continental expedition up the Missouri River, then on to the Pacific Coast undertaken by Meriwether Lewis and William Clark from May 14th, 1804, to Sept. 23, 1806." N Y Times Book Rev
"Explaining the politics of the expedition as well as its logistics, Lavender portrays the cast of characters with thoughtful detail and elucidates the explorers' findings about Indian cultures. The excitement and wonder of Lewis and Clark's remarkable adventure is vividly captured in this readable account." Booklist
Includes bibliography

Miller, John Chester, 1907-1991
The Federalist era, 1789-1801. Harper & Row 1960 304p il map (New American nation series) hardcover o.p. paperback available $15.25   **973.4**
   1. Federal Party (U.S.) 2. United States—History—1783-1809
   ISBN 0-06-133027-2 (pa)
A chronicle of the administrations of George Washington and John Adams, concentrating on the politics and diplomacy
Includes bibliography

973.5   United States—1809-1845

Bosco, Peter I.
The War of 1812. Millbrook Press 1991 128p il maps lib bdg $18.90   **973.5**
   1. United States—History—1812-1815, War of 1812
   ISBN 1-56294-004-X
"The causes of The War of 1812, the events surrounding it, and its various battles are described." SLJ
"Bosco provides an in-depth study of military strategy, with an emphasis on ships and sea battles. Black-and-white drawings and precise maps augment the excellent resource." Booklist
Includes glossary and bibliography

The **Era** of reform, 1830-1860; [documents; selected by] Henry Steele Commager. Krieger 1982 c1960 188p pa $11.50   **973.5**
   1. United States—Social conditions 2. United States—History—1815-1861
   ISBN 0-89874-498-9   LC 82-15190
"An Anvil original"

A reprint of the title first published 1960 by Van Nostrand
The fifty-five documents included in this volume begin with a letter from Thomas Jefferson at the end of his life and conclude with writings of Nathaniel Hawthorne and Horace Greeley
Includes bibliographical references

Hickey, Donald R., 1944-
The War of 1812; a forgotten conflict. University of Ill. Press 1989 457p il maps hardcover o.p. paperback available $14.95   **973.5**
   1. United States—History—1812-1815, War of 1812
   ISBN 0-252-06059-8 (pa)   LC 88-38928
"Hickey provides a well-researched and extensively documented overview of the causes and consequences of the War of 1812. In a penetrating analysis of prewar society, the author accumulates evidence suggesting that the war was ultimately unnecessary and unpopular. . . . Highly recommended as an inclusive political, military, and social treatment of a customarily neglected war." Booklist
Includes bibliography

Marrin, Albert, 1936-
1812: the war nobody won; illustrated with old prints & engravings, and diagrams & maps by Patricia A. Tobin. Atheneum Pubs. 1985 175p il maps $15.95   **973.5**
   1. United States—History—1812-1815, War of 1812
   ISBN 0-689-31075-7   • LC 84-21623
Describes the causes and leading events of the early nineteenth-century conflict between Great Britain and the United States
"A good introduction and overview of this often confusing chapter in American history." SLJ
Includes bibliography

Remini, Robert Vincent, 1921-
The Jacksonian era; [by] Robert V. Remini. 2nd ed. Davidson, H. 1997 150p il (American history series) pa $11.95   **973.5**
   1. Jackson, Andrew, 1767-1845 2. United States—Politics and government—1815-1861 3. United States—History—1815-1861
   ISBN 0-88295-931-X   LC 96-41307
First published 1989
The author "has masterfully summarized here the highlights of the Jacksonian era. The end product is fresh and insightful, with few flaws." Choice
Includes bibliographical references

Schlesinger, Arthur M., 1917-
The age of Jackson; by Arthur M. Schlesinger, Jr. Little, Brown 1945 577p hardcover o.p. paperback available $17.95   **973.5**
   1. United States—History—1815-1861 2. United States—Politics and government—1815-1861
   ISBN 0-316-77343-3 (pa)
The author shows the relation of Jacksonian democracy to law, industrialism, religion and literature, the beginning of the Free Soil movement and the growing intensity of sectional disputes
Includes bibliography

Sugden, John, 1947-
Tecumseh's last stand. University of Okla. Press
1985 298p il maps hardcover o.p. paperback
available $16.95   **973.5**
1. Tecumseh, Shawnee Chief, 1768-1813 2. United
States—History—1812-1815, War of 1812 3. Old
Northwest—History
ISBN 0-8061-2242-0 (pa)   LC 85-40480
"In this profile of the great Shawnee chief and general
Tecumseh, the characteristics of his remarkable personal-
ity are placed within the context of the role of the Indi-
ans in the War of 1812. . . . Sugden effectively utilizes
English and Canadian archives, court records, and other
source material to create a fascinating and much needed
addition to the literature." Booklist
Includes bibliography

Tocqueville, Alexis de
Democracy in America   **973.5**
1. United States—Social conditions 2. United
States—Politics and government 3. Democracy
4. American national characteristics
Hardcover and paperback editions available from various publishers
First part originally published in France, 1835; the
second in 1840
Based partly on the French author's observations of
American political and social conditions during a visit in
1831-1832. "It remains the best philosophical discussion
of Democracy illustrated by the experience of the United
States, up to the time when it was written, which can be
found in any language." Pratt Alcove

973.6   United States—1845-1861

Catton, William Bruce, 1926-
Two roads to Sumter; by William and Bruce
Catton. McGraw-Hill 1963 285p o.p.   **973.6**
1. Lincoln, Abraham, 1809-1865 2. Davis, Jefferson,
1808-1889 3. United States—History—1861-1865,
Civil War—Causes 4. United States—History—1815-
1861
"This study of the United States in the 1850's de-
scribes the thinking of Abraham Lincoln and Jefferson
Davis and their 'two roads' to the Civil War." Christ Sci
Monit

Johannsen, Robert Walter, 1925-
To the halls of the Montezumas; the Mexican
War in the American imagination; [by] Robert W.
Johannsen. Oxford Univ. Press 1985 363p il map
hardcover o.p. paperback available $17.95   **973.6**
1. Mexican War, 1846-1848
ISBN 0-19-504981-0 (pa)   LC 84-20696
This "is a scholarly but lively runthrough of the war
emphasizing the way it was portrayed in contemporary
newspapers, novels, and songs. Numerous passages from
letters and diaries enliven the text, which remains quite
readable in spite of its detail." Libr J
Includes bibliography

Lincoln, Abraham, 1809-1865
The Lincoln-Douglas debates of 1858; edited by
Robert W. Johannsen. Oxford Univ. Press 1965
330p pa $15.95   **973.6**
1. Lincoln-Douglas debates, 1858 2. United States—
Politics and government—1815-1861
ISBN 0-19-500921-5
With introductions to give perspective, this "includes
the seven debates of 1858 as well as Douglas's speech
in Chicago that set the tone for the debates." Guide to
Read in Am Hist
Includes bibliography

Nardo, Don, 1947-
The Mexican-American War. Lucent Press 1991
96p il maps (America's wars) lib bdg $24.95
     973.6
1. Mexican War, 1846-1848
ISBN 1-56006-402-1   LC 91-16728
This book "discusses the historical/cultural background
of the conflict, plus the major battles. Little exists for
this audience on the 1845-48 war; thus, the title should
be a boon to high school collections." SLJ
Includes glossary and bibliography

973.7   United States— Administration of Abraham Lincoln, 1861-1865. Civil War

Allen, Thomas B., 1929-
The Blue and the Gray; photography by Sam
Abell. National Geographic Soc. 1992 320p il map
$40   **973.7**
1. United States—History—1861-1865, Civil War
ISBN 0-87044-876-5   LC 92-13567
Also available with guidebook for $41.95 (ISBN 0-
87044-877-3)
This illustrated look at Civil War battlefields juxtaposes documentary photographs with recent shots of sites
and memorials
"The hurried, though crisply written, narrative is well
known, but the images of the war, several of them previously unpublished, summon powerful feelings about the
enduring and mystic chords of memory on war and its
costs." Libr J

Bailey, Ronald H.
Battles for Atlanta: Sherman moves east; by
Ronald H. Bailey and the editors of Time-Life
Books. Time-Life Bks. 1985 176p il maps (Civil
War) $19.95   **973.7**
1. Sherman, William T. (William Tecumseh), 1820-
1891 2. Atlanta Campaign, 1864 3. United States—
History—1861-1865, Civil War
     LC 85-24521
Details Sherman's march from Chattanooga through
Georgia, the events of the Atlanta campaign and siege,
with photographs and illustrations from the Civil War era
Includes bibliography

Bailey, Ronald H.—*Continued*

The bloodiest day: the battle of Antietam; by Ronald H. Bailey and the editors of Times-Life Books. Time-Life Bks. 1984 176p il (Civil War) $19.95 **973.7**
1. Antietam (Md.), Battle of, 1862

LC 84-8871
Details Lee's invasion of Maryland in his attempt to gain Union territory and foreign support, which ended in heavy losses on both sides, and Lee's forced retreat
Includes bibliography

Forward to Richmond: McClellan's peninsular campaign; by Ronald H. Bailey and the editors of Time-Life Books. Time-Life Bks. 1983 176p il (Civil War) $19.95 **973.7**
1. McClellan, George Brinton, 1826-1885 2. Peninsular Campaign, 1862

LC 83-5034
An illustrated look at the Peninsular Campaign of 1862 and the role of George Brinton McClellan
Includes bibliography

Battle chronicles of the Civil War; James M. McPherson, editor; Richard Gottlieb, managing editor. Macmillan 1989 6v il maps set $150 **973.7**
1. United States—History—1861-1865, Civil War—Campaigns
ISBN 0-02-920661-8 LC 89-8316
Contents: v1 1861; v2 1862; v3 1863; v4 1864; v5 1865; v6 Leaders, index
"A chronological history of the Civil War, this work focuses on military campaigns and battles. The first five volumes are each devoted to one year of 'America's bloodiest and most momentous war,' beginning with 1861 and ending with 1865. The sixth volume of the set consists of essays on Abraham Lincoln, Jefferson Davis, Ulysses S. Grant, William T. Sherman, Robert E. Lee, and Stonewall Jackson. The concluding volume also has a list of recommended readings on 'strategy, tactics, campaigns, battles, and military leaders,' as well as an index for the entire set." Booklist

Bishop, Jim, 1907-1987
The day Lincoln was shot; with illustrations selected and arranged by Stefan Lorant. Harper & Row 1955 304p il hardcover o.p. paperback available $6.50 **973.7**
1. Lincoln, Abraham, 1809-1865—Assassination
ISBN 0-06-080005-4 (pa)
"Here is an hour-by-hour account of April 14, 1865, alternating between Lincoln's activities and those in the plot to kill the Chief Executive and members of his Cabinet. . . . The author has permitted the reader to live through Lincoln's last hours and to share the grief of his contemporaries." Doors to More Mature Read
Includes bibliography

The **Blockade**; runners and raiders; by the editors of Time-Life Books. Time-Life Bks. 1983 176p il (Civil War) $19.95 **973.7**
1. United States—History—1861-1865, Civil War—Naval operations

LC 83-468
Surveys naval tactics and events of the Civil War, using photographs and other illustrations from that time
Includes bibliography

Boatner, Mark Mayo, 1921-
The Civil War dictionary; by Mark Mayo Boatner III; maps and diagrams by Allen C. Northrop and Lowell I. Miller. rev ed. McKay, D. 1988 974p maps $30; pa $20 **973.7**
1. United States—History—1861-1865, Civil War—Dictionaries
ISBN 0-8129-1689-1; 0-679-73392-2 (pa)

LC 87-40599
First published 1959
"With more than 4,000 entries . . . this dictionary remains the most comprehensive and consistently accurate reference tool on the American Civil War. In addition to the biographical sketches there are entries relating to campaigns and battles, naval engagements, weapons, issues and incidents, military terms and definitions, politics, literature, and statistics." Choice
Includes bibliography

Catton, Bruce, 1899-1978
The American Heritage new history of the Civil War; narrative by Bruce Catton; edited and with a new introduction by James McPherson; contributing editor, Noah Andre Trudeau. Viking 1996 630p il maps $50 **973.7**
1. United States—History—1861-1865, Civil War—Pictorial works
ISBN 0-670-86804-3 LC 96-8325
First published 1960 with title: The American Heritage picture history of the Civil War
Includes CD-ROM
McPherson "has enriched Catton's classical text with an extensive array of archival material culled from across the nation and abroad. . . . Newly developed three-dimensional maps illuminate the war's battles and campaigns." Publisher's note
Includes bibliographical references

Gettysburg; the final fury. Doubleday 1974 114p il maps hardcover o.p. paperback available $12.95 **973.7**
1. Gettysburg (Pa.), Battle of, 1863
ISBN 0-385-41145-6 (pa)
An account of the causes, events and consequences of the Civil War battle which turned the tide in favor of the Union forces
"What is truly distinguished about Catton's retelling of the Gettysburg story is his nearly total focus on the significant human and military details and, most important, the lucid serenity of his descriptive writing." Publ Wkly

Catton, Bruce, 1899-1978—*Continued*

Reflections on the Civil War; edited by John Leekley. Doubleday 1981 xxiv, 246p il o.p.; Berkley Bks. paperback available $12   **973.7**

1. United States—History—1861-1865, Civil War

ISBN 0-425-14141-1 (pa)   LC 79-6164

"In this work, Bruce [Catton] reflects on a wide range of subjects, including the cause and meaning of the Civil War; the actual experience of army life for the common soldier; and the major campaigns." Foreword

"If seldom profound, Catton is always evocative." Libr J

A stillness at Appomattox. Doubleday 1953 438p il hardcover o.p. paperback available $12.95   **973.7**

1. Appomattox Campaign, 1865 2. United States—History—1861-1865, Civil War—Campaigns

ISBN 0-385-04451-8 (pa)

Also available in hardcover from P. Smith

Concluding volume of trilogy which began with Mr. Lincoln's army (1951) and Glory road (1952). This final volume of the author's study of the Army of the Potomac covers the period from early 1864 to April, 1865

The author's "approach is judicious, his interpretation unbiased and his coverage comprehensive. . . . 'A Stillness at Appomattox' is a magnificent piece of writing." N Y Times Book Rev

Includes bibliography

Terrible swift sword. Doubleday 1963 559p maps (Centennial history of the Civil War) o.p.   **973.7**

1. United States—History—1861-1865, Civil War

The second book in a trilogy, preceded by: The coming fury (1961) and followed by: Never call retreat (1965)

This book begins just after the Battle of Bull Run in 1861 and continues until General McClellan was relieved of his command of the Army of the Potomac in 1862. The author makes two main points; how the war slowly but steadily got out of control, and how all out conflict changed the war's purpose and made it a war for human freedom

Includes bibliography

This hallowed ground; the story of the Union side of the Civil War. Doubleday 1956 437p maps (Mainstream of America series) o.p.   **973.7**

1. United States—History—1861-1865, Civil War

This history deals with the entire scope of the Civil War—from the months of unrest and hysteria that led to Fort Sumter through the Union victory

Includes bibliography

The **Causes** of the Civil War; edited by Kenneth M. Stampp. 3rd rev ed. Simon & Schuster 1991 255p pa $11   **973.7**

1. United States—History—1861-1865, Civil War—Causes 2. United States—History—1861-1865, Civil War—Sources

ISBN 0-671-75155-7   LC 91-36819

"A Touchstone book"

First published 1959 by Prentice-Hall

This book integrates the conclusions of various post-war historians with the thoughts of contemporary commentators like Jefferson Davis, Horace Greeley, and Lincoln. Political, cultural and economic aspects are emphasized

Includes bibliographical references

The **Civil** War; executive editor, Carter Smith. Facts on File 1989 various paging il (American historical images on file) $155   **973.7**

1. United States—History—1861-1865, Civil War—Pictorial works

ISBN 0-8160-1609-7   LC 86-32751

This looseleaf "volume of reproducible illustrations about the Civil War contains over 200 photographs, engravings, lithographs, paintings, and other visual representations. . . . The volume is divided into seven sections, one for the prelude to the war, one for each of the five war years, and one for Reconstruction. A biographical sketch or description of the event accompanies each picture. Indexed by subject. This set is an excellent source for research papers." Nichols. Guide to Ref Books for Sch Media Cent. 4th edition

The **Civil** War: opposing viewpoints; William Dudley, book editor. Greenhaven Press 1995 310p il (American history series) lib bdg $19.95; pa $11.95   **973.7**

1. United States—History—1861-1865, Civil War

ISBN 1-56510-225-8 (lib bdg); 1-56510-224-X (pa)
                                           LC 94-9510

"Dudley has arranged primary source, documentary evidence into six chapters that present differing views of issues and events surrounding the Civil War. For example, in the first chapter, which examines the roots of the war, two significant politicians of the time, Daniel Webster and John C. Calhoun, debate the preservation of the Union. . . . A valuable one-stop source of primary information." SLJ

Includes bibliography

Clark, Champ, 1923-

Gettysburg: the Confederate high-tide; by Champ Clark and the editors of Time-Life Books. Time-Life Bks. 1985 176p il maps (Civil War) $19.95   **973.7**

1. Gettysburg (Pa.), Battle of, 1863
                                           LC 85-1046

This book covers the 1863 Confederate campaign into the North culminating with the Union victory at the great three-day battle at Gettysburg

Includes bibliography

Davis, William C., 1946-

Brother against brother: the war begins; by William C. Davis and the editors of Time-Life Books. Time-Life Bks. 1983 176p il (Civil War) $19.95   **973.7**

1. United States—History—1861-1865, Civil War—Causes
                                           LC 82-17014

A look at the events leading up to the start of the Civil War. Contains numerous historical illustrations

Includes bibliography

Davis, William C., 1946—*Continued*

Death in the trenches: Grant at Petersburg; by William C. Davis and the editors of Time-Life Books. Time-Life Bks. 1986 176p il (Civil War) $19.95   **973.7**
1. Grant, Ulysses S. (Ulysses Simpson), 1822-1885
2. Petersburg (Va.)—History—Siege, 1864-1865
LC 86-5930
An illustrated look at the Union Army's Siege of Petersburg, Virginia, led by General Grant
Includes bibliography

First blood: Fort Sumter to Bull Run; by William C. Davis and the editors of Time-Life Books. Time-Life Bks. 1983 176p il (Civil War) $19.95   **973.7**
1. United States—History—1861-1865, Civil War— Campaigns
LC 82-19546
A pictorial survey of the early battles of the Civil War, from the Confederate attack on Fort Sumter to the Battle of Bull Run
Includes bibliography

Dear Mr. Lincoln; letters to the president; compiled and edited by Harold Holzer. Addison-Wesley 1993 380p il $26.95; pa $15
973.7
1. Lincoln, Abraham, 1809-1865 2. United States— History—1861-1865, Civil War
ISBN 0-201-63289-6; 0-201-40829-5 (pa)
LC 93-8083
"Lincoln was deluged with unoffical correspondence from ordinary citizens pertaining to a wide variety of topics: advice and instruction; compliments and congratulations; complaints and criticisms; family matters; and threats and warnings. For each letter, Holzer offers a brief explanatory note." Booklist
"The work is well organized and edited and provides additional insight into both Lincoln and public opinion at the time." Libr J
Includes bibliographical references

Encyclopedia of the Confederacy; Richard N. Current, editor in chief; editorial board, Paul D. Escott [et al.] Simon & Schuster 1993 4v set $365   **973.7**
1. Confederate States of America—Dictionaries
ISBN 0-13-275991-8   LC 93-4133
"Provides extensive coverage through more than 1,400 articles signed by scholars and emphasizing the role and perspective of the Confederacy. Offers accounts of campaigns and battles; biographical sketches; discussion of the government and its conduct of economic and foreign affairs; roles of ethnic minorities, women, and the free and slave African American; the cultural life of the South. Extensive cross-references and index. Illustrations include specially commissioned maps, contemporary etchings and photographs." Guide to Ref Books. 11th edition

Faust, Drew Gilpin
Mothers of invention; women of the slaveholding South in the American Civil War. University of N.C. Press 1996 326p il $29.95
973.7
1. United States—History—1861-1865, Civil War— Women 2. Women—Southern States
ISBN 0-8078-2255-8   LC 95-8896
Based on journals, letters and memoirs, this is an "analysis of the impact of secession, invasion and conquest on Southern white women. Antebellum images based on helplessness and dependence were challenged as women assumed an increasing range of social and economic responsibilities. . . . Faust's provocative analysis of a complex subject merits a place in all collections of U.S. history." Publ Wkly
Includes bibliographical references

Foner, Eric
A house divided; America in the age of Lincoln; [by] Eric Foner, Olivia Mahoney. Norton 1990 179p il hardcover o.p. paperback available $22.50
973.7
1. Lincoln, Abraham, 1809-1865 2. United States— History—1800-1899 (19th century)
ISBN 0-393-30612-7 (pa)   LC 89-9239
Issued in conjunction with an exhibit at the Chicago Historical Society, on view for a ten-year period, beginning in January 1990
The text gives an "overview of the antebellum U.S., the Civil War years, and the great conflict's aftermath. Best of all are the portrayed exhibit pieces, including clean reproductions of paintings, archival photos, and lithographs of famous people, places, and events as well as contemporary artifacts." Booklist
Includes bibliographical references

Gallman, J. Matthew (James Matthew)
The North fights the Civil War: the home front. Dee, I.R. 1994 211p (American ways series) $22.50; pa $14   **973.7**
1. United States—History—1861-1865, Civil War
ISBN 1-56663-049-5; 1-56663-050-9 (pa)
LC 93-47471
This is a study of "the impact of the Civil War on the political, social, and economic developments in the North as well as the South. . . . Gallman examines the traditions the North relied upon in preparing for war and the adjustments made to compensate for the large number of troops and supplies needed. The author disagrees with most historians on the war's impact upon economic growth in the late 19th century, arguing that economic growth actually slowed after the war. He also looks at the role that women, blacks, labor unions, and politicians played." Libr J
"A tenable thesis, capably rendered, on aspects of the epic seldom visited in the steady stream of Civil War books." Booklist
Includes bibliographical references

Gettysburg; by the editors of Time-Life Books. Time-Life Bks. 1995 180p il maps (Voices of the Civil War) $29.95   **973.7**
1. Gettysburg (Pa.), Battle of, 1863
LC 94-42303
"The story of the Battle of Gettysburg is told through the eyewitness accounts of the people who were at the scene. Diaries and letters of soldiers, officers, nurses and Gettysburg civilians are used. The book is well researched and . . . contains many excellent photos and maps as well as drawings and paintings done by the people who were in Gettysburg during the battle." Book Rep
Includes bibliographical references

Goolrick, William K.
Rebels resurgent: Fredericksburg to Chancellorsville; by William K. Goolrick and the editors of Time-Life Books. Time-Life Bks. 1985 176p il (Civil War) $19.95   **973.7**
1. United States—History—1861-1865, Civil War—Campaigns
LC 84-23984
Text and numerous illustrations portray the Confederate victories at Fredericksburg in 1862 and Chancellorsville in 1863
Includes bibliography

Hall, Richard, 1930-
Patriots in disguise; women warriors of the Civil War. Paragon House 1993 224p il o.p.; Marlowe & Co. paperback available $10   **973.7**
1. Women soldiers 2. United States—History—1861-1865, Civil War
ISBN 1-56924-864-8 (pa)   LC 92-17204
"This loosely organized narrative chronicle of the courageous exploits of numerous women who served in the Civil War as battlefield nurses, spies, and combat soldiers will make a lively addition to well-developed Civil War collections." Booklist
Includes bibliographical references

√ **Hansen, Joyce**
Between two fires; black soldiers in the Civil War. Watts 1993 160p il (African-American experience) lib bdg $22.70; pa $6.95   **973.7**
1. African American soldiers 2. United States—History—1861-1865, Civil War
ISBN 0-531-11151-2 (lib bdg); 0-531-15676-1 (pa)
LC 92-37381
Documents the recruitment, training, and struggles of African American soldiers during the Civil War and examines the campaigns in which they participated
This is a "well-researched and well-written volume. . . . Using primary-source material that is thoroughly documented within the text and in an excellent bibliography, Hansen has personalized this history." SLJ

√ **Hargrove, Hondon B., 1916-**
Black Union soldiers in the Civil War. McFarland & Co. 1988 250p il $35   **973.7**
1. United States. Army—History 2. United States—History—1861-1865, Civil War 3. African American soldiers
ISBN 0-89950-337-3   LC 88-42511
This volume "discusses the participation of Blacks in the Union Army during the Civil War. The chronologically arranged narrative covers Black soldiers in each battle. Special features include an extensive bibliography and nine appendixes that reprint documents and include rosters and statistics." Nichols. Guide to Ref Books for Sch Media Cent. 4th edition

Hattaway, Herman
How the North won; a military history of the Civil War; [by] Herman Hattaway and Archer Jones; illustrations by Jerry A. Vanderlinde. University of Ill. Press 1983 762p il maps hardcover o.p. paperback available $21.95   **973.7**
1. United States—History—1861-1865, Civil War—Campaigns
ISBN 0-252-06210-8 (pa)   LC 81-16332
In this examination of Civil War strategy "there is less description of battles than in standard accounts and much more attention to campaigns, command structure, and communications. . . . Books about strategy are often dull or incomprehensible, but this one combines clear exposition, numerous diagrams, and colorful anecdotes in a highly readable narrative." Choice
Includes bibliography

Jackson, Donald Dale, 1935-
Twenty million Yankees: the Northern home front; by Donald Dale Jackson and the editors of Time-Life Books. Time-Life Bks. 1985 176p il maps (Civil War) $19.95   **973.7**
1. United States—History—1861-1865, Civil War
LC 84-28030
An illustrated look at the social and political aspects of life in the North during the Civil War
Includes bibliography

Jaynes, Gregory
The killing ground: Wilderness to Cold Harbor; by Gregory Jaynes and the editors of Time-Life Books. Time-Life Bks. 1986 176p il maps (Civil War) $19.95   **973.7**
1. Virginia—History—1861-1865, Civil War
LC 86-1256
Text and numerous illustrations survey key Civil War battles in Virginia in early 1864
Includes bibliography

Katcher, Philip, 1941-
The Civil War source book. Facts on File 1992 318p il maps $35   **973.7**
1. United States—History—1861-1865, Civil War
ISBN 0-8160-2823-0   LC 92-8180
"Beginning with the campaigns and battles, the author explains the military technology of the day, troop organi-

Katcher, Philip, 1941—— *Continued*
zation, and life in the services. Biographies of important leaders and a thorough glossary that includes period terms are included. An abundance of photographs, charts, maps, and tables provide data that is invaluable. . . . This is a book that should be in every high school and public library." SLJ
Includes bibliographical references

Kirchberger, Joe H.
The Civil War and Reconstruction; an eyewitness history; [by] Joe Kirchberger. Facts on File 1991 389p il maps (Eyewitness history series) $45   **973.7**
1. United States—History—1861-1865, Civil War—Sources 2. Reconstruction (1865-1876)
ISBN 0-8160-2171-6   LC 90-40852
This work contains "quotations from eyewitnesses' memoirs, letters, diaries, newspapers, and official documents. Those quoted come from all walks of life. . . . Thirty-three documents are excerpted. Four appendixes contain valuable primary-source and reference materials. . . . Interspersed throughout are political cartoons, photographs, and paintings. . . . An excellent reference tool." SLJ
Includes bibliographical references

Korn, Jerry
The fight for Chattanooga: Chickamauga to Missionary Ridge; by Jerry Korn and the editors of Time-Life Books. Time-Life Bks. 1985 176p il maps (Civil War) $19.95   **973.7**
1. United States—History—1861-1865, Civil War
                                                LC 85-13981
An illustrated presentation of the key personalities and battle plans for the battles of Chickamauga, Chattanooga, Lookout Mountain and Missionary Ridge
Includes bibliography

War on the Mississippi: Grant's Vicksburg campaign; by Jerry Korn and the editors of Time-Life Books. Time-Life Bks. 1985 175p il maps (Civil War) $19.95   **973.7**
1. Grant, Ulysses S. (Ulysses Simpson), 1822-1885 2. Vicksburg (Miss.)—Siege, 1863
                                                LC 84-16206
An illustrated look at General Grant's campaign to wrest the strategically important Mississippi Valley from Confederate hands
Includes bibliography

Lee takes command: from Seven Days to Second Bull Run; by the editors of Time-Life Books. Time-Life Bks. 1984 176p il maps (Civil War) $19.95   **973.7**
1. Lee, Robert E. (Robert Edward), 1807-1870 2. Peninsular Campaign, 1862 3. Shenandoah Valley Campaign, 1862
                                                LC 83-24382
This volume describes how the Confederate army under the command of Robert E. Lee thwarted a drive against the capital in Richmond, Virginia, by Union forces under George McClellan in June, 1862. Driving

the enemy back in a series of battles called the Seven Days, Lee took the offensive and moved north in maneuvers climaxing in the second major battle at Bull Run in August, 1862. Illustrations include photographs, engravings, paintings and battle maps
Includes bibliography

Lincoln, Abraham, 1809-1865
The portable Abraham Lincoln; edited and with an introduction by Andrew Delbanco. Viking 1992 xxxvii, 341p il hardcover o.p. paperback available $12   **973.7**
1. United States—Politics and government—1815-1861 2. United States—Politics and government—1861-1865
ISBN 0-14-017031-6 (pa)   LC 91-37488
"The Viking portable library"
Material drawn from Speeches and writings, published by the Library of America (1989)
"This collection shows Lincoln at work in law, politics, and war. All the great Lincoln works are here, with the added bonus of several personal memos that show Lincoln's humor." Libr J
Includes bibliography

Wit & wisdom of Abraham Lincoln; a treasury of more than 650 quotations and anecdotes; [by] James C. Humes; with a foreword by Lamar Alexander. HarperCollins Pubs. 1996 250p $20
                                                      973.7
ISBN 0-06-017244-4   LC 95-38431
A collection of adages, quotations, anecdotes and speeches of Lincoln, accompanied by commentary from Humes. Also included are sections by Humes containing Lincoln lore and stories related to the assassination and to the Gettysburg address
Includes bibliography

Macdonald, John, 1945-
Great battles of the Civil War; foreword by John Keegan. Macmillan 1988 200p il maps hardcover o.p. paperback available $24.95   **973.7**
1. United States—History—1861-1865, Civil War—Campaigns
ISBN 0-02-034554-2 (pa)   LC 88-1782
The author "has selected 17 crucial Civil War engagements and applied computer mapping to their geography. . . . The cartography is accompanied by an intelligent text, clear graphs of force and loss ratios, and well-chosen illustrations. This unique Civil War atlas is valuable, if not indispensable, for library collections." Libr J

Marrin, Albert, 1936-
Unconditional surrender; U.S. Grant and the Civil War. Atheneum Pubs. 1994 200p il maps $21   **973.7**
1. Grant, Ulysses S. (Ulysses Simpson), 1822-1885 2. United States—History—1861-1865, Civil War
ISBN 0-689-31837-5   LC 93-20041
"Although this book tells of the early and post-war life of Ulysses Grant, it's not a biography so much as a Civil War chronicle that very successfully uses General

Marrin, Albert, 1936—_Continued_

Grant as a focus. . . . Using extensive eyewitness accounts, Marrin has distilled copious research into a history of living men and women who are complete with faults and contradictions (the racism of many of the Northern commanders, including Grant, is made clear); Grant seems here to be a man splendid in wartime and floundering in peace, except in his happy family life."
Bull Cent Child Books

Includes bibliography

McPherson, James M.

Abraham Lincoln and the second American Revolution. Oxford Univ. Press 1991 173p $18.75; pa $10.95 **973.7**
1. Lincoln, Abraham, 1809-1865 2. United States—History—1861-1865, Civil War
ISBN 0-19-505542-X; 0-19-507606-0 (pa)
LC 90-6885

The author "examines Lincoln's role in the transformation wrought by the Civil War—the liberation of four million slaves, the overthrow of the social and political order of the South." Publ Wkly

Includes bibliographical references

Battle cry of freedom; the Civil War era. Oxford Univ. Press 1988 904p il maps (Oxford history of the United States) $45 **973.7**
1. United States—History—1861-1865, Civil War
ISBN 0-19-503863-0   LC 87-11045
Also available in paperback from Ballantine Bks.

A narrative history of events from the Mexican War through Appomattox. The author describes military campaigns, tactics and leaders. How the war changed the American political, social and economic landscape is explored

This volume "is comprehensive yet succinct, scholarly without being pedantic, eloquent but unrhetorical. It is compellingly readable." N Y Times Book Rev

Includes bibliography

Drawn with the sword; reflections on the American Civil War. Oxford Univ. Press 1996 258p $25 **973.7**
1. Stowe, Harriet Beecher, 1811-1896. Uncle Tom's cabin 2. United States—History—1861-1865, Civil War
ISBN 0-19-509679-7   LC 95-38107
Analyzed in Essay and general literature index

A collection of "essays on some of the most thought-provoking questions of the Civil War. All of the essays were published earlier but have been updated and revised for this compilation. The topics deal with such subjects as the origins of the Civil War, the slavery question in both North and South, why the North won the war and why the South lost, President Abraham Lincoln, and the change in historical writing." Libr J

"These pieces provide a lively reminder that the best scholarship is also often a pleasure to read." N Y Times Book Rev

Marching toward freedom; blacks in the Civil War, 1861-1865. Facts on File 1991 142p il music (Library of American history) $17.95; pa $8.95 **973.7**
1. United States—History—1861-1865, Civil War
2. African Americans—History
ISBN 0-8160-2337-9; 0-8160-3092-8 (pa)
LC 90-13918
First published 1968 by Knopf in a different form

The author "focuses on the many roles played by blacks during the Civil War—slave, soldier, teacher, laundress, and abolitionist—and does an excellent job of incorporating primary-source material and first-person accounts by both black participants and contemporary white observers. The coverage is quite fair and impartial. . . . This is sure to be a well-used addition to any collection." SLJ

Includes bibliography

What they fought for, 1861-1865. Louisiana State Univ. Press 1994 88p (Walter Lynwood Fleming lectures in southern history) $16.95 **973.7**
1. United States—History—1861-1865, Civil War—Causes
ISBN 0-8071-1904-0   LC 93-36934
Also available in paperback from Anchor Bks.

Drawing on the letters and diaries of frontline troops, McPherson argues against what he sees as "the orthodox view that the typical Union and Confederate soldier . . . knew little and cared less about the issues of the Civil War, and so fought not out of a commitment to a cause but rather out of devotion to his comrades and desire to survive. On the contrary, McPherson maintains, . . . [Union and Confederate soldiers] tended to be politically aware and to possess strong convictions and patriotic motivations." Rev Am Hist

"McPherson's emphasis on moral and ideological factors in war gives his book a significance well beyond its specific subject." Publ Wkly

Includes bibliographical references

Nevin, David, 1927-

The road to Shiloh: early battles in the West; by David Nevin and the editors of Time-Life Books. Time-Life Bks. 1983 175p il (Civil War) $19.95 **973.7**
1. United States—History—1861-1865, Civil War—Campaigns
LC 83-4692

Surveys early Civil War battles in Kentucky and Tennessee, leading up to the Union's costly victory at Shiloh in April of 1862

Includes bibliography

Sherman's march: Atlanta to the sea; by David Nevin and the editors of Time-Life Books. Time-Life Bks. 1986 175p il maps (Civil War) $19.95 **973.7**
1. Sherman, William T. (William Tecumseh), 1820-1891 2. United States—History—1861-1865, Civil War
LC 86-5764

This volume portrays the destruction of civilian property and resources as Sherman marched across Georgia

Nevin, David, 1927——Continued
and through the Carolinas
Includes bibliography

Robertson, James I., Jr.
Tenting tonight; the soldier's life; by James I. Robertson, Jr., and the editors of Time-Life Books. Time-Life Bks. 1984 176p il map (Civil War) $19.95 **973.7**
1. United States. Army—Military life 2. Confederate States of America. Army 3. United States—History—1861-1865, Civil War

LC 84-8465

The non-fighting life of both Northern and Confederate soldiers is depicted in this book, which is illustrated throughout with photographs and other illustrations from the Civil War era
Includes bibliography

Sears, Stephen W.
Chancellorsville. Houghton Mifflin 1996 593p $35 **973.7**
1. Chancellorsville (Va.), Battle of, 1863
ISBN 0-395-63417-2   LC 96-31220
This work "covers not only the fierce battle but the whole campaign, from its prelude when Joseph Hooker took command of the Army of the Potomac to its best-known epilogue, the death of Stonewall Jackson. Along the way, Sears argues persuasively that Hooker restored the organization and morale of his troops and planned the campaign with great skill as he successfully executed its opening stages. A chain of errors, assumptions, and communications failures combined with the genuine brilliance and good luck of the Confederates to lead to a stinging if indecisive Union defeat." Booklist
Includes bibliographical references

Second Manassas; by the editors of Time-Life Books. Time-Life Bks. 1995 168p il maps (Voices of the Civil War) $29.95 **973.7**
1. Bull Run, 2nd Battle of, 1862

LC 94-48737

This illustrated look at the Second Battle of Bull Run is based on primary source material and details the assault on federal troops by Jackson and Longstreet and the ensuing Union retreat
Includes bibliographical references

Spies, scouts, and raiders: irregular operations; by the editors of Time-Life Books. Time-Life Bks. 1985 176p il maps (Civil War) $19.95 **973.7**
1. United States—History—1861-1865, Civil War

LC 85-21014

An account of the unconventional military operations employed during the Civil War including intelligence networks and misinformation campaigns
Includes bibliography

Stokesbury, James L.
A short history of the Civil War. Morrow 1995 354p maps $25; pa $14 **973.7**
1. United States—History—1861-1865, Civil War
ISBN 0-688-11523-3; 0-688-15129-9 (pa)

LC 95-7093

Focusing on military aspects of the war, the author "describes the Civil War as America's defining experience both for the causes involved and for the tremendous human and material costs. Stokesbury makes a solid case that participants thought the war was worth the effort and the sacrifice." Publ Wkly
Includes bibliographical references

The **War** the women lived; female voices from the Confederate South; edited by Walter Sullivan; with a foreword by George Core. Sanders & Co. 1995 xxix, 319p $24.95 **973.7**
1. United States—History—1861-1865, Civil War—Women 2. Confederate States of America 3. Women—Southern States
ISBN 1-879941-30-9   LC 95-36150
This volume presents "excerpts from the personal Civil War accounts of 20 Condederate women. Some come from well-known figues, such as Mary Chesnut and Belle Boyd, others from relative unknowns. . . . Some of the women were native Southerners, others immigrants, some sat out the war at home . . . others served as nurses and even spies." Booklist
"Fascinating and riveting reading, this book is strongly recommended for any Civil War or women's history collection." Libr J

Ward, Geoffrey C.
The Civil War; an illustrated history; [by] Geoffrey C. Ward with Ken Burns and Ric Burns. Knopf 1990 425p il maps $60; pa $35 **973.7**
1. United States—History—1861-1865, Civil War
ISBN 0-394-56285-2; 0-679-74277-8 (pa)

LC 89-43475

The authors aim to "present the war as the central defining event of American history and of the lives of those Americans caught up in it. In four separate, additional essays, professional historians briefly discuss the causes of the war, emancipation, the politics of the war, and its long-term meaning." Libr J
"A companion to a nine-part Public Broadcasting System documentary, this superbly designed book easily stands on its own." N Y Times Book Rev
Includes bibliographical references

Wheeler, Richard
Witness to Gettysburg. Harper & Row 1987 273p il maps o.p.; New Am. Lib. paperback available $11.95 **973.7**
1. Gettysburg (Pa.), Battle of, 1863
ISBN 0-452-00984-7 (pa)   LC 86-46108
Also available in hardcover from P. Smith
A "detailed, eyewitness version of the Battle of Gettysburg. The preparatory events by both civilians and soldiers, the skirmishes and marches, the agonizing three days of battle—all are authentically reenacted. The realism generated by the quotations that Wheeler cohesively

Wheeler, Richard—*Continued*

spins into his narrative is enhanced by period maps and illustrations adapted from sketches or photographs made at the time of battle." Booklist

Includes bibliography

973.8   United States—Reconstruction period, 1865-1901

Foner, Eric

America's Reconstruction; people and politics after the Civil War; [by] Eric Foner and Olivia Mahoney. HarperPerennial 1995 151p il maps hardcover o.p. paperback available $17.50   **973.8**

1. Reconstruction (1865-1876) 2. United States—History—1865-1898

ISBN 0-06-096989-X (pa)   LC 94-40387

Companion volume to an exhibit which originated at the Valentine Museum in Richmond, Virginia, in April 1995

This book "investigates the origins of Reconstruction during the Civil War, explores how black and white Southerners responded to the Confederacy's defeat and the destruction of slavery, and examines the policies of Reconstruction governments and the reasons for their overthrow." Publisher's note

Includes bibliographical references

Golay, Michael, 1951-

The Spanish-American War. Facts on File 1995 112p il maps (America at war) lib bdg $17.95

     973.8

1. Spanish-American War, 1898

ISBN 0-8160-3174-6   LC 94-39157

"Golay has chronicled the causes, major events, and crucial military strategies of the Spanish-American War, including the conflict's effects on the course of American history. . . . This book has a lengthy index; many enlightening archival photos, reproductions, and maps; and frequent, well-integrated quotations from primary sources, including some quotes from soldiers in battle. . . . It is a solid, well-researched account." SLJ

Includes bibliographical references

Reconstruction: opposing viewpoints; Brenda Stalcup, book editor. Greenhaven Press 1995 310p il (American history series) lib bdg $19.95; pa $11.95   **973.8**

1. Reconstruction (1865-1876)

ISBN 1-56510-227-4 (lib bdg); 1-56510-226-6 (pa)

     LC 94-28639

This volume presents opposing viewpoints on various aspects of Reconstruction. Andrew Johnson, Ulysses S. Grant, Frederick Douglass, Thaddeus Stevens and C. Vann Woodward are among those whose views are represented

Includes bibliography

Robinson, Charles M., 1949-

A good year to die; the story of the great Sioux War. Random House 1995 xxxi, 412p il maps $27.50   **973.8**

1. Dakota Indians—Wars

ISBN 0-679-43025-3   LC 95-7820

Also available in paperback from University of Okla. Press

In this history of the Plains War of 1876 the author "demonstrates that the initial balance of forces was by no means unequal. The U.S. Army did not have the numbers, the doctrine or the leadership to win the kinds of decisive battles it expected to win. Robinson is particularly critical of generals George Crook and George A. Custer and correspondingly complimentary toward such Lakota warrior-statesmen as Sitting Bull and Crazy Horse. The work's centerpiece is the Little Bighorn, where Robinson believes Custer's exhausted men panicked in the face of superior numbers." Publ Wkly

Includes bibliography

Roosevelt, Theodore, 1858-1919

The Rough Riders; new introduction by Elting E. Morison. Da Capo Press 1990 298p il pa $13.95   **973.8**

1. United States. Army. Volunteer Cavalry, 1st—History 2. Spanish-American War, 1898

ISBN 0-306-80405-0   LC 90-38860

A reprint of the title first published 1899 by Scribner

This is a history of the First United States Volunteer Cavalry, which fought in the Spanish-American War under the command of Theodore Roosevelt

Samuels, Peggy

Remembering the Maine; [by] Peggy and Harold Samuels. Smithsonian Institution Press 1995 358p il $29.95   **973.8**

1. Maine (Battleship) 2. Spanish-American War, 1898

ISBN 1-56098-474-0   LC 94-34649

The authors "have examined many previously secret contemporary documents on the *Maine* disaster and reached a plausible solution to the mystery. Moreover, their reasoned but vividly written narrative explores the colorful personalities behind the diplomacy and makes some telling points about the origins of U.S. gunboat diplomacy in the 20th century." Libr J

Includes bibliographical references

Sandoz, Mari, 1896-1966

The Battle of the Little Bighorn. Lippincott 1966 191p maps (Great battles of history series) o.p.; University of Neb. Press paperback available $7.95   **973.8**

1. Custer, George Armstrong, 1839-1876 2. Little Bighorn, Battle of the, 1876

ISBN 0-8032-9100-0 (pa)

Also available in hardcover from Amereon

"An account of the United States Army expedition against the Sioux Nation with emphasis on the political motives and ambitions of General Custer." Publ Wkly

Includes bibliography

Schlereth, Thomas J.
Victorian America; transformations in everyday life, 1876-1915. HarperCollins Pubs. 1991 363p (Everyday life in America) hardcover o.p. paperback available $14   **973.8**
    1. United States—Social life and customs
    ISBN 0-06-092160-9 (pa)   LC 89-46555
    The author surveys the objects, events, experiences, products and tastes that comprised what he terms America's Victorian culture (1876-1915) and shows how its values shaped modern life
    Includes bibliographical references

Shifflett, Crandall A.
Victorian America, 1876 to 1913; [by] Crandall Shifflett. Facts on File 1996 408p il maps (Almanacs of American life) $70   **973.8**
    1. United States—Social life and customs
    ISBN 0-8160-2531-2   LC 95-13553
    This illustrated overview of 19th century America contains sections on: historical geography; native American life; government; popular culture; urban development; influential personalities; and arts and letters
    Includes bibliographical references

Welch, James, 1940-
Killing Custer; the Battle of the Little Bighorn and the fate of the Plains Indians; by James Welch with Paul Stekler. Norton 1994 320p il $25
    973.8
    1. Little Bighorn, Battle of the, 1876 2. Indians of North America—Wars
    ISBN 0-393-03657-X   LC 94-5617
    "Welch produced this history of the Indian wars of the northern plains as a by-product of his work scripting a television documentary on the Battle of the Little Bighorn. In addition to military history, it contains long sections describing the life of the Plains Indians, accounts of contemporary Indian radical groups, and Welch's reactions while visiting the various historic sites in the area." Libr J
    "Welch and his coauthor provide an interesting perspective and offer some intriguing views of unresolved questions. . . . This is not a groundbreaking book, but it is both interesting and well written." Booklist
    Includes bibliographical references

973.9   United States—1901-

America in the 20th century. Marshall Cavendish 1995 11v il maps lib bdg set $439.95   **973.9**
    1. United States—Civilization 2. United States—History—1900-1999 (20th century)
    ISBN 1-85435-736-0   LC 94-10854
    Authors of individual volumes include: Ann Angel, Gini Holland, Janet McDonnell, Kelli Peduzzi, Carolyn Kott Washburne and David K. Wright
    Contents: v1. 1900-1909; v2. 1910-1919; v3. 1920-1929; v4. 1930-1939; v5. 1940-1949; v6. 1950-1959; v7. 1960-1969; v8. 1970-1979; v9. 1980-1989; v10. 1990s; v11 Index

This set "devotes one volume of approximately 144 pages to each of the century's 10 decades and an eleventh volume to a multi-faceted index. . . . Among the general topics covered in each of volumes 1-10 are social policy, politics, foreign relations, the economy, business and industry, literature and the arts, sports, education, family life, crime, and demographic change." Booklist
This compendium offers a solid, in-depth approach to its subject and would be a useful reference tool in school libraries and YA collections in public libraries." Libr J

American decades. Gale Res. 1994-1996 9v ea $79   **973.9**
    1. United States—Civilization 2. United States—History—1900-1999 (20th century)
    Also available CD-ROM version
    "A Manly, Inc. book"
    The set is divided as follows: 1900-1909 (ISBN 0-8103-5722-4); 1910-1919 (ISBN 0-8103-5723-2); 1920-1929 (ISBN 0-8103-5724-0); 1930-1939 (ISBN 0-8103-5725-9); 1940-1949 (ISBN 0-8103-5726-7); 1950-1959 (ISBN 0-8103-5727-5); 1960-1969 (ISBN 0-8103-8883-9); 1970-1979 (ISBN 0-8103-8882-0); 1980-1989 (ISBN 0-8103-8881-2)
    "A series of volumes covering the twentieth century by decades. . . . Fun to browse, each volume is divided into 13 sections covering topics such as the arts, government and politics, lifestyles and social trends, medicine and health, and sports. Each section opens with a chronology and overview and closes with short biographies, deaths, and a bibliography of important books published in the decade. Sidebars highlight events and prominent individuals." Am Libr

Gordon, Lois G.
The Columbia chronicles of American life, 1910-1992; [by] Lois Gordon and Alan Gordon. Columbia Univ. Press 1995 838p il $49.50 **973.9**
    1. United States—Civilization
    ISBN 0-231-08100-6   LC 95-18900
    First published 1987 with title: American chronicle: six decades in American life, 1920-1980 by Atheneum Pubs.
    This volume presents "in a browsable format the events, personalities, and elements of popular culture for each year of the period. . . . Among unique features of this chronology are its use of advertising slogans to capture the zeitgeist of an age. . . . There are three indexes: name, title (which includes books, poetry, movies, TV programs, etc.), and subject. Black-and-white illustrations appear every two or three pages." Booklist

Lemann, Nicholas
The promised land; the great black migration and how it changed America. Knopf 1991 401p hardcover o.p. paperback available $14   **973.9**
    1. African Americans—Social conditions 2. Internal migration
    ISBN 0-679-73347-7 (pa)   LC 90-52951
    An "account of the migration of 6.5 million black people from rural South to urban North between 1910-1970." N Y Times Book Rev
    The author "describes why the war on poverty did not succeed and why the civil rights movement yielded only

Lemann, Nicholas—*Continued*

partial victories in trying to win improvements. While Lemann's interviews establish the human drama of this process, his assessment of the consequences of this great movement both for African Americans and for the entire country raises substantial questions of justice and equality that cut to the heart of the social situation of the impoverished and oppressed today." Booklist

Includes bibliographical references

Manchester, William

The glory and the dream; a narrative history of America, 1932-1972. Little, Brown 1974 1397p o.p.; Bantam Bks. paperback available $27.95
973.9

1. United States—History—1900-1999 (20th century)
2. United States—Civilization 3. United States—Social conditions
ISBN 0-553-34589-3 (pa)

This is a history of "the major events, sensational happenings, and news-making personalities from the Great Depression through the second inauguration of Richard Nixon." Libr J

"What must impress any reader as he submerges himself in this chronicle is the prodigious energy with which Manchester keeps the narrative moving; the infinite details . . . which brighten the page; and last, and very important, the fairness of the reporting." Atl Mon

Includes bibliography

Terkel, Studs, 1912-

American dreams: lost and found. Pantheon Bks. 1980 xxv, 470p o.p.; Ballantine Bks. paperback available $6.99
973.9

1. United States—Civilization 2. United States—Social conditions
ISBN 0-345-32993-7 (pa)   LC 80-7703

A collection of statements by individual Americans expressing their personal aspirations and disappointments and feelings about the American dream, gathered by Terkel in his travels around the country

"This collection is a treasure, truly a valuable self-portrait of Americans, young and old, men and women. What is most remarkable about the entire collection is that it is never dull." Best Sellers

This fabulous century; by the editors of Time-Life Books. Time-Life Bks. 1969-1970 8v il maps
973.9

1. United States—Social life and customs—Pictorial works 2. United States—Civilization—Pictorial works 3. United States—History—1900-1999 (20th century)

For price and availability contact publisher

A "pictorial history of America's last 100 years. . . . History comes vibrantly alive through the carefully chosen photographs and illustrations of American life as it was and is. It's all here: the old hometown, all that jazz, boom and bust, radio, the movies, television, suburbia, culture, the youth trip, assassins, black emergence, doves and hawks." Libr J

Includes bibliography

Twentieth-century America; a primary source collection from the Associated Press; by the writers and photographers of the Associated Press. Grolier Educ. Corp. 1995 10v il set $349
973.9

1. United States—History—1900-1999 (20th century)
ISBN 0-7172-7494-2   LC 95-12550

Contents: v1 Reform, war, and peace, 1901-1929; v2 The Great Depression, 1929-1939; v3 World War, 1939-1945; v4 The Cold War home and abroad, 1945-1953; v5 The Eisenhower years, 1952-1960; v6 Civil Rights and the Great Society, 1961-1967; v7 From Woodstock to Watergate, 1968-1974; v8 The crisis of national confidence, 1974-1980; v9 The Reagan era, 1981-1988; v10 An uneasy peace, 1988-

"Political and social history, sports, legal and criminal happenings, and other areas of historical interest are related in chronological order and tied together by introductory comments and notes that place the stories in perspective. . . . Hundreds of photographs throughout the set make this a quality resource for pictures of the people and events of the period." Am Ref Books Annu, 1996

973.91   United States—1901-1953

Allen, Frederick Lewis, 1890-1954

The big change; America transforms itself, 1900-1950. Harper & Row 1952 308p hardcover o.p. paperback available $14.50
973.91

1. United States—History—1900-1999 (20th century)
2. United States—Social conditions 3. United States—Economic conditions—1900-1999 (20th century)
ISBN 0-06-132082-X (pa)

Sketches of "some of the major changes that took place in the United States during the years 1900-1950. Art, literature, manners, morals, sports, business, politics, and the everyday living that took place during this period come under the scrutiny of the author." Guide to Read in Am Hist

Includes bibliographical references

Only yesterday; an informal history of the nineteen-twenties. Harper & Row 1957 370p hardcover o.p. paperback available $7.50
973.91

1. United States—History—1919-1933 2. United States—Social conditions 3. United States—Economic conditions—1919-1933
ISBN 0-06-080004-6 (pa)

"An account of the years from the spring of 1919 to . . . [1931]. It is a kaleidoscopic picture of American politics, society, manners, morals, and economic conditions." Booklist

Includes bibliographical references

Since yesterday; the nineteen-thirties in America, September 3, 1929-September 3, 1939. Harper & Row 1940 362p il hardcover o.p. paperback available $14
973.91

1. United States—History—1919-1933 2. United States—History—1933-1945 3. United States—Social conditions 4. United States—Economic conditions
ISBN 0-06-091322-3 (pa)

Also available in hardcover from Borgo Press

Allen, Frederick Lewis, 1890-1954—*Continued*
A retrospective of the decade from September 3, 1929, when the great bull market reached its peak, to September 3, 1939, when England declared war on Germany. Since the years covered are those of the Great Depression, the chronicle contains more politics and economics and less of manners and customs and the arts

Burg, David F.
The Great Depression; an eyewitness history. Facts on File 1996 390p il (Eyewitness history series) $45   **973.91**
1. United States—Economic conditions—1933-1945
2. United States—Economic conditions—1919-1933
ISBN 0-8160-3095-2   LC 95-15830
The author "delivers a narrative summary and chronology of major events in the United States and throughout the world during the Depression. He offers seven chapters, each covering one or more years; brief contemporary quotations from politicians, journalists, authors, and advertisements; and 80 black-and-white photographs. The appendixes contain a selection of primary sources, mainly New Deal statutes and other documents, and capsule biographies." Libr J

Gregory, Ross
Modern America, 1914 to 1945. Facts on File 1995 455p il maps (Almanacs of American life) $75   **973.91**
1. United States—History—1900-1999 (20th century)
2. United States—Social life and customs
ISBN 0-8160-2532-0   LC 94-4168
The author "interweaves brief discussions with statistical tables to provide deeper perspectives of major themes in American history not found in annual almanacs. . . . Themes covered include population and immigration, transportation and communication, politics and government, religion, science, and the world wars." Libr J
Includes bibliographical references

Hofstadter, Richard, 1916-1970
The age of reform from Bryan to F.D.R. Knopf 1955 328, xxp $16.95; pa $10   **973.91**
1. United States—Politics and government—1900-1999 (20th century)
ISBN 0-394-41442-X; 0-394-70095-3 (pa)
This analysis of reform movements in American politics from 1890-1940 reviews: The agrarian uprising that found its expression in the Populist movement of the 1890's; The Progressive movement from about 1900-1914; The New Deal of the 1930's. Emphasis is placed upon the ideas of the leading political reformers
Includes bibliographical references

McElvaine, Robert S., 1947-
The Great Depression; America, 1929-1941. Times Bks. 1984 402p il hardcover o.p. paperback available $15   **973.91**
1. United States—History—1933-1945 2. United States—Economic conditions—1933-1945 3. Economic depressions
ISBN 0-8129-6343-1 (pa)   LC 82-40469
Among the topics discussed are "Herbert Hoover's Presidency, the banking crisis that greeted Roosevelt

when he entered office, the First Hundred Days, the so-called Second New Deal of 1935-36, the deep Government-inflicted 'recession' of 1937-38 and the subsequent shift from social spending to military preparedness." N Y Times Book Rev
Includes bibliographical references

Terkel, Studs, 1912-
Hard times; an oral history of the Great Depression. Pantheon Bks. 1970 462p hardcover o.p. paperback available $13   **973.91**
1. United States—Social conditions 2. United States—Economic conditions—1919-1933 3. United States—Economic conditions—1933-1945 4. Economic depressions
ISBN 0-394-74691-0 (pa)
"Persons of all ages, occupations, and classes scattered across the U.S. remember what they experienced or were told about the economic crisis of the 1930's. The result is a social document of immense interest." Booklist

Wormser, Richard, 1933-
Growing up in the Great Depression. Atheneum Pubs. 1994 124p il $15.95   **973.91**
1. Economic depressions 2. United States—Economic conditions—1933-1945
ISBN 0-689-31711-5   LC 93-20686
Historical background, interviews, and photographs combine to provide an impression of childhood during the Great Depression
"Wormser does an excellent job of providing the flavor of the Great Depression, making good use of oral histories by people who were young back then. . . . This book goes a long way toward presenting a sense of the deprivation which many people experienced." Voice Youth Advocates
Includes bibliographical references

973.917 United States— Administration of Franklin D. Roosevelt, 1933-1945

Heide, Robert, 1939-
Home front America; popular culture of the World War II era; by Robert Heide and John Gilman. Chronicle Bks. 1995 144p il pa $17.95
973.917
1. World War, 1939-1945—United States 2. Popular culture—United States
ISBN 0-8118-0927-7   LC 94-33722
This volume "looks nostalgically at everything from Victory Gardens and propaganda to Hollywood." Booklist
"The visual appeal of this book is striking and informative. Pages are on glossy paper with many colorful illustrations. Text is easy to read and does not distract the reader from the visual contents." Voice Youth Advocates
Includes bibliographical references

Leuchtenburg, William Edward, 1922-
Franklin D. Roosevelt and the New Deal,
1932-1940; [by] William E. Leuchtenburg. Harper
& Row 1963 393p il (New American nation
series) hardcover o.p. paperback available $16
973.917
1. Roosevelt, Franklin D. (Franklin Delano), 1882-
1945 2. United States—History—1933-1945 3. United
States—Economic conditions—1933-1945
ISBN 0-06-133025-6 (pa)

This treatment of Roosevelt's first two terms in office
emphasizes the economic crisis and New Deal reforms.
The author shows how social forces influenced government action: the San Francisco strike in 1934, the careers
of Huey Long and Father Coughlin, the sharecroppers'
revolt, and unemployment
This book "is comprehensive, logically organized, and
written with clarity and detachment." Am Hist Rev
Includes bibliography

973.918 United States—Administration of Harry S. Truman, 1945-1953

Klingaman, William K.
Encyclopedia of the McCarthy era. Facts on File
1996 502p il $50   **973.918**
1. McCarthy, Joseph, 1908-1957 2. Anticommunist
movements 3. United States—Politics and government—1945-1953—Dictionaries
ISBN 0-8160-3097-9   LC 95-23574
In addition to Senator McCarthy, this overview examines such figures as "Richard Nixon, Albert Einstein,
Frank Sinatra, The Hollywood Ten, Whittaker Chambers,
Roy Cohn, Lillian Hellman, Alger Hiss, and Owen Lattimore. Other entries focus on the government, organizations, court cases, and famous books and plays involving
McCarthyism. A chronology stretching from 1919 to
1960 and 18 appendixes bring together a selection of
hard-to-locate documents." Am Libr
For a fuller review see: Booklist, Sept. 1, 1996

973.92 United States—1953-

American culture after World War II; edited by
Karen L. Rood; associate editors: Kathryn
Bennett [et al.] Gale Res. 1994 xxx, 393p il
(Dictionary of twentieth-century culture) $90
973.92
1. United States—Civilization
ISBN 0-8103-8481-7   LC 93-51505
This work contains brief entries on people, terms,
movements, organizations, etc. associated with the arts in
the United States since World War II. "A topical table
of contents at the beginning of the volume lists articles
under such headings as *Art, Literature, Drama and Film,*
and *Music and Dance.* A time line from 1945 through
1993 lists, in parallel columns, historical events and
highlights in dance, drama, literature, TV, etc. The articles are well laid out in dictionary format and are easy
to read." Booklist

Dickson, Paul
Timelines. Addison-Wesley 1990 357p
hardcover o.p. paperback available $10.95 **973.92**
1. United States—History—1900-1999 (20th century)
2. Popular culture—United States
ISBN 0-201-56753-9 (pa)   LC 90-31597
This is "a compilation of events, statistics, names,
nostalgia, and trivia from 1945-1990, arranged by year
with selected events listed for some days of each
month." Libr J

Fariello, Griffin
Red scare; memories of the American
inquisition: an oral history. Norton 1995 575p
$29.95   **973.92**
1. Anticommunist movements 2. Internal security—
United States
ISBN 0-393-03732-0   LC 94-25859
Also available in paperback from Avon Bks.
"Here, in some 70 narratives, are the stories of the famous and the obscure who were the victims of McCarthyism—its indiscriminate allegations and unsubstantiated
charges—as well as the stories of high government officials, FBI agents, and informers paid to finger Communists. A useful addition to the literature of the period."
Libr J
Includes bibliographical references

Gitlin, Todd
The sixties; years of hope, days of rage. Bantam
Bks. 1987 513p hardcover o.p. paperback available
$16.95   **973.92**
1. United States—History—1961-1974 2. United
States—Social conditions 3. Students—Political activity
ISBN 0-553-37212-2 (pa)   LC 87-47575
"Though ex-SDS leader Gitlin occasionally falls prey
to the self-indulgence that snares most sixties' commentators, his analysis of the decade's politics is thought-
provoking and clearheaded. Rather than singing the familiar hymn of praise to youthful idealism, Gitlin carefully dissects why the activist spirit developed when it
did and what its legacy has been." Am Libr
Includes bibliography

Halberstam, David, 1934-
The fifties. Villard Bks. 1993 800p il o.p.;
Fawcett Bks. paperback available $15   **973.92**
1. United States—Social life and customs 2. United
States—Politics and government 3. Popular culture—
United States
ISBN 0-449-90933-6 (pa)   LC 92-56815
Also available Random House large print edition
This is a social history of the United States during the
1950s
The author's "sources are secondary and derivative,
but his instinct for the revealing anecdote, his ear for the
memorable quote, and his awesome powers of organiza-
tion add up to a variegated overview that moves seam-
lessly between the serious shenanigans of Chief Justice
Earl Warren and the frivolous ones of . . . Grace
Metalious." Natl Rev
Includes bibliographical references

Haskins, James, 1941-
The 60s reader; by James Haskins and Kathleen Benson. Viking Kestrel 1988 244p il o.p. **973.92**
1. United States—History—1961-1974 2. United States—Social conditions
LC 85-40886
A collection of essays, speeches, and reports which cover the social and political upheavals of the 1960s, including the Civil Rights movement, drugs, pop art, the generation gap, rock music, and ecology
"This book is an excellent look at the 60s and provides readers with a feeling of having been there." SLJ
Includes bibliography

A **History** of our time; readings on postwar America; edited by William H. Chafe, Harvard Sitkoff. 4th ed. Oxford Univ. Press 1995 588p pa $17.95 **973.92**
1. United States—History—1945-
ISBN 0-19-508277-X
LC 94-38349
First published 1983
This is an anthology of articles from differing political perspectives on issues in recent American history. Topics covered include the Cold War, McCarthyism, the movement for blacks' civil rights, the women's movement, the Vietnam War, Watergate, the Reagan revolution, and AIDS. Interspersed with articles written by historians are primary documents of the period, including Martin Luther King's "Letter from a Birmingham Jail," Lyndon B. Johnson's address "Why We Are in Vietnam," Mikhail Gorbachev's 1988 speech to the United Nations and Bill Clinton's 1994 State of the Union address
Includes bibliographical references

Kessler, Lauren
After all these years: sixties ideals in a different world. Thunder's Mouth Press 1990 209p pa $13.95 **973.92**
1. United States—Social conditions 2. Radicalism 3. United States—Politics and government—1900-1999 (20th century)
ISBN 0-938410-92-X
LC 90-10749
The author argues "that the Sixties ethos lives on in the hearts of many maturing hippies. . . . Forty-one 'survivors,' including four luminaries (Angela Davis, Tom Hayden, Gloria Steinem, and Arlo Guthrie), talk briefly about then and now, with emphasis on how they have kept the faith." Libr J
"Free of clichés and stereotypes, this is vital and affirmative social history." Booklist

Kuralt, Charles, 1934-1997
Charles Kuralt's America. Putnam 1995 279p il $24.95 **973.92**
1. United States—Description 2. United States—Social life and customs
ISBN 0-399-14083-2
LC 95-34785
Also available Thorndike Press large print edition and in paperback from Doubleday
"After serving 37 years as a reporter at CBS, Kuralt retired and set out on a trip to see his favorite American locations. . . . In this journal, the author records the people, places, and pets he encountered." Libr J

"Kuralt is not in search of crises or epiphanies; he values nature and good food, neighborliness and craftsmanship, quaintness and quirkiness. Though no literary match for American chroniclers like Calvin Trillin, the effable Kuralt does, in un-fancy style, convey his enthusiasm and his engagement." Publ Wkly

On the road with Charles Kuralt. Putnam 1985 316p il o.p.; Fawcett Bks. paperback available $5.95 **973.92**
1. United States—Social life and customs 2. United States—Description
ISBN 0-449-13067-3 (pa)
LC 85-6330
"As a CBS reporter specializing in 'soft' news, Kuralt has been roaming around the U.S. since 1967 in search of 'just plain folks.' Some 100 of the television interviews that resulted from that search have been transcribed for this collection. Loosely organized by themes emphasizing the individuality, altruism, and humor that characterize small town and rural Americans, the interviews and anecdotes are consistently entertaining." Booklist

Moyers, Bill
A world of ideas; conversations with thoughtful men and women about American life today and the ideas shaping our future. Doubleday 1989 513p il hardcover o.p. paperback available $25 **973.92**
1. United States—Civilization 2. United States—Politics and government—1989-
ISBN 0-385-26346-5 (pa)
LC 89-1109
"This book is a compilation of the 41 interviews that Moyers conducted for his 1988 PBS TV series, [a] mix of authors, scientists, educators, and philosophers, including the late Barbara Tuchman on the lessons of history; Tom Wolfe on political activism on the local scale; and former New York Public Library Director Vartan Gregorian." Libr J

A world of ideas II; public opinions from private citizens; Andie Tucher, editor. Doubleday 1990 284p il hardcover o.p. paperback available $22.95 **973.92**
1. United States—Civilization 2. United States—Politics and government—1989-
ISBN 0-385-41665-2 (pa)
LC 90-38334
"This collection encompasses 29 more interviews, including conversations with writer Maxine Hong Kingston, theater director Peter Sellars, medical researcher Jonas Salk, and journalist William L. Shirer." Libr J

White, Theodore H., 1915-1986
America in search of itself; the making of the President, 1956-1980. Harper & Row 1982 465p o.p.; Warner Bks. paperback available $9.95 **973.92**
1. United States—Politics and government—1900-1999 (20th century) 2. Presidents—United States—Election
ISBN 0-446-37098-3 (pa)
LC 81-47679
"A Cornelia & Michael Bessie book"
The author interprets "the forces that diminished our 'culture of hope' and led to the repudiation of liberality

White, Theodore H., 1915-1986—*Continued*
signaled by the 1980 election." Publ Wkly
"It is difficult to read this book . . . without being seduced by [White's] rare literary grace, his matchless knowledge of the political system." Harpers

973.921 United States— Administration of Dwight D. Eisenhower, 1953-1961

Branch, Taylor
Parting the waters: America in the King years, 1954-63. Simon & Schuster 1988 1064p il hardcover o.p. paperback available $16   **973.921**
1. King, Martin Luther, 1929-1968 2. United States—History—1953-1961 3. African Americans—Civil rights
ISBN 0-671-68742-5 (pa)   LC 88-24033
This history of the American civil rights movement from 1954 to 1963 focuses on the life of Dr. Martin Luther King
The author "has searched out the hidden reality and often tragic human drama of the King years. On his best pages, the past, miraculously, seems to spring back to life. King himself appears human, all too human. Yet when the reader is done, his remarkable virtues and ordinary vices seem of a piece, the component parts of a coherent, towering personality." Newsweek
Includes bibliography

973.922 United States— Administration of John F. Kennedy, 1961-1963

Finkelstein, Norman H., 1941-
Thirteen days/ninety miles; the Cuban missile crisis. Messner 1994 145p il $15   **973.922**
1. Cuban Missile Crisis, 1962
ISBN 0-671-86622-2   LC 93-29425
"Using information recently declassified by the U.S. government, Finkelstein effectively recounts events that led to the 1962 crisis, as well as the tense and confusing behind-the-scenes meetings that took place during it. . . . Richly detailed, well documented, and well written, this book dramatically sketches a crucial slice of 20th-century history." SLJ
Includes bibliography

Halberstam, David, 1934-
The best and the brightest. 20th anniversary ed. Random House 1992 xx, 688p $30   **973.922**
1. United States—Politics and government—1961-1974 2. United States—Foreign relations—Vietnam 3. Vietnam—Foreign relations—United States
ISBN 0-679-41062-7   LC 91-51020
Also available in paperback from Fawcett Bks.
First published 1972
"The author describes analytically rather than narratively, how the Kennedy-Johnson intellectual (McNa-

mara, Bundy, Rusk, Ball, Taylor, et al.) men praised as 'the best and the brightest' men of this century, became the architects of the disastrous American policy of Indochina." Libr J
Includes bibliography

Manchester, William
The death of a President, November 20—November 25, 1963. Harper & Row 1967 710p maps hardcover o.p. paperback available $18
    973.922
1. Kennedy, John F. (John Fitzgerald), 1917-1963—Assassination
ISBN 0-06-091531-5 (pa)
The book "offers the results of hundreds of interviews, the retracing of President Kennedy's last journey, and visits to all locations pertinent to the assassination and death of the President. The result is a multidetailed account which recreates the days, hours, and minutes of November 20-25, 1963, with an almost hypnotic effect." Booklist
Includes glossary and bibliography

Matthews, Christopher J.
Kennedy & Nixon; the rivalry that shaped postwar America; [by] Christopher Matthews. Simon & Schuster 1996 377p il $25; pa $14
    973.922
1. Kennedy, John F. (John Fitzgerald), 1917-1963 2. Nixon, Richard M. (Richard Milhous), 1913-1994 3. United States—Politics and government—1900-1999 (20th century)
ISBN 0-684-81030-1; 0-684-83246-1 (pa)
     LC 96-15677
"What caused the rift between Kennedy and Nixon, one-time friends and ideological soul mates, is the subject of this eminently readable dual political biography. Matthews, . . . shows how these two anti-New Dealers, anti-Communists, and freshmen members of Congress in 1946 became enemies as their political careers advanced." Libr J
Includes bibliographical references

973.924 United States— Administration of Richard Nixon, 1969-1974

Bernstein, Carl
All the President's men; by Carl Bernstein [and] Bob Woodward. Simon & Schuster 1974 349p il hardcover o.p. paperback available $12   **973.924**
1. Washington post 2. Watergate Affair, 1972-1974
ISBN 0-671-89441-2 (pa)
Also available in hardcover from Buccaneer Bks.
The two Washington Post reporters whose investigative journalism first revealed the Watergate scandal relate the story from the first suspicions, through the trail of false leads, lies, secrecy, and high-level pressure, to the final moments when they were able to put the pieces of the puzzle together and write the series that won the Post a Pulitzer Prize

Emery, Fred
Watergate; the corruption of American politics and the fall of Richard Nixon. Times Bks. 1994 555p il o.p.; Simon & Schuster paperback available $15 **973.924**
1. Nixon, Richard M. (Richard Milhous), 1913-1994
2. Watergate Affair, 1972-1974
ISBN 0-684-81323-8 (pa) LC 93-44736
"In addition to an introductory section on the cast of characters involved, Emery provides a detailed examination of the Committee To Re-elect the President (CRP) and its dirty tricks. . . . Riveting reading that is based on an unprecedented combing of the primary sources." Libr J
Includes bibliographical references

Greene, John Robert, 1955-
The limits of power; the Nixon and Ford administrations. Indiana Univ. Press 1992 296p $15.95 **973.924**
1. Nixon, Richard M. (Richard Milhous), 1913-1994
2. Ford, Gerald R., 1913- 3. United States—Politics and government—1961-1974 4. United States—Politics and government—1974-1989
ISBN 0-253-32637-0 LC 91-47014
This "analysis of eight years of Republican leadership (1969-1977) seeks to explain why the 'Myth of the Omnipotent President,' as Greene dubs it, came to an end. . . . Greene recounts the familiar Watergate story, then shows how Richard Nixon left the office of President 'infinitely more limited' than it had been when he was sworn in. He goes on to describe the populace's brief romance with Gerald Ford, which ended abruptly when Ford pardoned Nixon." Publ Wkly
Includes bibliographical references

Woodward, Bob, 1943-
The final days; [by] Bob Woodward, Carl Bernstein. Simon & Schuster 1976 476p il hardcover o.p. paperback available $14 **973.924**
1. Nixon, Richard M. (Richard Milhous), 1913-1994
2. Watergate Affair, 1972-1974 3. United States—Politics and government—1961-1974
ISBN 0-671-69087-6 (pa)
Also available in hardcover from Buccaneer Bks.
The title refers to the final days of the Nixon Presidency. The authors have "constructed a two-part narrative, the first half covering the period from April 30, 1973—the day John Dean was fired as White House counsel—until late July 1974, and the second half covering the last two weeks in detail." N Y Times Book Rev

973.927 United States—Administration of Ronald Reagan, 1981-1989

Levy, Peter B.
Encyclopedia of the Reagan-Bush years. Greenwood Press 1996 442p il $49.95 **973.927**
1. Reagan, Ronald, 1911- 2. Bush, George, 1924-
3. United States—Politics and government—1974-1989 4. United States—Politics and government—1989-
ISBN 0-313-29018-0 LC 95-37336
This "title covers the years between Reagan's first election to Clinton's victory over Bush. Each of more than 250 entries, listed in alphabetical order by subject, is from 100 to 1,000 words in length. More than focusing on the political climate, the book addresses social issues, popular culture, foreign concerns, and events of those years. Much of the terminology associated with these presidencies is explained." Book Rep
For a fuller review see: Booklist, July, 1996

Terkel, Studs, 1912-
The great divide; second thoughts on the American dream. Pantheon Bks. 1988 439p o.p.; Avon Bks. paperback available $4.95 **973.927**
1. United States—Social conditions
ISBN 0-380-70854-X (pa) LC 88-42543
"Ordinary people reflect on the issues of the 1980s—Reaganism, greed, farming, race relations, education, and religion. . . . The 'divide' exists when inner beliefs conflict with public policy; when family members harbor differing views on heartfelt issues; when the ideas of the 1960s are compared with those of the 1980s. . . . There are no answers here, just very timely and provocative commentary in Terkel's inimitable style." Libr J

Walsh, Kenneth T.
Feeding the beast; the White House versus the press. Random House 1996 340p $25 **973.927**
1. Press—Government policy 2. United States—Politics and government—1974-1989 3. United States—Politics and government—1989-
ISBN 0-679-44290-1 LC 95-41555
"Distilling his experience covering Reagan, Bush, and Clinton for U.S. *News*, Walsh details how animosity between the press and U.S. presidents has sprung up, devoting most space to the Clintons' case." Booklist
"What distinguishes this volume . . . is its thoroughness, its evenhandedness, and the author's willingness to chastise his colleagues." Libr J
Includes bibliographical references

974 Northeastern United States

Demos, John, 1937-
Entertaining Satan; witchcraft and the culture of
early New England; [by] John Putnam Demos.
Oxford Univ. Press 1982 543p il maps $41.75; pa
$16.95   **974**
1. Witchcraft 2. New England—History
ISBN 0-19-503131-8; 0-19-503378-7 (pa)
      LC 81-22463
"This is not simply a monograph on witchcraft but a
major attempt to understand the kind of society and the
kind of culture in which witchcraft had a place. To that
end Demos employs nearly every conceptual tool available to the historian, including those borrowed from psychology, anthropology, and sociology." N Y Rev Books
Includes bibliographical references

974.4 Massachusetts

Bradford, William, 1588-1657
Of Plymouth Plantation, 1620-1647; the
complete text, with notes and an introduction by
Samuel Eliot Morison. Knopf 1952 xliii, 448p
maps $25   **974.4**
1. Massachusetts—History—1600-1775, Colonial period 2. Pilgrims (New England colonists)
ISBN 0-394-43895-7
Written between 1630 and 1650; first published 1856
with title: History of Plymouth Plantation
"The opening book sketches the origin of the Separat-
ist movement, the flight from England to Holland, the
settlement at Leiden, the plans for the settlement in New
England, and the *Mayflower* voyage. The second book,
which includes the major part of the history, is in the
form of annals from 1620 to 1646, and describes every
aspect of the life of the Pilgrims. Besides being a primary historical source, the work has artistic value because
of its dignified, sonorous style, deriving from the Geneva
Bible." Oxford Companion to Am Lit. 5th edition

975 Southeastern United States. Southern States

Southern black leaders of the Reconstruction era;
edited by Howard N. Rabinowitz. University of
Ill. Press 1982 xxiv, 422p il (Blacks in the new
world) hardcover o.p. paperback available
$14.95   **975**
1. African Americans—Southern States—Biography
2. Reconstruction (1865-1876) 3. Southern States—
Politics and government
ISBN 0-252-00972-X (pa)   LC 81-11372
This volume of essays "examines the question of how
Southern black leaders functioned in Reconstruction politics and within the Republican party by looking at leaders on the national, state, and local level." Am Hist Rev
"The essayists deftly illustrate who the leaders were,
what their aims were and how they operated in the ambiguous, complex, and constraining post-Civil War envi-
ronment." Libr J
Includes bibliographical references

975.3 District of Columbia (Washington)

Brinkley, David
Washington goes to war. Knopf 1988 286p il
o.p.; Ballantine Bks. paperback available $12
      975.3
1. World War, 1939-1945—United States 2. Washington (D.C.)—History
ISBN 0-345-40730-X (pa)   LC 87-46017
"Brinkley's account of Washington, D.C., in the hal-
cyon days of World War II, when the capitol was the
fulcrum of world power and human folly, is exceptionally well written and enriched with wry wit and engaging
anecdotes." Libr J
Includes bibliography

Moore, John Leo, 1927-
Speaking of Washington; facts, firsts, and
folklore; [by] John L. Moore. Congressional
Quarterly 1993 307p il maps $36.95; pa $17.95
      975.3
1. United States—Politics and government 2. Washington (D.C.)
ISBN 0-87187-762-7; 0-87187-741-4 (pa)
      LC 93-30363
A "compendium of people, places, and events that
have shaped the presidency, the Congress, the Supreme
Court, and the political parties. Topics range from pets
at the White House to Congress's cemetery, but move on
to more political subjects such as third-party candidates
and campaign oratory." SLJ
"This is an inexpensive source packed with interesting
and entertaining information on the U.S. government. Libraries may want to put it in the circulating collection,
since it is not arranged for ready reference." Booklist

Our changing White House; edited by Wendell
Garrett. Northeastern Univ. Press 1995 xxii,
250p il map $40   **975.3**
1. White House (Washington, D.C.)
ISBN 1-55553-222-5   LC 94-43182
"In 10 wide-ranging essays by authorities in their
field, the executive mansion's evolution through two centuries is lovingly traced, including conception and design,
construction and later reconstruction, and original furnishings and many subsequent refurbishings, all related
with a wealth of detail. . . . The liberal presentation of
illustrations greatly augments the text." Booklist
Includes bibliographical references

Washington, D.C; a Smithsonian book of the
nation's capital. Smithsonian Bks. 1992 240p il
$39.95   **975.3**
1. Washington (D.C.)
ISBN 0-89599-032-6   LC 92-17647
This "book contains a series of essays by various authorities that captures the city's urban cultural mosaic
from its architecture, neighborhoods, and sports teams to
its various White House occupants and its unique
African-American experience. . . . An excellent and informative book for readers who want to look past the fa-
cade and into the heart of the nation's capital." SLJ

The **White** House; an historic guide. White House
Hist. Assn. il $12.95; pa $9.95 **975.3**
1. White House (Washington, D.C.)
First published 1962. (19th edition 1995) Periodically
revised
Published with the cooperation of the National Geographic Society
This book traces the changing appearance of the
White House through many administrations. It describes
life in the White House under different presidents as well
as its great furniture, paintings, collections of china, vermeil, and the furnishings of the official rooms

975.5 Virginia

Bridenbaugh, Carl, 1903-1992
Jamestown, 1544-1699. Oxford Univ. Press
1980 199p il $41.75 **975.5**
1. Jamestown (Va.)—History
ISBN 0-19-502650-0 LC 79-13989
This is an account of the earliest permanent English
settlement in the New World. The author relies almost
exclusively on the surviving original sources as he seeks
to revise the accepted ideas about Virginia and correct
many sentimental myths. He also deals with the economic and social life of the community, and assesses the early attempts at self-government in the town
"A short, clear study, by one of the most eminent historians." New Yorker
Includes bibliography

975.8 Georgia

Foxfire [1]-10. Anchor Press/Doubleday
1972-1993 10v il pa ea $14.95 **975.8**
1. Country life—Georgia 2. Appalachian region—Social life and customs 3. Handicraft
Editors: v1-6 Eliot Wigginton; v7 Paul F. Gillespie;
v8-9 Eliot Wigginton and Margie Bennett; v10 George P.
Reynolds and Susan Walker
First book in series has title: The Foxfire book
"A chronicle of the economic, historic, and cultural
changes of an Appalachian village as perceived through
the inquisitive minds of its younger generation. . . . Begun . . . as an experiment in getting students more directly involved in their classwork, the 'Foxfire' volumes
have developed into an enduring example of a practical
and effective educational philosophy." Booklist

Foxfire: 25 years; edited by Eliot Wigginton and
his students. Anchor Bks. (NY) 1991 xxi, 359p
il hardcover o.p. paperback available $14.95
975.8
1. Country life—Georgia 2. Appalachian region—Social life and customs 3. Handicraft
ISBN 0-385-41346-7 (pa) LC 90-22834
An "oral history of both the school and the publications whose educational philosophy sparked 25 years of
experimentation and achievement among the residents of
Appalachia." Booklist

976.1 Alabama

Agee, James, 1909-1955
Let us now praise famous men; three tenant
families; [by] James Agee, Walker Evans; with an
introduction to the new edition by John Hersey.
Houghton Mifflin 1988 c1941 liv, 471p il $29.95;
pa $16.95 **976.1**
1. Alabama—Social conditions 2. Farm tenancy
ISBN 0-395-48901-6; 0-395-48897-4 (pa)
LC 88-18110
First published 1941
This republication of the classic work based on a 1936
journalistic assignment contains "about twice as many
photographs [by Evans] as the original contained. These
photographs are all snapshots in black and white and
contain a story in themselves; they were not meant to illustrate but, as the original preface says, 'they and the
text are coequal, mutually independent, and fully collaborative.' The book is an account of the actual daily lives
of three families of tenant farmers." Best Sellers

976.2 Mississippi

Walton, Anthony
Mississippi; an American journey. Knopf 1996
279p il $24; pa $13 **976.2**
1. African Americans—Mississippi 2. Mississippi—
Race relations
ISBN 0-679-44600-1; 0-679-77741-5 (pa)
LC 95-32031
"Walton was born in Aurora, Illinois, in 1960 and
grew up there relatively untouched by racial prejudice.
However, in 1989, after the murder of Yusef Hawkins,
he was sent by a New York magazine to cover a protest
march in Bensonhurst. This event caused Walton to
question why his race was so hated. To understand, he
believed he had to go back to his beginnings in Mississippi. His book is the result of several years spent researching, traveling, and talking to friends and relatives
about their experiences in that state." Libr J

976.4 Texas

Reavis, Dick J.
The ashes of Waco; an investigation. Simon &
Schuster 1995 320p $24 **976.4**
1. Koresh, David 2. United States. Bureau of Alcohol,
Tobacco and Firearms 3. Branch Davidians 4. Waco
(Tex.) cult siege, 1993
ISBN 0-684-81132-4 LC 95-33125
In this examination of how federal law enforcement
agencies handled the attack on the Branch Davidian compound in Waco Texas the author is "scathing on the behavior of both the Bureau of Alcohol, Tobacco and Firearms and the Federal Bureau of Investigation, which took
charge after the initial assault failed." N Y Times Book
Rev
Includes bibliographical references

978   Western United States

Ambrose, Stephen E.

Undaunted courage; Meriwether Lewis, Thomas Jefferson, and the opening of the American West. Simon & Schuster 1996 511p il maps $27.50; pa $16   **978**
1. Lewis, Meriwether, 1774-1809 2. Lewis and Clark Expedition (1804-1806) 3. West (U.S.)—Exploration
ISBN 0-684-81107-3; 0-684-82697-6 (pa)
LC 95-37146

This treatment of the Lewis and Clark Expedition "is essentially a biography of Lewis, although the bulk of it is a lively retelling of the journey of the two captains—together with their party of soldiers and frontiersmen, Clark's black slave, York, and the legendary Shoshone Indian woman, Sacagawea, and her infant son—conveyed with passionate enthusiasm by Mr. Ambrose and sprinkled liberally with some of the most famous and vivid passages from the travelers' journals." N Y Times Book Rev

Includes bibliography

The **American** frontier: opposing viewpoints;

Mary Ellen Jones, book editor. Greenhaven Press 1994 306p il (American history series) lib bdg $19.95; pa $11.95   **978**
1. West (U.S.)—History 2. Frontier and pioneer life—West (U.S.)
ISBN 1-56510-086-7 (lib bdg); 1-56510-085-9 (pa)
LC 93-29898

"This book draws on many sources to present varied views of the American frontier. Each chapter represents aspects of a particular theme: the Native American, the pioneer, race and gender, the creation of mythic heroes, and popular culture. . . . An interesting compilation of source material on the frontier." Booklist

Includes bibliography

Brown, Dee Alexander

The American West; photos edited by Martin F. Schmitt. Scribner 1994 461p il maps $25   **978**
1. West (U.S.)—History
ISBN 0-02-517421-5   LC 94-37444

"This narrative history of westward expansion paints a vivid portrait of the settlers, pioneers, entrepreneurs, and Native Americans of the old West. Useful as collateral research material and for recreational reading." Booklist

Includes bibliography

Encyclopedia of the American West; Charles

Phillips and Alan Axelrod, editors. Simon & Schuster 1996 4v $325   **978**
1. West (U.S.)—Dictionaries
ISBN 0-02-897495-6   LC 96-1685

This reference set contains over 1700 alphabetically arranged entries and more than 1000 photographs. Biographies, histories of western states, and overview topical entries define traditional Western concerns within a social history framework

For a review see: Booklist, Dec. 1, 1996

Flanagan, Mike, 1950-

The Old West; day by day. Facts on File 1995 498p il $60   **978**
1. West (U.S.)—History
ISBN 0-8160-2689-0   LC 94-4663

First published 1987 by Renaissance House with title: Days of the West

"A guidebook to the trans-Mississippi West through 15,000 chronologically arranged and briefly described events, most of which occurred between 1848 and the closing of the frontier in 1890. Throughout the text are dozens of interesting sidebars about particular events. . . . This labor of love can serve as either a useful reference tool or an entertaining browse." Libr J

For a fuller review see: Booklist, Sept. 15, 1995
Includes bibliographical references

Morgan, Ted, 1932-

A shovel of stars; the making of the American West, 1800 to the present. Simon & Schuster 1995 559p il maps $30; pa $16   **978**
1. West (U.S.)—History 2. Frontier and pioneer life—West (U.S.)
ISBN 0-671-79439-6; 0-684-81492-7 (pa)
LC 94-43838

Companion volume Wilderness at dawn, entered in class 970

Morgan "looks at the settlement of each state during its territorial period from the Louisiana Purchase in 1803 to the admission of Alaska and Hawaii in 1959." Libr J

"This grandly inspired work—a completely satisfying read—embraces the texture and the drama of the West in all its heartbreak and heroism." Booklist

Includes bibliographical references

The **Oxford** history of the American West; edited

by Clyde A. Milner II, Carol A. O'Connor, Martha A. Sandweiss. Oxford Univ. Press 1994 872p il maps $49.95; pa $25   **978**
1. West (U.S.)—History
ISBN 0-19-505968-9; 0-19-511212-1 (pa)
LC 93-38829

"This book surveys the area's history and development from the time of the early natives up to the current day. The first three sections chronicle political, social, and economic history in roughly chronological order. . . . The final section examines how the West has been interpreted in art, literature, and popular entertainment. All the authors of the various chapters focus on the major events with just the right amount of interpretation and case-study illustration to give the reader a good sense of how the West developed." Libr J

Includes bibliographical references

Parkman, Francis, 1823-1893

The Oregon Trail   **978**
1. Oregon Trail 2. West (U.S.)—Description 3. Indians of North America 4. Frontier and pioneer life—West (U.S.)

Hardcover and paperback editions available from various publishers

First published 1847 in the "Knickerbocker Magazine." First published in book form, 1849, with title: The California and Oregon Trail

Parkman, Francis, 1823-1893—*Continued*

"An account of a trip made in 1846 by the author and his cousin Quincy Adams Shaw. They traveled together from St. Louis to Fort Laramie; there they separated, Parkman going to live for some weeks with a tribe of Sioux Indians. *The Oregon Trail* provides valuable descriptions of the prairies at the most fascinating period of their history and a remarkable ethnological study of the Indians." Benet's Reader's Ency of Am Lit

Includes bibliography

Schlissel, Lillian

Women's diaries of the westward journey; [compiled by] Lillian Schlissel; preface by Carl N. Degler; Gerda Lerner, supervising editor; expanded and with a new introduction by the author. Schocken Bks. 1992 278p il pa $14   **978**
1. Overland journeys to the Pacific 2. Frontier and pioneer life—West (U.S.) 3. West (U.S.)—Description 4. Women—Social conditions
ISBN 0-8052-1004-0

First published 1982

This account of the experiences, attitudes and perceptions of some hundred women who migrated West is based on their reminiscences, diaries, and letters. The book concerns their daily lives as they travelled the Overland Trail from the mid-west to California or Oregon between 1840 and 1870

"As compelling as the words are, the many photographs from the westward journey speak volumes by themselves. . . . Schlissel's book is a valuable research tool because of its thorough indexing, clear map, scholarly documentation, and superior organization and presentation." Voice Youth Advocates

Includes bibliography

Slatta, Richard W., 1947-

The cowboy encyclopedia. ABC-CLIO 1994 474p il $62.50   **978**
1. Cowhands—Dictionaries 2. West (U.S.)—Dictionaries 3. Frontier and pioneer life—Dictionaries
ISBN 0-87436-738-7   LC 94-19824

Also available in paperback from Norton

"Focusing on the cowboy experience in North and South America, *The Cowboy Encyclopedia* provides history, definitions, and commentary in an A-to-Z arrangement with major topics such as saddles and cowboy films receiving longer topical entries. Excellent cross-references and an extensive index provide easy access to all aspects of a topic." Am Libr

Cowboys of the Americas. Yale Univ. Press 1990 306p il (Yale Western Americana series) $45; pa $22   **978**
1. Cowhands 2. Frontier and pioneer life—West (U.S.)
ISBN 0-300-04529-8; 0-300-05671-0 (pa)
          LC 89-31880

The author presents a "comparative analysis of mounted herders, focusing on the cowboy of the United States and Canada, the *vaquero* of Mexico, the *gaucho* of Argentina, the *huaso* of Chile, and the *llanero* of Venezuela, showing how they all were similar in key values and characteristics." Libr J

"Slatta's colorful, extensive account of the cowboy mystique has value as a U.S. history reference text and will appeal to readers interested in the subject." Booklist

Includes glossary and bibliography

Thybony, Scott

The Rockies: pillars of a continent; photographed by Paul Chesley. National Geographic Soc. 1996 200p il map $16   **978**
1. Rocky Mountains
ISBN 0-7922-2940-1   LC 95-52391

An illustrated exploration of the Rockies from New Mexico into Canada. Desert, tundra and glaciers are some of the habitats encountered. Wildlife of the region is highlighted

Tunis, Edwin, 1897-1973

Frontier living; written and illustrated by Edwin Tunis. Crowell 1976 c1961 165p il maps $26
          978
1. Frontier and pioneer life—West (U.S.) 2. West (U.S.)—History
ISBN 0-690-01064-8

Companion volume to Colonial living, entered in class 973.2

A reprint of the title first published 1961 by World Publishing Company

This volume "portrays the manners and customs of the frontiersman and his family from the beginning of the westward movement through the 19th century in . . . text and more than 200 drawings." Wis Libr Bull

Turner, Frederick Jackson, 1861-1932

The frontier in American history   **978**
1. West (U.S.)—History 2. Frontier and pioneer life—West (U.S.)

Hardcover and paperback editions available from various publishers

First published 1920 by Holt and analyzed in Essay and general liteature index

This collection of studies presents the author's theory "that the westward-moving American frontier was a unique historical phenomenon which gave a special tincture to the development of American society. The theory provided a key to understanding the origins of American democracy, the American character, and the evolution of the American political system." Reader's Ency of the Am West

Westward expansion; an eyewitness history; [edited by] Sanford Wexler. Facts on File 1991 418p il maps (Eyewitness history series) $45
          978
1. Frontier and pioneer life—West (U.S.) 2. West (U.S.)—History 3. United States—Territorial expansion
ISBN 0-8160-2407-3   LC 90-42599

This work "includes primary-source material from various points of view, arranged chronologically from the French and Indian War through the settlement of the Great Plains. It presents stories of exploration, Indian-white relations, war and diplomacy, and settlers' experi-

Westward expansion—*Continued*

ences." Booklist

The accounts "are well chosen to portray the promises and realities of the frontier. Strongly recommended as a good introduction to source material." Libr J

Includes bibliographical references

Worster, Donald, 1941-

Dust bowl; the southern plains in the 1930s; [by] Donald Worster. Oxford Univ. Press 1979 277p il maps hardcover o.p. paperback available $11.95   **978**

1. Great Plains—History 2. Dust storms

ISBN 0-19-503212-8 (pa)   LC 78-27018

A "scholarly book on one of history's greatest ecological disasters. . . . The study . . . focuses on two counties, one in Oklahoma, the other in Kansas, and their people during the disaster; it next critically assesses New Deal policies with regard to the situation; and finally [it] carries its analysis to a perilous present and future. . . . Fine photographs and maps add to the strength of this book." Choice

Includes bibliographical references

978.1   Kansas

Stratton, Joanna L.

Pioneer women; voices from the Kansas frontier; introduction by Arthur M. Schlesinger, Jr. Simon & Schuster 1981 319p il hardcover o.p. paperback available $12.95   **978.1**

1. Women—Kansas 2. Frontier and pioneer life—Kansas 3. Kansas—History

ISBN 0-671-44748-3 (pa)   LC 80-15960

"A unique book based on the memoirs of nearly 800 pioneer women who lived in Kansas between 1854 and 1890. . . . The book presents personal and detailed accounts of life inside homes, the schools, and the social organizations of early Kansas." Choice

Includes bibliography

978.9   New Mexico

Bryan, Howard

Robbers, rogues, and ruffians; true tales of the Wild West in New Mexico; foreword by Tony Hillerman. Clear Light Pubs. 1991 318p il $22.95; pa $14.95   **978.9**

1. Frontier and pioneer life—West (U.S.) 2. Thieves 3. New Mexico—History

ISBN 0-940666-04-9; 0-940666-23-5 (pa)

LC 91-72481

The author "concentrates on some of the lesser-known desperadoes whose colorful stories have rarely been told. The stories center in and around the New Mexico Territory, where the reader meets such interesting characters as Joel Fowler, 'the human exterminator'; Charles Kennedy, proprietor of the Inn of Death; and Bronco Sue, a real 'black widow'; and many others." Booklist

979.4   California

Darlington, David

The Mojave; a portrait of the definitive American desert. Holt & Co. 1996 337p il maps $25   **979.4**

1. Mojave Desert (Calif.)

ISBN 0-8050-1631-7   LC 95-42056

"Besides exploring the natural history of the desert, Darlington also examines the human impact on the fragile desert environment. His travels through the Mojave bring him into contact with all sorts of people, including Sixties drop-outs, cowboy ranchers, dirt-bike racers, UFO watchers, scientists, and military personnel. Darlington captures the vastness and magnificence of the Mojave in his flowing narrative. His engaging writing style mixes information with anecdotes and provides a detailed, objective, and thorough look at one of the great American deserts." Libr J

Includes bibliographical references

Jackson, Donald Dale, 1935-

Gold dust. Knopf 1980 361p il maps $17.95

979.4

1. California—Gold discoveries 2. California—History 3. Frontier and pioneer life—California 4. Overland journeys to the Pacific

ISBN 0-394-40046-1   LC 79-22068

Also available in paperback from University of Neb. Press

Based "on diaries, journals, travelogues, and accounts of the California gold rush of the late 1840s and early 1850s. . . . It depicts the spread of gold mania throughout the United States and abroad; the great trek of some 80,000 forty-niners (and of a larger number of 1850 emigrants) by land and sea to the new El Dorado; and life in the mining camps and associated boomtowns." Christ Sci Monit

"Although [the book] is colorful and romantic, not analytical and profound, it is accurate." Choice

Includes bibliography

Muir, John, 1838-1914

The Yosemite; the original John Muir text; illustrated with photographs by Galen Rowell; each photograph accompanied by an excerpt from the works of John Muir and an annotation by Galen Rowell; introduction by the photographer. Sierra Club Bks. 1989 218p il hardcover o.p. paperback available $10   **979.4**

1. Yosemite National Park (Calif.)

ISBN 0-87156-782-2 (pa)   LC 88-34919

"A Yolla Bolly Press book"

New "photos complement the Sierra Club's edition of Muir's 1912 classic *The Yosemite*. . . . The combined artistry and shared passion of Muir and of Rowell . . . make this a stunning tribute to one of America's favorite national parks." Libr J

Includes bibliographical references

979.8 Alaska

Muir, John, 1838-1914
All the world over; notes from Alaska. Sierra Club Bks. 1996 87p pa $9   **979.8**
1. Alaska—Description
ISBN 0-87156-853-5   LC 95-25688
This account of the author's 1879 journey to southeastern Alaska was drawn from his Travels in Alaska, first published 1915 by Houghton Mifflin. The naturalist describes his voyages through the Alexander Archipelago, up the Stickeen River, and along the mainland coast

Scott, Alastair, 1954-
Tracks across Alaska; a dog sled journey. Atlantic Monthly Press 1990 247p il map (Traveler) hardcover o.p. paperback available $10.95   **979.8**
1. Alaska—Description
ISBN 0-87113-470-5 (pa)   LC 90-1022
"This is a true adventure account of a nature-lover's dog-sled journey in the freezing wilderness of the Iditarod trail." Booklist
"If libraries want one good contemporary arctic adventure story, this is it." Libr J
Includes glossary

980 South America. Latin America

✓ The **Cambridge** encyclopedia of Latin America and the Caribbean; general editors, Simon Collier, Thomas E. Skidmore, Harold Blakemore. 2nd ed. Cambridge Univ. Press 1992 479p il maps $69.95   **980**
1. Latin America—Dictionaries
ISBN 0-521-41322-2   LC 92-14496
First published 1985
"Broad coverage for the general reader of history and economic development, culture and society, and flora and fauna." N Y Public Libr. Book of How & Where to Look It Up
Includes bibliographical references

✓ **Chapman, Victoria L., 1956-**
Latin American history on file; [by] Victoria L. Chapman & David Lindroth. Facts on File 1996 various paging il maps $165   **980**
1. Latin America—History
ISBN 0-8160-3068-5   LC 95-30231
This looseleaf collection "is divided into ten sections covering cultures and modern eras in Mesoamerica, South America, and the Caribbean Basin, colonial Latin America and the wars of independence. Information is concise and clearly illustrated with drawings, maps and charts. The material sets Latin American cultures and events into an international and historical context." Book Rep

Dostert, Pierre Etienne
Latin America. Stryker-Post Publs. il maps (World today series) pa $11.50   **980**
1. Latin America
ISSN 0092-4148
Annual. First published 1967; prior to 1986 published under the authorship of Luis E. Aguilar
Surveys the history, politics, culture, and economy of the nations of Central and South America and the Caribbean region

Encyclopedia of Latin American history and culture; Barbara A. Tenenbaum, editor in chief; associate editors, Georgette Magassy Dorn [et al.] Scribner 1996 5v set $449   **980**
1. Latin America—Dictionaries
ISBN 0-684-19253-5   LC 95-31042
This work provides "coverage of Latin America from Mexico and the Caribbean to Tierra del Fuego and from prehistory to modern times. Written by scholars and edited by a specialist in Mexican culture at the Library of Congress, the 5,287 articles cover history, politics, art, literature, warfare, gender, class, and economics. Entries run from a paragraph to several pages for longer articles on such topics as education, slavery, and agriculture. Perhaps the work's strongest features are the 3,000 biographical entries, covering the individuals across all classes, occupations, and times." Libr J
For a fuller review see: Booklist, July, 1996

The **South** American handbook. Passport Bks. maps $39.95   **980**
1. Latin America 2. South America
Annual. First published 1924 by Rand McNally
"For each country, brief historical and socioeconomic information is followed by detailed descriptions of individual cities—their museums, libraries, art exhibitions, hotels (with rates), shops, transportation, etc. Though chiefly used for up-to-date travel information, the series has historical value in libraries." Booklist

Winn, Peter
Americas; the changing face of Latin America and the Caribbean. Pantheon Bks. 1993 639p il maps o.p.; University of Calif. Press paperback available $18   **980**
1. Latin America—History 2. Caribbean region—History
ISBN 0-520-20181-7 (pa)   LC 92-54114
This "companion volume to a PBS TV series uses a thematic rather than an encyclopedic approach to examine the 33 countries of Latin America and the Caribbean. Winn . . . integrates the PBS team's reportage with current scholarship in seven disciplines, ranging from anthropology to economics to sociology." Publ Wkly
"Recommended for all public and secondary libraries and junior colleges." Libr J

984   Bolivia

Klein, Herbert S.

Bolivia; the evolution of a multi-ethnic society.
Oxford Univ. Press 1982 318p maps (Latin
American histories) hardcover o.p. paperback
available $16.95   **984**

1. Bolivia—History

ISBN 0-19-505735-X (pa)   LC 81-9659

This history of Bolivia from the first agricultural villages of ca. 2500 B.C. emphasizes the dominant role of
the Indian peasantry, the effects of a mining economy,
and the vast changes brought about by the National Revolution of 1952

Includes bibliographical references

985   Peru

Bingham, Hiram, 1875-1956

Lost city of the Incas; the story of Machu
Picchu and its builders. Duell 1948 263p il o.p.;
Greenwood Press reprint available $69.75   **985**

1. Machu Picchu (Peru) 2. Peru—Antiquities 3. Incas

ISBN 0-313-22950-3

"In 1911 Bingham, an American explorer, found the
Inca city of Machu Picchu, which had been lost for 300
years. In this volume he tells of its origin, how it came
to be lost and how it was finally discovered." Libr J

Includes bibliography

Hemming, John, 1935-

The conquest of the Incas. Harcourt Brace
Jovanovich 1970 641p il maps hardcover o.p.
paperback available $21   **985**

1. Incas 2. Peru—History

ISBN 0-15-622300-7 (pa)

"This [study] focuses on relations of Spaniards and Incas during the Spanish conquest of Peru launched by Pi-
zarro and partners. Spaniards and Incas speak frequently
in their own words as preserved in Spanish documents.
. . . Inca ways and achievements, the empire's tragic
vulnerability because of rivalrous leaders and civil war,
and conquest aftermath are made sharply manifest."
Booklist

Includes bibliography

Incas: lords of gold and glory; by the editors of
Time-Life Books. Time-Life Bks. 1992 168p il
maps (Lost civilizations) $19.95   **985**

1. Incas

LC 92-5149

An illustrated look at the social, political, economic,
religious and cultural aspects of Inca civilization. The
Spanish conquest is also examined

Includes bibliography

McIntyre, Loren, 1917-

The incredible Incas and their timeless land;
photographs by the author; paintings by Louis S.
Glanzman; foreword by Eugenio Alarco; prepared
by the Special Publications Division, National
Geographic Society. National Geographic Soc.
1975 199p il maps $12.95; lib bdg $12.95   **985**

1. Incas 2. Peru—History

ISBN 0-87044-177-9; 0-87044-182-5 (lib bdg)

"The eight chapters present a history of the Incas and
their empire, a narrative of the Spanish conquest, and
portraits of the South American Indian today. Crafts, artifacts, ethnology, and archaeology are also well covered
in bright fashion." Booklist

Includes bibliography

Moseley, Michael Edward

The Incas and their ancestors; the archaeology
of Peru; [by] Michael E. Moseley. Thames &
Hudson 1992 272p il maps hardcover o.p.
paperback available $19.95   **985**

1. Incas 2. Peru—Antiquities

ISBN 0-500-27723-0 (pa)   LC 91-65309

This account of Andean prehistory and archaeology
takes us from the first settlement of 10,000 years ago to
the Spanish conquest

"Clearly presented, with a generous ration of maps
and illustrations, [the volume] is thoughtful and welcome." Times Lit Suppl

Sullivan, William, 1946-

The secret of the Incas; myth, astronomy, and
the war against time. Crown 1996 413p il maps
$35   **985**

1. Incas

ISBN 0-517-59468-4   LC 95-34627

The author argues that, through their precise astronomical observations and apocalyptic myths, the Incas
foretold their downfall at the hands of Spanish conquistadors in 1532. Inca society's martial nature and belief in
human sacrifice were attempts to stop time and avert
their demise

Includes bibliography

994   Australia

Harrell, Mary Ann

Surprising lands down under; prepared by the
Special Publications Division, National Geographic
Society. National Geographic Soc. 1989 199p il
maps lib bdg $12.95   **994**

1. Australia—Description 2. New Zealand—Description

ISBN 0-87044-719-X   LC 89-14499

An illustrated introduction to the geography, people,
and history of Australia and New Zealand

Includes glossary and bibliography

996 Polynesia and Micronesia

Heyerdahl, Thor
Easter Island—the mystery solved. Random House 1989 255p il $24.95 **996**
1. Easter Island
ISBN 0-394-57906-2 LC 88-32204
In this "book, the occasion for his return to Easter Island after 30 years, Heyerdahl tells the history of the island through the eyes of explorers and travelers, from its discovery by the Dutch in 1722, through Heyerdahl's . . . visit in 1986, during which he and his staff resumed limited excavations, and aided by residents and their recall of ancient myths, resolved the puzzle of how the statues had 'walked' from the quarries to their places on the island." Libr J
Includes bibliography

998 Arctic islands and Antarctica

Lopez, Barry Holstun, 1945-
Arctic dreams; imagination and desire in a northern landscape; [by] Barry Lopez. Scribner 1986 xxix, 464p maps o.p.; Bantam Bks. paperback available $12.95 **998**
1. Arctic regions 2. Natural history—Arctic regions
ISBN 0-553-34664-4 (pa) LC 85-24979
Based on the author's experiences in the Arctic. Lopez discusses "Arctic exploration, geography, weather, animal migration, and behavior." Libr J
"What compels the reader to enter this frozen world of the far north is Lopez's beautiful prose style and the breadth and strength of his understanding. He lavishes attention on and achieves precise expression of this world." Choice
Includes bibliography

Fic Fiction

A number of subject headings have been added to the books in this section to aid in curriculum work. It is not necessarily recommended that these subjects be used in the library catalog.

Achebe, Chinua, 1930-
Things fall apart; with an introduction by Kwame Anthony Appiah. Knopf 1995 xxi, 181p $15 **Fic**
ISBN 0-679-44623-0 LC 94-13429
Also available from Asher-Honor
"Everyman's library"
A reissue of the title first published 1958 in the United Kingdom and 1959 in the United States by McDowell, Obolensky
"The novel chronicles the life of Okonkwo, the leader of an Igbo (Ibo) community, from the events leading up to his banishment from the community for accidentally killing a clansman, through the seven years of his exile, to his return. The novel addresses the problem of the intrusion in the 1890s of white missionaries and colonial government into tribal Igbo society. It describes the simultaneous disintegration of its protaganist Okonkwo and of his village. The novel was praised for its intelligent and realistic treatment of tribal beliefs and of psychological disintegration coincident with social unraveling." Merriam-Webster's Ency of Lit

Adams, Douglas, 1952-
The Hitchhiker's Guide to the Galaxy. Harmony Bks. 1980 215p $15 **Fic**
1. Science fiction
ISBN 0-517-54209-9 LC 80-14572
Also available in paperback from Pocket Bks.
"Based on a BBC radio series, . . . this is the episodic story of Arthur Dent, a contemporary Englishman who discovers first that his unpretentious house is about to be demolished to make way for a bypass, and second that a good friend is actually an alien galactic hitchhiker who announces that Earth itself will soon be demolished to make way for an intergalactic speedway. A suitably bewildered Dent soon finds himself hitching . . . rides throughout space, aided by a . . . reference book, The Hitchhiker's Guide to the Galaxy, a compendium of 'facts,' philosophies, and wild advice." Libr J
Other titles featuring Arthur Dent are:
Life, the universe and everything (1982)
Mostly harmless (1992)
The restaurant at the end of the universe (1981)
So long, and thanks for all the fish (1984)

Adams, Richard, 1920-
Watership Down. Macmillan 1974 c1972 429p $40 **Fic**
1. Rabbits—Fiction 2. Allegories
ISBN 0-02-700030-3
Also available from Buccaneer Bks. and in paperback from Avon Bks.
First published 1972 in the United Kingdom
"Faced with the annihilation of its warren, a small group of male rabbits sets out across the English downs in search of a new home. Internal struggles for power surface in this intricately woven, realistically told adult adventure when the protagonists must coordinate tactics in order to defeat an enemy rabbit fortress. It is clear that the author has done research on rabbit behavior, for this tale is truly authentic." Shapiro. Fic for Youth. 3d edition

Agee, James, 1909-1955
A death in the family. McDowell, Obolensky 1957 339p o.p.; Bantam Bks. paperback available $5.99 **Fic**
1. Family life—Fiction 2. Death—Fiction 3. Tennessee—Fiction
ISBN 0-553-27011-7 (pa)
"Six-year-old Rufus Follet, his younger sister Catherine, his mother, and various relatives all react differently to the unexpected announcement that Rufus's father has been fatally injured in an automobile accident. The poignancy of sorrow, the strength of personal beliefs, and the comforting love and support of a family are all elements of this compassionate novel." Shapiro. Fic for Youth. 3d edition

Alcott, Louisa May, 1832-1888
A long fatal love chase. Random House 1995 242p $21 **Fic**
ISBN 0-679-44510-2 LC 95-6793
Also available Thorndike Press large print edition and in paperback from Dell
Written in 1866

Alcott, Louisa May, 1832-1888—*Continued*

This novel follows the "misfortunes of Rosamond Vivian, a young, impetuous Englishwoman who escapes a life of lonely dependence on her grandfather by running off with the charismatic adventurer Phillip Tempest. He is all unbridled male dominance and id, as well as a bigamist; Rosamond flees him in horror, from sanctuary to convent to madhouse, pursued relentlessly by Tempest." Libr J

"Alcott's portrayals of the pathological Phillip and of the conflicted Rosamond . . . show strong psychological insights. This absorbing novel revises our image of a complex and, it is now clear, prescient writer." Publ Wkly

Alder, Elizabeth

The king's shadow. Farrar, Straus & Giroux 1995 259p $17   **Fic**

1. Harold, King of England, 1022?-1066—Fiction
2. Orphans—Fiction 3. Great Britain—History—0-1066—Fiction

ISBN 0-374-34182-6   LC 93-34159

After he is orphaned and has his tongue cut out in a clash with the bullying sons of a Welsh noble, Evyn is sold as a slave and serves many masters, from the gracious Lady Swan Neck to the valiant Harold Godwinson, England's last Saxon king

"Readers will get their history almost without noticing it, but will come to understand the complex society and world within which these individuals functioned easily. Evyn is easy to identify with as both a victim and an outcast." Voice Youth Advocates

Alvarez, Julia

How the Garcia girls lost their accents. Algonquin Bks. 1991 290p $17.95   **Fic**

1. Dominican Americans—Fiction

ISBN 0-945575-57-2   LC 90-48575

Also available in paperback from New Am. Lib.

This novel "tells the story (in reverse chronological order) of four sisters and their family, as they become Americanized after fleeing the Dominican Republic in the 1960s. A family of privilege in the police state they leave, the Garcias experience understandable readjustment problems in the United States, particularly old world patriarch Papi. The sisters fare better but grow up conscious, like all immigrants, of living in two worlds." Libr J

"This is an account of parallel odysseys, as each of the four daughters adapts in her own way, and a large part of Alvarez's accomplishment is the complexity with which these vivid characters are rendered." Publ Wkly

In the time of the butterflies; a novel. Algonquin Bks. 1994 325p $21.95   **Fic**

1. Mirabel family 2. Sisters—Fiction 3. Dominican Republic—Fiction

ISBN 1-56512-038-8   LC 94-15004

Also available in paperback from New Am. Lib.

This novel is "based on the lives of the four Mirabel sisters (code name: 'Mariposas,' that is, butterflies), three of whom were martyred in 1960 during the liberation of the Dominican Republic from the dictator Trujillo. Through the surviving sister, Dedé, as well as memories of Minerva, Patria, and Maria Teresa, we discover the compelling forces behind each sister's role in the struggle for freedom." Libr J

"Alvarez captures the terrorized atmosphere of a police state, in which people live under the sword of terrible fear and atrocities cannot be acknowledged. As the sisters' energetic fervor turns to anguish, Alvarez conveys their courage and their desperation, and the full import of their tragedy." Publ Wkly

Anderson, Poul, 1926-

Harvest of stars. TOR Bks. 1993 395p hardcover o.p. paperback available $5.99   **Fic**

1. Science fiction

ISBN 0-8125-1946-9 (pa)   LC 93-15627

"A Tom Doherty Associates book"

"A future North America is dominated by the Avantist police state, while space is ruled by the vast Fireball corporation. Founded by entrepreneur Anson Guthrie, Fireball is devoted to a nearly libertarian ideal of individual freedom and laissez-faire economics, the antithesis of the Avantist policy. The original Guthrie is long dead, but his mind, downloaded into a computer, lives on to direct Fireball. When the Avantists capture a second copy of Guthrie . . . they have the power to destroy Fireball." Publ Wkly

"Sweeping, fast-paced, intricate, provocative, Anderson's latest will appeal to older, more sophisticated sf fans." Booklist

Other titles in the author's future history series are:
Harvest the fire (1995)
The stars are also fire (1994)

Anthony, Piers

If I pay thee not in gold; [by] Piers Anthony, Mercedes Lackey. Baen Pub. Enterprises 1993 398p $20; pa $5.99   **Fic**

1. Fantasy fiction

ISBN 0-671-72175-5; 0-671-87623-6 (pa)

LC 93-21473

"In the land of Mazonia where magic is the province of women and men are considered no better than slaves, a young sorceress sets out to defeat a curse upon her family and becomes the catalyst for changing her world. Veteran fantasy authors Anthony and Lackey join forces to produce a fantasy adventure that explores gender discrimination in a light-hearted fashion. The authors' styles complement each other and produce a story different in tone from either writer's individual efforts. Fans of both authors will demand this title." Libr J

Incarnations of immortality series   **Fic**

1. Fantasy fiction

This fantasy series speculates about the nature of good and evil, time, space, magic, and science

Titles in the series are:
And eternity (1990)
Bearing an hourglass (1984)
Being a green mother (1987)
For love of evil (1988)
On a pale horse (1983)
Wielding a red sword (1986)
With a tangled skein (1985)

Anthony, Piers—*Continued*

The Magic of Xanth series   Fic
1. Fantasy fiction

This fantasy series features magic as a weapon in the conservation of the universe
Titles in the series are:
Castle Roogna (1979)
Centaur Isle (1981)
The color of her panties (1992)
Crewel lye (1984)
Demons don't dream (1993)
Dragon on a pedestal (1983)
Geis of the Gargoyle (1995)
Harpy thyme (1994)
Isle of view (1990)
Night mare (1982)
Ogre, ogre (1982)
Question quest (1991)
Roc and a hard place (1995)
The source of magic (1979)
A spell for Chameleon (1977)
Yon ill wind (1996)

Arnow, Harriette Louisa Simpson, 1908-1986

The dollmaker; [by] Harriette Arnow. University Press of Ky. 1985 c1954 549p $30   Fic
1. Detroit (Mich.)—Fiction 2. Kentucky—Fiction
ISBN 0-8131-1544-2   LC 85-40073
Also available in paperback from Avon Bks.
A reissue of the title first published 1954 by Macmillan
"Arnow traces dislocations in the lives of Kentucky people transplanted to Michigan to work in the Willow Run bomber plant during World War II." Benet's Reader's Ency of Am Lit

Asimov, Isaac, 1920-1992

Fantastic voyage; a novel; based on the screenplay by Otto Klement and Joy Lewis Bixby. Houghton Mifflin 1966 239p hardcover o.p.; Bantam Bks. paperback available $5.99   Fic
1. Science fiction
ISBN 0-553-27572-0 (pa)
"Five people are sent on a rescue mission in a submarine, but this is no ordinary submarine moving through an ordinary sea. The people and the submarine are miniaturized. They are moving through a man's blood vessels to reach and break up a blood clot in his brain. The miniaturization will not last—they have only 60 minutes to do the job and leave the man's body, before they return to ordinary size." Publ Wkly

[The Foundation series]   Fic
1. Science fiction

This series narrates the fall of a great galactic empire and the efforts of the Foundations to combat the barbarism that follows
Titles in the series are:
Forward the Foundation (1993)
Foundation (1951)
Foundation and earth (1986)
Foundation and empire (1952)
Foundation's edge (1982)
Prelude to Foundation (1988)
Second Foundation (1986)

Atwood, Margaret, 1939-

Cat's eye. Doubleday 1989 c1988 446p hardcover o.p.; Bantam Bks. paperback available $10.95   Fic
1. Women artists—Fiction 2. Canada—Fiction
ISBN 0-553-37790-6 (pa)   LC 88-24345
Also available G.K. Hall large print edition
First published 1988 in Canada
Elaine Risley, the narrator of this novel, "is a Canadian painter of some renown who, at 50, has returned to her childhood city of Toronto for a retrospective of her work. The dull, provincial city of her youth has become world class in the intervening years . . . but in the week she is there her interest in the city's new galleries and restaurants and shops and, in many ways, in the retrospective itself, is only glancing. Her focus, and the novel's, is all on the past." N Y Times Book Rev
"Atwood's achievement is the decoding of childhood's secrets, and the creation of a flawed and haunting work of art." Time

The handmaid's tale. Houghton Mifflin 1986 311p hardcover o.p.; Fawcett Bks. paperback available $11   Fic
1. Allegories
ISBN 0-449-91153-5 (pa)
Also available G.K. Hall large print edition
"The time is the near future, the place is the Republic of Gilead—formerly known as the United States. A coup d'etat by religious fundamentalists has left the President and Congress dead, The Constitution suspended, and the borders sealed. . . . Atwood's storyteller, a 33-year-old woman known only as Offred, serves as a handmaid to one of the ruling Commanders of the Faithful, Fred, from whom she takes her name. . . . Her sole function . . . is to carry out a . . . version of Old Testament lore and bear a child for the aging Commander, with the collusion of his barren wife." Christ Sci Monit
"A gripping suspense tale, The Handmaid's Tale is an allegory of what results from a politics based on misogyny, racism, and anti-Semitism." Ms

Austen, Jane, 1775-1817

Emma   Fic
1. Great Britain—Fiction
Hardcover and paperback editions available from various publishers
First published 1815
"Emma is a pretty girl of sterling character and more will than she can properly manage. She thinks she knows what is best for everybody, and is a prey to many deceptions. She is imposed upon, and imposes upon herself; it is a long while before she sees things as they are, and recognizes where her own happiness lies. Her hero is one of Jane's sober, clear-eyed, and perfect men. The Fairfax and Churchill subplot furnishes a comedy of dissimulation contrasting didactically with Emma's honesty. A formidable snob and vulgarian, Mrs. Elton, and a good-natured bore, Miss Bates, who would be insufferable outside these pages, are among the more laughable characters." Baker. Guide to the Best Fic

Pride and prejudice   Fic
1. Great Britain—Fiction
Hardcover and paperback editions available from various publishers

Austen, Jane, 1775-1817—*Continued*

First published 1813

"Concerned mainly with the conflict between the prejudice of a young lady and the well-founded though misinterpreted pride of the aristocratic hero. The heroine's father and mother cope in very different ways with the problem of marrying off five daughters." Good Read

"The characters are drawn with humor, delicacy, and the intimate knowledge of men and women that Miss Austen always shows." Keller. Reader's Dig of Books

    Sense and sensibility   **Fic**

    1. Great Britain—Fiction

Hardcover and paperback editions available from various publishers

First published 1811

A story "in which two sisters, Elinor and Marianne Dashwood represent 'sense' and 'sensibility' respectively. Each is deserted by the young man from whom she has been led to expect an offer of matrimony. Elinor bears her deep disappointment with dignity and restraint while Marianne violently expresses her grief." Reader's Ency. 4th edition

Baldwin, James, 1924-1987

✓ Go tell it on the mountain. Knopf 1953 303p $14.50   **Fic**

    1. African Americans—Fiction 2. Harlem (New York, N.Y.)—Fiction

    ISBN 0-679-60154-6

Also available in paperback from Dell

This novel is an "autobiographical story of a Harlem child's relationship with his father against the background of his being saved in the pentecostal church." Benet's Reader's Ency of Am Lit

✓ If Beale Street could talk. Dial Press (NY) 1974 197p o.p.; Dell paperback available $5.99   **Fic**

    1. African Americans—Fiction 2. New York (N.Y.)—Fiction

    ISBN 0-440-34060-8 (pa)

Also available G.K. Hall large print edition

"Tish, aged 19, and Fonny, 22 years old, are in love and pledged to marry, a decision hastened by Tish's unexpected pregnancy. Fonny is falsely accused of raping a Puerto Rican woman and is sent to prison. The families of the desperate couple search frantically for evidence that will prove his innocence in order to reunite the lovers and provide a safe haven for the expected child. There is some explicit sex but it is not treated in a sensational manner, nor is the use of street language gratuitous." Shapiro. Fic for Youth. 3d edition

Ballard, J. G., 1930-

Empire of the Sun; a novel. Simon & Schuster 1984 279p o.p.; Pocket Bks. paperback available $5.99   **Fic**

    1. World War, 1939-1945—Fiction 2. Shanghai (China)—Fiction 3. Sino-Japanese Conflict, 1937-1945—Fiction

    ISBN 0-671-64877-2 (pa)   LC 84-10630

Also available in hardcover from Buccaneer Bks.

"The day after Pearl Harbor, Shanghai is captured by the Japanese, and 11-year-old Jim is separated from his parents and spends some months living on his own. Then he is captured and interned in a Japanese prison camp with other civilians. The story of the next four years is one of struggling to stay alive by any means possible." Libr J

"This novel is much more than the gritty story of a child's miraculous survival in the grimly familiar setting of World War II's concentration camps. There is no nostalgia for a good war here, no sentimentality for the human spirit at extremes. Mr. Ballard is more ambitious than romance usually allows. He aims to render a vision of the apocalypse, and succeeds so well that it can hurt to dwell upon his images." N Y Times Book Rev

Followed by The kindness of women (1991)

Balzac, Honoré de, 1799-1850

Old Goriot; translated from the French by Ellen Marriage. Knopf 1991 xxxiii, 237p $15   **Fic**

    1. Parent and child—Fiction 2. France—Fiction

    ISBN 0-679-40535-6   LC 91-52989

Also available in paperback from Penguin Bks.

"Everyman's library"

Original French edition, 1835. Part of the series: Scenes of Parisian life. This translation first published 1907. First Everyman's edition published 1908 by Dent

"Goriot, a retired manufacturer of vermicelli, is a good man and a weak father. He has given away his money in order to ensure the marriage of his two daughters, Anastasie and Delphine. Because of his love for them, he has to accept all kinds of humiliations from his sons-in-law, one a 'gentilhomme,' M. de Restaud, and the other a financier, M. de Nucingen. Both young women are ungrateful. They gradually abandon him. He dies without seeing them at his bedside, cared for only by young Rastignac, a law student who lives at the same boarding house, the pension Vauquer." Haydn. Thesaurus of Book Dig

Banks, Russell, 1940-

Rule of the bone; a novel. HarperCollins Pubs. 1995 390p $22; pa $10   **Fic**

    1. Adolescence—Fiction

    ISBN 0-06-017275-4; 0-06-092724-0 (pa)

                       LC 95-11701

The protagonist of this novel, fourteen-year-old Bone, "has a disturbed stepfather, a long-suffering mother, and a long-gone father. The first half of the book chronicles his willing but innocent drift into criminality. His life takes a turn for the better when he moves into an abandoned school bus with a Jamaican mystic. He travels to Jamaica with 'I-man,' and there he finds his self-centered druggie father, turns 15, is sexually initiated, and loses I-man in a violent drug deal." SLJ

"Intoxicating and unsparing, 'Rule of the Bone' is a romance for a world fast running out of room for childhood." N Y Times Book Rev

Beach, Edward Latimer, 1918-

Run silent, run deep; [by] Edward L. Beach. Holt & Co. 1955 364p o.p.; Naval Inst. Press reprint available $32.95 **Fic**

1. World War, 1939-1945—Fiction 2. Submarines—Fiction 3. Sea stories

ISBN 0-87021-557-4

"Commander Beach has taken the exciting material of a submarine war patrol in the Pacific in World War II and woven it into a novel. The author speaks and sees through the eyes of the book's central character, an Annapolis two-and-a-half striper with his first fleet submarine command, the Walrus." N Y Trib Books

"If ever a book has the ring of reality, this is it. From the moment the reader steps aboard a training boat in New London, Conn., to the time when the submarine Walrus dives deeply to avoid the depth charges of the enemy's destroyers, there is awe and respect for the author who created them." N Y Times Book Rev

Beagle, Peter S.

The last unicorn. Viking 1968 218p o.p.; New Am. Lib. paperback available $9.95 **Fic**

1. Unicorns—Fiction 2. Allegories

ISBN 0-451-45052-3 (pa)

"A beautiful and previously happy unicorn learns she may be the last unicorn left on earth. Wanting not to believe it, she sets off in quest of her fellows. In the course of her journey, she meets a carnival magician of little ability, has encounters with a Robin Hood-like band, a king presiding over a hate-filled and miserable land, with the aid of the mysterious Red Bull, and a glamorous, if previously ineffectual prince." Publ Wkly

"Beagle is a true magician with words, a master of prose and a deft practitioner in verse. He has been compared, not unreasonably, with Lewis Carroll and J. R. R. Tolkien, but he stands squarely and triumphantly on his own feet." Saturday Rev

Bellamy, Edward, 1850-1898

Looking backward: 2000-1887 **Fic**

1. Utopias—Fiction

Hardcover and paperback editions available from various publishers

First published 1888

"Julian West, a wealthy Bostonian, after spending the evening with his fiancée Edith Bartlett, finds that he cannot fall asleep. Hypnotized by Dr. Pillsbury, he awakens to find that it is 113 years later. Still retaining the vigor and appearance of his youth in 2000 A.D., he falls in love with another Edith, the great-granddaughter of his first fiancée. She guides him on a tour of the cooperative commonwealth which has come into existence. Labor is the cornerstone of society; all work and share alike. The State is the Great Trust. Economic security and a healthy moral environment have reduced crime. The cultural level has risen. Julian dreams that he is again in the old society, which now appalls him as ruthless, greedy, and unjust. To his relief, however, he awakens and finds himself still in the new Utopia." Haydn. Thesaurus of Book Dig

Bellow, Saul

The adventures of Augie March; with an introduction by Martin Amis. Knopf 1995 xxxvii, 616p $20 **Fic**

1. Jews—Fiction 2. Chicago (Ill.)—Fiction

ISBN 0-679-44460-2

Also available in paperback from Penguin Bks. "Everyman's library"

A reissue of the title first published 1953 by Viking

"It is a picaresque story of a poor Jewish youth from Chicago, his progress, sometimes highly comic, through the world of the 20th century, and his attempts to make sense of it." Merriam-Webster's Ency of Lit

Benchley, Peter

Jaws. Doubleday 1974 311p o.p.; Fawcett Bks. paperback available $5.99 **Fic**

1. Sharks—Fiction 2. Adventure fiction

ISBN 0-449-21963-1 (pa)

This is a "story about what happens when a great white shark terrorizes a small Long Island town. . . . A woman swimmer is devoured by the shark, and Police Chief Martin Brody insists on closing the beaches. But he's overruled by the town fathers who remind him that the community is dependent on summer visitors for economic survival. Two deaths later, the news can no longer be suppressed and Brody, an oceanographer and a fisherman go after the monster in an exciting chase." Publ Wkly

Bennett, James W., 1942-

The squared circle. Scholastic 1995 247p $14.95 **Fic**

1. Basketball—Fiction 2. Cousins—Fiction

ISBN 0-590-48671-3 LC 94-42283

Sonny, a university freshman and star basketball player, finds that the pressures of college life, NCAA competition, and an unsettling relationship with his feminist cousin bring up painful memories that he must face before he can decide what is important in his life

"The novel is full of symbolism, both sexual and mythological. Rough language and situations, such as a fraternity hazing, add a dimension of reality to the story but make this a selection for mature readers." Book Rep

Berry, James

Ajeemah and his son. Perlman Bks. 1992 c1991 83p $13.95; lib bdg $13.89; pa $3.95 **Fic**

1. Slavery—Fiction 2. Fathers and sons—Fiction 3. Jamaica—Fiction

ISBN 0-06-021043-5; 0-06-021044-3 (lib bdg); 0-06-440523-0 (pa) LC 92-6615

First published 1991 in the United Kingdom in a collection entitled The Future-telling lady

"Ajeemah and his son Atu are kidnapped and sold in West Africa, never to see home or family again. After the bitter journey to Jamaica, they are separated forever, sold off to plantations 20 miles apart. . . . The son's rebellion ends in heartbreak, flogging, suicide. The father is betrayed, but he survives to marry, sire a daughter, and celebrate when freedom comes." Booklist

"The power of Berry's writing places us in the story, confronted by the feelings of Ajeemah and Atu—and the author keeps us there until the last word." Horn Book

Blevins, Winfred

Stone song; a novel of the life of Crazy Horse; [by] Win Blevins. Forge 1995 400p $22.95   **Fic**

1. Crazy Horse, Sioux Chief, ca. 1842-1877—Fiction
2. Oglala Indians—Fiction

ISBN 0-312-85567-2   LC 95-6934

"A Tom Doherty Associates book"

A "biographical novel of the Sioux leader in command at the Battle of Little Big Horn. The author . . . evokes the mystical experiences that motivated the somber Crazy Horse from early childhood, depicting incidents from his subject's adult life that include a failed romance, successful military campaigns, and his final surrender to the U.S. Army in 1877." Libr J

"A deeply thoughtful and persuasive tribute. Blevins's novel offers the compelling story of a man destined for triumph and betrayal, but ultimately for glory." Publ Wkly

Block, Francesca Lia

Weetzie Bat. Harper & Row 1989 88p $12.95; lib bdg $14.89; pa $3.95   **Fic**

1. Friendship—Fiction 2. Los Angeles (Calif.)—Fiction

ISBN 0-06-020534-2; 0-06-020536-9 (lib bdg); 0-06-447068-7 (pa)   LC 88-6214

"A Charlotte Zolotow book"

Follows the wild adventures of Weetzie Bat and her Los Angeles punk friends, Dirk, Duck-Man, and Secret-Agent-Lover-Man

"A brief, off-beat tale that has great charm, poignancy, and touches of fantasy. . . . This creates the ambiance of Hollywood with no cynicism, from the viewpoint of denizens who treasure its unique qualities." SLJ

Other titles about Weetzie Bat and her friends are:
Baby Be-Bop (1995)
Cherokee Bat and the Goat Guys (1992)
Missing Angel Juan (1993)
Witch baby (1991)

Blume, Judy

Forever; a novel. Bradbury Press 1975 199p $16   **Fic**

ISBN 0-02-711030-3

Also available in paperback from Pocket Bks.

The "story of a teenage senior-year love affair based primarily on physical attraction. Once Katherine Danziger and Michael Wagner meet at a party, they have eyes only for each other, and their romance progresses rapidly from kissing to heavy petting to lying together and finally to frequent sexual intercourse after Kath gets the Pill from a Planned Parenthood officer. . . . Characters—including adults and friends of the protagonists—are well developed, dialog is natural, and the story is convincing; however, the explicit sex scenes will limit this to the mature reader." Booklist

Bonner, Cindy, 1953-

Lily; a novel. Algonquin Bks. 1992 336p $17.95   **Fic**

1. Texas—Fiction

ISBN 0-945575-95-5   LC 91-40237

"Lily DeLony, is 15, hardworking, and dutiful, having taken over the responsibilities of caring for her family af-

ter her mother's death. Life on the DeLonys' Texas farm in the 1880s is demanding, and her papa is a stern, humorless man. Lily has just blossomed into young womanhood, and the son of the only well-to-do family in the area has asked her to the church fair, but her heart has already been snared by Marion, the youngest of the notorious Beatty gang. Although Marion, nicknamed Shot, shares his brothers' outlaw life, he's sharp-witted, affectionate, and not without morals. Their attraction is as unavoidable as gravity." Booklist

"A fine first novel, making the timeworn theme of a responsible young girl's falling in love with an ne'er-do-well rascal new and fresh." Libr J

Followed by Looking after Lily (1994)

Bosse, Malcolm J., 1934-

The examination. Farrar, Straus & Giroux 1994 296p $17; pa $7.95   **Fic**

1. Brothers—Fiction 2. China—Fiction

ISBN 0-374-32234-1; 0-374-42223-0 (pa)   LC 93-50955

Fifteen-year-old Hong and his older brother Chen face famine, flood, pirates, and jealous rivals on their journey through fifteenth century China as Chen pursues his calling as a scholar and Hong becomes involved with a secret society known as the White Lotus

"Bosse has constructed a compelling, picaresque novel which blends adventure and history into a seamless fabric." Horn Book

Boulle, Pierre, 1912-1994

The bridge over the River Kwai; translated by Xan Fielding. Vanguard Press 1954 224p   **Fic**

1. Great Britain. Army—Officers—Fiction 2. World War, 1939-1945—Fiction 3. Thailand—Fiction

Available in hardcover from Amereon

Original French edition, 1952

"In 1942 the Japanese military under the command of Col. Saito orders its British prisoners of war to construct a bridge over the 400-foot-wide River Kwai in the Siamese jungle. Complications arise when prisoner Col. Nicholson insists that officers not be treated like regular lower-class soldiers. Medical officer Clipton is much more humane, and this difference brings the two fellow prisoners into frequent conflict. When the bridge is finally completed, a British demolition team prepares to destroy it." Shapiro. Fic for Youth. 3d edition

Bova, Ben, 1932-

Death dream. Bantam Bks. 1994 497p hardcover o.p. paperback available $5.99   **Fic**

1. Science fiction 2. Virtual reality—Fiction

ISBN 0-553-57256-3 (pa)   LC 93-46463

"Dan Santorini moves his family to Florida for a job with a young company working to create virtual reality games. At first, Dan is delighted to be reunited with his brilliant and eccentric former partner, Jase Lowrey. Yet Dan finds Jase uncomfortably manic, and Jase's playful barbs have a new, cruel sting. After Dan's company provides virtual reality teaching chambers to his daughter's school, his wife begins to observe a sinister effect on their daughter. Dan ignores his unease with his new company—and even his daughter's fainting spells—until

Bova, Ben, 1932-—*Continued*
two people die in a fighter pilot simulation he developed with Jase in their previous collaboration." Libr J

"Bova combines his usual deft writing with some imaginative bits of realistic science fiction, a riveting plot, plenty of nail-biting tension, and a surprising but satisifying ending." Booklist

Bradbury, Ray, 1920-
Dandelion wine; a novel. Knopf 1975 269p $24.95   Fic
1. Family life—Fiction 2. Illinois—Fiction
ISBN 0-394-49605-1
Also available in hardcover from Buccaneer Bks. and in paperback from Bantam Bks.
A reissue, with a new introduction by the author, of the title first published 1957 by Doubleday
A novel about one summer in the life of a twelve-year-old boy, Douglas Spaulding: the summer of 1928. The place is Green Town, Illinois, and Doug and his brother Tom wander in and out among their elders, living and dreaming, sometimes aware of things, again just having a wonderful time. Doug's big discovery that summer was that he was alive
"The writing is beautiful and the characters are wonderful living people. A rare reading experience—highly recommended to all libraries." Libr J

Something wicked this way comes. Knopf 1983 c1962 307p $24.95   Fic
1. Horror fiction
ISBN 0-394-53041-1   LC 82-48732
Also available in hardcover from Buccaneer Bks. and in paperback from Bantam Bks.
Reissue of the title first published 1962 by Simon & Schuster
"We read here of the loss of innocence, the recognition of evil, the bond between generations, and the purely fantastic. These forces enter Green Town, Illinois, on the wheels of Cooger and Dark's Pandemonium Shadow Show. Will Halloway and Jim Nightshade, two 13-year-olds, explore the sinister carnival for excitement, which becomes desperation as the forces of the dark threaten to engulf them. Bradbury's gentle humanism and lyric style serve this fantasy well." Shapiro. Fic for Youth. 3d edition

Bradford, Richard, 1932-
Red sky at morning; a novel. Lippincott 1968 256p o.p.; HarperCollins Pubs. paperback available $12   Fic
1. New Mexico—Fiction
ISBN 0-06-091361-4 (pa)
Also available in hardcover from Borgo Press
"Joshua Arnold and his mother move to their summer home in Corazon Sagrado, New Mexico, when the father joins the Navy during World War II. Josh copes with the Mexican and Anglo customs and is concerned with his mother's drinking. When his father dies in the war, he takes responsibility for his mother, his own life, and his father's business." Shapiro. Fic for Youth. 3d edition

Bradley, Marion Zimmer
The mists of Avalon. Knopf 1982 876p o.p.; Ballantine Bks. paperback available $14   Fic
1. Arthur, King—Fiction 2. Fantasy fiction 3. Great Britain—History—0-1066—Fiction
ISBN 0-345-35049-9 (pa)   LC 82-47810
This "retelling of the Arthurian legend is dominated by the character of Morgan le Fay (here called Morgaine), the powerful sorceress who symbolizes the historical clash betweeen Christianity and the early pagan religions of the British Isles." Publ Wkly
The author "deserves high praise for her work since this great and sweeping book successfully ties together legend and lore." Best Sellers

Bridgers, Sue Ellen, 1942-
Keeping Christina. HarperCollins Pubs. 1993 281p $15; lib bdg $14.89   Fic
1. Friendship—Fiction 2. School stories
ISBN 0-06-021504-6; 0-06-021505-4 (lib bdg)
        LC 92-22061
When she befriends Christina, the new girl in school, Annie does not suspect that there is more to her than meets the eye and that Christina will have a huge impact on Annie's family and her oldest friends
"Bridgers takes the reader into the lives of teenagers dealing with changeable emotions in a less-than-perfect world. Her skill in portraying realistic experiences makes this a book that will not collect dust on the library shelves. A quality book for young adults." Book Rep

Permanent connections. Harper & Row 1987 264p hardcover o.p. paperback available $3.95
        Fic
1. Family life—Fiction
ISBN 0-06-447020-2 (pa)   LC 86-45491
Forced to spend a semester in his father's small hometown up in the mountains, seventeen-year-old Rob finds his feelings of alienation and self-hatred diminishing as he forges relationships with relatives and new friends
"Narrated in understated but effective prose, the story relates with sympathy, but not sentimentality, one young pilgrim's progress toward maturity against the background of a well-realized rural setting." Horn Book

Brin, David, 1950-
The postman. Bantam Bks. 1985 294p hardcover o.p. paperback available $5.99   Fic
1. Science fiction 2. Nuclear warfare—Fiction 3. Oregon—Fiction
ISBN 0-553-27874-6 (pa)   LC 85-47647
This novel opens with the "familiar portrait of an America brought to the edge of extinction by nuclear war. An itinerant storyteller, Gordon Krantz, finds an old postman's uniform and bag and starts traveling across country, taking people's letters to loved ones and telling tales of a country on the road to recovery. Eventually he becomes a major force for that recovery, as the hope he gives the people rallies them." Booklist
"A well-crafted, realistic and often violent novel with diverse elements woven together in expert style." Best Sellers

Brontë, Charlotte, 1816-1855

Jane Eyre   **Fic**

1. Great Britain—Fiction

Hardcover and paperback editions available from various publishers

First published 1847

"In both heroine and hero the author introduced types new to English fiction. Jane Eyre is a shy, intense little orphan, never for a moment, neither in her unhappy school days nor her subsequent career as a governess, displaying those qualities of superficial beauty and charm that had marked the conventional heroine. Jane's lover, Edward Rochester, to whose ward she is governess, is a strange, violent man, bereft of conventional courtesy, a law unto himself. Rochester's moodiness derives from the fact that he is married to an insane wife, whose existence, long kept secret, is revealed on the very day of his projected marriage to Jane. Years afterward the lovers are reunited." Reader's Ency. 4th edition

Brontë, Emily, 1818-1848

Wuthering Heights   **Fic**

1. Great Britain—Fiction

Hardcover and paperback editions available from various publishers

First published 1847

Forced by a storm to spend the night at the home of the somber and unsociable Heathcliff, Mr. Lockwood has an encounter with the spirit of Catherine Linton. He gradually learns that Catherine's father, Mr. Earnshaw, had taken in Heathcliff as a young orphan. Heathcliff and Catherine began to fall in love, but after Mr. Earnshaw's death Catherine's brother treated Heathcliff in a degrading manner and Catherine married rich Edgar Linton. Heathcliff gradually worked his revenge against those who injured him

Brooks, Bruce, 1950-

The moves make the man; a novel. HarperCollins Pubs. 1984 280p $15; lib bdg $15.89; pa $4.50   **Fic**

1. African Americans—Fiction 2. Friendship—Fiction
ISBN 0-06-020679-9; 0-06-020698-5 (lib bdg); 0-06-440564-8 (pa)

"Jerome Foxworthy's consuming passion is 'hoops', and he gets excited when he sees a shortstop who has the same kind of love for baseball. 'Jayfox', 13, is the first and only black kid to integrate the junior high in Wilmington, N.C. His mother has a terrible accident, and in order to cook for his older brothers, he takes home economics, and finds that the only other male is that shortstop, Bix. Bix's mother is in a mental institution, and his stepfather will not allow Bix to visit her. Bix's problem becomes Jerome's with all sorts of consequences." BAYA Book Rev

This is an "excellent novel about values and the way people relate to one another." N Y Times Book Rev

Brooks, Terry, 1944-

The sword of Shannara; illustrated by the Brothers Hildebrandt. Ballantine Bks. 1991 726p il $17.95; pa $5.99   **Fic**

1. Fantasy fiction
ISBN 0-345-37143-7; 0-345-31425-5 (pa)

LC 90-43727

"A Del Rey book"

A reissue of the title first published 1977 by Random House

"Humans, trolls, dwarfs, elves, gnomes, sorcerers both good and evil, and battalions of knights and knaves populate this sweeping adult epic-fantasy. At the urging of a mysterious sorcerer, an adopted orphan named Shea reluctantly takes up the quest for the Sword of Shannara, a legendary elvin blade that alone can defeat the forces of evil engulfing the world." Booklist

This is an "engrossing saga of hardship and adventure with well-maintained action that will keep readers captive right up to a nicely-wrought finish." SLJ

Other titles in this epic-fantasy are:
The druids of Shannara (1991)
The Elfqueen of Shannara (1992)
The Elfstones of Shannara (1982)
First king of Shannara (1996)
The scions of Shannara (1990)
The talismans of Shannara (1993)
The wishsong of Shannara (1985)

Buchan, John, 1875-1940

The thirty-nine steps   **Fic**

1. Great Britain—Fiction 2. Secret service—Fiction 3. Spies—Fiction

Hardcover and paperback editions available from various publishers

First published 1915 by Doran

"A bored, well-to-do Englishman, Richard Hannay, returns home to England after growing up in South Africa. Drifting between his club and the sights of London, he is drawn into the confidences of a secret agent in the thick of espionage. The agent is murdered in Hannay's apartment and Richard finds himself on the run from Scotland Yard and the cult of the 'Black Stone.'" Shapiro. Fic for Youth. 3d edition

Buck, Pearl S. (Pearl Sydenstricker), 1892-1973

The good earth   **Fic**

1. China—Fiction

Hardcover and paperback editions available from various publishers

First published 1931 by Day

This novel set in pre-revolutionary China "describes the rise of Wang Lung, a Chinese peasant, from poverty to the position of a rich landowner, helped by his patient wife, O-lan. Their vigor, fortitude, persistence, and enduring love of the soil are emphasized throughout. Generally regarded as Pearl Buck's masterpiece, the book won universal acclaim for its sympathetically authentic picture of Chinese life." Reader's Ency. 4th edition

Bunyan, John, 1628-1688

The pilgrim's progress   **Fic**

1. Christian life—Fiction 2. Allegories

Hardcover and paperback editions available from various publishers

First published 1678

"The 'immortal allegory,' next to the Bible the most widely known book in religious literature. It was written in Bedford jail, where Bunyan was for twelve years a prisoner for his convictions. It describes the troubled journey of Christian and his companions through this life

Bunyan, John, 1628-1688—*Continued*

to a triumphal entrance into the Celestial city. Bunyan 'wrote with virgin purity utterly free from mannerisms and affectations; and without knowing himself for a writer of fine English, produced it.'" Pratt Alcove

Burnford, Sheila, 1918-1984

The incredible journey. Little, Brown 1961 145p

                                                   Fic
1. Cats—Fiction 2. Dogs—Fiction 3. Canada—Fiction

Available in hardcover from Amereon and in paperback from Bantam Bks.

"A half-blind English bull terrier, a sprightly yellow Labrador retriever, and a feisty Siamese cat have resided for eight months with a friend of their owners, who are away on a trip. Then their temporary caretaker leaves them behind in order to take a short vacation. The lonely trio decides to tackle the harsh 250-mile hike across the Canadian wilderness in search of home, despite the human and wild obstacles the group will encounter." Shapiro. Fic for Youth. 3d edition

Burns, Olive Ann

Cold Sassy tree. Ticknor & Fields 1984 391p $22.95   Fic
1. Georgia—Fiction
ISBN 0-385-31258-X   LC 84-8570
Also available in paperback from Dell

"Young Will Tweedy lives in a small Georgia town called Cold Sassy in the early 1900s. He is hard working (when pushed) because he has chores to do at home and work to do at his Grandpa Blakeslee's store. That still leaves him time to plan practical jokes with his pals and to overhear family dramas. The biggest drama begins when Grandpa, only three weeks after the death of his wife whom he had dearly loved, marries Miss Love Simpson—young enough to be his daughter. Miss Love has to face not only the town gossip, but also rejection from Will's Mother and Grandpa's other daughter. The story had humor, excitement, and realistic family confrontations." Shapiro. Fic for Youth. 3d edition

Followed by Leaving Cold Sassy, the unfinished sequel (1992)

Camus, Albert, 1913-1960

The fall; translated from the French by Justin O'Brien. Knopf 1957 147p o.p.; Vintage Bks. paperback available $10   Fic
ISBN 0-679-72022-7 (pa)
Original French edition, 1956

"A former Parisian lawyer explains to a stranger in an Amsterdam bar his current profession of judge-penitent. His bitter honesty prevented him first from winning his own self-esteem through good deeds, then from exhausting his own self-condemnation through debauchery. Knowing that no man is ever innocent, he is still trying to forestall personal judgment by confession, by judging others, and by avoiding any situation demanding action." Reader's Ency. 4th edition

The first man; translated from the French by David Hapgood. Knopf 1995 336p $23; pa $12
                                                   Fic
1. Algeria—Fiction
ISBN 0-679-43937-4; 0-679-76816-5 (pa)
                                          LC 95-2668
Also available G.K. Hall large print edition
Original French edition, 1994

"When Camus died in an automobile accident in 1960, a manuscript was found near him. It turned out to be the first chapters of his autobiographical novel. . . . The book covers the first 14 years of the life of Jacques Cormery, a.k.a. Albert Camus. First there is a 'search for the father,' the undercurrent of a boy's quest to fill a tragic vacuum created by his father's death when he is only a year old. The poverty and difficult circumstances in which he grows up in French Algeria make him feel like an outsider, even when he becomes an adult. Yet the memories of the child are filled with energy and physical intensity. The spontaneity of the narrative by an otherwise reserved writer makes this book a unique document for anyone interested in Camus." Libr J

The plague; translated from the French by Stuart Gilbert. Knopf 1948 278p $23   Fic
1. Plague—Fiction 2. Algeria—Fiction
ISBN 0-394-44061-7
Also available in paperback from Vintage Bks.
Original French edition, 1947

"Using an epidemic of bubonic plague in an Algerian city as a symbol for the absurdity of man's condition, Albert Camus has in this novel articulated his firm belief in mankind's heroism in struggling against the ultimate futility of life. The plague makes everyone in the city intensely aware both of mortality and of the fact that cooperation is the only logical consolation anyone will find in the face of certain death. Though each character, from doctor to priest, represents some aspect of mankind's attempts to deal with the absurd, none is a cardboard figure. The reader cares what happens to the men depicted here. One takes pleasure in the moments of deep human connection that leave us with the conviction that men are, on the whole, admirable." Shapiro. Fic for Youth. 3d edition

Capote, Truman, 1924-1984

Other voices, other rooms. Random House 1968 231p $19.95   Fic
1. Louisiana—Fiction
ISBN 0-394-43949-X
Also available in hardcover from Buccaneer Bks. and in paperback from New Am. Lib.

A novel describing the abnormal maturing of a loveless thirteen-year-old boy who goes to live with his father in a run-down Louisiana mansion peopled with eccentric characters

"It is knowledge of the human heart which 'Other Voices, Other Rooms' gives us; and this is genuine achievement. It is not only a work of unusual beauty, but a work of unusual intelligence." N Y Her Trib Books

The Thanksgiving visitor. Random House 1968 c1967 63p $19.95   Fic
1. Alabama—Fiction
ISBN 0-394-44824-3

This autobiographical story is about Buddy who was being raised by elderly relatives, and by his spinster cou-

Capote, Truman, 1924-1984—*Continued*
sin, Miss Sook Faulk. When Buddy is persecuted by a
bully, Odd Henderson, Miss Sook invites him to their
Thanksgiving dinner and precipitates the incident to
teach Buddy compassion

"If this volume seems thin . . . Capote has told his
story with such precise economy that once inside the
covers readers will no longer question the format. This
is storytelling in the classic tradition." Times Lit Suppl

Card, Orson Scott
Ender's game. TOR Bks. 1985 357p hardcover
o.p. paperback available $11.95   **Fic**
1. Science fiction
ISBN 0-312-85323-8 (pa)   LC 85-136148
"A Tom Doherty Associates book"
"Chosen as a six-year-old for his potential military genius, Ender Wiggin spends his childhood in outer space
at the Battle School of the Belt. Severed from his family,
isolated from his peers, and rigorously tested and trained,
Ender pours all his talent into the war games that will
one day repel the coming alien invasion." Libr J
"The key, of course, is Ender Wiggin himself. Mr.
Card never makes the mistake of patronizing or senti-
mentalizing his hero. Alternately likable and insufferable,
he is a convincing little Napoleon in short pants." N Y
Times Book Rev
Other titles in the author's distant future series about
Ender Wiggin are:
Children of the mind (1996)
Speaker for the Dead (1986)
Xenocide (1991)

Pastwatch; the redemption of Christopher
Columbus. TOR Bks. 1996 351p $23.95   **Fic**
1. Columbus, Christopher—Fiction 2. Space and
time—Fiction 3. America—Exploration—Fiction
ISBN 0-312-85058-1   LC 95-44927
"A Tom Doherty Associates book"
"Under the auspices of Pastwatch, a 23rd-century organization dedicated to viewing the past, three individuals journey to 15th-century Meso-America. They intend
to prevent the European conquest of the Americas by altering the circumstances surrounding Columbus's historic
voyage. Card's . . . novel posits a bold and compassionate alternative history filled with believable historical and
fictional characters." Libr J

Carmody, Isobelle
The gathering. Dial Bks. 1994 c1993 279p
hardcover o.p.; Penguin Bks. paperback available
$4.99   **Fic**
1. Horror fiction 2. Supernatural—Fiction
ISBN 0-14-036059-X (pa)   LC 93-31844
First published 1993 in Australia
When fifteen-year-old Nathaniel moves to a sinister
town that has been bruised by an ancient evil, he finds
himself one of those Chosen to fight the cycle of darkness
"The strongly atmospheric story includes enough suspense and unsettling violence to satisfy any horror fan
but is understated and thought-provoking in its psychological dimensions." Horn Book

Carter, Alden R.
Up country. Putnam 1989 256p $15.95   **Fic**
1. Alcoholism—Fiction 2. Wisconsin—Fiction
ISBN 0-399-21583-2   LC 88-37959
When his mother's drinking problem causes him to
spend several months with country relatives in upstate
Wisconsin, sixteen-year-old Carl begins to build a new
life for himself, only to see it threatened by a serious
mistake from his painful past
"The C.O.A. (children of alcoholics) explanations are
a bit overt at the end, but not enough to detract from the
solidly realistic positive ending. This would have been
melodramatic had it not been so carefully delineated."
Bull Cent Child Books

Cary, Lorene
The price of a child; a novel. Knopf 1995 317p
$23   **Fic**
1. Slavery—Fiction 2. African Americans—Fiction
ISBN 0-679-42106-8   LC 94-24667
"In 1855, Ginnie and two of her children set out with
their slave master for Nicaragua, where he has been appointed U.S. ambassador. Before boarding the ferry in
New York, Ginnie connects with operatives in the Underground Railroad who cleverly spirit her to Philadelphia, where she becomes freedwoman Mercer Gray.
While eluding slave catchers and struggling to earn a living, she grieves for her youngest child, left behind on the
plantation. Through the kindness of friends, she becomes
a lecturer in the cause for abolition." Libr J
"This delicate portrayal of a woman boldly opting to
explore the realities of liberty is a revealing depiction of
the struggles of free blacks during the decades of slavery." Booklist

Cather, Willa, 1873-1947
Death comes for the archbishop. Knopf 1927
303p hardcover o.p. paperback available $10 **Fic**
1. Catholic Church—Missions—Fiction 2. New Mexico—Fiction
ISBN 0-679-72889-9 (pa)
Also available reprint editions from various publishers
"Bishop Jean Latour and his vicar Father Joseph Vaillant together create pioneer missions and organize the
new diocese of New Mexico. . . . The two combine to
triumph over the apathy of the Hopi and Navajo Indians,
the opposition of corrupt Spanish priests and adverse climatic and topographic conditions. They are assisted by
Kit Carson and by such devoted Indians as the guide Ja-
cinto. When Vaillant goes as a missionary bishop to Colorado, they are finally separated, but Latour dies soon after his friend, universally revered and respected, to lie in
state in the great Santa Fe cathedral that he himself created." Oxford Companion to Am Lit. 5th edition

Early novels and stories. Library of Am. 1987
1336p $35   **Fic**
ISBN 0-940450-39-9   LC 86-10704
Omnibus edition of four novels: O pioneers! (1913);
The song of the lark (1915); My Antonia (1918); One of
ours (1922) and the story collection—The troll garden
(1905)

Cather, Willa, 1873-1947—*Continued*
My Ántonia; with illustrations by W. T. Benda.
Houghton Mifflin 1954 371p il $24.95; pa $5.95
Fic
1. Czech Americans—Fiction 2. Frontier and pioneer
life—Fiction 3. Nebraska—Fiction
ISBN 0-395-07514-9; 0-395-75514-X (pa)
Also available reprint editions from various publishers
First published 1918
"Told by Jim Burden, a New York lawyer recalling
his boyhood in Nebraska, the story concerns Antonia
Shimerda, who came with her family from Bohemia to
settle on the prairies of Nebraska. The difficulties related
to pioneering and the integration of immigrants into a
new culture are clearly portrayed." Shapiro. Fic for
Youth. 3d edition

O pioneers! **Fic**
1. Swedish Americans—Fiction 2. Frontier and pioneer life—Fiction 3. Nebraska—Fiction
Available in hardcover and paperback from various
publishers
First published 1913 by Houghton Mifflin
"The heroic battle for survival of simple pioneer folk
in the Nebraska country of the 1880's. John Bergson, a
Swedish farmer, struggles desperately with the soil but
dies unsatisfied. His daughter Alexandra resolves to vin-
dicate his faith, and her strong character carries her weak
older brothers and her mother along to a new zest for
life. Years of privation, are rewarded on the farm. But
when Alexandra falls in love with Carl Linstrum, and her
family objects because he is poor, he leaves to seek a
different career. After Alexandra's younger brother Emil
is killed by the jealous husband of the French girl Marie
Shabata, however, Carl gives up his plans to go to the
Klondike, returns to marry Alexandra and take up the
life of the farm." Haydn. Thesaurus of Book Dig

Cervantes Saavedra, Miguel de, 1547-1616
Don Quixote de la Mancha **Fic**
1. Spain—Fiction
Hardcover and paperback editions available from various publishers
Original Spanish edition, published in two parts, 1605
and 1615
"Treats of the pleasant manner of the knighting of that
famous gentleman, Don Quixote, of the dreadful and
never-to-be imagined adventure of the windmills, of the
extraordinary battle he waged with what he took to be a
giant, and of divers other rare and notable adventures
and strange enchantments which befell this valorous and
witty knight-errant." Carnegie Libr. of Pittsburgh
"The novel which obviously had for its genesis the
satire of romances of chivalry, gradually grew into a
most entertaining work of fiction, the first modern novel,
read and admired to this day as one of the world's great
literary achievements." Haydn. Thesaurus of Book Dig

Cherryh, C. J., 1942-
Foreigner; a novel of first contact. DAW Bks.
1994 378p $20; pa $5.99 **Fic**
1. Science fiction
ISBN 0-88677-590-6; 0-88677-637-6 (pa)
LC 94-179662
"Set on an alien world where the descendants of hu-
mans marooned in a long-ago starship accident live seg-

regated from the indigenous *atevi* on a remote island,
this [novel] . . . addresses the complicated issue of how
humans might have to compromise to survive on a planet
where they are barely tolerated by the original, humanoid
inhabitants." Publ Wkly
"Cherryh plays her strongest suit in this exploration of
human/alien contact, producing an incisive study-in-
contrast of what it means to be human in a world where
trust is nonexistent." Libr J

Childress, Alice, 1920-1994
A hero ain't nothin' but a sandwich. Coward,
McCann 1973 126p $15.95 **Fic**
1. Drug abuse—Fiction 2. African Americans—Fiction 3. Harlem (New York, N.Y.)—Fiction
ISBN 0-698-20278-3
Also available in paperback from Avon Bks.
"At the age of 13 Benjie Johnson is hooked on
'horse.' He believes that he can break the habit whenever
he is ready. When two of Benjie's teachers realize that
he is on drugs, they report him to the principal of the
school. Then begins his seesaw battle to break his addiction. Using Black English, the author draws a picture of
the urban drug scene." Shapiro. Fic for Youth. 3d edition

Christie, Agatha, 1890-1976
Murder on the Orient Express. Dodd, Mead
1985 c1933 263p il hardcover o.p.; HarperCollins
Pubs. paperback available $4.99 **Fic**
1. Mystery fiction
ISBN 0-06-100274-7 (pa) LC 84-72783
First United States edition published 1934 by Dodd,
Mead with title: Murder on the Calais Coach
A man is murdered on a train going from Istanbul to
Calais. The famous detective Hercule Poirot happens to
be on board and unravels the mystery
"This is the tour de force in which Agatha makes con-
spiracy believable and enlivens it by a really satisfying
description of the Taurus Express (part of the Orient sys-
tem)." Barzun. Cat of Crime. Rev and enl edition

Cisneros, Sandra
The house on Mango Street. Knopf 1994 134p
$21; pa $9 **Fic**
1. Chicago (Ill.)—Fiction 2. Mexican Americans—
Fiction
ISBN 0-679-43335-X; 0-679-73477-5 (pa)
LC 93-43564
"Originally published by Arte Público Press in 1984."
Verso of title page
Composed of a series of interconnected vignettes, this
"is the story of Esperanza Cordero, a young girl growing
up in the Hispanic quarter of Chicago. For Esperanza,
Mango Street is a desolate landscape of concrete and
run-down tenements, where she discovers the hard realities of life—the fetters of class and gender, the specter
of racial enmity, the mysteries of sexuality, and more."
Publisher's note
This is "a composite of evocative snapshots that manages to passionately recreate the milieu of the poor quarters of Chicago." Commonweal

Clancy, Tom, 1947-

The hunt for Red October. Naval Inst. Press 1984 387p $24.95   **Fic**

1. Nuclear submarines—Fiction 2. Spies—Fiction

ISBN 0-87021-285-0   LC 84-16569

Also available in paperback from Berkley Bks.

"Based on a true incident—the attempted defection of a Soviet destroyer in 1975—the plot concerns the defection of the 'Red October', a Soviet submarine carrying 26 Seahawk missiles able to destroy 200 cities. Russia's fleet is ordered to find and destroy the sub; the U.S. Navy wants to find it and get it to an American port. An 18-day, 4,000-mile hunt across the Atlantic ensues." Booklist

Clark, Mary Higgins

Where are the children? Simon & Schuster 1975 223p   **Fic**

1. Kidnapping—Fiction 2. Mystery fiction

Available in hardcover from Buccaneer Bks. and in paperback from Pocket Bks.

This tale is "set against a background of Cape Cod in the dead of winter. Nancy Eldredge's past hides a terrible secret. She was once tried and almost convicted of the murder of her two young children from a first marriage. . . . She is now happily married again with another little boy and girl. When these children vanish from their front yard in a snowstorm, Nancy's past is raked up and the local police are certain she has killed again." Publ Wkly

Clarke, Arthur C., 1917-

2001: a space odyssey. New Am. Lib. 1968 221p hardcover o.p. paperback available $12.95
                                                   Fic

1. Science fiction

ISBN 0-451-45273-9 (pa)

Also available in hardcover from Buccaneer Bks.

"Based on a screenplay by Stanley Kubrick and Arthur C. Clarke." Title page

Astronauts of the spaceship Discovery, aided by their computer, HAL, blast off in search of proof that extraterrestrial beings had a part in the development of intelligent life forms on Earth millions of years ago

"By standing the universe on its head, the author makes us see the ordinary universe in a different light. . . . [This novel becomes] a complex allegory about the history of the world." New Yorker

Followed by 2010: odyssey two (1982); 2061: odyssey three (1987); and 3001: the final odyssey (1997)

Childhood's end. Ballantine Bks. 1953 214p hardcover o.p. paperback available $5.99   **Fic**

1. Science fiction

ISBN 0-345-90988-7 (pa)

Also available in hardcover from Amereon and Buccaneer Bks.

This novel is "paradigmatic of Clarke's more speculative, transcendental novels. Structured as a succession of apocalytic revelations, it depicts the sudden metamorphosis of humanity, under the protective midwifery of the alien Overlords, into the next evolutionary stage, a group mind that ultimately merges with the cosmic Overmind, destroying the Earth in the process. . . . The alien other

that transcends humanity yet paradoxically represents humanity's destiny is a recurring theme in the author's speculative novels." New Ency of Sci Fic

Clavell, James

Shogun; a novel of Japan. Delacorte Press 1983 c1975 802p $25   **Fic**

1. Japan—Fiction

ISBN 0-385-29224-4

Also available in paperback from Dell

A reissue of the title first published 1975 by Atheneum

East and West meet in this "epic of feudal seventeenth-century Japan. When a gale casts John Blackthorne's ship ashore here, the English sea pilot and his crew must learn to sink or swim in an alien culture. Blackthorne's mentor is a feudal lord locked in a power struggle with another for control of all Japan. How Blackthorne makes himself useful and is rewarded with samurai status forms the bulk of this swashbuckler." Booklist

"Clavell creates a world: people, customs, settings, needs and desires all become so enveloping that you forget who and where you are. 'Shogun' is history infused with fantasy. It strives for epic dimension and occasionally it approaches that elevated state. It's irresistible, maybe unforgettable." N Y Times Book Rev

Cole, Brock, 1938-

Celine. Farrar, Straus & Giroux 1989 216p $15; pa $3.95   **Fic**

1. Adolescence—Fiction 2. Divorce—Fiction 3. Remarriage—Fiction

ISBN 0-374-31234-6; 0-374-41083-6 (pa)

                                     LC 89-45614

A "first-person narrative about a sixteen-year-old artist and her irresolute yearnings to find a center to her life. Living with her new stepmother while her father is on a lecture tour in Europe and her mother is trying to find herself, Celine has vague ambitions of finishing high school a year early so that she can join an older woman friend in Florence. She is convinced her father will allow her to do this if she can 'show a little maturity,' though, as events unfold, we come to see that the maturational status of the adults in the novel is just as much in question." Horn Book

"Here's a rare pleasure: Brock Cole's 'Celine' is a novel that doesn't set out deliberately to instruct, uplift, comfort, amuse or expand the horizons of those readers known . . . as 'young adults.' Yet it manages to accomplish all this and much more simply by telling a fine story about an unforgettable character." N Y Times Book Rev

Conrad, Joseph, 1857-1924

Heart of darkness   **Fic**

1. Africa—Fiction

Hardcover and paperback editions available from various publishers

Originally published 1902 in the collection Youth and two other stories

"Marlow tells his friends of an experience in the (then) Belgian Congo, where he once ran a river steamer

Conrad, Joseph, 1857-1924—*Continued*

for a trading company. Fascinated by reports about the powerful white trader Kurtz, Marlow went into the jungle in search of him, expecting to find in his character a clue to the evil around him. He found Kurtz living a depraved and abominable life, based on his exploitation of the natives. Without the pressures of society, and with the opportunity to wield absolute power, Kurtz succumbs to atavism." Reader's Ency. 4th edition

Lord Jim   **Fic**
1. Islands of the Pacific—Fiction
Hardcover and paperback editions available from various publishers
First published 1899
"A merciless analysis of a man who, branded as a coward among his fellows, found himself ultimately a demi-god among the Malay savages. Much of the incident of the Orient is drawn from scenes in the life of Rajah Brooke of Sarawak." Pratt Alcove

Conroy, Pat

The prince of tides. Houghton Mifflin 1986 567p $25   **Fic**
1. South Carolina—Fiction 2. New York (N.Y.)—Fiction
ISBN 0-395-35300-9   LC 86-10689
Also available in paperback from Bantam Bks.
"Savannah Wingo, a successful feminist poet who has suffered from hallucinations and suicidal tendencies since childhood, has never been able to reconcile her life in New York with her early South Carolina tidewater heritage. Her suicide attempt brings her twin brother, Tom, to New York, where he spends the next few months, at the request of Savannah's psychiatrist . . . helping to reconstruct and analyze her early life." Libr J

Cooney, Caroline B., 1947-

Flight #116 is down. Scholastic 1992 201p $14.95; pa $3.99   **Fic**
1. Aeronautics—Accidents—Fiction
ISBN 0-590-44465-4; 0-590-44479-4 (pa)
LC 91-9796
Teenager Heidi Landseth helps rescue people from a plane crash on her family's property, and the experience changes her life forever
"Using her trademark lightning pace, Cooney depicts the drama and human interest inherent in disaster. . . . This story will keep even the least bookish readers glued to their seats." Publ Wkly

Cooper, James Fenimore, 1789-1851

The last of the Mohicans   **Fic**
1. Frontier and pioneer life—Fiction 2. Indians of North America—Fiction
Hardcover and paperback editions available from various publishers
First published 1826
This Leatherstocking tale "presents Chingachgook and his son Uncas as the last of the Iroquois aristocracy. Natty Bumppo, the scout Hawkeye, is in the prime of his career in the campaign of Fort William Henry on Lake George under attack by the French and Indians. The

commander's daughters, Cora and Alice Munro, with the latter's fiancé Major Duncan Heyward, are captured by a traitorous Indian but rescued and conveyed to the fort by Hawkeye. Later Munro surrenders to Montcalm, and the girls are seized again by Indians. Uncas and Cora are killed, and the others return to civilization." Haydn. Thesaurus of Book Dig

Cormier, Robert

After the first death. Pantheon Bks. 1979 233p $7.95; lib bdg $14.99   **Fic**
1. Terrorism—Fiction
ISBN 0-394-84122-0; 0-394-94122-5 (lib bdg)
LC 78-11770
Also available in paperback from Dell
"A busload of children is hijacked by a band of terrorists whose demands include the exposure of a military brainwashing project. The narrative line moves from the teenage terrorist Milo to Kate the bus driver and the involvement of Ben, whose father is the head of the military operation, in this confrontation. The conclusion has a shocking twist." Shapiro. Fic for Youth. 2d edition

The chocolate war; a novel. Pantheon Bks. 1974 253p $20   **Fic**
1. School stories
ISBN 0-394-82805-4
Also available in hardcover from Buccaneer Bks. and in paperback from Dell
"In the Trinity School for Boys the environment is completely dominated by an underground gang, the Vigils. During a chocolate candy sale Brother Leon, the acting headmaster of the school, defers to the Vigils, who reign with terror in the school. Jerry Renault is first a pawn for the Vigils' evil deeds and finally their victim." Shapiro. Fic for Youth. 3d edition
Followed by: Beyond the chocolate war (1985)

I am the cheese; a novel. Pantheon Bks. 1977 233p $18.95   **Fic**
1. Intelligence service—Fiction 2. Organized crime—Fiction
ISBN 0-394-83462-3   LC 76-55948
Also available in paperback from Dell
"Adam Farmer's mind has blanked out; his past is revealed in bits and pieces—partly by Adam himself, partly through a transcription of Adam's interviews with a government psychiatrist. Adam's father, a newspaper reporter, gave evidence at the trial of a criminal organization which had infiltrated the government itself. He and his family, marked for death, came under the protection of the super-secret Department of Re-Identification, which changed the family's name and kept them under constant surveillance. Now an adolescent, Adam is finally let in on his parents' terrible secret." SLJ
"The suspense builds relentlessly to an ending that, although shocking, is entirely plausible." Booklist

Covington, Dennis

Lizard. Delacorte Press 1991 198p hardcover o.p. paperback available $3.99   **Fic**
1. Louisiana—Fiction
ISBN 0-440-21490-4 (pa)   LC 90-49789
Sent by his guardian to live at a Louisiana school for retarded boys, Lizard, a bright, deformed youngster, es-

Covington, Dennis—*Continued*

capes with the help of a visiting actor who gives him a role in his repertory company's production of "The Tempest"

This novel "addresses many themes which will make this title appealing to a wide audience of YAs: coming-of-age, romance, adventure, search for identity, handicaps, alcoholism, and grief." Voice Youth Advocates

Crane, Stephen, 1871-1900

The red badge of courage   **Fic**

1. Chancellorsville (Va.), Battle of, 1863—Fiction

Hardcover and paperback editions available from various publishers

First published 1895

"A young Union soldier, Henry Fleming, tells of his feelings when he is under fire for the first time during the battle of Chancellorsville. He is overcome by fear and runs from the field. Later he returns to lead a charge that re-establishes his own reputation as well as that of his company. One of the great novels of the Civil War." Cincinnati Public Libr

Craven, Margaret

I heard the owl call my name. Doubleday 1973 166p o.p.; Dell paperback available $3.50   **Fic**

1. Kwakiutl Indians—Fiction 2. Clergy—Fiction 3. Death—Fiction

ISBN 0-89966-854-2 (pa)

Also available in hardcover from Buccaneer Bks.

Not knowing that he has a fatal illness, a young Anglican priest is assigned to serve a parish of Kwakiutl Indians in the seacoast wilds of British Columbia. Among these vanishing Indians, Mark Brian learns enough of the meaning of life not to fear death

The author's "writing glows with delicate, fleeting images and a sense of peace. Her characters' hearts are bared by a few words—or by the fact that nothing is said at all." Christ Sci Monit

Crichton, Michael, 1942-

The Andromeda strain. Knopf 1969 295p $25   **Fic**

1. Science fiction

ISBN 0-394-41525-6

Also available in hardcover from Buccaneer Bks. and in paperback from Dell

"In these days of interplanetary exploration, this tale of the world's first space-age biological emergency may seem uncomfortably believable. When a contaminated space capsule drops to earth in a small Nevada town and all the town's residents suddenly die, four American scientists gather at an underground laboratory of Project Wildfire to search frantically for an antidote to the threat of a world-wide epidemic." Shapiro. Fic for Youth. 3d edition

Jurassic Park; a novel. Knopf 1990 399p $22.95   **Fic**

1. Science fiction 2. Dinosaurs—Fiction 3. Genetic engineering—Fiction

ISBN 0-394-58816-9   LC 90-52960

Also available G.K. Hall large print edition and in paperback from Ballantine Bks.

This novel "tells of a modern-day scientist bringing to life a horde of prehistoric animals." N Y Times Book Rev

"Crichton is a master at blending technology with fiction. . . . Suspense, excitement, and good adventure pervade this book." SLJ

Followed by The lost world (1995)

Crutcher, Chris, 1946-

Running loose. Greenwillow Bks. 1983 190p $17.95   **Fic**

1. School stories

ISBN 0-688-02002-X   LC 82-20935

Also available in paperback from Bantam Bks.

"Louie Banks tells what happened to him in his senior year in a small town Idaho high school. Besides falling in love with Becky and losing her in a senseless accident, Louie takes a stand against the coach when he sets the team up to injure a black player on an opposing team, and learns that you can't be honorable with dishonorable men." Voice Youth Advocates

"This is a story of honor and principles, messages that are achieved without preaching. An unusually fine first novel." Bull Cent Child Books

Staying fat for Sarah Byrnes. Greenwillow Bks. 1993 216p $15   **Fic**

1. Obesity—Fiction   2. Child abuse—Fiction 3. Friendship—Fiction 4. Swimming—Fiction

ISBN 0-688-11552-7   LC 91-40097

Also available Thorndike Press large print edition and in paperback from Dell

"An obese boy and a disfigured girl suffer the emotional scars of years of mockery at the hands of their peers. They share a hard-boiled view of the world until events in their senior year hurl them in very different directions. A story about a friendship with staying power, written with pathos and pointed humor." SLJ

Davis, Terry

If rock and roll were a machine. Delacorte Press 1992 209p hardcover o.p. paperback available $3.99   **Fic**

1. Motorcycles—Fiction   2. Authorship—Fiction 3. School stories

ISBN 0-440-21908-6 (pa)   LC 91-41807

The guidance of two adults and his interest in motorcycles and writing help high school junior Bert Bowden regain the sense of self that had been destroyed by his fifth-grade teacher

This novel "celebrates the fervor and robustness of a young man's passage to fulfillment through a superior, mature story." Voice Youth Advocates

Defoe, Daniel, 1661?-1731

Robinson Crusoe   **Fic**

1. Survival after airplane accidents, shipwrecks, etc.—Fiction

Hardcover and paperback editions available from various publishers

First published 1719

Defoe, Daniel, 1661?-1731—*Continued*

"A minutely circumstantial account of the hero's shipwreck and escape to an uninhabited island, and the methodical industry whereby he makes himself a comfortable home. The story is founded on the actual experiences of Alexander Selkirk, who spent four years on the island of Juan Fernandez in the early 18th century." Lenrow. Reader's Guide to Prose Fic

Dickens, Charles, 1812-1870

David Copperfield   **Fic**
1. Great Britain—Fiction
Hardcover and paperback editions available from various publishers
First published 1850
This novel "incorporates material from the autobiography Dickens had recently begun but soon abandoned and is written in the first person, a new technique for him. Although Copperfield differs from his creator in many ways, Dickens uses many early personal experiences that had meant much to him—his own period of work in a factory while his father was jailed, his schooling and reading, his passion for Maria Beadnell (a woman much like Dora Spenlow), and (more cursorily) his emergence from parliamentary reporting into successful novel writing." Merriam-Webster's Ency of Lit

Great expectations   **Fic**
1. Great Britain—Fiction
Hardcover and paperback editions available from various publishers
First published 1861
"The first-person narrative relates the coming-of-age of Pip (Philip Pirrip). Reared in the marshes of Kent by his disagreeable sister and her sweet-natured husband, the blacksmith Joe Gargery, the young Pip one day helps a convict to escape. Later he is sent to live with Miss Havisham, a woman driven half-mad years earlier by her lover's departure on their wedding day. . . . When an anonymous benefactor makes it possible for Pip to go to London for an education, he credits Miss Havisham. . . . Pips benefactor turns out to have been Abel Magwitch, the convict he once aided, who dies awaiting trial after Pip is unable to help him a second time. Joe rescues Pip from despair and nurses him back to health." Merriam-Webster's Ency of Lit

Hard times   **Fic**
1. Great Britain—Fiction
Hardcover and paperback editions available from various publishers
First published 1854
The proprietor of an experimental private school in an English manufacturing town, "Thomas Gradgrind, a fanatic of the demonstrable fact, has raised his children Tom and Louisa in an atmosphere of grimmest practicality. Louisa marries the banker Josiah Bounderby partly to protect her brother who is in Bounderby's employ, partly because her education has resulted in an emotional atrophy that makes her indifferent to her fate. Tom, shallow and unscrupulous, robs Bounderby's bank and contrives to frame Stephen Blackpool, an honest and long-suffering mill hand. Meanwhile, Louisa's dormant emotions begin to awaken, stimulated by disgust for the vulgar Bounderby, and the attentions of the charming, amoral

James Harthouse. When she runs away to her father and when Tom's guilt is discovered, Gradgrind realizes how his principles have blighted his children's lives. . . . The novel is Dickens' harshest indictment of practices and philosophical justifications of mid-19th-century industrialism in England." Reader's Ency. 4th edition

Oliver Twist   **Fic**
1. Great Britain—Fiction
Hardcover and paperback editions available from various publishers
First published 1837-1838
"A boy from an English workhouse falls into the hands of rogues who train him to be a pickpocket. The story of his struggles to escape from an environment of crime is one of hardship, danger and the severe obstacles overcome." Natl Counc of Teachers of Engl

A tale of two cities   **Fic**
1. France—History—1789-1799, Revolution—Fiction
Hardcover and paperback editions available from various publishers
First published 1859
"Although Dickens borrowed from Thomas Carlyle's history, *The French Revolution*, for his sprawling tale of London and revolutionary Paris, the novel offers more drama than accuracy. The scenes of large-scale mob violence are especially vivid, if superficial in historical understanding. The complex plot involves Sydney Carton's sacrifice of his own life on behalf of his friends Charles Darnay and Lucie Manette. While political events drive the story, Dickens takes a decidedly antipolitical tone, lambasting both aristocratic tyranny and revolutionary excess." Merriam-Webster's Ency of Lit

Dickinson, Peter, 1927-

A bone from a dry sea. Delacorte Press 1993 199p $16; pa $3.99   **Fic**
1. Prehistoric man—Fiction 2. Fossils—Fiction
ISBN 0-385-30821-3; 0-440-21928-0 (pa)
               LC 92-20491
Also available Thorndike Press large print edition
First published 1992 in the United Kingdom
"Li, a female child in a tribe of 'sea-apes' living some four million years ago, and Vinny, teenage daughter of a modern-day paleontologist, are the protagonists of alternating third-person stories, one extrapolating what life might have been like for an intelligent youngster in prehistoric times and the other demonstrating the difficulty of interpreting ancient shards." Booklist
"Basing his account of Li's people on an intriguing recent theory that we evolved from a semi-aquatic, apelike mammal, the author brilliantly suggests how we might have started along the road to what we are today. As readers have come to expect from him, the plot, characters, and background science are engrossing." SLJ

Eva. Delacorte Press 1989 219p hardcover o.p.; Bantam Bks. paperback available $4.50   **Fic**
1. Chimpanzees—Fiction 2. Science fiction
ISBN 0-440-207766-5 (pa)   LC 88-29435
"Eva wakes up from a deep coma that was the result of a terrible car accident and finds herself drastically altered. The accident leaves her so badly injured that her parents consent to a radical experiment to transplant her

Dickinson, Peter, 1927———Continued

brain and memory into the body of a research chimpanzee. With the aid of a computer for communication, Eva slowly adjusts to her new existence while scientists monitor her progress, feelings, and insight into the animal world." Voice Youth Advocates

"Raising ethical and moral questions, Dickinson creates a vision both profound and chilling." SLJ

Dijk, Lutz van, 1955-

Damned strong love; the true story of Willi G. and Stephan K.: a novel; translated from the German by Elizabeth D. Crawford. Holt & Co. 1995 138p $15.95   Fic

1. World War, 1939-1945—Fiction 2. Homosexuality—Fiction

ISBN 0-8050-3770-5   LC 94-42075

"Set in occupied Poland during World War II, this novel is based on the true story of Stefan K., a Polish boy who, at 16, fell in love with a German soldier. When their liaison was discovered by the Gestapo, the teen was tortured and sentenced to a labor camp. Readers learn how he managed to survive there until he escaped during the chaotic days before liberation. Stefan K.'s afterword, written in 1994, tells readers that he still doesn't know whether his lover survived." SLJ

"The novel, smoothly translated from the German, is told in the first person, providing the reader little distance from the subject." Horn Book

Doctorow, E. L., 1931-

Ragtime. Modern Lib. 1994 320p $15.50   Fic

1. New York (State)—Fiction

ISBN 0-679-60088-4   LC 93-43631

Also available in paperback from New Am. Lib.

This is a reissue of the title first published 1975 by Random House

"The lives of an upper-middle-class family in New Rochelle; a black ragtime musician who loses his love, his child, and his life because of bigotry; and a poor immigrant Jewish family are interwoven in this early-twentieth-century story. There are cameo appearances by well-known figures of that period: Houdini, anarchist Emma Goldman, actress Evelyn Nesbit, Henry Ford, and J.P. Morgan, whose magnificent library plays an important part in the story. The book mingles fact and fiction in portraying the era of ragtime." Shapiro. Fic for Youth. 3d edition

Dorris, Michael

A yellow raft in blue water. Holt & Co. 1987 343p $16.95   Fic

1. Mothers and daughters—Fiction 2. Indians of North America—Fiction

ISBN 0-8050-0045-3   LC 86-26947

Also available in paperback from Warner Bks.

"The bitter rifts and inevitable bonds between generations are highlighted as a teenaged daughter, mother, and grand matriarch of an American Indian family tell their life stories. Humorous and poignant, with unique characters." SLJ

Dostoyevsky, Fyodor, 1821-1881

Crime and punishment   Fic

1. Homicide—Fiction 2. Russia—Fiction

Hardcover and paperback editions available from various publishers

Written 1866

"The novel is a psychological analysis of the poor student Raskolnikov, whose theory that humanitarian ends justify evil means leads him to murder a St. Petersburg pawnbroker. The act produces nightmarish guilt in Raskolnikov. The narrative's feverish, compelling tone follows the twists and turns of Raskolnikov's emotions and elaborates his struggle with his conscience and his mounting sense of horror as he wanders the city's hot, crowded streets. In prison, Raskolnikov comes to the realization that happiness cannot be achieved by a reasoned plan of existence but must be earned by suffering." Merriam-Webster's Ency of Lit

The idiot   Fic

1. Epilepsy—Fiction 2. Russia—Fiction

Available in hardcover from Buccaneer Bks. and paperback from Penguin Bks.

Written 1868

"Dostoevsky puts into a world of foolishness, vice, pretence, and sordid ambitions, a being who in childhood had suffered from mental disease, and who with an intellect of more than ordinary power retains the simplicity and clear insight of a child. . . . The deeply absorbing drama in which he is a protagonist turns on the salvation of a woman, Nastasya Filipovna who had been corrupted in young girlhood." Baker. Guide to the Best Fic

Doyle, Sir Arthur Conan, 1859-1930

The hound of the Baskervilles   Fic

1. Mystery fiction 2. Great Britain—Fiction

Hardcover and paperback editions available from various publishers

First published 1902

This is the "case of the eerie howling on the moor and strange deaths at Baskerville. Sir Charles Baskerville is murdered, and Holmes and Watson move in to solve the crime." Haydn. Thesaurus of Book Dig

"By a miracle of judgment, the supernatural is handled with great effect and no letdown. The plot and subplots are thoroughly integrated and the false clues put in and removed with a master hand. The criminal is superb, Dr. Mortimer memorable, and the secondary figures each contribute to the total effect of brilliancy and grandeur combined. One wishes one could be reading it for the first time." Barzun. Cat of Crime. Rev and enl edition

Draper, Sharon M. (Sharon Mills)

Tears of a tiger. Atheneum Pubs. 1994 162p hardcover o.p. paperback available $3.95   Fic

1. Death—Fiction 2. African Americans—Fiction 3. Suicide—Fiction

ISBN 0-689-80698-1 (pa)   LC 94-10278

The death of African American high school basketball star Rob Washington in a drunk driving accident leads to the suicide of his friend Andy, who was driving the car

"The story emerges through newspaper articles, journal entries, homework assignments, letters, and conversations that give the book immediacy; the teenage conver-

Draper, Sharon M. (Sharon Mills)—*Continued*
sational idiom is contemporary and well written. Andy's perceptions of the racism directed toward young black males . . . will be recognized by African American YAs." Booklist

Dreiser, Theodore, 1871-1945
Sister Carrie   **Fic**
1. Chicago (Ill.)—Fiction 2. New York (N.Y.)—Fiction
Hardcover and paperback editions available from various publishers
First published 1900
"A powerful account of a young working girl's rise to the 'tinsel and shine' of worldly success, and of the slow decline of her lover and protector Hurstwood." Oxford Companion to Engl Lit

Du Maurier, Dame Daphne, 1907-1989
Rebecca. Doubleday 1938 457p $25   **Fic**
1. Great Britain—Fiction
ISBN 0-385-04380-5
Also available in paperback from Avon Bks.
"Rebecca, lovely and charming wife of English aristocrat Maxim de Winter, dies unexpectedly, and the mystery surrounding her death haunts all who remain at the Manderley country estate. Eight months after the sailing accident in which Rebecca lost her life Maxim remarries. Through his new wife's writing, the reader learns the truth about Rebecca's death and character." Shapiro. Fic for Youth. 3d edition

Dumas, Alexandre, 1802-1870
The Count of Monte Cristo   **Fic**
1. Adventure fiction 2. France—Fiction
Hardcover and paperback editions available from various publishers
Original French edition, 1844
"Edmond Dantés, a young sailor unjustly accused of helping the exiled Napoleon in 1815, has been arrested and imprisoned in the Chateau d'If, near Marseille. After fifteen years, he finally escapes by taking the place of his dead companion, the Abbé Faria; enclosed in a sack, he is thrown into the sea. He cuts the sack with his knife, swims to safety, is taken to Italy on a fisherman's boat. From Genoa, he goes to the caverns of Monte Cristo and digs up the fabulous treasures of which the dying Faria had told. He then uses the money to punish his enemies and reward his friends." Haydn. Thesaurus of Book Dig

The three musketeers   **Fic**
1. France—History—1589-1789, Bourbons—Fiction
Hardcover and paperback editions available from various publishers
Original French edition, 1844
"D'Artagnan arrives in Paris one day in 1625 and manages to be involved in three duels with three musketeers . . . Athos, Porthos and Aramis. They become d'Artagnan's best friends. The account of their adventures from 1625 on develops against the rich historical background of the reign of Louis XIII and the early part of that of Louis XIV, the main plot being furnished by the antagonism between Cardinal de Richelieu and Queen Anne d'Autriche." Haydn. Thesaurus of Book Dig

Duncan, Lois, 1934-
Killing Mr. Griffin. Little, Brown 1978 243p $15.95   **Fic**
1. School stories 2. Kidnapping—Fiction
ISBN 0-316-19549-9   LC 77-27658
Also available in paperback from Bantam Bks.
"Mr. Griffin, the stern high-school English teacher, is loathed by those who should appreciate his determination to educate them. Mark, a student, uses his cool glamour and cleverness to mesmerize classmates Jeff, David, Betsy and Sue, persuading them to kidnap Mr. Griffin, with the idea of scaring the teacher into handing out high grades for inferior work. They leave the man trussed and gagged in a remote spot, where he dies. Sue wants to go to the police with a confession, but Mark masterminds a frantic coverup." Publ Wkly
The author's "skillful plotting builds layers of tension that draws readers into the eye of the conflict. The ending is nicely handled in a manner which provides relief without removing any of the chilling implications." SLJ

Eliot, George, 1819-1880
Silas Marner   **Fic**
1. Great Britain—Fiction
Hardcover and paperback editions available from various publishers
First published 1861
"Silas Marner is a handloom weaver, a good man, whose life has been wrecked by false accusation of theft, which cannot be disproved. For years he lives a lonely life, with the sole companionship of his loom: and he is saved from his own despair by the chance finding of a little child. On this baby girl he lavishes the whole passion of his thwarted nature, and her filial affection makes him a kindly man again. After sixteen years the real thief is discovered, and Silas's good name is restored. On this slight framework are hung the richest pictures of middle and low class life that George Eliot has painted." Keller. Reader's Dig of Books

Ellison, Ralph
Invisible man; preface by Charles Johnson. Modern Lib. 1994 xxxiv, 572p $18.50   **Fic**
1. African Americans—Fiction
ISBN 0-679-60139-2   LC 94-176953
A reissue of the title first published 1952 by Random House
"Acclaimed as a powerful representation of the lives of blacks during the Depression, this novel describes the experiences of one young black man during that period. Dismissed from a Negro college in the South for showing one of the founders how Negroes live there, he is used later as a symbol of repression by a Communist group in New York City. After a Harlem race riot, he is aware that he must contend with both whites and blacks, and that loss of social identity makes him invisible among his fellow beings." Shapiro. Fic for Youth. 3d edition

Esquivel, Laura

Like water for chocolate; translated by Carol Christensen and Thomas Christensen. Doubleday 1992 245p hardcover o.p. paperback available $10.95   **Fic**
1. Women—Fiction 2. Cooking—Fiction 3. Mexico—Fiction
ISBN 0-385-42017-X (pa)   LC 91-47188
Original Spanish edition published 1989 in Mexico
Set in turn-of-the-century Mexico, this novel relates the story of Tita, "the youngest of three daughters. Practically raised in the kitchen, she is expected to spend her life waiting on Mama Elena and never to marry. Her habitual torment increases when her beloved Pedro becomes engaged to one of her sisters. Tita and he are thrown into tantalizing proximity and manage to communicate their affection through the dishes she prepares for him and his rapturous appreciation. Eventually, Tita's culinary wizardry unleashes uncontrollable forces, with surprising results." Booklist
"A poignant, funny story of love, life, and food which proves that all three are entwined and interdependent." Libr J

Faulkner, William, 1897-1962

Light in August. Random House 1967 c1959 480p $16.95; pa $12   **Fic**
1. Southern States—Fiction
ISBN 0-394-43335-1; 0-679-73226-8 (pa)
First published 1932 by Harrison Smith & Robert Haas, Inc.
The novel "reiterates the author's concern with a society that classifies men according to race, creed, and origin. Joe Christmas, the central character and victim, appears to be white but is really part black; he has an affair with Joanna Burden, a spinster whom the townsfold of Jefferson regard with suspicion because of her New England background. Joe eventually kills her and sets fire to her house; he is captured, castrated, and killed by the outraged townspeople, to whom his victim has become a symbol of the innocent white woman attacked and killed by a black man. Other important characters are Lena Grove, who comes to Jefferson far advanced in pregnancy, expecting to find the lover who has deserted her, and Gail Hightower, the minister who ignores his wife and loses his church because of his fanatic devotion to the past." Reader's Ency. 4th edition

The reivers; a reminiscence. Random House 1962 305p hardcover o.p. paperback available $12   **Fic**
1. Tennessee—Fiction
ISBN 0-679-74192-5 (pa)
"Told to his grandson as 'A Reminiscence,' Lucius Priest's monologue recalls his adventures in 1905 as an 11-year-old, when he, the gigantic but childish part-Indian Boon Hogganbeck, and a black family servant, Ned William McCaslin, become reivers (stealthy plunderers) of the automobile of his grandfather, the senior banker of Jefferson, Miss." Oxford Companion to Am Lit. 5th edition

Fielding, Henry, 1707-1754

The history of Tom Jones, a foundling   **Fic**
1. Great Britain—Fiction
Hardcover and paperback editions available from various publishers
First published 1749. Variant title: Tom Jones
"Squire Allworthy suspects that the infant whom he adopts and names Tom Jones is the illegitimate child of his servant Jenny Jones. When Tom is a young man, he falls in love with Sophia Western, his beautiful and virtuous neighbor. In the end his true identity is revealed and he wins Sophia's hand, but numerous obstacles have to be overcome, and in the course of the action the various sets of characters pursue each other from one part of the country to another, giving Fielding an opportunity to paint an incomparably vivid picture of England in the mid-18th century." Merriam-Webster's Ency of Lit

Fitch, Janet

Kicks. Clarion Bks. 1995 251p $15.95   **Fic**
1. Sexual ethics—Fiction 2. Los Angeles (Calif.)—Fiction
ISBN 0-395-69624-0   LC 94-18592
Laurie, a fifteen-year-old girl draws back from the false glamour of Los Angeles street life when Carla, an oft envied childhood friend becomes sexually promiscuous and overdoses on drugs
"The well-characterized Laurie exhibits the behaviors of a teen influenced by peer pressure. She doesn't understand her mother, longs for more than her family can afford, and is jealous of her older brother. The final confrontation between Laurie and Carla is realistic, emotional and believable." Book Rep

Fitzgerald, F. Scott (Francis Scott), 1896-1940

The Great Gatsby   **Fic**
1. Wealth—Fiction 2. Long Island (N.Y.)—Fiction
Hardcover and paperback editions available from various publishers
First published 1925
"The story takes place in the period from the First World War to the Depression. Nick Carraway, the narrator, comes to New York to make his fortune on Wall Street and becomes involved in the lives of his cousin Daisy Buchanan and her husband, Tom. Their marriage is failing, and becomes even more endangered when Daisy reencounters Jay Gatsby after a long separation. Gatsby is now wealthy with an income reputed to be derived from racketeering. He and Daisy had known and loved each other when they were younger, in the Midwest. When Tom's jealousy is aroused, there is a serious argument between Tom and Gatsby, with tragic consequences." Shapiro. Fic for Youth. 3d edition

Tender is the night   **Fic**

Hardcover and paperback editions available from various publishers
First published 1934
The story of Dick Diver, a young psychiatrist whose career was thwarted and his genius numbed through his marriage to the exquisite and wealthy Nicole Warren. On the outside their life was all glitter and glamour, but beneath the smooth, beautiful surface lay the corroding

Fitzgerald, F. Scott (Francis Scott), 1896-1940—
Continued
falseness of their social values and the tragedy of her disturbed mind

"Despite the book's many terrifying scenes, the warm tenderness of its writing lifts it into the realm of genuine tragedy." Reader's Ency. 4th edition

Flaubert, Gustave, 1821-1880
Madame Bovary   Fic
1. France—Fiction
Hardcover and paperback editions available from various publishers
Original French edition, 1857
A novel about the "life and fate of the Norman bourgeoise Emma Bovary. Unhappy in her marriage to a good-hearted but stupid village doctor, Emma finds her pathetic dreams of romantic love unfulfilled. A sentimental, discontented, and hopelessly limited person, she commits adultery, piles up enormous debts, and finally takes her own life in desperation. The novel's subject, the life of a very ordinary woman, and its technique, the amassing of precise detail, make Madame Bovary one of the crowning works in the development of the novel." Reader's Ency. 4th edition

Fletcher, Susan, 1951-
Flight of the Dragon Kyn. Atheneum Pubs.
1993 213p $15.95   Fic
1. Fantasy fiction 2. Dragons—Fiction
ISBN 0-689-31880-4   LC 92-44787
Prequel to Dragon's milk (1989)
"A Jean Karl book"
Fifteen-year-old Kara is summoned by King Orrik, who believes she has the power to call down the dragons that have been plundering his realm, and she is caught up in the fierce rivalry between Orrik and his jealous brother Rog
"This is a solid fantasy in a medieval Scandinavian-like setting, and there's plenty of drama, romance, and knavery to keep genre fans happy." Bull Cent Child Books

Forester, C. S. (Cecil Scott), 1899-1966
The African Queen. Little, Brown 1935 275p
hardcover o.p. paperback available $11.95   Fic
1. Christian missionaries—Fiction 2. Central Africa—Fiction 3. British—Central Africa—Fiction
ISBN 0-316-28910-8 (pa)
Also available G.K. Hall large print edition and in hardcover from Amereon and Buccaneer Bks.
"At her brother's death Rose Sayer is left alone in an isolated African mission. She is determined to fight against the Germans, who have taken her brother's black converts into custody. She joins forces with a Cockney, Alnutt, and they take a long and dangerous trip downriver in Alnutt's dilapidated launch in order to reach the German boat they intend to blow up. The journey points up the differences between this ill-matched pair, and their bravery as well." Shapiro. Fic for Youth. 3d edition

Forman, James D.
Becca's story. Scribner 1992 180p $14.95   Fic
1. United States—History—1861-1865, Civil War—Fiction
ISBN 0-684-19332-9   LC 92-1375
"Using his grandmother's letters and diary, the author recreates Becca Case's youth. The story takes place during the Civil War and emphasizes Becca's relationships with two suitors and how they competed for her love." Soc Educ
"This tender story of friendship and love is one that will endure. . . . The characters are strong and true, the conclusion stirring and poignant." SLJ

Forster, E. M. (Edward Morgan), 1879-1970
A passage to India   Fic
1. British—India—Fiction 2. India—Fiction
Hardcover and paperback editions available from various publishers
First published 1924
"Politics and mysticism are potent forces in India just after World War I. Ronald Heaslop, magistrate of Chandrapore, has asked his mother, Mrs. Moore, to visit him along with his fiancée, Adela Quested. To add to their knowledge of the real India, Dr. Aziz, a young Moslem doctor, offers to take them to the Marabar Caves outside the city. The visit is a shattering experience. Mrs. Moore is struck by the thought that all her ideas about life are no more than the hollow echo she hears in the cave. Adela, entering another cave alone, emerges in a panic and accuses Dr. Aziz of having attacked her in the gloom of the cave. The trial that results from her accusation divides the groups in the city so acutely that a reconciliation appears impossible." Shapiro. Fic for Youth. 3d edition

A room with a view. Putnam 1911 364p   Fic
1. Great Britain—Fiction 2. Italy—Fiction
Available in hardcover from Buccaneer Bks. and in paperback from Vintage Bks.
First published 1908
The novel "is set mostly in Italy, a country which represents for the author the forces of true passion. The heroine, upper-class Lucy Honeychurch, is visiting Italy with a friend. When she regrets that her hotel room has no view, lower-class Mr. Emerson offers the friends his own room and that of his son. Lucy becomes caught between the world of the Emersons and that of Cecil Vyse, the shallow, conventional young man of her own class to whom she becomes engaged on her return to England. Finally, she overcomes her own prejudice and her family's opposition and marries George Emerson." Reader's Ency. 4th edition

Fox, Paula
The moonlight man. Bradbury Press 1986 179p
$14.95   Fic
1. Fathers and daughters—Fiction 2. Alcoholics—Fiction 3. Nova Scotia—Fiction
ISBN 0-02-735480-6   LC 85-26907
Also available in paperback from Bantam Bks.
"A month's vacation with her estranged and sometimes alcoholic father becomes an emotional and, finally, liberating experience for 15-year-old Catherine Ames."

Fox, Paula—*Continued*
Soc Educ
"Fox's characters have great depth, and Catherine especially is notable for her realistic, yet ambiguous, feelings for her father. Her father's alcoholism is not treated in clinical detail but with great emotional sensitivity." Voice Youth Advocates

Francis, Dick
Come to grief. Putnam 1995 308p $23.95   **Fic**
1. Mystery fiction
ISBN 0-399-14082-4   LC 95-32377
"The champion jockey turned detective, Sid Halley, returns in this mystery to find the perpetrator of heinous crimes committed against prize-winning horses that are not insured. The horse community rejects his findings and does everything in its power to stop the investigation. . . . The reading is easy and descriptive. The story, set in the present, includes characters and situations that will appeal to teen readers . . . especially horse lovers." SLJ

Freedman, Benedict
Mrs. Mike; the story of Katherine Mary Flannigan; by Benedict and Nancy Freedman; drawings by Ruth D. McCrea. Coward-McCann 1947 312p   **Fic**
1. Flannigan, Katherine Mary O'Fallon—Fiction 2. Frontier and pioneer life—Fiction 3. Canada—Fiction
Hardcover available from Buccaneer Bks.
"At 16, Boston-reared Katherine Mary O'Fallon is sent north to Alberta, Canada, to find relief for the pleurisy from which she has been suffering. While residing with her Uncle John, she falls in love with Mike, a handsome Canadian Mounted Policeman. Life in the wilderness in the early 1900s is harsh, but the newly married couple finds joy and challenge in their adventures." Shapiro. Fic for Youth. 3d edition

Gaines, Ernest J., 1933-
The autobiography of Miss Jane Pittman. Dial Press (NY) 1971 245p o.p.; Bantam Bks. paperback available $4.99   **Fic**
1. African Americans—Fiction 2. Louisiana—Fiction
ISBN 0-553-26357-9 (pa)   LC 77-144380
"In the epic of Miss Jane Pittman, a 110-year-old ex-slave, the action begins at the time she is a small child watching both Union and Confederate troops come into the plantation on which she lives. It closes with the demonstrations of the sixties and the freedom walk she decides to make. This is a log of trials, heartaches, joys, love—but mostly of endurance." Shapiro. Fic for Youth. 3d edition

A lesson before dying. Knopf 1993 256p $23.50; pa $12   **Fic**
1. African Americans—Fiction 2. Mentally handicapped—Fiction 3. Prisoners—Fiction 4. Louisiana—Fiction
ISBN 0-679-41477-0; 0-679-74166-6 (pa)
                                        LC 92-20335
"The story of two African American men struggling to attain manhood in a prejudiced society, the tale is set in

Bayonne, La. . . in the late 1940s. It concerns Jefferson, a mentally slow, barely literate young man, who, though an innocent bystander to a shootout between a white store owner and two black robbers is convicted of murder, and the sophisticated, educated man who comes to his aid. When Jefferson's own attorney claims that executing him would be tantamount to killing a hog, his incensed godmother, Miss Emma, turns to teacher Grant Wiggins, pleading with him to gain access to the jailed youth and help him to face his death by electrocution with dignity." Publ Wkly
"YAs who seek thought-provoking reading will enjoy this glimpse of life in the rural South just before the civil rights movement." SLJ

Gallico, Paul, 1897-1976
The snow goose. Knopf 1940 57p $15   **Fic**
1. Geese—Fiction 2. Painters—Fiction 3. Dunkerque (France), Battle of, 1940—Fiction
ISBN 0-394-44593-7
Also available from Amereon
"In 1930 Philip Rhayader, a hunchbacked painter, moves to an abandoned lighthouse, where he devotes himself not only to his painting but to maintaining a bird sanctuary. Rejected by the world, he is a recluse until Fritha, a young girl, brings him a hurt Canadian snow goose to care for and heal. The bird becomes a bond in their deepening relationship. When Philip is killed in aiding the rescue at Dunkirk, Fritha continues to care for his birds until the lighthouse is destroyed." Shapiro. Fic for Youth. 3d edition

García Márquez, Gabriel, 1928-
Love in the time of cholera; translated from the Spanish by Edith Grossman. Knopf 1988 348p $27.50   **Fic**
1. Latin America—Fiction
ISBN 0-394-56161-9   LC 87-40484
Also available in paperback from Penguin Bks.
Original Spanish edition published 1985 in Colombia
"While delivering a message to her father, Florentino Ariza spots the barely pubescent Fermina Daza and immediately falls in love. What follows is the story of a passion that extends over 50 years, as Fermina is courted solely by letter, decisively rejects her suitor when he first speaks, and then joins the urbane Dr. Juvenal Urbino, much above her station, in a marriage initially loveless but ultimately remarkable in its strength. Florentino remains faithful in his fashion; paralleling the tale of the marriage is that of his numerous liaisons, all ultimately without the depth of love he again declares at Urbino's death." Libr J
"The poetry of the author's style, the humor in his voice, the joyous detail with which the plot is upholstered—all are reasons to live in this lush, luxurious novel for as long as you desire." Booklist

One hundred years of solitude; translated from the Spanish by Gregory Rabassa. Harper & Row 1970 422p $30; pa $13   **Fic**
1. Colombia—Fiction
ISBN 0-06-011418-5; 0-06-091965-5 (pa)
Also available G.K. Hall large print edition; Everyman's library edition and in paperback from Avon Bks.

García Márquez, Gabriel, 1928——*Continued*

Original Spanish edition published 1967 in Argentina

This novel "relates the founding of Macondo by Jose Arcadio Buendia, the adventures of six generations of his descendants, and, ultimately, the town's destruction. It also presents a vast synthesis of social, economic, and political evils plaguing much of Latin America. Even more important from a literary point of view is its aesthetic representation of a world in microcosm, that is, a complete history, from Eden to Apocalypse, of a world in which miracles such as people riding on flying carpets and a dead man returning to life tend to erase the thin line between objective and subjective realities." Ency of World Lit in the 20th Century

Garden, Nancy

Annie on my mind. Farrar, Straus & Giroux 1982 233p hardcover o.p. paperback available $3.95   Fic

1. Lesbians—Fiction

ISBN 0-374-40414-3 (pa)   LC 82-9189

"A few months into her freshman year at MIT, Liza Winthrop relives in reflective retrospect the past year, when she met and fell in love with Annie Kenyon." Booklist

"This is candid, dignified, perceptive, and touching; although the crux of the story line is the encounter that makes a physical relationship clear, it is the romantic element that dominates the book, with its strong characters and its tender love story." Bull Cent Child Books

Gilstrap, John

Nathan's run. HarperCollins Pubs. 1996 293p $22   Fic

1. Adventure fiction

ISBN 0-06-017385-8   LC 95-49136

Also available Thorndike Press large print edition

"Nathan isn't any old 12-year-old; he's a kid, shades of Dickens, who was unjustly thrown into a juvenile detention center and raped his first night there. Now the boy's on the lam, having escaped the center after killing a guard who for some mysterious reason tried to stab him to death. Crying for Nathan's blood are an ambitious politician and vengeful cops, as well as a sadistic mob hit man who aims to finish what the guard botched. . . . As the plucky kid fights against increasingly desperate odds, Gilstrap mixes sentiment and suspense with a wizard's touch." Publ Wkly

Golding, William, 1911-1993

Lord of the Flies; a novel. Coward-McCann 1955 243p hardcover o.p. paperback available $6.95   Fic

1. Allegories 2. Boys—Fiction 3. Survival after airplane accidents, shipwrecks, etc.—Fiction

ISBN 0-399-50148-7 (pa)

Also available in hardcover from Amereon and Buccaneer Bks.

First published 1954 in the United Kingdom

"Stranded on an island, a group of English schoolboys leave innocence behind in a struggle for survival. A political structure modeled after English government is set up and a hierarchy develops, but forces of anarchy and aggression surface. The boys' existence begins to degenerate into a savage one. They are rescued from their microcosmic society to return to an adult, stylized milieu filled with the same psychological tensions and moral voids. Adventure and allegory are brilliantly combined in this novel." Shapiro. Fic for Youth. 3d edition

Gordimer, Nadine, 1923-

My son's story. Farrar, Straus & Giroux 1990 277p $19.95   Fic

1. South Africa—Fiction 2. Race relations—Fiction 3. Fathers and sons—Fiction

ISBN 0-374-21751-3   LC 90-83232

Also available in paperback from Penguin Bks.

"Sonny is a teacher of mixed race. He and his wife are . . . sympathetic to the plight of the 'real blacks,' yet ambitious that they may someday be accepted by the whites. Sonny's political education begins when he's fired for helping black children demonstrate in their township. Jailed for promoting boycotts and participating in illegal gatherings, Sonny meets and falls in love with a blond, blue-eyed woman who works for a human-rights organization. Sonny's adolescent son, Will, tells the story of his father's political and erotic development, the resentments and betrayals that ensue." Newsweek

This is a "thoughtful, poised, quietly poignant novel that not only recognizes the value and cost of political commitment, but also takes account of recent developments in South Africa and Eastern Europe in a way that Gordimer's previous work did not." Christ Sci Monit

Gordon, Sheila, 1927-

Waiting for the rain; a novel of South Africa. Orchard Bks. 1987 214p $15.95   Fic

1. Race relations—Fiction 2. Friendship—Fiction 3. South Africa—Fiction

ISBN 0-531-05726-7   LC 87-7638

Also available in paperback from Bantam Bks.

"A Richard Jackson book"

Chronicles nine years in the lives of two South African youths—one black, one white—as their friendship ends in a violent confrontation between student and soldier

The author has "avoided the great pitfalls of such a story—caricature and sentiment. She writes with a determination to be fair and accurate, and, while she includes all the old stereotypes in their proper places . . . she does so in context and without hammering." N Y Times Book Rev

Grant, Cynthia D., 1950-

Mary Wolf. Atheneum Bks. for Young Readers 1995 166p $16; pa $4.50   Fic

1. Family life—Fiction 2. Unemployed—Fiction

ISBN 0-689-80007-X; 0-689-81251-5 (pa)

LC 95-2128

"As Mary Wolf turns 16, she and her family—mother, father, and three (soon to be four) younger siblings—have become nomads in their motor home. The father lost his insurance business in Nebraska in a business recession more than two years before. What began as a family vacation has become a downward spiral into pov-

Grant, Cynthia D., 1950——_Continued_
erty, emotional instability and petty crime." Book Rep

"The climax is violent but not exploitative—it delivers a strongly cathartic jolt as the author expertly releases the reader from her darkly absorbing story." Publ Wkly

Graves, Robert, 1895-1985
I, Claudius; from the autobiography of Tiberius Claudius, born B.C. 10, murdered and deified A.D. 54. Modern Lib. 1983 c1934 432p $15; pa $13
　　　　　　　　　　　　　　　　　　　Fic
1. Claudius, Emperor of Rome, 10 B.C.-54—Fiction 2. Augustus, Emperor of Rome, 63 B.C.-14 A.D.—Fiction 3. Rome—History—Fiction
ISBN 0-394-60811-9; 0-679-72477-X (pa)
Also available from Amereon
First published 1934 by Harrison Smith and Robert Haas

"Claudius is lame and a stammerer who seems unlikely to carry on the family tradition of power in ancient Rome. Immersing himself in scholarly pursuits, Claudius observes and lives through the plots hatched by his grandmother, Livia, political conspiracies, murders, and corruption, and he survives a number of emperors. He becomes emperor at last and is a just and well-liked ruler, in contrast to those who preceded him." Shapiro. Fic for Youth. 3d edition

Greene, Graham, 1904-1991
The heart of the matter. Viking 1948 306p o.p.; Penguin Bks. paperback available $10.95　　**Fic**
1. West Africa—Fiction
ISBN 0-14-018496-1 (pa)
Also available in hardcover from Amereon

"Set in West Africa, it is a suspense story ingeniously made to hinge on religious faith. . . . The hero is Scobie, an English Roman Catholic who has vowed to make his devout wife happy though he no longer loves her. He borrows money from a local criminal to send her out of harm's way to South Africa; then he falls in love with a young woman from a group of castaways whose ship has been torpedoed. The return of his wife, the development of an adulterous affair, and blackmail drive Scobie deeper into deception and lies. Forced to betray someone, he betrays his god and himself, and finally commits suicide." Reader's Ency. 4th edition

The power and the glory; introduction by John Updike. Viking 1990 295p hardcover o.p. paperback available $10.95　　　　　　**Fic**
1. Clergy—Fiction 2. Mexico—Fiction
ISBN 0-14-018499-6 (pa)　　　　　　LC 90-50052
Also available in hardcover from Amereon
First published 1940 with title: The labyrinthine ways
Set in Mexico, this novel "describes the desperate last wanderings of a whisky priest as outlaw in his own state, who, despite a sense of his own worthlessness (he drinks, and has fathered a bastard daughter), is determined to continue to function as priest until captured. . . . Like many of Greene's works, it combines a conspicuous Christian theme and symbolism with the elements of a thriller." Oxford Companion to Engl Lit

Grisham, John
The client. Doubleday 1993 422p $23.50　　**Fic**
1. Boys—Fiction 2. Mafia—Fiction
ISBN 0-385-42471-X　　　　　　　　LC 92-39079
Also available in paperback from Dell

"While sneaking into the woods to smoke forbidden cigarettes, preteen brothers Mark and Ricky find a lawyer committing suicide in his car. Mark tries to save the man but is instead grabbed by him and told the location of the body of a murdered U.S. senator—a murder for which the lawyer's Mafia-connected client is accused. Witnessing the successful suicide sends Ricky into shock and Mark into a web of lies, half-truths, and finally into refusal to tell the confided secret to the police. Mark accidentally but fortuitously hires a lawyer, Reggie Love, who steers him through a maze of FBI agents, legal proceedings, judges, ambitious lawyers, and hit men. . . . This thriller is unique in its theme and in its suspense mixed with humor. A sure 'all-night' read." SLJ

The runaway jury. Doubleday 1996 401p $26.95
　　　　　　　　　　　　　　　　　　　Fic
1. Mississippi—Fiction 2. Lawyers—Fiction
ISBN 0-385-47294-3　　　　　　　　LC 96-13872
Also available large print edition $30.95 (ISBN 0-385-48015-6)

"In a Mississippi Gulf Coast town, the widow of a lifelong smoker who died prematurely of lung cancer is suing Big Tobacco. Enter Rankin Fitch, a dark genius of jury fixing, who has won many such trials for the tobacco companies and who foresees no special problems here. Enter also a mysterious juror, Nicholas Easter, whom Fitch's army of jury investigators and manipulators can't quite seem to track—and his equally mysterious girlfriend Marlee. . . . The details of jury selection are fascinating." Publ Wkly

Guest, Judith
Ordinary people. Viking 1976 263p hardcover o.p. paperback available $6.95　　　　　**Fic**
1. Family life—Fiction
ISBN 0-14-006517-2 (pa)

"When his older brother drowns in a boating accident, seventeen-year-old Conrad Jarrett feels responsible and makes an unsuccessful attempt at suicide. After eight months in a mental institution, Conrad returns home to parents whose marriage is crumbling, friends who are wary of him, and a psychiatrist who works with him to help put the pieces together. The pain of adolescent anxiety and fragile family relationships are authentically depicted." Shapiro. Fic for Youth. 3d edition

Guthrie, A. B. (Alfred Bertram), 1901-1991
The big sky; [by] A. B. Guthrie, Jr. Sloane 1947 386p　　　　　　　　　　　　　　　　**Fic**
1. Frontier and pioneer life—Fiction 2. West (U.S.)—Fiction
Available in hardcover from Buccaneer Bks. and in paperback from Bantam Bks. and Houghton Mifflin

"After a quarrel and fight with his father, 17-year-old Boone Caudill leaves his home in Kentucky headed for St. Louis and the West. . . . The story follows his adventurous course, by foot and horseback, to the Mississippi, then by keel boat to the land of the big sky at the

Guthrie, A. B. (Alfred Bertram), 1901-1991—
Continued
headwaters of the Missouri, where for 13 years he leads the typical life of a mountain man of his period and in that short time sees the Indian degraded, the game killed off and the life he loved destroyed." Wis Libr Bull

Guy, Rosa
The disappearance. Delacorte Press 1979 246p hardcover o.p.; Bantam Bks. paperback available $3.99 **Fic**
1. Foster home care—Fiction 2. Mystery fiction 3. African Americans—Fiction
ISBN 0-440-92064-7 (pa) LC 79-50672
The disappearance of the seven-year-old daughter of a Brooklyn family casts suspicion on a juvenile offender from Harlem who has recently come to live with them
"Some readers might have difficulty with the Black and West Indian speech; others may not appreciate the 'down' ending. But, by story's close, each character has touched us and the fine delineation of all of them stands out as Guy's greatest strength." SLJ
Followed by New guys around the block (1983)

The friends. Holt & Co. 1973 203p $13.95 **Fic**
1. West Indians—New York (N.Y.)—Fiction 2. Harlem (New York, N.Y.)—Fiction 3. Friendship—Fiction
ISBN 0-03-007876-8
Also available in paperback from Bantam Bks.
"During early adolescence, friendship can be painful as well as joyful. Phyllisia learns this in her relationship with Edith Jackson. Having just arrived in Harlem from the West Indies, Phyllisia finds life difficult because she is new to the urban scene and because her father is a very strict disciplinarian. Because her accent marks her as different, she is treated with hostility by her classmates, and only Edith befriends her when she is involved in a fight. Phyllisia resists her father's authority when he forbids her to maintain her friendship with poor and slovenly Edith." Shapiro. Fic for Youth. 3d edition
Followed by Ruby, an adult novel, and Edith Jackson (1978)

Haggard, H. Rider (Henry Rider), 1856-1925
King Solomon's mines **Fic**
1. Adventure fiction 2. Central Africa—Fiction
Available in hardcover from Amereon and Buccaneer Bks.
First published 1885
"Highly coloured romance of adventure in the wilds of Central Africa in quest of King Solomon's Ophir; full of sensational fights, blood-curdling perils and extraordinary escapes." Baker. Guide to the Best Fic

Hahn, Mary Downing, 1937-
The wind blows backward. Clarion Bks. 1993 263p $13.95 **Fic**
1. Suicide—Fiction
ISBN 0-395-62975-6 LC 92-12245
Also available Thorndike Press large print edition and in paperback from Avon Bks.

"Since middle school, Spencer Adams has always held a special fascination for Lauren. Now that they are in high school and in love, however, the girl discovers that where there is light there must be shadow." Publ Wkly
"While Lauren's narration captures all the high emotions of first love, Hahn's writing is clean and unsentimental, her love scenes discreet but sexy, and her smooth fusion of serious themes of suicide and depression with a passionate love story has both dignity and wide appeal." Bull Cent Child Books

Hale, Edward Everett, 1822-1909
The man without a country **Fic**
1. Patriotism—Fiction 2. Prisoners—Fiction
Hardcover and paperback editions available from various publishers
"This long short-story concerns Philip Nolan, a young officer of the United States Army who is tried for the Aaron Burr conspiracy. During the court-martial he exclaims, 'Damn the United States! I wish I may never hear of the United States again!' The court thereupon sentences him to live out his life on a naval vessel, and never hear news of the United States. The story recounts the mental torments of the countryless prisoner, who after fifty-seven years finally learns that his nation is thriving, and dies happy." Haydn. Thesaurus of Book Dig

Hamilton, Virginia, 1936-
Sweet whispers, Brother Rush. Philomel Bks. 1982 215p $17.95 **Fic**
1. Single parent family—Fiction 2. African Americans—Fiction 3. Ghost stories
ISBN 0-399-20894-1 LC 81-22745
Also available in paperback from Avon Bks.
"Set in a contemporary urban locale, the reader is pulled into 14-year-old Tree's life. Confused emotions of love and anger toward her practical nurse mother for never being home and foisting off the care of her handsome 17-year-old retarded brother, lead to flashbacks via a mysterious lens manipulated by the attractive ghost of a dead uncle. Basic to the whole book is the disease porphyria, a metabolic defect from a genetic abnormality which becomes fatal when triggered by alcohol or certain drugs." Voice Youth Advocates

Hardy, Thomas, 1840-1928
The return of the native **Fic**
1. Great Britain—Fiction
Hardcover and paperback editions available from various publishers
First published 1878
"The novel is set on Egdon Heath, a barren moor in the fictional Wessex in southwestern England. The native of the title is Clym Yeobright, who has returned to the area to become a schoolmaster after a successful but, in his opinion, a shallow career as a jeweler in Paris. He and his cousin Thomasin exemplify the traditional way of life, while Thomasin's husband, Damon Wildeve, and Clym's wife, Eustacia Vye, long for the excitement of city life. Disappointed that Clym is content to remain on the heath, Eustacia, willful and passionate, rekindles her affair with the reckless Damon. After a series of coincidences Eustacia comes to believe that she is responsible

Hardy, Thomas, 1840-1928—*Continued*

for the death of Clym's mother. Convinced that fate has doomed her to cause others pain, Eustacia flees and is drowned (by accident or intent). Damon drowns trying to save her." Merriam-Webster's Ency of Lit

Tess of the D'Urbervilles   **Fic**
   1. Great Britain—Fiction

Hardcover and paperback editions available from various publishers

First published in complete form 1891

"The tragic history of a woman betrayed. . . . Tess the author contends, is sinned against, but not a sinner; her tragedy is the work of tyrannical circumstances and of the evil deeds of others in the past and the present, and more particularly of two men's baseness, the seducer, and the well-meaning intellectual who married her. . . . The pastoral surroundings, the varying aspects of field, river, sky, serve to deepen the pathos of each stage in the heroine's calamities, or to add beauty and dignity to her tragic personality." Baker. Guide to the Best Fic

Harris, Marilyn, 1931-

Hatter Fox. Random House 1973 241p hardcover o.p.; Ballantine Bks. paperback available $5.99   **Fic**
   1. Navajo Indians—Fiction 2. Reformatories—Fiction

ISBN 0-345-33137-5 (pa)

"Hatter Fox, a teenage Navajo girl, is a victim whose past is a series of virtually insufferable physical and mental tortures. As the novel opens, she is in jail for a minor offense. She stabs a young Indian Bureau doctor, Teague Summer, and is sent to a reformatory in the middle of New Mexico. The greater part of the story takes place there and describes her gradual and painful rehabilitation under the guidance of Summer. Finally released into his custody and beginning to learn to cope with the outside, Hatter Fox is killed by a tourist bus, her first paycheck still in her hand." Libr J

Harris, Mark, 1922-

Bang the drum slowly, by Henry W. Wiggen; certain of his enthusiasms restrained by Mark Harris. Knopf 1956 243p   **Fic**
   1. Baseball—Fiction

Available in hardcover from Amereon and Buccaneer Bks. and in paperback from Univ. of Neb. Press

"Henry Wiggen, star pitcher for the New York Mammoths, writes about his friend Bruce Pearson, who is slowly dying of Hodgkins Disease. Pearson, a third-string catcher, is ridiculed by his teammates for being stupid but strives to be a better player in order to help the team win the pennant." Shapiro. Fic for Youth. 3d edition

Harrison, Sue

Mother earth, father sky. Doubleday 1990 313p hardcover o.p.; Avon Bks. paperback available $6.50   **Fic**
   1. Indians of North America—Fiction 2. Prehistoric man—Fiction

ISBN 0-380-71592-9 (pa)   LC 89-25656

Also available Thorndike Press large print edition

"Harrison tells the story of an Aleutian woman living around 7000 B.C. When her village is destroyed by a hostile tribe, Chagak flees to her grandfather in the Whale Hunter tribe. Along the way, she finds safety with old Shuganan, but her trials do not end there. She endures brutalization and childbirth. . . . Harrison's fine first novel is based on thorough research into the lifestyle and beliefs of ancient Aleutians; exquisite detail imparts great viability to her characters." Booklist

Followed by My sister the moon

My sister the moon. Doubleday 1992 449p o.p.; Avon Bks. paperback available $6.50   **Fic**
   1. Indians of North America—Fiction 2. Prehistoric man—Fiction

ISBN 0-380-71592-9 (oa)   LC 91-29102

Also available Thorndike Press large print edition

"At her birth, Kiin's father had planned on killing her so that his wife might immediately produce a son. Her life, however, is saved when the chief claims her to be the wife for his infant son. Her life is one of difficulty and abuse—her father beats her regularly and gives her to traders for the night to improve his exchanges—but her inner strength enables her to survive through the turbulent, stormy times. This moving story keeps readers in its grip because every hint of peacefulness is upended by another difficulty." SLJ

Followed by Brother Wind (1994)

Hawthorne, Nathaniel, 1804-1864

The House of the Seven Gables   **Fic**
   1. Puritans—Fiction 2. New England—Fiction

Hardcover and paperback editions available from various publishers

First published 1851

"Set in mid-19th-century Salem, Mass., the work is a somber study in hereditary sin based on the legend of a curse pronounced on Hawthorne's own family by a woman condemned to death during the infamous Salem witchcraft trials. The greed and arrogant pride of the novel's Pyncheon family through the generations is mirrored in the gloomy decay of their seven-gabled mansion, in which the family's enfeebled and impoverished relations live. At the book's end the descendant of a family long ago defrauded by the Pyncheons lifts his ancestor's curse on the mansion and marries a young niece of the family." Merriam-Webster's Ency of Lit

The scarlet letter   **Fic**
   1. Puritans—Fiction 2. New England—Fiction

Hardcover and paperback editions available from various publishers

"Set in 17th-century Salem, the novel is built around three scaffold scenes, which occur at the beginning, the middle, and the end. The story opens with the public condemnation of Hester Prynne, and the exhortation that she confess the name of the father of Pearl, her illegitimate child. Hester's husband, an old and scholarly physician, just arrived from England, assumes the name of Roger Chillingworth in order to seek out Hester's lover and revenge himself upon him. He attaches himself as physician to a respected and seemingly holy minister, Arthur Dimmesdale, suspecting that he is the father of the child. *The Scarlet Letter* traces the effect of the actual and symbolic sin on all the characters." Benet's Reader's Ency of Am Lit

Heinlein, Robert A. (Robert Anson), 1907-1988

Stranger in a strange land. Putnam 1961 408p $21.95 **Fic**

1. Science fiction
ISBN 0-399-10772-X

Also available in hardcover from Buccaneer Bks. and in paperback from Ace Bks.

"The hero is a human born of space travelers from earth and raised by Martians. He is brought to the totalitarian post-World War III world that is in many ways depicted as a satire of the U.S. in the 1960s, marked by repressiveness in sexual morality and religion. The plot, which tells how the heroic stranger creates a Utopian society in which people preserve their individuality but share a brotherhood of community, made Heinlein and his novel cult objects for young people dedicated to a counterculture." Oxford Companion to Am Lit. 5th edition

Heller, Joseph

Catch-22; with an introduction by Malcolm Bradbury. Knopf 1995 xxxix, 568p $20 **Fic**

1. World War, 1939-1945—Fiction
ISBN 0-671-43722-3   LC 94-13984

Also available in paperback from Simon & Schuster "Everyman's library"

A reissue of the title first published 1961 by Simon & Schuster

"A comic, satirical, surreal, and apocalyptic novel . . . which describes the ordeals and exploits of a group of American airmen based on a small Mediterranean island during the Italian campaign of the Second World War, and in particular the reactions of Captain Yossarian, the protagonist." Oxford Companion to Engl Lit. 5th edition

"By way of some of the funniest dialogue ever, Heller takes shots at the hypocrisy, meanness, and stupidities of our society." Shapiro. Fic for Youth. 3d edition

Followed by Closing time (1994)

Hemingway, Ernest, 1899-1961

A farewell to arms. Scribner 332p $35 **Fic**

1. World War, 1914-1918—Fiction
ISBN 0-684-15562-1

Also available G.K. Hall large print edition and in paperback from Simon & Schuster

First published 1929; copyright renewed 1957

This novel "deals with a love-affair conducted against the background of the war in Italy. Its excellence lies in the delicacy with which it conveys a sense of the impermanence of the best human feelings; the unobstrusive force of its symbolism of mountain and plain; above all the vast scope of its vision of war—the retreat from Caporetto is one of the great war-sequences of literature." Penguin Companion to Am Lit

For whom the bell tolls. Scribner 471p $40 **Fic**

1. Spain—History—1936-1939, Civil War—Fiction
ISBN 0-684-10239-0

Also available G.K. Hall large print edition and in paperback from Simon & Schuster

First published 1940

"This war tale covers four tension-ridden days in the life of Robert Jordan, an American in the Loyalist ranks during the Spanish Civil War. Having accomplished his mission to blow up a bridge with the aid of guerilla bands, he is injured when his horse falls and crushes his leg. As enemy troops approach, he is left alone to meet their attack. Jordan's love for Maria, a young girl whom the Fascists had subjected to every possible indignity, adds another dimension to a story of courage, dedication—and treachery." Shapiro. Fic for Youth. 3d edition

The old man and the sea. Scribner 127p $14.95 **Fic**

1. Fishing—Fiction
ISBN 0-684-10245-5

Also available G.K. Hall large print edition

First published 1952; copyright renewed 1980

"The old fisherman Santiago had only one friend in the village, the boy Manolin. Everyone else thought he was unlucky because he had caught no fish in a long time. At noon on the eighty-fifth day of fishing, he hooked a large fish. He fought with the huge swordfish for three days and nights before he could harpoon it, but that battle came to nought when sharks destroyed the fish before Santiago could get back to the village." Shapiro. Fic for Youth. 3d edition

The sun also rises **Fic**

Available in hardcover and paperback from various publishers

First published 1926 by Scribner

This novel "deals with the lost generation of Americans who had fought in France during World War I and then had expatriated themselves from the America of Calvin Coolidge. The story is told by Jake Barnes, rendered impotent by a war wound. Lady Brett Ashley, a typical representative of the 'lost generation,' is divorcing her husband and diverts herself by her friendship, which sometimes seems like love, for Barnes. These two go to Spain with a group that includes Michael Campbell, whom Brett plans to marry; Bill Gorton, a friend of Jake; a Greek nobleman; and Robert Cohn, an American-Jewish writer." Reader's Ency. 4th edition

Herbert, Frank, 1920-1986

Dune. Putnam 1984 c1965 517p il $26.95 **Fic**

1. Science fiction
ISBN 0-399-12896-4   LC 83-16030

Also available in paperback from Ace Bks.

First published 1965 by Chilton

"Herbert combines several classic elements: a Machiavellian world of political intrigue worthy of fourteenth-century Italy, a huge cast of characters, and a detailed picture of a culture. Duke Leto Atreides and his family are coerced into exchanging their rich lands for a barren planet, Dune, which produces a unique drug. Duke's son, Paul, becomes the leader of a group that leads the Fremen of Dune against the enemy. This is a science fiction story with sociological and ecological import." Shapiro. Fic for Youth. 3d edition

Other titles about Dune are:
Chapterhouse: Dune (1985)
Children of Dune (1976)
Dune messiah (1969)
God Emperor of Dune (1981)
Heretics of Dune (1984)

Hersey, John, 1914-1993

A bell for Adano. Knopf 1944 269p $22.95; pa
$13   **Fic**
1. World War, 1939-1945—Fiction 2. Italy—Fiction
ISBN 0-394-41660-0; 0-394-75695-9 (pa)

Also available Thorndike Press large print edition and
in hardcover from Buccaneer Bks.

"As Major Victor Joppolo, newly appointed civil affairs officer for Amgot (Allied Military Government Occupied Territory), goes about the business of bringing order to the small Italian community of Adano, he learns
that the town has lost its 700-year-old bell and to replace
it becomes his preoccupation. . . . [The novel] shows
Joppolo assiduously making friends with the many odd
characters he encounters and bringing prosperity and
happiness to Adano." Bookmark

The wall. Knopf 1950 632p hardcover o.p.
paperback available $14   **Fic**
1. World War, 1939-1945—Fiction 2. Jews—Fiction
3. Warsaw (Poland)—Fiction
ISBN 0-394-75696-7 (pa)

"This novel is presented as a journal kept by a diarist
during World War II. It tells of life in the Warsaw Ghetto, depicting Jewish interdependence in a struggle for
survival. The writer's observations enrich our understanding of Jewish culture. Although the diarist dies of pneu-
monia in 1944, his escape from the enclosure within
which the Germans confined the Jews is a testament to
hope and courage." Shapiro. Fic for Youth. 3d edition

Hesse, Hermann, 1877-1962

Siddhartha; translated by Hilda Rosner. New
Directions 1951 153p $16.95; pa $5.95   **Fic**
1. Buddhism—Fiction 2. India—Fiction
ISBN 0-8112-0292-5; 0-8112-0068-X (pa)

Also available in hardcover from Buccaneer Bks. and
in paperback from Bantam Bks.

Original German edition, 1923

"The young Indian Siddhartha endures many experiences in his search for the ultimate answer to the question, what is humankind's role on earth? He is also looking for the solution to loneliness and discontent, and he
seeks that solution in the way of a wanderer, the company of a courtesan, and the high position of a successful
businessman. His final relationship is with a humble but
wise ferryman. This is an allegory that examines love,
wealth, and freedom while the protagonist struggles toward self-knowledge." Shapiro. Fic for Youth. 3d edition

Steppenwolf; translated from the German by
Basil Creighton. Holt & Co. 1929 309p $25; pa
$7.95   **Fic**
ISBN 0-8050-1317-2; 0-8050-1247-8 (pa)

Also available in hardcover from Amereon and Buccaneer Bks.

Original German edition, 1927

"The hero, Harry Haller . . . is torn between his own
frustrated artistic idealism and the inhuman nature of
modern reality, which, in his eyes, is characterized entirely by philistinism and technology. It is his inability to
be a part of the world and the resulting loneliness and
desolation of his existence that cause him to think of
himself as a 'Steppenwolf' (wolf of the Steppes). The
novel, which is rich in surrealistic imagery throughout,
ends in what is called the magic theater, a kind of allegorical sideshow. Here, Haller learns that in order to relate successfully to humanity and reality without sacrificing his ideals, he must overcome his own social and sexual inhibitions." Reader's Ency. 4th edition

Hillerman, Tony

Finding Moon. HarperCollins Pubs. 1995 319p
$24; pa $6.99   **Fic**
1. Vietnam War, 1961-1975—Fiction
ISBN 0-06-017772-1; 0-06-109261-4 (pa)

                                      LC 95-31309

Also available Thorndike Press large print edition

"Set mostly in Vietnam during the fall of Saigon in
1975, [this] is the tale of Moon Mathias, a self-described
third-rate editor of a third-rate Colorado newspaper who,
when his younger brother dies in Southeast Asia, discovers that there is a baby daughter missing somewhere in
Vietnam. Reluctantly drawn into a search for the child,
Moon is thereby drawn into a search for his own
values." Libr J

Skinwalkers. Harper & Row 1987 216p
hardcover o.p. paperback available $5.99   **Fic**
1. Mystery fiction 2. Navajo Indians—Fiction
ISBN 0-06-100017-5 (pa)

This is the first title to feature both of the author's
mystery series heroes Lieutenant Joe Leaphorn and Detective Jim Chee. Subsequent titles have featured the Navaho policemen individually as well as together

In this mystery "Leaphorn has three unsolved murders
to contend with, and then an attempt is made on Chee's
life. Much to Leaphorn's dismay bone head figures are
the sole clues found, indicating the work of a skinwalker
or witch. Hillerman's Leaphorn and Chee novels convey
the Navaho culture with all its intricacies set forth in a
meaningful way." Libr J

Hilton, James, 1900-1954

Lost horizon; a novel. Morrow 1995 c1933 262p
$23   **Fic**
1. Utopias—Fiction 2. Tibet (China)—Fiction
ISBN 0-688-14656-2   LC 96-160022

Also available in hardcover from Amereon and Buccaneer Bks. and in paperback from Pocket Bks.

A reissue of the title first published 1933

"Hugh Conway is a British consul at Baskul when
trouble erupts in 1931 and all civilians are evacuated. He
and three others board a plane lent by a Maharajah. After
they are airborne for several hours, they realize that they
are headed in the wrong direction. When the pilot finally
lands, the passengers find themselves in Shangri-La, a
utopian lamasery whose inhabitants know the secret of
attaining long life. Believing that war is going to destroy
all civilization, the High Lama summons the newcomers
to form the nucleus of a new civilization." Shapiro. Fic
for youth. 3d edition

Hinton, S. E.

The outsiders. Viking 1967 188p $14.99   **Fic**
1. Juvenile delinquency—Fiction
ISBN 0-670-53257-6

Also available in paperback from Bantam Bks.

Hinton, S. E.—*Continued*

"From the perspective of Ponyboy Curtis, the author relates the story of the Greasers, who are from the lower class, and their conflict with the Socs, who are their middle-class opposite number. For the Greasers, the gang comprises their street family, all the family that some of them have. In the collision between the two social factions, two buddies die, one as a hood, the other, a hero." Shapiro. Fic for Youth. 3d edition

"This remarkable novel by a seventeen-year-old girl gives a moving, credible view of the outsiders from the inside—their loyalty to each other, their sensitivity under tough crusts, their understanding of self and society." Horn Book

Tex. Delacorte Press 1979 194p hardcover o.p.; Bantam Bks. paperback available $8.95   **Fic**
1. Brothers—Fiction
ISBN 84-204-3924-X (pa)   LC 78-50448
"Fourteen-year-old Tex lives with his 17-year-old brother Mason in a rural area. Their father hasn't been home in five months, and the relationship between the two boys is tense. Each has his own problems, fears, and growing pains which keep him alienated from his brother, until a dramatic and terrifying experience forces them to seek comfort and support from each other." SLJ

"Many teens will empathize with Tex and his friends in their problems with parents, money, drugs, sex, and the law." Child Book Rev Serv

Ho, Minfong

Rice without rain. Lothrop, Lee & Shepard Bks. 1990 236p $14.95   **Fic**
1. Thailand—Fiction
ISBN 0-688-06355-1   LC 86-33745
In this story set in Thailand, "Jinda and her family are suspicious of the university students from Bangkok who have come to 'learn' in the drought-stricken northern village of Maekung. Their leader, Ned, . . . wins Jinda's heart and, eventually, the trust of the villagers. Ned convinces them to give just a third, not half, of their precious rice to the landlord. This resistance puts Jinda's father in prison and takes Jinda to Bangkok, where she is caught up in the student protest movement." Bull Cent Child Books

Ho's novel "gives an interesting and at times absorbing glimpse of class struggle in the Thailand of the 1970s. Village scenes are especially effective evocations of simple beauty and somnolence." SLJ

Hobbs, Valerie

How far would you have gotten if I hadn't called you back? a novel. Orchard Bks. 1995 306p $19.95; lib bdg $20.99   **Fic**
1. Automobile racing—Fiction 2. California—Fiction
ISBN 0-531-09480-4; 0-531-08780-8 (lib bdg)
      LC 94-48799
Also available in paperback from Penguin Bks.
"A Richard Jackson book"

"Sixteen-year-old Brownwyn Lewis is sure that the only way a displaced New Jersey person like herself will make it in rural California is to own a car. It will be her ticket to acceptance and excitement—and to boys—as well as a way of acting out against her father, whose al-

coholism and attempted suicide she's unwilling to forgive or forget. Although a car does enable her to find a group, it can't help her choose between two boys: solid, sensitive outsider Will Harding and cool, sexy bad boy JC. . . . Hobbs manipulates the elements (including the sex) with energy, confidence, and surprise. . . . An enticing coming-of-age story, unerringly accurate in both its passions and its scenery." Booklist

Hoffman, Alice

Second nature. Putnam 1994 254p hardcover o.p.; Berkley Pub. Group paperback available $6.50   **Fic**
ISBN 0-425-14681-2 (pa)   LC 93-11595
Also available Thorndike Press large print edition
"Robin Moore rescues a wild, unspeaking young man—called the Wolf Man because he was found, injured, in a wolf trap—from impending transfer to a mental hospital. In the process of teaching Stephen how to live in 'civilized' suburban society, she falls in love with him. Meanwhile, neighborhood animals are found with their throats slit, and a teenage girl is murdered; the Wolf Man is naturally a suspect." Libr J

"In the end, Ms. Hoffman suggests that it is love in all its wondrous forms, from a parent's love for a child to the most consuming sexual passion that truly delineates mankind. Her abiding vision of this ineluctable and uniquely human power informs 'Second Nature' with grace and beauty, making it at once her richest and wisest, as well as her boldest, novel to date." N Y Times Book Rev

Hogan, Linda

Solar storms; a novel. Scribner 1995 351p $22
      Fic
1. Canada—Fiction 2. Indians of North America—Fiction
ISBN 0-684-81227-4   LC 95-24563
"Angela Jensen, a frightened 17-year-old whose face is inexplicably scarred, has left her foster home in Oklahoma to return to the place of her birth, a desolate Indian village in northern Minnesota on a 'narrow finger of land called Adam's Rib.' There Angela meets her great-grandmother, Agnes; her great-great-grandmother, Dora-Rouge; and Bush, the strange and lonely woman who cared for her when she was just a baby. The four women pack two canoes, embarking on a voyage through the Northland's disjointed waterways in search of Dora-Rouge's birthplace, which is soon to be the site of a fierce struggle over a hydroelectric dam." N Y Times Book Rev

Holland, Isabelle

The man without a face. Harper & Row 1987 c1972 159p hardcover o.p. paperback available $4.50   **Fic**
1. Homosexuality—Fiction
ISBN 0-06-447028-8 (pa)   LC 88-140924
Reissue of the title first published 1972
"From his tutor, the badly scarred recluse Justice McLeod, 14-year-old Charles Norstadt learns much more than the meaning of homosexuality." Booklist
"The author handles the homosexual experience with

Holland, Isabelle—_Continued_

taste and discretion; the act of love between Justin and Charles is a necessary emotional catharsis for the boy within the context of his story, and is developed with perception and restraint. . . . A highly moral book, powerfully and sensitively written; a book that never loses sight of the humor and pain inherent in the human condition." Horn Book

Hugo, Victor, 1802-1885

The hunchback of Notre Dame　　　　Fic
1. France—History—1328-1589, House of Valois—Fiction 2. Middle Ages—Fiction

Hardcover and paperback editions available from various publishers

Original French edition, 1930. Variant title: Notre Dame de Paris

The hidden force of fate is symbolized by the superhuman grandeur and multitudinous imageries of the cathedral. "The first part . . . is a panorama of medieval life—religious, civic, popular, and criminal—drawn with immense learning and an amazing command of spectacular effect. These elements are then set in motion in a fantastic and grandiose drama, of which the personages are romantic sublimations of human virtues and passions—Quasimodo the hunchback, faithful unto death; Esmeralda, incarnation of innocence and steadfastness; Claude Frolla, Faust-like type of the antagonism between religion and appetite. Splendors and absurdities, the sublime and the grotesque are inextricably mingled in this strange romance. The date is fixed at the year 1482." Baker. Guide to the Best Fic

Les misérables　　　　　　　　Fic
1. Paris (France)—Fiction

Hardcover and paperback editions available from various publishers

Original French edition, 1862

"Set in the Parisian underworld and plotted like a detective story, the work follows Jean Valjean, a victim of society who has been imprisoned for 19 years for stealing a loaf of bread. A hardened criminal upon his release, he eventually reforms, becoming a successful industrialist and mayor of a northern town. Despite this he is haunted by an impulsive, regretted former crime and is pursued relentlessly by the police inspector Javert. Valjean eventually gives himself up for the sake of his adopted daughter, Cosette, and her husband, Marius. _Les Misérables_ is a vast panorama of Parisian society and its underworld, and it contains many famous episodes and passages." Merriam-Webster's Ency of Lit

Hurston, Zora Neale, 1891-1960

Novels and stories. Library of Am. 1995 1041p
$35　　　　　　　　　　　　　　Fic
1. African Americans—Fiction 2. Short stories
ISBN 0-940450-83-6　　　　　　　LC 94-25757

Companion volume to Folklore, memoirs, and other writings, entered in class 818

This collection contains Hurston's four novels: Jonah's gourd vine, Their eyes were watching God, Moses, man of the mountain, and Seraph on the Suwanee. Also included are nine short stories

"Libraries without a complete set of Hurston's fiction will find this volume a necessary and easy purchase to fill that unfortunate gap." Booklist

Their eyes were watching God　　　　Fic
1. African Americans—Fiction 2. Florida—Fiction

Hardcover and paperback editions available from various publishers

First published 1937 by Lippincott

This novel "treats social problems from a racial and feminist perspective. Janie Crawford, raised by her grandmother in rural poverty, flees her old and dictatorial husband with Joe Starks, an ambitious man who becomes the mayor of Florida's first town run by African Americans. When Joe dies, Janie falls in love with the younger Teacake and follows him to the truck farming area of the Florida swamps. In the floods following a hurricane, he is bitten by a rabid dog and, crazed, attacks Janie. She shoots him, is charged with murder, and finally exonerated. When she returns to the town she and Joe built, she tells her story to a friend." Benet's Reader's Ency of Am Lit

Hurwin, Davida, 1950-

A time for dancing. Little, Brown 1995 257p
$15.95　　　　　　　　　　　　Fic
1. Cancer—Fiction
ISBN 0-316-38351-1　　　　　　　LC 95-7169

Seventeen-year-old best friends Samantha and Juliana tell their stories in alternating chapters after Juliana is diagnosed with cancer

"Both friends confront the horrors of Julie's chemotherapy and other ramifications of her disease with courage, tenacity, and, finally, a sense of helplessness. Strong language could be problematic for some libraries, yet the novel resonates with grace and power." Booklist

Huxley, Aldous, 1894-1963

Brave new world. Harper & Row 1946 xx, 311p
hardcover o.p. paperback available $14　　Fic
1. Utopias—Fiction 2. Technology and civilization—Fiction
ISBN 0-06-090101-2 (pa)

Also available in hardcover from Amereon, Borgo Press and Buccaneer Bks.

First published 1932 by Doubleday, Doran & Company

"The ironic title, which Huxley has taken from Shakespeare's 'The Tempest,' describes a world in which science has taken control over morality and humaneness. In this utopia humans emerge from test tubes, families are obsolete, and even pleasure is regulated. When a so-called savage who believes in spirituality is found and is imported to the community, he cannot accomodate himself to this world and ends his life." Shapiro. Fic for Youth. 3d edition

Jackson, Shirley, 1919-1965

We have always lived in a castle. Viking 1962
214p hardcover o.p. paperback available $9.95
　　　　　　　　　　　　　　　Fic
1. Horror fiction
ISBN 0-14-007107-5 (pa)

Also available in hardcover from Amereon

"Since the time that Constance Blackwood was tried and acquitted of the murder of four members of her fam-

Jackson, Shirley, 1919-1965—*Continued*
ily, she has lived with her sister Mary Catherine and her
Uncle Julian in the family mansion. Mary Catherine
takes care of family chores and Uncle Julian is busy with
the writing of a detailed account of the six-year-old murders. Cousin Charles's arrival on the scene disrupts the
quiet peace of the family, and Mary Catherine's efforts
to get rid of him unloose a chain of events that bring
everything down in ruins." Shapiro. Fic for Youth. 3d
edition

James, Henry, 1843-1916
Novels, 1886-1890. Library of Am. 1989 1296p
$37.50   Fic
ISBN 0-940450-56-9   LC 88-82724
Contents: The Princess Casamassima (1886); The re-
verberator (1888); The tragic muse (1890)
Includes bibliographical references

The portrait of a lady   Fic
1. Europe—Fiction
Hardcover and paperback editions available from various publishers
First published 1881
"This is one of the best James's early works, in which
he presents various types of American characters transplanted into a European environment. The story centers
in Isabel Archer, the 'Lady,' an attractive American girl.
. . . Isabel refuses the offer of marriage of a typical
English peer, the excellent Lord Warburton, and of a
bull-dog-like New Englander, Casper Goodwood, to fall
a victim . . . to a worthless and spiteful dilettante, Gilbert Osmond, who marries her for her fortune and ruins
her life; but to whom she remains loyal in spite of her
realization of his vileness." Oxford Companion to Engl
Lit. 5th edition

The turn of the screw   Fic
1. Horror fiction 2. Ghost stories
Hardcover and paperback editions available from various publishers
First published 1898
This novella "is told from the viewpoint of the leading
character, a governess in love with her employer, who
goes to an isolated English estate to take charge of Miles
and Flora, two attractive and precocious children. She
gradually realizes that her young charges are under the
evil influence of two ghosts, Peter Quint, the ex-steward,
and Miss Jessel, their former governess. At the climax of
the story, she enters into open conflict with the children,
as a result of which Flora is alienated and Miles dies of
fright." Reader's Ency. 4th edition

Jones, James, 1921-1977
From here to eternity. Scribner 1951 861p o.p.;
Dell paperback available $7.50   Fic
1. Soldiers—United States—Fiction 2. World War,
1939-1945—Fiction 3. Hawaii—Fiction
ISBN 0-440-32770-9 (pa)
A story of Army life in Hawaii in the last months be-
fore Pearl Harbor. The chief characters are two sol-
diers—Pfc Robert Prewitt and First Sergeant Milton
Warden—and the women they love

"Mr. Jones has grappled with a variety of materials
and handles some of them less successfully than others.
There is a good deal of weak stuff in the two love affairs
and the characterizations of the women, and the sorties
into the field of general ideas are unimpressive. The
book as a whole, however, is a spectacular achievement;
it has tremendous vitality and driving power and graphic
authenticity." Atl Mon

Joyce, James, 1882-1941
A portrait of the artist as a young man   Fic
1. Ireland—Fiction
Hardcover and paperback editions available from vari-
ous publishers
First appeared serially, 1914-1915 in the United King-
dom; first United States edition published 1916 by
Huebsch
This autobiographical novel "portrays the childhood,
school days, adolescence, and early manhood of Stephen
Dedalus, later one of the leading characters in Ulysses.
Stephen's growing self-awareness as an artist forces him
to reject the whole narrow world in which he has been
brought up, including family ties, nationalism, and the
Catholic religion. The novel ends when, having decided
to become a writer, he is about to leave Dublin for Paris.
Rather than following a clear narrative progression, the
book revolves around experiences that are crucial to Stephen's development as an artist; at the end of each chapter Stephen makes some assertion of identity. Through
his use of the stream-of-consciousness technique, Joyce
reveals the actual materials of his hero's world, the components of his thought processes." Reader's Ency. 4th
edition

Kafka, Franz, 1883-1924
The trial; translated from the German by Willa
and Edwin Muir; revised, with additional notes, by
E. M. Butler. Knopf 1992 299p $17   Fic
ISBN 0-679-40994-7
Also available in hardcover from Buccaneer Bks. and
in paperback from Schocken Bks.
"Everyman's library"
Original edition 1924; first Everyman's Library edition, 1922
"Joseph K., a respected bank assessor, is arrested and
spends his remaining years fighting charges about which
he has no knowledge. The helplessness of an insignificant individual within a mysterious bureaucracy where
answers are never accessible is described in this provocative and disturbing book." Shapiro. Fic for Youth. 3d
edition

Kantor, MacKinlay, 1904-1977
Andersonville. World Pub. 1955 767p il o.p.;
New Am. Lib. paperback available $15.95   Fic
1. United States—History—1861-1865, Civil War—
Fiction 2. Confederate States of America—Fiction
ISBN 0-452-26956-3 (pa)
Also available in hardcover from Buccaneer Bks. and
P. Smith
"After twenty-five years of research Kantor wrote this
novel, which realistically portrays the atrocities of
Andersonville Prison, home of many Yankee soldiers

Kantor, MacKinlay, 1904-1977—*Continued*
during the Civil War. Ira Claffey, Georgia planter and
owner of the property on which Andersonville is built,
serves as a humane central character whose sorrows and
frustrations serve to point up the brutality of war. The
primitive, indeed horrible, existence of the prisoners is
described in detail." Shapiro. Fic for Youth. 3d edition

Kazantzakis, Nikos, 1883-1957
Zorba the Greek; translated by Carl Wildman.
Simon & Schuster 1952 311p hardcover o.p.
paperback available $11.95   **Fic**
1. Crete (Greece)—Fiction
ISBN 0-671-21132-3 (pa)
Also available in hardcover from Buccaneer Bks.
"An old Greek workman who is philosopher and he-
donist, raconteur and roué, Zorba goes to Crete with the
narrator, a rich and cultivated dilettante, who has been
stung into activity by being called a 'bookworm' as a
parting shot from his closest friend, en route to fight in
the Caucasus. He buys a mine and puts Zorba in charge
of the workmen. . . . Zorba accomplishes fantastic feats
of physical prowess, he tells wild stories of his erotic adventures, he misbehaves badly with his patron's money,
he dances, and sings, and talks." Times Lit Suppl
"Zorba the Greek is a novel sweet and elate with sunlight, friendship and happiness, with a life full of both
sensations and thoughts; it is in every sense a minor
classic, and Zorba, one feels, is among the significant
and permanent characters in modern fiction." New
Statesman

Keneally, Thomas
Schindler's list. Simon & Schuster 1982 400p
$25; pa $12   **Fic**
1. Schindler, Oskar, 1908-1974—Fiction 2. Holocaust,
1933-1945—Fiction 3. World War, 1939-1945—Fiction 4. Jews—Fiction
ISBN 0-671-51688-4; 0-671-88031-4 (pa)
                                         LC 82-10489
"An actual occurrence during the Nazi regime in Germany forms the basis for this story. Oskar Schindler, a
Catholic German industrialist, chose to act differently
from those Germans who closed their eyes to what was
happening to the Jews. By spending enormous sums on
bribes to the SS and on food and drugs for the Jewish
prisoners whom he housed in his own camp-factory in
Cracow, he succeeded in sheltering thousands of Jews,
finally transferring them to a safe place in Czechoslovakia. Fifty Schindler survivors from seven nations helped
the author with information." Shapiro. Fic for Youth. 3d
edition

Kennedy, William, 1928-
Ironweed. Viking 1983 227p hardcover o.p.
paperback available $11.95   **Fic**
1. Economic depressions—Fiction 2. New York
(State)—Fiction
ISBN 0-14-007020-6 (pa)   LC 82-40370
With this "tale of skid-row life in the Depression,
Kennedy adds another chapter to his 'Albany cycle'—a
group of novels set in the Albany, New York, under-
world from the 1920s onward. Following 'Legs' and

'Billy Phelan's Greatest Game,' 'Ironweed' tells the story
of Francis Phelan, a 58-year-old bum with muscatel on
his breath and hallucinations on his mind. Chief among
the latter is a vision of his infant son, who died after
falling out of Francis' arms. It is the desire to reconcile
himself to the memory of his dead son that brings Francis home to Albany, ultimately opening the door to a
possible reconciliation with his family." Booklist

Kerr, M. E., 1927-
Deliver us from Evie. HarperCollins Pubs. 1994
177p $15; lib bdg $14.89; pa $4.50   **Fic**
1. Lesbians—Fiction 2. Brothers and sisters—Fiction
ISBN 0-06-024475-5; 0-06-024476-3 (lib bdg);
0-06-447128-4 (pa)   LC 94-1296
Parr Burrman and his family face some difficult times
when word spreads through their rural Missouri town
that his older sister is a lesbian, and she leaves the family farm to live with the daughter of the town's banker
"The strong, multi-dimensional, well-plotted story addresses current issues with sensitivity, thoughtfulness,
and a touch of humor." Horn Book

Gentlehands. Harper & Row 1978 183p lib bdg
$16.89; pa $4.50   **Fic**
1. Grandfathers—Fiction 2. Social classes—Fiction
3. Criminals—Fiction
ISBN 0-06-023177-7 (lib bdg); 0-06-417067-9 (pa)
                                         LC 77-11860
"Buddy Boyle tries to impress rich, socially elite Skye
Pennington by introducing her to his refined and cultured
grandfather—and discovers that his grandfather is a Nazi
war criminal." Booklist
"The author's skill in conveying the conversation and
thought of this age is superb. The intrigue surrounding
Buddy's grandfather offers suspense and excitement to
the boy-meets-girl story line and adds some interesting
questions to the end. Told from Buddy's point of view,
this story will appeal to both boys and girls." Babbling
Bookworm

Kesey, Ken
One flew over the cuckoo's nest; a novel.
Viking 1962 311p hardcover o.p. paperback
available $10.95   **Fic**
1. Mentally ill—Fiction
ISBN 0-14-004312-8 (pa)
Also available Thorndike Press large print edition and
in paperback from New Am. Lib.
"Life in a mental institution is predictable and suffo-
cating under the iron rule of Nurse Ratched, who toler-
ates no disruption of routine on her all-male ward. Half-
Indian Chief Bromden, almost invisible on the ward because he is thought to be deaf and dumb, describes the
arrival of rowdy Randle Patrick McMurphy. McMurphy
takes on the nurse as an adversary in his attempt to organize his fellow inmates and breathe some self-esteem and
joy into their lives. The battle is vicious on the part of
the nurse, who is relentless in her efforts to break
McMurphy, but a spark of human will brings an element
of hope to counter the despotic institutional power." Shapiro. Fic for Youth. 3d edition

Keyes, Daniel, 1927-
Flowers for Algernon. Harcourt Brace & Co.
1995 c1966 286p $16 **Fic**
1. Mentally handicapped—Fiction 2. Science fiction
ISBN 0-15-100163-4 LC 95-148312
Also available Thorndike Press large print edition and
in hardcover from Buccaneer Bks.
"A Harcourt Brace modern classic"
First published 1966
"Charlie Gordon, aged 32, is mentally retarded and
enrolls in a class to 'become smart.' He keeps a journal
of his progress after an experimental operation that increases his I.Q. Although Charlie becomes brilliant, he is
unhappy because he cannot shed his former personality
and is tormented by his memories. In the end he begins
to lose the mental powers he has gained." Shapiro. Fic
for Youth. 3d edition

Kincaid, Jamaica
Annie John. Farrar, Straus & Giroux 1985 148p
$18.95 **Fic**
1. Antigua and Barbuda—Fiction
ISBN 0-374-10521-9
Also available in paperback from New Am. Lib.
"Episodes from the young life of Annie John, aged 10
to 17, as she grows up on the Caribbean island of Antigua. This is a magical coming-of-age tale, ripe with the
special ambience of its tropical setting and sustained by
Annie's far from naive awareness of the world around
her. Death, illness, and poverty intrude on the narrator's
perceptive sensibility from time to time, but even these
experiences instruct her and expand her understanding of
life and its shifting reality. . . . A poetic and intensely
moving work." Booklist

Autobiography of my mother. Farrar, Straus &
Giroux 1995 228p $20 **Fic**
1. Blacks—Fiction 2. Dominica—Fiction 3. Mothers
and daughters—Fiction
ISBN 0-374-10731-9 LC 94-24580
Also available in paperback from New Am. Lib.
The narrator of this novel is Xuela Claudette Richardson. "Raised without love and self-defined by her mother's death at the moment of her birth, Xuela regards life
in her Dominican villages with disturbing disinterest and
keen penetration. . . . Haunted by her mother's absence,
Xuela ensures her own barrenness, endures a loveless affair with and marriage to the English doctor Philip, who
loves her, and rejoices with stevedore Roland, whom she
loves—or claims to." Libr J
In Kincaid's "poised and crystalline prose, precise and
serene as a knife drawn through water, she now gives us
this starkly memorable 'self-portrait' of a calm, thoughtful, utterly alienated woman who has learned to lead a
life devoid of love, but not devoid of dignity." Christ Sci
Monit

King, Stephen, 1947-
Carrie. Doubleday 1974 199p $25 **Fic**
1. Extrasensory perception—Fiction 2. Horror fiction
3. Maine—Fiction
ISBN 0-385-08695-4
Also available G.K. Hall large print edition and in paperback from New Am. Lib.

"Carrie is 16, lonely, the butt of all her Maine classmates' tricks and jokes, an object of scorn even to her
own mother, who is fanatically religious and believes
anything remotely sexual is from the devil. Then one girl
becomes ashamed of the cruelty being vented on Carrie
and plans an act of kindness that will give her the first
happiness in her young life. The only trouble is the act
backfires horribly and Carrie is worse off than ever before. It is at this point, at the senior prom, that Carrie begins to put into effect her awesome telekinetic powers,
powers with which she has only toyed before." Publ
Wkly
"A terrifying treat for both horror and parapsychology
fans." SLJ

Christine. Viking 1983 526p $27.95 **Fic**
1. Horror fiction 2. Pennsylvania—Fiction
ISBN 0-670-22026-4 LC 82-20105
Also available in paperback from New Am. Lib.
"Arnie Cunningham—a teenager who has never fit
in—buys a dilapidated 1958 Plymouth Fury from an
equally broken-down Army veteran, Roland LeBay. But
Christine—and the soon-dead LeBay—have mysterious
regenerative powers; Christine's odometer runs backwards and the car repairs itself. Arnie becomes obsessed
by the car and possessed by its previous owner, losing
his girlfriend and his best friend as they work together
to save him from Christine's clutches." Publ Wkly
"As always, there is the sense of descriptive detail that
is the author's trademark. Yet the strength of King's
prose is best seen here in the remarkable accuracy of
language and attitude that captures the spirit of the
teenage characters." Libr J

Insomnia. Viking 1994 787p $27.95 **Fic**
1. Horror fiction
ISBN 0-670-85503-0 LC 94-784
Also available G.K. Hall large print edition and in paperback from New Am. Lib.
"On one of the long, exhausting walks old Ralph Roberts starts taking as a brain tumor slowly kills his wife,
he witnesses a friendly young neighbor, Ed Deepneau,
behaving totally out of character—indeed, like someone
possessed. About a year later and after his wife's death,
Ralph begins waking early and then earlier and earlier.
He also starts seeing things—intense colors streaming off
people and animals. Meanwhile, Ed has turned into an
antiabortion fanatic and wife-beater. Ralph intervenes to
help Helen Deepneau escape from Ed, for which Ed
threatens him. Or is it Ed? Ralph senses that someone or
something else is in control of the troubled man. Ralph's
right, of course. Ed has been involuntarily recruited on
one side, and, it develops, Ralph and his also-widowed
neighbor, Lois Chasse, on the other, of a supercosmic
struggle the import of which King reveals with delicious-
ly tantalizing gradualness." Booklist

Kingsolver, Barbara
Pigs in heaven; a novel. HarperCollins Pubs.
1993 343p $23; pa $13 **Fic**
1. Adoption—Fiction 2. Cherokee Indians—Fiction
3. Arizona—Fiction
ISBN 0-06-016801-3; 0-06-092253-2 (pa)
LC 92-54739
In this sequel to The bean trees (1988), Taylor Greer
and her adopted daughter Turtle "appear again in a ten-

Kingsolver, Barbara—*Continued*

der, funny exploration of the clashing demands of mother love and ethnic heritage. The plot turns on the Solomonic dilemma of choosing between two equally valid claims on a child's life. The issues of family and culture underlie a suspenseful, poignant narrative told by a born raconteur." Publ Wkly

Kinsella, W. P.

Shoeless Joe. Houghton Mifflin 1982 265p o.p.; Ballantine Bks. paperback available $11 **Fic**
1. Baseball—Fiction 2. Fantasy fiction
ISBN 0-345-41007-6 (pa)   LC 81-19196

In this fantasy, Iowan farmer Ray Kinsella "hears a voice say 'If you build it, he will come,' and knows that 'it' refers to a baseball park and 'he' to Shoeless Joe Jackson. . . . Ray builds his magic stadium and while watching Shoeless Joe and others play ball, hears the voice again, this time saying, 'Ease his pain.' The mission clearly means kidnapping J. D. Salinger and taking him to Fenway Park for a Red Sox game. Ray succeeds and Salinger . . . joins Ray on a further quest. Their odyssey culminates back at home plate in Iowa." Quill Quire

Klass, David

California Blue. Scholastic 1994 200p $14.95; pa $3.99 **Fic**
1. Butterflies—Fiction 2. Environmental protection—Fiction
ISBN 0-590-46688-7; 0-590-46689-5 (pa)
LC 93-13705

When seventeen-year-old John Rodgers discovers a new sub-species of butterfly which may necessitate closing the mill where his dying father works, they find themselves on opposite sides of the environmental conflict

"The absorbing first-person narration rings true, projecting the credible voice of a teenager just beginning to break free from his emotional ties at home, family and friends. The fears, excitement, anger and energy of this awkward psychological time are movingly captured here." Publ Wkly

Danger zone. Scholastic 1996 232p $16.95
Fic
1. Basketball—Fiction 2. Race relations—Fiction 3. African Americans—Fiction
ISBN 0-590-48590-3   LC 94-20234

When he joins a predominantly black "Teen Dream Team" that will be representing the United States in an international basketball tournament in Rome, Jimmy Doyle makes some unexpected discoveries about prejudice, racism, and politics

"The pace never lags, and Klass does a convincing job of capturing the feel of the game and depicting Doyle's attempts to be accepted by his teammates, as well as showing what happens when some terrorists add fear to the list of the team's opponents." Booklist

Klein, Norma, 1938-1989

No more Saturday nights. Knopf 1988 278p o.p.; Fawcett Bks. paperback available $3.95 **Fic**
1. Fathers and sons—Fiction
ISBN 0-449-70304-5 (pa)   LC 88-678

"Tim, a 17 year old unmarried father wins custody of his son in court. He later goes to college in New York where he and Mason, the baby, live with three girls willing to share their apartment with the odd couple. Tim has to come to terms with his relationship with his own father and with his son, always knowing that his baby is the most important thing in his life." Voice Youth Advocates

"Klein poses an interesting situation and deals with it perceptively and candidly; the first-person voice is convincing, the writing smooth and nicely paced." Bull Cent Child Books

Knowles, John, 1926-

A separate peace; a novel. Macmillan 1960 c1959 186p $40 **Fic**
1. School stories
ISBN 0-02-564850-0

Also available G.K. Hall large print edition and in paperback from Bantam Bks.

First published 1959 in the United Kingdom

"Gene Forrester looks back on his school days, spent in a New England town just before World War II. He both admires and envies his close friend and roommate, Finny, who is a natural athlete, in contrast to Gene's special competence as a scholar. When Finny suffers a crippling accident, Gene must face his own involvement in it." Shapiro. Fic for Youth. 3d edition

Koertge, Ronald

The Arizona kid; [by] Ron Koertge. Little, Brown 1988 228p o.p.; Avon Bks. paperback available $3.99 **Fic**
1. Rodeos—Fiction 2. Homosexuality—Fiction 3. Arizona—Fiction
ISBN 0-380-70776-4 (pa)   LC 87-35361

"Joy Street books"

Sixteen-year-old Billy comes to terms with his own values when he is sent to live with his gay uncle in Tucson and is introduced to the world of rodeos where he falls in love with an outspoken racehorse rider named Cara

This novel displays a "fine sensitivity to the insecurities of the adolescent male who's frequently called 'shorty,' the stresses of the gay lifestyle under the AIDS cloud of gloom, and the bittersweet playfulness of a summer romance." Voice Youth Advocates

Koestler, Arthur, 1905-1983

Darkness at noon; translated by Daphne Hardy. Macmillan 1987 267p $35 **Fic**
1. Communism—Fiction 2. Soviet Union—Fiction
ISBN 0-02-565210-9   LC 86-31273

Also available in paperback from Bantam Bks.

"A Macmillan Hudson River edition"

First published 1940 in the United Kingdom; this is a reissue of the 1941 edition

Koestler, Arthur, 1905-1983—*Continued*

This novel "deals with the arrest, imprisonment, trial, and execution of N. S. Rubashov in an unnamed dictatorship over which 'No.1' presides. Koestler describes Rubashov as 'a synthesis of the lives of a number of men who were victims of the so-called Moscow trials,' and the novel did much to draw attention to the nature of Stalin's regime." Oxford Companion to Engl. Lit. 5th edition

Koontz, Dean R. (Dean Ray), 1945-

Watchers. Putnam 1987 352p o.p.; Berkley Pub. Group paperback available $7.30 **Fic**
1. Horror fiction
ISBN 0-425-10746-9 (pa)   LC 86-22687
Also available Thorndike Press large print edition
"When the Russians sabotage a genetic research project in California, two mutated creatures escape from the lab. One is a golden retriever with high enough intelligence to think and communicate with humans; the other is the Outsider, a vicious monster created from a baboon and bred to kill. Both the man who befriends and adopts the dog and his new bride find themselves stalked by government agents anxious to find the dog, a particularly repulsive Mafia hit man intent on stealing him, and the Outsider, with whom the dog is linked telepathically." Libr J

La Farge, Oliver, 1901-1963

Laughing Boy. Houghton Mifflin 1929 302p o.p.; NAL/Dutton paperback available $3.50 **Fic**
1. Navajo Indians
ISBN 0-451-52244-3 (pa)
Also available in hardcover from Buccaneer Bks.
"This novel takes place in the early years of the twentieth century in Navajo country in the American Southwest. It is the story of the ill-fated love of Laughing Boy, worker in silver and maker of songs, and Slim Girl, whose education in American schools has embittered her. The reader is immersed in their tender romance but also learns a great deal about the culture and philosophical outlook of the Native American." Shapiro. Fic for Youth. 3d edition

L'Amour, Louis, 1908-1988

The Sacketts **Fic**
1. Western stories
This series explores the settling of the American West by focusing on the exploits of several generations of the Sackett family
Titles in the series are:
The daybreakers (1960)
Galloway (1974)
Jubal Sackett (1985)
Lando (1962)
The lonely men (1976)
Lonely on the mountain (1980)
Mojave crossing (1964)
Mustang man (1976)
Ride the dark trail (1972)
Ride the river (1983)
Sackett (1961)
The Sackett brand (1971)

Sackett's land (1975)
The sky-liners (1972)
To the far blue mountains (1976)
Treasure mountain (1979)
The warrior's path (1980)

Lawrence, D. H. (David Herbert), 1885-1930

Sons and lovers **Fic**
1. Mothers and sons—Fiction 2. Great Britain—Fiction
Available in hardcover and paperback from various publishers
First published 1913
"Paul Morel, adored youngest son of a middle-class mother who feels that her coal-miner husband was unworthy of her, has difficulty in breaking away from her. Mrs. Morel has given her son all her warmth and love for so long a time that Paul finds it impossible to establish a relationship with another women. Miriam is supportive and understanding of his artistic nature but appeals mainly to his higher nature; Clara Dawes becomes his mistress but she is married and will not divorce her husband. After the death of his mother, Paul arranges a reconciliation between Clara and her husband and, after months of grieving for his mother, at last finds the strength to strike out on his own." Shapiro. Fic For Youth. 3d edition

Le Carré, John, 1931-

The spy who came in from the cold. Coward-McCann 1964 c1963 256p o.p.; Ballantine Bks. paperback available $6.99 **Fic**
1. Spies—Fiction
ISBN 0-345-37737-0 (pa)
First published 1963 in the United kingdom
"The story of Alec Leamas, 50-year-old professional [secret agent] who has grown stale in espionage, who longs to 'come in from the cold'—and how he undertakes one last assignment before that hoped-for retirement. Over the years Leamas has grown unsure where his workday carapace ends and his real self begins. . . . Recalled from Berlin after the death of his last East German contact at the Wall, Leamas lets himself be seduced into a pretended defection—thereby providing the East Germans with data from which they can deduce that the head of their own spy apparatus is a double agent." N Y Times Book Rev

Lee, Gus

China boy; a novel. Dutton 1991 322p hardcover o.p. paperback available $11.95 **Fic**
1. Chinese Americans—Fiction 2. San Francisco (Calif.)—Fiction
ISBN 0-452-27158-4 (pa)   LC 90-21687
"The rough-and-tumble tale of Kai Ting, the only son of an aristocratic Shanghai couple whose escape from the Communists landed them in San Francisco's tough, predominantly black, Panhandle district. When Kai Ting's mother dies, his father marries a white woman who tries to eradicate her stepchildren's Chinese heritage. She sends the skinny, sheltered, and bewildered boy out into the neighborhood, where he becomes everyone's favorite punching bag." Am Libr

Lee, Gus—*Continued*

"Based on events in his own childhood, Mr. Lee's depiction of Kai's efforts to reconcile his Chinese heritage with the several equally bewildering worlds of American culture he is simultaneously exposed to . . . is vivid and moving." N Y Times Book Rev

Followed by Honor & duty (1994)

Lee, Harper, 1926-

To kill a mockingbird. 35th anniversary ed. HarperCollins Pubs. 1995 323p $17   Fic

1. Race relations—Fiction 2. Alabama—Fiction

ISBN 0-06-017322-X

Also available in paperback from Warner Bks.

A reissue with a new foreword by the author of the title first published 1960 by Lippincott

"Scout, as Jean Louise is called, is a precocious child. She relates her impressions of the time when her lawyer father, Atticus Finch, is defending a black man accused of raping a white woman in a small Alabama town during the 1930's. Atticus's courageous act brings the violence and injustice that exists in their world sharply into focus as it intrudes into the lighthearted life that Scout and her brother Jem have enjoyed until that time." Shapiro. Fic for Youth. 3d edition

LeMieux, A. C. (Anne Connelly)

Do angels sing the blues? Tambourine Bks. 1995 233p $14   Fic

1. Blues music—Fiction 2. Alcoholism—Fiction

ISBN 0-688-13725-3   LC 94-26411

Also available in paperback from Avon Bks.

A teenage boy sees his best friend and fellow band member begin a relationship with a girl who consistently lies and drinks too much

"This well-written book has realistic dialogue. Musical terminology and blues description enhance the realism but don't get in the way of the story. There are many themes here—coming of age, alcoholism, self-esteem, single parenting, death—all deftly interwoven to make a believable novel." Book Rep

L'Engle, Madeleine, 1918-

A wrinkle in time. Farrar, Straus & Giroux 1962 211p $17   Fic

1. Fantasy fiction

ISBN 0-374-38613-7

Also available Cornerstone Bks. large print edition and in paperback from Dell

Awarded the Newbery Medal, 1963

"A brother and sister, together with a friend, go in search of their scientist father who was lost while engaged in secret work for the government on the tesseract problem. A tesseract is a wrinkle in time. The father is a prisoner on a forbidding planet, and after awesome and terrifying experiences, he is rescued, and the little group returns safely to Earth and home." Child Books Too Good to Miss

"It makes unusual demands on the imagination and consequently gives great rewards." Horn Book

Followed by A wind in the door (1973)

Leroux, Gaston, 1868-1927

Phantom of the opera   Fic

1. Paris (France)—Fiction

Hardcover and paperback editions available from various publishers

This love story/thriller relates the tale of the mysterious masked terror who inhabits the cellars of the Paris Opera House

Lester, Julius

Othello; a novel. Scholastic 1995 151p $12.95   Fic

ISBN 0-590-41967-6   LC 94-12833

"An interpretation of Shakespeare's play in the form of a novel casts Othello, Iago, and Iago's wife as African immigrants in Elizabethan England. The first half of the book details the courtship and marriage of Othello and Desdemona; the second half closely follows the plot of the play and includes, in boldface, quotations and paraphrases from Shakespeare's play. An ambitious yet accessible reworking." Horn Book Guide

Levitin, Sonia, 1934-

Escape from Egypt; a novel. Little, Brown 1994 267p $16.95   Fic

1. Moses (Biblical figure)—Fiction 2. Bible stories 3. Jews—Fiction

ISBN 0-316-52273-2   LC 93-29376

Also available in paperback from Puffin Bks.

When Moses comes to lead the Israelites to the Promised Land, Jesse, a Hebrew slave, finds his life changed by his growing faith in God and his attraction to the half-Egyptian, half-Syrian Jennat

Levitin "has written a book that is troubling, moving, and sensual—and that forces its readers to think." Booklist

Lewis, C. S. (Clive Staples), 1898-1963

Out of the silent planet. Macmillan 1990 174p (Space trilogy series) $45   Fic

1. Mars (Planet)—Fiction 2. Science fiction

ISBN 0-02-570795-7   LC 89-13969

A reprint of the title first published 1938 in the United Kingdom

The first volume in a trilogy that includes Perelandra and That hideous strength (also available from Macmillan)

"The trilogy can be read on two levels: first for its exciting plot and second as a theological allegory, although Lewis denied this interpretation. The stories are about temptation. They concern the classic battle between good, as represented by Ransom, the philologist, and evil, as represented by Weston, the physicist. The battle is played out on the planets of Malacondra (Mars), Perelandra (Venus), and Earth." Shapiro. Fic for Youth. 3d edition

Lewis, Sinclair, 1885-1951

Babbitt   Fic

1. Middle classes—Fiction

Hardcover and paperback editions available from various publishers

Lewis, Sinclair, 1885-1951—*Continued*

First published 1922 by Harcourt, Brace

Satire on American middle-class life in a good-sized city. George F. Babbitt is a successful real estate man, a regular fellow, booster, Rotarian, Elk, Republican, who uses all the current catchwords, molds his opinions on those of the Zenith Advocate-Times and believes in 'a sound business administration in Washington'

Main Street   Fic

Hardcover and paperback editions available from various publishers

First published 1920 by Harcourt, Brace

"Carol Milford, a girl of quick intelligence but no particular talent, after graduation from college meets and marries Will Kennicott, a sober, kindly, unimaginative physician of Gopher Prairie, Minn., who tells her that the town needs her abilities. She finds the village to be a smug, intolerant, unimaginatively standardized place, where the people will not accept her efforts to create more sightly homes, organize a dramatic association, and otherwise improve the village life." Oxford Companion to Am Lit. 5th edition

Lipsyte, Robert

The brave. HarperCollins Pubs. 1991 195p $14.95; pa $4.50   Fic
1. Indians of North America—Fiction 2. Boxing—Fiction 3. New York (N.Y.)—Fiction
ISBN 0-06-023915-8; 0-06-447079-2 (pa)
LC 90-25396

Sequel to The contender

"A Charlotte Zolotow book"

Having left the Indian reservation for the streets of New York, seventeen-year-old boxer Sonny Bear tries to harness his inner rage by training with Alfred Brooks, who has left the sport to become a policeman

Lipsyte "avoids the inaccuracies so common to the genre and delivers a compelling and multidimensional story. His style is razor-sharp, and his imagery comes across with pounding clarity. The book fairly pulsates with energy, especially in the fight scenes, and ends with Sonny starting over in the grimy world of low-level professional boxing." SLJ

The chief. HarperCollins Pubs. 1993 226p lib bdg $14.89; pa $4.50   Fic
1. Indians of North America—Fiction 2. Boxing—Fiction
ISBN 0-06-021068-0 (lib bdg); 0-06-447097-0 (pa)
LC 92-54502

Sequel to The brave

This novel is "narrated by Marty Malcolm Witherspoon, a sensitive and earnest black aspiring writer who has become a confidant of (and publicist for) a half-Native American boxing hero, Sonny Bear. Lurking behind the action is a dispute involving political power and gambling that threatens to split the Moscondaga Indian Nation into warring factions. The major conflict is not who wins the boxing duels but how Sonny can use his hard-won fame to help his people resolve their problems." SLJ

"Dramatic doings, terse and thrilling language and deftly sketched characters produce a heart-pounding read." Publ Wkly

The contender. Harper & Row 1967 182p lib bdg $14.89; pa $4.50   Fic
1. Boxing—Fiction 2. Harlem (New York, N.Y.)—Fiction 3. African American athletes—Fiction
ISBN 0-06-023920-4 (lib bdg); 0-06-447039-3 (pa)

"After a street fight in which he is the chief target, Alfred wanders into a gym in his neighborhood. He decides not only to improve his physical condition but also to become a boxer. Because of this interest Alfred's life is completely changed. He assumes a more positive outlook on his immediate future, even within the confines of a black ghetto." Shapiro. Fic for Youth. 3d edition

Followed by The brave

One fat summer. Harper & Row 1977 152p lib bdg $14.89; pa $4.50   Fic
1. Reducing—Fiction 2. Obesity—Fiction
ISBN 0-06-023896-8 (lib bdg); 0-06-447073-3 (pa)
LC 76-49746

"Bobby Marks is 14 and fat. How fat, he doesn't know because he jumps off the scale when it hits 200 pounds. In one action-packed summer Bobby learns that altered physical appearance can bolster self-esteem. He's not sure he likes his friend Joanie's new nose and new ego, but he's certainly pleased with his own svelte new image. The slimming is a result of his summer job; tending the grounds of the town miser." West Coast Rev Books

"This is far superior to most of the summer-of-change stories; any change that takes place is logical and the protagonist learns by action and reaction to be both self-reliant and compassionate." Bull Cent Child Books

Followed by Summer rules (1981) and The summerboy (1982)

Llewellyn, Richard, 1906-1983

How green was my valley. Macmillan 1940 495p $40; pa $10   Fic
1. Coal mines and mining—Fiction 2. Wales—Fiction
ISBN 0-02-573420-2; 0-02-022372-2 (pa)

Also available in hardcover from Amereon

"Life in South Wales, where everyone depended on the coal mines for a livelihood, was not easy, but it had its happy moments. From the perspective of 50 years later, Huw Morgan remembers with much affection his family, friends, and neighbors in the valley. His father was something of a tyrant, while his mother was shrewd and impulsive. The love Huw shared with his many brothers and sisters was a sustaining force. One of his earliest memories is of the marriage of his eldest brother to Bronwen, beautiful, tender girl who was to prove to Huw that women's strength, though gentle, is equal to that of men." Shapiro. Fic for Youth. 3d edition

Followed by Up, into the singing mountain (1960)

London, Jack, 1876-1916

The call of the wild   Fic
1. Dogs—Fiction 2. Alaska—Fiction

Hardcover and paperback editions available from various publishers; including large print

First published 1903 by Macmillan

"Buck, half-St. Bernard, half-Scottish sheepdog, is stolen from his comfortable home in California and pressed into service as a sledge dog in the Klondike. At

London, Jack, 1876-1916—*Continued*
first he is abused by both man and dog, but he learns to
fight ruthlessly. He becomes lead dog on a sledge team,
after bettering Spitz, the vicious old leader, in a brutal
fight to the death. In John Thornton, he finally finds a
master whom he can respect and love. When Thornton
is killed by Indians, Buck breaks away to the wilds and
becomes the leader of a wolf pack, returning each year
to the site of Thornton's death." Reader's Ency. 4th edition

White Fang   Fic
1. Dogs—Fiction 2. Alaska—Fiction
Hardcover and paperback editions available from various publishers
First published 1906
White Fang "is about a dog, a cross-breed, sold to
Beauty Smith. This owner tortures the dog to increase
his ferocity and value as a fighter. A new owner
Weedom Scott, brings the dog to California, and, by kind
treatment, domesticates him. White Fang later sacrifices
his life to save Scott." Haydn. Thesaurus of Book Dig

Lord, Bette Bao
Spring Moon; a novel of China. Harper & Row
1981 464p hardcover o.p. paperback available
$5.99   Fic
1. Family life—Fiction 2. China—Fiction
ISBN 0-06-100105-8 (pa)
Also available in paperback from Avon Bks.
This novel "follows the history of a Mandarin Chinese
family from 1892 until 1927, with an epilogue that updates the story to 1972. Through the eyes of Spring
Moon, a lively and intelligent daughter of the house of
Chang, we see the beauty of the inner courtyard society
and observe its respect for family, order and harmony,
scholarship and poetry. But we see, too, how Chinese society's rigid etiquette hobbles the lives of its women as
surely as their bound feet." Saturday Rev

MacLean, Alistair, 1922-1987
The guns of Navarone. Doubleday 1957 320p
o.p.; Fawcett Bks. paperback available $5.99 Fic
1. World War, 1939-1945—Fiction
ISBN 0-449-21472-9 (pa)
Also available in hardcover from Buccaneer Bks.
"World War II is being fought, and the Germans control the island that guards the approaches to the eastern
Mediterranean with big guns. After all other attempts
have failed, a five-man British army team is chosen to
silence the guns of Navarone. They land on the island,
elude the Nazis, and scale a seemingly unclimbable
cliff." Shapiro. Fic for Youth. 3d edition
Followed by Force 10 from Navarone (1968)

Ice Station Zebra. Doubleday 1963 276p o.p.;
Fawcett Bks. paperback available $5.99   Fic
1. Spies—Fiction 2. Nuclear submarines—Fiction
3. Arctic regions—Fiction
ISBN 0-449-20576-2 (pa)
A novel of suspense and intrigue that begins on "a
bitter-cold morning in Holy Loch, Scotland, when a British doctor with top-level endorsements from the

American and British military forces seeks admission to
an American nuclear submarine. The submarine is slated
for a perilous trip to rescue the starving, freezing British
crew of a meteorological station situated on an ice floe
in the Arctic." Publ Wkly

Mahy, Margaret
The catalogue of the universe. Atheneum Pubs.
1986 c1985 185p $15.95   Fic
1. Fathers and daughters—Fiction
ISBN 0-689-50391-1   LC 85-72262
Also available in paperback from Penguin Bks.
First published 1985 in the United Kingdom
"As short, homely, brilliant Tycho contemplates the
stars and planets to understand his family problems and
hopeless love, Angela's confrontation with her father precipitates the emotional trauma of rejection. Through this
turmoil, she recognizes her romantic feelings for Tycho,
and the two have their first sexual encounter." SLJ
"Very tightly woven—the action takes place over two
days—richly textured, and abounding in fascinating and
eccentric characters, the book is another tour de force."
Horn Book

Memory. Margaret K. McElderry Bks. 1988
c1987 278p $16   Fic
1. Old age—Fiction 2. New Zealand—Fiction
ISBN 0-689-50446-2   LC 87-21427
Also available in paperback from Dell
First published 1987 in the United Kingdom
On the fifth anniversary of his older sister's death,
nineteen-year-old Jonny Dart, troubled by feelings of
guilt and an imperfect memory of the event, goes in
search of the only other witness to the fatal accident and,
through a chance meeting with a senile old woman, finds
a way to free himself of the past
This is "an original rites of passage story, in which
tenderness, rather than the traditional panoply of male-
ness, is the reward." Times Lit Suppl

Mailer, Norman
The naked and the dead. Holt & Co. 1948 721p
hardcover o.p. paperback available $14.95   Fic
1. Soldiers—United States—Fiction 2. World War,
1939-1945—Fiction
ISBN 0-8050-0521-8 (pa)
Also available in hardcover from Buccaneer Bks.
"In 1944 an American platoon takes part in the invasion and occupation of a Japanese-held island. The action
is divided into three parts: the landing on the island, the
counter-attack by night, and a daring patrol by the platoon behind enemy lines. The style is simple realism and
therefore the language is rough, in keeping with the army
setting." Shapiro. Fic for Youth. 2d edition
"The book is encyclopedic yet particular, both realistic
and symbolic. It is one of the best novels by an
American about World War II." Benet's Reader's Ency
of Am Lit

Malamud, Bernard, 1914-1986

The assistant; a novel. Farrar, Straus & Giroux 1957 246p o.p.; Avon Bks. paperback available $10 **Fic**

1. Jews—New York (N.Y.)—Fiction 2. Brooklyn (New York, N.Y.)—Fiction

ISBN 0-380-72085-X (pa)

This novel is "set in the prison of a failing grocery store, where Morris Bober, its elderly, long-suffering Jewish owner, teaches his assistant, Frankie Alpine, what it means to be a Jew, and what it means to be a man. After decades in which Jewish protagonists struggled to assimilate to the non-Jewish world around them, *The Assistant*

The fixer. Farrar, Straus & Giroux 1966 355p **Fic**

1. Jews—Fiction 2. Jews—Russia—Fiction 3. Russia—Fiction

Available in paperback from Penguin Bks. and Pocket Bks.

"Yakov Bok, a handyman, is arrested and charged with the killing of a Christian boy. Innocent of the crime, he is only guilty of being a Jew in Czarist Russia. In jail he is mentally and physically tortured as a scapegoat for a crime he insists he did not commit. Although his suffering and degradation are unrelenting, Bok emerges a hero as he maintains his innocence. Malamud has fashioned a powerful story of injustice and endurance based on a true incident." Shapiro. Fic for Youth. 3d edition

Mann, Thomas, 1875-1955

Buddenbrooks; the decline of a family; translated from the German by John E. Woods. Knopf 1993 648p $35 **Fic**

ISBN 0-679-41994-2   LC 92-18990

Also available Everyman's library edition

Original German edition, 1901. First United States edition translated by H. T. Lowe-Potter published 1924 in two volumes

"Mann's first novel, it expressed the ambivalence of his feelings about the value of the life of the artist as opposed to ordinary, bourgeois life. The novel is the saga of the fall of the Buddenbrooks, a family of merchants, from the pinnacle of their material wealth in 1835 to their extinction in 1877." Merriam-Webster's Ency of Lit

The magic mountain   **Fic**

1. Tuberculosis—Fiction   2. Hospitals—Fiction
3. Alps—Fiction

Some editions are:

Knopf $35, pa $17 translated from the German by John E. Woods (ISBN 0-679-44183-2; 0-679-73645-X)

Modern Lib. $19 translated by H. T. Lowe-Porter (ISBN 0-679-60041-8)

Original German edition, 1924

This novel "tells the story of Hans Castorp, a young German engineer, who goes to visit a cousin in a tuberculosis sanatorium in the mountains of Davos, Switz. Castorp discovers that he has symptoms of the disease and remains at the sanatorium for seven years, until the outbreak of World War I. During this time, he abandons his normal life to submit to the rich seductions of disease, introspection, and death. Through talking with other patients, he gradually becomes aware of and absorbs the predominant political, cultural, and scientific ideas of 20th-century Europe. The sanatorium comes to be the spiritual reflection of the possibilities and dangers of the actual world away from the magic mountain." Merriam-Webster's Ency of Lit

Markandaya, Kamala, 1924-

Nectar in a sieve; a novel. Day 1955 c1954 248p o.p.; New Am. Lib. paperback available $5.99 **Fic**

1. India—Fiction

ISBN 0-451-16836-4 (pa)

First published 1954 in the United Kingdom

"This realistic novel of peasant life in a southern Indian village portrays the struggle that Nathan and Rukmani must make to survive. Their first child is a daughter, Irawaddy, and there follow five other children, all sons, after an interval of seven years. Hardships are innumerable and insurmountable, whether they are disasters of nature such as drought, or such man-made catastrophes as the coming of a tannery to their village and a subsequent labor conflict. After many crises, Nathan and Rukmani come to the city to seek help from one of their sons, but he has disappeared. Nathan, finally destroyed by privation, dies, believing to the end that his life with Rukmani has been a happy one." Shapiro. Fic for Youth. 3d edition

Marsden, John, 1950-

Letters from the inside. Houghton Mifflin 1994 146p $14.95 **Fic**

1. Friendship—Fiction 2. Prisoners—Fiction 3. Australia—Fiction

ISBN 0-395-68985-6   LC 93-41185

Also available in paperback from Dell

First published 1991 in Australia

"Mandy and Tracey become penpals after Tracey places an ad for such in an Australian teen magazine. At first the missives are friendly and chatty . . . but gradually darker truths are revealed: Tracey is in prison, Mandy is becoming increasingly frightened of her older brother." Bull Cent Child Books

"The characters are vivid, each developed through her choice of language and response to the other girl's life. Marsden gives the reader a great deal to think about, exploring human responses to violence and victimization, Tracey's responsibility for her crime, and a justice system which abuses her." Horn Book

Tomorrow, when the war began. Houghton Mifflin 1995 286p $13.95 **Fic**

1. War stories 2. Australia—Fiction

ISBN 0-395-70673-4   LC 94-29299

Also available in paperback from Dell

First published 1993 in Australia

"Australian teenager Ellie and six of her friends return from a winter break camping trip to find their homes burned or deserted, their families imprisoned, and their country occupied by a foreign military force in league with a band of disaffected Australians. As their shock wears off, the seven decide they must stick together if they are to survive." SLJ

Marsden, John, 1950—— *Continued*
"The novel is a riveting adventure through which Marsden explores the capacity for evil and the necessity of working together to oppose it." Horn Book

Marshall, Catherine, 1914-1983
Christy. McGraw-Hill 1967 496p o.p.; Avon Bks. paperback available $6.99   **Fic**
1. Teachers—Fiction 2. Appalachian region—Fiction
ISBN 0-380-00141-1 (pa)
Also available in hardcover from Buccaneer Bks.
"A spirited young woman leaves the security of her home to become a teacher in Cutter Gap, Kentucky. It is 1912 and the needs of the Appalachian people are great. Christy learns much from the poverty and superstition of the mountain folk. Marshall's Christian faith and ideals are intertwined in the plot, which includes a love story." Shapiro. Fic for Youth. 3d edition

Martinez, Victor
Parrot in the oven; a novel. Cotler Bks. 1996 216p $14.95; lib bdg $14.89   **Fic**
1. Mexican Americans—Fiction 2. Family life—Fiction 3. Alcoholism—Fiction
ISBN 0-06-026704-6; 0-06-026706-2 (lib bdg)
              LC 96-2119
Manny relates his coming of age experiences as a member of a poor Mexican American family in which the alcoholic father only adds to everyone's struggle
The author "maintains the authenticity of his setting and characterizations through a razor-sharp combination of tense dialogue, coursing narrative and startlingly elegant imagery." Publ Wkly

Mason, Bobbie Ann
In country; a novel. Harper & Row 1985 247p hardcover o.p. paperback available $12   **Fic**
1. Veterans—Fiction 2. Vietnam War, 1961-1975—Fiction 3. Kentucky—Fiction
ISBN 0-06-091350-9 (pa)   LC 85-42579
"Sam, 17, is obsessed with the Vietnam War and the effect it has had on her life—losing a father she never knew and now living with Uncle Emmett, who seems to be suffering from the effects of Agent Orange. In her own forthright way, she tries to sort out why and how Vietnam has altered the lives of the vets of Hopewell, Kentucky. . . . A harshly realistic, well-written look at the Vietnam War as well as the story of a young woman maturing." SLJ

Maugham, W. Somerset (William Somerset), 1874-1965
Of human bondage   **Fic**

Hardcover and paperback editions available from various publishers
First published 1915
This novel's "hero is Philip Carey, a sensitive, talented, club-footed orphan who is brought up by an unsympathetic aunt and uncle. It is a study of his struggle for independence, his intellectual development, and his at-tempt to become an artist. Philip gets entangled and obsessed by his love affair with Mildred, a waitress. After years of struggle as a medical student, he marries a nice woman, gives up his aspirations, and becomes a country doctor. The first part of the novel is partly autobiographical, and the book is regarded as Maugham's best work." Reader's Ency. 4th edition

The razor's edge. Doubleday 1944 343p o.p.; Penguin Bks. paperback available $10.95   **Fic**
ISBN 0-14-018523-2 (pa)
"The novel is concerned in large part with the search for the meaning of life and with the dichotomy between materialism and spirituality. The main focus of the story is on Larry Darrell, who has returned from service as an aviator in World War I utterly rejecting his prewar values. He is concerned chiefly with discovering the meaning of human existence and eliminating evil in the world. To that end, he spends five years in India seeking—but not finding—answers." Merriam-Webster's Ency of Lit

Mazer, Norma Fox, 1931-
After the rain. Morrow 1987 291p $16   **Fic**
1. Grandfathers—Fiction 2. Death—Fiction
ISBN 0-688-06867-7   LC 86-33270
Also available G.K. Hall large print edition and in paperback from Avon Bks.
"Adolescent Rachel has always been a little afraid of Grandpa Izzy, her mother's father; sharp-tongued and irritable, the old man seems to have no kindness or softness in his nature. After the family learns that he has terminal cancer (which Izzy isn't told), Rachel begins to visit him and walk with him daily, and by the time he is near the end and hospitalized, she has come to love him." Bull Cent Child Books
"Izzy walks away with the story, his harsh, rough personality so realistic and recognizable that we feel we have known him and can understand the sorrow that overcomes Rachel. A powerful book, dealing with death and dying and the strength of family affection." Horn Book

McCaffrey, Anne
[The Pern series]   **Fic**
1. Fantasy fiction
"The people of Pern are in danger of the Threads, and look to the tamed dragons for protection from the thread-like spores. . . . McCaffrey has created a vivid and believable world, alive with interesting characters and events. There is plenty of action, a good plot, and the writing is excellent." Roman. Sequences
Fantasy titles set on Pern are:
All the Weyrs of Pern (1991)
The chronicles of Pern: first fall (1993)
The dolphins of Pern (1994)
Dragondrums (1979)
Dragonflight (1968)
Dragonquest (1971)
Dragonriders of Pern (1978)
Dragonsdawn (1988)
Dragonseye (1977)
Dragonsinger (1977)
Dragonsong (1976)

McCaffrey, Anne—*Continued*
The girl who heard dragons (1994)
Moreta: Dragonlady of Pern (1983)
Nerilka's story (1986)
Renegades of Pern (1989)
White dragon (1978)

McCarthy, Cormac, 1933-
All the pretty horses. Knopf 1992 301p $21; pa
$12   Fic
1. Mexico—Fiction 2. Cowhands—Fiction
ISBN 0-394-57474-5; 0-679-74439-8 (pa)
      LC 91-58560
First volume in the author's projected Border trilogy
In the spring of 1950, after the death of his grandfather, sixteen-year-old John Grady Cole "is evicted from
the Texas ranch where he grew up. He and another boy
Lacey Rawlins, head for Mexico on horseback, riding
south until they finally turn up at a vast ranch in moun-
tainous Coahuila, the Hacienda de la Purisima, where
they sign on as vaqueros. . . . John Grady's unusual talent for breaking, training and understanding horses becomes crucial to the *hacendado* Don Hector's ambitious
breeding program. For John Grady, La Purisima is a paradise, complete with its Eve, Don Hector's daughter,
Alejandra." N Y Times Book Rev
"Though some readers may grow impatient with the
wild prairie rhythms of McCarthy's language, others will
find his voice completely transporting." Publ Wkly
Followed by The crossing (1994)

McCullers, Carson, 1917-1967
The heart is a lonely hunter. Modern Lib. 1993
430p $15.50   Fic
1. Deaf—Fiction 2. Southern States—Fiction
ISBN 0-679-42474-1   LC 92-51062
Also available in hardcover from Buccaneer Bks. and
in paperback from Bantam Bks.
A reissue of the title first published 1940 by
Houghton Mifflin
"After his friend is committed to a hospital for the in-
sane, John Singer, a deaf mute, finds himself alone. He
becomes the pivotal figure in a strange circle of four oth-
er lonely individuals: Biff Brannon, the owner of a cafe;
Mick Kelly, a young girl; Jake Blount, a radical; and
Benedict Copeland, the town's black doctor. Although
Singer provides companionship for others, he remains
outside the warmth of close relationships." Shapiro. Fic
for Youth. 3d edition

The member of the wedding. Houghton Mifflin
1946 195p o.p.; New Directions paperback
available $7.95   Fic
1. Georgia—Fiction
ISBN 0-8112-0093-0 (pa)
"Twelve-year-old Frankie is experiencing a boring
summer until news arrives that her older brother will
soon be returning to Georgia from his Alaska home in
order to marry. Plotting to accompany the newlyweds on
their honeymoon occupies much of Frankie's waking
hours, while at the same time she is coping with the
pressures of puberty and its effects on her body and
mind. Particularly revealing are her conversations with
her six-year-old cousin and the nurturing black family
cook, Bernice." Shapiro. Fic for Youth. 3d edition

McCullough, Colleen, 1937-
The thorn birds. Harper & Row 1977 533p o.p.;
Avon Bks. paperback available $6.99   Fic
1. Family life—Fiction 2. Australia—Fiction
ISBN 0-380-01817-9 (pa)
"A multigenerational saga of life, love, and death on
an Australian sheep ranch." Reader's Ency. 3d edition
"The backdrop to this congested, sensational and often
bizarre plot, is the Australian outback, with its dramatic
landscapes, vast distances, isolation, bush camaraderie,
and natural hazards. The novel aroused lively literary
controversy. It was labelled by its critics as a 'potboiler':
crudely crafted, sensationally exaggerated, devised to ca-
ter to the florid expectations of the mass of undiscrimi-
nating readers of modern popular fiction. Its supporters
see it as a vigorously-written and racy narrative." Oxford
Companion to Australian Lit

McDermott, Alice
At weddings and wakes. Farrar, Straus &
Giroux 1992 213p $20   Fic
1. Family life—Fiction 2. Catholics—Fiction 3. Irish
Americans—Fiction 4. Brooklyn (New York, N.Y.)—
Fiction
ISBN 0-374-10674-6   LC 91-42070
Also available G.K. Hall large print edition and in paperback by Dell
Set in Brooklyn during the sixties, this novel "tells the
story of an extended Irish-American family observed primarily through the eyes of the children, a son and two
daughters. Time circles backwards and forwards around
a variety of family rituals: holiday meals, vacations at
the shore, the wedding of a favorite aunt. The poignant
middle-aged romance that develops between the aunt, a
former nun, and her suitor, a shy mailman, exacerbates
already pronounced family tensions. As they listen to oft-
repeated stories about poverty, disease, and early deaths,
the children are solemn witnesses to the Irish immigrant
experience in America." Libr J
"A formidably gifted prose stylist [McDermott] can
make each sentence a bell of sound, a prism of sight."
Publ Wkly

McKinley, Robin
Beauty; a retelling of the story of Beauty & the
beast. Harper & Row 1978 247p $16; lib bdg
$15.89; pa $4.95   Fic
1. Fairy tales
ISBN 0-06-024149-7; 0-06-024150-0 (lib bdg);
0-06-440477-3 (pa)   LC 77-25636
"McKinley's version of this folktale is embellished
with rich descriptions and settings and detailed characterizations. The author has not modernized the story but
varied the traditional version to attract modern readers.
The values of love, honor, and beauty are placed in a
magical setting that will please the reader of fantasy."
Shapiro. Fic for Youth. 3d edition

McMillan, Terry
Waiting to exhale. Viking 1992 409p $22   Fic
1. African American women—Fiction 2. Arizona—
Fiction 3. Friendship—Fiction
ISBN 0-670-83980-9   LC 91-46564
Also available G.K. Hall large print edition and in pa-
perback by Pocket Bks.

McMillan, Terry—*Continued*

This novel "tells the stories of four 30ish black women bound together in warm, supportive friendship and in their dwindling hopes of finding Mr. Right. Savannah, Bernadine, Robin and Gloria are successful professionals or self-employed women living in Phoenix. All are independent, upwardly mobile and 'waiting to exhale'—to stop holding their breaths waiting for the proper mate to come along." Publ Wkly

"Terry McMillan's heroines are so well drawn that by the end of the novel, the reader is completely at home with the four of them." N Y Times Book Rev

McMurtry, Larry

Lonesome dove; a novel. Simon & Schuster 1985 843p $24.95   **Fic**

1. West (U.S.)—Fiction 2. Frontier and pioneer life—Fiction

ISBN 0-671-50420-7   LC 85-2192

Also available in paperback from Pocket Bks.

"Two former Texas Rangers have been running a ramshackle stock operation near the Mexican border with a lot of work and not much success. When they hear rumors of freewheeling opportunities in the newly opened territory, they decide to break camp, pull up stakes, and head north. Their dusty trek is filled with troubles, violence, and unfulfilled yearning." Booklist

"'Lonesome Dove' shows, early on, just about every symptom of American Epic except pretentiousness. McMurtry has laconic Texas talk and leathery, slim-hipped machismo down pat, and he's able to refresh heroic clichés with exact observations about cowboy prudery, ignorance and fear of losing face." Newsweek

Followed by Streets of Laredo (1993) and Dead man's walk (1995)

Mehta, Gita

Raj; a novel. Simon & Schuster 1989 479p o.p.; Fawcett Bks. paperback available $12.50   **Fic**

1. India—Fiction

ISBN 0-449-90566=7 (pa)   LC 88-38504

An "historical novel that traces the life of an Indian princess from her birth during the year of Queen Victoria's Diamond Jubilee in 1897 until India wins its independence from the empire in the mid-twentieth century. Princess Jaya treads a path that leads from the ancient traditions of the maharajas—in which the woman was subjugated to the man—through the days in which India was held and exploited as a British possession; she becomes in the end a woman who has achieved her own independence and identity along with her country." Booklist

Melville, Herman, 1819-1891

Billy Budd, sailor   **Fic**

1. Sea stories

Hardcover and paperback editions available from various publishers

Written in 1891 but in a still "unfinished" manuscript stage when Melville died. First publication 1924 in the United Kingdom, as part of the Standard edition of Melville's complete works

"Narrates the hatred of petty officer Claggart by Billy, handsome Spanish sailor. Billy strikes and kills Claggart, and is condemned by Captain Vere even though the latter senses Billy's spiritual innocence." Haydn. Thesaurus of Book Dig

Moby-Dick; or, The whale   **Fic**

1. Whaling—Fiction 2. Sea stories

Hardcover and paperback editions available from various publishers

First published 1851

"Moby Dick is a ferocious white whale, who was known to whalers as Mocha Dick. He is pursued in a fury of revenge by Captain Ahab, whose leg he has bitten off; and under Melville's handling the chase takes on a significance beyond mere externals. Moby Dick becomes a symbol of the terrific forces of the natural universe, and Captain Ahab is doomed to disaster, even though Moby Dick is killed at last." Univ Handbook for Readers and Writers

"'Moby-Dick' had some initial critical appreciation, particularly in Britain, but only since the 1920s has it been recognized as a masterpiece, an epic tragedy of tremendous dramatic power and narrative drive." Oxford Companion to Engl Lit. 5th edition

Mendelsohn, Jane, 1965-

I was Amelia Earhart; a novel. Knopf 1996 145p $18   **Fic**

1. Earhart, Amelia, 1898-1937—Fiction

ISBN 0-679-45054-8   LC 96-4149

Also available Thorndike Press large print edition

The aviatrix tells the story of her final voyage. "Earhart's changing feelings dominate the novel, particularly during the flight itself, when the exhausted pilot and Noonan, her drunken navigator, fight heat, dehydration and each other in their . . . ill-equipped aeroplane. When they crash on an uninhabited island, fear, hatred and blinding whiteness are replaced by unbearable heat, silence and earthbound misery. At first, Earhart pines, sitting in the cockpit of her beautiful rusting Lockheed Electra and longing for rescue. Gradually, however, the charms of Noonan, fried coconut and utter peace prevail, and . . . they decide to risk a final, doomed flight." Times Lit Suppl

Michener, James A. (James Albert), 1907-

Hawaii. Random House 1959 937p   **Fic**

1. Hawaii—Fiction

Available in hardcover from Buccaneer Bks.

A "novel in which the racial origins of Hawaii are traced through several narrative strands that merge in contemporary history. The original Tahitian colonizers welcome the white missionaries who bring in Chinese and Japanese laborers, and all together make up the present-day 'golden' Hawaiian." Wis Libr Bull

Miller, Walter M., 1923-1996

A canticle for Leibowitz; a novel; by Walter M. Miller, Jr. Lippincott 1960 c1959 320p o.p.; Bantam Bks. paperback available $5.99   **Fic**

1. Science fiction

ISBN 0-553-27381-7 (pa)

Also available in hardcover from Buccaneer Bks.

Miller, Walter M., 1923-1996—*Continued*

"Here is science fiction of the highest literary excellence and thematic intelligence. A monastery founded by the scientist Leibowitz is discovered decades after an atomic war. In the first part of the book a young novice in the monastery is the protagonist; in the second part we see scholars in a new period of enlightenment; and in the final section we observe man's proclivity for repeating mistakes and the apparent inevitability of history's repeating itself." Shapiro. Fic for Youth. 3d edition

Mitchell, Margaret, 1900-1949

Gone with the wind; with a new preface by Pat Conroy and an introduction by James A. Michener. 60th anniversary ed. Scribner 1996 959p il $40   Fic

1. United States—History—1861-1865, Civil War—Fiction 2. Reconstruction (1865-1876)—Fiction 3. Southern States—Fiction

ISBN 0-684-82625-9   LC 95-52609

Also available Thorndike Press large print edition and in paperback from Avon Bks. and Warner Bks.

"The proud people of the South have been subjugated in the Civil War, the dreadful period of Reconstruction has followed, and Scarlett O'Hara, beautiful and headstrong, has been reduced to poverty and near-starvation. No longer the belle of the ball, she must do whatever possible to feed herself and her family, and she does not hesitate to use feminine wiles to accomplish her ends. When she finds a man she can respect, she discovers her real feelings too late and loses him. Scarlett and her plantation home, Tara, are among the most memorable names in fiction." Shapiro. Fic for Youth. 3d edition

Mori, Kyoko

Shizuko's daughter. Holt & Co. 1993 227p $15.95   Fic

1. Suicide—Fiction 2. Mothers and daughters—Fiction 3. Remarriage—Fiction 4. Japan—Fiction

ISBN 0-8050-2557-X   LC 92-26956

Also available in paperback from Fawcett Bks.

"Yuki is 12 when her mother, Shizuko, commits suicide, leaving Yuki to a distant father and a self-serving stepmother. Forbidden by custom from seeing her mother's family, Yuki is left to fend for herself; and she does, falling back on the artistic talent she inherited from her mother." Booklist

"Mori paints beautiful pictures with words, creating visual images that can be as haunting and elliptical as poetry." Horn Book

Morrison, Toni, 1931-

Beloved; a novel. Knopf 1987 275p $27.50   Fic

1. African Americans—Fiction 2. Slavery—Fiction 3. Mothers and daughters—Fiction

ISBN 0-394-53597-9

Also available in paperback from New Am. Lib.

This novel, "set in the third quarter of the 19th century, focuses on the life of the runaway slave woman Sethe and her struggle with the unspeakable pain of her past. Like Morrison's earlier novels, *Beloved* is marked by rich and lyrical language, narratives shot through with exotic and magical elements, and a fragmented structure that requires readers to participate in the telling." Benet's Reader's Ency of Am Lit

Jazz. Knopf 1992 229p $21   Fic

1. African Americans—Fiction 2. Harlem (New York, N.Y.)—Fiction

ISBN 0-679-41167-4   LC 91-58555

Also available G.K. Hall large print edition and in paperback from New Am. Lib.

This novel "tells the story of Violet and Joe Trace, married for over 20 years, residents of Harlem in 1926. . . . Violet works as an unlicensed hairdresser, doing ladies hair in their own homes, and Joe sells Cleopatra cosmetics door to door. . . . When the novel opens, Joe has shot his 18-year-old lover, Dorcas, and Violet has disfigured the dead girl's body at her funeral in a fit of rage. Joe, who was not caught, is in mourning, crying all day in his darkened apartment, and Violet has taken on the task of finding out whatever she can about Dorcas." Voice Lit Suppl

Mowry, Jess, 1960-

Way past cool. Farrar, Straus & Giroux 1992 309p $17   Fic

1. Juvenile delinquency—Fiction 2. California—Fiction

ISBN 0-374-28669-8   LC 91-42050

Also available in paperback from HarperCollins Pubs.

"Set in Oakland's mean streets, this novel is a . . . portrayal of gang life from the inside. It involves a group of young teens, the Friends, whose turf is threatened by a mysterious drive-by shooting. When the same thing happens to the Crew, a rival gang, the two groups band together, ultimately uncovering a plot by Deek, a drug dealer, to incite a gang war and move in on their territory." Libr J

"There is no glamour here, no celebration of the gang look or the gang life; Mowry is all compassion and fury. His streetwise dialogue has astonishing emotional depth. . . . Powerful, gritty, and transcendently hopeful." Booklist

Myers, Walter Dean, 1937-

Fallen angels. Scholastic 1988 309p $14.95; pa $4.50   Fic

1. Vietnam War, 1961-1975—Fiction 2. African American soldiers—Fiction

ISBN 0-590-40942-5; 0-590-40943-3 (pa)

       LC 87-23236

"Black, seventeen, perceptive and sensitive, Richie (the narrator) has enlisted and been sent to Vietnam; in telling the story of his year of active service, Richie is candid about the horror of killing and the fear of being killed, the fear and bravery and confusion and tragedy of the war." Bull Cent Child Books

"Except for occasional outbursts, the narration is remarkably direct and understated; and the dialogue, with morbid humor sometimes adding comic relief, is steeped in natural vulgarity, without which verisimilitude would be unthinkable. In fact, the foul talk, which serves as the story's linguistic setting, is not nearly as obscene as the events." Horn Book

Myers, Walter Dean, 1937—— *Continued*

Somewhere in the darkness. Scholastic 1992
168p $14.95; pa $3.50   Fic
1. Fathers and sons—Fiction 2. Prisoners—Fiction
ISBN 0-590-42411-4; 0-590-42412-2 (pa)
                                          LC 91-19295
A teenage boy accompanies his father, who has recently escaped from prison, on a trip that turns out to be
a time of, often painful, discovery for them both
"This is one of Myer's most memorable pieces of
writing: there is not an unnecessary word or phrase; the
scenes are vivid and emotionally powerful; and the characters are heartbreakingly realistic. A page-turner elevated to a higher plane by its theme of the universal quest
of a son for his father." Horn Book

Nathan, Robert, 1894-1985

Portrait of Jennie. Knopf 1940 c1939 212p
$19.95   Fic
1. Painters—Fiction
ISBN 0-394-44093-5
Also available Thorndike Press large print edition and
in hardcover from Amereon and Buccaneer Bks.
"Eban Adams, a struggling artist who is unable to sell
his art work, meets an unusual child named Jennie in the
park and immediately begins to prosper. He knows little
about her except that she belongs in the past and that every few months, when their paths cross, she has aged by
years. His finest painting is a portrait of her, a token of
his love, which ends in predestined tragedy." Shapiro.
Fic for Youth. 3d edition

Niven, Larry

The Mote in God's Eye; [by] Larry Niven &
Jerry Pournelle. Simon & Schuster 1974 537p o.p.;
Pocket Bks. paperback available $5.99   Fic
1. Science fiction
ISBN 0-671-74192-6 (pa)
"Superior space opera in which Earth's interstellar
navy contacts and does battle with an enormously hostile
alien race. The scenes of space warfare are well handled,
and the alien Moties are fascinating." Anatomy of Wonder
Followed by The gripping hand (1993)

Ringworld. Ballantine Bks. 1970 342p pa $5.95
                                                   Fic
1. Science fiction
ISBN 0-345-33392-6
"The Ringworld, a world shaped like a wheel so huge
that it surrounds a sun, is almost too fantastic to con-
ceive of. With a radius of 90 million miles and a length
of 600 million miles, the Ringworld's mystery is com-
pounded by the discovery that it is artificial. What phenomenal intelligence can be behind such a creation? Four
unlikely explorers, two humans and two aliens, set out
for the Ringworld, bound by mutual distrust and unsure
of each other's motives." Shapiro. Fic for Youth. 3d edition
Followed by The Ringworld engineers (1980) and The
Ringworld throne (1990)

Nordhoff, Charles, 1887-1947

The Bounty trilogy; by Charles Nordhoff and
James Norman Hall; illustrated by N. C. Wyeth.
Little, Brown 1982 691p il hardcover o.p.
paperback available $19.95   Fic
1. Bounty (Ship)—Fiction 2. Sea stories 3. Islands of
the Pacific—Fiction
ISBN 0-316-61166-2 (pa)
"An Atlantic Monthly Press book"
A reissue of the combined volume first published
1936
"Comprising the three volumes: Mutiny on the Bounty
[1932] Men Against the Sea [1934] & Pitcairn's Island
[1934]." Title page
Based on actual events stemming from a mutiny on a
British war vessel in 1787, "this great trilogy begins with
the story of the men who mutinied against the now famous Captain Bligh—'Mutiny on the Bounty.' In 'Men
Against the Sea' Bligh and his supporters, set adrift in
a small boat, made an incredible journey to safety. 'Pitcairn's Island' is the story of the mutineers who found
refuge on a remote Pacific island." Books for you

Norris, Frank, 1870-1902

The pit   Fic
Available in hardcover from Lightyear Press
Sequel to: The octopus (1901)
First published 1903 by Doubleday
The second volume of the author's unfinished The
epic of wheat trilogy "is a story of manipulations in the
Chicago Exchange. Curtis Jadwin, a stock speculator, is
so absorbed in making money that he neglects his emotionally starved wife Laura. Into this situation steps
Sheldon Corthell, dilettante artist, to console her. Laura
loves her husband, and postpones for awhile going away
with the aesthete. Meanwhile, Jadwin engages in a struggle with the Crookes gang of speculators. He beats them,
but is crushed by fluctuations in wheat production. He
and Laura effect a reconciliation." Haydn. Thesaurus of
Book Dig

Oneal, Zibby, 1934-

The language of goldfish; a novel. Viking 1980
179p hardcover o.p. paperback available $4.99
                                                   Fic
1. Mental illness—Fiction
ISBN 0-14-034540-X (pa)   LC 79-19167
Also available Cornerstone Bks. large print edition
"Thirteen-year-old Carrie, the middle child in an affluent and happy family, is full of fears about herself and
her relations with other people. . . . She attempts suicide
and then slowly, through therapy and through the creative stimulus of painting, begins to heal." SLJ
"Set in Chicago, this is an honest and gripping novel
that lingers long in memory." Booklist

Orczy, Emmuska, Baroness, 1865-1947

The Scarlet Pimpernel   Fic
1. France—History—1789-1799, Revolution—Fiction
Hardcover and paperback editions available from various publishers
First published 1905 by Putnam

Orczy, Emmuska, Baroness, 1865-1947—Continued

"An adventure story of the French Revolution. The apparently foppish young Englishman, Sir Percy Blakeney, is found to be the daring Scarlet Pimpernel, rescuer of distressed aristocrats." Reader's Ency. 4th edition

Orwell, George, 1903-1950

Animal farm   Fic

1. Animals—Fiction 2. Totalitarianism—Fiction

Hardcover and paperback editions available from various publishers

First published 1945 in the United Kingdom; first United States edition 1946

"The animals on Farmer Jones's farm revolt in a move led by the pigs, and drive out the humans. The pigs become the leaders, in spite of the fact that their government was meant to be 'classless.' The other animals soon find that they are suffering varying degrees of slavery. A totalitarian state slowly evolves in which 'all animals are equal but some animals are more equal than others.' This is a biting satire aimed at communism." Shapiro. Fic for Youth. 3d edition

Nineteen eighty-four   Fic

1. Totalitarianism—Fiction

Hardcover and paperback editions available from various publishers

First published 1949 by Harcourt, Brace

"A dictatorship called Big Brother rules the people in a collectivist society where Winston Smith works in the Ministry of Truth. The Thought Police persuade the people that ignorance is strength and war is peace. Winston becomes involved in a forbidden love affair and joins the underground to resist this mind control." Shapiro. Fic for Youth. 3d edition

Parks, Gordon

The learning tree. Harper & Row 1963 303p o.p.; Fawcett Bks. paperback available $5.99   Fic

1. African Americans—Fiction 2. Kansas—Fiction

ISBN 0-449-21504-0 (pa)

"At 12 years of age Newt is awakening to the world around him in his small town of Cherokee Flats, Kansas, in the 1920s. There is the impact of a first sexual experience and a first love, and because he is a Negro, special responsibility of behavior when one individual may represent an entire group in the eyes of the community." Shapiro. Fic for Youth. 3d edition

Pasternak, Boris Leonidovich, 1890-1960

Doctor Zhivago; [by] Boris Pasternak. Pantheon Bks. 1958 558p hardcover o.p. paperback available $15   Fic

1. Russia—Fiction

ISBN 0-679-73123-7 (pa)

Also available in hardcover from Buccaneer Bks. and in paperback from Ballantine Bks.

First published 1957 in Italy

"The account of the life of a Russian intellectual, Yurii Zhivago, a doctor and a poet, during the first three decades of the 20th c. A broad epic picture of Russia is developed as the background to Zhivago's family life, his creative ecstasies, his love for Lara (another man's wife), his emotional upheavals, wanderings, and moments of happiness. Though the novel ends with Zhivago's decline and death as a result of what the author saw as the dehumanization of life that prevailed in the postrevolution years, the epilogue is full of expectations of the freedom that is to come." Ency of World Lit in the 20th Century

Paterson, Katherine

Jacob have I loved. HarperCollins Pubs. 1980 216p $14.95; lib bdg $14.89; pa $4.50   Fic

1. Twins—Fiction 2. Sisters—Fiction 3. Chesapeake Bay (Md. and Va.)—Fiction

ISBN 0-690-04078-4; 0-690-04079-2 (lib bdg); 0-06-440368-8 (pa)

"Sara Louise, called Wheeze, felt like the unloved twin in competition with her sister Caroline. On a small Chesapeake Bay island Louise is isolated and denied the opportunity to fulfill her hopes and goals while everyone caters to her twin sister. The return of an old captain after a 50-year absence, and the advent of the war, gives Louise a chance to grow toward maturity and achieve her wish to work alongside her father." Shapiro. Fic for Youth. 3d edition

Paton, Alan

Cry, the beloved country   Fic

1. Race relations—Fiction 2. South Africa—Fiction

Hardcover and paperback editions available from various publishers

First published 1948 by Scribner

"Reverend Kumalo, a black South African preacher, is called to Johannesburg to rescue his sister. There he learns that his son Absalom has been accused of murdering a young white attorney whose interests and sympathies had been with the natives. Despite this, the attorney's father comes to the aid of the minister to help the natives in their struggle to survive a drought." Shapiro. Fic for Youth. 3d edition

Paton Walsh, Jill, 1937-

Grace. Farrar, Straus & Giroux 1992 255p $16   Fic

1. Darling, Grace—Fiction 2. Shipwrecks—Fiction 3. Great Britain—Fiction

ISBN 0-374-32758-0   LC 91-31054

After helping her father rescue the survivors of a shipwreck on the coast of England in 1838, Grace Darling finds her quiet life crumbling around her as she is unwillingly fashioned into a national hero

"This true event, and much of the aftermath, have been used by the author to blend fact and fiction with consummate skill in creating a narrative that is powerfully dramatic in its initial impact and sharply observant in describing the consequent events. . . . The characters are drawn with depth and nuance, the language and idiom are appropriate to the place and period, and the whole story has the tight-knit feel of a tapestry in word." Bull Cent Child Books

Paulsen, Gary

Harris and me; a summer remembered. Harcourt Brace & Co. 1993 157p $13.95   **Fic**
1. Farm life—Fiction 2. Cousins—Fiction
ISBN 0-15-292877-4   LC 93-19788

Sent to live with relatives on their farm because of his unhappy home life, an eleven-year-old city boy meets his distant cousin Harris and is given an introduction to a whole new world

"A hearty helping of old-fashioned, rip-roaring entertainment." Publ Wkly

Nightjohn. Delacorte Press 1993 92p $14.95
                                                Fic
1. Slavery—Fiction
ISBN 0-385-30838-8   LC 92-1222
Also available in paperback from Dell

Twelve-year-old Sarny's brutal life as a slave becomes even more dangerous when a newly arrived slave offers to teach her how to read

"Paulsen is at his best here: the writing is stark and bareboned, without stylistic pretensions of any kind. The narrator's voice is strong and true, the violence real but stylized with an almost mythic tone. . . . The simplicity of the text will make the book ideal for older reluctant readers who can handle violence but can't or won't handle fancy writing in long books. Best of all, the metaphor of reading as an act of freedom speaks for itself through striking action unembroidered by didactic messages." Bull Cent Child Books

Peck, Richard, 1934-

Father figure; a novel. Viking 1978 192p hardcover o.p. paperback available $3.99   **Fic**
1. Brothers and sisters—Fiction 2. Fathers and sons—Fiction
ISBN 0-14-037969-X (pa)   LC 78-7909
Also available in paperback from Dell

"When the mother of 17 year old Jim Atwater and his younger brother Byron dies, their father shows up unexpectedly at the funeral after an eight-year absence. He takes his two sons from their home in New York to his Florida residence. The friction between the father and older son, the pain and awkwardness of sharing, and the love that gradually emerges are well portrayed by the author." Shapiro. Fic for Youth. 3d edition

The last safe place on earth. Delacorte Press 1995 161p $15.95; pa $3.99   **Fic**
1. Censorship—Fiction 2. Family life—Fiction 3. Fundamentalism—Fiction
ISBN 0-385-32052-3; 0-440-22007-6 (pa)
                                      LC 94-446

Fifteen-year-old Todd sees his perfect suburban world start to unravel when his little sister has her mind poisoned by a member of a fundamentalist sect and he begins to notice signs of censorship in his community

"Peck writes with wit and warmth that will sweep teens into a world they'll recognize. He has a sharp eye for the poetic image that captures the contemporary scene." Booklist

Remembering the good times. Delacorte Press 1985 181p hardcover o.p. paperback available $4.50   **Fic**
1. Suicide—Fiction 2. Friendship—Fiction
ISBN 0-440-97339-2 (pa)   LC 84-19962

This novel focuses on "both friendship and suicide as a trio of adolescents becomes a pair when one of them kills himself. Buck, Kate & Trav have been friends for four years—since they were 12 or 13. . . . When Trav first shoplifts and then commits suicide, Kate and Buck wonder if they ever really knew him at all." Voice Youth Advocates

"This is a sad book but not a morbid one, and it's written with insight and a saving humor." Bull Cent Child Books

Peck, Robert Newton, 1928-

A day no pigs would die. Knopf 1973 c1972 150p $22; pa $4.99   **Fic**
1. Shakers—Fiction 2. Farm life—Fiction 3. Vermont—Fiction
ISBN 0-394-48235-2; 0-679-85306-5 (pa)

"Rob lives a rigorous life on a Shaker farm in Vermont in the 1920s. Since farm life is earthy, this book is filled with Yankee humor and explicit descriptions of animals mating. A painful incident that involves the slaughter of Rob's beloved pet pig is instrumental in urging him toward adulthood. The death of his father completes the process of his accepting responsibility." Shapiro. Fic for Youth. 3d edition

A part of the sky. Knopf 1994 163p $18   **Fic**
1. Shakers—Fiction 2. Farm life—Fiction 3. Vermont—Fiction
ISBN 0-679-43277-9   LC 93-41741
Sequel to A day no pigs would die

"Responsible for Mama and Aunt Carrie, the family farm, and the Peck animals, Rob bravely faces death, bankruptcy, and subsequent foreclosure during the hard times of the early Depression. Disheartened by ongoing problems—his ox dies, the cow's milk dries up, drought stunts the harvest—Rob cannot meet the family's $12 monthly mortgage payments, and the Pecks lose their home. Ultimately, Rob learns that wealth extends beyond money and that real values are priceless." Libr J

Pennebaker, Ruth

Don't think twice. Holt & Co. 1996 262p $15.95   **Fic**
1. Pregnancy—Fiction 2. Unmarried mothers—Fiction 3. Adoption—Fiction
ISBN 0-8050-4407-8   LC 95-20499

Seventeen years old and pregnant, Anne lives with other unwed mothers in a group home in rural Texas where she learns to be herself before giving her child up for adoption

"There is brutal honesty, tempered with sparkling adolescent wit throughout. . . . Some adults might react with anxiety to the sometimes frank language, to Anne's negative attitude towards religion, and to a minor segment in which one of the girls explains that she was molested by a clergyman. It would really be a shame, however, if those factors kept this moving book out of the hands of teen readers." Voice Youth Advocates

Pfeffer, Susan Beth, 1948-

The year without Michael. Bantam Bks. 1987 164p hardcover o.p. paperback available $3.99
Fic
1. Missing children—Fiction 2. Family life—Fiction
ISBN 0-553-27373-6 (pa)   LC 87-11474
"Thirteen year old Michael disappears on a Sunday afternoon. His family may never know what happened to him but they will hope and search until he's found. It falls upon Jody, Michael's older sister, to hold the family together as the stress and uncertainty mount." BAYA Book Rev

"Readers are held not only by the suspense of wanting to know what happened to Michael but also to a need to find out what happens to his family. While topical novels abound in literature for young adults, few offer the taut structuring, sound characterization, and honest dialogue that in this case turn a book about a contemporary problem into an exploration of more universal themes." SLJ

Plath, Sylvia

The bell jar; biographical note by Louis Ames; drawings by Sylvia Plath. Harper & Row 1971 296p il $18
Fic
1. Mental illness—Fiction
ISBN 0-06-013356-2
Also available in hardcover from Buccaneer Bks. and in paperback from Bantam Bks.
First published 1963 in the United Kingdom
"Esther Greenwood, having spent what should have been a glorious summer as guest editor for a young woman's magazine, came home from New York, had a nervous breakdown, and tried to commit suicide. Through months of therapy, Esther kept her rationality, if not her sanity. In telling the story of Esther Plath thinly disguised her own experience with attempted suicide and time spent in an institution." Shapiro. Fic for Youth. 3d edition

Pohl, Frederik, 1919-

The voices of heaven. TOR Bks. 1994 347p $21.95; pa $5.99
Fic
1. Science fiction
ISBN 0-312-85643-1; 0-8125-3518-9 (pa)
LC 94-2350
"A Tom Doherty Associates book"
"Shanghaied to a planet light-years away from his lunar home, fuelmaster Barry di Hoa is forced to adjust to life on the seismically unstable planet Pava, where a colony of religious fanatics awaits the end of the world. . . . He befriends indigenous aliens and gradually uncovers a malevolent plot to bring about 'the Millennium.'" Libr J

"With consummate craftsmanship, Pohl weaves suspenseful storytelling and memorable characterizations—including those of the native-to-Pava, caterpillarlike 'leps'—into a seamless, elegant whole." Booklist

Potok, Chaim, 1929-

The chosen; a novel; with a foreword by the author. 25th anniversary ed. Knopf 1992 c1967 295p $30
Fic
1. Jews—New York (N.Y.)—Fiction
ISBN 0-679-40222-5   LC 91-58551
A reissue of the title first published 1967 by Simon & Schuster

"Living only five blocks apart in the Williamsburg section of Brooklyn, New York, Danny and Reuven meet as opponents in a softball game. Out of this encounter evolves a strong bond of friendship between a brilliant Hasidic Jew and a scholar who is Orthodox in his religious thinking. During the course of their relationship Reuven becomes the means by which Danny's father a rabbi, can communicate with his son, who has been reared under a code of silence." Shapiro. Fic for Youth. 2d edition

Followed by The promise (1969)

My name is Asher Lev. Knopf 1972 369p $25
Fic
1. Jews—New York (N.Y.)—Fiction 2. Painters—Fiction
ISBN 0-394-46137-1
Also available in paperback from Fawcett Bks.

"Young Asher Lev is an obedient son of strict Jewish parents. When his artistic endeavors are discovered, he is sent to a religious leader for consultation because artists are not viewed favorably by the Hasidim. Asher's struggle for fulfillment and his ultimate rejection by his parents are poignantly drawn." Shapiro. Fic for Youth. 3d edition

Preston, Douglas

Relic; [by] Douglas Preston, Lincoln Child. Forge 1995 382p il $22.95
Fic
1. Horror fiction 2. Indians of South America—Fiction
ISBN 0-312-85630-X   LC 94-44321
"A Tom Doherty Associates book"
"A statue of the mad god Mbwun, a monstrous mix of man and reptile, was discovered by a Museum expedition to South America in 1987. Now, it is about to become part of the new Superstition Exhibition at the museum. . . . But as the exhibition's opening night approaches, the museum may have to be shut down due to a series of savage murders that seem to be the work of a maniac—or a living version of Mbwun." Publ Wkly

This thriller contains "just the right blend of gripping suspense, colorful characters, and credible science." Booklist

Pullman, Philip, 1946-

The golden compass. Knopf 1996 399p $20
Fic
1. Fantasy fiction 2. Arctic regions—Fiction
ISBN 0-679-87924-2   LC 95-33397
First published 1995 in the United Kingdom with title: Northern lights

This first title in a projected fantasy trilogy "introduces the characters and sets up the basic conflict, namely, a race to unlock the mystery of a newly discovered type of charged particles simply called *dust* that may be

Pullman, Philip, 1946——*Continued*
a bridge to an alternate universe. The action follows 11-year-old protagonist Lyra Belacqua from her home at Oxford University to the frozen wastes of the North on a quest to save dozens of kidnapped children from the evil 'Gobblers,' who are using them as part of a sinister experiment involving dust." Libr J

The ruby in the smoke. Knopf 1987 c1985 230p
lib bdg $11.99; pa $4.99   **Fic**
1. Mystery fiction 2. Orphans—Fiction 3. London (England)—Fiction
ISBN 0-394-98826-4 (lib bdg); 0-394-89589-4 (pa)
LC 86-20983
First published 1985 in the United Kingdom
This story "begins in 1872 on a 'cold, fretful' October afternoon in London. Sally Lockhart is the 16-year-old heroine who asks some innocent questions about her father's death that lead her into a world of stolen rubies and the opium trade." N Y Times Book Rev
"Pullman uses a cliff-hanger at the end of each chapter to keep readers enthralled in this fast-paced, intricate, and suspenseful novel. Sally's complex characterization as a resourceful, yet occasionally unsure, young woman, makes her both likable and memorable." Voice Youth Advocates

Pushkin, Aleksandr Sergeevich, 1799-1837
Eugene Onegin   **Fic**
1. Russia—Fiction
LC 80-511119
Hardcover and paperback editions available from various publishers
"The novel relates the experiences of its Byronic hero, Eugene. Bored with the social life in St. Petersburg, he visits his country estate and meets Tatyana, a young woman who falls in love with him and naively offers herself to him. The bored Eugene is not interested and rather bluntly tells her so. For lack of any other amusement, he then provokes a duel with Lensky, a young romantic poet who has become his friend. Lensky is killed, and Onegin goes back to the world of society. After his departure, Tatyana visits Eugene's country manor, browses through his library, and begins to realize how hollow and artificial he is. A few years later, when Eugene meets Tatyana, who is now the wife of a prince and a prominent member of St. Petersburg society, her beauty and charm, and perhaps her eminence in society, turn his head. He announces his love to her in a letter, as Tatyana had to him years before. Tatyana admits she still loves him but refuses him because of her duty to her husband." Reader's Ency. 4th edition

Rand, Ayn, 1905-1982
Atlas shrugged. 35th anniversary ed. Dutton 1992 1168p $39.95; pa $7.99   **Fic**
1. Individualism—Fiction 2. Capitalists and financiers—Fiction
ISBN 0-525-93418-9; 0-451-19114-5 (pa)
LC 91-36842
A reissue of the title first published 1957 by Random House
"In a technological civilization Rand's characters remain insecure and look to the government for protection.

In exchange they sacrifice their creativity and independence. The heroes, a copper tycoon and an inventor, reject this philosophy and fight for the individualist." Shapiro. Fic for Youth. 3d edition

The fountainhead. Macmillan 1943 754p $40
Fic
1. Individualism—Fiction 2. Architects—Fiction
ISBN 0-02-600910-2
Also available in paperback from New Am. Lib.
First published by Bobbs-Merrill
This novel "celebrates the achievements of an architect (presumably suggested by Frank Lloyd Wright) who is fiercely independent in pursuing his own ideas of design and who is therefore an example of the author's concept of Objectivism, which lauds individualism and 'rational self-interest.'" Oxford Companion to Am Lit. 5th edition

Remarque, Erich Maria, 1898-1970
All quiet on the western front; translated from the German by A. W. Wheen. Little, Brown 1929 291p $21.95   **Fic**
1. World War, 1914-1918—Fiction
ISBN 0-316-73992-8
Also available in hardcover from Amereon and in paperback from Fawcett Bks.
"Four German youths are pulled abruptly from school to serve at the front as soldiers in World War I. Only Paul survives, and he contemplates the needless violation of the human body by weapons of war. No longer innocent or lighthearted, he is repelled by the slaughter of soldiers and questions the usefulness of war as a means of adjudication. Although the young men in this novel are German, the message is universal in its delineation of the feelings of the common soldier." Shapiro. Fic for Youth. 3d edition
Followed by The road back (1931)

Renault, Mary, 1905-1983
The king must die. Pantheon Bks. 1958 338p hardcover o.p. paperback available $11   **Fic**
1. Theseus (Greek Mythology)—Fiction 2. Classical mythology—Fiction 3. Greece—Fiction
ISBN 0-394-75104-3 (pa)
"Retold by its hero, the legend of Theseus becomes a logical sequence of adventures that befell a slight, wiry, quick-witted youth impelled to prove his manhood in a semibarbaric society that put a premium on size and brawn. Although, at seventeen, he was already a king and a seasoned warrior, Theseus obeyed his patron god's prompting and voluntarily joined a company of young people conscripted for the bull-dances in Crete, became a renowned bull-leaper, and took advantage of an earthquake to overthrow the Cretan kingdom." Booklist
Followed by The bull from the sea (1962)

Rendell, Ruth, 1930-
Heartstones; illustrations by George Underwood. Harper & Row 1987 80p il o.p.; Ballantine Bks. paperback available $4.95   **Fic**
1. Horror fiction 2. Fathers and daughters—Fiction
ISBN 0-345-34800-1 (pa)   LC 86-46098
"The Harper short novel series"

Rendell, Ruth, 1930——*Continued*

"Adolescent Elvira is in intense spiritual communion with her father; she plans to devote all the rest of her life to him. Elvira's mother is dead, and her sister is outside the orbit that Elvira and her father have created for themselves. This arrangement works fine, as long as it lasts, but trouble arrives in the form of a woman Elvira's father wants to marry. Elvira is determined the marriage will not take place. And, alas, the fiancée dies—violently!" Booklist

"Such is Rendell's mastery of psychological suspense that throughout we remain unsure of the seriousness of Elvira's intentions." Libr J

Rice, Anne, 1941-

Interview with the vampire. Reset for anniversary ed. Knopf 1996 340p $25   Fic

1. Horror fiction 2. Vampires—Fiction

ISBN 0-394-49821-6   LC 96-232882

First published 1976

"In contemporary New Orleans a young reporter listens as Louis, a vampire, unfolds his tale. His story spans several hundred years . . . of a Faustian search for some meaning to his life-in-death existence, an existence complicated by his relationship to three other vampires. Lestat, the vampire who made him, is hated by Claudia, the five-year-old extraordinarily beautiful child-vampire Louis loves. . . . After Claudia attempts to kill Lestat she and Louis go to Europe in search of other vampires. In Paris they find Armand, Master Vampire, and he and Louis fall in love, remaining together for a time after Claudia's death in a state of meaningless immortality." Libr J

Followed by The vampire Lestat (1985); The queen of the damned (1988); The tale of the body thief (1992); Memnoch the Devil (1995)

Richter, Conrad, 1890-1968

The light in the forest. Knopf 1953 179p $23   Fic

1. Frontier and pioneer life—Fiction 2. Delaware Indians—Fiction

ISBN 0-394-43314-9   LC 52-12207

Also available in hardcover from Amereon and Buccaneer Bks. and in paperback from Fawcett Bks.

Companion volume to A country of strangers (1966)

"John Butler is kidnapped at the age of four and raised by Delaware Indians. Eleven years later, under a truce agreement between the Indians and the colonials, he is forcibly returned to his family. Irrevocably divided in his heart, he escapes and goes back to the Indians but is sent away after the failure of an Indian ambush." Shapiro. Fic for Youth. 3d edition

Rinaldi, Ann, 1934-

Wolf by the ears. Scholastic 1991 252p $13.95; pa $3.50   Fic

1. Jefferson, Thomas, 1743-1826—Fiction 2. Slavery—Fiction 3. African Americans—Fiction

ISBN 0-590-43413-6; 0-590-43412-8 (pa)
          LC 90-40563

"Set at Monticello from 1819-1822, this provocative historical novel deals with the conflicts of teenage Harriet Hemings, daughter of the slave Sally and allegedly of Thomas Jefferson. A member of two worlds, Harriet is confused about the truth of her parentage, her love of her master, her need to leave home and people she loves, and her eventual plan to pass as white." ALAN

Includes bibliographical references

Rodowsky, Colby F., 1932-

Remembering Mog. Farrar, Straus & Giroux 1996 135p $14   Fic

1. Homicide—Fiction 2. Death—Fiction 3. Family life—Fiction

ISBN 0-374-34663-1   LC 95-30616

After graduating from a private high school in Baltimore, Annie comes to terms with the loss of her sister who had been murdered two years earlier

"Rodowsky touchingly depicts the barrenness, anger, and yearning that are part of bereavement; the authentic twist of Annie's guilt and confusion at growing beyond her older sister . . . sets this title apart from many on the subject." Bull Cent Child Books

Rölvaag, Ole Edvart, 1876-1931

Giants in the earth; a saga of the prairie; [by] O. E. Rölvaag; translated from the Norwegian. Harper & Row 1927 465p hardcover o.p. paperback available $8   Fic

1. Norwegian Americans—Fiction 2. Frontier and pioneer life—Fiction 3. South Dakota—Fiction

ISBN 0-06-083047-6 (pa)

"In this epic tale of Norwegian settlers in the plains of South Dakota, the difficulties that they endure give the reader insight into those characteristics often thought of as typically American. Per Hansa and his wife, Beret, expect to make a living and a home for themselves by working the land. Per is pleased with his new life, proud of his successes with his farm and of his leadership in the small community of immigrants, Beret hates the hardships of frontier life and longs for the comforts of her life in Norway. Her religion, which is her chief consolation, gradually becomes an obsession and causes the tragedy with which the book ends." Shapiro. Fic for Youth. 3d edition

Followed by Peder Victorious (1929) and Their father's God (1931)

Saint-Exupéry, Antoine de, 1900-1944

The little prince; written and drawn by Antoine de Saint-Exupéry; translated from the French by Katherine Woods. Harcourt Brace & Co. 1943 91p il hardcover o.p. paperback available $9   Fic

ISBN 0-15-246503-0 (pa)   LC 67-1144

Also available in hardcover from Amereon

First published by Reynal & Hitchcock

"This many-dimensional fable of an airplane pilot who has crashed in the desert is for readers of all ages. The pilot comes upon the little prince soon after the crash. The prince tells of his adventures on different planets and on Earth as he attempts to learn about the universe in order to live peacefully on his own small planet. A spiritual quality enhances the seemingly simple observations of the little prince." Shapiro. Fic for Youth. 3d edition

Salinger, J. D. (Jerome David), 1919-

The catcher in the rye. Little, Brown 1951 277p
$22.95; pa $5.99   **Fic**
1. New York (N.Y.)—Fiction
ISBN 0-316-76953-3; 0-316-76948-7 (pa)
Also available in hardcover from Buccaneer Bks.

"The story of adolescent Holden Caulfield who runs
away from boarding-school in Pennsylvania to New York
where he preserves his innocence despite various attempts to lose it. The colloquial, lively, first-person narration, with its attacks on the 'phoniness' of the adult
world and its clinging to family sentiment in the form of
Holden's affection for his sister Phoebe, made the novel
accessible to and popular with a wide readership, particularly with the young." Oxford Companion to Engl Lit.
5th edition

Franny & Zooey. Little, Brown 1961 201p
$23.95; pa $4.99   **Fic**
1. Family life—Fiction 2. New York (N.Y.)—Fiction
ISBN 0-316-76954-1; 0-316-76949-5 (pa)

"At 20, Franny Glass is experiencing desperate dissat-
isfaction with her life and seems to be looking for help
via a religious awakening. Her brother Zooey tries to
help her out of this depression. He recalls the influence
on their growth and development of their appearance as
young radio performers on a network program called
'It's a Wise Child.' An older brother, Buddy, is also an
important component of the interrelationships in the
Glass family." Shapiro. Fic for Youth. 3d edition

Santiago, Danny

Famous all over town. Simon & Schuster 1983
284p o.p.; New Am. Lib. paperback available
$11.95   **Fic**
1. Mexican Americans—Fiction 2. Los Angeles
(Calif.)—Fiction
ISBN 0-452-25974-6 (pa)

"Mexican-American Rudy Medina [known as Chato]
looks back on his 14th year. 'Fourteen makes a man,' his
father says. Fourteen is also the year that Rudy's 'eco-
nomically viable household' (in the words of a social
worker) falls apart, and his closely knit neighborhood is
bulldozed to make way for the Southern Pacific Railroad." Libr J

This "is an honest, steady novel that presents some
hard cultural realities while not for a paragraph failing to
entertain." N Y Times Book Rev

Saroyan, William, 1908-1981

The human comedy; illustrated by Don
Freeman. Harcourt Brace Jovanovich 1989 c1943
242p il $15.95   **Fic**
1. California—Fiction 2. Family life—Fiction
ISBN 0-15-142301-6   LC 89-32785
Also available in paperback from Dell
"An HBJ modern classic"
A reissue of the title first published 1944

"Homer, the narrator, identifies himself in this novel
as a night messenger for the Postal Telegraph office. He
creates a view of family life in the 1940s in a small
town in California. His mother, Ma Macauley, presides
over the family and takes care of four children after her
husband dies. Besides Homer, there is Marcus, the

oldest, who is in the army; Bess; and Ulysses, the
youngest, who describes the world from his perspective
as a solemn four-year-old." Shapiro. Fic for Youth. 3d
edition

Saul, John

Creature. Bantam Bks. 1989 329p hardcover o.p.
paperback available $6.50   **Fic**
1. Horror fiction
ISBN 0-533-28411-8 (pa)   LC 88-7770

"When his family moves to idyllic Silverlake, Colorado, made over into a company town by his father
Blake's high-tech employer, Mark Tanner is a puny 16-
year-old stunted by a childhood illness. The town hosts
an experimental sports center that amazingly converts
weaklings into hulking jocks, and what's more, the company pushes its execs to get their boys into the program.
Blake's dreams for Mark are within reach. Of course,
there are some risks: a few athletes have gone berserk
and, after attacking their parents, have had to be locked
up. Despite his wife's misgivings—she thinks the whole
town's fishy—Blake signs Mark up, and risk becomes
reality." Booklist

Schaefer, Jack Warner, 1907-1991

Shane; [by] Jack Schaefer; illustrated by John
McCormack. Houghton Mifflin 1954 214p il
$15.95   **Fic**
1. Ranch life—Fiction 2. Wyoming—Fiction
ISBN 0-395-07090-2
Also available in hardcover from Buccaneer Bks and
in paperback from Bantam Bks.
Illustrated edition of the title first published 1949

"Wyoming in 1889 is the scene of conflict between
cattlemen and homesteaders when Shane mysteriously
disappears. He works hard as a hired hand for the
Starrett family, and young Bob Starrett grows to love
him, unaware that he is a feared gunfighter escaping his
past." Shapiro. Fic for Youth. 3d edition

Sheffield, Charles

Higher education; [by] Charles Sheffield & Jerry
Pournelle. TOR Bks. 1996 286p $21.95   **Fic**
1. Science fiction
ISBN 0-312-86174-5   LC 95-52875
"A Tom Doherty Associates book"

"In a politically correct world where the school system
fails to educate for fear of lawsuits, illiterate, ignorant
students face a bleak future of unemployment. When
Rick Luban is expelled for a minor prank, he joins Vanguard Mining and finds asteroid mining training to be a
more rigorous and demanding than school. This fast-
paced adventure begins the new 'Jupiter novels' series
with danger and intrigue in space." Libr J

Shelley, Mary Wollstonecraft, 1797-1851

Frankenstein   **Fic**

Hardcover and paperback editions available from various publishers
First published 1818

Shelley, Mary Wollstonecraft, 1797-1851—*Continued*

"The tale relates the exploits of Frankenstein, an idealistic Genevan student of natural philosophy, who discovers at the university of Ingolstadt the secret of imparting life to inanimate matter. Collecting bones from charnelhouses, he constructs the semblance of a human being and gives it life. The creature, endowed with supernatural strength and size and terrible in appearance, inspires loathing in whoever sees it." Oxford Companion to Engl Lit. 5th edition

Shute, Nevil, 1899-1960

On the beach. Morrow 1957 320p $22.95 **Fic**
1. Nuclear warfare—Fiction 2. Australia—Fiction
ISBN 0-688-02223-5

Also available in hardcover from Amereon and in paperback from Ballantine Bks.

"A nuclear war annihilates the world's Northern Hemisphere, and as atomic wastes are spreading southward, residents of Australia try to come to grips with their mortality. In spite of the inevitability of death, these people face their end with courage and live from day to day. They even plant trees they may never see mature." Shapiro. Fic for Youth. 3d edition

Sinclair, April

Ain't gonna be the same fool twice; a novel. Hyperion 1996 324p $19.95 **Fic**
1. African Americans—Fiction 2. College students—Fiction 3. Lesbians—Fiction
ISBN 0-7868-6069-3   LC 95-33051

In this sequel to Coffee will make you black, "Jean 'Stevie' Stevenson attends college before heading to San Francisco to seek a career in broadcasting. The irrepressible 'Stevie' continues to grapple with her self esteem and sexual orientation in this literary gem that, because of some frank language and lesbian love scenes, is best suited to mature readers." Booklist

Coffee will make you black. Hyperion 1994 239p $19.95 **Fic**
1. African Americans—Fiction 2. Chicago (Ill.)—Fiction
ISBN 1-56282-796-0   LC 93-13271

Also available in paperback from Avon Bks.

This novel's protagonist "is Jean ('Stevie') Stevenson, a spunky 11-year-old when the story begins, a high-school student when it concludes. The setting is Chicago, circa 1965-70. . . . Raised by a strict, if well-meaning, mother and an affectionate, if vague, father, Stevie soon finds herself caught up in one of the many riddles of youth: to be cool or be square. . . . Meanwhile, she is listening to Dr. Martin Luther King and Malcolm X and liberating herself from the confines of her upbringing and her fear of being 'different.'" Booklist

"Sinclair gives a realistic portrayal of personal awakening during a politically tumultuous time." Publ Wkly

Sinclair, Upton, 1878-1968

The jungle   **Fic**
1. Chicago (Ill.)—Fiction 2. Social problems—Fiction
Hardcover and paperback editions available from various publishers

First published 1906 by Doubleday, Page

"Jurgis Rudkus, an immigrant from Lithuania, arrives in Chicago with his father, his fiancée, and her family. He is determined to make a life for his bride in the new country. The deplorable conditions in the stockyards and the harrowing experiences of impoverished workers are vividly described by the author." Shapiro. Fic for Youth. 3d edition

Singer, Isaac Bashevis, 1904-1991

The certificate; translated by Leonard Wolf. Farrar, Straus & Giroux 1992 231p $22 **Fic**
1. Jews—Fiction 2. Warsaw (Poland)—Fiction
ISBN 0-374-12029-3   LC 92-054527

Also available in paperback from New Am. Lib./Dutton

Originally serialized 1967 in Yiddish newspaper

A novel about the "now-vanished universe of Polish Jewry between the world wars. Its narrator, David Bendiger, is a would-be writer, 'at eighteen and a half. . . no longer a day student' but still a dreamer, 'digging away at eternal questions' and trying to survive on his own in 1920s Warsaw. Offered the opportunity of a certificate that will permit him to emigrate to Palestine, he vacillates among three women—Sonya, a simple working girl; Edusha, a sexually active young Communist; and Minna, a daughter of the once-rich bourgeoisie—unable to decide whom he should choose." Publ Wkly

"Singer is the most magical of writers, transforming reality into art with seemingly effortless sleight of hand. His deceptively spare prose has a pristine clarity that is stunning in its impact." N Y Times Book Rev

Sleator, William

House of stairs. Dutton 1974 166p $14.95 **Fic**
1. Science fiction
ISBN 0-525-32335-X

Also available in paperback from Penguin Bks.

"Five 15-year-old orphans with widely ranging personality characteristics are involuntarily placed in a house of endless stairs and subjected to psychological experiments on conditioned human responses." Booklist

"The setting is bleak, dramatic and convincing; the interaction and development of the five young people as characters trapped in an abrasive situation are compelling. A very effective and provocative suspense story that can be read for plot alone or doubly enjoyed for the mystery and the message." Bull Cent Child Books

Smith, Betty, 1896-1972

A tree grows in Brooklyn; a novel. Harper & Row 1943 443p hardcover o.p. paperback available $7 **Fic**
1. Poverty—Fiction 2. Family life—Fiction 3. Brooklyn (New York, N.Y.)—Fiction
ISBN 0-06-080126-3 (pa)

Also available G.K. Hall large print edition and in hardcover from Buccaneer Bks.

"Life in the Williamsburg section of Brooklyn during the early 1900s is rough, but the childhood and youth of Francie Nolan is far from somber. Nurtured by a loving mother, Francie blossoms and reaches out for happiness despite poverty and the alcoholism of a father whose weakness is somewhat compensated for by his lovable disposition." Shapiro. Fic for Youth. 3d edition

Solzhenitsyn, Aleksandr, 1918-

One day in the life of Ivan Denisovich; translated from the Russian by H. T. Willets; with an introduction by John Bayley. Knopf 1995 xxvii, 159p (Everyman's library) $15   **Fic**

1. Soviet Union—Fiction 2. Political prisoners—Fiction

ISBN 0-679-44464-5

Also available in paperback From Farrar, Straus, Giroux

Original Russian edition, 1962; this is a reissue of the translation published 1991 by Farrar, Straus, Giroux

"Drawing on his own experiences, the author writes of one day, from reveille to lights-out, in the prison existence of Ivan Denisovich Shukhov. Innocent of any crime, he has been convicted of treason and sentenced to ten years in one of Stalin's notorious slave-labor compounds. The protagonist is a simple man trying to survive the brutality of a totalitarian system." Shapiro. Fic for Youth. 3d edition

Spark, Muriel

The prime of Miss Jean Brodie. Lippincott 1962 c1961 187p hardcover o.p. paperback available $11   **Fic**

1. Teachers—Fiction 2. Edinburgh (Scotland)—Fiction

ISBN 0-06-092398-9 (pa)

Also available in hardcover from Borgo Press and in paperback from New Am. Lib.

First published 1961 in the United Kingdom

"Miss Jean Brodie, teacher at the Marcia Blaine School for Girls in Edinburgh in the 1930s, gathers around herself a group of young girls who are set apart from other students as the Brodie set. . . . Miss Brodie will make these girls the 'crème de la crème,' especially if they will follow her advice to recognize their prime. Her teaching is unorthodox and her relationship with the students most informal, so that they are privy to her affair with the school's music teacher. We get glimpses into the future of these young girls and are made aware that students are capable of treachery as well as teacher-worship." Shapiro. Fic for Youth. 3d edition

Staples, Suzanne Fisher

Shabanu; daughter of the wind. Knopf 1989 240p $18; lib bdg $18.99; pa $14.99   **Fic**

1. Pakistan—Fiction 2. Sex role—Fiction

ISBN 0-394-84815-2; 0-394-94815-7 (lib bdg); 0-679-81030-7 (pa)   LC 89-2714

In a year that brings a destructive sandstorm, a feud with a rich landowner, and other disasters, Shabanu, the eleven-year-old daughter of a nomad in the Cholistan Desert of Pakistan, becomes a victim of her people's views of sex role and marriage

"Interspersing native words throughout adds realism, but may trip up readers, who must be patient enough to find meaning through context. This use of language is, however, an important element in helping Staples paint an evocative picture of life in the desert that includes references to the hard facts of reality." Booklist

Steinbeck, John, 1902-1968

Cannery Row. Viking 1945 208p hardcover o.p. paperback available $9.95   **Fic**

1. Monterey (Calif.)—Fiction

ISBN 0-14-018737-5 (pa)

"In this episodic work Steinbeck returned to the manner of Tortilla Flat (1935) and produced a rambling account of the adventures and misadventures of workers in a California cannery and their friends." Herzberg. Reader's Ency of Am Lit

Followed by Sweet Thursday (1954)

The grapes of wrath; introduction by Studs Terkel. Viking 1989 xx, 619p $25; pa $11.95   **Fic**

1. Migrant labor—Fiction 2. California—Fiction

ISBN 0-670-82638-3; 0-14-018640-9 (pa)

            LC 88-40296

Also available in Everyman's library edition

First published 1939

"Awarded the Pulitzer Prize in 1940, this moving and highly successful proletarian novel tells of the hardships of the Joad family. 'Okie' farmers forced out of their home in the Oklahoma dustbowl region by economic desperation, they drive to California in search of work as migrant fruitpickers. The grandparents die on the way; on their arrival the others are harassed by the police and participate in strike violence, during which Tom, the Joad son, kills a man. At the conclusion of the novel, throughout which descriptive and philosophical passages alternate with narrative portions, the family is defeated but still resolute." Reader's Ency. 4th edition

Of mice and men. Viking 1986 107p $19.95; pa $8.95   **Fic**

1. Migrant labor—Fiction 2. Ranch life—Fiction 3. Mentally handicapped—Fiction 4. California—Fiction

ISBN 0-670-52071-3; 0-14-018642-5 (pa)

            LC 86-1300

Also available G.K. Hall large print edition and in paperback from Dufour Eds.

First published 1937 by Covici-Friede

"Two uneducated laborers dream of a time when they can share the ownership of a rabbit farm in Califonia. George is a plotter and a schemer, while Lennie is a mentally deficient hulk of a man who has no concept of his physical strength. As a team they are not particularly successful, but their friendship is enduring." Shapiro. Fic for Youth. 3d edition

The pearl; with drawings by José Clemente Orozco. Viking 1947 122p il hardcover o.p. paperback available $8.95   **Fic**

1. Mexico—Fiction 2. Poverty—Fiction

ISBN 0-14-0818738-3 (pa)

"Kino, a poor pearl-fisher, lives a happy albeit spartan life with his wife and their child. When he finds a magnificent pearl, the Pearl of the World, he is besieged by dishonest pearl merchants and envious neighbors. Even a greedy doctor ties his professional treatment of their baby when it is bitten by a scorpion to the possible acquisition of the pearl. After a series of disasters, Kino throws the pearl away since it has brought him only unhappiness." Shapiro. Fic for Youth. 3d edition

Stendhal, 1783-1842
The red and the black   Fic
1. France—History—1815-1914—Fiction
Hardcover and paperback editions available from various publishers
Original French edition, 1830; first United States edition published 1898 by G.H. Richmond
"The author's most celebrated work, it is equally acclaimed for its psychological study of its protagonist—the provincial young romantic Julien Sorel—and as a satiric analysis of the French social order under the Bourbon restoration. Its intensely dramatic plot is purposively romantic in nature, while Stendhal's careful portraiture of Sorel's inner states is the work of a master realist, foreshadowing new developments in the form of the novel." Reader's Ency. 4th edition

Stevenson, Robert Louis, 1850-1894
Dr. Jekyll and Mr. Hyde   Fic

Hardcover and paperback editions available from various publishers
First published 1886 with title: The strange case of Dr. Jekyll and Mr. Hyde
"The disturbing tale of the dual personality of Dr. Jekyll, a physician. A generous and philanthropic man, he is preoccupied with the problems of good and evil and with the possibility of separating them into two distinct personalities. He develops a drug that transforms him into the demonic Mr. Hyde, in whose person he exhausts all the latent evil in his nature. He also creates an antidote that will restore him to his respectable existence as Dr. Jekyll. Gradually, however, the unmitigated evil of his darker self predominates, until finally he performs an atrocious murder. . . . The novel is of great psychological perception and strongly concerned with ethical problems." Reader's Ency. 4th edition

Treasure Island   Fic
1. Buried treasure—Fiction 2. Pirates—Fiction
Hardcover and paperback editions available from various publishers
First published 1882
Young Jim Hawkins discovers a treasure map in the chest of an old sailor who dies under mysterious circumstances at his mother's inn. He shows it to Dr. Livesey and Squire Trelawney who agree to outfit a ship and sail to Treasure Island. Among the crew is the pirate Long John Silver and his followers who are in pursuit of the treasure
"A masterpiece among romances. . . . Pew, Black Dog, and Long John Silver are a villainous trio, strongly individualized, shedding an atmosphere of malignancy and terror. The scenery of isle and ocean contrasts vividly with the savagery of the action." Baker. Guide to the Best Fic

Stewart, Mary, 1916-
Mary Stewart's Merlin trilogy. Morrow 1980 919p maps $19.95   Fic
1. Arthur, King—Fiction 2. Merlin (Legendary character)—Fiction 3. Great Britain—History—0-1066—Fiction
ISBN 0-688-00347-8   LC 80-21019
The three novels in this volume are also available separately in paperback from Fawcett Crest

An omnibus edition of: The crystal cave, The hollow hills and The last enchantment, first published 1970, 1973 and 1979 respectively
The first novel in this trilogy based on Arthurian legends concerns the difficult childhood and youth of the magician Merlin who grows up as a bastard at the court of the King of Wales where he is believed to be the offspring of the King's daughter and the devil. He gains much knowledge from a learned wizard and escapes to "Less Britain" where he becomes involved in efforts to unite all of Britain. The second novel tells of Merlin's involvement with the childhood of Arthur and Arthur's search for the magical sword, Caliburn. The last novel deals with Merlin's death and Arthur's turbulent reign
The author's "skill in creating colorful characters, suspense, and a brooding atmosphere serves her well in portraying England's Dark Ages, where witches, sorcerers, and tragic kings moved heroically through an enchanted land. Though Arthur's rise to power is the subject, the true star and narrator of the tale is Merlin the magician." Husband. Sequels
Includes bibliographical references

The prince and the pilgrim. Morrow 1995 292p map $23   Fic
1. Arthur, King—Fiction 2. Great Britain—History—0-1066—Fiction
ISBN 0-688-14538-8   LC 95-11366
Also available Thorndike Press large print edition
In this novel the author examines "two lesser-known characters from Malory's Le Morte d' Arthur. She enlarges upon and gives wonderful detail to Alexander, a young prince who sets off on a quest to avenge his father's assassination and to Alice, a gentle young lass who accompanies her father on pilgrimages to Holy shrines. Their stories are told in five alternating chapters until they meet, fall in love, and vanquish the foe in the exciting climax." SLJ

Stoker, Bram, 1847-1912
Dracula   Fic
1. Horror fiction 2. Vampires—Fiction
Hardcover and paperback editions available from various publishers
First published 1897
"Count Dracula, an 'undead' villain from Transylvania, uses his supernatural powers to lure and prey upon innocent victims from whom he gains the blood on which he lives. The novel is written chiefly in the form of journals kept by the principal characters—Jonathan Harker, who contacts the vampire in his Transylvanian castle; Harker's fiancée (later his wife), Mina, adored by the Count; the well-meaning Dr. Seward; and Lucy Westenra, a victim who herself becomes a vampire. The doctor and friends destroy Dracula in the end, but only after they drive a stake through Lucy's heart to save her soul." Merriam-Webster's Ency of Lit

Stone, Irving, 1903-1989
The agony and the ecstasy; a novel of Michelangelo. Doubleday 1961 664p o.p.; NAL/Dutton paperback available $6.99   Fic
1. Michelangelo Buonarroti, 1475-1564—Fiction 2. Italy—Fiction
ISBN 0-451-17135-7 (pa)
Available in hardcover from Buccaneer Bks.

Stone, Irving, 1903-1989—*Continued*

"Michelangelo's career is traced from his promising boyhood apprenticeships to the painter Ghirlandajo and the sculptor Bertoldo thru all the many years of his flowering genius. . . . Florence and Rome are the principal cities which serve as background for the development of the artist's life and work." Chicago Sunday Trib

"Stone's Michelangelo is an idealized version, purged not only of ambisexuality, but of the egotism, faultfinding, harsh irony, and ill temper that we know were characteristic of Michelangelo." Saturday Rev

Stowe, Harriet Beecher, 1811-1896

Uncle Tom's cabin   **Fic**
1. African Americans—Fiction 2. Slavery—Fiction
Hardcover and paperback editions available from various publishers
First published in book form 1852

"The book relates the trials, suffering, and human dignity of Uncle Tom, an old black slave. Cruelly treated by a Yankee plantation owner, Simon Legree, Tom dies as the result of a beating. Uncle Tom is devoted to Little Eva, the daughter of his white owner, Augustine St. Clare. Other important characters are the mulatto girl Eliza; the impish black child Topsy; Miss Ophelia St. Clare, a New England spinster; and Marks, the slave catcher. The setting is Kentucky and Louisiana." Reader's Ency. 4th edition

Styron, William, 1925-

The confessions of Nat Turner. Modern Lib. 1994 xliv, 428p $15.50; pa $13   **Fic**
1. Turner, Nat, 1800?-1831—Fiction 2. Slavery—Fiction 3. Southampton Insurrection, 1831—Fiction
ISBN 0-679-60101-5; 0-679-73663-8 (pa)
LC 94-9393

Also available from Buccaneer Bks.
A reissue of the title first published 1967 by Random House

This "account of an actual person and event is based on the brief contemporary pamphlet of the same title presented to a trial court as evidence and published in Virginia a year after the revolt of fellow slaves led by Turner in 1831. Imagining much of Turner's youth and early manhood before the rebellion that he headed at the age of 31, Styron in frequently rhetorical and pseudo-Biblical style has Turner recall his religious faith and his power of preaching to other slaves." Oxford Companion to Am Lit. 5th edition

Sophie's choice. Random House 1979 515p $29.95; pa $13   **Fic**
1. Authors—Fiction 2. Jews—United States—Fiction 3. Brooklyn (New York, N.Y.)—Fiction
ISBN 0-394-46109-6; 0-679-73637-9 (pa)

"Sophie Zawistowska is a Polish Catholic who has somehow survived Auschwitz and resettled in America after the war. Here, in a Jewish boarding house in Flatbush, she meets two men—Nathan Landau, a brilliant but dangerously unstable Jew who becomes her lover; and Stingo, a young Southern writer (and autobiographical simulacrum of Styron himself). The novel traces Stingo's intense involvement with the lovers—their euphoric highs as well as their cataclysmic descents into

psychopathy—and his growing fascination with the horror of Sophie's past." Libr J

"It was a daring act for Styron, whose sensibilities are wholly Southern, to venture into the territory of the American Jew, to say nothing of his plunge into European history. The book is powerfully moving." Burgess. 99 Novels

Sutcliff, Rosemary, 1920-1992

The Shining Company. Farrar, Straus & Giroux 1990 295p $14.95; pa $6.95   **Fic**
1. Great Britain—History—0-1066—Fiction 2. Adventure fiction
ISBN 0-374-36807-4; 0-374-46616-5 (pa)
LC 89-46142

This novel is "based on 'The Gododdin,' the earliest surviving poem set in Northern Britain. Set in A.D. 600, the story is told by Prosper who, with his bodyservant Conn, joins Prince Gorthyn as a shieldbearer when the prince enlists in a company formed by King Mynyddog of the Gododdin in an effort to unite the British kingdoms against the ever-present Saxon threat. The bulk of the story concerns the forging of men from disparate parts of Britain into a fighting unit, combined in a common cause. The rousing climax comes with their first mission when, sent deep into Saxon territory, they are abandoned by Mynyddog." SLJ

"The realistic telling of the tale makes Sutcliff's story interesting. She creates a setting so genuine that readers will find themselves transposed into another time and place." Voice Youth Advocates

Swarthout, Glendon Fred

Bless the beasts and children; [by] Glendon Swarthout. Doubleday 1970 205p o.p.; Pocket Bks. paperback available $5.99   **Fic**
1. Camps—Fiction
ISBN 0-671-52151-9 (pa)

"Six rich teenagers, rejected by their parents and avoided by their peers, group together at Box Canyon Summer Boys' Camp. Fragile egos and self-destructive personalities begin to heal under the leadership of Cotton, who gently pokes fun at their soft spots while building up their self-esteem. An effort on the part of the group to stop the wanton slaughter of buffalo provides a high point of suspense." Shapiro. Fic for Youth. 3d edition

Swift, Jonathan, 1667-1745

Gulliver's travels   **Fic**
1. Fantasy fiction
Hardcover and paperback editions available from various publishers
First published 1726

"In the account of his four wonder-countries Swift satirizes contemporary manners and morals, art and politics—in fact the whole social scheme—from four different points of view. The huge Brobdingnagians reduce man to his natural insignificance, the little people of Lilliput parody Europe and its petty broils, in Laputa philosophers are ridiculed, and finally all Swift's hatred and contempt find their satisfaction in degrading humanity to a bestial condition." Baker. Guide to the Best Fic

Tan, Amy

The hundred secret senses. Putnam 1995 358p $24.95 **Fic**

1. Chinese Americans—Fiction 2. Sisters—Fiction

ISBN 0-399-14114-6   LC 95-31791

Also available Thorndike Press large print edition and in paperback from Ivy Bks.

"Nearing divorce from her husband, Simon, Olivia Yee is guided by her elder half-sister, the irrepressible Kwan, into the heart of China. Olivia was five when 18-year-old Kwan first joined her family in the United States, and though always irritated by Kwan's oddities, Olivia was entranced by her eerie dreams of the ghost World of Yin. Only when visiting Kwan's home in Changmian does Olivia realize the dreams are, in Kwan's mind, memories from past lives. . . . Tan tells a mysterious, believable story and delivers Kwan's clipped, immigrant voice and engaging personality with charming clarity." Libr J

The Joy Luck Club. Putnam 1989 288p $22.95 **Fic**

1. Chinese Americans—Fiction 2. Mothers and daughters—Fiction

ISBN 0-399-13420-4   LC 88-26492

Also available Thorndike Press large print edition and in paperback from Vintage Bks. and Ivy Bks.

"Four aging Chinese women who knew life in China before 1949 and now live in San Francisco meet regularly to play mah-jongg and share thoughts about their American-born children. In alternating sections we learn about the cultural differences between the elderly 'aunties' and the younger generation. When one of the older women dies, her daughter is pressed to take her place in the Joy Luck Club. Her feeling of being out of place gradually gives way to an understanding of the need to retain cultural continuity and an appreciation for the strength and endurance of the older women." Shapiro. Fic for Youth. 3d edition

Temple, Frances, 1945-1995

Taste of salt; a story of modern Haiti. Orchard Bks. 1992 179p $15.95; lib bdg $16.99 **Fic**

1. Aristide, Jean-Bertrand—Fiction 2. Haiti—Fiction

ISBN 0-531-05459-4; 0-531-08609-7 (lib bdg)

     LC 92-6716

"A Richard Jackson book"

In the hospital after being beaten by Macoutes, seventeen-year-old Djo tells the story of his impoverished life to Jeremie, a young woman who, like him, has been working with the social reformer Father Aristide to fight the repression in Haiti

"Frequently in a political novel such literary elements as plot, character, motivation, and pacing are sacrificed to polemical discourse. Frances Temple doesn't make that mistake. . . . The book is a deeply felt, provocative statement of human courage." Horn Book

Tepper, Sheri S.

Beauty; a novel. Doubleday 1991 412p o.p.; Bantam Bks. paperback available $5.99 **Fic**

1. Fantasy fiction

ISBN 0-553-29527-6 (pa)   LC 90-22305

"A Foundation book"

This fantasy "takes the form of a diary, written by a 15-year-old girl of noble birth, begun in 1347 as the unsuspecting heroine is about to embark upon a harrowing journey through time and space. It is not long before readers recognize the writer as a familiar character, 'Sleeping Beauty'. Tepper's triumph in this novel is in turning Beauty simultaneously into a distinctive human character and a glowing symbol of humanity's hope. . . . Language, story, and setting combine to enliven the character and amplify the theme." SLJ

Tevis, Walter S., 1928-1984

The queen's gambit; [by] Walter Tevis. Random House 1983 243p **Fic**

1. Chess—Fiction 2. Orphans—Fiction

     LC 82-15058

Available in hardcover from Ultramarine

This is the "story of an orphan girl who is taught to play chess by the janitor of her orphanage. Beth Harmon has genius; she wins her first tournament when she is 14, becomes American champion at 18 and starts the international circuit. She may well be the second best player in the world. Only the world champion, a Russian . . . is stronger than she, and she is scared to death of him. The climax of the book comes when they meet over the board in a Moscow tournament." N Y Times Book Rev

"The suspense of [Beth's] confrontation with the European masters in Russia is so skillfully portrayed that even readers with no chess experience will feel the excitement." SLJ

Tey, Josephine, 1896-1952

The daughter of time. Macmillan 1952 c1951 204p o.p.; Simon & Schuster paperback available $9 **Fic**

1. Richard III, King of England, 1452-1485—Fiction 2. Mystery fiction 3. Great Britain—Fiction

ISBN 0-684-803386-0 (pa)

Also available in hardcover from Buccaneer Bks.

First published 1951 in England

"Alan Grant, injured policeman hospitalized and bored, is diverted by a photograph of Richard III, commonly conceded murderer of the princes in the Tower. With the invaluable assistance of a research student, Grant's convalescence becomes a lively pursuit of the truth as shown by records in Richard's time." Libr J

The author "not only reconstructs the probably historical truth, she re-creates the intense dramatic excitement of the scholarly research necessary to unveil it." N Y Times Book Rev

Thackeray, William Makepeace, 1811-1863

Vanity fair **Fic**

1. Great Britain—Fiction

Hardcover and paperback editions available from various publishers

First published 1848

"The book is a densely populated, multi-layered panorama of manners and human frailties. . . . The novel deals mainly with the interwoven fortunes of two women, the wellborn, passive Amelia Sedley and the ambitious, essentially amoral Becky Sharp, the latter perhaps the most memorable character Thackeray created. The adventuress Becky is the character around whom all the men play their parts." Merriam-Webster's Ency of Lit

Theroux, Paul
The Mosquito Coast; a novel; with woodcuts by
David Frampton. Houghton Mifflin 1982 374p
Fic
1. Honduras—Fiction 2. Inventors—Fiction 3. Allegories
LC 81-6787
Available in hardcover from Buccaneer Bks. and in
paperback from Avon Bks. and Penguin Bks.
"Allie Fox, a cantankerous Yankee inventor fed up
with an America gone soft, pursues his obsession with
total self-sufficency to the wild coast of Honduras, dragging
his devoted but uneasy family behind. His aim is to
make a 'slightly better job than God' of this poisoned
world, as far from cheeseburgers and drive-in churches
as possible. And his ingenious pioneer Eden actually
works, until his swelling egomania finally topples it."
Libr J
"The physical impact of the style, the exact observation,
the occasional intrusion of the hallucinatory make
this a remarkable work of art; its philosophical content
is profound." Burgess. 99 Novels

Tolkien, J. R. R. (John Ronald Reuel), 1892-1973
The hobbit; or, There and back again; illustrated
by the author. Houghton Mifflin 1938 310p il
hardcover o.p. paperback available $11.95   Fic
1. Fantasy fiction
ISBN 0-395-28265-9 (pa)
First published 1937 in the United Kingdom
"This fantasy features the adventures of hobbit Bilbo
Baggins, who joins a band of dwarves led by Gandalf
the Wizard. Together they seek to recover the stolen
treasure that is hidden in Lonely Mountain and guarded
by Smaug the Dragon. This book precedes the *Lord of
the Rings* trilogy." Shapiro. Fic for Youth. 3d edition

The lord of the rings. 2nd ed. Houghton Mifflin
1986 c1966 3v ea $21.95; pa $11.95   Fic
1. Fantasy fiction
Also available in a boxed set for $75, pa $45.95
(ISBN 0-395-19395-8; 0-395-48907-5)
The trilogy was first published 1954-55 in the United
Kingdom. This revised edition first published 1966 in the
United Kingdom
Contents: v1 The fellowship of the ring (ISBN 0-395-
48931-8; 0-395-27223-8); v2 The two towers (ISBN 0-
395-48933-4; 0-395-27222-X); v3 The return of the king
(ISBN 0-395-48930-X; 0-395-27221-1)
"This is a tale of imaginary gnomelike creatures who
battle against evil. Led by Frodo, the hobbits embark on
a journey to prevent a magic ring from falling into the
grasp of the powers of darkness. The forces of good succeed
in their fight against the Dark Lord of evil, and
Frodo and Sam bring the Ring to Mount Doom, where
it is destroyed." Shapiro. Fic for Youth. 3d edition

Tolstoy, Leo, graf, 1828-1910
Anna Karenina   Fic
1. Russia—Fiction
Hardcover and paperback editions available from various
publishers
Written in 1873-1876

This novel is "the story of a tragic, adulterous love.
Anna meets and falls in love with Aleksei Vronski, a
handsome young officer. She abandons her child and
husband in order to be with Vronski. When she thinks
Vronski has tired of her, she kills herself by leaping under
a train. . . . A subplot concerns the contrasting happy
marriage of Konstantin Levin and his young wife Kitty.
Levin's search for meaning in his life and his love for
a natural, simple existence on his estate are reflections of
Tolstoy's own moods and thoughts of the time." Reader's
Ency. 4th edition

War and peace   Fic
1. Napoleon I, Emperor of the French, 1769-1821—
Fiction 2. Russia—Fiction
Hardcover and paperback editions available from various
publishers
Original Russian edition, 1864-1869
"The story covers roughly the years between 1805 and
1820, centering on the invasion of Russia by Napoleon's
army in 1812 and the Russian resistance to the invader.
Over five hundred characters, all carefully rendered, populate
the pages of the novel. Every social level, from Napoleon
himself to the peasant Platon Karatayev, is represented.
Interwoven with the story of the war are narrations
of the lives of several main characters, especially
those of Natasha Rostova, Prince Andrey Bolkonsky, and
Pierre Bezukhov. These people are shown as they progress
from youthful uncertainties and searchings toward a
more mature understanding of life." Reader's Ency. 4th
edition

Traven, B.
The treasure of the Sierra Madre. Knopf 1935
366p o.p.; Hill & Wang paperback available
$10.95   Fic
1. Gold mines and mining—Fiction 2. Mexico—Fiction
ISBN 0-374-52149-2 (pa)
Also available Thorndike Press large print edition and
in hardcover from Amereon and Bentley
Original German edition, 1927
This novel analyzes the "psychology of greed in telling
of three Americans searching for a lost gold mine in
Mexican mountains." Oxford Companion to Am Lit. 5th
edition

Trumbo, Dalton, 1905-1976
Johnny got his gun. Stuart, L. 1970 c1959 309p
$9.95   Fic
1. World War, 1914-1918—Fiction 2. Physically
handicapped—Fiction
ISBN 0-8184-0110-9
Also available in paperback from Citadel Press
A reissue of the title published 1939 by Lippincott
"Far more than an antiwar polemic, this compassionate
description of the effects of war on one soldier is a
poignant tribute to the human instinct to survive. Badly
mutilated, blind, and deaf, Johnny fights to communicate
with an uncomprehending medical world debating his
fate." Shapiro. Fic for Youth. 3d edition

Twain, Mark, 1835-1910

The adventures of Huckleberry Finn   **Fic**
1. Mississippi River—Fiction 2. Missouri—Fiction
Hardcover and paperback editions available from various publishers
First published 1885. This is a companion volume to: The adventures of Tom Sawyer
This novel "begins with Huck's escape from his drunken, brutal father to the river, where he meets up with Jim, a runaway slave. The story of their journey downstream, with occasional forays into the society along the banks, is an American classic that captures the smells, rhythms, and sounds, the variety of dialects and the human activity of life on the great river. It is also a penetrating social commentary that reveals corruption, moral decay, and intellectual impoverishment through Huck and Jim's encounters with traveling actors and con men, lynch mobs, thieves, and Southern gentility." Reader's Ency. 4th edition

The adventures of Tom Sawyer   **Fic**
1. Mississippi River—Fiction 2. Missouri—Fiction
Hardcover and paperback editions available from various publishers
First published 1876. This is a companion volume to: The adventures of Huckleberry Finn
"Tom, a shrewd and adventurous boy, is at home in the respectable world of his Aunt Polly, as well as in the self-reliant, parentless world of Huck Finn. The two friends, out in the cemetery under a full moon, attempt to cure warts with a dead cat. They accidentally witness a murder, of which Muff Potter is later wrongly accused. Knowing that the true murderer is Injun Joe, the boys are helpless with fear; they decide to run away to Jackson's Island. After a few pleasant days of smoking and swearing, they realize that the townspeople believe them dead. Returning in time to hear their funeral eulogies, they become town heroes. At the trial of Muff Potter, Tom, unable to let an innocent person be condemned, reveals his knowledge. Injun Joe flees. Later Tom and his sweetheart, Becky Thatcher, get lost in the cave in which the murderer is hiding. They escape, and Tom and Huck return to find the treasure Joe has buried." Reader's Ency. 4th edition

A Connecticut Yankee in King Arthur's court
   Fic
1. Arthur, King—Fiction 2. Chivalry—Fiction
3. Great Britain—History—0-1066—Fiction
Hardcover and paperback editions available from various publishers
First published 1889; published in the United Kingdom with title: Yankee at the court of King Arthur
This satiric novel is a "tale of a commonsensical Yankee who is carried back in time to Britain in the Dark Ages, and it celebrates homespun ingenuity and democratic values in contrast to the superstitious ineptitude of a feudal monarchy." Merriam-Webster's Ency of Lit

The prince and the pauper   **Fic**
1. Edward VI, King of England, 1537-1553—Fiction
2. Great Britain—History—1485-1603, Tudors—Fiction
Hardcover and paperback editions available from various publishers
First published 1881

"Edward VI of England and a little pauper change places a few days before Henry VIII's death. The prince wanders in rags, while Tom Canty suffers the horrors of princedom. At the last moment, the mistake is rectified." Reader's Ency. 4th edition

Tyler, Anne, 1941-
Dinner at the Homesick Restaurant. Knopf 1982 303p $25   **Fic**
1. Family life—Fiction 2. Maryland—Fiction
ISBN 0-394-52381-4   LC 81-13694
Also available in paperback from Ivy Bks. and Fawcett Bks.
"Pearl Tull, an angry woman who vacillates between excesses of maternal energy and spurts of terrifying rage, has been deserted by her husband and has brought up her three children alone. Cody, the eldest, is handsome, wild, and in a lifelong battle of jealousy with his young brother, the sweet-tempered and patient Ezra. Their sister Jenny tries, through three marriages, to find a stability which was never present in Pearl's home. Ezra also tries to achieve a permanence through his homey Homesick Restaurant in Baltimore, but he is cruelly tricked by his brother and is unable to establish any unity in the family." Shapiro. Fic for Youth. 3d edition

Undset, Sigrid, 1882-1949
Kristin Lavransdatter; translated from the Norwegian. Knopf 1935 3v in 1 $40   **Fic**
1. Norway—Fiction
ISBN 0-394-43262-2
Also available in 3 paperback volumes ea $8.95 (ISBN v1 0-394-75299-6; v2 0-394-75293-7; v3 0-394-75291-0)
Although the "action takes place in the fourteenth century, the lives of the characters are marked by almost the same problems depicted in modern novels: passion, adultery, premarital pregnancy, ambition, conflict. Kristin, daughter of Lavrans and Ragnfrid, is betrothed to Simon Andressön but falls in love with Erlend Nikulassön and finally wins her father's approval to marry him. Her father realizes on their wedding night that they are already lovers. The book follows Kristin's life as she tries to manage her estate and as her husband loses his lands and leaves her after a bitter quarrel. After several attempts at reconciliation, Erlend returns, only to be killed in a fight. The six sons of Kristin follow different paths. Two die during the Black Plague, which was so dreadful a scourge in that era. The portrayal of this Norwegian woman is vivid and human." Shapiro. Fic for Youth. 3d edition

Updike, John
Rabbit, run. Knopf 1960 307p $25   **Fic**
1. Pennsylvania—Fiction
ISBN 0-394-44206-7
Also available in paperback from Fawcett Bks.
"A brilliant evocation of everyday life in America and the longings and frustrations of family life. Harry Angstrom ('Rabbit') is a salesman who, on an impulse, leaves home, his alcoholic wife, Janice, and his child, Nelson, to find freedom. After several escapades and a liaison with an ex-prostitute, he returns to his wife and

Updike, John—*Continued*

child and attempts to settle down again. Rabbit's malaise is not so much a yearning for freedom as, perhaps, a yearning for guiding spiritual values and meaning. At the end, still dissatisfied and guilt-ridden because of the responsibility he feels for the death of his second child, he begins running again." Reader's Ency. 4th edition

Followed by Rabbit redux (1971); Rabbit is rich (1981); and Rabbit at rest (1990)

Uris, Leon, 1924-

Exodus. Doubleday 1958 626p il   **Fic**

1. Zionism—Fiction

Available in hardcover from Buccaneer Bks. and in paperback from Bantam Bks.

"Following World War II the British forbade immigration of the Jews to Israel. European Jewish underground groups, aided by Palestinian agent Ari Ben Canaan, made every effort to aid these unfortunate victims of Nazi persecution. The novel provides insight into the heritage of the Jews and understanding of the danger involved in helping them reach a safe haven. It also includes the warm love story of Ari and a gentile nurse, Kitty Fremont, who cared very much for the welfare of the Jewish children caught in this nightmare." Shapiro. Fic for Youth. 3d edition

Verdelle, A. J., 1960-

The good negress. Algonquin Bks. 1995 298p $19.95   **Fic**

1. African Americans—Fiction 2. Detroit (Mich.)—Fiction

ISBN 1-56512-085-X   LC 94-40889

Also available in paperback from HarperCollins

Set in Virginia and Detroit during the 1950s and 1960s, this novel "is the coming-of-age story of Denise Palms, who leaves her grandmother's rural home to return to her family in Detroit. Denise's family expects her to concentrate on housework and childcare, but her teacher pushes her to spend time on afterschool lessons in diction and grammar in order to 'better' herself." Libr J

"Verdelle's truly fine debut novel belongs in the ranks of other classics in African American folk vernacular." Choice

Verne, Jules, 1828-1905

Around the world in eighty days   **Fic**

1. Voyages around the world—Fiction 2. Adventure fiction

Hardcover and paperback editions available from various publishers

Original French edition, 1873

"The hero, Phileas Fogg, undertakes his hasty world tour as the result of a bet made at his London club. He and his French valet Passepartout, meet with some fantastic adventures, but these are overcome by the loyal servant and the endlessly inventive Fogg. The feat they perform is incredible for its day; Fogg wins his bet, having circled the world in only eighty days." Reader's Ency. 4th edition

Twenty thousand leagues under the sea   **Fic**

1. Submarines—Fiction 2. Sea stories 3. Science fiction

LC 91-27739

Hardcover and paperback editions available from various publishers

Original French edition, 1870

"The voyage of the *Nautilus* permitted Verne to describe the wonders of an undersea world almost totally unknown to the general public of the period. Indebted to literary tradition for his Atlantis, he made his major innovation in having the submarine completely powered by electricity, although the interest in electrical forces goes back to Poe and Shelley. So far as the enigmatic ending is concerned, his readers had to wait for the three-part *The Mysterious Island* (1874-1875) to learn that Nemo had been the Indian warrior-prince Dakkar, who had been involved in the Sepoy Mutiny of 1857." Anatomy of Wonder 4

Vidal, Gore, 1925-

Lincoln. Modern Lib. 1993 712p $19   **Fic**

1. Lincoln, Abraham, 1809-1865—Fiction 2. United States—History—1861-1865, Civil War—Fiction

ISBN 0-679-60048-5   LC 92-27273

Also available in hardcover from Buccaneer Bks.

A reissue of the title first published 1984 by Random House

A volume in the author's American chronicle series

"In the atmosphere of intrigue that permanently settled over Washington City during the Civil War, the initially unpromising Lincoln, an unlikely hero, rises to greatness; despite almost insurmountable troubles that deteriorate his physical and mental well-being, Lincoln shows his true mastery of crisis leadership, necessary not only to save the Union but to refashion it." Booklist

This novel "is not so much an imaginative reconstruction of an era as an intelligent, lucid and highly informative transcript of it, never less than workmanlike in its blocking out of scenes and often extremely compelling." N Y Times Book Rev

Vinge, Joan D., 1948-

Psion. Delacorte Press 1982 346p o.p.; Warner Bks. paperback available $5.99   **Fic**

1. Science fiction 2. Telepathy—Fiction

ISBN 0-446-60354-6 (pa)   LC 82-70323

"Cat, an adolescent boy from the slums of spaceport Quarro is a survivor. Of mixed parentage, part alien, part human, he is an accomplished pickpocket and thief when he tangles with three Contract Labor recruiters. To escape conscription he 'volunteers' for an experimental program that teaches psychics to control and use their psychic powers. Cat soon finds himself involved in interplanetary intrigue as he becomes involved in a criminal plot to take over the crystal rich planet of Cinder." Voice Youth Advocates

"The book is written in the first person, cleverly alternating between thoughts, dreams and reality. It paints a grim and credible future with richness and psychological depth." Best Sellers

Voigt, Cynthia

Jackaroo. Atheneum Pubs. 1985 291p $18.95
Fic

1. Heroes and heroines—Fiction
ISBN 0-689-31123-0   LC 85-7954
Also available in paperback from Fawcett Bks.
"An Argo book"

"In a far-off feudal kingdom, where the people are hungry and oppressed by the lords, 16-year-old Gwyn, the innkeeper's daughter, takes on the identity of a masked legendary hero, Jackaroo, whose brave deeds for the poor have always inspired hope in harsh times." Booklist

"The style is fluid and consistent with the personalities of her characters; the setting is evoked through skillfully crafted description; the situations speak directly to the human condition. What is most notable, however, is the skill with which the social and political structures are described without interrupting the flow of the plot." Horn Book

The runner. Atheneum Pubs. 1985 181p $15.95
Fic

1. Running—Fiction 2. Track athletics—Fiction
ISBN 0-689-31069-2   LC 84-21663
Also available in paperback from Fawcett Bks. and Scholastic

As a dedicated runner, a teenage boy has always managed to distance himself from other people until the experience of coaching one of his teammates on the track team gradually helps him see the value of giving and receiving

"Told through the eyes of Bullet [featured in Dicey's song (1982) and Homecoming (1981)] the coming-of-age story is written in the third person. The technique, meant to distance the reader, is a subtle reflection of Bullet's purposeful disconnection from his feelings and his relationships with others. Cynthia Voigt has once again succeeded in crafting a powerful, intensely moving novel with a singular and memorable main character." Horn Book

Voltaire, 1694-1778

Candide
Fic

Hardcover and paperback editions available from various publishers
Original French edition, 1759

"In this philosophical fantasy, naive Candide sees and suffers such misfortune that he ultimately rejects the philosophy of his tutor Doctor Pangloss, who claims that 'all is for the best in this best of all possible worlds.' Candide and his companions—Pangloss, his beloved Cunegonde, and his servant Cacambo—display an instinct for survival that provides them hope in an otherwise somber setting. When they all retire together to a simple life on a small farm, they discover that the secret of happiness is 'to cultivate one's garden,' a practical philosophy that excludes excessive idealism and nebulous metaphysics." Merriam-Webster's Ency of Lit

Vonnegut, Kurt, 1922-

Cat's cradle; by Kurt Vonnegut, Jr. Holt, Rinehart & Winston 1963 223p o.p.; Dell paperback available $6.50
Fic

1. Atomic bomb—Fiction 2. Science fiction 3. Caribbean region—Fiction
ISBN 0-440-11149-8 (pa)

"In this mordant satire on religion, research, government, and human nature, a free-lance writer becomes the catalyst in a chain of events that unearths the secret of ice-nine. This is an element potentially more lethal than that produced by nuclear fission. The search leads to a mythical island, San Lorenzo, where the writer also discovers the leader of a new religion, Bokonon." Shapiro. Fic for Youth. 3d edition

Slaughterhouse-five; or, The children's crusade: a duty-dance with death. 25th anniversary ed. Delacorte Press; Lawrence, S. 1994 205p il $22.50; pa $6.50
Fic

1. World War, 1939-1945—Fiction 2. Science fiction
ISBN 0-385-31208-3; 0-440-18029-5 (pa)
LC 94-171120

A reissue of the title first published 1969

This novel "mixes a fictionalized account of the author's experience of the fire bombing of Dresden with a compensatory fantasy of the planet Tralfamadore, the science-fiction element is progressively dominated by the overall concerns of satire, black humor, and absurdism." Reader's Ency. 3d edition

"A masterpiece, in which Vonnegut penetrated to the heart of the issues developed in his earlier absurdist fabulations. A key work of modern SF." Anatomy of Wonder 4

Walker, Alice, 1944-

The color purple. 10th anniversary ed. Harcourt Brace Jovanovich 1992 290p il $19.95
Fic

1. African Americans—Fiction 2. Sisters—Fiction 3. Southern States—Fiction
ISBN 0-15-119154-9   LC 91-47202
Also available in hardcover from Buccaneer Bks. and in paperback from Pocket Bks.

A reissue of the title first published 1982

"A feminist novel about an abused and uneducated black woman's struggle for empowerment, the novel was praised for the depth of its female characters and for its eloquent use of black English vernacular." Merriam-Webster's Ency of Lit

Walker, Margaret, 1915-

Jubilee. Houghton Mifflin 1966 497p o.p.; Bantam Bks. paperback available $6.50
Fic

1. African Americans—Fiction 2. United States—History—1861-1865, Civil War—Fiction 3. Reconstruction (1865-1876)—Fiction
ISBN 0-553-27383-3 (pa)

"Vyry was a slave and the daughter of a slave. She suffered slavery's tribulations and looked forward to the time of freedom to bring her a home of her own and provide an education for her children. The Civil War and the Reconstruction period brought the possibility of that day of jubilation, but the attainment of her two desires

Walker, Margaret, 1915——*Continued*
still seemed remote. The author gives a clear picture of
the everyday life of slaves, their modes of behavior, and
the patterns and rhythms of their speech." Shapiro. Fic
for Youth. 3d edition

Warren, Robert Penn, 1905-1989
All the king's men   **Fic**

Hardcover and paperback editions available from various publishers
First published 1946 by Harcourt Brace
"In the South during the 1920s a young journalist,
Jack Burden, becomes involved in the drive for political
power by soon-to-be governor Willie Stark. The journey
is a rocky, disillusioning one, and involves exploitation,
deceit, and violence. When asked by Stark to uncover a
scandal in the past of Judge Irwin, Jack must weigh the
many consequences of such action." Shapiro. Fic for
Youth. 3d edition

Waugh, Evelyn, 1903-1966
Brideshead revisited; with an introduction by
Frank Kermode. Knopf 1993 xxxvii, 315p $17
                                                      Fic
1. Homosexuality—Fiction 2. Great Britain—Fiction
ISBN 0-679-42300-1   LC 93-1854
Also available in paperback from Little, Brown
"Everyman's library"
A reissue of the title first published 1945 by Little,
Brown
"The novel, which takes the form of an extended
flashback, is narrated by Charles Ryder, an army officer
billeted at the eponymous country house, owned by an
aristocratic Roman Catholic family headed by Lord and
Lady Marchman. Charles had visited Brideshead with
Sebastian Flyte, the Marchmains' younger son, when
both were Oxford undergraduates. In the course of the
narrative Ryder conveys his fascination with the family,
all of whom are eccentric or unhappy in some way." Oxford Companion to 20th Cent Lit in Engl

The loved one; an Anglo-American tragedy.
Little, Brown 1948 164p hardcover o.p. paperback
available $11.95   **Fic**
1. Funeral rites and ceremonies—Fiction 2. Hollywood (Calif.)—Fiction
ISBN 0-316-92608-6 (pa)
Available in hardcover from Buccaneer Bks.
"Depicting romance in a mortuary could be gruesome
but the author succeeds both in poking satirical fun at
the maudlin pretentiousness of the funeral industry and
in delighting the reader with a hilarious love story." Shapiro. Fic for Youth. 3d edition

Wells, H. G. (Herbert George), 1866-1946
The invisible man   **Fic**
1. Science fiction
Hardcover and paperback editions available from vari-
ous publishers
First published 1897

"The story concerns the life and death of a scientist
named Griffin who has gone mad. Having learned how
to make himself invisible, Griffin begins to use his invis-
ibility for nefarious purposes, including murder. When he
is finally killed, his body becomes visible again."
Merriam-Webster's Ency of Lit

Seven famous novels; with a preface by the
author. Knopf 1934 860p   **Fic**
1. Science fiction
Available in hardcover from Amereon and P. Smith
Contents: The time machine (1895); The island of Dr.
Moreau (1896); The invisible man (1897); The war of
the worlds (1898); The first men in the moon (1901);
The food of the gods (1904); In the days of the comet
(1906)

The time machine   **Fic**
1. Science fiction
Hardcover and paperback editions available from various publishers
First published 1895
"Wells advanced his social and political ideas in this
narrative of a nameless Time Traveller who is hurtled
into the year 802,701 by his elaborate ivory, crystal, and
brass contraption. The world he finds is peopled by two
races: the decadent Eloi, fluttery and useless, are dependent for food, clothing, and shelter on the simian subterranean Morlocks, who prey on them. The two races—
whose names are borrowed from the Biblical Eli and
Moloch—symbolize Wells's vision of the eventual result
of unchecked capitalism: a neurasthenic upper class that
would eventually be devoured by a proletariat driven to
the depths." Merriam-Webster's Ency of Lit

The war of the worlds   **Fic**
1. Science fiction
Available Thorndike Press large print edition and in
hardcover and paperback from various publishers
First published 1898
"The inhabitants of Mars, a loathsome though highly
organized race, invade England, and by their command
of superior weapons subdue and prey on the people." Baker. Guide to the Best Fic
In this novel the author "introduced the 'Alien' being
into the role which became a cliché—a monstrous invader of Earth, a competitor in a cosmic struggle for existence. Though the Martians were a ruthless and terrible
enemy, HGW was careful to point out that Man had
driven many animal species to extinction, and that human invaders of Tasmania had behaved no less callously
in exterminating their cousins." Sci Fic Ency

West, Dorothy, 1909-
✓ The wedding. Doubleday 1995 240p $20; pa
$9.95   **Fic**
1. African Americans—Fiction 2. Race relations—
Fiction 3. Martha's Vineyard (Mass.)—Fiction
ISBN 0-385-47143-2; 0-385-47144-0 (pa)
                                        LC 94-27285
Also available Thorndike Press large print edition
This novel is "set on Martha's Vineyard during the
1950s and focuses on the black bourgeois community
known as the Oval. Dr. Clark Coles and his wife,
Corrine, highly respected Ovalites, are preparing for the

West, Dorothy, 1909——Continued
wedding of their youngest daughter, Shelby, who, much
to their consternation, is marrying a white jazz musician.
Lute McNeil, a compulsive womanizer who has recently
made a fortune in the furniture business, is determined to
stop Shelby's wedding; he is confident that he can convince Shelby to marry him, which would bring him the
social acceptance he has always craved." Booklist
"Through the ancestral histories of the Coles family,
West . . . subtly reveals the ways in which color can
burden and codify behavior. The author makes her points
with a delicate hand, maneuvering with confidence and
ease through a sometimes incendiary subject." Publ Wkly

West, Jessamyn, d. 1984
The friendly persuasion. Harcourt Brace & Co.
1945 214p hardcover o.p. paperback available $10
                                                       Fic
1. Society of Friends—Fiction 2. Indiana—Fiction
ISBN 0-15-633606-5 (pa)
Available in hardcover from Buccaneer Bks.
"The Birdwell family of Indiana led a quiet life until
the Civil War came into their lives. They were Quakers
and tried to live according to the teachings of William
Penn. Jess Birdwell, a nurseryman, loved a fast horse as
well as his trees and the people he knew. Eliza, his wife,
was a Quaker minister and a gentle, albeit strict, soul.
When the war reached Indiana, Josh, the oldest son, was
torn between his Quaker upbringing and his belief in the
rightness of the Union cause; Mattie was at that difficult
age between childhood and womanhood; and Little Jess,
the youngest, ran into trouble with Eliza's geese. This is
a wonderful family chronicle, with the laughter, tears,
and tenderness that can be found in many families." Shapiro. Fic for Youth. 3d edition

West, Nathanael, 1903-1940
Miss Lonelyhearts. Liveright 1933 213p o.p.;
New Directions paperback available $9.95   Fic
1. Journalists—Fiction
ISBN 0-8112-0215-1 (pa)
"The story of a man who writes an 'advice to the
lovelorn' column, the theme of the book is the loneliness
of the individual in modern society. The hero tries to live
the role of omniscient counselor he has assumed for the
paper, but his attempts to reach out to suffering humanity
are twisted by circumstances, and he is finally murdered
by a man he has tried to help." Reader's Ency. 4th edition

Wharton, Edith, 1862-1937
The age of innocence; introduction by R. W. B.
Lewis. Scribner 361p $40; pa $12.95   Fic
1. New York (N.Y.)—Fiction
ISBN 0-684-14659-2; 0-684-71925-8 (pa)
Also available from Amereon
"Hudson River editions"
First published 1920 by D. Appleton & Co.; first
Scribner edition, 1968
"New York City in the 1920s was a place of tight so-
cial stratification with rituals for everything from ro-
mance to etiquette at the opera. The young attorney
Newland Archer was engaged to lovely, socially accept-
able May Welland. He faced the power of family and so-
cial mores when he became attracted to May's bohemian
cousin, Ellen." Shapiro. Fic for Youth. 3d edition

Ethan Frome   Fic

Hardcover and paperback editions available from various publishers
First published 1911
This is "an ironic tragedy of love, frustration, jealousy, and sacrifice. The scene is a New England village,
where Ethan barely makes a living out of a stony farm
and is at odds with his wife Zeena (short for Zenobia),
a whining hypochrondriac. Mattie, a cousin of Zeena's
comes to live with them, and love develops between her
and Ethan. They try to end their impossible lives by
steering a bobsled into a tree; instead ending up crippled
and tied to Zeena and the barren farm. Zeena, however,
is transformed into a devoted nurse and Mattie becomes
the nagging invalid." Benet's Reader's Ency of Am Lit

Wharton, William
Birdy. Knopf 1979 c1978 309p hardcover o.p.
paperback available $13   Fic
1. Mentally ill—Fiction 2. Birds—Fiction 3. Veterans—Fiction
ISBN 0-679-73412-0 (pa)   LC 77-28023
"At the close of World War II, in the mental ward of
a veteran's hospital, there is a patient whose behavior
quite baffles the psychiatrists. The patient's only childhood friend, another soldier who has a severe facial
wound, is transferred to the hospital in the hope he may
be of help. The friend instantly recognizes that the patient is behaving exactly like a bird. (The keeping of
birds had always been an obsession of the patient
throughout his adolescence.)" Choice
"Only the most rigorous imagination can make a story
of this sort work for a reader who is generally indifferent
to birds. Wharton has just such an imagination." Newsweek

White, Ellen Emerson
The road home. Scholastic 1995 469p $15.95
                                                       Fic
1. Vietnam War, 1961-1975—Fiction 2. Nurses—Fiction
ISBN 0-590-46737-9   LC 94-32173
Rebecca, a young nurse stationed in Vietnam during
the war, must come to grips with her wartime experiences once she returns home to the United States
"The dreadful realities of the war are forcefully conveyed, and Rebecca, who first appeared in the author's
Echo Company series, is an engaging character. The
lengthy novel is engrossing." Horn Book Guide

White, T. H. (Terence Hanbury), 1906-1964
The book of Merlyn; the unpublished conclusion
to The once and future king; prologue by Sylvia
Townsend Warner; illustrated by Trevor Stubley.
University of Tex. Press 1977 xx, 137p il
hardcover o.p. paperback available $10.95   Fic
1. Arthur, King—Fiction 2. Merlin (Legendary char-
acter)—Fiction 3. Great Britain—Fiction
ISBN 0-292-70769-X (pa)   LC 77-3454
Sequel to The once and future king

White, T. H. (Terence Hanbury), 1906-1964—
Continued

"White, who believed that the central theme of Malory's 'Morte d'Arthur' was to find an antidote to war, pursues that theme here, going to the animals for his answer. Old and defeated King Arthur is led by magician Merlyn into a badger's sett where a group of animals are discussing people. It's Merlyn, however, who becomes chief orator." Publ Wkly

"Writing during World War II, White vented his feelings about the futility of war with a fierceness that sometimes overwhelms the intriguing mixture of fantasy, humor, and rationality which pervaded the tetralogy." Booklist

The once and future king. Putnam 1958 677p
$23.95 Fic
1. Arthur, King—Fiction 2. Great Britain—History—0-1066—Fiction
ISBN 0-399-10597-2 LC 58-10760
Also available in paperback from Ace Bks.

An omnibus edition of four novels; The sword in the stone (1939), The witch in the wood (1939, now called The Queen of Air and Darkness) and The ill-made knight (1940). A number of alterations have been made in the earlier books. Previously unpublished, The candle in the wind "deals with the plotting of Mordred and his kinsmen of the house of Orkney, and their undying enmity to King Arthur." Times Lit Suppl

"White's contemporary retelling of Malory's *Le Morte d'Arthur* is both romantic and exciting." Shapiro. Fic for Youth. 3d edition

Wiesel, Elie, 1928-
Night, Dawn, The accident: three tales. Hill & Wang 1972 318p hardcover o.p. paperback available $11 Fic
1. Jews—Fiction
ISBN 0-374-52140-9 (pa)

In Dawn, Elisha, a young Jewish terrorist fighting for the creation of Israel in the 1940s is faced with an agonizing moral dilemma. He is to be the executioner of a British officer in reprisal for the hanging of a captured terrorist. A survivor of the concentration camps and a victim all of his life, Elisha considers whether he is any different from his oppressors if he can execute a helpless prisoner in cold blood. Night is a memoir. The accident concerns a survivor of Auschwitz who, recovering from a near-fatal accident, questions the meaning of man's existence and purpose, and death

Wilde, Oscar, 1854-1900
The picture of Dorian Gray Fic

Hardcover and paperback editions available from various publishers

First published 1891 in the United Kingdom; first United States edition published 1895 by G. Munro's Sons

"An archetypal tale of a young man who purchases eternal youth at the expense of his soul, the novel was a romantic exposition of Wilde's Aestheticism. Dorian Gray is a wealthy Englishman who gradually sinks into a life of dissipation and crime. Despite his unhealthy behavior, his physical appearance remains youthful and unmarked by dissolution. Instead, a portrait of himself catalogues every evil deed by turning his once handsome features into a hideous mask." Merriam-Webster's Ency of Lit

Wilder, Thornton, 1897-1975
The bridge of San Luis Rey; illustrated by Amy Drevenstedt. Boni, A. C. 1967 c1927 235p il o.p.; HarperCollins Pubs. paperback available $10 Fic
1. Peru—Fiction
ISBN 0-06-091341-X (pa)
Available in hardcover from Borgo Press and Buccaneer Bks.

First published 1927

"On Friday, July 20, 1714, high in the Andes of Peru, the famous bridge of San Luis Rey collapsed, killing the five people who were crossing it. A priest who was witness to the event decided that the tragedy provided the chance to prove the wisdom of God in that instance, and thereafter spent years investigating the lives of the people who had been killed." Shapiro. Fic for Youth. 3d edition

Williams-Garcia, Rita
Like sisters on the homefront. Lodestar Bks. 1995 165p $15.99 Fic
1. African Americans—Fiction 2. Family life—Fiction 3. Teenage mothers—Fiction
ISBN 0-525-67465-9 LC 95-3690

"It's bad enough that 14-year-old Gayle has one baby, but when she becomes pregnant again by another boy, Mama's had enough. She takes Gayle for an abortion and then ships her and her baby south to stay with religious relatives. . . . With the help of her dying great-grandmother, who leaves Gayle the family's African-American oral tradition, she begins to mature and understand her place in the family and her future." Child Book Rev Serv

"Beautifully written, the text captures the cadence and rhythm of New York street talk and the dilemma of being poor, black, and uneducated. This is a gritty, realistic, well-told story." SLJ

Wolfe, Thomas, 1900-1938
Look homeward, angel; a story of the buried life; with an introduction by Maxwell E. Perkins. Scribner 563p $45; pa $14 Fic
1. Family life—Fiction
ISBN 0-684-15158-8; 0-684-80443-3 (pa)
Also available in hardcover from Buccaneer Bks.

First published 1929

This novel, autobiographical in character, "describes the childhood and youth of Eugene Gant in the town of Altamont, state of Catawba (said to be Asheville, North Carolina). As Gant grows up, he becomes aware of the relations among his family, meets the eccentric people of the town, goes to college, discovers literature and ideas, has his first love affairs, and at last sets out alone on a mystic and romantic 'pilgrimage.'" Reader's Ency. 4th edition

Followed by Of time and the river (1935)

Wolff, Virginia Euwer
Make lemonade. Holt & Co. 1993 200p $15.95
                                                Fic
1. Teenage mothers—Fiction 2. Babysitters—Fiction
3. Poverty—Fiction
ISBN 0-8050-2228-7   LC 92-41182
Also available Thorndike Press large print edition and
in paperback by Scholastic
"Fourteen-year-old LaVaughn accepts the job of
babysitting Jolly's two small children but quickly realizes
that the young woman, a seventeen-year-old single mother, needs as much help and nurturing as her two neglected children. The four become something akin to a temporary family, and through their relationship each makes
progress toward a better life. Sixty-six brief chapters,
with words arranged on the page like poetry, perfectly
echo the patterns of teenage speech." Horn Book Guide

Probably still Nick Swansen. Holt & Co. 1988
144p $14.95   Fic
1. Learning disabilities—Fiction
ISBN 0-8050-0701-6   LC 88-13175
Sixteen-year-old learning-disabled Nick struggles to
endure a life in which the other kids make fun of him,
he has to take special classes, his date for the prom
makes an excuse not to go with him, and he is haunted
by the memory of his older sister who drowned while he
was watching
"It is a poignant, gentle, utterly believable narrative
that echoes with puzzlement and pain as Nick coura-
geously works through his personal crisis. It is also an
optimistic but real look at the difficulties faced by special kids caught between their limitations and their longing to experience life like everyone else." Booklist

Woodson, Jacqueline
I hadn't meant to tell you this. Delacorte Press
1994 115p $15.95   Fic
1. African Americans—Fiction 2. Friendship—Fiction
3. Incest—Fiction 4. Child sexual abuse—Fiction
ISBN 0-385-32031-0   LC 93-8733
Also available in paperback from Bantam Bks.
Marie, the only black girl in the eighth grade willing
to befriend her white classmate Lena, discovers that
Lena's father is doing horrible things to her in private
"Woodson's characters are deftly drawn, whole individuals; her spare prose and crystal images create a
haunting, poetic novel." Horn Book Guide

Woolf, Virginia, 1882-1941
To the lighthouse. Harcourt Brace & Co. 1927
310p $17; pa $9   Fic
1. Great Britain—Fiction
ISBN 0-15-190737-4; 0-15-690739-9 (pa)
Also available Everyman's Library edition from Knopf
Arranged in three sections, the first "called 'The window,' describes a day during Mr. and Mrs. Ramsay's
house party at their country home by the sea. Mr. Ramsay is a distinguished scholar . . . whose mind works ra-
tionally, heroically and rather icily. . . . The Ramsays
have arranged to take a boat out to the lighthouse, the
next morning, and their little son James is bitterly disappointed when a change in weather makes it impossible.
The second section, called 'Time passes' describes the

seasons and the house, unused and decaying, in the years
after Mrs. Ramsay's death. In the third section, the
'Lighthouse,' Mr. Ramsay and his friends are back at the
house. He takes the postponed trip to the lighthouse with
his now 16-year-old son, who is at last able to communicate silently with him and forgive him for being different
from his mother." Reader's Ency. 4th edition

Wouk, Herman, 1915-
The Caine mutiny; a novel of World War II.
Doubleday 1951 494p $27.50   Fic
1. United States. Navy—Fiction 2. World War, 1939-
1945—Fiction
ISBN 0-385-04053-9
Also available in hardcover from Buccaneer and Naval
Inst. Press and in paperback from Little, Brown
"The old American mine sweeper 'Caine' patrols the
Pacific during World War II. The action shifts from the
bridge of the ship to the wardroom and from scenes of
petty tyranny on the part of the skipper to incidents of
fierce action and heroism on the part of the men. Ensign
Willie Keith is assigned to the ship and leads a mutiny
against paranoid Captain Queeg, who is eventually
brought to trial in a scene that poses the difficulty of
weighing evidence to prove that the takeover by the men
was justifiable." Shapiro. Fic for Youth. 3d edition

The winds of war; a novel. Little, Brown 1971
885p $35; pa $6.99   Fic
1. World War, 1939-1945—Fiction
ISBN 0-316-95500-0; 0-316-95516-7 (pa)
"On the broadest of tapestries, Wouk weaves the effect of the preparation and the actual outbreak of World
War II upon the family of Commander 'Pug' Henry. The
affairs of the Henry family became intertwined with
those of others, in such varying scenes as Washington,
Berlin, Rome, London, and Moscow. . . . Despite the
novel's breadth, the development of Henry's character as
the middle-class military leader America needed in the
1940's is surprisingly credible." Choice
Followed by War and remembrance (1978)

Wright, Richard, 1908-1960
Native son; with an introduction: "How 'Bigger'
was born," by the author. Harper & Row 1969
c1940 xxxiv, 392p $24.95; pa $6.50   Fic
1. African Americans—Fiction 2. Race relations—
Fiction 3. Chicago (Ill.)—Fiction
ISBN 0-06-014762-8; 0-06-080977-9 (pa)
A reissue of the title first published 1940
"Bigger Thomas is black. He is driven by anger, hate,
and frustration, which are born out of the poverty that
has dominated his life. When he gets a job with the Dal-
tons, a white family, he is confused by their behavior
and misinterprets their patronizing friendship. Tragedy
follows when he accidentally kills Mary Dalton." Shapiro. Fic for Youth. 3d edition

Yolen, Jane
Briar Rose. Doherty Assocs. 1992 190p (Fairy
tale series) $17.95   Fic
1. Holocaust, 1933-1945 2. Fantasy fiction
ISBN 0-312-85135-9   LC 92-25456
"A TOR book"

Yolen, Jane—*Continued*

"Yolen takes the story of Briar Rose (commonly known as Sleeping Beauty) and links it to the Holocaust. . . . Rebecca Berlin, a young woman who has grown up hearing her grandmother Gemma tell an unusual and frightening version of the Sleeping Beauty legend, realizes when Gemma dies that the fairy tale offers one of the very few clues she has to her grandmother's past. . . . By interpolating Gemma's vivid and imaginative story into the larger narrative, Yolen has created an engrossing novel." Publ Wkly

Zindel, Paul

The Pigman; a novel. Harper & Row 1968 182p lib bdg $14.89 **Fic**

ISBN 0-06-026828-X

Also available in paperback from Bantam Bks.

"John Conlan and Lorraine Jensen, high school sophomores, are both troubled young people who have problems at home. They become friendly with an elderly widower, Mr. Pignati, who welcomes them into his home and shares with them his simple pleasures, including his collection of ceramic pigs, of which he is proud. When the Pigman, as the young people call him, goes to the hospital after a heart attack, they take advantage of his house for a party that becomes destructive. The consequences are tragic and propel the two young friends into more responsible behavior." Shapiro. Fic for Youth. 3d edition

Followed by The Pigman's legacy (1980)

S C Story Collections

Books in this class consist of short story collections that contain the works of a single author or the works of several authors. Literary collections that may include but are not limited to short stories are entered in classes 808.8, 810.8, 820.8, etc. Folk tales are entered in class 398.2.

African short stories; selected and edited by Chinua Achebe & C.L. Innes. Heinemann Educ. Bks. 1985 159p (African writers series) pa $10.95 **S C**

1. Africa—Fiction 2. Short stories

ISBN 0-435-90536-8 LC 84-218650

This collection of contemporary African fiction includes works by Ousmane, Ngugi, Gordimer, Mphahlele, Kibera, Achebe, and others. Writers from all parts of Africa are represented

This "is a fine anthology, well selected, well ordered, and altogether a pleasure to read." World Lit Today

Am I blue? coming out from the silence; edited by Marion Dane Bauer. HarperCollins Pubs. 1994 273p $15; lib bdg $14.89; pa $5.95 **S C**

1. Homosexuality—Fiction 2. Short stories

ISBN 0-06-024253-1; 0-06-024254-X (lib bdg); 0-06-440587-7 (pa) LC 93-29574

This "collection includes stories by Bruce Coville, Lois Lowry, Jane Yolen, Nancy Garden, and others. While all the pieces center on themes of coming to terms with homosexuality, they also are stories of love, coming of age, adventure, and self-discovery. A powerful commentary about our social and emotional responses to homosexuality and our human need for love and acceptance." Horn Book Guide

American eyes; new Asian-American short stories for young adults; edited by Lori M. Carlson; introduction by Cynthia Kadohata. Holt & Co. 1994 144p $15.95 **S C**

1. Asian Americans—Fiction 2. Short stories

ISBN 0-8050-3544-3 LC 94-22391

Also available in paperback from Fawcett Bks.

These ten stories reflect the conflict Asian Americans face in balancing an ancient heritage and an unknown future

"The stories are sensitive, realistic, humorous and eye-opening. The characters represent all facets of human behavior. . . . This well-balanced collection helps us see life through another's eyes no matter what our ancestry." Book Rep

American short story masterpieces; edited by Raymond Carver and Tom Jenks. Delacorte Press 1987 435p hardcover o.p. paperback available $7.50 **S C**

1. Short stories

ISBN 0-440-20423-2 (pa) LC 86-19964

"Thirty-six stories are presented here. . . . These are all stories written in a realistic vein, with strong narrative drive. They 'moved and exhilarated' the compilers, and readers will have equally positive reactions. Bernard Malamud, Ann Beattie, John Updike, Grace Paley, Flannery O'Connor, and James Baldwin are just a few of the superior practitioners of the form found here." Booklist

Andersen, Hans Christian, 1805-1875

Tales and stories; translated with an introduction by Patricia L. Conroy and Sven H. Rossel. University of Wash. Press 1980 xxxvi, 279p il hardcover o.p. paperback available $14.95 **S C**

1. Fairy tales 2. Short stories

ISBN 0-295-95936-3 (pa) LC 80-50867

This collection of 27 stories has been selected and translated with an adult audience in mind

Anderson, Sherwood, 1876-1941

Winesburg, Ohio **S C**

1. Short stories

Hardcover and paperback editions available from various publishers

First published 1919 by B. W. Huebsch

"A series of twenty-three vignettes, *Winesburg, Ohio* is a character study of a small town. It highlights individual residents and scrutinizes who they are and why this reality often conflicts with their dreams. The short stories are linked through George Willard, a young newspaper reporter who is disenchanted with the narrow-mindedness of small towns." Shapiro. Fic for Youth. 3d edition

Asimov, Isaac, 1920-1992

The complete stories. Doubleday 1990-1992 2v v1 pa $17.95; v2 o.p. **S C**

1. Science fiction 2. Short stories

ISBN 0-385-41627-X (v1 pa) LC 90-3136

"A Foundation book"

Asimov, Isaac, 1920-1992—*Continued*
This set contains all of Asimov's science fiction stories including the "collections 'Earth Is Room Enough' and 'Nine Tomorrows' from the 1950s as well as . . . 'Nightfall and Other Stories.'" SLJ

I, robot. Gnome Press 1950 253p o.p.; Bantam Bks. paperback available $6.50 **S C**
1. Science fiction 2. Robots—Fiction 3. Short stories
ISBN 0-553-29438-5 (pa)
"These loosely connected stories cover the career of Dr. Susan Calvin and United States Robots, the industry that she heads, from the time of the public's early distrust of these robots to its later dependency on them. This collection is an important introduction to a theme often found in science fiction: the encroachment of technology on our lives." Shapiro. Fic for Youth. 3d edition

Bad behavior; edited by Mary Higgins Clark. Harcourt Brace & Co. 1995 306p $20; pa $10
S C
1. Mystery fiction 2. Horror fiction 3. Short stories
ISBN 0-15-200179-4; 0-15-200178-6 (pa)
LC 94-43344
"Gulliver books"
At head of title: The International Association of Crime writers presents
A collection of twenty-two mystery stories, both new and previously published, by Thomas Adcock, Winifred Holtby, Joyce Carol Oates, Sara Paretsky, Barbara Steiner, Eric Weiner, and others
"What makes this collection work for young adults is the depiction of upfront moral dilemmas of ordinary people who easily slip into the underworld of crime. The manipulation of readers' expectations is carefully calculated so that subtlety is sacrificed for the punch of impact, but the stories will provide an adrenalin rush for teenagers who want their mysteries to cut to the chase." Bull Cent Child Books

The Best American short stories; selected from U.S. and Canadian magazines. Houghton Mifflin $25; pa $12.95 **S C**
1. Short stories
ISSN 0067-6233
Annual volumes 1993-1996 available
This annual series began in 1915 under the editorship of Edward J. O'Brien with title: Best short stories. Editors vary
An annual anthology of stories by American and Canadian writers culled from a variety of magazines. Authors represented include: Raymond Carver, Alice Munro, Tobias Wolff, John Updike, Rick Bass, Jamaica Kincaid, and Lynne Sharon Schwartz

The Best American short stories of the eighties; selected and with an introduction by Shannon Ravenel. Houghton Mifflin 1990 393p hardcover o.p. paperback available $12.95 **S C**
1. Short stories
ISBN 0-395-52223-4 (pa)
LC 90-30071
"These 20 stories were selected by series editor Ravenel from those printed in . . . *The Best American Short Stories*. . . . The variety of styles and themes in this collection ably reflects the talents and versatility of the short story writers of our day." Libr J

The Best crime stories of the 19th century; edited by Isaac Asimov, Charles G. Waugh, and Martin H. Greenberg. Dembner Bks. 1988 325p $16.95 **S C**
1. Mystery fiction 2. Short stories
ISBN 0-934878-99-4
LC 87-30581
At head of title: Isaac Asimov presents
Among the authors represented in this anthology of fifteen crime stories are well-known writers such as Poe, Conan Doyle, Twain, and Hawthorne. Among the lesser-known authors are William Russell, Israel Zangwill, and Robert Barr

The Best short stories by Negro writers; an anthology from 1899 to the present; edited and with an introduction by Langston Hughes. Little, Brown 1967 508p $19.95; pa $12.95 **S C**
1. African Americans—Fiction 2. Short stories
ISBN 0-316-38032-6; 0-316-38031-8 (pa)
Forty-seven stories by such authors as Charles W. Chesnutt, Paul Laurence Dunbar, Zora Neale Hurston, Richard Wright, and Alice Walker. The stories range "in locale from the Caribbean to Chicago, New York, California, the deep South. . . . Mr. Hughes has chosen stories that move, amuse, surprise. Some are complex, some not, but all are good reading. . . . Brief biographies of the authors are included." Publ Wkly

✓ **Black-eyed** Susans/Midnight birds; stories by and about black women; edited and with an introduction by Mary Helen Washington. Anchor Bks. (NY) 1990 398p pa $14 **S C**
1. African American women—Fiction 2. Short stories
ISBN 0-385-26015-6
LC 89-16799
This anthology of twenty-one short stories gathers together two collections: Black-eyed Susans, and Midnight birds, published 1975 and 1980 respectively
Authors represented include: Toni Cade Bambara, Toni Morrison, Paule Marshall, Gwendolyn Brooks, Alice Walker, and Ntozake Shange
Includes bibliography

Bova, Ben, 1932-
Challenges. TOR Bks. 1993 348p hardcover o.p. paperback available $4.50 **S C**
1. Science fiction 2. Short stories
ISBN 0-8125-1408-4 (pa)
LC 93-18413
"A Tom Doherty Associates book"
"A collection of 12 science-fiction short stories and 6 essays. . . . The dangers of war, ESP, and life in the near future are among the themes included. . . . Aspiring writers, YAs wanting to plunge into this genre for the first time, fans of Bova, and teens just looking for some short pieces worth their time should all find pleasure here." SLJ

Bradbury, Ray, 1920-
Fahrenheit 451. 40th anniversary ed. Simon & Schuster 1993 190p $21 **S C**
1. Short stories
ISBN 0-671-87036-X
LC 93-10885
Also available in paperback from Ballantine Bks.
First published 1953 in paperback by Ballantine Bks.
This edition includes a foreword by Ray Bradbury

Bradbury, Ray, 1920——Continued

The title story, a novelette, tells about a bookburner official in a future fascist state. The other stories are: The playground; And the rock cried out

The illustrated man. Doubleday 1951 251p o.p.; Bantam Bks. paperback available $5.99   **S C**
1. Science fiction 2. Short stories
ISBN 0-553-27449-X (pa)

Also available from Buccaneer Bks.

In this work "the stories are given a linking framework; they are all seen as magical tattoos becoming living stories, springing from the body of the protagonist." Sci Fic Ency

The Martian chronicles   **S C**
1. Science fiction 2. Short stories

Hardcover and paperback reprint editions available from various publishers

First published 1950 by Doubleday

This book's "closely interwoven short stories, linked by recurrent images and themes, tell of the repeated attempts by humans to colonize Mars, of the way they bring their old prejudices with them, and of the repeated, ambiguous meetings with the shape-changing Martians." Sci Fic Ency

The stories of Ray Bradbury; with an introduction by the author. Knopf 1980 xx, 884p $40   **S C**
1. Science fiction 2. Short stories
ISBN 0-394-51335-5   LC 80-7655

This is a collection of 100 of the author's short stories. There are Martian stories, stories of a midwestern childhood, Irish stories and stories from Mexico

"Bradbury has a distinctive voice, and with it he sings to us of magic, nostalgia, beauty, terror, tenderness, innocence, loss, love and wisdom. Here is a specifically American vision of wonder which will someday tell our descendants a great deal about this time and place and about the lives we lived in our imaginations." Publ Wkly

Brooks, Martha, 1944-

Paradise Café and other stories. Little, Brown 1990 c1988 124p $14.95   **S C**
1. Short stories
ISBN 0-316-10978-9   LC 90-4601

"Joy Street books"

First published 1988 in Canada

Fourteen short stories dealing with various aspects of love

"Brooks' stories are tiny masterpieces, each tenderly re-creating a point in time when a person experiences a realization so powerful that he or she is changed forever. . . . Each story reads just as its protagonist would speak, and her phrasing is continually delightful." SLJ

√ **Calling** the wind; twentieth century African-American short stories; edited and with an introduction by Clarence Major. HarperCollins Pubs. 1993 xxv, 622p hardcover o.p. paperback available $14   **S C**
1. African Americans—Fiction 2. Short stories
ISBN 0-06-098201-2 (pa)   LC 92-52620

"An Edward Burlingame book"

"Fifty-nine African American authors, including Terry McMillan, Arna Bontemps, Richard Wright, Langston Hughes, James Baldwin, Toni Morrison, Alice Walker and Rosa Guy, have each contributed one short story to this collection." Book Rep

This "could become *the* anthology of black American short fiction for wide use in the high school and college classroom as well as by the general reading public." Booklist

Capote, Truman, 1924-1984

Breakfast at Tiffany's: a short novel and three stories. Modern Lib. 1994 161p $13.50; pa $11
     S C
1. Short stories
ISBN 0-679-60085-X; 0-679-74565-3 (pa)
     LC 93-43633

First published 1958 by Random House

The novella which gives the book its title is the tale of a Manhattan playgirl, Holly Golightly. Completing the volume are three short stories: House of flowers, A diamond guitar, and A Christmas memory

Cheever, John, 1912-1982

The stories of John Cheever. Knopf 1978 693p $40   **S C**
1. Short stories
ISBN 0-394-50087-3   LC 78-160

Also available in paperback from Ballantine Bks.

A "bringing together of 61 Cheever stories in a single binding. . . . Most of these pieces were initially published in 'The New Yorker.'" Choice

"Readers will delight in the delineation of Cheever's mythical landscapes. . . . Resonant with feeling and meaning, this is a collection to treasure." Publ Wkly

Chekhov, Anton Pavlovich, 1860-1904

The image of Chekhov; forty stories in the order in which they were written; newly translated and with an introduction by Robert Payne. Knopf 1963 xxxvii, 344p $15   **S C**
1. Russia—Fiction 2. Short stories
ISBN 0-394-43009-3

These translations have been made from the twelve volume edition of Chekhov's collected works, edited by W. W. Yermilov and published in Moscow, 1950

"Payne has written an introductory essay on Chekhov's life and writings, including critical comments on many of the stories included in this volume. As a translator Payne has had his difficulties with Chekhov's idiomatic nineteenth-century Russian, but the effect is generally fresh and has a comparatively modern tone." Booklist

The Russian master and other stories; [by] Anton Chekhov; translated with an introduction and notes by Ronald Hingley. Oxford Univ. Press 1984 233p (World's classics) pa $5.95   **S C**
1. Russia—Fiction 2. Short stories
ISBN 0-19-281680-2   LC 83-23719

A collection of eleven short stories written between 1892 and 1899

Includes bibliography

Children of the night; the best short stories by black writers, 1967 to the present; edited by Gloria Naylor. Little, Brown 1996 c1995 xx, 569p $24.95   **S C**
1. African Americans—Fiction 2. Short stories
ISBN 0-316-59926-3   LC 95-16356
Companion volume to The Best short stories by Negro writers
"Organized by theme, these . . . stories offer a collective portrait of the black experience in the post-Civil Rights era. Included are works by Maya Angelou, Ralph Ellison, Terry McMillan, and others." Libr J
"In this brilliant collection of superb writing, each story provides keen insights told in heartbreakingly beautiful prose." Booklist

Chopin, Kate, 1851-1904
The awakening and selected stories; edited with an introduction by Nina Baym. Modern Lib. 1993 c1981 lviii, 354p $16.50   **S C**
1. Short stories
ISBN 0-679-42469-5   LC 92-51067
A reissue of the 1981 edition
In addition to the novel The awakening (1899) this volume also includes five stories from Bayou folk (1894) and seven from A night in Acadie (1897)
Includes glossary and bibliography

Christie, Agatha, 1890-1976
Miss Marple: the complete short stories. Dodd, Mead 1985 346p o.p.; Berkley Bks. paperback available $12   **S C**
1. Mystery fiction 2. Short stories
ISBN 0-425-09486-3 (pa)   LC 85-10220
This volume contains "all 20 short stories that Christie centered on the elderly sleuth. . . . The bulk of the stories are gathered from *The Tuesday Club* murders, chronicling the meetings of a group formed by Miss Marple and a handful of her friends." Publ Wkly

Cisneros, Sandra
Woman Hollering Creek and other stories. Random House 1991 165p $20; pa $10   **S C**
1. Mexican Americans—Fiction 2. Short stories
ISBN 0-394-57654-3; 0-679-73856-8 (pa)
    LC 90-52930
"Unforgettable characters march through a satisfying collection of tales about Mexican-Americans who know the score and cling to the anchor of their culture." N Y Times Book Rev

Classic American short stories; selected and introduced by Douglas Grant. Oxford Univ. Press 1989 398p pa $12.95   **S C**
1. Short stories
ISBN 0-19-282685-9   LC 89-16085
First published 1965 with title: American short stories
A chronologically arranged collection of fourteen short stories by such authors as Nathaniel Hawthorne, Edgar Allan Poe, Mark Twain, Ambrose Bierce, Henry James, Edith Wharton, Katherine Anne Porter, and Ernest Hemingway

Classic English short stories, 1930-1955; selected and introduced by Derek Hudson. Oxford Univ. Press 1990 362p pa $10.95   **S C**
1. Short stories
ISBN 0-19-281121-5   LC 89-16119
First published 1956 with title: Modern English short stories, second series
A collection of nineteen short stories by such authors as Somerset Maugham, Graham Greene, Virginia Woolf, Evelyn Waugh, and Elizabeth Bowen

Classic ghost stories; by Charles Dickens [et al.] Dover Publs. 1975 330p pa $7.95   **S C**
1. Ghost stories 2. Short stories
ISBN 0-486-20735-8
Contents: Sir Dominick Sarsfield, by J. S. LeFanu; The story of the bagman's uncle, by C. Dickens; The monkey's paw, by W. W. Jacobs; Wandering Willie's tale, by Sir W. Scott; Dracula's guest, by B. Stoker; The open door, by M. Oliphant; The mortal immortal, by M. Shelley; Dr. Heidegger's experiment, by N. Hawthorne; No. 1 Branch Line, the signalman, by C. Dickens; The tapestried chamber, by Sir W. Scott; The phantom coach, by A. B. Edwards; The dream woman, by W. Collins; The apparition of Mrs. Veal, by D. Defoe; The judge's house, by B. Stoker; The werewolf, by F. Marryat; The Horla, by G. de Maupassant; The upper berth, by F. M. Crawford; The haunted and the haunters, by Sir E. Bulwer-Lytton

Colette, 1873-1954
The collected stories of Colette; edited, and with an introduction by Robert Phelps; translated by Matthew Ward [et al.] Farrar, Straus & Giroux 1983 605p hardcover o.p. paperback available $18
    S C
1. Short stories
ISBN 0-374-51865-3 (pa)   LC 83-16449
"Includes two novellas that rank as classics, not only in Colette's canon, but in all of 20th century French literature. The Tender Shoot is the story of a singularly nasty middle-aged roué's pursuit of a 15-year-old peasant girl. . . . As Colette remarked of her writing, her 'great landscape was always the human face.' No work demonstrates this better than The Kepi, the portrait of a doomed 46-year-old French lieutenant." Time

Coming of age in America; a multicultural anthology; edited by Mary Frosch; foreword by Gary Soto. New Press (NY) 1994 274p $22.95; pa $11.95   **S C**
1. Short stories
ISBN 1-56584-146-8; 1-56584-147-6 (pa)
    LC 93-46921
This collection consists of sixteen short stories and excerpts from five novels, written by noted authors from a variety of ethnic backgrounds. Among the authors represented are Dorothy Allison, Cynthia Kadohata, Julia Alvarez, Frank Chin, Tobias Wolff, and Chaim Potok

Conrad, Joseph, 1857-1924

The complete short fiction of Joseph Conrad; edited with an introduction by Samuel Hynes. Ecco Press 1991-1993 4v   S C
1. Short stories

LC 91-27115

v1-2 available from Amereon
volume 1-2: stories, volume 3-4: tales
"This collection assembles Conrad's twenty-two short stories published between 1898 and 1925, and his longer tales, published between 1899 and 1915." Publisher's note

Crime classics; the mystery story from Poe to the present; edited by Rex Burns and Mary Rose Sullivan. Viking 1990 xxiv, 390p hardcover o.p. paperback available $12.95   S C
1. Mystery fiction 2. Short stories
ISBN 0-14-013128-0 (pa)   LC 90-50122
This anthology includes "Edgar Allan Poe's 'Murders in the Rue Morgue,' Arthur Conan Doyle's 'Scandal in Bohemia,' and Dashiell Hammett's 'House in Turk Street'—as well as several less-recognized delights. . . . The anthology is introduced by a trenchant essay surveying important developments in the history of the mystery story." Booklist

Crutcher, Chris, 1946-

Athletic shorts: six short stories. Greenwillow Bks. 1991 154p $16   S C
1. Short stories
ISBN 0-688-10816-4   LC 91-4418
Also available Thorndike Press large print edition and in paperback from Dell
"As the title suggests, athletics are part of the selections; and Crutcher, as usual, is best at accurately portraying the world of high school teammates and coaches—readers can practically smell the sweat. In the first story—a monologue by a fat guy who manages to keep his dignity—the author seamlessly blends humor with more serious elements. . . . The final entry, a gritty, no-holds-barred account of the fear surrounding AIDS, is especially effective. These *Athletic Shorts* will speak to YAs, touch them deeply, and introduce them to characters they'll want to know better." SLJ

Danticat, Edwidge, 1969-

Krik? Krak! Soho Press 1995 224p $20 S C
1. Haitian Americans—Fiction 2. Haiti—Fiction 3. Short stories
ISBN 1-56947-025-1   LC 94-41999
Also available in paperback from Vintage Bks.
The author "touches upon life both in Haiti and in New York's Haitian community, though we spend most of our time in Port-au-Prince and the country town of Ville Rose. The best of these stories humanize, particularize, give poignancy to the lives of people we may have come to think of as faceless emblems of misery, poverty and brutality." N Y Times Book Rev

Doyle, Sir Arthur Conan, 1859-1930

The complete Sherlock Holmes; with a preface by Christopher Morley. Doubleday 1960 c1930 1122p $25   S C
1. Mystery fiction 2. Short stories
ISBN 0-385-00689-6
Also available in a two-volume paperback edition from Bantam Bks.
First published 1930
Fifty-eight Sherlock Holmes stories which were originally published in nine separate volumes: A study in scarlet (1887); The sign of the four (1890); Adventures of Sherlock Holmes (1892); Memoirs of Sherlock Holmes (1894); The return of Sherlock Holmes (1905); The hound of the Baskervilles (1902); The valley of fear (1915); His last bow (1917); The case book of Sherlock Holmes (1927)

Faulkner, William, 1897-1962

Collected stories of William Faulkner. Random House 1950 900p $22.95; pa $19 S C
1. Short stories
ISBN 0-394-41967-7; 0-679-76403-8 (pa)
"Forty-two short stories, including all from These Thirteen (1931), all but two from Doctor Martino and other stories (1934) and seventeen published in magazines, 1932-1948. . . . Many of the stories deal with characters and incidents related to those in his novels set in the mythical Yoknapatawpha County, Mississippi." Libr J

Selected short stories of William Faulkner. Modern Lib. 1993 310p $15.50   S C
1. Short stories
ISBN 0-679-42478-4   LC 92-51072
A reissue of the 1961 edition
A variety of the author's output, diverse in method and subject matter, ranging in original publication dates from 1930 to 1955

Uncollected stories of William Faulkner; edited by Joseph Blotner. Random House 1979 716p hardcover o.p. paperback available $18 S C
1. Short stories
ISBN 0-394-74656-2 (pa)   LC 78-21803
Each of the forty-five stories collected here fall into one of three categories: stories which were revised after initial publication to become parts of later books; stories which were published in periodicals or limited editions but were never reprinted in any of Faulkner's short story collections; and stories which have not been previously published

Fitzgerald, F. Scott (Francis Scott), 1896-1940

The short stories of F. Scott Fitzgerald; a new collection; edited and with a preface by Matthew J. Bruccoli. Scribner 1989 775p $29.95; pa $17
              S C
1. Short stories
ISBN 0-684-19160-1; 0-684-80445-X (pa)
              LC 89-6351
"The 43 stories in this collection include both the famous ones and several that are less well known." Booklist

Fitzgerald, F. Scott (Francis Scott), 1896-1940—
Continued

The stories of F. Scott Fitzgerald; a selection of 28 stories; with an introduction by Malcolm Cowley. Scribner 1951 xxv, 473p $50   S C
1. Short stories
ISBN 0-684-15366-1
"The editor has attempted to make the best selection from all stages of Fitzgerald's career; the stories are arranged in chronological groups." Booklist

Gordimer, Nadine, 1923-
Crimes of conscience. Heinemann Educ. Bks. 1991 121p (African writers series) pa $8.95   S C
1. Africa—Fiction 2. Short stories
ISBN 0-435-90668-2
"This small retrospective collection of 11 short stories introduces teens to [the] Nobel Prize-winning writer, who shows with candor and humanity how racism affects people's personal lives." Booklist

Hawthorne, Nathaniel, 1804-1864
Tales and sketches, including Twice-told tales, Mosses from an old manse, and The snow-image; A wonder book for girls and boys; Tanglewood tales for girls and boys, being a second Wonder book. Library of Am. 1982 1493p $35   S C
1. Short stories
ISBN 0-940450-03-8   LC 81-20760
This volume contains all of Hawthorne's tales and sketches, which are arranged in order of their periodical publication

The Heinemann book of contemporary African short stories; edited by Chinua Achebe and C. L. Innes. Heinemann Educ. Bks. 1992 200p (African writers series) pa $10.95   S C
1. Africa—Fiction 2. Short stories
ISBN 0-435-90566-X   LC 93-106811
The twenty stories in this collection "are divided by region: five stories from Southern Africa; two from Central Africa; five from East Africa; two from Northern Africa; and six from West Africa. Region is important for, in many cases, the issues of the area are reflected in the selections. . . . The writing is mature, and the themes and moods are many, ranging from mystical to magical to supernatural to realistic. This anthology is a worthwhile addition to any library collection serving YAs." SLJ

Hemingway, Ernest, 1899-1961
The complete short stories of Ernest Hemingway; the Finca Vigía edition. Scribner 1987 650p $40; pa $18   S C
1. Short stories
ISBN 0-684-18668-3; 0-02-033200-9 (pa)
LC 87-12888
"To the 49 standard *Short stories of Ernest Hemingway*

In our time; stories. Scribner 156p $30; pa $9
S C
1. Short stories
ISBN 0-684-16480-9; 0-684-82276-8 (pa)
"Hudson River editions"
First published 1930. Copyright renewed 1958
Several of these "stories" picture episodes in the life of a growing boy in the timber country of the Middle West
"Of 'stories' in the commonly accepted sense of the word there are few. . . . Most of the others are psychological episodes, incidents, sketches . . . call them what you will. They are soundly and movingly done." Lit Rev

The Nick Adams stories; preface by Philip Young. Scribner 268p $40; pa $10.95   S C
1. Short stories
ISBN 0-02-550780-X; 0-684-16940-1 (pa)
"Hudson River editions"
First published 1972
Arranged chronologically, this collection of 24 tales contains all the semi-autobiographical Nick Adams stories
"The volume presents Nick as a child in the northern woods, as adolescent, as soldier, veteran, writer, husband and parent. The last Nick Adams story appeared in 1933, and what surprises here, in these . . . [stories] of varying length, quality and intent, is their freshness and immediacy." Publ Wkly

The short stories of Ernest Hemingway. Scribner 499p $50; pa $14   S C
1. Short stories
ISBN 0-684-15155-3; 0-684-80334-8 (pa)
Also available Scribner Classics edition $30 (ISBN 0-684-83786-2)
"Hudson River editions"
First published 1953
"Stories are mainly concerned with 'tough' people, either intelligent men and women who have dropped into an exhausted cynicism, or such primitives as frontiersmen, Indians, and professional athletes, whose essential courage and honesty are implicitly contrasted with the brutality of civilized society." Oxford Companion to Am Lit. 6th edition

Henry, O., 1862-1910
The best short stories of O. Henry; selected and with an introduction by Bennett A. Cerf, and Van H. Cartmell. Modern Lib. 1994 c1945 340p $20.50
S C
1. Short stories
ISBN 0-679-60122-8
Analyzed in Short story index
First Modern Library edition published 1945
O. Henry "is best known for his observations on the diverse lives of everyday New Yorkers, 'the four million ' neglected by other writers. He had a fine gift of humor and was adept at the ingenious depiction of ironic circumstances, in plots frequently dependent upon coincidence." Oxford Companion to Am Lit. 6th edition

Hesse, Hermann, 1877-1962

The fairy tales of Hermann Hesse; translated and with an introduction by Jack Zipes; woodcut illustrations by David Frampton. Bantam Bks. 1995 xxxi, 266p il hardcover o.p. paperback available $12.95 **S C**

1. Fairy tales 2. Short stories

ISBN 0-553-37776-0 (pa) LC 94-49166

"Quirky and evocative, Hesse's fairy tales stand alone, but also amplify the ideas and utopian longings of such counterculture avatars as *Siddhartha* and *Steppenwolf*." Publ Wkly

The **Horror** hall of fame; edited by Robert Silverberg and Martin H. Greenberg. Carroll & Graf Pubs. 1991 416p $21.95; pa $12.95 **S C**

1. Horror fiction 2. Short stories

ISBN 0-88184-692-9; 0-88184-880-8 (pa)

LC 91-12569

This collection "is made up of 18 mostly very famous stories by 18 very famous authors. 'The Fall of the House of Usher,' 'The Monkey's Paw,' 'The Damned Thing,' 'Pigeons from Hell,' 'Yours Truly, Jack the Ripper,' 'The Yellow Sign,' 'The Willows,' 'The Small Assassin,' 'The White People'—stories every horror fan just must read—are all here, along with effective but not-old-enough-to-be-classic tales by Ramsey Campbell, Harlan Ellison, Charles L. Grant, and Stephen King." Booklist

√ **Hughes, Langston, 1902-1967**

Short stories; edited by Akiba Sullivan Harper; with an introduction by Arnold Rampersad. Hill & Wang 1996 299p $25 **S C**

1. African Americans—Fiction 2. Short stories

ISBN 0-8090-8658-1 LC 95-19554

"Dating from 1919 to 1963, these pieces vary in theme, covering life at sea, the trials and tribulations of a young pianist and her elderly white patron, a visiting writer's experience in Cuba, a young girl's winning an art scholarship but losing it when it's learned she is black, and an ambitious black preacher trying to gain fame by being nailed to a cross. If you crave good reading don't pass up this gem." Libr J

√ **Hurston, Zora Neale, 1891-1960**

The complete stories; introduction by Henry Louis Gates, Jr. and Sieglinde Lemke. HarperCollins Pubs. 1995 xxiii, 305p hardcover o.p. paperback available $13.50 **S C**

1. African Americans—Fiction 2. Short stories

ISBN 0-06-092171-4 (pa) LC 91-50438

This collection of Hurston's short fiction contains nineteen stories originally published between 1921 and 1951, arranged in the order in which they were published, and seven previously unpublished stories

Includes bibliography

√ **Iguana** dreams; new Latino fiction; edited by Delia Poey and Virgil Suarez; with a preface by Oscar Hijuelos. HarperCollins Pubs. 1992 376p il hardcover o.p. paperback available $15 **S C**

1. Hispanic Americans—Fiction 2. Short stories

ISBN 0-06-096917-2 (pa) LC 92-52628

Also available in hardcover from Borgo Press

This "anthology brings together 29 short stories that reflect different aspects of Latino life from the despair of the barrio to the unease of working within the Anglo status quo, yet also embody humanity's archetypal dramas. . . . While each magnetic narrative is unique, they all radiate an aura of deliberateness, astuteness, and power." Booklist

√ **Invented** lives; narratives of black women, 1860-1960; [edited and with an introduction by] Mary Helen Washington. Anchor Press 1987 xxxi, 447p pa $11.95 **S C**

1. African American women—Fiction 2. Short stories

ISBN 0-385-24842-3 LC 86-24143

An anthology of novel excerpts and short stories from Gwendolyn Brooks, Frances Ellen Watkins Harper, Pauline Elizabeth Hopkins, Dorothy West, and others

Irving, Washington, 1783-1859

Bracebridge Hall; Tales of a traveller; The Alhambra. Library of Am. 1991 1104p $35 **S C**

ISBN 0-940450-59-3 LC 90-62267

This volume contains three collections of stories and sketches: Bracebridge Hall (1822); Tales of a traveller (1824); and The Alhambra (1832)

Jackson, Shirley, 1919-1965

The lottery; or, The adventures of James Harris. Farrar, Straus & Giroux 1949 306p hardcover o.p. paperback available $12 **S C**

1. Short stories

ISBN 0-374-51681-2 (pa)

Also available in hardcover from Bentley

The stories "in this collection seem to fall into three groups. There are the slight sketches, like genre paintings, dealing with episodes which are trivial in terms of plot but which by means of [the author's] precise, sensitive, and sharply focused style become luminous with meaning. . . . The second group comprises her social-problem sketches. . . . Her final group deals with fantasy, ranging from humorous whimsey to horrifying shock." Saturday Rev Lit

Joyce, James, 1882-1941

Dubliners **S C**

1. Ireland—Fiction 2. Short stories

Available in hardcover and paperback from various publishers

First published 1914 in the United Kingdom; in the United States 1916 by Huebsch

"This collection of 15 stories provides an introduction to the style and motifs found in Joyce's writing. The stories stand alone as individual scenes of Dublin society and are intertwined by the use of autobiography and symbolism." Shapiro. Fic for Youth. 3d edition

Kafka, Franz, 1883-1924

The complete stories; edited by Nahum N. Glatzer; with a new foreword by John Updike. Centennial ed. Schocken Bks. 1983 xxi, 486p il hardcover o.p. paperback available $15 **S C**

1. Short stories

ISBN 0-8052-1055-5 (pa) LC 83-3233

First published 1971

Kafka, Franz, 1883-1924—*Continued*
"All of Kafka's writing, with the exception of his three novels, is collected here and includes a number of fairly long stories followed by a group of shorter pieces varying in length from several pages to a single paragraph." Booklist

The metamorphosis and other stories; translated by Joachim Neugroschel. Scribner 1993 xxiii, 227p $25; pa $11   S C
1. Short stories
ISBN 0-684-19426-0; 0-684-80070-5 (pa)
                                          LC 92-43912
This is a collection of thirty stories, some of which are quite short. The stories are arranged in order of their original publication dates

King, Stephen, 1947-
Four past midnight. Viking 1990 763p $34.95
                                              S C
1. Horror fiction 2. Short stories
ISBN 0-670-83538-2   LC 90-50046
Also available in paperback from New Am. Lib.
This volume contains four novellas: The Langoliers; Secret window, secret garden; The library policeman; The sun dog
This book "is hard to put down, truly chilling, and sure to be enjoyed by YA horror afficionados everywhere." SLJ

Skeleton crew. Putnam 1985 512p o.p.; New Am. Lib. paperback available $6.99   S C
1. Horror fiction 2. Short stories
ISBN 0-451-16861-5 (pa)   LC 84-15947
This "collection of King's shorter work is a hefty sampler from all stages of his career, and demonstrates the range of his abilities. . . . There are several stories here that must rank among King's best." Publ Wkly

Kinsella, W. P.
Shoeless Joe Jackson comes to Iowa: stories. Southern Methodist Univ. Press 1993 141p il $19.95; pa $9.95   S C
1. Baseball—Fiction 2. Short stories
ISBN 0-87074-355-4; 0-87074-356-2 (pa)
                                          LC 93-3935
First published 1980 in Canada
"The title story contains the germ of Kinsella's novel Shoeless Joe; not as deep and rich as the longer work, it remains pure and perfect in itself. Among the other gems: 'Fiona the First,' a portrait of a man doomed to spend eternity picking up girls at airports, 'First Names and Empty Pockets,' in which a doll-mender saves the broken Janis Joplin; and 'The Grecian Urn,' a tale of people traveling in time by becoming part of works of art. Few writers can match Kinsella's ability to establish tone, character, and a complete reality in just a few paragraphs, then sweep the reader into his imagined world." Libr J

Kipling, Rudyard, 1865-1936
The best fiction of Rudyard Kipling; introduction by John Beecroft. Anchor Bks. (NY) 1989 627p hardcover o.p. paperback available $16.95   S C
1. Short stories
ISBN 0-385-26091-1 (pa)   LC 88-28317
Selected from: Kipling, a selection of his stories and poems (1956)
This compilation consists of the complete texts of Kim, The jungle book, Just so stories, Puck of Pook's Hill and seven stories including The man who would be king and Rikki-tikki-tavi

Koontz, Dean R. (Dean Ray), 1945-
Strange highways; [by] Dean Koontz. Warner Bks. 1995 561p $23.95; pa $6.99   S C
1. Horror fiction 2. Short stories
ISBN 0-446-51974-X; 0-446-60339-2 (pa)
                                          LC 94-49024
"A Brandon Tartikoff book"
This collection includes two novels: Strange highways and a revised version of Chase (1972). Also included are twelve novelettes and short stories
These stories "are well crafted and imaginative, with characters rarely taking second place to premise or plot device." Publ Wkly

L'Amour, Louis, 1908-1988
The outlaws of Mesquite; frontier stories. Bantam Bks. 1990 199p il hardcover o.p. paperback available $3.99   S C
1. Western stories 2. Short stories
ISBN 0-553-28714-1 (pa)   LC 89-18254
"Eight L'Amour classics fill this volume. . . . These terrific tales of the Old West are each introduced with black-and-white sketches as well as prefatory notes on cowboy customs." Booklist

Lardner, Ring, 1885-1933
The best short stories of Ring Lardner. Scribner 1976 c1957 346p $40   S C
1. Short stories
ISBN 0-684-14743-2
"Hudson River editions"
A reprint of the 1957 edition
"A selection of twenty-five stories by one of the most original figures in American literature, the colorful personality who was noted as a sports writer, humorist and columnist, as well as short-story writer." N Y Her Trib Books

Lawrence, D. H. (David Herbert), 1885-1930
The complete short stories. Viking 1961 3v hardcover o.p. paperbacks available v1-2 $8.95; v3 $8   S C
1. Short stories
ISBN 0-14-004382-9 (v1); 0-14-004255-5 (v2); 0-14-004383-7 (v3) (pa)
First published 1955 in the United Kingdom

Lawrence, D. H. (David Herbert), 1885-1930—
Continued

Lawrence's "consummate skill at incident or vignette
. . . helps to explain why many readers prefer his
shorter fiction. At their finest, Lawrence's novellas and
short stories combine meticulously accurate social settings with penetrating psychological analyses." Ency of
World Lit in the 20th Century

Le Guin, Ursula K., 1929-

A fisherman of the inland sea; science fiction
stories. HarperPrism 1994 191p il $19.99; pa $4.99
S C

1. Science fiction 2. Short stories
ISBN 0-06-105200-0; 0-06-105491-7 (pa)
LC 94-5397

This is a collection of eight stories which explore science fiction themes such as interplanetary visitors, space
colonies, and time travel

"Le Guin demonstrates her storytelling virtuosity in
each of these diverse tales." Voice Youth Advocates

Four ways to forgiveness. HarperPrism 1995
228p $20; pa $5.99   S C

1. Science fiction 2. Short stories
ISBN 0-06-105234-5; 0-06-105401-1 (pa)
LC 95-11459

"Four interrelated novellas deal with the Hainish culture on the twin planets of Werel and Yeowe and examine the relationship between love, freedom and forgiveness." Publ Wkly

"For YAs who have ever felt 'closed in' by society or
their parents, LeGuin's book is a wonderful choice." SLJ

The **Lightning** within; an anthology of
contemporary American Indian fiction; edited
and with an introduction by Alan R. Velie.
University of Neb. Press 1991 161p $25; pa
$9.95   S C

1. Indians of North America—Fiction 2. Short stories
ISBN 0-8032-4659-5; 0-8032-9614-2 (pa)
LC 90-12658

This anthology presents fiction by seven Native
American authors: Michael Dorris, Louise Erdrich, N.
Scott Momaday, Simon Ortiz, Leslie Marmon Silko, Ger-
ald Vizenor, and James Welch

The **Literary** ghost; great contemporary ghost
stories; edited and with an introduction by Larry
Dark. Atlantic Monthly Press 1991 369p
hardcover o.p. paperback available $13   S C

1. Ghost stories 2. Short stories
ISBN 0-87113-483-7 (pa)
LC 91-15052

The ghost story "is alive and more than well, as
proved by this anthology of 28 examples. . . . From the
U.S., Britain, Canada, South Africa, and India, the authors showcased here who have taken their fiction in the
direction of the supernatural are, specifically, such modern luminaries as Joyce Carol Oates, Nadine Gordimer,
Graham Greene, and Isaac Singer. . . . The variety of
approaches . . . represented here promises wide appeal."
Booklist

London, Jack, 1876-1916

The science fiction stories of Jack London;
edited by James Bankes. Carol Pub. Group 1993
211p pa $9.95   S C

1. Science fiction 2. Short stories
ISBN 0-8065-1407-8
LC 92-39510

Also available in hardcover from Buccaneer Bks.

"A Citadel Twilight book"

This is a collection of fifteen of the author's stories
which explore science fiction themes such as rejuvenation, bacteriological mutations, future societies, and a
postcatastrophic world

Short stories of Jack London; authorized
one-volume edition; edited by Earle Labor, Robert
C. Leitz, III, I. Milo Shepard. Macmillan 1990 xli,
738p hardcover o.p. paperback available $16 S C

1. Short stories
ISBN 0-02-022371-4 (pa)
LC 90-6175

This collection presents fifty stories "reprinted in the
form in which London originally delivered them for publication (without the changes and deletions performed by
magazine editors for serialization). . . . A splendid volume." Booklist

Includes bibliography

Malamud, Bernard, 1914-1986

The stories of Bernard Malamud. Farrar, Straus
& Giroux 1983 349p $17.95   S C

1. Short stories
ISBN 0-374-27037-6
LC 83-14100

Also available in paperback from New Am. Lib.

This is a collection of 25 tales "all selected by
Malamud himself and including some of his best-known
and loved stories: 'Idiots First,' 'The Jewbird,' 'Rembrandt's Hat,' 'Angel Levine.' This is the master storyteller at his best." Libr J

The **Mammoth** book of new world science fiction;
short novels of the 1960s; edited by Isaac
Asimov, Charles G. Waugh and Martin H.
Greenberg. Carroll & Graf Pubs. 1991 506p pa
$9.95   S C

1. Science fiction 2. Short stories
ISBN 0-88184-702-X

This "volume contains 10 of the most distinguished
novellas of the 1960s, one of the great creative times in
the history of modern science fiction and fantasy. Authors represented include Gordon Dickson ('Soldier Ask
Not'), Anne McCaffrey ('Weyr Search,' the first Pern
story), Roger Zelazny ('The Eve of Rumoko'), Mack
Reynolds ('Mercenary'), and others who flourished during the decade." Booklist

Masterpieces of fantasy and enchantment;
compiled by David G. Hartwell with the
assistance of Kathryn Cramer. St. Martin's Press
1988 622p $19.95   S C

1. Fantasy fiction 2. Short stories
ISBN 0-312-02250-6
LC 88-14752

Among the authors represented in this collection are
Ursula LeGuin, Horace Walpole, L. Frank Baum,
Michael Moorcock, and Poul Anderson

"A marvelous assortment of excerpts and stories that
will not only treat the confirmed fantasy lover but also
tempt the novice." Booklist

Masterpieces of mystery and suspense; compiled by Martin H. Greenberg. St. Martin's Press 1988 651p $19.95   **S C**
1. Mystery fiction 2. Short stories
ISBN 0-312-02251-4   LC 88-14753
A collection of 40 mystery and detective stories by such authors as Dorothy L. Sayers, Agatha Christie, Stephen King, and P. D. James
"Mystery fans, especially those who like hard-boiled detective yarns, will encounter many familiar authors among the contributors here—while uninitiated readers can sample some of the genre's best writers." Booklist

Maugham, W. Somerset (William Somerset), 1874-1965
Collected short stories. Penguin Bks. 1992-1993 4v v1 & v3 pa $11.95; v2 & v4 pa $12.95 **S C**
1. Short stories
ISBN 0-14-018589-5 (v1); 0-14-018590-9 (v2); 0-14-018591-7 (v3); 0-14-018592-5 (v4)
First published 1963 in the United Kingdom
"Two qualities of Maugham as a writer brought him mastery of the short story: an economical and exact means of fixing the sense of place, often exotic places; and an equally economical skill in realizing the crisis of a story." Penguin Companion to Engl Lit

Maupassant, Guy de, 1850-1893
The collected stories of Guy de Maupassant; ten volumes in one. Avenel Bks. 1985 1003p o.p.
     S C
1. Short stories
     LC 84-20316
A reissue of the 1903 edition published by Walter Black, Inc. with title: The complete short stories of Guy de Maupassant

McCullers, Carson, 1917-1967
The ballad of the sad café: the novels and stories of Carson McCullers. Houghton Mifflin 1951 791p o.p.; Bantam Bks. paperback available $5.50   **S C**
1. Short stories
ISBN 0-553-27254-3 (pa)
Contents: This volume contains three novels: The heart is a lonely hunter, The member of the wedding and Reflections in a golden eye (the first two titles are entered separately in the Fiction section); a novelette (the title story) and six short stories

Collected stories; including The member of the wedding and The ballad of the sad café; introduction by Virginia Spencer Carr. Houghton Mifflin 1987 392p hardcover o.p. paperback available $13.95   **S C**
1. Short stories
ISBN 0-395-44243-5 (pa)   LC 87-3944
"McCullers often wrote about grotesques, people afflicted physically and emotionally. Her themes include loneliness and the mental anguish that stems from love gone awry. Her style is unadorned, quietly rigorous. She's both charming and disquieting—an absorbing challenge to readers of serious fiction." Booklist

McKinley, Robin
A knot in the grain and other stories. Greenwillow Bks. 1994 195p $14   **S C**
1. Short stories
ISBN 0-688-09201-2   LC 93-17557
Also available in paperback from HarperCollins Pubs.
This collection "deals mainly with love: true, enduring love between apparently ill-matched lovers. Four of the stories share the setting of The Blue Sword and The Hero and the Crown while the title story is contemporary. McKinley has at her command a clear, apparently effortless style; fresh, original ideas; a romantic outlook; and a remarkable ability to evoke wonder and belief." Horn Book Guide

The **Merlin** chronicles; edited by Mike Ashley. Carroll & Graf Pubs. 1995 446p il pa $12.95
     S C
1. Merlin (Legendary character)—Fiction 2. Fantasy fiction 3. Short stories
ISBN 0-7867-0275-3   LC 96-154350
This collection of "stories by noted fantasy authors including Tanith Lee, Jane Yolen, and Charles de Lint focuses on the enigmatic figure of Merlin. Many of the stories are original to this volume." Libr J
"Particularly nice is the inclusion of works by both nineteenth and twentieth century writers. The anthology would be a good addition to a library with a large Arthurian collection." Voice Youth Advocates

Michener, James A. (James Albert), 1907-
Tales of the South Pacific. Macmillan 1986 c1947 326p $35   **S C**
1. Islands of the Pacific—Fiction 2. World War, 1939-1945—Fiction 3. Short stories
ISBN 0-02-584540-3   LC 86-28450
Also available in paperback from Fawcett Bks.
"Hudson River editions"
A reissue of the title first published 1947
These 18 tales describe "the strain and the boredom, the careful planning and heroic action, the color and beauty of the islands, and all that made up life during the critical days of the war in the Pacific." Wis Libr Bull

Mohr, Nicholasa, 1935-
In Nueva York. Dial Press (NY) 1977 192p o.p.; Arte Público Press paperback available $9.50
     S C
1. Puerto Ricans—New York (N.Y.)—Fiction 2. New York (N.Y.)—Fiction 3. Short stories
ISBN 0-934770-78-6 (pa)   LC 76-42931
"Set on New York City's Lower East Side, Nicholasa Mohr's 'In Nueva York' is a beautifully written montage of the lives of Puerto Rican immigrants who come to this country in search of a better life. Instead of the wealth and improved living conditions they had expected, they find themselves trapped in a slum area where filth and despair prevail. Lacking a central character, this collection of interrelated short stories creates a unifying tone by portraying the struggle of the various characters to overcome their surroundings and create a better life. Excellent characterization and Mohr's ability to evoke a feeling of the constant struggle both to survive and to be happy, contribute significantly to the strength of this book." ALAN

Nebula awards; SFWA's choices for the best science fiction and fantasy of the year. Harcourt Brace & Co.   **S C**
1. Science fiction 2. Short stories
ISSN 0741-5567
Volumes 25-31 available
First volume in this series, edited by Damon Knight, was published by Doubleday in 1965. Editors and publishers vary. Variant titles: Nebula award stories; Nebula winners
Included in this annual collection of award-winning stories and runners-up are essays on the writings and events in science fiction as well as lists of winners of Nebula Hugo awards, sponsored by Science Fiction Writers of America

The **Norton** book of American short stories; edited by Peter S. Prescott. Norton 1988 779p $27.50
     S C
1. Short stories
ISBN 0-393-02619-1   LC 88-14181
"The 70 stories Prescott chose for inclusion in this comprehensive anthology show to great effect the sterling quality of American short stories, from the dawn-days of Poe and Hawthorne to the . . . minimalism of Raymond Carver. A collection full of treasures." Booklist

The **Norton** book of science fiction; North American science fiction, 1960-1990; edited by Ursula K. Le Guin and Brian Attebery; Karen Joy Fowler, consultant. Norton 1993 869p $27.50   **S C**
1. Science fiction 2. Short stories
ISBN 0-393-03546-8   LC 93-16130
Damon Knight, Robert Silverberg, Connie Willis and Harlan Ellison are among the authors represented in this anthology of more than 60 stories
A "compilation of intelligent and entertaining sf that belongs in virtually every fiction collection." Booklist

Not the only one; lesbian and gay fiction for teens; Tony Grima, editor. Alyson Publs. 1995 c1994 237p pa $7.95   **S C**
1. Homosexuality—Fiction 2. Short stories
ISBN 1-55583-275-X   LC 94-39264
A collection of short stories portraying gay and lesbian teenagers at different moments in their lives
"Some readers may find some stories grim, or explicit (in that they refer in passing to sexual acts in a mild sort of way). Others will find humor, angst, and the other reactions that good fiction is supposed to bring out in the reader." Voice Youth Advocates

O'Brien, Tim, 1946-
The things they carried; a work of fiction. Houghton Mifflin 1990 273p o.p.; Penguin Bks. paperback available $10.95   **S C**
1. Vietnam War, 1961-1975—Fiction 2. Short stories
ISBN 0-14-014773-X (pa)   LC 89-39871
This is a collection of stories about American soldiers in Vietnam. . . . All of the stories "deal with a single platoon, one of whose members is a character named Tim O'Brien." N Y Times Book Rev
"This book may be self-conscious . . . but through its determination to treat these men with dignity and decency it proves immensely affecting." Newsweek

O'Connor, Flannery
Collected works. Library of Am. 1988 1281p $35   **S C**
1. Short stories
ISBN 0-940450-37-2   LC 87-37829
Contents: Wise blood; A good man is hard to find; The violent bear it away; Everything that rises must converge; Stories and occasional prose; Letters

The complete stories. Farrar, Straus & Giroux 1971 555p $37.50; pa $15   **S C**
1. Short stories
ISBN 0-374-12752-2; 0-374-51536-0 (pa)
This collection is "arranged in chronological order from the story she wrote for her master's thesis at the University of Iowa to 'Judgement Day.' . . . The stories here include the original openings and other chapters of her two novels 'Wise Blood' and 'The Violent Bear It Away.'" N Y Times Book Rev

O'Connor, Frank, 1903-1966
Collected stories; introduction by Richard Ellmann. Knopf 1981 701p hardcover o.p. paperback available $20   **S C**
1. Ireland—Fiction 2. Short stories
ISBN 0-394-71048-7 (pa)   LC 81-1253
The author "grew up with 'the troubles,' but the Ireland he evokes in these 72 stories . . . is the provincial life of his Cork boyhood." Libr J

Ortiz Cofer, Judith, 1952-
An island like you; stories of the barrio. Orchard Bks. 1995 165p $15.95; lib bdg $15.99
     S C
1. Puerto Ricans—United States—Fiction 2. Short stories
ISBN 0-531-06897-8; 0-531-08747-6 (lib bdg)
     LC 94-32496
Also available in paperback from Viking
"A Melanie Kroupa book"
"Twelve linked short stories explore teenage life in or about the Paterson, New Jersey barrio. . . . Cofer tells of various kids, such as a girl sent to spend the summer in Puerto Rico with her grandparents, a boy helped by his teacher to find unsuspected power in poetry, a girl uneasy about working with a mentally retarded man at her poolside summer job, a boy whose duty hour with his grandfather takes a suprising turn. . . . The combination of interweaving of characters, intensity of emotion, and deft control of language makes this a rewarding collection." Bull Cent Child Books

The **Other** side of heaven; postwar fiction by Vietnamese and American writers; edited by Wayne Karlin, Le Minh Khue and Truong Vu. Curbstone Press 1995 411p pa $17.95   **S C**
1. Vietnam—Fiction 2. Vietnam War, 1961-1975—Fiction 3. Short stories
ISBN 1-880684-31-4   LC 95-20869
The stories in this anthology "deal with the after-effects of the war on both sides. The stories present a number of interesting characters: a Ross Perot-like figure searching for the remains of his only son; a Puerto Rican

The Other side of heaven—*Continued*

mother who snaps when her only son is killed in Vietnam; the ghost of a soldier who resides under a rock. This book could be used in upper-level literature classes or in schools with Vietnamese-American students who would bring a special understanding to the culture described by the Vietnamese writers." Book Rep

The **Oxford** book of American detective stories; edited by Tony Hillerman, Rosemary Herbert. Oxford Univ. Press 1996 686p $25   **S C**
1. Mystery fiction 2. Short stories
ISBN 0-19-508581-7   LC 95-4504
This collection includes stories by B. Pronzini, E. A. Poe, E. S. Gardner, E. Queen and M. Muller

The **Oxford** book of American short stories; edited by Joyce Carol Oates. Oxford Univ. Press 1992 768p $30; pa $15.95   **S C**
1. Short stories
ISBN 0-19-507065-8; 0-19-509262-7 (pa)
                                       LC 92-1353
"Fifty-six short stories showcase this ever-vital and challenging art form's suppleness and power from Washington Irving's classic, 'Rip Van Winkle,' to the work of Sandra Cisneros. While Oates couldn't resist masterpieces such as Ernest Hemingway's 'A Clean, Well-Lighted Place,' her goal was 'familiar names, unfamiliar titles,' and her intention was to call our attention to works by the likes of Edgar Allan Poe, Harriet Beecher Stowe, Henry James, Kate Chopin, William Carlos Williams, and Saul Bellow that aren't anthologized to death. . . . Her standards of excellence are consistent throughout." Booklist

The **Oxford** book of English ghost stories; chosen by Michael Cox and R. A. Gilbert. Oxford Univ. Press 1987 c1986 504p $30; pa $13.95
                                       S C
1. Ghost stories 2. Short stories
ISBN 0-19-214163-5; 0-19-282666-2 (pa)
                                       LC 86-8690
First published 1986 in the United Kingdom
Arranged chronologically, the forty-two stories gathered here "date from the 1820s . . . to the 1980s. . . . In addition to featuring those writers one would expect to find here—Sheridan Le Fanu, M. R. James, and Walter de la Mare, for example—there is also a bounty of wonderful authors with whom U.S. audiences may not be familiar." Booklist

The **Oxford** book of gothic tales; edited by Chris Baldick. Oxford Univ. Press 1992 xxiii, 533p $35; pa $14.95   **S C**
1. Horror fiction 2. Short stories
ISBN 0-19-214194-5; 0-19-283117-8 (pa)
                                       LC 91-27290
This chronologically arranged anthology contains thirty-seven stories dating from the 18th to 20th century. Among the authors are Hawthorne, Poe, Stevenson, Hardy, Faulkner, Welty, Borges, Angela Carter and Isabel Allende

The **Oxford** book of Irish short stories; edited by William Trevor. Oxford Univ. Press 1989 567p $35; pa $13.95   **S C**
1. Ireland—Fiction 2. Short stories
ISBN 0-19-214180-5; 0-19-282845-2 (pa)
                                       LC 88-28147
"The great Irish writers—from Oliver Goldsmith and Oscar Wilde to James Joyce and Edna O'Brien—are represented in a collection for older advanced readers." Booklist

The **Oxford** book of modern fairy tales; edited by Alison Lurie. Oxford Univ. Press 1993 455p $30; pa $14.95   **S C**
1. Fairy tales 2. Short stories
ISBN 0-19-214218-6; 0-19-282385-X (pa)
                                       LC 92-28007
This volume is "full of old favorites and some priceless new gems, with a wonderful chronological arrangement that allows readers to absorb information on literary developments and trends, or simply to enjoy the well-told tales. . . . The whole collection is first rate and demonstrates beautifully that modern fairy tales are not just for kids." SLJ

The **Oxford** book of science fiction stories; edited by Tom Shippey. Oxford Univ. Press 1992 xxvi, 587p $25   **S C**
1. Science fiction 2. Short stories
ISBN 0-19-214204-6   LC 92-9512
This chronologically arranged anthology begins with The land ironclads, by H. G. Wells (1903) and ends with Piecework, by David Brin (1990). Other authors represented include Arthur C. Clarke, Frederik Pohl, Brian Aldiss, Ursula K. Le Guin, and Gene Wolfe
"Editor Shippey has cast his net widely as to themes, schools of sf writing, and authors. . . . He has also provided a generous and useful bibliography, making his effort a fine one for smaller collections and classroom use." Booklist

The **Oxford** book of short stories; chosen by V.S. Pritchett. Oxford Univ. Press 1981 547p $29.95; pa $14.95   **S C**
1. Short stories
ISBN 0-19-214116-3; 0-19-282113-X (pa)
                                       LC 81-156872
In addition to one of his own short stories, Pritchett has selected 40 others, written in English during the 19th and 20th centuries. Most of the authors are English, Irish or American and include Somerset Maugham, D. H. Lawrence, Faulkner, Twain, and Eudora Welty

Pilcher, Rosamunde, 1924-
Flowers in the rain & other stories. St. Martin's Press 1991 277p hardcover o.p. paperback available $6.99   **S C**
1. Short stories
ISBN 0-312-92774-6 (pa)   LC 91-18237
"A Thomas Dunne book"
"Hope, memory, love lost, and love regained are the major themes that thread their way through this easily read collection of short stories. Ranging in topic from a tale of a young woman who finds from a stranger the

Pilcher, Rosamunde, 1924——*Continued*
courage she never thought she had, to a portrait of a
bride-to-be who is forced to choose between two loves,
the sensitively written offerings portray a kaleidoscope of
human emotions that will touch the hearts of YA readers." SLJ

Poe, Edgar Allan, 1809-1849
The collected tales and poems of Edgar Allan
Poe. Modern Lib. 1992 1026p $20   **S C**
1. Mystery fiction 2. Horror fiction 3. Short stories
ISBN 0-679-60007-8   LC 92-50231
A reissue of The complete tales and poems of Edgar
Allan Poe published 1938
This volume contains short stories, poems, and a sampling of Poe's essays, criticism and journalistic writings

Tales of Edgar Allan Poe; illustrated by Barry
Moser; afterword by Peter Glassman. Books of
Wonder 1991 308p il $22   **S C**
1. Horror fiction 2. Short stories
ISBN 0-688-07509-6   LC 91-3277
This illustrated collection includes The gold bug; The
tell-tale heart; The fall of the House of Usher and The
pit and the pendulum
"Moser's watercolor paintings for 14 of Poe's best
stories are both macabre and understated. The best of
them make us further imagine the terrible things beyond
the edge." Booklist

Porter, Katherine Anne, 1890-1980
The collected stories of Katherine Anne Porter.
Harcourt Brace & World 1965 495p hardcover o.p.
paperback available $14   **S C**
1. Short stories
ISBN 0-15-618876-7 (pa)
Contains three collections of short stories: Flowering
Judas, and other stories (1935); The leaning tower, and
other stories (1944); Pale horse, pale rider (1939); and
four additional short stories: Virgin Violeta; The martyr;
The fig tree; and Holiday
"These are perfect examples of the short story and are
representative not only of the best American writing but
of the best in the world." SLJ

Pale horse, pale rider: three short novels.
Harcourt Brace Jovanovich 1990 c1939 208p $17
                                       S C
1. Short stories
ISBN 0-15-170755-3   LC 89-26886
First published 1939
"These three short novels include the title story, which
concerns a young newspaperwoman in love with a soldier who dies in the 1918 influenza epidemic; 'Noon
Wine,' the narrative of a shooting in the glare of a Texas
midday; and 'Old Mortality,' a three-stage account of a
Southern family that tries to believe its own myths about
itself." Good Read

Prize stories: The O. Henry Awards. Doubleday
$25.50; pa $10.95   **S C**
1. Short stories
ISSN 0079-5453
First collection, published in 1919 with title: O. Henry
Memorial Award prize stories, was edited by Blanche C.
Williams

Editors vary. 1967-1996: William Abrahams
This annual anthology of outstanding short stories by
American authors includes contributions by such authors
as John Updike, Joyce Carol Oates, Alice Adams, Raymond Carver, Bobbie Ann Mason, and T. Coraghessan
Boyle

Pushkin, Aleksandr Sergeevich, 1799-1837
Alexander Pushkin: complete prose fiction;
translated with an introduction and notes, by Paul
Debreczeny; verse passages translated by Walter
Arndt. Stanford Univ. Press 1983 545p $60; pa
$19.95   **S C**
1. Russia—Fiction 2. Short stories
ISBN 0-8047-1142-9; 0-8047-1800-8 (pa)
                                      LC 81-85450
"Aside from such well-known pieces as the 'Blackamoor of Peter the Great,' 'The Belkin Tales,' 'The
Queen of Spades,' and 'The Captain's Daughter,' [this
work] also includes several fictional fragments and the
important nonfictional 'A History of Pugachev.'" Libr J

Rites of passage; stories about growing up by
black writers from around the world; edited by
Tonya Bolden; with a foreword by Charles
Johnson. Hyperion Bks. for Children 1994 208p
hardcover o.p. paperback available $7.95 **S C**
1. African Americans—Fiction 2. Blacks—Fiction
3. Short stories
ISBN 0-7868-1076-9 (pa)   LC 93-31304
"Seventeen 'growing up' stories by noted black writers from the U.S., the Caribbean, Central America, England, Africa, and Australia. . . . The adolescent protagonists are well drawn, and their coming-of-age stories offer meaningful anecdotes on coping with, adapting to,
and interpreting life's experiences." SLJ
Includes bibliographical references

Robert Silverberg's worlds of wonder; edited and
with an introduction by Robert Silverberg.
Warner Bks. 1987 352p hardcover o.p.
paperback available $12.95   **S C**
1. Science fiction 2. Short stories
ISBN 0-446-39012-7 (pa)   LC 87-21603
This anthology contains thirteen classic SF stories
"that are still exciting reading today. . . . Silverberg's
analysis of these stories, and his recollections of their influence on his own development as a young writer, will
fascinate those who aspire to write science fiction. . . .
Any library that collects science fiction must have this
book." Voice Youth Advocates

Roth, Philip
Goodbye, Columbus, and five short stories.
Modern Lib. 1995 298p $13.50; pa $12   **S C**
1. Jews—United States—Fiction 2. Short stories
ISBN 0-679-60159-7; 0-679-74826-1 (pa)
                                      LC 94-44528
Also available in hardcover from Amereon and Buccaneer Bks.
A reissue of the title first published 1959 by
Houghton Mifflin

Roth, Philip—*Continued*

"The title story in this collection is about a young Radcliffe girl and a Rutgers boy who learn that there is more to love than exuberance and passion. All of the stories dramatize the dilemma of modern American Jews, torn between two worlds." Publ Wkly

Salinger, J. D. (Jerome David), 1919-

Nine stories. Little, Brown 1953 302p $22.95; pa $4.99   **S C**
1. Short stories
ISBN 0-316-76956-8; 0-316-76950-9 (pa)

This collection "introduced various members of the Glass family who would dominate the remainder of Salinger's work. Critical response divided itself between high praise and cult worship. Most of the stories deal with precocious, troubled children, whose religious yearnings—often tilting toward the East—are in vivid contrast to the materialistic and spiritually empty world of their parents. The result was a perfect literary formula for the 1950s." Benet's Reader's Ency of Am Lit

Saroyan, William, 1908-1981

My name is Aram; illustrated by Don Freeman. Harcourt Brace & Co. 1940 220p il o.p.; Dell paperback available $4.99   **S C**
1. Armenian Americans—Fiction 2. Short stories
ISBN 0-440-36205-9 (pa)

Sketches concerning Aram, an American-born Armenian boy and his mad cousin, his sad uncle, his reckless uncle, and other eccentric family members

Sholem Aleichem, 1859-1916

The best of Sholem Aleichem; edited by Irving Howe and Ruth R. Wisse. New Republic Bks. 1979 xxvii, 276p   **S C**
1. Jews—Fiction 2. Short stories

LC 79-9870

Available in large print edition from Walker & Co.

A collection of twenty-two of the author's stories translated from the Yiddish

Tevye the dairyman and The railroad stories; [by] Sholom Aleichem; translated from the Yiddish and with an introduction by Hillel Halkin. Schocken Bks. 1987 xli, 309p hardcover o.p. paperback available $15   **S C**
1. Jews—Fiction 2. Short stories
ISBN 0-8052-1069-5 (pa)   LC 86-24835

"Library of Yiddish classics"

"In the first eight stories of this collection, Tevye, the Russian Jew so familiar from *Fiddler on the Roof*, bemoans his fate. In these as well as the following 21 tales, the author displays his splendid storytelling skills." Booklist

Singer, Isaac Bashevis, 1904-1991

The death of Methuselah and other stories. Farrar, Straus & Giroux 1988 244p $17.95   **S C**
1. Jews—Fiction 2. Short stories
ISBN 0-374-13563-0   LC 87-21238

Also available in paperback from New Am. Lib.

This "collection of Singer's fiction displays his skill as a storyteller and his special ability to create a unique world of many possibilities. . . . As always, the confrontations exposed here—between love, and sex, man and woman, good and evil, life and death—achieve a magical palpability." Booklist

The image and other stories. Farrar, Straus & Giroux 1985 310p $17.95; pa $11   **S C**
1. Jews—Fiction 2. Short stories
ISBN 0-374-17465-2; 0-374-52079-8 (pa)

LC 85-4487

"These unabashedly traditional yarns, imbued with Jewish manners, customs, and syntax, range in setting from the Old World to the New and are cleanly humorous and poignant." Booklist

✓ The **Singing** spirit: early short stories by North American Indians; edited by Bernd C. Peyer. University of Ariz. Press 1989 xxi, 175p (Sun tracks) hardcover o.p. paperback available $11.95   **S C**
1. Indians of North America—Fiction 2. Short stories
ISBN 0-8165-1220-5 (pa)   LC 89-32419

"An anthology of short fiction written 'by Indians about Indians' during the complex social changes that occurred between 1888 and 1930. . . . The value of the stories lies as much in their historical context as it does in the charm of their individual content." Wilson Libr Bull

Includes bibliographical references

✓ **Somehow** tenderness survives; stories of Southern Africa; selected by Hazel Rochman. Harper & Row 1988 147p lib bdg $14.89; pa $4.50 **S C**
1. Short stories 2. South Africa—Fiction
ISBN 0-06-025023-2 (lib bdg); 0-06-447063-6 (pa)

LC 88-916

A collection of eight short stories and two "autobiographical accounts which vividly evoke what it means to come of age in South Africa under apartheid. The contributors, including Doris Lessing and Nadine Gordimer, as well as lesser-known writers, are of various races and their stories cover a time span of 35 years. . . . This title should be in every YA collection. A glossary and notes on contributors are included." Voice Youth Advocates

✓ **Song** of the turtle; American Indian literature, 1974-1994; edited with an introduction by Paula Gunn Allen. Ballantine Bks. 1996 353p $25

S C
1. Indians of North America—Fiction 2. Short stories
ISBN 0-345-37525-4   LC 95-39251

Companion volume to Voice of the turtle (1994)

"A One World book"

"This anthology of Native American literature includes strong, striking stories by such recognized contemporary writers as Susan Power, James Welch, and Joseph Bruchac." Booklist

Spider Woman's granddaughters; traditional tales and contemporary writing by Native American women; edited and with an introduction by Paula Gunn Allen. Beacon Press 1989 242p $19.95 **S C**

1. Indians of North America—Fiction 2. Short stories
ISBN 0-8070-8100-0   LC 88-47655

This is a collection of twenty-four stories by Native American women authors arranged in three thematic sections, 'The Warriors,' 'The Casualties,' and 'The Resistance.' The contributors include Marmon Silko, E. Pauline Johnson, Vickie L. Sears, Anna Lee Walters, Soge Track, LeAnne Howe and Louise Erdrich

"Each of the stories in this collection, whether traditional or modern, expresses the urgency of survival—of not vanishing either individually or politically. And the quality of the stories is stunning." Women's Rev Books

Includes bibliography

Streetlights: illuminating tales of the urban black experience; edited by Doris Jean Austin and Martin Simmons. Penguin Bks. 1996 515p pa $14.95   **S C**

1. City life—Fiction 2. African Americans—Fiction 3. Short stories
ISBN 0-14-017471-0   LC 94-24868

The editors present "stories by 49 black writers that evoke 49 distinctive interpretations of city life as lived today by African Americans. . . . These are stories about people in complicated relationships, relationships made even more difficult by the pressure, danger, and bleak indifference of the city. The plots involve painful or significant interactions between strangers; the fears of parents raising children in cities; conflicts between grown children and parents and between divorcing spouses; racism; money troubles; the disappointments and determination of immigrants; the pipe dreams of pregnant teenagers; and the pleasures and worries of homosexuals." Booklist

Styron, William, 1925-

A Tidewater morning; three tales from youth. Random House 1993 142p $17; pa $10   **S C**

1. Short stories
ISBN 0-679-42742-2; 0-679-75449-0 (pa)
LC 93-3639

"In each of these three stories, which originally appeared in *Esquire* magazine in the Seventies and Eighties, narrator Paul Whitehurst recalls significant episodes from his childhood in Virginia during the Depression and the Second World War." Libr J

"A teacher or librarian will be delighted to recommend this book to young readers who can appreciate the depths of its insights and the elegance of its style." Voice Youth Advocates

Tales from the planet Earth; created by Frederik Pohl and Elizabeth Anne Hull. St. Martin's Press 1986 268p hardcover o.p. paperback available $3.95   **S C**

1. Science fiction 2. Short stories
ISBN 0-312-90779-6 (pa)   LC 86-13832

"The aliens invade: not to conquer, but to sell. Earth becomes the Wall Street of the universe; humans become involuntary mediums through which the aliens communi-cate. The 19 variations on this theme by authors from 17 countries illustrate the international scope of science fiction and offer a strong sampling of familiar and unfamiliar talents." Libr J

Talking leaves; contemporary native American short stories; introduced and edited by Craig Lesley; associate editor, Katheryn Stavrakis. Dell 1991 xxvi, 385p pa $12.95   **S C**

1. Indians of North America—Fiction 2. Short stories
ISBN 0-385-31272-5   LC 92-139334

"A Laurel trade paperback"

This anthology includes contributions by such authors as Louise Erdrich, Diane Glancy, Michael Dorris, N. Scott Momaday, Paula Gunn Allen, and Mary Tallmountain

"All these stories have a strong sense of person and place and engagingly inform of the Native American condition." Libr J

Tolkien, J. R. R. (John Ronald Reuel), 1892-1973

The Silmarillion; edited by Christopher Tolkien. Houghton Mifflin 1977 365p hardcover o.p. paperback available $15.95   **S C**

1. Fantasy fiction 2. Short stories
ISBN 0-395-34646-0 (pa)   LC 77-8025

"J.R.R. Tolkien Quenta Silmarillion; (The history of the Silmarils) together with Ainudalë (The music of the Ainur) and Valaquenta; (Account of the Valar) To which is appended Akallabêth (The downfall of Númenor) and of the Rings of Power and the Third age." Facing title page

"Tolkien began writing these introductory legends in 1917 and, sporadically throughout his life, continued adding to them; his son Christopher has edited and compiled the various versions into a single cohesive work. Two brief tales, which outline the origin of the world and describe the gods who create and rule, precede the title story about the Silmarils—three brilliant, jewel-like creatures who are desired and fought over, setting up a clash between good and evil." Booklist

Unfinished tales of Númenor and Middle-earth; edited with introduction, commentary, index, and maps by Christopher Tolkien. Houghton Mifflin 1980 472p il hardcover o.p. paperback available $14.95   **S C**

1. Fantasy fiction 2. Short stories
ISBN 0-395-32441-6 (pa)   LC 80-83072

Title on spine: Unfinished tales

"This book was not planned by Tolkien and is a disparate collection held together by the continuing editorial presence of his son Christopher; his exhaustive commentary and countless footnotes are learned and helpful. . . . The nature and state of this material give us a rare glimpse of how Tolkien developed his fantasy world over the years." Publ Wkly

Tolstoy, Leo, graf, 1828-1910
Great short works of Leo Tolstoy; with an introduction by John Bayley; in the translations by Louise and Aylmer Maude. Harper & Row 1967 685p pa $7.50   **S C**
1. Russia—Fiction 2. Short stories
ISBN 0-06-083071-9
"A Perennial classic"
Contents: Family happiness; The Cossacks; The death of Ivan Ilych; The devil; The Kreutzer Sonata; Master and man; Father Sergius; Hadji Murád; Alyosha the Pot

Twain, Mark, 1835-1910
The complete short stories of Mark Twain; now collected for the first time; edited with an introduction by Charles Neider. Doubleday 1957 xxiv, 676p o.p.; Bantam Bks. paperback available $6.50   **S C**
1. Short stories
ISBN 0-553-21195-1 (pa)
Also available in hardcover from Amereon and Buccaneer Bks.
"The sixty pieces which are here hospitably called short stories illustrate both the weaknesses and the strengths of Mark Twain as a writer of fiction." N Y Times Book Rev

Updike, John
Pigeon feathers, and other stories. Knopf 1962 278p $19.95   **S C**
1. Short stories
ISBN 0-394-44056-0
Also available G.K. Hall large print edition and in paperback from Fawcett Bks.
These stories "are filled with gentle humor and irony. Youth, marriage, and family life provide most of the themes." Cincinnati Public Libr

Vampires: a collection of original stories; edited by Jane Yolen and Martin H. Greenberg. HarperCollins Pubs. 1991 228p $15; lib bdg $14.89; pa $4.50   **S C**
1. Vampires—Fiction 2. Short stories
ISBN 0-06-026800-X; 0-06-026801-8 (lib bdg); 0-06-440485-4 (pa)   LC 90-27888
A collection of thirteen original stories about vampires by a variety of authors
"In this collection of chilling, funny, and sensitive stories, the undead include piano teachers, mean old aunts, and even the girl next door." Booklist

Victorian ghost stories; an Oxford anthology; selected and introduced by Michael Cox and R.A. Gilbert. Oxford Univ. Press 1991 xx, 497p $31.25; pa $14.95   **S C**
1. Ghost stories 2. Short stories
ISBN 0-19-214202-X; 0-19-282999-8 (pa)
                                                    LC 91-2748
"This book contains 35 spine-tingling ghost stories, some written by such well-known authors as Charles Dickens, Robert Louis Stevenson, and Rudyard Kipling. The introduction provides an informative overview of the

development of the Victorian ghost story. These selections are sure to hook even the most reluctant reader." SLJ
Includes bibliographical references

The **Vintage** book of contemporary American short stories; edited and with an introduction by Tobias Wolff. Vintage Bks. 1994 558p pa $13
                                                         S C
1. Short stories
ISBN 0-679-74513-0   LC 94-15007
"A Vintage original"
"This collection gives us 33 well-chosen stories. Side by side with classics by favorite writers—Raymond Carver, Ann Beattie, Richard Ford—are recent contributions by Dennis Johnson, Allan Gurganus, Thom Jones, and others." Libr J

Vonnegut, Kurt, 1922-
Welcome to the monkey house; a collection of short works; by Kurt Vonnegut, Jr. Delacorte Press 1968 298p hardcover o.p. paperback available $6.50   **S C**
1. Short stories
ISBN 0-440-19478-4 (pa)
"A Seymour Lawrence book"
This collection "ranges in time from pieces written in 1950 to 1968 and in subject from observations on Barnstable Village on Cape Cod to a fictional exchange of letters between the fathers of deceased American and Soviet astronauts. In between, there's some semi-science fiction and even a fictional venture into cold war political psychology." Publ Wkly

We are the stories we tell; the best short stories by North American women since 1945; edited by Wendy Martin. Pantheon Bks. 1990 337p hardcover o.p. paperback available $15   **S C**
1. Women—Fiction 2. Short stories
ISBN 0-679-72881-3 (pa)   LC 89-39587
This anthology includes stories by Margaret Atwood, Ann Beattie, Sandra Cisneros, Louise Erdrich, Maxine Hong Kingston, Anne Tyler, Alice Walker, and nineteen other well-known women authors

Wells, H. G. (Herbert George), 1866-1946
The complete short stories of H. G. Wells. St. Martin's Press 1987 c1927 1038p $19.95   **S C**
1. Short stories
ISBN 0-312-15855-6   LC 87-27478
First published 1927 in the United Kingdom with title: The short stories of H. G. Wells
A collection of 62 short stories and the complete work: The time machine, first published 1895
"A fat, heavy volume packed with humour, strangeness, horror and imaginative stimulus." Daily Telegraph

Welty, Eudora, 1909-

The collected stories of Eudora Welty. Harcourt Brace Jovanovich 1980 622p $29.95; pa $15

S C

1. Short stories
ISBN 0-15-118994-3; 0-15-618921-6 (pa)

LC 80-7947

This volume contains four previously published collections: A curtain of green, and other stories; The wide net, and other stories; The golden apples and The bride of the Innisfallen, and other stories. Also included in this volume are two uncollected pieces: Where is the voice coming from? and The demonstrators

West, Dorothy, 1909-

The richer, the poorer: stories, sketches, and reminiscences. Doubleday 1995 254p $22; pa $12.95

S C

1. African Americans 2. Short stories
ISBN 0-385-47145-9; 0-385-47146-7 (pa)

LC 94-44013

"Two of the best stories included in this collection are 'The Roomer' and 'The Richer, the Poorer.' 'The Roomer' features a woman who has to explain to her tight husband an extravagant purchase—a new winter coat. 'The Richer, the Poorer' is a delicious parable about two sisters, one who saves for a rainy day, the other who doesn't; but it's the former sister not the latter who has regrets—that she has kept her money but has done no living. The autobiographical essays address issues of her childhood and of the present." Booklist

Westall, Robert, 1929-1993

Shades of darkness; more of the ghostly best stories of Robert Westall. Farrar, Straus & Giroux 1994 312p $17

S C

1. Ghost stories 2. Horror fiction 3. Short stories
ISBN 0-374-36758-2

LC 93-42229

This "collection of eleven stories by . . . Westall, gleaned from his earlier books and including one previously unpublished story, shows his uncanny way with eerie stories. His familiar themes—cats, schoolboys, World War II—are all represented here. The one new story, 'The Cats,' is a sophisticated tale of revenge by cats on a bullying, mean-spirited wife. A pleasure for Westall enthusiasts." Horn Book

Wharton, Edith, 1862-1937

The selected short stories of Edith Wharton; introduced and edited by R.W.B. Lewis. Scribner 1991 xxi, 390p $24.95

S C

1. Short stories
ISBN 0-684-19304-3

LC 91-11433

A "collection of 21 of the author's best stories. Lewis' excellent introduction explains Wharton's appeal and provides a brief overview of her life and prolific literary output." Booklist

Who do you think you are? stories of friends and enemies; selected by Hazel Rochman and Darlene Z. McCampbell. Little, Brown 1993 170p $16.95

S C

1. Friendship—Fiction 2. Short stories
ISBN 0-316-75355-6

LC 93-314

"Joy Street books"

"Louise Erdrich, John Updike, Ray Bradbury, Joyce Carol Oates, Sandra Cisneros, Tim O'Brien, Richard Peck, and Maya Angelou are among the 15 writers represented in this anthology of stories [two prose excerpts and a poem] about friendship and loss of friendship." Booklist

"Meticulously chosen and arranged, these works crystalize moments of vulnerability, sorrow and understanding; together, they serve as an excellent introduction to modern American writing." Publ Wkly

Wilson, Budge, 1927-

The leaving and other stories. Philomel Bks. 1992 c1990 207p o.p.; Scholastic paperback available $3.50

S C

1. Short stories 2. Nova Scotia—Fiction
ISBN 0-590-46933-9 (pa)

LC 91-28373

First published 1990 in Canada

A collection of nine short stories which capture a variety of experiences and feelings of young women growing up in Nova Scotia

"From their first sentences, the stories, models of understatement and evocation, proclaim the author's mastery of the form. . . . In all the stories the author's choice of themes and feel for the language and her precise and economic use of dialogue and detail to reveal character mark the emergence of an outstanding voice in young-adult literature." Horn Book

Wolfe, Thomas, 1900-1938

The complete short stories of Thomas Wolfe; edited by Francis E. Skipp; foreword by James Dickey. Scribner 1987 xxix, 621p $27.50; pa $15

S C

1. Short stories
ISBN 0-684-18743-4; 0-02-040891-9 (pa)

LC 86-13782

"All 58 of Wolfe's short stories . . . have been edited by Skipp in a way that represents what Wolfe himself may have wanted his audience to read." Booklist

Wright, Richard, 1908-1960

Uncle Tom's children; five long stories. Harper & Row 1938 xxx, 384p hardcover o.p. paperback available $7

S C

1. African Americans—Fiction 2. Short stories
ISBN 0-06-081251-6 (pa)

Also available in hardcover from Borgo Press

The stories in this collection deal with conflicts between whites and blacks in the South

PART 2

AUTHOR, TITLE, SUBJECT, AND ANALYTICAL INDEX

AUTHOR, TITLE, SUBJECT AND ANALYTICAL INDEX

This index to the books in the Classified Catalog includes author, title, subject, and analytical entries; added entries for joint authors, illustrators, and editors of works entered under title; and name and subject cross-references, all arranged in one alphabet.

The number in bold face type at the end of each entry refers to the Dewey Decimal Classification or to the Fiction or Story Collection section where the main entry for the book will be found. Works classed in 92 will be found under the name of the person written about.

For further information about this index and for examples of entries, see Directions for Use of the Catalog.

1/3, 1/3, 1/3. Brautigan, R.
In American short story masterpieces
S C

1/72nd scale. MacLeod, I.
In Nebula awards 26 p102-31 **S C**

4 plays. Inge, W. **812**

9 plays by black women **812.008**

The 13 clocks. Thurber, J.
In Thurber, J. Writings and drawings
818

15 short plays. McNally, T. **812**

20th-century arms and armor. Bull, S. **355.8**

20th century inventors. See Aaseng, N. Twentieth-century inventors **920**

21st century earth: opposing viewpoints
303.49

24 favorite one-act plays **808.82**

27 wagons full of cotton. Williams, T.
In 24 favorite one-act plays p94-116
808.82

50 chance of lightning. Salat, C.
In Am I blue? p227-43 **S C**

50 ways to fight censorship. Marsh, D.
323.44

50 ways to help your community. Fiffer, S.
361.3

The 60s reader. Haskins, J. **973.92**

65 years of the Oscar. Osborne, R. A.
791.43

100 best careers for the 21st century. Field, S.
331.7

100 days. See Schom, A. One hundred days
944.05

100 great Africans. Rake, A. **920**

100 great monologues from the neo-classical theatre **808.82**

100 great monologues from the Renaissance theatre **822.008**

100 key documents in American democracy
973

The 100 most influential women of all time. Felder, D. G. **920**

The 100 most popular young adult authors. Drew, B. A. **810.9**

100 questions and answers about AIDS. Ford, M. T. **616.97**

100 world-class thin books. Bodart, J. R.
028.1

150 ways teens can make a difference. Salzman, M. **302**

303 CD-ROMs to use in your library. Dewey, P. R. **025.2**

333 more science tricks & experiments. Brown, R. J. **507**

333 science tricks & experiments. Brown, R. J.
507

500 great books by women. Bauermeister, E.
016.3054

500 nations. Josephy, A. M. **970.004**

The 900 days. Salisbury, H. E. **940.54**

1,001 things everyone should know about American history. Garraty, J. A. **973**

1066: the year of the conquest. Howarth, D. A.
942.02

1300-1399 (14th century) *See* Fourteenth century

1500-1599 (16th century) *See* Sixteenth century

1700-1799 (18th century) *See* Eighteenth century

1776. Stone, P.
In Best American plays: 7th series—1967-1973 p199-244 **812.008**

1812: the war nobody won. Marrin, A. **973.5**

1984. See Orwell, G. Nineteen eighty-four
Fic

1984 revisited **823.009**

2000-2099 (21st century) *See* Twenty-first century

2001: a space odyssey. Clarke, A. C. **Fic**

2064, or thereabouts. Bunch, D. R.
In The Norton book of science fiction p93-97
S C

The $30,000 bequest. Twain, M.
In Twain, M. The complete short stories of Mark Twain **S C**

The £1,000,000 bank-note. Twain, M.
In Twain, M. The complete short stories of Mark Twain **S C**

A

A & P. Updike, J.
In Updike, J. Pigeon feathers, and other stories p187-96 **S C**

A-bomb victims *See* Atomic bomb victims

A.I.D.S. (Disease) *See* AIDS (Disease)

A+ projects in biology, Janice VanCleave's. VanCleave, J. P. **574**

A+ projects in chemistry, Janice VanCleave's. VanCleave, J. P. **540.7**

AAAS *See* American Association for the Advancement of Science

AACR *See* Anglo-American cataloguing rules

Aaron, Hank, 1934-
I had a hammer: the Hank Aaron story **92**

Aaron, Henry *See* Aaron, Hank, 1934-

Aaseng, Jay
(jt. auth) Aaseng, N. Head injuries **617.1**

Aaseng, Nathan, 1953-
Athletes **920**
Autoimmune diseases **616.97**
Cerebral palsy **616.8**
The common cold and the flu **616.2**
Great Justices of the Supreme Court **920**
Head injuries **617.1**
Invertebrates **592**
Science versus pseudoscience **001.9**
Twentieth-century inventors **920**
Vertebrates **596**

AASL *See* American Association of School Librarians

AAUW *See* American Association of University Women

Abandoned in the wasteland. Minow, N. N. **302.23**

Abbey, Edward, 1927-1989
The serpents of paradise **818**

Abbott, George
All quiet on the western front
In Best American screenplays **812.008**
Three men on a horse
In Twenty best plays of the modern American theatre p511-59 **812.008**

Abbott, R. Tucker (Robert Tucker), 1919-1995
A field guide to shells **594**

Abbott, Robert Tucker *See* Abbott, R. Tucker (Robert Tucker), 1919-1995

Abbreviations

Dictionaries

The Barnhart abbreviations dictionary **421.03**
Kleinedler, S. R. NTC's dictionary of acronyms and abbreviations **421.03**
Webster's guide to abbreviations **421.03**

The **ABC-CLIO** companion to the civil rights movement. Grossman, M. **323.1**

The **ABC-CLIO** companion to the environmental movement. Grossman, M. **363.7**

The **ABC-CLIO** world history companion to the industrial revolution. Stearns, P. N. **909.81**

The **ABC** of lettering. Biegeleisen, J. I. **745.6**

The **ABC's** of acting. Whelan, J. **792**

ABC's of the Bible **220**

Abdolah, Kader
Eagles
In Coming of age p29-42 **808.8**

Abdul-Jabbar, Kareem, 1947-
Black profiles in courage **920**

Abe Lincoln in Illinois. Sherwood, R. E.
In Best plays of the modern American theatre: 2nd series p725-73 **812.008**

Abel, Niels Henrik, 1802-1829
See/See also pages in the following book(s):
Bell, E. T. Men of mathematics p307-26 **920**

Abelard, Peter, 1079-1142
See/See also pages in the following book(s):
Durant, W. J. The age of faith p931-48 **940.1**

Abie's Irish Rose. Nichols, A.
In The Most popular plays of the American theater p159-222 **812.008**

Abiodun, Rowland
(jt. auth) Drewal, H. J. Yoruba **709.6**

Ablaze. Read, P. P. **363.1**

Abner, Allison, 1959-
Finding our way **305.23**

Abnormal growth *See* Growth disorders

Abnormal psychology
See also Compulsive behavior

Abnormalities, Human *See* Birth defects

Abodaher, David J.
Puerto Rico: America's 51st state? **972.95**

The **abolition** of man. Lewis, C. S.
In Lewis, C. S. The essential C. S. Lewis p428-66 **828**

Abolitionists
Coil, S. M. Harriet Beecher Stowe **92**
Douglass, F. Autobiographies **92**
Douglass, F. The life and times of Frederick Douglass **92**
Hedrick, J. D. Harriet Beecher Stowe **92**
Huggins, N. I. Slave and citizen: the life of Frederick Douglass **92**
McFeely, W. S. Frederick Douglass **92**
Ortiz, V. Sojourner Truth, a self-made woman **92**

Abominations. Raphael, L.
In Growing up gay p249-52 **808.8**

Abortion
Abortion **363.4**
The Abortion controversy **363.4**
Abortion: opposing viewpoints **363.4**
Day, N. Abortion **363.4**
Morowitz, H. J. The facts of life **612.6**
See/See also pages in the following book(s):
Alderman, E. The right to privacy p55-70 **323.44**
Bode, J. Kids still having kids p69-86 **362.7**
Mabie, M. C. J. Bioethics and the new medical technology **174**

Abortion **363.4**

Abortion. O'Neill, E.
In O'Neill, E. Complete plays v1 **812**

The **abortion.** Walker, A.
In We are the stories we tell **S C**

The **Abortion** controversy **363.4**

Abortion: opposing viewpoints **363.4**

About a woman named Nancy. West, D.
In West, D. The richer, the poorer: stories, sketches, and reminiscences **S C**

Adolescence—*Continued*
See/See also pages in the following book(s):
Galbraith, J. The gifted kids' survival guide
p243-55   **155.5**
Bibliography
Zvirin, S. The best years of their lives
                                           011.6
Fiction
Banks, R. Rule of the bone   **Fic**
Cole, B. Celine   **Fic**

Adolescence. Faulkner, W.
In Faulkner, W. Uncollected stories of William Faulkner p459-73   **S C**

Adolescent fathers *See* Teenage fathers

Adolescent mothers *See* Teenage mothers

Adolescent pregnancy *See* Teenage pregnancy

Adolescent prostitution *See* Juvenile prostitution

Adolescent psychiatry
Gutkind, L. Stuck in time   **616.89**

Adolescent psychology
Pratt, J. For real   **305.23**
See/See also pages in the following book(s):
Bettelheim, B. Surviving, and other essays
p350-69   **155.9**

Adolescents *See* Teenagers

Adolescents and ADD. Quinn, P. O.   **371.9**

Adoption
Adoption: opposing viewpoints   **362.7**
Gravelle, K. Where are my birth parents?
                                           362.7
Liptak, K. Adoption controversies   **362.7**
Fiction
Kingsolver, B. Pigs in heaven   **Fic**
Pennebaker, R. Don't think twice   **Fic**

Adoption, Interracial *See* Interracial adoption

Adoption controversies. Liptak, K.   **362.7**

Adoption: opposing viewpoints   **362.7**

Adrift. Callahan, S.   **910.4**

Advancing Luna and Ida B. Wells. Walker, A.
In Black-eyed Susans/Midnight birds p313-30
                                           S C

Adventure. Anderson, S.
In Anderson, S. Winesburg, Ohio   **S C**

Adventure and adventurers
Fiction
See Adventure fiction

Adventure fiction
See also Science fiction; Sea stories
Benchley, P. Jaws   **Fic**
Dumas, A. The Count of Monte Cristo   **Fic**
Gilstrap, J. Nathan's run   **Fic**
Haggard, H. R. King Solomon's mines   **Fic**
Sutcliff, R. The Shining Company   **Fic**
Verne, J. Around the world in eighty days
                                           Fic

Adventure heroes. Rovin, J.   **700**

The **adventure** of Abraham Lincoln's clue. Queen, E.
In Crime classics p299-316   **S C**
In The Oxford book of American detective stories p587-601   **S C**

The **adventure** of Black Peter. Doyle, Sir A. C.
In Doyle, Sir A. C. The complete Sherlock Holmes   **S C**

The **adventure** of Charles Augustus Milverton. Doyle, Sir A. C.
In Doyle, Sir A. C. The complete Sherlock Holmes   **S C**

The **adventure** of Shoscombe Old Place. Doyle, Sir A. C.
In Doyle, Sir A. C. The complete Sherlock Holmes   **S C**

The **adventure** of the Abbey Grange. Doyle, Sir A. C.
In Doyle, Sir A. C. The complete Sherlock Holmes   **S C**

The **adventure** of the Beryl Coronet. Doyle, Sir A. C.
In Doyle, Sir A. C. The complete Sherlock Holmes   **S C**

The **adventure** of the blanched soldier. Doyle, Sir A. C.
In Doyle, Sir A. C. The complete Sherlock Holmes   **S C**

The **adventure** of the Blue Carbuncle. Doyle, Sir A. C.
In Doyle, Sir A. C. The complete Sherlock Holmes   **S C**

The **adventure** of the Bruce-Partington plans. Doyle, Sir A. C.
In Doyle, Sir A. C. The complete Sherlock Holmes   **S C**

The **adventure** of the cardboard box. Doyle, Sir A. C.
In Doyle, Sir A. C. The complete Sherlock Holmes   **S C**

The **adventure** of the copper beeches. Doyle, Sir A. C.
In Doyle, Sir A. C. The complete Sherlock Holmes   **S C**

The **adventure** of the creeping man. Doyle, Sir A. C.
In Doyle, Sir A. C. The complete Sherlock Holmes   **S C**

The **adventure** of the dancing men. Doyle, Sir A. C.
In Doyle, Sir A. C. The complete Sherlock Holmes   **S C**

The **adventure** of the devil's foot. Doyle, Sir A. C.
In Doyle, Sir A. C. The complete Sherlock Holmes   **S C**

The **adventure** of the dying detective. Doyle, Sir A. C.
In Doyle, Sir A. C. The complete Sherlock Holmes   **S C**

The **adventure** of the empty house. Doyle, Sir A. C.
In Doyle, Sir A. C. The complete Sherlock Holmes   **S C**

The **adventure** of the engineer's thumb. Doyle, Sir A. C.
In Doyle, Sir A. C. The complete Sherlock Holmes   **S C**

The **Aeneid** of Virgil. Virgil   873
Æpyornis Island. Wells, H. G.
   In Wells, H. G. The complete short stories of
   H. G. Wells p260-72   S C
Aeronautics
   See also Airplanes; Rocketry
   Jane's all the world's aircraft   629.133
Accidents—Fiction
   Cooney, C. B. Flight #116 is down   Fic
Flights
   Earhart, A. Last flight   629.13
   Lindbergh, C. The Spirit of St. Louis
     629.13
   Lindbergh, C. "We"   92
   Saint-Exupéry, A. de. Wind, sand, and stars
     629.13
History
   Baker, D. Flight and flying   629.13
   Bilstein, R. E. Flight in America: from the
   Wrights to the astronauts   629.13
   Hallion, R. Test pilots   629.13
   Lopez, D. S. Aviation   629.13
   Scott, P. The shoulders of giants   629.13
Safety measures
   Nader, R. Collision course   363.1
Aeronautics, Military *See* Military aeronautics
Aerospace industries
   See also Airplane industry
   Jensen, C. No downlink   629.45
   Vaughan, D. The Challenger launch decision
     629.45
Aeschylus
   Agamemnon
     In Four Greek plays   882.008
     In Seven famous Greek plays   882.008
   Prometheus bound
     In Seven famous Greek plays   882.008
   See/See also pages in the following book(s):
   Hamilton, E. The Greek way p239-57
     880.9
Aesthetics
   See also Art appreciation
   Aristotle. Poetics   808.1
AFDC (Aid to families with dependent children)
   See Child welfare
The **affair**. Bredin, J.-D.   944.081
The **affair** at 7, rue de M—. Steinbeck, J.
   In Steinbeck, J. The portable Steinbeck
     818
The **affair** at the bungalow. Christie, A.
   In Christie, A. Miss Marple: the complete
   short stories   S C
The **affair** of the 'Avalanche Bicycle and Tyre
   Co., Limited'. Morrison, A.
   In The Best crime stories of the 19th century
   p217-40   S C
Affirmative action [At issue]   331.1
Affirmative action [Reference shelf]   342
Affirmative action programs
   Affirmative action [At issue]   331.1
   Affirmative action [Reference shelf]   342
The **affluent** society. Galbraith, J. K.   330
Africa
   Africa   960

Africa: opposing viewpoints   960
Dostert, P. E. Africa   960
Du Bois, W. E. B. W.E.B. Du Bois: a reader
     305.8
Antiquities
Africa's glorious legacy   960
Davidson, B. The lost cities of Africa   960
Biography
Rake, A. 100 great Africans   920
Description
See/See also pages in the following book(s):
Great rivers of the world p22-82   910
Exploration
Moorehead, A. The Blue Nile   962
Fiction
African short stories   S C
Conrad, J. Heart of darkness   Fic
Gordimer, N. Crimes of conscience   S C
The Heinemann book of contemporary African
   short stories   S C
Folklore
See Folklore—Africa
History
Davidson, B. Africa in history   960
Fage, J. D. A history of Africa   960
Jones, C. Africa, 1500-1900   960
Moorehead, A. The Blue Nile   962
Wepman, D. Africa: the struggle for indepen-
   dence   960
Maps
Africa on file   912
The Conservation atlas of tropical forests: Africa
     333.75
Africa, Central *See* Central Africa
Africa, South *See* South Africa
Africa, Sub-Saharan *See* Sub-Saharan Africa
Africa, West *See* West Africa
Africa   960
Africa, 1500-1900. Jones, C.   960
Africa in history. Davidson, B.   960
Africa in literature
Bibliography
Khorana, M. Africa in literature for children and
   young adults   016.9
Africa in literature for children and young adults.
   Khorana, M.   016.9
Africa on file   912
Africa: opposing viewpoints   960
Africa: the struggle for independence. Wepman,
   D.   960
African American actors
Jones, J. E. James Earl Jones: voices and si-
   lences   92
The **African** American almanac   305.8
African American artists
Bearden, R. A history of African-American art-
   ists   709.73
Harlem Renaissance: art of black America
     709.73
Henkes, R. The art of black American women
     709.73
African American arts
Creative fire   700

African American musicians

Basie, C. Good morning blues: the autobiography of Count Basie   92
Brooks, T. America's black musical heritage   780.89
Brown, S. Louis Armstrong   92
Collier, J. L. Duke Ellington   92
Collier, J. L. Louis Armstrong: an American success story   92
Ellington, D. Music is my mistress   92
Haskins, J. Black music in America   780.89
Haskins, J. Scott Joplin   92
Hopkins, J. Hit and run: the Jimi Hendrix story   92
Kirkeby, E. Ain't misbehavin': the story of Fats Waller   92
Otfinoski, S. Scott Joplin   92
Shirley, D. Everyday I sing the blues: the story of B.B. King   92
Southern, E. The music of black Americans   780.89
Terkel, S. Giants of jazz   920
We'll understand it better by and by   782.25

African American newspapers

Senna, C. The black press and the struggle for civil rights   071

African American poetry *See* American poetry—African American authors

African American singers

Brown, J. James Brown, the godfather of soul   92
De Veaux, A. Don't explain: a song of Billie Holiday   92
Gourse, L. Aretha Franklin   92
Gourse, L. Billie Holiday   92
Gourse, L. Unforgettable: the life and mystique of Nat King Cole   92
Haskins, J. Lena: a personal and professional biography of Lena Horne   92
Holiday, B. Lady sings the blues   92
Patterson, C. Marian Anderson   92
Wyman, C. Ella Fitzgerald   92

African American soldiers

Bloods: an oral history of the Vietnam War by black veterans   959.704
Burchard, P. "We'll stand by the Union": Robert Gould Shaw and the Black 54th Massachusetts Regiment   92
Hansen, J. Between two fires   973.7
Hargrove, H. B. Black Union soldiers in the Civil War   973.7
Powell, C. L. My American journey   92
Roth, D. Sacred honor: a biography of Colin Powell   92

Drama

Fuller, C. A soldier's play   812

Fiction

Myers, W. D. Fallen angels   Fic

African-American sports greats   920.003
African-American voices   810.8
African-American voices in young adult literature   810.9

African American women

Cary, L. Black ice   92
Chambers, V. Mama's girl   92
De Veaux, A. Don't explain: a song of Billie Holiday   92
Delany, S. Having our say   92
Gourse, L. Aretha Franklin   92
Gourse, L. Billie Holiday   92
Haskins, J. Lena: a personal and professional biography of Lena Horne   92
Holiday, B. Lady sings the blues   92
Hooks, B. Bone black: memories of girlhood   92
Lanker, B. I dream a world: portraits of black women who changed America   305.4
Mills, K. This little light of mine: the life of Fannie Lou Hamer   92
Ortiz, V. Sojourner Truth, a self-made woman   92
Parks, R. Quiet strength   92
Patterson, C. Marian Anderson   92
We are your sisters   305.4
Wyman, C. Ella Fitzgerald   92

Dictionaries

Notable black American women [bk I-II]   920.003

Drama

Shange, N. For colored girls who have considered suicide/when the rainbow is enuf   812

Fiction

Black-eyed Susans/Midnight birds   S C
Invented lives   S C
McMillan, T. Waiting to exhale   Fic

Health and hygiene

Mathis, D. Women of color   646.7

African Americans

The African American almanac   305.8
Baldwin, J. The fire next time   305.8
Baldwin, J. No name in the street   305.8
Baldwin, J. Nobody knows my name   305.8
Baldwin, J. Notes of a native son   305.8
Cleaver, E. Soul on ice   305.8
Crouch, S. The all-American skin game; or, The decoy of race   305.8
Du Bois, W. E. B. The Oxford W. E. B. Du Bois reader   305.8
Du Bois, W. E. B. The souls of black folk   305.8
Du Bois, W. E. B. W.E.B. Du Bois: a reader   305.8
Garza, H. African Americans and Jewish Americans   305.8
Hoobler, D. The African American family album   305.8
West, D. The richer, the poorer: stories, sketches, and reminiscences   S C
See/See also pages in the following book(s):
De Pauw, L. G. Founding mothers p70-98   305.4

Biography

Abdul-Jabbar, K. Black profiles in courage   920
Archer, J. They had a dream   920
Bearing witness: selections from African-American autobiography in the twentieth century   920
Bennett, L. What manner of man: a biography of Martin Luther King, Jr.   92

African Americans—Drama—_Continued_
Wilson, A. Joe Turner's come and gone
812
Wilson, A. The piano lesson
812
Wilson, A. Two trains running
812
Education
Black American colleges & universities
378.73
The Black student's guide to college success
378
Conroy, P. The water is wide
371.9
Kozol, J. Death at an early age
370.19
Fiction
Baldwin, J. Go tell it on the mountain
Fic
Baldwin, J. If Beale Street could talk
Fic
The Best short stories by Negro writers
S C
Brooks, B. The moves make the man
Fic
Calling the wind
S C
Cary, L. The price of a child
Fic
Children of the night
S C
Childress, A. A hero ain't nothin' but a sandwich
Fic
Draper, S. M. Tears of a tiger
Fic
Ellison, R. Invisible man
Fic
Gaines, E. J. The autobiography of Miss Jane Pittman
Fic
Gaines, E. J. A lesson before dying
Fic
Guy, R. The disappearance
Fic
Hamilton, V. Sweet whispers, Brother Rush
Fic
Hughes, L. Short stories
S C
Hurston, Z. N. The complete stories
S C
Hurston, Z. N. Novels and stories
Fic
Hurston, Z. N. Their eyes were watching God
Fic
Klass, D. Danger zone
Fic
Morrison, T. Beloved
Fic
Morrison, T. Jazz
Fic
Parks, G. The learning tree
Fic
Rinaldi, A. Wolf by the ears
Fic
Rites of passage
S C
Sinclair, A. Ain't gonna be the same fool twice
Fic
Sinclair, A. Coffee will make you black
Fic
Stowe, H. B. Uncle Tom's cabin
Fic
Streetlights: illuminating tales of the urban black experience
S C
Verdelle, A. J. The good negress
Fic
Walker, A. The color purple
Fic
Walker, M. Jubilee
Fic
West, D. The wedding
Fic
Williams-Garcia, R. Like sisters on the homefront
Fic
Woodson, J. I hadn't meant to tell you this
Fic
Wright, R. Native son
Fic
Wright, R. Uncle Tom's children
S C
Wright, R. Works
818
History
Asante, M. K. The historical and cultural atlas of African Americans
305.8
Bennett, L. Before the Mayflower: a history of black America
305.8
The Black Americans: a history in their own words, 1619-1983
305.8

Black firsts
305.8
Black history month resource book
305.8
Curtis, N. C. Black heritage sites
917.3
A Documentary history of the Negro people in the United States
305.8
Douglass, F. Frederick Douglass, in his own words
305.8
Franklin, J. H. From slavery to freedom
305.8
Harley, S. The timetables of African-American history
305.8
Historic speeches of African Americans
815.008
Hornsby, A., Jr. Chronology of African-American history
305.8
Jackson, K. A. America is me
305.8
King, M. L. Where do we go from here: chaos or community?
323.1
King, W. Stolen childhood
326
McPherson, J. M. Marching toward freedom
973.7
Perseverance
305.8
We are your sisters
305.4
The Young Oxford history of African Americans
305.8
History—Bibliography
Glover, D. M. Voices of the spirit
016.3058
Intellectual life
Gates, H. L. The future of the race
305.8
Language
Juba to jive
427
Music
See African American music
Pictorial works
The African Americans
779
Myers, W. D. One more river to cross
779
Poetry
Hughes, L. The collected poems of Langston Hughes
811
Quotations
Heart full of grace
808.88
Religion
See/See also pages in the following book(s):
Boorstin, D. J. The Americans: The national experience p190-99
973
Segregation
King, M. L. Stride toward freedom
323.1
Social conditions
Dyson, M. E. Between God and gangsta rap
305.8
Gates, H. L. The future of the race
305.8
Hacker, A. Two nations
305.8
Lemann, N. The promised land
973.9
Harlem (New York, N.Y.)
See/See also pages in the following book(s):
Glazer, N. Beyond the melting pot p24-85
305.8
Mississippi
Lomax, A. The land where the blues began
781.643
Walton, A. Mississippi
976.2
Southern States
Griffin, J. H. Black like me
305.8

Agay, Denes, 1911-
(ed) Best loved songs of the American people.
See Best loved songs of the American people
782.42

Age See Old age
The **age** of chivalry. Bulfinch, T.
In Bulfinch, T. Bulfinch's mythology
291

The **age** of fable. Bulfinch, T.
In Bulfinch, T. Bulfinch's mythology
291

The **age** of faith. Durant, W. J.   940.1
The **Age** of god-kings: timeframe 3000-1500 BC
930
The **age** of innocence. Wharton, E.   Fic
The **age** of Jackson. Schlesinger, A. M.
973.5
The **age** of Louis XIV. Durant, W. J.   940.2
The **age** of Napoleon. Durant, W. J.   940.2
The **age** of reason. Paine, T.
In Paine, T. Collected writings p663-830
320
The **age** of reason begins. Durant, W. J.
940.2
The **age** of reform from Bryan to F.D.R.
Hofstadter, R.   973.91
The **age** of revolution. Churchill, Sir W.
In Churchill, Sir W. A history of the English-speaking peoples v3   941
The **age** of Voltaire. Durant, W. J.   940.2
Age would be that does. Everett, P. L.
In Calling the wind p578-83   S C
Aged See Elderly
Agee, James, 1909-1955
A death in the family   Fic
Let us now praise famous men   976.1
The **ages** of Gaia. Lovelock, J.   574
Aggada
The Book of legends. Sefer ha-aggadah
296.1
Aggressiveness (Psychology)
Levy, B. In love and in danger   362.7
Lorenz, K. On aggression   152.4
Aging
Medina, J. J. The clock of ages   612.6
See/See also pages in the following book(s):
The Incredible machine p221-59   612
An **Aging** population: opposing viewpoints
305.26
Agnesi, Maria Gaetana, 1718-1799
See/See also pages in the following book(s):
Osen, L. M. Women in mathematics p39-48
920
The **agony** and the ecstasy. Stone, I.   Fic
Agosín, Marjorie, 1955-
Adelina
In Daughters of the fifth sun   810.8
Agosta, William C.
Bombardier beetles and fever trees   574.5
Chemical communication   591.5
Agricultural laborers
See also Peasantry

Ashabranner, B. K. Dark harvest: migrant farm-workers in America   331.5
Agricultural machinery
See/See also pages in the following book(s):
Langdon, W. C. Everyday things in American life, 1776-1876 p303-25   973
Agricultural pests
See also Insect pests
Agricultural products See Farm produce
Agriculture
See also Food supply
Patent, D. H. The vanishing feast   338.1
See/See also pages in the following book(s):
Emerson, R. W. The portable Emerson p558-68
818
Tudge, C. The time before history p264-79
573.2
United States
Goldberg, J. The disappearing American farm
338.1
Raeburn, P. The last harvest   338.1
Rhodes, R. Farm: a year in the life of an American farmer   630.9
See/See also pages in the following book(s):
Langdon, W. C. Everyday things in American life, 1607-1776 p273-98   973.2
Aguilar, Luis E.
Dostert, P. E. Latin America   980
Ah, wilderness!. O'Neill, E.
In O'Neill, E. Complete plays v3   812
Ahab [critical essays]   813.009
Aharoni, Yohanan, 1919-1976
The Macmillan Bible atlas   220.9
Ahoy, sailor boy!. Coppard, A. E.
In The Oxford book of English ghost stories p399-409   S C
Ahvel. Whittington, M. K.
In Vampires: a collection of original stories p121-33   S C
AI (Artificial intelligence) See Artificial intelligence
Aichele, Gary Jan
Oliver Wendell Holmes, Jr.—soldier, scholar, judge   92
Aickman, Robert, 1914-1981
The Cicerones
In The Oxford book of English ghost stories p477-86   S C
Aid to developing areas See Economic assistance
Aid to families with dependent children See Child welfare
Aidoo, Ama Ata, 1942-
Certain winds from the south
In African short stories   S C
The late bud
In Rites of passage p33-44   S C
Two sisters
In Daughters of Africa p532-42   808.8
Aidoo, Christina Ama Ata See Aidoo, Ama Ata, 1942-
AIDS (Disease)
Burkett, E. The gravest show on earth
362.1

Alaska
Description
Krakauer, J. Into the wild [biography of Christopher McCandless]   **92**
Muir, J. All the world over   **979.8**
Scott, A. Tracks across Alaska   **979.8**
See/See also pages in the following book(s):
White, E. B. Essays of E. B. White   **814**
Fiction
London, J. The call of the wild   **Fic**
London, J. White Fang   **Fic**
Natural history
See Natural history—Alaska
Alaska. Adams, A.
In The Oxford book of American short stories p571-81   **S C**
Alaska's wildlife treasures. Melham, T.   **599**
Alba, Alicia Gaspar de *See* Gaspar de Alba, Alicia, 1958-
Albee, Edward, 1928-
All over
In Best American plays: 7th series—1967-1973 p141-67   **812.008**
Three tall women   **812**
Tiny Alice
In Best American plays: 6th series—1963-1967 p1-45   **812.008**
Who's afraid of Virginia Woolf?   **812**
also in Best American plays: 5th series—1957-1963 p143-201   **812.008**
About
Edward Albee   **812**
Albert, Prince Consort of Victoria, Queen of Great Britain, 1819-1861
See/See also pages in the following book(s):
Strachey, L. Queen Victoria p134-203, 253-96   **92**
Albert Nobbs. Moore, G.
In The Oxford book of Irish short stories p109-51   **S C**
Album of American history   **973**
Albyn, Carole Lisa, 1955-
The multicultural cookbook for students   **641.5**
Alcestis. Euripides
In Four Greek plays   **882.008**
In Seven famous Greek plays   **882.008**
Alcindor, Lew *See* Abdul-Jabbar, Kareem, 1947-
Alcohol and teenagers *See* Teenagers—Alcohol use
Alcohol, Tobacco and Firearms Bureau (U.S.)
See United States. Bureau of Alcohol, Tobacco and Firearms
Alcoholic beverages
See also Drinking of alcoholic beverages
An **alcoholic** case. Fitzgerald, F. S.
In Fitzgerald, F. S. The stories of F. Scott Fitzgerald p436-42   **S C**
In The Oxford book of American short stories p301-09   **S C**
Alcoholics
See also Children of alcoholics
Seixas, J. S. Children of alcoholism   **362.29**

Fiction
Fox, P. The moonlight man   **Fic**
Alcoholism
See also Children of alcoholics; Drinking of alcoholic beverages
Alcoholism   **362.29**
Berger, G. Alcoholism and the family   **362.29**
Landau, E. Teenage drinking   **362.29**
Ryan, E. A. Straight talk about drugs and alcohol   **616.86**
Silverstein, H. Alcoholism   **616.86**
See/See also pages in the following book(s):
Berger, G. Addiction   **616.86**
Chemical dependency: opposing viewpoints   **362.29**
Landau, E. Hooked   **362.29**
Porterfield, K. M. Focus on addictions   **616.86**
Dictionaries
Encyclopedia of drugs and alcohol   **362.29**
Fiction
Carter, A. R. Up country   **Fic**
LeMieux, A. C. Do angels sing the blues?   **Fic**
Martinez, V. Parrot in the oven   **Fic**
Alcoholism   **362.29**
Alcoholism and the family. Berger, G.   **362.29**
Alcoran *See* Koran
Alcott, Louisa May, 1832-1888
A long fatal love chase   **Fic**
The selected letters of Louisa May Alcott   **92**
About
Anderson, W. T. The world of Louisa May Alcott   **92**
Alcuin, 735-804
See/See also pages in the following book(s):
Cantor, N. F. Medieval lives   **940.1**
Aldani, Lino
S is for snake
In Tales from the planet Earth   **S C**
Alder, Elizabeth
The king's shadow   **Fic**
Alderman, Ellen
In our defense: the Bill of Rights in action   **342**
The right to privacy   **323.44**
Aldersey-Williams, Hugh
The most beautiful molecule   **546**
Alderton, David
Foxes, wolves, and wild dogs of the world   **599.74**
Wild cats of the world   **599.74**
Aldiss, Brian Wilson, 1925-
Hothouse
In Robert Silverberg's Worlds of wonder   **S C**
Infestation
In Tales from the planet Earth   **S C**
Who can replace a man?
In The Oxford book of science fiction stories p278-86   **S C**

All over. Albee, E.
   In Best American plays: 7th series—1967-
     1973 p141-67   **812.008**

All quiet on the western front. Abbott, G.
   In Best American screenplays   **812.008**

All quiet on the western front. Firda, R. A.
                   833.009

All quiet on the western front. Remarque, E. M.
                        Fic

All rivers run to the sea. Wiesel, E.   **92**

All shall love me and despair. Thompson, J.
   In The Best American short stories, 1996
     p307-20   **S C**

All Souls'. Wharton, E.
   In Wharton, E. The selected short stories of
     Edith Wharton p366-84   **S C**

All summer in a day. Bradbury, R.
   In Bradbury, R. The stories of Ray Bradbury
     p532-36   **S C**

All terrain bicycles *See* Mountain bikes

All the dead pilots. Faulkner, W.
   In Faulkner, W. Collected stories of William
     Faulkner p511-31   **S C**

All the king's horses. Vonnegut, K.
   In Vonnegut, K. Welcome to the monkey
     house   **S C**

All the king's men. Warren, R. P.   **Fic**

All the President's men. Bernstein, C.
                    973.924

All the pretty horses. McCarthy, C.   **Fic**

All the troubles of the world. Asimov, I.
   In Asimov, I. The complete stories v1 p263-
     76   **S C**

All the way home. Mosel, T.
   In Best American plays: 5th series—1957-
     1963 p277-311   **812.008**

All the way in Flagstaff, Arizona. Bausch, R.
   In The Vintage book of contemporary
     American short stories p13-28   **S C**

All the Weyrs of Pern. McCaffrey, A. See note
   under McCaffrey, A. [The Pern series]
                     Fic

All the world over. Muir, J.   **979.8**

All things bright and beautiful. Herriot, J.   **92**

All things wise and wonderful. Herriot, J.   **92**

Allaby, Michael, 1933-
   Earth   **550**
   Fire   **541.3**
   How the weather works   **551.5**
   Water   **333.91**
   (ed) Illustrated dictionary of science. See Illus-
     trated dictionary of science   **503**

Allan, Tony
   (ed) Deserts. See Deserts   **574.5**

Allegories
   See also Fables
   Adams, R. Watership Down   **Fic**
   Atwood, M. The handmaid's tale   **Fic**
   Beagle, P. S. The last unicorn   **Fic**
   Bunyan, J. The pilgrim's progress   **Fic**
   Golding, W. Lord of the Flies   **Fic**
   Theroux, P. The Mosquito Coast   **Fic**

Allen, Frederick Lewis, 1890-1954
   The big change   **973.91**
   Only yesterday   **973.91**
   Since yesterday   **973.91**

Allen, Grant, 1848-1899
   The episode of the Mexican seer
   In The Best crime stories of the 19th century
     p202-16   **S C**

Allen, Paula Gunn
   Charlie
   In Song of the turtle p160-64   **S C**
   A deep purple
   In Spider Woman's granddaughters   **S C**
   Deer Woman
   In Talking leaves   **S C**
   Raven's road [excerpt]
   In Growing up gay p105-09   **808.8**
   (ed) Song of the turtle. See Song of the turtle
                   S C
   (ed) Spider Woman's granddaughters. See Spi-
     der Woman's granddaughters   **S C**
   See/See also pages in the following book(s):
   Coltelli, L. Winged words: American Indian
     writers speak   **897**

Allen, Thomas B., 1929-
   The Blue and the Gray   **973.7**
   War in the Gulf   **956.7**

Allen, Woody
   Play it again, Sam
   In Best American plays: 7th series—1967-
     1973 p563-85   **812.008**

Allende, Isabel
   If you touched my heart
   In The Oxford book of gothic tales p519-26
                 S C
   Paula   **92**

Allende family
About
   Allende, I. Paula   **92**

Allergies   **616.97**

Allergy
   Allergies   **616.97**
   Newman, G. Allergies   **616.97**
   See/See also pages in the following book(s):
   Clark, W. R. At war within p87-100
                 616.07
   Roueché, B. The medical detectives p302-16
                 616

Alleyne, Carla Debbie
   Hey Little Walter
   In Ten out of ten p205-35   **812.008**

Alligator. Michener, J. A.
   In Michener, J. A. Tales of the South Pacific
                 S C

Alligators
   Dow, L. Alligators and crocodiles   **597.9**

The alligators. Updike, J.
   In Who do you think you are? p64-72
                 S C

Alligators and crocodiles. Dow, L.   **597.9**

Allingham, Margery, 1904-1966
   See/See also pages in the following book(s):
   Modern mystery writers p1-15   **809.3**

Allison, Dorothy, 1949-
Bastard out of Carolina [excerpt]
In Coming of age in America p75-81
S C
River of names
In The Vintage book of contemporary
American short stories p3-12   S C

Allman, William F.
(ed) Newton at the bat. See Newton at the bat
796

Allocation of time *See* Time management

Allstetter, William D.
Speech and hearing   612.7

Allston, Washington, 1779-1843
See/See also pages in the following book(s):
Novak, B. American painting of the nineteenth
century p44-66   759.13

Allusions
Brewer's dictionary of phrase and fable
803
Cole, S. The Facts on File dictionary of 20th-
century allusions   031.02
Lass, A. H. The Facts on File dictionary of classical, biblical, and literary allusions   803

The **almanac** of American politics. Barone, M.
328.73

Almanac of American presidents   920

Almanacs
Barone, M. The almanac of American politics
328.73
Chase's calendar of events   394.2
Information please almanac   031.02
The People's almanac presents The twentieth
century   031.02
The Practical guide to practically everything
031.02
Tesar, J. E. The new view almanac   031.02
The Universal almanac   031.02
The World almanac and book of facts
031.02
The World almanac of U.S. politics   328.73

Almos' a man. Wright, R.
In The Best short stories by Negro writers
p91-103   S C

The **almost** white boy. Motley, W.
In The Best short stories by Negro writers
p134-44   S C

Alperovitz, Gar
The decision to use the atomic bomb and the architecture of an American myth   940.54

Alpha Ralpha Boulevard. Smith, C.
In The Norton book of science fiction p49-73
S C

Alphabets
See also Lettering

An **Alpine** idyll. Hemingway, E.
In Hemingway, E. The complete short stories
of Ernest Hemingway p262-66   S C
In Hemingway, E. The Nick Adams stories
p242-48   S C
In Hemingway, E. The short stories of Ernest
Hemingway p343-49   S C

Alps
        Fiction
Mann, T. The magic mountain   Fic
The **alternative**. Baraka, I. A.
In Calling the wind p261-74   S C
Alternative healing. Stewart, G.   615.8
Alternative medicine
Stewart, G. Alternative healing   615.8
Altruism
Meltzer, M. Who cares?   361
Altschiller, Donald
(ed) Affirmative action. See Affirmative action
[Reference shelf]   342
(ed) The Information revolution. See The Infor-
mation revolution   384.3
(ed) The United Nations' role in world affairs.
See The United Nations' role in world affairs
341.23

Alvarez, Julia
Customs
In Iguana dreams   S C
Daughter of invention
In Growing up Latino p3-15   810.8
How the Garcia girls lost their accents   Fic
How the García girls lost their accents [excerpt]
In Coming of age in America p226-38
S C
In the time of the butterflies   Fic
The kiss
In Daughters of the fifth sun   810.8
Snow
In Latina: women's voices from the border-
lands p127-28   810.8

Alvarez Quintero, Serafin, 1871-1938
Sunny morning
In Thirty famous one-act plays p243-50
808.82

Alvin Ailey American Dance Theater
Mitchell, J. Alvin Ailey American Dance The-
ater: Jack Mitchell photographs   792.8
See/See also pages in the following book(s):
Haskins, J. Black dance in America p166-74
792.8

Always, Rachel. Carson, R.   92
Always the young strangers. Sandburg, C.   92
Alyosha the Pot. Tolstoy, L., graf
In The Portable twentieth-century Russian
reader p3-9   891.7
In Tolstoy, L. Great short works of Leo Tol-
stoy p669-77   S C

Alzheimer's disease
Landau, E. Alzheimer's disease   362.1
Am I blue?   S C
Am I blue? [story] Coville, B.
In Am I blue? p1-16   S C
Am I thin enough yet?. Hesse-Biber, S. J.
616.85
The **amateur** naturalist. Durrell, G. M.   508
Amateur night at the Apollo. Cooper, R.
792.7

Amateur radio stations
        Handbooks, manuals, etc.
The ARRL handbook for the radio amateur
621.3841

The **amazing** brain. Ornstein, R. E.   **612.8**

Amazing grace. Kozol, J.   **362.7**

Amazing mysteries of the world. O'Neill, C.   **001.9**

Amazing Randi *See* Randi, James

Amazon River
Description
See/See also pages in the following book(s):
Great rivers of the world p299-330   **910**

Amber
Grimaldi, D. A. Amber   **553.2**

The **ambitious** guest. Hawthorne, N.
In Hawthorne, N. Tales and sketches; A wonder book for girls and boys; Tanglewood tales for girls and boys p299-307   **S C**

Ambler, Eric, 1909-
The case of the emerald sky
In Masterpieces of mystery and suspense p271-79   **S C**

Ambrose, Alison *See* Cole, Alison

Ambrose, Stephen E.
D-Day, June 6, 1944   **940.54**
Eisenhower   **92**
Undaunted courage   **978**

Ambuscade. Faulkner, W.
In Faulkner, W. Uncollected stories of William Faulkner p3-16   **S C**

Ambush. O'Brien, T.
In O'Brien, T. The things they carried   **S C**
In Who do you think you are? p152-55   **S C**

Amdur, Richard
Wilderness preservation   **333.7**

Amen. Hogan, L.
In Song of the turtle p141-46   **S C**

The **amen** corner. Baldwin, J.
In Black theatre USA   **812.008**

Amenhotep IV, King of Egypt *See* Akhenaton, King of Egypt, fl. ca. 1388-1358 B.C.

America
See also Latin America; North America; South America
Antiquities
America in 1492   **970.01**
Coe, M. D. Atlas of ancient America   **970.01**
Mysteries of the ancient Americas   **970.01**
Exploration
America in 1492   **970.01**
Christopher Columbus and his legacy: opposing viewpoints   **970.01**
Duncan, D. E. Hernando de Soto   **92**
Faber, H. The discoverers of America   **970.01**
Meltzer, M. Columbus and the world around him   **92**
Morison, S. E. The European discovery of America   **973.1**
Mysteries of the ancient Americas   **970.01**
The Search for El Dorado   **970.01**
Wright, R. Stolen continents   **970.004**

See/See also pages in the following book(s):
Boorstin, D. J. The Americans: The national experience p223-41   **973**
Exploration—Fiction
Card, O. S. Pastwatch   **Fic**

America. Card, O. S.
In The Norton book of science fiction p665-88   **S C**

America and Vietnam. Marrin, A.   **959.704**

America as story. Coffey, R. K.   **016.813**

America at 1750. Hofstadter, R.   **973.2**

America beyond 2001: opposing viewpoints   **303.49**

America by rivers. Palmer, T.   **551.48**

America in 1492   **970.01**

America in historical fiction. VanMeter, V.   **016.813**

America in search of itself. White, T. H.   **973.92**

America in the 20th century   **973.9**

America in Vietnam   **959.704**

America is me. Jackson, K. A.   **305.8**

American architecture
McAlester, V. A field guide to American houses   **728**
Nash, E. P. Frank Lloyd Wright   **720.973**
Wright, F. L. Frank Lloyd Wright: writings and buildings   **720.973**
See/See also pages in the following book(s):
Langdon, W. C. Everyday things in American life, 1607-1776 p1-17, 125-46   **973.2**

American art
Bearden, R. A history of African-American artists   **709.73**
Harlem Renaissance: art of black America   **709.73**
Henkes, R. The art of black American women   **709.73**
McElroy, G. C. Facing history   **704.9**
National Museum of American Art   **708**
See/See also pages in the following book(s):
Boorstin, D. J. The Americans: The democratic experience p502-14   **973**
Dictionaries
Baigell, M. Dictionary of American art   **709.73**
History
McLanathan, R. B. K. Art in America   **709.73**

American arts
Biography—Dictionaries
American cultural leaders   **920.003**

American Association for the Advancement of Science
Science Books & Films. See Science Books & Films   **016.5**

American Association of School Librarians
Information power   **027.8**

American Association of University Women
Orenstein, P. Schoolgirls   **305.23**

American authors, 1600-1900   **920.003**

American bison *See* Bison

The **American** blues. Just, W. S.
In The Other side of heaven p5-14   **S C**

American furniture
See/See also pages in the following book(s):
Langdon, W. C. Everyday things in American life, 1607-1776 p18-37, 147-57   **973.2**
American given names. Stewart, G. R.   **929.4**
American Heart Association cookbook   **641.5**
American Heritage   **973.05**
The **American** Heritage college dictionary   **423**
The **American** Heritage dictionary. See The American Heritage college dictionary   **423**
The **American** Heritage history of World War I   **940.3**
The **American** Heritage Larousse Spanish dictionary   **463**
The **American** Heritage new history of the Civil War. Catton, B.   **973.7**
The **American** Heritage picture history of the Civil War. See Catton, B. The American Heritage new history of the Civil War   **973.7**
An **American** hero: the true story of Charles A. Lindbergh. Denenberg, B.   **92**
American history. Corey, M.   **973.02**
American history. Ortiz Cofer, J.
In Iguana dreams   **S C**
In Who do you think you are? p36-46   **S C**
American homelessness. Hombs, M. E.   **362.5**
American Horse. Erdrich, L.
In Spider Woman's granddaughters   **S C**
The **American** Horticultural Society encyclopedia of garden plants   **635.9**
The **American** Horticultural Society encyclopedia of gardening   **635**
American idioms dictionary, NTC's. Spears, R. A.   **427**
American immigration. Leinwand, G.   **325.73**
An **American** in New York. Howe, L.
In Spider Woman's granddaughters   **S C**
American Indian medicine. Vogel, V. J.   **970.004**
American Indian Movement
Crow Dog, L. Crow Dog   **970.004**
See/See also pages in the following book(s):
Brave Bird, M. Lakota woman   **92**
Means, R. Where white men fear to tread   **92**
American Indian poetry *See* American poetry—American Indian authors
American Indian quotations   **808.88**
American Indian reference and resource books for children and young adults. Kuipers, B. J.   **016.97004**
American Indian voices   **810.8**
American Indians *See* Indians; Indians of Central America; Indians of Mexico; Indians of North America; Indians of South America
American Indians, American justice. Deloria, V.   **970.004**
American Indians and World War II. Bernstein, A. R.   **940.54**

American Kennel Club
The complete dog book   **636.7**
American Kennel Club dog care and training   **636.7**
The **American** kitchen, 1700 to the present. Plante, E. M.   **643**
American Library Association
See also American Association of School Librarians; Young Adult Library Services Association
American Library Association. Young Adult Services Division
See also Young Adult Library Services Association
The **American** Library Association guide to information access   **025.5**
American Library Association publications
American Association of School Librarians. Information power   **027.8**
The American Library Association guide to information access   **025.5**
Anglo-American cataloguing rules, 2d ed., 1988 revision   **025.3**
Automation for school libraries   **027.8**
Booklist   **028.1**
Bruwelheide, J. H. The copyright primer for librarians and educators   **346.04**
Carter, B. Best books for young adults   **028.1**
Coffey, R. K. America as story   **016.813**
Dewey, P. R. 303 CD-ROMs to use in your library   **025.2**
Edwards, M. A. The fair garden and the swarm of beasts   **027.62**
Excellence in library services to young adults   **027.62**
Genre favorites for young adults   **016.8**
Glover, D. M. Voices of the spirit   **016.3058**
Gorman, M. The concise AACR2, 1988 revision   **025.3**
Guide to reference books   **011**
Hit list: frequently challenged books for young adults   **098**
Hooper, B. Short story writers and their work   **809.3**
Intellectual freedom manual   **323.44**
Internet connections   **004**
Journal of Youth Services in Libraries   **027.6205**
Lynch, R. C. Musicals!   **792.6**
Readers' guide to twentieth-century science fiction   **809.3**
Rochman, H. Against borders   **011.6**
Rochman, H. Tales of love and terror   **028**
School Library Media Quarterly   **027.805**
Vandergrift, K. E. Power teaching   **027.8**
Videos for understanding diversity   **016.3713**
Williams, H. E. Books by African-American authors and illustrators for children and young adults   **016.3058**
Zvirin, S. The best years of their lives   **011.6**
American literary almanac   **810.9**

American literature—History and criticism—
Continued
The Cambridge history of American literature
810.9
Censored books   810.9
Magill's survey of American literature
810.9
Masterpieces of American literature   810.9
The New Moulton's library of literary criticism
820.9
Otfinoski, S. Nineteenth-century writers
810.9
 Mexican American authors—Collections
Growing up Chicana/o   810.8
Infinite divisions: an anthology of Chicana literature
810.8
 Women authors
Davis, C. J. Women writers in the United States
810.9
Modern American women writers   810.9
 Women authors—Bio-bibliography
The Feminist companion to literature in English
820.9
The Oxford companion to women's writing in
the United States   810.9
 Women authors—Collections
Circle of women: an anthology of contemporary
Western women writers   810.8
Grand mothers: poems, reminiscences, and short
stories about the keepers of our traditions
810.8
Infinite divisions: an anthology of Chicana literature
810.8
Latina: women's voices from the borderlands
810.8
The Norton anthology of literature by women
820.8
The Oxford book of women's writing in the
United States   810.8
Sister to sister   810.8
 Women authors—Dictionaries
The Oxford companion to women's writing in
the United States   810.9
American Loyalists
See/See also pages in the following book(s):
De Pauw, L. G. Founding mothers p124-49
305.4
The **American** Medical Association encyclopedia
of medicine   610.3
American Medical Association family medical
guide   616.02
The **American** Medical Association handbook of
first aid & emergency care   616.02
American Medical Women's Association
The Women's complete healthbook. See The
Women's complete healthbook   613
American men & women of science   920.003
American Museum of Natural History
Norell, M. Discovering dinosaurs in the
American Museum of Natural History
567.9
Rexer, L. American Museum of Natural History
508

The **American** Museum of Natural History's book
of dinosaurs and other ancient creatures. Wallace, J.   567.9
American music
 Dictionaries
The New Grove dictionary of American music
780.973
 History and criticism
Nichols, J. American music makers   920
American music makers. Nichols, J.   920
American musical theatre. Bordman, G. M.
792.6
American national characteristics
Boorstin, D. J. The Americans: The colonial experience   973.2
Boorstin, D. J. The Americans: The national experience   973
Tocqueville, A. de. Democracy in America
973.5
American nature writers   810.9
American newspapers
See/See also pages in the following book(s):
Langdon, W. C. Everyday things in American
life, 1776-1876 p152-82   973
American nicknames. Shankle, G. E.   929.4
American orations *See* American speeches
American painting
Lucie-Smith, E. American realism   759.13
Novak, B. American painting of the nineteenth
century   759.13
Yaeger, B. D. The Hudson River school
759.13
American painting of the nineteenth century.
Novak, B.   759.13
American photography, 1890-1965, from the Museum of Modern Art, New York   779
American poetry
 African American authors—Collections
Black sister   811.008
Every shut eye ain't asleep   811.008
I am the darker brother   811.008
In search of color everywhere   811.008
The Poetry of black America   811.008
Shimmy shimmy shimmy like my sister Kate
811.008
 American Indian authors—Collections
Day, A. G. The sky clears: poetry of the
American Indians   897
Harper's anthology of 20th century Native
American poetry   811.008
 Asian American authors—Collections
The Open boat   811.008
 Bio-bibliography
Contemporary poets   920.003
 Collections
American poetry: the nineteenth century
811.008
Beat voices   811.008
Ciardi, J. How does a poem mean?
821.008
The Columbia anthology of American poetry
811.008
The Columbia book of Civil War poetry
811.008
Drive, they said   811.008

Anderson, Maxwell, 1888-1959
Anne of the thousand days
In Best American plays: 3d series—1945-
1951 p547-91   **812.008**
High Tor
In Twenty best plays of the modern American
theatre p45-91   **812.008**
Winterset
In Twenty best plays of the modern American
theatre p1-43   **812.008**
Anderson, Paul, 1956-
Janet Reno   **92**
Anderson, Poul, 1926-
Harvest of stars   **Fic**
Harvest the fire. See note under Anderson, P.
Harvest of stars   **Fic**
Kyrie
In The Norton book of science fiction p201-
10   **S C**
Operation afreet
In Masterpieces of fantasy and enchantment
p593-622   **S C**
The stars are also fire. See note under Ander-
son, P. Harvest of stars   **Fic**
See/See also pages in the following book(s):
Science fiction writers of the golden age p1-16
    809.3
Anderson, Robert Woodruff, 1917-
Silent night, lonely night
In Best American plays: 5th series—1957-
1963 p313-39   **812.008**
Tea and sympathy
In Best American plays: 4th series—1951-
1957 p279-313   **812.008**
You know I can't hear you when the water's
running
In Best American plays: 6th series—1963-
1967 p335-65   **812.008**
Anderson, Rolf
Atlas of the American economy   **338.973**
Anderson, Sherwood, 1876-1941
Death in the woods
In The Norton book of American short stories
p220-30   **S C**
I want to know why
In Classic American short stories p307-18
    S C
In The Oxford book of short stories p238-46
    S C
The strength of God
In The Oxford book of American short stories
p256-63   **S C**
Winesburg, Ohio   **S C**
Anderson, Terry
Den of lions   **92**
Anderson, Terry H., 1946-
The movement and the sixties   **303.4**
Anderson, William T., 1952-
The world of Louisa May Alcott   **92**
Andersonville. Kantor, M.   **Fic**
Andes
Read, P. P. Alive   **910.4**
André Previn's guide to the orchestra. Previn, A.
    784

Andreas Vesalius the anatomist. Borel, P.
In The Oxford book of gothic tales p70-81
    S C
Andre's mother. McNally, T.
In McNally, T. 15 short plays p347-52
    812
Andrew Jackson and his America. Meltzer, M.
    92
Andrews, Charles McLean, 1863-1943
The colonial background of the American Revo-
lution   **973.2**
Andrews, Elaine K.
Indians of the Plains
In The First Americans series   **970.004**
Andrews, Robert, 1957-
The Columbia dictionary of quotations
    808.88
Androcles and the army. O'Connor, F.
In O'Connor, F. Collected stories p578-85
    S C
The **Andromeda** strain. Crichton, M.   **Fic**
Andryszewski, Tricia, 1956-
Immigration   **325.73**
What to do about nuclear waste   **363.7**
Anecdotes
See also Wit and humor
Angel, Ann, 1952-
America in the 20th century. See America in the
20th century   **973.9**
Angel. Chekhov, A. P.
In Chekhov, A. P. The Russian master and
other stories p172-82   **S C**
Angel, all innocence. Weldon, F.
In The Literary ghost p230-46   **S C**
The **angel** Esmeralda. DeLillo, D.
In The Best American short stories, 1995
p263-83   **S C**
Angel Levine. Malamud, B.
In Malamud, B. The stories of Bernard
Malamud p277-89   **S C**
The **angel** of the bridge. Cheever, J.
In Cheever, J. The stories of John Cheever
p490-97   **S C**
The **Angel** of the Odd. Poe, E. A.
In Poe, E. A. The collected tales and poems
of Edgar Allan Poe p376-83   **S C**
An **angel** on the porch. Wolfe, T.
In Wolfe, T. The complete short stories of
Thomas Wolfe p3-9   **S C**
Angel Street. Hamilton, P.
In The Most popular plays of the American
theater p567-624   **812.008**
Angela's ashes. McCourt, F.   **92**
Angelo, Joseph A.
The extraterrestrial encyclopedia   **574.999**
Angelou, Maya
The complete collected poems of Maya Angelou
    811
I know why the caged bird sings   **92**
I know why the caged bird sings [excerpt]
In Who do you think you are? p156-63
    S C

Animals—*Continued*
Infancy
See Animal babies
Migration
Waterman, T. H. Animal navigation   **591.1**
Poetry
Animal poems   **808.81**
North America
Stouffer, M. Marty Stouffer's wild America   **591.9**

Animals, Edible *See* Animal food

Animals, Extinct *See* Extinct animals

Animals, Fossil *See* Fossils

Animals, Habits and behavior of *See* Animal behavior

Animals as food *See* Animal food

Animals in research. McCoy, J. J.   **179**

Animals' rights *See* Animal rights

Animals without backbones   **592**

Animated films
Schneider, S. That's all folks!   **791.43**
Solomon, C. The Disney that never was   **741.5**
Thomas, B. Disney's art of animation   **741.5**

Aniwaya, Anikawa, and the killer teen-agers. Salisbury, R.
In Song of the turtle p136-40   **S C**

Ann, Martha
Goddesses in world mythology   **291.03**

"Anna Christie". O'Neill, E.
In O'Neill, E. Complete plays v1   **812**

Anna Karenina. Tolstoy, L., graf   **Fic**

Anna round the neck. Chekhov, A. P.
In Chekhov, A. P. The image of Chekhov p224-39   **S C**

The Annals of America   **973**

Anne, Queen of Great Britain, 1665-1714
See/See also pages in the following book(s):
Opfell, O. S. Queens, empresses, grand duchesses, and regents p121-29   **920**

Anne Frank remembered. Gies, M.   **940.53**

Anne Frank's Tales from the secret annex. Frank, A.   **839.3**

Anne of the thousand days. Anderson, M.
In Best American plays: 3d series—1945-1951 p547-91   **812.008**

Annette Estimé. LaForest, M. H.
In Streetlights: illuminating tales of the urban black experience p266-78   **S C**

The Annie Dillard reader. Dillard, A.   **818**

Annie John. Kincaid, J.   **Fic**

Annie on my mind. Garden, N.   **Fic**

Annie on my mind [excerpt] Garden, N.
In Growing up gay p64-68   **808.8**

Anniversary. Asimov, I.
In Asimov, I. The complete stories v2 p292-305   **S C**

Anniversary. Lardner, R.
In Lardner, R. The best short stories of Ring Lardner p239-48   **S C**

Annotated art. Cumming, R.   **750**

Anorexia nervosa
Kolodny, N. J. When food's a foe   **616.85**
Sacker, I. M. Dying to be thin   **616.85**
See/See also pages in the following book(s):
Maloney, M. Straight talk about eating disorders   **616.85**
Patterson, C. Eating disorders   **616.85**
Silverstein, A. So you think you're fat? p175-88   **616.85**
Sonder, B. Eating disorders   **616.85**

Another story. Cheever, J.
In Cheever, J. The stories of John Cheever p624-33   **S C**

Another story; or, A fisherman of the inland sea. Le Guin, U. K.
In Le Guin, U. K. A fisherman of the inland sea p147-91   **S C**

Another way out. Langer, L. L.
In Thirty famous one-act plays p433-46   **808.82**

Ansa, Tina McElroy
Willie Bea and Jaybird
In Calling the wind p558-65   **S C**

Anselm, Saint, Archbishop of Canterbury, 1033-1109
See/See also pages in the following book(s):
Jaspers, K. The great philosophers   **109**

Anshaw, Carol
Hammam
In The Best American short stories, 1994 p12-25   **S C**

Answer, please answer. Bova, B.
In Bova, B. Challenges p161-82   **S C**

The ant and the grasshopper. Maugham, W. S.
In Maugham, W. S. Collected short stories v1   **S C**

Antarctic regions
Davis, L. S. Penguin   **598**
See/See also pages in the following book(s):
Erickson, J. Glacial geology p153-75   **551.3**

The anthem sprinters. Bradbury, R.
In Bradbury, R. The stories of Ray Bradbury p569-78   **S C**

Anthology of contemporary Korean poetry   **895.7**

Anthology of Japanese literature from the earliest era to the mid-nineteenth century   **895.6**

Anthology of modern poetry, The Norton   **821.008**

Anthology of Shakespeare, An Oxford. Shakespeare, W.   **822.3**

Anthony, Piers
And eternity. See note under Anthony, P. Incarnations of immortality series   **Fic**
Bearing an hourglass. See note under Anthony, P. Incarnations of immortality series   **Fic**
Being a green mother. See note under Anthony, P. Incarnations of immortality series   **Fic**
Castle Roogna. See note under Anthony, P. The Magic of Xanth series   **Fic**
Centaur Isle. See note under Anthony, P. The Magic of Xanth series   **Fic**
The color of her panties. See note under Anthony, P. The Magic of Xanth series   **Fic**

Anthony, Piers—*Continued*

Crewel lye. See note under Anthony, P. The Magic of Xanth series   **Fic**

Demons don't dream. See note under Anthony, P. The Magic of Xanth series   **Fic**

Dragon on a pedestal. See note under Anthony, P. The Magic of Xanth series   **Fic**

For love of evil. See note under Anthony, P. Incarnations of immortality series   **Fic**

Geis of the Gargoyle. See note under Anthony, P. The Magic of Xanth series   **Fic**

Harpy thyme. See note under Anthony, P. The Magic of Xanth series   **Fic**

If I pay thee not in gold   **Fic**

Incarnations of immortality series   **Fic**

Isle of view. See note under Anthony, P. The Magic of Xanth series   **Fic**

The Magic of Xanth series   **Fic**

Night mare. See note under Anthony, P. The Magic of Xanth series   **Fic**

Ogre, ogre. See note under Anthony, P. The Magic of Xanth series   **Fic**

On a pale horse. See note under Anthony, P. Incarnations of immortality series   **Fic**

Question quest. See note under Anthony, P. The Magic of Xanth series   **Fic**

Roc and a hard place. See note under Anthony, P. The Magic of Xanth series   **Fic**

The source of magic. See note under Anthony, P. The Magic of Xanth series   **Fic**

A spell for Chameleon. See note under Anthony, P. The Magic of Xanth series   **Fic**

Wielding a red sword. See note under Anthony, P. Incarnations of immortality series   **Fic**

With a tangled skein. See note under Anthony, P. Incarnations of immortality series   **Fic**

Yon ill wind. See note under Anthony, P. The Magic of Xanth series   **Fic**

Anthony, Susan B., 1820-1906
About
Barry, K. Susan B. Anthony: a biography of a singular feminist   **92**

Anthropologists
Morell, V. Ancestral passions   **920**

Anthropology
See also Forensic anthropology

Anti-apartheid movement
See also Apartheid

Anti-war poetry *See* War poetry

The **antichrist**. Nietzsche, F. W.
In Nietzsche, F. W. The portable Nietzsche   **193**

Anticipation. Dove-Danquah, M.
In Daughters of Africa p223-26   **808.8**

Anticommunist movements
Fariello, G. Red scare   **973.92**
Klingaman, W. K. Encyclopedia of the McCarthy era   **973.918**

Antietam (Md.), Battle of, 1862
Bailey, R. H. The bloodiest day: the battle of Antietam   **973.7**

Antigone. Sophocles   **882**
also in Seven famous Greek plays   **882.008**

also in Sophocles. Electra, Antigone, Philoctetes   **882**

Antigua and Barbuda
Fiction
Kincaid, J. Annie John   **Fic**

The **antique** ring. Hawthorne, N.
In Hawthorne, N. Tales and sketches; A wonder book for girls and boys; Tanglewood tales for girls and boys p721-33   **S C**

Antiquities
See also Bible—Antiquities; Archeology
Rachlin, H. Lucy's bones, sacred stones, & Einstein's brain   **909**
Robbins, L. H. Stones, bones, and ancient cities   **930.1**

Antiquity of man *See* Human origins

Antisemitism
See also Jews—Persecutions
Arendt, H. Origins of totalitarianism   **321.9**
Bredin, J.-D. The affair   **944.081**
Goldhagen, D. Hitler's willing executioners   **940.53**
See/See also pages in the following book(s):
Carnes, J. Us and them p66-75   **305.8**
Magida, A. J. Prophet of rage: a life of Louis Farrakhan and his nation   **92**

Antivivisection movement *See* Animal rights movements

Antonello, Jean
Breaking out of food jail   **616.85**

Antoninus, Marcus Aurelius *See* Marcus Aurelius, Emperor of Rome, 121-180

Ants
Hoyt, E. The earth dwellers   **595.7**

Anxiety and phobias. Nardo, D.   **616.85**

Anyplace but here. Switzer, E. E.   **362.7**

Anyuta. Chekhov, A. P.
In Chekhov, A. P. The image of Chekhov p106-11   **S C**

Anzaldúa, Gloria, 1942-
Life line
In Growing up gay p90-92   **808.8**
People should not die in June in South Texas
In Growing up Latino p280-87   **810.8**

Anzovin, Steven, 1954-
(ed) Facts about the states. See Facts about the states   **973**
(ed) Speeches of the American presidents. See Speeches of the American presidents   **353.03**

Aouita, Said
See/See also pages in the following book(s):
Sandrock, M. Running with the legends p445-66   **796.42**

AP *See* Associated Press

Apache Indians
Debo, A. Geronimo   **92**
Sweeney, E. R. Cochise, Chiricahua Apache chief   **92**
See/See also pages in the following book(s):
Brown, D. A. The American West p124-31   **978**

Apache Indians—*Continued*
Brown, D. A. Bury my heart at Wounded Knee
p191-217, 392-413   **970.004**
Paths of life p61-90   **970.004**

Aparicio, Frances R.
(ed) Latino voices. See Latino voices   **810.8**

Apartheid
Bradley, C. The end of apartheid   **968.06**
Mandela, N. Nelson Mandela speaks
    968.06

Apel, Willi, 1893-1988
The New Harvard dictionary of music. See The
New Harvard dictionary of music   **780.3**

Apes
    See also Chimpanzees; Gorillas; Orangutan
Nichols, M. K. The great apes   **599.88**

Apiculture *See* Bees

Apollo 13 (Spacecraft)
Lovell, J. Lost moon: the perilous voyage of
Apollo 13   **629.45**

The **Apollo** of Bellac. Giraudoux, J.
In 24 favorite one-act plays p308-32
    808.82

Apollo project
Shepard, A. B., Jr. Moon shot   **629.45**
See/See also pages in the following book(s):
Man in space p60-81   **629.4**

Apollo Theatre (New York, N.Y.)
Cooper, R. Amateur night at the Apollo
    792.7

An **apology** to the moon furies. Vega, E.
In Growing up Latino p47-72   **810.8**

The **apostate**. London, J.
In London, J. The portable Jack London
p118-35   **818**
In London, J. Short stories of Jack London
p233-49   **S C**

Apostolic Church *See* Church history—30-600,
Early church

Appalachian Mountain region *See* Appalachian
region

Appalachian region
Fiction
Marshall, C. Christy   **Fic**
Social life and customs
Foxfire [1]-10   **975.8**
Foxfire: 25 years   **975.8**

The **apparition** of Mrs. Veal. Defoe, D.
In Classic ghost stories p207-10   **S C**

Appearance and reality. Maugham, W. S.
In Maugham, W. S. Collected short stories v1
    S C

Appearances. Anderson, G.
In Black theatre USA   **812.008**

Appel, Martin, 1948-
(jt. auth) Seaver, T. Great moments in baseball
    796.357

Appetite disorders *See* Eating disorders

Appiah, Anthony
(ed) Alice Walker: critical perspectives past and
present. See Alice Walker: critical perspectives past and present   **813.009**

(ed) Langston Hughes: critical perspectives past
and present. See Langston Hughes: critical
perspectives past and present   **818**
(ed) Richard Wright: critical perspectives past
and present. See Richard Wright: critical perspectives past and present   **813.009**
(ed) Toni Morrison: critical perspectives past
and present. See Toni Morrison: critical perspectives past and present   **813.009**
(ed) Zora Neale Hurston: critical perspectives
past and present. See Zora Neale Hurston:
critical perspectives past and present
    813.009

Appiah, Kwame Anthony *See* Appiah, Anthony

The **Applause/best** plays theater yearbook. See
The Best plays of [date]: The Otis Guern-
sey/Burns Mantle theater yearbook
    808.82

Apple, Hope
(jt. auth) Jacob, M. To be continued   **016.8**

Apple, Max
Bridging
In The Norton book of American short stories
p692-700   **S C**

The **apple**. Wells, H. G.
In Wells, H. G. The complete short stories of
H. G. Wells p394-402   **S C**

Apple Computer Inc.
Kendall, M. E. Steve Wozniak   **92**

The **apple** of contentment. Pyle, H.
In The Oxford book of modern fairy tales
p145-51   **S C**

The **apple** orchard. Anaya, R. A.
In Growing up Latino p292-304   **810.8**

Applications for college *See* College applications

Applications for positions
Résumés that get jobs   **650.14**

Applied arts *See* Decorative arts

Appomattox Campaign, 1865
Catton, B. A stillness at Appomattox   **973.7**

The **apprentice**. Balogun, F. O.
In African short stories   **S C**

April. Colette
In Colette. The collected stories of Colette
p601-05   **S C**

April, late April. Wolfe, T.
In Wolfe, T. The complete short stories of
Thomas Wolfe p323-31   **S C**

April twilights, and other poems. Cather, W.
In Cather, W. Stories, poems and other writings   **818**

The **April** witch. Bradbury, R.
In Bradbury, R. The stories of Ray Bradbury
p247-55   **S C**

Aptheker, Herbert, 1915-
(ed) A Documentary history of the Negro people in the United States. See A Documentary
history of the Negro people in the United
States   **305.8**

Aquarium fish. Mills, D.   **639.3**

Aquariums
Mills, D. Aquarium fish   **639.3**
Quinn, J. R. The fascinating fresh water fish
book   **639.3**

Architecture, Colonial *See* Colonial architecture

Architecture, Domestic *See* Domestic architecture

Architecture, Gothic *See* Gothic architecture

Architecture, Greek *See* Greek architecture

Architecture, Medieval *See* Medieval architecture

Architecture, Roman *See* Roman architecture

Architecture, from prehistory to post-modernism. Trachtenberg, M. **720.9**

Archy and Mehitabel. Marquis, D.
In Marquis, D. The lives and times of Archy & Mehitabel p19-166 **817**

Archy does his part. Marquis, D.
In Marquis, D. The lives and times of Archy & Mehitabel p279-477 **817**

Archy's life of Mehitabel. Marquis, D.
In Marquis, D. The lives and times of Archy & Mehitabel p169-276 **817**

Arctic dreams. Lopez, B. H. **998**

Arctic regions
Lopez, B. H. Arctic dreams **998**
See/See also pages in the following book(s):
Erickson, J. Glacial geology p132-52 **551.3**
Fiction
MacLean, A. Ice Station Zebra **Fic**
Pullman, P. The golden compass **Fic**
Natural history
See Natural history—Arctic regions

Ardley, Neil, 1937-
Dictionary of science **503**

Are these actual miles?. Carver, R.
In The Oxford book of American short stories p582-90 **S C**

Are we winning yet?. Nelson, M. B. **796**

An area in the cerebral hemisphere. Major, C.
In Children of the night p523-28 **S C**

Arem, Joel E., 1943-
Color encyclopedia of gemstones **553.8**

Arendt, Hannah
Eichmann in Jerusalem; criticism
In Bettelheim, B. Surviving, and other essays p258-73 **155.9**
The life of the mind **153**
On revolution **303.6**
On violence **303.6**
Origins of totalitarianism **321.9**
Thinking
In Arendt, H. The life of the mind **153**
Willing
In Arendt, H. The life of the mind **153**

Areopagitica. Milton, J.
In Milton, J. The portable Milton **828**

Argentina
Politics and government
Fraser, N. Eva Perón **92**
Page, J. A. Perón **92**

Argonauts (Greek mythology)
See/See also pages in the following book(s):
Hamilton, E. Mythology p159-79 **292**

The Argonauts of the air. Wells, H. G.
In Wells, H. G. The complete short stories of H. G. Wells p346-58 **S C**

Arguing euthanasia **179**

Arguing immigration **325.73**

Aria da Capo. Millay, E. S.
In Thirty famous one-act plays p465-78 **808.82**

Arias, Ron, 1941-
The castle
In Growing up Chicana/o p239-48 **810.8**

Arid regions
See also Deserts

Aristide, Jean-Bertrand
Fiction
Temple, F. Taste of salt **Fic**

Aristophanes
Birds
In Four Greek plays **882.008**
The frogs
In Seven famous Greek plays **882.008**
See/See also pages in the following book(s):
Hamilton, E. The Greek way p126-58 **880.9**

Aristotle, 384-322 B.C.
The basic works of Aristotle **888**
Metaphysics
In Aristotle. The basic works of Aristotle p689-926 **888**
Nicomachean ethics
In Aristotle. The basic works of Aristotle p927-1112 **888**
On generation and corruption
In Aristotle. The basic works of Aristotle p470-531 **888**
On the soul
In Aristotle. The basic works of Aristotle p535-603 **888**
Organon
In Aristotle. The basic works of Aristotle p1-212 **888**
Parva naturalia
In Aristotle. The basic works of Aristotle p607-30 **888**
Physica
In Aristotle. The basic works of Aristotle p213-394 **888**
Poetics **808.1**
In Aristotle. The basic works of Aristotle p1455-87 **888**
Politics
In Aristotle. The basic works of Aristotle p1127-1316 **888**
About
Adler, M. J. Aristotle for everybody **185**
Barnes, J. Aristotle **185**
See/See also pages in the following book(s):
Durant, W. J. The story of philosophy p41-74 **109**
Falcone, V. J. Great thinkers, great ideas **100**
Hamilton, E. The echo of Greece p94-103 **880.9**
Jaspers, K. The great philosophers **109**
Meadows, A. J. The great scientists **920**
Russell, B. A history of Western philosophy p159-207 **109**

Aristotle for everybody. Adler, M. J. **185**

Arizona
Fiction
Kingsolver, B. Pigs in heaven   **Fic**
Koertge, R. The Arizona kid   **Fic**
McMillan, T. Waiting to exhale   **Fic**
The **Arizona** kid. Koertge, R.   **Fic**
Armada, 1588 *See* Spanish Armada, 1588
The **Armada**. Mattingly, G.   **942.05**
Armaments *See* Military weapons
Armaments race *See* Arms race
Armande. Colette
    In Colette. The collected stories of Colette
      p455-68   **S C**
Armed forces
Sullivan, G. Elite warriors   **356**
Armed Services Vocational Aptitude Battery ba-
    sics. See Kappraff, R. M. ASVAB basics
      355
Armenian Americans
Fiction
Saroyan, W. My name is Aram   **S C**
Armenian massacres, 1915-1923
Kherdian, D. The road from home [biography of
    Veron Kherdian]   **92**
Armenians
Turkey
Kherdian, D. The road from home [biography of
    Veron Kherdian]   **92**
Armer, Karl Michael
On the inside track
    In Tales from the planet Earth   **S C**
Armesto, Felipe Fernández- *See* Fernández-
Armesto, Felipe
Armor, John
Manzanar   **940.53**
Armor
Bull, S. 20th-century arms and armor   **355.8**
Bull, S. An historical guide to arms & armor
      355.8
Arms, Thomas S.
Encyclopedia of the Cold War   **909.82**
Arms and armor *See* Armor; Weapons
Arms control
    See also Arms race
Nuclear proliferation: opposing viewpoints
      327.1
Arms race
See/See also pages in the following book(s):
Rhodes, R. Dark sun   **623.4**
Armstrong, Charlotte, 1905-1969
The splintered Monday
    In Masterpieces of mystery and suspense
      p339-55   **S C**
Armstrong, Karen
Jerusalem   **956.94**
Armstrong, Louis, 1900-1971
About
Brown, S. Louis Armstrong   **92**
Collier, J. L. Louis Armstrong: an American
    success story   **92**
See/See also pages in the following book(s):
Terkel, S. Giants of jazz p17-30   **920**
Army life *See* Soldiers

Army Nurse Corps *See* United States. Army
Nurse Corps
Arnason, Eleanor
The warlord of Saturn's moons
    In The Norton book of science fiction p305-
      12   **S C**
Arnason, H. Harvard
History of modern art: painting, sculpture, archi-
    tecture   **709.04**
Arnett, Ross H., Jr.
Simon and Schuster's guide to insects
      595.7
Arnold, Benedict, 1741-1801
About
Brandt, C. The man in the mirror: a life of Ben-
    edict Arnold   **92**
Arnold, Caroline, 1944-
Heart disease   **616.1**
Arnold, Denis
(ed) The New Oxford companion to music. See
    The New Oxford companion to music
      780.3
Arnold, H. J. P., 1932-
(ed) Man in space. See Man in space
      629.4
Arnold, Thomas, 1795-1842
See/See also pages in the following book(s):
Strachey, L. Eminent Victorians   **920**
Arnold Pentland. Wolfe, T.
    In Wolfe, T. The complete short stories of
      Thomas Wolfe p222-28   **S C**
Arnow, Harriette Louisa Simpson, 1908-1986
The dollmaker   **Fic**
Arobateau, Red Jordan
Nobody's people
    In Daughters of Africa p593-603   **808.8**
Aronson, Marc
(jt. auth) Leonard, T. M. Day by day: the seven-
    ties   **909.82**
(jt. auth) Meltzer, E. Day by day: the eighties
      909.82
Aros, J. W.
(ed) Balancing the federal budget. See Balanc-
    ing the federal budget   **336.3**
Around the world in eighty days. Verne, J.
      Fic
Arquette, Kaitlyn Clare, 1970-1989
About
Duncan, L. Who killed my daughter?   **364.1**
Arrian, ca. 96-ca. 180
Alexander the Great   **92**
Arrianus, Flavius *See* Arrian, ca. 96-ca. 180
Arrival and rehearsal. Colette
    In Colette. The collected stories of Colette
      p108-10   **S C**
The **ARRL** handbook for the radio amateur
      621.3841
Arsenic and old lace. Kesselring, J.
    In Best plays of the modern American the-
      atre: 2nd series p459-510   **812.008**
    In The Most popular plays of the American
      theater p429-504   **812.008**

Arthur, King

About

Ashe, G. The discovery of King Arthur   92
Day, D. The search for King Arthur
    942.01
Malory, Sir T. Le morte d'Arthur   398.2
Pyle, H. The story of King Arthur and his knights   398.2
Pyle, H. The story of the Grail and the passing of Arthur   398.2

Drama

Lerner, A. J. Camelot   812

Fiction

Bradley, M. Z. The mists of Avalon   Fic
Stewart, M. Mary Stewart's Merlin trilogy
    Fic
Stewart, M. The prince and the pilgrim   Fic
Twain, M. A Connecticut Yankee in King Arthur's court   Fic
White, T. H. The book of Merlyn   Fic
White, T. H. The once and future king   Fic

Arthur. Gordon, S.
  In Best American screenplays   812.008

Arthur Miller [critical essays]   812

Arthurian romances

See also Grail
Day, D. The search for King Arthur
    942.01
Pyle, H. The story of King Arthur and his knights   398.2
Pyle, H. The story of Sir Launcelot and his companions   398.2
Pyle, H. The story of the champions of the Round Table   398.2
Pyle, H. The story of the Grail and the passing of Arthur   398.2

Artificial intelligence

See/See also pages in the following book(s):
Fancher, R. E. Pioneers of psychology
    150.9
Horgan, J. The end of science p248-60
    501

Dictionaries

The McGraw-Hill illustrated encyclopedia of robotics & artificial intelligence   629.8

The artificial nigger. O'Connor, F.
  In O'Connor, F. Collected works p210-31
    S C
  In O'Connor, F. The complete stories p249-70
    S C

Artificial satellites

See/See also pages in the following book(s):
Man in space p200-27   629.4

Artist, Virginia A.
The clever Maakafi
  In The Big book of large-cast plays p248-56
    812.008

The artist. Falco, E.
  In The Best American short stories, 1995 p284-301   S C

Artist at home. Faulkner, W.
  In Faulkner, W. Collected stories of William Faulkner p627-46   S C

The artist of the beautiful. Hawthorne, N.
  In Hawthorne, N. Tales and sketches; A wonder book for girls and boys; Tanglewood tales for girls and boys p907-31
    S C

Artistic anatomy

See also Figure drawing
Gordon, L. How to draw the human figure
    743
Graves, D. R. Drawing portraits   743

Artistic photography

Adams, A. Ansel Adams   779
Adams, A. The portfolios of Ansel Adams
    779
American photography, 1890-1965, from the Museum of Modern Art, New York   779
Edwards, H. The art of dance   779
Evans, W. Walker Evans: the Getty Museum collection   779
Photographs that changed the world   779

Artists

See also African American artists; Architects; Illustrators; Painters; Women artists
Gilot, F. Matisse and Picasso   92
Kagan, A. Marc Chagall   92
The Oxford companion to twentieth-century art   709.04

Dictionaries

Authors & artists for young adults   920.003
A Biographical dictionary of artists
    920.003
Dictionary of the arts   700
International dictionary of art and artists
    703
The Oxford companion to art   703
The Oxford dictionary of art   703
World artists, 1950-1980   920.003
World artists, 1980-1990   920.003

Artists, American

Baigell, M. Dictionary of American art
    709.73
Berman, A. James McNeill Whistler   92
Bourdon, D. Warhol   92
Cikovsky, N., Jr. Winslow Homer   92
Hassrick, P. H. Charles M. Russell   92
Henkes, R. The art of black American women
    709.73
Henkes, R. Native American painters of the twentieth century   920
Hobbs, R. C. Edward Hopper   92
Mathews, N. M. Mary Cassatt   92
Meryman, R. Andrew Wyeth   92
Robinson, R. Georgia O'Keeffe   92
Taliaferro, J. Charles M. Russell   92
Wyeth, A. Andrew Wyeth, autobiography
    92
See/See also pages in the following book(s):
American cultural leaders   920.003

Artists, British

Ackroyd, P. Blake   92

Artists, Dutch

Schwartz, G. Rembrandt   92

Artists, French

Greenfeld, H. Paul Gauguin   92
Herrera, H. Matisse   92

Asian Americans—*Continued*
Fiction
American eyes   S C
Asian civilization
See also Buddhist civilization
Durant, W. J. Our Oriental heritage   950
Asian-Pacific folktales and legends   398.2
Asian philosophy *See* Oriental philosophy
Asimov, Isaac, 1920-1992
Asimov's Chronology of science and discovery
     509
Atom   539.7
Beginnings   577
The complete stories   S C
Contents: v1 The dead past; Franchise; Gimmicks three; Kid stuff; The watery place; Living space; The message; Satisfaction guaranteed; Hell-fire; The last trump; The fun they had; Jokester; The Immortal Bard; Someday; Dreaming is a private thing; Profession; The feeling of power; The dying night; I'm in Marsport without Hilda; The gentle vultures; All the troubles of the world; Spell my name with an S; The last question; The ugly little boy; Nightfall; Green patches; Hostess; "Breeds there a man . . . ?"; C-Chute; "In a good cause—"; What if—; Sally; Flies; "Nobody here but—"; It's such a beautiful day; Strikebreaker; Insert knob A in hole B; The up-to-date sorcerer; Unto the fourth generation; What is this thing called love?; The machine that won the war; My son, the physicist; Eyes do more than see; Segregationist v2 Not final!; The hazing; Death sentence; Blind alley; Evidence; The Red Queen's race; Day of the hunters; The deep; The Martian way; The monkey's finger; The singing bell; The talking stone; Each an explorer; Let's get together; Pâté de foie gras; Gallery slave; Lenny; A loint of paw; A statue for father; Anniversary; Obituary; Rain, rain, go away; Star light; Founding father; The key; The billiard ball; Exile to hell; Key item; Feminine intuition; The greatest asset; Mirror image; Take a match; Light verse; Stranger in paradise; That thou art mindful of him; The life and times of Multivac; The Bicentennial Man; Marching in; Old fashioned; The tercentenary incident
The Cross of Lorraine
In Masterpieces of mystery and suspense
    p570-85   S C
Fantastic voyage   Fic
Forward the Foundation. See note under Asimov, I. [The Foundation series]   Fic
Foundation. See note under Asimov, I. [The Foundation series]   Fic
Foundation and earth. See note under Asimov, I. [The Foundation series]   Fic
Foundation and empire. See note under Asimov, I. [The Foundation series]   Fic
[The Foundation series]   Fic
Foundation's edge. See note under Asimov, I. [The Foundation series]   Fic
Frontiers II   500
I, robot   S C
Contents: Robbie; Runaround; Reason; Catch the rabbit; Liar; Little lost robot; Escape; Evidence; The evitable conflict
Isaac Asimov's guide to earth & space   520
The march of the millennia   303.49
Prelude to Foundation. See note under Asimov, I. [The Foundation series]   Fic
Second Foundation. See note under Asimov, I. [The Foundation series]   Fic
The secret of the universe   520
Words from the myths   292
(ed) The Best crime stories of the 19th century. See The Best crime stories of the 19th century   S C
(ed) The Mammoth book of new world science fiction. See The Mammoth book of new world science fiction   S C

See/See also pages in the following book(s):
Science fiction writers of the golden age p17-46
     809.3
Asimov, Janet
(jt. auth) Asimov, I. Frontiers II   500
Asimov's Chronology of science and discovery. Asimov, I.   509
Asinof, Eliot, 1919-
Eight men out   796.357
ASPCA complete dog training manual. Fogle, B.
     636.7
Asphodel. Welty, E.
In Welty, E. The collected stories of Eudora Welty p200-08   S C
Aspirin
See/See also pages in the following book(s):
Roueché, B. The medical detectives p61-80
     616
Aspray, William
(jt. auth) Campbell-Kelly, M. Computer
     004
Assad, Hafez
See/See also pages in the following book(s):
Wakin, E. Contemporary political leaders of the Middle East p37-51   920
Assassination
Lindop, E. Assassinations that shook America
     364.1
Assassinations that shook America. Lindop, E.
     364.1
Assessment and the school library media center
     027.8
The **assignation.** Poe, E. A.
In Poe, E. A. The collected tales and poems of Edgar Allan Poe p293-302   S C
Assistance to developing areas *See* Economic assistance
The **assistant.** Malamud, B.   Fic
Assisted suicide *See* Euthanasia
Associated Press
Twentieth-century America. See Twentieth-century America   973.9
Association for Educational Communications and Technology
American Association of School Librarians. Information power   027.8
Association for the Study of American Indian Literatures (U.S.)
Returning the gift. See Returning the gift
     897
Associations
Directories
Student contact book   001.4
Assyria
See/See also pages in the following book(s):
Durant, W. J. Our Oriental heritage p265-84
     950
Asteroids
Desonie, D. Cosmic collisions   551.3
Astor, Gerald, 1926-
Crisis in the Pacific   940.54
The **Astrologer's** prediction; or, The maniac's fate
In The Oxford book of gothic tales p63-69
     S C

Astrology
See/See also pages in the following book(s):
Aaseng, N. Science versus pseudoscience p104-17   **001.9**
Dictionaries
Lewis, J. R. The astrology encyclopedia   **133.5**
The **astrology** encyclopedia. Lewis, J. R.   **133.5**

Astronautics
See also Space flight
Baker, D. Spaceflight and rocketry: a chronology   **629.4**
The First 25 years in space   **629.4**
Gibson, R. Space   **629.4**
Lee, W. To rise from earth   **629.4**
Man in space   **629.4**
Neal, V. Spaceflight   **629.4**
Space exploration: opposing viewpoints   **629.4**
Soviet Union
See/See also pages in the following book(s):
Man in space p26-39, 174-85   **629.4**
United States
See also Project Voyager
Bilstein, R. E. Flight in America: from the Wrights to the astronauts   **629.13**
Jensen, C. No downlink   **629.45**
Wolfe, T. The right stuff   **629.45**

Astronauts
Wolfe, T. The right stuff   **629.45**
The **astronomer**. Updike, J.
In Updike, J. Pigeon feathers, and other stories p179-86   **S C**

Astronomers
Christianson, G. E. Edwin Hubble: mariner of the nebulae   **92**

Astronomy
See also Constellations; Stars
Asimov, I. Isaac Asimov's guide to earth & space   **520**
Berman, B. Secrets of the night sky   **520**
The Cambridge atlas of astronomy   **523**
Chartrand, M. R. The Audubon Society field guide to the night sky   **523**
Florence, R. The perfect machine   **522**
Gallant, R. A. National Geographic picture atlas of our universe   **523**
Jastrow, R. God and the astronomers   **523.1**
Jastrow, R. Until the sun dies   **577**
Kals, W. S. Stars and planets   **523**
Levy, D. H. Skywatching   **520**
Miller, R. Making & enjoying telescopes   **522**
Mitton, J. Gems of Hubble   **520**
Moeschl, R. Exploring the sky   **523**
Moore, P. Stargazing   **523**
Norton's 2000.0   **523**
Pasachoff, J. M. A field guide to the stars and planets   **523**
Porcellino, M. R. Through the telescope   **522**
Sagan, C. Cosmos   **520**
Schaaf, F. Seeing the sky   **523**
The Universe explained   **523**

See/See also pages in the following book(s):
Sagan, C. Broca's brain p250-67   **500**
Atlases
See Stars—Atlases
Dictionaries
The Facts on File dictionary of astronomy   **520.3**
McGraw-Hill encyclopedia of astronomy   **520.3**
History
The Cambridge illustrated history of astronomy   **520**
North, J. D. The Norton history of astronomy and cosmology   **520**
See/See also pages in the following book(s):
Sullivan, W. The secret of the Incas   **985**

Astrophysics
Barrow, J. D. The origin of the universe   **523.1**
Calder, N. Einstein's universe   **530.1**
Goodstein, D. L. Feynman's lost lecture   **521**
Hawking, S. W. The nature of space and time   **530.1**
Parker, B. R. Chaos in the cosmos   **520**
Thorne, K. S. Black holes and time warps   **530.1**
Wentzel, D. G. The restless sun   **523.7**

ASVAB basics. Kappraff, R. M.   **355**

Asylum
See/See also pages in the following book(s):
Andryszewski, T. Immigration p71-85   **325.73**

Asylum. Jones, G.
In Black-eyed Susans/Midnight birds p130-34   **S C**

At Chênière Caminada. Chopin, K.
In Chopin, K. The awakening and selected stories p75-89   **S C**

At Chrighton Abbey. Braddon, M. E.
In Victorian ghost stories p163-89   **S C**

At the Burns-Coopers'. Brooks, G.
In Black-eyed Susans/Midnight birds p120-22   **S C**

At the end of the passage. Kipling, R.
In Victorian ghost stories p328-45   **S C**

At the landing. Welty, E.
In Welty, E. The collected stories of Eudora Welty p240-58   **S C**

At the pit's mouth. Kipling, R.
In Kipling, R. The best fiction of Rudyard Kipling p611-15   **S C**

At the post office. Chekhov, A. P.
In Chekhov, A. P. The image of Chekhov p57-58   **S C**

At the rendezvous of victory. Gordimer, N.
In Gordimer, N. Crimes of conscience p99-109   **S C**

At the Rialto. Willis, C.
In Nebula awards 25 p225-48   **S C**

At war within. Clark, W. R.   **616.07**

At weddings and wakes. McDermott, A.   **Fic**

Baker, Daniel B.
(ed) Explorers and discoverers of the world. See Explorers and discoverers of the world   **920.003**

Baker, David, 1944-
Flight and flying   **629.13**
Spaceflight and rocketry: a chronology   **629.4**

Baker, James R., 1925-
Critical essays on William Golding   **823.009**

Baker, James Thomas
Ayn Rand   **191**

Baker, Mark, 1950-
Nam   **959.704**

Baker, Patricia
Fashions of a decade, The 1940s   **391**
Fashions of a decade, The 1950s   **391**

Baker, Richard, 1925-
Richard Baker's companion to music   **780.9**

Baker, Russell, 1925-
The good times   **92**
Growing up   **92**
Inventing the truth. See Inventing the truth   **808**
There's a country in my cellar   **818**
(ed) The Norton book of light verse. See The Norton book of light verse   **821.008**
(ed) Russell Baker's book of American humor. See Russell Baker's book of American humor   **817.008**
See/See also pages in the following book(s):
Inventing the truth p21-38   **808**

Baker, Theodore, 1851-1934
Baker's biographical dictionary of musicians. See Baker's biographical dictionary of musicians   **920.003**

Baker, William J. (William Joseph), 1938-
Jesse Owens   **92**

Baker, William Lynn
Dancing honeybees and other natural wonders of science   **500**

Baker's biographical dictionary of musicians   **920.003**

Baker's bluejay yarn. Twain, M.
In Classic American short stories p141-47   **S C**

Bakich, Michael E.
The Cambridge guide to the constellations   **523.8**

Bakish, David
Richard Wright   **813.009**

Balaban, John, 1943-
Coming down again
In The Other side of heaven p245-51   **S C**

Balanced ecology. Schmitz, J. H.
In The Norton book of science fiction p98-114   **S C**

Balanchine, George, 1904-1983
About
Taper, B. Balanchine   **92**

Balancing the federal budget   **336.3**

Balay, Robert
(ed) Guide to reference books. See Guide to reference books   **011**

Balboa, Vasco Núñez de, 1475-1519
See/See also pages in the following book(s):
Faber, H. The discoverers of America p98-108   **970.01**

Bald eagle
Gerrard, J. M. The bald eagle   **598**

The bald soprano. Ionesco, E.
In Ionesco, E. Four plays p7-42   **842**

Baldick, Chris
(comp) The Concise Oxford dictionary of literary terms. See The Concise Oxford dictionary of literary terms   **803**
(ed) The Oxford book of gothic tales. See The Oxford book of gothic tales   **S C**

Baldock, Robert, 1950-
Pablo Casals   **92**

Baldwin, Dean R., 1942-
Virginia Woolf: a study of the short fiction   **823.009**

Baldwin, James, 1924-1987
The amen corner
In Black theatre USA   **812.008**
Blues for Mister Charlie
In Best American plays: 6th series—1963-1967 p47-96   **812.008**
Come out the wilderness
In Calling the wind p163-81   **S C**
Conversations with James Baldwin   **92**
The fire next time   **305.8**
Giovanni's room [excerpt]
In Growing up gay p85-89   **808.8**
Go tell it on the mountain   **Fic**
If Beale Street could talk   **Fic**
Jimmy's blues   **811**
No name in the street   **305.8**
Nobody knows my name   **305.8**
Notes of a native son   **305.8**
The price of the ticket   **814**
Sonny's blues
In American short story masterpieces   **S C**
In The Oxford book of American short stories p408-39   **S C**
Tell me how long the train's been gone
In Children of the night p324-51   **S C**
This morning, this evening, so soon
In The Best short stories by Negro writers p213-52   **S C**
About
Kenan, R. James Baldwin   **92**
Leeming, D. A. James Baldwin   **92**
See/See also pages in the following book(s):
Major modern black American writers p16-33   **810.9**
Modern black writers p57-69   **809**

The ballad of lost C'mell. Smith, C.
In The Oxford book of science fiction stories p302-21   **S C**

The ballad of Plastic Fred. Gansworth, E. L.
In Growing up Native American p325-33   **810.8**

Barthelme, Donald
The death of Edward Lear
In The Literary ghost p111-14   S C
The emerald
In The Best American short stories of the
eighties p57-84   S C
The glass mountain
In The Oxford book of modern fairy tales
p367-71   S C
Robert Kennedy saved from drowning
In The Norton book of American short stories
p587-95   S C
The school
In The Oxford book of American short stories
p556-59   S C

Bartholomew, Paul Charles, 1907-
Summaries of leading cases on the Constitution
342

Bartlett, John, 1820-1905
Familiar quotations   808.88

Bartlett's Roget's thesaurus   423

Barton, Clara, 1821-1912
About
Oates, S. B. A woman of valor: Clara Barton
and the Civil War   92

Barzini, Luigi Giorgio, 1908-1984
The Italians   945

Baseball
See also Softball; World series (Baseball)
Adair, R. K. The physics of baseball
796.357
Asinof, E. Eight men out   796.357
Baseball   796.357
The Baseball anthology   796.357
Chadwick, B. When the game was black and
white   796.357
Curran, W. Strikeout   796.357
Dickson, P. The joy of keeping score
796.357
Fox, S. R. Big leagues   796
Gilbert, T. W. Baseball and the color line
796.357
Gilbert, T. W. Superstars and monopoly wars
796.357
Gregorich, B. Women at play   796.357
Gutman, D. Baseball's greatest games
796.357
Gutman, D. The way baseball works
796.357
Hemphill, P. The heart of the game
796.357
Honig, D. Baseball: the illustrated history of
America's game   796.357
Kahn, R. The boys of summer   796.357
Kindall, J. Sports illustrated baseball
796.357
Seaver, T. Great moments in baseball
796.357
Smith, C. The storytellers   796.357
Williams, T. The science of hitting
796.357
Biography
Aaron, H. I had a hammer: the Hank Aaron sto-
ry   92
Creamer, R. W. Babe [Ruth]   92

Klapisch, B. High and tight: the rise and fall of
Dwight Gooden and Darryl Strawberry
92
Linn, E. Hitter: the life and turmoils of Ted
Williams   92
Macht, N. L. Roy Campanella   92
Mays, W. Say hey: the autobiography of Willie
Mays   92
Ribowsky, M. The power and the darkness: the
life of Josh Gibson in the shadows of the
game   92
Ritter, L. S. The glory of their times   920
Robinson, J. I never had it made   92
Robinson, R. Iron horse: Lou Gehrig in his time
92
Robinson, S. Stealing home: an intimate family
portrait by the daughter of Jackie Robinson
92
Rosenfeld, H. Iron man: the Cal Ripken, Jr., sto-
ry   92
Schoor, G. The illustrated history of Mickey
Mantle   92
Stengel, C. The gospel according to Casey
92
Stout, G. DiMaggio   92
Fiction
Harris, M. Bang the drum slowly, by Henry W.
Wiggen   Fic
Kinsella, W. P. Shoeless Joe   Fic
Kinsella, W. P. Shoeless Joe Jackson comes to
Iowa: stories   S C
Statistics
The Baseball encyclopedia   796.357
Neft, D. S. The sports encyclopedia: baseball
796.357
Reichler, J. L. The great all-time baseball record
book   796.357

Baseball   796.357

Baseball and the color line. Gilbert, T. W.
796.357

The **Baseball** anthology   796.357

The **Baseball** encyclopedia   796.357

Baseball's greatest games. Gutman, D.
796.357

The **basement** room. Greene, G.
In Classic English short stories, 1930-1955
p133-66   S C

Bashe, Philip
(jt. auth) Blanc, M. That's not all folks   92

Basic documents in American history   973

Basic electronics. Grob, B.   621.38

Basic life skills *See* Life skills

Basic rights *See* Civil rights; Human rights

The **basic** works of Aristotle. Aristotle   888

The **basic** writings of Sigmund Freud. Freud, S.
150.19

Basie, Count, 1904-1984
Good morning blues: the autobiography of
Count Basie   92
See/See also pages in the following book(s):
Terkel, S. Giants of jazz p109-19   920

Basie, William *See* Basie, Count, 1904-1984

Basil and Cleopatra. Fitzgerald, F. S.
    In Fitzgerald, F. S. The short stories of F.
       Scott Fitzgerald p431-48   **S C**

Basinger, Jeanine
    American cinema   **791.43**

Basketball
    Bird, L. Bird on basketball   **796.323**
    Blais, M. In these girls, hope is a muscle
                   796.323
    Douchant, M. Encyclopedia of college basket-
       ball   **796.323**
    Fox, S. R. Big leagues   **796**
    Frey, D. The last shot   **796.323**
    Joravsky, B. Hoop dreams   **796.323**
    Lieberman-Cline, N. Basketball for women
                   796.323
    Mikes, J. Basketball fundamentals   **796.323**
    Miller, F. Y. Winning basketball for girls
                   796.323
    The Official NBA basketball encyclopedia
                   796.323
    St. Martin, T. The art of shooting baskets
                   796.323

             Biography
    Bird, L. Drive: the story of my life   **92**
    Johnson, E. My life   **92**
    Krugel, M. Jordan   **92**
    Olajuwon, H. Living the dream   **92**
    Smith, S. Second coming: the strange odyssey
       of Michael Jordan—from courtside to home
       plate and back again   **92**
             Fiction
    Bennett, J. W. The squared circle   **Fic**
    Klass, D. Danger zone   **Fic**

Basketball for women. Lieberman-Cline, N.
                   796.323

Basketball fundamentals. Mikes, J.   **796.323**

Basque Hotel. Laxalt, R.
    In Where coyotes howl and wind blows free
       p30-37   **810.8**

Bass, Ellen
    Free your mind   **305.23**

Bass, Rick, 1958-
    Fires
    In The Best American short stories, 1996 p7-
       19   **S C**

Bassan, Maurice
    (ed) Stephen Crane: a collection of critical es-
    says. See Stephen Crane: a collection of criti-
    cal essays   **818**

Bastard out of Carolina [excerpt] Allison, D.
    In Coming of age in America p75-81
                   S C

Bastienne's child. Colette
    In Colette. The collected stories of Colette
       p147-53   **S C**

Bâtard. London, J.
    In London, J. The portable Jack London p69-
       81   **818**

Bate, Jonathan
    (ed) Shakespeare: an illustrated stage history.
    See Shakespeare: an illustrated stage history
                   792.9

Bates, Douglas
    The Pulitzer Prize   **071**

Bates, H. E. (Herbert Ernest), 1905-1974
    Never
    In The Oxford book of short stories p391-94
                   S C
    The woman who had imagination
    In Classic English short stories, 1930-1955
       p167-98   **S C**

Bates, Herbert Ernest *See* Bates, H. E. (Herbert
    Ernest), 1905-1974

Batey, Colleen E.
    Cultural atlas of the Viking world. See Cultural
    atlas of the Viking world   **948**

Bats
    Fenton, M. B. Bats   **599.4**
    Hill, J. E. Bats   **599.4**
    See/See also pages in the following book(s):
    Roueché, B. The medical detectives p40-48
                   616
    Wild animals of North America p47-75
                   599

Battered children *See* Child abuse

Battered women *See* Abused women

Battered women. Kosof, A.   **362.82**

Batting against Castro. Shepard, J.
    In The Best American short stories, 1994
       p277-92   **S C**

Battle chronicles of the Civil War   **973.7**

Battle cry of freedom. McPherson, J. M.
                   973.7

Battle of Britain, 1940 *See* Britain, Battle of,
    1940

The **Battle** of Britain. Hough, R. A.   **940.54**

The **Battle** of Hastings. Lace, W. W.   **942.02**

The **Battle** of Midway. Rice, E.   **940.54**

The **Battle** of the Little Bighorn. Sandoz, M.
                   973.8

Battle of Waterloo *See* Waterloo, Battle of, 1815

Battle royal. Ellison, R.
    In The Oxford book of American short stories
       p440-55   **S C**

The **battler.** Hemingway, E.
    In Hemingway, E. The complete short stories
       of Ernest Hemingway p97-104   **S C**
    In Hemingway, E. In our time p53-62
                   S C
    In Hemingway, E. The Nick Adams stories
       p47-57   **S C**
    In Hemingway, E. The short stories of Ernest
       Hemingway p127-38   **S C**

Battles
    Chandler, D. Battles and battlescenes of World
    War Two   **940.54**
            Dictionaries
    Eggenberger, D. An encyclopedia of battles
                   904

Battles and battlescenes of World War Two.
    Chandler, D.   **940.54**

Battles for Atlanta: Sherman moves east. Bailey,
    R. H.   **973.7**

Battles of the Revolutionary War, 1775-1781.
    Wood, W. J.   **973.3**

Bauchot, Roland
    (ed) Snakes. See Snakes   **597.9**

Bauer, Gerhard, 1940-
Soccer techniques, tactics & teamwork
796.334

Bauer, Marion Dane, 1938-
Dancing backwards
In Am I blue? p261-72 **S C**
'A writer's story **92**
(ed) Am I blue? See Am I blue? **S C**

Bauermeister, Erica
500 great books by women **016.3054**

Baughman, James L., 1952-
Henry R. Luce and the rise of the American news media **92**

Baughman, Judith
(ed) Modern women writers. See Modern women writers **016.813**

Baum, L. Frank (Lyman Frank), 1856-1919
The dummy that lived
In Masterpieces of fantasy and enchantment p419-25 **S C**
The glass dog
In Masterpieces of fantasy and enchantment p397-404 **S C**
The magic bonbons
In Masterpieces of fantasy and enchantment p413-18 **S C**
The queen of Quok
In Masterpieces of fantasy and enchantment p405-12 **S C**
In The Oxford book of modern fairy tales p215-23 **S C**

Baum, Lawrence
The Supreme Court **347**

Baum, Lyman Frank *See* Baum, L. Frank (Lyman Frank), 1856-1919

Baumfree, Isabella *See* Truth, Sojourner, d. 1883

Bausch, Richard, 1945-
All the way in Flagstaff, Arizona
In The Vintage book of contemporary American short stories p13-28 **S C**
Heat
In The Other side of heaven p353-78 **S C**

Bawden, Juliet
The art and craft of papier mâché **745.54**

Baxandall, Rosalyn Fraad, 1939-
(ed) America's working women. See America's working women **331.4**

Baxter, Charles
Gryphon
In The Best American short stories of the eighties p223-40 **S C**

Bay of Pigs. Persons, A. C. **972.91**

Bay of Pigs invasion *See* Cuba—History—1961, Invasion

Bayless, Deann Groen
(jt. auth) Bayless, R. Authentic Mexican **641.5**

Bayless, Rick
Authentic Mexican **641.5**

Bayly, C. A. (Christopher Alan)
Indian society and the making of the British Empire **954.03**

(ed) Atlas of the British Empire. See Atlas of the British Empire **912**

Bayly, Christopher Alan *See* Bayly, C. A. (Christopher Alan)

Baym, Nina
The scarlet letter **813.009**

Bayou Road Street [excerpt] Shaik, F.
In Streetlights: illuminating tales of the urban black experience p432-41 **S C**

BCCI *See* Bank of Credit and Commerce International SA

Be-ers and doers. Wilson, B.
In Wilson, B. The leaving and other stories **S C**

Beach, Edward Latimer, 1918-
Run silent, run deep **Fic**

Beach, Lewis
The clod
In Thirty famous one-act plays p451-60 **808.82**

The beach umbrella. Colter, C.
In The Best short stories by Negro writers p107-29 **S C**

Beachworld. King, S.
In King, S. Skeleton crew **S C**

Beaconsfield, Benjamin Disraeli, Earl of *See* Disraeli, Benjamin, Earl of Beaconsfield, 1804-1881

Beadwork
Taylor, C. Creative bead jewelry **745.58**

Beagle, Peter S.
The last unicorn **Fic**

Beagle Expedition (1831-1836)
Darwin, C. The voyage of the Beagle **508**

The beak of the finch. Weiner, J. **598**

Beale, Paul
(ed) Partridge, E. A concise dictionary of slang and unconventional English **427**

Beall, Julianne, 1946-
(ed) Dewey, M. Dewey decimal classification and relative index **025.4**

Bean, Roy, 1825?-1903
See/See also pages in the following book(s):
Walker, P. R. Great figures of the Wild West **920**

Bean, Suzanne M., 1957-
(jt. auth) Karnes, F. A. Girls & young women inventing **608**

Bear, Greg, 1951-
Moving Mars [excerpt]
In Nebula awards 30 p293-335 **S C**
Schrödinger's plague
In The Norton book of science fiction p477-84 **S C**

The bear. Faulkner, W.
In Faulkner, W. Uncollected stories of William Faulkner p281-95 **S C**

A bear hunt. Faulkner, W.
In Faulkner, W. Collected stories of William Faulkner p63-79 **S C**

Beard, Charles Austin, 1874-1948
An economic interpretation of the Constitution of the United States **342**

Beard, Jocelyn
(ed) 100 great monologues from the neo-classical theatre. See 100 great monologues from the neo-classical theatre **808.82**
(ed) 100 great monologues from the Renaissance theatre. See 100 great monologues from the Renaissance theatre **822.008**
(ed) The Best men's stage monologues of [date] See The Best men's stage monologues of [date] **808.82**
(ed) The Best women's stage monologues of [date] See The Best women's stage monologues of [date] **808.82**
(ed) Scenes from classic plays, 468 B.C. to 1970 A.D. See Scenes from classic plays, 468 B.C. to 1970 A.D. **808.82**

Bearden, Romare, 1914-1988
A history of African-American artists **709.73**

Beardsley, John
Pablo Picasso **92**

Bearing an hourglass. Anthony, P. See note under Anthony, P. Incarnations of immortality series **Fic**

Bearing the cross: Martin Luther King, Jr., and the Southern Christian Leadership Conference. Garrow, D. J. **92**

Bearing witness: selections from African-American autobiography in the twentieth century **920**

Bearing witness: stories of the Holocaust **808.8**

Bears
Domico, T. Bears of the world **599.74**

Bears. Bruchac, J.
In Song of the turtle p258-68 **S C**

Bears discover fire. Bisson, T.
In Nebula awards 26 p46-57 **S C**

Bears of the world. Domico, T. **599.74**

The **beast** in the jungle. James, H.
In Classic American short stories p155-212 **S C**

Beastly behaviors. Benyus, J. M. **591.5**

Beat the drum slowly . . . don't . . . too . . . fast. Bell, B. L.
In Song of the turtle p317-23 **S C**

Beat voices **811.008**

Beating the odds. Bode, J. **305.23**

Beatles
Hertsgaard, M. A day in the life **781.66**
MacDonald, I. Revolution in the head **781.66**

Beattie, Ann
Janus
In We are the stories we tell **S C**
A vintage Thunderbird
In The Vintage book of contemporary American short stories p29-47 **S C**
Weekend
In American short story masterpieces **S C**

Beauties and beasts. Hearne, B. G. **398.2**

The **beautiful** dream. Hesse, H.
In Hesse, H. The fairy tales of Hermann Hesse **S C**

Beautiful light and black our dreams. King, W.
In The Best short stories by Negro writers p438-47 **S C**

Beautiful origami. Aytüre-Scheele, Z. **736**

The **beautiful** suit. Wells, H. G.
In Wells, H. G. The complete short stories of H. G. Wells p139-43 **S C**

Beauty, Personal *See* Personal grooming

Beauty. McKinley, R. **Fic**

Beauty. Tepper, S. S. **Fic**

Beauty and the Beast
In Hearne, B. G. Beauties and beasts p3-13 **398.2**

Beauty lessons. Ortiz Cofer, J.
In Ortiz Cofer, J. An island like you p41-54 **S C**

The **beauty** mask. Reeve, A. B.
In The Oxford book of American detective stories p124-41 **S C**

The **beauty** trap. Landau, E. **155.6**

Beauvoir, Simone de, 1908-1986
The second sex **305.4**

Because of the dollars. Conrad, J.
In Conrad, J. The complete short fiction of Joseph Conrad v2 p218-48 **S C**

Becca's story. Forman, J. D. **Fic**

Beck, Earl R. (Earl Ray), 1916-
Under the bombs **940.54**

Beck, Jane Farrell- *See* Farrell-Beck, Jane

Beck, Warren A.
Historical atlas of the American West **911**

Becker, Marion Rombauer, 1903-1976
(jt. auth) Rombauer, I. von S. Joy of cooking **641.5**

Becker, Susan D.
The origins of the Equal Rights Amendment **305.4**

Becker, Udo
The Continuum encyclopedia of symbols **302.2**

Beckett, Samuel, 1906-1989
Waiting for Godot **842**
Waiting for Godot; criticism
In Samuel Beckett's Waiting for Godot **842**

About
Ben-Zvi, L. Samuel Beckett **848**
See/See also pages in the following book(s):
Esslin, M. The theatre of the absurd p29-91 **809.2**

Beckson, Karl E., 1926-
Literary terms **803**

Becky. Toomer, J.
In The Norton book of American short stories p324-26 **S C**

Bédé, Jean Albert
(ed) Columbia dictionary of modern European literature. See Columbia dictionary of modern European literature **803**

Best American plays: 6th series—1963-1967
812.008

Best American plays: 7th series—1967-1973
812.008

Best American plays: 8th series—1974-1982
812.008

Best American plays: 9th series—1983-1992
812.008

Best American screenplays **812.008**

The Best American short stories **S C**

The Best American short stories of the eighties
S C

The Best American sports writing **796**

The best and the brightest. Halberstam, D.
973.922

Best books *See* Books and reading—Best books

Best books for senior high readers **011.6**

Best books for young adults. Carter, B. **028.1**

The Best crime stories of the 19th century
S C

Best encyclopedias. See Kister, K. F. Kister's best
encyclopedias **016**

The best fiction of Rudyard Kipling. Kipling, R.
S C

Best-loved folktales of the world **398.2**

Best loved songs of the American people
782.42

Best-loved stories told at the National Storytelling
Festival **398.2**

Best magic, Bill Severn's. Severn, B. **793.8**

The best man. Vidal, G.
In Best American plays: 5th series—1957-
1963 p635-74 **812.008**

The Best men's stage monologues of [date]
808.82

The best of all possible worlds. Bradbury, R.
In Bradbury, R. The stories of Ray Bradbury
p625-30 **S C**

The best of enemies. Davidson, O. G. **305.8**

The Best of Free Spirit **305.23**

The best of Sholem Aleichem. Sholem Aleichem
S C

The Best of the West **818**

The Best plays of [date]: The Otis Guernsey/Burns
Mantle theater yearbook **808.82**

Best plays of the early American theatre
812.008

Best plays of the modern American theatre: 2nd
series **812.008**

The Best short stories by Negro writers **S C**

The best short stories of O. Henry. Henry, O.
S C

The best short stories of Ring Lardner. Lardner, R.
S C

The best side of heaven. Brooks, M.
In Brooks, M. Paradise Café and other stories
p45-54 **S C**

The Best women's stage monologues of [date]
808.82

The best years of their lives. Zvirin, S. **011.6**

Bester, Alfred, 1913-1987
Fondly Fahrenheit
In Robert Silverberg's Worlds of wonder
S C
See/See also pages in the following book(s):
Science fiction writers of the golden age p47-62
809.3

Bethune, Lebert
The burglar
In The Best short stories by Negro writers
p458-64 **S C**

Bethune, Mary Jane McLeod, 1875-1955
See/See also pages in the following book(s):
Black leaders of the twentieth century p191-219
920

The betrayal. Essop, A.
In African short stories **S C**

Betrayal. Woodard, L.
In Streetlights: illuminating tales of the urban
black experience p510-15 **S C**

Betrayals. Le Guin, U. K.
In Le Guin, U. K. Four ways to forgiveness
p1-34 **S C**

Bettelheim, Bruno
Freud and man's soul **150.19**
Surviving, and other essays **155.9**
The uses of enchantment **398**

Better Homes and Gardens new cook book
641.5

Better Homes and Gardens new garden book
635

A better mousetrap. Neuman, C.
In The Big book of large-cast plays p208-15
812.008

The better part of wisdom. Bradbury, R.
In Bradbury, R. The stories of Ray Bradbury
p822-31 **S C**

Betteridge, Harold T.
Cassell's German-English, English-German dictionary. See Cassell's German-English, English-German dictionary **433**

Betting *See* Gambling

Betty Crocker's Chinese cookbook. See Chin, L.
Betty Crocker's new Chinese cookbook
641.5

Betty Crocker's cookbook. Crocker, B. **641.5**

Betty Crocker's international cookbook. See
Crocker, B. Betty Crocker's new international
cookbook **641.5**

Betty Crocker's new Chinese cookbook. Chin, L.
641.5

Betty Crocker's new international cookbook.
Crocker, B. **641.5**

Between. Graver, E.
In Prize stories, 1996 p285-300 **S C**

Between God and gangsta rap. Dyson, M. E.
305.8

Between the pool and the gardenias. Danticat, E.
In Danticat, E. Krik? Krak! **S C**

Between two fires. Hansen, J. **973.7**

Beyer, Don E.
Castro! **92**

Beyle, Marie Henri *See* Stendhal, 1783-1842

Bicycling magazine's complete guide to riding and racing techniques. Matheny, F.   **796.6**

Biddle, Wayne
A field guide to germs   **616**

Biedermann, Hans, 1930-
Dictionary of symbolism   **302.2**

Biegeleisen, J. I. (Jacob Israel), 1910-
The ABC of lettering   **745.6**

Biegeleisen, Jacob Israel *See* Biegeleisen, J. I. (Jacob Israel), 1910-

Biely, Andrei *See* Bely, Andrey, 1880-1934

Bieman, Elizabeth
William Shakespeare: the romances   **822.3**

Bien pretty. Cisneros, S.
In Cisneros, S. Woman Hollering Creek and other stories   **S C**

Bierce, Ambrose, 1842-1914?
Chickamauga
In The Norton book of American short stories p74-79   **S C**
The coup de grâce
In Classic American short stories p148-55   **S C**
In The Oxford book of short stories p78-83   **S C**
The damned thing
In The Horror hall of fame p71-80   **S C**
A vine on a house
In The Oxford book of gothic tales p299-301   **S C**

Bierhorst, John
The mythology of Mexico and Central America   **299**
The mythology of North America   **299**
The mythology of South America   **299**
The way of the earth   **970.004**
(ed) The White deer and other stories told by the Lenape. See The White deer and other stories told by the Lenape   **398.2**

Big bang theory *See* Universe

Big Bertha stories. Mason, B. A.
In The Oxford book of American short stories p655-70   **S C**

The **big** black and white game. Bradbury, R.
In Bradbury, R. The stories of Ray Bradbury p272-81   **S C**

The **big** book of colleges. See Custard, E. T. The complete book of colleges   **378.73**

The **Big** book of large-cast plays   **812.008**

The **big** book of urban legends. Fleming, R. L.   **741.5**

Big boy leaves home. Wright, R.
In Wright, R. Uncle Tom's children   **S C**

The **big** change. Allen, F. L.   **973.91**

Big foot *See* Sasquatch

Big game hunting *See* Hunting

The **big** house. Behan, B.
In Behan, B. The complete plays   **822**

Big leagues. Fox, S. R.   **796**

Big meeting. Hughes, L.
In Hughes, L. Short stories   **S C**

The **big** sea: an autobiography. Hughes, L.   **92**

The **big** shot. Faulkner, W.
In Faulkner, W. Uncollected stories of William Faulkner p504-25   **S C**

The **big** sky. Guthrie, A. B.   **Fic**

Big two-hearted river. Hemingway, E.
In Hemingway, E. In our time p133-56   **S C**
In Hemingway, E. The Nick Adams stories p177-99   **S C**
In Hemingway, E. The short stories of Ernest Hemingway p207-32   **S C**

Big two-hearted river: part I. Hemingway, E.
In Hemingway, E. The complete short stories of Ernest Hemingway p163-69   **S C**

Big two-hearted river: part II. Hemingway, E.
In Hemingway, E. The complete short stories of Ernest Hemingway p173-80   **S C**

Big Volodya and Little Volodya. Chekhov, A. P.
In Chekhov, A. P. The image of Chekhov p204-18   **S C**

Big wheels: a tale of the laundry game (Milkman #2). King, S.
In King, S. Skeleton crew   **S C**

Big white fog. Ward, T.
In Black theatre USA   **812.008**

Bigfoot *See* Sasquatch

Bigotry *See* Toleration

BigWater. Sherman, C. W.
In Rites of passage p79-88   **S C**

The **bike.** Soto, G.
In Growing up Chicana/o p233-36   **810.8**

Bikes, Mountain *See* Mountain bikes

Biko, Stephen, 1946-1977
I write what I like   **968.06**
About
Woods, D. Biko   **92**

Bilingual books
English-Spanish
Cool salsa   **811.008**
The Tree is older than you are   **860.8**

Bill, Buffalo *See* Buffalo Bill, 1846-1917

The **bill.** Malamud, B.
In Malamud, B. The stories of Bernard Malamud p249-56   **S C**

Bill of rights (U.S.) *See* United States. Constitution. 1st-10th amendments

The **Bill** of Rights: opposing viewpoints   **342**

Bill Severn's best magic. Severn, B.   **793.8**

Billennium. Ballard, J. G.
In The Oxford book of science fiction stories p287-301   **S C**

The **billiard** ball. Asimov, I.
In Asimov, I. The complete stories v2 p362-76   **S C**

Billings, Charlene W., 1941-
Lasers   **621.36**
Supercomputers   **004**

The **billion** dollar skeleton. Phan, H. D.
In The Other side of heaven p223-30   **S C**

Billy, the Kid
See/See also pages in the following book(s):
Brown, D. A. The American West p301-09
        978
The Gunfighters p182-90   **364.3**
Walker, P. R. Great figures of the Wild West
        920

Billy Budd. Coxe, L. O.
In Best American plays: 3d series—1945-
   1951 p365-93   **812.008**
Billy Budd, sailor. Melville, H.   **Fic**
Biloxi blues. Simon, N.   **812**
  also in Simon, N. The collected plays of Neil
   Simon v3 p595-691   **812**

Bilstein, Roger E.
Flight in America: from the Wrights to the astronauts   **629.13**

Bing, Jon, 1944-
The Owl of Bear Island
In Tales from the planet Earth   **S C**

Binge-purge behavior *See* Bulimia

Bingen, Hildegard von *See* Hildegard, von Bing-
  en, Saint, 1098-1179

Bingham, George Caleb, 1811-1879
See/See also pages in the following book(s):
Novak, B. American painting of the nineteenth
  century p152-64   **759.13**

Bingham, Hiram, 1875-1956
Lost city of the Incas   **985**
The **bingo** van. Erdrich, L.
In Talking leaves   **S C**

Bioethics
Biomedical ethics: opposing viewpoints   **174**
Genetic engineering: opposing viewpoints
        174
Mabie, M. C. J. Bioethics and the new medical
  technology   **174**

Bioethics and the new medical technology. Mabie,
  M. C. J.   **174**

Biogeography
Quammen, D. The song of the dodo   **574.9**

Biograph. Martone, M.
In The Norton book of American short stories
  p749-63   **S C**

A **Biographical** dictionary of artists   **920.003**
The **Biographical** dictionary of scientists
        920.003
Biographical supplement and index. Freund, D.
  M.
In The Young Oxford history of African
  Americans   **305.8**

Biography
        Bibliography
Biography index   **920**
        Dictionaries
Abrams, I. The Nobel Peace Prize and the laure-
  ates   **920.003**
A Dictionary of twentieth-century world biogra-
  phy   **920.003**
Larousse biographical dictionary   **920.003**
Merriam-Webster's biographical dictionary
        920.003
Nobel Prize winners   **920.003**

        Indexes
Biography index   **920**
        Periodicals
Current biography yearbook   **920.003**
    Periodicals—Indexes
Current biography: cumulated index, 1940-1995
        920.003
        Technique
See Biography as a literary form

Biography as a literary form
Mungo, R. Your autobiography   **808**
Biography index   **920**

Biological diversity
Buchmann, S. The forgotten pollinators
        574.5
Margulis, L. What is life?   **577**
Patent, D. H. The vanishing feast   **338.1**
Raeburn, P. The last harvest   **338.1**
See/See also pages in the following book(s):
Rainis, K. G. Environmental science projects for
  young scientists p19-42   **574.5**

Biological parents *See* Birthparents
Biological rhythms
Bodyclock   **612**
Biological warfare
Taylor, C. L. Chemical and biological warfare
        358

Biology
   See also Adaptation (Biology); Life (Biolo-
  gy); Marine biology; Microbiology
Margulis, L. Five kingdoms   **574**
See/See also pages in the following book(s):
Naisbitt, J. Megatrends 2000 p241-69   **303.4**
        Dictionaries
Burnie, D. Dictionary of nature   **574.03**
Concise encyclopedia biology   **574.03**
Encyclopedia of life sciences   **574.03**
        Experiments
VanCleave, J. P. Janice VanCleave's A+
  projects in biology   **574**
        Periodicity
  See Biological rhythms
        Philosophy
Lovelock, J. The ages of Gaia   **574**
Margulis, L. What is life?   **577**
Thomas, L. The lives of a cell   **574**
Biomedical ethics: opposing viewpoints   **174**
Biorhythms *See* Biological rhythms
Biosphere
Lovelock, J. The ages of Gaia   **574**
Biotechnology
        Dictionaries
Bains, W. Biotechnology from A to Z   **660**
Steinberg, M. L. The Facts on File dictionary of
  biotechnology and genetic engineering
        660
Biotechnology from A to Z. Bains, W.   **660**
Bird, Gloria
Turtle Lake
  In Talking leaves   **S C**
Bird, Larry
Bird on basketball   **796.323**
Drive: the story of my life   **92**

The **bird** cage. White, P. C.
   In Black-eyed Susans/Midnight birds p45-53
   S C

The **bird** care book. Gerstenfeld, S. L.   **636.6**

The **bird** I fancied. Higgins, A.
   In The Oxford book of Irish short stories
   p445-54   **S C**

The **bird** like no other. West, D.
   In West, D. The richer, the poorer: stories,
   sketches, and reminiscences   **S C**

Bird of prey. Collier, J.
   In Masterpieces of fantasy and enchantment
   p189-96   **S C**

Bird on basketball. Bird, L.   **796.323**

Bird watching
   Birding   **598**

The **birder's** handbook. Ehrlich, P. R.   **598**

Birding   **598**

Birds
   See also Birds of prey; Finches; Water
   birds
   Brooks, B. On the wing   **598**
   Encyclopedia of birds   **598**
   Gerstenfeld, S. L. The bird care book
   636.6
   ### Fiction
   Wharton, W. Birdy   **Fic**
   ### Migration
   The Atlas of bird migration   **598**
   ### North America
   Book of North American birds   **598**
   Ehrlich, P. R. The birder's handbook   **598**
   Field guide to the birds of North America
   598
   Peterson, R. T. A field guide to the birds
   598
   ### West (U.S.)
   Peterson, R. T. A field guide to western birds
   598

Birds. Aristophanes
   In Four Greek plays   **882.008**

The **birds'** Christmas carol [adaptation] Gotwalt,
H. L. M.
   In The Big book of large-cast plays p339-51
   812.008

The **bird's** nest. Walpole, H.
   In Masterpieces of fantasy and enchantment
   p185-88   **S C**

The **birds** of God. Couto, M.
   In The Heinemann book of contemporary
   African short stories p67-71   **S C**

Birds of prey
   See also names of birds of prey
   Birds of prey   **598**

Birds of prey   **598**

Birdy. Wharton, W.   **Fic**

Birmingham (Ala.)
   ### Race relations
   King, M. L. Why we can't wait   **323.1**

Birnbaum, Jeffrey H., 1956-
   The lobbyists   **328.73**

Birnbaum, Max
   Cass & Birnbaum's guide to American colleges.
   See Cass & Birnbaum's guide to American
   colleges   **378.73**

Birth *See* Childbirth

Birth control
   Chesler, E. Woman of valor: Margaret Sanger
   and the birth control movement in America
   92
   Gay, K. Pregnancy   **363.9**
   Winikoff, B. The contraceptive handbook
   613.9
   See/See also pages in the following book(s):
   Bell, R. Changing bodies, changing lives p166-
   94   **613.9**

Birth defects
   See also Growth disorders
   Edelson, E. Birth defects   **616**
   Gravelle, K. Understanding birth defects
   618.92
   ### Dictionaries
   Wynbrandt, J. The encyclopedia of genetic dis-
   orders and birth defects   **616**

Birth injuries *See* Birth defects

The **birth** of Britain. Churchill, Sir W.
   In Churchill, Sir W. A history of the English-
   speaking peoples v1   **941**

The **birth** of the Republic, 1763-89. Morgan, E. S.
   973.3

Birtha, Becky, 1948-
   In the life
   In We are the stories we tell   **S C**
   Johnnieruth
   In Daughters of Africa p744-48   **808.8**
   In Growing up gay p18-22   **808.8**

The **birthday.** Wolfe, T.
   In Wolfe, T. The complete short stories of
   Thomas Wolfe p428-37   **S C**

The **birthday** party, and The room. Pinter, H.
   822

The **birthday** present. Jackson, L. S.
   In Streetlights: illuminating tales of the urban
   black experience p174-81   **S C**

The **birthday** present. Schulman, C.
   In Ten out of ten p1-31   **812.008**

The **birthmark.** Hawthorne, N.
   In Hawthorne, N. Tales and sketches; A won-
   der book for girls and boys; Tanglewood
   tales for girls and boys p764-80
   S C
   In The Oxford book of short stories p27-42
   S C

Birthmates. Jen, G.
   In The Best American short stories, 1995
   p110-25   **S C**

Birthparents
   Gravelle, K. Where are my birth parents?
   362.7

Birthrate
   See also Population

Birthright [excerpt] Stribling, T. S.
   In The Portable Harlem Renaissance reader
   p333-38   **810.8**

Bisatie, Mohamed el- *See* El-Bisatie, Mohamed

Bischoff, John
(jt. auth) Bird, L. Bird on basketball
796.323

Bisexuality
Pollack, R. The journey out 305.9

Bishop, Elizabeth, 1911-1979
The complete poems, 1927-1979 811
See/See also pages in the following book(s):
Voices & visions p395-426 811.009

Bishop, Jim, 1907-1987
The day Christ died 232.9
The day Lincoln was shot 973.7

Bishop, Michael, 1945-
The Bob Dylan Tambourine Software & Satori Support Services Consortium, Ltd.
In The Norton book of science fiction p616-27 S C
Life regarded as a jigsaw puzzle of highly lustrous cats
In Nebula awards 28 p207-27 S C
The ommatidium miniatures
In Nebula awards 25 p200-17 S C

Bishop, Morris, 1893-1973
The Middle Ages. See The Middle Ages [American Heritage] 940.1

Bishop, Paul
The framing game
In Bad behavior p21-35 S C

Bishop, Rudine Sims, 1937-
Presenting Walter Dean Myers 813.009

The **Bishop.** Chekhov, A. P.
In Chekhov, A. P. The image of Chekhov p304-22 S C
In The Portable twentieth-century Russian reader p12-28 891.7

Biskup, Michael D., 1956-
(ed) Criminal justice: opposing viewpoints. See Criminal justice: opposing viewpoints
345
(ed) Suicide: opposing viewpoints. See Suicide: opposing viewpoints 362.2

Biskupic, Joan
The Supreme Court and individual rights
342

Bismarck, Otto, Fürst von, 1815-1898
See/See also pages in the following book(s):
Carr, W. A history of Germany, 1815-1945 p87-171 943
Fulbrook, M. A concise history of Germany p126-37 943

Bison
The Buffalo hunters 970.004
See/See also pages in the following book(s):
Brown, D. A. Bury my heart at Wounded Knee p241-71 970.004

Bisson, Terry
Bears discover fire
In Nebula awards 26 p46-57 S C
England underway
In Nebula awards 29 p181-202 S C
They're made out of meat
In Nebula awards 27 p145-48 S C

The **bitch.** Colette
In Colette. The collected stories of Colette p417-20 S C

Bites and stings. Nichol, J. 591.6

Bitter cane. Lim, G.
In The Oxford book of women's writing in the United States p407-40 810.8

The **bitter** truth. Singer, I. B.
In Singer, I. B. The death of Methuselah and other stories p121-30 S C

Black, Henry Campbell, 1860-1927
Black's law dictionary 340.03

Black, Hugo LaFayette, 1886-1971
See/See also pages in the following book(s):
Aaseng, N. Great Justices of the Supreme Court p121-35 920

Black, Jeremy
The Cambridge illustrated atlas of warfare: Renaissance to revolution, 1492-1792 355

Black American colleges & universities
378.73

Black American poets and dramatists before the Harlem Renaissance 810.9

Black American poets and dramatists of the Harlem renaissance. See Black American poets and dramatists before the Harlem Renaissance
810.9

Black American prose writers before the Harlem Renaissance 810.9

Black American prose writers of the Harlem Renaissance 810.9

Black American women fiction writers
813.009

Black American women in Olympic track and field. Davis, M. D. 920

Black Americans *See* African Americans

The **Black** Americans: a history in their own words, 1619-1983 305.8

Black art (Magic) *See* Witchcraft

Black ass at the cross roads. Hemingway, E.
In Hemingway, E. The complete short stories of Ernest Hemingway p579-89 S C

Black authors
See also African American authors
Daughters of Africa 808.8
Bio-bibliography
Black writers 920.003
Dictionaries
The Schomburg Center guide to black literature from the eighteenth century to the present
809

The **Black** book of Bosnia 949.7

Black boy. Wright, R. 92
also in Wright, R. Works v2 818

The **Black** Bull of Norroway
In Hearne, B. G. Beauties and beasts p92-96
398.2

The **black** cat. Poe, E. A.
In Classic American short stories p25-37
S C
In Poe, E. A. The collected tales and poems of Edgar Allan Poe p223-30 S C

Black dance in America. Haskins, J. 792.8

Black death *See* Plague

The **black** death. Gottfried, R. S.   **616.9**

Black death. Hurston, Z. N.
 In Hurston, Z. N. The complete stories p202-08   **S C**

The **black** doctor. Aldridge, I.
 In Black theatre USA   **812.008**

Black drama (American) *See* American drama—African American authors

Black Elk, 1863-1950
 Black Elk speaks   **92**

Black-eyed Susans
 In Black-eyed Susans/Midnight birds   **S C**

Black-eyed Susans/Midnight birds   **S C**

The **black** ferris. Bradbury, R.
 In Bradbury, R. The stories of Ray Bradbury p851-57   **S C**

Black firsts   **305.8**

Black folktales. Lester, J.   **398.2**

Black heritage sites. Curtis, N. C.   **917.3**

Black history month resource book   **305.8**

Black holes (Astronomy)
 Thorne, K. S. Black holes and time warps   **530.1**
 See/See also pages in the following book(s):
 Hawking, S. W. Black holes and baby universes and other essays p101-25   **523.1**

Black holes and baby universes and other essays. Hawking, S. W.   **523.1**

Black holes and time warps. Thorne, K. S.   **530.1**

Black ice. Cary, L.   **92**

Black is my favorite color. Malamud, B.
 In Malamud, B. The stories of Bernard Malamud p73-84   **S C**

Black Jack. Kipling, R.
 In Kipling, R. The portable Kipling   **828**

Black Kettle, Cheyenne Chief, 1803?-1868
 See/See also pages in the following book(s):
 Brown, D. A. The American West p100-09   **978**

Black leaders of the nineteenth century   **920**

Black leaders of the twentieth century   **920**

Black like me. Griffin, J. H.   **305.8**

Black literature (American) *See* American literature—African American authors

The **black** mate. Conrad, J.
 In Conrad, J. The complete short fiction of Joseph Conrad v2 p63-89   **S C**

Black Moses [biography of Marcus Garvey] Cronon, E. D.   **92**

Black mother. See Davidson, B. The African slave trade   **967**

Black music
 See also African American music

Black music. Faulkner, W.
 In Faulkner, W. Collected stories of William Faulkner p799-821   **S C**

Black music in America. Haskins, J.   **780.89**

Black musicians
 See also African American musicians

Talamon, B. Bob Marley   **92**

Black Muslims
 Baldwin, J. The fire next time   **305.8**
 Brown, K. Malcolm X   **92**
 Gallen, D. Malcolm X: as they knew him   **92**
 Malcolm X. The autobiography of Malcolm X   **92**
 Myers, W. D. Malcolm X   **92**
 See/See also pages in the following book(s):
 Magida, A. J. Prophet of rage: a life of Louis Farrakhan and his nation   **92**

Black no more. Schuyler, G. S.
 In The Portable Harlem Renaissance reader p655-66   **810.8**

Black noise. Rose, T.   **781.64**

Black poetry (American) *See* American poetry—African American authors

Black powder. Wu, W. F.
 In American dragons: twenty-five Asian American voices p211-34   **810.8**

The **black** press and the struggle for civil rights. Senna, C.   **071**

Black profiles in courage. Abdul-Jabbar, K.   **920**

The **black** pumpkin. Koontz, D. R.
 In Koontz, D. R. Strange highways p155-73   **S C**

Black sister   **811.008**

The **Black** student's guide to college success   **378**

Black theatre USA   **812.008**

Black thunder [excerpt] Bontemps, A. W.
 In The Portable Harlem Renaissance reader p674-79   **810.8**

The **black** tradition in American modern dance. Long, R. A.   **792.8**

Black Union soldiers in the Civil War. Hargrove, H. B.   **973.7**

A **black** woman speaks. Richards, B.
 In 9 plays by black women   **811.008**

Black writers   **920.003**

The **blackamoor** of Peter the Great. Pushkin, A. S.
 In Pushkin, A. S. Alexander Pushkin: complete prose fiction p11-40   **S C**

The **blackberry** day. Pilcher, R.
 In Pilcher, R. Flowers in the rain & other stories   **S C**

The **blacker** the berry . . . [excerpt] Thurman, W.
 In The Portable Harlem Renaissance reader p636-49   **810.8**

Blackface. George, N.   **791.43**

The **blackguard.** McCarthy, M.
 In We are the stories we tell   **S C**

Blackham's Wimpy. Westall, R.
 In Westall, R. Shades of darkness p246-310   **S C**

A **blackjack** bargainer. Henry, O.
 In Henry, O. The best short stories of O. Henry   **S C**

Blackness. Kincaid, J.
 In Children of the night p381-84   **S C**

Blacks
See/See also pages in the following book(s):
Hook, J. N. Family names p284-301   **929.4**
Biography
See also African Americans—Biography
Mathabane, M. Kaffir boy   **92**
Mathabane, M. Kaffir boy in America   **92**
Fiction
Kincaid, J. Autobiography of my mother
Fic
Rites of passage   **S C**
Folklore
Lester, J. Black folktales   **398.2**
Quotations
Heart full of grace   **808.88**
My soul looks back, 'less I forget   **808.88**
United States
See African Americans
Blacks in art
See also African Americans in art
Feelings, T. The middle passage   **759.13**
Blacks in literature
See also African Americans in literature
The Schomburg Center guide to black literature from the eighteenth century to the present
809
Black's law dictionary. Black, H. C.   **340.03**
Black's medical dictionary   **610.3**
The **blacksmith** shop caper. Kinsella, W. P.
In Kinsella, W. P. Shoeless Joe Jackson comes to Iowa: stories   **S C**
Blackstone, Harry, 1885-1965
The Blackstone book of magic & illusion
793.8
The **Blackstone** book of magic & illusion. Blackstone, H.   **793.8**
Blackwell, Elizabeth, 1821-1910
See/See also pages in the following book(s):
Curtis, R. H. Great lives: medicine p185-94
920
Blackwood, Algernon, 1869-1951
The empty house
In The Oxford book of English ghost stories p222-35   **S C**
The kit-bag
In Victorian ghost stories p480-89   **S C**
The willows
In The Horror hall of fame p153-203
S C
Blain, Virginia, 1945-
(ed) The Feminist companion to literature in English. See The Feminist companion to literature in English   **820.9**
Blair, Clay, 1925-
The forgotten war   **951.9**
(jt. auth) Bradley, O. N. A general's life
92
Blair, Eric *See* Orwell, George, 1903-1950
Blais, Madeleine, 1947-
In these girls, hope is a muscle   **796.323**
Blake, Barbara Radke
Creating newsletters, brochures, and pamphlets
070.5

Blake, Nicholas J.
See/See also pages in the following book(s):
Modern mystery writers p16-30   **809.3**
Blake, William, 1757-1827
The complete poetry and prose of William Blake   **828**
Poems   **821**
The portable Blake   **828**
Songs of innocence and experience
In Blake, W. The portable Blake   **828**
William Blake   **828**
About
Ackroyd, P. Blake   **92**
See/See also pages in the following book(s):
Untermeyer, L. Lives of the poets p286-311
920
Blakemore, Harold
(ed) The Cambridge encyclopedia of Latin America and the Caribbean. See The Cambridge encyclopedia of Latin America and the Caribbean   **980**
Blanc, Mel, 1908-1989
That's not all folks   **92**
Blanchard, Paula
Sarah Orne Jewett   **92**
Blanco, Patricia
Rosario Magdaleno
In Latina: women's voices from the borderlands p90-95   **810.8**
Bland, Celia
The mechanical age   **941.08**
Blanning, T. C. W.
(ed) The Oxford illustrated history of modern Europe. See The Oxford illustrated history of modern Europe   **940.2**
Blas, Samuel
Revenge
In Bad behavior p37-46   **S C**
Bledsoe, Lucy Jane
Teamwork
In Growing up gay p240-43   **808.8**
Bleifeld, Maurice
Botany projects for young scientists   **581**
Bleiler, Everett Franklin, 1920-
(ed) Science fiction writers. See Science fiction writers   **809.3**
Bless the beasts and children. Swarthout, G. F.
Fic
Bless this house. Brand, C.
In Bad behavior p67-82   **S C**
Blessed assurance. Hughes, L.
In Hughes, L. Short stories   **S C**
The **blessed** man of Boston, my grandmother's thimble, and Fanning Island. Updike, J.
In Updike, J. Pigeon feathers, and other stories p227-45   **S C**
The **blessing.** Greene, G.
In Greene, G. The portable Graham Greene p414-20   **828**
Blevins, Winfred
Stone song   **Fic**

Blew, Mary Clearman, 1939-
(ed) Circle of women: an anthology of contemporary Western women writers. See Circle of women: an anthology of contemporary Western women writers **810.8**

Blind
Keller, H. The story of my life **92**
Lash, J. P. Helen and teacher: the story of Helen Keller and Anne Sullivan Macy **92**
Nicholson, L. Helen Keller **92**
See/See also pages in the following book(s):
Cheney, G. A. Teens with physical disabilities p51-61 **362.4**

Blind alley. Asimov, I.
In Asimov, I. The complete stories v2 p45-64 **S C**

The blind man. Lawrence, D. H.
In Lawrence, D. H. The complete short stories v2 **S C**

Blind watchers of the sky. Kolb, R. **523.1**
Blinder. Gordimer, N.
In Gordimer, N. Crimes of conscience p54-62 **S C**

Blish, James, 1921-1975
Common time
In Robert Silverberg's Worlds of wonder **S C**
How beautiful with banners
In The Norton book of science fiction p133-41 **S C**
In The Oxford book of science fiction stories p340-49 **S C**
See/See also pages in the following book(s):
Science fiction writers of the golden age p63-77 **809.3**

Blizzard!!!. Ponce, M. H.
In Iguana dreams **S C**

Blk love song #1. Kalamu ya Salaam
In Black theatre USA **812.008**

Bloch, Deborah Perlmutter
How to write a winning resume **650.14**

Bloch, Robert, 1917-1994
The man who collected Poe
In Masterpieces of mystery and suspense p426-39 **S C**
Yours truly, Jack the Ripper
In The Horror hall of fame p308-25 **S C**

Block, Francesca Lia
Baby Be-Bop. See note under Block, F. L. Weetzie Bat **Fic**
Cherokee Bat and the Goat Guys. See note under Block, F. L. Weetzie Bat **Fic**
Missing Angel Juan. See note under Block, F. L. Weetzie Bat **Fic**
Weetzie Bat **Fic**
Winnie and Tommy
In Am I blue? p29-44 **S C**
Witch baby. See note under Block, F. L. Weetzie bat **Fic**

Block, Lawrence, 1938-
Like a bug on a windshield
In Bad behavior p47-66 **S C**

One thousand dollars a word
In Masterpieces of mystery and suspense p645-51 **S C**

The Blockade **973.7**

Blom, Margaret Howard
Charlotte Brontë **823.009**

Blonde. Min, K.
In American eyes p3-7 **S C**

Blood

Circulation
See also Cardiovascular system
Avraham, R. The circulatory system **612.1**

Diseases
See also Leukemia

Blood at the root [excerpt] Simmons, M.
In Streetlights: illuminating tales of the urban black experience p452-65 **S C**

Blood-burning moon. Toomer, J.
In The Oxford book of American short stories p285-94 **S C**

Blood disease. McGrath, P.
In The Oxford book of gothic tales p502-18 **S C**

The blood-ghoul of Scarsdale. Friesner, E. M.
In Vampires: a collection of original stories p81-98 **S C**

Blood kin. Sherman, D.
In Vampires: a collection of original stories p35-63 **S C**

Blood libel. Hussey, L. A.
In Vampires: a collection of original stories p157-86 **S C**

Blood memory. Graham, M. **92**

Blood sister. Yolen, J.
In Am I blue? p191-212 **S C**

Blood, tears, and folly. Deighton, L. **940.54**

The bloodiest day: the battle of Antietam. Bailey, R. H. **973.7**

Bloodletters and badmen. Nash, J. R. **920**

Bloods: an oral history of the Vietnam War by black veterans **959.704**

The bloodstained pavement. Christie, A.
In Christie, A. Miss Marple: the complete short stories **S C**

Bloody Blanche. Schwob, M.
In The Oxford book of gothic tales p245-48 **S C**

The bloody countess. Pizarnik, A.
In The Oxford book of gothic tales p466-77 **S C**

Bloom, Harold, 1930-
(ed) Ahab. See Ahab [critical essays] **813.009**
(ed) Arthur Miller. See Arthur Miller [critical essays] **812**
(ed) Beowulf. See Beowulf [critical essays] **829**
(ed) Black American poets and dramatists before the Harlem Renaissance. See Black American poets and dramatists before the Harlem Renaissance **810.9**

Bloom, Harold, 1930——*Continued*

(ed) Black American prose writers before the Harlem Renaissance. See Black American prose writers before the Harlem Renaissance **810.9**

(ed) Black American prose writers of the Harlem Renaissance. See Black American prose writers of the Harlem Renaissance **810.9**

(ed) Black American women fiction writers. See Black American women fiction writers **813.009**

(ed) Carson McCullers. See Carson McCullers [critical essays] **813.009**

(ed) Cleopatra. See Cleopatra [critical essays] **822.009**

(ed) Contemporary black American fiction writers. See Contemporary black American fiction writers **813.009**

(ed) Contemporary black American poets and dramatists. See Contemporary black American poets and dramatists **810.9**

(ed) D.H. Lawrence's Sons and lovers. See D.H. Lawrence's Sons and lovers **823.009**

(ed) Daniel Defoe. See Daniel Defoe [critical essays] **823.009**

(ed) Edward Albee. See Edward Albee [critical essays] **812**

(ed) Franz Kafka's The metamorphosis. See Franz Kafka's The metamorphosis **833.009**

(ed) Franz Kafka's The trial. See Franz Kafka's The trial **833.009**

(ed) Fyodor Dostoevsky. See Fyodor Dostoevsky [critical essays] **891.7**

(ed) Gatsby. See Gatsby [critical essays] **813.009**

(ed) George Orwell's 1984. See George Orwell's 1984 **823.009**

(ed) Henry David Thoreau. See Henry David Thoreau [critical essays] **818**

(ed) Henry James's Daisy Miller, The turn of the screw, and other tales. See Henry James's Daisy Miller, The turn of the screw, and other tales **813.009**

(ed) Hester Prynne. See Hester Prynne [critical essays] **813.009**

(ed) Holden Caulfield. See Holden Caulfield [critical essays] **813.009**

(ed) J.D. Salinger. See J.D. Salinger [critical essays] **813.009**

(ed) James Dickey. See James Dickey [critical essays] **811**

(ed) Jean-Jacques Rousseau. See Jean-Jacques Rousseau [critical essays] **848**

(ed) John Dryden. See John Dryden [critical essays] **821**

(ed) John le Carré. See John le Carré [critical essays] **823.009**

(ed) John Steinbeck. See John Steinbeck [critical essays] **813.009**

(ed) John Updike. See John Updike [critical essays] **813.009**

(ed) Macbeth. See Macbeth [critical essays] **822.3**

(ed) Major modern black American writers. See Major modern black American writers **810.9**

(ed) Modern mystery writers. See Modern mystery writers **809.3**

(ed) The New Moulton's library of literary criticism. See The New Moulton's library of literary criticism **820.9**

(ed) Richard Wright's Native son. See Richard Wright's Native son **813.009**

(ed) Romantic poetry and prose. See Romantic poetry and prose **820.8**

(ed) Samuel Beckett's Waiting for Godot. See Samuel Beckett's Waiting for Godot **842**

(ed) Science fiction writers of the golden age. See Science fiction writers of the golden age **809.3**

(ed) Sinclair Lewis. See Sinclair Lewis [critical essays] **813.009**

(ed) Thomas Wolfe. See Thomas Wolfe [critical essays] **813.009**

The **Blue** and the Gray. Allen, T. B. **973.7**

Blue Bird's offering. Deloria, E. C.
In Spider Woman's granddaughters **S C**

The **blue** bottle. Bradbury, R.
In Bradbury, R. The stories of Ray Bradbury p804-11 **S C**

The **blue** cross. Chesterton, G. K.
In Masterpieces of mystery and suspense p26-43 **S C**

The **blue** geranium. Christie, A.
In Christie, A. Miss Marple: the complete short stories **S C**
In Crime classics p231-46 **S C**

Blue highways. Heat Moon, W. L. **917.3**

The **blue** moccasins. Lawrence, D. H.
In Lawrence, D. H. The complete short stories v3 **S C**

The **Blue** Nile. Moorehead, A. **962**

Bluebeard's daughter. Warner, S. T.
In The Oxford book of modern fairy tales p302-17 **S C**

Blueprint for life **573.2**

The **blues** begins. Leaks, S.
In The Best short stories by Negro writers p275-87 **S C**

Blues for Little Prez. Greenlee, S.
In Children of the night p414-22 **S C**

Blues for Mister Charlie. Baldwin, J.
In Best American plays: 6th series—1963-1967 p47-96 **812.008**

Blues for Pablo. Stewart, J.
In Calling the wind p205-19 **S C**

The **blues** I'm playing. Hughes, L.
In Hughes, L. Short stories **S C**
In The Portable Harlem Renaissance reader p619-27 **810.8**

Blues music
See also Jazz music; Soul music
Awmiller, C. This house on fire **781.643**
Davis, F. The history of the blues **781.643**
Lomax, A. The land where the blues began **781.643**
Nothing but the blues **781.643**
Oliver, P. The new Grove gospel, blues and jazz **780.89**

Blues music—*Continued*
Fiction
LeMieux, A. C. Do angels sing the blues?
             Fic

Blum, Daniel C.
(ed) Theatre world. *See* Theatre world 792

Blume, Judy
Forever   Fic
About
Weidt, M. N. Presenting Judy Blume
            813.009

Blumenson, Martin
Patton, the man behind the legend, 1885-1945
            92

Blumfeld, an elderly bachelor. Kafka, F.
In Kafka, F. The complete stories S C

Blumlein, Michael
The brains of rats
In The Norton book of science fiction p633-46   S C

A **blunder.** Chekhov, A. P.
In Chekhov, A. P. The image of Chekhov p96-98   S C

Bly, Carol
Talk of heroes
In American short story masterpieces
            S C
In The Vintage book of contemporary American short stories p48-68 S C

Bly, Nellie, 1867-1922
About
Kroeger, B. Nellie Bly   92
Boarder skirmish. Hamlett, C.
In The Big book of large-cast plays p291-98
            812.008

The **boarding** house. Joyce, J.
In Joyce, J. Dubliners   S C

Boardman, Edna M.
Censorship   025.2

Boardman, John, 1927-
(ed) The Oxford history of classical art. *See* The Oxford history of classical art 709.38
A **boar's** tooth. Michener, J. A.
In Michener, J. A. Tales of the South Pacific
            S C

Boas, Jacob
We are witnesses   940.53

Boatbuilding
See also Shipbuilding

Boatner, Mark Mayo, 1921-
The Civil War dictionary   973.7

Boats, Submarine *See* Submarines

Boats and boating
See also Sailing
Palmer, T. America by rivers 551.48

The **Bob** Dylan Tambourine Software & Satori Support Services Consortium, Ltd. Bishop, M.
In The Norton book of science fiction p616-27   S C

Bobby Fischer teaches chess. Fischer, B.
            794.1

Bober, Natalie
Abigail Adams   92

A restless spirit: the story of Robert Frost
            92
Thomas Jefferson: man on a mountain 92

Boccaccio, Giovanni, 1313-1375
See/See also pages in the following book(s):
Highet, G. The classical tradition p81-103
            809

Bochinski, Julianne Blair, 1966-
The complete handbook of science fair projects
            507.8

Bodart, Joni Richards
100 world-class thin books   028.1
Booktalk! 2-5. *See* Booktalk! 2-5 028.5
(ed) Booktalking the award winners. *See* Booktalking the award winners 028.5

Bodart-Talbot, Joni
See Bodart, Joni Richards

Bode, Janet
Beating the odds   305.23
Death is hard to live with   155.9
Hard time   364.3
Kids still having kids   362.7
New kids on the block: oral histories of immigrant teens   325.73
Truce: ending the sibling war 155.5
Trust & betrayal   158

Bodies in the moonlight. Hughes, L.
In Hughes, L. Short stories   S C

Bodmer, W. F. (Walter Fred), 1936-
The book of man   573.2

Bodmer, Walter Fred *See* Bodmer, W. F. (Walter Fred), 1936-

Body, Human *See* Human anatomy; Physiology

Body and mind *See* Mind and body

Body building basics. Kennedy, R. 613.7

Body language
Fast, J. Body language   153.6
Morris, D. Bodytalk   302.2

Body piercing
Reybold, L. Everything you need to know about the dangers of tattooing and body piercing
            617.9

The **body** politic. Weesner, T.
In Coming of age in America p32-51
            S C

The **body-snatcher.** Stevenson, R. L.
In Victorian ghost stories p303-18 S C

Bodybuilding
Kennedy, R. Bodybuilding basics 613.7

Bodybuilding (Weight lifting) *See* Weight lifting

Bodybuilding basics. Kennedy, R. 613.7

Bodyclock   612

Bodytalk. Morris, D.   302.2

Boer War, 1899-1902 *See* South African War, 1899-1902

The **Boer** War. Pakenham, T. 968.04

Boga, Steve, 1947-
Badminton   796.34

Bogard, Travis, 1918-1997
(comp) O'Neill, E. Complete plays 812

Bogs *See* Wetlands

Booktalking the award winners   028.5
Boole, George, 1815-1864
See/See also pages in the following book(s):
Bell, E. T. Men of mathematics p433-47
    920
Henderson, H. Modern mathematicians   920
Boom Town. Wolfe, T.
In Wolfe, T. The complete short stories of
Thomas Wolfe p120-41   S C
Boone, Daniel, 1734-1820
    About
Faragher, J. M. Daniel Boone   92
The **boor.** Chekhov, A. P.
In Thirty famous one-act plays p103-12
    808.82
Boorse, Henry A. (Henry Abraham), 1904-
The atomic scientists   539.7
Boorstin, Daniel J. (Daniel Joseph), 1914-
The Americans: The colonial experience
    973.2
The Americans: The democratic experience
    973
The Americans: The national experience
    973
Boothe, Clare *See* Luce, Clare Boothe, 1903-1987
Borchert, Donald M., 1934-
(ed) The Encyclopedia of philosophy: Supplement. See The Encyclopedia of philosophy: Supplement   103
Borden, Lizzie, 1860-1927
See/See also pages in the following book(s):
Aymar, B. A pictorial history of the world's greatest trials p173-91   345
Border crossings: emigration and exile   808.8
The **border** line. Lawrence, D. H.
In Lawrence, D. H. The complete short stories v3   S C
Bordewich, Fergus M.
Killing the white man's Indian   970.004
Bordman, Gerald Martin
American musical theatre   792.6
American theatre: a chronicle of comedy and drama, 1930-1969   792
The concise Oxford companion to American theatre   792.03
The Oxford companion to American theatre
    792.03
Borel, Pétrus, 1809-1859
Andreas Vesalius the anatomist
In The Oxford book of gothic tales p70-81
    S C
Borgatta, Edgar F., 1924-
(ed) Encyclopedia of sociology. See Encyclopedia of sociology   301
Borgatta, Marie L.
(ed) Encyclopedia of sociology. See Encyclopedia of sociology   301
Borges, Jorge Luis, 1899-1986
Death and the compass
In Crime classics p285-98   S C
The Gospel according to Mark
In The Oxford book of gothic tales p478-82
    S C

    About
Lindstrom, N. Jorge Luis Borges   863.009
Borgia family
    About
Cloulas, I. The Borgias   920
See/See also pages in the following book(s):
Durant, W. J. The Renaissance p404-40
    945
The **Borgias.** Cloulas, I.   920
Boriani, Maria Luisa
(jt. auth) Chiusoli, A. Simon & Schuster's guide to houseplants   635.9
Boris Yeltsin and the rebirth of Russia. Otfinoski, S.   92
Born free. Adamson, J.   599.74
Born naked. Mowat, F.   92
Born on the Fourth of July. Kovic, R.
    959.704
Born yesterday. Kanin, G.
In Best plays of the modern American theatre: 2nd series p181-227   812.008
Borneo
    Description
Galdikas, B. Reflections of Eden   599.8
Borowski, E. J. (Ephraim J.)
The HarperCollins dictionary of mathematics
    510.3
Borowski, Ephraim J. *See* Borowski, E. J. (Ephraim J.)
Borror, Donald Joyce, 1907-1988
A field guide to the insects of America north of Mexico   595.7
Bortolotti, Gary R.
(jt. auth) Gerrard, J. M. The bald eagle
    598
Borwein, Jonathan M.
(jt. auth) Borowski, E. J. The HarperCollins dictionary of mathematics   510.3
Boschung, Herbert T., Jr.
The Audubon Society field guide to North American fishes, whales, and dolphins. See The Audubon Society field guide to North American fishes, whales, and dolphins
    597
Bosco, Peter I.
The War of 1812   973.5
World War I   940.3
The **Boscombe** Valley mystery. Doyle, Sir A. C.
In Doyle, Sir A. C. The complete Sherlock Holmes   S C
Bosher, J. F. (John Francis)
The French Revolution   944.04
Bosher, John Francis *See* Bosher, J. F. (John Francis)
Boskind-White, Marlene
Bulimarexia   616.85
Boslough, John
Stephen Hawking's universe   523.1
Bosnia. Malcolm, N.   949.7
Bosnia and Hercegovina
    See also Sarajevo (Bosnia and Hercegovina)

Bosnia and Hercegovina—*Continued*
Maass, P. Love thy neighbor   949.7
Malcolm, N. Bosnia   949.7
Bosse, Malcolm J., 1934-
The examination   Fic
Bossy. Gurnah, A.
In African short stories   S C
Boston (Mass.)
History
Forbes, E. Paul Revere & the world he lived in
    92
Boston. Higdon, H.   796.42
Boston Marathon
Higdon, H. Boston   796.42
Boston Red Sox (Baseball team)
Halberstam, D. Summer of '49   796.357
Linn, E. Hitter: the life and turmoils of Ted
Williams   92
Boswell, James, 1740-1795
The life of Samuel Johnson   92
See/See also pages in the following book(s):
Durant, W. J. Rousseau and revolution p778-85
    940.2
Bosworth summit pound. Rolt, L. T. C.
In The Oxford book of English ghost stories
p430-37   S C
Botany
See also Plants
Attenborough, D. The private life of plants
    581.5
Dictionaries
Hyam, R. Plants and their names: a concise dictionary   581
Experiments
Bleifeld, M. Botany projects for young scientists
    581
Dashefsky, H. S. Botany   581
Hershey, D. R. Plant biology science projects
    581
Terminology
See also Popular plant names
Botany, Medical *See* Medical botany
Botany projects for young scientists. Bleifeld, M.
    581
The **Botathen** ghost. Hawker, R. S.
In Victorian ghost stories p65-73   S C
Botermans, Jack
The World of games. See The World of games
    794
Botticelli. McNally, T.
In McNally, T. 15 short plays p51-60
    812
The **bottle** of 1912. Raven, S.
In The Oxford book of English ghost stories
p471-76   S C
A **bottle** of Perrier. Wharton, E.
In Wharton, E. The selected short stories of
Edith Wharton p253-73   S C
Boucher, Anthony, 1911-1968
Crime must have a stop
In The Oxford book of American detective
stories p480-98   S C

Mr. Lupescu
In Masterpieces of fantasy and enchantment
p291-95   S C
Boucicault, Dion, 1820-1890
The octoroon
In Best plays of the early American theatre
p185-215   812.008
Boulle, Pierre, 1912-1994
The bridge over the River Kwai   Fic
Boulton, Alexander O.
Frank Lloyd Wright, architect   92
Bound east for Cardiff. O'Neill, E.
In O'Neill, E. Complete plays v1   812
Bound for glory. Guthrie, W.   92
Bounty (Ship)
Fiction
Nordhoff, C. The Bounty trilogy   Fic
The **Bounty** trilogy. Nordhoff, C.   Fic
Bouquet, Alan Coates
Everyday life in New Testament times
    225.9
Bourbon, House of *See* House of Bourbon
Bourdillon, Hilary
Women as healers   610.9
Bourdon, David, 1934-
Warhol   92
Bourgeoisie *See* Middle classes
Bourjaily, Vance, 1922-
The Amish farmer
In American short story masterpieces
    S C
Bourke-White, Margaret, 1904-1971
Portrait of myself   92
Boustani, Rafic
(jt. auth) Fargues, P. The atlas of the Arab
world   909
Bova, Ben, 1932-
Challenges   S C
Short stories included are: The man who hated gravity; Crisis
of the month; Sepulcher; Fitting suits; To touch a star; Brothers;
Interdepartmental memorandum; World War 4.5; Answer, please
answer; The mask of the Red Death; Bushido; Thy kingdom
come
Death dream   Fic
Inspiration
In Nebula awards 30 p86-98   S C
Bowden, Mary Weatherspoon
Washington Irving   818
Bowen, Catherine Drinker, 1897-1973
Miracle at Philadelphia   342
Bowen, Elizabeth, 1899-1973
The demon lover
In The Oxford book of short stories p346-52
    S C
Hand in glove
In The Oxford book of English ghost stories
p444-52   S C
Her table spread
In The Oxford book of Irish short stories
p311-18   S C
Maria
In Classic English short stories, 1930-1955
p304-19   S C

The **bowl**. Fitzgerald, F. S.
In Fitzgerald, F. S. The short stories of F. Scott Fitzgerald p390-411   **S C**

Bowlby, John
Charles Darwin   **92**

Bowler, Peter J.
Darwinism   **575.01**

Bowles, Paul, 1910-
The circular valley
In The Literary ghost p115-24   **S C**
A distant episode
In The Oxford book of American short stories p384-96   **S C**
In the red room
In The Best American short stories of the eighties p182-91   **S C**

Bowman, John Stewart, 1931-
(ed) The Cambridge dictionary of American biography. See The Cambridge dictionary of American biography   **920.003**

Bown, Deni
Encyclopedia of herbs & their uses   **581.6**

Bowring, Richard John, 1947-
(ed) The Cambridge encyclopedia of Japan. See The Cambridge encyclopedia of Japan   **952**

Los **Boxers**. Cisneros, S.
In Cisneros, S. Woman Hollering Creek and other stories   **S C**

Boxing
Biography
Barrow, J. L. Joe Louis   **92**
Foreman, G. By George   **92**
Frazier, J. Smokin' Joe   **92**
Hauser, T. Muhammad Ali   **92**
Lipsyte, R. Free to be Muhammad Ali   **92**
Mead, C. Champion: Joe Louis, black hero in white America   **92**
Fiction
Lipsyte, R. The brave   **Fic**
Lipsyte, R. The chief   **Fic**
Lipsyte, R. The contender   **Fic**

A **boy** and his dog. Brooks, M.
In Brooks, M. Paradise Café and other stories p11-17   **S C**
In Who do you think you are? p58-63   **S C**

Boy in Rome. Cheever, J.
In Cheever, J. The stories of John Cheever p452-66   **S C**

Boy meets girl. Spewack, B.
In Twenty best plays of the modern American theatre p371-413   **812.008**

Boy Scouts
Boy Scouts of America. Fieldbook   **369.43**

Boy Scouts of America
Fieldbook   **369.43**

Boy: tales of childhood. Dahl, R.   **92**

The **boy** who painted Christ black. Clarke, J. H.
In Rites of passage p71-78   **S C**

Boyce, Charles
Shakespeare A to Z   **822.3**

Boyd, Robert F.
(jt. auth) Fleming, R. L. The big book of urban legends   **741.5**

Boyden, Jo
Families   **306.8**

Boyer, Carl B. (Carl Benjamin), 1906-
A history of mathematics   **510**

Boyko, Carrie
(comp) Hold fast your dreams. See Hold fast your dreams   **815.008**

Boyle, Gregory J.
About
Fremon, C. Father Greg and the homeboys   **361.7**

Boyle, Patrick, 1905-1982
Pastorale
In The Oxford book of Irish short stories p363-74   **S C**

Boyne, Walter J., 1929-
Clash of Titans   **940.54**

Boys
Employment
See Children—Employment

Fiction
Golding, W. Lord of the Flies   **Fic**
Grisham, J. The client   **Fic**

Boys, Teenage *See* Teenagers

The **boys** in the band. Crowley, M.
In Best American plays: 7th series—1967-1973 p493-528   **812.008**

The **boys** of summer. Kahn, R.   **796.357**

Boys! Raise giant mushrooms in your cellar!. Bradbury, R.
In Bradbury, R. The stories of Ray Bradbury p589-601   **S C**

The **boys'** toilets. Westall, R.
In Westall, R. Shades of darkness p147-76   **S C**

Brace, Andrew H.
(ed) The International encyclopedia of dogs. See The International encyclopedia of dogs   **636.7**

Bracebridge Hall. Irving, W.
In Irving, W. Bracebridge Hall; Tales of a traveller; The Alhambra p1-377   **S C**

Bracebridge Hall; Tales of a traveller; The Alhambra. Irving, W.   **S C**

The **bracelet**. Colette
In Colette. The collected stories of Colette p297-99   **S C**

Bradbury, Ray, 1920-
And so died Riabouchinska
In Masterpieces of mystery and suspense p379-91   **S C**
Dandelion wine   **Fic**
Fahrenheit 451   **S C**
Contents: Fahrenheit 451; The playground; And the rock cried out
Good grief
In Who do you think you are? p3-13   **S C**

Bradbury, Ray, 1920——_Continued_
The illustrated man   **S C**
Contents: The veldt; Kaleidoscope; The other foot; The highway; The man; The long rain; The Rocket Man; The fire balloons; The last night of the world; The exiles; No particular night or morning; The fox and the forest; The visitor; The concrete mixer; Marionettes, Inc.; The city; Zero hour; The rocket
The Martian chronicles   **S C**
The ravine
  _In_ Read all about it! p252-71   **808.88**
The small assassin
  _In_ The Horror hall of fame p326-44   **S C**
Something wicked this way comes   **Fic**
The stories of Ray Bradbury   **S C**
Contents: The night; Homecoming; Uncle Einar; The traveler; The lake; The coffin; The crowd; The scythe; There was an old woman; There will come soft rains; Mars is heaven; The silent towns; The Earth men; The off season; The million-year picnic; The fox and the forest; Kaleidoscope; The Rocket Man; Marionettes, Inc.; No particular night or morning; The city; The fire balloons; The last night of the world; The veldt; The long rain; The great fire; The wilderness; A sound of thunder; The murderer; The April witch; Invisible boy; The golden kite, the silver wind; The fog horn; The big black and white game; Embroidery; The golden apples of the sun; Power-house; Hail and farewell!; The great wide world over there; The playground; Skeleton; The man upstairs; Touched with fire; The emissary; The jar; The small assassin; The next in line; Jack-in-the-box; The leave-taking; Exorcism; The happiness machine; Calling Mexico; The wonderful ice cream suit; Dark they were, and golden-eyed; The strawberry window; A scent of sarsaparilla; The Picasso summer; The day it rained forever; A medicine for melancholy; The shoreline at sunset; Fever dream; The town where no one got off; All summer in a day; Frost and fire; The anthem sprinters; And so died Riabouchinska; Boys! Raise giant mushrooms in your cellar!; The vacation; The illustrated woman; Some live like Lazarus; The best of all possible worlds; The one who waits; Tyrannosaurus Rex; The screaming woman; The terrible conflagration up at the place; Night call, collect; The Tombling day; The haunting of the new; Tomorrow's child; I sing the Body Electric!; The women; The inspired chicken motel; Yes, we'll gather at the river; Have I got a chocolate bar for you; A story of love; The parrot who met Papa; The October game; Punishment without crime; A piece of wood; The blue bottle; Long after midnight; The utterly perfect murder; The better part of wisdom; Interval in sunlight; The black ferris; Farewell summer; McGillahee's brat; The Aqueduct; Gotcha; The end of the beginning
There will come soft rains
  _In_ The Oxford book of American short stories p456-62   **S C**
Uncle Einar
  _In_ Masterpieces of fantasy and enchantment p310-17   **S C**
About
Mogen, D. Ray Bradbury   **813.009**
See/See also pages in the following book(s):
Science fiction writers of the golden age p78-93   **809.3**

Braddon, M. E. (Mary Elizabeth), 1835-1915
At Chrighton Abbey
  _In_ Victorian ghost stories p163-89   **S C**
The shadow in the corner
  _In_ The Oxford book of English ghost stories p51-68   **S C**
Braddon, Mary Elizabeth _See_ Braddon, M. E. (Mary Elizabeth), 1835-1915

Bradfield, Scott, 1955-
The darling
  _In_ The Vintage book of contemporary American short stories p69-88   **S C**

Bradford, Richard, 1932-
Red sky at morning   **Fic**

Bradford, Sarah, 1938-
Elizabeth   **92**
Bradford, William, 1588-1657
Of Plymouth Plantation, 1620-1647   **974.4**
Bradley, Bill
Time present, time past   **92**
Bradley, Catherine
The end of apartheid   **968.06**
Bradley, Fern Marshall
(ed) Rodale's all-new encyclopedia of organic gardening. See Rodale's all-new encyclopedia of organic gardening   **635**
Bradley, Marion Zimmer
Elbow room
  _In_ The Norton book of science fiction p412-26   **S C**
The mists of Avalon   **Fic**
The pledged word
  _In_ The Merlin chronicles   **S C**
Bradley, Omar Nelson, 1893-1981
A general's life   **92**
See/See also pages in the following book(s):
Oleksy, W. G. Military leaders of World War II   **920**

Brain
Aaseng, N. Head injuries   **617.1**
Metos, T. H. The human mind   **153**
Ornstein, R. E. The amazing brain   **612.8**
Powledge, T. M. Your brain   **612.8**
Sagan, C. The dragons of Eden   **153**
See/See also pages in the following book(s):
Frontline of discovery   **600**
The Incredible machine p325-75   **612**
The **brains** of rats. Blumlein, M.
  _In_ The Norton book of science fiction p633-46   **S C**
Brainwashing
Huxley, A. Brave new world revisited   **303.3**

Braithwaite, William Stanley, 1878-1962
See/See also pages in the following book(s):
Black American poets and dramatists before the Harlem Renaissance p1-13   **810.9**
Black American prose writers before the Harlem Renaissance p1-9   **810.9**
Brallier, Jess M.
Presidential wit and wisdom   **808.88**
Braly, David
The night watchman
  _In_ Read all about it! p244-51   **808.88**
Bramly, Serge, 1949-
Leonardo   **92**
Brancato, Robin F.
War of the words
  _In_ Center stage   **812.008**
Branch, Taylor
Parting the waters: America in the King years, 1954-63   **973.921**
Branch Davidians
Reavis, D. J. The ashes of Waco   **976.4**
Religious cults in America   **291**
Brand, Christianna, 1907-1988
Bless this house
  _In_ Bad behavior p67-82   **S C**

Brenner, Gerry, 1937-
(jt. auth) Rovit, E. H. Ernest Hemingway
813.009

Brennert, Alan
Ma qui
In Nebula awards 27 p53-72 **S C**

Breslin, James E. B., 1935-1996
From modern to contemporary **811.009**

Bressett, Kenneth E.
(ed) A Guide book of United States coins. See
A Guide book of United States coins
737.4

Brett, Simon, 1945-
The Nuggy Bar
In Masterpieces of mystery and suspense
p443-65 **S C**

Breughel, Pieter, the Elder *See* Brueghel, Pieter,
the Elder, 1522?-1569

Brewer, Ebenezer Cobham, 1810-1897
Brewer's dictionary of phrase and fable. See
Brewer's dictionary of phrase and fable
803

Brewer's dictionary of names. See Room, A.
Cassell dictionary of proper names **929.4**

Brewer's dictionary of phrase and fable **803**

Brewster, W. Herbert, d. 1987
See/See also pages in the following book(s):
We'll understand it better by and by
782.25

Brian, Denis
Einstein **92**

Briar Rose. Yolen, J. **Fic**

Brickell, Christopher
(ed) The American Horticultural Society encyclopedia of garden plants. See The American
Horticultural Society encyclopedia of garden
plants **635.9**
(ed) The American Horticultural Society encyclopedia of gardening. See The American
Horticultural Society encyclopedia of gardening **635**

Brickhill, Paul, 1916-1991
The great escape **940.54**

The **bridal** night. O'Connor, F.
In O'Connor, F. Collected stories p19-25
S C

The **bridal** party. Fitzgerald, F. S.
In Fitzgerald, F. S. The short stories of F.
Scott Fitzgerald p561-76 **S C**
In Fitzgerald, F. S. The stories of F. Scott
Fitzgerald p271-86 **S C**
In The Norton book of American short stories
p326-41 **S C**

The **bridal** wreath. Undset, S.
In Undset, S. Kristin Lavransdatter v1
Fic

The **bride**. Chekhov, A. P.
In Chekhov, A. P. The image of Chekhov
p323-[45] **S C**

The **bride** of the Innisfallen. Welty, E.
In Welty, E. The collected stories of Eudora
Welty p495-518 **S C**

The **bride** of the Innisfallen, and other stories.
Welty, E.
In Welty, E. The collected stories of Eudora
Welty p463-600 **S C**

The **bridegroom**. Gordimer, N.
In African short stories **S C**

Bridenbaugh, Carl, 1903-1992
Jamestown, 1544-1699 **975.5**

Brideshead revisited. Waugh, E. **Fic**

Bridge (Game)
Goren, C. H. Goren's new bridge complete
795.4

The **bridge** at Andau. Michener, J. A. **943.9**

Bridge complete, Goren's new. Goren, C. H.
795.4

The **bridge** of San Luis Rey. Wilder, T. **Fic**

The **bridge** over the River Kwai. Boulle, P.
Fic

Bridgers, Sue Ellen, 1942-
Keeping Christina **Fic**
Permanent connections **Fic**

Bridges
Petroski, H. Engineers of dreams **624**
Design and construction
Brown, D. J. Bridges **624**
History
See/See also pages in the following book(s):
Langdon, W. C. Everyday things in American
life, 1776-1876 p50-64 **973**

Bridging. Apple, M.
In The Norton book of American short stories
p692-700 **S C**

Bridwell, Raymond
Hydroponic gardening **635**

A **brief** history of the Caribbean. Rogoziński, J.
972.9

A **brief** history of time. Hawking, S. W.
523.1

A **brief** moment in the life of Angus Bethune.
Crutcher, C.
In Crutcher, C. Athletic shorts: six short sto-
ries p3-25 **S C**

The **brigadier** and the golf widow. Cheever, J.
In Cheever, J. The stories of John Cheever
p498-511 **S C**

Briggs, Asa, 1921-
(ed) A Dictionary of twentieth-century world biography. See A Dictionary of twentieth-
century world biography **920.003**

Bright and morning star. Wright, R.
In Calling the wind p94-122 **S C**
In Wright, R. Uncle Tom's children **S C**

Bright Eyes *See* La Flesche, Susette, 1854-1903

Bright Thursdays. Senior, O.
In Rites of passage p50-70 **S C**

Bright winter. Keesey, A.
In The Best American short stories, 1996
p177-94 **S C**

Brighton Beach memoirs. Simon, N. **812**
also in Best American plays: 9th series—
1983-1992 p1-39 **812.008**
also in Simon, N. The collected plays of Neil
Simon v3 p479-593 **812**

Brooke, Maxey, 1913-
Morte d'espier
  In The Merlin chronicles   S C
Brooke, Rupert, 1887-1915
Lithuania
  In Thirty famous one-act plays p361-74
      808.82
Brooklyn (New York, N.Y.)
  Fiction
Malamud, B. The assistant   Fic
McDermott, A. At weddings and wakes
      Fic
Smith, B. A tree grows in Brooklyn   Fic
Styron, W. Sophie's choice   Fic
Brooklyn. Marshall, P.
  In We are the stories we tell   S C
Brooklyn Dodgers (Baseball team)
Kahn, R. The boys of summer   796.357
Macht, N. L. Roy Campanella   92
Brooks, Bruce, 1950-
The moves make the man   Fic
On the wing   598
Brooks, Cleanth, 1906-1994
William Faulkner   813.009
(ed) Understanding poetry. See Understanding
  poetry   821.008
Brooks, Drex
Sweet medicine   970.004
Brooks, Gwendolyn
At the Burns-Coopers'
  In Black-eyed Susans/Midnight birds p120-22
      S C
The courtship and motherhood of Maud Martha
  In Invented lives p406-28   S C
If you're light and have long hair
  In Black-eyed Susans/Midnight birds p115-19
      S C
The rise of Maud Martha
  In Invented lives p429-32   S C
Selected poems   811
We're the only colored people here
  In The Best short stories by Negro writers
  p202-04   S C
  About
Kent, G. E. A life of Gwendolyn Brooks
      92
See/See also pages in the following book(s):
Major modern black American writers p53-69
      810.9
Brooks, James L., 1940-
Terms of endearment
  In Best American screenplays   812.008
Brooks, Martha, 1944-
A boy and his dog
  In Who do you think you are? p58-63
      S C
Paradise Café and other stories   S C
  Contents: Running with Marty; A boy and his dog; King of
  the roller rink; The way things are; Dying for love; The best side
  of heaven; In Orbit; Paradise Café; What I want to be when I
  grow up; Waiting for the carollers; Wild strawberries; Sunlight
  through organdy; Like Lauren Bacall; The crystal stars have just
  begun to shine
Brooks, Polly Schoyer
Beyond the myth: the story of Joan of Arc
      92

Brooks, Terry, 1944-
The druids of Shannara. See note under Brooks,
  T. The sword of Shannara   Fic
The Elfqueen of Shannara. See note under
  Brooks, T. The sword of Shannara   Fic
The Elfstones of Shannara. See note under
  Brooks, T. The sword of Shannara   Fic
First king of Shannara. See note under Brooks,
  T. The sword of Shannara   Fic
The scions of Shannara. See note under Brooks,
  T. The sword of Shannara   Fic
The sword of Shannara   Fic
The talismans of Shannara. See note under
  Brooks, T. The sword of Shannara   Fic
The wishsong of Shannara. See note under
  Brooks, T. The sword of Shannara   Fic
Brooks, Tilford
America's black musical heritage   780.89
Bro'r Abr'm Jimson's wedding: a Christmas story.
Hopkins, P. E.
  In Invented lives p130-46   S C
Brosman, Catharine Savage, 1934-
Jean-Paul Sartre   848
(ed) French culture, 1900-1975. See French cul-
  ture, 1900-1975   944.08
Brosnahan, Liam
The spelling lesson
  In Not the only one p26-36   S C
Brother against brother: the war begins. Davis, W.
  C.   973.7
Brother, can you spare a dime?. Meltzer, M.
      330.973
Brother Imás. Hinojosa, R.
  In Growing up Latino p250-58   810.8
Brother Square-Toes. Kipling, R.
  In Kipling, R. The portable Kipling   828
Brothers
  Fiction
Bosse, M. J. The examination   Fic
Hinton, S. E. Tex   Fic
Brothers. Bova, B.
  In Bova, B. Challenges p113-29   S C
The brothers. Collins, K.
  In 9 plays by black women   811.008
Brothers and sisters
  See also Twins
Bode, J. Truce: ending the sibling war
      155.5
  Fiction
Kerr, M. E. Deliver us from Evie   Fic
Peck, R. Father figure   Fic
Broughton, Rhoda, 1840-1920
The truth, the whole truth, and nothing but the
  truth
  In Victorian ghost stories p74-82   S C
Brower, David J.
See/See also pages in the following book(s):
Lucas, E. Naturalists, conservationists, and
  environmentalists   920
Brower, Kenneth, 1944-
Realms of the sea   574.92
Yosemite   917.9

Brown v. Board of Education. Tushnet, M. V.
344
Browne, Frances, 1816-1879
The story of Fairyfoot
In The Oxford book of modern fairy tales
p51-60 S C
Browne, Ray Broadus
(ed) Contemporary heroes and heroines. See
Contemporary heroes and heroines 920
Browne, Theodore
Natural man
In Black theatre USA 812.008
Browning, Elizabeth Barrett, 1806-1861
The poetical works of Elizabeth Barrett Brown-
ing 821
Sonnets from the Portuguese 821
About
Markus, J. Dared and done: the marriage of
Elizabeth Barrett and Robert Browning
92
See/See also pages in the following book(s):
Untermeyer, L. Lives of the poets p478-502
920
Drama
Besier, R. The Barretts of Wimpole Street
822
Browning, Robert, 1812-1889
The poetical works of Robert Browning
821
Robert Browning's poetry 821
About
Markus, J. Dared and done: the marriage of
Elizabeth Barrett and Robert Browning
92
See/See also pages in the following book(s):
Untermeyer, L. Lives of the poets p478-502
920
Drama
Besier, R. The Barretts of Wimpole Street
822
The **Browning** version. Rattigan, T.
In 24 favorite one-act plays p54-93
808.82
Brownmiller, Susan
Against our will 362.88
Brownstein, Samuel C., 1909-1996
How to prepare for SAT I 378.1
Brownstone, David M.
Timelines of the twentieth century 909.82
(jt. auth) Franck, I. M. The women's desk refer-
ence 305.4
(jt. auth) Franck, I. M. Women's world
305.4
Bruccoli, Matthew Joseph, 1931-
(ed) Modern women writers. See Modern wom-
en writers 016.813
Bruce, Sir David, 1855-1931
See/See also pages in the following book(s):
De Kruif, P. Microbe hunters 920
Bruce, James *See* Elgin, James Bruce, 8th Earl of,
1811-1863
Bruce Springsteen 92
Bruchac, Joseph, 1942-
Bears
In Song of the turtle p258-68 S C

Going home
In Talking leaves S C
(ed) Returning the gift. See Returning the gift
897
Bruegel, Pieter *See* Brueghel, Pieter, the Elder,
1522?-1569
Brueghel, Pieter, the Elder, 1522?-1569
About
Stechow, W. Pieter Bruegel the Elder
759.9493
Brugglesmith. Kipling, R.
In Kipling, R. The portable Kipling 828
Bruggmann, Maximilien, 1934-
(jt. auth) Acatos, S. Pueblos 970.004
Brulard, Henry *See* Stendhal, 1783-1842
Brunel Deschamps, Eliette
(jt. auth) Chauvet, J.-M. Dawn of art
759.01
Brunelli, Jean, 1934-
(jt. auth) Lindsay, J. W. Your pregnancy and
newborn journey 618.2
Bruno, Giordano, 1548-1600
See/See also pages in the following book(s):
Jaspers, K. The great philosophers 109
Bruno. Koontz, D. R.
In Koontz, D. R. Strange highways p309-35
S C
Brunsdale, Mitzi
James Joyce 823.009
Brunvand, Jan Harold
(ed) American folklore. See American folklore
398.2
(jt. auth) Fleming, R. L. The big book of urban
legends 741.5
Brush, Warren D.
(jt. auth) Collingwood, G. H. Knowing your
trees 582.16
The **brute**. Conrad, J.
In Conrad, J. The complete short fiction of
Joseph Conrad v2 p43-62 S C
Bruwelheide, Janis H., 1948-
The copyright primer for librarians and educa-
tors 346.04
Bryan, C. D. B. (Courtlandt Dixon Barnes)
Close encounters of the fourth kind 001.9
The National Geographic Society: 100 years of
adventure and discovery 910
Bryan, Courtlandt Dixon Barnes *See* Bryan, C.
D. B. (Courtlandt Dixon Barnes)
Bryan, Howard
Robbers, rogues, and ruffians 978.9
Bryan, T. Scott
Geysers: what they are and how they work
551.2
Bryan, William Jennings, 1860-1925
About
Ashby, L. William Jennings Bryan 92
Bryant, Cedric X., 1960-
(jt. auth) Peterson, J. A. Strength training for
women 613.7
Bryant, Dorothy, 1930-
The new sidewalk
In Where coyotes howl and wind blows free
p101-08 810.8

Bulgakov, Mikhail Afanas´evich, 1891-1940
The master and Margarita [excerpt]
In The Portable twentieth-century Russian
reader p189-201   **891.7**

Bulimarexia. Boskind-White, M.   **616.85**

Bulimia
Boskind-White, M. Bulimarexia   **616.85**
Kolodny, N. J. When food's a foe   **616.85**
Sacker, I. M. Dying to be thin   **616.85**
Sherman, R. T. Bulimia   **616.85**
See/See also pages in the following book(s):
Maloney, M. Straight talk about eating disorders
    616.85
Patterson, C. Eating disorders   **616.85**
Silverstein, A. So you think you're fat? p189-
202   **616.85**
Sonder, B. Eating disorders   **616.85**

Bull, Stephen
20th-century arms and armor   **355.8**
An historical guide to arms & armor   **355.8**

Bull-of-all-the-Land
In Hearne, B. G. Beauties and beasts p97-98
    398.2

Bull Run, 2nd Battle of, 1862
Second Manassas   **973.7**

Bullard, Sara
Free at last   **323.1**

Bulletin boards
Skaggs, G. Off the wall!   **027.8**

Bullins, Ed, 1935-
Goin' a buffalo
In Black theatre USA   **812.008**
See/See also pages in the following book(s):
Contemporary black American poets and drama-
tists p1-16   **810.9**

Bully for brontosaurus. Gould, S. J.   **508**

Bulwer-Lytton, Edward *See* Lytton, Edward Bulwer Lytton, Baron, 1803-1873

The **bum.** Maugham, W. S.
In Maugham, W. S. Collected short stories v2
    S C

The **bums** at sunset. Wolfe, T.
In Wolfe, T. The complete short stories of
Thomas Wolfe p274-78   **S C**

Bunch, Bryan H.
The timetables of technology   **609**
(jt. auth) Hellemans, A. The timetables of science   **509**

Bunch, David R.
2064, or thereabouts
In The Norton book of science fiction p93-97
    S C

A **Bunch** of laurel blooms for a present
In Hearne, B. G. Beauties and beasts p22-24
    398.2

Bunche, Ralph J. (Ralph Johnson), 1904-1971
About
Urquhart, B. E. Ralph Bunche   **92**

Bundy, McGeorge
See/See also pages in the following book(s):
Halberstam, D. The best and the brightest
    973.922

Bunin, Ivan Alekseevich, 1870-1953
Light breathing
In The Portable twentieth-century Russian
reader p59-65   **891.7**

Bunson, Margaret R.
The encyclopedia of ancient Egypt   **932**
Encyclopedia of ancient Mesoamerica   **972**

Bunson, Matthew
The encyclopedia of the Middle Ages
    940.1
Encyclopedia of the Roman Empire   **937**
Encyclopedia Sherlockiana   **823.009**
The vampire encyclopedia   **398**

Bunson, Stephen M.
(jt. auth) Bunson, M. R. Encyclopedia of ancient
Mesoamerica   **972**

Bunyan, John, 1628-1688
The pilgrim's progress   **Fic**

Buonarroti, Michel Angelo *See* Michelangelo
Buonarroti, 1475-1564

Buranelli, Vincent
Edgar Allan Poe   **818**

Burch, Jennings Michael
They cage the animals at night   **92**

Burchard, Peter, 1921-
"We'll stand by the Union": Robert Gould Shaw
and the Black 54th Massachusetts Regiment
    92

Burckhardt, Jacob, 1818-1897
The civilization of the Renaissance in Italy
    945

The **burden** of our time. See Arendt, H. Origins
of totalitarianism   **321.9**

Burford, Barbara
Dreaming the sky down
In Rites of passage p177-90   **S C**
Miss Jessie
In Daughters of Africa p676-80   **808.8**

Burg, David F.
The Great Depression   **973.91**
(ed) The World almanac of the American Revolution. See The World almanac of the
American Revolution   **973.3**

Burger, Warren E., 1907-1995
It is so ordered   **342**

Burgess, Anthony, 1917-1993
Cyrano de Bergerac   **822**

Burgess, Michael, 1948-
Reference guide to science fiction, fantasy, and
horror   **016.8**

The **burglar.** Bethune, L.
In The Best short stories by Negro writers
p458-64   **S C**

The **burglar.** Colette
In Colette. The collected stories of Colette
p270-73   **S C**

Burial at sea. Singer, I. B.
In Singer, I. B. The death of Methuselah and
other stories p25-35   **S C**

Buried child. Shepard, S.
In Best American plays: 8th series—1974-
1982 p277-311   **812.008**

The **buried** mirror. Fuentes, C.   **946**

Bush, Barbara, 1925-
    About
  Kilian, P. Barbara Bush   **92**
Bush, George, 1924-
    About
  Kilian, P. Barbara Bush   **92**
  Levy, P. B. Encyclopedia of the Reagan-Bush
    years   **973.927**
  See/See also pages in the following book(s):
  Character above all   **920**
  Walsh, K. T. Feeding the beast p77-99
     973.927
Bush River. Cary, J.
  In The Oxford book of Irish short stories
    p277-86   **S C**
Bushido. Bova, B.
  In Bova, B. Challenges p193-215   **S C**
Bushnaq, Inea
  (ed) Arab folktales. See Arab folktales
     398.2
Business
  See also Small business
Business and politics
  Birnbaum, J. H. The lobbyists   **328.73**
Business cycles
  See also Economic forecasting
  Galbraith, J. K. The Great Crash, 1929
     330.973
Business ethics
  Business ethics   **174**
  Ethics   **174**
Business ethics   **174**
Business letters
  Geffner, A. B. How to write better business let-
    ters   **651.7**
The **business** man. Poe, E. A.
  In Poe, E. A. The collected tales and poems
    of Edgar Allan Poe p413-20   **S C**
The **businessman.** Kafka, F.
  In Kafka, F. The metamorphosis and other
    stories p34-36   **S C**
But what if I don't want to go to college?. Unger,
  H. G.   **331.7**
Butch Cassidy and the Sundance Kid. Goldman,
  W.
  In Best American screenplays   **812.008**
Butler, Alban, 1711-1773
  Butler's lives of the saints   **920.003**
Butler, Dori Hillestad
  Interlude
    In Not the only one p127-33   **S C**
Butler, Octavia E.
  Speech sounds
    In The Norton book of science fiction p513-
    24   **S C**
Butler, Robert Olen
  Jealous husband returns in form of parrot
    In The Best American short stories, 1996
    p33-39   **S C**
  Letters from my father
    In The Other side of heaven p308-12
     S C

Salem
  In The Best American short stories, 1994
    p26-33   **S C**
Butler's lives of the saints. Butler, A.
     920.003
Buttercups. McKinley, R.
  In McKinley, R. A knot in the grain and oth-
    er stories p107-47   **S C**
Butterflies
  Pyle, R. M. The Audubon Society field guide to
    North American butterflies   **595.7**
  Taylor, B. Butterflies & moths   **595.7**
    Fiction
  Klass, D. California Blue   **Fic**
Butterflies & moths. Taylor, B.   **595.7**
The **butterfly.** Andersen, H. C.
  In Andersen, H. C. Tales and stories
     S C
The **butterfly** and the tank. Hemingway, E.
  In Hemingway, E. The complete short stories
    of Ernest Hemingway p429-36   **S C**
Butterworth, Rod R.
  Signing made easy   **419**
Buxton, E. M. Wilmot- *See* Wilmot-Buxton, E.
  M.
By George. Foreman, G.   **92**
By the way of morning fire. Weaver, M.
  In Children of the night p352-59   **S C**
Byatt, A. S. (Antonia Susan), 1936-
  The next room
    In The Literary ghost p257-81   **S C**
Byatt, Antonia Susan *See* Byatt, A. S. (Antonia
  Susan), 1936-
Bygone spring. Colette
  In Colette. The collected stories of Colette
    p449-51   **S C**
The **Byrds.** Coney, M.
  In The Norton book of science fiction p501-
    12   **S C**
Byrne, Deborah J.
  MARC manual   **025.3**
Byron, George Gordon Byron, 6th Baron, 1788-
  1824
  Byron   **821**
  See/See also pages in the following book(s):
  Untermeyer, L. Lives of the poets p383-417
     920
The **bystander.** Berriault, G.
  In American short story masterpieces
     S C
Byzantine Empire
  See/See also pages in the following book(s):
  Durant, W. J. The age of faith p118-35, 423-49
     940.1

C

C-chute. Asimov, I.
  In Asimov, I. The complete stories v1 p438-
    67   **S C**
Cabeza de Vaca, Alvar Nuñez *See* Nuñez Cabeza
  de Vaca, Alvar, 16th cent.

Cabinet officers
See also Prime ministers
Dolan, E. F. Shaping U.S. foreign policy
327.73

Cable, George Washington, 1844-1925
Belles Demoiselles plantation
In The Norton book of American short stories
p97-110 **S C**
Jean-ah Poquelin
In The Oxford book of gothic tales p165-82
S C

Cabot, John, 1450-1498
See/See also pages in the following book(s):
Faber, H. The discoverers of America p58-68
970.01

Cactus flower. Burrows, A.
In The Most popular plays of the American
theater p625-703 **812.008**

A **caddy's** diary. Lardner, R.
In Lardner, R. The best short stories of Ring
Lardner p321-36 **S C**

Cadigan, Pat
After the days of Dead-Eye 'Dee
In The Norton book of science fiction p605-
15 **S C**

Cady, Edwin Harrison, 1917-
Stephen Crane **813.009**

Cady, Jack, 1932-
The night we buried Road Dog
In Nebula awards 29 p242-96 **S C**

Caesar, Julius, 100-44 B.C.
See/See also pages in the following book(s):
Hamilton, E. The Roman way **870.9**

Caffeine
Gilbert, R. J. Caffeine, the most popular stimulant **615**

Caffeine, the most popular stimulant. Gilbert, R. J.
615

Cages. Gurnah, A.
In The Heinemann book of contemporary
African short stories p87-93 **S C**

Cages. Myers, W. D.
In Center stage **812.008**

Cagin, Seth
We are not afraid **323.1**

Cahill, Susan Neunzig
(ed) Wise women. See Wise women **200**

Caidin, Martin, 1927-1997
(jt. auth) Barbree, J. A journey through time
520

Cain, James M. (James Mallahan), 1892-1977
The baby in the icebox
In The Norton book of American short stories
p297-311 **S C**

Cain rose up. King, S.
In King, S. Skeleton crew **S C**

The **Caine** mutiny. Wouk, H. **Fic**

The **Caine** mutiny court-martial. Wouk, H.
In Best American plays: 4th series—1951-
1957 p439-77 **812.008**

Calasibetta, Charlotte Mankey
Fairchild's dictionary of fashion **391**

Calculus
Berlinski, D. A tour of the calculus **515**

Calder, Nigel, 1931-
Einstein's universe **530.1**

Caldwell, Ben, 1937-
Prayer meeting; or, The first militant preacher
In Black theatre USA **812.008**

Caldwell, Erskine, 1903-1987
Kneel to the rising sun
In The Norton book of American short stories
p374-94 **S C**

Calendar of literary facts **809**

A **calendar** of saints: the lives of the principal
saints of the Christian year. Bentley, J.
920.003

Calendars
Chase's calendar of events **394.2**
Kelly, A. A. Religious holidays and calendars
291.3

Calhoun, John C. (John Caldwell), 1782-1850
See/See also pages in the following book(s):
McPherson, J. M. Drawn with the sword p37-51
973.7

California
Fiction
Hobbs, V. How far would you have gotten if I
hadn't called you back? **Fic**
Mowry, J. Way past cool **Fic**
Saroyan, W. The human comedy **Fic**
Steinbeck, J. The grapes of wrath **Fic**
Steinbeck, J. Of mice and men **Fic**
Gold discoveries
Jackson, D. D. Gold dust **979.4**
History
Jackson, D. D. Gold dust **979.4**

The **California** and Oregon Trail. See Parkman, F.
The Oregon Trail **978**

California Blue. Klass, D. **Fic**

California Indians. Keyworth, C. L.
In The First Americans series **970.004**

California suite. Simon, N.
In Simon, N. The collected plays of Neil Simon v2 p549-632 **812**

The **Californian's** tale. Twain, M.
In Twain, M. The complete short stories of
Mark Twain **S C**

Calinger, Ronald S. (Ronald Steve), 1942-
(jt. auth) Shafritz, J. M. The dictionary of 20th-
century world politics **909.82**

Calisthenics *See* Gymnastics

The **call.** Westall, R.
In Westall, R. Shades of darkness p207-23
S C

The **call** of the wild. London, J. **Fic**
also in London, J. The portable Jack London
818

A **call** on Kuprin. Lawrence, J.
In Lawrence, J. The selected plays of Jerome
Lawrence and Robert E. Lee p303-68
812

Callaghan, Morley
The runaway
In The Oxford book of short stories p382-90
S C

Callahan, Steven
Adrift **910.4**

Calligraphy
Goffe, G. Calligraphy school 745.6
Harris, D. The art of calligraphy 745.6
Marsh, D. Calligraphy 745.6
Calligraphy school. Goffe, G. 745.6
Calling card. Campbell, R.
    In The Horror hall of fame p365-71
                                      S C
Calling Mexico. Bradbury, R.
    In Bradbury, R. The stories of Ray Bradbury
    p446-50   S C
Calling the wind   S C
Calloway, Colin G. (Colin Gordon), 1953-
    Indians of the Northeast
    In The First Americans series 970.004
Calvin, Jean, 1509-1564
    See/See also pages in the following book(s):
    Durant, W. J. The Reformation p459-90
                                940.2
Calvin, John *See* Calvin, Jean, 1509-1564
Calvin and Hobbes (Comic strip)
    Watterson, B. The Calvin and Hobbes tenth anniversary book 741.5
Calvocoressi, Peter
    Who's who in the Bible 220.9
Cambodia

Antiquities
See also Angkor (City)
History—1975-
Criddle, J. D. To destroy you is no loss
                                  959.6
Ngor, H. S. A Cambodian odyssey 92
A **Cambodian** odyssey. Ngor, H. S. 92
Cambodian refugees
Criddle, J. D. To destroy you is no loss
                                  959.6
The **Cambridge** ancient history 930
The **Cambridge** atlas of astronomy 523
Cambridge biographical dictionary. See Larousse biographical dictionary 920.003
The **Cambridge** dictionary of American biography 920.003
The **Cambridge** dictionary of philosophy 103
Cambridge dictionary of science and technology. See Larousse dictionary of science and technology 503
The **Cambridge** encyclopedia of China 951
The **Cambridge** encyclopedia of human evolution 573.2
The **Cambridge** encyclopedia of India, Pakistan, Bangladesh, Sri Lanka, Nepal, Bhutan, and the Maldives 954
The **Cambridge** encyclopedia of Japan 952
The **Cambridge** encyclopedia of language. Crystal, D. 400
The **Cambridge** encyclopedia of Latin America and the Caribbean 980
The **Cambridge** encyclopedia of Russia and the former Soviet Union 947
The **Cambridge** encyclopedia of the English language. Crystal, D. 420
The **Cambridge** encyclopedia of the Middle East and North Africa 956

The **Cambridge** gazetteer of the United States and Canada 917.3
Cambridge guide to American theatre 792.03
The **Cambridge** guide to literature in English 820.3
The **Cambridge** guide to the constellations. Bakich, M. E. 523.8
The **Cambridge** guide to world theatre 792.03
The **Cambridge** historical encyclopedia of Great Britain and Ireland 941
The **Cambridge** history of American literature 810.9
The **Cambridge** illustrated atlas of warfare: Renaissance to revolution, 1492-1792. Black, J. 355
The **Cambridge** illustrated atlas of warfare: the Middle Ages. Hooper, N. 355
The **Cambridge** illustrated history of astronomy 520
The **Cambridge** illustrated history of the British Empire 941.08
The **Cambridge** illustrated history of warfare 355
The **Cambridge** modern history. See The New Cambridge modern history 909.08
Camcorder tricks & special effects. Stavros, M. 778.59
Camcorders
Stavros, M. Camcorder tricks & special effects 778.59
Camelot. Lerner, A. J. 812
The **camera** at war. Lewinski, J. 779
The **camera** never blinks twice. Rather, D. 92
Cameras
See also Camcorders
Cameron, Peter
Jump or dive
    In Coming of age in America p58-72
                                   S C
Camp cooking *See* Outdoor cooking
Campaign fever. Sandock, F.
    In The Big book of large-cast plays p86-100
                             812.008
Campanella, Roy, 1921-1993
    About
Macht, N. L. Roy Campanella 92
Campbell, Andrew C. (Andrew Campbell)
(ed) The Encyclopedia of aquatic life. See The Encyclopedia of aquatic life 591.92
Campbell, Bebe Moore
Playing the game
    In Streetlights: illuminating tales of the urban black experience p44-55   S C
Campbell, James, 1935-
The Anglo-Saxons 942.01
Campbell, James Graham- *See* Graham-Campbell, James
Campbell, John Wood, 1910-1971
Night
    In The Oxford book of science fiction stories p95-114   S C

Carruth, Gorton
The encyclopedia of American facts and dates
973.02

The encyclopedia of world facts and dates
902

(jt. auth) Ehrlich, E. H. The Oxford illustrated literary guide to the United States **810.9**

Cars (Automobiles) See Automobiles

Carson, Clayborne, 1944-
(ed) The Eyes on the prize civil rights reader. See The Eyes on the prize civil rights reader
323.1

Carson, Kit, 1809-1868
Kit Carson's autobiography **92**

Carson, Rachel, 1907-1964
Always, Rachel **92**
The edge of the sea **574.92**
The sea around us **551.46**
Silent spring **363.7**
About
Hynes, H. P. The recurring silent spring
92

See/See also pages in the following book(s):
Lucas, E. Naturalists, conservationists, and environmentalists **920**

Carson, Rob, 1950-
Mount St. Helens: the eruption and recovery of a volcano **551.2**

Carson McCullers [critical essays] **813.009**

Cart, Michael
From romance to realism **028.5**
Presenting Robert Lipsyte **813.009**

Carter, Alden R.
Driver's test
In Center stage **812.008**
Up country **Fic**

Carter, Angela, 1940-1992
The courtship of Mr. Lyon
In The Oxford book of modern fairy tales p396-407 **S C**
The lady of the house of love
In The Oxford book of gothic tales p483-97 **S C**

Carter, Betty, 1944-
Best books for young adults **028.1**
Nonfiction for young adults **028.5**

Carter, Bruce See Hough, Richard Alexander, 1922-

Carter, James Earl See Carter, Jimmy, 1924-

Carter, Jimmy, 1924-
Talking peace **327.1**
See/See also pages in the following book(s):
Character above all **920**
White, T. H. America in search of itself
973.92

Carter, Julie
Cat
In Growing up gay p138-44 **808.8**

Cartier, Jacques, 1491-1557
See/See also pages in the following book(s):
Faber, H. The discoverers of America p143-54
970.01

Cartmell, Van Henry
(ed) 24 favorite one-act plays. See 24 favorite one-act plays **808.82**

(ed) Thirty famous one-act plays. See Thirty famous one-act plays **808.82**

Cartography See Map drawing; Maps

Cartoon history of United States foreign policy
327.73

Cartooning. Gerberg, M. **741.5**

Cartooning fundamentals. Ross, A. **741.5**

Cartoons, Animated See Animated films

Cartoons and caricatures
See also Comic books, strips, etc.
Gerberg, M. Cartooning **741.5**
Ross, A. Cartooning fundamentals **741.5**

Carver, George Washington, 1864?-1943
About
McMurry, L. O. George Washington Carver
92

Carver, Raymond
Are these actual miles?
In The Oxford book of American short stories p582-90 **S C**
Cathedral
In The Best American short stories of the eighties p126-41 **S C**
In The Vintage book of contemporary American short stories p108-24 **S C**
Fever
In American short story masterpieces
S C

What we talk about when we talk about love
In The Norton book of American short stories p651-61 **S C**
(ed) American short story masterpieces. See American short story masterpieces **S C**

Carwardine, Mark
Whales, dolphins, and porpoises **599.5**
(jt. auth) Adams, D. Last chance to see
591.5

Cary, Arthur Joyce Lunel See Cary, Joyce, 1888-1957

Cary, Joyce, 1888-1957
Bush River
In The Oxford book of Irish short stories p277-86 **S C**

Cary, Lorene
Black ice **92**
The price of a child **Fic**

Casablanca. Epstein, J. J.
In Best American screenplays **812.008**

Casals, Pablo, 1876-1973
About
Baldock, R. Pablo Casals **92**

The **case** book of Sherlock Holmes. Doyle, Sir A. C.
In Doyle, Sir A. C. The complete Sherlock Holmes **S C**

A **case** of identity. Doyle, Sir A. C.
In Doyle, Sir A. C. The complete Sherlock Holmes **S C**

The **case** of the caretaker. Christie, A.
In Christie, A. Miss Marple: the complete short stories **S C**

The **case** of the emerald sky. Ambler, E.
In Masterpieces of mystery and suspense p271-79 **S C**

The **case** of the perfect maid. Christie, A.
In Christie, A. Miss Marple: the complete short stories **S C**

The **case** of Vincent Pyrwhit. Pain, B.
In Victorian ghost stories p442-44 **S C**

Casey, Winifred Rosen *See* Rosen, Winifred, 1943-

The **cashier**. Colette
In Colette. The collected stories of Colette p157-59 **S C**

The **cask** of Amontillado. Poe, E. A.
In Poe, E. A. The collected tales and poems of Edgar Allan Poe p274-79 **S C**
In Poe, E. A. Tales of Edgar Allan Poe p51-59 **S C**

Cass, James, 1915-1992
Cass & Birnbaum's guide to American colleges. See Cass & Birnbaum's guide to American colleges **378.73**

Cass & Birnbaum's guide to American colleges **378.73**

Cassady, Marsh, 1936-
The book of scenes for aspiring actors **808.82**
(ed) The Book of monologues for aspiring actors. See The Book of monologues for aspiring actors **808.82**

Cassatt, Mary, 1844-1926
About
Mathews, N. M. Mary Cassatt **92**

Cassell, Dana K.
Encyclopedia of obesity and eating disorders **616.85**

Cassell dictionary of proper names. Room, A. **929.4**

Cassell's German-English, English-German dictionary **433**

Cassell's Italian dictionary: Italian-English, English-Italian **453**

Cassell's Latin dictionary **473**

Cassell's Spanish dictionary. See Cassell's Spanish-English, English-Spanish dictionary **463**

Cassell's Spanish-English, English-Spanish dictionary **463**

Casserly, Jack
(jt. auth) Goldwater, B. M. Goldwater **92**

Cassette tape recordings, Video *See* Videotapes

Cassette tapes, Audio *See* Sound recordings

Cassidy, Frederic Gomes, 1907-
(ed) Dictionary of American regional English. See Dictionary of American regional English **427**

Cassirer, Nadine Gordimer *See* Gordimer, Nadine, 1923-

Castedo, Elena
The white bedspread
In Iguana dreams **S C**

Castellano, Olivia, 1944-
Prologue for The Comstock journals (or Sotol City blues)
In Growing up Chicana/o p219-30 **810.8**

Castillo, Ana
Being Indian, a candle, and so many dying stars
In Daughters of the fifth sun **810.8**
On Francisco el Penitente's first becoming a santero and thereby sealing his fate
In Iguana dreams **S C**

Castillo, Richard Griswold del *See* Griswold del Castillo, Richard

Castillo-Speed, Lillian, 1949-
(ed) Latina: women's voices from the borderlands. See Latina: women's voices from the borderlands **810.8**

Casting the runes. James, M. R.
In The Horror hall of fame p204-25 **S C**

The **castle**. Arias, R.
In Growing up Chicana/o p239-48 **810.8**

The **castle** of Kerglas. Souvestre, E.
In The Merlin chronicles **S C**

Castle Roogna. Anthony, P. See note under Anthony, P. The Magic of Xanth series **Fic**

Castles
Gies, J. Life in a medieval castle **940.1**
Johnson, P. Castles of England, Scotland and Wales **941**
Macaulay, D. Castle **728.8**

Castles of England, Scotland and Wales. Johnson, P. **941**

Castro, Fidel, 1927-
About
Beyer, D. E. Castro! **92**
Geyer, G. A. Guerrilla prince: the untold story of Fidel Castro **92**

A **casual** affair. Maugham, W. S.
In Maugham, W. S. Collected short stories v4 **S C**

Cat. Carter, J.
In Growing up gay p138-44 **808.8**

The **cat** and the curmudgeon. Amory, C. **818**

The **cat** care book. Gerstenfeld, S. L. **636.8**

Cat in the rain. Hemingway, E.
In Hemingway, E. The complete short stories of Ernest Hemingway p129-31 **S C**
In Hemingway, E. In our time p89-94 **S C**
In Hemingway, E. The short stories of Ernest Hemingway p165-70 **S C**

Cat on a hot tin roof. Williams, T. **812**
also in Best American plays: 4th series— 1951-1957 p37-90 **812.008**

The **cat**, Spartan. Westall, R.
In Westall, R. Shades of darkness p224-45 **S C**

The **cat** that walked by himself. Kipling, R.
In Kipling, R. The portable Kipling **828**

The **cat** who came for Christmas. Amory, C. **818**

Catalano, Julie
Animal welfare **179**

Cataloging
Anglo-American cataloguing rules, 2d ed., 1988 revision **025.3**
Byrne, D. J. MARC manual **025.3**

Cataloging—*Continued*

Gorman, M. The concise AACR2, 1988 revision **025.3**

Intner, S. S. Standard cataloging for school and public libraries **025.3**

Catalogs *See* Postage stamps—Catalogs; School libraries—Catalogs; Videotapes—Catalogs

Catalogs, Classified *See* Classified catalogs

Catalogs, Subject *See* Subject catalogs

The **catalogue** of the universe. Mahy, M. **Fic**

Catanzarite, Gina, 1965-
(jt. auth) Treganowan, L. Lucille's car care **629.28**

A **catastrophe.** Wells, H. G.
In Wells, H. G. The complete short stories of H. G. Wells p502-11 **S C**

Catastrophes (Geology)
Dauber, P. M. The three big bangs **523.1**
Desonie, D. Cosmic collisions **551.3**

Catastrophic extinction of species *See* Mass extinction of species

Catch-22. Heller, J. **Fic**

Catch-22: antiheroic antinovel. Potts, S. W. **813.009**

Catch the moon. Ortiz Cofer, J.
In Ortiz Cofer, J. An island like you p55-65 **S C**

Catch the rabbit. Asimov, I.
In Asimov, I. I, robot **S C**

The **catcher** in the rye. Pinsker, S. **813.009**

The **catcher** in the rye. Salinger, J. D. **Fic**

Cathedral. Carver, R.
In The Best American short stories of the eighties p126-41 **S C**
In The Vintage book of contemporary American short stories p108-24 **S C**

Cathedral High School (Springfield, Mass.)
Blais, M. In these girls, hope is a muscle **796.323**

Cathedrals
Macaulay, D. Cathedral: the story of its construction **726**

Cather, Willa, 1873-1947
Alexander's bridge
In Cather, W. Stories, poems and other writings **818**
April twilights, and other poems
In Cather, W. Stories, poems and other writings **818**
Death comes for the archbishop **Fic**
A death in the desert
In The Oxford book of American short stories p264-84 **S C**
Early novels and stories **Fic**
The troll garden contains the following stories: Flavia and her artists; The sculptor's funeral; The garden lodge; "A death in the desert"; The marriage of Phaedra; A Wagner matinée; Paul's case
My Antonia **Fic**
also in Cather, W. Early novels and stories **Fic**
My mortal enemy
In Cather, W. Stories, poems and other writings **818**

Not under forty
In Cather, W. Stories, poems and other writings **818**
O pioneers! **Fic**
also in Cather, W. Early novels and stories **Fic**
Obscure destinies
In Cather, W. Stories, poems and other writings **818**
The old beauty, and others
In Cather, W. Stories, poems and other writings **818**
Old Mrs. Harris
In The Oxford book of women's writing in the United States p229-72 **810.8**
One of ours
In Cather, W. Early novels and stories **Fic**
Paul's case
In The Norton book of American short stories p203-20 **S C**
The song of the lark
In Cather, W. Early novels and stories **Fic**
Stories, poems, and other writings **818**
The troll garden
In Cather, W. Early novels and stories **Fic**
Youth and the bright Medusa
In Cather, W. Stories, poems and other writings **818**
About
Gerber, P. L. Willa Cather **813.009**
Keene, A. T. Willa Cather **92**
Lee, H. Willa Cather **92**
Wasserman, L. Willa Cather: a study of the short fiction **813.009**
See/See also pages in the following book(s):
Gombar, C. Great women writers, 1900-1950 **920**

Catherine II, the Great, Empress of Russia, 1729-1796
About
Alexander, J. T. Catherine the Great **92**
See/See also pages in the following book(s):
Durant, W. J. Rousseau and revolution p441-71 **940.2**
Opfell, O. S. Queens, empresses, grand duchesses, and regents p163-71 **920**

Catherine de Médicis, Queen, consort of Henry II, King of France, 1519-1589
See/See also pages in the following book(s):
Opfell, O. S. Queens, empresses, grand duchesses, and regents p93-100 **920**

Cathleen ni Houlihan. Yeats, W. B.
In 24 favorite one-act plays p391-402 **808.82**

Catholic Church
See/See also pages in the following book(s):
Durant, W. J. The age of faith p732-68 **940.1**
Russell, B. A history of Western philosophy p301-487 **109**
Dictionaries
The HarperCollins encyclopedia of Catholicism **282**

Champagne, Duane—*Continued*
(ed) The Native North American almanac. See
The Native North American almanac
970.004

Champion. Lardner, R.
In Lardner, R. The best short stories of Ring
Lardner p109-26 **S C**
In The Norton book of American short stories
p244-61 **S C**

Champion: Joe Louis, black hero in white America. Mead, C. **92**

Champlain, Samuel de, 1567-1635
See/See also pages in the following book(s):
Faber, H. The discoverers of America p161-69
970.01

Chance, Jane, 1945-
The lord of the rings **823.009**

A chance to make good. Grossman, J. R.
In The Young Oxford history of African
Americans **305.8**

Chancellorsville (Va.), Battle of, 1863
Sears, S. W. Chancellorsville **973.7**
Fiction
Crane, S. The red badge of courage **Fic**

Chandler, A. Bertram, 1912-1984
Don't knock the rock
In Tales from the planet Earth **S C**

Chandler, David, 1934-
Battles and battlescenes of World War Two
940.54

Chandler, Raymond, 1888-1959
I'll be waiting
In The Oxford book of American detective
stories p295-309 **S C**

Chaney, James Earl, 1943-1964
About
Cagin, S. We are not afraid **323.1**

Chang, Lan Samantha
The eve of the spirit festival
In The Best American short stories, 1996
p40-50 **S C**
Housepainting
In American eyes p13-27 **S C**
Pipa's story
In The Best American short stories, 1994
p34-51 **S C**

Chang. Nunez, S.
In Growing up Asian American p359-77
810.8

Change, Social *See* Social change

Changing bodies, changing lives. Bell, R.
613.9

The changing Supreme Court. Lindop, E.
347

The changing world of weather. Carpenter, C.
551.6

Chants (Plain, Gregorian, etc.)
See/See also pages in the following book(s):
Grout, D. J. A history of western music
780.9

Chaon, Dan
Fitting ends
In The Best American short stories, 1996
p51-68 **S C**

Chaos (Science)
Lampton, C. Science of chaos **003**
Parker, B. R. Chaos in the cosmos **520**
Peak, D. Chaos under control **003**
See/See also pages in the following book(s):
Horgan, J. The end of science p191-226
501

Chaos in the cosmos. Parker, B. R. **520**
Chaos under control. Peak, D. **003**
Chaotic behavior in systems *See* Chaos (Science)
Chapbooks
See also Comic books, strips, etc.

Chaplin, Charlie, 1889-1977
About
Milton, J. Tramp: the life of Charlie Chaplin
92
Smith, J. Chaplin **791.43**
See/See also pages in the following book(s):
Kerr, W. The silent clowns p74-97, 160-81,
337-64 **791.43**

Chapman, Richard
The complete guitarist **787.87**

Chapman, Robert L.
(ed) Roget A to Z. See Roget A to Z **423**
(ed) Roget's international thesaurus. See Roget's
international thesaurus **423**

Chapman, Vera, 1898-1996
A sword for Arthur
In The Merlin chronicles **S C**

Chapman, Victoria L., 1956-
Latin American history on file **980**

Chapman (Victoria) & Associates *See* Victoria
Chapman & Associates

Chappie [biography of Daniel James] Phelps, J.
A. **92**

A chapter in the history of a Tyrone family. Le
Fanu, J. S.
In The Oxford book of gothic tales p102-32
S C

Chapter two. Simon, N.
In Best American plays: 8th series—1974-
1982 p1-37 **812.008**
In Simon, N. The collected plays of Neil Simon v2 p635-737 **812**

Chapterhouse: Dune. Herbert, F. See note under
Herbert, F. Dune **Fic**

Chapters into verse **821.008**

Chapters: my growth as a writer. Duncan, L.
92

Character above all **920**

Characters and characteristics in literature
Cyclopedia of literary characters II **803**
Dictionary of American literary characters
810.3
Dictionary of British literary characters
820.3
Harris, L. L. Characters in 20th-century literature **809**
Hartman, D. K. Historical figures in fiction
016.8
Howes, K. K. Characters in 19th-century literature **809**
Swain, D. V. Creating characters **808.3**

Che ti dice la patria?. Hemingway, E.
In Hemingway, E. The complete short stories of Ernest Hemingway p223-30   **S C**
In Hemingway, E. The short stories of Ernest Hemingway p290-99   **S C**

Cheap in August. Greene, G.
In Greene, G. The portable Graham Greene p420-41   **828**

Cheap raw material. Meltzer, M.   **331.3**

Cheaper by the dozen [biography of Frank Bunker Gilbreth, 1868-1924] Gilbreth, F. B.   **92**

The **cheapjack**. O'Connor, F.
In O'Connor, F. Collected stories p56-66   **S C**

The **cheat**. O'Connor, F.
In O'Connor, F. Collected stories p515-24   **S C**

Cheating the gallows. Zangwill, I.
In The Best crime stories of the 19th century p151-64   **S C**

Check, William A.
Drugs & perception   **615**
The mind-body connection   **610**

The **checkerboard**. Anderson, A.
In The Best short stories by Negro writers p207-12   **S C**

The **cheerleaders** almanac. Kuch, K. D.   **791.6**

Cheerleading
French, S. B. The cheerleading book   **791.6**
Kuch, K. D. The cheerleaders almanac   **791.6**

The **cheerleading** book. French, S. B.   **791.6**

Chee's witch. Hillerman, T.
In The Oxford book of American detective stories p655-64   **S C**

Cheever, John, 1912-1982
The death of Justina
In The Oxford book of American short stories p541-51   **S C**
Goodbye, my brother
In The Oxford book of short stories p466-86   **S C**
The stories of John Cheever   **S C**
Contents: Goodbye, my brother; The common day; The enormous radio; O city of broken dreams; The Hartleys; The Sutton Place story; The summer farmer; Torch song; The pot of gold; Clancy in the Tower of Babel; Christmas is a sad season for the poor; The season of divorce; The chaste Clarissa; The cure; The superintendent; The children; The sorrows of gin; O youth and beauty!; The day the pig fell into the well; The five-forty-eight; Just one more time; The housebreaker of Shady Hill; The bus to St. James's; The worm in the apple; The trouble for Marcie Flint; The bella lingua; The Wrysons; The country husband; The Duchess; The scarlet moving van; Just tell me who it was; Brimmer; The golden age; The lowboy; The music teacher; A woman without a country; The death of Justina; Clementina; Boy in Rome; A miscellany of characters that will not appear; The chimera; The seaside houses; The angel of the bridge; The brigadier and the golf widow; A vision of the world; Reunion; An educated American woman; Metamorphoses; Mene, Mene, Tekel, Upharsin; Montraldo; The ocean; Marito in Città; The geometry of love; The swimmer; The world of apples; Another story; Percy; The fourth alarm; Artemis, the honest well digger; Three stories: I; Three stories: II; Three stories: III; The jewels of the Cabots
The swimmer
In The Norton book of American short stories p431-41   **S C**

Chekhov, Anton Pavlovich, 1860-1904
Anton Chekhov's plays—backgrounds, criticism   **891.7**
The bishop
In The Portable twentieth-century Russian reader p12-28   **891.7**
The boor
In Thirty famous one-act plays p103-12   **808.82**
The cherry orchard
In Chekhov, A. P. Anton Chekhov's plays—backgrounds, criticism   **891.7**
The image of Chekhov   **S C**
Contents: The little apples; St. Peter's Day; Green Scythe; Joy; The ninny; The highest heights; Death of a government clerk; At the post office; Surgery; In the cemetery; Where there's a will, there's a way; A report; The threat; The huntsman; The malefactor; A dead body; Sergeant Prishibeyev; A blunder; Heartache; Anyuta; The proposal; Vanka; Who is to blame; Typhus; Sleepyhead; The princess; Gusev; The peasant women; After the theater; A fragment; In exile; Big Volodya and Little Volodya; The student; Anna round the neck; The house with the mezzanine; In the horsecart; On love; The lady with the pet dog; The Bishop; The bride
The lady with the dog
In The Portable nineteenth-century Russian reader p534-49   **891.7**
A marriage proposal
In 24 favorite one-act plays p403-16   **808.82**
The Russian master and other stories   **S C**
Contents: His wife; A lady with a dog; The duel; A hard case; Gooseberries; Concerning love; Peasants; Angel; The Russian master; Terror; The Order of St. Anne
The sea gull
In Chekhov, A. P. Anton Chekhov's plays—backgrounds, criticism   **891.7**
The three sisters
In Chekhov, A. P. Anton Chekhov's plays—backgrounds, criticism   **891.7**
Uncle Vanya
In Chekhov, A. P. Anton Chekhov's plays—backgrounds, criticism   **891.7**
In The Portable nineteenth-century Russian reader p549-607   **891.7**
About
Kirk, I. Anton Chekhov   **891.7**
Pritchett, V. S. Chekhov   **92**

Chelton, Mary K., 1942-
(ed) Excellence in library services to young adults. See Excellence in library services to young adults   **027.62**

Chemical and biological warfare. Taylor, C. L.   **358**

Chemical communication. Agosta, W. C.   **591.5**

Chemical dependency: opposing viewpoints   **362.29**

Chemical elements
Atkins, P. W. The periodic kingdom   **541.2**
Newton, D. E. The chemical elements   **546**

Chemical engineering
See also Biotechnology

Chemical pollution *See* Pollution

Chemical warfare
Taylor, C. L. Chemical and biological warfare   **358**

Chiang, Kai-shek, 1887-1975
See/See also pages in the following book(s):
White, T. H. In search of history p154-61, 166-79   **92**

Chiang, Ted
Tower of Babylon
In Nebula awards 26 p58-83   **S C**

Chicago (Ill.)
Fiction
Bellow, S. The adventures of Augie March
   Fic
Cisneros, S. The house on Mango Street
   Fic
Dreiser, T. Sister Carrie   **Fic**
Sinclair, A. Coffee will make you black
   Fic
Sinclair, U. The jungle   **Fic**
Wright, R. Native son   **Fic**
Social conditions
Addams, J. Twenty years at Hull-House   **92**
Joravsky, B. Hoop dreams   **796.323**
Kotlowitz, A. There are no children here
   305.23

Chicago Historical Society
Foner, E. A house divided   **973.7**

The **Chicago** manual of style   **808**

Chicago poems. Sandburg, C.
In Sandburg, C. Complete poems of Carl Sandburg p3-76   **811**

Chicano literature *See* American literature—Mexican American authors

Chicanos *See* Mexican Americans

Chickamauga, Battle of, 1863
See/See also pages in the following book(s):
Korn, J. The fight for Chattanooga: Chickamauga to Missionary Ridge   **973.7**

Chickamauga. Bierce, A.
In The Norton book of American short stories p74-79   **S C**

Chickamauga. Wolfe, T.
In Wolfe, T. The complete short stories of Thomas Wolfe p381-96   **S C**

Chickenhawk. Mason, R.   **959.704**

The **chief. Lipsyte, R.**   **Fic**

Chief Joseph *See* Joseph, Nez Percé Chief, 1840-1904

Chief Joseph and the Nez Percés. Scott, R. A.
   92

Chigbo, Okey
The housegirl
In The Heinemann book of contemporary African short stories p149-64   **S C**

Child, Greg
(comp) Climbing: the complete reference. See Climbing: the complete reference   **796.5**

Child, Julia
The way to cook   **641.5**

Child, Lincoln
(jt. auth) Preston, D. Relic   **Fic**

Child abuse
See also Child sexual abuse
Child abuse: opposing viewpoints   **362.7**
Dolan, E. F. Child abuse   **362.7**

Hayden, T. L. Ghost girl   **362.7**
Hayden, T. L. The tiger's child   **155.5**
Mufson, S. Straight talk about child abuse
   362.7
Fiction
Crutcher, C. Staying fat for Sarah Byrnes
   Fic

Child abuse: opposing viewpoints   **362.7**

Child and father *See* Father and child

Child and parent *See* Parent and child

The **child** by tiger. Wolfe, T.
In Wolfe, T. The complete short stories of Thomas Wolfe p332-48   **S C**

Child care
See also Babysitting; Child rearing; Infants—Care
Stoppard, M. Complete baby and child care
   649

Child development
Stoppard, M. Complete baby and child care
   649
See/See also pages in the following book(s):
Bettelheim, B. Surviving, and other essays p338-49   **155.9**

A **child** is born. Nilsson, L.   **612.6**

Child labor *See* Children—Employment; Youth—Employment

Child molesting *See* Child sexual abuse

The **child** prodigy. Colette
In Colette. The collected stories of Colette p166-69   **S C**

Child prostitution *See* Juvenile prostitution

Child psychiatry
See also Mentally ill children
Gutkind, L. Stuck in time   **616.89**

Child psychology
See also Child rearing
Axline, V. M. Dibs: in search of self
   616.85
Bettelheim, B. The uses of enchantment
   398
Hayden, T. L. The tiger's child   **155.5**

Child rearing
See also Parenting
Lindsay, J. W. The challenge of toddlers
   649
Lindsay, J. W. Teen dads   **649**
Lindsay, J. W. Your baby's first year   **649**

Child sexual abuse
Kinnear, K. L. Childhood sexual abuse
   362.7
Mather, C. L. How long does it hurt?
   362.7
Fiction
Woodson, J. I hadn't meant to tell you this
   Fic

Child welfare
America's children: opposing viewpoints
   362.7

Childbirth
Hales, D. R. Pregnancy and birth   **618.2**
Nilsson, L. A child is born   **612.6**
Vaughan, C. How life begins   **612.6**

Children's literature—Bibliography—*Continued*
Holsinger, M. P. The ways of war   **016.8**
Khorana, M. Africa in literature for children and young adults   **016.9**
Miller-Lachmann, L. Our family, our friends, our world   **011.6**
Williams, H. E. Books by African-American authors and illustrators for children and young adults   **016.3058**
Stories, plots, etc.
Booktalking the award winners   **028.5**
Masterplots II: juvenile and young adult fiction series   **028.5**
Masterplots II: juvenile and young adult literature series supplement   **028.5**
The **children's** rights movement. Hawes, J. M.   **305.23**

Children's writings
Rising voices   **810.8**
Ten out of ten   **812.008**
Childress, Alice, 1920-1994
A hero ain't nothin' but a sandwich   **Fic**
The pocketbook game
In The Best short stories by Negro writers p205-06   **S C**
Wedding band
In 9 plays by black women   **811.008**
Wine in the wilderness
In Black theatre USA   **812.008**
A **child's** Christmas in Wales. Thomas, D.   **828**
A **child's** drawings. Shalamov, V. T.
In The Portable twentieth-century Russian reader p423-26   **891.7**
Chilton's auto repair manual   **629.28**
Chilvers, Ian
(ed) The Oxford dictionary of art. See The Oxford dictionary of art   **703**
The **Chimaera.** Hawthorne, N.
In Hawthorne, N. Tales and sketches; A wonder book for girls and boys; Tanglewood tales for girls and boys p1280-99   **S C**
The **chimera.** Cheever, J.
In Cheever, J. The stories of John Cheever p473-81   **S C**
Chimombo, Steve
The rubbish dump
In The Heinemann book of contemporary African short stories p72-80   **S C**
Chimpanzees
Goodall, J. The chimpanzees of Gombe   **599.88**
Goodall, J. In the shadow of man   **599.88**
Goodall, J. Through a window   **599.88**
Nichols, M. K. The great apes   **599.88**
Fiction
Dickinson, P. Eva   **Fic**
The **chimpanzees** of Gombe. Goodall, J.   **599.88**
Chimu Indians
See/See also pages in the following book(s):
Mysteries of the ancient Americas p272-81   **970.01**

Chin, Frank, 1940-
Railroad standard time
In Growing up Asian American p201-08   **810.8**
Yes, young daddy
In Coming of age in America p139-53   **S C**
Chin, Leeann
Betty Crocker's new Chinese cookbook   **641.5**
China
Antiquities
China's buried kingdoms   **931**
See/See also pages in the following book(s):
Builders of the ancient world p160-95   **930**
Civilization
China   **951**
See/See also pages in the following book(s):
Durant, W. J. Our Oriental heritage p635-823   **950**
Communism
See Communism—China
Description
Jenkins, P. Across China   **915.1**
Journey into China   **915.1**
Salzman, M. Iron & silk   **915.1**
See/See also pages in the following book(s):
Great rivers of the world p243-74   **910**
Dictionaries
The Cambridge encyclopedia of China   **951**
Fiction
Bosse, M. J. The examination   **Fic**
Buck, P. S. The good earth   **Fic**
Lord, B. B. Spring Moon   **Fic**
Foreign relations—United States
See/See also pages in the following book(s):
Tuchman, B. W. Practicing history p188-207   **907**
History
Fairbank, J. K. The great Chinese revolution: 1800-1985   **951**
Huang, R. China, a macro history   **951**
Seagrave, S. Dragon lady [biography of Tz'u-hsi]   **92**
Spence, J. D. The search for modern China   **951**
Stefoff, R. Mao Zedong   **92**
History—1912-1949
See/See also pages in the following book(s):
White, T. H. In search of history p62-101, 110-213, 231-42   **92**
History—1949-
Kort, M. China under communism   **951.05**
Terrill, R. China in our time   **951.05**
History—1976-
Woodruff, J. China in search of its future   **951.05**
History—1989, Tiananmen Square Incident
Salisbury, H. E. Tiananmen diary   **951.05**
Simmie, S. Tiananmen Square   **951.05**
Intellectual life
See/See also pages in the following book(s):
Durant, W. J. Our Oriental heritage p694-735   **950**

Chopin, Kate, 1851-1904
The awakening
In Chopin, K. The awakening and selected
stories p169-351   S C
The awakening and selected stories   S C
Includes the following short stories: Love on the Bon-Dieu;
Beyond the bayou; A visit to Avoyelles; La Belle Zoraïde; In Sa-
bine; Ozème's holiday; A matter of prejudice; At Chênière
Caminada; A respectable woman; Regret; Athénaïse; A night in
Acadie
A pair of silk stockings
In The Oxford book of women's writing in
the United States p63-67   **810.8**
The storm
In The Oxford book of American short stories
p129-35   S C
The story of an hour
In The Norton book of American short stories
p123-25   S C
About
Skaggs, P. Kate Chopin   **813.009**
Chopin in winter. Dybek, S.
In The Vintage book of contemporary
American short stories p141-61   S C
Choreographers
De Mille, A. Dance to the piper   92
Graham, M. Blood memory   92
Taper, B. Balanchine   92
The **chosen**. Potok, C.   Fic
Chou, En-lai *See* Zhou Enlai, 1898-1976
Chris Christophersen. O'Neill, E.
In O'Neill, E. Complete plays v1   812
Christ *See* Jesus Christ
Christabel. Pilcher, R.
In Pilcher, R. Flowers in the rain & other sto-
ries   S C
The **christening**. Lawrence, D. H.
In Lawrence, D. H. The complete short sto-
ries v1   S C
Christensen, Karen, 1957-
(ed) Encyclopedia of world sport. See Encyclo-
pedia of world sport   796
Christian art and symbolism
Snyder, J. Medieval art   709.02
Christian doctrine *See* Doctrinal theology
Christian life
Lewis, C. S. The Screwtape letters   248
Fiction
Bunyan, J. The pilgrim's progress   Fic
Christian missionaries
Fiction
Forester, C. S. The African Queen   Fic
The **Christian** roommates. Updike, J.
In American short story masterpieces
     S C
Christian saints
Brooks, P. S. Beyond the myth: the story of
Joan of Arc   92
Green, J. God's fool: the life and times of Fran-
cis of Assisi   92
Dictionaries
Bentley, J. A calendar of saints: the lives of the
principal saints of the Christian year
     920.003

Sandoval, A. The directory of saints
     920.003
Christianity
Lynch, P. A. Christianity   200
See/See also pages in the following book(s):
The World's religions p40-83   291
History
See Church history
Christianity comes to the Sioux. Power, S.
In Song of the turtle p307-16   S C
Christianson, Gale E.
Edwin Hubble: mariner of the nebulae   92
In the presence of the creator: Isaac Newton and
his times   92
Christianson, Stephen G.
Facts about the Congress   328.73
Christie, Agatha, 1890-1976
The blue geranium
In Crime classics p231-46   S C
Miss Marple: the complete short stories
     S C
Contents: The Tuesday night club; The Idol House of Astarte;
Ingots of gold; The bloodstained pavement; Motive v. opportuni-
ty; The thumbmark of St. Peter; The blue geranium; The com-
panion; The four suspects; A Christmas tragedy; The herb of
death; The affair at the bungalow; Death by drowning; Miss
Marple tells a story; Strange jest; The case of the perfect maid;
The case of the caretaker; Tape-measure murder; Greenshaw's
Folly; Sanctuary
Murder on the Orient Express   Fic
The submarine plans
In Masterpieces of mystery and suspense p44-
56   S C
About
Gill, G. Agatha Christie   92
Wagoner, M. Agatha Christie   823.009
Christine. King, S.   Fic
Christmas
Capote, T. One Christmas   92
Wales
Thomas, D. A child's Christmas in Wales
     828
The **Christmas** banquet. Hawthorne, N.
In Hawthorne, N. Tales and sketches; A won-
der book for girls and boys; Tanglewood
tales for girls and boys p849-67
     S C
Christmas is a sad season for the poor. Cheever,
J.
In Cheever, J. The stories of John Cheever
p128-36   S C
Christmas is for cops. Hoch, E. D.
In The Oxford book of American detective
stories p608-20   S C
A **Christmas** memory. Capote, T.
In Capote, T. Breakfast at Tiffany's: a short
novel and three stories   S C
Christmas morning. O'Connor, F.
In O'Connor, F. Collected stories p200-06
     S C
Christmas party. Stout, R.
In The Oxford book of American detective
stories p526-69   S C
A **Christmas** tragedy. Christie, A.
In Christie, A. Miss Marple: the complete
short stories   S C

Cinque, 1811?-1879
See/See also pages in the following book(s):
Abdul-Jabbar, K. Black profiles in courage p46-50; 57-67 **920**

Ciphers
Wrixon, F. B. Codes and ciphers **652**

Circe. Welty, E.
In Welty, E. The collected stories of Eudora Welty p531-37 **S C**

Circe's palace. Hawthorne, N.
In Hawthorne, N. Tales and sketches; A wonder book for girls and boys; Tanglewood tales for girls and boys p1382-1408 **S C**

A **circle** in the fire. O'Connor, F.
In O'Connor, F. Collected works p232-51 **S C**
In O'Connor, F. The complete stories p175-93 **S C**

A **circle** of friends. Voïnovich, V.
In The Portable twentieth-century Russian reader p574-99 **891.7**

Circle of women: an anthology of contemporary Western women writers **810.8**

The **circuit.** Jiménez, F.
In Growing up Chicana/o p137-44 **810.8**

The **circular** valley. Bowles, P.
In The Literary ghost p115-24 **S C**

Circulatory system *See* Cardiovascular system

The **circulatory** system. Avraham, R. **612.1**

Circumnavigation *See* Voyages around the world

Circus
Culhane, J. The American circus: an illustrated history **791.3**
Kunhardt, P. B. P.T. Barnum **92**

Circus. Saroyan, W.
In Saroyan, W. My name is Aram **S C**

Circus at dawn. Wolfe, T.
In Wolfe, T. The complete short stories of Thomas Wolfe p201-05 **S C**

The **circus** horse. Colette
In Colette. The collected stories of Colette p113-16 **S C**

Cisneros, Sandra
Eleven
In Growing up Chicana/o p155-59 **810.8**
Eyes of Zapata
In Daughters of the fifth sun **810.8**
Hairs
In We are the stories we tell **S C**
Hips
In We are the stories we tell **S C**
The house on Mango Street **Fic**
also in The Oxford book of American short stories p746-48 **S C**
The monkey garden
In Growing up Latino p288-91 **810.8**
My Lucy friend who smells like corn
In Who do you think you are? p119-21 **S C**
A rice sandwich
In We are the stories we tell **S C**
Salvador late or early
In Iguana dreams **S C**

Woman Hollering Creek and other stories **S C**

Contents: My Lucy friend who smells like corn; Eleven; Salvador late or early; Mexican movies; Barbie-Q; Mericans; Tepeyac; One holy night; My tocaya; Woman Hollering Creek; The Marlboro Man; La Fabulosa: a Texas operetta; Remember the Alamo; Never marry a Mexican; Bread; Eyes of Zapata; Anguiano religious articles rosaries statues . . .; Little miracles, kept promises; Los Boxers; There was a man, there was a woman; Tin tan tan; Bien pretty

Cities and towns
See also Inner cities
Cities of the world **910.3**
History
See/See also pages in the following book(s):
The Middle Ages [American Heritage] **940.1**
United States
America's cities: opposing viewpoints **307.7**
See/See also pages in the following book(s):
Boorstin, D. J. The Americans: The democratic experience p245-305 **973**

Cities and towns, ruined, extinct, etc. *See* Extinct cities

Cities of the world **910.3**

Citizen Hearst: a biography of William Randolph Hearst. Swanberg, W. A. **92**

Citizen Kane. Mankiewicz, H. J.
In Best American screenplays **812.008**

Citizens: a chronicle of the French Revolution. Schama, S. **944.04**

Citizens review. Honig, L.
In Prize stories, 1996 p144-62 **S C**

The **city.** Bradbury, R.
In Bradbury, R. The illustrated man **S C**
In Bradbury, R. The stories of Ray Bradbury p173-79 **S C**

The **city.** Hesse, H.
In Hesse, H. The fairy tales of Hermann Hesse **S C**

City: a story of Roman planning and construction. Macaulay, D. **711**

The **city** coat of arms. Kafka, F.
In Kafka, F. The complete stories **S C**

City for sale. Kanastoga, W.
In Iguana dreams **S C**

City life
Fiction
Streetlights: illuminating tales of the urban black experience **S C**
Poetry
Merriam, E. The inner city Mother Goose **811**

City lights pocket poets anthology **808.81**

'A **city** of the dead, a city of the living'. Gordimer, N.
In Gordimer, N. Crimes of conscience p1-17 **S C**

City of Truth. Morrow, J.
In Nebula awards 28 p228-317 **S C**

City planning
Rome
Macaulay, D. City: a story of Roman planning and construction **711**

Clark, John O. E. (John Owen Edward), 1937-
Matter and energy   **539**
(jt. auth) Darton, M. The Macmillan dictionary
of measurement   **389**
Clark, Kenneth, 1903-1983
Civilisation   **709**
Clark, Mary Higgins
Where are the children?   **Fic**
(ed) Bad behavior. See Bad behavior   **S C**
Clark, Thomas
(ed) The Writer's digest guide to good writing.
See The Writer's digest guide to good writing
    808
Clark, William, 1770-1838
About
Lavender, D. S. The way to the Western sea
    973.4
Clark, William R., 1938-
At war within   **616.07**
Clarke, Arthur C., 1917-
2001: a space odyssey   **Fic**
Childhood's end   **Fic**
Second dawn
In The Oxford book of science fiction stories
p198-227   **S C**
See/See also pages in the following book(s):
Science fiction writers of the golden age p94-
109   **809.3**
Clarke, Breena
The drill
In Streetlights: illuminating tales of the urban
black experience p56-60   **S C**
Clarke, Gerald
Capote   **92**
Clarke, John Henrik, 1915-
The boy who painted Christ black
In Rites of passage p71-78   **S C**
Santa Claus is a white man
In The Best short stories by Negro writers
p181-87   **S C**
Clarke, Michael, 1952-
Watercolor   **751.42**
Clarke, Peter B., 1940-
(ed) The World's religions. See The World's re-
ligions   **291**
Clarkson, Atelia
(ed) World folktales. See World folktales
    398.2
Clash of Titans. Boyne, W. J.   **940.54**
Classic American ghost stories   **133.1**
Classic American short stories   **S C**
Classic English short stories, 1930-1955   **S C**
Classic ghost stories   **S C**
Classic home cooking. Berry, M.   **641.5**
The Classic Noh theatre of Japan   **895.6**
Classical antiquities
See also Greece—Antiquities; Rome—An-
tiquities
Dictionaries
See Classical dictionaries
Classical art *See* Roman art
Classical ballet technique. Warren, G.   **792.8**

Classical dictionaries
Grant, M. A guide to the ancient world
    938.003
The Oxford classical dictionary   **938.003**
Radice, B. Who's who in the ancient world
    938.003
Classical literature
See also Greek literature; Latin literature
Highet, G. The classical tradition   **809**
Bio-bibliography
Grant, M. Greek and Latin authors, 800 B.C.-
A.D. 1000   **920.003**
Dictionaries
The Oxford companion to classical literature
    880.3
Classical music *See* Music
Classical music. Rushton, J.   **781.6**
Classical music. Stanley, J.   **780.9**
Classical music. Gammond, P.   **781.6**
Classical mythology
Asimov, I. Words from the myths   **292**
Fleischman, P. Dateline: Troy   **292**
Graves, R. Greek myths   **292**
Hamilton, E. Mythology   **292**
Dictionaries
Bell, R. E. Women of classical mythology
    292
Daly, K. N. Greek and Roman mythology A to
Z   **292**
Fiction
Renault, M. The king must die   **Fic**
Classical poetry
Collections
The Oxford book of classical verse in transla-
tion   **881.008**
The classical tradition. Highet, G.   **809**
Classification
Books
Intner, S. S. Standard cataloging for school and
public libraries   **025.3**
Classification, Dewey Decimal *See* Dewey Deci-
mal Classification
Classified catalogs
Middle and junior high school library catalog
    011.6
Claudius, Emperor of Rome, 10 B.C.-54
Fiction
Graves, R. I, Claudius   **Fic**
Clausius, Rudolf Julius Emmanuel, 1822-1888
See/See also pages in the following book(s):
Guillen, M. Five equations that changed the
world   **530.1**
Clavell, James
Shogun   **Fic**
Clawson, Calvin C.
The mathematical traveler   **513**
Clay, Cassius *See* Ali, Muhammad, 1942-
Clay. Joyce, J.
In Joyce, J. Dubliners   **S C**
Clay walls [excerpt] Kim, R.
In Growing up Asian American p301-18
    810.8

Clayman, Charles B.
(ed) The American Medical Association encyclopedia of medicine. See The American
Medical Association encyclopedia of medicine
610.3
(ed) American Medical Association family medical guide. See American Medical Association
family medical guide 616.02
(ed) The Human body: an illustrated guide to its
structure, function, and disorders. See The
Human body: an illustrated guide to its structure, function, and disorders 612

A **clean,** well-lighted place. Hemingway, E.
In Hemingway, E. The complete short stories
of Ernest Hemingway p288-91 S C
In Hemingway, E. The short stories of Ernest
Hemingway p379-83 S C
In The Oxford book of American short stories
p295-300 S C

Cleanliness
See also Hygiene

The **clearing** in the valley. Track, S.
In Spider Woman's granddaughters S C

Cleary, Beverly
My own two feet 92

Cleaver, Eldridge, 1935-
Soul on ice 305.8

Clemens, Samuel Langhorne See Twain, Mark,
1835-1910

Clementina. Cheever, J.
In Cheever, J. The stories of John Cheever
p438-51 S C

Clements, Kendrick A., 1939-
Woodrow Wilson 92

Clements, Patricia
(ed) The Feminist companion to literature in
English. See The Feminist companion to literature in English 820.9

Cleo. West, D.
In Invented lives p354-80 S C

Cleopatra, Queen of Egypt, d. 30 B.C.
About
Cleopatra 822.009
Cleopatra [critical essays] 822.009

Clergy
Fiction
Craven, M. I heard the owl call my name
Fic
Greene, G. The power and the glory Fic

Cleveland, Ray L., 1929-
The Middle East and South Asia 956

Clever dogs. Colette
In Colette. The collected stories of Colette
p163-66 S C

The **clever** Maakafi. Artist, V. A.
In The Big book of large-cast plays p248-56
812.008

The **client.** Grisham, J. Fic

Cliff, Michelle
Screen memory
In Calling the wind p566-77 S C

Cliffe, Roger W.
Woodworker's handbook 684

Clifford, Lucy Lane, 1853?-1929
The new mother
In Masterpieces of fantasy and enchantment
p280-90 S C
In The Oxford book of modern fairy tales
p120-39 S C

Clifford, Mike
(ed) The Harmony illustrated encyclopedia of
rock. See The Harmony illustrated encyclopedia of rock 781.66

Clifton, Lucille, 1936-
Quilting 811

Climate
See also Greenhouse effect; Meteorology;
United States—Climate; Weather
Carpenter, C. The changing world of weather
551.6
Encyclopedia of climate and weather 551.6
See/See also pages in the following book(s):
Frontline of discovery 600
Dictionaries
The Encyclopedia of climatology 551.5

Climbing: the complete reference 796.5

Cline, Nancy Lieberman- See Lieberman-Cline,
Nancy, 1958-

Clinton, Bill, 1946-
About
Maraniss, D. First in his class: a biography of
Bill Clinton 92
See/See also pages in the following book(s):
Walsh, K. T. Feeding the beast p127-56
973.927

Clinton, Hillary Rodham, 1947-
See/See also pages in the following book(s):
Walsh, K. T. Feeding the beast p157-75
973.927

Clinton, Michelle T.
Humiliation of the boy
In Song of the turtle p220-30 S C

Clinton, William Jefferson See Clinton, Bill,
1946-

Cloak and dagger fiction. Smith, M. J. 016.8

Cloak of anarchy. Niven, L.
In The Oxford book of science fiction stories
p400-19 S C

The **clock.** Harvey, W. F.
In The Oxford book of English ghost stories
p335-38 S C

The **clock** of ages. Medina, J. J. 612.6

The **clock** that struck thirteen. Sholem Aleichem
In Sholem Aleichem. The best of Sholem
Aleichem S C

The **clocks,** ribbons, mountain lakes, and clouds of
Jennifer Marginat Feliciano. Vega, E.
In Iguana dreams S C

The **clod.** Beach, L.
In Thirty famous one-act plays p451-60
808.82

Clod-Hans. Andersen, H. C.
In Andersen, H. C. Tales and stories
S C

Clones and cloning
See also Molecular cloning

Close encounters of the fourth kind. Bryan, C. D. B.   **001.9**

The **closed** shop. Maugham, W. S.
In Maugham, W. S. Collected short stories v2   **S C**

The **closet**. Chávez, D.
In Growing up Latino p85-98   **810.8**

The **closing** door [excerpt] Grimké, A. W.
In The Portable Harlem Renaissance reader p486-500   **810.8**

Closing the ring. Churchill, Sir W.   **940.53**

Clothing and dress
See also Costume; Fashion

Cloud, Stanley
The Murrow boys   **070.1**

Clouds
See/See also pages in the following book(s):
Weather p188-217   **551.5**

Clouk alone. Colette
In Colette. The collected stories of Colette p9-12   **S C**

Clouk's fling. Colette
In Colette. The collected stories of Colette p12-15   **S C**

Cloulas, Ivan
The Borgias   **920**

Clouse, Woody, 1965-
(jt. auth) Turner, E. T. Winning racquetball   **796.34**

Clute, John
Science fiction   **809.3**
(ed) The Encyclopedia of science fiction. See The Encyclopedia of science fiction   **809.3**

Clytie. Welty, E.
In The Oxford book of gothic tales p424-34   **S C**
In Welty, E. The collected stories of Eudora Welty p81-90   **S C**

Coal miner's daughter. See Lynn, L. Loretta Lynn: coal miner's daughter   **92**

Coal mines and mining
See/See also pages in the following book(s):
Lawrence, D. H. The portable D. H. Lawrence p613-23   **828**
Fiction
Llewellyn, R. How green was my valley   **Fic**

The **coast** is clear. Morales, E.
In Iguana dreams   **S C**

Cobb, Geraldyn M., 1931-
See/See also pages in the following book(s):
Yount, L. Women aviators   **920**

Cobb, Jerrie See Cobb, Geraldyn M., 1931-

Cobb, Jewel Plummer, 1924-
See/See also pages in the following book(s):
Yount, L. Contemporary women scientists   **920**

Coca-Cola culture   **306.4**

Cocaine
See also Crack (Drug)
See/See also pages in the following book(s):
Hermes, W. J. Substance abuse p59-70   **616.86**

Cocaine babies See Children of drug addicts

Cochise, Apache Chief, d. 1874
About
Sweeney, E. R. Cochise, Chiricahua Apache chief   **92**
See/See also pages in the following book(s):
Brown, D. A. The American West p124-31   **978**
Brown, D. A. Bury my heart at Wounded Knee p192-217   **970.004**

Cochran, Jacqueline, 1910?-1980
See/See also pages in the following book(s):
Oleksy, W. G. Military leaders of World War II   **920**
Yount, L. Women aviators   **920**

Cochrane, Elizabeth See Bly, Nellie, 1867-1922

Cock Robin Beale Street. Hurston, Z. N.
In Hurston, Z. N. The complete stories p122-26   **S C**

Cockcroft, James D.
The Hispanic struggle for social justice   **305.8**
Latinos in the making of the United States   **305.8**

The **cocktail** hour. Gurney, A. R.
In Best American plays: 9th series—1983-1992 p414-45   **812.008**

Cocktail party. Eliot, T. S.
In Eliot, T. S. The complete poems and plays, 1909-1950 p295-388   **818**

Code deciphering See Cryptography

Code three. Raphael, R.
In The Mammoth book of new world science fiction p251-300   **S C**

Codes See Ciphers

Codes and ciphers. Wrixon, F. B.   **652**

Cody, Iron Eyes, 1904-
See/See also pages in the following book(s):
Sonneborn, L. Performers   **920**

Cody, Liza
Lucky dip
In Bad behavior p91-117   **S C**

Cody, William Frederick See Buffalo Bill, 1846-1917

Cody's story. Olmstead, R.
In The Vintage book of contemporary American short stories p399-409   **S C**

Coe, Michael D.
Atlas of ancient America   **970.01**
Mexico   **972**

Coe, Sebastian
See/See also pages in the following book(s):
Sandrock, M. Running with the legends p289-324   **796.42**

Cofer, Judith Ortiz See Ortiz Cofer, Judith, 1952-

The **coffee-cart** girl. Mphahlele, E.
In African short stories   **S C**

Coffee will make you black. Sinclair, A.   **Fic**

Coffey, Rosemary K.
America as story   **016.813**

Coffey, Timothy
The history and folklore of North American wildflowers   **582.13**

Cole, Nat King, 1919?-1965
About
Gourse, L. Unforgettable: the life and mystique of Nat King Cole **92**

Cole, Sylvia
The Facts on File dictionary of 20th-century allusions **031.02**

Cole, Thomas, 1801-1848
See/See also pages in the following book(s):
Novak, B. American painting of the nineteenth century p61-79 **759.13**

Coleman, Bessie, 1896?-1926
See/See also pages in the following book(s):
Yount, L. Women aviators **920**

Coleman, Wanda
Eyes and teeth
In Coming of age in America p212-15 **S C**

Colen, Kimberly
(comp) Hold fast your dreams. See Hold fast your dreams **815.008**

Coleridge, Samuel Taylor, 1772-1834
The portable Coleridge **828**
The rime of the ancient mariner
In Coleridge, S. T. The portable Coleridge **828**
See/See also pages in the following book(s):
Untermeyer, L. Lives of the poets p338-70 **920**

Coleridge, Sara, 1802-1852
Phantasmion [excerpt]
In Masterpieces of fantasy and enchantment p455-64 **S C**

Coles, Joan M.
(jt. auth) Post, E. L. Emily Post's teen etiquette **395**

Colette, 1873-1954
The collected stories of Colette **S C**
Contents: The other table; The screen; Clouk alone; Clouk's fling; Chéri; The return; The pearls; Literature; My goddaughter; A hairdresser; A masseuse; My corset maker; The saleswoman; An interview; A letter; The Sémiramis Bar; "If I had a daughter . . ."; Rites; Newly shorn; Grape harvest; In the boudoir; The "master"; Morning glories; What must we look like?; The cure; Sleepless nights; Gray days; The last fire; A fable: The tendrils of the vine; The halt; Arrival and rehearsal; A bad morning; The circus horse; The workroom; Matinee; The starveling; Love; The hard worker; After midnight; "Lola"; Moments of stress; Journey's end; "The strike, oh, Lord, the strike!"; Bastienne's child; The accompanist; The cashier; Nostalgia; Clever dogs; The child prodigy; The misfit; "La Fenice"; "Gitanette"; The victim; The tenor; The quick-change artist; Florie; Gribiche; The hidden woman; Dawn; One evening; The hand; A dead end; The fox; The judge; The omelette; The other wife; Monsieur Maurice; The burglar; The advice; The murderer; The portrait; The landscape; The half-crazy; Secrets; "Châ"; The bracelet; The find; Mirror games; Habit; Alix's refusal; The seamstress; The watchman; The hollow nut; The patriarch; The sick child; The rainy moon; Green sealing wax; In the flower of age; The rivals; The respite; The bitch; The tender shoot; Bygone spring; October; Armande; The rendezvous; The kepi; The photographer's wife; Bella-Vista; April

Collected early poems, 1950-1970. Rich, A. **811**

The **collected** plays of Neil Simon v2-3. Simon, N. **812**

Collected poems. Aiken, C. **811**
Collected poems. Auden, W. H. **821**
Collected poems. Millay, E. S. **811**

The **collected** poems. Plath, S. **811**
Collected poems & translations. Emerson, R. W. **811**
Collected poems (1909-1935). Eliot, T. S.
In Eliot, T. S. The complete poems and plays, 1909-1950 **818**
Collected poems, 1909-1962. Eliot, T. S. **811**
Collected poems, 1917-1982. MacLeish, A. **811**
Collected poems, 1939-1989. Smith, W. J. **811**
Collected poems, 1947-1980. Ginsberg, A. **811**
Collected poems, 1948-1984. Walcott, D. **811**
The **collected** poems, 1952-1990. Yevtushenko, Y. A. **891.7**
Collected poems, 1953-1993. Updike, J. **811**
The **collected** poems of A. E. Housman. Housman, A. E. **821**
The **collected** poems of Dylan Thomas. Thomas, D. **821**
The **collected** poems of Langston Hughes. Hughes, L. **811**
The **collected** poems of Octavio Paz, 1957-1987. Paz, O. **861**
The **collected** poems of Primo Levi. Levi, P. **851**
The **collected** poems of Theodore Roethke. Roethke, T. **811**
The **collected** poems of Wallace Stevens. Stevens, W. **811**
The **collected** poems of Walter de la Mare. De la Mare, W. **821**
The **collected** poems of William Carlos Williams. Williams, W. C. **811**
Collected poems, prose, & plays. Frost, R. **818**
Collected short stories. Maugham, W. S. **S C**
Collected stories. McCullers, C. **S C**
Collected stories. O'Connor, F. **S C**
The **collected** stories of Colette. Colette **S C**
The **collected** stories of Eudora Welty. Welty, E. **S C**
The **collected** stories of Guy de Maupassant. Maupassant, G. de **S C**
The **collected** stories of Katherine Anne Porter. Porter, K. A. **S C**
Collected stories of William Faulkner. Faulkner, W. **S C**
The **collected** tales and poems of Edgar Allan Poe. Poe, E. A. **S C**
Collected works *See* Storytelling—Collections
Collected works. O'Connor, F. **S C**
Collected writings. Paine, T. **320**
A **collection** of favorite quilts. Florence, J. **746.46**
The **collection** program in schools. Van Orden, P. J. **027.8**
Collections of literature *See* Storytelling—Collections

The **color** of her panties. Anthony, P. See note under Anthony, P. The Magic of Xanth series
Fic

Color purple (Motion picture)
See/See also pages in the following book(s):
Walker, A. The same river twice   92
The **color** purple. Walker, A.   **Fic**
The **colored** girl. Williams, F. B.
In Invented lives p150-56   **S C**
The **colored** museum. Wolfe, G. C.
In Black theatre USA   **812.008**
Coltelli, Laura, 1941-
Winged words: American Indian writers speak
897
Colter, Cyrus, 1910-
The beach umbrella
In The Best short stories by Negro writers
p107-29   **S C**
The lookout
In Calling the wind p305-10   **S C**
Colton, Virginia
(ed) Reader's Digest complete guide to needlework. See Reader's Digest complete guide to needlework   **746.4**
Coltrane, John, 1926-1967
See/See also pages in the following book(s):
Terkel, S. Giants of jazz p173-79   **920**
The **Columbia** anthology of American poetry
811.008
The **Columbia** anthology of British poetry
821.008
The **Columbia** book of Civil War poetry
811.008
The **Columbia** chronicles of American life, 1910-1992. Gordon, L. G.   **973.9**
Columbia dictionary of modern European literature   **803**
The **Columbia** dictionary of modern literary and cultural criticism   **001.3**
The **Columbia** dictionary of quotations. Andrews, R.   **808.88**
The **Columbia** encyclopedia   **031**
The **Columbia** Granger's dictionary of poetry quotations   **808.88**
The **Columbia** Granger's guide to poetry anthologies. Katz, W. A.   **016.80881**
The **Columbia** Granger's index to poetry
808.81
The **Columbia** guide to standard American English. Wilson, K. G.   **428**
The **Columbia** history of American poetry
811.009
The **Columbia** history of British poetry
821.009
Columbus, Christopher
About
Christopher Columbus and his legacy: opposing viewpoints   **970.01**
Meltzer, M. Columbus and the world around him   **92**
See/See also pages in the following book(s):
Durant, W. J. The Reformation p258-68
940.2

Faber, H. The discoverers of America p27-78
970.01
Fiction
Card, O. S. Pastwatch   **Fic**
Columbus and the world around him. Meltzer, M.
92
Comanche Indians
Neeley, B. The last Comanche chief: the life and times of Quanah Parker   **92**
Come back, Little Sheba. Inge, W.
In Best American plays: 3d series—1945-1951 p251-80   **812.008**
In Inge, W. 4 plays p1-69   **812**
Come blow your horn. Simon, N.
In Simon N. The comedy of Neil Simon p11-102   **812**
Come dance with me in Ireland. Jackson, S.
In Jackson, S. The lottery   **S C**
Come home early, chile. Dodson, O.
In The Best short stories by Negro writers p171-80   **S C**
Come out the wilderness. Baldwin, J.
In Calling the wind p163-81   **S C**
Come to grief. Francis, D.   **Fic**
The **comeback** caper. Martens, A. C.
In The Big book of large-cast plays p115-35
812.008
Comedians
Kerr, W. The silent clowns   **791.43**
Comedy
See/See also pages in the following book(s):
Hamilton, E. The Greek way p126-58
880.9
The **comedy** of Neil Simon. Simon, N.   **812**
Comes now the power. Zelazny, R.
In The Norton book of science fiction p161-65   **S C**
Comets
See also Halley's comet
The Great comet crash   **523.6**
Sagan, C. Comet   **523.6**
Yeomans, D. K. Comets   **523.6**
See/See also pages in the following book(s):
Sagan, C. Cosmos p75-83   **520**
The **comforts** of home. O'Connor, F.
In Crime classics p317-38   **S C**
In O'Connor, F. Collected works p573-94
S C
In O'Connor, F. The complete stories p383-404   **S C**
The **comic** book reader's companion. Goulart, R.
741.5
Comic books, strips, etc.
See also Cartoons and caricatures
Daniels, L. Marvel   **741.5**
The Encyclopedia of American comics
741.5
Fleming, R. L. The big book of urban legends
741.5
Goulart, R. The comic book reader's companion
741.5
Goulart, R. The funnies   **741.5**
Harvey, R. C. The art of the comic book
741.5

The **complete** short stories of Ernest Hemingway. Hemingway, E.   **S C**

The **complete** short stories of Guy de Maupassant. See Maupassant, G. de. The collected stories of Guy de Maupassant   **S C**

The **complete** short stories of H. G. Wells. Wells, H. G.   **S C**

The **complete** short stories of Mark Twain. Twain, M.   **S C**

The **complete** short stories of Thomas Wolfe. Wolfe, T.   **S C**

The **complete** stories. Asimov, I.   **S C**

The **complete** stories. Hurston, Z. N.   **S C**

The **complete** stories. Kafka, F.   **S C**

The **complete** stories. O'Connor, F.   **S C**

Complete stories of the great operas, The new Milton Cross'. Cross, M.   **792.5**

The **complete** T. rex. Horner, J. R.   **567.9**

The **complete** tales and poems of Edgar Allan Poe. See Poe, E. A. The collected tales and poems of Edgar Allan Poe   **S C**

The **complete** twenty thousand leagues under the sea. See Verne, J. Twenty thousand leagues under the sea   **Fic**

Complete verse. Kipling, R.   **821**

The **Complete** woodworker   **684**

The **complete** works of William Shakespeare. Shakespeare, W.   **822.3**

Completely Mad. Reidelbach, M.   **741.5**

Complexity (Philosophy)
See/See also pages in the following book(s):
Horgan, J. The end of science p191-226   **501**

Complicities. Adams, A.
In The Best American short stories, 1996 p1-6   **S C**

Composers
Stanley, J. Classical music   **780.9**
Steinberg, M. The symphony   **784.2**
We'll understand it better by and by   **782.25**
See/See also pages in the following book(s):
Grout, D. J. A history of western music   **780.9**

Dictionaries
Composers since 1900   **920.003**
Great composers, 1300-1900   **920.003**
Roche, J. A dictionary of early music   **780.3**

Composers, American
Copland, A. Copland, since 1943   **92**
Haskins, J. Scott Joplin   **92**
Nichols, J. American music makers   **920**
Otfinoski, S. Scott Joplin   **92**

Composers since 1900   **920.003**

Composition (Art)
See/See also pages in the following book(s):
Canaday, J. E. What is art?   **701**

Composition (Rhetoric) *See* Rhetoric

The **Comprehensive** country music encyclopedia   **781.642**

Comprehensive health care organizations *See* Health maintenance organizations

Compton yearbook. See Compton's encyclopedia and fact-index   **031**

Compton's encyclopedia and fact-index   **031**

Compton's interactive encyclopedia. See Compton's encyclopedia and fact-index   **031**

Compulsion (Psychology) *See* Compulsive behavior

Compulsive behavior
Porterfield, K. M. Focus on addictions   **616.86**
Webb, M. Coping with compulsive behavior   **616.85**
See/See also pages in the following book(s):
Landau, E. Hooked   **362.29**

Compulsive gambling
Dolan, E. F. Teenagers and compulsive gambling   **362.7**

Compulsory labor *See* Slavery

Computer assisted instruction
Barron, A. E. The Internet and instruction   **004**
See/See also pages in the following book(s):
The Virtual school library   **027.8**

Computer-based information systems *See* Information systems

The **computer** glossary. Freedman, A.   **004**

Computer industry
Gates, B. The road ahead   **004**

Computer networks
See also Internet (Computer network)

Computer science
See also Electronic data processing

Computer simulation *See* Virtual reality

Computer software
Guide to free computer materials   **004**

Computers
See also Electronic data processing; Microcomputers; Supercomputers
Campbell-Kelly, M. Computer   **004**
Lampton, C. Science of chaos   **003**
See/See also pages in the following book(s):
Inventors and discoverers p246-73   **609**

Dictionaries
Downing, D. Dictionary of computer and Internet terms   **004**
Freedman, A. The computer glossary   **004**
Webster's New World dictionary of computer terms   **004**

Computers and civilization
Stoll, C. Silicon snake oil   **004**

Con artists *See* Swindlers and swindling

Conant, Roger, 1909-
A field guide to reptiles and amphibians, eastern and central North America   **597.6**
Peterson first guide to reptiles and amphibians   **597.6**

Conarroe, Joel, 1934-
(ed) Eight American poets. See Eight American poets   **811.008**

Conaway, James, 1941-
The Smithsonian   **069**

Concentration camps

See also Auschwitz (Poland: Concentration camp); Holocaust, 1933-1945; Japanese Americans—Evacuation and relocation, 1942-1945

Gill, A. The journey back from hell **940.53**

See/See also pages in the following book(s):

Bettelheim, B. Surviving, and other essays p3-124, 274-314 **155.9**

Conception

Prevention

See Birth control

Concerning love. Chekhov, A. P.

In Chekhov, A. P. The Russian master and other stories p136-43 **S C**

Concerning mold upon the skin, etc. Scott, J.

In The Best American short stories, 1993 p217-23 **S C**

Concha. Ponce, M. H.

In Growing up Chicana/o p147-51 **810.8**

The **concise** AACR2, 1988 revision. Gorman, M. **025.3**

The **Concise** Columbia encyclopedia **031**

The **concise** dictionary of national biography. See The Dictionary of national biography: the concise dictionary **920.003**

A **concise** dictionary of slang and unconventional English. Partridge, E. **427**

Concise encyclopedia biology **574.03**

The **concise** encyclopedia of the human body. Burnie, D. **612**

A **concise** history of Germany. Fulbrook, M. **943**

A **concise** history of modern painting. Read, Sir H. E. **759.06**

A **concise** history of modern sculpture. Read, Sir H. E. **735**

A **concise** history of posters: 1870-1970. Barnicoat, J. **741.6**

A **concise** history of the Russian Revolution. Pipes, R. **947.08**

The **concise** illustrated dictionary of science and technology. Gibilisco, S. **503**

The **concise** Oxford companion to American theatre. Bordman, G. M. **792.03**

The **Concise** Oxford companion to the theatre. See The Oxford companion to the theatre **792.03**

The **concise** Oxford dictionary of ballet. Koegler, H. **792.803**

The **Concise** Oxford dictionary of current English **423**

The **Concise** Oxford dictionary of English etymology. See The Oxford dictionary of English etymology **422.03**

The **Concise** Oxford dictionary of literary terms **803**

The **Concise** Oxford dictionary of quotations **808.88**

The **concrete** mixer. Bradbury, R.

In Bradbury, R. The illustrated man **S C**

Il **Conde.** Conrad, J.

In Conrad, J. The complete short fiction of Joseph Conrad v2 p90-104 **S C**

In Conrad, J. The portable Conrad **828**

The **cone.** Wells, H. G.

In Wells, H. G. The complete short stories of H. G. Wells p457-69 **S C**

Coney, Michael

The Byrds

In The Norton book of science fiction p501-12 **S C**

Confederate States of America

The War the women lived **973.7**

Dictionaries

Encyclopedia of the Confederacy **973.7**

Fiction

Kantor, M. Andersonville **Fic**

Confederate States of America. Army

Robertson, J. I., Jr. Tenting tonight **973.7**

The **conference.** Singer, I. B.

In Singer, I. B. The image and other stories p204-10 **S C**

Confession. Garcia, L. G.

In Iguana dreams **S C**

The **confession** of Charles Linkworth. Benson, E. F.

In The Oxford book of English ghost stories p253-65 **S C**

The **confession** stone. Dodson, O.

In Black theatre USA **812.008**

Confessions of an igloo dweller. Houston, J. A. **970.004**

Confessions of faith See Creeds

The **confessions** of Nat Turner. Styron, W. **Fic**

Conflict, Ethnic See Ethnic relations

Conflict of generations

Packer, A. J. Bringing up parents **306.8**

Confucianism

Hoobler, T. Confucianism **299**

See/See also pages in the following book(s):

Durant, W. J. Our Oriental heritage p658-79 **950**

Eastern wisdom **291**

Confucius

The wisdom of Confucius **181**

See/See also pages in the following book(s):

Jaspers, K. The great philosophers **109**

Confused. Singer, I. B.

In Singer, I. B. The image and other stories p270-94 **S C**

Congenital diseases See Medical genetics

Congress (U.S.) See United States. Congress

Congress A to Z **328.73**

Congress and the Nation **328.73**

Congressional Quarterly, Inc.

Baum, L. The Supreme Court **347**

Biskupic, J. The Supreme Court and individual rights **342**

Congress A to Z. See Congress A to Z **328.73**

Congress and the Nation. See Congress and the Nation **328.73**

Congressional Quarterly, Inc.—*Continued*
CQ's state fact finder. *See* CQ's state fact finder
    317.3
How Congress works. *See* How Congress works
    328.73
The Middle East. *See* The Middle East
    956
Presidential elections, 1789-1992. *See* Presidential elections, 1789-1992   324.6
Congressional Quarterly's guide to Congress
    328.73
Congressional Quarterly's guide to the presidency. *See* Guide to the presidency   353.03
Congressional Quarterly's guide to U.S. elections
    324.6
Congressional Quarterly's politics in America
    328.73
Congressional Quarterly's Soviet Union. *See* Russia and the independent states   947
Congreve, William, 1670-1729
The way of the world
  In The Oxford anthology of English literature
    v1   820.8
Conjuring *See* Magic tricks
Conley, Cort, 1944-
(ed) Modern American memoirs. *See* Modern American memoirs   810.8
Conley, Robert J.
Wili Woyi
  In Song of the turtle p52-70   **S C**
Connaroe, Joel
(ed) Six American poets. *See* Six American poets   811.008
A Connecticut Yankee in King Arthur's court. Twain, M.   **Fic**
Connell, Evan S., 1924-
The fisherman from Chihuahua
  In American short story masterpieces
    S C
Connelly, Marc, 1890-1980
Green pastures
  In Twenty best plays of the modern American theatre p191-231   812.008
The traveler
  In 24 favorite one-act plays p219-28
    808.82
Connelly, Thomas Lawrence
(ed) Almanac of American presidents. *See* Almanac of American presidents   920
Conner, Dennis
Learn to sail   797.1
Conner, Michael
Guide dog
  In Nebula awards 27 p16-52   **S C**
Connikie, Yvonne
Fashions of a decade, The 1960s   391
Connor, Richard C.
The lives of whales and dolphins   599.5
Conquering athletic injuries   617.1
The **conquest** of the Incas. Hemming, J.   985
Conrad, Barnaby, 1922-
The complete guide to writing fiction
    808.3

Conrad, Jim
Discover nature in the garden   **574.5**
Conrad, Joseph, 1857-1924
The complete short fiction of Joseph Conrad
    S C
  Contents: v1 The idiots; The lagoon; An outpost of progress; Karain; The return; Youth; Amy Foster; To-morrow; Gaspar Ruiz
  v2 An anarchist; The informer; The brute; The black mate; Il Conde; The secret sharer; Prince Roman; The partner; The Inn of the Two Witches; Because of the dollars; The warrior's soul; The tale
  v3 Heart of darkness; Typhoon; The end of the tether
  v4 Falk: a reminiscence; The duel; A smile of fortune; Freya of the seven isles: a story of shallow waters; The planter of Malata
Heart of darkness   **Fic**
Lord Jim   **Fic**
The Nigger of the "Narcissus"
  In Conrad, J. The portable Conrad   828
The portable Conrad   828
  Short stories included are: Prince Roman; Warrior's soul; Youth; Amy Foster; Outpost of progress; Heart of darkness; Il Conde; The lagoon; The secret sharer
The secret sharer
  In The Oxford book of short stories p109-46
    S C
Typhoon
  In Conrad, J. The portable Conrad   828
    About
Gillon, A. Joseph Conrad   823.009
Reilly, J. Joseph Conrad   92
See/See also pages in the following book(s):
Paterson, J. Edwardians   942.1
Conroy, Frank, 1936-
Midair
  In American short story masterpieces
    S C
  In The Norton book of American short stories p635-50   **S C**
Conroy, Pat
The prince of tides   **Fic**
The water is wide   371.9
The **conscience** of the court. Hurston, Z. N.
  In Hurston, Z. N. The complete stories p162-77   **S C**
Conscientious objectors
  See also Draft resisters
Consciousness
See/See also pages in the following book(s):
Horgan, J. The end of science p159-90
    501
The **conscription** of troops. Kafka, F.
  In Kafka, F. The complete stories   **S C**
The **Conservation** atlas of tropical forests: Africa
    333.75
Conservation movement *See* Environmental movement
Conservation of natural resources
    See also Nature conservation; Wildlife conservation
Amdur, R. Wilderness preservation   333.7
The Conservation atlas of tropical forests: Africa
    333.75
Patent, D. H. The vanishing feast   338.1
Conservation of water *See* Water conservation

Cowhands
Savage, W. W. The cowboy hero 973
Slatta, R. W. Cowboys of the Americas
978

See/See also pages in the following book(s):
Brown, D. A. The American West p59-76
978

Dictionaries
Slatta, R. W. The cowboy encyclopedia
978

Fiction
McCarthy, C. All the pretty horses Fic
Cowles, Frederick I., 1900-1948
The vampire of Kaldenstein
In The Oxford book of gothic tales p407-23
S C

Cox, Don Richard
Arthur Conan Doyle 823.009
Cox, James Melville, 1925-
(ed) Robert Frost: a collection of critical essays.
See Robert Frost: a collection of critical essays 811
Cox, Kathryn
(ed) The Good Housekeeping illustrated guide to women's health. See The Good Housekeeping illustrated guide to women's health 613
Cox, Michael, 1948-
(comp) The Oxford book of English ghost stories. See The Oxford book of English ghost stories S C
(comp) Victorian ghost stories. See Victorian ghost stories S C
Coxe, Louis Osborne, 1918-1993
Billy Budd
In Best American plays: 3d series—1945-1951 p365-93 812.008
A **coyote** is loping across the water. Golden, M.
In Circle of women: an anthology of contemporary Western women writers p300-14
810.8

Coyote learns a new trick. Brant, B.
In Song of the turtle p156-59 S C
Coyotes
Grady, W. The world of the coyote 599.74
Cozic, Charles P., 1957-
(ed) The Abortion controversy. See The Abortion controversy 363.4
(ed) An Aging population: opposing viewpoints. See An Aging population: opposing viewpoints 305.26
(ed) American values: opposing viewpoints. See American values: opposing viewpoints
306
(ed) America's cities: opposing viewpoints. See America's cities: opposing viewpoints
307.7
(ed) America's prisons: opposing viewpoints. See America's prisons: opposing viewpoints
365
(ed) Civil liberties: opposing viewpoints. See Civil liberties: opposing viewpoints 323
(ed) Education in America: opposing viewpoints. See Education in America: opposing viewpoints 370.9

(ed) Energy alternatives. See Energy alternatives
333.79
(ed) Gambling. See Gambling [Current controversies] 363.4
(ed) Gangs: opposing viewpoints. See Gangs: opposing viewpoints 364.1
(ed) Illegal immigration: opposing viewpoints. See Illegal immigration: opposing viewpoints
325.73
(ed) The Information highway. See The Information highway 004
(ed) Israel: opposing viewpoints. See Israel: opposing viewpoints 956.94
(ed) Nationalism and ethnic conflict. See Nationalism and ethnic conflict 305.8
(ed) Nuclear proliferation: opposing viewpoints. See Nuclear proliferation: opposing viewpoints 327.1
(ed) Pollution. See Pollution 363.7
(ed) Sexual values: opposing viewpoints. See Sexual values: opposing viewpoints
306.7
(ed) Space exploration: opposing viewpoints. See Space exploration: opposing viewpoints
629.4

Cozine, Andrew
Hand jive
In The Best American short stories, 1995 p175-94 S C
CQ *See* Congressional Quarterly, Inc.
CQ's state fact finder 317.3
Crabbe, Katharyn W., 1945-
J.R.R. Tolkien 823.009
Crack (Drug)
Berger, G. Crack 616.86
Crack babies *See* Children of drug addicts
Crack cocaine *See* Crack (Drug)
The **cracked** looking-glass. Porter, K. A.
In Porter, K. A. The collected stories of Katherine Anne Porter S C
Cracking the SAT & PSAT. Robinson, A.
378.1
Cracking the SAT II [subject tests] 378.1
Craft, William, 19th cent.
Running a thousand miles for freedom
In Great slave narratives p269-331 920
Crafts (Arts) *See* Handicraft
Craig, Albert M.
(jt. auth) Reischauer, E. O. Japan, tradition & transformation 952
Craig Claiborne's The New York Times food encyclopedia. Claiborne, C. 641.03
Craik, Dinah Maria Mulock, 1826-1887
The last house in C— Street
In Victorian ghost stories p44-54 S C
Merlin and Tom Thumb
In The Merlin chronicles S C
Crain, Esther
(jt. auth) Katz, W. A. The Columbia Granger's guide to poetry anthologies 016.80881
Cramer, Kathryn, 1962-
(comp) Masterpieces of fantasy and enchantment. See Masterpieces of fantasy and enchantment S C

Cran, William
(jt. auth) McCrum, R. The story of English
420

Cranberries (Musical group)
See/See also pages in the following book(s):
Reisfeld, R. This is the sound **781.66**

Cranch, Christopher Pearse, 1813-1892
The last of the Huggermuggers: a giant story
In Masterpieces of fantasy and enchantment
p339-67 **S C**

Crane, Hart, 1899-1932
See/See also pages in the following book(s):
Voices & visions p313-54 **811.009**

Crane, Nancy
(jt. auth) Li, X. Electronic styles **808**

Crane, Stephen, 1871-1900
The complete poems of Stephen Crane **811**
The little regiment
In The Oxford book of American short stories
p225-43 **S C**
Maggie: a girl of the streets; criticism
In Stephen Crane: a collection of critical essays p106-17 **818**
The open boat
In Classic American short stories p251-82
S C
In The Norton book of American short stories
p182-203 **S C**
In The Oxford book of short stories p179-201
S C
Prose and poetry **818**
The red badge of courage **Fic**
Red badge of courage; criticism
In Critical essays on Stephen Crane's The red
badge of courage **813.009**
In Stephen Crane: a collection of critical essays p95-105, 123-49 **818**
About
Cady, E. H. Stephen Crane **813.009**
Stephen Crane: a collection of critical essays
818

Crank, Dan L.
Neon powwow
In Song of the turtle p297-301 **S C**

Craters, caverns, and canyons. Erickson, J.
551.1

Craven, Margaret
Again calls the owl **92**
I heard the owl call my name **Fic**

Craver, Kathleen W.
School library media centers in the 21st century
027.8

Crawdaddy. Williams, D. A.
In Streetlights: illuminating tales of the urban
black experience p487-97 **S C**

Crawford, F. Marion (Francis Marion), 1854-1909
The upper berth
In Classic ghost stories p272-92 **S C**
In The Oxford book of English ghost stories
p69-86 **S C**

Crawford, Francis Marion *See* Crawford, F.
Marion (Francis Marion), 1854-1909

Crawford, Ruth *See* Seeger, Ruth Crawford,
1901-1953

Crayton, Pearl
The day the world almost came to an end
In The Best short stories by Negro writers
p325-31 **S C**
In Rites of passage p25-32 **S C**

Crazy Horse, Sioux Chief, ca. 1842-1877
About
Goldman, M. S. Crazy Horse **92**
Fiction
Blevins, W. Stone song **Fic**

Crazy Sunday. Fitzgerald, F. S.
In Fitzgerald, F. S. The short stories of F.
Scott Fitzgerald p698-713 **S C**
In Fitzgerald, F. S. The stories of F. Scott
Fitzgerald p403-18 **S C**

CRC handbook of chemistry and physics **540**

Creamer, Robert W.
Babe [Ruth] **92**

Created equal. Brodie, J. M. **920**

Creating characters. Swain, D. V. **808.3**

Creating newsletters, brochures, and pamphlets.
Blake, B. R. **070.5**

Creation
Eve, R. A. The creationist movement in modern
America **213**
Dictionaries
Leeming, D. A. Encyclopedia of creation myths
291.03

Creationism
See also Evolution
The **creationist** movement in modern America.
Eve, R. A. **213**

Creation's journey **709.73**

Creative ability
Edwards, B. Drawing on the right side of the
brain **741.2**
Grudin, R. The grace of great things **153.3**
Secrets of the inner mind **154**

Creative bead jewelry. Taylor, C. **745.58**

Creative fire **700**

The **creative** impulse. Maugham, W. S.
In Maugham, W. S. Collected short stories v2
S C

Creative mythology. Campbell, J.
In Campbell, J. The masks of God v4
291

Creative nonfiction. Gutkind, L. **808**

Creative writing
Dalton, R. The student's guide to good writing
808
O'Connor, S. Will my name be shouted out?
808

Creature. Saul, J. **Fic**

Creeds
The Encyclopedia of American religions: religious creeds **291**

Creel, Herrlee Glessner, 1905-1994
Chinese thought from Confucius to Mao Tsê-tung **181**

Crete (Greece)
See/See also pages in the following book(s):
Ceram, C. W. Gods, graves, and scholars p56-72 **930.1**

Crete (Greece)—*Continued*
Fiction
Kazantzakis, N. Zorba the Greek   Fic

Crevasse. Faulkner, W.
In Faulkner, W. Collected stories of William Faulkner p465-74   S C

Crewel lye. Anthony, P. See note under Anthony, P. The Magic of Xanth series   Fic

Crews: gang members talk to Maria Hinojosa. Hinojosa, M.   302.3

Cribb, Joe
The coin atlas   737.4

Crichton, Michael, 1942-
The Andromeda strain   Fic
Jurassic Park   Fic

Crick, Francis, 1916-
See/See also pages in the following book(s):
Brynie, F. H. Genetics & human health p58-65   616
Curtis, R. H. Great lives: medicine p250-60   920

Criddle, Joan D.
To destroy you is no loss   959.6

Crime
    See also Hate crimes; Homicide; Trials; White collar crimes
Bode, J. Hard time   364.3
Crime and criminals: opposing viewpoints   364
Criminal sentencing   345
Meltzer, M. Crime in America   364
Roth, M. The writer's complete crime reference book   808.3
See/See also pages in the following book(s):
Korem, D. Suburban gangs   364.1

Crime and criminals: opposing viewpoints   364

Crime and drugs *See* Drugs and crime

Crime and mystery: the 100 best books. Keating, H. R. F.   823.009

Crime and punishment. Dostoyevsky, F.   Fic

Crime classics   S C

Crime in America. Meltzer, M.   364

Crime must have a stop. Boucher, A.
In The Oxford book of American detective stories p480-98   S C

Crime syndicates *See* Organized crime

Crimes, White collar *See* White collar crimes

Crimes of conscience. Gordimer, N.   S C

Crimes of conscience [story] Gordimer, N.
In Gordimer, N. Crimes of conscience p82-87   S C

Crimes of the heart. Henley, B.   812
also in Best American plays: 8th series— 1974-1982 p518-48   812.008

A criminal act. Harrison, H.
In The Oxford book of science fiction stories p350-62   S C

Criminal investigation
    See also Forensic anthropology
Fisher, D. Hard evidence   363.2

Criminal justice, Administration of *See* Administration of criminal justice

Criminal justice: opposing viewpoints   345

Criminal sentencing   345

Criminals
    See also Thieves
Crime and criminals: opposing viewpoints   364
Nash, J. R. Bloodletters and badmen   920
Drug use
    See also Drugs and crime
Fiction
Kerr, M. E. Gentlehands   Fic

Crippen, Cynthia
(jt. auth) Leonard, T. M. Day by day: the seventies   909.82

The cripple. Andersen, H. C.
In Andersen, H. C. Tales and stories   S C

Criscoe, Betty L., 1940-
Award-winning books for children and young adults   011.6

Crisfield, Deborah
Pick-up games   790.1

Crisis in the Pacific. Astor, G.   940.54

Crisis of the month. Bova, B.
In Bova, B. Challenges p35-52   S C

Crispin, Edmund, 1921-1978
See/See also pages in the following book(s):
Modern mystery writers p61-74   809.3

The critic as artist. Wilde, O.
In Wilde, O. The portable Oscar Wilde p51-136   828

Critical essays on Eudora Welty   813.009

Critical essays on F. Scott Fitzgerald's Tender is the night   813.009

Critical essays on Franz Kafka   833.009

Critical essays on Henry David Thoreau's Walden   818

Critical essays on Henry James: the early novels   813.009

Critical essays on Henry James: the late novels   813.009

Critical essays on James Joyce   823.009

Critical essays on John Keats   821

Critical essays on Nadine Gordimer   823.009

Critical essays on Steinbeck's The grapes of wrath   813.009

Critical essays on Stephen Crane's The red badge of courage   813.009

Critical essays on Thomas Hardy   823.009

Critical essays on W.B. Yeats   821

Critical essays on Washington Irving   818

Critical essays on William Golding. Baker, J. R.   823.009

Critical essays on William Wordsworth   821

Critical survey of drama   822.009

Critical survey of short fiction   809.3

Criticism
    See also Books—Reviews
The New Moulton's library of literary criticism   820.9

Cruelty to animals See Animal welfare

'Cruiter. Matheus, J. F.
In Black theatre USA   **812.008**

Crumb, George
See/See also pages in the following book(s):
Nichols, J. American music makers p150-69
    920

Crusader Rabbit. Mowry, J.
In Children of the night p262-68   **S C**

Crusades
The Oxford illustrated history of the Crusades
    909.07
Runciman, Sir S. A history of the Crusades
    909.07
See/See also pages in the following book(s):
Durant, W. J. The age of faith p585-613
    940.1
Tuchman, B. W. A distant mirror p545-63
    944

        Maps
Riley-Smith, J. The atlas of the Crusades
    911

Crutcher, Chris, 1946-
Athletic shorts: six short stories   **S C**
Contents: A brief moment in the life of Angus Bethune; The pin; The other pin; Goin' fishin'; Telephone man; In the time I get
Running loose   **Fic**
Staying fat for Sarah Byrnes   **Fic**

Cruz, Victor Hernández, 1949-
(ed) Paper dance. See Paper dance   **811.008**

Cruzan, Nancy
See/See also pages in the following book(s):
Suicide p54-75   **362.2**

Cry, the beloved country. Paton, A.   **Fic**

Cryptography
Wrixon, F. B. Codes and ciphers   **652**

Crystal, David, 1941-
The Cambridge encyclopedia of language
    400
The Cambridge encyclopedia of the English language   **420**

The crystal cave. Stewart, M.
In Stewart, M. Mary Stewart's Merlin trilogy
    Fic

The crystal egg. Wells, H. G.
In Wells, H. G. The complete short stories of H. G. Wells p625-43   **S C**

The crystal stars have just begun to shine. Brooks, M.
In Brooks, M. Paradise Café and other stories p115-24   **S C**

Cuba
        History—1959-
See/See also pages in the following book(s):
Manchester, W. The glory and the dream p893-908, 958-71   **973.9**
        History—1961, Invasion
Persons, A. C. Bay of Pigs   **972.91**
        Pictorial works
Kufeld, A. Cuba   **972.91**
        Politics and government
Beyer, D. E. Castro!   **92**
Geyer, G. A. Guerrilla prince: the untold story of Fidel Castro   **92**

¡Cuba si!. McNally, T.
In McNally, T. 15 short plays p83-96
    812

Cuban Americans
Hoobler, D. The Cuban American family album
    305.8

Cuban Missile Crisis, 1962
Finkelstein, N. H. Thirteen days/ninety miles
    973.922

Cubism
See/See also pages in the following book(s):
Arnason, H. H. History of modern art: painting, sculpture, architecture   **709.04**
Read, Sir H. E. A concise history of modern painting   **759.06**

Cuddon, J. A. (John Anthony), 1928-
A dictionary of literary terms and literary theory
    803

Cuddon, John Anthony See Cuddon, J. A. (John Anthony), 1928-

Culhane, John
The American circus: an illustrated history
    791.3

Cullen, Countee, 1903-1946
My soul's high song   **818**
One way to heaven
In Cullen, C. My soul's high song p343-531
    818
One way to heaven [excerpt]
In The Portable Harlem Renaissance reader p680-93   **810.8**
See/See also pages in the following book(s):
Black American prose writers of the Harlem Renaissance p25-35   **810.9**

Cullen-DuPont, Kathryn
Elizabeth Cady Stanton and women's liberty
    92
The encyclopedia of women's history in America   **305.4**
(jt. auth) Frost-Knappman, E. Women's suffrage in America   **324.6**

The cult at the end of the world. Kaplan, D. E.
    291

Cultivated plants See House plants; Ornamental plants

Cults
    See also Satanism; Sects
Melton, J. G. Encyclopedic handbook of cults in America   **291**
Porterfield, K. M. Straight talk about cults
    291
Religious cults in America   **291**

Cultural anthropology See Ethnology

Cultural atlas of Mesopotamia and the ancient Near East. Roaf, M.   **935**

Cultural atlas of Spain and Portugal. Vincent, M.
    946

Cultural atlas of the Viking world   **948**

A cultural history of the French Revolution. Kennedy, E.   **944.04**

Cultural pluralism See Multiculturalism

Culturally deprived children See Socially handicapped children

A **curtain** of green, and other stories. Welty, E.
In Welty, E. The collected stories of Eudora
Welty p1-149   **S C**

Curtis, Nancy C.
Black heritage sites   **917.3**

Curtis, Robert H.
Great lives: medicine   **920**

Curtiss, Ursula Reilly, 1923-1984
The marked man
In Masterpieces of mystery and suspense
p526-36   **S C**

Cusanus, Nicolaus *See* Nicholas, of Cusa, Cardinal, 1401-1464

Cush, Cathie, 1957-
Depression   **616.85**

Cushi. Woodforde, C.
In The Oxford book of English ghost stories
p458-64   **S C**

Cushites
See/See also pages in the following book(s):
Splendors of the past p144-81   **930**

Cushman, Charlotte, 1816-1876
About
Faber, D. Love & rivalry   **920**

Cushman, Clare
(ed) The Supreme Court justices. See The Supreme Court justices   **920.003**

Cussans, Thomas
(ed) The Times atlas of European history. See
The Times atlas of European history   **911**

Custard, Edward T.
The complete book of colleges   **378.73**

Custer, George Armstrong, 1839-1876
About
Barnett, L. K. Touched by fire: the life, death,
and mythic afterlife of George Armstrong
Custer   **92**
Sandoz, M. The Battle of the Little Bighorn
                                               973.8
Wert, J. D. Custer   **92**

Custer died for your sins. Deloria, V.
                                               970.004

Customs, Social *See* Manners and customs

Customs. Alvarez, J.
In Iguana dreams   **S C**

Cuthbertson, Tom
Cuthbertson's all-in-one bike repair manual
                                               629.227

Cuthbertson's all-in-one bike repair manual.
Cuthbertson, T.   **629.227**

CyberHound's guide to Internet databases
                                               004

Cycles of life   **970.004**

Cycling
See also Bicycle touring; Bicycles; Motorcycles
Ballantine, R. Richards' ultimate bicycle book
                                               629.227

Cyclones
See also Hurricanes

Cyclopedia of literary characters II   **803**

Cyrano de Bergerac, 1619-1655
Drama
See/See also pages in the following book(s):
Burgess, A. Cyrano de Bergerac   **822**

Czars. Duffy, J. P.   **947**

Czech Americans
Fiction
Cather, W. My Antonia   **Fic**

D

D Day *See* Normandy (France), Attack on, 1944

D-Day, June 6, 1944. Ambrose, S. E.   **940.54**

D.H. Lawrence's Sons and lovers   **823.009**

D.N.A. *See* DNA

D.P.. Vonnegut, K.
In Vonnegut, K. Welcome to the monkey
house   **S C**

Da, Ngan
Above the woman's house
In The Other side of heaven p313-21
                                               S C

Da Vinci, Leonardo *See* Leonardo, da Vinci,
1452-1519

Dadaism
See/See also pages in the following book(s):
Arnason, H. H. History of modern art: painting,
sculpture, architecture   **709.04**
Read, Sir H. E. A concise history of modern
painting   **759.06**

Daddy Garbage. Wideman, J. E.
In The Vintage book of contemporary
American short stories p521-36   **S C**

The **daemon** lover. Jackson, S.
In Jackson, S. The lottery   **S C**

Dafydd ab Hugh
The Coon rolled down and ruptured his larinks,
a squeezed novel by Mr. Skunk
In Nebula awards 26 p195-221   **S C**

Dahl, Roald
Boy: tales of childhood   **92**
Going solo   **92**
About
West, M. I. Roald Dahl   **823.009**

Daily life in Chaucer's England. Singman, J. L.
                                               942.03

Daily life in colonial America   **973.2**

Daily life in Elizabethan England. Singman, J. L.
                                               942.05

Daily life in the world of Charlemagne. Riché, P.
                                               944

Daintith, John
(ed) The Facts on File dictionary of chemistry.
See The Facts on File dictionary of chemistry
                                               540.3

Dakota Indians
See also Oglala Indians
Anderson, G. C. Little Crow, spokesman for the
Sioux   **92**
Brave Bird, M. Lakota woman   **92**
Crow Dog, L. Crow Dog   **970.004**
Flood, R. S. Lost Bird of Wounded Knee
                                               92

Dante Alighieri, 1265-1321—*Continued*
The portable Dante   851
See/See also pages in the following book(s):
Durant, W. J. The age of faith p1056-81
   940.1
Highet, G. The classical tradition p70-80
   809

Danticat, Edwidge, 1969-
Krik? Krak!   **S C**
Contents: Between the pool and the gardenias; Caroline's wedding; Children of the sea; The missing peace; New York day women; Night women; Nineteen thirty-seven; Seeing things simply; A wall of fire rising
New York day women
In Children of the night p562-66   **S C**

Danube River valley
Description
See/See also pages in the following book(s):
Great rivers of the world p95-128   **910**

Darcy in the Land of Youth. O'Connor, F.
In O'Connor, F. Collected stories p262-82
   S C

The **dare**. Ellis, C.
In Bad behavior p125-31   **S C**

Dared and done: the marriage of Elizabeth Barrett and Robert Browning. Markus, J.   **92**

Darion, Joe, 1917-
Wasserman, D. Man of La Mancha   **812**

Dark, Alice Elliott
In the gloaming
In The Best American short stories, 1994 p61-78   **S C**

Dark, Larry
(ed) The Literary ghost. See The Literary ghost
   S C

The **dark**. Fowler, K. J.
In Nebula awards 27 p126-44   **S C**

Dark Ages *See* Middle Ages

The **dark** at the top of the stairs. Inge, W.
In Best American plays: 5th series—1957-1963 p105-42   **812.008**
In Inge, W. 4 plays p221-304   **812**

Dark harvest: migrant farmworkers in America. Ashabranner, B. K.   **331.5**

Dark in the forest, strange as time. Wolfe, T.
In Wolfe, T. The complete short stories of Thomas Wolfe p167-76   **S C**

The **dark** messiah. Wolfe, T.
In Wolfe, T. The complete short stories of Thomas Wolfe p459-64   **S C**

The **dark** princess [excerpt] Du Bois, W. E. B.
In The Portable Harlem Renaissance reader p511-35   **810.8**

Dark sun. Rhodes, R.   **623.4**

Dark they were, and golden-eyed. Bradbury, R.
In Bradbury, R. The stories of Ray Bradbury p469-80   **S C**

Darker than just before the dawn. MaGowan, J. H.
In Bad behavior p185-90   **S C**

Darkness at noon. Kingsley, S.
In Best American plays: 3d series—1945-1951 p505-43   **812.008**

Darkness at noon. Koestler, A.   **Fic**

Darling, Grace
Fiction
Paton Walsh, J. Grace   **Fic**

Darling, James David, 1950-
Whales, dolphins, and porpoises. See Whales, dolphins, and porpoises [National Geographic Soc.]   **599.5**

The **darling**. Bradfield, S.
In The Vintage book of contemporary American short stories p69-88   **S C**

Darlington, David
The Mojave   **979.4**

DARPA Internet (Computer network) *See* Internet (Computer network)

Darton, Michael
The Macmillan dictionary of measurement
   389

Darwin, Charles, 1809-1882
The Darwin reader   **575.01**
The essential Darwin   **575.01**
The portable Darwin   **575.01**
The voyage of the Beagle   **508**
About
Bowlby, J. Charles Darwin   **92**
Bowler, P. J. Darwinism   **575.01**
Milner, R. Charles Darwin   **92**
White, M. Darwin   **92**
See/See also pages in the following book(s):
Jastrow, R. Red giants and white dwarfs p218-30   **523.1**
Meadows, A. J. The great scientists   **920**
Tudge, C. The time before history   **573.2**

Darwinism *See* Evolution

Darwinism. Bowler, P. J.   **575.01**

Dasch, E. Julius (Ernest Julius), 1932-
(ed) Encyclopedia of earth sciences. See Encyclopedia of earth sciences   **550.3**

Dasch, Ernest Julius *See* Dasch, E. Julius (Ernest Julius), 1932-

Dash, Joan
The triumph of discovery: women scientists who won the Nobel Prize   **920**
We shall not be moved   **331.4**

Dashefsky, H. Steven
Botany   **581**
Environmental literacy   **363.7**
Environmental science   **574.5**
Microbiology: 49 science fair projects   **576**
Microbiology: high-school science fair experiments   **576**
Zoology: 49 science fair projects   **591**
Zoology: high school science fair experiments
   591

Data processing *See* Electronic data processing

Data storage and retrieval systems *See* Information systems

Dateline: Troy. Fleischman, P.   **292**

Dating (Social customs)
Landau, E. Interracial dating and marriage
   306.7
Levy, B. In love and in danger   **362.7**
Mufson, S. Straight talk about date rape
   362.88

Davis, Paul K., 1952-
Encyclopedia of invasions and conquests from ancient times to the present **355**

Davis, Rebecca Harding, 1831-1910
Life in the iron-mills
In The Oxford book of women's writing in the United States p198-228 **810.8**

Davis, Richard Harding, 1864-1916
Gallegher
In The Best crime stories of the 19th century p96-125 **S C**

Davis, Terry
If rock and roll were a machine **Fic**

Davis, William C., 1946-
Brother against brother: the war begins **973.7**
Death in the trenches: Grant at Petersburg **973.7**
First blood: Fort Sumter to Bull Run **973.7**

Davis, William Stearns, 1877-1930
A day in old Rome **937**

Davison, Michael Worth
(ed) Everyday life through the ages. See Everyday life through the ages **909**

Davita's harp [excerpt] Potok, C.
In Coming of age in America p239-53 **S C**

Dawidowicz, Lucy S.
The war against the Jews, 1933-1945 **940.53**

Dawn. Colette
In Colette. The collected stories of Colette p239-41 **S C**

Dawn. Purdy, J.
In Growing up gay p175-78 **808.8**

Dawn. Wiesel, E.
In Wiesel, E. Night, Dawn, The accident: three tales **Fic**

Dawn of art. Chauvet, J.-M. **759.01**

Dawson, Anthony B.
Watching Shakespeare: a playgoers' guide **822.3**

Day, A. Grove (Arthur Grove), 1904-
The sky clears: poetry of the American Indians **897**

Day, Arthur Grove *See* Day, A. Grove (Arthur Grove), 1904-

Day, David, 1944-
(jt. auth) Jackson, A. The complete manual of woodworking **684**

Day, David, 1949-
The search for King Arthur **942.01**

Day, John, 1948-
(ed) Oxford Bible atlas. See Oxford Bible atlas **220.9**

Day, Nancy
Abortion **363.4**
Sensational TV **791.45**

Day, Paul
(jt. auth) Bacon, T. The ultimate guitar book **787.87**

Day, Teresa Thurman
(ed) Automation for school libraries. See Automation for school libraries **027.8**

A day at Niagara. Twain, M.
In Twain, M. The complete short stories of Mark Twain **S C**

The day before America. MacLeish, W. H. **970.01**

Day by day: the eighties. Meltzer, E. **909.82**

Day by day: the seventies. Leonard, T. M. **909.82**

Day by day: the sixties. Parker, T. **909.82**

The day Christ died. Bishop, J. **232.9**

A day in old Rome. Davis, W. S. **937**

A day in the country. Jacobson, D.
In Somehow tenderness survives p37-47 **S C**

A day in the life. Hertsgaard, M. **781.66**

The day it rained forever. Bradbury, R.
In Bradbury, R. The stories of Ray Bradbury p497-505 **S C**

The day Lincoln was shot. Bishop, J. **973.7**

Day million. Pohl, F.
In The Norton book of science fiction p166-70 **S C**
In Robert Silverberg's Worlds of wonder **S C**

A day no pigs would die. Peck, R. N. **Fic**

Day of absence. Ward, D. T.
In Black theatre USA **812.008**

Day of infamy. Lord, W. **940.54**

Day of the hunters. Asimov, I.
In Asimov, I. The complete stories v2 p105-11 **S C**

The day the Cisco Kid shot John Wayne. Candelaria, N.
In Growing up Latino p115-30 **810.8**

The day the pig fell into the well. Cheever, J.
In Cheever, J. The stories of John Cheever p219-35 **S C**

The day the war ended. Gilbert, M. **940.54**

The day the world almost came to an end. Crayton, P.
In The Best short stories by Negro writers p325-31 **S C**
In Rites of passage p25-32 **S C**

A day with Conrad Green. Lardner, R.
In Lardner, R. The best short stories of Ring Lardner p127-38 **S C**

The daybreakers. L'Amour, L. See note under L'Amour, L. The Sacketts **Fic**

A daylight adventure. Stribling, T. S.
In The Oxford book of American detective stories p456-70 **S C**

A day's lodging. London, J.
In London, J. Short stories of Jack London p219-32 **S C**

Days of grace. Ashe, A. **92**

Days of judgment. Morin, I. V. **940.54**

The days of the French Revolution. Hibbert, C. **944.04**

Days of the West. See Flanagan, M. The Old West **978**

A day's wait. Hemingway, E.
In Hemingway, E. The complete short stories of Ernest Hemingway p332-34 **S C**

De Veaux, Alexis, 1948—_Continued_
The riddles of Egypt Brownstone
_In_ Black-eyed Susans/Midnight birds p180-91
S C

The tapestry
_In_ 9 plays by black women   **811.008**

De Vitis, A. A.
Graham Greene   **823.009**

De Vos, Gail, 1949-
Storytelling for young adults   **372.6**

The **deacon's** awakening. Richardson, W.
_In_ Black theatre USA   **812.008**

The **dead.** Joyce, J.
_In_ Joyce, J. Dubliners   **S C**
_In_ The Oxford book of Irish short stories
p228-66   **S C**

A **dead** body. Chekhov, A. P.
_In_ Chekhov, A. P. The image of Chekhov
p84-89   **S C**

A **dead** end. Colette
_In_ Colette. The collected stories of Colette
p249-51   **S C**

Dead end. Kingsley, S.
_In_ Twenty best plays of the modern American
theatre p681-738   **812.008**

The **dead** past. Asimov, I.
_In_ Asimov, I. The complete stories v1 p3-40
S C

Deaf
Keller, H. The story of my life   **92**
Lash, J. P. Helen and teacher: the story of
Helen Keller and Anne Sullivan Macy
92
Mango, K. N. Hearing loss   **617.8**
Nicholson, L. Helen Keller   **92**
See/See also pages in the following book(s):
Cheney, G. A. Teens with physical disabilities
p39-49   **362.4**
Drama
Medoff, M. H. Children of a lesser god
812
Education
Neimark, A. E. A deaf child listened: Thomas
Gallaudet, pioneer in American education
92
Fiction
McCullers, C. The heart is a lonely hunter
Fic

Means of communication
See also Sign language
Cohen, L. H. Train go sorry   **371.9**

A **deaf** child listened: Thomas Gallaudet, pioneer
in American education. Neimark, A. E.
92

A **deal** in ostriches. Wells, H. G.
_In_ Wells, H. G. The complete short stories of
H. G. Wells p225-29   **S C**

Dean, John Aurie, 1921-
(ed) Lange's handbook of chemistry. See
Lange's handbook of chemistry   **540**

DeAndrea, William L.
Encyclopedia mysteriosa   **809.3**

Dear, I. C. B. _See_ Dear, Ian, 1935-

Dear, Ian, 1935-
(ed) The Oxford companion to World War II.
See The Oxford companion to World War II
940.53

Dear Alexandros. Updike, J.
_In_ Updike, J. Pigeon feathers, and other stories p102-08   **S C**

Dear America: letters home from Vietnam
959.704

Dear author   **028.5**

Dear departed. Houghton, S.
_In_ Thirty famous one-act plays p269-81
808.82

Dear Mr. Lincoln   **973.7**

Dearly beloved. Fitzgerald, F. S.
_In_ Fitzgerald, F. S. The short stories of F.
Scott Fitzgerald p773-75   **S C**

The **dearly** beloved of Benjamin Cobb. Dane, C.
_In_ Classic English short stories, 1930-1955
p320-48   **S C**

Death
See also Terminal care
Bode, J. Death is hard to live with   **155.9**
Death and dying: opposing viewpoints
155.9
DiGiulio, R. C. Straight talk about death and
dying   **155.9**
Gootman, M. E. When a friend dies   **155.9**
Gravelle, K. Teenagers face to face with be-
reavement   **155.9**
Grollman, E. A. Straight talk about death for
teenagers   **155.9**
Kübler-Ross, E. Living with death and dying
155.9
Kübler-Ross, E. On death and dying   **155.9**
Nuland, S. B. How we die   **616.07**
What survives?   **133.9**
Fiction
Agee, J. A death in the family   **Fic**
Craven, M. I heard the owl call my name
Fic
Draper, S. M. Tears of a tiger   **Fic**
Mazer, N. F. After the rain   **Fic**
Rodowsky, C. F. Remembering Mog   **Fic**
Poetry
Stopping for death   **808.81**

Death. Anderson, S.
_In_ Anderson, S. Winesburg, Ohio   **S C**

Death and dying: opposing viewpoints   **155.9**

Death and the compass. Borges, J. L.
_In_ Crime classics p285-98   **S C**

Death and the librarian. Friesner, E. M.
_In_ Nebula awards 31 p59-73   **S C**

Death at an early age. Kozol, J.   **370.19**

Death be not proud [biography of his son] Gunther, J.   **92**

Death by drowning. Christie, A.
_In_ Christie, A. Miss Marple: the complete
short stories   **S C**

Death comes for the archbishop. Cather, W.
Fic

The **death** disk. Twain, M.
_In_ Twain, M. The complete short stories of
Mark Twain   **S C**

A **deep** purple. Allen, P. G.
  In Spider Woman's granddaughters   **S C**
Deer in the works. Vonnegut, K.
  In Vonnegut, K. Welcome to the monkey
  house   **S C**
Deer Woman. Allen, P. G.
  In Talking leaves   **S C**
The **defeat** of the city. Henry, O.
  In Henry, O. The best short stories of O.
  Henry   **S C**
The **defeat** of the Spanish Armada. See Mattingly,
  G. The Armada   **942.05**
Defender of the faith. Roth, P.
  In Roth, P. Goodbye, Columbus, and five
  short stories   **S C**
A **defense** of the social contracts. Soukup, M.
  In Nebula awards 30 p222-38   **S C**
Deffaa, Chip, 1951-
  Voices of the Jazz Age   **920**
Deficit financing
  Balancing the federal budget   **336.3**
Deficit spending See Deficit financing
Defoe, Daniel, 1661?-1731
  The apparition of Mrs. Veal
    In Classic ghost stories p207-10   **S C**
  Robinson Crusoe   **Fic**
About
  Daniel Defoe   **823.009**
DeFord, Miriam Allen, 1888-1975
  Who was when?   **902**
Degas, Edgar, 1834-1917
  Degas by Degas   **759.4**
About
  Meyer, S. E. Edgar Degas   **92**
Degas, Hilaire Germain Edgar See Degas, Edgar,
  1834-1917
Degas by Degas. Degas, E.   **759.4**
Deighton, Len, 1929-
  Blood, tears, and folly   **940.54**
Deities See Gods and goddesses
Deitsch, Jeremy Stafford- See Stafford-Deitsch,
  Jeremy
Del Castillo, Richard Griswold See Griswold del
  Castillo, Richard
Delaney, Edward J.
  The drowning
    In The Best American short stories, 1995
    p126-40   **S C**
Delany, Annie Elizabeth See Delany, Bessie
Delany, Bessie
  (jt. auth) Delany, S. Having our say   **92**
Delany, Martin R., 1812-1885
  See/See also pages in the following book(s):
  Black American prose writers before the Harlem
  Renaissance p35-48   **810.9**
Delany, Sadie
  Having our say   **92**
Delany, Samuel R.
  High weir
    In The Norton book of science fiction p183-
    200   **S C**
  Night and the loves of Joe Dicostanzo
    In Calling the wind p289-304   **S C**

The tale of dragons and dreamers
  In Masterpieces of fantasy and enchantment
  p426-54   **S C**
The tale of Gorgik
  In Children of the night p5-57   **S C**
See/See also pages in the following book(s):
  Contemporary black American fiction writers
  p15-29   **813.009**
Delany, Sarah Louise See Delany, Sadie
Delany family
About
  Delany, S. Having our say   **92**
Delaware
History
  Fisher, S. G. The Quaker colonies   **973.2**
Delaware Indians
Fiction
  Richter, C. The light in the forest   **Fic**
Legends
  The White deer and other stories told by the
  Lenape   **398.2**
DeLillo, Don
  The angel Esmeralda
    In The Best American short stories, 1995
    p263-83   **S C**
Delinquency, Juvenile See Juvenile delinquency
Delisle, James R.
  (jt. auth) Galbraith, J. The gifted kids' survival
  guide   **155.5**
Deliver us from Evie. Kerr, M. E.   **Fic**
Deloria, Ella Cara, 1888-1971
  Blue Bird's offering
    In Spider Woman's granddaughters   **S C**
  Waterlily [excerpt]
    In Growing up Native American p57-71
    810.8
Deloria, Vine
  American Indians, American justice
    970.004
  Custer died for your sins   **970.004**
  The nations within: the past and future of
  American Indian sovereignty   **323.1**
  Red earth, white lies   **398**
Delta autumn. Faulkner, W.
  In Faulkner, W. Uncollected stories of Wil-
  liam Faulkner p267-80   **S C**
A **delusion** of Satan. Hill, F.   **133.4**
Democracy
  Tocqueville, A. de. Democracy in America
    973.5
See/See also pages in the following book(s):
  Toffler, A. Future shock p416-30   **303.4**
Dictionaries
  The Encyclopedia of democracy   **321.8**
Democracy and education. Dewey, J.   **370.1**
Democracy in America. Tocqueville, A. de
    973.5
Democracy on trial. Smith, P.   **940.53**
The **democratic** experience. See Boorstin, D. J.
  The Americans: The democratic experience
    973

Democratic Party (U.S.)
See/See also pages in the following book(s):
White, T. H. America in search of itself
973.92

Democritus
See/See also pages in the following book(s):
Jaspers, K. The great philosophers **109**

Demographic yearbook. United Nations. Statistical Office **304.6**

The **demon-haunted** world. Sagan, C. **001.9**

The **demon** lover. Bowen, E.
In The Oxford book of short stories p346-52
S C

Demons don't dream. Anthony, P. See note under Anthony, P. The Magic of Xanth series
Fic

Demonstrations (Protest) *See* Protests, demonstrations, etc.

The **demonstrators.** Welty, E.
In Welty, E. The collected stories of Eudora Welty p608-22 **S C**

Demos, John, 1937-
Entertaining Satan **974**
The tried and the true
In The Young Oxford history of women in the United States **305.4**

Demosthenes, 384-322 B.C.
See/See also pages in the following book(s):
Hamilton, E. The echo of Greece p105-14
880.9

Den of lions. Anderson, T. **92**

Denckla, Tanya
The organic gardener's home reference **635**

Denenberg, Barry
An American hero: the true story of Charles A. Lindbergh **92**
The true story of J. Edgar Hoover and the FBI
363.2
Voices from Vietnam **959.704**

Denominations, Religious *See* Sects

Dental health. Siegel, D. S. **617.6**

Dentemaro, Christine
Straight talk about anger **152.4**

The **dentist.** O'Brien, T.
In O'Brien, T. The things they carried
S C

Dentistry
Siegel, D. S. Dental health **617.6**

The **denunciation.** Hemingway, E.
In Hemingway, E. The complete short stories of Ernest Hemingway p420-28 **S C**

Denyer, Ralph
The guitar handbook **787.87**

Departure. Anderson, S.
In Anderson, S. Winesburg, Ohio **S C**

Departures. L'Heureux, J.
In The Vintage book of contemporary American short stories p308-19 **S C**

Depression (Psychology)
Cush, C. Depression **616.85**
Hales, D. R. Depression **616.85**
Maloney, M. Straight talk about anxiety and depression **155.9**

McCoy, K. Life happens **616.85**
Newman, S. Don't be S.A.D.: a teenage guide to handling stress, anxiety & depression
155.9
Dictionaries
Roesch, R. The encyclopedia of depression
616.85

Depressions, Economic *See* Economic depressions

Deprogramming *See* Brainwashing

Deptula, Edward J.
(ed) Preparation for the SAT and PSAT. See Preparation for the SAT and PSAT
378.1

DeRose, David J.
Sam Shepard **812**

Des Pres, Terrence, 1939-1987
The survivor; criticism
In Bettelheim, B. Surviving, and other essays p284-98 **155.9**

Des Prez, Josquin *See* Josquin, des Pres, d. 1521

DeSalvo, Debra
(jt. auth) Mariotti, S. The young entrepreneur's guide to starting and running a business
658.1

Descartes, René, 1596-1650
See/See also pages in the following book(s):
Bell, E. T. Men of mathematics p35-55
920
Durant, W. J. The age of reason begins p636-47
940.2
Jaspers, K. The great philosophers **109**
Russell, B. A history of Western philosophy p557-68 **109**

A **descent** into the maelström. Poe, E. A.
In Poe, E. A. The collected tales and poems of Edgar Allan Poe p127-40 **S C**
In Poe, E. A. Tales of Edgar Allan Poe p27-50 **S C**

The **descent** of man. Wharton, E.
In Wharton, E. The selected short stories of Edith Wharton p49-65 **S C**

Deschamps, Eliette Brunel *See* Brunel Deschamps, Eliette

Description of a struggle. Kafka, F.
In Kafka, F. The complete stories **S C**

Desert ecology
Deserts **574.5**

Desert island. White, T. de V.
In The Oxford book of Irish short stories p401-11 **S C**

Desert Storm **956.7**

Desert Storm Operation *See* Persian Gulf War, 1991

Desertion. Simak, C. D.
In The Oxford book of science fiction stories p115-26 **S C**

Deserts
Flegg, J. Deserts **574.5**
The Sierra Club desert reader **808.8**

Deserts **574.5**

Design
Dictionaries
Pile, J. F. Dictionary of 20th-century design
745.4

Desire under the elms. O'Neill, E.
  In O'Neill, E. Complete plays v2   **812**
  In O'Neill, E. Nine plays p127-92   **812**

Desktop publishing
  Madama, J. Desktop publishing   **686.2**

Desonie, Dana
  Cosmic collisions   **551.3**

Desprès, Josquin *See* Josquin, des Pres, d. 1521

The **destructors.** Greene, G.
  In Greene, G. The portable Graham Greene
    p382-95   **828**

Desy, Jeanne, 1942-
  The princess who stood on her own two feet
  In The Oxford book of modern fairy tales
    p408-17   **S C**

The **detective** of dreams. Wolfe, G.
  In Masterpieces of fantasy and enchantment
    p197-213   **S C**

Detective story. Kingsley, S.
  In Best American plays: 3d series—1945-
    1951 p317-64   **812.008**

Detectives in mass media
        Dictionaries
  DeAndrea, W. L. Encyclopedia mysteriosa
        809.3

Determinism and indeterminism *See* Free will
  and determinism

Detroit (Mich.)
        Fiction
  Arnow, H. L. S. The dollmaker   **Fic**
  Verdelle, A. J. The good negress   **Fic**

Detweiler, Robert
  John Updike   **813.009**

Deutsch, Babette, 1895-1982
  Poetry handbook: a dictionary of terms
        808.1

Deutsch, Sarah
  From ballots to breadlines
  In The Young Oxford history of women in
    the United States   **305.4**

Developing countries
  Atlas of the Third World   **912**
  The Third World: opposing viewpoints
        330.9

        Dictionaries
  Kurian, G. T. Encyclopedia of the Third World
        903

Development *See* Growth disorders

The **Devil.** Tolstoy, L., graf
  In Tolstoy, L. Great short works of Leo Tol-
    stoy p303-51   **S C**

The **Devil** and Daniel Webster. Benét, S. V.
  In 24 favorite one-act plays p170-93
        808.82

The **Devil** and Tom Walker. Irving, W.
  In The Norton book of American short stories
    p25-35   **S C**

The **Devil** in manuscript. Hawthorne, N.
  In Hawthorne, N. Tales and sketches; A won-
    der book for girls and boys; Tanglewood
    tales for girls and boys p330-37
        S C

The **devil** in the belfry. Poe, E. A.
  In Poe, E. A. The collected tales and poems
    of Edgar Allan Poe p736-42   **S C**

The **devil** in the shape of a woman. Karlsen, C. F.
        133.4

Devil-worship *See* Satanism

The **Devil's** disciple. Shaw, B.
  In Shaw, B. The portable Bernard Shaw
        822

Dewey, John, 1859-1952
  Democracy and education   **370.1**
  See/See also pages in the following book(s):
  Durant, W. J. The story of philosophy p389-95
        109

Dewey, Melvil, 1851-1931
  Abridged Dewey decimal classification and rela-
    tive index   **025.4**
  Dewey decimal classification and relative index
        025.4

Dewey, Patrick R., 1949-
  303 CD-ROMs to use in your library
        025.2

Dewey Decimal Classification
  Dewey, M. Abridged Dewey decimal classifica-
    tion and relative index   **025.4**
  Dewey, M. Dewey decimal classification and
    relative index   **025.4**

Dewey decimal classification and relative index.
  Dewey, M.   **025.4**

Di Filippo, Paul
  The Great Nebula Sweep
  In Nebula awards 25 p218-24   **S C**
  Lennon spex
  In Nebula awards 28 p145-59   **S C**

Di Rienzo, Cola *See* Rienzo, Cola di, ca. 1313-
  1354

Diabetes
  Little, M. Diabetes   **616.4**

Diagnosing and treating mental illness. Lundy, A.
        616.89

Diagnosis
  Pinckney, C. The patient's guide to medical
    tests   **616.07**

Diagram Group
  Animal anatomy on file. See Animal anatomy
    on file   **591.4**
  Human body on file: anatomy. See Human body
    on file: anatomy   **611**
  The Macmillan visual desk reference. See The
    Macmillan visual desk reference   **031**
  Musical instruments of the world. See Musical
    instruments of the world   **784.19**
  Nature projects on file. See Nature projects on
    file   **508**
  Religions on file. See Religions on file
        291
  Rules of the game. See Rules of the game
        796
  Weapons. See Weapons   **623.4**

Diamant, Lincoln
  (jt. auth) Davidson, C. Stamping our history
        769.56

AUTHOR, TITLE, SUBJECT, AND ANALYTICAL INDEX
FIFTEENTH EDITION

The **diamond** as big as the Ritz. Fitzgerald, F. S.
  In Fitzgerald, F. S. The short stories of F.
    Scott Fitzgerald p182-216   **S C**
  In Fitzgerald, F. S. The stories of F. Scott
    Fitzgerald p5-38   **S C**
A **diamond** guitar. Capote, T.
  In Capote, T. Breakfast at Tiffany's: a short
    novel and three stories   **S C**
Diamond Island: Alcatraz. Wilson, D. B.
  In Talking leaves   **S C**
The **diamond** maker. Wells, H. G.
  In Wells, H. G. The complete short stories of
    H. G. Wells p252-59   **S C**
Diamond orchid. Lawrence, J.
  In Lawrence, J. The selected plays of Jerome
    Lawrence and Robert E. Lee p369-446
    812

Diaries
  Schiwy, M. A. A voice of her own   **808**
The **diary** of a young girl. Frank, A.   **92**
  also in Frank, A. The works of Anne Frank
    p25-240   **839.3**
The **diary** of a young girl: the definitive edition.
  Frank, A.   **92**
The **diary** of Adam and Eve. Twain, M.
  In Twain, M. The complete short stories of
    Mark Twain   **S C**
Diary of an African nun. Walker, A.
  In Children of the night p296-99   **S C**
The **diary** of Anne Frank. Goodrich, F.   **812**
Dias, Earl Joseph, 1916-
  Landslide for Shakespeare
  In The Big book of large-cast plays p152-67
    812.008
Diaz, Junot
  Ysrael
  In The Best American short stories, 1996
    p86-96   **S C**
Díaz de Vivar, Rodrigo *See* Cid, ca. 1043-1099
Dibs: in search of self. Axline, V. M.   **616.85**
DiCanio, Margaret
  The encyclopedia of violence   **303.6**
The **dice-box:** a fairy tale. Walpole, H.
  In Masterpieces of fantasy and enchantment
    p169-72   **S C**
Dice, brassknuckles & guitar. Fitzgerald, F. S.
  In Fitzgerald, F. S. The short stories of F.
    Scott Fitzgerald p237-58   **S C**
Dick, Harold G.
  The golden age of the great passenger airships,
    Graf Zeppelin & Hindenburg   **629.133**
Dick, Philip K.
  Colony
  In Robert Silverberg's Worlds of wonder
    S C
  Frozen journey
  In The Norton book of science fiction p386-
    401   **S C**
  The king of the elves
  In Masterpieces of fantasy and enchantment
    p375-94   **S C**
  In The Oxford book of modern fairy tales
    p321-40   **S C**

Dickens, Charles, 1812-1870
  David Copperfield   **Fic**
  Great expectations   **Fic**
  Hard times   **Fic**
  The magic fishbone
  In Masterpieces of fantasy and enchantment
    p13-22   **S C**
  In The Oxford book of modern fairy tales
    p99-108   **S C**
  No. 1 Branch Line, the signalman
  In Classic ghost stories p142-54   **S C**
  Oliver Twist   **Fic**
  The story of the bagman's uncle
  In Classic ghost stories p16-33   **S C**
  A tale of two cities   **Fic**
  To be taken with a grain of salt
  In Victorian ghost stories p55-64   **S C**
    About
  Kaplan, F. Dickens   **92**
  Martin, C. Charles Dickens   **92**
  Nelson, H. S. Charles Dickens   **823.009**
  Smith, G. Charles Dickens   **92**
Dickey, James
  The whole motion   **811**
    About
  James Dickey   **811**
Dickinson, Emily, 1830-1886
  The complete poems of Emily Dickinson
    811
  Final harvest   **811**
  New poems of Emily Dickinson   **811**
  The selected poems of Emily Dickinson
    811
    About
  Emily Dickinson: a collection of critical essays
    811
  Faber, D. Love & rivalry   **920**
  Ferlazzo, P. J. Emily Dickinson   **811**
  Longsworth, P. The world of Emily Dickinson
    92
  Wolff, C. G. Emily Dickinson   **92**
  See/See also pages in the following book(s):
  Untermeyer, L. Lives of the poets p578-90
    920
  Voices & visions p51-90   **811.009**
Dickinson, Lavinia
  See/See also pages in the following book(s):
  Faber, D. Love & rivalry p121-91   **920**
Dickinson, Peter, 1927-
  A bone from a dry sea   **Fic**
  Eva   **Fic**
Dickson, Gordon R., 1923-
  Soldier ask not
  In The Mammoth book of new world science
    fiction p148-200   **S C**
Dickson, Paul
  The joy of keeping score   **796.357**
  Timelines   **973.92**
  The Worth book of softball   **796.357**
Dictators
  Hoyt, E. P. Mussolini's empire   **92**
  Marrin, A. Stalin   **92**
  Radzinsky, E. Stalin   **92**
  Toland, J. Adolf Hitler   **92**
    Dictionaries
  Axelrod, A. Dictators and tyrants   **920.003**

Dictators and tyrants. Axelrod, A.   920.003
Dictionaries *See* Encyclopedias and dictionaries
Dictionaries, **Biographical** *See* Biography—Dictionaries
Dictionaries, **Classical** *See* Classical dictionaries
Dictionaries, **Multilingual** *See* Polyglot dictionaries
Dictionaries, **Picture** *See* Picture dictionaries
Dictionary of 20th-century design. Pile, J. F.
        745.4
The **dictionary** of 20th-century world politics. Shafritz, J. M.   909.82
Dictionary of acronyms and abbreviations, NTC's. Kleinedler, S. R.   421.03
Dictionary of Afro-American slang. *See* Juba to jive   427
Dictionary of American art. Baigell, M.
        709.73
Dictionary of American biography   920.003
Dictionary of American history   973.03
Dictionary of American history, Supplement
        973.03
Dictionary of American literary characters
        810.3
Dictionary of American regional English   427
Dictionary of architecture & construction
        720.3
A **dictionary** of battles. *See* Eggenberger, D. An encyclopedia of battles   904
Dictionary of British literary characters   820.3
Dictionary of catchphrases. Rees, N.   422.03
Dictionary of classical, biblical, and literary allusions, The Facts on File. Lass, A. H.
        803
Dictionary of computer and Internet terms. Downing, D.   004
Dictionary of computer terms. *See* Downing, D. Dictionary of computer and Internet terms
        004
The **dictionary** of costume. Wilcox, R. T.
        391
The **dictionary** of cultural literacy. Hirsch, E. D.
        031
Dictionary of daily life of Indians of the Americas
        970.004
A **dictionary** of early music. Roche, J.   780.3
The **Dictionary** of ecology and environmental science   363.7
Dictionary of English usage, Merriam-Webster's
        428
Dictionary of fictional characters   820.3
A **dictionary** of first names. Hanks, P.   929.4
Dictionary of first names. Kolatch, A. J.
        929.4
Dictionary of Hispanic biography   920.003
Dictionary of historic documents. Kohn, G. C.
        903
Dictionary of historical terms. Cook, C.   903
A **dictionary** of literary terms and literary theory. Cuddon, J. A.   803
Dictionary of mathematics terms. Downing, D.
        510.3

Dictionary of Mexican literature   860.3
A **dictionary** of modern English usage. *See* Fowler, H. W. The new Fowler's modern English usage   428
The **Dictionary** of national biography: the concise dictionary   920.003
Dictionary of Native American literature   897
Dictionary of Native American mythology. Gill, S. D.   299
Dictionary of nature. Burnie, D.   574.03
Dictionary of occupational titles   331.7
Dictionary of phrase and fable, Brewer's   803
Dictionary of Roman religion. Adkins, L.
        292
The **Dictionary** of science   503
Dictionary of science. Ardley, N.   503
Dictionary of scientific biography   920.003
A **dictionary** of slang and unconventional English. Partridge, E.   427
Dictionary of subject and symbols in art. Hall, J.
        704.9
Dictionary of symbolism. Biedermann, H.
        302.2
Dictionary of symbols. Liungman, C. G.
        302.2
Dictionary of symbols in Western art. Carr-Gomm, S.   704.9
A **dictionary** of the ancient Greek world. *See* Sacks, D. Encyclopedia of the ancient Greek world   938
Dictionary of the arts   700
Dictionary of the earth. Farndon, J.   550.3
The **dictionary** of the First World War. Pope, S.
        940.3
A **dictionary** of the Middle East. Hiro, D.
        956
A **dictionary** of the Second World War. Wheal, E.-A.   940.53
Dictionary of twentieth-century design. Pile, J. F.
        745.4
A **Dictionary** of twentieth-century world biography   920.003
The **Dictionary** of war quotations   808.88
The **Dictionary** of world myth   291.03
Diddling. Poe, E. A.
    In Poe, E. A. The collected tales and poems of Edgar Allan Poe p367-75   S C
Diderot, Denis, 1713-1784
    See/See also pages in the following book(s):
    Durant, W. J. The age of Voltaire p650-79
        940.2
Didrikson, Babe *See* Zaharias, Babe Didrikson, 1911-1956
Diefendorf, Elizabeth
    The New York Public Library's books of the century   028
Diet
    Brody, J. E. Jane Brody's nutrition book
        641.1
    Salter, C. A. The vegetarian teen   613.2
Dietrich, Richard F., 1936-
    British drama, 1890 to 1950   822.009

Diets, Reducing *See* Reducing

A different teacher. Wathen, E.
  In Not the only one p88-107   **S C**

Different values. Makhalisa, B.
  In Daughters of Africa p618-21   **808.8**

Different voices   **940.53**

The **difficult** path. Hesse, H.
  In Hesse, H. The fairy tales of Hermann Hesse   **S C**

Diff'rent. O'Neill, E.
  In O'Neill, E. Complete plays v2   **812**

DiGeronimo, Theresa Foy
  (jt. auth) DiSalvo, J. College admissions for the high school athlete   **378**

Digestion
  Avraham, R. The digestive system   **612.3**
  See/See also pages in the following book(s):
  The Incredible machine p55-97   **612**

The **digestive** system. Avraham, R.   **612.3**

DiGiulio, Robert C., 1949-
  Straight talk about death and dying   **155.9**

Dijk, Lutz van, 1955-
  Damned strong love   **Fic**

The **dilettante.** Wharton, E.
  In Wharton, E. The selected short stories of Edith Wharton p99-107   **S C**

Dilip Hiro *See* Hiro, Dilip

Dillard, Annie
  An American childhood   **92**
  The Annie Dillard reader   **818**
  Holy the firm
    In Dillard, A. The Annie Dillard reader   **818**
  The living [short story]
    In Dillard, A. The Annie Dillard reader   **818**
  Mornings like this   **811**
  Pilgrim at Tinker Creek   **818**
  (ed) Modern American memoirs. See Modern American memoirs   **810.8**
  See/See also pages in the following book(s):
  Inventing the truth p39-59   **808**

Dillen, Frederick G., 1946-
  Alice
    In Prize stories, 1996 p313-34   **S C**

Diller, Daniel C., 1959-
  (ed) Russia and the independent states. See Russia and the independent states   **947**

Dillon, Patrick M.
  Multimedia technology from A to Z   **006.6**

Dilov, Ljuben
  Contacts of a fourth kind
    In Tales from the planet Earth   **S C**

DiMaggio, Joe
                    About
  Stout, G. DiMaggio   **92**

Dinesen, Isak, 1885-1962
  The monkey
    In The Oxford book of gothic tales p344-85   **S C**
  Out of Africa and Shadows on the grass   **967.62**

Shadows on the grass
  In Dinesen, I. Out of Africa and Shadows on the grass   **967.62**

Dingus, Lowell
  (jt. auth) Norell, M. Discovering dinosaurs in the American Museum of Natural History   **567.9**

Dining
  Tannahill, R. Food in history   **641.3**

Dinner at the Homesick Restaurant. Tyler, A.   **Fic**

Dinosaur hunters. Spalding, D. A. E.   **567.9**

Dinosaur in a haystack. Gould, S. J.   **508**

The **Dinosaur** Society's dinosaur encyclopedia. Lessem, D.   **567.9**

Dinosaurs
  Fastovsky, D. E. The evolution and extinction of the dinosaurs   **567.9**
  Horner, J. R. The complete T. rex   **567.9**
  Norell, M. Discovering dinosaurs in the American Museum of Natural History   **567.9**
  Officer, C. B. The great dinosaur extinction controversy   **567.9**
  Psihoyos, L. Hunting dinosaurs   **567.9**
  Russell, D. A. An odyssey in time: the dinosaurs of North America   **567.9**
  Spalding, D. A. E. Dinosaur hunters   **567.9**
  Wallace, J. The American Museum of Natural History's book of dinosaurs and other ancient creatures   **567.9**
  Wilford, J. N. The riddle of the dinosaur   **567.9**
                    Dictionaries
  Lessem, D. The Dinosaur Society's dinosaur encyclopedia   **567.9**
                    Fiction
  Crichton, M. Jurassic Park   **Fic**

Direct action. Thelwell, M.
  In The Best short stories by Negro writers p470-78   **S C**

Direction (Theater) *See* Theater—Production and direction

Directory of American youth organizations. Erickson, J. B.   **369.4**

Directory of financial aids for minorities. Schlachter, G. A.   **378.3**

Directory of financial aids for women. Schlachter, G. A.   **378.3**

The **directory** of saints. Sandoval, A.   **920.003**

Dirty hands. Sartre, J. P.
  In Sartre, J. P. No exit, and three other plays   **842**

Disabled *See* Handicapped

Disadvantaged children *See* Socially handicapped children

DiSalvo, Jack
  College admissions for the high school athlete   **378**

The **disappearance.** Guy, R.   **Fic**

The **disappearance** of Lady Frances Carfax.
Doyle, Sir A. C.
In Doyle, Sir A. C. The complete Sherlock
Holmes **S C**

The **disappearing** American farm. Goldberg, J.
338.1

Disarmament *See* Arms control

Disaster relief
See also Food relief

Disasters
See also Natural disasters
Freiman, F. L. Failed technology **620**

Disch, Thomas M.
Problems of creativeness
In The Oxford book of science fiction stories
p363-84 **S C**

Discipline of children *See* Child rearing

Discover America. Little, C. E. **917.3**

Discover nature in the garden. Conrad, J.
574.5

The **discoverers** of America. Faber, H.
970.01

Discoveries (in geography) *See* Exploration

Discovering America's past **973**

Discovering ancient Egypt. David, A. R. **932**

Discovering dinosaurs in the American Museum
of Natural History. Norell, M. **567.9**

Discovering the wonders of our world **508**

The **discovery** of King Arthur. Ashe, G. **92**

The **discovery** of the Titanic. Ballard, R. D.
910.4

Discrimination
See also Hate crimes; Sex discrimination
Gillam, S. Discrimination **303.3**
Miller, M. Coping with a bigoted parent
303.3
Shapiro, J. P. No pity **323.3**
See/See also pages in the following book(s):
Sports in America: opposing viewpoints p131-53
796

Discrimination in education
See also Segregation in education
Finnegan, W. Crossing the line **968.06**
Kozol, J. Death at an early age **370.19**
See/See also pages in the following book(s):
Friendly, F. W. The Constitution—that delicate
balance **342**

Discrimination in employment
See also Affirmative action programs

Disease germs *See* Bacteria; Germ theory of disease

Diseases
See also names of specific diseases and
groups of diseases; and subjects with the sub-
division *Diseases*
Aaseng, N. Autoimmune diseases **616.97**
Kaufman, M. Easy for you to say **362.1**
LeVert, S. Teens face to face with chronic ill-
ness **362.1**

Disguised. Singer, I. B.
In Singer, I. B. The death of Methuselah and
other stories p48-60 **S C**

Disney, Walt, 1901-1966
About
Schickel, R. The Disney version **92**

Disney (Walt) Company *See* Walt Disney Company

The **Disney** that never was. Solomon, C.
741.5

Disneyland (Anaheim, Calif.)
Koenig, D. Mouse tales **791.06**

Disney's art of animation. Thomas, B. **741.5**

Dispatches from the front. Lande, N. **070.4**

The **displaced** person. O'Connor, F.
In O'Connor, F. Collected works p285-327
S C
In O'Connor, F. The complete stories p194-
235 **S C**

Displaced persons *See* Refugees

**Disraeli, Benjamin, Earl of Beaconsfield, 1804-
1881**
See/See also pages in the following book(s):
Strachey, L. Queen Victoria p327-66 **92**

Dissection
Berman, W. How to dissect **591.4**

Dissertations
Turabian, K. L. A manual for writers of term
papers, theses, and dissertations **808**
Using the Internet, online services & CD-ROMS
for writing research and term papers **004**

A **distant** episode. Bowles, P.
In The Oxford book of American short stories
p384-96 **S C**

A **distant** mirror. Tuchman, B. W. **944**

Distant signals. Weiner, A.
In The Norton book of science fiction p525-
37 **S C**

Distinguished African American scientists of the
20th century **920**

The **distributors.** Dumas, H.
In Calling the wind p232-41 **S C**

The **disuniting** of America. Schlesinger, A. M.
973

Ditsky, John
(ed) Critical essays on Steinbeck's The grapes
of wrath. See Critical essays on Steinbeck's
The grapes of wrath **813.009**

Diversity, Biological *See* Biological diversity

Diversity and the tropical rain forest. Terborgh, J.
574.5

The **divided** Carla. Nesvadba, J.
In Tales from the planet Earth **S C**

The **Divine** comedy. Dante Alighieri
In Dante Alighieri. The portable Dante
851

The **diviner.** Friel, B.
In The Oxford book of Irish short stories
p471-81 **S C**

Divorce
See also Children of divorced parents; Re-
marriage
Bolick, N. O. How to survive your parents' di-
vorce **306.89**
Fiction
Cole, B. Celine **Fic**

Dogs—Fiction—*Continued*
London, J. White Fang   **Fic**
Psychology
Thomas, E. M. The hidden life of dogs
    636.7
Training
Fogle, B. ASPCA complete dog training manual
    636.7
A **dog's** life. Mayle, P.   **828**
A **dog's** tale. Twain, M.
In Twain, M. The complete short stories of
Mark Twain   **S C**
Dolan, Edward F., 1924-
Child abuse   **362.7**
Illiteracy in America   **370.19**
The Old farmer's almanac book of weather lore
    398.2
Shaping U.S. foreign policy   **327.73**
Teenagers and compulsive gambling   **362.7**
The **dollmaker**. Arnow, H. L. S.   **Fic**
A **doll's** house. Ibsen, H.
In Ibsen, H. The complete major prose plays
    839.8
In Ibsen, H. Ibsen: four major plays
    839.8
The **doll's** house. Pilcher, R.
In Pilcher, R. Flowers in the rain & other sto-
ries   **S C**
Dolphins
The Audubon Society field guide to North
American fishes, whales, and dolphins
    597
Bonner, W. N. Whales of the world   **599.5**
Carwardine, M. Whales, dolphins, and porpoises
    599.5
Connor, R. C. The lives of whales and dolphins
    599.5
Hall, H. A charm of dolphins   **599.5**
Leatherwood, S. The Sierra Club handbook of
whales and dolphins   **599.5**
Whales, dolphins, and porpoises [Facts on File]
    599.5
Whales, dolphins, and porpoises [National Geo-
graphic Soc.]   **599.5**
The **dolphins** of Pern. McCaffrey, A. See note un-
der McCaffrey, A. [The Pern series]   **Fic**
The **domain** of Arnheim. Poe, E. A.
In Poe, E. A. The collected tales and poems
of Edgar Allan Poe p604-15   **S C**
Domestic architecture
McAlester, V. A field guide to American houses
    728
A **domestic** dilemma. McCullers, C.
In McCullers, C. The ballad of the sad café:
the novels and stories of Carson McCul-
lers   **S C**
In McCullers, C. Collected stories p148-57
    S C
Domestic finance *See* Personal finance
Domestic relations
    See also Family
Domestic violence *See* Family violence
Domestic violence   **362.82**
Domestic violence. McCue, M. L.   **362.82**

Domico, Terry
Bears of the world   **599.74**
Domínguez Ortiz, Antonio
Velázquez   **759.6**
Dominica
Fiction
Kincaid, J. Autobiography of my mother
    Fic
Dominican Americans
Fiction
Alvarez, J. How the Garcia girls lost their ac-
cents   **Fic**
Dominican Republic
Fiction
Alvarez, J. In the time of the butterflies
    Fic
Dominions, British *See* Commonwealth countries
Don Giovanni. Faulkner, W.
In Faulkner, W. Uncollected stories of Wil-
liam Faulkner p480-88   **S C**
Don José of La Mancha. Ortiz Cofer, J.
In Ortiz Cofer, J. An island like you p92-106
    S C
Don Juan in Hell. Shaw, B.
In Shaw, B. The portable Bernard Shaw
    822
Don Juan's temptation. O'Connor, F.
In O'Connor, F. Collected stories p167-75
    S C
Don Quixote de la Mancha. Cervantes Saavedra,
M. de   **Fic**
Doña Toña of Nineteenth Street. González, L.
In Growing up Chicana/o p59-66   **810.8**
Donadio, Stephen
(ed) The New York Public Library book of
twentieth-century American quotations. See
The New York Public Library book of twenti-
eth-century American quotations   **808.88**
Donald, David Herbert, 1920-
Lincoln   **92**
Donation of organs, tissues, etc.
See/See also pages in the following book(s):
Mabie, M. C. J. Bioethics and the new medical
technology   **174**
Donelson, Kenneth L.
(jt. auth) Nilsen, A. P. Literature for today's
young adults   **028.5**
Dongala, Emmanuel Boundzéki, 1941-
The man
In The Heinemann book of contemporary
African short stories p81-86   **S C**
Donne, John, 1572-1631
The complete English poems   **821**
The complete poetry and selected prose of John
Donne   **828**
About
Carey, J. John Donne, life, mind, and art
    821
Warnke, F. J. John Donne   **821**
See/See also pages in the following book(s):
Untermeyer, L. Lives of the poets p122-36
    920

Don't be S.A.D.: a teenage guide to handling stress, anxiety & depression. Newman, S. **155.9**

Don't explain: a song of Billie Holiday. De Veaux, A. **92**

Don't knock the rock. Chandler, A. B.
In Tales from the planet Earth **S C**

Don't know much about geography. Davis, K. C. **910.2**

Don't know much about history. Davis, K. C. **973**

Don't think twice. Pennebaker, R. **Fic**

Don't you want to be free?. Hughes, L.
In Black theatre USA **812.008**

The **Doomdorf** mystery. Post, M. D.
In The Oxford book of American detective stories p81-92 **S C**

The **Doonesbury** chronicles. Trudeau, G. B. **741.5**

The **door** in the wall. Wells, H. G.
In Wells, H. G. The complete short stories of H. G. Wells p144-61 **S C**

The **door** of opportunity. Maugham, W. S.
In Maugham, W. S. Collected short stories v2 **S C**

Doore, Gary
(ed) What survives? See What survives? **133.9**

The **Dorling** Kindersley history of the world. Somerset Fry, P. **909**

Dorling Kindersley ultimate visual dictionary **423**

The **Dorling** Kindersley visual encyclopedia **031**

Dorling Kindersley visual timeline of transportation. Wilson, A. **629.04**

The **Dorling** Kindersley world reference atlas **912**

Dorman, Sonya, 1924-
When I was Miss Dow
In The Norton book of science fiction p151-60 **S C**

Dornberg, John
Central and Eastern Europe **947**
Western Europe **940.55**

Dorothea Lange—a visual life **92**

Dorothea Lange's Ireland. Lange, D. **941.5**

Dorothy and my grandmother and the sailors. Jackson, S.
In Jackson, S. The lottery **S C**

Dorris, Michael
Groom service
In Song of the turtle p276-88 **S C**
Queen of diamonds
In Talking leaves **S C**
Rayona's seduction
In The Lightning within p133-61 **S C**
A yellow raft in blue water **Fic**
Yellow raft in blue water [excerpt]
In Growing up Native American p307-24 **810.8**

See/See also pages in the following book(s):
Coltelli, L. Winged words: American Indian writers speak **897**

Dorsey, Candas Jane
(Learning about) machine sex
In The Norton book of science fiction p746-61 **S C**

Dorsey, Thomas A.
See/See also pages in the following book(s):
We'll understand it better by and by **782.25**

Dostert, Pierre Etienne
Africa **960**
Latin America **980**

Dostoevskiĭ, Fedor Mikhaĭlovich *See* Dostoyevsky, Fyodor, 1821-1881

Dostoyevsky, Fyodor, 1821-1881
Crime and punishment **Fic**
The Grand Inquisitor
In The Portable nineteenth-century Russian reader p413-33 **891.7**
The idiot **Fic**
About
Fyodor Dostoevsky **891.7**
Leatherbarrow, W. J. Fedor Dostoevsky **891.7**

A **double-barreled** detective story. Twain, M.
In Twain, M. The complete short stories of Mark Twain **S C**

Double-edged sword. Drlica, K. **616**

A **double** life [excerpt] Pavlova, K.
In The Portable nineteenth-century Russian reader p282-91 **891.7**

Douchant, Mike, 1951-
Encyclopedia of college basketball **796.323**

The **Dough** prince
In Hearne, B. G. Beauties and beasts p151-53 **398.2**

Dougherty, Steve, 1948-
(jt. auth) Cooper, R. Amateur night at the Apollo **792.7**

Douglas, Aaron, 1898-1979
See/See also pages in the following book(s):
Harlem Renaissance: art of black America **709.73**

Douglas, Ellen
Grant
In Prize stories, 1996 p175-88 **S C**

Douglas, Marjory Stoneman
See/See also pages in the following book(s):
Lucas, E. Naturalists, conservationists, and environmentalists **920**

Douglas, Paul
The handbook of tennis **796.342**
Tennis **796.342**

Douglas, Stephen Arnold, 1813-1861
Lincoln, A. The Lincoln-Douglas debates of 1858 **973.6**

Douglass, Frederick, 1817?-1895
Autobiographies **92**
Frederick Douglass, in his own words **305.8**
The life and times of Frederick Douglass **92**
also in Douglass, F. Autobiographies **92**
My bondage and my freedom
In Douglass, F. Autobiographies **92**

Douglass, Frederick, 1817?-1895—*Continued*
Narrative of the life of Frederick Douglass, an American slave
 In Douglass, F. Autobiographies **92**
    About
Huggins, N. I. Slave and citizen: the life of Frederick Douglass **92**
McFeely, W. S. Frederick Douglass **92**
See/See also pages in the following book(s):
Abdul-Jabbar, K. Black profiles in courage p73-91 **920**
Archer, J. They had a dream p36-81 **920**
Black American prose writers before the Harlem Renaissance p49-61 **810.9**
Senna, C. The black press and the struggle for civil rights p39-47 **071**

Douglass, Jackie Leatherbury
Peterson first guide to shells of North America **594**

Dove, Rita
Mother love **811**
Second-hand man
 In Children of the night p255-61 **S C**
Selected poems **811**
The Zulus
 In Daughters of Africa p825-28 **808.8**
See/See also pages in the following book(s):
Contemporary black American poets and dramatists p17-31 **810.9**
Major modern black American writers p70-84 **810.9**

Dove (Sloop)
Graham, R. L. Dove **910.4**

Dove-Danquah, Mabel
Anticipation
 In Daughters of Africa p223-26 **808.8**

Dover, Kenneth James
(ed) Ancient Greek literature. See Ancient Greek literature **880.9**

Dow, Lesley
Alligators and crocodiles **597.9**

Down, Oliphant
The maker of dreams
 In 24 favorite one-act plays p256-71 **808.82**

Down at the dinghy. Salinger, J. D.
 In Salinger, J. D. Nine stories p111-30 **S C**

Down by the riverside. Wright, R.
 In Wright, R. Uncle Tom's children **S C**

Down in the darkness. Koontz, D. R.
 In Koontz, D. R. Strange highways p201-25 **S C**

Downer, Deborah A., 1954-
(ed) Classic American ghost stories. See Classic American ghost stories **133.1**

Downing, Douglas
Dictionary of computer and Internet terms **004**
Dictionary of mathematics terms **510.3**

The **Downing** Street years. Thatcher, M. **92**

The **downward** path to wisdom. Porter, K. A.
 In Porter, K. A. The collected stories of Katherine Anne Porter **S C**

Doyle, Sir Arthur Conan, 1859-1930
The adventure of the speckled band
 In Crime classics p77-102 **S C**
 In The Oxford book of gothic tales p264-85 **S C**
Adventures of Sherlock Holmes
 In Doyle, Sir A. C. The complete Sherlock Holmes **S C**
The captain of the "Pole-star"
 In Victorian ghost stories p283-302 **S C**
The case book of Sherlock Holmes
 In Doyle, Sir A. C. The complete Sherlock Holmes **S C**
The complete Sherlock Holmes **S C**
The collections included and their contents are as follows: Adventures of Sherlock Holmes: A scandal in Bohemia; The Red-headed League; A case of identity; The Boscombe Valley mystery; The five orange pips; The man with the twisted lip; The adventure of the Blue Carbuncle; The adventure of the speckled band; The adventure of the engineer's thumb; The adventure of the noble bachelor; The adventure of the Beryl Coronet; The adventure of the copper beeches
Memoirs of Sherlock Holmes: Silver Blaze; The yellow face; The stock-broker's clerk; The 'Gloria Scott'; The Musgrave ritual; The Reigate puzzle; The crooked man; The resident patient; The Greek interpreter; The naval treaty; The final problem
The return of Sherlock Holmes: The adventure of the empty house; The adventure of the Norwood builder; The adventure of the dancing men; The adventure of the solitary cyclist; The adventure of the priory school; The adventure of Black Peter; The adventure of Charles Augustus Milverton; The adventure of the six Napoleons; The adventure of the three students; The adventure of the golden pince-nez; The adventure of the missing three-quarter; The adventure of the Abbey Grange; The adventure of the second stain
The valley of fear: The tragedy of Birlstone; The Scrowrers
His last bow: The adventure of Wisteria Lodge; The adventure of the cardboard box; The adventure of the red circle; The adventure of the Bruce-Partington plans; The adventure of the dying detective; The disappearance of Lady Frances Carfax; The adventure of the Devil's foot; His last bow
The case book of Sherlock Holmes: The adventure of the illustrious client; The adventure of the blanched soldier; The adventure of the Mazarin stone; The adventure of the Three Gables; The adventure of the Sussex vampire; The adventure of the three Garridebs; The problem of Thor Bridge; The adventure of the creeping man; The adventure of the lion's mane; The adventure of the veiled lodger; The adventure of Shoscombe Old Place; The adventure of the retired colourman
The copper beeches
 In Masterpieces of mystery and suspense p3-25 **S C**
His last bow
 In Doyle, Sir A. C. The complete Sherlock Holmes **S C**
The hound of the Baskervilles **Fic**
 also in Doyle, Sir A. C. The complete Sherlock Holmes **S C**
Memoirs of Sherlock Holmes
 In Doyle, Sir A. C. The complete Sherlock Holmes **S C**
The Red-headed League
 In The Best crime stories of the 19th century p126-50 **S C**
The return of Sherlock Holmes
 In Doyle, Sir A. C. The complete Sherlock Holmes **S C**
A scandal in Bohemia
 In Crime classics p55-76 **S C**
The sign of the four
 In Doyle, Sir A. C. The complete Sherlock Holmes **S C**

Doyle, Sir Arthur Conan, 1859-1930—*Continued*
A study in scarlet
In Doyle, Sir A. C. The complete Sherlock
Holmes **S C**
The valley of fear
In Doyle, Sir A. C. The complete Sherlock
Holmes **S C**
About
Bunson, M. Encyclopedia Sherlockiana
823.009
Cox, D. R. Arthur Conan Doyle **823.009**
Jaffe, J. A. Arthur Conan Doyle **823.009**
Symons, J. Conan Doyle: portrait of an artist
92
Doyle, Conan *See* Doyle, Sir Arthur Conan, 1859-
1930
Doyle, Paul A., 1925-
Pearl S. Buck **813.009**
Doyle, Rodger
The atlas of contemporary America **304.6**
Doyle, William, 1942-
The Oxford history of the French Revolution
944.04
Dozois, Gardner R.
Solace
In Nebula awards 25 p63-73 **S C**
Dr. Bullivant. Hawthorne, N.
In Hawthorne, N. Tales and sketches; A won-
der book for girls and boys; Tanglewood
tales for girls and boys p34-41 **S C**
Dr. Heidegger's experiment. Hawthorne, N.
In Classic ghost stories p132-41 **S C**
In Hawthorne, N. Tales and sketches; A won-
der book for girls and boys; Tanglewood
tales for girls and boys p470-79
S C
Dr. Jekyll and Mr. Hyde. Stevenson, R. L.
Fic
Dr. Knoegle's end. Hesse, H.
In Hesse, H. The fairy tales of Hermann
Hesse **S C**
Dr. Martino. Faulkner, W.
In Faulkner, W. Collected stories of William
Faulkner p565-85 **S C**
Drabble, Margaret, 1939-
(ed) The Oxford companion to English litera-
ture. See The Oxford companion to English
literature **820.3**
Dracula *See* Vlad II, Dracul, Prince of Wallachia,
1431-1476
Dracula. Stoker, B. **Fic**
Dracula [biography of Vlad II] Florescu, R. R. N.
92
Dracula's guest. Stoker, B.
In Classic ghost stories p64-75 **S C**
Draft resisters
See also names of wars with the subdivi-
sion Draft resisters
Meltzer, M. Ain't gonna study war no more: the
story of America's peace seekers **322.4**
Dragon lady [biography of Tz'u-hsi] Seagrave, S.
92

Dragon on a pedestal. Anthony, P. See note under
Anthony, P. The Magic of Xanth series
Fic
Dragondrums. McCaffrey, A. See note under
McCaffrey, A. [The Pern series] **Fic**
Dragonflight. McCaffrey, A. See note under
McCaffrey, A. [The Pern series] **Fic**
The **dragonlover's** guide to Pern. Nye, J. L.
813.009
Dragonquest. McCaffrey, A. See note under
McCaffrey, A. [The Pern series] **Fic**
Dragonriders of Pern. McCaffrey, A. See note
under McCaffrey, A. [The Pern series]
Fic
Dragons
See/See also pages in the following book(s):
Nigg, J. Wonder beasts **398**
Fiction
Fletcher, S. Flight of the Dragon Kyn **Fic**
The **dragons** of Eden. Sagan, C. **153**
The **dragon's** teeth. Hawthorne, N.
In Hawthorne, N. Tales and sketches; A won-
der book for girls and boys; Tanglewood
tales for girls and boys p1356-81
S C
Dragonsdawn. McCaffrey, A. See note under
McCaffrey, A. [The Pern series] **Fic**
Dragonseye. McCaffrey, A. See note under
McCaffrey, A. [The Pern series] **Fic**
Dragonsinger. McCaffrey, A. See note under
McCaffrey, A. [The Pern series] **Fic**
Dragonsong. McCaffrey, A. See note under
McCaffrey, A. [The Pern series] **Fic**
Drake, Sir Francis, 1540?-1596
About
Cummins, J. G. Francis Drake **92**
Drama
See also American drama; Comedy; Eng-
lish drama; Motion picture plays; One act
plays; Tragedy
See/See also pages in the following book(s):
Highet, G. The classical tradition p127-43
809
Bio-bibliography
McGraw-Hill encyclopedia of world drama
809.2
Collections
24 favorite one-act plays **808.82**
The Actor's book of scenes from new plays
808.82
The Best plays of [date]: The Otis Guern-
sey/Burns Mantle theater yearbook
808.82
Cassady, M. The book of scenes for aspiring ac-
tors **808.82**
Great scenes for young actors from the stage
808.82
Latrobe, K. H. Readers theatre for young adults
808.5
Multicultural scenes for young actors
808.82
The Scenebook for actors **808.82**
Scenes from classic plays, 468 B.C. to 1970
A.D. **808.82**

Drama—*Continued*
Dictionaries
McGraw-Hill encyclopedia of world drama

809.2
History and criticism
Brockett, O. G. History of the theatre

792.09

Esslin, M. The theatre of the absurd   809.2

Masterplots II, drama series   809.2
Indexes
Play index   808.82
Stories, plots, etc.
Masterplots II, drama series   809.2
Technique
Catron, L. E. The elements of playwriting

808.2

Drama in education

Latrobe, K. H. Readers theatre for young adults

808.5

Poisson, C. L. Theater and the adolescent actor

792

Dramatists, American

Hellman, L. Three   92

Miller, A. Timebends   92

Williams, T. Conversations with Tennessee Williams   92

Draper, Sharon M. (Sharon Mills)

Tears of a tiger   Fic

Draper, Theodore, 1912-

A struggle for power   973.3

Drawing

   See also Artistic anatomy; Figure drawing; Pastel drawing

Edwards, B. Drawing on the right side of the brain   741.2

Graves, D. R. Drawing portraits   743

Horton, J. An introduction to drawing

   In The DK art school series   751

Smith, R. Drawing figures

   In The DK art school series   751

Smith, S. Drawing: the complete course

741.2

Drawing figures. Smith, R.

   In The DK art school series   751

Drawing on the right side of the brain. Edwards, B.   741.2

Drawing portraits. Graves, D. R.   743

Drawing: the complete course. Smith, S.

741.2

Drawn with the sword. McPherson, J. M.

973.7

Dray, Philip

   (jt. auth) Cagin, S. We are not afraid

323.1

A dream. Kafka, F.

   In Kafka, F. The complete stories   S C

   In Kafka, F. The metamorphosis and other stories p210-12   S C

The dream. Maugham, W. S.

   In Maugham, W. S. Collected short stories v2

S C

A dream about the gods. Hesse, H.

   In Hesse, H. The fairy tales of Hermann Hesse   S C

Dream children. Godwin, G.

   In American short story masterpieces

S C

Dream girl. Rice, E.

   In Best plays of the modern American theatre: 2nd series p365-409   812.008

The dream is better. Symons, J.

   In Masterpieces of mystery and suspense p232-45   S C

A dream of Armageddon. Wells, H. G.

   In Wells, H. G. The complete short stories of H. G. Wells p1010-38   S C

A dream of winter. Lehmann, R.

   In Classic English short stories, 1930-1955 p349-62   S C

Dream reader. Yolen, J.

   In The Merlin chronicles   S C

A dream sequence. Hesse, H.

   In Hesse, H. The fairy tales of Hermann Hesse   S C

The dream woman. Collins, W.

   In Classic ghost stories p183-206   S C

Dreaming is a private thing. Asimov, I.

   In Asimov, I. The complete stories v1 p149-61   S C

Dreaming the sky down. Burford, B.

   In Rites of passage p177-90   S C

Dreams

   See also Sleep

Parker, J. Parkers' complete book of dreams

154.6

Secrets of the inner mind   154

See/See also pages in the following book(s):

Freud, S. The basic writings of Sigmund Freud

150.19

Powledge, T. M. Your brain p103-11   612.8

Dreams of exile: Robert Louis Stevenson: a biography. Bell, I.   92

The dreamy kid. O'Neill, E.

   In O'Neill, E. Complete plays v1   812

Dreiser, Theodore, 1871-1945

Sister Carrie   Fic
About
Lundquist, J. Theodore Dreiser   813.009

Drenched in light. Hurston, Z. N.

   In Hurston, Z. N. The complete stories p17-25   S C

   In Hurston, Z. N. Novels and stories p940-48

Fic

   In The Portable Harlem Renaissance reader p695-702   810.8

Dressed like summer leaves. Dubus, A.

   In The Other side of heaven p172-81

S C

Dresser, Norine

Multicultural manners   395

Dresser, Peter D.

   (ed) Cancer sourcebook for women. See Cancer sourcebook for women   616.99

   (jt. auth) Kelly, A. A. Religious holidays and calendars   291.3

Dressmaking

   See also Needlework

Drew, Bernard A. (Bernard Alger), 1950-
The 100 most popular young adult authors
810.9

Drew, Charles Richard, 1904-1950
See/See also pages in the following book(s):
Curtis, R. H. Great lives: medicine p219-29
920

Drewal, Henry John
Yoruba **709.6**

Dreyfus, Alfred, 1859-1935
About
Bredin, J.-D. The affair **944.081**
See/See also pages in the following book(s):
Aymar, B. A pictorial history of the world's
greatest trials p201-19 **345**
Tuchman, B. W. The proud tower p171-226
909.82

Dreyfus in Kasrilevke. Sholem Aleichem
In Sholem Aleichem. The best of Sholem
Aleichem **S C**

The **drift.** L'Amour, L.
In L'Amour, L. The outlaws of Mesquite
p73-93 **S C**

The **drill.** Clarke, B.
In Streetlights: illuminating tales of the urban
black experience p56-60 **S C**

Drink. Anderson, S.
In Anderson, S. Winesburg, Ohio **S C**

Drinking of alcoholic beverages
Statistics on alcohol, drug & tobacco use
362.29

Drinking problem *See* Alcoholism; Drinking of
alcoholic beverages

Drive: the story of my life. Bird, L. **92**

Drive, they said **811.008**

Driver's test. Carter, A. R.
In Center stage **812.008**

Driving Miss Daisy. Uhry, A.
In Best American plays: 9th series—1983-
1992 p507-26 **812.008**

Driving the heart. Brown, J.
In The Best American short stories, 1996
p20-32 **S C**

Driving under the influence of alcohol *See*
Drunk driving

Drlica, Karl
Double-edged sword **616**
Understanding DNA and gene cloning
574.87

The **drop** of water. Andersen, H. C.
In Andersen, H. C. Tales and stories
S C

The **drowned** and the saved. Levi, P. **940.53**

Drowne's wooden image. Hawthorne, N.
In Hawthorne, N. Tales and sketches; A wonder book for girls and boys; Tanglewood
tales for girls and boys p932-44
S C

The **drowning.** Delaney, E. J.
In The Best American short stories, 1995
p126-40 **S C**

Drucker, Malka, 1945-
The widest heart
In Not the only one p9-17 **S C**

Drug abuse
See also Alcoholism; Drug addiction
Berger, G. Crack **616.86**
Drug abuse: opposing viewpoints **362.29**
Drugs in America **363.4**
Engel, J. Addicted: kids talking about drugs in
their own words **616.86**
Hermes, W. J. Marijuana **616.86**
Hermes, W. J. Substance abuse **616.86**
Ryan, E. A. Straight talk about drugs and alco-
hol **616.86**
Statistics on alcohol, drug & tobacco use
362.29
Winger, G. Valium and other tranquilizers
616.86
See/See also pages in the following book(s):
Berger, G. Addiction **616.86**
Chemical dependency: opposing viewpoints
362.29
Landau, E. Hooked **362.29**
Porterfield, K. M. Focus on addictions
616.86
Dictionaries
The Encyclopedia of drug abuse **616.86**
Encyclopedia of drugs and alcohol **362.29**
Fiction
Childress, A. A hero ain't nothin' but a sand-
wich **Fic**
Drug abuse: opposing viewpoints **362.29**
Drug addiction
See also Children of drug addicts
Go ask Alice **616.86**
Drug addicts
See also Children of drug addicts
Drug plants *See* Medical botany
Drug therapy
See also Mental illness—Drug therapy;
Pharmacology
Drug trade, Illicit *See* Drug traffic
Drug traffic
Drugs in America **363.4**
Drugs
See also Aspirin; Materia medica; Pharma-
cology; Psychotropic drugs; Steroids
Check, W. A. Drugs & perception **615**
Kittredge, M. Prescription and over-the-counter
drugs **615**
The PDR family guide to women's health and
prescription drugs **613**
Rodgers, J. E. Drugs & sexual behavior
615
Theodore, A. The origins & sources of drugs
615
Adulteration and analysis
See Pharmacology
Indexes
The Merck index **615**
Law and legislation
Drugs in America **363.4**
Legalizing drugs **363.4**
Marshall, E. Legalization **344**
Drugs, Nonprescription *See* Nonprescription
drugs
Drugs, Psychotropic *See* Psychotropic drugs

Drugs & perception. Check, W. A.   615
Drugs & sexual behavior. Rodgers, J. E.   615
Drugs and crime
See also Drug traffic
See/See also pages in the following book(s):
Meltzer, M. Crime in America p31-37   364
Drugs and youth *See* Youth—Drug use
Drugs in America   363.4
The **druids** of Shannara. Brooks, T. See note under Brooks, T. The sword of Shannara
Fic
Drums of Oude. Strong, A.
In Thirty famous one-act plays p287-301
808.82
Drunk driving
See/See also pages in the following book(s):
Landau, E. Teenage drinking p21-36
362.29
The **drunkard**. O'Connor, F.
In O'Connor, F. Collected stories p191-99
S C
Drury, John
The poetry dictionary   808.1
Druyan, Ann, 1949-
(jt. auth) Sagan, C. Comet   523.6
(jt. auth) Sagan, C. Shadows of forgotten ancestors   577
Dry rot. Michener, J. A.
In Michener, J. A. Tales of the South Pacific
S C
Dry September. Faulkner, W.
In Classic American short stories p344-59
S C
In Faulkner, W. Collected stories of William Faulkner p169-83   S C
In Faulkner, W. Selected short stories of William Faulkner   S C
In The Oxford book of short stories p330-40
S C
Dryden, John, 1631-1700
All for love; criticism
In Cleopatra   822.009
About
John Dryden   821
See/See also pages in the following book(s):
Durant, W. J. The age of Louis XIV p321-28
940.2
Untermeyer, L. Lives of the poets p193-209
920
Du Bois, W. E. B. (William Edward Burghardt), 1868-1963
The autobiography of W. E. B. DuBois   92
The dark princess [excerpt]
In The Portable Harlem Renaissance reader p511-35   810.8
Dusk of dawn
In Du Bois, W. E. B. Writings   818
The Oxford W. E. B. Du Bois reader
305.8
The souls of black folk   305.8
also in Du Bois, W. E. B. The Oxford W. E. B. Du Bois reader p97-240   305.8
also in Du Bois, W. E. B. Writings   818
Star of Ethiopia
In Black theatre USA   812.008

The suppression of the African slave-trade
In Du Bois, W. E. B. Writings   818
W.E.B. Du Bois: a reader   305.8
Writings   818
About
Gates, H. L. The future of the race   305.8
Lewis, D. L. W.E.B. DuBois   92
Marable, M. W.E.B. DuBois, black radical democrat   92
McKissack, P. C. W.E.B. DuBois   92
See/See also pages in the following book(s):
Black American prose writers before the Harlem Renaissance p62-77   810.9
Black leaders of the twentieth century p63-83
920
Du Bois, William Edward Burghardt *See* Du Bois, W. E. B. (William Edward Burghardt), 1868-1963
Du Châtelet-Lomont, Gabrielle Émilie, marquise, 1706-1749
See/See also pages in the following book(s):
Osen, L. M. Women in mathematics p49-69
920
Du Maurier, Dame Daphne, 1907-1989
Rebecca   Fic
About
Kelly, R. M. Daphne du Maurier   823.009
Du Pree, Carla R.
Believe
In Streetlights: illuminating tales of the urban black experience p83-92   S C
Duane, Daniel, 1967-
Caught inside   797.3
Duberman, Martin B.
In white America
In Best American plays: 6th series—1963-1967 p471-94   812.008
Dubious conceptions. Luker, K.   362.7
Dubliners. Joyce, J.   S C
Dubrovskii. Pushkin, A. S.
In Pushkin, A. S. Alexander Pushkin: complete prose fiction p145-210   S C
Dubus, Andre, 1936-
Dressed like summer leaves
In The Other side of heaven p172-81
S C
The fat girl
In American short story masterpieces
S C
In The Vintage book of contemporary American short stories p125-40   S C
The **Duc** de L'Omelette. Poe, E. A.
In Poe, E. A. The collected tales and poems of Edgar Allan Poe p708-10   S C
The **Duchess**. Cheever, J.
In Cheever, J. The stories of John Cheever p347-58   S C
The **duchess** and the jeweller. Woolf, V.
In Classic English short stories, 1930-1955 p33-41   S C
Ducker, Bruce
Ute Creek Pass
In Coming of age p109-25   808.8

Duncan, Dorée
(ed) Life into art: Isadora Duncan and her world. See Life into art: Isadora Duncan and her world **92**

Duncan, Isadora, 1878-1927
About
Life into art: Isadora Duncan and her world **92**

Duncan, John Alastair See Duncan, Alastair, 1942-

Duncan, Lois, 1934-
Chapters: my growth as a writer **92**
Killing Mr. Griffin **Fic**
Who killed my daughter? **364.1**
About
Kies, C. N. Presenting Lois Duncan **813.009**

Duncan, Phil
(ed) Congressional Quarterly's politics in America. See Congressional Quarterly's politics in America **328.73**

Duncan, Quince, 1940-
Swan song
In Rites of passage p89-90 **S C**

Dune. Herbert, F. **Fic**

Dune messiah. Herbert, F. See note under Herbert, F. Dune **Fic**

Dunham, Katherine
Afternoon into night
In The Best short stories by Negro writers p145-50 **S C**
See/See also pages in the following book(s):
Haskins, J. Black dance in America p93-105 **792.8**

Dunkerque (France), Battle of, 1940
Gelb, N. Dunkirk: the complete story of the first step in the defeat of Hitler **940.54**
Fiction
Gallico, P. The snow goose **Fic**

Dunkirk: the complete story of the first step in the defeat of Hitler. Gelb, N. **940.54**

Dunn, Charles James
Everyday life in traditional Japan **952**

Dunnahoo, Terry
How to survive high school **373**

Dunnigan, James F.
Victory at sea **940.54**

Dunning, Stephen
(comp) Reflections on a gift of watermelon pickle—and other modern verse. See Reflections on a gift of watermelon pickle—and other modern verse **811.008**

Dunsany, Edward John Moreton Drax Plunkett, Baron, 1878-1957
The jest of Hahalaba
In 24 favorite one-act plays p367-76 **808.82**

The kith of the Elf-folk
In The Oxford book of modern fairy tales p234-47 **S C**
Night at an inn
In Thirty famous one-act plays p255-63 **808.82**

The sword of Welleran
In Masterpieces of fantasy and enchantment p580-92 **S C**

Duplechan, Larry, 1956-
Zazoo
In Calling the wind p524-33 **S C**

The **duplicity** of Hargraves. Henry, O.
In Henry, O. The best short stories of O. Henry **S C**

DuPont, Kathryn Cullen- See Cullen-DuPont, Kathryn

Duppy get her. Adisa, O. P.
In Daughters of Africa p873-81 **808.8**

Dupuy, R. Ernest (Richard Ernest), 1887-1975
The Harper encyclopedia of military history **355**

Dupuy, Richard Ernest See Dupuy, R. Ernest (Richard Ernest), 1887-1975

Dupuy, Trevor N., 1916-1995
(jt. auth) Dupuy, R. E. The Harper encyclopedia of military history **355**

Durán, Manuel, 1925-
Cervantes **863.009**

Durand, Asher Brown, 1796-1886
See/See also pages in the following book(s):
Novak, B. American painting of the nineteenth century p80-91 **759.13**

Durant, Ariel, 1898-1981
(jt. auth) Durant, W. J. The age of Louis XIV **940.2**
(jt. auth) Durant, W. J. The age of Napoleon **940.2**
(jt. auth) Durant, W. J. The age of reason begins **940.2**
(jt. auth) Durant, W. J. The age of Voltaire **940.2**
(jt. auth) Durant, W. J. The lessons of history **901**
(jt. auth) Durant, W. J. Rousseau and revolution **940.2**

Durant, William James, 1885-1981
The age of faith **940.1**
The age of Louis XIV **940.2**
The age of Napoleon **940.2**
The age of reason begins **940.2**
The age of Voltaire **940.2**
The lessons of history **901**
The life of Greece **938**
Our Oriental heritage **950**
The Reformation **940.2**
The Renaissance **945**
Rousseau and revolution **940.2**
The story of philosophy **109**

Duration. Wharton, E.
In Wharton, E. The selected short stories of Edith Wharton p353-65 **S C**

Dürer, Albrecht, 1471-1528
See/See also pages in the following book(s):
Durant, W. J. The Reformation p311-20 **940.2**

Durham, Michael S., 1935-
The Mid-Atlantic States **917.4**
Powerful days **323.1**

Earling, Debra
Jules Bart, giving too much—August 1946
In Song of the turtle p212-15 **S C**
The old marriage
In Talking leaves **S C**
The **early** American sourcebook. Lawliss, C.
917.3

Early autumn. Hughes, L.
In Hughes, L. Short stories **S C**
Early church history *See* Church history—30-600, Early church
Early Europe **936**
The **Early** Middle Ages **940.1**
Early novels and stories. Cather, W. **Fic**
Earp, Wyatt, 1848-1929
See/See also pages in the following book(s):
Walker, P. R. Great figures of the Wild West **920**

Earth
Allaby, M. Earth **550**
Asimov, I. Isaac Asimov's guide to earth & space **520**
Earth energies **001.9**
Age
Smith, N. F. Millions and billions of years ago **551.7**
Internal structure
Vogel, S. Naked Earth **551.1**
Earth Day
Mowrey, M. Not in our back yard **363.7**
The **earth** dwellers. Hoyt, E. **595.7**
Earth energies **001.9**
Earth in the balance. Gore, A., Jr. **304.2**
The **Earth** men. Bradbury, R.
In Bradbury, R. The stories of Ray Bradbury p102-14 **S C**
Earth sciences
See also Geology
Erickson, J. Craters, caverns, and canyons **551.1**
Our awesome earth **508**
Planet earth **550**
Dictionaries
Encyclopedia of earth sciences **550.3**
Environmental encyclopedia **363.7**
Farndon, J. Dictionary of the earth **550.3**
Earth works. Dwyer, J. R. **016.3637**
Earthenware *See* Pottery
Earthquakes
Bolt, B. A. Earthquakes **551.2**
Bolt, B. A. Earthquakes and geological discovery **551.2**
Levy, M. Why the earth quakes **551.2**
Dictionaries
Ritchie, D. The encyclopedia of earthquakes and volcanoes **551.2**
Earthquakes and geological discovery. Bolt, B. A. **551.2**
Earth's holocaust. Hawthorne, N.
In Hawthorne, N. Tales and sketches; A wonder book for girls and boys; Tanglewood tales for girls and boys p887-906 **S C**

The **easiest** way. Walter, E.
In Best plays of the early American theatre p617-76 **812.008**
East *See* Asia
East (Far East) *See* East Asia
East (Near East) *See* Middle East
East Asia
Hinton, H. C. East Asia and the Western Pacific **950**
East Asia and the Western Pacific. Hinton, H. C. **950**
East Indians
United States
See/See also pages in the following book(s):
Takaki, R. T. Strangers from a different shore p294-314 **305.8**
East of the sun and west of the moon
In Hearne, B. G. Beauties and beasts p66-75 **398.2**
East to America: Korean American life stories **305.8**
Easter Island
Heyerdahl, T. Easter Island—the mystery solved **996**
See/See also pages in the following book(s):
Mysteries of mankind **930**
Eastern Europe
History
Russia and the independent states **947**
History—1989-
Dornberg, J. Central and Eastern Europe **947**
Politics and government
The Breakup of communism **947**
Stokes, G. The walls came tumbling down **947**
Eastern mysteries **291**
Eastern wisdom **291**
Eastman, Charles Alexander, 1858-1939
The Gray Chieftain
In The Singing spirit: early short stories by North American Indians p99-106 **S C**
The singing spirit
In The Singing spirit: early short stories by North American Indians p107-18 **S C**
Easton, Robert, 1940-
(jt. auth) Nabokov, P. Native American architecture **728**
Easy for you to say. Kaufman, M. **362.1**
Eating *See* Dining
Eating disorders
See also Anorexia nervosa; Bulimia
Abraham, S. Eating disorders **616.85**
Antonello, J. Breaking out of food jail **616.85**
Controlling eating disorders with facts, advice, and resources **616.85**
Epstein, R. S. Eating habits and disorders **616.85**
Hesse-Biber, S. J. Am I thin enough yet? **616.85**

Eating disorders—*Continued*
Maloney, M. Straight talk about eating disorders **616.85**
Moe, B. A. Coping with eating disorders **616.85**
Patterson, C. Eating disorders **616.85**
Silverstein, A. So you think you're fat? **616.85**
Sonder, B. Eating disorders **616.85**
See/See also pages in the following book(s):
Berger, G. Addiction **616.86**
Porterfield, K. M. Focus on addictions **616.86**
Dictionaries
Cassell, D. K. Encyclopedia of obesity and eating disorders **616.85**
Eating habits and disorders. Epstein, R. S. **616.85**
Eaton, Edith Maude *See* Sui Sin Far, 1865-1914
The **Eatonville** anthology. Hurston, Z. N.
In Hurston, Z. N. The complete stories p59-72 **S C**
In Hurston, Z. N. I love myself when I am laughing—and then again when I am looking mean and impressive p177-88 **818**
In The Norton book of American short stories p357-67 **S C**
Eban, Abba, 1915-
My people: the story of the Jews **909**
Ebenstein, Alan D.
Today's isms **335**
Ebenstein, William, 1910-
(jt. auth) Ebenstein, A. D. Today's isms **335**
Eberhart, Mignon G., 1899-1996
Spider
In The Oxford book of American detective stories p239-60 **S C**
Eble, Kenneth Eugene
F. Scott Fitzgerald **813.009**
Eblen, Ruth A.
(ed) The Encyclopedia of the environment. See The Encyclopedia of the environment **363.7**
Eblen, William R.
(ed) The Encyclopedia of the environment. See The Encyclopedia of the environment **363.7**
Ebola virus
Preston, R. The hot zone **614.5**
Ecclesiastical rites and ceremonies *See* Rites and ceremonies
The **echo** of Greece. Hamilton, E. **880.9**
Echoes. Ciardi, J. **811**
Eckert, Allan W.
A sorrow in our heart: the life of Tecumseh **92**
Eckler, A. Ross (Albert Ross), 1927-
Making the alphabet dance **793.73**
Eckler, Albert Ross *See* Eckler, A. Ross (Albert Ross), 1927-
Eckler, Ross *See* Eckler, A. Ross (Albert Ross), 1927-

Eckstrom, Christine K.
Forgotten Edens. See Forgotten Edens **508**
Ecological movement *See* Environmental movement
Ecology
See also Biogeography; Biological diversity; Environmental protection; Habitat (Ecology); types of ecology, e.g. Marine ecology
Agosta, W. C. Bombardier beetles and fever trees **574.5**
Bierhorst, J. The way of the earth **970.004**
Buchmann, S. The forgotten pollinators **574.5**
The Curious naturalist **508**
Ecology **574.5**
Gibbons, W. Keeping all the pieces **574.5**
Naar, J. This land is your land **333.7**
Dictionaries
The Dictionary of ecology and environmental science **363.7**
Environmental encyclopedia **363.7**
Experiments
Dashefsky, H. S. Environmental science **574.5**
Rainis, K. G. Environmental science projects for young scientists **574.5**
Ecology, Human *See* Human ecology
Ecology **574.5**
Economic assistance
See/See also pages in the following book(s):
Boorstin, D. J. The Americans: The democratic experience p568-79 **973**
Economic botany
Coffey, T. The history and folklore of North American wildflowers **582.13**
Lewington, A. Plants for people **581.6**
Economic conditions
See also Business cycles; racial and ethnic groups, classes of persons, and names of countries, cities, areas, etc., with the subdivision Economic conditions
Stearns, P. N. The ABC-CLIO world history companion to the industrial revolution **909.81**
Economic depressions
Galbraith, J. K. The Great Crash, 1929 **330.973**
McElvaine, R. S. The Great Depression **973.91**
Meltzer, M. Brother, can you spare a dime? **330.973**
Terkel, S. Hard times **973.91**
Wormser, R. Growing up in the Great Depression **973.91**
See/See also pages in the following book(s):
Heilbroner, R. L. The worldly philosophers **330.1**
Manchester, W. The glory and the dream p3-69 **973.9**
Fiction
Kennedy, W. Ironweed **Fic**
Economic development
See also Economic conditions
Economic entomology *See* Insect pests

Economic forecasting
   See also Employment forecasting
   Anderson, R. Atlas of the American economy
          338.973
An **economic** interpretation of the Constitution of
   the United States. Beard, C. A.   **342**
Economic zoology
   See also Beneficial insects; Insect pests
Economics
   Falcone, V. J. Great thinkers, great ideas
          100
   Galbraith, J. K. The affluent society   **330**
   Heilbroner, R. L. Economics explained   **330**
   Heilbroner, R. L. The worldly philosophers
          330.1
   Smith, A. The wealth of nations   **330.1**
Economics and the environment. Goldberg, J.
          333.7
Economics explained. Heilbroner, R. L.   **330**
Economics in America: opposing viewpoints
          338.973
Economists
   Heilbroner, R. L. The worldly philosophers
          330.1
Una **edad** muy tierna, m'ija. Reyna, T.
   In Growing up Chicana/o p203-08   **810.8**
An **eddy** on the floor. Capes, B.
   In Victorian ghost stories p403-30   **S C**
Edelman, Bernard
   (ed) Dear America: letters home from Vietnam.
   See Dear America: letters home from Viet-
   nam   **959.704**
Edelson, Edward, 1932-
   Birth defects   **616**
   The immune system   **616.07**
   The nervous system   **612.8**
   Sleep   **612.8**
   Sports medicine   **617.1**
Edey, Maitland Armstrong, 1910-1992
   (jt. auth) Johanson, D. C. Lucy: the beginnings
   of humankind   **573.2**
The **edge** of the sea. Carson, R.   **574.92**
Edgerton, William Benbow, 1914-
   (ed) Columbia dictionary of modern European
   literature. See Columbia dictionary of modern
   European literature   **803**
Edgeworth, Maria, 1767-1849
   The Limerick gloves
   In The Oxford book of Irish short stories p27-
   51   **S C**
Edible plants
   Livingston, A. D. Edible plants and animals
          641
Edible plants and animals. Livingston, A. D.
          641
Edinburgh (Scotland)
Fiction
   Spark, M. The prime of Miss Jean Brodie
          Fic
Edison, Thomas A. (Thomas Alva), 1847-1931
About
   Adair, G. Thomas Alva Edison   **92**

Edmo, Ed
   After Celilo
   In Talking leaves   **S C**
Edmonds, Margot
   Voices of the winds: native American legends
          398.2
Edmonds, Randolph, 1900-1983
   Old man Pete
   In Black theatre USA   **812.008**
Edmonds, Robin
   Pushkin   **92**
Edmonds, Sheppard Randolph *See* Edmonds,
   Randolph, 1900-1983
Edmunds, R. David (Russell David), 1939-
   Tecumseh and the quest for Indian leadership
          92
Edmunds, Russell David *See* Edmunds, R. David
   (Russell David), 1939-
An **educated** American woman. Cheever, J.
   In Cheever, J. The stories of John Cheever
   p521-35   **S C**
Education
   See also Colleges and universities; Elemen-
   tary education; Teaching
   See/See also pages in the following book(s):
   Toffler, A. Future shock p352-78   **303.4**
Curricula
   See also Colleges and universities—Curric-
   ula
Directories
   The High-school student's guide to study, travel,
   and adventure abroad   **370.19**
Philosophy
   Dewey, J. Democracy and education   **370.1**
Social aspects
   Kozol, J. Illiterate America   **370.19**
   O'Connor, S. Will my name be shouted out?
          808
Greece
   See/See also pages in the following book(s):
   Hamilton, E. The echo of Greece p49-103
          880.9
   Robinson, C. E. Everyday life in ancient Greece
          938
Rome
   See/See also pages in the following book(s):
   Davis, W. S. A day in old Rome p189-209
          937
United States
   America's children: opposing viewpoints
          362.7
   The Best of Free Spirit   **305.23**
   Education in America: opposing viewpoints
          370.9
   Postman, N. The end of education   **370.9**
United States—Dictionaries
   Unger, H. G. Encyclopedia of American educa-
   tion   **370.9**
United States—Directories
   American universities and colleges   **378.73**
   Barron's profiles of American colleges
          378.73
   Cass & Birnbaum's guide to American colleges
          378.73
   The College blue book   **378.73**

The **effect** of gamma rays on man-in-the moon marigolds. Zindel, P.   **812**

Eggenberger, David
An encyclopedia of battles   **904**

Egle̊, Queen of Serpents
In Hearne, B. G. Beauties and beasts p124-28   **398.2**

Egotism; or, The bosom-serpent. Hawthorne, N.
In Hawthorne, N. Tales and sketches; A wonder book for girls and boys; Tanglewood tales for girls and boys p781-94   **S C**

Egypt
       Antiquities
Aldred, C. The Egyptians   **932**
David, A. R. Discovering ancient Egypt   **932**
Egypt: land of the pharaohs   **932**
El Mahdy, C. Mummies, myth and magic in ancient Egypt   **393**
Hoffman, M. A. Egypt before the pharaohs   **932**
Mertz, B. Temples, tombs, and hieroglyphs   **932**
Romer, J. Ancient lives   **932**
See/See also pages in the following book(s):
Ceram, C. W. Gods, graves, and scholars p75-207   **930.1**
Durant, W. J. Our Oriental heritage p137-217   **950**
      Antiquities—Dictionaries
Bunson, M. R. The encyclopedia of ancient Egypt   **932**
      Civilization
Egypt: land of the pharaohs   **932**
Macaulay, D. Pyramid   **726**
Mertz, B. Temples, tombs, and hieroglyphs   **932**
Romer, J. Ancient lives   **932**
Taylor, J. H. Unwrapping a mummy   **932**
Weeks, J. The pyramids   **726**
      Civilization—Dictionaries
Bunson, M. R. The encyclopedia of ancient Egypt   **932**
      History
Aldred, C. The Egyptians   **932**

Egypt before the pharaohs. Hoffman, M. A.   **932**

Egypt: land of the pharaohs   **932**

Egyptian language
See/See also pages in the following book(s):
Mertz, B. Temples, tombs, and hieroglyphs   **932**

Egyptian mythology
See/See also pages in the following book(s):
El Mahdy, C. Mummies, myth and magic in ancient Egypt p139-74   **393**

Egyptian nights. Pushkin, A. S.
In Pushkin, A. S. Alexander Pushkin: complete prose fiction p249-60   **S C**

The **Egyptians**. Aldred, C.   **932**

Ehrenhaft, George
How to prepare for the ACT, American College Testing Assessment Program. See How to prepare for the ACT, American College Testing Assessment Program   **378.1**

Ehrlich, Anne H.
(jt. auth) Ehrlich, P. R. The population explosion   **304.6**

Ehrlich, Eugene H.
The Oxford illustrated literary guide to the United States   **810.9**
(comp) Oxford American dictionary. See Oxford American dictionary   **423**

Ehrlich, Paul, 1854-1915
See/See also pages in the following book(s):
Curtis, R. H. Great lives: medicine p46-53   **920**
De Kruif, P. Microbe hunters   **920**

Ehrlich, Paul R.
The birder's handbook   **598**
The population explosion   **304.6**

Ehrlich, Robert, 1938-
What if you could unscramble an egg?   **500**

Eichmann, Adolf, 1906-1962
See/See also pages in the following book(s):
Aymar, B. A pictorial history of the world's greatest trials p343-57   **345**

Eight American poets   **811.008**

Eight men out. Asinof, E.   **796.357**

Eighteen from Pereshchepena. Sholem Aleichem
In Sholem Aleichem. Tevye the dairyman and The railroad stories   **S C**

Eighteen twelve: the war nobody won. See Marrin, A. 1812: the war nobody won   **973.5**

Eighteenth century
  See also Enlightenment
Durant, W. J. Rousseau and revolution   **940.2**

The **eighty-yard** run. Shaw, I.
In The Norton book of American short stories p448-60   **S C**

Einstein, Albert, 1879-1955
The meaning of relativity   **530.1**
      About
Brian, D. Einstein   **92**
Goldberg, J. Albert Einstein   **92**
Hoffmann, B. Albert Einstein, creator and rebel   **92**
See/See also pages in the following book(s):
Guillen, M. Five equations that changed the world   **530.1**
Hawking, S. W. Black holes and baby universes and other essays p69-83   **523.1**
Jaspers, K. The great philosophers   **109**
Meadows, A. J. The great scientists   **920**
Sagan, C. Broca's brain p18-31   **500**

Einstein's universe. Calder, N.   **530.1**

Eisenheim the illusionist. Millhauser, S.
In The Literary ghost p284-303   **S C**

Eisenhower, Dwight D. (Dwight David), 1890-1969
      About
Ambrose, S. E. Eisenhower   **92**

Eisenhower, Dwight D. (Dwight David), 1890-1969—About—Continued
See/See also pages in the following book(s):
Character above all 920
Miller, M. Plain speaking: an oral biography of Harry S. Truman p337-45 92
Oleksy, W. G. Military leaders of World War II 920
White, T. H. In search of history p346-53, 403-10 92

El-Bisatie, Mohamed
A conversation from the third floor
In African short stories S C

El Cid *See* Cid, ca. 1043-1099

El-hi textbooks and serials in print 016.3713

El Mahdy, Christine
Mummies, myth and magic in ancient Egypt 393

Elbow room. Bradley, M. Z.
In The Norton book of science fiction p412-26 S C

Elder, John, 1947-
(ed) American nature writers. See American nature writers 810.9

Elder, Lonne, 1931-1996
Ceremonies in dark old men
In Best American plays: 7th series—1967-1973 p529-61 812.008
In Black theatre USA 812.008
Sounder
In Best American screenplays 812.008

Elderly
See also Aging; Old age
United States
An Aging population: opposing viewpoints 305.26
Terkel, S. Coming of age 305.26

Eldredge, Charles C.
Georgia O'Keeffe 759.13

Eleanor, of Aquitaine, Queen, consort of Henry II, King of England, 1122?-1204
See/See also pages in the following book(s):
Cantor, N. F. Medieval lives 940.1

Elections
See/See also pages in the following book(s):
Carter, J. Talking peace p126-47 327.1
United States
Congressional Quarterly's guide to U.S. elections 324.6
Congressional Quarterly's politics in America 328.73
Political parties & elections in the United States 324.2

Elections, Primary *See* Primaries

Electra. Sophocles
In Sophocles. Electra, Antigone, Philoctetes 882

Electra, Antigone, Philoctetes. Sophocles 882

Electric lines
See/See also pages in the following book(s):
Macaulay, D. Underground p67-77 624

Electric shock therapy
See/See also pages in the following book(s):
Roueché, B. The medical detectives p273-87 616

Electricity
Grob, B. Basic electronics 621.38
See/See also pages in the following book(s):
Inventors and discoverers p44-79 609
Experiments
Wong, O. K. Experimenting with electricity and magnetism 537

Electronic data processing
See also Artificial intelligence
Campbell-Kelly, M. Computer 004
Dictionaries
Freedman, A. The computer glossary 004
Webster's New World dictionary of computer terms 004

Electronic publishing
See also Desktop publishing

Electronic styles. Li, X. 808

Electronics
Grob, B. Basic electronics 621.38
Dictionaries
Turner, R. P. The illustrated dictionary of electronics 621.381

Electrotherapeutics
See also Electric shock therapy

Elementary education
Kidder, T. Among schoolchildren 372.1

Elementary school libraries
See also Children's libraries

The **elements** of expression. Plotnik, A. 808
The **elements** of playwriting. Catron, L. E. 808.2
The **elements** of style. Strunk, W. 808

Eleonora. Poe, E. A.
In Poe, E. A. The collected tales and poems of Edgar Allan Poe p649-53 S C

Elephant Man *See* Merrick, Joseph Carey, 1862 or 3-1890

The **Elephant Man.** Pomerance, B. 822
also in Best American plays: 8th series—1974-1982 p496-517 812.008

Elephants
Caras, R. A. A most dangerous journey 599.6
Chadwick, D. H. The fate of the elephant 599.6

The **elevator.** Sleator, W.
In Read all about it! p236-43 808.88

Eleven. Cisneros, S.
In Cisneros, S. Woman Hollering Creek and other stories S C
In Growing up Chicana/o p155-59 810.8

Eleven sons. Kafka, F.
In Kafka, F. The complete stories S C

The **Elfqueen** of Shannara. Brooks, T. See note under Brooks, T. The sword of Shannara Fic

The **Elfstones** of Shannara. Brooks, T. See note under Brooks, T. The sword of Shannara Fic

Ellis, Trey
Guess who's coming to Seder
In Calling the wind p534-38   **S C**
Ellison, Harlan
The man who rowed Christopher Columbus ashore
In The Best American short stories, 1993 p77-93   **S C**
In Nebula awards 29 p20-37   **S C**
Strange wine
In The Norton book of science fiction p350-56   **S C**
The whimper of whipped dogs
In The Horror hall of fame p345-64   **S C**
Ellison, Ralph
Backwacking, a plea to the Senator
In Children of the night p464-70   **S C**
Battle royal
In The Oxford book of American short stories p440-55   **S C**
Flying home
In The Best short stories by Negro writers p151-70   **S C**
In Calling the wind p135-50   **S C**
Invisible man   **Fic**
Invisible man; criticism
In Ralph Ellison: a collection of critical essays   **813.009**
See/See also pages in the following book(s):
Major modern black American writers p85-101   **810.9**
Ellmann, Richard, 1918-1987
James Joyce   **92**
(ed) The New Oxford book of American verse. See The New Oxford book of American verse   **811.008**
(ed) The Norton anthology of modern poetry. See The Norton anthology of modern poetry   **821.008**
Elly. Faulkner, W.
In Faulkner, W. Collected stories of William Faulkner p207-14   **S C**
Elocution *See* Public speaking
Elphick, Jonathan
(ed) The Atlas of bird migration. See The Atlas of bird migration   **598**
Elric at the end of time. Moorcock, M.
In Masterpieces of fantasy and enchantment p491-531   **S C**
El´tsin, Boris Nikolaevich *See* Yeltsin, Boris
Elul. Sholem Aleichem
In Sholem Aleichem. Tevye the dairyman and The railroad stories   **S C**
The **elusive** executive. See Ragsdale, L. Vital statistics on the presidency   **353.03**
Emancipation Proclamation (1863)
See/See also pages in the following book(s):
McPherson, J. M. Drawn with the sword p192-207   **973.7**
Emanoil, Mary
(ed) Encyclopedia of endangered species. See Encyclopedia of endangered species   **574.5**

Emanuel, James A.
Langston Hughes   **818**
Ember, Melvin
(ed) Encyclopedia of cultural anthropology. See Encyclopedia of cultural anthropology   **305.8**
Emblems *See* Signs and symbols
Embroidery. Bradbury, R.
In Bradbury, R. The stories of Ray Bradbury p281-84   **S C**
Embryology
See also Reproduction
Morowitz, H. J. The facts of life   **612.6**
Nilsson, L. A child is born   **612.6**
Vaughan, C. How life begins   **612.6**
The **emerald.** Barthelme, D.
In The Best American short stories of the eighties p57-84   **S C**
Emergency. Johnson, D.
In The Vintage book of contemporary American short stories p274-85   **S C**
Emergency medicine
Kittredge, M. Emergency medicine   **616.02**
Emerson, Ralph Waldo, 1803-1882
Collected poems & translations   **811**
English traits
In Emerson, R. W. The portable Emerson p395-518   **818**
Essays & lectures   **818**
Essays: first and second series
In Emerson, R. W. The portable Emerson p111-290   **818**
Nature
In Emerson, R. W. The portable Emerson p7-50   **818**
The portable Emerson   **818**
About
Yannella, D. Ralph Waldo Emerson   **818**
Emery, Fred
Watergate   **973.924**
Emigrants *See* Immigrants
Emigration *See* Immigration and emigration
Emily Dickinson: a collection of critical essays   **811**
Emily Post's etiquette. Post, P.   **395**
Emily Post's teen etiquette. Post, E. L.   **395**
Eminent Victorians. Strachey, L.   **920**
The **emissary.** Bradbury, R.
In Bradbury, R. The stories of Ray Bradbury p355-61   **S C**
Emma. Austen, J.   **Fic**
Emotional bankruptcy. Fitzgerald, F. S.
In Fitzgerald, F. S. The short stories of F. Scott Fitzgerald p546-60   **S C**
Emotional stress *See* Stress (Psychology)
Emotionally disturbed children
See also Mentally ill children
Hayden, T. L. The tiger's child   **155.5**
Emotions
Emotions [Time-Life Bks.]   **152.4**
Emotions [Time-Life Bks.]   **152.4**

Empedocles
See/See also pages in the following book(s):
Jaspers, K. The great philosophers 109
The Emperor Jones. O'Neill, E.
In O'Neill, E. Complete plays v1 812
In O'Neill, E. Nine plays p1-32 812
Emperors *See* Kings, queens, rulers, etc.
The empire. Hesse, H.
In Hesse, H. The fairy tales of Hermann
Hesse S C
The empire of the ants. Wells, H. G.
In Wells, H. G. The complete short stories of
H. G. Wells p92-108 S C
Empire of the Sun. Ballard, J. G. Fic
Empire State Building (New York, N.Y.)
Macaulay, D. Unbuilding 690
Empires ascendant: timeframe 400 BC-AD 200
930
Empires besieged: timeframe AD 200-600
930
Employment applications *See* Applications for
positions
Employment forecasting
Field, S. 100 best careers for the 21st century
331.7
Jones, L. K. Job skills for the 21st century
331.7
Employment guidance *See* Vocational guidance
Employment of children *See* Children—Employment
Employment of women *See* Women—Employment
Employment of youth *See* Youth—Employment
The empty house. Blackwood, A.
In The Oxford book of English ghost stories
p222-35 S C
Emshwiller, Carol
The start of the end of the world
In The Norton book of science fiction p466-
76 S C
The Enchanted prince
In Hearne, B. G. Beauties and beasts p109-14
398.2
The enchanted profile. Henry, O.
In Henry, O. The best short stories of O.
Henry S C
The Enchanted Tsarevitch
In Hearne, B. G. Beauties and beasts p14-17
398.2
Enchanted village. Van Vogt, A. E.
In Nebula awards 31 p231-45 S C
Encore!. Kehret, P. 812.008
An encounter. Joyce, J.
In Joyce, J. Dubliners S C
An encounter in the mist. Munby, A. N. L.
In The Oxford book of English ghost stories
p438-43 S C
The Encyclopedia Americana 031
Encyclopedia mysteriosa. DeAndrea, W. L.
809.3
Encyclopedia of African-American culture and
history 305.8

The Encyclopedia of American comics 741.5
Encyclopedia of American education. Unger, H.
G. 370.9
The encyclopedia of American facts and dates.
Carruth, G. 973.02
Encyclopedia of American family names. Robb,
H. A. 929.4
Encyclopedia of American Indian costume.
Paterek, J. 391
The encyclopedia of American intelligence and espionage. O'Toole, G. J. A. 327.12
The encyclopedia of American religions. Melton,
J. G. 200.9
The Encyclopedia of American religions: religious
creeds 291
Encyclopedia of American religious history.
Queen, E. L. 200.9
The encyclopedia of ancient Egypt. Bunson, M.
R. 932
Encyclopedia of ancient Mesoamerica. Bunson,
M. R. 972
The Encyclopedia of animal evolution 591.3
The Encyclopedia of aquatic life 591.92
Encyclopedia of art deco 709.04
An encyclopedia of battles. Eggenberger, D.
904
Encyclopedia of birds 598
Encyclopedia of card tricks. Hugard, J. 795.4
The Encyclopedia of careers and vocational guidance 331.7
The Encyclopedia of classical music. See Gammond, P. The Harmony illustrated encyclopedia of classical music 781.6
Encyclopedia of climate and weather 551.6
The Encyclopedia of climatology 551.5
Encyclopedia of college basketball. Douchant, M.
796.323
The Encyclopedia of colonial and revolutionary
America 973.3
Encyclopedia of constitutional amendments, proposed amendments, and amending issues,
1789-1995. Vile, J. R. 342
Encyclopedia of creation myths. Leeming, D. A.
291.03
Encyclopedia of cultural anthropology 305.8
The Encyclopedia of democracy 321.8
The encyclopedia of depression. Roesch, R.
616.85
The Encyclopedia of drug abuse 616.86
Encyclopedia of drugs and alcohol 362.29
Encyclopedia of earth sciences 550.3
The encyclopedia of earthquakes and volcanoes.
Ritchie, D. 551.2
Encyclopedia of endangered species 574.5
The encyclopedia of evolution. Milner, R.
573.2
Encyclopedia of gardening, The American Horticultural Society 635
The encyclopedia of gems and minerals. Holden,
M. 553.8

Encyclopedia Sherlockiana. Bunson, M.
823.009

Encyclopedias and dictionaries

See also Picture dictionaries; Polyglot dictionaries; names of languages and subjects with the subdivision *Dictionaries*

Academic American encyclopedia — 031
Collier's encyclopedia — 031
The Columbia encyclopedia — 031
Compton's encyclopedia and fact-index — 031
The Concise Columbia encyclopedia — 031
The Dorling Kindersley visual encyclopedia — 031
The Encyclopedia Americana — 031
Encyclopedic world atlas — 912
Kane, J. N. Famous first facts: a record of first happenings, discoveries, and inventions in American history — 031.02
Krantz, L. The peoplepedia — 031.02
The Larousse desk reference — 031
The Macmillan visual desk reference — 031
The New Encyclopaedia Britannica — 031
The New York Public Library desk reference — 031.02
Reader's Digest book of facts — 031.02
The World Book encyclopedia — 031

Bibliography

Kister, K. F. Kister's best encyclopedias — 016

The **Encyclopedic** dictionary of science. See Illustrated dictionary of science — 503

Encyclopedic handbook of cults in America. Melton, J. G. — 291

Encyclopedic world atlas — 912

Encylopedia of Russian history. Paxton, J. — 947

The **end** of apartheid. Bradley, C. — 968.06

The **end** of education. Postman, N. — 370.9

The **end** of science. Horgan, J. — 501

The **end** of something. Hemingway, E.
In Hemingway, E. The complete short stories of Ernest Hemingway p79-82 — S C
In Hemingway, E. In our time p31-35 — S C
In Hemingway, E. The Nick Adams stories p200-04 — S C
In Hemingway, E. The short stories of Ernest Hemingway p105-11 — S C

End of summer. Behrman, S. N.
In Twenty best plays of the modern American theatre p275-323 — 812.008

The **end** of the beginning. Bradbury, R.
In Bradbury, R. The stories of Ray Bradbury p880-84 — S C

The **end** of the flight. Maugham, W. S.
In Maugham, W. S. Collected short stories v4 — S C

The **end** of the party. Greene, G.
In Greene, G. The portable Graham Greene p29-36 — 828

The **end** of the tether. Conrad, J.
In Conrad, J. The complete short fiction of Joseph Conrad v3 — S C

End of the world. Kopit, A. L.
In Best American plays: 9th series—1983-1992 p95-125 — 812.008

Endangered peoples. Davidson, A. — 305.8

Endangered species

See also Rare animals; Wildlife conservation

Ackerman, D. The rarest of the rare — 574.5
Adams, D. Last chance to see — 591.5
Bergman, C. Wild echoes: encounters with the most endangered animals in North America — 591.5
Cohen, D. The modern ark — 333.95
Endangered species: opposing viewpoints — 574.5
Mann, C. C. Noah's choice — 574.5
The Official World Wildlife Fund guide to endangered species of North America — 574.5
Quammen, D. The song of the dodo — 574.9
Saving wildlife — 333.95

Dictionaries

Encyclopedia of endangered species — 574.5
Endangered wildlife of the world — 591.5
The Grolier world encyclopedia of endangered species — 591.5

Endangered species: opposing viewpoints — 574.5

Endangered wildlife of the world — 591.5

Ender's game. Card, O. S. — Fic

Endicott and the Red Cross. Hawthorne, N.
In Hawthorne, N. Tales and sketches; A wonder book for girls and boys; Tanglewood tales for girls and boys p542-48 — S C

Endings and beginnings. Pilcher, R.
In Pilcher, R. Flowers in the rain & other stories — S C

Endocrine glands

Little, M. The endocrine system — 612.4
Young, J. K. Hormones: molecular messengers — 612.4

The **endocrine** system. Little, M. — 612.4

Endres, Franz Carl, 1878-1954

Schimmel, A. The mystery of numbers — 133.3

Endrezze, Anita

The humming of stars and bees and waves
In Talking leaves — S C

Endurance, Physical *See* Physical fitness

The **enduring** chill. O'Connor, F.
In O'Connor, F. Collected works p547-72 — S C
In O'Connor, F. The complete stories p357-82 — S C

Enedina's story. Hernández-Avila, I.
In Latina: women's voices from the borderlands p229-39 — 810.8

Enemies. O'Brien, T.
In O'Brien, T. The things they carried — S C

The **enemy.** Singer, I. B.
In Singer, I. B. The image and other stories p91-101 — S C

The **enemy** of all the world. London, J.
   In London, J. The science fiction stories of
     Jack London p62-74   **S C**
An **enemy** of the people. Ibsen, H.
   In Ibsen, H. The complete major prose plays
         839.8
   In Ibsen, H. Ibsen: four major plays
         839.8
Energy *See* Force and energy
Energy alternatives   **333.79**
Energy resources
  See/See also pages in the following book(s):
  The Plains Indians of the twentieth century
   p219-35   **970.004**
      Government policy
  See/See also pages in the following book(s):
  Energy alternatives   **333.79**
The **engagement** party. Boles, R.
   In The Best short stories by Negro writers
    p479-89   **S C**
Engel, Joel, 1952-
  Addicted: kids talking about drugs in their own
   words   **616.86**
  (jt. auth) Foreman, G. By George   **92**
Engelmann, Larry
  Tears before the rain   **959.704**
Engels, Friedrich, 1820-1895
  (jt. auth) Marx, K. The Communist manifesto of
   Karl Marx and Friedrich Engels   **335.4**
  See/See also pages in the following book(s):
  Heilbroner, R. L. The worldly philosophers
         330.1
Engineering
    See also Steam engineering
  Freiman, F. L. Failed technology   **620**
  Magill's survey of science, applied science se-
   ries   **620**
       Experiments
  Goodwin, P. More engineering projects for
   young scientists   **620**
Engineering, Genetic *See* Genetic engineering
Engineering, Structural *See* Structural engineer-
  ing
Engineers
      Dictionaries
  Notable twentieth century scientists   **920.003**
Engineers of dreams. Petroski, H.   **624**
England
      History
    See Great Britain—History
England, my England. Lawrence, D. H.
   In Lawrence, D. H. The complete short sto-
    ries v2   **S C**
England underway. Bisson, T.
   In Nebula awards 29 p181-202   **S C**
Engle, Margarita
  Singing to Cuba [excerpt]
   In Latina: women's voices from the border-
    lands p222-27   **810.8**
  Uncle Teo's shorthand cookbook
   In Daughters of the fifth sun   **810.8**
Engle, Mary
  Internet connections. See Internet connections
         004

English arts
  See/See also pages in the following book(s):
  Durant, W. J. The age of Napoleon p376-85
         940.2
English authors
      Anecdotes
    See Authors, English—Anecdotes
English ballads
  The Oxford book of ballads   **821.008**
English drama
      Bio-bibliography
  Critical survey of drama   **822.009**
      History and criticism
  Critical survey of drama   **822.009**
  Dietrich, R. F. British drama, 1890 to 1950
         822.009
  Rusinko, S. British drama, 1950 to the present
         822.009
English fiction
      Bio-bibliography
  Contemporary novelists   **920.003**
      Dictionaries
  Dictionary of British literary characters
         820.3
      History and criticism
  A Reader's guide to the twentieth-century novel
         823.009
English language
  Crystal, D. The Cambridge encyclopedia of the
   English language   **420**
  Hayakawa, S. I. Language in thought and action
         412
  The Oxford companion to the English language
         420
      Acronyms
    See Acronyms
      Americanisms
    See Americanisms
      Composition and exercises
  Gutkind, L. Creative nonfiction   **808**
      Dictionaries
  The American Heritage college dictionary
         423
  The Concise Oxford dictionary of current Eng-
   lish   **423**
  Dictionary of American regional English
         427
  Dorling Kindersley ultimate visual dictionary
         423
  Hirsch, E. D. The dictionary of cultural literacy
         031
  Merriam-Webster's collegiate dictionary
         423
  Oxford American dictionary   **423**
  The Oxford desk dictionary: American edition
         423
  The Oxford dictionary of new words   **423**
  Random House compact unabridged dictionary
         423
  Random House unabridged dictionary   **423**
  Random House Webster's college dictionary
         423
  Third Barnhart dictionary of new English
         423
  Webster's II new college dictionary   **423**

Erdrich, Louise
American Horse
In Spider Woman's granddaughters   S C
The bingo van
In Talking leaves   S C
Fleur
In The Oxford book of American short stories
    p727-40   S C
In We are the stories we tell   S C
Lipsha's luck
In Song of the turtle p231-57   S C
Love medicine [excerpt]
In Growing up Native American p151-66
    810.8
In The Lightning within p108-30   S C
Old man Potchikoo
In The Oxford book of modern fairy tales
    p431-41   S C
The red convertible
In Who do you think you are? p134-45
    S C

See/See also pages in the following book(s):
Coltelli, L. Winged words: American Indian
    writers speak   **897**
Erickson, Jon, 1948-
Craters, caverns, and canyons   **551.1**
Dying planet   **575**
Glacial geology   **551.3**
A history of life on earth   **560**
The human volcano   **304.2**
Ice ages: past and future   **551.7**
An introduction to fossils and minerals   **560**
Marine geology   **551.46**
Quakes, eruptions, and other geologic cata-
    clysms   **550**
Erickson, Judith B.
Directory of American youth organizations
    369.4
Ermarth, Elizabeth, 1939-
George Eliot   **823.009**
Ernie's war. Pyle, E.   **940.53**
Ernst, Carl H.
Turtles of the world   **597.9**
Erotic literature
See/See also pages in the following book(s):
Lawrence, D. H. The portable D. H. Lawrence
    p646-71   **828**
An **error** in chemistry. Faulkner, W.
In The Oxford book of American detective
    stories p414-30   S C
Errors
Stein, G. Encyclopedia of hoaxes   **001.9**
Escape. Asimov, I.
In Asimov, I. I, robot   S C
The **escape.** Maugham, W. S.
In Maugham, W. S. Collected short stories v1
    S C
Escape from Egypt. Levitin, S.   Fic
Escape from freedom. Fromm, E.   **323.44**
Escape from Pharaoh. Hurston, Z. N.
In Hurston, Z. N. The complete stories p178-
    92   S C
The **escape;** or, A leap for freedom. Brown, W.
W.
In Black theatre USA   **812.008**

Escape to the blue planet. Boiko, C.
In The Big book of large-cast plays p101-14
    812.008
Escapes
Brickhill, P. The great escape   **940.54**
Eschatology
    See also Future life
Escher, M. C. (Maurits Cornelis), 1898-1972
The world of M. C. Escher   **769**
Escher, Maurits Cornelis *See* Escher, M. C.
    (Maurits Cornelis), 1898-1972
Eschmeyer, William N.
A field guide to Pacific coast fishes of North
    America   **597**
Eskimos *See* Inuit
Eskow, Dennis
Lyndon Baines Johnson   **92**
Eskridge, Kelley
Alien Jane
In Nebula awards 31 p74-92   S C
ESP *See* Extrasensory perception
Espenshade, Edward Bowman, 1910-
(ed) Goode's world atlas. See Goode's world at-
    las   **912**
Espionage
    See also Spies
Melton, H. K. The ultimate spy book
    327.12
Rogers, J. T. The secret war   **940.54**
Waller, J. H. The unseen war in Europe
    940.54
Espionage, American *See* American espionage
The **Esquimau** maiden's romance. Twain, M.
In Twain, M. The complete short stories of
    Mark Twain   S C
Esquivel, Laura
Like water for chocolate   Fic
Essay
Bender, S. Writing personal essays   **808**
Essay and general literature index   **080**
An **essay** concerning the true original, extent and
    end of civil government. Locke, J.
In Social contract p1-143   **320.1**
Essays
      Indexes
Essay and general literature index   **080**
Essays & lectures. Emerson, R. W.   **818**
Essays: first and second series. Emerson, R. W.
In Emerson, R. W. The portable Emerson
    p111-290   **818**
Essays of E. B. White. White, E. B.   **814**
The **essential** C. S. Lewis. Lewis, C. S.   **828**
The **essential** Darwin. Darwin, C.   **575.01**
The **essential** Darwin. See Darwin, C. The Darwin
    reader   **575.01**
The **essential** guide to nonprescription drugs. See
    Zimmerman, D. R. Zimmerman's Complete
    guide to nonprescription drugs   **615**
The **essential** Shakespeare. Shakespeare, W.
    822.3

Essex Institute
See/See also pages in the following book(s):
Aymar, B. A pictorial history of the world's greatest trials p81-95   **345**

Esslin, Martin
The theatre of the absurd   **809.2**

Essop, Ahmed
The betrayal
In African short stories   **S C**

Estes, Sally
(ed) Genre favorites for young adults. See Genre favorites for young adults   **016.8**

Estevan, d. 1539
See/See also pages in the following book(s):
Abdul-Jabbar, K. Black profiles in courage p5-13   **920**

Esther. Toomer, J.
In Calling the wind p25-29   **S C**

Esthetics *See* Aesthetics

Et in sempiternum pereant. Williams, C.
In The Oxford book of English ghost stories p421-29   **S C**

Eternal life. Sholem Aleichem
In Sholem Aleichem. The best of Sholem Aleichem   **S C**

Eternal triangle. O'Connor, F.
In O'Connor, F. Collected stories p328-37   **S C**

Ethan Brand. Hawthorne, N.
In Hawthorne, N. Tales and sketches; A wonder book for girls and boys; Tanglewood tales for girls and boys p1051-67   **S C**

Ethan Frome. Springer, M.   **813.009**

Ethan Frome. Wharton, E.   **Fic**
also in Wharton, E. Novellas and other writings   **818**

The ethical vegetarian. De Veaux, A.
In Streetlights: illuminating tales of the urban black experience p77-82   **S C**

Ethics
See also Business ethics

Ethics, Medical *See* Medical ethics

Ethics, Political *See* Political ethics

Ethics, Sexual *See* Sexual ethics

Ethics   **174**

Ethiopia
History
See/See also pages in the following book(s):
Moorehead, A. The Blue Nile   **962**

Ethnic dress. Kennett, F.   **391**

Ethnic groups
See also Minorities
Voices of multicultural America   **815.008**
Dictionaries
Gale encyclopedia of multicultural America   **305.8**
Harvard encyclopedia of American ethnic groups   **305.8**

Ethnic relations
See also Multicultural education; Multiculturalism; Race relations

Carnes, J. Us and them   **305.8**
Nationalism and ethnic conflict   **305.8**

Ethnology
Davidson, A. Endangered peoples   **305.8**
Dictionaries
Encyclopedia of cultural anthropology   **305.8**
Encyclopedia of world cultures   **306**
Polynesia
Heyerdahl, T. Kon-Tiki: across the Pacific by raft   **910.4**

Etiquette
Dresser, N. Multicultural manners   **395**
How to be a perfect stranger   **291.3**
Martin, J. Miss Manners' guide to excruciatingly correct behavior   **395**
Post, E. L. Emily Post's teen etiquette   **395**
Post, P. Emily Post's etiquette   **395**

Etruscans
Etruscans   **937**

Etruscans   **937**

Eudoxus, of Cnidus, ca. 400-ca. 350 B.C.
See/See also pages in the following book(s):
Bell, E. T. Men of mathematics p19-34   **920**

Eugene Onegin. Pushkin, A. S.   **Fic**

Euler, Leonhard, 1707-1783
See/See also pages in the following book(s):
Bell, E. T. Men of mathematics p139-52   **920**

The euphio question. Vonnegut, K.
In Vonnegut, K. Welcome to the monkey house   **S C**

Euripides, ca. 485-ca. 406 B.C.
Alcestis
In Four Greek plays   **882.008**
In Seven famous Greek plays   **882.008**
Medea
In Seven famous Greek plays   **882.008**
See/See also pages in the following book(s):
Hamilton, E. The Greek way p271-83   **880.9**

Europe
Antiquities
Early Europe   **936**
The Oxford illustrated prehistory of Europe   **936**
Church history
Bainton, R. H. Here I stand: a life of Martin Luther   **92**
The Oxford encyclopedia of the Reformation   **270.6**
Civilization
Durant, W. J. The age of Louis XIV   **940.2**
Durant, W. J. The age of Napoleon   **940.2**
Durant, W. J. The age of reason begins   **940.2**
Durant, W. J. The age of Voltaire   **940.2**
Durant, W. J. The Reformation   **940.2**
Durant, W. J. Rousseau and revolution   **940.2**
Description
Twain, M. The innocents abroad   **817**
See/See also pages in the following book(s):
Great rivers of the world p84-180   **910**

Europe—*Continued*
Fiction
James, H. The portrait of a lady   **Fic**
Folklore
See Folklore—Europe
Historical geography—Maps
Matthew, D. Atlas of medieval Europe   **911**
The Times atlas of European history   **911**
History
Dornberg, J. Western Europe   **940.55**
Opfell, O. S. Queens, empresses, grand duchesses, and regents   **920**
History—476-1492
Durant, W. J. The Reformation   **940.2**
The Oxford illustrated history of medieval Europe   **940.1**
Women's lives in medieval Europe: a sourcebook   **305.4**
History—1492-1789
Durant, W. J. The age of Louis XIV   **940.2**
Durant, W. J. The age of reason begins   **940.2**
Durant, W. J. The age of Voltaire   **940.2**
Durant, W. J. The Reformation   **940.2**
Durant, W. J. Rousseau and revolution   **940.2**
History—1789-1900
Doyle, W. The Oxford history of the French Revolution   **944.04**
Durant, W. J. The age of Napoleon   **940.2**
The Oxford illustrated history of modern Europe   **940.2**
Taylor, A. J. P. The struggle for mastery in Europe, 1848-1918   **940.2**
History—1900-1999 (20th century)
The Oxford illustrated history of modern Europe   **940.2**
History—1945-
See/See also pages in the following book(s):
White, T. H. In search of history p263-360   **92**
History—476-1492—Maps
Hooper, N. The Cambridge illustrated atlas of warfare: the Middle Ages   **355**
Intellectual life
Wilson, E. J. Encyclopedia of the Enlightenment   **940.2**
Social conditions
Tuchman, B. W. The proud tower   **909.82**
Europe, Central *See* Central Europe
Europe, Eastern *See* Eastern Europe
The **European.** Hesse, H.
   In Hesse, H. The fairy tales of Hermann Hesse   **S C**
European authors *See* Authors, European
European authors, 1000-1900   **920.003**
The **European** conquest of North America. Jones, C.   **970.01**
The **European** discovery of America. Morison, S. E.   **973.1**
European War, 1914-1918 *See* World War, 1914-1918
Euthanasia
   Arguing euthanasia   **179**
   Euthanasia: opposing viewpoints   **179**

Gay, K. The right to die   **179**
   See/See also pages in the following book(s):
   Hendin, H. Suicide in America p236-77   **179**
Landau, E. The right to die   **179**
Mabie, M. C. J. Bioethics and the new medical technology   **174**
Euthanasia: opposing viewpoints   **179**
Eva. Dickinson, P.   **Fic**
Evacuation and relocation of Japanese Americans, 1942-1945 *See* Japanese Americans—Evacuation and relocation, 1942-1945
Evangeline. Faulkner, W.
   In Faulkner, W. Uncollected stories of William Faulkner p583-609   **S C**
Evans, Elizabeth, 1935-
   Anne Tyler   **813.009**
Evans, Henry L.
   Firstborn
   In Streetlights: illuminating tales of the urban black experience p372-79   **S C**
Evans, Ivor H.
   (ed) Brewer's dictionary of phrase and fable. See Brewer's dictionary of phrase and fable   **803**
Evans, Lawrence Watt- *See* Watt-Evans, Lawrence, 1954-
Evans, Mary Lowe- *See* Lowe-Evans, Mary
Evans, Roger
   How to read music   **781.4**
Evans, Walker, 1903-1975
   Walker Evans: the Getty Museum collection   **779**
   (jt. auth) Agee, J. Let us now praise famous men   **976.1**
Eve, Raymond A., 1946-
   The creationist movement in modern America   **213**
The **eve** of Rumoko. Zelazny, R.
   In The Mammoth book of new world science fiction p1-50   **S C**
The **eve** of the spirit festival. Chang, L. S.
   In The Best American short stories, 1996 p40-50   **S C**
Eveline. Joyce, J.
   In Joyce, J. Dubliners   **S C**
Even the queen. Willis, C.
   In Nebula awards 28 p10-26   **S C**
Even unto death. London, J.
   In London, J. The science fiction stories of Jack London p35-39   **S C**
Events leading up to my death. Smith, H. K.   **92**
Ever such a nice boy. Plomer, W.
   In Classic English short stories, 1930-1955 p113-17   **S C**
Ever the winds of chance. Sandburg, C.   **92**
Everett, Percival L.
   Age would be that does
   In Calling the wind p578-83   **S C**
Everhart, Nancy
   How to write a term paper   **808**

Excavations (Archeology)—*Continued*
Iraq
Mesopotamia: the mighty kings   935
Israel
Shanks, H. Jerusalem   933

Excellence in library services to young adults
          027.62

Exchange value. Johnson, C.
In The Best American short stories of the
eighties p142-50   S C

Executions *See* Capital punishment

Executive power
See/See also pages in the following book(s):
Tuchman, B. W. Practicing history p294-303
          907

Exercise
See also Bodybuilding; Physical fitness;
Weight lifting
Soft workouts   613.7
White, T. P. The wellness guide to lifelong fit-
ness   613.7

Exercises, Reducing *See* Reducing

Exhibitions
See also Fairs

Exile to Hell. Asimov, I.
In Asimov, I. The complete stories v2 p377-
80   S C

Exiles *See* Refugees

The **exiles**. Bradbury, R.
In Bradbury, R. The illustrated man   S C

Exodus. Uris, L.   Fic

Exorcism. Bradbury, R.
In Bradbury, R. The stories of Ray Bradbury
p429-38   S C

Expanding universe *See* Universe

Expectation of life. O'Connor, F.
In O'Connor, F. Collected stories p431-44
          S C

Experience of the McWilliamses with membra-
nous croup. Twain, M.
In Twain, M. The complete short stories of
Mark Twain   S C

Experimentation on animals *See* Animal experimentation

Experimenting with electricity and magnetism.
Wong, O. K.   537

Experimenting with science in sports. Gardner, R.
          507.8

Experimenting with sound. Gardner, R.   534

Experimenting with time. Gardner, R.   529

Experimenting with water. Gardner, R.   553.7

Exploration
See also Africa—Exploration
Into the unknown   910
The Oxford book of exploration   910.4
Atlases
The Times atlas of world exploration   911
Dictionaries
Stefoff, R. The young Oxford companion to
maps and mapmaking   912

Explorers
Cummins, J. G. Francis Drake   92

Duncan, D. E. Hernando de Soto   92
Faber, H. The discoverers of America
          970.01
Heyerdahl, T. Green was the earth on the sev-
enth day   92
Into the unknown   910
Marks, R. L. Cortés   92
Meltzer, M. Columbus and the world around
him   92
Moorehead, A. The Blue Nile   962
Morison, S. E. The European discovery of
America   973.1
The Times atlas of world exploration   911
Dictionaries
Explorers and discoverers of the world
          920.003

Explorers and discoverers of the world
          920.003

Exploring the sky. Moeschl, R.   523

Exploring your world   910.3

Exposing a city slicker. Kafka, F.
In Kafka, F. The metamorphosis and other
stories p26-28   S C

Exposures. Benford, G.
In The Norton book of science fiction p445-
56   S C

Expressionism (Art)
See/See also pages in the following book(s):
Arnason, H. H. History of modern art: painting,
sculpture, architecture   709.04
Canaday, J. E. What is art?   701
Read, Sir H. E. A concise history of modern
painting   759.06

Extenuating circumstances. Oates, J. C.
In The Oxford book of women writing in the
United States p148-53   810.8

Extermination of pests *See* Pest control

Extinct animals
See also Mass extinction of species; Rare
animals
Erickson, J. Dying planet   575
Stanley, S. M. Extinction   574.5

Extinct cities
Splendors of the past   930
Stuart, G. S. America's ancient cities
          970.01

Extinct plants *See* Fossil plants

Extinction. Stanley, S. M.   574.5

Extinction of species, Mass *See* Mass extinction
of species

Extract from Captain Stormfield's visit to heaven.
Twain, M.
In Twain, M. The complete short stories of
Mark Twain   S C

Extraordinary origins of everyday things. Panati,
C.   031.02

Extrasensory perception
See also Telepathy
Secrets of the inner mind   154
Fiction
King, S. Carrie   Fic

Extraterrestrial communication *See* Interstellar
communication

The **extraterrestrial** encyclopedia. Angelo, J. A.
574.999

Exupéry, Antoine de Saint- *See* Saint-Exupéry,
Antoine de, 1900-1944

Eye
Hubel, D. Eye, brain, and vision   **612.8**
Samz, J. Vision   **617.7**

Eye, brain, and vision. Hubel, D.   **612.8**

Eye-hand coordination. Shange, N.
In Streetlights: illuminating tales of the urban
black experience p442-51   **S C**

The **Eye** of Allah. Kipling, R.
In Kipling, R. The portable Kipling   **828**

The **eyeless** dragons: a Chinese story. Morris, K.
In Masterpieces of fantasy and enchantment
p483-88   **S C**

The **eyes.** Wharton, E.
In Wharton, E. The selected short stories of
Edith Wharton p149-64   **S C**

Eyes and teeth. Coleman, W.
In Coming of age in America p212-15
S C

Eyes do more than see. Asimov, I.
In Asimov, I. The complete stories v1 p602-
04   **S C**

Eyes of Zapata. Cisneros, S.
In Cisneros, S. Woman Hollering Creek and
other stories   **S C**
In Daughters of the fifth sun   **810.8**

Eyes on the prize: America's civil rights years,
1954-1965. Williams, J.   **323.1**

Eyes on the prize: America's civil rights years, a
reader and guide. See The Eyes on the prize
civil rights reader   **323.1**

The **Eyes** on the prize civil rights reader
323.1

F

Faber, Doris, 1924-
Love & rivalry   **920**

Faber, Harold
The discoverers of America   **970.01**

A **fable.** Twain, M.
In Twain, M. The complete short stories of
Mark Twain   **S C**

A **fable:** the tendrils of the vine. Colette
In Colette. The collected stories of Colette
p100-01   **S C**

Fables
La Fontaine, J. de. Fifty fables of La Fontaine
841

Fabric painting. Innes, M.   **746.6**

La **Fabulosa:** a Texas operetta. Cisneros, S.
In Cisneros, S. Woman Hollering Creek and
other stories   **S C**

Face. Pineda, C.
In Daughters of the fifth sun   **810.8**

Face. Yamaguchi, Y.
In Border crossings: emigration and exile
p71-91   **808.8**

The **face** of the war. Wolfe, T.
In Wolfe, T. The complete short stories of
Thomas Wolfe p229-40   **S C**

Face value. Hamlett, C.
In The Big book of large-cast plays p185-96
812.008

Facing history. McElroy, G. C.   **704.9**

Facing the mariachis. Gaspar de Alba, A.
In Latina: women's voices from the border-
land p38-48   **810.8**

Facklam, Howard
(jt. auth) Facklam, M. Healing drugs   **615**

Facklam, Margery, 1927-
Healing drugs   **615**

The **fact** of a doorframe. Rich, A.   **811**

Facts, Miscellaneous *See* Curiosities and wonders

Facts about Canada, its provinces and territories.
Weihs, J. R.   **971**

Facts about the Congress. Christianson, S. G.
328.73

Facts about the presidents. Kane, J. N.   **920**

Facts about the states   **973**

Facts about the Supreme Court of the United
States. Paddock, L.   **347**

The **facts** concerning the recent carnival of crime
in Connecticut. Twain, M.
In The Norton book of American short stories
p51-65   **S C**

The **facts** in the case of M. Valdemar. Poe, E. A.
In Poe E. A. The collected tales and poems
of Edgar Allan Poe p96-103   **S C**

The **facts** in the great beef contract. Twain, M.
In Twain, M. The complete short stories of
Mark Twain   **S C**

The **facts** of life. Maugham, W. S.
In Maugham, W. S. Collected short stories v1
S C

The **facts** of life. Morowitz, H. J.   **612.6**

The **Facts** on File Asian political almanac. Cook,
C.   **950**

The **Facts** on File dictionary of 20th-century allusions. Cole, S.   **031.02**

The **Facts** on File dictionary of astronomy
520.3

The **Facts** on File dictionary of biotechnology and
genetic engineering. Steinberg, M. L.
660

The **Facts** on File dictionary of chemistry
540.3

The **Facts** on File dictionary of classical, biblical,
and literary allusions. Lass, A. H.   **803**

The **Facts** on File dictionary of science. See
Uvarov, E. B. The Penguin dictionary of science   **503**

The **Facts** on File dictionary of the theatre
792.03

The **Facts** on File encyclopedia of word and
phrase origins. Hendrickson, R.   **422.03**

The **Facts** on File encyclopedia of world mythology and legend. Mercatante, A. S.   **291.03**

The **Facts** on File history of the American people.
Scott, J. A.   **973**

Farrakhan, Louis
About
Magida, A. J. Prophet of rage: a life of Louis Farrakhan and his nation   **92**

Farrar, Ronald T.
(jt. auth) Worthington, J. F. The ultimate college survival guide   **378**

Farrell-Beck, Jane
(jt. auth) Payne, B. The history of costume   **391**

Farris, Lynne
Sewing fun stuff!   **746**

Farwell, Byron
Stonewall: a biography of General Thomas J. Jackson   **92**

The **fascinating** fresh water fish book. Quinn, J. R.   **639.3**

Fascinating people and astounding events from American history. Smith, R. D.   **973.02**

Fascism
Ebenstein, A. D. Today's isms   **335**
Laqueur, W. Fascism   **320.5**
Germany
See also National socialism
Hasselbach, I. Fuhrer-Ex   **943.087**
Italy
Hoyt, E. P. Mussolini's empire   **92**
See/See also pages in the following book(s):
Hearder, H. Italy p225-43   **945**

Fashion
See also Costume
History
Ewing, E. History of twentieth century fashion   **391**
Peacock, J. The chronicle of Western fashion   **391**
Yarwood, D. Fashion in the Western world, 1500-1900   **391**

Fashion. Ritchie, A. C. O. M.
In Best plays of the early American theatre p97-135   **812.008**

Fashion design
Dictionaries
Calasibetta, C. M. Fairchild's dictionary of fashion   **391**

Fashion in the Western world, 1500-1900. Yarwood, D.   **391**

Fashion models
Gross, M. Model   **659.1**

Fashions of a decade, The 1920s. Herald, J.   **391**

Fashions of a decade, The 1930s. Costantino, M.   **391**

Fashions of a decade, The 1940s. Baker, P.   **391**

Fashions of a decade, The 1950s. Baker, P.   **391**

Fashions of a decade, The 1960s. Connikie, Y.   **391**

Fashions of a decade, The 1970s. Herald, J.   **391**

Fashions of a decade, The 1980s. Carnegy, V.   **391**

Fashions of a decade, The 1990s. Feldman, E.   **391**

Fast, Cathy Carroll
(jt. auth) Fast, T. The women's atlas of the United States   **305.4**

Fast, Julius, 1918-
Body language   **153.6**

Fast, Timothy
The women's atlas of the United States   **305.4**

Fastovsky, David E.
The evolution and extinction of the dinosaurs   **567.9**

Fasts and feasts *See* Religious holidays

The **fat** girl. Dubus, A.
In American short story masterpieces   **S C**
In The Vintage book of contemporary American short stories p125-40   **S C**

The **fate** of the elephant. Chadwick, D. H.   **599.6**

Fated for misfortune. Sholem Aleichem
In Sholem Aleichem. Tevye the dairyman and The railroad stories   **S C**

Father and child
Popenoe, D. Life without father   **306.8**

Father and son. Hughes, L.
In The Portable Harlem Renaissance reader p599-618   **810.8**

Father figure. Peck, R.   **Fic**

Father Greg and the homeboys. Fremon, C.   **361.7**

Father Macclesfield's tale. Benson, R. H.
In Victorian ghost stories p459-65   **S C**

Father Sergius. Tolstoy, L., graf
In Tolstoy, L. Great short works of Leo Tolstoy p501-46   **S C**

Father water, Mother woods. Paulsen, G.   **799**

Fathers
See also Teenage fathers
Popenoe, D. Life without father   **306.8**

Fathers, Single parent *See* Single parent family

Fathers and daughters
Fiction
Fox, P. The moonlight man   **Fic**
Mahy, M. The catalogue of the universe   **Fic**
Rendell, R. Heartstones   **Fic**

Fathers and sons
Fiction
Berry, J. Ajeemah and his son   **Fic**
Gordimer, N. My son's story   **Fic**
Klein, N. No more Saturday nights   **Fic**
Myers, W. D. Somewhere in the darkness   **Fic**
Peck, R. Father figure   **Fic**

Fathers and sons. Hemingway, E.
In Hemingway, E. The complete short stories of Ernest Hemingway p369-77   **S C**
In Hemingway, E. The Nick Adams stories p256-68   **S C**
In Hemingway, E. The short stories of Ernest Hemingway p488-99   **S C**

Faulkner, William, 1897-1962
Collected stories of William Faulkner   **S C**
Contents: Barn burning; Shingles for the Lord; The tall men; A bear hunt; Two soldiers; Shall not perish; A rose for Emily; Hair; Centaur in brass; Dry September; Death drag; Elly; Uncle Willy; Mule in the yard; That will be fine; That evening sun; Red leaves; A justice; A courtship; Lo!; Ad astra; Victory; Crevasse; Turnabout; All the dead pilots; Wash; Honor; Dr. Martino; Fox hunt; Pennsylvania Station; Artist at home; The brooch; My Grandmother Millard; Golden land; There was a queen; Mountain victory; Beyond; Black music; The leg; Mistral; Divorce in Naples; Carcassonne

Dry September
In Classic American short stories p344-59
   S C
In The Oxford book of short stories p330-40
   S C
An error in chemistry
In The Oxford book of American detective stories p414-30   **S C**
Hand upon the waters
In Crime classics p269-84   **S C**
Light in August   **Fic**
The reivers   **Fic**
A rose for Emily
In The Oxford book of gothic tales p322-30
   S C
Selected short stories of William Faulkner
   S C
Contents: Barn burning; Two soldiers; A rose for Emily; Dry September; That evening sun; Red leaves; Lo!; Turnabout; Honor; There was a queen; Mountain victory; Beyond; Race at morning

That evening sun
In The Oxford book of American short stories p334-51   **S C**
Uncollected stories of William Faulkner
   S C
Contents: Ambuscade; Retreat; Raid; Skirmish at Sartoris; The unvanquished; Vendée; Fool about a horse; Lizards in Jamshyd's courtyard; The hound; Spotted horses; Lion; The old people; A point of law; Gold is not always; Pantaloon in black; Go down, Moses; Delta autumn; The bear; Race at morning; Hog pawn; Nympholepsy; Frankie and Johnny; The priest; Once aboard the Lugger (I); Once aboard the Lugger (II); Miss Zilphia Gant; Thrift; Idyll in the desert; Two dollar wife; Afternoon of a cow; Mr. Acarius; Sepulture South: gaslight; Adolescence; Al Jackson; Don Giovanni; Peter; Moonlight; The big shot; Dull tale; A return; A dangerous man; Evangeline; A portrait of Elmer; With caution and dispatch; Snow

Wash
In The Norton book of American short stories p342-52   **S C**
About
Brooks, C. William Faulkner   **813.009**
Hoffman, F. J. William Faulkner   **813.009**
Faurot, Jeannette L.
(ed) Asian-Pacific folktales and legends. See Asian-Pacific folktales and legends   **398.2**
Fauset, Jessie Redmon, 1882-1961
Mary Elizabeth
In Calling the wind p18-24   **S C**
Plum bun [excerpt]
In The Portable Harlem Renaissance reader p348-50   **810.8**
There is confusion [excerpt]
In The Portable Harlem Renaissance reader p340-48   **810.8**
See/See also pages in the following book(s):
Black American prose writers of the Harlem Renaissance p36-48   **810.9**

Black American women fiction writers p30-42
   813.009
Faust, Drew Gilpin
Mothers of invention   **973.7**
Fauvism
See/See also pages in the following book(s):
Arnason, H. H. History of modern art: painting, sculpture, architecture   **709.04**
Favorite folktales from around the world
   398.2
Fayer, Steve, 1935-
(jt. auth) Hampton, H. Voices of freedom
   323.1
FBI *See* United States. Federal Bureau of Investigation
The **FBI.** Kessler, R.   **363.2**
FBI Laboratory
Fisher, D. Hard evidence   **363.2**
Fear
See also Phobias
Ashley, J. Overcoming stage fright in everyday life   **616.85**
Dictionaries
Doctor, R. M. The encyclopedia of phobias, fears, and anxieties   **616.85**
Fear. Davies, R.
In Read all about it! p223-29   **808.88**
Fear of math. Zaslavsky, C.   **510.7**
Feast of fear. King, S.   **92**
Feather, Leonard
The encyclopedia of jazz   **781.65**
Feather tigers. Wolfe, G.
In The Norton book of science fiction p280-86   **S C**
Feathertop. Hawthorne, N.
In Hawthorne, N. Tales and sketches; A wonder book for girls and boys; Tanglewood tales for girls and boys p1103-23
   S C
In Masterpieces of fantasy and enchantment p31-48   **S C**
In The Oxford book of modern fairy tales p10-28   **S C**
Fechter, Charles, 1824-1879
The Count of Monte Cristo
In Best plays of the early American theatre p216-61   **812.008**
Federal budget *See* Budget—United States
Federal Bureau of Investigation (U.S.) *See* United States. Federal Bureau of Investigation
Federal courts *See* Courts—United States
Federal government
See/See also pages in the following book(s):
Boorstin, D. J. The Americans: The national experience p393-406   **973**
Federal Party (U.S.)
Miller, J. C. The Federalist era, 1789-1801
   973.4
The **Federalist**   **342**
The **Federalist** era, 1789-1801. Miller, J. C.
   973.4

Federici, Carlos M.
In the blink of an eye
In Tales from the planet Earth   **S C**

Feeding the beast. Walsh, K. T.   **973.927**

The **feeling** of power. Asimov, I.
In Asimov, I. The complete stories v1 p208-16   **S C**

Feelings, Dianne Johnson- *See* Johnson-Feelings, Dianne

Feelings, Tom, 1933-
The middle passage   **759.13**

Feiffer, Jules
Little murders
In Best American plays: 7th series—1967-1973 p467-91   **812.008**

Feinberg, Barbara Silberdick, 1938-
Harry S. Truman   **92**

Feinberg, Brian
The musculoskeletal system   **612.7**

Feinstein, John
A good walk spoiled   **796.352**

Felder, Deborah G.
The 100 most influential women of all time   **920**

Feldman, Andrew J.
The Sierra Club green guide   **363.7**

Feldman, David, 1950-
When do fish sleep? and other imponderables of everyday life   **031.02**
Why do clocks run clockwise? and other imponderables   **031.02**
Why do dogs have wet noses? and other imponderables of everyday life   **031.02**

Feldman, Elane
Fashions of a decade, The 1990s   **391**

Feldman, Robert S. (Robert Stephen), 1947-
Understanding stress   **155.9**

Fellow-creatures. Morris, W.
In The Best American short stories of the eighties p216-22   **S C**

The **fellowship** of the ring. Tolkien, J. R. R.
In Tolkien, J. R. R. The lord of the rings   **Fic**

Fellowships *See* Scholarships

Female role *See* Sex role

Feminine ingenuity. Macdonald, A. L.   **609**

Feminine intuition. Asimov, I.
In Asimov, I. The complete stories v2 p384-402   **S C**

The **feminine** mystique. Friedan, B.   **305.4**

Feminine psychology *See* Women—Psychology

Feminism
See also Women's movement
Banner, L. W. Elizabeth Cady Stanton   **92**
Barry, K. Susan B. Anthony: a biography of a singular feminist   **92**
Burns, S. Social movements of the 1960s   **303.4**
Cullen-DuPont, K. Elizabeth Cady Stanton and women's liberty   **92**
Feminism: opposing viewpoints   **305.4**
Friedan, B. The feminine mystique   **305.4**

Heilbrun, C. G. The education of a woman: the life of Gloria Steinem   **92**
Hooks, B. Bone black: memories of girlhood   **92**
Ireland, P. What women want   **92**
Ortiz, V. Sojourner Truth, a self-made woman   **92**
Steinem, G. Outrageous acts and everyday rebellions   **305.4**
Steinem, G. Revolution from within   **155.2**
See/See also pages in the following book(s):
A History of our time p243-77   **973.92**
Dictionaries
Cullen-DuPont, K. The encyclopedia of women's history in America   **305.4**

Feminism: opposing viewpoints   **305.4**

The **Feminist** companion to literature in English   **820.9**

A **fence** away from freedom. Levine, E.   **940.53**

Fences. Wilson, A.   **812**

"La Fenice". Colette
In Colette. The collected stories of Colette p180-83   **S C**

Fenollosa, Ernest Francisco, 1853-1908
(ed) The Classic Noh theatre of Japan. See The Classic Noh theatre of Japan   **895.6**

Fenton, M. Brock (Melville Brockett), 1943-
Bats   **599.4**

Fenton, Melville Brockett *See* Fenton, M. Brock (Melville Brockett), 1943-

Fenwick, Elizabeth, 1935-
Adolescence   **305.23**
How sex works   **613.9**

Ferber, Edna, 1887-1968
Stage door
In Twenty best plays of the modern American theatre p819-68   **812.008**

Fergus, Jan S., 1943-
Jane Austen   **92**

Fergus, Pamelia Dillin, b. 1824
See/See also pages in the following book(s):
Stefoff, R. Women pioneers   **920**

Ferguson, Margaret W., 1948-
(ed) The Norton anthology of poetry. See The Norton anthology of poetry   **821.008**

Ferguson, William, 1943-
The third voice
In The Literary ghost p125-26   **S C**

Ferlazzo, Paul J.
Emily Dickinson   **811**

Ferlinghetti, Lawrence
These are my rivers   **811**
(ed) City lights pocket poets anthology. See City lights pocket poets anthology   **808.81**

Fermat, Pierre de, 1601-1665
See/See also pages in the following book(s):
Bell, E. T. Men of mathematics p56-72   **920**

Fermi, Enrico, 1901-1954
About
Gottfried, T. Enrico Fermi, pioneer of the atomic age   **92**

A **field** guide to American houses. McAlester, V.
728

A **field** guide to animal tracks. Murie, O. J.
591.5

A **field** guide to eastern forests: North America. Kricher, J. C.
574.5

A **field** guide to freshwater fishes: North America north of Mexico. Page, L. M.
597

A **field** guide to germs. Biddle, W.
616

A **field** guide to mushrooms, North America. Mc-Knight, K. H.
589.2

A **field** guide to Pacific coast fishes of North America. Eschmeyer, W. N.
597

A **field** guide to Pacific coast shells. Morris, P. A.
594

A **field** guide to reptiles and amphibians, eastern and central North America. Conant, R.
597.6

A **field** guide to rocks and minerals. Pough, F. H.
549

A **field** guide to shells. Abbott, R. T.
594

A **field** guide to shells of the Pacific coast and Hawaii. See Morris, P. A. A field guide to Pacific coast shells
594

A **field** guide to the beetles of North America. White, R. E.
595.7

A **field** guide to the birds. Peterson, R. T.
598

Field guide to the birds of North America
598

A **field** guide to the insects of America north of Mexico. Borror, D. J.
595.7

A **field** guide to the mammals. Burt, W. H.
599

A **field** guide to the shells of our Atlantic coast. See Abbott, R. T. A field guide to shells
594

A **field** guide to the stars and planets. Pasachoff, J. M.
523

A **field** guide to trains of North America. Foster, G. L.
625.2

A **field** guide to venomous animals and poisonous plants. Foster, S.
574.6

A **field** guide to western birds. Peterson, R. T.
598

A **field** guide to western reptiles and amphibians. Stebbins, R. C.
597.6

A **field** guide to wildflowers of northeastern and north-central North America. Peterson, R. T.
582.13

The **field** of mustard. Coppard, A. E.
In The Oxford book of short stories p247-54
S C

Field trip. O'Brien, T.
In O'Brien, T. The things they carried
S C

Fieldbook. Boy Scouts of America
369.43

Fielding, Henry, 1707-1754
The history of Tom Jones, a foundling
Fic

Fields and pastures new. McCormack, J.
636.089

Fields of battle. Keegan, J.
973

Fiffer, Sharon Sloan, 1951-
(jt. auth) Fiffer, S. 50 ways to help your community
361.3

Fiffer, Steve
50 ways to help your community
361.3

Fifteen short plays. See McNally, T. 15 short plays
812

The **fifties.** Halberstam, D.
973.92

Fifty fables of La Fontaine. La Fontaine, J. de
841

Fifty-fafty. Westall, R.
In Westall, R. Shades of darkness p113-24
S C

Fifty grand. Hemingway, E.
In Hemingway, E. The complete short stories of Ernest Hemingway p231-49   S C
In Hemingway, E. The short stories of Ernest Hemingway p300-26   S C

Fifty ways to fight censorship. See Marsh, D. 50 ways to fight censorship
323.44

Fifty ways to help your community. See Fiffer, S. 50 ways to help your community
361.3

Fifty-yard dash. Saroyan, W.
In Saroyan, W. My name is Aram   S C

The **fight** for Chattanooga: Chickamauga to Missionary Ridge. Korn, J.
973.7

Figure drawing
Gordon, L. How to draw the human figure
743

Filipino Americans
See/See also pages in the following book(s):
Takaki, R. T. Strangers from a different shore p315-54
305.8

Filipovic, Zlata
Zlata's diary
92

Filisky, Michael, 1947-
Peterson first guide to fishes of North America
597

Film. Sklar, R.
791.43

Film industry (Motion pictures) *See* Motion picture industry

Filmer. Wells, H. G.
In Wells, H. G. The complete short stories of H. G. Wells p829-47   S C

Films *See* Motion pictures

Fimrite, Ron
The World Series
796.357

The **final** days. Woodward, B.
973.924

Final harvest. Dickinson, E.
811

The **final** problem. Doyle, Sir A. C.
In Doyle, Sir A. C. The complete Sherlock Holmes   S C

Finance
See also Deficit financing; Inflation (Finance)

Financial aid, Student *See* Student aid

Financial aid for college. Ordovensky, P.
378.3

Financial aid for the disabled and their families. Schlachter, G. A.
378.3

Financial planning, Personal *See* Personal finance

First conjugation. O'Faolain, J.
In The Oxford book of Irish short stories p515-25   **S C**

The **first** contact with the Gorgonids. Le Guin, U. K.
In Le Guin, U. K. A fisherman of the inland sea p13-21   **S C**

The **first** day. Jones, E. P.
In The Vintage book of contemporary American short stories p286-90   **S C**

First generation children *See* Children of immigrants

First in his class: a biography of Bill Clinton. Maraniss, D.   **92**

First king of Shannara. Brooks, T. See note under Brooks, T. The sword of Shannara   **Fic**

First ladies. Truman, M.   **920**

First love. Sasaki, R. A.
In Growing up Asian American p379-92   **810.8**

First love. Turgenev, I. S.
In The Portable nineteenth-century Russian reader p336-90   **891.7**

First love. Welty, E.
In Welty, E. The collected stories of Eudora Welty p153-68   **S C**

The **first** man. Camus, A.   **Fic**

The **first** man. O'Neill, E.
In O'Neill, E. Complete plays v2   **812**

The **first** men in the moon. Wells, H. G.
In Wells, H. G. Seven famous novels   **Fic**

First Monday in October. Lawrence, J.
In Lawrence, J. The selected plays of Jerome Lawrence and Robert E. Lee p507-69   **812**

First names and empty pockets. Kinsella, W. P.
In Kinsella, W. P. Shoeless Joe Jackson comes to Iowa: stories   **S C**

The **first** one. Hurston, Z. N.
In Black theatre USA   **812.008**

The **first** passage. Palmer, C. A.
In The Young Oxford history of African Americans   **305.8**

The **first** salute. Tuchman, B. W.   **973.3**

The **first** seven years. Malamud, B.
In Malamud, B. The stories of Bernard Malamud p13-25   **S C**

First sorrow. Kafka, F.
In Kafka, F. The complete stories   **S C**

The **First** World War. Gilbert, M.   **940.3**

Firstborn. Evans, H. L.
In Streetlights: illuminating tales of the urban black experience p372-79   **S C**

Fischer, Bobby, 1943-
Bobby Fischer teaches chess   **794.1**

Fischer, Susan H.
(jt. auth) Gravelle, K. Where are my birth parents?   **362.7**

Fish culture
See also Aquariums

Fish for Friday. O'Connor, F.
In O'Connor, F. Collected stories p458-69   **S C**

Fishbein, Seymour L.
Yellowstone country   **917.8**

Fisher, David, 1929-
(jt. auth) Read, A. The fall of Berlin   **940.54**

Fisher, David, 1946-
Hard evidence   **363.2**

Fisher, David E., 1932-
The scariest place on Earth   **551.55**

Fisher, Gary L.
(jt. auth) Cummings, R. W. The survival guide for teenagers with LD* (*learning differences)   **371.9**

Fisher, M. F. K. (Mary Frances Kennedy), 1908-1992
The lost, strayed, stolen
In The Literary ghost p5-30   **S C**

Fisher, Mary Frances Kennedy *See* Fisher, M. F. K. (Mary Frances Kennedy), 1908-1992

Fisher, Rudolph, 1897-1934
Miss Cynthie
In The Best short stories by Negro writers p35-47   **S C**
In Calling the wind p58-68   **S C**
The walls of Jericho [excerpt]
In The Portable Harlem Renaissance reader p537-47   **810.8**
See/See also pages in the following book(s):
Black American prose writers of the Harlem Renaissance p49-61   **810.9**

Fisher, Sydney George, 1856-1927
The Quaker colonies   **973.2**

Fisheries
See/See also pages in the following book(s):
Ocean planet   **574.92**

The **fisherman** from Chihuahua. Connell, E. S.
In American short story masterpieces   **S C**

A **fisherman** of the inland sea. Le Guin, U. K.   **S C**

Fishes
See also Aquariums
Mills, D. Aquarium fish   **639.3**
Quinn, J. R. The fascinating fresh water fish book   **639.3**

North America
The Audubon Society field guide to North American fishes, whales, and dolphins   **597**

Eschmeyer, W. N. A field guide to Pacific coast fishes of North America   **597**

Filisky, M. Peterson first guide to fishes of North America   **597**

Page, L. M. A field guide to freshwater fishes: North America north of Mexico   **597**

Fishing
See also Fly casting
Mason, B. Sports illustrated fly fishing   **799.1**

Paulsen, G. Father water, Mother woods   **799**

Flaubert, Gustave, 1821-1880—*Continued*
About
Buck, S. Gustave Flaubert   **843.009**
Lottman, H. R. Flaubert   **92**
Flavia and her artists. Cather, W.
   In Cather, W. Early novels and stories
            Fic
The **flax**. Andersen, H. C.
   In Andersen, H. C. Tales and stories
            S C
Flegg, Jim
Deserts   **574.5**
Fleischman, Paul
Dateline: Troy   **292**
Fleischmann, Wolfgang Bernard
Encyclopedia of world literature in the 20th century. See Encyclopedia of world literature in the 20th century   **803**
Fleming, Alexander, 1881-1955
See/See also pages in the following book(s):
Curtis, R. H. Great lives: medicine p77-90
            920
Fleming, John, 1919-
The Penguin dictionary of architecture
            720.3
Fleming, Louis B.
(jt. auth) Yamazaki, J. N. Children of the atomic bomb   **92**
Fleming, Robert E. (Robert Edward), 1936-
James Weldon Johnson   **818**
Fleming, Robert Loren
The big book of urban legends   **741.5**
Fletcher, Lucille, 1912-
Sorry, wrong number
   In 24 favorite one-act plays p117-32
            808.82
Fletcher, Marilyn P., 1940-
(ed) Readers' guide to twentieth-century science fiction. See Readers' guide to twentieth-century science fiction   **809.3**
Fletcher, Susan, 1951-
Flight of the Dragon Kyn   **Fic**
Fletcher, William P.
Recording your family history   **929**
Fleur. Erdrich, L.
   In The Oxford book of American short stories p727-40   **S C**
   In We are the stories we tell   **S C**
Flexner, James Thomas, 1908-
George Washington   **92**
Washington, the indispensable man   **92**
Flexner, Stuart Berg
(ed) Random House unabridged dictionary. See Random House unabridged dictionary
            423
(ed) Random House Webster's college thesaurus. See Random House Webster's college thesaurus   **423**
Flies. Asimov, I.
   In Asimov, I. The complete stories v1 p515-20   **S C**
The **flies**. Sartre, J. P.
   In Sartre, J. P. No exit, and three other plays
            842

Flight. Steinbeck, J.
   In Steinbeck, J. The portable Steinbeck
            818
Flight. Updike, J.
   In Updike, J. Pigeon feathers, and other stories p49-73   **S C**
Flight #116 is down. Cooney, C. B.   **Fic**
Flight and flying. Baker, D.   **629.13**
Flight in America: from the Wrights to the astronauts. Bilstein, R. E.   **629.13**
Flight of the Dragon Kyn. Fletcher, S.   **Fic**
Flintham, Victor
Air wars and aircraft   **358.4**
The **floating** world [excerpt] Kadohata, C.
   In Coming of age in America p122-35
            S C
   In Growing up Asian American p255-64
            810.8
Flodin, Mickey
(jt. auth) Butterworth, R. R. Signing made easy
            419
Flood, Renée S.
Lost Bird of Wounded Knee   **92**
The **flood**. Harjo, J.
   In Talking leaves   **S C**
The **flood**. Steinbeck, J.
   In Steinbeck, J. The portable Steinbeck
            818
Florence, Judy
A collection of favorite quilts   **746.46**
Florence, Ronald
The perfect machine   **522**
A **Florentine** tragedy. Wilde, O.
   In 24 favorite one-act plays p434-43
            808.82
Flores, Angel, 1900-1992
Spanish American authors   **920.003**
Florescu, Radu R. N.
Dracula [biography of Vlad II]   **92**
Florey, Howard, Baron Florey, 1898-1968
See/See also pages in the following book(s):
Curtis, R. H. Great lives: medicine p77-90
            920
Florida
Description
See/See also pages in the following book(s):
White, E. B. Essays of E. B. White   **814**
Fiction
Hurston, Z. N. Their eyes were watching God
            Fic
Florie. Colette
   In Colette. The collected stories of Colette p198-204   **S C**
Flotsam and Jetsam. Maugham, W. S.
   In Maugham, W. S. Collected short stories v2
            S C
Flower garden. Jackson, S.
   In Jackson, S. The lottery   **S C**
Flower gardening
Moggi, G. Simon and Schuster's guide to garden flowers   **635.9**

Flowering Judas. Porter, K. A.
  In The Oxford book of short stories p310-21
                                S C
  In Porter, K. A. The collected stories of Katherine Anne Porter   S C
Flowering Judas, and other stories. Porter, K. A.
  In Porter, K. A. The collected stories of Katherine Anne Porter   S C
The flowering of the strange orchid. Wells, H. G.
  In Wells, H. G. The complete short stories of H. G. Wells p203-11   S C
Flowers, A. R.
  De Mojo blues [excerpt]
  In Streetlights: illuminating tales of the urban black experience p129-35   S C
Flowers
  See also Wild flowers
Flowers for Algernon. Keyes, D.   Fic
Flowers for Marjorie. Welty, E.
  In Welty, E. The collected stories of Eudora Welty p98-106   S C
Flowers in the rain. Pilcher, R.
  In Pilcher, R. Flowers in the rain & other stories   S C
Flowers in the rain & other stories. Pilcher, R.
                              S C
Floyd, Samuel A.
  The power of black music   780.89
Floyd, Virginia
  The plays of Eugene O'Neill   812
Flu *See* Influenza
Fluff and Mr. Ripley. West, D.
  In West, D. The richer, the poorer: stories, sketches, and reminiscences   S C
Flute dream. Hesse, H.
  In Hesse, H. The fairy tales of Hermann Hesse   S C
Flute song. Smith, P. C.
  In Song of the turtle p94-114   S C
Fly casting
  Merwin, J. Fly fishing   799.1
Fly fishing. Merwin, J.   799.1
Flying home. Ellison, R.
  In The Best short stories by Negro writers p151-70   S C
  In Calling the wind p135-50   S C
The flying man. Wells, H. G.
  In Wells, H. G. The complete short stories of H. G. Wells p245-51   S C
Flying saucers *See* Unidentified flying objects
Flynn, Nigel
  George Orwell   92
Fo' dolla'. Michener, J. A.
  In Michener, J. A. Tales of the South Pacific   S C
The Focal encyclopedia of photography   770.2
Focus on addictions. Porterfield, K. M.
                          616.86
Fodor, Eugene, 1905-1991
  (ed) Fodor's travel guides. See Fodor's travel guides   910.2
Fodor's travel guides   910.2

Fog. O'Neill, E.
  In O'Neill, E. Complete plays v1   812
The fog horn. Bradbury, R.
  In Bradbury, R. The stories of Ray Bradbury p266-72   S C
Fogelman, Edwin
  (jt. auth) Ebenstein, A. D. Today's isms
                          335
Fogle, Bruce
  ASPCA complete dog training manual
                          636.7
  The encyclopedia of the dog   636.7
  Know your cat   636.8
  Know your dog   636.7
Folk and festival costume of the world. Wilcox, R. T.   391
Folk art
  See also Decorative arts
Folk art, Pennsylvania Dutch *See* Pennsylvania Dutch folk art
Folk lore *See* Folklore
Folk medicine *See* Traditional medicine
Folk medicine. Kusinitz, M.   615.8
Folk music
             United States
  See also Country music
Folk songs
             United States
  Lomax, A. The folk songs of North America in the English language   782.42
The folk songs of North America in the English language. Lomax, A.   782.42
Folklore
  See also Animals—Folklore; Dragons; Indians of North America—Folklore; Legends; topics as themes in folklore and names of ethnic or national groups with the subdivision *Folklore*
  Best-loved folktales of the world   398.2
  Best-loved stories told at the National Storytelling Festival   398.2
  Favorite folktales from around the world
                          398.2
  The Folklore of world holidays   394.2
  Hearne, B. G. Beauties and beasts   398.2
  World folktales   398.2
             Dictionaries
  Funk & Wagnalls standard dictionary of folklore, mythology, and legend   398.03
  Jones, A. Larousse dictionary of world folklore   398.03
  Mercatante, A. S. The Facts on File encyclopedia of world mythology and legend
                          291.03
             Africa
  African folktales   398.2
  Lester, J. Black folktales   398.2
  A Treasury of African folklore   398.2
             Asia
  Asian-Pacific folktales and legends   398.2
             Europe
  Bulfinch, T. Bulfinch's mythology   291
             France
  Pourrat, H. French folktales   398.2

Folklore—*Continued*

Iran
Picard, B. L. Tales of ancient Persia   **398.2**
Ireland
Irish folktales   **398.2**
Persia
See Folklore—Iran
United States
Fleming, R. L. The big book of urban legends   **741.5**

The Folklore of American holidays   **394.2**

Guiley, R. E. Atlas of the mysterious in North America   **398.2**
United States—Dictionaries
American folklore   **398.2**

Folklore, memoirs, and other writings. Hurston, Z. N.   **818**

The **Folklore** of American holidays   **394.2**

The **Folklore** of world holidays   **394.2**

Fondly Fahrenheit. Bester, A.
In Robert Silverberg's Worlds of wonder   **S C**

Foner, Eric
America's Reconstruction   **973.8**

A house divided   **973.7**

(ed) The Reader's companion to American history. See The Reader's companion to American history   **973.03**

Fonstad, Karen Wynn
The atlas of Middle-earth   **823.009**

The **Fontana** history of astronomy and cosmology. See North, J. D. The Norton history of astronomy and cosmology   **520**

The **Fontana** history of chemistry. See Brock, W. H. The Norton history of chemistry   **540.9**

The **Fontana** history of technology. See Cardwell, D. S. L. The Norton history of technology   **609**

Food
See also Animal food
Salter, C. A. Food risks and controversies   **641.1**

Trager, J. The food chronology   **641**
Dictionaries
Claiborne, C. Craig Claiborne's The New York Times food encyclopedia   **641.03**
History
Tannahill, R. Food in history   **641.3**

Food additives
See/See also pages in the following book(s):
Salter, C. A. Food risks and controversies p36-61   **641.1**
Dictionaries
Winter, R. A consumer's dictionary of food additives   **664**

Food assistance programs *See* Food relief

The **food** chronology. Trager, J.   **641**

Food in history. Tannahill, R.   **641.3**

Food industry
Love, J. F. McDonald's: behind the arches   **338.7**

The **food** of the gods. Wells, H. G.
In Wells, H. G. Seven famous novels   **Fic**

Food preparation *See* Cooking

Food relief
Hunger [Current controversies]   **363.8**

Food risks and controversies. Salter, C. A.   **641.1**

Food supply
See also Agriculture
Hunger [Current controversies]   **363.8**
See/See also pages in the following book(s):
Carter, J. Talking peace p68-75   **327.1**
Ehrlich, P. R. The population explosion p60-88   **304.6**

Fool about a horse. Faulkner, W.
In Faulkner, W. Uncollected stories of William Faulkner p118-34   **S C**

Fools. Simon, N.
In Simon, N. The collected plays of Neil Simon v3 p307-78   **812**

Fools crow [excerpt] Welch, J.
In Talking leaves   **S C**

Foot-prints on the seashore. Hawthorne, N.
In Hawthorne, N. Tales and sketches; A wonder book for girls and boys; Tanglewood tales for girls and boys p561-70   **S C**

Football
See also Soccer
Fox, S. R. Big leagues   **796**
Harrington, D. J. The Pro Football Hall of Fame   **796.332**
Jarrett, W. S. Timetables of sports history, football   **796.332**
Neft, D. S. The sports encyclopedia: pro football   **796.332**
Simms, P. Phil Simms on passing   **796.332**
Wilkinson, B. Sports illustrated football: winning defense   **796.332**
Wilkinson, B. Sports illustrated football: winning offense   **796.332**
Biography
Morris, J. Brian Piccolo   **92**

Foote, Horton
The widow Claire
In Best American plays: 9th series—1983-1992 p244-69   **812.008**
The young man from Atlanta   **812**

The **footprint** in the sky. Carr, J. D.
In The Oxford book of American detective stories p310-25   **S C**

Footprints in the jungle. Maugham, W. S.
In Maugham, W. S. Collected short stories v2   **S C**

For colored girls who have considered suicide/when the rainbow is enuf. Shange, N.   **812**
also in Best American plays: 8th series—1974-1982 p82-105   **812.008**

For colored girls who have considered suicide . . . [excerpt] Shange, N.
In Black theatre USA   **812.008**

For Esmé—with love and squalor. Salinger, J. D.
  In Salinger, J. D. Nine stories p131-73
                                      S C

For I have touched the sky. Resnick, M.
  In Nebula awards 25 p156-82   **S C**

For king and country: the maturing of George
  Washington, 1748-1760. Lewis, T. A.   **92**

For love of evil. Anthony, P. See note under Anthony, P. Incarnations of immortality series
                                        Fic

For Owen. King, S.
  In King, S. Skeleton crew   **S C**

For professional appearance. Wolfe, T.
  In Wolfe, T. The complete short stories of
    Thomas Wolfe p177-84   **S C**

For real. Pratt, J.   **305.23**

For the sake of Grace. Elgin, S. H.
  In The Norton book of science fiction p211-
    30   **S C**

For unborn children. Livingston, M. S.
  In Black theatre USA   **812.008**

For whom the bell tolls. Hemingway, E.   **Fic**

Forbes, Esther, 1891-1967
  Paul Revere & the world he lived in   **92**

Forbush, Edward Howe, 1858-1929
  Birds of Massachusetts and other New England
  states; criticism
  In White, E. B. Essays of E. B. White
                                        814
  See/See also pages in the following book(s):
  White, E. B. Essays of E. B. White   **814**

Force and energy
  Adair, R. K. The physics of baseball
                                    796.357
  Clark, J. O. E. Matter and energy   **539**
  Newton at the bat   **796**

The force of circumstance. Maugham, W. S.
  In Maugham, W. S. Collected short stories v2
                                        S C

Force of nature: the life of Linus Pauling. Hager,
  T.   **92**

Forced indoctrination *See* Brainwashing

Forced labor *See* Slavery

Ford, Ford Madox, 1873-1939
  See/See also pages in the following book(s):
  Paterson, J. Edwardians   **942.1**

Ford, Gerald R., 1913-
                About
  Cannon, J. M. Time and chance: Gerald Ford's
    appointment with history   **92**
  Greene, J. R. The limits of power   **973.924**
  See/See also pages in the following book(s):
  Character above all   **920**

Ford, Michael Thomas
  100 questions and answers about AIDS
                                    616.97
  The voices of AIDS   **362.1**

Ford, Richard, 1944-
  Rock Springs
  In American short story masterpieces
                                        S C
  In The Vintage book of contemporary
    American short stories p162-84   **S C**

Forecasting
  See also Economic forecasting; Weather
  forecasting
  21st century earth: opposing viewpoints
                                    303.49
  America beyond 2001: opposing viewpoints
                                    303.49
  Asimov, I. The march of the millennia
                                    303.49
  Cohen, J. E. How many people can the earth
    support?   **304.6**

Foreign aid program *See* Economic assistance

Foreign Policy Association
  Cartoon history of United States foreign policy.
  See Cartoon history of United States foreign
  policy   **327.73**

Foreign population *See* Immigrants

Foreign relations *See* International relations

Foreign study
                Directories
  The High-school student's guide to study, travel,
    and adventure abroad   **370.19**
  Study abroad   **378**

Foreign trade *See* International trade

Foreigner. Cherryh, C. J.   **Fic**

The **foreigner,** sister of the foreign woman.
  Djebar, A.
  In The Heinemann book of contemporary
    African short stories p121-28   **S C**

Foreigners *See* Immigrants

Foreignisms. Tuleja, T.   **422.03**

Foreman, George
  By George   **92**

Forensic anthropology
  Thomas, P. Talking bones   **614**
  See/See also pages in the following book(s):
  Massie, R. K. The Romanovs   **947.08**

Forensic medicine *See* Medical jurisprudence

The **forest** dweller. Hesse, H.
  In Hesse, H. The fairy tales of Hermann
    Hesse   **S C**

Forest ecology
  See also Rain forest ecology
  Kricher, J. C. A field guide to eastern forests:
    North America   **574.5**
  Maser, C. Forest primeval   **574.5**
  Walker, L. C. Forests   **582.16**

Forest primeval. Maser, C.   **574.5**

Forest reserves
  See also National parks and reserves

Forester, C. S. (Cecil Scott), 1899-1966
  The African Queen   **Fic**
  The hostage
  In Classic English short stories, 1930-1955
    p58-83   **S C**

Forester, Cecil Scott *See* Forester, C. S. (Cecil
  Scott), 1899-1966

Forests. Walker, L. C.   **582.16**

Forests and forestry
  See also Trees

Forever. Blume, J.   **Fic**

Forgiveness Day. Le Guin, U. K.
In Le Guin, U. K. Four ways to forgiveness
p35-92 **S C**
Forgotten Edens **508**
The **forgotten** plague. Ryan, F. **614.5**
The **forgotten** pollinators. Buchmann, S.
574.5
The **forgotten** war. Blair, C. **951.9**
Forman, Jack Jacob
Presenting Paul Zindel **813.009**
Forman, James D.
Becca's story **Fic**
Former Soviet republics
See also Eastern Europe—History—1989-;
Soviet Union
The Breakup of communism **947**
Dictionaries
The Cambridge encyclopedia of Russia and the
former Soviet Union **947**
Fornovo, Battle of, 1495
See/See also pages in the following book(s):
Barzini, L. G. The Italians p276-98 **945**
Forshay-Lunsford, Cin
Riding out the storm
In Center stage **812.008**
Forster, E. M. (Edward Morgan), 1879-1970
A passage to India **Fic**
A room with a view **Fic**
See/See also pages in the following book(s):
Paterson, J. Edwardians **942.1**
Forster, Edward Morgan *See* Forster, E. M. (Ed-
ward Morgan), 1879-1970
Forsyth, Adrian
Portraits of the rainforest **574.5**
Forsyth, Elizabeth Held
(jt. auth) Hyde, M. O. The violent mind
616.85
Forsyth, Frederick, 1938-
There are no snakes in Ireland
In Masterpieces of mystery and suspense
p317-38 **S C**
Fortification
Macaulay, D. Castle **728.8**
Fortune, Timothy Thomas, 1856-1928
See/See also pages in the following book(s):
Black leaders of the twentieth century p19-37
920
Senna, C. The black press and the struggle for
civil rights p76-83 **071**
Fortune teller. Minh, N. D.
In American eyes p80-107 **S C**
Fortyday. Knight, D. F.
In Nebula awards 30 p122-36 **S C**
Forward the Foundation. Asimov, I. *See* note un-
der Asimov, I. [The Foundation series]
Fic
Forward to Richmond: McClellan's peninsular
campaign. Bailey, R. H. **973.7**
Foss, Michael, 1937-
(ed) Poetry of the world wars. *See* Poetry of the
world wars **821.008**
Fossey, Dian
Gorillas in the mist **599.88**

About
Montgomery, S. Walking with the great apes
920
Mowat, F. Woman in the mists: the story of
Dian Fossey and the mountain gorillas of Af-
rica **92**
Fossil mammals
Johanson, D. C. Lucy: the beginnings of human-
kind **573.2**
Johanson, D. C. Lucy's child: the discovery of
a human ancestor **573.2**
Fossil man
Tattersall, I. The last Neanderthal **573.3**
Walker, A. The wisdom of the bones
573.2
Fossil plants
Stanley, S. M. Extinction **574.5**
Fossil reptiles
See also Dinosaurs
Fossils
See also Fossil mammals
The Encyclopedia of animal evolution
591.3
Erickson, J. An introduction to fossils and min-
erals **560**
The Historical atlas of the earth **551.7**
Johnson, K. R. Prehistoric journey **551.7**
Palmer, D. Fossils **560**
Pellant, C. Rocks, minerals & fossils of the
world **549**
Thompson, I. The Audubon Society field guide
to North American fossils **560**
Wallace, J. The American Museum of Natural
History's book of dinosaurs and other ancient
creatures **567.9**
See/See also pages in the following book(s):
Hecht, J. Vanishing life p22-32 **560**
Fiction
Dickinson, P. A bone from a dry sea **Fic**
Foster, Cecil
The scar
In Rites of passage p11-24 **S C**
Foster, Gerald L., 1936-
A field guide to trains of North America
625.2
Foster, Patricia
(ed) Sister to sister. *See* Sister to sister
810.8
Foster, Paul, 1931-
Tom Paine
In Best American plays: 7th series—1967-
1973 p393-423 **812.008**
Foster, R. F. (Robert Fitzroy), 1949-
Modern Ireland, 1600-1972 **941.5**
(ed) The Oxford illustrated history of Ireland.
See The Oxford illustrated history of Ireland
941.5
Foster, Robert Fitzroy *See* Foster, R. F. (Robert
Fitzroy), 1949-
Foster, Roy *See* Foster, R. F. (Robert Fitzroy),
1949-
Foster, Steven, 1957-
A field guide to venomous animals and poison-
ous plants **574.6**

Foster care. Davies, N. M.   362.7
Foster home care
  Burch, J. M. They cage the animals at night
                                   92
  Davies, N. M. Foster care   362.7
  See/See also pages in the following book(s):
  Bode, J. Kids still having kids p95-135
                            362.7
              Fiction
  Guy, R. The disappearance   Fic
The **foster** portfolio. Vonnegut, K.
  In Vonnegut, K. Welcome to the monkey
    house   S C
Foundation. Asimov, I. See note under Asimov, I.
  [The Foundation series]   Fic
Foundation and earth. Asimov, I. See note under
  Asimov, I. [The Foundation series]   Fic
Foundation and empire. Asimov, I. See note un-
  der Asimov, I. [The Foundation series]
                                   Fic
[The **Foundation** series]. Asimov, I.   Fic
Foundation's edge. Asimov, I. See note under
  Asimov, I. [The Foundation series]   Fic
The **founders** of the Western world. Grant, M.
                                   938
Founding father. Asimov, I.
  In Asimov, I. The complete stories v2 p331-
    36   S C
Founding mothers. De Pauw, L. G.   305.4
The **fountain.** O'Neill, E.
  In O'Neill, E. Complete plays v2   812
The **fountainhead.** Rand, A.   Fic
Four and twenty. Saville, N.
  In Streetlights: illuminating tales of the urban
    black experience p423-31   S C
Four beasts in one: The homo-camelopard. Poe, E.
  A.
  In Poe, E. A. The collected tales and poems
    of Edgar Allan Poe p510-16   S C
The **four** Dutchmen. Maugham, W. S.
  In Maugham, W. S. Collected short stories v4
                                  S C
Four, free, and illegal. Corpi, L.
  In Daughters of the fifth sun   810.8
Four Greek plays   882.008
Four in one. Knight, D. F.
  In Robert Silverberg's Worlds of wonder
                                   S C
The **four** lost men. Wolfe, T.
  In Wolfe, T. The complete short stories of
    Thomas Wolfe p106-19   S C
Four past midnight. King, S.   S C
Four plays. Ionesco, E.   842
Four plays. See Inge, W. 4 plays   812
Four quartets. Eliot, T. S.
  In Eliot, T. S. The complete poems and plays,
    1909-1950 p117-45   818
The **four** suspects. Christie, A.
  In Christie, A. Miss Marple: the complete
    short stories   S C
Four ways to forgiveness. Le Guin, U. K.
                                   S C

Fourier, Jean-Baptiste-Joseph, baron, 1768-1830
  See/See also pages in the following book(s):
  Bell, E. T. Men of mathematics p183-205
                                   920
The **fourposter.** De Hartog, J.
  In Best American plays: 4th series—1951-
    1957 p479-501   812.008
Fourteenth century
  Tuchman, B. W. A distant mirror   944
The **fourth** alarm. Cheever, J.
  In Cheever, J. The stories of John Cheever
    p645-49   S C
Fourth grade ukus. Hara, M.
  In Growing up Asian American p75-85
                                   810.8
Fourth World *See* Developing countries
Fowler, Alastair
  (ed) The New Oxford book of seventeenth
  century verse. See The New Oxford book of
  seventeenth century verse   821.008
Fowler, H. W.
  The new Fowler's modern English usage
                                   428
Fowler, Karen Joy
  The dark
  In Nebula awards 27 p126-44   S C
  The lake was full of artificial things
  In The Norton book of science fiction p580-
    90   S C
  Lieserl
  In Nebula awards 26 p132-40   S C
Fowler, Virginia C., 1948-
  Nikki Giovanni   811
Fox, Paula
  The moonlight man   Fic
Fox, Stephen C. (Stephen Carey)
  The unknown internment   940.53
Fox, Stephen R. (Stephen Russell)
  Big leagues   796
The **fox.** Colette
  In Colette. The collected stories of Colette
    p252-55   S C
The **fox** and the forest. Bradbury, R.
  In Bradbury, R. The illustrated man   S C
  In Bradbury, R. The stories of Ray Bradbury
    p131-43   S C
Fox hunt. Faulkner, W.
  In Faulkner, W. Collected stories of William
    Faulkner p587-607   S C
Foxes
  Alderton, D. Foxes, wolves, and wild dogs of
    the world   599.74
  Grambo, R. L. The world of the fox
                                   599.74
Foxes, wolves, and wild dogs of the world.
  Alderton, D.   599.74
Foxfire [1]-10   975.8
Foxfire: 25 years   975.8
The **Foxfire** book. See Foxfire [1]-10   975.8
FPA *See* Foreign Policy Association
Frady, Marshall
  Jesse: the life and pilgrimage of Jesse Jackson
                                   92

A **fragment**. Chekhov, A. P.
In Chekhov, A. P. The image of Chekhov
p191-92 **S C**

Fragment of a man. Ho, A. T.
In The Other side of heaven p33-50
S C

A **fragment** of stained glass. Lawrence, D. H.
In Lawrence, D. H. The complete short stories v1 **S C**

Fragments from the journal of a solitary man. Hawthorne, N.
In Hawthorne, N. Tales and sketches; A wonder book for girls and boys; Tanglewood tales for girls and boys p487-500
S C

Frame, Michael
(jt. auth) Peak, D. Chaos under control
003

The **framing** game. Bishop, P.
In Bad behavior p21-35 **S C**

France, Anatole, 1844-1924
Man who married a dumb wife
In Thirty famous one-act plays p5-24
808.82

France, Peter, 1935-
(ed) The New Oxford companion to literature in French. See The New Oxford companion to literature in French **840.3**

France
Civilization
Kennedy, E. A cultural history of the French Revolution **944.04**
Riché, P. Daily life in the world of Charlemagne **944**
See/See also pages in the following book(s):
Durant, W. J. The age of Napoleon p260-77
940.2
Durant, W. J. The age of reason begins p333-435 **940.2**
Civilization—Dictionaries
French culture, 1900-1975 **944.08**
Fiction
Balzac, H. de. Old Goriot **Fic**
Dumas, A. The Count of Monte Cristo **Fic**
Flaubert, G. Madame Bovary **Fic**
Folklore
See Folklore—France
History
See/See also pages in the following book(s):
Durant, W. J. The age of Louis XIV p3-86, 685-721 **940.2**
History—1328-1589, House of Valois
Brooks, P. S. Beyond the myth: the story of Joan of Arc **92**
Tuchman, B. W. A distant mirror **944**
History—1328-1589, House of Valois—Fiction
Hugo, V. The hunchback of Notre Dame
Fic
History—1589-1789, Bourbons
See/See also pages in the following book(s):
Durant, W. J. Rousseau and revolution p67-96, 845-72, 900-63 **940.2**
History—1589-1789, Bourbons—Fiction
Dumas, A. The three musketeers **Fic**

History—1789-1799, Revolution
Bernier, O. Words of fire, deeds of blood
944.04
Bosher, J. F. The French Revolution
944.04
Doyle, W. The Oxford history of the French Revolution **944.04**
Hibbert, C. The days of the French Revolution
944.04
Kennedy, E. A cultural history of the French Revolution **944.04**
Kirchberger, J. H. The French Revolution and Napoleon **944.04**
Paine, T. The rights of man **320**
Paine, T. Rights of man [and] Common sense
320
Rudé, G. F. E. The French Revolution
944.04
Schama, S. Citizens: a chronicle of the French Revolution **944.04**
Tocqueville, A. de. The old régime and the French Revolution **944.04**
See/See also pages in the following book(s):
Durant, W. J. The age of Napoleon p13-123
940.2
History—1789-1799, Revolution—Dictionaries
Paxton, J. Companion to the French Revolution
944.04
History—1789-1799, Revolution—Fiction
Dickens, C. A tale of two cities **Fic**
Orczy, E., Baroness. The Scarlet Pimpernel
Fic
History—1799-1815
See/See also pages in the following book(s):
Durant, W. J. The age of Napoleon p159-237
940.2
History—1815-1914—Fiction
Stendhal. The red and the black **Fic**
Politics and government—1815-1914
Bredin, J.-D. The affair **944.081**
Popular culture
See Popular culture—France
Social life and customs
See/See also pages in the following book(s):
Durant, W. J. The age of Napoleon p124-55
940.2

Franchise *See* Suffrage

Franchise. Asimov, I.
In Asimov, I. The complete stories v1 p43-56
S C

The **Franchise.** Kessel, J.
In Nebula awards 29 p203-41 **S C**

Francis, of Assisi, Saint, 1182-1226
About
Green, J. God's fool: the life and times of Francis of Assisi **92**

Francis, Dick
Come to grief **Fic**
Twenty-one good men and true
In Masterpieces of mystery and suspense p194-206 **S C**

Francis, Lee
Native time: an historical time line of native America **970.004**

Friends. O'Brien, T.
  In O'Brien, T. The things they carried
                                     S C

The **friends** of the friends. James, H.
  In The Oxford book of English ghost stories
    p150-71   S C

Friendship
  Bode, J. Trust & betrayal   158
  Stefoff, R. Friendship and love   155
              Fiction
  Block, F. L. Weetzie Bat   Fic
  Bridgers, S. E. Keeping Christina   Fic
  Brooks, B. The moves make the man   Fic
  Crutcher, C. Staying fat for Sarah Byrnes
                               Fic
  Gordon, S. Waiting for the rain   Fic
  Guy, R. The friends   Fic
  Marsden, J. Letters from the inside   Fic
  McMillan, T. Waiting to exhale   Fic
  Peck, R. Remembering the good times   Fic
  Who do you think you are?   S C
  Woodson, J. I hadn't meant to tell you this
                               Fic
              Poetry
  A Time to talk   808.81

Friendship and love. Stefoff, R.   155

Friesner, Esther M.
  The blood-ghoul of Scarsdale
  In Vampires: a collection of original stories
    p81-98   S C
  Death and the librarian
  In Nebula awards 31 p59-73   S C
  The death of Nimuë
  In The Merlin chronicles   S C

Frings, Ketti, d. 1981
  Look homeward, angel
  In Best American plays: 5th series—1957-
    1963 p237-76   812.008

Frink, Stephen
  Wonders of the reef   778.7

Frisch, Carlienne, 1944-
  Hearing the pitch   659.1

Frisco. Michener, J. A.
  In Michener, J. A. Tales of the South Pacific
                               S C

Frog hunt. Steinbeck, J.
  In Steinbeck, J. The portable Steinbeck
                               818

Frogs
    See also Toads
  Mattison, C. Frogs & toads of the world
                           597.8

The **frogs.** Aristophanes
  In Seven famous Greek plays   882.008

Frogs & toads of the world. Mattison, C.
                           597.8

From a raw deal to a new deal?. Trotter, J. W.
  In The Young Oxford history of African
    Americans   305.8

From another world. Rawson, C.
  In The Oxford book of American detective
    stories p431-55   S C

From ballots to breadlines. Deutsch, S.
  In The Young Oxford history of women in
    the United States   305.4

From Beirut to Jerusalem. Friedman, T. L.
                               956

From chocolate to morphine. Weil, A.
                           616.86

From fin de siecle to negritude. See Poems for the
  millennium v1   808.81

From here to eternity. Jones, J.   Fic

From Hinton to Hamlet. Herz, S. K.   809

From modern to contemporary. Breslin, J. E. B.
                         811.009

From Mottel the cantor's son. Sholem Aleichem
  In Sholem Aleichem. The best of Sholem
    Aleichem   S C

From peep show to palace. Robinson, D.
                         791.43

From Pocahontas to power suits. Mills, K.
                         305.4

From romance to realism. Cart, M.   028.5

From savage to nobleman. Hilger, M.   791.43

From Shanghai. Wilson, J.
  In The Best American short stories, 1994
    p316-28   S C

From slavery to freedom. Franklin, J. H.
                         305.8

From the cabby's seat. Henry, O.
  In Henry, O. The best short stories of O.
    Henry   S C

From the country of eight islands   895.6

From the heart   970.004

Frome, Keith W., 1960-
  (ed) The Columbia book of Civil War poetry.
  See The Columbia book of Civil War poetry
                         811.008

Fromm, Erich, 1900-1980
  The art of loving   152.4
  Escape from freedom   323.44

Frommer, Harvey
  (comp) Growing up Jewish in America. See
  Growing up Jewish in America   305.8

Frommer, Myrna
  (comp) Growing up Jewish in America. See
  Growing up Jewish in America   305.8

Frontier and pioneer life
  Faragher, J. M. Daniel Boone   92
  Sandburg, C. Abraham Lincoln: The prairie
    years and The war years   92
  Zochert, D. Laura: the life of Laura Ingalls Wil-
    der   92
           Dictionaries
  Slatta, R. W. The cowboy encyclopedia
                         978
             Fiction
  Cather, W. My Antonia   Fic
  Cather, W. O pioneers!   Fic
  Cooper, J. F. The last of the Mohicans   Fic
  Freedman, B. Mrs. Mike   Fic
  Guthrie, A. B. The big sky   Fic
  McMurtry, L. Lonesome dove   Fic
  Richter, C. The light in the forest   Fic
  Rölvaag, O. E. Giants in the earth   Fic

Fundamentalism

Fiction

Peck, R. The last safe place on earth   **Fic**

Funds, Scholarship *See* Scholarships

Funeral. West, D.

In West, D. The richer, the poorer: stories, sketches, and reminiscences   **S C**

Funeral rites and ceremonies

Fiction

Waugh, E. The loved one   **Fic**

Fungi

See also Mushrooms

Funk & Wagnalls standard dictionary of folklore, mythology, and legend   **398.03**

Funnies *See* Comic books, strips, etc.

The funnies. Goulart, R.   **741.5**

Funnyhouse of a Negro. Kennedy, A.

In Black theatre USA   **812.008**

Fur. Louis, L. G.

In The Best American short stories, 1994 p232-53   **S C**

Furey, Joan A.

(ed) Visions of war, dreams of peace. See Visions of war, dreams of peace   **811.008**

Furia, Philip, 1943-

The poets of Tin Pan Alley   **782.42**

The furnished room. Henry, O.

In Henry, O. The best short stories of O. Henry   **S C**

Furniture

See/See also pages in the following book(s):

Encyclopedia of art deco p48-65   **709.04**

Furniture, American *See* American furniture

Furst, Jill Leslie

(jt. auth) Furst, P. T. North American Indian art   **709.73**

Furst, Peter T.

North American Indian art   **709.73**

Furtaw, Julia C.

(ed) Native Americans information directory. See Native Americans information directory   **970.004**

Fury of the Northmen: timeframe AD 800-1000   **909.07**

Futrelle, Jacques, 1875-1912

The problem of cell 13

In Crime classics p103-38   **S C**

In The Oxford book of American detective stories p49-80   **S C**

The future is in eggs. Ionesco, E.

In Ionesco, E. Rhinoceros, and other plays   **842**

Future life

What survives?   **133.9**

The future of the race. Gates, H. L.   **305.8**

Future shock. Toffler, A.   **303.4**

A future we can't foresee. Steinbeck, J.

In Steinbeck, J. The portable Steinbeck   **818**

Futurology *See* Forecasting

Fyodor Dostoevsky [critical essays]   **891.7**

G

G.I. nightingales. Tomblin, B.   **940.54**

G.I.'s *See* Soldiers—United States

Gabo, Naum, 1890-1977

See/See also pages in the following book(s):

Read, Sir H. E. A concise history of modern painting   **759.06**

Gabriel, Ralph Henry, 1890-1987

(ed) Pageant of America. See Pageant of America   **973**

Gaddafi, Muammar *See* Qaddafi, Muammar al-, 1942-

Gaffers, grips, and best boys. Taub, E.   **791.43**

Gaffney, Eugene S.

(jt. auth) Norell, M. Discovering dinosaurs in the American Museum of Natural History   **567.9**

Gaines, Ernest J., 1933-

The autobiography of Miss Jane Pittman   **Fic**

Conversations with Ernest Gaines   **92**

A lesson before dying   **Fic**

A long day in November

In The Best short stories by Negro writers p359-402   **S C**

In Calling the wind p311-47   **S C**

See/See also pages in the following book(s):

Contemporary black American fiction writers p30-44   **813.009**

Gaines-Shelton, Ruth

The church fight

In Black theatre USA   **812.008**

Gaitskill, Mary, 1954-

The girl on the plane

In The Best American short stories, 1993 p10-24   **S C**

A romantic weekend

In The Vintage book of contemporary American short stories p185-206   **S C**

Galapagos Islands

See/See also pages in the following book(s):

Sammon, R. Seven underwater wonders of the world p93-117   **574.92**

Galassi, Peter, 1951-

(ed) American photography, 1890-1965, from the Museum of Modern Art, New York. See American photography, 1890-1965, from the Museum of Modern Art, New York   **779**

Galaxies

See/See also pages in the following book(s):

Sagan, C. Cosmos p246-56   **520**

Galbraith, John Kenneth, 1908-

The affluent society   **330**

The Great Crash, 1929   **330.973**

Galbraith, Judy

The gifted kids' survival guide   **155.5**

Galdikas, Biruté

Reflections of Eden   **599.8**

About

Montgomery, S. Walking with the great apes   **920**

Gale encyclopedia of multicultural America
305.8
Gale environmental almanac   363.7
Gale guide to Internet databases. See CyberHound's guide to Internet databases
004
Galens, Judy, 1968-
(ed) Gale encyclopedia of multicultural America. See Gale encyclopedia of multicultural America   305.8
Galilei, Galileo, 1564-1642
About
Reston, J., Jr. Galileo   92
See/See also pages in the following book(s):
Aymar, B. A pictorial history of the world's greatest trials p51-61   345
Durant, W. J. The age of reason begins p600-12
940.2
Meadows, A. J. The great scientists   920
Drama
Brecht, B. Galileo   832
Galileo See Galilei, Galileo, 1564-1642
Galileo. Reston, J., Jr.   92
Gall, Susan B.
(ed) The Asian-American almanac. See The Asian-American almanac   305.8
(ed) Notable Asian Americans. See Notable Asian Americans   920.003
Gall, Timothy L.
(ed) Statistics on alcohol, drug & tobacco use. See Statistics on alcohol, drug & tobacco use
362.29
Gallagher, Misha
Stories don't have endings
In Spider Woman's granddaughters   S C
Gallagher, Tess
The lover of horses
In American short story masterpieces
S C
Gallant, Mavis
Dédé
In The Best American short stories of the eighties p290-303   S C
Up north
In The Literary ghost p74-79   S C
Gallant, Roy A.
National Geographic picture atlas of our universe   523
Gallaudet, T. H. (Thomas Hopkins), 1787-1851
About
Neimark, A. E. A deaf child listened: Thomas Gallaudet, pioneer in American education
92
Gallaudet, Thomas Hopkins See Gallaudet, T. H. (Thomas Hopkins), 1787-1851
Gallegher. Davis, R. H.
In The Best crime stories of the 19th century p96-125   S C
Gállego, Julián
(jt. auth) Domínguez Ortiz, A. Velázquez
759.6
Gallen, David
Malcolm X: as they knew him   92

Gallenkamp, Charles
(jt. auth) Meyer, C. The mystery of the ancient Maya   972
Galleries, Art See Art museums
Galley slave. Asimov, I.
In Asimov, I. The complete stories v2 p244-71   S C
Gallico, Paul, 1897-1976
The snow goose   Fic
Gallman, J. Matthew (James Matthew)
The North fights the Civil War: the home front
973.7
Gallman, James Matthew See Gallman, J. Matthew (James Matthew)
Gallo, Donald R.
Presenting Richard Peck   813.009
(ed) Center stage. See Center stage
812.008
(jt. auth) Herz, S. K. From Hinton to Hamlet
809
Gallo, Robert C.
Virus hunting   616.97
See/See also pages in the following book(s):
Burkett, E. The gravest show on earth
362.1
Galloway. L'Amour, L. See note under L'Amour, L. The Sacketts   Fic
Galois, Évariste, 1811-1832
See/See also pages in the following book(s):
Bell, E. T. Men of mathematics p362-77
920
Galperin, Anne
Nutrition   612.3
(jt. auth) Hermes, W. J. Marijuana   616.86
Galsworthy, John, 1867-1933
The little man
In Thirty famous one-act plays p213-26
808.82
Galyan, Deborah
The Incredible Appearing Man
In The Best American short stories, 1996 p126-50   S C
The gambler, the nun, and the radio. Hemingway, E.
In Hemingway, E. The complete short stories of Ernest Hemingway p355-68   S C
In Hemingway, E. The short stories of Ernest Hemingway p468-87   S C
Gambling
See also Compulsive gambling
Gambling [Current controversies]   363.4
Gambling [Reference shelf]   363.4
Gambling [Current controversies]   363.4
Gambling [Reference shelf]   363.4
Game of chess. Goodman, K. S.
In Thirty famous one-act plays p347-56
808.82
A game of sixty-six. Sholem Aleichem
In Sholem Aleichem. Tevye the dairyman and The railroad stories   S C
Games
See also Sports; Word games; names of individual games

Games—*Continued*

Crisfield, D. Pick-up games   **790.1**

The World of games   **794**

Gamma, Karl

The handbook of skiing   **796.93**

Gammond, Peter

The Harmony illustrated encyclopedia of classical music   **781.6**

The Oxford companion to popular music   **781.64**

Gandhi, Mahatma, 1869-1948

All men are brothers   **92**

Gandhi on non-violence   **322.4**

Gandhi, Mohandas Karamchand *See* Gandhi, Mahatma, 1869-1948

Gandhi on non-violence. Gandhi, M.   **322.4**

Ganesan, Indira

The journey [excerpt]

In Growing up Asian American p393-98   **810.8**

Ganges River valley (India and Bangladesh)
Description
See/See also pages in the following book(s):

Great rivers of the world p195-228   **910**

Gangs

Fremon, C. Father Greg and the homeboys   **361.7**

Gangs: opposing viewpoints   **364.1**

Hinojosa, M. Crews: gang members talk to Maria Hinojosa   **302.3**

Korem, D. Suburban gangs   **364.1**

The **gang's** all here. Lawrence, J.

In Lawrence, J. The selected plays of Jerome Lawrence and Robert E. Lee p167-238   **812**

Gangs: opposing viewpoints   **364.1**

Gangsters *See* Mafia

Ganor, Solly, 1928-

Light one candle   **940.53**

Gans, Eric, 1941-

Madame Bovary   **843.009**

Gansworth, Eric L.

The ballad of Plastic Fred

In Growing up Native American p325-33   **810.8**

Ganz, Arthur F., 1928-

(jt. auth) Beckson, K. E. Literary terms   **803**

Garcia, Cristina

Lourdes Puente

In Latina: women's voices from the borderlands p58-68   **810.8**

Tito's good-bye

In Iguana dreams   **S C**

Garcia, Guy, 1955-

Frazer Avenue

In Iguana dreams   **S C**

Garcia, Lionel G.

Confession

In Iguana dreams   **S C**

Garcia, Richard A., 1941-

(jt. auth) Griswold del Castillo, R. César Chávez   **92**

Garcia, Rita Williams- *See* Williams-Garcia, Rita

García de Paredes, Angel

Cassell's Spanish-English, English-Spanish dictionary. *See* Cassell's Spanish-English, English-Spanish dictionary   **463**

García Márquez, Gabriel, 1928-

Love in the time of cholera   **Fic**

One hundred years of solitude   **Fic**

One hundred years of solitude; criticism

In Wood, M. Gabriel García Márquez: One hundred years of solitude   **863.009**
About
Bell-Villada, G. H. García Márquez   **92**

Garden, Nancy

Annie on my mind   **Fic**

Annie on my mind [excerpt]

In Growing up gay p64-68   **808.8**

Parents' Night

In Am I blue? p127-44   **S C**

Garden ecology

Conrad, J. Discover nature in the garden   **574.5**

The **garden** lodge. Cather, W.

In Cather, W. Early novels and stories   **Fic**

Garden of microbial delights. Sagan, D.   **576**

A **garden** party. Behan, B.

In Behan, B. The complete plays   **822**

Garden pests *See* Insect pests

The **gardener.** Kipling, R.

In Kipling, R. The portable Kipling   **828**

The **gardener** and the lord and lady. Andersen, H. C.

In Andersen, H. C. Tales and stories   **S C**

Gardening

See also Flower gardening; Indoor gardening

Better Homes and Gardens new garden book   **635**

Conrad, J. Discover nature in the garden   **574.5**
Dictionaries
The American Horticultural Society encyclopedia of gardening   **635**

Gardening, Organic *See* Organic gardening

Gardening at a glance. *See* Denckla, T. The organic gardener's home reference   **635**

Gardiner, John Rolfe

The voyage out

In The Best American short stories, 1994 p123-44   **S C**

Gardner, Erle Stanley, 1889-1970

Danger out of the past

In Masterpieces of mystery and suspense p259-70   **S C**

Leg man

In The Oxford book of American detective stories p261-94   **S C**

See/See also pages in the following book(s):

Modern mystery writers p75-93   **809.3**

Gardner, Helen, d. 1946

Gardner's art through the ages. *See* Gardner's art through the ages   **709**

Gassner, John, 1903-1967—*Continued*
(ed) Best American plays: 6th series—1963-1967. See Best American plays: 6th series—1963-1967 **812.008**
(ed) Best plays of the early American theatre. See Best plays of the early American theatre **812.008**
(ed) Best plays of the modern American theatre: 2nd series. See Best plays of the modern American theatre: 2nd series **812.008**
(ed) Twenty best plays of the modern American theatre. See Twenty best plays of the modern American theatre **812.008**

Gaster, Theodor Herzl, 1906-1992
(ed) Frazer, Sir J. G. The new golden bough **291**

Gates, Bill, 1955-
The road ahead **004**

Gates, David, 1947-
The mail lady
In The Best American short stories, 1994 p145-66 **S C**

Gates, Fay Carol
Judaism **296**

Gates, Henry Louis
The future of the race **305.8**
(ed) Alice Walker: critical perspectives past and present. See Alice Walker: critical perspectives past and present **813.009**
(ed) Bearing witness: selections from African-American autobiography in the twentieth century. See Bearing witness: selections from African-American autobiography in the twentieth century **920**
(ed) Langston Hughes: critical perspectives past and present. See Langston Hughes: critical perspectives past and present **818**
(ed) Richard Wright: critical perspectives past and present. See Richard Wright: critical perspectives past and present **813.009**
(ed) Toni Morrison: critical perspectives past and present. See Toni Morrison: critical perspectives past and present **813.009**
(ed) Zora Neale Hurston: critical perspectives past and present. See Zora Neale Hurston: critical perspectives past and present **813.009**
See/See also pages in the following book(s):
Inventing the truth p141-58 **808**

Gates, William H. See Gates, Bill, 1955-
Gather blue roses. Sargent, P.
In The Norton book of science fiction p250-54 **S C**
The **gathering**. Carmody, I. **Fic**
The **gathering** storm. Churchill, Sir W. **940.53**
Gatsby [critical essays] **813.009**
Gatti, Claudio, 1955-
(jt. auth) Cohen, R. In the eye of the storm: the life of General H. Norman Schwarzkopf **92**

Gauguin, Paul, 1848-1903
About
Greenfeld, H. Paul Gauguin **92**
Howard, M. Gauguin **759.4**

Gault, William Campbell
See no evil
In The Oxford book of American detective stories p471-79 **S C**

Gauss, Carl Friedrich, 1777-1855
See/See also pages in the following book(s):
Bell, E. T. Men of mathematics p218-69 **920**

Gautama Buddha
See/See also pages in the following book(s):
Jaspers, K. The great philosophers **109**

Gawain and the Grene Knight
Sir Gawain and the Green Knight **821**

Gay, John, 1685-1732
The beggar's opera
In The Oxford anthology of English literature v1 **820.8**

Gay, Kathlyn
Air pollution **363.7**
Caution! this may be an advertisement **659.1**
"I am who I am" **305.8**
Pregnancy **363.9**
Rainforests of the world **574.5**
The right to die **179**
Rights and respect **305.4**
Saving the environment **363.7**

Gay, Peter, 1923-
Freud **92**

Gay lifestyle See Homosexuality
Gay men
Chase, C. The hurry-up song **92**
Civil rights
Steffan, J. Honor bound **92**
Gay women See Lesbians
Gayle, Addison, 1932-1991
Richard Wright **92**
Gazetteers
See also Geographic names
The Oxford dictionary of the world **910.3**
The Statesman's year-book world gazetteer **910.3**
Webster's new geographical dictionary **910.3**

Gazzo, Michael V. (Michael Vincente), 1923-1995
A hatful of rain
In Best American plays: 4th series—1951-1957 p179-209 **812.008**

Gealt, Adelheid M.
(jt. auth) Cole, B. Art of the Western world **709**

Gebhardt, Richard H.
The complete cat book **636.8**
Geddes, Candida
(ed) The Complete horse book. See The Complete horse book **636.1**
Geese
Fiction
Gallico, P. The snow goose **Fic**
Geffner, Andrea B.
How to write better business letters **651.7**
Gehrig, Henry Louis See Gehrig, Lou, 1903-1941

Gehrig, Lou, 1903-1941
About
Robinson, R. Iron horse: Lou Gehrig in his time
92

Geis of the Gargoyle. Anthony, P. See note under Anthony, P. The Magic of Xanth series
Fic

Gelb, Norman
Dunkirk: the complete story of the first step in the defeat of Hitler   **940.54**

Geller, Larry, 1937-
If I can dream [biography of Elvis Presley]
92

Gemini project
See/See also pages in the following book(s):
Man in space p48-59   **629.4**

Gems
See also Precious stones
Dictionaries
Holden, M. The encyclopedia of gems and minerals   **553.8**

Gems of Hubble. Mitton, J.   **520**

The **gender** gap in schools. Hanmer, T. J.
376

Gender identity See Sex role

Gene mapping See Genetic mapping

Gene splicing See Genetic engineering; Recombinant DNA

Gene therapy
See/See also pages in the following book(s):
Mabie, M. C. J. Bioethics and the new medical technology   **174**

Genealogy
Doane, G. H. Searching for your ancestors
929
Fletcher, W. P. Recording your family history
929
Stryker-Rodda, H. How to climb your family tree   **929**

The **General** retires. Nguyen, H. T.
In The Other side of heaven p379-93
S C

General science index   **505**

Generals
Ambrose, S. E. Eisenhower   92
Barnett, L. K. Touched by fire: the life, death, and mythic afterlife of George Armstrong Custer   92
Blumenson, M. Patton, the man behind the legend, 1885-1945   92
Bradley, O. N. A general's life   92
Brandt, C. The man in the mirror: a life of Benedict Arnold   92
Catton, B. Grant moves south   92
Catton, B. Grant takes command   92
Cohen, R. In the eye of the storm: the life of General H. Norman Schwarzkopf   92
Farwell, B. Stonewall: a biography of General Thomas J. Jackson   92
Manchester, W. American Caesar: Douglas MacArthur, 1880-1964   92
Marrin, A. Virginia's general: Robert E. Lee and the Civil War   92

Phelps, J. A. Chappie [biography of Daniel James]   92
Powell, C. L. My American journey   92
Roth, D. Sacred honor: a biography of Colin Powell   92
Smith, G. Lee and Grant   92
Stoler, M. A. George C. Marshall: soldier-statesman of the American century   92
Thomas, E. M. Robert E. Lee   92
Wert, J. D. Custer   92

A **general's** life. Bradley, O. N.   92

Generation gap See Conflict of generations

Genet, Jean, 1910-1986
Deathwatch
In Genet, J. The maids [and] Deathwatch
842
The maids [and] Deathwatch   **842**
See/See also pages in the following book(s):
Esslin, M. The theatre of the absurd p200-33
809.2

Genetic engineering
See also Biotechnology; Molecular cloning; Recombinant DNA
Drlica, K. Double-edged sword   **616**
Drlica, K. Understanding DNA and gene cloning   **574.87**
Genetic engineering: opposing viewpoints
174
Genetics & society   **306.4**
Thro, E. Genetic engineering   **660**
Dictionaries
Steinberg, M. L. The Facts on File dictionary of biotechnology and genetic engineering
660
Fiction
Crichton, M. Jurassic Park   **Fic**

Genetic engineering: opposing viewpoints
174

Genetic fingerprints See DNA fingerprints

Genetic mapping
Bodmer, W. F. The book of man   **573.2**
Lee, T. F. The Human Genome Project
573.2

Genetics
See also Genetic mapping; Medical genetics
Blueprint for life   **573.2**
Genetics & society   **306.4**
Jones, S. The language of genes   **573.2**
Kitcher, P. The lives to come   **573.2**
Sagan, C. The dragons of Eden   **153**

Genetics & human health. Brynie, F. H.   **616**

Genetics & society   **306.4**

Genome mapping See Genetic mapping

Genre favorites for young adults   **016.8**

Genreflecting. Herald, D. T.   **016.8**

Gentiles and Jews See Jews and Gentiles

The **gentle** boy. Hawthorne, N.
In Hawthorne, N. Tales and sketches; A wonder book for girls and boys; Tanglewood tales for girls and boys p108-38
S C

The **gentle** vultures. Asimov, I.
In Asimov, I. The complete stories v1 p250-
62 **S C**

Gentlehands. Kerr, M. E. **Fic**

The **gentlemen** of the jungle. Kenyatta, J.
In African short stories **S C**

Gentlemen of the press. *See* Wolfe, T. The newspaper

Gentry, Curt, 1931-
(jt. auth) Bugliosi, V. Helter skelter **364.1**

Geoffrey, of Monmouth, Bishop of St. Asaph, 1100?-1154
Historia Britonum; criticism
In Ashe, G. The discovery of King Arthur
92

Geographic names
See also Gazetteers
United States
Shankle, G. E. American nicknames **929.4**
Shearer, B. F. State names, seals, flags, and symbols **929.9**

Geographical distribution of animals and plants
See Biogeography

Geography
See also Maps; Physical geography; Voyages and travels
Countries of the world and their leaders yearbook **910.3**
Davis, K. C. Don't know much about geography **910.2**
Geography on file **912**
Dictionaries
Encyclopedia of world geography **910.3**
Exploring your world **910.3**
Kurian, G. T. Encyclopedia of the First World **903**
Lands and peoples **910.3**
Webster's new geographical dictionary **910.3**
World geographical encyclopedia **910.3**
Worldmark encyclopedia of the nations **910.3**
Periodicals—Indexes
National geographic index, 1888-1988 **910**

Geography on file **912**

Geology
See also Catastrophes (Geology); Submarine geology
Erickson, J. An introduction to fossils and minerals **560**
Dictionaries
Farndon, J. Dictionary of the earth **550.3**
Experiments
Smith, B. G. Geology projects for young scientists **550**

Geology, Stratigraphic *See* Stratigraphic geology

Geology projects for young scientists. Smith, B. G. **550**

The **geometry** of love. Cheever, J.
In Cheever, J. The stories of John Cheever p594-602 **S C**

GeoNavigator. *See* World geographical encyclopedia **910.3**

Geophysics
Allaby, M. Earth **550**
Vogel, S. Naked Earth **551.1**

George, Henry, 1839-1897
See/See also pages in the following book(s):
Heilbroner, R. L. The worldly philosophers **330.1**

George, Nelson
Blackface **791.43**

A **George** Orwell companion. Hammond, J. R. **828**

George Orwell's 1984 **823.009**

George-Warren, Holly
(ed) The New Rolling Stone encyclopedia of rock & roll. *See* The New Rolling Stone encyclopedia of rock & roll **781.66**
(ed) The Rolling Stone album guide. *See* The Rolling Stone album guide **780.2**
(ed) The Rolling Stone illustrated history of rock & roll. *See* The Rolling Stone illustrated history of rock & roll **781.66**

George Washington's war. Leckie, R. **973.3**

Georges Seurat. Courthion, P. **759.4**

Georgia
Fiction
Burns, O. A. Cold Sassy tree **Fic**
McCullers, C. The member of the wedding **Fic**
History
See/See also pages in the following book(s):
Boorstin, D. J. The Americans: The colonial experience p71-96 **973.2**

Georgia on my mind. Sheffield, C.
In Nebula awards 29 p95-136 **S C**

The **geranium.** O'Connor, F.
In O'Connor, F. Collected works p701-13 **S C**
In O'Connor, F. The complete stories p3-14 **S C**

Gerber, John C.
Mark Twain **818**

Gerber, Peter R.
Indians of the Northwest coast **970.004**

Gerber, Philip L.
Robert Frost **811**
Willa Cather **813.009**

Gerberg, Mort
Cartooning **741.5**

Germ theory of disease
Biddle, W. A field guide to germs **616**
See/See also pages in the following book(s):
Clark, W. R. At war within p26-33 **616.07**

Germ warfare *See* Biological warfare

Germain, Sophie, 1776-1831
See/See also pages in the following book(s):
Osen, L. M. Women in mathematics p83-93 **920**

The **German** American family album. Hoobler, D. **305.8**

German Americans
Hoobler, D. The German American family album **305.8**
See/See also pages in the following book(s):
Hook, J. N. Family names p112-25 **929.4**

Get thee out. Sholem Aleichem
In Sholem Aleichem. The best of Sholem
Aleichem   S C
Getting in. Paul, W. H.   378
Getting real. Shwartz, S.
In Nebula awards 27 p212-31   S C
Getting the facts of life. White, P. C.
In Rites of passage p91-102   S C
Getty (J. Paul) Museum *See* J. Paul Getty Museum
Gettysburg (Pa.), Battle of, 1863
    Catton, B. Gettysburg   973.7
    Clark, C. Gettysburg: the Confederate high-tide
       973.7
    Gettysburg   973.7
    Wheeler, R. Witness to Gettysburg   973.7
Gettysburg   973.7
Gettysburg. Catton, B.   973.7
Geyer, Georgie Anne
    Guerrilla prince: the untold story of Fidel Castro
       92
Geysers
    Bryan, T. S. Geysers: what they are and how
       they work   551.2
Ghettoes, Inner city *See* Inner cities
The ghost. Sexton, A.
    In The Literary ghost p225-29   S C
Ghost and flesh, water and dirt. Goyen, W.
    In The Literary ghost p304-13   S C
Ghost dance
    See/See also pages in the following book(s):
    Brown, D. A. Bury my heart at Wounded Knee
    p416-38   970.004
Ghost girl. Hayden, T. L.   362.7
Ghost girls. Oates, J. C.
    In The Best American short stories, 1996
    p226-41   S C
The ghost in the mill. Stowe, H. B.
    In The Oxford book of American short stories
    p97-108   S C
The Ghost Maker. L'Amour, L.
    In L'Amour, L. The outlaws of Mesquite
    p51-72   S C
The ghost soldiers. O'Brien, T.
    In The Literary ghost p185-205   S C
    In O'Brien, T. The things they carried
       S C
Ghost stories
    Classic ghost stories   S C
    Hamilton, V. Sweet whispers, Brother Rush
       Fic
    James, H. The turn of the screw   Fic
    The Literary ghost   S C
    The Oxford book of English ghost stories
       S C
    Victorian ghost stories   S C
    Westall, R. Shades of darkness   S C
    See/See also pages in the following book(s):
    World folktales p188-213   398.2
A ghost story. Twain, M.
    In Twain, M. The complete short stories of
    Mark Twain   S C
The ghost who vanished by degrees. Davies, R.
    In The Literary ghost p54-63   S C

Ghostly populations. Matthews, J.
    In The Literary ghost p171-84   S C
Ghosts
    Classic American ghost stories   133.1
    Norman, M. Historic haunted America
       133.1
Dictionaries
    Guiley, R. E. The encyclopedia of ghosts and
    spirits   133.1
Ghosts. Ibsen, H.
    In Ibsen, H. The complete major prose plays
       839.8
    In Ibsen, H. Ibsen: four major plays
       839.8
Ghosts. O'Connor, F.
    In O'Connor, F. Collected stories p694-702
       S C
Giant panda
    Catton, C. Pandas   599.74
    Schaller, G. B. The last panda   599.74
    See/See also pages in the following book(s):
    Ward, P. Wild bears of the world   599.74
Giantism *See* Growth disorders
Giants in the earth. Rölvaag, O. E.   Fic
Giants of jazz. Terkel, S.   920
Gibaldi, Joseph, 1942-
    MLA handbook for writers of research papers
       808
Gibbon, Edward, 1737-1794
    See/See also pages in the following book(s):
    Durant, W. J. Rousseau and revolution p795-808
       940.2
Gibbons, Whit, 1939-
    Keeping all the pieces   574.5
Gibian, George
    (ed) The Portable nineteenth-century Russian
    reader. See The Portable nineteenth-century
    Russian reader   891.7
Gibilisco, Stan
    The concise illustrated dictionary of science and
    technology   503
    (ed) McGraw-Hill encyclopedia of personal
    computing. See McGraw-Hill encyclopedia of
    personal computing   004
    (ed) The McGraw-Hill illustrated encyclopedia
    of robotics & artificial intelligence. See The
    McGraw-Hill illustrated encyclopedia of
    robotics & artificial intelligence   629.8
    (jt. auth) Turner, R. P. The illustrated dictionary
    of electronics   621.381
Giblin, James, 1933-
    Three Mondays in July
    In Am I blue? p105-24   S C
    When plague strikes   614.4
Gibran, Kahlil, 1883-1931
    The Prophet   811
Gibson, Josh, 1911-1947
About
    Ribowsky, M. The power and the darkness: the
    life of Josh Gibson in the shadows of the
    game   92
Gibson, Kyle
    (jt. auth) Koppel, T. Nightline   791.45

Gill, Sam D., 1943-
Dictionary of Native American mythology
299

Gillam, Scott
Discrimination 303.3

Gillan, Jennifer
(ed) Unsettling America. See Unsettling America 811.008

Gillan, Maria
(ed) Unsettling America. See Unsettling America 811.008

Gillespie, Dizzy, 1917-1993
See/See also pages in the following book(s):
Terkel, S. Giants of jazz p147-61 920

Gillespie, John Birks *See* Gillespie, Dizzy, 1917-1993

Gillespie, John Thomas, 1928-
(ed) Best books for senior high readers. See Best books for senior high readers 011.6
(jt. auth) Morris, B. J. Administering the school library media center 027.8

Gillespie, Michael Patrick
(jt. auth) Fargnoli, A. N. James Joyce A to Z 823.009

Gillespie, Paul F.
(ed) Foxfire [1]-10. See Foxfire [1]-10 975.8

Gillette, J. Michael
Theatrical design and production 792

Gillette, William Hooker, 1853-1937
Secret service
In Best plays of the early American theatre p277-360 812.008

Gillispie, Charles Coulston
(ed) Dictionary of scientific biography. See Dictionary of scientific biography 920.003

Gillon, Adam, 1921-
Joseph Conrad 823.009

Gilman, Charlotte Perkins, 1860-1935
The yellow wallpaper
In The Norton book of American short stories p137-50 S C
In The Oxford book of American short stories p153-69 S C
In The Oxford book of gothic tales p249-63 S C
In The Oxford book of women's writing in the United States p41-55 810.8

Gilman, John, 1941-
(jt. auth) Heide, R. Home front America 973.917

Gilot, Françoise, 1921-
Matisse and Picasso 92

Gilpin, George H.
(ed) Critical essays on William Wordsworth. See Critical essays on William Wordsworth 821

Gilroy, Frank Daniel, 1925-
The subject was roses
In Best American plays: 6th series—1963-1967 p567-94 812.008

Gilstrap, John
Nathan's run Fic

Gimmicks three. Asimov, I.
In Asimov, I. The complete stories v1 p57-61 S C

Gimpel the fool. Singer, I. B.
In The Norton book of American short stories p394-406 S C

The gingerbread lady. Simon, N.
In Simon, N. The collected plays of Neil Simon v2 p149-227 812

Ginsberg, Allen, 1926-1997
Collected poems, 1947-1980 811
Cosmopolitan greetings 811
Howl; criticism
In Breslin, J. E. B. From modern to contemporary 811.009

Giovanna I, Queen of Naples, 1327?-1382 *See* Joanna I, Queen of Naples, 1327?-1382

Giovanni, Nikki
Conversations with Nikki Giovanni 92
Racism 101 814
Sacred cows—and other edibles 814
The selected poems of Nikki Giovanni (1968-1995) 811
(ed) Grand mothers: poems, reminiscences, and short stories about the keepers of our traditions. See Grand mothers: poems, reminiscences, and short stories about the keepers of our traditions 810.8
(ed) Shimmy shimmy shimmy like my sister Kate. See Shimmy shimmy shimmy like my sister Kate 811.008
About
Fowler, V. C. Nikki Giovanni 811
See/See also pages in the following book(s):
Contemporary black American poets and dramatists p32-46 810.9

Giovanni's room [excerpt] Baldwin, J.
In Growing up gay p85-89 808.8

Giraudoux, Jean, 1882-1944
The Apollo of Bellac
In 24 favorite one-act plays p308-32 808.82

Girl. Kincaid, J.
In Calling the wind p454-55 S C
In The Vintage book of contemporary American short stories p306-07 S C

A girl I used to know. Pilcher, R.
In Pilcher, R. Flowers in the rain & other stories S C

The girl on the plane. Gaitskill, M.
In The Best American short stories, 1993 p10-24 S C

The girl who heard dragons. McCaffrey, A. See note under McCaffrey, A. [The Pern series] Fic

The girl who loved graveyards. James, P. D.
In Bad behavior p145-62 S C

The girl who raised pigeons. Jones, E. P.
In Streetlights: illuminating tales of the urban black experience p219-38 S C

The girl with a pimply face. Williams, W. C.
In The Oxford book of American short stories p310-22 S C

Girls
Abner, A. Finding our way 305.23

Glory in the flower. Inge, W.
  In 24 favorite one-act plays p133-50
                                    808.82
The glory of their times. Ritter, L. S.   920
Gloss, Molly
  Interlocking pieces
  In The Norton book of science fiction p571-
    76   S C
  The jump-off creek [excerpt]
  In Circle of women: an anthology of contem-
    porary Western women writers p158-67
                                    810.8
Glossaries See Encyclopedias and dictionaries
A glossary of literary terms. Abrams, M. H.
                                    803
Glover, Denise Marie
  Voices of the spirit   016.3058
Gluck, Sherna Berger
  Rosie the Riveter revisited   331.4
Glut, Donald F.
  (jt. auth) Lessem, D. The Dinosaur Society's di-
    nosaur encyclopedia   567.9
Go ask Alice   616.86
Go back to your precious wife and son. Vonnegut,
  K.
  In Vonnegut, K. Welcome to the monkey
    house   S C
Go climb a tree if you don't like it. Sholem
  Aleichem
  In Sholem Aleichem. Tevye the dairyman and
    The railroad stories   S C
Go down, Moses. Faulkner, W.
  In Faulkner, W. Uncollected stories of Wil-
    liam Faulkner p256-66   S C
"Go in peace, Tobias son of Opperman". Tlali, M.
  In Daughters of Africa p432-7   808.8
Go tell it on the mountain. Baldwin, J.   Fic
God
  See/See also pages in the following book(s):
  Sagan, C. Broca's brain p128-36, 281-87
                                    500
God and the astronomers. Jastrow, R.   523.1
God Emperor of Dune. Herbert, F. See note under
  Herbert, F. Dune   Fic
God rest you merry, gentlemen. Hemingway, E.
  In Hemingway, E. The complete short stories
    of Ernest Hemingway p298-301
                                    S C
  In Hemingway, E. The short stories of Ernest
    Hemingway p392-96   S C
God sees the truth, but waits. Tolstoy, L., graf
  In Tolstoy, L. The portable Tolstoy p475-83
                                    891.7
God sends Sunday [excerpt] Bontemps, A. W.
  In The Portable Harlem Renaissance reader
    p667-74   810.8
Goddard, Donald Letcher
  (ed) Saving wildlife. See Saving wildlife
                                    333.95
Goddard, Robert Hutchings, 1882-1945
               About
  Coil, S. M. Robert Hutchings Goddard   92

See/See also pages in the following book(s):
  Aaseng, N. Twentieth-century inventors p27-38
                                    920
The goddess on the street corner. St. Clair, M.
  In Masterpieces of fantasy and enchantment
    p23-30   S C
Goddesses See Gods and goddesses
Goddesses in world mythology. Ann, M.
                                    291.03
Godliness. Anderson, S.
  In Anderson, S. Winesburg, Ohio   S C
Gods and goddesses
  See also Religions; names of individual
    gods and goddesses
  See/See also pages in the following book(s):
  Hamilton, E. Mythology p21-76   292
               Dictionaries
  Ann, M. Goddesses in world mythology
                                    291.03
  Bell, R. E. Women of classical mythology
                                    292
God's favorite. Simon, N.
  In Simon, N. The collected plays of Neil Si-
    mon v2 p475-545   812
God's fool: the life and times of Francis of Assisi.
  Green, J.   92
Gods, graves, and scholars. Ceram, C. W.
                                    930.1
God's trombones: seven Negro sermons in verse.
  Johnson, J. W.   811
God's wrath. Malamud, B.
  In Malamud, B. The stories of Bernard
    Malamud p257-65   S C
Godwin, Gail, 1937-
  Dream children
  In American short story masterpieces
                                    S C
Goeppert-Mayer, Maria, 1906-1972
  See/See also pages in the following book(s):
  Dash, J. The triumph of discovery: women sci-
    entists who won the Nobel Prize p1-33
                                    920
  McGrayne, S. B. Nobel Prize women in science
    p175-200   920
  Yount, L. Contemporary women scientists
                                    920
Goethe, Johann Wolfgang von, 1749-1832
  See/See also pages in the following book(s):
  Durant, W. J. Rousseau and revolution p555-67,
    580-628   940.2
Goetz, Diane M.
  (ed) The Good Housekeeping illustrated guide to
    women's health. See The Good Housekeeping
    illustrated guide to women's health   613
Goetzmann, William H.
  The first Americans   970.004
Goffe, Gaynor
  Calligraphy school   745.6
Gogh, Vincent van, 1853-1890
               About
  Bernard, B. Van Gogh   759.9492
  McQuillan, M. Van Gogh   759.9492
  Schapiro, M. Vincent Van Gogh   759.9492

Goldhagen, Daniel
Hitler's willing executioners   **940.53**
Golding, William, 1911-1993
Lord of the Flies   **Fic**
     About
Baker, J. R. Critical essays on William Golding
    823.009
Friedman, L. S. William Golding   **823.009**
Goldman, James, 1927-
The lion in winter
    In Best American plays: 6th series—1963-
     1967 p277-309   **812.008**
    In Best American screenplays   **812.008**
Goldman, Martin S.
Crazy Horse   **92**
Goldman, William, 1931-
Butch Cassidy and the Sundance Kid
    In Best American screenplays   **812.008**
Goldsmith, Donald
Supernova! the exploding star of 1987
    523.8
Goldsmith, Oliver, 1728-1774
Adventures of a strolling player
    In The Oxford book of Irish short stories p19-
     26   **S C**
Goldstein, Laura
Frankel, G. In the alleys   **779**
Goldstein, Lisa, 1953-
Alfred
    In Nebula awards 29 p68-81   **S C**
Midnight news
    In The Norton book of science fiction p819-
     29   **S C**
The Narcissus Plague
    In Nebula awards 31 p262-71   **S C**
Goldstein, Ruth M.
(jt. auth) Lass, A. H. The Facts on File dictio-
    nary of classical, biblical, and literary allu-
    sions   **803**
Goldwater, Barry M. (Barry Morris), 1909-
Goldwater   **92**
Golf
Ballingall, P. Golf   **796.352**
Campbell, M. Ultimate golf techniques
    796.352
Feinstein, J. A good walk spoiled   **796.352**
Golf rules in pictures   **796.352**
Golf, the greatest game   **796.352**
Mulvoy, M. Sports illustrated golf   **796.352**
Whitworth, K. Golf for women   **796.352**
Golf for women. Whitworth, K.   **796.352**
Golf rules in pictures   **796.352**
Golf, the greatest game   **796.352**
Goliah. London, J.
    In London, J. The science fiction stories of
     Jack London p83-103   **S C**
Gombar, Christina
Great women writers, 1900-1950   **920**
Gombe Stream National Park (Tanzania)
Goodall, J. The chimpanzees of Gombe
    599.88
Gombrich, E. H. (Ernst Hans), 1909-
The story of art   **709**

Gombrich, Ernst Hans *See* Gombrich, E. H.
    (Ernst Hans), 1909-
Gomez, Jewelle
Louisiana: 1850
    In Children of the night p109-51   **S C**
Gomm, Sarah Carr- *See* Carr-Gomm, Sarah
Goncharov, Ivan Aleksandrovich, 1812-1891
Oblomov's dream
    In The Portable nineteenth-century Russian
     reader p295-333   **891.7**
Gone with the wind. Mitchell, M.   **Fic**
Gonzalez, Genaro, 1949-
Un hijo del sol
    In Growing up Latino p38-46   **810.8**
González, Kathleen Ann
That was living
    In Latina: women's voices from the border-
     lands p97-106   **810.8**
González, Louie
Doña Toña of Nineteenth Street
    In Growing up Chicana/o p59-66   **810.8**
Gooch, Anthony
Cassell's Spanish-English, English-Spanish dic-
    tionary. See Cassell's Spanish-English, Eng-
    lish-Spanish dictionary   **463**
Good-by. London, J.
    In London, J. The portable Jack London
     p178-86   **818**
Good-bye, Mother. Piroli, W.
    In Coming of age p103-07   **808.8**
Good country people. O'Connor, F.
    In O'Connor, F. Collected works p263-84
     S C
    In O'Connor, F. The complete stories p271-91
     S C
The good doctor. Simon, N.
    In Simon, N. The collected plays of Neil Si-
     mon v2 p393-471   **812**
The good earth. Buck, P. S.   **Fic**
Good form. O'Brien, T.
    In O'Brien, T. The things they carried
     S C
Good grief. Bradbury, R.
    In Who do you think you are? p3-13
     S C
Good grooming *See* Personal grooming
Good health for African-American kids. Dixon, B.
M.   **649**
Good Housekeeping cookbook, The New
    641.5
Good Housekeeping family health & medical
    guide. See The New Good Housekeeping
    family health and medical guide   **616.02**
The Good Housekeeping illustrated guide to wom-
    en's health   **613**
The Good Housekeeping illustrated microwave
    cookbook   **641.5**
The good lion. Hemingway, E.
    In Hemingway, E. The complete short stories
     of Ernest Hemingway p482-84   **S C**
Good luck is better than gold. Ewing, J. H.
    In The Oxford book of modern fairy tales
     p140-44   **S C**

Gordimer, Nadine, 1923— *Continued*
Letter from his father
In The Literary ghost p314-29   S C
My son's story   Fic
About
Critical essays on Nadine Gordimer
823.009

Gordon, Alan, 1936-
(jt. auth) Gordon, L. G. The Columbia chronicles of American life, 1910-1992   973.9

Gordon, Charles George, 1833-1885
See/See also pages in the following book(s):
Strachey, L. Eminent Victorians   920

Gordon, Howard
After dreaming of President Johnson
In Children of the night p180-88   S C
I can't find my blackface
In Streetlights: illuminating tales of the urban black experience p146-57   S C
My Lucy
In Rites of passage p163-76   S C

Gordon, Jaimy, 1944-
A night's work
In The Best American short stories, 1995 p45-66   S C

Gordon, James Samuel
Stress management   155.9

Gordon, Linda
(ed) America's working women. See America's working women   331.4

Gordon, Lois G.
The Columbia chronicles of American life, 1910-1992   973.9

Gordon, Louise
How to draw the human figure   743

Gordon, Lyndall
Charlotte Brontë   92

Gordon, Mary, 1949-
The dancing party
In We are the stories we tell   S C
The important houses
In The Best American short stories, 1993 p335-58   S C
Intertextuality
In The Best American short stories, 1996 p151-58   S C
The neighborhood
In Coming of age in America p7-16   S C

Gordon, Matthew
Islam   297

Gordon, Roxy, 1945-
Pilgrims
In Song of the turtle p115-29   S C

Gordon, Ruth I., 1933-
(comp) Pierced by a ray of sun. See Pierced by a ray of sun   808.81

Gordon, Sheila, 1927-
Waiting for the rain   Fic

Gordon, Steve, d. 1982
Arthur
In Best American screenplays   812.008

Gore, Albert, Jr.
Earth in the balance   304.2

Goren, Charles Henry, 1901-1991
Goren's new bridge complete   795.4
Goren's new bridge complete. Goren, C. H.
795.4

Gorgas, William Crawford, 1854-1920
See/See also pages in the following book(s):
McCullough, D. G. The path between the seas
972.87

Gorge-purge syndrome See Bulimia
The **Gorgon's** head. Hawthorne, N.
In Hawthorne, N. Tales and sketches; A wonder book for girls and boys; Tanglewood tales for girls and boys p1169-89
S C

Gorilla, my love. Bambara, T. C.
In The Norton book of American short stories p675-80   S C

Gorillas
Fossey, D. Gorillas in the mist   599.88
Mowat, F. Woman in the mists: the story of Dian Fossey and the mountain gorillas of Africa   92
Nichols, M. K. The great apes   599.88
Gorillas in the mist. Fossey, D.   599.88

Goring, Rosemary
(ed) Larousse dictionary of beliefs and religions. See Larousse dictionary of beliefs and religions   291.03
(ed) Larousse dictionary of literary characters. See Larousse dictionary of literary characters   820.9
(ed) Larousse dictionary of writers. See Larousse dictionary of writers   803

Gorky, Maksim, 1868-1936
Recollections of Leo Tolstoy
In The Portable twentieth-century Russian reader p31-57   891.7
Twenty-six men and one girl
In The Portable nineteenth-century Russian reader p618-29   891.7

Gorman, Michael, 1941-
The concise AACR2, 1988 revision   025.3
(ed) Anglo-American cataloguing rules, 2d ed., 1988 revision. See Anglo-American cataloguing rules, 2d ed., 1988 revision   025.3

Gorog, Judith, 1938-
Those three wishes
In Read all about it! p475-78   808.88
The **gospel** according to Casey. Stengel, C.
92
The **Gospel** according to Mark. Borges, J. L.
In The Oxford book of gothic tales p478-82
S C

Gospel music
Oliver, P. The new Grove gospel, blues and jazz
780.89
We'll understand it better by and by
782.25

Goss, Clay, 1946-
(ed) Jump up and say! See Jump up and say!
810.8

Goss, Linda
(ed) Jump up and say! See Jump up and say!
810.8

Got a letter from Jimmy. Jackson, S.
In Jackson, S. The lottery   **S C**

Gotcha!. Bradbury, R.
In Bradbury, R. The stories of Ray Bradbury
p874-80   **S C**

Gothic architecture
Branner, R. Gothic architecture   **723**
Macaulay, D. Cathedral: the story of its construction   **726**

Gotlieb, Phyllis, 1926-
Tauf Aleph
In The Norton book of science fiction p427-44   **S C**

Gottesman, Greg
College survival   **378**

Gottfried, Robert S., 1949-
The black death   **616.9**

Gottfried, Ted, 1928-
Enrico Fermi, pioneer of the atomic age
     92

Gottschalk, Louis Moreau, 1829-1869
See/See also pages in the following book(s):
Nichols, J. American music makers p1-21
     920

Gotwalt, Helen Louise Miller
Bandit Ben rides again
In The Big book of large-cast plays p238-47
     812.008
The birds' Christmas carol [adaptation]
In The Big book of large-cast plays p339-51
     812.008
Name that book!
In The Big book of large-cast plays p299-312
     812.008

Goulart, Ron, 1933-
The comic book reader's companion   **741.5**
The funnies   **741.5**
(ed) The Encyclopedia of American comics. See
The Encyclopedia of American comics
     741.5

Gould, Gordon
See/See also pages in the following book(s):
Aaseng, N. Twentieth-century inventors p116-28
     920

Gould, Lewis L.
(ed) American first ladies. See American first
ladies   **920**

Gould, Stephen Jay, 1941-
Bully for brontosaurus   **508**
Dinosaur in a haystack   **508**
The flamingo's smile   **508**
(ed) The Historical atlas of the earth. See The
Historical atlas of the earth   **551.7**

Goulden, Joseph C.
Korea   **951.9**

Gourse, Leslie
Aretha Franklin   **92**
Billie Holiday   **92**
Unforgettable: the life and mystique of Nat
King Cole   **92**

Government *See* Political science

Government, Resistance to
See also Revolutions

Government and the press *See* Press—Government policy

Government by magic spell. Herzi, S. H.-D.
In The Heinemann book of contemporary
African short stories p94-99   **S C**

Government housing *See* Public housing

Government publications
    United States—Bibliography
Kelly, M. S. Using government documents
     015.73
United States. Superintendent of Documents.
U.S. Government books   **015.73**

Gow, James Ellis, 1907-1952
Tomorrow the world
In Best plays of the modern American theatre: 2nd series p597-640   **812.008**

Gowing, Sir Lawrence, 1918-1991
Matisse   **759.4**
(ed) A Biographical dictionary of artists. See A
Biographical dictionary of artists   **920.003**

Goya, Francisco, 1746-1828
    About
Gudiol, J. Goya   **759.6**
Waldron, A. Francisco Goya   **92**
See/See also pages in the following book(s):
Durant, W. J. Rousseau and revolution p300-09
     940.2

Goya y Lucientes, Francisco José de *See* Goya,
Francisco, 1746-1828

Goyen, William
Ghost and flesh, water and dirt
In The Literary ghost p304-13   **S C**

Graber, Eden
(ed) Staying healthy in a risky environment. See
Staying healthy in a risky environment
     613

Grace. Joyce, J.
In Joyce, J. Dubliners   **S C**
In The Oxford book of short stories p255-74
     S C

Grace. Paton Walsh, J.   **Fic**

Grace. Sears, V.
In Growing up Native American p279-98
     810.8
In Spider Woman's granddaughters   **S C**

The **grace** of great things. Grudin, R.   **153.3**

The **graduate.** Willingham, C.
In Best American screenplays   **812.008**

Gradwohl, Judith
(ed) Ocean planet. See Ocean planet
     574.92

Grady, Albert Wayne *See* Grady, Wayne, 1948-

Grady, Wayne, 1948-
The world of the coyote   **599.74**

Graf Zeppelin (Airship)
Dick, H. G. The golden age of the great passenger airships, Graf Zeppelin & Hindenburg
     629.133

Graff, Henry F. (Henry Franklin), 1921-
(ed) The Presidents: a reference history. See The
Presidents: a reference history   **920**

Grafton, Sue
The Parker shotgun
In Masterpieces of mystery and suspense p480-95   **S C**
In The Oxford book of American detective stories p639-54   **S C**

Graham, Andrew
(jt. auth) Hutchison, R. Meteorites   **523.5**

Graham, Martha
Blood memory   **92**

Graham, Robin Lee
Dove   **910.4**

Graham-Campbell, James
(ed) Cultural atlas of the Viking world. See Cultural atlas of the Viking world   **948**

Grahame, Kenneth, 1859-1932
The reluctant dragon
In The Oxford book of modern fairy tales p182-202   **S C**

Grail
Fiction
Pyle, H. The story of the Grail and the passing of Arthur   **398.2**

Grambo, Rebecca L., 1963-
The world of the fox   **599.74**

Gramma. King, S.
In King, S. Skeleton crew   **S C**

Grammar
See also English language—Grammar

Gramont, Sanche de *See* Morgan, Ted, 1932-

Grand, Gail L., 1943-
Student science opportunities   **507**

The **grand** alliance. Churchill, Sir W.   **940.53**

The **Grand** Inquisitor. Dostoyevsky, F.
In The Portable nineteenth-century Russian reader p413-33   **891.7**

Grand mothers: poems, reminiscences, and short stories about the keepers of our traditions   **810.8**

Grand slam. Chávez, D.
In Latina: women's voices from the borderlands p135-40   **810.8**

Grand Teton National Park (Wyo.)
See/See also pages in the following book(s):
Fishbein, S. L. Yellowstone country p126-53   **917.8**

The **Grand** Vizier's daughters. O'Connor, F.
In O'Connor, F. Collected stories p25-33   **S C**

Grandfathers
Fiction
Kerr, M. E. Gentlehands   **Fic**
Mazer, N. F. After the rain   **Fic**

Grandma Moses *See* Moses, Grandma, 1860-1961

Grandmothers
Grand mothers: poems, reminiscences, and short stories about the keepers of our traditions   **810.8**

Granger, Edith
The Columbia Granger's index to poetry. See The Columbia Granger's index to poetry   **808.81**

Gransden, K. W.
Virgil, the Aeneid   **873**

Grant, B. Rosemary
About
Weiner, J. The beak of the finch   **598**

Grant, Charles L.
Coin of the realm
In The Horror hall of fame p372-84   **S C**

Grant, Cynthia D., 1950-
Mary Wolf   **Fic**

Grant, Douglas, 1921-
(comp) Classic American short stories. See Classic American short stories   **S C**

Grant, Michael, 1914-
The founders of the Western world   **938**
Greek and Latin authors, 800 B.C.-A.D. 1000   **920.003**
A guide to the ancient world   **938.003**
A social history of Greece and Rome   **938**
(ed) Civilization of the ancient Mediterranean: Greece and Rome. See Civilization of the ancient Mediterranean: Greece and Rome   **938**

Grant, Peter R., 1936-
About
Weiner, J. The beak of the finch   **598**

Grant, Richard, 1948-
(jt. auth) Ballantine, R. Richards' ultimate bicycle book   **629.227**

Grant, Ulysses S. (Ulysses Simpson), 1822-1885
About
Catton, B. Grant moves south   **92**
Catton, B. Grant takes command   **92**
Davis, W. C. Death in the trenches: Grant at Petersburg   **973.7**
Korn, J. War on the Mississippi: Grant's Vicksburg campaign   **973.7**
Marrin, A. Unconditional surrender   **973.7**
Smith, G. Lee and Grant   **92**
See/See also pages in the following book(s):
McPherson, J. M. Drawn with the sword p159-73   **973.7**

Grant. Douglas, E.
In Prize stories, 1996 p175-88   **S C**

Grant moves south. Catton, B.   **92**

Grant takes command. Catton, B.   **92**

Grape harvest. Colette
In Colette. The collected stories of Colette p64-68   **S C**

The **grapes** of wrath. Steinbeck, J.   **Fic**
also in Steinbeck, J. The grapes of wrath and other writings, 1936-1941   **818**

The **grapes** of wrath and other writings, 1936-1941. Steinbeck, J.   **818**

Grass. Yourgrau, B.
In The Literary ghost p282-83   **S C**

Grassi, Battista
See/See also pages in the following book(s):
De Kruif, P. Microbe hunters   **920**

Grauer, Neil A.
Medicine and the law   **614**

Gravelle, Karen
Soaring spirits   **970.004**

Great Britain—Fiction—*Continued*

Fielding, H. The history of Tom Jones, a foundling   Fic

Forster, E. M. A room with a view   Fic

Hardy, T. The return of the native   Fic

Hardy, T. Tess of the D'Urbervilles   Fic

Lawrence, D. H. Sons and lovers   Fic

Paton Walsh, J. Grace   Fic

Tey, J. The daughter of time   Fic

Thackeray, W. M. Vanity fair   Fic

Waugh, E. Brideshead revisited   Fic

White, T. H. The book of Merlyn   Fic

Woolf, V. To the lighthouse   Fic

Historical geography—Maps

Gilbert, M. Atlas of British history   911

History

Churchill, Sir W. A history of the English-speaking peoples   941

The Oxford illustrated history of Britain   941

Saccio, P. Shakespeare's English kings   822.3

See/See also pages in the following book(s):

Durant, W. J. The age of Louis XIV p183-206, 244-311   940.2

Durant, W. J. The age of Napoleon p339-51, 512-27   940.2

History—0-1066

Ashe, G. The discovery of King Arthur   92

Campbell, J. The Anglo-Saxons   942.01

Day, D. The search for King Arthur   942.01

Salway, P. The Oxford illustrated history of Roman Britain   936.2

History—0-1066—Fiction

Alder, E. The king's shadow   Fic

Bradley, M. Z. The mists of Avalon   Fic

Stewart, M. Mary Stewart's Merlin trilogy   Fic

Stewart, M. The prince and the pilgrim   Fic

Sutcliff, R. The Shining Company   Fic

Twain, M. A Connecticut Yankee in King Arthur's court   Fic

White, T. H. The once and future king   Fic

History—1066-1154, Norman period

See also Hastings (East Sussex, England), Battle of, 1066

Howarth, D. A. 1066: the year of the conquest   942.02

Lace, W. W. The Battle of Hastings   942.02

History—1154-1399, Plantagenets

Singman, J. L. Daily life in Chaucer's England   942.03

See/See also pages in the following book(s):

Tuchman, B. W. A distant mirror p284-301   944

History—1455-1485, War of the Roses

Weir, A. The Wars of the Roses   942.04

History—1485-1603, Tudors

See also Spanish Armada, 1588

Kenny, A. J. P. Thomas More   92

McMurtry, J. Understanding Shakespeare's England   942.05

Singman, J. L. Daily life in Elizabethan England   942.05

Somerset, A. Elizabeth I   92

Weir, A. The children of Henry VIII   920

See/See also pages in the following book(s):

Mattingly, G. The Armada   942.05

History—1485-1603, Tudors—Drama

Bolt, R. A man for all seasons   822

History—1485-1603, Tudors—Fiction

Twain, M. The prince and the pauper   Fic

History—1603-1714, Stuarts

Fraser, A. Royal Charles: Charles II and the Restoration   92

Trevelyan, G. M. The English Revolution, 1688-1689   942.06

History—1642-1660, Civil War and Commonwealth

Fraser, A. Cromwell, the Lord Protector   92

History—1714-1837

See/See also pages in the following book(s):

Durant, W. J. Rousseau and revolution p669-745   940.2

History—1800-1899 (19th century)

See also Industrial revolution

The Encyclopedia of the Victorian world   941.081

Strachey, L. Queen Victoria   92

History—1900-1999 (20th century)

Longford, E. H. P., Countess of. The Queen: the life of Elizabeth II   92

Paterson, J. Edwardians   942.1

History—Dictionaries

The Cambridge historical encyclopedia of Great Britain and Ireland   941

Intellectual life

See/See also pages in the following book(s):

Durant, W. J. The age of Napoleon p386-407   940.2

Kings, queens, rulers, etc.

Ashe, G. The discovery of King Arthur   92

Bradford, S. Elizabeth   92

Cannon, J. The Oxford illustrated history of the British monarchy   941

Fraser, A. Royal Charles: Charles II and the Restoration   92

Longford, E. H. P., Countess of. The Queen: the life of Elizabeth II   92

Saccio, P. Shakespeare's English kings   822.3

Strachey, L. Queen Victoria   92

See/See also pages in the following book(s):

Durant, W. J. The age of Voltaire p89-115   940.2

Politics and government

Cannon, J. The Oxford illustrated history of the British monarchy   941

Politics and government—1952-

Thatcher, M. The Downing Street years   92

Great Britain. Army

Boulle, P. The bridge over the River Kwai   Fic

The **great** carbuncle. Hawthorne, N.

In Hawthorne, N. Tales and sketches; A wonder book for girls and boys; Tanglewood tales for girls and boys p435-49   S C

Great cats   599.74

Griffith Joyner, Florence
See/See also pages in the following book(s):
Davis, M. D. Black American women in Olympic track and field p63-72 **920**

Griffiths, Ralph A. (Ralph Alan)
(jt. auth) Cannon, J. The Oxford illustrated history of the British monarchy **941**

Griggs, Sutton Elbert, 1872-1930
See/See also pages in the following book(s):
Black American prose writers before the Harlem Renaissance p90-102 **810.9**

Grima, Tony
(ed) Not the only one. See Not the only one **S C**

Grimaldi, David A.
Amber **553.2**

Grimké, Angelina Emily, 1805-1879
Rachel
In Black theatre USA **812.008**

Grimké, Angelina Weld, 1880-1958
The closing door [excerpt]
In The Portable Harlem Renaissance reader p486-500 **810.8**

Grisham, John
The client **Fic**
The runaway jury **Fic**

The **grisly** folk. Wells, H. G.
In Wells, H. G. The complete short stories of H. G. Wells p607-21 **S C**

Griswold del Castillo, Richard
César Chávez **92**

Grmek, Mirko D.
History of AIDS **616.97**

Grob, Bernard
Basic electronics **621.38**

The **Grolier** multimedia encyclopedia. See Academic American encyclopedia **031**

The **Grolier** world encyclopedia of endangered species **591.5**

Grollman, Earl A.
Straight talk about death for teenagers **155.9**

Groom service. Dorris, M.
In Song of the turtle p276-88 **S C**

Grooming, Personal *See* Personal grooming

Gross, John J.
(ed) The Oxford book of essays. See The Oxford book of essays **824**

Gross, Michael, 1948-
Model **659.1**

Gross, Ruth V.
(ed) Critical essays on Franz Kafka. See Critical essays on Franz Kafka **833.009**

Grosseteste, Robert, 1175?-1253
See/See also pages in the following book(s):
Cantor, N. F. Medieval lives **940.1**

Grossman, James R.
A chance to make good
In The Young Oxford history of African Americans **305.8**

Grossman, Mark
The ABC-CLIO companion to the civil rights movement **323.1**

The **ABC-CLIO** companion to the environmental movement **363.7**

Groucho, Harpo, Chico and sometimes Zeppo. Adamson, J. **791.43**

The **Ground** Zero Club. Schulman, C.
In Ten out of ten p187-204 **812.008**

Group medical practice, Prepaid *See* Health maintenance organizations

Group values *See* Social values

Grout, Donald Jay, 1902-1987
A history of western music **780.9**

Grove, Sir George, 1820-1900
The New Grove dictionary of music and musicians. See The New Grove dictionary of music and musicians **780.3**

Groves, Donald G.
The oceans: a book of questions and answers **551.46**

Grove's dictionary of music and musicians. See The New Grove dictionary of music and musicians **780.3**

Growing up. Baker, R. **92**

Growing up Asian American **810.8**

Growing up Chicana/o **810.8**

Growing up gay **808.8**

Growing up in the Great Depression. Wormser, R. **973.91**

Growing up in twentieth-century America. West, E. **305.23**

Growing up Jewish **305.8**

Growing up Jewish in America **305.8**

Growing up Latino **810.8**

Growing up Native American **810.8**

Growth
Repair and renewal **612**

Growth disorders
See also Birth defects
Dictionaries
Wynbrandt, J. The encyclopedia of genetic disorders and birth defects **616**

The **growth** of the American Republic. Morison, S. E. **973**

Gruber, Gary R.
Gruber's complete preparation for the new SAT **378.1**

Grudin, Robert
The grace of great things **153.3**

Gruhzit-Hoyt, Olga, 1922-
They also served **940.54**

Grundy, Isobel
(ed) The Feminist companion to literature in English. See The Feminist companion to literature in English **820.9**

Grundy, Valerie
(ed) The Oxford-Hachette French dictionary. See The Oxford-Hachette French dictionary **443**

Gryphon. Baxter, C.
In The Best American short stories of the eighties p223-40 **S C**

Grzimek's encyclopedia of mammals **599**

The **guardeen**. Frost, R.
　In Frost, R. Collected poems, prose, & plays
　　p589-625　　　　　　　　　　　**818**
Guare, John
　The house of blue leaves
　In Best American plays: 7th series—1967-
　　1973 p309-36　　　　　　　**812.008**
Gubar, Susan, 1944-
　(comp) The Norton anthology of literature by
　women. See The Norton anthology of litera-
　ture by women　　　　　　　　**820.8**
Gudiol, José, 1904-1985
　Goya　　　　　　　　　　　　**759.6**
Guernsey, JoAnn Bren
　Pas de deux
　In Not the only one p108-16　　　**S C**
Guernsey, Otis Love, 1918-
　(ed) The Best plays of [date]: The Otis Guern-
　sey/Burns Mantle theater yearbook. See The
　Best plays of [date]: The Otis Guernsey/Burns
　Mantle theater yearbook　　　　**808.82**
Guerrilla prince: the untold story of Fidel Castro.
　Geyer, G. A.　　　　　　　　　**92**
Guess who's coming to Seder. Ellis, T.
　In Calling the wind p534-38　　　**S C**
Guest, Judith
　Ordinary people　　　　　　　　**Fic**
The **guest**. Sholem Aleichem
　In Sholem Aleichem. The best of Sholem
　Aleichem　　　　　　　　　　　**S C**
Guests of the nation. O'Connor, F.
　In O'Connor, F. Collected stories p3-12
　　　　　　　　　　　　　　　　S C
　In The Oxford book of Irish short stories
　　p342-53　　　　　　　　　　　**S C**
　In The Oxford book of short stories p371-81
　　　　　　　　　　　　　　　　S C
Guicciardini, Francesco, 1483-1540
　See/See also pages in the following book(s):
　Barzini, L. G. The Italians p157-75　　**945**
Guidance, Vocational *See* Vocational guidance
A **Guide** book of United States coins　**737.4**
Guide dog. Conner, M.
　In Nebula awards 27 p16-52　　　**S C**
Guide to American colleges, Cass & Birnbaum's
　　　　　　　　　　　　　　　378.73
Guide to Congress, Congressional Quarterly's
　　　　　　　　　　　　　　　328.73
Guide to free computer materials　　**004**
Guide to jobs and career planning. See Mitchell,
　J. S. The College Board guide to jobs and ca-
　reer planning　　　　　　　　**331.7**
Guide to reference books　　　　　**011**
A **guide** to the ancient world. Grant, M.
　　　　　　　　　　　　　　　938.003
Guide to the orchestra, André Previn's. Previn, A.
　　　　　　　　　　　　　　　784
Guide to the presidency　　　　**353.03**
Guide to U.S. elections, Congressional Quarterly's
　　　　　　　　　　　　　　　324.6
Guiley, Rosemary Ellen
　Atlas of the mysterious in North America
　　　　　　　　　　　　　　　398.2

The encyclopedia of ghosts and spirits
　　　　　　　　　　　　　　　133.1
The encyclopedia of witches and witchcraft
　　　　　　　　　　　　　　　133.4
Guillen, Michael
　Five equations that changed the world
　　　　　　　　　　　　　　　530.1
Guilt-edged blonde. Macdonald, R.
　In The Oxford book of American detective
　　stories p512-25　　　　　　　**S C**
Guin, Wyman
　The root and the ring
　In Masterpieces of fantasy and enchantment
　　p49-69　　　　　　　　　　　**S C**
Guinness book of records　　　**032.02**
The **Guinness** book of sports records　**796**
Guinness book of world records. See Guinness
　book of records　　　　　　**032.02**
The **Guinness** encyclopedia of popular music
　　　　　　　　　　　　　　　781.64
Guinness sports record book. See The Guinness
　book of sports records　　　　　**796**
The **guitar** handbook. Denyer, R.　**787.87**
Guitars
　Bacon, T. The ultimate guitar book　**787.87**
　Chapman, R. The complete guitarist　**787.87**
　Denyer, R. The guitar handbook　**787.87**
The **Gulag** archipelago, 1918-1956. Solzhenitsyn,
　A.　　　　　　　　　　　　　**365**
Gulf War, 1991 *See* Persian Gulf War, 1991
The **Gulf** war reader　　　　　**956.7**
Gullberg, Jan
　Mathematics　　　　　　　　　**510**
Gulliver, the story of a tall man. Wolfe, T.
　In Wolfe, T. The complete short stories of
　　Thomas Wolfe p241-49　　　　**S C**
Gulliver's travels. Swift, J.　　　　**Fic**
Gumption. Hughes, L.
　In Hughes, L. Short stories　　　**S C**
The **gun.** Carol, A.
　In Bad behavior p83-89　　　　**S C**
The **gun.** Hughes, L.
　In Hughes, L. Short stories　　　**S C**
Gun control *See* Firearms—Law and legislation
Gun control. Kruschke, E. R.　　**363.3**
The **Gunfighters**　　　　　　**364.3**
Gunn, Eileen
　Stable strategies for middle management
　In The Norton book of science fiction p705-
　　15　　　　　　　　　　　　　**S C**
The **guns** of August. Tuchman, B. W.　**940.3**
The **guns** of Navarone. MacLean, A.　**Fic**
Gunther, John, 1901-1970
　Death be not proud [biography of his son]
　　　　　　　　　　　　　　　92
Gunther, John, 1929-1947
　　　　　　　About
　Gunther, J. Death be not proud　　**92**
Guralnick, Peter
　Last train to Memphis: the rise of Elvis Presley
　　　　　　　　　　　　　　　92

Gurganus, Allan
Minor heroism
In The Vintage book of contemporary American short stories p207-28   **S C**
Gurnah, Abdulrazak
Bossy
In African short stories   **S C**
Cages
In The Heinemann book of contemporary African short stories p87-93   **S C**
Gurney, A. R. (Albert Ramsdell), 1930-
The cocktail hour
In Best American plays: 9th series—1983-1992 p414-45   **812.008**
The golden age
In Gurney, A. R. Love letters and two other plays p57-132   **812**
Love letters
In Gurney, A. R. Love letters and two other plays p1-55   **812**
Love letters and two other plays: The golden age, and What I did last summer   **812**
What I did last summer
In Gurney, A. R. Love letters and two other plays p133-209   **812**
Gurney, Albert Ramsdell *See* Gurney, A. R. (Albert Ramsdell), 1930-
Gusev. Chekhov, A. P.
In Chekhov, A. P. The image of Chekhov p154-70   **S C**
Guthrie, A. B. (Alfred Bertram), 1901-1991
The big sky   **Fic**
Guthrie, Alfred Bertram *See* Guthrie, A. B. (Alfred Bertram), 1901-1991
Guthrie, Woody, 1912-1967
Bound for glory   **92**
Gutkind, Lee
Creative nonfiction   **808**
Stuck in time   **616.89**
Gutman, Dan
Baseball's greatest games   **796.357**
The way baseball works   **796.357**
Guttmann, Allen
The Olympics, a history of the modern games   **796.48**
Guy, Rosa
The disappearance   **Fic**
The friends   **Fic**
Wade
In Calling the wind p242-50   **S C**
About
Norris, J. Presenting Rosa Guy   **813.009**
Gwala, Mafika Pascal, 1946-
Reflections in a cell
In African short stories   **S C**
Gymnastics
Ryan, J. Little girls in pretty boxes   **796.44**
Gynecology *See* Women—Diseases; Women—Health and hygiene

H

H bomb *See* Hydrogen bomb

H.M.O.'s *See* Health maintenance organizations
Haase, Ynez D.
(jt. auth) Beck, W. A. Historical atlas of the American West   **911**
Habit. Colette
In Colette. The collected stories of Colette p306-08   **S C**
Habitat (Ecology)
Robinson, M. Zoo animals   **591.5**
Hacienda. Porter, K. A.
In Porter, K. A. The collected stories of Katherine Anne Porter   **S C**
Hacker, Andrew
Two nations   **305.8**
Hackett, Albert, 1900-1995
(jt. auth) Goodrich, F. The diary of Anne Frank   **812**
Hackett, Sir John Winthrop, 1910-
(ed) Warfare in the ancient world. See Warfare in the ancient world   **355**
Hadden, Gerald
A great day of accounting
In Coming of age p77-88   **808.8**
Hadji Murád. Tolstoy, L., graf
In Tolstoy, L. Great short works of Leo Tolstoy p547-668   **S C**
Hadrian, Emperor of Rome, 76-138
About
Rome: echoes of imperial glory   **937**
Hagenston, Becky
Til death us do part
In Prize stories, 1996 p202-18   **S C**
Hager, Rachel
(ed) When they came to take my father—. See When they came to take my father—   **940.53**
Hager, Thomas
Force of nature: the life of Linus Pauling   **92**
Haggard, H. Rider (Henry Rider), 1856-1925
King Solomon's mines   **Fic**
Haggard, Henry Rider *See* Haggard, H. Rider (Henry Rider), 1856-1925
Hahn, Mary Downing, 1937-
The wind blows backward   **Fic**
Haig, Caroline MacDonald- *See* MacDonald-Haig, Caroline
Haigh, Christopher
(ed) The Cambridge historical encyclopedia of Great Britain and Ireland. See The Cambridge historical encyclopedia of Great Britain and Ireland   **941**
Haiku
Higginson, W. J. The haiku handbook   **808.1**
One man's moon   **895.6**
The **haiku** handbook. Higginson, W. J.   **808.1**
Hail and farewell. Bradbury, R.
In Bradbury, R. The stories of Ray Bradbury p296-302   **S C**
Haing S. Ngor *See* Ngor, Haing S.

Hard riding. McNickle, D.
  In The Singing spirit: early short stories by
    North American Indians p167-75
                                        S C
Hard time. Bode, J.   **364.3**
Hard times. Dickens, C.   **Fic**
Hard times. Terkel, S.   **973.91**
The **hard** worker. Colette
  In Colette. The collected stories of Colette
    p129-31   **S C**
Harding, Lee Emling
  (ed) Critical essays on Eudora Welty. See Criti-
    cal essays on Eudora Welty   **813.009**
Harding, Richard M.
  Survival in space   **616.9**
Harding, Vincent
  We changed the world
  In The Young Oxford history of African
    Americans   **305.8**
Hardshell. Koontz, D. R.
  In Koontz, D. R. Strange highways p344-70
                                        S C
Hardy, Oliver, 1892-1957
  See/See also pages in the following book(s):
  Kerr, W. The silent clowns p316-35   **791.43**
Hardy, Thomas, 1840-1928
  Barbara of the House of Grebe
  In The Oxford book of gothic tales p218-44
                                        S C
  Poems   **821**
  The return of the native   **Fic**
  Tess of the D'Urbervilles   **Fic**
  The three strangers
  In The Best crime stories of the 19th century
    p72-95   **S C**
                     About
  Critical essays on Thomas Hardy   **823.009**
Hare, R. M. (Richard Mervyn)
  Plato   **184**
Hare, Richard Mervyn *See* Hare, R. M. (Richard
  Mervyn)
The **hare-lip.** Ó Cadhain, M.
  In The Oxford book of Irish short stories
    p375-81   **S C**
Hargrove, Hondon B., 1916-
  Black Union soldiers in the Civil War
                                       973.7
Harjo, Joy, 1951-
  The flood
  In Talking leaves   **S C**
  Northern lights
  In Talking leaves   **S C**
  The woman who fell from the sky   **811**
    also in Song of the turtle p302-06 **S C**
  See/See also pages in the following book(s):
  Coltelli, L. Winged words: American Indian
    writers speak   **897**
Harjo, Lisa D.
  American Indian voices. See American Indian
    voices   **810.8**
Harlan, John Marshall, 1899-1971
  See/See also pages in the following book(s):
  Aaseng, N. Great Justices of the Supreme Court
    p55-69   **920**

Harlan, Louis R.
  Booker T. Washington: the making of a black
    leader, 1856-1901   **92**
  Booker T. Washington: the wizard of Tuskegee,
    1901-1915   **92**
Harlem (New York, N.Y.)
  Cooper, R. Amateur night at the Apollo
                                       792.7
                    Fiction
  Baldwin, J. Go tell it on the mountain **Fic**
  Childress, A. A hero ain't nothin' but a sand-
    wich   **Fic**
  Guy, R. The friends   **Fic**
  Lipsyte, R. The contender   **Fic**
  Morrison, T. Jazz   **Fic**
               Social conditions
  Brown, C. Manchild in the promised land
                                          92
Harlem Dance Theatre *See* Dance Theatre of
  Harlem
Harlem Renaissance
  Black American prose writers of the Harlem Re-
    naissance   **810.9**
  Haskins, J. The Harlem Renaissance   **700**
  The Portable Harlem Renaissance reader
                                       810.8
  Shimmy shimmy shimmy like my sister Kate
                                      811.008
  See/See also pages in the following book(s):
  Bearden, R. A history of African-American art-
    ists   **709.73**
Harlem Renaissance and beyond: literary biogra-
  phies of 100 black women writers, 1900-
  1945. Roses, L. E.   **920.003**
Harlem Renaissance: art of black America
                                      709.73
Harlem slanguage. Hurston, Z. N.
  In Hurston, Z. N. The complete stories p227-
    32   **S C**
A **Harlem** tragedy. Henry, O.
  In Henry, O. The best short stories of O.
    Henry   **S C**
Harley, Sharon
  The timetables of African-American history
                                       305.8
Harmful insects *See* Insect pests
Harmon, Charles T., 1960-
  (jt. auth) Symons, A. K. Protecting the right to
    read   **025.2**
  (ed) Using the Internet, online services & CD-
    ROMS for writing research and term papers.
    See Using the Internet, online services & CD-
    ROMS for writing research and term papers
                                        004
Harmon, Justin
  American cultural leaders. See American cultur-
    al leaders   **920.003**
Harmon, William, 1938-
  A handbook to literature   **803**
  (ed) The Oxford book of American light verse.
    See The Oxford book of American light verse
                                      811.008
  (ed) The Top 500 poems. See The Top 500 po-
    ems   **821.008**

Harmony. Lardner, R.
In Lardner, R. The best short stories of Ring
Lardner p149-66 **S C**
The **Harmony** illustrated encyclopedia of classical
music. Gammond, P. **781.6**
The **Harmony** illustrated encyclopedia of rock
781.66
Harnack, Andrew, 1937-
(ed) Adoption: opposing viewpoints. See Adoption: opposing viewpoints **362.7**
(ed) Animal rights: opposing viewpoints. See
Animal rights: opposing viewpoints **179**
The **harness.** Steinbeck, J.
In Steinbeck, J. The portable Steinbeck
818
Harnett, William Michael, 1848-1892
See/See also pages in the following book(s):
Novak, B. American painting of the nineteenth
century p221-34 **759.13**
Harold, King of England, 1022?-1066
Fiction
Alder, E. The king's shadow **Fic**
Harper, Frances Ellen Watkins, 1825-1911
Iola
In Invented lives p87-106 **S C**
See/See also pages in the following book(s):
Black American poets and dramatists before the
Harlem Renaissance p66-78 **810.9**
Harper, Michael S.
(ed) Every shut eye ain't asleep. See Every shut
eye ain't asleep **811.008**
See/See also pages in the following book(s):
Contemporary black American poets and dramatists p47-61 **810.9**
The **Harper** dictionary of music. See Ammer, C.
The HarperCollins dictionary of music
780.3
The **Harper** encyclopedia of military history.
Dupuy, R. E. **355**
The **HarperCollins** Bible dictionary **220.3**
The **HarperCollins** dictionary of mathematics.
Borowski, E. J. **510.3**
The **HarperCollins** dictionary of music. Ammer,
C. **780.3**
The **HarperCollins** dictionary of religion
200.3
The **HarperCollins** dictionary of sociology. Jary,
D. **301**
The **HarperCollins** encyclopedia of Catholicism
282
Harper's anthology of 20th century Native
American poetry **811.008**
Harper's Bible dictionary. See The HarperCollins
Bible dictionary **220.3**
Harpur, James
Revelations, the Medieval world **909.07**
Harpy thyme. Anthony, P. See note under Anthony, P. The Magic of Xanth series **Fic**
Harrap's new collegiate French and English dictionary **443**
Harrell, Mary Ann
Surprising lands down under **994**
Harrington, Denis J., 1932-
The Pro Football Hall of Fame **796.332**

Harris, David, 1929-
The art of calligraphy **745.6**
Harris, Jean
See/See also pages in the following book(s):
Aymar, B. A pictorial history of the world's
greatest trials p377-87 **345**
Harris, Joel Chandler, 1848-1908
The wonderful Tar-Baby story and How Mr.
Rabbit was too sharp for Mr. Fox
In The Norton book of American short stories
p111-14 **S C**
Harris, Kathy
(jt. auth) Pohl, C. Transracial adoption
362.7
Harris, Laurie Lanzen
Characters in 20th-century literature **809**
Harris, Marilyn, 1931-
Hatter Fox **Fic**
Harris, Mark, 1922-
Bang the drum slowly, by Henry W. Wiggen
Fic
Harris, Sherwood
(ed) The New York Public Library book of how
and where to look it up. See The New York
Public Library book of how and where to
look it up **025.5**
Harris and me. Paulsen, G. **Fic**
Harrison, David, 1938-
Canoeing **797.1**
Harrison, Harry, 1925-
A criminal act
In The Oxford book of science fiction stories
p350-62 **S C**
The view from the top of the tower
In Tales from the planet Earth **S C**
Harrison, Hazel
The encyclopedia of watercolor techniques
751.42
Pastel school **741.2**
Harrison, James, 1927-
Rudyard Kipling **828**
Harrison, John, 1693-1776
About
Sobel, D. Longitude **526**
Harrison, Max
(jt. auth) Oliver, P. The new Grove gospel,
blues and jazz **780.89**
Harrison, R. J. (Richard John), 1920-
(ed) Whales, dolphins, and porpoises. See
Whales, dolphins, and porpoises [Facts on
File] **599.5**
Harrison, Richard John See Harrison, R. J.
(Richard John), 1920-
Harrison, Sue
Mother earth, father sky **Fic**
My sister the moon **Fic**
Harrison Bergeron. Vonnegut, K.
In Vonnegut, K. Welcome to the monkey
house **S C**
Harrold, Francis B., 1948-
(jt. auth) Eve, R. A. The creationist movement
in modern America **213**

Hart, James David, 1911-1990
(ed) The Oxford companion to American literature. See The Oxford companion to American
literature   810.3

Hart, Moss, 1904-1961
Act one: an autobiography   92

Hart, Stephen
The language of animals   591.5

Harte, Bret, 1836-1902
The Iliad of Sandy Bar
In The Oxford book of short stories p67-77
    S C
The outcasts of Poker Flat
In The Norton book of American short stories
p65-74   S C
Selina Sedilia
In The Oxford book of gothic tales p158-64
    S C
The stolen cigar case
In The Oxford book of American detective
stories p40-48   S C

Harter, Carol C.
E. L. Doctorow   813.009

Harter, Penny
(jt. auth) Higginson, W. J. The haiku handbook
    808.1

Hartley, L. P. (Leslie Poles), 1895-1972
A visitor from down under
In The Oxford book of English ghost stories
p307-21   S C

Hartley, Leslie Poles *See* Hartley, L. P. (Leslie
Poles), 1895-1972

The **Hartleys.** Cheever, J.
In Cheever, J. The stories of John Cheever
p58-64   S C

Hartman, Donald K.
Historical figures in fiction   016.8

Hartnoll, Phyllis
(ed) The Oxford companion to the theatre. See
The Oxford companion to the theatre
    792.03

Hartog, Jan de *See* De Hartog, Jan, 1914-

Hartt, Frederick, 1914-1991
Art   709
Michelangelo   759.5

Hartwell, David G.
(comp) Masterpieces of fantasy and enchantment. See Masterpieces of fantasy and enchantment   S C

Hartz, Paula
Taoism   299

Harvard dictionary of music. See The New Harvard dictionary of music   780.3

Harvard encyclopedia of American ethnic groups
    305.8

Harvard guide to American history   973

The **harvest** gypsies. Steinbeck, J.
In Steinbeck, J. The grapes of wrath and other writings, 1936-1941   818

Harvest of stars. Anderson, P.   Fic

Harvest the fire. Anderson, P. See note under Anderson, P. Harvest of stars   Fic

Harvey, Henry Paul *See* Harvey, Sir Paul, 1869-
1948

Harvey, Karen D.
(ed) American Indian voices. See American Indian voices   810.8

Harvey, Liz
(ed) Shoot! See Shoot!   770

Harvey, Sir Paul, 1869-1948
The Oxford companion to classical literature.
See The Oxford companion to classical litera-
ture   880.3

Harvey, Robert C.
The art of the comic book   741.5

Harvey, W. F. (William Fryer), 1885-1937
The clock
In The Oxford book of English ghost stories
p335-38   S C

Harvey, William, 1578-1657
See/See also pages in the following book(s):
Curtis, R. H. Great lives: medicine p30-38
    920
Meadows, A. J. The great scientists   920

Harvey, William Fryer *See* Harvey, W. F. (William Fryer), 1885-1937

Harvey. Chase, M.
In The Most popular plays of the American
theater p223-88   812.008

Has anybody seen Miss Dora Dean?. Petry, A. L.
In Calling the wind p182-95   S C

Haskins, Charles
(jt. auth) Gravelle, K. Teenagers face to face
with bereavement   155.9

Haskins, James, 1941-
The 60s reader   973.92
Black dance in America   792.8
Black music in America   780.89
The Harlem Renaissance   700
I am somebody! a biography of Jesse Jackson
    92
Lena: a personal and professional biography of
Lena Horne   92
Scott Joplin   92
The Scottsboro Boys   345

Haslam, Alexandra R., 1963-
(ed) Where coyotes howl and wind blows free.
See Where coyotes howl and wind blows free
    810.8

Haslam, Gerald W., 1937-
The horned toad
In Growing up Chicana/o p103-13   810.8
(ed) Where coyotes howl and wind blows free.
See Where coyotes howl and wind blows free
    810.8

Hasselbach, Ingo
Fuhrer-Ex   943.087

Hassrick, Peter H.
Charles M. Russell   92

Hastings, Max
The Korean War   951.9

Hastings (East Sussex, England), Battle of, 1066
Howarth, D. A. 1066: the year of the conquest
    942.02
Lace, W. W. The Battle of Hastings
    942.02

Hawthorne, Nathaniel, 1804-1864—*Continued*
Rappaccini's daughter
  In The Oxford book of gothic tales p133-57
    S C
The scarlet letter **Fic**
Scarlet letter; criticism
  In Baym, N. The scarlet letter **813.009**
  In Hester Prynne **813.009**
  In Johnson, C. D. Understanding The scarlet
    letter **813.009**
Tales and sketches, including Twice-told tales,
  Mosses from an old manse, and The snow-
  image; A wonder book for girls and boys;
  Tanglewood tales for girls and boys, being a
  second Wonder book **S C**
  Contents: The hollow of the three hills; Sir William Phips;
  Mrs. Hutchinson; An old woman's tale; Dr. Bullivant; Sights
  from a steeple; The haunted quack; The wives of the dead; My
  kinsman, Major Molineux; Roger Malvin's burial; The gentle
  boy; The seven vagabonds; The Canterbury pilgrims; Sir William
  Pepperell; Passages from a relinquished work; Mr.
  Higginbotham's catastrophe; The haunted mind; Alice Doane's
  appeal; The village uncle; Little Annie's ramble; The gray champion; My visit to Niagara; Old news; Young Goodman Brown;
  Wakefield; The ambitious guest; A rill from the town-pump; The
  white old maid; The vision of the fountain; The Devil in manuscript; Sketches from memory; The wedding-knell; The may-pole
  of Merry Mount; The minister's black veil; Old Ticonderoga; A
  visit to the clerk of the weather; Monsieur du Miroir; Mrs. Bull-
  frog; Sunday at home; The man of Adamant; David Swan; The
  great carbuncle; Fancy's show box; The prophetic pictures; Dr.
  Heidegger's experiment; A bell's biography; Fragments from the
  journal of a solitary man; Edward Fane's rosebud; The toll-
  gatherer's day; Sylph Etherege; Peter Goldwaite's treasure; Endicott and the Red Cross; Night sketches; The Shaker bridal; Foot-
  prints on the seashore; Thomas Green Fessenden; Time's portraiture; Snow-flakes; The threefold destiny; Jonathan Cilley; Chip-
  pings with a chisel; Legends of the Province-House; The sister
  years; The lily's quest; John Inglefield's Thanksgiving; A virtuoso's collection; The old apple-dealer; The antique ring; The hall
  of fantasy; The new Adam and Eve; The birthmark; Egotism; or,
  The bosom-serpent; The procession of life; The celestial railroad;
  Buds and bird-voices; Little Daffydowndilly; Fire-worship; The
  Christmas banquet; A good man's miracles; The intelligence office; Earth's holocaust; The artist of the beautiful; Drowne's
  wooden image; A select party; A book of autographs;
  Rappaccini's daughter; P.'s correspondence; Main-street; Ethan
  Brand; The great stone face; The snow-image; Feathertop; The
  Gorgon's head; The Golden touch; The paradise of children; The
  three golden apples; The miraculous pitcher; The Chimaera; The
  Minotaur; The Pygmies; The dragon's teeth; Circe's palace; The
  pomegranate-seeds; The golden fleece
Tanglewood tales for girls and boys
  In Hawthorne, N. Tales and sketches; A won-
    der book for girls and boys; Tanglewood
    tales for girls and boys p1303-1470
    S C
The wives of the dead
  In The Oxford book of American short stories
    p62-68 **S C**
A wonder book for girls and boys
  In Hawthorne, N. Tales and sketches; A won-
    der book for girls and boys; Tanglewood
    tales for girls and boys p1159-1302
    S C
Young Goodman Brown
  In The Norton book of American short stories
    p35-46 **S C**
About
Martin, T. Nathaniel Hawthorne **813.009**
Miller, E. H. Salem is my dwelling place: a life
  of Nathaniel Hawthorne **92**
Readings on Nathaniel Hawthorne **813.009**
Haxton, Josephine *See* Douglas, Ellen

Hayakawa, Alan R.
  (jt. auth) Hayakawa, S. I. Language in thought
    and action **412**
Hayakawa, S. I.
  Language in thought and action **412**
Haycraft, Howard, 1905-1991
  (ed) American authors, 1600-1900. See
    American authors, 1600-1900 **920.003**
  (ed) British authors before 1800. See British au-
    thors before 1800 **920.003**
  (ed) British authors of the nineteenth century.
    See British authors of the nineteenth century
    920.003
Hayden, Palmer C., 1893-1973
  See/See also pages in the following book(s):
  Harlem Renaissance: art of black America
    709.73
Hayden, Thomas C.
  Peterson's handbook for college admissions
    378
Hayden, Torey L.
  Ghost girl **362.7**
  The tiger's child **155.5**
Haydn, Joseph, 1732-1809
  See/See also pages in the following book(s):
  Durant, W. J. Rousseau and revolution p373-81
    940.2
  Grout, D. J. A history of western music
    780.9
Hayslip, Le Ly
  When heaven and earth changed places: a Viet-
    namese woman's journey from war to peace
    92
Hayward, John, 1905-1965
  (comp) The Oxford book of nineteenth-century
    English verse. See The Oxford book of nine-
    teenth-century English verse **821.008**
Hazen, Edith P.
  (ed) The Columbia Granger's dictionary of poet-
    ry quotations. See The Columbia Granger's
    dictionary of poetry quotations **808.88**
  The Columbia Granger's index to poetry. See
    The Columbia Granger's index to poetry
    808.81
Hazen, Robert M., 1948-
  Science matters: achieving scientific literacy
    500
The hazing. Asimov, I.
  In Asimov, I. The complete stories v2 p16-29
    S C
He. Porter, K. A.
  In The Oxford book of American short stories
    p323-33 **S C**
  In Porter, K. A. The collected stories of Kath-
    erine Anne Porter **S C**
Head, Bessie, 1937-1986
  Snapshots of a wedding
  In African short stories **S C**
Head, Matthew *See* Canaday, John Edwin, 1907-
  1985
Head and shoulders. Fitzgerald, F. S.
  In Fitzgerald, F. S. The short stories of F.
    Scott Fitzgerald p3-24 **S C**
Head injuries. Aaseng, N. **617.1**

The **head** of the district. Kipling, R.
    In Kipling, R. The portable Kipling   **828**
Headache
    Kittredge, M. Headaches   **616.8**
Heade, Martin Johnson, 1819-1904
    See/See also pages in the following book(s):
    Novak, B. American painting of the nineteenth
        century p125-37   **759.13**
Heads of state
        See also Dictators; Kings, queens, rulers,
    etc.; Presidents; Prime ministers
    Opfell, O. S. Women prime ministers and presi-
        dents   **920**
    Wakin, E. Contemporary political leaders of the
        Middle East   **920**
Headwaiter. Himes, C.
    In Calling the wind p79-93   **S C**
Heafford, Philip Ernest
    Great book of math puzzles   **793.7**
The **healer.** McKinley, R.
    In McKinley, R. A knot in the grain and oth-
        er stories p1-39   **S C**
The **healer's** war [excerpt] Scarborough, E. A.
    In Nebula awards 25 p42-36   **S C**
Healing drugs. Facklam, M.   **615**
Health
        See also Hygiene; Physical fitness
    Check, W. A. The mind-body connection
        610
    Health and fitness: opposing viewpoints
        613
    Health on file   **613**
    Macmillan health encyclopedia   **610.3**
    The New Good Housekeeping family health and
        medical guide   **616.02**
        Dictionaries
    Isler, C. The Watts teen health dictionary
        610.3
    Tver, D. F. The nutrition and health encyclope-
        dia   **613.2**
        Environmental aspects
    See Environmental health
Health, Industrial *See* Occupational health and
    safety
Health, Public *See* Public health
Health. Williams, J.
    In The Best American short stories of the
        eighties p241-51   **S C**
Health and fitness: opposing viewpoints   **613**
Health and medicine projects for young scientists.
    O'Neil, K. E.   **610**
Health card. Yerby, F.
    In The Best short stories by Negro writers
        p192-201   **S C**
Health care *See* Medical care
Health care in America: opposing viewpoints
        362.1
The **Health** crisis: opposing viewpoints. See
    Health care in America: opposing viewpoints
        362.1
Health insurance
    Health care in America: opposing viewpoints
        362.1

Health maintenance organizations
    See/See also pages in the following book(s):
    Sherrow, V. The U.S. health care crisis p95-102
        362.1
Health on file   **613**
Health self-care
    American Medical Association family medical
        guide   **616.02**
Healthspeak. Freudenheim, E.   **362.1**
Healthy runner's handbook. Micheli, L. J.
        613.7
Healthy skin. MacKie, R. M.   **616.5**
Heaney, Seamus
    Selected poems, 1966-1987   **821**
    Station Island   **821**
Hearder, Harry
    Italy   **945**
Hearing
    Allstetter, W. D. Speech and hearing   **612.7**
Hearing impaired
        See also Deaf
Hearing loss. Mango, K. N.   **617.8**
Hearing the pitch. Frisch, C.   **659.1**
Hearne, Betsy Gould
    Beauties and beasts   **398.2**
    Includes the following stories: Beauty and the Beast; The en-
    chanted Tsarevitch; The princess and the pig; A bunch of laurel
    blooms for a present; The small-tooth dog; The fairy serpent;
    Monkey son-in-law; The lizard husband; Cupid and Psyche; The
    serpent and the grape-grower's daughter; The singing, soaring
    lark; East of the sun and west of the moon; Whitebear
    Whittington; The three daughters of King O'Hara; The Black
    Bull of Norroway; Bull-of-all-the-Land; Prince White Hog; The
    enchanted prince; The story of Five Heads; The ten serpents;
    Englè, Queen of Serpents; Sir Gawain and the loathly lady; The
    laidley worm of Spindleston Heughs; Kemp Owyne; Pinto Smal-
    to; The dough prince; Old Man Coyote, the young man and two
    otter sisters
Hearne, Elizabeth G. *See* Hearne, Betsy Gould
Hearst, William Randolph, 1863-1951
        About
    Swanberg, W. A. Citizen Hearst: a biography of
        William Randolph Hearst   **92**
Heart
        See also Blood—Circulation
        Diseases
    Arnold, C. Heart disease   **616.1**
Heart disease. Arnold, C.   **616.1**
Heart full of grace   **808.88**
The **heart** is a lonely hunter. McCullers, C.
        Fic
        also in McCullers, C. The ballad of the sad
            café: the novels and stories of Carson
            McCullers   **S C**
Heart of darkness. Conrad, J.   **Fic**
        also in Conrad, J. The complete short fiction
            of Joseph Conrad v3   **S C**
        also in Conrad, J. The portable Conrad
            828
Heart of Europe. Davies, N.   **943.8**
The **heart** of the brave. Jones, W.
    In The Singing spirit: early short stories by
        North American Indians p59-65   **S C**
The **heart** of the game. Hemphill, P.   **796.357**

The **heart** of the matter. Greene, G.   **Fic**
also in Greene, G. The portable Graham
    Greene p78-305   **828**
The **heart** of the park. O'Connor, F.
In O'Connor, F. The complete stories p81-94
                                                   S C
Heartache. Chekhov, A. P.
In Chekhov, A. P. The image of Chekhov
    p99-105   **S C**
Heartbreak house. Shaw, B.
In Shaw, B. The portable Bernard Shaw
                                                   822
Hearth, Amy Hill, 1958-
    (jt. auth) Delany, S. Having our say   **92**
Heartstones. Rendell, R.   **Fic**
Heat. Bausch, R.
In The Other side of heaven p353-78
                                                   S C
Heat. Oates, J. C.
In The Oxford book of American short stories
    p607-19   **S C**
Heat Moon, William Least
    Blue highways   **917.3**
The **heathen.** London, J.
In Classic American short stories p282-306
                                                   S C
In London, J. Short stories of Jack London
    p374-90   **S C**
Heaton, Eric William
    Everyday life in Old Testament times
                                                   221.9
Heaven to hell. Hughes, L.
In Hughes, L. Short stories   **S C**
The **heavenly** animal. Phillips, J. A.
In American short story masterpieces
                                                   S C
Hecht, Ann
    The art of the loom   **746.1**
Hecht, Jeff
    Aunt Horrible's last visit
In Vampires: a collection of original stories
    p187-201   **S C**
    Vanishing life   **560**
Heck, Alfons, 1928-
    (jt. auth) Ayer, E. H. Parallel journeys
                                                   940.53
Hedda Gabler. Ibsen, H.
In Ibsen, H. The complete major prose plays
                                                   839.8
In Ibsen, H. Ibsen: four major plays
                                                   839.8
Hedgecoe, John
    John Hedgecoe's complete guide to black &
    white photography and darkroom techniques
                                                   771
    John Hedgecoe's new book of photography
                                                   770.2
Hedrick, Joan D., 1944-
    Harriet Beecher Stowe   **92**
Hegel, Georg Wilhelm Friedrich, 1770-1831
See/See also pages in the following book(s):
    Durant, W. J. The story of philosophy p221-26
                                                   109
    Jaspers, K. The great philosophers   **109**

Russell, B. A history of Western philosophy
    p730-46   **109**
Heggen, Thomas, 1919-1949
    Mister Roberts
In Best American plays: 3d series—1945-
    1951 p415-53   **812.008**
Heide, Robert, 1939-
    Home front America   **973.917**
The **Heidi** chronicles. Wasserstein, W.
In Wasserstein, W. The Heidi chronicles and
    other plays   **812**
The **Heidi** chronicles and other plays. Wasserstein,
    W.   **812**
Heilbroner, Robert L.
    Economics explained   **330**
    The worldly philosophers   **330.1**
Heilbrun, Carolyn G., 1926-
    The education of a woman: the life of Gloria
    Steinem   **92**
Heinemann, Larry
    Paco's dreams
In The Other side of heaven p204-09
                                                   S C
The **Heinemann** book of African poetry in Eng-
    lish   **821**
Heinemann book of African women's poetry
                                                   896
The **Heinemann** book of contemporary African
    short stories   **S C**
Heinlein, Robert A. (Robert Anson), 1907-1988
    Our fair city
In Masterpieces of fantasy and enchantment
    p128-45   **S C**
    Stranger in a strange land   **Fic**
    About
    Stover, L. E. Robert A. Heinlein   **813.009**
See/See also pages in the following book(s):
    Science fiction writers of the golden age p110-
    25   **809.3**
Heiserman, David L., 1940-
    Build your own working robot   **629.8**
Helbig, Alethea
    This land is our land   **016.8**
Helen and teacher: the story of Helen Keller and
    Anne Sullivan Macy. Lash, J. P.   **92**
Helena, Saint, ca. 255-329
See/See also pages in the following book(s):
    Cantor, N. F. Medieval lives   **940.1**
Helena's husband. Moeller, P.
In Thirty famous one-act plays p307-22
                                                   808.82
Helga Crane. Larsen, N.
In Invented lives p174-231   **S C**
Hell-fire. Asimov, I.
In Asimov, I. The complete stories v1 p104-
    05   **S C**
Hellemans, Alexander, 1946-
    The timetables of science   **509**
    (jt. auth) Bunch, B. H. The timetables of tech-
    nology   **609**
Heller, Barbara R. (Barbara Rita), 1933-
    (jt. auth) Kogelman, S. The only math book
    you'll ever need   **513**

Heller, Joseph
Catch-22   **Fic**
Catch-22; criticism
  In Potts, S. W. Catch-22: antiheroic antinovel
                                                  813.009

Heller, Jules
(ed) North American women artists of the twentieth century. See North American women artists of the twentieth century   **920.003**

Heller, Nancy G.
Women artists   **920**
(ed) North American women artists of the twentieth century. See North American women artists of the twentieth century   **920.003**

Hellman, Lillian, 1906-1984
The autumn garden
  In Best American plays: 3d series—1945-
    1951 p205-49   **812.008**
The children's hour
  In Twenty best plays of the modern American
    theatre p561-98   **812.008**
Pentimento
  In Hellman, L. Three   **92**
Scoundrel time
  In Hellman, L. Three   **92**
Three   **92**
An unfinished woman
  In Hellman, L. Three   **92**
Watch on the Rhine
  In Best plays of the modern American the-
    atre: 2nd series p641-82   **812.008**

Hello out there. Saroyan, W.
  In Thirty famous one-act plays p549-61
                                                   808.82

Help wanted, male. Stout, R.
  In Masterpieces of mystery and suspense p94-
    131   **S C**

Help yourself: handbook for college-bound students with learning disabilities. Lewis, E.-L.
                                                      378

Helpful insects *See* Beneficial insects

Helping. Stone, R.
  In The Best American short stories of the
    eighties p304-32   **S C**
  In The Other side of heaven p95-117
                                                      S C
  In The Vintage book of contemporary
    American short stories p467-96   **S C**

Helping behavior
Miller, M. Everything you need to know about
  dealing with the police   **363.2**

Helprin, Mark
Letters from the Samantha
  In American short story masterpieces
                                                      S C
  In The Norton book of American short stories
    p722-32   **S C**

Helter skelter. Bugliosi, V.   **364.1**

Hemenway, Robert E., 1941-
Zora Neale Hurston   **92**

Hemingway, Ernest, 1899-1961
A clean, well-lighted place
  In The Oxford book of American short stories
    p295-300   **S C**

The complete short stories of Ernest Hemingway
                                                      S C
  Contents: The short happy life of Francis Macomber; The capital of the world; The snows of Kilimanjaro; Old man at the
  bridge; Up in Michigan; On the quai at Smyrna; Indian camp;
  The doctor and the doctor's wife; The end of something; The
  three-day blow; The battler; A very short story; Soldier's home;
  The revolutionist; Mr. and Mrs. Elliot; Cat in the rain; Out of
  season; Cross-country snow; My old man; Big two-hearted river:
  part I; Big two-hearted river: part II; The undefeated; In another
  country; Hills like white elephants; The killers; Che ti dice la
  patria?; Fifty grand; A simple enquiry; Ten Indians; A canary for
  one; An Alpine idyll; A pursuit race; Today is Friday; Banal story; Now I lay me; After the storm; A clean, well-lighted place;
  The light of the world; God rest you merry, gentlemen; The sea
  change; A way you'll never be; The mother of a queen; One
  reader writes; Homage to Switzerland; A day's wait; A natural
  history of the dead; Wine of Wyoming; The gambler, the nun,
  and the radio; Fathers and sons; One trip across; The tradesman's
  return; The denunciation; The butterfly and the tank; Night before battle; Under the ridge; Nobody ever dies; The good lion;
  The faithful bull; Get a seeing-eyed dog; A man of the world;
  Summer people; The last good country; An African story; A train
  trip; The porter; Black ass at the cross roads; Landscape with fig-
  ures; I guess everything reminds you of something; Great news
  from the mainland
A farewell to arms   **Fic**
For whom the bell tolls   **Fic**
Hills like white elephants
  In The Norton book of American short stories
    p352-57   **S C**
  In The Oxford book of short stories p341-45
                                                      S C
In our time   **S C**
  Contents: On the quai at Smyrna; Indian camp; The doctor and
  the doctor's wife; The end of something; The three-day blow;
  The battler; A very short story; Soldier's home; The revolution-
  ist; Mr. and Mrs. Elliot; Cat in the rain; Out of season; Cross-
  country snow; My old man; Big two-hearted river
A moveable feast   **92**
The Nick Adams stories   **S C**
  Contents: Three shots; Indian camp; The doctor and the doctor's wife; Ten Indians; The Indians moved away; The light of
  the world; The battler; The killers; The last good country; Crossing the Mississippi; Night before landing; Now I lay me; A way
  you'll never be; In another country; Big two-hearted river; The
  end of something; The three-day blow; Summer people; Wedding
  day; On writing; An Alpine idyll; Cross-country snow; Fathers
  and sons
The old man and the sea   **Fic**
The short happy life of Francis Macomber
  In Classic American short stories p359-98
                                                      S C
The short stories of Ernest Hemingway
                                                      S C
  Contents: The short happy life of Francis Macomber; The capi-
  tal of the world; The snows of Kilimanjaro; Old man at the
  bridge; Up in Michigan; On the quai at Smyrna; Indian camp;
  The doctor and the doctor's wife; The end of something; The
  three-day blow; The battler; A very short story; Soldier's home;
  The revolutionist; Mr. and Mrs. Elliot; Cat in the rain; Out of
  season; Cross-country snow; My old man; Big two-hearted river:
  The undefeated; In another country; Hills like white elephants;
  The killers; Che ti dice la patria; Fifty grand; A simple inquiry;
  Ten Indians; A canary for one; An Alpine idyll; A pursuit race;
  Today is Friday; Banal story; Now I lay me; After the storm; A
  clean, well-lighted place; The light of the world; God rest you
  merry, gentlemen; The sea change; A way you'll never be; The
  mother of a queen; One reader writes; Homage to Switzerland;
  A day's wait; A natural history of the dead; Wine of Wyoming;
  The gambler, the nun, and the radio; Fathers and sons
The sun also rises   **Fic**
Sun also rises; criticism
  In Reynolds, M. S. The sun also rises, a nov-
    el of the twenties   **813.009**
                     About
Baker, C. Hemingway: the writer as artist
                                                  813.009

Her mother's prayers on fire. Belton, D.
In Calling the wind p508-16 **S C**

Her sister's wedding. Stelboum, J. P.
In Not the only one p67-78 **S C**

Her table spread. Bowen, E.
In The Oxford book of Irish short stories p311-18 **S C**

Her turn. Lawrence, D. H.
In Lawrence, D. H. The complete short stories v1 **S C**

Heracles (Legendary character) *See* Hercules (Legendary character)

Herald, Diana Tixier
Genreflecting **016.8**

Herald, Earl Stannard
(jt. auth) Eschmeyer, W. N. A field guide to Pacific coast fishes of North America **597**

Herald, Jacqueline
Fashions of a decade, The 1920s **391**
Fashions of a decade, The 1970s **391**

Herb gardening
Bown, D. Encyclopedia of herbs & their uses **581.6**

The **herb** of death. Christie, A.
In Christie, A. Miss Marple: the complete short stories **S C**

Herb Society of America
Bown, D. Encyclopedia of herbs & their uses **581.6**

Herbal medicine *See* Medical botany

Herbal nightmare. Namioka, L.
In Center stage **812.008**

Herbert, F. Hugh (Frederick Hugh), 1897-1958
The moon is blue
In Best American plays: 3d series—1945-1951 p627-63 **812.008**

Herbert, Frank, 1920-1986
Chapterhouse: Dune. See note under Herbert, F. Dune **Fic**
Children of Dune. See note under Herbert, F. Dune **Fic**
Dune **Fic**
Dune messiah. See note under Herbert, F. Dune **Fic**
God Emperor of Dune. See note under Herbert, F. Dune **Fic**
Heretics of Dune. See note under Herbert, F. Dune **Fic**

Herbert, Frederick Hugh *See* Herbert, F. Hugh (Frederick Hugh), 1897-1958

Herbert, Rosemary
(ed) The Oxford book of American detective stories. See The Oxford book of American detective stories **S C**

Herbs
Bown, D. Encyclopedia of herbs & their uses **581.6**
Bremness, L. Herbs **581.6**
Rodale's illustrated encyclopedia of herbs **635**

Herbst, Dan
Sports illustrated soccer **796.334**

Herbst, Judith
Star crossing **629.4**

Hercegovina *See* Bosnia and Hercegovina

Hercules (Legendary character)
See/See also pages in the following book(s):
Hamilton, E. Mythology p224-43 **292**

Here I stand: a life of Martin Luther. Bainton, R. H. **92**

Here is my kingdom **810.8**

Here there be tygers. King, S.
In King, S. Skeleton crew **S C**

Here we are. Parker, D.
In 24 favorite one-act plays p210-18 **808.82**

Heredity
See also Genetic mapping
Blueprint for life **573.2**

Heretics of Dune. Herbert, F. See note under Herbert, F. Dune **Fic**

The **Heritage** of African poetry **896**

Herman, Woody
See/See also pages in the following book(s):
Terkel, S. Giants of jazz p133-45 **920**

Hermes, William J.
Marijuana **616.86**
Substance abuse **616.86**

Hermite, Charles, 1822-1901
See/See also pages in the following book(s):
Bell, E. T. Men of mathematics p448-65 **920**

Hernández-Avila, Inés
Enedina's story
In Latina: women's voices from the borderlands p229-39 **810.8**

A **hero** ain't nothin' but a sandwich. Childress, A. **Fic**

Herodotus
See/See also pages in the following book(s):
Hamilton, E. The Greek way p159-82 **880.9**

Heroes and heroines
Contemporary heroes and heroines **920**
See/See also pages in the following book(s):
Boorstin, D. J. The Americans: The national experience p327-62 **973**
Dictionaries
Rovin, J. Adventure heroes **700**
Fiction
Voigt, C. Jackaroo **Fic**

Heroes, monsters and other worlds from Russian mythology. Warner, E. **299**

Heroines *See* Heroes and heroines

Heroism *See* Courage

Heron, Ann
(ed) Two teenagers in twenty. See Two teenagers in twenty **305.23**

Herrera, Hayden
Matisse **92**

Herriot, James
All creatures great and small **92**
All things bright and beautiful **92**
All things wise and wonderful **92**
James Herriot's dog stories **636.7**
The Lord God made them all **92**

Herron, Carolivia
That place
  In Children of the night p532-61 **S C**
Herschel, Caroline Lucretia, 1750-1848
See/See also pages in the following book(s):
Osen, L. M. Women in mathematics p71-81
  920
Herself in love. Wiggins, M.
  In The Norton book of American short stories
  p732-41 **S C**
Hersey, John, 1914-1993
A bell for Adano **Fic**
Hiroshima **940.54**
The wall **Fic**
Armor, J. Manzanar **940.53**
(ed) Ralph Ellison: a collection of critical essays. See Ralph Ellison: a collection of critical essays **813.009**
Hershey, David R.
Plant biology science projects **581**
Herskowitz, Mickey
(jt. auth) Rather, D. The camera never blinks twice **92**
Herstory **920**
Hertsgaard, Mark, 1956-
A day in the life **781.66**
Hervey, Evelyn *See* Keating, H. R. F. (Henry Reymond Fitzwalter), 1926-
Herz, Sarah K.
From Hinton to Hamlet **809**
Herzegovina *See* Bosnia and Hercegovina
Herzi, Saida Hagi-Dirie
Government by magic spell
  In The Heinemann book of contemporary African short stories p94-99 **S C**
Herzog, Brad
The sports 100 **920**
Herzog, Chaim, 1918-1997
The Arab-Israeli wars **956**
Hesiod, fl. ca. 700 B.C.
See/See also pages in the following book(s):
Ancient Greek literature p10-28 **880.9**
Hess, Sonya Dorman *See* Dorman, Sonya, 1924-
Hesse, Hermann, 1877-1962
The fairy tales of Hermann Hesse **S C**
Contents: The dwarf; Shadow play; A man by the name of Ziegler; The city; Dr. Knoegle's end; The beautiful dream; The three linden trees; Augustus; The poet; Flute dream; A dream about the gods; Strange news from another planet; Faldum; A dream sequence; The forest dweller; The difficult path; If the war continues; The European; The empire; The painter; The fairy tale about the wicker chair; Iris
Siddhartha **Fic**
Steppenwolf **Fic**
About
Field, G. W. Hermann Hesse **833.009**
Hesse-Biber, Sharlene Janice
Am I thin enough yet? **616.85**
Hester Prynne [critical essays] **813.009**
Hettinga, Donald R.
Presenting Madeleine L'Engle **813.009**
Hey Little Walter. Alleyne, C. D.
  In Ten out of ten p205-35 **812.008**
Heyer, Paul, 1946-
Titanic legacy **910.4**

Heyerdahl, Thor
Easter Island—the mystery solved **996**
Green was the earth on the seventh day **92**
Kon-Tiki: across the Pacific by raft **910.4**
Heyes, Eileen
Children of the swastika **943.086**
Heyman, Neil M.
Western civilization **909**
Heymann, C. David (Clemens David), 1945-
A woman named Jackie: an intimate biography of Jacqueline Bouvier Kennedy Onassis
  92
Heymann, Clemens David *See* Heymann, C. David (Clemens David), 1945-
Hiatt, June
The principles of knitting **746.43**
Hibbard, Howard, 1928-1984
The Metropolitan Museum of Art **708**
Michelangelo **92**
Hibbert, Arthur Raymond *See* Hibbert, Christopher, 1924-
Hibbert, Christopher, 1924-
The days of the French Revolution **944.04**
Redcoats & Rebels **973.3**
Hickey, Donald R., 1944-
The War of 1812 **973.5**
Hickock, Richard, 1931-1965
About
Capote, T. In cold blood **364.1**
Hickok, Ralph
The encyclopedia of North American sports history **796**
A who's who of sports champions **920.003**
Hickok, Wild Bill, 1837-1876
About
Rosa, J. G. Wild Bill Hickok **92**
Hidden agendas. McNally, T.
  In McNally, T. 15 short plays p369-73
  812
Hidden attraction. Verschuur, G. L. **538**
The **hidden** life of dogs. Thomas, E. M.
  636.7
The **hidden** woman. Colette
  In Colette. The collected stories of Colette p235-38 **S C**
Hidden worlds of wildlife **591**
The **hiding** of Black Bill. Henry, O.
  In Henry, O. The best short stories of O. Henry **S C**
Hieroglyphics
  See also Picture writing; Rosetta stone inscription
See/See also pages in the following book(s):
Ceram, C. W. Gods, graves, and scholars p99-116 **930.1**
Mertz, B. Temples, tombs, and hieroglyphs
  932
Higdon, Hal
Boston **796.42**
Marathon **796.42**
Higgins, Aidan
The bird I fancied
  In The Oxford book of Irish short stories p445-54 **S C**

Hillerman, Tony—*Continued*
Finding Moon   Fic
Skinwalkers   Fic
(ed) The Best of the West. See The Best of the
 West   818
(ed) The Oxford book of American detective
 stories. See The Oxford book of American
 detective stories   S C
About
The Tony Hillerman companion   813.009
Hillman, Richard, 1949-
William Shakespeare: the problem plays
                                                822.3
Hills like white elephants. Hemingway, E.
 In Hemingway, E. The complete short stories
  of Ernest Hemingway p211-14   S C
 In Hemingway, E. The short stories of Ernest
  Hemingway p273-78   S C
 In The Norton book of American short stories
  p352-57   S C
 In The Oxford book of short stories p341-45
                                       S C
Hillway, Tyrus
Herman Melville   813.009
Hillyard, P. D.
The book of the spider   595.4
Hilton, James, 1900-1954
Lost horizon   Fic
Hilts, Philip J.
Smokescreen   364.1
Himes, Chester, 1909-1984
Headwaiter
 In Calling the wind p79-93   S C
Marihuana and a pistol
 In The Best short stories by Negro writers
  p104-06   S C
See/See also pages in the following book(s):
Modern mystery writers p94-108   809.3
Himmler, Heinrich, 1900-1945
About
Breitman, R. The architect of genocide: Himm-
 ler and the final solution   92
Hindenburg (Airship)
Dick, H. G. The golden age of the great passen-
 ger airships, Graf Zeppelin & Hindenburg
                                        629.133
Hinduism
Wangu, M. B. Hinduism   294.5
See/See also pages in the following book(s):
Eastern wisdom   291
The World's religions p124-43   291
The **hinge** of fate. Churchill, Sir W.   940.53
Hinojosa, Maria, 1961-
Crews: gang members talk to Maria Hinojosa
                                        302.3
Hinojosa, Rolando, 1929-
Brother Imás
 In Growing up Latino p250-58   810.8
The useless servants
 In Iguana dreams   S C
Hinshaw, John H., 1963-
(jt. auth) Stearns, P. N. The ABC-CLIO world
 history companion to the industrial revolution
                                        909.81

Hinton, Harold C., 1924-1993
East Asia and the Western Pacific   950
Hinton, S. E.
The outsiders   Fic
Tex   Fic
About
Daly, J. Presenting S. E. Hinton   813.009
Hips. Cisneros, S.
 In We are the stories we tell   S C
Hiro, Dilip
A dictionary of the Middle East   956
Hirohito, Emperor of Japan, 1901-1989
About
Behr, E. Hirohito   92
Hiroshima (Japan)
Bombardment, 1945
Alperovitz, G. The decision to use the atomic
 bomb and the architecture of an American
 myth   940.54
Hersey, J. Hiroshima   940.54
Lifton, B. J. A place called Hiroshima
                                         940.54
Lifton, R. J. Hiroshima in America   940.54
Takaki, R. T. Hiroshima   940.54
See/See also pages in the following book(s):
Yamazaki, J. N. Children of the atomic bomb
                                         92
Hiroshima in America. Lifton, R. J.   940.54
Hirsch, E. D. (Eric Donald), 1928-
The dictionary of cultural literacy   031
Hirsch, Eric Donald *See* Hirsch, E. D. (Eric Don-
 ald), 1928-
Hirschfelder, Arlene B.
The encyclopedia of Native American religions
                                         299
The Native American almanac   970.004
(comp) Rising voices. See Rising voices
                                         810.8
Hirshey, Gerri
Nowhere to run   781.644
Hirst, Michael
Michelangelo and his drawings   709.45
Hirst, Wolf Z.
John Keats   821
Hirunpidok, Visalaya
Yai
 In American dragons: twenty-five Asian
  American voices p168-84   810.8
His defense. Edwards, H. S.
 In The Best crime stories of the 19th century
  p253-65   S C
His Excellency. Maugham, W. S.
 In Maugham, W. S. Collected short stories v3
                                         S C
His father's Earth. Wolfe, T.
 In Wolfe, T. The complete short stories of
  Thomas Wolfe p206-13   S C
His last affair. Hughes, L.
 In Hughes, L. Short stories   S C
His last bow. Doyle, Sir A. C.
 In Doyle, Sir A. C. The complete Sherlock
  Holmes   S C

His last bow [short story] Doyle, Sir A. C.
In Doyle, Sir A. C. The complete Sherlock Holmes **S C**

His over-the-creek girl. Hurston, Z. N.
In Invented lives p255-79 **S C**

His vegetable wife. Murphy, P.
In The Norton book of science fiction p628-32 **S C**

His wife. Chekhov, A. P.
In Chekhov, A. P. The Russian master and other stories p1-6 **S C**

His women. Adams, A.
In Prize stories, 1996 p163-74 **S C**

Hispanic American art
Here is my kingdom **810.8**

Hispanic American poetry *See* American poetry—Hispanic American authors

Hispanic Americans
Cockcroft, J. D. The Hispanic struggle for social justice **305.8**
Cockcroft, J. D. Latinos in the making of the United States **305.8**
Garza, H. Latinas **305.4**
See/See also pages in the following book(s):
Hook, J. N. Family names p163-74 **929.4**
Dictionaries
Dictionary of Hispanic biography **920.003**
The Latino encyclopedia **305.8**
Notable Hispanic American women **920.003**
Fiction
Iguana dreams **S C**
History
Fernández-Shaw, C. M. The Hispanic presence in North America from 1492 to today **305.8**
Poetry
Paper dance **811.008**

Hispanic literature criticism **860.9**

The **Hispanic** presence in North America from 1492 to today. Fernández-Shaw, C. M. **305.8**

The **Hispanic** struggle for social justice. Cockcroft, J. D. **305.8**

Hispanic writers **920.003**

Historic buildings
See also Literary landmarks
United States
See also Colonial architecture

Historic haunted America. Norman, M. **133.1**

Historic places **917.3**

Historic sites
America's historic places **917.3**
Cantor, G. North American Indian landmarks **917.3**
Curtis, N. C. Black heritage sites **917.3**
Durham, M. S. The Mid-Atlantic States **917.4**
Historic places **917.3**
Lawliss, C. The early American sourcebook **917.3**
Parks directory of the United States **917.3**

Historic speeches of African Americans **815.008**

The **historical** and cultural atlas of African Americans. Asante, M. K. **305.8**

Historical atlas of the American West. Beck, W. A. **911**

The **Historical** atlas of the earth **551.7**

Historical atlas of the Holocaust **940.53**

Historical atlas of the United States **911**

Historical atlas of the Vietnam War. Summers, H. G. **959.704**

Historical atlases
Atlas of classical history **911**
Beck, W. A. Historical atlas of the American West **911**
Historical maps on file **911**
Matthew, D. Atlas of medieval Europe **911**
Riley-Smith, J. The atlas of the Crusades **911**
The Times atlas of the Second World War **911**
The Times atlas of world history **911**

Historical chronology
Carruth, G. The encyclopedia of American facts and dates **973.02**
Carruth, G. The encyclopedia of world facts and dates **902**
Chronicle of America **973.02**
Chronicle of the world **902**
The Chronology of world history **902**
DeFord, M. A. Who was when? **902**
Holidays and anniversaries of the world **394.2**
Smithsonian timelines of the ancient world **930**
Stewart, R. The illustrated almanac of historical facts **902**
The Timetables of American history **902**
Wetterau, B. The New York Public Library book of chronologies **902**
The World almanac of World War II **940.53**

Historical dictionary of modern Spain, 1700-1988 **946**

Historical dictionary of the Olympic movement. Buchanan, I. **796.48**

Historical fiction
Bibliography
Adamson, L. G. Recreating the past **016.8**
Coffey, R. K. America as story **016.813**
Hartman, D. K. Historical figures in fiction **016.8**
VanMeter, V. America in historical fiction **016.813**

Historical figures in fiction. Hartman, D. K. **016.8**

Historical first patents. Brown, T. **608**

Historical geology *See* Stratigraphic geology

An **historical** guide to arms & armor. Bull, S. **355.8**

Historical maps on file **911**

Historiography
See also United States—Historiography
Tuchman, B. W. Practicing history **907**

Hoffman, Alice
Second nature   Fic
Hoffman, Frederick J., 1909-1967
William Faulkner   813.009
Hoffman, Michael A., 1944-
Egypt before the pharaohs   932
Hoffman, William, 1925-
Stones
   In Prize stories, 1996 p51-64   S C
Hoffman, William M.
As is
   In Best American plays: 9th series—1983-
     1992 p184-209   812.008
Hoffmann, Banesh, 1906-1986
Albert Einstein, creator and rebel   92
Hoffmann, Roald, 1937-
Chemistry imagined   540
Hofstadter, Richard, 1916-1970
The age of reform from Bryan to F.D.R.
         973.91
America at 1750   973.2
Hog pawn. Faulkner, W.
   In Faulkner, W. Uncollected stories of Wil-
     liam Faulkner p311-30   S C
Hogan, Desmond
The Airedale
   In The Oxford book of Irish short stories
     p553-63   S C
Hogan, Linda
Amen
   In Song of the turtle p141-46   S C
Aunt Moon's young man
   In Talking leaves   S C
Making do
   In Spider Woman's granddaughters   S C
Mean spirit [excerpt]
   In Growing up Native American p203-14
         810.8
Solar storms   Fic
See/See also pages in the following book(s):
Coltelli, L. Winged words: American Indian
   writers speak   897
Hogan's goat. Alfred, W.
   In Best American plays: 6th series—1963-
     1967 p137-84   812.008
Hogarth, William, 1697-1764
See/See also pages in the following book(s):
Durant, W. J. The age of Voltaire p217-24
         940.2
Hohm, Charles F., 1947-
(ed) Population: opposing viewpoints. See Popu-
   lation: opposing viewpoints   304.6
Hoig, Stan
Night of the cruel moon   970.004
Hold fast your dreams   815.008
Holden, Amanda
(ed) The Viking opera guide. See The Viking
   opera guide   792.5
Holden, Martin
The encyclopedia of gems and minerals
         553.8
Holden Caulfield [critical essays]   813.009
Holding. Lowry, L.
   In Am I blue? p175-87   S C

Holding out. Sebestyen, O.
   In Center stage   812.008
Holding things together. Tyler, A.
   In We are the stories we tell   S C
Holdstock, Robert
Infantasm
   In The Merlin chronicles   S C
Hole (Musical group)
See/See also pages in the following book(s):
Reisfeld, R. This is the sound   781.66
Holiday, Billie, 1915-1959
Lady sings the blues   92
            About
De Veaux, A. Don't explain: a song of Billie
   Holiday   92
Gourse, L. Billie Holiday   92
See/See also pages in the following book(s):
Terkel, S. Giants of jazz p121-32   920
Holiday. Porter, K. A.
   In Porter, K. A. The collected stories of Kath-
     erine Anne Porter   S C
Holidays
   See also Christmas; Religious holidays
The American book of days   394.2
Chase's calendar of events   394.2
The Folklore of American holidays   394.2
The Folklore of world holidays   394.2
Holidays and anniversaries of the world
         394.2
Santino, J. All around the year   394.2
Thompson, S. E. Holidays, festivals, and cele-
   brations of the world dictionary   394.2
            Indexes
Holidays and festivals index   394.2
Holidays and anniversaries of the world
         394.2
Holidays and festivals index   394.2
**Holidays, festivals, and celebrations of the world
dictionary. Thompson, S. E.**   394.2
Holing, Dwight
Coral reefs   574.92
Holkeboer, Katherine Strand
Patterns for theatrical costumes   391
Holland, Gini
America in the 20th century. See America in the
   20th century   973.9
Holland, Isabelle
The man without a face   Fic
Holland *See* Netherlands
Hollander, John
(ed) American poetry: the nineteenth century.
   See American poetry: the nineteenth century
         811.008
(ed) Animal poems. See Animal poems
         808.81
(ed) The Literature of Renaissance England. See
   The Literature of Renaissance England
         820.8
(ed) The Oxford anthology of English literature.
   See The Oxford anthology of English litera-
   ture   820.8

Holley, Marietta, 1836-1926
A male Magdalene [excerpt]
In The Oxford book of women's writing in the United States p56-62   **810.8**

Holliday, Laurel, 1946-
(comp) Children in the Holocaust and World War II. See Children in the Holocaust and World War II   **940.53**

Hollier, Denis
(ed) A New history of French literature. See A New history of French literature   **840.9**

The **hollow** hills. Stewart, M.
In Stewart, M. Mary Stewart's Merlin trilogy   **Fic**

The **hollow** man. Burke, T.
In The Oxford book of English ghost stories p410-20   **S C**

The **hollow** men. Wolfe, T.
In Wolfe, T. The complete short stories of Thomas Wolfe p485-91   **S C**

The **hollow** nut. Colette
In Colette. The collected stories of Colette p319-20   **S C**

The **hollow** of the three hills. Hawthorne, N.
In Hawthorne, N. Tales and sketches; A wonder book for girls and boys; Tanglewood tales for girls and boys p7-11   **S C**

The **hollyhock** sowers. Wolfe, T.
In Wolfe, T. The complete short stories of Thomas Wolfe p465-68   **S C**

Hollywood (Calif.)
Fiction
Waugh, E. The loved one   **Fic**

Hollywood and the pits. Lee, C.
In American dragons: twenty-five Asian American voices p34-47   **810.8**

Holman, C. Hugh (Clarence Hugh), 1914-
(jt. auth) Harmon, W. A handbook to literature   **803**

Holman, Clarence Hugh *See* Holman, C. Hugh (Clarence Hugh), 1914-

Holmes, George, 1927-
(ed) The Oxford illustrated history of medieval Europe. See The Oxford illustrated history of medieval Europe   **940.1**

Holmes, Oliver Wendell, 1841-1935
About
Aichele, G. J. Oliver Wendell Holmes, Jr.—soldier, scholar, judge   **92**
See/See also pages in the following book(s):
Aaseng, N. Great Justices of the Supreme Court p71-85   **920**

Holmes, Safiya Henderson- *See* Henderson-Holmes, Safiya

Holmes, Sherlock (Fictitious character)
Bunson, M. Encyclopedia Sherlockiana   **823.009**

Holocaust, 1933-1945
See also World War, 1939-1945—Jews
Atkinson, L. In kindling flame: the story of Hannah Senesh, 1921-1944   **92**
Ayer, E. H. Parallel journeys   **940.53**
Bearing witness: stories of the Holocaust   **808.8**

Berenbaum, M. The world must know   **940.53**
Breitman, R. The architect of genocide: Himmler and the final solution   **92**
Dawidowicz, L. S. The war against the Jews, 1933-1945   **940.53**
Gies, M. Anne Frank remembered   **940.53**
Gilbert, M. The Holocaust   **940.53**
Goldhagen, D. Hitler's willing executioners   **940.53**
Linnea, S. Raoul Wallenberg: the man who stopped death   **92**
Meltzer, M. Never to forget: the Jews of the Holocaust   **940.53**
Nomberg-Przytyk, S. Auschwitz   **940.53**
Rogasky, B. Smoke and ashes: the story of the Holocaust   **940.53**
Senesh, H. Hannah Senesh, her life & diary   **92**
Spiegelman, A. Maus   **940.53**
Steiner, J. F. Treblinka   **940.53**
Weinberg, J. The Holocaust Museum in Washington   **940.53**
Yolen, J. Briar Rose   **Fic**
See/See also pages in the following book(s):
Bettelheim, B. Surviving, and other essays p84-104   **155.9**
Bibliography
Stephens, E. C. Learning about—the Holocaust   **016.94053**
Fiction
Keneally, T. Schindler's list   **Fic**
Maps
Historical atlas of the Holocaust   **940.53**
Personal narratives
Adler, D. A. We remember the Holocaust   **940.53**
Art from the ashes   **940.53**
Boas, J. We are witnesses   **940.53**
Children in the Holocaust and World War II   **940.53**
Different voices   **940.53**
Freeman, J. Job   **92**
Ganor, S. Light one candle   **940.53**
Gill, A. The journey back from hell   **940.53**
Gold, R. G. Ruth's journey   **940.53**
Horn, J. Mark it with a stone   **940.53**
Langer, L. L. Holocaust testimonies   **940.53**
Leitner, I. Isabella   **940.53**
Levi, P. The drowned and the saved   **940.53**
Levi, P. Survival in Auschwitz; and, The reawakening   **940.53**
Lindwer, W. The last seven months of Anne Frank   **940.53**
When they came to take my father—   **940.53**
Wiesel, E. All rivers run to the sea   **92**
Women in the resistance and in the Holocaust   **940.53**
Women of Theresienstadt   **940.53**
Pictorial works
Auschwitz   **940.53**
The Pictorial history of the Holocaust   **940.53**

Holocaust, 1933-1945—*Continued*
Poetry
Holocaust poetry   808.81
Psychological aspects
Epstein, H. Children of the Holocaust
                                                   940.53

Holocaust, 1933-1945 in literature
Art from the ashes   940.53
Holocaust Museum (U.S.) *See* United States
Holocaust Memorial Museum
The **Holocaust** Museum in Washington. Weinberg,
J.   940.53
Holocaust poetry   808.81
Holocaust testimonies. Langer, L. L.   940.53
Holsinger, M. Paul
The ways of war   016.8
Holtby, Winifred, 1898-1935
Why Herbert killed his mother
In Bad behavior p133-44   S C
The **Holy** Bible [King James Bible. Oxford Univ.
Press] Bible   220.5
Holy Bible: the new King James Version. Bible
                                                   220.5
Holy days *See* Religious holidays
Holy Grail *See* Grail
Holy matrimony. Johnson, N.
In Best American screenplays   812.008
Holy the firm. Dillard, A.
In Dillard, A. The Annie Dillard reader
                                                   818
Holzer, Harold
(ed) Dear Mr. Lincoln. See Dear Mr. Lincoln
                                                   973.7
Homage to Switzerland. Hemingway, E.
In Hemingway, E. The complete short stories
of Ernest Hemingway p322-31   S C
In Hemingway, E. The short stories of Ernest
Hemingway p422-35   S C
Hombs, Mary Ellen
American homelessness   362.5
Home. Maugham, W. S.
In Maugham, W. S. Collected short stories v1
                                                   S C
Home. Phillips, J. A.
In The Vintage book of contemporary
American short stories p410-25   S C
Home. Updike, J.
In Updike, J. Pigeon feathers, and other sto-
ries p151-68   S C
The **Home** book of modern verse   821.008
Home for Passover. Sholem Aleichem
In Sholem Aleichem. The best of Sholem
Aleichem   S C
Home front America. Heide, R.   973.917
Home instruction
See also Child development
Home is the hunter. Kuttner, H.
In Robert Silverberg's Worlds of wonder
                                                   S C
Home life *See* Family life
Home now. Oba, R.
In American eyes p28-36   S C

Home of the brave. Laurents, A.
In Best plays of the modern American the-
atre: 2nd series p557-96   812.008
Home to El Building. Ortiz Cofer, J.
In Ortiz Cofer, J. An island like you p131-43
                                                   S C
Home to Harlem [excerpt] McKay, C.
In The Portable Harlem Renaissance reader
p371-88   810.8
Home video cameras *See* Camcorders
Home video systems
See also Camcorders; Video recording
Homebase [excerpt] Wong, S.
In Growing up Asian American p327-34
                                                   810.8
Homecoming. Bradbury, R.
In Bradbury, R. The stories of Ray Bradbury
p9-19   S C
Homecooking. Woody, E.
In Talking leaves   S C
Homelanding. Atwood, M.
In The Norton book of science fiction p794-
96   S C
The **Homeless:** opposing viewpoints   362.5
Homeless persons
See also Refugees; Runaway teenagers
Hombs, M. E. American homelessness
                                                   362.5
The **Homeless:** opposing viewpoints   362.5
The **Homeless** problem   362.5
See/See also pages in the following book(s):
Mental illness: opposing viewpoints p164-92
                                                   362.2
Dictionaries
Fantasia, R. Homelessness: a sourcebook
                                                   362.5
The **Homeless** problem   362.5
Homelessness: a sourcebook. Fantasia, R.
                                                   362.5
Homer
The Iliad   883
The Odyssey   883
See/See also pages in the following book(s):
Ancient Greek literature p10-28   880.9
Iliad—Concordances
Willcock, M. M. A companion to the Iliad
                                                   883
Parodies, travesties, etc.
Vonnegut, K. Happy Birthday, Wanda June
                                                   812
Homer, Winslow, 1836-1910
About
Cikovsky, N., Jr. Winslow Homer   92
See/See also pages in the following book(s):
Novak, B. American painting of the nineteenth
century p165-90   759.13
The **homesick** Buick. MacDonald, J. D.
In Masterpieces of mystery and suspense
p246-58   S C
Homicide
See also Assassination
Bugliosi, V. Helter skelter   364.1
Capote, T. In cold blood   364.1

Hook, J. N. (Julius Nicholas), 1913-
Family names   **929.4**
Hook, Julius Nicholas See Hook, J. N. (Julius Nicholas), 1913-
Hooked. Landau, E.   **362.29**
Hooker, Joseph, 1814-1879
See/See also pages in the following book(s):
Sears, S. W. Chancellorsville   **973.7**
Hooks, Bell
Bone black: memories of girlhood   **92**
Hoop dreams. Joravsky, B.   **796.323**
Hooper, Brad
Short story writers and their work   **809.3**
Hooper, David, 1915-
The Oxford companion to chess   **794.1**
Hooper, Nicholas, 1956-
The Cambridge illustrated atlas of warfare: the Middle Ages   **355**
Hooray for peace, hurrah for war. Jantzen, S.   **940.3**
Hoover, Herbert, 1874-1964
See/See also pages in the following book(s):
McElvaine, R. S. The Great Depression   **973.91**
Hoover, J. Edgar (John Edgar), 1895-1972
About
Denenberg, B. The true story of J. Edgar Hoover and the FBI   **363.2**
Hoover, John Edgar See Hoover, J. Edgar (John Edgar), 1895-1972
Hoover, Paul, 1946-
(ed) Postmodern American poetry. See Postmodern American poetry   **811.008**
Hoover Dam (Ariz. and Nev.)
Dunar, A. J. Building Hoover Dam   **627**
Hop-Frog. Poe, E. A.
In Poe, E. A. The collected tale and poems of Edgar Allan Poe p502-09   **S C**
In Poe, E. A. Tales of Edgar Allan Poe p81-93   **S C**
Hopi Indians
See/See also pages in the following book(s):
Paths of life p237-66   **970.004**
Hopkins, Gerard Manley, 1844-1889
The poems of Gerard Manley Hopkins   **821**
See/See also pages in the following book(s):
Untermeyer, L. Lives of the poets p590-600   **920**
Hopkins, Jerry
Hit and run: the Jimi Hendrix story   **92**
Hopkins, Joseph G. E.
(ed) Album of American history. See Album of American history   **973**
Hopkins, Pauline Elizabeth, 1859-1930
Bro'r Abr'm Jimson's wedding: a Christmas story
In Invented lives p130-46   **S C**
Sappho
In Invented lives p109-29   **S C**
See/See also pages in the following book(s):
Black American prose writers before the Harlem Renaissance p103-14   **810.9**
Black American women fiction writers p43-55   **813.009**

Hopley-Woolrich, Cornell George See Woolrich, Cornell, 1903-1968
Hoppenstedt, Elbert M.
Shoo fly pudding
In The Big book of large-cast plays p168-84   **812.008**
Hopper, Edward, 1882-1967
Edward Hopper: the art and the artist   **759.13**
About
Berkow, I. G. Edward Hopper   **759.13**
Hobbs, R. C. Edward Hopper   **92**
Hopper, Grace
See/See also pages in the following book(s):
Yount, L. Contemporary women scientists   **920**
Horace
See/See also pages in the following book(s):
Hamilton, E. The Roman way   **870.9**
Horatius Flaccus, Quintus See Horace
Horemkenesi
About
Taylor, J. H. Unwrapping a mummy   **932**
Horgan, John
The end of science   **501**
The **Horizon** book of the Middle Ages. See The Middle Ages [American Heritage]   **940.1**
The **Horla.** Maupassant, G. de
In Classic ghost stories p249-71   **S C**
Hormones
See also Steroids
Little, M. The endocrine system   **612.4**
Young, J. K. Hormones: molecular messengers   **612.4**
Horn, Jane, 1945-
(ed) Cooking A to Z. See Cooking A to Z   **641.5**
Horn, Joseph, 1926-
Mark it with a stone   **940.53**
Hornblower, Simon
(ed) The Oxford classical dictionary. See The Oxford classical dictionary   **938.003**
Horne, Lena
About
Haskins, J. Lena: a personal and professional biography of Lena Horne   **92**
The **horned** toad. Haslam, G. W.
In Growing up Chicana/o p103-13   **810.8**
Horner, Jack See Horner, John R.
Horner, John R.
The complete T. rex   **567.9**
Hornsby, Alton, Jr.
Chronology of African-American history   **305.8**
Horovitz, Israel
Morning
In Best American plays: 7th series—1967-1973 p425-45   **812.008**
Horror fiction
Bad behavior   **S C**
Bradbury, R. Something wicked this way comes   **Fic**
Carmody, I. The gathering   **Fic**

Horror fiction—*Continued*

The Horror hall of fame	S C
Jackson, S. We have always lived in a castle	Fic
James, H. The turn of the screw	Fic
King, S. Carrie	Fic
King, S. Christine	Fic
King, S. Four past midnight	S C
King, S. Insomnia	Fic
King, S. Skeleton crew	S C
Koontz, D. R. Strange highways	S C
Koontz, D. R. Watchers	Fic
The Oxford book of gothic tales	S C
Poe, E. A. The collected tales and poems of Edgar Allan Poe	S C
Poe, E. A. Tales of Edgar Allan Poe	S C
Preston, D. Relic	Fic
Rendell, R. Heartstones	Fic
Rice, A. Interview with the vampire	Fic
Saul, J. Creature	Fic
Stoker, B. Dracula	Fic
Westall, R. Shades of darkness	S C

Bibliography

Burgess, M. Reference guide to science fiction, fantasy, and horror	**016.8**
Reginald, R. Science fiction and fantasy literature, 1975-1991	**016.8**

Bio-bibliography

Science fiction, fantasy, and horror writers	**809.3**

History and criticism

Horror: the 100 best books	**823.009**
Kies, C. N. Presenting young adult horror fiction	**813.009**
The Horror hall of fame	S C
Horror: the 100 best books	**823.009**

A **horse** and two goats. Narayan, R. K.
In The Oxford book of short stories p395-410
S C

The **horse-dealer's** daughter. Lawrence, D. H.
In Lawrence, D. H. The complete short stories v2
S C

The **horse** who would be king. Robinson, J.
In The Merlin chronicles
S C

Horsemanship
See also Rodeos

Horses

The Complete horse book	**636.1**
Edwards, E. H. The encyclopedia of the horse	**636.1**
Edwards, E. H. Horses	**636.1**
Morris, D. Horsewatching	**636.1**
Vogel, C. The complete horse care manual	**636.1**

Horses on a rooftop. Hawkins, C.
In Streetlights: illuminating tales of the urban black experience p158-66
S C

A **horse's** tale. Twain, M.
In Twain, M. The complete short stories of Mark Twain
S C

Horseshoes. Lardner, R.
In Lardner, R. The best short stories of Ring Lardner p205-26
S C

Horsewatching. Morris, D. **636.1**

Horton, George Moses, 1797?-1883?
See/See also pages in the following book(s):
Black American poets and dramatists before the Harlem Renaissance p79-90 **810.9**

Horton, James
An introduction to drawing
In The DK art school series **751**

Hoskin, Michael A.
(ed) The Cambridge illustrated history of astronomy. See The Cambridge illustrated history of astronomy **520**

Hospitals

Fiction

Mann, T. The magic mountain **Fic**

The **hostage.** Behan, B.
In Behan, B. The complete plays **822**

The **hostage.** Forester, C. S.
In Classic English short stories, 1930-1955 p58-83 **S C**

Hostages
Anderson, T. Den of lions **92**

Hostelling North America **647.9**

Hostess. Asimov, I.
In Asimov, I. The complete stories v1 p376-407 **S C**

Hostetler, John A., 1918-
Amish society **289.7**
(ed) Amish roots. See Amish roots **289.7**

Hot air. Kurtz, H. **791.45**

The **hot** zone. Preston, R. **614.5**

The **hotel.** Maja-Pearce, A.
In The Heinemann book of contemporary African short stories p146-48 **S C**

The **hotel.** Singer, I. B.
In Singer, I. B. The death of Methuselah and other stories p185-99 **S C**

The **hotel** child. Fitzgerald, F. S.
In Fitzgerald, F. S. The short stories of F. Scott Fitzgerald p598-615 **S C**

Hothouse. Aldiss, B. W.
In Robert Silverberg's Worlds of wonder **S C**

Houdini, Harry, 1874-1926
About
Brandon, R. The life and many deaths of Harry Houdini **92**

Hough, Richard Alexander, 1922-
The Battle of Britain **940.54**

Houghton, Stanley, 1881-1913
Dear departed
In Thirty famous one-act plays p269-81 **808.82**

Houghton, William Stanley *See* Houghton, Stanley, 1881-1913

The **hound.** Faulkner, W.
In Faulkner, W. Uncollected stories of William Faulkner p152-64 **S C**

The **hound** of the Baskervilles. Doyle, Sir A. C. **Fic**
also in Doyle, Sir A. C. The complete Sherlock Holmes **S C**

An **hour** with Abuelo. Ortiz Cofer, J.
In Ortiz Cofer, J. An island like you p66-71 **S C**

The **House** and Senate explained. Greenberg, E.
328.73

The **house** behind the Temple of Literature. Tran, V.
In The Other side of heaven p85-94
S C

A **house** divided. Foner, E. **973.7**

The **house** friend. Singer, I. B.
In Singer, I. B. The death of Methuselah and other stories p14-24 **S C**

The **house** in Turk Street. Hammett, D.
In Crime classics p181-200 **S C**

The **house** of blue leaves. Guare, J.
In Best American plays: 7th series—1967-1973 p309-36 **812.008**

House of Bourbon
See/See also pages in the following book(s):
Crow, J. A. Spain: the root and the flower p228-57 **946**

House of flowers. Capote, T.
In Capote, T. Breakfast at Tiffany's: a short novel and three stories **S C**

The **house** of Mapuhi. London, J.
In London, J. Short stories of Jack London p308-26 **S C**

The **house** of pride. London, J.
In London, J. Short stories of Jack London p296-307 **S C**

The **house** of quilts. Vásquez, E. C.
In Daughters of the fifth sun **810.8**

House of Romanov
About
Massie, R. K. The Romanovs **947.08**

House of stairs. Sleator, W. **Fic**

The **house** of the far and lost. Wolfe, T.
In Wolfe, T. The complete short stories of Thomas Wolfe p147-66 **S C**

The **House** of the Seven Gables. Hawthorne, N.
Fic

The **house** on Mango Street. Cisneros, S. **Fic**
also in The Oxford book of American short stories p746-48 **S C**

House plants
See also Indoor gardening
Chiusoli, A. Simon & Schuster's guide to houseplants **635.9**
Hodgson, L. All about houseplants **635.9**

The **house** the Blakeneys built. Davidson, A.
In The Norton book of science fiction p115-24 **S C**

The **house** with the mezzanine. Chekhov, A. P.
In Chekhov, A. P. The image of Chekhov p240-61 **S C**

The **housebreaker** of Shady Hill. Cheever, J.
In Cheever, J. The stories of John Cheever p253-69 **S C**

The **housegirl**. Chigbo, O.
In The Heinemann book of contemporary African short stories p149-64 **S C**

Household equipment and supplies
Maintenance and repair
How things work in your home (and what to do when they don't) **643**

Household pests
See also Insect pests

Housekeeping [excerpt] Robinson, M.
In Circle of women: an anthology of contemporary Western women writers p62-73
810.8

Housepainting. Chang, L. S.
In American eyes p13-27 **S C**

Houses
See also Domestic architecture
Maintenance and repair
How things work in your home (and what to do when they don't) **643**

Housing
See/See also pages in the following book(s):
Bettelheim, B. Surviving, and other essays p201-20 **155.9**

Housing projects, Government *See* Public housing

Housman, A. E. (Alfred Edward), 1859-1936
The collected poems of A. E. Housman
821

Housman, Alfred Edward *See* Housman, A. E. (Alfred Edward), 1859-1936

Housman, Laurence, 1865-1959
The rooted lover
In The Oxford book of modern fairy tales p170-77 **S C**

Houston, Charles Hamilton, 1895-1950
See/See also pages in the following book(s):
Black leaders of the twentieth century p221-40
920

Houston, James A., 1921-
Confessions of an igloo dweller **970.004**

Houston, Pam
In my next life
In Circle of women: an anthology of contemporary Western women writers p242-57
810.8

Houston, Samuel, 1793-1863
See/See also pages in the following book(s):
Kennedy, J. F. Profiles in courage p106-24
920

How beautiful with banners. Blish, J.
In The Norton book of science fiction p133-41 **S C**
In The Oxford book of science fiction stories p340-49 **S C**

How Congress works **328.73**

How does a poem mean?. Ciardi, J. **821.008**

How far would you have gotten if I hadn't called you back?. Hobbs, V. **Fic**

How green was my valley. Llewellyn, R. **Fic**

How I came West, and why I stayed. Baker, A.
In Circle of women: an anthology of contemporary Western women writers p326-40
810.8

How I contemplated the world from the Detroit House of Correction and began my life over again. Oates, J. C.
In The Norton book of American short stories p662-75 **S C**

Howe, Tina
Painting Churches
In Best American plays: 9th series—1983-1992 p40-69   **812.008**

Howell, Vernon *See* Koresh, David

Howells, William Dean, 1837-1920
The mouse-trap
In Best plays of the early American theatre p262-76   **812.008**

Howes, Kelly King
Characters in 19th-century literature   **809**

Hoxie, Frederick E., 1947-
(ed) Encyclopedia of North American Indians. See Encyclopedia of North American Indians   **970.004**

Hoyle, Jay, 1947-
Mark [biography of Mark Hoyle]   **92**

Hoyle, Mark, 1972-1986
About
Hoyle, J. Mark   **92**

Hoyle, Russ
(ed) Gale environmental almanac. See Gale environmental almanac   **363.7**

Hoyt, Edwin Palmer
The GI's war   **940.54**
Mussolini's empire   **92**

Hoyt, Erich, 1950-
The earth dwellers   **595.7**

Hoyt, Olga Gruhzit- *See* Gruhzit-Hoyt, Olga, 1922-

HUAC *See* United States. Congress. House. Committee on Un-American Activities

Huang, Ray
China, a macro history   **951**

Hubble, Edwin Powell, 1889-1953
About
Christianson, G. E. Edwin Hubble: mariner of the nebulae   **92**

Hubble Space Telescope
Barbree, J. A journey through time   **520**
Mitton, J. Gems of Hubble   **520**

Hubel, David (David Hunter), 1926-
Eye, brain, and vision   **612.8**

Huddle, David, 1942-
Past my future
In The Best American short stories, 1996 p159-76   **S C**

Hudson, Derek
(comp) Classic English short stories, 1930-1955. See Classic English short stories, 1930-1955   **S C**

The **Hudson** River school. Yaeger, B. D.   **759.13**

Huebsch, Bill
Loving Bobby
In Not the only one p191-204   **S C**

Huelle, Pawel
A miracle
In Coming of age p43-62   **808.8**

Huff, Betty Tracy
Spy for a day
In The Big book of large-cast plays p3-18   **812.008**

Hugard, Jean, 1872-1959
Encyclopedia of card tricks   **795.4**

Huggan, Isabel, 1943-
Celia behind me
In Who do you think you are? p73-82   **S C**

Huggins, Nathan Irvin, 1927-1989
Slave and citizen: the life of Frederick Douglass   **92**
(ed) Du Bois, W. E. B. Writings   **818**

Hughes, Charles Evans, 1862-1948
See/See also pages in the following book(s):
Aaseng, N. Great Justices of the Supreme Court p103-19   **920**

Hughes, Edward James *See* Hughes, Ted, 1930-

Hughes, James
(ed) The Larousse desk reference. See The Larousse desk reference   **031**

Hughes, Langston, 1902-1967
The big sea: an autobiography   **92**
The blues I'm playing
In The Portable Harlem Renaissance reader p619-27   **810.8**
The collected poems of Langston Hughes   **811**
Don't you want to be free?
In Black theatre USA   **812.008**
Father and son
In The Portable Harlem Renaissance reader p599-618   **810.8**
I wonder as I wander   **92**
Limitations of life
In Black theatre USA   **812.008**
Luani of the jungles
In The Portable Harlem Renaissance reader p585-92   **810.8**
Mulatto
In Black theatre USA   **812.008**
Not without laughter [excerpt]
In The Portable Harlem Renaissance reader p592-99   **810.8**
Red-headed baby
In The Oxford book of American short stories p365-70   **S C**
The return of Simple   **818**
Short stories   **S C**
Contents: Bodies in the moonlight; The young glory of him; The little virgin; Luani of the jungles; Slave on the block; Cora unashamed; The blues I'm playing; Why, you reckon?; Little old spy; Spanish blood; On the road; Gumption; Professor; Big meeting; Trouble with the angels; Tragedy at the baths; Slice him down; African morning; 'Tain't so; One Friday morning; Heaven to hell; Breakfast in Virginia; Saratoga rain; Who's passing for who?; On the way home; Name in the papers; Sailor ashore; Something in common; Mysterious Madame Shaghai; Never room with a couple; Powder-white faces; Pushcart man; Rouge high; Patron of the arts; Thank you, m'am'; Sorrow for a midget; Blessed assurance; Early autumn; Fine accommodations; The gun; His last affair; No place to make love; Rock, church; Mary Winosky; Those who have no turkey; Seventy-five dollars; The childhood of Jimmy
Slave on the block
In The Norton book of American short stories p367-74   **S C**
Thank you, m'am
In The Best short stories by Negro writers p70-73   **S C**
In Read all about it! p82-89   **808.88**

Human origins—*Continued*
Dictionaries
Milner, R. The encyclopedia of evolution
    573.2

Human relations
Bode, J. Trust & betrayal   **158**
Hill, M. Coping with family expectations
    158
Kuklin, S. Speaking out   **305.23**
See/See also pages in the following book(s):
Toffler, A. Future shock p86-111   **303.4**

Human rights
See/See also pages in the following book(s):
Carter, J. Talking peace p99-111   **327.1**
Human sexuality: opposing viewpoints   **306.7**
The **human** volcano. Erickson, J.   **304.2**

Humanism
Rogers, C. R. A way of being   **150.19**

Humanities
Dictionaries
The Columbia dictionary of modern literary and cultural criticism   **001.3**

Humbert, of Lorraine
See/See also pages in the following book(s):
Cantor, N. F. Medieval lives   **940.1**

Humboldt, Alexander, Freiherr von, 1769-1859
See/See also pages in the following book(s):
Meadows, A. J. The great scientists   **920**

Humboldt, Friedrich Wilhelm Heinrich Alexander *See* Humboldt, Alexander, Freiherr von, 1769-1859

Hume, David, 1711-1776
Of the original contract
In Social contract p145-66   **320.1**
See/See also pages in the following book(s):
Durant, W. J. The age of Voltaire p140-61
    940.2
Russell, B. A history of Western philosophy p659-74   **109**

Humes, Edward
No matter how loud I shout   **364.3**

Humes, James C.
Lincoln, A. Wit & wisdom of Abraham Lincoln
    973.7

Humez, Alexander
Zero to lazy eight   **513**

Humez, Nicholas D.
(jt. auth) Humez, A. Zero to lazy eight
    513

Humiliation of the boy. Clinton, M. T.
In Song of the turtle p220-30   **S C**

Humishuma *See* Mourning Dove, 1888-1936

The **humming** of stars and bees and waves. Endrezze, A.
In Talking leaves   **S C**

Humor *See* Wit and humor

Humorous poetry
The New Oxford book of English light verse
    821.008
The Norton book of light verse   **821.008**
The Oxford book of American light verse
    811.008

Humping the boonies. Mason, B. A.
In The Other side of heaven p300-07
    S C

The **hunchback** of Notre Dame. Hugo, V.
    Fic

The **hundred** secret senses. Tan, A.   **Fic**

Hungarian refugees
Michener, J. A. The bridge at Andau   **943.9**

Hungary
History—1956, Revolution
Michener, J. A. The bridge at Andau   **943.9**

Hunger
Hunger [Current controversies]   **363.8**
Hunger [Current controversies]   **363.8**

A **hunger** artist. Kafka, F.
In Kafka, F. The complete stories   **S C**

The **Hunsaker** blood. Mortenson, P.
In Circle of women: an anthology of contemporary Western women writers p315-25
    810.8

Hunt, Norman Bancroft- *See* Bancroft-Hunt, Norman

The **hunt** for hidden killers. Yancey, D.   **616**
The **hunt** for Red October. Clancy, T.   **Fic**

Hunter, Kristin, 1931-
An interesting social study
In The Best short stories by Negro writers p332-40   **S C**

The **Hunter** Gracchus. Kafka, F.
In Kafka, F. The complete stories   **S C**

The **Hunter** Gracchus: a fragment. Kafka, F.
In Kafka, F. The complete stories   **S C**

Hunters in the snow. Wolff, T.
In The Oxford book of American short stories p620-35   **S C**

Hunters of the northern forests   **970.004**

Hunting
Paulsen, G. Father water, Mother woods
    799

Great Britain
See/See also pages in the following book(s):
Gies, J. Life in a medieval castle p125-46
    940.1

A **hunting** accident. Gordimer, N.
In Gordimer, N. Crimes of conscience p42-53
    S C

Hunting dinosaurs. Psihoyos, L.   **567.9**

Hunting the deceitful turkey. Twain, M.
In Twain, M. The complete short stories of Mark Twain   **S C**

Huntington's chorea
See/See also pages in the following book(s):
Genetics & society p31-44   **306.4**

The **huntsman.** Chekhov, A. P.
In Chekhov, A. P. The image of Chekhov p72-77   **S C**

Hurley, Patrick J., 1883-1963
See/See also pages in the following book(s):
White, T. H. In search of history p197-205
    92

Hurlyburly. Rabe, D.
In Best American plays: 9th series—1983-1992 p126-83   **812.008**

Hussein, Ṣaddām—About—*Continued*
See/See also pages in the following book(s):
Wakin, E. Contemporary political leaders of the Middle East p19-35   **920**

Hussey, Leigh Ann
Blood libel
In Vampires: a collection of original stories p157-86   **S C**

Hussey, Mark, 1956-
Virginia Woolf A-Z   **823.009**

Huston, John, 1906-1987
The treasure of Sierra Madre
In Best American screenplays   **812.008**

The **Hutchinson** dictionary of world history   **903**

The **Hutchinson** dictionary of world myth. See The Dictionary of world myth   **291.03**

Hutchison, Robert, 1938-
Meteorites   **523.5**

The **Hutchison** dictionary of science. See The Dictionary of science   **503**

Huxley, Aldous, 1894-1963
Brave new world   **Fic**
Brave new world revisited   **303.3**

Hyam, R. (Roger)
Plants and their names: a concise dictionary   **581**

Hyam, Roger *See* Hyam, R. (Roger)

The **Hyannis** Port story. Vonnegut, K.
In Vonnegut, K. Welcome to the monkey house   **S C**

Hybridization *See* Plant breeding

Hyde, Margaret Oldroyd, 1917-
The violent mind   **616.85**

Hydrogen bomb
Rhodes, R. Dark sun   **623.4**

Hydroponic gardening. Bridwell, R.   **635**

Hydroponics
Bridwell, R. Hydroponic gardening   **635**

Hygiene
See also Health
McCoy, K. The new teenage body book   **613**

Hygiene, Industrial *See* Occupational health and safety

Hylton, William H.
(ed) Rodale's illustrated encyclopedia of herbs. See Rodale's illustrated encyclopedia of herbs   **635**

Hyman, Isabelle
(jt. auth) Trachtenberg, M. Architecture, from prehistory to post-modernism   **720.9**

Hynes, H. Patricia
The recurring silent spring [biography of Rachel Carson]   **92**

Hypatia, ca. 370-415
See/See also pages in the following book(s):
Osen, L. M. Women in mathematics p21-32   **920**

Hypatia's heritage. Alic, M.   **509**

Hyperactive children
See also Attention deficit disorder

Hysteria (Social psychology)
See/See also pages in the following book(s):
Roueché, B. The medical detectives p317-29   **616**

I

I am a camera. Van Druten, J.
In Best American plays: 4th series—1951-1957 p1-36   **812.008**

I am somebody! a biography of Jesse Jackson. Haskins, J.   **92**

I am the cheese. Cormier, R.   **Fic**

I am the darker brother   **811.008**

"I am who I am". Gay, K.   **305.8**

I can't breathe. Lardner, R.
In Lardner, R. The best short stories of Ring Lardner p11-21   **S C**

I can't find my blackface. Gordon, H.
In Streetlights: illuminating tales of the urban black experience p146-57   **S C**

I, Claudius. Graves, R.   **Fic**

I dream a world: portraits of black women who changed America. Lanker, B.   **305.4**

I feel a little jumpy around you   **808.81**

I guess everything reminds you of something. Hemingway, E.
In Hemingway, E. The complete short stories of Ernest Hemingway p597-601   **S C**

I had a hammer: the Hank Aaron story. Aaron, H.   **92**

I hadn't meant to tell you this. Woodson, J.   **Fic**

I have words to spend. Cormier, R.   **92**

I heard the owl call my name. Craven, M.   **Fic**

I know what the red clay looks like. Carroll, R.   **810.9**

I know what you're thinking. Wilhelm, K.
In Nebula awards 30 p205-21   **S C**

I know why the caged bird sings. Angelou, M.   **92**

I know why the caged bird sings [excerpt] Angelou, M.
In Who do you think you are? p156-63   **S C**

I love myself when I am laughing—and then again when I am looking mean and impressive. Hurston, Z. N.   **818**

I never even seen my father. Mohr, N.
In Mohr, N. In Nueva York   **S C**

I never had it made. Robinson, J.   **92**

I ought to be in pictures. Simon, N.
In Simon, N. The collected plays of Neil Simon v3 p217-305   **812**

I remember mama. Van Druten, J.
In Best plays of the modern American theatre: 2nd series p85-129   **812.008**

I, robot. Asimov, I.   **S C**

I sing the Body Electric!. Bradbury, R.
In Bradbury, R. The stories of Ray Bradbury p709-36   **S C**

If men played cards as women do. Kaufman, G. S.
In Thirty famous one-act plays p423-27
808.82

If rock and roll were a machine. Davis, T.
Fic

If the war continues. Hesse, H.
In Hesse, H. The fairy tales of Hermann Hesse
S C

If you sing like that for me. Sharma, A.
In The Best American short stories, 1996 p282-306
S C
In Prize stories, 1996 p25-50
S C

If you touched my heart. Allende, I.
In The Oxford book of gothic tales p519-26
S C

If you're light and have long hair. Brooks, G.
In Black-eyed Susans/Midnight birds p115-19
S C

Iguana dreams
S C

The **iguana** killer. Ríos, A.
In Growing up Chicano/o p41-55
810.8

Ikangaa, Juma, 1957-
See/See also pages in the following book(s):
Sandrock, M. Running with the legends p403-20
796.42

Ikhnaton *See* Akhenaton, King of Egypt, fl. ca. 1388-1358 B.C.

Ile. O'Neill, E.
In O'Neill, E. Complete plays v1
812

Ile forest. Le Guin, U. K.
In American short story masterpieces
S C

The **Iliad.** Homer
883

The **Iliad** of Sandy Bar. Harte, B.
In The Oxford book of short stories p67-77
S C

I'll be waiting. Chandler, R.
In The Oxford book of American detective stories p295-309
S C

The **ill-made** knight. White, T. H.
In White, T. H. The once and future king
Fic

Illegal aliens
Illegal immigration
325.73
Illegal immigration: opposing viewpoints
325.73
Immigration [Reference shelf]
325.73
See/See also pages in the following book(s):
Friendly, F. W. The Constitution—that delicate balance
342

Illegal immigration
325.73

Illegal immigration: opposing viewpoints
325.73

Illingworth, Valerie
(ed) The Facts on File dictionary of astronomy. See The Facts on File dictionary of astronomy
520.3

Illinois
Fiction
Bradbury, R. Dandelion wine
Fic

Illiteracy *See* Literacy

Illiteracy in America. Dolan, E. F.
370.19

Illiterate America. Kozol, J.
370.19

Illness *See* Diseases

Illumination of books and manuscripts
Wilson, E. B. Bibles and bestiaries
745.6

Illusions *See* Hallucinations and illusions

The **illustrated** almanac of historical facts. Stewart, R.
902

The **Illustrated** atlas of Jewish civilization
909

The **illustrated** dictionary of electronics. Turner, R. P.
621.381

Illustrated dictionary of science
503

The **illustrated** encyclopedia of classical music. See Gammond, P. The Harmony illustrated encyclopedia of classical music
781.6

The **Illustrated** encyclopedia of wildlife
591

The **illustrated** guide to the Bible. Porter, J. R.
220.6

The **Illustrated** history of country music
781.642

The **illustrated** history of Mickey Mantle. Schoor, G.
92

Illustrated history of South Africa
968

The **illustrated** man. Bradbury, R.
S C

The **Illustrated** New Musical Express encyclopedia of rock. See The Harmony illustrated encyclopedia of rock
781.66

The **illustrated** woman. Bradbury, R.
In Bradbury, R. The stories of Ray Bradbury p608-16
S C

Illustrations, Humorous *See* Cartoons and caricatures

Illustrators
Williams, H. E. Books by African-American authors and illustrators for children and young adults
016.3058

I'm in Marsport without Hilda. Asimov, I.
In Asimov, I. The complete stories v1 p239-49
S C

I'm not Rappaport. Gardner, H.
In Best American plays: 9th series—1983-1992 p210-43
812.008

I'm not stupid. Rodriguez, D. E.
In Ten out of ten p239-53
812.008

The **image.** Singer, I. B.
In Singer, I. B. The image and other stories p295-310
S C

The **image** and other stories. Singer, I. B.
S C

The **image** of Chekhov. Chekhov, A. P.
S C

Images of America: a panorama of history in photographs
973

Imaginary people. Pringle, D.
803

Imel, Dorothy
(jt. auth) Ann, M. Goddesses in world mythology
291.03

Immell, Myra
(ed) The Young adult reader's adviser. See The Young adult reader's adviser
011.6

Immigrants
Ungar, S. J. Fresh blood
305.8

Immigration. Andryszewski, T.
325.73

Immigration [Reference shelf]　　325.73
Immigration and emigration
　　See also Children of immigrants; Immigrants; Refugees; names of countries with the subdivision *Immigration and emigration*; names of countries, cities, etc. with the subdivision *Foreign population*; and names of nationality groups
　　Border crossings: emigration and exile　　**808.8**
　　The Settling of North America　　**911**
Immigration: opposing viewpoints　　325.73
Immigration to the U.S.　　325.73
The **Immortal** Bard. Asimov, I.
　　In Asimov, I. The complete stories v1 p135-37　　S C
Immortality
　　See also Future life
The **immune** system. Edelson, E.　　616.07
Immunity
　　Clark, W. R. At war within　　616.07
　　Edelson, E. The immune system　　616.07
　　See/See also pages in the following book(s):
　　The Incredible machine p157-219　　612
Immunization *See* Vaccination
The **imp** of the perverse. Poe, E. A.
　　In Poe, E. A. The collected tales and poems of Edgar Allan Poe p280-84　　S C
　　In Poe, E. A. Tales of Edgar Allan Poe p9-17　　S C
Impeaching the president. Morin, I. V.　　324.6
Impeachments
　　Morin, I. V. Impeaching the president　　324.6
Imperialism
　　Arendt, H. Origins of totalitarianism　　321.9
　　The Cambridge illustrated history of the British Empire　　**941.08**
　　See/See also pages in the following book(s):
　　Heilbroner, R. L. The worldly philosophers　　330.1
The **importance** of being Earnest. Wilde, O.　　822
　　also in The Oxford anthology of English literature v2　　820.8
　　also in Wilde, O. The portable Oscar Wilde p430-507　　828
The **important** houses. Gordon, M.
　　In The Best American short stories, 1993 p335-58　　S C
The **impossible** marriage. O'Connor, F.
　　In O'Connor, F. Collected stories p504-14　　S C
Impostors and imposture
　　Sifakis, C. Hoaxes and scams　　364.1
　　Stein, G. Encyclopedia of hoaxes　　001.9
The **impresario.** Singer, I. B.
　　In Singer, I. B. The death of Methuselah and other stories p131-45　　S C
Impressionism (Art)
　　Waldron, A. Claude Monet　　92
　　Welton, J. Impressionism　　759.05

　　See/See also pages in the following book(s):
　　Arnason, H. H. History of modern art: painting, sculpture, architecture　　**709.04**
In a far country. London, J.
　　In London, J. The portable Jack London p11-25　　**818**
　　In London, J. Short stories of Jack London p25-38　　S C
　　In The Oxford book of American short stories p190-205　　S C
"In a good cause—". Asimov, I.
　　In Asimov, I. The complete stories v1 p468-88　　S C
In a house of wooden monkeys. Youngblood, S.
　　In Children of the night p300-03　　S C
In a strange land. Maugham, W. S.
　　In Maugham, W. S. Collected short stories v2　　S C
In a thousand years' time. Andersen, H. C.
　　In Andersen, H. C. Tales and stories　　S C
In an art factory. Frost, R.
　　In Frost, R. Collected poems, prose, & plays p576-88　　**818**
In another country. Hemingway, E.
　　In Hemingway, E. The complete short stories of Ernest Hemingway p206-10　　S C
　　In Hemingway, E. The Nick Adams stories p168-74　　S C
　　In Hemingway, E. The short stories of Ernest Hemingway p267-72　　S C
In blue. Crowley, J.
　　In Nebula awards 25 p268-314　　S C
In camera. Westall, R.
　　In Westall, R. Shades of darkness p85-112　　S C
In cold blood. Capote, T.　　364.1
In country. Mason, B. A.　　Fic
In Dahomey. Dunbar, P. L.
　　In Black theatre USA　　**812.008**
In defense of American liberties: a history of the ACLU. Walker, S.　　323
In exile. Chekhov, A. P.
　　In Chekhov, A. P. The image of Chekhov p193-203　　S C
In kindling flame: the story of Hannah Senesh, 1921-1944. Atkinson, L.　　92
In-line skater's start-up. Werner, D.　　796.2
In-line skating
　　Werner, D. In-line skater's start-up　　796.2
In love. Lawrence, D. H.
　　In Lawrence, D. H. The complete short stories v3　　S C
In love and in danger. Levy, B.　　362.7
In my next life. Houston, P.
　　In Circle of women: an anthology of contemporary Western women writers p242-57　　**810.8**
In my own space. Glenn, C.
　　In Growing up gay p235-39　　**808.8**
In Nueva York. Mohr, N.　　S C

In Orbit. Brooks, M.
  In Brooks, M. Paradise Café and other stories
    p55-61   S C
In our defense: the Bill of Rights in action. Alder-
  man, E.   342
In our image. Karnow, S.   959.9
In our own image. Ritchin, F.   770.1
In our time. Hemingway, E.   S C
In Roseau. Kincaid, J.
  In The Best American short stories, 1996
    p195-212   S C
In Sabine. Chopin, K.
  In Chopin, K. The awakening and selected
    stories p41-52   S C
In search of Bernabe [excerpt] Limón, G.
  In Latina: women's voices from the border-
    lands p265-72   810.8
In search of color everywhere   811.008
In search of Epifano. Anaya, R. A.
  In Iguana dreams   S C
In search of history. White, T. H.   92
In search of the old ones. Roberts, D.
                                              970.004
In sight of the killing. McDowell, G.
  In Streetlights: illuminating tales of the urban
    black experience p306-17   S C
In the abyss. Wells, H. G.
  In Wells, H. G. The complete short stories of
    H. G. Wells p377-93   S C
In the alleys. Frankel, G.   779
In the American society. Jen, G.
  In The Oxford book of women's writing in
    the United States p176-89   810.8
In the arena: a memoir of victory, defeat, and re-
  newal. Nixon, R. M.   92
In the Avu observatory. Wells, H. G.
  In Wells, H. G. The complete short stories of
    H. G. Wells p212-19   S C
In the blink of an eye. Federici, C. M.
  In Tales from the planet Earth   S C
In the boudoir. Colette
  In Colette. The collected stories of Colette
    p69-71   S C
In the cemetery. Chekhov, A. P.
  In Chekhov, A. P. The image of Chekhov
    p64-66   S C
In the days of the comet. Wells, H. G.
  In Wells, H. G. Seven famous novels
                                              Fic
In the eye of the storm: the life of General H.
  Norman Schwarzkopf. Cohen, R.   92
In the family. Mitchison, N.
  In The Oxford book of modern fairy tales
    p341-51   S C
In the field. O'Brien, T.
  In O'Brien, T. The things they carried
                                              S C
In the flower of age. Colette
  In Colette. The collected stories of Colette
    p401-05   S C
In the gloaming. Dark, A. E.
  In The Best American short stories, 1994
    p61-78   S C

In the heart of the heart of the country. Gass, W.
  H.
  In The Norton book of American short stories
    p513-36   S C
In the horsecart. Chekhov, A. P.
  In Chekhov, A. P. The image of Chekhov
    p262-72   S C
In the life. Birtha, B.
  In We are the stories we tell   S C
In the modern vein. Wells, H. G.
  In Wells, H. G. The complete short stories of
    H. G. Wells p491-501   S C
In the name of his ancestor. Jones, W.
  In The Singing spirit: early short stories by
    North American Indians p52-58   S C
In the name of sorrow and hope [biography of
  Yitzhak Rabin] Ben Artzi-Pelossof, N.
                                              92
In the other half of time. Robles, M.
  In Daughters of the fifth sun   810.8
In the palm of your hand. Kowit, S.   808.1
In the park. Wolfe, T.
  In Wolfe, T. The complete short stories of
    Thomas Wolfe p250-59   S C
In the penal colony. Kafka, F.
  In Kafka, F. The complete stories   S C
In the presence of the creator: Isaac Newton and
  his times. Christianson, G. E.   92
In the red room. Bowles, P.
  In The Best American short stories of the
    eighties p182-91   S C
In the shadow of man. Goodall, J.   599.88
In the shadow of the glen. Synge, J. M.
  In 24 favorite one-act plays p377-90
                                              808.82
In the south. Lopez, J.
  In Iguana dreams   S C
In the time I get. Crutcher, C.
  In Crutcher, C. Athletic shorts: six short sto-
    ries p125-54   S C
In the time of the butterflies. Alvarez, J.   Fic
In the tunnels. Sleator, W.
  In Am I blue? p247-58   S C
In the zone. O'Neill, E.
  In O'Neill, E. Complete plays v1   812
  In Thirty famous one-act plays p405-18
                                              808.82
In the zoo. Stafford, J.
  In The Norton book of American short stories
    p472-90   S C
In their own words: a history of the American Ne-
  gro. See The Black Americans: a history in
  their own words, 1619-1983   305.8
In these girls, hope is a muscle. Blais, M.
                                              796.323
In white America. Duberman, M. B.
  In Best American plays: 6th series—1963-
    1967 p471-94   812.008
The **Inaugural** addresses of twentieth-century
  American presidents   353.03
Incarnations of immortality series. Anthony, P.
                                              Fic

Incas

Bingham, H. Lost city of the Incas   **985**

Hemming, J. The conquest of the Incas   **985**

Incas: lords of gold and glory   **985**

McIntyre, L. The incredible Incas and their timeless land   **985**

Moseley, M. E. The Incas and their ancestors   **985**

Sullivan, W. The secret of the Incas   **985**

See/See also pages in the following book(s):

Wright, R. Stolen continents   **970.004**

The **Incas** and their ancestors. Moseley, M. E.   **985**

Incas: lords of gold and glory   **985**

Incest

Mather, C. L. How long does it hurt?   **362.7**

See/See also pages in the following book(s):

Dolan, E. F. Child abuse p94-103   **362.7**

Fiction

Woodson, J. I hadn't meant to tell you this   **Fic**

An **incident** in the Ghobashi household. Rifaat, A.

In African short stories   **S C**

The **Incredible** Appearing Man. Galyan, D.

In The Best American short stories, 1996 p126-50   **S C**

The **incredible** Incas and their timeless land. McIntyre, L.   **985**

The **incredible** journey. Burnford, S.   **Fic**

The **Incredible** machine   **612**

Independent schools *See* Private schools

Index of majors and graduate degrees. College Entrance Examination Board   **378.73**

Index to the Wilson authors series   **920.003**

India

Antiquities

Ancient India   **934**

See/See also pages in the following book(s):

Builders of the ancient world p126-59   **930**

Durant, W. J. Our Oriental heritage p391-415, 440-502   **950**

Civilization

Ancient India   **934**

See/See also pages in the following book(s):

Durant, W. J. Our Oriental heritage p526-54, 613-33   **950**

Dictionaries

The Cambridge encyclopedia of India, Pakistan, Bangladesh, Sri Lanka, Nepal, Bhutan, and the Maldives   **954**

Fiction

Forster, E. M. A passage to India   **Fic**

Hesse, H. Siddhartha   **Fic**

Markandaya, K. Nectar in a sieve   **Fic**

Mehta, G. Raj   **Fic**

History

Collins, L. Freedom at midnight   **954.04**

Wolpert, S. A. A new history of India   **954**

History—1765-1947, British occupation

Bayly, C. A. Indian society and the making of the British Empire   **954.03**

Intellectual life

See/See also pages in the following book(s):

Durant, W. J. Our Oriental heritage p526-54   **950**

Politics and government

Gandhi, M. All men are brothers   **92**

Gandhi, M. Gandhi on non-violence   **322.4**

The **Indian** basket. Roberts, M.

In Talking leaves   **S C**

Indian camp. Hemingway, E.

In Hemingway, E. The complete short stories of Ernest Hemingway p67-70   **S C**

In Hemingway, E. In our time p15-19   **S C**

In Hemingway, E. The Nick Adams stories p16-21   **S C**

In Hemingway, E. The short stories of Ernest Hemingway p89-95   **S C**

Indian literature (American) *See* American literature—American Indian authors

Indian literature (East Indian) *See* Indic literature

Indian literature (North American Indian) *See* Indians of North America—Literature

Indian society and the making of the British Empire. Bayly, C. A.   **954.03**

Indiana

Fiction

West, J. The friendly persuasion   **Fic**

Indians

Wright, R. Stolen continents   **970.004**

See/See also pages in the following book(s):

Christopher Columbus and his legacy: opposing viewpoints   **970.01**

Antiquities

America in 1492   **970.01**

Coe, M. D. Atlas of ancient America   **970.01**

Mysteries of the ancient Americas   **970.01**

Stuart, G. S. America's ancient cities   **970.01**

Dictionaries

Dictionary of daily life of Indians of the Americas   **970.004**

Folklore

Bierhorst, J. The way of the earth   **970.004**

History

America in 1492   **970.01**

Indians (of India) *See* East Indians

Indians. Kopit, A. L.

In Best American plays: 7th series—1967-1973 p283-308   **812.008**

Indians in motion pictures

Hilger, M. From savage to nobleman   **791.43**

The **Indians** moved away. Hemingway, E.

In Hemingway, E. The Nick Adams stories p34-36   **S C**

The **Indians** of California   **970.004**

Indians of Central America

See also Mayas

Dictionaries

Bunson, M. R. Encyclopedia of ancient Mesoamerica   **972**

Inge, William, 1913-1973—*Continued*
Picnic
In Best American plays: 4th series—1951-
1957 p211-44   **812.008**
In Inge, W. 4 plays p71-148   **812**

Ingestion disorders *See* Eating disorders

Ingots of gold. Christie, A.
In Christie, A. Miss Marple: the complete
short stories   **S C**

Ingram, Willis J. *See* Harris, Mark, 1922-

The **ingrate**. Dunbar, P. L.
In Calling the wind p12-17   **S C**

The **ingredient**. Marzán, J.
In Iguana dreams   **S C**

Inherit the wind. Lawrence, J.
In Best American plays: 4th series—1951-
1957 p403-38   **812.008**
In Lawrence, J. The selected plays of Jerome
Lawrence and Robert E. Lee p1-69
    812

Injuries *See* First aid; Wounds and injuries

Inland. Muñiz, A.
In Border crossings: emigration and exile
p107-15   **808.8**

The **Inn** of the Two Witches. Conrad, J.
In Conrad, J. The complete short fiction of
Joseph Conrad v2 p193-217   **S C**

Inner cities
Kozol, J. Amazing grace   **362.7**

The **inner** city Mother Goose. Merriam, E.
    811

Innes, Catherine Lynette
(ed) African short stories. See African short stories   **S C**
(ed) The Heinemann book of contemporary
African short stories. See The Heinemann
book of contemporary African short stories
    S C

Innes, Michael, 1906-1994
See/See also pages in the following book(s):
Modern mystery writers p109-23   **809.3**

Innes, Miranda
Fabric painting   **746.6**
Jewelry   **745.594**

Innocens comes to Cotton. Mitchelson, T.
In Streetlights: illuminating tales of the urban
black experience p348-71   **S C**

The **innocent**. Greene, G.
In Greene, G. The portable Graham Greene
p43-46   **828**

The **innocents** abroad. Twain, M.   **817**

Innuit *See* Inuit

Inoculation *See* Vaccination

An **inquiry** into the nature and causes of the
wealth of nations. See Smith, A. The wealth
of nations   **330.1**

Insane *See* Mentally ill

Insanity *See* Mental illness—Jurisprudence

Inscriptions, Cuneiform *See* Cuneiform inscriptions

Insect pests
See/See also pages in the following book(s):
Berenbaum, M. R. Bugs in the system
    595.7

Insects
See also Ants; Butterflies; Moths
Arnett, R. H., Jr. Simon and Schuster's guide to
insects   **595.7**
Berenbaum, M. R. Bugs in the system
    595.7
Borror, D. J. A field guide to the insects of
America north of Mexico   **595.7**
The Encyclopedia of insects   **595.7**
Milne, L. J. The Audubon Society field guide to
North American insects and spiders
    595.7
Wootton, A. Insects of the world   **595.7**
See/See also pages in the following book(s):
Waldbauer, G. Insects through the seasons
    595.7

Insects, Injurious and beneficial *See* Beneficial
insects; Insect pests

Insects of the world. Wootton, A.   **595.7**

Insects through the seasons. Waldbauer, G.
    595.7

Insert knob A in hole B. Asimov, I.
In Asimov, I. The complete stories v1 p561-
62   **S C**

Inside edge. Brennan, C.   **796.91**

Inside Star trek. Solow, H.   **791.45**

Inside the Third Reich. Speer, A.   **943.086**

The **insiders**. Edwards, L.
In Streetlights: illuminating tales of the urban
black experience p93-101   **S C**

Insomnia. King, S.   **Fic**

Inspiration. Bova, B.
In Nebula awards 30 p86-98   **S C**

The **inspired** chicken motel. Bradbury, R.
In Bradbury, R. The stories of Ray Bradbury
p744-51   **S C**

Instant of the hour after. McCullers, C.
In McCullers, C. Collected stories p40-47
    S C

Instruction *See* Teaching

Instructional materials centers
See also School libraries
American Association of School Librarians. In-
formation power   **027.8**
Assessment and the school library media center
    027.8
Craver, K. W. School library media centers in
the 21st century   **027.8**
Loertscher, D. V. Taxonomies of the school li-
brary media program   **027.8**
Moody, R. B. Coming to terms   **027.8**
Morris, B. J. Administering the school library
media center   **027.8**
Stein, B. L. Running a school library media cen-
ter   **027.8**
Woolls, E. B. The school library media manager
    025.1

Periodicals
School Library Media Quarterly   **027.805**

Instrumental music
See/See also pages in the following book(s):
Grout, D. J. A history of western music
780.9

Insurance, Health *See* Health insurance

Intellect
Arendt, H. The life of the mind   **153**
Sagan, C. The dragons of Eden   **153**

Intellectual freedom
See also Academic freedom
Intellectual freedom manual   **323.44**
Symons, A. K. Protecting the right to read
025.2

Intellectual freedom manual   **323.44**

Intelligence *See* Intellect

Intelligence, Artificial *See* Artificial intelligence

Intelligence of animals *See* Animal intelligence

The **intelligence** office. Hawthorne, N.
In Hawthorne, N. Tales and sketches; A wonder book for girls and boys; Tanglewood tales for girls and boys p873-86
S C

Intelligence service
See also Espionage; Secret service
Melton, H. K. The ultimate spy book
327.12
Fiction
Cormier, R. I am the cheese   **Fic**

Intelligence tests
See also Educational tests and measurements

Intercultural education *See* Multicultural education

Intercultural studies *See* Cross cultural studies

Interdepartmental memorandum. Bova, B.
In Bova, B. Challenges p131-35   **S C**

Interest groups *See* Lobbying

An **interest** in life. Paley, G.
In We are the stories we tell   **S C**

An **interesting** social study. Hunter, K.
In The Best short stories by Negro writers p332-40   **S C**

Interlocking pieces. Gloss, M.
In The Norton book of science fiction p571-76   **S C**

Interlude. Butler, D. H.
In Not the only one p127-33   **S C**

Intermarriage
See also Interracial marriage

Internal migration
Lemann, N. The promised land   **973.9**

Internal security
United States
Fariello, G. Red scare   **973.92**

International arbitration
See/See also pages in the following book(s):
Carter, J. Talking peace p112-25   **327.1**

The **International** Association of Crime Writers presents Bad behavior. See Bad behavior
S C

The **International** atlas. See The New international atlas   **912**

International dictionary of art and artists
703

The **International** encyclopedia of dogs
636.7

International Military Tribunal for the Far East
See/See also pages in the following book(s):
Morin, I. V. Days of judgment p79-96
940.54

International politics *See* World politics

International relations
See also World politics
Carter, J. Talking peace   **327.1**
The United Nations' role in world affairs
341.23

The **international** thesaurus of quotations. Tripp, R. T.   **808.88**

International trade
Miller, E. W. America's international trade
382

Internet (Computer network)
Barron, A. E. The Internet and instruction
004
Downing, D. Dictionary of computer and Internet terms   **004**
The Information highway   **004**
Internet connections   **004**
Miller, E. B. The Internet resource directory for K-12 teachers and librarians   **004**
Stoll, C. Silicon snake oil   **004**
Using the Internet, online services & CD-ROMS for writing research and term papers   **004**
Directories
CyberHound's guide to Internet databases
004

Internet connections   **004**

The **Internet** resource directory for K-12 teachers and librarians. Miller, E. B.   **004**

Internment camps *See* Concentration camps

Interpersonal relations *See* Human relations

Interplanetary voyages
Herbst, J. Star crossing   **629.4**

The **interpretation** of dreams. Freud, S.
In Freud, S. The basic writings of Sigmund Freud   **150.19**

Interracial adoption
Pohl, C. Transracial adoption   **362.7**

Interracial America: opposing viewpoints
305.8

Interracial dating and marriage. Landau, E.
306.7

Interracial marriage
Landau, E. Interracial dating and marriage
306.7

Interracial relations *See* Race relations

The **interrogation.** Weiner, E.
In Bad behavior p289-98   **S C**

Interstellar communication
Dictionaries
Angelo, J. A. The extraterrestrial encyclopedia
574.999

Intertextuality. Gordon, M.
In The Best American short stories, 1996 p151-58   **S C**

Johnson, Clifford Vincent
Old blues singers never die
In The Best short stories by Negro writers
p414-27 **S C**

Johnson, Denis, 1949-
Emergency
In The Vintage book of contemporary
American short stories p274-85 **S C**

Johnson, Diane, 1934-
Great Barrier Reef
In The Best American short stories, 1993
p281-99 **S C**

Johnson, E. Pauline, 1861-1913
As it was in the beginning
In Spider Woman's granddaughters **S C**
A red girl's reasoning
In The Singing spirit: early short stories by
North American Indians p18-34 **S C**
The Tenas Klootchman
In The Singing spirit: early short stories by
North American Indians p35-42 **S C**

Johnson, Earvin, 1959-
My life **92**

Johnson, Emily Pauline, 1861-1913
See/See also pages in the following book(s):
Sonneborn, L. Performers **920**

Johnson, Georgia Douglas Camp, 1886-1966
A Sunday morning in the South
In Black theatre USA **812.008**

Johnson, Herschel, 1948-
Kingdom of night [excerpt]
In Streetlights: illuminating tales of the urban
black experience p196-206 **S C**

Johnson, Jack, 1878-1946
See/See also pages in the following book(s):
Lipsyte, R. Idols of the game p35-54 **920**

Johnson, Jacqueline
West wind
In Streetlights: illuminating tales of the urban
black experience p207-18 **S C**

Johnson, James Weldon, 1871-1938
God's trombones: seven Negro sermons in verse
811

About
Fleming, R. E. James Weldon Johnson **818**
See/See also pages in the following book(s):
Black American poets and dramatists before the
Harlem Renaissance p91-105 **810.9**
Black American prose writers before the Harlem
Renaissance p115-28 **810.9**
Black leaders of the twentieth century p85-103
920

Johnson, Joan J., 1942-
Teen prostitution **362.7**

Johnson, Kirk R.
Prehistoric journey **551.7**

**Johnson, Lyndon B. (Lyndon Baines), 1908-
1973**

About
Berman, L. Lyndon Johnson's war **959.704**
Eskow, D. Lyndon Baines Johnson **92**
Goodwin, D. K. Lyndon Johnson and the
American dream **92**
See/See also pages in the following book(s):
Character above all **920**

Halberstam, D. The best and the brightest
973.922

Johnson, Magic *See* Johnson, Earvin, 1959-

Johnson, Nunnally, 1897-1977
Holy matrimony
In Best American screenplays **812.008**

Johnson, Paul, 1928-
Castles of England, Scotland and Wales
941

Johnson, Robert, d. 1938
See/See also pages in the following book(s):
Davis, F. The history of the blues p124-33
781.643

Johnson, Samuel, 1709-1784
About
Boswell, J. The life of Samuel Johnson **92**
See/See also pages in the following book(s):
Durant, W. J. Rousseau and revolution p818-42
940.2

Johnson, Venice
(ed) Heart full of grace. See Heart full of grace
808.88

Johnson, William H., 1901-1970
See/See also pages in the following book(s):
Harlem Renaissance: art of black America
709.73

Johnson-Feelings, Dianne
Presenting Laurence Yep **813.009**

Joining the tribe. Due, L. A. **305.23**

The **joke** that made Ed's fortune. Twain, M.
In Twain, M. The complete short stories of
Mark Twain **S C**

Jokester. Asimov, I.
In Asimov, I. The complete stories v1 p123-
34 **S C**

Joliot-Curie, Irène, 1897-1956
See/See also pages in the following book(s):
McGrayne, S. B. Nobel Prize women in science
p117-43 **920**

Jonah's gourd vine. Hurston, Z. N.
In Hurston, Z. N. Novels and stories p1-171
Fic

Jonah's gourd vine [excerpt] Hurston, Z. N.
In Hurston, Z. N. I love myself when I am
laughing—and then again when I am
looking mean and impressive p189-96
818
In The Portable Harlem Renaissance reader
p719-28 **810.8**

Jonas, Gerald, 1935-
The living earth book of North American trees
582.16

Jonathan Cilley. Hawthorne, N.
In Hawthorne, N. Tales and sketches; A wonder book for girls and boys; Tanglewood
tales for girls and boys p607-15
S C

The **Jonathan** David dictionary of first names. See
Kolatch, A. J. Dictionary of first names
929.4

Jones, Alison
Larousse dictionary of world folklore
398.03

Jordan, William C. (William Chester), 1948-
(ed) The Middle Ages. See The Middle Ages
[Scribner] **909.07**

Jordan's end. Glasgow, E.
In The Oxford book of gothic tales p302-15
S C

Jorgensen, Paul A.
William Shakespeare: the tragedies **822.3**

Joris, Pierre
(ed) Poems for the millennium. See Poems for
the millennium v1 **808.81**

Joseph, Nez Percé Chief, 1840-1904
About
Scott, R. A. Chief Joseph and the Nez Percés
92

See/See also pages in the following book(s):
Brown, D. A. The American West p255-64
978
Brown, D. A. Bury my heart at Wounded Knee
p315-30 **970.004**

Josephine the Singer; or, The mouse folk. Kafka,
F.
In Kafka, F. The complete stories **S C**

Josephy, Alvin M., 1915-
500 nations **970.004**
(ed) America in 1492. See America in 1492
970.01
(ed) The American Heritage history of World
War I. See The American Heritage history of
World War I **940.3**

Josquin, des Pres, d. 1521
See/See also pages in the following book(s):
Grout, D. J. A history of western music
780.9

Jost, Kenneth
The Supreme Court yearbook **347**

Journal of researches into the geology and natural
history of the various countries visited by
H.M.S. Beagle. See Darwin, C. The voyage
of the Beagle **508**

Journal of Youth Services in Libraries
027.6205

Journalism
See also Broadcast journalism;
Photojournalism
Fallows, J. M. Breaking the news **302.23**
Kronenwetter, M. How to write a news article
808

Journalism in Tennessee. Twain, M.
In Twain, M. The complete short stories of
Mark Twain **S C**

Journalists
See also Women journalists
Baker, R. The good times **92**
Baker, R. Growing up **92**
Baughman, J. L. Henry R. Luce and the rise of
the American news media **92**
Cloud, S. The Murrow boys **070.1**
Hockenberry, J. Moving violations **92**
Kuralt, C. A life on the road **92**
Rather, D. The camera never blinks twice
92
Smith, H. K. Events leading up to my death
92

Swanberg, W. A. Citizen Hearst: a biography of
William Randolph Hearst **92**
Fiction
West, N. Miss Lonelyhearts **Fic**

Journals *See* Periodicals

Journals (Diaries) *See* Diaries

The **journals** of Sylvia Plath. Plath, S. **92**

A **journey**. Wharton, E.
In The Oxford book of American short stories
p244-55 **S C**
In Wharton, E. The selected short stories of
Edith Wharton p1-9 **S C**

The **journey** [excerpt] Ganesan, I.
In Growing up Asian American p393-98
810.8

The **journey** back from hell. Gill, A. **940.53**

Journey into China **915.1**

The **journey** out. Pollack, R. **305.9**

A **journey** through time. Barbree, J. **520**

Journey to Hanford. Saroyan, W.
In Saroyan, W. My name is Aram **S C**

Journeys *See* Voyages and travels

Journey's end. Colette
In Colette. The collected stories of Colette
p140-43 **S C**

Joy. Chekhov, A. P.
In Chekhov, A. P. The image of Chekhov
p45-47 **S C**

The **Joy** Luck Club. Tan, A. **Fic**

The **Joy** Luck Club [excerpt] Tan, A.
In Growing up Asian American p223-30
810.8

Joy of cooking. Rombauer, I. von S. **641.5**

The **joy** of keeping score. Dickson, P.
796.357

The **joy** of signing. Riekehof, L. L. **419**

Joyce, James, 1882-1941
The dead
In The Oxford book of Irish short stories
p228-66 **S C**
Dubliners **S C**
Contents: The sisters; An encounter; Araby; Eveline; After the
race; Two gallants; The boarding house; A little cloud; Counter-
parts; Clay; A painful case; Ivy day in the committee room; A
mother; Grace; The dead
Grace
In The Oxford book of short stories p255-74
S C
A portrait of the artist as a young man **Fic**
About
Brunsdale, M. James Joyce **823.009**
Critical essays on James Joyce **823.009**
Ellmann, R. James Joyce **92**
Fargnoli, A. N. James Joyce A to Z
823.009

Joyner, Florence Griffith *See* Griffith Joyner,
Florence

Joyner-Kersee, Jackie
See/See also pages in the following book(s):
Davis, M. D. Black American women in Olym-
pic track and field p82-93 **920**

Just dessert. Ponce, M. H.
In Latina: women's voices from the borderlands p185-98   **810.8**

Just don't never give up on love. Sanchez, S.
In Daughters of Africa p447-49   **808.8**

Just lather, that's all. Téllez, H.
In Bad behavior p281-88   S C

Just one more time. Cheever, J.
In Cheever, J. The stories of John Cheever
p248-52   S C

Just so stories. Kipling, R.
In Kipling, R. The best fiction of Rudyard
Kipling p347-97   S C

Just tell me who it was. Cheever, J.
In Cheever, J. The stories of John Cheever
p370-85   S C

Justice, Administration of *See* Administration of
justice

A **justice**. Faulkner, W.
In Faulkner, W. Collected stories of William
Faulkner p343-60   S C

Justice is blind. Wolfe, T.
In Wolfe, T. The complete short stories of
Thomas Wolfe p589-95   S C

Justinian I, Emperor of the East, 483?-565
See/See also pages in the following book(s):
Durant, W. J. The age of faith p103-17
    940.1

Justinianus, Flavius Anicius Julianus *See* Justinian I, Emperor of the East, 483?-565

Justman, Robert H.
(jt. auth) Solow, H. Inside Star trek   **791.45**

Juvenile courts
Humes, E. No matter how loud I shout
    364.3

Juvenile delinquency
    See also Gangs
Bode, J. Hard time   **364.3**
Fremon, C. Father Greg and the homeboys
    361.7
Humes, E. No matter how loud I shout
    364.3
Kinnear, K. L. Violent children   **305.23**
Lang, S. S. Teen violence   **364.3**
Marshall, J. E., Jr. Street soldier   **364.3**
Newton, D. E. Teen violence   **364.3**
See/See also pages in the following book(s):
Criminal sentencing p9-39   **345**
    Fiction
Hinton, S. E. The outsiders   Fic
Mowry, J. Way past cool   Fic

Juvenile prostitution
Johnson, J. J. Teen prostitution   **362.7**

K

Kaddafi, Muammar *See* Qaddafi, Muammar al-,
1942-

Kadohata, Cynthia
The floating world [excerpt]
In Coming of age in America p122-35
    S C

In Growing up Asian American p255-64
    810.8

Jack's girl
In The Literary ghost p247-56   S C
Singing apples
In American eyes p49-61   S C

Kaffir boy. Mathabane, M.   **92**

Kaffir boy [excerpt] Mathabane, M.
In Somehow tenderness survives p87-103
    S C

Kaffir boy in America. Mathabane, M.   **92**

Kafka, Franz, 1883-1924
The complete stories   S C
Contents: Description of a struggle; Wedding preparations in
the country; The judgment; The metamorphosis; In the penal colony; The village schoolmaster; Blumfeld, an elderly bachelor;
The warden of the tomb; A country doctor; The Hunter Gracchus; The Hunter Gracchus: a fragment; The Great Wall of China; A report to an Academy; A report to an Academy: two fragments; The refusal; A hunger artist; Investigations of a dog; A
little woman; The burrow; Josephine the Singer; or, The mouse
folk; Children on a country road; The tradesman; Unhappiness;
Unmasking a confidence trickster; A dream; A fratricide; A visit
to a mine; Jackals and Arabs; The bucket rider; An old manuscript; The knock at the manor gate; Eleven sons; My neighbor;
A crossbreed; The cares of a family man; The silence of the sirens; The city coat of arms; The problem of our laws; The conscription of troops; First sorrow; Advocates; The married couple
The metamorphosis; criticism
In Franz Kafka's The metamorphosis
    833.009
The metamorphosis and other stories   S C
The longer stories included are: Conversation with the wor-
shiper; Conversation with the drunk; Children on the highway;
Exposing a city slicker; The businessman; Unhappiness; The
judgment; The stoker; The metamorphosis; An ancient manu-
script; Jackals and Arabs; A fratricide; A dream; A report for an
Academy
The trial   Fic
The trial; criticism
In Franz Kafka's The trial   **833.009**
    About
Critical essays on Franz Kafka   **833.009**
Spann, M. Franz Kafka   **833.009**

Kagan, Andrew
Marc Chagall   **92**

Kagan, Donald
On the origins of war and the preservation of
peace   **355**

Kahn, Ada P.
(jt. auth) Doctor, R. M. The encyclopedia of
phobias, fears, and anxieties   **616.85**

Kahn, Leora
(ed) When they came to take my father—. See
When they came to take my father—
    940.53

Kahn, Roger
The boys of summer   **796.357**

Kalamu ya Salaam, 1947-
Blk love song #1
In Black theatre USA   **812.008**
Raoul's silver song
In Streetlights: illuminating tales of the urban
black experience p398-411   S C

Kaleidoscope. Bradbury, R.
In Bradbury, R. The illustrated man   S C
In Bradbury, R. The stories of Ray Bradbury
p143-50   S C

Kals, W. S.
Stars and planets   523

Kamerman, Sylvia E.
(ed) The Big book of large-cast plays. See The Big book of large-cast plays   812.008

Kaminer, Michael
(jt. auth) King, D. The mountain bike experience   796.6

Kamp, Jim
(ed) Notable Hispanic American women. See Notable Hispanic American women
    920.003

Kampuchea See Cambodia

Kanastoga, Wasabi
City for sale
In Iguana dreams   S C

Kanazawa, Tooru J.
Frontier home
In Growing up Asian American p37-51
    810.8

Kandinsky, Wassily, 1866-1944
See/See also pages in the following book(s):
Read, Sir H. E. A concise history of modern painting   759.06

Kane, Joseph Nathan, 1899-
Facts about the presidents   920
Famous first facts: a record of first happenings, discoveries, and inventions in American history   031.02
(ed) Facts about the states. See Facts about the states   973

Kanin, Garson, 1912-
Born yesterday
In Best plays of the modern American theatre: 2nd series p181-227   812.008

Kansas
        Fiction
Parks, G. The learning tree   Fic
        History
Stratton, J. L. Pioneer women   978.1

Kant, Immanuel, 1724-1804
See/See also pages in the following book(s):
Durant, W. J. Rousseau and revolution p531-51
    940.2
Durant, W. J. The story of philosophy p192-220
    109
Jaspers, K. The great philosophers   109
Russell, B. A history of Western philosophy p701-18   109

Kantor, MacKinlay, 1904-1977
Andersonville   Fic

Kaplan, David E., 1955-
The cult at the end of the world   291

Kaplan, Fred, 1937-
Dickens   92

Kaplan, Philip
Their finest hour: the Battle of Britain remembered   940.54

Kappraff, Ronald M.
ASVAB basics   355

Karain. Conrad, J.
In Conrad, J. The complete short fiction of Joseph Conrad v1 p62-99   S C

Karen. Killilea, M.   616.8

Karl V, Emperor of Germany See Charles V, Holy Roman Emperor, 1500-1558

Karl and the ogre. McAuley, P. J.
In The Oxford book of science fiction stories p535-49   S C

Karlen, Arno
Man and microbes   614.4

Karlin, Wayne
Point Lookout
In The Other side of heaven p294-99
    S C
(ed) The Other side of heaven. See The Other side of heaven   S C

Karls, John B.
The writer's handbook   808

Karlsen, Carol F., 1940-
The devil in the shape of a woman   133.4

Karnes, Frances A.
Girls & young women inventing   608

Karney, Robyn
(ed) Chronicle of the cinema. See Chronicle of the cinema   791.43

Karnow, Stanley
In our image   959.9
Vietnam   959.704

Karoff, Barbara, 1929-
South American cooking   641.5

Karolides, Nicholas J.
(ed) Censored books. See Censored books
    810.9

Karr, Mary
The Liar's Club   92

Karr, Phyllis Ann
A cold stake
In Vampires: a collection of original stories p134-56   S C
Merlin's dark mirror
In The Merlin chronicles   S C

Karst, Kenneth L.
(ed) Encyclopedia of the American Constitution. See Encyclopedia of the American Constitution   342

Karwatka, Dennis
Technology's past   609

Kaser, Michael Charles
(ed) The Cambridge encyclopedia of Russia and the former Soviet Union. See The Cambridge encyclopedia of Russia and the former Soviet Union   947

Kasinec, Denise, 1967-
(ed) The Schomburg Center guide to black literature from the eighteenth century to the present. See The Schomburg Center guide to black literature from the eighteenth century to the present   809

Kaspi, Andrè
(ed) Great dates in United States history. See Great dates in United States history
    973.02

Katamoto. Wolfe, T.
In Wolfe, T. The complete short stories of Thomas Wolfe p349-58   S C

Katcher, Philip, 1941-
The Civil War source book   973.7

Katō, Shūichi, 1919-
A history of Japanese literature   **895.6**

Katz, Bill *See* Katz, William A., 1924-

Katz, Judith A.
(jt. auth) Matson, K. The working actor
   792

Katz, Linda Sternberg
(jt. auth) Katz, W. A. The Columbia Granger's guide to poetry anthologies   **016.80881**
(ed) Magazines for libraries. See Magazines for libraries   **011**
(ed) Magazines for young people. See Magazines for young people   **011.6**

Katz, William A., 1924-
The Columbia Granger's guide to poetry anthologies   **016.80881**
(ed) Magazines for libraries. See Magazines for libraries   **011**
(ed) Magazines for young people. See Magazines for young people   **011.6**

Katzman, John
(jt. auth) Robinson, A. Cracking the SAT & PSAT   **378.1**

Katzner, Kenneth
The languages of the world   **400**

Kauffman, Henry J., 1908-
Pennsylvania Dutch American folk art   **745**

Kaufman, George S., 1889-1961
If men played cards as women do
In Thirty famous one-act plays p423-27
   808.82
The man who came to dinner
In Best plays of the modern American theatre: 2nd series p317-64   **812.008**
The solid gold Cadillac
In Best American plays: 4th series—1951-1957 p611-41   **812.008**
The still alarm
In 24 favorite one-act plays p229-37
   808.82
You can't take it with you
In Twenty best plays of the modern American theatre p233-73   **812.008**

Kaufman, Kate
(jt. auth) Bass, E. Free your mind   **305.23**

Kaufman, Miriam
Easy for you to say   **362.1**

Kawin, Bruce F., 1945-
(ed) Mast, G. A short history of the movies
   791.43

Kayaking. Krauzer, S. M.   **797.1**

Kazakov, Yuri Pavlovich, 1927-
Adam and Eve
In The Portable twentieth-century Russian reader p509-38   **891.7**

Kazantzakis, Nikos, 1883-1957
Zorba the Greek   **Fic**

Kazimiroff, Theodore L.
The last Algonquin [biography of Joe Two Trees]   **92**

Kazin, Alfred, 1915-
See/See also pages in the following book(s):
Inventing the truth p61-81   **808**

Kean, John M.
(ed) Censored books. See Censored books
   810.9

Keating, H. R. F. (Henry Reymond Fitzwalter), 1926-
Crime and mystery: the 100 best books
   823.009

Keating, Henry Reymond Fitzwalter *See* Keating, H. R. F. (Henry Reymond Fitzwalter), 1926-

Keaton, Buster, 1895-1966
See/See also pages in the following book(s):
Kerr, W. The silent clowns p117-50, 211-45
   791.43

Keaton, Joseph Francis *See* Keaton, Buster, 1895-1966

Keats, John, 1795-1821
Poems   **821**
Poetical works   **821**
About
Critical essays on John Keats   **821**
Hirst, W. Z. John Keats   **821**
See/See also pages in the following book(s):
Untermeyer, L. Lives of the poets p444-77
   920

Keats, Mark
Peter Salem, Minuteman
In The Big book of large-cast plays p216-27
   812.008

Keeble, John, 1944-
The chasm
In The Best American short stories, 1994 p202-25   **S C**

Keegan, John, 1934-
Fields of battle   **973**
A history of warfare   **355**
The Second World War   **940.53**
(ed) The Times atlas of the Second World War. See The Times atlas of the Second World War   **911**

Keela, the outcast Indian maiden. Welty, E.
In Welty, E. The collected stories of Eudora Welty p38-45   **S C**

Keene, Ann T.
Willa Cather   **92**

Keene, Donald, 1922-
(ed) Anthology of Japanese literature from the earliest era to the mid-nineteenth century. See Anthology of Japanese literature from the earliest era to the mid-nineteenth century
   895.6

Keeping all the pieces. Gibbons, W.   **574.5**

Keeping Christina. Bridgers, S. E.   **Fic**

Keesey, Anna
Bright winter
In The Best American short stories, 1996 p177-94   **S C**

Kehret, Peg
Encore!   **812.008**

Keino, Kip, 1940-
See/See also pages in the following book(s):
Sandrock, M. Running with the legends p37-65
   796.42

Kenny, Maurice, 1929-
Wet moccasins
In Talking leaves   **S C**
Kent, George E., 1920-1982
A life of Gwendolyn Brooks   **92**
Kentucky
          Fiction
Arnow, H. L. S. The dollmaker   **Fic**
Mason, B. A. In country   **Fic**
Kenya
Dinesen, I. Out of Africa and Shadows on the grass   **967.62**
          Description
Adamson, J. Born free   **599.74**
Kenyatta, Jomo, ca. 1891-1978
The gentlemen of the jungle
In African short stories   **S C**
          About
Wepman, D. Jomo Kenyatta   **92**
See/See also pages in the following book(s):
Aymar, B. A pictorial history of the world's greatest trials p331-37   **345**
The **kepi**. Colette
In Colette. The collected stories of Colette p498-531   **S C**
Kepler, Johannes, 1571-1630
See/See also pages in the following book(s):
Sagan, C. Cosmos p57-71   **520**
Keppler, Johannes See Kepler, Johannes, 1571-1630
The **kerastion**. Le Guin, U. K.
In Le Guin, U. K. A fisherman of the inland sea p69-73   **S C**
Kerfol. Wharton, E.
In Wharton, E. The selected short stories of Edith Wharton p210-28   **S C**
Kermode, Frank, 1919-
(ed) Modern British literature. See Modern British literature   **820.8**
(ed) The Oxford anthology of English literature. See The Oxford anthology of English literature   **820.8**
(ed) A Reader's guide to the twentieth-century novel. See A Reader's guide to the twentieth-century novel   **823.009**
Kern, Robert W., 1934-
The regions of Spain   **946**
(ed) Historical dictionary of modern Spain, 1700-1988. See Historical dictionary of modern Spain, 1700-1988   **946**
Kernfeld, Barry, 1950-
(ed) The New Grove dictionary of jazz. See The New Grove dictionary of jazz   **781.65**
Kerouac, Jack, 1922-1969
Pomes all sizes   **811**
The portable Jack Kerouac   **818**
          About
French, W. G. Jack Kerouac   **813.009**
Kerr, Jean
Mary, Mary
In Best American plays: 5th series—1957-1963 p379-417   **812.008**
In The Most popular plays of the American theater p289-356   **812.008**

Kerr, M. E., 1927-
Deliver us from Evie   **Fic**
Gentlehands   **Fic**
The Green Killer
In Bad behavior p163-70   **S C**
Night kites [excerpt]
In Growing up gay p190-95   **808.8**
We might as well all be strangers
In Am I blue? p19-26   **S C**
          About
Nilsen, A. P. Presenting M. E. Kerr   **813.009**
Kerr, Walter, 1913-1996
The silent clowns   **791.43**
Kerry, a teenage mother. Aitkens, M.   **362.7**
Kersee, Jackie Joyner- See Joyner-Kersee, Jackie
Kesey, Ken
One flew over the cuckoo's nest   **Fic**
Kessel, John
Buffalo
In Nebula awards 27 p193-211   **S C**
The Franchise
In Nebula awards 29 p203-41   **S C**
Invaders
In The Norton book of science fiction p830-50   **S C**
Kesselring, Joseph, 1902-1967
Arsenic and old lace
In Best plays of the modern American theatre: 2nd series p459-510   **812.008**
In The Most popular plays of the American theater p429-504   **812.008**
Kessler, James H.
Distinguished African American scientists of the 20th century. See Distinguished African American scientists of the 20th century   **920**
Kessler, Lauren
After all these years: sixties ideals in a different world   **973.92**
Kessler, Ronald
The FBI   **363.2**
Ketchum, William C., 1931-
Grandma Moses   **759.13**
Kett, Joseph F.
(jt. auth) Hirsch, E. D. The dictionary of cultural literacy   **031**
Kevorkian, Jack
See/See also pages in the following book(s):
Suicide p76-144   **362.2**
The **key**. Asimov, I.
In Asimov, I. The complete stories v2 p337-61   **S C**
The **key**. Vo, P.
In The Other side of heaven p252-57   **S C**
The **key**. Welty, E.
In Welty, E. The collected stories of Eudora Welty p29-37   **S C**
Key art terms for beginners. Yenawine, P.   **701**
Key item. Asimov, I.
In Asimov, I. The complete stories v2 p381-83   **S C**

Kincaid, Jamaica—*Continued*
Girl
  In Calling the wind p454-55   **S C**
  In The Vintage book of contemporary American short stories p306-07   **S C**
In Roseau
  In The Best American short stories, 1996 p195-212   **S C**
Xuela
  In The Best American short stories, 1995 p313-31   **S C**
The **kind** of light that shines on Texas. McKnight, R.
  In Coming of age in America p17-31   **S C**

Kindall, Jerry
Sports illustrated baseball   **796.357**

King, Ada *See* Lovelace, Ada King, Countess of, 1815-1852

King, B. B.
About
Shirley, D. Everyday I sing the blues: the story of B.B. King   **92**

King, Billie Jean
See/See also pages in the following book(s):
Lipsyte, R. Idols of the game p276-95   **920**

King, Coretta Scott, 1927-
My life with Martin Luther King, Jr   **92**

King, Dave, 1955-
The mountain bike experience   **796.6**

King, F. Wayne
(jt. auth) Behler, J. L. The Audubon Society field guide to North American reptiles and amphibians   **597.6**

King, Martin Luther, 1929-1968
Strength to love   **252**
Stride toward freedom   **323.1**
A testament of hope   **323.1**
Where do we go from here: chaos or community?   **323.1**
Why we can't wait   **323.1**
About
Bennett, L. What manner of man: a biography of Martin Luther King, Jr.   **92**
Branch, T. Parting the waters: America in the King years, 1954-63   **973.921**
Colaiaco, J. A. Martin Luther King, Jr   **92**
Garrow, D. J. Bearing the cross: Martin Luther King, Jr., and the Southern Christian Leadership Conference   **92**
King, C. S. My life with Martin Luther King, Jr   **92**
Martin Luther King, Jr.: a documentary—Montgomery to Memphis   **92**
Oates, S. B. Let the trumpet sound: the life of Martin Luther King, Jr   **92**
Schulke, F. King remembered   **92**
See/See also pages in the following book(s):
Archer, J. They had a dream p120-83   **920**
Black leaders of the twentieth century p277-303   **920**
Lindop, E. Assassinations that shook America p90-111   **364.1**

King, Stephen, 1947-
Carrie   **Fic**
Christine   **Fic**
Feast of fear   **92**
Four past midnight   **S C**
Contents: The Langoliers; Secret window, secret garden; The library policeman; The sun dog
Insomnia   **Fic**
The man in the black suit
  In Prize stories, 1996 p1-24   **S C**
Quitters, Inc.
  In Masterpieces of mystery and suspense p392-410   **S C**
The reach
  In The Horror hall of fame p385-407   **S C**
Skeleton crew   **S C**
Contents: The mist; Here there be tygers; The monkey; Cain rose up; Mrs. Todd's shortcut; The jaunt; The wedding gig; Paranoid: A chant; The raft; Word processor of the gods; The man who would not shake hands; Beachworld; The reaper's image; Nona; For Owen; Survivor type; Uncle Otto's truck; Morning deliveries (Milkman #1); Big wheels: a tale of the laundry game (Milkman #2); Gramma; The ballad of the flexible bullet; The reach
About
Magistrale, T. Stephen King   **813.009**
Reino, J. Stephen King   **813.009**

King, Thomas, 1943-
A seat in the garden
  In Song of the turtle p191-99   **S C**
  In Talking leaves   **S C**

King, Wilma, 1942-
Stolen childhood   **326**

King, Woodie, 1937-
Beautiful light and black our dreams
  In The Best short stories by Negro writers p438-47   **S C**

The **king** and his three daughters. Walpole, H.
  In Masterpieces of fantasy and enchantment p166-69   **S C**

The **king** must die. Renault, M.   **Fic**

The **king** of the cats. Benét, S. V.
  In Masterpieces of fantasy and enchantment p296-309   **S C**

The **king** of the elves. Dick, P. K.
  In Masterpieces of fantasy and enchantment p375-94   **S C**
  In The Oxford book of modern fairy tales p321-40   **S C**

The **King** of the Golden River; or, The Black Brothers. Ruskin, J.
  In The Oxford book of modern fairy tales p29-50   **S C**

King of the roller rink. Brooks, M.
  In Brooks, M. Paradise Café and other stories p18-24   **S C**

King Pest. Poe, E. A.
  In Poe, E. A. The collected tales and poems of Edgar Allan Poe p720-29   **S C**

King remembered. Schulke, F.   **92**

King Solomon's mines. Haggard, H. R.   **Fic**

Kingdom of night [excerpt] Johnson, H.
  In Streetlights: illuminating tales of the urban black experience p196-206   **S C**

Kiremidjian, David, 1936-
(jt. auth) Lass, A. H. The Facts on File dictionary of classical, biblical, and literary allusions   803
Kirinyaga. Resnick, M.
In The Norton book of science fiction p716-32   S C
Kirk, Irina
Anton Chekhov   891.7
Kirkeby, Ed
Ain't misbehavin': the story of Fats Waller   92
Kirkland, Jack, 1901-
Tobacco Road
In The Most popular plays of the American theater p89-158   812.008
In Twenty best plays of the modern American theatre p599-642   812.008
Kirkpatrick, D. L. (Daniel Lane)
(ed) Reference guide to English literature. See Reference guide to English literature   820.3
Kirkpatrick, Daniel Lane *See* Kirkpatrick, D. L. (Daniel Lane)
Kirshon, John W.
(ed) Chronicle of America. See Chronicle of America   973.02
The kiss. Alvarez, J.
In Daughters of the fifth sun   810.8
Kissinger, Henry, 1923-
Years of upheaval   92
Kister, Kenneth F., 1935-
Kister's best encyclopedias   016
Kister's best encyclopedias. Kister, K. F.   016
Kiswana Browne. Naylor, G.
In Calling the wind p428-37   S C
In Children of the night p240-51   S C
The kit-bag. Blackwood, A.
In Victorian ghost stories p480-89   S C
Kit Carson's autobiography. Carson, K.   92
Kitchens
Plante, E. M. The American kitchen, 1700 to the present   643
Kitcher, Philip, 1947-
The lives to come   573.2
The kite. Maugham, W. S.
In Classic English short stories, 1930-1955 p1-32   S C
In Maugham, W. S. Collected short stories v4   S C
The kith of the Elf-folk. Dunsany, E. J. M. D. P., Baron
In The Oxford book of modern fairy tales p234-47   S C
Kittens. Koontz, D. R.
In Koontz, D. R. Strange highways p371-76   S C
Kittredge, Mary, 1949-
The common cold   616.2
Emergency medicine   616.02
Headaches   616.8
The human body: an overview   612
Organ transplants   617.9

Pain   616
Prescription and over-the-counter drugs   615
The respiratory system   612.2
Kitzinger, Rachel, 1948-
(ed) Civilization of the ancient Mediterranean: Greece and Rome. See Civilization of the ancient Mediterranean: Greece and Rome   938
KKK *See* Ku Klux Klan
Klapisch, Bob
High and tight: the rise and fall of Dwight Gooden and Darryl Strawberry   92
Klass, David
California Blue   Fic
Danger zone   Fic
Klee, Paul, 1879-1940
See/See also pages in the following book(s):
Read, Sir H. E. A concise history of modern painting   759.06
Klein, Barry T.
(ed) Reference encyclopedia of the American Indian. See Reference encyclopedia of the American Indian   970.004
Klein, Herbert S.
Bolivia   984
Klein, Jeff Z.
Mario Lemieux, ice hockey star   92
Klein, Leonard S.
(ed) African literatures in the 20th century. See African literatures in the 20th century   896
(ed) Encyclopedia of world literature in the 20th century. See Encyclopedia of world literature in the 20th century   803
Klein, Norma, 1938-1989
No more Saturday nights   Fic
About
Phy, A. S. Presenting Norma Klein   813.009
Klein, Rachel
(jt. auth) Rexer, L. American Museum of Natural History   508
Kleinedler, Steven Racek
NTC's dictionary of acronyms and abbreviations   421.03
Kleiner, Fred S.
(ed) Gardner's art through the ages. See Gardner's art through the ages   709
Kliatt   028.1
Kline, Victoria
Last lines   808.81
Klingaman, William K.
Encyclopedia of the McCarthy era   973.918
Klinkowitz, Jerome
Kurt Vonnegut   813.009
Kluger, Jeffrey
(jt. auth) Lovell, J. Lost moon: the perilous voyage of Apollo 13   629.45
Kluger, Richard
Ashes to ashes   338.1
Knapp, Bettina Liebowitz, 1926-
The Brontës   823.009
Knappman, Elizabeth Frost- *See* Frost-Knappman, Elizabeth

Koolau the leper. London, J.
In London, J. The portable Jack London p164-77 **818**
In London, J. Short stories of Jack London p350-62 **S C**

Koontz, Dean R. (Dean Ray), 1945-
Strange highways **S C**
This collection includes the following: Strange highways [novel]; The black pumpkin; Miss Attila the Hun; Down in the darkness; Ollie's hands; Snatcher; Trapped; Bruno; We three; Hardshell; Kittens; The night of the storm; Twilight of the dawn; Chase [novel]
Watchers **Fic**

Kopit, Arthur L.
End of the world
In Best American plays: 9th series—1983-1992 p95-125 **812.008**
Indians
In Best American plays: 7th series—1967-1973 p283-308 **812.008**
Oh Dad, poor Dad, Mamma's hung you in the closet and I'm feelin' so sad
In Best American plays: 5th series—1957-1963 p483-508 **812.008**
Wings
In Best American plays: 8th series—1974-1982 p473-95 **812.008**

Koppel, Ted
Nightline **791.45**

Kopper, Philip
The Smithsonian book of North American Indians. See The Smithsonian book of North American Indians **970.004**

Koran
The Koran **297**

Korea
History
Yi, K.-B. A new history of Korea **951.9**
Korea. Goulden, J. C. **951.9**
Korea: the war before Vietnam. MacDonald, C. A. **951.9**

Korean Americans
East to America: Korean American life stories **305.8**
Lee, H. Still life with rice [biography of Hongyong Baek] **92**
See/See also pages in the following book(s):
Takaki, R. T. Strangers from a different shore p270-93, 436-45 **305.8**

Korean poetry
Anthology of contemporary Korean poetry **895.7**

Korean War, 1950-1953
Blair, C. The forgotten war **951.9**
Goulden, J. C. Korea **951.9**
Hastings, M. The Korean War **951.9**
Isserman, M. The Korean War **951.9**
MacDonald, C. A. Korea: the war before Vietnam **951.9**
Stokesbury, J. L. A short history of the Korean War **951.9**
Summers, H. G. Korean War almanac **951.9**
See/See also pages in the following book(s):
Feinberg, B. S. Harry S. Truman p107-20 **92**

Manchester, W. The glory and the dream p530-66 **973.9**
Miller, M. Plain speaking: an oral biography of Harry S. Truman p265-85 **92**
Truman, M. Harry S. Truman p454-97, 503-20 **92**

Korean War almanac. Summers, H. G. **951.9**

Korem, Danny
Suburban gangs **364.1**

Koresh, David
About
Reavis, D. J. The ashes of Waco **976.4**

Korn, Jerry
The fight for Chattanooga: Chickamauga to Missionary Ridge **973.7**
War on the Mississippi: Grant's Vicksburg campaign **973.7**

Kornbluth, C. M. (Cyril M.), 1923-1958
The little black bag
In Robert Silverberg's Worlds of wonder **S C**

Kornbluth, Cyril M. *See* Kornbluth, C. M. (Cyril M.), 1923-1958

Kornicki, Peter F. (Peter Francis)
(ed) The Cambridge encyclopedia of Japan. See The Cambridge encyclopedia of Japan **952**

Kort, Michael
China under communism **951.05**
Russia **947.085**

Kosof, Anna
Battered women **362.82**
Prison life **365**

Kotlowitz, Alex
There are no children here **305.23**

Kovalevskaîà, S. V. (Sof´íà Vasil´evna), 1850-1891
See/See also pages in the following book(s):
Bell, E. T. Men of mathematics p406-32 **920**
Henderson, H. Modern mathematicians **920**
Osen, L. M. Women in mathematics p117-40 **920**

Kovalevskaîà, Sof´íà Vasil´evna *See* Kovalevskaîà, S. V. (Sof´íà Vasil´evna), 1850-1891

Kovic, Ron
Born on the Fourth of July **959.704**

Kowalchik, Claire
(ed) Rodale's illustrated encyclopedia of herbs. See Rodale's illustrated encyclopedia of herbs **635**

Kowit, Steve
In the palm of your hand **808.1**

Kozol, Jonathan
Amazing grace **362.7**
Death at an early age **370.19**
Illiterate America **370.19**
Savage inequalities **371.9**

Kraft, Michael E.
(ed) Environmental policy in the 1990s. See Environmental policy in the 1990s **363.7**

Kuehl, John Richard, 1928-
F. Scott Fitzgerald   **813.009**

Kufeld, Adam
Cuba   **972.91**

Kuhlthau, Carol Collier, 1937-
(ed) Assessment and the school library media center. See Assessment and the school library media center   **027.8**
(ed) The Virtual school library. See The Virtual school library   **027.8**

Kuipers, Barbara J.
American Indian reference and resource books for children and young adults   **016.97004**

Kuklin, Susan
Speaking out   **305.23**
What do I do now?   **362.7**

Kumar, Mina, 1966-
How I made love to a Negro
In Streetlights: illuminating tales of the urban black experience p253-60   **S C**

Kummer, Ernst Edward, 1810-1893
See/See also pages in the following book(s):
Bell, E. T. Men of mathematics p510-25   **920**

Kunhardt, Peter W.
(jt. auth) Kunhardt, P. B. Lincoln   **92**
(jt. auth) Kunhardt, P. B. P.T. Barnum   **92**

Kunhardt, Philip B., 1928-
Lincoln   **92**
P.T. Barnum   **92**
(ed) Life in Camelot. See Life in Camelot [biography of John F. Kennedy]   **92**
(ed) Life laughs last. See Life laughs last   **779**
(ed) Life: the first 50 years, 1936-1986. See Life: the first 50 years, 1936-1986   **779**

Kunhardt, Philip B., 1951-
(jt. auth) Kunhardt, P. B. Lincoln   **92**
(jt. auth) Kunhardt, P. B. P.T. Barnum   **92**

Kunitz, Stanley, 1905-
Passing through   **811**
(ed) American authors, 1600-1900. See American authors, 1600-1900   **920.003**
(ed) British authors before 1800. See British authors before 1800   **920.003**
(ed) British authors of the nineteenth century. See British authors of the nineteenth century   **920.003**
(ed) European authors, 1000-1900. See European authors, 1000-1900   **920.003**

Kuralt, Charles, 1934-1997
Charles Kuralt's America   **973.92**
A life on the road   **92**
On the road with Charles Kuralt   **973.92**

Kurian, George Thomas
Encyclopedia of the First World   **903**
Encyclopedia of the Third World   **903**
(ed) Atlas of the Third World. See Atlas of the Third World   **912**

Kurtz, Howard, 1953-
Hot air   **791.45**

Kushites *See* Cushites

Kushner, Tony
Angels in America   **812**

Kusinitz, Marc
Folk medicine   **615.8**
Tropical medicine   **616.9**

Kutenplon, Deborah
Young adult fiction by African American writers, 1968-1993   **016.813**

Kutler, Stanley I.
(ed) Encyclopedia of the United States in the twentieth century. See Encyclopedia of the United States in the twentieth century   **973.03**
(ed) Encyclopedia of the Vietnam War. See Encyclopedia of the Vietnam War   **959.704**
(ed) The Supreme Court and the Constitution. See The Supreme Court and the Constitution   **342**

Kuttner, Henry, 1915-1958
The graveyard rats
In The Horror hall of fame p226-33   **S C**
Home is the hunter
In Robert Silverberg's Worlds of wonder   **S C**
See/See also pages in the following book(s):
Science fiction writers of the golden age p141-56   **809.3**

Kuttner, Paul
Science's trickiest questions   **500**

Kutzer, M. Daphne
(ed) Writers of multicultural fiction for young adults. See Writers of multicultural fiction for young adults   **813.009**

Kuwait
History—1991, Persian Gulf War
See Persian Gulf War, 1991

Kwakiutl Indians
Fiction
Craven, M. I heard the owl call my name   **Fic**

Kyrie. Anderson, P.
In The Norton book of science fiction p201-10   **S C**

L

La Farge, Oliver, 1901-1963
Laughing Boy   **Fic**

La Flesche, Francis, d. 1932
The story of a vision
In The Singing spirit: early short stories by North American Indians p69-73   **S C**

La Flesche, Susette, 1854-1903
Nedawi
In The Singing spirit: early short stories by North American Indians p3-13   **S C**

La Fontaine, Jean de, 1621-1695
Fifty fables of La Fontaine   **841**

La Salle, René Robert Cavelier *See* La Salle, Robert Cavelier, sieur de, 1643-1687

La Salle, Robert Cavelier, sieur de, 1643-1687
See/See also pages in the following book(s):
Faber, H. The discoverers of America p228-37   **970.01**

LaMay, Craig L.
(jt. auth) Minow, N. N. Abandoned in the wasteland **302.23**

Lamb, Wendy
(ed) Ten out of ten. See Ten out of ten **812.008**

Lamb, William See Melbourne, William Lamb, 2nd Viscount, 1779-1848

The **lame** shall enter first. O'Connor, F.
In O'Connor, F. Collected works p595-632 **S C**
In O'Connor, F. The complete stories p445-82 **S C**

Lammers, Susan M.
(jt. auth) Hodgson, L. All about houseplants **635.9**

L'Amour, Louis, 1908-1988
The daybreakers. See note under L'Amour, L. The Sacketts **Fic**
Education of a wandering man **92**
Galloway. See note under L'Amour, L. The Sacketts **Fic**
Jubal Sackett. See note under L'Amour, L. The Sacketts **Fic**
Lando. See note under L'Amour, L. The Sacketts **Fic**
The lonely men. See note under L'Amour, L. The Sacketts **Fic**
Lonely on the mountain. See note under L'Amour, L. The Sacketts **Fic**
Mojave crossing. See note under L'Amour, L. The Sacketts **Fic**
Mustang man. See note under L'Amour, L. The Sacketts **Fic**
The outlaws of Mesquite **S C**
Contents: The outlaws of Mesquite; Love and the Cactus Kid; The Ghost Maker; The drift; No rest for the wicked; That Packsaddle affair; Showdown on the Tumbling T; The sixth shotgun
Ride the dark trail. See note under L'Amour, L. The Sacketts **Fic**
Ride the river. See note under L'Amour, L. The Sacketts **Fic**
Sackett. See note under L'Amour, L. The Sacketts **Fic**
The Sackett brand. See note under L'Amour, L. The Sacketts **Fic**
The Sacketts **Fic**
Sackett's land. See note under L'Amour, L. The Sacketts **Fic**
The sky-liners. See note under L'Amour, L. The Sacketts **Fic**
To the far blue mountains. See note under L'Amour, L. The Sacketts **Fic**
Treasure mountain. See note under L'Amour, L. The Sacketts **Fic**
The warrior's path. See note under L'Amour, L. The Sacketts **Fic**

Lampton, Christopher
DNA fingerprinting **614**
Science of chaos **003**
Telecommunications: from telegraphs to modems **621.382**

Lancelot (Legendary character)
Pyle, H. The story of Sir Launcelot and his companions **398.2**

The **land** ironclads. Wells, H. G.
In The Oxford book of science fiction stories p1-21 **S C**
In Wells, H. G. The complete short stories of H. G. Wells p115-38 **S C**

Land use
See also Wetlands

The **land** where the blues began. Lomax, A. **781.643**

Landau, Elaine
Alzheimer's disease **362.1**
The beauty trap **155.6**
Breast cancer **616.99**
Hooked **362.29**
Interracial dating and marriage **306.7**
The right to die **179**
Sexual harassment **305.4**
Teenage drinking **362.29**
The white power movement **322.4**

Lande, Nathaniel
Dispatches from the front **070.4**

The **landing** on Kuralei. Michener, J. A.
In Michener, J. A. Tales of the South Pacific **S C**

Landis, Geoffrey A.
Ripples in the Dirac sea
In Nebula awards 25 p12-26 **S C**

Landmarks, Literary See Literary landmarks

Lando. L'Amour, L. See note under L'Amour, L. The Sacketts **Fic**

Landon, Perceval, 1869-1927
Thurnley Abbey
In Victorian ghost stories p466-79 **S C**

Landor's cottage. Poe, E. A.
In Poe, E. A. The collected tales and poems of Edgar Allan Poe p616-25 **S C**

Lands and peoples **910.3**

The **landscape.** Colette
In Colette. The collected stories of Colette p285-87 **S C**

Landscape and dream. Krusoe, N.
In The Best American short stories, 1994 p226-31 **S C**

Landscape painting
Yaeger, B. D. The Hudson River school **759.13**

Landscape with figures. Hemingway, E.
In Hemingway, E. The complete short stories of Ernest Hemingway p590-96 **S C**

Landslide for Shakespeare. Dias, E. J.
In The Big book of large-cast plays p152-67 **812.008**

Landynski, Jacob W.
(ed) The Living U.S. Constitution. See The Living U.S. Constitution **342**

Lane, Eric
(ed) The Actor's book of scenes from new plays. See The Actor's book of scenes from new plays **808.82**

Lane, Fitz Hugh, 1804-1865
See/See also pages in the following book(s):
Novak, B. American painting of the nineteenth century p110-24 **759.13**

Large print books—*Continued*

Crutcher, C. Athletic shorts: six short stories   **S C**

Crutcher, C. Staying fat for Sarah Byrnes   **Fic**

Delany, S. Having our say   **92**

Dickinson, P. A bone from a dry sea   **Fic**

Forester, C. S. The African Queen   **Fic**

Frank, A. The diary of a young girl: the definitive edition   **92**

García Márquez, G. One hundred years of solitude   **Fic**

Gill, G. Agatha Christie   **92**

Gilstrap, J. Nathan's run   **Fic**

Grisham, J. The runaway jury   **Fic**

Hahn, M. D. The wind blows backward   **Fic**

Halberstam, D. The fifties   **973.92**

Harrison, S. Mother earth, father sky   **Fic**

Harrison, S. My sister the moon   **Fic**

Hemingway, E. A farewell to arms   **Fic**

Hemingway, E. For whom the bell tolls   **Fic**

Hemingway, E. The old man and the sea   **Fic**

Herriot, J. The Lord God made them all   **92**

Hersey, J. A bell for Adano   **Fic**

Hersey, J. Hiroshima   **940.54**

Hillerman, T. Finding Moon   **Fic**

Hoffman, A. Second nature   **Fic**

Keller, H. The story of my life   **92**

Kennedy, J. F. Profiles in courage   **920**

Kesey, K. One flew over the cuckoo's nest   **Fic**

Keyes, D. Flowers for Algernon   **Fic**

Kidder, T. Among schoolchildren   **372.1**

Kilian, P. Barbara Bush   **92**

King, M. L. Strength to love   **252**

King, S. Carrie   **Fic**

King, S. Insomnia   **Fic**

Knowles, J. A separate peace   **Fic**

Koontz, D. R. Watchers   **Fic**

Kuralt, C. Charles Kuralt's America   **973.92**

L'Engle, M. A wrinkle in time   **Fic**

London, J. The call of the wild   **Fic**

Lord, B. B. Legacies: a Chinese mosaic   **951.05**

Mayle, P. A dog's life   **828**

Mazer, N. F. After the rain   **Fic**

McCormack, J. Fields and pastures new   **636.089**

McDermott, A. At weddings and wakes   **Fic**

Mendelsohn, J. I was Amelia Earhart   **Fic**

Mitchell, M. Gone with the wind   **Fic**

Morrison, T. Beloved   **Fic**

Morrison, T. Jazz   **Fic**

Nathan, R. Portrait of Jennie   **Fic**

Oneal, Z. The language of goldfish   **Fic**

Powell, C. L. My American journey   **92**

Robinson, R. Iron horse: Lou Gehrig in his time   **92**

Sholem Aleichem. The best of Sholem Aleichem   **S C**

Smith, B. A tree grows in Brooklyn   **Fic**

Steinbeck, J. Of mice and men   **Fic**

Stewart, M. The prince and the pilgrim   **Fic**

Stryker-Rodda, H. How to climb your family tree   **929**

Tan, A. The hundred secret senses   **Fic**

Tan, A. The Joy Luck Club   **Fic**

Thomas, E. M. The hidden life of dogs   **636.7**

Thomas, E. M. The tribe of tiger   **599.74**

Traven, B. The treasure of the Sierra Madre   **Fic**

Tuchman, B. W. The first salute   **973.3**

Updike, J. Pigeon feathers, and other stories   **S C**

Wells, H. G. The war of the worlds   **Fic**

West, D. The wedding   **Fic**

Wiesel, E. All rivers run to the sea   **92**

Wolff, V. E. Make lemonade   **Fic**

Larkin, Colin
(ed) The Guinness encyclopedia of popular music. See The Guinness encyclopedia of popular music   **781.64**

Larkin, Philip
(comp) The Oxford book of twentieth-century English verse. See The Oxford book of twentieth-century English verse   **821.008**

Larner, Jeremy
The candidate
In Best American screenplays   **812.008**

Larocca, Félix E. F.
(jt. auth) Cassell, D. K. Encyclopedia of obesity and eating disorders   **616.85**

Larousse, Pierre, 1817-1875
Petit Larousse illustré. See Petit Larousse illustré   **443**

Larousse biographical dictionary   **920.003**

Larousse concise French-English, English-French dictionary   **443**

Larousse concise Spanish-English, English-Spanish dictionary   **463**

The **Larousse** desk reference   **031**

Larousse dictionary of beliefs and religions   **291.03**

Larousse dictionary of literary characters   **820.9**

Larousse dictionary of science and technology   **503**

Larousse dictionary of world folklore. Jones, A.   **398.03**

Larousse dictionary of world history   **903**

Larousse dictionary of writers   **803**

Larousse English-Spanish Spanish-English dictionary   **463**

Larry Bird's Basketball Birdwise. See Bird, L. Bird on basketball   **796.323**

Larsen, Jesse
(jt. auth) Bauermeister, E. 500 great books by women   **016.3054**

Larsen, Nella
Freedom
In The Oxford book of women's writing in the United States p95-99   **810.8**
Helga Crane
In Invented lives p174-231   **S C**

Larsen, Nella—*Continued*
Passing [excerpt]
In The Portable Harlem Renaissance reader
p460-85 **810.8**
Quicksand [excerpt]
In The Portable Harlem Renaissance reader
p410-60 **810.8**
Sanctuary
In Calling the wind p34-38 **S C**
See/See also pages in the following book(s):
Black American prose writers of the Harlem Renaissance p94-107 **810.9**
Black American women fiction writers p103-16 **813.009**
Larsen, Rebecca, 1944-
Paul Robeson, hero before his time **92**
Larson, Erik
Lethal passage **364.1**
Larson, Gary
The far side **741.5**
The prehistory of the Far side **741.5**
Lasers
Billings, C. W. Lasers **621.36**
Lash, Joseph P., 1909-1987
Eleanor and Franklin **92**
Helen and teacher: the story of Helen Keller and Anne Sullivan Macy **92**
Laska, Vera, 1923-
(ed) Women in the resistance and in the Holocaust. See Women in the resistance and in the Holocaust **940.53**
Laskin, David, 1953-
Braving the elements **551.6**
Lass, Abraham Harold, 1907-
The Facts on File dictionary of classical, biblical, and literary allusions **803**
(jt. auth) Cole, S. The Facts on File dictionary of 20th-century allusions **031.02**
The **last** Algonquin [biography of Joe Two Trees] Kazimiroff, T. L. **92**
The **last** analysis. Bellow, S.
In Best American plays: 6th series—1963-1967 p97-136 **812.008**
The **last** battle. Ryan, C. **940.54**
Last chance to see. Adams, D. **591.5**
The **last** clear definite function of man. Steinbeck, J.
In Steinbeck, J. The portable Steinbeck **818**
The **last** Comanche chief: the life and times of Quanah Parker. Neeley, B. **92**
The **last** enchantment. Stewart, M.
In Stewart, M. Mary Stewart's Merlin trilogy **Fic**
The **last** fire. Colette
In Colette. The collected stories of Colette p97-99 **S C**
Last flight. Earhart, A. **629.13**
The **last** flower. Thurber, J.
In Thurber, J. Writings and drawings **818**
The **last** gaze. Singer, I. B.
In Singer, I. B. The death of Methuselah and other stories p220-32 **S C**

The **last** good country. Hemingway, E.
In Hemingway, E. The complete short stories of Ernest Hemingway p504-44 **S C**
In Hemingway, E. The Nick Adams stories p70-132 **S C**
The **last** harvest. Raeburn, P. **338.1**
The **last** house in C— Street. Craik, D. M. M.
In Victorian ghost stories p44-54 **S C**
Last kiss. Fitzgerald, F. S.
In Fitzgerald, F. S. The short stories of F. Scott Fitzgerald p757-72 **S C**
The **last** laugh. Lawrence, D. H.
In Lawrence, D. H. The complete short stories v3 **S C**
The **last** leaf. Henry, O.
In Henry, O. The best short stories of O. Henry **S C**
Last lines. Kline, V. **808.81**
"The **last** minstrel in California". Villarreal, J. A.
In Iguana dreams **S C**
The **last** Mohican. Malamud, B.
In Malamud, B. The stories of Bernard Malamud p46-72 **S C**
Last morning. Pilcher, R.
In Pilcher, R. Flowers in the rain & other stories **S C**
The **last** Neanderthal. Tattersall, I. **573.3**
The **last** night of the world. Bradbury, R.
In Bradbury, R. The illustrated man **S C**
In Bradbury, R. The stories of Ray Bradbury p193-96 **S C**
The **last** of the belles. Fitzgerald, F. S.
In Fitzgerald, F. S. The short stories of F. Scott Fitzgerald p449-63 **S C**
In Fitzgerald, F. S. The stories of F. Scott Fitzgerald p240-53 **S C**
The **last** of the Huggermuggers: a giant story. Cranch, C. P.
In Masterpieces of fantasy and enchantment p339-67 **S C**
The **last** of the Mohicans. Cooper, J. F. **Fic**
Last of the red hot lovers. Simon, N.
In Simon N. The comedy of Neil Simon p583-657 **812**
The **last** panda. Schaller, G. B. **599.74**
Last post. O'Connor, F.
In O'Connor, F. Collected stories p679-86 **S C**
The **last** question. Asimov, I.
In Asimov, I. The complete stories v1 p290-300 **S C**
The **last** safe place on earth. Peck, R. **Fic**
The **last** seven months of Anne Frank. Lindwer, W. **940.53**
The **last** shot. Frey, D. **796.323**
Last summer at Mars Hill. Hand, E.
In Nebula awards 31 p272-320 **S C**
Last train to Memphis: the rise of Elvis Presley. Guralnick, P. **92**
The **last** trump. Asimov, I.
In Asimov, I. The complete stories v1 p106-19 **S C**

The **last** unicorn. Beagle, P. S.   **Fic**

The **last** Yankee. Miller, A.
   In Miller, A. The portable Arthur Miller
   p447-88   **812**

Late and posthumous poems, 1968-1974. Neruda,
P.   **861**

The **late** bud. Aidoo, A. A.
   In Rites of passage p33-44   **S C**

Late developments. Mullins, T.
   In Bad behavior p191-204   **S C**

A **late** encounter with the enemy. O'Connor, F.
   In O'Connor, F. Collected works p252-62
    S C
   In O'Connor, F. The complete stories p134-44
    S C
   In The Oxford book of American short stories
   p397-407   **S C**
   In The Oxford book of women's writing in
   the United States p126-34   **810.8**

The **late** Henry Conran. O'Connor, F.
   In O'Connor, F. Collected stories p13-19
    S C

The **Late** Middle Ages   **940.1**

Latimer, Lewis Howard, 1848-1928
See/See also pages in the following book(s):
   Abdul-Jabbar, K. Black profiles in courage
   p178-96   **920**

Latin America
   See also South America
   Dostert, P. E. Latin America   **980**
   The South American handbook   **980**
Biography—Dictionaries
   Dictionary of Hispanic biography   **920.003**
Civilization
   Fuentes, C. The buried mirror   **946**
Dictionaries
   The Cambridge encyclopedia of Latin America
   and the Caribbean   **980**
   Encyclopedia of Latin American history and cul-
   ture   **980**
Fiction
   García Márquez, G. Love in the time of cholera
    Fic
History
   Chapman, V. L. Latin American history on file
    980
   Winn, P. Americas   **980**
See/See also pages in the following book(s):
   Christopher Columbus and his legacy: opposing
   viewpoints   **970.01**

Latin American art
   Latin American artists of the twentieth century
    709.8

Latin American artists of the twentieth century
    709.8

Latin American authors *See* Authors, Latin
American

Latin American cooking
   Karoff, B. South American cooking   **641.5**

Latin American history on file. Chapman, V. L.
    980

Latin American literature
   See also Mexican literature

Bio-bibliography
   Flores, A. Spanish American authors
    920.003
History and criticism
   Hispanic literature criticism   **860.9**
   The Latin American short story   **863.009**
   Masterpieces of Latino literature   **860.9**
The **Latin** American short story   **863.009**

Latin authors *See* Authors, Latin

Latin language
Dictionaries
   Cassell's Latin dictionary   **473**
   Oxford Latin dictionary   **473**

Latin literature
   See also Classical literature
Collections
   The Norton book of classical literature
    880.8
   The Portable Roman reader   **870.8**
History and criticism
   Hamilton, E. The Roman way   **870.9**

Latina: women's voices from the borderlands
    810.8

Latinas. Garza, H.   **305.4**

The **Latino** encyclopedia   **305.8**

Latino voices   **810.8**

Latinos (U.S.) *See* Hispanic Americans

Latinos in the making of the United States. Cockcroft, J. D.   **305.8**

Latrobe, Kathy Howard
   Readers theatre for young adults   **808.5**

Laughing Boy. La Farge, O.   **Fic**

The **laughing** man. Salinger, J. D.
   In Salinger, J. D. Nine stories p83-110
    S C

Laughlin, Mildred, 1922-1994
   (jt. auth) Latrobe, K. H. Readers theatre for
   young adults   **808.5**

"The **laughter** of my father". Villarreal, J. A.
   In Iguana dreams   **S C**

Laughton, Charles, 1899-1962
   (jt. auth) Brecht, B. Galileo   **832**

Laumer, Keith, 1925-1993
   The night of the trolls
   In The Mammoth book of new world science
   fiction p51-96   **S C**

Laurel, Stan, 1890-1965
See/See also pages in the following book(s):
   Kerr, W. The silent clowns p316-35   **791.43**

Laurent, Monique
   Rodin   **92**

Laurents, Arthur, 1918-
   Home of the brave
   In Best plays of the modern American the-
   atre: 2nd series p557-96   **812.008**

Lautrec, Henri de Toulouse- *See* Toulouse-
Lautrec, Henri de, 1864-1901

Lavender, David Sievert, 1910-
   The way to the Western sea   **973.4**

Lavin, Mary, 1912-1996
   My vocation
   In The Oxford book of short stories p432-42
    S C

Layman, Nancy S., 1942-
Sexual harassment in American secondary
schools **344**

Lazarus, John
The opera handbook **792.5**

Lazarus laughed. O'Neill, E.
In O'Neill, E. Complete plays v2 **812**
In O'Neill, E. Nine plays p359-458 **812**

LC *See* Library of Congress

Lê, Minh Khuê
Tony D.
In The Other side of heaven p210-22
S C
(ed) The Other side of heaven. See The Other
side of heaven **S C**

Le Carré, John, 1931-
The spy who came in from the cold **Fic**
About
John le Carré **823.009**

Le Fanu, Joseph Sheridan, 1814-1873
An account of some strange disturbances in
Aungier Street
In Victorian ghost stories p19-36 **S C**
A chapter in the history of a Tyrone family
In The Oxford book of gothic tales p102-32
S C
Green tea
In The Horror hall of fame p37-70 **S C**
In The Oxford book of Irish short stories p78-
108 **S C**
Sir Dominick Sarsfield
In Classic ghost stories p1-15 **S C**
Squire Toby's will
In The Oxford book of English ghost stories
p25-50 **S C**

Le Guin, Ursula K., 1929-
A fisherman of the inland sea **S C**
Contents: The first contact with the Gorgonids; Newton's
sleep; The ascent of the north face; The rock that changed things;
The kerastion; The Shobies' story; Dancing to Ganam; Another
story; or, A fisherman of the inland sea
Four ways to forgiveness **S C**
Contents: Betrayals; Forgiveness Day; A man of the people; A
woman's liberation
Ile forest
In American short story masterpieces
S C
The matter of Seggri
In Nebula awards 30 p253-92 **S C**
May's lion
In The Oxford book of women's writing in
the United States p190-96 **810.8**
The new Atlantis
In The Norton book of science fiction p317-
36 **S C**
The ones who walk away from Omelas
In The Norton book of American short stories
p566-71 **S C**
The rule of names
In Masterpieces of fantasy and enchantment
p3-12 **S C**
Semley's necklace
In The Oxford book of science fiction stories
p322-39 **S C**
She unnames them
In We are the stories we tell **S C**

The Shobies' story
In Nebula awards 26 p19-45 **S C**
Solitude
In Nebula awards 31 p29-58 **S C**
Sur
In The Best American short stories of the
eighties p157-73 **S C**
Texts
In The Oxford book of American short stories
p552-55 **S C**
The wife's story
In The Oxford book of modern fairy tales
p418-21 **S C**
(ed) The Norton book of science fiction. See
The Norton book of science fiction **S C**

Le Vert, Suzanne *See* LeVert, Suzanne

Leach, Maria, 1892-1977
(ed) Funk & Wagnalls standard dictionary of
folklore, mythology, and legend. See Funk &
Wagnalls standard dictionary of folklore, mythology, and legend **398.03**

Leadbelly, 1885-1949
See/See also pages in the following book(s):
Davis, F. The history of the blues p164-71
781.643

The leader. Ionesco, E.
In Ionesco, E. Rhinoceros, and other plays
842

The leader of the people. Steinbeck, J.
In Steinbeck, J. The portable Steinbeck
818

Leadership [African Americans: voices of tri-
umph] **920**

Leaf by Niggle. Tolkien, J. R. R.
In Tolkien, J. R. R. Poems and stories p193-
220 **828**

The league of the old men. London, J.
In London, J. Short stories of Jack London
p155-68 **S C**

Leahy, Christopher W.
Borror, D. J. A field guide to the insects of
America north of Mexico **595.7**

Leakey, Louis Seymour Bazett, 1903-1972
About
Morell, V. Ancestral passions **920**

Leakey, Mary D., 1913-1996
About
Morell, V. Ancestral passions **920**

Leakey, Richard E., 1944-
The origin of humankind **573.2**
Origins **573.2**
Origins reconsidered **573.2**
The sixth extinction **304.2**
About
Morell, V. Ancestral passions **920**

Leaks, Sylvester
The blues begins
In The Best short stories by Negro writers
p275-87 **S C**

The leaning tower. Porter, K. A.
In Porter, K. A. The collected stories of Katherine Anne Porter **S C**

The leaning tower, and other stories. Porter, K. A.
In Porter, K. A. The collected stories of Katherine Anne Porter **S C**

Learn to sail. Conner, D.   **797.1**

Learning, Art of *See* Study skills

Learning, Psychology of *See* Psychology of learning

(Learning about) machine sex. Dorsey, C. J.
In The Norton book of science fiction p746-61   **S C**

Learning about—the Holocaust. Stephens, E. C.
    016.94053

Learning and scholarship
See also Education
See/See also pages in the following book(s):
Durant, W. J. The age of faith p903-30
    940.1
Durant, W. J. The age of Louis XIV p481-94
    940.2
Durant, W. J. The Reformation p230-57
    940.2
Emerson, R. W. The portable Emerson p51-71
    818

Learning disabilities
See also Attention deficit disorder
Cummings, R. W. The survival guide for teenagers with LD* (*learning differences)
    371.9
Knox, J. M. Learning disabilities   **618.92**
Lewis, E.-L. Help yourself: handbook for college-bound students with learning disabilities
    378
Peterson's colleges with programs for students with learning disabilities   **378.73**
Fiction
Wolff, V. E. Probably still Nick Swansen
    Fic

Learning resource centers *See* Instructional materials centers

The **learning tree**. Parks, G.   **Fic**

Least Heat Moon, William *See* Heat Moon, William Least

Leatherbarrow, William J.
Fedor Dostoevsky   **891.7**

Leatherwood, Stephen
The Sierra Club handbook of whales and dolphins   **599.5**

The **leave-taking**. Bradbury, R.
In Bradbury, R. The stories of Ray Bradbury p425-28   **S C**

Leaves of grass. Whitman, W.   **811**
also in Whitman, W. Poetry and prose
    818

Leaving. Vassanji, M. G.
In The Heinemann book of contemporary African short stories p114-20   **S C**

The **leaving**. Wilson, B.
In Wilson, B. The leaving and other stories
    S C

The **leaving** and other stories. Wilson, B.
    S C

Leavitt, David, 1961-
Gravity
In The Oxford book of American short stories p741-45   **S C**
The lost language of cranes [excerpt]
In Growing up gay p110-16   **808.8**

Leavitt, Judith Walzer
Typhoid Mary   **614.5**

Lebanon
History
Friedman, T. L. From Beirut to Jerusalem
    956

Lebow, Irwin
Information highways and byways   **302.2**

LeBow, Michael D.
Overweight teenagers   **613.2**

Lechery. Phillips, J. A.
In The Norton book of American short stories p742-48   **S C**

Leckie, Robert
George Washington's war   **973.3**
Okinawa   **940.54**

The **lecture**. Singer, I. B.
In The Oxford book of American short stories p488-503   **S C**

Ledbetter, Huddie *See* Leadbelly, 1885-1949

The **ledge**. Hall, L. S.
In American short story masterpieces
    S C

Lee, Andrea, 1953-
Mother
In Children of the night p163-71   **S C**
Winter barley
In The Best American short stories, 1993 p199-216   **S C**

Lee, Cherylene
Hollywood and the pits
In American dragons: twenty-five Asian American voices p34-47   **810.8**

Lee, Don L. *See* Madhubuti, Haki R.

Lee, Gus
China boy   **Fic**
Toussaint
In Growing up Asian American p87-108
    810.8

Lee, Harper, 1926-
To kill a mockingbird   **Fic**

Lee, Helen Elaine
Silences
In Children of the night p269-79   **S C**

Lee, Helie
Still life with rice [biography of Hongyong Baek]   **92**

Lee, Hermione
Willa Cather   **92**

Lee, Marie G.
Summer of my Korean soldier
In American eyes p37-48   **S C**

Lee, Robert E. (Robert Edward), 1807-1870
About
Lee takes command: from Seven Days to Second Bull Run   **973.7**
Marrin, A. Virginia's general: Robert E. Lee and the Civil War   **92**
Smith, G. Lee and Grant   **92**
Thomas, E. M. Robert E. Lee   **92**
See/See also pages in the following book(s):
Catton, B. Gettysburg p72-107   **973.7**

Lessem, Don
The Dinosaur Society's dinosaur encyclopedia
567.9
(jt. auth) Horner, J. R. The complete T. rex
567.9

Lesseps, Ferdinand Marie de, vicomte, 1805-1894
See/See also pages in the following book(s):
McCullough, D. G. The path between the seas
972.87

Lessing, Doris May, 1919-
African laughter 968.91
Mrs. Fortescue
In The Oxford book of short stories p487-500
S C
The old chief Mshlanga
In Somehow tenderness survives p19-35
S C

Lessing, Gotthold Ephraim, 1729-1781
See/See also pages in the following book(s):
Durant, W. J. Rousseau and revolution p508-17
940.2
Jaspers, K. The great philosophers 109
The **lesson.** Bambara, T. C.
In Calling the wind p348-54 S C
In Children of the night p232-39 S C
The **lesson.** Ionesco, E.
In Ionesco, E. Four plays p43-78 842
A **lesson** before dying. Gaines, E. J. Fic
A **lesson** from the heart. Yabu, J.
In American dragons: twenty-five Asian American voices p161-65 810.8
The **lessons** of history. Durant, W. J. 901
Lester, Julius
Black folktales 398.2
Othello Fic
To be a slave 326
Let history judge. Medvedev, R. A. 947.084
Let my people go. White, D. G.
In The Young Oxford history of African Americans 305.8
Let the trumpet sound: the life of Martin Luther King, Jr. Oates, S. B. 92
Let us now praise famous men. Agee, J.
976.1
Lethal passage. Larson, E. 364.1
Let's get together. Asimov, I.
In Asimov, I. The complete stories v2 p217-30 S C
A **letter.** Colette
In Colette. The collected stories of Colette p45-50 S C
The **letter.** Malamud, B.
In Malamud, B. The stories of Bernard Malamud p155-61 S C
The **letter.** Maugham, W. S.
In Maugham, W. S. Collected short stories v4
S C
Letter from a dogfighter's aunt, deceased. Powell, P.
In The Literary ghost p216-24 S C
Letter from his father. Gordimer, N.
In The Literary ghost p314-29 S C

Letter of Fus Fixico, January 11, 1907. Posey, A.
In The Singing spirit: early short stories by North American Indians p123-24
S C
Letter of Fus Fixico, March 23, 1906. Posey, A.
In The Singing spirit: early short stories by North American Indians p121-22
S C
Letter writing
See also Business letters
Lettering
Biegeleisen, J. I. The ABC of lettering
745.6
Letters
Dear author 028.5
Letters from a World War II GI. Winston, K.
940.54
Letters from my father. Butler, R. O.
In The Other side of heaven p308-12
S C
Letters from the inside. Marsden, J. Fic
Letters from the Samantha. Helprin, M.
In American short story masterpieces
S C
In The Norton book of American short stories p722-32 S C
Letters of the sun, letters of the moon. Levy, I.
In Coming of age p139-53 808.8
Letters to America 811.008
Leuchtenburg, William Edward, 1922-
Franklin D. Roosevelt and the New Deal, 1932-1940 973.917
(jt. auth) Morison, S. E. The growth of the American Republic 973
Leukemia
Personal narratives
Lund, D. H. Eric 92
Levenson, J. C. (Jacob Claver), 1922-
(ed) Crane, S. Prose and poetry 818
Levenson, Jacob Claver *See* Levenson, J. C. (Jacob Claver), 1922-
Leventhal, Alice Walker *See* Walker, Alice, 1944-
LeVert, Marianne
AIDS 616.97
The welfare system 361.6
LeVert, Suzanne
Huey Long 92
Teens face to face with chronic illness
362.1
Levertov, Denise, 1923-
Sands of the well 811
See/See also pages in the following book(s):
Breslin, J. E. B. From modern to contemporary
811.009
Levi, Peter, 1931-
Atlas of the Greek world 938
The life and times of William Shakespeare
822.3
Levi, Primo, 1919-1987
The collected poems of Primo Levi 851
The drowned and the saved 940.53

Life sciences
Dictionaries
Encyclopedia of life sciences   **574.03**

Life skills
Abner, A. Finding our way   **305.23**
Bode, J. Beating the odds   **305.23**
Cummings, R. W. The survival guide for teenagers with LD* (*learning differences)   **371.9**
Kohl, C. The string on a roast won't catch fire in the oven   **305.23**
Santamaria, P. High performance through self-management   **640**

Life styles *See* Lifestyles

Life: the '60s   **779**

Life: the first 50 years, 1936-1986   **779**

Life, the universe and everything. Adams, D. See note under Adams, D. The Hitchhiker's Guide to the Galaxy   **Fic**

Life with father. Lindsay, H.
In Best plays of the modern American theatre: 2nd series p131-80   **812.008**
In The Most popular plays of the American theater p11-88   **812.008**

Life without father. Popenoe, D.   **306.8**

The life you save may be your own. O'Connor, F.
In O'Connor, F. Collected works p172-83   **S C**
In O'Connor, F. The complete stories p145-56   **S C**

Lifeguard. Updike, J.
In The Oxford book of short stories p539-44   **S C**
In Updike, J. Pigeon feathers, and other stories p211-20   **S C**

Lifesaving
See also First aid

Lifestyles
See/See also pages in the following book(s):
Naisbitt, J. Megatrends 2000 p118-53   **303.4**

Lifton, Betty Jean
A place called Hiroshima   **940.54**

Lifton, Robert Jay, 1926-
Hiroshima in America   **940.54**

Ligeia. Poe, E. A.
In Poe, E. A. The collected tales and poems of Edgar Allan Poe p654-66   **S C**

Light breathing. Bunin, I. A.
In The Portable twentieth-century Russian reader p59-65   **891.7**

Light in August. Faulkner, W.   **Fic**

The light in the forest. Richter, C.   **Fic**

Light of other days. Shaw, B.
In Robert Silverberg's Worlds of wonder   **S C**

The light of the world. Hemingway, E.
In Hemingway, E. The complete short stories of Ernest Hemingway p292-97   **S C**
In Hemingway, E. The Nick Adams stories p39-46   **S C**
In Hemingway, E. The short stories of Ernest Hemingway p384-91   **S C**

Light one candle. Ganor, S.   **940.53**

The light princess. MacDonald, G.
In The Oxford book of modern fairy tales p61-98   **S C**

Light verse. Asimov, I.
In Asimov, I. The complete stories v2 p437-40   **S C**

Lighter, J. E. (Jonathan E.)
(ed) Random House historical dictionary of American slang. See Random House historical dictionary of American slang v1   **427**

Lighter, Jonathan E. *See* Lighter, J. E. (Jonathan E.)

The Lightning within   **S C**

Lights, camera, poetry!   **811.008**

Like a bug on a windshield. Block, L.
In Bad behavior p47-66   **S C**

Like Argus of the ancient times. London, J.
In London, J. Short stories of Jack London p667-89   **S C**

Like Lauren Bacall. Brooks, M.
In Brooks, M. Paradise Café and other stories p106-14   **S C**

Like mother used to make. Jackson, S.
In Jackson, S. The lottery   **S C**

Like sisters on the homefront. Williams-Garcia, R.   **Fic**

Like that. McCullers, C.
In McCullers, C. Collected stories p47-57   **S C**

Like water for chocolate. Esquivel, L.   **Fic**

Lilly's hunger. Lacy, B. A.
In Streetlights: illuminating tales of the urban black experience p261-65   **S C**

Lily. Bonner, C.   **Fic**

Lily Daw and the three ladies. Welty, E.
In Welty, E. The collected stories of Eudora Welty p3-11   **S C**

The lily's quest. Hawthorne, N.
In Hawthorne, N. Tales and sketches; A wonder book for girls and boys; Tanglewood tales for girls and boys p685-91   **S C**

Lim, Genny
Bitter cane
In The Oxford book of women's writing in the United States p407-40   **810.8**

Limerick, Patricia Nelson, 1951-
Brooks, D. Sweet medicine   **970.004**

The Limerick gloves. Edgeworth, M.
In The Oxford book of Irish short stories p27-51   **S C**

Limitations of life. Hughes, L.
In Black theatre USA   **812.008**

The limits of independence. Salmon, M.
In The Young Oxford history of women in the United States   **305.4**

The limits of power. Greene, J. R.   **973.924**

Limón, Graciela
In search of Bernabe [excerpt]
In Latina: women's voices from the borderlands p265-72   **810.8**

Lin, Julia C.
Modern Chinese poetry   **895.1**

The little mermaid. Andersen, H. C.
In Andersen, H. C. Tales and stories
S C

Little miracles, kept promises. Cisneros, S.
In Cisneros, S. Woman Hollering Creek and
other stories S C

The little mother. O'Connor, F.
In O'Connor, F. Collected stories p355-80
S C

Little mother up the Morderberg. Wells, H. G.
In Wells, H. G. The complete short stories of
H. G. Wells p575-86 S C

Little murders. Feiffer, J.
In Best American plays: 7th series—1967-
1973 p467-91 812.008

A little night music. Wheeler, H. C.
In Best American plays: 8th series—1974-
1982 p182-227 812.008

Little old spy. Hughes, L.
In Hughes, L. Short stories S C

A little place off the Edgware Road. Greene, G.
In The Literary ghost p336-41 S C

The little prince. Saint-Exupéry, A. de Fic

The little regiment. Crane, S.
In The Oxford book of American short stories
p225-43 S C

Little terror. Barnard, R.
In Masterpieces of mystery and suspense
p222-31 S C

The little virgin. Hughes, L.
In Hughes, L. Short stories S C

The little willow. Towers, F.
In Classic English short stories, 1930-1955
p42-57 S C

A little woman. Kafka, F.
In Kafka, F. The complete stories S C

Littlefield, Daniel C.
Revolutionary citizens
In The Young Oxford history of African
Americans 305.8

Littleton, C. Scott
(ed) Eastern wisdom. See Eastern wisdom
291

Litwack, Leon F.
(ed) Black leaders of the nineteenth century. See
Black leaders of the nineteenth century
920

Litz, A. Walton
(ed) Modern American women writers. See
Modern American women writers 810.9

Liungman, Carl G., 1938-
Dictionary of symbols 302.2

Live (Musical group)
See/See also pages in the following book(s):
Reisfeld, R. This is the sound 781.66

Lively, Penelope, 1933-
Revenant as typewriter
In The Literary ghost p156-70 S C

Liver
Diseases
See/See also pages in the following book(s):
Roueché, B. The medical detectives p218-35,
345-60 616

The lives and times of Archy & Mehitabel. Marquis, D. 817

The lives of a cell. Thomas, L. 574

The lives of the dead. O'Brien, T.
In O'Brien, T. The things they carried
S C

Lives of the great songs 782.42

Lives of the poets. Untermeyer, L. 920

The lives of whales and dolphins. Connor, R. C.
599.5

The lives to come. Kitcher, P. 573.2

The living [short story] Dillard, A.
In Dillard, A. The Annie Dillard reader
818

The living and the dead. Hendrickson, P.
959.704

The living earth book of North American trees.
Jonas, G. 582.16

Living snakes of the world in color. Mehrtens, J.
M. 597.9

Living space. Asimov, I.
In Asimov, I. The complete stories v1 p77-88
S C

Living the dream. Olajuwon, H. 92

Living together *See* Unmarried couples

The Living U.S. Constitution 342

Living with death and dying. Kübler-Ross, E.
155.9

Living with multiple sclerosis. Shuman, R.
616.8

Livingston, A. D., 1932-
Edible plants and animals 641

Livingston, Helen
(jt. auth) Livingston, A. D. Edible plants and
animals 641

Livingston, Myra Cohn
(comp) A Time to talk. See A Time to talk
808.81

Livingston, Myrtle Smith
For unborn children
In Black theatre USA 812.008

Livingstone, Marco
Pop art: a continuing history 709.04

Livvie. Welty, E.
In Welty, E. The collected stories of Eudora
Welty p228-39 S C

Lizard. Covington, D. Fic

The Lizard husband
In Hearne, B. G. Beauties and beasts p35-38
398.2

Lizards in Jamshyd's courtyard. Faulkner, W.
In Faulkner, W. Uncollected stories of William Faulkner p135-51 S C

LJ/Library Journal. See Library Journal
020.5

Llewellyn, Richard, 1906-1983
How green was my valley Fic

Llewellyn-Jones, Derek
(jt. auth) Abraham, S. Eating disorders
616.85

Llosa, Ricardo Pau- *See* Pau-Llosa, Ricardo,
1954-

London, Jack, 1876-1916—*Continued*
of John Harned; The night-born; War; Told in the drooling ward; The Mexican; The pearls of Parlay; Wonder of woman; The red one; On the Makaloa mat; The tears of Ah Kim; Shin bones; When Alice told her soul; Like Argus of the ancient times; The princess; The water baby

To build a fire (1908)
In The Norton book of American short stories p231-44   **S C**
White Fang   **Fic**
About
Labor, E. Jack London   **813.009**

London, Jonathan, 1947-
Hands
In Am I blue? p215-23   **S C**

London (England)
Fiction
Pullman, P. The ruby in the smoke   **Fic**
Intellectual life
Paterson, J. Edwardians   **942.1**

Loneliness. Anderson, S.
In Anderson, S. Winesburg, Ohio   **S C**

The **lonely** men. L'Amour, L. See note under L'Amour, L. The Sacketts   **Fic**

Lonely on the mountain. L'Amour, L. See note under L'Amour, L. The Sacketts   **Fic**

Lonesome dove. McMurtry, L.   **Fic**

Long, David E.
The anatomy of terrorism   **303.6**

Long, Huey Pierce, 1893-1935
About
LeVert, S. Huey Long   **92**
Williams, T. H. Huey Long   **92**
See/See also pages in the following book(s):
Lindop, E. Assassinations that shook America p57-68   **364.1**

Long, Richard A., 1927-
The black tradition in American modern dance   **792.8**

Long, Robert Emmet, 1934-
(ed) Banking scandals: the S&Ls and BCCI. See Banking scandals: the S&Ls and BCCI   **364.1**
(ed) Censorship. See Censorship [Reference shelf]   **323.44**
(ed) Criminal sentencing. See Criminal sentencing   **345**
(ed) Drugs in America. See Drugs in America   **363.4**
(ed) Immigration. See Immigration [Reference shelf]   **325.73**
(ed) Immigration to the U.S. See Immigration to the U.S.   **325.73**
(ed) Religious cults in America. See Religious cults in America   **291**
(ed) Suicide. See Suicide   **362.2**

Long after midnight. Bradbury, R.
In Bradbury, R. The stories of Ray Bradbury p812-16   **S C**

Long black song. Wright, R.
In Wright, R. Uncle Tom's children   **S C**

A **long** day in November. Gaines, E. J.
In The Best short stories by Negro writers p359-402   **S C**
In Calling the wind p311-47   **S C**

Long day's journey into night. O'Neill, E.   **812**
also in O'Neill, E. Complete plays v3   **812**

Long distances. Rhodes, J. P.
In Children of the night p172-79   **S C**

A **long** fatal love chase. Alcott, L. M.   **Fic**

Long Island (N.Y.)
Fiction
Fitzgerald, F. S. The Great Gatsby   **Fic**

The **long** rain. Bradbury, R.
In Bradbury, R. The illustrated man   **S C**
In Bradbury, R. The stories of Ray Bradbury p208-19   **S C**

The **long** road to Ummera. O'Connor, F.
In O'Connor, F. Collected stories p48-55   **S C**

The **long** run. Wharton, E.
In Wharton, E. The selected short stories of Edith Wharton p229-52   **S C**

The **long** valley. Steinbeck, J.
In Steinbeck, J. The grapes of wrath and other writings, 1936-1941   **818**

The **long** voyage home. O'Neill, E.
In O'Neill, E. Complete plays v1   **812**

Long walk to forever. Vonnegut, K.
In Vonnegut, K. Welcome to the monkey house   **S C**

Long walk to freedom: the autobiography of Nelson Mandela. Mandela, N.   **92**

The **long** way out. Fitzgerald, F. S.
In Fitzgerald, F. S. The stories of F. Scott Fitzgerald p443-47   **S C**

A **long** way up. See Valens, E. G. The other side of the mountain: the story of Jill Kinmont   **92**

Longevity
See also Aging; Old age

Longford, Elizabeth Harman Pakenham, Countess of, 1906-
The Queen: the life of Elizabeth II   **92**

Longitude
Sobel, D. Longitude   **526**

Longman dictionary of 20th century biography. See A Dictionary of twentieth-century world biography   **920.003**

Longsworth, Polly
The world of Emily Dickinson   **92**

Lonsdale, Roger H.
(ed) The New Oxford book of eighteenth century verse. See The New Oxford book of eighteenth century verse   **821.008**

Look homeward, angel. Frings, K.
In Best American plays: 5th series—1957-1963 p237-76   **812.008**

Look homeward, angel. Wolfe, T.   **Fic**

Looking backward: 2000-1887. Bellamy, E.   **Fic**

The **lookout.** Colter, C.
In Calling the wind p305-10   **S C**

Lookout Mountain, Battle of, 1863
See/See also pages in the following book(s):
Korn, J. The fight for Chattanooga: Chickamauga to Missionary Ridge   **973.7**

Loos, Anita, 1893-1981
Liquor makes you smart
In The Norton book of American short stories
p311-18 **S C**

Loose ends. Weller, M.
In Best American plays: 8th series—1974-
1982 p337-68 **812.008**

Lopez, Barry Holstun, 1945-
Arctic dreams **998**

Lopez, Donald S., 1923-
Aviation **629.13**

Lopez, Jack
In the south
In Iguana dreams **S C**

Lopez, Luis E. *See* Kanastoga, Wasabi

López, Tiffany Ana
(ed) Growing up Chicana/o. See Growing up
Chicana/o **810.8**

Lord, Bette Bao
Legacies: a Chinese mosaic **951.05**
Spring Moon **Fic**

Lord, Walter, 1917-
Day of infamy **940.54**
The night lives on **910.4**
A night to remember **910.4**

The **Lord** God made them all. Herriot, J. **92**

Lord Jim. Conrad, J. **Fic**

Lord Mountdrago. Maugham, W. S.
In Maugham, W. S. Collected short stories v2
S C

The **lord** of the Dynamos. Wells, H. G.
In Wells, H. G. The complete short stories of
H. G. Wells p284-93 **S C**

Lord of the Flies. Golding, W. **Fic**

The **lord** of the rings. Chance, J. **823.009**

The **lord** of the rings. Tolkien, J. R. R. **Fic**

Lorde, Audre
See/See also pages in the following book(s):
Contemporary black American poets and drama-
tists p90-105 **810.9**

Lorenz, Konrad
On aggression **152.4**

Loring, F. G.
The tomb of Sarah
In Victorian ghost stories p431-41 **S C**

Los Angeles (Calif.)
Fiction
Block, F. L. Weetzie Bat **Fic**
Fitch, J. Kicks **Fic**
Santiago, D. Famous all over town **Fic**
Social conditions
Fremon, C. Father Greg and the homeboys
361.7

Loser. Mulkerns, V.
In The Oxford book of Irish short stories
p437-44 **S C**

Loshikl. Singer, I. B.
In Singer, I. B. The image and other stories
p128-39 **S C**

Loss of breath. Poe, E. A.
In Poe, E. A. The collected tales and poems
of Edgar Allan Poe p395-404 **S C**

Loss of Eden: a biography of Charles and Anne
Morrow Lindbergh. Milton, J. **92**

Lost Bird, d. 1920
About
Flood, R. S. Lost Bird of Wounded Knee
92

Lost Bird of Wounded Knee. Flood, R. S.
92

The **lost** blend. Henry, O.
In Henry, O. The best short stories of O.
Henry **S C**

The **lost** boy. Wolfe, T.
In Wolfe, T. The complete short stories of
Thomas Wolfe p359-80 **S C**

Lost children *See* Missing children

The **lost** cities of Africa. Davidson, B. **960**

Lost city of the Incas. Bingham, H. **985**

The **lost** decade. Fitzgerald, F. S.
In Fitzgerald, F. S. The short stories of F.
Scott Fitzgerald p747-50 **S C**
In Fitzgerald, F. S. The stories of F. Scott
Fitzgerald p470-73 **S C**

Lost face. London, J.
In London, J. Short stories of Jack London
p339-49 **S C**

The **lost** ghost. Freeman, M. E. W.
In The Oxford book of English ghost stories
p190-204 **S C**

Lost horizon. Hilton, J. **Fic**

Lost in place. Salzman, M. **92**

Lost in the city. Jones, E. P.
In Children of the night p385-93 **S C**

Lost in Yonkers. Simon, N. **812**

The **lost** inheritance. Wells, H. G.
In Wells, H. G. The complete short stories of
H. G. Wells p512-19 **S C**

Lost kingdoms of the Maya. Stuart, G. S.
972

The **lost** language of cranes [excerpt] Leavitt, D.
In Growing up gay p110-16 **808.8**

Lost moon: the perilous voyage of Apollo 13.
Lovell, J. **629.45**

The **lost,** strayed, stolen. Fisher, M. F. K.
In The Literary ghost p5-30 **S C**

Lost treasure **910.4**

The **lost** world. Jarrell, R.
In Jarrell, R. The complete poems **811**

Loteria: La Rosa. Milligan, M. G.
In Daughters of the fifth sun **810.8**

Lott, David Newton
(comp) The Presidents speak. See The Presidents speak **353.03**

The **lottery.** Jackson, S. **S C**

The **lottery** [story] Jackson, S.
In Jackson, S. The lottery **S C**
In The Norton book of American short stories
p490-97 **S C**

Lottman, Herbert R.
Flaubert **92**

The **lotus** eater. Maugham, W. S.
In Maugham, W. S. Collected short stories v4
S C

Louis, Father *See* Merton, Thomas, 1915-1968
Louis, Joe, 1914-1981
About
Barrow, J. L. Joe Louis   92
Mead, C. Champion: Joe Louis, black hero in white America   92
See/See also pages in the following book(s):
Lipsyte, R. Idols of the game p138-61   920
Louis, Laura Glen
Fur
  In The Best American short stories, 1994 p232-53   S C
Louise. Maugham, W. S.
  In Maugham, W. S. Collected short stories v1   S C

Louisiana
Fiction
Capote, T. Other voices, other rooms   Fic
Covington, D. Lizard   Fic
Gaines, E. J. The autobiography of Miss Jane Pittman   Fic
Gaines, E. J. A lesson before dying   Fic
Louisiana: 1850. Gomez, J.
  In Children of the night p109-51   S C
Lourdes Puente. Garcia, C.
  In Latina: women's voices from the borderlands p58-68   810.8
Love, Catherine E.
  (ed) Larousse concise French-English, English-French dictionary. See Larousse concise French-English, English-French dictionary   443
  (ed) Larousse concise Spanish-English, English-Spanish dictionary. See Larousse concise Spanish-English, English-Spanish dictionary   463
Love, John F.
  McDonald's: behind the arches   338.7
Love
  Fromm, E. The art of loving   152.4
  Lindsay, J. W. Teenage couples, caring, commitment and change   306.8
  Stefoff, R. Friendship and love   155
Love. Colette
  In Colette. The collected stories of Colette p126-28   S C
Love. O'Brien, T.
  In O'Brien, T. The things they carried   S C
Love & rivalry. Faber, D.   920
Love and death at the mall. Peck, R.   808.06
Love and sex among the invertebrates. Murphy, P.
  In Nebula awards 26 p91-101   S C
Love and the Cactus Kid. L'Amour, L.
  In L'Amour, L. The outlaws of Mesquite p25-50   S C
Love day. Styron, W.
  In Styron, W. A Tidewater morning p1-38   S C
Love in the night. Fitzgerald, F. S.
  In Fitzgerald, F. S. The short stories of F. Scott Fitzgerald p302-16   S C
Love in the time of cholera. García Márquez, G.   Fic

Love letters. Gurney, A. R.
  In Gurney, A. R. Love letters and two other plays p1-55   812
Love letters and two other plays: The golden age, and What I did last summer. Gurney, A. R.   812
Love medicine [excerpt] Erdrich, L.
  In Growing up Native American p151-66   810.8
  In The Lightning within p108-30   S C
Love nest. Lardner, R.
  In Lardner, R. The best short stories of Ring Lardner p167-77   S C
Love of life. London, J.
  In London, J. The portable Jack London p82-99   818
  In London, J. Short stories of Jack London p169-85   S C
Love on the Bon-Dieu. Chopin, K.
  In Chopin, K. The awakening and selected stories p3-18   S C
Love oranges. Senior, O.
  In Daughters of Africa p565-67   808.8
The love-philtre of Ikey Schoenstein. Henry, O.
  In Henry, O. The best short stories of O. Henry   S C
Love poems   808.81
Love poetry
  A Book of love poetry   808.81
  Love poems   808.81
Love thy neighbor. Maass, P.   949.7
Lovecraft, H. P. (Howard Phillips), 1890-1937
  The outsider
  In The Oxford book of gothic tales p316-21   S C
Lovecraft, Howard Phillips *See* Lovecraft, H. P. (Howard Phillips), 1890-1937
The loved one. Waugh, E.   Fic
Lovejoy's college guide   378.73
Lovelace, Ada King, Countess of, 1815-1852
See/See also pages in the following book(s):
Henderson, H. Modern mathematicians   920
Lovell, Jim
  Lost moon: the perilous voyage of Apollo 13   629.45
Lovell, Mary S.
  The sound of wings: the life of Amelia Earhart   92
  Straight on till morning: the biography of Beryl Markham   92
Lovelock, James
  The ages of Gaia   574
The lovely lady. Lawrence, D. H.
  In Lawrence, D. H. The complete short stories v3   S C
The lovely Myfanwy. De la Mare, W.
  In The Oxford book of modern fairy tales p251-77   S C
A lovely Sunday for Creve Coeur. Williams, T.
  In Best American plays: 8th series—1974-1982 p106-32   812.008
The lover of horses. Gallagher, T.
  In American short story masterpieces   S C

The **luncheon**. Maugham, W. S.
In Maugham, W. S. Collected short stories v1
S C

Lund, Doris Herold
Eric **92**

Lund, Eric
About
Lund, D. H. Eric **92**

Lundquist, James
Theodore Dreiser **813.009**

Lundwall, Sam J.
Time everlasting
In Tales from the planet Earth **S C**

Lundy, Allan
Diagnosing and treating mental illness
616.89

Lunsford, Cin Forshay- *See* Forshay-Lunsford, Cin

Lurie, Alison
(ed) The Oxford book of modern fairy tales. *See* The Oxford book of modern fairy tales
S C

Lust. Minot, S.
In We are the stories we tell **S C**

Luther, Martin, 1483-1546
About
Bainton, R. H. Here I stand: a life of Martin Luther **92**
See/See also pages in the following book(s):
Durant, W. J. The Reformation p341-79, 447-53
940.2

Luu, Le
The rucksack
In The Other side of heaven p118-21
S C

Lychack, William
A stand of fables
In The Best American short stories, 1996 p220-25 **S C**

Lying *See* Truthfulness and falsehood

Lyme disease
Mactire, S. P. Lyme disease and other pest-borne illnesses **616.9**
See/See also pages in the following book(s):
Rouché, B. The medical detectives p390-405
616
Yancey, D. The hunt for hidden killers p25-32
616

Lyme disease and other pest-borne illnesses.
Mactire, S. P. **616.9**

Lynch, Patricia Ann
Christianity **200**

Lynch, Richard Chigley, 1932-
Musicals! **792.6**

Lyndon Johnson and the American dream. Goodwin, D. K. **92**

Lyndon Johnson's war. Berman, L. **959.704**

Lynn, Elizabeth A.
The red hawk
In Masterpieces of fantasy and enchantment p224-51 **S C**

Lynn, Elizabeth Cook- *See* Cook-Lynn, Elizabeth

Lynn, Loretta
Loretta Lynn: coal miner's daughter **92**

Lyons, Mary E.
Sorrow's kitchen: the life and folklore of Zora Neale Hurston **92**

Lyons, Michael J., 1930-
World War II: a short history **940.53**

Lyricists
Furia, P. The poets of Tin Pan Alley
782.42

Lysandra's Poem. Wilson, B.
In Wilson, B. The leaving and other stories
S C

Lytle, Clifford M.
(jt. auth) Deloria, V. American Indians, American justice **970.004**
(jt. auth) Deloria, V. The nations within: the past and future of American Indian sovereignty **323.1**

Lyttle, Richard B.
Ernest Hemingway **92**

Lytton, Edward Bulwer Lytton, Baron, 1803-1873
The haunted and the haunters
In Classic ghost stories p293-330 **S C**

M

Ma, Christopher
(ed) The Practical guide to practically everything. *See* The Practical guide to practically everything **031.02**

Ma, Van Khang
Mother and daughter
In The Other side of heaven p340-52
S C

Ma and Tom. Steinbeck, J.
In Steinbeck, J. The portable Steinbeck
818

Ma qui. Brennert, A.
In Nebula awards 27 p53-72 **S C**

Maass, Peter, 1960-
Love thy neighbor **949.7**

Mabel. Maugham, W. S.
In Maugham, W. S. Collected short stories v4
S C

Mabie, Margot C. J.
Bioethics and the new medical technology
174

Mabinogion
See/See also pages in the following book(s):
Bulfinch, T. Bulfinch's mythology **291**

Mabry, Marcus
White bucks and black-eyed peas **92**

Mabunda, L. Mpho
(ed) The African American almanac. *See* The African American almanac **305.8**
(ed) Dictionary of Hispanic biography. *See* Dictionary of Hispanic biography **920.003**

Mabuza, Lindiwe
Wake . . .
In The Heinemann book of contemporary African short stories p33-56 **S C**

MacLean, Katherine, 1925-
Night-rise
In The Norton book of science fiction p376-
85   S C

MacLeish, Archibald, 1892-1982
Collected poems, 1917-1982   811
The fall of the city
In Twenty best plays of the modern American
theatre p764-74   812.008
J.B.
In Best American plays: 5th series—1957-
1963 p589-633   812.008

MacLeish, William H., 1928-
The day before America   970.01

MacLeod, Ian
1/72nd scale
In Nebula awards 26 p102-31   S C

MacMahon, Bryan, 1909-
The ring
In The Oxford book of Irish short stories
p388-91   S C

The **Macmillan** Bible atlas. Aharoni, Y.
     220.9

The **Macmillan** dictionary of measurement.
Darton, M.   389

Macmillan encyclopedia of earth sciences. See
Encyclopedia of earth sciences   550.3

Macmillan health encyclopedia   610.3

The **Macmillan** illustrated encyclopedia of myths
and legends. Cotterell, A.   291.03

The **Macmillan** visual desk reference   031

The **Macmillan** visual dictionary   413

MacNee, Marie J.
(ed) Science fiction, fantasy, and horror writers.
See Science fiction, fantasy, and horror writers   809.3

MacNeil, Robert, 1931-
(jt. auth) McCrum, R. The story of English
     420

Mactire, Sean P.
Lyme disease and other pest-borne illnesses
     616.9

Macy, Anne Sullivan *See* Sullivan, Anne, 1866-
1936

Macy, Sue, 1954-
Winning ways   796.09

Mad (Periodical)
Reidelbach, M. Completely Mad   741.5

The **mad** Lomasneys. O'Connor, F.
In O'Connor, F. Collected stories p98-120
     S C

Madama, John
Desktop publishing   686.2

Madame Bovary. Flaubert, G.   Fic

Madame Bovary. Gans, E.   843.009

Madame de Troyes. Wharton, E.
In Wharton, E. Novellas and other writings
     818

Madame Zena's séance. Hanson, M. E.
In The Big book of large-cast plays p277-90
     812.008

Madame Zilensky and the King of Finland. Mc-
Cullers, C.
In McCullers, C. The ballad of the sad café:
the novels and stories of Carson McCul-
lers   S C
In McCullers, C. Collected stories p110-18
     S C

Ma'dear. McMillan, T.
In Children of the night p423-33   S C

Madhubuti, Haki R.
See/See also pages in the following book(s):
Contemporary black American poets and drama-
tists p106-19   810.9

The **madness** of John Harned. London, J.
In London, J. The portable Jack London
p249-62   818
In London, J. Short stories of Jack London
p464-76   S C

Maelzel's Chess-Player. Poe, E. A.
In Poe, E. A. The collected tales and poems
of Edgar Allan Poe p421-39   S C

Maeterlinck, Maurice, 1862-1949
A miracle of Saint Anthony
In Thirty famous one-act plays p169-85
     808.82

Mafham, Ken Preston- *See* Preston-Mafham, Ken

Mafham, Rod Preston- *See* Preston-Mafham, Rod

Mafia
Fiction
Grisham, J. The client   Fic

Magazine-writing—Peter Snook. Poe, E. A.
In Poe, E. A. The collected tales and poems
of Edgar Allan Poe p564-73   S C

Magazines *See* Periodicals

Magazines for libraries   011

Magazines for school libraries. See Magazines for
young people   011.6

Magazines for young people   011.6

Magellan, Ferdinand, 1480?-1521
See/See also pages in the following book(s):
Faber, H. The discoverers of America p129-42
     970.01

Maggie of the green bottles. Bambara, T. C.
In Daughters of Africa p384-89   808.8

Magic. Porter, K. A.
In Porter, K. A. The collected stories of Katherine Anne Porter   S C

The **magic** barrel. Malamud, B.
In American short story masterpieces
     S C
In Malamud, B. The stories of Bernard
Malamud p124-43   S C

The **magic** bonbons. Baum, L. F.
In Masterpieces of fantasy and enchantment
p413-18   S C

The **magic** fishbone. Dickens, C.
In Masterpieces of fantasy and enchantment
p13-22   S C
In The Oxford book of modern fairy tales
p99-108   S C

The **magic** mountain. Mann, T.   Fic

The **Magic** of Xanth series. Anthony, P.   Fic

The **mail** lady. Gates, D.
  In The Best American short stories, 1994
  p145-66   **S C**

Mailer, Norman
  The naked and the dead   **Fic**

Main-street. Hawthorne, N.
  In Hawthorne, N. Tales and sketches; A wonder book for girls and boys; Tanglewood
  tales for girls and boys p1023-50
                      S C

Main Street. Lewis, S.   **Fic**

Maine
             Fiction
  King, S. Carrie   **Fic**

Maine (Battleship)
  Samuels, P. Remembering the Maine   **973.8**

The **Maine** woods. Thoreau, H. D.
  In Thoreau, H. D. A week on the Concord
  and Merrimack rivers; Walden; The
  Maine woods; Cape Cod   **818**

Mainiero, Lina
  (ed) American women writers. See American
  women writers   **810.9**

Maisel, Louis Sandy, 1945-
  (ed) Political parties & elections in the United
  States. See Political parties & elections in the
  United States   **324.2**

Maja-Pearce, Adewale
  The hotel
  In The Heinemann book of contemporary
  African short stories p146-48   **S C**
  (ed) The Heinemann book of African poetry in
  English. See The Heinemann book of African
  poetry in English   **821**

Majesty. Fitzgerald, F. S.
  In Fitzgerald, F. S. The short stories of F.
  Scott Fitzgerald p464-80   **S C**

The **majesty** of the law. O'Connor, F.
  In O'Connor, F. Collected stories p320-27
                      S C
  In The Oxford book of Irish short stories
  p354-62   **S C**

Major, Clarence
  An area in the cerebral hemisphere
  In Children of the night p523-28   **S C**
  My mother and Mitch
  In Rites of passage p191-202   **S C**
  Scat
  In Calling the wind p399-404   **S C**
  (ed) Calling the wind. See Calling the wind
                      S C
  (ed) Juba to jive. See Juba to jive   **427**
See/See also pages in the following book(s):
  Contemporary black American fiction writers
  p88-103   **813.009**
  Contemporary black American poets and drama-
  tists p120-31   **810.9**

Major, Devorah, 1952-
  Nzinga's treasure
  In Streetlights: illuminating tales of the urban
  black experience p289-93   **S C**

Major, Roberta Olsen
  Melodrama at Mayfair Meadows
  In The Big book of large-cast plays p228-37
                      812.008

Major characters in American fiction   **813.009**
Major modern black American writers   **810.9**
The **Major** poets: English and American
                      821.008

Make lemonade. Wolff, V. E.   **Fic**

The **maker** of dreams. Down, O.
  In 24 favorite one-act plays p256-71
                      808.82

Makes me wanna holler. McCall, N.   **92**

Makeup, Theatrical *See* Theatrical makeup

Makeup (Cosmetics) *See* Cosmetics

Makhalisa, Barbara
  Different values
  In Daughters of Africa p618-21   **808.8**

Making & enjoying telescopes. Miller, R.
                      522

Making and using scientific equipment. Newton,
  D. E.   **507.8**

Making art safely. Spandorfer, M.   **702.8**

Making do. Hogan, L.
  In Spider Woman's granddaughters   **S C**

Making it all the way into the future on Gaxton
  Falls of the red planet. Malzberg, B. N.
  In The Norton book of science fiction p313-
  16   **S C**

Making it in the music business. Wilson, L.
                      780

The **making** of a New Yorker. Henry, O.
  In Henry, O. The best short stories of O.
  Henry   **S C**

The **making** of the atomic bomb. Rhodes, R.
                      623.4

The **making** of the president, 1960. White, T. H.
                      324.6

Making peace with the planet. Commoner, B.
                      304.2

Making peace with the PLO. Makovsky, D.
                      956.94

Making the alphabet dance. Eckler, A. R.
                      793.73

Making their mark   **709.04**

Making waves: an anthology of writings by and
  about Asian American women   **305.4**

Makovsky, David
  Making peace with the PLO   **956.94**

Malamud, Bernard, 1914-1986
  The assistant   **Fic**
  The fixer   **Fic**
  Idiots first
  In The Norton book of American short stories
  p460-64   **S C**
  The Jewbird
  In The Oxford book of modern fairy tales
  p352-60   **S C**
  The magic barrel
  In American short story masterpieces
                      S C
  My son the murderer
  In The Oxford book of American short stories
  p504-10   **S C**

Mammon and the archer—*Continued*
In The Norton book of American short stories
p151-56   **S C**

The **Mammoth** book of new world science fiction
    S C

Mammy. West, D.
In West, D. The richer, the poorer: stories, sketches, and reminiscences   **S C**

Man

Influence on nature
See Human influence on nature

Origin
See Human origins

Man, Fossil *See* Fossil man

Man, Prehistoric *See* Prehistoric man

The **man.** Bradbury, R.
In Bradbury, R. The illustrated man   **S C**

The **man.** Dongala, E. B.
In The Heinemann book of contemporary African short stories p81-86   **S C**

Man about the house. Urquhart, F.
In Classic English short stories, 1930-1955 p266-73   **S C**

Man about town. Henry, O.
In Henry, O. The best short stories of O. Henry   **S C**

Man and microbes. Karlen, A.   **614.4**

A **man** by the name of Ziegler. Hesse, H.
In Hesse, H. The fairy tales of Hermann Hesse   **S C**

A **man** for all seasons. Bolt, R.   **822**

The **man** from Buenos Aires. Sholem Aleichem
In Sholem Aleichem. Tevye the dairyman and The railroad stories   **S C**

A **man** from Glasgow. Maugham, W. S.
In Maugham, W. S. Collected short stories v1   **S C**

The **man** I killed. O'Brien, T.
In O'Brien, T. The things they carried   **S C**
In Who do you think you are? p146-51   **S C**

Man in space   **629.4**

The **man** in the black suit. King, S.
In Prize stories, 1996 p1-24   **S C**

Man in the drawer. Malamud, B.
In Malamud, B. The stories of Bernard Malamud p193-239   **S C**

The **man** in the mirror: a life of Benedict Arnold. Brandt, C.   **92**

Man, myth, & magic   **133**

The **man** of Adamant. Hawthorne, N.
In Hawthorne, N. Tales and sketches; A wonder book for girls and boys; Tanglewood tales for girls and boys p421-28   **S C**

A **man** of ideas. Anderson, S.
In Anderson, S. Winesburg, Ohio   **S C**

Man of La Mancha. Wasserman, D.   **812**

The **man** of science. Jerome, J. K.
In Victorian ghost stories p379-84   **S C**

The **man** of the crowd. Poe, E. A.
In Poe, E. A. The collected tales and poems of Edgar Allan Poe p475-81   **S C**

The **man** of the house. O'Connor, F.
In O'Connor, F. Collected stories p183-90   **S C**

A **man** of the people. Le Guin, U. K.
In Le Guin, U. K. Four ways to forgiveness p93-144   **S C**

A **man** of the world. Hemingway, E.
In Hemingway, E. The complete short stories of Ernest Hemingway p492-95   **S C**

Man-size in marble. Nesbit, E.
In The Oxford book of English ghost stories p125-36   **S C**

The **man** that corrupted Hadleyburg. Twain, M.
In The Best crime stories of the 19th century p266-315   **S C**
In Twain, M. The complete short stories of Mark Twain   **S C**

The **man** that was used up. Poe, E. A.
In Poe, E. A. The collected tales and poems of Edgar Allan Poe p405-12   **S C**

The **man** to send rain clouds. Silko, L.
In The Lightning within p48-52   **S C**

The **man** upstairs. Bradbury, R.
In Bradbury, R. The stories of Ray Bradbury p336-45   **S C**

The **man** who came to dinner. Kaufman, G. S.
In Best plays of the modern American theatre: 2nd series p317-64   **812.008**

The **man** who collected Poe. Bloch, R.
In Masterpieces of mystery and suspense p426-39   **S C**

The **man** who could not see devils. Russ, J.
In Masterpieces of fantasy and enchantment p149-61   **S C**

The **man** who could work miracles. Wells, H. G.
In Wells, H. G. The complete short stories of H. G. Wells p807-25   **S C**

The **man** who counted. Tahan, M.   **793.7**

The **man** who had seen the rope trick. Aiken, J.
In The Oxford book of modern fairy tales p387-95   **S C**

The **man** who hated gravity. Bova, B.
In Bova, B. Challenges p15-33   **S C**

The **man** who loved islands. Lawrence, D. H.
In Lawrence, D. H. The complete short stories v3   **S C**

Man who married a dumb wife. France, A.
In Thirty famous one-act plays p5-24   **808.82**

The **man** who mistook his wife for a hat and other clinical tales. Sacks, O. W.   **616.8**

The **man** who put up at Gadsby. Twain, M.
In Twain, M. The complete short stories of Mark Twain   **S C**

The **man** who rowed Christopher Columbus ashore. Ellison, H.
In The Best American short stories, 1993 p77-93   **S C**
In Nebula awards 29 p20-37   **S C**

The **man** who saw through Heaven. Steele, D.
In The Norton book of American short stories
p261-76   **S C**

The **man** who stained his soul. Vu, B.
In The Other side of heaven p166-71
    S C

The **man** who was almost a man. Wright, R.
In The Oxford book of American short stories
p371-83   **S C**

The **man** who would be king. Kipling, R.
In Kipling, R. The best fiction of Rudyard
Kipling p562-88   **S C**
In Kipling, R. The portable Kipling   **828**

The **man** who would not shake hands. King, S.
In King, S. Skeleton crew   **S C**

A **man** with a conscience. Maugham, W. S.
In Maugham, W. S. Collected short stories v4
    S C

The **man** with the scar. Maugham, W. S.
In Maugham, W. S. Collected short stories v2
    S C

The **man** with the twisted lip. Doyle, Sir A. C.
In Doyle, Sir A. C. The complete Sherlock
Holmes   **S C**

The **man** without a country. Hale, E. E.   **Fic**

The **man** without a face. Holland, I.   **Fic**

Man, woman and boy. Dixon, S.
In The Best American short stories, 1993
p187-98   **S C**

The **management** of grief. Mukherjee, B.
In The Best American short stories of the
eighties p333-50   **S C**
In The Oxford book of American short stories
p697-713   **S C**

Manahan, Anna Anderson *See* Anderson, Anna,
d. 1984

Manchester, William
American Caesar: Douglas MacArthur, 1880-
1964   **92**
The death of a President, November 20—No-
vember 25, 1963   **973.922**
The glory and the dream   **973.9**
One brief shining moment: remembering Kenne-
dy   **92**

Manchild in the promised land. Brown, C.
    92

Mancini, Richard E.
Indians of the Southeast
In The First Americans series   **970.004**

Mandela, Nelson
Long walk to freedom: the autobiography of
Nelson Mandela   **92**
Mandela   **92**
Nelson Mandela speaks   **968.06**
About
Hoobler, D. Mandela   **92**
Otfinoski, S. Nelson Mandela   **92**
See/See also pages in the following book(s):
Sparks, A. Tomorrow is another country
    968.06

Mandela, Winnie
About
Hoobler, D. Mandela   **92**

Mandelbrot, Benoit B.
See/See also pages in the following book(s):
Henderson, H. Modern mathematicians   **920**

Mandelman, Avner
Pity
In The Best American short stories, 1995
p67-79   **S C**

Mandelstam, Osip, 1891-1938
Theodosia
In The Portable twentieth-century Russian
reader p171-83   **891.7**

Mandishona, Daniel
A wasted land
In The Heinemann book of contemporary
African short stories p57-66   **S C**

Manet, Édouard, 1832-1883
About
Courthion, P. Edouard Manet   **759.4**
Wright, P. Manet   **92**

Mango, Karin N., 1936-
Hearing loss   **617.8**

Manhoff, Bill
The owl and the pussycat
In Best American plays: 6th series—1963-
1967 p495-525   **812.008**

Manic-depressive psychoses
See also Depression (Psychology)

Mankiewicz, Herman J., 1897-1953
Citizen Kane
In Best American screenplays   **812.008**

Mankiewitz won't be bowling Tuesday nights
anymore. Kinsella, W. P.
In Kinsella, W. P. Shoeless Joe Jackson
comes to Iowa: stories   **S C**

Mann, Abby, 1927-
Judgment at Nuremberg
In Best American screenplays   **812.008**

Mann, Charles C.
Noah's choice   **574.5**
(jt. auth) Menzel, P. Material world   **306.8**

Mann, Thomas, 1875-1955
Buddenbrooks   **Fic**
The magic mountain   **Fic**

The **manned** missiles. Vonnegut, K.
In Vonnegut, K. Welcome to the monkey
house   **S C**

Manners *See* Etiquette

Manners and customs
See also Country life; names of ethnic
groups, countries, cities, etc. with the subdivision *Social life and customs*
Dresser, N. Multicultural manners   **395**

Manning, Henry Edward, Cardinal, 1808-1892
See/See also pages in the following book(s):
Strachey, L. Eminent Victorians   **920**

Mansfield, Katherine, 1888-1923
The woman at the store
In The Oxford book of short stories p300-09
    S C

Mansfield, Kathleen Beauchamp *See* Mansfield,
Katherine, 1888-1923

Manslaughter *See* Homicide

Mars (Planet)—*Continued*
Fiction
Lewis, C. S. Out of the silent planet   **Fic**

Mars is heaven. Bradbury, R.
In Bradbury, R. The stories of Ray Bradbury p81-94   **S C**

Marsalis, Wynton
Marsalis on music   **780**
See/See also pages in the following book(s):
Crouch, S. The all-American skin game; or, The decoy of race p192-204   **305.8**

Marsalis on music. Marsalis, W.   **780**

Marsden, John, 1950-
Letters from the inside   **Fic**
Tomorrow, when the war began   **Fic**

Marsh, Dave
50 ways to fight censorship   **323.44**

Marsh, Don, 1957-
Calligraphy   **745.6**

Marsh, Geoffrey *See* Grant, Charles L.

Marsh, George Perkins, 1801-1882
See/See also pages in the following book(s):
Lucas, E. Naturalists, conservationists, and environmentalists   **920**

Marsh, Dame Ngaio, 1899-1982
Death on the air
In Masterpieces of mystery and suspense p67-93   **S C**
See/See also pages in the following book(s):
Modern mystery writers p124-38   **809.3**

Marsh ecology
Wetlands in danger   **574.5**

Marshall, Andrew
(jt. auth) Kaplan, D. E. The cult at the end of the world   **291**

Marshall, Catherine, 1914-1983
Christy   **Fic**

Marshall, Eliot
Legalization   **344**

Marshall, George C. (George Catlett), 1880-1959
About
Stoler, M. A. George C. Marshall: soldier-statesman of the American century   **92**
See/See also pages in the following book(s):
Halberstam, D. The best and the brightest   **973.922**

Marshall, John, 1755-1835
About
Stites, F. N. John Marshall, defender of the Constitution   **92**
See/See also pages in the following book(s):
Aaseng, N. Great Justices of the Supreme Court p17-37   **920**

Marshall, Joseph E., Jr.
Street soldier   **364.3**

Marshall, Paule, 1929-
Barbados
In The Best short stories by Negro writers p309-24   **S C**
Brooklyn
In We are the stories we tell   **S C**

Reena
In Black-eyed Susans/Midnight birds p85-105   **S C**
To Da-duh, in memoriam
In Calling the wind p275-83   **S C**
In Daughters of Africa p348-55   **808.8**
See/See also pages in the following book(s):
Black American women fiction writers p131-45   **813.009**

Marshall, S. L. A. (Samuel Lyman Atwood), 1900-1977
The American Heritage history of World War I. See The American Heritage history of World War I   **940.3**

Marshall, Samuel Lyman Atwood *See* Marshall, S. L. A. (Samuel Lyman Atwood), 1900-1977

Marshall, Sarah Catherine Wood *See* Marshall, Catherine, 1914-1983

Marshall, Thurgood
About
Davis, M. D. Thurgood Marshall   **92**

Marta del Angel. Feyder, L.
In Latina: women's voices from the border p172-78   **810.8**

Martens, Anne Coulter
The comeback caper
In The Big book of large-cast plays p115-35   **812.008**

Martes. Pau-Llosa, R.
In Iguana dreams   **S C**

Martha, Henry *See* Harris, Mark, 1922-

Martha's Vineyard (Mass.)
Fiction
West, D. The wedding   **Fic**

Martial arts
See also Self-defense for women
Corcoran, J. The martial arts sourcebook   **796.8**
Salzman, M. Iron & silk   **915.1**

The **martial** arts sourcebook. Corcoran, J.   **796.8**

The **Martian** child. Gerrold, D.
In Nebula awards 30 p151-88   **S C**

The **Martian** chronicles. Bradbury, R.   **S C**

A **Martian** odyssey. Weinbaum, S. G.
In The Oxford book of science fiction stories p70-94   **S C**

The **Martian** way. Asimov, I.
In Asimov, I. The complete stories v2 p129-65   **S C**

Martin, Christopher, 1939-
Charles Dickens   **92**
H.G. Wells   **92**

Martin, Colin, 1939-
The Spanish Armada   **942.05**

Martin, George R. R.
The way of cross and dragon
In The Oxford book of science fiction stories p454-71   **S C**

Martin, Judith, 1938-
Miss Manners' guide to excruciatingly correct behavior   **395**

Martin, Linda Wagner- *See* Wagner-Martin, Linda

Mason, Bobbie Ann—*Continued*
Shiloh
  In American short story masterpieces
                                                  S C
  In We are the stories we tell   S C
Mason, Robert, 1942-
Chickenhawk   959.704
The **masque** of the Red Death. Poe, E. A.
  In Poe, E. A. The collected tales and poems
    of Edgar Allan Poe p269-73   S C
  In Poe, E. A. Tales of Edgar Allan Poe p117-
    25   S C
Mass communication *See* Communication; Tele-
  communication
Mass extinction of species
Hecht, J. Vanishing life   560
Leakey, R. E. The sixth extinction   304.2
Officer, C. B. The great dinosaur extinction con-
  troversy   567.9
Mass hysteria *See* Hysteria (Social psychology)
The **Mass** island. O'Connor, F.
  In O'Connor, F. Collected stories p644-54
                                        S C
Mass media
Fallows, J. M. Breaking the news   302.23
Mass media: opposing viewpoints   302.23
McLuhan, M. Understanding media   302.23
The Media and politics   302.23
Sherrow, V. Violence and the media   303.6
Violence in the media   303.6
                  Dictionaries
Weiner, R. Webster's New World dictionary of
  media and communications   302.23
Mass media: opposing viewpoints   302.23
Massachusetts
  History—1600-1775, Colonial period
Bradford, W. Of Plymouth Plantation, 1620-
  1647   974.4
A **masseuse.** Colette
  In Colette. The collected stories of Colette
    p33-36   S C
Massie, Robert K., 1929-
Nicholas and Alexandra   92
Peter the Great   92
The Romanovs   947.08
**Masson, J. Moussaieff (Jeffrey Moussaieff),
  1941-**
When elephants weep   591.5
Masson, Jeffrey Moussaieff *See* Masson, J.
  Moussaieff (Jeffrey Moussaieff), 1941-
Mast, Gerald, 1940-1988
A short history of the movies   791.43
The **"master".** Colette
  In Colette. The collected stories of Colette
    p71-74   S C
Master and man. Tolstoy, L., graf
  In The Portable nineteenth-century Russian
    reader p489-529   891.7
  In Tolstoy, L. Great short works of Leo Tol-
    stoy p451-500   S C
  In Tolstoy, L. The portable Tolstoy p602-52
                                        891.7

The **master** and Margarita [excerpt] Bulgakov, M.
  A.
  In The Portable twentieth-century Russian
    reader p189-201   891.7
The **master** builder. Ibsen, H.
  In Ibsen, H. The complete major prose plays
                                        839.8
"**Master** Harold"—and the boys. Fugard, A.
                                        822
Masterpieces of African-American literature
                                        810.9
Masterpieces of American literature   810.9
Masterpieces of fantasy and enchantment
                                        S C
Masterpieces of Latino literature   860.9
Masterpieces of mystery and suspense   S C
Masterpieces of women's literature   809
Masterpieces of world literature   809
Masterpieces of world philosophy   100
Masterpieces: the best-loved paintings from
  America's museums. Frankel, D.   750
Masterplots   808.8
Masterplots II, drama series   809.2
Masterplots II: juvenile and young adult fiction
  series   028.5
Masterplots II: juvenile and young adult literature
  series supplement   028.5
Masterplots II, short story series 809.3
Masters, Edgar Lee, 1868-1950
Spoon River anthology   811
Masterson, Martha Gay, 1838-1916
See/See also pages in the following book(s):
Stefoff, R. Women pioneers   920
Masterton. Maugham, W. S.
  In Maugham, W. S. Collected short stories v4
                                        S C
The **matchmaker.** Wilder, T.
  In Best American plays: 4th series—1951-
    1957 p535-72   812.008
  In Wilder, T. Three plays: Our town, The
    skin of our teeth, The matchmaker
                                        812
Materia medica
  See also Drugs
                  Indexes
The Merck index   615
Material world. Menzel, P.   306.8
Materialism
What survives?   133.9
The **math** entertainer. *See* Heafford, P. E. Great
  book of math puzzles   793.7
Math in science and nature. Gardner, R.   510
Math on file   510
Math projects in the computer age. Thomas, D. A.
                                        510
Mathabane, Mark
Kaffir boy   92
Kaffir boy [excerpt]
  In Somehow tenderness survives p87-103
                                        S C
Kaffir boy in America   92

Mattison, Christopher
The care of reptiles and amphibians in captivity
639.3
The encyclopedia of snakes 597.9
Frogs & toads of the world 597.8
Mattson, Mark T.
Atlas of the 1990 census 304.6
(jt. auth) Asante, M. K. The historical and cultural atlas of African Americans 305.8
Maugham, Somerset *See* Maugham, W. Somerset (William Somerset), 1874-1965
Maugham, W. Somerset (William Somerset), 1874-1965
Collected short stories S C
Contents: v1 Rain; The fall of Edward Barnard; Honolulu; The luncheon; The ant and the grasshopper; Home; The pool; Mackintosh; Appearance and reality; The three fat women of Antibes; The facts of life; Gigolo and Gigolette; The happy couple; The voice of the turtle; The lion's skin; The unconquered; The escape; The judgement seat; Mr. Know-all; The happy man; The romantic young lady; The point of honour; The poet; The mother; A man from Glasgow; Before the party; Louise; The promise; A string of beads; The yellow streak
v2 The vessel of wrath; The force of circumstance; Flotsam and Jetsam; The alien corn; The creative impulse; Virtue; The man with the scar; The closed shop; The bum; The dream; The treasure; The colonel's lady; Lord Mountdrago; The social sense; The verger; In a strange land; The Taipan; The consul; A friend in need; The round dozen; The human element; Jane; Footprints in the jungle; The door of opportunity
v3 Miss King; The hairless Mexican; Giulia Lazzari; The traitor; His Excellency; Mr. Harrington's washing; Sanatorium
v4 The book-bag; French Joe; German Harry; The four Dutchmen; The back of beyond; P. & O.; Episode; The kite; A woman of fifty; Mayhew; The lotus eater; Salvatore; The wash-tub; A man with a conscience; An official position; Winter cruise; Mabel; Masterton; Princess September; A marriage of convenience; Mirage; The letter; The outstation; The portrait of a gentleman; Raw material; Straight flush; The end of the flight; A casual affair; Red; Neil MacAdam
The kite
In Classic English short stories, 1930-1955 p1-32 S C
Of human bondage Fic
An official position
In The Oxford book of short stories p219-37 S C
The razor's edge Fic
The taipan
In The Oxford book of English ghost stories p283-88 S C
About
Burt, F. D. W. Somerset Maugham
823.009
Maugham, William Somerset *See* Maugham, W. Somerset (William Somerset), 1874-1965
Mauki. London, J.
In London, J. The portable Jack London p187-99 818
In London, J. Short stories of Jack London p391-403 S C
Maule, Jeremy
(ed) The Oxford book of classical verse in translation. See The Oxford book of classical verse in translation 881.008
Maupassant, Guy de, 1850-1893
The collected stories of Guy de Maupassant S C
The Horla
In Classic ghost stories p249-71 S C

Mauro, Robert A.
The Mother Goose Olympics
In The Big book of large-cast plays p267-76 812.008
Maus. Spiegelman, A. 940.53
Maus II [excerpt] Spiegelman, A.
In Bearing witness p40-47 808.8
Maxims *See* Proverbs
May, Charles E. (Charles Edward), 1941-
The short story 809.3
May, Elaine Tyler
Pushing the limits
In The Young Oxford history of women in the United States 305.4
May, Herbert Gordon, 1904-
(ed) Oxford Bible atlas. See Oxford Bible atlas 220.9
May day. Fitzgerald, F. S.
In Fitzgerald, F. S. The short stories of F. Scott Fitzgerald p97-141 S C
In Fitzgerald, F. S. The stories of F. Scott Fitzgerald p83-126 S C
The may-pole of Merry Mount. Hawthorne, N.
In Hawthorne, N. Tales and sketches; A wonder book for girls and boys; Tanglewood tales for girls and boys p360-70 S C
Mayas
The Magnificent Maya 972
Meyer, C. The mystery of the ancient Maya 972
The Route of the Mayas 972
Stuart, G. S. Lost kingdoms of the Maya 972
See/See also pages in the following book(s):
Builders of the ancient world p70-89 930
Ceram, C. W. Gods, graves, and scholars p348-416 930.1
Mysteries of the ancient Americas p144-65 970.01
Wright, R. Stolen continents 970.004
Mayer, Barbara, 1939-
How to succeed in high school 373
Mayer, Maria Goeppert- *See* Goeppert-Mayer, Maria, 1906-1972
Mayhew. Maugham, W. S.
In Maugham, W. S. Collected short stories v4 S C
Mayle, Peter
A dog's life 828
Mayo, Edith
(ed) The Smithsonian book of the First Ladies. See The Smithsonian book of the First Ladies 920
Mayor, F. M. (Flora Macdonald), 1872-1932
Miss de Mannering of Asham
In The Oxford book of gothic tales p386-406 S C
Mayor, Flora Macdonald *See* Mayor, F. M. (Flora Macdonald), 1872-1932
Mays, Willie, 1931-
Say hey: the autobiography of Willie Mays
92

McClatchy, J. D., 1945-
(ed) The Vintage book of contemporary American poetry. See The Vintage book of contemporary American poetry **811.008**

McClellan, George Brinton, 1826-1885
About
Bailey, R. H. Forward to Richmond: McClellan's peninsular campaign **973.7**

McClintock, Barbara
See/See also pages in the following book(s):
Dash, J. The triumph of discovery: women scientists who won the Nobel Prize p67-97 **920**
McGrayne, S. B. Nobel Prize women in science p144-74 **920**

McCloskey, Susan
(jt. auth) Davidson, W. Writing a winning college application essay **378**

McCloud, Scott
Understanding comics **741.5**

McCluskey, John (John A.), 1944-
Top of the game
In Calling the wind p539-51 **S C**

McCormack, John
Fields and pastures new **636.089**

McCormick, Jim, 1920-
(jt. auth) Krantz, L. The peoplepedia **031.02**

McCourt, Frank
Angela's ashes **92**

McCourt family
About
McCourt, F. Angela's ashes **92**

McCoy, J. J. (Joseph J.), 1917-
Animals in research **179**

McCoy, Joseph J. See McCoy, J. J. (Joseph J.), 1917-

McCoy, Kathleen, 1945-
Life happens **616.85**
The new teenage body book **613**

McCoy, Kathy See McCoy, Kathleen, 1945-

The McCoy Hotel. Chávez, D.
In Growing up Chicana/o p251-69 **810.8**

McCrum, Robert
The story of English **420**

McCuan, Walter R., 1947-
(ed) 21st century earth: opposing viewpoints. See 21st century earth: opposing viewpoints **303.49**
(ed) America beyond 2001: opposing viewpoints. See America beyond 2001: opposing viewpoints **303.49**

McCue, Margi Laird
Domestic violence **362.82**

McCuen, Jo Ray, 1929-
(jt. auth) Winkler, A. C. Writing the research paper **808**

McCullers, Carson, 1917-1967
The ballad of the sad café
In McCullers, C. The ballad of the sad café: the novels and stories of Carson McCullers **S C**
In McCullers, C. Collected stories p195-253 **S C**

The ballad of the sad café: the novels and stories of Carson McCullers **S C**
Short stories included are: Wunderkind; The jockey; Madame Zilensky and the King of Finland; The sojourner; A domestic dilemma; A tree. A rock. A cloud

Collected stories **S C**
Short stories included are: Sucker; Court in the West eighties; Poldi; Breath from the sky; The orphanage; Instant of the hour after; Like that; Wunderkind; The aliens; Untitled piece; The jockey; Madame Zilensky and the King of Finland; Correspondence; A tree. A rock. A cloud; Art and Mr. Mahoney; The sojourner; A domestic dilemma; The haunted boy; Who has seen the wind

The heart is a lonely hunter **Fic**
also in McCullers, C. The ballad of the sad café: the novels and stories of Carson McCullers **S C**

The member of the wedding **Fic**
also in McCullers, C. The ballad of the sad café: the novels and stories of Carson McCullers **S C**
also in McCullers, C. Collected stories p255-392 **S C**

The member of the wedding [play] **812**
also in Best American plays: 3d series— 1945-1951 p171-203 **812.008**

Reflections in a golden eye
In McCullers, C. The ballad of the sad café: the novels and stories of Carson McCullers **S C**

Sucker
In Who do you think you are? p122-33 **S C**

About
Carson McCullers **813.009**

McCullough, Colleen, 1937-
The thorn birds **Fic**

McCullough, David G., 1933-
The path between the seas **972.87**
Truman **92**

McCutcheon, Marc
Roget's superthesaurus **423**

McDaniel, Melissa
Stephen Hawking **92**

McDermott, Alice
At weddings and wakes **Fic**

McDonald, Elvin
(ed) The American Horticultural Society encyclopedia of gardening. See The American Horticultural Society encyclopedia of gardening **635**

McDonald's: behind the arches. Love, J. F. **338.7**

McDonald's Corp.
Love, J. F. McDonald's: behind the arches **338.7**

McDonnell, Janet, 1962-
America in the 20th century. See America in the 20th century **973.9**

McDowell, Garrett
In sight of the killing
In Streetlights: illuminating tales of the urban black experience p306-17 **S C**

McDowell, Margaret B.
Edith Wharton **813.009**

McElroy, Colleen J.
Jesus and Fat Tuesday
In Calling the wind p466-79   **S C**
The woman who would eat flowers
In Children of the night p471-501   **S C**
McElroy, Guy C., d. 1990
Facing history   **704.9**
McElvaine, Robert S., 1947-
The Great Depression   **973.91**
McFarland, David
(ed) The Oxford companion to animal behavior.
See The Oxford companion to animal behavior   **591.5**
McFeely, William S.
Frederick Douglass   **92**
McGahern, John, 1934-
The beginning of an idea
In The Oxford book of Irish short stories p526-40   **S C**
McGillahee's brat. Bradbury, R.
In Bradbury, R. The stories of Ray Bradbury p864-72   **S C**
McGrath, Patrick, 1950-
Blood disease
In The Oxford book of gothic tales p502-18   **S C**
Marmilion
In The Literary ghost p127-43   **S C**
McGrath, Tom
MTV: the making of a revolution   **791.45**
McGraw-Hill concise encyclopedia of science & technology   **503**
McGraw-Hill encyclopedia of astronomy **520.3**
McGraw-Hill encyclopedia of personal computing   **004**
McGraw-Hill encyclopedia of physics   **530**
McGraw-Hill encyclopedia of science & technology   **503**
McGraw-Hill encyclopedia of world drama   **809.2**
The **McGraw-Hill** illustrated encyclopedia of robotics & artificial intelligence   **629.8**
McGraw-Hill yearbook of science & technology.
See McGraw-Hill encyclopedia of science & technology   **503**
McGrayne, Sharon Bertsch
Nobel Prize women in science   **920**
McGreal, Ian Philip, 1919-
(ed) Great thinkers of the Eastern world. See Great thinkers of the Eastern world   **181**
(ed) Great thinkers of the Western world. See Great thinkers of the Western world   **190**
McGuire, Paula
(ed) American cultural leaders. See American cultural leaders   **920.003**
McHugh, Maureen F.
The Lincoln Train
In Nebula awards 31 p131-45   **S C**
Virtual love
In Nebula awards 30 p99-110   **S C**
McIntyre, Loren, 1917-
The incredible Incas and their timeless land   **985**

McIntyre, Vonda N.
The mountains of sunset, the mountains of dawn
In The Norton book of science fiction p287-99   **S C**
McKay, Claude
Banana bottom [excerpt]
In The Portable Harlem Renaissance reader p395-408   **810.8**
Banjo [excerpt]
In The Portable Harlem Renaissance reader p389-94   **810.8**
Home to Harlem [excerpt]
In The Portable Harlem Renaissance reader p371-88   **810.8**
Truant
In Calling the wind p39-49   **S C**
See/See also pages in the following book(s):
Black American prose writers of the Harlem Renaissance p108-22   **810.9**
McKay, David W.
(jt. auth) Smith, B. G. Geology projects for young scientists   **550**
McKenny, Margaret
(jt. auth) Peterson, R. T. A field guide to wildflowers of northeastern and north-central North America   **582.13**
McKie, J. R.
Oda Rainbow
In Streetlights: illuminating tales of the urban black experience p318-39   **S C**
McKie, Robin
(jt. auth) Bodmer, W. F. The book of man   **573.2**
McKinley, Robin
Beauty   **Fic**
A knot in the grain and other stories   **S C**
Contents: The healer; The stagman; Touk's house; Buttercups; A knot in the grain
McKinley, William, 1843-1901
See/See also pages in the following book(s):
Lindop, E. Assassinations that shook America p45-56   **364.1**
McKissack, Fredrick, 1939-
(jt. auth) McKissack, P. C. W.E.B. DuBois   **92**
McKissack, Pat See McKissack, Patricia C., 1944-
McKissack, Patricia C., 1944-
W.E.B. DuBois   **92**
McKnight, Kent H.
A field guide to mushrooms, North America   **589.2**
McKnight, Reginald, 1956-
The kind of light that shines on Texas
In Coming of age in America p17-31   **S C**
Mali is very dangerous
In Calling the wind p498-507   **S C**
McKnight, Vera B.
(jt. auth) McKnight, K. H. A field guide to mushrooms, North America   **589.2**
McLanathan, Richard B. K.
Art in America   **709.73**

McLaughlin, Dean, 1931-
Hawk among the sparrows
In The Mammoth book of new world science
fiction p409-53   **S C**

McLaughlin, Jack, 1926-
Jefferson and Monticello   **92**

McLaughlin, Ruth
Seasons
In Circle of women: an anthology of contem-
porary Western women writers p199-211
    810.8

McLaverty, Michael
The poteen maker
In The Oxford book of Irish short stories
p382-87   **S C**

McLean, David
Marine Corps issue
In The Other side of heaven p327-39
    S C

McLean, Will
(jt. auth) Singman, J. L. Daily life in Chaucer's
England   **942.03**

McLuhan, Marshall, 1911-1980
Understanding media   **302.23**

McLynn, F. J.
Robert Louis Stevenson   **92**

McMahon, Pat *See* Hoch, Edward D., 1930-

McManners, Hugh
The backpacker's handbook   **796.5**

McManners, John
(ed) The Oxford illustrated history of Christianity. *See* The Oxford illustrated history of
Christianity   **270**

McMillan, Terry
Ma'dear
In Children of the night p423-33   **S C**
Quilting on the rebound
In Calling the wind p597-608   **S C**
Touching
In Streetlights: illuminating tales of the urban
black experience p340-47   **S C**
Waiting to exhale   **Fic**
See/See also pages in the following book(s):
Black American women fiction writers p117-30
    813.009
Contemporary black American fiction writers
p74-87   **813.009**

McMurray, Emily
(ed) Notable twentieth century scientists. *See*
Notable twentieth century scientists
    920.003

McMurry, Linda O.
George Washington Carver   **92**

McMurtry, Jo, 1937-
Understanding Shakespeare's England
    942.05

McMurtry, Larry
Lonesome dove   **Fic**

McNally, Raymond T., 1931-
(jt. auth) Florescu, R. R. N. Dracula [biography
of Vlad II]   **92**

McNally, T. M.
Skin deep
In Prize stories, 1996 p65-84   **S C**

McNally, Terrence, 1939-
15 short plays   **812**
Contents: Bringing it all back; Noon; Botticelli; Next; ¡Cuba
si!; Sweet Eros; Witness; Whiskey; Bad habits; The Ritz; Prelude
& Liebestod; Andre's mother; The wibbly, wobbly, wiggly dance
that Cleopatterer did; Street talk; Hidden agendas
Frankie and Johnny in the Clair de Lune
In Best American plays: 9th series—1983-
1992 p350-79   **812.008**
Noon
In Best American plays: 7th series—1967-
1973 p445-56   **812.008**
The Ritz
In Best American plays: 8th series—1974-
1982 p369-400   **812.008**

McNamara, Robert S., 1916-
About
Hendrickson, P. The living and the dead
    959.704
See/See also pages in the following book(s):
Halberstam, D. The best and the brightest
    973.922

McNamee, Gregory
(ed) The Sierra Club desert reader. *See* The Sierra Club desert reader   **808.8**

McNamer, Deirdre
Rima in the weeds [excerpt]
In Circle of women: an anthology of contem-
porary Western women writers p341-55
    810.8

McNeil, Barbara
(ed) Twentieth-century author biographies master index. *See* Twentieth-century author biographies master index   **920.003**

McNickle, D'Arcy, 1904-1977
Going to school
In Coming of age in America p154-65
    S C
Hard riding
In The Singing spirit: early short stories by
North American Indians p167-75
    S C
Train time
In The Singing spirit: early short stories by
North American Indians p162-66
    S C

McPartland, Jimmy, 1907-1991
See/See also pages in the following book(s):
Deffaa, C. Voices of the Jazz Age p150-73
    920

McPhee, Penelope
Martin Luther King, Jr.: a documentary—Montgomery to Memphis. *See* Martin Luther King,
Jr.: a documentary—Montgomery to Memphis
    92
(jt. auth) Schulke, F. King remembered   **92**

McPherson, James Alan, 1943-
A loaf of bread
In Children of the night p445-63   **S C**
The story of a scar
In American short story masterpieces
    S C
In Calling the wind p355-65   **S C**

McPherson, James M.
Abraham Lincoln and the second American
Revolution   **973.7**

Medicine—*Continued*
See/See also pages in the following book(s):
Davis, W. S. A day in old Rome p160-69
    937
Data processing
Oleksy, W. G. Science and medicine   **502**
Dictionaries
The American Medical Association encyclopedia
  of medicine   **610.3**
Black's medical dictionary   **610.3**
Isler, C. The Watts teen health dictionary
    610.3
Magill's medical guide, health and illness
    610.3
Merriam-Webster's medical desk dictionary
    610.3
The Oxford medical companion   **610.3**
Stedman's medical dictionary   **610.3**
Experiments
O'Neil, K. E. Health and medicine projects for
  young scientists   **610**
Handbooks, manuals, etc.
Merck manual of diagnosis and therapy
    610.3
History
Encyclopedia of plague and pestilence
    614.4
See/See also pages in the following book(s):
Boorstin, D. J. The Americans: The colonial ex-
  perience p209-39   **973.2**
Durant, W. J. The age of Voltaire p586-602
    940.2

Law and legislation
See also Medical jurisprudence
Physiological effect
See Pharmacology
Research
Gallo, R. C. Virus hunting   **616.97**
Henig, R. M. A dancing matrix   **576**
See/See also pages in the following book(s):
Weinberg, R. A. Racing to the beginning of the
  road   **616.99**
Medicine, Nuclear *See* Nuclear medicine
Medicine, Veterinary *See* Veterinary medicine
Medicine and the law. Grauer, N. A.   **614**
A **medicine** for melancholy. Bradbury, R.
  In Bradbury, R. The stories of Ray Bradbury
  p505-13   **S C**
**Médicis, Catherine de, Queen, consort of Henry
II, King of France, 1519-1589** *See* Catherine de
  Médicis, Queen, consort of Henry II, King of
  France, 1519-1589
Medieval architecture
Snyder, J. Medieval art   **709.02**
Medieval art
Snyder, J. Medieval art   **709.02**
See/See also pages in the following book(s):
Durant, W. J. The age of faith p845-62
    940.1
The Middle Ages [American Heritage]
    940.1
Medieval art. Snyder, J.   **709.02**
Medieval church history *See* Church history—
  600-1500, Middle Ages

Medieval civilization
Cantor, N. F. Medieval lives   **940.1**
Durant, W. J. The age of faith   **940.1**
The Early Middle Ages   **940.1**
Gies, F. Life in a medieval village   **940.1**
The Late Middle Ages   **940.1**
Matthew, D. Atlas of medieval Europe   **911**
The Middle Ages [American Heritage]
    940.1
The Middle Ages: a concise encyclopaedia
    940.1
Tuchman, B. W. A distant mirror   **944**
See/See also pages in the following book(s):
Crow, J. A. Spain: the root and the flower
  p113-38   **946**
Medieval English literature
  In The Oxford anthology of English literature
  v1   **820.8**
Medieval history *See* Middle Ages—History
Medieval literature
See/See also pages in the following book(s):
Durant, W. J. The age of faith p1018-55
    940.1
History and criticism
Burrow, J. A. Medieval writers and their work
    820.9
Medieval lives. Cantor, N. F.   **940.1**
Medieval philosophy
See/See also pages in the following book(s):
Durant, W. J. The age of faith p949-83
    940.1
A **medieval** romance. Twain, M.
  In Twain, M. The complete short stories of
  Mark Twain   **S C**
Medieval writers and their work. Burrow, J. A.
    820.9
Medina, John J., 1956-
The clock of ages   **612.6**
Medina, Pablo, 1948-
Spider's bite
  In Iguana dreams   **S C**
Meditations on history. Williams, S. A.
  In Black-eyed Susans/Midnight birds p230-77
    S C
  In Children of the night p58-99   **S C**
Mediterranean region
Gazetteers
Grant, M. A guide to the ancient world
    938.003
Medley. Bambara, T. C.
  In Black-eyed Susans/Midnight birds p356-74
    S C
Medoff, Mark Howard
Children of a lesser god   **812**
Medvedev, Roy Aleksandrovich, 1925-
Khrushchev: the years in power   **947.085**
Let history judge   **947.084**
The October Revolution   **947.084**
Medvedev, Zhores Aleksandrovich
(jt. auth) Medvedev, R. A. Khrushchev: the
  years in power   **947.085**
Mee, Charles L.
Meeting at Potsdam   **940.53**

The **member** of the wedding [play] McCullers, C.
    812
> *also in* Best American plays: 3d series—
> 1945-1951 p171-203   **812.008**

Memoirs. Sakharov, A. D.   **92**

Memoirs of Sherlock Holmes. Doyle, Sir A. C.
> *In* Doyle, Sir A. C. The complete Sherlock
> Holmes   **S C**

Memory
> *See also* Amnesia
> *See/See also pages in the following book(s):*
> Ornstein, R. E. The amazing brain p133-50
>   **612.8**

Dictionaries

Noll, R. The encyclopedia of memory and memory disorders   **153.1**

Memory. Mahy, M.   **Fic**

A **memory.** Welty, E.
> *In* Welty, E. The collected stories of Eudora
> Welty p75-80   **S C**

A **memory** of two Mondays. Miller, A.
> *In* 24 favorite one-act plays p13-53
>   **808.82**

Men against the sea. Nordhoff, C.
> *In* Nordhoff, C. The Bounty trilogy p297-438
>   **Fic**

Men in sports   **796**

Men of mathematics. Bell, E. T.   **920**

Men of old Catawba. See Wolfe, T. Old Catawba

Men of our time   **811.008**

Men on the moon. Ortiz, S. J.
> *In* The Lightning within p99-106   **S C**

Men under water. Lombreglia, R.
> *In* The Vintage book of contemporary
> American short stories p320-41   **S C**

Men with their big shoes. Jackson, S.
> *In* Jackson, S. The lottery   **S C**

Menaker, Daniel
> Influenza
> *In* Prize stories, 1996 p120-43   **S C**

Menander, of Athens, 343?-291? B.C.
> *See/See also pages in the following book(s):*
> Hamilton, E. The echo of Greece p139-54
>   **880.9**

Menaseh's dream. Singer, I. B.
> *In* The Oxford book of modern fairy tales
> p361-66   **S C**

Mendel, Gregor, 1822-1884
> *See/See also pages in the following book(s):*
> Brynie, F. H. Genetics & human health p30-44
>   **616**

Mendel, Johann Gregor *See* Mendel, Gregor, 1822-1884

Mendelsohn, Jane, 1965-
> I was Amelia Earhart   **Fic**

Mendoza, Durango
> Summer water and Shirley
> *In* Coming of age in America p100-10
>   **S C**

Mene, Mene, Tekel, Upharsin. Cheever, J.
> *In* Cheever, J. The stories of John Cheever
> p554-60   **S C**

Meneseteung. Munro, A.
> *In* The Best American short stories of the
> eighties p351-72   **S C**

Menez, Joseph Francis, 1917-
> (jt. auth) Bartholomew, P. C. Summaries of
> leading cases on the Constitution   **342**

Menninga, Gysbert
> The visitation
> *In* Not the only one p61-66   **S C**

Mennonites
> *See also* Amish

Mental illness
> Lundy, A. Diagnosing and treating mental illness   **616.89**
> Mental illness: opposing viewpoints   **362.2**
> Smith, D. W. Schizophrenia   **616.89**
> *See/See also pages in the following book(s):*
> Powledge, T. M. Your brain p151-58   **612.8**
> #### Drug therapy
> Veggeberg, S. Medication of the mind
>   **616.89**
> #### Fiction
> Oneal, Z. The language of goldfish   **Fic**
> Plath, S. The bell jar   **Fic**
> #### Jurisprudence
> *See/See also pages in the following book(s):*
> Friendly, F. W. The Constitution—that delicate
> balance   **342**

Mental illness: opposing viewpoints   **362.2**

Mental suggestion
> *See also* Brainwashing

Mental telepathy *See* Telepathy

Mental tests *See* Psychological tests

Mentally handicapped
> #### Fiction
> Gaines, E. J. A lesson before dying   **Fic**
> Keyes, D. Flowers for Algernon   **Fic**
> Steinbeck, J. Of mice and men   **Fic**

Mentally ill
> #### Fiction
> Kesey, K. One flew over the cuckoo's nest
>   **Fic**
> Wharton, W. Birdy   **Fic**

Mentally ill children
> Gutkind, L. Stuck in time   **616.89**

Menus
> Karoff, B. South American cooking   **641.5**
> The New Good Housekeeping cookbook
>   **641.5**

Menzel, Donald Howard, 1901-1976
> (jt. auth) Pasachoff, J. M. A field guide to the
> stars and planets   **523**

Menzel, Peter
> Material world   **306.8**

Mercatante, Anthony S.
> The Facts on File encyclopedia of world mythology and legend   **291.03**

Mercenary. Reynolds, M.
> *In* The Mammoth book of new world science
> fiction p97-147   **S C**

Micheaux, Oscar, 1884-1951
See/See also pages in the following book(s):
Black American poets and dramatists before the
Harlem Renaissance p106-18   **810.9**
Black American prose writers before the Harlem
Renaissance p129-39   **810.9**
Michelangelo and his drawings. Hirst, M.
709.45

Michelangelo Buonarroti, 1475-1564
About
Hartt, F. Michelangelo   **759.5**
Hibbard, H. Michelangelo   **92**
Hirst, M. Michelangelo and his drawings
709.45
Murray, L. Michelangelo   **709.45**
See/See also pages in the following book(s):
Labella, V. A season of giants: Michelangelo,
Leonardo, Raphael, 1492-1508   **709.45**
Fiction
Stone, I. The agony and the ecstasy   **Fic**
Micheli, Lyle J., 1940-
Healthy runner's handbook   **613.7**
Michelin guides   **910.2**
Michener, James A. (James Albert), 1907-
The bridge at Andau   **943.9**
Hawaii   **Fic**
Tales of the South Pacific   **S C**
Contents: Coral Sea; Mutiny; An officer and a gentleman; The
cave; The milk run; Alligator; Our heroine; Dry rot; Fo' dolla';
Passion; A boar's tooth; Wine for the mess at Segi; The airstrip
at Konora; Those who fraternize; The strike; Frisco; The landing
on Kuralei; A cemetery at Hoga Point
Mickey Mouse (Cartoon character)
The Art of Mickey Mouse   **741.5**
Microbe hunters. De Kruif, P.   **920**
Microbes *See* Bacteria
Microbiology
See also Biotechnology
Biddle, W. A field guide to germs   **616**
Dixon, B. Power unseen   **576**
Microorganisms from smallpox to Lyme disease
616
Sagan, D. Garden of microbial delights
576
Experiments
Dashefsky, H. S. Microbiology: 49 science fair
projects   **576**
Dashefsky, H. S. Microbiology: high-school sci-
ence fair experiments   **576**
Microcomputers
Consumer reports guide to personal computers
004
Dictionaries
Margolis, P. E. Random House personal com-
puter dictionary   **004**
McGraw-Hill encyclopedia of personal comput-
ing   **004**
Micromegas. Voltaire
In Voltaire. The portable Voltaire   **848**
Microorganisms
See also Bacteria
Microorganisms from smallpox to Lyme disease
616
Microscopes
Stewart, G. Microscopes   **502**

Microsoft Corporation
Gates, B. The road ahead   **004**
Microwave cooking
The Good Housekeeping illustrated microwave
cookbook   **641.5**
Microwave cooking   **641.5**
Microwave cooking   **641.5**
The **Mid-Atlantic** States. Durham, M. S.
917.4
Midair. Conroy, F.
In American short story masterpieces
S C
In The Norton book of American short stories
p635-50   **S C**
Middle age
See also Aging
Middle Ages
See also Church history—600-1500, Middle
Ages; Fourteenth century; Medieval civiliza-
tion
Dictionaries
Bunson, M. The encyclopedia of the Middle
Ages   **940.1**
The Middle Ages [Scribner]   **909.07**
The Middle Ages: a concise encyclopaedia
940.1
Fiction
Hugo, V. The hunchback of Notre Dame
Fic
History
See also Europe—History—476-1492
Cantor, N. F. Medieval lives   **940.1**
Durant, W. J. The age of faith   **940.1**
The Early Middle Ages   **940.1**
Fury of the Northmen: timeframe AD 800-1000
909.07
Gies, F. The knight in history   **940.1**
Gies, F. Life in a medieval village   **940.1**
Gies, F. Women in the Middle Ages   **305.4**
Gies, J. Life in a medieval castle   **940.1**
Harpur, J. Revelations, the Medieval world
909.07
The Late Middle Ages   **940.1**
The March of Islam: timeframe AD 600-800
909
The Middle Ages [American Heritage]
940.1
Runciman, Sir S. A history of the Crusades
909.07
History—Pictorial works
Smithsonian timelines of the ancient world
930
Maps
Hooper, N. The Cambridge illustrated atlas of
warfare: the Middle Ages   **355**
The **Middle** Ages [American Heritage]   **940.1**
The **Middle** Ages [Scribner]   **909.07**
The **Middle** Ages: a concise encyclopaedia
940.1
Middle and junior high school library catalog
011.6
Middle classes
Fiction
Lewis, S. Babbitt   **Fic**

Middle East

See also Arab countries

The Cambridge encyclopedia of the Middle East and North Africa   956

Cleveland, R. L. The Middle East and South Asia   956

The Middle East: opposing viewpoints   956

Roaf, M. Cultural atlas of Mesopotamia and the ancient Near East   935

Antiquities

Reader's Digest atlas of the Bible   220.9

Civilization

Civilizations of the ancient Near East   939

Description

Twain, M. The innocents abroad   817

Dictionaries

Hiro, D. A dictionary of the Middle East   956

Foreign relations—United States

The Middle East   956

History

Lewis, B. The Middle East   956

Politics and government

Friedman, T. L. From Beirut to Jerusalem   956

The Middle East   956

Wakin, E. Contemporary political leaders of the Middle East   920

The **Middle** East   956

The **Middle** East and South Asia. Cleveland, R. L.   956

The **Middle** East: opposing viewpoints   956

Middle East War, 1991 *See* Persian Gulf War, 1991

The **middle** kingdom. Tong Enzheng

In Tales from the planet Earth   S C

The **middle** passage. Feelings, T.   759.13

The **middle** years. James, H.

In The Norton book of American short stories p80-96   S C

In The Oxford book of American short stories p170-89   S C

Middleton, Alex L. A.

(ed) Encyclopedia of birds. See Encyclopedia of birds   598

Middleton, Richard Barham, 1882-1911

On the Brighton Road

In The Oxford book of English ghost stories p266-69   S C

Midnight birds

In Black-eyed Susans/Midnight birds   S C

Midnight blue. Macdonald, R.

In Masterpieces of mystery and suspense p132-59   S C

Midnight news. Goldstein, L.

In The Norton book of science fiction p819-29   S C

Midrash

The Book of legends. Sefer ha-aggadah   296.1

A **midsummer** knight's dream. Henry, O.

In Henry, O. The best short stories of O. Henry   S C

Midway, Battle of, 1942

Rice, E. The Battle of Midway   940.54

Midwinter. Sutton, D.

In The Merlin chronicles   S C

A **midwinter's** tale. Swanwick, M.

In The Norton book of science fiction p733-45   S C

The **Mighty** chieftains   920

Migrant labor

Ashabranner, B. K. Dark harvest: migrant farmworkers in America   331.5

Griswold del Castillo, R. César Chávez   92

Fiction

Steinbeck, J. The grapes of wrath   Fic

Steinbeck, J. Of mice and men   Fic

Migrant people. Steinbeck, J.

In Steinbeck, J. The portable Steinbeck   818

Migration *See* Immigration and emigration

Migration, Internal *See* Internal migration

Migration of animals *See* Animals—Migration

Mikes, Jay, 1953-

Basketball fundamentals   796.323

Mikkelsen, Nina

Virginia Hamilton   813.009

Milady bigamy. De la Torre, L.

In Masterpieces of mystery and suspense p630-44   S C

Milanes, Cecilia Rodriguez- *See* Rodriguez-Milanes, Cecilia

Milestones in science and technology. Mount, E.   509

Military aeronautics

See also World War, 1939-1945—Aerial operations

Flintham, V. Air wars and aircraft   358.4

Military airplanes

Flintham, V. Air wars and aircraft   358.4

Military art and science

See also Military aeronautics

Black, J. The Cambridge illustrated atlas of warfare: Renaissance to revolution, 1492-1792   355

The Cambridge illustrated history of warfare   355

Hooper, N. The Cambridge illustrated atlas of warfare: the Middle Ages   355

Toffler, A. War and anti-war   355

Warfare in the ancient world   355

Warry, J. Warfare in the classical world   355

Military history

See also names of countries with the subhead *Army* or the subdivision *Military history;* and names of wars, battles, sieges, etc.

Black, J. The Cambridge illustrated atlas of warfare: Renaissance to revolution, 1492-1792   355

Flintham, V. Air wars and aircraft   358.4

Kagan, D. On the origins of war and the preservation of peace   355

Keegan, J. A history of warfare   355

Warfare in the ancient world   355

The **misfit**. Colette
In Colette. The collected stories of Colette
p170-79 **S C**

The **misfits**. Miller, A.
In American short story masterpieces
S C

Mishler, Clifford
(jt. auth) Krause, C. L. Standard catalog of
world coins **737.4**

Miss Attila the Hun. Koontz, D. R.
In Koontz, D. R. Strange highways p174-200
S C

Miss Butterfly. Mori, T.
In American dragons: twenty-five Asian
American voices p26-33 **810.8**

Miss Clairol. Viramontes, H. M.
In Latina: women's voices from the borderlands p120-25 **810.8**
In The Oxford book of women's writing in
the United States p154-58 **810.8**

Miss Cynthie. Fisher, R.
In The Best short stories by Negro writers
p35-47 **S C**
In Calling the wind p58-68 **S C**

Miss de Mannering of Asham. Mayor, F. M.
In The Oxford book of gothic tales p386-406
S C

Miss Emily's roses. Zambreno, M. F.
In Vampires: a collection of original stories
p64-80 **S C**

Miss Jéromette and the clergyman. Collins, W.
In Victorian ghost stories p198-217 **S C**

Miss Jessie. Burford, B.
In Daughters of Africa p676-80 **808.8**

Miss Julie. Strindberg, A.
In Thirty famous one-act plays p29-58
808.82

Miss King. Maugham, W. S.
In Maugham, W. S. Collected short stories v3
S C

Miss Lonelyhearts. West, N. **Fic**

Miss Luhester gives a party. Fair, R. L.
In The Best short stories by Negro writers
p403-07 **S C**

Miss Manners' guide to excruciatingly correct behavior. Martin, J. **395**

Miss Marple tells a story. Christie, A.
In Christie, A. Miss Marple: the complete
short stories **S C**

Miss Marple: the complete short stories. Christie,
A. **S C**

Miss Temptation. Vonnegut, K.
In Vonnegut, K. Welcome to the monkey
house **S C**

Miss Winchelsea's heart. Wells, H. G.
In Wells, H. G. The complete short stories of
H. G. Wells p991-1009 **S C**

Miss Zilphia Gant. Faulkner, W.
In Faulkner, W. Uncollected stories of William Faulkner p368-81 **S C**

Missing Angel Juan. Block, F. L. See note under
Block, F. L. Weetzie Bat **Fic**

Missing children
Fiction
Pfeffer, S. B. The year without Michael
Fic

The **missing** line. Singer, I. B.
In Singer, I. B. The death of Methuselah and
other stories p176-84 **S C**

Missing: page thirteen. Green, A. K.
In The Oxford book of American detective
stories p93-123 **S C**

The **missing** peace. Danticat, E.
In Danticat, E. Krik? Krak! **S C**

Missing persons
See also Runaway teenagers

Missing you [excerpt] Petersen, I.
In Circle of women: an anthology of contemporary Western women writers p103-07
810.8

The **mission** of Jane. Wharton, E.
In Wharton, E. The selected short stories of
Edith Wharton p66-81 **S C**

Missionaries, Christian *See* Christian missionaries

Missionaries of Charity
Teresa, Mother. My life for the poor **92**

Missionary Ridge, Battle of, 1863
See/See also pages in the following book(s):
Korn, J. The fight for Chattanooga:
Chickamauga to Missionary Ridge **973.7**

Missions
India
Teresa, Mother. My life for the poor **92**

Mississippi
Fiction
Grisham, J. The runaway jury **Fic**
Race relations
Cagin, S. We are not afraid **323.1**
Walton, A. Mississippi **976.2**

Mississippi River
Fiction
Twain, M. The adventures of Huckleberry Finn
Fic
Twain, M. The adventures of Tom Sawyer
Fic

Mississippi River valley
Twain, M. Life on the Mississippi **818**
Description
See/See also pages in the following book(s):
Great rivers of the world p361-98 **910**

Mississippi valley *See* Mississippi River valley

Missouri
Fiction
Twain, M. The adventures of Huckleberry Finn
Fic
Twain, M. The adventures of Tom Sawyer
Fic

Missouri River valley
Description
See/See also pages in the following book(s):
Great rivers of the world p361-98 **910**

The **mist**. King, S.
In King, S. Skeleton crew **S C**

The **mistake**. Singer, I. B.
In Singer, I. B. The image and other stories
p258-69 **S C**

Monterey (Calif.)
Fiction
Steinbeck, J. Cannery Row   **Fic**

Montesquieu, Charles de Secondat, baron de, 1689-1755
See/See also pages in the following book(s):
Durant, W. J. The age of Voltaire p340-60
    940.2

Montgomery, Robert, 1904-1981
Subject to fits
In Best American plays: 7th series—1967-1973 p369-91   **812.008**

Montgomery, Sy
Walking with the great apes   **920**

Montgomery (Ala.)
Race relations
King, M. L. Stride toward freedom   **323.1**

Montraldo. Cheever, J.
In Cheever, J. The stories of John Cheever p561-66   **S C**

Moody, Regina B.
Coming to terms   **027.8**

Moody, William Vaughn, 1869-1910
The great divide
In Best plays of the early American theatre p361-97   **812.008**

Moon
See/See also pages in the following book(s):
Jastrow, R. Red giants and white dwarfs p104-15   **523.1**

Moon, Voyages to *See* Space flight to the moon

Moon-face. London, J.
In London, J. The portable Jack London p63-68   **818**

A moon for the misbegotten. O'Neill, E.
In Best American plays: 4th series—1951-1957 p133-78   **812.008**
In O'Neill, E. Complete plays v3   **812**

The moon is blue. Herbert, F. H.
In Best American plays: 3d series—1945-1951 p627-63   **812.008**

Moon Lake. Welty, E.
In Welty, E. The collected stories of Eudora Welty p342-74   **S C**

The moon of the Caribbees. O'Neill, E.
In 24 favorite one-act plays p238-55
    808.82
In O'Neill, E. Complete plays v1   **812**

The moon pool. Merritt, A.
In Masterpieces of fantasy and enchantment p540-79   **S C**

Moon shot. Shepard, A. B., Jr.   **629.45**

Moonlight. Faulkner, W.
In Faulkner, W. Uncollected stories of William Faulkner p495-503   **S C**

The moonlight man. Fox, P.   **Fic**

Moonwalk. Power, S.
In The Vintage book of contemporary American short stories p426-44   **S C**

Moorcock, Michael, 1939-
Elric at the end of time
In Masterpieces of fantasy and enchantment p491-531   **S C**

Moore, C. L. (Catherine Lucille), 1911-
No woman born
In Robert Silverberg's Worlds of wonder
    S C
See/See also pages in the following book(s):
Science fiction writers of the golden age p141-56   **809.3**

Moore, Catherine Lucille *See* Moore, C. L. (Catherine Lucille), 1911-

Moore, Charles
About
Durham, M. S. Powerful days   **323.1**

Moore, Freddie, 1900-1992
See/See also pages in the following book(s):
Deffaa, C. Voices of the Jazz Age p174-87
    920

Moore, George, 1852-1933
Albert Nobbs
In The Oxford book of Irish short stories p109-51   **S C**

Moore, Gerald, 1924-
(ed) The Penguin book of modern African poetry. See The Penguin book of modern African poetry   **896**

Moore, J. J. Smith- *See* Smith-Moore, J. J., 1955-

Moore, John, 1907-1967
Local boy makes good
In Classic English short stories, 1930-1955 p199-220   **S C**

Moore, John Leo, 1927-
Speaking of Washington   **975.3**

Moore, Lorrie
Terrific mother
In The Best American short stories, 1993 p300-34   **S C**

Moore, Marianne, 1887-1972
The complete poems of Marianne Moore
    811
See/See also pages in the following book(s):
Voices & visions p243-76   **811.009**

Moore, Patrick
Stargazing   **523**

Moorehead, Alan, 1910-1983
The Blue Nile   **962**

Moragas, Elvira D.
(ed) Larousse English-Spanish Spanish-English dictionary. See Larousse English-Spanish Spanish-English dictionary   **463**

Moral and philosophic stories *See* Fables

Moral education
See/See also pages in the following book(s):
Bettelheim, B. Surviving, and other essays p127-41   **155.9**

Morales, Ed
The coast is clear
In Iguana dreams   **S C**

Moramarco, Fred S., 1938-
(jt. auth) Shucard, A. Modern American poetry, 1865-1950   **811.009**

Moravians
See/See also pages in the following book(s):
Langdon, W. C. Everyday things in American life, 1607-1776 p87-109   **973.2**

Morris, Richard Brandon, 1904-1989
(ed) Basic documents in American history. See
Basic documents in American history
973

Morris, William, 1834-1896
Lindenborg Pool
In Masterpieces of fantasy and enchantment
p532-39 **S C**
Ogier the Dane
In The Merlin chronicles **S C**

Morris, Wright, 1910-
Fellow-creatures
In The Best American short stories of the
eighties p216-22 **S C**

Morrison, Arthur, 1863-1945
The affair of the 'Avalanche Bicycle and Tyre
Co., Limited'
In The Best crime stories of the 19th century
p217-40 **S C**

Morrison, Jaydene
Coping with ADD/ADHD **616.85**

Morrison, Jim, 1943-1971
About
Jones, D. Jim Morrison, dark star **92**

Morrison, Toni, 1931-
Beloved **Fic**
Conversations with Toni Morrison **92**
Jazz **Fic**
"Recitatif"
In Calling the wind p438-53 **S C**
In The Oxford book of women's writing in
the United States p159-75 **810.8**
Seemothermotherisverynice
In Black-eyed Susans/Midnight birds p60-76
S C
About
Toni Morrison: critical perspectives past and
present **813.009**
See/See also pages in the following book(s):
Black American women fiction writers p146-63
813.009
Contemporary black American fiction writers
p104-21 **813.009**
Inventing the truth p83-102 **808**
Major modern black American writers p119-36
810.9

Morrow, James
City of Truth
In Nebula awards 28 p228-317 **S C**

Morsberger, Robert Eustis, 1929-
James Thurber **817**

The **mortal** immortal. Shelley, M. W.
In Classic ghost stories p118-31 **S C**

Le **morte** d'Arthur. Malory, Sir T. **398.2**

Morte d'espier. Brooke, M.
In The Merlin chronicles **S C**

Mortenson, Pauline
The Hunsaker blood
In Circle of women: an anthology of contemporary Western women writers p315-25
810.8

Morton, William Thomas Green, 1819-1868
See/See also pages in the following book(s):
Curtis, R. H. Great lives: medicine p54-65
920

Mosel, Tad
All the way home
In Best American plays: 5th series—1957-
1963 p277-311 **812.008**

Moseley, Michael Edward
The Incas and their ancestors **985**

Mosenfelder, Donn
(jt. auth) Fischer, B. Bobby Fischer teaches
chess **794.1**

Moser, Diane, 1944-
(jt. auth) Spangenburg, R. The history of science
from the ancient Greeks to the scientific revolution **509**
(jt. auth) Spangenburg, R. The history of science
in the 18th century **509**
(jt. auth) Spangenburg, R. The history of science
in the nineteenth century **509**
(jt. auth) Spangenburg, R. The history of science
from 1895 to 1945 **509**
(jt. auth) Spangenburg, R. The history of science
from 1946 to the 1990s **509**
(jt. auth) Spangenburg, R. Wernher von Braun
92

Moses (Biblical figure)
Fiction
Levitin, S. Escape from Egypt **Fic**

Moses, Anna Mary Robertson *See* Moses,
Grandma, 1860-1961

Moses, Grandma, 1860-1961
About
Ketchum, W. C. Grandma Moses **759.13**

Moses, man of the mountain. Hurston, Z. N.
In Hurston, Z. N. Novels and stories p335-
595 **Fic**

Moses, man of the mountain [excerpt] Hurston, Z.
N.
In Hurston, Z. N. I love myself when I am
laughing—and then again when I am
looking mean and impressive p219-45
818

Moslem countries *See* Islamic countries

Moslemism *See* Islam

Mosley, Walter
The thief
In Prize stories, 1996 p270-84 **S C**

The **Mosquito** Coast. Theroux, P. **Fic**

Moss, Alfred A., 1943-
(jt. auth) Franklin, J. H. From slavery to freedom **305.8**

Moss, Joyce, 1951-
Profiles in American history **973**

Moss, Leonard, 1931-
Arthur Miller **812**

Moss, Thylias
See/See also pages in the following book(s):
Contemporary black American poets and drama-
tists p132-42 **810.9**
Going where I'm coming from **920**

Mossman, Jennifer
(ed) Holidays and anniversaries of the world.
See Holidays and anniversaries of the world
394.2

The **most** beautiful molecule. Aldersey-Williams,
H. **546**

Municipal planning *See* City planning

A **municipal** report. Henry, O.
In Henry, O. The best short stories of O.
Henry   **S C**

Munitions *See* Military weapons

Muñiz, Angelina, 1936-
Inland
In Border crossings: emigration and exile
p107-15   **808.8**

Munn, H. Warner (Harold Warner), 1903-1981
The sleeper and the seer
In The Merlin chronicles   **S C**

Munn, Harold Warner *See* Munn, H. Warner
(Harold Warner), 1903-1981

Muñoz, Elías Miguel
The movie maker
In Iguana dreams   **S C**

Munro, Alice
Meneseteung
In The Best American short stories of the
eighties p351-72   **S C**
A real life
In The Best American short stories, 1993
p25-48   **S C**
Royal beatings
In We are the stories we tell   **S C**

Munro, David
(ed) The Oxford dictionary of the world. See
The Oxford dictionary of the world
                                    910.3

Munro, H. H. (Hector Hugh) *See* Saki, 1870-
1916

Murder *See* Homicide

Murder at the automat. Woolrich, C.
In Crime classics p247-68   **S C**

Murder in the cathedral. Eliot, T. S.
In Eliot, T. S. The complete poems and plays,
1909-1950 p173-221   **818**

Murder on the Calais Coach. See Christie, A.
Murder on the Orient Express   **Fic**

Murder on the Orient Express. Christie, A.
                                    Fic

Murder under the microscope. Russell, W.
In The Best crime stories of the 19th century
p51-71   **S C**

The **murderer**. Bradbury, R.
In Bradbury, R. The stories of Ray Bradbury
p241-47   **S C**

The **murderer**. Colette
In Colette. The collected stories of Colette
p278-80   **S C**

Murderers. Michaels, L.
In American short story masterpieces
                                    S C
In The Vintage book of contemporary
American short stories p342-46   **S C**

The **murders** in the Rue Morgue. Poe, E. A.
In Crime classics p3-34   **S C**
In The Oxford book of American detective
stories p10-39   **S C**
In Poe, E. A. The collected tales and poems
of Edgar Allan Poe p141-68   **S C**
In Poe, E. A. Tales of Edgar Allan Poe p169-
216   **S C**

Murie, Margaret E.
See/See also pages in the following book(s):
Lucas, E. Naturalists, conservationists, and
environmentalists   **920**

Murie, Olaus Johan, 1889-1963
A field guide to animal tracks   **591.5**
See/See also pages in the following book(s):
Lucas, E. Naturalists, conservationists, and
environmentalists   **920**

Murowchick, Robert E., 1956-
(ed) China. See China   **951**

Murphy, Bruce, 1962-
(ed) Benet's reader's encyclopedia. See Benet's
reader's encyclopedia   **803**

Murphy, Jack J.
(jt. auth) Murphy, W. B. Nuclear medicine
                                    616.07

Murphy, Pat, 1955-
His vegetable wife
In The Norton book of science fiction p628-
32   **S C**
Love and sex among the invertebrates
In Nebula awards 26 p91-101   **S C**

Murphy, Virginia Reed, d. 1921
See/See also pages in the following book(s):
Stefoff, R. Women pioneers   **920**

Murphy, Wendy B.
Nuclear medicine   **616.07**

Murray, Albert
(jt. auth) Basie, C. Good morning blues: the autobiography of Count Basie   **92**

Murray, Joseph Edward
See/See also pages in the following book(s):
Curtis, R. H. Great lives: medicine p302-10
                                    920

Murray, Linda
Michelangelo   **709.45**

Murray, Robert F., Jr.
(ed) The Human Genome Project and the future
of health care. See The Human Genome
Project and the future of health care   **174**

Murray, Thomas H., 1946-
(ed) The Human Genome Project and the future
of health care. See The Human Genome
Project and the future of health care   **174**

Murrow, Edward R.
See/See also pages in the following book(s):
Cloud, S. The Murrow boys   **070.1**

The **Murrow** boys. Cloud, S.   **070.1**

Musa, Mark
(ed. & tr) Dante Alighieri. The portable Dante
                                    851

Muscular dystrophy
See/See also pages in the following book(s):
Cheney, G. A. Teens with physical disabilities
p29-37   **362.4**

Musculoskeletal system
Feinberg, B. The musculoskeletal system
                                    612.7

Museum of Modern Art (New York, N.Y.)
American photography, 1890-1965, from the
Museum of Modern Art, New York   **779**

Museum of Natural History (New York, N.Y.)
See American Museum of Natural History

Museums

  See also Art museums

The **Musgrave** ritual. Doyle, Sir A. C.

  In Doyle, Sir A. C. The complete Sherlock
  Holmes   **S C**

Mushrooms

  McKnight, K. H. A field guide to mushrooms,
  North America   **589.2**

Music

  See also music of particular countries, e.g.
  American music; types of music; subjects
  with the subdivision Songs; and ethnic groups
  with the subdivision Music

  Marsalis, W. Marsalis on music   **780**

Analysis, appreciation

  See Music appreciation

Bio-bibliography

Baker's biographical dictionary of musicians
      920.003

Composers since 1900   **920.003**

Great composers, 1300-1900   **920.003**

Musicians since 1900   **920.003**

Dictionaries

Ammer, C. The HarperCollins dictionary of music   **780.3**

Baker, R. Richard Baker's companion to music
      780.9

Kennedy, M. The Oxford dictionary of music
      780.3

The New Grove dictionary of music and musicians   **780.3**

The New Harvard dictionary of music
      780.3

The New Oxford companion to music
      780.3

Roche, J. A dictionary of early music
      780.3

History and criticism

Gammond, P. The Harmony illustrated encyclopedia of classical music   **781.6**

Grout, D. J. A history of western music
      780.9

Rushton, J. Classical music   **781.6**

Slonimsky, N. Music since 1900   **780.9**

Spence, K. The young people's book of music
      780

Stanley, J. Classical music   **780.9**

Swafford, J. The Vintage guide to classical music   **781.6**

Law and legislation

Wilson, L. Making it in the music business
      780

Study and teaching

Evans, R. How to read music   **781.4**

Music, African American *See* African American
  music

Music, Gospel *See* Gospel music

Music, Vocal *See* Vocal music

Music appreciation

  See also Music—History and criticism

Copland, A. What to listen for in music
      781.1

Stanley, J. Classical music   **780.9**

Steinberg, M. The symphony   **784.2**

Music education *See* Music—Study and teaching

Music from Spain. Welty, E.

  In Welty, E. The collected stories of Eudora
  Welty p393-426   **S C**

Music industry

  Powell, S. Hit me with music   **781.66**

  Wilson, L. Making it in the music business
      780

Music is my mistress. Ellington, D.   **92**

The **music** of black Americans. Southern, E.
      780.89

The **Music** of what happens   **811.008**

Music since 1900. Slonimsky, N.   **780.9**

The **music** teacher. Cheever, J.

  In Cheever, J. The stories of John Cheever
  p413-22   **S C**

Music videos

  McGrath, T. MTV: the making of a revolution
      791.45

Musical instruments

  Previn, A. André Previn's guide to the orchestra
      784

Dictionaries

Musical instruments of the world   **784.19**

Musical instruments of the world   **784.19**

Musical notation

  Evans, R. How to read music   **781.4**

The **musical** theatre. Lerner, A. J.   **792.6**

Musicals

  Bordman, G. M. American musical theatre
      792.6

  Lerner, A. J. The musical theatre   **792.6**

Directories

  Lynch, R. C. Musicals!   **792.6**

Musicians

  See also Composers; Women musicians

  Baldock, R. Pablo Casals   **92**

  Guthrie, W. Bound for glory   **92**

Dictionaries

Baker's biographical dictionary of musicians
      920.003

Contemporary musicians   **920.003**

Kennedy, M. The Oxford dictionary of music
      780.3

Musicians since 1900   **920.003**

The New Grove dictionary of music and musicians   **780.3**

The New Oxford companion to music
      780.3

Musicians, African American *See* African
  American musicians

Musicians, American

  Off the record   **781.64**

Musicians, Black *See* Black musicians

Musicians since 1900   **920.003**

Musil, Muzette

  Screaming

  In Not the only one p117-26   **S C**

The **Muslim** almanac   **297**

Muslim countries *See* Islamic countries

Muslim women

  See/See also pages in the following book(s):

  Islam: opposing viewpoints p63-98   **320.5**

Muslimism *See* Islam

My roomy. Lardner, R.
   In Lardner, R. The best short stories of Ring Lardner p283-302   **S C**

My sister the moon. Harrison, S.   **Fic**

My son the murderer. Malamud, B.
   In Malamud, B. The stories of Bernard Malamud p85-92   **S C**
   In The Oxford book of American short stories p504-10   **S C**

My son, the physicist. Asimov, I.
   In Asimov, I. The complete stories v1 p598-601   **S C**

My son's story. Gordimer, N.   **Fic**

My soul looks back, 'less I forget   **808.88**

My soul's high song. Cullen, C.   **818**

My tocaya. Cisneros, S.
   In Cisneros, S. Woman Hollering Creek and other stories   **S C**

My traitor's heart. Malan, R.   **968.06**

My visit to Niagara. Hawthorne, N.
   In Hawthorne, N. Tales and sketches; A wonder book for girls and boys; Tanglewood tales for girls and boys p244-50   **S C**

My vocation. Lavin, M.
   In The Oxford book of short stories p432-42   **S C**

My watch. Twain, M.
   In Twain, M. The complete short stories of Mark Twain   **S C**

Myers, Joan, 1944-
   (il) Okihiro, G. Y. Whispered silences   **940.53**

Myers, Walter Dean, 1937-
   Cages
      In Center stage   **812.008**
   Fallen angels   **Fic**
   Malcolm X   **92**
   One more river to cross   **779**
   Somewhere in the darkness   **Fic**
   About
   Bishop, R. S. Presenting Walter Dean Myers   **813.009**

Myerson, Joel
   (ed) Critical essays on Henry David Thoreau's Walden. See Critical essays on Henry David Thoreau's Walden   **818**

Myhrvold, Nathan P.
   (jt. auth) Gates, B. The road ahead   **004**

Mysteries of mankind   **930**

Mysteries of the ancient Americas   **970.01**

Mysterious Madame Shanghai. Hughes, L.
   In Hughes, L. Short stories   **S C**

The **mysterious** stranger. Twain, M.
   In Twain, M. The complete short stories of Mark Twain   **S C**

The **Mysterious** world   **133**

Mystery and detective stories *See* Mystery fiction

Mystery fiction
   Bad behavior   **S C**
   The Best crime stories of the 19th century   **S C**

Christie, A. Miss Marple: the complete short stories   **S C**

Christie, A. Murder on the Orient Express   **Fic**

Clark, M. H. Where are the children?   **Fic**

Crime classics   **S C**

Doyle, Sir A. C. The complete Sherlock Holmes   **S C**

Doyle, Sir A. C. The hound of the Baskervilles   **Fic**

Francis, D. Come to grief   **Fic**

Guy, R. The disappearance   **Fic**

Hillerman, T. Skinwalkers   **Fic**

Masterpieces of mystery and suspense   **S C**

The Oxford book of American detective stories   **S C**

Poe, E. A. The collected tales and poems of Edgar Allan Poe   **S C**

Pullman, P. The ruby in the smoke   **Fic**

Tey, J. The daughter of time   **Fic**
   Bibliography
Keating, H. R. F. Crime and mystery: the 100 best books   **823.009**
   Bio-bibliography
Modern mystery writers   **809.3**
   Dictionaries
DeAndrea, W. L. Encyclopedia mysteriosa   **809.3**
   History and criticism
Modern mystery writers   **809.3**
   Technique
Roth, M. The writer's complete crime reference book   **808.3**

The **mystery** of Marie Roget. Poe, E. A.
   In Poe, E. A. The collected tales and poems of Edgar Allan Poe p169-207   **S C**

The **mystery** of numbers. Schimmel, A.   **133.3**

The **mystery** of the ancient Maya. Meyer, C.   **972**

Mystification. Poe, E. A.
   In Poe, E. A. The collected tales and poems of Edgar Allan Poe p354-60   **S C**

The **myth** of Sisyphus, and other essays. Camus, A.   **844**

Mythical animals
   See also Animals—Folklore; Dragons

Mythology
   See also Gods and goddesses; mythology of particular national or ethnic groups or of particular geographic areas, e.g. Celtic mythology
Bulfinch, T. Bulfinch's mythology   **291**
Campbell, J. The masks of God   **291**
Campbell, J. The power of myth   **291**
Eliot, A. The universal myths   **291**
Frazer, Sir J. G. The golden bough   **291**
Frazer, Sir J. G. The new golden bough   **291**
Hearne, B. G. Beauties and beasts   **398.2**
Leeming, D. A. The world of myth   **291**
World mythology   **291**
See/See also pages in the following book(s):
Highet, G. The classical tradition p520-40   **809**

Mythology—*Continued*
Dictionaries
Ann, M. Goddesses in world mythology
291.03
Cotterell, A. The Macmillan illustrated encyclopedia of myths and legends **291.03**
The Dictionary of world myth **291.03**
Funk & Wagnalls standard dictionary of folklore, mythology, and legend **398.03**
Leeming, D. A. Encyclopedia of creation myths
291.03
Man, myth, & magic **133**
Mercatante, A. S. The Facts on File encyclopedia of world mythology and legend
291.03
Mythology, Egyptian *See* Egyptian mythology
Mythology, Japanese *See* Japanese mythology
Mythology, Norse *See* Norse mythology
Mythology, Slavic *See* Slavic mythology
Mythology. Hamilton, E. **292**
Mythology in literature
Campbell, J. The masks of God **291**
The **mythology** of Mexico and Central America. Bierhorst, J. **299**
The **mythology** of North America. Bierhorst, J. **299**
The **mythology** of South America. Bierhorst, J. **299**
Myths. See Eliot, A. The universal myths
291

N

Naar, Alex J.
(jt. auth) Naar, J. This land is your land
333.7
Naar, Jon
This land is your land **333.7**
Nabhan, Gary Paul
(jt. auth) Buchmann, S. The forgotten pollinators
574.5
Nabokov, Peter
Native American architecture **728**
Nabokov, Vladimir Vladimirovich, 1899-1977
The return of Chorb
In The Portable twentieth-century Russian reader p381-90 **891.7**
The visit to the museum
In The Portable twentieth-century Russian reader p391-402 **891.7**
Nada. Ortiz Cofer, J.
In Daughters of the fifth sun **810.8**
In The Other side of heaven p25-32
S C
Nader, Ralph
Collision course **363.1**
Nāgārjuna
See/See also pages in the following book(s):
Jaspers, K. The great philosophers **109**
Nagasaki (Japan)
Bombardment, 1945
See/See also pages in the following book(s):
Yamazaki, J. N. Children of the atomic bomb
92

Nairobi. Oates, J. C.
In The Best American short stories of the eighties p174-81 **S C**
Naisbitt, John
Megatrends **303.4**
Megatrends 2000 **303.4**
Nakamura, Joyce
(ed) Writers for young adults: biographies master index. See Writers for young adults: biographies master index **920.003**
The **naked** and the dead. Mailer, N. **Fic**
Naked Earth. Vogel, S. **551.1**
Naked ladies. Nelson, A.
In The Best American short stories, 1993 p169-86 **S C**
Naked masks. Pirandello, L. **852**
Nam. Baker, M. **959.704**
Nam-Bok the unveracious. London, J.
In London, J. The portable Jack London p42-55 **818**
Name in the papers. Hughes, L.
In Hughes, L. Short stories **S C**
Name that book!. Gotwalt, H. L. M.
In The Big book of large-cast plays p299-312
812.008
The **nameless** man. Ottolengui, R.
In The Best crime stories of the 19th century p241-52 **S C**
Namer of beasts, maker of souls. Salmonson, J. A.
In The Merlin chronicles **S C**
Names
See also Geographic names
Dictionaries
Room, A. Cassell dictionary of proper names
929.4
Names, Personal *See* Personal names
The **names** of the nation. Wolfe, T.
In Wolfe, T. The complete short stories of Thomas Wolfe p185-94 **S C**
Namioka, Lensey
Herbal nightmare
In Center stage **812.008**
Who's Hu? [excerpt]
In American dragons: twenty-five Asian American voices p48-64 **810.8**
See/See also pages in the following book(s):
Going where I'm coming from **920**
Nanji, Azim
(ed) The Muslim almanac. See The Muslim almanac **297**
Napier of Magdala, Robert Cornelis Napier, 1810-1890
See/See also pages in the following book(s):
Moorehead, A. The Blue Nile **962**
Napoleon I, Emperor of the French, 1769-1821
About
Durant, W. J. The age of Napoleon **940.2**
Kirchberger, J. H. The French Revolution and Napoleon **944.04**
Schom, A. One hundred days **944.05**
See/See also pages in the following book(s):
Emerson, R. W. The portable Emerson p325-45
818

Nationalism and ethnic conflict 305.8

The **nations** within: the past and future of American Indian sovereignty. Deloria, V. 323.1

Native America. Mather, C. 970.004

Native America in the twentieth century 970.004

The **Native** American almanac. Hirschfelder, A. B. 970.004

Native American architecture. Nabokov, P. 728

The **Native** American experience 970.004

Native American myths and legends 299

Native American painters of the twentieth century. Henkes, R. 920

Native Americans See Indians of North America

The **Native** Americans 970.004

Native Americans information directory 970.004

The **Native** North American almanac 970.004

Native North American literature 810.9

Native son. Wright, R. Fic
  also in Wright, R. Works v1 818

Native son [play] Wright, R.
  In Black theatre USA 812.008

Native time: an historical time line of native America. Francis, L. 970.004

Natividad, Irene, 1948-
  (ed) The Asian-American almanac. See The Asian-American almanac 305.8

Natkiel, Richard
  (jt. auth) Ferrell, R. H. Atlas of American history 911

Natural disasters
  See also Storms
  Davis, L. A. Natural disasters 904
  Erickson, J. Quakes, eruptions, and other geologic cataclysms 550
  Great disasters 904
  Raging forces: earth in upheaval 904
  Watson, B. A. Acts of God 551.6

Natural gardening See Organic gardening

Natural history
  See also Biogeography
  Baker, W. L. Dancing honeybees and other natural wonders of science 500
  The Curious naturalist 508
  Darwin, C. The voyage of the Beagle 508
  Discovering the wonders of our world 508
  Few, R. The atlas of wild places 508
  Forgotten Edens 508
  Gibbons, W. Keeping all the pieces 574.5
  Gould, S. J. Bully for brontosaurus 508
  Gould, S. J. Dinosaur in a haystack 508
  Gould, S. J. The flamingo's smile 508
  Nature projects on file 508
  Our awesome earth 508
  Seff, P. Our fascinating earth 508
  Dictionaries
  The New book of popular science 503
  Maps
  Wood, R. M. Atlas of the natural world 508

Alaska
  Melham, T. Alaska's wildlife treasures 599
  Arctic regions
  Lopez, B. H. Arctic dreams 998
  Canada
  Canada's incredible coasts 971
  Corfu Island (Greece)
  Durrell, G. M. My family & other animals 574.9
  North America
  MacLeish, W. H. The day before America 970.01
  The Walker's companion 508
  Virginia
  Dillard, A. Pilgrim at Tinker Creek 818

The **natural** history of seals. Bonner, W. N. 599.74

A **natural** history of the dead. Hemingway, E.
  In Hemingway, E. The complete short stories of Ernest Hemingway p335-41 S C
  In Hemingway, E. The short stories of Ernest Hemingway p440-49 S C

Natural man. Browne, T.
  In Black theatre USA 812.008

Natural monuments
  Dictionaries
  Reader's Digest natural wonders of the world 910.3

Natural parents See Birthparents

Natural resources
  See also Conservation of natural resources; Energy resources; Marine resources; Mines and mineral resources

Natural selection
  See also Evolution
  Bowler, P. J. Darwinism 575.01
  Darwin, C. The Darwin reader 575.01
  Darwin, C. The essential Darwin 575.01
  Darwin, C. The portable Darwin 575.01
  Quinn, J. R. Wildlife survivors 574.5

Naturalism in literature See Realism in literature

Naturalists
  Axelrod, A. The environmentalists 920.003
  Bowlby, J. Charles Darwin 92
  Lucas, E. Naturalists, conservationists, and environmentalists 920
  Milner, R. Charles Darwin 92
  White, M. Darwin 92
  Wilkins, T. John Muir 92

Naturalists, conservationists, and environmentalists. Lucas, E. 920

Nature
  Bierhorst, J. The way of the earth 970.004
  Earth energies 001.9

Nature, Effect of man on See Human influence on nature

Nature. Emerson, R. W.
  In Emerson, R. W. The portable Emerson p7-50 818

Nature. Swenson, M. 811

Nature conservation
  See also Wildlife conservation
  Commoner, B. Making peace with the planet 304.2

Nelson, Alice Moore Dunbar- *See* Dunbar-Nelson, Alice Moore, 1875-1935

Nelson, Andrew Nathaniel
The modern reader's Japanese-English character dictionary **495.6**

Nelson, Antonya
Naked ladies
In The Best American short stories, 1993 p169-86 **S C**

Nelson, Douglas
(jt. auth) Parker, T. Day by day: the sixties **909.82**

Nelson, Gaylord
See/See also pages in the following book(s):
Lucas, E. Naturalists, conservationists, and environmentalists **920**

Nelson, Glenn C.
Ceramics **738.1**

Nelson, Harland S.
Charles Dickens **823.009**

Nelson, Mariah Burton
Are we winning yet? **796**

Nelson, Michael, 1949-
(ed) Guide to the presidency. See Guide to the presidency **353.03**
(ed) The Presidency A to Z. See The Presidency A to Z **353.03**

Nelson Mandela speaks. Mandela, N. **968.06**

Nemerov, Howard
Trying conclusions **811**

Nemiroff, Robert, d. 1991
Hansberry, L. To be young, gifted and black **92**

Neo-fascism *See* Fascism

Neo-Nazis
See/See also pages in the following book(s):
Laqueur, W. Fascism **320.5**

Neon powwow. Crank, D. L.
In Song of the turtle p297-301 **S C**

Nepal
See/See also pages in the following book(s):
The Cambridge encyclopedia of India, Pakistan, Bangladesh, Sri Lanka, Nepal, Bhutan, and the Maldives **954**

Nerilka's story. McCaffrey, A. See note under McCaffrey, A. [The Pern series] **Fic**

Neruda, Pablo, 1904-1973
Late and posthumous poems, 1968-1974 **861**
Selected odes of Pablo Neruda **861**
Twenty love poems and a song of despair **861**

Nervous system
Edelson, E. The nervous system **612.8**
Diseases
See also Epilepsy; Huntington's chorea; Multiple sclerosis
Sacks, O. W. The man who mistook his wife for a hat and other clinical tales **616.8**

Nesbit, E. (Edith), 1858-1924
The book of beasts
In The Oxford book of modern fairy tales p203-14 **S C**

Hurst of Hurstcote
In The Oxford book of gothic tales p286-96 **S C**
John Charrington's wedding
In Victorian ghost stories p360-66 **S C**
Man-size in marble
In The Oxford book of English ghost stories p125-36 **S C**

Nesbit, Edith *See* Nesbit, E. (Edith), 1858-1924

A **nest** egg for paradise. Singer, I. B.
In Singer, I. B. The image and other stories p176-203 **S C**

Nesvadba, Josef
The divided Carla
In Tales from the planet Earth **S C**

Netherlands
Civilization
See/See also pages in the following book(s):
Durant, W. J. The age of reason begins p436-94 **940.2**

History
See/See also pages in the following book(s):
Durant, W. J. The age of Louis XIV p164-80 **940.2**

History—1940-1945, German occupation
Frank, A. The diary of a young girl **92**
Frank, A. The diary of a young girl: the definitive edition **92**
Frank, A. The works of Anne Frank **839.3**
Gies, M. Anne Frank remembered **940.53**
Lindwer, W. The last seven months of Anne Frank **940.53**
Reiss, J. The upstairs room **92**
History—1940-1945, German occupation—Drama
Goodrich, F. The diary of Anne Frank **812**

Networks, Information *See* Information networks

Neuman, Colleen
A better mousetrap
In The Big book of large-cast plays p208-15 **812.008**

Neurology *See* Nervous system

Never. Bates, H. E.
In The Oxford book of short stories p391-94 **S C**

Never bet the Devil your head. Poe, E. A.
In Poe, E. A. The collected tales and poems of Edgar Allan Poe p482-89 **S C**

Never marry a Mexican. Cisneros, S.
In Cisneros, S. Woman Hollering Creek and other stories **S C**

Never quite a Hollywood star. Revard, C.
In Talking leaves **S C**

Never room with a couple. Hughes, L.
In Hughes, L. Short stories **S C**

Never shake a family tree. Westlake, D. E.
In Masterpieces of mystery and suspense p514-25 **S C**

Never to forget: the Jews of the Holocaust. Meltzer, M. **940.53**

Nevin, David, 1927-
The road to Shiloh: early battles in the West **973.7**
Sherman's march: Atlanta to the sea **973.7**

New, Gregory R.
(ed) Dewey, M. Dewey decimal classification and relative index **025.4**

New & selected poems, 1940-1986. Shapiro, K. J. **811**

The **new** accelerator. Wells, H. G.
In Wells, H. G. The complete short stories of H. G. Wells p927-42 **S C**

The **new** Adam and Eve. Hawthorne, N.
In Hawthorne, N. Tales and sketches; A wonder book for girls and boys; Tanglewood tales for girls and boys p746-63 **S C**

The **new** American Bible. Bible **220.5**

New and selected poems. Oliver, M. **811**

New and selected poems. Soto, G. **811**

New and selected poems, 1923-1985. Warren, R. P. **811**

A **new** Arabian night's entertainment. Walpole, H.
In Masterpieces of fantasy and enchantment p162-66 **S C**

The **new** Atlantis. Le Guin, U. K.
In The Norton book of science fiction p317-36 **S C**

The **New** book of popular science **503**

New bridge complete, Goren's. Goren, C. H. **795.4**

The **New** Cambridge modern history **909.08**

The **New** Cassell's German dictionary. See Cassell's German-English, English-German dictionary **433**

The **New** Columbia encyclopedia. See The Columbia encyclopedia **031**

The **new** complete babysitter's handbook. Barkin, C. **649**

The **new** comprehensive American rhyming dictionary. Young, S. **423**

The **New** Cosmopolitan world atlas. See Rand McNally cosmopolitan world atlas **912**

A **new** day. Wright, C. S.
In The Best short stories by Negro writers p341-46 **S C**
In Calling the wind p284-88 **S C**

New dictionary. Vonnegut, K.
In Vonnegut, K. Welcome to the monkey house **S C**

The **New** Encyclopaedia Britannica **031**

New England
Description
New England, land of scenic splendor **917.4**
Fiction
Hawthorne, N. The House of the Seven Gables **Fic**
Hawthorne, N. The scarlet letter **Fic**
History
Demos, J. Entertaining Satan **974**
History—1600-1775, Colonial period
Karlsen, C. F. The devil in the shape of a woman **133.4**
New England, land of scenic splendor **917.4**
The **new** English Bible. See Bible. The revised English Bible **220.5**

A **New** English-Chinese dictionary **495.1**

New Eve and old Adam. Lawrence, D. H.
In Lawrence, D. H. The complete short stories v1 **S C**

The **new** Fowler's modern English usage. Fowler, H. W. **428**

New garden book. See Better Homes and Gardens new garden book **635**

New geographical dictionary, Webster's **910.3**

The **new** golden bough. Frazer, Sir J. G. **291**

The **New** Good Housekeeping cookbook **641.5**

The **New** Good Housekeeping family health and medical guide **616.02**

The **New** Grove dictionary of American music **780.973**

The **New** Grove dictionary of jazz **781.65**

The **New** Grove dictionary of music and musicians **780.3**

The **new** Grove gospel, blues and jazz. Oliver, P. **780.89**

The **New** Harvard dictionary of music **780.3**

A **New** history of French literature **840.9**

A **new** history of India. Wolpert, S. A. **954**

A **new** history of Korea. Yi, K.-B. **951.9**

The **New** international atlas **912**

New Jersey
History
Fisher, S. G. The Quaker colonies **973.2**
The **new** Jerusalem Bible. Bible **220.5**

New kids on the block: oral histories of immigrant teens. Bode, J. **325.73**

A **new** leaf. Fitzgerald, F. S.
In Fitzgerald, F. S. The short stories of F. Scott Fitzgerald p634-47 **S C**

The **new** life [La vita nuova] Dante Alighieri
In Dante Alighieri. The portable Dante **851**
In Emerson, R. W. Collected poems & translations **811**

New Mexico
Fiction
Bradford, R. Red sky at morning **Fic**
Cather, W. Death comes for the archbishop **Fic**
History
Bryan, H. Robbers, rogues, and ruffians **978.9**

The **new** Milton Cross' complete stories of the great operas. Cross, M. **792.5**

The **new** Milton Cross' more stories of the great operas. Cross, M. **792.5**

The **new** mother. Clifford, L. L.
In Masterpieces of fantasy and enchantment p280-90 **S C**
In The Oxford book of modern fairy tales p120-39 **S C**

The **New** Moulton's library of literary criticism **820.9**

The **New** our bodies, ourselves **613**

The **New** Oxford book of American verse **811.008**

The New Oxford book of eighteenth century verse
821.008

The New Oxford book of English light verse
821.008

The New Oxford book of English verse, 1250-1950 **821.008**

The New Oxford book of Irish verse **821.008**

The New Oxford book of seventeenth century verse **821.008**

The New Oxford book of Victorian verse
821.008

The New Oxford companion to literature in French
840.3

The New Oxford companion to music **780.3**

New paths to power. Smith, K. M.
In The Young Oxford history of women in the United States **305.4**

The new Penguin dictionary of modern history, 1789-1945. Townson, D. **903**

New poems of Emily Dickinson. Dickinson, E.
811

The new prime. Vance, J.
In Robert Silverberg's Worlds of wonder
S C

New republic (Periodical)
The Black book of Bosnia **949.7**

The New Rolling Stone encyclopedia of rock & roll **781.66**

New selected poems. Hughes, T. **821**

New selected poems. Levine, P. **811**

The new sidewalk. Bryant, D.
In Where coyotes howl and wind blows free p101-08 **810.8**

The new teenage body book. McCoy, K. **613**

New Testament *See* Bible. N.T.

The new view almanac. Tesar, J. E. **031.02**

New words
Dictionaries
The Oxford dictionary of new words **423**
Third Barnhart dictionary of new English
423

The new world. Churchill, Sir W.
In Churchill, Sir W. A history of the English-speaking peoples v2 **941**

New World dictionary of computer terms, Webster's **004**

The New world order: opposing viewpoints
327

New Year's Day. Wharton, E.
In Wharton, E. Novellas and other writings
818

New Year's Eve. Wein, E. E.
In Not the only one p54-60 **S C**

New York (N.Y.)
Description
See/See also pages in the following book(s):
White, E. B. Essays of E. B. White **814**
Fiction
Baldwin, J. If Beale Street could talk **Fic**
Conroy, P. The prince of tides **Fic**
Dreiser, T. Sister Carrie **Fic**
Lipsyte, R. The brave **Fic**

Mohr, N. In Nueva York **S C**
Salinger, J. D. The catcher in the rye **Fic**
Salinger, J. D. Franny & Zooey **Fic**
Wharton, E. The age of innocence **Fic**
Foreign population
Glazer, N. Beyond the melting pot **305.8**
History
See/See also pages in the following book(s):
Langdon, W. C. Everyday things in American life, 1607-1776 p38-47 **973.2**

New York (State)
Fiction
Doctorow, E. L. Ragtime **Fic**
Kennedy, W. Ironweed **Fic**

New York day women. Danticat, E.
In Children of the night p562-66 **S C**
In Danticat, E. Krik? Krak! **S C**

The New York idea. Mitchell, L. E.
In Best plays of the early American theatre p398-457 **812.008**

New York in June. Sloan, B.
In Not the only one p215-33 **S C**

New York Public Library
Books for the teen age **011.6**
Corey, M. American history **973.02**

The New York Public Library book of chronologies. Wetterau, B. **902**

The New York Public Library book of how and where to look it up **025.5**

The New York Public Library book of twentieth-century American quotations **808.88**

The New York Public Library desk reference
031.02

The New York Public Library performing arts desk reference **791**

The New York Public Library science desk reference. Barnes-Svarney, P. **500**

The New York Public Library writer's guide to style and usage **808**

The New York Public Library's books of the century. Diefendorf, E. **028**

The New York Times atlas of the world **912**

New York Times Company
The New York Times Index **071**

The New York Times food encyclopedia, Craig Claiborne's. Claiborne, C. **641.03**

The New York Times Index. New York Times Company **071**

The New York Times selective guide to colleges. See Fiske, E. B. The Fiske guide to colleges
378.73

New York University. Medical Center
Staying healthy in a risky environment. See Staying healthy in a risky environment
613

New York Vietnam Veterans Memorial Commission
Dear America: letters home from Vietnam. See Dear America: letters home from Vietnam
959.704

New York Yankees (Baseball team)
Halberstam, D. Summer of '49 **796.357**

Nguyen, Quang Lap
The sound of harness bells
In The Other side of heaven p287-93
S C

Nguyen, Quang Thieu
Two village women
In The Other side of heaven p65-72
S C

Nguyen, Xuan Hoang
The autobiography of a useless person
In The Other side of heaven p235-44
S C

Nguyen Duc Minh *See* Minh, Nguyen Duc

Niatum, Duane, 1938-
Crow's sun
In Talking leaves   S C
(ed) Harper's anthology of 20th century Native
American poetry. See Harper's anthology of
20th century Native American poetry
811.008

Nice old-fashioned romance, with love lyrics and
everything. Saroyan, W.
In Saroyan, W. My name is Aram   S C

A **nice** place to stay. Tyre, N.
In Masterpieces of mystery and suspense
p620-29   S C

Nichol, John, 1939-
Bites and stings   591.6

Nicholas II, Emperor of Russia, 1868-1918
About
Massie, R. K. Nicholas and Alexandra   92
Massie, R. K. The Romanovs   947.08

Nicholas, of Cusa, Cardinal, 1401-1464
See/See also pages in the following book(s):
Jaspers, K. The great philosophers   109

Nicholls, Peter, 1939-
(ed) The Encyclopedia of science fiction. See
The Encyclopedia of science fiction
809.3

Nichols, Anne, 1891?-1966
Abie's Irish Rose
In The Most popular plays of the American
theater p159-222   812.008

Nichols, Janet, 1952-
American music makers   920

Nichols, Michael K., 1953-
The great apes   599.88

Nicholson, Lois, 1949-
Helen Keller   92

The **Nick** Adams stories. Hemingway, E.
S C

Nicknames
Shankle, G. E. American nicknames   929.4

Nicodemus Bluff. Hannah, B.
In The Best American short stories, 1994
p167-88   S C

Nicolaus Cusanus *See* Nicholas, of Cusa, Cardinal, 1401-1464

Nicomachean ethics. Aristotle
In Aristotle. The basic works of Aristotle
p927-1112   888

Niering, William A.
The Audubon Society field guide to North
American wildflowers: eastern region
582.13

Nietzsche, Friedrich Wilhelm, 1844-1900
The antichrist
In Nietzsche, F. W. The portable Nietzsche
193
Nietzsche contra Wagner
In Nietzsche, F. W. The portable Nietzsche
193
The portable Nietzsche   193
Thus spoke Zarathustra
In Nietzsche, F. W. The portable Nietzsche
193
Twilight of the idols
In Nietzsche, F. W. The portable Nietzsche
193

See/See also pages in the following book(s):
Durant, W. J. The story of philosophy p301-35
109
Jaspers, K. The great philosophers   109
Russell, B. A history of Western philosophy
p760-73   109
Nietzsche contra Wagner. Nietzsche, F. W.
In Nietzsche, F. W. The portable Nietzsche
193

Nigg, Joe
Wonder beasts   398
The **Nigger** of the "Narcissus". Conrad, J.
In Conrad, J. The portable Conrad   828
The **night**. Bradbury, R.
In Bradbury, R. The stories of Ray Bradbury
p3-8   S C
Night. Campbell, J. W.
In The Oxford book of science fiction stories
p95-114   S C
Night. Melfi, L.
In Best American plays: 7th series—1967-
1973 p457-65   812.008
Night. Wiesel, E.
In Wiesel, E. Night, Dawn, The accident:
three tales   Fic
Night and the loves of Joe Dicostanzo. Delany, S.
R.
In Calling the wind p289-304   S C
Night at an inn. Dunsany, E. J. M. D. P., Baron
In Thirty famous one-act plays p255-63
808.82
Night before battle. Hemingway, E.
In Hemingway, E. The complete short stories
of Ernest Hemingway p437-59   S C
Night before landing. Hemingway, E.
In Hemingway, E. The Nick Adams stories
p137-42   S C
The **night-born**. London, J.
In London, J. The portable Jack London
p263-75   818
In London, J. Short stories of Jack London
p477-88   S C
Night call, collect. Bradbury, R.
In Bradbury, R. The stories of Ray Bradbury
p670-79   S C
Night, Dawn, The accident: three tales. Wiesel, E.
Fic

Nixon, Richard M. (Richard Milhous), 1913-1994

In the arena: a memoir of victory, defeat, and renewal   **92**

RN: the memoirs of Richard Nixon   **92**

About

Aitken, J. Nixon, a life   **92**

Emery, F. Watergate   **973.924**

Greene, J. R. The limits of power   **973.924**

Matthews, C. J. Kennedy & Nixon   **973.922**

White, T. H. The making of the president, 1960   **324.6**

Woodward, B. The final days   **973.924**

See/See also pages in the following book(s):

Cannon, J. M. Time and chance: Gerald Ford's appointment with history   **92**

Character above all   **920**

No. 1 Branch Line, the signalman. Dickens, C.

In Classic ghost stories p142-54   **S C**

No coward soul is mine. Brontë, E.   **821**

No cure for it. Wolfe, T.

In Wolfe, T. The complete short stories of Thomas Wolfe p533-36   **S C**

No door. Wolfe, T.

In Wolfe, T. The complete short stories of Thomas Wolfe p67-105   **S C**

No downlink. Jensen, C.   **629.45**

No exit. Sartre, J. P.

In Sartre, J. P. No exit, and three other plays   **842**

No exit, and three other plays. Sartre, J. P.   **842**

No living voice. Millington, T. S.

In Victorian ghost stories p190-97   **S C**

No matter how loud I shout. Humes, E.   **364.3**

No more masks!   **811.008**

No more rivers. Wolfe, T.

In Wolfe, T. The complete short stories of Thomas Wolfe p596-611   **S C**

No more Saturday nights. Klein, N.   **Fic**

No name in the street. Baldwin, J.   **305.8**

No nature. Snyder, G.   **811**

No ordinary time [biography of Franklin D. Roosevelt] Goodwin, D. K.   **92**

No particular night or morning. Bradbury, R.

In Bradbury, R. The illustrated man   **S C**

In Bradbury, R. The stories of Ray Bradbury p165-73   **S C**

No pity. Shapiro, J. P.   **323.3**

No place for you, my love. Welty, E.

In We are the stories we tell   **S C**

In Welty, E. The collected stories of Eudora Welty p465-81   **S C**

No place to make love. Hughes, L.

In Hughes, L. Short stories   **S C**

Nō plays

The Classic Noh theatre of Japan   **895.6**

No rest for the wicked. L'Amour, L.

In L'Amour, L. The outlaws of Mesquite p95-112   **S C**

No time for sergeants. Levin, I.

In Best American plays: 4th series—1951-1957 p573-609   **812.008**

No woman born. Moore, C. L.

In Robert Silverberg's Worlds of wonder   **S C**

Noah's choice. Mann, C. C.   **574.5**

The **Nobel** Peace Prize and the laureates. Abrams, I.   **920.003**

Nobel Prize winners   **920.003**

Nobel Prize women in science. McGrayne, S. B.   **920**

Nobel Prizes

Abrams, I. The Nobel Peace Prize and the laureates   **920.003**

Dash, J. The triumph of discovery: women scientists who won the Nobel Prize   **920**

McGrayne, S. B. Nobel Prize women in science   **920**

Nobel Prize winners   **920.003**

Noble, William, 1932-

Bookbanning in America   **098**

Nobody ever dies. Hemingway, E.

In Hemingway, E. The complete short stories of Ernest Hemingway p470-81   **S C**

Nobody has to know. Macdonald, J.

In Vampires: a collection of original stories p3-7   **S C**

"Nobody here but—". Asimov, I.

In Asimov, I. The complete stories v1 p521-30   **S C**

Nobody knows. Anderson, S.

In Anderson, S. Winesburg, Ohio   **S C**

Nobody knows my name. Baldwin, J.   **305.8**

Nobody's people. Arobateau, R. J.

In Daughters of Africa p593-603   **808.8**

Noether, Amalie Emmy *See* Noether, Emmy, 1882-1935

Noether, Emmy, 1882-1935

See/See also pages in the following book(s):

Henderson, H. Modern mathematicians   **920**

McGrayne, S. B. Nobel Prize women in science p64-89   **920**

Osen, L. M. Women in mathematics p141-52   **920**

Nofi, Albert A.

(jt. auth) Dunnigan, J. F. Victory at sea   **940.54**

A **noise** of war. Langguth, A. J.   **937**

Noll, A. Michael

(jt. auth) Pierce, J. R. Signals   **621.382**

Noll, Richard

The encyclopedia of memory and memory disorders   **153.1**

Nomberg-Przytyk, Sara, 1915-

Auschwitz   **940.53**

Non-proliferation of nuclear weapons *See* Arms control

Non-violence in peace and war; excerpts. *See* Gandhi, M. Gandhi on non-violence   **322.4**

Nona. King, S.

In King, S. Skeleton crew   **S C**

Nonbook materials *See* Audiovisual materials

The **Norton** book of light verse   821.008
The **Norton** book of science fiction   S C
The **Norton** book of women's lives   920
The **Norton** history of astronomy and cosmology. North, J. D.   520
The **Norton** history of chemistry. Brock, W. H.   540.9
The **Norton** history of technology. Cardwell, D. S. L.   609
Norton's 2000.0   523
Norway
    Fiction
    Undset, S. Kristin Lavransdatter   Fic
Norwegian Americans
    Fiction
    Rölvaag, O. E. Giants in the earth   Fic
Norwich, John Julius, 1929-
  (ed) Oxford illustrated encyclopedia of the arts. See Oxford illustrated encyclopedia of the arts   700
A **nose** for news. Sale, R.
  In The Oxford book of American detective stories p217-38   S C
Nostalgia. Colette
  In Colette. The collected stories of Colette p159-62   S C
Nostradamus, 1503-1566
    About
    Randi, J. The mask of Nostradamus   92
Not final!. Asimov, I.
  In Asimov, I. The complete stories v2 p1-15   S C
Not in our back yard. Mowrey, M.   363.7
Not like other boys—growing up gay. Shyer, M. F.   92
Not the only one   S C
Not under forty. Cather, W.
  In Cather, W. Stories, poems and other writings   818
Not without laughter [excerpt] Hughes, L.
  In The Portable Harlem Renaissance reader p592-99   810.8
Notable American women, 1607-1950   920.003
Notable American women: the modern period   920.003
Notable Asian Americans   920.003
Notable black American women [bk I-II]   920.003
Notable Hispanic American women   920.003
Notable native Americans   920.003
Notable twentieth century scientists   920.003
A **note** on experts: Dexter Vespasian Joyner. Wolfe, T.
  In Wolfe, T. The complete short stories of Thomas Wolfe p438-46   S C
Notes. O'Brien, T.
  In O'Brien, T. The things they carried   S C
Notes of a native son. Baldwin, J.   305.8
Nothing but the blues   781.643

The **notorious** jumping frog of Calaveras County. Twain, M.
  In Twain, M. The complete short stories of Mark Twain   S C
Nourse, Alan Edward, 1928-
  The virus invaders   616
Nourse, Kenneth A.
  How to write your college application essay   378
Nouveau petit Larousse illustré. See Petit Larousse illustré   443
Nova Scotia
    Fiction
    Fox, P. The moonlight man   Fic
    Wilson, B. The leaving and other stories   S C
Novak, Barbara
  American painting of the nineteenth century   759.13
Novak, William
  (jt. auth) Johnson, E. My life   92
Novallo, Annette
  (ed) Student contact book. See Student contact book   001.4
A **novel** in letters. Pushkin, A. S.
  In Pushkin, A. S. Alexander Pushkin: complete prose fiction p50-61   S C
Novelists, American
    Dictionaries
    Contemporary novelists   920.003
Novelists, English
    Dictionaries
    Contemporary novelists   920.003
Novellas and other writings. Wharton, E.   818
Novels, 1886-1890. James, H.   Fic
Novels and stories. Hurston, Z. N.   Fic
The **novels** of Henry James. Wagenknecht, E.   813.009
Now I ask you. O'Neill, E.
  In O'Neill, E. Complete plays v1   812
Now I lay me. Hemingway, E.
  In Hemingway, E. The complete short stories of Ernest Hemingway p276-82   S C
  In Hemingway, E. The Nick Adams stories p144-53   S C
  In Hemingway, E. The short stories of Ernest Hemingway p363-71   S C
Now is the time. Brown, C.
  In Calling the wind p405-20   S C
Now you cookin' with gas. Hurston, Z. N.
  In Hurston, Z. N. The complete stories p233-41   S C
Nowak, Ronald M.
  Walker, E. P. Walker's mammals of the world   599
Nowhere to run. Hirshey, G.   781.644
NTC's American idioms dictionary. Spears, R. A.   427
NTC's dictionary of acronyms and abbreviations. Kleinedler, S. R.   421.03
Nubes. Romero, O.
  In Growing up Chicana/o p95-100   810.8

O

Ó Cadhain, Máirtín
The hare-lip
  In The Oxford book of Irish short stories
  p375-81   **S C**

O city of broken dreams. Cheever, J.
  In Cheever, J. The stories of John Cheever
  p42-57   **S C**

Ó Conaire, Pádraic, 1883-1928
My little black ass
  In The Oxford book of Irish short stories
  p267-70   **S C**

O pioneers! Cather, W.   **Fic**
  also in Cather, W. Early novels and stories
       Fic

O Yes. Olsen, T.
  In The Oxford book of women's writing in
  the United States p111-25   **810.8**

O youth and beauty! Cheever, J.
  In Cheever, J. The stories of John Cheever
  p210-18   **S C**

Oates, Joyce Carol, 1938-
Extenuating circumstances
  In The Oxford book of women writing in the
  United States p148-53   **810.8**
Ghost girls
  In The Best American short stories, 1996
  p226-41   **S C**
Heat
  In The Oxford book of American short stories
  p607-19   **S C**
How I contemplated the world from the Detroit
House of Correction and began my life over
again
  In The Norton book of American short stories
  p662-75   **S C**
Mark of Satan
  In Prize stories, 1996 p105-19   **S C**
Nairobi
  In The Best American short stories of the
  eighties p174-81   **S C**
The others
  In The Literary ghost p64-68   **S C**
The premonition
  In Bad behavior p205-22   **S C**
Secret observations on the goat-girl
  In The Oxford book of gothic tales p498-501
       S C
Where are you going, where have you been?
  In American short story masterpieces
       S C
  In The Vintage book of contemporary
  American short stories p347-65   **S C**
  In We are the stories we tell   **S C**
  In Who do you think you are? p14-35
       S C
(ed) The Oxford book of American short stories.
See The Oxford book of American short sto-
ries   **S C**

Oates, Stephen B., 1936-
Abraham Lincoln, the man behind the myths
       92
Let the trumpet sound: the life of Martin Luther
King, Jr   **92**

With malice toward none: the life of Abraham
Lincoln   **92**
A woman of valor: Clara Barton and the Civil
War   **92**

Oates, Whitney Jennings, 1904-1973
(ed) Seven famous Greek plays. See Seven famous Greek plays   **882.008**

Oba, Ryan
Home now
  In American eyes p28-36   **S C**

Obejas, Achy, 1956-
Polaroids
  In Latina: women's voices from the border-
  lands p162-70   **810.8**

Obesity
LeBow, M. D. Overweight teenagers   **613.2**
Silverstein, A. So you think you're fat?
       616.85

See/See also pages in the following book(s):
Maloney, M. Straight talk about eating disorders
       616.85
Sonder, B. Eating disorders   **616.85**
Control
  See Reducing
Dictionaries
Cassell, D. K. Encyclopedia of obesity and eat-
ing disorders   **616.85**
Fiction
Crutcher, C. Staying fat for Sarah Byrnes
       Fic
Lipsyte, R. One fat summer   **Fic**

Obituary. Asimov, I.
  In Asimov, I. The complete stories v2 p306-
  19   **S C**

Object lesson. Queen, E.
  In Read all about it! p53-66   **808.88**

The object stares back. Elkins, J.   **152.14**

Oblomov's dream. Goncharov, I. A.
  In The Portable nineteenth-century Russian
  reader p295-333   **891.7**

The oblong box. Poe, E. A.
  In Poe, E. A. The collected tales and poems
  of Edgar Allan Poe p711-19   **S C**

O'Brien, Edna
Irish revel
  In The Oxford book of Irish short stories
  p495-514   **S C**

O'Brien, Robert, 1932-
(ed) The Encyclopedia of drug abuse. See The
Encyclopedia of drug abuse   **616.86**

O'Brien, Tim, 1946-
Ambush
  In Who do you think you are? p152-55
       S C
The ghost soldiers
  In The Literary ghost p185-205   **S C**
The man I killed
  In Who do you think you are? p146-51
       S C
Speaking of courage
  In The Other side of heaven p155-65
       S C

O'Connor, Flannery—*Continued*
  In The Oxford book of women's writing in
    the United States p126-34   **810.8**
Parker's back
  In The Oxford book of short stories p501-19
                                        S C
Revelation
  In The Norton book of American short stories
    p536-54   **S C**
A view of the woods
  In We are the stories we tell   **S C**
The violent bear it away
  In O'Connor, F. Collected works p329-479
                                        S C
Wise blood
  In O'Connor, F. Collected works p1-131
                                        S C
See/See also pages in the following book(s):
  Gombar, C. Great women writers, 1900-1950
                                        920

O'Connor, Frank, 1903-1966
  Collected stories   **S C**
  Contents: Guests of the nation; The late Henry Conran; The
  bridal night; The Grand Vizier's daughters; Song without words;
  The shepherds; The long road to Ummera; The cheapjack; The
  Luceys; Uprooted; The mad Lomasneys; News for the church;
  Judas; The babes in the wood; The frying-pan; The miracle; Don
  Juan's temptation; First confession; The man of the house; The
  drunkard; Christmas morning; My first Protestant; Legal aid; The
  masculine principle; The sentry; The lady of the sagas; Darcy in
  the Land of Youth; My Oedipus complex; The pretender; Freedom; Peasants; The majesty of the law; Eternal triangle; Masculine protest; The sorcerer's apprentice; The little mother; A sense
  of responsibility; Counsel for Oedipus; The old faith; Unapproved route; The study of history; Expectation of life; The ugly
  duckling; Fish for Friday; A set of variations on a borrowed
  theme; The American wife; The impossible marriage; The cheat;
  The weeping children; An out-and-out free gift; The Corkerys; A
  story by Maupassant; A great man; Androcles and the army; Public opinion; Achilles' heel; The wreath; The teacher's Mass; The
  martyr; Requiem; An act of charity; The Mass island; There is
  a lone house; The story teller; Last post; The cornet player who
  betrayed Ireland; Ghosts
  Guests of the nation
    In The Oxford book of Irish short stories
      p342-53   **S C**
    In The Oxford book of short stories p371-81
                                        S C
  The majesty of the law
    In The Oxford book of Irish short stories
      p354-62   **S C**
  A minority
    In Bearing witness p86-97   **808.8**
O'Connor, Mary Flannery *See* O'Connor,
  Flannery
O'Connor, Stephen, 1952-
  Will my name be shouted out?   **808**
Octavian *See* Augustus, Emperor of Rome, 63
  B.C.-14 A.D.
October. Colette
  In Colette. The collected stories of Colette
    p452-54   **S C**
The October game. Bradbury, R.
  In Bradbury, R. The stories of Ray Bradbury
    p787-92   **S C**
The October Revolution. Medvedev, R. A.
                                        947.084
The octoroon. Boucicault, D.
  In Best plays of the early American theatre
    p185-215   **812.008**

Oda Rainbow. McKie, J. R.
  In Streetlights: illuminating tales of the urban
    black experience p318-39   **S C**
The odd couple. Simon, N.
  In Best American plays: 6th series—1963-
    1967 p527-65   **812.008**
  In Simon N. The comedy of Neil Simon
    p215-302   **812**
Odd couple (female version). Simon, N.
  In Simon, N. The collected plays of Neil Si-
    mon v3 p379-475   **812**
Oddities *See* Curiosities and wonders
Odets, Clifford, 1906-1963
  Golden boy
    In Twenty best plays of the modern American
      theatre p775-818   **812.008**
  Waiting for Lefty
    In Thirty famous one-act plays p521-45
                                        808.82
Odlum, Jacqueline Cochran *See* Cochran, Jac-
  queline, 1910?-1980
O'Donnol, Shirley Miles, 1915-
  American costume, 1915-1970   **792**
O'Donovan, Michael *See* O'Connor, Frank, 1903-
  1966
Odour of chrysanthemums. Lawrence, D. H.
  In Lawrence, D. H. The complete short sto-
    ries v2   **S C**
Odysseus (Greek mythology)
  See/See also pages in the following book(s):
  Asimov, I. Words from the myths p201-11
                                        292
  Hamilton, E. Mythology p291-318   **292**
The Odyssey. Homer   **883**
An odyssey in time: the dinosaurs of North Amer-
  ica. Russell, D. A.   **567.9**
Odyssey of an egg. West, D.
  In West, D. The richer, the poorer: stories,
    sketches, and reminiscences   **S C**
An odyssey of the north. London, J.
  In London, J. Short stories of Jack London
    p39-64   **S C**
Oedipus Rex. Sophocles
  In Four Greek plays   **882.008**
Oedipus the King. Sophocles   **882**
  also in Seven famous Greek plays
                                        882.008
Oeiras, Sebastião José de Carvalho e Melo,
  Conde de *See* Pombal, Sebastião José de
  Carvalho e Melo, Marquês de, 1699-1782
Oermann, Robert K.
  America's music   **781.642**
  (jt. auth) Bufwack, M. A. Finding her voice
                                        781.642
Of course. Jackson, S.
  In Jackson, S. The lottery   **S C**
Of human bondage. Maugham, W. S.   **Fic**
Of mice and men. Steinbeck, J.   **Fic**
  also in Steinbeck, J. The portable Steinbeck
                                        818
Of mice and men [play] Steinbeck, J.
  In Twenty best plays of the modern American
    theatre p643-80   **812.008**

Okimoto, Jean Davies, 1942-
Hum it again, Jeremy
In Center stage   **812.008**

Okinawa. Leckie, R.   **940.54**

Okpewho, Isidore
(ed) The Heritage of African poetry. See The Heritage of African poetry   **896**

Okri, Ben
Converging city
In The Heinemann book of contemporary African short stories p134-45   **S C**

Oktoberfest. Wolfe, T.
In Wolfe, T. The complete short stories of Thomas Wolfe p308-15   **S C**

Okudzhava, Bulat S., 1924-1997
Unexpected joy
In Border crossings: emigration and exile p1-15   **808.8**

Olajuwon, Akeem *See* Olajuwon, Hakeem

Olajuwon, Hakeem
Living the dream   **92**

Olalla. Stevenson, R. L.
In The Oxford book of gothic tales p183-217   **S C**

The **old** Adam. Lawrence, D. H.
In Lawrence, D. H. The complete short stories v1   **S C**

Old age
See also Aging
Fiction
Mahy, M. Memory   **Fic**

Old and new poems. Hall, D.   **811**

The **old** apple-dealer. Hawthorne, N.
In Hawthorne, N. Tales and sketches; A wonder book for girls and boys; Tanglewood tales for girls and boys p714-20   **S C**

The **old** beauty, and others. Cather, W.
In Cather, W. Stories, poems and other writings   **818**

Old blues singers never die. Johnson, C. V.
In The Best short stories by Negro writers p414-27   **S C**

Old Catawba. Wolfe, T.
In Wolfe, T. The complete short stories of Thomas Wolfe p214-21   **S C**

The **old** chief Mshlanga. Lessing, D. M.
In Somehow tenderness survives p19-35   **S C**

Old country advice to the American traveler. Saroyan, W.
In Saroyan, W. My name is Aram   **S C**

Old English literature *See* Anglo-Saxon literature

The **old** faith. O'Connor, F.
In O'Connor, F. Collected stories p404-12   **S C**

Old farmer's almanac
Watson, B. A. Acts of God   **551.6**

The **Old** farmer's almanac book of weather lore. Dolan, E. F.   **398.2**

Old-fashioned. Asimov, I.
In Asimov, I. The complete stories v2 p530-37   **S C**

Old folks' Christmas. Lardner, R.
In Lardner, R. The best short stories of Ring Lardner p139-48   **S C**

The **old** forest. Taylor, P. H.
In The Best American short stories of the eighties p1-56   **S C**

Old Goriot. Balzac, H. de   **Fic**

The **old** maid. Wharton, E.
In Wharton, E. Novellas and other writings   **818**

The **old** man and the sea. Hemingway, E.   **Fic**

Old man at the bridge. Hemingway, E.
In Hemingway, E. The complete short stories of Ernest Hemingway p57-58   **S C**
In Hemingway, E. The short stories of Ernest Hemingway p78-80   **S C**

Old Man Coyote, the young man and two otter sisters
In Hearne, B. G. Beauties and beasts p154-56   **398.2**

Old man of the temple. Narayan, R. K.
In The Literary ghost p330-35   **S C**

Old man Pete. Edmonds, R.
In Black theatre USA   **812.008**

Old man Potchikoo. Erdrich, L.
In The Oxford book of modern fairy tales p431-41   **S C**

Old Man Rivers. Wolfe, T.
In Wolfe, T. The complete short stories of Thomas Wolfe p563-88   **S C**

Old man's beard. Wakefield, H. R.
In The Oxford book of English ghost stories p339-53   **S C**

An **old** manuscript. Kafka, F.
In Kafka, F. The complete stories   **S C**

The **old** marriage. Earling, D.
In Talking leaves   **S C**

Old Mary. Mohr, N.
In Mohr, N. In Nueva York   **S C**

Old mortality. Porter, K. A.
In Porter, K. A. The collected stories of Katherine Anne Porter   **S C**
In Porter, K. A. Pale horse, pale rider: three short novels   **S C**

Old Mr. Marblehall. Welty, E.
In Welty, E. The collected stories of Eudora Welty p91-97   **S C**

Old Mrs. Harris. Cather, W.
In The Oxford book of women's writing in the United states p229-72   **810.8**

Old New York. Wharton, E.
In Wharton, E. Novellas and other writings   **818**

Old news. Hawthorne, N.
In Hawthorne, N. Tales and sketches; A wonder book for girls and boys; Tanglewood tales for girls and boys p251-75   **S C**

Old Northwest
History
Sugden, J. Tecumseh's last stand   **973.5**

The **old** nurse's story. Gaskell, E. C.
In Victorian ghost stories p1-18   **S C**

The **omelette**. Colette
In Colette. The collected stories of Colette p259-62   **S C**

Omeros. Walcott, D.   **811**

The **ommatidium** miniatures. Bishop, M.
In Nebula awards 25 p200-17   **S C**

On a pale horse. Anthony, P. See note under Anthony, P. Incarnations of immortality series   **Fic**

On account of a hat. Sholem Aleichem
In Sholem Aleichem. The best of Sholem Aleichem   **S C**

On aggression. Lorenz, K.   **152.4**

On cassette. See Words on cassette   **011**

On death and dying. Kübler-Ross, E.   **155.9**

On discovery. Kingston, M. H.
In We are the stories we tell   **S C**

On Francisco el Penitente's first becoming a santero and thereby sealing his fate. Castillo, A.
In Iguana dreams   **S C**

On generation and corruption. Aristotle
In Aristotle. The basic works of Aristotle p470-531   **888**

On Gold Mountain. See, L.   **920**

On Golden Pond. Thompson, E.
In Best American screenplays   **812.008**

On Greenhow Hill. Kipling, R.
In Kipling, R. The portable Kipling   **828**

On guard. Waugh, E.
In Classic English short stories, 1930-1955 p118-32   **S C**

On leprechauns. Wolfe, T.
In Wolfe, T. The complete short stories of Thomas Wolfe p537-41   **S C**

On love. Chekhov, A. P.
In Chekhov, A. P. The image of Chekhov p273-83   **S C**

On revolution. Arendt, H.   **303.6**

On strivers row. Hill, A.
In Black theatre USA   **812.008**

On the beach. Shute, N.   **Fic**

On the Brighton Road. Middleton, R. B.
In The Oxford book of English ghost stories p266-69   **S C**

On the inside track. Armer, K. M.
In Tales from the planet Earth   **S C**

On the Makaloa mat. London, J.
In London, J. Short stories of Jack London p599-619   **S C**

On the market day. Mativo, K.
In The Heinemann book of contemporary African short stories p104-13   **S C**

On the origins of war and the preservation of peace. Kagan, D.   **355**

On the quai at Smyrna. Hemingway, E.
In Hemingway, E. The complete short stories of Ernest Hemingway p63-64   **S C**
In Hemingway, E. In our time p11-12   **S C**
In Hemingway, E. The short stories of Ernest Hemingway p87-88   **S C**

On the rainy river. O'Brien, T.
In O'Brien, T. The things they carried   **S C**

On the road. Hughes, L.
In Hughes, L. Short stories   **S C**

On the road to Texas: Pete Fonseca. Rivera, T.
In Growing up Latino p147-54   **810.8**

On the road with Charles Kuralt. Kuralt, C.   **973.92**

On the soul. Aristotle
In Aristotle. The basic works of Aristotle p535-603   **888**

On the way home. Hughes, L.
In Hughes, L. Short stories   **S C**

On the way to the poorhouse. Singer, I. B.
In Singer, I. B. The image and other stories p117-27   **S C**

On the wing. Brooks, B.   **598**

On violence. Arendt, H.   **303.6**

On wings of joy. Garfunkel, T.   **792.8**

On writing. Hemingway, E.
In Hemingway, E. The Nick Adams stories p233-41   **S C**

On writing well. Zinsser, W. K.   **808**

Onassis, Jacqueline Kennedy
About
Heymann, C. D. A woman named Jackie: an intimate biography of Jacqueline Bouvier Kennedy Onassis   **92**

Once aboard the Lugger (I). Faulkner, W.
In Faulkner, W. Uncollected stories of William Faulkner p352-58   **S C**

Once aboard the Lugger (II). Faulkner, W.
In Faulkner, W. Uncollected stories of William Faulkner p359-67   **S C**

The **once** and future king. White, T. H.   **Fic**

Once there were four. Sholem Aleichem
In Sholem Aleichem. The best of Sholem Aleichem   **S C**

One act plays
24 favorite one-act plays   **808.82**
The Big book of large-cast plays   **812.008**
Center stage   **812.008**
Garner, J. Stagings   **812.008**
Play it again!   **812.008**
Ten out of ten   **812.008**

One brief shining moment: remembering Kennedy. Manchester, W.   **92**

One Christmas. Capote, T.   **92**

One day in the life of Ivan Denisovich. Solzhenitsyn, A.   **Fic**

One day of happiness. Singer, I. B.
In Singer, I. B. The image and other stories p14-31   **S C**

One day, then another. Warren, O.
In Streetlights: illuminating tales of the urban black experience p484-86   **S C**

One evening. Colette
In Colette. The collected stories of Colette p242-45   **S C**

One fat summer. Lipsyte, R.   **Fic**

One flew over the cuckoo's nest. Kesey, K.   **Fic**

One Friday morning. Hughes, L.
In Hughes, L. Short stories   **S C**
One holy night. Cisneros, S.
In Cisneros, S. Woman Hollering Creek and other stories   **S C**
One hundred days. Schom, A.   **944.05**
One hundred fifty ways teens can make a difference. See Salzman, M. 150 ways teens can make a difference   **302**
One hundred great Africans. See Rake, A. 100 great Africans   **920**
One hundred great monologues from the neo-classical theatre   **808.82**
One hundred great monologues from the Renaissance theatre. See 100 great monologues from the Renaissance theatre   **822.008**
One hundred key documents in American democracy. See 100 key documents in American democracy   **973**
The one hundred most influential women of all time. See Felder, D. G. The 100 most influential women of all time   **920**
The one hundred most popular young adult authors. See Drew, B. A. The 100 most popular young adult authors   **810.9**
One hundred poems from the Chinese   **895.1**
One hundred poems from the Japanese   **895.6**
One hundred questions and answers about AIDS. See Ford, M. T. 100 questions and answers about AIDS   **616.97**
One hundred world-class thin books. See Bodart, J. R. 100 world-class thin books   **028.1**
One hundred years of solitude. García Márquez, G.   **Fic**
One in a million. Sholem Aleichem
In Sholem Aleichem. The best of Sholem Aleichem   **S C**
One man's moon   **895.6**
One more river to cross. Myers, W. D.   **779**
One of our future poets, you might say. Saroyan, W.
In Saroyan, W. My name is Aram   **S C**
One of ours. Cather, W.
In Cather, W. Early novels and stories   **Fic**
One of the girls in our party. Wolfe, T.
In Wolfe, T. The complete short stories of Thomas Wolfe p195-200   **S C**
One parent family *See* Single parent family
One reader writes. Hemingway, E.
In Hemingway, E. The complete short stories of Ernest Hemingway p320-21   **S C**
In Hemingway, E. The short stories of Ernest Hemingway p420-21   **S C**
One teenager in ten. See Two teenagers in twenty   **305.23**
One-third, one-third, one-third. See Brautigan, R. 1/3, 1/3, 1/3
One thousand dollars a word. Block, L.
In Masterpieces of mystery and suspense p645-51   **S C**
The one thousand dozen. London, J.
In London, J. Short stories of Jack London p97-111   **S C**

One trip abroad. Fitzgerald, F. S.
In Fitzgerald, F. S. The short stories of F. Scott Fitzgerald p577-97   **S C**
One trip across. Hemingway, E.
In Hemingway, E. The complete short stories of Ernest Hemingway p381-409   **S C**
One way to heaven. Cullen, C.
In Cullen, C. My soul's high song p343-531   **818**
One way to heaven [excerpt] Cullen, C.
In The Portable Harlem Renaissance reader p680-93   **810.8**
The one who waits. Bradbury, R.
In Bradbury, R. The stories of Ray Bradbury p630-35   **S C**
The one who watches. Ortiz Cofer, J.
In Ortiz Cofer, J. An island like you p72-81   **S C**
One writer's beginnings. Welty, E.   **92**
Oneal, Elizabeth *See* Oneal, Zibby, 1934-
Oneal, Zibby, 1934-
The language of goldfish   **Fic**
O'Neil, Doris C.
(ed) Life: the '60s. See Life: the '60s   **779**
O'Neil, Karen E.
Health and medicine projects for young scientists   **610**
O'Neill, Catherine, 1950-
Amazing mysteries of the world   **001.9**
O'Neill, Eugene, 1888-1953
All God's chillun got wings
In O'Neill, E. Nine plays p83-126   **812**
Complete plays   **812**
Contents v1: Abortion; "Anna Christie"; Before breakfast; Beyond the horizon; Bound east for Cardiff; Bread and butter; Chris Christophersen; The dreamy kid; The Emperor Jones; Fog; Gold; Ile; In the zone; The long voyage home; The moon of the Caribbees; The movie man; Now I ask you; The personal equation; Recklessness; The rope; Servitude; Shell shock; The sniper; The straw; Thirst; Warnings; The web; Where the cross is made; A wife for life; v2: All God's chillun got wings; Desire under the elms; Diff'rent; Dynamo; The first man; The fountain; The great God Brown; The hairy ape; Lazarus laughed; Marco millions; Mourning becomes Electra: Homecoming; Mourning becomes Electra: The haunted; Mourning becomes Electra: The hunted; Strange interlude; Welded; v3: Ah, wilderness!; Days without end; Hughie; The iceman cometh; Long day's journey into night; A moon for the misbegotten; More stately mansions; A touch of the poet
Desire under the elms
In O'Neill, E. Nine plays p127-92   **812**
The Emperor Jones
In O'Neill, E. Nine plays p1-32   **812**
The great god Brown
In O'Neill, E. Nine plays p289-358   **812**
The hairy ape
In O'Neill, E. Nine plays p33-82   **812**
Hughie
In Best American plays: 6th series—1963-1967 p311-23   **812.008**
The iceman cometh   **812**
also in Best American plays: 3d series—1945-1951 p95-171   **812.008**
In the zone
In Thirty famous one-act plays p405-18   **808.82**

O'Neill, Eugene, 1888-1953—*Continued*
Lazarus laughed
  In O'Neill, E. Nine plays p359-458   **812**
Long day's journey into night   **812**
Marco millions
  In O'Neill, E. Nine plays p193-288   **812**
A moon for the misbegotten
  In Best American plays: 4th series—1951-
    1957 p133-78   **812.008**
The moon of the Caribbees
  In 24 favorite one-act plays p238-55
    808.82
Mourning becomes Electra
  In O'Neill, E. Nine plays p657-829   **812**
Nine plays   **812**
Strange interlude
  In O'Neill, E. Nine plays p459-656   **812**
A touch of the poet
  In Best American plays: 5th series—1957-
    1963 p1-53   **812.008**
(ed) Seven famous Greek plays. See Seven fa-
  mous Greek plays   **882.008**
            About
Carpenter, F. I. Eugene O'Neill   **812**
Floyd, V. The plays of Eugene O'Neill
    812

O'Neill, Michael, 1953-
Percy Bysshe Shelley   **92**

O'Neill, Terry, 1944-
(ed) Biomedical ethics: opposing viewpoints.
  See Biomedical ethics: opposing viewpoints
    174
(ed) Economics in America: opposing viewpoints. See Economics in America: opposing
  viewpoints   **338.973**
(ed) Immigration: opposing viewpoints. See Immigration: opposing viewpoints   **325.73**
(ed) Paranormal phenomena: opposing viewpoints. See Paranormal phenomena: opposing
  viewpoints   **133**

The ones who walk away from Omelas. Le Guin,
  U. K.
  In The Norton book of American short stories
    p566-71   **S C**

Onions, Charles Talbut, 1873-1965
A Shakespeare glossary   **822.3**
(ed) The Oxford dictionary of English etymology. See The Oxford dictionary of English etymology   **422.03**

Onions, Oliver, 1873-1961
The cigarette case
  In The Oxford book of English ghost stories
    p236-46   **S C**

Online reference services *See* Reference services
  (Libraries)

Only in America. Lawrence, J.
  In Lawrence, J. The selected plays of Jerome
    Lawrence and Robert E. Lee p239-301
    812

The **only** man on Liberty Street. Kelley, W. M.
  In The Best short stories by Negro writers
    p428-37   **S C**
  In Calling the wind p155-62   **S C**

The **only** math book you'll ever need. Kogelman,
  S.   **513**

Only the dead know Brooklyn. Wolfe, T.
  In Wolfe, T. The complete short stories of
    Thomas Wolfe p260-64   **S C**

Only yesterday. Allen, F. L.   **973.91**

Ooka, Shohei, 1909-1988
Taken captive   **940.54**

The **Open** boat   **811.008**

The **open** boat. Crane, S.
  In Classic American short stories p251-82
    S C
  In The Norton book of American short stories
    p182-203   **S C**
  In The Oxford book of short stories p179-201
    S C

The **open** door. Oliphant, M.
  In Classic ghost stories p76-117   **S C**
The **open** door. Riddell, J. H., Mrs.
  In Victorian ghost stories p256-82   **S C**

Opera
The Oxford illustrated history of opera
    792.5
See/See also pages in the following book(s):
Grout, D. J. A history of western music
    780.9
        Bio-bibliography
Musicians since 1900   **920.003**
        Stories, plots, etc.
Cross, M. The new Milton Cross' complete sto-
  ries of the great operas   **792.5**
Cross, M. The new Milton Cross' more stories
  of the great operas   **792.5**
Freeman, J. W. The Metropolitan Opera stories
  of the great operas   **792.5**
Lazarus, J. The opera handbook   **792.5**
The Viking opera guide   **792.5**
The **opera** handbook. Lazarus, J.   **792.5**

The **operation**. Mohr, N.
  In Mohr, N. In Nueva York   **S C**

Operation afreet. Anderson, P.
  In Masterpieces of fantasy and enchantment
    p593-622   **S C**

Operation Desert Storm *See* Persian Gulf War,
  1991

Operetta
    See also Musicals

Opfell, Olga S.
Queens, empresses, grand duchesses, and regents
    920
Women prime ministers and presidents   **920**

Opie, Iona Archibald
(ed) The Oxford book of narrative verse. See
  The Oxford book of narrative verse
    821.008

Opie, Peter, 1918-1982
(ed) The Oxford book of narrative verse. See
  The Oxford book of narrative verse
    821.008

Oppenheimer, J. Robert, 1904-1967
See/See also pages in the following book(s):
Rhodes, R. Dark sun   **623.4**
Oppenheimer, Robert *See* Oppenheimer, J. Rob-
  ert, 1904-1967

Opposing viewpoints in American history
    973

Overweight teenagers. LeBow, M. D.   613.2

Overy, R. J. (Richard James), 1947-
The road to war   940.53
Why the Allies won   940.53

Overy, Richard James *See* Overy, R. J. (Richard James), 1947-

Ovid, 43 B.C.-17 or 18
Metamorphoses   873

Owens, Jesse, 1913-1980
About
Baker, W. J. Jesse Owens   92

Owens, Louis
Soul-catcher
In Song of the turtle p147-55   S C

The owl and the pussycat. Manhoff, B.
In Best American plays: 6th series—1963-1967 p495-525   812.008

The Owl of Bear Island. Bing, J.
In Tales from the planet Earth   S C

Owls
Sparks, J. Owls   598

Owoyele, David
The will of Allah
In African short stories   S C

The Oxford 50th anniversary book of the United Nations. Patterson, C.   341.23

Oxford American dictionary   423

The Oxford anthology of English literature   820.8

An Oxford anthology of Shakespeare. Shakespeare, W.   822.3

Oxford Bible atlas   220.9

The Oxford book of American detective stories   S C

The Oxford book of American light verse   811.008

The Oxford book of American short stories   S C

Oxford book of American verse, The New   811.008

The Oxford book of ballads   821.008

The Oxford book of classical verse in translation   881.008

The Oxford book of eighteenth century verse. See The New Oxford book of eighteenth century verse   821.008

The Oxford book of English ghost stories   S C

Oxford book of English light verse, The New   821.008

The Oxford book of essays   824

The Oxford book of exploration   910.4

The Oxford book of gothic tales   S C

The Oxford book of humorous quotations   808.88

The Oxford book of Irish short stories   S C

The Oxford book of literary anecdotes   828

The Oxford book of modern fairy tales   S C

The Oxford book of money   808.8

The Oxford book of narrative verse   821.008

The Oxford book of nineteenth-century English verse   821.008

The Oxford book of science fiction stories   S C

The Oxford book of seventeenth century verse. See The New Oxford book of seventeenth century verse   821.008

The Oxford book of short stories   S C

The Oxford book of twentieth-century English verse   821.008

Oxford book of Victorian verse, The New   821.008

The Oxford book of war poetry   808.81

The Oxford book of women's writing in the United States   810.8

The Oxford classical dictionary   938.003

The Oxford companion to American literature   810.3

The Oxford companion to American theatre. Bordman, G. M.   792.03

The Oxford companion to animal behavior   591.5

The Oxford companion to art   703

The Oxford companion to chess. Hooper, D.   794.1

The Oxford companion to classical literature   880.3

The Oxford companion to English literature   820.3

The Oxford companion to French literature. See The New Oxford companion to literature in French   840.3

The Oxford companion to German literature. Garland, H. B.   830.3

The Oxford companion to Irish literature   820.9

The Oxford companion to medicine. See The Oxford medical companion   610.3

The Oxford companion to popular music. Gammond, P.   781.64

The Oxford companion to Spanish literature   860.3

The Oxford companion to the Bible   220.3

The Oxford companion to the English language   420

The Oxford companion to the Supreme Court of the United States   347

The Oxford companion to the theatre   792.03

The Oxford companion to twentieth-century art   709.04

The Oxford companion to twentieth-century literature in English   820.3

The Oxford companion to twentieth-century poetry in English   821.009

The Oxford companion to women's writing in the United States   810.9

The Oxford companion to World War II   940.53

The Oxford desk dictionary: American edition   423

The Oxford desk thesaurus: American edition. Urdang, L.   423

The Oxford dictionary of art   703

Palestine
Civilization
Porter, J. R. The illustrated guide to the Bible
220.6
See/See also pages in the following book(s):
Durant, W. J. Our Oriental heritage p299-349
950

Maps
Aharoni, Y. The Macmillan Bible atlas
220.9
Social life and customs
Bouquet, A. C. Everyday life in New Testament
times
225.9
Heaton, E. W. Everyday life in Old Testament
times
221.9
Palestine problem, 1917- *See* Israel-Arab conflicts; Jewish-Arab relations
Palestinian Arabs
Israel: opposing viewpoints
956.94
Paley, Grace
An interest in life
In We are the stories we tell
S C
A subject of childhood
In The Norton book of American short stories
p506-12
S C
The used-boy raisers
In American short story masterpieces
S C
Palgrave, Francis Turner, 1824-1897
(comp) The Golden treasury of the best songs &
lyrical poems in the English language. See
The Golden treasury of the best songs & lyrical poems in the English language
821.008
Palisca, Claude V.
(jt. auth) Grout, D. J. A history of western music
780.9
Palmer, Arnold, 1929-
See/See also pages in the following book(s):
Lipsyte, R. Idols of the game p201-17   920
Palmer, Colin A., 1942-
The first passage
In The Young Oxford history of African
Americans
305.8
Palmer, Douglas
Fossils
560
Palmer, Laura
Shrapnel in the heart
959.704
Palmer, Tim
America by rivers
551.48
Palmerston, Henry John, Viscount, 1784-1865
See/See also pages in the following book(s):
Strachey, L. Queen Victoria p204-52   92
Palmisano, Joseph M.
(ed) Environmental career directory. See Environmental career directory
363.7
Pamphlets
Blake, B. R. Creating newsletters, brochures,
and pamphlets
070.5
Bibliography
Vertical file index
015.73
Indexes
Vertical file index
015.73

Panama Canal
McCullough, D. G. The path between the seas
972.87
Panati, Charles, 1943-
Extraordinary origins of everyday things
031.02
Panati's extraordinary origins of everyday things.
See Panati, C. Extraordinary origins of everyday things
031.02
Pancake, Breece D'J, d. 1979
The honored dead
In The Other side of heaven p73-80
S C
Panda *See* Giant panda
Pandas. Catton, C.
599.74
Pankhurst, R. J. (Richard John), 1940-
(jt. auth) Hyam, R. Plants and their names: a
concise dictionary
581
Pankhurst, Richard John See Pankhurst, R. J.
(Richard John), 1940-
Panozzo, Michael E.
(jt. auth) Mizerak, S. Steve Mizerak's complete
book of pool
794.7
Pantaloon in black. Faulkner, W.
In Faulkner, W. Uncollected stories of William Faulkner p238-55
S C
Papa, snake & I. Honwana, L. B.
In African short stories
S C
Papacy
See also Popes
Papago Indians
See/See also pages in the following book(s):
Paths of life p115-40
970.004
Paper crafts
See also Origami
Bawden, J. The art and craft of papier mâché
745.54
Paper dance
811.008
Paper dolls. Jackson, E.
In 9 plays by black women
811.008
Paper lantern. Dybek, S.
In The Best American short stories, 1996
p113-25
S C
Paper money
Friedberg, R. Paper money of the United States
769.5
Paper money of the United States. Friedberg, R.
769.5
Paper pills. Anderson, S.
In Anderson, S. Winesburg, Ohio
S C
Paperback books
Bibliography
Kies, C. N. Supernatural fiction for teens
016.8
Reviews
Kliatt
028.1
Parables
See also Fables
Paradise Café. Brooks, M.
In Brooks, M. Paradise Café and other stories
p62-69
S C
Paradise Café and other stories. Brooks, M.
S C

Paradise lost. Milton, J.
  In Milton, J. The portable Milton   **828**
The **paradise** of bachelors. Melville, H.
  In The Oxford book of American short stories
    p69-77   **S C**
The **paradise** of children. Hawthorne, N.
  In Hawthorne, N. Tales and sketches; A wonder book for girls and boys; Tanglewood tales for girls and boys p1215-29   **S C**
Paradise regained. Milton, J.
  In Milton, J. The portable Milton   **828**
Parallel journeys. Ayer, E. H.   **940.53**
Paraná River valley (Brazil and Argentina)
  Description
  See/See also pages in the following book(s):
  Great rivers of the world p333-48   **910**
Paranoid: a chant. King, S.
  In King, S. Skeleton crew   **S C**
Paranormal phenomena: opposing viewpoints
    133
Parapsychology
    See also Extrasensory perception; Occultism
  Cavendish, R. The world of ghosts and the supernatural   **133**
  Earth energies   **001.9**
  The Mysterious world   **133**
  Paranormal phenomena: opposing viewpoints
    133
  See/See also pages in the following book(s):
  Aaseng, N. Science versus pseudoscience p53-60   **001.9**
  Sagan, C. The demon-haunted world   **001.9**
  Dictionaries
  Encyclopedia of occultism & parapsychology
    133
  Guiley, R. E. The encyclopedia of ghosts and spirits   **133.1**
Parasites
    See also Insect pests
Parasitic diseases
  See/See also pages in the following book(s):
  Roueché, B. The medical detectives p14-25, 81-104, 124-37   **616**
Paredes, Angel García de *See* García de Paredes, Angel
Paredez, Deborah
  Tia Maria
    In Daughters of the fifth sun   **810.8**
Parent and child
    See also Children of alcoholics; Children of divorced parents; Children of drug addicts; Children of immigrants; Conflict of generations; Father and child
  Fenwick, E. Adolescence   **305.23**
  Miller, M. Coping with a bigoted parent
    303.3
  Packer, A. J. Bringing up parents   **306.8**
  See/See also pages in the following book(s):
  Galbraith, J. The gifted kids' survival guide p228-42   **155.5**
  Fiction
  Balzac, H. de. Old Goriot   **Fic**

Parenting
    See also Child rearing
  Lindsay, J. W. Teen dads   **649**
Parents, Biological *See* Birthparents
Parents, Single *See* Single parent family
Parents, Teenage *See* Teenage fathers; Teenage mothers
Parents, Unmarried *See* Unmarried mothers
Parents' Night. Garden, N.
  In Am I blue? p127-44   **S C**
Paretsky, Sara
  The Maltese cat
    In Bad behavior p223-57   **S C**
Parezo, Nancy J.
  (ed) Paths of life. See Paths of life
    970.004
Parini, Jay
  John Steinbeck   **92**
  (ed) The Columbia anthology of American poetry. See The Columbia anthology of American poetry   **811.008**
  (ed) The Columbia history of American poetry. See The Columbia history of American poetry   **811.009**
Paris (France)
  Description
  Hemingway, E. A moveable feast   **92**
  Fiction
  Hugo, V. Les misérables   **Fic**
  Leroux, G. Phantom of the opera   **Fic**
  History
  See/See also pages in the following book(s):
  Tuchman, B. W. A distant mirror p155-63
    944
  Intellectual life
  Stein, G. The autobiography of Alice B. Toklas
    92
Park, Robert, 1927-
  The inventor's handbook   **608**
Parker, Barry R.
  Chaos in the cosmos   **520**
Parker, Charlie, 1920-1955
  See/See also pages in the following book(s):
  Terkel, S. Giants of jazz p163-71   **920**
Parker, Derek
  (jt. auth) Parker, J. Parkers' complete book of dreams   **154.6**
Parker, Dorothy, 1893-1967
  Here we are
    In 24 favorite one-act plays p210-18
    808.82
  The standard of living
    In The Norton book of American short stories p318-22   **S C**
Parker, Ely Samuel, 1828-1895
  See/See also pages in the following book(s):
  Brown, D. A. Bury my heart at Wounded Knee p176-90   **970.004**
Parker, Geoffrey, 1943-
  (ed) The Cambridge illustrated history of warfare. See The Cambridge illustrated history of warfare   **355**
  (jt. auth) Martin, C. The Spanish Armada
    942.05

Peasants. O'Connor, F.
In O'Connor, F. Collected stories p313-20
S C

Peavy, Linda Sellers, 1943-
Pioneer women **305.4**

The **pebble** people. Jack, R.
In Talking leaves **S C**

Peck, David R.
American ethnic literatures **016.8**

Peck, Richard, 1934-
Father figure **Fic**
The last safe place on earth **Fic**
Love and death at the mall **808.06**
Priscilla and the wimps
In Who do you think you are? p92-95
S C
Remembering the good times **Fic**
About
Gallo, D. R. Presenting Richard Peck
813.009

Peck, Robert Newton, 1928-
A day no pigs would die **Fic**
A part of the sky **Fic**

Pedagogy *See* Teaching

Peden, Margaret Sayers
(ed) The Latin American short story. See The
Latin American short story **863.009**

Pediatric psychiatry *See* Child psychiatry

Pediatrics *See* Children—Health and hygiene

The **pedlar's** revenge. O'Flaherty, L.
In The Oxford book of Irish short stories
p287-99 **S C**

Peduzzi, Kelli
America in the 20th century. See America in the
20th century **973.9**

The **peeler.** O'Connor, F.
In O'Connor, F. The complete stories p63-80
S C

A **peephole** in the gate. Singer, I. B.
In Singer, I. B. The death of Methuselah and
other stories p93-120 **S C**

Peery, Janet
What the thunder said
In The Best American short stories, 1993
p161-68 **S C**

The **pelican.** Wharton, E.
In Wharton, E. The selected short stories of
Edith Wharton p10-25 **S C**

Pellant, Chris
Rocks, minerals & fossils of the world **549**

Pelossof, Noa Ben Artzi- *See* Ben Artzi-Pelossof,
Noa

Pemberton, John, 1928-
(jt. auth) Drewal, H. J. Yoruba **709.6**

Pemberton, William E., 1940-
Harry S. Truman **92**

The **pen** pal. Wilson, B.
In Wilson, B. The leaving and other stories
S C

Pendergast family
See/See also pages in the following book(s):
Truman, M. Harry S. Truman p61-73 **92**

The **pendulum.** Henry, O.
In Henry, O. The best short stories of O.
Henry **S C**

The **Penguin** book of interviews. See The Norton
book of interviews **920**

The **Penguin** book of Irish verse **821.008**

The **Penguin** book of love poetry. See A Book of
love poetry **808.81**

The **Penguin** book of modern African poetry
896

The **Penguin** book of twentieth-century speeches
808.85

The **Penguin** book of women's humor **808.87**

The **Penguin** dictionary of architecture. Fleming,
J. **720.3**

The **Penguin** dictionary of science. Uvarov, E. B.
503

Penguins
Davis, L. S. Penguin **598**

Penguins (Hockey team) *See* Pittsburgh Penguins
(Hockey team)

Peninsular Campaign, 1862
Bailey, R. H. Forward to Richmond: McClellan's peninsular campaign **973.7**
Lee takes command: from Seven Days to Second Bull Run **973.7**

Penn, William, 1644-1718
See/See also pages in the following book(s):
Langdon, W. C. Everyday things in American
life, 1607-1776 p48-62 **973.2**

Pennebaker, Ruth
Don't think twice **Fic**

Pennington, James W. C., 1809-1870
The fugitive blacksmith
In Great slave narratives p193-267 **920**

Pennsylvania
Fiction
King, S. Christine **Fic**
Updike, J. Rabbit, run **Fic**
History
Fisher, S. G. The Quaker colonies **973.2**
See/See also pages in the following book(s):
Langdon, W. C. Everyday things in American
life, 1607-1776 p48-124 **973.2**

Pennsylvania Dutch
See/See also pages in the following book(s):
Langdon, W. C. Everyday things in American
life, 1607-1776 p63-73 **973.2**

Pennsylvania Dutch American folk art. Kauffman,
H. J. **745**

Pennsylvania Dutch folk art
Kauffman, H. J. Pennsylvania Dutch American
folk art **745**

Pennsylvania Station. Faulkner, W.
In Faulkner, W. Collected stories of William
Faulkner p609-25 **S C**

The **penny.** West, D.
In West, D. The richer, the poorer: stories,
sketches, and reminiscences **S C**

Penrose, Roger
(jt. auth) Hawking, S. W. The nature of space
and time **530.1**

Pentimento. Hellman, L.
In Hellman, L. Three **92**

Personal computer buying guide. See Consumer reports guide to personal computers **004**

The **personal** equation. O'Neill, E.
In O'Neill, E. Complete plays v1 **812**

Personal finance
Rendon, M. Straight talk about money
332.4

Personal grooming
Landau, E. The beauty trap **155.6**
Mathis, D. Women of color **646.7**

Personal hygiene *See* Hygiene
Personal life skills *See* Life skills
Personal names
Hanks, P. A dictionary of first names
929.4
Kolatch, A. J. Dictionary of first names
929.4
Stewart, J. African names **929.4**
United States
Hook, J. N. Family names **929.4**
Robb, H. A. Encyclopedia of American family names **929.4**
Shankle, G. E. American nicknames **929.4**
Stewart, G. R. American given names
929.4

Personal time management *See* Time management

Personality
The Enigma of personality **155.2**

Personality fabulosa. Palacios, M.
In Latina: women's voices from the borderlands p200-07 **810.8**

Persons, Albert C., 1915-
Bay of Pigs **972.91**

Perspective
Smith, R. An introduction to perspective
In The DK art school series **751**

Pert, Candace, 1946-
See/See also pages in the following book(s):
Yount, L. Contemporary women scientists
920

Peru
Antiquities
Bingham, H. Lost city of the Incas **985**
Moseley, M. E. The Incas and their ancestors
985
Fiction
Wilder, T. The bridge of San Luis Rey **Fic**
History
Hemming, J. The conquest of the Incas
985
McIntyre, L. The incredible Incas and their timeless land **985**
See/See also pages in the following book(s):
Sullivan, W. The secret of the Incas **985**

Peshkov, Aleksei Maksimovich *See* Gorky, Maksim, 1868-1936

Pest control
See/See also pages in the following book(s):
Berenbaum, M. R. Bugs in the system p284-300
595.7

Pesticides
See/See also pages in the following book(s):
Salter, C. A. Food risks and controversies p62-77 **641.1**

Environmental aspects
Carson, R. Silent spring **363.7**
Pesticides and wildlife
Carson, R. Silent spring **363.7**
Pests
See also Insect pests

Peter I, the Great, Emperor of Russia, 1672-1725
About
Massie, R. K. Peter the Great **92**
See/See also pages in the following book(s):
Durant, W. J. The age of Louis XIV p391-410
940.2

Peter. Faulkner, W.
In Faulkner, W. Uncollected stories of William Faulkner p489-94 **S C**
Peter Goldwaite's treasure. Hawthorne, N.
In Hawthorne, N. Tales and sketches; A wonder book for girls and boys; Tanglewood tales for girls and boys p522-41
S C
Peter Rugg, the missing man. Austin, W.
In The Oxford book of American short stories p33-61 **S C**
Peter Salem, Minuteman. Keats, M.
In The Big book of large-cast plays p216-27
812.008
Peter Shaffer's Amadeus. Shaffer, P. **822**
Petersburg (Va.)
History—Siege, 1864-1865
Davis, W. C. Death in the trenches: Grant at Petersburg **973.7**
Petersburg [excerpt] Bely, A.
In The Portable twentieth-century Russian reader p81-89 **891.7**
Petersen, Inez
Missing you [excerpt]
In Circle of women: an anthology of contemporary Western women writers p103-07
810.8
Peterson, Dawn Micklethwaite
(jt. auth) Connor, R. C. The lives of whales and dolphins **599.5**
Peterson, James A., 1943-
Strength training for women **613.7**
Peterson, Leslie
(jt. auth) Gravelle, K. Teenage fathers
306.8
Peterson, Levi S., 1933-
The newsboy
In Where coyotes howl and wind blows free p57-73 **810.8**
Peterson, Louis
Take a giant step
In Black theatre USA **812.008**
Peterson, Owen, 1924-
(comp) Representative American speeches. See Representative American speeches
815.008
Peterson, Richard F.
William Butler Yeats **821**
Peterson, Roger Tory, 1908-1996
A field guide to the birds **598**

The **Picasso** summer. Bradbury, R.
   In Bradbury, R. The stories of Ray Bradbury
   p493-97   **S C**

Piccolo, Brian, 1943-1970
        About
   Morris, J. Brian Piccolo   **92**

Pichon & Sons, of the Croix Rousse
   In Victorian ghost stories p100-14   **S C**

Pick-up games. Crisfield, D.   **790.1**

Pickering, David, 1958-
   (ed) The Facts on File dictionary of the theatre.
   See The Facts on File dictionary of the theatre   **792.03**

Picketing *See* Strikes

Pickford, Nigel
   The atlas of shipwrecks & treasure   **910.4**

Picnic. Inge, W.
   In Best American plays: 4th series—1951-
   1957 p211-44   **812.008**
   In Inge, W. 4 plays p71-148   **812**

The **Pictorial** history of the Holocaust   **940.53**

A **pictorial** history of the world's greatest trials.
   Aymar, B.   **345**

Picture dictionaries
   Dorling Kindersley ultimate visual dictionary
       423
   The Macmillan visual dictionary   **413**
   The Oxford-Duden pictorial English-Japanese
   dictionary   **495.6**

The **picture** of Dorian Gray. Wilde, O.   **Fic**
   also in Wilde, O. The portable Oscar Wilde
   p138-391   **828**

A **picture** of the virgin. Kinsella, W. P.
   In Kinsella, W. P. Shoeless Joe Jackson
   comes to Iowa: stories   **S C**

Picture writing
     See also Hieroglyphics
   Liungman, C. G. Dictionary of symbols
       302.2

A **piece** of news. Welty, E.
   In Welty, E. The collected stories of Eudora
   Welty p12-16   **S C**

A **piece** of steak. London, J.
   In London, J. The portable Jack London
   p232-48   **818**
   In London, J. Short stories of Jack London
   p448-63   **S C**

A **piece** of wood. Bradbury, R.
   In Bradbury, R. The stories of Ray Bradbury
   p800-04   **S C**

Piecework. Brin, D.
   In The Oxford book of science fiction stories
   p550-76   **S C**

Piecework. Hamill, P.   **814**

Pied Piper's land. Norcross, E. B.
   In The Big book of large-cast plays p197-207
       812.008

Pierce, John Robinson, 1910-
   Signals   **621.382**

Pierce, Trudy Griffin- *See* Griffin-Pierce, Trudy

Pierced by a ray of sun   **808.81**

Pierre Auguste Renoir. Pach, W.   **759.4**

Pieter Bruegel the Elder. Stechow, W.
       759.9493

Pigeon feathers. Updike, J.
   In Updike, J. Pigeon feathers, and other stories p116-50   **S C**

Pigeon feathers, and other stories. Updike, J.
       S C

Pigeons from hell. Howard, R. E.
   In The Horror hall of fame p234-64
       S C

Piggott, Juliet
   Japanese mythology   **299**

The **Pigman.** Zindel, P.   **Fic**

Pigs in heaven. Kingsolver, B.   **Fic**

Pilbeam, David R.
   (ed) The Cambridge encyclopedia of human
   evolution. See The Cambridge encyclopedia
   of human evolution   **573.2**

Pilcher, Rosamunde, 1924-
   Flowers in the rain & other stories   **S C**
   Contents: The doll's house; Endings and beginnings; Flowers
   in the rain; Playing a round with love; Christabel; The blackberry
   day; The red dress; A girl I used to know; The watershed; Mari-
   gold garden; Weekend; A walk in the snow; Cousin Dorothy;
   Whistle for the wind; Last morning; Skates

Pile, John F.
   Dictionary of 20th-century design   **745.4**

Pilgrim at Tinker Creek. Dillard, A.   **818**

Pilgrims (New England colonists)
   Bradford, W. Of Plymouth Plantation, 1620-
   1647   **974.4**

Pilgrims. Gordon, R.
   In Song of the turtle p115-29   **S C**

The **pilgrims.** Kiely, B.
   In The Oxford book of Irish short stories
   p412-24   **S C**

The **pilgrim's** progress. Bunyan, J.   **Fic**

Pillar of salt. Jackson, S.
   In Jackson, S. The lottery   **S C**

Pillars of society. Ibsen, H.
   In Ibsen, H. The complete major prose plays
       839.8

Pilon. Steinbeck, J.
   In Steinbeck, J. The portable Steinbeck
       818

Pilots, Airplane *See* Air pilots

Pima Indians
   See/See also pages in the following book(s):
   Paths of life p115-40   **970.004**

Pimples (Acne) *See* Acne

The **pin.** Crutcher, C.
   In Crutcher, C. Athletic shorts: six short stories p27-49   **S C**

Pinckney, Cathey
   The patient's guide to medical tests   **616.07**

Pinckney, Edward R.
   (jt. auth) Pinckney, C. The patient's guide to
   medical tests   **616.07**

Pindar
   See/See also pages in the following book(s):
   Hamilton, E. The Greek way p85-103
       880.9

The **Plains** Indians of the twentieth century
970.004

Planet earth **550**
Planets
    See also names of planets
    Kals, W. S. Stars and planets **523**
    Mammana, D. Other suns, other worlds?
523.2
    Watters, T. R. Planets **523.4**
    See/See also pages in the following book(s):
    Jastrow, R. Red giants and white dwarfs p130-
78 **523.1**
    Exploration
    See/See also pages in the following book(s):
    Man in space p160-73 **629.4**
Planned parenthood *See* Birth control
Plant biology science projects. Hershey, D. R.
581
Plant breeding
    Raeburn, P. The last harvest **338.1**
Plant conservation
    See also Rare plants
Plant names, Popular *See* Popular plant names
Plant propagation
    See also Plant breeding
Plante, Ellen M.
    The American kitchen, 1700 to the present
643
The **planter** of Malata. Conrad, J.
    In Conrad, J. The complete short fiction of
      Joseph Conrad v4 **S C**
Plants
    See also House plants; Rare plants; Tropi-
cal plants
    Attenborough, D. The private life of plants
581.5
    Gray, A. Gray's Manual of botany **581**
    Experiments
    Hershey, D. R. Plant biology science projects
581
    Fertilization
    See Fertilization of plants
    Soilless culture
    See Hydroponics
Plants, Edible *See* Edible plants
Plants, Fossil *See* Fossil plants
Plants, Ornamental *See* Ornamental plants
Plants, Poisonous *See* Poisonous plants
Plants and their names: a concise dictionary.
    Hyam, R. **581**
Plants for people. Lewington, A. **581.6**
Plants of the tropics. Reading, S. **581.5**
Plas, Rob van der, 1938-
    The bicycle repair book **629.28**
Plastic surgery
    See/See also pages in the following book(s):
    Stoppard, M. The breast book p103-14
612.6
Plath, Sylvia
    The bell jar **Fic**
    The collected poems **811**

Crossing the water **811**
    The journals of Sylvia Plath **92**
Plato
    The Republic **888**
    About
    Hare, R. M. Plato **184**
    See/See also pages in the following book(s):
    Durant, W. J. The story of philosophy p5-40
109
    Emerson, R. W. The portable Emerson p295-
    324 **818**
    Falcone, V. J. Great thinkers, great ideas
100
    Hamilton, E. The echo of Greece p79-93
880.9
    Jaspers, K. The great philosophers **109**
    Russell, B. A history of Western philosophy
    p104-59 **109**
Platonov, Andreĭ Platonovich, 1899-1951
    The Potudan River
    In The Portable twentieth-century Russian
      reader p118-52 **891.7**
The **Plattner** story. Wells, H. G.
    In Wells, H. G. The complete short stories of
      H. G. Wells p325-45 **S C**
Plautus, Titus Maccius
    Amphitryon
    In The Portable Roman reader p22-74
870.8
Play direction (Theater) *See* Theater—Production
and direction
Play index **808.82**
Play it again! **812.008**
Play it again, Sam. Allen, W.
    In Best American plays: 7th series—1967-
      1973 p563-85 **812.008**
Play production *See* Theater—Production and di-
rection
Play writing *See* Drama—Technique
Players. Kriegel, L.
    In Prize stories, 1996 p301-12 **S C**
The **playground.** Bradbury, R.
    In Bradbury, R. Fahrenheit 451 **S C**
    In Bradbury, R. The stories of Ray Bradbury
      p312-24 **S C**
Playgrounds
    See also Parks
Playing a round with love. Pilcher, R.
    In Pilcher, R. Flowers in the rain & other sto-
      ries **S C**
Playing courier. Twain, M.
    In Twain, M. The complete short stories of
      Mark Twain **S C**
Playing the game. Campbell, B. M.
    In Streetlights: illuminating tales of the urban
      black experience p44-55 **S C**
Playing with dynamite. Updike, J.
    In The Best American short stories, 1993
      p1-9 **S C**
Plays *See* Drama—Collections; One act plays
The **plays** of Eugene O'Neill. Floyd, V. **812**
Plaza suite: Visitor from Forest Hills. Simon, N.
    In Simon N. The comedy of Neil Simon
      p560-82 **812**

Police brutality
See/See also pages in the following book(s):
Criminal justice: opposing viewpoints p172-99
345

Poliomyelitis vaccine
See/See also pages in the following book(s):
Sherrow, V. Jonas Salk **92**

Political action committees *See* Lobbying

Political campaigns *See* Politics

Political conventions
See/See also pages in the following book(s):
White, T. H. America in search of itself
973.92

Political economy. Twain, M.
In Twain, M. The complete short stories of
Mark Twain **S C**

Political ethics
Machiavelli, N. The prince **320**

Political extremism *See* Radicalism

Political handbook of the world **324.025**

Political parties
Political handbook of the world **324.025**
Wattenberg, M. P. The decline of American political parties, 1952-1994 **324.2**
See/See also pages in the following book(s):
Politics in America: opposing viewpoints
320.4
Dictionaries
Political parties & elections in the United States
324.2

Political parties & elections in the United States
324.2

Political prisoners
Solzhenitsyn, A. The Gulag archipelago, 1918-1956 **365**
Fiction
Solzhenitsyn, A. One day in the life of Ivan
Denisovich **Fic**

Political science
Countries of the world and their leaders yearbook **910.3**
Falcone, V. J. Great thinkers, great ideas
100
Hobbes, T. Leviathan **320.1**
Machiavelli, N. The prince **320**
Paine, T. Collected writings **320**
Paine, T. The rights of man **320**
Paine, T. Rights of man [and] Common sense
320
Plato. The Republic **888**
Social contract **320.1**
The Statesman's year-book **310.5**
See/See also pages in the following book(s):
Durant, W. J. The lessons of history p68-80
901
Dictionaries
Shafritz, J. M. The dictionary of 20th-century
world politics **909.82**
Handbooks, manuals, etc.
Political handbook of the world **324.025**

Politicians
Countries of the world and their leaders yearbook **910.3**

United States
Havel, J. T. U.S. presidential candidates and the
elections **324.6**
Kennedy, J. F. Profiles in courage **920**
LeVert, S. Huey Long **92**
Williams, T. H. Huey Long **92**

Politics
See/See also pages in the following book(s):
White, T. H. America in search of itself
973.92

Politics, Practical *See* Politics

Politics. Aristotle
In Aristotle. The basic works of Aristotle
p1127-1316 **888**

Politics and business *See* Business and politics

Politics and Islam *See* Islam and politics

Politics and students *See* Students—Political activity

Politics in America, Congressional Quarterly's
328.73

Politics in America: opposing viewpoints
320.4

Pollack, Frank L.
Finis
In The Oxford book of science fiction stories
p22-32 **S C**

Pollack, Rachel
The journey out **305.9**

Pollination *See* Fertilization of plants

Pollock and the Porroh man. Wells, H. G.
In Wells, H. G. The complete short stories of
H. G. Wells p430-46 **S C**

Pollution
See also Air pollution; Environmental protection; Marine pollution; Radioactive pollution; Water pollution
Commoner, B. Making peace with the planet
304.2
Erickson, J. The human volcano **304.2**
Pollution **363.7**
Water: opposing viewpoints **333.91**

Pollution **363.7**

Pollution control industry
See also Recycling

Polmar, Norman
(jt. auth) Allen, T. B. War in the Gulf
956.7

Polo, Marco, 1254-1323?
The travels of Marco Polo **915**

Polo. Brown, C.
In Streetlights: illuminating tales of the urban
black experience p34-36 **S C**

Poltergeists. Shapiro, J.
In The Best American short stories, 1993
p94-112 **S C**

Polyglot dictionaries
The Macmillan visual dictionary **413**

Polyphemus. Wolfe, T.
In Wolfe, T. The complete short stories of
Thomas Wolfe p265-70 **S C**

Population—*Continued*
Ehrlich, P. R. The population explosion

                              304.6
Erickson, J. The human volcano   **304.2**
Population: opposing viewpoints   **304.6**
See/See also pages in the following book(s):
21st century earth: opposing viewpoints

                             303.49

Statistics

United Nations. Statistical Office. Demographic yearbook   **304.6**
The **population** explosion. Ehrlich, P. R.

                             304.6

Population: opposing viewpoints   **304.6**
The **porcelain** man. Kennedy, R.
  In The Oxford book of modern fairy tales p427-30   **S C**

Porcellino, Michael R.
  Through the telescope   **522**

Pornography
See/See also pages in the following book(s):
Dolan, E. F. Child abuse p104-14   **362.7**
Human sexuality: opposing viewpoints

                             306.7

Porpoises
Carwardine, M. Whales, dolphins, and porpoises

                             599.5
Whales, dolphins, and porpoises [Facts on File]
                             599.5
Whales, dolphins, and porpoises [National Geographic Soc.]   **599.5**
The **portable** Abraham Lincoln. Lincoln, A.

                             973.7

The **portable** Arthur Miller. Miller, A.   **812**
The **portable** Bernard Shaw. Shaw, B.   **822**
The **portable** Blake. Blake, W.   **828**
The **portable** Chaucer. Chaucer, G.   **821**
The **portable** Coleridge. Coleridge, S. T.   **828**
The **portable** college adviser. Robbins, W. H.

                             378

The **portable** Conrad. Conrad, J.   **828**
The **portable** D. H. Lawrence. Lawrence, D. H.

                             828

The **portable** Dante. Dante Alighieri   **851**
The **portable** Darwin. Darwin, C.   **575.01**
The **portable** Emerson. Emerson, R. W.   **818**
The **portable** Graham Greene. Greene, G.

                             828

The **Portable** Greek reader   **880.8**
The **Portable** Harlem Renaissance reader

                             810.8

The **portable** Jack Kerouac. Kerouac, J.   **818**
The **portable** Jack London. London, J.   **818**
The **portable** Kipling. Kipling, R.   **828**
The **portable** Milton. Milton, J.   **828**
The **portable** Nietzsche. Nietzsche, F. W.

                             193

The **Portable** nineteenth-century Russian reader
                             891.7
The **portable** Oscar Wilde. Wilde, O.   **828**
The **Portable** Roman reader   **870.8**

The **portable** Steinbeck. Steinbeck, J.   **818**
The **portable** Tolstoy. Tolstoy, L., graf   **891.7**
The **Portable** twentieth-century Russian reader

                             891.7

The **portable** Voltaire. Voltaire   **848**
Porter, David L., 1941-
  (ed) African-American sports greats. See African-American sports greats   **920.003**
Porter, Harold Everett, 1887-1936
  The valiant
    In Thirty famous one-act plays p379-99

                             808.82

Porter, J. R. (Joshua Roy), 1921-
  The illustrated guide to the Bible   **220.6**
Porter, Joshua Roy *See* Porter, J. R. (Joshua Roy), 1921-
Porter, Katherine Anne, 1890-1980
  The collected stories of Katherine Anne Porter
                             S C

    Contents: Flowering Judas, and other stories: María Concepción; Virgin Violeta; The martyr; Magic; Rope; He; Theft; That tree; The jilting of Granny Weatherall; Flowering Judas; The cracked looking-glass; Hacienda
    Pale horse, pale rider: Old mortality; Noon wine; Pale horse, pale rider
    The leaning tower, and other stories: The old order; The downward path to wisdom; A day's work; Holiday; The leaning tower
  A days work
    In Classic American short stories p319-43

                             S C

  Flowering Judas
    In The Oxford book of short stories p310-21

                             S C

  Flowering Judas, and other stories
    In Porter, K. A. The collected stories of Katherine Anne Porter   **S C**
  He
    In The Oxford book of American short stories p323-33   **S C**
  The leaning tower, and other stories
    In Porter, K. A. The collected stories of Katherine Anne Porter   **S C**
  Pale horse, pale rider
    In Porter, K. A. The collected stories of Katherine Anne Porter   **S C**
  Pale horse, pale rider: three short novels

                             S C

    Contents: Old mortality; Noon wine; Pale horse, pale rider
  Theft
    In The Norton book of American short stories p292-97   **S C**

About

Givner, J. Katherine Anne Porter   **92**
Hendrick, W. Katherine Anne Porter

                             813.009

See/See also pages in the following book(s):
Gombar, C. Great women writers, 1900-1950
                             920
Porter, Roy, 1946-
  (ed) The Biographical dictionary of scientists. See The Biographical dictionary of scientists
                             920.003
Porter, William Sydney *See* Henry, O., 1862-1910
The **porter**. Hemingway, E.
  In Hemingway, E. The complete short stories of Ernest Hemingway p571-78   **S C**

Princeton Review Inc.—*Continued*
Spencer, J. Visiting college campuses
   378.73

The **principles** of knitting. Hiatt, J.   **746.43**

Pringle, David
Imaginary people   **803**
(ed) St. James guide to fantasy writers. See St.
James guide to fantasy writers   **809.3**

Printing
Greenfeld, H. Books: from writer to reader
   070.5

History
See/See also pages in the following book(s):
Boorstin, D. J. The Americans: The colonial ex-
perience p319-40   **973.2**

Printmaking techniques. Ayres, J.   **760**

Prints
Ayres, J. Printmaking techniques   **760**
Ross, J. The complete printmaker   **760.2**
See/See also pages in the following book(s):
Canaday, J. E. What is art?   **701**

Priscilla and the wimps. Peck, R.
In Who do you think you are? p92-95
   S C

The **prison** cell. Greene, G.
In Greene, G. The portable Graham Greene
p60-77   **828**

Prison life. Kosof, A.   **365**

The **prisoner** of Second Avenue. Simon, N.
In Best American plays: 7th series—1967-
1973 p73-102   **812.008**
In Simon, N. The collected plays of Neil Simon v2 p231-99   **812**

Prisoners
See also Political prisoners
Fiction
Gaines, E. J. A lesson before dying   **Fic**
Hale, E. E. The man without a country   **Fic**
Marsden, J. Letters from the inside   **Fic**
Myers, W. D. Somewhere in the darkness
   Fic

Prisoners of war, Japanese *See* Japanese prisoners of war

Prisoners without trial. Daniels, R.   **940.53**

Prisons
United States
America's prisons: opposing viewpoints
   365
Kosof, A. Prison life   **365**
See/See also pages in the following book(s):
Criminal sentencing p46-69   **345**
Meltzer, M. Crime in America p137-47
   364

Pritchard, Melissa
Spirit seizures
In The Literary ghost p144-55   **S C**

Pritchett, V. S. (Victor Sawdon), 1900-1997
Chekhov   **92**
Many are disappointed
In The Oxford book of short stories p353-61
   S C
A story of Don Juan
In The Literary ghost p69-73   **S C**

In The Oxford book of English ghost stories
p453-57   **S C**
The voice
In Classic English short stories, 1930-1955
p105-12   **S C**
(ed) The Oxford book of short stories. See The
Oxford book of short stories   **S C**

Pritchett, Victor Sawdon *See* Pritchett, V. S.
(Victor Sawdon), 1900-1997

Privacy, Right of *See* Right of privacy

The **private** life of plants. Attenborough, D.
   581.5

Private schools
Directories
The Handbook of private schools   **370.25**
Peterson's private secondary schools   **373.2**

The **private** war of Private Jacob. Haldeman, J.
W.
In The Norton book of science fiction p300-
04   **S C**

Privateering
Marley, D. F. Pirates and privateers of the
Americas   **910.4**

Prize stories: The O. Henry Awards   **S C**

Prizes, Literary *See* Literary prizes

Prizes (Rewards) *See* Awards

Pro Football Hall of Fame
Harrington, D. J. The Pro Football Hall of Fame
   796.332

Probably still Nick Swansen. Wolff, V. E.
   Fic

Problem children *See* Emotionally disturbed children

Problem drinking *See* Alcoholism

The **problem** of cell 13. Futrelle, J.
In Crime classics p103-38   **S C**
In The Oxford book of American detective
stories p49-80   **S C**

The **problem** of Old Harjo. Oskison, J. M.
In The Singing spirit: early short stories by
North American Indians p128-35
   S C

The **problem** of our laws. Kafka, F.
In Kafka, F. The complete stories   **S C**

The **problem** of Thor Bridge. Doyle, Sir A. C.
In Doyle, Sir A. C. The complete Sherlock
Holmes   **S C**

Problems of creativeness. Disch, T. M.
In The Oxford book of science fiction stories
p363-84   **S C**

The **procession** of life. Hawthorne, N.
In Hawthorne, N. Tales and sketches; A wonder book for girls and boys; Tanglewood
tales for girls and boys p795-807
   S C

Product safety
Welsh, H. J. Animal testing and consumer products   **670**

Products, Commercial *See* Commercial products

Profession. Asimov, I.
In Asimov, I. The complete stories v1 p162-
207   **S C**

The **Professional** secretary's handbook   **651.3**

Professions
  See also Occupations
  Specialty occupational outlook: professions
      331.7

Professor. Hughes, L.
  In Hughes, L. Short stories   **S C**

The **professor's** yarn. Twain, M.
  In Twain, M. The complete short stories of
    Mark Twain   **S C**

Profiles in American history. Moss, J. **973**

Profiles in courage. Kennedy, J. F. **920**

De **profundis.** Wilde, O.
  In Wilde, O. The portable Oscar Wilde p508-
    658   **828**

Programmed instruction
  See also Computer assisted instruction

Programming (Computers)
  See also Computer software

Programs, Computer *See* Computer software

Programs, Television *See* Television programs

Progressive movement, 1900-1915
  Schneider, D. American women in the Progres-
    sive Era, 1900-1920   **305.4**

Project Apollo *See* Apollo project

Project Gemini *See* Gemini project

Project Mercury *See* Mercury project

Project Voyager
  See/See also pages in the following book(s):
  Sagan, C. Cosmos p150-56, 159-61   **520**

Proliferation of arms *See* Arms race

Prologue for The Comstock journals (or Sotol
  City blues). Castellano, O.
  In Growing up Chicana/o p219-30   **810.8**

A **prologue** to America. Wolfe, T.
  In Wolfe, T. The complete short stories of
    Thomas Wolfe p409-19   **S C**

Prometheus bound. Aeschylus
  In Seven famous Greek plays   **882.008**

Prominent women of the 20th century
      920.003

The **promise.** Maugham, W. S.
  In Maugham, W. S. Collected short stories v1
      S C

The **promise.** Steinbeck, J.
  In Steinbeck, J. The portable Steinbeck
      818

The **promise** of America. Wolfe, T.
  In Wolfe, T. The complete short stories of
    Thomas Wolfe p482-84   **S C**

The **promised** land. Lemann, N. **973.9**

Promises, promises. Simon, N.
  In Simon N. The comedy of Neil Simon
    p393-494   **812**

Pronzini, Bill
  Cat's-paw
  In Masterpieces of mystery and suspense
    p600-19   **S C**
  Words do not a book make
  In The Oxford book of American detective
    stories p602-607   **S C**

Propaganda
  Huxley, A. Brave new world revisited
      303.3

Proper library. Ferrell, C.
  In The Best American short stories, 1994
    p107-22   **S C**
  In Children of the night p280-95 **S C**

Prophecies (Occultism)
  Randi, J. The mask of Nostradamus **92**
  See/See also pages in the following book(s):
  Reader's Digest mysteries of the unexplained
    p12-33   **001.9**

The **Prophet.** Gibran, K. **811**

The **prophet** from Jupiter. Earley, T.
  In The Best American short stories, 1994
    p90-106   **S C**

Prophet of rage: a life of Louis Farrakhan and his
  nation. Magida, A. J. **92**

The **prophetess.** Ndebele, N. S.
  In The Heinemann book of contemporary
    African short stories p8-24   **S C**

The **prophetic** pictures. Hawthorne, N.
  In Hawthorne, N. Tales and sketches; A won-
    der book for girls and boys; Tanglewood
    tales for girls and boys p456-69
      S C

The **proposal.** Chekhov, A. P.
  In Chekhov, A. P. The image of Chekhov
    p111-12   **S C**

Prose, Francine, 1947-
  Other lives
  In We are the stories we tell **S C**

Prose and poetry. Crane, S. **818**

Prosody *See* Versification

Prosthetic appliances. Shalamov, V. T.
  In The Portable twentieth-century Russian
    reader p420-22   **891.7**

Prostitution
  See also Juvenile prostitution

Prostitution, Juvenile *See* Juvenile prostitution

Protecting the right to read. Symons, A. K.
      025.2

Protection of environment *See* Environmental
  protection

Protection of wildlife *See* Wildlife conservation

Protestant Reformation *See* Reformation

Protests, demonstrations, etc.
  See also Riots
  Anderson, T. H. The movement and the sixties
      303.4

Prothero, Stephen R.
  (jt. auth) Queen, E. L. Encyclopedia of
    American religious history **200.9**

Protista. Marechera, D.
  In African short stories   **S C**

The **proud** tower. Tuchman, B. W. **909.82**

Provence (France)
    Social life and customs
  Mayle, P. A dog's life   **828**

Proverbs
  The Oxford dictionary of English proverbs
      398.9

Proverbs—*Continued*
Titelman, G. Y. Random House dictionary of popular proverbs & sayings   **398.9**

Prussia
See/See also pages in the following book(s):
Spencer, W. Germany then and now p36-59
943

The **Prussian** officer. Lawrence, D. H.
In Lawrence, D. H. The complete short stories v1   **S C**

Pryor, Kelli
(jt. auth) Pratt, J. For real   **305.23**

Przytyk, Sara Nomberg- *See* Nomberg-Przytyk, Sara, 1915-

Psihoyos, Louis
Hunting dinosaurs   **567.9**

Psion. Vinge, J. D.   **Fic**

Psychiatrists
Gay, P. Freud   **92**

Psychiatry
See also Adolescent psychiatry; Child psychiatry
Veggeberg, S. Medication of the mind
616.89

Psychical research *See* Parapsychology

Psychoactive drugs *See* Psychotropic drugs

Psychoanalysis
Bettelheim, B. Freud and man's soul
150.19
Freud, S. The basic writings of Sigmund Freud
150.19

Psychological tests
See also Educational tests and measurements
See/See also pages in the following book(s):
Alderman, E. The right to privacy p277-89
323.44

Psychologists
See also Psychiatrists
Fancher, R. E. Pioneers of psychology
150.9

Psychology
See also Adjustment (Psychology); Adolescent psychology; Aggressiveness (Psychology); Behaviorism; Child psychology; Social psychology
Rogers, C. R. A way of being   **150.19**
History
Fancher, R. E. Pioneers of psychology
150.9

Psychology, Comparative *See* Comparative psychology

Psychology of learning
Metos, T. H. The human mind   **153**
See/See also pages in the following book(s):
Bettelheim, B. Surviving, and other essays p142-68   **155.9**

Psychopathology of everyday life. Freud, S.
In Freud, S. The basic writings of Sigmund Freud   **150.19**

Psychopharmaceuticals *See* Psychotropic drugs

Psychotropic drugs
See also Cocaine

Weil, A. From chocolate to morphine
616.86

PTSD *See* Post-traumatic stress disorder

Public debts
See also Deficit financing

Public documents *See* Government publications

Public figures *See* Celebrities

Public health
Leavitt, J. W. Typhoid Mary   **614.5**
See/See also pages in the following book(s):
Carter, J. Talking peace p78-86   **327.1**

Public housing
Kotlowitz, A. There are no children here
305.23

Public Information Dept. (United Nations) *See* United Nations. Dept. of Public Information

Public lands
See also National parks and reserves

Public opinion. O'Connor, F.
In O'Connor, F. Collected stories p585-92
S C

Public relations
Libraries
Blake, B. R. Creating newsletters, brochures, and pamphlets   **070.5**
Schaeffer, M. Library displays handbook
021.7

Public schools
Kozol, J. Savage inequalities   **371.9**
Boston (Mass.)
Kozol, J. Death at an early age   **370.19**
South Carolina
Conroy, P. The water is wide   **371.9**

Public speaking
Ashley, J. Overcoming stage fright in everyday life   **616.85**
Leeds, D. Powerspeak   **808.5**
Ryan, M. How to give a speech   **808.5**

Public utilities
Macaulay, D. Underground   **624**

Public welfare
See also Food relief
Kronenwetter, M. Welfare state America
361.6
LeVert, M. The welfare system   **361.6**
Poverty: opposing viewpoints   **362.5**

Publishers and publishing
See also Book industries
Baughman, J. L. Henry R. Luce and the rise of the American news media   **92**
The Chicago manual of style   **808**
Swanberg, W. A. Citizen Hearst: a biography of William Randolph Hearst   **92**
The Writer's handbook   **808**
The Writer's market   **808**

Publius Terentius Afer *See* Terence

Puck of Pook's Hill. Kipling, R.
In Kipling, R. The best fiction of Rudyard Kipling p399-530   **S C**

Puckett, Barry
(ed) Holidays and festivals index. See Holidays and festivals index   **394.2**

Pyramids—*Continued*
Weeks, J. The pyramids   726

Q

Qaddafi, Muammar al-, 1942-
See/See also pages in the following book(s):
Wakin, E. Contemporary political leaders of the Middle East p71-89   920

Quacks and quackery
Gilbert, S. K. Medical fakes and frauds   615.8

The **Quaker** colonies. Fisher, S. G.   973.2

Quakers *See* Society of Friends

Quakes, eruptions, and other geologic cataclysms. Erickson, J.   550

The **quality** of silence. Golden, M.
In Streetlights: illuminating tales of the urban black experience p136-45   S C

Quammen, David, 1948-
The song of the dodo   574.9
Walking out
In American short story masterpieces   S C

Quantum theory
Hawking, S. W. The nature of space and time   530.1
Lindley, D. Where does the weirdness go?   530.1

The **quare** fellow. Behan, B.
In Behan, B. The complete plays   822

Quayle, Dan
See/See also pages in the following book(s):
Walsh, K. T. Feeding the beast p100-12   973.927

Queen, Edward L.
Encyclopedia of American religious history   200.9

Queen, Ellery
Abraham Lincoln's clue
In Masterpieces of mystery and suspense p160-75   S C
The adventure of Abraham Lincoln's clue
In Crime classics p299-316   S C
In The Oxford book of American detective stories p587-601   S C
Object lesson
In Read all about it! p53-66   808.88
See/See also pages in the following book(s):
Modern mystery writers p154-72   809.3

The **Queen** of Air and Darkness. White, T. H.
In White, T. H. The once and future king   Fic

Queen of diamonds. Dorris, M.
In Talking leaves   S C

The **queen** of Quok. Baum, L. F.
In Masterpieces of fantasy and enchantment p405-12   S C
In The Oxford book of modern fairy tales p215-23   S C

The **queen** of spades. Pushkin, A. S.
In Pushkin, A. S. Alexander Pushkin: complete prose fiction p211-33   S C

The **Queen:** the life of Elizabeth II. Longford, E. H. P., Countess of   92

Queen Wintergreen. Fulton, A.
In The Best American short stories, 1993 p63-76   S C

Queens *See* Kings, queens, rulers, etc.

Queens, empresses, grand duchesses, and regents. Opfell, O. S.   920

The **queen's** gambit. Tevis, W. S.   Fic

"Queer". Anderson, S.
In Anderson, S. Winesburg, Ohio   S C

Quentin, Patrick *See* Wheeler, Hugh Callingham, 1912-1987

A **quest** must end. Goodridge Roberts, T.
In The Merlin chronicles   S C

Question quest. Anthony, P. *See* note under Anthony, P. The Magic of Xanth series   Fic

Questions and answers
See also Examinations
Davis, K. C. Don't know much about geography   910.2
Ehrlich, R. What if you could unscramble an egg?   500
Feldman, D. When do fish sleep? and other imponderables of everyday life   031.02
Feldman, D. Why do clocks run clockwise? and other imponderables   031.02
Feldman, D. Why do dogs have wet noses? and other imponderables of everyday life   031.02
Jackson, K. A. America is me   305.8
Sutton, C. More how do they do that?   031.02

The **quick-change** artist. Colette
In Colette. The collected stories of Colette p196-97   S C

Quicksand [excerpt] Larsen, N.
In The Portable Harlem Renaissance reader p410-60   810.8

Quiet strength. Parks, R.   92

Quietus. Russell, C.
In The Best short stories by Negro writers p347-55   S C

Quiller-Couch, Sir Arthur Thomas, 1863-1944
The roll-call of the reef
In The Oxford book of English ghost stories p137-49   S C

Quilting
Florence, J. A collection of favorite quilts   746.46

Quilting. Clifton, L.   811

Quilting on the rebound. McMillan, T.
In Calling the wind p597-608   S C

Quinn, John R.
The fascinating fresh water fish book   639.3
Wildlife survivors   574.5

Quinn, Patricia O.
Adolescents and ADD   371.9

Quinn, Susan
Marie Curie   92

Quintana, Leroy V.
La yerba sin raíz (The weed without a root)
In Iguana dreams   S C

Racism—*Continued*
Landau, E. The white power movement
    322.4

Racism 101. Giovanni, N.   **814**

Racquetball
Turner, E. T. Winning racquetball   **796.34**

Radetsky, Peter
The invisible invaders   **616**

Radicalism
Anderson, T. H. The movement and the sixties
    303.4
Burns, S. Social movements of the 1960s
    303.4
Kessler, L. After all these years: sixties ideals in
    a different world   **973.92**

Radice, Betty, 1912-1985
Who's who in the ancient world   **938.003**

Radio
See/See also pages in the following book(s):
Inventors and discoverers p182-213   **609**
    Handbooks, manuals, etc.
The ARRL handbook for the radio amateur
    621.3841

Radio broadcasting
Smith, C. The storytellers   **796.357**

Radio industry *See* Radio broadcasting

Radio journalism *See* Broadcast journalism

Radio programs
    See also Talk shows
Lackmann, R. W. Same time—same station
    791.44

Radio stations, Amateur *See* Amateur radio stations

Radioactive fallout
See/See also pages in the following book(s):
White, E. B. Essays of E. B. White   **814**

Radioactive pollution
Read, P. P. Ablaze   **363.1**

Radioactive waste disposal
    See also Radioactive pollution
Andryszewski, T. What to do about nuclear
    waste   **363.7**
See/See also pages in the following book(s):
Gay, K. Air pollution p80-88   **363.7**

Radner, Gilda, 1946-1989
It's always something   **92**

Radzinsky, Edvard
Stalin   **92**

Raeburn, Paul
The last harvest   **338.1**

The raft. King, S.
    In King, S. Skeleton crew   **S C**

Rage in the streets. Archer, J.   **303.6**

Raging forces: earth in upheaval   **904**

Rags Martin-Jones and the Pr-nce of W-les. Fitzgerald, F. S.
    In Fitzgerald, F. S. The short stories of F.
    Scott Fitzgerald p273-88   **S C**

Ragsdale, Lyn, 1954-
Vital statistics on the presidency   **353.03**

Ragtime. Doctorow, E. L.   **Fic**

Rahman, Aishah
The mojo and the sayso
    In Black theatre USA   **812.008**
Unfinished women cry in no man's land while
a bird dies in a gilded cage
    In 9 plays by black women   **811.008**

Raid. Faulkner, W.
    In Faulkner, W. Uncollected stories of William Faulkner p37-57   **S C**

The raid. Tolstoy, L., graf
    In Tolstoy, L. The portable Tolstoy p169-99
    891.7

Railroad standard time. Chin, F.
    In Growing up Asian American p201-08
    810.8

The railroad stories. See Sholem Aleichem. Tevye
the dairyman and The railroad stories
    S C

Railroads
Foster, G. L. A field guide to trains of North
    America   **625.2**
See/See also pages in the following book(s):
Langdon, W. C. Everyday things in American
    life, 1776-1876 p326-67   **973**
White, E. B. Essays of E. B. White   **814**
    Models
Schleicher, R. H. The HO model railroading
    handbook   **625.1**

Rain
    See also Acid rain

Rain. Chiu, C.
    In Not the only one p205-14   **S C**

Rain. Maugham, W. S.
    In Maugham, W. S. Collected short stories v1
    S C

The rain came. Ogot, G.
    In Daughters of Africa p365-71   **808.8**

Rain forest ecology
Forsyth, A. Portraits of the rainforest   **574.5**
Gay, K. Rainforests of the world   **574.5**
Newman, A. Tropical rainforest   **574.5**
Reading, S. Plants of the tropics   **581.5**
Terborgh, J. Diversity and the tropical rain forest   **574.5**

Rain forests
The Conservation atlas of tropical forests: Africa
    333.75

Rain in the heart. Taylor, P. H.
    In The Oxford book of American short stories
    p463-80   **S C**

Rain music. Nguyen, L.
    In American dragons: twenty-five Asian
    American voices p155-60   **810.8**

Rain, rain, go away. Asimov, I.
    In Asimov, I. The complete stories v2 p320-26   **S C**

Rainey, Anson F., 1930-
(ed) Aharoni, Y. The Macmillan Bible atlas
    220.9

Rainforests of the world. Gay, K.   **574.5**

Rainis, Kenneth G.
Environmental science projects for young scientists   **574.5**

Rappaccini's daughter. Hawthorne, N.
In Hawthorne, N. Tales and sketches; A wonder book for girls and boys; Tanglewood tales for girls and boys p975-1005
S C
In The Oxford book of gothic tales p133-57
S C

Rare animals
See also Endangered species; Extinct animals
Ackerman, D. The rarest of the rare **574.5**
The Official World Wildlife Fund guide to endangered species of North America
574.5

Rare plants
See also Endangered species
The Official World Wildlife Fund guide to endangered species of North America
574.5
The **rarest** of the rare. Ackerman, D. **574.5**

Rashad. Wideman, J. E.
In The Other side of heaven p279-86
S C

Rasmussen, R. Kent
Mark Twain A to Z **818**

Rasmussen, Waldo
(ed) Latin American artists of the twentieth century. See Latin American artists of the twentieth century **709.8**

Rasputin, Grigoriĭ Efimovich, 1871-1916
About
Fuhrmann, J. T. Rasputin **92**
See/See also pages in the following book(s):
Massie, R. K. Nicholas and Alexandra **92**

Rassam, Hormuzd
See/See also pages in the following book(s):
Moorehead, A. The Blue Nile **962**

Rat. Kelly, J. P.
In The Norton book of science fiction p654-64
S C

Rather, Dan
The camera never blinks twice **92**

Rationalism
See also Enlightenment

Rattigan, Terence
The Browning version
In 24 favorite one-act plays p54-93
808.82

Raven, Simon, 1927-
The bottle of 1912
In The Oxford book of English ghost stories p471-76
S C

Ravenel, Shannon
(comp) The Best American short stories of the eighties. See The Best American short stories of the eighties
S C

Raven's road [excerpt] Allen, P. G.
In Growing up gay p105-09 **808.8**

Ravenscroft, Anna
(jt. auth) Goffe, G. Calligraphy school
745.6

The **ravine.** Bradbury, R.
In Read all about it! p252-71 **808.88**

Ravnitzki, Yehoshua Ḥana, 1859-1944
(ed) The Book of legends. Sefer ha-aggadah. See The Book of legends. Sefer ha-aggadah
296.1

Raw material. Maugham, W. S.
In Maugham, W. S. Collected short stories v4
S C

Rawdon's roof. Lawrence, D. H.
In Lawrence, D. H. The complete short stories v3
S C

Rawlings, Marjorie Kinnan, 1896-1953
About
Silverthorne, E. Marjorie Kinnan Rawlings
92

Rawson, Clayton, 1906-1971
From another world
In The Oxford book of American detective stories p431-55
S C

Raymond's run. Bambara, T. C.
In Rites of passage p1-10 **S C**
In Who do you think you are? p47-57
S C

Rayona's seduction. Dorris, M.
In The Lightning within p133-61 **S C**

The **razor's** edge. Maugham, W. S. **Fic**

The **reach.** King, S.
In The Horror hall of fame p385-407
S C
In King, S. Skeleton crew **S C**

Read, Anthony
The fall of Berlin **940.54**

Read, Sir Herbert Edward, 1893-1968
A concise history of modern painting
759.06
A concise history of modern sculpture **735**

Read, Phyllis J.
The book of women's firsts **920.003**

Read, Piers Paul, 1941-
Ablaze **363.1**
Alive **910.4**

Read all about it! **808.8**

The **Reader's** adviser **011**

The **Reader's** companion to American history
973.03

Reader's Digest Association, Inc.
ABC's of the Bible. See ABC's of the Bible
220
America's fascinating Indian heritage. See America's fascinating Indian heritage
970.004
America's historic places. See America's historic places **917.3**
Book of North American birds. See Book of North American birds **598**
Discovering America's past. See Discovering America's past **973**
Everyday life through the ages. See Everyday life through the ages **909**
Great disasters. See Great disasters **904**
Harrison, H. Pastel school **741.2**
Historic places. See Historic places **917.3**
How in the world? See How in the world?
600

Recombinant DNA
Drlica, K. Understanding DNA and gene cloning **574.87**

Recommended reference books for small and medium-sized libraries and media centers **011**

The reconciliation. Wells, H. G.
In Wells, H. G. The complete short stories of H. G. Wells p551-58 **S C**

Reconstruction (1865-1876)
Foner, E. America's Reconstruction **973.8**
Kirchberger, J. H. The Civil War and Reconstruction **973.7**
Reconstruction: opposing viewpoints **973.8**
Southern black leaders of the Reconstruction era **975**
See/See also pages in the following book(s):
Senna, C. The black press and the struggle for civil rights p63-74 **071**
Fiction
Mitchell, M. Gone with the wind **Fic**
Walker, M. Jubilee **Fic**

Reconstruction (1939-1951)
See/See also pages in the following book(s):
Miller, M. Plain speaking: an oral biography of Harry S. Truman p233-49 **92**
White, T. H. In search of history p263-306 **92**

Reconstruction: opposing viewpoints **973.8**

The record of Badalia Herodsfoot. Kipling, R.
In The Oxford book of short stories p147-66 **S C**

Recording your family history. Fletcher, W. P. **929**

Recordings, Sound *See* Sound recordings

Recreating the past. Adamson, L. G. **016.8**

Recreation
See also Amusements

The recurring silent spring [biography of Rachel Carson] Hynes, H. P. **92**

Recycling
See/See also pages in the following book(s):
Rainis, K. G. Environmental science projects for young scientists p43-74 **574.5**

Red. Maugham, W. S.
In Maugham, W. S. Collected short stories v4 **S C**

The red and the black. Stendhal **Fic**

The red badge of courage. Crane, S. **Fic**

Red Bird *See* Zitkala-Ša, 1876-1938

Red bonnet. Patterson, L.
In The Best short stories by Negro writers p448-57 **S C**

Red Cloud, Sioux Chief, 1822-1909
See/See also pages in the following book(s):
Brown, D. A. The American West p78-98 **978**
Brown, D. A. Bury my heart at Wounded Knee p23-49 **970.004**

The red convertible. Erdrich, L.
In Who do you think you are? p134-45 **S C**

The red dress. Pilcher, R.
In Pilcher, R. Flowers in the rain & other stories **S C**

Red earth, white lies. Deloria, V. **398**

Red giants and white dwarfs. Jastrow, R. **523.1**

A red girl's reasoning. Johnson, E. P.
In The Singing spirit: early short stories by North American Indians p18-34 **S C**

The red hawk. Lynn, E. A.
In Masterpieces of fantasy and enchantment p224-51 **S C**

Red-headed baby. Hughes, L.
In The Oxford book of American short stories p365-70 **S C**

The Red-headed League. Doyle, Sir A. C.
In The Best crime stories of the 19th century p126-50 **S C**
In Doyle, Sir A. C. The complete Sherlock Holmes **S C**

The Red House clock. Westall, R.
In Westall, R. Shades of darkness p177-206 **S C**

Red leaves. Faulkner, W.
In Faulkner, W. Collected stories of William Faulkner p313-41 **S C**
In Faulkner, W. Selected short stories of William Faulkner **S C**

Red lipstick. Barnes, Y.
In Streetlights: illuminating tales of the urban black experience p24-33 **S C**

Red moccasins. Power, S.
In The Best American short stories, 1993 p113-26 **S C**

The red one. London, J.
In London, J. The portable Jack London p314-35 **818**
In London, J. The science fiction stories of Jack London p191-211 **S C**
In London, J. Short stories of Jack London p578-98 **S C**

Red pony. Steinbeck, J.
In Steinbeck, J. The grapes of wrath and other writings, 1936-1941 **818**
In Steinbeck, J. The portable Steinbeck **818**

The Red Queen's race. Asimov, I.
In Asimov, I. The complete stories v2 p85-104 **S C**

The red room. Wells, H. G.
In The Oxford book of English ghost stories p172-79 **S C**
In Wells, H. G. The complete short stories of H. G. Wells p447-56 **S C**

Red scare. Fariello, G. **973.92**

Red Sea
See/See also pages in the following book(s):
Sammon, R. Seven underwater wonders of the world p67-91 **574.92**

Red sky at morning. Bradford, R. **Fic**

Red Sox (Baseball team) *See* Boston Red Sox (Baseball team)

Redcoats & Rebels. Hibbert, C. **973.3**

Redemption. Gardner, J.
In American short story masterpieces
S C

Redmond, Tim
(jt. auth) Mowrey, M. Not in our back yard
363.7

Reducing
LeBow, M. D. Overweight teenagers   613.2
Weight Watchers healthy life-style cookbook
641.5

Fiction
Lipsyte, R. One fat summer   Fic

Reed, Gregory J.
(jt. auth) Parks, R. Quiet strength   92

Reed, Ishmael, 1938-
See/See also pages in the following book(s):
Contemporary black American fiction writers
p137-53   813.009
Contemporary black American poets and drama-
tists p143-58   810.9
Major modern black American writers p137-51
810.9

Reed, Jean
(ed) Résumés that get jobs. See Résumés that
get jobs   650.14

Reed, Kenneth T.
Truman Capote   813.009

Reed, Mark, 1947-
Yes, my darling daughter
In Twenty best plays of the modern American
theatre p467-510   812.008

Reed, Mary Hutchings
(jt. auth) Bruwelheide, J. H. The copyright
primer for librarians and educators
346.04

Reed, Virginia *See* Murphy, Virginia Reed, d.
1921

Reed, W. L.
(ed) National anthems of the world. See National anthems of the world   782.42

Reed, Walter, 1851-1902
See/See also pages in the following book(s):
De Kruif, P. Microbe hunters   920

Reef, Catherine
John Steinbeck   92
Walt Whitman   92

Reef. Stafford-Deitsch, J.   574.92

Reel women. Acker, A.   920

Reena. Marshall, P.
In Black-eyed Susans/Midnight birds p85-105
S C

Rees, Nigel, 1944-
Dictionary of catchphrases   422.03

Reesman, Jeanne Campbell
(jt. auth) Labor, E. Jack London   813.009

Reeve, Arthur Benjamin, 1880-1936
The beauty mask
In The Oxford book of American detective
stories p124-41   S C

Reeves, Bass
See/See also pages in the following book(s):
Abdul-Jabbar, K. Black profiles in courage
p126-39   920

Reeves, Randall R.
(jt. auth) Leatherwood, S. The Sierra Club handbook of whales and dolphins   599.5

Reeves, Thomas C., 1936-
The life and times of Joe McCarthy   92

Reeves-Stevens, Garfield
(jt. auth) Reeves-Stevens, J. The art of Star Trek
791.45

Reeves-Stevens, Judith
The art of Star Trek   791.45

Reference books
Bibliography
American reference books annual   011
Guide to reference books   011
The New York Public Library book of how and
where to look it up   025.5
The Reader's adviser   011
Recommended reference books for small and
medium-sized libraries and media centers
011
Reviews
American reference books annual   011
Recommended reference books for small and
medium-sized libraries and media centers
011

Reference Books Bulletin. See Booklist
028.1

Reference encyclopedia of the American Indian
970.004

Reference guide to English literature   820.3

Reference guide to science fiction, fantasy, and
horror. Burgess, M.   016.8

Reference guide to short fiction   809.3

Reference services (Libraries)
The American Library Association guide to information access   025.5

Reference shelf
Abortion   363.4
Affirmative action   342
Animal rights and welfare   179
Balancing the federal budget   336.3
Banking scandals: the S&Ls and BCCI
364.1
The Breakup of communism   947
Censorship   323.44
Criminal sentencing   345
Drugs in America   363.4
Gambling   363.4
The Greenhouse effect   363.7
The Homeless problem   362.5
Immigration   325.73
Immigration to the U.S.   325.73
The Information revolution   384.3
Religious cults in America   291
Representative American speeches   815.008
Suicide   362.2
The United Nations' role in world affairs
341.23
Women's issues   305.4

Reflections in a cell. Gwala, M. P.
In African short stories   S C

Reflections in a golden eye. McCullers, C.
In McCullers, C. The ballad of the sad café:
the novels and stories of Carson McCullers   S C

Reflections of Eden. Galdikas, B.   **599.8**

Reflections on a gift of watermelon pickle—and other modern verse   **811.008**

Reflections on the Civil War. Catton, B.   **973.7**

Reformation
> *See also* Sixteenth century
>
> Bainton, R. H. Here I stand: a life of Martin Luther   **92**
> Durant, W. J. The Reformation   **940.2**
> The Oxford encyclopedia of the Reformation   **270.6**
>
> *See/See also pages in the following book(s):*
> Tuchman, B. W. The march of folly   **909.08**

Reformatories
> **Fiction**
> Harris, M. Hatter Fox   **Fic**

Reformers
> American reformers   **920.003**

Refugees
> Sawyer, K. K. Refugees   **362.87**
> *See/See also pages in the following book(s):*
> Andryszewski, T. Immigration p71-85   **325.73**

Refugees, Cambodian *See* Cambodian refugees

Refugees, Hungarian *See* Hungarian refugees

Refuges, Wildlife *See* Wildlife refuges

The **refusal**. Kafka, F.
> *In* Kafka, F. The complete stories   **S C**

Refuse and refuse disposal
> *See also* Radioactive waste disposal; Recycling

The **regent** of the North. Morris, K.
> *In* Masterpieces of fantasy and enchantment p473-83   **S C**

Reginald, R., 1948-
> Science fiction and fantasy literature, 1975-1991   **016.8**

Regionalism *See* Nationalism

The **regions** of Spain. Kern, R. W.   **946**

Regret. Chopin, K.
> *In* Chopin, K. The awakening and selected stories p96-101   **S C**

Reich, Jerome R.
> Colonial America   **973.2**

Reich, Steve
> *See/See also pages in the following book(s):*
> Nichols, J. American music makers p170-91   **920**

Reichler, Joseph L., 1915-1988
> The great all-time baseball record book   **796.357**

Reichman, Henry, 1947-
> Censorship and selection   **025.2**

Reid, Suzanne Elizabeth
> Presenting Cynthia Voigt   **813.009**

Reidelbach, Maria
> Completely Mad   **741.5**

The **Reigate** puzzle. Doyle, Sir A. C.
> *In* Doyle, Sir A. C. The complete Sherlock Holmes   **S C**

Reilly, Jim
> Joseph Conrad   **92**

Reino, Joseph
> Stephen King   **813.009**

Reischauer, Edwin O. (Edwin Oldfather), 1910-1990
> Japan, tradition & transformation   **952**

Reiser, Bob
> (jt. auth) Seeger, P. Everybody says freedom   **323.1**

Reisfeld, Randi
> This is the sound   **781.66**

Reisgies, Teresa, 1966-
> (jt. auth) Salzman, M. 150 ways teens can make a difference   **302**

Reiss, Johanna
> The upstairs room   **92**

Reiss, Tom
> (jt. auth) Hasselbach, I. Fuhrer-Ex   **943.087**

The **reivers**. Faulkner, W.   **Fic**

The **rejected** buppie. Baraka, I. A.
> *In* Streetlights: illuminating tales of the urban black experience p20-23   **S C**

The **rejuvenation** of Major Rathbone. London, J.
> *In* London, J. The science fiction stories of Jack London p25-34   **S C**

Relations among ethnic groups *See* Ethnic relations

Relative distances [excerpt] Jenkins, V.
> *In* Circle of women: an anthology of contemporary Western women writers p271-77   **810.8**

Relativity (Physics)
> Calder, N. Einstein's universe   **530.1**
> Einstein, A. The meaning of relativity   **530.1**
> Osserman, R. Poetry of the universe   **530.1**
> Thorne, K. S. Black holes and time warps   **530.1**
>
> *See/See also pages in the following book(s):*
> Goldberg, J. Albert Einstein   **92**
> Hawking, S. W. Black holes and baby universes and other essays p69-83   **523.1**

Relic. Preston, D.   **Fic**

A **relic** of the Pliocene. London, J.
> *In* London, J. The portable Jack London p32-41   **818**
> *In* London, J. The science fiction stories of Jack London p40-48   **S C**
> *In* London, J. Short stories of Jack London p75-83   **S C**

Religion
> *See also* Theology
> Durant, W. J. The age of faith   **940.1**
> Eerdmans' handbook to the world's religions   **291**
>
> *See/See also pages in the following book(s):*
> Emerson, R. W. The portable Emerson p72-91   **818**
> The Middle Ages [American Heritage]   **940.1**
> Naisbitt, J. Megatrends 2000 p270-97   **303.4**
> Sagan, C. Broca's brain p281-91, 308-11   **500**

Religion—*Continued*
Dictionaries
The Encyclopedia of religion   **200.3**
The HarperCollins dictionary of religion
    200.3
Larousse dictionary of beliefs and religions
    291.03
Man, myth, & magic   **133**
History
Monroe, C. E. World religions   **291**
Religion and politics
    See also Islam and politics
Religion and science
Deloria, V. Red earth, white lies   **398**
Jastrow, R. God and the astronomers   **523.1**
Religions
    See also Gods and goddesses; Occultism; Sects
Eerdmans' handbook to the world's religions
    291
Frazer, Sir J. G. The golden bough   **291**
Frazer, Sir J. G. The new golden bough
    291
Religions on file   **291**
The World's religions   **291**
Dictionaries
The HarperCollins dictionary of religion
    200.3
Larousse dictionary of beliefs and religions
    291.03
Religions of Japan. Earhart, H. B.   **291**
Religions on file   **291**
Religious art and symbolism
    See also Christian art and symbolism
Campbell, J. The power of myth   **291**
Religious ceremonies *See* Rites and ceremonies
Religious cults *See* Cults
Religious cults in America   **291**
Religious freedom *See* Freedom of religion
Religious holidays
Kelly, A. A. Religious holidays and calendars
    291.3
Religious holidays and calendars. Kelly, A. A.
    291.3
Religious life
    See also Celibacy
Religious orders
See/See also pages in the following book(s):
Durant, W. J. The age of faith p785-818
    940.1
Religious poetry
Collections
Chapters into verse   **821.008**
Relocation of Japanese Americans, 1942-1945
    See Japanese Americans—Evacuation and relocation, 1942-1945
The **reluctant** dragon. Grahame, K.
    In The Oxford book of modern fairy tales p182-202   **S C**
The **remarkable** case of Davidson's eyes. Wells, H. G.
    In Wells, H. G. The complete short stories of H. G. Wells p273-83   **S C**

Remarque, Erich Maria, 1898-1970
All quiet on the western front   **Fic**
All quiet on the western front; criticism
    In Firda, R. A. All quiet on the western front
    833.009
Remarriage
Fiction
Cole, B. Celine   **Fic**
Mori, K. Shizuko's daughter   **Fic**
Rembrandt Harmenszoon van Rijn, 1606-1669
About
Schwartz, G. Rembrandt   **92**
Rembrandt's hat. Malamud, B.
    In Malamud, B. The stories of Bernard Malamud p266-76   **S C**
Remedial English. Smith, E.
    In Ten out of ten p157-86   **812.008**
Remember him a outlaw. De Veaux, A.
    In Black-eyed Susans/Midnight birds p192-205   **S C**
    In Children of the night p152-62   **S C**
Remember the Alamo. Cisneros, S.
    In Cisneros, S. Woman Hollering Creek and other stories   **S C**
Remembering Mog. Rodowsky, C. F.   **Fic**
Remembering the good times. Peck, R.   **Fic**
Remembering the Maine. Samuels, P.   **973.8**
Remini, Robert Vincent, 1921-
The Jacksonian era   **973.5**
Remnants. Singer, I. B.
    In Singer, I. B. The image and other stories p102-16   **S C**
Renaissance
    See also Sixteenth century
Burckhardt, J. The civilization of the Renaissance in Italy   **945**
Durant, W. J. The Renaissance   **945**
Walker, P. R. The Italian Renaissance   **945**
See/See also pages in the following book(s):
Crow, J. A. Spain: the root and the flower p139-60   **946**
Highet, G. The classical tradition p104-26, 219-54   **809**
Maps
Black, J. The Cambridge illustrated atlas of warfare: Renaissance to revolution, 1492-1792
    355
The **Renaissance.** Cole, A.   **709.02**
Renaissance art
Cole, A. The Renaissance   **709.02**
Cooper, T. E. Renaissance   **709.45**
Labella, V. A season of giants: Michelangelo, Leonardo, Raphael, 1492-1508   **709.45**
The **renaissance** at Charleroi. Henry, O.
    In Henry, O. The best short stories of O. Henry   **S C**
Renault, Mary, 1905-1983
The king must die   **Fic**
Rendell, Ruth, 1930-
The fever tree
    In Masterpieces of mystery and suspense p179-93   **S C**
Heartstones   **Fic**

Riley-Smith, Jonathan—*Continued*
(ed) The Oxford illustrated history of the Crusades. See The Oxford illustrated history of the Crusades **909.07**

Rilke, Rainer Maria, 1875-1926
Selected poems of Rainer Maria Rilke **831**

A **rill** from the town-pump. Hawthorne, N.
In Hawthorne, N. Tales and sketches; A wonder book for girls and boys; Tanglewood tales for girls and boys p308-13 **S C**

Rima in the weeds [excerpt] McNamer, D.
In Circle of women: an anthology of contemporary Western women writers p341-55 **810.8**

Rimbaud, Arthur, 1854-1891
Poems **841**

Rimbaud, Jean Nicolas Arthur See Rimbaud, Arthur, 1854-1891

The **rime** of the ancient mariner. Coleridge, S. T.
In Coleridge, S. T. The portable Coleridge **828**

Rinaldi, Ann, 1934-
Wolf by the ears **Fic**

Rinearson, Peter, 1954-
(jt. auth) Gates, B. The road ahead **004**

Rinehart, Mary Roberts, 1876-1958
The lipstick
In The Oxford book of American detective stories p356-74 **S C**

The **ring**. MacMahon, B.
In The Oxford book of Irish short stories p388-91 **S C**

Ringworld. Niven, L. **Fic**

Rio Grande valley
Description
See/See also pages in the following book(s):
Great rivers of the world p429-42 **910**

Ríos, Alberto
The iguana killer
In Growing up Chicano/o p41-55 **810.8**
Saturnino el Magnifico
In Iguana dreams **S C**

Riots
See/See also pages in the following book(s):
Carnes, J. Us and them p120-27 **305.8**

Rip-roaring reads for reluctant teen readers. Sherman, G. W. **028.5**

Rip Van Winkle. Irving, W.
In The Oxford book of American short stories p17-32 **S C**

Ripken, Cal, Jr.
About
Rosenfeld, H. Iron man: the Cal Ripken, Jr., story **92**

Ripples in the Dirac sea. Landis, G. A.
In Nebula awards 25 p12-26 **S C**

The **rise** and fall of the British Empire. James, L. **909**

The **rise** and fall of the Third Reich. Shirer, W. L. **943.086**

The **rise** of Japan and the Pacific Rim. Ross, S. **952.04**

The **rise** of Maud Martha. Brooks, G.
In Invented lives p429-32 **S C**

Rising of the moon. Gregory, Lady
In Thirty famous one-act plays p91-98 **808.82**

Rising voices **810.8**

Riskin, Robert, 1897-1955
Meet John Doe
In Best American screenplays **812.008**

Ritchie, Anna Cora Ogden Mowatt, 1819-1870
Fashion
In Best plays of the early American theatre p97-135 **812.008**

Ritchie, David, 1952-
The encyclopedia of earthquakes and volcanoes **551.2**
Shipwrecks **910.4**
UFO **001.9**

Ritchie, Donald A.
The young Oxford companion to the Congress of the United States **328.73**

Ritchin, Fred
In our own image **770.1**

The **rite** of challenge. Timlett, P. V.
In The Merlin chronicles **S C**

Rites. Colette
In Colette. The collected stories of Colette p59-61 **S C**

Rites and ceremonies
How to be a perfect stranger **291.3**

Rites of passage **S C**

Ritter, Lawrence S.
The glory of their times **920**

Rittner, Carol Ann, 1943-
(ed) Different voices. See Different voices **940.53**

Ritual See Rites and ceremonies

The **Ritz**. McNally, T.
In Best American plays: 8th series—1974-1982 p369-400 **812.008**
In McNally, T. 15 short plays p269-332 **812**

The **rivals**. Colette
In Colette. The collected stories of Colette p406-10 **S C**

The **rivals**. Sheridan, R. B. B. **822**

The **river**. O'Connor, F.
In O'Connor, F. Collected works p154-71 **S C**
In O'Connor, F. The complete stories p157-74 **S C**

The **river**. Wagner, P.
In Streetlights: illuminating tales of the urban black experience p471-83 **S C**

The **river** maid. Yolen, J.
In The Oxford book of modern fairy tales p422-26 **S C**

The **River** Niger. Walker, J. A.
In Best American plays: 8th series—1974-1982 p228-76 **812.008**

River of names. Allison, D.
In The Vintage book of contemporary American short stories p3-12 **S C**

Rivera, Tomás
On the road to Texas: Pete Fonseca
In Growing up Latino p147-54   **810.8**

Rivero, Eliana S. (Eliana Suárez), 1940-
(ed) Infinite divisions: an anthology of Chicana
literature. See Infinite divisions: an anthology
of Chicana literature   **810.8**

Rivers, Conrad Kent
Mother to son
In The Best short stories by Negro writers
p356-58   **S C**

Rivers
See also Amazon River; Mississippi River;
Nile River
Great rivers of the world   **910**
Palmer, T. America by rivers   **551.48**

RN: the memoirs of Richard Nixon. Nixon, R. M.
92

Roaches. Rodriguez, A.
In Iguana dreams   **S C**

The road ahead. Gates, B.   **004**

Road block. Mahjoub, J.
In The Heinemann book of contemporary
African short stories p129-33   **S C**

The road from Coorain. Conway, J. K.   **92**

The road from home [biography of Veron
Kherdian] Kherdian, D.   **92**

The road home. White, E. E.   **Fic**

The road to equality. Chafe, W. H.
In The Young Oxford history of women in
the United States   **305.4**

The road to Shiloh: early battles in the West.
Nevin, D.   **973.7**

The road to war. Overy, R. J.   **940.53**

Roads
See/See also pages in the following book(s):
Langdon, W. C. Everyday things in American
life, 1776-1876 p19-37, 66-89   **973**

Roads of destiny. Henry, O.
In Henry, O. The best short stories of O.
Henry   **S C**

Roaf, Michael
Cultural atlas of Mesopotamia and the ancient
Near East   **935**

Robb, H. Amanda
Encyclopedia of American family names
929.4

Robbers and outlaws *See* Thieves
Robbers, rogues, and ruffians. Bryan, H.
978.9

The robbery. Mohr, N.
In Mohr, N. In Nueva York   **S C**

Robbie. Asimov, I.
In Asimov, I. I, robot   **S C**

Robbins, Lawrence H.
Stones, bones, and ancient cities   **930.1**

Robbins, Wendy H.
The portable college adviser   **378**

Robert, Henry Martyn, 1837-1923
The Scott, Foresman Robert's Rules of order
newly revised   **060.4**

Robert, Sarah Corbin
(ed) Robert, H. M. The Scott, Foresman Robert's Rules of order newly revised   **060.4**

Robert Browning's poetry. Browning, R.   **821**

Robert Frost. Gerber, P. L.   **811**

Robert Frost: a collection of critical essays
811

Robert Gardner's challenging science experiments.
Gardner, R.   **507.8**

Robert Kennedy saved from drowning. Barthelme,
D.
In The Norton book of American short stories
p587-95   **S C**

Robert Silverberg's worlds of wonder   **S C**

Roberts, David, 1943-
In search of the old ones   **970.004**

Roberts, Edgar V.
Writing themes about literature   **808**

Roberts, J. M. (John Morris), 1928-
History of the world   **909**

Roberts, John Morris *See* Roberts, J. M. (John
Morris), 1928-

Roberts, Mickey
The Indian basket
In Talking leaves   **S C**
It's all in how you say it
In Talking leaves   **S C**

Roberts, Robin
(jt. auth) Lieberman-Cline, N. Basketball for
women   **796.323**

Roberts, Royston M.
Serendipity: accidental discoveries in science
500

Roberts, Sam
Who we are   **304.6**

Roberts, Sheryl Lindsell- *See* Lindsell-Roberts,
Sheryl

Roberts, Theodore Goodridge *See* Goodridge
Roberts, Theodore, 1877-1953

Robert's Rules of order. Robert, H. M.
060.4

Robertson, Dougal
Survive the savage sea   **910.4**

Robertson, James I., Jr.
Tenting tonight   **973.7**

Robeson, Paul, 1898-1976
About
Larsen, R. Paul Robeson, hero before his time
92

Robinson, Adam
Cracking the SAT & PSAT   **378.1**

Robinson, Charles M., 1949-
A good year to die   **973.8**

Robinson, Cyril Edward, b. 1884
Everyday life in ancient Greece   **938**

Robinson, David, 1930-
From peep show to palace   **791.43**

Robinson, Douglas Hill, 1918-
(jt. auth) Dick, H. G. The golden age of the
great passenger airships, Graf Zeppelin &
Hindenburg   **629.133**

Robinson, Francis
(ed) The Cambridge encyclopedia of India, Pakistan, Bangladesh, Sri Lanka, Nepal, Bhutan, and the Maldives. See The Cambridge encyclopedia of India, Pakistan, Bangladesh, Sri Lanka, Nepal, Bhutan, and the Maldives
954

Robinson, Jackie, 1919-1972
I never had it made 92
About
Robinson, S. Stealing home: an intimate family portrait by the daughter of Jackie Robinson
92

See/See also pages in the following book(s):
Lipsyte, R. Idols of the game p162-84 920
Robinson, Jennifer
The horse who would be king
In The Merlin chronicles S C
Robinson, Joy D. Marie
Antoine de Saint-Exupéry 848
Robinson, Julia B., 1919-1985
See/See also pages in the following book(s):
Henderson, H. Modern mathematicians 920
Robinson, Kim Stanley
Festival night
In Nebula awards 29 p47-67 S C
The lucky strike
In The Norton book of science fiction p538-68 S C
Vinland the dream
In Nebula awards 28 p195-206 S C
Robinson, Marilynne
Housekeeping [excerpt]
In Circle of women: an anthology of contemporary Western women writers p62-73
810.8

Robinson, Michael
Zoo animals 591.5
Robinson, Ray, 1920-
Iron horse: Lou Gehrig in his time 92
Robinson, Roxana
Georgia O'Keeffe 92
Mr. Sumarsono
In The Best American short stories, 1994 p264-76 S C
Robinson, Sharon, 1950-
Stealing home: an intimate family portrait by the daughter of Jackie Robinson 92
Robinson, Spider
User friendly
In Tales from the planet Earth S C
Robinson Crusoe. Defoe, D. Fic
Robles, Mireya
In the other half of time
In Daughters of the fifth sun 810.8
Robotics
Heiserman, D. L. Build your own working robot
629.8
Thro, E. Robotics 629.8
Dictionaries
The McGraw-Hill illustrated encyclopedia of robotics & artificial intelligence 629.8
Robots
Thro, E. Robotics 629.8

Fiction
Asimov, I. I, robot S C
Roc and a hard place. Anthony, P. See note under Anthony, P. The Magic of Xanth series
Fic
Roche, Elizabeth
(jt. auth) Roche, J. A dictionary of early music
780.3
Roche, Jerome
A dictionary of early music 780.3
Rochman, Hazel
Against borders 011.6
Tales of love and terror 028
(ed) Bearing witness: stories of the Holocaust. See Bearing witness: stories of the Holocaust
808.8
(comp) Somehow tenderness survives. See Somehow tenderness survives S C
(comp) Who do you think you are? See Who do you think you are? S C
The **rock** & roll almanac. Bego, M. 781.66
Rock and roll music See Rock music
Rock, church. Hughes, L.
In Hughes, L. Short stories S C
Rock drawings, paintings, and engravings
See also Cave drawings
Rock music
Bego, M. The rock & roll almanac 781.66
Nite, N. N. Rock on almanac 781.66
Powell, S. Hit me with music 781.66
Reisfeld, R. This is the sound 781.66
The Rolling Stone illustrated history of rock & roll 781.66
Dictionaries
The Harmony illustrated encyclopedia of rock
781.66
The New Rolling Stone encyclopedia of rock & roll 781.66
Poetry
Sweet nothings 811.008
The **Rock** musician. See The Jazz musician
920
Rock musicians
Bruce Springsteen 92
Geller, L. If I can dream [biography of Elvis Presley] 92
Guralnick, P. Last train to Memphis: the rise of Elvis Presley 92
The Harmony illustrated encyclopedia of rock
781.66
Hopkins, J. Hit and run: the Jimi Hendrix story
92
Jones, D. Jim Morrison, dark star 92
Rock on almanac. Nite, N. N. 781.66
Rock Springs. Ford, R.
In American short story masterpieces
S C
In The Vintage book of contemporary American short stories p162-84 S C
The **rock** that changed things. Le Guin, U. K.
In Le Guin, U. K. A fisherman of the inland sea p57-67 S C
The **rocket**. Bradbury, R.
In Bradbury, R. The illustrated man S C

The **Rocket** Man. Bradbury, R.
In Bradbury, R. The illustrated man   **S C**
In Bradbury, R. The stories of Ray Bradbury
p150-59   **S C**

Rocketry
Baker, D. Spaceflight and rocketry: a chronology   **629.4**
Spangenburg, R. Wernher von Braun   **92**

The **Rockies:** pillars of a continent. Thybony, S.   **978**

The **rocking-horse** winner. Lawrence, D. H.
In Lawrence, D. H. The complete short stories v3   **S C**
In The Oxford book of short stories p275-89   **S C**

Rockne, Knute, 1888-1931
See/See also pages in the following book(s):
Lipsyte, R. Idols of the game p78-94   **920**

Rocks
Chesterman, C. W. The Audubon Society field guide to North American rocks and minerals   **549**
Pellant, C. Rocks, minerals & fossils of the world   **549**
Pough, F. H. A field guide to rocks and minerals   **549**

Rocky Mountains
Thybony, S. The Rockies: pillars of a continent   **978**

Rodale's all-new encyclopedia of organic gardening   **635**
Rodale's encyclopedia of organic gardening. See Rodale's all-new encyclopedia of organic gardening   **635**
Rodale's illustrated encyclopedia of herbs   **635**

Rodda, Harriet Stryker- *See* Stryker-Rodda, Harriet

Rodeos
See/See also pages in the following book(s):
Brown, D. A. The American West p377-89   **978**

Fiction
Koertge, R. The Arizona kid   **Fic**

Rodgers, Bill, 1947-
See/See also pages in the following book(s):
Sandrock, M. Running with the legends p97-131   **796.42**

Rodgers, Carolyn M., 1945-
See/See also pages in the following book(s):
Contemporary black American poets and dramatists p159-70   **810.9**

Rodgers, Joann Ellison
Cancer   **616.99**
Drugs & sexual behavior   **615**

Rodgers, Richard, 1902-1979
Lindsay, H. The sound of music   **812**

Rodin, Auguste, 1840-1917
About
Laurent, M. Rodin   **92**

Rodowsky, Colby F., 1932-
Remembering Mog   **Fic**

Rodriguez, Abraham, 1961-
Roaches
In Iguana dreams   **S C**

Rodriguez, David E.
I'm not stupid
In Ten out of ten p239-53   **812.008**

Rodriguez, Luis J.
See/See also pages in the following book(s):
Going where I'm coming from   **920**

Rodriguez-Milanes, Cecilia
Abuela Marielita
In Iguana dreams   **S C**

Roelofs, Gerrit Hubbard
(ed) The Major poets: English and American. See The Major poets: English and American   **821.008**

Roesch, Roberta
The encyclopedia of depression   **616.85**

Roethke, Theodore, 1908-1963
The collected poems of Theodore Roethke   **811**

Rogal, Samuel J.
(ed) Calendar of literary facts. See Calendar of literary facts   **809**

Rogasky, Barbara
Smoke and ashes: the story of the Holocaust   **940.53**

Roger Malvin's burial. Hawthorne, N.
In Hawthorne, N. Tales and sketches; A wonder book for girls and boys; Tanglewood tales for girls and boys p88-107   **S C**

Rogers, Carl R. (Carl Ransom), 1902-1987
A way of being   **150.19**

Rogers, Deborah Webster
J.R.R. Tolkien   **823.009**

Rogers, Ivor A.
(jt. auth) Rogers, D. W. J.R.R. Tolkien   **823.009**

Rogers, James T.
The secret war   **940.54**

Rogers, Will, 1879-1935
About
Yagoda, B. Will Rogers   **92**
See/See also pages in the following book(s):
Sonneborn, L. Performers   **920**

Rogerson, J. W. (John William), 1935-
Atlas of the Bible   **220.9**

Rogerson, John William *See* Rogerson, J. W. (John William), 1935-

Roget, Peter Mark, 1779-1869
Kipfer, B. A. Roget's 21st century thesaurus in dictionary form   **423**

Roget A to Z   **423**
Roget's 21st century thesaurus in dictionary form. Kipfer, B. A.   **423**
Roget's II   **423**
Roget's international thesaurus   **423**
Roget's international thesaurus. See Roget A to Z   **423**
Roget's superthesaurus. McCutcheon, M.   **423**

Rogoziński, Jan
A brief history of the Caribbean   **972.9**

Rogoziński, Jan—*Continued*
Pirates! **910.4**

Roleff, Tamara L., 1959-
(ed) Abortion: opposing viewpoints. See Abortion: opposing viewpoints **363.4**
(ed) Business ethics. See Business ethics **174**
(ed) The Homeless: opposing viewpoints. See The Homeless: opposing viewpoints **362.5**
(ed) The Legal system: opposing viewpoints. See The Legal system: opposing viewpoints **347**

Rolfe, John, 1585-1622
See/See also pages in the following book(s):
Woodward, G. S. Pocahontas p160-67 **92**

The **roll-call** of the reef. Quiller-Couch, Sir A. T.
In The Oxford book of English ghost stories p137-49 **S C**

Rollerblading *See* In-line skating

The **Rolling** Stone album guide **780.2**

The **Rolling** Stone encyclopedia of rock & roll. See The New Rolling Stone encyclopedia of rock & roll **781.66**

The **Rolling** Stone illustrated history of rock & roll **781.66**

Rolt, L. T. C. (Lionel Thomas Caswell), 1910-1974
Bosworth summit pound
In The Oxford book of English ghost stories p430-37 **S C**

Rolt, Lionel Thomas Caswell *See* Rolt, L. T. C. (Lionel Thomas Caswell), 1910-1974

Rölvaag, Ole Edvart, 1876-1931
Giants in the earth **Fic**

Roman architecture
Brown, F. E. Roman architecture **722**
Macaulay, D. City: a story of Roman planning and construction **711**

Roman art
The Oxford history of classical art **709.38**

Roman Catholic Church *See* Catholic Church

Roman cooking
See/See also pages in the following book(s):
Davis, W. S. A day in old Rome p100-21 **937**

Roman Empire *See* Rome

Roman fever. Wharton, E.
In Classic American short stories p234-51 **S C**
In Wharton, E. The selected short stories of Edith Wharton p342-52 **S C**

Roman mythology *See* Classical mythology

The **Roman** way. Hamilton, E. **870.9**

The **romance** of a busy broker. Henry, O.
In Henry, O. The best short stories of O. Henry **S C**

The **romance** of certain old clothes. James, H.
In Victorian ghost stories p83-99 **S C**

Romances
See also Arthurian romances
See/See also pages in the following book(s):
Highet, G. The classical tradition p162-77 **809**

Romano, Clare
(jt. auth) Ross, J. The complete printmaker **760.2**

Romanov, Nikolaï *See* Nicholas II, Emperor of Russia, 1868-1918

Romanov, House of *See* House of Romanov

The **Romanovs.** Massie, R. K. **947.08**

Romanowski, Patricia
(jt. auth) Geller, L. If I can dream [biography of Elvis Presley] **92**
(ed) The New Rolling Stone encyclopedia of rock & roll. See The New Rolling Stone encyclopedia of rock & roll **781.66**

Romans
Great Britain
Salway, P. The Oxford illustrated history of Roman Britain **936.2**

Romantic poetry and prose
In The Oxford anthology of English literature v2 **820.8**

A **romantic** weekend. Gaitskill, M.
In The Vintage book of contemporary American short stories p185-206 **S C**

The **romantic** young lady. Maugham, W. S.
In Maugham, W. S. Collected short stories v1 **S C**

Rombauer, Irma von Starkloff, 1877-1962
Joy of cooking **641.5**

Rome
Antiquities
See/See also pages in the following book(s):
Builders of the ancient world p38-69 **930**
Biography
Radice, B. Who's who in the ancient world **938.003**
Civilization
Adkins, L. Handbook to life in ancient Rome **937**
Civilization of the ancient Mediterranean: Greece and Rome **938**
Cornell, T. J. Atlas of the Roman world **937**
Davis, W. S. A day in old Rome **937**
Hamilton, E. The Roman way **870.9**
Rome: echoes of imperial glory **937**
See/See also pages in the following book(s):
Russell, B. A history of Western philosophy p270-83 **109**
History
Cornell, T. J. Atlas of the Roman world **937**
Grant, M. The founders of the Western world **938**
Grant, M. A social history of Greece and Rome **938**
Langguth, A. J. A noise of war **937**
Rome: echoes of imperial glory **937**
History—Dictionaries
Bunson, M. Encyclopedia of the Roman Empire **937**
History—Fiction
Graves, R. I, Claudius **Fic**

Running
Higdon, H. Marathon   **796.42**
Micheli, L. J. Healthy runner's handbook
                                             613.7
Rosen, M. Sports illustrated track: championship
running   **796.42**
Fiction
Voigt, C. The runner   **Fic**
Running. Howard, E.
In Am I blue? p85-101   **S C**
Running a school library media center. Stein, B.
L.   **027.8**
Running a thousand miles for freedom. Craft, W.
In Great slave narratives p269-331   **920**
Running for president   **324**
Running loose. Crutcher, C.   **Fic**
Running with Marty. Brooks, M.
In Brooks, M. Paradise Café and other stories
p3-10   **S C**
Running with the legends. Sandrock, M.
                                             796.42
Rural life *See* Country life; Farm life
Rushton, Julian
Classical music   **781.6**
Rusinko, Susan
British drama, 1950 to the present   **822.009**
Tom Stoppard   **822**
Rusk, Dean, 1909-1994
See/See also pages in the following book(s):
Halberstam, D. The best and the brightest
                                             973.922
Ruskin, John, 1819-1900
The King of the Golden River; or, The Black
Brothers
In The Oxford book of modern fairy tales
p29-50   **S C**
Russ, Joanna, 1937-
A few things I know about Whileaway
In The Norton book of science fiction p337-
49   **S C**
The man who could not see devils
In Masterpieces of fantasy and enchantment
p149-61   **S C**
Russell, Bertrand, 1872-1970
A history of Western philosophy   **109**
See/See also pages in the following book(s):
Durant, W. J. The story of philosophy p357-64
                                             109
Russell, Charles M. (Charles Marion), 1864-
1926
About
Hassrick, P. H. Charles M. Russell   **92**
Taliaferro, J. Charles M. Russell   **92**
Russell, Charlie
Quietus
In The Best short stories by Negro writers
p347-55   **S C**
Russell, Dale A.
An odyssey in time: the dinosaurs of North
America   **567.9**
Russell, Percy, 1926-
(jt. auth) Tver, D. F. The nutrition and health
encyclopedia   **613.2**

Russell, Ray
Sardonicus
In The Oxford book of gothic tales p435-65
                                             S C
Russell, Sandi
Render me my song   **810.9**
Sister
In Daughters of Africa p694-98   **808.8**
Russell, William
Murder under the microscope
In The Best crime stories of the 19th century
p51-71   **S C**
Russell Baker's book of American humor
                                             817.008
Russia
See also Russia (Republic); Soviet Union
Dictionaries
The Cambridge encyclopedia of Russia and the
former Soviet Union   **947**
Paxton, J. Encylopedia of Russian history
                                             947
Fiction
Chekhov, A. P. The image of Chekhov
                                             S C
Chekhov, A. P. The Russian master and other
stories   **S C**
Dostoyevsky, F. Crime and punishment   **Fic**
Dostoyevsky, F. The idiot   **Fic**
Malamud, B. The fixer   **Fic**
Pasternak, B. L. Doctor Zhivago   **Fic**
Pushkin, A. S. Alexander Pushkin: complete
prose fiction   **S C**
Pushkin, A. S. Eugene Onegin   **Fic**
Tolstoy, L., graf. Anna Karenina   **Fic**
Tolstoy, L., graf. Great short works of Leo Tol-
stoy   **S C**
Tolstoy, L., graf. War and peace   **Fic**
Historical geography—Maps
Gilbert, M. Atlas of Russian history   **911**
History
Alexander, J. T. Catherine the Great   **92**
Great dates in Russian and Soviet history
                                             947
Kort, M. Russia   **947.085**
Massie, R. K. Nicholas and Alexandra   **92**
Massie, R. K. Peter the Great   **92**
Pipes, R. A concise history of the Russian Rev-
olution   **947.08**
Riasanovsky, N. V. A history of Russia
                                             947
Russia and the independent states   **947**
Sakharov, A. D. Memoirs   **92**
See/See also pages in the following book(s):
Durant, W. J. The age of Napoleon p672-89
                                             940.2
Kings, queens, rulers, etc.
Alexander, J. T. Catherine the Great   **92**
Duffy, J. P. Czars   **947**
Massie, R. K. Nicholas and Alexandra   **92**
Massie, R. K. Peter the Great   **92**
Massie, R. K. The Romanovs   **947.08**
Russia (Republic)
See also Russia; Soviet Union
The Breakup of communism   **947**
The Breakup of the Soviet Union: opposing
viewpoints   **947.086**

Russia (Republic)—*Continued*
Politics and government
Otfinoski, S. Boris Yeltsin and the rebirth of
Russia **92**
Social conditions
Adelman, D. The "children of perestroika" come
of age **947.086**
Russia and the independent states **947**
Russian authors *See* Authors, Russian
The **Russian** duck. Smith, M. C.
In Song of the turtle p269-75 **S C**
Russian Empire *See* Russia
Russian history atlas. See Gilbert, M. Atlas of
Russian history **911**
Russian language
Dictionaries
The Oxford English-Russian dictionary
491.7
The Oxford Russian dictionary **491.7**
Russian literature
Collections
The Portable nineteenth-century Russian reader
891.7
The Portable twentieth-century Russian reader
891.7
Dictionaries
Handbook of Russian literature **891.7**
The **Russian** master. Chekhov, A. P.
In Chekhov, A. P. The Russian master and
other stories p183-202 **S C**
The **Russian** master and other stories. Chekhov,
A. P. **S C**
Russian revolution *See* Soviet Union—History—
1917-1921, Revolution
Ruth, Babe, 1895-1948
About
Creamer, R. W. Babe **92**
See/See also pages in the following book(s):
Lipsyte, R. Idols of the game p95-116 **920**
Ruth, George Herman *See* Ruth, Babe, 1895-
1948
Ruth's journey. Gold, R. G. **940.53**
Rux, Paul Philip
(ed) Skills for life: library information literacy
for grades 9-12. See Skills for life: library in-
formation literacy for grades 9-12 **025.5**
Ryan, Betsy *See* Ryan, Elizabeth A. (Elizabeth
Anne), 1943-
Ryan, Bob
(jt. auth) Bird, L. Drive: the story of my life
92
Ryan, Bryan
(ed) Hispanic writers. See Hispanic writers
920.003
Ryan, Cornelius
The last battle **940.54**
Ryan, Elizabeth A. (Elizabeth Anne), 1943-
Straight talk about drugs and alcohol
616.86
Ryan, Frank, 1944-
The forgotten plague **614.5**

Ryan, Halford Ross
(ed) The Inaugural addresses of twentieth-
century American presidents. See The Inaugu-
ral addresses of twentieth-century American
presidents **353.03**
Ryan, Joan
Little girls in pretty boxes **796.44**
Ryan, Margaret, 1950-
How to give a speech **808.5**
Ryder, Albert Pinkham, 1847-1917
See/See also pages in the following book(s):
Novak, B. American painting of the nineteenth
century p211-20 **759.13**
Rylant, Cynthia
Something permanent **811**
Ryskind, Morrie, 1895-1985
My man Godfrey
In Best American screenplays **812.008**

S

S.A.T. *See* Scholastic aptitude test
S is for snake. Aldani, L.
In Tales from the planet Earth **S C**
Saari, Peggy
(ed) Prominent women of the 20th century. See
Prominent women of the 20th century
920.003
Saavedra, Miguel de Cervantes *See* Cervantes
Saavedra, Miguel de, 1547-1616
Sabbath in Gehenna. Singer, I. B.
In Singer, I. B. The death of Methuselah and
other stories p212-19 **S C**
Sabin, Albert
See/See also pages in the following book(s):
Curtis, R. H. Great lives: medicine p281-92
920
Sabin vaccine *See* Poliomyelitis vaccine
Saccio, Peter
Shakespeare's English kings **822.3**
Sacco-Vanzetti case
See/See also pages in the following book(s):
Aymar, B. A pictorial history of the world's
greatest trials p229-45 **345**
Sachar, Howard Morley, 1928-
A history of the Jews in America **305.8**
Sachare, Alex
(ed) The Official NBA basketball encyclopedia.
See The Official NBA basketball encyclope-
dia **796.323**
Sacker, Ira M.
Dying to be thin **616.85**
Sackett. L'Amour, L. See note under L'Amour, L.
The Sacketts **Fic**
The **Sackett** brand. L'Amour, L. See note under
L'Amour, L. The Sacketts **Fic**
The **Sacketts.** L'Amour, L. **Fic**
Sackett's land. L'Amour, L. See note under
L'Amour, L. The Sacketts **Fic**
Sackler, Howard, d. 1982
The great white hope
In Best American plays: 7th series—1967-
1973 p1-72 **812.008**

Sacks, David
Encyclopedia of the ancient Greek world
938

Sacks, Oliver W.
The man who mistook his wife for a hat and other clinical tales **616.8**

The **sacred** and the profane. Sykes, C.
In Classic English short stories, 1930-1955 p221-49 **S C**

Sacred art *See* Christian art and symbolism

Sacred cows—and other edibles. Giovanni, N.
814

Sacred honor: a biography of Colin Powell. Roth, D. **92**

Sacred music *See* Church music

Sacred numbers *See* Symbolism of numbers

The **sad** story of a dramatic critic. Wells, H. G.
In Wells, H. G. The complete short stories of H. G. Wells p520-28 **S C**

Ṣaddām Hussein *See* Hussein, Ṣaddām

Sadie, Stanley
(ed) The New Grove dictionary of American music. See The New Grove dictionary of American music **780.973**
(ed) The New Grove dictionary of music and musicians. See The New Grove dictionary of music and musicians **780.3**

Sadie when she died. McBain, E.
In Crime classics p357-88 **S C**

Sadler, A. E., 1961-
(ed) Affirmative action. See Affirmative action [At issue] **331.1**
(ed) The Environment: opposing viewpoints. See The Environment: opposing viewpoints **363.7**
(ed) Family violence. See Family violence **362.82**

Safer, Morley
Flashbacks: on returning to Vietnam
959.704

Safety, Industrial *See* Occupational health and safety

Safire, William
(comp) Lend me your ears. See Lend me your ears **808.85**

Safrai, Ze'ev
(ed) Aharoni, Y. The Macmillan Bible atlas
220.9

Sagan, Carl, 1934-1996
Broca's brain **500**
Comet **523.6**
Cosmos **520**
The demon-haunted world **001.9**
The dragons of Eden **153**
Pale blue dot **520**
Shadows of forgotten ancestors **577**

Sagan, Dorion, 1959-
Garden of microbial delights **576**
(jt. auth) Margulis, L. What is life? **577**

Sagarin, Edward, 1913-1986
(jt. auth) Aymar, B. A pictorial history of the world's greatest trials **345**

Sahadi, Lou
(jt. auth) Mays, W. Say hey: the autobiography of Willie Mays **92**

Sailing
Conner, D. Learn to sail **797.1**

Sailor ashore. Hughes, L.
In Hughes, L. Short stories **S C**

Sailors' life *See* Seafaring life

Saint-Aubin, Horace de *See* Balzac, Honoré de, 1799-1850

Saint-Exupéry, Antoine de, 1900-1944
The little prince **Fic**
Wind, sand, and stars **629.13**
About
Robinson, J. D. M. Antoine de Saint-Exupéry
848

Saint Helens, Mount (Wash.) *See* Mount Saint Helens (Wash.)

Saint Joan. Shaw, B.
In The Oxford anthology of English literature v2 **820.8**

Saint Lawrence River valley
Description
See/See also pages in the following book(s):
Great rivers of the world p415-26 **910**

Sainte-Marie, Buffy, 1941-
See/See also pages in the following book(s):
Sonneborn, L. Performers **920**

Saints
See also Christian saints
Dictionaries
Butler, A. Butler's lives of the saints
920.003

Sakharov, Andreĭ Dmitrievich, 1921-1989
Memoirs **92**

Saki, 1870-1916
Sredni Vashtar
In The Oxford book of short stories p174-78
S C
Tobermory
In Masterpieces of fantasy and enchantment p368-74 **S C**

Sakyamuni *See* Gautama Buddha

Salaam, Kalamu ya *See* Kalamu ya Salaam, 1947-

Salamanca, Daniel, 1869?-1935
See/See also pages in the following book(s):
Klein, H. S. Bolivia p181-96 **984**

Salat, Cristina
50% chance of lightning
In Am I blue? p227-43 **S C**

Sale, Richard, 1911-1993
A nose for news
In The Oxford book of American detective stories p217-38 **S C**

Salem (Mass.)
Drama
Miller, A. The crucible **812**
History
Hansen, C. Witchcraft at Salem **133.4**
Hill, F. A delusion of Satan **133.4**

Salem (Mass.). Essex Institute *See* Essex Institute

Same time, next year—*Continued*
In The Most popular plays of the American theater p505-65   **812.008**

Same time—same station. Lackmann, R. W.   **791.44**

Samelson, Ken
(ed) Reichler, J. L. The great all-time baseball record book   **796.357**

Samjatin, Jewgenij *See* Zamíàtin, Evgeniĭ Ivanovich, 1884-1937

Sammon, Rick
Seven underwater wonders of the world   **574.92**

Samson Agonistes. Milton, J.
In Milton, J. The portable Milton   **828**
In The Oxford anthology of English literature v1   **820.8**

Samson and Delilah. Lawrence, D. H.
In Lawrence, D. H. The complete short stories v2   **S C**

Samuel. London, J.
In London, J. The portable Jack London p214-31   **818**
In London, J. Short stories of Jack London p431-47   **S C**

Samuel Beckett's Waiting for Godot   **842**

Samuels, Harold
(jt. auth) Samuels, P. Remembering the Maine   **973.8**

Samuels, Peggy
Remembering the Maine   **973.8**

Samuelson, Joan
See/See also pages in the following book(s):
Sandrock, M. Running with the legends p421-44   **796.42**

Samz, Jane
Vision   **617.7**

San Francisco (Calif.)
Fiction
Lee, G. China boy   **Fic**

Sanatorium. Maugham, W. S.
In Maugham, W. S. Collected short stories v3   **S C**

Sánchez, Alfonso E. Pérez *See* Pérez Sánchez, Alfonso E. (Alfonso Emilio)

Sanchez, Sonia, 1934-
Just don't never give up on love
In Daughters of Africa p447-49   **808.8**
See/See also pages in the following book(s):
Contemporary black American poets and dramatists p171-85   **810.9**

Sanctuaries, Wildlife *See* Wildlife refuges

Sanctuary (Law) *See* Asylum

Sanctuary. Christie, A.
In Christie, A. Miss Marple: the complete short stories   **S C**

Sanctuary. Larsen, N.
In Calling the wind p34-38   **S C**

Sanctuary movement
See also Refugees

Sand Creek, Battle of, 1864
See/See also pages in the following book(s):
Brown, D. A. Bury my heart at Wounded Knee p68-102   **970.004**

Sandburg, Carl, 1878-1967
Abraham Lincoln: The prairie years and The war years   **92**
Always the young strangers   **92**
Chicago poems
In Sandburg, C. Complete poems of Carl Sandburg p3-76   **811**
The complete poems of Carl Sandburg   **811**
Cornhuskers
In Sandburg, C. Complete poems of Carl Sandburg p79-147   **811**
Ever the winds of chance   **92**
Good morning, America
In Sandburg, C. Complete poems of Carl Sandburg p315-435   **811**
Honey and salt
In Sandburg, C. Complete poems of Carl Sandburg p706-71   **811**
The people, yes
In Sandburg, C. Complete poems of Carl Sandburg p439-617   **811**
The prairie years [condensation]
In Sandburg, C. Abraham Lincoln: The prairie years and The war years   **92**
Selected poems   **811**
Slabs of the sunburnt West
In Sandburg, C. Complete poems of Carl Sandburg p271-314   **811**
Smoke and steel
In Sandburg, C. Complete poems of Carl Sandburg p149-268   **811**
The story of Blixie Bimber and the power of the gold buckskin whincher
In The Oxford book of modern fairy tales p248-50   **S C**
The war years [condensation]
In Sandburg, C. Abraham Lincoln: The prairie years and The war years   **92**
About
Crowder, R. Carl Sandburg   **818**
Niven, P. Carl Sandburg   **92**

Sanders, Andrew
The short Oxford history of English literature   **820.9**

Sandock, Frank
Campaign fever
In The Big book of large-cast plays p86-100   **812.008**

Sandoval, Annette
The directory of saints   **920.003**

Sandoz, Mari, 1896-1966
The Battle of the Little Bighorn   **973.8**

Sandrock, Michael, 1958-
Running with the legends   **796.42**

Sands of the well. Levertov, D.   **811**

Sandstorms: days and nights in Arabia. Theroux, P.   **953**

Sandweiss, Martha A.
(ed) The Oxford history of the American West.
See The Oxford history of the American West   **978**

Satchell, Mary—*Continued*
The secret gifts
In The Big book of large-cast plays p136-51
812.008

Satellites, Artificial *See* Artificial satellites

Satire
Lewis, C. S. The Screwtape letters   **248**
See/See also pages in the following book(s):
Highet, G. The classical tradition p303-21
809

Satisfaction guaranteed. Asimov, I.
In Asimov, I. The complete stories v1 p91-
103   **S C**

Sato, Hiroaki, 1942-
(ed) From the country of eight islands. See
From the country of eight islands   **895.6**

Saturnino el Magnifico. Ríos, A.
In Iguana dreams   **S C**

Saul, John
Creature   **Fic**

Savage, Candace, 1949-
Peregrine falcons   **598**
Wild cats   **599.74**
The world of the wolf   **599.74**

Savage, William W.
The cowboy hero   **973**

Savage inequalities. Kozol, J.   **371.9**

Savannah. Jones, W.
In Streetlights: illuminating tales of the urban
black experience p239-52   **S C**

Savidge, Charlotte
(ed) The Facts on File dictionary of the theatre.
See The Facts on File dictionary of the theatre   **792.03**

Saville, Nan
Four and twenty
In Streetlights: illuminating tales of the urban
black experience p423-31   **S C**

Saving the environment. Gay, K.   **363.7**

Saving wildlife   **333.95**

Savings and loan associations
Banking scandals: the S&Ls and BCCI
364.1

Sawyer, Kem Knapp
Refugees   **362.87**

Sawyer, Robert J., 1960-
You see but you do not observe
In Nebula awards 31 p188-205   **S C**

Saxons *See* Anglo-Saxons

Say hey: the autobiography of Willie Mays. Mays,
W.   **92**

Say it loud!. Jones, K. M.   **781.64**

Sayer, Jeffrey
(ed) The Conservation atlas of tropical forests:
Africa. See The Conservation atlas of tropical
forests: Africa   **333.75**

Sayers, Dorothy L. (Dorothy Leigh), 1893-1957
The adventurous exploit of the cave of Ali Baba
In Crime classics p201-30   **S C**
The necklace of pearls
In Masterpieces of mystery and suspense p57-
66   **S C**

The **scandal** detectives. Fitzgerald, F. S.
In Fitzgerald, F. S. The stories of F. Scott
Fitzgerald p309-25   **S C**

A **scandal** in Bohemia. Doyle, Sir A. C.
In Crime classics p55-76   **S C**
In Doyle, Sir A. C. The complete Sherlock
Holmes   **S C**

Scandinavian Americans
See/See also pages in the following book(s):
Hook, J. N. Family names p136-53   **929.4**

Scandinavians
See also Vikings

Scanners live in vain. Smith, C.
In Robert Silverberg's Worlds of wonder
S C

The **scapegoat.** Dunbar, P. L.
In The Best short stories by Negro writers
p17-29   **S C**

The **scar.** Foster, C.
In Rites of passage p11-24   **S C**

Scarborough, Elizabeth Ann
The healer's war [excerpt]
In Nebula awards 25 p42-36   **S C**

The **scarecrow.** MacKaye, P.
In Best plays of the early American theatre
p677-716   **812.008**

Scariano, Margaret
(jt. auth) Dolan, E. F. Illiteracy in America
370.19
(jt. auth) Dolan, E. F. Shaping U.S. foreign policy   **327.73**

The **scariest** place on Earth. Fisher, D. E.
551.55

The **scarlet** letter. Baym, N.   **813.009**

The **scarlet** letter. Hawthorne, N.   **Fic**

The **scarlet** moving van. Cheever, J.
In Cheever, J. The stories of John Cheever
p359-69   **S C**

The **Scarlet** Pimpernel. Orczy, E., Baroness
Fic

The **scarlet** plague. London, J.
In London, J. The science fiction stories of
Jack London p149-90   **S C**

Scarre, Christopher
(ed) Smithsonian timelines of the ancient world.
See Smithsonian timelines of the ancient
world   **930**

Scat. Major, C.
In Calling the wind p399-404   **S C**

Scenarios *See* Motion picture plays

Scene design and stage lighting. Parker, W. O.
792

The **Scenebook** for actors   **808.82**

Scenes from classic plays, 468 B.C. to 1970 A.D.
808.82

A **scent** of sarsaparilla. Bradbury, R.
In Bradbury, R. The stories of Ray Bradbury
p487-92   **S C**

Schaaf, Fred
Seeing the sky   **523**

Schaefer, Jack Warner, 1907-1991
Shane   **Fic**

Scott, John Anthony, 1916-
The Facts on File history of the American people 973
Settlers on the Eastern Shore 973.2
The story of America 973
Scott, Mark W.
(ed) Shakespeare for students. See Shakespeare for students 822.3
Scott, Peter W.
The complete aquarium 639.3
Scott, Phil, 1961-
The shoulders of giants 629.13
Scott, Robert Alan
Chief Joseph and the Nez Percés 92
Scott, Thomas, 1935-
(ed) Concise encyclopedia biology. See Concise encyclopedia biology 574.03
Scott, Sir Walter, 1771-1832
The tapestried chamber
In Classic ghost stories p155-68 S C
In The Oxford book of English ghost stories p1-12 S C
The two drovers
In The Oxford book of short stories p1-26 S C
Wandering Willie's tale
In Classic ghost stories p45-63 S C
The Scott, Foresman Robert's Rules of order newly revised. Robert, H. M. 060.4
Scott-Kilvert, Ian
(ed) British writers. See British writers 920.003
Scottish Americans
See/See also pages in the following book(s):
Hook, J. N. Family names p86-96 929.4
Scottish ballads
The Oxford book of ballads 821.008
Scott's specialized catalogue of United States stamps 769.56
Scott's standard postage stamp catalogue 769.56
The Scottsboro Boys. Haskins, J. 345
Scottsboro case
Haskins, J. The Scottsboro Boys 345
Scoundrel time. Hellman, L.
In Hellman, L. Three 92
Scranton, Robert L.
Greek architecture 722
Screaming. Musil, M.
In Not the only one p117-26 S C
The screaming woman. Bradbury, R.
In Bradbury, R. The stories of Ray Bradbury p646-57 S C
The screen. Colette
In Colette. The collected stories of Colette p6-9 S C
Screen memory. Cliff, M.
In Calling the wind p566-77 S C
Screen plays *See* Motion picture plays
The screwfly solution. Sheldon, R.
In The Oxford book of science fiction stories p435-53 S C
The Screwtape letters. Lewis, C. S. 248

The Scrowrers. Doyle, Sir A. C.
In Doyle, Sir A. C. The complete Sherlock Holmes S C
Scuba duba. Friedman, B. J.
In Best American plays: 7th series—1967-1973 p169-97 812.008
Scull, Christina
(jt. auth) Hammond, W. G. J.R.R. Tolkien, artist & illustrator 92
The sculptor's funeral. Cather, W.
In Cather, W. Early novels and stories Fic
Sculpture
See/See also pages in the following book(s):
Canaday, J. E. What is art? 701
Durant, W. J. The age of faith p863-94 940.1
Sculpture, Modern *See* Modern sculpture
Sculpture I. Patrinos, A.
In The Best American short stories, 1996 p242-55 S C
The scythe. Bradbury, R.
In Bradbury, R. The stories of Ray Bradbury p55-66 S C
Sea animals *See* Marine animals
The sea around us. Carson, R. 551.46
The sea change. Hemingway, E.
In Hemingway, E. The complete short stories of Ernest Hemingway p302-05 S C
In Hemingway, E. The short stories of Ernest Hemingway p397-401 S C
The sea gull. Chekhov, A. P.
In Chekhov, A. P. Anton Chekhov's plays—backgrounds, criticism 891.7
Sea life *See* Seafaring life
Sea lions *See* Seals (Animals)
Sea monsters
Ellis, R. Monsters of the sea 591.92
Sea otter *See* Otters
The sea raiders. Wells, H. G.
In Wells, H. G. The complete short stories of H. G. Wells p418-29 S C
Sea shells *See* Shells
Sea stories
Beach, E. L. Run silent, run deep Fic
Melville, H. Billy Budd, sailor Fic
Melville, H. Moby-Dick; or, The whale Fic
Nordhoff, C. The Bounty trilogy Fic
Verne, J. Twenty thousand leagues under the sea Fic
A sea worry. Kingston, M. H.
In American dragons: twenty-five Asian American voices p112-17 810.8
Seabright, Idris *See* St. Clair, Margaret, 1911-1995
Seafaring life
Dana, R. H. Two years before the mast 910.4
Graham, R. L. Dove 910.4
See/See also pages in the following book(s):
Ocean planet p36-81 574.92
Seagrave, Sterling
Dragon lady [biography of Tz'u-hsi] 92

The **seal** in the bedroom. Thurber, J.
   In Thurber, J. Writings and drawings
        818

Seals (Animals)
  Bonner, W. N. The natural history of seals
        599.74
  Bonner, W. N. Seals and sea lions of the world
        599.74
  See/See also pages in the following book(s):
  Wild animals of North America p283-307
        599

Seals (Numismatics)
  Shearer, B. F. State names, seals, flags, and
    symbols   **929.9**

Seals and sea lions of the world. Bonner, W. N.
        599.74

Sealskin trousers. Linklater, E.
  In Classic English short stories, 1930-1955
    p84-104   **S C**

The **seamstress**. Colette
  In Colette. The collected stories of Colette
    p311-13   **S C**

The **search** for Africa. Davidson, B.   **967**

The **Search** for El Dorado   **970.01**

The **search** for King Arthur. Day, D.   **942.01**

The **search** for modern China. Spence, J. D.
        951

Search for peace. Jacobs, W. J.   **341.23**

Searching for your ancestors. Doane, G. H.
        929

Sears, Stephen W.
  Chancellorsville   **973.7**

Sears, Vickie, 1941-
  Dancer
    In Talking leaves   **S C**
  Grace
    In Growing up Native American p279-98
        810.8
    In Spider Woman's granddaughters   **S C**

Sears list of subject headings   **025.4**

Seashore
  Carson, R. The edge of the sea   **574.92**

Seashore ecology
  The World's wild shores   **574.5**

The **seaside** houses. Cheever, J.
  In Cheever, J. The stories of John Cheever
    p482-89   **S C**

The **season** of divorce. Cheever, J.
  In Cheever, J. The stories of John Cheever
    p137-46   **S C**

A **season** of giants: Michelangelo, Leonardo, Raphael, 1492-1508. Labella, V.   **709.45**

Seasons. McLaughlin, R.
  In Circle of women: an anthology of contemporary Western women writers p199-211
        810.8

A **seat** in the garden. King, T.
  In Song of the turtle p191-99   **S C**
  In Talking leaves   **S C**

Seaton, George, 1911-1979
  Miracle on 34th Street
    In Best American screenplays   **812.008**

Seaver, Tom
  Great moments in baseball   **796.357**

Seay family
        About
  See, L. On Gold Mountain   **920**

Sebestyen, Ouida, 1924-
  Holding out
    In Center stage   **812.008**

The **Second** Barnhart dictionary of new English.
  See Third Barnhart dictionary of new English
        423

Second best. Lawrence, D. H.
  In Lawrence, D. H. The complete short stories v1   **S C**

Second coming: the strange odyssey of Michael Jordan—from courtside to home plate and back again. Smith, S.   **92**

Second dawn. Clarke, A. C.
  In The Oxford book of science fiction stories p198-227   **S C**

Second Foundation. Asimov, I. See note under Asimov, I. [The Foundation series]   **Fic**

Second-hand man. Dove, R.
  In Children of the night p255-61   **S C**

Second Manassas   **973.7**

Second nature. Hoffman, A.   **Fic**

The **second** night of summer. Schmitz, J. H.
  In The Oxford book of science fiction stories p171-97   **S C**

The **second** sex. Beauvoir, S. de   **305.4**

The **Second** World War. Keegan, J.   **940.53**

Secondary education
        Law and legislation
  Layman, N. S. Sexual harassment in American secondary schools   **344**

Secondary schools *See* High schools

The **secret**. Singer, I. B.
  In Singer, I. B. The image and other stories p161-75   **S C**

The **secret** gifts. Satchell, M.
  In The Big book of large-cast plays p136-51
        812.008

Secret observations on the goat-girl. Oates, J. C.
  In The Oxford book of gothic tales p498-501
        S C

The **secret** of cartwheels. Henley, P.
  In Circle of women: an anthology of contemporary Western women writers p17-34
        810.8

The **secret** of the Incas. Sullivan, W.   **985**

The **secret** of the universe. Asimov, I.   **520**

Secret service
    See also Espionage; Intelligence service; Spies
        Fiction
  Buchan, J. The thirty-nine steps   **Fic**

Secret service. Gillette, W. H.
  In Best plays of the early American theatre p277-360   **812.008**

The **secret** sharer. Conrad, J.
  In Conrad, J. The complete short fiction of Joseph Conrad v2 p105-43   **S C**

The secret sharer—*Continued*
In Conrad, J. The portable Conrad **828**
In The Oxford book of short stories p109-46
S C
The secret war. Rogers, J. T. **940.54**
Secret window, secret garden. King, S.
In King, S. Four past midnight p247-399
S C
Secret writing *See* Cryptography
Secretaries
Handbooks, manuals, etc.
Lindsell-Roberts, S. The secretary's quick reference handbook **651.3**
Merriam-Webster's secretarial handbook
651.3
The Professional secretary's handbook
651.3
The secretary's quick reference handbook.
Lindsell-Roberts, S. **651.3**
Secrets. Colette
In Colette. The collected stories of Colette p291-93 **S C**
Secrets of the inner mind **154**
Secrets of the night sky. Berman, B. **520**
Sects
Mead, F. S. Handbook of denominations in the United States **280**
Dictionaries
Melton, J. G. The encyclopedia of American religions **200.9**
Secularism
See also Atheism
Sedeen, Margaret
Star-spangled banner **929.9**
See, Lisa
On Gold Mountain **920**
See how they run. Vroman, M. E.
In The Best short stories by Negro writers p253-74 **S C**
See no evil. Gault, W. C.
In The Oxford book of American detective stories p471-79 **S C**
Seeger, Pete
Everybody says freedom **323.1**
Seeger, Ruth Crawford, 1901-1953
See/See also pages in the following book(s):
Nichols, J. American music makers p90-107
920
Seeing Ellie. Ormand, E.
In Not the only one p159-69 **S C**
Seeing the sky. Schaaf, F. **523**
Seeing things simply. Danticat, E.
In Danticat, E. Krik? Krak! **S C**
Seemothermotherisverynice. Morrison, T.
In Black-eyed Susans/Midnight birds p60-76
S C
Seff, Nancy R.
(jt. auth) Seff, P. Our fascinating earth **508**
Seff, Philip
Our fascinating earth **508**
Segregation
See also Apartheid; Discrimination

Segregation in education
Kozol, J. Savage inequalities **371.9**
Tushnet, M. V. Brown v. Board of Education
344
Segregationist. Asimov, I.
In Asimov, I. The complete stories v1 p605-09 **S C**
Seidensticker, John
(ed) Great cats. See Great cats **599.74**
Seismology *See* Earthquakes
Seitz, Blair
(il) Seitz, R. H. Amish ways **289.7**
Seitz, Ruth Hoover
Amish ways **289.7**
Seixas, Judith S.
Children of alcoholism **362.29**
Séjour, Victor
The brown overcoat
In Black theatre USA **812.008**
Seko, Toshihiko, 1956-
See/See also pages in the following book(s):
Sandrock, M. Running with the legends p345-68
796.42
Selby, David
(jt. auth) Willson, Q. The ultimate classic car book **629.222**
A select party. Hawthorne, N.
In Hawthorne, N. Tales and sketches; A wonder book for girls and boys; Tanglewood tales for girls and boys p945-58
S C
The selected letters of Louisa May Alcott. Alcott, L. M. **92**
Selected odes of Pablo Neruda. Neruda, P.
861
The selected plays of Jerome Lawrence and Robert E. Lee. Lawrence, J. **812**
Selected poems. Brooks, G. **811**
Selected poems. Dove, R. **811**
Selected poems. Jarrell, R.
In Jarrell, R. The complete poems **811**
Selected poems. Lowell, R. **811**
Selected poems. Pasternak, B. L. **891.7**
Selected poems. Paz, O. **861**
Selected poems. Pound, E. **811**
Selected poems. Rexroth, K. **811**
Selected poems. Sandburg, C. **811**
Selected poems, 1946-1985. Merrill, J. **811**
Selected poems, 1957-1987. Snodgrass, W. D.
811
Selected poems, 1966-1987. Heaney, S. **821**
The selected poems of Emily Dickinson. Dickinson, E. **811**
The selected poems of Nikki Giovanni (1968-1995). Giovanni, N. **811**
Selected poems of Rainer Maria Rilke. Rilke, R. M. **831**
The selected short stories of Edith Wharton. Wharton, E. **S C**
Selected short stories of William Faulkner. Faulkner, W. **S C**

Shakespeare, William, 1564-1616—Criticism, interpretation, etc.—*Continued*

Jorgensen, P. A. William Shakespeare: the tragedies   **822.3**

Readings on the tragedies of William Shakespeare   **822.3**

Rowse, A. L. Shakespeare the man   **822.3**

Saccio, P. Shakespeare's English kings   **822.3**

Shakespeare for students   **822.3**

Spurgeon, C. F. E. Shakespeare's imagery and what it tells us   **822.3**

Vaughn, J. A. Shakespeare's comedies   **822.3**

Dictionaries

Boyce, C. Shakespeare A to Z   **822.3**

Onions, C. T. A Shakespeare glossary   **822.3**

Shewmaker, E. F. Shakespeare's language   **822.3**

Dramatic production

Shakespeare: an illustrated stage history   **792.9**

Parodies, travesties, etc.

Stoppard, T. Rosencrantz and Guildenstern are dead   **822**

Stage history

Hodges, C. W. The Globe restored   **792.09**

Technique

Spurgeon, C. F. E. Shakespeare's imagery and what it tells us   **822.3**

Shakespeare A to Z. Boyce, C.   **822.3**

Shakespeare: an illustrated stage history   **792.9**

Shakespeare for students   **822.3**

A **Shakespeare** glossary. Onions, C. T.   **822.3**

Shakespeare of London. Chute, M. G.   **822.3**

Shakespeare the man. Rowse, A. L.   **822.3**

Shakespeare's comedies. Vaughn, J. A.   **822.3**

Shakespeare's English kings. Saccio, P.   **822.3**

Shakespeare's imagery and what it tells us. Spurgeon, C. F. E.   **822.3**

Shakespeare's language. Shewmaker, E. F.   **822.3**

Shalamov, Varlam Tikhonovich

A child's drawings

In The Portable twentieth-century Russian reader p423-26   **891.7**

Lend-lease

In The Portable twentieth-century Russian reader p427-34   **891.7**

Prosthetic appliances

In The Portable twentieth-century Russian reader p420-22   **891.7**

Shale, Richard, 1947-

The Academy Awards index   **791.43**

Shall not perish. Faulkner, W.

In Faulkner, W. Collected stories of William Faulkner p101-15   **S C**

Shane. Schaefer, J. W.   **Fic**

Shange, Ntožake

Aw, babee, you so pretty

In Black-eyed Susans/Midnight birds p345-49   **S C**

Comin to terms

In Black-eyed Susans/Midnight birds p340-44   **S C**

Eye-hand coordination

In Streetlights: illuminating tales of the urban black experience p442-51   **S C**

For colored girls who have considered suicide/when the rainbow is enuf   **812**

also in Best American plays: 8th series—1974-1982 p82-105   **812.008**

For colored girls who have considered suicide . . . [excerpt]

In Black theatre USA   **812.008**

Oh she gotta head fulla hair

In Children of the night p529-31   **S C**

Spell #7

In 9 plays by black women   **811.008**

See/See also pages in the following book(s):

Contemporary black American poets and dramatists p186-200   **810.9**

Major modern black American writers p152-66   **810.9**

Shanghai (China)

Fiction

Ballard, J. G. Empire of the Sun   **Fic**

Shankle, George Earlie

American nicknames   **929.4**

Shanks, Hershel

Jerusalem   **933**

Shaping U.S. foreign policy. Dolan, E. F.   **327.73**

Shapiro, James S., 1955-

(ed) The Columbia anthology of British poetry. See The Columbia anthology of British poetry   **821.008**

Shapiro, Jane, 1942-

Poltergeists

In The Best American short stories, 1993 p94-112   **S C**

Shapiro, Joseph P.

No pity   **323.3**

Shapiro, Karl Jay, 1913-

New & selected poems, 1940-1986   **811**

Sharks

Fiction

Benchley, P. Jaws   **Fic**

Sharma, Akhil

If you sing like that for me

In The Best American short stories, 1996 p282-306   **S C**

In Prize stories, 1996 p25-50   **S C**

Sharpe, Genell J. Subak- *See* Subak-Sharpe, Genell J.

Sharrar, Jack F., 1949-

(ed) Great monologues for young actors. See Great monologues for young actors   **812.008**

(ed) Great scenes for young actors from the stage. See Great scenes for young actors from the stage   **808.82**

Shiloh. Mason, B. A.
In American short story masterpieces
S C
In We are the stories we tell
S C
Shilts, Randy
And the band played on
362.1
Shimmy shimmy shimmy like my sister Kate
811.008

Shin bones. London, J.
In London, J. Short stories of Jack London
p633-51
S C
Shine, Ted, 1931-
Contribution
In Black theatre USA
812.008
(ed) Black theatre USA. See Black theatre USA
812.008
Shiner, Lewis
The war at home
In The Norton book of science fiction p577-
79
S C
Shingles for the Lord. Faulkner, W.
In Faulkner, W. Collected stories of William
Faulkner p27-43
S C
The **Shining** Company. Sutcliff, R.
Fic
Shinto
See/See also pages in the following book(s):
Eastern wisdom
291
Ship. Macaulay, D.
387.2
Shipbuilding
See/See also pages in the following book(s):
Langdon, W. C. Everyday things in American
life, 1607-1776 p229-40
973.2
Shipman, Pat
(jt. auth) Walker, A. The wisdom of the bones
573.2
Shippey, T. A. (Tom A.)
(ed) The Oxford book of science fiction stories.
See The Oxford book of science fiction sto-
ries
S C
Shippey, Tom A. *See* Shippey, T. A. (Tom A.)
Shipping
See/See also pages in the following book(s):
Langdon, W. C. Everyday things in American
life, 1607-1776 p211-28
973.2
Ships. Henry, O.
In Henry, O. The best short stories of O.
Henry
S C
Shipwrecks
Ballard, R. D. The discovery of the Titanic
910.4
Callahan, S. Adrift
910.4
Heyer, P. Titanic legacy
910.4
Lord, W. The night lives on
910.4
Lord, W. A night to remember
910.4
Macaulay, D. Ship
387.2
Pickford, N. The atlas of shipwrecks & treasure
910.4
Dictionaries
Ritchie, D. Shipwrecks
910.4
Fiction
Paton Walsh, J. Grace
Fic
Shirer, William L. (William Lawrence)
The rise and fall of the Third Reich
943.086

See/See also pages in the following book(s):
Cloud, S. The Murrow boys
070.1
Shirley, Dame, 1819-1906
See/See also pages in the following book(s):
Stefoff, R. Women pioneers
920
Shirley, David, 1955-
Everyday I sing the blues: the story of B.B.
King
92
Shizuko's daughter. Mori, K.
Fic
The **Shobies'** story. Le Guin, U. K.
In Le Guin, U. K. A fisherman of the inland
sea p75-105
S C
In Nebula awards 26 p19-45
S C
A **shocking** accident. Greene, G.
In Greene, G. The portable Graham Greene
p400-05
828
Shockley, Ann Allen, 1927-
The world of Rosie Polk
In Calling the wind p480-97
S C
Shockley, William
See/See also pages in the following book(s):
Aaseng, N. Twentieth-century inventors p91-102
920
Shoeless Joe. Kinsella, W. P.
Fic
Shoeless Joe Jackson comes to Iowa. Kinsella, W.
P.
In Kinsella, W. P. Shoeless Joe Jackson
comes to Iowa: stories
S C
Shoeless Joe Jackson comes to Iowa: stories.
Kinsella, W. P.
S C
Shoes. Henry, O.
In Henry, O. The best short stories of O.
Henry
S C
Shogun. Clavell, J.
Fic
Sholem Aleichem, 1859-1916
The best of Sholem Aleichem
S C
Contents: The haunted tailor; A Yom Kippur scandal; Eternal
life; Station Baranovich; The pot; The clock that struck thirteen;
Home for Passover; On account of a hat; Dreyfus in Kasrilevke;
Two anti-semites; A Passover expropriation; If I were Rothschild;
Tevye strikes it rich; The bubble bursts; Chava; Get thee out;
From Mottel the cantor's son; Bandits; The guest; The
Krushniker delegation; One in a million; Once there were four
Tevye the dairyman and The railroad stories
S C
Includes the following stories: Tevye strikes it rich; Tevye
blows a small fortune; Today's children; Hodl; Chava; Shprintze;
Tevye leaves for the land of Israel; Lekh-Lekho; To the reader;
Competitors; The happiest man in all Kodny; Baranovich Station;
Eighteen from Pereshchepena; The man from Buenos Aires; Elul;
The slowpoke express; The miracle of Hoshana Rabbah; The
wedding that came without its band; The tallis koton; A game of
sixty-six; High school; The automatic exemption; It doesn't pay
to be good; Burned out; Hard luck; Fated for misfortune; Go
climb a tree if you don't like it; The tenth man; Third class
Sholom Aleichem *See* Sholem Aleichem, 1859-
1916
Shoo fly pudding. Hoppenstedt, E. M.
In The Big book of large-cast plays p168-84
812.008
Shoot!
770
Shore, Edward A.
(jt. auth) Gardner, R. Math in science and nature
510
The **shoreline** at sunset. Bradbury, R.
In Bradbury, R. The stories of Ray Bradbury
p513-20
S C

The **short** happy life of Francis Macomber. Hemingway, E.

 In Classic American short stories p359-98
  S C

 In Hemingway, E. The complete short stories of Ernest Hemingway p5-28 S C
 In Hemingway, E. The short stories of Ernest Hemingway p3-37 S C

A **short** history of Ireland. Ranelagh, J.
  941.5

A **short** history of philosophy. Solomon, R. C.
  109

A **short** history of the American Revolution. Stokesbury, J. L. **973.3**

A **short** history of the Civil War. Stokesbury, J. L.
  973.7

A **short** history of the Korean War. Stokesbury, J. L. **951.9**

A **short** history of the movies. Mast, G.
  791.43

A **short** history of World War I. Stokesbury, J. L.
  940.3

A **short** history of World War II. Stokesbury, J. L.
  940.53

The **short** Oxford history of English literature. Sanders, A. **820.9**

Short plays *See* One act plays

Short stories
 African short stories S C
 Am I blue? S C
 American eyes S C
 American short story masterpieces S C
 Andersen, H. C. Tales and stories S C
 Anderson, S. Winesburg, Ohio S C
 Asimov, I. The complete stories S C
 Asimov, I. I, robot S C
 Bad behavior S C
 The Best American short stories S C
 The Best American short stories of the eighties
  S C
 The Best crime stories of the 19th century
  S C
 The Best short stories by Negro writers
  S C
 Black-eyed Susans/Midnight birds S C
 Bova, B. Challenges S C
 Bradbury, R. Fahrenheit 451 S C
 Bradbury, R. The illustrated man S C
 Bradbury, R. The Martian chronicles S C
 Bradbury, R. The stories of Ray Bradbury
  S C
 Brooks, M. Paradise Café and other stories
  S C
 Calling the wind S C
 Capote, T. Breakfast at Tiffany's: a short novel and three stories S C
 Cheever, J. The stories of John Cheever
  S C
 Chekhov, A. P. The image of Chekhov
  S C
 Chekhov, A. P. The Russian master and other stories S C
 Children of the night S C
 Chopin, K. The awakening and selected stories
  S C

Christie, A. Miss Marple: the complete short stories S C
Cisneros, S. Woman Hollering Creek and other stories S C
Classic American short stories S C
Classic English short stories, 1930-1955
  S C
Classic ghost stories S C
Colette. The collected stories of Colette
  S C
Coming of age in America S C
Conrad, J. The complete short fiction of Joseph Conrad S C
Crime classics S C
Crutcher, C. Athletic shorts: six short stories
  S C
Danticat, E. Krik? Krak! S C
Doyle, Sir A. C. The complete Sherlock Holmes
  S C
Faulkner, W. Collected stories of William Faulkner S C
Faulkner, W. Selected short stories of William Faulkner S C
Faulkner, W. Uncollected stories of William Faulkner S C
Fitzgerald, F. S. The short stories of F. Scott Fitzgerald S C
Fitzgerald, F. S. The stories of F. Scott Fitzgerald S C
Gordimer, N. Crimes of conscience S C
Hawthorne, N. Tales and sketches, including Twice-told tales, Mosses from an old manse, and The snow-image; A wonder book for girls and boys; Tanglewood tales for girls and boys, being a second Wonder book S C
The Heinemann book of contemporary African short stories S C
Hemingway, E. The complete short stories of Ernest Hemingway S C
Hemingway, E. In our time S C
Hemingway, E. The Nick Adams stories
  S C
Hemingway, E. The short stories of Ernest Hemingway
Henry, O. The best short stories of O. Henry
  S C
Hesse, H. The fairy tales of Hermann Hesse
  S C
The Horror hall of fame S C
Hughes, L. Short stories S C
Hurston, Z. N. The complete stories S C
Hurston, Z. N. Novels and stories **Fic**
Iguana dreams S C
Invented lives S C
Jackson, S. The lottery S C
Joyce, J. Dubliners S C
Kafka, F. The complete stories S C
Kafka, F. The metamorphosis and other stories
  S C
King, S. Four past midnight S C
King, S. Skeleton crew S C
Kinsella, W. P. Shoeless Joe Jackson comes to Iowa: stories S C
Kipling, R. The best fiction of Rudyard Kipling
  S C
Koontz, D. R. Strange highways S C
L'Amour, L. The outlaws of Mesquite S C

Short stories—_Continued_
History and criticism
The American short story, 1900-1945/1945-1980
    813.009
Critical survey of short fiction   **809.3**
Hooper, B. Short story writers and their work
    809.3
The Latin American short story   **863.009**
Masterplots II, short story series   **809.3**
May, C. E. The short story   **809.3**
Reference guide to short fiction   **809.3**
Indexes
Short story index   **808.83**
The **short** stories of Ernest Hemingway. Hemingway, E.   **S C**
The **short** stories of F. Scott Fitzgerald. Fitzgerald, F. S.   **S C**
The **short** stories of H. G. Wells. See Wells, H. G. The complete short stories of H. G. Wells   **S C**
Short stories of Jack London. London, J.   **S C**
The **short** story. May, C. E.   **809.3**
Short story index   **808.83**
Short story writers and their work. Hooper, B.   **809.3**
A **short** trip home. Fitzgerald, F. S.
    _In_ Fitzgerald, F. S. The short stories of F. Scott Fitzgerald p372-89   **S C**
Shorter, Frank, 1947-
    See/See also pages in the following book(s):
    Sandrock, M. Running with the legends p133-70   **796.42**
Shorthand
    Gregg shorthand dictionary   **653**
Shortwave radio
    See also Amateur radio stations
Shoshoni Indians
    See/See also pages in the following book(s):
    People of the western range   **970.004**
Should wizard hit mommy?. Updike, J.
    _In_ Updike, J. Pigeon feathers, and other stories p74-82   **S C**
The **shoulders** of giants. Scott, P.   **629.13**
A **shovel** of stars. Morgan, T.   **978**
Show business _See_ Performing arts
Showalter, Elaine
    (ed) Modern American women writers. See Modern American women writers   **810.9**
Showdown on the Tumbling T. L'Amour, L.
    _In_ L'Amour, L. The outlaws of Mesquite p133-77   **S C**
Shower of gold. Welty, E.
    _In_ Welty, E. The collected stories of Eudora Welty p263-74   **S C**
Shprintze. Sholem Aleichem
    _In_ Sholem Aleichem. Tevye the dairyman and The railroad stories   **S C**
Shrapnel in the heart. Palmer, L.   **959.704**
Shreeve, James
    (jt. auth) Johanson, D. C. Lucy's child: the discovery of a human ancestor   **573.2**

Shucard, Alan, 1935-
    American poetry   **811.009**
    Modern American poetry, 1865-1950   **811.009**
Shuman, Robert
    Living with multiple sclerosis   **616.8**
Shute, Nevil, 1899-1960
    On the beach   **Fic**
Shuttles, Space _See_ Space shuttles
Shwartz, Susan, 1949-
    Getting real
    _In_ Nebula awards 27 p212-31   **S C**
Shyer, Christopher
    (jt. auth) Shyer, M. F. Not like other boys—growing up gay   **92**
Shyer, Marlene Fanta
    Not like other boys—growing up gay   **92**
Siberia (Russia)
Description
See/See also pages in the following book(s):
    Great rivers of the world p231-40   **910**
Siblings _See_ Brothers and sisters
Sicherman, Barbara
    (ed) Notable American women: the modern period. See Notable American women: the modern period   **920.003**
The **sick** child. Colette
    _In_ Colette. The collected stories of Colette p327-46   **S C**
The **sick** child. DeCora, A.
    _In_ The Singing spirit: early short stories by North American Indians p45-47   **S C**
A **sick** collier. Lawrence, D. H.
    _In_ Lawrence, D. H. The complete short stories v1   **S C**
Sickle cell anemia
    Beshore, G. W. Sickle cell anemia   **616.1**
Sickness _See_ Diseases
Siddhārtha _See_ Gautama Buddha
Siddhartha. Hesse, H.   **Fic**
Siegel, Dorothy Schainman
    Dental health   **617.6**
Sierra Club
    Feldman, A. J. The Sierra Club green guide   **363.7**
    Turner, T. Sierra Club   **333.95**
The **Sierra** Club desert reader   **808.8**
The **Sierra** Club green guide. Feldman, A. J.   **363.7**
The **Sierra** Club handbook of whales and dolphins. Leatherwood, S.   **599.5**
Sifakis, Carl
    Hoaxes and scams   **364.1**
Sifakis, Stewart
    Who was who in the Civil War   **920.003**
Sifry, Micah L.
    (ed) The Gulf war reader. See The Gulf war reader   **956.7**
Sigerman, Harriet
    Laborers for liberty
    _In_ The Young Oxford history of women in the United States   **305.4**

Sigerman, Harriet—*Continued*
An unfinished battle
In The Young Oxford history of women in
the United States   **305.4**

Sight *See* Vision

Sights from a steeple. Hawthorne, N.
In Hawthorne, N. Tales and sketches; A wonder book for girls and boys; Tanglewood
tales for girls and boys p42-48   **S C**

The **sign** in Sidney Brustein's window. Hansberry,
L.
In Best American plays: 6th series—1963-
1967 p227-75   **812.008**

Sign language
See also Deaf—Means of communication
Butterworth, R. R. Signing made easy   **419**
Costello, E. Random House American sign lan-
guage dictionary   **419**
Costello, E. Signing   **419**
Riekehof, L. L. The joy of signing   **419**
Sternberg, M. L. A. American sign language: a
comprehensive dictionary   **419**

The **sign** of the four. Doyle, Sir A. C.
In Doyle, Sir A. C. The complete Sherlock
Holmes   **S C**

Signals. Pierce, J. R.   **621.382**

Signing. Costello, E.   **419**

Signing made easy. Butterworth, R. R.   **419**

The **signing-up** of 59200/5. Greene, G.
In Greene, G. The portable Graham Greene
p405-14   **828**

Signs and symbols
See also Sign language
The Barnhart abbreviations dictionary
    421.03
Becker, U. The Continuum encyclopedia of
symbols   **302.2**
Biedermann, H. Dictionary of symbolism
    302.2
Liungman, C. G. Dictionary of symbols
    302.2

Silas Marner. Eliot, G.   **Fic**

Silberman, Neil Asher, 1950-
(ed) Invisible America. See Invisible America
    973

Silence—a fable. Poe, E. A.
In Poe, E. A. The collected tales and poems
of Edgar Allan Poe p459-61   **S C**

The **silence** of the sirens. Kafka, F.
In Kafka, F. The complete stories   **S C**

Silences. Lee, H. E.
In Children of the night p269-79   **S C**

The **silent** clowns. Kerr, W.   **791.43**

Silent night, lonely night. Anderson, R. W.
In Best American plays: 5th series—1957-
1963 p313-39   **812.008**

Silent passengers. Woiwode, L.
In The Best American short stories, 1993
p49-62   **S C**

Silent snow, secret snow. Aiken, C.
In The Norton book of American short stories
p277-91   **S C**

Silent spring. Carson, R.   **363.7**

The **silent** towns. Bradbury, R.
In Bradbury, R. The stories of Ray Bradbury
p94-102   **S C**

Silicon muse. Schenck, H.
In The Oxford book of science fiction stories
p516-34   **S C**

Silicon snake oil. Stoll, C.   **004**

The **silken-swift.** . . Sturgeon, T.
In Masterpieces of fantasy and enchantment
p261-79   **S C**

Silko, Leslie, 1948-
A Geronimo story
In The Lightning within p53-66   **S C**
The man to send rain clouds
In The Lightning within p48-52   **S C**
Tony's story
In Song of the turtle p31-37   **S C**
Uncle Tony's goat
In Growing up Native American p299-305
    810.8
Yellow Woman
In The Oxford book of American short stories
p591-600   **S C**
In Spider Woman's granddaughters   **S C**
In We are the stories we tell   **S C**
See/See also pages in the following book(s):
Coltelli, L. Winged words: American Indian
writers speak   **897**

The **Silmarillion.** Tolkien, J. R. R.   **S C**

Silver Blaze. Doyle, Sir A. C.
In Doyle, Sir A. C. The complete Sherlock
Holmes   **S C**

The **silver** crown. Malamud, B.
In Malamud, B. The stories of Bernard
Malamud p307-28   **S C**

The **Silver** Screen. Davies, P. H.
In The Best American short stories, 1996
p69-85   **S C**

Silvera, John D.
Liberty deferred
In Black theatre USA   **812.008**

Silverberg, Robert
Good news from the Vatican
In The Norton book of science fiction p242-
49   **S C**
How it was when the past went away
In The Mammoth book of new world science
fiction p301-55   **S C**
(ed) The Horror hall of fame. See The Horror
hall of fame   **S C**
(ed) Robert Silverberg's worlds of wonder. See
Robert Silverberg's worlds of wonder
    S C

Silverstein, Alvin
So you think you're fat?   **616.85**

Silverstein, Herma
Alcoholism   **616.86**

Silverstein, Robert A.
(jt. auth) Silverstein, A. So you think you're fat?
    616.85

Silverstein, Virginia B.
(jt. auth) Silverstein, A. So you think you're fat?
    616.85

Silverthorne, Elizabeth, 1930-
Marjorie Kinnan Rawlings   **92**

Silverwork
See/See also pages in the following book(s):
Langdon, W. C. Everyday things in American
life, 1607-1776 p176-91   **973.2**

Silvester, Christopher
(ed) The Norton book of interviews. See The
Norton book of interviews   **920**

Simak, Clifford D., 1904-1988
Desertion
In The Oxford book of science fiction stories
p115-26   **S C**
Over the river and through the woods
In The Norton book of science fiction p125-
32   **S C**

Sime, Ruth Lewin, 1939-
Lise Meitner   **92**

Simmie, Scott
Tiananmen Square   **951.05**

Simmons, Martin
Blood at the root [excerpt]
In Streetlights: illuminating tales of the urban
black experience p452-65   **S C**
(ed) Streetlights: illuminating tales of the urban
black experience. See Streetlights: illuminating tales of the urban black experience
     S C

Simms, Phil, 1955-
Phil Simms on passing   **796.332**

Simon, Neil
Barefoot in the park
In The Most popular plays of the American
theater p357-428   **812.008**
In Simon N. The comedy of Neil Simon
p103-214   **812**
Biloxi blues   **812**
also in Simon, N. The collected plays of Neil
Simon v3 p595-691   **812**
Brighton Beach memoirs   **812**
also in Best American plays: 9th series—
1983-1992 p1-39   **812.008**
also in Simon, N. The collected plays of Neil
Simon v3 p479-593   **812**
Broadway bound   **812**
also in Simon, N. The collected plays of Neil
Simon v3 p693-803   **812**
California suite
In Simon, N. The collected plays of Neil Si-
mon v2 p549-632   **812**
Chapter two
In Best American plays: 8th series—1974-
1982 p1-37   **812.008**
In Simon, N. The collected plays of Neil Si-
mon v2 p635-737   **812**
The collected plays of Neil Simon v2-3
     812
Come blow your horn
In Simon N. The comedy of Neil Simon p11-
102   **812**
The comedy of Neil Simon   **812**
Fools
In Simon, N. The collected plays of Neil Si-
mon v3 p307-78   **812**
The gingerbread lady
In Simon, N. The collected plays of Neil Si-
mon v2 p149-227   **812**

God's favorite
In Simon, N. The collected plays of Neil Si-
mon v2 p475-545   **812**
The good doctor
In Simon, N. The collected plays of Neil Si-
mon v2 p393-471   **812**
I ought to be in pictures
In Simon, N. The collected plays of Neil Si-
mon v3 p217-305   **812**
Last of the red hot lovers
In Simon N. The comedy of Neil Simon
p583-657   **812**
Little me
In Simon, N. The collected plays of Neil Si-
mon v2 p13-145   **812**
Lost in Yonkers   **812**
The odd couple
In Best American plays: 6th series—1963-
1967 p527-65   **812.008**
In Simon N. The comedy of Neil Simon
p215-302   **812**
Odd couple (female version)
In Simon, N. The collected plays of Neil Si-
mon v3 p379-475   **812**
Plaza suite: Visitor from Forest Hills
In Simon N. The comedy of Neil Simon
p560-82   **812**
Plaza suite: Visitor from Hollywood
In Simon N. The comedy of Neil Simon
p538-59   **812**
Plaza suite: Visitor from Mamaroneck
In Simon N. The comedy of Neil Simon
p497-537   **812**
The prisoner of Second Avenue
In Best American plays: 7th series—1967-
1973 p73-102   **812.008**
In Simon, N. The collected plays of Neil Si-
mon v2 p231-99   **812**
Promises, promises
In Simon N. The comedy of Neil Simon
p393-494   **812**
The star-spangled girl
In Simon N. The comedy of Neil Simon
p303-92   **812**
The Sunshine Boys
In Simon, N. The collected plays of Neil Si-
mon v2 p303-89   **812**
Sweet Charity
In Simon, N. The collected plays of Neil Si-
mon v3 p1-113   **812**
They're playing our song
In Simon, N. The collected plays of Neil Si-
mon v3 p115-215   **812**

Simon & Schuster's guide to houseplants.
Chiusoli, A.   **635.9**
Simon and Schuster's guide to garden flowers.
Moggi, G.   **635.9**
Simon and Schuster's guide to insects. Arnett, R.
H., Jr.   **595.7**
A **simple** enquiry. Hemingway, E.
In Hemingway, E. The complete short stories
of Ernest Hemingway p250-52   **S C**
In Hemingway, E. The short stories of Ernest
Hemingway p327-30   **S C**
Simple foods for the pack. Axcell, C.   **641.5**
The **simplest** game. Gardner, P.   **796.334**

Sinners. O'Faoláin, S.
In The Oxford book of short stories p362-70
    S C

Sino-Japanese Conflict, 1937-1945
    Fiction
Ballard, J. G. Empire of the Sun   **Fic**

Sinyavsky, Andrei, 1925-1997
Pkhentz
    In The Portable twentieth-century Russian reader p485-506   **891.7**

Siobhan La Rue in color. Renville, D.
    In Song of the turtle p331-40   **S C**

Siouan Indians
    See also Dakota Indians; Oglala Indians

Sioux Indians *See* Dakota Indians

Sippy, Shana
    (jt. auth) Dobkin, R. The college woman's handbook   **378**

Sir Bertrand. Barbauld, A. L. A.
    In The Oxford book of gothic tales p3-6
    S C

Sir Dominick Sarsfield. Le Fanu, J. S.
    In Classic ghost stories p1-15   **S C**

Sir Gawain and the Green Knight *See* Gawain and the Grene Knight

Sir Gawain and the loathly lady
    In Hearne, B. G. Beauties and beasts p131-38
    398.2

Sir Rabbit. Welty, E.
    In Welty, E. The collected stories of Eudora Welty p331-41   **S C**

Sir William Pepperell. Hawthorne, N.
    In Hawthorne, N. Tales and sketches; A wonder book for girls and boys; Tanglewood tales for girls and boys p166-73
    S C

Sir William Phips. Hawthorne, N.
    In Hawthorne, N. Tales and sketches; A wonder book for girls and boys; Tanglewood tales for girls and boys p12-17   **S C**

Sister. Russell, S.
    In Daughters of Africa p694-98   **808.8**

Sister Ann of the Cornfields. Kinsella, W. P.
    In Kinsella, W. P. Shoeless Joe Jackson come to Iowa: stories   **S C**

Sister Carrie. Dreiser, T.   **Fic**

Sister Katherine. Monreal, D. N.
    In Growing up Chicana/o p175-98   **810.8**

Sister to sister   **810.8**

The **sister** years. Hawthorne, N.
    In Hawthorne, N. Tales and sketches; A wonder book for girls and boys; Tanglewood tales for girls and boys p678-84
    S C

Sisters
    Fiction
Alvarez, J. In the time of the butterflies
    Fic
Paterson, K. Jacob have I loved   **Fic**
Tan, A. The hundred secret senses   **Fic**
Walker, A. The color purple   **Fic**
The **sisters.** Joyce, J.
    In Joyce, J. Dubliners   **S C**

Sisters and brothers *See* Brothers and sisters

Sitkoff, Harvard
    (ed) A History of our time. See A History of our time   **973.92**

Sitting around the pool, soaking up the rays. Pohl, F.
    In Tales from the planet Earth   **S C**

Sitting Bull, Dakota Chief, 1831-1890
    About
Vestal, S. Sitting Bull, champion of the Sioux
    92

    See/See also pages in the following book(s):
Brown, D. A. The American West p215-27
    978
Walker, P. R. Great figures of the Wild West
    920

Sivananda Yoga Vedanta Center (London, England)
Yoga, mind & body. See Yoga, mind & body
    294.5

Six American poets   **811.008**

Six characters in search of an author. Pirandello, L.
    In Pirandello, L. Naked masks p211-76
    852

Six of one—. Fitzgerald, F. S.
    In Fitzgerald, F. S. The short stories of F. Scott Fitzgerald p667-79   **S C**

A **six-pack** and a fake I.D.: teens look at the drinking question. Cohen, S.   **616.86**

Sixteenth century
The Oxford encyclopedia of the Reformation
    270.6

The **sixth** extinction. Leakey, R. E.   **304.2**

The **sixth** shotgun. L'Amour, L.
    In L'Amour, L. The outlaws of Mesquite p179-99   **S C**

The **sixties.** Gitlin, T.   **973.92**

The **sixties** reader. See Haskins, J. The 60s reader
    973.92

Sixty-five years of the Oscar. See Osborne, R. A. 65 years of the Oscar   **791.43**

Sixty years after Hiroshima thirteen years after Rodney King. Henderson-Holmes, S.
    In Streetlights: illuminating tales of the urban black experience p167-73   **S C**

Skaggs, Gayle, 1952-
Off the wall!   **027.8**

Skaggs, Peggy
Kate Chopin   **813.009**

Skal, David J.
V is for Vampire   **398**

Skates. Pilcher, R.
    In Pilcher, R. Flowers in the rain & other stories   **S C**

Skating *See* Ice skating

Skeleton. Bradbury, R.
    In Bradbury, R. The stories of Ray Bradbury p324-36   **S C**

Skeleton crew. King, S.   **S C**

The **smuggler**. Singer, I. B.
   In Singer, I. B. The death of Methuselah and
     other stories p85-92   **S C**

Smuggling of drugs *See* Drug traffic

Smurthwaite, David
   The Pacific war atlas   **940.54**

The **snail** and the rosebush. Andersen, H. C.
   In Andersen, H. C. Tales and stories
     S C

The **snake**. Steinbeck, J.
   In Steinbeck, J. The portable Steinbeck
     818

The **snakeman**. Tapahonso, L.
   In Song of the turtle p71-75   **S C**

Snakes
   Mattison, C. The encyclopedia of snakes
     597.9
   Mehrtens, J. M. Living snakes of the world in
     color   **597.9**
   Snakes   **597.9**

Snakes   **597.9**

Snapshots of a wedding. Head, B.
   In African short stories   **S C**

Snatched away. TallMountain, M.
   In Talking leaves   **S C**

Snatcher. Koontz, D. R.
   In Koontz, D. R. Strange highways p243-58
     S C

The **sniper**. O'Neill, E.
   In O'Neill, E. Complete plays v1   **812**

Snodgrass, Mary Ellen
   (ed) Black history month resource book. See
     Black history month resource book   **305.8**
   (ed) Celebrating women's history. See Celebrat-
     ing women's history   **305.4**

Snodgrass, W. D. (William De Witt), 1926-
   Selected poems, 1957-1987   **811**

Snodgrass, William De Witt *See* Snodgrass, W.
   D. (William De Witt), 1926-

Snow, Dean R., 1940-
   (jt. auth) Coe, M. D. Atlas of ancient America
     970.01

Snow. Alvarez, J.
   In Latina: women's voices from the border-
     lands p127-28   **810.8**

Snow. Crowley, J.
   In The Norton book of science fiction p591-
     604   **S C**

Snow. Faulkner, W.
   In Faulkner, W. Uncollected stories of Wil-
     liam Faulkner p665-77   **S C**

Snow-flakes. Hawthorne, N.
   In Hawthorne, N. Tales and sketches; A won-
     der book for girls and boys; Tanglewood
     tales for girls and boys p593-97
     S C

The **snow** goose. Gallico, P.   **Fic**

The **snow-image**. Hawthorne, N.
   In Hawthorne, N. Tales and sketches; A won-
     der book for girls and boys; Tanglewood
     tales for girls and boys p1087-1102
     S C

The **snow** queen. Andersen, H. C.
   In Andersen, H. C. Tales and stories
     S C

The **snows** of Kilimanjaro. Hemingway, E.
   In Hemingway, E. The complete short stories
     of Ernest Hemingway p39-56   **S C**
   In Hemingway, E. The short stories of Ernest
     Hemingway p52-77   **S C**

Snyder, Gary
   No nature   **811**

Snyder, James
   Medieval art   **709.02**

Snyder, Zilpha Keatley
   The three men
     In Where coyotes howl and wind blows free
     p20-29   **810.8**

So I guess you know what I told him. Dobyns, S.
   In The Best American short stories, 1995
     p195-209   **S C**

So long, and thanks for all the fish. Adams, D.
   See note under Adams, D. The Hitchhiker's
     Guide to the Galaxy   **Fic**

So this is man. Wolfe, T.
   In Wolfe, T. The complete short stories of
     Thomas Wolfe p478-81   **S C**

So you have to give a speech! See Ryan, M. How
   to give a speech   **808.5**

So you have to write a term paper! See Everhart,
   N. How to write a term paper   **808**

So you think you're fat?. Silverstein, A.
     616.85

A **Soaring** spirit: timeframe 600-400 BC   **930**

Soaring spirits. Gravelle, K.   **970.004**

Sobel, Dava
   Longitude   **526**

Soccer
   Bauer, G. Soccer techniques, tactics & team-
     work   **796.334**
   Gardner, P. The simplest game   **796.334**
   Herbst, D. Sports illustrated soccer   **796.334**
   Rosenthal, G. Soccer skills and drills
     796.334

Soccer skills and drills. Rosenthal, G.
     796.334

Soccer techniques, tactics & teamwork. Bauer, G.
     796.334

Social action
   Fiffer, S. 50 ways to help your community
     361.3
   Meltzer, M. Who cares?   **361**

Social anthropology *See* Ethnology

Social change
   Naisbitt, J. Megatrends   **303.4**
   Naisbitt, J. Megatrends 2000   **303.4**
   Toffler, A. Future shock   **303.4**
   Toffler, A. Powershift   **303.4**

Social classes
   See also Middle classes
             Fiction
   Kerr, M. E. Gentlehands   **Fic**

Social contract   **320.1**

The **social** contract. Rousseau, J.-J.
   In Social contract p167-307   **320.1**

Social customs *See* Manners and customs

Social democracy *See* Socialism

Social drinking *See* Drinking of alcoholic beverages

Social ethics

    See also Bioethics

A **social** history of Greece and Rome. Grant, M.
    938

Social justice: opposing viewpoints   **323**

Social life and customs *See* Manners and customs

Social movements

  Burns, S. Social movements of the 1960s
    303.4

Social movements of the 1960s. Burns, S.
    303.4

Social problems
Fiction
  Sinclair, U. The jungle   **Fic**

Social psychology

    See also Alienation (Social psychology); Hysteria (Social psychology)

  Bettelheim, B. Surviving, and other essays
    155.9

  Fromm, E. Escape from freedom   **323.44**

Social sciences

  See/See also pages in the following book(s):

  Horgan, J. The end of science p143-58
    501

The **social** sense. Maugham, W. S.

  In Maugham, W. S. Collected short stories v2
    S C

Social values

  American values: opposing viewpoints   **306**

Socialism

  Ebenstein, A. D. Today's isms   **335**

  See/See also pages in the following book(s):

  Naisbitt, J. Megatrends 2000 p93-117   **303.4**

  Tuchman, B. W. The proud tower p407-62
    909.82

History

  See/See also pages in the following book(s):

  Durant, W. J. The lessons of history p56-67
    901

Socially handicapped children

  Conroy, P. The water is wide   **371.9**

  Kozol, J. Amazing grace   **362.7**

  Kozol, J. Savage inequalities   **371.9**

Societies

    See also Associations

Society of Friends

  Fisher, S. G. The Quaker colonies   **973.2**

  See/See also pages in the following book(s):

  Boorstin, D. J. The Americans: The colonial experience p33-69   **973.2**

  Carnes, J. Us and them p6-13   **305.8**

  Langdon, W. C. Everyday things in American life, 1607-1776 p48-62   **973.2**

  Meltzer, M. Ain't gonna study war no more: the story of America's peace seekers p24-39
    322.4

Fiction

  West, J. The friendly persuasion   **Fic**

Sociology
Dictionaries
  Encyclopedia of sociology   **301**

  Jary, D. The HarperCollins dictionary of sociology   **301**

Socrates

  See/See also pages in the following book(s):

  Aymar, B. A pictorial history of the world's greatest trials p1-13   **345**

  Jaspers, K. The great philosophers   **109**

  Russell, B. A history of Western philosophy p82-93   **109**

The **soft-hearted** Sioux. Zitkala-Ša

  In The Singing spirit: early short stories by North American Indians p78-85   **S C**

Soft voices at Passenham. White, T. H.

  In The Oxford book of English ghost stories p487-94   **S C**

Soft workouts   **613.7**

Softball

  Dickson, P. The Worth book of softball
    796.357

Software, Computer *See* Computer software

The **sojourner**. McCullers, C.

  In McCullers, C. The ballad of the sad café: the novels and stories of Carson McCullers   **S C**

  In McCullers, C. Collected stories p138-47
    S C

Sojourner Truth *See* Truth, Sojourner, d. 1883

Sojourner Truth, a self-made woman. Ortiz, V.
    92

Sokolov, Sasha, 1943-

  A school for fools [excerpt]

  In The Portable twentieth-century Russian reader p602-11   **891.7**

Solace. Dozois, G. R.

  In Nebula awards 25 p63-73   **S C**

Solar radiation

    See also Greenhouse effect

Solar storms. Hogan, L.   **Fic**

Solar system

  Asimov, I. The secret of the universe   **520**

  Kolb, R. Blind watchers of the sky   **523.1**

  Mammana, D. Other suns, other worlds?
    523.2

  See/See also pages in the following book(s):

  Goodstein, D. L. Feynman's lost lecture p145-70   **521**

  Levy, D. H. Skywatching p228-63   **520**

Soldier ask not. Dickson, G. R.

  In The Mammoth book of new world science fiction p148-200   **S C**

Soldiers

    See also Women soldiers; names of countries with the subdivision *Army—Military life*
United States
  Hoyt, E. P. The GI's war   **940.54**
United States—Fiction
  Jones, J. From here to eternity   **Fic**

  Mailer, N. The naked and the dead   **Fic**

Soldiers. Southerland, E.

  In Calling the wind p366-69   **S C**

Songs
See also National songs; Popular music
Lives of the great songs   **782.42**
Songs, American *See* American songs
Songs of innocence and experience. Blake, W.
In Blake, W. The portable Blake   **828**
Songwriters *See* Composers; Lyricists
Songwriter's market   **782.42**
Sonneborn, Liz
Performers   **920**
Sonnets. Shakespeare, W.   **821**
Sonnets from the Portuguese. Browning, E. B.
    821
Sonny's blues. Baldwin, J.
In American short story masterpieces
    S C
In The Oxford book of American short stories
p408-39   **S C**
Sons and fathers *See* Fathers and sons
Sons and lovers. Lawrence, D. H.   **Fic**
Sons and mothers *See* Mothers and sons
Sontag, Susan, 1933-
The way we live now
In The Best American short stories of the
eighties p252-70   **S C**
Soper, Tony, 1939-
(jt. auth) Sparks, J. Owls   **598**
Sophie's choice. Styron, W.   **Fic**
Sophistication. Anderson, S.
In Anderson, S. Winesburg, Ohio   **S C**
Sophocles
Antigone   **882**
also in Seven famous Greek plays
    882.008
also in Sophocles. Electra, Antigone,
Philoctetes   **882**
Electra
In Sophocles. Electra, Antigone, Philoctetes
    882
Electra, Antigone, Philoctetes   **882**
Oedipus Rex
In Four Greek plays   **882.008**
Oedipus the King   **882**
also in Seven famous Greek plays
    882.008
Philoctetes
In Sophocles. Electra, Antigone, Philoctetes
    882
About
Scodel, R. Sophocles   **882**
See/See also pages in the following book(s):
Hamilton, E. The Greek way p258-70
    880.9
The **sorcerer's** apprentice. O'Connor, F.
In O'Connor, F. Collected stories p345-55
    S C
Sorrow, Barbara
CD-ROM for librarians and educators
    025.2
Sorrow for a midget. Hughes, L.
In Hughes, L. Short stories   **S C**
A **sorrow** in our heart: the life of Tecumseh.
Eckert, A. W.   **92**

Sorrow's kitchen: the life and folklore of Zora
Neale Hurston. Lyons, M. E.   **92**
The **sorrows** of gin. Cheever, J.
In Cheever, J. The stories of John Cheever
p198-209   **S C**
Sorry, wrong number. Fletcher, L.
In 24 favorite one-act plays p117-32
    808.82
Soto, Gary
The bike
In Growing up Chicana/o p233-36   **810.8**
Broken chain
In Read all about it! p29-39   **808.88**
The jacket
In Coming of age in America p3-6   **S C**
New and selected poems   **811**
See/See also pages in the following book(s):
Going where I'm coming from   **920**
Soto, Hernando de, ca. 1500-1542
About
Duncan, D. E. Hernando de Soto   **92**
See/See also pages in the following book(s):
Faber, H. The discoverers of America p214-24
    970.01
Soukup, Martha
A defense of the social contracts
In Nebula awards 30 p222-38   **S C**
Over the long haul
In Nebula awards 26 p172-94   **S C**
Soul-catcher. Owens, L.
In Song of the turtle p147-55   **S C**
Soul music
Brown, J. James Brown, the godfather of soul
    92
Hirshey, G. Nowhere to run   **781.644**
Soul on ice. Cleaver, E.   **305.8**
Soul to soul. Khanga, Y.   **92**
Souls belated. Wharton, E.
In Wharton, E. The selected short stories of
Edith Wharton p26-46   **S C**
The **souls** of black folk. Du Bois, W. E. B.
    305.8
also in Du Bois, W. E. B. The Oxford W. E.
B. Du Bois reader p97-240   **305.8**
also in Du Bois, W. E. B. Writings   **818**
Sound
Experiments
Gardner, R. Experimenting with sound   **534**
The **sound** of harness bells. Nguyen, Q. L.
In The Other side of heaven p287-93
    S C
The **sound** of music. Lindsay, H.   **812**
A **sound** of thunder. Bradbury, R.
In Bradbury, R. The stories of Ray Bradbury
p231-41   **S C**
The **sound** of wings: the life of Amelia Earhart.
Lovell, M. S.   **92**
Sound recordings
Bibliography
Words on cassette   **011**
Reviews
The Rolling Stone album guide   **780.2**
Sounder. Elder, L.
In Best American screenplays   **812.008**

Southey, Robert, 1774-1843
See/See also pages in the following book(s):
Untermeyer, L. Lives of the poets p338-70
   920

Southwest, New *See* Southwestern States
Southwestern States
   Antiquities
Acatos, S. Pueblos   970.004
Cordell, L. S. Ancient Pueblo peoples
   970.004
Roberts, D. In search of the old ones
   970.004

Souvenir. Phillips, J. A.
In We are the stories we tell S C

Souvestre, Emile, 1806-1854
The castle of Kerglas
In The Merlin chronicles S C

Sovereigns *See* Kings, queens, rulers, etc.
Soviet Union
 See also Former Soviet republics; Russia; Russia (Republic)
   Dictionaries
The Cambridge encyclopedia of Russia and the former Soviet Union 947
Paxton, J. Encylopedia of Russian history
   947
   Fiction
Koestler, A. Darkness at noon Fic
Solzhenitsyn, A. One day in the life of Ivan Denisovich Fic
   Historical geography—Maps
Gilbert, M. Atlas of Russian history 911
   History
The Breakup of the Soviet Union: opposing viewpoints 947.086
Russia and the independent states 947
   History—1917-1921, Revolution
Medvedev, R. A. The October Revolution
   947.084
   History—Chronology
Great dates in Russian and Soviet history
   947
   Politics and government
Marrin, A. Stalin 92
Medvedev, R. A. Khrushchev: the years in power 947.085
Medvedev, R. A. Let history judge
   947.084
Otfinoski, S. Boris Yeltsin and the rebirth of Russia 92
Radzinsky, E. Stalin 92
Solzhenitsyn, A. The Gulag archipelago, 1918-1956 365

Soyinka, Akinwande Oluwole *See* Soyinka, Wole
Soyinka, Wole
(ed) Poems of black Africa. See Poems of black Africa 896
See/See also pages in the following book(s):
Modern black writers p388-98 809

Space, Outer *See* Outer space
Space. Gibson, R. 629.4
Space and time
Hawking, S. W. The nature of space and time
   530.1

   Fiction
Card, O. S. Pastwatch Fic
Space exploration: opposing viewpoints 629.4
Space exploration projects for young scientists. Vogt, G. 520
Space flight
 See also Mercury project
Harding, R. M. Survival in space 616.9
Lee, W. To rise from earth 629.4
Man in space 629.4
Space flight to the moon
Lovell, J. Lost moon: the perilous voyage of Apollo 13 629.45
Shepard, A. B., Jr. Moon shot 629.45
Space medicine
Harding, R. M. Survival in space 616.9
Space probes
See/See also pages in the following book(s):
Man in space p82-99 629.4
Space sciences
Vogt, G. Space exploration projects for young scientists 520
Space shuttles
See/See also pages in the following book(s):
Man in space p128-49 629.4
Space stations
See/See also pages in the following book(s):
Man in space p100-09 629.4
Space Telescope *See* Hubble Space Telescope
Space-time for springers. Leiber, F.
In Masterpieces of fantasy and enchantment p318-29 S C
Space travel *See* Interplanetary voyages
Space vehicles
 See also Artificial satellites; Space shuttles
Spaceflight. Neal, V. 629.4
Spaceflight and rocketry: a chronology. Baker, D.
   629.4
Spain
Vincent, M. Cultural atlas of Spain and Portugal
   946
   Biography—Dictionaries
Dictionary of Hispanic biography 920.003
   Civilization
Crow, J. A. Spain: the root and the flower
   946
Fuentes, C. The buried mirror 946
Kern, R. W. The regions of Spain 946
See/See also pages in the following book(s):
Durant, W. J. The age of reason begins p274-332 940.2
   Fiction
Cervantes Saavedra, M. de. Don Quixote de la Mancha Fic
   History
 See also Spanish Armada, 1588
Historical dictionary of modern Spain, 1700-1988 946
See/See also pages in the following book(s):
Durant, W. J. Rousseau and revolution p273-97
   940.2
   History—1898, War of 1898
See Spanish-American War, 1898

Speaking of Washington. Moore, J. L.   975.3

Speaking out. Kuklin, S.   305.23

Spears, Richard A.
NTC's American idioms dictionary   427
(ed) Kleinedler, S. R. NTC's dictionary of acronyms and abbreviations   421.03

Special collections in libraries *See* Libraries—Special collections

Specialty occupational outlook: professions   331.7

Specialty occupational outlook: trade & technical   331.7

The spectacles. Poe, E. A.
In Poe, E. A. The collected tales and poems of Edgar Allan Poe p688-707   S C

Spector, Joel
(jt. auth) Geller, L. If I can dream [biography of Elvis Presley]   92

Speech
Allstetter, W. D. Speech and hearing   612.7

Speech and hearing. Allstetter, W. D.   612.7

The speech of Polly Baker. Franklin, B.
In The Norton book of American short stories p23-25   S C

Speech sounds. Butler, O. E.
In The Norton book of science fiction p513-24   S C

Speeches
Lend me your ears   808.85
The Penguin book of twentieth-century speeches   808.85
Speeches of the American presidents   353.03

Speeches, addresses, etc., American *See* American speeches

Speeches of the American presidents   353.03

Speed, Lillian Castillo- *See* Castillo-Speed, Lillian, 1949-

Speer, Albert, 1905-1981
Inside the Third Reich   943.086

Speleology *See* Caves

Spell #7. Shange, N.
In 9 plays by black women   811.008

A spell for Chameleon. Anthony, P. *See* note under Anthony, P. The Magic of Xanth series   Fic

Spell my name with an S. Asimov, I.
In Asimov, I. The complete stories v1 p277-89   S C

A spell of kona weather. Watanabe, S.
In Coming of age in America p166-74   S C

Spellenberg, Richard
The Audubon Society field guide to North American wildflowers: western region   582.13
Familiar flowers of North America: eastern region   582.13
Familiar flowers of North America: western region   582.13

The spelling lesson. Brosnahan, L.
In Not the only one p26-36   S C

Spence, Eulalie, 1894-1981
Undertow
In Black theatre USA   812.008

Spence, Jonathan D.
The search for modern China   951

Spence, Keith
The young people's book of music   780

Spencer, Donald D., 1931-
(comp) Webster's New World dictionary of computer terms. See Webster's New World dictionary of computer terms   004

Spencer, Herbert, 1820-1903
See/See also pages in the following book(s):
Durant, W. J. The story of philosophy p265-300   109

Spencer, Janet
Visiting college campuses   378.73

Spencer, John R.
(ed) The Great comet crash. See The Great comet crash   523.6

Spencer, Pamela G.
What do young adults read next?   016.8

Spencer, William
Germany then and now   943

Spender, Dale
(ed) British women writers. See British women writers   820.8

Spewack, Bella, 1899-1990
Boy meets girl
In Twenty best plays of the modern American theatre p371-413   812.008

The Sphinx. Poe, E. A.
In Poe, E. A. The collected tales and poems of Edgar Allan Poe p471-74   S C

The Sphinx without a secret. Wilde, O.
In The Oxford book of Irish short stories p152-56   S C

Spider. Eberhart, M. G.
In The Oxford book of American detective stories p239-60   S C

Spider Woman's granddaughters   S C

Spiders
Hillyard, P. D. The book of the spider   595.4
Milne, L. J. The Audubon Society field guide to North American insects and spiders   595.7

Spider's bite. Medina, P.
In Iguana dreams   S C

The spider's web. Kibera, L.
In African short stories   S C

Spiegelman, Art
Maus   940.53
Maus II [excerpt]
In Bearing witness p40-47   808.8

Spiegelman, Vladek
About
Spiegelman, A. Maus   940.53

Spielberg, Steven, 1947-
About
Sanello, F. Spielberg   92

Spieler, Marlena
(jt. auth) Berry, M. Classic home cooking   641.5

States' rights *See* State rights

The **Statesman's** year-book   310.5

The **Statesman's** year-book world gazetteer
                                                 910.3

Statesmen
    See also Heads of state; Politicians
    Dolan, E. F. Shaping U.S. foreign policy
                                                 327.73

Station Baranovich. Sholem Aleichem
    In Sholem Aleichem. The best of Sholem
    Aleichem   S C

Station Island. Heaney, S.   821

Statistical abstract of the United States. United
    States. Bureau of the Census   317.3

Statistical abstract of the world   310.5

Statistical yearbook. United Nations. Statistical
    Office   310.5

Statistics
    Information please almanac   031.02
    The Statesman's year-book   310.5
    Statistical abstract of the world 310.5
    United Nations. Statistical Office. Statistical
    yearbook   310.5
    United States. Bureau of the Census. Statistical
    abstract of the United States   317.3
    The World almanac and book of facts
                                                 031.02

Statistics on alcohol, drug & tobacco use
                                                 362.29

A **statue** for father. Asimov, I.
    In Asimov, I. The complete stories v2 p286-
    91   S C

Staupers, Mabel Keaton, 1890-1989
    See/See also pages in the following book(s):
    Black leaders of the twentieth century p241-57
                                                 920

Stavans, Ilan
    (ed) Growing up Latino. See Growing up Latino
                                                 810.8

Stavros, Michael
    Camcorder tricks & special effects 778.59

Stay, Byron L.
    (ed) Censorship: opposing viewpoints. See Cen-
    sorship: opposing viewpoints   323.44

Staying fat for Sarah Byrnes. Crutcher, C.
                                                 Fic

Staying healthy in a risky environment   613

Steady going up. Angelou, M.
    In Children of the night p223-31 S C

Stealing home: an intimate family portrait by the
    daughter of Jackie Robinson. Robinson, S.
                                                 92

Stealth at sea. Van der Vat, D.   359

Steam engineering
    See/See also pages in the following book(s):
    Inventors and discoverers p14-43   609

Stearns, Peter N.
    The ABC-CLIO world history companion to the
    industrial revolution   909.81

Stebbins, Robert C. (Robert Cyril), 1915-
    A field guide to western reptiles and amphibians
                                                 597.6

    (jt. auth) Conant, R. Peterson first guide to rep-
    tiles and amphibians   597.6

Stechow, Wolfgang, 1896-1974
    Pieter Bruegel the Elder   759.9493

Stedman's medical dictionary   610.3

Steele, Daniel, 1824-1914
    The man who saw through Heaven
    In The Norton book of American short stories
    p261-76   S C

Steele, Mary
    Aunt Millicent
    In Read all about it! p12-28   808.88

Steffan, Joseph
    Honor bound   92

Steffens, Roger
    (jt. auth) Talamon, B. Bob Marley 92

Stefoff, Rebecca, 1951-
    The American environmental movement
                                                 363.7
    Friendship and love   155
    Herman Melville   92
    Mao Zedong   92
    Saddam Hussein   92
    Women pioneers   920
    The young Oxford companion to maps and
    mapmaking   912

Stein, Barbara L.
    Running a school library media center
                                                 027.8
    (jt. auth) Blake, B. R. Creating newsletters, bro-
    chures, and pamphlets   070.5

Stein, Gertrude, 1874-1946
    The autobiography of Alice B. Toklas 92
    See/See also pages in the following book(s):
    Gombar, C. Great women writers, 1900-1950
                                                 920

Stein, Gordon
    Encyclopedia of hoaxes   001.9

Stein, Jess M., 1914-1984
    (ed) Random House Webster's college thesau-
    rus. See Random House Webster's college
    thesaurus   423

Stein, Joseph, 1912-
    Fiddler on the roof
    In Best American plays: 6th series—1963-
    1967 p399-433   812.008

Steinbeck, John, 1902-1968
    Cannery Row   Fic
    Conversations with John Steinbeck 92
    The grapes of wrath   Fic
    also in Steinbeck, J. The grapes of wrath and
    other writings, 1936-1941   818
    Grapes of wrath; criticism
    In Critical essays on Steinbeck's The grapes
    of wrath   813.009
    The grapes of wrath and other writings, 1936-
    1941   818
    The long valley contains the following short stories: Chrysan-
    themums; White quail; Flight; Snake; Breakfast; Raid; Harness;
    Vigilante; Johnny Bear; Murder; St. Katy the virgin; Leader of
    the people
    The harvest gypsies
    In Steinbeck, J. The grapes of wrath and oth-
    er writings, 1936-1941   818

Stevens, Garfield Reeves- *See* Reeves-Stevens, Garfield

Stevens, Gregory I.
(ed) Videos for understanding diversity. See Videos for understanding diversity
    016.3713

Stevens, John F. (John Frank), 1853-1943
See/See also pages in the following book(s):
McCullough, D. G. The path between the seas
    972.87

Stevens, Judith Reeves- *See* Reeves-Stevens, Judith

Stevens, R. L. *See* Hoch, Edward D., 1930-

Stevens, Wallace, 1879-1955
The collected poems of Wallace Stevens
    811

See/See also pages in the following book(s):
Voices & visions p123-56   **811.009**

Stevenson, Burton Egbert, 1872-1962
(comp) The Home book of modern verse. See The Home book of modern verse
    821.008

Stevenson, Robert E.
(ed) Islands. See Islands   **508**

Stevenson, Robert Louis, 1850-1894
The body-snatcher
  In Victorian ghost stories p303-18   **S C**
Dr. Jekyll and Mr. Hyde   **Fic**
Olalla
  In The Oxford book of gothic tales p183-217
    S C
The song of the morrow
  In The Oxford book of modern fairy tales p178-81   **S C**
Thrawn Janet
  In The Oxford book of short stories p99-108
    S C
Treasure Island   **Fic**
About
Bell, I. Dreams of exile: Robert Louis Stevenson: a biography   **92**
McLynn, F. J. Robert Louis Stevenson   **92**
Saposnik, I. S. Robert Louis Stevenson
    828

Stevick, Philip
(ed) The American short story, 1900-1945/1945-1980. See The American short story, 1900-1945/1945-1980   **813.009**

Stewart, Elinore Pruitt, 1878-1933
See/See also pages in the following book(s):
Stefoff, R. Women pioneers   **920**

Stewart, Gail, 1949-
Alternative healing   **615.8**
Microscopes   **502**

Stewart, George Rippey, 1895-1980
American given names   **929.4**

Stewart, Ian, 1945-
Nature's numbers   **510**

Stewart, John
Blues for Pablo
  In Calling the wind p205-19   **S C**

Stewart, Julia
African names   **929.4**

Stewart, Mary, 1916-
The crystal cave
  In Stewart, M. Mary Stewart's Merlin trilogy
    Fic
The hollow hills
  In Stewart, M. Mary Stewart's Merlin trilogy
    Fic
The last enchantment
  In Stewart, M. Mary Stewart's Merlin trilogy
    Fic
Mary Stewart's Merlin trilogy   **Fic**
The prince and the pilgrim   **Fic**

Stewart, Mary Elinore Pruitt *See* Stewart, Elinore Pruitt, 1878-1933

Stewart, Robert, 1941-
The illustrated almanac of historical facts
    902

Stewart, Susan C.
(ed) The Women's complete healthbook. See The Women's complete healthbook   **613**

The **stick** up. Killens, J. O.
  In The Best short stories by Negro writers p188-91   **S C**

Sticks and bones. Rabe, D.
  In Best American plays: 7th series—1967-1973 p245-82   **812.008**

Stiegel, Henry William, 1729-1785
See/See also pages in the following book(s):
Langdon, W. C. Everyday things in American life, 1607-1776 p199-210   **973.2**

The **still** alarm. Kaufman, G. S.
  In 24 favorite one-act plays p229-37
    808.82

Still life. Updike, J.
  In Updike, J. Pigeon feathers, and other stories p27-48   **S C**

Still life with rice [biography of Hongyong Baek] Lee, H.   **92**

A **still** moment. Welty, E.
  In Welty, E. The collected stories of Eudora Welty p189-99   **S C**

A **stillness** at Appomattox. Catton, B.   **973.7**

A **stillness** heard round the world. Weintraub, S.
    940.4

Stilwell, Joseph Warren, 1883-1946
See/See also pages in the following book(s):
White, T. H. In search of history p132-44, 166-79   **92**

The **sting.** Ward, D. S.
  In Best American screenplays   **812.008**

Stinson, Katherine, 1891-1977
See/See also pages in the following book(s):
Yount, L. Women aviators   **920**

Stites, Francis N.
John Marshall, defender of the Constitution
    92

The **stock-broker's** clerk. Doyle, Sir A. C.
  In Doyle, Sir A. C. The complete Sherlock Holmes   **S C**

Stockings. O'Brien, T.
  In O'Brien, T. The things they carried
    S C

Streetlights: illuminating tales of the urban black experience   **S C**

The **strength** of God. Anderson, S.
   In Anderson, S. Winesburg, Ohio   **S C**
   In The Oxford book of American short stories p256-63   **S C**

The **strength** of the strong. London, J.
   In London, J. The portable Jack London p200-13   **818**
   In London, J. The science fiction stories of Jack London p131-43   **S C**
   In London, J. Short stories of Jack London p404-16   **S C**

Strength to love. King, M. L.   **252**

Strength training for women. Peterson, J. A.   **613.7**

Stress (Psychology)
   Feldman, R. S. Understanding stress   **155.9**
   Gordon, J. S. Stress management   **155.9**
   Maloney, M. Straight talk about anxiety and depression   **155.9**
   McCoy, K. Life happens   **616.85**
   Nardo, D. Anxiety and phobias   **616.85**
   Newman, S. Don't be S.A.D.: a teenage guide to handling stress, anxiety & depression   **155.9**

Stress management. Gordon, J. S.   **155.9**

Stribling, T. S. (Thomas Sigismund), 1881-1965
   Birthright [excerpt]
   In The Portable Harlem Renaissance reader p333-38   **810.8**
   A daylight adventure
   In The Oxford book of American detective stories p456-70   **S C**

Stribling, Thomas Sigismund *See* Stribling, T. S. (Thomas Sigismund), 1881-1965

Strictly diplomatic. Carr, J. D.
   In Masterpieces of mystery and suspense p280-94   **S C**

Stride toward freedom. King, M. L.   **323.1**

Strider. Tolstoy, L., graf
   In Tolstoy, L. The portable Tolstoy p435-74   **891.7**

The **strike.** Michener, J. A.
   In Michener, J. A. Tales of the South Pacific   **S C**

"The **strike,** oh, Lord, the strike!". Colette
   In Colette. The collected stories of Colette p143-46   **S C**

Strike-pay. Lawrence, D. H.
   In Lawrence, D. H. The complete short stories v1   **S C**

Strikebreaker. Asimov, I.
   In Asimov, I. The complete stories v1 p550-60   **S C**

Strikeout. Curran, W.   **796.357**

Strikes
   Dash, J. We shall not be moved   **331.4**

Strindberg, August, 1849-1912
   Miss Julie
   In Thirty famous one-act plays p29-58   **808.82**

A **string** of beads. Maugham, W. S.
   In Maugham, W. S. Collected short stories v1   **S C**

The **string** on a roast won't catch fire in the oven. Kohl, C.   **305.23**

Stringer, Jenny
   (ed) The Oxford companion to twentieth-century literature in English. See The Oxford companion to twentieth-century literature in English   **820.3**

Strisik, Paul, 1918-
   Capturing light in oils   **751.45**

Stroebel, Leslie D.
   (ed) The Focal encyclopedia of photography. See The Focal encyclopedia of photography   **770.2**

A **stroke** of good fortune. O'Connor, F.
   In O'Connor, F. Collected works p184-96   **S C**
   In O'Connor, F. The complete stories p95-107   **S C**

Strong, Austin, 1881-1952
   Drums of Oude
   In Thirty famous one-act plays p287-301   **808.82**

Strong as death is love. Singer, I. B.
   In Singer, I. B. The image and other stories p70-79   **S C**

Strothers, Ronald
   You can't have greens without a neck bone
   In Streetlights: illuminating tales of the urban black experience p466-70   **S C**

Structural engineering
   Morgan, S. Structures   **624.1**

Structures. Morgan, S.   **624.1**

The **struggle** for mastery in Europe, 1848-1918. Taylor, A. J. P.   **940.2**

A **struggle** for power. Draper, T.   **973.3**

Strunk, William, 1869-1946
   The elements of style   **808**

Stryker-Rodda, Harriet
   How to climb your family tree   **929**

Stuart, Gene S., 1930-1993
   America's ancient cities   **970.01**
   Lost kingdoms of the Maya   **972**

Stuart, George E.
   (jt. auth) Stuart, G. S. Lost kingdoms of the Maya   **972**

Stuart, Ian, 1922-1987 *See* MacLean, Alistair, 1922-1987

The **stucco** house. Gilchrist, E.
   In The Best American short stories, 1995 p31-44   **S C**

Stuck in time. Gutkind, L.   **616.89**

Stucky, Richard Keith
   (jt. auth) Johnson, K. R. Prehistoric journey   **551.7**

The **student.** Chekhov, A. P.
   In Chekhov, A. P. The image of Chekhov p219-23   **S C**

Student access guide to America's top internships. See Oldman, M. Student advantage guide to America's top internships   **331.5**

Surrealism
See/See also pages in the following book(s):
Arnason, H. H. History of modern art: painting, sculpture, architecture   **709.04**
Read, Sir H. E. A concise history of modern painting   **759.06**

Surrogate mothers
See/See also pages in the following book(s):
Mabie, M. C. J. Bioethics and the new medical technology   **174**
Reproductive technologies   **176**

Survival after airplane accidents, shipwrecks, etc.
Callahan, S. Adrift   **910.4**
Read, P. P. Alive   **910.4**
Robertson, D. Survive the savage sea   **910.4**
Fiction
Defoe, D. Robinson Crusoe   **Fic**
Golding, W. Lord of the Flies   **Fic**

The **survival** guide for teenagers with LD* (*learning differences). Cummings, R. W.   **371.9**

Survival in Auschwitz; and, The reawakening. Levi, P.   **940.53**
Survival in space. Harding, R. M.   **616.9**
Survival of the fittest *See* Natural selection
Survive the savage sea. Robertson, D.   **910.4**
Surviving, and other essays. Bettelheim, B.   **155.9**

Survivor type. King, S.
   In King, S. Skeleton crew   **S C**

Sutcliff, Rosemary, 1920-1992
The Shining Company   **Fic**

Sutherland, Fraser
(ed) Random House Webster's college thesaurus. See Random House Webster's college thesaurus   **423**

Sutherland, James
(ed) The Oxford book of literary anecdotes. See The Oxford book of literary anecdotes   **828**

Sutton, Caroline
More how do they do that?   **031.02**

Sutton, Dave *See* Woolls, E. Blanche

Sutton, David, 1944-
Midwinter
   In The Merlin chronicles   **S C**

The **Sutton** Place story. Cheever, J.
   In Cheever, J. The stories of John Cheever p65-78   **S C**

Svarney, Patricia Barnes- *See* Barnes-Svarney, Patricia

Swafford, Jan
The Vintage guide to classical music   **781.6**

Swain, Dwight V.
Creating characters   **808.3**

Swain, E. G. (Edmund Gill), 1861-1938
Bone to his bone
   In The Oxford book of English ghost stories p270-76   **S C**

Swain, Edmund Gill *See* Swain, E. G. (Edmund Gill), 1861-1938

Swamps *See* Wetlands

Swan song. Duncan, Q.
   In Rites of passage p89-90   **S C**

Swanberg, W. A., 1907-1992
Citizen Hearst: a biography of William Randolph Hearst   **92**

Swann, Brian
(ed) Coming to light. See Coming to light   **897**

Swanwick, Michael
A midwinter's tale
   In The Norton book of science fiction p733-45   **S C**

Swarm. Sterling, B.
   In The Oxford book of science fiction stories p472-95   **S C**

Swarthout, Glendon Fred
Bless the beasts and children   **Fic**

Sweat. Hurston, Z. N.
   In Hurston, Z. N. The complete stories p73-85   **S C**
   In Hurston, Z. N. I love myself when I am laughing—and then again when I am looking mean and impressive p197-207   **818**
   In Hurston, Z. N. Novels and stories p955-65   **Fic**
   In The Oxford book of American short stories p352-64   **S C**
   In The Oxford book of women's writing in the United States p101-10   **810.8**

Swedish Americans
Fiction
Cather, W. O pioneers!   **Fic**

Sweeney, Edwin R. (Edwin Russell), 1950-
Cochise, Chiricahua Apache chief   **92**

Sweet, Jeffrey, 1950-
(ed) The Best plays of [date]: The Otis Guernsey/Burns Mantle theater yearbook. See The Best plays of [date]: The Otis Guernsey/Burns Mantle theater yearbook   **808.82**

Sweet Charity. Simon, N.
   In Simon, N. The collected plays of Neil Simon v3 p1-113   **812**

Sweet Eros. McNally, T.
   In McNally, T. 15 short plays p97-112   **812**

Sweet medicine. Brooks, D.   **970.004**
Sweet nothings   **811.008**
Sweet whispers, Brother Rush. Hamilton, V.   **Fic**

Sweetheart of the Song Tra Bong. O'Brien, T.
   In O'Brien, T. The things they carried   **S C**

The **sweethearts.** Andersen, H. C.
   In Andersen, H. C. Tales and stories   **S C**

Swenson, May, 1919-1989
Nature   **811**

Świebocka, Teresa
(ed) Auschwitz. See Auschwitz   **940.53**

Swift, Jonathan, 1667-1745
Gulliver's travels   **Fic**

Syria
See/See also pages in the following book(s):
Mertz, B. Temples, tombs, and hieroglyphs
932
The **system** of Doctor Tarr and Professor Fether.
Poe, E. A.
In Poe, E. A. The collected tales and poems
of Edgar Allan Poe p307-21 **S C**
System theory
See also Chaos (Science)
Szenes, Hannah *See* Senesh, Hannah, 1921-1944
Szumski, Bonnie, 1958-
(ed) Interracial America: opposing viewpoints.
See Interracial America: opposing viewpoints
305.8
Szymanski, Ronald
(jt. auth) Karls, J. B. The writer's handbook
808

T

The **tablets** of the law. Hurston, Z. N.
In Hurston, Z. N. The complete stories p193-
201 **S C**
Tadpoles *See* Frogs
Tafolla, Carmen, 1951-
Chencho's cow
In Daughters of the fifth sun **810.8**
Taft, Robert A., 1889-1953
See/See also pages in the following book(s):
Kennedy, J. F. Profiles in courage p221-35
920
Tahan, Malba, 1895-
The man who counted **793.7**
Taine, John *See* Bell, Eric Temple, 1883-1960
'Tain't so. Hughes, L.
In Hughes, L. Short stories **S C**
The **Taipan**. Maugham, W. S.
In Maugham, W. S. Collected short stories v2
S C
In The Oxford book of English ghost stories
p283-88 **S C**
Takaki, Ronald T., 1939-
Hiroshima **940.54**
Strangers from a different shore **305.8**
Take a giant step. Peterson, L.
In Black theatre USA **812.008**
Take a match. Asimov, I.
In Asimov, I. The complete stories v2 p422-
36 **S C**
Take pity. Malamud, B.
In Malamud, B. The stories of Bernard
Malamud p3-12 **S C**
Taken captive. Ooka, S. **940.54**
Taking care of business. Hill, K. S.
In Talking leaves **S C**
Taking care of your cat. See Gerstenfeld, S. L.
The cat care book **636.8**
Talamon, Bruce
Bob Marley **92**
Talbert, Richard J. A., 1947-
(ed) Atlas of classical history. See Atlas of clas-
sical history **911**

Talbot, Frank
(ed) Islands. See Islands **508**
The **tale**. Conrad, J.
In Conrad, J. The complete short fiction of
Joseph Conrad v2 p268-84 **S C**
The **tale** of dragons and dreamers. Delany, S. R.
In Masterpieces of fantasy and enchantment
p426-54 **S C**
The **tale** of Gorgik. Delany, S. R.
In Children of the night p5-57 **S C**
A **tale** of Jerusalem. Poe, E. A.
In Poe, E. A. The collected tales and poems
of Edgar Allan Poe p467-70 **S C**
A **tale** of the Ragged Mountains. Poe, E. A.
In Poe, E. A. The collected tales and poems
of Edgar Allan Poe p679-87 **S C**
A **tale** of two cities. Dickens, C. **Fic**
Tales and sketches, including Twice-told tales,
Mosses from an old manse, and The snow-
image; A wonder book for girls and boys;
Tanglewood tales for girls and boys, being a
second Wonder book. Hawthorne, N.
S C
Tales and stories. Andersen, H. C. **S C**
Tales from the planet Earth **S C**
Tales from the secret annex, Anne Frank's. Frank,
A. **839.3**
Tales of a traveller. Irving, W.
In Irving, W. Bracebridge Hall; Tales of a
traveller; The Alhambra p379-717
S C
Tales of ancient Persia. Picard, B. L. **398.2**
Tales of Edgar Allan Poe. Poe, E. A. **S C**
The **tales** of Henry James. Wagenknecht, E.
813.009
Tales of love and terror. Rochman, H. **028**
Tales of space and time. Wells, H. G.
In Wells, H. G. The complete short stories of
H. G. Wells p623-825 **S C**
Tales of the South Pacific. Michener, J. A.
S C
Taliaferro, John, 1952-
Charles M. Russell **92**
The **talismans** of Shannara. Brooks, T. See note
under Brooks, T. The sword of Shannara
Fic
Talk of heroes. Bly, C.
In American short story masterpieces
S C
In The Vintage book of contemporary
American short stories p48-68 **S C**
Talk shows
Day, N. Sensational TV **791.45**
Kurtz, H. Hot air **791.45**
Talk to the deaf. See Riekehof, L. L. The joy of
signing **419**
Talking bones. Thomas, P. **614**
Talking horse. Malamud, B.
In Malamud, B. The stories of Bernard
Malamud p329-50 **S C**
Talking leaves **S C**
Talking peace. Carter, J. **327.1**

Taylor, A. J. P. (Alan John Percivale), 1906-1990
The struggle for mastery in Europe, 1848-1918
940.2

Taylor, Alan John Percivale *See* Taylor, A. J. P. (Alan John Percivale), 1906-1990

Taylor, Barbara, 1954-
Butterflies & moths   595.7

Taylor, C. L.
Chemical and biological warfare   358

Taylor, Carol, 1943-
Creative bead jewelry   745.58

Taylor, Colin F.
(ed) Native American myths and legends. See Native American myths and legends   299

Taylor, David, 1934-
The ultimate cat book   636.8
The ultimate dog book   636.7

Taylor, Diane K., 1946-
(ed) Conquering athletic injuries. See Conquering athletic injuries   617.1

Taylor, John H.
Unwrapping a mummy   932

Taylor, Kamala Purnaiya *See* Markandaya, Kamala, 1924-

Taylor, L. B., 1932-
(jt. auth) Taylor, C. L. Chemical and biological warfare   358

Taylor, Maxwell D., 1901-1987
See/See also pages in the following book(s):
Halberstam, D. The best and the brightest
973.922

Taylor, Michael R.
Cave passages   796.5

Taylor, Paul M., 1946-
(ed) Conquering athletic injuries. See Conquering athletic injuries   617.1

Taylor, Peter Hillsman, 1917-1994
The old forest
In The Best American short stories of the eighties p1-56   S C
Rain in the heart
In The Oxford book of American short stories p463-80   S C

Taylor, Rich, 1946-
Indy   796.7

Tea and sympathy. Anderson, R. W.
In Best American plays: 4th series—1951-1957 p279-313   812.008

The **teacher**. Anderson, S.
In Anderson, S. Winesburg, Ohio   S C

Teachers
See also Educators
Unger, H. G. Teachers and educators   920
Fiction
Marshall, C. Christy   Fic
Spark, M. The prime of Miss Jean Brodie
Fic

Teachers and educators. Unger, H. G.   920

The **teacher's** Mass. O'Connor, F.
In O'Connor, F. Collected stories p612-20
S C

Teaching
Kidder, T. Among schoolchildren   372.1

Teaching, Freedom of *See* Academic freedom

Teaching young adult literature. Brown, J. E.
809

Teamwork. Bledsoe, L. J.
In Growing up gay p240-43   808.8

Tears before the rain. Engelmann, L.
959.704

Tears of a tiger. Draper, S. M.   Fic

The **tears** of Ah Kim. London, J.
In London, J. Short stories of Jack London p620-32   S C

Technology
See also Engineering
Barnes-Svarney, P. The New York Public Library science desk reference   500
Freiman, F. L. Failed technology   620
How in the world?   600
Macaulay, D. The way things work   600
Mount, E. Milestones in science and technology
509
Science and technology desk reference   500
The Way science works   500
See/See also pages in the following book(s):
21st century earth: opposing viewpoints
303.49
Dictionaries
Ardley, N. Dictionary of science   503
Gibilisco, S. The concise illustrated dictionary of science and technology   503
Larousse dictionary of science and technology
503
McGraw-Hill concise encyclopedia of science & technology   503
McGraw-Hill encyclopedia of science & technology   503
The New book of popular science   503
Oxford illustrated encyclopedia of invention and technology   603
Van Nostrand's scientific encyclopedia   503
History
Bunch, B. H. The timetables of technology
609
Cardwell, D. S. L. The Norton history of technology
609
Inventors and discoverers   609
James, P. Ancient inventions   609
Karwatka, D. Technology's past   609
Williams, T. I. The history of invention
609
History—Dictionaries
Great scientific achievements   509

Technology and a technocrat. Steinbeck, J.
In Steinbeck, J. The portable Steinbeck
818

Technology and civilization
See also Computers and civilization
America beyond 2001: opposing viewpoints
303.49
Asimov, I. The march of the millennia
303.49
McLuhan, M. Understanding media   302.23
Toffler, A. Future shock   303.4
See/See also pages in the following book(s):
Postman, N. The end of education   370.9

Telepathy
Fiction
Vinge, J. D. Psion **Fic**
A **telephone** call on Yom Kippur. Singer, I. B.
In Singer, I. B. The image and other stories
p235-48 **S C**
Telephone man. Crutcher, C.
In Crutcher, C. Athletic shorts: six short sto-
ries p105-23 **S C**
Telereference *See* Information networks
Telescopes
See also Hubble Space Telescope
Florence, R. The perfect machine **522**
Design and construction
Miller, R. Making & enjoying telescopes
522
Television
Minow, N. N. Abandoned in the wasteland
302.23
Equipment and supplies
See also Video recording
Television actors *See* Actors
Television and children
Minow, N. N. Abandoned in the wasteland
302.23
Television in politics
See/See also pages in the following book(s):
White, T. H. America in search of itself
973.92
Television journalism *See* Broadcast journalism
Television programs
See also Talk shows
Day, N. Sensational TV **791.45**
Thompson, R. J. Television's second golden age
791.45
Television's second golden age. Thompson, R. J.
791.45
Telgen, Diane
(ed) Notable Hispanic American women. See
Notable Hispanic American women
920.003
Tell freedom [excerpt] Abrahams, P.
In Somehow tenderness survives p7-18
S C
Tell me how long the train's been gone. Baldwin,
J.
In Children of the night p324-51 **S C**
Tell my horse. Hurston, Z. N.
In Hurston, Z. N. Folktales, memoirs, and
other writings **818**
The **tell-tale** heart. Poe, E. A.
In The Norton book of American short stories
p47-51 **S C**
In The Oxford book of American short stories
p91-96 **S C**
In Poe, E. A. The collected tales and poems
of Edgar Allan Poe p303-06 **S C**
In Poe, E. A. Tales of Edgar Allan Poe p19-
25 **S C**
Teller, Edward, 1908-
See/See also pages in the following book(s):
Rhodes, R. Dark sun **623.4**

Teller's ticket. Flanagan, R.
In The Norton book of American short stories
p681-92 **S C**
Téllez, Hernando, 1908-1966
Just lather, that's all
In Bad behavior p281-88 **S C**
Temperance
See also Drinking of alcoholic beverages
Temple, Frances, 1945-1995
Taste of salt **Fic**
Temple, Ruth Zabriskie
(ed) Modern British literature. See Modern Brit-
ish literature **820.9**
A **temple** of the Holy Ghost. O'Connor, F.
In O'Connor, F. Collected works p197-209
S C
In O'Connor, F. The complete stories p236-48
S C
Temples, tombs, and hieroglyphs. Mertz, B.
932
The **temptation** of Harringay. Wells, H. G.
In Wells, H. G. The complete short stories of
H. G. Wells p239-44 **S C**
The **temptations** of Merlin. Tremayne, P.
In The Merlin chronicles **S C**
Ten Indians. Hemingway, E.
In Hemingway, E. The complete short stories
of Ernest Hemingway p253-57 **S C**
In Hemingway, E. The Nick Adams stories
p27-33 **S C**
In Hemingway, E. The short stories of Ernest
Hemingway p331-36 **S C**
Ten out of ten **812.008**
The **Ten** serpents
In Hearne, B. G. Beauties and beasts p120-23
398.2
Tenant farming *See* Farm tenancy
The **Tenas** Klootchman. Johnson, E. P.
In The Singing spirit: early short stories by
North American Indians p35-42 **S C**
Tender is the night. Fitzgerald, F. S. **Fic**
The **tender** shoot. Colette
In Colette. The collected stories of Colette
p421-48 **S C**
Tender street. TallMountain, M.
In Song of the turtle p130-35 **S C**
Tenenbaum, Barbara A., 1946-
(ed) Encyclopedia of Latin American history
and culture. See Encyclopedia of Latin
American history and culture **980**
Tenison, Robin Hanbury- *See* Hanbury-Tenison,
Robin
Tennent, Gilbert, 1703-1764
See/See also pages in the following book(s):
Hofstadter, R. America at 1750 **973.2**
Tennessee
Fiction
Agee, J. A death in the family **Fic**
Faulkner, W. The reivers **Fic**
Tennis
Douglas, P. The handbook of tennis
796.342
Douglas, P. Tennis **796.342**

Tewodros II, Negus of Ethiopia *See* Theodore II, Negus of Ethiopia, d. 1868

Tex. Hinton, S. E.   **Fic**

Texas

Fiction
Bonner, C. Lily   **Fic**

Textbooks

Bibliography
El-hi textbooks and serials in print   **016.3713**

Textile industry

History
Macaulay, D. Mill   **690**
See/See also pages in the following book(s):
Langdon, W. C. Everyday things in American life, 1776-1876 p240-73   **973**

Textile painting
Innes, M. Fabric painting   **746.6**

Texts. Le Guin, U. K.
In The Oxford book of American short stories p552-55   **S C**

Tey, Josephine, 1896-1952
The daughter of time   **Fic**
See/See also pages in the following book(s):
Modern mystery writers p188-201   **809.3**

Thacker, John
(jt. auth) Brodman, M. Straight talk about sexually transmitted diseases   **616.95**

Thackeray, William Makepeace, 1811-1863
Vanity fair   **Fic**

Thailand

Fiction
Boulle, P. The bridge over the River Kwai   **Fic**
Ho, M. Rice without rain   **Fic**

Thames River valley (England)

Description
See/See also pages in the following book(s):
Great rivers of the world p153-64   **910**

Thanhha, Lai
The walls, the house, the sky
In The Other side of heaven p258-65   **S C**

Thank you, m'am. Hughes, L.
In The Best short stories by Negro writers p70-73   **S C**
In Hughes, L. Short stories   **S C**
In Read all about it! p82-89   **808.88**

The Thanksgiving visitor. Capote, T.   **Fic**

That championship season. Miller, J.
In Best American plays: 8th series—1974-1982 p133-57   **812.008**

That evening sun. Faulkner, W.
In Faulkner, W. Collected stories of William Faulkner p289-309   **S C**
In Faulkner, W. Selected short stories of William Faulkner   **S C**
In The Oxford book of American short stories p334-51   **S C**

That Packsaddle affair. L'Amour, L.
In L'Amour, L. The outlaws of Mesquite p113-31   **S C**

That place. Herron, C.
In Children of the night p532-61   **S C**

That thou art mindful of him. Asimov, I.
In Asimov, I. The complete stories v2 p463-82   **S C**

That tree. Porter, K. A.
In Porter, K. A. The collected stories of Katherine Anne Porter   **S C**

That was living. González, K. A.
In Latina: women's voices from the borderlands p97-106   **810.8**

That will be fine. Faulkner, W.
In Faulkner, W. Collected stories of William Faulkner p265-88   **S C**

Thatcher, Margaret
The Downing Street years   **92**
The path to power   **92**

That's all folks!. Schneider, S.   **791.43**

That's not all folks. Blanc, M.   **92**

Theater
See also Acting; Musicals

Dictionaries
The Cambridge guide to world theatre   **792.03**
The Facts on File dictionary of the theatre   **792.03**
The Oxford companion to the theatre   **792.03**

History
Brockett, O. G. History of the theatre   **792.09**
The Oxford illustrated history of theatre   **792.09**

Production and direction
Poisson, C. L. Theater and the adolescent actor   **792**

Great Britain—History
Hodges, C. W. The Globe restored   **792.09**

Japan
See also Nō plays

United States
The Best plays of [date]: The Otis Guernsey/Burns Mantle theater yearbook   **808.82**
Bordman, G. M. American theatre: a chronicle of comedy and drama, 1930-1969   **792**
Hart, M. Act one: an autobiography   **92**
Theatre world   **792**

United States—Dictionaries
Bordman, G. M. The concise Oxford companion to American theatre   **792.03**
Bordman, G. M. The Oxford companion to American theatre   **792.03**
Cambridge guide to American theatre   **792.03**

United States—History
Henderson, M. C. Theater in America   **792.09**

Theater and the adolescent actor. Poisson, C. L.   **792**

Theater in America. Henderson, M. C.   **792.09**

Theaters

Stage setting and scenery
Gillette, J. M. Theatrical design and production   **792**

Theaters—Stage setting and scenery—*Continued*
James, T. The what, where, when of theater props **792**
Parker, W. O. Scene design and stage lighting **792**

The **theatre** of the absurd. Esslin, M. **809.2**

Theatre world **792**

Theatrical costume *See* Costume

Theatrical design and production. Gillette, J. M. **792**

Theatrical makeup
Corson, R. Stage makeup **792**

Thebes (Egypt: Extinct city)
See/See also pages in the following book(s):
Mertz, B. Temples, tombs, and hieroglyphs **932**

Theft. Porter, K. A.
In The Norton book of American short stories p292-97 **S C**
In Porter, K. A. The collected stories of Katherine Anne Porter **S C**

The **theft** of the four of spades. Hoch, E. D.
In Masterpieces of mystery and suspense p466-79 **S C**

Their eyes were watching God. Hurston, Z. N. **Fic**
also in Hurston, Z. N. Novels and stories p173-333 **Fic**

Their eyes were watching God [excerpt] Hurston, Z. N.
In Hurston, Z. N. I love myself when I am laughing—and then again when I am looking mean and impressive p246-95 **818**

Their finest hour. Churchill, Sir W. **940.53**

Their finest hour: the Battle of Britain remembered. Kaplan, P. **940.54**

Theism
See also Atheism

Thelwell, Michael, 1939-
Direct action
In The Best short stories by Negro writers p470-78 **S C**

Theodore II, Negus of Ethiopia, d. 1868
See/See also pages in the following book(s):
Moorehead, A. The Blue Nile **962**

Theodore, Alan
The origins & sources of drugs **615**

Theodore Roosevelt and his America. Meltzer, M. **92**

Theodosia. Mandelstam, O.
In The Portable twentieth-century Russian reader p171-83 **891.7**

Theology
See also Doctrinal theology
Great thinkers of the Western world **190**

Theology, Doctrinal *See* Doctrinal theology

Therapeutics
See also Gene therapy

Therapy, Gene *See* Gene therapy

There are no children here. Kotlowitz, A. **305.23**

There are no snakes in Ireland. Forsyth, F.
In Masterpieces of mystery and suspense p317-38 **S C**

There are smiles. Lardner, R.
In Lardner, R. The best short stories of Ring Lardner p227-37 **S C**

There is a lone house. O'Connor, F.
In O'Connor, F. Collected stories p654-72 **S C**

There is confusion [excerpt] Fauset, J. R.
In The Portable Harlem Renaissance reader p340-48 **810.8**

There was a man, there was a woman. Cisneros, S.
In Cisneros, S. Woman Hollering Creek and other stories **S C**

There was a queen. Faulkner, W.
In Faulkner, W. Collected stories of William Faulkner p727-44 **S C**
In Faulkner, W. Selected short stories of William Faulkner **S C**

There was an old woman. Bradbury, R.
In Bradbury, R. The stories of Ray Bradbury p66-76 **S C**

There will come soft rains. Bradbury, R.
In Bradbury, R. The stories of Ray Bradbury p76-81 **S C**
In The Oxford book of American short stories p456-62 **S C**

There's a country in my cellar. Baker, R. **818**

There's no reason to get romantic. Slater, A. T.
In American dragons: twenty-five Asian American voices p185-99 **810.8**

There's no such thing. De Lint, C.
In Vampires: a collection of original stories p8-18 **S C**

Thernstrom, Stephan
(ed) Harvard encyclopedia of American ethnic groups. See Harvard encyclopedia of American ethnic groups **305.8**

Theroux, Paul
The Mosquito Coast **Fic**

Theroux, Peter
Sandstorms: days and nights in Arabia **953**

The **thesaurus** of slang. Lewin, E. **427**

These are my rivers. Ferlinghetti, L. **811**

Theseus (Greek mythology)
See/See also pages in the following book(s):
Hamilton, E. Mythology p209-23 **292**
Fiction
Renault, M. The king must die **Fic**

They all laughed. Flatow, I. **609**

They also served. Gruhzit-Hoyt, O. **940.54**

They cage the animals at night. Burch, J. M. **92**

They had a dream. Archer, J. **920**

They that sit in darkness. Burrill, M. P.
In Black theatre USA **812.008**

They're made out of meat. Bisson, T.
In Nebula awards 27 p145-48 **S C**

They're playing our song. Simon, N.
  In Simon, N. The collected plays of Neil Simon v3 p115-215   **812**
Thibault, Jacques Anatole *See* France, Anatole, 1844-1924
The **thief.** Mosley, W.
  In Prize stories, 1996 p270-84   **S C**
Thieves
  Bryan, H. Robbers, rogues, and ruffians
                                          978.9
  The Gunfighters   **364.3**
A **thing** of beauty. Spinrad, N.
  In The Oxford book of science fiction stories p420-34   **S C**
Things. Lawrence, D. H.
  In Lawrence, D. H. The complete short stories v3   **S C**
Things fall apart. Achebe, C.   **Fic**
Things left undone. Tilghman, C.
  In The Best American short stories, 1994 p293-315   **S C**
The **things** they carried. O'Brien, T. **S C**
The **things** they carried [story] O'Brien, T.
  In The Best American short stories of the eighties p271-89   **S C**
  In O'Brien, T. The things they carried
                                          S C
  In The Oxford book of American short stories p636-54   **S C**
  In The Vintage book of contemporary American short stories p366-84   **S C**
Think like a dinosaur. Kelly, J. P.
  In Nebula awards 31 p93-113   **S C**
The **thinker.** Anderson, S.
  In Anderson, S. Winesburg, Ohio   **S C**
Thinking *See* Thought and thinking
Thinking. Arendt, H.
  In Arendt, H. The life of the mind   **153**
Thiong'o, Ngũgĩ wa *See* Ngũgĩ wa Thiong'o, 1938-
Third Barnhart dictionary of new English
                                          423
Third class. Sholem Aleichem
  In Sholem Aleichem. Tevye the dairyman and The railroad stories   **S C**
The **third** man. Greene, G.
  In Greene, G. The portable Graham Greene p306-81   **828**
Third Street. Colman, R.
  In Ten out of ten p33-47   **812.008**
The **third** voice. Ferguson, W.
  In The Literary ghost p125-26   **S C**
Third World *See* Developing countries
The **Third** World: opposing viewpoints **330.9**
Thirst. O'Neill, E.
  In O'Neill, E. Complete plays v1   **812**
Thirteen days/ninety miles. Finkelstein, N. H.
                                          973.922
Thirty famous one-act plays   **808.82**
The **thirty-nine** steps. Buchan, J.   **Fic**
This boy's life [excerpt] Wolff, T.
  In Coming of age in America p197-211
                                          S C

  In Who do you think you are? p83-91
                                          S C
This boy's life: a memoir. Wolff, T.   **92**
This fabulous century   **973.9**
This hallowed ground. Catton, B.   **973.7**
This house on fire. Awmiller, C.   **781.643**
This is Lagos. Nwapa, F.
  In Daughters of Africa p400-06   **808.8**
This is the sound. Reisfeld, R.   **781.66**
This is what it means to say Phoenix, Arizona. Alexie, S.
  In The Best American short stories, 1994 p1-11   **S C**
This land is our land. Helbig, A.   **016.8**
This land is your land. Naar, J.   **333.7**
This little light of mine: the life of Fannie Lou Hamer. Mills, K.   **92**
This morning, this evening, so soon. Baldwin, J.
  In The Best short stories by Negro writers p213-52   **S C**
This same sky   **808.81**
Thomas, Aquinas, Saint, 1225?-1274
  See/See also pages in the following book(s):
  Falcone, V. J. Great thinkers, great ideas
                                          100
  Russell, B. A history of Western philosophy p452-63   **109**
Thomas, Augustus, 1857-1934
  The witching hour
  In Best plays of the early American theatre p511-56   **812.008**
Thomas, Bob, 1922-
  Disney's art of animation   **741.5**
Thomas, Clarence
  See/See also pages in the following book(s):
  Landau, E. Sexual harassment p12-25
                                          305.4
Thomas, David A. (David Allen), 1946-
  Math projects in the computer age   **510**
Thomas, David Hurst
  The Native Americans. See The Native Americans   **970.004**
Thomas, Dylan, 1914-1953
  A child's Christmas in Wales   **828**
  The collected poems of Dylan Thomas   **821**
  The poems of Dylan Thomas   **821**
  Under milk wood   **822**
Thomas, Elizabeth Marshall, 1931-
  The hidden life of dogs   **636.7**
  The tribe of tiger   **599.74**
Thomas, Emory M., 1939-
  Robert E. Lee   **92**
Thomas, Joyce Carol
  Young Reverend Zelma Lee Moses
  In Children of the night p304-23   **S C**
Thomas, Lewis, 1913-1993
  The lives of a cell   **574**
Thomas, Peggy
  Talking bones   **614**
Thomas, Robert Joseph *See* Thomas, Bob, 1922-
Thomas, Sam
  (ed) Best American screenplays. See Best American screenplays   **812.008**

The **three** big bangs. Dauber, P. M.   **523.1**

Three contributions to the theory of sex. Freud, S.
In Freud, S. The basic writings of Sigmund
Freud   **150.19**

The **Three** daughters of King O'Hara
In Hearne, B. G. Beauties and beasts p84-91
398.2

The **three-day** blow. Hemingway, E.
In Hemingway, E. The complete short stories
of Ernest Hemingway p85-93   **S C**
In Hemingway, E. In our time p39-49
S C
In Hemingway, E. The Nick Adams stories
p205-16   **S C**
In Hemingway, E. The short stories of Ernest
Hemingway p113-25   **S C**

Three faces of Vietnam. Wormser, R.
959.704

The **three** fat women of Antibes. Maugham, W. S.
In Maugham, W. S. Collected short stories v1
S C

The **three** golden apples. Hawthorne, N.
In Hawthorne, N. Tales and sketches; A wonder book for girls and boys; Tanglewood
tales for girls and boys p1236-53
S C

Three hours between planes. Fitzgerald, F. S.
In Fitzgerald, F. S. The stories of F. Scott
Fitzgerald p464-69   **S C**

Three hundred thirty-three more science tricks &
experiments. See Brown, R. J. 333 more science tricks & experiments   **507**

Three hundred thirty-three science tricks & experiments. See Brown, R. J. 333 science tricks &
experiments   **507**

The **three** linden trees. Hesse, H.
In Hesse, H. The fairy tales of Hermann
Hesse   **S C**

The **three** men. Snyder, Z. K.
In Where coyotes howl and wind blows free
p20-29   **810.8**

Three men on a horse. Abbott, G.
In Twenty best plays of the modern American
theatre p511-59   **812.008**

Three Mondays in July. Giblin, J.
In Am I blue? p105-24   **S C**

The **three** musketeers. Dumas, A.   **Fic**

Three o'clock. Wolfe, T.
In Wolfe, T. The complete short stories of
Thomas Wolfe p447-50   **S C**

Three plays: Our town, The skin of our teeth, The
matchmaker. Wilder, T.   **812**

Three shots. Hemingway, E.
In Hemingway, E. The Nick Adams stories
p13-15   **S C**

The **three** sisters. Chekhov, A. P.
In Chekhov, A. P. Anton Chekhov's plays—
backgrounds, criticism   **891.7**

Three stories: I. Cheever, J.
In Cheever, J. The stories of John Cheever
p672-75   **S C**

Three stories: II. Cheever, J.
In Cheever, J. The stories of John Cheever
p675-78   **S C**

Three stories: III. Cheever, J.
In Cheever, J. The stories of John Cheever
p678-80   **S C**

The **three** strangers. Hardy, T.
In The Best crime stories of the 19th century
p72-95   **S C**

Three Sundays in a week. Poe, E. A.
In Poe, E. A. The collected tales and poems
of Edgar Allan Poe p730-35   **S C**

Three swimmers and the grocer from Yale. Saroyan, W.
In Saroyan, W. My name is Aram   **S C**

Three tall women. Albee, E.   **812**

The **threefold** destiny. Hawthorne, N.
In Hawthorne, N. Tales and sketches; A wonder book for girls and boys; Tanglewood
tales for girls and boys p598-606
S C

Thrift. Faulkner, W.
In Faulkner, W. Uncollected stories of William Faulkner p382-98   **S C**

Thro, Ellen
Genetic engineering   **660**
Robotics   **629.8**
Volcanoes of the United States   **551.2**

Through a window. Goodall, J.   **599.88**

Through a window. Wells, H. G.
In Wells, H. G. The complete short stories of
H. G. Wells p230-38   **S C**

Through anger and love. Mori, T.
In Growing up Asian American p53-64
810.8

Through Indian eyes   **970.004**

Through the telescope. Porcellino, M. R.   **522**

Thrown-away child. Adcock, T.
In Bad behavior p1-20   **S C**

Thucydides
See/See also pages in the following book(s):
Ancient Greek literature p88-104   **880.9**
Hamilton, E. The Greek way p183-203
880.9

The **thumbmark** of St. Peter. Christie, A.
In Christie, A. Miss Marple: the complete
short stories   **S C**

Thurber, James, 1894-1961
The 13 clocks
In Thurber, J. Writings and drawings
818
The last flower
In Thurber, J. Writings and drawings
818
The male animal
In Best plays of the modern American the-
atre: 2nd series p267-316   **812.008**
My life and hard times
In Thurber, J. Writings and drawings
818
The seal in the bedroom
In Thurber, J. Writings and drawings
818
The Thurber carnival   **817**
The unicorn in the garden
In The Norton book of American short stories
p323-24   **S C**

Thurber, James, 1894-1961—*Continued*
In The Oxford book of modern fairy tales
p300-01   **S C**
Writings and drawings   **818**
About
Morsberger, R. E. James Thurber   **817**
The **Thurber** carnival. Thurber, J.   **817**

Thurman, Wallace, 1902-1934
The blacker the berry . . . [excerpt]
In The Portable Harlem Renaissance reader
p636-49   **810.8**
Cordelia the crude
In The Portable Harlem Renaissance reader
p629-33   **810.8**
Infants of the spring [excerpt]
In The Portable Harlem Renaissance reader
p649-53   **810.8**
See/See also pages in the following book(s):
Black American prose writers of the Harlem Renaissance p123-33   **810.9**

Thurnley Abbey. Landon, P.
In Victorian ghost stories p466-79   **S C**

Thurow, Lester C.
(jt. auth) Heilbroner, R. L. Economics explained
330

The **Thursday** events. Ye Yonglie
In Tales from the planet Earth   **S C**

Thurston, Herbert
(ed) Butler, A. Butler's lives of the saints
920.003

Thus spoke Zarathustra. Nietzsche, F. W.
In Nietzsche, F. W. The portable Nietzsche
193

Thutmose III, King of Egypt, ca. 1504-1450 B.C.
See/See also pages in the following book(s):
Mertz, B. Temples, tombs, and hieroglyphs
932

Thy kingdom come. Bova, B.
In Bova, B. Challenges p217-70   **S C**

Thybony, Scott
The Rockies: pillars of a continent   **978**

Thyroid gland
See/See also pages in the following book(s):
Roueché, B. The medical detectives p375-89
616

Tia Maria. Paredez, D.
In Daughters of the fifth sun   **810.8**

Tiananmen diary. Salisbury, H. E.   **951.05**

Tiananmen Square. Simmie, S.   **951.05**

Tiananmen Square Incident, China, 1989 *See*
China—History—1989, Tiananmen Square Incident

Tibet (China)
Dalai Lama XIV. Freedom in exile   **92**
Fiction
Hilton, J. Lost horizon   **Fic**

Tiburzi, Bonnie, 1948-
See/See also pages in the following book(s):
Yount, L. Women aviators   **920**

Tickets, please. Lawrence, D. H.
In Lawrence, D. H. The complete short stories v2   **S C**

Ticks
See also Lyme disease

A **Tidewater** morning. Styron, W.   **S C**
A **Tidewater** morning [story] Styron, W.
In Styron, W. A Tidewater morning p79-142
S C

Tien-an men Massacre, 1989 *See* China—History—1989, Tiananmen Square Incident

Tigers
Thomas, E. M. The tribe of tiger   **599.74**
The **tiger's** child. Hayden, T. L.   **155.5**

Til death us do part. Hagenston, B.
In Prize stories, 1996 p202-18   **S C**

Tilghman, Christopher
Things left undone
In The Best American short stories, 1994
p293-315   **S C**

Till, Emmett
See/See also pages in the following book(s):
Abdul-Jabbar, K. Black profiles in courage
p199-206   **920**

Time
Gardner, R. Experimenting with time   **529**
Price, H. Time's arrow & Archimedes' point
523.1
Dictionaries
Encyclopedia of time   **529**

Time. Téffi, N. A.
In The Portable twentieth-century Russian reader p67-73   **891.7**

Time and chance: Gerald Ford's appointment with history. Cannon, J. M.   **92**

Time and space *See* Space and time

The **time** before history. Tudge, C.   **573.2**

Time detectives. Fagan, B. M.   **930.1**

Time everlasting. Lundwall, S. J.
In Tales from the planet Earth   **S C**

A **time** for dancing. Hurwin, D.   **Fic**

Time-Life Books
Africa's glorious legacy. See Africa's glorious legacy   **960**
The Age of god-kings: timeframe 3000-1500 BC. See The Age of god-kings: timeframe 3000-1500 BC   **930**
Algonquians of the East Coast. See Algonquians of the East Coast   **970.004**
Anatolia. See Anatolia   **939**
Ancient India. See Ancient India   **934**
Bailey, R. H. Battles for Atlanta: Sherman moves east   **973.7**
Bailey, R. H. The bloodiest day: the battle of Antietam   **973.7**
Bailey, R. H. Forward to Richmond: McClellan's peninsular campaign   **973.7**
Barbarian tides: timeframe 1500-600 BC. See Barbarian tides: timeframe 1500-600 BC
930
Birding. See Birding   **598**
The Blockade. See The Blockade   **973.7**
Blueprint for life. See Blueprint for life
573.2
The Buffalo hunters. See The Buffalo hunters
970.004

To Da-duh, in memoriam. Marshall, P.
  In Calling the wind p275-83   **S C**
  In Daughters of Africa p348-55   **808.8**
To destroy you is no loss. Criddle, J. D.
        959.6
To hell with dying. Walker, A.
  In The Best short stories by Negro writers
    p490-96   **S C**
To kill a mockingbird. Lee, H.   **Fic**
"To let". Croker, B. M.
  In Victorian ghost stories p346-59   **S C**
To market, to market. West, D.
  In West, D. The richer, the poorer: stories,
    sketches, and reminiscences   **S C**
To-morrow. Conrad, J.
  In Conrad, J. The complete short fiction of
    Joseph Conrad v1 p210-36   **S C**
To rise from earth. Lee, W.   **629.4**
To the far blue mountains. L'Amour, L. See note
  under L'Amour, L. The Sacketts   **Fic**
To the halls of the Montezumas. Johannsen, R. W.
        973.6
To the lighthouse. Woolf, V.   **Fic**
To the man on trail. London, J.
  In London, J. The portable Jack London p3-
    10   **818**
  In London, J. Short stories of Jack London
    p17-24   **S C**
To the reader. Sholem Aleichem
  In Sholem Aleichem. Tevye the dairyman and
    The railroad stories   **S C**
To touch a star. Bova, B.
  In Bova, B. Challenges p87-111   **S C**
Toads
  Mattison, C. Frogs & toads of the world
        597.8
Tobacco
  See also Tobacco industry
Tobacco habit
  Hilts, P. J. Smokescreen   **364.1**
  Kluger, R. Ashes to ashes   **338.1**
  Statistics on alcohol, drug & tobacco use
        362.29
  See/See also pages in the following book(s):
  Porterfield, K. M. Focus on addictions
        616.86
Tobacco industry
  Hilts, P. J. Smokescreen   **364.1**
  Kluger, R. Ashes to ashes   **338.1**
Tobacco Road. Kirkland, J.
  In The Most popular plays of the American
    theater p89-158   **812.008**
  In Twenty best plays of the modern American
    theatre p599-642   **812.008**
Tobermory. Saki
  In Masterpieces of fantasy and enchantment
    p368-74   **S C**
Tobias, Sheila
  Overcoming math anxiety   **510**
Tocqueville, Alexis de
  Democracy in America   **973.5**
  The old régime and the French Revolution
        944.04

Today is Friday. Hemingway, E.
  In Hemingway, E. The complete short stories
    of Ernest Hemingway p271-73   **S C**
  In Hemingway, E. The short stories of Ernest
    Hemingway p356-59   **S C**
Today's children. Sholem Aleichem
  In Sholem Aleichem. Tevye the dairyman and
    The railroad stories   **S C**
Today's isms. Ebenstein, A. D.   **335**
Todd, Janet M., 1942-
  (ed) British women writers. See British women
    writers   **820.8**
Toffler, Alvin
  Future shock   **303.4**
  Powershift   **303.4**
  War and anti-war   **355**
Toffler, Heidi
  (jt. auth) Toffler, A. War and anti-war   **355**
The toilet. Baraka, I. A.
  In Best American plays: 6th series—1963-
    1967 p325-34   **812.008**
The toilet. Mhlophe, G.
  In Somehow tenderness survives p77-86
        S C
Toklas, Alice B.
        About
  Stein, G. The autobiography of Alice B. Toklas
        92
Toland, John
  Adolf Hitler   **92**
Told in the drooling ward. London, J.
  In London, J. The portable Jack London
    p282-90   **818**
  In London, J. Short stories of Jack London
    p494-501   **S C**
Toleration
  Miller, M. Coping with a bigoted parent
        303.3
Tolkien, J. R. R. (John Ronald Reuel), 1892-
  1973
  The fellowship of the ring
    In Tolkien, J. R. R. The lord of the rings
        Fic
  The hobbit   **Fic**
  The lord of the rings   **Fic**
  Lord of the rings; criticism
    In Chance, J. The lord of the rings
        823.009
  Poems and stories   **828**
  Short stories included are: Leaf by Niggle; Farmer Giles of
  Ham; Smith of Wootton Major
  The return of the king
    In Tolkien, J. R. R. The lord of the rings
        Fic
  The Silmarillion   **S C**
  Contents: Ainulindale; Valaquenta; Quenta Silmarillion: Of the
  beginning of days; Quenta Silmarillion: Of Autë and Yavanna;
  Quenta Silmarillion: Of the coming of the elves and the captivity
  of Melkor; Quenta Silmarillion: Of Thingol and Melian; Quenta
  Silmarillion: Of Eldamar and the princes of the Eldalië; Quenta
  Silmarillion: Of Fëanor and the unchaining of Melkor; Quenta
  Silmarillion: Of the Silmarils and the unrest of the Noldor;
  Quenta Silmarillion: Of the darkening of Valinor; Quenta
  Silmarillion: Of the flight of the Noldor; Quenta Silmarillion: Of
  the Sindar; Quenta Silmarillion: Of the sun and moon and the
  hiding of Valinor; Quenta Silmarillion: Of men; Quenta

Tolkien, J. R. R. (John Ronald Reuel), 1892-1973—*Continued*

Silmarillion: Of the return of the Noldor; Quenta Silmarillion: Of Beleriand and its realms; Quenta Silmarillion: Of the Noldor in Beleriand; Quenta Silmarillion: Of Maeglin; Quenta Silmarillion: Of the coming of men into the West; Quenta Silmarillion: Of the ruin of Beleriand and the fall of Fingollin; Quenta Silmarillion: Of Beren and Lúthien; Quenta Silmarillion: Of the fifth battle: Niraeth Arnoediad; Quenta Silmarillion: Of Turin Turambar; Quenta Silmarillion: Of the ruin of Doriath; Quenta Silmarillion: Of Tuor and the fall of Gondolin; Quenta Silmarillion: Of the voyage of Eärendil and the war of wrath; Akallabeth; Of the Rings of Power and the Third Age

The two towers

   In Tolkien, J. R. R. The lord of the rings

                                 Fic

Unfinished tales of Númenor and Middle-earth

                                 S C

Contents: Of Tuor and his coming to Gondolin; The childhood of Túrin; The words of Húrin and Morgoth; The departure of Túrin; Túrin in Doriath; Túrin among the outlaws; Of Mim the dwarf; The return of Túrin to Dor-lómin; The coming of Túrin into Brethil; The journey of Morwen and Nienor to Nargothrond; Nienor in Brethil; The coming of Glaurung; The death of Glaurung; The death of Túrin; A description of the Island of Númenor; Aldarion and Erendis; The disaster of the Gladden Fields; The Northmen and the Wainriders; The ride of Eorl; Cirion and Eorl; The tradition of Isildur; The quest of Erebor; Of the journey of the Black Riders according to the account that Gandalf gave to Frodo; Concerning Gandalf, Saruman and the Shire; The battles of the Fords of Isen; The Drúedain; The Istari; The Palantiri

About

Crabbe, K. W. J.R.R. Tolkien   **823.009**

Fonstad, K. W. The atlas of Middle-earth

                                 823.009

Hammond, W. G. J.R.R. Tolkien, artist & illustrator   **92**

Rogers, D. W. J.R.R. Tolkien   **823.009**

Tolkien, John Ronald Reuel *See* Tolkien, J. R. R. (John Ronald Reuel), 1892-1973

The **toll-gatherer's** day. Hawthorne, N.

   In Hawthorne, N. Tales and sketches; A wonder book for girls and boys; Tanglewood tales for girls and boys p508-13

                                 S C

Tolstoy, Leo, graf, 1828-1910

Alyosha the Pot

   In The Portable twentieth-century Russian reader p3-9   **891.7**

Anna Karenina   **Fic**

The Cossacks [excerpt]

   In Tolstoy, L. The portable Tolstoy p358-434

                                 891.7

The death of Ivan Ilych

   In The Portable nineteenth-century Russian reader p440-89   **891.7**

God sees the truth, but waits

   In Tolstoy, L. The portable Tolstoy p475-83

                                 891.7

Great short works of Leo Tolstoy   **S C**

Contents: Family happiness; The Cossacks; The death of Ivan Ilych; The devil; The Kreutzer Sonata; Master and man; Father Sergius; Hadji Murád; Alyosha the Pot

How much land does a man need?

   In Tolstoy, L. The portable Tolstoy p506-22

                                 891.7

The Kreutzer sonata

   In Tolstoy, L. The portable Tolstoy p523-601

                                 891.7

Master and man

   In The Portable nineteenth-century Russian reader p489-529   **891.7**

   In Tolstoy, L. The portable Tolstoy p602-52

                                 891.7

The portable Tolstoy   **891.7**

The power of darkness [play]

   In Tolstoy, L. The portable Tolstoy p747-825

                                 891.7

The raid

   In Tolstoy, L. The portable Tolstoy p169-99

                                 891.7

Sevastopol

   In Tolstoy, L. The portable Tolstoy p239-93

                                 891.7

Strider

   In Tolstoy, L. The portable Tolstoy p435-74

                                 891.7

Two Hussars

   In Tolstoy, L. The portable Tolstoy p294-357

                                 891.7

War and peace   **Fic**

What men live by

   In Tolstoy, L. The portable Tolstoy p484-505

                                 891.7

The wood-felling

   In Tolstoy, L. The portable Tolstoy p200-38

                                 891.7

About

Rowe, W. W. Leo Tolstoy   **891.7**

Toltecs

   See also Aztecs

Tom Edison's shaggy dog. Vonnegut, K.

   In Vonnegut, K. Welcome to the monkey house   **S C**

Tom Jones. See Fielding, H. The history of Tom Jones, a foundling   **Fic**

Tom Paine. Foster, P.

   In Best American plays: 7th series—1967-1973 p393-423   **812.008**

Tom Quartz. Twain, M.

   In Twain, M. The complete short stories of Mark Twain   **S C**

The **tomb** of Sarah. Loring, F. G.

   In Victorian ghost stories p431-41   **S C**

Tomblin, Barbara

G.I. nightingales   **940.54**

The **Tombling** day. Bradbury, R.

   In Bradbury, R. The stories of Ray Bradbury p679-84   **S C**

Tomorrow and tomorrow and tomorrow. Vonnegut, K.

   In Vonnegut, K. Welcome to the monkey house   **S C**

Tomorrow is another country. Sparks, A.

                                 968.06

Tomorrow the world. Gow, J. E.

   In Best plays of the modern American theatre: 2nd series p597-640   **812.008**

Tomorrow, when the war began. Marsden, J.

                                   Fic

Tomorrow's child. Bradbury, R.

   In Bradbury, R. The stories of Ray Bradbury p697-709   **S C**

Tom's husband. Jewett, S. O.
In The Oxford book of women's writing in
the United States p10-20   **810.8**

Tong Enzheng
The middle kingdom
In Tales from the planet Earth   **S C**

Toni Morrison: critical perspectives past and
present   **813.009**

Tony D. Lê, M. K.
In The Other side of heaven p210-22
S C

Tony, Grammy, Emmy, Country. See Franks, D.
Entertainment awards   **792**

The **Tony** Hillerman companion   **813.009**

Tony's story. Silko, L.
In Song of the turtle p31-37   **S C**

Tony's wife. Dunbar-Nelson, A. M.
In The Oxford book of women's writing in
the United States p21-26   **810.8**

Toomai of the Elephants. Kipling, R.
In Kipling, R. The portable Kipling   **828**

Toomer, Jean, 1894-1967
Balo
In Black theatre USA   **812.008**
Becky
In The Norton book of American short stories
p324-26   **S C**
Blood-burning moon
In The Oxford book of American short stories
p285-94   **S C**
Cane [excerpt]
In The Portable Harlem Renaissance reader
p318-32   **810.8**
Esther
In Calling the wind p25-29   **S C**
Fern
In The Best short stories by Negro writers
p30-34   **S C**
See/See also pages in the following book(s):
Black American prose writers of the Harlem Re-
naissance p134-46   **810.9**

The **tooth.** Jackson, S.
In Jackson, S. The lottery   **S C**

The **top** 10 of everything. Ash, R.   **031.02**

The **Top** 500 poems   **821.008**

Top of the game. McCluskey, J.
In Calling the wind p539-51   **S C**

Top of the News. See Journal of Youth Services
in Libraries   **027.6205**

Topeka (Kan.). Board of Education
Tushnet, M. V. Brown v. Board of Education
344

Topographical drawing
See/See also pages in the following book(s):
Boorstin, D. J. The Americans: The national ex-
perience p241-48   **973**

Torch song. Cheever, J.
In Cheever, J. The stories of John Cheever
p89-102   **S C**

Tories, American *See* American Loyalists

Torrence, Vivian F.
(jt. auth) Hoffmann, R. Chemistry imagined
540

Torsvan, Traven *See* Traven, B.

Tortillas and beans. Steinbeck, J.
In Steinbeck, J. The portable Steinbeck
818

Tortoises *See* Turtles

Tosamah's story. Momaday, N. S.
In The Lightning within p4-18   **S C**

Totalitarianism
See also Dictators
1984 revisited   **823.009**
Arendt, H. Origins of totalitarianism   **321.9**
Fromm, E. Escape from freedom   **323.44**
Huxley, A. Brave new world revisited
303.3
Fiction
Orwell, G. Animal farm   **Fic**
Orwell, G. Nineteen eighty-four   **Fic**
Psychological aspects
See/See also pages in the following book(s):
Bettelheim, B. Surviving, and other essays
p317-32   **155.9**
"A **totally** alien life-form". Lewis, S.   **305.23**

Totem and taboo. Freud, S.
In Freud, S. The basic writings of Sigmund
Freud   **150.19**

Totten, Herman L., 1938-
Culturally diverse library collections for youth
011.6

A **touch** of the poet. O'Neill, E.
In Best American plays: 5th series—1957-
1963 p1-53   **812.008**
In O'Neill, E. Complete plays v3   **812**

Touched by fire: the life, death, and mythic afterlife of George Armstrong Custer. Barnett, L.
K.   **92**

Touched with fire. Bradbury, R.
In Bradbury, R. The stories of Ray Bradbury
p346-55   **S C**

Touching. McMillan, T.
In Streetlights: illuminating tales of the urban
black experience p340-47   **S C**

Touk's house. McKinley, R.
In McKinley, R. A knot in the grain and other stories p73-105   **S C**

Toulouse-Lautrec, Henri de, 1864-1901
About
Lucie-Smith, E. Toulouse-Lautrec   **759.4**

A **tour** of the calculus. Berlinski, D.   **515**

Touring, Bicycle *See* Bicycle touring

Toussaint. Hansberry, L.
In 9 plays by black women   **811.008**

Toussaint. Lee, G.
In Growing up Asian American p87-108
810.8

Tower of Babel *See* Babel, Tower of

Tower of Babylon. Chiang, T.
In Nebula awards 26 p58-83   **S C**

Towers, Frances
The little willow
In Classic English short stories, 1930-1955
p42-57   **S C**

Towle, Tony, 1939-
(jt. auth) Mariotti, S. The young entrepreneur's
guide to starting and running a business
658.1

Town planning *See* City planning

Town smokes. Benedict, P.
  In The Oxford book of American short stories
    p750-64   **S C**

The **town** where no one got off. Bradbury, R.
  In Bradbury, R. The stories of Ray Bradbury
    p526-32   **S C**

Towne, Stuart *See* Rawson, Clayton, 1906-1971

Towns *See* Cities and towns

Townsend, Richard F.
  The Aztecs   **972**

Townson, Duncan
  The new Penguin dictionary of modern history,
  1789-1945   **903**

Townson, W. D. (William Duncan) *See* Townson, Duncan

Toxic plants *See* Poisonous plants

Toxic substances *See* Poisons and poisoning

A **toy** princess. De Morgan, M.
  In The Oxford book of modern fairy tales
    p109-19   **S C**

Toynbee, Arnold, 1852-1883
  A study of history [abridged]   **909**

Trachtenberg, Marvin
  Architecture, from prehistory to post-modernism   **720.9**

Trachtman, Paul
  The Gunfighters. See The Gunfighters   **364.3**

Track, Soge
  The clearing in the valley
  In Spider Woman's granddaughters   **S C**

Track athletics
  See also Running
      Fiction
  Voigt, C. The runner   **Fic**

Tracks across Alaska. Scott, A.   **979.8**

Trade, International *See* International trade

Trade unions *See* Labor unions

Trades *See* Occupations

The **tradesman**. Kafka, F.
  In Kafka, F. The complete stories   **S C**

The **tradesman's** return. Hemingway, E.
  In Hemingway, E. The complete short stories
    of Ernest Hemingway p410-19   **S C**

Traditional medicine
  Kusinitz, M. Folk medicine   **615.8**

Traditions *See* Manners and customs

Traffic accidents
  See also Drunk driving

Trafficking in drugs *See* Drug traffic

Trafzer, Clifford E.
  Cheyenne revenge [excerpt]
  In Talking leaves   **S C**

Tragedy
See/See also pages in the following book(s):
  Hamilton, E. The Greek way p227-38   **880.9**

Tragedy at the baths. Hughes, L.
  In Hughes, L. Short stories   **S C**

The **tragedy** of Birlstone. Doyle, Sir A. C.
  In Doyle, Sir A. C. The complete Sherlock
    Holmes   **S C**

Trager, James
  The food chronology   **641**

Trager, Oliver
  (ed) Sports in America. See Sports in America   **796**

The **tragic** muse. James, H.
  In James, H. Novels, 1886-1890   **Fic**

The **Trail** of Tears across Missouri. Gilbert, J.   **970.004**

Trailside (Television program)
  Merwin, J. Fly fishing   **799.1**

The **train**. O'Connor, F.
  In O'Connor, F. Collected works p753-62   **S C**
  In O'Connor, F. The complete stories p54-62   **S C**

Train. Williams, J.
  In The Vintage book of contemporary
    American short stories p537-52   **S C**

The **train** and the city. Wolfe, T.
  In Wolfe, T. The complete short stories of
    Thomas Wolfe p10-29   **S C**

Train go sorry. Cohen, L. H.   **371.9**

Train time. McNickle, D.
  In The Singing spirit: early short stories by
    North American Indians p162-66   **S C**

A **train** trip. Hemingway, E.
  In Hemingway, E. The complete short stories
    of Ernest Hemingway p557-70   **S C**

Training, Occupational *See* Occupational training

Training of children *See* Child rearing

Trains, Railroad *See* Railroads

The **traitor**. Maugham, W. S.
  In Maugham, W. S. Collected short stories v3   **S C**

Tramp: the life of Charlie Chaplin. Milton, J.   **92**

Tran, Vu
  The house behind the Temple of Literature
  In The Other side of heaven p85-94   **S C**

Transaction. James, K. C.
  In Children of the night p434-44   **S C**

Transcultural studies *See* Cross cultural studies

Transients in Arcadia. Henry, O.
  In Henry, O. The best short stories of O.
    Henry   **S C**

Transplantation of organs, tissues, etc.
  See also names of organs of the body with
  the subdivision Transplantation
  Kittredge, M. Organ transplants   **617.9**
See/See also pages in the following book(s):
  Clark, W. R. At war within p175-220   **616.07**

Transportation
  Wilson, A. Dorling Kindersley visual timeline of
  transportation   **629.04**

Transportation—*Continued*
See/See also pages in the following book(s):
Langdon, W. C. Everyday things in American
life, 1607-1776 p241-54   **973.2**

Transracial adoption. Pohl, C.   **362.7**

The **trap**. Singer, I. B.
In Singer, I. B. The death of Methuselah and
other stories p68-84   **S C**

Trapp, J. B. (Joseph Burney), 1925-
(ed) Medieval English literature. See Medieval
English literature   **820.8**

Trapp, Joseph Burney *See* Trapp, J. B. (Joseph
Burney), 1925-

Trapp family
Drama
Lindsay, H. The sound of music   **812**

Trapped. Koontz, D. R.
In Koontz, D. R. Strange highways p259-308
    S C

Travel tips from Aunt Augusta. Greene, G.
In Greene G. The portable Graham Greene
p441-45   **828**

The **traveler**. Bradbury, R.
In Bradbury, R. The stories of Ray Bradbury
p25-35   **S C**

The **traveler**. Connelly, M.
In 24 favorite one-act plays p219-28
    808.82

The **traveling** companion. Andersen, H. C.
In Andersen, H. C. Tales and stories
    S C

Travelogue. Lardner, R.
In Lardner, R. The best short stories of Ring
Lardner p261-72   **S C**

Travels *See* Voyages and travels

The **travels** of Marco Polo. Polo, M.   **915**

Travels with Charley. Steinbeck, J.   **973**

Traven, B.
The treasure of the Sierra Madre   **Fic**

Travers, Bridget
(ed) World of invention. See World of invention
    609

The **treasure**. Maugham, W. S.
In Maugham, W. S. Collected short stories v2
    S C

The **treasure** hunt. Steinbeck, J.
In Steinbeck, J. The portable Steinbeck
    818

The **treasure** in the forest. Wells, H. G.
In Wells, H. G. The complete short stories of
H. G. Wells p313-21   **S C**

Treasure Island. Stevenson, R. L.   **Fic**

Treasure mountain. L'Amour, L. See note under
L'Amour, L. The Sacketts   **Fic**

The **treasure** of Sierra Madre. Huston, J.
In Best American screenplays   **812.008**

The **treasure** of the Sierra Madre. Traven, B.
    Fic

A **Treasury** of African folklore   **398.2**

Treating acne. Walzer, R. A.   **616.5**

Treblinka (Poland: Concentration camp)
Steiner, J. F. Treblinka   **940.53**

A **tree**. A rock. A cloud. McCullers, C.
In McCullers, C. The ballad of the sad café:
the novels and stories of Carson McCullers   **S C**
In McCullers, C. Collected stories p125-33
    S C

A **tree** grows in Brooklyn. Smith, B.   **Fic**

The **Tree** is older than you are   **860.8**

Trees, Joe Two *See* Two Trees, Joe

Trees
North America
Familiar trees of North America: eastern region
    582.16
Familiar trees of North America: western region
    582.16
Jonas, G. The living earth book of North
American trees   **582.16**
United States
Collingwood, G. H. Knowing your trees
    582.16
Walker, L. C. Forests   **582.16**

Trefil, James S., 1938-
(jt. auth) Hazen, R. M. Science matters: achieving scientific literacy   **500**
(jt. auth) Hirsch, E. D. The dictionary of cultural literacy   **031**
(jt. auth) Morowitz, H. J. The facts of life
    612.6

Treganowan, Lucille
Lucille's car care   **629.28**

Tregear, Mary
Chinese art   **709.51**

Trelease, Jim
(ed) Read all about it! See Read all about it!
    808.8

Tremayne, Peter
The temptations of Merlin
In The Merlin chronicles   **S C**

Trevelyan, George Macaulay, 1876-1962
The English Revolution, 1688-1689   **942.06**

Trevor, William, 1928-
Death in Jerusalem
In The Oxford book of Irish short stories
p455-70   **S C**
Going home
In The Oxford book of short stories p520-38
    S C
(ed) The Oxford book of Irish short stories. See
The Oxford book of Irish short stories
    S C

The **trial**. Kafka, F.   **Fic**

A **trial**. Twain, M.
In Twain, M. The complete short stories of
Mark Twain   **S C**

Trial by combat. Jackson, S.
In Jackson, S. The lottery   **S C**

Trial marriage *See* Unmarried couples

Trials
Haskins, J. The Scottsboro Boys   **345**
Hill, F. A delusion of Satan   **133.4**
Wice, P. B. Miranda v. Arizona   **345**
History
Aymar, B. A pictorial history of the world's
greatest trials   **345**

Twenty million Yankees: the Northern home front. Jackson, D. D. **973.7**

Twenty-one good men and true. Francis, D.
In Masterpieces of mystery and suspense p194-206 **S C**

Twenty-six men and one girl. Gorky, M.
In The Portable nineteenth-century Russian reader p618-29 **891.7**

Twenty thousand leagues under the sea. Verne, J. **Fic**

Twenty years at Hull-House. Addams, J. **92**

Twice shy. Neff, D. T.
In Ten out of ten p115-52 **812.008**

Twilight. Hoang, K. P.
In The Other side of heaven p266-74 **S C**

Twilight of the dawn. Koontz, D. R.
In Koontz, D. R. Strange highways p400-29 **S C**

Twilight of the idols. Nietzsche, F. W.
In Nietzsche, F. W. The portable Nietzsche **193**

Twins
See also Brothers and sisters
Fiction
Paterson, K. Jacob have I loved **Fic**

Twitchett, Denis Crispin
(ed) The Cambridge encyclopedia of China. See The Cambridge encyclopedia of China **951**

Two anti-semites. Sholem Aleichem
In Sholem Aleichem. The best of Sholem Aleichem **S C**

Two blue birds. Lawrence, D. H.
In Lawrence, D. H. The complete short stories v2 **S C**

Two dollar wife. Faulkner, W.
In Faulkner, W. Uncollected stories of William Faulkner p412-23 **S C**

The **two** drovers. Scott, Sir W.
In The Oxford book of short stories p1-26 **S C**

Two for the seesaw. Gibson, W.
In Best American plays: 5th series—1957-1963 p341-78 **812.008**

Two gallants. Joyce, J.
In Joyce, J. Dubliners **S C**

Two Hussars. Tolstoy, L., graf
In Tolstoy, L. The portable Tolstoy p294-357 **891.7**

Two kinds. Tan, A.
In The Oxford book of American short stories p714-26 **S C**

Two little tales. Twain, M.
In Twain, M. The complete short stories of Mark Twain **S C**

Two nations. Hacker, A. **305.8**

Two plays. Brecht, B. **832**

Two roads to Sumter. Catton, W. B. **973.6**

Two sisters. Aidoo, A. A.
In Daughters of Africa p532-42 **808.8**

Two soldiers. Faulkner, W.
In Faulkner, W. Collected stories of William Faulkner p81-99 **S C**
In Faulkner, W. Selected short stories of William Faulkner **S C**

Two teenagers in twenty **305.23**

Two Thanksgiving Day gentlemen. Henry, O.
In Henry, O. The best short stories of O. Henry **S C**

Two thousand and one: a space odyssey. See Clarke, A. C. 2001: a space odyssey **Fic**

The **two** towers. Tolkien, J. R. R.
In Tolkien, J. R. R. The lord of the rings **Fic**

Two trains running. Wilson, A. **812**

Two Trees, Joe
About
Kazimiroff, T. L. The last Algonquin **92**

Two village women. Nguyen, Q. T.
In The Other side of heaven p65-72 **S C**

Two wrongs. Fitzgerald, F. S.
In Fitzgerald, F. S. The short stories of F. Scott Fitzgerald p513-30 **S C**
In Fitzgerald, F. S. The stories of F. Scott Fitzgerald p287-304 **S C**

Two years before the mast. Dana, R. H. **910.4**

Tyco model railroad manual. See Schleicher, R. H. The HO model railroading handbook **625.1**

Tyler, Anne, 1941-
Dinner at the Homesick Restaurant **Fic**
Holding things together
In We are the stories we tell **S C**
About
Evans, E. Anne Tyler **813.009**

Tyler, Royall, 1757-1826
The contrast
In Best plays of the early American theatre p1-37 **812.008**

The **typewriter.** West, D.
In The Portable Harlem Renaissance reader p501-09 **810.8**
In West, D. The richer, the poorer: stories, sketches, and reminiscences **S C**

Typhoid fever
Leavitt, J. W. Typhoid Mary **614.5**
See/See also pages in the following book(s):
Roueché, B. The medical detectives p26-38 **616**

Typhoid Mary, d. 1938
About
Leavitt, J. W. Typhoid Mary **614.5**

Typhoon. Conrad, J.
In Conrad, J. The complete short fiction of Joseph Conrad v3 **S C**
In Conrad, J. The portable Conrad **828**

Typhoons
See also Hurricanes

Typhus. Chekhov, A. P.
In Chekhov, A. P. The image of Chekhov p123-30 **S C**

Typography *See* Printing

Tyrannosaurus Rex. Bradbury, R.
  In Bradbury, R. The stories of Ray Bradbury
    p636-46   S C
Tyre, Nedra, 1921-
  A nice place to stay
    In Masterpieces of mystery and suspense
      p620-29   S C
Tz'u-hsi, Empress dowager of China, 1835-1908
                About
  Seagrave, S. Dragon lady   92

U

U.F.O.'s *See* Unidentified flying objects
U.S. Chess Federation's official rules of chess.
  United States Chess Federation   **794.1**
U.S. Government books. United States. Superinten-
  dent of Documents   **015.73**
The **U.S.** health care crisis. Sherrow, V.
                                          362.1
U.S. Holocaust Memorial Museum *See* United
  States Holocaust Memorial Museum
U.S. presidential candidates and the elections. Ha-
  vel, J. T.   **324.6**
U.S.S.R. *See* Soviet Union
U-2 Incident, 1960
  See/See also pages in the following book(s):
  Manchester, W. The glory and the dream p867-
    76   **973.9**
Udhari, Abdullah al- *See* Al-Udhari, Abdullah
UFO. Ritchie, D.   **001.9**
UFOs *See* Unidentified flying objects
The **ugliest** house in the world. Davies, P. H.
  In The Best American short stories, 1995
    p94-109   S C
Ugly. Luczak, R.
  In Not the only one p150-58   S C
The **ugly** duckling. Andersen, H. C.
  In Andersen, H. C. Tales and stories
                                             S C
The **ugly** duckling. Milne, A. A.
  In 24 favorite one-act plays p347-66
                                         808.82
The **ugly** duckling. O'Connor, F.
  In O'Connor, F. Collected stories p444-58
                                             S C
The **ugly** little boy. Asimov, I.
  In Asimov, I. The complete stories v1 p301-
    33   S C
Uhry, Alfred
  Driving Miss Daisy
    In Best American plays: 9th series—1983-
      1992 p507-26   **812.008**
Ujifusa, Grant
  (jt. auth) Barone, M. The almanac of American
    politics   **328.73**
Ulam, Stanislaw M.
  See/See also pages in the following book(s):
  Henderson, H. Modern mathematicians   **920**
The **ultimate** cat book. Taylor, D.   **636.8**
The **ultimate** classic car book. Willson, Q.
                                         629.222

The **ultimate** college survival guide. Worthington,
  J. F.   **378**
The **ultimate** dog book. Taylor, D.   **636.7**
Ultimate golf techniques. Campbell, M.
                                         796.352
The **ultimate** guitar book. Bacon, T.   **787.87**
The **ultimate** motorcycle book. Wilson, H.
                                         629.227
The **ultimate** safari. Gordimer, N.
  In Gordimer, N. Crimes of conscience p110-
    21   S C
The **ultimate** spy book. Melton, H. K.
                                         327.12
UN *See* United Nations
Un-American Activities Committee *See* United
  States. Congress. House. Committee on Un-
  American Activities
Unapproved route. O'Connor, F.
  · *In* O'Connor, F. Collected stories p412-22
                                             S C
Unbegaun, B. O.
  (ed) The Oxford Russian dictionary. See The
    Oxford Russian dictionary   **491.7**
Unbuilding. Macaulay, D.   **690**
Uncle Cornelius his story. MacDonald, G.
  In Victorian ghost stories p130-49   S C
Uncle David's nonsensical story about giants and
  fairies. Sinclair, C.
  In The Oxford book of modern fairy tales
    p1-9   S C
Uncle Einar. Bradbury, R.
  In Bradbury, R. The stories of Ray Bradbury
    p19-25   S C
  In Masterpieces of fantasy and enchantment
    p310-17   S C
Uncle Monday. Hurston, Z. N.
  In Hurston, Z. N. The complete stories p106-
    16   S C
Uncle Otto's truck. King, S.
  In King, S. Skeleton crew   S C
Uncle Teo's shorthand cookbook. Engle, M.
  In Daughters of the fifth sun   **810.8**
Uncle Tom's cabin. Aiken, G.
  In Best plays of the early American theatre
    p136-84   **812.008**
Uncle Tom's cabin. Stowe, H. B.   **Fic**
Uncle Tom's children. Wright, R.   S C
  also in Wright, R. Works v1   **818**
Uncle Tony's goat. Silko, L.
  In Growing up Native American p299-305
                                         810.8
Uncle Vanya. Chekhov, A. P.
  In Chekhov, A. P. Anton Chekhov's plays—
    backgrounds, criticism   **891.7**
  In The Portable nineteenth-century Russian
    reader p549-607   **891.7**
Uncle Wiggily in Connecticut. Salinger, J. D.
  In Salinger, J. D. Nine stories p27-56
                                             S C
Uncle Willy. Faulkner, W.
  In Faulkner, W. Collected stories of William
    Faulkner p225-47   S C

Uncollected stories of William Faulkner. Faulkner, W.   **S C**

Uncommon women and others. Wasserstein, W.
In Wasserstein, W. The Heidi chronicles and other plays   **812**

Unconditional surrender. Marrin, A.   **973.7**

The **unconquered**. Maugham, W. S.
In Maugham, W. S. Collected short stories v1   **S C**

Undaunted courage. Ambrose, S. E.   **978**

The **undefeated**. Hemingway, E.
In Hemingway, E. The complete short stories of Ernest Hemingway p183-205   **S C**

In Hemingway, E. The short stories of Ernest Hemingway p233-66   **S C**

Under milk wood. Thomas, D.   **822**

Under the bombs. Beck, E. R.   **940.54**

Under the knife. Wells, H. G.
In Wells, H. G. The complete short stories of H. G. Wells p403-17   **S C**

Under the moon. Yeats, W. B.   **821**

Under the ridge. Hemingway, E.
In Hemingway, E. The complete short stories of Ernest Hemingway p460-69   **S C**

Undercover. Wright, E.
In Bad behavior p299-306   **S C**

Underdeveloped areas *See* Developing countries

Undergraduates *See* College students

Underground. Macaulay, D.   **624**

Underprivileged children *See* Socially handicapped children

Understanding birth defects. Gravelle, K.   **618.92**

Understanding comics. McCloud, S.   **741.5**

Understanding DNA and gene cloning. Drlica, K.   **574.87**

Understanding entropy. Malzberg, B. N.
In Nebula awards 30 p199-204   **S C**

Understanding Islam. Lippman, T. W.   **297**

Understanding media. McLuhan, M.   **302.23**

Understanding multiple sclerosis. See Shuman, R. Living with multiple sclerosis   **616.8**

Understanding poetry   **821.008**

Understanding Shakespeare's England. McMurtry, J.   **942.05**

Understanding stress. Feldman, R. S.   **155.9**

Understanding The scarlet letter. Johnson, C. D.   **813.009**

Undertow. Cornell, J. C.
In The Best American short stories, 1995 p210-30   **S C**

Undertow. Spence, E.
In Black theatre USA   **812.008**

Underwater exploration
Ballard, R. D. The discovery of the Titanic   **910.4**

Macaulay, D. Ship   **387.2**

Underwater photography
Frink, S. Wonders of the reef   **778.7**

Underwood, John, 1934-
(jt. auth) Williams, T. The science of hitting   **796.357**

Undocumented aliens *See* Illegal aliens

Undset, Sigrid, 1882-1949
The bridal wreath
In Undset, S. Kristin Lavransdatter v1   **Fic**

The cross
In Undset, S. Kristin Lavransdatter v3   **Fic**

Kristin Lavransdatter   **Fic**
The mistress of Husaby
In Undset, S. Kristin Lavransdatter v2   **Fic**

Unemployed
Fiction
Grant, C. D. Mary Wolf   **Fic**

Unexpected joy. Okudzhava, B. S.
In Border crossings: emigration and exile p1-15   **808.8**

An **unfinished** battle. Sigerman, H.
In The Young Oxford history of women in the United States   **305.4**

An **unfinished** story. Henry, O.
In Henry, O. The best short stories of O. Henry   **S C**

Unfinished tales of Númenor and Middle-earth. Tolkien, J. R. R.   **S C**

An **unfinished** woman. Hellman, L.
In Hellman, L. Three   **92**

Unfinished women cry in no man's land while a bird dies in a gilded cage. Rahman, A.
In 9 plays by black women   **811.008**

Unforgettable: the life and mystique of Nat King Cole. Gourse, L.   **92**

Ungar, Sanford J.
Fresh blood   **305.8**

Unger, Harlow G., 1931-
But what if I don't want to go to college?   **331.7**

Encyclopedia of American education   **370.9**
Teachers and educators   **920**

Unger, Leonard
(ed) American writers. See American writers   **920.003**

Unhappiness. Kafka, F.
In Kafka, F. The complete stories   **S C**
In Kafka, F. The metamorphosis and other stories p50-55   **S C**

The **unicorn** in the garden. Thurber, J.
In The Norton book of American short stories p323-24   **S C**
In The Oxford book of modern fairy tales p300-01   **S C**

Unicorns
See/See also pages in the following book(s):
Nigg, J. Wonder beasts   **398**
Fiction
Beagle, P. S. The last unicorn   **Fic**

Unidentified flying objects
Bryan, C. D. B. Close encounters of the fourth kind   **001.9**
Ritchie, D. UFO   **001.9**

The **victim**. James, P. D.
In Masterpieces of mystery and suspense p207-21 **S C**

The **victim**. Sinclair, M.
In The Oxford book of English ghost stories p289-306 **S C**

Victims of atomic bombings *See* Atomic bomb victims

Victims of crime
See also Abused women

Victoria, Queen of Great Britain, 1819-1901
About
Strachey, L. Queen Victoria **92**
See/See also pages in the following book(s):
Opfell, O. S. Queens, empresses, grand duchesses, and regents p201-08 **920**

Victoria Chapman & Associates
Health on file. See Health on file **613**

Victorian America. Schlereth, T. J. **973.8**

Victorian America, 1876 to 1913. Shifflett, C. A. **973.8**

Victorian ghost stories **S C**

Victorian prose and poetry
In The Oxford anthology of English literature v2 **820.8**

Victory. Faulkner, W.
In Faulkner, W. Collected stories of William Faulkner p431-64 **S C**

Victory at sea. Dunnigan, J. F. **940.54**

Victory over Japan. Gilchrist, E.
In The Norton book of American short stories p626-34 **S C**

Vidal, Gore, 1925-
The best man
In Best American plays: 5th series—1957-1963 p635-74 **812.008**
Lincoln **Fic**

Video. Lewis, R. **778.59**

Video cameras, Home *See* Camcorders

Video cassette recorders and recording *See* Video recording

Video recording
See also Camcorders
Handbooks, manuals, etc.
Lewis, R. Video **778.59**

Videorecorders *See* Video recording

Videos, Music *See* Music videos

Videos for understanding diversity **016.3713**

Videotape recorders and recording *See* Video recording

Videotapes
Maltin, L. Leonard Maltin's movie and video guide **791.43**
Catalogs
Videos for understanding diversity **016.3713**

Vietnam
Description
Safer, M. Flashbacks: on returning to Vietnam **959.704**
Fiction
The Other side of heaven **S C**

Foreign relations—United States
Halberstam, D. The best and the brightest **973.922**
History
Karnow, S. Vietnam **959.704**
Politics and government
FitzGerald, F. Fire in the lake **959.704**
Summers, H. G. Historical atlas of the Vietnam War **959.704**

Vietnam Veterans Memorial (Washington, D.C.)
Palmer, L. Shrapnel in the heart **959.704**

Vietnam War, 1961-1975
America in Vietnam **959.704**
Berman, L. Lyndon Johnson's war **959.704**
Denenberg, B. Voices from Vietnam **959.704**
Encyclopedia of the Vietnam War **959.704**
Everything we had **959.704**
FitzGerald, F. Fire in the lake **959.704**
Hendrickson, P. The living and the dead **959.704**
Isserman, M. The Vietnam War **959.704**
Karnow, S. Vietnam **959.704**
Marrin, A. America and Vietnam **959.704**
Summers, H. G. Historical atlas of the Vietnam War **959.704**
Summers, H. G. Vietnam War almanac **959.704**
The Vietnam war: opposing viewpoints **959.704**
Wormser, R. Three faces of Vietnam **959.704**
See/See also pages in the following book(s):
Carroll, J. An American requiem **92**
A History of our time p297-349 **973.92**
Manchester, W. The glory and the dream p1045-57 **973.9**
Tuchman, B. W. The march of folly **909.08**
Tuchman, B. W. Practicing history p256-66 **907**
Aerial operations
Mason, R. Chickenhawk **959.704**
Draft resisters
See/See also pages in the following book(s):
Meltzer, M. Ain't gonna study war no more: the story of America's peace seekers p221-57 **322.4**
Fiction
Hillerman, T. Finding Moon **Fic**
Mason, B. A. In country **Fic**
Myers, W. D. Fallen angels **Fic**
O'Brien, T. The things they carried **S C**
The Other side of heaven **S C**
White, E. E. The road home **Fic**
Personal narratives
Baker, M. Nam **959.704**
Bloods: an oral history of the Vietnam War by black veterans **959.704**
Dear America: letters home from Vietnam **959.704**
Engelmann, L. Tears before the rain **959.704**
Hayslip, L. L. When heaven and earth changed places: a Vietnamese woman's journey from war to peace **92**

Violence—*Continued*
Bode, J. Hard time   364.3
Hyde, M. O. The violent mind   616.85
Kinnear, K. L. Violent children   305.23
Lang, S. S. Teen violence   364.3
Newton, D. E. Teen violence   364.3
Sherrow, V. Violence and the media   303.6
Violence against women   362.83
Violence in the media   303.6
Violence: opposing viewpoints   303.6
See/See also pages in the following book(s):
Bettelheim, B. Surviving, and other essays
p185-200   155.9
Dictionaries
DiCanio, M. The encyclopedia of violence
    303.6
Violence against women   362.83
Violence and the media. Sherrow, V.   303.6
Violence in the media   303.6
Violence: opposing viewpoints   303.6
The **violent** bear it away. O'Connor, F.
In O'Connor, F. Collected works p329-479
    S C
Violent children. Kinnear, K. L.   305.23
The **violent** mind. Hyde, M. O.   616.85
Viramontes, Helena Maria, 1954-
Miss Clairol
In Latina: women's voices from the border-
lands p120-25   810.8
In The Oxford book of women's writing in
the United States p154-58   810.8
The moths
In Growing up Chicana/o p117-24   810.8
In Growing up Latino p32-37   810.8
Viren, Lasse, 1949-
See/See also pages in the following book(s):
Sandrock, M. Running with the legends p171-
202   796.42
Virgil
Aeneid; criticism
In Gransden, K. W. Virgil, the Aeneid
    873
The Aeneid of Virgil   873
See/See also pages in the following book(s):
Hamilton, E. The Roman way   870.9
Virgil, the Aeneid. Gransden, K. W.   873
Virgin Violeta. Porter, K. A.
In Porter, K. A. The collected stories of Kath-
erine Anne Porter   S C
Virginia
Church history
See/See also pages in the following book(s):
Bridenbaugh, C. Jamestown, 1544-1699 p61-75
    975.5
History
See/See also pages in the following book(s):
Boorstin, D. J. The Americans: The colonial ex-
perience p97-143, 301-06   973.2
History—1861-1865, Civil War
Jaynes, G. The killing ground: Wilderness to
Cold Harbor   973.7
Natural history
See Natural history—Virginia
Virginia Woolf: a study of the short fiction. Bald-
win, D. R.   823.009

Virginia Woolf A-Z. Hussey, M.   823.009
The **Virginia** Woolf reader. Woolf, V.   828
Virginia's general: Robert E. Lee and the Civil
War. Marrin, A.   92
Virtual love. McHugh, M. F.
In Nebula awards 30 p99-110   S C
Virtual reality
Weiss, A. E. Virtual reality   006
Fiction
Bova, B. Death dream   Fic
The **Virtual** school library   027.8
Virtue. Maugham, W. S.
In Maugham, W. S. Collected short stories v2
    S C
A **virtuoso's** collection. Hawthorne, N.
In Hawthorne, N. Tales and sketches; A won-
der book for girls and boys; Tanglewood
tales for girls and boys p697-713
    S C
Virus hunting. Gallo, R. C.   616.97
The **virus** invaders. Nourse, A. E.   616
Viruses
See also Ebola virus
Henig, R. M. A dancing matrix   576
Nourse, A. E. The virus invaders   616
Radetsky, P. The invisible invaders   616
See/See also pages in the following book(s):
Biddle, W. A field guide to germs   616
Drlica, K. Understanding DNA and gene cloning
p225-47   574.87
Vision
Elkins, J. The object stares back   152.14
Hubel, D. Eye, brain, and vision   612.8
Vision disorders
Samz, J. Vision   617.7
A **vision** of judgment. Wells, H. G.
In Wells, H. G. The complete short stories of
H. G. Wells p109-14   S C
The **vision** of the fountain. Hawthorne, N.
In Hawthorne, N. Tales and sketches; A won-
der book for girls and boys; Tanglewood
tales for girls and boys p324-29
    S C
A **vision** of the world. Cheever, J.
In Cheever, J. The stories of John Cheever
p512-17   S C
Visions of war, dreams of peace   811.008
A **visit** from Reverend Tileston. Cook-Lynn, E.
In Talking leaves   S C
A **visit** of charity. Welty, E.
In The Oxford book of short stories p411-16
    S C
In Welty, E. The collected stories of Eudora
Welty p113-18   S C
A **visit** to a mine. Kafka, F.
In Kafka, F. The complete stories   S C
A **visit** to Avoyelles. Chopin, K.
In Chopin, K. The awakening and selected
stories p28-32   S C
A **visit** to the clerk of the weather. Hawthorne, N.
In Hawthorne, N. Tales and sketches; A won-
der book for girls and boys; Tanglewood
tales for girls and boys p390-94
    S C

Watercolor painting—*Continued*
Technique
Harrison, H. The encyclopedia of watercolor techniques **751.42**
Smith, R. C. The art of watercolor **751.42**
Wiegardt, E. Watercolor free & easy **751.42**

Watercolor still life. Lloyd, E. J.
In The DK art school series **751**

Waterford, Helen, 1909-
(jt. auth) Ayer, E. H. Parallel journeys **940.53**

Watergate. Emery, F. **973.924**

Watergate Affair, 1972-1974
Bernstein, C. All the President's men **973.924**
Emery, F. Watergate **973.924**
Woodward, B. The final days **973.924**
See/See also pages in the following book(s):
Cannon, J. M. Time and chance: Gerald Ford's appointment with history **92**
A History of our time p415-34 **973.92**

Waterlily [excerpt] Deloria, E. C.
In Growing up Native American p57-71 **810.8**

Waterloo, Battle of, 1815
Schom, A. One hundred days **944.05**

Waterman, Talbot H. (Talbot Howe), 1914-
Animal navigation **591.1**

Waters *See* Russell, William

Waters, Benny, 1902-
See/See also pages in the following book(s):
Deffaa, C. Voices of the Jazz Age p28-51 **920**

Waters, Muddy, 1915-1983
See/See also pages in the following book(s):
Davis, F. The history of the blues p192-99 **781.643**

Waters, Thomas *See* Russell, William

The watershed. Pilcher, R.
In Pilcher, R. Flowers in the rain & other stories **S C**

Watership Down. Adams, R. **Fic**

Waterways
See/See also pages in the following book(s):
Langdon, W. C. Everyday things in American life, 1776-1876 p90-114 **973**

The watery place. Asimov, I.
In Asimov, I. The complete stories v1 p73-76 **S C**

Wathen, Elisabeth
A different teacher
In Not the only one p88-107 **S C**

Watkin, David, 1941-
A history of Western architecture **720.9**

Watkins, Frances Ellen *See* Harper, Frances Ellen Watkins, 1825-1911

Watkins, Gloria Jean *See* Hooks, Bell

Watkins, Mel
(ed) Canada. *See* Canada **971**

Watson, Benjamin A.
Acts of God **551.6**

Watson, Burton, 1925-
(ed) From the country of eight islands. *See* From the country of eight islands **895.6**

Watson, James D., 1928-
See/See also pages in the following book(s):
Brynie, F. H. Genetics & human health p58-65 **616**
Curtis, R. H. Great lives: medicine p250-60 **920**

Watson, Noelle
(ed) Reference guide to short fiction. *See* Reference guide to short fiction **809.3**

Watt-Evans, Lawrence, 1954-
Richie
In Vampires: a collection of original stories p211-25 **S C**

Wattenberg, Martin P., 1956-
The decline of American political parties, 1952-1994 **324.2**

Watters, Thomas R.
Planets **523.4**

Watterson, Bill
The Calvin and Hobbes tenth anniversary book **741.5**

Watts book of music. *See* Spence, K. The young people's book of music **780**

The Watts teen health dictionary. Isler, C. **610.3**

Waugh, Charles G. (Charles Gordon), 1943-
(ed) The Best crime stories of the 19th century. *See* The Best crime stories of the 19th century **S C**
(ed) The Mammoth book of new world science fiction. *See* The Mammoth book of new world science fiction **S C**

Waugh, Evelyn, 1903-1966
Brideshead revisited **Fic**
The loved one **Fic**
On guard
In Classic English short stories, 1930-1955 p118-32 **S C**

Wax, Nina
Occupational health **616.9**

The way baseball works. Gutman, D. **796.357**

Way down deep in the jungle. Jones, T.
In The Best American short stories, 1995 p7-30 **S C**

The way it was. Freeman-Villalobos, T. M.
In Talking leaves **S C**

The way life works. Hoagland, M. B. **574**

A way of being. Rogers, C. R. **150.19**

The way of cross and dragon. Martin, G. R. R.
In The Oxford book of science fiction stories p454-71 **S C**

The way of the earth. Bierhorst, J. **970.004**

The Way of the warrior **970.004**

The way of the world. Congreve, W.
In The Oxford anthology of English literature v1 **820.8**

A way out. Frost, R.
In Frost, R. Collected poems, prose, & plays p565-75 **818**

Weber, R. David, 1941-
  (jt. auth) Schlachter, G. A. Directory of financial aids for minorities **378.3**
  (jt. auth) Schlachter, G. A. Financial aid for the disabled and their families **378.3**
  (jt. auth) Schlachter, G. A. High school senior's guide to merit and other no-need funding **378.3**

Webster, Daniel, 1782-1852
  See/See also pages in the following book(s):
  Kennedy, J. F. Profiles in courage p64-84 **920**

Webster's collegiate thesaurus. See Merriam-Webster's collegiate thesaurus **423**
Webster's dictionary of English usage. See Merriam-Webster's dictionary of English usage **428**
Webster's dictionary of synonyms. See Merriam-Webster's dictionary of synonyms **423**
Webster's geographical dictionary. See Webster's new geographical dictionary **910.3**
Webster's guide to abbreviations **421.03**
Webster's II new college dictionary **423**
Webster's medical desk dictionary. See Merriam-Webster's medical desk dictionary **610.3**
Webster's new biographical dictionary. See Merriam-Webster's biographical dictionary **920.003**
Webster's new geographical dictionary **910.3**
Webster's New World dictionary of computer terms **004**
Webster's New World dictionary of media and communications. Weiner, R. **302.23**
Webster's New World thesaurus. Laird, C. **423**
Webster's ninth new collegiate dictionary. See Merriam-Webster's collegiate dictionary **423**
Webster's secretarial handbook. See Merriam-Webster's secretarial handbook **651.3**
Webster's standard American style manual. See Merriam-Webster's standard American style manual **808**
Webster's third new international dictionary of the English language **423**
Webster's word histories. See Merriam-Webster's word histories **422.03**

The **wedding**. Chávez, D.
  In Daughters of the fifth sun **810.8**
The **wedding**. West, D. **Fic**
The **wedding**. Williams, J.
  In American short story masterpieces **S C**

Wedding band. Childress, A.
  In 9 plays by black women **811.008**
Wedding day. Bennett, G.
  In The Portable Harlem Renaissance reader p363-69 **810.8**
Wedding day. Hemingway, E.
  In Hemingway, E. The Nick Adams stories p231-32 **S C**
The **wedding** gig. King, S.
  In King, S. Skeleton crew **S C**

The **wedding-knell**. Hawthorne, N.
  In Hawthorne, N. Tales and sketches; A wonder book for girls and boys; Tanglewood tales for girls and boys p352-59 **S C**

Wedding preparations in the country. Kafka, F.
  In Kafka, F. The complete stories **S C**
The **wedding** reception. Greene, G.
  In Greene G. The portable Graham Greene p446-50 **828**
The **wedding** that came without its band. Sholem Aleichem
  In Sholem Aleichem. Tevye the dairyman and The railroad stories **S C**
Wee Willie Winkie. Kipling, R.
  In Kipling, R. The best fiction of Rudyard Kipling p554-61 **S C**
A **week** on the Concord and Merrimack rivers. Thoreau, H. D.
  In Thoreau, H. D. A week on the Concord and Merrimack rivers; Walden; The Maine woods; Cape Cod **818**
Weekend. Beattie, A.
  In American short story masterpieces **S C**
Weekend. Pilcher, R.
  In Pilcher, R. Flowers in the rain & other stories **S C**
Weeks, John
  The pyramids **726**
Weep for our pride. Plunkett, J.
  In The Oxford book of Irish short stories p425-36 **S C**
The **weeping** children. O'Connor, F.
  In O'Connor, F. Collected stories p525-37 **S C**
Weesner, Theodore
  The body politic
  In Coming of age in America p32-51 **S C**
Weetzie Bat. Block, F. L. **Fic**
Weglyn, Michi, 1926-
  Years of infamy **940.53**
Weidman, Jerome, 1913-
  My father sits in the dark
  In The Norton book of American short stories p460-64 **S C**
Weidt, Maryann N.
  Presenting Judy Blume **813.009**
Weierstrass, Karl, 1815-1897
  See/See also pages in the following book(s):
  Bell, E. T. Men of mathematics p406-32 **920**

Weight control See Reducing
Weight lifting
  See also Bodybuilding
  Baechle, T. R. Fitness weight training **613.7**
  Peterson, J. A. Strength training for women **613.7**
Weight Watchers healthy life-style cookbook **641.5**

Weights and measures
Dictionaries
Darton, M. The Macmillan dictionary of measurement **389**

Weihs, Jean Riddle
Facts about Canada, its provinces and territories **971**

(jt. auth) Intner, S. S. Standard cataloging for school and public libraries **025.3**

Weil, Andrew
From chocolate to morphine **616.86**

Wein, Elizabeth E., 1964-
New Year's Eve
In Not the only one p54-60 **S C**

Weinbaum, Stanley G., 1902-1935
A Martian odyssey
In The Oxford book of science fiction stories p70-94 **S C**

Weinberg, Jeshajahu, 1918-
The Holocaust Museum in Washington **940.53**

Weinberg, Robert A.
Racing to the beginning of the road **616.99**

Weiner, Andrew, 1949-
Distant signals
In The Norton book of science fiction p525-37 **S C**

Weiner, Eric
The interrogation
In Bad behavior p289-98 **S C**

Weiner, Jonathan
The beak of the finch **598**

Weiner, Mitchel, 1907-
(jt. auth) Brownstein, S. C. How to prepare for SAT I **378.1**

Weiner, Richard, 1927-
Webster's New World dictionary of media and communications **302.23**

Weinreich, Beatrice
(ed) Yiddish folktales. See Yiddish folktales **398.2**

Weintraub, Stanley, 1929-
A stillness heard round the world **940.4**

Weir, Alison
The children of Henry VIII **920**
The Wars of the Roses **942.04**

Weishampel, David B., 1952-
(jt. auth) Fastovsky, D. E. The evolution and extinction of the dinosaurs **567.9**

Weiss, Ann E., 1943-
Money games **796**
Virtual reality **006**

Weiss, Carl, 1905-1935
See/See also pages in the following book(s):
Williams, T. H. Huey Long p865-72 **92**

Wekesser, Carol, 1963-
(ed) Africa: opposing viewpoints. See Africa: opposing viewpoints **960**
(ed) Alcoholism. See Alcoholism **362.29**
(ed) American foreign policy: opposing viewpoints. See American foreign policy: opposing viewpoints **327.73**

(ed) America's children: opposing viewpoints. See America's children: opposing viewpoints **362.7**
(ed) The Breakup of the Soviet Union: opposing viewpoints. See The Breakup of the Soviet Union: opposing viewpoints **947.086**
(ed) Ethics. See Ethics **174**
(ed) Euthanasia: opposing viewpoints. See Euthanasia: opposing viewpoints **179**
(ed) Feminism: opposing viewpoints. See Feminism: opposing viewpoints **305.4**
(ed) Genetic engineering: opposing viewpoints. See Genetic engineering: opposing viewpoints **174**
(ed) Health care in America: opposing viewpoints. See Health care in America: opposing viewpoints **362.1**
(ed) Politics in America: opposing viewpoints. See Politics in America: opposing viewpoints **320.4**
(ed) Reproductive technologies. See Reproductive technologies **176**
(ed) Sexual harassment. See Sexual harassment **331.4**
(ed) Social justice: opposing viewpoints. See Social justice: opposing viewpoints **323**
(ed) Suicide: opposing viewpoints. See Suicide: opposing viewpoints **362.2**
(ed) Violence against women. See Violence against women **362.83**
(ed) Violence in the media. See Violence in the media **303.6**
(ed) Water: opposing viewpoints. See Water: opposing viewpoints **333.91**

Welch, James, 1940-
Fools crow [excerpt]
In Talking leaves **S C**
Killing Custer **973.8**
The marriage of White Man's Dog
In The Lightning within p21-45 **S C**
Yellow Calf
In Song of the turtle p38-51 **S C**
See/See also pages in the following book(s):
Coltelli, L. Winged words: American Indian writers speak **897**

Welch, Priscilla
See/See also pages in the following book(s):
Sandrock, M. Running with the legends p67-96 **796.42**

Welch, Robert, 1947-
(ed) The Oxford companion to Irish literature. See The Oxford companion to Irish literature **820.9**

Welcome to the monkey house. Vonnegut, K. **S C**

Welcome to the monkey house [story] Vonnegut, K.
In Vonnegut, K. Welcome to the monkey house **S C**

Welded. O'Neill, E.
In O'Neill, E. Complete plays v2 **812**

Weldon, Fay
Angel, all innocence
In The Literary ghost p230-46 **S C**

Welfare state America. Kronenwetter, M. **361.6**

The **welfare** system. LeVert, M.   **361.6**

The **well** of loneliness [excerpt] Hall, R.
   In Growing up gay p34-35   **808.8**

"**We'll** stand by the Union": Robert Gould Shaw and the Black 54th Massachusetts Regiment. Burchard, P.   **92**

We'll understand it better by and by   **782.25**

Weller, Archie
   Johnny Blue
     In Rites of passage p143-50   **S C**

Weller, Michael
   Loose ends
     In Best American plays: 8th series—1974-1982 p337-68   **812.008**
   Spoils of war
     In Best American plays: 9th series—1983-1992 p446-76   **812.008**

Wellesley, Charles *See* Brontë, Charlotte, 1816-1855

The **wellness** guide to lifelong fitness. White, T. P.   **613.7**

Wells, H. G. (Herbert George), 1866-1946
   The complete short stories of H. G. Wells
       S C

Short stories included are: The empire of the ants; A vision of judgment; The land ironclads; The beautiful suit; The door in the wall; The pearl of love; The country of the blind; The stolen bacillus; The flowering of the strange orchid; In the Avu observatory; The triumphs of a taxidermist; A deal in ostriches; Through a window; The temptation of Harringay; The flying man; The diamond maker; Æpyornis Island; The remarkable case of Davidson's eyes; The Lord of the Dynamos; The Hammerpond Park burglary; The moth; The treasure in the forest; The Plattner story; The Argonauts of the air; The story of the late Mr. Elvesham; In the abyss; The apple; Under the knife; The sea raiders; Pollock and the Porroh man; The red room; The cone; The purple pileus; The jilting of Jane; In the modern vein; A catastrophe; The lost inheritance; The sad story of a dramatic critic; A slip under the microscope; The reconciliation; My first aeroplane; Little mother up the Morderberg; The story of the last trump; The grisly folk; The crystal egg; The star; A story of the stone age; A story of the days to come; The man who could work miracles; Filmer; The magic shop; The valley of spiders; The truth about Pyecraft; Mr. Skelmersdale in Fairyland; The inexperienced ghost; Jimmy Goggles the god; The new accelerator; Mr. Ledbetter's vacation; The stolen body; Mr. Brisher's treasure; Miss Winchelsea's heart; A dream of Armageddon

   The first men in the moon
     In Wells, H. G. Seven famous novels
       Fic

   The food of the gods
     In Wells, H. G. Seven famous novels
       Fic

   In the days of the comet
     In Wells, H. G. Seven famous novels
       Fic

   The invisible man   **Fic**
     also in Wells, H. G. Seven famous novels
       Fic

   The island of Dr. Moreau
     In Wells, H. G. Seven famous novels
       Fic

   The land ironclads
     In The Oxford book of science fiction stories p1-21   **S C**

   The magic shop
     In The Oxford book of modern fairy tales p224-33   **S C**

   The red room
     In The Oxford book of English ghost stories p172-79   **S C**

   Seven famous novels   **Fic**

   The stolen bacillus, and other incidents
     In Wells, H. G. The complete short stories of H. G. Wells p193-321   **S C**

   Tales of space and time
     In Wells, H. G. The complete short stories of H. G. Wells p623-825   **S C**

   The time machine   **Fic**
     also in Wells, H. G. The complete short stories of H. G. Wells p9-91   **S C**
     also in Wells, H. G. Seven famous novels
       Fic

   The time machine, and other stories
     In Wells, H. G. The complete short stories of H. G. Wells p7-192   **S C**

   Twelve stories, and a dream
     In Wells, H. G. The complete short stories of H. G. Wells p827-1038   **S C**

   The war of the worlds   **Fic**
     also in Wells, H. G. Seven famous novels
       Fic

About
Costa, R. H. H.G. Wells   **823.009**
Martin, C. H.G. Wells   **92**
See/See also pages in the following book(s):
Paterson, J. Edwardians   **942.1**

Wells, Herbert George *See* Wells, H. G. (Herbert George), 1866-1946

Wells, Ida B. *See* Wells-Barnett, Ida B., 1862-1931

Wells-Barnett, Ida B., 1862-1931
See/See also pages in the following book(s):
Black leaders of the twentieth century p39-61   **920**

Welsh, Heidi J.
   Animal testing and consumer products   **670**

Welton, Jude, 1955-
   Impressionism   **759.05**

Welty, Eudora, 1909-
   The bride of the Innisfallen, and other stories
     In Welty, E. The collected stories of Eudora Welty p463-600   **S C**
   Clytie
     In The Oxford book of gothic tales p424-34   **S C**
   The collected stories of Eudora Welty   **S C**

Contents: Lily Daw and the three ladies; A piece of news; Petrified man; The key; Keela, the outcast Indian maiden; Why I live at the P.O.; The whistle; The hitch-hikers; A memory; Clytie; Old Mr. Marblehall; Flowers for Marjorie; A curtain of green; A visit of charity; Death of a traveling salesman; Powerhouse; A worn path; First love; The wide net; A still moment; Asphodel; The winds; The purple hat; Livvie; At the landing; Shower of gold; June recital; Sir Rabbit; Moon Lake; The whole world knows; Music from Spain; The wanderers; No place for you, my love; The burning; The bride of the Innisfallen; Ladies in spring; Circe; Kin; Going to Naples; Where is the voice coming from?; The demonstrators

   A curtain of green, and other stories
     In Welty, E. The collected stories of Eudora Welty p1-149   **S C**
   The golden apples
     In Welty, E. The collected stories of Eudora Welty p259-461   **S C**
   More conversations with Eudora Welty   **92**

Wheal, Elizabeth-Anne—*Continued*
(jt. auth) Pope, S. The dictionary of the First World War **940.3**

Wheatcroft, Andrew
(jt. auth) Overy, R. J. The road to war **940.53**

Wheatley, Phillis, 1753-1784
About
Jensen, M. Phillis Wheatley **92**
See/See also pages in the following book(s):
Black American poets and dramatists before the Harlem Renaissance p119-32 **810.9**

Wheeler, Daniel
(ed) Arnason, H. H. History of modern art: painting, sculpture, architecture **709.04**

Wheeler, Hugh Callingham, 1912-1987
A little night music
In Best American plays: 8th series—1974-1982 p182-227 **812.008**

Wheeler, Lonnie
(jt. auth) Aaron, H. I had a hammer: the Hank Aaron story **92**
(jt. auth) Marshall, J. E., Jr. Street soldier **364.3**

Wheeler, Marcus
(ed) The Oxford Russian dictionary. See The Oxford Russian dictionary **491.7**

Wheeler, Richard
Witness to Gettysburg **973.7**

Whelan, Jeremy
The ABC's of acting **792**

When a friend dies. Gootman, M. E. **155.9**

When Alice told her soul. London, J.
In London, J. Short stories of Jack London p652-66 **S C**

When do fish sleep? and other imponderables of everyday life. Feldman, D. **031.02**

When elephants weep. Masson, J. M. **591.5**

When everyone was pregnant. Updike, J.
In The Norton book of American short stories p618-22 **S C**

When food's a foe. Kolodny, N. J. **616.85**

When heaven and earth changed places: a Vietnamese woman's journey from war to peace. Hayslip, L. L. **92**

When I was Miss Dow. Dorman, S.
In The Norton book of science fiction p151-60 **S C**

When I was Puerto Rican. Santiago, E. **92**

When plague strikes. Giblin, J. **614.4**

When the bough breaks. Corser, K. **618.3**

When the game was black and white. Chadwick, B. **796.357**

When the Revolution comes. Patterson, L.
In Streetlights: illuminating tales of the urban black experience p392-79 **S C**

When the train comes. Wicomb, Z.
In Somehow tenderness survives p61-76 **S C**

When the world was young. London, J.
In London, J. The science fiction stories of Jack London p116-30 **S C**

When they came to take my father— **940.53**

When we dead awaken. Ibsen, H.
In Ibsen, H. The complete major prose plays **839.8**

Where are my birth parents?. Gravelle, K. **362.7**

Where are the children?. Clark, M. H. **Fic**

Where are you going, where have you been?. Oates, J. C.
In American short story masterpieces **S C**
In The Vintage book of contemporary American short stories p347-65 **S C**
In We are the stories we tell **S C**
In Who do you think you are? p14-35 **S C**

Where coyotes howl and wind blows free **810.8**

Where do we go from here: chaos or community?. King, M. L. **323.1**

Where does the weirdness go?. Lindley, D. **530.1**

Where I live. Vonnegut, K.
In Vonnegut, K. Welcome to the monkey house **S C**

Where I work. Cummins, A.
In The Best American short stories, 1994 p52-60 **S C**

Where is it written?. Schwartz, A.
In Coming of age in America p82-99 **S C**

Where is the voice coming from?. Welty, E.
In The Oxford book of American short stories p481-87 **S C**
In Welty, E. The collected stories of Eudora Welty p603-07 **S C**

Where next, Columbus? **629.4**

Where the cross is made. O'Neill, E.
In O'Neill, E. Complete plays v1 **812**

Where there's a will, there's a way. Chekhov, A. P.
In Chekhov, A. P. The image of Chekhov p67-69 **S C**

Where white men fear to tread. Means, R. **92**

Wherever home begins **811.008**

Wheye, Darryl
(jt. auth) Ehrlich, P. R. The birder's handbook **598**

The **whimper** of whipped dogs. Ellison, H.
In The Horror hall of fame p345-64 **S C**

The **whirligig** of life. Henry, O.
In Henry, O. The best short stories of O. Henry **S C**

Whiskey. McNally, T.
In McNally, T. 15 short plays p139-97 **812**

A **whisper** in the veins. Wolverton, T.
In Growing up gay p196-207 **808.8**

Whispered silences. Okihiro, G. Y. **940.53**

A **white** horse. Jones, T.
In The Vintage book of contemporary American short stories p291-305
S C

White House (Washington, D.C.)
Our changing White House 975.3
The White House 975.3

The **White** House 975.3

The **white** old maid. Hawthorne, N.
In Hawthorne, N. Tales and sketches; A wonder book for girls and boys; Tanglewood tales for girls and boys p314-23
S C

White on black. Slesinger, T.
In The Norton book of American short stories p412-20 **S C**

White-out. Wolf, P.
In Talking leaves **S C**

The **white** people. Machen, A.
In The Horror hall of fame p113-52
S C

The **white** power movement. Landau, E.
322.4

White rat. Jones, G.
In Calling the wind p374-80 **S C**

The **white** silence. London, J.
In London, J. Short stories of Jack London p8-16 **S C**

The **white** stocking. Lawrence, D. H.
In Lawrence, D. H. The complete short stories v1 **S C**

Whitebear Whittington
In Hearne, B. G. Beauties and beasts p76-83
398.2

Whitefield, George, 1714-1770
See/See also pages in the following book(s):
Hofstadter, R. America at 1750 **973.2**

Whitehead, Fred
(ed) Culture wars: opposing viewpoints. See Culture wars: opposing viewpoints **306**

Whiteley, Sandra, 1943-
(ed) The American Library Association guide to information access. See The American Library Association guide to information access
025.5

Whiteman, Roberta Hill, 1947-
Summer girl
In Talking leaves **S C**

Whitfield, Philip J.
(ed) The Human body explained. See The Human body explained **612**

Whitman, Albery Allson, 1851-1901
See/See also pages in the following book(s):
Black American poets and dramatists before the Harlem Renaissance p133-45 **810.9**

Whitman, Alden, 1913-1990
(ed) American reformers. See American reformers **920.003**

Whitman, Ann H.
(ed) Familiar trees of North America: eastern region. See Familiar trees of North America: eastern region **582.16**

(ed) Familiar trees of North America: western region. See Familiar trees of North America: western region **582.16**

Whitman, Walt, 1819-1892
Leaves of grass **811**
also in Whitman, W. Poetry and prose
818
Poetry and prose **818**
Works. See Whitman, W. Poetry and prose
818

About
Miller, J. E. Walt Whitman **811**
Reef, C. Walt Whitman **92**
See/See also pages in the following book(s):
Untermeyer, L. Lives of the poets p558-77
920
Voices & visions p3-50 **811.009**

Whitney, David C., 1921-
The American presidents **920**

Whittington, Mary K.
Ahvel
In Vampires: a collection of original stories p121-33 **S C**

Whitworth, Kathy, 1939-
Golf for women **796.352**

Who am I this time?. Vonnegut, K.
In Vonnegut, K. Welcome to the monkey house **S C**

Who believes in ghosts!. London, J.
In London, J. The science fiction stories of Jack London p9-15 **S C**

Who can replace a man?. Aldiss, B. W.
In The Oxford book of science fiction stories p278-86 **S C**

Who cares?. Meltzer, M. **361**

Who dealt?. Lardner, R.
In Lardner, R. The best short stories of Ring Lardner p273-82 **S C**
In The Oxford book of short stories p290-99
S C

Who do you think you are? **S C**

Who has seen the wind?. McCullers, C.
In McCullers, C. Collected stories p171-94
S C

Who is to blame. Chekhov, A. P.
In Chekhov, A. P. The image of Chekhov p118-22 **S C**

Who killed my daughter?. Duncan, L. **364.1**

Who was when?. DeFord, M. A. **902**

Who was who in America **920.003**

Who was who in America: historical volume, 1607-1896 **920.003**

Who was who in Native American history. Waldman, C. **920.003**

Who was who in the American revolution. Purcell, L. E. **920.003**

Who was who in the Civil War. Sifakis, S.
920.003

Who we are. Roberts, S. **304.6**

The **whole** motion. Dickey, J. **811**

The **Whole** world book of quotations **808.88**

Wiesel, Elie, 1928-
The accident
In Wiesel, E. Night, Dawn, The accident: three tales   **Fic**
All rivers run to the sea   **92**
Dawn
In Wiesel, E. Night, Dawn, The accident: three tales   **Fic**
Night
In Wiesel, E. Night, Dawn, The accident: three tales   **Fic**
Night, Dawn, The accident: three tales   **Fic**

Wife abuse
See also Abused women
A **wife** for a life. O'Neill, E.
In O'Neill, E. Complete plays v1   **812**
Wife-wooing. Updike, J.
In Updike, J. Pigeon feathers, and other stories p109-15   **S C**
The **wife's** story. Le Guin, U. K.
In The Oxford book of modern fairy tales p418-21   **S C**

Wiget, Andrew
(ed) Dictionary of Native American literature. See Dictionary of Native American literature   **897**

Wiggen, Henry W. *See* Harris, Mark, 1922-
Wiggins, Colin
Post-impressionism   **759.05**
Wiggins, Marianne
Herself in love
In The Norton book of American short stories p732-41   **S C**

Wigginton, B. Eliot
(ed) Foxfire [1]-10. See Foxfire [1]-10   **975.8**
(ed) Foxfire: 25 years. See Foxfire: 25 years   **975.8**

Wigginton, Eliot *See* Wigginton, B. Eliot
Wight, James Alfred *See* Herriot, James
Wigoder, Geoffrey, 1922-
(ed) The Encyclopedia of Judaism. See The Encyclopedia of Judaism   **296**
Wilbur, Richard, 1921-
See/See also pages in the following book(s):
Breslin, J. E. B. From modern to contemporary   **811.009**

Wilcox, R. Turner, 1888-1970
The dictionary of costume   **391**
Folk and festival costume of the world   **391**
Wild America, Marty Stouffer's. Stouffer, M.   **591.9**
Wild animals of North America   **599**
Wild bears of the world. Ward, P.   **599.74**
Wild cats
See also Cats; Lions; Pumas; Tigers
Alderton, D. Wild cats of the world   **599.74**
Great cats   **599.74**
Savage, C. Wild cats   **599.74**
Wild cats of the world. Alderton, D.   **599.74**
The **wild** duck. Ibsen, H.
In Ibsen, H. The complete major prose plays   **839.8**

Wild echoes: encounters with the most endangered animals in North America. Bergman, C.   **591.5**
Wild flowers
Coffey, T. The history and folklore of North American wildflowers   **582.13**
Niering, W. A. The Audubon Society field guide to North American wildflowers: eastern region   **582.13**
Peterson, R. T. A field guide to wildflowers of northeastern and north-central North America   **582.13**
Spellenberg, R. The Audubon Society field guide to North American wildflowers: western region   **582.13**
Spellenberg, R. Familiar flowers of North America: eastern region   **582.13**
Spellenberg, R. Familiar flowers of North America: western region   **582.13**
Wild meat and the bully burgers [excerpt] Yamanaka, L.-A.
In American eyes p8-12   **S C**
Wild strawberries. Brooks, M.
In Brooks, M. Paradise Café and other stories p89-95   **S C**
Wildcat. O'Connor, F.
In O'Connor, F. Collected works p725-31   **S C**
In O'Connor, F. The complete stories p26-32   **S C**

Wilde, Oscar, 1854-1900
The critic as artist
In Wilde, O. The portable Oscar Wilde p51-136   **828**
A Florentine tragedy
In 24 favorite one-act plays p434-43   **808.82**
The importance of being Earnest   **822**
also in The Oxford anthology of English literature v2   **820.8**
also in Wilde, O. The portable Oscar Wilde p430-507   **828**
The picture of Dorian Gray   **Fic**
also in Wilde, O. The portable Oscar Wilde p138-391   **828**
The portable Oscar Wilde   **828**
De profundis
In Wilde, O. The portable Oscar Wilde p508-658   **828**
Salome
In Thirty famous one-act plays p63-85   **808.82**
In Wilde, O. The portable Oscar Wilde p392-429   **828**
The selfish giant
In The Oxford book of modern fairy tales p166-69   **S C**
The Sphinx without a secret
In The Oxford book of Irish short stories p152-56   **S C**
See/See also pages in the following book(s):
Aymar, B. A pictorial history of the world's greatest trials p193-99   **345**
Wilder, Billy, 1906-
Some like it hot
In Best American screenplays   **812.008**

Williams, Fannie Barrier, 1855-1944
The colored girl
In Invented lives p150-56   **S C**

Williams, Helen Elizabeth, 1933-
Books by African-American authors and illustrators for children and young adults
    016.3058

Williams, Hugh Aldersey- *See* Aldersey-
Williams, Hugh

Williams, Jack, 1936-
The weather book   **551.6**

Williams, Jay, 1914-1978
Petronella
In The Oxford book of modern fairy tales
p380-86   **S C**

Williams, Jeanne, 1930-
(ed) Animal rights and welfare. See Animal
rights and welfare   **179**

Williams, John Alfred, 1925-
Mothersill and the foxes [excerpt]
In Streetlights: illuminating tales of the urban
black experience p498-509   **S C**
Son in the afternoon
In The Best short stories by Negro writers
p288-94   **S C**
In Calling the wind p220-25   **S C**

Williams, Joy, 1944-
Health
In The Best American short stories of the
eighties p241-51   **S C**
Honored guest
In The Best American short stories, 1995
p141-55   **S C**
Train
In The Vintage book of contemporary
American short stories p537-52   **S C**
The wedding
In American short story masterpieces
    S C

Williams, Juan
Eyes on the prize: America's civil rights years,
1954-1965   **323.1**

Williams, Michael W. (Michael Warren)
(ed) The African American encyclopedia. See
The African American encyclopedia
    305.8

Williams, Miller
(jt. auth) Ciardi, J. How does a poem mean?
    821.008

Williams, Peter W.
(ed) Encyclopedia of the American religious experience. See Encyclopedia of the American
religious experience   **200.9**

Williams, Phil, 1948-
(jt. auth) Shafritz, J. M. The dictionary of 20th-
century world politics   **909.82**

Williams, Sherley Anne, 1944-
Meditations on history
In Black-eyed Susans/Midnight birds p230-77
    S C
In Children of the night p58-99   **S C**

Williams, T. Harry (Thomas Harry), 1909-1979
Huey Long   **92**

Williams, Ted, 1918-
The science of hitting   **796.357**
About
Linn, E. Hitter: the life and turmoils of Ted
Williams   **92**

Williams, Tennessee, 1911-1983
27 wagons full of cotton
In 24 favorite one-act plays p94-116
    808.82
Cat on a hot tin roof   **812**
also in Best American plays: 4th series—
1951-1957 p37-90   **812.008**
Conversations with Tennessee Williams   **92**
The glass menagerie   **812**
also in Best plays of the modern American
theatre: 2nd series p1-38   **812.008**
A lovely Sunday for Creve Coeur
In Best American plays: 8th series—1974-
1982 p106-32   **812.008**
The night of the iguana
In Best American plays: 5th series—1957-
1963 p55-104   **812.008**
Orpheus descending
In Best American plays: 5th series—1957-
1963 p509-51   **812.008**
The rose tattoo
In Best American plays: 4th series—1951-
1957 p91-132   **812.008**
A streetcar named Desire   **812**
also in Best American plays: 3d series—
1945-1951 p49-93   **812.008**
Summer and smoke
In Best American plays: 3d series—1945-
1951 p665-701   **812.008**
About
Falk, S. L. Tennessee Williams   **812**

Williams, Thomas Harry *See* Williams, T. Harry
(Thomas Harry), 1909-1979

Williams, Thomas Lanier *See* Williams, Tennessee, 1911-1983

Williams, Trevor Illtyd
The history of invention   **609**

Williams, William Appleman, 1921-1990
(ed) America in Vietnam. See America in Vietnam   **959.704**

Williams, William Carlos, 1883-1963
The collected poems of William Carlos Wil-
liams   **811**
The girl with a pimply face
In The Oxford book of American short stories
p310-22   **S C**
See/See also pages in the following book(s):
Voices & visions p157-204   **811.009**

Williams-Garcia, Rita
Like sisters on the homefront   **Fic**

Williamson, Jack, 1908-
The metal man
In The Oxford book of science fiction stories
p59-69   **S C**

Willie Bea and Jaybird. Ansa, T. M.
In Calling the wind p558-65   **S C**

Willing. Arendt, H.
In Arendt, H. The life of the mind   **153**

Winchell, Donna Haisty
Alice Walker 813.009

The **wind** blows backward. Hahn, M. D. **Fic**

Wind, sand, and stars. Saint-Exupéry, A. de
629.13

Window gardening
See also House plants

The **winds.** Welty, E.
In Welty, E. The collected stories of Eudora
Welty p209-21 **S C**

Winds of renewal 970.004

The **winds** of war. Wouk, H. **Fic**

Wine for the mess at Segi. Michener, J. A.
In Michener, J. A. Tales of the South Pacific
S C

Wine in the wilderness. Childress, A.
In Black theatre USA 812.008

Wine of Wyoming. Hemingway, E.
In Hemingway, E. The complete short stories
of Ernest Hemingway p342-54 **S C**
In Hemingway, E. The short stories of Ernest
Hemingway p450-67 **S C**

Winesburg, Ohio. Anderson, S. **S C**

Winged words: American Indian writers speak.
Coltelli, L. 897

Winger, Gail
Valium and other tranquilizers 616.86

Wings. Kopit, A. L.
In Best American plays: 8th series—1974-
1982 p473-95 812.008

Wings of morning. Childers, T. 940.54

Wings of the dove. Bennett, H.
In Calling the wind p517-23 **S C**

Winikoff, Beverly
The contraceptive handbook 613.9

Winkler, Anthony C.
Writing the research paper 808

Winkler, Paul W. (Paul Walter)
(ed) Anglo-American cataloguing rules, 2d ed.,
1988 revision. See Anglo-American cataloguing rules, 2d ed., 1988 revision 025.3

Winn, Peter
Americas 980

Winnie and Tommy. Block, F. L.
In Am I blue? p29-44 **S C**

Winning basketball for girls. Miller, F. Y.
796.323

Winning racquetball. Turner, E. T. 796.34

Winning ways. Macy, S. 796.09

Winston, Keith, 1912-1970
Letters from a World War II GI 940.54

Winter, Frank H.
(jt. auth) Neal, V. Spaceflight 629.4

Winter, Laurel
Somebody's boyfriend
In Not the only one p18-25 **S C**

Winter, Ruth, 1930-
A consumer's dictionary of food additives
664

Winter adventure. Stark, P. 796.9

Winter barley. Lee, A.
In The Best American short stories, 1993
p199-216 **S C**

Winter cruise. Maugham, W. S.
In Maugham, W. S. Collected short stories v4
S C

Winter dreams. Fitzgerald, F. S.
In Fitzgerald, F. S. The short stories of F.
Scott Fitzgerald p217-36 **S C**
In Fitzgerald, F. S. The stories of F. Scott
Fitzgerald p127-45 **S C**

The **winter** flies. Leiber, F.
In The Norton book of science fiction p171-
82 **S C**

The **winter** of our discontent. Wolfe, T.
In Wolfe, T. The complete short stories of
Thomas Wolfe p451-58 **S C**

Winter sports
See also Olympic games
Stark, P. Winter adventure 796.9

Winterdance. Paulsen, G. 798

Winters, Paul A., 1965-
(ed) Crime and criminals: opposing viewpoints.
See Crime and criminals: opposing viewpoints
364
(ed) The Death penalty: opposing viewpoints.
See The Death penalty: opposing viewpoints
364.6
(ed) Gambling. See Gambling [Current contro-
versies] 363.4
(ed) Hate crimes. See Hate crimes 364.1
(ed) Islam: opposing viewpoints. See Islam: opposing viewpoints 320.5
(ed) The Media and politics. See The Media and
politics 302.23
(ed) Race relations: opposing viewpoints. See
Race relations: opposing viewpoints
305.8

Winterset. Anderson, M.
In Twenty best plays of the modern American
theatre p1-43 812.008

Winterson, Jeanette, 1959-
Oranges are not the only fruit [excerpt]
In Growing up gay p166-74 808.8

Wintle, Justin, 1949-
(ed) The Dictionary of war quotations. See The
Dictionary of war quotations 808.88

Wintry peacock. Lawrence, D. H.
In Lawrence, D. H. The complete short stories v2 **S C**

Wisconsin
Fiction
Carter, A. R. Up country **Fic**

The **wisdom** of Confucius. Confucius 181

The **wisdom** of the bones. Walker, A. 573.2

Wise blood. O'Connor, F.
In O'Connor, F. Collected works p1-131
S C

Wise women 200

The **wish** house. Kipling, R.
In Kipling, R. The portable Kipling 828

Wishengrad, Morton, 1913-1963
The rope dancers
In Best American plays: 5th series—1957-
1963 p203-35   **812.008**

The **wishsong** of Shannara. Brooks, T. See note
under Brooks, T. The sword of Shannara
          Fic

Wit & wisdom of Abraham Lincoln. Lincoln, A.
          973.7

Wit and humor
See also American wit and humor; Come-
dy; English wit and humor; Humorous poetry
The Oxford book of humorous quotations
          808.88
The Penguin book of women's humor
          808.87
See/See also pages in the following book(s):
World folktales p351-83   **398.2**

Wit and its relation to the unconscious. Freud, S.
In Freud, S. The basic writings of Sigmund
Freud   **150.19**

The **wit** of Porportuk. London, J.
In London, J. Short stories of Jack London
p250-69   **S C**

Witalec, Janet, 1965-
(ed) Native North American literature. See Native North American literature   **810.9**

The **witch**. Jackson, S.
In Jackson, S. The lottery   **S C**

The **witch** à la mode. Lawrence, D. H.
In Lawrence, D. H. The complete short stories v1   **S C**

Witch baby. Block, F. L. See note under Block,
F. L. Weetzie bat   **Fic**

The **witch** in the wood. See White, T. H. The
Queen of Air and Darkness

Witchbird. Bambara, T. C.
In Black-eyed Susans/Midnight birds p375-92
          S C

Witchcraft
Demos, J. Entertaining Satan   **974**
Hansen, C. Witchcraft at Salem   **133.4**
Hill, F. A delusion of Satan   **133.4**
Karlsen, C. F. The devil in the shape of a wom-
an   **133.4**
          Dictionaries
Guiley, R. E. The encyclopedia of witches and
witchcraft   **133.4**
          Drama
Miller, A. The crucible   **812**
Witchcraft at Salem. Hansen, C.   **133.4**
Witches
          Fiction
See/See also pages in the following book(s):
World folktales p173-87   **398.2**

The **witching** hour. Thomas, A.
In Best plays of the early American theatre
p511-56   **812.008**

With a tangled skein. Anthony, P. See note under
Anthony, P. Incarnations of immortality series
          Fic

With caution and dispatch. Faulkner, W.
In Faulkner, W. Uncollected stories of William Faulkner p642-64   **S C**

With malice toward none: the life of Abraham
Lincoln. Oates, S. B.   **92**

Without benefit of clergy. Kipling, R.
In Kipling, R. The best fiction of Rudyard
Kipling p593-610   **S C**
In Kipling, R. The portable Kipling   **828**

Witlieb, Bernard, 1939-
(jt. auth) Read, P. J. The book of women's firsts
          920.003

Witness. McNally, T.
In McNally, T. 15 short plays p113-38
          812

The **witness.** Petry, A. L.
In Children of the night p205-22   **S C**

Witness to Gettysburg. Wheeler, R.   **973.7**

Witt, Elder
(jt. auth) Biskupic, J. The Supreme Court and
individual rights   **342**
(ed) The Supreme Court A to Z. See The Supreme Court A to Z   **347**

The **wives** of the dead. Hawthorne, N.
In Hawthorne, N. Tales and sketches; A wonder book for girls and boys; Tanglewood
tales for girls and boys p61-67   **S C**
In The Oxford book of American short stories
p62-68   **S C**

Woiwode, Larry
Silent passengers
In The Best American short stories, 1993
p49-62   **S C**

Wolf, Marvin J.
(jt. auth) Means, R. Where white men fear to
tread   **92**

Wolf, Phyllis
White-out
In Talking leaves   **S C**

Wolf, R. Craig
(jt. auth) Parker, W. O. Scene design and stage
lighting   **792**

Wolf, Stephanie Grauman
As various as their land   **973.2**

The **wolf** almanac. Busch, R.   **599.74**

Wolf by the ears. Rinaldi, A.   **Fic**

Wolfe, Daniel
T.E. Lawrence   **92**

Wolfe, Gene
The detective of dreams
In Masterpieces of fantasy and enchantment
p197-213   **S C**
Feather tigers
In The Norton book of science fiction p280-
86   **S C**
How the whip came back
In The Oxford book of science fiction stories
p385-99   **S C**

Wolfe, George C.
The colored museum
In Black theatre USA   **812.008**

Wolfe, Thomas, 1900-1938
The complete short stories of Thomas Wolfe
S C

Contents: An angel on the porch; The train and the city; Death the proud brother; No door; The four lost men; Boom town; The sun and the rain; The house of the far and lost; Dark in the forest, strange as time; For professional appearance; The names of the nation; One of the girls in our party; Circus at dawn; His father's earth; Old Catawba; Arnold Pentland; The face of the war; Gulliver, the story of a tall man; In the park; Only the dead know Brooklyn; Polyphemus; The far and the near; The bums at sunset; The bell remembered; Fame and the poet; Return; Mr. Malone; Oktoberfest; 'E: a recollection; April, late April; The child by tiger; Katamoto; The lost boy; Chickamauga; The company; A prologue to America; Portrait of a literary critic; The birthday; A note on experts: Dexter Vespasian Joyner; Three o'clock; The winter of our discontent; The dark Messiah; The hollyhock sowers; Nebraska Crane; So this is man; The promise of America; The hollow men; The anatomy of loneliness; The lion at morning; The plumed knight; The newspaper; No cure for it; On leprechauns; The return of the prodigal; Old Man Rivers; Justice is blind; No more rivers; The Spanish letter

Look homeward, angel   **Fic**
About
Thomas Wolfe   **813.009**

Wolfe, Tom
The right stuff   **629.45**

Wolff, Cynthia Griffin
Emily Dickinson   **92**

Wolff, Tobias, 1945-
Hunters in the snow
In The Oxford book of American short stories
p620-35   **S C**
The liar
In American short story masterpieces
S C
This boy's life [excerpt]
In Coming of age in America p197-211
S C
In Who do you think you are? p83-91
S C
This boy's life: a memoir   **92**
(ed) The Vintage book of contemporary American short stories. See The Vintage book of contemporary American short stories
S C

Wolff, Virginia Euwer
Make lemonade   **Fic**
Probably still Nick Swansen   **Fic**

Wolpert, Stanley A., 1927-
A new history of India   **954**

Wolsey, Thomas, Cardinal, 1475?-1530
See/See also pages in the following book(s):
Durant, W. J. The Reformation p525-42
940.2

Wolverton, Terry
A whisper in the veins
In Growing up gay p196-207   **808.8**

Wolves
Alderton, D. Foxes, wolves, and wild dogs of the world   **599.74**
Busch, R. The wolf almanac   **599.74**
Savage, C. The world of the wolf   **599.74**
Steinhart, P. The company of wolves
599.74

The **woman**. Dunbar-Nelson, A. M.
In Daughters of Africa p161-63   **808.8**

Woman and home. Westall, R.
In Westall, R. Shades of darkness p3-22
S C

The **woman** at the store. Mansfield, K.
In The Oxford book of short stories p300-09
S C

The **woman** at the Washington Zoo. Jarrell, R.
In Jarrell, R. The complete poems   **811**

A **woman** doctor's guide to skin care. Bergfeld, W. F.   **616.5**

Woman Hollering Creek. Cisneros, S.
In Cisneros, S. Woman Hollering Creek and other stories   **S C**

Woman Hollering Creek and other stories. Cisneros, S.   **S C**

The **woman** in Gaul. Hurston, Z. N.
In Hurston, Z. N. The complete stories p261-83   **S C**

Woman in the mists: the story of Dian Fossey and the mountain gorillas of Africa. Mowat, F.
92

A **woman** named Jackie: an intimate biography of Jacqueline Bouvier Kennedy Onassis. Heymann, C. D.   **92**

A **woman** of fifty. Maugham, W. S.
In Maugham, W. S. Collected short stories v4
S C

A **woman** of valor: Clara Barton and the Civil War. Oates, S. B.   **92**

Woman of valor: Margaret Sanger and the birth control movement in America. Chesler, E.
92

The **woman** warrior. Kingston, M. H.   **92**

The **woman** warrior: memoirs of a girlhood among ghosts [excerpt] Kingston, M. H.
In Growing up Asian American p319-26
810.8

The **woman** who fell from the sky. Harjo, J.
811
also in Song of the turtle p302-06   **S C**

The **woman** who had imagination. Bates, H. E.
In Classic English short stories, 1930-1955 p167-98   **S C**

The **woman** who rode away. Lawrence, D. H.
In Lawrence, D. H. The complete short stories v2   **S C**

The **woman** who would eat flowers. McElroy, C. J.
In Children of the night p471-501   **S C**

A **woman** with a past. Fitzgerald, F. S.
In Fitzgerald, F. S. The stories of F. Scott Fitzgerald p364-80   **S C**

A **woman** without a country. Cheever, J.
In Cheever, J. The stories of John Cheever p423-28   **S C**

A **woman's** liberation. Le Guin, U. K.
In Le Guin, U. K. Four ways to forgiveness p145-208   **S C**

Woman's Party *See* National Woman's Party

The **Woman's** way   **970.004**

Women
See also Abused women; women of particular racial or ethnic groups, e.g. *African American women;* and women in various occupations and professions

Yolen, Jane—*Continued*
The river maid
In The Oxford book of modern fairy tales
p422-26   **S C**
(ed) Favorite folktales from around the world.
See Favorite folktales from around the world
    398.2
(ed) Vampires: a collection of original stories.
See Vampires: a collection of original stories
    S C

A **Yom** Kippur scandal. Sholem Aleichem
In Sholem Aleichem. The best of Sholem
Aleichem   **S C**

Yon ill wind. Anthony, P. See note under Anthony, P. The Magic of Xanth series   **Fic**

Yoon, Steve Chan-No
Stoplight
In American dragons: twenty-five Asian
American voices p14-25   **810.8**

Yoruba (African people)
Drewal, H. J. Yoruba   **709.6**

Yosemite National Park (Calif.)
Brower, K. Yosemite   **917.9**
Muir, J. The Yosemite   **979.4**

You can't be any poorer than dead. O'Connor, F.
In O'Connor, F. The complete stories p292-
310   **S C**

You can't have greens without a neck bone.
Strothers, R.
In Streetlights: illuminating tales of the urban
black experience p466-70   **S C**

You can't take it with you. Kaufman, G. S.
In Twenty best plays of the modern American
theatre p233-73   **812.008**

You can't tell a man by the song he sings. Roth,
P.
In Roth, P. Goodbye, Columbus, and five
short stories   **S C**

You know I can't hear you when the water's running. Anderson, R. W.
In Best American plays: 6th series—1963-
1967 p335-65   **812.008**

You see but you do not observe. Sawyer, R. J.
In Nebula awards 31 p188-205   **S C**

You touched me. Lawrence, D. H.
In Lawrence, D. H. The complete short stories v2   **S C**

Youcha, Geraldine
(jt. auth) Seixas, J. S. Children of alcoholism
    362.29

You'll never know, dear, how much I love you.
Updike, J.
In Updike, J. Pigeon feathers, and other stories p172-78   **S C**

Young, Al, 1939-
Going for the moon
In Calling the wind p584-96   **S C**

Young, Faye *See* Miller, Faye Young

Young, John K.
Hormones: molecular messengers   **612.4**

Young, Patrick
Schizophrenia   **616.89**

Young, Peter, 1915-
(ed) The World almanac of World War II. See
The World almanac of World War II
    940.53

Young, Robyn V.
(ed) Gale encyclopedia of multicultural America.
See Gale encyclopedia of multicultural America   **305.8**

Young, Stuart, 1938-
Allergies. See Allergies   **616.97**

Young, Sue
The new comprehensive American rhyming dictionary   **423**

Young, Whitney Moore, 1921-1971
See/See also pages in the following book(s):
Black leaders of the twentieth century p331-58
    920

Young adult fiction by African American writers,
1968-1993. Kutenplon, D.   **016.813**

Young Adult Library Services Association
Carter, B. Best books for young adults
    028.1
Outstanding books for the college bound. See
Outstanding books for the college bound
    011.6

Young Adult Library Services Association. Intellectual Freedom Committee
Hit list: frequently challenged books for young
adults. See Hit list: frequently challenged
books for young adults   **098**

The **Young** adult reader's adviser   **011.6**

Young adults' library services
De Vos, G. Storytelling for young adults
    372.6
Edwards, M. A. The fair garden and the swarm
of beasts   **027.62**
Excellence in library services to young adults
    027.62

Periodicals
Journal of Youth Services in Libraries
    027.6205
VOYA: Voice of Youth Advocates
    027.6205

Young adults' literature
African-American voices in young adult literature   **810.9**
Carter, B. Nonfiction for young adults
    028.5
Read all about it!   **808.8**

Bibliography
Adamson, L. G. Recreating the past   **016.8**
Best books for senior high readers   **011.6**
Bodart, J. R. 100 world-class thin books
    028.1
Books for you   **011.6**
Carter, B. Best books for young adults
    028.1
Criscoe, B. L. Award-winning books for children and young adults   **011.6**
Genre favorites for young adults   **016.8**
Hartman, D. K. Historical figures in fiction
    016.8
Helbig, A. This land is our land   **016.8**
Holsinger, M. P. The ways of war   **016.8**

PART 3

SELECT LIST OF RECOMMENDED CD-ROM REFERENCE WORKS

SELECT LIST OF RECOMMENDED CD-ROM REFERENCE WORKS

A.D.A.M. essentials. A.D.A.M. Software Inc., 1600 RiverEdge Parkway, Suite 800, Atlanta, GA 30328 2 computer optical discs sd., col. $129.95

System requirements for Windows: 486 or higher; 8MB RAM; 12.5MB free hard drive space; Windows 3.1 or higher; double-speed CD-ROM drive; SVGA; sound card; modem for online access

System requirements for Macintosh: 68030 processor or higher; 8MB RAM; 10MB free hard drive space; System 7.1 or higher; double-speed CD-ROM drive; 14-in. or larger 256-color monitor; modem for online access

High school bundle combines A.D.A.M. (Animated Dissection of Anatomy for Medicine) The Inside Story and the Cardiovascular Module from the A.D.A.M./Benjamin-Cummings Interactive Physiology series to create an interactive software tool for exploring the 12 major body systems. Includes structure-related terms, descriptions, and pronunciations; sound detailing normal and abnormal physiological processes; and health-related career information. Also provides access to 100 medical websites

The **American** Indian: a multimedia encyclopedia. version 2.0. Facts on File 1995 1 computer optical disc sd., col. $149.95

System requirements for DOS: IBM compatible PC; 640K RAM; 2MB free hard drive space; DOS 5.0; double-speed CD-ROM drive; color monitor

System requirements for Windows: 386 or higher; 8MB RAM; 2MB free hard drive space; Windows 3.1 or higher; double-speed CD-ROM drive; color monitor; sound card; mouse

System requirements for Macintosh: 68030 processor or higher; 2MB RAM; 1.3MB free hard drive space; System 7.1 or higher; double-speed CD-ROM drive; 13-in. 256-color monitor

Provides overviews of more than 150 Native American groups and the address directories of tribes, museums, and societies; the full text of prominent historical documents, including rare maps, treaties, land grants, and letters; over 1,000 biographical profiles; audio and video clips; maps, photos, and drawings

Bodyworks. version 6.0. The Learning Company, One Athenaeum St., Cambridge, MA 02142 1 computer optical disc sd., col. $49.95

System requirements for Windows: 486 or higher; 8MB RAM; 20MB free hard drive space; Windows 3.1 or Windows 95; double-speed CD-ROM drive; SVGA; sound card; mouse

System requirements for Macintosh: 68040 processor or higher; 8MB RAM; System 6.0.7 or higher; double-speed CD-ROM drive (quad-speed recommended); 13-in. 256-color monitor; mouse

This multimedia journey through the human body features 25 rotating virtual reality models (with 360-degree views); live-action videos and animations of body processes; x-rays, a sonogram and childbirth; audio pronunciations and definitions for more than 1,200 medical terms; over 300,000 words of text covering all aspects of anatomy and physiology

The **Columbia** world of quotations. Columbia Univ. Press 1996 1 computer optical disc sd., col. $350

System requirements for DOS: IBM compatible 386 or higher; 640K RAM; DOS 5.0 or higher; CD-ROM drive; MSCDEX 2.0 or higher

System requirements for Windows: 386 or higher; 8MB RAM; Microsoft Windows 3.1; CD-ROM drive; MSCDEX 2.0 or higher

System requirements for Macintosh: 68030 processor or higher; 8MB RAM; CD-ROM drive

This database features over 60,000 quotations by about 5,000 authors. It is searchable by keyword and assigned subject heading, author or speaker's name, gender, nationality, occupation, birthdate or century

Encarta encyclopedia, deluxe edition. Microsoft Corp., One Microsoft Way, Redmond, WA 98052 1997 2 computer optical discs sd., col. $79.95

System requirements for Windows: 486DX or higher; 8MB RAM (Windows 3.1/Windows 95), 12MB RAM (Windows NT); 20MB (Windows 3.1), 15MB (Windows 95), 13MB (Windows NT) free hard drive space; 1MB video RAM; double-speed CD-ROM drive; SVGA; sound card; mouse; speakers or headphones; modem (14.4 kbps or higher recommended)

System requirements for Macintosh: IIci or higher; 8MB RAM; 16MB free hard drive space; System 7.1 or higher; 256-color monitor

This deluxe edition, contains over 30,000 articles, 14,000 photos and illustrations, 2,300 audio clips and 150 videos and animations. Other features include a multimedia collage section, 360-degree panoramic views, web links, monthly updates, and access to a news and periodical database

Famous American speeches: a multimedia history—1850 to the present. Oryx Press 1996 1 computer optical disc sd., col. $129.95

System requirements for Windows: 386SX or higher; 4MB RAM; 2MB free hard drive space; Windows 3.1; double-speed CD-ROM drive; SVGA; sound card; speakers or headphones

Contains the full text of more than 300 speeches made by presidents; government, military, and civil rights leaders; and other influential people. Includes photos, a timeline, audio and video clips, and hypertext links built into each document

Great artists. Cambrix Publishing Inc., 9304 Deering Avenue, Chatsworth, CA 91311 1994 1 computer optical disc sd., col. $49.95

System requirements for Windows: 386 or higher; 4MB RAM; 4MB free hard drive space; Windows 3.1 or 95; DOS 3.1 or higher; MSCDEX 2.2 or higher; CD-ROM drive; SVGA; sound card; mouse

Developed with the National Gallery of London, this explores the paintings, lives and times of major European artists. Students can navigate by artist, painting, time or geography. Includes a timeline, an art atlas, and a "behind the scenes" video tour of the National Gallery

Her heritage: a biographical encyclopedia of famous American women. Pilgrim New Media, 132 Adams St., #10, Newton, MA 02158 1994 1 computer optical disc sd., col. $49.95

System requirements for Windows: 486 or Pentium-class processor; 8MB RAM; Windows 3.1 or Windows 95 (may require more memory and faster microprocessor); double-speed CD-ROM drive; SVGA; sound card

System requirements for Macintosh: 68000-series processor or PowerPC; 4MB RAM; System 7; double-speed CD-ROM drive; 256-color monitor

Profiles over 1,000 American women who achieved fame in the arts, science, health, law, politics, religion, and social reform. Includes photographs, etchings, newsreel and video footage

How your body works. Mindscape, 88 Rowland Way, Novato, CA 94945 1996 1 computer optical disc sd., col. $29.99

System requirements for Windows: 486SX; 8MB RAM; 5MB free hard drive space (11.5MB recommended); Windows 3.1 or higher; double-speed CD-ROM drive; SVGA; sound card; mouse

System requirements for Macintosh: LC series or higher; 8MB RAM; 4MB free hard drive space; System 7.1 or higher; CD-ROM drive; 13-in. or larger 256-color monitor

This interactive encyclopedia of the human body features 3-D animations of the 12 body systems, over one hour of full-motion video, advice from medical experts, and pertinent information on such topics as disorders, medications and first aid

Junior DISCovering authors. version 2.0. U.X.L. 1997 1 computer optical disc sd., col. $325

System requirements for Windows: 386 or higher (486DX or higher recommended); 8MB RAM; 5MB free hard drive space; Windows 3.1 or higher; DOS 5.0 or higher; double-speed CD-ROM drive; MSCDEX 2.2 or higher; SVGA; 8-bit or higher sound card; mouse

System requirements for Macintosh: Color Mac; 8MB Ram; 3MB free hard drive space; System 6.0.8 or higher; CD-ROM drive; Macintosh CD-ROM extensions

Provides information on the lives and works of over 450 most-studied writers. Search options allow navigation by author, ethnicity, gender, title, subject, time period or character name. Includes plotlines of authors' best known works as well as author portraits

Landmark documents in American history. Facts on File 1995 1 computer optical disc sd., col. $149.95

System requirements for DOS: IBM compatible PC; 640K RAM; 2MB free hard drive space; DOS 5.0 or higher; double-speed CD-ROM drive; color monitor

System requirements for Windows: 386 or higher; 8MB RAM; 2MB free hard drive space; Windows 3.1 or higher; double-speed CD-ROM drive; color monitor; sound card; mouse

System requirements for Macintosh: 68030 processor or higher; 8MB RAM; 2MB free hard drive space; System 7.1; double-speed CD-ROM drive; 13-in. 256-color monitor

Coverage includes Supreme Court decisions; treaties; essays; letters; legislation; speeches; government charters and constitutions; debates; party platforms; and all presidential inaugurals. Features introductions for every document, photos, video clips, biographies, and bibliographic information

Magazine article summaries. EBSCO Publishing, 10 Estes Street, Ipswich, MA 01938 2 computer optical discs sd., col. prices vary according to update service

System requirements for DOS: IBM compatible 386 or higher; 640K RAM; 5MB free hard drive space; DOS 5.0 or higher; MSCDEX version 2.1 or higher; CD-ROM player with interface card

System requirements for Windows: 386 or higher (486 recommended); 16MB RAM; 15MB free hard drive space; Windows 3.1 or higher; CD-ROM player with interface card

System requirements for Macintosh: any Classic II or Color Classic, SE/30, LC, LC II and LC III, or any MAC II, Quadra, Centris, Performa, or PowerBook series; 1.5MB RAM; 1MB free hard drive space; CD-ROM player

This database contains abstracts for over 400 different general interest magazines, the New York Times, and nearly 5,000 Magill's Book Reviews

Masterplots complete CD-ROM. Salem Press 1997 1 computer optical disc sd., col. $750

System requirements for Windows: 386SX (486 recommended); 4MB RAM; 3MB hard drive space; Windows 3.1 or higher; CD-ROM drive; VGA

System requirements for Macintosh: 68030 processor (68040 or higher recommended); 4MB RAM; 3MB hard drive space; System 7.0 or higher; CD-ROM drive; monitor

Contains the complete contents from Masterplots and all Masterplots II series. Features hypertext links to author biographies and detailed character descriptions

Mayo Clinic Family Health. version 3.0 (WIN); 2.0 (MAC). IVI Publishing, Inc., 7500 Flying Cloud Dr., Minneapolis, MN 55344-3739 1997 1 computer optical disc sd., col. $39.95 (WIN); $29.95 (MAC)

System requirements for Windows: 486DX or higher; 8MB RAM (16MB RAM recommended); 19MB (minimum)-25MB free hard drive space; Windows 3.1 or higher; DOS 5.0 or higher; double-speed CD-ROM drive (quad-speed recommended); VGA; 16-bit sound card; mouse; speakers; 14.4 kbps modem (28.8 recommended) required for Internet access

System requirements for Macintosh: Centris, Quadra, Performa, or higher or Power Mac; 8MB RAM; System 7.0.1 or higher; color monitor; mouse; speakers or headphones

Mayo Clinic Family Health—*Continued*

Health resource with information on medical conditions, drug and prescription reference, first aid and disease prevention. Provides access to Mayo Health O@sis

Microsoft bookshelf. Microsoft Corp., One Microsoft Way, Redmond, WA 98052 1 computer optical disc sd., col. $54.95

System requirements for Windows: 486SX or higher; 8MB RAM; 4.5MB free hard drive space; Windows 3.1 or higher; double-speed CD-ROM drive; SVGA; sound card; mouse; speakers or headphones

System requirements for Macintosh: IIcx or higher; 8MB RAM; 4MB free hard drive space; System 7 or higher; 13-in. 256-color monitor

A multimedia reference library that provides access to updated versions of The American Heritage Dictionary, The Columbia Dictionary of Quotations, The National Five-Digit Zip Code and Post Office Directory, The Hammond World Atlas, The Original Roget's Thesaurus, The Concise Columbia Encyclopedia, The Peoples' Chronology, and The World Almanac and Book of Facts. In addition, provides access to The Microsoft Bookshelf Internet Directory 96 and The Microsoft Concise Encarta 96 World Atlas (modem required)

PC Globe maps 'n' facts. Broderbund Software, Inc., 500 Redwood Blvd., Novato, CA 94948 1994 1 computer optical disc sd., col. $34.95

System requirements for Windows: 386SX or higher (486DX for Windows 95); 2MB RAM (8MB for Windows 95); 6MB free hard drive space; Windows 3.1 or higher; DOS 5.0 or higher; CD-ROM drive; VGA (SVGA recommended); sound card; mouse

System requirements for Macintosh: 68030 processor or higher; 4MB RAM; 6MB free hard drive; System 7.0 or higher; CD-ROM drive; 13-in. or larger 256-color monitor; sound card; mouse

This comprehensive resource provides access to full-color maps and data for 227 countries, as well as information on groups of countries and individual cities. Features include comparison charts on such subjects as agriculture, crime, economics, education, health, manufacturing, and travel; automatic distance calculations; and local times worldwide

Peterson's career & college quest. Peterson's 1 computer optical disc sd., col. $695

System requirements for Windows: 486DX; 8MB RAM (16MB recommended); 35MB free hard drive space (65MB recommended); Windows 3.1 or higher; double-speed CD-ROM drive or better; SVGA; 8-bit sound card or higher

System requirements for Macintosh: 68030 processor (Power Mac recommended), 8MB RAM (16MB for Power Mac), 35MB free hard drive space (70MB recommended), System 7.0 or higher and QuickTime 1.5 (System 7.5.3 and QuickTime 2.5 recommended); double-speed CD-ROM drive or better; 13-in. color monitor

Updated annually, this interactive program covers career choices, college selection, vocational-technical school options, and financial aid planning options

Picture atlas of the world. National Geographic Soc. 1992 (DOS); 1995 (WIN/MAC) 1 computer optical disc sd., col. $79.95

System requirements for DOS: 286 or higher; 2MB RAM; DOS 4.0 or higher; CD-ROM drive; MSCDEX 2.1 or higher; VGA; sound card; mouse; speakers or headphones

System requirements for Windows: 386 or higher; 4MB RAM; Windows 3.1 or higher; DOS 5.0 or higher; double-speed CD-ROM drive; 256-color monitor

System requirements for Macintosh: Color Mac; 4MB RAM; System 6.0.8 or higher; double-speed CD-ROM drive; 256-color monitor

Includes over 800 world, continental, and regional maps; audio and video clips; essays, captions, an index and glossary

RedShift 2. Maris Multimedia, Inc., 4040 Civic Center Drive, Suite 200, San Rafael, CA 94903 1995 1 computer optical disc sd., col. $39.95

System requirements for Windows: 386SX or higher; 8MB RAM; Windows 3.1/3.11 or higher; DOS 3.3; double-speed CD-ROM drive; SVGA; sound card; mouse

System requirements for Macintosh: LC, Performa, Centris, or Quadra series (System 7.0 or higher) or Power Mac 6100 (System 7.1.2 or higher); 8MB RAM; QuickTime 2.0 or higher; double-speed CD-ROM drive; 14-in. or larger color monitor; mouse

This interactive planetarium includes virtual reality 3-D simulations of planetary orbits and star fields; tutorials and narrated tours; over 200,000 stars, asteroids, and comets; 700 full-screen photographs with cross-referenced captions. The full text of Penguin's Dictionary of Astronomy is also included

SIRS Government Reporter. SIRS, Inc., P.O. Box 2348, Boca Raton, FL 33427-2348 1 computer optical disc sd., col. $800

System requirements for DOS: IBM compatible PC; 512K RAM; 14MB free hard drive space; DOS 3.3 or higher; CD-ROM drive with device driver; VGA

This database contains information published by and about our federal government. Coverage includes U.S. Government Documents, Historic Documents, U.S. Supreme Court Decisions, Justices' Directory, Congressional Directory, and the Federal Agency Directory

SIRS Researcher. SIRS, Inc., P.O. Box 2348, Boca Raton, FL 33427-2348 1 computer optical disc sd., col. $1,350

System requirements for DOS: IBM compatible PC; 512K RAM; 16MB free hard drive space; DOS 3.3 or higher; CD-ROM drive with device driver; MSCDEX 2.0 or higher; VGA

System requirements for Windows: IBM compatible PC; 4MB RAM; 20MB free hard drive space; Windows 3.1; CD-ROM drive with device driver; MSCDEX 2.0 or higher; VGA; mouse

System requirements for Macintosh: Color Mac; 4MB RAM; 20MB free hard drive space; System 7 or higher; CD-ROM drive; 256 color monitor; mouse

This general reference database provides access to thousands of full-text articles from more than 1,200 newspapers, magazines, journals and government publications exploring social, scientific, historic, economic, political and global issues. Dating from 1988 to the present, many of the articles are accompanied by graphics, including charts, maps, diagrams and drawings

SuperTom. Information Access Company, 362 Lakeside Drive, Foster City, CA 94404 2 computer optical discs sd., col.

System requirements for DOS: IBM compatible PC (486 or higher recommended); 640K RAM; DOS 3.3 or higher (5.0 or higher recommended); 2 CD-ROM drives; MSCDEX 2.0 or higher; monitor (VGA recommended)

System requirements for Macintosh: MacPlus or higher (LC or Quadra series recommended); 2MB RAM (4MB recommended); System 6.05-6.08; 2 CD-ROM drives; monitor

This multi-source database indexes over 180 periodicals; more than 100 are full text. Includes selected full text newspaper articles and four reference books

Time magazine multimedia almanac. The Learning Company, One Athenaeum St., Cambridge, MA 02142 1995 1 computer optical disc sd., col. $39.95

System requirements for Windows: 486 or higher; 4MB RAM (8MB recommended); Windows 3.1 or Windows 95; DOS 5.0 or higher; double-speed CD-ROM; MSCDEX 2.2 or higher; SVGA; sound card; mouse; speakers or headphones

System requirements for Macintosh: 68040 processor or higher; 4MB RAM (8MB recommended); System 7.1 or higher; double-speed CD-ROM drive; 13-in. 256-color monitor; mouse

Includes full coverage of Time magazine from January 1989 through June 1995 as well as selected historical articles from 1923 through 1989. The almanac features tables and charts from the *U.S. Statistical Abstract* plus full-color maps and charts. The *CIA World Factbook* includes world organizations, vital statistics on every country, abbreviations, and other key facts and figures

U.S. News & World Report Getting into college. Creative Multimedia, 225 SW Broadway, Suite 600, Portland, OR 97205 1 computer optical disc sd., col. $29.95

System requirements for Windows: 486DX or higher; 8MB RAM, 5MB free hard drive space (18MB recommended); Windows 3.1 or higher; double-speed CD-ROM drive; SVGA; sound card; 14.4 modem for online access

System requirements for Macintosh: 68040 or higher; 8MB RAM (16MB recommended); 5MB free hard drive space; System 7.1 or higher; double-speed CD-ROM drive; 256-color monitor; 14.4 modem for online access

Users can explore 1,400 colleges by location, size, academics, athletics and more. Includes photos, slide shows, advice from college counselors and students, testing and financial aid information, and Internet access to colleges and organizations needed for the college search

The **ultimate** human body. version 2.0. DK Multimedia, Inc. 1996 1 computer optical disc sd., col. $39.95

System requirements for Windows: 486DX or higher; 8MB RAM (12MB recommended for Windows 95); Windows 3.1 or higher; double-speed CD-ROM drive; SVGA; 8- or 16-bit sound card; mouse; speakers or headphones

System requirements for MMX version for Windows: Pentium processor; 16MB RAM; 1MB video RAM; Windows 95; quad-speed CD-ROM drive; SVGA; 16-bit sound card; mouse; speakers or headphones

System requirements for Macintosh: 68040 (LC II) or higher; 8MB RAM; 12MB free hard drive space; System 7.0 or higher, double-speed CD-ROM drive; 256-color monitor; 8-bit sound card; mouse; speakers or headphones

Three search paths: "The Body Machine," "The Body Organs," and "The Body Systems" make it easy to discover what every part of the human body looks like, where it is situated, what it is called and how it works. Includes microphotography, 3-D images, illustrations, animations, sound and text. Provides access to Body Online on the World Wide Web

Women in America. Primary Source Media, 12 Lunar Drive, Woodridge, CT 06525 1995 1 computer optical disc sd., col. (American journey: history in your hands) $149

System requirements for DOS: 386 IBM compatible or higher; 640K RAM (510K free); 5MB free hard drive space; DOS 5.0 or higher; double-speed CD-ROM drive; SVGA; Vesa driver installed; sound card, mouse, and speakers are optional

System requirements for Windows: 486 or higher; 8MB RAM; 5MB free hard drive space; double-speed CD-ROM drive; SVGA; mouse; sound card and speakers are optional

System requirements for Macintosh: 68040 processor or higher; 8MB RAM; 5MB free hard drive space; System 7.0 or higher; double-speed CD-ROM drive; 256-color monitor; mouse

Chronicles the history of women in America from the earliest settlements through the suffrage and feminist movements to the testimony of Anita Hill in the 1990s

PART 4

DIRECTORY OF PUBLISHERS AND DISTRIBUTORS

DIRECTORY OF PUBLISHERS AND DISTRIBUTORS

21st Cent. Bks. (NY): 21st Cent. Bks., 115 W. 18th St., New York, N.Y. 10011-4113 Tel 212-886-9200 Fax 212-633-0748

Abbeville Press Inc., 488 Madison Ave., New York, N.Y. 10022 Tel 212-888-1969; 800-278-2665 Fax 212-644-5085

ABC-CLIO Inc., 130 Cremona Dr., Santa Barbara, Calif. 93117 Tel 805-968-1911 Fax 805-685-9685

Abingdon Press, 201 8th Ave. S., P.O. Box 801, Nashville, Tenn. 37202-0801 Tel 615-749-6000; 800-251-3320 (orders) Fax 615-749-6512; 749-6577 (orders)

Abrams: Harry N. Abrams Inc., 100 5th Ave., New York, N.Y. 10011 Tel 212-206-7715; 800-345-1359 Fax 212-645-8437

Adams Pub., 260 Center St., Holbrook, Mass. 02343-1074 Tel 617-767-8100; 800-872-5627 Fax 617-767-0994

Addison-Wesley See Addison Wesley Longman

Addison Wesley Longman Inc., 1 Jacob Way, Reading, Mass. 01867 Tel 617-944-3700; 800-447-2226 Fax 617-944-9351

Aladdin Paperbacks, 1230 Ave. of the Americas, New York, N.Y. 10020 Tel 212-698-7000; 800-223-2336 (orders only)

Alaska Northwest Bks., 2208 N.W. Market St., Suite 300, Seattle, Wash. 98107 Tel 206-784-5071; refer orders to Graphic Arts Center Pub. Co., P.O. Box 10306, Portland, Or. 97210 Tel 503-226-2402; 800-452-3032 Fax 503-223-1410

Algonquin Bks.: Algonquin Bks. of Chapel Hill, 307 W. Weaver St., Carrboro, N.C. 27510 Tel 919-967-0108 Fax 919-933-0272; refer orders to Workman Pub. Co. Inc., 708 Broadway, New York, N.Y. 10003 Tel 212-254-5900; 800-722-7202 Fax 212-254-8098; 800-521-1832 (orders)

Allyn & Bacon Inc., 160 Gould St., Needham Heights, Mass. 02194-2310 Tel 617-455-1200; 800-223-1360 Fax 617-455-1220; refer orders to Simon & Schuster, 200 Old Tappan Rd., Old Tappan, N.J. 07675 Tel 201-767-5937; 800-223-1360 Fax 800-445-6991

Alyson Publs. Inc., 40 Plympton St., Boston, Mass. 02118 Tel 617-542-5679; 800-825-9766 (orders only) Fax 617-542-9189; refer orders to Consortium Bk. Sales & Distr., 1045 Westgate Dr., Suite 90, St. Paul, Minn. 55114-1065 Tel 612-221-9035; 800-283-3572 (orders) Fax 612-221-0124

AMACOM, 135 W. 50th St., New York, N.Y. 10020 Tel 212-903-8315 Fax 212-903-8168; refer orders to P.O. Box 169, Saranac Lake, N.Y. 12983 Tel 518-891-5510; 800-250-5308 Fax 518-891-3653

American Assn. for the Advancement of Science, 1333 H St. N.W., 11th Floor, Washington, D.C. 20005 Tel 202-326-6400

American Assn. of School Adm., 1801 N. Moore St., Arlington, Va. 22209-9988 Tel 703-528-0700 Fax 703-875-0731

American Bk. Co., 125 Spring St., Lexington, Mass. 02173; refer orders to Heath

American Forestry Assn., 1516 P St. N.W., Washington, D.C. 20005 Tel 202-667-3300 Fax 202-667-7751

American Heritage, 60 5th Ave., New York, N.Y. 10011 Tel 212-206-5500

American Indian Pubs. Inc., 177 F Riverside Dr., Newport Beach, Calif. 92663

American Lib. Assn., 50 E. Huron St., Chicago, Ill. 60611 Tel 312-280-2425; 800-545-2433 Fax 312-280-2422

American Quilter's Soc., 5801 Kentucky Dam Rd., Paducah, Ky. 42003 Tel 502-898-6211; 800-626-5420 Fax 502-898-8890

American Radio Relay League Inc., 225 Main St., Newington, Conn. 06111 Tel 203-666-1541 Fax 203-665-1166

American Youth Hostels Inc., P.O. Box 37613, Washington, D.C. 20013-7613 Tel 202-783-6161 Fax 202-783-6171

Amherst Media, 418 Homecrest Dr., Amherst, N.Y. 14226 Tel 716-874-4450; 800-622-3278; refer orders to Independent Pubs. Group, 814 N. Franklin St., Chicago, Ill. 60610 Tel 312-337-0747; 800-888-4741 Fax 312-337-5985

Amistad Press Inc., Time & Life Bldg., Rockefeller Center, Room 3845, New York, N.Y. 10020 Tel 212-522-6936; refer orders to Viking Penguin, 375 Hudson St., New York, N.Y. 10014-3657 Tel 212-366-2000; 800-331-4624

AMPHOTO, 1515 Broadway, New York, N.Y. 10036 Tel 212-536-5121 Fax 212-536-5359; refer orders to 1695 Oak St., Lakewood, N.J. 08701 Tel 908-363-4511; 800-451-1741

Anchor Bks. (NY): Anchor Bks., 1540 Broadway, New York, N.Y. 10036-4094 Tel 212-354-6500; 800-223-6834 Fax 212-492-9698

Anchor Press See Anchor Bks. (NY) 10036 Tel 212-354-6500; 800-223-6834 Fax 212-492-9698

Anchor Press/Doubleday, 1540 Broadway, New York, N.Y. 10036 Tel 212-354-6500; 800-223-6834 Fax 212-492-9698

Andrews & McMeel See Andrews McMeel Pub.

Andrews McMeel Pub. 4520 Main St., Kansas City, Mo. 64111 Tel 816-360-6700; 800-826-4216 Fax 816-932-6820

Aperture Foundation Inc., 20 E. 23rd St., New York, N.Y. 10010 Tel 212-505-5555; 800-631-3577 Fax 212-979-7759; refer orders to Farrar, Straus & Giroux Inc., 19 Union Sq. W., New York, N.Y. 10003 Tel 212-741-6900; 800-788-6262

Applause Theatre Bk. Pubs., 211 W. 71st St., New York, N.Y. 10023 Tel 212-595-4735 Fax 212-721-2856

Arcade Pub., 141 5th Ave., New York, N.Y. 10010 Tel 212-475-2633; 800-343-9204 Fax 212-353-8148; refer orders to Little, Brown & Co., 200 West St., Waltham, Mass. 02254 Tel 617-890-0250; 800-343-9204 Fax 617-890-0875

Archon Bks., 2 Linsley St., North Haven, Conn. 06473-2517 Tel 203-239-2702 Fax 203-239-2568

Arco Pub. Inc., Simon & Schuster Bldg., 1230 Ave. of the Americas, New York, N.Y. 10020 Tel 212-698-7000; 800-223-2348; refer orders to Simon & Schuster, 200 Old Tappan Rd., Old Tappan, N.J. 07675 Tel 800-223-2336 (orders) Fax 800-445-6991

Aris Bks., 1621 5th St., Berkeley, Calif. 94710 Tel 415-527-5171; 800-447-2226

Arte Público Press, University of Houston, 4800 Calhoun, Houston, Tex. 77204 Tel 713-743-2841; 800-633-2783 Fax 713-743-2847

Association for Educ. Communications & Technology, 1025 Vermont Ave. N.W., Suite 820, Washington, D.C. 20005 Tel 202-347-7834

Atheneum Bks. for Young Readers, 1230 Ave. of the Americas, New York, N.Y. 10020 Tel 212-698-7000; 800-223-2348 Fax 800-445-6991; refer orders to Simon & Schuster, 200 Old Tappan Rd., Old Tappan, N.J. 07675 Tel 800-223-2336 (orders) Fax 800-445-6991

Atheneum Pubs., 1230 Ave. of the Americas, New York, N.Y. 10020 Tel 212-698-7000; 800-223-2348 Fax 800-445-6991; refer orders to Simon & Schuster, 200 Old Tappan Rd., Old Tappan, N.J. 07675 Tel 800-223-2336 (orders) Fax 800-445-6991

Atlantic Monthly Press, 841 Broadway, New York, N.Y. 10003-4793 Tel 212-614-7850; 800-638-6460 Fax 212-614-7886; refer orders to Publishers Group West, P.O. Box 8843, Emeryville, Calif. 94662 Tel 800-788-3123

August House Inc., P.O. Box 3223, Little Rock, Ark. 72203-3223 Tel 501-372-5450; 800-284-8784 Fax 501-372-5579

Avenel Bks., 40 Engelhard Ave., Avenel, N.J. 07001 Tel 908-827-2700; 800-223-6804; refer orders to Random House

Avon Bks., 1350 Ave. of the Americas, 2nd Floor, New York, N.Y. 10019 Tel 212-261-6800; 800-238-0658 Fax 212-261-6895; refer orders to P.O. Box 767, Dresden, Tenn. 38225 Tel 800-223-0690

Baen Pub. Enterprises, P.O. Box 1403, Riverdale, N.Y. 10471 Tel 718-548-3100 Fax 718-548-3102; refer orders to Simon & Schuster, 200 Old Tappan Rd., Old Tappan, N.J. 07675 Tel 800-223-2336 (orders) Fax 800-445-6991

Ballantine Bks., 201 E. 50th St., New York, N.Y. 10022 Tel 212-751-2713; 800-638-6460 Fax 212-572-4912; refer orders to 400 Hahn Rd., Westminster, Md. 21157 Tel 800-726-0600

Bantam Bks. Inc., 1540 Broadway, New York, N.Y. 10036 Tel 212-354-6500; 800-323-9872; 800-223-6834 (outside NY) Fax 212-492-9698

Barnes & Noble Bks., 4720 Boston Way, Lanham, Md. 20706 Tel 301-306-0400; 800-462-6420 Fax 301-459-3366

Barricade Bks. Inc., 150 5th Ave., New York, N.Y. 10011 Tel 212-627-7000; 800-592-6657 Fax 212-627-7028

Barron's Educ. Ser. Inc., 250 Wireless Blvd., Hauppauge, N.Y. 11788 Tel 516-434-3311; 800-257-5729; 800-645-3476 (outside NY) Fax 516-434-3723

Basic Bks. Inc. Pubs., 10 E. 53rd St., New York, N.Y. 10022-5299 Tel 212-207-7057 Fax 212-207-7203; refer orders to HarperCollins Pubs., 1000 Keystone Ind. Park, Scranton, Pa. 18512-0588 Tel 717-941-1500; 800-982-4377 Fax 800-822-4090

Beacham Pub., 740 N. Casey Key Rd., P.O. Box 830, Osprey, Fla. 34229-0830 Tel 813-918-0620; 800-466-9644

Beacon Press, 25 Beacon St., Boston, Mass. 02108 Tel 617-742-2110; 800-788-6262 Fax 617-723-3097; refer orders to Farrar, Straus & Giroux Inc., 19 Union Sq. W., New York, N.Y. 10003 Tel 212-741-6900; 800-631-8571 Fax 212-633-9385

Bedford Arts Pubs., 301 Brannan St., Suite 410, San Francisco, Calif. 94107 Tel 415-882-7870; refer orders to Publisher Resources Inc., 1224 Heil Quaker Blvd., P.O. Box 7001, La Vergne, Tenn. 37086-7001 Tel 615-793-5090; 800-937-5557

Bedrick Bks.: Peter Bedrick Bks. Inc., 2112 Broadway, Room 318, New York, N.Y. 10023 Tel 212-496-0751 Fax 212-496-1158

Beekman House, 40 Engelhard Ave., Avenel, N.J. 07001 Tel 908-827-2700; 800-223-6804; refer orders to Random House

Belknap Press, 79 Garden St., Cambridge, Mass. 02138 Tel 617-495-2480

Benziger Pub. Co., 936 Eastwind Dr., Westerville, Ohio 43081 Tel 614-890-1111; 800-848-1567 Fax 614-899-4304

Berg Pubs. Ltd., 150 Cowley Rd., Oxford OX4 1JJ, Eng. Tel (01865) 245 104 Fax (01865) 791 165; refer orders to Biblios Pubs. Distr. Services Ltd., Star Rd., Partridge Green, Horsham, W. Sussex RH13 8LD, Eng. Tel (01403) 710 971; 710 851 (orders) Fax (01403) 711 143
Branch offices
U.S.: Berg Pubs., 13950 Park Center Rd., Herndon, Va. 22071 Tel 703-435-9326; 800-546-9326 Fax 703-689-0660

Berkley Bks., 200 Madison Ave., New York, N.Y. 10016 Tel 212-951-8800; 800-631-8571 Fax 212-545-8917; refer orders to P.O. Box 506, E. Rutherford, N.J. 07073 Tel 201-933-9292; 800-223-0510 (orders) Fax 201-933-4927

Berkley Pub. Group (The), 200 Madison Ave., New York, N.Y. 10016 Tel 212-951-8800; 800-631-8571 Fax 212-213-6706; refer orders to P.O. Box 506, E. Rutherford, N.J. 07073 Tel 201-933-9292; 800-223-0510 (orders) Fax 201-933-4927

Betterway Bks., 1507 Dana Ave., Cincinnati, Ohio 45207 Tel 513-531-2690; 800-289-0963 Fax 513-531-7107

Betterway Publs. Inc., 1507 Dana Ave., Cincinnati, Ohio 45207 Tel 513-531-2222; 800-289-0963 Fax 513-531-4082

Biblo & Tannen Booksellers & Pubs. Inc., 321 Sandbank Rd., Cheshire, Conn. 06410; refer orders to Biblo-Moser Bk. Pubs. & Distributors, P.O. Box 302, Cheshire, Conn. 06410

Bicycle Bks. Pub. Inc., 1282 7th Ave., San Francisco, Calif. 94122 Tel 415-665-8214 Fax 415-753-8572

Blackbirch Press Inc., 260 Amity Rd., Woodbridge, Conn. 06525 Tel 203-387-7525; 800-831-9183 Fax 203-389-1596

Blackwell Ref., 108 Cowley Rd., Oxford OX4 1JF, Eng. Tel (01865) 791 100 Fax (01865) 791 347; refer orders to Marston Bk. Services Ltd., P.O. Box 87, Osney Mead, Oxford OX2 0DT, Eng. Tel (01865) 791 155 Fax (01865) 791 927
Branch offices
U.S.: Blackwell Ref., 238 Main St., Suite 501, Cambridge, Mass. 02142 Tel 617-547-7110 Fax 617-547-0789; refer orders to American Int. Distr. Corp., 64 Depot Rd., Colchester, Vt. 05446 Tel 802-878-0315; 800-488-2665 (outside Vt.) Fax 802-878-1102

Blair: John F. Blair Pub., 1406 Plaza Dr., Winston-Salem, N.C. 27103-1470 Tel 910-768-1374; 800-222-9796 Fax 910-768-9194

Bluejay Bks. Inc., 26 Douglas Rd., Chappequa, N.Y. 10514 Tel 914-238-3491; refer orders to St. Martin's Press

BOA Eds. Ltd., 260 East Ave., Rochester, N.Y. 14604 Tel 716-546-3410 Fax 716-546-3913

Body Press/Perigee, 200 Madison Ave., New York, N.Y. 10016 Tel 212-951-8400; 800-631-8571; refer orders to P.O. Box 506, E. Rutherford, N.J. 07073 Tel 800-223-0510

Bonanza Bks., 40 Engelhard Ave., Avenel, N.J. 07001 Tel 908-827-2700; 800-223-6804; refer orders to Random House

Bonaventure Press, 25 Tulip, Aliso Viejo, Calif. 92656 Tel 714-643-1599 Fax 714-643-1599

Bonus Bks., 160 E. Illinois St., Chicago, Ill. 60611 Tel 312-467-0580; 800-225-3775 Fax 312-467-9271

Booklist Publs., 50 E. Huron St., Chicago, Ill. 60611 Tel 312-280-2424; 800-545-2433 Fax 312-944-2641 (orders only)

Books of Wonder, 132 7th Ave., New York, N.Y. 10011 Tel 212-989-3475; 800-207-6968 Fax 212-989-1203

Bowker: R. R. Bowker Co., 121 Chanlon Rd., New Providence, N.J. 07974 Tel 908-464-6800; 800-521-8110 Fax 908-464-3553; refer orders to Reed Ref. Pub., P.O. Box 31, New Providence, N.J. 07974

Boy Scouts of Am., P.O. Box 152079, 1325 W. Walnut Hill Lane, Irving, Tex. 75038-3096 Tel 214-659-2273; refer orders to National Distr. Center, 2109 Westinghouse Blvd., P.O. Box 7143, Charlotte, N.C. 28241-7143 Tel 704-588-4260

Bradbury Press Inc., 1230 Ave. of the Americas, New York, N.Y. 10020 Tel 212-698-7200; 800-223-2348; refer orders to Simon & Schuster Children's Order Dept., 200 Old Tappan Rd., Old Tappan, N.J. 07675 Tel 800-223-2336 Fax 800-445-6991

Brassey's U.K., 33 John St., London WC1N 2AT, Eng. Tel (0171) 753 7777; 753 7791 (orders) Fax (0171) 753 7795; refer orders to Marston Bk. Services Ltd., P.O. Box 269, Abingdon, Oxfordshire OX14 4YN, Eng. Tel (01235) 465 500 Fax (01235) 465 555
Branch offices
U.S.: Brassey's (US) Inc., 22883 Quicksilver Dr., No. 100, Dulles, Va. 20166 Tel 703-260-0602 Fax 703-260-0701; refer orders to P.O. Box 960, Herndon, Va. 20172 Tel 800-775-2518 Fax 703-661-1501

Braziller: George Braziller Inc., 171 Madison Ave., Suite 1103, New York, N.Y. 10016 Tel 212-889-0909 Fax 212-689-5405

Browndeer Press, 525 B St., Suite 1900, San Diego, Calif. 92101 Tel 619-699-6707; 800-831-7799

Bullseye Bks., 201 E. 50th St., New York, N.Y. 10022 Tel 212-751-2600; 800-726-0600; refer orders to 400 Hahn Rd., Westminster, Md. 21157 Tel 301-848-2436; 800-733-3000 Fax 800-659-2436

Cambridge Univ. Press, Edinburgh Bldg., Shaftesbury Rd., Cambridge CB2 2RU, Eng. Tel (01223) 312 393 Fax (01223) 315 052
Branch offices
U.S.: Cambridge Univ. Press, 40 W. 20th St., New York, N.Y. 10011-4211 Tel 212-924-3900; refer orders to 110 Midland Ave., Port Chester, N.Y. 10573-4930 Tel 914-937-9600; 800-872-7423 (orders only) Fax 914-937-4712

Camden House (Camden East): Camden House Pub. Ltd., 7 Queen Victoria Rd., Camden East, Ont., Can. K0K 1J0 Tel 613-378-6661 Fax 613-378-6123

Candlewick Press, 2067 Massachusetts Ave., Cambridge, Mass. 02140 Tel 617-661-3330 Fax 617-661-0565; refer orders to Penguin USA, P.O. Box 120, Bergenfield, N.J. 07621-0120 Tel 800-526-0275 Fax 201-385-6521; 800-227-9604

Career Press Inc. (The), 3 Tice Rd., P.O. Box 687, Franklin Lakes, N.J. 07417 Tel 201-848-0310; 800-227-3371 Fax 201-848-1727

Carol Pub. Group, 120 Enterprise Ave., Secaucus, N.J. 07094 Tel 201-866-0490 Fax 201-866-8159

Carroll & Graf Pubs. Inc., 260 5th Ave., New York, N.Y. 10001 Tel 212-889-8772 Fax 212-545-7909; refer orders to Publishers Group West, P.O. Box 8843, Emeryville, Calif. 94662 Tel 800-788-3123

Center for African Art (The), 593 Broadway, New York, N.Y. 10012 Tel 212-966-1313 Fax 212-966-1432

Chapman & Hall Ltd., 2-6 Boundary Row, London SE1 8HN, Eng. Tel (0171) 865 0066 Fax (0171) 522 9623; refer orders to International Thomson Pub. Services Ltd., Cheriton House, North Way, Andover, Hampshire SP10 5BE, Eng. Tel (01264) 332 424 Fax (01264) 364 418

Chelsea House Pubs., P.O. Box 914, 1974 Sproul Rd., Suite 400, Broomall, Pa. 19008-0914 Tel 610-353-5166; 800-362-9786 Fax 610-359-1439

Chicago Review Press, 814 N. Franklin St., Chicago, Ill. 60610 Tel 312-337-0747; 800-888-4741 (orders only) Fax 312-337-5985

Chilton Bk. Co., 201 King of Prussia Rd., Radnor, Pa. 19089-0230 Tel 610-964-4000; 800-695-1214 Fax 610-694-4745; refer orders to 1 Chilton Way, Radnor, Pa. 19089-0230

Christian Classics Inc., 77 W. Main St., P.O. Box 30, Westminster, Md. 21158 Tel 410-848-3065; 800-888-3065 Fax 410-857-2805

Chronicle Bks., 85 2nd St., 6th Floor, San Francisco, Calif. 94105 Tel 415-537-3730; 800-722-6657 (orders) Fax 415-537-4470; 800-858-7787 (orders)

Churchill Livingstone, Robert Stevenson House, 1-3 Baxter's Pl., Leith Walk, Edinburgh EH1 3AF, Scotland Tel (0131) 535 1021; (0500) 556 242 Fax (0131) 535 1022
Branch offices
U.S.: Churchill Livingstone Inc., 650 Ave. of the Americas, New York, N.Y. 10011 Tel 212-206-5000 Fax 212-727-7808; refer orders to Churchill Livingstone Fulfillment Center, 5 S. 250 Frontenac Rd., Naperville, Ill. 60563-1711 Tel 708-416-3939; 800-553-5426 Fax 708-983-5576

Citadel Press, 120 Enterprise Ave., Secaucus, N.J. 07094 Tel 201-866-0490 Fax 201-866-8159

City Lights Bks., 261 Columbus Ave., San Francisco, Calif. 94133 Tel 415-362-1901 Fax 415-362-4921; refer orders to The Subterranean Co., P.O. Box 160, 265 S. 5th St., Monroe, Or. 97456 Tel 541-847-5274; 800-274-7826 Fax 541-847-6018

Clarion Bks., 215 Park Ave. S., New York, N.Y. 10003 Tel 212-420-5800 Fax 212-420-5855; refer orders to Houghton Mifflin Co., 181 Ballardville St., Wilmington, Mass. 01887 Tel 508-661-1300; 800-225-3362

Clear Light Pubs., 823 Don Diego, Santa Fe, N.M. 87501 Tel 505-989-9590; 800-253-2747 (orders only) Fax 505-989-9519

Coin & Currency Inst. Inc (The), P.O. Box 1057, Clifton, N.J. 07014 Tel 201-471-1441

Cole Group Inc., 1330 N. Dutton Ave., Suite 103, Santa Rosa, Calif. 95401 Tel 707-526-2682; 800-959-2717 Fax 707-526-2687

College Entrance Examination Bd., 45 Columbus Ave., New York, N.Y. 10023-6992 Tel 212-713-8000 Fax 212-713-8184; refer orders to College Bd. Publs., P.O. Box 886, New York, N.Y. 10101-0886 Tel 800-323-7155 (credit card orders)

Collier Bks., 1230 Ave. of the Americas, New York, N.Y. 10020 Tel 212-698-7000; 800-223-2348; refer orders to Simon & Schuster Order Dept., 200 Old Tappan Rd., Old Tappan, N.J. 07675 Tel 800-223-2336 Fax 800-445-6991

Collier, P.F.: P. F. Collier Inc., 866 3rd Ave., New York, N.Y. 10022 Tel 212-702-3550 Fax 212-605-3019

Colorado Associated Univ. Press, P.O. Box 849, Niwot, Colo. 80544 Tel 303-530-5337; 800-268-6044 Fax 303-530-5306

Columbia Univ. Press, 562 W. 113th St., New York, N.Y. 10025 Tel 212-666-1000 Fax 212-316-3100; refer orders to 136 S. Broadway, Irvington, N.Y. 10533 Tel 914-591-9111; 800-944-8648 Fax 914-591-9201; 800-944-1844

Compton's Learning Co., 310 S. Michigan Ave., 11th Floor, Chicago, Ill. 60604 Tel 312-347-7959; 800-554-9862 Fax 312-294-2199

Conari Press, 2550 9th St., Suite 101, Berkeley, Calif. 94710 Tel 510-649-7175; 800-685-9595 (orders) Fax 510-649-7190; refer orders to Publishers Group West, P.O. Box 8843, Emeryville, Calif. 94662 Tel 800-788-3123

Congdon & Weed, 180 N. Michigan Ave., Chicago, Ill. 60601-7401 Tel 312-782-9181; 800-221-7945; refer orders to Contemporary Bks.

Congressional Quarterly Inc., 1414 22nd St. N.W., Washington, D.C. 20037-1003 Tel 202-887-8500; 800-638-1710 (orders) Fax 202-887-6706

Consumer Repts. Bks., 101 Truman Ave., Yonkers, N.Y. 10703 Tel 914-378-2000 Fax 914-378-2901; refer orders to St. Martin's Press Inc., 175 5th Ave., Room 1715, New York, N.Y. 10010 Tel 212-674-5151; 800-221-7945 Fax 212-420-9314

Contemporary Bks. Inc., 2 Prudential Plaza, Suite 1200, Chicago, Ill. 60601 Tel 312-540-4500; 800-621-1918 Fax 312-540-4687

Contemporary Res. Assocs., P.O. Box 7240, Dallas, Tex. 75209 Tel 214-690-5882

Continuum, 370 Lexington Ave., Suite 1700, New York, N.Y. 10017-6550 Tel 212-953-5858; 800-937-5557; refer orders to Publisher Resources Inc., 1224 Heil Quaker Blvd., P.O. Box 7001, La Vergne, Tenn. 37086 Tel 615-793-5090; 800-937-5557 Fax 615-793-3915; 800-774-6733

Conway Greene Pub. Co., 11000 Cedar Ave., Cleveland, Ohio 44106 Tel 216-721-0077; 800-977-2665 Fax 216-721-8256

Cornell Univ. Press, 512 E. State St., P.O. Box 250, Ithaca, N.Y. 14851-0250 Tel 607-277-2338; refer orders to C.U.P. Services, 750 Cascadilla St., Ithaca, N.Y. 14850 Tel 800-666-2211 (outside NY) Fax 607-277-2374; 800-688-2877

Cotler Bks.: Joanna Cotler Bks., 10 E. 53rd St., New York, N.Y. 10022-5299 Tel 212-207-7000; 800-331-3761 Fax 212-207-7145

Council of State Govts., Iron Works Pike, P.O. Box 11910, Lexington, Ky. 40578 Tel 606-231-1939; 800-800-1910 (orders only) Fax 606-231-1858

Coward-McCann Inc., 200 Madison Ave., New York, N.Y. 10016 Tel 212-951-8400; 800-631-8571; refer orders to 390 Murray Hill Parkway, East Rutherford, N.J. 07073

CQ Press, 1414 22nd St. N.W., Washington, D.C. 20037-1003 Tel 202-887-8500; 800-638-1710 (orders) Fax 202-887-6706

Cranbury Publs., P.O. Box 2260, Norwalk, Conn. 06852-2260 Tel 203-847-8029

CRC Press Inc., 2000 Corporate Blvd. N.W., Boca Raton, Fla. 33431 Tel 407-994-0555; 800-272-7737 (orders) Fax 407-997-7249; 998-9114 (orders)

Creative Educ. Inc., 123 S. Broad St., P.O. Box 227, Mankato, Minn. 56001 Tel 507-388-6273; 800-445-6209 Fax 507-388-2746

Crowell See HarperCollins Pubs.

Crown Pubs. Inc., 201 E. 50th St., New York, N.Y. 10022 Tel 212-751-2600; refer orders to 400 Hahn Rd., Westminster, Md. 21157 Tel 410-848-1900; 800-733-3000 Fax 800-659-2436

Crown Trade Paperbacks, 201 E. 50th St., New York, N.Y. 10022 Tel 212-751-2600 Fax 212-572-6192; refer orders to 400 Hahn Rd., Westminster, Md. 21157 Tel 410-848-1900; 800-733-3000 Fax 800-659-2436

CSA Publs., Binghamton Univ., P.O. Box 6000, Binghamton, N.Y. 13902-6000 Tel 607-777-6048 Fax 607-777-4000

Curbstone Press, 321 Jackson St., Willimantic, Conn. 06226 Tel 203-423-5110 Fax 203-423-9242

Da Capo Press Inc., 233 Spring St., New York, N.Y. 10013 Tel 212-620-8000; 800-221-9369; 800-321-0050 (orders only) Fax 212-463-0742

Davidson, H.: Harlan Davidson Inc., 773 Glenn Ave., Wheeling, Ill. 60090-6000 Tel 708-541-9720 Fax 708-541-9830

DAW Bks. Inc., 375 Hudson St., New York, N.Y. 10014 Tel 212-366-2096; refer orders to Penguin USA, 375 Hudson St., New York, N.Y. 10014 Tel 212-366-2000 Fax 212-366-2666

De Gruyter: Walter de Gruyter & Co., Postfach 30 34 21, 10728 Berlin, Germany Tel (030) 260050 Fax (030) 26005251
Branch offices
U.S.: Walter De Gruyter Inc., 200 Saw Mill River Rd., Hawthorne, N.Y. 10532 Tel 914-747-0110 Fax 914-747-1326

Dee, I.R.: Ivan R. Dee Inc., 1332 N. Halsted St., Chicago, Ill. 60622-2637 Tel 312-787-6262 Fax 312-787-6269; refer orders to 62 Imlay St., Brooklyn, N.Y. 11231-1227 Tel 800-634-0226 (orders only)

Delacorte Press, 1540 Broadway, New York, N.Y. 10036 Tel 212-354-6500; 800-323-9872 Fax 212-765-3869

Dell Pub. Co. Inc., 1540 Broadway, New York, N.Y. 10036 Tel 212-354-6500; 800-323-9872; 800-223-6834 (outside NY) Fax 212-492-9698

Dembner Bks., 61 4th Ave., New York, N.Y. 10011 Tel 212-228-8828; 800-365-3453; refer orders to Publishers Group West, P.O. Box 8843, Emeryville, Calif. 94662 Tel 800-788-3123

Dial Bks., 375 Hudson St., New York, N.Y. 10014 Tel 212-366-2000 Fax 212-366-2020; refer orders to Penguin USA, P.O. Box 120, Bergenfield, N.J. 07261 Tel 201-387-0600; 800-526-0275

Dial Bks. for Young Readers, 375 Hudson St., New York, N.Y. 10014 Tel 212-366-2000 Fax 212-366-2020; refer orders to Penguin USA, P.O. Box 120, Bergenfield, N.J. 07261 Tel 201-387-0600; 800-526-0275

Dial Press (NY): The Dial Press, 1540 Broadway, New York, N.Y. 10036 Tel 212-354-6500; 800-323-9872; 800-223-6834 (outside NY) Fax 212-492-9698

Dioscorides Press Inc., 133 S.W. 2nd Ave., Suite 450, Portland, Or. 97204 Tel 503-227-2878; 800-327-5680 (U.S. & Can.) Fax 503-227-3070

DK Pub. Inc., 95 Madison Ave., New York, N.Y. 10016 Tel 212-213-4800; 888-342-5357 Fax 212-213-5240; refer orders to Publishers Resources, 1224 Heil Quaker Blvd., La Vergne, Tenn. 37086-7001 Tel 615-793-5090; 800-937-5557 Fax 800-774-6733

Dodd, Mead Out of business; list acquired by Putnam Pub. Group and others

Doherty Assocs.: Tom Doherty Assocs. Inc., 175 5th Ave., New York, N.Y. 10010 Tel 212-388-0100; 800-221-7945 Fax 212-420-9314; refer orders to St. Martin's Press Inc., 175 5th Ave., Room 1715, New York, N.Y. 10010 Tel 212-674-5151; 800-221-7945 Fax 212-420-9314

Donnelley: R. R. Donnelley & Sons Co., 2223 Martin Luther King Dr., Chicago, Ill. 60616 Tel 312-326-8000

Dorling Kindersley See DK Pub.

Doubleday, 1540 Broadway, 18th Floor, New York, N.Y. 10036 Tel 212-354-6500; 800-223-6834 (outside NY); 800-223-5780 (orders) Fax 212-302-7985; 800-258-4233 (orders)

Dover Publs. Inc., 180 Varick St., 9th Floor, New York, N.Y. 10014 Tel 212-255-3755 Fax 212-626-9670; refer orders to 31 E. 2nd St., Mineola, N.Y. 11501 Tel 516-294-7000; 800-223-3130 Fax 516-742-5049

Drama Bk. Pubs., 260 5th Ave., New York, N.Y. 10001 Tel 212-725-5377 Fax 212-725-8506

Duke Univ. Press, P.O. Box 90660, Durham, N.C. 27708-0660 Tel 919-687-3600 Fax 919-688-4574

Dutton, 375 Hudson St., New York, N.Y. 10014-3657 Tel 212-366-2000 Fax 212-366-2020; refer orders to Penguin USA, P.O. Box 999, Dept. 17109, Bergenfield, N.J. 07621 Tel 800-253-6476

Dutton Children's Bks., 375 Hudson St., New York, N.Y. 10014-3657 Tel 212-366-2000 Fax 212-366-2020; refer orders to Penguin USA, P.O. Box 120, Bergenfield, N.J. 07261 Tel 201-387-0600; 800-526-0275

Eastman Kodak. Professional Photography Div., 343 State St., Bldg. 10, 6th Floor, Rochester, N.Y. 14650-0132 Tel 716-724-1580 Fax 716-724-0774

Ecco Press, 100 W. Broad St., Hopewell, N.J. 08525 Tel 609-466-4748; 800-223-2584; refer orders to W. W. Norton & Co. Inc., 500 5th Ave., New York, N.Y. 10110 Tel 212-354-5500; 800-233-4830 (orders) Fax 212-869-0856; 800-458-6515 (orders)

Educational Directories Inc., P.O. Box 199, Mount Prospect, Ill. 60056-0346

Eerdmans: Wm. B. Eerdmans Pub. Co., 255 Jefferson Ave. S.E., Grand Rapids, Mich. 49503 Tel 616-459-4591; 800-253-7521 (U.S. & Can. orders only) Fax 616-459-6540

Elliott & Clark Pub. Inc., 1745 Kalorama St. N.W., Suite B1, Washington, D.C. 20009 Tel 202-387-9805; 800-789-7733 Fax 202-328-3204

Encyclopaedia Britannica Inc., 310 S. Michigan Ave., Chicago, Ill. 60604 Tel 312-347-7000; 800-554-9862 Fax 312-294-2191

Encyclopaedia Britannica Educ. Corp., 310 S. Michigan Ave., Chicago, Ill. 60604 Tel 312-347-7900; 800-554-9862

Enslow Pubs., 44 Fadem Rd., Springfield, N.J. 07081-0699 Tel 201-379-8890; 800-398-2504 Fax 201-379-7940

Eriksson: Paul S. Eriksson Pub., P.O. Box 62, Forest Dale, Vt. 05745 Tel 802-247-4210 Fax 802-247-4256; refer orders to Independent Pubs. Group, 814 N. Franklin, Chicago, Ill. 60610 Tel 312-337-0747; 800-888-4741 Fax 312-337-5985

Evans & Co.: M. Evans & Co. Inc., 216 E. 49th St., New York, N.Y. 10017 Tel 212-688-2810; 800-879-4214 Fax 212-486-4544; refer orders to National Bk. Network, 4720 Boston Way, Lanham, Md. 20706 Tel 301-459-8696; 800-462-6420 Fax 301-459-2118

Faber & Faber Ltd., 3 Queen Sq., London WC1N 3AU, Eng. Tel (0171) 465 0045 Fax (0171) 465 0034; refer orders to Burnt Mill, Elizabeth Way, Harlow, Essex CM20 2HX, Eng. Tel (01279) 417 134 Fax (01279) 417 366

Branch offices

U.S.: Faber & Faber Inc., 53 Shore Rd., Winchester, Mass. 01890-2821 Tel 617-721-1427 Fax 617-729-2783; refer orders to C.U.P. Services, 750 Cascadilla St., Ithaca, N.Y. 14851 Tel 607-277-2211; 800-666-2211 Fax 607-277-6292

Facts on File Inc., 11 Penn Plaza, New York, N.Y. 10001 Tel 212-967-8800; 800-322-8755 (except Alaska & Hawaii) Fax 212-683-3633; 800-678-3633 (except Alaska & Hawaii)

Fairchild Publs. Inc., 7 W. 34th St., New York, N.Y. 10001 Tel 212-630-3880; 800-247-6622 Fax 212-630-3868

Farrar, Straus & Giroux Inc., 19 Union Sq. W., New York, N.Y. 10003 Tel 212-741-6900; 800-631-8571 Fax 212-633-9385

Fawcett Bks., 201 E. 50th St., New York, N.Y. 10022 Tel 212-572-2713; 800-733-0600 Fax 212-572-6046; refer orders to 400 Hahn Rd., Westminster, Md. 21157 Tel 800-733-3000

Feminist Press: The Feminist Press at the City Univ. of N.Y., 311 E. 94th St., New York, N.Y. 10128-5684 Tel 212-360-5790 Fax 212-348-1241

Ferguson, J.G.: J. G. Ferguson Pub. Co., 200 W. Monroe, Suite 250, Chicago, Ill. 60606 Tel 312-580-5480 Fax 312-580-4948

Fine, D.I.: Donald I. Fine Inc., 375 Hudson St., New York, N.Y. 10014-3657 Tel 212-366-2570 Fax 212-366-2933; refer orders to Penguin USA, P.O. Box 999, Dept. 17109, Bergenfield, N.J. 07621 Tel 800-253-6476

Firefly Bks. (Buffalo): Firefly Bks., P.O. Box 1338, Ellicott Station, Buffalo, N.Y. 14205 Tel 800-387-5085

Fireside Bks., 1230 Ave. of the Americas, New York, N.Y. 10020 Tel 212-698-7000; 800-223-2348; refer orders to Simon & Schuster, 200 Old Tappan Rd., Old Tappan, N.J. 07675 Tel 800-223-2336 (orders) Fax 800-445-6991

Focal Press Inc., 313 Washington St., Newton, Mass. 02158 Tel 617-928-2500; refer orders to 225 Wildwood Ave., Woburn, Mass. 01801 Tel 800-366-2665 Fax 617-933-6333

Fodor's Travel Publs. Inc., 201 E. 50th St., New York, N.Y. 10022 Tel 212-572-8784; 800-733-3000 Fax 212-572-2248; refer orders to 400 Hahn Rd., Westminster, Md. 21157 Tel 410-848-1900; 800-733-3000 Fax 800-659-2436

Foreign Policy Assn. Inc., 470 Park Ave. S., 2nd Floor, New York, N.Y. 10016-6819 Tel 212-481-8100; 800-628-5724 Fax 212-481-9275; refer orders to C.U.P. Services, P.O. Box 6525, Ithaca, N.Y. 14851 Tel 607-277-6292; 800-688-2788 Fax 800-477-5836

Forest Press (Albany): Forest Press, 85 Watervliet Ave., Albany, N.Y. 12206 Tel 518-489-8549

Forge, 175 5th Ave., New York, N.Y. 10010 Tel 212-388-0100 Fax 212-388-0191; refer orders to St. Martin's Press Inc., 175 5th Ave., Room 1715, New York, N.Y. 10010 Tel 212-674-5151; 800-221-7945 Fax 212-420-9314

Fortress Press, 426 S. 5th St., P.O. Box 1209, Minneapolis, Minn. 55440-1209 Tel 612-330-3300; 800-328-4648 Fax 612-330-3455

Four Winds Press, 1230 Ave. of the Americas, New York, N.Y. 10020 Tel 212-698-7000; 800-257-5755; refer orders to Simon & Schuster Children's Ordering Dept., 200 Old Tappan Rd., Old Tappan, N.J. 07675 Tel 800-223-2336 (orders) Fax 800-445-6991

Franklin Sq. Press, 666 Broadway, New York, N.Y. 10012 Tel 212-614-6500 Fax 212-228-5889; refer orders to LPC/InBook, 1436 W. Randolph St., Chicago, Ill. 60607 Tel 312-432-7650; 800-243-0138 Fax 312-432-7603

Free Press, 1230 Ave. of the Americas, New York, N.Y. 10020 Tel 212-698-7000; 800-223-2348; refer orders to Simon & Schuster Order Dept., 200 Old Tappan Rd., Old Tappan, N.J. 07675 Tel 800-223-2336 Fax 800-445-6991

Free Spirit Pub. Inc., 400 1st Ave. N., Suite 616, Minneapolis, Minn. 55401 Tel 612-338-2068; 800-735-7323 Fax 612-337-5050

Freeman, W.H.: W. H. Freeman & Co., 41 Madison Ave., 37th Floor, New York, N.Y. 10010 Tel 212-576-9400 Fax 212-689-2383; refer orders to 4419 W. 1980 S., Salt Lake City, Utah 84104 Tel 801-973-4660; 800-877-5351 Fax 801-977-9712

French & Spanish Bk. Corp. (The), 115 5th Ave., New York, N.Y. 10003

Fromm Int. Pub. Corp., 560 Lexington Ave., New York, N.Y. 10022 Tel 212-308-4010 Fax 212-371-5187

Frontier Press (Columbus): The Frontier Press Co., P.O. Box 1098, Columbus, Ohio 43216 Tel 614-864-3737

Funk & Wagnalls Inc., 1 International Blvd., Suite 444, Mahwah, N.J. 07495-0017 Tel 201-529-6900 Fax 201-529-6906

Gale Res. Co., 835 Penobscot Bldg., 645 Griswold St., Detroit, Mich. 48226-4094 Tel 313-961-2242; 800-877-4253 Fax 313-961-6083

Garland Pub. Inc., 717 5th Ave., Suite 2500, New York, N.Y. 10022 Tel 212-751-7447 Fax 212-308-9399; refer orders to 1000A Sherman Ave., Hamden, Conn. 06514 Tel 203-281-4487; 800-627-6273 (orders only) Fax 203-230-1186

Genealogical Pub. Co. Inc., 1001 N. Calvert St., Baltimore, Md. 21202 Tel 410-837-8271; 800-296-6687

Getty Mus.: The J. Paul Getty Mus., 17985 Pacific Coast Highway, Malibu, Calif. 90265 Tel 310-459-7611 Fax 310-454-6633; refer orders to P.O. Box 2112, Santa Monica, Calif. 90407-2112 Tel 310-453-5352; 800-223-3431 Fax 310-453-7966

Gnomon Press, P.O. Box 475, Frankfort, Ky. 40602-0475 Tel 502-223-1858

Goodheart-Willcox Co. Inc., 123 W. Taft Dr., South Holland, Ill. 60473-2089 Tel 708-333-7200; 800-323-0440 Fax 708-333-9130

Gospel Pub. House, 1445 Boonville Ave., Springfield, Mo. 65802 Tel 417-831-8000; 800-641-4310 (orders) Fax 417-862-2781; 800-328-0294 (orders)

Greenhaven Press Inc., 10911 Technology Pl., San Diego, Calif. 92128-9009 Tel 619-485-7424; 800-231-5163 Fax 619-485-9549

Greenwillow Bks., 1350 Ave. of the Americas, New York, N.Y. 10019 Tel 212-261-6500; 800-237-0657 Fax 212-261-6549; refer orders to William Morrow & Co. Inc., 39 Plymouth St., P.O. Box 1219, Fairfield, N.J. 07007 Tel 800-843-9389

Greenwood Press, 88 Post Rd. W., P.O. Box 5007, Westport, Conn. 06881 Tel 203-226-3571; 800-225-5800 (orders only) Fax 203-222-1502

Grey Heron Bks., P.O. Box 69552, Portland, Or. 97201 Tel 503-294-7939 Fax 503-294-7973

Grolier Inc., Sherman Turnpike, Danbury, Conn. 06816 Tel 203-797-3500; 800-356-5590

Grolier Educ. Corp., Sherman Turnpike, Danbury, Conn. 06816 Tel 203-797-3500; 800-356-5590 Fax 203-797-3197

Grove / Atlantic , 841 Broadway, New York, N.Y. 10003-4793 Tel 212-614-7850; 800-521-0178 Fax 212-614-7915; refer orders to Publishers Group West, P.O. Box 8843, Emeryville, Calif. 94662 Tel 800-788-3123

Grove Press See Grove/Atlantic

Grove Weidenfeld See Grove/Atlantic

Grove's Dictionaries of Music Inc., 345 Park Ave. S., New York, N.Y. 10010 Tel 212-689-9200 Fax 212-689-9711

Gylantic Pub. Co., 6024 S. Pearl St., Littleton, Colo. 80121 Tel 303-797-6093

Hall, G.K. & Co.: G. K. Hall & Co., P.O. Box 159, Thorndike, Me. 04921 Tel 800-223-6121; lib. & general ref. bks. available from 866 3rd Ave., New York, N.Y. 10022 Tel 212-702-6789; 800-257-5755

Hammond Inc., 515 Valley St., Maplewood, N.J. 07040-1396 Tel 201-763-6000; 800-526-4953 Fax 201-763-7658

Harcourt Brace & Co., 523 B St., Suite 1900, San Diego, Calif. 92101 Tel 619-699-6707; 800-831-7799 Fax 619-699-6542

Harcourt Brace College Pubs., 301 Commerce St., Suite 3700, Fort Worth, Tex. 76102 Tel 800-447-9479; refer orders to 6277 Sea Harbor Dr., Orlando, Fla. 32887 Tel 800-782-4479 (orders)

Harcourt Brace Jovanovich See Harcourt Brace & Co.

Harmony Bks., 201 E. 50th St., New York, N.Y. 10022 Tel 212-751-2600 Fax 212-572-6192; refer orders to Random House Inc., 400 Hahn Rd., Westminster, Md. 21157 Tel 410-848-1900; 800-733-3000 Fax 800-659-2436

Harper & Row See HarperCollins Pubs.

HarperCollins College Pubs., 10 E. 53rd St., New York, N.Y. 10022-5299 Tel 212-207-7021; 800-782-2665; refer orders to 1900 E. Lake, Glenview, Ill. 60025 Tel 708-657-3900

HarperCollins Pubs., 10 E. 53rd St., New York, N.Y. 10022-5299 Tel 212-207-7000; 800-242-7737 Fax 212-207-7145; refer orders to 1000 Keystone Ind. Park, Scranton, Pa. 18512-0588 Tel 717-941-1500; 800-982-4377 Fax 800-822-4090

HarperPerennial, 10 E. 53rd St., New York, N.Y. 10022-5299 Tel 212-207-7000; 800-242-7737 Fax 212-207-7145; refer orders to 1000 Keystone Ind. Park, Scranton, Pa. 18512-0588 Tel 717-941-1500; 800-982-4377 Fax 800-822-4090

HarperPrism, 10 E. 53rd St., New York, N.Y. 10022-5299 Tel 212-207-7000; 800-242-7737 Fax 212-207-7145; refer orders to 1000 Keystone Ind. Park, Scranton, Pa. 18512-0588 Tel 717-941-1500; 800-982-4377 Fax 800-822-4090

HarperSanFrancisco, 1160 Battery St., San Francisco, Calif. 94111-1213 Tel 415-477-4400; 800-328-5125 Fax 415-477-4444; refer orders to 1000 Keystone Ind. Park, Scranton, Pa. 18512-0588 Tel 717-941-1500; 800-982-4377 Fax 800-822-4090

Harvard Univ. Press, 79 Garden St., Cambridge, Mass. 02138 Tel 617-495-2600; 495-2480 (orders) Fax 617-495-8924; 800-962-4983

Hearst Bks., 1350 Ave. of the Americas, New York, N.Y. 10019 Tel 212-261-6500; 800-237-0657 Fax 212-261-6549; refer orders to North Light Bks., 1507 Dana Ave., Cincinnati, Ohio 45207 Tel 513-531-2222; 800-289-0963 Fax 513-531-4082

Heinemann Educ. Bks. Ltd., Halley Ct., Jordan Hill, Oxford OX2 8EJ, Eng. Tel (01865) 314 301 Fax (01865) 314 029

Branch offices

U.S.: Heinemann Educ. Bks. Inc., 361 Hanover St., Portsmouth, N.H. 03801-3912 Tel 603-431-7894; 800-541-2086 Fax 603-431-7840

Hill & Wang Inc., 19 Union Sq. W., New York, N.Y. 10003 Tel 212-741-6900 Fax 212-741-6973; refer orders to P.O. Box 506, E. Rutherford, N.J. 07073 Tel 800-788-6262 Fax 201-933-2316

Holiday House Inc., 425 Madison Ave., New York, N.Y. 10017 Tel 212-688-0085 Fax 212-421-6134

Holt & Co.: Henry Holt & Co., 115 W. 18th St., New York, N.Y. 10011 Tel 212-886-9200; 800-488-5233 Fax 212-633-0748

Horizon Press, P.O. Box 402, Times Sq. Station, New York, N.Y. 10108 Tel 212-757-4420

Houghton Mifflin Co., 222 Berkeley St., Boston, Mass. 02116 Tel 617-351-5000 Fax 617-227-5409; refer orders to 181 Ballardville St., Wilmington, Mass. 01887 Tel 508-661-1300; 800-225-3362

Howell Bk. House Inc., 1633 Broadway, New York, N.Y. 10019 Tel 212-654-8295 Fax 212-654-4717; refer orders to Macmillan Pub., 201 W. 103rd St., Indianapolis, Ind. 46290 Tel 800-428-5331 Fax 800-882-8583

Human Kinetics Pubs. Inc., 1607 N. Market St., P.O. Box 5076, Champaign, Ill. 61825-5076 Tel 217-351-5076; 800-747-4457 Fax 217-351-2674; 217-351-1549 (orders)

Hyperion, 114 5th Ave., New York, N.Y. 10011 Tel 212-633-4400 Fax 212-633-4833; refer orders to Little, Brown & Co. Inc., 200 West St., Waltham, Mass. 02254 Tel 617-890-0250; 800-343-9204 Fax 617-890-0875

Hyperion Bks. for Children, 114 5th Ave., New York, N.Y. 10011 Tel 212-633-4400 Fax 212-633-4833; refer orders to Little, Brown & Co. Inc., 200 West St., Waltham, Mass. 02254 Tel 617-890-0250; 800-343-9204 Fax 617-890-0875

Hyperion Press (Westport): Hyperion Press Inc., 47 Riverside Ave., Westport, Conn. 06880 Tel 203-226-1091

IEEE Press, 445 Hoes Lane, P.O. Box 1331, Piscataway, N.J. 08855-1331 Tel 908-562-3967; 800-678-4333 Fax 908-981-8062

Indiana Univ. Press, 601 N. Morton St., Bloomington, Ind. 47404-3797 Tel 812-855-6804; 800-842-6796 (orders) Fax 812-855-7931

Information Today Inc., 143 Old Marlton Pike, Medford, N.J. 08055 Tel 609-654-6266 Fax 609-654-4309

Insight Bks., 233 Spring St., New York, N.Y. 10013-1578 Tel 212-620-8000; 800-221-9369 Fax 212-463-0742

International Focus Press, P.O. Box 1587, Richardson, Tex. 75083

International Pubs. (NY): International Pubs. Co. Inc., 239 W. 23rd St., 5th Floor, New York, N.Y. 10011 Tel 212-366-9816 Fax 212-366-9820

Investor Responsibility Res. Center Inc., 1755 Massachusetts Ave. N.W., Suite 600, Washington, D.C. 20036 Tel 202-234-7500

Island Press (Covelo): Island Press, Star Route 1, Box 38, Covelo, Calif. 95428 Tel 707-983-6432; refer orders to P.O. Box 7, Covelo, Calif. 95428 Tel 800-828-1302

Ivy Bks., 201 E. 50th St., New York, N.Y. 10022 Tel 212-572-2572; 800-733-3000 (orders)

Jane's Information Group, Sentinel House, 163 Brighton Rd., Coulsdon, Surrey CR5 2NH, Eng. Tel (0181) 763 1030 Fax (0181) 763 1005
Branch offices
U.S.: Jane's Information Group, 1340 Braddock Pl., Suite 300, Alexandria, Va. 22314-1651 Tel 703-683-3700 Fax 703-836-0029

Jewish Lights Pub., P.O. Box 237, Sunset Farm Offices, Route 4, Woodstock, Vt. 05091 Tel 802-457-4000; 800-962-4544 Fax 802-457-4004

Jewish Publ. Soc., 1930 Chestnut St., Philadelphia, Pa. 19103-4599 Tel 215-564-5925; 800-234-3151 Fax 215-564-6640; refer orders to JPS, O'Neil Highway, Dunmore, Pa. 18512 Tel 800-355-1165 Fax 717-348-9297

Johns Hopkins Univ. Press (The), 2715 N. Charles St., Baltimore, Md. 21218-4319 Tel 410-516-6990; 800-537-5487 (orders only) Fax 410-516-6998

Johnson Pub., 820 Michigan Ave., Chicago, Ill. 60605

Jossey-Bass Inc. Pubs., 350 Sansome St., San Francisco, Calif. 94104 Tel 415-433-1767; 888-378-2537 Fax 415-433-0499

Jugglebug, 7506 J Olympic View Dr., Edmonds, Wash. 98026 Tel 206-774-2127; 800-523-1776 Fax 206-774-5811

Kendall/Hunt Pub. Co., 4050 Westmark Dr., Dubuque, Iowa 52004-1840 Tel 319-589-1000; 800-228-0810 Fax 319-589-2955; 800-772-9165

Kessler Bks.: Martin Kessler Bks., 1230 Ave. of the Americas, New York, N.Y. 10020 Tel 212-698-7000; 800-223-2348; refer orders to Simon & Schuster Order Dept., 200 Old Tappan Rd., Old Tappan, N.J. 07675 Tel 800-223-2336 Fax 800-445-6991

Key Porter Bks., 70 The Esplanade, 2nd Floor, Toronto, Ont., Can. M5E 1R2 Tel 416-862-7777; 800-387-8032 Fax 416-862-2304

Kitchen Sink Press, 320 Riverside Dr., Northampton, Mass. 01060 Tel 413-586-9525; 800-365-7465 Fax 413-586-7040

Knopf: Alfred A. Knopf Inc., 201 E. 50th St., New York, N.Y. 10022 Tel 212-751-2600; 800-726-0600 Fax 212-572-2593; refer orders to Random House Inc., 400 Hahn Rd., Westminster, Md. 21157 Tel 410-848-1900; 800-733-3000 Fax 800-659-2436

Kodansha Am. Inc., 114 5th Ave., 18th Floor, New York, N.Y. 10011 Tel 212-727-6460; 800-631-8571 Fax 212-727-9177; refer orders to Farrar, Straus & Giroux, 19 Union Sq. W., New York, N.Y. 10003 Tel 212-741-6900; 800-631-8571 Fax 212-633-9385

Kodansha Int./USA See Kodansha Am.

Krause Publs. Inc., 700 E. State St., Iola, Wis. 54990 Tel 715-445-2214 Fax 715-445-4087

Krieger: Robert E. Krieger Pub. Co. Inc., P.O. Box 9542, Melbourne, Fla. 32902-9542 Tel 407-724-9542; 727-7270 (orders only) Fax 407-951-3671

Langford Bks., P.O. Box 88, South Bend, Ind. 46624 Tel 219-287-5008

Larousse Kingfisher Chambers Inc., 95 Madison Ave., New York, N.Y. 10016 Tel 212-686-1060; 800-497-1657 Fax 212-686-1082

Lawrence, S.: Seymour Lawrence Inc., 222 Berkeley St., Boston, Mass. 02116 Tel 617-351-5000; refer orders to Wayside Rd., Burlington, Mass. 01803 Tel 617-272-1500; 800-225-3362

Leisure Press, P.O. Box 5076, Champaign, Ill. 61820-5076 Tel 217-351-5076; 800-747-4457 Fax 217-351-2674

Lerner Publs. Co., 241 1st Ave. N., Minneapolis, Minn. 55401 Tel 612-332-3344; 800-328-4929 Fax 612-332-7615

Levin Assocs.: Hugh Lauter Levin Assocs. Inc., 2507 Post Rd., Southport, Conn. 06490 Tel 203-254-7733 Fax 203-254-7586

Lexington Bks., 1230 Ave. of the Americas, New York, N.Y. 10020 Tel 212-698-7000; 800-223-2348; refer orders to Simon & Schuster Order Dept., 200 Old Tappan Rd., Old Tappan, N.J. 07675 Tel 800-223-2336 Fax 800-445-6991

Libraries Unlimited Inc., P.O. Box 6633, Englewood, Colo. 80155-6633 Tel 303-770-1200; 800-237-6124 Fax 303-220-8843

Library of Am. (The), 14 E. 60th St., New York, N.Y. 10022 Tel 212-308-3360; 800-631-3577 Fax 212-750-8352; refer orders to Penguin USA, P.O. Box 999, Dept. 17109, Bergenfield, N.J. 07621 Tel 800-253-6476

Library of Congress, Washington, D.C. 20540 Tel 202-707-6095 Fax 202-707-9898; refer orders to U.S. Govt. Ptg. Office, Washington, D.C. 20402 Tel 202-783-3238

Library Professional Publs., 2 Linsley St., North Haven, Conn. 06473-2517 Tel 203-239-2702 Fax 203-239-2568

Limelight Eds., 118 E. 30th St., New York, N.Y. 10016 Tel 212-532-5525; 800-426-0489 Fax 212-532-5526; refer orders to Whitehurst Clark Fulfillment Inc., 100 Newfield Ave., Edison, N.J. 08837 Tel 908-225-2727; 800-488-8040 Fax 908-225-1562

Linnet Bks., 2 Linsley St., North Haven, Conn. 06473-2517 Tel 203-239-2702 Fax 203-239-2568

Linworth Pub. Inc., 480 E. Wilson Bridge Rd., Suite L, Worthington, Ohio 43085-2372 Tel 614-436-7107 Fax 614-436-9490

Lion Bks., 210 Nelson Rd., Suite B, Scarsdale, N.Y. 10583 Tel 914-725-2280

Lippincott See HarperCollins Pubs.

Little, Brown & Co. Inc., 34 Beacon St., Boston, Mass. 02108 Tel 617-227-0730 Fax 617-227-0790; refer orders to 200 West St., Waltham, Mass. 02154 Tel 617-890-0250; 800-343-9204 Fax 617-890-0875

Littlefield, Adams & Co., 4720 Boston Way, Lanham, Md. 20706 Tel 301-459-3366

Liveright Pub. Corp., 500 5th Ave., New York, N.Y. 10110 Tel 212-354-5500; 800-233-4830 Fax 212-869-0856

Lodestar Bks., 375 Hudson St., New York, N.Y. 10014 Tel 212-366-2000 Fax 212-366-2020; refer orders to Penguin USA, P.O. Box 120, Bergenfield, N.J. 07261 Tel 201-387-0600; 800-526-0275

Longman Group Ltd., Longman House, Burnt Mill, Harlow, Essex CM20 2JE, Eng. Tel (01279) 426 721 Fax (01279) 431 059; refer orders to P.O. Box 88, Harlow, Essex CM19 5SR, Eng. Tel (01279) 623 928 Fax (01279) 414 130

Branch offices

U.S.: Longman Pub., Longman Bldg., 10 Bank St., White Plains, N.Y. 10606-1951 Tel 914-993-5000; refer orders to Addison-Wesley Pub. Co., Jacob Way, Reading, Mass. 01867 Tel 617-944-3700; 800-447-2226 (orders only)

Lothrop, Lee & Shepard Bks., 1350 Ave. of the Americas, New York, N.Y. 10019 Tel 212-261-6500; 800-843-9389 Fax 212-261-6549

Louisiana State Univ. Press, P.O. Box 25053, Baton Rouge, La. 70894-5053 Tel 504-388-6294; 800-861-3477 Fax 504-388-6461

LPC/InBook, 1436 W. Randolph St., Chicago, Ill. 60607 Tel 312-432-7650; 800-243-0138 Fax 312-432-7603

Lucent Bks., P.O. Box 289011, San Diego, Calif. 92198-9011 Tel 619-485-7424 Fax 619-485-9549; refer orders to Greenhaven Press, 10911 Technology Pl., San Diego, Calif. 92127 Tel 619-485-7424; 800-231-5163 Fax 619-485-9549

Lucent Press, P.O. Box 289011, San Diego, Calif. 92198-9011

Lyons & Burford, 31 W. 21st St., New York, N.Y. 10010 Tel 212-620-9580 Fax 212-929-1836

Macmillan, 1633 Broadway, New York, N.Y. 10019 Tel 212-654-3000; refer orders to 201 W. 103rd St., Indianapolis, Ind. 46290 Tel 800-858-7674 Fax 317-871-6728; 800-835-3202

Macmillan Lib. Ref. USA, 1633 Broadway, New York, N.Y. 10019 Tel 212-654-8464; 800-223-2336 Fax 212-654-4745; refer orders to Simon & Schuster, 200 Old Tappan Rd., Old Tappan, N.J. 07675 Tel 800-223-2336 (orders)

Madison Press Bks., 40 Madison Ave., Toronto, Ont., Can. M5R 2S1 Tel 416-923-5027 Fax 416-923-7169

Magination Press, 19 Union Sq. W., New York, N.Y. 10003 Tel 212-924-3344; 800-825-3089 (orders) Fax 212-242-6339

Margaret K. McElderry Bks., 1230 Ave. of the Americas, New York, N.Y. 10020 Tel 212-698-7000; 800-257-5755; refer orders to Simon & Schuster Children's Ordering Dept., 200 Old Tappan Rd., Old Tappan, N.J. 07675 Tel 800-223-2336 (orders)

Marlowe & Co., 632 Broadway, 7th Floor, New York, N.Y. 10012 Tel 212-460-5742 Fax 212-460-5796; refer orders to Publishers Group West, P.O. Box 8843, Emeryville, Calif. 94662 Tel 800-788-3123

Marquis Who's Who Inc., 121 Chanlon Rd., New Providence, N.J. 07974 Tel 908-464-6800; 800-521-8110 Fax 908-464-3553

Marshall Cavendish Bks. Ltd., 119 Wardour St., London W1V 3TD, Eng. Tel (0171) 734 6710 Fax (0171) 734 6221
Branch offices
U.S.: Marshall Cavendish Corp., 99 White Plains Rd., Tarrytown, N.Y. 10591-9001 Tel 914-332-8888; 800-821-9881 Fax 914-332-1888

Mayfield Pub. Co., 1240 Villa St., Mountain View, Calif. 94041 Tel 415-960-3222; 694-2815 (orders); 800-433-1279 (orders) Fax 415-960-0328

McFarland & Co. Inc. Pubs., P.O. Box 611, Jefferson, N.C. 28640-0611 Tel 910-246-4460; 800-253-2187 (orders only) Fax 910-246-5018

McGraw-Hill Int. Bk. Co., 1221 Ave. of the Americas, New York, N.Y. 10020 Tel 212-512-2000; 800-722-4726; refer orders to McGraw-Hill/Tab Direct Marketing Orders, 860 Taylor Station Rd., Blacklick, Ohio 43004 Tel 800-262-4729 Fax 614-759-3641

McKay, D.: David McKay Co. Inc., 201 E. 50th St., New York, N.Y. 10022 Tel 212-751-2600; 800-638-6460 Fax 212-872-8026; refer orders to Random House Inc., 400 Hahn Rd., Westminster, Md. 21157 Tel 410-848-1900; 800-733-3000 Fax 800-659-2436

Medical Economics Data Inc., 5 Paragon Dr., Montvale, N.J. 07645-1742 Tel 201-358-7500; 800-442-6657 Fax 201-573-4956

Merck & Co. Inc., P.O. Box 2000, Rahway, N.J. 07065 Tel 201-574-5403

Meredith Corp., 1716 Locust St., Des Moines, Iowa 50309-3023 Tel 515-284-3000; 800-678-8091 Fax 515-284-2700

Meriwether Pub. Ltd., P.O. Box 7710, Colorado Springs, Colo. 80933 Tel 719-594-4422; 800-937-5297 Fax 719-594-9916

Merriam-Webster Inc., 47 Federal St., P.O. Box 281, Springfield, Mass. 01102 Tel 413-734-3134; 800-828-1880 Fax 413-731-5979

Messner: Julian Messner, 299 Jefferson Rd., P.O. Box 480, Parsippany, N.J. 0754-0480 Tel 201-739-8000

Methuen & Co. Ltd., Michelin House, 81 Fulham Rd., London SW3 6RB, Eng. Tel (0171) 581 9393 Fax (0171) 589 8419; refer orders to Reed Bk. Services, P.O. Box 5, Rushden, Northamptonshire NN10 6XJ, Eng. Tel (01933) 58521 Fax (01933) 50284
Branch offices
U.S.: Methuen Inc., 29 W. 35th St., New York, N.Y. 10001 Tel 212-244-3336

Metropolitan Mus. of Art, 1000 5th Ave., New York, N.Y. 10028 Tel 212-879-5500 Fax 212-535-4830

Metropolitan Opera Guild, 1865 Broadway, New York, N.Y. 10023 Tel 212-582-3285

Michelin Tire Corp., P.O. Box 3305, Spartanburg, S.C. 29304-3305

Milkweed Eds., 430 1st Ave. N., Suite 400, Minneapolis, Minn. 55401-1743 Tel 612-332-3192 Fax 612-332-6248

Millbrook Press Inc. (The), 2 Old New Milford Rd., Brookfield, Conn. 06804 Tel 203-740-2220; 800-462-4703 Fax 203-740-2526; 740-2526

Minnesota Hist. Soc. Press, 345 Kellogg Blvd. W., St. Paul, Minn. 55102-1906 Tel 612-296-2264; 800-647-7827 (orders only) Fax 612-297-1345

MIT Press (The), 55 Hayward St., Cambridge, Mass. 02142 Tel 617-625-8569; 800-356-0343 Fax 617-258-6779; refer orders to 48 Grove St., Suite 101, Somerville, Mass. 02144 Tel 617-625-8569 Fax 617-625-6660

Modern Lang. Assn. of Am. (The), 10 Astor Pl., New York, N.Y. 10003-6981 Tel 212-475-9500 Fax 212-477-9863

Modern Lib. (The), 201 E. 50th St., New York, N.Y. 10022 Tel 212-751-2600; 800-726-0600

Morning Glory Press, 6595 San Haroldo Way, Buena Park, Calif. 90620-3748 Tel 714-828-1998 Fax 714-828-2049

Morrow: William Morrow & Co. Inc., 1350 Ave. of the Americas, New York, N.Y. 10019 Tel 212-261-6500; 800-843-9389 Fax 212-261-6595; refer orders to Wilmor Warehouse, P.O. Box 1219, 39 Plymouth St., Fairfield, N.J. 07007 Tel 201-227-7200

Morrow Junior Bks., 1350 Ave. of the Americas, New York, N.Y. 10019 Tel 212-261-6500; 800-237-0657 Fax 212-261-6689; refer orders to Wilmor Warehouse, P.O. Box 1219, 39 Plymouth St., Fairfield, N.J. 07007 Tel 201-227-7200

Museum of Modern Art (The), 11 W. 53rd St., New York, N.Y. 10019 Tel 212-708-9733 Fax 212-708-9779

Mysterious Press, 1271 Ave. of the Americas, New York, N.Y. 10020 Tel 212-522-7200 Fax 212-522-7158; refer orders to Little, Brown & Co. Inc., 200 West St., Waltham, Mass. 02254 Tel 617-890-0250; 800-343-9204 Fax 617-890-0875

NAL/Dutton, 375 Hudson St., New York, N.Y. 10014-3657 Tel 212-366-2000

National Council of Teachers of English, 1111 W. Kenyon Rd., Urbana, Ill. 61801-1096 Tel 217-328-3870; 800-369-6283 Fax 217-328-9645

National Educ. Assn., 1201 16th St. N.W., Washington, D.C. 20036-3290 Tel 202-822-7252 Fax 202-822-7206; refer orders to P.O. Box 509, West Haven, Conn. 06516 Tel 203-934-2669; 800-229-4200 Fax 203-933-5276

National Geographic Soc., 1145 17th St. N.W., Washington, D.C. 20036 Tel 202-857-7000; 800-368-2728; refer orders to P.O. Box 1640, Washington, D.C. 20013-9861 Tel 301-921-1200; 800-638-4077

National Journal, 1730 M St. N.W., Washington, D.C. 20036 Tel 202-857-1400; 800-424-2921 Fax 202-833-8069; refer orders to Macmillan Pub. Co. Inc., 201 W. 103rd St., Indianapolis, Ind. 46290 Tel 800-858-7674 Fax 317-871-6728; 800-835-3202

National Science Teachers Assn., 1840 Wilson Blvd., Arlington, Va. 22201 Tel 703-243-7100 Fax 703-243-7177

National Storytelling Press, 216 Headtown Rd., Jonesborough, Tenn. 37659 Tel 423-753-2171; 800-525-4514 Fax 423-753-9331

National Textbook Co., 4255 W. Touhy Ave., Lincolnwood, Ill. 60646-1975 Tel 708-679-5500; 800-323-4900 Fax 708-679-2494

Native Am. Bk. Pubs., 5884 Winans Lake Rd., Brighton, Mich. 48116

Naval Inst. Press, U.S. Naval Inst., Preble Hall, 118 Maryland Ave., Annapolis, Md. 21402-5035 Tel 410-268-6110 Fax 410-269-7940; refer orders to 2062 Generals Highway, Annapolis, Md. 21401-6780 Tel 410-224-3378; 800-233-8764 Fax 410-224-2406

Neal-Schuman Pubs. Inc., 100 Varick St., New York, N.Y. 10013 Tel 212-925-8650 Fax 212-219-8916

Nelson, T.: Thomas Nelson Pubs., P.O. Box 14100, Nashville, Tenn. 37214 Tel 615-889-9000; 800-251-4000 Fax 615-883-7619; 391-5225 (orders)

New Am. Lib. Inc. (The), 375 Hudson St., New York, N.Y. 10014 Tel 212-366-2000; refer orders to Penguin USA, P.O. Box 120, Bergenfield, N.J. 07621 Tel 201-387-0600; 800-526-0275

New Directions Pub. Corp., 80 8th Ave., New York, N.Y. 10011 Tel 212-255-0230 Fax 212-255-0231; refer orders to W. W. Norton & Co. Inc., 500 5th Ave., New York, N.Y. 10110 Tel 212-354-5500; 800-233-4830 (orders) Fax 212-869-0856; 800-458-6515 (orders)

New Discovery Bks., 299 Jefferson Rd., P.O. Box 480, Parsippany, N.J. 07054-0480 Tel 201-739-8000; 800-848-9500 Fax 201-739-8503

New Press (NY), 450 W. 41st St., New York, N.Y. 10036 Tel 212-629-8802 Fax 212-268-6349; refer orders to W. W. Norton & Co. Inc., 500 5th Ave., New York, N.Y. 10110 Tel 212-354-5500; 800-233-4830 (orders) Fax 212-869-0856; 800-458-6515 (orders)

New Republic Bks., 1220 19th St. N.W., Suite 205, Washington, D.C. 20036; refer orders to Simon & Schuster

New York Graphic Soc., 34 Beacon St., Boston, Mass. 02106 Tel 617-227-0730; refer orders to Little, Brown

New York Public Lib. Astor, Lenox & Tilden Foundations, 5th Ave. & 42nd St., New York, N.Y. 10018 Tel 212-512-0203; refer orders to Publications Office, 8 W. 40th St., 3rd Floor, New York, N.Y. 10018 Tel 212-512-0202

New York Review of Bks. Inc., 250 W. 57th St., Room 1321, New York, N.Y. 10107 Tel 212-757-8070 Fax 212-333-5374; refer orders to Consortium Bk. Sales & Distr., 1045 Westgate Dr., Suite 90, St. Paul, Minn. 55114-1065 Tel 612-221-9035; 800-283-3572 (orders) Fax 612-221-0124

New York Times Co. (The), 229 W. 43rd St., New York, N.Y. 10036 Tel 212-556-3664; 800-631-2580

New York Univ. Press, 70 Washington Sq. S., New York, N.Y. 10012 Tel 212-998-2575; 800-996-6987 (orders) Fax 212-995-3833

Newmarket Press, 18 E. 48th St., New York, N.Y. 10017 Tel 212-832-3575; 800-669-3903 Fax 212-832-3629; refer orders to Random House Inc., 400 Hahn Rd., Westminster, Md. 21157 Tel 410-848-1900; 800-733-3000 Fax 800-659-2436

NewSage Press, 825 N.E. 20th Ave., Suite 150, Portland, Or. 97232 Tel 503-232-6794; refer orders to Publishers Group West, P.O. Box 8843, Emeryville, Calif. 94662 Tel 800-788-3123

Noonday Press, 19 Union Sq. W., New York, N.Y. 10003 Tel 212-741-6900; 800-631-8571 Fax 212-633-9385

North Light Bks., 1507 Dana Ave., Cincinnati, Ohio 45207 Tel 513-531-2690; 800-289-0963 Fax 513-531-4082

North Point Press, 19 Union Sq. W., New York, N.Y. 10003 Tel 212-741-6900; 800-631-8571 Fax 212-633-9385

Northeastern Univ. Press, 360 Huntington Ave., 416 Columbus Pl., Boston, Mass. 02115 Tel 617-373-5480 Fax 617-373-5483; refer orders to P.O. Box 6525, Ithaca, N.Y. 14851 Tel 607-277-2211

NorthWord Press Inc., P.O. Box 1360, Minocqua, Wis. 54548 Tel 715-356-7644; 800-336-6398 (orders only) Fax 715-356-9762

Norton: W. W. Norton & Co. Inc., 500 5th Ave., New York, N.Y. 10110 Tel 212-354-5500; 800-233-4830 (orders) Fax 212-869-0856; 800-458-6515 (orders)

NTC Pub. Group, 4255 W. Touhy Ave., Lincolnwood, Ill. 60646-1975 Tel 847-679-5500; 800-323-4900 (orders) Fax 847-679-2494

Odessa, 111 Virginia Ave., Cocoa, Fla. 32922 Tel 407-636-4361

Ohio State Univ. Press, 1070 Carmack Rd., 180 Pressey Hall, Columbus, Ohio 43210-1002 Tel 614-292-6930 Fax 614-292-2065

Oliver Press Inc. (The), Charlotte Sq., 5707 W. 36th St., Minneapolis, Minn. 55416-2510 Tel 612-926-8981; 800-865-4837 Fax 612-926-8965

Omnigraphics Inc., Penobscot Bldg., Detroit, Mich. 48226 Tel 313-961-1340; 800-234-1340 Fax 800-875-1340

Orchard Bks., 95 Madison Ave., 7th Floor, New York, N.Y. 10016 Tel 212-951-2600; 800-621-1115 Fax 212-213-6435

Orion Bks. (NY): Orion Bks., 201 E. 50th St., New York, N.Y. 10022 Tel 212-751-2600 Fax 212-572-6192; refer orders to Random House

Ortho Bks., P.O. Box 5006, San Ramon, Calif. 94583-0906 Tel 510-355-3372 Fax 510-842-5518; refer orders to The Solaris Group, Customer Service, 2527 Camino Ramon, Suite 200, San Ramon, Calif. 94583-0906 Tel 800-457-6900

Oryx Press (The), 4041 N. Central Ave., 7th Floor, Phoenix, Ariz. 85012-3397 Tel 602-265-2651; 800-279-6799 Fax 602-265-6250; 800-279-4663

Overlook Press (The), 149 Wooster St., 4th Floor, New York, N.Y. 10012 Tel 212-477-7162 Fax 212-477-7525; refer orders to 2568 Route 212, Woodstock, N.Y. 12498 Tel 914-679-6838 Fax 914-679-8571

Oxford Univ. Press, Walton St., Oxford OX2 6DP, Eng. Tel (01865) 556 767 Fax (01865) 556 646
Branch offices
U.S.: Oxford Univ. Press Inc., 198 Madison Ave., New York, N.Y. 10016-4314 Tel 212-726-6000; 800-334-4249 Fax 212-725-2972; refer orders to 2001 Evans Rd., Cary, N.C. 27513 Tel 919-677-1303; 800-451-7556 Fax 919-677-1303

Oxmoor House Inc., P.O. Box 2262, Birmingham, Ala. 35201 Tel 205-877-6000; 800-633-4910 Fax 205-877-6078; refer orders to Leisure Arts (Little Rock), 5701 Ranch Dr., Little Rock, Ark. 72212 Tel 501-868-8800; 800-643-8030 Fax 501-868-8937

Pantheon Bks. Inc., 201 E. 50th St., New York, N.Y. 10022 Tel 212-872-8238; 800-638-0600 Fax 212-572-6030; refer orders to Random House Inc., 400 Hahn Rd., Westminster, Md. 21157 Tel 410-848-1900; 800-733-3000 Fax 800-659-2436

Paradox Press, 1700 Broadway, New York, N.Y. 10019 Tel 212-636-5400 Fax 212-636-5443

Paragon House Pubs., 370 Lexington Ave., New York, N.Y. 10016 Tel 212-953-5950; 800-937-5557 Fax 212-953-5940; refer orders to Continuum Pub. Co., 370 Lexington Ave., Suite 1700, New York, N.Y. 10017-6550 Tel 212-953-5858; 800-937-5557

Parkwest Publs. Inc., 451 Communipaw Ave., Jersey City, N.J. 07304 Tel 201-432-3257 Fax 201-432-3708; 800-727-5937

Passport Bks., 4255 W. Touhy Ave., Lincolnwood, Ill. 60646-1975 Tel 847-679-5500; 800-323-4900 (orders) Fax 847-679-2494

Pathfinder Press, 410 West St., New York, N.Y. 10014 Tel 212-741-0690 Fax 212-727-0150

Penguin Bks. See Penguin USA

Penguin USA, 375 Hudson St., New York, N.Y. 10014 Tel 212-366-2000; refer orders to Penguin USA P.O. Box 120, Bergenfield, N.J. 07621 Tel 201-387-0600; 800-526-0275

Penguin Studio See Penguin USA

Perennial Lib., 10 E. 53rd St., New York, N.Y. 10022-5299 Tel 212-207-7000; refer orders to HarperCollins Pubs., Keystone Ind. Park, Scranton, Pa. 18512 Tel 800-982-4377; 800-242-7737 (outside Pa.)

Perigee Bks., 200 Madison Ave., New York, N.Y. 10016 Tel 212-951-8400; 800-631-8571; refer orders to P.O. Box 506, East Rutherford, N.J. 07073 Tel 800-223-0510 (orders)

Perlman Bks.: Willa Perlman Bks., c.o. HarperCollins Pubs., 10 E. 53rd St., New York, N.Y. 10022-5299 Tel 212-207-7000; 800-331-3761 Fax 212-207-7145; refer orders to 1000 Keystone Ind. Park, Scranton, Pa. 18512 Tel 717-941-1500; 800-982-4377; 800-242-7737 (outside Pa.) Fax 800-822-4090

Persea Bks. Inc., 171 Madison Ave., New York, N.Y. 10016 Tel 212-779-7668 Fax 212-689-5405

Peterson's, 202 Carnegie Center, P.O. Box 2123, Princeton, N.J. 08543-2123 Tel 609-243-9111; 800-338-3282 (orders) Fax 609-243-9150; 452-0966 (orders)

Peterson's Guides Inc., 202 Carnegie Center, P.O. Box 2123, Princeton, N.J. 08543-2123 Tel 609-243-9111; 800-338-3282 (orders) Fax 609-243-9150; 452-0966 (orders)

Phaidon Press Ltd., Regent's Wharf, All Saints St., London N1 9PA, Eng. Tel (0171) 843 1234 Fax (0171) 843 1111
Distributors
U.S.: Chronicle Bks.

Phillips: S. G. Phillips Inc., P.O. Box 83, Chatham, N.Y. 12037 Tel 518-392-3068

Philomel Bks., 200 Madison Ave., New York, N.Y. 10016 Tel 212-951-8400; 800-631-8571; refer orders to 390 Murray Hill Parkway, E. Rutherford, N.J. 07073

Pinnacle Bks. (NY): Pinnacle Bks., 475 Park Ave. S., New York, N.Y. 10016 Tel 212-889-2299; 800-221-2647 Fax 212-779-8073; refer orders to Penguin USA, P.O. Box 120, Bergenfield, N.J. 07621-0120 Tel 201-387-0600; 800-526-0275

Plays Inc., 120 Boylston St., Boston, Mass. 02116 Tel 617-423-3157 Fax 617-423-2168

Plenum Press, 233 Spring St., New York, N.Y. 10013-1578 Tel 212-620-8000; 800-221-9369 (orders) Fax 212-463-0742; 807-1047 (orders)

Pocket Bks., Simon & Schuster Bldg., 1230 Ave. of the Americas, New York, N.Y. 10020 Tel 212-698-7000; 800-223-2348 Fax 800-445-6991; refer orders to Simon & Schuster Inc., 200 Old Tappan Rd., Old Tappan, N.J. 07675 Tel 201-767-5937; 800-223-2336

Potter: Clarkson N. Potter Inc. Pubs., 201 E. 50th St., New York, N.Y. 10022 Tel 212-751-2600 Fax 212-572-6192; refer orders to Random House Inc., 400 Hahn Rd., Westminster, Md. 21157 Tel 410-848-1900; 800-733-3000 Fax 800-659-2436

Praeger Pubs., 88 Post Rd. W., P.O. Box 5007, Westport, Conn. 06881 Tel 203-226-3571; 800-225-5800 Fax 203-222-1502

Prakken Publs. Inc., 275 Metty Dr., Suite 1, Ann Arbor, Mich. 48103 Tel 313-769-1211; 800-530-9673 (orders)

Prentice-Hall Inc., 1 Lake St., Upper Saddle River, N.J. 07428 Tel 201-236-7000; refer orders to Prentice-Hall/Allyn & Bacon, 200 Old Tappan Rd., Old Tappan, N.J. 07675 Tel 800-223-1360 Fax 800-445-6991

Prentice Hall General Ref. refer orders to Simon & Schuster Ordering Dept., 200 Old Tappan Rd., Old Tappan, N.J. 07675 Tel 201-767-5937; 800-223-2336 Fax 201-767-5852 (orders)

Prentice-Hall Int. Inc., 1 Lake St., Upper Saddle River, N.J. 07428 Tel 201-236-7000

Presidio Press, 505 B San Marin Dr., Suite 300, Novato, Calif. 94945-1340 Tel 415-898-1081; 800-966-5179 Fax 415-898-0383; refer orders to Berkley Pub. Group, P.O. Box 506, E. Rutherford, N.J. 07073 Tel 201-933-9292; 800-223-0510 (orders) Fax 201-933-4927

Prima Pub., 3875 Atherton Rd., Rocklin, Calif. 95765 Tel 916-632-4400 Fax 916-632-4405; refer orders to Random House Inc., 400 Hahn Rd., Westminster, Md. 21157 Tel 410-848-1900; 800-733-3000 Fax 800-659-2436

Princeton Univ. Press, 41 William St., Princeton, N.J. 08540 Tel 609-258-4900 Fax 609-258-6305; refer orders to California-Princeton Fulfillment Services, 1445 Lower Ferry Rd., Ewing, N.J. 08618 Tel 609-883-1759; 800-777-4726 Fax 609-883-7413; 800-999-1958

Prometheus Bks., 59 John Glenn Dr., Amherst, N.Y. 14228-2197 Tel 716-691-0133; 800-421-0351 (orders only) Fax 716-564-2711; 716-691-0137 (orders)

Puffin Bks., 27 Wright's Lane, London W8 5TZ, Eng. Tel (0171) 416 3000 Fax (0171) 416 3099; refer orders to Penguin Bks. Ltd., Bath Rd., Harmondsworth, W. Drayton, Middlesex UB7 0DA, Eng. Tel (0181) 899 4000 Fax (0181) 899 4099

Branch offices
U.S.: Puffin Bks., 375 Hudson St., New York, N.Y. 10014-3657 Tel 212-366-2000

Putnam: G. P. Putnam's Sons, 200 Madison Ave., New York, N.Y. 10016 Tel 212-951-8400; 800-631-8571; refer orders to 390 Murray Hill Parkway, E. Rutherford, N.J. 07073

Putnam Pub. Group (The), 200 Madison Ave., New York, N.Y. 10016 Tel 212-951-8400; 800-631-8571; refer orders to 390 Murray Hill Parkway, East Rutherford, N.J. 07073

Raintree Pubs. See Raintree Steck-Vaughn

Raintree Steck-Vaughn, 466 Southern Blvd., Chatham, N.J. 07928 Tel 201-514-1525 Fax 201-514-1612; refer orders to P.O. Box 26105, Austin, Tex. 78755 Tel 512-343-8227; 800-531-5015 Fax 512-343-6854

Rand McNally, 8255 N. Central Park, Skokie, Ill. 60076-2970 Tel 708-673-9100 Fax 708-673-0813

Random House Inc., 201 E. 50th St., 22nd Floor, New York, N.Y. 10022 Tel 212-751-2600; 800-726-0600; refer orders to 400 Hahn Rd., Westminster, Md. 21157 Tel 410-848-1900; 800-733-3000 Fax 800-659-2436

Random House Value Pub. Inc., 40 Engelhard Ave., Avenel, N.J. 07001 Tel 908-827-2700; 800-223-6804 Fax 908-827-2641

RB Bks., 1006 N. 2nd St., Harrisburg, Pa. 17102 Tel 717-232-7944; 800-497-1497 Fax 717-238-3280

Reader's Digest Assn. Inc. (The), 260 Madison Ave., New York, N.Y. 10016 Tel 212-850-7007 Fax 212-850-7079; refer orders to Reader's Digest Rd., Pleasantville, N.Y. 10570 Tel 800-431-1246 Fax 914-238-7620

Rebus Inc., 632 Broadway, New York, N.Y. 10012 Tel 212-505-2255 Fax 212-505-5462

Reference Service Press, 1100 Industrial Rd., Suite 9, San Carlos, Calif. 94070 Tel 415-594-0743 Fax 415-594-0411

Regnery Bks., 422 1st St. S.E., Washington, D.C. 20003 Tel 202-546-5005; 800-462-6420 Fax 202-546-8759

Riverhead Bks., 200 Madison Ave., New York, N.Y. 10016 Tel 212-951-8444; 800-631-8571 Fax 212-799-8236

Rizzoli Int. Publs. Inc., 300 Park Ave. S., New York, N.Y. 10010 Tel 212-387-3400; 800-462-2387 Fax 212-387-3535; refer orders to St. Martin's Press Inc., 175 5th Ave., Room 1715, New York, N.Y. 10010 Tel 212-674-5151; 800-221-7945 Fax 212-420-9314

Roberts Rinehart Pubs., 5455 Spine Rd., Mezzanine W., Boulder, Colo. 80301 Tel 303-530-4400; 800-352-1985 Fax 303-530-4488; refer orders to Publishers Group West, P.O. Box 8843, Emeryville, Calif. 94662 Tel 800-788-3123

Robson/Parkwest Publs., 451 Communipaw Ave., Jersey City, N.J. 07304 Tel 201-432-3257

Rodale Press Inc., 33 E. Minor St., Emmaus, Pa. 18098 Tel 610-967-8411; 800-527-8200 Fax 610-967-8962

Rosen Pub. Group Inc. (The), 29 E. 21st St., New York, N.Y. 10010 Tel 212-777-3017; 800-237-9932 Fax 212-777-0277

Rourke: R. Rourke Pub. Co., P.O. Box 3328, Vero Beach, Fla. 32964 Tel 561-234-6001

Routledge, 11 New Fetter Lane, London EC4P 4EE, Eng. Tel (0171) 583 9855 Fax (0171) 583 0701; refer orders to International Thomson Pub. Services Ltd., Cheriton House, North Way, Andover, Hampshire SP10 5BE, Eng. Tel (01264) 332 424 Fax (01264) 364 418

Branch offices

U.S.: Routledge, 29 W. 35th St., New York, N.Y. 10001-2299 Tel 212-244-6412; 800-634-7064 Fax 212-563-2269; 800-248-4724 (orders)

Running Press Bk. Pubs., 125 S. 22nd St., Philadelphia, Pa. 19103-4399 Tel 215-567-5080; 800-345-5359 (orders only) Fax 800-453-2884

Rutgers Univ. Press, 109 Church St., New Brunswick, N.J. 08901 Tel 908-932-7764; 932-1070 (orders); 800-446-9323 Fax 908-932-7039; 932-1074 (orders)

Salem Press Inc., P.O. Box 1097, Englewood Cliffs, N.J. 07632 Tel 201-871-3700; 800-221-1592 Fax 201-871-8668

Sanders & Co.: J. S. Sanders & Co. Inc., 238 Public Sq., Franklin, Tenn. 37064 Tel 615-790-8951; 800-350-1101 Fax 615-790-2594; refer orders to National Bk. Network, 4720 Boston Way, Lanham, Md. 20706 Tel 301-459-8696; 800-462-6420 Fax 301-459-2118

Sargent Pubs.: Porter Sargent Pubs. Inc., 11 Beacon St., Suite 1400, Boston, Mass. 02108 Tel 617-523-1670 Fax 617-523-1021

Sasquatch Bks., 1008 Western Ave., Suite 300, Seattle, Wash. 98104 Tel 206-467-4300; 800-775-0817 Fax 206-467-4338; refer orders to Pacific Pipeline Inc., 8030 S. 228th St., Kent, Wash. 98032-3898 Tel 206-872-5523; 800-444-7323; 800-677-2222 (orders)

Scarborough House, 4720 Boston Way, Lanham, Md. 20706 Tel 301-459-5308; 800-462-6420 Fax 301-459-2118; refer orders to National Bk. Network

Scarecrow Press Inc., 4720 Boston Way, Suite A, Lanham, Md. 20706 Tel 301-459-3366; 800-462-6420 Fax 301-459-2118

Schirmer Bks., 1633 Broadway, New York, N.Y. 10019 Tel 212-654-8464; 800-223-2336 Fax 212-654-4745; refer orders to Simon & Schuster, 200 Old Tappan Rd., Old Tappan, N.J. 07675 Tel 800-223-2336 (orders) Fax 800-445-6991

Schocken Bks. Inc., 201 E. 50th St., New York, N.Y. 10022 Tel 212-572-2559; 800-726-0600 Fax 212-572-6030; refer orders to Random House Inc., 400 Hahn Rd., Westminster, Md. 21157 Tel 410-848-1900; 800-733-3000 Fax 800-659-2436

Scholastic Inc., 555 Broadway, New York, N.Y. 10012-3999 Tel 212-343-6100 Fax 212-343-4535; refer orders to 2931 E. McCarty, Jefferson City, Mo. 65101 Tel 800-325-6149

Scientific Am. Lib., 41 Madison Ave., E. 26th, 35th Floor, New York, N.Y. 10010 Tel 212-576-9400 Fax 212-689-2383; refer orders to W. H. Freeman & Co., 4419 W. 1980 S., Salt Lake City, Utah 84104 Tel 801-973-4660; 800-877-5351 Fax 801-977-9712

Scolar Press, Ashgate Pub. Ltd., Gower House, Croft Rd., Aldershot, Hampshire GU11 3HR, Eng. Tel (01252) 331 551 Fax (01252) 344 405; refer orders to Ashgate Distr. Services, Unit 3, Lower Farnham Rd., Aldershot, Hampshire GU12 4DY, Eng. Tel (01252) 331 551

Branch offices

U.S.: Scolar Press, Old Post Rd., Brookfield, Vt. 05036-9704 Tel 802-276-3162; 800-535-9544 Fax 802-276-3837

Scott, Foresman & Co., 1900 E. Lake Ave., Glenview, Ill. 60025 Tel 708-729-3000 Fax 708-729-8910

Scott Pub. Co. (Sidney): Scott Pub. Co., 911 Vandemark Rd., Sidney, Ohio 45365 Tel 937-498-0802; refer orders to P.O. Box 828, Sidney, Ohio 45365 Tel 800-572-6885

Scribner See Simon & Schuster

Seal Press (The), 3131 Western Ave., Suite 410, Seattle, Wash. 98121-1028 Tel 206-283-7844 Fax 206-285-9410; refer orders to Inland Bk. Co., 140 Commerce St., East Haven, Conn. 06512 Tel 203-467-4257; 800-243-0138 Fax 203-467-8364

Seattle Art Mus., P.O. Box 22000, Seattle, Wash. 98112-9700 Tel 206-654-3120 Fax 206-654-3135; refer orders to University of Wash. Press, P.O. Box 50096, Seattle, Wash. 98145-5096 Tel 206-543-8870; 800-441-4115 Fax 206-543-3932; 800-669-7993

Sharpe, M.E.: M. E. Sharpe Inc., 80 Business Park Dr., Armonk, N.Y. 10504 Tel 914-273-1800; 800-541-6563 Fax 914-273-2106

Sheridan House Inc., 145 Palisade St., Dobbs Ferry, N.Y. 10522 Tel 914-693-2410 Fax 914-693-0776

Sierra Club Bks., 100 Bush St., 13th Floor, San Francisco, Calif. 94103 Tel 415-291-1600 Fax 415-291-1602; refer orders to Random House Inc., 400 Hahn Rd., Westminster, Md. 21157 Tel 410-848-1900; 800-733-3000 Fax 800-659-2436

Silver Burdett Press, 299 Jefferson Rd., P.O. Box 480, Parsippany, N.J. 07054-0480 Tel 201-739-8000; 800-848-9500 Fax 201-739-8503

Simon & Schuster Inc. Pubs., Simon & Schuster Bldg., 1230 Ave. of the Americas, New York, N.Y. 10020 Tel 212-698-7000; 800-223-2348; refer orders to Simon & Schuster, 200 Old Tappan Rd., Old Tappan, N.J. 07675 Tel 800-223-2336 (orders) Fax 800-445-6991

Simon & Schuster Bks. for Young Readers, 1230 Ave. of the Americas, New York, N.Y. 10020 Tel 212-698-7000; 800-257-5755; refer orders to Simon & Schuster Children's Ordering Dept., 200 Old Tappan Rd., Old Tappan, N.J. 07675 Tel 800-223-2336 (orders) Fax 800-445-6991

Smith & Kraus Inc., 1 Main St., Lyme, N.H. 03768 Tel 603-795-4331; 800-895-4331 Fax 603-795-4427

Smithmark Pubs. Inc., 115 W. 18th St., New York, N.Y. 10011 Tel 212-519-1304 Fax 212-519-1310

Smithsonian Bks., 470 L'Enfant Plaza, Room 7100, Washington, D.C. 20560 Tel 202-287-3738; 800-223-2584

Smithsonian Institution Press, 470 L'Enfant Plaza, Suite 7100, Washington, D.C. 20560 Tel 202-287-3738 Fax 202-287-3184; refer orders to P.O. Box 960, Herndon, Va. 20172-0960 Tel 800-782-4612 Fax 703-689-0660

Soho Press Inc., 853 Broadway, New York, N.Y. 10003 Tel 212-260-1900 Fax 212-260-1902; refer orders to Farrar, Straus & Giroux Inc., 19 Union Sq. W., New York, N.Y. 10003 Tel 212-741-6900; 800-631-8571 Fax 212-633-9385

Southern Methodist Univ. Press, 314 Fondren Lib. W., Dallas, Tex. 75275 Tel 214-768-1432 Fax 214-768-1428; refer orders to Texas A&M Univ. Press, John H. Lindsey Bldg., Drawer C, College Station, Tex. 77843-4354 Tel 409-845-1436; 800-826-8911 (orders) Fax 409-847-8752

Sports Illustrated, Time & Life Bldg., 1271 Ave. of the Americas, New York, N.Y. 10020 Tel 212-522-1212; refer orders to National Bk. Network, 4720 Boston Way, Lanham, Md. 20706-4310 Tel 301-459-8696; 800-462-6420

St. James Press, c.o. Gale Res. Inc., 835 Penobscot Bldg., Detroit, Mich. 48226-4094 Tel 313-961-2242; 800-877-4253 Fax 313-961-6083

St. Martin's/Marek, 175 5th Ave., New York, N.Y. 10010 Tel 212-674-5151; 800-221-7945

St. Martin's Press Inc., 175 5th Ave., Room 1715, New York, N.Y. 10010 Tel 212-674-5151; 800-221-7945 Fax 212-420-9314

ST Publs., 407 Gilbert Ave., Cincinnati, Ohio 45202 Tel 513-421-2050; 800-925-1110 (orders) Fax 513-421-5144

Stackpole Bks. Inc., 5067 Ritter Rd., Mechanicsburg, Pa. 17055 Tel 717-796-0411; 800-732-3669 Fax 717-796-0412

Stanford Univ. Press, Stanford, Calif. 94305-2235 Tel 415-723-1593 Fax 415-725-3457

Starwood Pub., 5230 MacArthur Blvd. N.W., Washington, D.C. 20016 Tel 202-362-7404 Fax 202-362-6001

Sterling Pub. Co. Inc., 387 Park Ave. S., New York, N.Y. 10016-8810 Tel 212-532-7160; 800-367-9692 Fax 212-213-2495; 800-542-7567

Stewart, Tabori & Chang Inc., 575 Broadway, 6th Floor, New York, N.Y. 10012 Tel 212-941-2929 Fax 212-941-2982; refer orders to Publisher Resources Inc., 1224 Heil Quaker Blvd., P.O. Box 7001, La Vergne, Tenn. 37086-7001 Tel 615-793-5090; 800-937-5557

Stockton Press, 345 Park Ave. S., New York, N.Y. 10010 Tel 212-689-9200 Fax 212-689-9711

Storey Communications Inc., Schoolhouse Rd., Pownal, Vt. 05261-9990 Tel 802-823-5200; 800-441-5700 Fax 802-823-5819; refer orders to HarperCollins Pubs., 1000 Keystone Ind. Park, Scranton, Pa. 18512-0588 Tel 717-941-1500; 800-982-4377 Fax 800-822-4090

Story Press (Cincinnati): Story Press, 1507 Dana Ave., Cincinnati, Ohio 45207 Tel 513-531-2690; 800-289-0963 Fax 513-531-4744

Stravon Educ. Press, 845 3rd Ave., New York, N.Y. 10022 Tel 212-371-2880

Stryker-Post Publs., P.O. Drawer 1200, Harpers Ferry, W.Va. 25445 Tel 304-535-2593; 800-995-1400 Fax 304-535-6513

Stuart, L.: Lyle Stuart, Inc., 120 Enterprise Ave., Secaucus, N.J. 07094 Tel 201-866-4199; 800-572-6657

Studio Mus. in Harlem, 144 W. 125th St., New York, N.Y. 10027 Tel 212-864-4500

Summit Bks., 1230 Ave. of the Americas, New York, N.Y. 10020 Tel 212-698-7501; 800-223-2336; refer orders to Prentice Hall Trade, Simon & Schuster Inc., 200 Old Tappan Rd., Old Tappan, N.J. 07675 Tel 201-767-5937; 800-223-2336 (orders only)

Superintendent of Docs., U.S. Govt. Ptg. Office, Washington, D.C. 20402

TAB Bks., P.O. Box 40, Blue Ridge Summit, Pa. 17294-0850 Tel 717-794-2191; 800-233-1128 Fax 717-794-2080

Tambourine Bks., 1350 Ave. of the Americas, New York, N.Y. 10019 Tel 212-261-6500; 800-237-0657 Fax 212-261-6549; refer orders to Wilmor Warehouse, P.O. Box 1219, 39 Plymouth St., Fairfield, N.J. 07007 Tel 201-227-7200

Tarcher, J.P.: Jeremy P. Tarcher Inc., 5858 Wilshire Blvd., Suite 200, Los Angeles, Calif. 90036 Tel 213-935-9980; refer orders to 1 Grosset Dr., Kirkwood, NY 13795 Tel 800-847-5515

Taylor Pub. Co., 1550 W. Mockingbird Lane, Dallas, Tex. 75235 Tel 214-819-8100; 800-677-2800 (orders only) Fax 214-819-8580

Teacher Ideas Press, P.O. Box 6633, Englewood, Colo. 80155-6633 Tel 303-770-1200; 800-237-6124 Fax 303-220-8843

Ten Speed Press, P.O. Box 7123, Berkeley, Calif. 94707 Tel 510-559-1600; 800-841-2665 Fax 510-524-1052

Thames & Hudson Ltd., 30 Bloomsbury St., London WC1B 3QP, Eng. Tel (0171) 636 5488 Fax (0171) 636 1695; refer orders to 44 Clockhouse Rd., Farnborough, Hampshire GU14 7QZ, Eng. Tel (01252) 541 602 Fax (01252) 377 380

Branch offices

U.S.: Thames & Hudson Inc., 500 5th Ave., New York, N.Y. 10110 Tel 212-354-3763 Fax 212-398-1252; refer orders to W. W. Norton & Co. Inc., 500 5th Ave., New York, N.Y. 10110 Tel 212-354-5500; 800-233-4830 (orders) Fax 212-398-1252; 800-458-6515 (orders)

Theatre Communications Group Inc., 355 Lexington Ave., New York, N.Y. 10017 Tel 212-697-5230 Fax 212-983-4847

Thomasson-Grant Pub., 1 Morton Dr., Charlottesville, Va. 22903-6806 Tel 804-977-1780 Fax 804-977-1696

Thunder's Mouth Press, 632 Broadway, 7th Floor, New York, N.Y. 10012 Tel 212-780-0380 Fax 212-780-0388; refer orders to Publishers Group West, P.O. Box 8843, Emeryville, Calif. 94662 Tel 800-788-3123

Ticknor & Fields, 215 Park Ave. S., New York, N.Y. 10003 Tel 212-420-5800; 800-225-3362 Fax 212-420-5855; refer orders to Houghton Mifflin Co., Wayside Rd., Burlington, Mass. 01803 Tel 617-272-1500; 800-225-3362

Tilbury House, 132 Water St., Gardiner, Me. 04345 Tel 207-582-1899; 800-582-1899 Fax 207-582-8227; refer orders to Consortium Bk. Sales & Distr., 1045 Westgate Dr., Suite 90, St. Paul, Minn. 55114-1065 Tel 612-221-9035; 800-283-3572 Fax 612-221-0124

Time-Life Bks. Inc., 777 Duke St., Alexandria, Va. 22314 Tel 703-838-7000 Fax 703-684-5224; refer orders to 1450 E. Parham Rd., Richmond, Va. 23280 Tel 800-621-7026

Times Bks., 201 E. 50th St., New York, N.Y. 10022 Tel 212-751-2600; 800-726-0600; refer orders to Random House Inc., 400 Hahn Rd., Westminster, Md. 21157 Tel 410-848-1900; 800-733-3000 Fax 800-659-2436

Times Business, 201 E. 50th St., New York, N.Y. 10022 Tel 212-751-2600; 800-726-0600

Todd Publs., 18 N. Greenbush Rd., W. Nyack, N.Y. 10994 Tel 914-358-6213

TOR Bks., 175 5th Ave., New York, N.Y. 10010 Tel 212-388-0100; 800-221-7945 Fax 212-420-9314; refer orders to St. Martin's Press Inc., 175 5th Ave., Room 1715, New York, N.Y. 10010 Tel 212-674-5151; 800-221-7945 Fax 212-420-9314

Tracks Pub., 140 Brightwood Ave., Chula Vista, Calif. 91910 Tel 619-476-7125 Fax 619-476-8173; refer orders to Independent Pubs. Group, 814 N. Franklin, Chicago, Ill. 60610 Tel 312-337-0747; 800-888-4741 Fax 312-337-5985

Trafalgar Sq. Inc., Howe Hill Rd., N. Pomfret, Vt. 05053 Tel 802-457-1911; 800-423-4525 Fax 802-457-1913

Turner Pub. (Atlanta): Turner Pub. Inc., 1050 Techwood Dr. N.W., Atlanta, Ga. 30318 Tel 404-885-4038 Fax 404-885-4066; refer orders to Andrews & McMeel Inc., 4520 Main St., Kansas City, Mo. 64111 Tel 816-360-6700; 800-826-4216 Fax 816-932-6820

Tuttle: Charles E. Tuttle Co. Inc., 153 Milk St., 5th Floor, Boston, Mass. 02109 Tel 617-951-4080 Fax 617-951-4045; refer orders to Rural Route 1, Box 231-5, North Clarendon, Vt. 05759-9700 Tel 802-773-8930; 800-526-2778 Fax 800-329-8885

Twayne Pubs., 1633 Broadway, New York, N.Y. 10019 Tel 212-654-3000; refer orders to 201 W. 103rd St., Indianapolis, Ind. 46290 Tel 800-858-7674 Fax 317-871-6728; 800-835-3202

U.N. Publs., Palais des Nations, CH-1211 Geneva 10, Switzerland Tel (022) 9172614 Fax (022) 9170027

Branch offices

U.S.: U.N. Publs., 2 United Nations Plaza, Room DC2-853, New York, N.Y. 10017 Tel 212-963-8302; 800-253-9646 Fax 212-963-3489

U.S. Govt. Ptg. Office, USGPO Stop SSMR, Washington, D.C. 20401; refer orders to Superintendent of Docs., Washington, D.C. 20402-9325 Tel 202-783-3238

U.X.L, 835 Penobscot Bldg., Detroit, Mich. 48226-4094 Tel 313-961-2242; 800-877-4253 Fax 313-961-6348

Ungar See Continuum

U PUB, 4611-F Assembly Dr., Lanham, Md. 20706-4391 Tel 301-459-7666; 800-274-4888 (U.S.); 800-233-0504 (Can.)

University of Ariz. Press (The), 1230 N. Park Ave., No. 102, Tucson, Ariz. 85719 Tel 520-621-1441; 800-426-3797 (orders only) Fax 520-621-8899

University of Ark. Press, 201 Ozark St., Fayetteville, Ark. 72701 Tel 501-575-3246; 800-525-1823 Fax 501-575-6044; 800-626-0090 (orders)

University of Calif. Press, 2120 Berkeley Way, Berkeley, Calif. 94720 Tel 510-642-4247; 800-777-4726 Fax 510-642-7127

University of Chicago Press, 5801 S. Ellis Ave., 4th Floor, Chicago, Ill. 60637 Tel 312-702-7700 Fax 312-702-9756; refer orders to 11030 S. Langley Ave., Chicago, Ill. 60628 Tel 312-568-1550; 800-621-2736 Fax 312-660-2235; 800-621-8476

University of Ga. Press (The), 330 Research Dr., Suite B-100, Athens, Ga. 30602-4901 Tel 706-369-6130 Fax 706-369-6131

University of Ill. Press, 1325 S. Oak St., Champaign, Ill. 61820 Tel 217-333-0950 Fax 217-244-8082; refer orders to P.O. Box 4856, Baltimore, Md. 21211 Tel 800-545-4703 Fax 410-516-6969

University of Iowa Press, 100 Kuhl House, Iowa City, Iowa 52242-1000 Tel 319-335-2000 Fax 319-335-2055; refer orders to Publications Order Dept., 100 Oakdale Campus, No. M1050H, Iowa City, Iowa 52242-5000 Tel 319-335-4645; 800-235-2665 Fax 319-335-4039

University of Minn. Press, 111 3rd Ave. S., Suite 290, Minneapolis, Minn. 55401-2520 Tel 612-627-1970; 800-388-3863 Fax 612-627-1980

University of Mo. Press (The), 2910 LeMone Blvd., Columbia, Mo. 65201 Tel 314-882-7641; 800-828-1894 (orders only) Fax 314-884-4498

University of N.C. Press (The), P.O. Box 2288, Chapel Hill, N.C. 27515-2288 Tel 919-966-3561; 800-848-6224 (orders) Fax 919-966-3829; 800-272-6817 (orders)

University of N.M. Press, 1720 Lomas Blvd. N.E., Albuquerque, N.M. 87131-1591 Tel 505-277-4810; 800-249-7737 Fax 505-277-3350; 800-622-8667 (orders)

University of Neb. Press, 312 N. 14th St., Lincoln, Neb. 68588-0484 Tel 402-472-3581; 472-3584 (orders) Fax 402-472-6214; 800-526-2617 (orders)

University of Nev. Press, Mail Stop 166, Reno, Nev. 89557-0076 Tel 702-784-6573 Fax 702-784-6200

University of Okla. Press, 1005 Asp Ave., Norman, Okla. 73019-0445 Tel 405-325-5111 Fax 405-325-4000; refer orders to P.O. Box 787, Norman, Okla. 73070-0787 Tel 405-325-2000; 800-627-7377 Fax 405-364-5798; 800-735-0476

University of Pa. Press, 423 Guardian Dr., Blockley Hall, 13th Floor, Philadelphia, Pa. 19104-6097 Tel 215-898-6261 Fax 215-898-0404; refer orders to P.O. Box 4836, Hampden Station, Baltimore, Md. 21211 Tel 410-516-6948; 800-445-9880 Fax 410-516-6998

University of Pittsburgh Press, 127 N. Bellefield Ave., Pittsburgh, Pa. 15260 Tel 412-624-7391 Fax 412-624-7380; refer orders to C.U.P. Services, P.O. Box 6525, Ithaca, N.Y. 14851 Tel 800-666-2211 Fax 800-688-2877

University of S.C. Press, 937 Assembly St., Carolina Plaza, 8th Floor, Columbia, S.C. 29208 Tel 803-777-5243; 800-777-5243 Fax 803-777-0160; refer orders to 205 Pickens St., Columbia, S.C. 29208 Tel 803-251-6309; 800-768-2500 Fax 800-868-0740

University of S. Fla. Press, 4202 E. Fowler Ave., Tampa, Fla. 33620 Tel 813-974-2011; refer orders to University Presses of Fla., 15 N.W. 15th St., Gainesville, Fla. 32603 Tel 904-392-1351

University of Tex. Press, P.O. Box 7819, Austin, Tex. 78713-7819 Tel 512-471-7233; 800-252-3206 Fax 512-320-0668

University of Toronto Press, 10 St. Mary St., Suite 700, Toronto, Ont., Can. M4Y 2W8 Tel 416-978-2239 Fax 416-978-4738; refer orders to 5201 Dufferin St., Downsview, Ont., Can. M3H 5T8 Tel 416-667-7791; 800-565-9523 Fax 416-667-7832
Branch offices
U.S.: University of Toronto Press, 340 Nagel Dr., Cheektowaga, N.Y. 14225 (warehouse) Tel 716-683-4547

University of Wash. Press, P.O. Box 50096, Seattle, Wash. 98145-5096 Tel 206-543-4050; 800-441-4115 Fax 206-543-3932; 800-669-7993; refer orders to School of Am. Res. Press, P.O. Box 2188, Santa Fe, N.M. 87504-2188 Tel 505-984-0741

University of Wis. Press (The), 114 N. Murray St., Madison, Wis. 53715-1199 Tel 608-262-4928; 262-8782 (orders) Fax 608-262-7560

University Press of Fla., 15 N.W. 15th St., Gainesville, Fla. 32611-2079 Tel 904-392-1351; 800-226-3822 Fax 904-392-7302

University Press of Kan., 2501 W. 15th St., Lawrence, Kan. 66049-3904 Tel 913-864-4154; 864-4155 (orders) Fax 913-864-4586

University Press of Ky., 663 S. Limestone St., Lexington, Ky. 40508-4008 Tel 606-257-8442 Fax 606-257-2984; refer orders to C.U.P. Services, P.O. Box 6525, Ithaca, N.Y. 14851 Tel 607-277-2211; 800-666-2211

University Press of Miss., 3825 Ridgewood Rd., Jackson, Miss. 39211-6492 Tel 601-982-6205; 800-737-7788 Fax 601-982-6217

Van Nostrand Reinhold Co. Inc., 115 5th Ave., New York, N.Y. 10003 Tel 212-254-3232 Fax 212-254-9499; refer orders to 7625 Empire Dr., Florence, Ky. 41042-0668 Tel 606-525-6600; 800-842-3636 Fax 606-525-7778

Vanguard Press Inc., 424 Madison Ave., New York, N.Y. 10017 Tel 212-753-3906

VGM Career Horizons, 4255 W. Touhy Ave., Lincolnwood, Ill. 60646-1975 Tel 708-679-5500; 800-323-4900 Fax 708-679-2494

Viking See Penguin USA

Viking Kestrel See Penguin USA

Viking Studio Bks. See Penguin USA

Villard Bks., 201 E. 50th St., New York, N.Y. 10022 Tel 212-572-2720; 800-726-0600 Fax 212-572-6026; refer orders to Random House Inc., 400 Hahn Rd., Westminster, Md. 21157 Tel 410-848-1900; 800-733-3000 Fax 800-659-2436

Vintage Bks., 201 E. 50th St., New York, N.Y. 10022 Tel 212-751-2600; 800-726-0600; refer orders to Random House Inc., 400 Hahn Rd., Westminster, Md. 21157 Tel 410-848-1900; 800-733-3000 Fax 800-659-2436

Wadsworth Pub. Co., 10 Davis Dr., Belmont, Calif. 94002-2978 Tel 415-595-2350; refer orders to Wadsworth Distr. Center, 7625 Empire Dr., Florence, Ky. 41042 Tel 606-525-2230; 800-354-9706 Fax 606-525-0978

Walker & Co., 435 Hudson St., New York, N.Y. 10014 Tel 212-727-8300; 800-289-2553 Fax 212-727-0984

Warner Bks., Time & Life Bldg., 1271 Ave. of the Americas, New York, N.Y. 10020 Tel 212-522-7200 Fax 212-522-7158; refer orders to Little, Brown & Co. Inc., 200 West St., Waltham, Mass. 02254 Tel 617-890-0250; 800-343-9204 Fax 617-890-0875

Washington Sq. Press, Simon & Schuster Bldg., 1230 Ave. of the Americas, New York, N.Y. 10020 Tel 212-698-7000; 800-223-2348; refer orders to Prentice Hall Trade, Simon & Schuster Inc., 200 Old Tappan Rd., Old Tappan, N.J. 07675 Tel 201-767-5937; 800-223-2336 (orders only)

Watson-Guptill Publs., 1515 Broadway, New York, N.Y. 10036 Tel 212-536-5121 Fax 212-536-5055; refer orders to 1695 Oak St., Lakewood, N.J. 08701 Tel 908-363-4511; 800-451-1741 Fax 908-363-0338

Watts: Franklin Watts Inc., Sherman Turnpike, Danbury, Conn. 06813 Tel 203-797-3500; 800-621-1115 Fax 203-797-3143

Wayne State Univ. Press, Leonard N. Simons Bldg., 4809 Woodward Ave., Detroit, Mich. 48201-1309 Tel 313-577-4606; 800-978-7323 (orders only) Fax 313-577-6131

Wesleyan Univ. Press, 110 Mt. Vernon St., Middletown, Conn. 06459 Tel 860-685-2420; refer orders to University Press of New England, 23 S. Main St., Hanover, N.H. 03755 Tel 603-643-7100; 643-7110 (orders); 800-421-1561 (orders) Fax 603-643-1540; 643-1560 (orders)

West Pub. Co., 620 Opperman Dr., P.O. Box 64526, St. Paul, Minn. 55164-0526 Tel 612-687-7000; 800-328-9424

Western Pub. Co. Inc., 1220 Mound Ave., Racine, Wis. 53404 Tel 414-633-2431

Westview Press Inc., 5500 Central Ave., Boulder, Colo. 80301-2877 Tel 303-444-3541; 800-456-1995 Fax 303-449-3356; refer orders to HarperCollins Pubs., 1000 Keystone Ind. Park, Scranton, Pa. 18512-0588 Tel 717-941-1500; 800-982-4377 Fax 800-822-4090

White House Hist. Assn., 740 Jackson Pl. N.W., Washington, D.C. 20503 Tel 202-737-8292; refer orders to Independent Pubs. Group, 814 N. Franklin, Chicago, Ill. 60610 Tel 312-337-0747; 800-888-4741 Fax 312-337-5985

White, J.T.: James T. White & Co., 1700 State Highway 3, Clifton, N.J. 07013

Wiley: John Wiley & Sons Inc., 605 3rd Ave., New York, N.Y. 10158-0012; refer orders to 1 Wiley Dr., Somerset, N.J. 08873-1272 Tel 908-469-4400; 800-225-5945 Fax 908-302-2300

Williams & Wilkins, 351 W. Camden St., Baltimore, Md. 21201-2436 Tel 410-528-4000; 800-527-5597 Fax 410-528-4422; refer orders to P.O. Box 1496, Baltimore, Md. 21203

Wilson, H.W.: The H. W. Wilson Co., 950 University Ave., Bronx, N.Y. 10452 Tel 718-588-8400; 800-367-6770 Fax 718-590-1617

Wings Bks., 201 E. 50th St., 22nd Floor, New York, N.Y. 10022 Tel 212-751-2600; 800-726-0600; refer orders to 400 Hahn Rd., Westminster, Md. 21157 Tel 410-848-1900; 800-733-3000 Fax 800-659-2436

Woodbridge Press Pub. Co., 815 De La Vina St., Santa Barbara, Calif. 93101 Tel 805-965-7039; 800-237-6053 Fax 805-963-0540

Workman Pub. Co. Inc., 708 Broadway, New York, N.Y. 10003 Tel 212-254-5900; 800-722-7202 Fax 212-254-8098; 800-521-1832 (orders)

World Almanac See World Almanac Bks.

World Almanac Bks., 1 International Blvd., Suite 444, Mahwah, N.J. 07495-0017 Tel 201-529-6900 Fax 201-529-6901

World Bk. Inc., 525 W. Monroe, 20th Floor, Chicago, Ill. 60661 Tel 312-258-3700; 800-621-8202 Fax 312-258-3950

Writer Inc. (The), 120 Boylston St., Boston, Mass. 02116-4615 Tel 617-423-3157 Fax 617-423-2168

Writers & Readers Pub. Inc., 625 Broadway, 10th Floor, New York, N.Y. 10012 Tel 212-982-3158 Fax 212-529-7399; refer orders to Publishers Group West, P.O. Box 8843, Emeryville, Calif. 94662 Tel 800-788-3123

Writer's Digest Bks., 1507 Dana Ave., Cincinnati, Ohio 45207 Tel 513-531-2222; 800-289-0963 Fax 513-531-4744; 531-4082 (orders)

Yale Univ. Press, 302 Temple St., New Haven, Conn. 06520 Tel 203-432-0960; 800-987-7323 Fax 203-432-0948; refer orders to P.O. Box 209040, New Haven, Conn. 06520-9040 Tel 203-432-0940

Yankee Bks., 33 E. Minor St., Emmaus, Pa. 18098 Tel 610-967-5171; 800-527-8200 Fax 610-967-8963

Zondervan Pub. House, 5300 Patterson Ave. S.E., Grand Rapids, Mich. 49530 Tel 616-698-6900; 800-727-1309 Fax 616-698-3255; 800-934-6381 (orders)